The New York Times
Theater Reviews

**THE UNIVERSITY OF MEMPHIS
LIBRARIES**

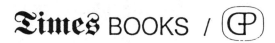

Times Books & Garland Publishing, Inc. / New York 1992

Published by TIMES BOOKS,
The New York Times Book Co., Inc.
130 Fifth Avenue, New York, N.Y. 10011
and by
GARLAND PUBLISHING, INC.
New York & London

ISBN 0-8240-7574-9

Printed on acid-free, 250-year-life paper

Manufactured in the United States of America

Contents

Foreword

All theater reviews published in The New York Times between 1870–1988 have been assembled and reproduced in book form under the title THE NEW YORK TIMES THEATER REVIEWS.

This collection is accompanied by computer-generated indexes which cover the periods 1870–1919, 1920–1970, 1971–1972, 1973–1974, 1975–1976, 1977–1978, 1979–1980, 1981–1982, 1983–1984, 1985–1986, and 1987–1988. Each index is divided into three sections: Titles, Personal Names, and Corporate Names.

The present volume updates the collection by reproducing all of the Times theater reviews published in 1989–1990. It also includes articles about the shows that won Pulitzer Prizes, New York Drama Critics Circle Awards, and Antoinette Perry (Tony) Awards. The volume is completed by a three-part index, prepared along the same lines as the earlier indexes.

New compilations will be published periodically to keep the collection constantly updated.

The New York Times
Theater Reviews
1989

1989

STAGE VIEW/Mel Gussow

Dramatizing the Woes of Yuppies

IN THE THEATER, AS IN LIFE, PEOple have been discovering that the fast track can be a treadmill. They are forced to confront what could be called the Yuppie Trauma: early success leading to young-life crisis. If you rise to the top of a profession before you are 30 — as stockbroker, movie producer, publisher, theater director — burnout may result when you are 30 something.

Increasingly on stage — and in films and on television — the Yuppie Trauma has become a subject for dramatic and comedic contemplation as audiences are asked to understand the vicissitudes of being young and prosperous. For many, sympathies stop short; in a world beset by terrorism, acid rain, hunger and earthquakes, the problems of young upwardly mobile careerists seem

In three new plays the species is at least human, a microcosm of an endangered society.

marginal, perhaps even incomprehensible. But our concern can of course be deepened by the seriousness of the artistic approach. Coincidentally, the three most striking new plays I have seen so far this season deal revealingly with the subject: Richard Greenberg's "Eastern Standard," which opens at the Golden Theater on Thursday after its engagement at Manhattan Theater Club; Wendy Wasserstein's "The Heidi Chronicles" now at Playwrights Horizons and maybe headed for Broadway, and Dennis McIntyre's "National Anthems," presently at the Long Wharf Theater in New Haven and a strong candidate for transfer to New York.

Each of the plays takes a disparate view of the brat race, but in common the authors are able to hold their characters at arm's length, to be ironic as well as sympathetic. None of them accepts any pretension; all are concerned with broader, human issues, such as the loss of individualism in the cogs of the system. To the question, does one care about yuppies, we can answer, only when they are as human as they are in these plays. For these three thoughtful playwrights, yuppies are a microcosm of an endangered society. They are just succeeding earlier and crashing more quickly. In each

case, the message is enhanced in the delivery. The playwrights have been given assured productions in which the actors mirror the perspicacity of the plays.

The perspective is partly a reflection of the playwrights' ages. Ms. Wasserstein is 38; Mr. McIntyre, 46. The youngest of them, Mr. Greenberg, is 30 and he is the one most deeply immersed in the world and speaks from front-line experience. He has already explored the subject in a number of plays. In his melancholic "Life Under Water," adolescents idle richly in the Hamptons before swimming in the mainstream. "The Maderati" was a gleeful assault on the glittering celebrity of publishing, posing the question, "What does being good have to do with getting published?" In the hilarious one-act "The Author's Voice," Mr. Greenberg carried the premise into surrealism. A handsome, suave new novelist has all the qualities for success — except for the fact that he has absolutely no talent. The actual author, his ghostwriter, could be Quasimodo's identical twin. He is confined in a locked room, from which he secretly produces the author's art. Personality, self-presentation, sex appeal are all important conditions of yuppiehood.

Then there is the reverse side: sudden, sometimes insincere, altruism. The high-flyers in "Eastern Standard" have a spasm of self-doubt and social remorse. Stephen (Dylan Baker), the central character, is an architect who designs high-rise monoliths all over Manhattan, until he realizes the social responsibility he bears. He *is* urban blight. His girlfriend, Phoebe (Patricia Clarkson), a stockbroker, finally faces the fact that her co-workers may be evil (and that she shares in the complicity). Drew (Peter Frechette), an artist and the most naturally cynical in the group, feels that his peers, the Julian Schnabels and the David Salles, are on "the cutting edge of the passé" — and where does that leave him?

The characters respond by inviting a homeless person to the Hamptons. Responding to their innate hypocrisy, the bag lady steals their valuables. Possessions are themselves amulets of success, as in Mr. McIntyre's "National Anthems." In that bitter play, Arthur and Leslie Reed (Tom Berenger and Mary McDonnell), a wealthy Midwestern couple, buy the brand names and memorize the buzz words of their times. Their life style is a glossy photographic spread in House & Garden magazine. They do not simply have a stereo; they have a Bang & Olufsen music system with RL140 speakers. In their driveway is a silver BMW, which the husband is thinking of upgrading to a Porsche.

The Reeds are startled from their false paradise by a visit from a confrontational neighbor, Ben Cook (Kevin Spacey). After a late-night housewarming party, he unloads an unwelcome wagon of disparaging remarks about the complacent couple, their life and their unseen friends, all of whom seem to spend their time hang-gliding, ice-boating and making money. For a long stretch the hosts are unfailingly courteous — company manners even for the unmannerly. The living room war begins with the neighbor's casual assault on the expensive Milanese furniture and continues with a bruising scrimmage of tackle football. The neighbor, who is a fireman, eventually poses his sense of civic duty opposite their acquisitiveness and quest for status.

■

That fireman would have been far more gracious to the heroine of Ms. Wasserstein's play. Heidi (Joan Allen) is a good girl of the 1960's, someone who demonstrated for feminism, campaigned for Senator Eugene McCarthy and could be enlisted in any

Our concern can deepen with the seriousness of the artistic approach.

ecological emergency. In her personal life, she is wary about settling for any prescribed goal, whether it is marrying well or seeking worldly advantage. Meanwhile her friends are leaping prematurely into positions of prestige and power. A faithless lover and former liberal activist ends up publishing a trendy magazine called Boomer. One could imagine the characters in all three plays sitting down with the latest issue of Boomer to see how the other fellow got there first, if indeed he did.

Heidi herself is an art historian, woefully aware of the neglect suffered by women artists who painted in secrecy. An epiphany comes to her in an aerobics class, where she is surrounded by overachievers in mind and body. Cowed by her sisters, but not blaming them for her depression, Heidi feels stranded, and, almost, out of ideals. She finds a renewed strength in her independence, in her willingness to forego competition in the mainstream. She also achieves an additional sense of purpose by adopting a child, adding single motherhood to her other concerns.

■

Similarly, in "Eastern Standard" the characters look to marriage for stability — to coupling and to friends as family (a recurrent theme in many yuppie plays). The Reeds in "National Anthems" have no such solace — not even intimate friends to keep their fireside warm. When the neighbor leaves, after his anguished recounting of his own failed attempt at heroism, the couple's elegant home is in disarray. The host and hostess sit silently as if at the end of a siege.

Though it begins with wry humor, "National Anthems" has the most mordant conclusion. That is not to suggest that the other two plays end on an upbeat note. Each leaves theatergoers — and the other characters in the plays — in a state of sobering inquietude. For Heidi, motherhood is more of a challenge than a solution. In "Eastern Standard," the architect and the stockbroker may marry as planned, but the stockbroker's brother is, as we know, dying of AIDS. The anguish of AIDS is also a backdrop in

"The Heidi Chronicles," as the heroine's gay soulmate (Boyd Gaines), a successful pediatrician, confronts losses in his own life.

These three plays deal directly with the yuppie experience, but each raises more universal issues that are also reflected in current works on other stages. The suburban country club world of A.R. Gurney, Jr.'s "Cocktail Hour" is very far removed from yuppiedom, but the hero's primary concern — how to justify his life to his parents — is something that would be immediately recognized by his younger compatriots in the plays by Mr. Greenberg and others.

Craig Lucas's "Reckless" (which closes its run today at the Circle Repertory Company) deals with characters of a similar age, but of a different social standing. They do, however, face related problems such as entrapment by apparent comfort. In this fanciful comedy, a husband takes out a contract on his wife's life (partly because she talks too much) and then warns her of the danger. She leaves home on Christmas Eve in search of sanctuary, self and fulfillment, which is of course also Heidi's aim.

Last season, in "Serious Money," Caryl Churchill decried the quick-rich life in London's financial world. Howard Korder's "Boys' Life" of last spring was a pre-yuppie comedy about rampant young Sybarites who, one assumes, will soon stop the partying and dive into the marketplace.

■

More and more films and television programs are also charting the upward — and sometimes immediately downward — mobility of early risers, as in "Broadcast News," "Wall Street" and almost anything starring Michael J. Fox ("The Secret of My Success," "Bright Lights, Big City"). One could trace an arc from "The Graduate" in 1967 to "Working Girl" in 1988 (both Mike Nichols films), marking each as endemic of its time.

In "The Graduate," Benjamin Braddock (Dustin Hoffman) is beset by a man boasting of the supremacy of plastics and the young man reacts with irony. Were that movie to be made today, Benjamin might be the head of a plastics empire, edging his elders into early retirement. In "Working Girl," Tess (Melanie Griffiths), as a Cinderella secretary, outwits all suppressive opposition, those who are male, those who are older and, most tellingly, her immediate superior (Sigourney Weaver), who is the same age.

Ms. Weaver's character is the ultimate yuppie, and, as such, is a sister to Phoebe in "Eastern Standard," although, we are led to believe, Phoebe eventually comes to her senses and realizes the shallowness of h / world while Ms. Weaver scurries to get back on the track after her derailment.

On television, there is "thirtysomething," in which couples try to have it all, and, often do, but at great personal expense. Watching these characters try to balance family and career, one thinks of Ms. Wasserstein's Heidi as a new single mother, soon to search for daycare. If she brings the baby to the office, Heidi

would turn into Diane Keaton in the movie "Baby Boom" (briefly a television situation comedy), in which the simple fact of parenting makes it difficult for a woman to continue as an executive.

On "Murphy Brown," Candice Bergen plays an anchorwoman still short of fortysomething, but already faced with the threat of obsolescence. In the television studio that is her habitat, she is challenged by an Eve Harrington, who is younger and more ambitious (but not too smart), and a post-adolescent producer in the Michael J. Fox tradition.

With the exception of "thirtysomething," which takes a more realistic approach, the television shows are

lightheaded to the point of being frivolous; a laugh track can certainly mitigate against social concern. In contrast, "Eastern Standard," "The Heidi Chronicles" and "National Anthems" are witty comedies with a socially redemptive purpose, and each is written from a mature perspective. Avoiding sentimentality and free from a facile resolution, the playwrights treat the Yuppie Trauma with trenchancy. At the end of "Eastern Standard," Stephen toasts his friends and the "sadly infrequent — accidental — happinesses of all the rest of our lives." And in a typical Greenberg coda, the wine they drink turns out to be sour. []

1989 Ja 1, II:5:1

STAGE VIEW/Michael Billington

Five Ways to Be Prospero

LONDON

"**T**HE TEMPEST" HAS ALWAYS been one of Shakespeare's most popular plays. It also possesses a mythical power that seems to inspire other artists. As the Shakespearean scholar Anne Barton points out in the New Penguin edition, Mozart sketched out an opera based upon it, Hollywood plundered its story for a science fiction film ("The Silent Planet"), T.S. Eliot used fragments of it in "The Waste Land" and W. H. Auden wrote a long

Recent productions of 'The Tempest' have radically reinterpreted the deposed duke.

poem, "The Sea and the Mirror," dwelling on the destinies of its principal characters.

But it has never enjoyed such a theatrical boom as it did in 1988 when playgoers in Britain were confronted by no fewer than five separate productions of the play. Peter Hall, who made his debut with it at the National Theater in 1973, ended his 15-year directorship with a radically different version. John Wood is currently playing Prospero in a Royal Shakespeare Company production at Stratford-on-Avon, which will later transfer to London. Jonathan Miller directed the work at the Old Vic with the screen's former exorcist, Max von Sydow. Tokyo's Ninagawa Company imported a boldly theatrical version to the Edinburgh Festival last autumn, and Cheek by Jowl, an innovative London-based touring company, is currently performing the work in repertory with Sophocles' "Philoctetes" (another play about a desert island hero).

Shakespeare once defined love as a quality that "looks on tempests and is never shaken." In 1988 playgoers in England and Scotland looked on more "Tempests" than ever before. Whether they were shaken is another matter.

Why should there be so many productions in one year? In part it is a reflection of renewed interest in Shakespeare's late plays. Once seen as fairy-tale romances with a Tennysonian aura, they are now viewed as much tougher, harsher plays in which Shakespeare balances his preoccupation with loss and recovery with visions of unregenerate humanity.

Even the much-maligned "Cymboline" turned up both in Mr. Hall's season of late plays at the National and at the R.S.C. and proved itself not to be the hodgepodge so disliked by Dr. Johnson and Shaw but a boldly experimental play about sexual torment, national discord and the good and base aspects of humanity.

But the real reason for the popularity of "The Tempest" is not hard to see. In an age of director's theater, it allows every interpretative artist to conjure up his or her own world on stage just as Prospero controls the elements on his enchanted isle.

Indeed the play can be seen as a metaphor for the theatrical process itself with Prospero equipping himself with the artist's power to raise the winds and darken the sun, shake the earth and command spirits while at the same time confronting the dangers of playing God. It is no accident that two of the recent productions (the Ninagawa Company's and Cheek by Jowl's) both seized on the idea of a play-within-a-play with Prospero presented either as a benevolent impresario or a dictatorial surrogate-author.

Paradoxically, although "The Tempest" is a director's play, the most striking feature of the recent productions is the drastic revision of Prospero as a character. Stage tradition usually sees him as a benign schoolmaster or a wizened sage who is a mixture of Santa Claus and Michelangelo's Noah and approximately four times as old as his brother Antonio.

Michael Bryant at the National, however, played Prospero as a tetchy autocrat turning purple with fury at the mention of his brother and looking back in anger at his usurpation. When he described to Miranda how the two of them were "heaved" out of Milan, Bryant leaned on the verb as if still obsessed by his humiliation.

But the major insight of both director and actor came in Prospero's famous renunciation of his magic: a speech often taken on a rising melodic curve so that we ignore what is being said. When, however, Bryant came to "Graves at my command have waked their sleepers, oped and let 'em forth by my so potent art," he stopped dead in his tracks as if haunted by his practice of Faustian necromancy. And when he "required some Heavenly music" (an achingly long time in coming), it was in the tones of a diabolist urgently seeking absolution.

◼

Mr. Wood, returning to the R.S.C. after a gap of 16 years, also got away from the idea of Prospero as an old conjurer in decreasing demand at Masonic banquets. In his open-necked shirt, baggy trousers and gardening boots (what else would he be wearing after 12 years on a desert island?), Mr. Wood presented us with an angry hermit who uses supernatural power to shield himself from human contact.

Prospero lost his dukedom, Mr. Wood forcefully reminded us, because he was "all dedicated to close-

ness," and you sensed his tormented, bookish solitude in the nervous jocularity with which he greeted his old enemies and in the tentative way he donned his restored crown. But Mr. Wood, as the most exciting Prospero of the year, also invested the character with a wealth of sardonic irony. When Ferdinand assured Prospero

No longer is he the benign schoolmaster or wizened sage, a mix of Noah and Santa Claus.

that Miranda's "virgin snow abated the ardor of his liver," Mr. Wood greeted his reassurance with a deeply cynical "Well," as if he had heard that one before.

◼

If recent productions have laid to rest the idea of Prospero as an old bore, they have also rediscovered in the text an almost Pirandellian essay on the nature of illusion and reality. Obviously a play that demands a shipwreck, masques, dissolving banquets, Ovidian spirits, prancing nymphs and grim reapers lends itself to fantasy and spectacle. But Japan's Ninagawa Company (which visited New York's Central Park two years ago with a production of "Medea") thrillingly showed how "The Tempest" not only can be accommodated to Oriental styles but also can become a complex meditation on the nature of theater itself.

Clive Barda

John Wood performing with the Royal Shakespeare Company—the year's most exciting Prospero

Yukio Ninagawa, the director, calculatedly set the action on the Japanese island of Sado: a historic refuge for political exiles and the place where noh drama was virtually invented in the 15th century. Mr. Ninagawa's elegant device was to mount the play on a straw-thatched stage on the edge of a crashing sea as though being rehearsed by an amateur group of noh performers today. Haruhiko Jo (looking oddly like a young Mr. Hall) both stage-managed the action and inevitably assumed the role of Prospero.

◼

But the striking element was the way one gradually forgot about the rehearsal framework, as if the whole Sado company had been transformed into the creatures of Prospero's imagination. This led to moments of pure magic, as when masked harpies entered bearing lacquered trays and teapots, descended from the noh platform to join the entrapped courtiers in a grave and solemn dance and then slowly enticed them into Prospero's circle of power. And when Prospero invoked "ye elves of hills, brooks, standing lakes and groves," everyone silently encircled Prospero as though diurnal reality had been metamorphosed by theatrical illusion and the magic of language. The Ninagawa Company proved that there is no business like noh business.

Declan Donnellan's production for Cheek by Jowl employed a similar device. An autocratic young actor-manager created the storm out of an improvisation session, assumed the role of Prospero and beadily supervised the action from an on-stage dressing room. But where the Japanese production opened up imaginative horizons, this one reduced the play to a banal comment on the nature of performance.

As he does so often, it was Dr. Miller — arguably the best-read director on the British stage — who provided the most mentally bracing production, reminding us that "The Tempest" directly reflects Jacobean intellectual concerns. Dr. Miller saw the play as stemming from a period when the occult philosophy of the Renaissance was giving way to mod-

ern scientific thought. His Prospero was both an old-fashioned magus and a post-Copernican with an astronomer's telescope in his cell.

But Dr. Miller also stressed that Shakespeare was drawing on the literature of discovery and exploration — in particular William Strachey's account of the wreck and miraculous recovery of the Sea-Adventure off the Bermudan coast in 1609 — and the Jacobean fascination with colonialism. Thus Mr. von Sydow's Prospero became a white overlord manipulating a mutinous black Caliban and a collaborative Ariel keenly mimicking the gestures of the island's invaders. The colonial metaphor was pushed through to its logical conclusion so that finally Ariel gathered up the pieces of Prospero's abandoned staff and, watched by awe-struck tribesmen, fitted them back together to hold his wand of office aloft before an immobilized Caliban. "The Tempest" suddenly acquired a new political dimension unforeseen by Shakespeare.

◼

They say there is a perfect production of "Twelfth Night" laid up for us in Heaven; and maybe "The Tempest" is too intractable a drama ever to yield up all its secrets in one production. What the recent storm of "Tempest"'s has done, however, is to banish the sentimental notion of the play as Shakespeare's farewell to his art and a thinly disguised piece of autobiography. Instead what has emerged is a play about a Faustian despot that combines myth, magic and the occult with a reflection of Jacobean realities including power structures, philosophy, science and the exploration of the New World. It seems a much bigger play than it did a year ago and, in the words of Anne Barton, an infinitely obliging work of art. ☐

1989 Ja 1, II:5:1

Present to Past, Fact to Fantasy

PHANTASIE, by Sybille Pearson; directed by John Rubinstein; scenic design, William Barclay; lighting design, Phil Monat; costume design, Deborah Shaw; sound design, Phil Lee; production stage manager, Shannon Graves. Presented by the Vineyard Theater, 309 East 26th Street.

D	Diane Salinger
Leah	Elzbieta Czyzewska
Michael	Michael French
Valerie	Laurinda Barrett

WITH: Myra Taylor and Ryan Cutrona

By MEL GUSSOW

An adoptee searches for her natural mother in Sybille Pearson's "Phantasie," but that search is less for a new parent than it is for clues to the character's buried self. Without knowledge of the circumstances of her birth or of her parentage, the woman (Diane Salinger) has had to fantasize possibilities. In her imaginative musings, she is everything from the child of a mother who was raped to the unacknowledged daughter of a Rothschild.

In this perceptive new play, the woman's adoptive mother (Elzbieta Czyzewska) is close, maternal and caring. There are no serious mother-daughter conflicts, except, perhaps, on the daughter's side. She has a tendency to be reserved to the point of seeming cold, erecting a wall of defensiveness, a wall that even her well-meaning husband finds difficult to overcome.

As skillfully directed, by John Rubinstein at the Vineyard Theater, "Phantasie" is the opposite of a made-for-television problem movie, in which, in quasi-documentary fashion, a drama moves step by step toward resolution. Ms. Pearson's play is inward and elliptical, at times enigmatic. The central character's quest will continue long after the play has ended. There are no sudden emotional outbursts or last-minute revelations. The drama remains interior; the playwright seems as reserved as her protagonist and, in a strange way, that intensifies the interest.

One can feel the character's tentativeness, her frustration and her growing hope, as she embarks on her investigation. With the help of various agencies, she canvasses hospitals and combs telephone directories and is gradually led back into her early history. The search becomes her self-analysis, as she realizes that her adult air of apology can be traced to her childhood insecurity. Without justification, she was afraid of being sent

An interior drama without a resolution.

back, of losing her adopted life. She has always tried to live up to a superimposed ideal — and found herself wanting.

As relief, she has adopted various personas. Her name varies. To her mother, she is Dorothy; to her husband she is "D" (for daughter?), and a third name with that initial letter awaits her in her past. Despite her apparent timidity, she has clownish instincts, revealed in direct conversation with the audience. Ms. Pearson,

the author of "Sally and Marsha," follows the stream of experience from present to past, from fact to fantasy. Even as the daughter learns something about her antecedents, she never loses her trepidation, deepened by the fact that she herself is about to become a mother.

There is no denouement as in Shakespeare, with prodigal children and regretful parents locked in a family embrace. Though it occupies much of the second act, the eventual encounter with her birth mother seems to pass in an instant. Trying hard to recall specifics of that meeting and regretting the missed opportunity, she says, "No one should go to a reunion without a paid impartial observer." In a sense, the audience acts as that observer. We read the mother-daughter meeting for all its nuances.

Unanswered questions still abound, but the daughter has emanations of her origin, finding a semblance of herself in stories about her natural grandmother, who seemingly shared with her a youthful wildness, a gift of imagination, or "phantasie." In the play's most touching scene, the protagonist imagines a meeting with her adoptive mother in which they finally are able to move past silences to an exchange of confidences. Although the play does not achieve the emotional heights of the recent Gillian Armstrong movie on a similar subject, "Hide Tide," it finds a truthfulness within a natural reserve. "Phantasie" is small and quietly affecting.

In Ms. Salinger's sometimes brittle performance, the daughter is always trying to arm herself against rejection, even as Ms. Czyzewska offers love as well as kinship. Laurinda Barrett and Michael French are helpful in supporting roles and Ryan Cutrona and Myra Taylor fill out the canvas as all the doctors, social workers and desk clerks encountered on this intimate journey of discovery.

1989 Ja 4, C15:5

Crying Over Unspilled Milk

FOR DEAR LIFE, by Susan Miller; directed by Norman René; set by Loy Arcenas; costumes by Walker Hicklin; lighting by Arden Fingerhut; dance by Theodore Pappas; fight staged by B. H. Barry; associate producer, Jason Steven Cohen. Presented by Joseph Papp. At the Public Theater, Martinson Hall, 425 Lafayette Street.

Jake	Tony Shalhoub
Maggie	Bellina Logan
Catherine	Laila Robins
Dottie	Christine Estabrook
Peter	Joseph Lambie
Sam	Stephen Mailer
Emily	Jennifer Aniston

By FRANK RICH

The relentlessly right-thinking and ferociously articulate characters in Susan Miller's new play, "For Dear Life," are the kind of people who can't contemplate the change of seasons without anticipating nuclear winter. They can't pour a glass of milk without crying over the snapshot of a missing child on the carton. They can't go to the bathroom without worrying about the depletion of the ozone layer.

They're not exactly a fun crowd, and they wear out their welcome quickly at the Public Theater. Were "For Dear Life" a satirical dissection of its pretentious characters or a serious discussion of the social issues to which the dialogue pays lip service, it might at least qualify as an attenuated revue sketch or, failing that, as a syllabus for the New School. But Ms. Miller, the author of "Nasty Rumors and Final Remarks" and "Flux," has so little distance on her material that "For Dear Life" is as smug and narcissistic as the indolent dilettantes who inhabit it.

The play's ostensible subject is marriage. Jake (Tony Shalhoub), a disk jockey infatuated with old standards and major league baseball, and Catherine (Laila Robins), a film critic, seem perfectly happy, but Jake is worried. The world is falling apart, so why shouldn't their marriage follow suit? "Maybe it's just that you and Catherine are impatient with each other's gestalt," says their helpful friend Dottie (Christine Estabrook), a West Coast film maker.

Then again, maybe not. By Act II, set almost two decades later, the marriage has indeed broken up, though we don't know why; Jake and Catherine, both devoted to their mildly rebellious teen-age son (Stephen Mailer), still seem to be in love. In Act III, Ms. Miller flashes back to the son's first birthday, but once again she withholds any explanation of the couple's divorce, announcing instead that it's a waste of time to "look for reasons." Why should Ms. Miller do the hard work of examining her characters when she can end her play with a laundry list of buzzwords (Hitler, the atomic bomb, Vietnam, AIDS) that so efficiently illustrate how deeply concerned a citizen she is?

Early on, Jake and Catherine speak of the "long-researched phrases" they use in their writing, and apparently this is Ms. Miller's literary method as well. There isn't a spontaneous line in the script, which, like some of the playwright's previous work, seems an unintentional parody of J. D. Salinger's Glass-family stories. Jake is a happy man because his life "is made up of shimmering minor moments," while the impossibly erudite Catherine is so "tired of syllables" she yearns to have a low-class New Jersey accent. My favorite howler is Jake's poetically expressed fear, while vacationing at his country house, that "a tree could fall into our happiness," though a close second is the unanswered question "Where's the tabula rasa here?"

Such vague phrasemaking ducks the introspection that the play disingenuously purports to provide; even the details that might give the characters a superficial reality are fuzzy. While "For Dear Life" emulates Michael Weller's "Loose Ends," it's all just loose ends. Jake and Catherine's generation is unclear — they eventually seem to be late-fortysomething, though cast a fashionable decade younger — and the shifts in time are apparent only from the Playbill, so completely does the writing blur any distinctions between the play's various periods. No wonder that the talented director, Norman René, can't breathe life, dear or cheap, into any of it, and that some good actors (and not-so-good ones) look consistently silly.

Between the splintery scenes, the audience is treated to Jake's radio program: performers like Sinatra, Astaire and Ella Fitzgerald singing such great songs as "A Foggy Day" and "I Guess I'll Have to Change My

Plan." For trapped theatergoers, unfortunately, plans are not so easily changed.

1989 Ja 11, C17:1

Looking Back

SKIN — A STATE OF BEING, conceived and directed by Ping Chong, in collaboration with John Fleming, Jeannie Hutchins, Dan Froot, Allan Tung and Daryl; set designer, Mr. Chong; lighting designer, Howard Thies; costume designer, Matthew Yokobosky; projections designer, Jan Hartley; sound designer, Brian Hallas; production coordinator, Mery Vladimer; set realized by the La Mama Set Construction Group, David Adams, Mark Tambella and Jun Maeda. Presented by La Mama E.T.C., Ellen Stewart, artistic director. At La Mama E.T.C. Annex, 64 East Fourth Street.

WITH: John Fleming, Dan Froot, Jeannie Hutchins, Allan Tung, Louise Smith and Daryl.

By MEL GUSSOW

In "Skin — a State of Being" (at La Mama Annex), Ping Chong takes his audience aloft into a cloudland of airy activities. As cumulus images drift by in the background, offstage voices of polite flight attendants settle us into our seats, preparing travelers for an armchair theatrical adventure. A real airline should be so soothing and accommodating. Ping Chong Airways is not about to overbook or to fly in an endless holding pattern.

There are clues that this will be an unusual journey, beginning with the scenery. We are told that on one side of the plane is Mount Fuji and on the opposite side, Grant's Tomb. Fastening our metaphorical seat belts, we await all eventualities and discover surprises along with occasional irritations. What follows is an hour of Mr. Chong at his most abstruse. The show is evocative, especially in the visual design, but it is not as enticing as the author's "Kind Ness" and "A Race," although it expands on aspects of both and of other of his experimental works.

On the current journey, created in collaboration with Mr. Chong's company of actors, he moves backward from supersonic civilization to primitive times. In flight, we encounter a race of humanoids with froglike heads, and in a series of episodes they re-enact a life process, from birth through education and courtship.

The play is intended as a reminder of the uniqueness of our existence. In actuality, it is a reminder of the uniqueness of Ping Chong. In contrast with many other performance artists, he is a wry cultural annotator, fond of puns and conundrums. The waggish humor enlivens the trip but does not entirely alleviate the obscurities. Repeatedly, one wants to ask the playwright-pilot to explain the mission.

The best approach, of course, is to play along with the celestial circumnavigation and to select and reject images. For me, there were a few too many froggy leaps by the actors around the stage. The voices on the imaginary plane's sound system and the Bunraku-like puppeteers manipulating sculptural birds were more intriguing.

Along the way to Xanadu, Mr. Chong offers random comments on the suppression of the weak by the powerful and the enslavement of women by men — and vice versa. But principally, he seems concerned with shamans and symbols. If I understand it correctly — and with Mr. Chong there is always room for interpretation — "Skin" is a play about nostalgia, about the baggage of informed memory that is passed down through generations of passengers on their life flight.

1989 Ja 12, C15:1

Turgenev, With License

By MEL GUSSOW

Special to The New York Times

HARTFORD, Jan. 11 — Brian Friel labeled his recent adaptation of the novel "Fathers and Sons" "after Turgenev" to indicate that he had taken certain artistic liberties with the original. In his version, "Nothing Sacred" (at Hartford Stage), the Canadian playwright George F. Walker has assumed artistic license.

Since its premiere last January in Toronto, "Nothing Sacred" has become one of the most popular new plays in American regional theaters; Hartford Stage is one of six to schedule productions. In the program, Mr. Walker announces that this is not an adaptation, but a play inspired by the novel, adding, "I think you can't approach these dead guys with unreserved reverence." One would have hoped at least for a little reserved reverence.

•

Although there were alterations, Mr. Friel's adaptation (presented last season at the Long Wharf Theater in New Haven) was faithful to "Fathers and Sons" both in details and in spirit. Mr. Walker's play is an entirely different samovar, but just close enough in outline as to make the playwright's disclaimer ingenuous. His iconoclastic view is summarized by the title of his play, borrowed from the 1937 Fredric March-Carole Lombard film.

Despite his statement that "Nothing Sacred" is a "Canadian comedy not a Russian tragedy," it takes place in the novel's time and place. The playwright refers to the characters — the ones he retains — by their original names and they share relationships as in Turgenev.

The novel, Turgenev's acknowledged masterpiece, focuses on the character of Bazarov, the proud nihilist (and doctor) who challenges traditional values — those held by his parents, by the father of his acolyte, Arkady, and in particular by Arkady's Uncle Pavel, a Russian dandy irrepressibly infatuated with Western culture.

•

In Mr. Walker's version, Bazarov (Christian Baskous) becomes a diabolical clown as well as something of a vulgarian and Pavel (Richard M. Davidson) a ridiculous fop. Both characters veer into caricature. In the novel, Pavel challenges Bazarov to a duel, in which the older man is superficially wounded. In the play, Pavel kills Bazarov in that duel, and Bazarov's body is thrown on the trash heap (an accumulation of broken tables, wheels and spare parts that line the open stage like an automobile graveyard).

Dying such a fool's death robs Bazarov of his tragic dimension and vitiates the political weight of the novel. It also eliminates one of the most moving death scenes in all literature.

The tragedy of Bazarov is that he — a confirmed skeptic — succumbs to an unfulfilled romantic love for a wealthy widow and later pays the price for his own awakened idealism. He dies of an infection contracted while treating peasants for typhoid fever. Mr. Walker's changes include the suggestion that Bazarov's relationship with the widow is an affair that precedes the events of the play by several years. The playwright has also elected to keep Bazarov's parents offstage, weakening the generational conflict between fathers and sons.

In quest of comedy, he moves his play dangerously close to whimsy. Flowers repeatedly sprout on cue through the floorboards of the stage and at one point a character proclaims, "I ain't going up against the wood demon," as if the adapter had momentarily confused Turgenev with a cowboy version of Chekhov. Though Mr. Walker's exact purpose remains undefined, one might surmise that his interest is at least partly deflationary.

•

The play is effective in two respects: in showing the alliance between Bazarov and Arkady (they wander through the landscape like Rosencrantz and Guildenstern) and in picturing the subjugation of servants, who are beset by social as well as physical abuse.

The acting wavers with, under the playwright's guidelines, the most persuasive performances coming from Mr. Baskous (a brusque, arrogant Bazarov) and Robert Stanton as Arkady. James Simpson, as director, and his set designer, Michael Yeargan, have given the play a fluid physical production, including a wheat field backdrop that further anchors the adaptation in Russia — even as the adapter keeps prodding it toward limbo.

It was Isaiah Berlin who said that by exploring man's moral predicament Turgenev's novels, especially "Fathers and Sons," are basic documents "for the understanding of the Russian past and of our present." In his eccentric dramatization, Mr. Walker has made Turgenev seem remote.

1989 Ja 13, C5:1

Tom Lehrer's Words, 20 Years Later

TOMFOOLERY, words, music and lyrics by Tom Lehrer; adapted by Cameron Mackintosh and Robin Ray; director and choreographer, Pamela Hunt; musical arrangements by Chris Walker and Robert Fisher; additional arrangements and orchestrations by Bob McDowell; set design, Randolph Alexander; light design, Kenneth J. Lapham; costume design, Thomas Lee Keller; musical director, Bob McDowell; production stage manager, Jon Roger Clark. Presented by Equity Library Theater. 103d Street and Riverside Drive.

WITH: Don Bradford, Jack Doyle, Patricia Masters and John Remme.

By STEPHEN HOLDEN

More than two decades after many of them were written, the songs of Tom Lehrer still feel remarkably contemporary. Writing about politics and culture in a relatively optimistic time, Mr. Lehrer distilled a snobbish, cold-blooded misanthropy that went sharply against the cultural grain.

In the Equity Library Theater's revival of "Tomfoolery," a revue of Lehrer songs performed eight years ago at the Village Gate, several of the songs have the ring of predictions that came true. "Pollution," "George Murphy," "National Brotherhood Week," "Smut" and "The Old Dope Peddler," respectively anticipated syringe-littered beaches, the Reagan Presidency, the "not in my backyard" syndrome, and the glut of pornography and drugs.

The production, directed by Pamela Hunt and featuring Don Bradford, Jack Doyle, Patricia Masters and John Remme, is set in an Ivy League campus coffee shop in the early 1960's. The setting underscores a tone of academic smugness that runs through Mr. Lehrer's lyrics, whose rhymes are as impeccable as the sentiments are icy. Among the players, Mr. Remme most closely evokes the composer. Tweedy and snooty, he gives his numbers the same gleeful twist of cynicism that Mr. Lehrer used to give them in his performances.

1989 Ja 14, 10:4

Through a Keyhole, Darkly

ULYSSES IN NIGHTTOWN, adapted from a chapter of James Joyce's novel "Ulysses." Dramatized by Marjorie Barkentin; directed by Wayne Martens; production stage manager, Carol Venezia; assistants to the director, Monique Miller and James Sullivan; lighting designer, Edward R.F. Matthews; technical director, Betsy J. Wingfield. Presented by Mr. Martens, in association with the Harold Clurman Theater. At the Samuel Beckett Theater, 410 West 42d Street.

WITH: Leslie Block, Stephen Vincent Brennan, James Burke, Cheryl Clifford, Steve Coats, Jayne Amelia Larson, Joseph McKenna, Erin McLaughlin, Robert Molnar, David Teschendorf, Steve Varnum, Carol Venezia, Michele Winslow and Kurt Ziskie.

By STEPHEN HOLDEN

If evocative language were the cornerstone of compelling drama, "Ulysses in Nighttown," Marjorie Barkentin's dramatization of the Walpurgisnacht episode from Joyce's "Ulysses" might qualify as a modern classic. Faithful to the letter of Joyce's prose, the play — a mosaic of scenes connected by a narrator — follows Leopold Bloom and Stephen Dedalus on a June evening in 1904 into the fleshpots of Dublin where they find themselves in a phantasmagoric brothel.

But language alone cannot carry a drama, and "Ulysses in Nighttown" has not worn well since its 1958 production gained instant recognition for Zero Mostel, who originated the role of Bloom and repeated it on Broadway in 1974. In its latest revival by the Harold Clurman Theater Production Company at the Samuel Beckett Theater, the play unfolds as a choppy sequence of dramatized illustrations for a work whose meanings are too richly layered to reveal themselves readily on the stage. Directed by Wayne Martens and featuring a cast of 13 actors, most of whom play multiple roles, the production is scrupulously acted but lacks a dramatic center.

•

Foremost among the missing ingredients is a commanding central performance. As portrayed by Steve Coats, Leopold Bloom, a mild-mannered milquetoast in his day-to-day relations, appears equally taciturn when acting out his deepest fantasies of sexual abasement and personal glory.

The role offers an actor a chance to change instantaneously from shrinking violet to imperious egomaniac as he fantasizes himself a national hero. During explicit scenes of sadomasochistic humiliation in the brothel, his Bloom remains an inert lump whose clownish mugging reveals neither en-

Leslie Block and Steve Coats in "Ulysses in Nighttown."

joyment nor pain. Mr. Mostel's oversized vaudevillian Bloom may not have been true to Joyce, but at least it offered a sense of larger-than-life subconscious forces roiling beneath the character's placid exterior.

•

Without a magnetic center, the production's virtues seem tangential. David Teschendorf's portrayal of the rowdy Buck Mulligan; Kurt Ziskie's cheerfully priapic song and dance man, Blazes Boylan; Leslie Block's sensuous Molly Bloom, and James

Burke's questing Stephen Dedalus glimmer with light and poetry, but the play gives neither Molly nor Stephen enough space for an actor to develop them as more than sketches.

The setting is very spare. Robert Molnar, as the narrator, sits perched atop a high judge's bench, the legs of which form a giant keyhole. Mr. Molnar's muted delivery sets the tone for an evening in which dramatic excitement is subjugated to literary earnestness.

1989 Ja 15,44:1

THEATER VIEW

By FRANK RICH

West End Risks and Rewards

LONDON

A N EXPATRIATE AMERICAN FRIEND OF mine who has devoted five years to voracious London theatergoing is thinking of moving home to New York. I asked him what he would miss most about the theater in London and wasn't surprised when he failed to answer "musicals on roller skates." But I was wrong to assume that he would rhapsodize about "the classics" or the Royal Shakespeare Company or the National Theater. "I'm beginning to worry that there can be too much Shakespeare," he said, referring to the five not altogether distinguished productions of "The Tempest" he'd already seen this year. "What I'll really miss most," he said, "is Vanessa Redgrave. I've seen her give a half-dozen performances that I'll never forget."

Miss Redgrave is giving one of those performances right now in a West End revival of Tennessee Williams's "Orpheus Descending." Will homebound Americans ever see it? One can hardly assume so; Miss Redgrave, whose vocal support for the Palestine Liberation Organization is repugnant to many, has been conspicuously absent from our stages since the Boston Symphony Orchestra canceled her engagement as a narrator for Stravinsky's "Oedipus Rex" in 1982. In the meantime, Americans are missing the creative prime of the greatest actress in the English-speaking theater.

But "Orpheus Descending," as directed by Peter Hall, is not merely a platform for Miss Redgrave's personal triumph. It is a landmark production full of implications for the American theater. When originally produced on Broadway in 1957, "Orpheus Descending," a revision of its author's 1940 "Battle of Angels," lasted only two months, in spite of sensitive collaborators that included the director Harold Clurman, the actress Maureen Stapleton and the designer Boris Aronson. Once the film version ("The Fugitive Kind") came and went, the play was largely forgotten. To much of the American theater — the high-minded nonprofit theater included — a Broadway flop is an untouchable, no matter who wrote it. How many American companies would think of dusting off "Orpheus Descending"? There's more cachet in rejiggering a Pirandello text yet one more time than in attempting an adventurous re-examination of a Broadway failure by a native writer.

Enter Miss Redgrave and Mr. Hall, who lavish such passion and imagination on Williams's mongrel play that their efforts would be heroic and touching even if the results were not as thrilling as they are. While Mr. Hall's staging retains a semblance of the

work's ostensible setting, a dry-goods store in the sleepy deep South, the director elevates the action and language to the fever-pitch of Gothic hallucination with expressionist lighting, understated electronic music and lurid B-movie imagery drawn from Hollywood film noir. By unearthing the play's modern, anti-naturalistic theatricality, Mr. Hall not only salvages "Orpheus Descending" — which some London critics assumed to be a widely circulated classic back home — but also may have found an esthetic route into some of the obstinate works that subsequently derailed the playwright's career.

Miss Redgrave makes her contribution to the reclamation by finding a classic Williams heroine in the role of Lady Torrance, the lonely middle-aged daughter of an Italian immigrant murdered by the Ku Klux Klan. When Lady Torrance is liberated from the oppression of her mean, cancer-ridden husband by the arrival of her Orpheus, an Elvis-like drifter played by Jean-Marc Barr, the actress blossoms from a dour storekeeper into an incandescent spirit determined "not to be defeated." When defeat inexorably comes, at the hands of the mendacious and bigoted bullies who invariably crush Williams's angels, the bloody demise of the tall, festively dressed Miss Redgrave is a harrowing sight — as if the most towering and verdant tree in a forest were slowly toppling to the ground.

■

What makes the Hall-Redgrave "Orpheus Descending" doubly daring by American standards is its presentation under commercial auspices. This is the first attraction of the new Peter Hall Company, a London-New York producing venture that the director undertook this fall, upon retiring as head of the National Theater after a 15-year rule. Certainly Mr. Hall could have inaugurated this precarious operation with a safer project; Miss Redgrave could have starred in "A Streetcar Named Desire." It says much about the director's courage — and his belief in Tennessee Williams — that he would gamble his new company on an experimental production of an American play that few American directors would consider staging even as part of a nonprofit subscription season.

This is consistent with Mr. Hall's career; he approaches Williams today with the same pioneering vigor he brought to Shakespeare when he was creating the Royal Shakespeare Company a generation ago. (Miss Redgrave appeared in one of his early Stratford-upon-Avon productions, the Laurence Olivier "Coriolanus" of 1959.) Mr. Hall is also a longtime champion of American writers, their neglected works included. An old poster

'Orpheus Descending' is a both a landmark production and a personal triumph for Vanessa Redgrave.

Shakespeare's present London base reawakened my memory of Mr. Hall's restoration of another Broadway failure, Edward Albee's "All Over," with Peggy Ashcroft and Angela Lansbury, at the Aldwych Theater in 1972. And Mr. Hall's affection for American playwrights is now shared by Miss Redgrave. Early this year, she and Timothy Dalton made a powerful case for O'Neill's rarely seen "Touch of the Poet." The actress's next

Photographs by Alastair Muir

Ms. Redgrave in "Orpheus Descending"

stage assignment is a new play by the London-based American writer Martin Sherman (the author of "Bent").

Necessity demands that the Peter Hall Company balance risks like "Orpheus Descending" with box-office sure things. (Next up is a Dustin Hoffman "Merchant of Venice.") Mr. Hall is a showman, after all; one of his less fondly remembered American projects at the National was the ill-fated musical biography of Jean Seberg. Whether he can survive the ruthless economic realities of the commercial theater over the long run in London, let alone in New York, will depend on the depth of his company's pockets and perhaps the availability of stars. If "Orpheus Descending" had failed, would the Peter Hall Company already be scrambling to keep its backers from deserting?

To a visitor, the West End theatrical marketplace hardly seems hospitable territory for even as shrewd an impresario as Mr. Hall. Shaftesbury Avenue continues to sink to the same tourists' common denominator as Broadway. With the exception of such anomalous attractions as the Jonathan Miller season of classics at the Old Vic and Derek Jacobi's repertory of "Richard II" and "Richard III" at the Phoenix, the commercial theater of London is almost all déjà vu for the American visitor. Of the 33 plays and musicals running in the West End in mid-December, well more than half have been seen in New York (from "Sugar Babies" to "A Walk in the Woods" to "Cats" and even "Can-Can"). The number of brand-new plays to arrive in the West End since the summer, roughly half a dozen, only

slightly exceeds the dismal Broadway total. In weak dollars, top London ticket prices are now approaching Broadway's. And, for all the blather about the English musical's renaissance, London, like New York, hasn't seen a new musical hit since "The Phantom of the Opera."

The only two new serious plays I found in the West End originated in institutional theaters, just like such Broadway equivalents as "Spoils of War" and "Eastern Standard." Nicholas Wright's "Mrs. Klein" is a transfer from the National Theater, where Mr. Wright is literary manager. "Henceforward," Alan Ayckbourn's latest, was first produced at the playwright's home company in Scarborough.

Both works have been enthusiastically received — a phenomenon an American theatergoer can comprehend without necessarily endorsing. The three-character "Mrs. Klein" is a chamber docudrama (complete with its own tasteful offstage chamber-music quartet for scene changes) in the mold of such West End hits as "Duet for One," "84 Charing Cross Road" and "Breaking the Code." The real-life figure at center stage, the iconoclastic psychoanalyst Melanie Klein (Gillian Barge), is diagrammatically revealed as a physician who should have healed herself before lecturing anyone else on how not to be a Jewish mother. While Miss Barge embodies her part perfectly, she fails to deliver the fiery star performance that can galvanize talky middlebrow drama of this type. For me, the evening's fascination came in the second act, when Zoë Wanamaker, stuck with an omnipresent but frequently mute role, demonstrated how many different contemplative poses it is possible for an actress to strike, with and without cigarette in hand, while patiently waiting for infrequent cues.

The prolific Mr. Ayckbourn, whose two major works of the 1980's ("A Chorus of Disapproval" and "A Small Family Business") appeared under Mr. Hall's aegis at the National (and remain unproduced in New York), continues to bend theatrical form and to delve into the spiritual void he finds beneath the bucolic surface of the English middle class.

But "Henceforward" is slight: a cautionary tale about the future in which a blocked electronic composer (Ian McKellen) proves so alienated that he opts for machines over people. With its apocalyptic urban violence and heavy ironies about humanity and technology, the play seems an already dated rehash of "A Clockwork Orange," the film "Brazil" and Jules Feiffer's "Little Murders." Perhaps the text would seem sharper in another production; this is not one of Mr. Ayckbourn's more graceful directing jobs. The gimcrack-filled set doesn't evoke future-shock so much as a playboy pad of 1959; Mr. McKellen seems completely ill at ease, as if he weren't sure whether he had landed in a boulevard comedy or "Krapp's Last Tape." Only Jane Asher, contributing a striking double-turn as a domestic robot and a flesh-and-blood estranged wife, rescues "Henceforward" from its own mechanical cleverness.

∎

The exciting new plays in London so far this season have been in repertory at the National — even if only passing through that institution on their way to the West End and points beyond. Harold Pinter's "Mountain Language," Alan Bennett's "Single Spies" and David Hare's "Secret Rapture" — each elegantly produced as well as written — augur well for the company's post-Hall vitality under the new artistic director, Richard Eyre.

All three plays are ineffably English, which is to say that they are political. (And austerely so by American standards: AIDS, now a fixture of socially concerned New York plays, went unmentioned in the London plays I saw.) The bleakest of the National's

Jill Baker in David Hare's "Secret Rapture"

trio was Mr. Pinter's 20-minute work — a harsh series of glimpses into an unidentified police state (surely not Northern Ireland) whose underworld of officially sanctioned torture takes one back full-circle to the creepy mental asylum of the author's early drama of bureaucratic menace, the 1958 "Hothouse." In "Single Spies," Mr. Bennett, who first found prominence in the Cambridge-spawned "Beyond the Fringe," looks at the earlier Cambridge generation that nurtured the traitors Guy Burgess (played by Simon Callow) and Anthony Blunt (played by Mr. Bennett). Even audiences who have tired of this profusely documented case may find "Single Spies" a riveting dramatization of that juncture where national, class, intellectual and sexual loyalties all come into ludicrously comic conflict. For added fun, Prunella Scales offers an uncanny impersonation of Queen Elizabeth II, who seems even more enigmatic than the Soviet spies in her midst.

"The Secret Rapture," Mr. Hare's sorrowful parable of Thatcher-era England, will reach the New York Shakespeare Festival next fall in a new production starring Blair Brown, to whom the author dedicates the published script. Ms. Brown's role, well filled by Jill Baker at the National, is the angelic flip side of Susan Traherne in "Plenty" she only wants to do the moral, even

saintly, thing in a society of unbridled greed. Of course, she is destroyed, in an act of violence comparable to that which martyrs Miss Redgrave's heroine in "Orpheus Descending."

There are two other principal women, each compelling, in "The Secret Rapture"; few male playwrights since Williams have written female characters to match Mr. Hare's. But what does it say about our theater that an English writer's latest work, however welcome, is certain to reach New York while our own master dramatist's reborn tragic heroine remains in exile, with no guarantee of safe passage home?

1989 Ja 15, II:1:4

Correction

Because of a mechanical error, the Theater View column on page 5 of the Arts and Leisure section today appears with a sentence omitted. The sentence should have read, "An old poster behind a refreshment stand at the Royal Shakespeare's present London base reawakened my memory of Mr. Hall's restoration of another Broadway failure, Edward Albee's 'All Over,' with Peggy Ashcroft and Angela Lansbury, at the Aldwych Theater in 1972."

1989 Ja 15, 3:1

Macho Memories

By STEPHEN HOLDEN

"Guys like to fight — it's like petting but it's hard and very fast," observes John O'Keefe in "Shimmer," a rivetingly kinetic solo performance piece in which he remembers his troubled adolescence in Iowa in the mid-1950's.

Mr. O'Keefe, a playwright and actor whose surreal family drama "All Night Long" was produced in 1984 in New York at Second Stage, might be described as the Clint Eastwood of performance artists. Wearing a plain white T-shirt with rolled-up sleeves, jeans and work boots, the writer, now in his mid-40's, exudes the crackling machismo of an archetypal American rebel-fighter. Reminiscing about life on a juvenile detention farm in 1955, he re-creates an entire gallery of surly adolescents and their grim custodians.

•

In those days, Mr. O'Keefe recalls, his nickname was Captain Spacey because he had dreams of becoming an astronaut. The title of the piece refers to the crude mystical philosophy that he and his best friend Gary invent to describe their spooky spiritual apprehensions. They imagine that everything from radio static to smoke curling off a cigarette embodies a secret code they call "Shimmer."

Arranged as a series of dramatically lighted blackout scenes, Mr. O'Keefe's hour-and-15-minute monologue begins with pungent descriptions of life on the farm and gathers momentum as the narrator and his best friend conceive and carry out a risky escape plan. The diction and imagery of Mr. O'Keefe's prose recaptures with astounding fidelity the turbulent, quick-changing emotions and the acute sensory experience of adolescence.

Gliding and shadowboxing around the stage, Mr. O'Keefe physically re-enacts fights and confrontations with an edgy ferocity that feels so spontaneous one can almost forget the fact that every moment of the piece, which is to be performed through Jan. 29 at Performance Space 122 (150 First Avenue, at Ninth Street) has been carefully rehearsed. And at key emotional moments, Mr. O'Keefe's speaking voice shades into song. If his work lacks ultimately lacks the sociological weight of Eric Bogosian's performance pieces or the layered ironies of Spalding Gray's monologues, it is bravura storytelling that etches itself on the mind.

1989 Ja 16, C15:1

One Man, 2 Cities And a Baby

A TALE OF TWO CITIES, by Charles Dickens; adapted by Everett Quinton; directed by Kate Stafford; sets by Jan Bell, James Eckerle and Daphne Groos; costumes by Susan Young; lights by Richard Currie. Presented by the Ridiculous Theatrical Company, at the Charles Ludlam Theater, 1 Sheridan Square.

WITH: Everett Quinton

By FRANK RICH

"What in the gay hell?" asks a startled Everett Quinton upon opening his apartment door during the early moments of the new Ridiculous Theatrical Company production, "A Tale of Two Cities." In true Dickensian fashion, Mr. Quinton, playing the role of an aspiring transvestite club performer, has just discovered that he is the recipient of an abandoned baby in a milk crate. The infant is sobbing; the new adoptive father takes it personally. "He's a straight baby," Mr. Quinton concludes. "But we can coexist. I know it can be done."

How it is done is the premise of this 90-minute one-man farce, as both written and performed by Mr. Quinton. Hoping so to quiet the child so he can dress up for his big break, a rock-singing gig that night, Mr. Quinton tries telling a fairy tale. The Grimms won't do. "It was the best of times, it was the worst of times," says Mr. Quinton in frustration. Before long, he is acting out Dickens's novel of the French Revolution, from the passing

8

of the coded message "recalled to life" on a Dover-bound coach to Sydney Carton's final assignation with the Paris guillotine.

•

But there are really three tales being told in this "Tale of Two Cities," and it is their constant interplay that makes for an always fascinating, sometimes funny and finally moving evening. At face value, the piece is a stunt resembling the Ridiculous's "Mystery of Irma Vep," a mock-Victorian "penny dreadful" in which Mr. Quinton and Charles Ludlam played all the roles. Yet this time the period melodrama is always enclosed within the frame of the contemporary cold-water-flat setting,

The theater's first work without a text by Ludlam since he died.

with its microwave oven and ringing telephone: we never forget that Mr. Quinton is playing a drag performer (and sometime wigmaker) who is in turn undertaking his many Dickensian characters. And arcing inevitably over the entire enterprise is another, real-life drama. While there have been other Ridiculous productions since Mr. Ludlam, the company's inventor, died at age 44 in 1987, this is the first not to use a Ludlam text — the first in which Mr. Quinton, the new artistic leader, steps out fully on his own.

•

Some of the evening is what Ridiculous fans expect. Though Mr. Quinton doesn't have Mr. Ludlam's range as a performer, and his impersonations can be strained, his wittiest turns are riotous. As Mme. Defarge, psychotic revolutionary and "vendor of wine," he not only knits up a malevolent storm but also does a stunning burlesque of Blanche Yurka's portrayal of the role in the 1935 David O. Selznick film. No less enjoyable are Mr. Quinton's readings of the animated maid Miss Pross, the lisping informer John Bassad and the loathsome aristocrat St. Evrémonde (with his withering contempt for the "sickness that labels itself humanitarianism").

By choosing a classic novel as a source and remaining true to it in his fashion (his Caedmon Records diction included), Mr. Quinton is following the Ludlam example of such past Ridiculous plays as "Camille," "Medea" and "Le Bourgeois Avant-Garde." By making delighted use of simple found objects as props and costumes — a Murphy bed for the Bastille, bird cages for the heroine Lucie Manette's skirt — he is also upholding the let's-put-on-a-show spirit that has always linked the Ridiculous to classic traditions in theater. But it's not just theatrical paraphernalia that tumbles out of the closet in "A Tale of Two Cities," and it isn't only the French Revolution that gives the play its political content.

•

Without being preachy about it, Mr. Quinton does, after all, take us into the heart of a man, unnamed, who dreams of acting the role of a woman. Though the Dickens narrative never subsides, the performer delivers

Anita and Steve Shevett

Everett Quinton in a scene from the new Ridiculous Theatrical Company production, "A Tale of Two Cities."

some of it nude, some of it while shaving in a bathtub, some of it in racy black lingerie. By the time he gets to the final prison encounter in which Sydney Carton martyrs himself by switching identities with the doomed Charles Darnay, Mr. Quinton has accomplished his own identity switch as well. High-heeled shoes, a glittering gown, a red wig and elaborate makeup successfully complete his metamorphosis from a bald, funny-looking man, a sort of cartoonish Hume Cronyn, into a glamorous chanteuse.

The transformation is not flamboyantly comic, as might be expected, but as earnest and straightforward as the contrapuntal one in Dickens. The audience recognizes that it is witnessing a serious act of self-revelation that makes intriguing connections between role-playing in the theater and elsewhere. Though such issues have always been implicit in Ridiculous theatricals, Mr. Quinton pushes them

center stage. And he does so without sentimentality. It's a joyful gay performer, as dignified as Sydney Carton, who emerges at the end of the tale, and one too honest to pretend to be what he's not. The baby must inevitably go the way of the bathwater.

One can easily pick at "A Tale of Two Cities." Both the star and his new director, the performance art stalwart Kate Stafford, might have trimmed a good 20 minutes of stalled characterizations and repetitions. There are trashy gags, many of them at the infant's expense, that pander to the gallery. But there is also an independent sensibility hard at work here, honoring Charles Ludlam's legacy while putting a personal stamp on it. I left Sheridan Square with the high feeling that the Ridiculous Theatrical Company had been recalled to life.

1989 Ja 18, C15:4

A Lion in Love

MAX AND MAXIE, by James McLure; directed by D. Lynn Meyers; sets and costume design, Eduardo Sicangco; lighting design, Kirk Bookman and David Neville; production stage manager, Victor Lukas; technical director, Serge Hunkins. Presented by the York Theater Company, Janet Hayes Walker, producing director; Molly Pickering Grose, managing director. At 2 East 90th Street.

Max .... John Newton
Maxie .... Sandy Roveta
The Boy .... Robin Haynes

By MEL GUSSOW

A famous clown named Max Luck is in Florida rehearsing a role in an avant-garde tragicomedy (very much like "Waiting for Godot"), and his insecurity in the play sends him into a swirl of memories about his early days in vaudeville. For many years, he and his partner, Maxie (later his first wife), had been struggling troupers. As Max began to be successful on his own, Maxie was overcome by mental illness. Eventu-

ally she was institutionalized, leaving her celebrated husband with feelings of remorse and guilt.

If that summary of the events in James McLure's new play, "Max and Maxie," seems to parallel the actual story of Bert Lahr and his first wife, Mercedes Delpino, it is no accident. In an earlier version at the Denver Center Theater Company, the play was entitled "Lahr and Mercedes."

Though "Max and Maxie" at the York Theater is fictionalized, it follows the outline of Lahr's life, from his youthful clowning to "Waiting for Godot," which he played in Florida before he opened in it on Broadway. It is difficult to watch the play without thinking about the Bert Lahr behind the Max Luck. While those thoughts enhance our interest, they also make us increasingly cognizant of the play's shortcomings. The character Mr. McLure has created is never as sizable or as funny as Lahr was, and the "Waiting for Godot" tryout is an awkward framing device.

•

Up to a point, the play is an intriguing character study, through a combi-

nation of factors, including Mr. McLure's own talent for writing comic dialogue (previously demonstrated in "Lone Star," among other plays) and a flavorful performance by John Newton as Max. In one of the play's oddities, Mr. Newton looks and sounds less like Lahr than like Tom Ewell, who co-starred with the comedian in that first American "Godot."

"Max and Maxie" captures the flair of old vaudeville, as the team travels around the country sharpening routines while living at a penurious level. As Max later says, the two hardest things in life are, one, breaking into vaudeville and, two, breaking into vaudeville. When he is reminded that by this time vaudeville is dead, he responds that then life is even harder.

Through his playwright's eye, Mr. McLure views the awakening romance between the partners, a comic and a dancer. He shows us the cheerful adaptability of the young Maxie (an appealing and unaffected performance by Sandy Roveta) and the obsessiveness of Max, who gets up in the middle of the night to work on the act, a scene that is reminiscent of one in "Notes on a Cowardly Lion," John Lahr's revealing biography of his father.

Skating the surface, the playwright telescopes a career and rushes past the Broadway and Hollywood fame in order to deposit the sad clown in limbo in Florida, to have him indicate that he can't go on, and then, of course, go on. The "Godot" passages are further weakened by the presence on stage of a young man as admiring, attitudinizing interviewer. A glimpse of the later Maxie lost in a dream world is not enough. We want to know so much more about the clown's rise and his partner's collapse — and about their interior lives.

Sandy Underwood

John Newton and Sandy Roveta in "Max and Maxie."

D. Lynn Meyers's compact production was initially staged at the Cincinnati Playhouse in the Park, and has been brought to the York with its original cast (Robin Haynes plays the interviewer as well as other minor characters). With the help of Eduardo Sicangco's set and costume design, "Max and Maxie" conveys the theatrical atmosphere and the comedy of early vaudeville. But the play remains an incohesive amalgam of fact and fiction.

1989 Ja 18, C14:6

And the Lord Said . . .

GENESIS: MUSIC AND MIRACLES FROM THE MEDIEVAL MYSTERY PLAYS, book and lyrics by A. J. Antoon and Robert Montgomery; music by Michael Ward; directed by Mr. Antoon; choreography by Lynne Taylor-Corbett; scenery and costumes by John Conklin; lighting by Jan Kroeze; sound by David A. Schnirman and Gene Ricciardi; associate producer, Jason Steven Cohen. Presented by Joseph Papp. At the Public Theater/Lu-Esther Hall, 425 Lafayette Street.

WITH: Stephen Bogardus, Bill Christopher-Myers, Mindy Cooper, Braden Danner, Raymond G. del Barrio, Melissa De Sousa, Ty Granaroli, David Patrick Kelly, Mary Munger, Tina Paul, Russ Thacker and Christine Toy.

By MEL GUSSOW

Handed down through centuries, the Medieval Mystery Plays are a native folk art in England, France and Germany. There are so many cycles and so many directorial interpretations of Bible stories that one always looks for a fresh perspective. This, unfortunately, is not forthcoming in "Genesis: Music and Miracles from the Medieval Mystery Plays," an unimaginative storybook version of biblical highlights that opened last night at the Public Theater.

The bland music was written by Michael Ward, the book and lyrics (which vie with each other in banality) are by A. J. Antoon and Robert Montgomery, and the direction is by Mr. Antoon. One's disappointment is deepened by the fact that Mr. Antoon and Mr. Montgomery have both done such rewarding work in the past.

Were it not for the auspices, "Genesis" might pass for a mild Sunday-school entertainment. As each of the five tales unfolds on stage, one recalls other, more interesting versions, including the Open Theater's "Serpent," Martha Clarke's "Garden of Earthly Delights" and the musical "The Apple Tree."

•

Most of the visual touches are familiar — the obligatory swirls of stage fog simulating clouds and a large, rippling sheet to denote the Flood. There are a few variations. Adam and Eve (Stephen Bogardus and Mary Munger) are seduced by a boyish Lucifer (Russ Thacker, who doubles as a bishop) offering them a crystal apple. It is the announced intention of the authors to make the tales seem more modern as the show progresses. As a result, Abraham is dressed like a Hasidic rabbi, and he and his wife have a neat little house and a rocking chair.

The dialogue and lyrics are more doggerel than verse, and finds room for clinkers like "Cain, Cain, come here at once/Obey the old man's grunts." The music, played by a three-piece combo sitting offstage south of Eden, suddenly has a calypso beat when Noah begins building the ark, as if his destination might be the Caribbean. In this version, Noah's wife wants to bring along a lady friend for company, but her husband will not let her. Breaking the two-by-two rule, he decides that one nag is enough.

With Noah, one fondly recalls the Bill Cosby comedy sketch in which an incredulous Noah builds an ark to the Lord's measurements. For the record, the ark at the Public is meant to be 300 cubits long and 50 cubits high, and still leaves one with the Cosby question: what's a cubit?

George Joseph

Apple Polishing

Mary Munger plays Eve in "Genesis: Music and Miracles for a New Age," with book and lyrics by A.J. Antoon and Robert Montgomery and music by Michael Ward.

The actors are earnest, if not overly expressive, although Braden Danner makes us feel Isaac's peril as Abraham threatens him with a menacing knife. Whenever Isaac is otherwise unavailable, a pathetic-looking stuffed lamb is brought out and sacrificed.

John Conklin's pastoral backdrops are an asset, as are the uncredited offstage voices, which sound like Richard Kiley and Irene Worth. They play God and an unidentified woman. The two actors bring a genuine authority to the otherwise commonplace adaptation. At one point, Adam acknowledges to God that there is "full mickle in Your might." The musical "Genesis" is certainly lacking in mickle.

1989 Ja 18, C20:5

Reality Confessed But Not Embraced

ENRICO IV, by Luigi Pirandello; translated by Robert Cornthwaite; directed by J. Ranelli; scenic design by Marjorie Bradley Kellogg; costume design by Andrew B. Marlay; lighting design, John Gleason; sound design by Philip Campanella. Presented by the Roundabout Theater Company, Gene Feist, artistic director; Todd Haimes, executive director. At 100 East 17th Street.

Landolfo	Peter Francis James
Arialdo	Joshua Worby
Ordulfo	Lazaro Perez
Bertholdo	Richard Hicks
Giovanni	Frank Nastasi
Marchese Carlo di Nolli	Brian Cousins
Donna Matilde Spina	Diane Kagan
Frida	Karen Chapman
Doctor Dionisio Genoni	Robert Stattel
Barone Tito Belcredi	Jack Ryland
Enrico IV	Paul Hecht

By MEL GUSSOW

As a philosophical comedy, Pirandello's "Enrico IV" (at the Roundabout Theater Company) deals with the limits of logic and the possibilities of artifice. In keeping with other Pirandello plays, it encapsulates a truth within an illusion.

While in a costume pageant, a man falls from a horse. When he awakens, he believes he is the character he is representing — the 11th-century German Emperor Enrico IV. His concerned relatives regard him as a madman. They indulge his fantasy and reinforce his delusions by turning his villa into a fully staffed emperor's castle. Twelve years later, he suddenly recovers his sanity but keeps that information to himself. As the play begins, people from his past — and a psychiatrist — come to cure him, not knowing that he is already cured.

Within this outline there are countless Pirandellian twists, involving a lost love, double images of people, an act of violent retribution and, principally, the act of pretension itself. Speaking of art, Pirandello said a character's drama is his "vital function; without it he would cease to exist." At all costs, Enrico wants to maintain his fantasy, and even when he confesses his sanity, he leaves a little doubt in the air.

Because the plot is so layered, it takes the full first act to set it in motion, by which time theatergoers — as well as characters in the play — may succumb to confusion. As with other major Pirandello, this is a play with rewards worth savoring, and it is just as pertinent today as when the author wrote it in 1922. Enrico has lost time; Pirandello has not.

In his production at the Roundabout, starring Paul Hecht in the title role, J. Ranelli begins on a broad note. The director makes it too clear that Enrico's attendants are stagehands, setting the scene for the charade with lights, props and costumes. The intention is to illuminate; the result is to sacrifice subtlety. But once Mr. Hecht is on stage, the whirligig of a play begins to spin.

Mr. Hecht, who played Enrico's archrival, Belcredi, in the 1973 Broadway revival starring Rex Harrison, moves up effortlessly to Mr. Harrison's role. With intelligence and an exact proportion of diabolical wit, he plays with his attendants as he informs them of his recovery while still keeping them off balance.

•

Heading toward the play's sudden and dramatic conclusion, Mr. Hecht makes one feel the character's vulnerability. Enrico has been playing the game too long — and too convincingly. It is as if he has been imprisoned in a gulag and on his return is an alien in his own land. When his attendants suggest that he might want to take advantage of the accouterments of 20th-century civilization, literally to turn on the electricity, Mr. Hecht declines, saying feelingly that it "would only blind me," and asks for his oil lamp.

Martha Swope

Paul Hecht in "Enrico IV."

Time itself has wounded Enrico, an injury that the actor makes tangible. During the period when the character was mad, his hair turned gray. Sane, he wonders whose hair it was — the emperor's or the man who pretended to that role. Awakening to reality and prolonging the masquerade, the character is like a patient in a psychological case history described by Oliver Sachs, as in Harold Pinter's play "A Kind of Alaska."

In this play and others, Pirandello foreshadowed Pinter, Ionesco and Genet. One can see in "Enrico IV" the roots of Ionesco's "Exit the King" and Genet's "Balcony." As an experimentalist, Pirandello was not only prescient; he is also imperishable.

Robert Cornthwaite's translation is felicitous, so much so that one wishes all the actors were as articulate as Mr. Hecht. Most of them are at least adequate, but only two others have an extra edge of authority — Peter Francis James in a small role as an attendant and Robert Stattel as the psychiatrist.

Eric Bentley has suggested that "Enrico" parodies "Hamlet." If so, then the psychiatrist is Polonius. Amusingly played by Mr. Stattel, he is a fussbudget filled with pretentious jargon, as in his notion that the case is an example of "analogical elasticity." Within the doctor's diagnosis, there is more than a degree of truth. He knows, for example, that Enrico's obsession has become a fixation. As conceived by Pirandello and as acted by Mr. Hecht, that fixation remains, in revival, as tantalizing as the emperor himself.

1989 Ja 19, C22:3

Room With Goat

AT THE CHELSEA, production manager, William H. Lang; stage manager, Elise-Ann Konstantin; design consultant, Scott Bradley; produced by Anne Hamburger. Presented by En Garde Arts. At 222 West 23d Street.

LITTLE HOUSE ON THE PRAIRIE, by Stephan Balint.

Mary	Alexandra Auder
Laura	Rebecca Major
Man	Mr. Balint

A QUIET EVENING WITH SID AND NANCY

Nancy	Penny Arcade
Sid	Steven Wastell
Interviewer	Mitch Markowitz
Delivery Boy	Giorgio Deus

THE ROOM, by David Van Tieghem with Tina Dudek. Portions of this piece were derived from the play "Legend of Sarah" by James Gow and Arnaud d'Usseau.

By MEL GUSSOW

In her quest for novel "site specific" locations for environmental theater, Anne Hamburger has taken intrepid audiences into abandoned storefronts, converted warehouses and city streets, from which we watched a play enacted on and around the facade of a high-rise apartment building. The latest excursion of Ms. Hamburger's En Garde Arts company is to the Chelsea Hotel, with a series of performance-art events featuring downtown artists and evoking the hotel's bohemian past.

For each of the three plays on the opening bill (repeated this weekend), theatergoers are packed into tiny one-room apartments to watch — really to overhear — private conversations. The plays do not necessarily benefit from being seen on location; each could be staged in a theater on a single set. But in varying degrees, the work is intriguing, especially so in the case of the final event, a collaboration between David Van Tieghem, the performance-art percussionist and composer, and the dancer Tina Dudek.

Tom Brazil

Penny Arcade and Stephen Wastell in "At the Chelsea," a series of performance-art events at the Chelsea Hotel.

Warned that the elevators in the Chelsea are not reliable, theatergoers are shepherded up the staircase to a third-floor apartment, which appears to be in the process of being converted into a farmhouse. There is grass on the carpet. The title of the play, written by Stephan Balint of Squat Theater, is "Little House on the Prairie." This is, in fact, a relocated, urbanized version of that popular television show, as enacted by Alexandra Auder, Rebecca Major, Mr. Balint and a live goat standing in for a third "Little House" sister.

There is a certain wackiness within the whimsy, especially when the actresses play scenes directly with the goat, which peers over the edge of a child's playpen to regard the audience with quizzical detachment, as if to ask what we are doing in this stuffy little room. We could return the question. In the background, on a television screen, is an episode of the real "Little House," should one want to check for authenticity.

The second play, the creation of Penny Arcade, takes place in a nearby apartment and puts us up close (too close when the pizza starts flying) to the last sad days of Sid Vicious and Nancy Spungen (Stephen Wastell and Ms. Arcade). Spaced out and wired, the two are lounging on an unmade bed watching television and waiting for something, anything, to happen.

•

A rock journalist awkwardly interviews them, but when they speak — Ms. Arcade with a natural flamboyance, Mr. Wastell in a stupor — the play succeeds in approximating the ennui of the real-life characters (as in the film "Sid and Nancy"). Both actors achieve a verisimilitude, shared by the trash-filled setting. Coming after the goat version of "Little House," this play raises serious questions about the housekeeping standards on the third floor of the Chelsea.

The final play, "The Room," moves theatergoers to a neat, relatively hospitable apartment for a domestic argument between Mr. Van Tieghem

The audience at the Chelsea Hotel overhears private conversations.

and Ms. Dudek as a couple breaking up. After Ms. Dudek leaves in anger, Mr. Van Tieghem expresses his pent-up anxieties by orchestrating the apartment into an acoustical environment, inventively tap-tapping a table, a bed and a fireplace.

With the return of Ms. Dudek, the two dance on the table and then she moves to the mantle where she lurks like a wingless bird. Employing electronic sounds as well as a television screen, the show evokes an eeriness as if in preparation for a robotic invasion. On the screen, there is a scene that could have been clipped out of "Close Encounters of the Third Kind."

Though paying a price for audience discomfort, the plays hold one's attention. But as the goat bleats, as Sid and Nancy squabble and as the percussionist's sounds reverberate, one wonders what the neighbors are thinking — perhaps that this is a night like any other night at the Chelsea. En Garde Arts' first expedition into the hotel could awaken the ghosts of Sid, Nancy, Jimi Hendrix and Dylan Thomas.

1989 Ja 20, C3:1

Telling on Selling

AD HOCK, music by Ralph Affoumado; lyrics by David Curtis and Alice Whitfield; directed by Sue Lawless; stage manager, Rachel S. Levine. Presented by Eric Krebs. At Theater Cabaret at Caffe Bonnell, 432 42d Street.

WITH: Philip Hernandez, Susan J. Jacks and Jana Robbins.

By STEPHEN HOLDEN

The world of advertising, as scores of novels and movies have insisted

over the years, is populated with sensitive artists prostituting their creative talents in order to live well. For those who make it big in the business, the cliché has it, success and self-flagellation often go hand in hand.

•

"Ad Hock," an acidic 90-minute revue about the advertising business, at the Theater Cabaret of Caffe Bonnelle, does nothing to dispel the stereotype of copywriters, media handlers and jingle producers as cynical, guilt-ridden sellouts. Its creators, the composer Ralph Affoumado and lyricists David Curtis and Alice Whitfield, are all veterans of the Madison Avenue wars. And the insiders' portrait of the business presented by their songs is far from rosy. As the title of one of the show's 21 numbers puts it, they belong to "The World's Second Oldest Profession."

Philip Hernandez, Susan J. Jacks and Jana Robbins, the revue's three performers, are presented by the director Sue Lawless as typical younger members of their profession — fashionably overdressed, ambitious and self-pitying. Together they portray a cross-section of advertising world personnel, from the anonymous, chameleon-voiced jingle singer with pop-star aspirations (Ms. Jacks) to the art director who identifies with Gauguin (Mr. Hernandez), to the copy writer who likes to think of her story boards as extensions of her favorite children's literature (Ms. Robbins).

Though briskly paced and snappily performed, "Ad Hock" devotes far too much time to reflecting on the anxieties of ad agency life and not nearly enough to satirizing commercials. But when the authors turn their Madison Avenue-honed talents to creating zany ads, the show becomes amusing. The evening's funniest number, "Moscow Goes Madison Avenue," imagines the kind of ads that a Russian agency might create for imaginary products like Potato Helper and ears of Chernobyl-grown corn that can double as night lights. The ads are broadcast on the mythical WKGB, "the station that listens to you."

1989 Ja 20, C11:1

A Winter Wonderland, Plus a Dog Act

ICE CAPADES, produced and directed by Willy Bietak and Tom Scallen; choreography by Sarah Kawahara; production designed by Robert W. Rang; costumes designed by Jef Billings; musical direction and supervision by Kevin Nadeau; lighting designed by Robert Schultz; musical arrangements by Ardell Hake. Presented by Mr. Scallen. At Madison Square Garden, 34th Street and Seventh Avenue.

WITH: Jill and Peter, Robert Wagenhoffer, Simone Grigorescu, Terry Head, Kristan and Chip, Brad Doud, Kevin Parker, Bob and Julie, Jean Pierre Boulas, Kitty Kelly, Danny Nicholson, David Jamison and Gerard Soules.

By RICHARD F. SHEPARD

The Ice Capades has returned to Madison Square Garden in a new edition, , a show that is brilliant in color, fast on the ice and imaginative in décor. It is not, to be sure, Harold Pinter, and rather than judge it for its significant silences and inner meaning, neither of which were in attendance, it lends itself very nicely to a gee-whiz rating.

On the gee-whiz scale, Ice Capades merits a loud 10. There are the usual brilliantly executed skating acts, the

expected assortment of breathtaking expertise and the anticipated backflips, somersaults, mad dashes, dervish-whirling and other hazardous and/or graceful tours de force. Like opera, ice shows have their essentials and the question is not what is done but how it is done.

The theme this year is "Return to Romance," and Willy Bietak and Tom Scallen, the producers and directors, have adorned the skating with lavish backdrops that will divert even those whose ideas of entertainment do not extend to two and a half hours of unalloyed skating.

The show opens with a Hollywood-musical sort of setting, the performers descending from two attractive staircases. Later on, a large and cumbersome but effective galleon "sails" about the icy arena with a full crew, bound on an adventurous exploration that culminates in a cannonade. The final segment, set in 1905 Paris, evokes "Sunday in the Park With George" and is a picturesque postcard warmly drawn.

The music is most pleasant, with an eclectic program ranging from rock-and-roll, for the California Raisins, to "The Blue Danube," for the waltzing ensemble. As for the skaters, they transform the Garden into a veritable palace of talent. Robert Wagenhoffer, a man of tremendous and energetic dexterity, virtually tears up the arena with his ice choreography framed in music and in dramatic blue and red lighting. Kitty Kelly is a charmer whose skates and smile both flash as she does her turns. Brad Doud is funny as the ineptly debonair skater whose suavity comes a cropper.

The dancing couples, among them Julie Patterson and Bob Moskalyk, Jill Watson and Peter Oppegard, and Kristan Lowery and Chip Rossbach, recreate the skill and sensitivity that have won them awards.

The Ice Capades will be at the Garden through Jan. 29 and will then move to the Meadowlands Arena in New Jersey, from which it will travel to Nassau Coliseum on Long Island. Oh yes, shades of the old Roxy, there's also a dog act; nobody minded that the dogs worked on carpet. At any rate, this show is the best ice, and one hopes it's the only ice, we'll witness this winter.

1989 Ja 21, 17:4

Next Year, In Moscow

THREE SISTERS, by Anton Chekhov; directed by Eve Adamson; production design by Christopher Martin; costume design by Jonathan Bixby; stage manager, Jonathan Bank; technical director, Randy Alexander. Presented by the Jean Cocteau Repertory, 330 Bowery.

Andrei Prozorov	Joseph Menino
Natasha Ivanova	Carol Dearman
Olga	Elise Stone
Masha	Gretchen Krich
Irina	Jeanne Demers
Fyodor Kuligin	Harris Berlinsky
Aleksandr Vershinin	Craig Cook
Baron Tusenbach	Robert Ierardi
Vasily Solyony	Christopher Oden
Ivan Chebutykin	Coral S. Potter
Aleksei Fedotik	Mark Schulte
Ferapont	Craig Smith
Anfisa	Wynne Kaufman

By WILBORN HAMPTON

When Stanislavsky first read Chekhov's "Three Sisters," written especially for the Moscow Art Theater, he was disappointed. There were no real characters, the director complained, only hints of them. Yet nearly a century later the characters who inhabit Chekhov's drawing rooms and gardens in provinical Russia speak more clearly to the eternal yearnings and frustrations of the human condition than those in a hundred contemporary plays.

For its third offering of the season, the Cocteau Repertory company, 330 Bowery, has mounted a worthy revival of "Three Sisters," though some of the actors' performances give only hints at the fullness of the characters.

Stanislavsky later said it was only after re-reading Chekhov's plays that one could begin "to realize the depths hidden beneath the surface," and he offered some advice to future actors of the plays. "All those who try to 'act' or 'pretend' when taking part in Chekhov's plays are making a sad mistake," the Russian director said. "One should become part of his plays. One should live them, have one's being in them."

•

It's a tall order, and Eve Adamson, the Cocteau's director, has only partly succeeded in coaxing such involvement from her cast. The interpretations are strong on philosophy but give little sense of the despair that life is slipping by. The production captures the sadness of the play but rarely finds either the humor or the tragedy.

There is much to admire in most of the performances. But the portrayals, thoughtful as they are from time to time, are incomplete. In the language of the theater, the actors are in and out, which is to say some scenes work well while others never quite reach their potential. Some in the cast might perhaps have taken Stanislavsky's advice and read the play one more time.

One of the best performances is Carol Dearman's Natasha, who makes a seamless transition from shy fiancée to lady of the manor, proving that anyone with a strong will and a smattering of French can become a tyrannical bourgeoise. And Harris Berlinsky finds a touching pathos in the role of Kuligin, Masha's long-suffering husband.

Of the sisters, Gretchen Krich's Masha is believably bitter over her unhappy marriage, but her kindled passion for Vershinin never quite catches fire. Part of this problem is Craig Cook's rather stiff Vershinin, whose ruminations on the elusiveness of happiness are poignant but who is unconvincing as a prospective lover. Jeanne Demers's Irina is exuberant in her dreams of Moscow and work, but there is little sense of grief in her realization that these dreams will be unfulfilled. Of her suitors, Robert Ierardi's Baron Tusenbach is a credible dreamy Romantic. And Christopher Oden's Solyony is a vengefully angry young man.

The real delight of the production is Craig Smith in the small role of Ferapont, the aged porter who appears from time to time carrying papers to be signed. It is a gem of a performance and makes one wish to see Mr. Smith as Chebutykin, Vershinin, or just about any other Chekhov character he would care to play.

Despite the reservations, there are few more enjoyable evenings in the theater than returning to the Prozorov's house (or the country estates of Mme. Ranevskaya, Serebryakov or Ivanov), and one is grateful to the Cocteau company for the chance for a visit.

1989 Ja 24, C16:4

In the Beginning

SONGS OF PARADISE, based on the biblical poetry of Itsik Manger; book by Miriam Hoffman and Rena Berkowicz Borow; music by Rosalie Gerut; directed by Avi Hoffman; music arrangements by Bevan Manson; musical director, James Mironchik; musical staging, Eleanor Reissa; set design by Steven Perry; lighting design by Anne Militello. A production of the Joseph Papp Yiddish Theater, company based in the Riverdale section of the Bronx, in association with the YIVO Institute for Jewish Research. At the Public Theater, 425 Lafayette Street.

WITH: Adrienne Cooper, Rosalie Gerut, Avi Hoffman, David Kener and Eleanor Reissa.

By RICHARD F. SHEPARD

There is surely nothing now onstage in New York that is more sprightly in any of our city's many tongues than "Songs of Paradise," the first production of the Joseph Papp Yiddish Theater. Recounting the story of Genesis, "Songs of Paradise," now playing at the Public Theater, is witty, tuneful, contemporary and traditional.

Offered in English and in Yiddish (they don't step on each other), it is poetic in the style of Itsik Manger, the Yiddish writer on whose biblical verse the authors Miriam Hoffman and Rena Berkowicz Borow have based the book. The music, by Rosalie Gerut, arranged by Bevan Manson and played on piano by James Mironchik, the musical director, draws on everything from rock-and-roll and gospel to traditional Jewish beats. An unusually gifted cast of five brings everything to a polished gleam onstage.

•

If you wanted, you could call the show something of a Yiddish "Green Pastures," but it is very much its own thing, a mélange of folksiness and sophistication, of veteran Yiddish expressions and modern American allusion. It runs less than two hours, including intermission, and the brevity proves that when it comes to sparkle, less is more — that is, more or less.

The company that has borrowed the name of the artistic director of the New York Shakespeare Festival as well as one of his theaters, undertakes to tell, in its own terms, the story of the Bible's first chapter. You will find that this version of Genesis adds new dimensions, often hilarious, never blasphemous.

Here is Adam, seen immediately after his creation, reclining in a beach chair, sun reflector under his chin and bored until he hands over a rib and receives a shapely Eve. Eve also gets bored and hangs out with the snake and the apple tree (all in one person), and the rest is tsoris. Then comes Cain, the older, twisted son, and Abel, the younger, spoiled son, who is irritating enough to make the murder seem more like manslaughter than an explanation.

•

Then there is Abraham, the pipe-smoking Father of a Nation, burdened, as the script puts it, with "one God, one wife and one shiksa with a child." And here are Jacob, so bright that as a baby, he "knew commodities and the Ten Commandments," and Esau, a motorcyclist in the Marlon Brando vein, who sells the birthright for a bowl of lentils.

The cast, directed with knowing humor and quick pacing by Avi Hoffman, has a wonderful sense of spoof that imparts the flavor of a revue and the style of an operetta. They do everything in a multiplicity of roles and bring to the parts an inspired

sense of silliness, along with good voices for the songs. In addition to Mr. Hoffman and Miss Gerut, whose onstage talent matches their offstage creativity, the players are Adrienne Cooper, whose operatic training superbly supplements her good-humored acting; David Kener, a comedian who adapts brilliantly to any situation, and Eleanor Reissa, who not only did the show's musical staging but also knows how to evoke merriment in dialogue.

Do you have to know Yiddish to appreciate "Songs of Paradise"? No, you don't have to, there's enough English to keep you abreast of what's happening. On the other hand, if you don't know a bit of Yiddish, you will be in the situation of someone using dietetic substitutes: the illusion may be there, but the substance is lacking. Still, on yet another hand, King James managed to make a readable Torah in English, and after a while many didn't know the language could be different. So go to the Public and catch this happy Genesis while it lasts.

1989 Ja 24, C16:3

Martha Swope

Rosalie Gerut and Avi Hoffman in "Songs of Paradise."

Stunted Aspirations, Lasting Obsessions

THE NIGHT HANK WILLIAMS DIED, by Larry L. King, directed by Christopher Ashley; setting by Edward T. Gianfrancesco; lighting by Craig Evans; costumes by Jess Goldstein; sound by Aural Fixation; production stage manager, Greta Minsky. Presented by the WPA Theater, Kyle Renick, artistic director; Donna Lieberman, managing director. At 519 West 23d Street.

Thurmond Stottle	Matt Mulhern
Gus Gilbert	Barton Heyman
Nellie Bess Powers Clark	Betsy Aidem
Moon Childers	J. R. Horne
Sheriff Royce Landon Jr.	Steve Rankin
Vida Powers	Phyllis Somerville

By MEL GUSSOW

As "The Night Hank Williams Died" moves to its conclusion, a theatergoer may ponder the question of how a play can be so amusing and ultimately so poignant. For the answer, look back at the inspiration: those country music songs that encouraged so many singers and songwriters to fantasize about conquering Nashville.

In a Hank Williams song (like "Your Cheatin' Heart"), there is an abiding sorrow as love gone wrong turns a man to drinking, thinking and longing about what might have been. "The Night Hank Williams Died," a fine new play by Larry L. King, captures the spirit of Hank Williams's

homely poetry while adding a generous helping of Mr. King's Texas geniality and humor. The play is itself a plaintive country-western song. All that is missing from the landscape is the lonesome whistle of a train.

Mr. King once wrote a magazine article suggesting that country music commemorated the people and places known by children of the Depression, "our pitifully few conquests" and "our impoverished and isolated lives." The play, which opened last night at the WPA Theater, is testimony to the author's idea. In it, the title character remains an offstage idol; the play is about a man who would be Hank Williams.

Nashville could be a continent away from Stanley, Tex., a town so tiny that it has no last picture show to close. When the highway was built, it carefully skirted Stanley, leaving its citizens adrift. There is only one jukebox, the centerpiece in the Sundowner bar, where we learn all we need to know about the people of Stanley — their stunted aspirations as well as their few lingering obsessions.

The town's hope may have once been Thurmond Stottel, a former high school football hero and would-be country singer. Now a disgruntled gas pump jockey, Thurmond has come down with a case of "the donothings and the don't cares." The re-

Martha Swope

Matt Mulhern and Betsy Aidem in "The Night Hank Williams Died."

His first song is a self-parody that asks for "a little bitty bit of love," but by the time he offers his choicest tune, it turns out to be touching as well as relevant to the play's central theme. In his words, "Yesterday seemed too early but now tomorrow's too late." Mr. King is the composer and lyricist of Thurmond's songs — and there may still be room for him in Nashville.

Under Mr. Ashley's direction, there are heartfelt performances from the three principals, Mr. Heyman, Mr. Mulhern and Ms. Aidem, and complementary ones in supporting roles from J. R. Horne, Phyllis Somerville and Steve Rankin (as the sheriff).

Mr. King comes to playwriting (he was co-author of the book for "The Best Little Whorehouse in Texas") after a career as a novelist and journalist. On the strength of "The Night Hank Williams Died," it is clear that he has a natural gift for the theater.

1989 Ja 25, C16:4

Acting on Impulse

HEDDA GABLER, by Henrik Ibsen; translated by Henry Beissel; directed by Richard Fancy; set design, Robert Joel Schwartz; lighting design, Stephen Petrilli; costume design, Barbara A. Bell; sound design, Kenn Dovel; stage manager, Jennifer E. Boggs; technical director, Mr. Petrilli. Presented by the Pearl Theater Company, 122 West 22d Street.

Miss Juliane Tesman	Joan Matthiessen
Bertha	Sylvia Davis
George Tesman	Stuart Lerch
Hedda Tesman	Joanne Camp
Mrs. Thea Elvsted	Robin Leslie Brown
Assessor Brack	Frank Geraci
Eilert Lovborg	James Nugent

By WILBORN HAMPTON

Fresh from lampooning Ibsen and his "new woman" in a production of Shaw's early play "The Philanderer," the Pearl Theater Company has turned its attention to the playwright himself with a workable revival of "Hedda Gabler."

Among Ibsen's last plays, written at the time of his return to Norway after 27 years in Italy, "Hedda Gabler" is difficult to classify. It addresses none of the social concerns with which his earlier plays dealt nor does it examine the spiritual conflicts of the later plays. "Hedda Gabler" is primarily a psychological case study of the title character, though one hopes General Gabler's daughter is not Ibsen's ideal for the "new woman."

Hedda has always been a favorite role for actresses. The challenge is in keeping the playing of Romantic tragedy that borders on madness within the realm of believability. Hedda Gabler is a knot of contradictions. She flees reality, demands that her heroes wear garlands of vine leaves in their hair and cannot bear to think of anything ugly, like illness or death. Yet she is also a woman who would kill the poet if she cannot be his inspiration.

Any successful production hinges on a strong performance in the title role because it is she who sets everything in motion. The Pearl's Hedda is Joanne Camp, who is taking a leave from "The Heidi Chronicles" at Playwrights Horizon to play with those pistols and bring havoc to the lives of everyone around her.

Ms. Camp begins rather low-key, a rather pouty and difficult-to-please newlywed who seems genuinely sorry

Rosegg/Martha Swope Associates

Joanne Camp in the title role of "Hedda Gabler."

that she may have offended her husband's favorite aunt. Hedda becomes more a wheedling manipulator than a cruel seducer who could talk a man into buying a house for her because she could think of nothing else to say. Ms. Camp's Hedda is not so much a tragic figure as an impulsive one, a mischief-maker driven as much by childish jealousy and pique as by boredom.

Her final, fatal gesture seems as much a tantrum to gain attention as it is a sacrifice to some high Romantic ideal. It is not a portrait of Hedda Gabler that everyone will immediately recognize, but it is a convincing one.

If the tragic dimensions of the play have been somewhat reduced in the Pearl production, part of the reason is in Richard Fancy's direction. At times the approach is more like a domestic melodrama about compulsion and tawdry affairs, perhaps more suitable for daytime television. But it uncovers the basic selfishness of all the characters and suggests that "Hedda Gabler" may have been Ibsen's idea of a happy ending.

The other performances similarly begin small in scope yet build to a strong end. James Nugent's Lovborg, the object of Hedda's obsession and her husband's rival, is powerful and moving in his grief over the lost manuscript, although there are only hints of a wasted genius in the early scenes. Stuart Lerch gives a sympathetic Tesman, whose idea of excitement is to cut the pages of a new book. And Robin Leslie Brown is quite good as Thea, the runaway wife who is as much a slave to Romance as Hedda but without the destructive flaw.

Robert Joel Schwartz has again designed a delightful set, all full of period furniture, doilies, old photos and fringed lamp shades. It is a marvel how Mr. Schwartz converts the Pearl's small stage into such striking sets, whether they be London clubs or Oslo drawing rooms.

1989 Ja 25, C18:5

---

turn to Stanley of his married, high school sweetheart, Nellie Bess, reactivates his ambition and is a catalyst for the plot of the play.

A play that is itself a plaintive country-western song.

Mr. King knows these people from their Stetsons to their toes, and he obviously has an affection for them (except for the mean, small-minded sheriff). The audience shares that feeling in abundance, as the author artfully avoids sentimentality and any hint of situation comedy. These are real people, and the play, performances and set design (by Edward T. Gianfrancesco) are resonant of a specific time and place. The emotions are also identifiable to people far from Texas.

There is one moment that approaches melodrama, but it is well-motivated within the context of the play. On all counts, Christopher Ashley's production is marked by its modesty and its down-home authenticity. In the tradition of the WPA, the play is staged with scrupulous attention to realistic detail.

The avuncular center is Gus, the philosophical bar owner, whom Bar-

ton Heyman personifies with a precision that must come from empathy. Wearing a bottle opener on a string around his neck (one of the many signs of the period; there were no screwtop caps on beer bottles in 1952), he is as much a part of the bar as the pool table, the five bar stools and the other talismans of the clublike environment.

•

Dutifully, Gus guards his beer supply while insisting that he offers customers no credit. What customers? The only ones we see are Thurmond, Nellie Bess and Gus's crony, Moon Childers — and Thurmond hardly ever pays. For Gus, the bar is more a home than a business. From here, as a kind of town crier, he has watched the decline of Stanley and of his own dreams. Wishing better for the younger people, especially Nellie Bess (Betsy Aidem), he knows progress is only achieved through risk. Explaining his hesitation about movin' on, Thurmond (Matt Mulhern) refers self-consciously to having roots in Stanley, though he would not know roots if he stumbled over them.

All Thurmond really wants is to return to his high school days, and when he dances with Nellie Bess, he rests his chin on her head, nestling as they must have done at so many adolescent dances. At no point is there is an attempt to idealize the couple. Nellie is no prom queen, though she probably was the prettiest girl in Stanley High. Similarly, Thurmond is not presented as a country star in the rough.

From Superman To Spin Doctors

MANHATTAN PUNCH LINE'S FIFTH ANNUAL FESTIVAL OF ONE-ACT COMEDIES, Series A, Steve Kaplan, artistic director. Set design by James Wolk; lighting design by Danianne Mizzy; costume design by Fontilla Boone; sound design by Scott David Sanders. At Judith Anderson Theater, 422 West 42d Street. WONDERFUL PARTY!, by Howard Korder; directed by Val Hendrickson; original music, David Yazbeck. THE GETTYSBURG SOUND BITE, by Ted Tally; directed by Louis Scheeder. ONE MONDAY, by Matt Cutugno; directed by Scott Rubsam. SEVEN MENUS, by David Ives; directed by Fred Sanders. SEX LIVES OF SUPERHEROES, by Stephen Gregg; directed by Paul Lazarus.

By MEL GUSSOW

The theme music from "Superman" is a prelude to Stephen Gregg's "Sex Lives of Superheroes," a tale of craven cowardice. A hero-worshiping young man (Barry Miller) allows his former girlfriend (Andrea Weber) to strip their apartment, item by item, of all its furnishings. Finally all that remains is a poster of Superman. Deep in despondency, the antihero fantasizes that he is giving lectures on the title subject, with Ms. Weber as his heckler.

In the course of this intermittently amusing comedy, the worm turns, with the help of a new woman (Elaine Rinehart). They are introduced through the kindness of their shared psychiatrist. She has her own obsession — rewriting romantic stories so they have dismally unhappy endings. Though the play is a modest effort, the writing, Paul Lazarus's staging and the acting (especially that of Mr. Miller) put it several cuts above the other four plays in Evening A at Manhattan Punch Line. This is the company's fifth annual festival of one-act comedies.

Two other works, Ted Tally's "Gettysburg Sound Bite" and David Ives's "Seven Menus," at least begin with a promising idea, but both would benefit from sharper writing and performing. The remaining two comedies are negligible.

•

The Tally skit may aspire to a spot on "Saturday Night Live," as the author imagines that Abraham Lincoln had handlers and spin doctors who tried to rewrite the Gettysburg Address into a snappy sound bite. Mr. Tally (the author of "Terra Nova" and the most accomplished playwright on the evening's bill) looks for political satire in anachronisms. Dan Desmond's Lincoln looks Lincolnesque, but he drinks Rolling Rock from the bottle. His aides are clones from a 1988 convention. Their goal is make Lincoln seem presidential (a hopeless task). The play is never as funny as it sounds; it lacks bite.

Mr. Ives has no follow-through in "Seven Menus," a "La Ronde"-style comedy about couples changing partners in a trendy restaurant. The play is both overlong and undernourished; among other things, this restaurant comedy has no sense of food. Mr. Ives was on much surer comic ground in "Sure Thing," his mirthful entry in last season's Punch Line festival.

The evening's principal disappointment is the curtain-raiser, "Wonderful Party!" by Howard Korder, about a party in which the hostess (Ann Talman) knows none of the guests. The tiny stage at the Judith Anderson Theater is filled with actors, gossiping, arguing and bumping into one another. A somewhat similar idea was attempted several seasons ago — with far funnier results — in Wallace Shawn's "Hotel Play."

Mr. Korder's talent for dialogue (demonstrated in "Boys' Life") is lost in the melee. In one of the few moments that deserve a laugh, the hostess offers her guests blue tropical drinks and asks if they want them with or without tiny decorative umbrellas.

The slightest play, Matt Cutugno's "One Monday" is a brief blackout sketch about the hazards of Wall Street. Two highly competitive yuppie traders confront a crash in their fortunes in a scene that dwindles in comparison to others of its ilk. Fortunately, the quintet ends with a comic-book smile — "Sex Lives of Superheroes."

The production is one of two evenings of one-act comedies presented in repertory. Evening B will be performed tonight.

1989 Ja 26, C16:1

American Music, Latin Perspective

BLACK AND BLUE, conceived and directed by Claudio Segovia and Héctor Orezzoli; choreographers, Cholly Atkins, Henry LeTang, Frankie Manning and Fayard Nicholas; lighting designed by Neil Peter Jampolis and Jane Reisman; scenery, costumes designed and lighting designed by Mr. Segovia and Mr. Orezzoli; musical supervision, arrangements and orchestrations by Sy Johnson; additional arrangements and orchestrations by Luther Henderson; sound designed by Abe Jacob; assistant choreographer, Dianne Walker; associate producer, Marilynn LeVine; production stage manager, Alan Hall. Presented by Mel Howard and Donald K. Donald. At the Minskoff Theater, 200 West 45th Street.

WITH: Ruth Brown, Linda Hopkins, Carrie Smith, Bunny Briggs, Ralph Brown, Lon Chaney, Jimmy Slyde, Dianne Walker, Rashamella Cumbo, Tanya Gibson, Germaine Goodson, Angela Hall, Kyme, Valerie Macklin, Deborah Mitchell, Valerie E. Smith, Frederick J. Boothe, Eugene Fleming, Ted Levy, Bernard Manners, Van Porter, Kevin Ramsey, Ken Roberson, Melvin Washington, Cyd Glover, Savion Glover and Dormeshia Sumbry.

By FRANK RICH

"Black and Blue," the new revue at the Minskoff, is a festive tribute to great black American jazz and blues artists as only a madcap pair of Argentine set and costume designers could have imagined it.

The entrepreneurs in question — they conceived, directed and designed the entire affair — are Claudio Segovia and Héctor Orezzoli, whose previous spectacles include "Tango Argentino" and "Flamenco Puro." They mean well. Their revue is a weird, at times diverting, crosscultural mishmash. While bursting with talent worthy of the Cotton Club or the Apollo or Birdland, "Black and Blue" looks like the bloated nightclub floor shows that used to flourish in decadent Latin American capitals just before dictatorships collapsed.

When Mr. Segovia and Mr. Orezzoli stay out of the way, some beloved performers strut their stuff to beguiling effect. Ruth Brown, the rhythm-and-blues chanteuse, applies sarcastic varnish and two-a-day burlesque timing to the ribald Andy Razaf lyrics of "If I Can't Sell It, I'll Keep Sittin' on It." In the sole number choreographed by Fayard Nicholas, of the legendary Nicholas brothers, the young dancers Kevin Ramsey, Eugene Fleming and Ted Levy make time stop with their time steps accompanying Carrie Smith's smoky rendition of "I Want a Big Butter and Egg Man." To watch these lithe men skip in place or buoyantly bob their arms while tucking back their feet is to see show-biz dancing stake its claim to grace.

An even younger trio of dancers — the teen-age Cyd Glover, Savion Glover and Dormeshia Sumbry, all clad in formal Astaire white — bring down the house as they tap up and down stairs in Henry LeTang's choreography for "Rhythm Is Our Business." Much later, the elfin, silver-haired Bunny Briggs, who has been a professional hoofer since 1931, puts us "In a Sentimental Mood" by slyly illustrating the miniaturist techniques, particularly the "paddle and roll," of the first generations of tap masters. In every number, the music — whether by Ellington or Arlen or Waller or Handy — is in the authentic hands of an onstage band overflowing with top soloists like the pianist Sir Roland Hanna, the alto saxophonist Jerome Richardson and the drummer Grady Tate.

Authenticity is not always the order of the long night, however. Mr. Segovia and Mr. Orezzoli don't seem to understand that the power of blues and jazz often rests in their unadorned simplicity. In "Black and Blue," the lily isn't just painted and gilded; it's smothered in whipped cream and encased in marzipan. That fine singer Linda Hopkins wails a heartfelt "After You've Gone" only to give way to dancers who wrest the song's emotion away from her and provide a soupy, upbeat Vegas finish. Ellington's "Black and Tan Fantasy," so lovingly played by the band, serves as a platform for some utterly unerotic interpretive dancing (choreographed by Frankie Manning) that might be the June Taylor Dancers' answer to "Slaughter on Tenth Avenue."

•

At times it's hard to tell where the directors' innocent vulgarity leaves off and intentional camp begins. An arch, competitive duet between Miss Brown and Miss Hopkins on "T'Ain't Nobody's Bizness If I Do" kids the song into oblivion. When Miss Smith sings "I've Got a Right to Sing the Blues," she unaccountably leans back on a large tilted black disk as if she were awaiting root canal work. Miss Brown's rendition of "Body and Soul," inexplicably set against a gray slab of Stonehenge proportions, is so oddly inflected and lispy that it could pass for a Carol Channing impersonation. When Miss Smith later sings "Am I Blue," her vocal interpretation is beside the point; she's perched precariously on a swing, from which dangles a glittery white train high and wide enough to shroud at least half of the Big Apple Circus.

Perhaps "Black and Blue" intends to dazzle us with its lavishness, but the production is lavish by Crazy Horse revue standards, not Broadway's. Ever-falling crimson velour curtains and flashing proscenium lights suggest the busy environments of television game shows rather than the chic opulence of the Harlem Renaissance. The metallic, bejeweled outfits wrapped around the three voluminous leading ladies seem like imprisoning carapaces; the patchwork suits given the older male tap dancers are patronizingly clownish. And what is one to make of the rows of nondescript monochromatic compartments, one per chorus dancer, that are rolled out with much fanfare in the finale? For a few minutes,

Martha Swope

Ruth Brown during "St. Louis Blues" in "Black and Blue."

"Black and Blue" seems to have landed in a large international airport's restroom.

•

It's too bad that Mr. Segovia and Mr. Orezzoli didn't turn over more of

Two Argentines put together a madcap revue on Broadway.

their show to Mr. LeTang, who stages its wittiest numbers and also played a key role in the artistically overlapping and far superior "Sophisticated Ladies." The failings of "Black and Blue" are a function not only of a cultural gap but also of its creators' apparent inability to edit and pace their material. The numbers occur in no particular order, rarely segue into each other and never build toward a cumulative point or feeling. The evening seems much longer than its two and a half hours because its energy is diffuse rather than concentrated. While a revue doesn't require a script, it must have its own internal theatrical logic if the whole is to equal, let alone transcend, the sum of the parts.

In this case, the parts are not to be sniffed at. One can enjoy the real American gems in "Black and Blue" as long as one has the patience to pick them out of their gaudy settings of tourist-trap kitsch.

1989 Ja 27, C3:1

The Ties That Fail to Bind

WHEN WE ARE MARRIED, by J. B. Priestley; directed by Kenneth Frankel; set design by Hugh Landwehr; costume design by Jess Goldstein; lighting design by David F. Segal; production stage manager, Anne Keefe. Presented by Long Wharf Theater, Arvin Brown, artistic director; M. Edgar Rosenblum, executive director. At New Haven.

Ruby Birtle .... Jill Tasker
Gerald Forbes .... Robertson Dean
Mrs. Northrop .... Joyce Ebert
Nancy Holmes .... Leslie Simons
Fred Dyson .... William Youmans
Henry Ormonroyd .... George Hearn
Alderman Joseph Helliwell .... Howard Witt

Councillor Albert Parker	Donal Donnelly
Herbert Soppitt	Ralph Williams
Annie Parker	Margaret Hilton
Clara Soppitt	Laurie Kennedy
Maria Helliwell	Patricia Conolly
Lottie Grady	Marylouise Burke
Rev. Clement Mercer	William Swetland

By MEL GUSSOW
Special to The New York Times

NEW HAVEN, Jan. 26 — When J. B. Priestley's "When We Are Married" was revived in London in 1956, the production was a tribute to the eloquent art of English character acting. Enlisting such expert farceurs as Prunella Scales and Bill Fraser, the director Ronald Eyre turned a period comedy into a blithe evening of turnabout fair play. To the sound of laughter, timid souls became emboldened to talk back and stuffed shirts lost their starch.

Along the way, the production disguised the thinness of the story line. Three Yorkshire couples, married in the same ceremony, gather 25 years later to celebrate their anniversary, only to discover that their ties were not legally binding. The momentary unhitching sends the characters scrambling in different directions, all of which lead to a happy conclusion.

"When We Are Married" is very much a company play; this is a key to its durability and to the fact that it is becoming a popular choice in American regional theaters. At the Long Wharf Theater, Kenneth Frankel has armed the farce with a primarily American company. Unsurprisingly, the production lacks the world-class polish of its London predecessor, but, of course, not everyone saw that revival.

On its own terms, Mr. Frankel's production has its assets (including Hugh Landwehr's atmospheric setting) as well as a few drawbacks. Not all of the actors are comfortable in their definably English roles. In one specific case, however, the produc-

T. Charles Erickson

Donal Donnelly as Albert Parker, in "When We Are Married."

tion manages to improve upon the London version. That is in the performance of Donal Donnelly as Albert Parker, the self-important local councilman.

Mr. Donnelly delivers a rich and variegated portrayal, investing a small role with a full range of quirks and crotchets. As he delineates the character's blind spots, each becomes a motif. His wife, a suddenly rebellious doormat, calls him stingy, and every time the epithet is repeated, Mr. Donnelly flinches, as if his ego has been struck by a sharp blow.

Eventually, the flinch becomes a cringe, so that by the end of the evening the actor seems somehow stooped and bowed by the criticism. It is Parker who has misguidedly thought of himself as "an exciting sort of a chap." As personified by Mr. Donnelly, a boring man is raised to a height of mirthfulness.

•

The two spouses who turn against their overbearing mates — Parker's wife and the mousey husband of the town battleax — are also given zesty characterizations. Margaret Hilton and Ralph Williams (smiling at his own new bravery) earn the audience's favor. Gently, they prove that there are decent folk in the small-minded town of Clecklewyke.

In contrast, Mr. Williams's shrewish mate, a woman only a George Bernard Shaw could find attractive, is played by Laurie Kennedy with artificial sourness. Unpersuasively she pretends to a dowager's manner and look. Howard Witt, as a philandering alderman, is one of several in the cast who seems closer to Connecticut than to Yorkshire — although Patricia Conolly is a welcome presence as his complacent wife.

Complacency is at the root of much of the comedy, as Priestley spoofs the smugness of people who ascend from shopkeeping to positions of minor local authority. Pomposity and piety are the author's twin targets.

Priestley's spokesman is Henry Ormonroyd, a newspaper photographer called in to commemorate the supposedly blissful anniversary. Even in an alcoholic haze, Ormonroyd is an astute observer of human behavior, noticing the uneasiness of the haughty people around him, their insecurity about facing his camera.

In London, Mr. Fraser was incomparable in the role of Ormonroyd, a perfect portrait of a rumpled old reprobate. At Long Wharf, George Hearn strikes an alternate but creditable note, making the photographer a hearty ham actor in life and a wily scamp in someone else's living room. While tippling, Mr. Hearn's character always seems on the verge of a song, and by the end of the evening he and Marylouise Burke, as the alderman's gaudy girlfriend, engagingly harmonize on an old music-hall tune.

Seeing the play again, one more fully appreciates Priestley's agility in constructing — and tumbling — his Yorkshire house of cards and in commenting on the unmannerly side of the marital state at the turn of the century. A set-up is succeeded by a follow-through. Running gags do not run down and acts have amusing curtain lines (even though there is no actual curtain on the open Long Wharf stage). For those who missed the vintage London revival, Mr. Frankel's production, led by Mr. Donnelly, offers ample pleasure.

1989 Ja 28, 14:3

Sex and Surrealism

BETTY BENDS THE BLUES, written and composed by Ellen Maddow; directed by Paul Zimet; set design, Janie Geiser, light design, Carol Mullins; costume design, Gabriel Berry; choreography by Anne Hammel; the Talking Band presented by Theater for the New City, George Bartenieff, artistic and managing director; Crystal Field, executive artistic director. At 155 First Avenue.

WITH: Ellen Maddow and Harry Mann.
THE MALADY OF DEATH, by Marguerite Duras; music by Blue Gene Tyranny; directed by Richard Armstrong.
WITH: Tina Shepard and Rosemary Quinn.

By STEPHEN HOLDEN

With its distilled oracular diction, repetitious imagery, and use of narrative indirection to grasp at the profound, the prose of Marguerite Duras strikes one as simultaneously poetic and pretentious. Such self-conscious writing would also seem to resist dramatization. But in "The Malady of Death," one of two new theater pieces by the Talking Band, the experimental company founded by veterans of Joseph Chaikin's Open Theater in 1974, the author's dreamy erotic novella has been turned into an allusive, visually striking tone poem for the stage.

An extended meditation on sex, death and emotion, "The Malady of Death" is the story of a man who, believing himself incapable of love, hires a woman to teach him how to love. Their sojourn, during which she gently upbraids him while making herself entirely available, unfolds in a house by the sea over several days.

In the Talking Band's piece, at Theater for the New City, the man's melancholy reflections on the interlude are read by Tina Shepard to a mostly reclining Rosemary Quinn in a setting whose white-sheeted walls and shifting light evoke a procession of enchanted days and nights. Oceanic sound effects and an unobtrusively lovely keyboard score by Blue Gene Tyranny help to evoke a strong sense of place and the way the rhythms of nature affect mood.

The theatrical atmosphere is so attuned to the language that the author's images of love and the sea, of desire and despair, are reinforced. Ms. Shepard's readings, which build to a cry of spiritual emptiness, suggest that the novella may be an extended suicide note, though its meanings remain open to other interpretations.

"Betty Bends the Blues," the piece that begins the evening, is the third part of a musical trilogy featuring its author and composer, Ellen Maddow, as a housewife named Betty Suffer. In the earlier plays, "Bedroom Suite" and "Betty and the Blenders," appliances, furniture and household bric-a-brac became musical instruments.

In "Betty Bends the Blues," the plucky title character is visited by an East Village neighbor, Benny (Harry Mann), who plays the saxophone and keyboard. The two make music together and swap personal observations on the small absurdities of life in New York. They end their visit by asking such philosophical questions as, "How you do know this is not a dream?" and, "What would you like to do if you knew you wouldn't get caught?"

With its rambling anecdotes, its surreal kitchen set by Janie Geiser and music performed by a toy synthesizer, "Betty Bends the Blues" portrays apartment life as a domestic science-fiction story that you make up as you go along.

1989 Ja 28, 13:1

The Way America Saw The Way America Was

BORN YESTERDAY, by Garson Kanin; directed by Josephine R. Abady; production supervised by John Tillinger; setting by David Potts; costumes by Ann Roth; lighting by Jeff Davis; sound by Lia Vollack; hair by J. Roy Helland; production stage manager, Don

Walters; associate producer, Martha Wilson. Presented by Jay H. Fuchs, Columbia Artists Management, A. Joseph Tandet and the Cleveland Play House, in association with Little Prince Productions Ltd. At the 46th Street Theater, 226 West 46th Street.

Helen	Heather Ehlers
Paul Verrall	Daniel Hugh Kelly
Bellhop and a bootblack	Gregory Jbara
Bellhop, barber and waiter	Paul Hebron
Eddie Brock	Joel Bernstein
The Assistant Manager	Ron Johnston
Harry Brock	Edward Asner
Billie Dawn	Madeline Kahn
Ed Devery	Franklin Cover
A Manicurist	Charlotte Booker
Senator Norval Hedges	John Wylie
Mrs. Hedges	Peggy Cosgrave

By FRANK RICH

Theatergoers who were born yesterday can only speculate about why Garson Kanin's "Born Yesterday" caused a sensation on Broadway in 1946. The play's flat new revival at the 46th Street Theater, enlivened solely by Madeline Kahn's game stab at the heroine, Billie Dawn, refuses to yield many clues. Nor can the ritualistic explanation for the comedy's initial runaway success — the emergence of Judy Holliday, the original Billie, as a star — be the entire story. If one eliminates musicals, "Born Yesterday" is the seventh-longest running play in Broadway history, eclipsing even Neil Simon's most popular works in the record books. Mr. Kanin didn't merely write a hit; he created a phenomenon.

A phenomenon very much of its day, perhaps. Mr. Kanin set his play in the nation's capital at a time of bustling transition that makes our current change of Presidents seem of little historical moment. Washington, a sleepy town before World War II, was suddenly a booming metropolis, itself born again in the new prosperity of peacetime. The country it governed was up for grabs. "Born Yesterday" — which shared its Broadway season with such other civic-minded plays as Howard Lindsay and Russel Crouse's "State of the Union" and Arthur Laurents's "Home of the Brave" — asked what kind of democracy a rich, victorious United States was going to be, and it phrased the question in a vigorous, wisecracking way.

•

The play's high-minded concerns are tucked into a brassy Pygmalion tale redolent of both Damon Runyon and George Abbott, Mr. Kanin's theatrical mentor. The pugnacious Harry Brock (Edward Asner), a self-made scrap-metal tycoon, has come to Washington to expand his business empire by buying a Senator. He also hires a New Republic reporter (those were the days!) to teach cultured Capitol Hill manners to his mistress Billie, a mink-clad "dumb blonde" who once labored in the "Anything Goes" chorus line.

To Harry's horror, Billie turns into a whistle-blowing crusader once her tutor has awakened her to Tom Paine and Dickens. "This country and its institutions belong to the people who inhabit it!" she says after seeing the light, and she means it. "Born Yesterday" believes there's nothing wrong with America that cannot be righted by an informed citizenry. Mr. Kanin's comedy is far more sanguine about the prospects of purging greed and corruption than are such related postwar dramas as Robert Sherwood's screenplay for "The Best Years of Our Lives" and Arthur Miller's "All My Sons."

The innocence of Mr. Kanin's patriotism, as expressed through the ingenuous spirit of Billie, must be recaptured like lightning in a bottle if ''Born Yesterday'' is to charm an audience today. The required freshness is entirely absent from the elephantine current production, which, arriving in New York after an extended road tour, lumbers about the stage like a dusty old Packard in search of a 100,000-mile overhaul.

The show has two directors — Josephine R. Abady and a so-called production supervisor, John Tillinger — and not one sustained spell of spontaneity. Miss Kahn at least offers the polished comic turn one expects, complete with funny walks and pouting double takes. If the Holliday cadences still can be heard in her voice, the actress has her own ditsy ways to hum ''Anything Goes'' and to exit Harry's $235-a-day hotel suite in a wiggly Mae West huff. The evening's one claim to passion arrives when she angrily tells off her keeper in the second act, in a heartfelt feminist revolt that prefigures speeches Mr. Kanin and Ruth Gordon would soon write for Katharine Hepburn in the movies ''Adam's Rib'' and ''Pat and Mike.''

Such is the staging's bumpy gait that even Miss Kahn is left hanging a beat after every joke, waiting with a self-conscious half-smile for the audience's laughter. And the rest of the casting conspires against her and Mr. Kanin. Daniel Hugh Kelly, as the New Republic reporter, is as robotically genial as a department store floorwalker, thereby rendering Billie's sudden infatuation with him ludicrous as well as sexless. The supporting players, most crucially the proper Washington types scandalized by Billie's faux pas, are stock mannequins who deprive Miss Kahn of worthy farcical foils even as they accentuate the situation-comedy contrivances in the script.

•

Mr. Asner also hails from a sitcom, but his lovably gruff television character of Lou Grant, first created for ''The Mary Tyler Moore Show,'' had all the depth the buffoons lurking about him in ''Born Yesterday'' lack. Yet his Harry Brock is disastrous.

Barking his dems-and-dose lines in an accent that alternately sounds like Anthony Quinn's Zorba the Greek and Popeye, Mr. Asner plays the junk magnate as a one-note heavy. Villains are not this actor's forte (remember him in ''Roots''?), and even if they were, his characterization would still violate the play's spirit.

Harry is a bully, to be sure — he's a racketeer who slaps people around — but there must be something likeable about him if we are to believe that he and Billie have been together for over eight years and, more important, if his final comeuppance is to give the evening its essential comic payoff. Mr. Asner's excessively sinister fixer imposes a post-Watergate malevolence on a light comedy that wasn't built to carry such weighty baggage. In place of Mr. Kanin's innocent 1946 valentine to democracy's resilience, we're left with a morality play that leaves us feeling as jaded and dispirited as if we'd stayed home to watch tonight's network news.

1989 Ja 30, C11:1

Life for Laughs

THE KATHY AND MO SHOW: PARALLEL LIVES, written and performed by Mo Gaffney and Kathy Najimy; directed by Paul Benedict; set design by David Jenkins; costume design by Gregg Barnes; lighting design by Frances Aronson; executive producer, James B. Freydberg. Kenneth F. Martel and Ellen M. Krass present a Martel Media Enterprises Production, in association with Home Box Office and Kenneth M. Weinstock. At the Westside Arts Theater, Downstairs, 407 West 43d Street.

By MEL GUSSOW

Kathy Najimy and Mo Gaffney, the authors and stars of ''The Kathy and Mo Show: Parallel Lives,'' are San Diego's amusing answer to Cagney and Lacey, Kate and Allie and other strong-minded pair-bonded women. Kathy and Mo are not detectives or careerists but playful post-feminist satirists.

The revised and expanded version of their two-person show, which opened last night at the Westside Arts Theater, begins with Kathy and Mo wearing wings and lolling on a cloud. They are angels, looking down from heaven and organizing the world, post-Genesis. The first question to be decided is which gender should bear babies. The two consider their possible choices and then, as a whim, casually agree to give that role to women. To equalize the sexes, they bestow large egos on men. Such is the luck of the divine draw.

From here, Kathy and Mo sweep down to earth and assume their often ambiguous identities in contemporary society. They march from adolescence (two girls who watch their favorite movie, ''West Side Story,'' on television and suddenly realize that it is ''a lot like 'Romeo and Juliet' '') to midlife in crisis.

Together they turn clichés into malapropisms and skewer stereotypes wherever they find them, in the performing arts as well as in real life. Playing two club ladies of mature years though not mature minds, they tell us about their women-studies group, which combines tours with such subjects as ''Women in Terrorism,'' for them only a small step from macramé.

Some of the targets are easy (including repressed Roman Catholic schoolgirls) and there is a distinct dip at the beginning of the second act. But as directed by Paul Benedict, the two share an engaging sense of absurdism as they switch roles and, occasionally, sexes.

More than Kathy, Mo — a k a Maureen — portrays men as well as women. Mo, who can assume a manly swagger, has the edge in terms of character transformation: Even as a man, in her case a good ol' Texas boy with a cigarette permanently affixed to his lower lip, Kathy is recognizable (her figure is a factor). But in most of their disguises they are a funny pair, especially so when they are playing siblings or best friends (who can turn into rivals).

The maniacal look in Kathy's eyes matches her hairdo, and she has the manners (if not the musicality) of a chanteuse. As a would-be bar singer, she bleats ''Little Lamb'' so loudly that it could rouse Ethel Merman into a duel. Mo may have a more inclusive acting talent, as demonstrated in her virtuosic mime about a woman's daily ablutions, which, in her hands, seems like a cross between endless aerobics and Chinese water torture.

The program for ''The Kathy and Mo Show'' names dozens of the characters portrayed on stage and also enumerates many of the foods, junk and otherwise, mentioned in the course of performance. The list omits the team's humorous commentary, as in the diet-conscious order of a B.L.T. — ''No B,'' or lasagna ''with egg, spinach and kelp.'' Kelp lasagna is a pasta peer of the grouper tortellini on the menu in Richard Greenberg's ''Eastern Standard.'' With Kathy and Mo, food is a subtext. The text for the day is sexism and parochialism in all its forms. The comedy team is as wry as it is ecumenical.

1989 F 1, C21:1

Of Murders Most Foul On the Moors

In ''Breakfast With the Moors Murderers,'' a performance piece by Torture Chorus, a Los Angeles-based ensemble, Stephen Holman and Laura Richmond caricature Ian Brady and Myra Hindley, the seemingly respectable young lovers who randomly murdered five children in England in the 1960's and buried them on the moors.

The piece, which the group staged at Franklin Furnace on Friday and Saturday nights, paints the couple as the psychopathic forerunners of the punk rocker Sid Vicious and his girlfriend Nancy Spungen, who were also misfits with grotesque delusions of grandeur. While Ian furiously smashes dolls stuffed with newspaper and canned spaghetti, Myra, who dreams of celebrity, sulks about the fact that the victims are getting all the publicity. Demureness alternates with frenzy.

•

When Ian starts to show home movies of their mildly kinky sex life, Myra becomes skittish, and he shuts off the projector. Periodically the couple sing snippets from ''The Sound of Music.'' ''My Favorite Things'' is murmured in a childish monotone while they finger giant slices of foam rubber toast. Moments later, Ian enthusiastically attempts to persuade members of the audience to kill the people sitting next to them.

Torture Chorus's brand of surreal comedy, which the group calls ''splattervillian,'' is closely related to the messy rituals of the Kipper Kids, and Mr. Holman's Ian is a descendant of Alfred Jarry's surreal theater character, Ubu. Tradition notwithstanding, ''Breakfast With the Moors Murderers'' says nothing about human nature and social repression that hasn't been addressed more powerfully by punk rockers and screaming comedians. STEPHEN HOLDEN

1989 F 2, C18:4

Edward Asner and Madeline Kahn in ''Born Yesterday,'' a revival at the 46th Street Theater.

Reality vs. Existence

THE CÉZANNE SYNDROME, by Normand Canac-Marquis; directed by Liz Diamond; translated by Louison Danis; set design, Anne Servanton; costume design, Sally J. Lesser; lighting design, Donald Holder; sound design, Phil Lee; stage manager, Casandra Scott; production manager, David Waggett. The SoHo Rep, Marlene Swartz, artistic director, presents the New Wave of Quebec Festival. At Greenwich House, 27 Barrow Street.

Gilbert	David Strathairn
Suzanne	Caris Corfman
Thomas Wancicovski	Edward Baran

By MEL GUSSOW

"The Cézanne Syndrome," the opening play in the SoHo Rep's three-week festival of new French-Canadian drama, is a brief hallucinatory chronicle of a death retold. A mother and child have died in an automobile accident and the grief-stricken father goes through daily domestic routines while his mind wanders in time and fantasy. He imagines that his wife has returned from the grave to help explain the apparent inexplicability of the collision.

The Normand Canac-Marquis play, a prize winner in the playwright's native Montreal, is intended to move the audience to pity. Instead it fills the air with ennui. Digressions defuse whatever momentum exists on stage. As we watch the husband (David Strathairn) in his cluttered kitchen, his self-conscious, perhaps shock-induced, eccentricities add to the chaos.

•

After welding an automobile fender on the kitchen table, he prepares to sit down to a solitary dinner. When the telephone rings, he puts it in the stove. He stuffs his work pants in the refrigerator. His late wife (Caris Corfman) appears, and she putters around the kitchen. Becoming angry, she throws the silverware on the floor. Periodically, the husband is interrupted by flashing red lights, denoting the accident, and by questions from an investigating officer (Edward Baran).

The play's core, the husband's interior monodrama, silent and spoken, lacks the intensity of Franz Xaver Kroetz's wordless "Request Concert" (a paradigm of this dramatic species) and is in doleful contrast to the Dario Fo-Franca Rame comedy sketches about a woman alone.

•

The fault is not primarily in the performances. Under Liz Diamond's direction, Mr. Strathairn conveys a measure of the character's obsessiveness and Ms. Corfman plays the wife with a cheerfulness that is supposed to make the accident seem even more tragic. As translated from the French by Louison Danis, the play is burdened by circumlocutions; the mood as well as the language seem resistant to translation.

The title is a reference to Cézanne's statement that what is important is less the subject painted than "the state of mind of the observer." As a demonstration of the Cézanne syndrome, the play is elliptical without being especially mysterious, increasing one's impatience to arrive at the destination.

1989 F 3, C3:5

On the Waterfront

HENRY LUMPER, by Israel Horovitz; directed by Grey Cattell Johnson; set design by David Condino; lighting design by Douglas Kirkpatrick; production stage manager, Elizabeth Heeden; assistant stage managers, Douglas Gettel and Elaine O'Donnell. Presented by the Working Theater/Gloucester Stage Company, in association with Actor's Outlet Theater. At 120 West 28th Street.

WITH: Ralph Bell, Carol Bradley, Brian Delate, Randy Frazier, Joseph Jamrog, Cullen Johnson, Jordan Lund, Paul O'Brien, Courtney Peldon and Roger Serbagi.

By MEL GUSSOW

In "Henry Lumper," Israel Horovitz's working-class Massachusetts version of "Henry IV, Part 1 and Part 2," Hal and Hotspur (Harry Percy) were high school classmates. Hal, a star quarterback, fell in love with a pretty cheerleader, who later married Harry. This makes the Hal-Hotspur feud a triangle as well as a duel to the death.

Years after graduating from Princeton University, Hal returns to his native Glossop (a stand-in for Gloucester) to work as a lumper, or longshoreman. He idles his time boozing with Jack (Tubby) Silva, Petey, Bardolph and other layabouts (and wenches) while his father, Henry Boley, is fighting to retain control of his two-fisted union, the Waterfront Workers and Fisherman's Benevolent Association (the W.W.F.B.A.).

In the Horovitz chronicle (at the Actor's Outlet) one is asked to believe that the W.W.F.B.A. is as consequential as a kingdom and that one ascends to its head by right of primogeniture. In the coronation ceremony, the golden gavel of office passes from father to son. Making the story of waterfront greed and corruption fit Shakespeare's history play is almost as difficult as sorting out scrambled pieces from two jigsaw puzzles.

Additionally crowding the offstage landscape is a fleet of tuna boats, price-cutting and jeopardizing the Cape Ann fishing trade. They are op-

Martha Swope Associates/Carol Rosegg
Brian Delate

erated by the Moon-like Church of the New Way, whose members are referred to as "lilies." Mr. Horovitz's War of the Lilies is no laughing matter, but there are moments when "Henry Lumper" drifts into self-parody.

The odd thing is that when the play diverges from "Henry IV," as in the romance between Hal and Lady Percy and in several scenes on the Glossop docks and between fathers and sons, it reveals an intrinsic strength. Mr. Horovitz, an accomplished playwright, has an interesting story to tell about the decline of a port town's industry and morality, and apparently much of it is based on fact. But just as "Henry Lumper" disarms Shakespeare, Shakespeare strains "Henry Lumper."

One is also unavoidably aware of the omissions from the original. Fal-

staff, for one, has been shortchanged. Missing, for example, is the scene in which he and Hal playact as Henry IV and son. Other important characters are excused from duty, minimalized or distorted (the Earl of Worcester is now a cocaine kingpin). In other words, "Henry IV" is subject to the vagaries of the central fish story.

Except in the role of the Chorus, who begins and ends the play on a note of irony, the author has made no attempt to approximate Shakespeare's poetry. In that sense, it is closer to "On the Waterfront" than it is to "Henry IV." When Hal makes his pledge to his dying father, he vows: "Things are going to be different, Pop. I swear it to ya." Later, newly gaveled as "No. 1" of the union, he bluntly banishes Tubby Silva with, "I don't know you, fat man."

While some of this has an earthy pungency, there are moments of silliness. The final one-on-one knife fight between Hal and Harry Percy is tautly acted and staged, but it is vitiated by Harry's last words, as he fondly remembers shared Percy-Boley family vacations in New Hampshire.

The play was first presented at Mr. Horovitz's Gloucester Stage Company. It has been restaged in New York by Grey Cattell Johnson, the company's associate artistic director, as a co-production with the Working Theater. The set designer, David Condino, has turned the Actor's Outlet into an evocative environment of planks and decks, simulating a waterfront inhabited by actors and theatergoers.

The enthusiastic and uneven cast leaps into "Henry Lumper" as if it really were "Henry IV." Roger Serbagi and Ralph Bell bring authority to the roles of Henry Boley and the Chorus, Brian Delate is a stalwart all-American Hal and Jordan Lund has Falstaffian proportions in both manner and look. Little Courtney Peldon, who is very appealing as Percy's 6-year-old daughter, may be the only person in the theater unaware of the play's Shakespearean lineage.

This is the third Horovitz play about contemporary social disorders in Gloucester. It was preceded by an original, "North Shore Fish," and by "The Year of the Duck" (a Horovitz variation on Ibsen's "Wild Duck"). By far the most rewarding is "North Shore Fish," which, unshadowed by a masterpiece, allowed the playwright to pursue his own theatrical imagination.

1989 F 5, 53:1

Hometown Girl Makes Bad

THE VISIT, by Friedrich Dürrenmatt; directed by Warren Manzi; set design by Jay Stone; lighting design by Ben Solotaire; costume design by Maud Kernsnowski; sound design by David Lawson; production stage manager, Tom Canary; produced by Catherine Russell. Presented by the Actors Collective, at the Courtyard Playhouse, 39 Grove Street.

Mayor	Nicholas Saunders
Schoolmaster	Jed Krascella
Priest Marcus	Powell
Alfred Ill	Drew Eliot
Claire Zachanassian	Francine Farrell
Boby	Howard Katz
Doctor	James Farrell
Karl	Kevin McGinn
Otillie	Marian Chamow

By WILBORN HAMPTON

The town of Guellen has fallen on hard times. Rich in cultural heritage

(Goethe once spent the night in the local inn and Brahms composed a quartet there), Guellen has sold its one museum to America and its only asset is a broken typewriter in the Town Hall. There is nothing even left to tax.

As the lights come up on "The Visit," Friedrich Dürrenmatt's macabre moralistic fable of hypocrisy and greed, which the Actors Collective is presenting at the Courtyard Theater, the entire town has gathered at the train station to await the return of Claire Zachanassian, Guellen's most famous daughter and now a multimillionaire. When Mme. Zachanassian arrives, her baggage includes a coffin, a sedan chair and a black panther. Among her entourage are her seventh husband, two blind eunuchs and a couple of hoods from Sing Sing. She has plans for the coffin.

•

The people of Guellen are hoping Mme. Zachanassian will make a small donation to save her hometown from bankruptcy. They are relying on one Alfred Ill, the local shopkeeper who was Claire's childhood sweetheart, to kindle her generosity. But Claire has an old score to settle.

Mme. Zachanassian offers to bail out the town and throw in something extra for each Guellener if one of them will kill Alfred for her. It seems Alfred left Claire pregnant and penniless when he jilted her all those years ago, and she is back in town to buy a little justice. When the Mayor haughtily rejects her offer, Mme. Zachanassian replies, "I'll wait."

Dürrenmatt's comedy is of the blackest sort, and anyone considering a revival should give some serious study to the darkest side of human nature. Yet in the Actors Collective production, more thought seems to have been given to passing a little bell (which rang to indicate Alfred's shop door opening and closing) between actors entering and leaving the shop than to characterization.

•

The production boasts a cast of 35. There were certainly a lot of people traipsing up and down the aisles and sidling around the backs of the audience at the Courtyard's small arena stage. Some scenes were played directly behind one section of the audience, and the entire arrival scene at the train station was played in the theater's entryway.

For the most part, the acting was not above the level of an extended classroom exercise. Nicholas Saunders as the Mayor and Jed Krascella as the schoolmaster gave credible performances. As Alfred, Drew Eliot was plausible in his own set speeches, but he never seemed involved with the other actors. And one could never quite believe in Francine Farrell's constantly smiling Mme. Zachanassian. Warren Manzi directed.

1989 F 5, 56:5

Blizzards Without And Within

BRILLIANT TRACES, by Cindy Lou Johnson; directed by Terry Kinney; sets by John Lee Beatty; costume design by Laura Crow; lights by Dennis Parichy; sound design by Chuck London/Stewart Werner; production stage manager, Fred Reinglas. Presented by Circle Repertory Company, Tanya Berezin, artistic director; Connie L. Alexis, managing director. At the Cherry Lane Theater, 38 Commerce Street.

Henry Harry	Kevin Anderson
Rosannah DeLuce	Joan Cusack

By FRANK RICH

We are, as the Playbill announces, "in the state of Alaska, in the middle of nowhere" in Cindy Lou Johnson's new play, "Brilliant Traces." The setting is a wood cabin more forbidding than Charlie Chaplin's in "The Gold Rush." Outside is a howling blizzard; inside is one indistinct occupant, sleeping beneath a bundle of blankets. And soon comes a fierce knocking on the door. The sleeper, a young man played by Kevin Anderson, awakens to admit a distraught young woman, played by Joan Cusack, who invades his cabin in full bridal regalia, from silver satin slippers to ice-encrusted veil.

Even if Ms. Johnson had few other talents — and she seems to have many — one couldn't dispute her ability to grab an audience's immediate attention. The opening moments of "Brilliant Traces," a Circle Repertory Company production staged at the Cherry Lane Theater, possess the same kind of tall-tale abandon that marked the company's previous (and equally snow-dusted) play, Craig Lucas's "Reckless." Like Mr. Lucas, Ms. Johnson has spun an alternately comic and anguished fable about contemporary men and women who run away from home — whether from parents, children or mates — and she has written it with an imaginative disregard for pedantic reality. While these new Circle Rep plays deal with common issues of love and family, they do so with characters, stories and dialogue so fantastic that they could exist only within the enchanted realm of the stage.

Ms. Johnson is not yet as experienced or accomplished a writer as Mr. Lucas, but there is much to enjoy during her play's intermissionless 90 minutes, starting with a powerful per-

formance by Ms. Cusack. Best known now for her flamboyant turn as Melanie Griffith's close friend in the film "Working Girl," this actress demonstrated last spring, in the English play "Road," that she can also convey the wary fragility of a lost girl-woman terrified of being crushed by men. The role of Rosannah DeLuce, as Ms. Johnson's heroine is named, capitalizes on Ms. Cusack's full range. The bride blown in by the blizzard is dizzy — she has driven to Alaska arbitrarily, after abruptly fleeing her wedding 3,000 miles away — and yet she is also disfigured by "brilliant traces," the playwright's conceit for the scars of love.

No less wounded is Rosannah's involuntary host, Henry, another refugee from civilization. For reasons that Ms. Johnson too teasingly withholds until the play's final moments — and which will remain undisclosed here — Henry has sworn off the "roller coaster" of a personal life forever, to hide out in a hermit's isolation. To him, people are "wild cards" who serve only to wreck a man's tranquillity and bring him grief. To Rosannah, people who "touch your soul" and get "under your skin" inevitably leave you "ruined and alone." It's only a matter of time, of course, before these two strangers fall into each other's arms, ready to try once more to connect.

•

Henry and Rosannah's fusion comes about as it usually does in romantic comedies. Their chance meeting is followed by an angry misunderstanding, a lowering of defenses, an exchange of confessions and a final embrace.

But the conventions are transformed by the absurdity of the setting and the situation and by the raw articulation of the characters' pain. Henry and Rosannah not only journey

to the end of the world to escape the traumas of intimacy — a feat many can accomplish while staying put — but they also express themselves in heightened language that veers without warning between hardened, comic cynicism and naked, life-and-death panic. "Brilliant Traces" redefines the familiar by recasting it in histrionic extremes and poetic images (from those of ice to charred shoes) that are as theatrical as the Alaskan weather that establishes the play's tone.

It's when the author pushes her metaphors self-consciously that her characters cease to be people and become the pawns of a claustrophobic literary scheme. So much is made of the metaphysical properties of nourishing food, winter whiteouts and aimless highway driving that "Brilliant Traces" can sound like a joint parody of Anne Tyler, Don DeLillo and Joan Didion. Ms. Johnson's more straightforward speeches can sometimes dip into sentimental cliché as well. Hearts are too often hurting or breaking or pounding, especially as the play pants too hard in order to force its conclusion.

That "Brilliant Traces" usually holds the stage in even its arch passages is in part a tribute to the alert production. It was a smart idea to entrust a playwright who aims for the emotional jugular and the esthetically rambunctious to a director, Terry Kinney, from Chicago's artistically like-minded Steppenwolf Company. In league with the usual Circle Rep designers — notably Dennis Parichy (lighting) and Chuck London and Stewart Werner (sound) — Mr. Kinney gives "Brilliant Traces" a volatile atmosphere of mystery and danger that recalls Steppenwolf's "Orphans."

Mr. Anderson, who acted with Mr. Kinney in "Orphans," is a compelling presence as Henry, though the role is limited by Ms. Johnson's coy insistence on protecting the character's privacy for most of the evening. The playwright's spirit seems more heavily invested in Rosannah — who, in Henry's accurate account, keeps "flinging out wild kinds of energy at everything in her path." In Ms. Cusack's performance, that energy is piercing, whether she is thrashing madly like a bird with a broken wing or arranging her pale features into a vacant passivity, hoping that protective coloration will save her from being wiped out by love once more. "I'm hovering," says Rosannah, in her most frequent description of her exile from the world. Ms. Cusack's hovering is such a convincing emotional highwire act that "Brilliant Traces" becomes overwhelming when she makes her final, cathartic descent through the blizzard for a warm sanctuary that may yet be home.

1989 F 6, C11:1

Bob Marshak

Kevin Anderson and Joan Cusack in "Brilliant Traces," a Circle Repertory Company production staged at the Cherry Lane Theater.

Greenhorn Greengrocer

THE IMMIGRANT: A HAMILTON COUNTY ALBUM, by Mark Harelik, conceived by Mr. Harelik and Randal Myler; set designer, Randy Benjamin; lighting designer, Susan A. White; costume designer, Victoria Lee; sound designer, J. Wise; production stage manager, Rick Lucero; production coordinator, Lisa Forman; general manager, Lawlor/Shovestull; language/dialect coach, Ari Roussimoff. Presented by the American Jewish Theater, Stanley Brechner, artistic director. At the Susan Bloch Theater, 307 West 26th Street.

Ima Perry	Ann Hillary
Haskell Harelik	Lonny Price
Milton Perry	Nesbitt Blaisdell
Leah Harelik	Lisa Pelikan

By MEL GUSSOW

Looking as formal and out of place as a penguin at the Equator, a young, Jewish refugee from Russia arrives in Hamilton, Tex., in 1909 and begins to build a new life. Many years later, the man's grandson, Mark Harelik, would write a play about his grandfather's experience. The result, "The Immigrant," at the American Jewish Theater, is a dramatized oral history chronicling the Americanization of Haskell Harelik.

There is a disarming ingenuousness to the play that compensates for the familiarity of the story. At moments, we think we are watching a fairy tale. Except for one momentary brush with local rednecks, Haskell is unhampered as he earns his way into the hearts of his neighbors. While there must have been other pressures on the actual immigrant, the author is less concerned with details of ostracism than with the story of Haskell's personal growth and his own quest for assimilation.

As written by Mr. Harelik and played by Lonny Price, Haskell is a very appealing figure. The play, within its self-limiting boundaries, is an affectionate character study that also delineates the friendship between a green immigrant and a small-town Texas banker and his wife, who take him under their wing and become his protectors.

•

With Haskell established in Hamilton — his wheelbarrow has evolved into a fruit and vegetable market — and with his wife newly arrived from Russia, the first act ends on an uplifting note. Once again we are told that through hard work and determination anything is possible.

In the second act, in a schematic series of vignettes, the playwright condenses the rest of the character's life. Three sons are born and, in an instant, they are serving in World War II. The business thrives and changes. Then, unconvincingly, Haskell and the banker have an argument about United States immigration policy — and the friendship is severed.

The momentum that advanced the first act is missing. As is often the case, the journey proves to be more interesting than what happens once the destination is reached. Fortunately, the act is brief and the playwright regains his poise in an epilogue in which the youngest Harelik son brings us up to date on the family fortunes and touchingly describes the aged Haskell's eventual retreat into a vision of his boyhood. Under the direction of John Driver, the actors — Mr. Price, Nesbitt Blaisdell, Ann Hillary and Lisa Pelikan — sustain the play through its dramatic lapses.

Mr. Price's Haskell is a quick learner, filled with common sense and an intuitive awareness that transcends cultural and linguistic differences. The banker's wife (Ms. Hillary) speaks English loudly and clearly to the immigrant as if he were deaf rather than Russian. Later, when he is not understood by her, Mr. Price amusingly imitates her response to him, shouting Yiddish at exactly the same level of loudness.

•

When the banker suggests that Haskell add grapefruit to his fruit line, he gruffly explains that they are

Martha Swope Associates/Carol Rosegg

Lonny Price and Lisa Pelikan in "The Immigrant: A Hamilton County Album," at the Susan Bloch Theater.

cover papers disclosing that Mama has real estate back in Argentina.

Mama recovers her strength, but nobody is happy about that and the play moves on to a macabre conclusion.

As seen in an English translation by Myra Gann, as it is done Wednesdays through Fridays (weekends it is played in Spanish), the performance, under the direction of Vicente Castro, is convincing, although the action

Peter Krupenye

Rubén Pla in Roberto Cossa's "Happy Birthday, Mama."

cannot meet for dinner without debating the moral and psychological complexities of Hedda Nussbaum, who needs a bland, earnest drama dedicated to the unsurprising proposition that the wounds of child abuse don't easily heal? "Dalton's Back" is a topical play in the way that the daily weather report is front-page news.

The author is Keith Curran, who is clearly writing out of honest concern. His protagonist, Dalton (John Dossett), is a young, sensitive schoolteacher haunted by a childhood spent in fear of an unloving and at times violent mother. Unless Dalton reconciles himself with his past, he cannot forge a stable relationship with Teresa (Colleen Davenport), the warm woman he wants to marry. He will be doomed instead to replay his traumatic youth in nightmares and in life, even to the point of inflicting violence on himself or on those he loves.

To accentuate the obvious — that the maltreated boy is father to the troubled man — Mr. Curran makes literal the parallelism between his

'Dalton's Back' points out that the maltreated boy is father to the troubled man.

hero's present and past: As the grown-up Dalton and Teresa carry out their volatile affair, they share the stage with the younger Dalton (Matt McGrath), who is doing simultaneous battle with his mother (Lisa Emery). While no one can dispute the psychological linkages that ensue, it isn't particularly revelatory or theatrical to draw straight lines between related events from childhood and adulthood as if they were column A and column B.

•

Mr. Curran's paired scenes — the young and the mature Daltons need their backs stroked to fall asleep, for example — may give the play recurrent images, but they don't tell the audience what it yearns to know. We learn more about Dalton's back than we do about the monstrous but superficially sketched mother responsible for his insomnia. We never even meet Dalton's father, who, however frequently absent from home, surely must be a major part of the story; the playwright would rather give stage time to Dalton's colorfully hip best friend (Jayce Bartok), a source of forced comic relief. The romance between Teresa and Dalton is also emotionally and erotically cloudy, despite much bounding in and out of the bed that dominates William Barclay's perfunctory set.

With the exception of one gratuitous though welcome interlude in which past and present characters fantasize singing the euphoric rock song "Ain't No Mountain High Enough," Mark Ramont's staging is either prosaic or jumbled. The acting ranges from the affable (the two Daltons) to the grating (everyone else). The incidental music is of the wistful easy-listening variety, as befits a play that achieves its reconciliatory ending as effortlessly as one might flip a light switch.

"big yellow things; grow on trees!" With astonishment, Mr. Price repeats, "Big yellow things?" Much of the actor's considerable humor comes from his mimicry, which is the character's method of becoming a Texan. Slowly, a slight drawl creeps into his accented speech.

Mr. Blaisdell contains himself within his crusty role as the banker, a man who relinquishes his natural reserve when confronted with the openness of the stranger. Though in the second-act argument Haskell insists that he has paid his debt to the banker, that debt of friendship could never be fully paid. At least as we see on stage, without the banker — or someone similarly forthcoming — the immigrant would have had a far more

difficult time of adjustment. Ms. Hillary and Ms. Pelikan (as Haskell's wife) are helpful as the women who offer their husbands emotional sustenance.

Without the benefit of elaborate scenery or of projections, Mr. Driver has given the play a reasonably flavorful production (at the Susan Bloch Theater). The production emphasizes the storytelling quality of the narrative. Even as the second act slackens, one continues to feel the sincerity of the effort — as a look into a family album of photographs and as a portrait of a self-made American.

1989 F 8, C19:1

What to Do About Mama?

HAPPY BIRTHDAY, MAMA, by Roberto Cossa, translated by Myra Gann; directed by Vicente Castro; producer, Miriam Colon Valle, set design, Robert Klingelhoefer; lighting design, Bill Simmons; costume design, Stephen Pardee; production stage manager, Uriel Menson. Presented by the Puerto Rican Traveling Theater, 304 West 47th Street.

Esther	Marta Vidal
Pedro	Mateo Gómez
Osvaldo	Nelson Landrieu
Graciela	Eugenia Cross
Gabriel	Rubén Pla
Luisa	Carmen Rosario

By RICHARD F. SHEPARD

One of the sturdiest bridges between Spanish-writing dramatists and English-speaking audiences is the Puerto Rican Traveling Theater, which has been offering New Yorkers bilingual theater since 1967.

The company's newest offering at its West 47th Street house is a short

work, "Happy Birthday, Mama," by an Argentine playwright, Roberto Cossa. In little more than an hour, Mr. Cossa, with savage sarcasm, creates a flow chart of greed, depicting the way it triumphs over family ties and such tenuous bonds as affection and love.

The play, which has been done in South America, is now set in an apartment in a Spanish-speaking neighborhood of the Bronx, where a 70-year-old mother (Carmen Rosario) has just fainted at the start of a surprise party for her birthday. Her three grown sons and two daughters-in-law manifest genuine concern as they wait for the doctor.

Soon, there are practical intrusions. The one couple, who live in a crowded apartment, "volunteer" to move into Mama's spacious apartment. The other couple "volunteers" to sell the apartment and take Mama in. The third son says Mama should take in boarders and live off the rent. The concern of all is money, and there is riotous celebration when they dis-

jumps from happy highs to malevolent lows almost without shifting gears. Marta Vidal is persuasive as a manipulative daughter-in-law, and Rubén Pla is amusing as the bachelor son — imaginative, avaricious and wrapped up in physical fitness, until a crisis sends him back to smoking. Mateo Gómez, Nelson Landrieu and Eugenia Cross complete a cast that works together very nicely.

The play, while interesting, lacks a certain consistency, as though it is not sure whether to be comedy or tragedy. As a result, the onlooker is not sure how far to let emotion take over for fear of being brought up short a moment later. But as staged, with the fateful tango theme in the background, "Happy Birthday, Mama" may be an attractive experience for audiences eager to explore approaches to familiar topics by writers from other backgrounds.

1989 F 9, C22:3

Bad Deeds

DALTON'S BACK, by Keith Curran; directed by Mark Ramont; set design by William Barclay; costume design by Susan Lyall; lighting design by Dennis Parichy; sound design by Robert J. Rick Jr.; production stage manager, Denise Yaney. Presented by Circle Repertory, Tanya Berezin, artistic director; Connie L. Alexis, managing director. At 99 Seventh Avenue South, at Fourth Street.

Dalton Possil	John Dossett
Teresa MacIntyre	Colleen Davenport
Dalty	Matt McGrath
Mom	Lisa Emery
Hiram	Jayce Bartok

By FRANK RICH

If social consciousness were all, the Circle Repertory Company would deserve a brace of humanitarian citations for presenting "Dalton's Back," a play about child abuse. But at a time when two or more New Yorkers

If anything, "Dalton's Back" is a reversion to the polite, realistic television drama that the Circle Repertory has admirably avoided this season in its other parent-and-child plays, "Reckless" and the current "Brilliant Traces" (which continues

Gerry Goodstein

John Dossett in Keith Curran's "Dalton's Back," at the Cherry Lane Theater.

at the Cherry Lane while Mr. Curran's play runs at the company's home base). But perhaps such judgments are unfair to television. After returning home from the Circle Rep, I watched a videotape replay of the night's episode of "Thirtysomething," which by coincidence used the same two-tiered time scheme employed by "Dalton's Back" to far more sophisticated effect.

The author of the "Thirtysomething" episode, I discovered upon rewinding to the opening credits, was Joseph Dougherty, who hasn't been heard from as a playwright since his promising "Digby" was presented at the Manhattan Theater Club a few seasons ago. I'm not sure exactly what the moral of this story is for the New York theater, but it is probably more timely than anything "Dalton's Back" has to say about child abuse.

1989 F 10, C3:1

Short Snacks

MANHATTAN PUNCH LINE'S FESTIVAL OF ONE-ACT COMEDIES, Series B. Steve Kaplan, artistic director. Set design by James Wolk; lighting design by Danianne Mizzy; costume design by Michael Schler; sound design by Scott David Sanders; production stage manager, Jonathan D. Secor. At the Judith Anderson Theater, 422 West 42d Street.

SEEING SOMEONE, by Laurence Klavan, directed by Steve Kaplan; stage manager, Steven Spulick.

REQUIEM FOR A HEAVYWEIGHT, by Mark O'Donnell; directed by Robin Saex; stage manager, Cathy D. Tomlin.

NEWS FROM ST. PETERSBURG, by Rich Orloff; directed by Adam Zahler; stage manager, Padraic Fisher.

PILLOW TALK, by Peter Tolan; directed by Jason McConnell Buzas; stage manager, Valerie Roux.

GOOD HONEST FOOD, by Bill Bozzone; directed by Steve Kaplan; stage manager, Stephen Spulick.
WITH: Larry Block, Bill Cohen, Steven Gilborn, Daniel Hagen, Cady Huffman, Jack Kenny, Nicholas Levitin, Christiane McKenna, Steve Marcus, Kathrin King Segal, Constance Shulman and Victor Slezak.

By MEL GUSSOW

The festival of one-act comedies at the Manhattan Punch Line is something of a cliffhanger, as we wait for a funny play to come along. Actually, the 10th and final play in the two-part repertory — Bill Bozzone's "Good Honest Food" — qualifies for that label, and the ninth play, Peter Tolan's "Pillow Talk," also has its comedic merits.

Mr. Bozzone, a proven talent at the Ensemble Studio Theater as well as at the Punch Line, is in mirthful form with this sketch about the world's greasiest spoon. The woman in charge of the restaurant is an ill-tempered waitress (Kathrin King Segal), who is so busy insulting the customers and playing practical jokes that she has no time to remove the dirty dishes from the counter. The service is catch-as-catch-can, but the writing and acting are precise.

Into this dingy diner comes the slick, smart-suited Victor Slezak, carrying his briefcase and eager to make a computer deal with a client (Steve Gilborn). Desperately, Mr. Slezak tries to hold on to his dignity, but wherever he turns he is threatened by gravy stain — or worse. To the newcomer's amazement, the food turns out to be good, but in contrast to the regulars, he prefers cleanliness and a kind word for the price.

•

Amid the clutter there are sharp-edged performances by Mr. Slezak, Mr. Gilborn and, especially, Ms. Segal, who makes the waitress as slovenly as a housewife in a George Price cartoon. The brisk direction is by Steve Kaplan.

"Pillow Talk" puts two heterosexual male friends (Daniel Hagen and Jack Kenny) in embarrassing proximity. On a transcontinental automobile trip they stay overnight in the mobile home of Mr. Hagen's grandmother, and are forced to share a bed. The author works infinite variations on the bedding arrangement, beginning with Mr. Kenny's acute dis-

Martha Swope Associates/Carol Rosegg

Kathrin King Segal in "Good Honest Food," a one-act comedy at the Manhattan Punch Line.

comfort and Mr. Hagen's equally acute desire for sleep.

This is more a vaudeville sketch than a play, with Mr. Hagen playing

the convivial but suffering host and Mr. Kenny the apoplectic guest in the trailer. The comedy is attenuated, but Mr. Kenny can write clever dialogue, and the actors (as directed by Jason McConnell Buzas) are a clownish team.

In order to see the final two plays in Evening B, one must endure three disposable curtain-raisers. Laurence Klavan's "Seeing Someone" is the closest to having a funny idea. On a date, a young man (Mr. Kenny) cannot stop thinking about his former girlfriend, who, through a kind of ESP, he sees consorting with other men. The play has a certain cartoon sensibility, but not much humor.

Rich Orloff's "News From St. Petersburg" is a heavy-handed spoof of all things Russian, including the unamusing observation that Russians address each other formally by their long names. In Mark O'Donnell's "Requiem for a Heavyweight," Larry Block (wearing a small trunk on his nose) plays a slothful circus elephant hanging around an apartment as if he were a couch potato. In all three cases, whimsy wanes.

Evening B (featuring "Good Honest Food") alternates with Evening A at the Judith Anderson Theater.

1989 F 11, 12:3

History With Fiction

PLAY BALL, by R. A. Shiomi; directed by Ernest H. Abuba; set design, Atsushi Moriyasu; lighting design, Victor En Yu Tan; sound design, Joseph Tornabene; costume design, Toni-Leslie James; stage manager, Sue Jane Stoker; dramaturge, Robert Graham Small. Presented by Pan Asian Repertory Theater, Tisa Chang, artistic director. At the Apple Corps Theater, 336 West 20th Street.

John A. Wildman .... Ed Easton
Karl Warden .... James Jenner
Gordon Hirabayashi .... Ron Nakahara

Kazuo Yoshida .... Steve Park
Harry Nakamura .... Norris M. Shimabuku
John Warden .... Kelley Hinman

By MEL GUSSOW

Most dramatizations of the United States Government's internment of Japanese-Americans during World War II fall into one of two categories. They are either documentaries or they are based on personal memories. In contrast to previous treatments of the subject at the Pan Asian Repertory Theater, R. A. Shiomi takes a third approach.

His work "Play Ball," is inspired by the story of Gordon Hirabayashi, who was found guilty of violating a curfew in 1942 and of protesting his evacuation to an internment camp. Mr. Hirabayashi, one of the few Japanese-Americans to fight the Government order, carried his case through the courts and after many years managed to get a reversal of his convictions. Though Mr. Hirabayashi is a character in the play (as portrayed by Ron Nakahara), other aspects of the story are fictional, including a melodramatic confrontation with the military authorities that becomes the catalyst for the drama.

Having chosen this risk-filled approach, the playwright seasons his realism with a measure of abstraction. There is a dreamlike quality in the storytelling and in Ernest H. Abuba's stylized staging that enhances the audience's curiosity. But by trying to reach the heart of the central character's cause without holding to the facts of the case, "Play Ball" raises questions similar to those asked about the film "Mississippi Burning": questions about a dramatist's obligation to specifics of contemporary history.

At the same time, the play is not the imaginative leap that it is intended to be. The dialogue is occasionally marked by a kind of italicized pronouncement that Mr. Shiomi so effectively spoofed in his private-eye caper, "Yellow Fever." The baseball imagery, indicated by the title, seems superimposed, and while focusing on that single invented incident, the author averts the intricacies of the legal battle itself.

Martha Swope Associates/Carol Rosegg

Ron Nakahara, left, and Norris M. Shimabuku in "Play Ball."

Researching the story, Mr. Shiomi apparently became fascinated by the fact that some people (including Earl Warren, then the Attorney General of California) who were instrumental in support of internment later became known for their liberalism. In the play, Hirabayashi's nemesis is a collage of such men, a military official who, decades after the war, becomes a judge respected for his role in civil rights cases.

The collision between the judge-to-be and the play's Hirabayashi ends with the killing of one of Hirabayashi's boyhood friends. As written by Mr. Shiomi and as played by James Jenner, the interrogator seems like a caricature villain. Seen over a period of three decades, he never loses his sinister look and his smug smile. Equally unrealized is the character's strong-arm assistant (Ed Easton), who unconvincingly repents his racism.

•

What partly sustains interest — in addition to the urgency of the theme — is Mr. Shiomi's conception of Hirabayashi and Mr. Nakahara's carefully controlled performance in that role. From his first entrance into the lonely cabin that is the setting for the play, the actor exudes a quiet confidence, as if that alone could vanquish discrimination. Were it not for the Government's policy, a man like this might have achieved a position of public authority.

Though Hirabayashi in the play, as in life, leaves the United States to find a livelihood (as a professor of sociology), he does not lapse into self-pity. Nor does he regard himself as stateless. Instead, as one of the dispossessed, he never stops looking for an ameliorative future. Mr. Shiomi has been unable to create a play commensurate with that challenging character and his real-life story.

1989 F 12, 68:4

Mädchens à Trois

TRIPLETS IN UNIFORM, by Jeffrey Essmann; directed by David Warren; original music composed and performed by Michael-John LaChiusa; sets designed by James Youmans; costumes designed by Mary Beth Kilkelly; lighting designed by Howard Thies; hair designs by Carl Wilson; artistic director, Liz Dunn; production stage manager, Meryl Vladimer; stage manager, Jenny Peek. Presented by La Mama E.T.C. at 74A East Fourth Street.

Frau Fotze	Ann Mantel
Frau Nietzsche/Eileen	Mary Shultz
Frau Gimmel	Cornelia Kiss
Herr Gimmel/Putz/Herr Fokschmidt/Pastor Adolphus	Bob Koherr
Jana Gimmel	Kim Sykes
Jena Gimmel	Jeffrey Essmann
Jinna Gimmel	Kathy Kinney
Ilse	Susan Finch

By STEPHEN HOLDEN

When we first meet Jana, Jena and Jinna Gimmel, the identical triplets who reek mischief in Jeffrey Essmann's madcap comedy "Triplets in Uniform," the scene is Prussia and the year 1919. The simpering adolescent trio has just returned for another semester to the forbidding Kaiserina Wilhelmina School for Girls, whose stern headmistress, Frau Fotze, has an inexplicable phobia about mirrors. Moments before the triplets' arrival, Frau Fotze has engaged a mysterious young woman, Frau Nietzsche, to be the school's new penmanship teacher.

Roy Blakey

Kathy Kinney, left, Jeffrey Essmann and Kim Sykes in a scene from the comedy "Triplets in Uniform."

To Frau Fotze's astonishment, the demure young instructor has informed her that she is a hermaphrodite, and in spite of herself the poor headmistress finds herself inflamed by the confession.

The triplets, who are much more interested in seducing the school's handsome idiot stable boy than in pursuing their studies, soon find themselves in hot water. During a jealous spat with Ilse, an abused scholarship student who earns her tuition cleaning rain gutters, they accidentally behead her. Carrying the head in a hatbox, the sisters flee to Turkey where they become a vaudeville act on a freak farm. Their big song, one of the high points of the play, is a Turkish hootchy-kootchy number performed for an audience whose identical cutout heads are borrowed from Edvard Munch's famous painting "The Scream."

"Triplets in Uniform," which plays Thursdays through Saturdays at The Club at La Mama, is the first full-length play by Mr. Essmann, whose cabaret act there last season included an extended comic monologue also set in Eastern Europe. The play, which explicitly parodies the German cult film "Mädchen in Uniform," "The Children's Hour" and the Hayley Mills movie "The Trouble With Angels," weaves those plots into an amusing assault on European Expressionism in all its manifestations. Among the targets are Fritz Lang movies, the operas "Salome" and "Wozzeck," German Expressionist paintings and the prurient side of Freudian thinking that looks for truth in the churning depths of the unconscious.

If Mr. Essmann's play is strongly indebted to Ridiculous Theatrical Company conventions, he brings his own refined literary spin to a tradition that celebrates cross-dressing (the playwright himself plays one of the triplets), broad generic parody and elaborate corkscrew plots that turn on mistaken identity and magical hocus-pocus. The whimsical tone of the play is established early in the evening when the headmistress airily describes the Gimmel sisters as being "as alike as three little drops of blood."

•

Under David Warren's directorial hand, the pacing of a play that would benefit from some judicious trimming is a bit too leisurely, and the performances shy away from full-out caricature. But if the show has its dry patches, on the whole it is very diverting. The two strongest performances belong to Ann Mantel as Frau Fotze, an indefatigable pillar of respectability engaged in a perpetual struggle to repress her assorted kinks and compulsions, and Mary Shultz as Frau Nietzsche, a woman with at least two other identities besides the dainty, dutiful self she presents to her employer.

James Youmans's spare, economical sets use German Expressionist paintings as witty backdrops, and the feverish atmosphere is underscored by original post-Wagnerian-style background music played continuously but very lightly by its composer, Michael-John LaChiusa.

1989 F 12, 70:4

Loose Tongue
On the Skids

THE UNGUIDED MISSILE, by David Wolpe; directed by Fred Kolo; set and lighting design, Holger; costume design, Gail Cooper-Hecht; audio/visual producer, Matthew Heineman; production stage manager, Richard Hester; general manager, Mickey Rolfe. Presented by the American Place Theater, Wynn Handman, director. At 111 West 46th Street.

Martha Mitchell	Estelle Parsons
John Mitchell	Jerome Dempsey
The Photographer, Alan Webster and others	Nick Searcy
Mike Madden, Todd Peterson and others	Barry Cullison
Sherri Peterson	Lezlie Dalton
Cathy Ried, Dr. Kramer and others	Mary Jo Salerno

By MEL GUSSOW

Speaking her mind during the depths of Watergate, Martha Mitchell was either a virago gone haywire or a

protector of democratic principles. David Wolpe's play "The Unguided Missile" bolsters the first description, while making it clear that Mrs. Mitchell kept her tunnel vision fixed firmly on the interests of herself and her husband, John N. Mitchell, the indicted former Attorney General.

The Martha Mitchell portrayed on stage by Estelle Parsons at the American Place Theater is no closet liberal. She is also far too shallow a figure to justify a play about her, or, at least, to justify this play about her. Expecting a vivid display of character coloration or at least an amusing political comedy, one finds a tiresome story about a scold who is victimized by her own bluntness.

The woman's unpredictability, Martha Mitchell as "unguided missile," momentarily holds the audience's interest, which is quenched by the lameness of Mr. Wolpe's dramaturgy and of Fred Kolo's direction. Filling the stage with a camera crew and television monitors only makes one curious to know what programs are being broadcast on other channels.

•

Patched together from public record and private guesswork, "The Unguided Missile" introduces Mrs. Mitchell on the day of the break-in at the Democratic National Committee headquarters at the Watergate. As crucial political events begin to happen around her, she seems mostly concerned with her relatively insignificant position in the Washington pecking order. As she says, proudly, "I'm the seventh most respected woman in the whole world." One would hesitate to think who the first six were at the time.

The source of her supposed respect was her husband's brief authority, lit-

Estelle Parsons as Martha Mitchell in David Wolpe's play "The Unguided Missile."

tle of which is exhibited on stage. The role of John Mitchell is insubstantial and, in common with the play, unrevealing. Playing Mr. Mitchell, Jerome Dempsey is called upon to puff a pipe, look impassive and stonewall questions.

Other actors ineffectively pretend to be specific members of the Senate Watergate Committee, as well as pseudonymous characters. Congressional interrogation is cross cut with domestic scenes, in which the Mitchells address each other with a cloying effusiveness ("my little sugar dish," "rum raisin"), endearments that call for a quick kick from W. C. Fields.

With melodramatic fanfare, Mrs. Mitchell is held prisoner in her quarters. When she tries to use the telephone, it is ripped out. With no outlet for her anger except to shout from the window, she drinks heavily and behaves raucously (she is drugged by those who are presumably guarding her). The downhill slide is steep.

With the help of makeup, Ms. Parsons manages a fair physical resemblance to her character, though her voice wanders afar from Mrs. Mitchell's native Arkansas. The actress is a proven expert at commanding a stage by herself, as she did in "Miss Margarida's Way" and the Dario Fo-Franca Rame monologues. But her role as Martha Mitchell is not cut from similar dramatic or comedic cloth.

It is unclear whether Mr. Wolpe intends to spoof his protagonist or to present a sympathetic portrait of her. Instead, "The Unguided Missile" lapses into self-parody. In one blistering argument, Mr. Mitchell accuses his wife of being "emasculating," and she counterattacks with the most withering assault she knows: "You don't know how to use the media like I do." Within minutes, her husband is maundering around the stage, the Big Enchilada and self-acknowledged Old Stone Face, asking himself, "How did I become made of sand?"

The most theatrical character is off stage and that of course is Richard M. Nixon, "King Richard" as Mrs. Mitchell calls him. She hopes that he will rescue them, but he will not even answer his telephone. Mr. Nixon himself achieved a fictional life on stage in "Secret Honor" by Donald Freed and Arnold M. Stone. With its eccentric humor and penetrating analysis of the misuses of power, "Secret Honor" is everything that "The Unguided Missile" is not.

1989 F 13, C16:3

Moral Conundrums

BITTER FRIENDS, by Gordon Rayfield; directed by Allen Coulter; set design, Michael C. Smith; costume design, Laura Drawbaugh; lighting design, Dan Kinsley; sound design, Gary and Timmy Harris; production stage manager, D. C. Rosenberg. Presented by Jewish Repertory Theater, Ran Avni, artistic director; Edward M. Cohen, associate director. At 344 East 14th Street.

David Klein .... Ben Siegler
Rachel Klein .... Farryl Lovett
Rabbi Arthur Schaefer .... Sam Gray
Ambassador Ezra Ben-Ami ...... Yosi Sokolsky
Helen Klein .... Viola Harris
Congressman Frank Fitzgerald .... Bill Nelson
Wingate Whitney .... Dan Pinto
Embassy employee, headwaiter and guard
.... Andrew Thain

By STEPHEN HOLDEN

Gordon Rayfield's political melodrama "Bitter Friends" is a play so charged with incident and moral debate that by the end one is left almost breathless from chasing its labyrinthine arguments.

The troubling issues around which Mr. Rayfield's fictional account of espionage and American-Israeli relations revolves are deep, knotty questions of ethnic identity, commitment to country versus religious heritage, and much more. The plot is an ingeniously constructed moral puzzle. After the United States has refused to help Israel build an air defense system, David Klein (Ben Siegler), a young idealist who was brought up to care passionately about the fate of Israel, slips classified defense information to an Israeli intelligence agent.

•

David is convicted of treason, but Rabbi Arthur Schaefer (Sam Gray), an experienced power broker who was a close friend of the young man's deceased father, arranges a deal involving the Israeli Ambassador (Yosi Sokolsky), a Justice Department lawyer (Dan Pinto) and a friendly Congressman (Bill Nelson), by which he can get off with a light sentence instead of life imprisonment. When the deal falls through at the last second, Schaefer tries desperately to salvage the situation, but in pulling every string he discovers that all the ties that once bound family, friends, colleagues and countries no longer hold.

The drama, at the Jewish Repertory Theater, unfolds as a series of bruising clashes interspersed with Schaefer's musings to the audience. At the center of the storm stands David, an idealistic hothead who battles everyone attempting to help him, including his wife, Rachel (Farryl Lovett), and his mother, Helen (Viola Harris).

In building the play's argumentative structure, Mr. Rayfield often stretches credibility. The turn in the story by which the deal falls through is especially shaky and the plot is so thick that, except for Rabbi Schaefer, the mere unfolding of it leaves little room for character development. Played by Mr. Gray with a powerful authority, Schaefer is an immensely likable, complex man with a streak of the entertainer in him. Discussing Jewish history and law, he extracts amusing nuggets of folk wisdom from the stories of Abraham, Moses and Joshua and weaves them into a rich open-ended meditation on Jewish identity.

The Jewish Repertory Theater production, directed by Allen Coulter, makes do with a minimum of scenery and props. Facsimiles of square stone pillars on either side of the stage suggest official Washington. While the acting is a bit too high-pitched, several of the performances have real gravity. Besides Mr. Gray's rabbi, the most impressive portrayal is Miss Harris's as David's mother, a stiff-backed widow driven by a taut, dignified rage.

"Bitter Friends" has holes, but they are faults of ambition. The issues with which it grapples are simply too various to be contained in a single drama. But one must also admire the intellectual energy and courage of a play that seizes the political moment and engages it with such thrashing intensity.

1989 F 14, C16:3

Gelbart's Scorn for Scandals

By FRANK RICH

Special to The New York Times

CAMBRIDGE, Mass., Feb. 12 — Maybe it was foolish to hope that Congress, the press or the courts could ever explain the Iran-contra scandal to anyone's satisfaction. From Fawn Hall's shredder to Robert McFarlane's planned birthday cake for the Ayatollah, this Washington escapade was a farce whose lunatic logic only Hollywood could understand — and only a Hollywood-trained President could have presided over.

Perhaps this is also why a Hollywood writer, Larry Gelbart, has written what may be the most penetrating, and is surely the funniest, exegesis of the fiasco to date. "Mastergate," as Mr. Gelbart calls his satirical comedy at Harvard's American Repertory Theater, takes the form of a Capitol Hill hearing in which self-aggrandizing Congressmen windily seek to answer such questions as "What does the President know, and does he have any idea that he knew it?" The nominally fictionalized conspiracy under investigation — the latest incident of "governmental self-abuse," appropriately known as "Mastergate" — puts a film studio, Master Pictures, in cahoots with the White House. This time the C.I.A. has illicitly armed Central American guerrillas by laundering $800 million through the budget of the forthcoming epic "Tet: The Movie."

•

Mr. Gelbart was born for this endeavor. In its scornful attitude toward official bureaucracy, "Mastergate" overlaps with his television series "M*A*S*H"; in its cynical view of show-biz chicanery, it recalls "Tootsie," which he co-wrote. Running 90 mostly breathless minutes, "Mastergate" has the frenzied tone and topical perishability of old-time Sid Caesar sketches (some of which Mr. Gelbart also wrote) as well as the heartlessness essential to nasty satire (as one expects from a writer who adapted "Volpone" into Broadway's "Sly Fox").

Just as crucial to "Mastergate" as the author's comic bent, however, is his moral outrage. Mr. Gelbart is furious, and not just at wrongdoers in public life. Even as he ridicules his Oliver North stand-in, the excessively decorated Maj. Manley Battle (played with the perfect mix of Boy Scout earnestness and sanctimonious arrogance by Daniel Von Bargen), the playwright mocks camera-hogging Congressmen of both the smug left and the "gung-holier than thou" right (each acted, in an impressive about-face, by Alvin Epstein). Nor does Mr. Gelbart spare the medium that shaped his career. "Mastergate" is flanked by television monitors and narrated with surpassing fatuousness by Merry Chase (Cherry Jones) of the Total News Network. As has been true at least since Tet (the battle, not the movie), the distorted televised images of news events often matter more than the events themselves.

To Mr. Gelbart, language is a principal casualty in the post-Vietnam era of government by press conference and photo opportunity. And when language is corrupted, so is what the play's George Bush figure (Joseph Daly) genially dismisses as the "so-called truth." The oxymoronic officials of "Mastergate" follow the tradition of those who coined phrases like "pacification program" and "modified limited hangout" for obfuscating ends. Mr. Gelbart's politicos can invert the meaning of nearly any word.

Richard Feldman
Daniel Von Bargen as Maj. Manley Battle in "Mastergate."

One witness protects the national interest by being "steadfastly evasive and selectively honest." Another defends his Administration's dreadful mistakes by pleading "they were honest mistakes, honestly made — honestly dreadful." The pro-American country "San Elvador" is described as having "a democratic form of government that has been run by its army for the past 40 years." We learn where clandestine meetings that did not take place took place; we hear what was discussed in "nondiscussions." A Congressman delivers the lesson of Watergate: "Those that forget the past are certain to be subpoenaed."

The play's priceless doublespeak is more reminiscent of "Catch-22" than of "M*A*S*H." (Mr. Gelbart's Major Battle is surely a descendant of Joseph Heller's Major Major.) Sometimes "Mastergate" buckles under its linguistic weight, but even when the fictive witnesses become as tiresome as their real-life counterparts, the inventive director Michael Engler puts on a bustling show.

In 'Mastergate,' the wrongdoers can do nothing right.

The gifts that Mr. Engler brought to "Eastern Standard" are irrelevant here. Mr. Gelbart doesn't require character development or any emotion other than malice. He demands — and is given — the vivid strokes of an editorial cartoon. Philipp Jung's environmental set, with mannequins for extras and the painting of the signing of the Declaration of Independence as an ironic backdrop, is a three-ring Washington circus buffeted by flashbulb firestorms. Among the most delightful clowns are Jerome Kilty, as a committee chairman whose patrician elegance is matched only by his stupidity, and Jeremy Geidt as a schedule-pressed Secretary of State who brusquely informs his inquisitors that "the truth will have to wait until after I finish testifying."

"Mastergate" leaves its audience wondering how much longer the truth can wait and how many more coinages using the syllable "gate" the nation can absorb. Mr. Gelbart brings down the curtain with the chilling specter of more clandestine plans being hatched by yet another crew of fanatical nobodies passing through the Government on their way to either jail or higher office. Though it's natural to wish that a play of this quality might travel to New York, the national interest in this case should dictate a detour. "Mastergate" could be the most valuable contribution to public policy that Harvard has sent to Washington in years.

1989 F14, C17:1

The Maltese Magpie

IN A PIG'S VALISE, book and lyrics by Eric Overmyer; music by August Darnell; directed and choreographed by Graciela Daniele; set design by Bob Shaw; lighting design by Peggy Eisenhauer; costume design by Jeanne Button; musical direction, Peter Schott; sound design, Gary and Timmy Harris; hair design, Antonio Soddu; production stage manager, Robert Mark Kalfin; stage manager, Paula Gray. Presented by the Second Stage Theater, Robyn Goodman and Carole Rothman, artistic directors. At 2162 Broadway, at 76th Street.

James Taxi .... Nathan Lane
Dolores Con Leche .... Ada Maris
Zoot Alors and Gut Bucket .... Jonathan Freeman
Root Choyce .... Thom Sesma
The Bop Op .... Reg E. Cathey
Blind Sax .... Charlie Lagond
Shrimp Bucket .... Michael McCormick
Mustang Sally .... Lauren Tom
Dizzy Miss Lizzy .... Dian Sorel

By FRANK RICH

"In a Pig's Valise," the "hard-boiled yarn with music" at the Second Stage, is an homage to detective fiction by a playwright whose affection for Raymond Chandler and Dashiell Hammett may be second only to his love for the sound of his own voice. The playwright is Eric Overmyer, the author of the widely produced "On the Verge," a work of such relentless erudition that its icy intricacies of diction linger long after the play's subject and human mouthpieces have evaporated. "In a Pig's Valise" offers more of the same showy verbiage, but, as they say, "with music." Nonetheless, one is most likely to leave the theater humming the similes.

New musicals are so rarely produced, let alone by companies as ambitious as the Second Stage, that the wastefulness of "In a Pig's Valise" is dispiriting. The premise, though not original, promises fun. Mr. Overmyer propels his hero, the trench-coated private eye James Taxi (a rumpled Nathan Lane), through every cliché twist known to his pulp genre. As Taxi stalks the Heartbreak Hotel at the corner of Neon and Lonely in the "kiss-me-deadly night air," he encounters femmes fatales, red herrings and unanswered questions that mount up "like a stack of unpaid utility bills."

The trench-coated hero encounters femmes fatales and a few red herrings.

Mr. Overmyer's compulsive, unedited wordplays mount up more precipitously still. Along with similes, ethnic food references and double entendres, his favorite tic is to tinker idly with familiar phrases: "a cut and blow-dried case" or "I get the driftwood." One must do more to parody a literary style that is already, in the hands of its wittiest practitioners, something of a put-on. Mr. Overmyer is clever to a fault, as if he were trying to imitate Tom Stoppard with the aid of a thesaurus. By Act II, the mere mention of the words neon, noir, genre or gumshoe, however linguistically fractured the usage, makes one squirm.

Aside from a funny replay of the slapping scene from "Chinatown," the only amusing riffs are those in which the characters deconstruct their own tale, commenting self-consciously on how vintage detective fiction (and films) rely on the past tense, "ominous underscoring" and narrative dissolves. Unfortunately, the plot — something an audience may want even in a mock-detective story — is dismantled by the same academic knowingness. The villains of "In a Pig's Valise" are trying to steal American dreams, which leads to an avalanche of secondhand, Leslie Fiedleresque ruminations on the metaphysical, political and erotic implications of national myths perpetrated by the likes of Walt Disney and John Dillinger.

•

As a musical — or a play with music, or whatever — "In a Pig's Valise" seems an uneasy compromise among strong personalities who never found the essential common ground for collaboration. The composer, August Darnell of the band Kid Creole and the Coconuts, is the kind of pop recruit the musical theater desperately needs, but his own style meets the material halfway only in some sultry saxophone solos. While the music and the onstage band are agreeable, the score seems irrelevant to the show's milieu. So do Mr. Overmyer's amateurish lyrics, with their dead words and inevitable rhymes ("I'm a talent scout without a doubt/ I'm the one who's got the clout.")

The director and choreographer, Graciela Daniele, goes her own way as well by evoking the smoky atmosphere of her last theater piece, "Tango Apasionado," without the tangos. Without any drama to propel it, "In a Pig's Valise" would have benefited from a galvanizing style. But Ms. Daniele fails to impose a theatrical order that might integrate the seemingly arbitrary musical numbers into the script. Two dancing girls often sashay about for little reason other than a temporary cessation of puns.

Though Mr. Lane is a fine comic actor, he is, as Mr. Overmyer might say, a stalled Taxi — an uncomfortable and unvaried singing detective. The rest of the cast can charitably be described as campy, with the striking exception of Ada Maris, who plays Delores Con Leche, a comic yet sexy lady in red, with more musical-comedy verve than the rest of the company combined. I also enjoyed the usher who deposited me in my seat with the request that I "laugh really hard, because the critics are here tonight." If the response of most of my neighbors was any indication, everybody these days is a critic.

1989 F 15, C15:1

Susan Cook
Nathan Lane and Ada Maris in a scene from "In a Pig's Valise."

A Return To the Beginning

FIFTH OF JULY, by Lanford Wilson; directed by Andrew Glant-Linden; scenery by Richard Ellis; lighting by A. C. Hickox; costumes by Hilarie Blumenthal; sound by Steven Osgood; production stage managers, Jon Roger Clark and John Frederick Sullivan. Presented by Equity Library Theater, 103d Street and Riverside Drive.

Kenneth Talley Jr. .... Jack L. Davis
Shirley Talley .... Cate Damon
Jed Jenkins .... Laurence Overmire
John Landis .... Kevin Jeffries
Gwen Landis .... Susanna Frazer
June Talley .... Rebecca Hoodwin
Sally Friedman .... Joan Mann
Weston Hurley .... Don Weingust

By D. J. R. BRUCKNER

No Talley, in Lanford Wilson's trilogy about the Talley family, ages gracefully — and a revival of "Fifth of July" at the Equity Library Theater reveals that the first play in the series has aged considerably, if not well, in 11 years. The Talleys are not as fascinating here as they would become in "Talley's Folly" and "Talley and Son," and Mr. Wilson's skeptical, sometimes caustic, reflections on the illusions of the 1960's, so startling when the Circle Repertory Company first produced the play in 1978, have lost some of their punch.

Andrew Glant-Linden, the director, and his cast bring great energy to the Equity performance. And the second act retains its emotional power as an aging group of former radicals, reunited in a small Missouri town, recognize how empty was the reality behind their romantic memories and how treacherous they have become to one another. But too much of the humor in the long first act was so topical that by now it has disappeared with the headlines of a gone decade.

As Kenneth Talley Jr., the Vietnam War veteran with two artificial legs, Jack L. Davis is a wry and fragile man whose surface candor and wit conceal an inner terror that bursts out in a harrowing moment at the end — although this Kenneth has none of the sense of menace that William Hurt brought to the role originally. Laurence Overmire, as Jed, Kenneth's lover, has the right mixture of affection, resentment, silence and confidence to keep you guessing until the last moment about whether his apparent strength is not mere pretence.

•

Joan Mann makes a delightfully nutty, and wise, Sally, the widowed Talley aunt who sees space ships and constantly misplaces her husband's ashes. And Kevin Jeffries and Susanna Frazer as John and Gwen Landis, Kenneth's old college friends, are a well-matched pair of noisy, phony and selfish schemers who set your nerves on edge the moment they walk on stage.

If there is a bit of miscasting, it is Cate Damon as Shirley, the precocious 13-year-old daughter of June, Kenneth's sister. Miss Damon is engaging and she can extort laughter with some of the daydreaming girl's sillier lines. But she is no teen-ager, and the character she creates here reminds you at every turn that she is a grown-up comic imitating an adolescent.

1989 F 16, C34:3

The Prey Deserves The Predator

OTHER PEOPLE'S MONEY, by Jerry Sterner; directed by Gloria Muzio; scenic designer, David Jenkins; costume designer, Jess Goldstein; lighting designer, F. Mitchell Dana; sound designer, David Budries; production stage manager, Stacey Fleischer. A Hartford Stage Company production presented by Jeffrey Ash and Susan Quint Gallin in association with Dennis Grimaldi. At the Minetta Lane Theater, 18 Minetta Lane.

William Coles .... James Murtaugh
Andrew Jorgenson .... Arch Johnson
Lawrence Garfinkle .... Kevin Conway
Bea Sullivan .... Scotty Bloch
Kate Sullivan .... Mercedes Ruehl

By MEL GUSSOW

New England Wire and Cable, a solidly established but outmoded Rhode Island business, is ripe for a takeover. Here comes Lawrence Garfinkle, Larry the Liquidator, riding into town in his stretch limo and plotting to annihilate the company. Later, when Garfinkle (Kevin Conway) is about to assume control, he cuts up with a chorus of "The Farmer and the Cowman" from "Oklahoma!" The song reminds us that, for all its stock-market timeliness, Jerry Sterner's "Other People's Money" is a kind of Eastern western (the corporate raider is the carpetbagger) as well as board room melodrama.

Although "Other People's Money," which opened last night at the Minetta Lane Theater, follows a dramatic formula, it is a swift straight line of a play. This is in contrast to the more complex "Serious Money," which crisscrossed so many financial bridges that it entangled itself in its own plotting. Mr. Sterner's work could serve as an explanatory guide for anyone who wants to know more about such Wall Street subjects as white knights, shark repellents and poison pills.

Peter Cunningham

Kevin Conway in "Other People's Money" at Minetta Lane Theater.

Those buzzwords themselves say something about the cutthroat nature of Garfinkle's world. He is a piranha. Money breeds more money, and he wants as much as he can get — for the power that it possesses and for the pleasure it provides.

What gives the play its drive, besides the acuity of some of the dialogue, is Mr. Conway's authoritative performance. The amoral Garfinkle wastes no time on charm, yet in the actor's portrayal the character has a certain likability, beginning with his frankness. He is neither more nor less than he says he is, and he communicates an Olympian pride in his skill as a predator. To a great extent, his foes deserve him

Mr. Conway is an unusual choice for this richly ethnic role except for the fact that he seems to revel in playing obsessive figures. As research for the transformation, he must have been studying Jackie Mason, emulating his accent and the drollness of his delivery. In keeping with that role model, many of his lines are like stand-up comedy (lawyers, in particular, are the target of

his disdain). The actor has also fattened — or padded — himself for the role, emphasizing Garfinkle's self-satisfaction.

•

One might legitimately ask whether it is necessary for the author to have a character that reinforces an ethnic stereotype. But Mr. Conway's intensity keeps Garfinkle from becoming a caricature.

The raider's primary rival is not the owner (Arch Johnson) but the savvy Wall Street attorney (Mercedes Ruehl) hired to block the takeover. In an overly pat touch, the lawyer happens to be the daughter of the company boss's longtime assistant. The role itself has a manufactured quality, which Ms. Ruehl partly cosmetizes with her ebullience. The lawyer is smart, tough and eager to play big league hardball with someone of Garfinkle's stature. Their confrontations are at the core of the play. Between them there is gamesmanship as well as malice — and, unconvincingly, an air of mutual sexual attraction.

The other characters, though well played, are less vivid. The company owner is so rigidly uncompromising that he wears out our patience (he infuriates his attorney). James Murtaugh is the firm's heir apparent, for whom promises of succession are as tangible as rainbows, and Scotty Bloch is the boss's faithful aide. The actors are allied under Gloria Muzio's fluid direction.

The author himself seems less concerned with delineating character than with arranging for argument and advancing the story, which leads unwaveringly to a climactic stockholder's meeting in which the owner and the outsider each make a pitch for support. The speeches are summations to the audience as jury. Mr. Johnson's plea for loyalty is as reasonable as it is impractical — and it is no competition for Mr. Conway's appeal to the pragmatic self-interest of the stockholders. "Other People's Money" offers no surprises, but it is buoyed by Mr. Conway's performance and, as a play about the cannibalistic nature of big business, it has a heart of irony.

1989 F 17, C3:4

Oppressed Housewife As 'Missing Person'

SHIRLEY VALENTINE, by Willy Russell; directed by Simon Callow; designed by Bruno Santini; lighting by Nick Chelton. Presented by the Really Useful Theater Company and Bob Swash. At the Booth Theater, 222 West 45th Street.

Shirley Valentine .... Pauline Collins

By FRANK RICH

It's commonplace to watch star actresses impersonate forlorn working-class women — they almost always win awards for it — but Willy Russell's one-woman play "Shirley Valentine" takes the truly brave risk of asking an audience to spend an evening with a performer who is unmistakably as unglamorous as her humble role.

Pauline Collins, the actress in question, has not dressed down to appear as Mr. Russell's monologuist, Shirley Bradshaw (née Valentine), an oppressed 42-year-old Liverpudlian

housewife who talks nonstop to the walls of her humdrum suburban kitchen. Miss Collins's rag-doll features, bouncy blue eyes excepted, are handsome but anonymous. Her curly reddish hair has no luster. Her voice is emphatic but only in the manner of a burdened weekend shopper asking directions from a bus driver. When the script calls upon Miss Collins to take some sun, she doesn't disguise the fold of flab between her bikini top and her chinos.

Authenticity like this cannot be faked, and neither can the chatty inti-

Pauline Collins finds freedom with a Greek waiter.

macy, robust humor and intense conviction with which the actress holds the stage at the Booth Theater for more than two hours. Audiences will adore Pauline Collins — not because she can match the brilliant acting of the week's other oppressed-English-housewife soliloquy (Maggie Smith in Alan Bennett's "Bed Among the Lentils" on public television), but because she radiates the genuine, unpretentious vitality of a warm old friend giving us the real lowdown. That Miss Collins captivates us with her honesty is all the more amazing given how frequently her vehicle seems contrived.

•

As a play, "Shirley Valentine" is feminism West End style; it intends to titillate and perhaps even shock matinee theatergoers with a mild level of ideological daring that will be familiar to those who have seen "Steaming," "Song & Dance," "Woman in Mind" or Mr. Russell's own "Educating Rita." In these British plays, women discover that many

Catherine Ashmore

Pauline Collins in "Shirley Valentine" at the Booth Theater.

men are pigs, children are ungrateful and autonomy is a birthright. A New York theatergoer can fully agree with the message and still be perplexed by the astonished cries of "Eureka!" with which it is presented at this late date.

Though Miss Collins often addresses us like a stand-up comic, Mr.

Russell's heroine is tamer than equivalent contemporary Middle American women played by Roseanne Barr or Lily Tomlin. Indeed, Shirley Valentine is an updated variant on the sentimentalized, indomitable doormats once regularly assigned by Hollywood to Shirley MacLaine (Charity Hope Valentine, of "Sweet Charity," included). The difference is that Mr. Russell's Shirley can free herself from subservience to a bad man (her callous husband, Joe) — as long as the catalyst for that liberation is a hot-blooded "good man" (a taverna waiter she meets during a two-week jaunt to Greece). Mr. Russell isn't about to risk offending customers of either gender. If he had written "A Doll's House," Nora would have waltzed back through the door and asked Torvald out for a drink.

The playwright is a slick craftsman even so, and his first act, which Shirley delivers while preparing Joe's dinner, bubbles along professionally. Though the setups and punch lines follow a rhythmic formula — and though the mocking complaints about Joe are of Phyllis Diller bluntness — one laughs at Shirley's riesling-fueled explanations of why sex is like shopping at Safeway and why marriage resembles the Middle East. The Erma Bombeck-esque domestic anecdotes are jolly, and Miss Collins does a vibrant job of filling out the characters who inhabit them: the kids in a school Nativity play, a patronizing headmistress, a braggart neighbor.

By Act II, Shirley has achieved her promised leap of rebellion: She has traveled to the foreign land of self-realization by running away to join her best friend on a Mediterranean vacation. The trip instantly accomplishes for Shirley what an education did for Mr. Russell's Rita, prompting her to deliver a fervent pitch for taking charge of one's unused (or wasted) life. "Why do we get all these feelings and dreams and hopes if we don't ever use them?" asks Shirley rhetorically. She announces that she has "fallen in love with the idea of living" and that "it's nice to like yourself." These aren't postcards from Greece — they're inspirational greeting cards.

"It's the same for everyone; I know it is," Shirley says. Mr. Russell spells out his messages to advertise the universality of his heroine's plight and subsequent triumph. But, as Mr. Bennett and Miss Smith so handily demonstrated in their television portrait of a vicar's miserable wife, the universality and pathos of a wasted existence are most touchingly conveyed by that existence's specific details, not by superimposed sermons.

The director and designer of "Shirley Valentine," Simon Callow and Bruno Santini, happen to be Mr. Bennett's collaborators on his current London stage hit, "Single Spies." They have done a sensitive job by Mr. Russell as well. The contrast between Shirley's kitchen imprisonment and Greek liberation is graphically abstracted by Mr. Santini's vivid sets, evocatively lighted by Nick Chelton. Mr. Callow, himself an excellent actor, undoubtedly played an important role in facilitating the seamless ease of Miss Collins's performance.

For most of the play, that performance is highly likable without being moving; the practiced, jokey writing can be as confining for the protagonist as a bad marriage. Yet when Shirley abruptly breaks comic stride in her kitchen, self-disgustedly demanding to know how and when she became a "missing person," or when she later celebrates her stretch marks as proud badges of maturity, Miss Collins does dig deeper. While Mr. Russell's valentine to ordinary women may otherwise seem candied, there is never anything false or ordinary about the actress's heart beating so irrepressibly within.

1989 F 17, C3:1

Words at Odds With Deeds

THE ESTATE, written and directed by Ray Aranha; original music composed by Robert P. Mills; set design by Maurice C. Dana; lighting design by Sean Dolan; costume design by Kathryn J. Foust; production stage manager, Dominque J. Cook; assistant stage manager, Christine Cullen. Presented by Blue Heron Theater Inc., Ardelle Striker, artistic director. At Westbeth Theater Center, 151 Bank Street.

Garth	James Fleming
Will	Tyrone Murphy
Minta	Donna-Marie Peters
Benjamin Banneker	Donald Lee Taylor
Thomas Jefferson	George McGrath
Sally Hemmings	Rhianna Jean Waters
Martha Jefferson	Elizabeth Striker
John Walker	Noel Craig
Cal	Ennis Smith
Tom	Greig Sargeant
Abigail Adams	Jane Moore

By MEL GUSSOW

"The Estate," Ray Aranha's probing drama about a crisis in the life of Thomas Jefferson, was first presented at Hartford Stage in 1976, one of the rare theatrical recognitions of the Bicentennial season. Thirteen years later the play has finally arrived in New York (produced by the Blue Heron Theater at the Westbeth Theater Center), its passions — and its problems — intact.

Mr. Aranha, best known as the author of "My Sister, My Sister," and as the actor who played James Earl Jones's friend Bono in August Wilson's "Fences," is disturbed by the many Jeffersonian contradictions. Jefferson, who in the play has not yet become President, is regarded here as a man of principle but not of moral courage.

•

Though Jefferson is outraged by injustices against blacks, he is himself a slaveholder and he expresses a patrician double standard in his own household. In the play he has been having a long-term affair with his mulatto slave, Sally Hemmings, the half-sister of his deceased wife. In Jefferson's book, "Notes on Virginia," quoted by Mr. Aranha, he speculates that blacks are intellectually inferior to whites. His response to Sally is ambiguous in the extreme.

The crux of the drama is Jefferson's meeting with a self-taught, freed black astronomer, Benjamin Banneker, who has come to Jefferson to have his scientific studies certified (in real life, the two merely corresponded). While respecting Banneker's persistence, he is unwilling to accept him as his equal, in a scene that ends with Banneker's poignant realization of his own irreconcilable dilemma. He can never be recognized in his time.

•

Racism is studied in various shadings — from a bigoted neighbor who firmly supports slavery but, unlike Jefferson, can allow for the veracity

of Banneker's work, to Abigail Adams, a fervent abolitionist with a moralistic attitude toward Sally Hemmings.

There is enough material here for a trilogy of plays. In his revised version, Mr. Aranha has trimmed "The Estate" to two emotion-filled acts, but he has not eliminated the rant and the excessive verbiage. "The Estate" is inflated with speechifying, much of which was disguised in Paul Weidner's original Hartford Stage production.

That production was headed by Josef Sommer as Jefferson, the playwright himself as Banneker and Seret Scott as Sally Hemmings — and one could not envision a more persuasive cast. The New York production is far less secure, especially in the performances by George McGrath and Donald Lee Taylor (as Jefferson and Banneker). In supporting roles, Jane Moore has a quiet professionalism as Abigail Adams, and Ennis Smith has a definite power as a rebellious slave who may be on his way to becoming a Nat Turner.

Even in this journeyman production, it is heartening to see the play again and to feel the surge of history that inspired Mr. Aranha. Though roughhewn and still in need of editing, "The Estate" is a play rooted in conviction and dramatic truth.

1989 F 18, 18:1

Somebody Up There Likes Billie and Heidi

HEAVEN WILL PROTECT THE working girl, but only up to a point.

I don't honestly suppose that we can consider Billie Dawn a working girl. Billie, as you'll surely recall, is the blonde and feisty mistress of wealthy junk dealer Harry Brock in Garson Kanin's comedy "Born Yesterday." And, at the time we get to know her, she isn't really working for hire. For mink coats, yes; but not for hire. Billie makes distinctions of this kind.

When Harry Brock's lawyer, a man who's shucked his ideals but always has time for Billie, mentions to her — almost admiringly — that she's come a long way since her days in the chorus, Billie is quick to correct him. She was not just a girl in the chorus line when she decorated "Anything Goes." In that musical, she had five lines to say. She will even recite them for you. Example: "He *was* here but he is gone now."

"I could of been a star," she informs her friend — "probably," she adds. What is most splendid about Billie, a trimly turned-out presence from the tips of her circus-pony toes to the outer edges of her deep black eyelashes, is her pride. And her doubt. She is a dreamy realist.

Suddenly, however, she is not good enough for Harry Brock because Harry has come to Washington, D.C., to buy himself a Senator and he can't have a "stupid" girl on his arm as he mixes with the tonier set. Where-

Madeline Kahn and Edward Asner in "Born Yesterday"—someone Harry can't belt around anymore

Peter Cunningham

upon he hires a young reporter from the New Republic to give Billie a little class. The heroine of the current film "Working Girl" starts her corporate ascent by wearing designer dresses and deciding that she needs more "serious" hair. So she goes out and has her hair done. Billie Dawn is having her brain done.

Well, you knew the plot. The question I kept asking myself, as the curtain went up on the posh mulberry-tinted walls of a Washington hotel suite, was whether or not Billie's — or, more correctly, Garson Kanin's — play was going to hold up. After all, "Born Yesterday" wasn't born yesterday. It was born 43 years ago, and nothing dates like politics. I'm kidding.

The answer to that question is that Mr. Kanin's very funny, sometimes touching, gleefully sardonic and immaculately crafted play holds up absolutely, solid as a rock. Strangely, one reason you can tell just how indestructible it is lies in the determination of one of its principals to put it through a vocal shredder. If the play *could* be destroyed, it would have been.

Edward Asner, a fine actor, has unaccountably been persuaded, or permitted, to punctuate his marauding as Harry Brock with a series of shattering bullroars that invariably rip holes in the rhythmic texture of the comedy. The Harry we hear about

Beset by various vicissitudes, the heroines of 'Born Yesterday' and 'The Heidi Chronicles' call on special resources.

seems to be a boor with a certain practiced charm. The one we get is straight out of Lower Slobbovia.

Madeline Kahn's Billie, on the other hand, has the early disadvantage of looking and sounding rather too much like Judy Holliday — the effect is eerie, sometimes — but she gradually creates an interior presence that is just right for the needs of the play. She is attractively sensual: The first, inevitable kiss she bestows upon Daniel Hugh Kelly as the New Republic's man has some dramatic energy to it, enough to drive these two rebels toward a palace coup. And, behind Billie's accumulated shellac, you hear and feel an intelligence that is both wistful and tough-minded steadily stretching its wings. I think we could say that she *becomes* a working girl, i.e. someone Harry can't belt around anymore.

Meantime, Mr. Kelly perfectly gauges the moment-by-moment support she needs. His own performance is knowledgeable, as it must be, but there's never any sense that he's slumming.

Brace yourself for some bumps and you'll have a good time.

The witty, self-effacing, stunningly played heroine of Wendy Wasserstein's "The Heidi Chronicles" is a working girl of sorts — having got through late adolescence, she becomes a teacher of art — but she is not the Cinderella who gets to the ball. She is the Cinderella who has to sit home in the ashes.

Figuratively, not literally. We first meet Joan Allen, who fills the part with such mysterious authority, at a school dance in the mid-1960's. She hovers. She evades. She tells little social lies. She doesn't finish her gestures. She explains, when pressed, that she came with a friend for whom she is now waiting.

We also meet, quite quickly, the two men whose paths will cross hers down the years, pleasantly if not profitably. Boyd Gaines, describing himself as "a small noise from Winnetka," while the sounds of Glen Miller purr through the loudspeakers, slips onto a bench beside her and regales her with imitations of old movies ("We have this one night before the ship docks at Portsmouth"). But she needn't dream of any such nights, for this dedicated medical student whom she would very much like to touch is gay.

Peter Friedman plays a chap named Scoop who is a great deal more direct. He wants her to stop edging to the outside of every occa-

Gerry Goodstein

Joan Allen and Peter Friedman in the "Heidi Chronicles"—She has valuables.

sion and to come on in. He further wants her to stop fibbing and to face up to home truths ("You're going home with 15 virgins in a station wagon.") He would like to have sex with her — she doesn't rule it out — but she's not to be foolish enough to think he'd marry her ("I don't want to come home to an A-plus" is his credo). Still friends, though.

Playwright Wasserstein, in her chronicle-style journey that will be transferring to Broadway on March 9, escorts us through the protest movements of the 70's and then looks in on their aftermath (their betrayal?) in the 80's. Whatever is going on, Heidi is always present, with her freshness, her reticence, her waiting.

Asked whether she supports the lesbian life style of a youngster with a serape draped over her shoulders and fronds of hair falling into her eyes, Heidi replies "I'm just visiting." When the members of a circle take to hugging each other by way of declaring their solidarity, Heidi accepts a hug but doesn't hug back.

■

Visiting a den of wives who aren't precisely enchanted with their husbands ("Why should an educated woman spend the rest of her life making him and his children tunafish sandwiches?"), Heidi cocks her head, puzzled. When she goes to Scoop's wedding, why does Scoop spend so much time dancing with *her*? We see her intense, questioning eyes over Scoop's shoulder as the two sway gently, and whatever she is seeing has some alarm in it.

The evening covers a great deal of territory — including one hilarious sendup of TV talk-show hostesses — but none of it is territory to which Heidi is willing to commit herself, not for real. What freezes Heidi into hold-back position? I don't know. I can only tell you that I believed in Heidi all the time I was watching her. And I was both intrigued and moved by a two-line exchange between a drop-in Scoop and a hearth-bound Heidi near the end of the unfinished quest. Scoop, still watching Heidi, is still acting as goad, as gadfly. He cautions her:

"Heidi, you're clutching your purse."

Fingers tightening on the bag just a trace, she replies:

"I have valuables."

I think she does. I do think she does.

Did I say that Miss Allen is wonderful? □

1989 F 19, II:5:1

Some Dressing On the Salad Days

WITHOUT APOLOGIES, by Thom Thomas; directed by Edgar Lansbury; set design by John Wulp; light design by Paul Wonsek; costume design by Karen Hummel; scenery supervised by Lynn Pecktal; sound design by Aural Fixation; stage manager, Fredrick Hahn; incidental music composed by Tamara Kline. Presented by the Hudson Guild, Geoffrey Sherman, producing director; Steven Ramay, associate dierctor, in cooperation with American Theater Works, John Nassivera and Sandra C. Mintz. At 441 West 26th Street.

Algy Beaumont	Kurt Knudson
Gwen	Pauline Flanagan
Ernie Beaumont	Peter Pagan
Cecily	Carrie Nye
Brenda	Laura Brutsman
Willie Jukes	Edmund Lewis

By MEL GUSSOW

When we left the characters in "The Importance of Being Earnest," Jack and Algernon had discovered that they were long-lost brothers. Each was about to marry the woman of his choice — Jack matched with Gwendolyn and Algernon with Cecily. Thirty-four years later, in Thom Thomas's sequel, "Without Apologies," each brother is married to the other's intended, and they have all settled down to a life of middle-class dullness.

An octogenarian, Lady Bracknell, is living in an upstairs room. She never appears on stage and neither does Miss Prism. The other characters are less fortunate — as are those theatergoers who agree with James Agate that "Earnest" is "probably the best light comedy" in the English language, an assessment that has remained unchallenged for more than 40 years.

"Without Apologies," at the Hudson Guild Theater, may not be the worst light comedy in the English language, but it is probably the most unnecessary. Watching without laughter, one can only wonder at the reasons for Mr. Thomas's rashness. Perhaps he thought that Oscar Wilde did not get it right in the first place.

Ostensibly the play is about the real people who were the basis for Wilde's characters, and in support of that whimsical notion, the last names of the characters have been changed. Happily, their past lives remain immutable and undamaged by the imitation.

•

In search of revisionism, the playwright turns Algernon into a stout, cranky writer of obituaries and Western romances, makes Gwendolyn a middle-aged flibbertigibbet and deposits a bankrupt Jack (born Ernest) and Cecily on their doorstep seeking shelter.

Seven years pass in the course of the play, during which time the couples change partners again and Mr. Thomas offers historical signposts — a bad joke about Hitler and recordings of Edward VIII's abdication and Edward R. Murrow covering the London blitz. In this regard, there are indications that Mr. Thomas's model is less Wilde than Sir Noël Coward in his English chronicles, like "Cavalcade." "Without Apologies" falls far short of both, as Algernon and Jack look back wistfully on their salad days from the vantage point of their increasingly wilted present.

As a subplot, the unappealing daughter of Algernon and Gwendolyn marries a young man who dreams about being Jimmy Durante. He sings several Durante songs and salutes Mrs. Calabash "wherever you are." Possibly she is upstairs with Lady Bracknell.

•

Doubling Mr. Thomas's jeopardy is the casting. Kurt Knudson, who was a very funny pseudo-Hemingway in the comedy "Geniuses," is not by a long shot an English Algernon, and Pauline Flanagan and Peter Pagan offer merely a hint of Gwendolyn and Jack. Only Carrie Nye as Cecily could pass for her character at an older age. The single other asset in Edgar Lansbury's production is John Wulp's set design, especially the music-hall décor over the proscenium arch, which promises a diversion that is not forthcoming.

Though Tom Stoppard managed to celebrate "The Importance of Being Earnest" in his play "Travesties," an actual sequel to a classic should be undertaken only with the greatest trepidation. There is no need to know what Huckleberry Finn and Tom Sawyer were like in later years, though in "The Boys in Autumn," Bernard Sabath insisted on telling us. Similarly, there is no need to know anything more about the characters in "The Importance of Being Earnest." It would have been no loss if "Without Apologies" had been left in a handbag in a cloakroom at Victoria Station — the Brighton line.

1989 F 19, 74:4

Soulful Assortment

STEP INTO MY WORLD, music and lyrics by Micki Grant; conceived, developed and directed by Ronald G. Russo; choreography by Jeffrey Dobbs; musical director, George Caldwell; musical arrangements, William McDaniel; lighting design, Jeffrey Hubbell; costume design, Mary Ann Lach; production manager, Christophe Pierre; stage manager Teri Thorpe; wardrobe supervisor, Migdalia Ferrand. Presented by Amas Repertory Theater, Rosetta Le Noire, founder and artistic director; Jeffrey Solis, managing director. At 1 East 104th Street.

WITH: Jennifer Bell, Jean Cheek, Ellen De Verne, Jeffrey Dobbs, Martron Gales, David Girolmo, Evan Mattews and Deborah Woodsono.

By STEPHEN HOLDEN

Few theater composers can claim as broad a stylistic grasp as Micki Grant, whose body of work is being celebrated in a new revue, "Step Into My World," at the Amas Repertory Theater.

Miss Grant who made her reputation in 1972 with the successful Off-Broadway show, "Don't Bother Me, I Can't Cope" was represented briefly on Broadway in 1980 with "It's So Nice to Be Civilized," which had originated a year earlier at the Amas. She also contributed songs to the Broadway shows "Your Arm's Too Short to Box With God" (1976) and "Working" (1978). But these have been only the most visible projects in a prolific career.

•

"Step Into My World" collects over two dozen songs from assorted shows and divides them into thematic blocks: "emotions," "women," "faith," "dreams deferred," "working" and "love." The subjects are as varied as Miss Grant's music, which embraces Rodgers and Hammerstein, Bessie Smith, Jacques Brel and Motown, among other influences. A fluent melodist, Miss Grant writes songs through which characters speak directly and dramatically. Though not a highly refined technician, she usually manages to avoid the clichés of the genres she chooses; both her music and lyrics are permeated with a warm, sometimes luminously compelling sense of humanity.

But unfortunately, as has been the case with Miss Grant's lesser-known shows, by far the best thing about "Step Into My World" is the songwriting. The Amas Theater production, directed by Ron Russo, is one of the company's typically crude, homemade efforts. None of show's eight singers possesses anything close to a first-class voice, and when the singers try to blend, their harmonies remain woefully out of tune.

The female singers tend to fare better than the men. The show's two strongest performances are Deborah Woodson's rendition of Miss Grant's torch song, "Bright Lights," and Jan Cheek's version of "I've Still Got My Bite," a rollicking Bessie Smith-style anthem for a swinging grandmother.

1989 F 19, 76:4

Dreams, Desire And Desperation

SUENOS, adapted by Ruth Maleczech from the writings of Sor Juana Inés de la Cruz, Eduardo Galeano and Homero Aridjis; directed by Ms. Maleczech; music composed by Herschel Garfein; original lyrics by Ms. Maleczech with George Emilio Sanchez; additional lyrics by Mr. Garfein; choreographer, Pat Hall Smith; music director and conductor, Richard Pittman; mural designer and painter, Eduardo Carrillo; lighting designer, Clay Shirky; sound designer, L. B. Dallas; costume designer, Toni-Leslie James; set designer, Michael Deegan; production manager, Monica Bowin; technical director, David Bruné; company manager, David Baron; stage manager, Anthony Gerber; associate music director, Jonathan Knight. Presented by Mabou Mines and Intar Hispanic American Arts Center, produced in association with the Boston Musica Viva. At the Triplex Theater, 199 Chambers Street.

WITH: John Arrucci, Luz Bermejo, James Coelho, Eric Culver, Charles Davis, Jeffrey Dooley, Ratzo B. Harris, Lorraine Hunt, Clinton Chinyelu Ingram, Itabora, Irma-Estel LaGuerre, Maribel Lizardo, Julissa Marquez, Barbara Martinez, Tomas Milian, Theresa Patton, Erica Payne, Gustavo Pereira, Claudio Ragazzi, William Reinert, Isabel Saez, Renoly Santiago, Nairobi Smith, Roger Guenveur Smith, Rohan Smith, Jennifer Sobotka, Eduardo Uribe and Terence Yancey.

By MEL GUSSOW

"Sueños," the new Ruth Maleczech-Herschel Garfein musical, draws inspiration from the murals by Eduardo Carrillo that decorate the stage at the Triplex Theater. The sweeping canvases have a somber, impressionistic quality until we look closely at the figures in the setting. In one painting, a pack of emaciated dogs stares hollow-eyed — the hounds of war about to destroy their victims.

As in the Carillo paintings, beneath the surface of the drama is an imminent threat of violence. For example, a story is told about a tyrant who killed all the black dogs in his country simply because he believed his enemy had turned himself into a black dog. The musical, a co-production of Mabou Mines and Intar, is about dreams (as in the title) and also about desire and the desperation to which it can lead.

As conceived and written by Ms. Maleczech, the play is a diffuse collage of three dramatic strands. There is, most evocatively, the tale of Sor Juana Inés de la Cruz, a 17th-century Mexican nun, celebrated as one of her nation's foremost poets. As we see in the play, Sor Juana faced a crisis that was intellectual as well as moral and eventually led to her abandonment of her art.

Paralleling this specific story is a less interesting archetypal portrait of a Latin American dictator through the centuries, and both are counterpointed by excerpts, sung and spoken, from the work of Latin American poets and revolutionaries.

•

One's curiosity about Sor Juana is whetted at the same time attention is diverted by the scenes with the nameless dictator (Tomas Milian), whose relationship with a teen-age bride is shadowed by that of Juan and Eva Perón. In common with other theatrical pieces by Ms. Maleczech and her Mabou Mines colleagues, the show is intended to be layered rather than linear, but in this case the layers need more elucidation.

The nun's story is enhanced by Mr. Garfein's music, drawn freely from diverse Hispanic rhythms, and by the singing and acting of Lorraine Hunt as Sor Juana (she alternates in the role with Irma-Estel LaGuerre). Ms. Hunt, a 1986 Metropolitan Opera Auditions winner, has a presence to match her commanding voice. She heads a large cast of wavering ability.

As director, Ms. Maleczech adds a touch of fluidity by placing the orchestra (small, with the accent on plucked strings) in a central pit surrounded by platforms on which the play takes place. Many of the words are in Spanish, which is either immediately translated or is simple enough to be understood by theatergoers with a rudimentary knowledge of the language.

"Sueños" has some of the spontaneity and political verve of the San Francisco Mime Troupe. But despite the workshops that have preceded the New York production, it still seems to be a work in progress. Ms. Maleczech, one of our more innovative experimentalists, has not yet been able to integrate all of the show's kaleidoscopic elements.

1989 F 23, C13:3

Couples

LOVE'S LABOR'S LOST, by William Shakespeare; directed by Gerald Freedman; set design by John Ezell; costume design by James Scott; lighting design by Natasha Katz; music composed by John Morris; choreography by Tina Paul; associate producer, Jason Steven Cohen. Presented by Joseph Papp. At the Public/Newman Theater, 425 Lafayette Street.

Ferdinand	Mark Moses
Longaville	Mark Hymen
Dumaine	Spike McClure
Berowne	William Converse-Roberts
Anthony Dull	Steve Ryan
Costard	Steve Routman
Don Adriano de Armado	Richard Libertini
Moth	P. J. Ochlan
Jaquenetta	Julia Gibson
Boyet	John Horton
Princess of France	Christine Dunford
Maria	Kate Fuglei
Katharine	Juliette Kurth
Rosaline	Roma Downey

A Forester and Attendant	Brian Dykstra
Sir Nathaniel	Ronn Carroll
Holofernes	Joseph Costa
Marcade	Davis Hall
Attendants	

Peter Carlton Brown, Andrew Colteaux and Michael Gerald

By MEL GUSSOW

The freshness of Gerald Freedman's production of "Love's Labor's Lost" at the Public Theater extends from John Ezell's verdant setting to the cast, which is filled with talented newcomers. It is Don Adriano de Armado, the fantastical Spaniard, who suggests that green is "the color of lovers," and by green he means the innocence that accompanies immaturity.

In this, the seventh production in Joseph Papp's continuing marathon of Shakespeare, Mr. Freedman has, as intended, moved beyond the traditional reading of the play as dealing with the "game of love." Studying the "truth of love," he shoots arrows into frippery of all kinds. In this perfectly titled comedy, love conquers all, especially its own pretensions.

When Ferdinand, the King of Navarre, persuades his friends to become his allies in a year of retreat, contemplation and enforced celibacy, he does not know that the Princess of France and her entourage are in town. Two by two, all conveniently unattached and mutually attracted, they will soon be matched in a lightsome romantic roundelay.

The octet of lovers is counterpointed by the mischief-making subplot about pedants and parsons who prattle on as if words had no diminishing returns. As we are told, they have "been at a great feast of language and stolen the scraps." With hope, they might aspire to the dubious heights of Don Adriano, who, more than anyone else in Navarre, is in love with the idea of love.

To emphasize the air of affectation, Mr. Freedman has transposed the play to the 1930's. Ferdinand and his friends are dressed for the country club, where they play badminton and practical jokes. Dumaine toots a saxophone, as if it had been left over from an after-hours lounge party. They could be fraternity brothers interrupting a sweet tune in order to sign a bond of self-denial.

Although the princess and her friends are also dressed for a weekend party, the updating lacks a costume consistency, a curious divergence in an otherwise well-coordinated outing. Wearing a top hat and white gloves, the princess's attendant looks as if he is applying for the position of Mandrake the Magician (he does, after all, have a few verbal tricks up his sleeve, but he is not a prestidigitator). Don Adriano (Richard Libertini) is a tall, plumed bird. In his raiment, he looks like other inperiod Don Adrianos. If this is the 1930's, he must be on his way to a costume party.

Mr. Libertini is one of the show's two familiar players (the other is William Converse-Roberts, outstanding in the pivotal role of Berowne). Because of Mr. Libertini's gift for comic

In the Public's 'Love's Labor's Lost,' pretensions are punctured.

lunacy, one expects his cavalier to be a zany. In collaboration with his director, the actor has something more melancholic in mind, a Don Quixote lost in an illusory world of literary ideals. He is awakened from his dreams by his wry page (P. J.

Ochlan). Mr. Libertini does become funnier as the play proceeds — to the point where he confesses that he has no shirt under his jacket and therefore goes "woolward for penance," a line that has always had a curiously contemporary, five-and-dime ring to it.

At the same time, the paired lovers bring a renewed ingenuousness to their roles. Allied on one side are Mark Moses, Mark Hymen, Spike McClure (the saxophonist who also croons like Bing Crosby) and Mr. Converse-Roberts; on the other, Christine Dunford, Kate Fuglei, Juliette Kurth and Roma Downey. As is customarily the case, Berowne and Rosaline (Ms. Downey) go the furthest in winning the audience's favor. Both are as engaging as Shakespeare calls for them to be in conveying the impetuousness of their liaison.

Love's labor leads the men to conceal their epistolary ardor for the ladies. Although this scene seems surefire, it demands the headstrong passion that it receives from the present company. The women have their moment of superiority when the swains pretend to be rude Muscovite dancers and are intentionally confused, each one for another. As choreographed by Tina Paul, the men are activated into a Cossack kick chorus.

In only one area does the otherwise graceful performance slacken, and that is in the playing of the bombastic pretenders. Though they were drawn from life in Shakespeare's time, we know their counterparts in the world of media as well as academia. The actors cast in the roles (Ronn Carroll and Joseph Costa) sacrifice flair in search of fustian, and Steve Ryan is a commonplace Dull. It is left to Steve Routman's well-remunerated Costard and Julia Gibson's Jacquenetta to add a note of country clownishness.

Despite the production's three-hour length, the actors are quick on their feet and with their responses. As he did in last summer's "Much Ado About Nothing" in Central Park, Mr. Freedman reaffirms his position as one of our most reliable and nimble directors of Shakespeare.

1989 F 23, C15:1

A Koch Predecessor

HIZZONER!, by Paul Shyre; directed by John Going; set design by Eldon Elder; costume design by Patrizia von Brandenstein; lighting design by John McLain; sound design by Abe Jacob; general manager, Ralph Roseman; production stage manager, Michael A. Bartuccio; production assistant, Doug Lange. Presented by Unicorn Entertainment in association with Warner/Chappel Music and Patricia Di Benedetto, executive producer. At the Longacre Theater, 220 West 48th Street.

Fiorello H. La Guardia .... Tony Lo Bianco

By MEL GUSSOW

Impersonation is not simply the art of mimicking mannerisms but of reaching to the heart of the manner, creating, even for an instant, an incarnation rather than an imitation. Such is not the case with Tony Lo Bianco's Fiorello La Guardia in "Hizzoner!," the one-man show that opened last night at the Longacre Theater.

As a muckraking, progressive, fiercely independent mayor of New York City, La Guardia left a valuable political legacy as well as proof that

Martha Swope

Tony Lo Bianco

flamboyance is not necessarily antithetical to accomplishment. He was a masterly politician and manipulator of his own image. The La Guardia represented on stage in Paul Shyre's monodrama is, instead, a buffoon. He would win few votes either as a candidate or as a comedian.

In attempting to mimic La Guardia's distinctive high-pitched voice, Mr. Lo Bianco wanders from James Cagney to Elmer Fudd. The cartoon aspect of his performance is underscored by his conclusion of a press conference with a New York-accented version of Porky Pig's signoff, "D-d-d-dat's all folks."

An injury sustained during a performance has forced Mr. Lo Bianco to perform with a cast on his foot. One sympathizes with the actor's predicament, and Eldon Elder's cluttered and unsightly set offers additional obstacles. But there is no dramatic justification for Mr. Lo Bianco to bounce around the stage as he does. One fully expects him to be catapulted trampoline-style into the audience. Actually there is one direct involvement with the audience. In an ill-advised moment, he entices a theatergoer to come on stage with him, breaking whatever small sense of period and credibility he has achieved.

As an actor, Mr. Lo Bianco has been most adept in naturalistic roles, as in the revival of Arthur Miller's "View From the Bridge." But he is not a chameleon. His performance as

Martha Swope
A scene from Gerald Freedman's production of Shakespeare's "Love's Labor's Lost."

La Guardia is a busy gathering of poses, stances and tics. Working energetically and perspiring profusely, he quickly becomes a wilted Little Flower.

Mr. Shyre and the director, John Going, share in the liability. As a monodrama, "Hizzoner!" is in direct contrast to Willy Russell's recently opened "Shirley Valentine," in which the actress Pauline Collins gradually unfolds the fullness of a character. "Hizzoner!" is less a play than a diversionary action, as the playwright raids the cupboard of clichés in an attempt to disguise the fact that there is only one actor in the cast.

The stage La Guardia repeatedly talks on the telephone, shouts to unseen assistants, answers unseen reporters and re-creates his fireside-style radio show. Eventually there is an obligatory reading of the funnies during a newspaper strike, one of La Guardia's more memorable activities. As performed, it is merely childish.

Ostensibly the show takes place on La Guardia's last day as Mayor, in 1945. As he packs his belongings in large wooden crates, each item leads to a reminiscence. A tabletop Trylon and Perisphere sparks a memory of the 1939 World's Fair. There are enough mementoes and empty cases for him to re-enact his entire term of office, although we never receive an adequate impression of the complexity of this dynamic figure.

Hats are aligned on the wall and at various points he pretends to be a fireman, cowboy and Indian chief. Wearing a soldier's helmet, he declares that Dec. 7, 1941, was "a day that will live in infamy." Because of

his falsely cherubic countenance, it might have been more appropriate if he had borrowed "blood, sweat and tears."

Mr. Shyre has written a number of interesting stage documentaries, including his adaptations of Sean O'Casey's memoirs. This time he unwisely ambles away from his central subject to embrace anecdotes from others — for example, Dorothy Parker on Calvin Coolidge — padding an already overlong show.

At one point the Mayor lists his accomplishments, as if offering a résumé for a future campaign. He names the bridges, tunnels, highways and airports that surround our city. As one may have forgotten, they derived from La Guardia's time in office and were largely the handiwork of Robert Moses. Mr. Shyre seeks extra dramatic mileage and wins a few smiles by casting a 1980's perspective on these public-works projects. When they are all completed, predicts the Mayor, "driving your car in New York City will be a pleasure."

For all of La Guardia's contributions, New York's urban problems have intensified. With a mayoral election approaching, his unflaggable spirit is certainly worth re-evoking, perhaps with a revival of the musical "Fiorello!"

Though the current portrait is intended to be admiring, a curious distortion takes place. The Mayor's iconoclasm becomes mean-spirited and his political acumen seems accidental. "Hizzoner!" succeeds in diminishing La Guardia's stature.

1989 F 24, C3:1

By FRANK RICH

Special to The New York Times

NEW HAVEN, Feb. 21 — John Guare, the author of "The House of Blue Leaves" and "Landscape of the Body," was not born to write neat plays. So the good news from the Yale Repertory Theater is that Mr. Guare has abandoned the sober classical style he lavished on his "Lydie Breeze" trilogy during much of this decade and has instead brought forth a completely uninhibited comic mess.

Mr. Guare's new play goes by the title "Moon Over Miami," and since the author's wit informs every line, it almost never ceases to tickle the intelligence. Mess is a term of approval rather than censure in Mr. Guare's case. If this nearly three-hour jape is to have a further, more persuasively stageworthy life — and one hopes so — the trick will be to boil down the chaos to its essence, not to tidy it up into the kind of theater commonly applauded as well made.

It is precisely Mr. Guare's willingness to free associate in language, theatrical style and content that makes his best work figuratively (and, in this instance, literally) sing. "Moon Over Miami" so beggars coherent description that it's easier to catalogue its overstuffed contents than rationally explain them.

•

The play opens with a mysterious theft at the Anchorage Museum of Fine Arts in Alaska and closes with a chorus line at Miami's Fountaine Moon Hotel. Its characters include an undercover F.B.I. agent (Oliver Platt), a gangster visibly obsessed with his own genitals (Stanley Tucci), Miami's foremost Jewish-Cuban Congressman (Lewis J. Stadlen) and an Arab sheik (Tony Shalhoub) who wants to rebuild Israel in Florida. ("I don't mind Israel," he explains. "I just don't like where it is.") Among the love interests is a leggy femme fatale (Susan Kellermann) who correctly predicts stock-market trends

'Moon Over Miami' is playing at Yale.

whenever she reaches orgasm, and the innocent Corleen (Julie Hagerty), who hopes to bring culture to millionaire drug runners through the Everglades Light Opera.

As with Mr. Guare's screenplay for the Louis Malle film "Atlantic City," the truly dominant character in "Moon Over Miami" is the fast-changing, drug-infested beach town of the title. Mr. Guare's Miami is a malevolent, all-American frontier for "the pilgrims from the lost places," with more moons, metaphorical and otherwise, than have been seen since the early plays of Tom Stoppard. The city's ethos is a surreal mélange of 1950's resort kitsch and 1980's corruption. While "Moon Over Miami" can resemble a campy Hotel Fontainebleau floorshow, complete with band and a chorus of ludicrously buxom "mermaids," its main plot is a satirical rehash of the Abscam scandal, with mimed videotape replays of public officials receiving attaché cases of cash.

The play originated as a film project for John Belushi, and its Abscam gags now seem to have exhausted their shelf life. When the script narrows its focus to politics (especially in Act II), the writing goes flat. Mr. Guare's conventional polemical point — that overzealous F.B.I. agents, entrapped Congressmen and mobsters are morally interchangeable — doesn't justify the laborious efforts devoted to making it. The jokes about the dispirited post-Watergate F.B.I. are much fresher. Mr. Guare may be the first satirist to make fun of J. Edgar Hoover in part by insisting that law enforcement's most gossiped-about bachelor was in fact a flaming heterosexual.

Even so, the tacky Miami flora and fauna are usually more fun than the Feds. The most hilarious fixture of the Fountaine Moon Hotel is Fran Farkas, an obese, middle-aged, gold-lamé-wrapped singer with a riotous repertory of obscene songs, all delivered by Laurel Cronin with a low-key, deadpan sincerity appropriate to husky saloon renditions of elegant Rodgers-and-Hart ballads. Fran, who always carries a hand mike in her purse, is a grotesque hybrid of Arnie, the songwriting zookeeper of "Blue Leaves," and the self-parodistic Robert Goulet of "Atlantic City." Her outrageous songs — with words and music by Mr. Guare — skirt bona fide classics just enough to avoid risking litigation. "Hey there/You with the scars on your thighs," goes one of the few lyrics remotely repeatable in polite company.

•

In addition to Miss Cronin's, the other memorable performances are by the forever dazed Mr. Platt, a very promising comic actor whom some may recall as the pudgy trader who fixes up Melanie Griffith with a lecher in "Working Girl," and Miss Hagerty, who played the deaf Hollywood star in the Lincoln Center "Blue Leaves" and who here must lip-sync songs and speeches that her shy character feels compelled to record privately in advance on cassette. Mr. Platt and Miss Hagerty are also the play's only real innocents — typical Guare nobodies in forlorn search of gaudy American dreams — and, in the end, its light-opera romantic couple.

One cannot envy the director, Andrei Belgrader, and designer, Judy Gailen, charged with keeping this multi-scene, multi-character, multi-genre reverie afloat. The production's cinematic gears and more hysterical performances (notably Mr. Tucci's barking gangster) often sputter — sometimes because they need more practice but also because of obvious script repetitions and dead spots that should have been caught in rehearsal. In contrast to "Atlantic City," this work frequently seems more burdened than liberated by the author's far-flung inventiveness, as if five or six plays were constantly fighting for the audience's attention. Fascinating as most of those plays are, they will somehow have to coalesce if Mr. Guare's "Moon" is to rise.

1989 F 24, C3:1

Gerry Goodstein

Julie Hagerty and Oliver Platt in "Moon Over Miami."

Slumming Around With Abscam

MOON OVER MIAMI, by John Guare; directed by Andrei Belgrader; set design by Judy Gailen; costume design by Candice Donnelly; lighting design by Scott Zielinski; sound design by G. Thomas Clark and Ann Johnson; musical direction, incidental music and arrangements by Lawrence Yurman; dances by Wesley Fata; words and music by Mr. Guare; music for "Osvaldo's Song" by Galt MacDermot. Presented by Yale Repertory Theater, Lloyd Richards, artistic director; Benjamin Mordecai, managing director. At New Haven.

Otis Presby	Oliver Platt
Giselle Saint Just	Susan Kellermann
Reggie	Richard Spore
Sheldon S. Slutsky	Stanley Tucci
Mermaids	Frances Barney, Dana Morosini, Jacquelyn Mari Roberts, Ali Sharaf and Mary Walden
Osvaldo Muñoz	Lewis J. Stadlen
Fran Farkas	Laurel Cronin
Bobby Devine	Lawrence Yurman
Senator Wayne Bentine	Sam Stoneburner
Maître d' and TV Anchor	Walker Jones
Manager	Roger Bechtel
Belden	Dennis Reid
Walt Wilcox	Richard Riehle
Sheik of Akbahran	Tony Shalhoub
Mambo Instructor	Robert Russell
Ida Mendelssohn	Mary Walden
Vicky and Flor	Mary Mara
Policeman	Jim MacLaren
Corleen	Julie Hagerty
Congressman Clasnowski	John R. Conway
F.B.I. Agents	Martin Blanco and Robin Selfridge
Corleen's Voice	Ann Whitney

Not Just Books

GOOD, by C. P. Taylor; directed by Robert Hupp; costume design by Jonathan Bixby; lighting design by Craig Smith; music directed and arranged by Ned Ginsberg. Presented by the Jean Cocteau Repertory. At the Bouwerie Lane Theater, 330 Bowery.

John Halder	Craig Smith
Maurice	Harris Berlinsky
Major	Craig Cook
Helen	Gretchen Krich
Mother	Elise Stone
Anne	Jeanne Demers
Bouller	Joseph Menino
Eichmann	Robert Ierardi
Bok	Mark Schulte
Nurse and Elizabeth	Carol Dearman
Hitler, doctor and dispatch rider	Christopher Oden

By WILBORN HAMPTON

William James once wrote that the difference between a good man and a bad one is the choice of a cause. John Halder, a mild-mannered professor of German literature, takes up the National Socialist Party.

Halder, the antihero of C. P. Taylor's "Good," which is being given a

Gerry Goodstein
Craig Smith as John Halder in C. P. Taylor's "Good."

compelling revival by the Jean Cocteau Repertory Company, has a senile mother in an asylum, a wife who can neither clean nor cook and a best friend named Maurice who is a Jew. Around 1933, Halder begins to hear bands — jazz bands, swing bands, the Berlin Philharmonic — that provides a mental sound track to his life. He also starts an affair with one of his students and joins the Nazi Party, although he admits he's "not 100 percent sure about Hitler."

The rest of this troubling play is an exercise in Halder's rationalizing his subsequent betrayal of everything he presumably holds dear as he metamorphoses from a rather ordinary and humdrum college professor into an SS officer who will send millions to their deaths. "They got me at a bad time," Halder says in one of the many explanations he offers for what happens to him.

Halder keeps assuring Maurice that the Nazi campaign against the Jews is just a passing phase that will soon be halted. "Hitler will be out in six months," he says confidently, while refusing to get his friend exit papers for Switzerland.

Halder's first assignment for the party is to organize a book burning at the university. The professor's initial

distress at this task ("Oh, I like him," he says as he studies the list of proscribed authors.) is quickly salved when he is told that he can keep his own copies of the condemned works. His mistress, Anne, helps assuage his misgivings. "It's just books," she observes.

Underneath all the double talk is the premise that these characters were, at one time, good people. That is nonsense, of course. Any claim Halder might stake to virtue suffocates in the smoke from that first pyre of books. Yet for all the play's weaknesses, "Good" is frightening and mesmerizing. And lest there be any doubt that it is timely, one need only witness the initial trepidation with which Ayatollah Khomeini's

death threat against Salman Rushdie was met.

The Cocteau is fortunate in having Craig Smith as John Halder. Mr. Smith, one of the more consistently fine actors around town, makes no attempt to cloak Halder with sympathy, as did Alan Howard, the English actor who created the role in London and played it on Broadway in 1982. Mr. Smith's honest, unvarnished performance brings home the full horror of this "good" man. Harris Berlinsky as Maurice and Jeanne Demers as Anne are both commendable. And Mark Schulte provides an excellent turn in the cameo role of the SS officer Bok. Robert Hupp directed.

1989 F 25, 18:4

The Best of the Best

JEROME ROBBINS'S BROADWAY, by James M. Barrie, Irving Berlin, Leonard Bernstein; Jerry Bock, Sammy Cahn, Moose Charlap; Betty Comden, Larry Gelbart, Morton Gould; Adolph Green, Oscar Hammerstein 2d, Sheldon Harnick, Arthur Laurents, Carolyn Leigh; Stephen Longstreet, Hugh Martin, Jerome Robbins, Richard Rodgers, Burt Shevelove, Stephen Sondheim, Joseph Stein and Jule Styne. Entire production choreographed and directed by Mr. Robbins; production scenic designer, Robin Wagner; supervising costume designer, Joseph G. Aulisi; lighting designer, Jennifer Tipton; scenery by Boris Aronson, Jo Mielziner, Oliver Smith, Mr. Wagner and Tony Walton; costumes by Mr. Aulisi, Alvin Colt, Raoul Pene du Bois, Irene Sharaff, Mr. Walton, Miles White and Patricia Zipprodt; sound by Otts Munderloh; orchestrations by Sid Ramin and William D. Brohn; musical continuity by Scott Frankel; produced in association with the Pace Theatrical Group; musical director, Paul Gemignani; assistants to the choreographer, Cynthia Onrubia, Victor Castelli and Jerry Mitchell; co-director, Grover Dale. Presented by

the Shubert Organization, Roger Berlind, Suntory International Corporation, Byron Goldman and Emanuel Azenberg. At the Imperial Theater, 249 West 45th Street.

WITH: Jason Alexander, Richard Amaro, Dorothy Benham, Jeffrey Lee Broadhurst, Christophe Caballero, Mindy Cartwright, Irene Cho, Jamie Cohen, Charlotte d'Amboise, Camille de Ganon, Donna Di Meo, Donna Marie Elio, Mark Esposito, Susann Fletcher, Scott Fowler, Angelo H. Fraboni, Ramon Galindo, Nicholas Garr, Gregorey Garrison, Carolyn Goor, Michael Scott Gregory, Andrew Grose, Alexia Hess, Nancy Hess; Louise Hickey, Eric A. Hoisington, Barbara Hoon, JoAnn M. Hunter, Scott Jovovich, Pamela Khoury, Susan Kikuchi, Michael Kubala, Robert La Fosse, Mary Ann Lamb, Jane Lanier, David Lowenstein, Michael Lynch, Greta Martin, Joey McKneely, Julio Monge, Troy Myers, Maria Neenan, Jack Noseworthy, Steve Ochoa, Kelly Patterson, Luis Perez, Faith Prince, James Rivera, Tom Robbins, George Russell, Greg Schanuel, Debbie Shapiro, Renée Stork, Mary Ellen Stuart, Linda Talcott, Leslie Trayer, Ellen Troy, Andi Tyler, Scott Wise, Elaine Wright, Barbara Yeager and Alice Yearsley.

Charlotte d'Amboise as Peter Pan in "Jerome Robbins's Broadway."

By FRANK RICH

For any child who ever fell in love with the Broadway musical, there was always that incredible moment of looking up to see the bright marquees of Times Square for the first time. I had always assumed it was an unrepeatable thrill until I saw the show that Jerome Robbins officially unveiled at the Imperial Theater last night.

•

In "Jerome Robbins's Broadway," the American musical theater's greatest director and choreographer doesn't merely bring back the thunderous excitement of songs and

Martha Swope
Jason Alexander in a scene from "A Funny Thing Happened on the Way to the Forum," from "Jerome Robbins's Broadway."

dances from classic musicals like "West Side Story" and "Peter Pan" and "Gypsy." For an encore, he pulls off the miracle of re-creating that ecstatic baptism, that first glimpse of Broadway lights, of every Broadway theatergoer's youth.

The moment occurs as Mr. Robbins's show ends. The three World War II sailors of "On the Town," winding down from their dizzy 24-hour pass through the pleasures of New York, New York, come upon a dazzling, crowded skyscape of twinkling signs heralding the smash musicals Mr. Robbins staged between 1944 and his withdrawal from Broadway in 1964. Some of the theaters' (the Adelphi, the New Century) are gone now; some of the shows are forgotten. But the awe that seizes those innocent young sailors of 1944 overwhelms the jaded Broadway audience of 1989, too — and not because of the simple scenic effect. While "Jerome Robbins's Broadway" may celebrate a vanished musical theater, it does so with such youthful exuberance that nostalgia finally gives way to a giddy, perhaps not even foolish, dream that a new generation of Broadway babies may yet be born.

Most certainly a new generation is visible on the Imperial's stage. For this 15-number anthology, Mr. Robbins has recruited 62 remarkable performers: most from the Broadway ranks, a few from ballet, and all too young to have seen their predecessors in these roles. They perform with a skill, sexiness and zest that sometimes eclipses the originals, throwing off the cobwebs and camp that almost always attend Broadway revivals.

•

When the sailors Robert La Fosse, Scott Wise and Michael Kubala go girl-chasing in their helluva town — and the girls include beauties like Mary Ellen Stuart and Alexia Hess — one doesn't think of every other cast to play "On the Town" (or its ballet precursor, "Fancy Free"). One instead feels the charge of fresh talent cockily strutting its stuff. What comes through is not an imitation of the original production but presumably an equivalent to the electricity with which the upstart creative team of Mr. Robbins, Leonard Bernstein, Betty Comden and Adolph Green first took Broadway by storm.

"Jerome Robbins's Broadway" even succeeds in reclaiming legendary star roles for its young company. Jason Alexander, the evening's delightful narrator, accomplishes the seemingly impossible: he banishes the memory of Zero Mostel from the

Old delights and fresh pleasures of a vanished era.

" Singing "New York, New York," from "On the Town." are, from left, Scott Wise, Robert La Fosse and Michael Kubala. Martha Swope

role of Pseudolus in "A Funny Thing Happened on the Way to the Forum." Charlotte d'Amboise brings her own insouciant pixiness to "Peter Pan." Debbie Shapiro, the production's lead singer, at once recalls and reinvents the jazzy comic vocal attack once owned by Nancy Walker.

As Mr. Robbins demonstrates that young performers can hold their own with Broadway's past, so he proves that his way of doing musicals has gone into hiding but not out of style. Audiences inured to the hydraulic scenic gizmos, formless acrobatics, deafening amplification and emotional vacuity of this decade's Broadway spectaculars will find Mr. Robbins's musical theater a revelation. Many of the numbers in "Jerome Robbins's Broadway" are performed before simple or blank backdrops, and most of them prompt laughter or tears. While the show is undeniably lavish — the sumptuous costume reproductions are of museum-exhibition quality — it is the extravagance of taste, not money, that generates the joy.

•

That taste belongs to the arena of theater, not to the serious dance world to which Mr. Robbins turned permanently after "Fiddler on the Roof." Nowhere is this more apparent than in the 25-minute suite of dances from "West Side Story" that rocks the audience at the conclusion of the first act. It is not the steps of the dances — least of all the classic lifts of the "Somewhere" ballet — that get to us so much as Mr. Robbins's ability to propel a story, mood and characters over music and space. The self-destructiveness of the warring Jets and Sharks is all the more poignant because the gangs' violent movements evolve out of the benign, timeless playground antics of urban teen-agers. A born showman's brilliant theatrical lighting effect, even more than the choreography and lush Bernstein melody, boosts the "Somewhere" fantasy to a heavenly paradise.

"Hold my hand, and I'll take you there," goes a Stephen Sondheim lyric in that song. In "Tradition" (from "Fiddler") and "I'm Flying" (from "Peter Pan"), as in the "Somewhere" ballet, characters take hands, often forming a circle as they do so, to suggest an idealized sense of family that will eventually be ripped apart. Yet the touching — some might say sentimental — side of Mr. Robbins is always balanced by a hearty affection for the knockabout show-biz traditions of unalloyed burlesque.

•

"Comedy Tonight" (the incomparable opening number of "Forum"), the "Charleston" from "Billion Dollar Baby" and the Keystone Kops ballet from "High Button Shoes" are riotous, self-contained, swinging-door farces rendered entirely as nonstop dance. On a smaller scale, but no less witty, are Mr. Robbins's evocations of the lost vaudeville worlds of the soft-shoe (Mr. Alexander and Faith Prince's duet to "I Still Get Jealous" from "High Button Shoes") and the striptease ("You Gotta Have a Gimmick" from "Gypsy"). It's only when Mr. Robbins's choreography reaches self-consciously from the theater into hifalutin dance that it seems more arty than artistic. "The Small House of Uncle Thomas" ballet from "The King and I" and "Mr. Monotony," a jazz ballet cut from two Irving Berlin musicals during their out-of-town tryouts, look like period curiosities now — though they are so beautifully performed that it's hardly torture to wait them out.

A more inherent limitation of "Jerome Robbins's Broadway" is its anthology form. However wonderful Mr. Robbins's show stoppers were, his most influential legacy to the musical theater was his gradual blurring of the halts between musical numbers and scenes. The last Robbins musicals were steamrollers in which script, movement, scenery, song and dance all surged forward at once to create a seamless dramatic adventure.

In "Jerome Robbins's Broadway," that gift for relentless theatrical flow

comes through in the "West Side Story" suite and "Comedy Tonight," as well as in "I'm Flying" at that moment when the Darling house pulls away so Peter Pan and his recruits can soar above London to Never Land. But the constant movement that was "Gypsy" — perhaps the quintessentially cinematic Robbins production — cannot be captured here, and, for some reason, the "Fiddler" suite in Act II is precise in its self-contained dances (the comic nightmare, the wedding bottle-dance) but warped in overall shape. The communal fight that breaks out in the middle of "Tradition" and the pogrom that flows out of the wedding dance have both been eliminated — which is tantamount to removing the rumbles from "West Side Story." The sanitization leaves "Fiddler" looking more conventional and saccharine than it was when it first played the Imperial.

At no other time does "Jerome Robbins's Broadway," to my knowledge, violate the spirit of the original works. So faithful is the production to Broadway's past that it becomes a one-evening tour of an entire era, highlighting not just composing giants like Jule Styne but also such bright asterisks to Broadway music as Moose Charlap. With the exception of a synthetic overture, the sound of the pit band, conducted by Paul Gemignani and orchestrated by Sid Ramin and William D. Brohn, is exhilaratingly authentic, down to the contributions made by the dance arrangers Betty Walberg and Trude Rittman.

Through the lyrics and snippets of dialogue, one rediscovers an era's wiseguy Broadway comic style, which united writers as disparate as Arthur Laurents and Sammy Cahn. Thanks to the extraordinary efforts of the overall designers Robin Wagner (scenery), Joseph G. Aulisi (costumes) and Jennifer Tipton (lighting), "Jerome Robbins's Broadway" also offers what will probably remain a once-in-a-lifetime survey of Broadway theater design, from early Tony Walton to middle Jo Mielziner and late Boris Aronson. The dominant de-

signer is Oliver Smith, whose glorious palette can encompass New Yorks as antithetical as those of "On the Town" and "West Side Story," and whose collaborations with the costume designers Irene Sharaff, Miles White and Alvin Colt have no present-day match in technicolor Fauvist verve.

•

If "Jerome Robbins's Broadway" is history, it is history that pulses and reverberates. The "West Side Story" suite alone harks back to Agnes de Mille's Broadway dream ballets even while anticipating the gyrating phalanxes of Michael Bennett's "Company" and "A Chorus Line." No doubt Mr. Robbins's anthology won't mean the same thing to theatergoers who didn't grow up with his shows, but it may well attract new converts to traditions whose hold on the musical theater are as shaky as that fiddler on the roof. After seeing "Jerome Robbins's Broadway" at Thursday's press preview, I hurried back to the Saturday matinee with two young boys roughly the same age I was when I saw my first Robbins musical, "Peter Pan." Long after Peter told them "to think lovely, wonderful thoughts," they were still flying.

1989 F 27, C13:1

Critics? Boo!

GUS AND AL, by Albert Innaurato; directed by David Warren; set by James Youmans; costumes by David C. Woolard; lighting by Robert Jared; sound by John Gromada; musical arrangements by Ted Sperling; production stage manager, Allison Sommers; production manager, Carl Mulert. Presented by Playwrights Horizons, Andre Bishop, artistic director; Paul S. Daniels, executive director. At 416 West 42d Street.

Kafka and Sigmund Freud ......Charles Janasz
Al ....Mark Blum
Mrs. Briggs ....Helen Hanft
Gustav Mahler .... Sam Tsoutsouvas
Natalie Bauer Lechner
                          Cara Duff-MacCormick
Justine Mahler ....Christina Moore
Alma Schindler .... Jennifer Van Dyck
Camillo .... Bradley White

By FRANK RICH

It's hard to believe that four years have passed since Albert Innaurato, the author of "Gemini" and "The Transfiguration of Benno Blimpie," last had a new play in New York. As a writer, Mr. Innaurato has an intense operatic voice, by turns comic and sentimental, that lingers in the ear. Even "Coming of Age in SoHo," his jumbled comedy of 1985, retains a vivid afterlife. Among other distinctive traits, it may be the only play ever to have changed the gender of its protagonist (from female to male) during previews.

"Gus and Al," Mr. Innaurato's pleasant new work, is in part a response to the poor reception that greeted "Coming of Age" (a play that was itself, in part, a response to the disappointing Broadway fate of "Passione"). He is hardly the only New York playwright obsessed with his critics; this seems to be the theme at the Playwrights Horizons studio theater this season, where "Gus and

Responding to response to a response.

Al" was preceeded by Tom Mardirosian's "Saved From Obscurity," an actor's account of hard knocks. And Mr. Innaurato, like Mr. Mardirosian, isn't really bitter. The protagonist of his play, a South Philadelphia-bred playwright named Al Innaurato (Mark Blum), takes consolation in shopping sprees at Tower Records and a solitary mixed review, from The New York Times.

•

The Gus of "Gus and Al" is another victim of critical disfavor, Gustav

Paul Kolnik

Mark Blum in "Gus and Al."

Mahler (Sam Tsoutsouvas). Through circumstances that shouldn't be examined too seriously, Al travels from Manhattan, 1989, to Vienna, 1901, where he becomes the composer's friend and temporary housemate. Gus is glad to meet Al because he is blocked on his Fifth Symphony and is "surrounded by silly women," includ-

ing his ambitious sister Justine (Christina Moore) and his friend and chronicler Natalie Bauer Lechner (Cara Duff-MacCormick). Both men's lives are soon complicated further by the intrusions of Alma Schindler (Jennifer Van Dyck), Gus's bride-to-be, and the consultations of Sigmund Freud (Charles Janasz).

Next to Mr. Innaurato's usual theatrical eruptions, "Gus and Al" is decidedly a chamber piece. The jokes are mild (while sometimes very amusing), the emotions are muted, and the tone is often ruminative. Having just turned 40, Al worries that he is "a preposterous homosexual fat man who has nothing to offer." Mr. Innaurato's play is the story of Al's redemption. The writer finds solace in the past both by taking Gus's inspirational advice and by surviving a "Death in Venice"-like infatuation with a young Italian man (Bradley White) whose family name sparks the evening's funniest double-whammy gag.

•

Though "Gus and Al" lacks dramatic glue and periodically falls into discursive doldrums, it is flecked with sweetly written passages. In Mr. Blum's appealing, weary-eyed portrayal, Al's self-pity isn't self-martyrdom so much as a rueful hypersensitivity to the modern world with which he is perpetually at odds. It's tough for Al to be a playwright in an age in which, as he tells a baffled Gus, "we do Shakespeare with TV actors and break-dancing and rock-and-roll." Mahler has his own problems, not the least of which is his pivotal position in a farcical love triangle whose collisions give the evening its sporadic theatrical shape.

Mr. Innaurato is far less pungent when he moves from his specific characters to general observations about the 20th-century charnel-house horrors that evolved from fin-de-siècle Vienna. As usual, his happy ending, in which Al abruptly learns to rise above his own cynicism and "hug life," seems forced and treacly. The platitudes disperse, however briefly, when Al returns home to confront his abusive landlady (played by Helen Hanft in a wheelchair) and his roommate, a runaway laboratory ape known as Kafka.

David Warren's smart production, with its mock-period designs by James Youmans (set) and David C. Woolard (costumes), is in the appropriate low key. Not all the acting is at Mr. Blum's level, though Ms. Moore is a vinegary Justine Mahler and Ms. Van Dyck, who has few New York credits, is a find as Alma. "Her rudeness is like an aphrodisiac," is how Gus describes his sweetheart, and that is exactly the odd erotic quality, at once fetching and obnoxious, supplied by Ms. Van Dyck's acidic performance.

•

In a smaller, more conventional turn, Miss Hanft gets her laughs as the landlady, telling Al upon his return home that "anyone who can put up with an ape and travel through time can't be all bad." Roughly the same tentative sentiments apply to the erratic Mr. Innaurato, who, for a playwright struggling through a mid-career crisis of confidence, is looking pretty good.

1989 F 28, C17:1

No Resistance

THE NEST, by Franz Xaver Kroetz; directed by Bartlett Sher; translated by Roger Downey; set designer, Rob Murphy; costumes by Marina Draghici; lighting by Pat Dignan; sound by Mark Bennett; production stage manager, Elizabeth Valsing; production manager, William H. Lang. New York Theater Workshop presents the New Directors Series. At the Perry Street Theater, 31 Perry Street.

Martha	Alma Cuervo
Kurt	Matt Craven
Stefan	Michael Pryor

By MEL GUSSOW

Marriage for Kurt and Martha is the sheerest bliss, despite the fact that Kurt's income as a truckdriver is limited. In "The Nest" by Franz Xaver Kroetz, the two go through their daily routine. When Kurt comes home from work, his wife automatically gives him a bottle of beer. They have dinner and settle down with television, then convert their couch into a bed and go to sleep. The scene is West Germany but it could be any small town in the United States.

Martha is about to have her first baby. Sitting at their dining table, they tick off an endless list of expenses, refrained by Kurt's confident response to every financial request, "You got it." In the play, as directed by Bartlett Sher for the New York Theater Workshop, Kurt and Martha are a portrait of contentment, but with a gentle edge of self-parody. Significantly, they begin the play by watching a situation comedy on television, which is, in fact, a mirror image of their own story. Television reflects life, or vice versa.

•

It is easy to enjoy the mock banalities of these early scenes and the deft performances of Alma Cuervo and Matt Craven. Having seen the play before, in 1986, at the Bush Theater in London, my amusement was tempered by the fact that I knew what was coming — the sudden swerve of fate that would turn a situation comedy into an ecological nightmare. At that point, humor flees the stage.

To make extra money, Kurt does a special job for his boss, which entails disposing of toxic wastes. That disposal leads directly to the illness of the couple's new baby — and the happy world of Kurt and Martha spins awry. The change is total, and deleterious to the marriage as well as to the environment. Mr. Kroetz chronicles the decline with deliberation, as life's cruelty destroys an idyll.

Though understated, the commentary on industrial recklessness is embittered. "The Nest" attacks an urgent contemporary problem and identifies a cause, the casualness with which a faceless technocracy can poison a community, and the blindness with which people accept the status quo, whatever it may be.

At her most aggrieved, Martha accuses her husband of being nothing more than "a trained ape." As he realizes, there is a certain truth to the charge. He has followed his boss's suggestion — not even an order — without challenging its effect. It does not take much imagination to look behind the theme of the play and to uncover deeper parallels, including the rise of Nazism itself. The question posed is one of inaction in the face of evil.

Kurt, the ultimate blue-collar drone, eventually raises his voice, beginning with a mea culpa but ending with a charge of complicity. In

this brief but compelling play, Mr. Kroetz strikes a vengeful blow against civilization's power to self-destruct. In contrast to Sarah Pia Anderson's starkly minimal London production, Mr. Sher's version at the Perry Street Theater averts some of the terror of the story; the first half is almost too funny. There is no need to make the nest quite so cozy.

At the same time, the staging is as crisp as Rob Murphy's setting. Mr. Craven subtly moves his inarticulate truckdriver from amiability to anger to overwhelming guilt, and Ms. Cuervo is a portrait of shocked awareness as she watches her household disintegrate.

Using Roger Downey's conversational translation, Mr. Sher makes one useful addition in the New York production. The baby, played in London by inanimate bunting, is portrayed here by a real infant. Michael Pryor, who alternates in that role with Justin Musumeci, is a real charmer. He meets every cue and he is never at a loss for silence. Years from now, one may look back on his auspicious stage debut at 8 months in Mr. Kroetz's horrific domestic tragedy.

1989 Mr 2, C26:

Famous Poet, Infamous Politics

INCOMMUNICADO, by Tom Dulack; directed by Blanka Zizka; lighting design by Jerold R. Forsyth; set design by Andrei Efremoff; costume design by Lara Ratnikoff; original score by Adam Wernick; stage manager, Kathryn Bauer. Presented by the Wilma Theater, Jiri Zizka, artistic and producing director; Ms. Zizka, artistic and producing director; W. Courtenay Wilson, managing director. At 2030 Sansom Street, Philadelphia.

Ezra Pound	David Hurs
M.P.	Anthony Chisholm
Till	Reginald Flowers
Lawyer	Peter Wray
Doctor	David Simon

By MEL GUSSOW

Special to The New York Times

PHILADELPHIA, Feb. 28 — Of all the great contemporary literary figures, Ezra Pound is the most contradictory. He was a poetic genius (by his measure and that of others) and an inspiration behind modernism in the arts — as well as a fanatical racist and anti-Semite. In "Incommunicado" (at the Wilma Theater here) Tom Dulack makes a bold dramatic assault on Pound's outrageous life and myth. Though the play has rough edges, it has an urgency and a seriousness of purpose in dealing with an exceedingly controversial subject.

The playwright has performed that most difficult task of humanizing an artist — and, in this case, a monster — and he has done so through an exercise of his own artistic imagination.

Re-creating a genius and an undisguised bigot.

not by patching together a play from published sources.

•

Mr. Dulack (the author of "Solomon's Child," a 1981 Broadway play about deprogramming) has imagined what might have happened when the poet was arrested in Pisa in 1945 before he was brought back to the United States to face charges of treason. Pound had remained in Italy during World War II and delivered a series of virulent radio broadcasts. Imprisoned in a cage, he was treated like an animal, which is of course what many people thought he was.

In "Incommunicado," Pound (David Hurst) is an undisguised bigot (in direct response to his guard, a black M.P.). At the same time, he demonstrates his immense intelligence and erudition. Without seeking the audience's sympathy, the character becomes a man to be pitied, especially as one sees art jeopardized by the perversity of his politics.

The playwright raises crucial questions — about the reasons for Pound's ravings (partly paranoia resulting from literary slights); the legality of the charges and the punishment, and the literary repercussions, including the attempts of fellow writers to save Pound from himself. When Pound is told that Hemingway and others are encouraging a plea of insanity so that he can escape hanging, he is furious at what he considers to be an insult.

But even as he affirms his sanity, we see him overcome by a kind of dementia. As an undercurrent, the play asks if it is possible for someone to be a major artist and such an offensive human being.

The poet offers no defense for his acts while suggesting that he had no awareness of their effect. When he sees a photograph of Holocaust horrors — in one of the playwright's apparent additions — he is momentarily overcome. This is not to suggest that Pound on stage, or in life, ever had recriminations, but in the play there is at least a touch of self-examination.

Theatergoers may find themselves seduced by diabolical Old Ez, as he calls himself. But Mr. Dulack is not about to abdicate his moral responsibility. In a scorching finale, we suddenly hear several of Pound's self-incriminating broadcasts, and they are even more vile than one expected.

"Incommunicado" is most effective when Pound speaks his mind or is in direct confrontation with his guard (Anthony Chisholm). The work is less secure in encounters with a legalistic defense attorney and a psychiatrist. But these scenes do not vitiate the larger picture, the portrait of a galvanic artist in purgatory.

Using a dirt-floor scenic design by Andrei Efremoff, Blanka Zizka, as director, is unrelenting in her depiction of Pound's deprivation in confinement; "Incommunicado" can be a discomforting play to watch.

Mr. Hurst does not resemble Pound either in looks or in voice, and he lacks the poet's ability to assume regional American dialects, all of which he compensates for with his acting skill. He strikes to the heart of his character — his unabated arrogance as well as his fiendish sense of humor. Presented with a dictionary by his guard, the poet can barely express his appreciation, finally acknowledging that "a dictionary is a wonderful thing even if you know all the words."

Some may question the propriety of creating a play about such a figure. As justification, "Incommunicado" astutely reconsiders an ugly chapter in literary and political history and offers a cautionary warning against the possibility of reccurrence — especially apt in a time when freedom of literature is threatened by terrorism. In confinement, Pound often quotes Confucius, as in the statement,

"When a man is universally disliked, inquiry is necessary." Mr. Dulack's inquiry is both judicious and unflinching.

1989 Mr 3, C3:1

Low Jinks Among The Ruthless

LEND ME A TENOR, by Ken Ludwig; directed by Jerry Zaks; setting by Tony Walton; costumes by William Ivey Long; lighting by Paul Gallo; sound by Aural Fixation; hair by Angela Gari; music coordinator, Edward Strauss; general manager, Robert Kamlot; production stage manager, Steven Beckler. Presented by Martin Starger and the Really Useful Theater Company. At the Royale Theater, 242 West 45th Street.

Maggie	J. Smith-Cameron
Max	Victor Garber
Saunders	Philip Bosco
Tito Merelli	Ron Holgate
Maria	Tovah Feldshuh
Bellhop	Jeff Brooks
Diana	Caroline Lagerfelt
Julia	Jane Connell

By FRANK RICH

A farce should be cleverly built, energetically directed and buoyantly acted, but there is one thing it absolutely must be: consistently funny. As staged by Jerry Zaks and performed by a cast led by Philip Bosco and Victor Garber, "Lend Me a Tenor," the jolly play by Ken Ludwig at the Royale, is an impeccable example of how to construct and mount a farce — up to a point. "Lend Me a Tenor" is all things farcical except hilarious.

•

There are some scattered big laughs, certainly, though one must wait through most of Act I for the first of them to arrive. The prime buffoon is Mr. Bosco, attired in the white tie, top hat and tails of a Cleveland opera impresario in 1934. Mr. Bosco

Buffoonery, trickery, vanity and greed.

has just learned that his imported star for the night's sold-out performance of Verdi's "Otello," the legendary Italian tenor Tito Merelli (Ron Holgate), is too ill to go on. The news that $50,000 worth of tickets may have to be refunded does not sit well. Mr. Bosco turns comatose from the shock, then reddens with apoplexy, then flies into a shrieking, violent rage, and finally subsides into an open-mouthed stupor, looking like a bloated marlin just after the fisherman has removed the hook. It's the second priceless display of technique this season — the first, also partnered by Mr. Garber, was in "The Devil's Disciple" — by one of the best comic actors we have.

Nearly as splendid are both Mr. Holgate, who gets Mr. Bosco into this jam, and Mr. Garber, who must get him out of it. More than 25 years after he played Miles Gloriosus in "A Funny Thing Happened on the Way to the Forum," Mr. Holgate still makes a fine comic specialty of vain ladies' men; his Tito, known to his adoring fans as "Il Stupendo," is a paragon of temperamental matinee-idol hamminess from his silver mane to his preposterously thick Italian accent.

Martha Swope

Victor Garber, left, and Philip Bosco in "Lend Me a Tenor."

Mr. Garber is his charming antithesis: Max, the nerdy, bespectacled Cleveland Grand Opera Company gofer who harbors Walter Mitty fantasies of being a great tenor himself. When he is drafted by Mr. Bosco to impersonate the ailing star in "Otello," Mr. Garber carries out the hoax in high style, mimicking Mr. Holgate's personality (and singing voice) as effortlessly as Clark Kent turns into Superman.

Such is Mr. Ludwig's unabashedly silly, highly workable premise. In "Lend Me a Tenor," two Otellos (in identical costumes and chocolate makeup) pop in and out of six slamming doors in a two-room hotel suite, all the while pursued by a bevy of understandably confused Desdemonas that includes Tito's long-suffering Italian wife (an insufferably mannered Tovah Feldshuh), Max's would-be fiancée (J. Smith-Cameron) and an ambitious soprano determined to sleep her way to the Met (Caroline Lagerfelt). What's more, Mr. Ludwig, who is a lawyer as well as a playwright, has done the hard work of crafting the machinery of farce. Unlike the lackadaisical Neil Simon of "Rumors," he carefully maps out his mistaken identities and close shaves, even to the extent of making certain that each Otello clocks the same time at lovemaking (15 minutes, if you must know).

•

So why does "Lend Me a Tenor" fail to rise into comic pandemonium? The trouble is not Mr. Zaks's timing or slapstick choreography, which are as fast and stylish as one expects from the director of "Anything Goes" and "The Front Page." Nor should one look too critically at the credibility of Mr. Ludwig's plot or characters. As is demonstrated in the evening's breathless coda — a silent-movie frenzy — farcical clowning has little to do with reality and a lot to do with the illogical lunacy of wind-up toys.

The play's real comic shortfall is in its details rather than in its master plan. The lines are almost never witty, settling instead for the hoary double-entendres that so titillate the West End (where "Tenor" was a hit in another production). Worse, too many of the farcical situations seem like pale echoes of those in similar works from the play's period (notably Broadway's "Room Service" and Hollywood's "Night at the Opera," both of 1935). While farces always

trade in stock elements, and while the author's homage to a Marx Brothers past is intentional, the old tricks must be augmented by new inventions if the audience is to be ambushed into riotous laughter. A final scene — or third act — that might have topped the traditional set-ups with fresh, hysterical surprises never arrives.

•

One must also ask whether Mr. Zaks is too kind to direct killer farce fueled by the basest human traits. The warmth that the director brings to comedies like "The House of Blue Leaves" and "Wenceslas Square" is misplaced in a piece in which every character will stop at nothing to get what he wants. Jane Connell (in the Margaret Dumont role of the Opera Guild dowager who might fire Mr. Bosco), Ms. Lagerfelt and at times Mr. Garber seem benign rather than ruthless as they pursue their selfish ends. The softening of the characters' malice deflates the cartoonishness of a farce much as a Looney Tune might crumble if Tweety weren't placed in real jeopardy by Sylvester the cat.

With its speedy gait, gleaming lighting (by Paul Gallo) and wildly luxurious Art Deco sets and costumes (by Tony Walton and by William Ivey Long), the play looks so much like a prime example of its genre that one is all the more frustrated by the shortage of belly laughs. But the evening provides professional, painless fluff even so. If, as "Lend Me a Tenor" would have us believe, a Cleveland audience of 1934 can mistake a rank impostor for the world's most celebrated opera star, it would be foolish to underestimate the prospects of a simulated farce on Broadway in 1989.

1989 Mr 3, C3:1

Transcending A Bleak Reality

THE PAPER GRAMOPHONE, based on a screenplay by Aleksandr Chervinsky; adapted for the stage by Yuri Yeremin and Mr. Chervinsky; English translation by Micael Yeargan; lighting by Ken Tabachnik; sound by David Budries; dance movement by Kathryn Posin; dramaturge, Greg Leaming; production interpreter, Alexander Gelman; production stage manager, Wendy Cox. Presented by Mark Lamos, artistic director; David Hawkanson, managing director. At Hartford.

Lidiya Ivanovna	Kathleen Chalfant
Viktoriya	Ann Dowd
Semyon	Ray Virta
Oscar Borisovich	Jack Bittner
Student	Evan Blackford

By MEL GUSSOW
Special to The New York Times

HARTFORD — "The Paper Gramophone," which is having its American premiere at Hartford Stage, is both an artifact of Stalinist Russia and a gentle love story about the purity that can survive in a repressive environment. Given its dramatic limitations, it is a touching evocation of a young woman's attempt to reach beyond despair to a kind of idealism.

Aleksandr Chervinsky originally wrote "The Paper Gramophone" as a screenplay, but, for political reasons, it was not filmed. As adapted to the stage by the author and Yuri Yeremin, it was presented in the Soviet Union in 1982 and has become a continuing favorite during perestroika. At the invitation of Mark Lamos, artistic director of Hartford Stage, Mr. Yeremin has staged it here with an American company.

The play is small in scale, small enough so that, at times, it seems to float away from the wide Hartford stage. The expansiveness of a film would, in fact, be an advantage. Then one could see, as well as hear about, the barrenness of Stalinist times. As a work for the theater, "The Paper Gramophone" does not have the narrative drive or the rich canvas of characters of "Stars in the Morning Sky," the modern Russian play that was presented in New York's international festival last year.

•

But there is a convincing truthfulness about the work, as well as a strong central character, the aptly named Viktoriya — and Ann Dowd, an actress making her East Coast debut, is very appealing in the role. Viktoriya is an orphan, whose parents

were dissidents — in other words, "enemies of the people" — and her parents' background continues to haunt her. She has become the ward of a family friend who is principal of a boys' school in a provincial town. With time on her hands as a caretaker at the school, Viktoriya has dreams that carry her into a fantasy world.

An avid reader, she has gone through the school's library, and she is searching for self-fulfillment as in fiction (the school, significantly, is located on Tolstoy Street). Her desire for motherhood — an assurance of a future life through a child — leads her into a liaison with a handsome sailor (Ray Virta). To his surprise, he falls in love with this plain young woman.

Reaching beyond despair to idealism.

The play deals principally with the difficulty of pursuing their shared passion while avoiding surveillance and with Viktoriya's role as an outsider in a rigid society. Like an Anne Frank, she is simply too vibrant (actress as well as character) to be confined in what in her case is an emotional attic. Her enthusiasms are irrepressible, and the sailor quickly becomes her co-conspirator.

•

Ms. Dowd and Mr. Virta seem endemic to this bleak environment. The actress finds a radiance within her character's drabness and Mr. Virta moves effortlessly from the required early surliness to an empathy with Viktoriya in her predicament.

Counterpointing the couple are the school principal (Kathleen Chalfant) and an aged teacher (Jack Bittner),

who has been broken in rank and in spirit because of his own dissidence. These two characters are only glancingly observed, although the principal also acts as the heroine's conscience.

Tentatively, the author tries to be experimental by having the principal appear as a talking picture on the wall of Viktoriya's miniscule bedroom. The device is awkward, as is Mr. Yeremin's use of the small, repeatedly revolving set. But neither is injurious to the intimate portrait of a young woman trying — against odds — to embrace life in its fullness. Viktoriya's hope is expressed by her paper gramophone, a rudimentary phonograph that momentarily enlivens her existence with music, dancing and the joy of an unattainable world.

1989 Mr 4, 11:4

Mystery and Power

MYTHOS OEDIPUS and DIONYSUS FILIUS DEI, text and direction by Ellen Stewart; light design by John P. Dodd; special effects by Rob Vivona; The Great Jones Repertory Company, presented by La Mama E.T.C. At 66 East Fourth Street.

MYTHOS OEDIPUS, music by Eliabeth Swados, Sheila Dabney, Genji Ito, David Sawyer and Michael Sirotta; musical direction by Ms. Dabney and Mr. Sirotta; choreography by Min Tanaka, Manhong Kang, Maureen Fleming Odo and the ensemble; set design by Jun Maeda; costume design by Eiko Yamaguchi; masks by Gretchen Green.

DIONYSUS FILIUS DEI, vocal score by Ms. Swados; music and orchestrations by Ms. Dabney, Mr. Ito and Mr. Sirotta; choreography by Ms. Stewart and the company; set design by David Adams, Ms. Stewart, Mark Tambella and Watoku Ueno; costume design by Sally J. Lesser; masks by Stephen Loebel; Greek translation by Eleni Petratos.

WITH: John Kelly, Alan Bezozi, Du-Yee Chang, Sheila Dabney, Rose Davis, Ron Dreyer, Abba Elethea, Maureen Fleming Odo, Henry Freeman, Susan Huffaker, Genji Ito, Manhong Kang, John Kelly, Hulya Kuser, Bob Morffi, David Phillips, Federico Restrepo, Cynthia Rogers, Tony Scheitinger, Shigeko, Michael Sirotta, Frances Ellen Thorpe, Ching Valdes/Aran, Valois, Lou Zeldis and Sam Zuckerman.

By D. J. R. BRUCKNER

There may be more to Dionysian ecstasy than meets the eye in Ellen Stewart's "Dionysus Filius Dei," performed by the Great Jones Repertory Company at La Mama. But since there are no words in this "dance opera" except a minimal vocal score in Greek provided by Elizabeth Swados, what eludes the eye often escapes comprehension and baffles the emotions.

"Dionysus" is on a double bill with Miss Stewart's "Mythos Oedipus," first performed in Greece and then at La Mama last year. In that dance opera, Miss Stewart used Sophocles' plays about Oedipus, along with other material, to create an exalted vision of the triumph of suffering over fate and divine manipulation. It compels an audience to approach the well-known story with a fresh imagination.

The god Dionysus is especially seductive to actors and playwrights since, historically, theater in the West either developed out of the Dionysian cult or grew up alongside it. But the many stories about and references to this often terrifying god that are scattered through ancient literature are not widely known now, and in "Dionysus Filius Dei" they are not explained or given a dramatic structure. Some of the stories are given no structure at all; in one long sequence we are

taken on a tour of Dionysus' progress through eight kingdoms as he drives people to orgies of lust and madness, but we are given no hint about how his bloody adventures inspired a powerful sinister religion or how they lead to his apotheosis at the end.

There are some spectacular scenes in this piece; the appropriately barbaric music is haunting; and at times the sensuous energy of the dancing suggests the frightening and orgiastic power the ancients said Dionysian ceremonies had.

But there is entirely too much mystery here. This version of the legends omits the most dramatic story about the god: eventually Apollo, the god of reason, accepted Dionysus into his own temple and from this union rose the tension underlying much of Western art and philosophy. Miss Stewart's play has some emotional power — none of the ancient Dionysus myths is innocent, after all — but the hero here is Dionysus before he was drawn into the Apollonian circle of light, and at the end he remains only what he was at the beginning: a shadowy alien.

1989 Mr 5, 69:1

Chinese History

WHITE BONED DEMON, created and directed by Leslie Mohn; visual design by Barbara Abramson and Gabriel Bäcklund; original music and arrangements by James Harry and Chris Abajian; ballet choreography by Alan Lindblad; light design by Vaclav Kucera; costume design and fabrication by Mary Cricket Smith; production manager, Steve Paul. Red Eye Collaboration presented by the Theater for the New City, George Bartenieff, artistic director/managing director; Crystal Field, executive artistic director. At 155 First Avenue, at 10th Street.

WITH: Mark Amdahl, Daniel Boone, Andrea Dickerson, Bettina Geyer, Barbara Hiesiger, Lisa Hurst, Miriam Must, Stepehn Peabody, Catherine Seltz and Zhang Xin.

By MEL GUSSOW

Before she became the wife of Mao Zedong and, subsequently, the most powerful woman in China, Jiang Qing was an actress. One of her favorite roles was Nora in "A Doll's House," which she played in Shanghai in 1935. Beginning with these facts and Jiang's trial as one of the notorious Gang of Four, Leslie Mohn has created an irreverent, freewheeling political escapade titled "White Boned Demon." The title refers to Jiang, who, after her downfall, was attacked as a Circe-like temptress. The play, a production of the Red Eye Collaboration — a Minneapolis equivalent of the Mabou Mines — is now at Theater for the New City.

From her prison cell, Jiang (played by Zhang Xin) dreams about her early days on stage and re-creates a performance of the Ibsen play. Her "Doll's House" is a continent away from naturalism. It has the panoply, in miniature, of the Peking Opera and the insouciance of the Ridiculous Theatrical Company.

Playing Jiang as Ibsen's heroine, Miriam Must affects a dumb-Nora, doll-like voice and a mincing manner, while Stephen Peabody's Torvald Helmer is so heavily masked that he could be mistaken for a Chinese dragon. He becomes a stand-in for Mao himself, lecturing — and hectoring — his oppressed wife from a little red book. Though the play-within-a-play holds to the outline of Ibsen, it

T. Charles Erickson

Ann Dowd and Ray Virta in "The Paper Gramophone."

Daniel Boone and Miriam Must in "White Boned Demon."

Vaclav Kucero

adds occasional references to imperialists and other running dogs.

Balletic interludes turn the work into a kind of "Small House of Uncle Henrik." Dance and drama are further interrupted by a pushy director (doubling on stage as an oily Dr. Rank), who insists on reblocking the play in performance, and also by Jiang commenting from her imprisoned present. Finally she steps back into the past to put the Helmer house in order. Jiang is quick to parallel Nora's plight with her own. As she sees it, both are victims of male supremacy, and they triumph by becoming door-slamming counterrevolutionaries.

the same time, the jealous Jiang, he actress, hastens to rewrite

In prison, Jiang Qing re-creates her performance in 'A Doll's House.'

her own apparently devastating reviews so that she can be a star in several firmaments. In a flash-forward she has her original theater director arrested, and abuses him like her own private running dog.

The comedy is the stage approximation of a series of Chinese boxes — plays within plays, jokes within jokes — disappearing into infinity behind a strobe-lit scrim where we see a masked Mao, looking like a Madame Tussaud waxwork and speaking like an automaton. The show operates on so many frequencies at once that one is not always sure who is ridiculing whom and whether the portrait (of Nora as well as Jiang) is meant to be sympathetic. But as playwright and director, Ms. Mohn has an oddly engaging theatricality. The work is playful rather than pretentious, and it awakens one's interest in the tyrannical central subject.

The actors are attuned to the double-edge art of self-mockery, and include, most prominently, Ms. Must,

Catherine Seltz, Mr. Peabody, Daniel Boone and Mark Amdahl (as Ibsen's Krogstad, who is treated as a capitalist villain). Threaded through the show is a clanging pastiche of Chinese music by James Harry and Chris Abajian. The attractive dancers are dressed as for a Red Army detachment. The costumes, opulent in the case of the principals, are designed by Mary Cricket Smith.

Ms. Mohn footnotes the performance with slides, asides and feminist fortune cookies distributed to the audience during the intermission. Mine read, "Women are one half of the sky," a sentiment that was later reiterated in the dialogue. Other quotations according to Madame Mao include, "All art is political" and "Women are the true revolutionaries." Those two statements sum up the message of "White Boned Demon," a play that re-evaluates Chinese history from the provocative perspective of anarchic comedy.

1989 Mr 5, 68:1

On the Bright Side, He Wasn't a Worm

METAMORPHOSIS, adapted and directed by Steven Berkoff from a short story by Franz Kafka. Musical director, Larry Spivack; costume designer, Jacques Schmidt; scenic supervisor, Duke Durfee; costume supervisor, Susan O'Donnell; lighting supervisor, Brian Nason; production stage manager, Patrick Horrigan; general manager, Ralph Roseman; music performed by Mr. Spivack. Presented by Lars Schmidt and Roger L. Stevens. At the Ethel Barrymore Theater, 243 West 47th Street.

Gregor	Mikhail Baryshnikov
Mr. Samsa	René Auberjonois
Mrs. Samsa	Laura Esterman
Greta	Madeleine Potter
Chief Clerk	Mitch Kreindel
The Lodger	T. J. Meyers

By FRANK RICH

It's hard to guess who will suffer most at Steven Berkoff's theatrical version of "Metamorphosis": devotees of Franz Kafka, whose story is

distorted into Marxist kitsch by this adaptation, or fans of Mikhail Baryshnikov, whose stage debut as a dramatic actor, however dignified, amounts to little more than a sideshow to the loud circus surrounding him. But at least one constituency, albeit a smaller one, should be happy — the Berkoff cult. The director doesn't even have to appear in the flesh to upstage Kafka and Mr. Baryshnikov throughout this piece's interminable (and intermissionless) 100 minutes.

•

Actually, Mr. Berkoff does have a surrogate on stage at the Barrymore, in the form of the show's true leading man, the actor René Auberjonois. With his greased-back hair and grizzly, scowling mien, Mr. Auberjonois barks out the role of Gregor Samsa's father as if he were doing an impersonation of Mr. Berkoff's impersonation of Hitler on the recent television mini-series "War and Remembrance." And in that performance lies the message of this "Metamorphosis." In Mr. Berkoff's retelling, Gregor Samsa, the commercial traveler who awakens one morning to find himself transformed into a gigantic dung beetle, is no longer a lost, alienated soul consumed by the terror of living. He is instead the martyred victim of a greedy, parasitic bourgeois society symbolized by his father. Let Kafka worry about man's eternal, complex private war with himself and his family; Mr. Berkoff reduces "Metamorphosis" to a class struggle between the bug and the pigs.

Both in its ideology and in its once avant-garde Expressionist theatrical style, this "Metamorphosis" is very much a product of the late 1960's (when it was first produced in London, with Mr. Berkoff as Gregor). The stark setting is a gray void on which has been erected a spare, skeletal jungle gym that fans out like a spider's legs. While delivering a condensed choral recitation of Kafka's text, Gregor's father, mother (Laura Esterman) and sister (Madeleine Potter) perform mimed routines front and center, most of which reveal them to be grotesquely materialistic vulgarians. "Cash! ... Cigars! ... Shoes!" they yell at the prospect of any new income. At mealtime, they chomp away with a slobbering relish that might offend the residents of "Animal Farm."

Mr. Baryshnikov, always wearing the workaday suit and rimless spectacles of the pre-metamorphosed Gregor, is never allowed to leave the stage, but neither is he often given the opportunity to dominate the action. He is usually sequestered in the shadowy background, on the cagelike platform that represents Gregor's room. There he performs contortionist stunts, all executed with exquisite grace and precision, that simulate the beetle's perambulations: hanging upside down from the ceiling, whirring his legs in helpless panic, masticating his food, scuttling across the floor. When Mr. Baryshnikov must speak, his accent gives "Metamorphosis" one of its few connections to the frayed Old World that spawned Kafka, but the emotional tone of his acting is no less facetious than that of his fellow players.

There is nothing embarrassing about Mr. Baryshnikov's work here. The real question is why he picked a stage assignment that, for all its High Culture trappings, makes no more demands on his great talent than would the title role of "Legs Diamond."

Steven Berkoff's version of the Kafka story.

Only once does "Metamorphosis" allow Mr. Baryshnikov to reveal the deep artistic soul that informs his gestural poetry. When Mr. Auberjonois throws the apple that penetrates Gregor's carapace, we not only see a dancer's delicate rendition of an insect's slow, crumpled fall to the ground but we also find, in the innocence of Mr. Baryshnikov's baffled expression, a man's far steeper descent into the clutches of mortality.

The rest of the evening's acting is so consistently clownish that the performers cannot be held accountable. Outrageous caricature is what Mr. Berkoff needs to make his polemical point, and, since that point requires that representatives of commerce be still more disgusting than the Samsa family, the crude portrayals of the chief clerk and the single, porky

Mikhail Baryshnikov in Steven Berkoff's staging of Franz Kafka's story "Metamorphosis."

Martha Swope

lodger (in lieu of the three in Kafka) are unwatchably gross. His strident ideological scheme notwithstanding, however, Mr. Berkoff can waffle for sentimental effect. Gregor's mother and sister, though previously presented as interchangeably heartless, weep their way through the beetle's death rattles.

In Mr. Berkoff's vibrant staging of "Coriolanus," seen at the New York Shakespeare Festival this season, his martial theatrical techniques were well matched to a play dealing with politics, war and civic behavior. Those same techniques are like jackboots when stamped upon Kafka's intimate journey into one man's soul. Larry Spivack, who provided the tingling electronic score for "Coriolanus," fills "Metamorphosis" with percussion and piano poundings suitable for a silent horror movie. Mr. Berkoff's typically hyperbolic lighting scheme emerges as more florid than Brechtian: when the Samsa family imagines happier times (in slow motion, no less), grays and blacks give way to gooey floods of blue and yellow.

Such grand theatrical gestures are anathema to fiction whose power derives precisely from its author's ability to cloak terror within the dry, homely details of humdrum daily life. As written by Kafka, "Metamorphosis" is "realism pure and simple, so realistic as to be hard to bear," writes the biographer Ernst Pawel in a wise program essay whose nearly every sentence rebukes the production on stage. Mr. Berkoff's bombastic "Metamorphosis" is hard to bear not because it locks us into Gregor Samsa's nightmare, but because it cavalierly crushes two sensitive artists, like so many insects, underfoot.

1989 Mr 7, C15:1

Without Slamming Doors

RUN FOR YOUR WIFE! written and directed by Ray Cooney; set supervision by Michael Anania; costumes by Joseph G. Aulisi; lighting by Marilyn Rennagel; production stage manager, Amy Pell. The Theater of Comedy production presented by Don Taffner, Paul Elliott and Strada Entertainment Trust. Virginia Theater, 245 West 52d Street.

John Smith	Ray Cooney
Detective Sgt. Troughton	Gareth Hunt
Barbara Smith	Hilary Labow
Detective Sgt. Porterhouse	Dennis Ramsden
Bobby Franklyn	Gavin Reed
The reporter	Doug Stender
Mary Smith	Kay Walbye
Stanley Gardner	Paxton Whitehead

By MEL GUSSOW

Every season, at least one British farce takes a long lease on a West End theater under a marquee festooned with effusive comments ("I loved it!" Daily Mail). One can tell almost everything about the plays from the apparently interchangeable titles: "No Sex Please, We're British," "Not Now, Darling," "Move Over, Mrs. Markham" and "Run for Your Wife!" The last three were written or co-written by Ray Cooney.

Last night, "Run for Your Wife!" opened at the Virginia Theater, in a production directed by Mr. Cooney heading a cast composed primarily of English actors. This is the show as tourists might see it in London (the original production has just passed its 2,500th performance in the West

End). On Broadway, "Run for Your Wife!" puts America's fondness for British comedy to a stress test.

Accepting the ground rules for allowable contrivances in farce, the play is still burdened with blind alleys, limp jokes, forced puns and troubled entendres. Even the four doors on stage are not used to farcical advantage; they are locked or blocked rather than slammed.

In this comedy about bigamy, a dull man turns out to have a hyperactive romantic life. That is the beginning and the slowly approached end of the evening's tomfoolery. John Smith, a London taxi driver(played by Mr. Cooney), maintains two separate households, one in Wimbledon, the other a few minutes away in Streatham. Because of an accident too complicated to explain, his worlds collide, and the police are called in to investigate.

With increasing ineptitude, the taxi driver tries to keep one wife from learning about the other. To extend his comedy, Mr. Cooney uses every subterfuge in the joke book, including the pretense of his being homosexual. Whenever possible, the play makes fun of stereotypes (dumb cops, swishy gays and prefeminist women who think only of getting their man into bed).

The central idea has comic possibilities, as was proved years ago in the Alec Guinness movie "The Captain's Paradise," but Mr. Cooney's play founders while rushing between ports. The sole attempt at ingenuity is to have both homes on stage at the same time, so we see the wives simultaneously though they remain invisible to each other. Alan Ayckbourn used this device with panache in "How the Other Half Loves." Mr. Cooney uses it inattentively. The double occupancy comes and goes at whim.

To complicate the plot, almost everyone is mistaken for someone else, one wife for a nun, the other for a transvestite, and that leads to two more subjects for ridicule. Sex appears to be on everyone's mind, though there is an ingenuousness in that department. Much of the confu-

A dull cabdriver has a hyperactive romantic life.

sion derives from the cute terms of endearment characters use for their mates. It does not pay to ask questions — to wonder why the two policemen are so incredibly gullible, and why they are devoting so much time to a minor case, or what the two attractive women see in the colorless cabdriver.

The play might have been enlivened in performance — as is certainly the case with that other new farce, Ken Ludwig's "Lend Me a Tenor" — but, with one exception, the acting is as ordinary as John Smith is supposed to be. Because the cabdriver has suffered a blow to his head, Mr. Cooney has to walk around in a daze, which is no excuse for his lack of expression.

It has often been said that the key to comedy is to play it for its reality, and some of the actors seem to take that advice — to no avail, because there is scant comedy to begin with. Faced with an errant husband, Kay Walbye (as the Wimbledon wife) comes close to hysteria. Her Streatham counterpart, Hilary Labow, is simply treated as décor, and the two police sergeants, Gareth Hunt and Dennis Ramsden, fade to blandness.

Paxton Whitehead, as the hero's friend who unwittingly becomes his accomplice, is the only actor able to exercise a sustained comedic impulse (although Gavin Reed is effective at conjuring comic clichés). With the look of a benign giraffe, Mr. Whitehead stumbles through the two apartments and the obstacles of the plot.

Quick on the double take and even quicker on the response, he is an agile physical comedian. With the unexpected arrival of the police, he dives for cover behind a couch and emerges with a wastebasket over his head. This, as it turns out, is one of the show's more risible moments, which should say something about the quality of the humor.

In tune with his writing, Mr. Cooney's staging is mechanical, as characters watch one another watching. As designed by Michael Anania, both homes could stand refurbishing. As a playwright, Mr. Cooney carries on a tradition created in the 1950's by Brian Rix. Since that time, there has been a revolution — and a revitalization — in British comedy on stage and in movies and television, led by Joe Orton, Tom Stoppard, Michael Frayn and the members of the Monty Python troupe, among others. In contrast, "Run for Your Wife!" aspires to mediocrity and achieves it.

1989 Mr 8, C17:1

Deborah Gray Mitchell

Paxton Whitehead in "Run for Your Wife!," at the Virginia Theater.

An Eyeful

WHAT THE BUTLER SAW, by Joe Orton; directed by John Tillinger; scenery by John Lee Beatty; costumes by Jane Greenwood; lighting by Ken Billington; sound by John Gromada; production stage manager, James Harker. Presented by Manhattan Theater Club, Lynne Meadow, artistic director, and Barry Grove, managing director. At City Center Stage 1, 131 West 55th Street.

Dr. Prentice	Charles Keating
Geraldine Barclay	Joanne Whalley-Kilmer
Mrs. Prentice	Carole Shelley
Nicholas Beckett	Bruce Norris
Dr. Rance	Joseph Maher
Sergeant Match	Patrick Tull

By FRANK RICH

There are no butlers in "What the Butler Saw," the play the English writer Joe Orton completed only

weeks before he was murdered in 1967. Orton's title, with its prurient whiff of Edwardian peep shows, is generic: it announces a low farce rife with fallen trousers, sexual indiscretions, mistaken identities, lewd puns. And in John Tillinger's riotous production at the Manhattan Theater Club — New York's first exposure to Orton's unexpurgated text — "What the Butler Saw" doesn't disappoint. Here at last are the two hours of nonstop laughter that theatergoers have been pursuing all season.

But to settle for calling Orton's comedy funny is not to do it justice. In this work, the author of "Entertain-

In 'What the Butler Saw,' all is undermined and nothing's what it seems.

ing Mr. Sloane" and "Loot" wrote that rare thing, a truly revolutionary play. Orton is scrupulous in honoring the rules of classic farce — no small achievement in itself — and yet he subversively uses those rules to demolish the even stricter rules governing the civilization beyond the theater's walls. "What the Butler Saw" undermines psychiatry, religion, marriage, government, definitions of gender and even simple language. By the time he reaches his breathless conclusion, Orton has transported us to a Cloudcuckooland of his own fiercely imagined invention. It's a place where girls have switched identities (and wardrobes) with boys, yes can mean no, and inmates are freely running the asylum.

The setting is a middle-class psychiatric clinic specializing in "the complete nervous breakdown and its byproducts." The action begins with the oldest gag in the book: the very proper Dr. Prentice (Charles Keating) is interrupted by his spouse (Carole Shelley) just as he tries to seduce a bosomy young secretarial applicant (Joanne Whalley-Kilmer) sent over by the Friendly Faces Employment Bureau. The rest of the play's frenzied plot springs entirely from that simple setup. The more strenuously Dr. Prentice attempts to cover up his transgression, the more disastrous the consequences. For added mix-ups, Orton stirs in such unexpected visitors as Dr. Rance (Joseph Maher), a Government inspector representing the clinic's "immediate superiors in madness," and a randy pageboy from the Station Hotel (Bruce Norris) attempting to sell compromising photographs of Dr. Prentice's nymphomaniacal wife.

"Why are there so many doors?" asks Dr. Rance upon arrival. "Was this house designed by a lunatic?" At the lunatic farcical level, "What the Butler Saw" is ingeniously conceived. Characters constantly tear through swinging doors to catch one another in compromising states of undress, until finally Dr. Prentice, an utter nonentity, stands circumstantially

Gerry Goodstein

Carole Shelley and Joseph Maher in "What the Butler Saw," completed by Joe Orton only weeks before he was murdered in 1967.

accused of being "a transvestite, fetishist, bisexual murderer." Comic props (stray high-heel shoes, straitjackets, pistols, underwear, even some seemingly benign roses) are choreographed into ricocheting running gags, which are then topped by Orton's Wildean zingers. When Mrs. Prentice suspects her husband of taking up transvestism, she coolly tells him, "I'd no idea our marriage teetered on the edge of fashion."

The playwright even goes so far as to give "What the Butler Saw" a farce's traditional finale. Orphaned twins are reunited with their family with the aid of a reconstructed birth trinket; a deus ex machina (a policeman, played by Patrick Tull, in Dionysian drag) literally descends from the heavens. But if this happy ending is as old as the theater, it has been sneakily rejiggered by Orton to lock us into a new, inverted view of the world. To reach the play's celebratory reconciliation, the audience must tolerate incest, homoeroticism ("The world is full of naked men running in all directions!" cries Mrs. Prentice) and a mocking of all kinds of authority. The prop that brings the play's characters, themes and plot into final unity is nothing less than a large brass phallus that a gas-main explosion had severed from a statue of Sir Winston Churchill.

•

"What the Butler Saw" could only be the artistic act of a gay man taunting a repressive society, yet the freedom for which it proselytizes is ecumenical and timeless. When Dr. Rance is accused of concocting severe psychoanalytic diagnoses from skimpy facts, he retorts that "civilizations have been founded and maintained on theories that refuse to obey facts." But as Orton liberates his characters from their clothes, so he intends to liberate theatergoers of all persuasions from exactly those theories that keep civilization straitjacketed in prejudice. Not only does "What the Butler Saw" dismiss doctrinaire religion as "the last ditch stand of a man on the brink of disaster" but it also repeatedly defines ideal psychotherapy as that which "liberates and exploits madness," permitting nonconformity instead of "curing" it.

One can argue with Orton's specific ideological stands after leaving the theater. In Mr. Tillinger's fast-paced production, "What the Butler Saw" is simply too dizzy and high-spirited to quarrel with in the ample flesh. As was true of his restorative New York revivals of "Sloane" and "Loot," the director plays the comedy straight, not for camp. Orton's people, after all, are entirely real. It's this playwright's mission — and genius — to demonstrate that the world, not its most independent inhabitants, is bent.

•

In a fine cast that includes past Orton masters (Miss Shelley, Mr. Keating) and first-rate newcomers (notably Ms. Whalley-Kilmer), the catalytic performance, unsurprisingly, comes from Mr. Maher, who has played the authority figure in each of Mr. Tillinger's Orton revivals. Dr. Rance, a self-proclaimed "representative of order" who sows nothing but chaos (and commitment papers), is the looniest Maher turn yet — a psychiatrist who misinterprets every bit of evidence before him even as he swings between maniacal jigs of rage and pompous effusions of nonsensical scientific erudition ("The insane are famous for their wild ways").

The only sadness in the mirthful evening comes from the knowledge that this masterwork, in which Orton's elegance of execution at last matched his anarchy of intent, was the end of the line. While "What the Butler Saw" could stand as the crowning achievement of most playwriting careers, from a red-hot writer of 34 it was surely an augury of much more, much of it unimaginable, yet to come.

1989 Mr 9, C21:1

Immaculate Conception

MEASURE FOR MEASURE, by William Shakespeare; directed by Mark Lamos; sets and costumes by John Conklin; lighting by Pat Collins; sound by David Budries; original music by Mel Marvin; general manager, Steven C. Callahan; production manager, Jeff Hamlin; stage manager, Wendy Chapin; assistant stage manager, Fredric H. Orner. Presented by Lincoln Center Theater, Gregory Mosher, director; Bernard Gersten, executive producer. At the Mitzi E. Newhouse Theater, 150 West 65th Street.

Vincentio	Len Cariou
Escalus	George Hall
Angelo	Campbell Scott
Lucio	Reggie Montgomery
First gentleman and Varrius	Marcus Giamatti
Second gentleman and Abhorson	Philip Moon
Mistress Overdone	Lois Smith
Pompey	Jack Weston
Claudio	Bradley Whitford
Provost	Deryl Caitlyn
Father Thomas and Barnardine	Mario Arrambide
Isabella	Kate Burton
Francisca	Marceline Hugot
Elbow	Thomas Ikeda
Froth	Ethyl Eichelberger
Justice and Friar Peter	Don Mayo
Secretary to Angelo	Koji Okamura
Juliet	Gabriella Diaz-Farrar
Boy	Joel E. Chaiken
Mariana	Lorraine Toussaint
Secretaries Robert Bella and Jonathan Baker	

Officers
Jonathan Baker, Paul S. Eckstein, Jonathan Nichols and Ascanio Sharpe

---

By FRANK RICH

The setting of "Measure for Measure" is a city teeming with vice. Prostitution and alcohol plague the populace, unchecked by the state's lax law enforcement. Although the city is Vienna, we recognize the scene from closer to home. The questions raised — primarily, Where does justice intersect with morality, and how can it be obtained? — are always with us. And so one initially assumes that the director Mark Lamos is up to something smart in his staging of "Measure for Measure" at the Mitzi Newhouse Theater at Lincoln Center. The reigning Duke (Len Cariou) wears a dark suit and summons aides with a Touch-Tone phone. The production's "Vienna" is represented by a stage wall splattered with contemporary graffiti. Its inhabitants are racially diverse.

The beginning of Mr. Lamos's inventiveness, unfortunately, also proves to be its sum. While his "Measure for Measure" remains in present-day costume — the prisoners seem to be sentenced to wearing sportswear from the Gap — the production never achieves a specificity that might conjure up the atmosphere of the gritty world we live in. The play instead languishes in an antiseptic void: the standard-issue vacuum of Modern Dress Theater.

The cool gray color scheme seems to have been chosen for decorative rather than substantive ends, and it is preserved at all costs. The sole glimpses Mr. Lamos offers of a decadent society are a few flashing police lights and a bohemian espresso bar that only the denizens of Disney World might consider a fleshpot.

Though Mr. Lamos has told interviewers that his graffiti wall was inspired by the abstract artist Cy Twombly, he hasn't re-created Mr. Twombly's agitated canvases; he's re-created the hushed chicer-than-thou ambiance of a downtown gallery where those canvases might be for sale. Coincidence or not, "Measure for Measure" is color coordinated with Lincoln Center's Broadway production of "Our Town" and, with its two chairs and one table, is even more sparsely furnished.

•

The town Shakespeare presents in this comedy may be our town, but it's a social realm closer to "Bonfire of

Brigitte Lacombe

Len Cariou as Duke Vincentio in "Measure for Measure."

the Vanities" than to Mr. Lamos's tranquil environment — a crucible of enormous moral ambiguities. Let the people in "Measure for Measure" try to do the right thing (according to their consciences and to benefit their brethren), and they almost invariably come up short.

When the Duke turns over his legal authority to his puritanical deputy, Angelo (Campbell Scott), the outcome is a resurgence of strict law-and-order but a collapse of mercy-tempered justice. Even Angelo can't live up to his own high standards, and neither can the heroine who sparks his lust, the fledgling novice Isabella (Kate Burton). Devout to a fault, Isabella would rather preserve her virtue than trade her body for the life of the brother, Claudio (Bradley Whitford), unjustly condemned by Angelo. So complex are Shakespeare's characterizations that nearly everyone on stage is variously wrong and right. By the reconciliatory finale, Angelo and Isabella have infused their rigid moral codes with true charity even as the previously sensible Duke embraces his own forms of self-contradiction.

•

Mr. Lamos, who is the artistic director of the Hartford Stage, has a high reputation as a Shakespearean director. Whether that reputation is deserved or merely an instance of resident-theater-movement hyperbole cannot be measured from the scanty evidence here. That Mr. Lamos is sensitive to the intellectual issues in this "problem play" is beyond question. He doesn't flatten Angelo into an abject hypocrite or Isabella into a one-note prig. He never misreads the text even as he threatens to present it as a staged reading.

His "Measure for Measure" doesn't miss Shakespeare's point; it's simply beside the point. Why stage

Flashing police lights and an espresso bar signify decadence.

this fascinating play — whose so-called problems are challenges to theatrical exploration — if one has nothing burning to say about it? Like the "Midsummer Night's Dream" that was my first exposure to the director's work in Hartford last fall, his "Measure" prizes pristine imagery over the hurly-burly of passion. Rarely have Shakespeare's comedies, even as nominal a comedy as this one, seemed so humorless. The production's emotional tone, like Angelo's blood, is "very snow-broth."

•

Because of the intimate theater and minimalist design, Mr. Lamos does allow us to focus on the acting, which generally doesn't stand up to the close scrutiny. Aside from Pat Collins's expressionist lighting, Mr. Cariou gives the play its only aura of mystery when he first appears as the enigmatic Duke; when he re-emerges in disguise as a friar, the performance settles into bland geniality. Mr. Scott and Ms. Burton simulate the anguish of Angelo and Isabella with whining rather than summoning it from within. Mr. Whitford's doomed Claudio contemplates his fear of death with more conviction.

While some of the major comic turns are embarrassing (Reggie Montgomery's Lucio, Thomas Ikeda's Elbow), the brightest specks on the drab canvas are the bit clowns Jack Weston (a baggy-pants Pompey), Lois Smith (Mistress Overdone) and, until he opens his mouth, Ethyl Eichelberger (Froth). Rowdy and unkempt, they're the only ones in Mr. Lamos's immaculate contemporary village who seem like people we might actually know.

1989 Mr 10, C3:1

Sex and More Sex

MANHATTAN CLASS COMPANY, ONE-ACT PLAY FESTIVAL, SERIES A. Set design by Dan Conway and Gregory Mercurio; lighting design by John Hastings; costume design by Dianne-Finn Chapman; sound design by Lia Vollack; production manager, Laura Kravets; associate producers, Maggie Lear and Eric Berkal; general manager, W. D. Cantler. Presented by Manhattan Class Company, Robert LuPone, executive director; Bernard Telsey, executive director. At the Nat Horne Theater, 440 West 42d Street.
THE LOST COLONY, by Wendy MacLeod; directed by Michael Greif.
WITH: Ken Marks, Robin Morse, Joe Ponazecki and Jane Summerhays.

RED SHEETS, by Erik Ehn; directed by Daniel Wilson.
WITH: Kent Adams, Cara Buono, Jarlath Conroy and Melora Walters.

BIKINI SNOW, by Anna Theresa Cascio; directed by Jimmy Bohr.
WITH: Mark W. Conklin, Linda Larson, Stephen Schnetzer and Leif Tilden.

By WILBORN HAMPTON

According to its stated credo, the Manhattan Class Company is "dedicated to finding, developing and producing a new generation of playwrights and theater artists." Such goals and objectives are to be heartily applauded, but judging by Evening A of the company's 1989 festival of new one-acts, someone needs to organize a search party.

The writing in all three plays on the bill, while showing occasional glimmers of promise, seldom rises above the level of a workshop script in progress.

The best of the trio, Wendy MacLeod's "Lost Colony," is also the most conventional play. Stevie Lang (Robin Morse) is vacationing with her parents and fiancé, Jack (Ken Marks), on the North Carolina shore. The family spends time sitting on a deck watching turtles, listening to frogs or flying a kite on the beach in between discussions about a mystery man who keeps calling Stevie on the phone and who is giving her second thoughts about marrying Jack. Stevie, who says she "never loved anyone as much as I loved my cat," is looking for excitement. The audience knows what she means.

•

"The Lost Colony" is written in a series of fade-in, fade-out scenes that would be best suited to television (appropriate breaks for commercials), and much of the dialogue (conversations about the merits of different suntan lotions and the relative intelligence of Dalmatians) serves only to pad the play to half an hour. Ms. Morse as Stevie and Joe Ponazecki as her father give fine performances.

Erik Ehn's "Red Sheets" is probably meant to be shocking but succeeds only in being tedious. It opens with Donna (Melora Walters) telling an image of the Madonna how her father (Kent Adams) sexually abused her. The recitation is occasionally interrupted while Donna shouts encouragement to an offstage boyfriend who is taking pot shots at Daddy as he returns home. Next we see Daddy, full of bullet holes but still alive and kicking, as he drives off with daughter No. 2. (Donna now being in jail). There are some symbolic references to dogs, and automobile jumper cables also come into play.

•

The last piece, Anna Theresa Cascio's "Bikini Snow," takes place in a fallout shelter in the basement of B. Altman's, circa 1957. Tracy (Linda Larson), a socialite whose father plays golf with President Eisenhower, and a Bikinian (Mark W. Conklin) kidnap the beatnik son of the man who detonated the Bravo H-bomb on the Bikini atoll. They plan to hold him hostage until Ike gives the Bikinians Maui in reparation.

The plight of the Bikinians is a sad chapter in the brief history of the nuclear age, yet "Bikini Snow" never aims much higher than the zany sophistication of a college skit. The humor picks up with the arrival of Ms. Larson, who brings an appealing lunacy to the character of Tracy. Jimmy Bohr has directed with a fondness for slapstick and a firm belief in the theory that the louder a line is blurted, the funnier it is. There are also a lot of jokes about sexual organs.

1989 Mr 11, 16:1

Road to Mongolia

THE SUNDAY PROMENADE, by Lars Forssell; directed by Steve Stettler; set by Russell Parkman; lighting by Pat Dignan; costumes by C. Jane Epperson; sound by Tom Gould; production stage manager, Denise Laffer. Presented by TNT, The New Theater of Brooklyn, Deborah J. Pope and Mr. Stettler, artistic directors. At 465 Dean Street, Brooklyn.

With: Caitlin Hart, John Jiler, Marty Lodge, Innes-Fergus McDade, Cate McNider, Owen S. Rackleff, Jeff Rose, Christopher Shaw, Allan Stevens and Trinity Thompson.

By D. J. R. BRUCKNER

The whole is not as good as parts of "The Sunday Promenade" by Lars Forssell, but the good parts make this strange play at the New Theater of Brooklyn an amusing evening. Mr. Forssell's imagination is more poetic than dramatic; he can make you find connections among wildly conflicting ideas and his dialogue often reminds you of the snipped and elliptical lines of song lyrics.

Actors and directors must approach this play with some trepidation. It is a highly literary piece that borrows situations not only from other plays but also from novels and films, and its emotional twists are treacherous. But with the exception of an awkward final scene — in which a haunting vision that is beautifully talked about would be better unseen — the New Theater's cast under Steve Stettler's direction gives a performance that sends you away smiling, if puzzled.

At the turn of the century a Swedish merchant with an uncontrolled sense of humor and an absurdly unworldly vision of life tries so hard to make his family and friends see the comedy in human existence that he leads half of them to a bizarre end — in Outer Mongolia. Where it happens hardly matters because, by the end, Mr. Forssell has got the audience so involved in his exploration of how many improbabilities one can believe in that it would not be surprising if they disappeared on the moon or in some unknown dimension.

Along the way, the town's pastor, who discovers to his astonishment that he believes in God, pursues the merchant's wife, who teases his passion without knowing she is doing it; a shop employee elopes with the merchant's deaf-mute daughter in a scene that is funny and deeply sentimental at the same time; the merchant's older son dies twice, and the younger one, who is a bit retarded, turns out to be not only the toughest and most resilient member of this menagerie, but by far the wisest. So the play is an odd soup of comedy, melodrama, farce and burlesque, but much of it is delicious going down.

Since the playwright's game is intellectual sleight of hand, most of the characters are merely two-dimensional. The only one given a chance to grow is the younger son, Willy, mischievously and winningly played by Jeff Rose. As the merchant's mother, Trinity Thompson is a fierce old number with a terrifying wit but a heart that melts with every breath. And as the eloping clerk, Marty Lodge is delightful when he pours out his frustrations and hopes to a young woman who cannot hear or speak but who, he realizes, understands his every word and answers all his questions about his own worth.

1989 Mr 12, 68:1

Casting Stones

RENO: IN RAGE AND REHAB, written and performed by Reno; directed by John Ferraro; lighting design by Jackie Manassee; associate producer, Jacqueline Judd; executive producer, James B. Freydberg. Presented by Ellen M. Krass and Home Box Office. At Actor's Playhouse, 100 Seventh Avenue South, at Bleecker Street.

By STEPHEN HOLDEN

When Reno, a punkish young comedienne with a rock-and-roll attitude,

Jessica Katz

Cast members in "The Sunday Promenade." From left are Jeff Rose, Marty Lodge, Innes-Fergus McDade and Trinity Thompson.

performs, she becomes a swaggering perpetual-motion machine. Delivering a nonstop 90-minute monologue that focuses on the absurdities of life in New York, she is like a kid pretending to be an airplane out of control. At any second, one senses, there could be a crash landing right into the audience.

Much of the impact of "Reno: In Rage and Rehab," her solo show at the Actor's Playhouse, comes out of this restless, charged physicality. Her tireless energy helps her to land jokes on such overly familiar subjects as yuppies and nouvelle-cuisine restaurants. Recalling an expensively dressed young woman standing behind her in line at the bank, she exclaims, "I burned my bra so this 24-year-old broad could trade futures on Wall Street?" Some of Reno's other targets include overweight policemen, $2,800 designer dogs, the Canal Bar, Details magazine and New York politicians.

Among Reno's longer bits, the most incisive has to do with her alienated Long Island childhood. The child of Hispanic parents, brought up by all-American adoptive parents in a fancy suburb "nestled in the Caucasoid mountains," she remembers her family as being "on the cutting edge of dullness." Their fondness for Jell-O was matched by an obsession with cleanliness. Cries of "Don't put the stainless on the stainless!" resounded around the house. In recalling this sanitized upbringing, Reno slips out of her punchy Lower East Side bohemian mode to offer an amusing caricature of genteel speech. One wishes she indulged her talents for mimicry more generously throughout the evening.

In other extended bits, Reno works with interesting concepts, but doesn't nail them down with enough telling personal details. Reflecting on her guilt about receiving gifts or on the pitfalls of what she calls "co-dependent relationships," she avoids being specific by blowing up everyday emotions into generalized absurdist fantasies.

It is in her sexual humor that Reno is the most audacious. Memories of the time a director asked her to portray a male role segue into an analysis of sexual slang and its implications. The bit goes way beyond George Carlin in challenging taboos. Reno is at her funniest when saying the unprintable and parodying macho body language. Like a streetwise Bette Midler, she lights up when it comes time to clear the air, go over the line, and burst some polite bubbles.

1989 Mr 16, C20:4

Misery Loves Misery

THE MAGIC ACT, by Laurence Klaven; directed by Peter Zapp; produced by Kate Baggott; scenic design, Martha Fay; design concept, Brian Martin; lighting design, David Higham; sound design, Bruce Ellman; costume design, David Sawaryn; special make-up effects, Ben-Efex Inc.; production stage manager, Jana Llynn. Presented by The Ensemble Studio Theater, Curt Dempster, artistic director; Peter Shavitz, managing director. At 549 West 52d Street.

Mona Kale .... Anne O'Sullivan
Young Alan/Todd .... Rick Lawless
Young Annabelle/Linda ..... Cordelia Richards
Mother/Older Annabelle/Newswoman
Frederica Meister
Father/Older Alan/Newsman ..Sam Schacht

By WILBORN HAMPTON

Mona Kale is one of those blissfully unhappy souls who revel in the misery of solitude. She lives and loves vicariously through her friends, most of whom wish she would just go away. Mona also has a little trouble separating reality from fantasy, but then who doesn't.

As the lights come up on "The Magic Act," Laurence Klavan's whimsical if predictable new play at the Ensemble Studio Theater, Mona is in the dock accused of murdering Alan and Annabelle, two old high-school chums on whom Mona had once doted and who had been so in love as teen-agers they nearly pined to death when separated by summer camp.

The prosecution contends that Mona, visiting Alan and Annabelle after losing touch for many years, killed them because they were so happy, in revenge for her own loneliness. Mona has another explanation for what happened.

Television has a field day with the case and thanks to the blanket coverage on the evening news, Mona becomes a national symbol for the lonely and insane. Viewers can even call in to vote on her guilt or innocence (50 cents a call; the verdict at the end of the news).

Mr. Klavan has an eye and ear for satire, but in "The Magic Act" he is better at defining a scene than he is at moving it toward some particular point. The first act, in which Alan and Annabelle meet and fall in love, and with whom Mona ingratiates herself, has a certain effervescent appeal. But the second, in which Mona visits the couple many years later, fizzles. For one thing, nothing very surprising happens, at least nothing the audience hasn't guessed during intermission.

There is some promising writing in "The Magic Act" and some humorous observations on the absurdities of modern life and the people it has produced. But Mr. Klavan tries to pull a whole warren of rabbits out of his script. He has a fondness for simile, for example, but often strings several together in one line of dialogue, weakening the effect.

Peter Zapp has directed with some real sleight of hand, keeping his industrious actors, most of whom play a variety of roles, moving swiftly and smoothly backward and forward in time, through a score or so of scenes, so there's little time to dwell on the paucity of content. Brian Martin and Martha Fay have collaborated on a pragmatic set that quickly shifts among a dozen places.

Anne O'Sullivan gives a credible and energetic performance as Mona, although she allows the character's exuberance a fairly free rein in some scenes. Rick Lawless and Cordelia Richards, as the young Alan and Annabelle, present a boy and girl next door who recall the magic of young love. Sam Schacht and Frederica Meister's adult Alan and Annabelle so shatter that illusion, they might provide a motive for murder.

1989 Mr 16, C21:1

Mystery, Before, During and After

SUNSPOT, written, directed and designed by John Jesurun. Lighting by Jeff Nash; production stage manager, Brad Phillips; assistant director, Johannes Frick. Presented by the Kitchen, 512 West 19th Street.

WITH: Larry Tighe, Katrin Brinkmann, Black Eyed Susan, Michael Tighe, Steve Buscemi, Jane Smith, Helena White and Sanghi Wager.

By MEL GUSSOW

The mystery in a John Jesurun play invariably begins before the performance, as the audience tries to find its equilibrium in a nebulous theatrical space. Often this turns out to be a simulated moviedrome or television studio, where actors talk back to their own images. With "Black Maria" (in 1987), the entire floor space of the theater was filled with chairs. There was no stage and there were no live actors. The "play" appeared entirely on screens around and above the audience.

In the case of Mr. Jesurun's new performance piece, "Sunspot" (at the Kitchen), the mystery continues throughout the show and after it has ended. In question is the author's purpose. It is scant help to be informed that the play is "a comedy about 'foreign' language and the problems of translation." That part is self-evident. The perplexity is what Mr. Jesurun is trying to translate and how much of it is decipherable.

This time the stage is set with five brightly lighted tables of varying dimension — white planes in an architectural environment. These could be tables in a surrealistic billiard parlor (Formica rather than felt). Because of Mr. Jesurun's previous experimentations in mixing film, television and theater and in distorting the audience's perspective, one fully expects the tabletops to become horizontal screens for projections. This is not the case.

As the actors cluster around one table, it appears as if they have entered a room for surgery or autopsy. While waiting for news from a satellite, they listen to the unheard heartbeat of an unseen creature that has entered their dimension, perhaps through a sunspot.

At the behest of the author, who is also the director (as well as the designer), the actors speak their lines in the manner of automatons. Some words are in German, most are in barely inflected English. As a refrain, there is talk about an elusive concierge who is somehow connected to the sunspot.

Occasionally the actors (Black-Eyed Susan and Steve Buscemi, among others) interrupt the dialogue with sudden movements. Baseball bats are bashed against the tops of the tables, which are lassoed as if for a roundup, and performers splash one another with buckets of water. There are also sounds of Sousa and other composers in the background. In contrast to other Jesurun pieces, none of this is invigorating. Through choice, the usually imaginative playwright has limited his instrumentation. As a result, the play is etherized upon a table.

1989 Mr 18, 14:4

Love vs. Art

NIEDECKER, by Kristine Thatcher; directed by Julianne Boyd; set designer, James Noone; lighting designer, Frances Aronson; costume designer, Deborah Shaw; sound designer, Bruce Ellman; production stage manager, Linda Carol Young. Presented by the Women's Project and Productions, Julia Miles, artistic director. At the Apple Corps Theater, 336 West 20th Street.

WITH: Mary Diveny, Jane Fleiss, Frederick Neumann and Helen Stenborg.

By STEPHEN HOLDEN

"Niedecker," Kristine Thatcher's earnest low-key drama celebrating the life and work of the late poet Lorine Niedecker, contemplates the artist with such intense reverence that its subject emerges an almost saintly symbol of integrity, simplicity and devotion.

When Niedecker died in 1970 at the age of 66, she was an obscure literary figure. Since then, her knotty, distilled poetry, revolving on crystalline images of the natural world, has acquired a small but solid reputation. In Ms. Thatcher's play, we see the poet applying her technique, which she called "condensery," to editing the writings of a young admirer who visits her for informal instruction.

This method involved getting rid of prepositions and connectives, leaving only the bare bones of essential words. It helped to give her verse a concentrated power that some have compared to Emily Dickinson's.

Martha Holmes

Helen Stenborg and Frederick Neumann in "Niedecker."

One reason for Niedecker's obscurity was the fact that this very diffident woman found the promotion of her own work abhorrent. For most of her life she lived a spare rustic existence in a one-and-a-half-room cabin on Black Hawk Island, near Fort Atkinson, Wis. Ms. Thatcher's play, which is set in the vicinity of the cabin, begins the day after the assassination of President John F. Kennedy and concludes six years and two months later on the afternoon of Niedecker's funeral.

During this period, Niedecker married for the second time to a hard-drinking local working man with no interest in what he called her "scribbling." Years earlier, she had divorced her first husband after he burned her notebooks.

The play, directed by Julianne Boyd at the Apple Corps Theater, puts the shy, enigmatic poet (Helen Stenborg) in the middle of a triangle where she is again nearly forced to choose between her art — the key to her psychic survival — and her happy marriage.

Tugging on one side, the naïvely adoring student, Mary (Jane Fleiss), stimulates Niedecker's latent ambitions for artistic recognition, going so far as to send some of the poet's work to New York City publishers. Mary's antagonist is Niedecker's husband Al (Frederick Neumann), an unlettered

Lorine Niedecker's poems are woven into a drama celebrating her life.

fisherman who erupts in furious humiliation when Mary foolishly persuades him to read some of his wife's poems.

•

With fragments of Niedecker's poetry woven into the action in as natural a way as possible, the evening unfolds as a well-acted, if overly tidy, domestic drama. Ms. Stenborg gives a strong, still performance in the title role that is at once deeply sympathetic and suffused with enigma. Mr. Neumann's affectionately loutish Al matches Ms. Stenborg's Lorine in depth. Together, the two create a fully realized portrait of a marriage that flourishes because certain uncrossable boundaries on each side are tacitly respected.

1989 Mr 19, 61:1

The Bough Breaks

CRADLE SONG, book and lyrics by Mary Bracken Phillips; music by Jan Mullaney; directed by Anthony J. Stimac; set design, Richard Ellis; lighting design, Clarke W. Thornton; costume design, Amanda J. Klein; sound design, Daryl Borenstein; musical direction, Keith Levenson and Mr. Mullaney; production stage manager, Sandra M. Franck; arrangements and orchestrations, Mr. Levenson. Presented by Musical Theater Works, Mr. Stimac, artistic director; Mark S. Herko, associate artistic director. At St. Peter's Lutheran Church, Lexington Avenue at 54th Street.

WITH: Keith Charles, Mary Bracken Phillips, Carole Schweid and Paul E. Ukena Jr.

By RICHARD F. SHEPARD

Almost like a puppy pulling at one's trouser leg, "Cradle Song," a new

musical that opened for a limited run Wednesday night at the Theater at Saint Peter's Church, is doing its best to be liked. It is an unabashedly sentimental story about a modern young

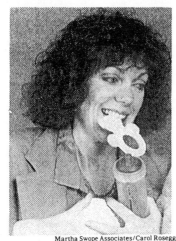

Mary Bracken Phillips in a scene from "Cradle Song."

upwardly mobile couple and how they discovered, the hard way, what the best things in life really are.

The show, with music by Jan Mullaney and book and lyrics by Mary Bracken Phillips, is presented by Musical Theater Works, which, in keeping with its aim, has developed it from a staged reading to its present state.

In the most simple and direct manner, the show addresses the audience and practically insists on establishing a rapport. It often succeeds, with some clever and pretty songs to be found among others that are less winning. The cast of four is perky and persuasive, and under Anthony J. Stimac's direction it conveys an air of earnest honesty.

•

Jonathan (Paul E. Ukena Jr.) and Paula (Ms. Phillips, the playwright) are a hard-working pair who have dedicated their lives to their careers and — with whatever is left over — to each other, for they are sincerely in love. Their relationship turns to marriage and somewhat unexpectedly to parenthood. First mother, then father (who dreaded having a child), dote on the baby. While they are at work, the baby dies of sudden infant death syndrome, an incident depicted here with dramatic understatement. They feel guilty and decide to separate. Finally, they understand that life is more than immolation in the job, and they are reunited as better people.

The script is by no means a morality play, and the ambiance is more light than grim, even when it comes to the pathos. This is reflected in such songs as "Father's Day," in which Mr. Ukena, a pleasant-looking and pleasant-voiced performer, tells of his detestation of sports and other trappings that seem to be part of fatherhood. In "Nobody's Perfect," Ms. Phillips, who is attractive and versatile, reflects a maturity that recognizes fallibility.

•

The leads are augmented by Carole Schweid, who plays Paula's elder sister and who puts over a colorful ditty, "Is It Anybody's Business but My Own?," and by Keith Charles as Paula's single-minded boss.

"Cradle Song," one suspects, has not yet reached full flower. Some of

the music is ordinary and forgettable, and the device of having the lead characters speak to the audience reflectively and retrospectively just before the script fades back in time does not work all that well. The show also manifests occasional dragginess, and an optimism that seems too ebullient for its circumstances. But it does have promise.

1989 Mr 19, 61:1

Secrets on the Podium

MANHATTAN CLASS ONE-ACTS, SERIES B. Set design by Dan Conway and Gregory Mercurio; lighting design by John Hastings; costume design by Dianne-Finn Chapman; sound design by Lia Vollack; production manager, Laura Kravets; associate producers, Maggie Lear and Eric Berkal; general manager, W. D. Cantler. Presented by Manhattan Class Company, Robert LuPone and Bernard Telsey, executive directors. At the Nat Horne Theater, 440 West 42d Street.

DAKOTA'S BELLY, WYOMING, by Erin Cressida Wilson; directed by Brian Mertes.

CATFISH LOVES ANNA, by Constance Ray; directed by Kevin Kelley.

PRELUDE AND LIEBESTOD, by Terrence McNally; directed by Paul Benedict.
WITH: Simon Brooking, Larry Bryggman, Dominic Cuskern, Leslie Denniston, Cass Morgan, Panchali Null, Constance Ray, Gordana Rashovich, Kyra Sedgwick and Victor Slezak.

By WILBORN HAMPTON

Stream of consciousness is always a tricky business in the theater. Shakespeare was a master, and the Greeks employed choruses to similar effect. Sam Shepard and Lanford Wilson are among the modern playwrights who can seamlessly weave asides to the audience into their dramas.

But devoting a whole play to nothing but the mental meanderings of its five characters and keeping the audience engaged, even for one act, is quite a task. It is one, however, that Terrence McNally undertakes with mostly successful results in "Prelude and Liebestod," the acerbic final work of Evening B in the Manhattan Class Company's festival of one-act plays.

The setting is the concert hall where a famous conductor (Larry Bryggman) is scheduled to lead the orchestra (the theater audience) in a program of Isolde's Act III love-death aria from "Tristan und Isolde" and Bruckner's Fourth Symphony. We never get to the Bruckner, although the Wagner is reprised.

Throughout the performance the audience is privy to the secret reflections of the conductor, the concertmaster, the soprano, the conductor's wife (seated in a box) and a young man (in the orchestra's fifth row) who has not escaped the conductor's roving eye.

•

Mr. McNally exposes the hypocrisy of our outward actions in relation to our inward thoughts, as well as the inconstancy of our own emotions. As the conductor goes over his life on the podium, he alternately feels affection and loathing for his wife. He turns once to cast a loving glance at her only to find her looking at the fashion ads in the program. ("I love you. She's reading!"). He both derides and praises the musicians and spends so much time thinking about himself that he loses his place in the score.

"Prelude and Liebestod" is very clever and witty, and Mr. McNally's conductor could be any of us trying to orchestrate our lives. Mr. Bryggman gives an excellent and sharply defined reading of the conductor and is ably supported by the rest of the cast.

The other two plays are rather uneven. The curtain-raiser, Erin Cressida Wilson's "Dakota's Belly, Wyoming," badly needs an editor. Vern (Victor Slezak) has caught his wife, Trixie (Kyra Sedgwick), in an affair with the ranch foreman and doesn't know what to do except go see his sister (Gordana Rashovich), who doesn't know what to do either. There is some promising writing in the play, like Vern's account of foaling a colt with the man who had cuckolded him.

Martha Swope Associates/Carol Rosegg

Larry Bryggman in "Prelude and Liebestod."

But there is a lot of extended business (looking in mirrors or one another's mouths, mutilating one another, adolescent sex) that simply becomes boring.

Sandwiched between these pieces is Constance Ray's "Catfish Loves Anna," an amusing scene involving two sisters, Betsy and Anna, who have gone fishing so Anna can tell Betsy a secret in private. Betsy, played with disarming charm by Ms. Ray, is scandalized. "I'm the one with children and a husband and a beautiful home," she tells her sister. "You're the one who was Teacher of the Year." The exercise is little more than a character study, but Ms. Ray writes bright dialogue.

1989 Mr 19, 61:4

2 Plays, Lean and Hungry

MACBETH, by William Shakespeare; directed by Nick Ward; designer, Fred Pilbrow; company stage manager, Sonia Friedman; American stage manager, Sarah Cornelia Koeppe; fight director, Malcolm Ranson. The touring productions from the Education Department of the National Theater, Royal National Theater of Great Britain presented by Zebra Promotions, Julian Ellison, executive producer; Herman LeVern Jones, associate producer. At the Harry De Jur Playhouse, 466 Grand Street.
WITH: Alan Bennion, Amelda Brown, Katrin Cartlidge, Ken Drury, Paul Higgins, Cyril Nri, Matthew Scurfield and Paul Stacey.
APART FROM GEORGE, written and directed by Mr. Ward, designer, Mr. Pilbrow; music, Richard Heacock.
WITH: Mr. Bennion, Miss Brown, Miss Cartlidge and Mr. Scurfield.

By D. J. R. BRUCKNER

'Voice, gesture and expression are about all Nick Ward allows the actors to use in two plays he is directing at the Harry De Jur Playhouse during the second American tour of the Education Department troupe of Britain's Royal National Theater. Some characters in "Macbeth" wield knives (not swords) in battle; in Mr. Ward's own play, "Apart From George," two chairs, a walking stick, a bucket and a notebook are all the props. Four actors take on the five roles in Mr. Ward's play and eight actors perform 27 parts in the Shakespeare. Even the costumes in both plays seem little more than suggestions to stimulate the viewer's imagination.

The actors take such pleasure in meeting the challenge of what Mr. Ward calls "creative constraints" that it is impossible not to admire them, even when you disagree with their interpretations. That is really the point of these tours. In the cities it visits, the British troupe gives workshops for students and professional actors as well as performances of the two plays on alternating nights.

This stripped-down "Macbeth" has tremendous power. There are times when you want it to slow down — the entire play is done in just under two hours — but this company approaches it like epic poetry, and what a poem it is. One of their specialties is regional accents and they use them here to produce the effect of music.

Some scenes are overwrought, notably the killing of Macbeth and the vision of the long line of Scottish kings destined to spring from the doomed Banquo. In others, like the knocking on the door in the banquet scene, the almost breathless delivery of lines accents the uneasy humor of the situations and at the same time raises the level of apprehension.

The decision of this group to emphasize the language, the images and ideas of this play and to act out little of the combat or the emotional struggle is a gamble that pays off on the whole. Their performance reminds you forcefully of the deep sense of mystery that builds throughout the play, giving it a tragic dimension far greater than its toll of murders adds up to.

•

"Apart From George" is Mr. Ward's play about what happens to a family in the Fen country along England's eastern coast when the father loses his job as a farm laborer. Mr. Ward grew up in that area and his feeling for its remoteness, its accents and its haunting silences is affecting.

In the performance Amelda Brown, Matthew Scurfield and Katrin Cartlidge create a mother, father and young daughter whose fear, suffering and rebellion against life itself put you in mind of the darker visions of Thomas Hardy. And Alan Bennion is so impressive as an old landowner whose passions — revealed in his eyes and expressions — have a volcanic life his words cannot conceal, and as a vicar who tries to keep others from despair only to fall into it himself, that you find it difficult to remember the two roles are not played by two actors.

The play, however, is less compelling than the acting. Written two years ago, it is an achievement for a man who is now only 26 years old. His theatrical imagination, his gifted use of language and his compassion make you hope he will write many more.

Amelda Brown in "Macbeth."

But the fate of this play's characters, no matter how dreadful it is to watch as it unfolds, never really touches the audience. With few words and in little more than an hour these people gain depth and stature before your eyes, but they live and die at a cool distance from you. In the end it is Miss Brown, Miss Cartlidge, Mr. Scurfield and Mr. Bennion who stay with you, not the hapless Fen country villagers they portray.

1989 Mr 21, C19:1

Regal Suffering, Humble Rebirth

THE WINTER'S TALE, by William Shakespeare; directed by James Lapine; set design by John Arnone; costume design by Franne Lee; lighting design by Beverly Emmons; music by William Finn and Michael Starobin; musical director, David Evans; choreography by Diane Martel; fights staged by B. H. Barry; associate producer, Jason Steven Cohen. Presented by Joseph Papp. At the Public/Anspacher Theater, 425 Lafayette Street.

Polixenes	Christopher Reeve
Leontes	Mandy Patinkin
Hermione	Diane Venora
Camillo	James Olson
A Sicilian Lady and Mopsa	Kathleen McNenny
Mamillius	Jesse Bernstein
Emilia and Dorcas	Bertina Johnson
A Sicilian Lord and Time	Michael Cumpsty
Antigonus	Graham Brown
Paulina	Alfre Woodard
Jailer and Officer	Frank Raiter
Cleomenes, Mariner and a Servant of the Old Shepherd	Albert Farrar
Dion	Peter Jay Fernandez
Old Shepherd	MacIntyre Dixon
Clown	Tom McGowan
Autolycus	Rocco Sisto
Florizel	Graham Winton
Perdita	Jennifer Dundas
A Sicilian Gentleman	Dan Cordle
Harlequin	Rob Besserer
The Players, Lords and Ladies Rob Besserer, Cynthia Friberg and Raymond Kurshal	
Shepherdess	Denise Faye

By FRANK RICH

When Mandy Patinkin is on stage emoting — or, these days, on record crooning — there is always a second suspenseful drama percolating just beneath the official script. Will the actor keep his volatile emotions within the bounds of the character he's playing, or will he fly over the rainbow into an unedited orgy of tears and strangled tenor sobs that call more attention to his own over-wrought sensitivity than to his role? The tension between the two Patinkins — the one in control, the other not — is the main reason he divides audiences as violently as any star around.

As Leontes, King of Sicilia, in James Lapine's inspired production of "The Winter's Tale" at the Public Theater, the actor is handed his greatest opportunities yet for self-in-

---

Mandy Patinkin in James Lapine's 'Winter's Tale.'

---

dulgence. More irrationally than Othello, Leontes rises to a jealous rage in the opening scene, imagining without cause that his pregnant wife, Hermione (Diane Venora), is carrying a child fathered by his own life-long best friend, the Bohemian King, Polixenes (Christopher Reeve). And at first Mr. Patinkin does let his feelings run away with him. Perhaps to avoid lachrymose hysteria, he beats out the neurotically short-circuited verse with a professorial waving of his hands and clamps his eyes shut to convey his paranoid consternation.

•

When the stakes are at their highest, however, Mr. Patinkin comes through with the most mature work of his career, never to retreat thereafter. The leap occurs at the moment Leontes, having refused to heed Hermione's pleas of innocence, suffers an abrupt double punishment: His young son dies, and so, or so he is told, does Hermione. As Mr. Patinkin hears the wails of mournful news from a balcony above, he reels in grief by merely leaning a delicate step backward. And then he stands utterly still, his eyes wide open. His suffering is regal in its imposing aura of silence, not in histrionics. When he speaks again, it is in a new, broken, sweet voice; the arrogant ruler has become the humblest penitent.

Any successful production of "The Winter's Tale" must make that metamorphosis deeply moving — though few do — because Leontes's transformation is the play's fulcrum and its essence. In this late romance, Shakespeare takes his characters into the winter of destructiveness and death, then allows them to redeem themselves in a spring of both figurative and actual resurrection. It takes 16 years for Leontes to pay penance for his needless transgressions. Only then can Hermione, disguised as a statue, miraculously be reborn as well. "The Winter's Tale" is an in-credible play in every way — from Shakespeare's magical, affirmative denouement to his awesome interweaving of high tragedy, low pastoral clowning and the mistaken identities and familial reunions of classic farce.

•

If Mr. Lapine has been a helpful influence on Mr. Patinkin — they also collaborated on "Sunday in the Park With George" — he is even more impressive in his ability to knit Shakespeare's many moods into elegant unity. While one wouldn't have predicted this happy result from Mr. Lapine's muddy Central Park "Midsummer Night's Dream," much of his other work, one realizes now, could have been preparation for "The Winter's Tale."

The director's fascination with archetypal images of death and rebirth has been apparent since "Twelve Dreams," his play about Carl Jung. He pursued the theme further when writing "Sunday in the Park" and "Into the Woods" with Stephen Sondheim. To achieve their characters' renewal, both musicals take a post-intermission flash-forward comparable to the 16-year jump in "The Winter's Tale." As Leontes is redeemed only after embracing a living statue of his "dead" wife, so George in "Sunday" can move on only after embracing a beloved woman who is "reborn" by stepping out of a painting.

There are echoes of the Sondheim-Lapine musicals in this "Winter's Tale," from the accentuation of parent-child bonds to the injection of a storybook motif (a Harlequin, played by the graceful dancer Rob Besserer, sets the fairy-tale tone) to the tingling music-box score by Michael Starobin, the Sondheim orchestrator, and William Finn. But it is the director's keen eye for every detail, a rarity in the New York Shakespeare Festival marathon, that really tells the tale.

Using handsome late-18th-century sets (by John Arnone) and costumes (by Franne Lee), Mr. Lapine piles up the action on platforms, allowing for the highly dramatic vertical choreography of pivotal scenes of eavesdropping, trial and flight. Beverly Emmons's lighting completes the poetic transition from the wintry candle-light of a mournful Sicilia to the vernal greenery of a festive Bohemia, with a chilling stop along the way for the coastal storm that leads a courtier to his grizzly death and a changeling baby to her adoptive home.

Mr. Lapine's precision extends to his casting. Though Ms. Venora's Hermione starts by mothering the audience as much as her child, this fine actress's intelligence eventually burns away the saccharine excesses. The play's problematic, second-half comic antics are in hilarious hands.

Martha Swope Associates/Rebecca Lesher

Diane Venora, Christopher Reeve, center, and Mandy Patinkin in "The Winter's Tale."

Rocco Sisto, as the irrepressible, ballad-singing rogue Autolycus, is a sneering yet likable cynic; his quick wit is the perfect foil for the slow burns of his most easily bamboozled victims, the bumpkin shepherd and son played with Laurel-and-Hardy vaudeville verve by MacIntyre Dixon and Tom McGowan. Mr. Reeve, though mirthless in comic disguise, is a surprisingly vulnerable Polixenes. Alfre Woodard's feisty Paulina, the play's conscience, and Graham Winton's Florizel and Jennifer Dundas's Perdita, its fairy-tale prince and princess, are the other standouts in a company that only occasionally sinks to the merely competent.

By the time he reaches the statue scene, Mr. Lapine has everything he needs to put the evening's complexities together. Mr. Patinkin, now serene and silver-templed, buries his head in Ms. Venora's neck, consummating a reconciliation that is the more rending for its simple stillness and its formal, indeed statuary, beauty. Perched above the idyllic embrace is a dark dream tableau invented by the director but consistent with a dream-fixated text: the dead characters stand in a flurry of snow, as if frozen within a child's crystalline paperweight. With this gesture, the cycles of life and of seasons merge in Mr. Lapine's staging as they so hauntingly do in Shakespeare's play. And the audience is left with just enough of winter's cruel chill to be intoxicated anew by the discovery that spring is here.

1989 Mr 22, C19:4

Scoundrel With Charm

SLEEPING DOGS, by Neal Bell; directed by Thomas Babe; scenery by Michael Boak; lighting by Greg MacPherson; costumes by Claudia Brown; sound by Tom Gould; stage manager, Jess Lynn. Presented by New Arts Theater, Joshua Astrachan, artistic director. At Intar, 420 West 42d Street.

Park	Richmond Hoxie
Sling	Christopher Fields
Sally	Leslie Lyles
Nana	Cynthia Kaplan
Miner	John P. Connolly
Evelyn Keestro	Jodie Markell
Bartender	David Briggs
Capp	Richard Council

By MEL GUSSOW

In Neal Bell's "Sleeping Dogs," the insurance executive portrayed by Richmond Hoxie has made millions by juggling his company's books. He has sold policies to bogus clients (masquerading under the names of Judge Crater, Jimmy Hoffa and Amelia Earhart). As a result, the value of the company's stock has risen. Then, to pad his own income, he has declared the clients dead and collected the premiums. Even allowing for the naïveté of his young employees, one might have expected someone to notice the names.

Beginning with this farfetched premise, the play (presented at Intar by New Arts Theater) moves into the inevitable collapse of Mr. Hoxie's scam. Federal agents are about to invade his office and he is desperately seeking ways to remove incriminating documents. What follows is a moderately interesting but self-consciously artificial yarn about chicanery in high places.

The subject is a provocative one, as has been the case with previous plays by Mr. Bell (dealing with such public issues as C.I.A. surveillance and

F.B.I. entrapment), but the execution leaves little breathing space for humanity — in spite of Mr. Hoxie's trenchant performance.

●

As he has demonstrated on a number of other occasions, Mr. Hoxie is an expert at mocking stuffed shirts, and he takes comic advantage of his single-edged character in "Sleeping Dogs." The actor finds humor in and around the dialogue, as in the self-corrective statement, "When I was a kid . . . when I was a smaller capitalist." But there is little he can do with such awkward — and more common — phrasings as, "I had my soon-dashed hopes."

To heighten the symbolism (and the whimsy), there is a title character, a dog named Nana (as in "Peter Pan"), played by the actress Cynthia Kaplan. Shuffling and sniffling, the dog is on its last legs. Though Ms. Kaplan is reasonably convincing in canine costume (how will that read on her résumé?), as a playwright Mr. Bell has yet to perfect the art of writing dog dialogue. Albert Innaurato is far more adept creating lines for his actor-as-ape in "Gus and Al." Add the actor playing a bear in "The Winter's Tale," and one can spot an anthropomorphic trend in the making.

In Mr. Bell's play, a modicum of amusement is provided by two minor characters, a shamus with scruples (John P. Connolly) and a secretary with resources (Jodie Markell). The two are more colorful than the principal characters. If only Mr. Hoxie had been able to win their confidence, the outcome of his dilemma might have been different. But he is, as we see him, a man alone on a pinnacle, and his dispassionate attitude toward his wife, best friend and others bars him from any sympathy.

Under the assured direction of Thomas Babe, the play moves, with small scenic changes, from the top of the office tower to a sub-basement complete with underground stream. In the increasingly long line of plays about the wages of greed, "Sleeping Dogs" has a certain novelty but few surprises. It is a shaggy-dog story fitfully stirring with life.

1989 Mr 23, C17:1

Football and Boys

LEAVE IT TO JANE, music and lyrics by Jerome Kern; book by Guy Bolton and P. G. Wodehouse; production staged and choreographed by Lynnette Barkley and Niki Harris; music director, Ethyl Will; conductor, Paul Johnson; scene design, John Shimrock; lighting design, Kenneth Posner; costume design, Lillian Glasser; sound design, Hector Melia. Presented by Equity Library Theater, 103d Street and Riverside Drive.

Ollie Mitchell	Tom Brown
Coach Matty McGowan	R. Bruce Elliott
Stubby Talmadge	Nick Corley
Silent Murphy	Caroll Van Cleave
Dr. Witherspoon	Rob Donohoe
Bessie Tanner	Susan Hartley
Flora Wiggins	Heidi Joyce
Professor Talbot	Michael Iannucci
Hiram Bolton	Marcus Powell
Billy Bolton	Peter Reardon
Jane Witherspoon	Wendy Oliver

By STEPHEN HOLDEN

The Equity Library Theater's revival of the 1917 musical "Leave It to Jane" opens with a bang, as cheerleaders and athletes parade through the aisles drumming up support for the football team of the fictional Atwater College.

College romance and football rivalry — between Atwater and its sis-

ter school, Bingham — are about the only things on the mind of a cheerfully fluffy show with music and lyrics by Jerome Kern and a book by Guy Bolton and P. G. Wodehouse. Though "Leave It to Jane" is stylistically considered to be one of Kern's Princess Theater musicals, it actually opened on Broadway at the Longacre Theater, where it ran for 167 performances.

Mildly progressive in its time, the show interweaves its story and songs more cohesively than many other Broadway musicals of the period. While its score includes no enduring Kern standards, its academic setting inspired Kern to write three witty numbers with mythological and historical references: "The Siren's Song," "Cleopatterer" and "Sir Galahad."

The story poses two less-than-burning questions, whose answers are not hard to guess. Can Jane Witherspoon, Atwater's irresistible campus flirt, lure Billy Bolton to bring his athletic skills to Atwater instead of to his father's alma mater, Bingham? And will her treachery prevent her and Billy from finding true love once her schemes are revealed?

●

The Equity Library Theater revival, staged and directed by Lynnette Barkley and Niki Harris, dispatches the story efficiently but without providing a truly snappy set piece save for the opening number. The cast includes Wendy Oliver as an ingenuous flaxen-haired Jane and Peter Reardon as the instantly smitten Billy. The production's most confident performance belongs to Nick Corley, who gives the role of Stubby Talmadge, Atwater's resident Casanova, a crackling joie de vivre.

1989 Mr 23, C17:1

Back on the Track

THE WIZARD OF OZ, adapted, produced and directed by Michel M. Grilikhes; choreographer, Onna White; associate choreographer, Jim Taylor; costume designer, Bill Campbell; art director, Jeremy Railton; music supervisor, Tom Worrall; scenic designer, Stephen Ehlers, dimensional sound designer, John Neal; dance arranger, Jackie Shaw O'Neill; original music, Harold Arlen; original lyrics, E. Y. Harburg; original incidental music, Herbert Stothart. Presented by M. M. G. Arena Productions. At Radio City Music Hall, 50th Street and Sixth Avenue.

Dorothy	Grace Greig
Aunt Em and Glinda	Linda Johnson
Uncle Henry	John Sovec
Zeke and Cowardly Lion	Guy Allen
Hunk and Scarecrow	Joe McDonough
Hickory and Tin Woodsman	Joe Giuffre
Miss Gulch and Wicked Witch	Polly Seale
Professor Marvel, Wizard and Gate Keeper	Bart Williams

By RICHARD F. SHEPARD

First of all, it must be reported that that critical mass known as small fry gave every evidence of a warm reaction to the enactment of "The Wizard of Oz" that opened Wednesday night at Radio City Music Hall. The children applauded when familiar songs resounded over the sound system and tensed when Dorothy and her eccentric friends appeared to be in a tight corner.

This musical extravaganza is a live — well, mostly live — spectacle that, admittedly, even proudly, patterns itself on the classic 1939 film whose cast included Judy Garland, Ray Bolger, Bert Lahr, Jack Haley and Frank Morgan, with wonderful music

by Harold Arlen and E. Y. Harburg. It is a show that will travel, after performances at Radio City through April 9, to large arenas elsewhere.

Leonard Kamsler

Grace Greig, as Dorothy, in "The Wizard of Oz," at Radio City Music Hall through April 9.

The show is an amiable, colorful and at times even spectacular affair. Without a survey, it is not possible to say whether the young in the audience enjoyed it more because they had seen the movie or because they had not. To an older and therefore crankier spectator, it did not come close to the film, although what it does on its own is pleasant enough and even prompted pleasurable recollections of Judy and the gang on the screen.

The sets are attractive, with a natural-looking Kansas landscape, a fairytale Munchkinland and a verdant Emerald City. The Music Hall's huge stage does not move around in this production, which is self-contained, but a farmhouse is lofted during the tornado (it blew a bit overlong, probably to allow time to shift the scene to Oz). There is considerable movement up and down, what with wafting witches, fierce flying monkeys (one actually soars away with Dorothy), and a clever, eye-catching transformation of three high-flying performers into snowdrops. The appearance of the big and ominous face of the wizard was appropriately scary. The mechanicals merit a good rating.

The cast of 42, maneuvered by the producer and director, Michel M. Grilikhes, also cut familiar and attractive figures on the vast platform. Grace Greig, a 23-year-old who plays Dorothy, has a young girl's profile and manner. Joe McDonough's dancing was particularly adroit as the Scarecrow.

A picky graybeard might have felt that there were two separate events taking place around him. The music and the dialogue are all on boomingly played tape that, with its stereophonic virtuosity, seemed sufficient unto itself. The performers took on the aspect of dancers carefully choreographed to the sound track. The vast arena did not allow for the intimate emergence of personality that the motion picture camera permits, and to a seasoned eye Dorothy's story seemed to be an animated comic strip, deftly done, to be sure, but not the film.

But that's the sort of talk that keeps up-and-coming generations bored to tears and, in self-defense, straitjack-eted in headphones. To the customers approaching their teens, this "Wiz-ard" was accorded the status old-timers give to grand opera.

1989 Mr 24, C3:1

Star Animal Trainer's Farewell

By RICHARD F. SHEPARD

The circus came to Madison Square Garden on Thursday with the fare-well tour of its star animal trainer, Gunther Gebel-Williams, as its focus. The celebration outshone any con-ceivable office retirement party.

Mr. Gebel-Williams, who has been working out with his animals at Ring-ling Brothers and Barnum & Bailey for 21 years, hardly looks like a man who is ready to hang up his whip. The blond 54-year-old trainer never looked more radiant. He wasn't walk-ing on air, but he rode a white horse, a gray elephant and a striped tiger.

In the smash finale, with his name glowing in big lights above the arena, he directed, with the aplomb of a vet-eran tank commander, a herd of per-forming elephants. He even mounted a teeterboard and had one of them hurl him up to its back.

In his first time out during the show, Mr. Gebel-Williams served as choreographer for 18 high-stepping white horses. In the second act, he re-turned in the role we all will remem-ber him in. He entered a cage with 18 Bengal tigers, rough-looking custom-ers, each and every one, and had them leaping through flames, rolling over and posing on hind legs on a re-volving pedestal. To judge from the handouts he slipped some of them, the tigers worked on a merit system.

There was more to the circus, of course, than the popular animal im-presario, who, in any event, will not leave the big top but will only retire from the road. The rest of this year's spectacle is a well-produced affair. Even though the opening act and theme of the show is Hollywood's golden years, the circus had no Holly-wood pretensions of Busby Berkeley proportions — as it has striven for in some previous editions, to its detri-ment. The theme is carried out amus-ingly and colorfully, but befitting cir-cus standards.

This year's production, the circus's 119th, has its quota of thrills. The Flying Lunas and the Flying Alejan-dros live up to their names, spinning about like spacecraft and accom-plishing three and even three and a half airborne somersaults at ridicu-lous hazard. The three Carillo Broth-ers are undaunted as they soft-shoe on a high wire, doing acrobatics one would not attempt on a sidewalk.

Gunther Gebel-Williams serves as choreographer for 18 white horses.

It was only a matter of time before the circus got around to building an indoor ski slope and the one they have provided for the Royal Canadian Aerial Ski Squadron lets them slalom down a steep slant, whirl in midair and land on what appears to be the biggest water bed in town. The Ayak brothers, who get along well, do aerial gymnastics that rely only on the most tenuous of hand- and foot-holds.

The clowns are now treated as an important ingredient, as they should be, and receive lots of time for their own acts and for turns between other acts.

The big show is a standard, tradi-tional circus and it will be here through April 23, which should give you ample time to get into spring training for craning your neck up-ward and swiveling your torso to-ward three rings.

1989 Mr 25, 13:1

Coming Home

SOME SWEET DAY, by Nancy Fales Garrett, directed by Seret Scott; set design by Michael H. Yeargan; costume design by David Murin; lighting design by Pat Collins; production stage manager, Robin Kevrick. Presented by Long Wharf Theater, New Haven. Arvin Brown, artistic director; M. Edgar Rosen-blum, executive director.

Vernard Morgan Jr.	Terry Alexander
Ben (Preach) Morgan	Damien Leake
Raymond Morgan	Herb Lovelle
Vernard Morgan Sr.	Mike Hodge
Shug	Yvette Hawkins
Elizabeth Morgan McKee	Rosanna Carter
Annie Mae Morgan	Cynthia Belgrave
Elijah Morgan	Clebert Ford
Judy Miller	Cynthia Mace
Mr. Abercrombie	Jack R. Marks

By MEL GUSSOW

Special to The New York Times

NEW HAVEN, March 23 — The aged matriarch has died, and mem-bers of her large family have re-turned to the homestead for the fu-neral. Sooner than expected, they will divide the estate. In Nancy Fales Garrett's absorbing new play, "Some Sweet Day" (at the Long Wharf Theater), the Morgan family is de-fined by individual self-interest.

Except for a shared heritage and upbringing, the relatives have little in common. Brothers, fathers and sons, cousins — they have all dispersed across the United States and, in the words of the frequently refrained title hymn, it will be "Some Sweet Day" before they can achieve the kinship that comes with understanding. Over two days, several do gain a tentative awareness of the meaning of the family bond. In that sense the play re-affirms traditional values but not be-fore it has raised some challenging questions.

Though there are moments of im-precision and the play does not yet earn its three-act length, it has a natural flow and in terms of charac-ter and atmosphere it has the breadth of a good novel. The work is made doubly intriguing by the fact that the Morgans are black and the play-wright happens to be white.

•

Ms. Garrett's promising "Playing in Local Bands" has not adequately prepared us for the artistic assurance of "Some Sweet Dreams." In it, she has written a play that is filled with down-home authenticity and humor, deepened by Seret Scott's unobtru-sive direction and by a finely meshed cast. Michael H. Yeargan's indoor-outdoor set design is an additional asset.

It is the evening's oddity that the most insecure characterization is that of a white woman (married to a Morgan grandson). While the daugh-ter-in-law is definably an outsider in this environment, that is not justifica-tion for the artificiality of some of her dialogue.

The Morgans are an evocative ex-tended family, brought to life with stresses and dreams intact. Three brothers have come home, including Vernard Morgan Sr. (Mike Hodge), who is the only one of his generation with a feeling for the family home-stead. Vernard's wife (Cynthia Bel-grave) is a black equivalent of a Jew-ish mother, irrepressibly optimistic and busily placing food before not al-ways receptive relatives, a fact that never deters her. Her waspish sister-in-law (Rosanna Carter) is a portrait of subdued embitterment.

All these characters are written and acted with fond and humorous de-tail, but they are, in effect, back-ground to the younger generation — Vernard Jr. (Terry Alexander) and his home-boy cousin (Damien Leake). It is their story that emerges and begins to dominate the family tapestry.

Mr. Alexander's character, mar-ried to a white woman, is a dashing, outwardly successful television cam-eraman. But he is shadowed by fears and insecurities. One passing sugges-tion that he has aspirations of making movies is worth developing. His char-acter (as well as that of his wife) could be strengthened.

In contrast, Mr. Leake plays the grandson who has stayed on the farm — and is treated as the family fool. At first, theatergoers may also regard him as a slow-witted eccentric, a man drinking moonshine and worrying about his hogs. Gradually it becomes clear that he knows exactly what he wants — to turn the farm into a viable

The fate of the homestead lies in the balance.

business — and that no one is pre-pared to listen to him. Like an Uncle Vanya, he is the family mainstay who is given no credit for his accomplish-ment.

As delineated by Mr. Leake, who gives the evening's most moving per-formance, the character is, in fact, the hope of the family, and, by infer-ence, the hope of a disappearing agrarian economy — and it is he who makes the most heartfelt plea for progress. The other characters, we are told, are walking through life backward.

Ms. Garrett is subtle about her symbolism. A jetliner screeches by. A white entrepreneur, a man with his own reasonableness, offers to buy the farm in order to extend a housing development. Changes are occurring in this sleepy South Carolina town,

Gunther Gebel-Williams and friends have arrived with the circus at Madison Square Garden.

T. Charles Erickson

Damien Leake, left, and Terry Alexander in Nancy Fales Garrett's new play, "Some Sweet Day."

but the author resolutely keeps those changes just out of dramatic range.

•

The focus is up close on the family. By choice, Ms. Garrett has staked out a landscape that is familiar from fiction and drama (from William Faulkner through Beth Henley): a death in the family and an inhospitable homecoming. Helped by her director and actors (who also include Herb Lovelle and Clebert Ford), she brings to that subject her own sense of humanity as well as her growing skill as a playwright.

1989 Mr 27, C13:1

Of Life and Death In a Small Place

OUR TOWN, by Thornton Wilder; directed by Gregory Mosher; sets by Douglas Stein; costumes by Jane Greenwood; lighting by Kevin Rigdon; musical director, Michael Barrett; general manager, Steven C. Callahan; production manager, Jeff Hamlin. Presented by Lincoln Center Theater, Mr. Mosher, director; Bernard Gersten, executive producer. At the Lyceum Theater, 149 West 45th Street.

Stage Manager	Don Ameche
Dr. Gibbs	James Rebhorn
Joe Crowell	Atticus Brady
Howie Newsome	John Griesemer
Mrs. Gibbs	Frances Conroy
Mrs. Webb	Roberta Maxwell
George Gibbs	Jason Gedrick
Rebecca Gibbs	Amanda Weeden
Wally Webb	Shane Culkin
Emily Webb	Helen Hunt
Professor Willard	Bill Alton
Mr. Webb	Peter Maloney
Woman in the Balcony	Marilyn Hamlin
Man in the Auditorium	Steven Goldstein
Lady in the Box	Joan MacIntosh
Simon Stimson	Jeff Weiss

By MEL GUSSOW

To a younger generation, Don Ameche is best known as a lively old fellow in movies like "Cocoon," but those with longer memories will think of him as the young man who invented the telephone in the movie "Alexander Graham Bell" and who, in moments of crisis, remained loyal to his friend, Tyrone Power, in "Alexander's Ragtime Band" and other films. In other words, he brought with him considerable artistic baggage and nostalgia as he stepped into the role of the Stage Manager in the Lincoln Center Theater revival of "Our Town" at the Lyceum Theater.

The actor could have drawn from his cinematic background and his identification with the small-town American landscape. But the first step toward that goal would be for Mr. Ameche to remember his lines. At Saturday's matinee, the prompter was the actor's valuable ally in his performance.

At times, he managed to disguise his tentativeness with an improvisatory manner, as if he were making up his dialogue as he went along. The Stage Manager is meant to be informal, but there are limits to his spontaneity. On the other hand, when Mr. Ameche was called upon to pretend to be Mr. Morgan serving strawberry ice cream sodas to the young lovers, Emily and George, he assumed a studied cracker-barrel accent. This is in contrast to the approach of his predecessor, Spalding Gray, who played the Stage Manager with simplicity.

By the end of "Our Town," as the Stage Manager leads Emily from her grave back into an ordinary day in her life, Mr. Ameche began to demonstrate his suitability in the role. He is approaching 81, which means that he was born during the time of the events of the play. That fact in itself adds a dimension to his portrayal.

Gregory Mosher's production is otherwise in confident hands. Helen Hunt (following Penelope Ann Miller) has the dewy innocence necessary for Emily. Though somewhat less engaging than his predecessor, Eric Stoltz, Jason Gedrick is comfortable in the role of George, and the couple's scene of first love at the soda fountain continues to have its overwhelming effect on theatergoers. Emily's confession, "I am now; I always have been," must be seven of the most loving words ever spoken on the stage.

Other cast changes are minor. Among those actors continuing in their roles, Peter Maloney, Frances Conroy, James Rebhorn, Roberta Maxwell, Jeff Weiss and Bill Alton are authoritative. As Emily's father, Mr. Maloney delivers an exceedingly knowing portrayal, enhancing a small role with sagacity as well as skepticism.

Under Mr. Mosher's direction, the revival offers moving proof that Thornton Wilder had something sobering (rather than sentimental) to say in "Our Town" — about the brevity of life, the shadow of death and the need to live every moment to its fullest. The production ends its run on Sunday.

1989 Mr 28, C15:1

With Doors Slamming, The Farce Is Back and Loud

By MEL GUSSOW

In expressing his admiration for "The Importance of Being Earnest," Max Beerbohm wrote: "What differentiates this farce from any other, and makes it funnier than any other, is the humorous contrast between its style and matter. To preserve its style fully, the dialogue must be spoken with grave unction." One might add that the graver the unction, the funnier the performance, a fact that is as true of Joe Orton as it is of Oscar Wilde.

Orton is currently represented at the Manhattan Theater Club with an insouciant revival of his posthumous "What the Butler Saw," the most recent in a quartet of farces of varying quality in New York this season. On Broadway are Ken Ludwig's "Lend Me a Tenor," Neil Simon's "Rumors" and Ray Cooney's "Run for Your Wife." Their simultaneous appearance may be a coincidence, or it may signify a trend — the need for laughter as a tonic, not as a social statement. Satire may indeed be what closes on Saturday night, but farce is timeless.

For centuries, people have been trying to define it. Orton himself, not known as a theorizer, said his comedy "Loot" "takes a farcical view of things normally treated as tragic." Taking a cue from the playwright, farce could be regarded as tragedy spilled backward. If Oedipus had skidded on a banana peel, would people have laughed?

•

The Oxford Companion to Theater offers one of the more useful descriptions of farce by saying that it is "an extreme form of comedy in which laughter is raised at the expense of probability, particularly by horseplay and bodily assault." One word in that definition is in question — probability. Events in farce can be extremely far-fetched, but within the context of the work, they also have to be believable.

Farce is the upstart of comedy, less concerned with developing character than with provoking mirth; one portal to that destination is a door that slams. Farce could be arbitrarily de-

---

A quartet of shows may signify the need for laughter as a tonic.

---

fined as a comedy with at least five doors. Five are ideal for hasty entrances and exits (and in this case less is not more).

This principle is demonstrated by the season's two funniest farces, "What the Butler Saw" and "Lend

Me a Tenor." Actually, "What the Butler Saw" has only four doors but it also has a drawstring curtain, behind which lurk many of the evening's heartiest laughs. In "Lend Me a Tenor," one of the six doors separates two adjacent hotel rooms and is therefore a double door of humor. "Rumors" also has six doors, but not enough farcical traffic. "Run for Your Wife," with four doors, has the fewest laughs.

A large share of the success of the productions of "What the Butler Saw" and "Lend Me a Tenor." belongs to the directors, John Tillinger and Jerry Zaks, respectively. They are arguably our two finest directors of theatrical comedy. Neither limits himself to farce, but each has made it something of a specialty. It is no coincidence that both began their careers as actors, which is also true of Gene Saks, the director of "Rumors." Mr. Cooney, of course, is also an actor (as well as a playwright and director) but he is not on that level. Capitalizing on their intuitive understanding of acting, the other three directors find shortcuts to comic explosiveness.

Both "Rumors" and "Run for Your Wife" are encumbered with unanswered questions. With Mr. Simon's play, one wonders why the first guests at the suburban dinner party are so adamant about not telling the next guests that their host has apparently tried to kill himself. There is no point in the secrecy, except to set the plot in motion. With Mr. Cooney's play, one wonders how two bumbling policemen could afford to spend so much time worrying about a minor incident (the hero, played by the author, has had a brush with a mugger).

In the case of "Lend Me a Tenor," the problem is simple and the setup is neatly motivated. A famous Italian tenor is apparently indisposed for a performance of Verdi's "Otello" in Cleveland and the local impresario, pressed by time, must come up with an alternate solution. From this, the comedy spirals.

The premise of "What the Butler Saw" is far more devious, dealing with a lustful psychiatrist, his wanton wife and characters of different sexes switching clothes and also dealing with the search for missing body parts from a statue. But on its own absurdist terms, the play is clear-cut, and leads headlong to its mock Shakespearean denouement. This is perhaps less a true farce than a parody of a farce, using traditional devices for a new-fashioned black comic purpose.

Both shows benefit from expert farceurs with clockwork timing. In "Lend Me a Tenor," Philip Bosco and Victor Garber, who were recently paired on stage in Shaw's "Devil's Disciple," are a quickly reflexive team. Each knows exactly when to fume, fret and keep his silence — and how to react to the other to the greatest comic effect.

Watch the cloud fall over Mr. Bosco's face when he is confronted with the possibility that his mild-mannered assistant, Mr. Garber, may become a substitute Otello. The line, spoken by Mr. Bosco with perfect pauses, is: "Otello. Big black fellow. You?" Similarly, there is the ecstatic expression on Mr. Garber's heavily made-up face when he realizes that he has completely fooled his girlfriend into thinking he is the real tenor.

The two actors and Ron Holgate (as the preening tenor) make the play seem funnier than it is, although there is the possibility that "Lend Me a Tenor" is a sturdier vehicle than

Martha Swope

A scene from Ken Ludwig's "Lend Me a Tenor." From left are Jane Connell, Philip Bosco, Jeff Brooks and J. Smith-Cameron.

one imagines. Before coming to Broadway, this American farce was a hit in London and is currently playing in Paris. As has often been said, farce travels better than other forms of comedy.

•

Joseph Maher and Charles Keating are droll personifiers of the bizarre world of Orton. Their partnership began three years ago — under Mr. Tillinger's hand — in the revival of "Loot." Previously, Mr. Maher starred in "Entertaining Mr. Sloane," also staged by Mr. Tillinger. This means that the actor and director share a triple Orton crown.

In "What the Butler Saw," Mr. Maher and Mr. Keating play mad psychiatrists (or psychiatrically inclined madmen). Wryly assisted by Carole Shelley and Joanne Whalley-Kilmer, they are the soul of reasonableness, underplaying every eccentricity even as it ascends to aberrant heights. From their first encounter, they spar with subtlety, playing Orton as dryly as if they were playing Noël Coward. Along with Mr. Bosco and Mr. Garber, they are paradigms of the art of grave unction.

•

For all its fun, farce has always had its detractors, beginning with Shaw, who said, "I go to the theater to be moved to laughter, not to be tickled or bustled into it; and that is why, though I laugh as much as anybody at a farcical comedy, I am out of spirits before the end of the third act." He concluded, with a certain snobbery, "If the public ever becomes intelligent enough to know when it is really enjoying itself and when it is not, there will be an end of farcical comedy."

There is, one might suggest, a substantial difference between being tickled and being bustled. The first denotes an act of amusement, the second an act of manipulation. Contrary to Shaw's hope, there is no end in sight for farce. It extends from Aristophanes through Feydeau and Joe Orton to this week in New York theater.

1989 Mr 29, C17:1

Tried in the Court Of Public Opinion

COBB, by Lee Blessing; directed by Lloyd Richards; set design by Rob Greenberg; costume design by Joel O. Thayer; lighting design by Ashley York Kennedy; sound design by G. Thomas Clark; production stage manager, Maureen F. Gibson. Presented by Yale Repertory Theater, Mr. Richards, artistic director; Benjamin Mordecai, managing director. At New Haven.

Mr. Cobb .... Josef Sommer
The Peach .... James E. Reynolds
Ty .... Chris Cooper
Oscar Charleston .... Delroy Lindo

By FRANK RICH

Special to The New York Times

NEW HAVEN, March 28 — Having written "A Walk in the Woods," a high-minded comedy about Soviet-American arms negotiations, Lee Blessing would seem to be retreating into nostalgic escapism with "Cobb," his new play about the Detroit Tigers centerfielder who tore up opponents and record books in the 20th century's early innings. But on the eve of our new baseball season, the name Ty Cobb, by chance, is back in the news. Pete Rose, the player who in 1985 at last surpassed Cobb's career record for hits, is under investigation, reportedly for gambling activities eerily echoing a scandal that engulfed Cobb in the 1920's.

Cobb was found not guilty. Mr. Rose's fate will be decided by the Commissioner-designate of Baseball, A. Bartlett Giamatti, among others. "Cobb," meanwhile, is having its premiere at Yale, the farm club where Mr. Giamatti got his training for the big leagues. And though there's no way Mr. Blessing could have known that his play would dovetail with the Rose sadness, the resonance is there. The play's format vaguely resembles a trial — in the court of public opinion — in which the hero pleads with the audience (and posterity) to understand the vanity, greed and anger that shaped his controversial life off the field as much as on.

•

The setting is a faded baseball stadium that, as evocatively designed by Rob Greenberg, seems ripped from an old newspaper. There we meet the ghost of the retired Cobb (who died in 1961), in the form of Josef Sommer, and two younger Cobbs: the fresh peach just out of Georgia (James E. Reynolds) and the cynical star at maturity (Chris Cooper). Together the trio spins an unconventional biographical tale. Cobb's life was defined by a highly educated father, a mother who shot and killed the father, a series of violent encounters with strangers (especially black strangers) and lots of money. Cobb was the first professional athlete to parlay his earnings, modest by contemporary standards, into millions. A true son of Georgia and Michigan, he was an early investor in Coca-Cola and General Motors.

There's no new information in "Cobb" for baseball addicts who have read Charles C. Alexander's definitive "Ty Cobb" (1984). But Mr. Blessing knows how to talk baseball in the form of flavorful theatrical dialogue. In a small tour de force of writing, we're even taken with words on a trip around the bases — no video replay required — with a player whose naked aggression added a frightening dimension to the phrase "stealing home."

Gerry Goodstein
Josef Sommer, front, and Delroy Lindo in "Cobb" at the Yale Repertory Theater in New Haven.

Aided by an excellent cast directed by Lloyd Richards, the playwright is also adept at keeping the man's character in focus and in balance. For all Cobb's racism, arrogance and rage, he still is intelligent, if hardly likable. "Marriage was created so even the greatest of men could have the opportunity to fail," Cobb says as he describes his pathetic domestic life. Forced to spend his last 33 years in retirement — unable "to do the one thing that made me special" — Cobb becomes a forlorn figure out of a Lardner story or, in Mr. Sommer's richly textured performance, a Beckett loner passing time in a folding chair at each year's Hall of Fame rites, playing out his end game with cancer.

It's when Mr. Blessing steps from the specifics of Cobb's story to grand themes that "Cobb" becomes intellectually shallow and dramatically inert. Too often we are told that Cobb, with his sharpened spikes, is a symbol of American power in the American century — a paradigmatic figure to stand with Carnegie or Rockefeller. The pretentious announcements of this message and the superficial analogies used to draw it do not make the thesis convincing or stimulating enough to tranform Cobb into Citizen Kane.

Mr. Blessing's other broad concerns are American mythology and racism. His protagonist, like the real Cobb, gropes to figure out why his statistically superior baseball record and exemplary business career would eventually be eclipsed by the Horatio Alger legend of the home-run-slugging Babe Ruth, whom he regarded as a freak. While the question is interesting, the stagy debates it prompts about cultural myth-making are static, with or without a hokey projection of Ruth's ghostly face as a backdrop.

An even more palpable specter haunting Mr. Blessing's Cobb is the great Negro League player Oscar Charleston, known during his career as "the black Cobb." Delroy Lindo, the actor who played the mysterious stranger in August Wilson's "Joe Turner's Come and Gone," is a mesmerizing presence in the role. Yet the burden of representing all victims of racism and segregation — in Cobb's society and in baseball — robs the character of his individuality, turning him into a blandly angelic archetype. Worse, Mr. Blessing implies that Cobb's and baseball's deep-rooted bigotry might have been ameliorated if only a Cobb and a Charleston had faced each other on the field or on the bench. This is the same sentimental if crowd-pleasing stand, unencumbered by the mean realities of history, that Mr. Blessing took on the Russians and the Americans in "A Walk in the Woods."

Poor Cobb! Mr. Blessing is going to have to give this promising play more drama and less preaching if the baseball giant who was usurped by Ruth in life is not to be upstaged by Pete Rose in death.

1989 Mr 31, C3:3

Loosing Faith In the Tooth Fairy

A. WHITNEY BROWN'S BIG PICTURE (IN WORDS), written and performed by A. Whitney Brown; directed by Wynn Handman; lighting design, Brian MacDevitt. Presented by American Place Theater, Mr. Handman, director. At 111 West 46th Street.

By STEPHEN HOLDEN

A. Whitney Brown, whose cynical news commentaries are a regular feature on "Saturday Night Live," has carved out a comic identity as the quintessential disillusioned baby boomer.

The 37-year-old humorist, who admits to having once been a dedicated hippie, affects a mock professorial knowingness as he admits to being "part of a whole generation so starved for meaning we were able to read significance into Donovan lyrics." From there, he traces his alienation to the assassination of President John F. Kennedy. After 1963, he muses, his generation's feelings about its ability to affect America's future changed from "Ask not what your country can do for you; ask what you can do for your country," to a shrug and a nihilistic, "Hey, man, what can I do?"

The mordant wit and wisdom that animate Mr. Brown's "Saturday Night Live" appearances in the "Weekend Update" segments are now a one-man show, "A. Whitney Brown's Big Picture (in Words)," which plays at the American Place Theater through April 8. The evening is an augmented collection of Mr. Brown's best commentaries, very loosely structured by the director Wynn Handman into a parody of a serious academic lecture.

In appearance and dress, Mr. Brown suggests a patrician rake, a black-sheep cousin of Chevy Chase who, having wasted too many years following the Grateful Dead, has elegantly cleaned up his act. His tone is supercilious on the surface and bitter underneath, with glints of sweetness amid the acidity. The main running theme of the evening is his loss of faith in everything from the tooth fairy and Santa Claus to humanity itself. Twirling a globe, he offers witty generalizations about the major superpowers. "In China, even if you're a one-in-a-million type guy, there are still a thousand just like you," he says. The paranoia of the Soviet Union is attributed in part to its neighbors, "mellow" Iranians, excitable Germans and "750 million ravenous Hindus."

Mr. Brown also aims some clever zingers at the Bush Administration. "In 200 years, we've come from George to George — from 'I cannot tell a lie' to 'I cannot tell,'" he says. In the mind of Vice President Dan Quayle, he surmises, "Rowe vs. Wade are alternative ways to cross the Potomac."

Pulling against Mr. Brown's disgust with the world is a strain of old-fashioned nostalgia. Remembering the moon landing on July 20, 1969, he comments: "We were the toast of the ecosystem! The very slime we evolved from stood up and took a bow." Though he goes on to castigate Neil A. Armstrong for mouthing banalities, one senses that this was one American accomplishment of which Mr. Brown approves. Another was the Declaration of Independence, from which he quotes admiringly, lingering on the implications of the words, "a decent respect to the opinions of mankind."

Despite his towering misanthropy, Mr. Brown still harbors a sense of the good old days. In 1952, the year he was born, he recalls, "cars had fins, fish were cooked, pasta was spaghetti and everything was black and white."

1989 Mr 31, C36:1

Relationships Asunder

THE MEMBER OF THE WEDDING, by Carson McCullers; directed by Harold Scott; set design by Thomas Cariello; costume design by Andrew B. Marlay; lighting design by Shirley Prendergast; sound design by Philip Campanella; production stage manager, Kathy J. Faul. Presented by Roundabout Theater Company, Gene Feist, artistic director; Todd Haimes, executive director. At 100 East 17th Street.

Berenice Sadie Brown .... Esther Rolle
Frankie Addams .... Amelia Campbell
John Henry West ..... Calvin Lennon Armitage
Jarvis Addams .... David Whalen
Janice .... Jeri Leer
Honey Camden Brown .... William Christian
Mr. Addams .... Drew Synder
Mrs. West .... Deborah Strang
Helen Fletcher .... Donna Eskra
Club Members .... Jeanne Bucci; Susan Honey
T. T. Williams .... Lou Ferguson
Barney MacKean .... Steven Douglas Cook

By MEL GUSSOW

Frankie Addams, the 12-year-old title character in "The Member of the Wedding," shares her dreams and fantasies with her two friends — her 12-year-old cousin, John Henry, and Berenice, the family cook. The three are a family unto themselves and, within the Addams kitchen, Frankie's fancy can take flight. To her, the outside world, the real world, is a fiction.

Any faithful production of the Carson McCullers play should capture the isolation and the evanescence of Frankie's sanctuary, which in its own way is as fragile as Tennessee Williams's "Glass Menagerie." As adapted by McCullers from her novella, "The Member of Wedding" is very much a play of its time, 1945 in a small Southern town, and its distinction rests in its specificity, its eccentricity and the author's lyrical language. In an attempt to re-evaluate the play, Harold Scott's revival at the Roundabout Theater takes a more naturalistic approach instead of treating the work as a wistful period piece. As a result, "The Member of the Wedding" loses a great deal of its charm.

•

Frankie was conceived of as a spritelike tomboy (incarnated by Julie Harris in the original production and in the movie), going through a difficult rite of passage. In the words of Harold Clurman, who directed the Broadway production in 1950, Frankie is aching with growing pains. As played by Amelia Campbell in Mr. Scott's revival, Frankie is a far more tangible creature. As she intrudes herself into her brother's wedding, she is less the ethereal spirit of McCullers's play than a willful and stubborn child. Although Ms. Campbell (herself an adult actress) is earnest in her portrayal, she does not strike the necessary imaginative chords.

Esther Rolle's Berenice is a stolid matriarchal presence, instructive but not censorious. As with her younger colleague, this is a respectable performance, but it is one that falls short of Berenice's magnetism. Ms. Rolle does not have the embracing air that would make Frankie believe that with Berenice in charge one is eternally safe. As Ms. Rolle sings "His Eye Is on the Sparrow," one unavoidably recalls the power of Ethel Waters, the first Berenice.

•

Of the three principals, only Calvin Lennon Armitage, who alternates with Lindsay Gordon in the role of John Henry, seems completely at home in the McCullers environment. This bespectacled 7-year-old is line-perfect and natural in his characterization of the impressionable youngster. Dressing up in Berenice's high-

heeled shoes or rushing across the stage in a tutu, he brings a sense of wonderment to an otherwise earthbound production.

Martha Swope

Esther Rolle and Calvin Lennon Armitage in "The Member of the Wedding," at the Roundabout Theater through April 30.

As the three sit around the kitchen table and as Berenice rambles through the lessons of her love life, there are moments that testify to the author's assessment that the play's subject is "togetherness," but more often the performances themselves seem disconnected. As director, Mr. Scott has been unable to recapture the magical pulse of McCullers's excursion into autobiography. The staging is further marred by a languidness that extends the play to three hours.

The other characters are sketchily drawn (Frankie's surly, widowed father; her brother), with the possible exception of Berenice's angry foster brother, Honey, who in the course of the play goes through his own violent rite of passage. As played by William Christian, this role achieves a certain resilience, making it even clearer how crucially the character affects Berenice. The central fabric of the play is the intimate bond between Frankie and Berenice. Without that kinship, there cannot be a memorable "Member of the Wedding."

1989 Ap 1, 16:3

When Two's a Crowd

QUINTUPLETS, by Luis Rafael Sanchez; English translation by Alba Oms and Ivonne Coll; directed by Ms. Oms; producer, Miriam Colon; set design by Robert Klingelhoefer; lighting design, Bill Simmons; costume design, Laura Drawbaugh; sound design, Gary and Timmy Harris; production stage manager, D. C. Rosenberg. Presented by the Puerto Rican Traveling Theater, 304 West 47th Street.

Daphne, Bianca and Carlotta Morrison ....
.... Ivonne Coll
Baby and Mandrake Morrison, and El Gran Divo Papa Morrison .... Roberto Medina

By D. J. R. BRUCKNER

Two actors search out the vanity, rascality, self-delusion and sheer lunacy of six characters in Luis Rafael Sanchez's "Quintuplets." And in the production at the Puerto Rican Traveling Theater, the actors, Ivonne Coll and Roberto Medina, do create the illusion that they are six people. In fact, a seventh pops up briefly in one scene.

Running almost two hours, the play is too long by about half and its abrupt conclusion in a little dialogue about theater and reality leaves the impression that even the playwright may have grown weary.

But appearing alternately in six episodes, Miss Coll and Mr. Medina share a lot of fun with the audience as a set of middle-aged quintuplets from Puerto Rico — Carlotta, Bianca and Daphne Morrison and their brothers Mandrake and Baby — and the father of the five, El Gran Divo Papa.

An enormously pregnant Carlotta litters the place with pill bottles and enlists from the audience a dozen volunteers to assist her if she should go into labor right on stage. As she

Metamorphosis from scene to scene.

lumbers around, you forget that, minutes before, the same actress was an elegantly dressed Bianca coming apart at the seams while she struggles for self-control. Bianca's attempts to give up smoking are wonderfully farcical and the collapse of her icy reserve as she confesses her passion for a "fire-eating princess from Cathay" in a circus troupe is a tickling bit of comedy.

•

Were it not for the physical resemblance, it would be hard to believe either of these women could be related to the sensuous Daphne of the first scene. Her every movement suggests sex and when she talks about men her hands seem to reach out and grab them. Her meditation on kissing fairly sets the stage on fire and her burning description of a man on a beach makes lust seem a shining virtue.

Peter Krupenye

Ivonne Coll in "Quintuplets."

On the whole, the male characters offer an actor fewer opportunities. Mr. Medina does have some funny moments as the shy Baby Morrison, but the only role that lets him show what he can do is Mandrake, a fast-talking, sleazy magician with a large repertory of funny stories. Mandrake has a problem: his magical powers and "incredible charm" come from the devil. When this is revealed, Mr. Medina branches into two characters at once — a skeptical, swaggering Mandrake and an annoyed devil who protests, "I swear to God, I am the devil," and tells a hilarious version of the fall of the angels from heaven. Mr. Medina's presentation of this confrontation is very adroit; it has the incredible charm Mandrake aspires to.

1989 Ap 2, 51:1

A 3-Day Immersion in New Plays

By MEL GUSSOW

Special to The New York Times

LOUISVILLE, Ky., April 2 — An intensive three days at the Actors Theater of Louisville, seeing plays that often dealt with family and fraternal bonds, brought to mind the company's own past tie with new and developing talent, the founding tradition of the Humana Festival of New American Plays. Under the direction of Jon Jory, the Actors Theater has deservedly won a place as a valuable nurturer of Beth Henley, Marsha Norman, Jane Martin and many other playwrights.

Two years ago, in an effort to inject new vitality into his organization, Mr. Jory announced that he would commission writers from other disciplines to write plays. In principle, the position could be defensible; in practice, it has also meant the signing of name theatrical novices who probably need the commissioning fee (reportedly around $20,000) about as much as Louisville needs the importation of bourbon.

First on the firing line last year was Jimmy Breslin with the woeful "Queen of the Leaky Roof Circuit."

This year, the celebrity author passing through Louisville was William F. Buckley Jr., with "Stained Glass," an adaptation of his 1978 espionage novel. Though Mr. Buckley has proven himself in a plethora of endeavors, as a playwright he is a total tyro.

•

"Stained Glass" and two other works in this year's festival did not earn their place on the Actors Theater stage, but they were offset by three plays — Harry Crews's "Blood Issue," Charlene Redick's "Autumn Elegy" and, most enjoyably, Arthur Kopit's savage put-down of Hollywood, "Bone-the-Fish."

Mr. Buckley was the only one of the commissioned writers to be absent during the marathon. He had been at the opening several weeks ago in the company of some 50 of his friends, who were flown from New York for the occasion. A theater party from New York was undoubtedly a first for Louisville.

Were it not for the author's eminence, "Stained Glass" would have been lost in the slush pile. Dramaturgically, it is stiff and stately, with a posture of erudition. The dialogue in the B-movie scenario is seasoned with words like excogitate and vermiform appendices.

The play is Mr. Buckley's rewriting of the Cold War, circa 1952, with villainy attributed to an alliance between the C.I.A. and the K.G.B. Together, they plot to assassinate the democratically elected new head of a unified Germany, an exclamatory sort who shouts, eureka-style, "To defy gravity!" For that alone, he deserves his fate.

•

On one side of the stage there are waxwork dialogues between actors pretending to be Dean Acheson and Allen Dulles. There are several awkward romantic scenes and some strong language, though not enough to cause the posting of the sign to that

Richard Trigg
Anne Pitoniak in the Actors Theater of Louisville production of Harry Crews's "Blood Issue."

effect, as is the case with several other plays. "Stained Glass" is not helped by its production, but then the production is not helped by the play. The lesson learned: Even with the greatest of excogitation, one cannot create a play out of vermiform appendices.

But behind the "Stained Glass" window, this was a festival with considerable merit. Mr. Kopit aroused audiences with his acerbity, his pitch-black humor and his sheer virulence. As expertly staged by James Simpson, "Bone-the-Fish" was also the festival's most polished effort, though it would benefit from some revisions in the second act. "Bone-the-Fish" is that rarity in Louisville — a New York play.

Beginning with the title, it could be regarded as Mr. Kopit's response to David Mamet's "Speed-the-Plow." In fact, the plays share much more than two hyphens. Mr. Kopit asks how far a film director will go in demeaning

himself in quest of work. His answer is not printable in this newspaper. "Bone-the-Fish" makes "Speed-the-Plow" seem genteel in comparison.

•

At the core of the comedy is the blood oath between a hotshot producer (Joseph Ragno) and his out-of-work former partner (Bruce Adler). They agree to film the life story of a

From William F. Buckley, a work for the stage.

rock star with one name and memoirs entitled "Moby Dick." Though one might question the parallels with Mr. Mamet as well as the importance of Mr. Kopit's purpose, there is no mistaking the freshness and the pungency of the writing. The two actors are a very funny comedy team, Mr. Adler acceding to the most bizarre requests, Mr. Ragno speaking with a permanently forked tongue, as in his statement, "To be crass just for a moment, if I may."

An exit poll probably would have confirmed Mr. Crews's "Blood Issue" as the festival favorite. An acclaimed novelist, Mr. Crews is a playwright in the rough, a fact that is probably in keeping with his persona as a renegade of the arts. "Blood Issue" is a Georgia homecoming play about family skeletons and a battle between brothers, one a redneck, the other a writer whose career seems to follow that of the author.

The weakest element is the writer, who delivers such bottom-of-the-bottle explanations as, "I drink to make it all go away." The symbolism of blood ties is overly refrained, and when the writer uncovers the skeletons, they are exactly the ones that have been rattling throughout the play.

On the other hand, the house is overflowing with colorful characters. At the center is the grandmother, a kind of matriarchal version of Big Daddy. Playing the role in Mr. Jory's production is Anne Pitoniak, delivering the festival's most impressive performance. There is vivid support by Bob Burrus, Nancy Niles Sexton and John Dennis Johnston, among others.

•

Ms. Redick's "Autumn Elegy" is a quiet, understated play about an elderly, reclusive country couple facing the imminent death of the wife. Filled with pauses, "Autumn Elegy" has moments of poignancy, but it is a sketch for a play yet to be written. For one thing, it is missing a confrontation between the principal characters.

In the audience were Hume Cronyn and Jessica Tandy, who discovered "The Gin Game" on their last visit to the festival. One had to consider the possibility that if the Cronyns had acted in "Autumn Elegy," it might have moved the play, despite its flaws, to a deeper emotional level.

There is always at least one play that divides the festival, and this year it was Constance Congdon's "Tales of the Lost Formicans," a satirical look at suburbia as seen through the eyes of extra-terrestrials. In performance, the play was almost impossible to follow, switching from humans to aliens (the same actors in both roles). Intending to be arresting, it was instead enervating.

At least "The Lost Formicans" did not run on empty, as was the case with two other noncommissioned works, Steven Dietz's "God's Country," a seemingly unprocessed collage of data about neo-Nazism in America, and "The Bug," Richard Strand's unamusing look at computerism. As Keith Reddin battled manfully with the leading role in "The Bug," one wished that Christopher Durang, sitting in the audience, might rise from his seat and give Mr. Strand a lesson in comic playwriting. Following Mr. Kopit, Mr. Durang is the single playwright commissioned for next year's festival — along with two novelists, E. L. Doctorow and Tama Janowitz.

1989 Ap 5, C19:4

Warding Off Evil

AMULETS AGAINST THE DRAGON FORCES, by Paul Zindel; directed by B. Rodney Marriott; sets by David Potts; costumes by Walker Hicklin; lights by Dennis Parichy; sound design by Chuck London Media/Stewart Werner; original music by Norman L. Berman; fight director, Rick Sordelet; production stage manager, M. A. Howard. Presented by Circle Repertory Company, Tanya Berezin, artistic director; Connie L. Alexis, managing director. At 99 Seventh Avenue South, at Fourth Street.

Chris	Matt McGrath
Harold	Loren Dean
Floyd	John Spencer
Mrs. Boyd	Deborah Hedwall
Mrs. Dipardi	Ruby Holbrook
Attendant No. 1/Leroy	Jerome Preston Bates
Attendant No. 2/Joey	John Viscardi
Richie	Robert Gladding
Roochie	James Gregory Smith
Rosemary	Carrena Lukas

By FRANK RICH

While most of François Truffaut's "Small Change" has receded in memory, I can't imagine forgetting the scene in which a baby tumbles from a high apartment-house window and survives. Truffaut made an indel-

ible image out of profound questions that had defined his career from "The 400 Blows" and that never leave most of us: By what miracle do some children survive? What happens to those victims of cruel, lonely, loveless childhoods who do grow up but don't bounce back?

These questions also animate the far different work of Paul Zindel, whose breakthrough play of 1970, "The Effect of Gamma Rays on Man-in-the-Moon Marigolds," told of two sisters trying to escape the suffocating grip of their bitter mother. Mr. Zindel's new play at the Circle Repertory Company, "Amulets Against the Dragon Forces," returns to the same themes, a similar mother, another Staten Island household (of 1955) and, as the title indicates, some of the same overwriting. It's easy to mock Mr. Zindel's unshapely hothouse drama, whose occupants are variously afflicted by cancer, dipsomania, kleptomania, bisexual nymphomania and poetic excess. Then we see the child at center stage trying to ward off the horrors, the child too genuine to dismiss as fiction, and "Amulets" becomes gripping and disturbing despite its Gothic overkill.

The child is the teen-age Chris (Matt McGrath), who travels with his mother (Deborah Hedwall), an itinerant practical nurse, from house to house as she takes on live-in assignments with terminal patients. Chris was long ago abandoned by his father, who fled to St. Augustine, Fla. ("near the Ripley's Believe It or Not Museum"). Now the boy finds himself carrying his suitcase and shopping bags into a dingy household populated entirely by abandoned souls. The dying widow (Ruby Holbrook) in the care of Chris's mother is ignored by her son, a brutish, alcoholic longshoreman named Floyd (John Spencer). The middle-aged Floyd reserves most of his love and abuse for the young Harold (Loren Dean), a sweet hustler who had been abandoned by his own parents before finding his way into Floyd's bed.

Gerry Goodstein
Matt McGrath, left, and John Spencer in the Circle Repertory Company production of "Amulets Against the Dragon Forces."

Though they have not all been created with equal depth by Mr. Zindel, the characters are invariably fascinating — even the ravaged, nearly comatose patient who bites anyone who comes near her. But "Amulets" is primarily a Tennessee Williams-like standoff between the sensitive Chris and the bellicose Floyd, who

Paul Zindel's 'Amulets' studies some survivors.

will not rest until he has brutalized the vulnerabilities of everyone around him. Floyd not only hates women — his mother, Chris's mother, his discarded wife — but he also likes to fire up the local male roughnecks by inviting them over for booze and whores.

The struggle between the frail Chris and the destructive Floyd would seem no contest. Chris has no defenses — only a collection of carved figures, his amulets, that provides him with a fantasy world of escapist storytelling. Floyd has ready fists and an abusive tongue poised to spill anyone's most shameful secrets. But as the compassionate Mr. Zindel avoided simple moral judgments with the mother in "Marigolds," so he does with Floyd: we can still find the abused child who was father to the vicious man. In Mr. Spencer's volatile performance, the longshoreman is alternately a "slobbering, horrendous freak" and an articulate student of human nature, with equally devastating results.

As nakedly acted by the brave and talented Mr. McGrath, Chris is an open wound, almost painful to watch. A gawky, delicate misfit with an epicene voice, he tries to head off rejection by chattily advertising his own precociousness. The only teacher who ever thought the boy anything but "completely deranged" had decided that he was a writer. Chris clings to this diagnosis even though the teacher, a Shakespeare scholar, herself suffered a nervous breakdown after being ridiculed by students.

•

In this teacher's class, Chris learned that "everyone loved action and suspense." Mr. Zindel, a popular author of fiction for adolescents, knows the same lesson, but he piles on too much florid action in "Amulets": Do we need a smashed chandelier, a gay love triangle, a sudden financial windfall *and* an orgy? None of these events are underplayed by the director, B. Rodney Marriott, or are left unaccompanied by Norman L. Berman's creepy incidental score. One must also quarrel with the overworked mythology of Chris's amulets, with the psychoanalytical symmetry of the parent-child relationships and with the unlikely Act II exchange of confessional monologues (however well written) between Floyd and Chris's mom, who otherwise hate each other.

Ms. Hedwall, despite some uneasiness with her lines, becomes rending in that scene, the starchy mother's one chance to reveal how she went from being one women's-magazine cliché (the model 1950's housewife) to another ("the desperate divorcée") without ever finding the woman she might have been. Mr. Dean's lost boy

of the streets also commands attention — with his ethereal ingenuousness, if not with his mumbling.

But Chris is the child crashing toward earth in Mr. Zindel's play, and it is for him that the playwright holds out the blind hope denied the others. As the pitiful Mr. McGrath cries into a phone, begging his dismissive father in vain for love, it's hard to imagine how he can possibly grow up intact. "It's all in the timing" is Floyd's explanation of how Chris might yet survive the same dragon forces that maimed him, and who knows? It's not without wisdom that Mr. Zindel situates the searing drama of childhood, like Chris's absent father, in the mysterious, macabre neighborhood of Ripley's Believe It or Not.

1989 Ap 6, C17:4

Assimilation

THE EDUCATION OF H*Y*M*A*N K*A*P*L*A*N, book by Benjamin Bernard Zavin; music and lyrics by Oscar Brand and Paul Nassau; based on the stories by Leo Rosten. Directed by Lonny Price; musical director, Nicholas Levin; set designer, Randy Benjamin; costume designer, Gail Cooper-Hecht; lighting designer, Betsy Adams; production stage manager, Jon Roger Clark; production coordinator, Lisa Forman. Presented by the American Jewish Theater, Stanley Brechner, artistic director. At the Susan Bloch Theater, 307 West 26th Street.

Hyman Kaplan	Jack Hallett
Sam Pinsky	Norman Golden
Rose Mitnick	Laura Patinkin
Mr. Parkhill	Stephen McNaughton
Sadie Moskowitz/Mrs. Mitnick	Molly Stark
Stanislaus Wilkomirski/Officer Callahan/ Judge Mahon	Michael Shelle
Reuben Plonsky/Yissel Fishbein	Neal Ben-Ari

By RICHARD F. SHEPARD

When Hyman Kaplan speaks, everybody listens, but few understand. Kaplan's tin ear produces a pidgin English so revisionary that it is foreign even to the immigrants who are his fellow students of English in night school on the Lower East Side.

Kaplan may be anarchic in his approach to English but he is an American patriot, right off the boat. You can tell that because he signs his name in stars as in the title of the musical that opened Tuesday night at the American Jewish Theater's Susan Bloch Theater: "The Education of H*Y*M*A*N K*A*P*L*A*N."

The show, a revival of the 1968 Broadway production, is by Benjamin Bernard Zavin, who wrote the book, with music and lyrics by Oscar Brand and Paul Nassau. The musical was inspired by the hilarious stories of Leo Rosten (who wrote them under the name of Leonard Q. Ross).

•

In weaving a musical from such material, the creators came up with a relative of the book: not a sibling but more of a cousin. They installed a plot: Kaplan falls in love with Miss Mitnick, the bright student, who is betrothed to a repulsive stranger. The Palmer raids of the early 1920's that arbitrarily deported aliens on suspicion of radicalism has a piece of the action as well.

One can have a very nice time at this musical, although it is not the strongest evening of theater in sight. It is amusing but not uproarious, and its score is sprinkled with some clever tunes. Under Lonny Price's sure-handed direction, the personable cast of 11 moves about the Lower East Side schoolroom setting quite

nimbly. The second act is appreciably livelier than the first, perhaps because the characters begin to emerge as personalities rather than as quaint Yiddish equivalents of the little folk of "Brigadoon."

There is high humor in the class's analysis of Macbeth's line, "tomorrow and tomorrow..." when Kaplan, somehow injecting Julius Scissor into the play, explains how he chose the wrong way. Kaplan's letter, with its grammatically debatable usages ("If your eye falls on a bargain, pick it up") is hilarious. "An Old-Fashioned Husband," as sung by Neal Ben-Ari, playing the repugnant groom-to-be, is among the more appealing songs. Others are "Ooee Ooere," which illustrates the pronunciation of "W's"; "Anything Is Possible," which is romantic and upbeat, and the rousing "All American," which brings down the curtain.

•

Jack Hallett, in the title role, is versatile, a knowing performer who catches Kaplan's beatific smile as well as the deferential demeanor toward those whom he respects. But the actor does not achieve the forcefully dominating character of Kaplan that one somehow expects of this embryo American. Laura Patinkin, as the good-looking Miss Mitnick, has a strong and sweet voice, although her Yiddish accent with its shades of latter-day Wellesley needs work.

Stephen McNaughton is wholly convincing as the well-bred Bostonian Mr. Parkhill, who chooses to dedicate himself to teaching English to immigrants and suffers for it. Molly Stark is excellent as Sadie Moskowitz, a mature student of healthy girth and a wonderfully comic flirtatious manner. Norman Golden, as Kaplan's best friend, lends an unmistakable flavor of Yiddishkeit. Michael Shelle proves to be a valuable man for all seasons, first as a non-Jewish Polish student, second as a brogue-laden cop and finally as sober judge.

The work is funny and bright for much of the way, and it is ingratiating, even with its failings. The run has been extended through May 21 and, to put it Kaplanesquely, that adds up to dollars and sense.

1989 Ap 6, C22:4

The Man They Love

DON JUAN OF SEVILLE, by Tirso de Molina; translation by Lynne Alvarez; directed by Carey Perloff; scenic design, Donald Eastman; costume design, Gabriel Berry; lighting design, Frances Aronson; composer, Elizabeth Swados. Presented by the Classic Stage Company, Ms. Perloff, artistic director, Ellen Novack, managing director, and Intar, Hispanic American Arts Center, Max Ferrá, artistic director, James DiPaola, managing director. At 136 East 13th Street.

Don Juan	Jeffrey Nordling
Catalinon	Michael Perez
Don Gonzalo	Robert Langdon Lloyd
Tisbea	Kim Yancey
Isabella	Denise B. Mickelbury
Octavio	Jack Stehlin
Don Pedro and King Alphonso	Ron Faber

WITH: Royce M. Becker, Sara Erde, Don Gettinger, Michael Jayce, Norberto Kerner, Winter Mead, Hope Nye, Al Rodriguez, Jack Stehlin, John Wendes Taylor, Jill Williams and Sarah Williams.

By WILBORN HAMPTON

The stage has produced a number of playwrights whose place in dramatic literature rests as much on the

influence they have exerted on other writers as on any work of their own. Few, however, have provided more enduring inspiration for later artists than Tirso de Molina, an early-17th-century Spanish ecclesiastic who created the character of Don Juan.

Tom Chargin

Jeffrey Nordling

Tirso claimed to have written some 400 plays, but his fame rests almost solely on "El Burlador de Sevilla y Convidado de Piedra," a tale of seduction and retribution that is known mostly through Molière, Mozart, Byron, Pushkin and Shaw, to name a few of the authors who employed Tirso's infamous character to their own ends. The CSC Theater, in collaboration with Intar, is offering a new translation of Tirso's play, retitled "Don Juan of Seville."

It is hard to tell from the CSC production what merits the original work might hold for late-20th-century theatergoers. The director, Carey Perloff, has so camped up this version that it is more a burlesque of the Don Juan legend than a serious attempt to stage Tirso's morality play of repentance delayed.

•

From the start, there is little sense of purpose to the production. The action moves from episode to episode, the cast relying on gimmickry and sight gags to try to grab a laugh. Ms. Perloff either encourages or allows

A 17th-century work is given a new translation.

her actors to indulge in excesses of gesturing, shouting and stomping about the stage. It's as though the director doesn't trust her text and has turned to absurd costuming, farcical wigs and even silly walks to keep our attention.

Lynne Alvarez's new translation is mostly rhymed couplets that are delivered in the singsong cadence of rap lyrics. Gabriel Berry's costumes range, for no obvious reason, from 17th-century hose and ruff to leather motorcycle jackets, zoot suits and Spandex tights. Donald Eastman's sets include scaffolding, catwalks, ramps, ladders, a garden bench and, of course, a tomb. The prop list includes an Instamatic camera, a World War II bayonet, flashlights and a couple of rapiers.

The hodgepodge of accouterments aside, the real puzzle of the CSC production is in some of the characterizations Ms. Perloff and her actors have drawn. The modest fisherwoman Tisbea, for example, is introduced as little more than a strumpet making lewd suggestions with her fishing pole and sensuously crawling all over the shipwrecked Don Juan when he washes onto her beach. As played by Kim Yancey, one must seriously question who is seducing whom. Tisbea's chaste admonition to Don Juan, moments later, that "God exists and so does death" thus becomes ludicrous.

The rest of the cast, while energetic, does not for the most part help the credibility of the production. Happily, the two main exceptions are Jeffrey Nordling, who gives a dashing, wicked and reasoned reading to the title role, and Michael Perez, who ably plays his servant Catalinon. Together they salvage some meaning from this ill-conceived exercise. Robert Langdon Lloyd provides a passable Don Gonzalo. Elizabeth Swados has composed some pleasant music for the show.

1989 Ap 7, C3:5

Mommy Dearest

THE FORBIDDEN CITY, by Bill Gunn; directed by Joseph Papp; set design by Loren Sherman; costume design by Judy Dearing; lighting design by Peter Kaczorowski; music supervision by Sam Waymon; associate producer, Jason Steven Cohen. Presented by Mr. Papp. At the Public Theater/LuEsther Hall, 425 Lafayette Street.

Nick Hoffenburg Jr.	Akili Prince
Molly Hoffenburg	Gloria Foster
Nick Hoffenburg Sr.	Frankie R. Faison
Ivan Trumbull	P. Jay Sidney
Cupid Trumbull	Cortez Nance Jr.
Abel Trumbull	Guy Davis
Loretta	Erika Alexander
Smitty	Allie Woods Jr.
Whistlin' Billy	Mansoor Najee-Ullah
David	Demitri Corbin
Hodge	William Cain

By MEL GUSSOW

It takes almost three hours, but the infantile 16-year-old hero of "The Forbidden City" finally talks back to his oppressive mother. "Ogress!" he shouts. "Bête noire!" and even "Fee, fo, fum!" If there were any doubt that the mother was a dragon, it has long since been dispelled by the fire-breathing performance of Gloria Foster. Both she and the play, which opened last night at the Public Theater, go way overboard. The Wicked Witch of the West is in "The Forbidden City," and her name is Molly Hoffenburg, as played by Ms. Foster.

From the opening minutes of Bill Gunn's tortured family trauma set in

The playwright Bill Gunn died Wednesday at the age of 54.

the 1930's, Molly is on the warpath to destroy her son (Akili Prince). She tells him he is as "dumb as dishwater," whipping him indiscriminately and humiliating him before his teen-age girlfriend.

The final sign that Molly is severely disturbed is the way she switches from child abuse to cloying sentimentality when three railroad workers stop by her kitchen seeking a hand-out. With strangers, Molly is the soul of beneficence, and she prides herself on her membership in ladies' clubs with other black women, a fact that leads her to have tea with Eleanor Roosevelt. But at home, Molly would offer a field day for Freudians. As the wildly uncontrollable center of Mr. Gunn's overwritten play, she is miserable company — for the other characters and for theatergoers who are asked to endure her fiendish behavior.

Such a woman is beyond tragedy (and beyond Tennessee Williams).

Martha Swope
Gloria Foster in "The Forbidden City," at the Public Theater.

She can exist only in a Gothic horror story. We keep waiting for her son to stalk her, Norman Bates style, but when death knocks, the victim is someone else, and like so much else in the play, it is aberrant.

Molly and her husband (Frankie R. Faison) have come north to Philadelphia seeking opportunity. The husband is a member of the working class while his wife envies the Main Line. She has several overwhelming enthusiasms — for herself (as in mirror, mirror on the wall) and for Hollywood movies. As she says, "I would rather live in the movies than die in Philadelphia."

•

She eventually confesses that she has always wanted to be Gloria Swanson. Her real role model, of course, is Joan Crawford, even to her insistence that her son call her Mother Dear when there is company. The son responds by giggling, wetting his bed and talking to his dead brother. A would-be poet, he quotes the poetry of Paul Laurence Dunbar. Everyone quotes Paul Laurence Dunbar.

While the mother runs her monstrous path through the house, the father sits placidly, without lifting a helping finger. As he says to his son, "Anything your mother does short of killing you is all right with me." Occasionally, he offers an aphorism. When told that life is hard, he responds, "Hard as lard and twice as greasy." One can see where his son gets his gift for poetry.

As director, Joseph Papp has allowed — or encouraged — Ms. Foster into acts of histrionic excess. She preens and poses and delivers her lines with affectation.

•

"Forbidden City" momentarily comes down to earth when the father's poker-playing friends stop by for a game and when the son has a conversation with his girlfriend. These outsiders are islands of sanity. But soon the plot thickens with more Hoffenburg horrors. Things get even worse as Molly undertakes an assignation with an elderly white man, who interrupts the play with a boring monologue.

At the end of "The Forbidden City," there is that showdown between mother and son, with Mr. Prince joining Ms. Foster in acting at the top of his fervor. Mr. Faison does what little

he can with the role of the weakling father, but his co-stars — and the play itself — are swamped in a sea of rant and pretension.

1989 Ap 7, C3:1

Urban Nomads

LADIES, by Eve Ensler; directed by Paul Walker; music by Joshua Shneider; set designed by Victoria Petrovich; lighting designed by Debra Dumas; costumes designed by Donna Zakowska; sound designed by John Kilgore; production manager, Steven Ehrenberg; stage manager, Michele Steckler. Presented by Music-Theater Group, Lyn Austin, producing director; Diane Wondisford and Mark Jones, associate producing directors, and the Women's Project and Productions Inc., Julia Miles, artistic director. At St. Clement's, 423 West 46th Street.

Dot	Margaret Barker
Prince	Denise Delapenha
Alpha	Alexandra Gersten
Nickie	Allison Janney
Allegro	Marcella Lowery
Mary	Isabell Monk
Monetty	Novella Nelson
Rosa	ChingValdes/Aran
Ama	Beverly Wideman

By MEL GUSSOW

In Eve Ensler's collage "Ladies," nine homeless women drift and dream through nomadic lives. The play (at St. Clement's) has an evident authenticity, having been drawn from the author's experience working in New York City shelters. The scene is appropriately stark but the play is schematic, with monologues failing to merge into a moving dramatic portrait. Though the play lasts barely one hour, it seems longer, perhaps because of its lack of momentum.

Some of the moments touch responsive chords, as the women speak about their lives before and after they lost their homes. Novella Nelson, playing a woman who had three children by the time she was 17, explains the difference between those who are crazy and those who are insane. "People get crazy," she says, "to protect themselves from people who are insane."

The craziness of the characters on stage is sometimes concealed. Isabell Monk, dressed in a neatly tailored suit, does not look like a shopping-bag lady. With an apparent rationality, she declares that she does not belong in such depressed surroundings. Eventually, she reveals a fearfulness bordering on hysteria.

Marcella Lowery talks about inspecting an apartment and finding that it is a sewer with walls: in other words, a home for the homeless. She and others in the shelter that is the setting for "Ladies" share a desperation and an incapacity to alter their lives. In most cases, they have suffered abuse at the hands of men, one of the more sustained aspects of the fragmented show.

The problem of the homeless is a difficult one to dramatize. To her credit, Ms. Ensler avoids sentimentality. At the same time, there is a self-limitation in her method. The play does not seem more than a reproduction of the reality as the author found it. The stories are not so different from ones that might be overheard in a bus terminal or on the street, and several of them are whimsical, like one woman's story about her love for Liberace.

"Ladies" does benefit from an atmospheric production, under the direction of Paul Walker. The actresses seem sensitive to the material. In re-

pose, they look like sculptural figures, waiting in limbo for a reclamation that will never arrive. Victoria Petrovich's set design and Debra Dumas's lighting are additional assets. The lighting shifts from dreamlike shadows to bright white as social workers offer offstage announcements about unnecessary (for these women) subjects like sex education. In the background, a combo plays midnight jazz by Joshua Schneider.

The characters in "Ladies" (co-produced by the Music-Theater Group and the Women's Project) are not only homeless, they are also rootless and rudderless, clinging to frayed mementoes and memories that signify their existence. The play remains in need of further definition.

1989 Ap 7, C3:1

No Place Like London

SWEENEY TODD: THE DEMON BARBER OF FLEET STREET, music and lyrics by Stephen Sondheim; boook by Hugh Wheeler; from an adaptation by Christopher Bond; directed by Susan H. Schulman; scenic design and graphics, James Morgan; costume design, Beba Shamash; lighting design, May Jo Dondlinger; technical director, James E. Fuller Jr.; production stage manager, Trey Hunt; music director, David Krane; choreographer, Michael Lichtefeld. Presented by the York Theater Company, Janet Hayes Walker, producing director; Molly Pickering Grose, managing director. At the Church of the Heavenly Rest, 2 East 90th Street.

Jonas Fogg	Tony Gilbert
Policeman	David E. Mallard
Bird Seller	Ted Keegan
Dora	Dawn Stone
Mrs. Mooney	Mary Ellen Phillips
Anthony Hope	Jim Walton
Sweeney Todd	Bob Gunton
Beggar Woman	SuEllen Estey
Mrs. Lovett	Beth Fowler
Judge Turpin	David Barron
The Beadle	Calvin Remsberg
Johanna	Gretchen Kingsley-Weihe
Tobias Ragg	Eddie Korbich
Pirelli	Bill Nable

By STEPHEN HOLDEN

In the 10 years since it first opened on Broadway, "Sweeney Todd," Stephen Sondheim and Hugh Wheeler's Grand Guignol musical of revenge run amok, has only grown in stature.

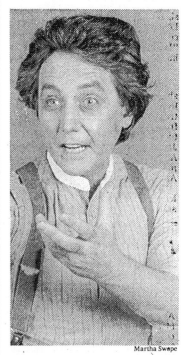

Martha Swope
Bob Gunton in "Sweeney Todd."

Among other things, "Sweeney Todd" anticipated darker times. New York City today, with its homelessness and municipal corruption scandals, feels a lot more like the show's grim 19th-century London setting than it did a decade ago. That's why the show's railing misanthropy hits so much closer to home. In 10 years, the somewhat forbidding Sondheim score has also been absorbed into the culture. Music that echoes composers as disparate as Gilbert and Sullivan, Puccini and Bernard Herrmann has been recognized as one of the most majestic of modern operatic scores.

One of the questions surrounding the future of "Sweeney Todd" has been how much weight it could carry if given a drastically scaled-down production from the one on Broadway that used a gigantic set incorporating parts from an iron foundry. The York Theater Company's stunning revival happily proves the show can be just as gripping when done as a small chamber opera. In some ways it even benefits from the more intimate scale.

•

Susan H. Schulman, the director of the York Theater revival, has ingeniously re-conceived "Sweeney Todd" as an environmental theater piece in which the floor in front of the audience is a painted cobblestone street. At one end stands the shop where the demon barber dispenses bloody murder. Opposite looms the headquarters of the diabolical Judge Turpin. The theater walls are a painted set of shabby tenements and clotheslines. Inside this ominous shadowy environment, one has a real sense of social constriction and lurking danger. During the course of the evening, the company sweeps back and forth between the two sites, stopping occasionally to make accusatory, threatening eye contact with the audience.

The director has assembled a cast almost as impressive as the Broadway company, with the brilliant performance of Bob Gunton in the title role, surpassing even Len Cariou's iron portrayal in the original cast. Hollow-eyed and zombie-like, ignited by an unappeasable lust for vengeance, Mr. Gunton projects an intensity that at moments borders on seizure. Even in the show's lighter moments, he remains a tense, quivering hulk, wracked with demons. And as his murderous fury escalates into a literal foaming at the mouth, he becomes a terrifying, pitiable creature who still retains enough humanity to engage compassion. Vocally Mr. Gunton has a harder, more gravelly tone than Mr. Cariou's more mellifluous baritone. But this harsher quality gives his solos an extra edge of crazy determination.

As his doting accomplice, Mrs. Lovett, Beth Fowler is quite different from Angela Lansbury and in her own way as convincing. Instead of a savage comic caricature of an avaricious shopkeeper with dime-novel dreams, she is a more conventional, self-deluded woman with a streak of genuine tenderness. Jim Walton and Gretchen Kingsley-Weihe as the young lovers are less satisfying. Though both have fine singing voices, their stage encounters are clumsy and rushed. But David Barron imbues the role of Judge Turpin with just the right air of corrupt self-righteousness. And Eddie Korbich and Calvin Remsberg are outstanding as Tobias Ragg and the Beadle.

•

Not the least of the production's accomplishments is the musical director David Krane's reduction of the original orchestral score into full-bodied arrangements for three synthesizers whose textural subtleties range from birdsong to snare drum. And the colder, pricklier electronic textures that frequently sound like pipe organ and harpsichord eerily complement the play's fiendish imagery of glinting, lethal razor blades.

Five years ago, the York Theater mounted an incandescent revival of "Pacific Overtures," another complicated Sondheim show that one would have thought impossible to revive effectively in a small church theater. In "Sweeney Todd," the company has more than matched that impressive accomplishment.

1989 Ap 8, 11:5

Betrayal All Around

NIGHT BREATH, by Dennis Clontz; directed by Richard Bly; production stage manager, Elaine O'Donnell; lighting designer, Brian Aldous; costume designer, Elizabeth Huffman; hair designer, Brian Grace. Presented by the Beacon Project Inc. At the Pelican Studio, 750 Eighth Avenue, at 46th Street.

Woman No. 1	Geraldine Singer
Woman No. 2	Elizabeth Huffman
Woman No. 3	Nancy Learmonth
Man	Brian Markinson

By WILBORN HAMPTON

Before the lights come up on "Night Breath," a curious play by Dennis Clontz that is being staged by the Beacon Project, a medley of recorded folk songs is played as a sort of prelude. One of the songs is "Wayfaring Stranger," and it pretty much sets the tone for what follows.

Three women of divergent backgrounds and experience find themselves together in a burned barn in rural California one night in 1907. The covered body of a fourth woman lies in the barn with them, and this proximity of death elicits a defensive yet searching self-examination from each survivor in the hour before dawn, the "night breath" of the title.

Mr. Clontz is a playwright who works hard at maintaining the enigmatic nature of his characters. He indulges in quite a bit of symbolism, some of it forced and some of it effective, and intersperses the women's personal reflections with such trivial conversations as a discussion of crickets. And there is the odd conundrum thrown in for the audience to ponder, such as whether a trifurcated road "is one road going off three ways or three roads coming together." As if to underscore the Everywoman quality of the play, Mr. Clontz has brought a San Francisco businesswoman (identified only as Woman No. 1), a woman of easy virtue (No. 2), and a farmer's daughter (No. 3) together in his burned barn.

Each in her turn tells her story, and each story involves betrayal at the hands of a man (the character named, Man, of course, and ably played in all three incarnations by Brian Markinson.) Each of the women identifies with the dead woman and begins her narrative in the third person, as though she was talking about the deceased, until it becomes clear she is telling her own story and the monologue segues into an active scene.

Under Richard Bly's direction, this device, which could prove awkward, works quite smoothly. Two of these three vignettes are fully realized and provide the foundation for the drama of the play. The first scene (gamely acted by Geraldine Singer as Woman No. 1) fails to rise above the level of bad melodrama. But the second and third, despite the occasional cliché in the script, turn into real conflict. Elizabeth Huffman (Woman No. 2) and Nancy Learmonth (No. 3) have pared their performances to basic emotions and in so doing succeed in

Patrick J. Dougherty

Elizabeth Huffman

turning a pair of faintly sketched characters into credible portraits of women whose night of soul-searching gains our attention and sympathy.

The play is also not without humor, especially from Ms. Huffman, and this alleviates some of the more tedious passages. "Night Breath" is an interesting evening, but it would be a stronger one if it were trimmed to just that one hour before dawn instead of the 100 minutes of playing time (without intermission) in the Beacon production.

1989 Ap 9, 57:2

Repression

TEMPTATION, by Vaclav Havel; translated by Marie Winn; directed by Jiri Zizka; scenery by Jerry Rojo; costumes by Hiroshi Iwasaki; lighting by Jerold R. Forsyth; music by Adam Wernick; sound effects by Charles Cohen; projection design by Jeffrey S. Brown; choreography by Raymond G. del Barrio; associate producer, Jason Steven Cohen. Presented by Joseph Papp. At the Public Theater, 425 Lafayette Street.

Dr. Libby Lorencova	Tanny McDonald
Dr. Kotrly	David Schechter
Dr. Neuwirth	Joel McKinnon Miller
Marketa	Katherine Hiler
Dr. Henry Foustka	David Strathairn
The Deputy Director	Larry Block
Petrushka	Marla Sucharetza
The Director	Bill Moor
The Special Secretary	Ronnie West
Vilma	Margaret Gibson
Mrs. Mulch	Sarah Melici
Fistula	Bille Brown
The Lovers	
	Angel David and Annie Rae Etheridge
The Dancer	Raymond G. del Barrio

By FRANK RICH

There is no glasnost for the dissident Czechoslovak playwright Vaclav Havel, who has once again been thrown in prison for championing human rights in Prague, and there is no glasnost in "Temptation," the Havel play now having its American premiere at the Public Theater.

Set in the malevolent scientific institute of a totalitarian state, "Temptation" is a reworking of "Faust" in which the devil you don't know is always worse than the devil you do know, and the devil you do know is at best a party apparatchik, at worst a thug. In "Temptation," as in such past Havel plays as "The Memorandum" and "A Private View," even simple words (starting with "morality") are inverted in meaning by a state that demands intellectual conformity and that governs by fear. It's Mr. Havel's incredible gift — all the more incredible given his inability to see his own works in production — that he spins out the nightmare of repression in intricate verbal comedy to match that of Tom Stoppard, his longtime friend and admirer.

•

Perhaps it's a small mercy that Mr. Havel cannot see the Public's shabby version of "Temptation," because it might break his heart. The director is the Czechoslovak-born Jiri Zizka of the Wilma Theater in Philadelphia. As was demonstrated in his grotesque production of "1984," which appeared at the Joyce Theater as part of the American Theater Exchange two seasons ago, Mr. Zizka loves theatrical toys (slide shows, electronic music, fluorescent lighting, high-tech scenery) and scantily clad female bodies. Words, ideas and actors don't concern him too much.

Mr. Zizka reset Orwell's novel in an almost unrecognizable burlesque rendering of the United States. "Temptation" might as well be floating through the outer space that is periodically and pretentiously projected on the production's front curtain. Mr. Havel's dialogue, as translated by Marie Winn, is often rapid-fire bureaucratic double-speak demanding the hard-edged style of a Terry Gilliam satire like "Brazil." As lethargically delivered here, the lines evaporate long before the jokes register. The tricky metaphysical monologues fare no better; the actors, like the audience, seem to lose their way in

Martha Swope

David Strathairn as Foustka in "Temptation," at Public Theater.

---

mid-conundrum. Even the nonverbal theatrics, notably a witches' sabbath finale, are choreographed with a clunkiness that takes the fun out of the fairly continuous display of black-lace stockings and brassieres.

•

Under such circumstances, it's hard to know whether to blame the director or the cast for the poor quality of the performance. The intelligent David Strathairn should have been ideal as the evening's Faust — a scientist who is captivated by black magic and sadistic sexual fantasies during his doomed search for the truth that might set him free. Under Mr. Zizka's guidance, Mr. Strathairn's voice and personality are so weightless that the actor would be unidentifiable without the Playbill. As the villains of the piece — a tatty old mock-Shavian Mephistopheles and a fascist institute director prone to extorting sexual favors from male syco-

Havel, imprisoned again, attacks totalitarianism in 'Temptation.'

phants — Bille Brown and Bill Moor are, at least, articulate in their hamminess. The rest of the company, Larry Block's unctuous deputy director excepted, is robotic.

The listless production only accentuates the author's repetitions and the laborious setup of his less-than-startling final twist. But if "Temptation" seems lesser Havel, it would be absurd to make any conclusive judgment on the basis of this staging — just as it was impossible to evaluate the Havel play "Largo Desolato" on the basis of the distorted rendering it, too, received (under Richard Foreman's egocentric direction) at the New York Shakespeare Festival in 1985.

•

"Temptation" is actually the second Havel presentation at the Public this year. Shortly after the writer was arrested in Prague in January, leading American playwrights joined representatives of Helsinki Watch and the American Center of PEN in a celebrity-studded program of readings to demand his release. It might be worthwhile if these influential citizens returned to the Public to bear witness, as Mr. Havel cannot, to this production of "Temptation." While the plight of the playwright in Czechoslovakia may be beyond the reach of concerned Americans, the plight of his plays in New York, at least, is not.

1989 Ap 10, C13:1

T. Charles Erickson

Richard Thomas in the title role of "Peer Gynt" at the Hartford Stage.

Peeling Ibsen's Existential Onion

By MEL GUSSOW

Special to The New York Times

HARTFORD, April 8 — "Peer Gynt" represented, as Ibsen wrote, "a process of spiritual liberation and catharsis," for the title character as well as for the playwright. Though Ibsen himself regarded it as his play least likely to be understood outside of his country, it has become one of his most universal works. Along with "Brand," "Peer Gynt" is a poetic masterpiece, fraught with dangers for theatrical mountaineers daring to climb its craggy peaks (and to descend into its earthy valleys). For this reason, the play is seldom performed, rarer still in its entirety.

Mark Lamos's two-part, five-hour production, starring Richard Thomas, is monumental, both as risk and as achievement, drawing upon the artistic resources of the director and the Hartford Stage and inspiring Mr. Thomas to a feat of acting. Following his "Hamlet" last season in Hartford, his fearless performance in this most challenging role further validates his position as one of America's leading classical actors.

The last two productions of the play that I have seen, both admirable, both spare, were at the CSC and at Stratford-on-Avon (with Derek Jacobi in the title role). In contrast, Mr. Lamos's more ambitious version has a visual richness that is itself transporting. It is, one might add, in direct

A panoramic 'Peer Gynt,' with Richard Thomas.

antithesis to his recent, muted production of "Measure for Measure" at Lincoln Center.

Mr. Lamos has a clear-sighted view of "Peer Gynt" as both timeless and timely. As Peer undertakes his journey to find his innermost self, peeling an onion to its nonexistent core, one can find contemporary existential parallels. And in Peer's penchant for troll-ery can be read all the self-indulgences that deflect man from a truer purpose.

The sweep of "Peer Gynt" is cinematic, for which the director and his designer, John Conklin, have found imaginative theatrical equivalents. Peer's journey is visualized with a sequence of striking scenic alterations, using perspective-distorting panoramas; sculptural figures (a huge pig, a small Sphinx), landscapes in miniature; and stage-filling dropcloths of sharply varying color. In characteristic Lamos fashion, individual scenes conjure painterly images that run all the way from Bruegel to Manet (a picnic on the beach).

In one of several coups de théâtre, the director turns the stage into the deck of a ship during a storm, then instantly transforms it into the roiling sea itself (Peer fights a diabolical fellow passenger for possession of a toy-size lifeboat), and, finally, into the bleak Norwegian landscape. In such a fashion, the director repeatedly stimulates the audience's imagination.

This is not to suggest that the production (or the play) is flawless. There is a dramatic ebb toward the end of the first act of the second half, as Peer wanders through several continents, scenes that in other productions are often abridged. More in question is the translation by Gerry Bamman and Irene B. Berman. Though it is in verse, it is not always poetic and there is often an awkward slanginess, as in the use of words like phooey and hunky-dory. At other times, however, the translation has a flow that overrides such eccentricities, and there are several interesting variations. For example, the symbolic Great Boyg becomes the Great Between.

Mr. Thomas's Peer is a kind of anti-Hamlet, a man of action who refuses to be introspective. A fantasizer and an improviser, he is not to be trusted, yet women repeatedly put their faith in him. Any actor playing Peer must capture both the recklessness and the charm. Mr. Thomas has both in abundance.

The production opens inside Peer's home rather than outdoors, as is customary. The room is decorated as a nursery, with Magritte-like hanging objects. Peer and his mother (Patricia Conolly) are rumaging through the attic of memory. Then Peer begins to spin his story about his wild ride on the back of a reindeer. His mother — as well as the audience — is spellbound by the fabulous tale. It is, of course, a fiction, a fact that does not vitiate the storytelling.

In subsequent scenes, Mr. Thomas maintains that high level of excitement, as he seduces a bride on her wedding day; provokes a second woman, Solveig, to become his lifelong muse, and flees through the wilderness. His adventure in the kingdom of the trolls is, as it should be, vulgar, comic and threatening, and he escapes with his humanity barely intact. In the second half of the play, which theatergoers can see on alternate evenings or on marathon days after a dinner break, Peer circumnavigates the world.

•

In Mr. Thomas's older Peer, the weight of his worldliness is reflected in his stance and in his voice. Even as he becomes an international robber baron and sinks more deeply into cynicism, he retains his curious sense of honesty. He never fools himself, ultimately realizing that "life is too high a price to pay for birth," and persisting on a path to enlightenment.

Ms. Conolly finds endearing qualities in Peer's mother and there are also persuasive performances, in a variety of roles, by Stephen Rowe, Philip Goodwin, Wyman Pendleton, Leslie Geraci and Tara Hugo (as the saintly Solveig). For Mr. Lamos and Mr. Thomas, "Peer Gynt" is a virtuosic accomplishment, precisely the kind of work institutional theaters should be attempting.

1989 Ap 11, C17:1

Paying One's Dues

WELCOME TO THE CLUB, music by Cy Coleman; lyrics by Mr. Coleman and A. E. Hotchner; book by Mr. Hotchner; directed by Peter Mark Schifter; musical numbers staged by Patricia Birch; scenery by David Jenkins; costumes by William Ivey Long; lighting by Tharon Musser; sound by Otts Munderloh; orchestrations by Doug Katsaros; vocal arrangements by Mr. Coleman and David Pogue; musical director, Mr. Pogue; production stage manager, Mary Porter Hall; associate producer, Robert R. Larsen. Presented by Mr. Coleman, Mr. Hotchner, William H. Kessler Jr. and Michael M. Weatherly in association with Raymond J. Greenwald. At the Music Box, 239 West 45th Street.

Arlene Meltzer	Marilyn Sokol
Milton Meltzer	Avery Schreiber
Gus Bottomly	Bill Buell
Aaron Bates	Scott Wentworth
Bruce Aiken	Samuel E. Wright
Kevin Bursteter	Scott Waara
Betty Bursteter	Jodi Benson
Carol Bates	Marcia Mitzman
Eve Aiken	Terri White
Winona Shook	Sally Mayes

By FRANK RICH

Handed a free night and 90 bucks of mad money, would any couple choose to see a Broadway musical comedy set in a prison for alimony deadbeats? Apparently the creators of "Welcome to the Club," the new attraction at the Music Box, think so, for they have actually put on a show with songs like "Pay the Lawyer" and "Love Behind Bars" and a production number about a jail break. I didn't laugh, but maybe that's my problem. Until Mel Brooks proved otherwise, who would have believed in the song-and-dance possibilities of Adolf Hitler and Eva Braun?

Even so, A. E. Hotchner, the evening's author, and Cy Coleman, the composer and lyricist, are not Mel Brooks, and they are working on a budget that allows for few Busby Berkeley extravagances. "Welcome to the Club" looks as if it cost less than a typical bout of divorce litigation. Its wit is largely restricted to ethnic jokes ("I was out of there faster than a matzoh from the Vatican!"), a reference to Vanna White and the usual variations on "Take my wife; please." The most raucous response at a critics' preview was reserved for a lyric that placed the term mother-in-law in repeated, one might say obsessive, proximity to a sexual epithet.

•

If mother-in-law jokes sound antediluvian in 1989, they are all too typical of a musical that, though "set in the present," according to the Playbill, is embarrassingly out of touch with the present-day realities of men, women, sex, marriage and divorce. Comedy must have some basis in truth to be funny, yet every detail in Mr. Hotchner's book seems to have wafted down from a mysogynist time warp where women are all castrating kvetches and the ideal marriage resembles the one embalmed on top of a wedding cake.

The male inmates of "Welcome to the Club" are a demographic cross section of clichés: a henpecked middle-aged Jewish pharmacist (Avery Schreiber), a sensitive young writer (Scott Wentworth), a black insurance salesman (Samuel E. Wright) and a yuppie in suspenders (Scott Waara). We are asked to believe that these middle-class careerists would all rather stay in jail than pay up, even though three of the four long to return to their wives in time for the happy ending promised by the opening song. In Mr. Hotchner's view, divorce not only leads to marital reconciliation but it also has no impact on children (who are invisible here) and no deeper causes than a wife's overuse of a Bloomingdale's charge card. Even the slammer is a lark — a spacious health club where one can order out for pizza and be coddled by a lovesick, soon-to-be-wed corrections officer named Gus.

•

Granted, it might be preposterous for a musical comedy to emulate "Scenes From a Marriage," but "Welcome to the Club" offers less in the way of gritty domestic reality than most television commercials for leading headache remedies. Reflecting the absence of credible characters or drama or emotions, Mr. Hotchner's book dispenses with scenes and story for idle song cues.

Let someone say the word incommunicado and there will be a song about communicating; let someone take a swig of Southern Comfort, and a fantasy sequence will re-enact the Civil War. For no convincing reason, there are two campy fantasy numbers (one per act) about resort towns: "Rio" and "Miami Beach." Country-western numbers are

dragged in with the belated arrival of a female inmate, a cowgirl recording star who also serves as the convenient love interest for the sole male prisoner who can't go home again.

Sally Mayes, a firm-voiced performer new to New York, underplays the role of the Dolly Parton clone, and she is easily the most charming surprise in Peter Mark Schifter's production. With the exception of Marcia Mitzman, who delivers a gratuitous pull-out-the-stops ballad with warmth and poise, the rest of the company is either wasted (Terri White and Jodi Benson), bland or, in the case of the repellently stereotyped Jewish couple (Mr. Schreiber and Marilyn Sokol), unwatchable. Nearly as hid-

Peter Cunningham

Terri White in Cy Coleman's new musical, "Welcome to the Club," at the Music Box Theater.

eous is David Jenkins's set, the most conspicuous feature of which, prison bars aside, is a well-marked entrance to a rest room.

•

Patricia Birch's modest musical staging, Tharon Musser's lighting and William Ivey Long's costumes brighten up the scene when they can, and so, on occasion, does Mr. Coleman's first score for the stage since "Barnum" in 1980. Mr. Coleman writes music with a Tin Pan Alley bounce that makes one feel good to be in a Broadway theater. In common with "Wildcat," "Seesaw" and "I Love My Wife," this Coleman project has a better score than the material merits, but the quality is too inconsistent to galvanize the show. Several numbers sound like retreads — among them, an opera parody reminiscent of "On the Twentieth Century" — and, given the night's subject, every song would benefit from lyrics by either of Mr. Coleman's brilliant women collaborators of the past, Carolyn Leigh ("Little Me") and Dorothy Fields ("Sweet Charity").

But Leigh and Fields are dead now, and Mr. Coleman must make do with prosaic words of his own. As a season almost bereft of new musicals nears its end, "Welcome to the Club" leaves one feeling far more disturbed about the extinction of the songwriting teams that once electrified Broadway than about the humdrum breakups of husbands and wives.

1989 Ap 14, C3:1

Mysterious Ways

EARLY ONE EVENING AT THE RAINBOW BAR AND GRILLE, by Bruce Graham; directed by Pamela Berlin; setting by Edward T. Gianfrancesco; lighting by Craig Evans; costumes by Mimi Maxmen; sound by Aural Fixation; production stage manager, Carol Fishman. Presented by WPA Theater, Kyle Renick, artistic director; Donna Lieberman, managing director. At 519 West 23d Street.

Shep .... Dan Butler
Roy .... Gregory Grove
Willy .... Jay Patterson
Jake Bullard .... Kent Broadhurst
Shirley .... Sharon Ernster
Virginia .... Julie White
Joe .... William Wise

By MEL GUSSOW

God is just a guy named Joe in Bruce Graham's apocalyptical comedy, "Early One Evening at the Rainbow Bar and Grille." As played by William Wise, He is an amiable fellow, but the concept is at least as old as George Burns — and the playwright does not offer an excess of interesting variations. The play, which was first presented at the Philadelphia Festival Theater for New Plays, is at the WPA.

The long first act is devoted to setting the scene, a bar in a small Pennsylvania town — one of Edward T. Gianfrancesco's most vivid environments. Anyone who wants to open a bar or a grille should contact this imaginative scenic designer.

The town is beset by a sudden, world-threatening disaster, but life seems to go on as usual. The bartender (Dan Butler), a hopeful writer of fiction and a patient listener, appears to be undiscouraged even when he is considering suicide. For the versatile Mr. Butler, the mild-mannered character is the reverse of the roguish producer he played recently in "The Emerald City."

Momentarily enlivening the scene are a gas pump jockey, a rifle-bearing marksman and a gym teacher (Julia White) soon to be the bartender's love interest. The play circles the main issue (death and destruction) while the playwright (the author of "Burkie") paints local color and the characters exchange small talk. Under the direction of Pamela Berlin, the actors — especially Mr. Butler and Ms. White — help to pass the time.

Finally God arrives, expresses an uncommon familiarity with the personal lives of the other characters and orders a gin and tonic. Being divine, He knows where the missing lime is — behind the ketchup bottle. So much for miracles, at least for the moment. His theological approach is summarized by the line, "I adlib a lot."

Mr. Butler and Ms. White seem rather too easily convinced of His powers, but the others remain more skeptical. While awaiting their fate, the characters (including God) tell jokes about religion and other matters, some of them ungodly. Donald Trump and Barry Manilow, among others, are the subjects of punchlines. In a moment of crisis, Mr. Wise even attempts a knock-knock joke that would be spotted by a 6-year-old. No wonder He eventually drinks Maalox straight from the bottle.

The humor comes largely from showing how down to earth a divinity can be. In other words, the play is like a comedy sketch that outwears its welcome. Despite occasional smiles and ingratiating performances in the leading roles, "Early One Evening" drifts idly to its conclusion, which is no way for an end-of-the-world play to end.

1989 Ap 14, C34:5

STAGE VIEW/Benedict Nightingale

Success Blunts The Fangs Of a Biting Spoof

"FORBIDDEN BROADWAY." The very title is clearly meant to suggest something clandestine and a bit wicked. And in its early years, in 1983 or 1984, Gerard Alessandrini's revue did indeed leave you feeling that you'd been sharing the evening murk with a cabal of performing witches and warlocks, assembled to stick verbal pins into effigies of their theatrical enemies — and inflict pain, if not on their bodies, at least on their egos. Nothing more entertainingly malignant was to be found on any New York stage. The art of satire, dead elsewhere, had been surreptitiously resurrected at Palsson's supper club on Manhattan's Upper West Side.

The voodoo seems less forbidden and more public these days. There are currently productions of the revue in Boston and Del Ray Beach, Fla. Starting next month, a national road company will take it to St.

Louis and Louisville, Ky., among other destinations. And the show is by now so firmly ensconced in its new Manhattan base — at Theater East, where it moved from Palsson's last fall — that it is wise to book tickets a good month in advance.

On top of all this, a London version has recently opened, its American title unchanged, in the very heart of the West End. "Forbidden Broadway" has become an institution, and not just a New York one.

Alastair Mui

Michael Fenton Stevens and Jenny Michelmore send up "The Phantom of the Opera" in London's "Forbidden Broadway."

That, of course, is the problem. Another feeling the show gave one in the early 1980's, less fanciful than that of being present at some occult rite, was that one was watching the revenge of Restaurant Row. Broadway's unwilling waiters and alienated waitresses were making it clear what they really thought of the musicals for which they'd unsuccessfully auditioned and of the successful people they hence had to serve with a smile. It was a way of pouring hot soup over a smug star's head without getting fired. At Theater East they still encourage this comparison.

The show actually begins with an actress emerging from the audience, wearing an

In London and New York, the vengeful voodoo of 'Forbidden Broadway' has mellowed into an institution.

apron, to share her bewilderment:

Sarah Brightman is fine,
Peter Allen divine,
But I ask myself till I turn blue,
Who do they know?
Who gets them where they want to go?

But somehow it has become hard to believe she remembers very much about waiting on tables.

It is even harder to sense resentment, envy and the other unlovely emotions that once spiced "Forbidden Broadway" in the company newly arrived in the West End. There are at least two reasons for this. First, the London theater community is less fiercely competitive than its New York counterpart, and the city's restaurants are considerably less dependent on "resting" actors.

Second, the company at the Fortune Theater is often required to spend its already rather slim talent for mimicry on performers far less familiar to it than to any American: Mary Martin, Carol Channing, Ann Miller, Chita Rivera, the late Ethel Merman. One no longer gets a burlesque of "La Cage aux Folles" in the latest Manhattan version of "Forbidden Broadway." Yet a travesty George Hearn is to be found intoning "I ham what I ham" in London, even though the musical itself folded there many moons ago and was no great success in the first place. Little wonder his impassioned boast comes across so wanly.

Not that Mr. Alessandrini — director and lyricist in London, as in New York — has altogether neglected local targets. A spoof Roger Moore, the actor who was expected to star in Andrew Lloyd Webber's new musical, "Aspects of Love," sings a James Bond theme while the celebrated composer creeps balefully above the stage, stroking a fluffy white cat: "Lloyd Webber, he's the man with the Midas touch, the man with the spider's touch."

There's a nice parody of the song, "It's Almost Like Being in Love," aimed at the current West End craze for reviving American musicals: " 'Brigadoon' is in town, 'South Pacific' has closed down, it's almost like 1948." Nor has Mr. Alessandrini failed to notice — who could? — the curious proliferation of Shakespeare history plays right now in London. "Brush up your Richard, start wearing your hump," chant three identical Crookbacks, leering and buckling in lopsided unison.

One of the current productions of "Richard III" is being staged by the Royal Shakespeare Company, which itself becomes the subject of a burlesque of the racecourse song from the movie of "My Fair Lady." Snooty nobs in Ascot finery ask one another, "Don't you feel good if you've seen John Gielgud?" and then coldly watch a passing play, blandly proclaiming the experience "orgasmic, Jacobi outdid Olivier."

But the shot misses its victims' viscera. It's not just that John Gielgud does not perform for the R.S.C. The quintessential company supporter is earnestly middle class and far more likely to wear jeans and a jersey than morning dress. What makes the R.S.C. vulnerable to satire is that it's intellectually fashionable, not that it's socially chic.

■

The New York company's collective fingers remain more confidently on their world's theatrical pulse. Its members have a deadly feel for the mannered stutterings and stammerings of David Mamet's dialogue, and they have some pertinent questions to ask about the sexual plausibility of "M. Butterfly." They seem more streetwise, sharper and also more skillful than their British cousins, even when they're singing the same lyrics about the same British shows: "Cats," say, or what they call "Starlight Excess," with its "computer laser effects, hydraulic scenic design and wireless headset sound."

The most effective parody on each side of the Atlantic is of "Les Misérables," which is amiably accused of being long, ineptly plotted, confusing, scruffy, depressing, too British, too French, musically boring and mercenary in its offstage marketing: "Rich folks pay 20 bucks [for] a shirt that has a starving pauper on it." The American version of the number is, however, the more memorably gawky and bedraggled.

■

It doesn't help the British performers that the Fortune, though small, is a conventionally shaped playhouse, less informal and intimate than Theater East. Again, it doesn't help them that the London theater itself is so much less circumscribed and more productive than Broadway — how can they be sure that their audiences will be familiar with the local counterparts of "Speed-the-Plow" or "Legs Diamond"?

Yet one still wonders if the New York cast is fully exploiting its advantages, either of place or of professional flair. Isn't there something just a bit, well, cozy about "Forbidden Broadway" as it has evolved in its own hometown?

For those who like a bit of venom in their revues, it's not especially en-

There's a touch of vitriol left in this satire, but no one's flesh is rawly exposed.

couraging to read in one of the show's brochures that "the stars themselves can't help loving the stylish parodies and in one or two cases — Stephen Sondheim amongst them — have helped by providing material and real support."

Maybe that's why a number called "Into the Words" comes across more as a compliment to that songwriter's convoluted originality than a nose thumbed at it. Certainly, it's hard to believe that Anthony Quinn "loved" the parody of him that trundled and creaked onstage back in 1984, looking like a geriatric man-elephant: "Zorba's what he'll do while he's waiting to die; Zorba is his last big try." There's a touch of vitriol in the show's portrayals of Sarah Brightman, "a nightingale on LSD," and of Liza "one-note" Minnelli. But it doesn't eat very far into any performer's skin; it doesn't leave anyone's flesh rawly exposed.

This is, of course, a familiar enough development, similar to what happened to "All in the Family" and several other television shows at first praised for their bite. The teeth get blunter; the fun becomes more and more affectionate; attack becomes narcissistic celebration. The audience begins to react as the audience reacted at a recent matinee at Theater East, as if it were reviving its acquaintance with likable if eccentric old friends.

This would matter more, one supposes, if politicians or bureaucrats or a class of person more powerful than singers or actors were being parodied. But these days there is so little satire of any sort in America, on stage, film or television, that one feels bound to voice some regret — and, with it, a not altogether facetious suggestion. Perhaps the servers and dishwashers of Restaurant Row should turn their attention to the successful performers so solidly established at Theater East. Perhaps it's time for a forbidden "Forbidden Broadway." □

1989 Ap 16, II:7:1

Blood on the Drawing-Room Floor

THE THIRTEENTH CHAIR, by Bayard Veiller; directed by Maggie Jackson; scenic design, James A. Bazewicz; lighting design, Douglas Cox; costume design, Lisa LoCurto; sound design, Hector Milia; production stage manager, Carol Venezia. Presented by Equity Library Theater, 103d Street and Riverside Drive.

Helen O'Neill	Malia Ondrejka
Will Crosby	T. Ryder Smith
Mrs. Crosby	Maxine Taylor-Morris
Roscoe Crosby	Daniel Nalbach
Edward Wales	Bob Horen
Mary Eastwood	Mare Kenney
Helen Trent	Rosemary Keough
Grace Standish	Ellen Orchid
Braddish Trent	David Rose
Howard Standish	Peter Blaxill
Philip Mason	Tom Spivey
Elizabeth Erskine	Alison Trattner
Pollock	Joseph Scott
Rosalie LaGrange	Babs Hooyman
Inspector Tim Donohue	Hewitt Brooks
Sergeant Dunn	Bernard Ferstenberg
Policeman and Doolan	Mike Kimmel

By RICHARD F. SHEPARD

Years ago, when movies were in their infancy and television was not even a gleam in an inventor's eye, theater had a stranglehold on what is now called light entertainment. But as the new Equity Library Theater production of a 1916 mystery, "The Thirteenth Chair," indicates, stylish drama like other fashion goes out of style.

Ned Synder

Babs Hooyman in a scene from "The Thirteenth Chair."

"The Thirteenth Chair" is as rusty a vehicle as has creaked across a stage in current seasons, but there is no mystery about why this whodunit by Bayard Veiller was attractive to the company, which is commendably dedicated to serving as a showcase for professional talent: it has 18 roles. It is a period piece, the kind that came to a full stop years ago, a wordy drawing-room murder in which almost nothing you see gives you a clue until the guilty party collapses at the finale.

•

The son of a wealthy family intends to marry a pretty but poor young woman whose mother is déclassé Irish in that old New York of the setting. A friend of the family asks that the announcement be delayed one day and has arranged for Rosalie LaGrange, a raffish, outspoken and distinctly un-Gallic Irish medium, to conduct a seance. She's a character who reveals tricks of her trade but promises to play things straight on this evening.

She and the 12 guests sit in the usual hand-holding circle; lights dim; voices discuss the recent murder of a man known to all present; a gasp is heard; the lights go on, and the meddlesome family friend is dead of a stab in the back. Whodunit? That is what Inspector Tim Donohue, dap-

per, talkative and deductive as all get-out, intends to learn. That is the play.

•

Maggie Jackson's direction of this cast of attractive performers provides occasional light moments and an overall patina of good-natured forbearance, humor and affection. Babs Hooyman, as the medium, gives a robust performance that creates fun out of the essential hamminess of the part. Malia Ondrejka, as the romantic lead, is beauteous and also may be the one who comes closest to fashioning a real person out of her role. Hewitt Brooks makes an urbane inspector and, considering the tonnage of verbiage he has to deliver, injects a welcome undertone of playfulness to the part.

"The Thirteenth Chair" is a museum piece and only the mood in which you approach it will determine whether it comes across as hopeless melodrama or as light mellow drama.

1989 Ap 16, 61:1

Anatomy Of an Explosion

WALKERS, by Marion Isaac McClinton; directed by Steven Ramay and Mr. McClinton; set and light design by Paul Wonsek; costume design by Elsa Ward; sound design by Craig R. Zaionz; stage manager, Fredrick Hahn. Presented by the Hudson Guild Theater, Geoffrey Sherman, producing and artistic director; Mr. Ramay, associate director. At 441 West 26th Street.

Walker Gillette Walker	Terry E. Bellamy
Woman	Iona Morris
Annalisa Walker	Faye M. Price
Boston Westinghouse (Wes Jr.) Walker	Ron Dortch
Boston Westinghouse Walker Sr.	John Henry Redwood
Danny Skynner	James A. Williams

By STEPHEN HOLDEN

"Walkers," an enraged but exasperatingly sketchy new drama by Marion Isaac McClinton, a Minnesota-based playwright, tackles so many serious themes that only a four-

hour epic tragedy could begin to develop them into a cohesive dramatic tapestry. Racism, black self-hatred and inherited patterns of family violence are only the three most obvious issues among those raised by the play, at the Hudson Guild Theater, 441 West 26th Street.

Instead of creating a sprawling family history, the playwright has telescoped a story with overtones of Greek tragedy into a two-hour psychological mystery that makes a lot of noise but conveys little emotional resonance. The unhappy story of the Walkers, a poor black family from Virginia, is revealed in melodramatic flashbacks as a prison psychiatrist interrogates Walker Gillette Walker (Terry E. Bellamy), a young policeman who has gone berserk and killed his wife and children.

•

The psychiatrist, Danny Skynner (James A. Williams), is a hollow dramatic contrivance whose psychic soundings of a prisoner who can't remember his crimes consist of asking him to reconstruct past events as though they were scenes in a movie. In addition to Walker and the psychiatrist, we eventually meet Walker's retired boxer father, Boston (John Henry Redwood), his older brother, Boston Jr. (Ron Dortch) and his adored younger sister, Annalisa (Faye M. Price).

The Walker children have been indoctrinated in despair. Boston Sr., who once fought Sonny Liston, philosophizes in portentous boxing metaphors and describes life as "a knockout punch." Remembering his past, the killer, who is given to blustery poetic diatribes, becomes an oratorical mouthpiece for the playwright. Soliloquies about trout fishing, Disneyland and the Holy Trinity are meant to evoke what might otherwise be inexpressible. But the language and imagery are so heavy-handed and at times incoherent that they retard the drama and quickly come to seem like the playwright's ill-advised shortcuts to constructing a dramatic narrative.

•

Co-directed by the playwright with Steven Ramay, the drama unfolds on

Gerry Goodstein

Terry E. Bellamy, left, and James A. Williams in "Walkers."

a nearly bare interrogation-room set. As Walker's memory returns, the characters drift in from the wings to do psychological battle with one another. But the gaps in the story are so enormous that we never become familiar with any of the Walker family members.

The production's most sensitive performance belongs to Ms. Price, who projects an enormous bitterness and vulnerability. But far too much about her life remains unexplained. When we first meet Annalisa, she is a youngster about to attend her mother's funeral. In her next appearance, she has just been released from prison. All we are told about the intervening years is something vague about drugs.

In its present form, "Walkers" plays like an outline for a much larger work.

1989 Ap 16, 60:1

Love and Deceit in Old Spain

THE PHANTOM LADY, by Pedro Calderón de la Barca; translated by Edwin Honig; directed by Julian Webber; set design by Stephan Olson; costume design, Patricia Adshead; lighting design, Donald Holder; fight director, Jim Manley; music composed, selected and arranged by Jared Walker, stage manager, Nina L. Heller; production manager, David Waggett. Presented by SoHo Repertory Theater, Marlene Swartz, artistic director. At Greenwich House, 27 Barrow Street.

Don Manuel	Donald Berman
Cosme	Gregor Paslawsky
Doña Angela	Monique Fowler
Isabel	Anne O'Sullivan
Don Luis	Brian P. Glover
Don Juan	Richard McMillan
Doña Beatriz	Valerie Charles
Guitar	Jared Walker

By RICHARD F. SHEPARD

"The Phantom Lady," which is now being offered by the SoHo Rep as an American debut, has a certain documented durability about it. The comedy was written by the great Spanish playwright Pedro Calderón de la Barca in 1629, when New York was still New Amsterdam and a Broadway house was a tepee. In an eloquent and often poetic English translation by Edwin Honig, this new production captures what was surely the robust spirit of the original.

The story is about, well, it's one of those 300-year-old comedies with a complicated plot, lots of people running from room to room and mistaking what they've seen and jumping to false conclusions. Doña Angela, boldly and handsomely portrayed by Monique Fowler, is the widowed sister of Don Juan (Richard McMillan) and Don Luis (Brian P. Glover), two patrician traditionalists who keep her sequestered and in basic mourning-black. She is a strong-minded woman who wants as much freedom to choose men as men have to choose women.

In her attempts at flight from austerity she meets Don Manuel (Donald Berman), the dashing friend of Don Juan. Love naturally results, although he doesn't know who she is, and that establishes the runabout format of everything that follows. Not quite as hilarious as when the Marx Brothers, who followed Calderón de la Barca, did it, but quite amusing just the same.

The director Julian Webber gives highest tribute to the venerable

work; that is, he does not ossify it but breathes life into it, even as the trappings of Old Spain are preserved. The characters, clad in 1600's speech and garb, have a universality about them and there is a genial mood that laughs with the play rather than at it.

For one thing, the performers are affectionately immersed in their parts. The two noble brothers particularly manifest a comic presence with their posturing and their romantic hyperbole. Mr. McMillan gives us a pompously pinch-faced and verbose character who can roll his eyes and pull a word out of the air by grasping with his long, theatrical fingers. Mr. Glover is funnily lugubrious as the brother who can get nowhere with the ladies and who sneers, "The last resort of jealousy is to destroy the happiness of others." Mr. Berman, in the more prosaic role of the hero, bravely stands up to the comic competition.

A hallmark of comedy, particularly the more antique kind, is the part for a faithful servant who is trustworthy, loyal, wise, completely irreverent and capable of winning a laugh at a moment of crisis. Here the two servants are ebulliently created — sweetly by Anne O'Sullivan, as the lady's maid, and tartly by Gregor Paslawsky, as the servant of the hero. The cast is filled out by Valerie Charles, as Don Juan's beloved, and Jared Walker, who sits on one side of the stage and strums tunes that provide an attractive audio backdrop for Stephan Olson's simple yet effective sets and Patricia Adshead's eyecatching costumes.

1989 Ap 16, 60:1

Malice Aforethought

BRIMSTONE AND TREACLE, by Dennis Potter; directed by Rosemary Hay; scenic design, Christina Weppner; lighting design, Frances Aronson; costume design, Martha Bromelmeier; sound design, Vito Ricci; still photography, Ruby J. Levesque; production stage manager, Debora E. Kingston; assistant director, John Bjostad; supervising producer, Richard Husson. Presented by Margot Lewitin, artistic director. At the Interart Theater, 549 West 52d Street.

Pattie	Shula Van Buren
Mrs. Bates	Maggie Soboil
Mr. Bates	Frank Lazarus
Martin	Rudy Caporaso

By MEL GUSSOW

Demonism is the subject, hypocrisy the subtext in Dennis Potter's "Brimstone and Treacle." This is Mr. Potter's own stage adaptation of his television play, which later became a movie starring Sting, Denholm Elliott and Joan Plowright. As directed by Rosemary Hay at the Interart Theater, "Brimstone and Treacle" is a distinctive Potter's brew, concocted from a recipe of insidious ingredients. The play, staged in sharp, mock-Gothic fashion, is grotesquely amusing.

A young man named Martin Taylor (Rudy Caporaso) insinuates himself into a seemingly ordinary English household. He is even weirder than other opportunistic English outsiders in plays by writers like Joe Orton and Harold Pinter. As the husband (Frank Lazarus) says to Martin, "You might be a pickpocket or the devil himself." He is correct on both counts.

The family's daughter has been incapacitated as the result of an automobile accident. Unable to communicate, she twitches violently. Martin introduces himself to her parents as

her loving friend — and offers to assist in her care as well as in the housework. Having just encountered God as an ordinary Joe in Bruce Graham's "Early Evening in the Rainbow Bar and Grille," we now see Satan as a super-nanny. The wife (Maggie Soboil), a mass of worry lines furrowing her brow, is happy to share her overburdening responsibility, but the husband is suspicious of a man with no credentials or means of support.

In the 1982 film version, it was clear from the opening minutes that Martin was a confidence man. The play leaves that question up in the air at least for a time, though more than in the movie it is obvious that he is the devil incarnate or at least a fiendish facsimile, a fact that is occasionally telegraphed by the actor to the audience. The film was more intent on picturing the mundane realities of the

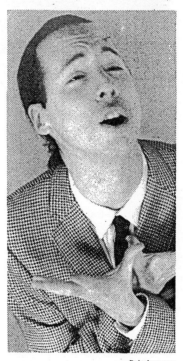

Ruby Levesque

Rudy Caporaso in a scene from "Brimstone and Treacle."

family life and in posing parallels between the stranger's sorcery and the husband's pseudopieties (he writes evangelical homilies).

At least in Ms. Hay's production, the play is more interested in the

comedy, underscored in Mr. Caporaso's malicious performance. The theatrical version, confined to a sin-

Inviting in a stranger who's really *strange*.

gle room, is tighter and, in a good sense, more claustrophobic. In place of Sting's film score, between the scenes are heard popular songs dealing with witchcraft, magic and deviltry as sources of romance, which is Martin's attitude in the play itself.

When backs are turned, lightning crashes and that old black magic begins to weave its spell. Martin plays a cat and mouse game with the couple, wooing the wife with endearments like Mumsy. The husband keeps his distance until he realizes that Martin is a gourmet cook. Apparently, the way to his soul is through boeuf bourguignon.

Although "Brimstone and Treacle" does not aspire to the depth of "The Singing Detective" and Mr. Potter's other more notable work, it has its own macabre charm and more than a measure of social commentary about middle-class morality.

Under Ms. Hay's direction, the couple is as drab as the faded wallpaper (but more fun to watch). Even the husband's neo-Nazism is presented as a banality and his wife is a walking tea cozy. Christina Weppner's set design suitably accents the dreariness. Both Mr. Lazarus and Ms. Soboil are resourceful and Shula Van Buren choreographs her spasms as the ailing daughter.

The fork-tongued center of this menage is Mr. Caporaso's Martin (the role played on screen by Sting). In contrast to his predecessor, the stage Martin is more closely approximate to the father's low opinion of the character. Only the gullible mother could imagine that the daughter would have had a relationship with him. Mr. Caporaso deftly manages the difficult task of being both sinister and sentimental, as in the title of the play. "Brimstone and Treacle" leaves a scent of sulfur in the air — and we can hear the dogs of hell barking — as the author sardonically suggests that diabolism is not necessarily deleterious to one's mental health.

1989 Ap 18, C15:3

On Stage, the Feminist Message Takes on a Sly and Subtle Tone

By FRANK RICH

On Friday night I joined a capacity audience at the Plymouth Theater to hear the lectures of the art historian Dr. Heidi Holland, as performed by the actress Joan Allen in Wendy Wasserstein's play "The Heidi Chronicles." Although I'd seen "The Heidi Chronicles" before, I hadn't quite noticed how comprehensively Dr. Hol-

land — and the author who created her — folded a feminist art history lesson, with slides, into the creases of a play that is otherwise an unpedagogical account of a woman's life in the far-from-academic world of 1965 to 1989.

Dr. Holland's lesson may not be new, but her presentation of it is spirited. She reminds her students — and us — that female artists were until recently absent from textbooks and that even now they are underrepresented. And as Dr. Holland stands at the lectern, flashlight pointer in hand, she illuminates how a woman's mind and soul are at work in the paintings

The women have equal weight in a new 'Sweeney Todd'

of several centuries. Ms. Allen does this with such humor that no one in the audience could possibly mistake the Plymouth Theater for the New School.

"The Heidi Chronicles," of course, is itself an artwork by a woman, and, had I not known the author since roughly Act I, Scene 5 (New York, 1977) in the play's chronology, journalistic ethics would not forbid me from going on about it. But I can say that the lessons taught by Dr. Heidi Holland and Wendy Wasserstein were very much with me the day after my visit to the Plymouth when I saw an altogether extraordinary production of "Sweeney Todd," directed by Susan H. Schulman and presented by the York Theater Company in its playhouse at the Church of the Heavenly Rest on the Upper East Side.

•

Like most of the people in the York's audience, I suspect, I have seen "Sweeney Todd" many times with various casts. But I had never seen "Sweeney Todd" — or, if memory serves, any Sondheim musical — directed by a woman. (With very occasional exceptions, women have been welcome as choreographers but not as directors of Broadway musicals.) Ms. Schulman's production raises many issues about Mr. Sondheim's piece, starting most obviously with the matter of scale. Her "Sweeney Todd" is in one of the tiniest Off Off Broadway theaters, while Harold Prince's initial staging of a decade ago was in the largest Broadway house, the Gershwin (then the Uris). Still, it is from the human point of view rather than the theatrical perspective that Ms. Schulman most radically rethinks the tale of the demon barber of Fleet Street.

That rethinking is evident in the treatment of two female characters: the major role of the pie-shop proprietress, Mrs. Lovett, originated by Angela Lansbury on Broadway, and the secondary role of an anonymous, foul-mouthed beggar who haunts the action mysteriously until the finale, whereupon, in the satisfying manner of Victorian fiction, she is revealed to be the mad long-lost wife of Sweeney Todd himself.

•

Angela Lansbury's Mrs. Lovett will probably never be equaled. (Those who missed it can rent the exemplary video version of "Sweeney Todd," made during the post-Broadway road tour, with George Hearn in the title role). As the crude, love-starved and amoral purveyor of meat pies made from Sweeney's victims, Ms. Lansbury careered from finely etched Dickensian caricature (with face by Phiz) to grotesque dementia with the same larger-than-life comic savagery that has always distinguished her villains, whether Mr. Sondheim's (the Mayoress of "Anyone Can Whistle") or not (the mother of the Manchurian Candidate). While Ms. Lans-

Martha Swope Associates/Carc
Bob Gunton and Beth Fowler in the York Theater Company production of "Sweeney Todd."

bury's presentation of evil was too witty to be hateful, her Mrs. Lovett was unmistakably a cannibalistic capitalist. She deserved her final push into the oven nearly as much as does the witch in "Hansel and Gretel."

Beth Fowler, an experienced Sondheim performer who has the role at the York, goes about the assignment in another way. Her Mrs. Lovett is more pathetic than conniving, more lost in vague and doomed romantic fantasies about Sweeney Todd than obsessed with making a killing in the meat-pie racket. To put it more concretely, she's closer to Tennessee Williams's Amanda Wingfield than to Ethel Merman's Mama Rose in "Gypsy."

•

Where Ms. Lansbury cagily tried to exploit Sweeney's murderous rampage for her own mercenary ends, Ms. Fowler just goes dully along with his psychotic scheme until she's bonkers herself. Ms. Lansbury's performance found its perfect expression in the Act I finale ("A Little Priest"), a ghoulish duel of jokes with Sweeney. By contrast, Ms. Fowler's intellectual symbiosis with Sweeney seems limited; her maternal relationship with the shop apprentice, Tobias, is more potent, with the result that their song of devotion, "Not While I'm Around," becomes the emotional apex of the second act. Eddie Korbich, who plays and sings Tobias beautifully, completes the picture by treating Mrs. Lovett as the mother he presumably never had.

By the end, Tobias, one of the few survivors of the show's carnage, is consumed by the deep fog of familial loss. And so, strangely enough, given his responsibility for all the bloodshed, is Sweeney Todd, as acted by Bob Gunton. When Mr. Gunton discovers that the beggar woman he murdered was the wife who was raped and stolen from him all those years earlier by the evil Judge Turpin, he cradles her corpse in his arms, sobbing, unable to let go.

The moment would make no sense if the beggar had been the shrill hag she was in the Prince production. SuEllen Estey, the actress now in the part, is as feral as her predecessor,

but there is a sadness in her eyes as she slips along the fringes of the action; a suffering woman lives beneath the rags and derelict's makeup. Dead, she is indeed someone worth mourning, and, in the arms of Mr. Gunton, she is as much his wife as his murder victim. As Sweeney cradles her on the blood-splattered cobblestone road that we look down upon from bleachers, "Sweeney Todd" embraces tragedy.

I have usually been moved by "Sweeney Todd," but never in the way Ms. Schulman's rendering moved me. It is not that the director set out to create a feminist interpretation — which the text cannot support in any case — but that she gives equal weight to female characters who originally came off as stylized slatterns in a man's story. It may be simply that she sees the play's women more fully or has more compassion for them. Whatever the explanation, the balance of "Sweeney Todd" has subtly shifted; the musical

The musical is warmer without being sentimentalized.

is warmed up without being sentimentalized. The audience at the York is held spellbound, and in my experience that wasn't always the case at the Uris.

Some of the credit belongs to the incandescent rage of Mr. Gunton, whose brooding eyes and scalding voice command us, like the victims of his vengeance, to the horrors of the grave. The small theater plays its role as well. Its intimacy, which places the audience cheek by jowl with the throat slittings, turns "Sweeney Todd" into a hot box of passion. But even one who found the Broadway production overblown must concede that Ms. Schulman's staging, resourceful as it often is, sticks fairly close to Mr. Prince's original ideas.

(As did the York's miniaturized "Pacific Overtures," by another director of several seasons back.) Ms. Schulman's most radical staging revision has been to remove the thematic scenic frame of the Prince version — a huge foundry that symbolized the dehumanization and class oppression of the Industrial Revolution — and t keep the focus on the pie shop.

By stripping the Brechtian from the physical production and from Mrs. Lovett (who now has lost what resemblance she once had to Mrs. Peachum and Mother Courage), Ms. Schulman doesn't rob the work of its class politics, which are taken care of by the libretto anyway, but she reclaims it as an arena for its characters, men and women and children alike. The dark heart of the play, the story of a man's revenge against a society that destroyed his wife and daughter, stands revealed.

Susan H. Schulman's "Sweeney Todd" ends its limited run at the York on April 29. Is there no way to prolong its life so that more of Heidi Holland's students — and Stephen Sondheim's for that matter — might be able to discover its revelations?

1989 Ap 19, C15:

Speaker and Listener

SERIOUS COMPANY — AN EVENING OF ONE ACT PLAYS, directed by Susan Flakes; sets b Shelley Barclay; lighting by Joshua Star buck; costumes by Jennifer Straniere; production stage manager, Gigi Rivkin; general manager, Michael Stotts. Presented by th Source Foundation, Ms. Flakes, artistic director. At the Apple Corps Theater, 336 West 20t Street.

SWAN SONG, by Anton Chekhov.
Vasily Svetlovidov .... Conrad L. Osborn
Nikita .... Frank Gerac

THE STRONGER, by August Strindberg.
Mlle. Y .... Katina Comming
Mrs. X .... Diane Salinge
Waitress .... Gigi Rivki

HUGHIE, by Eugene O'Neill.
Erie Smith .... Austin Pendleto
A Night Clerk .... Mr. Gerac

By MEL GUSSOW

Each of the one-act plays grouped under the title "Serious Company" is a monologue, or near-monologue, and a natural for an actor's audition. Play the proper notes and they would seem to be three easy pieces.

In the current production at the Apple Corps Theater, however, only Eugene O'Neill's "Hughie" comes to life and that because of Austin Pendleton's performance in the central role. The two other plays — Chekhov's brief vaudeville "Swan Song" and Strindberg's study of a marital triangle, "The Stronger" — are given desultory performances. The plays are a production of the Source Foundation, and are directed by Susan Flakes.

•

As Erie Smith, the small-time Broadway gambler, Mr. Pendleton emphasizes the character's seediness and his loneliness. Having staked his confidence on the admiration of the hotel night clerk, Hughie, Erie is bereft without him. With a new clerk in Hughie's place, Erie tries to get the old magic working again, but he is condemned to a life of solitaire. In his heart he knows that he is jinxed, an aspect that Mr. Pendleton captures with a kind of nervous bravado.

The performance is in contrast to that of Jason Robards, who created the role on Broadway in 1964. Mr.

Pendleton's Erie has clearly depleted his resilience; he is fueled only by his remembrance of the time when Hughie was the audience for his pipe dreams.

Each of the plays has two characters — a speaker and a listener. Both are essential and it is with the listener that the production of "Hughie" falters. Frank Geraci's dapper night clerk seems out of place in this flea-bag midtown hotel.

"Swan Song," Chekhov's first vaudeville sketch, is a Russian fore-bear of "A Life in the Theater," an aging actor's lament recounted to a prompter who inhabits the stage like a theater cat. As performed by Conrad L. Osborne (as the actor) and Mr. Geraci, the play loses its humor. Though it lasts barely 20 minutes, it seems long and somber.

The production of "The Stronger" is more promising, but Diane Salinger, in the speaking role, occasionally overacts and Katina Commings, perhaps in response, overreacts. In each case, the words and the absence of words should speak for themselves. This was certainly the case some years ago when Geraldine Page and Amy Wright played the enigmatic Mlle. Y and the loquacious Mrs. X. Through no fault of the authors, the Chekhov and the Strindberg become time-consuming curtain-raisers to "Hughie."

1989 Ap 19, C19:1

Cartoon Characters, Real and Imagined

YOUNG RUBE, book by George W. George and Matty Selman; music and lyrics by Mr. Selman; directed by Mark Herko; set design consultant, David Mitchell; lighting design, Richard Latta; costume design, Amanda J. Klein; musical director, Bryan Louiselle; production stage manager, Alan Fox; choreographer, Margie Castleman. Presented by Musical Theater Works, Anthony J. Stimac, artistic director, Mr. Herko, associate artistic director. At St. Peter's Church, 54th Street and Lexington Avenue.

WITH: Adinah Alexander, Maria Bostick, Kenneth Boys, Hal Hudson, Joan Jaffe, Skip Lackey, Gary Kirsch, Mike O'Carroll, Robert Polenz, Keith Savage, Don Stephenson and Miki Whittles.

By STEPHEN HOLDEN

Near the end of the first act of "Young Rube," a new musical that focuses on the adolescence of the legendary cartoonist Rube Goldberg, a bunch of the wacky characters who have been percolating in his mind surround him onstage and urge him to pursue his artistic aspirations. "We can't draw ourselves; you've got to try," they plead in the song "We're Counting On You." For a moment, one hopes that what until then has been a lifeless paint-by-number show will demonstrate a spark of life and that the inner world of the cartoonist's imagination will at last be revealed. But the leap is never made.

Instead of finding witty theatrical and musical corollaries to Goldberg's fantastic contraptions, "Young Rube," a presentation of Musical Theater Works at St. Peter's Church, concentrates on the adolescent cartoonist's conflicts with his boorish father and his difficulties holding a job. When we first meet him, he is awkwardly cavorting with one of his characters, the clownish Boob McNutt. But the real people in the young

man's life — his placard-toting feminist girlfriend, Tillie (Maria Bostick); his father, Max (Mike O'Carroll), and the dictatorial editor of The San Francisco Chronicle, Harry Mayo Bunker (Robert Polenz) — are as one-dimensional as the imaginary ones.

The biggest deficit of the show, whose book was written by the cartoonist's son, George W. George, in collaboration with Matty Selman, who also provided the music and lyrics, is a sense of humor. The strictly expository dialogue lacks any kind of wit, and under Mark Herko's direction, the actors move and talk like stick figures. Skip Lackey, the young actor afflicted with the title role, has a hard time carrying a tune and in all the exuberance he displays there is not an ounce of charm.

Mr. Selman's score is a simplified pastiche of turn-of-the-century styles, from ragtime to Gilbert and Sullivan. The musical arrangements for a small ensemble are crammed with cartoonish sound effects that jar the ear as they try to inject a sense of fun. "Young Rube" makes the fatal mistake of presenting the maturation of a sophisticated comic artist as a singing Saturday morning cartoon.

1989 Ap 21, C3:4

Ivory Tower

ARISTOCRATS, by Brian Friel; directed by Robin Lefèvre; scenery by John Lee Beatty; costumes by Jane Greenwood; lighting by Dennis Parichy; sound by John A. Leonard; production stage manager, Tom Aberger. Presented by Manhattan Theater Club, Lynne Meadow, artistic director; Barry Grove, managing director. At Theater Four, 424 West 55th Street.

Willie Diver	John Christopher Jones
Tom Hoffnung	Peter Crombie
Uncle George	Thomas Barbour
Casimir	Niall Buggy
Alice	Margaret Colin
Eamon	John Pankow
Claire	Haviland Morris
Judith	Kaiulani Lee
Father	Joseph Warren
Anna's Voice	Roma Downey

By FRANK RICH

Audiences arriving at Brian Friel's "Aristocrats" are all but enfolded within a panorama of lush Irish greenery. The setting, a heaven-sent assignment for the designer John Lee Beatty, is a Georgian mansion in provincial County Donegal. Moss and ivy crawl over every wall; a towering tree spills leaves from above; an expanse of bright lawn flows from the house's exposed parlor to the stage's edge. It is summer, the mid-1970's, and the sun is out.

What we see is Ireland at its most ravishing, but Ireland being Ireland, and Mr. Friel being arguably the most penetrating Irish playwright of his generation, the skies cannot remain cloudless for long. "Aristocrats," a Manhattan Theater Club presentation at Theater Four, is Mr. Friel's Chopin-flecked "Cherry Orchard" or "Three Sisters," in which the ache of one family becomes a microcosm for the ache of a society. While Mr. Friel's touch in this 1979 work isn't always as subtle as Chekhov's, "Aristocrats" is a lovely play, funny and harrowing. Though the abrupt juxtapositions of the beautiful and the tragic may be any Irish writer's birthright, Mr. Friel makes the Irish condition synonymous with the human one.

Margaret Colin and Niall Buggy in a scene from the Manhattan Theater Club production of "Aristocrats," by Brian Friel.

To be sure, the house on stage, which belongs to a once-powerful district judge, is haunted by the country's troubles, as well as by the literary ghosts of Yeats and O'Casey, who, we're told, may have visited the mansion in its salad days. But if "Aristocrats" expresses the national political concerns hinted at by its ironic title, the politics follow rather than dictate what is largely the intimate drama of a family reunion prompted by an impending wedding and overtaken by illness. Judge O'Donnell has suffered a stroke, and four of his five adult children have gathered at his deathbed.

The O'Donnells are not a happy clan. The engaged daughter, Claire (Haviland Morris), is to marry a drab greengrocer twice her age. Her sister Alice (Margaret Colin) is an alcoholic who lives discontentedly in London with her embittered, lapsed activist of a husband, Eamon (John Pankow). Another sister, Judith (Kaiulani Lee), has given up an illegitimate child to an orphanage even as she is forced to cope with the second, incontinent childhood of her father. Though the lone brother, Casimir (Niall Buggy), purports to have a wife and three children in Hamburg, no one in the family has seen them. "It has the authentic ring of phony fiction," Eamon says of Casimir's obsessive boasts of domestic bliss.

What went wrong? We learn of a mother, long dead, who committed suicide. We sense the tyranny of the Lear-like father, who even now, in near-delirium, bellows humiliating commands through his sickroom intercom. And in the isolation of each

character we see a reflection of the entire household's alienation from Ireland. Even at home, this family is in exile. The judge, a Roman Catholic aristocrat with "a greed for survival," never bothered himself with the civil-rights concerns of his plebeian fellow Catholics in the village below, and yet could never be a part of the Protestant Establishment either. He sent his children abroad to school. He administered the law for whoever happened to be in power.

"Aristocrats" has the ring of phony fiction only when Mr. Friel pounds his Chekhovian notes of decay, notably in the neat final-act resolutions and particularly when he brings on a visiting American academic (Peter Crombie) who is studying the local folkways. The rest of the evening offers the blend of psychological ambiguity and crackling theatrical instinct that has been Mr. Friel's signature since "Philadelphia, Here I Come!" more than 20 years ago. Leave it to this writer to inject the esthetics of Beckett into a heartbreak house by creating an elderly uncle in an elegant white-linen suit (Thomas Barbour) who remains mute as a matter of principle. Mr. Friel's feel for absurdist black comedy is given even fuller vent when the characters sit obediently in lawn chairs before a boom box to listen to a taped, unwittingly callous message from the one absent sister, an insufferably pious nun who fled to Africa 17 years earlier.

This writer's plays must be a joy for actors, and those assembled by the director, Robin Lefèvre (a vistor from London's Hampstead Theater), blossom in impressive tandem with roles that keep turning inside out. It's typical of Mr. Friel's paradoxical way that he would make his most anti-establishment character — the cynical, working-class Eamon — the most nostalgic upholder of Irish cultural tradition by the final curtain. It's typical of Mr. Lefèvre's superb production that Mr. Pankow, an amazingly versatile American actor, is so sensitive to every nuance that the metamorphosis is entirely credible.

All three sisters, also first-rate, undergo similar transformations. The initially sunny Ms. Morris, though too gorgeous to pass for the brood's ugly duckling, gradually comes to resemble her departed, depressive mother. Ms. Colin swings between alcoholic hostility and sweetness, at last to reach an affecting middle ground when she describes how she could reach accommodation with her fearful father only when he could no longer recognize her. Ms. Lee's moment to dazzle comes when she suddenly tightens her voice and jaw, forsaking her previous maternal lilt, to describe her crippled diurnal existence caring for the dying.

•

But it is Casimir, the son, most stifled by the father, who is indelible. The role was originated at the Abbey Theater by John Kavanagh, the brilliant Joxer of the Gate Theater's "Juno and the Paycock" seen in New York. Mr. Buggy, the one-time Abbey actor imported from London for the role here, is another true original. Bald, round and often boasting a child's moony grin, he gives us an excitable, overgrown mother's boy who in middle age retains vast illusions about his heritage (he plays an imaginary croquet game on the lawn) but none about himself.

Casimir knows he has always been a figure of fun, ridiculed by others as either the village idiot or a homosexual. But with his factory job and presumed family in Germany, he has found a way to feel and give happiness without risking "exposure to too much hurt." His hands frequently flying about, his boisterous laughter just one note below hysteria, Mr. Buggy becomes the most fragile Humpty Dumpty; Casimir is a jolly life of the party clinging to that role because his own life depends on it. Only his father, of course, still has the power to send him tumbling back into the terrors of childhood. When the fall comes, as it must, we, too, experience terror, as a grown man collapses into pieces on that beautiful Irish sod and waters it with his tears.

1989 Ap 26, C15:1

Star Lures

STARMITES, music and lyrics by Barry Keating; book by Stuart Ross and Mr. Keating; choreography by Michele Assaf; directed and staged by Larry Carpenter; sets by Lowell Detweiler; costumes by Susan Hirschfeld; lighting by Jason Kantrowitz; sound by John Kilgore; musical direction and dance arrangements by Henry Aronson; orchestrations and sound effects by James McElwaine; associate musical direction and vocal arrangements by Dianne Adams; assistant choreographer, T. C. Charlton; production stage manager, Zoya Wyeth; associate producers, Peter Bogyo, John Burt and Severn Sandt. Presented by Hinks Shimberg, Mary Keil and Steven Warnick. At the Criterion Center Stage Right, Broadway and 45th Street.

Eleanor and Bizarbara	Liz Larsen
Mother and Diva	Sharon McNight
Shak Graa	Ariel Grabber
Spacepunk	Brian Lane Green
Trinkulus	Gabriel Barre
Ack Ack Ackerman	Bennett Cale
Herbie Harrison	Victor Trent Cook
Dazzle Razzledorf	Christopher Zelno
Shotzi	Mary Kate Law
Canibelle	Gwen Stewart
Balbraka	Freida Williams
Maligna	Janet Aldrich
Droids	John-Michael Flate and Ric Ryder

By MEL GUSSOW

"Starmites," the most microcosmic of intergalactic epics, arrived on Broadway last night after a nine-year odyssey through the outer reaches of Off Broadway and regional theater. Despite changes, the show remains what it always was — a space-age "Peter Pan" of particular interest to Trekkies, star warriors and sci-fi fans of all generations.

The Barry Keating comic-book musical that inaugurated the new Criterion Center Stage Right theater is a polished high-tech version of the original that first amused audiences at the Ark Theater in SoHo. The show has been slightly enlarged, although even on Broadway it retains a convivial Off Broadway feeling. In that and other senses, it has some of the appeal of "Little Shop of Horrors" and is the very opposite of Andrew Lloyd Webber's "Starlight Express." This is a vest-pocket rather than a fast-track musical.

What "Starmites" has is a childlike fancifulness and a genuine affection for its genre, for its labyrinthine detail as well as its exclamatory dialogue. Mr. Keating, who conceived the show, composed the score and co-wrote the book with Stuart Ross, is clearly a comic-book fanatic.

•

The cast is headed by the lithesome Liz Larsen, playing a teen-age earthling with a passion for comics. In a time and space warp, she turns out to be the legendary Milady, a potential queen of the universe who can finger snap a foe into a state of suspended animation. Her adventures lead her into the nether regions of Innerspace to rescue the solar system from self-destruction — and from such societal impediments as tabloid television. The show has its share of social commentary, although it still does not have a sharply satiric storyline. At times, "Starmites" veers perilously close to the subject it is spoofing.

The heroine is a neo-feminist version of all those storybook young women who were flown — or blown away — to kingdom come. In this case, the "lost boys" are street urchins in sneakers and ragged dungarees. Their mini-membership includes a lead singer and a backup trio that needs absolutely no encouragement to break into a song like the catchy title number. Milady's comrade in arms is the lead Starmite, clean-cut despite his name, Spacepunk. He is a variation on Luke Skywalker (the actor, Brian Lane Green, bears a certain resemblance to Harrison Ford).

The quest leads the couple to a Darth Vader-land in search of a totemic super weapon called the Cruelty. In the first version of the show, the Cruelty looked like a cross between a French horn and a kewpie doll. On Broadway, it becomes a glistening heavy-metal guitar. In neither instance is it as imaginative as it should be. The book is also burdened by too many references by Ms. Larsen to chapter and verse in her comic-book collection back on earth. If she really knew how every episode was going to turn out, she could have cut to the chase.

The most salutary approach is to sit back in the comfortable new Criterion Center theater and enjoy the show's assets. These include Mr. Keating's eclectic pop-rock score, which occasionally pauses for a sweet ballad or a gospel number between the hard-driving 60's-style melodies. Some of Mr. Keating's lyrics are simplistic, but others have a cartoon cleverness, which is something that could also be said about the show itself.

•

To its credit, "Starmites" never takes itself too seriously and is always tongue in cheek. It remains a light-hearted space flight. Ms. Larsen, in particular, is appealing as the damsel who can single-handedly overcome distress but does not want to push her pluck too far. Zestfully, she sets her character in her opening anthem, "Superhero Girl."

The actress also doubles as her other self, a homely Innerspace teenager on a postnasal trip. In both her guises, she is arm in arm with Mr. Green, playing a super hero who is sometimes so busy expressing himself rhetorically that he forgets he is

'Starmites' combines comics and pop-rock with special effects.

meant to be a man of action. Ms. Larsen and Mr. Green are nicely matched for duets, and Bennett Cale, Victor Trent Cook and Christopher Zelno are their helpful support team.

The plot cauldron bubbles with the character of Diva, the Queen of the Banshees and an enemy who becomes friendly under fire. In a role that might have been made to order for Bette Midler, Sharon McNight is power-packed. Her signature song, "Hard to Be Diva," is a lowdown growl of cheerful discontent with celebrity. As she sings, "It's hard to be Diva, but so much harder not to be." Ms. McNight also plays Diva's opposite, the earthling's nagging mother.

The Banshees are Diva's women warriors. Unfortunately, these backup belters are beyond camp, with the lead singer a dominatrix who might be more at home in an operatic version of "Springtime for Hitler." "Starmites" goes too far at times, but perhaps that is in the nature of the comic-book style. The fantasy elements are enhanced in Larry Carpenter's resourceful production. In its extended program credits, the show lists not only a chief pyrotechnician but also an apprentice pyrotechnician. Whenever there is a momentary lapse, special effects — laser beams, a shower of stars — and Ms. Larsen herself come to the rescue.

1989 Ap 28, C3:1

Banality of Evil

GHETTO, by Joshua Sobol; in a version by David Lan; directed by Gedalia Besser; English lyrics by Jeremy Sams; musical direction by William Schimmel; movement by Nir Ben Gal and Liat Dror; sets by Adrian Vaux; costumes by Edna Sobol; lighting by Kevin Rigdon; production stage manager, William Hare. Presented by Circle in the Square Theater, Theodore Mann, artistic director; Paul Libin, producing director. At 50th Street, west of Broadway.

Srulik	Avner Eisenberg
Kittel	Stephen McHattie
Hayyah	Helen Schneider
The Dummy	Gordon Joseph Weiss
Gens	George Hearn
Weiskopf	Donal Donnelly
Kruk	Jarlath Conroy

With: Marshall Coid, Alma Cuervo, Richard M. Davidson, Julie Anne Eigenberg, Julie Goell, David Hopkins, Andrea Clark Libin, Brian Maffitt, Jonathan Mann, Jerry Matz, Spike McClure, Barry Mitterhoff, Matthew P Mutrie, Angelo Ragonesi, Jon Rothstein, David Rosenbaum, Ahvi Spindell, William Swindler and William Verderber.

By FRANK RICH

At the bare minimum, dramatic works about the Holocaust have an obligation to restore vivid immediacy to horrors that scoundrels and the passing of time would have the world forget. As presented in good conscience but with scant competence by the Circle in the Square, Joshua Sobol's "Ghetto" is too lifeless to

Martha Swope Associates

Gabriel Barre, left, Liz Larsen and Brian Lane Green in "Starmites," at the Criterion Center.

meet this minimal requirement. A tedious stage treatment of the Holocaust, however well intentioned, is a trivialization of the Holocaust. One need only look at all the dozing faces in the audience to see that "Ghetto" is aiding rather than combating historical amnesia.

Presumably something has happened to Mr. Sobol's play on its circuitous route from Israel to New York. "Ghetto" has received acclaim on several continents in other stagings, starting with the initial one directed by Gedalia Besser for the Haifa Municipal Theater in 1984. Though Mr. Besser is in charge of the Circle in the Square version, he is entirely at sea with his locally recruited company. Working with a bizarrely chosen cast that includes actors one associates with the Irish playwright Brian Friel (Donal Donnelly, Jarlath Conroy) and variety performers with little acting experience (the cabaret singer Helen Schneider, the clown Avner Eisenberg), Mr. Besser has fielded perhaps the most ineptly performed production of the Broadway season.

A highly viable dramatic idea has been buried beneath the wreckage. Using a mixture of fact and justifiable poetic license, Mr. Sobel tells the story of the theater that incongruously flourished in the ghetto of Vilna, Lithuania, from 1942 to 1943. Though "Ghetto" takes place a few weeks after a majority of Vilna's 70,000 residents had been exterminated by the Nazis, the remaining Jews still "put on their finery and come to the show." Why? Mr. Sobol sees the survival of the theater at Vilna as a testament to the perseverance of the human spirit in the face of unfathomable evil and certain doom.

The point is well taken, but the dramatization of it is diffuse. "Ghetto" frequently breaks down into predictable soliloquies delivered by stereotyped ghetto residents. There's an austere socialist librarian (Mr. Conroy) who reads his diary entries to the recorded accompaniment of a pecking typewriter; an oily, ranting entrepreneur who puts his own survival before his community's (Mr. Donnelly), and the German-appointed Jewish leader who endlessly attempts to square his conscience with his collaborationist expediencies (George Hearn). The minor figures are even more anonymous: as played by a large contingent of often-expressionless extras, they seem less like victims of the Nazis than like refugees from an exhausted summerstock tour of "Oliver!"

⚫

To an extent, "Ghetto" aspires to be a musical in the Brecht-Weill mode. Songs that survived Vilna's liquidation are intermingled with the dialogue scenes, both as ironic commentary and as a simulation of the shows presented in the ghetto. But this promising format is destroyed by the seeming arbitrariness of the songs' placement and by the campy delivery of Ms. Schneider, who, one is not surprised to discover in the Playbill, has appeared in "Cabaret." (There's a rouged Joel Grey impersonator in "Ghetto" as well.)

Though it's to be assumed that Mr. Sobol's play would have more heft in a better production, some of the writing gives one pause. In David Lan's translation, at least, "Ghetto" is a fount of clichéd rhetoric, with speeches often beginning with constructions like "No one has the moral authority to decide..." and "History will judge..." Theatergoers can't be blamed if they tune out before the end

Martha Swope

Helen Schneider and Stephen McHattie in "Ghetto" at Circle in the Square.

of such sentences, or if they refuse to pay diligent attention to canned debates about the nature of art or the validity of the resistance movement.

Even the violent episodes don't create much of a stir in Mr. Besser's desultory staging, which often places the crucial action at the distant end of the arena stage. The evening's sole spurts of energy can be found in a stylized dance of Nazi uniforms (reminiscent of the Polish director Tadeusz Kantor's Holocaust hallucinations) and in the performance of Stephen McHattie, whose German commandant, a sadist of exceptional wit and elevated musical tastes, is drawn in far more specific detail than any of his victims.

Of the other actors, Mr. Hearn is notable for his ability to sustain a single note of sour befuddlement for nearly three hours, while Mr. Eisenberg may be remembered for his ability to speak of the massacre of 50,000 Jews with the offhand annoyance of someone inconvenienced by a minor traffic accident. "Ghetto" is almost perverse in its ability to make the true nightmare of our century ring completely false.

1989 My 1, C11:1

Machines? Phooey!

LARGELY NEW YORK, written and directed by Bill Irwin; scenery by Douglas Stein; costumes by Rose Pederson; lighting by Nancy Schertler; sound by Bob Bielecki; video design by Dennis Diamond and Video Studios; collaborator and production stage manager, Nancy Harrington; original steps and routines by Margaret Eginton, Leon Chesney and Steve Clemente; choreography by Mr. Irwin and Kimi Okada; executive producer, Robin Ullman. Presented by James B. Freydberg, Kenneth Feld, Jerry L. Cohen, Max Weitzenhoffer, the John F. Kennedy Center for the Performing Arts and the Walt Disney Studios. At the St. James Theater, 246 West 44th Street.

The Post-Modern Hoofer .... Bill Irwin
The Poppers
         .... Leon Chesney and Steve Clemente
The Soloist .... Margaret Eginton
The Videographer .... Dennis Diamond
The Video Assistant .... Debra Elise Miller
The Dean .... Jeff Gordon
The Ensemble
   Michael Barber, Jon E. Brandenberg, Chris Quay Davis, Patti Dobrowolski, Raymond Houle, Amy Mack, Karen Omahen, Lori Vadino, Cindy Sue Williams, Toni Wisti and Christina Youngman.

Joan Marcus

Bill Irwin in a scene from "Largely New York."

By FRANK RICH

Any fears that Bill Irwin, having arrived on Broadway, might have gone Broadway are quickly dispelled in "Largely New York," the sweet, brief show that the invaluable New Vaudeville clown brought to the St. James last night. While Mr. Irwin may now be playing across the street from "The Phantom of the Opera," he is congenitally incapable of succumbing to high-tech glitz. Not that he doesn't make a good-natured try. "Largely New York" opens with Mr. Irwin attempting to manipulate the theater's many curtains with an elaborate remote control. One is relieved to see that he need merely push a few buttons to gum up the works entirely (and hilariously) before retreating to his natural terrain, the bare stage.

⚫

Mr. Irwin holds that stage for 65 minutes with affable innocence, bravura comic talent and a little help from some gifted friends. Still traveling with a burlesque performer's classic gear — a steamer trunk of tricks, a top hat, horn-rimmed glasses, baggy pants, a cane — Mr. Irwin is the earnest soul of blond, blue-eyed passivity. Then the world, whether of inanimate objects or animated people, comes crashing in. "Largely New York," which was first seen in a workshop presentation at City Center a year ago, resembles the previous Irwin pieces "The Regard of Flight" and "The Courtroom." It's a loose-limbed web of vignettes in which a well-meaning, spectacularly elastic outsider searches for physical and mental equilibrium in the nuthouse that passes for civilization.

This time, Mr. Irwin plays a character called the the Post-Modern Hoofer, restricting his language to the facial and the physical. The New York he encounters is largely inhabited by equally mute dancers: a former member of the Merce Cunningham company (Margaret Eginton), a pair of boom-box-bearing "poppers" (as the upwardly mobile break dancers Leon Chesney and Steve Clemente are known) and an entire troupe of terminally severe mock

Twyla Tharpists. An irrepressible mimic, Mr. Irwin can't help but adopt the terpsichorean technique of any and all comers — however incongruous the discrepancy between his white-bread personality and the wild idiosyncracies of his adopted ethnic or avant-garde dance styles. Eventually, and no less amusingly, the others take a stab at Mr. Irwin's own favored routine: a buck-and-wing "Tea for Two," to Wurlitzer accompaniment.

⚫

Though dance is the primary medium of "Largely New York," the message often pertains to technology. The first remote control we see is not the last, and the show is full of updated variants on "Modern Times" and Jacques Tati's "Mon Oncle." The independent-minded theatrical and music-making machinery of "Largely New York" repeatedly breaks down, defying the cures offered by a much-consulted instruction manual. For added future shock, a ubiquitous video cameraman, trailing his monitor and an assistant behind him, is constantly inviting one and all (audience included) to mug for the camera in the name of performance art.

While Mr. Irwin's moralizing about technological dehumanization can be ponderous — he darkly reveals that people prefer the televised picture of violent reality to reality itself — some of the video sequences are so lively as to dispute his point. Both as comedy and technology, Mr. Irwin's duet with a videotaped image of himself is dazzling; what's more, the sketch is

Chaos is available at the press of a few buttons.

topped by a magic stunt that can honestly be called a post-modern reincarnation of the spirit of Harry Houdini.

⚫

Most of the show's other highlights are of a more visceral nature: the joyously syncopated rap-beat gymnastics of Mr. Chesney and Mr. Clemente, and the extraordinary running (and leaping) gags executed by the one-time Big Apple Circus clown Jeff Gordon, who leads a mysterious flock of formally robed academics around the fringes of the action. On stage and off, Mr. Irwin's collaborators throughout are first-rate, including the video designer Dennis Diamond and the co-choreographer Kimi Okada, who has obviously drawn on her own experiences in the next-wave dance world when distilling fashionable choreographic attitudes down to their self-parodistic essence.

•

It's typical of "Largely New York" that more passion is lavished on the satire of downtown esthetics than on the comic romance that Mr. Irwin gingerly carries out (often by video) with the lovely, resolutely deadpan Ms. Eginton. The bewildered Mr. Irwin cuts a most human figure on stage and even allows himself a final-curtain kiss, but his clowning, however slapstick, often remains austerely intellectual in its preoccupations. Along with the repetition of beloved past bits (the invisible staircase and the human vacuum cleaner, among others), this may be why his show seems too even in tempo and a shade overlong, even at 65 minutes. Though no one can accuse Bill Irwin of bending to meet Broadway demands in this charming entertainment, neither can one say that "Largely New York" offers a great talent or his audience the exhilaration of an artistic stretch.

1989 My 2, C15:1

_____

Music From Detroit

A THRILL A MOMENT, by William (Mickey) Stevenson; production choreographed and directed by Edward Love; musical director, Grenoldo Frazier; production stage manager, Lisa L. Watson; set design, Richard Harmon; costume design, Fontella Boone; light design, William H. Grant 3d and Jerry Forsyth. Presented by Henry Street Settlement's New Federal Theater, Woodie King Jr., producer. At the Louis Abrons Arts for Living Center, 466 Grand Street.

WITH: Adrian Bailey, Irene Datcher, Dwayne Grayman, Kelly Rice, Kiki Shepard, Gina Taylor and Allison Williams.

By STEPHEN HOLDEN

"A Thrill a Moment," a new musical revue built around the work of the veteran Motown songwriter William (Mickey) Stevenson, resurrects an era of black music that, given today's aggressive hard-edged rap, seems downright quaint in its innocence.

Though not as famous as the Motown songwriting and producing team of Holland-Dozier-Holland, Mr. Stevenson had a hand in creating a number of significant hits for the company in the early 1960's. They include the Marvelettes' "Playboy" and "Beechwood 4-5789," the early Marvin Gaye hits "Stubborn Kind of Fellow" and "Pride and Joy," and the Martha and the Vandellas song "Dancing in the Street." He also co-wrote Mitch Ryder and the Detroit Wheels' full-tilt 1966 hit "Devil With a Blue Dress On." All these songs are included in the show.

•

The obvious way to stage an anthology of Mr. Stevenson's songs would be to mount a nostalgic revue. But Edward Love, who choreographed

and directed the evening at the Henry Street Settlement's New Federal Theater, doesn't even go that far. A cast of seven singers drifts aimlessly about a makeshift barroom setting of no particular flavor.

In a show that has no theatrical vision beyond its basic premise, all you're left with is the music. The singers are adequate but not outstanding, and the musical arrangements faithful in spirit to the period. The strongest voice belongs to Adrian Bailey, who pours his heart into "Love Me All the Way," a pop-gospel duet with Irene Datcher. Vocally, however, he is a long way from Mr. Gaye or the Four Tops' Levi Stubbs.

"A Thrill a Moment" is so undeveloped that it is still essentially a show in search of a production.

1989 My 4, C23:1

_____

A Ménage à Trois For Starters

NO LIMITS TO LOVE, by David Mercer; directed by Hilary Blecher; set by Russell Parkman; lighting by David Noling; costumes by Elsa Ward; sound by Tom Gould; production stage manager, Jana Llynn. Presented by the New Theater of Brooklyn, Deborah J. Pope and Steve Stettler, artistic directors. At 465 Dean Street, Brooklyn.

Marna Croft	Donna Davis
Edward Croft	Richard Bekins
Hugh Bainbridge	Robert Burke
Otto Neumann	Jeremiah Sullivan

By WILBORN HAMPTON

Early in David Mercer's "No Limits to Love," which is being given its New York premiere at the New Theater of Brooklyn, there is some light banter about the inanities of the British theater of the 1970's. Three characters are discussing a play they recently saw. Why, one asks, was everyone in the cast having sex with one another in the second act? The answer (something about socioeconomic conditions in Britain) is unimportant. But it is the sort of question one might ask leaving "No Limits to Love."

No one actually has sex with anyone else in Mr. Mercer's 1980 play. But sex is a topic that preoccupies each of the four characters. And not without reason. Edward (Richard Bekins) and Marna (Donna Davis) are a married couple involved in a ménage à trois with Hugh (Robert Burke), an Oxford history don who has a secret past and a catatonic wife somewhere.

•

The time is pre-Thatcher Britain and this trio has set up house in an area of northern London that sounds a lot like Hampstead. A new neighbor, Otto (Jeremiah Sullivan), turns out to be Edward's former pyschoanalyst, who left his patients and ran away to Canada with a young Italian boy who just happens to be an old flame of Hugh's as well. From there, the plot gets as complicated as a soap opera. By the time the ghosts of former lovers are dragged into it, we are essentially dealing with a ménage à sept (or possibly huit).

The incumbent jealousies and frustrations in such a situation provide ample ammunition for a barrage of sniping among the quartet (literally, at one point), and Mr. Mercer's dialogue can be wickedly witty. The danger is in trying to read a socioeconomic "Whither Britain?" text between the lines. At most, "No Limits

to Love" is one of those "How Did We Get Here and What Do We Do Now?" plays that work best if the audience doesn't have time to think too much about what's being said. For one thing, none of the characters are people you would actually want to know. These are people who think it terribly funny to pretend to scrape dog excrement from one's shoes with a mate's toothbrush and whose favorite pastime is to spy on a neighbor's trips to the loo through binoculars.

•

The humor of the play, Mr. Mercer's last before his death in 1980, comes mostly in the very literate insults that fly about the stage, or at least should fly. In the New Theater production, they sort of meander. Hilary Blecher has directed as though there were a serious answer to that original question about sexual excesses if we would only take the time to find it. The action thus fairly plods along, and what should be a quick-paced two-hour comedy plays out to two and a half hours. The result is similar to staging Joe Orton's "What the Butler Saw" as a dramatic treatise on the declining state of mental-health care in Britain. There are also a few duds in the script, and some of the lines should be cut — jokes about bisexual men that were written before AIDS, for starters.

The cast, while energetic, is only partly successful. The best scenes are between Mr. Bekins and Mr. Burke, both of whom give fine performances and who are not afraid to let the egocentric shallowness of their characters draw the laughs they deserve.

1989 My 4, C21:1

_____

Portents And Epiphanies

APPROACHING ZANZIBAR, by Tina Howe; directed by Carole Rothman; set design, Heidi Landesman; lighting design, Dennis Parichy; costume design, Susan Hilferty; sound design, Gary and Timmy Harris; hair design, Antonio Soddu; production stage manager, Pamela Edington; stage manager, Ken Simmons. Presented by Second Stage Theater, Robyn Goodman and Ms. Rothman, artistic directors. At 2162 Broadway, at 76th Street.

Wallace Blossom	Harris Yulin
Charlotte Blossom	Jane Alexander
Turner Blossom	Clayton Barclay Jones
Pony Blossom	Angela Goethals
Old Man, Randy Wands and Scotty Childs	Jamie Ross
Palace St. John and Dr. Sybil Wren	Maggie Burke
Fletcher St. John and Amy Childs	Damien Jackson
Joy Ballad and Dalia Paz	Aleta Mitchell
Olivia Childs	Bethel Leslie

By FRANK RICH

Tina Howe is one of the smartest playwrights we have, but does she really believe she can outsmart death? That seems to be the case in "Approaching Zanzibar," her new play at the Second Stage. In this determinedly uplifting comedy, an American nuclear family confronts its mortality, then bounces back at once with renewed hope. And I mean literally bounces back. The evening ends with the characters jumping around an aged matriarch's death bed shouting ecstatic cries of "Paradise!"

The woman whose imminent passing inspires such life-affirming joy is Olivia Childs (Bethel Leslie), a legendary 81-year-old artist who combines the personal ethos of Georgia O'Keeffe with the avant-garde esthet-

ics of Christo. Olivia is in the terminal throes of cancer in Taos, N.M.; "Approaching Zanzibar" tells of how her middle-aged niece Charlotte Blossom (Jane Alexander) journeys by car from Westchester with her husband, Wallace (Harris Yulin), and their son and daughter to pay last repects. Where the rest of us might find Burger Kings or speed traps en route cross-country, the Blossoms have a habit of stumbling upon portents, metaphors and epiphanies that raise intimations of their own mortality.

A mysterious, unidentified old man in black wanders into the family's camping ground. Charlotte takes to having a recurrent nightmare about an abandoned baby. When Wallace and the 12-year-old Turner (Clayton Barclay Jones) go fishing in a North Carolina mountain stream, the father instructs his son to regard their catch not as a potential dinner but as "departed human souls." (Babies, we're later told, "start out as fish" as well.) In the Blue Ridge Mountains, fellow tourists accentuate the biological chain: the Blossoms no sooner meet an infant than they encounter a deaf boy with psychic powers to predict the infant's path from cradle to grave.

Ms. Howe has always been a poetic writer fascinated by the connections between parents and children, art and life, love and death. But in her most luminous plays, the imagery grows out of character and incident. While the most fanciful soliloquy in "Coastal Disturbances" was also fishy (it was about dolphins), the monologue was grounded by the accompanying erotic spectacle of a life-guard expressing his love for the heroine by burying her in sand. "Approaching Zanzibar," by contrast, puts its inspirational message ahead of drama, burying its people in symbols and tall cautionary tales.

•

We learn more about the cosmic implications of electric eels and figurative trips to Zanzibar than about the Blossoms' marriage or about the couple's feelings toward their fairly generic children. Though Wallace is identified as a composer, Charlotte's profession or nonfamilial passions (if any) are left vague, and both adults are defined superficially by their position on a pop-psychology time line (menopause for her, midcareer crisis for him). Olivia, too, is just a type, summed up by her canned bohemian philosophy of life rather than by her relationships to anyone in her life.

The reason Ms. Howe would rather embrace general homilies than delineate specific people is both transparent and human. It's easier to neutralize the trauma of death if one removes it from intimate range and places it instead in the abstract context of the universe. "Approaching Zanzibar" hopes that death will be easier to contemplate if we remember that babies perpetuate the race, that departed souls and beautiful mountains are forever, that we (like Aunt Olivia) can "realize" ourselves in what time we have. In a hokey Act I finale nearly as sentimental as its Act II counterpart, the Blossom children overcome their first fears of mortality by gazing at the eternal stars.

Perhaps those who take cheer from condolence cards will find hope in these tableaux and in such lines as "We're all flowing into each other" and "Nature is very beautiful; it's so logical." Yet the familiar ring of these words suggests how mechanical Ms. Howe's optimism is. What Wallace calls "the fine art of letting

Jane Alexander
Susan Cook

After 'Coastal Disturbances,' Tina Howe heads for the heartland.

go" in his own musical compositions is missing in the willed platitudes of "Approaching Zanzibar." Ms. Howe's typically bracing humor and pathos break through only in early scenes showing the spats endemic to long family car trips and in Charlotte's sudden flash of specific rage at the passing of her childbearing years.

Ms. Alexander is touching at that moment but otherwise is adrift in a vague role. Carole Rothman, who is the director and Ms. Howe's highly sensitive longtime collaborator, also seems flummoxed; her production is not well cast. Mr. Yulin offers superficial disgruntlement as Wallace, and Ms. Leslie appears too young and stolid to embody the ravaged, ethereal, sporadically ga-ga Olivia. The child actors fail to remove the curse of the cutes from precocious kids who say far too many of the darndest things. In one redundant comic scene requiring the parents and children to reverse roles, the acting sinks to the skin-crawling level of "The Brady Bunch."

As with the impressionistic "Painting Churches," Heidi Landesman has designed an imaginative set in the style of the play's own artist. Huge sheets of canvas fly and fall to suggest mountains, rivers and the open road in between. But we are acutely aware that the intricate, constantly shifting scenery, like Ms. Howe's flowery overwriting, is straining very hard to achieve its glimpses of paradise. While the Blossoms may blithely make their peace with death in "Approaching Zanzibar," the audience pays the price of inheriting the anxiety they discard.

1989 My 5, C3:1

A Different Road To Wonderland

NOIRESQUE: THE FALLEN ANGEL, written and directed by Ping Chong; created in collaboration with the cast; set design, Mr. Chong; lighting design, Howard Thies; costume design, Matthew Yokobosky; sound de-

sign, Brian Hallas; stage management, Arthur C. Catricala and Sue Jane Stoker. Presented by the Pan Asian Repertory Theater, Tisa Chang, artistic-producing director. At Playhouse 46, 423 West 46th Street.

Alice .... Lauren Tom
Herr Hasenpfeffer and Citoyen
                    Ron Nakahara
Katz, Jammer and Citoyen
                  Mel Duane Gionson
Mme.L'Argent and Citoyenne ..... Kati Kuroda
The Angel and Citoyen .... Du-Yee Chang
C. E. O'Donnell, Rag and Bottle Man and Citoyen .... Norris M. Shimabuku
Nadine Nadine and Citoyenne .... Mary Lee

By MEL GUSSOW

In his theatrical work, Ping Chong draws together ingredients from various arts, both performance and graphic, and then offers his own sardonic commentary. His puckish wit would seem to be most appropriate to a freehand interpretation of "Alice in Wonderland," and so it is — up to a point.

The difficulty with his new play, "Noiresque: The Fallen Angel," begins with the fact that it is double-edged. This is a case of Lewis Carroll dipped in film noir. Though both aspects occasionally mesh, more often they seem to clash — the whimsicality of Carroll interrupted by the intentional banalities in the spoof of detective movies.

The play, Mr. Chong's first collaboration with the Pan Asian Repertory Theater, begins promisingly, as Alice (Lauren Tom) embarks on her journey. Instead of tumbling down a rabbit hole, she takes a mysterious train — the All Points Far East Local. In the background are heard echoing voices — her parents warning her not to talk to strangers, a conductor announcing various symbolic points of debarkation, like Vale of Tears. The final destination is Terminal City, whose inhabitants are Terminites.

•

The first person Alice meets in her travels is Herr Hasenpfeffer, who, beneath the pfeffer, is of course our old friend, the White Rabbit. In the present inversion, he may be early rather than late. Ron Nakahara plays the character with a scatterbrained sense of absurdism, deriving humor not only from his lines but even from his odd costume. His hat is circled by a broad brim with large holes in it. Merrily rushing across the stage at St. Clement's, the actor looks as if he has a flying saucer sitting on his head.

As other characters enter, the play moves sideways rather than in a direct line. Vaudeville dialogue ("Have you got the time?," "What do you have in mind?") alternates with film noir references. Lost in the shuffle is the central theme, which is, one would have thought, Alice's own confusion. The conception of Alice, as played by the talented Ms. Tom, verges on coyness.

"Noiresque" is often playful with its literary source and with foreign languages. But it does not have the humor of, for example, the author's "Kind Ness," a fanciful excursion into anthropology and adolescence. Except for the railroad motif (which includes signal lights simulating moving trains) and a top-hatted dancing chorus, the production does not take ample advantage of Mr. Chong's imagination.

•

The show is enlivened by the appearance of an angel (Du-Yee Chang), Alice's guardian seraph. His wistful presence suggests that it

might have been rewarding had Mr. Chong chosen to emphasize his subtitle to an even greater degree.

"Noiresque" is interesting as a creative link between this experimental theater artist and the Pan Asian troupe, which has earned its reputa-

Martha Swope Associates/Carol Rosegg
Ron Nakahara

tion principally through its presentation of new plays with a naturalistic base. Stylistically, this is a definite change of pace for the company and its actors. Under Mr. Chong's direction, they reveal previously concealed clownish instincts, especially so in the case of Mr. Nakahara.

This accomplished actor has often moved audiences with his performances as stoical survivors of Nisei camps and other troubled husbands and paterfamilias. It is liberating to see him cavort amusingly as a creature crossbred by the imaginations of Lewis Carroll and Ping Chong. The play itself might most properly be regarded as an idea in progress.

1989 My 5, C3:4

A Backstage Journey

NEW CITIES, written by Paul Zimet, in collaboration with the Talking Band: William Badgett, Ellen Maddow, Lizzie Olesker and Tina Shepard. Directed by Mr. Zimet; music by Ms. Maddow and Harry Mann; lighting and scenery by Arden Fingerhut; costumes by Gabriel Berry; choreography by Rocky Bornstein; production stage manager Ben Voorhies; associate director, Mr. Bornstein. Presented by La Mama E.T.C., 74A East Fourth Street.

By D. J..R. BRUCKNER

In "New Cities," performed by the Talking Band at La Mama, music is bread, not the food of love, for a string quartet on a world concert tour. A problem is that the bread provides not much sustenance most of the time for the weary and homesick musicians.

The point is made comically early on in this whimsical piece when the four players go into a restaurant in some remote city halfway around the world and find themselves eating out of flowerpots and buckets, using wrenches, a towel rack and a fur-covered fan instead of forks and spoons. As they travel through variously hostile climates, cramped into tiny hotel cubicles and rattling train compartments, they become increasingly starved for the sound of their own language, for their friends and lovers and pets, and even for the chance to play their own music instead of Beethoven, Schubert and Brahms.

•

Paul Zimet directs this backstage journey of souls with a light touch. You can laugh at these hapless tune makers in every one of the play's quick sketches, and end up with an affectionate sympathy for them.

As is usual with the Talking Band, music, words and at times dance movements create effects that tease you with the illusion that they refer to something familiar that you cannot quite remember. The technique does not always work, but when it does, it is delightful, as in a song for four voices about the way a person talks when he is trying to make a pass, or a duet in which a cellist describing perfect love alternates lines with a violinist recounting the adventures of an explorer in New Guinea.

There are nodding moments when the onlooker may feel the strain of the tortuous tour, but at the end, when the audience is let out of the dressing rooms and into the auditorium as the characters in shimmering formal

The Talking Band, a group that performs in "New Cities."

dress give their last concert, the ovation that greets the cast seems heartfelt.

The Talking Band members making up the quartet — William Badgett, Ellen Maddow, Lizzie Olesker and Tina Shepard — create distinctive, eccentric characters with almost no dialogue and very few lines that make much ordinary sense. But there are four other presences on stage that should be listed as characters, too: Dennis McHugh's sublime instruments on which the actors mimic performance while recorded music plays.

They are velvet, satin and felt-covered objects that suggest violins, a viola and a cello and that are played with silk, fringed bows that end in fantastic scrolls (the cello has a large hand at the end of its fingerboard). They are every bit as odd, and almost as substantial, as the characters wielding them.

1989 My 7, 74:3

Buried Secrets

THE SPEED OF DARKNESS, by Steve Tesich; directed by Robert Falls; set by Thomas Lynch, costumes by Nan Cibula, lighting by Michael S. Philippi; sound and original music by Rob Milburn; production stage manager, Lois Griffing; stage manager, Jill Larmett. The Goodman Theater of the Art Institute of Chicago presents a Chicago Theater Group production. Mr. Falls, artistic director; Roche Schulfer, producing director. At Chicago.

Joe	Bill Raymond
Anne	Lee Guthrie
Mary	Brigitte Bako
Lou	Stephen Lang
Eddie	Andy Hirsch

By FRANK RICH

Special to The New York Times

CHICAGO, May 6 — Joe, a prominent building contractor and apostle of the American Dream, worked his way up from scratch after returning from decorated service in Vietnam. He had to start out in garbage. In "The Speed of Darkness," Steve Tesich's first new play since 1980, Joe (Bill Raymond) pays thanks for his success at the televised award ceremony naming him South Dakota's Man of the Year. As he tells his fellow citizens, he owes everything to "your trash and filth and waste that you wanted to be taken anywhere and buried out of sight."

The mystery at the core of Mr. Tesich's play, now having its premiere at the Goodman Theater here, is the exact nature of that "trash and filth and waste," both literally and metaphorically. Set in the present but preoccupied with the 1960's, "The Speed of Darkness" is the most as-

The dark residues of Vietnam and other grimes that won't be cleansed.

tringent work in years by a writer whose previous play. "Division Street," took a farcical slant on the Vietnam legacy, and whose best-

Tom Lascher

Brigitte Bako and Stephen Lang in Steve Tesich's new play, "The Speed of Darkness."

known script, for the film "Breaking Away," is an immigrant's celebration of American virtues. Though not without humor, Mr. Tesich's new play is structured like a tragedy. When the buried filth in Joe's past — and his neighbors' — finally rises to the surface, it oozes over the landscape like an inky national stain, as if to represent all that is shameful and greedy and lethal in our recent history.

•

With its exposure of covered-up crimes against society, its absurdist portrait of an all-American family and its abundant use of a symbolic baby, "The Speed of Darkness" can seem like Mr. Tesich's attempt to meld "All My Sons," "Sticks and Bones" and "Buried Child" with "Oedipus the King." But if this is at times its author's most pretentious play, it is also his most ambitious and, potentially, a major breakthrough. The powerful scenes and images resonate so deeply that they linger in spite of the self-indulgent textual excesses and some murkiness of tone in the production, directed by Robert Falls.

The evening's highest achievement in writing and performance is the character of Lou, a war buddy of Joe's played by Stephen Lang. Now a tramp — he prefers the term "urban homeless" — Lou turns up in South Dakota without warning and triggers the events that rock Joe's heretofore contented family. A garrulous street philosopher caked in dirt, Mr. Lang may be unrecognizable to those who recall him as John Malkovich's brother in the Dustin Hoffman "Death of a Salesman." He is shattering in a speech in which Lou recounts his arrest at the Vietnam Veterans Memorial in Washington for attempting to scratch his name into the wall of the dead.

•

Lou was told by the marines who arrested him that the wall was "only for those who died, not those who survived." But as he says, "I didn't survive." A feral cur of a man, driven half-mad by a country that alternately treats Vietnam veterans as "garbage" and heroes, he is reduced to bumming around the country trailing what he calls "son of wall," the traveling replica of the Washington original. One could say, too, that the wall travels with him and other vet-

erans who are, in his phrase, "M.I.A., Missing in America." As "The Speed of Darkness" accelerates, we gradually realize that th enormous rear wall of Thomas Lynch's spooky living room set is itself an echo of the wedged, pitch-black war memorial.

The family occupying that living room is not so clearly drawn. In the first act, Joe, his wife (Lee Guthrie) and his teen-age daughter (Brigitte Bako) are presented almost as a parodistically complacent sitcom family out of "Father Knows Best." Is this facetious stylization Mr. Tesich's intentional setup for the fall to come, or an unwanted byproduct of the fey female performances? Either

way, the family is stripped of the weight required for it to carry the heavy burdens of Act II. While Mr. Raymond's Joe, a character with "the problems of a great man and the inner resources of an ordinary guy," is sometimes compelling, he is the biggest victim of the production's mixed signals. It's impossible for the actor to build the emotional foundation that might justify the pull-out-the-stops soliloquy that yanks Joe and the play to catharsis.

Among the other dramaturgical issues Mr. Tesich might reconsider are the pileup of melodramatic incidents (a suicide, a questioned paternity, a rape of the environment) and the excess of "violent thoughts," prairie storms and other premonitions of their imminent arrival. The playwright also has a tendency to assign highfalutin authorial digressions to his characters, at one point asking us to believe that an otherwise ordinary high-school boy would find "something Greek" in the forces swirling about him.

I also quarrel with Mr. Tesich's insistence here, as in "Division Street," to reach for a sentimentally hopeful finale. Just before he does so, there is a far more effective scene in which an enraged Joe takes his daughter's fantasy infant — several pounds of earth wrapped in a white blanket — and stomps it violently into his green living room carpet. What makes the moment wrenching in context is its power to suggest the interred filth and waste of the Vietnam era at last erupting from darkness into light. Having achieved this painful exorcism, Mr. Tesich should know that there is no longer any way to sweep the dirt back under the rug.

1989 My 9, C15:1

The Right To Be Extraordinary

ELEEMOSYNARY, by Lee Blessing; directed by Lynne Meadow; sets by John Lee Beatty; costumes by William Ivey Long; lighting by Dennis Parichy; production stage manager, Ruth Kreshka. Presented by the Manhattan Theater Club, Ms. Meadow, artistic director; Barry Grove, managing director; in association with Spoleto Festival U.S.A. At the Manhattan Theater Club Stage II, City Center, 131 West 55th Street.

Dorothea	Eileen Heckart
Artie	Joanna Gleason
Echo	Jennie Moreau

By FRANK RICH

There are some absent friends you don't realize how much you've been

missing until they suddenly pop up again. Eileen Heckart, who has been away from the New York stage throughout this decade, is definitely one of them.

One of the first times I saw Ms. Heckart, about 25 years ago, she was good-naturedly choosing to ignore a chorus of boos from a disgruntled Broadway audience at Terrence McNally's memorably disastrous "And Things That Go Bump in the Night." In "Eleemosynary," the Lee Blessing play prompting her current Off Broadway appearance at the tiny Manhattan Theater Club Stage II, she looks and sounds exactly the same as she did way back then. Ms. Heckart is what one might describe as a long actress — long of face, of torso, of tongue. There is mischief in her big

Gerry Goo

Joanna Gleason, left, and Eileen Heckart star in Lee Blessing's "Eleemosynary."

glistening eyes. And when she speaks, it is in the low, crystalline, merry rasp of a wise aunt who has seen and understood everything (perhaps with cigarette in hand), relished most of it and can't wait for the next adventure.

Ms. Heckart's role in "Eleemosynary" fits her profile. She plays Dorothea Westbrook, flintiness personified, an independent-minded matriarch who believes that women have the inalienable right to be extraordinary and who lives by the credo, "There isn't anything the mind can't do." Dorothea chooses to be eccentric because the choice allows her to be a wife and mother and "still talk to animals." She also tries to invent a new way of flying and takes to conversing with the dead with an alacrity that might impress Shirley MacLaine. Happening upon James Monroe ("the last President to wear short pants"), Dorothea asks him if the Era of Good Feelings was really "as good as all that." His response? "He said it was *fair*," says Ms. Heckart, as matter-of-factly as if she were describing the weather.

•

"Eleemosynary" is a three-woman, three-generation family play about the havoc someone like the well-meaning but fundamentally selfish Dorothea can inflict on those closest to her. Her daughter, Artie (Joanna Gleason), is a perpetual malcontent, unable to be intimate with anyone, including her own daughter, Echo (Jennie Moreau). Dorothea raises Echo devotedly after Artie abandons her, only to discover that Echo, too, has become as brainy but difficult as the Westbrook women before her. Telling the story on a bare, platformed stage, Mr. Blessing takes us back and forth in time, through the characters' various childhoods and marriages and illnesses and rages, until his trio can find some common ground.

As is the case with such other recent Blessing plays as "A Walk in the Woods," seen on Broadway last season, and "Cobb," at the Yale Repertory Theater earlier this spring, "Eleemosynary" is distinguished by its brevity (75 minutes or so), its clever dialogue, its unassailable ideology (this play is as vehemently in favor of feminism as its predecessors were for disarmament and against racism) and its reconciliatory conclusion. Mr. Blessing can make familial relationships seem as uncomplicated as he does East-West arms negotiations. For the sake of psychological tidiness and theatrical compactness, he keeps the men in the women's lives not just offstage but virtually uncharacterized, and withholds his one dramatic confrontation until the waning minutes.

•

What we get in place of emotional or intellectual depth are words, lots of them. The play's title refers to the charity and forgiveness that ultimately overtake the Westbrooks, but it is also a crucial word for Echo, who overcompensates for her mother's inattention by devoting herself to winning spelling bees. Echo is forever showing off by reciting her favorite arcane dictionary entries. Those in the audience who recognize the words and know the spellings are given ample opportunity to join her orgy of self-congratulation.

The cast, under the fluid direction of Lynne Meadow, makes the most of its own opportunities. Ms. Gleason, another of our most distinctive comic actresses, makes a congenitally sour character funny and finally sympathetic; Ms. Moreau achieves the same feat for a brat. When "Eleemosynary" induces restlessness, as it does at least half the time, it's because the writing, not the acting, lacks the human reality that might root the play in the theater or in the audience's psyche. As the friend who attended a press preview with me said on the phone a day later, "I can't remember what that play was about or even the one thing I thought I had learned from it — how to pronounce 'eleemosynary.' "

Eileen Heckart, however, is just too dear to forget.

1989 My 10, C15:3

Murder and Honesty, Seeming and Being

PLAYBOY OF THE WEST INDIES, by Mustapha Matura; directed by Dennis Scott; set design by Michael Yeargan; costume design by Mary Myers; lighting design by William B. Warfel; production stage managers, Margaret Adair Quinn and Maureen F. Gibson. Presented by Yale Repertory Theater, Lloyd Richards, artistic director; Benjamin Mordecai, managing director. At New Haven.

Peggy	Suzzanne Douglas
Stanley	Jeffrey Wright
Phil	A. Benard Cummings
Jim	Michael Rogers
Mikey	Vince Williams
Ken	Kevin Jackson
Mama Benin	Fanni Green
Ivy	Jacquelyn Mari Roberts
Alice	Kathi Kennedy
Mac	Richard Gant

By MEL GUSSOW

Special to The New York Times

NEW HAVEN, May 8 — In "The Playboy of the Western World," John Millington Synge wrote about an Ireland in which the "springtime of local life" had not been forgotten. The same is certainly true of Trinidad in 1950, as richly represented in Mustapha Matura's affectionate Caribbean salute to Synge, "The Playboy of the West Indies." The play is running at the Yale Repertory Theater after productions at other regional theaters.

Mr. Matura's play is an almost direct transcription of the original — in terms of narrative and content — but with the substitution of an island patois. The events are the same; the words are different, though equally flavorful. Despite a glossary in the program, however, some of the language is difficult to understand.

Though Mayaro, Trinidad, is thousands of miles and a half-century away from Synge's Mayo, the two are connected by bonds of custom as well as humor. Substituting a Caribbean lilt for an Irish brogue, the play retains its roguish charm as well as its more provocative social dimensions. With its gentle satire, the play is also related to the early Trinidadian fiction of V. S. Naipaul (in particular, the novel "The Suffrage of Elvira"). On one level, both authors comment on an emerging nation's mimicry of the icons and aspirations of North America.

Christy Mahon, renamed Ken, is now a sugar-cane worker and "de fella who killed he fadder." Ken, like Christy, is idolized for his apparently patricidal act. Pegeen Mike, her name abbreviated to Peggy, runs her father's rum shop rather than a pub. She is still the pretty country lass who, through her own rigidity, loses her one opportunity at romance with

the single free spirit in this tightly knit community.

Ken's confession that he killed his tyrannical father is enough to give him immediate heroic status. The young man (Kevin Jackson) quickly becomes the center of all admiration, especially from women who are bored by the dullness of the everyday men in their lives. The first to succumb is Peggy (Suzzanne Douglas), who is affianced to an eligible but wimpish suitor.

Inspired by his love for Peggy, Ken begins to relish his new role and is swept away into athletic feats and rhapsodic flights of poetry. He achieves such an aura of confidence that when his disreputable father — not dead but furious — arrives, the older man almost does not recognize his offspring. As in the original, the play mocks the hypocrisy that allows a community to elevate appearance over reality and to honor a murderer but not an honest man.

•

Though the Synge and the Matura operate on parallel lines, there are, of course, cultural differences. Mayaro believes in superstitions as exemplified by an Obeah woman, the Trinidadian approximation of the original

Gerry Goodstein

Kevin Jackson and Suzzanne Douglas in Mustapha Matura's "Playboy of the West Indies" at the Yale Repertory Theater.

play's Widow Quin. As engagingly personified by Mr. Jackson, Ken seems content to be a swaggerer, whereas one thinks of Christy embarking on more self-fulfilling adventures. But perhaps that shift in emphasis is more in the eye of the beholder. The author plays fair with his borrowed source, and in basic human terms Ken and Christy are twins.

Mr. Jackson and Ms. Douglas share a youthful romantic appeal, so much so that, as in any good production of "The Playboy of the Western World," one roots for them to countermand their plot and seek happiness together. There is vivid support from the other actors, especially Fanni Green, Jacquelyn Mari Roberts and Kathi Kennedy as the women who are variously energized by the hero's presence. In his assured production, Dennis Scott captures the West Indian atmosphere without overdoing the steel-band rhythms.

Although he speaks in his own voice — as previously heard in such plays as "Meetings" and "Play Mas" — Mr. Matura succeeds in demonstrating Synge's transportability and his continuing universality.

1989 My 11, C17:1

'On the Town' Is Revived in Washington

By MEL GUSSOW

Special to The New York Times

WASHINGTON, May 10 — "Jerome Robbins's Broadway," with its artfully selected collage of musical excerpts, arouses the audience's eagerness to see fresh revivals of the individual shows. The Arena Stage is the first to oblige, with a return engagement of "On the Town," that high-spirited, ingenuous evocation of a dreamland New York, circa 1944.

Sans crime, sans drugs, with spotless subways and no traffic on the streets, New York New York is a helluva town. Was there ever a city like this? Only on Broadway and in the movies. Douglas C. Wager, as director, is to be commended for his reinvention of our mythical musical past.

Mr. Wager, who had a double Arena Stage success with the Marx Brothers musicals, "Animal Crackers" and "The Cocoanuts," uses a similar approach for "On the Town." He evidently regards it — correctly — as a period piece, a fanciful rather than a believable musical comedy, and he has accentuated both the music and the comedy.

•

The score (music by Leonard Bernstein, lyrics by Betty Comden and Adolph Green) is filled with youthful verve. For all three it was a Broadway first, and it manages to combine innocence with audacity. The songs are as diverse as the city itself, ranging from the ecstatic "New York, New York" to the plaintive "Lonely Town," which movingly indicates how lost one can be in a crowd.

Along the path from the Bronx to the Battery, there are other vintage show tunes, like "Lucky to Be Me" and "I Get Carried Away," a hymn to impetuousness. "Carried Away" might itself be an alternate title for a show in which three sailors on leave swing headlong into a 24-hour celebration of urban romance.

Some of that celebration is giddy to the point of being silly, but the songs help one glide past the jokes. The Comden and Green storyline is the thinnest thread unifying a tour of hot and cool spots of the era. A sailor

The musical is set in an ingenuous New York of 1944

named Gabey searches for his dream girl, Miss Turnstiles, quickly finds her in Carnegie Hall and then leaves her until they meet again at 11 P.M. in Times Square. To its credit, the plot does not intrude and the cast regards it with a properly offhand manner.

•

The one aspect of "On the Town" that is missing is Mr. Robbins's choreography (the musical was inspired by his ballet "Fancy Free"). According to the Arena Stage, it was not possible to adapt the original choreography to the arena-style staging. The new choreography by Marcia Milgrom Dodge is serviceable — liveliest, as one might expect, with the sailors chorus. With dancing diminished, the focus is on the songs.

For his production, Mr. Wager has enlisted a team of newcomers, all of whom are appropriately energetic — and some of whom provide more fun than others. Paul Binotto and Valerie Wright are neatly matched as the central couple, Gabey and Miss Turnstiles. Ms. Wright, who has a gamin-like appeal, stresses the comic side of her character. Adriane Lenox is amusing as a street-smart cabdriver, the role originated by Nancy Walker. She has an easy spontaneity that charms her initially reluctant suitor, the handsome John Scherer.

It is only with the third couple, the fast-talking Ozzie and a polysyllabic anthropologist, that the show momentarily lapses. Gordon Paddison's gee-whiz dialogue is an encumbrance, as is Kathleen Mahony-Bennett's mugging. Both actors have good singing voices, but Ms. Mahony-Bennett does not seem to be a natural comedienne.

Zack Brown has given the show a crisp, storybook setting, with model mockups of bridges and skyscrapers. There is a glittering Times Square and, for extra pleasure, there is a cute convertible toy Checker cab (so much for reality). In revival, "On the Town" remains resolutely upbeat and carefree. With its blissful air of nostalgia, it is a very nice place to visit.

1989 My 12, C3:4

None of this is overstated, but it is apparent enough to give the play an added edge of recognition.

•

This is not to suggest that Mr. Kahn has shortchanged Shakespeare or neglected other aspects of the play. Floyd King's top-hatted Touchstone is a particular asset, with the actor adopting a wry, almost Noël Coward-like stance that makes his alliance with that country wench, Audrey, all the more amusing. As performed, Rosalind, Celia and Touchstone are a congenial, mutually affectionate trio of travelers seeking enlightenment in Arden.

Melancholy to his weary bones, Ted van Griethuysen does not overplay Jaques's lamentation, but keeps the character as the cautionary opposite of Rosalind and her idealism. Lawrence Redmond is in fine voice as Amiens; Bellina Logan is a forthright Phebe, lovestruck at the sight of Ganymede, and Paris Peet finds an elegance in an effete courtier.

One could wish for a more threatening Charles the Wrestler, too easily outmanned by Mr. Philpot. Doubling as the unfraternal Duke Frederick and Duke Senior, Emery Battis is more at home as the banished than as the banisher. And there is a ubiquitous gentlewoman peering around corners like a baleful wanderer from "Macbeth." But in almost all respects, Mr. Kahn is agile in capturing the mercurial spirit of the play, especially as personified by Ms. Le Beauf and Ms. Gallagher.

The director stresses the theatricality of the work, placing it in a proscenium within a proscenium — a neatly framed architectural design by Andrew Jackness. Before Rosalind delivers the epilogue, the stage is stripped to its austerity. She addresses the audience informally as the actress behind the character, pleading affectingly for a common understanding between men and women, a charge that is the essence of "As You Like It."

1989 My 13, 10:5

Shakespearean Comedy With an American Tone

By MEL GUSSOW
Special to The New York Times

WASHINGTON, May 10 — The forest of Arden is transporting, magically turning the urbanized into the countrified and uniting lovers of contrasting guises. "As You Like It" is a blithe pastoral comedy that draws its strength primarily from the character of Rosalind, that most attractive and witty of Shakespearean heroines.

For his production in the Shakespeare Theater at the Folger, Michael Kahn has cast Sabrina Le Beauf in the central role. Those who know her only as Sondra Huxtable, the oldest daughter on "The Cosby Show," may be surprised to realize that she is an articulate, classically trained actress quite adept at playing Shakespeare.

As required by Rosalind, she has the talent to alter her personality as well as her appearance, exchanging her flouncy costume and courtly manners for the boyish appeal of the runaway Ganymede. In Arden, she finds her fulfillment in the eyes of her suitor, Orlando, that compulsive poetaster who has the odd habit of pinning verses to trees.

Though Mark Philpot is a congenial partner for Ms. Le Beauf, it is the actress who gives their romance its momentum. She is so headstrong that sometimes her quick tongue trips her up, but the character and the actress prove to have an inner resourcefulness.

Mr. Kahn has enhanced the production (the last at the Folger this season) with a subtly American tone. In the city, Rosalind and Celia (Melissa Gallagher) are best friends as well as

cousins, trading secrets and encouraging each other in romantic endeavors. It is only when she is afoot in the forest that Rosalind comprehends the rhapsodic extent of Orlando's ardor and his ability to sustain his half of the dialogue.

Joan Marcus

Sabrina Le Beauf in Michael Kahn's production of Shakespeare's "As You Like It."

Similarly, Mr. Philpot and Edward Gero as his insidious (but ultimately redeemable) brother maintain a rivalry that may strike home with younger Folger theatergoers more used to movies than to Shakespeare.

STAGE VIEW/Walter Kerr

Largely Chaplin? Or Is It Indiana Jones?

ONE OF BILL IRWIN'S CONstant companions in the immensely funny entertainment known as "Largely New York" is a cane, a perfectly ordinary walking cane with which he does certain wondrous things. Actually, he does even more wondrous things with one of those remote controls that make television sets so obedient, but we'll get to that.

At one point, just to give you a preliminary inkling, Mr. Irwin is cheerfully performing a duet with himself — he's right out there on the St. James stage and his image is alongside him on a television monitor — to a ragged-up tune that may or may not be "Tea for Two." Sometimes it is, sometimes it isn't. Either way, both of the Irwins who are shuffling rhythmically about in such perfect unison carry canes.

Gradually it seems that Mr. Irwin, the real one, is beginning to bring too much enthusiasm to his work. Whereupon the one inside the television set gets a firm grip on the bot-

Bill Irwin offers chills, spills, suspense, snakes, passion, corpses and miraculous rescues, and bravest of all, mime.

tom of *his* cane and uses it to produce three sharp raps for attention on the edge of the set that contains him. Enough to bring that other fellow to a submissive, if mystified, halt. The contretemps that now springs up between them is hilarious. No, it's better than that. It's choice.

In addition to the cane, Mr. Irwin wears his trousers baggy, and perhaps it is this familiar combination of factors — cane, baggy trousers — that causes some people to describe him as Chaplinesque. Before we go I must issue a correction here. Mr. Irwin is not Chaplinesque. Chaplin is Chaplinesque. Mr. Irwin is Irwinesque.

If we have got that point straight, we can proceed to the next question.

What *is* Irwinesque?

I could give you a list of the man's qualities as a courteous, trustworthy, clean and thrifty model citizen, bespeaking an early association with the Boy Scouts, though that won't exactly bring us to the point. Oh, let's do it anyway:

Irwin is certainly courteous. He is possessed of supernatural powers whenever he whips out his magical remote control, but is most deferential when it comes to exercising those powers over a lighter-than-air dancer in a shocking-pink leotard, whom he loves. He doesn't mind being ruthless with lights, say, jabbing the electronic gadget at them to make them come on, just as he makes passes at billowing stage curtains when he wants them closed or whipped upwards. A masterly fellow. However, when he does conjure up that fleeting, enchanted girl, he gives no further orders. He looks at her with dream in his eyes and gives her the run of the stage.

Thinking how nice it would be if they could take a little walk in the snow, he not only arranges for a snowfall to take place on the St. James stage, he arranges a snowfall built for two — no more, very private. The snow comes fluttering down, that is to say, in an area approximately two feet square, a good fit for them. That's thoughtfulness. Alas, when the birdlike pink creature is offered a stroll, she shakes her head slowly, if not exactly ruefully, and slips off into the wings. Does Irwin, bitterly disappointed and still yearning, linger idly among the falling flakes, hoping that he looks rather like Ronald Colman in "A Tale of Two Cities"? He does not, not he. Nor does he leave the scene abruptly, taking his bile out on the city. Instead he whips out his all-purpose vacuum cleaner

d vacuums up the snowfall he has created.
neither litters nor loiters.
rwin is helpful, in all matters large or
all. I am now thinking of a moment on
ge when the omnipresent (almost) televi-
1 camera is aimed directly at the audience
t left idle, its technicians having tempo-
ily vanished. Mr. Irwin strolls curiously to
camera, looks into the lens to see the vast
lience staring at him, and promptly and
sibly raises his hands to make that famil-
photographer's gesture of "Closer, come
ser together."

■

And he is singularly brave, though it does
n no good whatsoever. It does not bother
n at all that the great rear stage door
uld open a crack, mysteriously allowing a
cious academic in cap and gown to slith-
nto the proceedings, spy-like. He gives in-
ers elbow room because he is polite, not
wing that they will multiply on him, as the
demics do, until they form a great pie-
ped wedge and advance upon him, poor
ow.
He does not hesitate to look into, or even
mb into, his backstage trunk, even though
s bigger than Pandora's box and presum-
y even more dangerous. A few bod-
turn up in it as the evening proceeds. And
en he is using his TV doodad to summon
sh guests into being, he risks becoming too
olved in the astoundingly agile antics of
o breakdancers headed directly for ner-
us breakdowns. He watches these perform-
s in awe. So do we. One of them — they are
lled poppers on the program, which is all
ht with me — seems to notice that the mu-
al soundtrack which Mr. Irwin has also
mmoned up is now turning vaguely Egypt-
n. This popper, whose real name is
on Chesney, at once begins to writhe as
ugh an oversized snake had entered one of
s arms. As both poppers — the other one is
eve Clemente — now stretch and slither-
gly link arms, fingertips to fingertips, they
otion to Irwin to come join them. It is clear
at he does not — absolutely does not — wish
join them, though, being such a gentle-
an, he does. The minute his fingertips are in
e circuit, the snake — undulating ferocious-
— enters his arm. I saw it.
I think it must have been along about here
that I began to wonder if, instead of
calling his show "Largely New
York," Mr. Irwin mightn't have been
well advised to call it something like
"Bill Irwin and the Temple of Doom."
The film of almost that name, with all

of its snakes, did very good business, I
understand, and it must be said that
in just one hour and 15 minutes the
exhibit at the St. James provides an
audience with all of the very qualities
that made the movie so successful:
chills, spills, suspense, snakes, passion, corpses, miraculous rescues. (I
may have forgotten to mention that
at one point in the goings-on Mr. Irwin
is abruptly whooshed upward to the
roof of the playhouse, there to dangle
by one foot. And I believe I caught a
glimpse of Mr. Irwin plucking from a
suitcase the very same pink dancer's
costume we'd grown so accustomed
to, now empty. The possibly baleful
implications of this left me personally
disturbed until the fetching creature
was rescued.).

■

It now occurs to me that my little
catalogue of Irwinesque qualities
may be of some use to us, after all. It
may have come to your attention that
I haven't quoted anything as being
spoken aloud. That is to say, Bill
Irwin is that very strange beast, a
mime.
What's a mime?
Funny thing. Although practically
everybody knows that mime is some
sort of imitation that is performed
without words, mime didn't really
start that way. Would you believe
that, in the form's ancient beginnings,
the performers actually talked?
Furthermore, mime still hasn't
firmly made up its mind whether to
be totally silent or only occasionally
on such good behavior. Our old friend
Marcel Marceau, of course, is totally
silent. But Bill Irwin wasn't always as
silent as he is these nights at the St.
James. Nor am I thinking of his brilliant performance in someone else's
play (the character Lucky in Beckett's "Waiting for Godot") but of his
work in his own contrivances. I swear
I heard him chattering away during
portions of the pieces he did early on,
over at the American Place. Now he's
really clammed up. What we're getting on Broadway in "Largely New
York" is Irwin plain, Irwin "pure."
But whence this straining after purity, this sometime insistence on a
world gone mute? If I had to give a
capsule answer, my guess would be

something like this: When words are
used, the brain takes charge and the
body is neglected. Mime gives us a
rap on the knuckles to remind us that
there's a body to be accounted for. We
need to remember what it's like.
You may recall that each time you
went to see Marcel Marceau, and no
matter how new the evening's program may have been, the proceedings usually began with the mime's
basic exercise, "Walking Against the
Wind." And you saw, for the first and
only time really, a man walk against
the wind. You don't normally see such
a thing on the street. You're too busy
holding on to your hat. You don't even
see it in a movie. In a movie you
mostly see the wind that is being
walked against.

■

But while Marceau was doing what
was partly a warmup for him, we
were busy making discoveries, seeing
tendons, seeing the moving frame,
seeing bones find their sockets.
And whenever the present poppers
wander into view, you'll instantly —
no, sooner than instantly — see tendons and frames and sockets shivering their timbers giddily, manically,
unmistakably. They all dance, and
good for them.
Of course if you want to dig more

Irwin exhibits all the best qualities of Boy Scouts.

deeply into this mime-show's special
significance you can always say that
what Irwin is showing us is modern
man's last-ditch battle with all the
electronic gadgetry going. Probably
he's doing just that. I was laughing
too much to tell, having begun to
double up as Mr. Irwin first flipped
his remote control at every drop-
curtain and draw-curtain in the
place; by the time they seemed about
to drown him in a tidal wave of swirling velure, I wasn't bothering my
head about meanings. I was a bit
worried about that dancer, missing
from what I took to be her costume,
and was mightily relieved along
about 9:25 to see her lining up for a
bow, costume unwrinkled. I was also
relieved when Mr. Irwin got to kiss
her, kind and courteous, clean and
reverent as ever. It was on the last
curtain call, but when better?
Once more, the names. The truly
stupendous poppers are Leon Chesney and Steve Clemente. The former
is said to have taught Baryshnikov to
breakdance. They tell me Baryshnikov is all right now. The delectable
Margaret Eginton is the nonelectron-
ic sprite, mobile as a sparkler's point
on the Fourth of July. Jeff Gordon is
an academic who dives into the orchestra pit, unconcerned about landing on his mortarboard. All Bill Irwins are Bill Irwin. □

1989 My 14, II:5:1

Alcohol and Autos

CROSSIN' THE LINE, by Phil Bosakowski; directed by Sonya Baehr; set by Michael C.
Smith; lights by Dave Feldman; costumes by
Debra Stein; production stage manager, Denise Nations; general manager, Stephen Nebgen. Presented by the Lamb's Theater Company, Carolyn Rossi Copeland, producing director. At the Little Theater, 130 West 44th
Street.

Ellie Burke	Brenda Thomas
Bette	Judy Malloy
Trudee Waits	Talia Paul
Mitch Kohler	John Speredakos
Sergeant Martin/Richie	Michael Francis Boyle
Hayden Doyle	Josh Mosby

By WILBORN HAMPTON

Of all the perils of modern life, none
casts the net of destruction further
than drug and alcohol abuse. Phil
Bosakowski examines one tragedy of
such abuse in his short, taut play
"Crossin' the Line," which is being
presented at the Lamb's Little Theater.
Three teen-agers — a boy and two
girls — are out for a ride to celebrate
the young man's birthday. They have
a few beers. Roadwork has closed one
lane of a highway and their car plows
into a row of cement-filled oil drums.
One girl is killed and the other is injured so badly she cannot speak. Hayden Doyle, the boy who was driving,
suffers a broken wrist. The damage
to the survivors' lives, of course, does
not end there.
Clara, the girl who is killed, was a
class president, a cheerleader and
chairman of the local chapter of Students Against Driving Drunk. Everyone blames Hayden for Clara's death,
including Hayden himself, but none
more virulently than Clara's brother,
Mitch, who was also Hayden's close
friend. But as even most teen-agers
know, guilt and innocence are never
so easily defined. In fact, Mr. Bosakowski has dealt the hands very
evenly and avoids pat answers. Hayden is found guilty on three charges
arising from the accident, but on a
technicality he is acquitted of the
charge of driving under the influence.
A big question is whether Clara herself had been drinking and what happened in the car at the time of the accident.
Mr. Bosakowski's play is more a
documentary than a drama, and that
is not intended as a criticism. The
writing is straight to the point and
never lapses into sermonizing. But
there is little real conflict to turn the
story into a drama for the stage.
Playing at just over an hour, "Crossin' the Line" should find a home in
school drama clubs and church theaters.
Sonya Baehr has directed an able
cast and keeps the story moving
unobtrusively through a series of
quick scene changes, forward and
backward in time, in and out of court-
rooms, police stations, hospital
wards, an ambulance and a lonely
stretch of highway. Brenda Thomas
is especially good as the lawyer and
Josh Mosby gives a credible performance as Hayden.

1989 My 14, 48:1

Warring Friends

THE SUNSHINE BOYS, by Neil Simon; directed
by Marilyn Chris; sets, Ray Recht; costumes,
Karen Hummel; lights, Dan Kinsley; sound,
Jonathan Rigg; stage manager, Saylor Cres-
well. Presented by the Jewish Repertory Thea-
ter, Ran Avni, artistic director; Edward M.
Cohen, associate director. At 344 East 14th
Street.

Willie Clark	Lee Wallace
Al Lewis	Bernie Passeltiner
Ben Silverman	Fred Einhorn
Roxie O'Neill, R.N.	Miriam Burton
Phil Schaefer/Patient	Edwin Bordo
Eddie	Patrick Cognetta
Nursey	Amy Gordon

By RICHARD F. SHEPARD

Among the more audacious ventures in theatrical circles is the revival of a play that, through the
medium of film, has gained such
popularity that it becomes the stand-

*Bill Irwin with, from left, Jeff Gordon, Steve Clemente, Leon Chesney
and Margaret Eginton in "Largely New York"—Mime gives us a rap
on the knuckles to remind us that there's a body to be accounted for.
We need to remember what it's like.*

ard against which later productions of it are bound to be measured.

For one who has never seen Neil Simon's hilarious comedy "The Sunshine Boys" in either the stage version of 1972 or the 1975 film, which lives on in fairly frequent rerun, the revival by the Jewish Repertory Theater will be a completely satisfying, enjoyable evening. For others, with views colored particularly by memories of Walter Matthau and George Burns as the film's cranky antiquated vaudeville team, "The Sunshine Boys" on East 14th Street will still seem amusing, if somewhat less rollicking.

The Jewish Repertory, which says this is the first Off Broadway revival of the play, has delivered an attractive staging of the comedy, under the direction of Marilyn Chris. The production briskly pursues a gag-strewn script to tell the story of the two old and virtually retired one-time show biz headliners who hate each other but who are brought together to revive their comedy routine on a television special.

Lee Wallace, as Willie Clark, the team member who keeps up the illusion of still being at work, projects a strong voice and personality and is genuinely funny. He has a vague resemblance to Mayor Koch, and the irascible character he portrays is the essence of the familiar old-style New York comic. If one must make comparisons, one must say he doesn't achieve the saturnine malevolence that Mr. Matthau did in the film, but, all right, he's a different sort of hysteric.

Bernie Passeltiner is no less effective as the more philosophical partner, Al Lewis, who is happily retired and living with his daughter in New Jersey. Mr. Passeltiner also grasps the more logical and serene nature of his role, yet very nicely nurtures it into the exasperated anger that his confederate generates in him.

Fred Einhorn admirably fits into the part of Willie's long-suffering nephew, the unavailing peacemaker who contains his exasperation even when Willie forgets the names of his two small children. Miriam Burton is appealing and attractive as the nurse who attends to Willie after his heart attack, eats his candy and puts him in his place.

Theater lovers will appreciate one advantage this presentation of "The Sunshine Boys" has over the film. It is live theater, and there are all sorts of undertows between audience and cast that a movie projector filters out. All that, and the fact that Mr. Simon has given us a classically funny bit of business, a comedy with an understanding of human frustration, makes a visit to the Jewish Rep a worthy pilgrimage.

1989 My 14, 49:1

Las Vegas Afterlife

LEGENDS IN CONCERT, created and directed by John Stuart; lighting design and production consultant, Dennis Condon; choreography by Inez Mourning; musical director, Kerry McCoy; costumes by Betty Lurenz; technical consultant, Ron Popp; multi-media design, Media Innovations/Joseph Jarred; technical director, Alan Murphy; lasers, Mark Fisher; supervisor in charge of production, Steve Yuhasz; associate producers, Don Saxon, Robert R. Blume and Malcolm Allen. Presented by Mr. Stuart. At the Academy Theater, 234 West 43d Street.

WITH: Clive Baldwin, Eddie Carroll, Randy Clark, Donny Ray Evins, Katie LaBourdette, Tony Roi, Julie Sheppard, George Trullinger and Daryl Wagner.

By STEPHEN HOLDEN

"Legends in Concert," the glitzy Las Vegas revue that opened at the Academy Theater on Wednesday evening, presents nine performers doing mechanical impersonations of stars who have little in common beyond the fact that they are all dead.

With its discothèque lighting, cheerleaders' choreography and a slide show that contrasts blown-up images of the stars being remembered with their imitators' live contortions, the revue is one of those ghoulish concoctions that probably could have emanated only from the Nevada desert.

●

As directed by John Stuart, who also produced, the performers capture only the surface qualities of the stars they impersonate. The one exception is Tony Roi's Elvis Presley. Mr. Roi, who physically resembles the 1950's Elvis, injects passion and humor into "All Shook Up," "My Way," "Jailhouse Rock" and "Trilogy" — a medley of "Dixie," "All My Trials" and "Battle Hymn of the Republic" that became a Presley staple. Though his leg gyrations are not Presley's, he at least seems to be alive, alert and having fun.

The same can't be said of the other homages, which have all the enthusiasm of an animated wax museum. Eddie Carroll's Jack Benny is a mugging, eyeball-rolling caricature. George Trullinger's Buddy Holly leads a pom-pom-waving cheering squad. As Al Jolson, Clive Baldwin dons blackface, does a little jig and exclaims, "Eat your heart out, Michael Jackson!" Daryl Wagner's Liberace has a shrill Southern accent. Julie Sheppard, as Judy Garland, sings with a grating nasality. And Katie LaBourdette, as Marilyn Monroe, has no heart.

●

The most accurate impersonation, Donny Ray Evins's Nat King Cole, is spoiled by some vocal grandstanding. The most inaccurate is Randy Clark's burly gum-chewing travesty of John Lennon.

At the end of "Legends in Concert," the cast lines up to sing a chorus of "Rock-and-Roll Heaven," an odd choice seeing as only three of the nine legends — Holly, Lennon and Presley — had anything to do with rock-and-roll. But then, almost everything about "Legends in Concert" rings false.

1989 My 14, 49:3

Go Along to Get Along, Or Demand to Be Real?

YANKEE DAWG YOU DIE, by Philip Kan Gotanda; directed by Sharon Ott; set and projection by Kent Dorsey; costumes by Jess Goldstein; lighting by Dan Kotlowitz; music and sound by Stephen LeGrand and Eric Drew Feldman; production stage manager, Robin Rumpf; production manager, Carl Mulert. Presented by Playwrights Horizons, Andre Bishop, artistic director; Paul S. Daniels, executive director. At 416 West 42d Street.

Vincent .... Sab Shimono
Bradley .... Stan Egi

By FRANK RICH

"Yankee Dawg You Die" — a cartoon exclamation tinged with both genuine anger and Hollywood camp — is the perfect title for Philip Kan Gotanda's piquant comedy at Playwrights Horizons. Mr. Gotanda's subject, soberly put, is the humiliation

that Asian-American actors have suffered when enslaved by screen stereotyping, whether during the glamorous reign of Anna May Wong or in Michael Cimino's "Year of the Dragon." Yet his tone is anything but preachy. Mr. Gotanda is a polemicist who sees both sides of a question, a writer whose grievances are balanced by a wicked sense of humor. He gladly embraces the ludicrous clichés of "Godzilla" or World War II P.O.W. potboilers if that's what it takes to turn their racism inside out.

●

Though there are only two characters in "Yankee Dawg You Die," they encapsulate an entire subchapter in Hollywood history. Vincent (Sab Shimono) is an elegant silver-haired one-time Oscar nominee (best supporting actor, of course) who has always been willing to play subserviently by the industry's rules, which required endless appearances as waiters, houseboys, sadistic Japanese officers and "dumb North Vietnamese generals." Bradley (Stan Egi), Vincent's young new-found friend and colleague, in jeans and leather jacket, is a third-generation Japanese-American trained at the tony American Conservatory Theater in San Francisco. While Vincent was bowing and scraping and affecting a caricatured accent, Bradley was paying his dues in introspective, independent Asian-American films suitable for exhibition at the New York Film Festival.

When we meet them at a glittery Hollywood Hills party, Vincent is dressed in white, Bradley in black, and that's how they tend to see things. The cynical, successful older actor still refers to himself as an "Oriental"; he takes pride in having never turned down a role. Bradley is at once condescending and naïve, uncompromising and ambitious. He has little doubt that a William Morris agent will land him a leading part in a television series, and he vows never to play characters that demean his race.

●

Mr. Gotanda is poised between his two men. There is enormous affection in his presentation of Vincent, whose show-business past in vaudeville's so-called Chop Suey Circuit and in stage musicals like "Tea Cakes and Moon Songs" is fondly evoked. Vincent

teaches Bradley a shuffling soft-shoe and happily remembers a long-ago standing ovation from Sessue Hayakawa. In those days, he reminds his young protégé, "there was no Asian-American consciousness or Asian-American theater" but only "a handful of Orientals who wanted to perform." In Vincent's own unquenchable delight in performing — conveyed with priceless authority by Mr. Shimono, who himself labored as the original houseboy in Broadway's musical-comedy "Mame" — we see what kept him going, no matter what the sellouts required for steady employment.

Bradley makes a strong case against Vincent, reminding him that every screen stereotype comes with a price: some child somewhere will be taunted as a "gook" or worse. But Mr. Gotanda doesn't give his young upstart a monopoly on wisdom or virtue. As "Yankee Dawg" contains a hilarious satire of the white-man's-burden epic in which Vincent gained his Academy Award nomination — he played Peter O'Toole's servant, inevitably named Saki — so it offers a devilish send-up of a monologue in Bradley's first Asian-American play. As spoken by an alienated youth driving the freeways and misguidedly fantasizing about the Asian roots of Neil Sedaka, the anti-assimilationist soliloquy is not without its echoes of David Henry Hwang's early "F.O.B."

A realist befriends an idealist in 'Yankee Dawg You Die.'

Once Vincent and Bradley meet each other halfway, "Yankee Dawg" finds an even broader generosity of spirit. The men impersonate their Caucasian Hollywood heroes, from Fred Astaire to Mickey Rourke, and work devotedly at an acting-class scene from Shakespeare. Vincent may never concede that he was a "Chinese Stepin Fetchit," but neither does he forget his "dead dreams,"

Gerry Goodstein

Stan Egi, left, and Sab Shimono, the only characters in "Yankee Dawg You Die" at Playwrights Horizons. The play deals with the stereotyping Asian-American actors have had to endure on the big screen.

slain by the dream factory. When he reminisces about the interracial romance edited out of his role in a Sam Fuller police melodrama, a black-and-white still of his phantom triumph is projected behind him, a celluloid specter of Hollywood's shame rising up from the cutting-room floor.

Unfortunately, the men's delicate symbiosis becomes diagrammatic in Act II. The moment that the older man decides that the younger one resembles him 35 years earlier, Vincent and Bradley start to learn from each other with unconvincing patness, to the point of exchanging polemical positions, rhetorical phrases and even wardrobe colors. Worse, Vincent is revealed to have a second buried identity that plunges the play into ideological overload and accentuates the superficiality with which Mr. Gotanda treats both men's private lives.

Though the director, Sharon Ott, struggles with the play's latent shift to a more metaphysical tone, her production is otherwise as sharp as the writing. "Yankee Dawg" opens with a mock credits sequence redolent of B drive-in movies and proceeds at a stylish clip in a handsome set (by Kent Dorsey) that bridges Asian austerity and American pop. Mr. Shimono and Mr. Egi do the same with their beguiling acting partnership, in which not only does East meet West, but also father meets son and pathos meets comedy. While Mr. Gotanda has rewarded both actors with the roles denied Vincent in his Hollywood heyday — "human beings with honest emotions" — the fun comes from watching them grow directly out of the ashes of the inhuman roles that came before.

1989 My 15, C13:4

Coming of Age

OVER FORTY, book by Celeste Walker; music, lyrics, musical arrangments and direction by Weldon; directed by Mikell Pinkney; scenic and costume designs by Felix E. Cochren; lighting design by Christian Epps; production stage management by Avan. Presented by Marjorie Moon, owner. At the Billie Holiday Theater, 1368 Fulton Street, at Restoration Plaza, in the Bedford-Stuyvesant section of Brooklyn.

Gwen Matthews .... Eunice Newkirk
Patricia Ellen Shaw .... Janyse M. Singleton
Beryl Paige .... Marisa Francesca Turner
Annie Ruth Johnson .... Lady Peachena

By RICHARD F. SHEPARD

There's no plot to speak of in "Over 40," a charmer of a musical playing at the intimate Billie Holiday Theater at the Restoration Plaza in Brooklyn, but there is certainly no dearth of stories.

This show, with a book by Celeste Walker and music and lyrics by Weldon Irvine, places four women onstage to celebrate — or mourn — as the fourth joins the others in that great sorority of women who have attained their 40th birthday.

Each of these four personable women represents a somewhat different outlook on life. Three are career women raised in the city, although one is divorced, another is unfruitfully married and concentrating on fertility pills, and the last is single only because she doesn't want to leave her mother. The fourth, older than the others, is a homemaker from Georgia whose thoughts run to the Lord and to her children.

The women speak and sing about the 1960's, about careers, about men, about the various states of womanhood. That's not a plot, but it is certainly a topic. What with good music sung, crooned or belted by these four singers, and with the help of dialogue that is perceptive, sharp and good-humored, "Over 40" achieves a spirited intimacy that is appealing.

Under Mikell Pinkney's direction, the quartet switches from comedy to spiritual fervor without clashing gears. The four go into a reverie about the Lone Ranger, the Mouseketeers and Shirley Temple — the latter recalled in a short mincing delivery of "The Good Ship Lollipop" by Marisa Francesca Turner, whose powerful vocals and flair for comedy make her a hit of the show.

•

Act I concludes with the four singing "We Shall Overcome" in an unusual and riveting arrangement that embraces several musical styles and reflects the finely attuned sensitivity of Mr. Irvine; it engaged the entire audience, which sang along and applauded loudly. As Annie Ruth Johnson from the rural South, Lady Peachena delivered a well-received folksy commentary in a manner that was funny yet touching and dignified. Her songs, mostly in the gospel format, are loud and clear and heartfelt.

Eunice Newkirk, as the recently divorced birthday person, gives depth to a song called "Why Did We Part?" and otherwise also communicates the mixed emotions of a woman who wants her independence but also needs love. Janyse M. Singleton, as another 40-year-old, conveys the air of an efficient woman who has come to realize that there is more to life than putting feet on the corporate ladder. She gives a poignant edge to her solo, "Ignite My Love."

"Over 40" is by no means a presentation in the traditional mold of what makes a play. But as it wryly or sentimentally retraces American social history of the last several decades from a black perspective, it is a musical entertainment within whose bounds pop, rock-and-roll, reggae, rap, doo-wop, jazz and gospel freely roam. With a sensitive ear, one may hear more than music at this pleasant offering.

1989 My 16, C17:1

Replaying the Music

BLAME IT ON THE MOVIES, musical sequences compiled and conceived by Ron Abel, Billy Barnes and David Galligan, from an original idea by Franklin R. Levy. Directed by Mr. Galligan; original music and lyrics by Mr. Barnes; musical direction and arrangements by Mr. Abel; musical staging and choreography Larry Hyman; set design, Fred Duer; costume design, Bonnie Stauch; lighting design, Michael Gilliam; sound design Jon Gottlieb; production stage manager, Elsbeth M. Collins. Presented by Roger Berlind, Franklin R. Levy and Gregory Harrison. At the Criterion Center Stage Left, 1530 Broadway, at 45th Street.

WITH: Sandy Edgerton, Kathy Garrick, Bill Hutton, Christine Kellogg, Peter Marc, Dan O'Grady, Barbara Sharma and Patty Tiffany.

By STEPHEN HOLDEN

"Blame It on the Movies" the perky new revue of movie songs at the Criterion Center, springs from a nearly sure-fire theatrical premise. Put eight singers and dancers on a set that evokes the velvet twilight of an old-time movie palace, hand them 40 years of mostly familiar film songs to perform, and somewhere along the way everyone will have at least one nostalgic button pushed. The concept is so enticing in fact that watching this innocuously pleasant entertainment, one is continually nagged by a realization of the many ways in which a terrific opportunity has been squandered.

Directed by David Galligan and staged and choreographed by Larry Hyman, "Blame It on the Movies" compacts more than 75 songs, song fragments and excerpts from sound tracks into a cheerful musical cavalcade that spans four decades, beginning in the late 1930's. The songs, many of which are glossed in elaborate medleys that offer only snatches of particular tunes, are grouped in thematic blocks. Some are chronological ("The 40's," "The War Years") and others conceptual ("Fox in Love," "Foreign Film Tribute").

•

Were "Blame It on the Movies" everything it might have been, the show would present a constantly

Marc Bryan-Brown

Barbara Sharma as an usher in "Blame It on the Movies."

changing kaleidoscope of looks, moods and sounds resurrecting various movie genres and period flavors. Instead, what one gets is a crisply paced but blandly performed procession of songs delivered by singers who have decent voices but very little personality or sense of style.

Though the two best vocal performances — of "My Foolish Heart" and "The Long Hot Summer" — both belong to sultry voiced Patty Tiffany, one could easily name a score of young New York theater and cabaret singers with stronger voices and more expression. And Ron Abel's arrangements for the tinny-sounding quintet backing the singers barely distinguish between 40's swing and 80's pop-rock. Everything is homogenized into the same jangly, streamlined television-variety-show idiom.

The show's one moment of genuine movie magic is a ballet tribute to the Hollywood film score, in which Christine Kellogg and Dan O'Grady do an anguished pas de deux to a recording of Franz Waxman's score for "A Place in the Sun." The emotionally jagged dancing, the lush overripe score and the garish jail-cell lighting conjure up the movie's aura of doomed romance and bring back strong memories of Montgomery Clift and the young Elizabeth Taylor. The revue's most astutely conceived segment, "Fox in Love," pays

tribute to the floridly oratorical love songs embellishing the romantic films released by 20th Century-Fox in the 1950's and early 1960's. The genre's most exaggeratedly stylized ballads — "April Love," and "Love Is a Many Splendored Thing" — had stentorian melodies by Sammy Fain and lyrics by Paul Francis Webster that were declaimed like scripture: love the "April rose that only grows in the early spring." But though the segment presents obvious possibilities for parody, the opportunity isn't pursued.

Mr. Hyman's choreography strongly echoes Tommy Tune's far wittier staging for "A Day in Hollywood/A Night in the Ukraine," the show that "Blame It on the Movies" most closely resembles. In the most inventive bit, an unglamorous young couple attending "A Man and a Woman" disappear behind their theater sets and rise seconds later transformed into sexy icons of 60's Continental sophistication. The show could do with a dozen more moments this clever.

1989 My 18, C22:3

The Impossible Dream

ALIVE BY NIGHT, by Reine Bartève; translated by Alex Gross; directed by Françoise Kourilsky; set and lights by Watoku Ueno; music and sound by David Simons; costumes by Carol Ann Pelletier; stage manager, Lamis Khalaf. Presented by Ubu Repertory Theater, Ms. Kourilsky, artistic director. At 15 West 28th Street.

Ray and Geslin .... T. Scott Lilly
Nick and Beaurepaire .... Joseph McKenna
Marina and Cécile Dudion ...... Corliss Preston
The Watchman .... Thomas Carson
Margot and De Lalance .... René Houtrides

By D. J. R. BRUCKNER

Reine Bartève sifts through the trash heap of history in her new play, "Alive by Night," being presented by Ubu Repertory Theater to celebrate the bicentenary of the French Revolution. Up to a point the play is about the surrender of the city of Verdun to Prussian forces in September 1792, when a number of European monarchs tried to stop the revolution and restore Louis XVI to the throne. The French version of the play will open in Verdun on Saturday as part of the official bicentennial festivities.

Ms. Bartève's choice of which revolutionary event to celebrate tells you what she is up to. Gen. Nicolas de Beaurepaire, commanding the defense of Verdun, committed suicide when the civil authorities voted to open the gates to the enemy. Even though Beaurepaire eventually ended up in the Pantheon in Paris as a hero, what the city councilors did was not glorious.

•

But then glory does not go far in this play. Ray, a young vagabond (T. Scott Lilly), and his girlfriend, Marina (Corliss Preston), find a down-and-out musician, Nick (Joseph McKenna), poring over a tattered diary he has found — one written by Cécile Dudion, who left a Carmelite convent to join the revolution and was in Verdun at its fall. As they read her account aloud, Nick becomes Beaurepaire, Ray one of his officers and Marina the renegade nun. Soon the three are engulfed in the agony of the beleaguered city.

Not for long. The junkyard's watchman (Thomas Carson), a lonely clown, bursts in with a loaded gun and

67

only reluctantly agrees to join in the game. Finally, a rich woman named Margot. (René Houtrides) comes along looking for her dog, Lulu, and, while she makes a valiant effort to take on the role of an 18th-century noblewoman who is infatuated with Beaurepaire, she never quite gets into it. In fact, she brings the others back to the present and you are left wondering whether the meek dreaming of noble revolt can ever stand a chance against the seductions of wealth and empty-headed fun.

Ms. Bartève sends up a lot of pieties of French patriotism along the way and even throws in a few lyrical outbursts that, in David Simons's arrangements, are amusing parodies of French art songs.

There are some laughs in "Alive by Night," which continues at the Ubu Repertory Theater, 15 West 28th Street, until Saturday. But all in all, the idea is better than the execution. The role of the watchman, as the easily duped guardian of reality, is not clearly drawn. And the subversive function of the flighty Margot is never exploited enough to make the character the destructive comic she could be, even though Ms. Houtrides makes her as funny as she can. But it's a nice thought, to celebrate a nation's founding event with a little deconstruction.

1989 My 18, C22:3

And the Winner Is . . .

PRIZES, music and lyrics by Charles DeForest; book by Raffi Pehlivanian; directed by Lee Minskoff; choreography by Margo Sappington; musical direction and arrangements, Ned Ginsburg; set design, Jane Sablow; lighting design, Beau Kennedy; production manager, Christophe Pierre; stage manager, John Rainwater; costume coordinator, Robert Griggs. Presented by AMAS Repertory, Rosetta LeNoire, artistic director and founder; Jeffrey Solis, managing director. At 1 East 104th Street.

WITH: Bruce Barbaree, Nick Corley, Natania Cox, Peter Ermides, Luther Fontaine, Martron Gales, Nancy Groff, Paul Hoover, Dexter Jones, Allen Walker Lane, Heidi Mollenhauer, Kari Nicolaisen, Doug Okerson, Rita Renha, Troy Rintala, Mary Stout, Darcy Thompson and Karen Ziemba.

By STEPHEN HOLDEN

"Prizes," the new musical at the AMAS Repertory Theater, offers the discomfiting sight of marginally talented singers, actors and dancers portraying fictional musical comedy legends at the peak of their powers.

The show, whose book attempts to condense several novels' worth of plot into just over two hours, flashes back on the lives of some half-dozen performers who have been nominated for a mythical musical-comedy award. Together, they embody a cross section of modern Broadway star types.

Leda Farrell (Nancy Groff) suggests a hybrid of Rosalind Russell, Angela Lansbury and Carol Channing, but with a strong dash of vitriol. Milton Gershe (Allen Walker Lane), is a roly-poly Zero Mostel type, and Edie Winters (Heidi Mollenhauer) recalls the fledgling Barbra Streisand. Rounding out the contestants are Shoo-Fly Lewis (Luther Fontaine), a veteran black vaudevillian, and Jess and Maggie Lincoln (Doug Okerson and Karen Ziemba), a song-and-dance team on the comeback trail.

At its best, "Prizes," suggests a pale shadow of "Merrily We Roll Along" and "Follies" in the way it tries to sum up Broadway musical history through generic songs and production numbers. The better-than-average score, by Charles DeForest, shows the composer's stylistic grasp of theater song styles as varied as those of Cole Porter and Jerry Herman. His lyrics, however, often clunk in their attempt at super-sophisticated wordplay.

•

The show's best moments are its tap-dance routines, executed by Mr. Fontaine and Martron Gales, who plays Shoo-Fly's son. Mr. Fontaine, unfortunately, has no singing voice. Nor does Ms. Groff, who gives a gorgonlike portrayal of an aging Broadway diva. Under the direction of Lee Minskoff, the level of most of the acting is unintentional caricature.

1989 My 18, C22:4

Performer Portrays A Nonperformer

S. J. PERELMAN IN PERSON, by Bob Shanks, based on the published works of S. J. Perelman; directed by Ann Shanks; sets by Wes Peters; costumes by Leon I. Brauner; lights by Mal Sturchio. Presented by Comco Productions Inc. At the Cherry Lane Theater, 38 Commerce Street.

S. J. Perelman .... Lewis J. Stadlen

By MEL GUSSOW

Though S. J. Perelman was pigeonholed as a humorist, he was, first of all, a literary artist — an acrobat with language — and his wit and erudition are imperishable. Feeling low? Enervated by ennui? Read Perelman and rejoice.

These and other thoughts arise in hindsight (as in "The Hindsight Saga," the author's regrettably unfinished memoirs) after seeing "S. J. Perelman in Person," a monodrama drawn — and, one might suggest, quartered — from his published work. Starring Lewis J. Stadlen, the Bob Shanks play opened last night at the Cherry Lane Theater.

The first obstacle is that Perelman was not himself a performer. Some of his pieces have, of course, been performed (by the Marx Brothers and others), but in person he was a man to whom histrionics did not come naturally. His clowning was reserved for print. His essays — his feuilletons — were written to be read, privately or aloud. His comedy sketches, though not easy to act, are stageworthy (as in his play "The Beauty Part").

•

Mr. Shanks freely mixes both aspects of Perelman, and Mr. Stadlen — perhaps "button cute" but not exactly "rapier keen" — acts everything. This means that, playing Perelman, he cavorts and does voices: Groucho Marx, George S. Kaufman and even James Cagney and Peter Lorre. The imitations are impressive (except for the women), but they are also self-depleting. One voice that seems to elude the actor is that of Perelman himself, missing his Rhode Island twang and sounding closer to Groucho.

Mr. Stadlen achieved his own first celebrity impersonating Groucho in the musical "Minnie's Boys" (and went on to play many other roles successfully). The inescapable conclusion is that within his Perelman lurks a Groucho eager to get out — to light a cigar, raise his eyebrows and scurry across the stage at a crouch. That probably would have resulted in a funnier show. But this is Perelman, and for believability the delivery should be low-key and marked by savoir-faire.

As a framework, there is Mr. Stadlen inhabiting a book-lined study. He begins at a recline, then leaps to his feet and into action, which means he clips an article from a newspaper — an attempted illustration of the Perelman method of creativity. The actor then embarks on a discursive journey, occasionally accompanied by visual aids.

He holds up a murky copy of an early Perelman cartoon ("I've got Bright's disease and he has mine") and projects random slides from a Perelman family album (pictures of his wife and his brother-in-law, Nathanael West), without furnishing especially illuminating commentary. Relentlessly, the show raises subjects that it is unprepared to develop, including the author's relationship with the Marx Brothers and his own proclivity for global peregrinations.

Any compilation of Perelman is bound to strike some comic chords, although, oddly, some of the funnier moments in the play deal not with the author but with others. There are one-liners from Dorothy Parker as well as words from Groucho, as in the comedian's blurb for the book jacket of one Perelman collection: "From the moment I picked up your book until I laid it down, I was convulsed with laughter. Some day I intend reading it."

Mr. Shanks and Ann Shanks, as director, have clouded the literary waters by surrounding the actor with props — a skeleton for a sketch about a doctor; funny hats (including a pithy one suitable for Captain Spaulding), and a gorilla, which leads unwisely to the title character dancing with an anthropoid. Were Perelman alive, undoubtedly he would have stirred from his alembics and retorts and cast an onomatopoetic aspersion.

1989 My 18, C22:4

Of Men and Women

EQUAL 'WRIGHTS, three one-act plays. Set design, Matthew Moore and James Wolk; lighting design, Brian MacDevitt; costume design, Michael Schler; sound design, Scott Sanders; production stage manager, Denise Laffer; production manager, Jonathan Dimock Secor; associate producer, Christina Rosati; stage manager, Cathy D. Tomlin. Presented by Manhattan Punch Line, Steve Kaplan, artistic director. At the Judith Anderson Theater, 422 West 42d Street.

THE AGREEMENT, by Janet Neipris; directed by Steven Kaplan; assistant director, Catherine Curtin.
WITH: Susan Pellegrino, Richmond Hoxie, Ilana Levine, Pat Nesbit, Brian Keeler and David Wasson.

MARATHONS, by Terri Wagener; directed by Robin Saex.
WITH: Ellen Tobie and Michael French

HOW IT HANGS, by Grace McKeaney; directed by Melia Bensussen.
WITH: Caris Corfman, Robin Groves, Beth Dixon, Peggity Price and Miles Herter.

By D. J. R. BRUCKNER

The most energetic of three one-act plays in Manhattan Punch Line's "Equal 'Wrights" (by playwrights who are women) also has the snappiest lines. "Marathons" by Terri Wagener is, of course, about the New York City Marathon — and the other marathons of life endured by the play's two characters, She (No. 8,219 in the 1988 marathon) and He (No. 13,099).

Ellen Tobie and Michael French actually run, mostly in place, through the 35 minutes of this piece, and they end up a little damp. But these actors, Ms. Wagener and the director, Robin Saex, make the running seem as natural as any stage movement. What you remember is not foot patter, but a middle-aged divorced sperm-bank manager from Iowa teaching a middle-aged, wisecracking and womanizing man from the Bronx a few lessons about honesty, tenderness, endurance and, most important, competition as they trot through the five boroughs.

"You know, this isn't as much fun as I thought it would be," He says halfway through this, his first long race. The play is much more fun than one imagined it could be.

•

"The Agreement," by Janet Neipris, jumps from California to New York City and from a courthouse to a cafe in 10 short scenes running 55 minutes. Ten or 15 minutes could probably be cut to the play's advantage, but this is a funny and wise play about a separated couple approaching their final divorce decree — with little help from the people they are gamely trying to date or from their lawyers, who compete not only with each other but also with their clients.

Ms. Neipris's imagination runs to sitcom at times, but she has a wonderful ear for the way people talk when they are trying to say the right thing in an unfamiliar and unnerving situation; the writing is this play's great strength. It must be said that Steve Kaplan, the director, and an experienced cast do not always do justice to it. Some wonderful lines seem to float out of the characters impersonally, as though their emotions and at times even their bodies were elsewhere.

•

Grace McKeaney's "How It Hangs" is supposed to take place in Wyoming, but the accents adopted by the actors often make you think it must be the deep southern part of the state. No matter. Ms. McKeaney is exploring the self-doubts and mutual distrusts of four battered women trying to give one another support in a makeshift shelter, and their courage, anger, humor and suffering would be compelling in any inflection.

This is still a messy play that cries out for some rewriting, but in this performance under the direction of Melia Bensussen, it develops force when it turns from the corny and awkward humor of the opening scene to the wrenching departure of one woman, who is leaving to marry the man who had once beat her. The passage from the loud and sometimes treacherous laughter of the first few minutes to the quiet sad smiles at the end is a journey filled with surprising emotional turns.

1989 My 18, C20:3

The Mating And Unmating Game

ANCIENT HISTORY, by David Ives; directed by Jason McConnell Buzas; scenery by Philipp Jung; lighting by Deborah Constantine; costumes by Claudia Stephens; sound design, David Ferdinand; production stage manager, Greg Weiss; stage manager, Tony Luna; producing associate, Herbert H. O'Dell; general manager, Gordon Farrell. Presented by

Primary Stages Company, Casey Childs, artistic director; Janet Reed, associate artistic director. At the 45th Street Theater, 354 West 45th Street.

Ruth .... Beth McDonald
Jack ....Christopher Wells

By MEL GUSSOW

As a playwright, David Ives is the inventor of what could be called stop-and-go comedies. A scene begins, then is interrupted by a bell or a buzzer, and the scene starts again, with the characters revising, rejecting or repeating what was said before. This approach can work with splendid comic precision, as it did last year in Mr. Ives's one-act "Sure Thing," in which he offered infinite variations on a young couple's first meeting.

The author uses a similar approach in his first full-length play, "Ancient History" (at Primary Stages), a two-character comedy dealing with a couple who have been living together for six months. Though the play never quite succeeds in accomplishing its aim, it gives added evidence of the author's originality and his special brand of comic bravura.

The play begins and ends in a bedroom and, consequently, is not without its farcical and sexual implications. Ruth and Jack, both in their mid-30's, start by convincing us of their similarities — as "tall, thin, funny people" who adore each other — and gradually convince themselves of their irreconcilable differences.

Together, the two create their own apparently invulnerable fortress. Like Spencer Tracy and Katharine Hepburn, they call each other by the same nickname, Pinky (one of a number of film references in the play). Their shared routines and buzzwords become amulets against outsiders, such as family. They are so in tune that one will tell a story and both will know the punch line. For most of the first act, they are companionable company for the audience as well as for each other, with the credit shared by the playwright, his director, Jason McConnell Buzas, and the actors, Beth McDonald and Christopher Wells.

Quite early, they speak about the apparent durability of their relationship and what it might lead to, meaning marriage. Jack has been married once and is divorced. Ruth is tempted by the prospect (and encouraged by parental and peer pressure). She suggests, "We could make wonderful kids." He responds, intuitively, "We *are* wonderful kids."

On one level, it is that perpetuation of enforced adolescence that holds them together. At work, as he is with Ruth, Jack is a man without responsibilities, although one would not say that he is irresponsible. He just wants to continue indulging his pleasures. Ruth becomes insistent about growing up, but her motivations are mixed, deriving at least as much from a sense of propriety as from psychological need.

The growing disparity is symbolized — and also dramatically simplified — by the fact that they are of different faiths. She is Jewish. He is an "ex-lapsed Catholic," with no defined religious belief. She begins to make familial demands even before they can agree on marriage in principle.

•

As the two move through their mating — and unmating — ritual, the telephone periodically rings, the stop-and-go aspect of the play signifying a change in conversation. Sometimes,

after a ring, the characters switch subjects (from harmony to jealousy, from themselves to an earlier generation). Sometimes they repeat or rephrase the dialogue. Occasionally, one will even answer the telephone. If the playwright has a distinct use in mind for the device, he has not communicated it to the audience (as he did in "Sure Thing"). The two acts also occur, somewhat predictably, before and after a party. Nevertheless, the play retains its ingenuity and is given ingratiating, carefully modulated performances by the two actors (on a nicely understated bedroom set by Philipp Jung).

As encouraged by the author, we wonder how two people who are evidently so "crazy about each other" can move so far apart. Jack explains the shift by saying that they are characters in a new genre — "screwball tragedy," which is not an inappropriate label for the play itself. As the title of the tantalizing comedy suggests, the divisiveness between men and women is, of course, ancient history.

1989 My 18, C29:3

A Noh Blend of the Medieval and Modern

•

By ALLAN KOZINN

Ryo Noda, a young Japanese composer and instrumentalist, has written several works in which he has tried to find common ground between his country's traditional music and its Western-influenced contemporary school. It is not an easy task: each language has its own sense of tonality and timbre, reflected in its instrumentation, and its own kind of rhythmic and harmonic movement.

One of Mr. Noda's endeavors in this direction, "Kiyotsune: The Death of a Warrior," had its American premiere on Wednesday at the Japan Society, 333 East 47th Street, where it is running through tonight.

Sung and chanted in Japanese and lasting nearly two hours without an intermission, the work can seem long to a Western listener, even with the aid of the libretto in the program book. Yet Mr. Nodo's score succeeds in bringing together the distant traditions that interest him, and his blend of medieval Japanese elements with modern chromaticism produced music of great beauty.

"Kiyotsune," composed in 1981, is a Noh play based on a 12th-century episode recorded in the "Tales of the Heike." Its protagonist is a warrior who, confronted with the certainty that his clan will be defeated, commits suicide in the hope of attaining future bliss.

Kiyotsune's wife, Miyako, left with only a lock of her warrior husband's hair, is naturally distraught, and also resentful, since she does not fully apprehend his motive for drowning himself. Kiyotsune appears to her in a sequence of dream scenes, and in a final dance, he evokes the wartorn world and shows that in his death he has been purified and will enter paradise.

Mr. Noda used the original 15th-century Japanese text by Zeami Motokiyo, and directed the production, which takes place in a spare,

Jack Vartoogian

Ryo Noda, foreground, and Noriyoshi Umewaka in "Kiyotsune: The Death of a Warrior," tonight at the Japan Society.

Oriental-abstract set designed by Hiroshi Shimokawa, with the small band of musicians deployed to either side of the stage.

The tale unfolds in the glacial, highly stylized manner of a traditional Noh play, and was choreographed by Noriyoshi Umewaka (who also portrayed Kiyotsune). Mr. Umewaka delivered the title characters' few chanted lines himself, from behind his mask; but Miyako, who was portrayed by Koichi Okada, had more florid music, which was provided by a vocal stand-in, Toshiko Matsudaira, a soprano.

The plot was furthered by a chanted narration, delivered by Yukio Tanaka, one of the stage musicians. Mr. Noda's music seemed to succeed in his goal of melding styles. Not fully Japanese, but hardly Western, and neither traditional nor particularly modern, the score mixed Western tonality and even a touch of atonality (Miyako's lament had, at certain times, the same eerie edge as Schoenberg's "Erwartung") with music that otherwise seemed to be bound to ancient forms.

The scoring was similarly trans-Pacific, amid the textures of two kotos, a biwa (lute), a shakuhachi (bamboo flute), percussion and sho (a reed-based mouth organ), Mr. Noda played a haunting and timbrally varied saxophone part.

1989 My 19, C3:4

STAGE VIEW/Mel Gussow

When New Plays Are Made From Old

AT LEAST SINCE SHAKESPEARE, playwrights have been tempted to rewrite the works of others. Usually they resist that temptation; if not, they should take on that role with trepidation. Michael Frayn, who has translated Chekhov's four major plays and has also written his own freehanded adaptation of Chekhov, "Wild Honey," admonishes that it is "a presumptuous enterprise" to rewrite someone else's play. This, of course, has not deterred him or any of his colleagues. They do it for diverse reasons — as an act of homage to a favorite writer; to complete a play that was left unfinished (as was the case with "Wild Honey"); as commentary; to improve upon a flawed original; or simply out of envy.

That last reason, naturally the most unprofitable, can also lead a playwright to write a sequel to another's original work, as happened earlier this season to "The Importance of Being Earnest" (the play was "Without Apologies," the author, Thom Thomas). In the mail I once received a manuscript from a playwright anxious to follow up — and to contradict — Samuel Beckett with a play entitled "Godot Arrives."

In rewriting the work of another, three approaches are possible — translation (which can be literal); adaptation (which allows for latitude), and the writing of a new play that can transpose the original material to a different environment. Of the three, the third has the most pitfalls and can end in self-defeating competition. But if a true connection exists between the authors, the results can be rewarding, as it is with Brian Friel's "Aristocrats," a Chekhovian look at Ireland's faded gentry.

"Aristocrats" (which is running at Manhattan Theater Club's Theater Four) was inspired by Chekhov, in particular by "The Three Sisters." In his play, Mr. Friel shares themes with his Russian mentor — the decline of the aristocracy and the rise of the working class; lingering romanticism on both sides of the fence; illusion as an instrument for survival. Mr. Friel's wistfully disoriented brother is a converging of several Chekhovian characters (the brother in "The Three Sisters" and Uncle Vanya himself), but the playwright has not been slavish about his source. Actually there are four sisters in his play (the one who is absent is, in the Irish tradition, a nun). His divergences give the play a consistent fascination.

This dramatization of a prominent family's decline is brought movingly to life by an American cast (with the addition of the Irish actor Niall Buggy as the brother), under the direction of Robin Lefèvre. Heightening the international applicability of the play, several American actors (Kaiulani Lee, John Pankow and Haviland Morris) offer especially evocative performances. It is Mr. Pankow's character, a man of the working class, who turns out to have the strongest feeling for the family legacy.

Though he is a distinctly Irish playwright, Mr. Friel has often expressed his affinity for Russian writers — in his original plays and in his translations and adaptations. Among his works are a translation of "The Three Sisters" and an adaptation of Turgenev's novel "Fathers and Sons." Mr. Friel candidly labeled that adaptation "after Turgenev," though, in fact, it was faithful to the spirit of the novel. On the other hand, in his eccentric version of "Fathers and Sons," entitled "Nothing Sacred," the Canadian playwright George F. Walker offers no such disclaimer, though one would seem necessary. "Nothing Sacred" takes place in Russia in Turgenev's time and uses a number of the characters in the novel, but it is often self-consciously anachronistic. When the play was presented earlier this season at Hartford Stage, Mr. Walker was quoted in the program as saying, in reference to Turgenev and others, "You can't approach these dead guys with unreserved reverence." If not reverence, at least it demands sympathetic understanding — and a greater gift for language than is apparent in Mr. Walker.

This is certainly the case with Mr. Friel and with others, beginning with Mr. Frayn, Tom Stoppard and Christopher Hampton, all of whom have divided their time between original work and translations and adapta-

Spinning off from someone else's work could be an inspiration, an act of homage or simply pure envy.

tions. Both Mr. Stoppard and Mr. Hampton have adapted others (Arthur Schnitzler for Mr. Stoppard, Odon von Horvath for Mr. Hampton) while also working creatively at that third approach, writing a new play inspired by a classic. Mr. Stoppard retold "Hamlet" through the eyes of Rosencrantz and Guildenstern, and Mr. Hampton turned "The Misanthrope" inside out and called it "The Philanthropist."

■

The Trinidadian playwright Mustapha Matura has taken still another — and a novel — approach to John Millington Synge with a play entitled "The Playboy of the West Indies" (along with Mr. Walker's "Nothing Sacred," this is one of the most popular works in American regional theaters this season). Mr. Matura's comedy borrows themes, events and characters from "The Playboy of the Western World," while transporting the play from Ireland at the turn of the century to Trinidad in 1950. Irish dialect is replaced by a Caribbean patois.

It is a surprise to realize — in Dennis Scott's production at the Yale Repertory Theater (which closed yesterday) — that the play can exist independent of Synge's dialogue. The new play draws vitality from Mr. Matura's own unabashed, Syngian love of character and local language. Coincidentally, the playwright has also rewritten Chekhov in a play called "Trinidad Sisters." With the exception of Shakespeare, Chekhov may be the dramatist most universally rewritten. In the United States, there have been translations and adaptations by, among others, Lillian Hellman, Lanford Wilson, David Mamet, Jean-Claude Van Itallie and Tennessee Williams (a neglected version of "The Seagull").

Shakespeare, of course, has been a frequent source for musical theater ("West Side Story," "Kiss Me Kate") as well as for drama. In "Henry Lumper," Israel Horovitz transplanted "Henry IV, Parts One and Two" to Gloucester, Mass., for a drama about labor and familial battles in a waterfront union. In this case, the farther the playwright moved from Shakespeare, the more interesting his play became.

"Macbeth" was remade as political satire (Barbara Garson's "Macbird") and as absurdist comedy (Ionesco's "Macbett," a serio-comic attempt to understand the roots of mass murder). "King Lear" was reinterpreted in Edward Bond's "Lear" and Ethyl Eichelberger's "Leer" (in which the actor-author played all the roles, including the king and Cordelia). In Lee Breuer's forthcoming Mabou Mines, gender-switching version (also entitled "Lear"), the king is a queen.

■

The two most remarkable reinventors of Shakespeare are primarily known as film directors — Ingmar Bergman and Akira Kurosawa, the former with his stage adaptation of "Hamlet," the latter with his films, "Ran" ("King Lear" with sons) and "Throne of Blood" ("Macbeth"). The Kurosawa adaptations are exemplary instances of the cross-cultural transportability of masterpieces — also true with Kurosawa's cinematic version of Gorky's "Lower Depths."

Whether the auteur or adapter is Bergman or Kurosawa, Mr. Friel or Mr. Matura, inspiration has to begin with admiration and even symbiosis. In his analysis of the plays of Mr. Friel, the critic and poet Seamus Deane relates him to other Irish playwrights by saying that the "atmosphere of permanent crisis and of unshakable apathy is as much a feature of Friel's as it is of Beckett's or O'Casey's plays." And, he might have added, of Chekhov's plays as well. What Mr. Friel demonstrates in "Aristocrats" is that he is Chekhovian and that Chekhov himself has a deep kinship with the Irish.   □

1989 My 21, II:5:1

The Vice of Meekness

THE HEART OUTRIGHT, by Mark Medoff; directed by Mike Rutenberg; set designer, Peter R. Feuche; costume designer, Traci DiGesu; lighting designer, K. Robert Hoffman; production stage manager, Kathleen Mary. Presented by Theater for the New City, George Bartenieff, executive director; Crystal Field, executive artistic director. At 155 First Avenue, at 10th Street.

Stephen (Red) Ryder	David Andrews
Angel Childress	Anjanette Comer
Dickie Turpin	Kim McCullum
Ray Fowler	Kevin O'Connor

By STEPHEN HOLDEN

One would have to search hard to find a playwright more obsessed with machismo, heroism and psychic emasculation than Mark Medoff. In his first successful play, "When You Comin' Back, Red Ryder?" a gun-toting drifter terrorizes the occupants of a roadside diner into confronting "the truth" about themselves. The title character, Stephen Ryder, is a 19-year-old milquetoast whose James Dean-like self-image is savagely assailed.

Mr. Medoff's new play, "The Heart Outright," at Theater for the New City, picks up Stephen's story eight years later, in 1977. A Vietnam veteran with an artificial hand, he is the manager of a movie theater in Austin, Tex., that has recently begun showing pornography. The play's first act, "The Dirty Picture Man," is a monologue in which the well-meaning, pathetically credulous Stephen (David Andrews) describes his boring life as a candy concessioner, custodian and manager of a theater whose change in policy has earned him the derisive nickname of the act's title.

The playwright reserves most of the vital information about his character for the second act, "Terminal," which is set four years later in a bus station in Stephen's southern New Mexico hometown. While waiting for the bus back to Austin after his mother's funeral, he confronts his former sweetheart, Angel (Anjanette Comer), his brutal stepfather, Ray (Kevin O'Connor), and Dickie (Kim McCullum), an envious, mentally disturbed high school classmate.

Like the original play, the sequel is a psychological melodrama in which Stephen's fighting spirit is severely tested and found wanting. After Ray and Dickie both pick fistfights and Angel offers herself to him, Stephen confesses his fear and cowardice in such anguished tones as to suggest that meekness is for him the most unmentionable of vices. Having brought up the themes of machismo and cowardice in American life, the playwright doesn't explore their ramifications. Stephen, while not a terribly interesting character, is quite sympathetic. A gentle soul in a barbaric cowboys-and-Indians environment, he merely wants to do the decent thing. But if the play's message is merely to suggest how hard it is for the mild-mannered to make their way in such a macho environment, that's hardly news.

Gerry Goodstein

Richard Grant and Fanni Green, above, in Mustapha Matura's "Playboy of the West Indies," recently at the Yale Repertory Theater. At right, Haviland Morris, Kaiulani Lee, John Pankow and Niall Buggy in the Manhattan Theater Club's production of "Aristocrats" by Brian Friel—modeled after Synge and Chekhov

As Stephen, Mr. Andrews offers a detailed but very self-conscious portrayal in which he never fully blends into the character. Mr. McCullum and Mr. O'Connor offer broad, physical performances in roles that are already written as caricatures. The calmest performance belongs to Ms. Comer's Angel, but she too is a bit twitchy. Mr. Medoff's often overwrought dialogue requires a more understated approach than the emotion-drenched treatment of the director, Mike Rutenberg. The action should explode from beneath tautly composed surfaces like sudden thunder in the desert.

1989 My 21, 68:2

Pulling Whiskers

LAUGHING MATTERS, by Linda Wallem and Peter Tolan; production directed by Martin Charnin; music and lyrics by Mr. Tolan; scenery and lighting designed by Ray Recht; production stage manager, Jonathan Dimock Secor; costumes coordinated by Jade Hobson; general management, Robert V. Straus Productions Inc. Presented by Zev Guber and Sanford H. Fisher, Beluga Entertainment Corporation. At St. Peter's Church, Lexington Avenue at 54th Street.

WITH: Linda Wallem and Peter Tolan

By MEL GUSSOW

At the very end of their two-person revue, "Laughing Matters" (in the Theater at St. Peter's Church), Linda Wallem and Peter Tolan perform three brief, delirious musical spoofs of widely divergent Broadway songwriters.

First in line is Irving Berlin's version of Kafka's "Metamorphosis," with "You're Not Sick, You're Just a Bug," sung Ethel Merman style. Next is a Stephen Sondheim storybook that could be called "Fun With Dick and Jane (and Spot)," which, weirdly, manages to sound like "Sunday Into the Woods With George and Sweeney Todd." Finally, and perhaps oddest of all, is an upbeat musical "Iliad," attributed to John Kander and Fred Ebb, in which a Liza Minnelli-like Helen offers a high-kicking command to "open the gates" to Troy, as if it were a Greek cabaret.

●

Unfortunately, the preceding material in the show is only moderately amusing. The show principally deals with people out of town and newcomers to New York City, and includes several sketches about an unsophisticated bridge-playing husband and wife from Illinois who joke about 7-Eleven stores and other supposed icons of Middle America. When they come to Manhattan, they stay at the Plaza — the *Milford* Plaza — and readily pay a $1 camera tax on demand in order to photograph natives on the city streets.

Though there are occasional smiles, much of the material is closer to sitcom than to Second City. The partners, who write all of their own material, find a bit more humor in a street-corner exchange between a yuppie and a homeless person, who turn out to be high school friends. The comedy is most secure in a scene between a fast-talking Hollywood agent and a nymphet singing star who suddenly takes herself seriously. She wants to follow Madonna and do a play by that Mamet person (pronounced Mamay).

Martha Swope

Linda Wallem and Peter Tolan in the revue "Laughing Matters."

As actors and singers, Ms. Wallem and Mr. Tolan strike an amiably improvisatory air. To their credit, they never seem to be working too hard. Conversely, one wishes that in some of the scenes they would try harder. Onstage, they are congenial collaborators, with Mr. Tolan specializing in characters wryly removed from battle (even when they are bums) and Ms. Wallem posing as women on the verge — but never over the edge — of a nervous breakdown. The music, lyrics and piano playing are all by Mr. Tolan.

An earlier version of the show was presented at Manhattan Punch Line. With the help of Martin Charnin as director, the act has moved Off Broadway. Despite a number of changes of scenery, it has the appearance more of cabaret than of theater, and rises to its comic potential only in the closing collage. If Mr. Tolan would only concoct takeoffs on other aspects of our musical theater, and if the two could keep the level of the rest of the show on or near that of the coda, "Laughing Matters" might deserve its title.

1989 My 21, 68:1

Rest Home Romp

THE BLESSING, by Clare Coss; directed by Roberta Sklar; set design, Donald Eastman; costume design, Sally J. Lesser; lighting design, Frances Aronson; sound design, Daniel Moses Schreier; production stage manager, Richard Hester; literary adviser, Christopher Breyer; general manager, Mickey Rolfe. Presented by American Place Theater, Wynn Handman. At 111 West 46th Street.

Claudine	Louisa Horton
Kathleen	Beth Fowler
Marilyn	Leila Boyd
Flora	Olga Merediz
Restive	Anita Gillette
Nan	Kelly Bishop
Miss Mary	Anne Shropshire

By MEL GUSSOW

"The Blessing," a new play by Clare Coss at the American Place Theater, is intended to be a penetrating drama about the complex relationship between an aging mother and her divorced daughter who is a lesbian. Instead, it is an exceedingly tiresome visit with two self-serving and unlikable characters.

As much as anything the mother, Claudine (Louisa Horton), and the daughter, Restive (Anita Gillette), are separated by a language barrier. Claudine, a well-to-do Louisiana widow confined to a Long Island rest home, speaks platitudes that could have appeared on greeting cards ("Where there is room in the heart, there is room in the home") In other words, she has second thoughts about her living arrangements and would prefer to move in with her daughter.

●

The appropriately named Restive is a globe-trotting photojournalist who covered the war in Vietnam but who should not be trusted to write a photo caption. She describes the ocean as "the vasty deep" and "the majestic main," calls her mother "a people person" and refers to herself, at least professionally, as "a kicking, flailing original."

While the haughty Claudine offers the other residents unsolicited advice on geriatric sex, the daughter keeps tight control over her mother's estate. When they communicate, they often compare notes on their husbands. With the mother that means a paragon named Mix (as in Tom), with the daughter, a heel commonly referred to as the Rat. On the other hand, Restive and her lesbian lawyer lover (Kelly Bishop) have an idealized relationship.

Bored by the bickering, one tries to focus on the contradictory nature of the rest home itself. Seemingly expensive, so overstaffed that three nurses can spend their time lounging in the mother's room watching "Ryan's Hope," the place serves Spam for dinner and strawberry Kool-Aid as an afternoon refreshment. No wonder the mother daydreams about life back on the bayou.

Throughout the play there are undercurrents about the difficulty of the mother's adjustment to the daughter's lesbianism, but the issue is never seriously confronted. Dealing with that subject, the author repeatedly falls back on jokes. The daughter says that a majority of people suffer from homophobia and the mother responds, "I'm *not* afraid of high places."

Trapped by the limits of the characters, the actresses (who include Beth Fowler, wasted in a role as a nurse) are reduced to giving one-dimensional performances. With the least help from the author, Ms. Bishop is the closest to developing a character. Roberta Sklar has staged the play slowly as if the people persons really had something interesting to say. By the end of the evening, in a prolonged death scene, the mother is using words like vasty deep and majestic main. One supposes this means that, in common with her daughter, she is now a kicking, flailing original.

1989 My 22, C12:1

A Bang, No Whimpers And Conversation

THE INVESTIGATION OF THE MURDER IN EL SALVADOR, by Charles L. Mee Jr.; directed by David Schweizer; original music by Peter Gordon; set designer, Tom Kamm; costume designer, Gabriel Berry; lighting designer, Anne Militello; sound designer, Eric Liljestrand; production stage manager, Carol Fishman; production manager, William H. Lang. Presented by the New York Theater Workshop, at the Perry Street Theater, 31 Perry Street.

Stanton	Paul Schmidt
D'Costa	Thom Christopher
Lady Aitkin	Kathleen Chalfant
Butler	Isiah Whitlock Jr.
Meridee	Leslie Nipkow
Peter	Greg Mehrten
Howard	Tom McDermott
Maid	Shona Tucker
Bodyguard	Freddie Frankie

Musicians
Peter Gordon, Eric Liljestrand and Ned Sublette

Martha Holmes

Explorers

Kelly Bishop, left, and Anita Gillette are part of the cast in "The Blessing," a comedy of self-discovery by Clare Coss, opening today at the American Place Theater.

By MEL GUSSOW

Lounging on an elegant terrace of a beach house, the characters in "The Investigation of the Murder in El Salvador" are exemplars of an aristocracy of wealth. As they watch the sun set on several empires, they drink, talk and sometimes do not even pretend to listen to one another, exchanging half-remembered, bizarre anecdotes and interrupted dreams.

Offstage are heard helicopters, gun shots and, finally, explosions. Seeing Charles L. Mee Jr.'s new play (the final work in an extremely auspicious season for the New York Theater Workshop, at the Perry Street Theater), one necessarily thinks of T. S. Eliot — in particular, of "The Cocktail Party." But this is a "Cocktail Party" with a contemporary political punch — Eliot crossbred with Wallace Shawn. In Mr. Mee's El Salvador, the world ends with a loud bang.

•

On the surface, this is almost a drawing-room comedy. Neatly attired in a white linen suit, the host, D'Costa (played by Thom Christopher), manipulates his servants as well as his guests. Anyone who accepts his hospitality or his employment must also be prepared to accept his abuse.

Swathed in a burnoose, the elderly Lady Aitkin (Kathleen Chalfant) resembles Louise Nevelson and is filled with outrageous comments about life and art. Her relic of a husband (Tom McDermott), dormant in a wheelchair comfortably close to his portable oxygen, makes rude remarks about old-line liberals, sounding like one of those sidelong commentators in Warren Beatty's "Reds."

A jaded young couple (Greg Mehrten and Leslie Nipkow) casually pass the time with alcohol, drugs and the smallest of small talk — until Mr. Mehrten is viciously attacked by Lady Aitkin's Lhasa apso. A banker (Paul Schmidt), less well defined than the other guests, idles solipistically.

In language and attitude, Mr. Mee has captured the death-in-life decadence of his characters. They are not so much above the battle as superfluous. The host himself is the kind of banana-republic robber baron for whom revolutions are made. As he says, "If you're going to have excess wealth" — and he certainly has it — "you must exploit someone."

•

At moments the vacuity of the people is overstated, as in Lady Aitkin's laundry list of what is in and what is out in popular culture. But Mr. Mee, who is an historian as well as a playwright, is closely attuned to the self-parodying aspects of our civilization, and there is always a political undercurrent in the conversation (as insistent as the lapping waves heard in the background).

The dialogue is as literate as it is self-revealing. As he demonstrated in his brief text for Martha Clarke's "Vienna: Lusthaus," and in his own "Imperialists at the Club Cave Canem," Mr. Mee has a keen eye for verbal imagery. In his new play, the fanciful stories often end before reaching a conclusion, a fact that succeeds in extending the aura of mystery. Information is withheld (there

Paula Court

Thom Christopher and Shona Tucker are in Charles L. Mee Jr.'s "Investigation of the Murder in El Salvador"

is a murder but no investigation), and that feeling is heightened by the intrusion of the servant (Isiah Whitlock Jr. and Shona Tucker), walking on stage with blood suddenly spilled on their clothes, but still ready to perform household duties with their customary haughtiness.

•

The crispness of Mr. Mee's text is reflected in the precision of the performances and of David Schweizer's production. Tom Kamr's stylish scenery would be as at home in the Hamptons as in El Salvador (a statement in itself). The setting is cleanly and almost uncomfortably modern. On a second level of the house, in a sound studio behind glass, sits a small combo led by Peter Godon, who also wrote the score (which moves from electronically inclined modernism to classical guitar). Eric Liljestrand's sound design adds another articulate dimension.

At one point, a character refers to the anesthetizing of England through food, drink and self-indulgence. It is a word that could be applied with accuracy to the characters in Mr. Mee's provocative play. They are amoral and inhumane, and in his cautionary but all too credible fable, they have inherited the earth.

1989 My 23, C14:4

Playing With Food

EMPIRES AND APPETITES, created, designed and directed by Theodora Skipitares; lyrics by Andrea Balis; music by Pat Irwin; technical design by Michael Cummings; lighting by Pat Dignan; "Wheat," "Brand Names" and "How to Grow a Car" choreographed by Gail Conrad; stage manager, David Flanigan; technical director, Kyle Chepulis; scenic artists: Holly Laws, Read Baldwin, Mr. Chepulis, Isabelle DuFour, David Flanigan, Elba Lugo, Oisaa Mbonika and Tom Moore. Presented by Theater for the New City, Bartenieff-Field, in association with Skysaver Productions. At 155 First Avenue, at Ninth Street.

Narrators . Tom Costello and Trinket Monsod
Manipulators
Isabelle DuFour, Preston Foerder, Cora Hook and Stephen Kaplin

---

By MEL GUSSOW

Theodora Skipitares has taken her brief puppet play with music, "A History of Food," and reconstituted it. The result is an improved and expanded version entitled "Empires

and Appetites." Both works have Ms. Skipitares's characteristic piquancy, but the new musical play is more nourishing and more clearly the work of a social commentator. It is also a case of an artist realizing the potential of her art.

As in her earlier pieces (which include "The Age of Invention" and "Defenders of the Code"), Ms. Skipitares takes puppetry on a scientific and historical expedition. The subject is food through the ages, an arc that transports us from myth through modern methods of nutrition.

The play, at the Theater for the New City, uses a galaxy of puppets of varying dimension — early man (or late ape) as an Atlas-high robot; hand puppets; tiny shadow puppets and life-size figures that are as realistic as the trompe l'oeil sculpture of Duane Hansen. These inanimate objects are brought startlingly to life by an expert troupe of manipulators under Ms. Skipitares's direction.

•

The first act of the show recapitulates "A History of Food" in more polished form, moving from a hologrammatic Cronus eating his young (except for Zeus) to Pharaoh's dream of wheat. In a typical Skipitares tilt, the Pilgrims' first Thanksgiving is seen in an aerial — or over — view. The madcap first-act finale is a musicalization of Malthus.

A chorus of brand-name household products, in altered form, now highlights the second act. Uncle Ben remains but with Aunt Jemima, Quaker Oats and Chiquita Banana replacing such fast-food predecessors as Colonel Sanders, who has been banished to the attic along with Betty Crocker. Clacking their hands and feet, the new food-town quartet does a rap dance to one of Pat Irwin's merriest tunes. The author then undertakes a campaign for better foods and farms. A lecture on home economics is illustrated by a miniaturized chef slicing squash — an ingenious action that might be envied by Bunraku puppeteers.

•

Suddenly an ancient car wheels on stage carrying Henry Ford, who praises the American farm as "the heartland of the country" at the same time he asks for the replacement of farm animals by machinery. From here the canvas becomes more political, with Presidents beginning with Franklin D. Roosevelt taking their turn in the nutritional spotlight. Oddly, the show stops with President Richard M. Nixon (who, as a puppet, is amusingly made to resemble the man in the moon). Jimmy Carter — President and peanut farmer — would have been a natural next stop.

The show is enhanced by Ms. Irwin's music, Andrea Balis's lyrics (although some of them are too crammed with information) and Ms. Skipitares's design. Narration is supplied by Tom Costello, who mimics all the presidents, and Trinket Monsod, who sings the score in a sweet, softly shaded voice. "Empires and Appetites" feeds the mind at the same time it stirs the senses.

1989 My 25, C18:4

All the King's Courters

LOVE'S LABOR'S LOST, by William Shakespeare; directed by Paul Giovanni; sets by Robert Klingelhoefer; costumes by Jess Goldstein; lights by Stephen Strawbridge; dance consultation by Patricia Birch; songs and incidental music by Bruce Adolphe; staff repertory director, Jennifer McCray; production stage manager, C. A. Clark; stage manager, Richard Feldman. Presented by the Acting Company, John Houseman, founder; Margot Harley, executive producers; Gerald Gutierrez, artistic director. At Marymount Manhattan Theater, 221 East 71st Street.

King Ferdinand of Navarre
                            Spencer Beckwith
Berowne .... Gary Sloan
Longaville .... Ken Sawyer
Dumaine .... Larry Green
Boyet .... David Rainey
Marcade and Sir Nathaniel . Gregory Wallace
Don Adriano de Armado ...... Douglas Krizner
Holofernes .... John Tillotson
Dull .... Michael MacCauley
Costard .... Anthony Cummings
Moth .... John Greenleaf
The Princess of France .... Laura Perrotta
Maria .... Theresa McCarthy
Katharine .... Martha Thompson
Rosaline .... Alison Stair Neet
Jaquenetta .... Gayla Finer

By MEL GUSSOW

In Paul Giovanni's production for the Acting Company, "Love's Labor's Lost," that most literate of Shakespearean comedies, has been turned into a tedious exercise in artifice. The poetry is sacrificed along with the impetuousness of the romance, which should proceed magically, four by four — the King of Navarre and the Princess of France, each accompanied by a trio of followers who conveniently fall in love with one another.

"Love's Labor's Lost" begins a brief New York season for this touring company (in residence at Marymount Manhattan Theater), a season to be followed by the Bella and Sam Spewack comedy, "Boy Meets Girl," and an adaptation of a children's story, "The Phantom Tollbooth."

The weaknesses of Mr. Giovanni's staging would be self-evident, but they are made even clearer by the coincidence of Gerald Freedman's recent engaging production of the play for the New York Shakespeare Festival. In all respects, the Acting Company version suffers by comparison.

•

The first of the director's mistakes is to introduce the king and his friends clothed in gauzy gowns that make them look like animated statuary, a determinedly silly appearance for nobles about to embark on a sequestered period of enforced celibacy. It is no help to have Browne, the wittiest of the group, trip over his hem or, later, do a pratfall from a park bench. Gary Sloan, who was an authoritative Faust several seasons ago at the Classic Stage Company, is an overly capricious Berowne. His laughs and those of others should come from the lines and not from superimposed stage business involving banana peels and rubber snakes.

Frippery, within reason, is usually reserved for the clowns and the fantastic Don Adriano de Armado. In this production they are carried into caricature. Clutching his heart and swooning, Douglas Krizner misses Don Adriano's melancholy and, in addition, is encumbered with a burlesque Hispanic accent. Among the clowns, only Anthony Cummings is amusing as a relatively straightforward Costard.

It is left to the ladies to restore a certain equilibrium. Alison Stair Neet and Laura Peretta as Rosaline and the princess (they alternate in the roles) bring a needed elegance to a production that is often merely mannered. When the princess learns of the death of her father, the play becomes more somber and the actors, including Spencer Beckwith as the king, rise to the occasion.

•

In this final scene it is obvious that a number of the actors are capable of playing Shakespeare — if only the director had provided more of an opportunity. For 16 years, the Acting Company has been a valuable national resource, traveling the country with classics. But, to borrow Costard's word, this production offers the audience scant remuneration.

1989 My 26, C4:5

Other New York Stories

SHOWING OFF, by Douglas Bernstein and Denis Markell; directed by Michael Leeds; sets and prop designers, Joseph Varga and Penny Holpit; costume designer, Jeanne Button; lighting and sound designer, Josh Starbuck; musical director, Stephen Flaherty; associate producer, Howard Deutsch. Presented by Suzanne J. Schwartz and Jennifer Manocherian. At Steve McGraw's, 158 West 72d Street.

WITH: Mr. Bernstein, Veanne Cox, Donna Murphy and Mark Sawyer.

By RICHARD F. SHEPARD

Enthusiasts of the perky cabaret revues once so prevalent in New York who — in an access of ungrammatical nostalgia — like to say "They just don't make 'em like they used to," should take note: a visit to "Showing Off" shows that they do.

Indeed, "Showing Off" is as brisk and bright a revue as one can find.

And it is in a proper setting: the newly redone and enlarged cabaret room of Steve McGraw's, an establishment once known as Palsson's Supper Club (158 West 72d Street), where "Forbidden Broadway" grew to fame.

This is a show as New York as a Woody Allen movie, a West Side show that is laughable testimony to the culture of a neighborhood steeped in serious reform and Chinese restaurants. The show is not consumed with politics or sex. There are other things in life, like the addictive videotape-rental disease, Michele Marsh on the 5 o'clock and 11 o'clock Channel 2 news, the New York sophisticates who plan never to see "Me and My Girl" or "The Fantasticks" and the slick, show-biz rabbi whose Temple for the Performing Arts sums up the High Holy Days as "the big blast and the big fast."

•

Not everything is spun gold. A few items, like the rabbi's spiel and a number about Jacques Cousteau's underwater photography, are a bit overdrawn. But Denis Markell and Douglas Bernstein, the writers, usually hit the mark, and the cast — which includes Mr. Bernstein, Veanne Cox, Donna Murphy and Mark Sawyer, directed by Michael Leeds, with Steven Flaherty at piano — is top-drawer.

The ensemble numbers are particularly lively and funny, from the title song, which explains why people perform, to the concluding "Old-Fashioned Song," in which the cast rakes over those shows that force an embarrassed audience to sing along.

There's also a paean to West 72d Street ("You're going out there a youngster, but you've got to come back a store") and a dynamic song about the people who get "Ninas" hidden in their caricatures by Al Hirschfeld in The New York Times.

Mr. Bernstein evokes a comically sad, lonely man whose joy each

evening is watching Ms. Marsh give the news on television, sympathizing with murder victims and glowing at kittens who have found a home. Ms. Murphy has an extraordinary talent for satirizing passion, as when she is caught by her husband in the act of smuggling videotapes into the house after they have sworn to kick the habit. Ms. Murphy also puts across a torch song lamenting the days when one could enjoy Amos 'n' Andy on radio and when nobody minded seal pups getting clubbed for their skins.

As for Ms. Cox, she has all the manner of the established comedienne whose eyes stare with guileless innocence at a perverse world, whose body is as easily eloquent as her words, whose big number (about a boy who kissed her) is beautifully simple yet humorous.

"Showing Off," is a colorful set of caricatures of the way we live.

1989 My 28, 57:1

Remembering It Well

GIGI, book and lyrics by Alan Jay Lerner; music by Frederick Loewe; based on a novel by Colette; directed by Gerard Alessandrini; choreography by John Carrafa; musical direction by Paul Johnson; sets by Nicholas Lundy; costumes by Bruce Goodrich; lighting by Nancy Collings; production stage manager, Jess Lynn. Presented by Equity Library Theater, Jeffrey R. Costello, producing director. At 310 Riverside Drive, at 103d Street.

Gigi .... Pamela Shafer
Honoré .... Russell Costen
Gaston .... Bob Cuccioli
Clothilde .... Jamie Martin
Liane .... Donna Ramundo
Mamita .... D'Yan Forest
Lucille .... Marylin Monaco
Aunt Alicia .... Lynette Bennett
Charles .... John Byron
Sandomir .... Toby Reivant
Alphonse/Count André/Maître DuClos/telephone installer John Patti
Maître d'/ .... Bernard Granville
WITH: Nicholas Augustus, Kevin Brunner, Jonathan Cerullo, Terrence DuBay, Julie Jirousek, Kathleen LoGiudice, Andrea Lyman, Robert Paolucci, Joanna Polinsky, Gilbert Marc Polt, Lin Snider, Eileen Woods.

By STEPHEN HOLDEN

Any musical that depends as much upon evoking a high-style period ambiance as Lerner and Loewe's "Gigi" is bound to be compromised by a production that fails to offer at least a modicum of opulence. In the Equity Library Theater's cheery but threadbare revival, the few props chosen to suggest turn-of-the-century Parisian grandeur look like moth-eaten relics from a second-hand shop. By the end of the show, one feels starved for the spectacle of glamorous sophisticates wallowing in luxury.

The theater version of "Gigi" has never cast the spell of the 1958 movie. When the mechanical stage adaptation opened on Broadway in 1973, it ran for only 103 performances. Even though it used seven of the original film's nine songs and added four new numbers, the effervescent score, which includes such Lerner and Loewe standards as "I Remember It Well," "The Night They Invented Champagne," "Thank Heaven for Little Girls" and the title song couldn't overcome the sense of its being a scissors-and-paste version of the movie.

Among other structural flaws, the scenes of the play proceed choppily, and its Cinderella ending feels rushed and perfunctory.

•

Directed by Gerard Alessandrini, the mastermind of "Forbidden

Broadway," the Equity Library Theater revival is a janglingly noisy affair whose performances are stylistically unsynchronized. Russell Costen's Honoré is a twinkly but ineffectual vaudevillian who accentuates his dialogue with self-conscious hand movements as though he were treading water.

Bob Cuccioli's Gaston is dashing enough for the role, but the tone of his performance is more operatically Italian than suavely Gallic. Although Pamela Shafer's aggressively ingenuous Gigi is not without charm, the actress is too mature to be convincing as a teen-ager.

1989 My 28, 57:1

Send In the Witches

THE LARK, by Jean Anouilh; adapted by Lillian Hellman; directed by Janet Hayes Walker; scenic design, Deborah Scott; costume design, Holly Hynes; lighting design, Brian Mac Devitt; technical director, James E. Fuller Jr.; production stage manager, Victor Lukas. Presented by the York Theater Company, Ms. Walker, producing director; Molly Pickering Grose, managing director. At the Church of the Heavenly Rest, 2 East 90th Street.

Warwick .... Dennis Parlato
Cauchon .... Mel Boudrot
Joan .... Ann Dowd
Joan's Mother and Yolande .... Marie Wallace
Joan's Father and Executioner .... Ralph David Westfall
Joan's Brother and English soldier .... Tom Nichols
The Promoter .... Joel Swetow
The Inquistor .... Neil Vipond
Brother Ladvenu .... Russell Lawyer
Robert de Beaudricourt .... John Camera
Agnes Sorel .... Lisa Fugard
The Little Queen .... Laura Carden
Charles, the Dauphin .... Benjamin White

By STEPHEN HOLDEN

In "The Lark," Jean Anouilh's drama about Joan of Arc, the playwright's sharpest image of his heroine is expressed by the worldly Englishman, Warwick, who sits as one of her judges. The character, who represents the voice of secular reason in a play that steams with religious fervor, compares Joan to a lark that sings "a joyous, crazy song of courage." Warwick is the only character who recognizes that Joan's execution might elevate her into a martyr with far more mythic power than any force she could wield were her life spared.

When it opened on Broadway in 1955 with Julie Harris as Joan, the play bore obvious analogies to the Communist witch hunts of the era. In its current revival at the York Theater — its first New York production since then — the play doesn't have any convenient metaphorical resonance. Somewhat old-fashioned in tone, the drama is an unabashedly admiring meditation on the phenomenon of Joan. In rhetorical dialogue that often verges on the flowery, the playwright paints her as a miraculous exemplar of spiritual perfection and courage in a dark age.

•

Set during Joan's official interrogation, the play recounts Joan's exploits in episodic flashbacks. Her father is a brute. Her mother, seeing that her daughter is intractably set in her ways, proposes she become a prostitute. Fueled by faith in her unseen voices and employing a brash mixture of common sense and a blindly infectious enthusiasm, Joan charms her way to the French court and ultimately to victory on the battlefield against England.

Performers in the revue "Showing Off." Clockwise from top left, Donna Murphy, Mark Sawyer, Veanne Cox and Douglas Bernstein.

Martha Swope Associates/Rebecca Lesher

The play's staging in the impressively arched, echoey Church of the Heavenly Rest gives the York Theater's revival an extra fillip of religiosity. The director, Janet Hayes Walker, has assembled an appropriately grave and scowling committee of clergymen and officials whose debates resound with windy pomposity. The most colorful supporting performances belong to Neil Vipond as an agitated Inquisitor and to Benjamin White as the petulant, cowering Dauphin who, thanks to Joan's battlefield victories, ascends to the French throne.

As Joan, Ann Dowd captures a broad range of emotion, from abject fear to fanatical determination, and in evoking her spiritual faith, the actress exudes a low-keyed radiance. While her performance is appealing, it is a bit too muted to convey the bewitching intensity that would move cynical aristocrats, effete Dauphins and brutish officers alike to allow Joan to cut such a swath.

1989 My 29, 20:5

Absurdist Parody Of Current Attitudes

MARATHON '89, SERIES A, producer, Kate Baggott; associate producer, Peter Glatzer; set design, Maurice Dana; lighting design, Greg MacPherson; costume design, Deborah Shaw; sound design, Gayle Jeffrey; production stage manager, Stephen Vallillo. Presented by the Ensemble Studio Theater, Curt Dempster, artistic director; Peter Shavitz, managing director. At 549 West 52d Street.

THE ESSENCE OF MARGROVIA, by Jenny Lombard; directed by Lisa Peterson.

Lizzy	Cody Conklin
Terry	Lizabeth Zindel

SELF-TORTURE AND STRENUOUS EXERCISE, by Harry Kondoleon; directed by Max Mayer.

Carl	Donald Berman
Alvin	John Michael Higgins
Bethany	Alexandra Gersten
Adele	Caroline Aaron

WINK-DAH, by William Yellow Robe Jr.; directed by Richard Lichte.

Two Shoe	Kohl Miner
Death	Randy Mantooth
Virgil	Philip Moon
Jeremy	Eagle-Eye Cherry
Earnest	Cochise Anderson
Victor Young	Frank Girardeau

By WILBORN HAMPTON

In the advanced state of self-absorption in which modern life exists, it is sometimes hard to determine with any degree of accuracy whether the emotion one feels toward another person is love or hate. It is even difficult to remember whether one is alive or dead.

These are only some of the complexities facing the two couples in Harry Kondoleon's "Self-Torture and Strenuous Exercise," which was written several years ago and which is now being presented in Series A of the Ensemble Studio Theater's Marathon '89. Mr. Kondoleon's absurdist study is the most polished of three works in the opening bill of the ensemble's one-act festival. The other two — Jenny Lombard's "Essence of Margrovia" and William Yellow Robe Jr.'s "Wink-Dah" — have their moments, but both are in need of serious editing.

In "Self-Torture," Carl (Donald Berman), a novelist whose book "Motel of the Heart" has just won a national award, confesses over dinner to Al (John Michael Higgins) that he and Al's wife, Beth (Alexandra

Gersten) are planning to run away together that very night. Al, a golly-gosh kind of guy and a gourmet cook whose main concern at this news is that he will now have to wash the dinner dishes, thinks this is understandable considering that Carl's wife, Adele, has just died. That Adele (Caroline Aaron) is very much alive and hellbent on revenge will not deter Al from his innate optimism.

The able cast, directed at roller-coaster speed by Max Mayer, brings a lot of energy to the play and mostly masks the fact that there is little significance behind the cleverness of the writing. Mr. Kondoleon is a keen observer of contemporary attitudes, and "Self-Torture" is more than anything else a parody of them. It says something about the substance of the play that the biggest laugh comes when Adele, badly in need of a Valium and her wrists bandaged, smashes her fist into a cheesecake. The quartet of actors is first-rate, especially Mr. Higgins's Al and Ms. Gersten's Beth.

The opening play, "The Essence of Margrovia," concerns a pair of pubescent schoolgirls who have slipped into the woods one evening during their summer vacation so that Lizzy (Cody Conklin) can invoke some black magic that will give Terry (Lizabeth Zindel) breasts and with them the love of her heartthrob back home.

There is a lot more going on with Lizzy, however, than dabbling in the dark arts, but we don't get to that until the last five minutes or so of the work. The rest of the play, while charming and occasionally funny, would probably gain greater appreciation with a younger audience. Ms. Lombard has a fine ear for dialogue, but she needs to find a more direct route to the heart of her matter. Both performances are credible, especially Ms. Zindel's Terry, and Lisa Peterson has directed with a sure hand that keeps the audience involved through the tedious moments.

Wink-dah, we learn from Mr. Yellow Robe's play, is an Indian word for homosexual. When Jeremy (Eagle-Eye Cherry) returns to the tepee badly beaten from an encounter with a young white man on the eve of a festival, his brother, Virgil (Philip Moon), sets out to avenge him and protect him from the white man's father.

There is some taut drama in Mr. Yellow Robe's play, most fully realized in a confrontation between Jeremy and Virgil over traditional Indian values against the impurities of the white man's society. But there is also a lot of excess baggage in the script and at an hour, "Wink-Dah" is too long by half. For starters, any play with a character called Death should probably reduce the cast by one.

Mr. Yellow Robe would have a stronger play if he kept to the realities of his drama and left the metaphysics to campfire tales. Mr. Cherry and Mr. Moon give strong performances. Richard Lichte directed.

1989 My 30, C19:1

'In the Midst Of Celtic Ruins'

CYMBELINE, by William Shakespeare; directed by JoAnne Akalaitis; set design by George Tsypin; costume design by Ann Hould-Ward; lighting design by Pat Collins; original music by Philip Glass; music direction by Alan Johnson; fight direction by

David Leong; choreography by Diane Martel; associate producer, Jason Steven Cohen. Presented by Joseph Papp. At the Public/Newman Theater, 425 Lafaeytte Street.

Queen	Joan MacIntosh
Imogen	Joan Cusack
Posthumus	Jeffrey Nordling
Cymbeline	George Bartenieff
Pisanio	Peter Francis James
Cloten	Wendell Pierce
Iachimo	Michael Cumpsty
Philario and Second Jailer	John Madden Towey
Caius Lucius	Earl Hindman
Soothsayer	Rajika Puri
Belarius	Frederick Neumann
Guiderius	Jesse Borrego
Arviragus	Don Cheadle

WITH: Teagle F. Bougere, Ethan T. Bowen, Tom Fervoy, Clement Fowler, Richard Hicks, Tom-Dale Keever, Wendy Lawless, Devon Michaels, David Neumann, David Ossian, William Parry, Mary Beth Peil, Stefan Schnabel, Sharon Washington, Eloise Watt, Jacob White and Joe Zaloom.

By FRANK RICH

"Cymbeline," the late Shakespeare romance, is an exuberantly confusing play that has never wanted for detractors. Samuel Johnson famously dismissed it as "unresisting imbecility," while Shaw, no Shakespeare fan, found it "stagy trash." Such critics have a new ally in the director JoAnne Akalaitis, who has mounted a travesty of "Cymbeline" at the Public Theater. This is the most reckless entry in the Shakespeare Festival's Marathon, a waste not only of a powerful, seldom produced text but also of such major artists as the composer Philip Glass, who wrote the arresting score, and the actress Joan Cusack, who is secure but stranded in the star role of Imogen.

Ms. Akalaitis also wastes her own not inconsiderable intelligence. A tart director of experimental theater pieces ("Dead End Kids") and intimate dramas by the West German writer Franz Xaver Kroetz ("Request Concert," "Through the Leaves"), she puts naïve stock in the value of changing the settings of classic plays. At Harvard's American Repertory Theater, she angered Samuel Beckett by revising the setting of "Endgame" and then mounted a production of Jean Genet's "Balcony" that trendily and pointlessly unfolded in Latin America. Even Ms. Akalaitis's Kroetz stagings have been marred by the unconvincing trans-

planting of German types to American environments like Queens.

For "Cymbeline," the director's conceit, stated in the program, is to stage the play "in the midst of Celtic ruins — a Romantic fantasy in Victorian England." Shakespeare, particularly the experimental Shakespeare of the crazy-quilt final phase, won't brook such nonsense. "Cymbeline" unfolds all over the map, geographically and culturally, from pre-Christian Britain (of which the title character was king) to Renaissance Italy to a fairy-tale vision of Wales. To set it down in Celtic ruins (represented primarily by cloudy slide projections of Stonehenge) and then straitjacket it in the cloak of Victorian England is to annihilate a work that belongs to the full spectrum of a playwright's autumnal imagination rather than to any narrow directorial idée fixe.

Like "The Winter's Tale," which follows it in the canon, "Cymbeline" tells a riotously complicated story (two dozen last-minute revelations in the final scene alone) featuring banished children, the dead returning to life and, finally, hard-won repentence and reconciliation. For spice, there is a full-scale war, sexual intrigue out of Boccaccio, a wicked stepmother worthy of the Grimms and a deus ex machina dream in which Jupiter descends. How does a director knit it together? There is no substitute for riding Shakespeare's every dexterous change of mood and style, as demonstrated by James Lapine in his magical recent "Winter's Tale."

•

Ms. Akalaitis, by contrast, levels everything to the low common denominator of her campy evocation of Victorian melodrama, as represented by George Tsypin's inky, Edward Gorey-esque set, wandering ghosts out of "The Addams Family," crashing organ chords and antique stage machinery. But Shakespearean romance is hardly synonymous with Ms. Akalaitis's Victorian romance. In place of the play's tingling admixture of sorrow, wit and fantasy, Ms. Akalaitis provides sniggling music-hall gags at the text's expense. "Cymbeline" becomes a parodistic penny dreadful like the Ridiculous Theatrical Company's "Mystery of Irma Vep" or the Shakespeare Festival's own "Mystery of Edwin Drood," but

Martha Swope

Jeffrey Nordling and Joan Cusack in "Cymbeline."

without even the saving grace of first-rate farceurs or an audience plebiscite (unless one counts those theatergoers who vote with their feet before the more than three hours have expired).

It's typical of the production that Iachimo, a schemer resembling Iago, becomes a hissable, pose-striking villain who, as portrayed by Michael Cumpsty, both looks and acts like Robert Goulet. Meanwhile, a character who is supposed to be funny, Cloten, the cloddish son of the evil Queen, is mirthless as mugged by Wendell Pierce. Humor has never been Ms. Akalaitis's forte, and neither is her marshaling of crowds. The prissy slow-motion battle scenes seem sanitized, and the highly populated denouement has all the spontaneity of a high-school commencement pageant.

•

The casting is bizarre. George Bartenieff makes one of the most forgettable titular roles in Shakespeare indelible by mauling every line. While one can applaud Ms. Akalaitis for casting a black actor as Cloten, doesn't credibility (and coherence for a hard-pressed audience) demand that his mother also be black? Apparently not, since the Queen is reserved instead for a favored Akalaitis leading lady, Joan MacIntosh. We are also supposed to believe, in a celebrated scene, that Imogen would mistake Cloten's decapitated torso for her husband's, yet the scene and Imogen are rendered ridiculous here by the conflicting races of the confused corpses. It's productions like this, which practice arbitrary tokenism rather than complete and consistent integration, that mock the dignified demands of the nontraditional casting movement.

The few sincere performances, in ascending order of interest, come from Jeffrey Nordling as the husband Posthumus, Peter Francis James as the loyal servant Pisanio and Ms. Cusack. As she demonstrated on stage in "Road" and "Brilliant Traces" and on film in "Working Girl," this actress has many colors; she is potentially ideal as a heroine who travels between two genders and nations, not to mention between life and death, on her way to redemption. But a facetious and bloodless "Cymbeline" robs Imogen of any emotional context, imprisoning her in the bland, demeaning Victorian role of a damsel in distress. For Ms. Cusack and the audience alike, her rescue couldn't arrive soon enough.

1989 Je 1, C15:1

In Protest

NOW AND AT THE HOUR OF OUR DEATH, inspired by Nell McCafferty's "The Armagh Women." Researched and written by members of the company. Director, Abigail Morris. Presented by the Irish Arts Center and Trouble and Strife Theater Company. At 553 West 51st Street.

Aine	Maeve Murphy
Geraldine	Finola Geraghty
Emer	Gaby Chiappe
Margaret	Caroline Seymour

By MEL GUSSOW

In 1980, in response to a Government ruling criminalizing the role of political prisoners, a group of women staged the so-called dirty protest at the Armagh jail in Northern Ireland.

Sylvie Tata

Members of the Trouble and Strife theater company in a scene from "Now and at the Hour of Our Death."

The prisoners were locked in their cells for 23 hours every day and did not bathe or use the toilets.

This extraordinarily self-demeaning exercise in civil protest lasted for more than a year, an experience that has been condensed into a brief pungent play entitled "Now and at the Hour of Our Death." Previously presented at the Young Vic in London and at the Dublin Theater Festival, the play is the collaborative work of the women's collective Trouble and Strife. It is running through Sunday at the Irish Arts Center.

•

As intended, the piece is a minute by minute look at bare-minimum existence. Though the episodic play does not have the artistic shape of prison dramas like Athol Fugard's "Island" or Manuel Puig's "Kiss of the Spider Woman," it is, on its own terms, an exceedingly graphic slice of horrific life.

The audience is up close as the characters go through their daily nonablutions, reach for distractions (some of them fanciful) and argue the relative merits of peaceful and violent protest. Immersing themselves in their roles, the four actresses convey the impulsive dedication of their characters. The details of prison life are not so much planned as they are a lesson in adaptation to dehumanization. As the work demonstrates, there are no outer limits to endurance when a moral issue is at stake.

•

The characters represent various faces of Irish womanhood, ranging from a mother separated from her children to a teen-ager who seasons her political commitment with enthusiasm for rock. An outside point of view is provided by a middle-class feminist who has chosen to join her sisters in protest.

Paired in adjoining cells, the women share conflicts as well as allegiances. Occasionally, there is a wistfulness about the life they are missing by following their conscience. The bond among the inmates is conveyed with conviction by the actresses —

Maeve Murphy, Finola Geraghty, Gaby Chiappe and Caroline Seymour — who created the work with their director, Abigail Morris. "Now and at the Hour of Our Death" is an angry cry provoking our sympathy as well as our respect.

1989 Je 1, C18:4

Spender in the Grass

FLORIDA CRACKERS, by William S. Leavengood; directed by John Bishop; sets by John Lee Beatty; costumes by Connie Singer; lights by Dennis Parichy; sound by Chuck London and Stewart Werner; music by Jonathan Brielle; production stage manager, Fred Reinglas. Presented by Circle Repertory Company, Tanya Berezin, artistic director; Connie L. Alexis, managing director. At 99 Seventh Avenue South, at West Fourth Street.

Joe	John C. McGinley
Russell	Scott Rymer
Grant	Michael Piontek
Lori	Kim Flowers
Dean	Joel Anderson
Strings	Brian Jensen
Tracey	Cyndi Coyne

By FRANK RICH

Back in that innocent time when drugs were "reefers" rather than a national tragedy, Tom Lehrer wrote a hilarious ballad singing the praises of that pillar of American folklore, "The Old Dope Peddler." Mr. Lehrer's song was a put-on, of course, but William S. Leavengood, who expresses much the same sentiments in a new play titled "Florida Crackers," doesn't appear to be joking. "Florida Crackers," the wan finale to a robust Circle Repertory Company season, is a nostalgia piece about the old dope peddlers of 1979. It takes us back to the days when the good ole boys of St. Petersburg could still run soft drugs for big laughs and small bucks.

Boys will be boys, especially when they're good ole boys. The three brothers we meet in "Florida Crackers" are the most adorable of scamps. Joe (John C. McGinley), the rambunctious 30-year-old leader of the brood, thirsts for women and Jack Daniels in equal measure. Russell (Scott Rymer) is terribly sensitive; he wants to return to school for a postgraduate degree in philosophy and, to this end, carries around a dog-eared copy of "The Portable Nietzsche." Grant (Michael Piontek) is a misunderstood but ineffably gentle drifter, and what do you expect? These guys come from a broken middle-class home, for gosh sake.

•

"Florida Crackers" interweaves the melodramatic story of Joe's largest and riskiest drug deal — it's "going down," as they say — with elegiac heart-to-heart conversations in which the brothers speak of their aspirations for a better life, exchange confidences with their doltish girlfriends and lament their betrayal of the once-proud family legacy (as crudely symbolized by a discarded land inheritance and a grandparent's ring). One brother or another is forever "waiting for something more" or hoping "to do something with my life." Out of such dreams can grow a floundering playwright's second act.

Lest Mr. Leavengood be judged by post-1979 standards and accused of being an apologist for drug dealers, his Act II rushes to assure us that crime indeed does not pay. A junkie's onstage overdose, a harsh offstage jail sentence and a soupçon of violence remind us that the halcyon precrack era is fast drawing to a close. As one smuggler darkly warns, "It's

Gerry Goodstein

John C. McGinley and Kim Flowers in the Circle Repertory Company production of William S. Leavengood's "Florida Crackers."

not the way it used to be.'' Organized crime and more sophisticated law enforcement are about to push philosophers out of the drug trade and back to the nation's campuses, with consequences that linger to this day.

●

Writing in the sincere, naturalistic style that was a staple at the Circle Rep before its recent literary rebirth, Mr. Leavengood is not without some talent for telling anecdotes and jokes. But his characters remain either mawkish or comic stereotypes, no matter how many of the lighting designer Dennis Parichy's poetic sunsets they admire or how much Nietzsche they read. Under the uncharacteristically heavy-handed direction of John Bishop, the play's punchlines are hit too hard, and both the performances and brawling lack authenticity. Mr. McGinley, most crucially, never convinces us that he's either a cracker, a natural leader of all the men on stage or an irresistible magnet for every woman between St. Pete and Disney World.

In the rest of the company, only Kim Flowers, as one of Mr. McGinley's most inexplicably loyal paramours, possesses the radiance required to shine through the torpor. The production's other asset is a splendidly tacky John Lee Beatty set, which captures the crackers' bachelor pad in every detail, from the salmon-colored paint on the stucco walls to the indeterminately hideous shade of the shag carpet. The set is surrounded by a moat of golden sand, which the audience must cross on the way to its seats. If you're in the market for a cheap, legal summertime high, be sure to wear your sandals.

1989 Je 2, C3:1

Decisions, Decisions

HAMLET, by William Shakespeare; directed by Linda J. K. Masson. Presented by the Riverside Shakespeare Company, Timothy W. Oman, artistic director. At 165 West 86th Street.

Francisco, Gravedigger No. ♭, Player and Osric .... Jeff Shoemaker
Bernado, Gravedigger No. 2 and Sailor .... William Schenker
Horatio .... Robert Emmet
Ghost, Player King and 2d English Ambassador .... Richmond Johnson
Claudius .... Andrew Jarkowksy
Laertes .... Todd Loweth
Polonius .... R. Bruce Elliott
Gertrude .... Sonja Lanzener
Hamlet .... Austin Pendleton
Ophelia .... Lisa Nicholas
Rosencrantz .... Woody Sempliner
Guildenstern .... Gene Santarelli
Player Queen and Attendant
.... Paula Eschweiler

By WILBORN HAMPTON

Locked somewhere in the heart of any actor worth his greasepaint is the ambition to play Hamlet. The chance to undertake the role, however, is mercifully not given to every actor in his lifetime. And, as Winston Churchill said in another context, even when such an opportunity presents itself, it should not necessarily be taken.

Austin Pendleton, one of our more consistently fine actors, has now taken on the role in a respectable if uneven production by the Riverside Shakespeare Company.

At the outset, it should be said that Mr. Pendleton gives an intelligent, articulate and reasoned reading of the title role. And he brings an under-

standing to the character that eludes many Hamlets. But there are factors that work against the complete credibility of Mr. Pendleton's Hamlet.

●

For one thing, Mr. Pendleton is known primarily, perhaps unfairly, as a comic actor and his impish countenance at first makes one think more of a Puck than a melancholic Danish Prince. Further, it is an irony of the stage that by the time an actor is old enough to begin to grasp the depths of the role, he is often too old to play it. It asks for suspending a lot of disbelief to accept Mr. Pendleton at this stage of his career as a college student preparing to return to another semester at Wittenberg. Another disconcerting aspect to Mr. Pendleton's performance is his tendency to keep a half-mocking grin fixed on his face, especially in his early parries with the residents and visitors to the Danish court, as though he himself were somewhat bemused to be playing the role.

But there is much to commend in his interpretation. Mr. Pendleton does not miss a line or nuance, of Hamlet's sarcastic humor, and when the moment for passion comes, he summons a fury that is focused and gripping. And Mr. Pendleton follows the playwright's own advice on acting in delivering Hamlet's soliloquies, speaking them simply, letting his own discretion be his tutor and suiting his action to the word.

Other forces are at work in Elsinore, of course, and in the Riverside production some are good, some are bad, and some are simply indifferent. Lisa Nicholas is a convincing Ophelia, touching in her naïveté and her affection for Hamlet and pitiable in her final confusion and madness. Sonja Lanzener as Gertrude and Andrew Jarkowsky as Claudius give strong performances, providing the fulcrum on which Hamlet's fate finally turns. Jeff Shoemaker plays the parts of Gravedigger No. 1, Player, Osric and Francisco well.

●

Other roles are less happily realized. The Ghost of Hamlet's father swaggers onstage, gazing around the theater as though he were a late arrival looking for his seat. Horatio smiles like a game-show host at everything that happens. And Polonius, looking younger and more fit than Hamlet, is simply miscast. Linda J. K. Masson directed. Should she undertake another "Hamlet," she should not to wait until the middle of Act IV to call an intermission.

1989 Je 2, C3:5

Jungle Terror

CONVERSATION AMONG THE RUINS, by Emilio Carballido; English translation by Dr. Myra Gann; directed by Alejandra Gutiérrez; set design, Robert Klingelhoefer; lighting design, Bill Simmons; costume designer, Laura Drawbaugh; sound design, Gary and Timmy Harris; production stage manager, Mark Wagenhurst; producer, Miriam Colón. Presented by the Puerto Rican Traveling Theater, 304 West 47th Street.

Anarda .... Elizabeth Ruiz Clemens
Enedina .... Teresa Yenque
Antonio .... Mark Morant

By D. J. R. BRUCKNER

Emilio Carballido's passion for torrents of words and his taste for exposing the underside of life might make

Peter Krupenye

Elizabeth Ruiz Clemens in "Conversation Among the Ruins," Emilio Carballido's play which opens Thursday at Puerto Rican Traveling Theater, 304 West 47th Street

"Conversation Among the Ruins" an appropriate title not only for his latest play but also for his collected works. "Conversation," however, lacks much of the humor that has given bite to the Mexican playwright's other scripts, and the language becomes a murky flood that sinks his story.

The play — now in performance at the Puerto Rican Traveling Theater, 304 West 47th Street — starts off promisingly with two women competing for the same man, a situation Mr. Carballido has exploited before, often hilariously. But as the man and the younger of the two women recall their past together, so many tortured and brutal characters get tangled up in their story without ever putting in an appearance on stage that one gives up trying to understand or even care. Eventually this somber recitation roars and gasps its way to an impressively exasperating end in a murder that is violent but unaffecting.

All this happens in a remote jungle area of Mexico in the 1950's. Much of the dialogue sounds more like a social-conscience Hollywood movie of the 1930's or 40's. The concerns voiced here — about political corruption, the exploitation of the poor, the ignorant, children and women, and many other themes — have lurked under the surface in previous Carballido plays, even comic ones, giving them a subtle resonance. In "Conversation" they reach out like the roots and tendrils of Robert Klingelhoefer's ominous jungle set to trip and strangle the characters.

The cast, under the direction of Alejandra Gutiérrez, struggles honorably with this material. Elizabeth Ruiz Clemens, as a corrupt old millionaire's young, adulterous wife, who takes off for the jungle in search of a young man she betrayed, is pitiable at times, contemptible at others and almost always infuriating. Mark Morant, as the man she is after, turns from a cold and distant figure into a hunted and frightened one who is more terrified of his own feelings than of the life he has fled or the love he cannot bring himself to acknowledge.

●

In many ways, Teresa Yenque has the most enviable role — as an older Indian woman who becomes the young man's housekeeper, and in her imagination much more. She alone is given the gift of occasional silences, and Ms. Yenque knows how to be a powerful presence in quiet isolation on a stage filled with a pounding cataract of words.

1989 Je 4, 64:6

War and Love

ARMS AND THE MAN, by George Bernard Shaw; directed by Frank Hauser; set design by Franco Colavecchia; costume design by A. Christina Giannini; lighting design by F. Mitchell Dana; sound design by Philip Campanella; production stage manager, Roy W. Backes. Presented by Roundabout Theater, Gene Feist, artistic director; Todd Haimes, executive director. At 100 East 17th Street.

Raina Petkoff .... Roma Downey
Catherine Petkoff .... Barbara Andres
Captain Bluntschli .... Daniel Gerroll
Nicola .... Yusef Bulos
Petkoff .... MacIntyre Dixon
Louka .... Catherine Christianson
Sergius Saranoff .... Christopher Noth
Major Plechanoff .... Richard Buckley

Martha Swope

By WILBORN HAMPTON

When "Arms and the Man" opened in London in 1894, a wildly cheering audience demanded that the author take a bow. As Shaw stepped onstage, one man in the balcony shouted a loud, long "Boo!" Shaw looked up at the gallery and said, "My dear fellow, I couldn't agree with you more, but what are we against so many?"

In fact, Shaw was never entirely comfortable with the success of "Arms and the Man," his second play to be produced. He would later describe it as flimsy and fantastical and call the first production a ghastly failure.

Revival
Roma Downey and Daniel Gerroll are in George Bernard Shaw's "Arms and the Man," directed by Frank Hauser.

But who is the playwright against so many? "Arms and the Man" remains one of Shaw's most popular plays and the Roundabout Theater has mounted an attractive and delightfully amusing production that has been pruned to its plot and philosophical essentials yet retains its acerbic ridicule of Romantic notions, some of which persist to this day.

•

Frank Hauser has assembled a mostly fine cast that rarely misses a nuance of the mockery Shaw makes of conventional Victorian views, not only the obvious ones of war and soldiering, but also those of love, chivalry, class structure and women. Mr. Hauser has kept the action at a relaxed pace that allows his actors, for the most part, to develop characters rather than caricatures.

Shaw himself found great sympathy in the character of Sergius, the Bulgarian major who leads an ill-advised cavalry charge into the face of a Serbian machine-gun nest and inadvertently becomes a hero only because the Serbs had the wrong ammunition and could not open fire. But it is Captain Bluntschli, the sensible Swiss mercenary and son of a hotelier who carries chocolate in his cartridge belt instead of spare bullets, whom modern audiences have come to admire most.

•

The Roundabout production is fortunate in Daniel Gerroll as Bluntschli. Mr. Gerroll presents a dashing figure at Raina's second-floor bedroom window, and there is just enough of a desperate, hunted man in his opening scene to excite the young Bulgarian woman's affection. Later, after he has become her "chocolate-cream soldier" and has offered her his pistol "to protect yourself from me," he becomes the play's voice of sanity and reason against the marshaled armies of hypocrisy.

Mr. Gerroll's transition from a soldier of fortune to a Swiss hotel keeper is deft. It begins at the end of the second act when he sits down to write out his address, which he does with the meticulous precision of a desk clerk copying a passport number on a registration card. By the time Bluntschli gets around to proposing to Raina by reciting a list of his holdings (4,000 bed sheets, 10,000 knives and forks, etc.) he has, as Raina observes, "a low shopkeeper's mind." He replies, "That's the Swiss national character," and coming from Mr. Gerroll it is neither a boast nor a confession, but a simple statement of fact. Mr. Gerroll resists the temptation to turn Bluntschli into a Romantic hero, as actors often do.

Roma Downey is an enticing Raina who can match wits with Bluntschli almost every time. She is more attracted to gunfire than frightened of it. She wants to be Romantic, but is sensible enough to recognize the truth when she hears it. She may not be sure whether she fell in love with Bluntschli because he was the "first man not to take her seriously" or because he once pointed a gun at her head, but she accepts its result. And she will not be the object of an auction.

•

Christopher Noth captures the strutting buffoon in the character of Sergius, a man devoted to the idea of Higher Love although his passion for the maid Louka makes it difficult for him to live up to it for any length of time, but the more pitiable side to the Bulgarian is lost in his performance.

Catherine Christianson is a coquettish and appealing Louka, the know-

ing maid who disdains the "soul of a servant." MacIntyre Dixon and Barbara Andres, as Raina's parents, the proud Petkoffs who own the only two-story house and the only library in rural Bulgaria, and Yusef Bulos as their butler round out the solid cast.

Franco Colavecchia has provided charming sets, evoking a wood-paneled Balkan hunting lodge, an ivy-covered garden and a library consisting of a couple of bookshelves with only half a dozen slim volumes on them. And A. Christina Giannini has designed a wardrobe of colorful costumes ranging from rustic peasant dirndls to the finest frocks in Sofia.

1989 Je 5, C12:4

Callas: The Grail

THE LISBON TRAVIATA, by Terrence McNally; directed by John Tillinger; sets by Philipp Jung; costumes by Jane Greenwood; lighting by Ken Billington; sound by Gary and Timmy Harris; production stage manager, Pamela Singer; fights staged by B. H. Barry. Presented by Manhattan Theater Club, Lynne Meadow, artistic director; Barry Grove, managing director. At City Center Stage I, 131 West 55th Street.

Stephen	Anthony Heald
Mendy	Nathan Lane
Mike	Dan Butler
Paul	John Slattery

By MEL GUSSOW

In "The Lisbon Traviata," Terrence McNally has written the theatrical equivalent of an operatic double bill — an opéra bouffe followed by a tragic denouement. The first act, in the play's newly revised version, is a savagely amusing and empathetic study of two men whose lives have been lost in opera. The second act is discordant, as it was in the play's earlier showcase production in 1985.

Since the play was first presented, it has gone through alterations, all of which are improvements and help to bridge the difference between the two acts. John Tillinger's new production,

which opened last night at the Manhattan Theater Club, is even sharper than his original at Theater Off Park. The performances by Anthony Heald and, in particular, by Nathan Lane, are among the finest offered by these estimable actors. But the author has not solved the play's structural problems.

In the first act, we are sequestered in a richly baroque apartment — itself a kind of red plush opera box — with the host, Mendy (Mr. Lane), and his guest, Stephen (Mr. Heald). Both are addicted to the genius and the memory of Maria Callas, almost to the point of exclusion of all other singers, whom they dismiss with the most excoriating remarks. One does not have to be a music critic to appreciate Mr. McNally's wit and his encyclopedic knowledge of the art form under scrutiny.

When Mr. Heald mentions an obscure pirated recording of a Callas "Traviata" performed in Lisbon, Mr. Lane is swept away in anticipation. That recording, still unheard by him, becomes a kind of Holy Grail.

In the first version of the play, the dialogue between the two men was almost too funny. Though Mr. McNally still cannot resist ridiculing his artistic peers (past and present), the act has been reshaped so that laughter is underscored with portent. As the two reveal themselves through their references to opera and to their own relationship, we can sense the abject loneliness and the desperation of both characters. The first act is tragedy in the guise of comedy.

Mr. Lane, formerly married and the father of a son (as he says, "Callas was named in my divorce for alienation of affections") is, for all his campiness, filled with feelings of immense insecurity. He is, one might say, all show and no follow-through. In contrast, Mr. Heald's character is as obsessed by love as he is by opera, to the point of confusing the two.

The play is an ambitious attempt to confront demons absent or suppressed in the playwright's other, engaging work. Mr. McNally is taking

himself and his subject with the utmost seriousness. For a long time, we are held by his acuity — and by the intensity of Mr. Tillinger's direction. The audience's anticipation at the end of the first act almost equals that of Mr. Lane awaiting the recording of "The Lisbon Traviata."

•

The second act moves to the apartment Mr. Heald shares with Dan Butler, an apartment that is the absolute opposite of Mr. Lane's — cleanly and stylishly modern (two splendid set designs by Philipp Jung). As is soon evident, the two halves of the play are as disparate as the settings.

In his home, Mr. Heald is unable to come to terms with what he considers to be Mr. Butler's betrayal. The latter is involved in a new liaison, which Mr. Heald, with carefully orchestrated malevolence, tries to torpedo. Though the confrontation retains the play's earlier vituperativeness, it swims into banal dramatic waters, as the homosexual characters echo clichés from fiction about heterosexual couples. Mr. Heald becomes the spurned "wife" deserted for a younger love and crazed in a pursuit of retribution. While the violent conclusion may seem inevitable in the context of opera, it is not convincing in this domestic drama.

The two minor roles, though deftly played by Mr. Butler and John Slattery, are undeveloped. Mr. Heald's character is, in the new version of the play, a book editor rather than a struggling playwright, but he still courts self-pity. Despite his supposed revelations, emotionally we learn little more about him than we knew in the first act.

At the same time, Mendy (Mr. Lane) does not appear after the first act. Mendy, the ultimate opera lover, the man who by his own admission is "too much for most people," becomes a supporting player in a drama in which he has earned a starring role. In a difficult assignment, Mr. Heald artfully avoids overstatement. But it is Mr. Lane who deserves the highest praise for a brilliant performance as a man doomed to live an ordinary life while aspiring to the ecstasy of opera.

1989 Je 7, C21:1

Gerry Goodstein

Nathan Lane, left, and Anthony Heald in "The Lisbon Traviata."

A Broadway Legend, Fondly Remembered

CALL ME ETHEL!, by Christopher Powich and Rita McKenzie; directed by Mr. Powich; musical direction, Peter Blue; set designer, Russell Pyle; lighting designer, Robert Bessoir; costume designer, Dale Wibbin; sound designer, Phillip Allen; special costumes, Georgia Reese; assistant lighting designer, Stefan Jacobs; associate artistic director, Lonny Price. Presented by the American Jewish Theater, Stanley Brechner, artistic director. At 307 West 26th Street.

WITH: Rita McKenzie

By STEPHEN HOLDEN

"Hollywood shoots too many movies and not enough blondes," Ethel Merman once quipped when commenting on the movie "There's No Business Like Show Business," in which she received top billing but Marilyn Monroe won all the attention. The crack is one of many brassy Merman one-liners that pepper "Call Me Ethel!", the tribute to the star at the American Jewish Theater in which Rita McKenzie re-creates Merman's voice and body language with an uncanny accuracy.

With her braying trumpet of a voice and her blunt, smart-aleck humor, Merman, who died in 1984 at age 75, is remembered more as a natural phenomenon of the Broadway musical than as a glamorous woman of the theater. And that is how Ms. McKenzie plays her. The two-act show, an enlargement of Ms. McKenzie's successful cabaret act, is an affectionate remembrance of the star that portrays her as a tough, unrefined trouper with an essentially kind heart.

"Call Me Ethel!" is structured around the conceit of having Merman regale her longtime agent, Lou Irwin, with remarks and anecdotes in preparation for a possible film biography. The device works well enough to hold together a rough biographical chronology interspersed with Merman-identified songs. The show imagines the star displaying her legendary chutzpah during an audition for the Gershwins' "Girl Crazy," the musical that made her famous, by suggesting they "jazz up" her big number, "I Got Rhythm." Her memories of Cole Porter, in whose shows she scored a succession of triumphs, are tinged with a romantic nostalgia. Act I ends with a medley from "Annie Get Your Gun."

The second act is mostly devoted to the shows "Call Me Madam" and "Gypsy." The 1950 Irving Berlin show, inspired by the life of the Washington party-giver Perle Mesta, prompts reminiscences of Merman's personal and social life during the 1950's. Ms. McKenzie's re-creation of "Rose's Turn," the star's penultimate song from "Gypsy," is more than an impressive feat of mimickry. She gives the number a ferocious, snapping passion that brings the scene dramatically to life.

"Call Me Ethel!", which was written and directed by Christopher Powich, doesn't try to probe Merman's psyche any more deeply than "Tallulah," a similar star biography that ran theatrically after originating in a cabaret. The decision to keep a light touch was probably wise, since Merman, like Bankhead, was a self-created caricature conceived for public consumption.

What gives "Call Me Ethel!" the edge over similar shows is the fidelity with which Ms. McKenzie captures Merman's vocal personality. If she lacks Merman's seemingly unlimited vocal projection, her stamina is still impressive. Especially when Ms. McKenzie is performing the material from "Gypsy," the strength and accuracy of her re-creation are matched by a depth of feeling.

1989 Je 10, 14:3

True Confessions

FRIENDS, written and directed by Lee Kalcheim; set design by Richard Meyer; lighting design by Steve Rust; production stage manager, Denise Laffer. Presented by Manhattan Punch Line, Steve Kaplan, artistic director. At the Judith Anderson Theater, 422 West 42d Street.

Howard (Okie) Peterson .... Richard Lenz
Mel .... David Spielberg

By STEPHEN HOLDEN

In Lee Kalcheim's play "Friends," two men in their late 40's who have been close since their days as Yale undergraduates reunite in a Vermont cabin to share their midlife crises.

Mel (David Spielberg), a man of many talents, has yet to find a successful niche for himself in the world. Jewish and from New York City, he is smart, funny and capable, but unable to commit himself to either an occupation or a woman. And the rustic life he has chosen in the New England countryside has begun to pall.

Mel's best friend, Howard (Richard Lenz), a taciturn Oklahoman of Swedish descent, is a born winner. He has a beautiful high-powered wife, whom Mel admits to coveting, and he drives a Mercedes-Benz. At the United Nations, where he works, he is about to be named the American delegate.

●

The production, presented at the Manhattan Punch Line Theater under the author's direction, is not the play's first New York appearance. Five years ago, it opened at the Manhattan Theater Club to mixed reviews and has since been extensively rewritten.

Carefully crafted and acted with a fine sense of psychological detail, "Friends" is so doggedly intent on seeming true to life that it feels like a textbook exercise in realistic television scriptwriting. Mr. Lenz and Mr. Spielberg deliver subtle, convincing portraits of men of almost opposite personalities who share a nagging disappointment and emptiness.

●

The drama is awfully slow in building. Scenes in which the pair play parlor games and impulsively try to telephone Mel's secret teen-age love attenuate a story that loses momentum the longer its confrontations are post-poned. The realism is so scrupulous that the predictable crux of the drama is telegraphed too clearly for there to be much suspense. No sooner has the grim and hollow-eyed Howard arrived and plunked down a hunting rifle whose presence makes Mel nervous, than one anticipates future revelations of Howard's repressed rage and suicidal inclinations.

When those confesssions finally come, they are accompanied by convincing explanations of the family dynamics that have driven him to his present state.

That's the trouble with "Friends." Everything is prepared and explained so that it makes too much sense. Life is messier and reality more mysterious than "Friends" would have us believe.

1989 Je 11, 67:1

Martha Swope Associates/Carol Rosegg

David Spielberg, left, and Richard Lenz in "Friends."

Stratford Offers Majesty, Mirth and Gore

By MEL GUSSOW

Special to The New York Times

STRATFORD, Ontario, June 4 — When John Neville began his reign as artistic director of the Stratford Festival, he vowed to restore the company to a position of artistic and financial stability. Through a combination of theatrical acumen and pragmatism — seasoned with a dash of audacity — the director has gone a long way toward accomplishing that goal.

Mr. Neville's fourth and final season (he is to be succeeded by David William) begins on several eye-opening notes. Henry V and his infantrymen fight World War I in the trenches around Agincourt, "Kiss Me Kate" almost becomes a tap-dance musical and, for an extra fillip, "Titus Andronicus" and "The Comedy of Errors" share a tragical-comical double bill.

While theatergoers may be attracted to Stratford by "Kiss Me Kate," the production that will undoubtedly linger longest in their minds is "Henry V," as boldly staged by John Wood (the Canadian director, not the English actor with the same name). Mr. Wood has moved the play 500 years forward to the outbreak of World War I.

That transplantation may seem eccentric, but it has been undertaken with exuberance and imagination by Mr. Wood and his cast, headed by Geraint Wyn Davies in the title role. Mr. Wood's historical point is provocative, tracing the supreme self-confidence of the English and their empire through the ages. By 1915, patriotism might still be confused with jingoism.

Mr. Wyn Davies's Henry exudes a military and moral authority. He is a handsome aristocrat with an iron hand, through his person sending out a message of his nation's invulnerability. He has a regal bearing — with a touch of Winston Churchill in the night. In the background are interludes of Gilbert and Sullivan, reinforcing the feeling of noblesse oblige.

The tone of the production is set by William Needle's Chorus, dressed like a World War I pensioner. He tells the story matter-of-factly, as if he is lecturing on a celebrated battle. Effortlessly, he is woven into the action. In contrast to the English are the lofty French — complacent, decadent and, we are led to believe, absolutely incapable of winning.

Along the path to English victory, there are awkward atmospheric moments — though guns are fired, soldiers also draw short swords for close combat — but Mr. Wood's approach works with surprising efficacy. The production is buoyed by the supporting performances (including that of Antoni Cimolino, who plays the Dauphin like a French Hotspur) and by John Ferguson's design, which captures the smoke and siege of English films about the Great War.

When Henry woos Katherine of France — an amiably romantic exchange between Mr. Wyn Davies and Kim Horsman — one awaits the King's unstated suggestion, "Kiss me, Kate," words that are heard with musical fervor in Stratford's other Festival Theater.

Tapping 'Kate'

In each of his seasons, Mr. Neville has presented a lavish musical production. "Kiss Me Kate" is a natural choice, offering audiences both a précis of "The Taming of the Shrew" and a bounteous Cole Porter score, including clever variations on Shakespeare, soaring ballads, ethnic pastiches and some of the wittiest lyrics the composer ever devised. This is a rare show that has the audience humming along with the overture.

The musical is on insecure ground only with the Sam and Bella Spewack backstage book, which creaks enough to need pruning. Though Donald Saddler, as director and choreographer, offers a polished production — superior to the recent one staged by the Royal Shakespeare Company — it lacks that extra éclat that Jerry Zaks brought to "Anything Goes" at Lincoln Center.

There is one inspired musical number, a stylish tap version of "Too Darn Hot" that begins the second act. The song is choreographed by Mr. Saddler and Dirk Lumbard, who plays Lucentio. Through a stage door erupts a chorus of male dancers, led by Mr. Lumbard, giving a dazzling demonstration of close-order choreography.

Oddly, "Too Darn Hot" is one of the more extraneous numbers. In the movie version, Ann Miller danced it

Jayne Lewis as Lilli Vanessi and Victor A. Young as Fred Graham in "Kiss Me Kate" at the Stratford Festival in Ontario.

in the opening scene and then was told it had been cut from the show. Mr. Lumbard uses it to enhance the modern theatrical side of "Kiss Me Kate."

Several songs later, Douglas Chamberlain and Dale Mieske offer a hearty vaudeville rendition of the musical's second deserved showstopper, "Brush Up Your Shakespeare." The leading players, Victor A. Young and Jayne Lewis, add their own panache. "Kiss Me Kate," a Stratford adornment, is overdue for a major New York revival.

A Gableresque Sister

Mr. Neville is himself represented as the director of "The Three Sisters," in which Lucy Peacock and Allan Gray (as Masha and Vershinin)

'Titus Andronicus' contrasts with 'The Comedy of Errors.'

are the striking center of an otherwise uneven production. Before a formal, lacework background, several of the other actors lack subtlety — as is the case with Larissa Lapchinski as Natasha. But Ms. Peacock is a Masha with a tinge of Hedda Gabler, a figure of glamour stifling amid boredom, and Mr. Gray captures the rhapsodic, reflective nature of Vershinin.

Scheduling during a three-day visit did not permit attendance at "A Midsummer Night's Dream" and "The Merchant of Venice," among the other early-season openings. "Merchant" is a restaging of the Michael Langham production, starring Brian Bedford, seen last year at the Shakespeare Theater at the Folger in Washington. Mr. Bedford's eloquent

Shylock must be a high point at this season's festival — along with Mr. Wyn Davies's Henry and Ms. Peacock and Mr. Gray in "The Three Sisters."

Blood and Farce

The theory behind the matching of "Titus Andronicus" and "The Comedy of Errors" is that, staged back to back in abbreviated form, the plays will shed light on each other. What they share is their immense disparity — "Titus" as the bloodiest of tragedies, "Comedy of Errors" as Shakespeare's most farcical comedy.

Necessarily, "Titus" suffers more in the abridgement — and in contrast to Deborah Warner's stunning production for the Royal Shakespeare Company. Jeannette Lambermont's 90-minute, quick-script version rushes from mayhem to murder, littering the stage with lost digits and limbs. The director uses Kabuki techniques, indicating that she may have an interesting approach for a full-length version. As adapted and directed into a brisk 70-minute clown show by Richard Monette, "The Comedy of Errors" poses no such problems. Cut to the funnybone, the show is, as intended, a mirthful divertissement.

The principal advantage of the doubling is that it allows actors to demonstrate their versatility. After the intermission, Keith Dinicol, the Satanic emperor in "Titus," does a deft turn as two low-comedy Dromios, and Geordie Johnson, his good brother in "Titus," cavorts as two faces of Antipholus. Similarly, Goldie Semple, a fierce Tamora, easily becomes the merrily flummoxed wife of Antipholus.

At one point, as a cue to the audience that there is irreverence afoot, a tribune from "Titus" wanders onstage in "The Comedy of Errors." He glares at the audience like a samurai warrior, then realizes that he is in the wrong play and sheepishly exits. With

the help of his actors and directors, John Neville has brushed up his Shakespeare festival.

1989 Je 12, C13:1

Locker Room Romp With Lewd Lyrics

UP 'N' UNDER, by John Godber; directed by Geoffrey Sherman; set and light design by Paul Wonsek; costume design by Pamela Scofield; sound design by Craig R. Zaionz; stage manager, Gary M. Zabinski. Presented by the Hudson Guild Theater, Mr. Sherman, producing-artistic director; Steven Ramay, associate director. At 441 West 26th Street.

Hazel Scott	Elaine Rinehart
Frank Rowley	Ivar Brogger
Phil Hopley	Ray Collins
Tony Burtoft	Fredrick Hahn
Arthur Hoyle	John Curless
Reg Welsh and Steve Edwards	
	Edmund Lewis

By WILBORN HAMPTON

If "Rocky" had been written about the dreams and fantasies of a Yorkshire rugby coach instead of a Philadelphia prizefighter, the result might have been "Up 'n' Under," John Godber's play now at the Hudson Guild Theater.

The comparison, in fact, is rather forced on the audience since Arthur Hoyle (John Curless), the protagonist of this slight comedy, tells anyone who will listen how much he loves all four of the "Rocky" movies, and the film's theme song is used as incidental inspirational music in the play.

Arthur, who was banned from Rugby League play for such unorthodox tactics as poking the opposing center in the eye in the scrum, is now a trainer of pub teams. He makes a £3,000 wager with Reg, an old rival who is now the coach of a gang of toughs (with "only four teeth between them") who play rugby as the Cobblers, that he can train any team of Reg's choosing to beat the Cobblers within five weeks. Reg chooses the Wheatsheafs, a motley collection of ill-equipped weekend players who can muster only four of their seven members on any given day and who hold the distinction of being the worst rugby team in Yorkshire.

●

The rest of the play, which won an Olivier Award when it was first produced in Britain five years ago, consists of Arthur persuading the team to play the match, their training for it and the game itself. Mr. Godber employs a grab bag of styles to tell this story, including a bad imitation of Shakespearean monologues (even stealing the occasional line) that provide a running commentary on the team's progress. The rhymes are more the quality of team fight songs than poetry. There are a lot of locker room gags, such as pulling down one another's shorts, jokes about passing wind and silly pub chatter.

The subject is not without dramatic possibilities, since one of the last bastions of class distinction in Britain can be found on its playing fields. Rugby, the forebear of American football, is generally regarded as a sport for young gentlemen of the upper class, as opposed to soccer, which is a working-class game. An exception is in the north of England, where Rugby League is an enduring passion of all classes.

But for the most part, there is little real drama, or humor for that matter, in "Up 'n' Under." Apart from the ac-

tual rugby match, which is played out in the second act, complete with slow motion and instant replay, not much happens onstage to capture the audience's imagination or attention.

●

There are occasional bright moments. A three-mile cross-country run by the team as it begins training is cleverly and amusingly done, and the one bawdy song (rugby teams are notorious for devising lewd lyrics for popular melodies), in which the team sings a lusty rendition of "Bye-Bye Blackbird," is a howl. There is one touching scene in which Frank, a divorced butcher with two children he rarely sees, explains to Hazel, a young woman who takes over the team's training, why he still plays rugby at the age of 35. Ivar Brogger gives a moving reading of the lonely rugger, ably assisted by Elaine Rinehart as Hazel. The play needs more such character study and less horseplay.

The rest of the cast is energetic and gives a good example of ensemble acting. No one drops the ball. The accents are fairly uniform, even if there is more Midlands than Yorkshire in them. Geoffrey Sherman, the director, keeps things jogging along nicely, and his staging of the game is skillful, especially with the same six actors playing both teams.

1989 Je 13, C17:1

Teacher of the Year, With Reservations

THE GOOD COACH, by Ben Siegler; directed by Michael Bloom; setting by Edward T. Gianfrancesco; lighting by Craig Evans; costumes by Deborah Shaw; sound by Aural Fixation. WPA Theater, Kyle Renick, artistic director. At 519 West 23d Street.

Joe LaPorte	Tom Mardirosian
Frank	Richard Council
Sally	Mary Kane
Man	Jace Alexander
Student	Sal Barone
Chuck	Bill Cwikowski
Hooker and Karen	Kathryn Rossetter

By MEL GUSSOW

The story is familiar in life as well as fiction: An outwardly upright citizen conceals a dark secret that contradicts his present respectability. One need only recall Alfred Hitchcock's "Shadow of a Doubt" and other films to realize the renewable dramatic possibilities, but in his first play, "The Good Coach," Ben Siegler barely gives the premise a workout.

In the play (at the WPA Theater), the title character (Tom Mardirosian) coaches dodgeball and other sports in a small-town school. Because of his altruism and an avuncular concern for his students, he has just been named teacher of the year. Then his world collapses. The catalyst for this upheaval is a rapist who has been terrorizing the community. In a letter to a local newspaper, the rapist reaches out for someone to share his culpability with him — and the self-accusatory coach, obsessed by his own past, responds.

The coach's secret, when it is revealed, is so negligible as to be laughable. It is an indiscretion not serious enough to haunt a man for so many years and it would be naïve to think it could have turned a grade-school student into an adult psychopath.

The other characters are simplistic, including the rapist and the coach's friends, who are unbelievably resistant to his attempts at confession. The playwright has tried to diversify the narrative by flashing back to scenes between the coach and the child he thinks he corrupted, but these scenes — as well as others — lack tautness. The tale briefly holds our attention in the beginning, when the coach speaks mockingly about what it means to be a gym teacher.

Michael Bloom, the director, underplays the melodramatic aspects of the story. Within the constraints of the play, the performances are effective, especially so in the case of the two pivotal roles. Mr. Mardirosian moves skillfully from congeniality to self-incrimination and Jace Alexander is insidious as the small-town Jack the Ripper.

The play is supposedly a psychological thriller dealing with, in the author's words, "crossing the line" — between acceptable and aberrant behavior. Actually, "The Good Coach" is an unconvincing entry in the standard Book of Plots.

1989 Je 13, C18:5

Life and Death In a Bathtub

MARATHON '89, Series B. Set designer, Linda Giering Balmuth; production supervisor, David M. Mead; lighting design, Greg MacPherson; costume design, Teresa Snider-Stein; production stage manager, Ira Mont; sound design, Gayle Jeffery. Presented by the Ensemble Studio Theater, Curt Dempster, artistic director; Peter Shavitz, managing director. At 549 West 52d Street.

WOMAN FLOATING OUT A WINDOW, by Jacklyn Maddux; directed by Charles Karchmer; stage manager, Judy Sostek.

Parker	Carmen de Lavallade
Meredith	Jody Gelb
Oswald	Sam Gray

PATHOLOGICAL VENUS, by Brighde Mullins; directed by Jimmy Bohr; music compsed by Charles Goldbeck.

Venus	Merri Blechler
Betty Butchko	Susan Greenhill
Kenwigs	John Scanlan

THE OPEN BOAT, by Neal Bell; directed by Curt Dempster; stage manager, Dean Gray.

John-John	Phillip Casnoff
Marcus	John Ottavino
Jane	Debra Stricklin
Vincent	John MacKay

By MEL GUSSOW

Neal Bell takes the title and central image of his one-act play, "The Open Boat," from Stephen Crane. As Crane wrote about the shipwreck in his short story of the same name, "Many a man ought to have a bathtub larger than the boat which rode upon the sea." Mr. Bell plays upon the idea of a tub as boat and vice versa, with, in this macabre case, both becoming vessels of death.

As directed by Curt Dempster, Mr. Bell's play is the only interesting one of the three works in Series B of the Ensemble Studio Theater's Marathon '89, the company's 12th annual series of short plays. "The Open Boat" is overly elliptical, but it is stageworthy — in contrast to the two other neophyte efforts, Brighde Mullins's "Pathological Venus" and Jacklyn Maddux's "Woman Floating Out a Window."

One could consider "The Open Boat" a nightmare remembered as a daydream, as two old friends, one a policeman (John Ottavino), the other, a criminal (Phillip Casnoff) vie with each other for supremacy. One source of their conflict is Mr. Casnoff's sister (Debra Stricklin), but the basic differences are deeper and hinge on matters of morality.

The underlying narrative is like a chapter from television's "Wiseguys," although Mr. Bell seems more concerned with withholding information than with delineating motivation. In this and other plays, he has a way of treating malicious intent with matter-of-fact ease. Here his fearful visions include corpses putrefying in bathtubs. Among the dead is an older policeman, a family friend of all the other characters. The reason for his death remains one of the show's mysteries.

•

Mr. Dempster has staged the sprawling work with fluidity, switching from dry land to lake, and he has drawn intriguing off-center performances from his actors, especially Mr. Casnoff. Even as the play remains elusive, it holds one's attention, which is not the case with Ms. Mullins's self-conscious absurdist cartoon.

"Pathological Venus" is set on a fat farm in Nevada, a "home for eating disorders" whose sole patient seems to be a woman who would prefer to remain overweight (Merri Biechler.) The play itself is burdened with an unnutritious surfeit of words and whimsy; it desperately needs slimming. As the head of the home (Susan Greenhill) correctly observes, "Excess is excess."

"Woman Floating Out a Window" also deals — even more unprofitably — with nursing and nurturing. Ms. Maddux's one-act centers on the imminent death of a celebrated artist, Maggie Flowers, also known as Toots. The artist is ensconsced in an off-stage bedroom. We hear about her from her young protégée (Jody Gelb) and her former companion (Sam Gray). The latter has a habit of describing Toots's art in exclamatory terms, like, "Exquisite! Such movement! The colors!" In criticism as well as art, excess is excess.

•

Mr. Gray is an even more irritating presence than the artist's nurse (Carmen de Lavallade), who, if she is the angel of death, is decidedly an undemonstrative one, and the moody protégée who proudly boasts that critics have compared her work to that of her mentor.

In the course of this 40-minute theatrical chestnut, we learn very little about the aged artist, beyond the fact that she has dubious judgment in her choice of friends. It is the play rather than the patient that quietly floats out the window.

1989 Je 15, C14:5

Falling in Love With a Dowry

THE HEIRESS, by Ruth and Augustus Goetz; directed by Kenneth Frankel; set design by Loy Arcenas; costume design, Jess Goldstein; lighting design by David F. Segal; production stage manager, Anne Keefe. Presented by the Long Wharf Theater, Arvin Brown, artistic director; M. Edgar Rosenblum, executive director. At New Haven.

Maria	Ann Sheehy
Dr. Sloper	Richard Kiley
Mrs. Penniman	Margaret Hilton
Catherine Sloper	Jayne Atkinson
Mrs. Almond	Gloria Maddox
Arthur Townsend	Peter Mackenzie
Marian Almond	Wendee Pratt
Morris Townsend	Michel R. Gill
Mrs. Montgomery	Jeanne Ruskin

By MEL GUSSOW

Special to The New York Times

NEW HAVEN, June 14 — Despite Henry James's own reservations about the complexity of his short novel "Washington Square," it has proven to be one of the author's most durable works. That popularity has been further enhanced by Ruth and Augustus Goetz's engrossing adaptation (on stage and as a film). The Goetz version, "The Heiress," manages the difficult feat of dramatizing James without overdramatizing James — as is clearly demonstrated in Kenneth Frankel's production at the Long Wharf Theater.

Richard Kiley, who played the role of Dr. Sloper in the 1976 Broadway revival, is the striking center of the Long Wharf production. He offers an illuminating portrait of a proud, uncompromising father who is ineluctably driven to diminish the life of his daughter, the painfully shy Catherine Sloper. The actor keeps the doctor from becoming a villain (an evident pitfall). Instead, he emphasizes his authority and his austerity. Once again, Mr. Kiley is a commanding presence in a role in which that attribute is an absolute essential.

Both the doctor and his daughter (Jayne Atkinson) are helpless within their natures. They are destined to disappoint one another, and, as Sloper realizes, in some respects they are more alike than they care to admit. As was the case in the novel, the adapters do not apportion guilt, not even to the scoundrel, Morris Townsend (Michel R. Gill).

It is unimaginable to the father that this handsome suitor would consider Catherine to be desirable, except in anticipation of her inheritance. The doctor is unable to see that happiness of a sort might be achievable for his daughter in marriage to Morris. At the same time, he is brutal in his declaration to her that Morris's motives are mercenary.

The doctor has truth on his side — Morris is, of course, an opportunist — but he does not have the humanity to temper that honesty. As Catherine gradually comes to realize, her father's coldness has deep psychological roots, tracing back to the death of her mother. Eventually, they each behave with cruelty; it is Catherine who suffers the most.

Just as Mr. Kiley keeps the doctor from becoming a tyrant, Ms. Atkinson averts self-pity. With a downcast look of discomfort and a severity that goes beyond a feeling of insufficiency, the actress allows no sentimentality to intrude on her portrayal. That fact in itself strengthens the character and it makes her rebellion even more moving. By the end of the play, Catherine is sharpsighted about her predicament and about her need for resilience in self-sacrifice.

Morris is the most problematic of the three characters. In the William Wyler film, Montgomery Clift earned one's sympathy by revealing a boyish insecurity beneath the bravado. In Mr. Gill's more direct portrayal, Morris's motivations seem transparent: there is no question that he has fallen in love with Catherine's potential dowry. Nevertheless, the actor makes Morris seem — in Catherine's eyes — a most attractive and attainable match.

As director, Mr. Frankel has neatly meshed the three pivotal performances while also drawing helpful characterizations from Margaret Hilton as Catherine's aunt, Mrs. Penniman, and from Jeanne Ruskin as Morris's forthright sister. With her fluttering encouragement of the romance, Mrs. Penniman is the closest the play comes to having a comic character, partly because she has more than a touch of cynicism about her niece's prospects.

The Jamesian reserve of the performances is reflected in Loy Arcenas's setting (an elegant version of the Sloper parlor) and Jess Goldstein's costume design, both of which are tastefully in period. With its measured sense of proportion and atmosphere, Mr. Frankel's production is akin to the Merchant-Ivory film adaptations "The Europeans" and "The Bostonians."

While telescoping events, the adapters have made one significant addition — Catherine's artful deception in her final rejection of Morris. That scene gives the work more of a confrontation before the climax, without vitiating the nuances of the novel. In this rewarding revival, "The Heiress" evokes a time of gentility and restraint, when a rigid code of acceptable behavior could stifle self-realization.

1989 Je 16, C3:1

Bicker, Bicker

APOCALYPTIC BUTTERFLIES, by Wendy MacLeod; directed by Marcus Stern; sets by Nephelie Andonyadis; lighting by Scott Zielinski; costumes by Melina Root; sound by John Huntington; production manager, Phineas Perkins; production stage manager, James Mountcastle; music composed by Mr. Stern. Presented by New Arts Theater, Joshua Astrachan, artistic director. At Intar, 420 West 42d Street.

Hank Tater	Greg Germann
Muriel	Colette Kilroy
Francine	Marylouise Burke
Dick	Matthew Lewis
Trudi	Susan Knight

By MEL GUSSOW

Beneath its fanciful title, Wendy MacLeod's "Apocalyptic Butterflies" is earthbound. In this domestic comedy-drama (presented at Intar by the New Arts Theater), Ms. MacLeod is preoccupied with the marital strife of a young couple, cutely named Hank and Muriel Tater, who live in a small Maine town with their as yet unnamed infant daughter. During the brief play, the Taters bicker to such a degree that one may question what brought them together in the first place.

•

Muriel (Colette Kilroy) has become prematurely dowdy and unresponsive to her husband's romantic solicitations. Hank (Greg Germann) is brusquely dismissive of his wife's feelings and his father's gift of a lawn full of totem poles. When it comes to sharing household responsibilities, he is totally inept. He confuses Lysol with Ajax and, to his wife's extreme consternation, puts coffee grounds in the sink. Some of the arguments move the play a step beyond sitcom into the world of television commercials. One keeps waiting for Mr. Clean or Roto Rooter to come to the rescue.

Hank's funk leads him precipitately into an affair, and that liaison momentariy brightens the play as well as the husband's life. As portrayed by Susan Knight, making her New York debut, the character is refreshingly candid in her response. Ending their affair, Hank wonders if

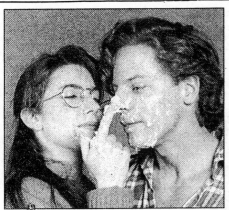

Martha Swope Associates/Rebecca Lesher

Rediscovery
Colette Kilro and Greg Germann are in "Apocalyptic Butterflies," a new comedy by Wendy MacLeod about a couple who find a way to recognize the miraculous in the monotonous.

she would ever have considered marrying him. She answers, "Who wants to marry a guy who cheats on his wife?"

•

If the play had more of this insouciance and less of the husband's bluntness, it might have offered a more reflective picture of a troubled marriage. Through a choice of split-level scenic design, the director Marcus Stern has unmoored the play from strict naturalism. Mr. Germann awkwardly climbs down from one setting to another, from what appears to be a trailer home in the sky to the Taters's chaotic kitchen. With the exception of Ms. Knight and Marylouise Burke (as Hank's indulgent mother), the actors lack a certain lightness, with Mr. Germann stressing his character's surliness.

"Apocalyptic Butterflies" arrives in New York after productions in the Yale Repertory Theater Winterfest and at the Greenwich Theater in London. Despite its credentials, the play deals, in mundane fashion, with what is referred to as the "ebb and flow" of the Tater marriage. There is too much ebb and not enough flow.

1989 Je 17, 12:3

Romance, Romance

THE PASSION OF NARCISSE MONDOUX, by Gratien Gélinas; English version by Linda Garboriau and Mr. Gélinas; directed by Peter Moss; sets by Michael Egan; costumes by François Barbeau; lighting by Susan Chute; sound design, Wayne Tepley; technical director, Andy Calamates; stage manager, Brian A. Kaufman. Presented by Samuel Gesser. At the Apple Corps Theater, 336 West 20th Street.

Laurentienne Robichaud .... Huguette Oligny
Narcisse Mondoux .... Gratien Gélinas

By D. J. R. BRUCKNER

As long as there is life, there is romance, as all the French know, and one point Gratien Gélinas seems to be making in "The Passion of Narcisse Mondoux" is that as masters of the rituals of the great Gallic religion of romance, the Québécois surpass everyone.

Mr. Gélinas, a Quebec playwright who has been a Canadian institution as a popular broadcast and stage entertainer in both French and English for 50 years, tells his story with a good deal of humor — and personal passion. Indeed, he says he wrote the comedy for his wife, the actress Huguette Oligny, and the two of them make up the entire cast of the production at the Apple Corps Theater (performed in French on Tuesdays and in English Wednesdays through Sundays).

•

The play tells an old story, often in familiar words. In a Quebec village, Mondoux, a retired master plumber, comes to "the chic Belhumeur Funeral Home" to pay his respects to the town's mayor, and immediately begins a campaign to win the mayor's widow, Laurentienne. Whether he succeeds hardly matters; both people are old enough and, in their very different ways, wise enough to know that the pursuit is more important than the capture.

Eventually, of course, the hunter and his quarry change places and the game becomes more complicated than either suspected it would be. But along the way, both rediscover their own lives and histories and confess things to each other that they had hardly admitted to themselves. This is all good old-fashioned fun.

There are times in the English version when you would like to know the lines in French, as when Mondoux says, "I could listen to the voice of my conscience, but it always agrees with me" or when Laurentienne says that "if women were only interested in important men there wouldn't be many men women would be interested in." The irony, sentiment and humor come over all right in English, but the tone is foreign.

•

At 79 years old, Mr. Gélinas is wiry and agile, with a voice that could fill a theater much larger than the Apple Corps. He creates a very odd and delightful character who talks with his hands as much as with his mouth — the hands tellingly contradicting what the mouth says half the time.

Mondoux will talk, so much so that at first it seems doubtful that the play can really be the vehicle for Miss Oligny it is supposed to be. But after a while, her silences and hesitations, her glances and smiles become voices beyond speech that reveal Laurentienne's character more than anything spoken does. Miss Oligny is a beautiful and powerful presence; the tribute, even the adulation, the playwright and his Mondoux give her seem quite right.

1989 Je 18, 50:1

The James Brothers, Henry and Jesse

PLAYS IN THE PARK, sets, props and sound designed by Kyle Chepulis; site coordinator, William H. Lang. Presented by En Garde Arts; produced by Anne Hamburger. Three plays performed at Belvedere Castle, midpark at 79th Street; Bow Bridge, and the Dairy, midpark at 64th Street.

BABEL ON BABYLON, written and directed by Matthew Maguire; stage manager, Jennifer McDowall. Creation Company.

Jacob .... Kevin Davis
Ruth .... Tessie Hogan

BAD PENNY, written by Mac Wellman; directed by Jim Simpson; composer, Michael Roth; assistant director, Jeff Sichel; stage manager, Dan M. Weir.
WITH: Reg E. Cathey, Zivia Flomenhaft, Jan Leslie Harding, Jeffrey M. Jones, Mitch Markowitz and Stephen Mellor.

MINNY AND THE JAMES BOYS, written by Anna Theresa Cascio; directed by Kevin Kelley; stage manager, Eddie Phillips.

Minny .... Augusta Allen-Jones
Jesse James .... Thomas Gibson
Henry James .... Bill Kux

By MEL GUSSOW

Moving environmentally through the streets and buildings of Manhattan, En Garde Arts is an invigorating urban presence. With its current "Plays in the Park" trilogy, Anne Hamburger's nomadic troupe takes a venturesome stride forward. Mac Wellman's "Bad Penny," the centerpiece of the company's current experiment in site-specific theater, encapsulates the lunacy of Central Park and the city that surrounds it.

"Bad Penny" is a sharply satiric comedy as well as an on-location performance event, a play that earns its setting on and around Bow Bridge on the Lake. Sitting on a lakeside rock, two strangers (Jan Leslie Harding and Stephen Mellor) have a conversation that reveals their obsessive personalities. Ms. Harding is playing an

Strange things happen on and around the Lake.

outer-borough New Yorker with an ardent belief in the power of myth, while Mr. Mellor, as a visitor from Big Ugly, Mont., is a "freelance memory fabulist." He has been trudging through the park with a flat tire, heading west to find someone to fix it. As the audience eavesdrops on the dialogue, strange things happen.

In the middle of the Lake, a man sits on a tiny island and shouts rude remarks through a megaphone. A woman on Bow Bridge adds her own vocal challenge and, across the water, Reg E. Cathey, who may be a homeless person, orates in company with a 12-member chorus carrying umbrellas. In oblique fashion, the conversation accrues a stereophonic richness.

Ms. Harding warns Mr. Mellor about the "hideous Boatman of Bow Bridge." But in true New York spirit, he remains complacent, even as the masked Boatman appears, rowing a boat that is shrouded as if it had just come from a five-alarm pyre. The Boatman could be Charon himself crossing our local Styx. Mr. Mellor calmly disregards his danger as he is beckoned to the play's diabolical conclusion.

As ingeniously directed by Jim Simpson, "Bad Penny" is nurtured by its outdoor landscape, but it is good enough that it could also be staged indoors (if a theater could float the Boatman across a stage). Alternatively, the play could be portaged from park to pool.

•

The opening play on the En Garde triple bill, Matthew Maguire's "Babel on Babylon," a modernized retelling

Tom Brazil

Stephen Mellor, left, Mitch Markowitz, center, and Jan Leslie Harding in Central Park in a scene from "Bad Penny," a segment of the En Garde Arts "Plays in the Park" trilogy.

of the Tower of Babel story, is verbose to the point of rant. But it is elevated by two factors — the evident sincerity of the acting by Kevin Davis and Tessie Hogan and the location of the drama. Standing in for Babel is the tower of Belvedere Castle on a promontory overlooking the Delacorte Theater.

The third play, staged by Kevin Kelley on the lawn adjoining the Dairy, is an entirely different dramatic matter. Anna Theresa Cascio's play is entitled "Minny and the James Boys," the James Boys referring to Henry and Jesse. Ms. Cascio has imagined an afterlife rivalry between the two over Minny Temple, Henry's adored cousin and tragic muse (the model for Isabel Archer and Milly Theale, among other James heroines).

As Jesse and Henry vie for Minny, each of the three reveals endemic traits — Jesse's volatility, Henry's febrility and Minny's fervor. The author and her actors (Thomas Gibson, Bill Kux and Augusta Allen-Jones) share a theatrical flair and an enthu-

siasm for the characters. The play raises interesting questions about varieties of passion. It might be developed into a longer play, dealing even more perceptively with the odd triangle — and with Minny in particular.

•

Weather permitting, the plays are performed individually at 7 P.M. on Wednesday, Thursday and Friday evenings. On weekends they are staged consecutively at 3 and 6 P.M. Each lasts about 30 minutes, with added time to walk from one site to another.

As the unabashed actors went through their public, highly emotive artistic endeavors at a twilight performance on Saturday, a few passersby (on foot and in boats) stared. But most seemed oblivious or at least unmindful of the theater happening around them, as if this were just another average evening in Central Park. This is, of course, one of the salient points of En Garde Arts, and, in particular, of "Bad Penny."

1989 Je 20, C15:4

Alastair Muir

Daniel Day-Lewis as Hamlet in Richard Eyre's production for the National Theater.

Alastair Muir

John Wood, left, in "The Tempest" and Dustin Hoffman as Shylock in "The Merchant of Venice."

Fourfold View of London's Shakespeare

By FRANK RICH

Special to The New York Times

LONDON, June 18 — The rage for Shakespeare among Hollywood movie stars is now a trans-Atlantic affair. Dustin Hoffman, a career-long stage actor but never before a Shakespearean, is dominating London theater-lobby chat, if not exactly London theater, with his Shylock in Peter Hall's staging of "The Merchant of Venice" at the Phoenix Theater in the West End. After "Rain Man," the production has predictably sold out its three-month run, and, at the performance I attended, flash cameras augmented the lighting design. This prompted an usher to run down the aisle at the final curtain demanding one poor theatergoer's film and shrieking "Ignorant people!" at the fans who violated decorum.

When theatrical events spark this much hysteria, tradition demands that they be classified as either triumphs or disasters. Mr. Hoffman's Shylock refuses to conform. A quick study as always, the actor has mastered the verse, which he projects comfortably in a nasal bray of indeterminate accent. But who is his Shylock? As if to sidestep the troubling dilemma of the role — is he a victim or an embodiment of anti-Semitism? — Mr. Hoffman provides a neutral characterization that arouses no strong feelings, whether of compassion or pity or anger.

•

Too fond of wagging his fingers when engaged in self-debate, the actor sometimes seems as genially Talmudic as Tevye — an impression abetted by his silver-streaked beard and yarmulke. He greets the gobs of contemptuous spit from Venetian Christians with sardonic grins rather than outrage. His distress over his daughter's departure arouses the hyperventilation but not the deep sor-

row of the similarly afflicted father in "Kramer vs. Kramer." And when this Shylock takes his humiliated leave in the trial scene, leather suitcase and hat in hand, we find in Mr. Hoffman's stooped shoulders and shambling walk a pale ghost of Willy Loman.

Dustin Hoffman's Shylock dominates theater talk.

While this isn't the blandest Shylock of recent English seasons (that was Alec Guinness's at Chichester), it is overshadowed for many audiences by Antony Sher's highly impassioned interpretation for the Royal Shakespeare Company. The effect of Mr. Hoffman's mild Shylock is to shift the play's emphasis from the dark doings in Venice to the romantic couplings of Belmont. Mr. Hall directs accordingly, taking fond care of the ring machinations of the fifth act and fielding an exceptionally fervent supporting cast, from Portia (Geraldine James) to Gratiano (Michael Siberry, who played the title role in the second New York visit of "Nicholas Nickleby"). Though Mr. Hoffman presents himself as a company member — he receives no billing and joins in a mass curtain call — his remoteness from his fellow actors in performance seems larger than that warranted by Shylock's social status as a despised outsider.

'Hamlet' at the National

After the revival of Tennessee Williams's "Orpheus Descending," Mr. Hall's "Merchant" is the second offering of his new British-American venture in the commercial theater. At the director's former domain, the Na-

tional Theater, his successor, Richard Eyre, has now presented his first major Shakespeare production: "Hamlet," with Daniel Day-Lewis, an actor whose previous National appearance under Mr. Eyre's guidance, in Dusty Hughes's "Futurists," anticipated his movie stardom in "My Beautiful Laundrette" and "The Unbearable Lightness of Being."

Mr. Eyre, who staged a celebrated "Hamlet" with Jonathan Pryce at the Royal Court in 1980, has this time brought forth the most unfashionable production imaginable. Romantic and straightforward in what one imagines to have been the John Barrymore manner, it is the antithesis of the previous "Hamlet" I encountered at the National, Ingmar Bergman's. The prince's only real neurosis is his Oedipal fixation on Gertrude (Judi Dench), as expressed in a torrid closet scene; he grows in heroic stature instead of disintegrating into madness as the nearly uncut text unfolds.

•

Such an unexceptional interpretation would be impossible to support without the right Hamlet, but in Mr. Day-Lewis, Mr. Eyre has his man. With his Byronic profile and mistiness, the actor is sexy, emotionally high strung and intellectually cocksure in the athletic style of an American star like Kevin Kline. This may explain in part why Mr. Day-Lewis received mixed reviews from English critics, a few of whom measured him unfavorably against Roger Rees's drier, more cerebral Hamlet of a few seasons back. It's also possible that

his performance has grown, since he now savors the soliloquies instead of rattling through them as he reportedly did at the March opening.

On its own terms, Mr. Eyre's wintry staging, with its shadowy corridors of court intrigue, is impeccable. His crucial collaborators include the designer John Gunter, who was also the director's partner on the company's legendary "Guys and Dolls," and such supporting players as Miss Dench and David Bamber (whose sensitive Horatio is a far cry from the hilarious Tory twit-next-door he plays in Mike Leigh's film "High Hopes"). Michael Bryant's Polonius, a Deng-like politician by turns steely and doddering, sets a new standard for the part. His callous treatment of his daughter adds to the horror of her eventual destruction, even if Stella Gonet's Ophelia isn't up to the challenge.

'John' and 'Tempest'

At the Royal Shakespeare Company, where Terry Hands is approaching the end of his tenure as artistic director on a high note, young directors rather than actors are often the stars. Deborah Warner has followed her acclaimed "Titus Andronicus" and "Electra" with a lucid "King John" that emulates Peter Brook in its intimacy (at the company's smaller London space, the Pit) and in its stripping away of any theatrical paraphernalia that might distract from the text or the actors. The costumes belong to no period; the settings are primarily conveyed by arrangements of ladders and chairs.

The most discussed director of the moment at the Royal Shakespeare's main house at the Barbican Center is Nicholas Hytner, whose staging of Shakespeare's valedictory work, "The Tempest," runs simultaneously with his National Theater production of "Ghetto." In the fall, he will follow Mr. Hands and Trevor Nunn into the commercial musical theater by directing "Miss Saigon," the new epic by the authors of "Les Misérables," for the producer Cameron Mackintosh at the Drury Lane.

Mr. Hytner's "Tempest" unfolds on a large tilted oval disc. Like Miss Warner's "King John," its supporting cast boasts too many indistinguishable English actors declaiming with their throats, and one is surprised by how little is made of both Caliban and the second-half spectacles. But John Wood, returning to the English stage after a decade often spent in New York, is a compelling Prospero, ruling the enchanted isle of his exile by conscience and imagination rather than by brute histrionic force.

Simply dressed in tweedy slacks and an open-necked white shirt, Mr. Wood cracks his large staff over his knee when he relinquishes his magic in the final scene. As he stands alone with his fractured stick on the huge darkening disc, we're left not with the outsize image of an egotistical star turn but with the diminutive figure of a modest mortal, a human compass taking Shakespeare's final measure of the world.

1989 Je 21, C15:3

Ayckbourn's England And Its Dark Laughter

By FRANK RICH

Special to The New York Times

SCARBOROUGH, England, June 15 — In this Yorkshire seaside resort, where pensioners practice ballroom dancing at the Victorian Grand Hotel while teen-agers hang out at a shiny Pizza Hut, one can see the contradictions of England today. Pressing hard on the cozy English landscape that Americans still romanticize is the hard-edged environment of economic expansion, the Thatcher England of progress or soullessness, depending on one's point of view. There is nothing unique about Scarborough, and that's why it is a fitting home for Alan Ayckbourn. The most extraordinary career in contemporary English playwriting is built entirely of the stuff of ordinary lives.

At a time when England boasts

'The Revengers' Comedies': part mirth, part chill.

very few dramatists as vital as the dominant American playwrights of this decade, Mr. Ayckbourn is a one-man renaissance. As the artistic director of the 300-seat Stephen Joseph Theater in the Round in Scarborough, he spends most of each year directing other writers' scripts, then directs a new play of his own. This summer's production, "The Revengers' Comedies," an epic achievement that opened here this week and runs until Sept. 23, coincides with his 50th birthday and his 30th year in Scarborough. It is, incredibly, his 37th play — an output, English commentators fondly point out, that equals Shakespeare's.

Mr. Ayckbourn's plays eventually make their way south to London, whether to the West End or the National Theater, sometimes recast with stars, again under the author's direction. "Henceforward ...," seen in Scarborough in 1987, is now in its second West End cast, and "Man of the Moment," last year's Scarborough premiere, is scheduled for London production next winter, with Michael Gambon in the lead. Mr. Gambon, the brilliant actor known primarily to American audiences for "The Singing Detective," has appeared in two Ayckbourn triumphs in London in recent seasons, "A Chorus of Disapproval" and "A Small Family Business," as well as in Mr. Ayckbourn's stunning revival of Arthur Miller's "View From the Bridge." Yet the Ayckbourn-Gambon collaboration has yet to be seen in the United States.

Were it not for the fine Manhattan Theater Club production of "Woman in Mind," a relatively minor work of 1985, New York audiences would have no idea of this writer's remarkable growth through the 1980's. Mr. Ayckbourn's American reputation largely rests instead on the Broadway productions of "Absurd Person Singular," "The Norman Conquests" and "Bedroom Farce" — none written later than 1976, all but the last erratically performed in New York and all still showing the author's boulevard-comedy roots. Mr. Ayckbourn's later, most ambitious writing scares away many American commercial producers and resident theaters with rare exceptions like the Alley Theater in Houston, Arena Stage in Washington and A Contemporary Theater in Seattle. These plays demand large, versatile casts — John Gay's "Beggar's Opera" is folded within "A Chorus of Disapproval" — and also audiences who can stomach middle-class characters miserably lonely in marriage and consumed by greed.

•

For his 50th-birthday play, Mr. Ayckbourn decreed by press release that "something rather ambitious was in order." But what could he do to top his previous experiments in theatrical form and character? Mr. Ayckbourn's earlier works include a 2-actor play cycle whose 16 variants require 8 different scripts ("Intimate Exchanges"), a trilogy about the same people in different locations of the same house over a single weekend ("The Norman Conquests"), a comedy in which two couples occupy different settings but the same stage space ("How the Other Half Loves"), and a play occurring in one of four different versions as determined at each performance by a coin toss ("Sisterly Feelings").

Now Mr. Ayckbourn has outdone himself, making "The Revengers' Comedies" a work in two parts — one riotously funny, one chilling — that can be seen, "Nicholas Nickleby" style, in either two nights or in a six-hour marathon with a dinner break. At the marathon performance I attended, the playwright never lost the rapt attention of an audience widely heterogeneous in age and class. "The Revengers' Comedies" begins at a heavily plotted, hugely entertaining pitch that recalls the old movies to which it frequently pays homage — "Strangers on a Train," "Rebecca," "Kind Hearts and Coronets" — then expands after intermission to reveal an immensely disturbing vision of contemporary middle-class England poisoned by the rise of economic ruthlessness and the collapse of ethics.

•

Though there are two dozen characters, all indelibly portrayed by the Scarborough cast, "The Revengers' Comedies" is primarily about two strangers who meet by chance on a fog-bound London bridge late one night while each attempts suicide. Karen Knightly (Christine Kavanagh) is a young, attractive, rapacious heiress who has been jilted by her lover. Henry Bell (Jon Strickland) is her social opposite: a "piddling" 42-year-old clerk who has lost his job in a multi-national corporation by refusing to play office politics. Abandoning suicide, Karen and Henry make a pact to get revenge on each other's nemeses. Karen, impersonating a temporary secretary, goes to work for Henry's former employer while Henry goes undercover among Karen's horsey set in Dorset.

As these two characters burrow into their hilarious Machiavellian schemes, Mr. Ayckbourn's portrait of urban and rural England grows darker. The multi-national corporation in London is a nightmare out of Caryl Churchill's "Top Girls" — a cesspool of sexism and careerism, epitomized by a boorish, burping and leering executive with the memorable name of Bruce Tick (Jeff Shankley). In the country, where the landed gentry have names like Imogen Staxton-Billing (Elizabeth Bell), we meet the spookily daft Knightly servants and hear about a "mysterious accident," perhaps pyromaniacal, of long ago. Poor, nebbishy Henry finds himself dragged into a shotgun duel tacitly sanctioned by the local police. "This is the 20th century, not the Dark Ages!" he cries.

•

Or is it? By the end of Part 1, in which Bruce Tick is driven to a heart attack in a London wine bar, the fun of justifiable revenge has been replaced by the excruciating spectacle of watching lives, some of them innocent, being cruelly destroyed. One begins to feel compassion even for the loathsome Tick. Yet Karen cannot let go of the game and, in Part 2 of "The Revengers' Comedies," the game has become synonymous with the national sport of hostile corporate takeovers, wholesale job "redundancies" and industrial destruction of the countryside. "Being good is never enough in itself," says Karen by way of rationalization for her expedient behavior. With a subtlety beyond the reach of many polemical English playwrights, Mr. Ayckbourn does not shy away from presenting the alternative to good as pure evil.

While "The Revengers' Comedies" has a few false endings before arriving at its devastating, though not hopeless, conclusion, it is hard to speak highly enough of a work whose elegant writing and staging is accompanied by an utter lack of pretension. Mr. Ayckbourn would as soon make reference to the Everly Brothers' song "Cathy's Clown" as to Cyril Tourneur's Jacobean "Revenger's Tragedy." That's in keeping with a writer who chooses to work on a small stage in a small town but whose talent and theatrical ambitions increasingly seem without limit.

1989 Je 22, C17:1

The Girls He Left Behind

ARRIVEDERCI PAPA, by Richard Iorio, Tony Bondi and Sal Piro; directed by Mr. Piro; scenic design by Peter Hruska; lighting by Amy A. C. Coombs; costumes by Chickie Pinto; general manager, John Glines; stage manager, Philip Goldstein; assistant director, Charlie Catanese. Presented by Arrivederci Papa Company. At the Actors' Playhouse, 100 Seventh Avenue South, between Grove and Bleecker Streets.

Giuseppe LaMorte .... Michael H. Pritchard
Bella Mattarazza .... Richard (Bella) Iorio
Gemma Mattarazza .... Tony Bondi
Philomena Mattarazza .... Phillip McDowell
Tootsie Mattarazza .... Razor Sharp
Anthony Mattarazza .... Anthony Linzalone
Serafina Mattarazza .... Tommy Phillips
Katie O'Malley Mattarazza ...... Thom Hansen
Father Morosa .... Vincent Bandille
Nicolina Mauda .... Lou Valentino

By STEPHEN HOLDEN

Gemma, Philomena and Tootsie Mattarazza, who gather at the Casa de la Morte funeral parlor with their obese mother, Bella, may be the noisiest three sisters ever to have shouted across a New York stage. Convened for the funeral of their father, whose body lies in an open coffin, they preen and bicker and dish the dirt in a style that might best be described as camp fortissimo.

The oldest daughter, Gemma (Tony Bondi), we learn, has dreamed of stardom ever since finishing as runner-up in a Miss Ronzoni contest. Philomena (Phillip McDowell) aspires to be a gypsy fortune teller. Their pregnant younger sister, Tootsie (Razor Sharp), was recently thrown out of Chickie Pinto's School for Wayward Girls.

•

Also on hand are their gay brother Anthony (Anthony Linzalone), a beautician who is both the apple of his mother's eye and the object of his grandmother Serafina's desire, and Katie O'Malley Mattarazza (Thom Hansen), a whisky-swilling in-law with a towering beehive hairdo. Katie is alone, her husband having recently changed his identity for the Government's witness protection program. But it is Mama Bella (Richard Iorio) who dominates the gathering with oversized emotional outbursts that match her immense girth.

"Arrivederci Papa" — created by Mr. Iorio, Mr. Bondi, and the director Sal Piro, at the Actors' Playhouse — is the latest example of what is rapidly becoming a full-fledged genre,

Remains

Richard (Bella) Iorio, right, plays a grieving widow whose only son played by Arthur Linzalone, left, has more boyfriends than her three daughters combined in "Arrivederci Papa."

Gerry Goodstein

the anything-for-a-laugh drag farce in which nothing is held sacred, least of all plot and character. The play, which blends the style of Charles Busch's partly transvestite comedies with environmental theater tricks borrowed from "Tony 'n' Tina's Wedding," is diverting in its raucous way but too chaotic really to hold together.

•

In the plot, such as it is, everyone in the party is furtively trying to wrest possession of the key to the dead man's vault. But periodically, the play stops in its tracks for the audience to be handed cards for a game of Fingertip Bingo, or to vote for which

of the sisters should be named Miss Casa de la Morte, or to be regaled with truly tasteless jokes. And when Father Morosa (Vincent Bandille) belatedly arrives, he delivers a eulogy constructed of pop song titles, from "The Way We Were" to "Up, Up and Away."

While the production's overall level of wit is a notch below that of Mr. Busch's plays, the cast's drag caricatures convey an exuberant playfulness. Those who wish not to be accosted by the actors are advised to avoid sitting in the front rows.

1989 Je 22, C15:3

'Death of a Salesman' As an Upbeat Musical

THE LOMAN FAMILY PICNIC, by Donald Margulies; directed by Barnet Kellman; scenery by G. W. Mercier; costumes by Jess Goldstein; lighting by Debra J. Kletter; music by David Shire; musical director, Mark Goodman; sound by Aural Fixation; choreography by Mary Jane Houdina; production stage manager, Renée Lutz. Presented by Manhattan Theater Club, Stage II, Lynne Meadow, artistic director, Barry Grove, managing director. At City Center, 131 West 55th Street.

Doris .... Marcia Jean Kurtz
Mitchell .... Michael Miceli
Stewie .... Judd Trichter
Herbie .... Larry Block
Marsha .... Wendy Makkena

By MEL GUSSOW

Donald Margulies's new play, "The Loman Family Picnic" at Manhattan Theater Club's Stage II, is a catalogue of clichés about middle-class Jewish family life. In it, the playwright is practicing on ground already well tilled by Woody Allen and Philip Roth, among many others. In that talented company, "The Loman Family Picnic" is an interloper.

The mother (Marcia Jean Kurtz) could be Mr. Allen's airborne mother in "New York Stories" — but with less humor as she rambles on in anticipation of her older son's bar mitzvah. She is, she tells us, a very happy person; actually she is miserable. When we meet her in the mid-1960's she is ripping up her wedding gown to turn it into a Halloween costume of the Bride of Frankenstein.

The father (Larry Block) is a drone who sells lighting fixtures and has nothing whatever to say to his wife or their two sons. The sons are also hackneyed characters — the bar mitzvah boy is a self-centered opportunist while the 11-year-old is a prospective playwright and misunderstood genius. They all live in "a high-

rise ghetto" near Coney Island and strive to keep up with their equally acquisitive neighbors.

The plot turns around the bar mitzvah, a gross affair that brings more than $2,700 in cash and bonds to the celebrant, who is immediately confronted by his greedy father. In an especially distasteful scene, the father grabs the money as if it were his share of the box-office receipts and then gets into a wrestling match with his sons. To diversify the storytelling, the playwright conjures the ghost of a favorite aunt. In a final attempt at a twist, he stages four variations on a showdown between husband and wife, each one less rewarding than the one before.

Ms. Kurtz and Mr. Block are accomplished comic actors who have done far more interesting work in related roles in other plays (Ms. Kurtz in Israel Horovitz's "Today I Am a Fountain Pen"). Sporadically the playwright offers an amusing line. But more often the characters banter banalities while the play aspires to black comedy.

The younger son has been writing an upbeat musical version of "Death of a Salesman" called "Willy!," and eventually the family sings a chorus of the intended show stopper, "What a Perfect Day for a Picnic." Unfortunately, this proves to be a mediocre song (even if it were written by an 11-year-old), and it is sung by actors who are decidedly unmusical. Although the play is ably staged by Barnet Kellman, it works neither as parody nor as social commentary. Despite its title, it has little to do with the Arthur Miller play.

Mr. Margulies's attitude toward his characters (except the 11-year-old) is mean-spirited and unforgiving. Art can elevate characters above caricatures, but in the case of "The Loman Family Picnic," the aim is lower, and the result is a reinforcement of stereotypes.

1989 Je 22, C24:1

Urban Anxiety

WORKING ONE-ACTS '89, scenery and costume design by Anne C. Patterson; production stage manager, Mihaly Kerenyi; lighting design by Spencer Mosse; assistant stage manager, Christine Schanda; sound design supervisor, Mark Bennett. Presented by the Working Theater, Bill Mitchelson, artistic director; Laurie Grossman, general manager. At the Henry Street Settlement, 466 Grand Street.

THE CLOSER, by Will Holtzman; directed by R. J. Cutler; sound design by John Gromada.

Howard .... Murry Rubinstein
Al .... Earl Hagan Jr.

FLOOR ABOVE THE ROOF, by Daniel Therriault; directed by John Pynchon Holms; sound design by Tom Gould.

Cantor .... Mark Kenneth Smaltz
Jay .... David Wolos-Fonteno
Swifty .... Richard Fiske
Elroy .... Randy Frazier

FREEZE TAG, by Jackie Reingold; directed by Evan Handler; sound design, Mark Bennett; assistant to the director, Diane Wheeler-Nicholson.

Aldrich .... Lyn Greene
Andrea .... Julie Boyd

SAND MOUNTAIN MATCHMAKING, written and directed by Romulus Linney; sound design, Mark Bennett; assistant to the director, Ellen Melaver.

Rebecca Tull .... Adrienne Thompson
Clink Williams .... Earl Hagan Jr.
Slate Foley .... Paul O'Brien
Radley Nollins .... Robert Arcaro
Little Stiles .... Mary Foskett
Vester Stiles .... John Karol
Sam Bean .... Scott Sowers

By D.J.R. BRUCKNER

Humor is the dominant mood of four plays making up the Working Theater's "Working One-Acts '89" at the Henry Street Settlement Arts for Living Center — even though two of the four take slightly sinister turns. Modern urban anxiety is the theme of three; the fourth, a nice tonic at the end of the program, is about romantic shenanigans in the Cumberland Mountains long ago when life was simpler but by no means more innocent.

In "The Closer" by Will Holtzman, Howard, an aggressive deal maker in the business world, arrives at his new apartment from a trip to find it filled with movers' boxes and a stranger named Al.

Al is no everyday intruder but "the neighbor from here," a man who lived in the apartment at one time and who has wandered back searching for a life and the memory of the wife he lost. Suddenly he becomes a menace to Howard's life and to his very identity. In the end Mr. Holtzman gives his tale a melodramatic twist that deflates its tension, but Murray Rubenstein and Earl Hagan Jr., under R. J. Cutler's direction, create two compelling characters adrift in the city's sea of loneliness.

•

Daniel Therriault's "Floor Above the Roof" brings together four laborers in a Manhattan warehouse. The playwright touches some sensitive issues: black-white antagonism, ethnic strife, resentment of immigrants — too many, perhaps. But his real interest is in how men deal with their hunger for women, a hunger that drives all four of his characters, from a drunken Lothario who has been tossed out by his lover to an elevator operator who loves all women and regrets only that there is not time to make love to them all. Randy Frazier as the elevator man and David Wolos-Fonteno as a Jamaican immigrant give moving and eloquent performances, directed by John Pynchon Holms.

Lyn Greene as Aldrich, an East Village newspaper vendor, and Julie Boyd as Andrea, her old schoolmate turned yuppie, make Jackie Reingold's "Freeze Tag," directed by Evan Handler, the most gripping play of the quartet. The two women have not seen each other in years, but as part of a mail-order course in how to be a private detective, Aldrich investigates Andrea and, as she sells her a newspaper, demonstrates that Andrea does not know everything, or even much, about her own life. The revelations rise from the amusing to the hilarious until the newspaper vendor admits there are things in her own life she does not understand or even recognize, and suddenly one sees the entire story in a darker, disturbing light.

•

Finally, Romulus Linney as director shapes seven well-matched actors into an ensemble that fairly dances its way through his "Sand Mountain Matchmaking," a wicked little comedy about love among simple country folk that is told like a subversive morality tale. Compared with the other three plays, this one is all surface, but what a bright surface it is — a mirror that reveals both the base reality underlying the noblest intentions and the common humanity that makes us at least tolerable to one another.

1989 Je 25, 45:4

Down the Drain

UBU, by Alfred Jarry; adapted by Larry Sloan and Doug Wright; based on a literal translation by Jacqueline de la Chaume; directed by Mr. Sloan; original score by Greg Cohen; sets by Douglas Stein; costumes by Susan Hilferty; lights by Stephen Strawbridge; sound by Bill Dreisbach; musical director/orchestrator, Mr. Cohen; production manager, Jeff Hamlin; production stage manager, Matthew T. Mundinger; stage manager, Sarah Manley; movement director, Tim Carryer. Presented by Lincoln Center Theater, Gregory Mosher, director; Bernard Gersten, executive producer. At the Mitzi E. Newhouse, Lincoln Center.

Père Ubu .... Oliver Platt
Mère Ubu .... Jodie Markell
Captain Bordure .... Olek Krupa
Pile .... Ramiro Carrillo
Cotice .... Trip Hamilton
King Venceslas, Stanislas Leczinski and General Lasky .... Bill Alton
Queen Rosamund .... Kristine Nielsen
Bougrelas .... Barnabas Miller
Boleslas, Michel Federovitch and a Russian Soldier ..... K. Todd Freeman
Ladislas, the Czar and a Bear . Ralph Marrero
Ubu's Conscience .... Christopher Durang
The Imagemaker and the Younger Peasant .... Patrick Garner
The Nobles and Nicola Rensky ...... Tom Aulino

By MEL GUSSOW

When it was first presented in Paris more than 100 years ago, Alfred Jarry's "Ubu" was a scandal, offending the public (and critics) with its savagery and its Rabelaisian language. The riotous opening night reception was indicative of the effectiveness of Jarry's assault. The play was a frontal attack on the audience's complacency as well as a prophetic statement about man's potential for bestiality.

Even in controversy "Ubu" has always had its ardent defenders, including poets, playwrights and actors like Sacha Guitry, who ranked it "first among excessive caricatures." Eventually the play became a cornerstone of the avant-garde, influencing Cubism and Dadaism as well as absurdist theater.

•

Over the years "Ubu" has been more studied and talked about than performed — for reasons that are readily apparent in the new Lincoln Center Theater production. As adapted by Larry Sloan and Doug Wright, and as directed by Mr. Sloan, the play opened last night at the Mitzi E. Newhouse Theater. In this version, Jarry's mock "Macbeth" seems almost relentlessly unfunny. Seeing the play for the first time, a theatergoer may wonder if it is producible.

It can, of course, be staged, but it has to be done with the comic zeal and imagination that Peter Brook brought to it in his 1980 production. In that knockabout interpretation "Ubu" became a clown show, thumbing its nose at convention and never forgetting that the objective was derisive laughter. The Brook version was performed (at La Mama) in a fractured collage of French and English, a fact that in itself gave Jarry's earthiness a lunatic variety.

•

In direct contrast, Mr. Sloan's version is simply blunt, reminding us that, in its earliest form, "Ubu" was actually a youthful prank, written when Jarry was 15 years old. Without directorial flair — in terms of setting, costumes, performance and pacing — the production itself seems like a schoolboy scrawl.

The minimalist setting (by Douglas Stein) is the equivalent of a large locker room shower. There is a gurgling drain in the center of the room, used as an all-purpose receptacle. Other props like Jarry's disembraining machine are wheeled on and off stage without adding the necessary macabre humor.

Prodded by his ambitious wife, Ubu murders the King of Poland and usurps his crown. Soon he is slaughtering friends as well as enemies, crippling himself politically with every cruel act. Because he is a comic figure, he is as inept as he is corrupt, but in the current version he lacks a leavening sense of self-ridicule.

Several of the actors, notably Oliver Platt in the title role, have appeared to comic advantage in other

Oliver Platt in the title role of Alfred Jarry's "Ubu," at the Mitzi E. Newhouse Theater.

plays. Padded into pear shape, Mr. Platt looks like Ubu, but, under Mr. Sloan's direction, he seems to work very hard to very little effect. The rampage itself becomes repetitious. The supporting players are either broad (Jodie Markell as Ubu's wife), bland or, in several cases, barely intelligible — in this production, that is not necessarily a drawback.

•

The adapters have made alterations in the text, which now runs a brief (but not brisk) 80 minutes. They have invented a character called Ubu's Conscience, partly by borrowing lines from other characters. In an intriguing casting note, the role is played by Christopher Durang,

dressed in a skimpy nightshirt and looking as if it were "time to retire."

In character as Ubu's Jiminy Cricket, Mr. Durang has a pleasantly pedantic approach to matters of morality and he provokes a few smiles — greatly needed in the circumstances. The actor-playwright also succeeds in reminding one how hilarious he was as the Infant of Prague in his own comedy, "Laughing Wild."

By being first as well as outrageous, Jarry could claim his place in modern theatrical history. He deserves something other than manhandling.

1989 Je 26, C14:1

Some West End Efforts to Repel The New American Invasion

By FRANK RICH

Special to The New York Times

LONDON — If anyone wonders why the British invasion of Broadway dwindled to a single play last season ("Shirley Valentine"), the answer is to be found here. The most popular drama in the West End is an American import, "M. Butterfly." Visitors to London can also see "Steel Magnolias," "Speed-the-Plow," "Frankie and Johnny in the Clair de Lune," "Brigadoon" "To Kill a Mockingbird," Beth Henley's "Debutante Ball," Steppenwolf's "Grapes of Wrath" and Lincoln Center's "Anything Goes." Just departed are Jackie Mason, "A Walk in the Woods" and "Forbidden Broadway." The Royal Shakespeare Company will soon open a new play by the American writer Richard Nelson and

Vanessa Redgrave and Larry Lamb in "A Madhouse in Goa."

a revival of "The Man Who Came to Dinner" directed by Gene Saks.

This shift in the cultural balance-of-trade reflects reality. English playwriting is somnambulant next to the dynamic American writing of recent seasons. Were it not for the National Theater, serious contemporary plays would be hard to find in London this summer. The National is responsible for Alan Bennett's "Single Spies" (now in the West End), David Hare's "Secret Rapture" (now in its second cast) and David Storey's "March on Russia" — estimable works in which established writers return to past themes with results ranging from the elegantly entertaining (Mr. Bennett) to the combative (Mr. Hare) to the elegiac (Mr. Storey). Startling, though, these plays are not, at least to audiences familiar with the same authors' "The Old Country," "Plenty" and "In Celebration."

'Madhouse' and Others

For the unexpected, audiences might turn to Martin Sherman, the expatriate American author of "Bent." Mr. Sherman's new play at the Apollo Theater is a pair of interconnected one-act comedies titled "A Madhouse in Goa." It has its obvious flaws, but it also has Vanessa Redgrave and guts. The first half, a letter-perfect homage to Tennessee Williams set in Corfu in 1966, is about an encounter between a jabbering Southern widow named Mrs. Honey ("Solitary travelers are the most despised race on earth") and a young American writer awakening to his literary and sexual persuasions. After intermission, the action jumps years, to 1990, and islands, to Santorini, where we meet a dying novelist whose sole best seller turns out to have been the source of Mr. Sherman's first act. Now a Hollywood producer comes calling to adapt the novel yet again — this time into a musical.

However predictable the show-business jokes, Mr. Sherman has pertinent points to make about American writers who are "famous too soon, thrown aside too quickly" and about those who smooth out life into commercial fiction that favors so-called universal truths over unpleasant political imperatives. One only wishes that Mr. Sherman didn't dilute his own message by using his play's apocalyptic denouement as an excuse to wrap himself in every right-minded cause known to the planet. The American director Robert Allan Ackerman is unerringly sensitive to the intellectual playfulness, humor and tenderness that precede the evening's literal and figurative flameout, and he has elicited superb performances in double roles from Rupert Graves, Larry Lamb and the incredible Miss Redgrave, whose mock Williams widow is far removed from her bona-fide Williams heroine of "Orpheus Descending."

•

Elsewhere in the West End, the non-American choices tend to be starry Shakespeare (whether Dustin Hoffman as Shylock or Alan Bates and Felicity Kendal as Benedick and Beatrice) or fluff. Visitors who don't care about impressing friends back home could put together a madcap week of theatergoing that mixes such antiques as "Run for Your Wife," "The Mousetrap," "Blood Brothers" and Tommy Steele's "Singin' in the Rain" with such new contenders for midweek matinee approbation as "The Royal Baccarat Scandal," "Over My Dead Body" (with Donald Sinden), "The Secret of Sherlock

Holmes'' (with Jeremy Brett) and Leslie Bricusse's "Sherlock Holmes — the Musical" (with Ron Moody).

Such enterprises can flourish in a commercial theater where producing costs are still relatively reasonable and showmanship can still prevail. Only in London, perhaps, do producers have the temerity to run advertisements with critics' quotations like "Sizzles with homoeroticism!" (to sell "As You Like It" at the Old Vic) and "The audience laughed so much they nearly did themselves a mischief" ("Over My Dead Body").

'Vortex' and 'Aspects'

Critics were even more enthusiastic about Philip Prowse's revival of "The Vortex," the young Noël Coward's once-notorious breakthrough play of 1926. A moralistic condemnation of a vain mother who takes lovers the same age as her 24-year-old drug-infatuated son, the work is more camp than shocking now. It is performed with appropriately bared fangs by Maria Aitken and Rupert Everett, tall embodiments of debauchery both, in Mr. Prowse's striking, nearly hallucinatory black-and-white Art Deco décor.

May-September romances, spiced with soupçons of lesbianism and "Lolita," are also the preoccupation of the season's Andrew Lloyd Webber musical, "Aspects of Love," an adaptation of David Garnett's 1955 novel in which a tempestuous French actress (Ann Crumb) bounces between a younger roué (Michael Ball) and his much older uncle (Kevin Colson) for 17 years of soap operatics and nearly three hours of stage time. While the show is completely sung, it is not always musical. Then again, pity the poor composer who must confront recitative like "Shall I order an espresso or a capuccino?"

The libretto, which weds the services of Don Black ("Song and Dance") and Charles Hart ("Phantom of the Opera"), puts great store by the mood-setting properties of Champagne. The evening's opening (and, for that matter, perpetual) melody announces the deeper theme: "Love changes everything/hands and faces, earth and sky .../how you live and how you die." For those left unmoved by romantic metamorphoses, there is a gratuitous visit to a Parisian circus headlining a Dolly Parton impersonator and an existential funeral dance in which the director, Trevor Nunn, and choreographer, Gillian Lynne, pay their respects to Harold Prince's "Zorba."

It's hard to imagine that Mr. Prince, who collaborated with Mr. Lloyd Webber on "Evita" and "Phantom," would have made the mistake of undercasting the stars of a show dependent on sexual energy. Though American, Miss Crumb is in the strident mold of such local Lloyd Webber heroines as Elaine Paige, Marti Webb and Sarah Brightman while Mr. Ball is a baby-cheeked juvenile who has what it takes to lead "Singin' in the Rain" should Tommy Steele ever retire. Mr. Colson, who famously took over for Roger Moore in rehearsals, is an able actor whose suave continental charm might be more persuasive to an American viewer if he didn't so uncannily resemble William Kunstler.

•

The real point of the exercise may be to demonstrate that Mr. Lloyd Webber isn't merely a purveyor of conspicuously costly spectacles but can instead write an intimate, Mozart-scaled operetta like Lerner and Loewe's "Gigi" or Stephen Sondheim's "Little Night Music," both of which are specifically evoked. The effort has succeeded with London critics like Michael Coveney of The Financial Times, who found the musical "remarkably daring" and applauded its "great stretches of lyric beauty." Those who find instead that great stretches of "Aspects of Love" amount to a thinking man's cautious "Run for Your Wife" may still enjoy the incessant movements of Maria Bjornson's monochromatic Gallic sets. The early coupling of a train, more passionate than that of its passengers, sizzles with asexual eroticism.

1989 Je 27, C15:4

A Civil War Panorama In 'John Brown's Body'

• By MEL GUSSOW

Special to The New York Times

WILLIAMSTOWN, Mass., June 25 — Stephen Vincent Benét's "John Brown's Body" was written as a story in verse to be read aloud. For that and other reasons, it comes resonantly to life on stage, as is evident in Peter Hunt's current version at the Williamstown Theater Festival. As directed by Mr. Hunt and as performed by a fine three-person cast — Christopher Reeve, Robert Lansing and Laurie Kennedy — the adaptation is an enlightening and deeply felt drama about the Civil War, seen through the prism of the author's comprehensive historical perspective.

Despite "Gone With the Wind," "The Andersonville Trial" and all the other cinematic and dramatic treatments that came after the 1928 work, "John Brown's Body" retains its freshness and its epic sweep. In it, Benét contemplates North and South with a compassionate sense of the losses suffered by both sides as well as the immeasurable gains. As Benét's Robert E. Lee says, with irony intended, "It is well that war should be so terrible; if it were not we might become too fond of it."

With John Brown's raid as catalyst and recurrent motif, the adaptation moves from Bull Run to Gettysburg, from home front to prison camp. Through monologues, dialogues, letters home and lyrical descriptions of countrymen in combat, it captures the anguish as well as the panoply of the war.

•

Following the guidelines established by Charles Laughton in his 1953 Broadway adaptation, Mr. Hunt has his cast formally attired. Behind the actors, a large chorus provides a musical and, occasionally, a spoken background. There is a minimum of added theatricality — a backdrop by Hugh Landwehr that looks like an aerial view of a Civil War battlefield. The adaptation reduces the poem to its essence and, through the performers, achieves a dramatic immediacy. Though it begins ceremonially, "John Brown's Body" is soon in the heat of the conflict.

With Mr. Lansing offering a narrative context, the actors move with agility among the characters, both fictional and historical. Mr. Reeve plays the author's two contrasting fictional heroes — the Northerner, Jack Ellyat, and, shading his voice into a gentle Georgian lilt, Clay Wingate, the Southern patriot who remains equally loyal to his roots. Mr. Reeve brings a great conviction to his roles in this staged dramatization.

Something similar could be said about Mr. Lansing, who stands in for John Brown, Lee and Lincoln, among others, with a modesty that does not

Christopher Reeve in "John Brown's Body," at the Williamstown Theater Festival in Williamstown, Mass.

vitiate the authority of these leaders. In a long interior monologue, his Lincoln is revealed as a down-to-earth man thrust into a position of national morality. Ms. Kennedy plays the women romantically involved with both Ellyat and Wingate, as well as the elderly doyenne of Wingate Hall, who becomes a bitter remnant and conscience of the war itself.

All three actors studiously avoid rhetorical flourishes and anything that might be confused with the stentorian. With apparent effortlessness, they step away from their lecterns to act out scenes. Filtered through the evening are balladlike songs and hymns delivered by the chorus, with Clark Morgan and B. J. Ward (singing a tender lament) as the excellent soloists. In a relatively brief period, we receive a full picture of the turmoil of a cataclysmic event that the author calls "a crack in time itself."

It is left to Mr. Reeve to strike one of the show's most plaintive chords as Jack Ellyat manages, after the war, to track down the woman he loved and was forced to leave. That moment, in common with so much else in the dramatization, is stoical rather than sentimental. Finally, Mr. Lansing offers a moving coda, suggesting tragic emanations that will linger long after the end of the war.

With the death this year of Nikos Psacharopoulos, the founder and for more than three decades the artistic director of the Williamstown Theater Festival, there was some question about the future of this summer playhouse, which is being run this season by Mr. Hunt and Austin Pendleton. "John Brown's Body" begins the company's 35th season on a note of eloquence.

1989 Je 27, C14:5

Faustian Footwear

THE RED SNEAKS, a musical based on the story of "The Red Shoes." Written by Elizabeth Swados; inspired by improvisations with the Company; directed and composed by Ms. Swados; sets and costumes by G. W. Mercier; lighting by M. L. Geiger; choreography by Arthur Fredric and the Company; stage manager, Frank Dalrymple; music performed by Paul O'Keefe and Lewis Robinson. Presented by Theater for a New Audience, Jeffrey Horowitz, artistic and producing director. At the Perry Street Theater, 31 Perry Street.

Shawn	Shawn Benjamin
James	James Sheffield-Dewees
Dedre	Dedre Guevara
Kenny	Kenny Lund
Raquel	Raquel Richard
Valerie	Valerie Evering
Shun	Donald (Shun) Faison
Teresina	Teresina Sullo

By STEPHEN HOLDEN

The most refreshing thing about "The Red Sneaks," Elizabeth Swados's contemporary musical adaptation of "The Red Shoes," is the chance to hear youths rather than adults talk about the nightmarish pressures of urban life.

A loose allegorical montage of monologues, songs and dances, the 70-minute show expands upon a small section of Ms. Swados's "Swing," a music-theater work that opened two years ago at the Brooklyn Academy of Music. The new piece, now at the Perry Street Theater, was developed by Ms. Swados and a multi-ethnic cast of eight young people during a six-week training period of improvisatory and musical exercises.

•

The goal was to explore those themes of the story that had personal relevance to the performers. What they came up with is an exuberant Faustian tale about a welfare-hotel resident named Dedre (Dedre Guevara) who is persuaded by Shawn (Shawn Benjamin), a young Mephistophelean drifter, to accept a pair of glitter-encrusted red sneakers that can grant to their wearer any desire.

The plot, such as it is, spins off from two matching monologues delivered by the predator and his prey. After ticking off a list of recent local news stories involving racism and teen-age violence, Shawn, who is attracted to evil, reflects on how "there's got to be power in giving out fear." Dedre, after describing a wretched home life that has caused her to move 20 times in 3 years, says she wants to be as beautiful and rich as LaToya Jackson and Robin Givens.

Though the exact circumstances of Dedre's fast trip to an early death are not spelled out, the shoes could represent any desperate remedy for teen-age misery, from drugs to casual sex to prostitution. In the show's rough-housing ensemble numbers, the cast, which appears to range in age from 10 to 17, alternates between identifying with Dedre and commenting on her predicament. They perform Ms. Swados's perky bare-bones songs, which run a familiar gamut of styles, from rap to folk-pop, with an unaffected animation.

"The Red Sneakers" has the deliberately sloppy, unfinished feel of a teen-age bull session with music. One has the sense that whatever interesting material the ensemble developed was thrown in, even if it didn't quite fit. That's certainly the case in a darkly humorous monologue, delivered by a towheaded child actor, Kenny Lund. Mordantly assessing his career as a youthful model, he analyzes his occupation in terms of profit venture and boasts that his looks would make him perfect for dealing crack because no one would suspect him.

1989 Je 29, C13:1

Three in One

MARATHON '89, SERIES C, set design, Sharon Sprague; production supervisor, David M. Mead; lighting, Gil Danieli; costumes, David E. Sawaryn; production stage manager, Ken Simmons; sound, Gayle Jeffery. Kate Baggott, producer; Peter Glatzer, associate producer. Presented by the Ensemble Studio Theater, Curt Dempster, artistic director; Peter Shavitz, managing director. At 549 West 52d Street.

OUTSIDE THE RADIO, by Kermit Frazier; directed by Oz Scott; stage manager, Fran Levin.
Wilbur .... Herb Downer
Iris .... Seret Scott
Rachel .... Tamika Tamara-Tucker-Cole
Arlene .... Katherine Leask

BIG FROGS, by David Golden; directed by Matthew Penn; stage manager, Peggy Laurel.
Dennis .... Barry Sherman
Harley .... Thomas Kopache

WATER MUSIC, by Michael Erickson; directed by Beth A. Schachter; stage manager, Tom Roberts.
Luis .... Zach Grenier
Abungi .... Tyrone Wilson
Charles .... James G. Macdonald

By MEL GUSSOW

The three plays in Series C of the Ensemble Studio Theater's Marathon '89 are diffuse, episodic works. Two of them have a degree of promise but would benefit from further development and, in particular, from an avoidance of the pitfall of predictability. Both deal with the potentially explosive rivalry between an older and a younger man.

Michael Erickson's "Water Music" has the guise of a political thriller. A mysterious young man (James G. Macdonald) shows up unannounced at the home of a Portuguese expatriate (Zach Grenier) in the Central African Empire. His host is a shady character with an autocratic attitude toward his servant (Tyrone Wilson).

The end of the play is no surprise, but the relationship between the guest and the host has a certain barely concealed malevolence, enhanced in the performances by Mr. Grenier and Mr. Macdonald. Mr. Grenier has a Peter Lorre-like slyness, as he tries to manipulate his guest to his convenient purposes. As director, Beth A. Schachter has given a semblance of order to the play's clutter.

In David Golden's "Big Frogs," a young college student takes a job in the security office of a large department store. The chief security man (Thomas Kopache) thinly disguises his arrogance as perfectionism. He is an impossibly demanding supervisor and the young man (Barry Sherman)

has a nonchalance that is bound to aggravate their differences. Mr. Kopache shows Mr. Sherman how to catch shoplifters, while offering his cynical motto: "Nobody takes what you don't want to give."

One can spot the twist of the play without the benefit of surveillance — the younger man will of course beat the older man at his own sinister game — but the author undercuts his work by having Mr. Sherman become overly imitative. As directed by Matthew Penn, there is a tautness in the acting — and Mr. Golden's writing has an occasional humor. As intended, the audience feels a justifiable antagonism against the older character, a man who certainly deserves his comeuppance.

Kermit Frazier, the best known of the three playwrights, has written the least interesting play, "Outside the Radio." A black doctor, practicing in a small Northern community, desperately wants to be assimilated. On the other hand, his wife feels adrift and alone, and would like to return to a more ethnically diverse area.

The incredibly pompous doctor (Herb Downer) refers to himself as "a man in my position" and says such ridiculous things as, "Obsessed, she was obsessing with her past." Nevertheless he remains popular with his patients; presumably his diagnoses are more straightforward. His wife (Seret Scott) seems down to earth, but she has her own difficulties, spending her days clipping coupons from magazines and saying that she is "becoming invisible." Though she insists, "I want to be in the world again," she is, in fact, losing her mind.

With overripe dialogue and transparent emotions, the play falls into soap opera. Under Oz Scott's direction, there are helpful performances by Mr. Downer and Ms. Scott and an appealing one by a child actress with the melodic name Tamika Tamara-Tucker-Cole. In all three plays, acting cannot overcome the weaknesses of the writing.

1989 Je 29, C14:5

Three Men And a Bottle

CINZANO, by Lyudmila Petrushevskaya; Theater Chelovek, U.S.S.R., directed by Roman Kozak; artistic director, Lyudmila Roshchkovan; literary manager, Arkadi Tsimbler; set design, Valery Firsov; light design, Viktor Platonov; sound design, Aleksandr Krichevsky; scenery; Vladimir Vozdayev; props, Irina Kozak. Staller Center for the Arts presents the Norstar Bank International Theater Festival. At SUNY, Stony Brook.

Pasha .... Sergei Zemtsov
Kostya .... Igor Zolotovitsky
Valya .... Grigory Manukov

By MEL GUSSOW

Special to The New York Times

STONY BROOK, L.I., June 27 — Theater Chelovek is an Off Broadway-size Moscow theater that specializes in work that is both naturalistic and humanistic (chelovek means man in Russian). The company is currently on its first North American tour, beginning with a production of "Cinzano" at the Norstar Bank International Theater Festival at the State University at Stony Brook.

Although it is novel to see a non-classic Soviet studio theater that emphasizes everyday events, "Cinzano" is not a particularly enlivening play. It is a slice of contemporary life without metaphor or political reverberations. Written by Lyudmila Petrushevskaya, the play compares unfavorably with such bold Soviet efforts by other companies as "Cerceau," seen several seasons ago in London, and "Stars in the Morning Sky," presented last year in the First New York International Festival of the Arts.

In Miss Petrushevskaya's work, three young men meet in an empty Moscow apartment and share a number of bottles of Cinzano while comparing notes on their lives. It is never explained why they drink Cinzano rather than vodka, although one may assume it is an attempt to imitate Western ways. Their problems with wives and parents are, depending on one's point of view, familiar or universal. The conclusion is easily anticipated.

The point of the play is apparently the community of feeling shared by the three men. But the dialogue is rambling and repetitious. Some of this may be a result of the simultaneous English translation, provided through headsets and seemingly not always in synchronization with what is seen on stage.

What gives the play a rationale is the acting. All three — Sergei Zemtsov, Igor Zolotovitsky and Grigory Manukov — have an easy informality that makes it seem as if they are living rather than acting their roles. Together they drink, eat, banter and eventually become morose, as any young men might in similar circumstances.

Each has a clownish instinct, amusing the audience with moments of physical comedy — trying to sit without sliding off a steeply raked modern chair and, most cleverly, flipping over a full glass of Cinzano so quickly that not one drop is spilled. They also reveal a musical penchant, at one point joining in a jam by tapping their feet and every object in sight.

One would like to see the actors in an improvisatory situation. Here they are restricted by the dialogue. As director, Roman Kozak emphasizes the reality of the play, although the setting is perhaps too sparse for this wide stage. At moments, the director reaches for a kind of artiness, posing the actors in brightly lighted doorways, which they fill with clouds of cigarette smoke.

It would be inappropriate to assess the work of Theater Chelovek on the basis of this brief effort. There are other works in the current repertory, including the internationally acclaimed play, "The Emigrants," which would perhaps show the company off to better artistic advantage.

"Cinzano" will be performed at Staller Center for the Arts through Saturday, to be followed next week by Jozef van den Berg of the Netherlands with his play "Waited Long Enough," a response to "Waiting for Godot."

1989 Je 29, C15:1

Love Triumphs, Twice

DOUBLE BLESSING, by Brenda Shoshanna Lukeman; directed by Edward M. Cohen; set design, Ray Recht; costume design, Karen Hummel; lighting design, Dan Kinsley; sound design, Paul Garrity; original music, Marshall Coid; production stage manager, D. C. Rosenberg. Presented by the Jewish Repertory Theater, Ran Avni, artistic director; Mr. Cohen, associate director. At 344 East 14th Street.

Martha Snitofsky .... Rosalind Harris
Chana Snitofsky .... Helen Greenberg
Manny Hagoodnick ...... Victor Raider-Wexler
Morris Blavatsky .... Mark Ethan

By D. J. R. BRUCKNER

True love among the innocent is the theme of Brenda Shoshanna Lukeman's "Double Blessing" at the Jewish Repertory Theater. And even though perfect moral simplicity in ordinary adults becomes utterly preposterous after a while, the actors in this production bring a warmth and

Martha Swope Associates/Carol Rosegg
Rosalind Harris, left, and Helen Greenberg in "Double Blessing."

good humor to their roles that make you want to go on believing in their characters.

In Borough Park in Brooklyn a widow descended from generations of rabbis — whose forbidding portraits glower from every wall of her living room — has called together her family and friends once again to meet a young man who might marry her willful and decidedly secularized daughter. As has happened previously, the expected prey does not show up. But unlike others who have pulled a disappearing act, this young man sends along a friend, a total stranger who climbs in the window while the noisy family is gathering outside the house and promptly falls in love with the daughter.

The widow, whose husband died in a traffic accident on their honeymoon, has been pursued for a decade by an old friend who seizes the opportunity of all this confusion to press his own case. Eventually love triumphs over the widow's religious and social objections to her daughter's new, indeed first, suitor and it even dissolves a lifetime of frosty superiority as she falls into the arms of her own long-suffering admirer.

•

Some situations in this old-fashioned drawing room comedy are quite funny, and Ms. Lukeman gives a couple of characters good lines about such familiar embarrassments as virginity and piety. But the outcome is obvious 10 minutes into the play and the writer simply does not create enough twists and turns in her plot to keep one interested. The second act is especially clumsy as the mother and daughter overcome a lifetime of emotional separation and fear of each other. The play has them practically talking themselves out of their spiritual isolation — a singularly undramatic device.

Lively direction by Edward M. Cohen and inspired casting conceal many of the problems in this play. Rosalind Harris and Helen Greenberg create a mother and daughter who radiate passion but who are more afraid of themselves and of each other than of the menacing world outside Borough Park. Victor Raider-Wexler makes an appealing and comical middle-aged bachelor who would probably be happier if there were no such thing as sex but who submits to its uncomfortable demands to get what he wants: tender, undying love. And Mark Ethan can make one believe there really could be in this age a young man who has talked to God on Brighton Beach and who is utterly stunned by the power of his own feelings for a woman. This cast delivers a group of people who are wonderfully attractive without being glamorous, or mysterious, or even strange.

1989 Jl 2, 38:1

Sidelong Aspersions And Mini-Spoofs

HERD OF BUFFALO, written and directed by Ethyl Eichelberger; costumes by Gerard Little; lighting by Pedro Rosado; technical adviser, Matt Baylor. Presented by Performance Space 122, Mark Russell, executive director; Robin Schatell, managing director. At 150 First Avenue, at Ninth Street.

Doctor	Ethyl Eichelberger
Sidney	Jonathan Baker
Beulah	Helen Shumaker
Prunella/Mr. Hill	Gerard Little
Faelitia	Katy Dierlam
Mystery	Joan Moossy

By MEL GUSSOW

Wearing a white fright wig for his role as a mad doctor, Ethyl Eichelberger looks like the Ghost of Christmas Past. Behind that disguise, he remains a compulsive parodist, accordionist and fire-eater (even on the most humid of summer nights). His new play, "Herd of Buffalo," at Performance Space 122, is a rambling revenger's comedy that defies logic and is at least a half-hour too long to sustain its minimal premise. But in the author-director's signature fashion, it has its amusing interludes.

In his improvisational approach, Mr. Eichelberger seems to direct and to rewrite the play as it moves along. He responds to the audience's reaction and to his own free-flowing thought process. As a result, the show may vary from night to night.

"Herd of Buffalo" deals with a backstage vendetta between the mad doctor and a diva-like performance artist (Katy Dierlam) who he thinks has stolen his rightful role as Solange in "The Maids." With insufficient cause, he plots to blow up his nemesis, a startling thought when one considers Ms. Dierlam's amplitude. In this case, the doctor's assistant (Jonathan Baker) is not kidding when he warns, "It ain't over till the fat lady sings."

Fortunately, the plot digresses, allowing the star and company to offer sidelong aspersions and mini-spoofs of such experimental artists as Mark

Paula Court

Ethyl Eichelberger

Morris and Bill Irwin as well as a passing salute to the Flying Karamazov Brothers, with whom Mr. Eichelberger shared a Lincoln Center stage in "The Comedy of Errors."

As was clear in such previous entertainments as his one-man version of "King Lear" and his send-up of Corneille, Mr. Eichelberger is a closet academician. In the second act he borrows scenes from Thomas Kyd's "Spanish Tragedy" and T. S. Eliot's "Family Reunion." To those unprepared for such intellectual intrusions, he identifies the source in the middle of the performance, adding critical comments. As Helen Shumaker gives her rotelike recitation from Eliot, he says, "I bet she doesn't have the slightest idea what she is talking about." He is equally quick to poke fun at himself and to declare all ulterior motives. When the dialogue momentarily is in Spanish, he explains, "This is a blatant appeal for a grant."

•

His actors are his anxious allies, joining him in exercising the artifice of Eichelberger. This is especially true of Mr. Baker and Gerard Little who doubles in roles as a femme fatale and a stagehand, and, hermaphroditically, brings both characters on stage simultaneously.

Whenever there is a lapse in laughter, the star takes up his accordion or sits at the piano and leads his cast in a jovial, handmade tune, like the finale, "Happy Ending." One wishes that Mr. Eichelberger would take the extra time to refine his work while still communicating that irrepressible feeling of spontaneous combustion.

1989 Jl 6, C18:4

The Cutting Edge

CYRANO DE BERGERAC, by Edmond Rostand; translated by Brian Hooker; directed by Robert Mooney and Timothy W. Oman; produced by Gus Kaikkonen; sets by David P. Gordon; costumes by Martha Hally; music and lyrics by Shoukoufeh-Azari; fight choreographer, Ian Rose; technical director, James E. Fuller Jr.; production stage manager, Matthew G. Marholin. Presented by Riverside Shakespeare Company, Mr. Oman, artistic director. At parks throughout New York City.

Cyrano	Frank Muller
Christian	Robert Sedgwick
Roxane	Susan Pellegrino
De Guiche	Weston Blakesley
Ragueneau	Daniel Timothy Johnson
Le Bret	James Maxson
Lignière	William Michie
Valvert	Jared Hammond
Cuigy	Edward Henzel
D'Artagnan	Christopher Mixon
Duenna/Mother Marguerite	Maggie McClellan

WITH: Gregory Lamont Allen, Russ Cusick, Brian Dykstra, Fred Fahmie, Belynda Hardin, Jane Macfie, Matt McLain, Carine Monthertrand, Herbert Mark Parker, Ian Rose, Melinda Wade, Gregory Linus Weiss and Grover Zucker.

By D. J. R. BRUCKNER

During the final scene of the Riverside Shakespeare Company's production of "Cyrano de Bergerac" in Riverside Park, stars shone through the trees and squadrons of fireflies twinkled in the night. It is the moon dying that Cyrano invokes during the scene, but no matter; the show of tiny lights above and below set the right mood. Presumably, at some point in the company's monthlong tour of Edmond Rostand's play through 16

Marc Bryan-Brown

Frank Muller

parks in all five boroughs of the city, Cyrano's lunar goddess will come out on cue. Not that the moon alone could rescue the awkwardly melodramatic last act, but a little light distraction of any kind helps.

There are a hundred good reasons why "Cyrano" should not succeed as a play, but it almost always does, and this company's presentation of the comic romance about a fearless 17th-century French captain whose pride is almost as big as his huge nose and whose gift of poetry is inexhaustible provides laughter, sentiment and spectacle for a summer's evening.

•

Robert Mooney and Timothy W. Oman, the directors, keep their colorfully costumed cast moving so swiftly and rhythmically through scenes of brawls, assignations, sword fights, battles and love scenes that one thinks immediately of a musical. That is the right approach.

Despite its very large cast — some of the little roles can be great fun — the success of the play depends heavily on a few characters, mostly on Cyrano and the woman he secretly loves, Roxane. The Cyrano role is very taxing. This poet speaks brilliantly for three hours; he can talk weary soldiers out of their hunger, women out of their modesty and opponents out of their wits. There were times when Frank Muller in this production grew hoarse from the effort. But on the whole he created a Cyrano with the right mix of effrontery, vanity, passion and perverse charm.

Susan Pellegrino is a complex and believable Roxane. It is not easy to create a woman who can keep our sympathy even though she prefers a dolt to a genius and needs 15 years to recognize the difference. But Miss Pellegrino gives Roxane enough frivolity to make her ignorance seem natural and enough passion to make her mistakes forgivable.

Weston Blakesley as De Guiche is just the perfectly pompous martinet he ought to be and Daniel Timothy Johnson is merriment personified as Ragueneau the baker; his verse recipe for a cake is a hilarious and memorable moment. One could wish Robert Sedgwick would make the handsome but slow-witted Christian a more powerful presence; after all, Roxane must have seen *something* in him if he could so blind her to Cyrano's superior love for so long.

There are two serious annoyances in this production. The sword fighting is utterly inadequate. When, in a famous scene, Cyrano composes and recites a ballad while finishing off an opponent, the point is that his wit is lethal; he must be a superb swordsman. Here he looked as though he could not put a blade through a paper silhouette. And the directors unfortunately are too faithful to Rostand in the last act. This play is a case in which prudent trimming and changes in the playwright's emphases in the final minutes are necessary. In the first place, a dying man, even one delirious from a skull fracture, cannot leap all over the stage as this Cyrano does. And unless his remarks are given a certain cutting, ironic edge, the hero ends up pitiable, shrunken at the very moment when he should grow into a giant.

1989 Jl 6, C19:1

Oh Well, O Will

TWELFTH NIGHT, by William Shakespeare, directed by Harold Guskin; scenery by John Lee Beatty; costumes by Jeanne Button; lighting by Richard Nelson; music by Peter Golub; production stage manager, James Harker. Presented by New York Shakespeare Festival, Joseph Papp, president. At Delacorte, Central Park, enter at 81st Street and Central Park West or 79th Street and Fifth Avenue.

Feste	Gregory Hines
Orsino	Stephen Collins
Curio	L. Peter Callender
Valentine	Frank Raiter
Viola	Mary Elizabeth Mastrantonio
Sea Captain	Stephen Mendillo
Sir Toby Belch	John Amos

Maria	Charlaine Woodard
Sir Andrew Aguecheek	Fisher Stevens
Olivia	Michelle Pfeiffer
Malvolio	Jeff Goldblum
Antonio	Andre Braugher
Sebastian	Graham Winton
Servant	Mary Mara

Officers

John Hickey, Dan Berkey, Jake Weber
Priest ....James Cahill
Waiter ....Bill Camp
WITH: Gigi Bermingham, David Borror, Lisa Gay Hamilton, Mari Nelson, Patrick Rameau, Rainn Wilson.

By FRANK RICH

Not all movie stars are created equal. Some are born great, some achieve greatness and some have greatness thrust upon them, to para phrase William Shakespeare's "Twelfth Night," the play serving as a Central Park summer camp for some visitors from Hollywood. Some stars, one might add, are not so great at all. But as visitors to the Delacorte Theater can discover, every variety of star, however dim, is welcome in the New York Shakespeare Festival production of a comedy that has rarely lived up so well to its full title, "Twelfth Night, or What You Will."

This is a crazy-quilt evening that tells us more about show business — public relations, career advancement, egomania — than it does about the lovesick passions of Illyria. Given that the personalities involved include Michelle Pfeiffer, Jeff Goldblum and Gregory Hines — not to mention the impresario who recruited them, Joseph Papp — the production is not without interest of an extra-theatrical sort. As a night of Shakespeare, however, this "Twelfth Night" may most please audiences whose expectations have been sunk by exposure to the most star-laden of the previous Shakespeare Marathon productions, "Julius Caesar." The

Michelle Pfeiffer, Jeff Goldblum, Gregory Hines . . .

idylls of July have it by a nose or two over the ides of March.

For that, we can mainly thank Mary Elizabeth Mastrantonio, whose Viola would be a treasure in any "Twelfth Night." Central Park regulars may recall that as Katherine of France she was a dazzling sparring partner for Kevin Kline in the 1984 "Henry V" and that as the conscience-torn Isabella she was the sole life in the "Measure for Measure" of a summer later. As Viola, the shipwrecked young woman driven to disguise her true feelings and gender, Ms. Mastrantonio is given far wider territory and conquers it all.

Equally agile of tongue and limb, the actress-is at home in the verse, heightening its most lyrical passages ("Make me a willow cabin at your gate. . . .") without adding artificial sweetener. In Edwardian cap, jacket, trousers and bow tie as the page Cesario, she conveys boyishness without burying her own sexuality in androgyny; we never doubt how women and men alike might fall for her. And when the time comes for Viola to try to untangle the knot of mistaken identities that place her in the excruciating center of several interlocking, unrequited love affairs, Ms. Mastrantonio turns what might be a moment of whining histrionics into human high

comedy. She tumbles to the ground and madly tries to draw a chart of all the confusions before finally turning her predicament over to a more effective arbiter, Time.

●

While Ms. Mastrantonio does not quite have to perform solo in "Twelfth Night," she receives solid partnering only from Stephen Collins as Orsino, a duke who knows when the time has come to forsake his fatuous mooniness and turn on the charm, and from Graham Winton as her dashing twin brother, Sebastian. In the more important role of Olivia, the countess who pines in vain for the disguised Viola, Ms. Pfeiffer offers an object lesson in how gifted stars with young careers can be misused by those more interested in exploiting their celebrity status than in furthering their artistic development.

Did anyone connected with "Twelfth Night" see Ms. Pfeiffer's delightful Carole Lombard turn in Jonathan Demme's screwball comedy "Married to the Mob"? It's unfortunate that the actress has been asked to make both her stage and Shakespearean comic debut in a role chained to melancholy and mourning. It's also unclear why the director, Harold Guskin, a prominent acting

Martha Swope

Stephen Collins and Mary Elizabeth Mastrantonio in Shakespeare's "Twelfth Night".

coach, failed to come to the rescue of Ms. Pfeiffer's vocal delivery, shaky and wan even when miked. Only when the actress gives out an uninhibited yelp of lust in Sebastian's arms does she seem comfortably herself onstage.

Mr. Guskin's direction isn't entirely laissez-faire. The contradictory spirit of "Twelfth Night" lives in Peter Golub's rain-flecked score and in John Lee Beatty's set, an imaginative evocation of both the cliffside villas and beachfront pleasure domes of the fin-de-siècle Riviera. But as an acting coach, Mr. Guskin seems more of a cheerleader, allowing seasoned performers to reach heights of self-indulgence that would make an Oscar presenter blush.

Easily the most shocking offender is Mr. Goldblum, who gets no laughs in the heretofore foolproof scene in which Olivia's puritanical steward, Malvolio, is duped into romantic lightheadedness by a forged letter. Fracturing every line into unintelligibility with eye and tongue poppings, racing his voice up and down the octave, Mr. Goldblum fails to define Malvolio's pomposity in the first place, thereby rendering his subsequent fall and cruel humiliation meaningless. Malvolio may be "sick of self love," as Olivia says, but Mr. Goldblum's egotism is of another order entirely. This is a star appearance at the esthetic level of an autograph signing.

With the exception of Charlaine Woodard's sprightly Maria, the other comic players are just as mirthless. John Amos has none of the carousing Sir Toby's aura of ruined nobility, and Fisher Stevens, a little too young to be impersonating the "What me worry?" deadpan of Joey Bishop, misses the vulnerability that makes Olivia's hapless suitor, Sir Andrew Aguecheek, funny and pathetic. As the clown, Feste, the joyous Mr. Hines has his sweet moments but is often used as patronizingly as Ms. Pfeiffer. Mr. Hines's great talents as a dancer are constantly mocked — not for real laughs but to advertise his show-biz identity — and his bittersweet role is flattened into an obsequious and incessantly smiling jester, as if to dismiss his acting prowess. True, the clown's final lyric says that "we'll strive to please you every day," but pleasure is one thing, pandering another. Mr. Hines is at one point asked to bare his rump.

Though it would be pretentious to talk about Shakespeare in considering a "Twelfth Night" in which such discussions were probably kept to a minimum, the author does peek through here and there. This is palpably true when Ms. Mastrantonio, her tears of longing still gleaming in her wide eyes, leaps on Mr. Collins's back to celebrate the long-delayed reciprocation of her affections. Love, the gesture reminds us, requires a brave, selfless, potentially foolish leap beyond one's narcissistic romantic fantasies and into the unknown. In Illyria as elsewhere, it's only that lesser and passing thing, infatuation, that is written in the stars.

1989 Jl 10, C13:1

A Polish Perspective On an Elusive Reality

PEPSICO SUMMERFARE, two United States premieres, directed by Andrzej Wajda. Presented by Stary Theater of Cracow, Stanislaw Radwan, artistic director. At the State University College at Purchase.

THE DYBBUK, by Szymon Anski; in Polish, with a simultaneous translation over headphones; costumes by Krystyna Zachwatowicz; music by Zygmunt Konieczny; choreographer, Januez Jozefowicz.
WITH: Izabela Olszewska, Jerzy Trela, Krzysztof Globisz, Jerzy Radziwilowicz, Aldona Grochal, Dorota Pomykala, Dariusz Drozdz, Staniszaw Gronkowski, Jan Peszek, Ryszard Lukowski, Jan Monczka, Marek Kalita, Tadeusz Huk, Stefan Szramel, Kazimierz Borowiec, Tadeusz Malak, Pawel Kruszelnicki, Krzysztof Stawowy, Ewa Kolasinska, Grazyna Laszczyk, Marta Jurasz.

HAMLET, by Shakespeare; translated into the Polish by Stanislaw Baranczak, with a simultaneous translation back into English over headphones; art director, Krystyna Zachwatowicz; composer, Stanislaw Radwan.

Hamlet	Teresa Budziscz-Krzyzanowska
King	Jerzy Gralek
Queen	Ewa Lassek
Polonius	Jerzy Binczycki
Ophelia	Dorota Segda
Horatio	Krzysztof Globisz
Laertes	Marek Kalita
Rosencrantz	Aleksander Fabisiak
Guildenstern	Jan Monczka
Fortinbras	Jerzy Radziwilowicz

WITH: Jan Peszek, Ryszard Lukowski, Pawel Kruszelnicki

By STEPHEN HOLDEN

In the powerfully imaginative theater of Andrzej Wajda, the characters are forever slipping from world to world, between stages within stages. It is a theater in which unseen forces and historical ghosts exert as much control over life as the most powerful of the living, in which those who seek to know their fates must grapple with spirits in order to understand the past.

Both in "Hamlet" and "The Dybbuk," which the eminent Polish director and his Stary Theater of Cracow have brought to the Pepsico Summerfare festival, the stage is halved into foreground and background spaces, each representing a different plane of reality. For Shakespeare's "Hamlet," by far the more experimental of the two productions, the basic elements of a conventional theatrical presentation are physically reversed.

Much of the action of the drama, presented in Polish with a simultaneous translation available on headphones, is set in a backstage dressing room in which the Danish prince, portrayed by the brilliant Polish actress Teresa Budziscz-Krzyzanowska, is preparing for a performance. The audience, seated behind the backstage area at the extreme rear of a literally empty theater, faces that theater's footlights, which can be seen through a center-stage entrance from Hamlet's dressing room. Periodically, the players turn toward the empty house with their backs to the audience, moving in and out of view of the doorway as they emote into the bare echoing hall.

The empty seats for "Hamlet" are the same ones that an actual audience fills for performances of Szymon Anski's 1914 classic, "The Dybbuk." In this majestic, visually stunning production of the most famous of all Jewish dramas, a nearly transparent scrim separates the audience from the actors. Through a second scrim behind a large window at the rear of the stage can be seen a very animated-looking graveyard of towering tombstones and curling smoke that suggests a world of hovering spirits. At key moments during the drama, the characters plunge into this steamy, treacherous netherworld to communicate with the dead.

The stage, in more than one sense of the word, is the central metaphor of Mr. Wajda's enigmatic, deeply political "Hamlet." There is the actual theater setting, in which Hamlet is shown preparing his role and where he reads his "to be or not to be" soliloquy from a script on his makeup table. The other stage is the global arena in which the Danish royal family act out their national drama.

In setting "Hamlet" backstage, the director seems to be asking the most fundamental questions about the role of the theater in national and world affairs as well as what, if any, political impact it might have in Communist countries like Poland.

Wojciech Plewinski

Dorota Segda, left, as Ophelia, and Teresa Budziscz-Krzyzanowska as Hamlet in Andrzej Wajda's production for the Pepsico Summerfare.

At the same time, the concept of Hamlet as an actor preparing to go on the stage profoundly undermines the character's veracity. What if his fuming and fussing is all literally make-believe as it sometimes seems? Miss Budzisz-Krzyanowska plays the role as a hot-tempered paranoiac who wears a glittering, twisted smile much of the time. The director doesn't make anything of the role's being played by a woman. Dorota Segda's dithering Ophelia is a doting, credulous girlfriend who takes Hamlet's whimsical fantasies — suicide, for instance — seriously enough to act them out. The most hot-blooded character in the production is Laertes (Marek Kalita).

On a contemporary political level, the director's use of "Hamlet" to suggest the disparity between public acts and behind-the-scenes machinations has cynically fatalistic overtones. When the visiting thespians enact "The Death of Gonzago" for Claudius and Gertrude, Hamlet instructs Horatio to gauge Claudius's expression through a backstage video monitor that is also visible to the audience.

•

As we watch the same scene from two radically different perspectives — one a televised closeup of Claudius's expressionless face, the other a stage performance with his back to us with the players circled around him glaring accusingly — neither vantage point offers anything close to a definitive view. All through the drama, the director ponders the conflicting interpretations presented by different physical perspectives of events. In one of the production's more startling images, Claudius, on his knees before a statue of Christ on the cross, literally flagellates himself in a maudlin act of public penance.

But the most bravura touch comes at the end with the arrival of the victorious Fortinbras. Stealing into the dressing room, he puts on Hamlet's clothes, and the play, rather than ending, begins again with Fortinbras playing Hamlet's role. Where in Ingmar Bergman's "Hamlet," at the

Brooklyn Academy of Music last year, Fortinbras led a totalitarian police brigade that swept onto the scene of carnage like a blast of bitter air, in Mr. Wajda's "Hamlet" the new players who arrive only repeat the same cycles of the past. The secret crimes go on.

While the company's "Hamlet" is an enigmatic investigation of theatrical and political truth in which emotions are not to be trusted, "The Dybbuk" is suffused with an almost stately passion. The story of an impoverished young yeshiva student who dies and, in the form of an evil spirit (a dybbuk), enters the body of the young woman he believed was predestined as his bride, unfolds as a luminous mystery play, filled with a sense of the accumulated weight of history, law and spiritual teaching. During most of the drama, the stage is half in shadow. Moving slowly through the dusky atmosphere, haloed in light that seems to emanate from unseen sources, the actors have the depth of allegorical figures in a 17th-century painting.

The performances, especially those of Jan Peszek, the holy man who exorcizes the spirit, and Aldona Grochal, as Lea, from whom he attempts to wrest the demon, have an anguished dignity. Krystyna Zachwatowicz's dark, luxuriant costumes and Zygmunt Konieczny's ritualistic music deepen the atmosphere of visionary solemnity.

1989 Jl 11, C13:1

A Woman's Life

SPIRIT TIME, by Wilfred Cartey; adapted by Lumengo Joy Hooks; directed by Meachie Jones; original music by Stephen Hooks; set by Felix E. Cochren; costumes by Fontella Boone; lights by Kathy Perkins; company manager, Daniel Wynne, Jr.; stage manager, Juliet Warner; technical director, Dwayne Perryman III. Presented by National Black Touring Circuit, Inc., Woodie King, Jr., producer. At the Arts for Living Center of the Henry Street Settlement, 466 Grand Street.

With Lumengo Joy Hooks, Kathy Smith and Stephen Hooks.

By RICHARD F. SHEPARD

When theater is harnessed to poems, there is always a question about how well they will work together. In the case of Wilfred Cartey's poetry and the performance of a gifted trio in "Spirit Time" at the Arts for Living Center of the Henry Street Settlement, on the Lower East Side, the match works quite effectively.

Mr. Cartey, a professor of black studies at the City University of New York, is a Trinidad-born poet whose latest published work is a book of lyric verse, "Choreographers of the Dawn." In this adaptation of his poems to the stage by Lumengo Joy Hooks, who is also its star, music and dance have been blended with his words and the result is an hour and a quarter of earnest and passionate lyricism.

"Spirit Time" is not exactly a play, but that is by no means a dismissal of it. Like a poem itself, it has moments that seize the viewer's emotions and imagination and others that leave the onlooker awash in vigorous imagery. For one not attuned to poetry or imagery, it may be difficult of access, for want of a linear story line, but for those in tune with its title it can be as moving as a piece of music.

•

In essence, the work is about a black woman, Womanchile and her progress through life, her childhood, her age of romance, her hardships, her aspirations, all the time calling upon her kindred ethereal spirit, Watunga. We follow through from innocent babyhood, with toys and pristine goodness, to the more corrupting and difficult stages of living. The themes range from the primeval Great Rift of Africa (very movingly memorialized in a chant) to an old woman at a Harlem window and to oppressed blacks in South Africa.

Ms. Hooks gives a finely tuned performance as an actress who has obviously infused the very essence of the poet's emotions. She steers the play, under the sensitive direction of Meachie Jones, from primal awe to great boundless grief, to anger, to recurrent joy and faith. It is difficult, given the sheer power of a poet's words, for an actor to avoid emoting and although Ms. Hooks occasionally succumbs, her performance is so immersed in the sense of the writing that it would be churlish to carp at an otherwise heartfelt interpretation.

•

Kathy Smith, as the spirit, is a lithe and ethereal presence, her dancing slimness in striking counterpoint to the generously proportioned Ms. Hooks, who, it must be emphasized, demonstrates an energetic agility in her own right.

Stephen Hooks, who rounds out the cast, is a versatile musician, playing guitar and drums and other accessory instruments needed for the music he has written to provide exclamation points to the words.

"Spirit Time" is not an easy time, perhaps, for your run-of-the-mill playgoer, but those in search of art and theater should find in it something stimulating.

1989 Jl 14, C18:1

Dem Bums, Singing

PLAY TO WIN, book by Carles Cleveland and James de Jongh; lyrics by Mr. Cleveland, Mr. de Jongh and Jimi Foster; music by Mr. Foster; directed by Ken Nixon; choreographed by Leslie Dockery; musical arrangements by Harrison Fisher; original staging by Regge Life; costumes by Linda Geley; settings by Tom Barnes; sound consultants, Gary and Timmy Harris; lighting by Mathew J. Williams; production stage manager, Kathy Alden McGowan. Presented by Theaterworks USA, Jay Harnick, artistic director; Charles Hull, managing director. At the Promenade Theater, Broadway at 76th Street.

Satchel	Bruce Butler
Jackie	Michael-David Gordon
Rickey	Peter Schmitz
Colonel	Barry J. Tarallo
Rachel	Shona Tucker

By D. J. R. BRUCKNER

Theaterworks/USA has opened its first monthlong season of free summer theater for young and family audiences with "Play to Win," a snappy one-hour musical about how baseball became a truly all-American game when Jackie Robinson won a contract with the Brooklyn Dodgers in 1947.

•

The play, by Carles Cleveland and James de Jongh, is a joyous and very smart celebration not only of one man but of a nation and its favorite pastime as well. There are dark moments of bigotry, struggle and failure in it. But Robinson's triumph at the end — his first home run in the majors — is a victory for humanity, and the last song sung by the cast in praise of baseball might well be a hymn to everybody.

In many ways there is far too much to say about the 1947 season, but these playwrights are not distracted. They do not take the story through the Dodgers' capture of the pennant or Robinson's Most Valuable Player award or the heart-stopping subway series that year. They concentrate on Robinson's sassy determination not to be held back by white prejudice — in college, in the Army or in sports — and on the sheer guts it took for him to become the first black player in major league baseball.

But it was not his courage alone that did it, and in "Play to Win," Branch Rickey, the Dodgers' general manager who hired Robinson, comes across as a good-humored, flinty, shrewd and combative character.

Jimi Foster's music, to lyrics by himself and the two playwrights, is upbeat, bouncy and memorable. There is something especially satisfying about coming out of a musical about baseball and being able to hum the music from it.

Under Ken Nixon's very energetic direction, the five members of the cast fill not only the principal roles listed in the program, but many others, and they have a delightful time changing race by simply donning white or black baseball caps. Bruce Butler is a fine Satchel Paige, who acts as the narrator, and he doubles as a fussy white hotel clerk refusing Robinson a room during spring training.

Michael-David Gordon and Shona Tucker make an attractive pair as Robinson and his wife, Rachel, and if Mr. Gordon is not always able to suggest how much Robinson suffered from bigotry, he evokes very well the great player's anger and his superb discipline. Peter Schmitz is an admirably confident, even blustery, Rickey and Barry J. Tarallo creates a couple of mean but ridiculous racists in and out of baseball.

There are painful memories in the Jackie Robinson story, but on the whole it is one of the best stories Americans can tell about themselves. "Play to Win" tells it economically, with a lot of feeling.

1989 Jl 21, C3:2

Kings, Queens And Dolls

THE PIXIE LED, by Christopher Harris; directed by Julian Richards; set designers, Michael T. Roberts and John Pope; costume designer, Tim Heywood; lighting designer, Clifton Taylor; production stage manager, John Handy; assistant director, Kate Chate. Produced by Union 212, Geoffrey M. Freeman, Jonathan Willis, Beatie Edney, Mr. Richards, Cole Theatrical Enterprises and Darren Lee Cole, in association with Krystyna and David Winn and Susan and Richard Madris. At the Judith Anderson Theater, 422 West 42d Street.

WITH: John Wylie, Amanda Boxer and Steven Crossley.

By WILBORN HAMPTON

Early on in "The Pixie Led," a play by Christopher Harris that opened last night at the Judith Anderson Theater, a denizen of an asylum the program identifies as Bedlam, circa 1850, asks two other inmates, "Am I surrounded by an invisible mist, or is it something we are all just imagining?"

Actually, this play is enveloped in something more akin to one of those pea soup fogs for which Victorian London was famous — murky, impenetrable and befuddling to any hapless wayfarer trapped in it.

Most of what passes as plot occupies a day in the life of three inmates of that notorious asylum. For reasons too complicated to explain briefly (or coherently), a mad astronomer is persuaded that he is the logical claimant to the vacant throne of Spain. He is then convinced that if he is to be a King, he must have a Queen, and a woman who was ostensibly committed for prostitution is enlisted to be his bride. There is also a doll whose nose has been lost. Beginning playwrights should be discouraged from writing parts for dolls.

Mr. Harris is reported to have loosely based his play (very loosely, one might add) on Gogol's "Diary of a Madman" and "Nose," two of the Russian's so-called St. Petersburg stories set in a mad city where nothing was what it seemed. "The Pixie Led," which was first performed on

Martha Swope Associates/ Carole Rosegg

Amanda Boxer and Steven Crossley in "The Pixie Led," a play by Christopher Harris.

London's Fringe, is set in a madhouse where, for all the talk on stage, nothing really happens.

Perhaps a master Absurdist like Samuel Beckett, or a brilliant wordsmith like Tom Stoppard, could use such a situation to explore the limits of madness against the confines of sanity. But "Pixie Led" offers little more than sophomoric double talk that is only occasionally mildly diverting. If there is a point somewhere, it is exceedingly well hidden in an excess of verbiage. Mr. Harris is a writer who will not use one figure of speech when four or five come to mind.

Only briefly, toward the end, when the inmates begin to question one another as to why they are in the asylum, is there a breath of life in these characters. But Mr. Harris quickly abandons this pursuit to return to the wellspring from which he draws most of his wit, namely the cleverness and vulgarity of insults the inmates can hurl at one another. There are also a lot of scatological metaphors and one crude monologue describing a brutal and lurid execution that would make a sadist wince.

The cast works very hard. John Wylie is striking as the would-be King of Spain; Amanda Boxer is convincing as the coarse-tongued tart, and Steven Crossley is sympathetic as their foil.

"The Pixie Led" is the kind of play that may sound pretty good while discussing it with friends over a few jars down at the pub. But the paucity of intellectual, dramatic or comedic content should have become fairly apparent by the second rehearsal.

1989 Jl 21, C3:5

London Festival Rivals Edinburgh's

By MATT WOLF

LONDON

BEYOND THE APPETITE HERE for American exports — which produced the well-timed July 4 opening of "Anything Goes," and continues unabated — London's theatrical life has taken an international turn

of late. Such imported fare is traditional at the Edinburgh International Festival, which occasionally sends its best offerings south for further exposure. But this year, even before Edinburgh opens its 43d season on Aug. 12, London theatergoers have been able to broaden their cultural horizons closer to home. This, in fact, may be the year in which London takes the lead in an area that Edinburgh has long dominated by default.

The prime force in this upheaval is the biennial London International Festival of Theater, which ends its fifth season next Sunday, having presented 15 shows. Since it began in 1981, L.I.F.T. has become an increasingly prominent fixture on Europe's festival circuit. In addition, the capital is host through October to the more modest International '89 series at the National Theater, which brings foreign works to the house for

> ## This may be the year in which London takes the lead in an area long dominated by Edinburgh.

the first time since 1987. That event has already brought "The Grapes of Wrath" to the South Bank in the well-received production by Chicago's Steppenwolf Theater Company. Still to come are Anton Chekhov's "Uncle Vanya," performed by the Moscow Art Theater, and Matsuyo Akimato's "Suicide for Love," performed by Tokyo's Ninagawa Company.

■

All of this adds up to heady competition for Edinburgh, although it may be unfair to prejudge a Scottish institution that has historically provided so many adventures. As recently as 1987, after all, Edinburgh offered the British premiere of the Gate Theater of Dublin's "Juno and the Paycock," acclaimed on Broadway last summer. But the festival's selections this year include several works that, at least to American eyes, must seem fairly old hat: Claudio Segovia and Hector Orezzoli's "Tango Argentino," for example, or "The Garden of Earthly Delights," presented by Martha Clarke's Music Theater Group.

In addition, Edinburgh has come under increasing criticism that its vitality is waning. Last September, Alex Renton wrote in The Independent, "Edinburgh as playground will survive — but as an international forum for excellence, it is under serious challenge." And John Peter, in The Sunday Times of London, echoed, "I think we're now reaching a point where hard decisions are needed about [the festival's] purpose and survival."

No such decisions have yet been forced on the flourishing London International Festival of Theater. It has the advantage, of course, of having to prove its excellence not annually, but only every other year. Nor are the two events comparable in scale. While Edinburgh presses an entire city and its tourist industry into action, spending millions of pounds in the process, L.I.F.T. has this year spent £560,000 (about $900,000) to bring its various companies to venues that are mostly off the beaten tourist path.

The International Festival doesn't pretend to dominate the London theater. Indeed, during the event's first week, several of its entries received scant coverage because of the back-to-back arrivals of three American musicals: "Anything Goes"; a production of "On the Town" at the Guildhall School of Music and Drama, and a summertime revival of the Tommy Steele vehicle, "Singin' in the Rain."

Also unlike Edinburgh, L.I.F.T. announces no theme beyond the self-evident goal, as defined by the festival's co-director, Rose de Wend Fenton, of bringing "the best of contemporary theater from all over the world." Striving toward a similar overall end, Edinburgh gives each season a focus. This year it's Spain, and Edinburgh's schedule is laced with classics from the Spanish repertory. In addition, the Barcelona-based Els Comediants will offer two shows, one of which, "The Devils," was staged in London's Battersea Park as part of L.I.F.T. in 1985.

This sort of collaboration is something Ms. Fenton would like to encourage. "I'm always saying to Edinburgh, 'Please, let's work together,'" she remarked.

Edinburgh organizers, however, prefer to keep their distance. "Edinburgh has certainly considered London part of its audience," said Christopher Barron, the general manager of the festival, "and I don't believe there's much point in the same thing being seen in London and then in Edinburgh." As for Els Comediants, Mr. Barron added, "while we've known of this company from L.I.F.T., we would have known of it anyway." He attributed the Edinburgh booking to the fact that "the major companies of the world are getting many more opportunities to travel."

These opportunities are reflected in the itineraries of some of this season's L.I.F.T. productions that have made their way to New York. Moscow's Chelovek Studio production of Lyudmila Petrushevskaya's "Cinzano" ended an engagement July 1 at SUNY-Stony Brook prior to its London run. The Soviet director Anatoly Vasiliev's staging of Pirandello's "Six Characters in Search of an Author," which played in London simultaneously with "Cinzano," completes its four-performance run tomorrow at the Pepsico Summerfare at SUNY-Purchase. Summerfare also has an Edinburgh connection this year: The Stary Theater of Cracow's "Dybbuk," directed by Andrzej Wajda, which played in Purchase earlier this month, opens in Scotland on Aug. 28.

As more and more festivals compete worldwide, a certain interchangeability is inevitable, and this is part of the reason for a shift away from L.I.F.T.'s original identity. According to Ms. Fenton, who is 32 years old, the festival has departed from the purpose she and her co-director, Lucy Neal, laid out at its inception, two years after they graduated from the University of Warwick in 1979.

"Initially, we started with the idea of doing much more visual theater, and then text crept into it," said Ms. Fenton, marking the distinction between plays that depend for their impact primarily on the image and those that depend heavily on the word. "The British theater was so dominated by text that performance and visual artists tended to be relegated to black boxes on the fringe."

∎

But over the years, the primacy of the word has reasserted itself, alongside — as in the case of Mr. Vasiliev's "Six Characters" — a striking visual style. "Quite simply, one couldn't be perverse and say no to a wonderful production because it happens to be based on a text," Ms. Fenton said.

Often, definitions of "text" can be problematic. In Fiona Templeton's "You — The City," which opened the L.I.F.T. season on July 3, individual theatergoers in London's East End were taken through a two-hour series of encounters with actors playing cab drivers, prostitutes, evangelists and the like. Seemingly spontaneous, the meetings were in fact fully written and staged. The invited participation, beginning with a printed form that asked patrons, "Are you now, or have you ever been?" was merely a front for a production whose mock-Piran-

Some of this season's L.I.F.T. productions have made their way to New York.

dellian pretensions were cruelly exposed by the real thing in the form of "Six Characters" three nights later.

"Song of Lawino," also from New York, was a buoyant piece of feminist and cultural affirmation by a Ugandan poet, Okot p'Bitek, an effusion of sound and color whose energy demolished any potential stridency.

L.I.F.T.'s biggest box-office success so far this year has been a celebrated Irish play: Tom Murphy's "Whistle in the Dark" (1961) in the Abbey Theater of Dublin production of 1986, directed by Garry Hynes. Ironically, text almost does this play in. Using the Irish community in the English Midlands to explore man's instinct for violence, "A Whistle in the Dark" is so schematic and telescoped a piece of writing that it precludes any possibility of surprise.

∎

Besides "Six Characters," the classics this year include Gogol's "Government Inspector" and Chekhov's "Three Sisters," both presented by the Katona Jozsef Theater of Hungary (see box). These plays depart from L.I.F.T.'s recent penchant for contemporary plays, whether George C. Wolfe's Off Broadway hit "The Colored Museum" (1987) or Poland's Teatr Nowy in "The End of Europe" (1985). Evidently, any sort of material is up for grabs, as the festival consolidates its eclectic reputation.

The International Festival's current situation is considerably improved from the poverty-stricken optimism of its first year, when it produced 10 shows on a budget of £125,000 (about $230,000 at the time), and Ms. Fenton admitted to occasional nostalgia for her initial enthusiasm and naïveté.

"If you don't know how impossible the mountain is to climb, you set off quite gaily," she said, laughing. "It's only when you anticipate and look up that you see the crags gazing down at you threateningly." □

1989 Jl 23, II:5:1

— Standing Ovation —

It can't be common for four hours of Chekhov in Hungarian to bring a Western audience to its feet, but such was the case July 13 at "Three Sisters," performed by Hungary's Katona Jozsef Theater at the Old Vic. The five-minute standing ovation honored a production of rare emotional richness and psychological ruthlessness. Although earphones were available to guide audiences at the London International Festival of Theater presentation through each scene, the lucidity and force of the performances soon made interpretation unnecessary. As Michael Billington wrote in The Guardian, "Acting of this force cuts through the language barrier."

What stunned throughout the evening was the director Tamás Ascher's thorough embrace of this work's despair. Not for him the elegantly pained gentility of recent British productions of the play. These sisters were caught on a ceaselessly wounding and anxious treadmill, and in one typically shocking moment of fury, Irina dumped a jug of water over herself to calm her raging discontent.

Katona Jozsef had opened its London season two days earlier with Gogol's "Government Inspector," but this work's belligerently farcical tone did not prepare for the Chekhov.

Chicago is reportedly interested in bringing the company to its international theater festival next year, in which case Americans may encounter the kind of dramatic jolt that reaches across continents. — M. W.

1989 Jl 23, II:5:5

A Show by the Pickle Family, Starring Clowning

By JENNIFER DUNNING

Special to The New York Times

STONY BROOK, L.I., July 21 — The Pickle Family Circus is so refreshingly unassuming and so lively that to call it a landmark institution sounds overly solemn. But the San Francisco-based circus, now in its 15th year, spawned Bill Irwin and Geoff Hoyle. An offspring of the San Francisco Mime Troupe, the Pickles were also the first in this country to establish a one-ring, intimate show on the order of European circuses.

The bad news is that the closest they have got to New York City is here, where they performed on Friday night at the Staller Center on the campus of the State University in the Norstar Bank International Theater Festival. The good news is that they are a dream of a circus with even greater simplicity and refinement than New York's Big Apple Circus and all the artistry but none of the preciousness of Cirque du Soleil.

By group decision there are no animal acts in this circus commune. Instead, the stage is taken over in swift and neatly paced succession by jugglers, acrobats, wire-walkers and acrobats in an evening that culminates in a surprisingly successful one-act theater piece based on a turn-of-the-century vaudeville act set in a French café. The glue that holds all this together is the inspired clowning for which the circus has become known.

The star clown is Queenie Moon. Loud mouthed, gregarious and a le-

A one-ring, intimate show at Stony Brook.

thal punster, she opens the show with an act that sets the tone for the entire evening, when she is forced to take care of a disastrously misbehaving baby. Joan Rankin, who plays Queenie, and Diane Wasnak, the wonderfully observed baby, reappear throughout the night in various guises. But this opening act showcases their expert, wittily timed acting and mime and prepares us for what is to come.

Jens Larson communicates the exaltation of flight in "If I Had Wings," an act on the Roman rings in which, performing without a net, he soars out over the audience in tights that could have been designed by Picasso for "Parade." Pretty young Ayin De Sela walks and dances along a wire in the poetic "Tale From the Sea," and 10 of the circus's 14 performers turn out for a knockabout acrobatics act.

John Gilkey and Karen Quest are jugglers who bounce through the most complicated routines without once losing the individuality that makes it all an art.

The Pickles start young, apparently, for Lorenzo John Pisoni and Miriam De Sela, two of their star acrobats, are 12 years old. Mr. Pisoni, the son of Larry Pisoni and Peggy Snider, co-founders of the circus, tumbles with a dancer's grace. Everyone comes together in the closing "Café Chaotique," a finely worked riot of plots and circus acts

put together by Judy Finelli, the circus's artistic director.

The cast was completed by Jean-Luc Martin, Noah Chomy, Rosalinda Rojas, Heather Basarab and Shana Carroll, Ryszard Ostrowski and Abdulkadir Ouled-Sidi-Ali. Throughout, the music was performed by a zany onstage jazz band that included Bill Belasco, Richard Harmon, Helena Jack, Rocky Klemenak and Harvey Robb. May all the Pickles soon return.

1989 Jl 24, C12:3

Soviet Version of Pirandello Puts Audience in the Play

By FRANK RICH

Special to The New York Times

PURCHASE, N.Y., July 21 — It's not just six characters who are in search of an author in Anatoly Vasiliev's imaginative staging of Luigi Pirandello's comedy. By Act II -- and by the Soviet director's design — roughly 200 theatergoers are in the same fix.

Like Pirandello's six abandoned fictional figures, who invade a theatrical rehearsal hoping to be brought to completion by actors, the audience watching Mr. Vasiliev's "Six Characters" at Pepsico Summerfare finds itself on a stage in the middle of a rehearsal of a seemingly fatuous play. Mr. Vasiliev's actors sit indiscriminately among the spectators. The house lights are up. And, to make an American audience's disorientation complete, the simultaneous translation piped into our headsets is abruptly shut off.

What do the theatergoers do? Their behavior is naturally Pirandellian. At the opening performance on Friday night, some pounded and shook their headsets even after the translator, yet another lost character, appeared on stage to render the occasional line in English. Two women behind me developed an unstoppable case of the giggles. Another woman, announcing a bit too loudly to her companion that she planned to beat the intermission rush to the restroom, marched conspicuously and solemnly to the exit. Then there were the scattered men in the audience who found themselves fondled by actresses representing the prostitutes of Madame Pace's salon, a setting of the play rehearsing within Pirandello's play. Asked to behave like pigs in heat, these impromptu performers sank to the occasion with smarmy, lascivious hamminess.

These are trivial happenings, to be sure, but they cut to the heart of Pirandello's intent. "Six Characters" does not merely demand a re-examination of the relationship between theater and life — or between those dreary academic poles of illusion and truth — but it also asks, far more profoundly, that each member of the audience examine his own singular relationship to existence. "Who are you?" is the question that confronts the theater director in Pirandello's

third act. Well, who are we? Do we, like the men in Mr. Vasiliev's audience Friday night, play any character, however degrading, demanded of us by others? Do we rebel against our roles, like the woman who marched out? Do we play the part of "audience" and sit there as passively as, say, a drama critic? Are we our own authors or the creations of Someone Else?

Mr. Vasiliev cannot resolve these existential dilemmas anymore than can Pirandello or anyone short of a religious absolutist. This production, whose brief touring engagement here ends with Monday night's performance, does reopen the right questions. While by definition there can be no such thing as an orthodox production of "Six Characters," Mr. Vasiliev's is more unorthodox than most; it is a tireless deconstruction of a play that is itself a demolition of reality.

•

Where Pirandello's text gives us six characters and the troupe of actors who are gradually recruited to act the roles of those characters, Mr. Vasiliev exponentially increases the variables in the equation. His actors switch roles among themselves throughout the evening, emphasizing that the actors visited by the six characters of "Six Characters" are themselves characters played by actors in yet another open-ended drama. The Chinese-box-like conception of the production, which steadily obliterates the theater's fourth wall, gives fresh life to Eric Bentley's observation that "with Pirandello, you always have the irony within the irony."

A deconstruction of a play that demolishes reality.

There is a historical twist to Mr. Vasiliev's "Six Characters" as well. When Pirandello's play had its premiere in Italy in 1921, the Russian theater was in the midst of its greatest period of experimentation, a revolution against stage realism parallel to the one championed by "Six Characters." But Pirandello's play did not make it to the Soviet Union during

that hospitable decade before Stalin snuffed out avant-garde esthetics in favor of Socialist Realism.

Grigory Gladi in "Six Characters in Search of an Author."

Now, of course, the climate in the Soviet Union is right once more for "Six Characters," and Mr. Vasiliev's staging achieves the mating of experimental Soviet stagecraft and Pirandello that, if history had been different, could have been accomplished in Moscow six decades ago. Certainly this production, like the work of such other liberated contemporary Soviet directors as Yuri Lyubimov, is in the tradition of an adventurous Soviet director of the 1920's like Aleksandr Tairov, who overthrew realism to revel in the naked, unabashed theatricality of theater. The audience at "Six Characters" shares the stage at Summerfare in every way with Mr. Vasiliev's company; the backstage machinery and scenic fragments are exposed, as are the wings where actors sit and wait for their cues. Improvisational clowning, gestural repetition and music (from hot jazz to a gently weeping Spanish guitar) are as much a part of the show as Pirandello's text is.

•

In Moscow, the Vasiliev company reportedly performs in a cramped basement room. That claustrophobia is missing in the more diffuse environment at Summerfare, and not all the acting carried to my vantage spot in the bleachers. One must also add that, moments of Buñuelian eroticism aside, Mr. Vasiliev's approach sometimes stresses Pirandello the dry theoretician over Pirandello the passionate Sicilian dramatist. We are given perhaps too much time to meditate on the fact that there wouldn't be a "Largely New York" or an "M. Butterfly" or even a "Who Framed Roger Rabbit" without Pirandello.

When, in the final act, Mr. Vasiliev reverts to a formal proscenium staging to dramatize the familial violence that engulfs the six characters, he bursts through the boundary between thought and feeling. The events of the

play-within-the-play's denouement — a child's drowning, a young man's suicide — are all too transparently an author's melodramatic fictions. But the ensuing wails of grief sound so true that, paradoxically, for the first time all night the power of theater makes us forget that we are in a theater. Then the illusion fades, and the audience is again left in limbo. We know Mr. Vasiliev is true to Pirandello because even as the curtain falls on "Six Characters," we are left with the terrifying sensation that another curtain is going up.

1989 Jl 24, C13:1

In Which the Lady Is No Gentleman

THE LADY IN QUESTION, written by Charles Busch; directed by Kenneth Elliott; set design by B. T. Whitehill; costume design by Robert Locke and Jennifer Arnold; lighting design by Vivien Leone; production stage manager, Robert Vandergriff. Presented by Kyle Renick and Mr. Elliott. At the Orpheum Theater, 126 Second Avenue, at Eighth Street.

Gertrude Garnet .... Mr. Busch
Voice of the Announcer .... James Cahill
Professor Mittelhoffer/Dr. Maximilian
                                          Mark Hamilton
Heidi Mittelhoffer .... Theresa Marlowe
Karel Freiser .... Robert Carey
Prof. Erik Maxwell .... Arnie Kolodner
Hugo Hoffmann/Lotte Elsner
                                          Andy Halliday
Baron Wilhelm von Elsner .... Mr. Elliot
Kitty, the Countess de Borgia ..... Julie Halston
Augusta von Elsner/Raina Aldric
                                          Meghan Robinson

By FRANK RICH

Selfish is too kind a word for Gertrude Garnet, "the leading concert pianist of the international stage" and the all-American heroine of "The Lady in Question," Charles Busch's latest celebration of Hollywood kitsch. Hitler may be on the march, but Gertrude, on tour in Bavaria, can't worry her pretty head about politics. She finds the Germans "so warm, so friendly" and reassures the Nazis' victims that patience will reward them with an afterlife of "Champagne and caviar." For Gertrude, art comes first, then her wardrobe, then her cosmetics bag (Suzette, the maid, has stolen it) and then, of course, love. To paraphrase Lorenz Hart, the lady in question is a tramp.

As both written and acted by Mr. Busch, she is also hilarious company. This performer's Theater-in-Limbo company, best known for the long-running "Vampire Lesbians of Sodom," has found its most assured style and, I suspect, its biggest hit in the new play at the Orpheum Theater. Not that "The Lady in Question" can precisely be called a new play. A saga of war-torn romance and intrigue set in 1940, the piece has been distilled from such patriotic Hollywood potboilers of the period as "Escape," "Reunion in France" and "Above Suspicion." These were movies in which determined American women wearing Adrian gowns (Joan Crawford, Norma Shearer) joined with square-jawed Joes (Robert Taylor, Fred MacMurray) to beat suave Nazi swine (Conrad Veidt, Basil Rathbone) in a perilous midnight dash to the Swiss border.

As always, Mr. Busch knows his M-G-M schlock, but never previously has he or his director, Kenneth Elliott, dished it out with such sustained, well-paced discipline. Along with its double-entendre groaners, "The Lady in Question" actually offers some melodramatic chills and, thanks to the witty production design, the backlot shock effects allotted movies with B budgets. It's all here: the overblown soundtrack score, in which Wagner and Strauss enjoy a shotgun collaboration with Max Steiner; the propagandistic asides identifying the American cause with both God and Joe Stalin; the fake snow powdering the Alpine ski slopes; the stern, omniscient narrator who warns the audience that "yes, human life is cheap in the fatherland."

•

While Mr. Busch's plays are often linked with Charles Ludlam's lighter efforts, such generalizing distorts the artistry of both. Mr. Ludlam, a theatrical classicist and a political iconoclast, usually had a second agenda, ideological or esthetic, percolating within his gender-flipped sendups. Mr. Busch's attitude is the simpler one of "Hooray for Hollywood!" The man revels in trash. "The Lady in Question" mimics its source material so accurately and affectionately that it is as much homage as parody; the tone is closer to "Dames at Sea" or a Mel Brooks film than it is to the Ridiculous Theatrical Company. I'm not sure the show would play much differently if Mr. Busch took the radical step of casting a woman as Gertrude Garnet.

But what actor of either gender could top Mr. Busch? Last seen as Chicklet, a teen-age girl with a multiple-personality disorder in the lesser "Psycho Beach Party," he continues to be the Sybil of camp. With red Rita Hayworth hair and a low voice that variously recalls Bankhead, Bacall, Stanwyck, Davis and Russell, Mr. Busch is a walking anthology of feminine Hollywood legends. Yet the performance is not another cabaret drag act in which the breathless quick changes are the oppressively showy

point. His Gertrude is a seamless, often subtle characterization, ready to meet any challenge, including the Greer Garson-like inspirational speeches that transform the heroine from a Stork Club hedonist into a selfless patriot by the final clinch. So complex is the illusion created by Mr. Busch that when Gertrude appears in Dietrich-esque blazer and pants to go riding at Baron von Elsner's schloss, we don't even stop to think that we are watching a man impersonate a woman impersonating a man.

•

Mr. Busch's fellow clowns easily exceed their past Theater-in-Limbo

---

For Gertrude, art comes first, then her wardrobe.

---

turns. In the other cross-gender performance, Andy Halliday offers a vicious blond Nazi youth in braids and bows — a psychotic hybrid of a Trapp Family Singer and Patty McCormack in "The Bad Seed." Julie Halston, as Gertrude's sidekick since vaudeville days in Sandusky, Ohio, is the apotheosis of wisecracking second bananas of the Joan Blondell-Eve Arden era. In the evening's most amusing double act, Meghan Robinson plays two disparate mothers, a Führer-worshipping Baroness and a high-minded anti-Nazi actress so self-dramatizing that one often feels she would rather win an Oscar than get out of Germany alive. "I must walk to freedom!" is Ms. Robinson's histrionic vow, and how she does so, her wheelchair and a steep staircase notwithstanding, gives "The Lady in Question" its funniest excursion into physical comedy.

It's a tribute to Mr. Busch that, without raising his voice, he is never upstaged by this riotous crew. Like the actresses he emulates, he rules by force of personality, often proving the

cool, elegant, just slightly off-center eye of the farcical storm around him. That the lady in question is a man soon becomes beside the point. What matters here is that the performer in question is a star.

1989 Jl 26, C17:1

A Lot of Fireworks, Then a Great Race

THE STORY OF KUFUR SHAMMA, by Jackie Lubeck and François Abu Salem; directed by Mr. Salem; sets, costumes and masks designed by Francine Gaspar; lighting design by Philippe Andrieux; music montage by Mr. Salem; original music composed by Sheikh Imam; language consultant, Mohammed Batrawi. El-Hakawati Theater Company, presented by Dance Theater Workshop's Suitcase Fund, in association with International Performing Arts Consultants Inc. At the Bessie Schönberg Theater, 219 West 19th Street.

Walid	Nabil El-Hajjar
Ka'wash	Amer Khalil
Nijmeh	Jackie Lubeck
Abed	Edward Muallem
Hajeleh	Iman Aoun
Karim	Akram Tallawi

By WILBORN HAMPTON

Toward the end of the first act of "The Story of Kufur Shamma," the six cast members of El-Hakawati troupe huddle close together at the front of the sand-covered stage, a lone spotlight dimly illuminating their faces. As much as anything else in the work that opened Wednesday night for a week's run at the Dance Theater Workshop, that tableau captures the cramped and desperate existence of displaced men and women forced to live in refugee camps by powers beyond their control.

"Kufur Shamma" is actually more a saga than a play, a sort of oral narrative of a fictitious village acted out with music, mime, masks and songs as well as the scenes. The tale is as old as the expulsion from Eden. It is about refugees, and if one changed the names of the cast of characters, it could just as easily concern the plight of Armenians, Chinese, Tibetans, Jews, Vietnamese or Cambodians — and that's only a partial list for this century.

This story, however, is about Palestinians. It specifically concerns Walid, who returns to his home village of Kufur Shamma in 1948 from Cairo with a university degree only to find the town deserted except for chickens, flies and Ka'wash, the village idiot. Ka'wash explains that one day there were a lot of fireworks followed by a great race in which the entire village took part. "Everyone ran in a different direction," Ka'wash recalls. "Strange race, huh?" Walid decides to search for villagers who fled the fighting and vows to "turn the world upside down until we find them." With Ka'wash in tow he sets out on a 40-year odyssey that ranges from Kuwait to Massachusetts via refugee camps and the desert, picking up followers along the way.

•

El-Hakawati, which translates as the Storytellers, is a 12-year-old Palestinian theater company from East Jerusalem that is more in the tradition of a troupe of strolling players. Each member of the cast performs several roles and together they offer a good example of ensemble acting. Amer Khalil is a delight as Ka'wash, bringing a humorous and touching quality to the idiot, and

Amer Khalil

Nabil El-Hajjar presents a sympathetic Walid, full of patience with a world that has gone awry. Polished performances are also given by Jackie Lubeck, Edward Muallem, Iman Aoun and Akram Tallawi. Ms. Lubeck is also co-author of the work with the director, François Abu Salem.

"Kufur Shamma" is not without problems, the foremost of which is the need for some serious editing. There are ample opportunities for tightening the script, which plays at just under three hours, and Mr. Salem could speed up the pace of the journey without damaging the effect. The physical production, however, is a small marvel, especially considering that the company is on tour. Set and costume changes are woven seamlessly together, using a few doors, curtains and rugs, robes and scarves and some old jerrycans, and fit the workshop's space as if they had been tailored for it.

El-Hakawati, which is making its first North American tour this summer, very nearly did not get to New York. A planned engagement was canceled at the last minute for reasons that presumably involved some political sensibilities concerning Israel and the Palestinians. If there is any political villain in "Kufur Shamma," it might just as well be the English, who built the first road to the village and introduced white bread into the diet. That road was the beginning of the end for Kufur Shamma.

Of course, one would have to be more of an idiot than Ka'wash not to know that someone flew the planes and fired the guns that dispersed nearly a million Palestinians. But "The Story of Kufur Shamma" is about those refugees, not the armies that put them to flight, and El-Hakawati tells it with humor and skill. One should be grateful to Dance Theater Workshop for giving them a stage from which to tell their story.

1989 Jl 28, C17:1

The Glory of Love

THE ROSE TATTOO, by Tennessee Williams; directed by Irene Lewis; setting by Hugh Landwehr; costumes by Candice Donnelly; lighting by Pat Collins; production stage manager, Tree O'Halloran. Presented by the Williamstown (Mass.) Theater Foundation; George Morfogen, executive director; Peter Hunt and Austin Pendleton, artistic directors. At the Williamstown Theater Festival Main stage.

Serafina Delle Rose	Maria Tucc
Rosa Delle Rose	Marisa Tome
Alvaro Mangiacavallo	James Naughton
Assunta	Anne Pitonia
Jack Hunter	Dan Cordle

With: Ariane Brandt, Michael Branton, Angela Bullock, Marianne Ferrari, June Gable, Christopher George, Frank Gerac, Dana Morosini, Jane O'Malley, Molly Regan, Isa Thomas, Elizabeth Ware, Jody Watson, Celia Weston, Ralph Williams.

T. L. Boston

Meghan Robinson, left, and Charles Busch in "The Lady in Question" at the Orpheum Theater.

Charlie Erickson

Maria Tucci and James Naughton in the Williamstown Theater production of "The Rose Tattoo."

By WILBORN HAMPTON

Perhaps the most exacting measure of a playwright's enduring place in dramatic literature is the scrutiny of time on the writer's secondary works. Even in the critical and commercial decline of his later years, the masterpieces of Tennessee Williams were never questioned. Now, six years after his death, revivals of some of the second-rank plays, like "Night of the Iguana" and "Orpheus Descending," serve as a testament to the abiding power of Williams's voice.

The latest evidence is a vibrant and boisterous production of "The Rose Tattoo," running through this weekend at the Williamstown Theater Festival as part of its 35th-anniversary season.

Written 40 years ago, the poignant comedy of a young Sicilian seamstress in Louisiana who, suddenly widowed, stubbornly clings to her illusion of her dead husband's fidelity while fiercely guarding her daughter's chastity, might have proved anachronistic. But Williams did not create characters to the cut and fashion of the time. Rather he tailored them to the more demanding dimensions of human needs and desire. With a poet's economy of language Williams could more clearly define a character's fears, dreams and heartaches in one line than most writers can achieve in two or three acts. For actors adroit enough to seize them, the characters in Williams's plays provide opportunities for real tours de force.

•

In the Williamstown "Rose Tattoo," Maria Tucci takes her opportunity and soars. Quite simply, Ms. Tucci is superb as Serafina, the mercurial dressmaker for whom time does not exist except for the clock in her heart — "and it don't go tick, tick; it says 'love, love.'" Serafina's great fear is that her love for her slain husband, and thus her life, may have been made insignificant by his infidelity. Her dignity, even when she

becomes the butt of her neighbors' jokes, is that of one who can hold steadfastly to her own set of moral values in the face of the fickleness of time.

Obviously no stranger to Italian, Ms. Tucci slips back and forth between the languages with an unselfconscious facility that is lyrical. No shade of Serafina's passion escapes Ms. Tucci. When she hides her daughter Rosa's clothes and keeps her locked naked in the house so she won't run off to meet a young sailor, it seems the only natural thing for a concerned mother to do. When Serafina at last meets the sailor and forthrightly demands: "My daughter is a virgin; or was. I want to know which," it is the only logical question to ask before forcing him to kneel before a plaster Madonna and swear his honorable intentions. And when she disdains her mocking neighbors as women who "got no more use for the marriage bed — they sleep on their bellies and make love without the glory," it is a condemnation of all the loveless sex that a more permissive society tolerates.

•

James Naughton adds a splendid performance as Alvaro Mangiacavallo (Al Eat-a-horse), the buffone with big ears and a touch of the poet who woos Serafina with a four-year-old box of chocolates and a new rose tattoo on his chest to remind her of her husband. If Mr. Naughton's Italian accent, which at times sounds like Don Novello's Father Guido Sarducci, could use some work, his characterization is hilarious and touching. Mangiacavallo is searching only "for love and affection in a world that is lonely and cold," and it is this grandson of a Sicilian village idiot who stirs from the ashes of Serafina's shattered illusions the fire still smoldering in her heart.

•

In the other two main roles, Marisa Tomei as Rosa is a headstrong spitfire who is every inch her mother's daughter, and Dan Cordle is humor-

ous and bashful as the sailor boyfriend. An exception to a generally weak supporting cast is Anne Pitoniak, who offers an excellent turn as Assunta, the old seller of love potions who hears "star noises" in the night. If her name wasn't in the program, one would swear Ms. Pitoniak had just wandered onstage from a piazza in Palermo.

Irene Lewis directed from a solid understanding of the play and its characters.

1989 Jl 28, C3:4

Barking Guards For Ushers

WARD NO. SIX, an improvisation on Anton Chekhov's short story. Director, Yuri Yeremin; designer, Stepan Zograbian; stage manager, Yuri Fainkin; lights, Valery Fomin; script, Mr. Yeremin; literary adaptation, Olga Shvedova; company management, Vyacheslav Orlov. In Russian with simultaneous translation via headphones. The Pushkin Theater of Moscow, Mr. Yeremin, artistic director, presented by Pepsico Summerfare, at the State University College at Purchase, N.Y.

Doctor	Gennady Krynkin
Nobleman	Votaly Stremovsky
Guard	Aleksandr Mikhailushkin
Friend	Andrei Maiovor
New Doctor	Aleksandr Yermakov
Jew	Yuri Rumyantsev
Silent Man	Andrei Dubrosky
Mail sorter	Romualdas Vildanas
Fat Man	Vladimir Sokolov
Maid	Galina Moracheva

Ward attendants
    Valery Barinov and Aleksandr Borovikov

By STEPHEN HOLDEN

PURCHASE, N.Y., July 27 — Environmental theater depicting simulated brutality and degradation has a built-in limitation for an audience. As much as we are encouraged to imagine ourselves involved in the surrounding unpleasantness, we still know we are merely spectators who, barring an accident, will soon exit the scene unharmed. Even if we are yelled at, caressed and prodded to move around, we feel essentially safe.

"Ward No. Six," an ambitious environmental piece by the Pushkin Theater of Moscow, which runs until Tuesday at the Pepsico Summerfare festival, ingeniously works off this contradiction. It goes to greater lengths than most environmental pieces to create a nightmarish setting, but instead of pretending that we are participants in the drama, it treats the audience of only 70 people at each performance as voyeuristic observers.

•

The setting of the piece, based on Chekhov's short story, is the mental ward of a clinic in a small provincial Russian town. A straw-floored shed that houses five patients who are bullied by a sadistic guard and tended by a mostly absent doctor, it is a filthy, stifling animal shelter unfit for human habitation. To reach the scene, which is air-conditioned and does not literally reek, the audience is herded by barking guards through the bowels of the Summerfare theater complex and distributed on numbered chairs placed around all four sides of the shed.

Activities inside the ward can be viewed by peering through wooden slats that form the walls of the structure. A guard and two attendants patrolling the premises stalk the perimeter, moving behind the audience's backs. Although a scene occasionally erupts outside the shed, most of the action is contained within.

Votaly Stremovsky in "Ward No. Six," being presented by the Pushkin Theater of Moscow at the Pepsico Summerfare festival.

An eerie effect of the setup is that the audience seated on one side faces the disembodied glares of those sitting opposite. The sight of so many staring eyes evokes a chilly, paranoid climate of faceless spies and informants. At the same time, watching the actors through gaps in a wall underscores the voyeuristic impulse that is an inevitable ingredient of theatergoing. Because we are physically shielded from the cast members, who are sometimes just inches away from our gazes, we feel the slightly creepy sense of witnessing covert actions.

The political implications of the production design are obvious and certainly intended by the director, Yuri Yeremin, and the Pushkin company. Their grubby ward stands as a symbolic microcosm of the Soviet society before its recent liberalization, with the Chekhov story bent into a metaphor for totalitarian paranoia and oppression.

•

At the center of the drama are the philosophical and theological conversations between a nobleman (Votaly Stremovsky), who has been incarcerated for 12 years for a persecution complex, and the doctor who has witnessed so much agony that he has ceased to feel any compassion. Why should we relieve human suffering when it is through suffering that we think about our souls and God and philosophy? he asks. Pain, he maintains, is a concept that, once it is understood as a concept, will disappear through an effort of will.

The doctor is drawn to the nobleman because he is the only educated person in the region, and he is desperate for an intellectual sparring partner. The nobleman, who insists on the reality of pain, invokes a passionate, well-reasoned humanism. On an intellectual level, at least, he is the most rational person in sight. Mr. Stremovsky's nobleman leaves it tantalizingly unclear just how unstrung the character really is. Though he goes momentarily berserk when the guard tries to cut his hair, the conditions would seem to warrant the most extreme acts of rebellion. Gennady Krynkin, a ruddy, barrel-chested actor with thick eyebrows and a hard, impenetrable gaze, imbues the doctor

The sadism of the mental ward as a paradigm for repression.

with an ominous solidity that makes the character all the more pathetic when he finally crumbles.

The play compresses the several weeks of Chekhov's story into an hour and 20 minutes of scenes separated by blackouts in which the actual time between events is not always clear. Developed through improvisation, the play's dialogue, spoken in Russian with simultaneous translation via headphones, lifts the story out of the 1890's and into an abstract, more modern time that still feels like the past.

•

The drama's scenes of physical abuse are sparing and well executed. Though there are a couple of thrashing melees and two scenes of inmates being brutally kicked, the sense of oppression is ultimately more psychic than physical. That is as it should be.

For the overwhelming concept dramatized by "Ward No. Six" is the complete irrationality and arbitrariness of totalitarian rule and the insanity of any notion that suffering and self-sacrifice are in some way good for the soul.

Although very different in style from the work of Andrzej Wajda's Stary Theater of Cracow and from the Antoly Vasiliev Theater Company of Moscow's "Six Characters in Search of an Author," which the Summerfare festival also presented this season, "Ward No. Six" shares many of the same preoccupations as the other productions that arrived at the festival in the spirit of glasnost. Two of the four productions — "Six Characters" and "Ward No. Six" — dropped the fourth wall dividing actors and audience, allowing the companies to translate the new openness literally in their theatrical vocabulary. The Stary Theater's "Hamlet IV" and "The Dybbuk" demonstrated similar aspirations by experimenting with theatrical perspective.

In this impressive festival-within-a-festival of Soviet and Eastern European theater, one felt a sense of the theater artists not only revealing themselves to the West but also concentratedly mulling over the role of their art in a climate that for the moment at least has allowed them an exhilarating — and challenging — freedom of expression.

1989 Jl 29, 16:1

Spiffy Piffle

MADAME SHERRY, book and lyrics by Otto Harbach; music by Karl Hoschna; choreography and musical staging by Dan Siretta; directed and adapted by Martin Connor; scenery designed by Eduardo Sicangco; costumes designed by José Lengson; lighting designed by Kirk Bookman; assistant choreographer, Keith Savage; assistant musical director; John McMahon; technical director, John Hugh Minor; resident dramaturg, Tommy Krasker; stage manager, Michael Brunner; associate artistic director, Mr. Siretta; associate producer, Sue Frost; musical supervision by Lynn Crigler; musical direction by Ted Kociolek; dance music by G. Harrell; produced by Michael P. Price. Presented by the Goodspeed Opera House, East Haddam, Conn.

WITH: Adinah Alexander, Heather Berman, Teri Bibb, Molly Brown, Leonard Drum, Douglas Fisher, Tim Foster, Joanna Glushak, Donna Hagan, Gary Kirsch, Renée Laverdiere, Robert R. McCormick, David Monzione, Elizabeth Nackley Aurelio Padron, Rodney Pridgen, Maureen Sadusk and Kevin Weldon.

By STEPHEN HOLDEN

Special to The New York Times

EAST HADDAM, Conn., July 23 — The Manhattan dance studio that is the setting for the first act of the Otto Harbach-Karl Hoschna musical "Madame Sherry" is a place where twittery socialites play at being budding Isadora Duncans. In "Aesthetic Dancing/Every Little Movement," the opening number of the Goodspeed Opera House's glowing revival of the 1910 show, half a dozen students waft about the stage, their chiffon-draped arms spread like giant butterfly wings in an interpretive dance that looks at once silly and sensuous.

The number sets the perfect tone for a musical that, like virtually every other Broadway show of its period, never keeps its feet on the ground. Crammed with mistaken identities and amorous complications, the plot of "Madame Sherry" tells how the studio's playboy proprietor, Edward Sherry (Robert R. Mc-

Diane Sobolewski

Robert R. McCormick and Teri Bibb in "Madame Sherry," at the Goodspeed Opera House in East Haddam, Conn.

Cormick) has to scuffle when his straitlaced benefactor, Uncle Theophilus (Douglas Fisher), unexpectedly arrives on the premises. An archeologist who has spent years scouring Greek antiquities in search of the Venus de Milo's missing arms, the pompous old windbag has subsidized Edward's profligate life in the mistaken assumption that his nephew is a proper family man. It is a fiction that Edward has carefully cultivated in correspondence in which he has described an imaginary wife and two children.

•

Desperate not to be discovered and financially cut off, Edward enlists his sassy dance instructor Lulu (Joanna Glushak) and her Venezuelan suitor Leonardo (Aurelio Padron) to pose as his children and his blowsy housekeeper Catherine (Maureen Sadusk) to act as his wife. Further complicating matters are the appearances of Theophilus's beautiful niece Yvonne (Teri Bibb), fresh from a convent, and Pepita (Adinah Alexander) the dagger-wielding Venezuelan spitfire whom Leonardo left behind. Pepita's dagger, which used to belong to her mother, once killed "three faithless lovers in one swell poop," she boasts ominously.

It takes a lot of ingenuity to make this sort of piffle fly, but the Goodspeed Opera production, directed by Martin Connor with musical staging by Dan Siretta, maintains a spirit of continuous levity. In the show's original production, the most famous song, "Put Your Arms Around Me, Honey," by Albert Von Tilzer and Junie McCree, was interpolated into the show shortly after it opened on Broadway. And the Goodspeed production has added "Oh! You Beautiful Doll" (by Nat D. Ayer and Seymour Brown), "Ciribiribin," (the 1898

waltz by A. Pestalozza and Nathan Haskell Dole), and "Cuddle Up a Little Closer, Lovey Mine," from the 1908 Hoschna-Harbach show "Three Twins," among others.

•

These interpolations are in keeping with the history of a musical that, in steering away from operetta, was constructed to accommodate performances of the hits of the day in vaudeville fashion. The added songs bolster the plot, underscoring the show's warm-blooded point of view toward erotic expression while remaining true to the spirit of the period. And together they offer a delightful pastiche of turn-of-the-century pop styles. In the show's most exhilarating number, "Walking the Dog," Mr. Siretta, the Goodspeed's gifted choreographer, has outdone himself with a witty set piece in which the members of the ensemble are dragged slinkily around the stage by imaginary canines on leashes.

The cast of unknowns provides some snappy performances, most notably the sharp, high-spirited caricatures by Miss Glushak, Miss Alexander and Miss Sadusk. Mr. McCormick's Edward exudes the right glint of rakishness, and Miss Bibb displays a strong lyric soprano. Without straining for opulence, Eduardo Sicangco's scenery, José Lengson's spiffy costumes and Kirk Bookman's lighting design evoke an oldtime New York glamour that is especially effective in rippling, blue-lighted scenes aboard Uncle Theophilus's yacht.

1989 Jl 30, 57:1

Sex and Unhappiness

BOOCHIE and EVERY GOODBYE AIN'T GONE
... , two one-act plays directed by Mikell
Pinkney; scenic and costume design by Felix
E. Cochren; lighting by Christian Epps; production stage manager, Avan. Presented by
the Billie Holiday Theater, executive director,
Marjorie Moon. At 1368 Fulton Street, Brooklyn.

BOOCHIE, by Mari Evans.

Joy .... Denise Burse-Mickelbury

EVERY GOODBYE AIN'T GONE.... , by Bill
Harris.

Frank Dandridge .... Marcus Naylor
Rula Payton .... Gwendolyn Roberts Frost

By D. J. R. BRUCKNER

"On my honor I will do my best/To
take what they give me and steal the
rest" is the motto of Frank Dandridge, a soldier who, against all
odds, persuades an aloof nightclub
singer to marry him in "Every Goodbye Ain't Gone...." by Bill Harris.
But the wedding is hardly a victory.
Rula Payton, the singer he marries,
will give love only when she feels like
it, and when she finally does, he finds
he cannot take it.

"Every Goodbye," a bittersweet
look at two bright and frightened people trapped in themselves, is the second of two one-act plays sharing a bill
at the Billie Holiday Theater, 1368
Fulton Street, in the Bedford-Stuyvesant section of Brooklyn. The plot is
nothing new, but Mr. Harris concentrates on creating two engaging characters who are never quite in step as
they perform an elaborate dance of
seeking and escaping each other.

The principal weakness in this play
is that Frank has to act as the narrator as well as the protagonist; this is
a clumsy dramatic device, and Marcus Naylor in the role seems at times
distracted by the narrative mono-

logues. Once he is engaged in the battle of wit and affection that Frank
carries on with Rula, he is more comfortable with his lines and at times
manages to give Frank something of
a tragic dimension.

Rula, as portrayed by Gwendolyn
Roberts-Frost, is an intelligent and
passionate woman whose seductiveness is all the more dangerous because she has no control over it. The
Billie Holiday has given us the chance
to see Ms. Roberts-Frost in very different roles in the last few years, and
one of the pleasures of watching her
comes from her ability to reveal the
actor at work without ever stepping
out of character. There is a tension
between two powerful personalities,
her own and her character's, that is
almost palpable.

"Boochie" by Mari Evans, which
opens the evening, is a tough acting
challenge. Joy, a woman who has
loved too deeply and too blindly, has
to let an audience see two lovers, a
couple of other adults and her small
son as these ghosts in her memory
slowly and painfully force her to yield
up an appalling secret she has hidden
from herself for years.

As an essay on child abuse, the play
is a poignant but predictable piece.
But Denise Burse-Mickelbury as Joy
remembering all those other people
turns it into an entrancing descent
into horror, made all the more painful
by the moments of domestic peace
and laughter. There is little action in
this one-woman piece; Ms. Burse-
Mickelbury has to rely entirely on her
voice. More accurately: voices — and
resonant voices they are. The last
minute of the play is a stunning vision
of Joy sitting in her kitchen which
has become her hell, but the echoes of
those voices go on haunting one long
after that vision has faded.

1989 Jl 30, 57:2

John Wood in "The Man Who Came to Dinner," playing in London's West End.
Alastair Muir

On London Stage, the 'A's' Are Rather Flat

By MEL GUSSOW

Special to The New York Times

LONDON, July 31 — This summer
the West End is giving its regards to
Off Broadway as well as to Broadway, with "Frankie and Johnny in the
Clair de Lune" and "Steel Magnolias" joining "Anything Goes" and
other musicals. Opening in August is
a new American play, Donald Freed's
"Veteran's Day," starring Jack Lem-
mon and Michael Gambon.

Swimming with the current, the
Royal Shakespeare Company is hav-
ing its own American season with
Moss Hart and George S. Kaufman's
1939 comedy, "The Man Who Came to
Dinner" (starring John Wood) and
the premiere of Richard Nelson's
"Some Americans Abroad."

Though "The Man Who Came to
Dinner" has been treated to an elaborate production on the main Barbican
stage, it is Mr. Nelson's small, unpretentious comedy in the Pit that offers
the greater diversion. This is a light
comedy with an underlying mordancy about America's ambiguous
love affair with everything English.

Fifty years after its Broadway premiere and during Kaufman's own
centenary year, "The Man Who Came
to Dinner" is less than historical. The
character of Sheridan Whiteside was
intended as a lampoon of the critic
and curmudgeon Alexander Woolcott,
but was so admiring of its protagonist
that Woolcott himself eventually
played the role on stage. The character's sallies, most of them directed
against small-town America and
Whiteside's reluctant hosts, today
seem abusive rather than acerbic.

In response to his doctor's question,
"May I call in later this afternoon?"
the wheelchair-bound Whiteside says,
"If you do, I will spit right in your
eye." There is no way such bluntness
can be made to seem humorous. It is
not until much later in the play when
Whiteside reveals the humanity (or,
rather, the sentimentality) behind his
irascibility that Mr. Wood locates the
comedy.

Before that, one must endure an in-
tricate, unfunny first act during
which one remembers other sounder
Kaufman-Hart collaborations ("You
Can't Take It With You," "Once in a
Lifetime"). "The Man Who Came to

Dinner" is less a social comedy than
an idle commentary on celebrity worship, with enough names dropped to
make it a 1930's trivia test.

A measure of fun is provided by two
cameo characters — a theatrical bon
vivant with more than a passing
resemblance to Noël Coward, and a
comedian named Banjo who cavorts
in films with his brothers Wacko and
Sloppo. Desmond Barrit plays Banjo
as if he were Zero (as in Mostel), one
of the production's two novelties; the

An Americanized season includes Richard Nelson as well as Moss Hart.

other is that Mr. Wood is a thin rather
than a fat Whiteside, looking more
like a saturnine Shaw.

Although Mr. Wood is not a natural
clown, he is funniest in moments of
physical comedy, simultaneously
wagging his eyebrows and his whiskers and doing a double take by suddenly wheeling his chair backward on
stage. For Mr. Wood, Whiteside is
clearly a busman's holiday between
acting in "The Tempest" and the
forthcoming "Master Builder."

The play is well-made, if contrived,
and it becomes more amusing as it
proceeds — although a collage of
Christmas tunes at the start of each
act adds unnecessary time to the
evening. Led by Gene Saks, as guest
American director, supporting actors
add their own deft touches, especially
so in the case of Barrie Ingham as the
mock Coward and Cherry Morris as
an ex-ax murderer maneuvered into
the plot.

At least one British critic was quick
to accuse the Royal Shakespeare
Company of doing the play to cater to
American tourists. Though certainly
many Americans will see it, the appeal, I think, is primarily to English
audiences, which seem to like their
comedy emphatic.

In one of many funny moments in
"Some Americans Abroad," an expatriate American, with increasing futility, tries to describe the humor of a
broad television farce to her visiting
countrymen. She ends with the observation: "What's amazing about Eng-

land is that in time you begin to find
this sort of thing funny as well. Or so
I'm told."

In common with "The Man Who
Came to Dinner," "Some Americans
Abroad" drops names, but to greater
comic advantage, as, for example, in
telling about a retired American couple choosing to settle in Jamesian
Rye rather than Dickensian London.

Following a group of academics on
a whirlwind theatrical tour, the
comedy moves briskly through all the
required stops — from the Lyttleton
buffet at the National Theater to
Foyles bookstore to Stratford-Upon-
Avon, making astute comments at
each point about the customs and
crotchets of both English and Americans. What makes the play especially entertaining are Mr. Nelson's
thrusts at academia. The dialogue
has some of the sardonic feeling of
David Lodge's comic novels. Each of
the characters is gently self-spoofing.

In earlier Richard Nelson plays,
one could often hear the political
gears grinding. Here there is an assurance in the storytelling, and political points are made with subtlety,
especially in reference to the contradictions between the morality of the
art the characters are teaching and
the apparent lack of morality in their
own lives.

Anton Lesser, as the new head of
the English department, poses as a
deep thinker, but he is a borrower and
a blender of the ideas of others. Professionally, he is a coward who
speaks with permanently forked
tongue, offering small bribes (expenses for dinner) in lieu of reward
for services rendered — an attitude
that is of course not limited to the
teaching profession.

In the course of the play, Mr.
Lesser bungles two crises. A fellow
teacher is accused of molesting a student in the tour group and the chairman has the assignment of dismissing a congenial colleague (Simon
Russell Beale, who alternates at the
Pit as a hilarious fop in "The Man of
Mode," a Restoration comedy by Sir
George Etherege.) Mr. Beale, who is
a born victim, may in fact be the only
true teacher of the group. The others
are so mired in careerism that they
scarcely have time to read books.

Under Roger Michell's nimble direction, the production moves fluidly
from scene to scene. The actors are
precisely in character and are also
secure with their American accents.
Mr. Nelson could flesh out a few more

of the characters, including a misanthropic retired professor (John Bott) — in contrast to Sheridan Whiteside, his insults are funny — and the one American (Joe Melia) not involved in the tour. He could act more as a chorus.

The play delightfully skewers cant and intellectual pomposity, while also making a mockery of such tourist customs as check-splitting and pence-pinching. Even as we enjoy "Some Americans Abroad," one question remains: Can the play travel to the United States? The most receptive audience would seem to be those very people Mr. Nelson is satirizing, Americans eager to be at home in England.

1989 Ag 1, C13:3

Far-Flung Stories

THE PEOPLE WHO COULD FLY, conceived and directed by Joe Hart; sets, Ron Kadri; costumes, Vicki Esposito; lights, Chris Gorzelik; assistant director, Jackie Gill. The Warp and Woof Theater Company presented by Eric Krebs, in association with South Street Theater. At 424 West 42d Street.

WITH: Rich Bianco, Heide Brehm, Michael Calderone, Caprice Cosgrove, John DiMggio, Jacqueline Gregg, Jennifer Krasnansky, Christopher Petit, Anne Shapiro, Steve Siegler, Kristina Swedlund and Scott Wasser.

By D. J. R. BRUCKNER

Right at the beginning of "The People Who Could Fly," an addled potter in India mistakes an enormous tiger for his donkey and captures the surprised beast. From that moment this fantastic enactment of six tales from around the world soars into strange and enchanting places of the imagination.

The Shoestring Players, an ensemble created by the Warp and Woof Theater Company, using almost no props other than a few pieces of cloth, are wizards of illusion in this magical entertainment at the South Street Theater. A pair of hands becomes a dripping roof, another pair the splash the drip makes below. A group of actors forms a rosebush whose blossoms beckon an unwary young girl to pluck them.

•

Fairies in a glen appear and disappear like fireflies; elfin wolves and elfin serpents menace lovers in the moonlight; two rows of seated actors are transformed into a babbling river where a massive wrestler in medieval Japan meets a trio of women he cannot refuse; a hilarious barbarian army roars over a mountain pass only to be routed by a simple fool; a crazy devil living in a garden in which the trees are all steel and the soil all rubber is outwitted by a smart aleck who elopes with the devil's daughter.

This troupe is especially fond of birds. Mysterious birds fly into a well in Majorca and create a fabulous banquet, complete with a Madeira fountain, for a prince who is himself a bird; the son of a witch doctor remembers a secret word that turns slaves in the American South into birds that fly away to freedom; in one astonishing scene a man mounts a giant eagle composed of a dozen actors and flies it over the oceans.

•

There is obviously a special appeal for children in these stories from India, Majorca, Haiti, Scotland, Japan and America, but anyone who is too old to be delighted by them is too old altogether. Under the direc-

Suzanne Karp

Scott Wasser in "The People Who Could Fly."

tion of Joe Hart, and to the accompaniment of muted, beautiful percussion sounds, the Shoestring Players tell them with the precision, grace and energy of a speaking ballet company.

But Mr. Hart has trained his crew in a good deal more than movement and pantomime. The people, animals, apparitions and, in some cases, even plants and rocks in these stories are strong characters brought fully to life by the actors with wonderful economy. Mr. Hart is an ingenious storyteller; the brief dialogue he has written for each piece is spare, eloquent and often very funny. Even in the one tale that gets a little heavy-handed, the one that gives the evening its name, the language has the simplicity, directness and resonance one associates with the oldest and best folk stories.

"The People Who Could Fly" is two hours of theatrical magic that seems to pass in a few moments of happy dreaming.

1989 Ag 3, C20:3

Parents' Pin Hopes On Son's Rooster

EL CORONEL NO TIENE QUIEN LE ESCRIBA (NO ONE WRITES TO THE COLONEL) from a story by Gabriel García Márquez; adapted and directed by Carlos Giménez; translated by Nina Miller; set and costume design by Rafael Reyeros; lighting design by José Jimenez; original music by Federico Ruiz. Presented by Joseph Papp. At the Public/Newman Theater, 425 Lafayette Street.

The Colonel	José Tejera
The Colonel's Wife	Aura Rivas
Best Friend	Anibal Grunn
Postal Administrator	Francisco Alfaro
Doctor	Daniel Lopez
Lawyer	Pedro Pineda
Alvaro	Aitor Gaviria
German	Eric Wildpret
Alfonso	José Borges
Friend of Agustín	Rolando Felizola
Wife of Sabas and Wife of Black Man	
	Mimi Sills
Assassin	Norman Santana
Friends of the Colonel's Son	
Carlos Garcia, Garbriel Flores and Fabian Rodriguez	

By STEPHEN HOLDEN

In the fiction of Gabriel García Márquez, the weight of history hangs like a stone in the sweltering atmosphere, and the spirits of the dead haunt the living in feverish dreams. Time stands still in the sense that the dead continue to stir as long as the tiniest memory of them persists. For the living, dreams of the distant past are often more vivid than the grinding physical realities of the present. Nothing essentially changes. In an atmosphere simmering with political unrest, the revolutions that sweep the land leave conditions only worse than before.

Finding theatrical corollaries for Mr. García Márquez's static, time-warped dream world of ghosts, rain and memories isn't the easiest task facing a director. But in "El Coronel No Tiene Quien Le Escriba" ("No One Writes to the Colonel"), a dramatic adaptation by the Venezuelan theater troupe Rajatabla of a García Márquez story, the rhythms and moods of the author's prose are illuminated with precision and economy.

•

The drama, which opened the Festival Latino at the Public Theater on Tuesday, begins and ends with a surrealistic, rain-drenched funeral procession that symbolizes the playwright's vision of a Latin America somnolent with mourning. By the end of the evening, about the only thing that has happened is that the main characters, a retired army colonel (José Tejera) and his wife (Aura Rivas) who are slowly dying from hunger in a distant, unnamed army outpost, are closer to death. They are losing the ability to distinguish between food and excrement.

"El Coronel No Tiene Quien Le Escriba," directed and adapted by Carlos Giménez, is one of Mr. García Márquez's darker stories, for it is unleavened by the loamy eroticism that gives much of the author's work an added emotional tug. As the play opens, Agustín, the couple's son, who was assassinated while passing out revolutionary leaflets, is being mourned by the town where he grew up. As the play unfolds, Agustín's proud, ailing parents bicker over what to do with their son's fighting rooster, whose sale may be their best hope for a life-sustaining annuity.

•

Sensing that the rooster doesn't really belong to him but to the town whose dormant life force it represents, the colonel is reluctant to go through with the sale. For more than 15 years he has been counting on receiving the pension that was once promised to him as a fighter in a revolution that has sunk the nation further into poverty and repression. Although friends remind him that many presidents and scores of bureaucracies have come and gone in the faraway capital city, he still remains certain of imminent restitution. And every Friday when the mail arrives by coastal riverboat, he visits the port expecting good news.

Efficiently and with a minimum of flash, the director creates a world in which natural forces, social traditions and sorrowful memories reinforce a feeling of overwhelming spiritual stagnation. Periodically, claps of thunder and torrential rains erupt outside the door of the colonel's barrackslike house, whose walls are expanded by the play's end to suggest

Miguel Garcia

José Tejera in "El Coronel No Tiene Quien Le Escriba"

the borders of the world. The downpours, the recurrent toll of church bells, swelling organ music and the slow-motion movements of silently observant ghosts give the drama a solemn, ritualistic flow.

The tone of the acting, stage design and hallucinatory lighting matches dialogue in which the characters complain about the endless rainy season, their physical aches and pains and the prices of things. Some of the most striking recurrent images are of half-naked people sitting in metal tubs and gazing skyward as they wring soaking clothes over their bodies to try to cool themselves.

Mr. Tejera's portrayal of the colonel, though very low-key, still gives him the dimensions of a Marquezian everyman. A dreamer who cowers under his dignified exterior, he is an ironic comic hero because of his blind faith. As his practical, penny-pinching wife, Miss Rivas gives a performance that starts out muted and slowly rises in desperation. Like so many of Mr. García Márquez's characters, they would rather entrust their destinies to fate than break the spell of expectation.

"El Coronel No Tiene Quien Le Escriba" is being performed through Saturday at the Newman Theater. All performances are in Spanish; simultaneous translation via headphones is available for the Saturday matinee and evening performances. The play is the first of seven Latin American dramas to be presented during the monthlong festival.

1989 Ag 3, C17:1

Life and Dreams

EL GRAN CIRCO E.U. CRANIANO (THE GREAT U.S. KRANIAL CIRCUS) written, directed and translated by Myrna Casas; set design by José M. Llompart; costume design by Wayne Thomas Seitz; lighting design by Toni Fernandez; makeup by Migdalia Correa; stage manager, Mr. Llompart. Producciones Cisne. Festival Latino in New York, Oscar Ciccone and Cecilia Vega, directors, presented by Joseph Papp. Associate producer, Jason Steven Cohen. At the Public/Anspacher Theater, 425 Lafayette Street.

By RICHARD F. SHEPARD

When midsummer torpor imbues the theatergoer with a sense of overwork at the mere mention of the word experimental, the arrival of a Puerto Rican company with just such a production at the start of the Festival Latino in New York should banish all such forebodings.

The show is different. It is refreshing. It is funny. It is lifelike and warm. And don't be frightened by "experimental"; it is intelligible, both in its spoken Spanish for the cognoscenti and in its simultaneous English translation via earpiece for the uninitiated. The play's author and director is Myrna Casas, and it is being staged through Sunday at the Public Theater by Producciones Cisne, a 25-year-old nonprofit theater company.

It is called "El Gran Circo E.U. Cranio," a title that is translated in the program as "The Great U.S. Kranial Circus." This is a tip-off on the approach of this ingenious presentation. It is set in a small circus in Puerto Rico (actually, it could be anywhere) and the acts are all inventions of the performers, seemingly improvised stories.

●

The stories smack of reality: a woman in a crowded airplane recalling her sojourn with her daughter in Hartford; another woman telling of the violent death of a young man who may or may not be her son. Are the stories really true? No matter; they reflect realities of life far more effectively than a documentary could. There is a theme here but not a plot: the piece is about life and dreams and the blurriness of self-perception.

Do not for a minute think this is all sobersided stuff; just when you are taking things mournfully to heart there is something to jerk you back to wry — there we go again — reality. Above all, there is a kind of Saroyanesque humanity and buoyancy that pervades the production.

Under the ministrations of Ms. Casas, the eight-member cast performs in a natural, earthy manner. The company not only works well together but it also establishes an intimate rapport with its audience.

Josie Perez, a Puerto Rican television and stage personality who is also president of the Cisnes troupe, portrays the circus owner with considerable dignity and forbearance, a sort of mother hen whose own troubles emerge as the play progresses. Angel Domenech catches the quality of uncertainty buried within a man whose exterior is tough and streetwise.

Elsa Roman, as one of the performers in the circus, is particularly appealing as a mature woman, with a peasant earthiness and the hint of better days in the past. Everyone concerned, as a matter of fact, contributes to the sense of humanity and warmth that pervade the piece. Experimental it may be, but you won't need a seat belt to keep you from nodding off.

1989 Ag 4, C15:1

Stratford's 'Silent Woman' Speaks Volumes

CASUAL DRESS IS THE MODE ON stage at Stratford this summer. Hamlet lounges around the castle at Elsinore in his pajamas, as if he had brought the wrong clothes home from Wittenberg. Still wearing pajamas, he sleepwalks through "To be or not to be," redirects the Players and enters Gertrude's bedchamber looking as if it were time for him to retire. In his mother's room, he suddenly extracts a dagger from his pajama bottoms in order to slay Polonius. Inexplicably, Polonius is hiding under the covers in Gertrude's bed, despite the fact that there is an appropriate arras in the background. Not until he is shipped away to England does Hamlet change his costume, and then he simply puts on an overcoat over his pajamas.

Bedding down for the night in the forest, the lovers in "A Midsummer Night's Dream" change to their own varieties of night dress. If Oberon had only told Puck to look for the Athenian in the striped pajamas, there might have been no confusion of identities. I am not sure what the directors (Ron Daniels for "Hamlet," John Caird for "A Midsummer Night's Dream") are trying to say with this odd costuming choice, but in neither case is it helpful to an understanding of the play.

As it turns out, "A Midsummer Night's Dream" is by far the most rewarding of the three productions on the main stage ("Cymbeline" is being performed in addition to "Hamlet"). The principal attractions at Stratford this summer are both at the smaller Swan Theater — an exuberant revitalization of Ben Jonson's seldom performed comedy, "The Silent Woman or Epicoene," and an articulate evocation of Christopher Marlowe's "Dr. Faustus." The third production at the Swan, "Romeo and Juliet," is not without its own eccentricities.

In Stratford soon after the death of Lord Olivier, it was difficult to watch the plays in the current repertory without being aware of the shadow cast by the great English actor. The most challenging assignment is undertaken by Mark Rylance, who plays both Hamlet and Romeo. In each case, he is wide of the mark established by Lord Olivier and contenders for his acting crown. Actually, there is not a great difference between Mr. Rylance's two characterizations. When Juliet asks, "Wherefore art thou, Romeo?," the most reasonable answer would be, "Elsinore."

Mr. Rylance's Romeo is moody and petulant, the very soul of inaction in a role that calls for impetuousness. The approach, naturally, is used to better advantage as Hamlet. But the production of "Hamlet" forces the actor to suffer a series of indignities, not all of which concern those ubiquitous bedclothes. At one point, for example, Claudius immerses Hamlet head first in a small washtub, making it look as if Hamlet is dunking for apples. It must be said in Mr. Rylance's defense that he has a command of Shakespearean language, leading one to think that in less aberrant and self-indulgent circumstances he might prove equal to his roles.

This is more than can be said for David O'Hara, who is equally ineffectual as Mercutio

'Silent Woman' and 'Dr. Faustus' are principal attractions at Stratford this summer.

and Posthumus (in "Cymbeline"). In both of these roles he speaks with a thick Scottish burr,

a fact that blurs his already blunted diction. In "Romeo and Juliet," he is an earthbound Mercutio, a bogus Brando to Mr. Rylance's variation on James Dean.

Assuming an air of forced intensity, Mr. Rylance and his Juliet, Georgia Slowe, do not convince us of their passionate relationship. He seems to be avoiding eye contact with all the other actors, while, in her exceedingly mannered performance, she appears to be trying to stare everyone into submission.

In both "Hamlet" and "Romeo and Juliet" there are mitigating factors. Mr. Daniels's production of "Hamlet," as designed by Antony McDonald, is visually striking. With all angles at a tilt, Elsinore looks to be in mortal jeopardy, as if the ship of state were sinking. Heightening the image, cycloramic views of clouds and turbulent seas are seen through large picture windows. The older actors are stalwart — Clare Higgins as Gertrude, Peter Wight as Claudius and, in particular, Patrick Godfrey as Polonius. Rebecca Saire also offers a touching lost-girl portrait of Ophelia, a refreshing contrast to Ms. Slowe's Juliet.

In "Romeo" it is also the older actors who stabilize the play, beginning with Patrick Godfrey, who makes Friar Laurence far less an interfering busybody than he often seems. There is some question whether or not "Romeo" belongs on the Swan stage, supposedly reserved for lesser-known plays of the period. But, as directed by Terry Hands, the work benefits from being enacted in such close proximity to the audience, especially in the slashing dueling scenes.

■

In all respects, Danny Boyle's version of "The Silent Woman" is the most assured and stylish production at Stratford. This neglected comedy resoundingly merits revival, at least when it is done with such humor and conviction. A bitter, even dire, comedy about marriage and miserliness, it has a decided absence of heroes. The ostensible villain is an old bachelor suitably named Morose who has a pathological hatred of noise in a world in which cacophony is a way of life. Posed against him are three playful young worthies, including Morose's nephew, who covets his uncle's money. In order to produce an alternate heir, Morose decides to marry and chooses a silent, shy and

Alastair Muir

Members of the Stratford-on-Avon cast of "The Silent Woman"—an assured and stylish production that stimulates an ensemble jauntiness from its actors.

subservient woman. In a hilarious hoax, all tables are turned. Nothing is what it seems to be, beginning with that not-so-silent woman.

The besieged Morose is amusingly played in self-spoofing, Scrooge-like manner by David Bradley, who wears a large pillow around his head as an oversize earmuff. As one of his crotchets, he insists that his servant, Mute, answer his questions not with words but by pawing the ground with his right foot, which makes Mute seem like a vaudeville horse doing its arithmetic. This leads to a mirthful motif, including a wonderful sight gag in which the servant enters bearing a three-tiered wedding cake. Responding to his master's question, he bobs his head right into the frosting. The joke is of course not in the script, but, I imagine, Jonson, Marlowe and Shakespeare all would have laughed.

The catalyst for the comedy is a rogue named Truewit, who, in Richard McCabe's diabolical performance, lives up to his name. Mr. McCabe, the most virtuosic actor currently at Stratford, merrily manipulates everyone to his purpose (although Morose's greedy nephew has a major surprise saved for the play's ending). The rest of the cast, all roles well acted, include an outrageous fop (Sir Amorous La Foole), a pretentious poetizer and a chorus of flibbertygibbets.

This is exactly the kind of play one looks forward to seeing at the Swan. It belies its obscurity, offers provocative commentary on social injustices of the times (especially in regards to women) and stimulates an ensemble jauntiness from its actors. Of all the plays at Stratford, it also has the most splendiferous use of costumes for scenic effect.

In contrast, though with commensurate success, Barry Kyle's production of "Dr. Faustus" has a suitable starkness. The director and his company, headed by Gerard Murphy giving a powerful performance in the title role, distills the play to its essence, freeing it from pretension while emphasizing the philosophical argument. David Bradley's Mephistopheles is matter-of-fact, a visiting professor who has wandered into Faust's study with a nefarious, soul-searching offer.

■

Mr. Murphy's youthful Faust is swept away by his own yearning for knowledge and experience (one could imagine Richard Thomas, in a similar production, undertaking the role in America). Richard McCabe, as the clownish servant Wagner, is a leavening presence. The deadly sins are unembellished — clever, choreographic impressions performed by adept actors. In this all-male production, actors play Faust's fantasy women, adding a dimension of dementia to the nightmarish surroundings. There is one other curious note — again in the area of costuming. Beneath their robes, the academicians wear Reeboks.

Watching "Dr. Faustus," one is reminded of Jan Kott's tantalizing suggestion that Faust and Hamlet may have been at Wittenberg at the same time. With this in mind, it might be interesting to see paired productions of the plays, revealing the divergent effects of the Wittenberg University experience.

The seasonal crowd-pleaser — as it often is — is "A Midsummer Night's Dream," in a light-hearted, jovial version by Mr. Caird. This is in direct contrast to the darker and more magical tones of Benjamin Britten's opera, as staged again this summer by Peter

Alastair M▮

Gerard Murphy in the title role of Dr. Faustus and behind him David Bradley as Mephistopheles in Stratford-on-Avon production.

Hall at Glyndebourne. Mr. Caird's eclectic modernization does almost anything for a laugh -- and sometimes goes too far. But the play maintains its refreshing guilelessness, appealing to the youngest (as well as older) theatergoers.

This is one production in which all three comic aspects are equally amusing — the mechanicals led by David Troughton's boastful Bottom; the lovers (in particular, Amanda Bellamy's Hermia and Sarah Crowden's Helena) and Richard McCabe's Puck. Mr. McCabe plays Puck as an English schoolboy prankster, a class cut-up who savors his mischief almost as much as we do. As with other plays at Stratford, the production suffers in the design area, in this case because of its cluttered staircase set that looks as if it were left over from a production of "Nicholas Nickleby."

■

There is one production at Stratford that is totally missable — Bill Alexander's version of "Cymbeline." Had I not seen Peter Hall's version of the play last year at the National Theater (featuring an extraordinary performance by Geraldine James as Imogen) or Mark Lamos's earlier, imaginative production at the Hartford Stage, I might think that there was a curse on the play. Call it "the British tragedy," and do not mention it by name, especially in an actor's dressing room. Superstition aside, "Cymbeline" can be staged effectively, but it demands considerably more insight and far better casting than is currently exhibited at Stratford.

Though the production is more coherent than the one directed by JoAnne Akalaitis for the New York Shakespeare Festival, it is also misguided. The performances veer from histrionics to lassitude. In his limited appearances, Cymbeline brusquely shoves aside anyone who gets in his way while Iachimo seems to have no zest for his duplicity. As Imogen, a role that needs an authoritative presence, Naomi Wirthner is unassertive, certainly not

the nonpareil of Shakespeare's imagination. David Troughton, as the luckless villain, Cloten, provides the production's single auspicious note, enhancing a role with a clownish deviltry.

Highlighted by Mr. Troughton (as Cloten and Bottom), Mr. Bradley (Morose coupled with Mephistopheles), the lovers in "A Midsummer Night's Dream," Mr. Murphy's Faust and Mr. McCabe's triple-witted Puck, Wagner and Truewit, the Stratford season is rich in character acting.   □

1989 Ag 6, II:5:1

Madcap Rome

A FUNNY THING HAPPENED ON THE WAY TO THE FORUM, book by Burt Shevelove and Larry Gelbart; music and lyrics by Stephen Sondheim; direction and musical staging by Albert Takazauckas; music direction by John Johnson; scenery by Ralph Funicello; costumes by Beaver Bauer; lighting by Derek Duarte; wigs and hair by Rick Echols; sound by Daryl Bornstein. The American Conservatory Theater presented by the American Festival Theater. At 1850 Elm Street, Stratford, Conn.

Senex	Peter Donat
Domina	Ruth Kobart
Hero	Mark Daniel Cade
Hysterium	Howard Swain
Pseudolus	Michael McShane
Erronius	Dan Kremer
Miles Gloriosus	Michael X. Martin
Lycus	Drew Eshelman
Tintinabula	Karen Lew
Panacea	Cathy Thomas-Grant
Gemini Twins	
	Paula Markowitz and Marcia Pizzo
Vibrata	Velina Brown
Gymnasia	Gina Ferrall
Philia	Nancy Carlin
Proteans	
Michael Scott Ryan, Stephen Weingartner and John Furse	

By RICHARD F. SHEPARD

Special to The New York Times

STRATFORD, Conn., Aug. 3 — The funny thing that is happening near Interstate 95, a road otherwise outstanding for tragically bottlenecked traffic on the New England trade

route, is the musical that is opening the season for the American Festival Theater here.

The presentation is a revival of "A Funny Thing Happened on the Way to the Forum," with music and lyrics by Stephen Sondheim and book by Burt Shevelove and Larry Gelbart (adapted, quite loosely, from the comedies of Plautus, who worked in ancient Rome). "Forum" first opened on Broadway in 1962, and with the formidable Zero Mostel prancing about in the madcap lead, the show ran for more than two years. For those who may remember only Mr. Mostel's joyfully dominating presence, a visit to Stratford may remind them how tuneful the show is on its own.

●

The American Conservatory Theater is producing "Forum," which will run through Aug. 13 in the comfortable playhouse on the grounds of the Festival Theater, which used to be known as the American Shakespeare Theater. The company, directed by Albert Takazauckas, brings considerable talent and requisite humor to this fast-moving, wisecracking farce so redolent of old burlesque comedy. When it is good, it is very, very good, but when it is slow, mostly during the romantic interludes, it is as dead-stopped as the traffic on the nearby highway.

The whole thing hangs on a plot that the writers have fashioned more as a line on which to hang their wiseguy dialogue than as a story intended to make you fear for the outcome. The outcome runs, even gallops, right through the two acts. What happens is that a slave, Pseudolus, wants his freedom and is promised it by his handsome young owner, Hero, if he arranges a union with Philia, a virgin already presold by her owner to a military man who is on his way to fetch her.

Micheal McShane is splendid as the quick-thinking, unprincipled slave. He recalls, in girth and energy, Mr. Mostel, but he is very much his own interpreter, with his own way of feigning servility, registering duplicity and generally bringing together this glorious collage of loose

Micheal McShane as Pseudolus in "A Funny Thing Happened on the Way to the Forum."

ends. Howard Swain, as Hysterium, chief slave of the house, is a hands-on comic — that is, he uses his hands as much as his mouth to express what he is up to and he is very funny while doing it. Peter Donat, as the lecherous father of the house, is a Roman version of a comic-strip Jiggs, henpecked by his Maggie of a wife, overwhelmingly portrayed by Ruth Kobart, and he is at his best in the song called "Everybody Ought to Have a Maid."

Michael X. Martin, as the captain come for his bride, is handsome, with a good voice and an aptitude for comedy, as he shows in vaunting the military man's egotism and love of war.

Whether the songs will be immortal, only time will tell, but many of them have survived tunefully for a quarter of a century now: "Comedy Tonight," "Impossible" and "Lovely," to mention a few.

All of which is to say that if you are headed north and east on the Interstate and there is gridlock ahead, pull out at Exit 32 and head for the American Festival Theater. There's comedy tonight.

1989 Ag 6, 49:3

Departure of 'Oh! Calcutta!,' And Attitudes of an Old Era

By FRANK RICH

On a sweltering August night when the entire population was looking for any excuse to take off its clothes, "Oh! Calcutta!" threw in the towel at last.

Sunday night was the 5,959th and final Broadway performance of "the world's longest running erotic stage musical" — the show that began its career in 1969 as a chic, notorious avatar of what was once called "the sexual revolution" but that in recent years settled into the anonymity of those New York tourist spots patronized mainly by visitors who don't speak English too well. "Oh! Calcutta!" has been running a very, very long time. As I took my seat in the Edison Theater on Sunday, the armrest came off in my hand. Then the entertainment began with a striptease dance baring a truly hard-core anatomical fact: Even "Oh! Calcutta!" is not immune to cellulite.

As Broadway closings go, this one was hardly a sentimental occasion. The house was not packed to overflowing; as the ads used to say, there were good seats available at all

"Oh! Calcutta!," which opened in 1976, is actually a revival. The original "Oh! Calcutta!" ran roughly 1,300 performances from 1969 to 1972, first at the Eden Theater (lately the Second Avenue Theater) Off Broadway, then at the Belasco Theater uptown. So thorny are the statistics that even Variety misplaced about 700 of the pre-Edison performances in its front-page farewell.

In the careers of its distinguished authors, "Oh! Calcutta!" is an asterisk as well. The show was conceived as a jape — "an entertainment in the erotic area in the best possible taste" — by the critic Kenneth Tynan, who rounded up such tony friends as Samuel Beckett, Sam Shepard, John Lennon and Jules Feiffer to contribute sketches, songs and poetry. (Kathleen Tynan says in her invaluable 1967 biography of her husband, "The Life of Kenneth Tynan," that other participants he considered were Peter Brook, Edna O'Brien, Jean-Luc Godard, Federico Fellini, Michael Bennett, Elaine May, Joe Orton, Har-

old Pinter and Tennessee Williams.) It was part of the revue's tongue-in-cheek tone that the Playbill did not identify who wrote what. It's a measure of the writing's slight quality that the authors never made a move of their own to divvy up credit.

"We are not trying to make a revolution," Tynan told reporters before the opening. He wanted to make mischief, fun and money. But 1969 was a time of social upheaval in the United States on all fronts, and "Oh! Calcutta!," with its full nudity and simulated sexual activity, was inevitably seen in the context of such contemporaneous stage and film breakthroughs in erotic frankness as "Hair," "I Am Curious (Yellow)," "Dionysus in 69" and the briefly censored "Che!" Caught in the ideological crossfire, Tynan's show was labeled too mild and schoolboyish silly by serious critics and yet reviled as "hard-core pornography" by The Daily News. Only the public loved it.

"Oh! Calcutta!" must have done something right. A theatrical production doesn't run off and on for 20 years at Broadway ticket prices well into the era of video porn, simply by exposing a few breasts, buttocks and penises. At the closing, the show looked shabby and was performed with the aggressive gaiety one normally encounters only in West End sex farces approaching their 10th anniversaries. Anachronistic dialogue references to Pee-wee Herman, Smurfs and Famous Amos cookies made it clear that strict textual fidelity was not a pressing concern of the management. But the shell of the original, at least, remained, and to see "Oh! Calcutta!" in 1989 was to have an inkling of what once captivated so many theatergoers.

What I saw was a throwback to the "Bob & Carol & Ted & Alice" America of two decades ago — a land of would-be "swinging" couples, newfangled sex therapy and the Playboy Philosophy. It was a place where

women were erotic appendages to men, where the mere mention of euphemisms for sexual organs or acts caused blushing and eye-popping and where masturbation was viewed not as a form of safe sex but as a naughty embarrassment. Two sketches are built around the second and third oldest jokes in creation — lecherous doctors and a farmer's randy son. Male homosexuality, explicitly forbidden from the show by Tynan, is alluded to once, with the word "weirdo." The evening's erotic ballets, accompanied by disco lighting, soft-rock music (some of it by Peter Schickele) and confessional Lenore Kandel poetry, could be a Feiffer parody of a Greenwich Village interpretive dance recital, circa 1964.

Is this an America where many of us would want to live now? Perhaps not, which explains why the native audience of "Oh! Calcutta!" was long ago supplanted by visitors from the Far East. Not only is the show less erotically daring than the advertising spreads in a typical present-day fashion magazine, but "Oh! Calcutta!" also subscribes to social attitudes, whether juvenile or sexist or unknowingly bigoted, that many, the original authors likely included, would now consider antideluvian. It is appropri-

The show's native audience left years ago.

ate that the revue would have finished its New York run in a worn Art Deco building, the Edison Hotel, that is the largest relic of old New York left standing in its typically half-demolished Times Square block. At Sunday's performance, I felt I had

The show set many records, all with qualifications.

prices. A desultory television camera crew loitered about, attracting little curiosity as it went through the motions of recording a slow night's News Event. Most of the audience — respectable-looking couples of all ages and non-New York points of origin — didn't realize it was a witness to history until the producer informed the crowd of the fact in pre-performance remarks from the stage.

Yet history of what import, exactly? In theater history, "Oh! Calcutta!" is an asterisk. For the moment, it is the longest-running production to appear on Broadway, outstripping "A Chorus Line" by 127 performances. But "Oh! Calcutta!" achieved this temporary record in a theater with only one-third as many seats to fill as its competitor, and it stacked the deck by frequently jamming two or three extra performances into the standard eight-performance Broadway week. What's more, the Edison

The New York Times/Ruby Washington

The cast of "Oh! Calcutta!" at the Edison Theater on Sunday as the long-running erotic musical closed.

stepped back into the past like the hero of Jack Finney's time-travel novel, "Time and Again."

Of course, one doesn't want to be carried away by nostalgia. Following the Mapplethorpe uproar and the erosion of Roe v. Wade, there is reason to wonder whether the clock may yet be turned back until the social climate is hospitable again for "Oh! Calcutta!," with its celebration of strict erotic orthodoxy and unchallenged male supremacy. Should that time arrive, there will no doubt be another revival to chalk up still more asterisked performances. For now, however, "Oh! Calcutta!" is closed, and perhaps only its newly unemployed actors have real cause to mourn.

1989 Ag 8, C13:4

Old-Time Machismo, Soulful Communion

SHENANDOAH, book by James Lee Barrett, Peter Udell and Philip Rose; lyrics by Mr. Udell; directed by Mr. Rose; music by Gary Geld; choreographed by Robert Tucker; set design by Kurt Lundell; costumes by Guy Geely; lighting design by Stephen Ross; production stage manager, Mortimer Halpern. Presented by Howard Hurst, Sophie Hurst and Peter Ingster. At the Virginia, 245 West 52d Street.

Charlie Anderson	John Cullum
Jacob	Burke Lawrence
James	Christopher Martin
Nathan	Nigel Hamer
John	Stephen McIntyre
Jenny	Tracey Moore
Henry	Robin Blake
Robert (The Boy)	Jason Zimbler
Anne	Camilla Scott
Gabriel	Roy McKay
Reverend Byrd, Engineer	Donald Saunders
Sam	Thomas Cavanagh
Sgt. Johnson	Jim Selman
Lieutenant	Casper Roos
Tinkham	Richard Liss
Carol	Jim Bearden
Corporal	Stephan Simms
Marauder	Sam Mancuso
Confederate Snipers	
David Connolly, Gerhard Kruschke	

By STEPHEN HOLDEN

Many of the qualities associated with the term old-fashioned musical are abundant in the 1975 show "Shenandoah," which is back on Broadway for a limited run at the Virginia Theater.

A Civil War yarn adapted from a 1965 movie that starred James Stewart, "Shenandoah" has a red-blooded ambiance, and its homey folk-pop score by Gary Geld with lyrics by Peter Udell grasps at the essence of Americana. But it misses.

The best thing about "Shenandoah" is its main character, Charlie Anderson. A rugged John Wayne type who rules firmly over a family of six boys and one girl, he is a cranky, opinionated widower with a warm heart under his leathery exterior. When things get too tough, he repairs to the family plot for soulful communion with his revered dead wife.

Because Charlie is the only figure in "Shenandoah" who is more than a sketch, any production of the show demands a leading actor who crackles with the craggy machismo of a stubborn frontiersman. John Cullum, who reprises his original Tony Award-winning performance, fits the bill perfectly. In Mr. Cullum's detailed, vocally forceful performance, Charlie is thunderously willful, maddeningly superstitious and hot-tempered, but also strong, caring and likable.

The wrinkle in Charlie's personality is that he doesn't believe in fighting other people's wars. When the Civil War comes to the Shenandoah Valley of Virginia, where he and his children tend a prosperous farm, he refuses to let anybody in the family enter the fray. Lest anyone think the Anderson boys are shrinking violets, however, they assure us in the song "Next to Lovin' (I Like Fightin')" that they are just itching to raise some hell on the battlefield.

The Andersons ultimately learn the hard way that when everything around you is in flames, you are bound to catch some of the heat. One day Union soldiers abduct the youngest boy, Robert, because he happens to be wearing a Confederate cap. All but one of the Anderson men leave home to look for him. James, Charlie's oldest son, is instructed to stay on the farm and care for his wife and newborn child, and they become the victims of scavenging soldiers.

Both musically and in its moral tone, "Shenandoah" aspires to be the equal of "Oklahoma!" or "South Pa-

The New York Times/Marilynn K. Yee
John Cullum in the Broadway musical "Shenandoah."

cific," two Rodgers and Hammerstein shows that celebrate American machismo while exploring the meaning of courage and the nature of the male fighting spirit.

The score, though tuneful, lacks any songs with the kind of majesty so abundant in Rodgers and Hammerstein. And the more closely Geld and Udell try to follow Rodgers and Hammerstein, the more they stumble, as in "It's a Boy," a feeble echo of the "Soliloquy" from "Carousel." Ballads like "Violets and Silverbells," the wedding song of Charlie's daughter, Jenny, and her soldier husband, Sam, strive for a classic simplicity but sound only self-consciously cutesy.

When "Shenandoah" opened on Broadway 14 years ago, it had a historical resonance. America's divided emotions over the Vietnam War were still fresh and its wounds were just beginning to mend. In the new production, that resonance is lost.

Because the book, by James Lee Barrett, who wrote the original screenplay, succeeds in developing

only one full-blown character, the show generates no strong sense of family or community. The other members of the Anderson clan have little more substance than the tacky painted scenery through which they move.

•

"Shenandoah" is well constructed in a paint-by-numbers sort of way. The songs are carefully folded into the book's copious dialogue. Instead of an overture, the show uses a martial prologue, "Raise the Flag of Dixie," to set the scene. The story itself is symmetrically framed by scenes of the Anderson family in church. Hearty set pieces on the Anderson homestead are interwoven with Charlie's graveside soliloquies and with playful conversations between Robert (Jason Zimbler) and Gabriel (Roy McKay), his black playmate.

Except for the quavery-voiced performance of Thomas Cavanagh in the role of a shy husband who marries into the family, the supporting cast is adequate. But while the singing and occasional dancing are smooth, the acting under the direction of Philip Rose seems strictly by rote, the exception being Mr. Cullum.

That may help explain why a show that deals with the passions of war feels so cold, mechanical and morally weightless. "Shenandoah" never acquires the dramatic urgency of a serious musical play.

1989 Ag 9, C13:1

Winsome Fugitive From the Humdrum

SHIRLEY VALENTINE, by Willy Russell; directed by Simon Callow; designed by Bruno Santini; lighting by Nick Chelton. Presented by the Really Useful Theater Company and Bob Swash, in association with Paramount Pictures. At the Booth Theater, 222 West 45th Street.

Shirley Valentine .... Ellen Burstyn

By MEL GUSSOW

Willy Russell's "Shirley Valentine" is a monologue that becomes a monodrama, or, more accurately, a monocomedy, offering a resonant portrait of a 42-year-old Liverpool housewife who learns to live more fully by taking a fugitive holiday in Greece. The title role was first played in London and in New York by Pauline Collins, who deservedly won a Tony Award as best actress last season. She has now been succeeded on Broadway by Ellen Burstyn. In the English tradition, one major actress has followed another in a role in which the original has left her imprint.

Ms. Collins's Shirley was a perfect match of actress and character (something that could also be said about Ms. Burstyn's performance as the waitress in the film "Alice Doesn't Live Here Anymore," for which she won an Academy Award). It would be unrewarding to belabor the differences between the two except to say that Ms. Collins is, of course,

Martha Swope
Ellen Burstyn, who has replaced Pauline Collins in "Shirley Valentine."

definably English and that she exuded working-class charm and vulnerability. Her performance has been preserved in the forthcoming film version, co-starring Tom Conti.

•

Ms. Burstyn is a widely accomplished and versatile actress. Emotionally, Shirley is well within her range, and though her Liverpool accent wavers, the spirit of the character remains intact. She is a sweet-tempered survivor, filled with candid and amusing remarks about family, friends and sex, but without an ounce of malice or vulgarity. In contrast to her predecessor, Ms. Burstyn adds a note of gentility and worldliness. She portrays the character unaffectedly and wisely avoids reaching for laughs (they are endemic to the play) or accenting the sentiment.

"Shirley Valentine' is not a play to be taken too seriously. It is not, like Alan Ayckbourn's "Woman in Mind," about a wife going mad, but about a repressed woman realizing how much she has allowed herself to be shortchanged by life. As performed by Ms. Burstyn, Mr. Russell's play remains a blithe and touching character study.

It is the strength of the character that carries the actress, rather than the reverse. Trapped in humdrum domesticity, Shirley is so appealing in

The actress adds gentility to Pauline Collins's role.

her plight and in her growing resolve to do something about it that she becomes disarming. The story of her rite of passage is gracefully told. No other characters appear, but she populates the stage with her imaginative powers of description and her gift for self-dramatization.

Occasionally she speaks for others, including her self-involved husband, her children and, especially, Costas, the Corfu taverna keeper who leads her gently on a romantic voyage of discovery. She even manages to lend character to her favorite sounding board, the wall of her kitchen. "Wall," along with the audience, becomes her confidant, and we silently urge her to proceed on her path to self-realization.

As a play, "Shirley Valentine" is seemingly filled with digressions, with anecdotes about her children in school as well as her life in Liverpool. But as the character correctly observes, everything is linked. This is a one-woman show that earns its stage time.

•

One indication of an actress's absorption in a role is how well she manages the small moments as well as the turning points. When Ms. Burstyn confesses that for once in her life she would like to sip "a glass of wine in a country where the grape is grown," she underscores that line with a look of longing, as if making a promise to herself.

It might have been possible to Americanize Shirley — her story is relevant to an international audience — but that would have been unfair to the character. So much of her heart and her humor derive from her specificity as an Englishwoman. The integrity of the character has been preserved in the present production.

As before, Simon Callow's direction is, in the best sense, unobtrusive, and Bruno Santini's scenic design strikingly pictures the character's disparate habitats. When the second act curtain rises, there is a sigh of sympathy from theatergoers as fellow conspirators. Shirley has broken away, although as Ms. Burstyn artfully communicates, there are further steps to be taken by this endearing character before the play can reach its destination.

1989 Ag 10, C13:1

Drip-Painted Art And Personal Demons

FESTIVAL LATINO: PEGGY AND JACKSON, libretto by Michael Alasa; directed by Mr. Alasa; co-director and stage manager, Mary Lisa Kinney; music by David Welch; set design by Design Associates; costume design by Natalie Barth Walker; sound by Bronwen Jones.

Jackson	Michael Alasa
Peggy	Ann Marie Milazzo
Lee	Wendy Clifford
Ruth	Catherine Lippencott
Howard	Luciano Valerio
Ted	Jon Spano
Gloria	Pamela Scott

ADIOS, TROPICANA, book and lyrics by Chuck Gomez; directed and choreographed by Mark Pennington; music by Mr. Pennington; set design by Tom Crisp; costume design by Paul Mantell; sound by Bronwen Jones; stage manager, Mary Lisa Kinney. Festival Latino in New York, Oscar Ciccone and Cecilia Vega, directors, presented by Joseph Papp. Associate producer, Jason Steven Cohen. At the Public/Martinson, 425 Lafayette Street.

La China	Elaine M. Carinci
Aidita	Iliana Guibert
Angelina	Francesca MacAaron
Claudia	Elizabeth Acosta
Soldier	zRolando Gomez

By STEPHEN HOLDEN

"I am in command of every drip I make," Jackson Pollock says in one of many seemingly endless sung monologues about the art world in the 80-minute one-act musical, "Peggy and Jackson."

The first of two one-act musicals to be presented at the New York Shakespeare Festival by the Duo Theater, a 20-year-old Hispanic-American theater company as part of the Festival Latino, "Peggy and Jackson," explores the relationships between Pollock, the legendary Abstract Expressionist painter, his wife, Lee Krasner, and the art collector Peggy Guggenheim.

Michael Alasa, who plays Pollock, wrote the libretto and directed the show, which unintentionally parodies "Sunday in the Park With George." Wandering in and out of a set made of drip-painting canvases, the characters maunder on about art and their personal demons. Jackson moans about his drinking. Peggy is obsessed with the decay of Venice, the emptiness of society and her role as an art-world power broker. Lee describes a courtship and marriage that began as a partnership and deterioriated as her husband became famous. The single emotion that runs through the humorless show is tortured self-pity.

"Peggy and Jackson," which is almost entirely sung, has a ghastly score, played on electric keyboards, that mixes overwrought romantic clichés with bubbly new-age textures intended to suggest the musical equivalent of painterly drips and swirls. Nothing could be further from the spirit of so-called action painting than this saccharine bilge. The performances of Mr. Alasa, Ann Marie Milazzo as Peggy and Wendy Clifford as Lee are painfully inept. Posing self-consciously, the performers gaze up at the rafters and spew out interminable psychobabble.

•

Those who have the fortitude to endure "Peggy and Jackson" will find the 50-minute "Adios, Tropicana," which follows, to be at least unpretentious. The show, with a book and lyrics by Chuck Gomez and music by Mark Pennington, who also directed, is set in 1980, backstage at the Tropicana Nightclub in Havana.

La China (Elaine M. Carinci) and Angelina (Francesca MacAaron),

---

A twin bill is offered by the Festival Latino.

---

two of the three showgirls who are performing that evening, have decided to leave Cuba by seeking asylum in the Peruvian Embassy in Havana. The third dancer, Aidita (Iliana Guibert) is tempted to go with them but declines. The crux of the drama is Angelina's attempts to persuade her mother, Claudia (Elizabeth Acosta) to flee with her.

"Adios, Tropicana" plays like a very rough sketch for one act of a larger show about Cuban life. Though crude at the seams, Mr. Gomez's book at least begins to capture some backstage flavor. Mr. Pennington's conga-flavored pop songs are shapely and tuneful. And Miss Acosta, who plays Angelina's mother, has a strong, almost operatic voice. Still, "Adios, Tropicana" is just a fragment.

1989 Ag 10, C16:5

How Well We Know What We Know

NO + (NO MORE), written and directed by Raul Osorio; music by Andreas Bodenhoffer; sound and light design by Taller de Investigación Teatral. Festival Latino in New York, Oscar Ciccone and Cecilia Vega, directors, presented by Jason Cohen. At the Public Theater/LuEsther Hall, 425 Lafayette Street.

Pupils
    Rebeca Ghigliotto, Juan Carlos Montagna and Patricio Strahovsky Villagran
Tutor ....Manuel Peña
Musicians
    Andreas Bodenhoffer, Marcelo Witto, Jorge Alejandro and Florencio Jaramillo

By D. J. R. BRUCKNER

Learning is what "No + (No More)" is all about, but who — including the audience — learns what, is anybody's guess. Taking his inspiration from "The Students Want to Teach," a short story about role reversal by the Austrian writer Peter Handke, the Chilean playwright Raul Osorio has created a wordless play that repeatedly tempts a viewer into imagining he knows what is going on and then makes him question his own judgment.

The performance — by the Chilean experimental theater group Taller de Investigación Teatral, as part of the Festival Latino at the Public Theater — begins with a hilarious sketch on apples. Waiting for their teacher, three students standing against a wall spattered with graffiti solemnly eat apples — cores, seeds, stems and all. When they have finished, each reaches into a pocket, pulls out another apple and eats that. Only the arrival of the teacher, when these three are munching on their third apples, rescues the tittering audience from nervous hysteria.

Mr. Osorio's intentions are far from anything as innocent as a classroom game. The students do present apples to the teacher finally -- and everything else in their pockets, including ridiculous toys, tiny books and huge pens. And they fly paper airplanes and throw balls that stick to the teacher.

Ines Paulino Mori

Rebecca Ghigliotto, Jaime Lorca and Juan Carlos Montagna, right, performing in a scene from "No + (No More)."

But this theater company was established in the harshest days of the Pinochet regime in Chile when the "No +" of the title was a common graffito on walls in that country. Protesters could add whatever they wanted no more of, like "death." And the absurd action of this unspoken play produces eventually a sense of menace; the struggle between the teacher and students turns into a battle over life itself.

Who wins the battle is up to the audience to figure out, if it can. The many upendings of the arrogant teacher are fun. But he has the last word when he paints "viva" over the students' "No +" scrawled on a wall. Is he simply canceling out their slogan with a hurrah to authority? Is it possible he means to suggest we read the superimposed words as "live no more?" In any case, is the struggle worthwhile? Not even that is settled; in the end all four characters lie in a circle of blood — are they dead? — under sheets made of old newspapers.

If the mental teasing of this strange piece is at times irritating, the sights and sounds are captivating. There is sound: a metronome, the crash of dinner plates hurled against a wall, and the occasional intrusion of incongruous chamber music. Latin American theater is usually much richer in spectacle and more sensuous in balletic movement than ours, and Mr. Osorio and this cast let us see on a stark black and white set how some of that luxury is produced.

One may leave this play puzzled about what it means but with a deepened appreciation of what performance is, and with admiration for these actors who, without a word, leave no doubt that they understand one another, and their art, perfectly.

1989 Ag 12, 14:4

Dreaming the Dream

CHINESE CHARADE, by Manuel Pereiras; directed by Susana Tubert; composers, Sergio Garcia Marruz and Saul Spangenberg; musical director, Mr. Garcia Marruz; Spanish lyrics, Emilia Conde and Anita Velez; choreography, Poli Rogers; dance captain, Marianella Crispin; set design by Robert Klingelhoefer; costume design, Maria Ferreira-Contessa; sound design, Gary Harris; dramaturge, Manuel Martin; production stage manager, Lisa Ledwich; producer, Miriam Colon Valle. Presented by the Puerto Rican Traveling Theater. At various locations. For information: 354-1293.

The Dream Bookie	Bonnie Diaz
Lele	Cintia Cruz
Guanche	Jorge Oliver
La Contessa	Eileen Galindo
Menelio	Jack Landron

By RICHARD F. SHEPARD

The New York most visitors never get to is the playing field for the Puerto Rican Traveling Theater, an agile bilingual troupe that is spending August performing in mostly working-class neighborhoods of all the boroughs as well as Westchester and New Jersey.

The company has been making these outdoor theater rounds for more than 20 years, performing in one place in Spanish and in another in English. That is not easy, and one may take pride that New York is home to a group as versatile as this one.

This year's offering, "Chinese Charade" ("El Chino de la Charada"), had its official opening Wednesday, in English, in a New York almost every visitor knows, the spacious Fountain Plaza at Lincoln Center. The brightly colored set, a rickety skyline and dingy Lower East Side tenement, was backed by a real and regal skyline of which the centerpiece was the reproduction of the Statue of Liberty that tops a building opposite the center.

•

All of this helped to make the musical production a festive, lighthearted occasion, a felicitous point of departure for the tour of 23 parks, playgrounds and street locations in the metropolitan area.

The show is in the tradition of street theater, that is, it is direct in plot, audible, and filled with body movement. It is, however, more sophisticated than so much of the genre because it does not rely on slapstick; it has wistful themes among the comic ones and might even give an audience something to chew on. It is also imaginatively staged on a fully designed theatrical platform with sound equipment and props.

The story is simplicity itself. A young Puerto Rican couple (Jorge Oliver and Cintia Cruz) — he makes flags, she is a dressmaker — are persuaded by "the dream bookie" (Bonnie Diaz) to invest in a lottery ticket that is sure to win. Life is hard, and the villainous bodega proprietor (Jack Landron) demands payment of the bills and the nagging "Contessa" (Eileen Galindo) tries to get out of paying hers for alterations. The couple are even robbed by a housebreaker who chuckles as he advises them to be realists, like himself, and not dreamers.

•

It is a story about aspiration, not achievement, of dreams of success in New York, he as a taxi driver, she as a fancy-neighborhood dress designer.

Each member of the cast is amiable and nimble under the lively direction of Susana Tubert, who makes sure no one is immobile for long. More important, the actors bring life and probability to the broadly drawn characters they portray. Ms. Diaz is particularly attractive and bouncy as the dream bookie, always upbeat and full of hope. The music, by Sergio Garcia Marruz and Saul Spangenberg, has an eclectic Latin beat, and the words to "Money," "At the Bodega," and "Dreamers Lie" are very cleverly to the point.

"Chinese Charade" is theatrically streetwise, and even on a still, hot summer's day it provides its own pleasant breeziness.

1989 Ag 13, 57:3

Jokes and Maxims

BEST FRIENDS, by John Voulgaris; directed by Donald L. Brooks; music by Mark Barkin and Peter Storm; stage manager, Bill Maloney. Presented by Paul Carlton Productions, in association with T.O.T.A.L. At Actors' Playhouse, 100 Seventh Avenue South, at Sheridan Square.

Andrew Turner	David Conaway
Greg Meadows	Chris A. Kelly

By D. J. R. BRUCKNER

In "Best Friends," John Voulgaris toys with scores of questions about the nature of friendship, the rewards and perils of fame, the futility of intelligence, the emptiness of self-satisfaction and many other ordinary concerns that fill the dialogue of soap operas and romantic fiction — but he provides no answers and doesn't even make the questions very interesting.

It must be said that Donald L. Brooks, the director, and Chris A. Kelly and David Conaway, who play the friends of the title, bring a lot of energy to the performance of Mr. Voulgaris's play at the Actors Playhouse. It is a pity to see it so misspent.

Mr. Kelly as Greg, the star of a popular television series, returns to New York from Hollywood to visit his lifelong friend Andrew (Mr. Conaway), a failed painter whose wife and children have recently abandoned him. In his bitter desperation, Andrew decides the only way he will ever achieve recognition is by murdering someone famous, so he ties his best friend to a chair and rehearses several ways of doing him in.

•

But Greg tricks Andrew into freeing him and gives him abuse for abuse until Andrew regains his sanity. At last, in a clumsy piece of irony, Andrew's worst hallucinations come true — by accident. It is the kind of plot one doesn't have to pay attention to, to get the point.

And the actors are given very little with which to create interesting characters. There are many tired and juvenile jokes about sex, airlines, drinking, Hollywood and New York, tirades about the art market, money, success, drugs and the horrors of city life, and a scattering of maxims of homely philosophy.

•

But despite some reminiscences about their youth and their families, there is very little to give one a sense of who these characters are, or to make one care about them. If they did not keep repeating their names, it would be possible to forget which is which. Andrew has a life history, but no life to speak of, and there is only one brief stretch in the second act when Mr. Kelly has enough material to turn Greg into an eccentric and somewhat interesting person.

That comes too late. When Greg, looking down the barrel of a .45-caliber automatic, says, "Do it and get it over with," the first response that springs to mind is, "Amen."

1989 Ag 13, 57:6

Another Time, Another Dream

SUENO DE UNA NOCHE DE VERANO (A MIDSUMMER NIGHT'S DREAM), by William Shakespeare, directed by Ramon Pareja; adapted by Manuel Rueda; translated by Melia Bensussen; music by Dante Cucurullo; setting by Soucy De Pellerano; costumes by Ramon Pareja. Presented by Theater of Fine Arts of the Dominican Republic and New York Shakespeare Festival, Joseph Papp, president. At the Public/Newman, 425 Lafayette Street.

Matilde Capitán	
Luna	
Teseo	Pepito Guerra
Hipolita	Monina Sola
Egeo	Miguel Angel Martínez
Hermia	Oleka Fernández
Demetrio	Osvaldo Añez
Lisandro	Kenny Grullon
Elena	Elvira Tavéras
Cartabon	Rosemary Echevarría
Lanzadera	Angel Mejía
Flauta	Micky Montilla
Barbiqui	Víctor López
Hada	Lourdes Ozuna
Puck	Reynaldo Disla
Oberon	Juan María Almonte
Titania	Miriam Bello

WITH: Garibaldi Reyes, Francisco Manzueta, Genaro Ozuna, Jackson Delgado, Jenny De La Rosa, Thana Olmos, Lina Lorenzo, Jorge Bello-Joa, Ricardo Bella-Joa.

By RICHARD F. SHEPARD

When it is set in a Caribbean city William Shakespeare may never have heard of, in a future not even this age has reached and in a language that is not English, "A Midsummer Night's Dream" runs considerable risk of turning into a nightmare. Well, the National Theater of the Dominican Republic has done all this with the Bard's comedy and, far from rudely awakening, the company has created an adaptation that sails amusingly along in its own Spanish dreamboat.

This "Midsummer Night's Dream" ("Sueño de una Noche de Verano") has a surrealistic quality about it, something that carries the imagination a level or two beyond the simplicity of the original, which has all the elements of straightaway street comedy that is elevated by a magnificence of language.

•

In his Spanish adaptation for the Festival Latino at the Public Theater, Manuel Rueda has kept the main body of the play, and even the lines generally seem to be literal translations of the Shakespearean words. But he has tacked on a prologue, eliminated the delightful final performance of "Pyramus and Thisby" and tinkered mildly with the ending.

The changes involve the setting, a Santo Domingo of the future, with a spiritless population living in a graveyard of rusting automobiles. A boy is washed ashore from the sea, clutching papers that a leading citizen reads — and repeats and repeats — in English as "A Midsummer Night's Dream."

The play takes off immediately, with the people of this dead city changing character and costume but not the setting to indulge in this optimistic adventure that may set a new note for the despairing. As a device, this approach may be more meaningful to an audience not brought up on Shakespeare than it may be to one reared in the tradition. But this presentation has its dramatic rewards for almost any theatergoer.

•

For one thing, there is the wondrous set that is the handiwork of Soucy de Pellerano, a well-established Dominican artist. She has fashioned a three-level setting for the dexterous performers. It is ingenious scenery, a seemingly random pile of automotive junk that quite cunningly is a warren of stage entrances and exits.

Ramon Pareja, the director, has carried through the surreal concept of the story of misdirected spells and intentions good and evil. His interpretation involves loud noises punctuating the prose, a good deal of tumbling and a rather dreamy musical score by Dante Cucurullo that emphasizes the unreality of what is going on. It establishes, within the 90 minutes of the show, which is done in one act, the essential quality of fun that Shakespeare achieved.

Reynaldo Disla, as Puck, is a nimble chap, with rough beard, motorcycle helmet, glasses and a devilish sense of humor as he sows confusion. Angel Mejía, as Bottom (Lanzadera), one of the workers rehearsing a play for the king, catches the comic naïveté of a fellow who is given an ass's head to wear by Puck and who attracts the attentions of the passionate fairy queen, Titania.

•

Pepito [illegible] gives his Theseus the dignity and forcefulness worthy of a kind and just king who is about to be married and who finds himself having to make a severe decision. As Oberon, the king of the fairies, Juan María Almonte is wise and, at the same time, a wiseacre.

For an Anglophone who checked the goings-on by listening to the English translation on headphones, there was a loss of effect in the delivery of the lines, as though one were hearing a familiar friend over a static-studded long-distance line. That is perhaps inevitable, as any Spanish speaker might say to one who is trying to fully savor Don Quixote in English. A visitor to the visiting company's production should find that what may be missed by the ear is compensated for by what meets the eye.

1989 Ag 16, C16:1

Mechanic-Midwife

THE YEAR OF THE BABY, by Quincy Long, directed by Joumana Rizk; dramaturg, Kathleen Dimmick; setting by Geoffrey Makstutis; lighting by Clay Shirky; costumes by Pamela Korp; sound by Jeffrey Tayor; stage manager-assistant director, Tamara Holt. Presented by Home for Contemporary Theater and Art, 44 Walker Street.

Kenny	Quincy Long
Donna	Kathleen Dimmick
Cashier/Storekeeper	Viki Boyle
Bartender/Mechanic	Patrick Kerr
Luther	Edward Baran
Martha	Verna Hampton

By MEL GUSSOW

"The Year of the Baby" is vaguely reminiscent of "Raising Arizona," but has little of that movie's vagrant humor. This new Quincy Long play, at Home for Contemporary Theater and Art, aims for shagginess and settles for loose ends.

The central characters, an ingenuous young married couple played by the author and Kathleen Dimmick, hurriedly leave town after the wife has briefly "borrowed" a neighbor's baby. On the run, the nomadic pair try to have a baby of their own while settling down in a backwater hotel that could be part of a Norman Bates chain of hostelries.

The proprietors are creepy though uninteresting people, nosing into the guests' affairs. Despite the apparent lack of amenities, the husband and wife stay on for what seems like an interminable period. Rarely does Mr. Long reveal his own quirky sense of humor, previously evidenced in such comedies as "Something About Baseball," seen in one of the Ensemble Studio Theater's annual festivals of one-acts.

•

A few smiles arise from a character with a most unusual hyphenate; he is a mechanic-midwife. In the play's most bizarre sequence, he mixes his two occupations, examining the pregnant wife as if she were a vehicle brought into his body shop for repair. At such times, it is clear that "The Year of the Baby" could have a feminist backlash.

Joumana Rizk has staged the play in environmental fashion, with the audience surrounding the action as it unfolds in a number of spaces. With such an episodic story, the approach has possibilities, but, in practice, it proves to be self-defeating. Walking to their seats, theatergoers loudly crunch motel gravel under their feet, disordering the neat paths arranged by the set designer, Geoffrey Makstutis. During the performance, those sitting in back rows have to stand up and crane their necks to see what is happening across the room. Ms. Rizk's direction is the opposite of brisk.

Mr. Long and Patrick Kerr, as the mechanic, are capable performers, and Ms. Dimmick has a certain angelic fragility that makes her character bearable even as the play wades knee-deep into a pool of whimsy.

1989 Ag 17, C14:6

Before Its Time

MY BIG LAND, by Alexander Galich; directed by Oleg P. Tabakov; translated by Alexander Gelman; scenery by S. Kutsevalov; costume design, E. Pechenkina; lighting design, N. Kurdyumova; sound design, N. Koloskov. Joseph Papp presents the Vladimir I. Nemirovich-Danchenko Studio-School under the auspices of The M. Gorky Moscow Art Theater, U.S.S.R. At the Public Theater/Susan Stein Shiva Theater, 425 Lafayette Street.

David Shvartz	Filip Yankovsky
Abram Shvartz	Vladimir Mashkov
Meyer Wolf	Roman Kuznechenko
Tanya	Alyona Khovanskaya
Hanna	Irina Apeksemova
Roza Gurevich	Liya Yelshevskaya
Mitya/Odintsova	Dmitri Stolbtsov
Slavka/Smorodin	Yuri Yekimov
Chernyshov	Igor Kozlov
Lyudmila Shutova	Irina Gordina
Lapshin	Sergei Shentalinsky
Zhenka	Yevgeny Mironov
Arisha	Nina Muzhikova

By RICHARD F. SHEPARD

"My Big Land," the Soviet play being presented in Russian by the Moscow Art Theater School at the Public Theater, is so thought-provoking that the mind continually flits from the play on hand to the heavy-handed world in which it was created 30 years ago.

The drama by Alexander Galich is about Jews in the Soviet Union, specifically about Jews from a town in the Ukraine. The story sprawls through three acts that take the audience from the late 1920's through the paranoid days of mid-30's Moscow and to the grim Holocaust years of World War II.

The central figures are David Shvartz, a young man who gives great promise of being a virtuoso violinist, and his father, Abram, a heavy drinker who seems to be in business of a very marginal sort. The father's ambitions rest entirely in the future of his son, who is sensitive and self-centered where the parent is plebeian, outspoken and given to expressing his emotions loudly and embarrassingly.

•

Into their lives flow a stream of people: an old friend, just returned in 1929 from Palestine, where he felt he had nothing in common with Zion; a rather benevolent commissar at David's music academy who says, "I believe that everything the party does is singularly wise and, if I ever doubt that, I'll probably put a bullet through my head"; a neighborhood housewife who seems to be imbued with the most Yiddishkeit, or Jewish feeling, of anyone in the show (when she suspects the reticent returnee of having money, she says, "When Jews become officers, everybody stops saluting").

David goes to the Moscow school, where his best friend loses his scholarship and is ousted from the Communist youth organization because his father is an "enemy of the state." David's father visits, and comes across as an inept loudmouth bumpkin, bearing only money and love for

Martha Swope Associates/Carol Rosegg

Vladimir Mashkov

the son. The third act finds David as a wounded officer encountering his yellow-starred father in a dream. The father was killed by the Nazis during a round-up in their hometown.

The curtain comes down on a sad song by the author called "When I Return," with lyrics that tie everything together and imply that sons return to their fathers, and even authors to their people; it gives point to the roar of passing trains that punctuates the dialogue, creating a mood of transience that may or may not characterize the impermanence of Jewish life in hostile surroundings. The message is not that you can't go home again, but that you must. Mr. Galich, who died in exile in the 1970's, has written a play with characters who are fully dimensional humans rather than cardboard figures, and despite a tendency to avoid polemics, he has taken a strong moral stand in touchy circumstances.

•

The play is movingly acted by its young cast, under the direction of Oleg Tabakov, who acted in it in Moscow in 1958 until the censors closed it during dress rehearsals. The youthful players are sincere and passionate and persuasive; the sets, particularly the scene for the hospital train with its crowded cargo of wounded, are not spectacular but are the more real for that. Vladimir Mashkov, the 25-year old who plays the grizzled father, gives a stellar performance in a role that has had its counterpart here in immigrant theater dealing with the conflict between older newcomers and their American-born offspring. Filip Yankovsky, as David, brings a brooding forcefulness to his part.

If there is a rhythm to the piece it is one of laconic quietudes broken by emotional outbursts, and it works very well. Each act has a short prologue that frames the action to come. (The excellent English translation is by Alexander Gelman.) Whatever the play lacks in dramatic continuity — there is a sporadic, episodic quality about it — is compensated by its intense and poetic manner.

There is something else striking about the play, which runs through Saturday: it is the knowledge that one is seeing in 1989 in New York a work that was suppressed in Moscow in 1958. It makes one wonder what the author was really saying at a time when Jews were scapegoats of a ruthless government, a dozen years after the leading lights of the Yiddish arts had been killed by order of Stalin.

It often seems as if the author is making the point that the Jew is like anyone else in his country, that he doesn't want to go to Palestine, that Jews can be as stupid as the next dolt, that Jews were not the only ones to bear the burden of Russian bigotry. But 30 years ago, Soviet writers knew caution; Jewish writers in particular had been charged not long before with being "rootless cosmopolitans" and of using "Aesopian" language.

A tendency to be critical of "My Big Land" because it plays down Jewishness even as it condemns anti-Semitism must be tempered by the knowledge that Galich had done a gutsy, anti-Government play, one that the Government honored by closing it. What may appear to be negative today might well have been forthright and positive — it certainly was daring — in the yesterday of its genesis.

"My Big Land" is a provocative play in which the idiom is not only Russian but also one that recalls a time when direct messages were sent at one's peril. It is as interesting theater as one can find in New York at the moment.

1989 Ag 17, C15:1

Honesty, Honesty

THE QUINTESSENTIAL IMAGE, by Jane Chambers; directed by Peg Murray; costumes by Charles Catanese; lighting by Tracy Dedrickson; stage managers, Kathleen Mary and Courtney Flanagan. Presented by the Glines. At the Courtyard Playhouse, 39 Grove Street, near Bleecker Street.

Margaret Foy	Rochelle DuBoff
Lacy Lanier	Ruth Kulerman

IN HER OWN WORDS (A PORTRAIT OF JANE), arranged and directed by Ms. Murray.

WITH: Mary Kay Adams, Shelley Conger, Rochelle DuBoff, Ruth Kulerman and Judy Tate.

By STEPHEN HOLDEN

In "The Quintessential Image," a jaunty one-act comedy by Jane Chambers, photography and a telegenic appearance become pointed metaphors for the masks assumed by people who wish to conceal homosexual identities.

As the play opens, Margaret Foy (Rochelle DuBoff), a sleek young talk-show hostess boasts to the audience about her latest journalist coup. In a few moments, she announces, she will conduct the first television interview ever with her idol, Lacy Lanier (Ruth Kulerman), a Nobel Prize-winning photojournalist. But no sooner has Lacy slouched onto the stage and sat in the wrong chair than Margaret's enthusiasm turns to chagrin.

•

The eminent photographer proves to be the furthest thing from an artistic grande dame dispensing anecdotal nuggets about generals and heads of state. Blowsy and eccentric, she rattles on about how she could never please her ailing mother with whom she lives in Louisiana. After recalling that she was bald until the age of 3, she casually confesses her lifelong obsession with Belinda, the local Mayor's daughter who had beautiful blond finger curls.

When Margaret points to blowups of some of Lacy's most famous wartime photos and asks her to comment on them, it turns out that all were in some way inspired by Belinda. Asked to recall some of her big romances,

Lacy regales Margaret with tales of her lesbian escapades in a women's hotel. By the end of the interview, Lacy has thoroughly punctured her own mystique and offhandedly revealed that Margaret herself is a closeted lesbian.

"The Quintessential Image" is nothing more or less than a Norman Lear-style comedy that makes its case for honesty and self-acceptance with confidence and good humor. The dialogue shows a sure command of the swift comic rhythms and brittle tone of sitcom writing. Peg Murray, who directed the production at the Courtyard Playhouse, has kept the pace lively. And Ms. DuBoff and Ms. Kulerman imbue their roles with a subtle sense of caricature.

•

"In Her Own Words (A Portrait of Jane)," the work that opens the evening, is a biographical portrait of Ms. Chambers compiled largely from her own writings by John Glines and performed by five actresses. The material is arranged chronologically into a collage that interweaves biographical data with excerpts from plays. While the piece offers many details of Ms. Chambers's life, its elaborate musical structure, in which cast members adopt formal testimonial voices, gives it the feel of a political portrait rather than of an intimate personality profile.

The most dramatic moment is Judy Tate's thrashing portrayal of an angry feminist bag lady from the Chambers play "Mine." It is also the piece's most generous excerpt from a Chambers work.

•

The story ends on a note of eerie poignancy. In 1983, three years after her most successful play, "Last Summer at Bluefish Cove," was first produced, the playwright died of a brain tumor at age 45. Coincidentally, the main character in "Bluefish Cove" also died of a brain tumor. When she wrote the drama, Ms. Chambers's illness had not been diagnosed. In a late journal entry, she compares her own experience of facing death with that of her character, Lil, and finds the work "honest and real."

"In Her Own Words" concludes with an inspirational epitaph by the playwright, who was not religious. "Life is not a crapshoot," she wrote. "It is what we who love each other do together. And that is, in itself, sufficient."

1989 Ag 17, C18:3

Real or Not, Visions Have Value

SAINT JOAN, by George Bernard Shaw; directed by Michael Smuin; scenery by Ralph Funicello; costumes by Sandra Woodall; lighting by Derek Duarte; music composed by Stephen LeGrand and Eric Drew Feldman; sound by Mr. LeGrand; hair and makeup by Rick Echols; sound adapted by Daryl Bornstein; dramaturge, Dennis Powers. The American Conservatory Theater, presented by The American Festival Theater, 1850 Elm Street, Stratford, Conn.

Robert de Baudricourt and Warwick's Page .... Stephen Weingartner
Steward and De Courcelles .... Liam O'Brien
Joan .... Andrea Marcovicci
Bertrand de Poulengey .... Kelvin Han Yee
Archbishop of Rheims .... Daniel Kremer
La Trémouille .... Garland J. Simpson
Court Page, D'Estivet and English Soldier .... Tom Todoroff
Gilles de Rais .... Richard Butterfield
Captain La Hire .... Mark Daniel Cade
The Dauphin .... Howard Swain
Duchesse de la Trémouille ....
.... Cathy Thomas-Grant

Dunois .... Lawrence Hecht
Richard de Beauchamp .... Peter Donat
Chaplain de Stogumber .... David Maier
Peter Cauchon .... William Paterson
The Inquisitor .... Sydney Walker
Brother Martin Ladvenu .... Kelvin Han Yee
Executioner .... John Furse

By RICHARD F. SHEPARD

George Bernard Shaw never let a show stand in the way of social comment and, more often than not, put the two together in witty theatrical exegesis.

He had so much on his mind when he wrote "Saint Joan" that it is one of the more difficult stage chores to get it all out of the actors' mouths. This is evident in the handsomely staged, but not inspirationally performed, production of the play by the American Conservatory Theater at the American Festival Theater in Stratford, Conn., where it may be seen through Aug. 27.

Joan, who listened to her inner voices, rallied the French, defeated the English occupiers and was burned at the stake by the enemy after being condemned for heresy by the Inquisition. In 1920, she was canonized and in 1923 the Shaw play had its opening in a Theater Guild production in New York.

It is to the credit of the company at Stratford that they have very delicately pruned the original script so that the missing parts are difficult to pinpoint.

Andrea Marcovicci, in the title role, has the talent to present a credible Joan, but as others have found, it is a difficult part in which to establish a presence. Shaw did not want a Joan who was either a pretty heroine or an overwhelming mystic. She was a country girl but not a peasant and she accepted her visions as a fact of life. It is not easy to establish such a character and, at the same time, have her as one who can persuade kings and prelates of her strength. Ms. Marcovicci is perhaps a mite too handsome, a speck too country-fresh and a bit short on creating a woman who must have been a rare and compelling nuisance.

Marty Sohl

Andrea Marcovicci in the title role of "Saint Joan" at the American Festival Theater.

Under Michael Smuin's direction, the cast members wade into the dialogue with conviction, tackling their parts with an earnestness that makes the characters come alive. The flow of words at times is caught up in too swift a current and certain voices are less easily distinguished than others.

Peter Donat, as the Earl of Warwick, is English gentlemanly in the best Shaw tradition of a rather pleasant man doing unpleasant jobs. Howard Swain is excellent as the Dauphin, whom Joan establishes as King; he plays the part of the cowardly and poverty-stricken prince in a fitting clownish style.

The churchly roles are well cast. Daniel Kremer, makes the Archbishop of Rheims into a suitably sophisticated political clergyman who understands that visions, whether real or not, have value, that "a miracle is an event that creates faith." William Paterson is thoroughly convincing as the Bishop of Beauvais, a dedicated church legalist who puts everything next to justice. And Sydney Walker makes a fair-minded Inquisitor, practical, merciful and devoted to his principles.

"Saint Joan" is a thoroughly absorbing play and this production is one that pays it sufficient tribute. A play should be judged on what it has to say without further commentary, but it is hard to resist a line of commentary from the author himself, who wrote as an explanatory preface to the work:

"There are no villains in the piece. Crime, like disease, is not interesting: it is something to be done away with by general consent, and that is all about it. It is what men do at their best, with good intentions, and what normal men and women find that they must and will do in spite of their intentions, that really concern us."

1989 Ag 19, 14:1

STAGE VIEW/Mel Gussow

English Actors Win the Classics Challenge

LONDON

IN RICHARD EYRE'S PRODUCTION of "Hamlet" at the National Theater (starring Daniel Day-Lewis in the title role), Polonius (Michael Bryant) was giving instructions to his aide Reynaldo. Suddenly Mr. Bryant stopped speaking, then said, as if in a daze, "I was about to say something," and searched his mind for his place in the play. Finally, after an extended pause, he asked, "Where did I leave?" The actor playing Reynaldo reminded him, "At 'closes in the consequence,' at 'friends or

Testing themselves, versatile performers elevate their plays with astonishing consistency.

so,' and 'gentlemen,' " and Mr. Bryant picked up the thread of the conversation.

The moment, of course, is direct from the text. I have heard many actors play this scene with believable absent-mindedness, but when Mr. Bryant did it, it was startling. The actor waited so long between the apparent memory loss and his request for help that there was an audible murmur in the audience. Was it Polonius or Mr. Bryant who had forgotten his lines? Actually Mr. Bryant was word perfect in his Shakespeare. Soon after the performance I happened to see an English actress of my acquaintance and described the moment to her. She said, admiringly, "Michael does that every night!"

■

Something similar happened years ago when Laurence Olivier was playing in Strindberg's "Dance of Death." At one point, the actor — in character — fell to the floor as if struck by lightning. The moment was so sudden and convincing that theatergoers thought the actor had suffered a stroke in mid-performance, a fact that, as I remember, was reported in the daily press. Lord Olivier was able to repeat that "stroke" night after night. Some years later, in Harold Pinter's "No Man's Land," Ralph Richardson was also called upon to fall down and he stumbled with such verisimilitude that it seemed as if Sir Ralph, not the character, had toppled.

With all three actors, Lord Olivier, Sir Ralph and Mr. Bryant, life seemed to be imitating art when actually the reverse was true in the extreme. Each of the actors was swept away by his role onto a mysterious plane where theater could not be distinguished from reality. The result is a performance of intense identification.

Because of Mr. Bryant's impassioned portrayal of Polonius, we hear some lines as if for the first time, an unusual thing to say about Polonius, who is of course one of the most familiar figures in all of dramatic literature. No longer is Polonius a fussbudget; in Mr. Bryant's interpretation he is an immensely concerned parent in great distress about both of his offspring. One feels that concern not only in his admonition to Laertes but in his irate charge to Ophelia that she is being naïve in accepting Hamlet's "tenders of affection." It is possible, in Mr. Bryant's remarkable performance, to view the events at Elsinore through the eyes of Polonius.

In this production there is a second commanding performance — by Judi Dench as Gertrude. She is sensual with Claudius, ma-

ternal with Hamlet, confused about her identity and dazzled by her son's evident dementia. Although Mr. Day-Lewis has several striking moments as Hamlet, his performance does not have the riveting immediacy exemplified by his two older colleagues.

Both Mr. Bryant and Dame Judi are among a phalanx of experienced English actors who with an astonishing consistency seem to elevate whatever production they happen to be in — Mr. Bryant last year as Prospero at the National, Dame Judi the previous year as Cleopatra. It is heartening to realize in a season marked by the death of Lord Olivier that the great English acting tradition survives, as versatile actors continue to challenge themselves in classics on stage. This summer, one could see — and enjoy — Alan Bates and Felicity Kendal, Juliet Stevenson, Edward Petherbridge, Jim Broadbent and, in a modern play, Prunella Scales.

When such actors return for a single play or a seasonal repertory, the English are eager to receive them. On Broadway, actors of this stature would be more hesitant about ♦

John Haynes (Bryant); Alastair Muir (Petherbridge and Broadbent)

Among the British actors for whom art seems to imitate life are Michael Bryant as Polonius, above left, in "Hamlet" at the National Theater; Edward Petherbridge, top right, as Alceste in "The Misanthrope" and Jim Broadbent in "A Flea in Her Ear" at the Old Vic.

making a commitment — a hesitancy shared by producers — and audiences would want to be sure that the production itself was a critical success.

In London, theatergoers are more willing to go along with proven favorites, especially, one might add, with actresses like Ms. Kendal and Ms. Scales who are television stars as well as theater artists. There is of course a reverse side — actors may choose a vehicle, spin-offs of television roles, stage sitcoms or creaky thrillers, all of which are staples in London. It was not so long ago that Donald Sinden triumphed on the West End as King Lear. This year he is appearing in "Over My Dead Body," which, undiminished by disastrous notices, continues to cater to a nondiscriminating public.

Coming to the West End next month is a Jeffrey Archer mystery, starring Paul Scofield and Alec McCowen. When actors of this caliber choose to do more demanding work, there are obstacles to be encountered. The performances may have to transcend a misguided or arbitrary production, or, at least, they may have to ignore weak elements in the supporting cast or in scenic design.

■

Mr. Bates and Ms. Kendal shared star billing in a repertory pairing of "Much Ado About Nothing" and "Ivanov" (recently closed), both staged by Elijah Mojinsky. For "Much Ado," the director transposed the play to a sunny land that resembled the border between Mexico and Texas, with bare wood furniture that might have been at home at a taco stand.

In spite of the disconcerting décor and a vaguely modernized directorial approach, the two actors pitched themselves into their roles with gusto, even to playing upon the fact that each was a bit too old for Benedick and Beatrice, peering with feigned myopia at each other's love letters. After enduring performances by attitudinizing young actors in the title roles of "Hamlet" and "Romeo and Juliet" at Stratford-on-Avon, it was refreshing to be greeted by the assurance and articulation of Mr. Bates and Ms. Kendal.

At the National, Ms. Stevenson is playing a particularly headstrong "Hedda Gabler," clearly the most charismatic person in her conservative community. Howard Davies's production is in the Olivier Theater, the largest of the company's three houses, and the director has unwisely filled the stage with a set that looks more like a public library reading room than the parlor of the Tesman home. In the middle of the stage is a towering — and teetering — staircase, which creaks every time Hedda goes upstairs. But Ms. Stevenson's performance overrides such distractions, and she is ably abetted by Suzanne Burden, who lends a vitality to the often colorless role of Thea Elvsted.

In his book, "Being an Actor," Simon Callow expresses an actor's lament: the subjugation of the performer in a theater increasingly dominated by directors who place concept above all and regard themselves as the theatrical equivalent of auteurs on film. Mr. Callow refers to this as a rule by "directocracy."

That comment came to mind while watching Richard Jones's new production of Georges Feydeau's "Flea in Her Ear" at the Old Vic, which is under the aegis of the determinedly iconoclastic Jonathan Miller. Last season, Mr. Jones offered a radicalized version of Ostrovsky's "Too Clever by Half," turning a naturalistic Russian play into a diabolical farce. That production was bizarre but fascinating and it was heightened by the virtuosic performance by Alex Jennings in the central role (Mr. Jennings is presently appearing in "Ghetto" at the National).

■

This season, the director has attempted a related re-invention of Feydeau, trying to transform a boulevard farce into a ferocious nightmare out of Kafka or Krafft-Ebing, both of whom are quoted in the program. Though Ostrovsky survived the onslaught, Feydeau succumbs. The approach is provocative but it is also self-defeating and ignores the first and second rules of farce (it should be fast and funny).

In spite of this fact, Mr. Broadbent, doubling in roles as a frazzled husband and bumbling porter, is amusing, as are several of his colleagues, including Phelim McDermott as a man with a wavering speech defect. One might suggest that either the roles or the actors are director-proof. Americans can look forward to a presumably more authentic revival of the play, using the same John Mortimer translation, directed by John Tillinger and opening the season at the Long Wharf Theater in New Haven.

Far preferable to the Old Vic Feydeau is the Molière at the National, "The Misanthrope," a co-production with the Bristol Old Vic, directed by Paul Unwin and starring Edward Petherbridge. Mr. Petherbridge is an elegant Alceste, the self-wounding truth-teller in a world of hypocrites. Sian Thomas is charming as Celimene, the woman he adores in spite of all evidence of nonreciprocity. The primary obstacle is the scenery, designed by Richard Hudson — a less effective variation on his perspective-distorting setting for "Too Clever by Half." But the production lets Molière (in the Tony Harrison adaptation) speak for himself.

One of the most delightful performances in London this season is given by Ms. Scales in "Single Spies," Alan Bennett's double package of espionage stories. The two plays are staged by Mr. Bennett and Mr. Callow, each of whom are also actors. As directors, they disarm the directocracy; they are less superimposers than the actors' encouragers and accomplices. In the second play, Ms. Scales, best known for playing Sybil Fawlty on television's "Fawlty Towers," transforms herself into Queen Elizabeth II. Marching through the Queen's picture gallery with that titled traitor, Sir Anthony Blunt (Mr. Bennett), she gives a performance that is both a spoof and a tribute. Impersonating Her Majesty with regal humor, she exemplifies the actor's art as well as acting at its most English. □

1989 Ag 20, II:5:1

Alastair Muir

Juliet Stevenson in the title role of "Hedda Gabler" at the National Theater—clearly the most charismatic person in her community

An Intrusion of Power

FESTIVAL LATINO: EL PASO o PARABOLA DEL CAMINO (EL PASO or PARABLE OF THE PATH) A collective creation of La Candelaria; directed by Santiago García; translated by Nina Miller; set design by Jorge Ardila and Mr. García; music by Ignacio Rodríguez; lighting by Mr. García; set by Mr. Ardila; costumes by the company. Presented by Joseph Papp; associate producer, Jason Steven Cohen. At the Public/Anspacher Theater, 425 Lafayette Street.

Emiro	César Badillo
Don Blanco	Francisco Martínez
Musician 1	Fernando Peñuela
Musician 2	Hernando Forero
Chela	Nohora Ayala
Doris	Martha Osorio
Obdullo	Alvaro Rodríguez
Prostitute	Inés Prieto
Taxi Driver	Fernando Mendoza
The Lady (Fernanda)	Patricia Ariza
The Lover	Rafael Giraldo
Stranger 1	Carolina Vivas
Stranger 2	Ignacio Rodríguez

By D. J. R. BRUCKNER

The world intrudes on the habitués of a Colombian crossroads tavern in "El Paso o Parábola del Camino" (The Parable of the Path), and they learn in a brutal moment that they might be fortunate, after all, to live where "news comes from other places," as the innkeeper says.

It is a sign of the sheer sense of theater, the energy and the acting ability of the members of the Colombian theater company, La Candelaria, that they keep their audience at the Public Theater laughing right up to the final violent scene of this play and that the violence does not seem out of place.

There is a pun in the title. In the theater, "el paso" refers not to walking but to a skit or improvisation, and this play is a collective creation of La Candelaria and its director, Santiago

García. It is performed in Spanish as part of the Festival Latino, with English translation through earphones supplied Sunday afternoon and evening.

There is something of everything here — comedy, tragedy, melodrama, music, farce. Magically, it all fits together. A giggling prostitute, a rich woman with her gigolo and a taxi driver whose cab broke down in a rainstorm take refuge in the tavern and get into uproarious confrontations with the innkeeper, her employees, a dipsomaniacal old man and a hilarious gay waiter named Obdulio. Throughout, a pair of somewhat sodden musicians find excuses to perform popular songs that obliquely and comically comment on the action.

•

This circus is interrupted by two silent men who arrive in a truck loaded with wooden cases, later found to be filled with guns. While the pair are a little sinister, their solemn silence is ridiculed by the others and they become part of the fun, up to a point. At the end, one of them is wounded offstage in a mysterious confrontation, a helicopter descends to collect the guns and one of the two gun runners leaves a pile of money on the bar, saying: "Nothing happened here."

Who were they? Guerrillas? Government agents? Cocaine suppliers? It doesn't matter. They are from the world of power, where the news comes from, all of it bad. The realities this ingenious company examines in "Parábola del Camino" don't need names.

The members of the cast love these characters, and the warmth of their feelings reaches the audience. Everyone in the play is slightly mad in his or her own special way, but their lunacies become first familiar and then lovable. Even the gun runners have a peculiar attractiveness.

1989 Ag 20, 62:1

Blood and Gore At the Barbecue

TITUS ANDRONICUS, by William Shakespeare; directed by Michael Maggio; scenery by John Lee Beatty; costumes by Lewis D. Rampino; lighting by Jennifer Tipton; music by Louis Rosen; fights staged by B. H. Barry; associate producer, Jason Steven Cohen. Presented by Joseph Papp. At the Delacorte Theater, Central Park, enter at 81st Street and Central Park West or 79th Street and Fifth Avenue.

Titus Andronicus	Donald Moffat
Lucius	David Purdham
Mutius and Publius	Steve Pickering
Quintus	Deryl Caitlyn
Martius	Rainn Wilson
Lavinia	Pamela Gien
Tamora	Kate Mulgrew
Chiron	Bill Camp
Demetrius	Don Harvey
Alarbus	Armand Schultz
Aaron	Keith David
Saturninus	Don R. McManus
Bassianus and Goth 3	Robert Curtis-Brown
Marcus Andronicus	Jon DeVries
Young Lucius	Bradley Kane
Aemilius	Joseph M. Costa
Nurse	Tanny McDonald
Clown	Peter Appel
Goth 1 and Messenger	Armand Schultz
Goth 2	Deryl Caitlyn

Senators, Soldiers and Attendants
N. Richard Aarif, Daniel Berkey, Bryan Hicks, Susan Knight, William Langan, James McCauley, Cameron Miller, Erik Oñate, Joshua Perl, Andrew Prosky, Guy S. Wagner and William Wheeler.

By FRANK RICH

The first sight to greet the audience at the Central Park "Titus Andronicus" is a small, flaming barbecue grill propped up on a slender tripod at center stage. "Titus Andronicus" is a revenge-begets-revenge tragedy of rape, dismemberment and decapitations whose body count runs so high even scholars don't always jibe on the final tally. It ends with a cannibalistic feast in which a mother unwittingly eats a pie containing the innards of her sons. So why are we greeted by a wimpy barbecue that is less evocative of the barbarous human stew of Shakespeare's ancient Rome than of last weekend's hot-dogs-and-marshmallows cookout in Great Neck?

The answer arrives soon enough.

What the New York Shakespeare Festival has decided to present is a genteel "Titus Andronicus," which is kind of like doing "The Texas Chain Saw Massacre" without the chain saw or "Sweeney Todd" with an electric razor. Not particularly heartfelt or grotesque or long (the text is butchered more persuasively than the play's victims), this is a "Titus" that serves little purpose beyond filling another slot in the Shakespeare marathon and reconvening the increasingly numbing debate about the marathon's purpose and direction. It's a routine sandal-and-toga recital of an early, infelicitously written work that, more than its betters in the canon, demands extravagant imagination and passion to rouse audiences.

•

As usual, there is talent on display at the Delacorte Theater, and, as usual, much of it is misused. The great wastes this time are the director, Michael Maggio, and the star, Donald Moffat. In his "Romeo and Juliet" at the Goodman Theater in Chicago last season, Mr. Maggio revealed a gentle sensitivity that brought both eroticism and innocence to the poetic love scenes. Mr. Maggio was less at home with the larger-scale conflicts of the Montagues and Capulets. It's perverse that his first Shakespeare assignment in New York would play precisely to the weakness of his "Romeo" rather than to his gifts for handling introspective characters, poetry and intimacy of feeling (all of which are in short supply in "Titus"). When Mr. Maggio directed a Sondheim musical at the Goodman, after all, his choice was "Sunday in the Park With George," not "Sweeney Todd."

•

If Mr. Maggio is an intelligent director stuck with the wrong play, he nonetheless makes a modest go of it, using an unobtrusive doom-and-gloom set by John Lee Beatty and a lot of cello sawing for incidental music. Mr. Maggio aims to be lucid, if not lurid, and, less successfully, tries

Sandal and toga revenge in Grand Guignol style.

to ward off the ridiculousness induced by the plot's nonstop gore. (Charles Ludlam, Joseph Papp's original directorial choice for "Titus" two summers ago, would have made the ridiculous its own reward.) But the

Martha Swope

Donald Moffat in the title role of "Titus Andronicus."

Grand Guignol of Shakespeare's revenge tragedy doesn't respond to Mr. Maggio's level-headed approach. A play whose increasingly unhinged hero anticipates Lear — and whose writing excesses emit the savage energy of a young playwright — "Titus Andronicus" needs a mad foot stomping on the pedal. Such was the tack apparently taken by Peter Brook and Laurence Olivier in the breakthrough 1955 Stratford production that allowed audiences to see that the senseless carnage of Shakespeare's most belittled play was not far-fetched any longer in the aftermath of World War II.

Without a go-for-broke sensibility inflating it into high theater, "Titus" devolves into merely a shallow play — variously a poor man's "Lear," "Coriolanus" and "Othello," devoid of the major tragedies' sophisticated ideas, rich language, psychological complexities and true catharses. No wonder Mr. Moffat, who is in principle well cast in the title role, seems a bit lost. With his bushy white eyebrows, trim beard, bristling hair and imposing physique, he looks every inch a battle-scarred Roman general on the warpath for retribution. But the performance, like the production, is too muted and patrician in adversity. Though Mr. Moffat is tender in comforting his ravaged daughter, Lavinia, his paternal affection is never matched by the bloodcurdling rage that might plunge him credibly into the homicidal.

The evening's other performance of authority, by Keith David as the villainous Moor, Aaron, suffers similarly. Here is a conscienceless devil so cruel that hanging is considered too light a punishment for him. But the production doesn't allow Mr. David, who was a fearsome Aufidius in the Steven Berkoff "Coriolanus," the histrionic room to unleash the irrational evil of a motiveless mass murderer. The actor is instead at his firmest in Aaron's one atypically sentimental scene — his expression of affection for his own newborn child.

•

Given the context, there are a few other acceptable performances, notably from Jon DeVries and David Purdham, as Titus's brother and most prominent son. Steve Pickering, Mr. Maggio's Mercutio from Chicago, does well by small roles, but some of the weaker acting is so typical of the marathon that one wonders how much freedom of choice the visiting director had in casting. When Pamela Gien's Lavinia, in the play's most grievous incident, is raped, then loses her tongue and hands, only her diction seems to suffer. Even worse is the production's nominal Hollywood "star," Kate Mulgrew, whose scarlet-clad Tamora, Queen of the Goths, combines the sibilant diction of Tammy Grimes with the brazen red-headed hussiness of Rhonda Fleming. Put this Tamora in close proximity to that fateful barbecue, and the atmosphere of "Titus Andronicus" switches instantly from fourth-century Rome to present-day Tony Roma's.

1989 Ag 21, C13:1

Horror Meets The Musical

BUZZSAW BERKELEY, by Doug Wright; music and lyrics by Michael John LaChiusa; conceived by Christopher Ashley and Mr. Wright; directed by Mr. Ashley; setting by Edward T. Gianfrancesco; lighting by Craig Evans; costumes by Don Newcomb; sound by Aural Fixation; choreography by Joe Lanteri; properties by Regina B. Santore; production stage manager, Greta Minsky. The Silly Series II presented by WPA Theater, Kyle Renick, artistic director; Donna Lieberman, managing director. At 519 West 23d Street.

Martha Swope

Ethyl Eichelberger and Shauna Hicks in "Buzzsaw Berkeley."

Mr. Krupps, James Looney, Zack Fleece and Ace	Peter Bartlett
Judy Gorgon	Shauna Hicks
Mickey Looney	Keith Reddin
Edgore Soames and Howie Stubbs	John Hickok
Old Miss Soames, Mary Looney and Buzzsaw Berkeley	Ethyl Eichelberger
Mona Starch	Becky Gelke
Prudy Doody	Vicki Lewis

By MEL GUSSOW

Remember those M-G-M musicals in which Mickey Rooney and Judy Garland found love, happiness and a Broadway or Hollywood future by putting on a show in a barn? Actually several of those movies starred Gene Kelly and Judy Garland, but the spirit was similarly ingenuous and in the end show business conquered all.

In the new musical spoof "Buzzsaw Berkeley" (the latest in the so-called Silly Series at the WPA Theater), show business — or rather a serial killer known as Mr. Show Biz — runs amok, as the authors crossbreed "Babes in Arms" and "Summer Stock" with "The Texas Chain Saw Massacre" as well as other horror movies of recent times.

The idea has some promise, but the show is paltry as a musical satire. Aspiring to comic invention, Doug Wright, as author, and Michael John LaChiusa, as composer and lyricist, settle for opening a trunk filled with trivia. "Buzzsaw Berkeley" becomes a catch-all anthology of Hollywood over 50 years, moving eclectically from "The Wizard of Oz" to "The Exorcist," while also finding time to make fun of Shirley Temple tapping and to borrow a falling chandelier from "The Phantom of the Opera." The show wilts next to "Little Shop of Horrors" (a WPA creature feature) as well as countless examples of the genre by Charles Ludlam.

•

The musical begins teasingly as Mickey Looney and Judy Gorgon (Keith Reddin and Shauna Hicks) sit at a soda fountain and plot to catch the killer who is slashing a swath through the singers and dancers of Grave Hollow, U.S.A. "Making music in this town," the audience is told, "is tantamount to suicide."

Mickey and Judy and their equally stage-struck friends will be the bait, a fact that leads to one of Mr. Wright's funnier parody lines. On opening night of the barn show, Mickey tells the other actors, "We're all going out on the stage tonight, but we're not all coming back."

More often, the author and composer seem content with identifying the object to be ridiculed and forget about ironic commentary. Many of the jokes begin and end with the names of the characters; Buzzsaw himself is a Hollywood choreographer who happens to have a buzz saw instead of a hand? Mr. LaChiusa's lyrics do not measure up to the titles of the songs, with the exception of "I'm Taking This Show to Hell," in which a variation on Stephen Sondheim gradually changes to Cole Porter.

•

The second act is a show within a show, "The History of Human Civilization," which is meant to be transporting but is instead diversionary, wandering from the rape of the Sabine women to the American Revolution. These tableaux give the actors a chance to wear garish costumes. In a change of pace, the WPA's resident scenic designer, Edward T. Gianfrancesco, places the play behind a curtain on a proscenium stage.

As director, Christopher Ashley (who conceived the show with Mr. Wright) stresses campiness; characters are broadly caricatured. One exception is Ms. Hicks's Judy. The actress is pretty and demure and can hold a high note. She also projects an underlying feeling of instability, as associated with Judy Garland at a later age. When Mickey momentarily rejects her in favor of the Mayor's pushy daughter, Prudy Doody (Vicki Lewis), Ms. Hicks looks as if she might resort to serial murder.

Mr. Reddin is appropriately boyish and a little sly as Mickey, and Ethyl Eichelberger has a few amusing moments as the mother and father of the murderer (for the patriotic finale, he also impersonates the Statue of Liberty). But as an evening of mock nostalgia, "Buzzsaw Berkeley" is a musical of diminishing returns.

1989 Ag 21, C14:3

When Hollywood Ruled Britannia

PRIVATES ON PARADE, book and lyrics by Peter Nichols; music by Denis King; directed by Larry Carpenter; choreography by Daniel Pelzig; set design by Loren Sherman; costume design by Lindsay W. Davis; lighting design by Marcia Madeira; sound design by Robert E. Casey; production stage manager, Kathy J. Faul. Presented by the Roundabout Theater, Gene Feist, artistic director; Todd Haimes, producing director. At 100 East 17th Street.

Pvt. Steven Flowers	Jim Fyfe
Cpl. Len Bonny	Ross Bickell
Acting Capt. Terri Dennis	Jim Dale
Flight Sgt. Kevin Cartwright	Gregory Jbara
Lance Cpl. Charles Bishop	John Curry
Leading Aircraftman Eric Young-Love	Edward Hibbert
Sylvia Morgan	Donna Murphy
Sgt. Maj. Reg Drummond	Donald Burton
Maj. Giles Flack	Simon Jones
Lee	Tom Matsusaka
Cheng	Stephen Lee

By MEL GUSSOW

With his gymnastic wit and droll body, Jim Dale places his signature on whatever character he chooses to play, as he demonstrates anew in the New York premiere of Peter Nichols's "Privates on Parade." In the comedy, which opened last night at the Roundabout Theater Company, he is Acting Capt. Terri Dennis, a vaudevillian who specializes in female impersonation. It is an exceedingly flamboyant role that benefits from Mr. Dale's bold brand of clowning.

As an actor, he is not satisfied with anything halfhearted. Cast grandly against type, he dives into the character, putting on feminine airs and costumes and transforming himself into a preening powderpuff of a song and dance man. Terri is the queenpin of the Middlesex Regiment, a special service unit of military misfits on hyperactive duty in Malaysia several years after the end of World War II.

Mr. Dale first played the role 10 years ago at the Long Wharf Theater in New Haven and he returns to it with artful abandon, unearthing fresh humor in familiar material. The comedy in "Privates on Parade" is an amalgam of old jokes and music hall routines, but none of this matters much when Mr. Dale is center stage.

Jim Dale plays the vaudevillian captain in 'Privates on Parade'.

Despite its occasional suggestions of seriousness, the play is outranked by other works by the author, beginning with "Joe Egg" and "Forget-Me-Not Lane" (which has still not been presented in New York). As a satiric commentary on colonialism, "Privates on Parade" is shadowed by Caryl Churchill's "Cloud 9."

•

In its favor, it has an easygoing spontaneity. The characters are unabashed about their own amateurism as performers. Repeatedly, the dialogue stops for a song, with enough parody numbers to make the play a musical revue. The score (music by Denis King and lyrics by Mr. Nichols), is a nostalgic pastiche of a period when Hollywood ruled Britannia.

Terri and his conscripted countrymen are doomed to perform their vaudeville shows in theaters filled with non-English-speaking natives. At one point, the troupe — at the behest of its misguided major — puts on a show in a hostile section of the Malaysian interior. When guerrillas cut the power circuit, one actor does his magic act in the dark. More than anything, this reverse sight gag is representative of the lack of communication between the actors and their audience, between the English army and Malaysians.

In the late 1940's, the playwright was himself a member of such a special service unit. His alter ego in the

Martha Swope

Simon Jones, left, and Jim Dale in Peter Nichols's "Privates on Parade."

play is a young recruit quick to mimic his elders while undergoing his own rite of passage. In the role, Jim Fyfe personifies innocence eager for experience. Ross Bickel, Donald Burton and Edward Hibbert are exactingly English in contrasting roles, Mr. Hibbert as a blusterer who repeatedly threatens fisticuffs (watch out or he will respond with a "bunch of fives").

●

Next to Mr. Dale, the most amusing performance is given by Simon Jones as the bumbling commanding officer, Major Flack. As was evident in Alan Ayckbourn's "Woman in Mind," Mr. Jones excels at playing characters whose outward rationality thinly disguises dottiness. In the case of Major Flack, he can blithely lead his men to slaughter while maintaining an attitude of sanctimonious zeal. Major Flack is dangerous as well as unpredictable.

As director, Larry Carpenter has nimbly managed the many transitions, as the actors move back and forth between barracks room banter and vaudeville performance. The musical direction is by Philip Campanella, who leads a busy offstage combo.

Along his path to inimitability, Mr. Dale is called upon to imitate Marlene Dietrich, Carmen Miranda and Noël Coward, which he does with characteristic panache. Each impersonation is a salute as well as a deft act of criticism. His Dietrich is especially diabolical. Wearing silvery tights, he gingerly straddles a chair and, with intentional malice, murmurs his way through a spoof of sensuality. In this scene and others, he adds hilarity to the burlesque antics of "Privates on Parade."

1989 Ag 23, C13:3

Letter of the Lore

LOVE LETTERS, by A. R. Gurney; directed by John Tillinger; lighting design by Dennis Parichy; production stage manager, William H. Lang. Presented by Roger L. Stevens, Thomas Viertel, Steven Baruch and Richard Frankel. At the Promenade Theater, Broadway at 76th Street.

Andrew Makepeace Ladd 3d ....John Rubinstein
Melissa Gardner ....Stockard Channing

By MEL GUSSOW

In "Love Letters," A. R. Gurney has written an evocative epistolary account of two charter members of the privileged set. In less than two hours, we see Andrew Makepeace Ladd 3d and Melissa Gardner over a period of 50 years, as the author carries them from second grade through the trauma of adulthood, marriage, divorce and middle age. Despite the scope of the story, this is a work of modest intentions and modest achievement.

The play, which opened last night at the Promenade Theater, is not to be confused with Mr. Gurney's more fully realized efforts (plays that include "The Dining Room" and, more recently, "The Cocktail Hour"). It is a staged reading and, at the same time, a theatrical contrivance. But within self-imposed limitations, it has dramatic assets. Written with Mr. Gurney's customary authenticity, it becomes an often humorous Baedecker to a place and time, America — and an American elite — at mid-century.

John Rubinstein and Stockard Channing in "Love Letters," at the Promenade Theater.

Not least of all, it is, in performance, a testimony to the actor's art, a theatrical exercise in which actors, far more than in less schematic surroundings, have to draw upon their own intuitive resources — without the benefit of physical interaction or scenic effects — in order to create character and conflict.

"Love Letters" is unadorned theater, what the English would describe as a platform piece. It has been presented for limited performances since last February, with actors alternating in the roles. It is now being performed for a special eight-week engagement, with a new cast each week, beginning with John Rubinstein and Stockard Channing.

It would be difficult to imagine a finer pair of performances (although one of the rewards of the play would be to see the dimensions brought to it by different actors). Mr. Rubinstein and Ms. Channing are persuasively in character as these ultimate WASPs — Andy, already stuffy at the age of 7 and sometimes insufferable when he becomes a United States Senator, and Melissa, an undisciplined and unhappy woman all of her life. As Melissa observes late in the play, it is astonishing that the two of them could have come from such similar backgrounds yet turn out to be so radically different.

Through the eyes of the two characters, the author offers a cross-section of Gurney country, a rigidly stratified society that is defined by the proper schools, parental expectation and a kind of benign paternalism toward those less fortunate. Neither character is especially admirable, a fact that may limit the audience's sympathy, but the actors, as directed by John Tillinger, enhance one's interest.

The play works precisely because there are only two people on stage, sitting at a table and reading to each other from a book of letters. Were the reading to be fully staged, one would be even more aware of the banalities of the shared lives.

At first, the two exchange notes and Valentines in grade school, soon replaced by letters and picture postcards, each of which retains the characters' idiosyncracies. Andy remains instructive; Melissa is defined by her spontaneity, by her ability to speak her mind in print. Even in adulthood she fills her letters with childish effusions, some of which, to the play's advantage, could be excised (as letter writers, both are oceans away from

such correspondents as George Bernard Shaw and Mrs. Campbell). That Ms. Channing manages to find meaning in these lines is a tribute to her own acting art.

In several minor senses, the play challenges credibility. The mail arrives with unimaginable dispatch -- letters are never delayed or go astray. Furthermore, some letters are so brief as to become dialogue (which is, of course, the point). A character asks a question, then, posthaste, comes the answer, followed by the next question.

For all one's reservations about the chain-letter aspect of the evening, something dramatic occurs. The two characters connect. As one actor reads, the other reacts, communicating fathoms beneath the words, especially so in the case of Ms. Channing, who gives her character surprising richness. When Mr. Rubinstein reads a particularly self-serving account of his academic accomplishments, her face moves from bemusement to boredom to chagrin. She can scarcely wait for the letter to end so that she can offer her criticism of his literary style and of his lack of self-knowledge.

Similarly, as Ms. Channing describes her casual romantic alliances, one can see in Mr. Rubinstein's expressions his disapproval along with his curiosity. As opposites, each provides the other with what is needed. The irony is that they do not understand this until late in life. These are, in fact, star-crossed love letters. The play concludes on a poignant note, as we realize that the letters — the root of their lifelong relationship — are actually the instrument that keeps them apart.

1989 Ag 25, C3:1

In London, Hot Plays and Hot Weather

By MEL GUSSOW

Special to The New York Times

LONDON — On one of the hottest nights of the summer, the tiny pub theater in the East Dulwich Tavern

was filled to overflowing. Without a hint of air-conditioning or ventilation, the temperature rose as if someone were turning up the steam in a sauna. The play, "In Lambeth," written and directed by Jack Shepard, dealt with a meeting between William Blake and Tom Paine, after Paine had helped foment the American Revolution.

The first act took place in Blake's garden in Lambeth, where we encountered Blake and his wife (Michael Maloney and Lesley Clare O'Neill), up a tree, naked. When Paine (Bob Peck) arrived for an unexpected visit, the Blakes remained unclothed for a time, then with the announcement of a chill in the air, the couple went indoors to dress — to the sound of laughter from the uncomfortable theatergoers.

"In Lambeth" is an informative and thought-provoking dialogue about the uses of revolution, and the varieties of radical commitment. The cross-purposes of art and politics are scrutinized by the two contrasting Englishmen and by Mrs. Blake, who can say — ingenuously, not condescendingly — to their guest, "And what were you doing in America?" To which the play's Paine answers forthrightly, "Fighting the war of independence."

All three performances added luster to the work, especially so in the case of Mr. Peck, celebrated for his virtuosic doubling as the villainous Sir Mulberry Hawk and the heroic John Browdie in "Nicholas Nickelby." He has the zeal to play Paine and the boldness to do it for two sweltering weeks on the Fringe, far away from the center of London theater. One reason for Mr. Peck's appearance in such offbeat surroundings is that, in common with the playwright, he lives in nearby Dulwich. Because of the critical and audience response, it is expected that "In Lambeth" will return, presumably in less humid circumstances.

Heat and Strikes

The weather — the warmest in 13 years — and repeated transit strikes were blamed for a drop in London box-office receipts. Trying to combat that loss, box-office personnel in at least one theater were told to lie when asked if the theater was air-conditioned. As theatergoers discovered, one could count on coolness only at the institutional theaters, the National, the Royal Shakespeare Company, and — a refreshing newcomer to audience comfort — the Royal Court.

The theaters themselves remain London's pride, even as one is occasionally threatened, as in New York, by urban redevelopers. They are jewelbox reminders of English theatrical history. I thought I had been in all the active West End houses, but, sitting in the Strand (the play was "Much Ado About Nothing") I realized that I had never been in this splendid theater before. The reason was self-evident. For 10 years the Strand was the home of "No Sex Please, We're British."

A Tom Murphy Revival

As it turned out, "In Lambeth" was one of the few rewarding new plays of the summer, along with Richard Nelson's "Some Americans Abroad" (at the Royal Shakespeare Company). Another recent Royal Shakespeare opening proved to be less auspicious — the London premiere of Robert Holman's "Across Oka." The play is an ornithological epic, centering on an almost extinct crane whose eggs are transported across continents (and the Oka preserve in the Soviet Union). A Russian scientist is trying to propagate the bird, but makes the mistake of entrusting the eggs to two teen-age boys, who, as the audience suspects, will soon shatter their Anglo-Soviet détente. Though high-minded, the play manages to be both predictable and unbelievable.

The most powerful contemporary play, though not a new one, was Tom Murphy's "Whistle in the Dark," which, in the Abbey Theater production, was presented at the Royal Court as part of the London International Festival of Theater. Written in 1960, when Mr. Murphy was 25 years old, the play has lost none of its riveting sense of menace. This is an excoriating drama about family and country, offering an uncompromisingly harsh group portrait of Irishmen at war with themselves. The Carneys are a family of braggarts and brawlers, brought up by their father to battle one another but never to question his authority. Beneath the father's prideful boasts, he is a coward, and his sons are in various ways failures.

Garry Hynes's volatile production begins in chaos, as the men of the family crowd the stage. Once the emotion subsides, individual identities emerge — the eldest brother, who is regarded as an intellectual but is as ineffectual and as cowardly as his father; and his brutish brothers, who live by their wits and their fists.

The most moving in a fine cast was Sean McGinley as the one brother who, beneath his vulgarity, has the strongest sense of fidelity and family. When the father (Godfrey Quigley) blathers excuses for not joining his sons in their blood feud against their rivals, Mr. McGinley signals with his silence that he understands the deficiencies and the self-defeats of the warring Carneys.

Though only a guest production, "A Whistle in the Dark" seems a definitive Royal Court play of the naturalistic school, reminiscent of the early work of John Osborne and David Storey. Mr. Murphy, an unjustly neglected playwright, has written a dozen plays in the intervening years, few of which have been presented in the United States.

One of them, the provocative "Conversations on a Homecoming," briefly appeared several seasons ago at the Summerfare festival in Purchase, N.Y. New Yorkers will have another chance to see "A Whistle in the Dark" if, as planned, the Irish Repertory Theater is able to bring its recent revival for an extended engagement this fall.

The two most popular shows in London — with ticket sales unaffected by the weather — are "The Merchant of Venice," with Dustin Hoffman and Geraldine James, and Andrew Lloyd Webber's "Aspects of Love," both of which are scheduled to go to Broadway. In direct contrast to the play "In Lambeth," "The Merchant of Venice" has the most elaborate costumes, making it for the actors the warmest play in London.

Pique Over Sondheim

As usual in London, some of the most theatrical events took place off-stage, as was the case with the announcement that Stephen Sondheim

had been chosen to fill the first Oxford University chair in theater, a professorship endowed by the producer Cameron Mackintosh, who gave Oxford $2.8 million to expand the university's theater program.

The London press greeted the selection with chagrin, as if by accepting the money and the appointment Oxford had made a Faustian pact with the commercial theater. If Mr. Sondheim's equivalent in England — Harold Pinter or Tom Stoppard — were appointed to a chair at an American university, there certainly would not be a similar outcry.

Sheik Zubayr

A minor theatrical contretemps arose when it was reported in the London newspapers that Col. Muammar el-Qaddafi had claimed that Shakespeare was an Arab and that his real name was Sheik Zubayr, a reference to a seventh-century convert to Islam. Actually, Colonel Qaddafi had simply repeated a joke he had first made in a speech last year, but Elizabethan scholars were quick to take up their Shakespeares and to reiterate counterclaims that Bacon, Marlowe and the Earl of Oxford were the real authors of Shakespeare's plays.

Should Colonel Quaddafi's candidate be certified, it would, of course, necessitate a name change for the Royal Shakespeare Company. It would become the Royal Sheik Zubayr Company — the R.S.Z.C.

1989 Ag 28, C13:4

Arias Without Music

BEFORE DAWN, by Terence Rattigan; directed by Will Lieberson; set, Adrienne Brockway; costumes, Christine Vlasak; lighting design, Deborah Matlack; sound, George Jacobs; production stage manager, Winifred H. Powers. Presented by the Quaigh Theater, Mr. Lieberson, artistic director; Patricia Kearney, managing director; Judith Rubin, producer. At Theater 808, 808 Lexington Avenue, at 62d Street.

Scarpia	Lee Moore
Schiarrone	Eddie Lane
Tosca	Elizabeth Karr
Mario	Steven Colantti

By MEL GUSSOW

Should there ever be a revival of interest in the plays of Terence Rattigan, "Before Dawn" will certainly not be in the vanguard of rediscoveries. In fact, by offering the New York premiere of this flaccid sendup of "Tosca," the Quaigh Theater is doing the late English playwright a disservice.

Initially written as one half of the double bill entitled "In Praise of Love," the play was excised before the work was presented on Broadway in 1974. Exhumed, it demonstrates the author's heavyhanded humorlessness and the perverse pleasure he seemed to take in mocking both Puccini and the original Sardou play on which the opera is based.

Reversing tragedy, Rattigan has given the story a happy ending. Tosca still stabs the villainous police chief Scarpia, but in the Rattigan version Scarpia is wearing a knife-proof vest. He lives — and demands that Tosca fulfill their bargain ("What is your price?" "My price is you.") before he agrees to free her lover from prison. In a curious and unpersuasive turnabout, Scarpia and Tosca end the play in each other's arms.

The dialogue is burdened with dubious double entendres and a prolonged vaudeville routine in which Scarpia and his bumbling aide confuse orders. Tosca is prone to speak in epithets, as in "Villain, perfidious villain" and "Lustful spawn of Satan." Scarpia's lovestruck response to such terms of endearment is, "Come, O constellation of my universe." The dialogue might sound better in Italian — with music.

When the play was first presented in London, the leading roles were undertaken by Donald Sinden and Joan Greenwood. Though one could imagine their deftness, the play was still a failure. At the Quaigh, in a production directed by Will Lieberson, the actors work hard to fretful effect.

As Scarpia, Lee Moore looks as if he is holding his breath in anticipation of an aria that never arrives. Elizabeth Karr's attractive Tosca lacks the requisite worldliness and, as Scarpia's henchman, Eddie Lane trips awkwardly over the furniture and his sword. When Tosca faints, Scarpia revives her by waving a burnt feather under her nose. A flock of flaming feathers could not bestir this play. As the audience watches, "Before Dawn" dies.

1989 Ag 31, C20:5

Wages of Gluttony

LA NONNA, by Roberto Cossa; directed by Braulio Villar; assistant director, Beatriz Cordoba; production designer, Robert Weber Federico. Presented by Repertorio Español, René Buch, artistic director; Gilberto Zaldivar, producer. At the Gramercy Arts, 138 East 27th Street.

La Nonna	Ofelia Gonzalez
Carmelo	Rene Sanchez
Mari	Tatiana Vecinos
Marta	Adriana Sananes
Chico	Ricardo Barber
Anyula	Lilia Veiga
Don Francisco	George Bass

By D. J. R. BRUCKNER

Roberto Cossa's comedy "La Nonna" is sometimes dark, and often its humor may be too robust for delicate sensibilities. But in the production by Repertorio Español, the Argentinian writer's play at the Gramercy Arts Theater is very funny; the laughter it brings from the audience is gleeful and utterly unashamed.

Mr. Cossa toys with some dangerous themes. How many playwrights would risk making a 100-year-old matriarch a comic monster? There are rough ethnic jokes; people fall victim to nothing more blameworthy than their own innocence; calamities are made ridiculous. The play is a formidable challenge to a director and cast.

In this case, seven regulars from the Repertorio Español, under the direction of Braulio Villar, create characters whose absurdities ward off an audience's sympathy and keep the action moving so swiftly that there is no time for ethical reflection. And they do it without turning the characters into cartoon figures even though some of the pranks here put one in mind of the mayhem of Saturday morning television.

The story is simple enough: A family of Italian extraction in Buenos Aires is driven into poverty and desperation by its centenarian grandmother, who is eating them out of house and home. Her language is a hilarious mixture of Italian and Span-

Sheila Burnett

Bob Peck, left, and Michael Maloney in "In Lambeth," at the theater in the East Dulwich Tavern in London.

ish, but she is easy to comprehend; every word is about food and she does nothing but eat.

Her family's efforts to avoid ruin become schemes to get rid of Nonna. But the great survivor is as impervious to their plots as she has been to time for a century. Each trap they lay for her springs on one of them. In the end, every stick of furniture may be gone, even the lampshades, but Nonna remains, still eating.

Ofelia Gonzalez, as Nonna, is the key to the comedy. Every time the play seems to be coming a little too close to dangerous emotions like sorrow, compassion or indignation, she rolls on stage just a bit more imperious, and hungry, than before. There is not a pitiable bone in this character's old body. There are ways for an actor to fake eating, but Ms. Gonzalez cannot fake them all. Nonna gorges on bags of popcorn and potato chips, pots of stew, loaves of bread, pecks of apples, plates of sausage and cheese, jars of jam and mayonnaise and a basket of flowers. And as others eat around her, Ms. Gonzalez's eyes seem able to watch the hands of half a dozen people at once as they lift a bite from plate to mouth.

George Bass, as an 80-year-old man tricked as much by his own greed as by the wiles of Nonna's family into marrying her, only to have her devour his entire candy shop in a few days, turns a small role into a large comic performance. And Ricardo Barber, as one of Nonna's sons, whose absurd schemes for avoiding work and solving the Nonna problem

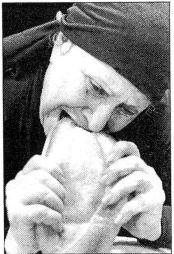

Gerry Goodstein

Ofelia Gonzalez of Repertorio Español in "La Nonna" at the Gramercy Arts Theater.

lead to the family's downfall, is the kind of rascal whose just rewards at the end make you feel warm inside even as you laugh at him.

Altogether, this cast is as nimble as an acrobatic troupe performing in a mine field. Nothing is too sacred, or fearful, to be ridiculed by them and yet they give no offense.

1989 S 1, C12:1

Kabuki's Whirl of Illusions and Disguises

By JACK ANDERSON

Two men claim to be the same warrior. One is not only an impostor, but also a fox. Both fox and man clamber over railings and pop in and out of windows with astonishing ease. And the roles of the fox, the fox disguised as the warrior and the real warrior are played by the same nimble actor — Ichikawa Ennosuke 3d, whose company, Ennosuke's Kabuki, opened Wednesday night at the Metropolitan Opera House in a remarkable display of virtuosity.

The story of the fox is told in "Yoshitsune Senbonzakura" ("Yoshitsune and the Thousand Cherry Trees"), one of two works the group from Tokyo is offering on its programs. Kabuki, which dates from the 16th century, combines acting with singing, dancing and spectacle and is one of the glories of Japanese theater. This company offers particularly lively examples of it, thanks to the showmanship of its star and artistic director, Ennosuke, who, like all great Kabuki actors, is professionally known by a single name. He calls himself 3d to distinguish himself from his grandfather, Ennosuke 2d, another illustrious actor. A member of a theatrical family, Ennosuke is the son of Danshiro 3d.

Ennosuke must be one of the world's greatest quick-change artists. Sudden appearances and disappearances are among his specialties. Therefore, "Yoshitsune Senbonza-

kura," with its illusions and disguises, is ideally suited to his talents.

During its three acts, he disappears through a trapdoor, only to return moments later, his noble robes replaced by a fox's fur. Then he vanishes and becomes a warrior again. And after all the characters are told of his true nature, this fox flies off, with the aid of wires, into the heavens.

Ennosuke's magic involves more than stagecraft; he does more than change costumes. He reveals the metamorphoses of man and fox through his acting and dancing. Portraying the real warrior, he looks dignified. But when the fox impersonates the warrior, he grows oddly twitchy. Discarding human apparel, Ennosuke as fox hops about, holding his hands like paws and speaking with animal-like squeaks.

The fox is attracted by the sound of a small drum, and the audience learns that this is because the drum is made from the hides of his parents. Receiving the drum as a gift, Ennosuke, as fox, rolls about with it and holds it between his teeth, looking extraordinarily like a puppy frisking with a toy.

Ennosuke may be the star of this show, but he is not its only attraction. He is capably supported by a company of 24 musicians and 36 actors and dancers. Ichikawa Danshiro, Ennosuke's brother in real life, was especially effective as a scowling villain.

Johan Elbers

Ichikawa Ennosuke 3d in "Yoshitsune Senbonzakura," at the Metropolitan Opera House.

As is customary in Kabuki presentations, female roles are played by men. The action includes many of the frozen poses characteristic of this theatrical form. Again following tradition, a runway has been built into the audience, along which actors make entrances and exits.

Other effects result from 20th-century technology and the imagination of Shunichiro Kanai, the troupe's set designer. Cherry blossoms fall on palace roofs. Buildings sink into the earth and slide from sight and a temple rises out of nowhere. "Yoshitsune Sebonzakura" is one theatrical conjuring trick after another.

"Kurozuka" ("The Black Mound"), which completes the program, is less flamboyant. Yet its subtleties allow Ennosuke to emphasize other aspects of his artistry. The story concerns wandering priests who are given lodging by an old woman. She, in turn, receives religious instruction from them. Ignoring her explicit commands, however, one of the priests' servants peers into an inner room of her dwelling. The pile of human bones he beholds there makes it clear that this is no ordinary woman. Growing dismayed that a member of a religious group could be disobedient, she rejects the priests' teachings and announces that she is really a ferocious demon.

•

What makes the production remarkable is Ennosuke's portrayal of the woman. At first, she looks totally innocent. The way Ennosuke walks feebly, with lowered gaze, suggests that this is a venerable, weary peasant, exhausted by a hard life in the wilderness. A quick, suspicious glance backward at the priests hints that she may not be entirely guileless. Yet she does appear to derive comfort from the priests' wisdom. Happy to learn that she may achieve salvation, she totters while attempting to dance to a children's song.

As a demon, however, Ennosuke becomes a wild-haired, frenzied monster. Nevertheless, the way he slowly but inexorably grows weaker in his

movements convincingly represents the ultimate triumph of religious truth over evil.

Transistor headsets offering translations of both plays can be rented in the lobby. The dialogue is recited quietly and does not drown out the sounds from the stage. These translations help emphasize that Kabuki plays possess serious meanings as well as dazzling visual effects.

1989 S 8, C3:4

The Right Action For the Wrong Reason

MURDER IN THE CATHEDRAL, by T. S. Eliot; directed by Peter Royston; stage manager, Eileen McGill; costumes supplied by Play Troupe of Port Washington, the Earl Hall Center; masks by Lisa Rosenthal. Presented by the Royston Company. At St. Paul's Chapel, Columbia University, 116th Street and Broadway; Friday and next Saturday at the Church of the Holy Trinity, 316 East 88th Street; Sept. 22 and 23 at St. Malachy's — the Actor's Chapel, 239 West 49th Street.

Thomas à Becket .... Henry Fandel
Women of Canterbury
    Melissa Kalt, Melanie Kane and Pamela Davis
Priests of Canterbury
    Dudley Stone, Eric Barkan and John Royston
Messenger .... Mark Walthers
Tempters/Knights
    Gretchen Michelfeld, Charlie Fersko, Jeff Callan and Gregory St. John

By WILBORN HAMPTON

In December 1170, Thomas à Becket returned to England from seven years' exile in France to reclaim his archbishopric at Canterbury. In doing so, Becket knew he faced almost certain death at the wrathful hands of King Henry II, embittered at his former Chancellor for switching his allegiance to a Higher Power. A scant 764 years later, also in December, T. S. Eliot undertook a commission to write a play for the Canterbury Festival. Eliot chose Becket's martyrdom as his subject and the result was "Murder in the Cathedral," a play intended for a special audience of churchgoers to be performed for a limited run in the cathedral's Chapter House the next summer. To Eliot's admitted amazement, the play soon became a popular success in the commercial theater and is now considered one of the poet's most enduring works.

•

It is not, however, a play one would immediately recommend to fledgling theater companies looking for a sure-fire hit to open a new venture. Yet the Royston Company has chosen this brooding introspection on life and immortality as its first production, which is being performed through tonight at St. Paul's Chapel at Columbia University and at other churches in Manhattan for the next two weekends. It is a bold selection, and while the overall result is somewhat uneven, the central conflict is well argued through two quite good performances by Henry Fandel as Becket and Gregory St. John as the Fourth Tempter. The production, enhanced by the chapel setting, mostly holds the audience's involvement, although one's attention occasionally flags.

This is no small feat in itself for a play in which there is virtually no action and the main conflict is the internal struggle in a saint's soul. At the time he wrote "Murder in the Cathedral," Eliot's own life was in serious transformation. The poet had finally separated from his first wife, Vivienne, who would spend her last years in a mental sanitarium, and he had become Vicar's Warden at St. Stephen's Church, attending daily prayers. He had also broken with his friend and onetime mentor, Ezra Pound, and had not produced any serious work for some time. Eliot, perhaps feeling a certain martyrdom of his own, was undergoing a spiritual reawakening.

The play is in two parts — the first the visitation of Becket by four tempters and the second his confrontation with four knights who will be his assassins — separated by a Christmas sermon delivered by Becket. A chorus of Canterbury women and a trio of priests provide a running commentary.

The heart of the drama, however, is in Becket's temptations. The first three tempters are the usual ones of pleasure, glory and power and are easily dismissed. The fourth is more insidious — the lure of martyrdom itself, to die for the sake of gaining immortality on earth. This is what Eliot feared most (the poet played the role of the Fourth Tempter in the film of the play). The scene between Becket and the Fourth Tempter is strong drama, and Mr. Fandel and Mr. St. John make the most of it. "The last temptation is the greatest treason," Becket declares as he finally rejects it. "To do the right deed for the wrong reason."

•

Peter Royston, the director and the company's founder, has gotten the most out of the chapel setting. The Fourth Tempter, for example, enters from the pulpit, suggesting the sin he represents originates in the church itself. And Becket's wonderful sermon on the true meaning of God's promise of peace, delivered with simplicity and humility by Mr. Fandel, is likewise given from the pulpit. Mr. Royston has cast a woman as the First Tempter, a clever idea that works well enough in Gretchen Michelfeld's reading of the role as a strumpet, and the lines of the chorus of three women, of whom Pamela Davis stood out, are broken into individual speeches.

Although there are occasional lapses into the histrionics of coffeehouse poetry recitations from some of the cast, Mr. Royston has fashioned a mostly straightforward and thoughtful production. It will be performed Friday and next Saturday at the Church of the Holy Trinity, and on Sept. 22 and 23 at St. Malachy's church.

1989 S 9, 13:1

Anthropomorphic Acrobats From Japan

By JACK ANDERSON

Puppets served tea and performed acrobatic tricks Tuesday morning when the Japan Society offered "Karakuri Ningyo: Ancient Festival Puppets," a presentation that was both unusual and delightful.

The program consisted of a display of mechanical puppets that are traditionally shown at outdoor festivals in communities near the Japanese city of Nagoya. The ornately robed figures dated from the 18th and 19th centuries. Most were just slightly bigger than baby dolls. All could perform feats of virtuosity and one of the pleasures of "Karakuri Ningyo" was that of enjoying intricate actions for their own sake.

The remarkably agile motions were made possible by strings pulled by ingenious puppeteers and by clockwork devices embedded in the puppets.

One puppet performed acrobatic balancing tricks on a pedestal. Another passed through ocean waves without getting wet by stepping across a set of wooden piles of varying heights. Still another dipped a pen into an inkwell and wrote calligraphic characters on a small banner. The show's greatest virtuoso swung from one trapeze to another.

A very dignified puppet served tea. When a cup was placed in his hands he would glide slowly with it toward a human guest at the other side of the space. Then, when the guest accepted the cup, the puppet would turn around and glide back. This automaton behaved like a robot, but had the manners of an aristocrat.

The program, produced by Teruaki Hori, was occasionally accompanied by live music and featured members of four groups: the Community Association for the Preservation of Festival Floats in Kamezaki (Ishibashi-gumi), the Community Association for the Preservation of Festival Floats in Kamezaki (Nishigumi), the Community Association for the Preservation of Festival Floats in Inuyama and the Fraternity Society for the Preservation of Temmansha Shrine Festival Floats in Arimatsu.

Most of the time, the puppeteers were out of sight, just as they would be when the puppets performed at the festivals. But protective coverings were occasionally raised to allow audiences a view backstage. The puppeteers' intense concentration and alertness added a touch of drama to the spectacle.

1989 S 15, C28:4

Learning to Identify With Internal Demons

SWEENEY TODD, music and lyrics by Stephen Sondheim; book by Hugh Wheeler; from an adaptation by Christopher Bond; directed by Susan H. Schulman; scenic design, James Morgan; costume design, Beba Shamash; lighting design, Mary Jo Dondlinger; production stage manager, Perry Cline; music direction and design, David Krane; choreography by Michael Lichtefeld. Presented by Circle in the Square Theater, Theodore Mann, artistic director; Paul Libin, producing director. At 1633 Broadway, at 53d Street.

Jonas Fogg	Tony Gilbert
Policeman	David E. Mallard
3ird Seller	Ted Keegan
Dora	Sylvia Rhyne
Mrs. Mooney	Mary Phillips
Anthony Hope	Jim Walton
Sweeney Todd	Bob Gunton
Beggar Woman	SuEllen Estey
Mrs. Lovett	Beth Fowler
Judge Turpin	David Barron
The Beadle	Michael McCarty
Johanna	Gretchen Kingsley
Tobias Ragg	Eddie Korbich
Pirelli	Bill Nabel

By FRANK RICH

Of all the powerful moments in the American musical theater, there may be none more perverse than the Act I apex of "Sweeney Todd." That moment has never seemed either more moving or more sick than as played by Bob Gunton, the Demon Barber of Fleet Street, in the revival of Stephen Sondheim's musical that has arrived at the Circle in the Square.

Let others move us with tales of love among men and women. Mr. Sondheim in this scene writes of the passion of a man for murder. Having spent 15 years in exile on a trumped-up prison charge, Sweeney has just returned to Victorian London to plot revenge on the judge who destroyed him and his family. The chalky-faced Mr. Gunton, his evenly parted hair shot with silver and his raccoon eyes rattling around their red-rimmed sockets, knows that the instruments of that revenge will be his old "friends" — the razors with which he has been reunited at long last. Sweeney sings affectionately to his razors, then stands up to raise one to the sky. "At last my right arm is complete again!" Mr. Gunton cries in surging, ecstatic voice as his long silver blade glints high in a spotlight, poised to slash through the night.

Homicidal rage may not be a pretty emotion, but who can deny that it is deeply felt? In "Sweeney Todd," Mr. Gunton's soaring anger, the crowning feature of a blazing characterization, seizes us as surely as his razor will have at the throats of his many victims; this actor earns our sympathy even as he threatens to welcome us to the grave. One of the canards about Mr. Sondheim has always been that his musicals are longer on intellect than feeling. In keeping with the performance at its heart, Susan H. Schulman's production of "Sweeney Todd," a remounting of her searing York Theater Company staging of last spring, reveals the nonsense of that assumption. No one writes more passionately for the musical theater than Stephen Sondheim. It's the nature of those passions that makes frightened audiences want to shunt them aside by dismissing them as "intellectual." Mr. Sondheim fearlessly explores psychic caverns where civilized people are not dying to go.

•

Unlike Harold Prince's original 1979 Broadway production of "Sweeney Todd" — which inhabited the huge Gershwin Theater (then the Uris) upstairs from Circle in the Square — Ms. Schulman's won't keep an audience at a safe remove from Sweeney's bloodthirstiness. The director eliminates the physical distance from the executioner's scalding soul by obliterating the proscenium arch and locking us in a gloomy arena set (by James Morgan) that surrounds us with the characters' sooty, squalid nocturnal London. But greater proximity does not alone explain why this "Sweeney Todd" is more upsetting than the first. Ms. Schulman's new take on Mr. Sondheim's musical has less to do with her staging — some of which owes a debt

Bob Gunton and Beth Fowler in "Sweeney Todd."

Martha Swope

to Mr. Prince's in any case — than with her distinctive reading of what the show is about.

Mr. Prince's "Sweeney Todd," amply supported by the Hugh Wheeler-Christopher Bond book as well as by the Sondheim lyrics, emphasized the dehumanizing horror of the Industrial Age. The first thing the audience saw was a front curtain depicting the oppressive British beehive, or social pecking order; the hulking set included part of an actual iron foundry. Sweeney was the victim of Darwinian class struggle; he was a wronged representative of "the lower zoo" rising up against "the privileged few." While such sentiments remain in the text, Ms. Schulman has played down the simplistically stated ideology of "Sweeney Todd" by removing Mr. Prince's Brechtian theatrical trappings and with them any trace of Brechtian alienation. We are instead asked to identify point-blank with Sweeney and his partner in crime, the pie-baking Mrs. Lovett (Beth Fowler), as tragic figures caught in conundrums of sex and death. The characters' universal internal demons, rather than the remote demons of their Dickensian London, are center stage.

While the original production had some of the tone of "The Threepenny Opera," Ms. Schulman's is more like a penny-dreadful "Macbeth." One misses the savage comic attack of Mr. Prince's version (and of Angela Lansbury's Mrs. Lovett) but receives in exchange a played-for-keeps tale of love and innocence thwarted and twisted into hate and destruction, of cannibalism with a shockingly human face.

Ms. Schulman's route into "Sweeney" begins with her superb cast, then blossoms through Mr. Sondheim's score. Ms. Fowler makes us believe in Mrs. Lovett's maternal heart, even as she grinds up Sweeney's victims for meat-pie filling, because we see a lonely woman hopelessly in love with the barber she first met years ago. If Mr. Gunton loves his razors more than the deluded Mrs. Lovett, his longing for his lost wife and his daughter is an overwhelming obsession, finally to reach a rending catharsis in his sobbing embrace of his wife's corpse.

The heated acting, if not always the authenticity of accents, extends to the key supporting players: SuEllen Estey as a feral beggar woman with a secret, David Barron's sadomasochistic Judge Turpin, Michael McCarty's mercurial Beadle and especially Eddie Korbich's forlorn pie-shop assistant. They not only sing well (without amplification) but also infuse the stereotypes of 19th-century melodrama with pathos and madness. Though the strong-voiced young lovers, Jim Walton and Gretchen Kingsley, remain mannequins, they are somewhat shackled by the writing. Mr. Sondheim's forte is not dewy-eyed Romeo-and-Juliet couples (unless he's mocking them, as in "A Funny Thing Happened on the Way to the Forum").

Thanks to the performances, the larger quarters at Circle in the Square do not entirely dismantle the cheek-by-jowl relationship the show enjoyed with its audience in the York's tiny quarters last spring. The ghostly atmosphere is inevitably dissipated, however, and some of it might have been reclaimed by stronger musical accompaniment. David Crane's clever synthesizer arrangements, effective at the York, lack the presence essential to deliver

the score's Bernard Herrmann-like horror effects in the larger house.

Yet the beauty and drama of Mr. Sondheim's songs remain, and Ms. Schulman and company make us listen to them anew. Like his protagonist, Mr. Sondheim hears "the music that nobody hears": the music by which people act out their basest grand passions. We're increasingly aware that the plot's ugliest incidents inspire Mr. Sondheim's most gorgeous melodies. Rape comes with a minuet and murder with a rhapsodic ode to "Pretty Women." When Ms. Fowler fantasizes about domestic bliss with Sweeney — in a cozy resort hideaway equally suitable for lovemaking and throat-slitting — she expresses her deranged hopes in a cheery mock-Beatrice Lillie ditty, "By the Sea."

By forcing us to face Mr. Sondheim's music and the feelings it contains so intensely, Ms. Schulman doesn't obliterate the Prince production; she creates an alternative. Such is the depth of Mr. Sondheim's achievement that "Sweeney Todd" can support radically different interpretations (not to mention intervening assaults by opera companies) and easily hold its own without elaborate stage machinery. Stripped of its giant set, its politics, its orchestra, much of its chorus and its dazzling original stars, this troubling musical still refuses to leave us alone and, if anything, insinuates its way further into the audience's own private darkness. A naked "Sweeney Todd" stands revealed as a musical of naked rage, chewing up everyone in its path as it spits out blood and tears.

1989 S 15, C3:1

Alphabet Soup

ANULAH, LET THEM EAT CAKE, directed and designed by Karen William and Tom Andrews; written by Ms. Williams and Mark Bradford; music composed by Mickele Navazio and Tonny Prabowo; film by Peter von Ziegesar; video by Scott Anderson and Peter von Ziegesar, Chutes and Ladders Theater Company, in collaboration with Indonesian Artists; presented by the Theater for the New City, George Bartenieff, executive director; Crystal Field, executive artistic director. At 155 First Avenue, at Ninth Street.

John	Arswendi Nasution
Priyo	Fien Herman
Wilson	Tom Andrews
Dr. Ben Gigi	Roderick Murray
Putu 1	Maria Sriningsih
Putu 2	Derrick McQuee
Putu 3	Karen Williams
Agus	Agus Tono

By D. J. R. BRUCKNER

Mixed media in the theater can be a mixed blessing. In "Anulah, Let Them Eat Cake" at the Theater for the New City, the music of Tonny Prabowo and Mickele Navazio is as light and loony as most of the dialogue, giving this little play the air of comic opera. But symbolic film and video sequences running throughout the performance mostly add further confusion to a mystifying story.

The work, concocted by the Chutes and Ladders Theater Company in collaboration with Indonesian actors associated with the noted Indonesian poet Rendra, had its premiere in June in Jakarta. The self-indulgent influence of the poet is evident in this piece, but theatergoers who wilted through four hours of his "Ritual of Solomon's Children" here in 1988 should know that "Anulah" occupies only one hour and even when it is not understandable, it is entertaining.

It is an exploration of cultural confusion, mostly the West's misunderstanding of South Pacific cultures in its single-minded pursuit of material prosperity. But Indonesians' understanding of themselves gets bruised too. The dialogue is a mixture of English and Malay. The actors or the television screen translate everything, but that hardly matters; the script is pretty much alphabet soup in any language.

The play acknowledges as much when, during one particularly impenetrable part of the story, a menacing woman in an outlandish cloak looms over a knot of prostrate actors and utters in both languages a hilarious sibylline speech that turns out to be nothing more than a litany on the word "whatchamacallit" (that is what "anulah" means).

●

If there is a failure in translation, it is deeper than words. Despite funny skits, haunting music and a few gaudily spectacular scenes, there is a fundamental dramatic flaw. The misunderstood Indonesian is personified in a character named John. No matter what happens to anyone else, John is the focus, and in the end the play fails to make one care much about him. The wit of this work is distant and a bit cold.

With one exception. There is noth-

The New York Times/Neal Boenzi

Agus Tono rehearsing "Anulah, Let Them Eat Cake," at the Theater for the New City.

ing cold about the Indonesian actor Agus Tono. This minute mischiefmaker (his character is himself) pulverizes every scene, bouncing mutely through them like a Charlie Chaplin on a trampoline. Nothing can hold him down, certainly not the arms, legs or sprawling bodies of other actors. He can leap twice his own height from a standstill to somersault right over people's heads. And when he decides to make up to other characters, to hug their knees and deck them with flowers — with only a hint of a conspiratorial glance at the audience — he can bring them down to size in the blink of an eye. When he springs into action, the muddle of everything going on around him does not seem important.

1989 S 17, 79:4

A TV Evangelist With Las Vegas Values

CARNAGE, A COMEDY, by Adam Simon and Tim Robbins; directed by Mr. Robbins; scenic design by Catherine Hardwicke; costume design by Neil Spisak; lighting design by Robert Wierzel; backdrop artist, Ethan Johnson; original music and arrangements performed by Anarchestra; musical director, David Robbins; production stage manager, Michel Chenelle. The Actors' Gang production presented by Joseph Papp. At the Public/Susan Stein Shiva Theater, 425 Lafayette Street.

WITH: Lee Arenberg, Ned Bellamy, Jack Black, Cynthia Ettinger, Jeff Foster, Kyle Gass, Brent Hinkley, Shannon Holt, Lisa Moncure, Dean Robinson and Cari Dean Whittemore.

By FRANK RICH

If there are still any innocents who fantasize that movie actors make up their own dialogue, they will quickly be disabused of the notion at "Carnage, a Comedy," the new play at the Public Theater. The co-author (with Adam Simon) and director of "Carnage" is the gifted actor Tim Robbins, who was in every way the winning pitcher in the jazzily written baseball movie "Bull Durham." But the author of "Bull Durham" was Ron Shelton. Mr. Robbins's performance as a writer for the theater, let alone as a director, is far less persuasive. There may have been a more amateurish work than "Carnage" on a professional stage in New York this year, but somehow the gods spared me from seeing it.

The production was developed by a Los Angeles-based company known as the Actors' Gang, of which Mr. Robbins, who remains offstage in "Carnage," is artistic director. The script is a series of blackout sketches about the Rev. Dr. Cotton Slocum (Lee Arenberg), a television evangelist of apocalyptic beliefs and Las Vegas values, and the gun-worshiping, book-burning paranoids in and beyond his flock who confuse jingoistic notions of Manifest Destiny with divine wisdom. The authors wish to impress upon the audience the connections between religious and political fanaticism, between church and governmental corruption. In the era of Jim Bakker, Jimmy Swaggart and Oliver North, "Carnage" may strike only the truest PTL believers as controversial.

What makes the evening ludicrous, however, is not that its authors state the obvious incoherently (or, as they would have it, surrealistically) but that they give the audience the idiot treatment. The play doesn't so much preach as condescend to the converted, and its overweening arrogance is far harder to take than its routine ineptitude. The Actors' Gang seems to assume that no one in the theater has read a newspaper or even watched "Nightline" for several years; it repeatedly presents stale news as thunderous revelation, from the cynicism of latter-day Elmer Gantrys to the paramilitary fantasies of the far right to the greedy hucksterism of religious theme parks. A long sequence parodying a televised revival meeting is so tame that one longs to pick up a remote control and switch the channel to the real thing.

As patronizing as the play is to the audience, it is even more so to its characters. They are uniformly acted at a hysterical pitch that recalls the comic-book style used by the avant-garde theater in the late 1960's to caricature Middle Americans as

Cynthia Ettinger, left, Jeff Foster and Jack Black in "Carnage, a Comedy," at the Public Theater.

Martha Swope

homogeneous yahoos. Slocum's followers live in tract homes, dress in gaudy K Mart fashions and sound like Gomer Pyle. They are usually made up in clownish white face, and their aggregate I.Q. is probably lower than that of a losing contestant on "Wheel of Fortune."

By contrast, the members of the Actors' Gang are very smart and terminally hip. In their Playbill biographies, they crack jokes and reveal their clever nicknames, like Tim (Daddy Fresh) Robbins. They thank "inspirators" eclectically ranging from Jackie Gleason to the Théâtre du Soleil. They graciously acknowledge the contributions of such celebrity supporters as Hollywood studio executives, Kevin Costner, Anjelica Huston and Robin Williams. Its title notwithstanding, "Carnage" is not a comedy. But that this preening exercise in show-biz self-indulgence would occupy a rare Public Theater platform for new American playwrights is surely a farce.

1989 S 18, C14:1

Correction

A picture caption yesterday with a review of the play "Carnage, a Comedy" referred incorrectly in some copies to the performer at the center. She was Lisa Moncure.

1989 S 19, A3:1

The Black Experience

IMPERCEPTIBLE MUTABILITIES IN THE THIRD KINGDOM, by Suzan-Lori Parks; directed by Liz Diamond; set design, Alan Glovsky; set design consultants, Deborah Scott and Kyle Chepulis; lighting design, Pat Dignan; costume design, Laura Drawbaugh; slide photography, Phil Perkis; sound design, Pam Peterson; composer, Daniel Goode; production stage manager, Jennifer McDowall. Presented by BACA Downtown, in association with Y in Terms of X. At 111 Willoughby Street, Brooklyn.

Naturalist/Overseer/Charles/Duffy
.... Peter Schmitz
Veronica/Us-Seer/Aretha/Mrs. Smith
.... Pamala Tyson
Robber/Soul-Seer/Miss Faith/Mr. Smith
.... Jasper McGruder
Molly/Kin-Seer/Blanca/Muffy ....Kenya Scott
Charlene/Shark-Seer/Anglor/Buffy
.... Shona Tucker

By MEL GUSSOW

Behind the imposing title "Imperceptible Mutabilities in the Third Kingdom," there is the voice of a thoughtful young playwright, Suzan-Lori Parks. In a quartet of thematically related scenes (at BACA Downtown in Brooklyn), the author demonstrates a historical perspective and a theatrical versatility. The title of the piece is entirely applicable. In this study of the black experience from slavery to the present, the changes are almost invisible — like geological shifts in the earth.

Ms. Parks's heightened, dreamlike approach is occasionally reminiscent of the work of Adrienne Kennedy and Ntozake Shange (the evening begins with a young woman considering suicide). But there is substantial evidence of the playwright's originality; ironically this occurs in a play that deals partly with the loss of identity. Ms. Parks's identity as an artist is clear. In her four "Mutabilities," she is earnest about making political points but has a playful sense of language and a self-effacing humor that leavens the work whenever it threatens to become pretentious.

In the opening scene, "Snails," three contemporary black women have their privacy invaded by a nosy naturalist masquerading as an exterminator. Insinuating himself into their habitat, he spies on them with the help of a camera hidden inside a mechanical mock-up of a giant cockroach. Too large to step on, the bug lurks like a killer mutant. Despite the invasion, the women continue to converse, in dialogue that achieves an unconscious urban lyricism.

"Snails" is concerned with such vital matters as education, literacy, domestic violence and, tangentially, the preservation of wildlife. One of the characters habitually watches the television show "Wild Kingdom," and is astonished when she sees the peaceful Marlin Perkins carrying a gun on camera. The world, as we soon see, is falling apart, or, in the words of the pompous exterminator, "the great cake of civilization is beginning to crumble."

"Open House" is a symbolic case of open-heart surgery, an exploration into the life and mind of a former slave who is dying. In a collage of nightmarish images, she relives events from her plantation past, including her disparagement at the

hands of the white girls whom she raised for her master.

In the climactic piece, "Greeks," a black Marine sergeant plays the role of good soldier far beyond the call of duty. He is all starch and polish, mimicking the white man and debasing himself as he waits for his unknown and perhaps irrelevent "distinction" to arrive. His family at home extols him in his absence, maintaining a happy facade while falling into blindness (literally, in the case of the sergeant's wife).

This is a double-edged comedy, mocking stereotypes while leaving us with a bitter message about the pitfalls of assimilation. As in the other scenes, the work is shadowed by myth and metaphor, in this instance, Icarus, whose story is woven into the narrative.

There are occasional rough patches in the writing and some of the projected photographs (by Phil Perkis) impede the flow of the play. One scene, "The Third Kingdom," about the rocky passage of slave ships, is as brief as an interlude. But "Imperceptible Mutabilities" is filled with surprising turns that demonstrate the playwright's ingenuity and humanity.

Within the somewhat austere confines of the BACA stage, Liz Diamond, the director, has given the work a striking production, drawing on the talents of a fine cast and taking advantage of the imaginations of the set designer, Alan Glovsky, and the costume designer, Laura Drawbaugh.

The five actors (Jasper McGruder, Pamala Tyson, Kenya Scott, Shona Tucker and Peter Schmitz) inhabit the various worlds of Ms. Parks's play with sensitivity. Mr. McGruder and Ms. Tyson are especially moving — Mr. McGruder as the sergeant who calmly embraces self-sacrifice, Ms. Tyson as the soldier's dutiful wife and as the former slave. On her deathbed, haunted by ancient memories, she embodies the anguish of a life in subjugation.

1989 S 20, C24:4

A Vehicle For a Leading Lady

THE SOLID GOLD CADILLAC, by Howard Teichmann and George S. Kaufman; directed by Gitta Honegger; set design by Ed Check; costume design by James A. Schuette; lighting design by Jennifer Tipton; production stage manager, Karen L. Carpenter; resident stage manager, Margaret Adair Quinn. Presented by Yale Repertory Theater, Lloyd Richards, artistic director; Benjamin Mordecai, managing director. At New Haven.

Narrator .... Henry Winkler
T. John Blessington .... Earl Hindman
Alfred Metcalfe .... James Lally
Warren Gillie .... Joseph Fuqua
Clifford Snell .... Tom McGowan
Laura Partridge .... Anne Pitoniak
Amelia Shotgraven .... Deborah Offner
Mark Jenkins.............. Christopher Centrella
Miss L'Arriere .... Claudia Feldstein
Edward L. McKeever .... Tommy Hollis
Miss Logan, Estelle Evans and Reporter
.... Zoey Zimmerman
Anchors .... Al Terzi and Diane Smith
Reporters .... Sean Cullen and William Langan

By MEL GUSSOW

Special to The New York Times

NEW HAVEN, Sept. 15 — As a playwright and director, George S. Kaufman was the great collaborator of the popular American theater. But some of his collaborations were far less re-

warding than others, as is demonstrated by his partnership with Howard Teichmann in writing "The Solid Gold Cadillac." This 1953 Broadway comedy about chicanery in big business has been revived at the Yale Repertory Theater for the centennial of Kaufman's birth.

The comedy is halfhearted in its cynicism and only randomly representative of Kaufman's considerable wit. The construction is surprisingly schematic given his reputation for well-made plays. Cinematic techniques are awkwardly used, as if the authors could not decide whether they were writing a play or a scenario.

On Broadway and in the movies, "The Solid Gold Cadillac" was a vehicle for its leading lady, and whatever liveliness exists in Gitta Honegger's production at Yale is principally a credit to Anne Pitoniak, who plays the pivotal role of Laura Partridge. With her grandmotherly appearance, she is a most unprepossessing — but persuasive — giant killer.

As a small stockholder who topples an empire, Miss Pitoniak is not quite the little-old-lady patented by Josephine Hull on Broadway or the Billie Dawn-influenced upstart played by Judy Holliday in the film version. She is instead a feisty and determined idealist, elderly but never fragile, and quite the professional actress the character is supposed to be when she is not challenging corporate politics. Her digressions about the theater are, in fact, the most Kaufmanesque aspect of the script, as in her comment on how tiring it is to perform Shakespeare: "You never get to sit down unless you're a king."

From the moment Miss Pitoniak speaks out at the annual stockholders meeting of the General Products Corporation and questions the high executive salaries, the company's complacency is in jeopardy. Soon she has organized the other small stockholders into a rebellious family.

Once having established the conflict, the authors are at sea about how far they are prepared to go in mocking corruption — and settle for easy targets. The executives become interchangeable fools. Practicing their hobbies (carpentry, golf) on company time, they are too obviously mindless. Such sequences should have been played down rather than given center stage, as is the case in Ms. Honegger's production.

At the heart of the plot is the relationship between Mrs. Partridge and the company's former boss, Edward L. McKeever, now in Washington in the Cabinet. At Mrs. Partridge's urging he returns to corporate battle. The scenes between the two offer Miss Pitoniak an opportunity to demonstrate her disarming spontaneity and her character's intuitive use of her wiles.

Tommy Hollis is a dapper, almost wistful McKeever, making him a titan of industry who has never lost his youthful ebullience. Mr. Hollis's delivery of his schoolboy oration, "Spartacus to the Gladiators" and Miss Pitoniak's abashed reaction to its histrionics provide one of the show's zestful interludes. The other actors, limited by their one-dimensional roles, try to compensate by playing broadly.

The portrait of big business has a nostalgic period quality. There is an innocence not only about Mrs. Partridge but also about the executives who unthinkingly put one of their own subsidiary companies out of business.

Today such a move would probably be intentional for a self-serving purpose.

"The Solid Gold Cadillac" is presented as a fairy tale, with Mrs. Partridge as Cinderella and McKeever as her equally elderly Prince Charming. That framework is underscored by a narrator, in this case, Henry Winkler (his predecessors on Broadway and in the movie were Fred Allen and George Burns). Mr. Winkler appears on film, projected over the heads of the other actors. The narration serves as a self-conscious apology for the mildness of the satire.

1989 S 21, C28:1

The Younger Set

THE 1989 YOUNG PLAYWRIGHTS FESTIVAL, sets by Allen Moyer; costumes by Jess Goldstein; lighting by Karl E. Haas; sound by Janet Kalas; production manager, Carl Mulert; production stage manager, Mimi Apfel. Presented by the Foundation of the Dramatists Guild, Nancy Quinn, producing director; Sheri M. Goldhirsch, managing director. At Playwrights Horizons, 416 West 42d Street.

TWICE SHY, by Debra Neff; directed by Mark Brokaw.

PETER BREAKS THROUGH, by Alejandro Membreno; directed by Thomas Babe.

PAINTED RAIN, by Janet Allard; directed by Mary B. Robinson.

FINNEGAN'S FUNERAL PARLOR AND ICE CREAM SHOPPE, by Robert Kerr; directed by Mr. Babe. WITH: Ray Cochran, Mark W. Conklin, Allison Dean, David Eigenberg, David Barry Gray, Katherine Hiler, Kimble Joyner, Lauren Klein, David Lansbury, James McDonnell, Debra Monk, Christopher Shaw, Jill Tasker and Mary Testa.

By MEL GUSSOW

The four writers in this season's Young Playwrights Festival are among the most talented to emerge in the eight years of the annual series. Their short plays opened last night at Playwrights Horizons (three by other playwrights will be given staged readings in October). As was also true last year, there are definite signs that the young playwrights — they have to be under the age of 19 when they submit their work to the Dramatists Guild competition — are exploring ideas that move far beyond the problems of adolescence.

This is certainly the case in Debra Neff's "Twice Shy." With its sophistication and understanding of the emotional stress within the closest of relationships, the play would stand out in any one-act festival.

Assuring that fact, Mark Brokaw has given the play an excellent production. Under his direction, the actors are exactingly in character — with special credit to Katherine Hiler, who is very appealing in the central role. They avoid all opportunities for caricature, which could be a possibility with the heroine's manipulative mother (Lauren Klein). But as written and performed, the scenes between mother and daughter should provoke laughs of recognition among theatergoers with similar tense but loving familial situations.

●

At the same time, we see Ms. Hiler relating differently to three men in her life: her best friend and roommate (who is a homosexual); his lover, who invariably causes Ms. Hiler to be late for class because he is

practicing tai chi in her bathroom, and a new man who enters her life courtesy of her mother.

Each of the three is a vivid character, and they are nimbly portrayed by a trio of disparate actors (Ray Cochran, David Lansbury and Mark W. Conklin, respectively). Wisely, Ms. Neff is unafraid to end her play on a note of tentativeness — as in life. "Twice Shy" is a poignant look at a young woman trying to regain her equilibrium in her imbalanced world.

Mr. Cochran, who is amiably subdued in "Twice Shy," soars into stratospheric comedy in Alejandro Membreno's "Peter Breaks Through," in which urban decadence collides with airy fantasy. It would be unfair to reveal the twists of the author's exceedingly clever plot, except to say that the ending is a turnabout in which one character receives a most justified comeuppance. Under Thomas Babe's artful direction, Mary Testa and James McDonnell join Mr. Cochran in making this a mischievous romp.

"Painted Rain" by Janet Allard — at 15 the youngest of the playwrights — is the most traditional of the quartet. This is a sweet, sad vignette about two lonely boys growing up in an orphanage, one of whom dreams about being a painter. There is a gentle poetic quality in the writing and the imagery. Led by their director, Mary B. Robinson, Christopher Shaw and Kimble Joyner communicate the empathy that binds the boys in friendship and the strains that constantly threaten to put them at arm's distance.

At last year's festival, Robert Kerr was represented by "And the Air Didn't Answer," an absurdist comedy about a free-thinking Catholic schoolboy. This season he returns with a macabre cartoon called "Finnegan's Funeral Parlor and Ice Cream Shoppe," directed by Mr. Babe. The title character (Mr. McDonnell) is an undertaker who has decided to put "the fun back in funerals." In addition to his new soda fountain, Finnegan is contemplating "theme funerals."

The funniest moments in this pitch-black comedy do not deal with deadly events, but with family matters concerning Finnegan's sons. One is an insanely disreputable dropout (David Eigenberg) whose favorite pastime is "rioting by himself"; the other is a shy homebody (David Barry Gray) who is unable to speak until encouraged by an attractive young woman (Allison Dean) applying for a job. As enacted by Mr. Gray, the boy's speech lessons are wryly amusing. In this and other moments, it is evident — as it was in his play last year — that the author has an outrageous sense of humor. This is one Young Playwrights Festival that warrants an extended engagement.

1989 S 22, C5:4

Shakespeare On the Beach

MIDSUMMER NIGHTS, music by Kevin Kuhn; book and lyrics by Bryan D. Leys; directed by David Saint; musical director, Seth Rudetsky; set design, James Noone; lighting design, Mark London; costume design, Amanda J. Klein; production stage manager, Ira Mont; choreography by Jonathan Cerullo. Presented by Musical Theater Works, Anthony J. Stimac, artistic director. At the Theater at St. Peter's Church, 54th Street and Lexington Avenue.

Penelope Quince	Judith Moore
Fred Bottom	George Merritt
Theseus T. Duke	Wally Dunn
Hippolyta Thrace	Kristine Nevins
Oberon	Eric Kornfeld
Titania	Tracey Berg
Puck	Harold Perrineau Jr.
Hermia Thrace	Traci Lyn Thomas
Lysander Duke	Peter Marc
Helena Bottom	Brenda Braxton
Demetrius J. Quince	Howard Samuelsohn
Cobweb	Joyce P. King
Blossom	Jamie Martin
Moth	Stacy Morze

By WILBORN HAMPTON

Few plays travel more easily to different times and places than "A Midsummer Night's Dream." The Public Theater moved it to fin de siècle Brazil to open its Shakespeare Marathon and the Royal Shakespeare Company put it somewhere in limbo in its new staging at Stratford-on-Avon last spring. Now the Musical Theater Works has, with not a few liberties, plopped it down in Laguna Beach, Calif., circa 1965, and set it to music under the title "Midsummer Nights." Like the 60's, the result turns out to be a very mixed bag of tricks.

That is not to say "Midsummer Nights," which is being presented at the Theater at St. Peter's Church, Lexington Avenue at 54th Street, is without its merits. It is a frothy show with lively tunes by Kevin Kuhn and some sassy and clever lyrics by Bryan D. Leys. But once the game of matching Shakespeare's characters to their namesakes in Laguna Beach is exhausted, there is little to fill the gaps between songs.

●

The cast is divided into two groups — the "adults" and the "teen-agers" — and the working premise is, as Puck (a beach boy) puts it, "For every teen-ager looking for a good time, there is a parent who hopes he doesn't find it." The crossed lovers are stereotyped to fit any high school yearbook. Hermia is a four-eyed bookworm who wears her sweater to the beach; Helena is a leather-jacketed hell-raiser; Demetrius is a nerd with a slide rule in his belt, and Lysander is the king of the beach bums. Cobweb, Blossom and Moth form a bikini-clad backup trio. On the adult side, Oberon and Titania are a couple of diehard beatniks, and the mechanicals, Theseus and Hippolyta, double as a community theater company and the teen-agers' parents.

As songwriters, Mr. Kuhn and Mr. Leys are a promising team. The music will appeal mostly to those who have a fondness for 1960's pop, although there are a ballad or two and a couple of rousing production numbers to keep your foot tapping. One can hear contemporary influences here and there, but one would also like to hear some of Mr. Kuhn's songs again. The finale, "Magic Midsummer Nights," lingers in the mind. Mr. Leys's witty lyrics contribute considerably. In fact, Mr. Leys employs most of his invention in the lyrics,

using them to define characters (as in Titania and Oberon's duet "What Good Is Being a Beatnik?") and rarely repeating a line.

●

The main weakness of "Midsummer Nights" is the book, which is also by Mr. Leys and which seems to be guided by the misconception that the mere mention of a television show or brand name from the 1960's is somehow funny in itself. There should be a strict limit of one Tupperware joke per nostalgia show.

Carol Rosegg

Brenda Braxton in the musical "Midsummer Nights."

The 14 energetic cast members moves briskly between numbers and, under David Saint's direction, avoid running into each other on the small stage at St. Peter's. Brenda Braxton as Helena and Howard Samuelsohn as Demetrius get the most out of their matchup. Ms. Braxton's opening-act solo, "He's Gonna Be My Boyfriend" is belted like a threat rather than a lovesick ballad.

Ms. Braxton is commanding on the stage. When the trio behind her encroaches on her spotlight, she wheels and barks, "You're supposed to be backup girls, now back up!" Mr. Samuelsohn turns his solo "I'm a Square" into a rocking showstopper that is a credit to the memory of Elvis. Judith Moore can take a song like "A Small Affair" and make it a confidential confession to the audience, and can milk a ditty like "Bright and New" for all it's worth. Traci Lyn Thomas is also winning, especially in her duet with Ms. Braxton, "Guys Will Be Guys."

It is distracting to hear an apology for a show before the lights dim, but Anthony J. Stimac, the Musical Theater Works' artistic director, informed the audience at the outset that "Midsummer Nights" is a work in progress and that "changes are made every night." One hopes they don't change the good bits.

1989 S 24, 71:3

A Homoerotic Twist For an Old Tale

I & I, by Else Lasker-Schüler; directed by Judith Malina; translated by Beate Hein Bennett; music by Carlo Altomare; set by Ilion Troya; lighting by Michael Smith and 14th Street Stage Lighting; costumes by Bénédicte Leclerc. Presented by the Living Theater, 272 East Third Street. WITH: Alan Arenius, Carlo Altomare, Elena

Jandova, Gary Brackett, Ilion Troya, Initia, Jerry Goralnick, Joanie Fritz, Laura Kolb, Laurence Frommer, Lillian Jenkins, Lois Kagan, Lola Ross, Michael Saint Clair, Philip Brehse, Rain House, Robert Projansky, Sander Van Dam, Sheila Dabney, Thomas Walker, Tim Wright, Victoria Murphy and Willie C. Barnes.

By D. J. R. BRÜCKNER

Faust and Mephistopheles go to heaven together, embraced by God, in Else Lasker-Schüler's "I & I," a wild play that upends not only Goethe but also many Western literary, religious and historical traditions. Lasker-Schüler, a Jewish poet who fled Germany when the Nazis took over in 1933, wrote the play in Jerusalem in the early 40's and was still revising it when she died in 1945. Now the first English translation of the German text, by Beate Hein Bennett, is being staged by Judith Malina at the Living Theater, 272 East Third Street.

Lasker-Schüler seems to have wanted to write a new plot for all of human history and to use every theatrical technique from Goethe's classicism to Dada. Her large cast of characters includes Max Reinhardt, the Ritz Brothers, Kings Saul, David and Solomon along with the Canaanite god Baal from the Bible (here an ally, of God, not an enemy). Hitler, with a platoon of big Nazis, and a scarecrow also put in appearances.

•

Her purpose, in a text filled with hundreds of literary echoes, is serious. Behind the bizarre antics of her characters and the often scorching humor of her lines is a tremendous longing for mercy and reconciliation, for a way out of the labyrinth of human evil. It is a longing one feels all the more at the end of the play because she could not extend it to Hitler and the Nazis, who all sink into a sea of fire as Faust and the devil go to heaven.

"I & I" is a play within a play. Unfortunately, Miss Malina takes it a step further. She puts the audience at tables in a cafe called Gehenna where actors in devil suits prance around with trays like bunnies in the old Playboy Clubs. And she often threads the action through this cramped little piece of pretense, forcing the audience to stretch, crane around and even occasionally jump up to see. This play would have much greater force at a distance, as Lasker-Schüler indicated clearly when she set it in an outdoor theater under a tower.

It would also have greater force if its ideas were not smothered in endless, usually erotic tangles of flesh. For instance, Lasker-Schüler has Faust discover to his surprise that his jousting with the devil has made him love his adversary and even become one with him; but the philosophical point she makes about the transformation of hatred and fear by love and tolerance is lost when, as happens in this performance, man and devil are portrayed as intensely homoerotic throughout. Lasker-Schüler was herself a relentless subverter of accepted ideas, but she, as much as Goethe, saw the Faust-Mephistopheles story as something a little deeper than a sensual romp.

Nonetheless, this last exotic work of a most exotic poet is a compelling and disorienting experience. With its exalted vision, its distracting mixture of farce, tragedy and music hall skit, it is like a great ruin that baffles one's every effort to comprehend it. There is a lot to be said for a fine ruin.

1989 S 24, 72:3

Sibling Rivalry On a Historic Scale

THE MAN WHO SHOT LINCOLN, by Luigi Creatore; directed by Crandall Diehl; scenery and costumes by Michael Bottari and Ronald Case; lighting by Craig Miller; production stage manager, Renée F. Lutz. Presented by William De Silva, in association with Claridge Productions. At the Astor Place Theater, 434 Lafayette Street.

Edwin Booth	Sam Tsoutsouvas
Mary Devlin	Marcia Gay Harden
The Player	Eric Tull
John Wilkes Booth	Conan McCarty

By HERBERT MITGANG

The great American game of discovering the "real" assassin of a President or other major public figure is stretched to its most absurd limit in "The Man Who Shot Lincoln," a play by Luigi Creatore that opened Thursday night at the Astor Place Theater.

Why was Lincoln shot? Not simply because a fanatical Southern sympathizer wanted to kill him in the belief that doing so would somehow help the

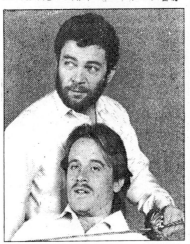

Brothers Booth Sam Tsoutsouvas, top, and Conan McCarty will appear in "The Man Who Shot Lincoln," a play by Luigi Creatore about events surrounding the historic event as told by John Wilkes Booth's brother Edwin

Confederacy. No, according to the proceedings on stage, it all had to do with sibling rivalry between Edwin Booth and John Wilkes Booth.

For the last 124 years, the culprit who killed Lincoln at Ford's Theater in 1865 has been known to be John Wilkes Booth. The egomaniacal young actor, an inveterate plotter, self-dramatizer and sometime spy for the Confederacy, has come down in history as an American Judas. But Mr. Creatore has turned history on its head; his play barely seems interested in what the Civil War was all about.

And despite all the flashbacks and ghosts in "The Man Who Shot Lincoln," Lincoln himself is missing.

The setting of the two-act drama, which is directed by Crandall Diehl, is described in the program notes as "Backstage at a theater. Perhaps." There are a lot of perhapses in the plot. Without quite giving the plot away (since it builds up to a trick ending), it can be revealed that Mr. Creatore's play is really about the Booths.

The patriarch of the acting family, Junius Brutus Booth (Eric Tull, who

also plays other minor roles), appears as a ghostly presence. Edwin Booth (Sam Tsoutsouvas) and his brother, John Wilkes Booth (Conan McCarty), both seem like drunken, womanizing weirdos, which may be one of the few truthful elements in the play. Edwin was regarded as a fine Shakespearean actor in his time, but that is not visible here. The most important prop is a whisky bottle.

Edwin is married to Mary Devlin (Marcia Gay Harden), a prompter and young actress. But he suspects that earlier in her career she had an affair with John Wilkes. Edwin's jealousy is boundless; he vows revenge. But John Wilkes seems more interested in his press notices, which he reads on stage. Edwin's wife also returns as a ghost after he has practically hounded her to death.

1989 S 24, 72:6

The History Lesson

GOREE, by Matsemela Manaka; directed by John Kani; choreographed by Nomsa Manaka; lighting design by Siphiwe Khumalo; set by Mr. Manaka; music conceived, composed and arranged by Motsumi Makhene, Mr. Manaka, Peter Boroko and Sibongile Khumalo. Costumes by Kate Manaka. Presented by New Federal Theater, Woodie King Jr. producer. At the Riverside Church, 120th Street and Riverside Drive.

WITH: Nomsa Manaka and Sibongile Khumalo

By WILBORN HAMPTON

If enthusiasm were all it took, most shows would be hits and "Goree," a homily about self-discovery told primarily through African song and dance, would be a smash.

Although the two-woman cast of "Goree," which is being offered by the New Federal Theater at the Riverside Church, brings a lot of energy onstage, the work is little more than an 80-minute variety show loosely held together by the story of a South African girl who travels to Senegal in search of a woman renowned as the best singer and dancer in Africa. The girl finds herself stranded on Goree, a small island off Dakar from whence slave ships once sailed, where she is befriended by a woman who teaches her to dance and sing, and who throws in some rudimentary African history between numbers.

Nomsa Manaka gives a charming innocence to the girl and dances with feeling, using her upper torso, arms and hands to movingly convey the yearning of an enslaved people, as well as, in one number, the cavorting of an ostrich. Sibongile Khumalo has a big voice with a plaintive quality that faintly resembles Odetta's, and is sympathetic and maternal as the woman who becomes the girl's teacher. Ms. Khumalo also plays the violin, but she sings better than she fiddles.

Matsemela Manaka, who wrote the book and, along with Ms. Khumalo, Motsumi Makhene and Peter Boroko, composed the music, also plays percussion behind a scrim. One distraction to "Goree" is that the songs and dances are performed to taped music backed by live drums or violin, a mix that would be best suited for a house party or school program. An accompaniment of solo drums without the canned sound track would be more effective, especially since the tape sounds like it was recorded from scratchy old 78's.

Art From Apartheid Nomsa Manaka will appear in "Goree," a South African musical with book by Matsemela Manaka and music by Motsumi Makhene that explores the experience of apartheid

The story, such as it is, is simplistic, and Mr. Manaka tries to force a history lesson, complete with dates, onto the dialogue. The fact that the Portuguese first landed in West Africa in 1444, or that the French drove the British out of Senegal in 1885, adds nothing to understanding the oppression Africa has suffered through centuries of colonialism and slavery. Such lessons are better taught in human terms, as the South African musical "Sarafina!" was told through the lives of a Soweto high school class. No actor should have lines like "Jazz has its origins in Africa" or "Johannesburg is a human jungle."

"Goree" was directed by John Kani, the actor and playwright who is associate director of the Market Theater in Johannesburg, where it was first presented.

As a celebration of African culture, the singing and dancing in "Goree" are entertaining. But as theater, it more resembles a "Sesame Street" segment sponsored by the letter A, for Africa. Children should enjoy the show and get the most from it.

1989 S 24, 72:3

Othello Is Othello, But Whatever Got Into Iago?

STAGE VIEW/Benedict Nightingale

Willard White as Othello and Imogen Stubbs as Desdemona— proving elusive

STRATFORD-ON-AVON, England WHAT DOES THE EXPERIence of directing "Chess" do to the brain? Can there conceivably be creative life after "Starlight Express"? Is it possible to stage even so fine a musical as "Les Misérables" and easily readjust to the intricacies of Shakespearean verse? Trevor Nunn's revival of Heywood's obscure "Fair Maid of the West" in 1986 was modestly reassuring; but it was still difficult to settle into one's seat for his new "Othello" without internally voicing such worries. The West End and Broadway's current Kublai Khan was returning to the Royal Shakespeare Company, whose artistic director he used to be, for his first important classical production in seven years. Were his nerve ends sensitive enough to cope?

The answer is yes, emphatically yes. Both the Stratford playhouse in which Mr. Nunn's 'Othello' is receiving its premiere and the London theater to which it's soon moving — the Other Place and the Young Vic, respectively — are tiny, informal, somewhat makeshift places. They stand in roughly the same relation to the Minskoff or Broadway as egg boxes to the Pyramids. But in that tight space Mr. Nunn has extracted an imposing Othello from the opera singer Willard White, a splendidly original Desdemona from a rising young actress called Imogen Stubbs — and the Iago is as striking, in its quiet way, as anything Ian McKellen has done.

It's not the first time that Mr. McKellen, an actor who can become mannered and overblown on grander stages, has successfully adapted to the Other Place. Some still rate the stealthy, hungry Macbeth he performed there 13 years ago, also for Mr. Nunn, as the finest of its generation. But his Iago is more understated even than that. With his pale, arid face, cropped hair and small, neat mustache, he looks very much the professional NCO, and most of the time he sounds equally blunt and businesslike. Even when he's imprecating against "raging motions, carnal stings and unbitted lusts" he's pretty matter-of-fact, as if those feelings were somewhat unmilitary objects he'd found in an inventory of the quartermaster's stores. It's scarcely surprising that no one suspects or fears him. He's part of the barrack-room furniture, as anonymous and unthreatening as the iron bedsteads and tin washbowls sparsely spread across the Stratford stage.

◾

Indeed, the performance is not just muted, it's perilously so. When Iago finally works out how best to bad-mouth Desdemona, turning "her virtue into pitch" in Othello's eyes, Mr. McKellen displays no sense of triumph, no self-congratulatory excitement. On the contrary, he gives a minuscule smile and a still smaller shrug, stifles a yawn and readies himself for sleep. He's cool and unobtrusive in everything he does, whether it's lighting his pipe, setting the sentries or organizing the ruin of the Othellos.

Yet never for a moment does one feel that,

In Trevor Nunn's unpretentious revival, the characters act in new ways and get some odd notions.

downbeat acting is actually deadbeat acting. Things are happening inside the apparent human vacuum, plenty of them. With this Iago, offhandedness is partly camouflage, and partly his way of distancing himself from a strange subterranean pain. Coleridge famously commented on the character's "motiveless malignity"; but deftly, at times almost invisibly, Mr. McKellen suggests that he has a reason for his vindictiveness. The sight of love, indeed the very thought of it, troubles him, fascinates him, obsesses him, and at some fathomless level enrages him, because he cannot feel or understand it.

That's not an original interpretation, but Mr. McKellen approaches it from a new angle. For one, Iago's relationship with his wife Emilia, usually just the butt of his disdain, becomes central to the play. Several times he kisses her fulsomely, only to push her away in puzzled disappointment, like a man who has found cherry soda in a glass he hoped was brimming with claret. Why can't he so much as taste what others seem able to enjoy? The idea that's several times expressed in the text, and is commonly regarded as one of the feebler ways Iago rationalizes evil, begins to eat into his mind or, as he himself says, "gnaw my inwards." Othello can love and be loved: maybe he's loved and been loved by Emilia. Mr. McKellen's mouth twists, his hands tighten, his voice gulps and darkens, as the fantasy possesses him and refuses to let go.

In other words, Iago is more the victim of jealousy than Othello himself, and the emotion becomes irresistible, boundless. This stranger to Venice, this black man, has clearly experienced feelings he himself hasn't — how, why, and what can they be? At the end he just can't stop staring at the couple he's destroyed, Othello and Desdemona, reunited on their deathbed. And it's not satisfaction, not murderous glee that one sees in his eyes. He still desperately hopes at last to discover the emotional secrets that have nourished them and maddened him, and they're still proving elusive.

By comparison Mr. White seems somewhat external: strong, authoritative and charismatic, but a bit more declamatory than even Othello, who is prone to grandiloquence, should properly be. One doesn't sense that maggots are hatching in his guts or seething in his head. One does however feel something unusual and genuinely helpful to the play, which is that his mistrust of Desdemona is not altogether unreasonable.

Ian McKellen (right) as Iago with Imogen Stubbs and Willard White—more a victim than Othello himself

That's because Imogen Stubbs plays her as a gauche, callow girl, apt to express her affection for him by leaping into his arms or, with a whoop of joy, onto his back. It's hard to understand how her father can call her "a maiden of spirit so still and quiet that her motion blushed at itself," but it's easy enough to see why Othello should buy Iago's lies. Might not someone so effervescent yet unformed guilelessly bounce into another man's bed?

Mr. Nunn has not lost his thoughtfulness — or, for that matter, his feeling for atmosphere and telling detail. In this, he's much aided by the intimacy of his stage and the economy of his 19th-century furniture and props. Here's a place where soldiers shave and drink spiked wine in chipped mugs and play rough jokes on each other, and women sew and pack their luggage and eat sultanas and listen to the crickets chirruping outside.

Not only does all this add to the authenticity; it reminds you that, unlike the other great Shakespearean tragedies, "Othello" is a domestic play, more about the eternal triangle than the eternal verities. As Mr. Nunn unpretentiously stages it, it could be unfolding at any time in anyone's bedroom, living room and kitchen. That's what makes it so immediate. That's what makes the evil it shows so alarming. □

1989 S 24, II:5:1

A Crucible Of Contradictions

ORPHEUS DESCENDING, by Tennessee Williams; directed by Peter Hall; designed by Alison Chitty; lighting by Paul Pyant with Neil Peter Jampolis; American costumes in association with Richard Schurkamp; electronic score, Stephen Edwards; sound design, Paul Arditti; associate producer, Nicki Frei. The Peter Hall Company presented by James M. Nederlander and Elizabeth Ireland McCann, by arrangement with Duncan C. Weldon and Jerome Minskoff. At the Neil Simon Theater, 250 West 52d Street.

Dolly Hamma .... Patti Allison
Beulah Binnings .... Sloane Shelton
Pee Wee Binnings .... Pat McNamara
Dog Hamma .... Mitch Webb
Carol Cutrere .... Anne Twomey
Eva Temple .... Bette Henritze
Sister Temple .... Peg Small
Uncle Pleasant .... Doyle Richmond
Val Xavier .... Kevin Anderson
Vee Talbott .... Tammy Grimes
Lady Torrance .... Vanessa Redgrave
Jabe Torrance .... Brad Sullivan
Sheriff Talbott .... Manning Redwood
Mr. Dubinsky and 1st Man ... Thomas Kopache
Woman .... Constance Crawford
David Cutrere .... Lewis Arlt
Nurse Porter .... Marcia Lewis
Clown and 2d Man .... Stephen Mendillo
Townspeople
Lynn Cohen and Richard McWilliams

By FRANK RICH

The fusion of Vanessa Redgrave and Tennessee Williams is an artistic explosion that was bound to happen, and the wonder is that we had to wait until Peter Hall's revival of "Orpheus Descending." Williams and Miss Redgrave were made for each other because they are brilliant theater artists in the same way. They run at life bravely, openly, without defenses and without fear of their inevitable destruction, like great, beautiful deer bounding across a highway after dark.

You don't go to Williams and Redgrave for an elegant intellectual evening or for a show of classical

Vanessa Redgrave and Kevin Anderson in "Orpheus Descending."

The New York Times/Fred R. Conrad

technique. You go to watch what the playwright once called a world lit by lightning. At the Neil Simon Theater, where Mr. Hall's production has arrived on Broadway via the West End, the flashes of gut-deep humor and pain sear the night as Miss Redgrave takes complete, perhaps eternal possession of the role of Lady Torrance, the middle-aged proprietor of a dry-goods store somewhere in a fetid Deep South.

Lady Torrance is an archetypal Williams outcast. The lonely daughter of an immigrant Sicilian bootlegger murdered long ago by the Ku Klux Klan, she has been married unhappily for 20 years to a bigoted tyrant now riddled by cancer. The Orpheus who descends to rescue her is Val Xavier (Kevin Anderson), a guitar-toting drifter of 30 whom Williams wrote with Elvis Presley in mind. That Val and Lady will end up sharing a bed is never in question. It's how Miss Redgrave gets there, how she melts from a barren, rigid businesswoman to a radiant celebrator of the "life in my body," that astonishes. What Miss Redgrave does is fill out each moment, however tiny, with the dramatic (if sometimes funny) conflict of emotions, taking any risk she can that might allow her character to seep into every crevice of the play.

Early on, when hypocritical neighbors tell Lady that they pray for her doomed husband, she responds not with stoic silence but with a mocking, spiraling laugh that establishes her contempt for her spouse even as it reveals the buried humanity that her marriage could not snuff out. Once Val appears seeking work, Miss Redgrave greets him with a barking inquisition in her guttural Italian accent, and yet again she subtly reveals the countervailing forces tugging within. As Val empties his pockets trying to find a former employer's letter of reference, Miss Redgrave's eyes scour the floor desperately, as if the stranger's each discarded scrap of paper might be a harbinger of hope.

By Act II, Lady is sitting rigidly in a chair, trying to ward off Val's sexual pull by keeping her back to him. But Miss Redgrave's glowing eyes and nervously grinning mouth are yanked as if by gravity in his direction anyway. Mr. Anderson helps bring Lady's body in line with her spirit by means of a neck massage that loosens her hair, voice and torso until finally this tall woman seems to have merged with the play's central image of liberation — a floating, legless bird that lives "all its life on its wings in the sky." When Miss Redgrave then takes off her silk robe to join Val in

his itinerant's bed under the shop's staircase, the nudity seems completely natural. This Lady has long since been stripped of everything, including at least 20 years of age.

The grotesque fate that Williams holds in store for his lovers thereafter, and that brings Miss Redgrave's performance to its devastating, tragic peak, is the substance not only of "Orpheus Descending" but of the playwright's life work as well. Lady and Val are sensitive nonconformists who, like that sweet bird and like most Williams protagonists, must be destroyed by the bullying real world as soon as they come down to earth. A two-month flop when staged by Harold Clurman on Broadway in 1957, "Orpheus Descending" can now be seen as a pivotal chapter in the author's canon, reverberating throughout his career. Under the title "Battle of Angels," an early version of the play was Williams's first, unsuccessful attempt to storm New York in 1940. (It closed during its Boston tryout.) In 1957, "Orpheus" was the boundary between Williams's biggest successes and saddest theatrical travails.

•

That Mr. Hall and Miss Redgrave would choose to revive this sprawling, problematic piece rather than one of the preceding, established Williams classics is heroic. What's more, the director has brought his full wide-ranging imagination to bear on the text. Abandoning any pretense of realism, Mr. Hall stages the play in a hallucinatory set (by Alison Chitty) that floats against a spooky, cloud-streaked azure sky. The lighting, by Paul Pyant with Neil Peter Jampolis, mixes theatrical expressionism with Hollywood film noir; blinding car headlights frequently sweep through the general store's rain-streaked windows. Stephen Edwards's electronic score, punctuated by the upstairs cane bangings of Lady's dying husband and the howling of flesh-hungry dogs, provides ominous underscoring to expository speeches delivered directly to the audience by the town's quasi-Greek chorus of ghoulish, gossipy harpies.

The hothouse imagery fits a play set in a Southern Gothic Hades belonging to a corrupt America "sick with neon." In "Orpheus," characters are burned alive, babies are killed in the womb and racist mob violence always threatens to erupt. Like Miss Redgrave, Mr. Hall has the guts to embrace and explore the contradictions in Williams's play rather than to attempt to reconcile them in one rigid style or another. "Orpheus" is an unwieldy mix of myth, ritual (a conjure man included), social realism and bluesy poetry. Why not revel in the author's imagination instead of trying, as the original production apparently did, to domesticate it?

The production casts new light on the play's place in Williams's work.

To pull off his balancing act, however, Mr. Hall needs a consistent level of acting that is left unfulfilled by his new New York supporting cast.

One would expect American actors to do better by Williams than their London counterparts, but whether through miscasting or underrehearsing, that's not the case here. Anne Twomey, as a ghostly drug-and-sex-eviscerated Cassandra of plantation's past, and Tammy Grimes, as a sheriff's wife pathetically lost in spiritual visions, bring actressy technique rather than Miss Redgrave's transparency of emotion to roles that should be affecting, not campy. Though Mr. Anderson, a much more honest actor, is a tender Val, he never emits the animalistic erotic charge of a character Williams likened to "a fox in a chicken coop." With the exception of Sloane Shelton, the many evil Delta denizens are comic-book rednecks, most crucially Lady's husband (Brad Sullivan) and her former lover (Lewis Arlt).

As a result, this "Orpheus" is more of a triumph for Miss Redgrave than for Williams, whose script reveals its seams when in the other actors' hands. But since everything the star does is in the playwright's service, her spirit always comes through, even when passages of his play do not. Nowhere is that spirit more powerfully conveyed than when Miss Redgrave twirls about in a red and gold party dress in Act II, defiantly savoring her hard-won freedom by imitating the monkey that long ago danced to her beloved father's hand organ.

Such happiness is at most transitory in a Williams play — notably one that takes as its credo "We're all sentenced to solitary confinement for life" — and Miss Redgrave knows it. The intensity of her joy is so overwhelming that when the dance abruptly ends, as it must, the void in its wake is all the more unexpectedly shocking. It's as if the lights are blown out on stage, and our fellow theatergoers notwithstanding, we are plunged into Williams's solitary confinement, grief-stricken and alone.

1989 S 25, C15:4

Candide School Of Innocents Abroad

INDIANA DOG, by Jeffrey Klayman; directed by Mervyn Willis; costume design, Mary Myers; set design, Constanza Romero; light design, Brian Aldous; sound design/music, Jeffrey Taylor; music and lyrics, Mr. Klayman; stage manager, Tamara Holt. Presented by Cucaracha Theater, artistic directors, Richard Caliban and David Simonds; producing director, Janet Paparazzo; associate director, Hugh Palmer. At 429 Greenwich Street.

WITH: Kathryn Atwood, Les Baum, Maureen Bradley, Marko Dillahunt, Joey L. Golden, Daniel Kohl, Vivian Lanko, David B. McConeghey, Nickalaus, Chris Oldcorn, Mollie O'Mara, Hugh Palmer, David Phillips, Glen M. Santiago, David Simonds, Suzanne Steele, Sally Stewart, Jeffrey Taylor, Will Hamilton Thayer, Elizabeth Thompson, Loreen Tyrrel, Robert Walch and Damian Young.

By MEL GUSSOW

The approach to global travel taken by Armand, the peripatetic hero of Jeffrey Klayman's "Indiana Dog," is the opposite of that of Phileas Fogg in "Around the World in 80 Days." Fogg wants to move as fast as he can; Armand has a surfeit of time. As he sees the world, he ages from a young rebel to a veteran of foreign voyages.

The play itself (at the Cucaracha Theater) is a shaggy-dog comedy, the kind of digressionary journey where one flies to Japan solely to catch a freighter to China. As in any such meandering trip, "Indiana Dog" has its ups, downs and plateaus — and there are nagging questions about the plot. But the show has a verve that is infectious, caught by theatergoers as well as by the actors, who number 22 plus that title dog. Positive energy flows back and forth across the open stage.

The journey begins on a satiric note as Armand, apparently at the end of his story, wanders into Central Park and finds himself surrounded by the oddest of urban fauna, beginning with two world-class joggers who compare notes on New York high and low life. This is, they explain, the city where $4,000 a month is the going rate for a "new slum" dwelling on Tompkins Square. As with subsequent episodes, this scene could stand as a self-contained comedy sketch.

From here, Armand (Glen M. Santiago, who looks like a flaky-haired Gene Wilder) begins to roam in mind and body, taking us back through his worldly jaunt with his International Student Fly-Drive-and-Swim Pass. The younger version of the character is played by David Simonds. Armand is straight from the Candide school of innocents abroad. Things happen all around him — banditry, terrorism and war — but he blithely passes through and emerges unscathed until the very end.

Asked what he does, he considers the question, then answers truthfully, "I write postcards." He also sends gifts home and they become objects of mistaken identification (his parents use a pair of antique maracas as ashtrays). The play itself is like a series of animated postcards.

On this excursion, there is no time to enjoy today because one always has to book tomorrow. Everyone competes for frequent-flier points. Armand accumulates five million, enough for him to fly to Jupiter and back, although misguidedly following his "derelict star," he takes a different, disastrous route. Or does he? Even allowing for Mr. Klayman's whirligig view of the world, "Indiana Dog" fogs its mirror especially in matters dealing with Armand's childhood. He may or may not have run over his playmate's parents while driving their car. Furthermore, the author's borrowing of Beckett (Armand can't go on; he will go on) is facile.

The comedy is at its most entertaining when it is freewheeling, as in a sideshow interlude with a customs agent dressed as a clown. While snooping through luggage, he extracts an object from a handbag and is told by the owner that she never travels anywhere without her hand-carved Etruscan vase.

Though there is a minimum of scenery and there are no projections, Mervyn Willis's production achieves a vividness. As director, he relies on the author's conjuring ability and the comedic instincts of his actors, who double and triple in roles. In addition to Mr. Santiago's sweet-tempered performance, there are playful contributions from, among others, Elizabeth Thompson, Kathryn Atwood, Damian Young and David Phillips. Playing a guitarist who seems to have stayed on from the 1960's, Mr. Phillips sings a few amiable tunes, with music and lyrics by Mr. Klayman.

Beneath the sprawling surface, there are impertinent reflections on travel and the nomadic life. Armand, like others of his itinerant ilk, is unable to resist a cathedral, a cemetery (he reads Voltaire at Père Lachaise) or a sandy beach, hoping that each vista may be more buena than the one before. Even as the last train is leaving town, he is tempted by the thought of visiting one more castle off the map. In his eclectic desire to see everything and never go home again, Armand is the ultimate Occidental tourist.

1989 S 26, C17:1

The M-G-M Movie This Is Not

BIG HOTEL, by Charles Ludlam; directed by Everett Quinton; scenery by Mark Beard; costumes by Susan Young; lighting by Richard Currie; music and sound by James S. Badrak, Alan Gregorie and Jan Bell; properties by Daphne Groos and James Eckerle; hair by Joe Anthony. Presented by the Ridiculous Theatrical Company. At the Charles Ludlam Theater, 1 Sheridan Square.

Mafonga and Norma Desmond
.... Everett Quinton
Magic Mandarin and Mata Hari
.... Bryan Webster
God and Mr. X .... Stephen Pell
Devil and Chocha Caliente ...Terence Mintern
Elwynn Chamberpot and Waiter ...Gary Mink
Cramwell, Masie Madigan and Santa Claus
.... Bobby Reed
Ballerina .... Sophie Maletsky
Bellhop and Lupe Velez ...James Robert Lamb
Drago Rubles and Martok .... Eureka
Trilby and Blondine Blondell .Christine Weiss
Svengali and a Gypsy .... H. M. Koutoukas
Cobra Slaves
...... James Robert Lamb and Gary Mink
Bride and Assorted Guests .. Teresa McIntyre

By FRANK RICH

In Act II of the Ridiculous Theatrical Company's "Big Hotel," a bellhop starts sobbing over esthetics. "I've lost the thread of the narrative!" he cries over and over, and no wonder. Wandering about the Big Hotel in his call-for-Philip-Morris costume, the bellhop has stumbled upon a crucifixion. The victim bears an uncanny resemblance to Charlie Chan.

Nor do the confusions of this particularly busy day end there. Among the hotel's guests are Svengali and Trilby, the legendary Hollywood stars Norma Desmond and Lupe Velez, and a great Russian ballerina whose penchant for suicide is so obsessive that she makes the Greta Garbo of "Grand Hotel" seem like Rebecca of Sunnybrook Farm. A gorilla enters the lobby, and so does a young bride whose wedding gown is promptly ripped off by the revolving door.

•

As for the narrative, forget it. "Big Hotel," which was first seen by a very few people on occasional nights in the late 1960's, was Charles Ludlam's first playwriting venture and, we can see now, an unofficial manifesto of the Ridiculous artistic creed. A collage of transvestite clowning and classical references (whether to Aristotle or Cecil B. DeMille), it owes far more to the shaggy blackout sketches of burlesque than it does to the taut threads of the well-made play. Yet for all its storytelling anarchy and St. Marks Baths locker-room humor,

The guests include Norma Desmond and Svengali.

"Big Hotel" is the outpouring of a playwright well schooled in the dramatic conventions he wanted either to invert or deconstruct. Ludlam knew almost everything about the theater and, as young writers are wont to do, did not hesitate to remind the audience of his precocity, sometimes in verse.

•

That Everett Quinton, serving as director and star, would now revive this youthful potpourri is another example of the shrewd leadership he has brought to the Ridiculous company since Ludlam's death three summers ago. Mr. Quinton's mission is to keep the Ridiculous past alive while creating the troupe's future. By mixing revivals of forgotten or little-seen Ludlam plays like this with new works (like last season's "Tale of Two Cities"), he gives the company and its audience essential continuity. The densely packed "Big Hotel" is almost a Rosetta stone of Ridiculousness; it sets the Ridiculous plays that followed — and presumably those to come — within a historical context.

While Mr. Quinton has obviously cut and, on occasion, updated the

Anita and Steve Shevett

Eureka, left, and Everett Quinton in Charles Ludlam's first play, "Big Hotel"

121

original text, "Big Hotel" is still far too arcane and attenuated to serve as a happy baptism for Ridiculous newcomers. But the half-hour of dead weight notwithstanding, the play is essential viewing, as cultural anthropology if not consistently as entertainment, for those who know and care about the rest of the Ludlam canon.

•

Here, in embryonic state, are the author's fascination with traditional dramatic forms (farce, tragedy), his affection for old-fashioned theatrical stunts (many involving life-size dummies) and his utter refusal to accept the status quo of so-called good taste. In "Big Hotel," a woman's orgasmic screams shatter glass, a toy poodle (an actual toy in fact) relieves itself on stage, and the pages of a Bible serve as toilet paper. Some of the funnier gags are not reportable in a family newspaper, but the Playbill happily notes that, pace Jesse Helms, they have all been underwritten in part by the National Endowment for the Arts.

Working with witty, resourceful sets (by Mark Beard) and typically outrageous costumes (by Susan Young), Mr. Quinton stages "Big Hotel" in the exaggerated house style, which is not to be confused with M-G-M's. In or out of drag, the standout performers include the Ridiculous stalwarts known as Eureka and H. M. Koutoukas as well as the newcomer Bryan Webster, who leads a chorus line at the hotel's Fire Pit restaurant in "The Lady in Red" when he's not on the cross.

•

If there's anything to regret about Mr. Quinton's own performance, it is only its brevity. As a Norma stranded in identity somewhere between Swanson and Callas, he performs the final scene of "Sunset Boulevard" with a hilarious twist worthy of a lighter Billy Wilder classic like "Some Like It Hot." Somewhat later, for reasons that I can't explain any better than that bellhop, Mr. Quinton appears as a cobra woman in a headdress overrun by green plastic snakes. Ludlam lives in such moments and so, heaven help us, does Maria Montez.

1989 S 29, C3:1

High Tec

HOLLYWOOD SCHEHERAZADE, by Charlie Peters; directed by Gregory Lehane; scenic design, Herbert H. O'Dell; lighting design, Deborah Constantine; costume design, Claudia Stephens; music and sound design, Michael Keck. Presented by Primary Stages Company, Casey Childs, artistic director. At the 45th Street Theater, 354 West 45th Street.

Barney	Michael Keck
Peter Fortune	Daniel Ahearn
Morley Waxman	Herbert Rubens
Boyd	Tom McBride
Jurgen Sallow	Robert Verlaque
Daria Freehandle	Jennifer Ashe
William Prole	Christopher Randolph
Telia	Cynthia Mace

By D. J. R. BRUCKNER

Charlie Peters's new little comedy, "Hollywood Scheherazade," is an innocent piece of nonsense. Utterly innocent. It is over soon enough, in little more than an hour, but it could have made its points and won all its laughs in a quarter of that time.

In the performance, at Primary Stages, the cast, under the direction

of Gregory Lehane, gives as much life as it can to Mr. Peters's cartoon characters, but even they cannot long sustain interest in the playwright's sendup of detective-story plays and films. "Hollywood Scheherazade" does not go much beyond the kind of skits people might think up to enliven a house party.

•

The story is about a private detective, Peter Fortune (Daniel Ahearn), who is hired by a Hollywood mogul, Morley Waxman (Herbert Rubens) to find something — but he will not say what it is. Obviously, the heavy-drinking, flat-voiced Fortune, who is eternally lucky despite his protestations that he is "not a happy man," runs up against a strong-arm thug, a gorgeous seductress, a woman who has been cheated and is seeking vengeance, an oily lawyer and a sinister assassin with a Middle European accent.

Any viewer with a slight knowledge of old detective yarns can supply his own lines and incidents for such a caper. The humor here runs to lines like, "It was autumn in Hollywood, when the air turns brown and falls to the ground."

•

Mr. Ahearn gives a special meaning to "deadpan." As he moves without even a flicker of emotion through the mayhem the other characters try to pull him into, his Peter Fortune seems not so much world-weary as in a state of nirvana, quite above the ridiculous intrigues, greed and lust of his clients. Even the power-mad Waxman — whom Mr. Rubens turns into the one true comic creation of the evening — is unable to bring him down to earth.

For about 10 minutes, while the audience is taking seats, Michael Keck, at a piano bar on the set, reminds one of the scores of ivory ticklers in the bar scenes of all the old detective films, while Mr. Keck's electronic music on the sound system carries one into a dreamy world of nostalgia. It is the best part of the show.

1989 O 1, 60:5

Verbal Tennis

ABEL AND BELA and ARCHITRUC, by Robert Pinget; translated by Barbara Wright and Barbara Bray, respectively; directed by Nicholas Kepros; set design, Paul Steinberg; costume design, Gabriel Berry; lighting design, Pat Dignan; stage manager, Rachel S. Levine; sound design, Phil Lee; music by David Bushler. Presented by Ubu Repertory Theater Inc. At 15 West 28th Street.

Abel/Cook	Robert Burke
Bela	Peter Mackenzie
King	Tom Lacy
Baga	Jarlath Conroy

By MEL GUSSOW

Although Robert Pinget's reputation as an experimental novelist — as a leader of the nouveau roman movement in France — is secure, his role as a playwright is more problematic. These problems are not resolved by the Ubu Repertory Theater production of two Pinget one-acts, "Abel and Bela" and "Architruc."

A friend and artistic follower of Samuel Beckett, Mr. Pinget shares with him a playful intellect and a sense of the comic ravages of time. At least in the United States, his work is rarely performed. Significantly, one

of his finest short plays, "La Manivelle," was adapted into English by Beckett himself. Under the title "The Old Tune," the comedy shifted its setting from France to Ireland — and it gained Irish wit. The two plays at the Ubu theater are of interest as examples of French absurdism, but neither has the charm or theatricality of "The Old Tune."

In "Abel and Bela," two unsuccessful playwrights — or two aspects of a single psyche — conspire to share authorship of a play. As if engaged in a verbal tennis match, they serve and volley and criticize each other's strokes. Studiously they invent a complex political plot while avoiding any profundity or, in Mr. Pinget's word, essence. They agree that such seri-

Carol Rosegg/Martha Swope Associates

Tom Lacy in "Architruc," half of a double bill by Robert Pinget at Ubu Repertory Theater.

ousness would be the route to still another theatrical failure.

•

Gradually they forsake invention and look into their own lives for inspiration, but some psychological barrier forces them back to their wandering imaginations. In the play, there is a genial sense of self-mockery. Whenever Abel becomes too pompous, Bela reawakens him to reality. In a sense, the dialogue becomes a self-criticism, exemplifying Mr. Pinget's apparent reluctance to explore his own deeper emotions.

Using Barbara Wright's translation, the director, Nicholas Kepros, tries to instill theatricality into the play by placing his two characters in the audience of a theater. They face an unseen stage, and we face them. This gives the comedy a tantalizing double-edged quality. Are we on stage and are the actors in the audience? But even as the actors change their seats, the play remains stationary. It is an aural rather than a visceral experience, reminding one that Mr. Pinget has frequently written for the radio.

•

There is more overt stage life in "Architruc" (translated by Barbara Bray), in which a bored King treats his Prime Minister as if he were the court Fool. The Prime Minister is made to perform theatrical games, which fill the time and delay the inevitable end — the arrival of the figure of death as the final guest in this mock masquerade. As with other plays by Mr. Pinget ("The Old Tune,"

"Dead Letter"), "Architruc" seems at least partly a refraction of "Waiting for Godot."

The actors offer assured performances (Robert Burke and Peter Mackenzie in "Abel and Bela", Tom Lacy and Jarlath Conroy in "Architruc"). But none of them, with the possible exception of Mr. Conroy as the Prime Minister, is distinguished by his humor. They, along with the plays, lack that essence that would help transform the dialogue into more than intriguing intellectual exercises.

1989 O1, 61:1

On the Bench

HOME GAMES, by Tom Ziegler; directed by Roderick Cook; set design by Paul Wonsek; light design by Stuart Duke; costume design by Barbara Forbes; sound design by Aural Fixation; production stage manager, Melissa L. Burdick. Presented by Hudson Guild Theater, Geoffrey Sherman, producing artistic director; Steven Ramay, associate director. At 441 West 26th Street.

Anton Tucker	John Braden
Mertle Mae Tucker	Kymberly Dakin
Frank Whitfield	Michael E. Knight

By MEL GUSSOW

It is the premise of Tom Ziegler's "Home Games" (which opened last night at the Hudson Guild Theater) that behind Yogi Berra and Elston Howard, the 1955 New York Yankees had a third, reserve catcher, a bush leaguer named Tony Tucker, who spent exactly one year in the majors. Actually that year, Howard was generally in the outfield and the Yankees had another backup catcher, Charlie Silvera, who was not — by any stretch of the imagination — the basis for Tucker.

Although the fictional Tucker was with the pennant-winning team through its World Series loss to the Brooklyn Dodgers, he never came to bat. For him, it was a long dry season and when the Yankees traded him to the Cleveland Indians, he quit baseball and went into the trucking business. Lucky Cleveland, unlucky theatergoers.

When we meet him in 1985, Tucker (John Braden) is insane, a result of an unexplained accident. He thinks that his pert daughter (Kymberly Dakin) is Casey Stengel and that their cluttered apartment is Yankee Stadium. For the duration of the play, he relives the 1955 World Series, strapping on his shinguards and badgering his daughter manager to bench Berra, and put him in the lineup. He humors him (strike one).

A stranger arrives — a prosperous young businessman (Michael E. Knight) who has met the daughter in a night-school class in American literature, and who wants her to help him with his compositions. She tells her father that he is Mickey Mantle, and he plays the role (strike two).

Although he is engaged to someone else, Mr. Knight repeatedly comes to call. He writes terrible poetry and quotes Thoreau. When Ms. Dakin hears that line about quiet desperation, she identifies with it and suggests that Thoreau must have had a bad day, which is what she is having with her crazy father and her blind cat (strike three).

Although Mr. Ziegler has an occasional facility for writing one-line jokes, his characters are dreary. The play is as insubstantial as the corn chips the heroine munches throughout the evening. Except for random references to Casey Stengel, baseball lore is at a minimum and the heroine's martyrdom is overstated. "Home Games" hammers home the metaphor, as in the case of the title of the play, which refers to baseball, the family household and the nursing home that may be in the father's future.

The most pretentious lines are awarded to Mr. Knight, as in a speech urging Ms. Dakin to leave home and become a truck driver ("Out there somewhere is a whole world"). There is little the actors can do except to accent each character's one note — the daughter's apparent placability, the suitor's stuffiness and the old codger's whimsy. Roderick Cook's production fits awkwardly on the Hudson Guild's small stage, forcing the daughter to close a curtain on her father in his bedroom whenever her guest comes to call. In the case of "Home Games," Yogi Berra was wrong: sometimes it's over *before* it's over.

1989 O 2, C16:3

Kelly McGillis Stars In 'Twelfth Night'

By FRANK RICH

Special to The New York Times

WASHINGTON, Oct. 1 — Though there are movie stars who regard classic roles as a careerlong mission instead of a one-shot summer vacation — Kevin Kline and Mary Elizabeth Mastrantonio among them — New York audiences have lately seen too many Hollywood visitors treat Shakespeare like a cheap tart. These are the stars who milk the Bard for all the self-serving publicity he's worth during rehearsal, then turn their backs on him by self-indulgently goofing their way through his plays in performance. The audience, asked to bask in the empty glow of celebrity rather than the deep illumination of Shakespeare, goes home with the gloomy feeling of having been had.

It is a different feeling — call it joy — that Washington theatergoers are taking away from the new production of "Twelfth Night" that has opened the 20th season of the Shakespeare Theater at the Folger Library. Like the misbegotten "Twelfth Night" in Central Park last summer, this one has its Hollywood import: Kelly McGillis, the charming if hardly riveting leading lady in such hit films as "Top Gun" and "The Accused." But there all comparisons end, both in intent and achievement. Ms. McGillis isn't passing through Washington between "projects" on the other coast. Having played Portia here last year, Ms. McGillis has returned for the entire Folger season. She'll appear in four plays, all but one (Schiller's "Mary Stuart") by Shakespeare, in a schedule that keeps her in Washington until mid-June.

Impressive as Ms. McGillis's professional commitment to the classics and to a resident theater company may be, her acting is more so. While other stars may give out interviews

---

A classic with a lead who isn't just passing through.

---

about how classical stage experience enriches their art, this actress is actually providing an object lesson on stage. From her first entrance as the shipwrecked Viola, in which she sounds wrenching notes of grief at the loss of her twin brother, Sebastian, Ms. McGillis is in command of a psychologically complex, technically expert performance that reveals a range scarcely tapped by her screen roles to date.

Disguised as the page Cesario, Ms. McGillis pines for the unobtainable Orsino (Peter Webster) with such rapt, consuming desire that the duke need only idly graze her with his arm to fill the house with the hot currents of frustrated sexual tension. Yet the actress does not convey comically erotic desire at the expense of the poignant, "blank" quality of a woman forced to hide both her love and gender. It's only after Viola at last reunites with Mark Philpot's sweet Sebastian — with whom she really does seem to share "one face, one voice, one habit" — that Ms. McGillis emerges from blank boyishness into womanhood. And even that happy ending comes with a sorrowful undertone: This Viola seems better suited for her mirror-image brother than for the fatuously romantic duke of her dreams. By the time the clown Feste (Yusef Bulos) sings his melancholy final song, the androgyny at the center of both the play and Ms. McGillis's performance has raised unresolved mysteries as potent as the evening's considerable laughter.

The unerring direction is by Michael Kahn, who is the artistic director of the Folger and who began his association with Ms. McGillis when he taught her at Juilliard. Like his star, he explores the contradictions of a play in which the lyrical ideal of love is always tempered by the cruel reality of men and women. Mr. Kahn sets his evocatively designed production in a Last Days of the Raj outpost of English colonialism. His Sir Toby Belch (David Sabin) and Sir Andrew Aguecheek (Floyd King) are the idle Edwardian boors, pickled in Gordon's Gin and armed with golf clubs, that one might laugh at in Waugh or Coward, while Malvolio (Philip Goodwin) could well be their stuffy, long-suffering gentlemen's club steward. They are all extremely funny, but only to that pathetic point when the terrified Mr. King finds himself in an unwonted duel and Mr. Goodwin appears in a straitjacket, reduced by a prank to a humiliated, bedraggled wreck in a madhouse.

Leading a cast whose other standouts include Franchelle Steward Dorn (whose mock-Indian Maria recalls the mischievous Eleanor Bron in the Beatles' movie "Help!") and David Medina (that rare thing, a vivid Fabian), Mr. Kahn has achieved a consistency of performance that cannot be bettered by any Shakespeare company I've seen in this country or England this year. Ms. McGillis couldn't turn this "Twelfth Night" into a star turn even if she were the lesser kind of star who would be tempted to try.

'Midsummer Night'

At Arena Stage, Washington's preeminent resident theater company, another, more austere variety of Shakespeare is in residence. The

Joan Marcus

Kelly McGillis in "Twelfth Night."

Rumanian-born director Liviu Ciulei is staging "A Midsummer Night's Dream" in a spare, almost sceneryless production that doesn't relocate Shakespeare's Athens and its neighboring wood to another locale so much as transport it to a cerebral stratosphere.

There are some striking interludes. The erotic fantasies and nightmares of the confused lovers are made palpable in a rapid series of mimed tableaux played out within a large silk bubble. When Titania awakens from her infatuation with an ass, the transformed Bottom rises above her on a clear plastic bower, his silhouette lingering beside her as a shadow, like the morning-after image of a vanishing dream. Mr. Ciulei, notably aided by David Marks's matronly but portly Thisbe, also has a farcical field day with the tradesmen's play-within-the-play.

The production would be above intellectual reproach were it not for some odd lapses: a homophobic opening gag about an epicene court couturier, an earthbound Puck who caricatures the tomboyishness of Mary Martin's Peter Pan, and the amateurish use of canned, evergreen Philip Glass recordings instead of a freshly commissioned score (whether by Mr. Glass or a stand-in). A more pervasive flaw of Mr. Ciulei's "Dream," however, has nothing to do with the intellect. One cannot escape the dry tone of the acting, which recalls that of the "Hamlet" he staged with Kevin Kline in New York.

With or without magic drops, no character seems to lose himself in love in this "Dream." One leaves the play keenly aware that the director regards both the Athenian and fairy kingdoms as fascist states — the militaristic royal costumes and brandished switchblades tell us so — but the human passions that can overthrow social oppression, at least for one long midsummer night, never flare brighter than a tepid lovers' spat. As was the case in the similarly imaginative yet chilly "Dream" Mark Lamos directed at the Hartford Stage last year, Mr. Ciulei seems to relegate his skilled performers to the role of cogs rather than use them as full collaborators in his vision. Leading directors are no less capable than leading Hollywood actors of turning Shakespeare's plays into self-absorbed star turns.

1989 O 4, C17:1

Of Mouths and Muffins

THE IMPORTANCE OF BEING EARNEST, by Oscar Wilde; directed by Robert Perillo; sets and lights designed by Giles Hogya; costumes designed by Jonathan Bixby; original music composed by Ellen Mandel; stage manager, Isabel Lopez. Presented by Jean Cocteau Repertory, 330 Bowery, at Second Street.

John Worthing	Christopher Oden
Algernon Moncrieff	Robert Ierardi
The Rev. Canon Chasuble	Zenon Zelenich
Merriman and Lane	Harris Berlinsky
Lady Bracknell	Joseph Menino
Gwendolen Fairfax	Carol Dearman
Cecily Cardew	Lyn Wright
Miss Prism	Angela Vitale

By WILBORN HAMPTON

There are few more enjoyable evenings in the theater than to accompany those Oscar Wilde dandies John Worthing and Algernon Moncrieff as they pursue, both in town and the country, love and earnestness. In "The Importance of Being Earnest," which is being presented by the Jean Cocteau Repertory company, Wilde uses his epigrams like a rapier, slashing his way through Mayfair drawing rooms and Hertfordshire gardens and leaving the cloak of hypocrisy that covered Victorian manners in tatters of laughter.

By re-creating on stage a society in which only the superficial and trivial are treated with seriousness, Wilde became the forerunner of England's most wickedly iconoclastic playwrights — from Shaw, a more social-minded fellow traveler, to Joe Orton, perhaps Wilde's most direct literary descendent.

To present Wilde's last play as nothing more than a silly comedy of manners, however, is to fall prey to the very earnestness Wilde ridicules.

●

The Cocteau staging amounts to little more than a campy burlesque of manners. Lady Bracknell, for example, is played in drag, and it says something of the level of sophistication of this production that Joseph Menino gives one of the better performances. Mr. Menino at least grasps the nature of his character and delivers Lady Bracknell's pronouncements (such as "To lose one parent may be regarded as a misfortune, but to lose both seems like carelessness") with the straightforward haughtiness they demand.

For the most part, the other portrayals are broad to the point of parody. Jack Worthing is played as a fop given to pulling faces and talking with his mouth full of muffin. The objects of Jack's and Algernon's affections

Jonathan Slaff

Lyn Wright and Robert Ierardi

are less a caricature, but neither is fully developed. Little Cecily (Lyn Wright), she who calls a spade and spade, more often resembles a spirited Cockney waif than the despirited Cockney waif than the demure ward of a country gentleman. And Gwendolyn (Carol Dearman), she who is glad to say she has never seen a spade, is more a headstrong vixen than a Victorian debutante. The scene at tea between them has all the subtlety of a cat fight.

These are the excesses of a director who does not entirely trust his material. Robert Perillo appears to have been given more attention to the timing of sight gags, such as the ravenous consumption of tea cakes and cucumber sandwiches or Cecily playing on a garden swing, than to characterization or the linguistic delights of the text.

Robert Ierardi gives a passable Algernon that improves in each act, and Harris Berlinsky has his moments doubling as both manservants, as when Algernon idly expresses his hopes that tomorrow will be a fine day, and his valet quietly observes, "It never is, sir."

"The Importance of Being Earnest" is a play in which less is infinitely more. But as Algernon says in another context, "It is awfully hard work doing nothing."

1989 O 5, C19:1

Laurie Anderson, All Alone in America

By STEPHEN HOLDEN

In Laurie Anderson's performance piece "Empty Places," the song that goes the furthest in distilling its mood and summing up its themes is a witty new ballad called "Hiawatha."

Borrowing its opening lines from Longfellow's poem, the song goes on to quote from Chuck Berry's "Memphis" and then to imagine mythical American couples, "Geromino and Little Nancy, Marilyn and John F." dancing. Punctuating the verses is an eerie cry of "Yoo hoo!" It is one of many leitmotifs in a work that, above all, evokes an American sense of loneliness, of cowboys calling through wide open spaces.

•

Although the 90-minute work, which is the opening event of the Next Wave Festival of the Brooklyn Academy of Music, is staged somewhat differently from Ms. Anderson's epic "United States," it is essentially a continuation of the earlier piece. Interweaving songs, film, slides, electronic music and anecdotes in an extended series of interconnected fragments, Ms. Anderson creates a loosely knit collage of images, sounds and phrases that collectively compile her latest vision of the American spirit.

For "Empty Spaces," the single large screen before which Ms. Anderson used to perform has been replaced by a series of screens on which images appear and vanish in a fluid stream. Used in conjunction, they also create what Ms. Anderson calls "instant sets," such as the re-appearing interior of a recording studio. Since "United States," Ms. Anderson has experimented by performing with other musicians on the stage. But in "Empty Spaces," she has returned to a solo format, in which, alone with just a violin and a keyboard, she appears to conjure up the visuals and some of the music as if by magic.

Martha Swope Associates/Linda Alaniz

Laurie   Anderson

Although Ms. Anderson has said that "Empty Spaces" is more political than her past performance pieces, its politics are anything but doctrinaire. In the past she has always made her points by allusion and ironic juxtaposition, and here she is only somewhat more direct. In an amusing mock-academic lecture, she finds musical metaphors for the speaking styles of world leaders. Hitler's speeches were the sound of drums; Mussolini's, Italian arias, and Ronald Reagan's quieter speeches, variations on "When You Wish Upon a Star."

Entering the realm of sexual politics, she recalls attending a feminist demonstration at a Playboy club and having a conversation with one of the women who worked there that made her think twice about protesting. Reflecting on urban blight, she tells an uncharacteristically self-flagellating anecdote in which she finds it difficult to look at the human misery in a hospital emergency room.

Whether talking (often through a device that lowers her voice), singing in a lilting folkish soprano, or playing a tape-bow violin that creates a rich spectrum of animal cries and subterranean growls, Ms. Anderson commands the stage with an easy grace. "Empty Spaces," which includes more personal anecdotes than any previous Anderson work, is also her funniest work. Her cool, deadpan delivery of punchlines shows her to be a natural comic talent in the low-keyed manner of performers like Steven Wright. Musically, "Empty Spaces" continues the idiom that Ms. Anderson refined in "United States," of a kind of minimalist electronic folk song. Fragment after fragment suggests space-age hoedown music, slowed-down until it sounds strangely doleful.

•

Where "Empty Spaces" seems thin is in some of its imagery. In using Elvis Presley and John F. Kennedy as recurrent symbols, Ms. Anderson fails to glean any new slant or resonance. In the past, she has usually been more original. And her reliance on them suggests that a certain fatigue may have overtaken her in the search for fresh iconography. The time may have come for Ms. Anderson to take a break from imagining the United States.

1989 O 6, C3:1

Biblical Twist

II SAMUEL 11, ETC., written and directed by David Greenspan; lighting design by David Bergstein; set design by William Kennon. Presented by Home for Contemporary Theater and Art, 44 Walker Street.

Character 1	Ron Bagden
Character 2	Mary Shultz

By MEL GUSSOW

Lounging in a bathrobe and speaking conversationally, the actress Mary Shultz recalls the story of David and Bathsheba. She tells it as her own story, as the victim of a king who seduced her and had her husband killed. As she explains in David Greenspan's "II Samuel 11, Etc." (at Home for Contemporary Theater and Art), she was a woman completely without choice. If Bathsheba did not accede to David's offensive demands, she would have been stoned to death by the people.

In this interior monologue, Mr. Greenspan cleverly merges biblical phrasings with a modern-day Bathsheba's confessional musings, as in the remark "David, chosen by God, was not the healthiest influence on his children." Bathsheba is quietly but relentlessly critical of David, as in her remembrance that, post-seduction, he suggested that they pray together. In this suggestion, one can naturally see contemporary evangelical correlatives.

The sad fate of the unsung Bathsheba, who by her own admission "sort of disappears" from the story once her son Solomon has inherited the throne, is the most intriguing aspect of Mr. Greenspan's bifurcated play. As it turns out, it is only one of several principal strands. Among other things, the "Etc." of the title refers to the difficulty of the artistic process. The playwright himself is represented on stage by a character (portrayed by Ron Bagden) who is supposedly writing the play we are seeing.

While Ms. Shultz speaks, Mr. Bagden is seen in the background at his desk, silently contemplating his creative infertility. Trying to will himself into inspiration, he is repeatedly interrupted by intimate homoerotic fantasies, which are recounted in graphic detail by Ms. Shultz acting as the author's ego. These fantasies not only impede the playwright's creativity, they also delay the telling of the far more interesting Bathsheba story.

In the second act, Mr. Bagden becomes the speaker, delivering a convoluted monologue about the various heterosexual involvements of a woman named Margot (and her friends) over a period of many years. Further clouding the question of gender, Mr. Bagden tells his story from the female point of view. With a plethora of unseen characters, the monologue seems almost as intricate a three-dimensional chess. The character of the playwright admits to creating confusion but does not alleviate it. Except for the fact that Mr. Bagden is still playing the role of the writer, the second act has only a tangential thematic relevance to Bathsheba, who has disappeared from the narrative along with Ms. Shultz.

•

Although both halves of the play are self-concerned to the point of solipsism, in each half there is, at odd moments, a wry detachment. At the height of orgasmic release, the playwright says to himself, "I've got to find a way to get this down on paper," and in so saying, records it for his audience. The play becomes a mirror within a mirror — within a mirror.

Doubling as his own director, Mr. Greenspan has given his work an appropriately austere production, a feeling of reserve — rather than flamboyance — that is reflected by the actors. Mr. Bagden carefully understates his lines, communicating the idea that he can follow his circuitous path even as it leads us into a labyrinth. Ms. Shultz is matter of fact and amusingly indelicate as Bathsheba. Though burdened by too many nonlinear levels of perception and an overload of sexual imagery, "II Samuel 11, Etc." is indicative of a playwright with an intense, idiosyncratic turn of mind and a playfulness about the possibilities of theater.

1989 O 7, 13:

Eileen and Company

WONDERFUL TOWN, book by Joseph Fields and Jerome Chodorov; based on the play "My Sister Eileen" by Mr. Fields and Mr. Chodorov and the stories by Ruth McKenney; music by Leonard Bernstein; lyrics by Betty Comden and Adolph Green; directed by Adrienne Weiss; musical director, Barbara Irvine; choreographer, Jonathan Cerullo; set designer, Wendy Ponte; costume designer, Claudia Stephens; lighting designer, Brian MacDevitt; sound designer, Hector Milla; production stage managers, Bernita Robinson and Jill Cordle. Presented by Equity Library Theater (310 Riverside Drive, at 103d Street), Jeffrey R. Costello, producing director.

WITH: Robert Bianca, Eric Brooks, Christine Campbell, Lucio Fernandez, Allen Fitzpatrick, Margaret Fung, Deborah Genevieve Walker Jones, Colette Kilroy, Nancy Leach, Stacey Logan, Bill Martel, Michael Metzel, Terry Reaner, Roger Rifkin, Mason Roberts, Blair Ross, Greg Templeton, Ovidio Vargas.

By STEPHEN HOLDEN

Has New York ever been so innocent a place as the grimy but effervescent city depicted in the 1953 musical "Wonderful Town"? That question pertains crucially to the Equity Library Theater's revival of the show, in which the director Adrienne Weiss has unwisely cast members of the ensemble as homeless people and punks in the street scenes. The insertion of contemporary references confuses the mood without adding any ironic resonance.

From a late-1980's perspective, "Wonderful Town" — which Joseph Fields and Jerome Chodorov based on their play "My Sister Eileen" and the stories by Ruth McKenney — is strictly a period piece. Its story of two Ohio sisters — one beautiful and flighty, the other plain and smart — who arrive in the big city with lofty career ambitions and settle into a crummy Greenwich Village apartment, is an archetypal coming-to-New York comedy of another era.

•

The main interest of the Equity Library Theater revival is in re-discovering the score composed by Leonard Bernstein with lyrics by Betty Comden and Adolph Green. Mr. Bernstein's unprepossessing music contemplates New York from two opposite perspectives. Deliberately homespun songs like "Ohio," "A Quiet Girl" and "It's Love" evoke a wide-eyed out-of-towner's idealism, while numbers like "Christopher Street," "Conga!" and "Let It Come Down/Ballet at the Village Vortex" anticipate "West Side Story," which was to open only four years later. In them, the composer fastened on cool jazz and Latin American dance music as the two idioms most expressive of the city's musical melting pot.

Ideally, "Wonderful Town" should be staged as a singing and dancing sitcom reminiscent of "I Love Lucy" but with a smart literary gloss. In the two leading roles, Stacey Logan and Colette Kilroy both display charm, though Miss Logan's Eileen overemphasizes standard "dumb blonde" comic shtick, and Miss Kilroy has none of the half-suppressed antic fire of Rosalind Russell, who originated the role.

•

The chaotic production lacks consistency of tone and a sure sense of comic rhythm. The staging seems arbitrary and the entrances and exits feel unprepared. Vocally, only Allen Fitzpatrick as the staid young editor Robert Baker is impressive.

The dancing varies from embarrassing to competent. For the delirious "Conga!" the male chorus members struggle to get Miss Kilroy off the ground and keep her safely aloft. Somewhat more assured is the witty "Ballet at the Village Vortex," in which the choreographer Jonathan Cerullo and the company poke fun at the more tarnished clichés of slinky, seductive nightclub dance.

1989 O 8, 64:1

Dancing and Delay

THE AUNTS, by Gary Bonasorte; directed by Charles Maryan; set design, Atkin Pace, lighting design, John Gleason; costume design, Lana Fritz; production stage manager, Bill McComb; sound design by Brian Ronan; dances by Bertram Ross. Presented by Ervin Litkei, in association with Ethel Gabriel and Larry Lipp, at the 47th Street Theater, 304 West 47th Street.

Meg	Bethel Leslie
Nan	Ann Wedgeworth
Pita	Mia Dillon
Chuck	Christopher Wynkoop

By MEL GUSSOW

When Mia Dillon, wearing a voluminous dress, makes her first entrance in "The Aunts," it is immediately clear to everyone in the theater that her character is supposed to be pregnant — to everyone, that is, except the other characters on stage. For unexplained reasons, the young woman's two aunts are oblivious to her condition.

It is not simply that the aunts are self-involved. They are manipulated into their blindness by the playwright, Gary Bonasorte, who is trying to withhold information and delay a dramatic surprise. As it slowly evolves, the play at the 47th Street Theater is all delay — and the only surprise is that anyone would choose to produce it or act in it.

In this story of domestic strife, one aunt (Ann Wedgeworth) is facing the imminent death of her invalid husband and the other (Bethel Leslie) is struggling to extract herself from the misery of her marriage. Complicating their concerns is the behavior of their unmarried, orphaned niece. The three are gathered in Ms. Wedgeworth's house for what becomes a prolonged death watch.

To pass the time of the play, the women turn on the radio and phonograph, offering theatergoers an almost continuous "Make Believe Ballroom" of old ballads. They dance with each other, drink, bake marijuana brownies (to relieve the dying husband's pain) and manage to fill the emptiness of the dialogue with another kind of emptiness.

Acting can sometimes transcend ʳ°ᵈⁱ, ·ʲⁿᵍ, but in this instance the actresses and the author descend to bathos together. The three accomplished performers are misled by their material and, presumably, by their director, Charles Maryan, into the land of self-parody.

•

Rushing around the small stage in a brightly colored dressing gown, Ms. Wedgeworth is in a perpetual dither, acting absentminded and frivolous as if she has already begun her merry widowhood. Ms. Dillon hides her talent behind the squeaks and squeals of arrested adolescence. Ms. Leslie, marginally more watchable than her co-stars, stresses her character's severity and is as sour as an unripe crab apple. Christopher Wynkoop adds bluster in a supporting role as Ms. Leslie's errant husband.

A modicum of interest — far short of tension — is supplied by the fact that the unseen invalid has a bell in his bedroom, which he has vowed to ring three times when agony calls and he wants help in ending his life. At one point, the doorbell rings loudly, three times, causing the women to leap to attention. Unfortunately, this is a false alarm.

1989 O 8, 64:1

Stacey Logan, left, and Colette Kilroy in "Wonderful Town."

The New York Times/Michelle V. Agins

Christine Lahti as an Angry Heidi in 'Chronicles'

By LAURIE WINER

Christine Lahti has stepped into the role of Heidi Holland, the art historian from whom stand-up comics could take a lesson. When she begins her witty lecture at the top of Wendy Wasserstein's lavishly awarded play "The Heidi Chronicles," at the Plymouth Theater, Ms. Lahti, who took over the role last month, wastes no time in banishing all traces of her predecessor Joan Allen's fawnlike, reactive presence.

The new Heidi plants both hands on either side of the podium in an upright, defiant stance; she's a woman warrior going into battle for her sisters. Eyes flashing behind academic standard-order wire-rim glasses, Ms. Lahti bitingly reminds her audience that in her day, the traditional art textbook included no women at all, "from the dawn of history to the present."

Unlike Ms. Allen's sorrowful failed reformer, Ms. Lahti's Heidi gets angry, and her defensive habit of reaching for the clever quip is fueled by an acidic sarcasm. With virtually a completely new cast (Anne Lange is the holdover from the original), "The Heidi Chronicles" has lost some of its subtlety in the smaller roles. But that's hardly the bad news.

In the title role, Ms. Lahti's fierce interpretation has the unintentional effect of exposing the play's critical flaw, one that previously had been camouflaged by Ms. Allen's more oblique approach. "The Heidi Chronicles" suffers from a severe credibility gap. Its heroine is not the woman she — and others — claim she is.

•

Just why is Heidi Holland so angry, or sorrowful, as the case may be? According to the play the reasons are these: As a Vassar student in the late 1960's, Heidi attends a college mixer where she met an overbearingly arrogant but charismatic young Eugene McCarthy canvasser with the unlikely name of Scoop Rosenbaum (Tony Shalhoub). Scoop immediately assesses his soon-to-be conquest as a "serious good person" — the characters often offer Heidi unsolicited, admiring descriptions of herself; in another prescient moment, Scoop informs Heidi that she will be "interesting, exemplary, even sexy, but basically unhappy." "The ones who open doors usually are," he explains soberly.

While Heidi does try to help open some doors for women in the 1970's, she is hardly the martyred warrior that Ms. Wasserstein and Ms. Lahti would have us believe. It's true, however, that she dutifully attends a women's consciousness-raising group at which she reluctantly confesses to four cloyingly supportive group members her demoralizing secret: she is in love with a man, Scoop, who is ambivalent toward her.

At the same time, this serious good person begins to develop the ungenerous trait of sitting in judgment — always by way of a cleverly bitchy zinger — on any woman who has something she does not: a husband, higher earning power, a more recent birth date. Yet Ms. Wasserstein sidesteps the issue of Heidi's need to condemn. The playwright constantly stacks the deck against the characters to whom Heidi feels superior, and, with one exception, she never imagines the play from anyone else's perspective.

•

When Scoop marries a pampered Southerner named Lisa (Ms. Lange) who illustrates children's books (read: an intellectual lightweight), Heidi attends the wedding with her best friend, a homosexual pediatrician named Peter (played with crisp comic assurance by David Pierce). Peter is Heidi's equal in acerbity, and he's the only character in the play Ms. Wasserstein seems to regard as Heidi's equal in suffering. He, too, is a serious good person. We know this because Ms. Wasserstein has given him an impeccable cause: he specializes in helping children with AIDS.

But while Peter may be a good-hearted doctor, he's a rude wedding guest. He and Heidi waste no time in trashing the bride — always wittily — whether she's in the room or not. When Lisa dares to refer to her new husband as "sweetie," Heidi and Peter immediately pick up the ball, addressing each other as "sweetie," with just the right mock ironic tone. Not to worry, though: the bride is not hip enough to realize she's being insulted.

It should come as no surprise that Scoop concurs with Heidi's assessment of his wife. And when the band strikes up the bride and groom's favorite song (Sam Cooke's "You Send Me"), Scoop lingers in the anteroom with Heidi rather than return to the wedding. With the connecting door open (read: anyone could walk in), Scoop kisses Heidi and sways her tightly to the music in an intimate embrace.

That this man would risk his minutes-old marriage for the sake of a last kiss from Heidi could only mean that he is absurdly arrogant, psychic or that the playwright is mythologizing her heroine's charms.

John Updike once said of the English writer Henry Greene, "He never asks us to side with him against a character, and he never dramatizes his own prodigious acceptance of human incorrigibility." Ms. Wasserstein, on the other hand, is guilty on both counts. As Heidi gets older, her generosity evaporates toward younger women — those she and her friends see as ungratefully reaping the rewards of their hard-fought battles.

In a scene at a baby shower, a younger woman who "took women's studies at Brown" is proved, ipso facto, to be a representative bubblehead of the coming generation. When a shower guest describes the young woman with whom Scoop is now illicitly involved, the unfortunate adultress is elevated to a symbol. "She's like that entire generation," confides the guest conspiratorially to her friends. "They have opinions on everything and have done nothing."

While Ms. Wasserstein does not put that sentence in Heidi's mouth, Heidi soon enough reveals her own bias. In a pivotal monologue, Heidi finally examines her own growing unease. She describes a kind of breakdown she had in the locker room at her gym. While stripping for aerobics class, Heidi becomes almost immobilized with depression as she listens to the other women jabbering around her. Her observations about these women center on what they're wearing, how old they are, where they shop and what they own.

One woman has "perfect red nails," another shops at Lord & Taylor, another likes brown rice and women's fiction. Most offensive, however, are "two 27-year-old hotshots," both wearing purple and green leather, who have busy careers, alligator datebooks and who bring their own heavier weights to class.

●

For once, Heidi's barbed tongue is rendered impotent by these women and their possessions; paradoxically, she feels their own judgments weighing heavily upon her. She imagines that they view her as having chosen "the wrong road." Childless, single and unhappy, Heidi says she feels stranded. She looks for the source of her unhappiness, but doesn't find it. "I don't blame the ladies in the locker room for how I feel," she says, after blaming them all.

This monologue, which many people take as an indictment of the failure of the women's movement, has al-

A fierce interpretation of a heroine.

ways puzzled me. Ms. Allen brought an exquisite sadness to it; she seemed to have realized that she had failed herself in some profound way, although it was never quite clear how. A person is not made unhappy by sticking close to her values in life, even as others fall by the wayside, corrupt and impure in purple and green leather. Ms. Allen's sadness seemed to imply that it was not merely the world at large that had disappointed Heidi.

In Ms. Lahti's hands, and despite the actress's tears, Heidi is more blameful than guilty. Ms. Lahti's is a more active but less sophisticated reading of the character. By demanding that Heidi retain her halo, the actress has denied the play the possibility that its heroine might be imperfect. Without that possibility, "The Heidi Chronicles" is dishonest — witty, but empty.

●

At the play's conclusion, Heidi adopts a baby. Ms. Wasserstein avoids the question of motivation (was the adoption a reaction to the women in the locker room?), and the logistics of exactly how Heidi acquired the child. But Heidi's wish for her daughter, Judy, is simple and universal: that for Judy, "maybe, just maybe, things will be a little better."

Perhaps Ms. Wasserstein believes that in writing this scene, she has finally bestowed upon Heidi that generosity of spirit so lacking before. But if Heidi resents younger women who appear to have it easier than she did, how will she shield her own daughter from that resentment? When she blames the women's movement for leaving her stranded and alone, she chooses to ignore the real culprit. The person who has let Heidi down is none other than Heidi herself.

1989 O 9, C13:1

Monster Mash

FRANKIE, book by George Abbott; lyrics by Gloria Nissenson; music by Joseph Turrin; co-directed by Mr. Abbott and Donald Saddler; based on "Frankenstein" by Mary Shelley; scenic design, James Morgan; costume design, Beba Shamash; lighting design, Stuart Duke; technical director, James E. Fuller Jr.; production stage manager, William J, Buckley 3d; music director, Arthur M.

Greene. Presented by the York Theater Company, Janet Hayes Walker, producing director; Molly Pickering Grose, managing director. At the Church of the Heavenly Rest, 2 East 90th Street.

Victor Stanford	Richard White
Elizabeth Blake	Elizabeth Walsh
Flora	Ellia English
Frankie	Gil Rogers
Burton Stanford	Casper Roos
Henry Green	Mark Zimmerman
Jake/Nurse	Kim Moore
Fred/Nurse	Howard Pinhasik
Joe/Sheriff	Ron Wisniski
Tracy Green	Colleen Fitzpatrick

By MEL GUSSOW

Before settling into marital bliss, Dr. Victor Stanford has decided to devote himself to an ambitious scientific experiment. Embracing his fiancée, he sings to her of his dream of becoming famous: "I'll be cited in schools with Hippocrates and Darwin." If by Darwin he means "survival of the fittest," the doctor is out of luck — as is the show in which he appears, "Frankie," George Abbott's modern musical version of "Frankenstein." For the York Theater Company, the new musical is a steep comedown after its revivals of "Sweeney Todd" and other shows by Stephen Sondheim.

Certainly there are many alternative approaches to the familiar tale — as a Boris Karloff horror movie, a David Cronenberg-style investigation of psychopathology or a Mel Brooks romp (a chorus of Peter Boyle singing "Puttin' on the Ritz" would be particularly welcome in "Frankie"). With "The Phantom of the Opera" staring balefully over their shoulders, Mr. Abbott and his collaborators (Joseph Turrin, composer, and Gloria Nissenson, lyricist) misguidedly approach "Frankenstein" as a love story with a happy ending. The result is as simple-minded as if told from the monster's point of view.

●

Along the way, the musical borrows freely from scores of its betters. Having succeeded in reanimating a convict's corpse, Dr. Stanford (Richard White) and his equally smug medical partner suddenly sing and dance like Henry Higgins and Colonel Pickering. The object of their attention — a glum, gray-haired Gil Rogers — is, of course, at the furthest remove from Eliza Dolittle.

Contemplating this poor hulk, the doctor's maid (Ellia English) sings a lullaby, as if he were a homeless orphan instead of a monster about to run amok. Later she calms him by feeding him soul food, "collard greens and buttered beans," which is the height of Ms. Nissenson's poetic invention. Mr. Turrin's music is a match in blandness. As for the recitative ("I had a corpse, I gave it blood, I gave it a pacemaker") it would sound better if translated in Transylvanian.

In his many years in the theater as director and author, Mr. Abbott has of course provided us with countless evenings of entertainment. But his book for "Frankie" lacks any sense of Gothic surprise, and the staging (by Mr. Abbott and Donald Saddler) is sedentary, except for those occasional moments when the monster lumbers from side to side. There is not even a single enlivening special effect in the doctor's laboratory, like those in the otherwise unlamented Broadway "Frankenstein" of several seasons ago.

●

Mr. White and Elizabeth Walsh, who plays his fiancée, might be engaging in other theatrical circumstances. Here they have to pretend

Peter Cunningham

Christine Lahti in "The Heidi Chronicles."

that they are in a real romance instead of a mock monster musical. The actors manage to conceal what must be their embarrassment, except for Casper Roos, as the doctor's elderly brother, who seems understandably disconcerted by the fact that he has to play one scene in his undershorts. The only performer almost to rise above the material is Ms. English as the maid, a role that is so stereotypical that one fully expects her to say, "I don't know nothin' about birthin' monsters."

As for Frankie of the woeful countenance, Mr. Rogers, whose lines are intentional gibberish, is often seen peeping from behind a curtain. Eventually he kidnaps and ties up Ms. Walsh, preparing for his own scientific experiment. It is at that moment that one realizes that all Frankie has learned in his second life is how to tie a knot.

Despite all the ineptitude that has preceded it, nothing could possibly prepare the audience for the incredible finale. After several murders and that assault on the leading lady — and on the American musical — Frankie is belatedly put to sleep. A prayerful Ms. English leads the company in singing a spiritual in honor of the monster, in which she confuses the River Jordan with the River Styx. Of all the afflictions suffered by Mary Shelley's creature, the musical "Frankie" is undoubtedly the most onerous.

1989 O 10, C18:3

Taking Wilde At His Word

THE IMPORTANCE OF BEING EARNEST, by Oscar Wilde; directed by Mark Lamos; assistant director, Rob Bundy; set design, Michael Yeargan; costume design, Jess Goldstein; lighting design, Peter Kaczorowski; sound design, David Budries; dramaturge, Greg Leaming; production stage manager, Ruth E. Sternberg; assistant stage manager, Barbara Reo. Presented by Hartford Stage, Mr. Lamos, aristic director; David Hawkanson, managing director. At Hartford, Conn.

Algernon Moncrieff .... Victor Slezak
Lane, Merriman .... John Scanlan
John Worthing .... Mark Lamos
Lady Bracknell .... Barbara Bryne
Hon. Gwendolen Fairfax .... Mary Layne
Miss Prism .... Helen Carey
Cecily Cardew .... Mary-Louise Parker
Rev. Canon Chasuble .... Benjamin Stewart

By LAURIE WINER

"In matters of grave importance, style, not sincerity, is the vital thing," says Gwendolen, one of the perceptive if frivolous dilettantes in Oscar Wilde's "Importance of Being Earnest." In his new production of the play at the Hartford Stage, Mark Lamos has taken Gwendolen's dictum to heart, staging an "Earnest" that delivers the bon mots born of boredom in turn-of-the-century British drawing rooms and country estates. But in his production, the characters rarely emerge as much more than stylish mouthpieces for Wilde's famous wit.

Mr. Lamos, who has been the artistic director of Hartford Stage since 1980, has forgone his custom of re-imagining the settings of classic plays ("Hamlet" in a banana republic, "Twelfth Night" in 1930's America). With "Earnest" he takes a straightforward approach and casts himself in the lead role of Jack Wor-

thing, the love-struck and very earnest aristocrat of questionable parentage.

•

Mr. Lamos has acted before, both in Hartford and around the country (he makes his screen debut in a coming film about AIDS, "Longtime Companion"), and he is not a bad actor exactly. A small man with a handsome, expressive face, he attracts instant sympathy in the way that Harry Langdon did in his silent film comedies. But when his character gets caught in a bit of tricky slapstick choreography, such as an attempted kiss that ends in a pratfall, Mr. Lamos falls short of the physical grace his woeful demeanor promises. Similarly, while his voice is pleasing and his accent dead on, he projects a stilted presence that says he has the equipment to be a natural actor but lacks the gift.

Two other major roles are likewise marred. Mary Layne as Gwendolen reveals only the character's superficiality; she never acknowledges that even London debutantes might suffer from a sincere emotion. When she wishes to communicate to Jack her intention to accept his proposal, she thrusts her chest toward him with a sigh that looks like it was borrowed from a bad opera. Her Gwendolen will all too obviously become, as Jack fears, just like her mother, and in far less than the 150 years he calculates. Victor Slezak approximates the ennui of Jack's best friend, Algernon, with a lazy insolence that doesn't translate to upper class. He slouches rather than lounges, and when he falls in love with Jack's young ward, Cecily, he smiles at her with the same self-satisfied smirk he flashed earlier when Jack threatened to eat the cucumber sandwiches he had earmarked for himself.

T. Charles Erickson

Mary-Louise Parker in "The Importance of Being Earnest."

Almost by default, Mary-Louise Parker, as Cecily, becomes the stand-in for the spirit of Wilde — a role usually reserved for Algernon or Jack. Fresh-faced and impish, Miss Parker doesn't judge her character's affections to be silly and useless; she imbues this country girl with a mind sharp enough to shear any sophisicated city rival who dares to cross

Delighting in a life with little more to do than be witty.

her, as Gwendolen briefly does. In this interpretation, Cecily seems to be a slightly less serious cousin of Jane Austen's Elizabeth Bennett in "Pride and Prejudice." And when Algernon asks her to clip a flower for his button hole, she brandishes the scissors at him with a breezy sexual knowingness that suggests that her life in the country may not have been so cloistered after all. Like Wilde, this Cecily delights in a life in which she has little more to do than be witty, fall in love and be fallen in love with.

•

Sailing in like a battleship in an elaborately bustled brown-and-pink gown (one of the many lavish costumes designed by Jess Goldstein), Barbara Bryne is a formidible Lady Bracknell. She uses the full range of her distinctive voice, which rings rather gratingly in the upper registers but which sounds deadly matter-of-fact in the lower, to launch both the inanities and pure nuggets of social truth that Lady Bracknell delivers. When she attempts to calculate whether Jack's holdings make him an eligible match for her Gwendolen, she stares off into the distance, narrowing her eyes and silently moving her lips; she looks like a top-notch accountant on a complex tax case.

"Nothing is easier than to handle this play without noticing what it contains," wrote the critic Eric Bentley, of "Earnest." While Mr. Lamos and company have taken note of Wilde's wit and wisdom, they could go further in liberating it from the purely abstract quality of the epigram on the page.

1989 O 11, C15:1

Souls Sing Out

GOD'S TROMBONES, a gospel musical adaptation of James Weldon Johnson's writings; directed by Woodie King Jr.; musical director, Grenoldo Frazier; set designer, Llewellyn Harrison; production stage manager, Dwayne B. Perryman 3d; lighting designer, William H. Grant 3d; movement, Dianne McIntyre. Presented by New Federal Theater at Theater of the Riverside Church. Mr. King, producer. At 120th Street and Riverside Drive.

The Rev. Bradford Parham .... Lex Monson
The Rev. Sister Rena Pinkston
                                        Theresa Merritt
Sister Odessa Jackson .... Rhetta Hughes
The Rev. Sister Marion Alexander
                                       Trazana Beverley
The Rev. Ridgley Washington ..... Cliff Frazier
Jackson Family
    Deborah Blackwell-Cook, Sabrynaah Pope,
Rhetta Hughes and Don Corey Washington

By STEPHEN HOLDEN

In the sermons of James Weldon Johnson, whose writings form the heart of the 1969 gospel musical

"God's Trombones," famous Bible stories are told in fervent oratorical cadences and embellished with story-book imagery that turns them into stirring folk tales. An early 20th-century poet, civil-rights leader, diplomat and preacher, Johnson likened the sound of gospel voices to fanfares of trombones.

His version of the Creation evokes a God who is very human in His loneliness and who vows, "I'll make me a man, but first I'll make me a world!" It goes on to picture God as a perfectionistic sculptor "toiling on a lump of clay" to refine the human form.

Johnson's retelling of the Creation is one of more than half a dozen of his sermons that have been stitched together with familiar gospel hymns to make "God's Trombones," which has been revived by the New Federal Theater at the Theater of Riverside Church. The show is more than a celebration of Johnson's powers as an old-time gospel preacher.

Its introduction, which places him in the distinguished company of Harriet Tubman, the Rev. Dr. Martin Luther King Jr., Malcolm X, Jesse Jackson and Archbishop Desmond Tutu, stresses the central role of the clergy in shaping and holding together black curlture throughout history.

•

"God's Trombones" is structured as a church meeting, at which four preachers take turns delivering Johnson's messages. Most of the words are spoken, though occasionally an invocation is sung in semi-improvisatory, gospel recitative with keyboard accompaniment.

The four preachers are sharply different in personality. Serenely paternalistic, the Rev. Bradford Parham (Lex Monson) delivers a tear-jerking sermon in which a woman's death is pictured as an achingly tender reconciliation with Jesus on whose breast she lays her head for eternal rest.

The Rev. Sister Marion Alexander (Trazana Beverley), alternates a scolding tone with one of tearful outrage as she recounts the story of the Crucifixion. The angriest preacher, the Rev. Ridgley Washington (Cliff Frazier), literally shakes his fist at the heavens as he recounts the book of Exodus. The most benign sounding is the Rev. Sister Rena Pinkston (Theresa Merritt), who sings the gospel message in a rich but slightly worn gospel alto.

•

The between-sermon hymns, which include such favorites as "Amen," "How Great Thou Art" and "Were You There," are sung with verve and feeling by the Jackson Family Quartet (Rhetta Hughes, Deborah Blackwell-Cook, Sabrynaah Pope and Don Corey Washington). None possess a genuinely roof-raising voice.

Woodie King Jr.'s staging on a spare church set decorated by a single stained-glass window treats the show as a straightforward gospel service. Given the passion of Johnson's language, which explodes with fire, brimstone and tears, the tone of the production is quite subdued. Although the singers and speakers move about the stage, the feel of the show is still static. In both Johnson's language and in the voices of the performers, one senses another level of energy that remains untapped.

1989 O 11, C17:1

Tongue in Cheek And Foot in Mouth

MASTERGATE, by Larry Gelbart; directed by Michael Engler; scenery by Philipp Jung; costumes by Candice Donnelly; lighting by Stephen Strawbridge; sound by Marc Salzberg; video by Dennis Diamond; video music by Glen Roven; stage manager, Cathy B. Blaser; general manager, Steven Suskin. Presented by Gene Wolsk. At the Criterion Center Stage Right, Broadway and 45th Street.

Senator Bowman	Jerome Kilty
Representative Proctor and Secretary of State Bishop	Tom McDermott
Shepherd Hunter	John Dossett
Representative Byers, Senator Knight and Steward Butler	Wayne Knight
Senator Bunting, Representative Sellers and Wyle Slaughter	Jeff Weiss
Abel Lamb	Steve Hofvendahl
Major Manley Battle	Daniel von Bargen
Vice President Burden and Clay Fielder	Joseph Daly
Mr. Child, Mr. Picker, Mr. Boyle and Mr. Carver	Zach Grenier
Merry Chase	Melinda Mullins
TNN Director	Katrina Stevens
TNN Cameramen	Merrill Holtzman and Harold Dean James
Senior Staffer	William Cain
The Wives	Ann McDonough

Pages
Charles Geyer, Isiah Whitlock Jr. and Priscilla C. Shanks

By FRANK RICH

How do you write a truthful play in which everyone is a liar? Set it on Capitol Hill, of course. In "Mastergate," Larry Gelbart's excoriating satire of the Iran-contra hearings, the witnesses before a Congressional committee aspire only to be "steadfastly evasive and selectively honest," and they don't even succeed at that. They speak in nonsensical double talk and official bureaucratese redolent of such past Gelbart writings as Sid Caesar's shtick and television's "M*A*S*H." As Maj. Manley Battle — a lunatic amalgam of Oliver North, Alexander Haig and Joseph Heller's Major Major — says, "I prefer to call a spade by its code word."

Yet Mr. Gelbart, unlike his obfuscating characters, speaks the harsh truth. "Mastergate" isn't subtitled "A Play on Words" for nothing. Its subject is not just Washington's scandals but the destruction of language that accompanies those scandals, for language is the first casualty of official mendacity. American voters have now lived through two decades of "pacification programs," "modified limited hangouts," "stonewalling," "non-denial denials" and other euphemisms for covert criminal actions or their subsequent cover-ups. What has this relentlessly corrupt coinage done to our society? Mr. Gelbart, mad as hell and unable to take it anymore, has written a comedy in which the laughter derives almost entirely from the linguistic pratfalls taken by public officials to avoid taking responsibility for their betrayal of the public trust.

•

Set in the Sherman Adams Room of the John Mitchell Building — in Philipp Jung's environmental design, a Congressional circus ringed by television monitors — "Mastergate" is "an exhausting inquiry" into the latest example of "debilitating governmental self-abuse." The scandal in question was an attempt to divert arms to Central American guerrillas by funneling a billion dollars through Master Pictures' high-budget action film, "Tet!, the Movie." But the inquiry's most pressing question — "What did the President know, and does he have any

idea that he knew it?" — is soon swamped by the testimony's oxymorons, mixed metaphors, mangled idioms and dizzying jargon.

Officials testify about their non-participation in "non-discussions" and applaud the ally of San Elvador for practicing "a democratic form of government that's been run by its army for the past 40 years." One inquisitor promises to "broadly narrow down the scope" of the hearings while a harried Secretary of State (Tom McDermott) sonorously assures the committee that "the truth will have to wait until I finish testifying." To thicken the smoke screen separating citizens from the facts, "Mastergate" has another overlay of falsehood provided by the fatuous gavel-to-gavel coverage of Total News Network. It's part of Mr. Gelbart's point that the fictive media event, or in the historian Daniel Boorstin's phrase, "the pseudo-event," and the actual news event have blurred into a single impenetrable morass. Everyone is showboating for the camera, whether in Congressional tribunals or in the real or faked battle scenes that have brought war, from Tet on, into our living rooms each night.

•

In Michael Engler's production at the Criterion Center, this point is accentuated by asking the theater audience to choose between watching the live action and its simultaneous closed-circuit broadcast on the video monitors. Mr. Engler, the young director who did so well by the human comedy of Richard Greenberg's "Eastern Standard" last season, is equally gifted at delivering a heartless comic barrage consistent with Mr. Gelbart's Broadway adaptations of Plautus ("A Funny Thing Happened on the Way to the Forum") and Ben Jonson ("Sly Fox").

"Mastergate" is staged as a Herblock cartoon come to life, with bright caricatures to match from a vivid acting ensemble led by Jerome Kilty as a Sam Ervinesque committee chairman, Jeff Weiss doubling as posturing Congressmen of both the "gung-holier than thou" right and the Jane Fonda left, Daniel von Bargen as the overdecorated major and Joseph Daly as a down-home Vice President who applauds "the Revolution thing" in American history even while failing to recall exactly when it was.

•

What Mr. Engler cannot do is disguise the fact that "Mastergate," however smart, is not the Broadway show its venue suggests but a sketch — and one that feels stretched to fill 90 minutes. There are times when Mr. Gelbart's compulsive wordplays, whether malapropisms or pun-ridden proper names, run off into wheel-spinning overdrive, and there are a few missed satiric opportunities that might have served in their place. It seems a waste to have a television correspondent who sounds exactly like Diane Sawyer (Melinda Mullins) and not have fun with her real-life counterpart's role as a press officer in the waning days of the Nixon White House. Nor does Mr. Gelbart, a co-author of "Tootsie" and a veteran of show-biz wars, get all the juice out of the Hollywood corruption that makes the budget-padding of "Tet!, the Movie" echo "Heaven's Gate" as much as Watergate.

By outliving Oliver North's trial and the front-page prominence of figures like George Shultz and William Casey, "Mastergate" has also lost immediacy since its premiere at the

Martha Swope
Daniel von Bargen as Maj. Manley Battle in "Mastergate."

American Repertory Theater in Cambridge last spring. Satire can have the shelf life of yesterday's newspapers. But if "Mastergate" leaves the audience a bit unsatisfied, especially by its lack of resolution, that is consistent with the Iran-contra affair itself, which refuses to follow the well-made scenario of Watergate. As Theodore Draper wrote in The New York Review of Books over the summer, "Without a full disclosure of the President's responsibility, the [North] trial took on the appearance of 'Hamlet' without the Prince." In The New Yorker this week, Frances FitzGerald similarly likens the scandal, with its shuffled events and shredded subplots, to "modernist drama": "The simple, old-fashioned questions cannot be answered directly, and the most serious questions have jokes for answers."

Mr. Gelbart has sharpened those black jokes and demands that we take seriously the "squandered lives and laundered dollars" that are their constant punch lines. "Mastergate" concludes with an angry warning of "the next, inevitable Whatever-Gate," with its fresh crowd of "photo-opportunistic nobodies who grab the limelight before either being sent on to jail or up to higher office." And with Noriegate and HUD-gate looming, the warning sticks. When "Mastergate" is funny, it is very funny. When it is not, it still stands up for a patriotic integrity beyond the understanding of the clowns who parade across its national stage.

1989 O 13, C3:1

Adultery Fare

A FLEA IN HER EAR, by Georges Feydeau; translated by John Mortimer; directed by John Tillinger; set design by John Lee Beatty; costume design by Jane Greenwood; lighting design by Marc B. Weiss; production stage managers, Robin Kevrick and Anne Keefe. Presented by Long Wharf Theater (Arvin Brown, artistic director; M. Edgar Rosenblum, executive director), in New Haven.

Camille Chandebise	Edmund Lewis
Carlos Homenides de Histangua	Ramiro Carrillo
Victor Emmanuel Chandebise/Poche	Donal Donnelly
Raymonde Chandebise	Harriet Harris
Lucienne Homenides de Histangua	Nancy Mette
Dr. Finache	George Guidall
Romain Tournel	Frank Muller
Etienne Plucheux	John Rothman
Antoinette Plucheux	Kristine Nielsen
Eugénie	Veanne Cox
Augustin Feraillon	Larry Block
Olympe	Aideen O'Kelly
Baptistin	William Preston
Herr Schwarz	Clement Fowler

With: A. J. Glassman, Ann Hutchinson, David Scott Meikle, Katlyn McNeill, Jody Rowell.

By MEL GUSSOW

Special to The New York Times

NEW HAVEN, Oct. 6 — John Tillinger's production of "A Flea in Her Ear," which is opening the 25th season at the Long Wharf Theater, is performed with split-second synchronicity. The mechanics of the farce never show as the actors and audience are swept away by the sport of the chase — the slammed doors, the revolving beds, the frazzled looks and the mistaken identities that confuse an irate husband and a drunken hotel porter.

With all gears meshed the comedy flows, unimpeded by any thought of credibility and unhampered by the fact that a few of the performances are not as amusing as they should be. This "Flea" is not perfect, but it is fast, mirthful and, when necessary, frenetic.

As the director reminds us, Feydeau's humor is linguistic as well as physical. Words, especially when they are misunderstood, matter as much as pratfalls and doubletakes. This is the case with Camille Chandebise, a scamp with a pronounced speech impediment, and Carlos Homenides de Histangua, a Spanish gentleman who is fiercely afraid of being cuckolded.

•

At Long Wharf, those two roles are played by Edmund Lewis and Ramiro Carrillo, respectively, add the lightness of helium to an already aerated production. Camille, the nephew of the play's protagonist, Victor Emmanuel Chandebise (Donal Donnelly), is unable to sound a consonant for most of the play. This means that his comedy derives from mime and doubletalk, with occasional bursts of intelligibility. Mr. Lewis deftly acts his lines as if they all should be understood. To him, the others are aliens who have not yet learned his language.

As for Mr. Carrillo, his role is the opposite; he discovers consonants where they do not exist. The actor never allows his accent to become a burlesque. He is Castillian to the core, and his outrage at what he thinks is his wife's infidelity is palpable.

These two actors inspire the heartiest laughter, but they are players on a team, mobilized to a single purpose — to keep "Flea" flying. The first act sets the devious plot in motion, as the suspicious wife (Harriet Harris) tries to catch her husband (Mr. Donnelly) on an errant night. The second act causes a commotion, as the innocent husband and almost all of the play's other characters are entrapped in the scandalous Hotel Coq d'Or. Parenthetically, a more recent purveyor of stage comedy, Tom Stoppard, paid homage to Feydeau by placing the indelicacies of "Dirty Linen" in an English version of the Coq d'Or.

•

In Mr. Tillinger's "Flea," there is a brief second-act letdown. This is at least partly attributable to Mr. Donnelly's other persona. He is suitably stuffy as the husband, but, doubling as the hotel porter, Poche, he misses the low-comedy lurchings that add wit to this bumbler. Mr. Donnelly is a fine character actor, but he is not a natural clown. Such is the strength of the other performances, including Mr. Donnelly's increasingly frazzled Victor Emmanuel, that the comedy gathers momentum, reaching a delirious conclusion as everyone seems to be in the wrong room at the wrong time.

"A Flea in Her Ear" has a panoply of character roles — philandering husbands, promiscuous wives and deceitful servants — almost all of whom are drawn to dabble in adultery. Ms. Harris, Nancy Mette, George Guidall and Frank Muller each contribute handily to the evening's diversion. In Feydeau, even a cameo can be a scene-stealer, as is true with the valet, a role that Laurence Olivier reserved for himself in a National Theater production. At Long Wharf, the valet is played by John Rothman with a deadpan sense of drollery. John Mortimer's translation is felicitous and John Lee Beatty's ingenious scenery is a free adaptation of Hector Guimard's designs for the Paris Metro.

Despite appearances, Feydeau is not foolproof, as was demonstrated by the recent revival of "A Flea in Her Ear" at the Old Vic in London. The director, Richard Jones, tried to reinvent the play as a cross between Kafka and Krafft-Ebing. This was too much weight for the farce to bear. Mr. Tillinger, with his effortless, effervescent staging, adds Feydeau to his comedy successes, which already include the collected works of Joe Orton.

1989 O 13, C15:1

Subdividing The Dachas

SUMMERFOLK, by Maxim Gorky; adapted from the translation by John Tillinger and Edward Gilbert; music by Debussy, Rachmaninoff and Wihtol; directed by Anne Bogart; music adapted and directed by Jeff Halpern; set adapted from designs by Victoria Petrovich; lighting designed by Robert Murphy; costumes designed by William Lane; sound designed by Stephen Santomena. Presented by Trinity Repertory Company, Ms. Bogart, artistic director; Timothy Langan, managing director. At Providence, R.I.

Bassov	Bill Damkoehler
Varvara	Cynthia Strickland
Kaleria	Theresa McCarthy
Vlass	Ed Shea
Suslov	Timothy Crowe
Yulia	Becca Lish
Dudakov	Andy Weems
Olga	Janice Duclos
Shalimov	Brian McEleney
Ryumin	Henry Stram
Maria Lvovna	Barbara Orson
Sonya	Josephine Chavez
Dvoetochie	Peter Gerety
Zamislov	Jonathan Fried
Maxim Zimin	Derek Stearns
Kropilkin	Elizabeth Stott
Sasha	Marni Rice
Semyonov	Barney O'Hanlon

Grey People
Brooke Berman, Stephanie Bond, Peter Kendall, Stephanie Paul and Michael Peterson.

By MEL GUSSOW
Special to The New York Times

PROVIDENCE, Oct. 12 — It is clear from her debut as artistic director of the Trinity Repertory Company that Anne Bogart is not satisfied with halfway measures. Her unorthodox production of Gorky's "Summerfolk," which opened Wednesday night, is an ambitious attempt to reinvent the play as a radical and relevant comedy about the complacency and ennui of the new Russian bourgeoisie. In pursuit of her bold concept, she loses sight of the specific humanity of Gorky's characters and she obscures the heartline of the play itself.

"Summerfolk," written in 1904, was conceived as a kind of postscript to Chekhov's "Cherry Orchard." In Gorky's terms, this is a world of "false hopes and unfulfilled promises." Dachas have been subdivided into summer colonies, where the newly rich idle away their time in unhappy romantic alliances. In common with Chekhov's characters, they still dream about a better life. In contrast to Chekhov, Gorky had both a harshness and a cynicism.

When the Royal Shakespeare Company presented its masterful production of the play, it was like the discovery of a great novel on stage, welcoming the audience into a landscape of richly observed characters in collision.

Wisely, Ms. Bogart has chosen not to transport the play out of its time. In language and design, her "Summerfolk" is ensconced in its period, although in a starker version than is customary; there is not a samovar or a sofa in sight. Her primary alterations are in style and emotion. Instead of naturalistic drama, she offers something close to farce, and, for counterpoint, she reorders and overlaps some scenes.

•

It is one thing to take the character of Vlass, an amiable, foolish young man, and turn him into an approximation of a Shakespearean clown (Ed Shea is very funny and agile in the role). But it is quite another thing to have so many sight gags and to turn a passing reference into a running joke, as is the case with a sad alcoholic engineer. His remark "Have you seen my wife?" is repeated so often that it assumes Henny Youngman proportions. In pursuit of humor, the director frequently distracts us from the play's essential strains of longing and despair. "Summerfolk" certainly has its comic side, but it is not vaudeville comedy.

The approach is very different from that of Peter Brook in his production of "The Cherry Orchard" (which was performed in Brooklyn in 1988). Mr. Brook stripped Chekhov to essentials, as if he were restoring a valuable wood to its natural finish. Ms. Bogart is a refinisher and refurbisher. Admiration for her effort will necessarily be tempered by the degree of one's enthusiasm for the original play.

For me, the strength of the eccentric production is in the resilience of Gorky, the way he shines through all the stylization, as in the relationship between the foolish Vlass and the older woman he loves (Barbara Orson). In contrast to the pettiness of their friends, they seem to have a genuine connection, touchingly transmitted in the two performances.

There is also the case of Cynthia Strickland's Varvara, who is the closest the group portrait comes to having a central character. She is stifled in her marriage to a boorish lawyer. Ms. Strickland conveys Varvara's confusion without overdoing the anxiety. In addition, Theresa McCarthy has the necessary tremulous quality for her role as the eternally hopeful poet of the group.

•

On the other hand, there is Brian McEleney's flaccid portrait of Shalimov, the "celebrity" writer who has joined the summerfolk for this season. As with many others on stage, he too easily becomes a figure of mockery. The director is so insistent about picturing a widespread ineffectuality that she reduces our empathy.

Visually, the production is expressive. The summer colony sprawls over a broad open stage, an intricate sculptural environment with events occurring on many different levels. To add an additional — but obvious — political dimension, several nonspeaking peasants occupy the set as metaphorical figures.

The entire play is underscored by a musical collage of Debussy and Rachmaninoff, among others, played and sung by talented instrumentalists and singers (Ms. McCarthy has a particularly lilting voice). The purpose, one assumes, is to parallel the emptiness of the lives of the characters with the rhapsodic art of the composers. Arranged and conducted by Jeff Halpern, the music adds luster to the evening.

As Ms. Bogart demonstrated in "No Plays No Poetry," her dramatization of Brecht's nontheatrical writings, she can be both thought-provoking and imaginative at conjuring large-scale canvases. Her "Summerfolk" reaffirms that ability, while raising questions about her interest in allowing a play to speak in its own voice.

1989 O 14, 15:4

A Visit to the Forest

A MIDSUMMER NIGHT'S DREAM, by William Shakespeare; directed by Shepard Sobel; set design, Robert Joel Schwartz; lighting design, Douglas O'Flaherty; costume design, Phillip Contic; sound design, Richard L. Sirois; choreogrpahy, Alice Teirstein; original music, Thom Tilney; stage manager, Judith Sostek; technical director, Richard A. Kendrick. Presented by the Pearl Theater Company, 125 West 22d Street.

Theseus and Oberon	Frank Geraci
Hippolyta and Titania	Robin Leslie Brown
Egeus and Peter Quince	Dugg Smith
Hermia	Donnah Welby
Demetrius Stuart Lerch	
Lysander	Michael John McGuinness
Helena	Joanne Camp
Nick Bottom	James Nugent
Francis Flute and Peaseblossom	Richard Hart
Robin Starveling and Mustardseed	Eric Walstedt
Tom Snout and Moth	John Will
Snug and Cobweb	Andrew W. Sellon
Puck and Philostrate	Laura Rathgeb

By WILBORN HAMPTON

There is, of course, no such thing as a foolproof play, but "A Midsummer Night's Dream" comes about as close as anything written in the last 400 years. Shakespeare's confection of farce and fantasy can survive virtually any conceit or time warp visited on it and provide a measure of mirth in at least one of the three plots.

For its first offering of the season, the Pearl Theater Company has mounted a lively and charming staging that mostly succeeds, in varying degrees, in all three parts of the forest.

It is always a curiosity in any production of "A Midsummer Night's Dream" to discover which of the three separate casts — the lovers, the rustics or the fairies — will emerge as the most winning. When the Public Theater opened its Shakespeare Marathon with the play early last year, F. Murray Abraham's Bottom and his cohorts stole the show. In the new Royal Shakespeare Company staging this summer in Stratford-on-Avon, Richard McCabe's Puck and his band of fairies wove the major enchantment. In the Pearl's version, it is Donnah Welby and Joanne Camp who provide most of the merriment as those alternately wooed and spurned young ladies, Hermia and Helena.

•

Ms. Welby's Hermia can in almost the same breath express her passionate yearnings to Lysander while ordering him "to lie yet further off" when they bed for the night in the woods. She accepts as only her due the ardent proclamations of love from both Demetrius and Lysander, yet when she becomes the woman scorned, she is a feisty hellcat, quite capable of scratching out the eyes of her lifelong friend. It's an assured and funny performance.

No less confident or humorous is Ms. Camp's Helena. More accustomed to the role of rejected lover, she is confounded by her consternation at suddenly being the object of two men's affections. When Helena protests that she does not deserve such ill usage as to have declarations of love heaped on her, Ms. Camp is genuinely outraged.

Under Shepard Sobel's frolicsome direction, the two women grasp, snatch and almost literally fall head over heels in their zeal to hold onto their respective swains. Stuart Lerch as Demetrius and Michael John McGuinness as Lysander provide good foils.

•

Mr. Sobel has not neglected the other two plots, though they are less consistently successful. The rustics' actual performance of Pyramus and Thisbe is a romp, though the rehearsals and malapropisms fall a bit flat. James Nugent's Bottom is best at its most physical. As an ass, Mr. Nugent suffers from a donkey's head that covers his mouth, making him somewhat unintelligible. Of the other good rustics, Andrew W. Sellon's Snug is noteworthy.

Robin Leslie Brown is a lusty Titania, especially as she makes love to Bottom's donkey, and Laura Rathgeb is a sprightly Puck, bounding up and down ladders and tumbling around the stage, full of mischievous glee. Frank Geraci's Oberon is rather stern.

Philip Contic's costumes are opulent, full of satin and ribbons, and Alice Teirstein has choreographed a lot of movement on a small stage while managing to keep the actors from colliding with one another. Thom Tilney has composed some pleasant original lullabies.

1989 O 15, 67:1

Prostitute as Heroine

NELSON 2 RODRIGUES, two plays by Nelson Rodrigues; directed by Antunes Filho; assistants to the director, Beatriz Cordoba and Rita Martins; scenery and costumes by J. C. Serroni; corporal training, Miss Martins; sound track by Mr. Filho and Mario Gregio; Senhorinha's costume by José Nunes; lighting by Robert Weber Federico; waltzes and tangos by Carmen Baker-Clark; narrator's voice, Francisco Rivela; additional wardrobe by Maria Ferreira Contesa, Boamerses Rubio and Zunilda Brites. Presented by Repertorio Español, Gilberto Zaldivar, producer; René Buch, artistic director. At Gramercy Arts Theater, 138 East 27th Street.

WITH: Maria José Alvarez, Ana Paula Aquino, Ricardo Barber, George Bass, Birgit Bofarull, José Luis Ferrer, Dody Fogel, Betsy Kenyon, Katerina Llado, Alfonso Manosalvas, Antonio Melián, Luis Alberto Nuñez, José Cheo Oliveras, Virginia Rambal, René Sánchez, Diego Taborda, Marta Vidal and Juan Villarreal.

By D. J. R. BRUCKNER

If there ever was a playwright who could find evil in a bright field of wild flowers or corruption in a baby's breath, it was that scourge of Brazil, Nelson Rodrigues. There could hardly be a better introduction to his work than the two plays — "Family Album" and "All Nudity Will Be Punished" — that the Brazilian director Antunes Filho has combined under the title "Nelson 2 Rodrigues."

The program was a sensation when Mr. Filho and his Brazilian troupe took it on tour in Europe seven years ago. Now the Repertorio Español has brought the director here to re-create it for the company.

This is, every minute, intense and triumphant theater; it sends one away with a chill running up the back of the neck and unsure of the reality of anything outside the magic enclosure of the stage. This version is in Spanish (along with a few final phrases of the original Portuguese), and someone without the language will miss the scalding jokes and insults that were Rodrigues's vocabulary. But the theater supplies excellent plot summaries, and Mr. Filho uses movement, light and music brilliantly to convey the passion, perversion and menace in the plays. There is a great deal more than words here to fill the imagination of an audience.

•

"Family Album," which was banned in Brazil for 22 years after it was written in 1945, uses the contrast between the serenity of seven posed portraits of a wealthy provincial family and the reality of its mem-

bers' lives to expose the greed, lust, hatred and thirst for vengeance that consume these powerful people. Rodrigues's slashing and often very funny ridicule of prevailing social pieties keeps one laughing, if somewhat nervously, amid increasingly horrifying revelations of treachery, incest and murder.

In "All Nudity Will Be Punished" (1965) the humor is more scathing and unrelenting and the vision even darker. The brother of a rich widower in Rio de Janeiro maneuvers his sibling into marrying a prostitute, scandalizing his son, his friends, his aunts, the church, everyone. In this tale of deception, rape, homosexuality and suicide, only the prostitute is a heroine, and a most memorable one. The unnerving balance of hilarity and horror is sustained to the end.

The program says Mr. Filho has "adapted" these plays. His principal adapting tool is a pair of scissors, which he has used wisely, making a stunning production that is also something of an homage to Rodrigues (it is rather moving to hear the recorded voice of the writer, who died in 1981, protesting briefly before each play that he really was romantic and deeply sentimental).

On an elegant set of Art Nouveau glass panels created by J. C. Serroni, Mr. Filho creates gorgeous scenes — wedding marches down a long staircase, waltzes and tangos sweeping across the stage, wakes and funeral processions — which serve as sumptuous backgrounds to the sordid couplings, deaths and empty triumphs of

the characters. And he uses recordings of love songs, dance music, Bach chorales and baroque masses to set off their mockery, rage and cries of agony. He keeps the plays moving elegantly, but very fast. And given the subject matter, he is almost a model of restraint; except for one scene in which four women appear bare-breasted, there is little in this profoundly sensuous performance that could not be presented in a church.

Through the years the members of the Repertorio Español have demonstrated admirable versatility in plays from old classics to contemporary comedies. They can do pretty much what they want to — and they are up to the challenges posed by this visionary director. They deserve the roar of approval that greets them at the end of each of these plays.

1989 O 15, 65:1

One Kooky Family

THE GLASS MENAGERIE, by Tennessee Williams; directed by Tazewell Thompson; setting by Loy Arcenas; costumes by Marjorie Slaiman; lighting by Nancy Schertler; sound by Susan R. White; technical director, David M. Glenn; stage manager, Maxine Krasowski Bertone; assistant stage manager, Tara Galvin. Presented by Arena Stage, Zelda Fichandler, producing director; Douglas C. Wager, associate producing director; Guy Bergquist, associate producer. At the Kreeger Theater, Washington.

Amanda Wingfield	Ruby Dee
Tom Wingfield	Jonathan Earl Peck
Laura Wingfield	Tonia Rowe
Jim Connors	Ken LaRon

By LAURIE WINER

Special to The New York Times

WASHINGTON, Oct. 12 — Imagine a television sitcom writer adapting a Tennessee Williams play for a network executive: "We've got this mother, named Amanda, she's a terrible nag; she drives her children crazy. The son, Tom, he's a stand-in for a henpecked husband; he's constantly rolling his eyes because Amanda won't get off his back. We'll get endless mileage out of that routine. The daughter, Laura — and here's what makes our idea so special — is a serious, shy girl with a gimpy leg, a glass collection and a hilarious tendency to faint when her bossy Ma and browbeaten brother insist on bringing home a gentleman caller!"

That is pretty much the level of sensitivity that Tazewell Thompson brings to his production of "The Glass Menagerie," which opened tonight at the Arena Stage. His all-black cast features Ruby Dee as Amanda Wingfield, whose fortunes are traditionally thought to limn the collapse of the old white south. Forget the improbability that a black woman in the 1930's would recall long-ago beaux who were prominent young planters on the Mississippi Delta and who went on to become vice presidents of banks. The main problem with this production is not race-related. No, this "Menagerie" tramples on the internal poetry of the characters, on the very heart of the play itself.

•

As Tom Jonathan, Earl Peck veers between excessive reverence for the text, when his character steps back to

narrate the action, and broad comedy of an unusually inappropriate nature. When Tom brings home the Gentleman Caller, for example, Mr. Peck takes a full minute to gape with open-mouthed incredulity at the furniture, which Amanda has reupholstered for the occasion. Similarly, when Tom rails at his mother for invading his privacy, Mr. Peck covers his forehead with his hand, stamps his foot, jumps on a chair and shouts. Ms. Dee, who can also be seen as the sage Mother Sister in Spike Lee's film "Do the Right Thing", answers his most vicious attack ("You ugly, babbling, old witch") with what looks and sounds like an asthma attack. This is one kooky family.

As Laura, Tonia Rowe has almost no chance of establishing poignancy. Indeed, the play gets laughs in places one could never have imagined. When Amanda brings out "gay deceivers" to pad Laura's bra, she flaunts them as if she were playing a Benny Hill routine. And when the Gentleman Caller arrives, Laura hides behind the front door as he enters and then dexterously scoots out before he sees her (so much for that gimpy leg). That the audience continually laughs with these hijinks and not at them makes the entire cast complicit in this travesty against Williams.

Loy Arcenas has designed an evocative set that could have been effective if any real people had inhabited it. Under Nancy Schertler's lighting, its thickly plastered, copper-colored walls seem to disintegrate at the play's end into a ghostly, decaying ruin. By that point in the evening, however, it's like asking the audience to find pathos in the household of "Three's Company."

1989 O 16, C19:1

Parallel Lives

BESIDE HERSELF, by Joe Pintauro; directed by John Bishop; sets by John Lee Beatty; costumes by Ann Emonts; lights by Dennis Parichy; sound by Chuck London and Stewart Werner; music by Jonathan Brielle; hair design by Bobby H. Grayson; production stage manager, Denise Yaney; production supervisor, Mark Ramont. Presented by Circle Repertory Company, Tanya Berezin, artistic director, Connie L. Alexis, managing director. At 99 Seventh Avenue South, at Fourth Street.

Mary	Lois Smith
Harry	Edward Seamon
Alexandra	Melissa Joan Hart
Skidie	Calista Flockhart
Violet	Susan Bruce
Angie-Jake	William Hurt
Bear	Edward Seamon

By FRANK RICH

The image that lingers from Joe Pintauro's new play, "Beside Herself," is that of four women in white negligees, each representing the same heroine at a different age, as they comb out their hair and prepare for sleep. The setting is a cozy house in the woods on an isolated island; the light is the dim glow of a harvest moon. While there is nothing prurient about the scene, its appeal recalls the calendar art that was yesteryear's soft-core pornography. The idealized women are golden icons intended to be worshiped from a distance by an audience of men.

Gerry Goodstein

Virginia Rambal and Ricardo Barber in a scene from "All Nudity Will Be Punished."

Gerry Goodstein

Lois Smith and William Hurt in Joe Pintauro's "Beside Herself."

It's a tableau that can stand for the entire evening. While Mr. Pintauro is a serious writer with a sincere mission, his play apotheosizes women from afar while pretending to understand them from within. "Beside Herself" is a character study that says more about its author than the woman at center stage. Not even the four excellent actresses in the Circle Repertory Company's production can rescue Mary, Mr. Pintauro's middle-aged poet of the woods, from the fog of sentimental male abstraction.

•

A soupy fog it is. As befits a play set near a peat bog and inhabited by the ghosts of Mary's past selves, waves of dry-ice smoke roll persistently through the scenery. A more lethal kind of fog permeates Mr. Pintauro's dialogue as he calls attention to the "smoky river" of mist or the "miraculous illumination" of the moon or the many symbolic animals that are mowed down by passing cars on the highway beyond Mary's cabin.

When the playwright turns to specifics, he reveals how hollow the metaphors and fabulist flourishes are. The crisis faced by the lonely present-day Mary (Lois Smith) has to do with a long-ago misbegotten marriage. Betrayed by the man she loved, she had instead married his lackluster brother. Now both men are dead, and the barren Mary, unfulfilled as a writer, schoolteacher, mother and wife, must decide whether life is worth living. Enter Augie-Jake (William Hurt), a U.P.S. deliveryman much her junior. Mary thinks the gentleman caller is a double for the man she really loved. Augie-Jake, whose own troubled history is littered with betrayals, is looking for the mother he never really had. Anyone need a road map?

•

Perhaps if Mr. Pintauro brought on the brothers in Mary's past, her soap-opera travails and their resolution might seem more compelling and less schematic. As it stands, the heroine's story seems yanked off the ready-to-wear rack from the dramaturgical store of middle Williams and early Inge. The omnipresent trio of younger Marys — pre-teen (Melissa Joan Hart), post-teen (Calista Flock-hart) and pre-middle-age (Susan Bruce) — is exploited mainly for time-travel jokes (some amusing), expository convenience and open-and-shut debates about past and present motives. Though Mary's corporeal presence is quadrupled, the audience's knowledge of her interior life is not. She remains a blurry masculine fantasy of womanhood, a playwright's conceit without psychological substance.

No blame can be placed on John Bishop's deft, well-cast staging, which uses a leaf-strewn John Lee Beatty set and velvety Dennis Parichy lighting to transport the audience into the dreamy woods of a contemporary fairy tale (complete with Grimm bear played by the unlucky Edward Seamon). Ms. Smith is her usual honest, peppery self in a role that is at best a holding action for the Ma Joad she plays in the Steppenwolf "Grapes of Wrath" expected on Broadway next spring. Among the younger alter egos, Ms. Flockhart, in her New York debut, shows unusual promise. She brings consistent emotional clarity to messy post-pubescent effusions, not the least of which is the line "No wonder this place is such a slushy dung heap of a horror!"

•

Mr. Hurt, after an absence of seven years, has chosen to return to the Circle Rep in an assignment far less demanding than even the minor roles of his apprenticeship. With his gruff monosyllables and burly demeanor, he meets the modest requirements of the small-town U.P.S. man perfectly: William Bendix impersonations don't get much better than this.

1989 O 18, C15:1

Delving Into Russian Theater in Louisville

By MEL GUSSOW

Special to The New York Times

LOUISVILLE, Oct. 15 — Several hundred stage directors, teachers and scholars specializing in Russian studies, including visitors from the Soviet Union, took part this weekend in a marathon of plays, lectures and panels at the Actors Theater of Louisville. The events were a climax to a citywide "Classics in Context" celebration of the arts in Russia, initiated by Jon Jory, artistic director of the Louisville theater.

The participants reflected on the "Moscow Art Theater: Past, Present and Future," with specific reference to the tantalizing kinship and rivalry between Anton Chekhov and Konstantin Stanislavsky, which began with "The Seagull."

Two years after its devastating failure in St. Petersburg, "The Seagull" opened at the Moscow Art Theater in a triumphant new production directed by Stanislavsky. That night, Dec. 17, 1898, was to alter the course of theatrical history, establishing the careers of both the playwright and the director and certifying the company's role as one of the most influential theaters of its time.

•

As speakers in Louisville suggested, the combined success was also the catalyst in raising controversies that have continued to exist for more than 90 years. Crucial to the artistic relationship is the question of whether Chekhov was a great playwright because of Stanislavsky or despite him.

There is the related issue of whether Chekhov's plays are comedies or dramas.

The original failure of "The Seagull" was partly attributable to the fact that it was performed on a gala benefit night between two light entertainments. The audience came to laugh — and did. When Stanislavsky undertook the play, starring himself as Trigorin and Chekhov's future wife, Olga Knipper, as Arkadina, he staged it as serious drama. He approached Chekhov's subsequent masterworks in a similar vein, an approach that was too serious for some, apparently, including Chekhov. After seeing "The Seagull," Chekhov wrote Maxim Gorky that the play was "performed horribly." But speakers in Louisville made it clear that Chekhov could be self-contradictory. In letters to friends, he expressed both admiration and criticism about Stanislavsky's direction.

•

Dr. Laurence Senelick, an American educator and author, took a revisionist approach to Stanislavsky by linking this theatrical revolutionary with the Victorians. He quoted the director's acknowledged fondness for "cheap effects" and enumerated the times he had tried to introduce horses and trains into Chekhovian productions. It was Chekhov who strove for simplicity.

Directors since Stanislavsky have taken persuasive positions on one side or the other. The same thing could be said about Gorky, as demonstrated by Anne Bogart's radical reinterpretation of "Summerfolk," now at the Trinity Repertory Company in Providence.

Hearing all the vigorous discussion, which took place in the theater's lobby and bar as well as on stage, a visitor looked forward to the Actors Theater productions of "The Seagull" and Gorky's "Children of the Sun." Both, however, added to the irresolution.

David Talbott

Beth Dixon and John Pielmeier in Anton Chekhov's "Seagull," in the "Classics in Context" celebration at the Actors Theater of Louisville.

Gloria Muzio's production of this difficult Gorky play was poorly acted (with the definite exception of Randy Danson) and floundered between the extremes of farce and melodrama. Mr. Jory's production of "The Seagull," though more stable in terms of style and acting (especially in John Pielmeier's portrait of Trigorin), occasionally went too far in the direction of comedy. Before the performance, Mr. Jory announced his self-consciousness at facing an audience of people who had already directed their own versions of the play.

•

One must add that no production could possibly equal the expectations aroused by consideration of earlier seminal productions, seen in photographs in an exhibition prepared by the Stanislavsky Museum in Moscow. Some of that first-hand feeling was evoked by a screening of Pudovkin's 1928 silent film version of Gorky's novel "The Mother." Shown on a small screen placed on the set for "Children of the Sun," the film had an astonishing clarity. With its attention to detail, its panoramic imagery and virtuosic command of cinematic techniques, "The Mother" acted as an introduction to the kind of art created at the Moscow Art Theater.

A half-hearted personalized view of Chekhov came in Karen Sunde's brief monodrama, "Anton, Himself," in which William McNulty unconvincingly played the author in his study at Yalta, alternately writing a story and talking about events at home. With all of Chekhov's life and letters to draw from, this play must be accounted as a missed opportunity.

•

A historical perspective was offered by Norris Houghton, who announced that he was probably the only person at the conference who had known the director and had watched him work, later recounted in his book, "Moscow Rehearsals." Describing the view from 1934, Mr. Houghton said it was the director's credo that artists should learn to serve their art and not the reverse.

Speaking from his position as one of the founders of the Group Theater and the Actors Studio, Robert Lewis talked about the uses and abuses of the Stanislavsky system of acting, reinterpreted in America as the Method. In reference to the use of one's own private emotions in performance, Mr. Lewis drew laughter by saying, "If crying were acting, my Aunt Rivka would be Duse." He added that the true Stanislavskian should not ask himself what he would do if he were in that dramatic situation, but what he would do if he were that character in that period in that play.

In his lecture on the "Visionary Sons of Stanislavsky," Dr. Paul Schmidt said that Chekhov was "the first playwright to write a play whose dramatic effect depended crucially and continually on more than just the words spoken by the actors." He added that it was Vsevolod Meyerhold, not Stanislavsky, who "first recorded the newness of the notion," and developed it in his theory of physical action, in which performers interacted with properties and scenery.

•

The contribution of Meyerhold as director and others who followed was detailed in an exhibition of Russian Constructivist theater design at the J. B. Speed Museum. The Russian alliance with American theater reached all the way back to productions of early plays of Eugene O'Neill (represented by vivid scenic sketches) and forward to experiments that could be linked to contemporary performance art.

In a lively panel, three members of the current Moscow Art Theater traced the evolution of the company. Oleg Yefremov, the theater's director for the last 20 years, said that the "artistic theater" in Russia had always played the role of "truth-teller, particularly during the period of restriction of public opinion." He added that theater in the Soviet Union now faced the problem of "the absence of prohibition," and wondered if writers might find it difficult to be provocative in a nonrepressive environment.

Any questions one might have about the current state of Soviet theater were answered by the production of "Cinzano," a raw and amusing slice of contemporary Soviet life, written by Lyudmila Petrushevskaya and acted by three talented young Russians.

When this Moscow Art studio theater production was first presented at Stony Brook, L.I., in June, it seemed well acted but unenlightening. At Louisville, it appeared to undergo a transformation. On an intimate stage and with heightened theatrical energy, "Cinzano" proved to be an engrossing look at the economic, social and sexual problems of Russian youth. Watching it, one could detect Stanislavskian psychological elements, as well as Meyerholdian principles of physical action. In common with so much else on this valuable weekend, "Cinzano" benefited from being experienced in context.

1989 O 19, C19:3

The Best Defense Is Being Offensive

THE HOUSE OF HORROR, written, directed and performed by Paul Zaloom. House design, Joseph John and Mr. Zaloom; lighting design, Lori A. Dawson; house and furnishing built by Mr. John; projection design, Jan Hartley; slide photography, Paul Sharratt; puppet heads sculptured by Mr. Zaloom. Presented by the Vineyard Theater, 108 East 15th Street.

By STEPHEN HOLDEN

Almost as soon as the Smiths, a family of six from the Bronx, have been shown a cozy new suburban home in Garden City, L.I., their allergies begin to act up. First they begin to sneeze. Soon their quarrelsome twin sons have developed itchy rashes, and before long Grandma is suffering from schizophrenic seizures. Ultimately, the family cannot survive the trial live-in period they have been given by the real-estate agent, for the chemicals in the rugs, furniture and air freshener have turned the place into a death trap.

In "The House of Horror," the opening piece of Paul Zaloom's new show of satirical fun at the Vineyard Theater, the Smiths are porcine-faced hand puppets sneezing and scratching on a set that resembles a cross section of a large doll house. Mr. Zaloom, the clown and puppeteer who manipulates and speaks for them, is a longtime member of the Bread and Puppet Theater. For years, he has satirized our consumer culture using trash and found materials and in the process turning himself into a performance-art relative of the Toxic Avenger.

The dream home in which "The House of Horror" unfolds is also essentially trash. It was made, its developer boasts to the Smiths, out of "4,000 man-made petrochemical substances." Its amenities include a doorbell programmed to rotate 6,780 tunes, "hyperplaid" covered furniture chemically treated so that anything that spills literally bounces onto the floor, and mushroom-shaped deodorizers in every room.

Mr. Zaloom's style of puppetry is blunt and indelicate in the street-theater mode of the Bread and Puppet Theater. His creations look and talk like cartoons. Manipulating them, he is much less interested in showing off his technical skills than in sustaining a raucous Punch-and-Judy atmosphere as he gleefully twits us with unpleasant truths. He reminds us that our chemically dependent lives are permeated with hazards that we would prefer to think are outside the house but that are really everywhere. Even our homes — our chemically fortified little havens of security — can do us in if we're not careful.

In "Yikes!," the evening's other extended piece, Mr. Zaloom manipulates found objects to create cheerfully nihilistic essays on peace, justice, nature and religion. Mr. Zaloom has a wonderful knack for making

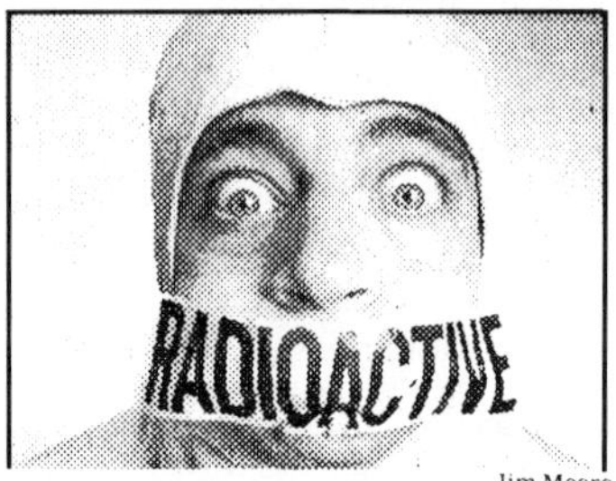

Jim Moore

Paul Zaloom

junky objects into irreverent metaphors for powerful people. The military brass at an international peace conference are represented by trophies stiffly mounted on pedestals. President and Mrs. Bush become two miniature fir trees, the smaller one sprayed white.

In the essay on justice, the bribed jurors in a corrupt drug-trafficking case are symbolized by a dozen eggs of varying colors. Over the course of the trial the brown ones are replaced until all 12 are white. The religion essay portrays a contentious global ecumenical conference whose host is a plastic Santa Claus.

"The House of Horror" and "Yikes!" are connected by an appalling but funny demonstration, "Safety Begins Here," which interweaves slides of actual items in a catalogue of nuclear-waste-disposal equipment with recipes from an imaginary nuclear cookbook called "Einstein's Edibles."

"The House of Horror" doesn't pretend to play fair with the issues it raises. It is rude, agitprop street-style theater that grinds our noses into the mountains of our own trash.

1989 O 19, C26:1

Hot Time

MILL FIRE, by Sally Nemeth; directed by David Petrarca; set design, Linda Buchanan; costume design, Laura Cunningham; lighting design, Robert Christen; sound design, Rob Milburn; production stage manager, Nancy Harrington. Presented by the Women's Project and Productions, Julia Miles, artistic director. At the Apple Corps Theater, 336 West 20th Street.

Widows
Martha Lavey, Mary Ann Thebus and Jacqueline Williams

Marlene .... Kelly Coffield
Champ .... James Krag
Sunny .... Kate Buddeke
Bo .... B. J. Jones
Jemison .... Paul Mabon
Minister/OSHA Investigator Timothy Grimm

By LAURIE WINER

Three widows stare ominously from behind black tulle veils while the audience files in to Sally Nemeth's play "Mill Fire" at the Apple Corps Theater. "Mill Fire" is, thankfully, not as grim as the visages of those three women: its young heroine, Marlene, another widow, refuses to grieve in the conventional, quiet mode thought proper in Birmingham, Ala., in 1978. But in Ms. Nemeth's image-laden, often heavy-handed language, the play is as relentlessly portentous as that opening image promises it will be.

Marlene's husband, Champ, works nights at the local steel mill. On the eve of the mill fire that will claim his life, Marlene tries repeatedly to keep her husband home. She pleads with him to call in sick or to claim car trouble; anything to get him to stay in their cozy connubial bed.

If Marlene has had a premonition, she doesn't say; she seems concerned solely with quenching her own desire. But in "Mill Fire," which weaves backward and forward in time, that fateful preamble echoes with a grinding regularity throughout the play.

•

Serving both as a Greek chorus and as the extended voice of Marlene and other women in the community, the three widows periodically declaim in homespun poetry that should be incantatory but that remains stubbornly pedestrian and self-conscious. Ms. Nemeth uses atmospheric descriptions as metaphors for her heroine's state of mind; when Champ leaves for work, for instance, and Marlene's sexual desire begins to wane, the women will say something like, "It's the rain, makes it cooler, darker." Or, later, when Marlene first gets a handle on her overwhelming grief, the women will report, "It cleared that mornin', cleared, and the sun came out hot and bright." After a while, these women become as dependable (and as interesting) as the evening weather report.

Still, "Mill Fire," which had its premiere this year at the Goodman Theater in Chicago, conveys with some sensitivity the shifting tone of its heroine's grief. Kelly Coffield makes Marlene admirable and fiery even as she travels from hysteria to unforgiving anger to a tentative re-embracing of emotion and life.

Too often, though, Ms. Nemeth shortchanges her heroine by drawing her spirited nature in generic terms. Marlene's passion for Champ, for instance, never transcends newlywed sex play of the nudge, nudge, wink, wink variety. "You know how I get when it rains," she tells Champ, in one of their milder exchanges.

•

Some suspense is built into a subplot concerning Marlene's brother Bo, the mill foreman, who was taking medication for pain on the night of the fire. Could he have employed bad judgment by sending Champ to work on a possibly malfunctioning fur-

…ace? Ms. Nemeth leaves hanging the question of Bo's culpability. But this subplot takes on a touching and unexpected turn when it provides the impetus for a reconciliation between Bo and his neglected, bourbon-loving wife, Sunny.

Under David Petrarca's direction, the production achieves moments of power only when the writing is at its most simple, as when Marlene takes the dreaded middle-of-the-night phone call on the morning of the accident. Its final image, which involves the spreading of Champ's ashes on the marital bed, is too reminiscent of a similar moment in Sam Shepard's 1985 production of "A Lie of the Mind." Like most of "Mill Fire," the moment strives for an originality it never quite attains.

1989 O 19, C22:3

Springtime for Black Shirts

DANGEROUS GAMES, conceived, written, directed and choreographed by Graciela Daniele; music by Astor Piazzolla; lyrics by William Finn; book by Jim Lewis and Ms. Daniele; scenic design, Tony Straiges; costume design, Patricia Zipprodt; lighting design, Peggy Eisenhauer; sound design, Otts Munderloh; musical direction and arrangements, James Kowal; musical consultant and arrangements, Rodolfo Alchourron; fight direction, B. H. Barry and Luis Perez; production stage manager, Robert Mark Kalfin; music coordinator, John Monaco; co-choreographed by Tina Paul. Presented by Jules Fisher, James M. Nederlander and Arthur Rubin, in association with Mary Kantor. Nederlander Theater, 208 West 41st Street.

WITH: Richard Amaro, Ken Ard, René Ceballos, Adrienne Hurd-Sharlein, Philip Jerry, Diana Laurenson, John Mineo, Gregory Mitchell, Dana Moore, Elizabeth Mazer, Tina Paul, Luis Perez, Malinda Shaffer, Marc Villa and Danyelle Weaver.

Musicians: Rodolfo Alchourron, Jorge Alfano, Miguel Arrabal, Adrian Brito, Jon Kass and James Kowal

By FRANK RICH

If theater people want to make a spectacle of themselves on a Broadway stage, that is their inalienable right, but whatever happened to the poor audience's right to enjoy a few laughs in the face of such disaster? "Dangerous Games," a new musical misfire at the Nederlander, extinguishes all opportunities for fun by shrouding its inanities in stern sermonettes on sexual politics, dour images from Greek mythology and real-life South American state terrorism. Mel Brooks notwithstanding, it's hard to have a hoot when the advancing chorus line consists of goose-stepping Black Shirts.

The production was conceived, co-written, directed and choreographed

The musical was conceived and directed by Graciela Daniele.

by Graciela Daniele, an artisan of show-biz perkiness who has folded simulated Bob Fosse struts into entertainments like "Drood" and "The Pirates of Penzance." Since Jerome Robbins, there have been no Broad-

way choreographers, Fosse included, with the imagination and varied dance vocabulary necessary to sustain a full theatrical evening of dancing. Ms. Daniele would seem an unlikely candidate even to make the attempt — her previous musicals have been neither dominated nor distinguished by their choreography. And yet, presumably inspired by serious dance-theater experimenters like Pina Bausch and Martha Clarke, she has slammed together two hours of mediocre Broadway routines padded by repetition and crushed by pretense.

•

With its fetching Astor Piazzolla tango music and "Evita"-like political posturing, "Dangerous Games" should in all candor be titled "Don't Cry for Me, Tango Argentino." Act I, called "Tango" and seen in more atmospheric form Off Broadway two years ago under the title "Tango Apasionado," is a meditation on masculine sexual brutality; it looks like a bus-and-truck tour of Fosse's "Chicago" and is acted in New Yorkese redolent of his "Sweet Charity." Even so, the setting purports to be an Argentine brothel of the 1930's where a tango involving two brothers and the newest virgin on the block (unaccountably played by the oldest-looking dancer on stage) spirals violently out of hand.

Ms. Daniele's game, more insidious than dangerous, is to give theatergoers a little erotic titillation and then hector them for surrendering to such base instincts. She and her co-author, Jim Lewis, are reminiscent of those public censors who used to insist on viewing every last X-rated movie before imposing a ban. But even if "Tango" weren't a hypocritical exploitation of the machismo it purports to condemn, it would still fail as both sex show and morality play. The tango theatrics are so prim that even the bordello in "Les Misérables" offers rougher trade. The resolution of the heroine's nightmare is so perfunctorily attained that "Tango" could be a public-service skit about date rape.

Martha Swope

Gregory Mitchell, left, and René Ceballos

Act II of "Dangerous Games," titled "Orfeo," is a retelling of the Orpheus myth dedicated to "all the desaparecidos" — the victims who disappeared during the reign of Argentina's junta in the late 1970's. The horrors of a police state are reduced to the symbolic figure of a mediocre rock singer (Ken Ard) brandishing a whip; the gatekeepers of the fascist hell tell the incarcerated to "have a nice day." Here, too, there is a happy ending to sanitize the unspeakably cruel acts ostensibly under examination: a precocious child actor raises her arms to greet the dawn of a new and brighter day. Along the way to that finale, there are interludes of tepid folk dancing, more gringo than

gaucho in style, and a wobbly lovers' pas de deux that might look corny in a June Allyson-Dick Powell musical.

As Ms. Daniele exposes the limits of her own talent by stretching it over too much time and space, so she exposes those of her cast. The company is composed largely of competent Broadway chorus performers, John Mineo and René Ceballos prominent among them, whose dancing, singing and acting cannot withstand the ruthless scrutiny of a center-stage spotlight.

Nor are the offstage collaborators at their best. The set designer Tony Straiges has put the red back into red-light district for "Tango" and given "Orfeo" an underworld that looks more like a bargain basement. Mr. Piazzolla's score, attractively played by James Kowal's band, cannot escape its sameness. When occasional lyrics are called for, and sometimes when they're not, they have been written in a ham-fisted pseudo-Brecht manner by the gifted William Finn, author of "March of the Falsettos." The humor of a late-evening song about "the joys of torture" seems especially lost on the audience at "Dangerous Games."

1989 O 20, C3:3

The Law of the Street

A BRONX TALE, written and performed by Chazz Palminteri; directed by Mark W. Travis; set designer, James Noone; lighting designer, Jeffrey Schissler; original music by Glenn Mehrbach; executive producer, Arthur Cantor. Presented by Peter Gatien and Dan Lauria. At Playhouse 91, 316 East 91st Street.

By STEPHEN HOLDEN

Chazz Palminteri's one-man play "A Bronx Tale" is the theatrical equivalent of sprawling streetwise rock songs like Bruce Springsteen's "Jungleland" and Billy Joel's "Scenes From an Italian Restaurant." Performing on a set that impressionistically re-creates the corner of 187th Street and Belmont Avenue in 1960, the New York-born actor and writer spins a vivid true story of his own childhood and adolescence when he was taken under the wing of a neighborhood gangster named Little Johnny.

Interspersed with musical snippets by Dion and the Belmonts (the legendary Bronx-based harmony group) and some portentous keyboard filler, the 90-minute monologue is really an extended rock-and-roll ballad in words. Street characters with colorful nicknames like Eddie Mush, Frankie Coffee Cake and Gigi the Whale pop in and out of this sentimental morality tale that pits the law-abiding values of the narrator's bus-driver father against Little Johnny's amoral street code.

•

The drama, at the 91st Street Playhouse, begins when the narrator, age 9, witnesses a shooting involving the gangster and afterward lies to the police about what he saw. Much to the chagrin of the boy's father, Little Johnny, a bachelor, becomes the child's mentor, introducing him to a life of crap games and easy money. "The working man is a sucker," says Little Johnny, explaining his philosophy.

The story reaches a melodramatic crescendo in 1968 when racial ten-

Chazz Palminteri

sions in the neighborhood and strains within Little Johnny's criminal world all erupt on a single night. The climax involves the narrator's first crush on a girl, his borrowing of Little Johnny's bright red Cadillac, and the violent denouement eight years later of the incident he witnessed as a boy.

•

"A Bronx Tale" is a good yarn, the basic credibility of which lies in its author's knack for recalling details like the absurd, complicated tests of character and loyalty to which the boys in the neighborhood subjected their unsuspecting girlfriends. And in describing a social microcosm of urban blue-collar Sicilian-American life, the play makes it perfectly clear how the law of the street in a tightly bound community can be more compelling than the law of the land.

Mr. Palminteri and the director, Mark W. Travis, have wisely decided not to embellish the piece with arty frills beyond a judicious use of musical fragments to deepen a mood that is essentially nostalgic. Although Mr. Palminteri is not a rivetingly kinetic actor, he puts enough body language into his performance to give the evening an easy physical fluidity. And where the piece contains ample material that other actors might turn into splashy ethnic caricature, Mr. Palminteri tells his story plainly. His understatement enhances the believability of a tale that seems a perfect vehicle for the movies.

1989 O 22, 63:5

Defection, But Where?

THE AMBASSADOR, by Slawomir Mrozek; translated by Ralph Manheim and Mr. Mrozek; directed by Mac Ewing; lighting design, Terry Wuthrich; set design, George Allison; costume design, Deborah Rooney; sound design, Ben Adam; production stage manager, Anne Marie Hobson. Presented by the

Vietnam Veterans Ensemble Theater Company, Thomas Bird, artistic director. At the South Street Theater, 424 West 42d Street.

The Ambassador	David Adamson
Othello	Anthony Chisholm
Amelia	Sharon Ernster
The Deputy	James Gleason
The Man	Michael Manetta

By MEL GUSSOW

In his plays, Slawomir Mrozek mixes art and polemics. Sometimes, as in "Tango" and "Emigrés," his sense of theater is as strong as his political awareness. This is not the case with "The Ambassador," receiving its United States premiere at the Vietnam Veterans Ensemble Theater Company. With politics taking precedence, the narrative becomes a thin thread on which to hang the author's inquiry into the nature of dissidence and diplomacy during a time of subversion.

The beginning of the play is intriguing. The Ambassador of a country very much like the United States is stationed in an unidentified totalitarian nation. Through the windows of George Allison's compact set, one can see the barbed wire surrounding the embassy, and soon we can hear the rabble outside.

●

The Ambassador (David Adamson) is discovered on the floor, where he appears to be searching frantically for a hidden microphone. Gradually, it is revealed that the Ambassador is not trying to debug his lair, but is simply looking for a lost cufflink. An observant theatergoer would have noticed the clue — his flapping French cuff.

The joke is a good one, and who is to say whether the cufflink itself is not bugged. In this country, nothing is secret. The audience's interest continues with the appearance of the host nation's Deputy Prime Minister, who is as guileful as the Ambassador is ingenuous; he seems to know the Ambassador's moves before they're made.

The comedy gradually lessens, almost depleting itself by intermission, although the second act is momentarily stirred by the announcement to the Ambassador that his Government has "ceased to exist." It is one thing to be an ambassador without portfolio, quite another to be an ambassador without a country. Questions remain as to who will defect where.

●

Eventually the play becomes didactic. The work never has the wit of Mr. Mrozek's earlier efforts — or the fierceness of Fernando Arrabal's political parables. More agile actors would have helped, but only James Gleason, as the deputy minister, and Anthony Chisholm, as the Ambassador's aide, come close to having the necessary lightness of touch. Under the direction of Mac Ewing, the play and performances are less than synergistic.

For the Veterans Ensemble (known as Vetco), "The Ambassador" is a step toward diversification. In its previous nine years, this company has specialized in plays relating to the Vietnam War. The choice of Mr. Mrozek helps to expand Vetco's political perspective, which is to be admired even as the play disappoints.

1989 O 22, 63:1

A Family Reunion

GOD'S POLICEMEN, by Richard Lay; directed and designed by Judy Strawn. Presented by the Sage Theater Company. St. John's Episcopal Church, 224 Waverly Place.

Billy	Derek Conte
Cornelius	Dennis Dooley
Miss June	Bonnie Haagenbuch
Miss July	Angie Kristic
Chip	Donald Lowe
Betty	Helene Abrams
Ma	Lynn Guberman
Miss August	Victoria Taylor
Manicurist	Louise Elm

By D. J. R. BRUCKNER

At one point in "God's Policemen," two serial killers force a captive salesman to mimic Elvis Presley performing the song "Don't Be Cruel." By then, the song is a plea that might well be taken up by the audience and addressed to the playwright, Richard Lay.

This strange piece — being presented by the Sage Theater Company at St. John's Episcopal Church in Greenwich Village — is described by its author as a sinister comedy. But last Sunday it was neither sinister nor comic. The serial killers, played by Derek Conte and Dennis Dooley, are lunatic brothers whose mother (Lynn Guberman), having committed suicide, appears alive in flashbacks and as a ghost in the present. Her daughter, Betty (Helene Abrams), is even crazier than the brothers, but less homicidal.

The murderous brothers have fantasy love affairs with two skin-magazine pinups played by Bonnie Haagenbuch and Angie Kristic, and, of course, the women eventually fall into their clutches. There is nothing sinister about that. These two would like to make their clutches evil, but they are only clumsy.

No one is killed, or even kicked around, in this play, which desperately tries to achieve comic effects. Mr. Lay throws almost every available clichéd situation and device into it — aerobic exercises, a costume party, a beauty-parlor scene, eating frenzies, sex in a closet, barbaric imitations of Latin American dances, awful sight gags and a few dozen terrible and tasteless sexual and scatological jokes.

None of it works. In fact, the only really funny moment is a ghostly speech by the mother about war, hunger and what it is like to be dead. Evidently some heavy irony was intended, but it did not come out that way and one could see a smile flickering about among the audience as all this bombast echoed from the stage.

1989 O 22, 64:4

Hero's Own Story

ALL GOD'S DANGERS, by Theodore Rosengarten, Michael Hadley and Jennifer Hadley; based on the novel "All God's Dangers: The Life of Nate Shaw," by Mr. Rosengarten; directed by William Partlan; scenery and costumes by G. W. Mercier; lighting by Tina Charney; sound by Greg Sutton; production stage manager, Tom Aberger; associate producer, Rick Azar. Presented by John Cullen, Ms. Hadley and Mr. Hadley. At the Lamb's Theater, 130 West 44th Street.

Nate Shaw	Cleavon Little

By FRANK RICH

Of all American storytellers, few are more popular than those elderly men and women whose memories

Scarsbrook/Alabama Shakespeare Festival

Cleavon Little in "All God's Dangers," a stage version of the 1974 book based on the reminiscences of Nate Shaw, an Alabama cotton farmer.

reach back into the ashes of the Old South. And few deserve that popularity more than the 84-year-old Alabama cotton farmer whose reminiscences were published in 1974 under the title "All God's Dangers: The Life of Nate Shaw."

Unlike Ernest J. Gaines's Miss Jane Pittman or Allan Gurganus's Oldest Living Confederate Widow, Nate Shaw is not a fictional creation. He was discovered by the historian Theodore Rosengarten while doing research on the Depression-era Alabama Sharecroppers Union. What Mr. Rosengarten preserved on tape was a black witness to rural Southern history with incredible recall, hard-won wisdom and the verbal gifts of a Faulknerian storyteller. Though Shaw died the year before "All God's Dangers" was published, he is alive in every one of the 550 pages Mr. Rosengarten distilled from his raw 1,500-page transcript. An illiterate man's oral history not only sings as autobiographical literature but also serves as a detailed, indigenous record of a feudal, racially divided society struggling to emerge from the shadow of slavery.

In the stage adaptation of "All God's Dangers" at the Lamb's Theater, Mr. Rosengarten and two collaborators, Michael Hadley and Jennifer Hadley, have boiled down Nate Shaw's recollections further, to the two-hour contours of a one-man show starring Cleavon Little. The result is a conscientious, if often undramatic, précis of the book that touches on the major elements of Shaw's narrative while preserving his voice and free-ranging anecdotal gait. Mr. Little, adopting the stooped walk and white beard of the elderly Shaw, addresses the audience from a plain set suggesting a sepia scrapbook photograph of the Alabama tool shed where Mr. Rosengarten conducted his interviews. Though the words are all Shaw's, the format allows Mr. Little to mimic the voices of other characters who enter the tale, from white scoundrels to black wives.

The tale takes Nate from his first days behind a plow at age 9 to a proud maturity that includes the fathering of 10 children and the achievement of a measure of worldly success. The dangers he must overcome begin but

do not end with racism. When Nate isn't being cheated by a Jim Crow school system or the criminal chicanery of bankers, he finds his crop ravaged by the boll weevil. But if he has few tools with which to battle nature, he gradually invents the means to defy an oppressive social order. "All God's Dangers" is in no small part an archetypal account of the forging of a courageous, self-made black resistance fighter in the unsung years before civil-rights activism became a mass movement.

That's why the crucial event in "All God's Dangers" is Shaw's heroic confrontation with gun-toting white sheriffs who were trying to dispossess a neighboring farmer in 1932. While the incident is used as the play's hokey framing device, both the event itself and Shaw's consequent, unjust 12-year prison sentence are too cloudily presented on stage to have much impact. At such times one wishes that an experienced playwright had worked on the adaptation. Mr. Rosengarten and the Hadleys do not always seem to realize that editing a book to manageable theatrical length is not the same as shaping it into theater. "All God's Dangers" might be more stageworthy if its authors had presented a few episodes in depth and full context rather than attempting a sampler of so many in Reader's Digest-style condensation.

A commanding and funny actor, Mr. Little prevents languor by creating an intimate rapport with the audience. But his inclination to milk laughs — unchecked by the director, William Partlan — combines with the script's shapelessness to shift the balance in Shaw's story. By italicizing the very occasional sexual references and by pouring too much burlesque energy into the female impersonations, Mr. Little perhaps inadvertently emphasizes the domestic humors of the character above all else.

●

To be sure, the militant champion of dignity and justice is still visible in this show, but he is upstaged by an amiable old codger, a professional entertainer performing "Nate Shaw Tonight." That will not be a bad thing if Nate Shaw, the entertainer, can in turn draw new readers to the real and far more stirring Nate Shaw who resides in Mr. Rosengarten's remarkable book.

1989 O 23, C15:3

Pigtails and Pastiches

SLAY IT WITH MUSIC, book and lyrics by Michael Colby; directed by Charles Repole; choreography by Dennis Dennehy; music by Paul Katz; scenery by James Wolk; costumes by Michele Reisch; lighting by Dan Kotlowitz; musical director, Phil Reno; production stage manager, Paul J. Smith. Presented by Broadway Tomorrow, Elyse Curtis, artistic director, in association with Mr. Colby. At Actors Outlet Theater, 120 West 28th Street.

WITH: Susan Benstein, J. P. Dougherty, Louisa Flaningam, Janet Metz, Virginia Sandifur and Barry Williams.

By STEPHEN HOLDEN

"Slay It With Music" is the latest and far from the cleverest in a seemingly endless torrent of camp musicals inspired by old movies. Although shows of this sort usually send up vintage genre films, "Slay It With Music," dares to set its satirical sights a bit higher by compresssing plot elements from "Whatever Happened to Baby Jane?," "Sunset Boulevard" and "The Bad Seed." The result is a lighthearted mishmash of a show lacking in drive and focus.

In looking beyond the world of B-movies toward films that are inseparable in our memory from their star performances, "Slay It With Music" fails to come to grips with the Hollywood legends associated with those movies. Its cast members don't begin to suggest the hysterical intensity or the mannerisms of Joan Crawford, Bette Davis, Gloria Swanson, Erich von Stroheim, or even Patty McCormack, whose original movie roles are crudely cartooned in Michael Colby's book. As a result, the overall tone of a show that has many amusing comic details is hollow and uncertain.

The musical, at the Actors Outlet, tells the story of two actress sisters, the reclusive Edna Beaucoup (Virginia Sandifur) and her Pollyanna-like younger sister, Marcy Beaumont (Louisa Flanigam) who share a bitter sibling rivalry. Edna, a hybrid of characters made famous by Bette Davis and Gloria Swanson, is guarded by a fanatically devoted servant named Zachary Von Zell (J. P. Dougherty).

As the story begins, Edna is desperate to make her movie comeback as an ax-wielding murderer in a movie called "Chop Chop." When her younger sister, who has been starring in a soap opera called "Poughkeepsie," comes to visit, she turns her into a prisoner in her creaky old mansion. Spying on the house is Jill Litle (Susan Bernstein), a nosy pigtailed next-door neighbor. Not the least of the show's flaws is the clumsy, desperate insertion of allusions to "The Bad Seed," mostly at the end of the show.

"Slay It With Music" still has its charming moments. Its two best numbers, the title song and "More Than Just a Movie Fan," are deft, witty pastiches of 1940's Hollywood production numbers. And in the small role of a tour guide to the homes of the stars, Janet Metz steals what little is to be grabbed of the show. But

under the direction of Charles Repole, the main performances by Miss Sandifur and Miss Flanigam are scattered and unsatisfactory. Like the rest of "Slay It With Music," they lack a forceful comic vision.

1989 O 24, C20:6

The Passions Win

THE SECRET RAPTURE, written and directed by David Hare; scenery by Santo Loquasto; costumes by Jane Greenwood; lighting by Richard Nelson; music composed by Nick Bicât; associate producer, Jason Steven Cohen. Presented by Joseph Papp and the Shubert Organization. At the Ethel Barrymore Theater, 243 West 47th Street.

Isobel Glass	Blair Brown
Marion French	Frances Conroy
Tom French	Stephen Vinovich
Katherine Glass	Mary Beth Hurt
Irwin Posner	Michael Wincott
Rhonda Milne	Jennifer Van Dyck

By FRANK RICH

In the one moving scene in David Hare's new play, "The Secret Rapture" — the last — the audience is suddenly overwhelmed by pity for a young woman it has hated all night long. The woman is Marion French, a Tory junior cabinet minister whose faith in dog-eat-dog capitalism is so unshakable and whose contempt for her adversaries is so patronizing that she makes Margaret Thatcher seem like Mary Poppins. But Marion has been shaken now. The home of her recently deceased father, a provincial bookseller, is being dismantled. Someone she loves has been murdered in a crime of passion. And so Frances Conroy, the actress who plays Marion in a progression of starchy yuppie business suits, cracks apart, her once stony face streaked by tears.

What consumes Marion, and what touches even those who despise her, is not her specific losses so much as her feeling of utter helplessness. She has been engulfed by the chaos that comes when people's passions spin out of control, and she realizes that there is nothing in her philosophy to save her. In "The Secret Rapture," Mr. Hare uses the tragic story of Marion and her very different sister, Isobel (Blair Brown), as an ecumenical parable of the failure of all religions, temporal and spiritual, to offer salvation in the world we have made. The saintly Isobel, a free-spirited graphics artist who is as selfless as

Martha Swope

Mary Beth Hurt, left, and Blair Brown in "The Secret Rapture," at the Ethel Barrymore Theater.

Marion is materialistic, is also crushed by the uncontrollable passions around her. So is the play's one true believer in old-time faith, Marion's sad-eyed husband, Tom (Stephen Vinovich), a born-again Christian entrepreneur who cannot find Jesus at the moment when he needs Him most.

•

Mr. Hare, the author of "Plenty" and "A Map of the World," is not merely the flip socialist ideologue that he is so often taken for, and in "The Secret Rapture" he has gone further than before in marrying political thought to the compelling drama of lives that refuse to conform to any ideology's utopian plan. Framing his play with a pair of funerals, he tells a story of a warring family and obsessive love even as he folds in a polemical "Other People's Money"-style case history of corporate cannibalism and greed in the Thatcher-Reagan era. But Mr. Hare, serving as his play's director for its Broadway premiere at the Barrymore, is his own worst enemy. The passion and wit that reside in his script — and that are essential to engage an audience and lead it to his ideas — are left unrealized in this production.

Those who did not see last season's London staging of "The Secret Rapture," directed by Howard Davies ("Les Liaisons Dangereuses"), are blameless if they find Mr. Hare's New York version baffling right up to that final scene. The textual tinkering since London may be minor, but the wholesale changes of casting and design have flattened the play's subtleties into coarse agitprop and tossed its overall intentions into confusion. It's a measure of how poorly "The Secret Rapture" has been mounted here that a designer as gifted as Santo Loquasto has provided a dingy black-and-tan set that makes England, as much a character in the play as its people, indistinguishable from, say, metropolitan Cleveland. Between the drab set and the leaden staging that often reduces people to poseurs standing around at a cocktail party, we might as well be home listening to Mr. Hare's words on radio or reading them in a book.

•

The colorless presentation is of a piece with most of the acting. One of the delights of Mr. Hare's best writing is his ability to offer fully rounded views of characters of either political pole. He gives his ideological devils their due as magnetic leaders (the

V. S. Naipaul figure in "A Map of the World," the Rupert Murdoch stand-in of "Pravda") and is not afraid to mock the self-indulgence of would-be martyrs sharing his own leftist credo (Susan Traherne in "Plenty"). Such ambiguities are ignored by both lead actresses in "The Secret Rapture," who instead perform a dull, diagrammatic bad sister versus good sister act. Until her final scene, the talented Ms. Conroy is a desexed martinet — a humorless heavy. (Penelope Wilton, the Marion in London, was feminine and funny as well as forbidding.) In Ms. Brown's bland reading, Isobel's purity is a matter of lofty smiles and holier-than-thou vocal posturing; the

---

Ideology fails. Religion fails. So does love.

---

inner fire of deep conviction is replaced by a skin-deep air of self-satisfaction.

It's no secret that Mr. Hare created Isobel for Ms. Brown; the published text of "The Secret Rapture" is dedicated to her. But judging from this production and Mr. Hare's new movie, "Strapless," in which Ms. Brown also stars as a good sister, it is clear that another director will have to help the actress realize the dream performances that remain locked in the playwright's imagination. Mr. Hare has undermined his leading lady further by assigning the role of her lover to an idiosyncratic character actor, Michael Wincott, who is never convincing as either her love object or, later, as a romantic obsessive whose behavior drives the play's entire second act. When Mr. Wincott and Ms. Brown come to emotional blows at the pivotal opening of that act, the display of yelling and hand-waving is so embarrassingly empty that it earns unwanted laughter.

•

Under these underinhabited circumstances, "The Secret Rapture" is up for grabs, and Mary Beth Hurt runs away with the show in the secondary role of Katherine, an abusive, foul-mouthed alcoholic who was the much younger second wife of Isobel's and Marion's father. As she accomplished in Michael Frayn's thematically related play, "Benefactors," Ms. Hurt inexorably exposes the buried violence of the eccentric Englishwoman-next-door who also happens to be insane. It's part of Mr. Hare's point that people like Katherine, one of two characters in the play who brandish lethal weapons, practice an evil that is eternally beyond the reach of both a virtuous do-gooder like Isobel and a public scold like Marion. The world has become a place where no good deed, let alone bad one, goes unpunished.

"I hate all this human stuff!" says Marion at one point, frustrated by the way people with their "endless complications" insist on gumming up the best-laid plans by which she and all other right-thinking citizens would have society run smoothly. The beauty of "The Secret Rapture," whose title refers to a nun's ecstatic unity with Christ at death, is that Mr. Hare embraces the human, messy though it may be. To do otherwise is to forestall rapture until death — or to settle for a soulless existence that one character calls a "perfect imitation of life." What I don't understand is how a dramatist so deep in human stuff could allow so pallid an imitation of life to represent his play on a Broadway stage.

1989 O 27, C3:1

Glitter, With Gusto

TAKARAZUKA, producer, Kohei Kobayashi; president, Haruhiko Saka; artistic directors, Shinji Ueda and Hirotoshi Ohara; composers and arrangers, Takio Terada, Kenji Yoshizaki, Kaoru Irie, Kazuakira Hashimoto and Toshiko Yonekawa; conductor, Kazuakira Hashimoto; choreographers, Yoshijiro Hanayagi, Mayumi Nishizaki, Eiken Fujima, Hagi Hanayagi, Kiyomi Hayama, Taku Yamada and Roger Minami; set designers, Hideo Ishihama and Toshiaki Sekiya; costume designers, Harumi Tokoro, Kikue Nakagawa and Ikuei Touda; lighting designer, Naoji Inai; lighting supervisor, Ken Billington; assistant directors, Masazumi Tani and Masaya Ishida. Radio City Music Hall Productions presents a Mitsubishi special event.

WITH: Yuri Matsumoto, Junko Takara, Akira Ban, Mizuki Oura, Kae Segawa, Mito Hibiki, Yu Shion, Ai Kodama, Mira Anju and Yuki Amami.

By STEPHEN HOLDEN

One of the first laws of stage entertainment — one that made Florenz Ziegfeld a Broadway legend — is that there is something intrinsically awesome in the sight of rows of showgirls, decked out like floats, descending a grand staircase in formation.

As the 61-member Takarazuka Revue Company from Japan re-enacted that ritual in the finale of its show at Radio City Music Hall on Wednesday evening, the glitz and pomp momentarily matched anything that has been seen on a stage specifically designed for such extravaganzas. The show, which runs through Sunday, is the company's first American appearance in three decades.

Composed of women, Takarazuka is Japan's answer to the Ziegfeld Follies, the Folies-Bergère, Las Vegas floor shows, and the Music Hall's own spectaculars all rolled into one glittering unwieldy package.

While the revue delivers a lot of flash in its blaring orchestrations, in the performers' phonetic pronunciations of American lyrics and in its re-hashed Broadway choreography, it is an odd, sometimes monotonous cross-cultural hybrid. Its first half — the Japanese section — is a slow-moving sequence of dance-theater tableaux combining traditional Japanese dance and modern Japanese songs with Las Vegas-style production values.

The music, most of it composed and arranged by Takio Terada, is a relentless, overbearing hodgepodge, far more Western than Asian in style. It frequently suggests an imitation of Bill Conti's bombastic movie scores for the "Rocky" series. When used in a production number celebrating cherry blossoms, which waft onto the stage from the wings, the juxtaposition of floral delicacy and the two-fisted music seems not just silly but also jarring.

The show's second half, which salutes American show business, should amuse those with a taste for gaudy camp fun and cross-dressing, though the transvestism completely lacks the erotic tension one associates with Marlene Dietrich or even Judy Garland cavorting in top hat and cane. Although dressed as men, the perform-

ers in the ensemble numbers don't pretend to seem masculine, at least by the standards of body language in Western choreography. And the absence of sharp sexual differentiation gives the production numbers the ethereality of a children's pageant.

The one notable exception is Mizuki Oura, the show's most charismatic performer and its closest thing to a star. Slinking about the stage and huskily singing songs like "A Pretty Girl Is Like a Melody" and "Too Close for Comfort" (the latter during a sequence called "An Arabian Dream," which involves the dragging onto the stage of a wood camel), she suggests a softer echo of Miss Dietrich or Grace Jones.

Perhaps the show's most amusing number, "Flower Fantasy," finds the cast costumed as garish Southern belles, creating an expressionistic parody of the picnic scene from "Gone With the Wind." Its least effective moments are those that try too hard for a specifically New York feel — a production number danced to a cheesy pastiche of "Rhapsody in Blue" and a chirpy all-cast-member version of "Manhattan."

1989 O 27, C21:1

Eye of the Beholder

BEAUTY MARKS, by Kim Merrill; directed by Peter Askin; produced by Melanie Webber; set design by Roy Hine; lighting design by Greg MacPherson; costume design by Laura Drawbaugh; sound design by Bruce Ellman; production stage manager, Ken Simmons. Presented by Alley Cat Productions. At Intar Theater, 420 West 42d Street.

Henry	Bernie Barrow
Margaret	Elizabeth Lawrence
Daphne	Kim Merrill
June	Colleen Quinn

By STEPHEN HOLDEN

"Everyone needs a place to dance and sing," observes a character at the end of Kim Merrill's play "Beauty Marks." The pronouncement is one of many mawkishly sentimental observations that punctuate a drama so aswirl in tearful memories, accusations and reconciliations that it has the feel of a high-pitched soap opera.

"Beauty Marks," at the Intar Theater, is set in a Nebraska farming community and focuses on the seesawing relationship between teen-age sisters who live in a shack with their grandfather and his new wife. They make a wildly eccentric quartet. Granddad (Bernie Barrow) is a former football hero who, having lost the family farm, works as a guard at a chemical plant and makes foolish investments. His new wife, Margaret (Elizabeth Lawrence), longs to travel but can't afford it, and so contents herself with cooking exotic foreign dishes while playing Edith Piaf tapes.

•

Older sister June (Colleen Quinn) is a beautiful, haughty teen-ager who, as the drama opens, expects momentarily to be crowned the local Corn Husk queen. Her plain but brainy younger sister, Daphne (Miss Merrill) is a future anthropologist who envies her prettier sibling and lectures her on esoteric fertility ceremonies. The drama revolves around a freak accident during the Miss Corn Husk pageant that leaves June disfigured and brings to the surface the girls' painful memories of their mother, who died of breast cancer.

The closest equivalents of "Beauty Marks" are the family dramas of Paul Zindel, which have a similar blend of sentimentality and turbulence. But where Mr. Zindel's plays can have a basic credibility, "Beauty Marks" rings essentially false. The plotting is overly schematic, and its characters' paint-by-numbers changes of heart culminate in a saccharine resolution.

The drama might have more credibility if the dialogue and acting displayed an ear for the vernacular of Plains States farmers. But though the four actors, especially Miss Quinn as the unfortunate beauty queen, give vivid performances, the play, directed by Peter Askin, sounds like it's set somewhere between Pine Valley and Springfield, in the never-never land of daytime drama.

1989 O 29, 63:5

From Victims To Villains

ANTHONY ROSE, by Jules Feiffer; directed by Paul Benedict; set design by James Wolk; lighting by Curt Senie; costumes by Vickie Esposito; sound by Conny M. Lockwood; production manager, Cynthia Hart; stage manager, Paul Lockwood. Presented by the Philadelphia Festival Theater for New Plays, Dr. Carol Rocamora, artistic and producing director. Harold Prince Theater, Annenberg Center, Philadelphia.

Anthony Rose	Bob Balaban
Chester	Reed Birney
Alec	Anthony Fusco
Nick	Tony Musante
Anita	Socorro Santiago

By LAURIE WINER

Special to The New York Times

PHILADELPHIA, Oct. 25 — Anthony Rose, the playwright and title character in Jules Feiffer's dark comedy at the Philadelphia Festival Theater for New Plays, is a refugee from the treacherous domestic battles fought in such former Feiffer works as "Grown-Ups" and "Little Murders." In "Anthony Rose," Mr. Feiffer has shifted the battleground on which his characters fight for their identities from the Upper West Side of Manhattan to a rehearsal hall in Kansas City. Long a man of the theater, Mr. Feiffer knows that cast members can forge bonds as tight — and as damaging — as any family.

Once a Broadway playwright ranked with Neil Simon, now an embittered Hollywood screenwriter, Rose wanders from regional theater to regional theater, disrupting rehearsals of his ever-popular comedy "The Parent Lesson," which was a hit on Broadway 25 years ago. Rose longs to "write dialogue again," but instead of starting a new play, he's obsessed with rewriting "The Parent Lesson." The regional theaters that are reviving it, however, want the original hit, and they evict the playwright from the premises. In Kansas City, Anthony Rose gets his way.

Alec, the director of "The Parent Lesson," is only too pleased to have the playwright on hand. It gives him a chance to air his elaborate thesis, which places Rose in the pantheon of American dramatists right alongside Eugene O'Neill and Arthur Miller. But Rose ignores Alec and everyone else (except for Anita, the show's pretty ingénue). He sets out to rewrite "The Parent Lesson" to fit his present mood.

A neglected, angry son when he first wrote the play, Rose is now a neglected, angry husband and father. "My wife wouldn't take me seriously, so I left," he says. "Now she takes me seriously." His son, he believes, only wants his money. The actors protest in vain as Rose brings in new scenes, transforming the sons in the play from victims to villains and thereby justifying the father's abandonment of his own family. Ignoring their objections, Rose states that "the play is now word for word true." "Fathers exist to be hated," he insists. "Families aren't about fathers — they're about mothers and children."

But Rose isn't simply a playwright getting revenge on his family through his work. He insinuates himself into the company with a diffident presence, and the actors compete like sib-

Suzanne Rochelle
Bob Balaban

lings for his approval. Before long the real Rose emerges. He's arrogant and vicious, and his seemingly offhand wisecracks are in fact search-and-destroy darts that shatter the fragile show-biz egos of every actor in sight. Anita positively glows with confidence, however. Rose may have succeeded in seducing her, but she has succeeded in getting herself a much larger role.

But "The Parent Lesson" gets better as Rose transforms it; it takes on heft and substance and the actors, now fighting for their dignity, say their lines as if they matter. You can't have art without pain, Mr. Feiffer seems to be saying. But you likewise can't ask an audience to care about a character's pain if you have not revealed its source.

•

As conceptually interesting — and often funny — as his play is, Mr. Feiffer has left out the heart that could have made "Anthony Rose" really moving. Aside from some tantrums directed at the actors, Rose's despair is rendered in shallow psychological terms. "All I could do to survive was to make jokes," he explains at one point. By then the actors in the play within a play have been so battered down by his malevolence that they don't even care. The audience doesn't care much either.

Bob Balaban is best when establishing Rose's enigmatic, sinister quality in the early scenes, before the audience or the other characters have got a fix on him. He peers through Neil Simon-like glasses (surely a coincidence!) and answers people's questions with a shy — or is it stingy — smile. There's no payoff, though, to this promising setup. Once his character's intentions are revealed, Mr. Balaban simply gets red in the face and yells like a petty tyrant.

Paul Benedict has directed a strong cast with a firm sense of pace; Mr. Feiffer's short, taut scenes are kept crackling. Until the final, disappointingly moralistic coda in which the actors have their revenge on Rose, the play always feels as if it's going someplace.

James Wolk's simple set captures the atmosphere of the rehearsal room. With its tacky, castoff sofa, folding chairs and plain work table, it's a loathsome, barren place at first sight. Inhabited by actors, it becomes almost cozy and familiar, like a shaggy old bathrobe.

•

Reed Birney, as an inexperienced actor named Chester, snares the only emotional moment of the evening. Stung by a dead-on and particularly cruel Rose insult, Chester must gather his splintered pride and go on with a scene. Red-eyed and trembling, he fights to hide his humiliation as he steps forward to recite a line of dialogue. For the first time Chester connects with a real emotion and is something other than callow and stiff in his role. Mr. Birney manages a neat trick here: he reveals Chester's personal leap in maturity without making him a better actor.

Perhaps Mr. Feiffer should do what Anthony Rose did: go back to his play and flesh out the mean-spirited protagonist. In "Anthony Rose," it's not only the play within a play that needs some tinkering.

1989 O 30, C16:3

Tappers and Topers

OH, KAY!, music by George Gershwin; lyrics by Ira Gershwin; original book by Guy Bolton and P. G. Wodehouse; directed by Martin Connor; musical direction by David Evans; choreography and musical staging by Dan Siretta; adaptation by James Racheff; produced by Michael P. Price; scenery designed by Kenneth Foy; costumes designed by Judy Dearing; lighting designed by Craig Miller; artistic consultant, Sheldon Epps; assistant choreographer, Keith Savage; dance arrangements and orchestrations by Donald W. Johnston; additional orchestrations by Larry Moore and Danny Troob; technical director, John Hugh Minor; stage manager, Michael Brunner; associate producer, Sue Frost. At the Goodspeed Opera House, East Haddam, Conn.

WITH: Alexander Barton, Tracey M. Bass, Keith Robert Bennett, Marion J. Caffey, Helmar Augustus Cooper, Yvette Curtis, Denise Heard, Lynise Heard, Pamela Isaacs, Larry Johnson, Dexter Jones, Sara Beth Lane, Stanley Wayne Mathis, Sharon Moore, Brenda Pressley, Ron Richardson, Ken Leigh Rogers, Mark Kenneth Smaltz, Lynn Sterling and Horace Turnbull.

By STEPHEN HOLDEN

Special to The New York Times

EAST HADDAM, Conn., Oct. 29 — Early in the second act of the Goodspeed Opera House revival of "Oh, Kay!" comes a moment of delicious fun, when Duke (Stanley Wayne Mathis), a happy-go-lucky young bootlegger, succumbs to an ailment that a Gershwin song identifies as "Fidgety Feet." With his legs tugging him about the stage, Mr. Mathis flails and gyrates in a funky acrobatic Charleston that is so infectious it instantly galvanizes the ensemble into a lurching, tapping frenzy. The fever doesn't subside until everyone is nearly breathless.

"Fidgety Feet," the most uplifting of several exuberant dance numbers in the show, was masterminded by Dan Siretta, the Goodspeed's talented choreographer, whose production numbers for the Opera House's revivals of old musicals have provided many of their liveliest moments.

Diane Sobolewski
Pamela Isaacs in "Oh, Kay!"

There is, however, a crucial difference between this new production of George and Ira Gershwin's 1926 musical spoofing Prohibition and previous Goodspeed revivals. The setting has been moved from Long Island to Harlem and the production has been given an all-black cast. Though the concept, credited to Mr. Siretta, results in a few awkwardnesses, it is by and large quite successful.

The relocation of "Oh, Kay!" to Harlem makes sense. The urban setting injects a dash of realism to a story, by Guy Bolton and P. G. Wodehouse, that is essentially frivolous. And much of the Gershwins' score, which includes the jazzy pop spiritual, "Clap Yo' Hands," also has a Cotton Club ambiance. The production — directed by Martin Connor, with a cast headed by Ron Richardson — steers a careful middle ground in tone between vintage Broadway and oldtime Harlem music hall.

The further it veers from Broadway formality, the more relaxed and enjoyable the show becomes. As Duke and Larry Potter, a song and dance team who also deal in contraband, Mr. Mathis and Marion J. Caffey all but steal the show. Mr. Mathis's virtuosic "Fidgety Feet" is nearly matched in verve by Mr. Caffey's leading of the ensemble in "Clap Yo' Hands," whose choreography figuratively takes the Charleston to church. And in the title role of Kay Jones, a music-hall performer who wears several disguises, Pamela Isaacs has only to raise an eyebrow to strike sparks. Her brassy comic charisma recalls Patti LuPone as Reno Sweeney in the Lincoln Center Theater production of "Anything Goes."

The weakest elements in the production are the miscasting of Mr. Richardson as a debonair playboy and musical direction that at moments pits the orchestra against singers who often seem rhythmically adrift. The decision was apparently made to cast for dancers rather than singers. Vocally, the biggest disappointment is Mr. Richardson, whose rough delivery and lumbering sense of rhythm combine to trample "Someone to Watch Over Me."

Performances continue through Dec. 23.

1989 N 1, C22:3

A Lesson Learned: Life Isn't Opera

THE LISBON TRAVIATA, by Terrence McNally; directed by John Tillinger; sets by Philipp Jung; costumes by Jane Greenwood; lighting by Ken Billington; sound by Gary and Timmy Harris; fight staging by B. H. Barry; production stage manager, Pamela Singer. Presented by the Manhattan Theater Club, Lynne Meadow, artistic director; Barry Grove, managing director. At the Promenade Theater, 2162 Broadway, at 76th Street.

Stephen	Anthony Heald
Mendy	Nathan Lane
Mike	Dan Butler
Paul	John Slattery

By MEL GUSSOW

With his new, nonviolent ending to "The Lisbon Traviata," Terrence McNally recognizes that life is not grand opera. In the final scene, Anthony Heald is called on to internalize his anguish over his lover's departure rather than to melodramatize it as he did in the earlier version of the play. In the end, he is alone, without life support, a victim of self-abandonment. As a result, the denouement — and the play itself — has become more moving.

But "The Lisbon Traviata" retains its basic problems of structure and motivation. Except for that improved conclusion, the play, now at the Promenade Theater, is not perceptibly different from the version that was reviewed last June at the Manhattan Theater Club. The superbly matched performances of Mr. Heald and Nathan Lane and the intelligent direction of John Tillinger remain a constant.

The first act is still a savagely amusing dialogue between two friends who are obsessively concerned with opera, in particular with the singing of Maria Callas. One does not have to be an opera expert to appreciate the wit and the mordancy of the remarks about the failings of all singers except for the formidable Callas. As performed by Mr. Heald and by Mr. Lane (as a kind of one-man opéra bouffe), the first act leaves the audience in a state of heightened anticipation, almost equal to that of Mr. Lane's looking forward to the pirated recording of Callas's "Lisbon Traviata."

•

With a stark change of scenery (by Philipp Jung), the second act moves from Mr. Lane's plush, boudoir-style home to the sleekly modern apartment that Mr. Heald shares with a doctor (Dan Butler) who is about to leave him for a younger man (John Slattery). Reaching for tragedy, the play embraces domestic banality, as

Except for the denouement, the play is the same in its new run.

homosexuals repeat clichés from fiction about heterosexual couples, with Mr. Heald cast in the role of the spurned wife, Mr. Butler as the unfaithful husband.

But Mr. Lane still does not appear in the final act — and his absence is deeply felt. The character and the

actor remain the most vivid aspects of the play. Despite the mask of comedy, the first act has already achieved a seriousness and even an urgency to which the second act can only aspire. As Mr. Lane and Mr. Heald reveal themselves through their involvement in opera, one can sense the desperation of each character. This is especially evident in the case of Mr. Lane, who still deserves the highest praise for his performance as a man who has chosen to play the clown and has submerged his own life in a world of operatic passion.

1989 N 1, C22:3

Old Work, New Look, Thanks to Masks

STUFF AS DREAMS ARE MADE ON. Presented by the Brooklyn Academy of Music, Harvey Lichtenstein, president and executive producer. At Lepercq Space, 30 Lafayette Avenue, at Ashland Place, Fort Greene section.

WITH: Fred Curchack

By MEL GUSSOW

In Fred Curchack's "Stuff as Dreams Are Made On," a one-man show becomes a stage-filling phantasmagoria. This freehand reinvention of "The Tempest," in which Mr. Curchack plays all the roles and assumes all directorial and scenic responsibility, opened Tuesday at the Brooklyn Academy of Music as part of the Next Wave festival.

With lightning dexterity and to the sound of his own thundersheet, he quick-changes from Prospero to Ariel to Caliban, sometimes managing to keep several characters on stage at once. When he is playing Caliban, his Prospero mask and his Miranda doll (acting as ventriloquist's dummy) are watching and commenting. One of his feats is in changing and throwing his voice.

Diverging from "The Tempest," he conducts conversations among the characters on such subjects as Shakespeare, the pretensions of performance art and the fact that after touring the world, he has finally — sigh of relief — arrived in Brooklyn. Miranda warns him to watch his step or he may lose his audience.

Mr. Curchack is a clown as well as a commentator. On one level, his play is an act of criticism — of the artist himself as well as of his source. Repeatedly he interrupts his own performance with a comic aside in an attempt to demystify the event. His art is created as we watch it. Apparently he is opposed to atavism — and he is also not happy about late-comers to his show and people unfamiliar with the plot of "The Tempest."

•

While remaining faithful to his text in principle, he omits characters and inserts occasional contemporary dialogue. For all his apparent informality, he comes up with evocative interpretations of a Curchack kind, like his investigation of the relationship between Caliban and Miranda. They may have been closer than one suspected, despite the fact that Miranda can dismiss Caliban as an illiterate representative of the third world. This Caliban refuses to cringe; in his monstrous mask, he could frighten Freddy from "Nightmare on Elm Street."

The masks are themselves a chimerical gallery of distorted faces, often caught as in stop-action photography. As for Prospero, he is a top-hatted, white-masked Mephisto, an actor conducting a backstage tour of his magical island. There are different voices for each of the characters, including a singing voice for the androgynous Ariel and an amusingly broad Neapolitan accent for Ferdinand. Miranda is smitten by this preening "biceptual" pinhead but re-

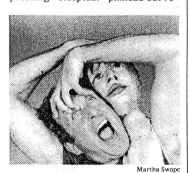

Martha Swope

Fred Curchack

tains her self-parodying intellectualism, as in her description of her world as a "deconstructed Jungian paradise."

In response to Mr. Curchack's diverse talents, one is most captivated by his role as designer in motion. Wielding a battery of handheld lights (flashlight, cigarette lighter, floor lamp), he uses himself as a shadow puppet. In giant silhouette, he becomes fearsome specters and demons, populating a Rorschach landscape of images. At one climactic point, his shadow looms larger and more menacing and then levitates into space. At such moments, it is clear that when Mr. Curchack is on stage, imagination knows no limitations.

His art is firmly rooted in technique, ranging from Noh to kathakali, from classic mime to Method acting (his Caliban has elements of Brando). The fact that he has condensed "The Tempest" into 80 minutes, while adding extras, should come as no surprise to anyone who has seen his previous shows, such as "Fred Breaks Bread with the Dead," which was a collage of "Hamlet" with music, "The Hairy Ape," "Ulysses" and other literary works.

Mr. Curchack is so polymorphous in performance that at the end of the show, one might expect to see a dozen participating artists take a bow instead of one unmasked, seraphic-looking theatrical virtuoso.

1989 N 2, C22:4

Yes, Sometimes

SID CAESAR & COMPANY: DOES ANYBODY KNOW WHAT I'M TALKING ABOUT?, directed by Martin Charnin; scenery and lighting, Neil Peter Jampolis; costumes, Karen Roston;

sound, Bruce Cameron; musical director, Elliot Finkel; original songs, Mr. Charnin; production stage manager, Frank Hartenstein; associate producers, J. Scott Broder, Sonny Bloch and Robert Courson. Presented by Ivan Bloch and Harold Thau, in association with Larry Spellman. At the John Golden Theater, 252 West 45th Street.

WITH: Sid Caesar, Lee Delano, Linda Hart, Lubitza Gregus, Peter Shawn, Laura Turnbull, Erick Devine and Carolyn Michel.

By FRANK RICH

When a show-biz legend returns to Broadway after a long absence, especially a legend who has written a memoir about his hard times, he always runs the risk of being upstaged by an audience's memories of his youth. But Sid Caesar, it can happily be reported, looks and sounds the same as ever in his new revue, "Sid Caesar & Company: Does Anybody Know What I'm Talking About?" at the Golden. His clown's arsenal is intact, too: the eyeballs and eyelids that can fly and bulge in at least four different directions while mimicking a slot machine, the manic tongue that can fracture any foreign language into ear-bending double talk, the weary skepticism that makes even an elaborately costumed Spanish matador sound like a put-upon waiter at the Carnegie Deli.

No, there's no need to worry about finding a shadow of the Sid Caesar we've loved for 40 years in "Sid Caesar & Company." There is, however, good reason to worry about his show, for it is so misconceived that it turns the guest of honor into a beggar at his own feast. What good is Mr. Caesar's remarkable comic instrument if no one has given him a score? The star who enjoyed the writing services of Mel Brooks, Larry Gelbart, Neil Simon, Mel Tolkin, Lucille Kallen and Woody Allen, among others, on television's "Your Show of Shows" and its progeny has no billed writers in this outing. Nor does he have any second bananas who might remotely rival Imogene Coca, Carl Reiner, Howard Morris or even the somewhat less-than-immortal "Show of Shows" dance team of Mata and Hari.

What Mr. Caesar does have is a director, Martin Charnin, responsible for juicing up a Caesar nightclub act seen last summer Off Broadway. To Mr. Charnin, going Broadway apparently means spending money. He has commissioned a handsome set from Neil Peter Jampolis — a black box framed by a band of light, like the old Sylvania television screens. He has hired a supporting cast of seven, top-heavy with toupées and large breasts, of whom only one (Lee Delano, a Reiner stand-in) is steadily employed by the sketches and only one other (the wasted Linda Hart, last of "Anything Goes") has discernible talent. Mr. Charnin also hired himself to write three songs, or at least to retrieve them from a trunk of all-purpose Special Material. These numbers, one of which makes vast satirical sport of the task of sweeping a messy stage, are irrelevant to the star but do require the employment of onstage musicians as well as the aggressively winsome smiles of every last featherbedder in the company.

In the middle of this "production" stands Mr. Caesar, straitjacketed by a chalk-striped suit but always eager to please. Among the dozen or so bits he performs are some golden oldies, including a finger-bashing performance of the Grieg Piano Concerto, the "Show of Shows" sketch "At the Movies" and the Germanic pseudo-intellectual non sequiturs of that instant expert on everything and nothing, the Professor.

It's representative of this revue that even these gems are undermined by Mr. Charnin, who lets each selec-

tion run on until it expires of exhaustion. "At the Movies," in which Mr. Caesar's innocent moviegoer finds himself trapped in a marital brawl, is further dented by the weak players and by a juvenile updating of its punch line to accommodate out-of-the-closet times. The baggy-pants Professor — the granddaddy of so many classic comedy shticks, including Mel Brooks's 2,000-Year-Old Man — is denied a punch line altogether. Mr. Caesar must instead segue into the final Charnin choral musical number, an uplifting anthem to positive thinking titled "Make a New Now, Now!" By the second chorus, you may well begin to fear that "Now" will never turn into Then.

Other sketches, all introduced by stilted patter about comic truths, demonstrate that some of Mr. Caesar's comedy is shackled to passing half-truths of a distant America. His notions about forbidding mothers-in-law, henpecked husbands and preening teen-agers are of a piece with the rest of television's Golden Age, including "I Love Lucy" and "The Honeymooners." What we don't see is the sophisticated material — the cultural parodies, the articulate marital warfare of the Hickenloopers — that made Mr. Caesar and "Your Show of Shows" a dominant influence on mass American comedy for a genera-

tion. It's not coincidence that Caesar alumni created such movies, plays and television series as "Blazing Saddles," "Annie Hall," "Love and Death," "The Odd Couple," "The Dick Van Dyke Show," "All in the Family," "M*A*S*H" and the current "Mastergate." You can see vestiges of vintage Caesar sketches in all of them.

•

At the Golden, the man himself looks so fit and ready to amuse that he could probably still perform "Little Me," his brilliant Broadway marathon of 1962, in which Neil Simon let him fly in seven hilarious roles of "Show of Shows" caliber. By contrast, the show at hand frustrates the audience, which has come to praise Caesar, by burying him.

1989 N 2, C19:3

Peter Cunningham

Sid Caesar in his new Broadway music and comedy revue.

A Sidekick For the Elephant

GRANDMA GOES WEST, conceived and directed by Paul Binder; musical director, Rik Albani; original music, Linda Hudes; clown coordinator, Michael Christensen; scenery design by James Leonard Joy; lighting design, Jan Kroeze; costume design by Donna Zakowska; associate director, Dominique Jando; choreographer, Monica Lévy; production manager, Robert Libbon; ring director, Guillaume Casaly; shadow puppet design, Stephen Kaplin. Presented by The Big Apple Circus, Mr. Binder, founder and artistic director; James C. McIntyre, executive director. At Lincoln Center.

The Puppeteers: Jenny Klion, with David Casey, John Lepiarz, Melinda and Olivier Merlier.
WITH: Katja Schumann, Barry Lubin, Vanessa Thomas, Pedro Reis, David Rosaire, Cesar Aedo, Vince Bruce, Taso Stavrakis, Guillaume and Mireille Casaly, Ben Williams, the Rios Brothers and The Loyal-Suarez Troupe.

By MEL GUSSOW

After last season's collaboration with the Nanjing Acrobatic Troupe, the Big Apple Circus has done an about-face. Its new show, "Grandma Goes West," is a rambunctious but not-so-wild version of a cowboy jamboree. As usual, the entertainment (in a heated tent at Lincoln Center) is intimate and unpretentious. Children in the front rows reach out as if to touch the animals.

Nothing is overstated, and hardly any act goes on too long. Suitably, the show begins with a riderless white horse galloping around the circus's one ring. What follows is the Big Apple's customary parade of aerialists, tumblers and trained animals, interspersed with the shenanigans of the resident clowns. The lead clown this year is Barry Lubin's Grandma, a country cousin of Jonathan Winters's Grandma Frickett. This is one assertive old lady who never finds herself at wits' end.

•

Along with a return visit from that prodigious pachyderm, Anna May, there are Katja Schumann's graceful horses, the Loyal-Suarez family troupe riding and jumping bareback, and — this season's innovation — a bison. Admittedly, one's performance expectations for a bison are not exceedingly high. At the Big Apple, an elephant can dance to its own tam-

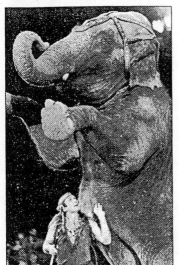

Patricia Lanza

Anna May, right, and Ben Williams are part of the Big Apple Circus now at Lincoln Center.

bourine, a monkey can hold the reins of a Dalmatian-drawn firewagon and David Rosaire's pets are a peppy pride of performing Pekingese. But what can a bison do besides look ugly?

The Big Apple's bison (unnamed) steps into the center of the ring and takes a bow (bending at the knees, snout to the ground), which is worth a round of applause. Later, the bison snuffles and then stands, all four feet close together, on a small platform. With more training, perhaps it could play straight bison in that drunk act with Anna May, one of many scenes well remembered from previous shows and not reprised. One is forced to the irrefutable conclusion that anything a bison can do, an elephant can do better.

•

This year the equilibrists do not seem quite as daring (the Flying Gaonas are flying somewhere other than the Big Apple) and at least one of the variety numbers is excisable — a whip-cracking cancan involving Vanessa Thomas and several clowns. On the other hand, the Rios Brothers are a particular audience favorite. As one satisfied circusgoer was heard to say, "I especially liked it when that one man lay on his back and the other man jumped all over him." Technically this is a Risley act, which is identified in the souvenir program as "acrobatic foot juggling with a human partner." As one Rios spins through the legs of the other, the effect is like that of a human windmill or a perpetual-motion machine. Could you imagine the pandemonium if the Flying Karamazov Brothers tried a Risley?

Under the direction of Paul Binder, the Big Apple Circus is in residence through the Christmas season until Jan. 7.

1989 N 3, C4:1

An Era Suggested

MEET ME IN ST. LOUIS, songs by Hugh Martin and Ralph Blane; book by Hugh Wheeler; based on "The Kensington Stories" by Sally Benson and the M-G-M movie "Meet Me in St. Louis." Directed by Louis Burke; choreography by Joan Brickhill; production design, Keith Anderson; lighting, Ken Billington; musical supervisor, Milton Rosenstock; musical director, Bruce Pomahac; orchestrations, Michael Gibson; dance arranger, James Raitt; sound, Alan Stieb and James Brousseau; vocal arrangers, Mr. Martin and Mr. Pomahac; ice choreographer, Michael Tokar; production stage manager, Robert Bennett; assistant director, Lonnie Chase; associate choreographer, Herman-Jay Muller. Presented by Brickhill-Burke Productions, Christopher Seabrooke and EPI Products. At the Gershwin Theater, 222 West 51st Street.

Lon Smith	Michael O'Steen
Randy Travis	Brian Jay
Katie	Betty Garrett
Motorman	Jim Semmelman
Tootie Smith	Courtney Peldon
Mrs. Smith	Charlotte Moore
Grandpa Prophater	Milo O'Shea
Esther Smith	Donna Kane
Rose Smith	Juliet Lambert
John Truitt	Jason Workman
Agnes Smith	Rachael Graham
Mr. Alonzo Smith	George Hearn
Warren Sheffield	Peter Reardon
Ida Boothby	Naomi Reddin
Douglas Moore	Gregg Whitney
Eve Finley	Shauna Hicks
Dr. Bond	Gordon Stanley
Lucille Ballard	Karen Culliver
Clinton A. Badger	Craig A. Meyer

By FRANK RICH

It's hard not to feel stirred when the lights dim in a Broadway theater, the

curtain rises on a picture-postcard frontcloth, and a confident pit band splashes through an overture heralding "The Trolley Song," "The Boy Next Door" and "Have Yourself a Merry Little Christmas." Do these songs affect us because their authors, Hugh Martin and Ralph Blane, touched something eternal in the American character when they wrote them for the M-G-M film musical "Meet Me in St. Louis" during the wartime of 1944? Or is it because the songs were first delivered by Judy Garland, that difficult cultural icon about whom our complicated feelings remain forever unresolved?

I'm not sure. In any case, Judy Garland isn't coming back and the original "Meet Me in St. Louis" is available on videocassette. So what's the mission of the stage replica at the Gershwin Theater? To spread the good will earned by the overture, I guess. And that task, if not a lot else, is accomplished by this lavish show despite such obstacles as insipid acting, an inane book and a complete lack of originality. While it's not high praise to say so, "Meet Me in St. Louis" is superior to the other latter-day Broadway adaptations of M-G-M musicals, "Seven Brides for Seven Brothers" and "Singin' in the Rain." Unlike its predecessors, this show respects its source and knows its audience. It also benefits from the fact that the original material — Sally Benson's stories of domestic bliss and teen-age romance on the eve of the 1904 Louisiana Purchase Exposition — is too Kensington Avenue-bound to insist upon cinematic sweep.

•

The driving force behind the stage version is the director-and-choreographer team of Louis Burke and Joan Brickhill. They have put on many musicals in South Africa, and I don't mean "Sarafina!" (Though they do list one "all black African musical" in their Playbill biographies, their St. Louis is conspicuously all white.) Given the familiar titles in their credits, it's clear that Mr. Burke and Miss Brickhill have a particular passion for vintage Broadway musicals. After seeing "Meet Me in St. Louis," it's equally clear that they have not witnessed many of those musicals in their original productions.

Their show, so reminiscent of "American" musicals in London, is the work of people who know what Broadway hits are supposed to look and sound like — information gleaned from the close study of original-cast recordings and production photographs — but who can only guess at what makes such shows tick. "Meet Me in St. Louis" comes with turntables of lantern-lighted Victorian scenery (by Keith Anderson) that mimics the opulence of Oliver Smith's designs in a show like "Hello, Dolly!" without recapturing their glamorous, advanced taste. The costumes — boaters and suspenders for men, petticoats galore for women — could be slightly faded wash-and-wear knockoffs of Miles White's clothes for "High Button Shoes." Miss Brickhill's energetic (and well executed) dance routines — struts, cakewalks, square dances, dream ballets — have no internal drive but look like compilations of souvenir-program freeze-frames of the Broadway choreography of Michael Kidd and Onna White. Even Hilary Knight's poster art for the show suggests an enervated hybrid of his posters for "Sugar Babies" and "Half a Sixpence."

What prevents the derivative from becoming boring (except in a Halloween fantasy sequence) is the conviction and hard cash behind it. "Meet Me in St. Louis," in contrast to most Broadway revivals, doesn't look cheap. There's not only a trolley but also an ice rink to employ a skater or two still loitering in the Gershwin

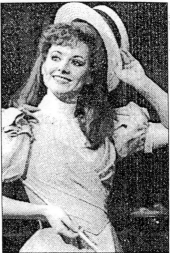

The New York Times/Bill Swersey

Donna Kane, as Esther Smith, in "Meet Me in St. Louis," at the Gershwin Theater.

from "Starlight Express." What's more, Mr. Burke and Miss Brickhill have drilled their company and collaborators to produce the sound that goes with the show's look. Bruce Pomahac's conducting, Michael Gibson's orchestrations and all the voices have the brash snap of another era.

Yet this rigorous paint-by-numbers attempt to manufacture a Broadway hit is also the show's main trap. The mechanical technique precludes the imaginative spontaneity that might allow "Meet Me in St. Louis" to soar above the lumpy sum of its parts. As a result, this production desperately needs an exciting creative force on stage to ignite it — a Robert Lindsay, a Debbie Allen, a star-to-be — and that spark never comes. The Smith family and their neighbors are played by performers whose personalities are as generic as the production around them.

Donna Kane sings the Garland numbers with clarion tone, but she and her sibling partner in boy-chasing, Juliet Lambert, act like well-schooled Miss America contestants; only the different colors of their wigs permit us to tell them apart. (The boys are so interchangeable that the one next door might as well be addressed as "occupant.") As the Smith patriarch, a role identical to his ill-fated turn in Richard Rodgers's "I Remember Mama," George Hearn can only rail at the "newfangled" telephone and condescend to his wife (Charlotte Moore). Milo O'Shea, a silver-haired grandfather in a progression of funny hats, deserves combat pay for the stage time he must share with the robotic little girl impersonating Margaret O'Brien's Tootie.

In the Marjorie Main role of the cook, Betty Garrett offers the genuine brio of the 1940's musical comedy performer she was. The evening's other real links to the past are Mr. Martin and Mr. Blane, who have written 10 new songs for the occasion. The lyrics for these numbers, which variously apotheosize banjos, the Irish,

New York City and ice, are as laughably silly as the ginger peachy Hugh Wheeler dialogue. (When the chorus sings "ice is twice as nice," one wants to counter, "But liquor is quicker!") The music, while no patch on the original "St. Louis" score, is consistent with the 1940's Tin Pan Alley sound that is so endearing in Mr. Martin's output, with and without Mr. Blane, in the musicals "Best Foot Forward," "Look Ma, I'm Dancin'," "Love From Judy" and "High Spirits."

•

But "Meet Me in St. Louis" isn't a throwback to those old Martin shows, any more than it transports us to turn-of-the-century St. Louis or to Arthur Freed's heyday at M-G-M. A synthetic approximation of old-fashioned Broadway crowd-pleasers rather than the real thing, it most resembles the many professional, second-rate shows a musical-comedy fanatic would settle for seeing in the 1950's or 60's when there were no tickets to be had at a "Music Man" or "Dolly." (There's even a march, "Paging Mr. Sousa," written and staged like "76 Trombones.") No doubt "Meet Me in St. Louis" can serve the same function today for matinee audiences shut out of Broadway's current reigning hits. It's hardly an unpleasant way to kill an afternoon in the theater, especially if you have a high tolerance for camp and are in the company of wide-eyed kids.

1989 N 3, C3:1

Joyce and Lenin, Cecily and Gwendolen

TRAVESTIES, by Tom Stoppard; directed by Robert Hupp; set and lighting designed by Giles Hogya; costumes designed by Jonathan Bixby; music composed by Ellen Mandel; choreography by Nicole Fosse; stage manager, Isabel Lopez. Presented by the Jean Cocteau, 330 Bowery, at Second Avenue.

Henry Carr .... Harris Berlinsky
Tristan Tzara .... Christopher Oden
James Joyce .... Joseph Menino
Lenin .... James Sterling
Bennett .... Robert Ierardi
Gwendolen .... Carol Dearman
Cecily .... Lyn Wright
Nadya .... Angela Vitale

By WILBORN HAMPTON

History has long made footnote of the fact that James Joyce, Lenin and Tristan Tzara were all neighbors in Zurich just as the Great War was reaching its apex and the Russian Revolution was getting under way. But it is thanks to Tom Stoppard that those titans of literature, politics and art have come to be inexorably linked with a fourth resident of Zurich at that time — one Henry Carr, a junior British consular official and amateur thespian.

In "Travesties," Mr. Stoppard's dazzling display of perception and nonsense that is enjoying a rollicking revival at the Cocteau Repertory, Carr recounts his memories of the three men through anecdote and digression ("the saving grace of senile reminiscence"). Carr's disjointed memoir is spun around an amateur production of "The Importance of Being Earnest," directed by Joyce, in which Carr played a leading role ("not Ernest, the other one"), and that landed both men in the law courts.

It is soon clear that Carr's memory is at best inexact. He recalls Lenin as

a blond Scandinavian sailor, then dismisses him as a minor figure ("who would have thought big oaks from a corner room at No. 14 Spiegelgasse?"). Joyce, he remembers, wore mismatched suits, talked in limericks and was always trying to borrow a pound. But Carr himself confesses, "I stand open to correction on all points."

Mr. Stoppard's play is woven directly onto the framework of Wilde's. Tzara and Carr, for example, are direct stand-ins for Jack and Algernon ("that's the one"). Mr. Stoppard uses lines from Wilde as lead-ins to his own scenes, and it is helpful, though by no means essential, to have some knowledge of "Earnest" to catch all the humor in "Travesties." The Cocteau is now offering both plays in repertory.

The Cocteau production of "Travesties" races forward on Mr. Stoppard's verbal roller coaster, leaving one dizzy yet exhilarated by its sudden semantic twists, turns, dips and loops. For the most part, the Cocteau cast provides a fast and amusing ride. There is only one stretch, when Lenin offers his view on art and the revolution, when the action drags noticeably.

Harris Berlinsky, a Cocteau veteran, gives a fine performance as the vain, inept and pompous Carr. Switching seamlessly from the older to the younger Carr through changes in voice and movement, Mr. Berlinsky creates a humorous yet sympathetic petty bureaucrat. One might wish only for a dash more acerbity to sharpen the characterizaton. Christopher Oden's exaggerations are well suited to the flamboyant Tzara ("my art belongs to Dada"), who pulls his poems out of a hat, and Joseph Menino offers a whimsical Joyce that, despite a slip or two in his Irish accent, never trips over a bad rhyme. Robert Ierardi has a nice turn as Carr's Swiss manservant.

Carol Dearman as Gwendolyn and Lyn Wright as Cecily are fun to watch. Gwendolyn, who is helping Joyce write "Ulysses" (or "Elasticated Bloomers," as it was originally titled) by jointly researching Homer, and the Dublin Street Directory of 1904, and Cecily, the radical librarian, mirror their roles in the Wilde play. Their tea party scene, sung to a music hall ditty in "Travesties," is a delight.

Robert Hupp, the director, has come up with some flourishes of his own. For what Mr. Stoppard calls the "time slips" of Carr's memory, in which a scene reverses itself and starts over, Mr. Hupp inverts the lighting and has his characters waddle rapidly backward to their starting marks. The effect is like pressing the rewind/search button on a VCR to back up the action.

Following all the conversations in "Travesties" is, as Carr observes, "like hearing every other line of the Catechism." A lot of it may be nonsense, but it is very clever nonsense indeed, and the Cocteau production is worth a trip to the Bowery.

1989 N 3, C29:1

Killed in Battle And in Flagrante

NEW MUSIC, a trilogy by Reynolds Price; scene design by Dan Conway; lighting design by John Hastings; costume design by C. L. Hundley; sound design by Jeffrey Montgomerie; production stage managers, Jean Bruns

for "August Snow" and "Night Dance" and Benjamin Gutkin for "Better Days." Assistant stage manager, Morgan F. Kennedy; dramaturge, Roger T. Danforth. Presented by the Cleveland Playhouse, Josephine R. Abady, artistic director; Dean R. Gladden, managing director.

AUGUST SNOW and NIGHT DANCE directed by David Esbjornson.

BETTER DAYS directed by Ms. Abady.
WITH: David Adkins, John Carpenter, Barbara eda-Young, Jody Gelb, Kelly Gwin, John Hickey, James Hurdle, Susan Knight, Sonja Lanzener, Kathleen Mahony-Bennett, Bill Raymond and Richard Thomsen.

By MEL GUSSOW
Special to The New York Times

CLEVELAND — In the final play of Reynolds Price's trilogy, "New Music," a father reveals a closely guarded family secret to his son. The moment is both intimate and wryly amusing — and it is followed by other personal intimations. After almost six hours in the company of an extended family in a small North Carolina town, we come to recognize the characters as old friends and to feel the tautness of the bonds of blood, marriage and acquaintanceship.

The audience at the Cleveland Play House is asked to enter this world as if it were one of the author's novels. Like the fine writer he is, Mr. Price is not interested in manipulating theatergoers. As a novelist, he has been compared with Faulkner. As a dramatist, he is related to Horton Foote and Romulus Linney. All these writers, rooted in specific rural environments, share a gift for revealing character through atmosphere, and vice versa, and they have a natural love for the intricacies and the lyricism of local language. In the plays, as in his fiction, Mr. Price deals with stressful families whose energies are marshaled by strong, individualistic women.

The trilogy is leisurely in its unfolding. Each of the three connected plays takes place at a pivotal point in the lives of the Averys — in 1937, as Neal and his wife, Taw, face their first marital crisis; in 1945, as they and other townspeople try to overcome the effects of World War II, and finally in 1975, with the death of Neal's mother and with war in Vietnam as an additional shadow over the Avery household.

The first play, "August Snow," is slight and anecdotal; in the second, "Night Dance," the story becomes more dramatic and diverges from naturalism. The third, "Better Days," is the most fully realized. It could stand on its own, but it is nurtured by our knowledge of earlier events. Seeing the play by itself, one would not know about the Huck-and-Tom skylarking days of Neal and his best friend, Porter Farwell; or about the hurtful truthtelling of Neal's embittered mother. These are two issues of increasing importance in understanding all of the characters. In true trilogy fashion, the plays work best when seen in sequence, as at one of the Cleveland Play House's regularly scheduled Sunday marathons.

•

We hear about wars and domestic violence in harrowing — and sometimes black comic — detail. Men are killed in battle and in flagrante. There are few sad songs in "New Music," but rather a rejuvenating sense that things will improve, that succeeding generations will dance to new emotional rhythms. Mr. Price is evenhanded about apportioning responsibility. Even the most overtly unsympathetic of the characters — Neal's mother — is admired after her death

for her loyalty and her common sense. Loyalty is the overweening attribute in the play, and the most difficult to maintain.

The principal themes are love and loss and the salving effects of time. This is not idealism but a kind of pragmatic acceptance of the fact that the weather will eventually change, if only the characters are not overwhelmed by their thoughts of suicide.

Even as one is warmed at Mr. Price's imaginative hearth, he maintains a novelist's quiescence, as if to say that dialogue and action will take care of themselves. It is not so much the literary quality of the dialogue — although as a stylist he can use three figures of speech in a row when one would be ample. The difficulty is in the avoidance of confrontations, so that it seems as if characters are traveling on separate tracks. They are revealed less in collision than in contrasting soliloquies, especially so in the case of Neal and his wife, who habitually sidestep showdowns.

Neal is meant to be the golden boy of this small town, the object of everyone's love and admiration. But there is little in the writing and even less in Kelly Gwin's performance to justify such a supposition. Perhaps that is the author's point, that Neal does not really stand out, except in the eyes of his beholders. But it is in these areas that one wishes Mr. Price had been more forthcoming as a playwright. In the third play, we finally receive a more complex picture of Neal, as played in middle age by Bill Raymond. His telling portrait is that of a man approaching the other side of the hill, and, to his astonishment, maturing into an optimist.

Richard Termine.
Bill Raymond in "Better Days," the final play in Reynolds Price's trilogy, "New Music."

From Reynolds Price, a trilogy on the tautness of human bonds.

Until that final play, Neal and Taw are upstaged by minor characters — their flirtatious young landlady (Kathleen Mahony-Bennett), the landlady's crusty father-in-law (John Carpenter) and Neal's best friend

(John Hickey). Each of these three is artfully delineated both in the writing and in the performance. In the case of Mr. Carpenter, he is so colorful he may deserve a subsidiary play of his own, so he could tell us more about his reprobate days and nights and about his singing dog Dave, who could only manage to get through the first verse of "The Star Spangled Banner" before breaking down in sobs.

A strength of the plays is in their shaggy humor and tall, tangential ruminations, but the trilogy has a sense of dramatic momentum, culminating in a poignant moment of honesty as survivors make their peace and try to face their inextricably linked future.

This trilogy would be a daunting prospect for any theater. Josephine R. Abady and David Esbjornson, as co-directors, have undertaken the assignment with resourcefulness, though the plays would be improved with sharper casting and a more inventive scenic design (and some further definition by the author). In common with Mr. Price's novels, "New Music" is indigenous to its time, place and characters, seemingly ordinary country people who rise, in what Anne Tyler has accurately called "startling, almost incongruous eloquence."

1989 N 4, 16:3

Of Thee I Kvetch

THE PRISONER OF SECOND AVENUE, by Neil Simon; directed by John Driver; set designer, Scott Bradley; lighting designer, Susan A. White; costume designer, Victoria Lee; sound designer, J. Wise, production stage manager, Patrick Ward. Presented by the American Jewish Theater, Stanley Brechner, artistic director. At the Susan Bloch Theater, 307 West 26th Street.

Mel Edison .... Mike Burstyn
Edna Edison .... Lyn Greene
Harry Edison .... Ronald Hunter
Jessie .... Madelyn Cates
Pearl .... Sylvia Kauders
Pauline .... Estelle Harris

By WILBORN HAMPTON

To be sure, life in New York City has its drawbacks. Crime is rampant, pollution is everywhere and nothing works: if the hospitals or the garbage men aren't on strike, the water is turned off. But it could be worse. You could have Mel Edison as a neighbor.

Mel is a 43-year-old (47 in the original production) advertising executive who lives on the 14th floor of a high-rise on 88th Street at Second Avenue. He is also the angry central force around which everyone else moves in "The Prisoner of Second Avenue," Neil Simon's billet-doux to Gotham that has been revived by the American Jewish Theater.

Mel is a complainer. The air-conditioner is too cold, the couch has too many pillows, and if he puts his ear to the too-thin walls of his too-small apartment, he can just hear that the music is too loud next door. To add to Mel's woes, his Valium doesn't work anymore, the company he works for is losing money and his shrink has died. His only consolation is to yell at his wife and to bully her into banging on the neighbors' wall for him.

•

The foundation on which Mr. Simon built this play is one long kvetch about the hazards and tribulations of life in New York, circa 1971. Even the background radio broadcasts that come on during scene changes are a litany of violence and hardship that describe the unraveling of the social fabric of our society. In short, they're not much different from this morning's newscast.

To make such bellyaching work as a full-length play, and a comedy at that, an actor must somehow find a saving grace in Mel's character that will gain the audience's empathy, if not sympathy. Mike Burstyn, the Mel in the American Jewish Theater revival, presents a man, however, who is angry to the point of belligerence. He berates his wife with such virulence that one begins to fear for her safety, and he harangues his neighbors with such menace that one wonders why someone doesn't call the police. When he brings home a shovel to wreak revenge on an upstairs neighbor, one is simply relieved it isn't an AK-47.

Mr. Burstyn's Mel is so disagreeable that by the time he loses his job, returns home to a burgled apartment and finally isolates himself into a nervous breakdown, one may feel only that justice has finally been served.

•

As Edna, Mel's long-suffering wife, Lyn Greene makes the most of what could at best be described as a bad marriage. But her character is never fully developed.

In the only really funny scene, when Mel's brother and three sisters gather to debate how much money they should contribute to help him recover from his breakdown, Estelle Harris is hilarious and pretty much steals the show.

John Driver directed.

1989 N 5, 96:1

Hypocrites And Capitalists

THREEPENNY OPERA, book and lyrics by Bertolt Brecht; music by Kurt Weill; translated by Michael Feingold; directed by John Dexter; musical staging, Peter Gennaro; scenery and costumes by Jocelyn Herbert; associate scenic design by Duke Durfee; lighting by Andy Phillips and Brian Nason; hair by Phyllis Della; sound by Peter Fitzgerald; music director, Julius Rudel; associate producers, Margo Lion, Hiroshi Sugawara, Lloyd Phillips, Kiki Miyake and Nancy Ellison; production stage manager, Bob Borod. Presented by Jerome Hellman, in association with Haruki Kadokawa and James M. Nederlander. At the Lunt-Fontanne Theater, 205 West 46th Street.

A ballad singer .... Ethyl Eichelberger
Jenny Diver .... Suzzanne Douglas
Jonathan Jeremiah Peachum ...Alvin Epstein
Filch .... Jeff Blumenkrantz
Mrs. Peachum ....Georgia Brown
Polly Peachum ....Nancy Ringham
Macheath .... Sting
Matt of the Mint .... Josh Mostel
Crook-Finger Jack ....Mitchell Greenberg
Sawtooth Bob .... David Schechter
Ed .... Philip Carroll
Walter .... Tom Robbins
Jimmy .... Alex Santoriello
Tiger Brown .... Larry Marshall
Dolly .... Anne Kerry Ford
Betty .... Jan Horvath
Vixen .... Teresa De Zarn
Molly .... Leslie Castay
Suky Tawdry .... K. T. Sullivan
Old Whore .... Fiddle Viracola
Smith .... David Pursley
Policemen, Beggars and Bystanders
     MacIntyre Dixon, Michael Piontek, Philip Carroll, David Schechter and Steven Major West
Lucy ....Kim Criswell

By FRANK RICH

After emerging from the inert gray mass that is Broadway's "Three-

Nancy Ellison

Sting in "Threepenny Opera" at the Lunt-Fontanne Theater.

penny Opera," the first thing you want to do — assuming you don't drink — is run home and listen to any available recording of its score. The reason is not to revisit the evening's high points — there are none — but to make sure you are still among the living. How could these scathing songs, forged in the crucible of the century's apocalypse, sound as numbing as they do from the stage? One would have to be lobotomized not to respond to the blasted fusion of jazz, classicism and political rage with which Kurt Weill and Bertolt Brecht first rocked Berlin in 1928.

As it happens, nearly any "Threepenny Opera" recording (Bobby Darin's possibly excepted) will resuscitate the spirit absent at the Lunt-Fontanne. One album of particularly relevant note is the 1985 anthology "Lost in the Stars," in which contemporary musicians of many idioms take on the Weill canon. Among the recording's participants is Sting, Broadway's new Macheath. On record, he sings a monotonous "Ballad of Mack the Knife" — not his number now, but all too consistent with his current performance.

Yet a few cuts away on the same record, Tom Waits performs a nasty, pulsating "What Keeps Mankind Alive?" — a number Sting does puncture at the Lunt — and the incendiary Brecht-Weill spirit comes at you like a slap in the face. Mr. Waits even helps one understand the promising notion behind the mating of a serious pop icon and "Threepenny Opera": the raw aggression of Brecht can indeed overlap with the outlaw pose in contemporary rock.

But this idea, like the evening's other sincere intentions, is fumbled in the execution. A plausible actor in the films "Plenty" and "Stormy Monday," Sting is a stiff onstage. He seems to hope that a large cane and a smug, insistent pout will somehow convey the menace of a character who is a murderer, rapist, thief and arsonist — Brecht's idea of a ruthless capitalist. Not that the star's Macheath should be put on the gallows as the scapegoat for all the production's ills. So tepid is the level of performance throughout the company that one must wonder if another director might have coaxed more out of Sting and everyone else.

The director at hand is John Dexter, whose past forays into epic theater ("M. Butterfly") and Brecht-Weill (the Metropolitan Opera's "Mahagonny") would seem to make him ideal for "Threepenny Opera." Like Richard Foreman, who staged the blistering 1976 revival with Raul Julia, he would rather be faithful to original Brechtian practice than to the 1954 Marc Blitzstein "Threepenny" adaptation that ran Off Broadway for seven years.

Mr. Dexter uses an unbowdlerized (if not uncut) translation by Michael Feingold that restores Brecht's scatology and the complete, correctly ordered score. Jocelyn Herbert's scenic rendition of lowlife Victorian London — a few scraps of wood that might have been left out in the rain — leaves acres of room to expose the stage's machinery. The lighting is harsh and white, the projected scene titles all in place. Far from trying to tart up "Threepenny Opera" for Broadway, Mr. Dexter makes the show look so spartan that by contrast "Our Town" might seem decadent.

•

Even so, the outward faithfulness to Brechtian alienation does not pay off, because the trappings are never harnessed to the theatrical energy that might animate Brecht's lacerating view of a bourgeois hell in which hypocrisy is the daily bread. The scalding style and passion required in the acting and music are absent. There's no visual focus to the staging, no Hogarthian imaginative verve to enliven the drab palette of Ms. Herbert's sets and costumes. Foolproof sequences pass without the bite of black humor: the Peachums' entrepreneurial display of the five pitiful beggars' costumes their employees use for cadging money from the guilty rich; Macheath and Polly's wedding amid posh stolen furnishings; the tango reunion of Macheath and the prostitute Jenny. Julius Rudel's onstage band, sitting on top of the squat and cluttered playing area, renders the familiar orchestrations with a lassitude more appropriate to a hotel-lobby tea service than a Weimar cabaret.

It says much about this production that the neighboring "Sweeney Todd," a musical influenced by Weill and Brecht that shares the setting of

"Threepenny Opera" but not its rigorous banishment of sentimentality, comes across as a more vitriolic assault on capitalism's inequities. Lacking any clear line of attack or variations in pace, Mr. Dexter's staging often seems to leave his cast milling about aimlessly waiting for the next cue.

One never has the sense of a company unified in its effort to put across a show and its acidic ideology. Each performer occupies a different, yet equally inappropriate, theatrical universe, from Kim Criswell's campy Lucy to Larry Marshall's deadly earnest Tiger Brown to Suzanne Douglas's saccharine Jenny, who elocutes the nihilistic "Solomon Song" as if she were instructing the audience in "Getting to Know You."

At least some drama is provided by the predicament of Nancy Ringham, an understudy abruptly asked to fill in for Maureen McGovern, whose vocal ailments required her to vacate the role of Polly for several weeks. But here, as when she was similarly elevated to stardom on the opening-night eve of the last Rex Harrison revival of "My Fair Lady," Ms. Ringham proves simply a competent ingénue.

Not that a Stratas or a Lenya might have made a difference. The company's experienced Brecht-Weill hands, Alvin Epstein and Georgia Brown as the Peachums, seem as tired and mechanical as the others, as if *this* "Threepenny" had been running for seven years. (They might at least bother to look at each other.) Though Ethyl Eichelberger's bald head and wicked scowl do make the Ballad Singer an arresting George Grosz caricature, he, too, wears out his early welcome by pursuing his shtick to unchecked, self-indulgent excess in the hours to come.

It is when Mr. Eichelberger first greets the audience that Mr. Dexter's production makes its one stab at a statement: he announces that we are to see a "new American version" of the piece "played by the poorest of the poor for an audience of their own." In the English-accented staging that follows, this conceit is more or less forgotten until a post-curtain-call coda, in which chorus members, apparently representing the homeless of New York, bed down for the night in cardboard boxes.

These "homeless" look more like hippies from "Hair" than the battered souls visible just outside the theater; they might well have received their ersatz beggars' costumes from the hypocritical Peachums. And who exactly are the hypocrites here? The creators of this "Threepenny Opera" aren't helping the poor by dragging them on clownishly to provide a boffo finale to a torpid show; like the Peachums, they are merely exploiting the poor to serve their own commercial enterprise. Not for the first time does Brecht get the last — and, in this production, the only — laugh.

1989 N 6, C13:4

Modern Types

CLOSER THAN EVER, directed by Richard Maltby Jr.; conceived and co-directed by Steven Scott Smith; lyrics by Mr. Maltby; music by David Shire; musical direction and additional vocal arrangements by Patrick Scott Brady; musical staging by Marcia Milgrom Dodge; scenery, Philipp Jung; costumes, Jess Goldstein, lighting, Natasha Katz. Presented by Janet Brenner, Michael Gill and Daryl Roth. At the Cherry Lane Theater, 38 Commerce Street.

WITH: Brent Barrett, Sally Mayes, Richard Muenz and Lynne Wintersteller.

By LAURIE WINER

"Closer Than Ever," a revue of songs by David Shire and Richard Maltby Jr. that opened last night at the Cherry Lane Theater, offers a gallery of contemporary people struggling with the usual dilemmas. They're all here: men who can't commit to women, women who wish they could do without men, two-career couples who are too busy to stay home with the baby when the au pair gets sick. After spending an evening with them, however, they immediately fade, like faces we've encountered at a cocktail party and can only dimly remember the next day.

Mr. Maltby and Mr. Shire are a team in search of a book musical. When focused tightly on a subject, as in their charming 1983 Broadway collaboration "Baby," they use wit and musical brio to illuminate extraordinary terrors and joys in ordinary lives. By contrast, with no theme to hold the evening together, their tunes rarely rise above the pleasantly boring. If you need a song to remind you of the ubiquitousness of health clubs or Muzak in elevators, this is the revue for you.

The four cast members are not required to provide between-song patter or informative stories about the authors' 30-odd years together. Each song they deliver is a self-contained story in a familiar setting. The show's best song gives a character her due with a refreshing absence of buzzwords. In "Miss Byrd," (first heard at the Manhattan Theater Club's song-and-sketch revue "Urban Blight"), a prim real estate agent squirms in her swivel chair as she relives a sexual encounter of "not more than 20 minutes ago" with the superintendent in a basement apartment that she should have been busy renting. Played by the endearing Sally Mayes, Miss Byrd is dizzy with her secret.

More often than not, though, the characters in "Closer Than Ever" are only too willing to share their dreams and woes, however banal. True to its title, "Like a Baby," for example, is an icky emotional outpouring with a Top 40-style lyric:

Like a baby
I'm hungry till you feed me
I just want you to need me
Be here and be mine.

Two rather dreary songs, "Patterns," which was cut from "Baby," and "Life Story," seem almost dutiful in their depiction of middle-aged women who contemplate their mildly disappointing lives.

Mr. Shire's melodies range from the cool jazz of "Back on Base" (in which Ms. Mayes seduces the on-stage bass player with some sultry moves that might have been borrowed from Jerome Robbins's "Mr. Monotony") to the jittery, Sondheimesque opening number, "Doors." In its exhortation to bravely face life's scariest minefields, "Doors" recalls Mr. Sondheim's more richly worded "Into the Woods."

Wide-eyed and unguarded, Ms. Mayes brings a nervous individuality to the proceedings and she's also given the best songs. Brent Barrett, Richard Muenz and Lynne Wintersteller, though good singers, do not rescue their underimagined characters from blandness. It's a relief when Ms. Mayes hops on the piano and engages the pianist, Patrick Scott

Brady, in a witty duet for a high-strung woman and her unfocused former boyfriend.

Played against Philipp Jung's airy, cloud-filled backdrop, Mr. Maltby's staging is simple and efficient. To paraphrase one of Mr. Maltby's characters and Gertrude Stein, one wishes there was more there there.

1989 N 7, C19:1

Stomping at The Baling Plant

THE WIDOW'S BLIND DATE, written and directed by Israel Horovitz; scenery by Edward Gianfrancesco; lighting by Craig Evans; costumes by Janet Irving; fight sequences, B. H. Barry; production stage manager, Crystal Huntington. Presented by David Bulasky, Barbara Darwall and Peter von Mayrhauser. At the Circle in the Square Downtown, 159 Bleecker Street, between Thompson and Sullivan Streets.

George Ferguson	Tom Bloom
Archie Crisp	Paul O'Brien
Margy Burke	Christine Estabrook

By LAURIE WINER

At "The Widow's Blind Date," the Israel Horovitz play that opened last night at the Circle in the Square Downtown, audiences may wonder what they're seeing: is this an attempt to explore the deepest roots and causes of misogyny, or a gratuitously violent and sexually titillating revenge fantasy in the manner of an early Charles Bronson movie?

Margy, a widowed New York University English professor, returns to her working-class hometown in Massachusetts as her brother lies dying in a local hospital. But instead of keeping vigil at her brother's side, she has made a date with George, a friend from high school, who works, as he has since he was 12, tying and pressing huge stacks of paper in a baling plant run by his uncle.

As they await Margy's arrival, George and his buddy, Archie, drink Budweiser out of cans. Though in their late 30's, they cling to teen-age male bonding rituals, reviewing events from high school (there's an ominous reference to an incident that took place at a senior dance beach party) and appraising Margy's sexual assets and liabilities as they imagine what her life might be like since she moved away.

George is a lumpish philosopher, dispensing thoughtful gems like "Death is a part of life." With his high-pitched giggle and ferretlike grin, Archie is the more menacing of the two. When he delivers a monologue about the agony of watching his dog die — it took 4 hours and 22 minutes — the audience might think it's getting a glimpse into the pain of a lonely loser, but Mr. Horovitz has something else in mind.

Margy arrives, and the pieces start to come together. While the men hope that the reunion will provide a sexual payoff for one or both of them, Margy immediately disarms them and keeps them guessing. One moment she's icy and stern, the next warm; one moment she's flirtatious, the next she's flaunting her superior education (she answers a question with a snappish, "The antecedent to the pronoun is not exactly clear, Archie").

In the first hint of the melodrama to come, Margy reveals that she once drove a 1951 powder-blue Studebaker, the very car that ran down Archie's poor dead mutt. After that, events begin to spin out of control. By then no

one should be surprised to learn that on the night of the beach party Margy was the 17-year-old victim of a gang rape in which Archie and George participated.

The playwright does his most sophisticated work in dramatizing the foundation of the men's friendship. In a world that's never given them a foothold, George and Archie form a bond that they sense might somehow empower them. Archie, like Murph in Mr. Horovitz's 1968 play, "The Indian Wants the Bronx," initiates the violence. George, like the earlier play's Joey, is the more sensitive follower, desperate to be loved, who dissolves in tears at the first hint of savagery, but who is unable to stop himself from joining in.

Under Mr. Horovitz's direction, the actors cannot breathe life into the events that unfold. Even B. H. Barry's fight choreography looks phony, though Edward Gianfrancesco's set, with its dingy brick walls, low-hanging lamps and huge bundles of paper, makes an ideal stomping ground.

Tom Bloom is undistinguished in the role of George, the play's least intelligent but most emotionally complicated character. Paul O'Brien makes Archie truly creepy. Christine Estabrook emphasizes Margy's smug side, making her less sympathetic than she should be.

In the play's final and most incredible moment, Mr. Horovitz asks us to believe that Margy masterminded the evening's bloody outcome, and that she's leaving to finish off the other men who violated her. When she screams, "I would very much like to watch you suffer and die," you might wonder if next season will bring a scary Horovitz sequel: "The Widow's Blind Date, Part II: The Revenge Continues."

1989 N 8, C23:1

Correction

A theater review on Wednesday about the Israel Horovitz play "The Widow's Blind Date" reversed the descriptions of the personalities of the two male characters. George (played by Tom Bloom) is the more menacing character with the high-pitched giggle and ferretlike grin who starts the violence. Archie (played by Paul O'-Brien) is the sensitive one who dissolves in tears at the first hint of savagery but is unable to keep from joining it.

1989 N 14, A3:2

A Celebration of Romance And Bravura on the Ice

By ANNA KISSELGOFF

The growth of skating as an art form was manifest again on Monday night in "Skating for Life — A Celebration of Champions," a benefit performance that included Olympic champions as disparate in style as John Curry and Scott Hamilton. An unexpected treat was a rare appearance by Oleg and Ludmilla Protopopov, Soviet defectors who were Olympic gold medalists in 1964 and 1968.

The performance, which included new choreography, was a benefit for AIDS victims and AIDS support groups, organized by the Design Industries Foundation for AIDS, which is made up of professionals in the fashion, textile, interior design and related fields. The 24 skaters scooted out on a makeshift rectangular rink in the New York State Armory at Lexington Avenue and 26th Street. A winter wonderland effect to go with the ice was provided by white cutouts of Christmas trees, complete with electric lights.

Although conventional skating moves were common among the performers, as in the case of Lisa-Marie Allen, an American who led off, there was also a fine creative edge among others.

•

Mr. Curry, a Briton who was a 1976 Olympic gold medalist and who has done more than anyone to promote the artistic side of skating, was seen in two atypical numbers. In the first, he appeared — hair slicked back and all in black — like a futuristic anti-Pierrot with a touch of Marcel Marceau. Trapped inside an invisible box, he escaped to bounce or throw an equally invisible balloon. The jazz music was a surprise but the solo had the subtlety and wistfulness expected from Mr. Curry.

It was a bigger surprise later to see him in a romantic duet with Judy Blumberg, an American national champion who usually performs with her ice-dance partner, Michael Seibert.

The image of Mr. Curry as the epitome of a ballroom dancer is new. But unwinding in and out of embraces, he and Miss Blumberg, a first-rate dramatic skater, made for a picture in tenderness.

JoJo Starbuck and Ken Shelley, an ever-popular American pair, were a perfect prom couple — he in a 1950's white dinner jacket and glasses, she a vision of loveliness in pink chiffon.

Characterization was pushed even further by Robin Cousins, affecting casualness with a hands-in-the-pockets, Gene Kelly style but actually offering daredevil bravura, and Mr. Hamilton as the all-American kid in a virtuosic duet with a chair. Both were magnificent showstoppers. Toller Cranston, the Canadian Rudolf Nureyev of the ice, was his marvelous moody, idiosyncratic self in a solo.

The Protopopovs, in pale blue, may no longer be in their prime. Nevertheless they demonstrated the balletic style they pioneered in a simple flowing duet in which their unity of line was remarkably striking.

The duos known as pairs skaters in competitions were all spectacular. The Americans included Lea Ann Miller and Bill Fauver in a witty calypso number and Tai Babilonia and Randy Gardner in a sensual adagio act. The Canadians included Barbara Underhill and Paul Martini in a dream sequence and Tracy Wilson and Robert McCall as a flapper and drunk during Prohibition.

Other soloists were Rosalynn Sumners, Caryn Kadavy, Denise Biellmann, Elizabeth Manley and the young Katherine Healy, whose high leg extensions and purity infused her gracious glide through "The Rose Adagio" of "The Sleeping Beauty."

1989 N 8, C25:1

Methods Of Destruction

MOUNTAIN LANGUAGE and THE BIRTHDAY PARTY, by Harold Pinter; directed by Carey Perloff; scenic design by Loy Arcenas; costume design by Gabriel Berry; lighting design by Beverly Emmons; sound design by Daniel Moses Schreier; music for "Mountain Language" by Wayne Horvitz; production stage manager, Richard Hester. Presented by CSC Theater, 136 East 13th Street.

MOUNTAIN LANGUAGE

Elderly Woman	Jean Stapleton
Young Woman	Wendy Makkena
Sergeant	Richard Riehle
Officer	David Strathairn
Prisoner	Peter Riegert
Guard	Miguel Perez
Second Guard	Thomas Delling

THE BIRTHDAY PARTY

Petey	Bill Moor
Meg	Jean Stapleton
Stanley	David Strathairn
Lulu	Wendy Makkena
Goldberg	Peter Riegert
McCann	Richard Riehle

By FRANK RICH

Though written three decades apart, Harold Pinter's first full-length work, the 1958 "Birthday Party," and his latest play, the 20-minute "Mountain Language," build to the same grotesque conclusion: a defenseless man is reduced to a quivering, speechless wreck by properly dressed thugs serving an unnamed organization. Mr. Pinter hasn't changed that much in 30 years, but neither has the world around him. This is still a century in which terror can arrive with a stranger's knock at the door. The silence that follows — the deadly silence of abject fear — is the ultimate Pinter pause.

Carey Perloff, the artistic director of the Classic Stage Company, has performed a useful service by pairing these two plays, allowing the audience to see the continuity of the playwright's career in a single night. One wishes only that Ms. Perloff had chosen a stronger early Pinter play to achieve this mission (like "The Hothouse" or "The Caretaker") or had at least directed the one she did choose with a harder edge. After the opening jolt of "Mountain Language," a slack "Birthday Party" turns the double bill's thematic parallels into an academic exercise.

•

Even "Mountain Language" must be approached with the right attitude. Those who go with grand expectations of "the new Pinter play" should recall that the last new Pinter play was also a one-act work about state terrorism, the 1984 "One for the Road." More a political activist than an active dramatist in recent years, Mr. Pinter has again written a sketch whose unobjectionable championship of human rights is amplified by the tough wit of his voice. Such is the effectiveness of "Mountain Language" that one wishes Mr. Pinter might serve his cause with a major, more easily disseminated work.

The current play consists of four scenes, strobe flashes of totalitarian cruelty, in which women visit a political prison and confront the military guards who incarcerate their husbands and sons. "Mountain Language" could take place anywhere and everywhere freedom is denied. What makes the landscape quintessentially Mr. Pinter's is the author's skill at compressing so much black laughter and blacker action into so few words.

•

He does so, as usual, by working between the lines. When an elderly woman is mauled by an attack dog, a Gestapo-like bureaucrat is concerned only with the official procedure that requires the listing of the dog's name. A younger woman sent through a wrong door by mistake, discovers her hooded husband in mid-torture and soon learns, again in offhand bureaucratese, just what gruesome price she must pay to save him.

Throughout the play, language is the oppressors' weapon of choice. The fascist captors speak in lies, scatology and double talk; the enemies of the state find their language has been declared dead and outlawed altogether. Only the victims' thoughts — conveyed on tape — can escape the reach of the thought police.

While Ms. Perloff does not have access to Michael Gambon, Eileen Atkins and the other stars available to Mr. Pinter in the play's National Theater debut in London last year, her lucid production does not require them. The stark low-key staging is marred only by the sentimental use of music at play's end. The outstanding performance comes from Jean Stapleton, who fleshes out the nearly wordless role of a suffering mother with an unflinching gaze of pain and bereavement.

•

Ms. Stapleton is also first-rate in "The Birthday Party," in which she brings supreme comic obtuseness to Meg, the pathetic proprietor of a shabby seaside boarding house whose only lodger, Stanley (David Strathairn), is inexorably destroyed by two sinister visitors, Goldberg (Peter Riegert) and McCann (Richard Riehle). Oblivious to the malevolent events around her, and even to the implications of her own confused maternal and sexual impulses, Ms. Stapleton turns Meg into an absurdist creation more reminiscent of Ruth White, her memorable predecessor in this role on Broadway in 1967, than her broadly drawn Edith Bunker. Ms. Stapleton's Meg is the kind of spiritually bankrupt modern survivor who makes one question the value of survival.

•

The trouble is that Meg's bad taste — accentuated by tacky period pop songs, furnishings and costumes — becomes the animus of the play, as if Mr. Pinter were Joe Orton, spoofing middle-class kitsch for wicked farcical ends. But "The Birthday Party" isn't as funny or sociologically specific as Ms. Perloff seems to think it is. Like "Mountain Language," its vicious cat-and-mouse games of destruction could be set in any Kafkaesque environment and are played for keeps.

Paula Court

Jean Stapleton in Harold Pinter's "Mountain Language."

While Mr. Riegert and Mr. Strathairn, both fine actors, always deliver their characters' legitimate gags, they rarely delineate the danger and anxiety of a violent struggle between the hunter and the hunted. In this "Birthday Party," the words are all there, but the Pinter language, the eternal terror beneath the words, seems to have been outlawed.

1989 N 9, C21:3

A Revolution Ends, Not With a Bang

THE TALENTED TENTH, by Richard Wesley; directed by M. Neema Barnette; scenery by Charles McClennahan; costumes by Alvin B. Perry; lighting by Anne Militello; sound by James Mtume; production stage manager, Diane Ward. Presented by Manhattan Theater Club, Stage I at City Center. At 131 West 55th Street.

Father/Sam Griggs	Graham Brown
Bernard	Richard Lawson
Pam	Marie Thomas
Marvin	Richard Gant
Rowena	LaTanya Richardson
Irene	Elain Graham
Ron	Rony Clanton
Tanya	Lorraine Toussaint

By MEL GUSSOW

"The talented tenth," in W. E. B. Du Bois's memorable phrase, were those exceptional blacks who were destined to save their people from "contamination and death." In Richard Wesley's ambitious, unwieldy new play, "The Talented Tenth," his present-day equivalents of this leadership class are black urban professionals obsessively dedicated to their own self-interest.

Now in their early 40's, they are far more concerned about not being trapped in middle management than they are about reawakening their youthful idealism. The attitude of the playwright is both cynical and recriminatory: this is how the black revolution ends, not with a bang, but with "buppies."

For much of the play, which opened last night at the Manhattan Theater Club, the intention is comic. With acerbic wit, Mr. Wesley is out to assail what V. S. Naipaul referred to as "the mimic men." In this case, it is American blacks emulating the worst of their white countrymen, fired by an almost tangible craving for the assets of economic advantage.

The six principal characters, three married couples who have been best friends since their days at Howard University in the early 1960's, luxuriate on the beach in Jamaica and compare condos and stock options while planning future holidays in Abidjan. Mr. Wesley is scalpel-sharp in his satire of this highly selective, single-minded group.

•

It is when the author views the terrain with a more serious purpose that the play moves into troubled and banal waters. The central character, Bernard, once the best of Howard University's brightest, has allowed his radical zeal and his personal relationships to deteriorate during years of compromise as a broadcasting executive. Mr. Wesley tries to suggest that Bernard can still carry a banner in the army of Du Bois.

Trying to convert Bernard's burnout into tragedy, Mr. Wesley over-reaches, as in by the protagonist's recitation of the lineage of his legacy (the names of his teachers and of

their teachers) and a long aside about a failed revolutionary idol. Eventually, Mr. Wesley seems reluctant to bring his play to a conclusion and offers several alternative endings.

While Bernard's sudden re-emergence as an activist is not persuasive, other characters are rendered with remarkable vividness. At its strongest, the play opens the audience's eyes to a many-layered, contradictory world, a kind of black "Big Chill" of life's winners and love's losers. The people evoked range from a paragon of early black capitalism who lived his life "by everyone's expectations but his own" to a fast-climbing young black journalist whose expectations are *only* her own.

Beginning with his early plays ("The Past Is the Past," "The Last Street Play"), Mr. Wesley has had a natural gift for expansive storytelling, one reason why his long employment as a Hollywood screenwriter has been a loss for the theater. On his return, he reveals that his narrative skills are undiminished, as is his keen sense of historical perspective.

He demonstrates this in fascinating chronicles about high times at Howard, marching to Montgomery with Martin Luther King and the explosive growth of a black business class. And in one urban epiphany, Bernard elucidates his loss of empathy for the disadvantaged. One of these stories — about Bernard's abandonment of a Howard revolutionary named Habiba, who died fighting in Angola — eventually acquires dramatic prominence. Habiba is the lingering symbol of Bernard's lost illusions.

Gerry Goodstein

Richard Lawson in "The Talented Tenth" at City Center.

The most perceptive scene is not Bernard's soul-searching, nor the climactic — and obvious — confrontations with his wife and his mistress, but an earlier encounter in a health club between his wife (Marie Thomas) and a friend (LaTanya Richardson) in which they accept the chasm that has always existed between them — one of skin tone, social background and genealogy. There is an intimacy in this scene that is too often lacking in other aspects of the play.

With the play having gone through a workshop last season, one would have expected it to have a greater cohesiveness. For that, the director M. Neema Barnette bears a partial responsibility, as she does for the drab scenic design.

The actors are allied in delivering consanguine performances. With his

intelligent concern, Richard Lawson almost succeeds in making the audience care about Bernard's angst. Ms. Thomas and Lorraine Toussaint each have a forceful presence as wife and mistress, and there is helpful work by Rony Clanton, Elain Graham, Graham Brown and Richard Gant. Ms. Richardson gives a striking performance as Mr. Gant's outspoken, shrewd wife. It is she who offers the playwright's most telling observation about his "Talented Tenth": the problem is not so much the pain that others cause black people, but "the pain we cause ourselves."

1989 N 10, C3:1

New York Neverland

PRINCE OF CENTRAL PARK, by Evan H. Rhodes; directed and choreographed by Tony Tanner; music by Don Sebesky; lyrics by Gloria Nissenson; scenery and costumes by Michael Bottari and Ronald Case; lighting by Norman Coates; musical direction by Joel Silberman; production stage manager, Steven Ehrenberg. Presented by Abe Hirschfeld and Jan McArt. Karen Poindexter, executive producer; Belle M. Deitch, associate producer. At the Belasco Theater, 111 West 44th Street.

Margie Miller	Jo Anne Worley
Jay-Jay	Richard H. Blake
Elmo	Anthony Galde
Sally	Chris Callen

WITH: Adrian Bailey, Jody Keith Barrie, Stephen Bourneuf, Terry Eno, Anne-Marie Gerard, Ruth Gottschall, Sko, Marilyn Hudgins, Terry Iten, Jason Ma, Bonnie Perlman, Sel Vitella, Alice Yearsley

By FRANK RICH

"Prince of Central Park," the new musical at the Belasco, is a numbing evening of such guileless amateurism that it will probably have a future as a Harvard Business School case study, whatever its fate in the annals of drama. Even modest Broadway shows like this cost more money than the gross national product of some third world nations. People put up this money. As long as there are people as gullible as the sponsors of "Prince of Central Park," the theater need never fear for its survival.

The author of the book is Evan H. Rhodes, whose novel of the same title also served as the basis for a Ruth Gordon made-for-television movie. He tells the "Harold and Maude"-ish story of Jay-Jay (Richard H. Blake), a 12-year-old foster-home runaway who lives by his wits in a tree house in Central Park until he encounters Margie Miller (Jo Anne Worley), a jogger of late middle-age who has just lost her husband to a younger woman and her adult daughter to the career track.

Since Jay-Jay and Margie must meet cute — through chalk messages left on a pristine park bench — Act I is all exposition. In Act II, Jay-Jay and Margie bravely overcome outmoded legal obstacles and moral attitudes to get married. They adopt five children, two of whom become the first sibling astronauts and together head a successful manned space mission to Pluto.

Actually, I am lying. Something else entirely happens in Act II. But I assure you that my version is more interesting.

The soft rock score, by Don Sebesky, is insistently cheery even when muggers are singing about ripping off little old ladies; the tunes don't so much linger in the mind as pound it

senseless. Though in one number ("Zap") Gloria Nissenson's lyrics make nearly as much use of a four-letter synonym for excrement as does "Threepenny Opera," her more typical phrases deal with "turning a new leaf," "setting myself free," "growing my dreams" and discovering that "here's where I belong." Tony Tanner's choreography doesn't just resemble aerobics. It *is* aerobics.

And the jokes? On her first entrance, Ms. Worley cups both breasts and says, "Gravity, gravity, what did I ever do to you?" Shortly after that she wishes to a star that her estranged husband's penis will "fall off in bed tonight." And to think that family entertainment had begun to appear a lost cause in the American musical.

Martha Swope

Jo Anne Worley in "Prince of Central Park," at the Belasco Theater.

The performances are nothing if not strenuous. The young Mr. Blake belts out every song mechanically and interchangeably, seeming less like a refugee of the streets than an aging Mouseketeer. Wearing a series of colored jogger headbands and novelty T-shirts, Ms. Worley plunges through the show like a Mack truck, mowing down everything before her with a personality undiminished in bulk or pitch since the halcyon days of "Laugh-In." Among the supporting players, a dancer named Alice Yearsley proves to be the production's entire store of grace and style. Though her roles are several and small, she never fails to carve out her own delicate space from the crass spectacle around her.

Much of that spectacle has to do with celebrating the city of New York. This would be swell if one actually believed that anyone connected with "Prince of Central Park" had spent much time in the city lately. (The show originated in south Florida, and there are a few gratuitous but knowing jokes about "retirement villages.")

Among the Manhattanites onstage are a friendly park ranger out of a Smokey Bear promotional campaign, an adorably cuckoo bag lady and, for a dash of malevolence, a gang of well-scrubbed crack dealers whose ethnic makeup is so demographically balanced that they might have first convened at the United Nations. But the biggest unintentional laugh for a New York audience arrives when Ms. Worley ventures into Bloomingdale's and is immediately welcomed by a kindly silver-haired saleswoman who offers her complete undivided attention.

"Prince of Central Park" also has a serious obsession with Tavern on the Green, whose name is dragged into nearly every scene before and after serving as a setting for a dance number. Given the vehicle for these insistent plugs, it's hard to know whether the restaurant should consider itself the beneficiary of free advertising or the victim of a dissatisfied customer's personal vendetta.

1989 N 10, C3:1

Thwarted Sexuality And Devious Curves

A DANCE LESSON, by David Wiltse, directed by Gordon Edelstein; set design by Hugh Landwehr; costume design by David Murin; lighting design by Pat Collins; production stage manager, Ruth M. Feldman. Presented by the Long Wharf Theater, Arvin Brown, artistic director; M. Edgar Rosenblum, executive director. At the Long Wharf, Stage II, New Haven.

Jason	Eric Conger
Dan Hauser	John Cunningham
Susan Hauser	Debra Mooney
Jay Hauser	Josh Charles
Jack Stone	Quentin O'Brien
Smitty	Rob Kramer

By MEL GUSSOW
Special to The New York Times

NEW HAVEN, Nov. 7 — "A Dance Lesson," by David Wiltse, begins as a gently amusing genre piece about an average Nebraska family in the mid-1950's. As the work unfolds (at the Long Wharf Theater's Stage II), it is evident that the author has something more sobering in mind — a bitterly regretful play dealing with guilt and retribution.

Mr. Wiltse is concerned with individual small-mindedness and with a community's inability to allow for the existence of any aberrant or even eccentric behavior. In the play, a son, discovering incriminating truths about his supposedly upright father, has to come to terms with his own responsibility in shattering his parents' marriage.

There are moments of irresolution in the writing and a superimposed framework that leaves the play less than fully dramatized. As in "The Glass Menagerie," a narrator reflects on his distant family trauma. Where Tennessee Williams allowed his play to be enveloped by its characters, Mr. Wiltse holds too firmly to his narrator as commentator and observer.

Some of the narrator's comments — his attempt, in effect, to rewrite family history and to warn his younger incarnation against his harmful acts — give the play a meaningful subtext. But "A Dance Lesson" is strongest when narration subsides and scenes are played out to their wounding conclusion.

At first, the wife (Debra Mooney), repressed but still hopeful about having a career of her own on a local radio station, is flattered by the attentions of a handsome young neighbor (Quentin O'Brien). To her, he is an engaging free spirit and a welcome contrast to the stuffiness of the community. Other characters, beginning with her son, are suspicious of his motives. Soon the plot is filled with devious curves involving thwarted sexuality, especially that of the father (John Cunningham), a prosecuting attorney who has a moralistic sense of propriety — and of self-denial. With a rotelike rigidity he hectors his son about improving his habits.

As the characters accrue complexity, points are missed. One definite oversight is the fact that the neighbor, the catalyst for all that occurs, is banished too early in the play. He is never allowed to justify himself and remains the single object of the narrator's animosity. The others are forgiven for their weaknesses, as, for example, when the son is finally able to accept the fallibility of his father.

•

Mr. Wiltse (the author of "Suggs" and "Doubles," and a novelist as well as a playwright) weaves an intriguing web around his characters and around the town itself. Increasingly, it starts to resemble an environment like that in the movie "Blue Velvet." Closed doors do not necessarily lead to concealment.

Under Gordon Edelstein's direction, the actors are well-orchestrated in a low-key manner. Though some of the events might lend themselves to melodrama, the focus is on the reality of the circumstances and the routine of family life.

Josh Charles and Rob Kramer, as the son and his best friend, convey the awkwardness of their age with deftness and humor; they never seem able to come to rest indoors. Mr. O'Brien enhances the neighbor with a certain sinister quality as he insinuates himself into several lives, and, in the central roles, Mr. Cunningham and Ms. Mooney create a sharp-edged portrait of a couple whose apparent compatability is itself a fabrication that derives from familiarity and necessity. "A Dance Lesson" becomes a discerning memory play in which each of the characters is entrapped by a confluence of time, place and morality.

1989 N 11, 16:5

Faithful Platonically

YOUR HANDSOME CAPTAIN, by Simone Schwarz-Bart; translated by Jessica Harris and Catherine Temerson; directed by Françoise Kourilsky; set and lighting by Watoku Ueno; costume design by Carol Ann Pelletier; composer, Henry Threadgill; stage manager, Rachel S. Levine; music performed by Wayne Kirton. Presented by Ubu Repertory Theater Inc. At 15 West 28th Street.

Wilnor	Reg E. Cathey
Marie-Ange	Sharon McGruder

By STEPHEN HOLDEN

"Your Handsome Captain," Simone Schwarz-Bart's drama at the Ubu Repertory Theater, is less a play than a poetic dialogue for two voices, one of which is only heard offstage in a simulation of a recording. The play is the first by Ms. Schwarz-Bart, a novelist from Guadeloupe. It relies primarily on its incantatory language and repetitious imagery to create a dreamlike portrait of a couple struggling to maintain a long-distance relationship. But the story is too vague and the characters too unformed for a deep chord to be struck.

•

For reasons that are only dimly explained, Wilnor (Reg E. Cathey), a young Haitian farmer, and his wife Marie-Ange (Sharon McGruder), live apart and communicate by audiocassette. Wilnor, who works in Guadeloupe, has been sending money along with his aural missives to his wife in Port-au-Prince through a friend. The bulk of the one-hour drama consists of Wilnor's playing of a long cassette message from Marie-Ange in which

she coyly discloses that she has been made pregnant by the go-between. Her excuse is that though unfaithful in body, she has remained true to Wilnor in spirit by keeping the image of him in her mind during lovemaking.

•

While taping his response, Wilnor experiences feelings that range from fury to forgiveness. In his correspondence he has been painting a much rosier picture of his life in Guadeloupe than the desolate stage setting reveals his true circumstances to be. For revenge, part of him would like to invent a fantastic story of opulence and sensuality. But another part would rather cling to the relationship, which seems to be the only thing he has.

Mr. Cathey, a lean, vocally expressive actor, does what he can to dramatize Wilnor's desperation. But both the situation and the language of the play, which Jessica Harris and Catherine Temerson has translated from French into English, are too abstract and fuzzy to carry much weight.

1989 N 12, 71:6

The Face of Jesus

HEAVEN ON EARTH, by Robert Schenkkan; directed by Mark Brokaw; setting by Edward T. Gianfrancesco; lighting by Craig Evans; costumes by Ellen McCartney; sound by Aural Fixation; production stage manager, Liz Small. Presented by WPA Theater, Kyle Renick, artistic director; Donna Lieberman, managing director. At 519 West 23d Street.

Bobby Jr.	Jay O. Sanders
Martha	Helen Stenborg
Jessie	Bobo Lewis
Miguel	Steven Rodriguez
John Morrow	Arthur Hanket
Tom Dooley	Raynor Scheine

By MEL GUSSOW

Robert Schenkkan's "Heaven on Earth" (at the WPA Theater) is a minor, miracle play of limited scope and familiar intent. Over the playwright's shoulder is the shadow of déjà vu, as he tells the story of how the tiny town of Waylon briefly became the Lourdes of West Texas.

An amiable grandmother (Helen Stenborg) quotes Scripture when she and her next-door neighbor are not working at a beauty salon that sounds like a local franchise of the "Steel Magnolia" chain. She shares her house and a failing second-hand appliance business with her prodigal grandson (Jay O. Sanders).

The discovery of a face resembling that of Jesus Christ on the side of an old freezer in the backyard alters their lives. Mr. Sanders awakens to an evangelical calling, which includes selling souvenirs. An epiphany will eventually follow but not before — in the play's single evocative scene — there is a moment of truth between the elderly woman and her grandson in which they talk about the accidental death of the young man's parents. In this and other scenes, Miss Stenborg is a sympathetic presence, but the moment fades as quickly as that heavenly image, which the audience never sees because the freezer is conveniently facing in the other direction.

•

The rest of the play is preoccupied with the neighbor's jokes (with topical references to her favorites on television) and by a bantering rivalry

Martha Swope Associates/Carol Rosegg

Salvation In Robert Schenkkan's "Heaven on Earth," Bobo Lewis plays the wisecracking neighbor of a grandmother who hopes to save the soul of a cynical young drifter in a Texas town.

between Mr. Sanders and a fellow night watchman at a Piggly Wiggly warehouse. One of the work's failings is its inability to convey the West Texas atmosphere despite the drawling accents (the word yes has two syllables). "Heaven on Earth" dwindles in authenticity next to plays by Larry L. King, Beth Henley and others.

The director Mark Brokaw has drawn capable performances from his cast, with particularly effective work by Mr. Sanders, Bobo Lewis (as the garrulous neighbor) and Miss Stenborg, who lends the grandmother a purity that is insufficiently represented in the text. Edward T. Gianfrancesco's set makes the family yard look like a cluttered tag sale, which is an appropriate metaphor for this shopworn play.

1989 N 12, 71:5

Three Romances And Two Sports

HYDE PARK, by James Shirley; directed by Michael R. Fife; production stage manager, Elaine R. O'Donnell; set designer, Miguel Lopez-Castillo; lighting designer, Brian Aldous; costume designer, Austin Sanderson; original music composed by Raymond Benson. Presented by the Beacon Project Inc. At the Pelican Studio Theater, 750 Eighth Avenue, at 46th Street.

Trier	Marc F. Nohe
Lacy	Richard Falklen
Venture	Anthony John Lizzul
Lord Bonvile	Robert L. Rowe
Jenny, Runner, Milkmaid and Musician	Nina Minton
Page, Runner and Jockey	Jerry Priori
Rider	Warren Watson
Mistress Carol	Elizabeth Huffman
Mistress Bonavent	Leah Cartmell
Fairfield	Stuart Laurence
Bonavent	Richard Bourg
Julietta	Nancy Learmonth
Waiting Woman	Jaime Sheedy

By WILBORN HAMPTON

The period between the end of the Renaissance and the beginning of the Restoration has provided little more than a footnote in the history of the

English-speaking theater. Marlowe, Shakespeare and Jonson were gone, and in their place such playwrights as Richard Brome, William D'Avenant and James Shirley took over London's stages in the years just before the Puritans closed the theaters.

For the most part, their plays are but pale shadows of their Elizabethan forebears, and it is no accident that few of them have been staged in more than 300 years. Two summers ago the Royal Shakespeare Company mounted Shirley's 1632 comedy "Hyde Park" with success at the Swan Theater in Stratford-on-Avon, and now the Beacon Project is offering the same play in what is probably its American premiere.

"Hyde Park" is a sort of 17th-century soap opera, updated to 1912 in the Beacon production, spun out around three interwoven romances that treat on two of man's favorite sports — wenching and horse racing. Behind some weak puns and bawdy humor, the emphasis is on plot contrivance rather than characterization and the plot relies heavily on coincidence — misdirected missives, hidden identities and timely eavesdropping. To be sure, other playwrights, including Shakespeare, employ similar devices. But it is easier to suspend disbelief for a poet, and when it comes to poetry, Shirley was no

Patrick James Dougherty

Elizabeth Huffman in a scene from "Hyde Park."

Shakespeare. Both writers, for example, offer similar advice to scorned suitors on the virtue of patience. Shakespeare, in "Much Ado About Nothing," says: " 'Tis all men's office to speak patience/To those that wring under the load of sorrow." Shirley's rejected lover says simply, "Have patience, spleen."

Many of Shirley's characters, in fact, find antecedents in Shakespeare. In "Hyde Park," for example, Mistress Carol is a feisty flirt who would "rather hear tedious tales of Holinshed than talk of love" and who passes on the gifts of one admirer as her own token to another. And if Mistress Carol is a mirror of Beatrice in "Much Ado," then Fairfield stands in as her Benedict.

The director, Michael R. Fife, keeps the action moving at a brisk canter, and the Beacon's cast, at least in the main roles, coaxes some fun and humor from Shirley's comedy by virtue of sheer energy and enthusiasm. Elizabeth Huffman is a pert Mistress Carol, taunting in her disdain for her three suitors yet coy

when she finally succumbs to love. As Fairfield, Stuart Laurence presents both a lovesick wooer and a cunning courter who well understands that "what women are forbidden, they are mad to execute." Robert L. Rowe gives an accomplished performance as Lord Bonvile, a dashing nobleman who sets out to seduce a maiden and ends up married. Nancy Learmonth and Leah Cartmell, as Julietta and Mistress Bonavent, are charmers who would turn any gallant's eye.

1989 N 12, 73:1

Lodgers and Motion

GRAND HOTEL, book by Luther Davis; songs by Robert Wright and George Forrest; based on Vicki Baum's novel. Directed and choreographed by Tommy Tune; additional music and lyrics by Maury Yeston; orchestrations, Peter Matz; musical and vocal direction, Jack Lee; music supervision and additional music, Wally Harper; associate director, Bruce Lumpkin; setting, Tony Walton; costumes, Santo Loquasto; lighting, Jules Fisher. Presented by Martin Richards, Mary Lee Johnson, Sam Crothers, Sander Jacobs, Kenneth D. Greenblatt, Paramount Pictures, Jujamcyn Theaters, in association with Patty Grubman and Marvin A. Krauss. At the Martin Beck Theater, 302 West 45th Street.

Colonel Doctor Otternschlag .... John Wylie
The Countess and the Gigolo
        Yvonne Marceau and Pierre Dulaine
General Director Preysing .. Timothy Jerome
Flaemmchen .... Jane Krakowski
Otto Kringelein .... Michael Jeter
Raffaela .... Karen Akers
Elizaveta Grushinskaya Liliane Montevecchi
Felix von Gaigern .... David Carroll
With
  Jennifer Lee Andrews, Keith Crowningshield, Gerrit de Beer, David Elledge, Ben George, Henry Grossman, Rex D. Hays, Suzanne Henderson, David Jackson, Mitchell Jason, Ken Jennings, J. J. Jepson, Charles Mandracchia, Michel Moinot, Kathi Moss, Lynnette Perry, Hal Robinson, William Ryall, Bob Stillman, Danny Strayhorn, Walter Willison.

By FRANK RICH

The director and choreographer Tommy Tune may have the most extravagant imagination in the American musical theater right now, and there isn't a moment, or a square inch of stage space, that escapes its reach in "Grand Hotel." The musical at the Martin Beck Theater is an uninterrupted two hours of continuous movement, all dedicated to creating the tumultuous atmosphere of the setting: an opulent way station at a distant crossroads of history in Berlin — that of 1928. Think of a three-dimensional collage — or a giant Joseph Cornell box two tall stories high — filled with the smoky light, faded gilt fixtures, dirty secrets, lost mementos and ghostly people of its time and place. Then imagine someone shaking the whole thing up as if waves were tossing around the Titanic. That's Mr. Tune's "Grand Hotel."

•

Is that enough to make a musical? Not really, as it happens, but "Grand Hotel" should satisfy those with a boundless appetite for showmanship untethered to content. Visual craftsmanship doesn't get much more accomplished than this on Broadway. In a departure from the current fashion in theatrical spectaculars, Mr. Tune creates a world on stage without resorting to rococo naturalism or substituting money for creativity. Tony Walton's stunning set, in which an orchestra occupies the lofty second tier, is but a deep, dilapidated shell in which dreamy abstract imagery (strings of pearls floating inside

transparent structural pillars) stands in for a literal hotel floor plan. Santo Loquasto's costumes and Jules Fisher's lighting — equally brilliant evocations of Expressionism — don't try to wow the audience with Technicolor eruptions but instead hold to a dark crimson-to-sepia palette that suggests the vanished luxury pictured on frayed antique postcards and the fever dreams of a world on the brink of Depression and war.

Mr. Tune's restless manipulation of these resources is often inspired. In the opening number — a directorial tour de force to match the equivalent prologue, "Wilkommen," in Harold Prince's Weimar Berlin musical "Cabaret" — phalanxes of performers crisscross the stage in ever-changing configurations, the characters individually singing of their lots, until finally the audience sees the panorama of lives, upstairs and down, intersecting throughout the vast hotel.

•

Though the effect is that of cinematic crosscutting, there's never an intrusion of scenic machinery to yank the characters about. "Grand Hotel" finds its kaleidoscopic activity and churning pace in the constant rearrangement of the dozens of straight-backed chairs that are the set's dominant furnishing, or in the sudden appearance of a quartet of desperate phone callers in a cacophonous downstage tableau, or in the hallucinatory fragments of period dance steps along the shadowy periphery of main events. As in Mr. Tune's "Nine," the large cast is omnipresent and usually on the run. So dense is the atmosphere that finally it can be stilled only by eradication — an effect Mr. Tune accomplishes in the coup de théâtre that brings the evening to a close.

Even then, one remains haunted by this show's imagery. One does, however, forget nearly everything else. "Grand Hotel" never delivers those other, conventional elements one might want in a musical — attractive songs, characters to care about, an exciting cast. Nor does it work up the good cry achieved by the all-star 1932 M-G-M film. This "Grand Hotel" impresses the audience without engaging it, and, when the titillating dramatic promises of the opening sequence lead nowhere, monotony and impatience set in. One would have to go back past "Nine" to Michael Bennett's "Ballroom" to find a Broadway musical with so large a discrepancy between the mediocre quality of the material and the flair of its presentation.

Martha Swope

Jane Krakowski and Michael Jeter in "Grand Hotel."

The first instinct might be to blame the book, which in this case is not an adaptation of the Hollywood "Grand Hotel," but of the Vicky Baum novel that was its source. Yet the author, Luther Davis, and the unbilled book doctor, Peter Stone, have done an efficient, clever job of compressing a complicated narrative into a scenario that recalls the movie's solid structure while altering some of its details. What's missing is the flesh that, in a musical, must be filled in by songs and performances.

A stage kaleidoscope of intersecting and transient lives.

Mr. Tune is presumably responsible for the evening's central failing, the miscasting of the doomed lovers at its center. Liliane Montevecchi, as a "dying swan" of a ballerina facing the end of her career, is unconvincing in or out of a tutu as a "great artist" of transparent vulnerability; her thin physique and Russian character name do not camouflage the temperament of a brassy French cabaret chanteuse. While David Carroll, as a count reduced to cat burglary, has a beautiful voice, his silver cigarette case seems more aristocratic and Continental than its owner. One doesn't have to make invidious comparisons to Greta Garbo and John Barrymore to see that the romantic and sexual chemistry between their stage heirs is nil.

Most of the other principals are only adequate: Jane Krakowski as a secretary who fantasizes about sleeping her way to Hollywood stardom, Timothy Jerome as a business tycoon in crisis, John Wylie as a bitter World War I veteran. As Ms. Montevecchi's devoted confidante, Karen Akers could pass as a dark-haired impersonator of Carol Channing's Lorelei Lee — with height, kewpie-doll makeup and bangs to match. But when Ms. Akers sings it's as if Lorelei Lee were on Quaaludes: taking her catch-in-the-throat vocal style to a fetishistic extreme, Ms. Akers slurs every lyric into unintelligibility. Were she not dressed as a man, even the love she feels for the ballerina would dare not speak its name.

•

Perhaps a stronger score would have buoyed the acting. One can see what might have been when Michael Jeter, as the dying clerk Otto Kringelein on a last fling, is given a musical number that expresses a character's emotion. Celebrating his liberation from clerkdom into high living by stepping out, Mr. Jeter lets loose like a human top gyrating out of control — literally breaking out of his past into a new existence. Fine as the performer is, it is because a song and choreography for once dramatize a character dynamically that this song is touching as the evening's others are not.

Though emphatically arranged (by Peter Matz and Wally Harper) and conducted (by Jack Lee), the rest of the score leaves the characters stranded in banalities. The only catchy melody is a cabaret number, "le jazz hot" style, for a dance team (David Jackson and Danny Strayhorn), and it doesn't build, even choreographically, as similar turns did in Mr. Tune's "My One and Only." While that number is by Robert Wright and George Forrest ("Kismet"), many others are by Maury Yeston ("Nine"). Mr. Yeston could not resist writing a solo for Ms. Montevecchi titled "Bonjour Amour," and his big love ballad may give Andrew Lloyd Webber his first opportunity to accuse another songwriter of being derivative.

Mr. Tune also has his odd derivative moments. When he uses a pair of ballroom bolero dancers as metaphors for love and death or a chorus of advancing scullery workers to symbolize proletarian rage, he skirts the conceits of the Prince musicals "Follies" and "Sweeney Todd." Like the book's allusions to growing anti-Semitism or ponderous stabs at moralizing ("We're *all* dying, Otto"), such pretentious themes seem out of place in Mr. Tune's show and hardly substitute for the more basic ingredients that are missing. But even such lapses fail to obscure the director's own original gifts. Mr. Tune has built the grandest hotel imaginable in "Grand Hotel." It would be a happier occasion if so many of its rooms weren't vacant.

1989 N 13, C13:3

More Is More

THE CHRISTMAS SPECTACULAR, originally conceived, produced and directed by Robert F. Jani; executive producers, David J. Nash and Patricia M. Morinelli; general manager, Steven Rivellino; staging director, Frank Wagner; scenic designer, Charles Lisanby; lighting designer, Ken Billington; costume designers, Jose Lengsen and Frank Spencer; staging and choreography, Violet Holmes, Linda Lemac and Marianne Selbert. Presented by Radio City Music Hall Productions. At 50th Street and Avenue of the Americas.

Narrator, Scrooge and Santa ..... Charles Edward Hall
Mr. Cratchit ..... Steven Edward Moore
Mrs. Cratchit ..... Ann-Marie Blake
Sarah Cratchit ..... Stacy Latham
Tiny Tim ..... Alex Myers
Peter Cratchit ..... Bradley Latham
Belinda ..... Amy Gear
Martha ..... Christiane Farr
Coachman ..... Marty McDonough
Poultry Man ..... LeRoi Freeman
Mrs. Claus ..... Marty Simpson
Skaters
Laurie Welch, Randy Coyne, Amy Tolbert and Keith Davis
WITH: The New Yorkers and the Rockettes

By RICHARD F. SHEPARD

With the reliability of the holiday it celebrates, "The Christmas Spectacular" rolled into Radio City Music Hall Friday night and will be ensconced there through Jan. 3. For those who feel the need to cling to eternal verities, like Coca-Cola that is less than classic, the reassuring news is that this year's production is virtually the same as the one last year.

"The Christmas Spectacular," whose title cannot be accused of inflating the magnitude of the show, offers everything a family might need for stimulation in the way of sound or sight. Not one of its 90 minutes can be described as cogitative, and its spirits, which are high, should not be confused with spirituality. It is colorful, ingenious and, even in its more intimate moments, as gorgeously mammoth as a Roman holiday.

The 12 scenes pass by efficiently; it is a show that has the exquisite timing of a space shot. Here are the Rockettes, 36 precisionists in a breathtaking march-shuffle to "The Parade of the Wooden Soldiers." Here they are again, this time dancing around a brilliantly lit carousel on a revolving stage.

•

The mood is set from the start by 32 costumed dancers offering a parody of classical ballet to the music of "Nutcracker." And who should come onstage but Ebenezer Scrooge, transformed from something of a cost accountant to the type of fellow who has just inherited an unlimited expense account. Beautiful settings abound, including one with a horse-drawn carriage.

Santa flies above the stage en route to delivering his bounty. The New Yorkers, a dozen or more clean-cut vocalists, perform golden oldies. And for the grand finale, there is "The Living Nativity," a pageant that has been on the Music Hall's stage for more than 55 years and that has been retained as a capstone to this particular production, which dates to 1985.

The tableau depicts the first Christmas and the procession of kings and others to Bethlehem. Behind a gauzy curtain that lends a mystic aura, people cross the vast, desertlike stage with their live sheep, camels and donkeys. It is a magnificent testimony to the imagination of ingenious show people.

•

The show pays tribute to Robert F. Jani, who conceived, produced and directed this version of the Music Hall perennial and who died this year. "The Christmas Spectacular" employs 117 performers, including members of the orchestra, who are carried onstage, above stage and below stage on a flight-decklike platform. The show involves 350 costumes, an ice rink and scenery that towers 45 feet high and is 95 feet long. The Music Hall is a place for outsize planning, and the gifted Mr. Jani understood the difference between merely big and truly colossal.

1989 N 13, C20:5

Mage and Monster: An Odd Couple

THE TEMPEST, by William Shakespeare; directed by Jude Kelly; set design by Franco Colavecchia; costume design by Lindsay W. Davis; lighting by Dennis Parichy; music composed by Michael Ward; sound design by Eric Santaniello; production stage manager, Roy W. Backes. Presented by the Roundabout Theater Company, Gene Feist, artistic director; Todd Haimes, producing director. At 100 East 17th Street.

A Boatswain ..... Evan O'Meara
The Master of a Ship ..... Craig Wroe
Alonso ..... Jack Ryland
Antonio ..... Rocco Sisto
Sebastian ..... Gabriel Barre
Gonzalo ..... Robert Stattel
Ferdinand ..... John Wittenbauer
Adrian ..... Erik Knutsen
Miranda ..... Angela Sherrill
Prospero ..... Frank Langella
Ariel ..... B. D. Wong
Caliban ..... Jay Patterson
Trinculo ..... Michael Countryman
Stephano ..... Michaeljohn McGann
Sailors, spirits and goddesses
Vincent Dopulos, Ed Hart, Jason MacDonald, Jack Smith, Dave Spauling and Buddy Stoccardo

By LAURIE WINER

The British director Jude Kelly might have a vibrant "Tempest" in her, but the production that opened last night at the Roundabout Theater isn't it.

Her version of Shakespeare's drama is filled with conceptions that, while not necessarily contradictory, seem unrelated. Prospero is a stern biblical figure in a flowing robe. The shipwrecked royals en route to Naples are 18th-century gentlemen in powdered wigs, skirted coats and knee breeches; the most jaded ones among them snort cocaine. The spirits that Prospero summons to help him perform his magic are bandaged mummies, and the slave Caliban is a green-tongued reptile. Ariel might be an American Indian; long black braids flow down his bare back. He also occasionally sports a long Isadora Duncan scarf around his neck. There's nothing really objectionable about any of this, but, you want to ask, what does it mean?

•

The actors, too, are rarely in tune with one another. Powerfully built and rich of voice, Frank Langella is a physically imposing Prospero. He fixes the audience with a hypnotic stare, but he's reluctant to glance for very long at any human being on the stage with him. He exists only for Prospero's monologues, which he delivers with a messianic intensity. But when called upon to make a paternal gesture toward his daughter, Miranda, like a simple pat on her head, he seems to resent the interruption in the rapport he is trying to establish with the audience.

Mr. Langella makes Prospero an isolated and lonely figure, which is a fair interpretation. Caliban notes that others hate him "as rootedly as I do." But Mr. Langella's detachment leaves the play unmoored and ill-equipped to move us at the end. Prospero may be, as scholars have noted, a stand-in for Shakespeare as he approached the end of his life. Wise but weary with all he knows about human nature, he is a reclusive magician, capable of manipulating man and nature. But he is also a man who renews himself through an act of forgiveness, and he must still have some stake in flesh and blood passions, however self-sufficient he may be.

Prospero's neglect of his daughter is a pity because it looks as if Angela Sherrill could have made a fine Miranda, had she found a connection with either Mr. Langella or with John Wittenbauer, this production's insipid Ferdinand (the shipwrecked prince with whom she falls instantly in love). Ms. Sherrill perhaps overstresses Miranda's waiflike innocence, and Mr. Langella doesn't help by appearing to regard her love for Ferdinand as a silly indulgence. But the actress has a lack of guile that makes most of the performances around her look forced. Ms. Kelly should have assured her that a more sophisticated and confident reading of the verse would not have marred the appealing simplicity she brings to the role.

As Ariel, B. D. Wong undoes himself in trying to energize Prospero's austere island (designed by Franco Colavecchia). He's forever springing on and off stage, or up and down Prospero's Stonehenge-shaped mountain, arms raised for balance like a robotic ballet dancer. He answers his master with an incessantly piercing voice and a brittle smile. Prospero may call him a brave, dainty or airy spirit, but Mr. Wong's Ariel is more of a pest.

•

As Caliban, Jay Patterson is also encumbered by the physical manifestation of his character, which in this case, since he seems to be one of the living lizard people, means darting tongue, hunched shoulder and twitching neck. When this despised creature, whom Prospero has enslaved, reveals that he has a soul and a beautiful dream of a better life, Mr. Patterson offers his inspired verse ("Be not afeard: the isle is full of noises") as if Calaban is a chronically slow student who's hoping he's stumbled upon the correct answer.

●

As the drunken butler Stephano, Michaeljohn McGann, who sings and dances with a grace to match Fatty Arbuckle, provides a few moments of levity. As Antonio, who first masterminded his brother Prospero's exile from Milan, Rocco Sisto proves that he is a master of sneering villainy. But when Prospero pardons him with a brotherly embrace, his Antonio is incapable of experiencing redemption: Mr. Sisto hangs his head and pouts at Mr. Langella with an insincere, moony stare.

Ms. Kelly has not so much directed the play as applied unnecessary cosmetic surgery. Consequently, when Mr. Langella steps forward in the play's epilogue to ask for our indulgence, there may be some reluctance to grant it.

1989 N 15, C18:3

Correction

A theater review on Nov. 15 about the Roundabout Theater Company's production of Shakespeare's "Tempest" misinterpreted a gesture. The actors' intent was to portray 18th-century gentlemen taking snuff, not cocaine.

1989 D 9, 3:2

Familiar Conventions In New Workout

A FEW GOOD MEN, by Aaron Sorkin; directed by Don Scardino; set design by Ben Edwards; costume design by David C. Woolard; lighting design by Thomas R. Skelton; sound score and design by John Gromada; production stage manager, Dianne Trulock. Presented by David Brown, Lewis Allen, Robert Whitehead, Roger L. Stevens, Kathy Levin, the Suntory International Corporation and the Shubert Organization. At the Music Box, 239 West 45th Street.

Sentry .... Ron Ostrow
Lance Cpl. Harold W. Dawon .... Victor Love
Pfc. Louden Downey .... Michael Dolan
Lieut. (j.g.) Sam Weinberg .... Mark Nelson
Lieut. (j.g.) Daniel A. Kaffee .... Tom Hulce
Lieut. Comdr. Joanne Galloway
                                        Megan Gallagher
Capt. Isaac Whitaker .... Edmond Genest
Capt. Matthew A. Markinson .... Robert Hogan
Pfc. William T. Santiago .... Arnold Molina
Lieut. Col. Nathan Jessep .... Stephen Lang
Lieut. Jonathan James Kendrick
                                        Ted Marcoux
Lieut. Jack Ross .... Clark Gregg
Cpl. Jeffrey Owen Howard .. Geoffrey Nauffts
Capt. Julius Alexander Randolph .Paul Butler
Comdr. Walter Stone .... Fritz Sperberg
Marines, sailors, M.P.'s, lawyers, et al.
Stephen Bradbury, Jeffrey Dreisbach, Michael Genet, George Gerdes and Joshua Malina

By FRANK RICH

Even if the stage were not a battleground of tables and chairs in gunmetal gray, it wouldn't take long to recognize the terrain in "A Few Good Men," Broadway's new play about a court-martial. "It's an open-and-shut case," goes an early line. "I suspect there's more to this case than what's reported in the division report," goes another. The cast of antagonists includes a sarcastic Navy defense attorney who doesn't want to be a hero (Tom Hulce), a tightly wound com-

manding officer who insists on being one (Stephen Lang) and some cowed enlisted men caught in the crossfire. Let the scene change, and more than a few good marching men in crew cuts and khaki will sound off, "One, two, three-four!"

So pronounced is the déjà vu at the Music Box that one can only assume that the author, Aaron Sorkin, is invoking "The Caine Mutiny Court-Martial" and its brethren intentionally. And why not? It's reassuring to watch familiar conventions being

---

Are the accused marines covering up for higher-ups?

---

given a new workout. The Music Box Theater, after all, is where an even older genre of boulevard drama was made fun again in "Sleuth" and "Deathtrap." When the evidence of a "conspiracy to commit murder" piles up in the opening hour of "A Few Good Men" — and when that evidence is buttressed by some very good acting under the direction of Don Scardino — one sits back in confidence that Mr. Sorkin is laying land mines for 10 o'clock explosions.

But it's nearly 11 when the play ends, and Mr. Sorkin never does reward one's expectations. "A Few Good Men" is too predictable to satisfy as courtroom entertainment, and its attempts to tie its plot to some larger moral issues, in the manner of Charles Fuller's "Soldier's Play," are lightweight. The evening's message is: "You don't need to wear a patch on your arm to have honor." There is a higher code than the Marine code, and there are times when good soldiers must disobey orders. If that lesson isn't news, at least it might have been made compelling. But despite passing allusions to Nuremberg and My Lai, "A Few Good Men" doesn't argue its unarguable point in the gripping context of history.

Mr. Sorkin's talky case is instead merely a generic one about bullying and conformity in the barracks of the peacetime Marines. Though the play's fictional crime was committed in 1986 at the American naval base at Guantánamo Bay, Cuba, the time and place seem irrelevant. The co-defendants are accused of overdoing the unofficial punishment of an unpopular private. The most pressing question raised by their trial is whether they might be covering up for higher-ups.

While it is announced that the Marine Corps itself is on trial, the story turns on much narrower grounds. The why-and-whodunit solutions prove unsurprising, and to reach them the author force-feeds laborious clues into the action, some errant luggage tags among them. For a subplot, Mr. Sorkin charts the slowly blossoming alliance of three ill-matched defense lawyers, each of whom comes with a single psychological characteristic whose cause (a domineering father, for instance) may also be affixed like a luggage tag.

Since one of the trio is a woman, a crusading special investigator played by Megan Gallagher, there might have been a love triangle within the defense team. But that possibility for drama is foreclosed early, when one of her male colleagues (Mark Nelson) is revealed to be a devoted new

Joan Marcus
Mark Nelson and Tom Hulce in "A Few Good Men."

dad. This leaves any possible romantic activity to Mr. Hulce, who is schematically presented as Ms. Gallagher's contentious opposite: as he is afraid to fight a serious case, so she loves to fight yet doesn't know how to win. They're made for each other, of course, but they are the last people in the theater to figure that out.

Despite the handicap of a Hollywood coiffure, Mr. Hulce draws on his considerable stores of humor and sensitivity to portray his character's fast conversion from arrogant goof-off to daredevil legal-eagle. Ms. Gallagher forcefully sounds her one note of two-fistedness, and the impassioned Mr. Nelson professionally snaps Mr. Sorkin's one-liners, some of which are so redolent of show business they seem to have wandered in from a Johnny Carson monologue instead of "Mister Roberts."

No less fine are such supporting players as Victor Love and Michael Dolan as the stoical defendants, Clark Gregg as a legal defender of the military faith, Paul Butler as a no-nonsense judge and Geoffrey Nauffts as the witness inevitably called upon to

provide comic relief in Act II. In a class by himself is Mr. Lang, the base commander, whose spectacular performance as a feral Vietnam veteran in Steve Tesich's "Speed of Darkness" in Chicago this year is matched here by his mesmerizing turn as a post-Vietnam military strongman with a smile and tongue as fierce as his muscles.

For all Mr. Scardino's accomplished direction of actors, his staging makes hokey use of tacky lightning-and-thunder effects to try to simulate the riveting suspense missing in the plot. One result is to make "A Few Good Men" look dated, and that impression is compounded by a script that has been unluckily ambushed by current events. "We live in a world that has walls, and those walls have to be guarded by men with guns," says Mr. Lang at one point — a perfectly plausible statement for his character to make in 1986. But to an audience in November 1989, the historical imperatives underlying "A Few Good Men" may seem almost as ancient as its courtroom theatrics.

1989 N 16, C23:4

The Enemy Within

SEEING DOUBLE, script: Sinai Peter, Joan Holden, Emily Shihadeh, Jody Hirsh, Henri Picciotto, Nabil al-Hadithy and Isa Nidal Totah with Harvey Varga, Arthur Holden and Nidal Nazzal; directed by Daniel Chumley; composers, Bruce Bathol, Randy Craig and Dan Hart; lyrics by Mr. Barthol, with Mr. Craig and Mr. Totah; musical direction, Mr. Hart; costume design, Callie Floor; set and backdrop design, Kent Mathieu and Ellen Callas; stage design, David Brune, Mr. Chumley and Harvey Varga/Concept Fabrication; lighting design, Gregory R. Tate. Presented by the San Francisco Mime Troupe. Through Nov. 22 and Dec. 1 to 10 at the Triplex Theater, 199 Chambers Street.

WITH: Keiko Shimosato, Jeri Lynn Cohen, Harry Rothman, Ed Holmes, Michael Sullivan, Rebecca Klingler, Warren Sata, Isa Nidal Totah, Harry Rothman, Elliot Kavee and Dan Hart.

By MEL GUSSOW

By courting controversy, the San Francisco Mime Troupe has remained in the vanguard of political theater during its entire 27-year history. The company's new show, "Seeing Double," certainly must be rated as one of its most outspoken efforts. This is nothing less than a bitterly satiric musical sendup of the conflict between Israelis and Palestinians. The traveling show (presented at the Triplex Theater) is so evenhanded in

its criticism as to offend extremists on both sides. At the same time, it has a pronounced moral position.

In characteristic Mime Troupe manner, the story is a far-fetched farcical melodrama performed street-theater style. Two young Californians fly to Israel to assert conflicting claims to a specific piece of disputed land. One, an American of Palestinian origin, has a family deed to the property, while the other, who is Jewish, has discovered biblical proof that the land was ceded to his people thousands of years ago.

●

Each of the two characters is easygoing and individualized. Salim Razalis is a laid-back Californian addicted to MTV and oblivious to anything political — the opposite of his fervid Palestinian parents. David Goldberg is a back-to-kosher, neo-Talmudic scholar — to the horror of his parents. They hope he will grow out of it and will share the multi-ethnic diversity of assimilation (as he complains over dinner, "Thai takeout again?"). The story is made doubly chaotic and amusing by the fact that both young men are played by the same actor (Michael Sullivan), deftly switching roles, attitudes and accents.

Their coincident flight to Israel (on Trump Fly-by-Night Airlines) averts a hijacking attempt by the Smokers Liberation Lobby and culminates in a crash landing. In a rollicking comedy of errors, Salim and David are mistaken for each other and each is accidently transported to an enemy camp. Naturally, neither can distinguish friend from foe, with David momentarily finding an ally among the Palestinians in a young woman who shares his ardor for computer hard- and software.

Mocking militancy, the show is populated by such self-parodies as an Arab soldier who will not let her father enter his home until he remembers the password and the fierce spiritual leader of an Israeli outpost, an émigré from Brooklyn, who sings a rap song that sounds like kibitzing on the kibbutz.

The acrobatic cast dives in and out of beards and battle fatigues. Roles are cast without regard to gender or nationality (Mr. Sullivan, playing Arab and Jew, is black), which adds to the work's ecumenical absurdism. Most of the actors have mastered the company's comic-strip style of performance, especially so in the case of Mr. Sullivan. There is no trouble telling his two look-alikes apart, even when they are caught up in a quick-changing vaudeville chase around the soapbox scenery. All Middle Eastern problems would be solved if only the doubles could meet.

At various points, members of the four-piece combo are caught up in the action, catching flying briefcases and being distracted from their hybrid musical chores (the songs alternate between an Arab and an Israeli beat). Under the direction of Daniel Chumley, the show is, in every sense, a collaboration. The Mime Troupe's customary creation by committee (10 people are credited with authorship) results in a surprisingly unified cartoon in which nothing is held sacred except human lives and principles of freedom. The hardest thing for the characters to say is the dreaded C word, compromise. Beneath its outrageous surface, "Seeing Double" is a political satire with an urgent cautionary message.

1989 N 16, C28:4

Rewriting a Story That Never Changes

JACQUES AND HIS MASTER, by Milan Kundera; translated by Simon Callow; directed by Deborah J. Pope; set by Daniel Conway; lighting by Pat Dignan; costumes by C. Jane Epperson; fight director, Jason Kuschner; sound by Tom Gould; production stage manager, Dean Gray. Presented by The New Theater of Brooklyn, 466 Dean Street, Brooklyn.

Jacques .... Ray Virta
Master .... Gregory Salata
Agathe/Daughter .... Katherine Selverstone
Saint-Ouen .... Robin Tate
Justine/Mother .... Nancy A. Mayans
Young Bigre/Marquis .... Mark Diekmann
Old Bigre/Agathe's Father .... Jack Straw
Innkeeper/Marquise .... Monica Merryman

By WILBORN HAMPTON

At the outset of Milan Kundera's "Jacques and His Master," which is being presented at The New Theater of Brooklyn, Jacques informs the audience that he and his master are on a journey, but he confides that neither has any idea of their destination. "No one knows where he's going," the master points out defensively, and from this Beckettian observation the two men try to find some meaning to their existence.

To amuse themselves on the way, Jacques and his master swap stories about their amorous adventures in the manner of Chaucer's "Canterbury Tales" and Boccaccio's "Decameron." These tales, which are acted out as plays within the play, treat on the loss of virginity, cuckoldry and even true love. In between, master and servant discourse on the nature of guilt and the thorny problem of who is ultimately responsible for one's bad behavior and bad luck.

•

In fact, the best parts of "Jacques and His Master," which Mr. Kundera based on Diderot's "Jacques le Fataliste" and which draws inspration not only from Beckett but also from Pirandello and another Czechoslovak-born writer, Tom Stoppard, are these metaphysical discussions. "We are not to blame for what we do," Jacques asserts at one point, "because it is written Up There." Later on, both men begin to question the talent of their creator. "Perhaps our master was a bad poet," the master suggests. "Would we be any better if someone else had invented us?"

Soon Jacques and his master begin to catch on that not only do they keep repeating themselves ("It's always the same story that never changes," Jacques complains), but that someone Up There is doing some major rewriting of their lives. "Who's been allowed to rewrite our story?" the master demands to know. "Death to people who rewrite stories!" And Jacques comments: "Everything that's happened down here has been rewritten hundreds of times. Who's ever going to check to find out what really happened?" Jacques observes that "nothing is certain in this world." His master commands, "No useless truths!"

The weakness of "Jacques and His Master" as a work for the stage is in the narration of the bawdy tales of seduction and deceit, which are rather modestly presented in the Brooklyn production. Although Jacques and his master step into the scenes as characters in their own tales, these playlets never really come to life, and the audience becomes only a third-party spectator to a storytelling session.

Ray Virta is droll and worldly-wise as Jacques, and Gregory Salata provides him with an intelligent foil as the master. The Brooklyn production flags noticeably when Mr. Virta and Mr. Salata are not at center stage, although Robin Tate and Monica Merryman give credible performances as characters in the story sequences. Deborah J. Pope has directed with an understanding of Mr. Kundera's philosophical wit, but the pace tends to plod from time to time, and the blocking, especially in placing actors behind the audience, is somewhat awkward.

The translation by Simon Callow is smoothly idiomatic, although the slang ranges from the odd Briticism to American cowboy.

1989 N 16, C28:5

How Escapism Courts Disaster

POSITIVE ME, written and composed by Lisa Edelstein; directed by Ethan Silverman; choreography by Robert La Fosse; music arranged, produced and recorded by Peter Millrose; set design by John de Fazio; costumes by Michelle Freedman; lighting by Howard Thies; wigs and makeup by Bobby Miller; sound by Tony Meola; stage management by Steve Wildern. Presented by La Mama E.T.C., 74A East Fourth Street.

WITH: Stephanie Berry, Lisa Edelstein, Thomas Gibson, Margaux Guerard, Robert I., Mark Anthony Wade, Joe Warfield and Mary Lou Wittmer.

By STEPHEN HOLDEN

Lisa Edelstein's AIDS-education musical, "Positive Me," at La Mama E.T.C., is a buoyant, frisky show whose main purpose is to convince teen-agers that they are not invulnerable to AIDS. In the opening scene, Ms. Edelstein portrays a teen-ager who asks her boyfriend (Thomas Gibson) to use a condom during sex. Refusing, he offers a litany of reasons, including the fact that he is neither gay nor an intravenous drug user. But as the show makes perfectly clear, anyone who is sexually active is at some risk of infection.

Other characters in the show include a prostitute who is wise in the ways of protection, a drag queen who laments, "What ever happened to no responsibility?," a young heroin addict who scoffs at the notion of using fresh syringes (they're too expensive) and a smug chorus of religious moralists who see the AIDS epidemic as God's punishment. A parody of a television game show makes fun of the false notion that it is possible to turn one's back on the AIDS crisis by fleeing the city.

The songs in "Positive Me" are simple, direct messages expressed in a grade-school rap and pop vocabulary. With its nonstop pace and rough-and-tumble choreography by Robert La Fosse, the show has something of the chaotic energy of a junior high school playground. In talking about sex and drugs, the matter-of-fact lyrics and dialogue don't euphemize, but neither do they strain after a streetwise hipness.

"Positive Me" plays Thursdays to Sundays through Nov. 26 at the first-floor theater at La Mama, 74A East Fourth Street. Miss Edelstein hopes to showcase the musical in high schools and junior colleges across the country.

1989 N 16, C28:5

A Maiden, a Gypsy And a Shlimazl

THE WITCH, based on Abraham Goldfaden's musical "The Witch"; book adaptation and English lyrics by Amielle Zemach; additional lyrics by Itzik Manger and Dennis Perman; additional music by Max Helfman, Lori McKelvey and Henoch Cohn; directed and choreographed by Benjamin Zemach; musical director/arranger, Ms. McKelvey; set designer, Ray Recht; costume designer, Frances Blau; lighting designer, Kevin Connaughton; associate director, Ms. Zemach; assistant choreographer, Karen Sevenoff; stage manager, Ellen-Stuart Plotnick; assistant stage managers, Danny Ashkenasi and Ms. Sevenoff. Presented by Jewish Repertory Theater, Ran Avni, artistic director; Edward M. Cohen, associate director. At 344 East 14th Street.

Witch No. 1, Miriam and Little Girl .... Elizabeth McDonough
Witch No.2, Leah, Horse Dancer and Belly Dancer .... Giulietta Lavezzo
Witch No. 3, Rachel and Babkelah Boy .... Lori Wilner
Bobbe Yachne .... Priscilla Quinby
Mirele .... Emily Loesser
Abraham .... Joseph Travers
Batya and Baile .... Anna Bess Lank
Elyakum .... Samuel D. Cohen
Hotzmach No.1 .... Daniel Neiden
Hotzmach No. 2 and Leo, the Gypsy .... Avery Saltzman
Hotzmach No.3 .... Bruce Connelly

By RICHARD F. SHEPARD

In addition to own attractions, the production of "The Witch" by the Jewish Repertory Theater carries with it a few items of historical hoo-ha that add a dash of significance to this jolly tale, one of the hardiest theater perennials.

This version, in English, is based on the original musical by Abraham Goldfaden, who is the zayder — grandpa, to those who rely on the Jewish Rep's mother tongue — of Yiddish theater. "The Witch" was the first Yiddish play presented professionally in America, little more than a century ago, on the Lower East Side.

Also, for record keepers, this is the first time that the Jewish Rep has injected Yiddish to the extent that it has in "The Witch," where perhaps about half the lyrics are in the old-country idiom, enough to lend flavor but not enough to block continuity for those not in the know.

This "Witch" is a new adaptation, conceived, directed and choreographed by Benjamin Zemach, an 87-year-old actor, choreographer and teacher whose credits include work with the original Habimah troupe, Max Reinhardt and Martha Graham. His daughter, Amielle Zemech, is associate director and writer of the adaptation, which incorporates lyrics by Itzik Manger, the poet and all-around man of Yiddish letters. "The Witch" is, in short, a Jewish theater experience, not quite bewitching, but a classically satisfying combination of folklore and performing arts.

No sooner has the curtain gone up than one realizes that affairs are indeed in the hands of a choreographer whose sense of drama is heightened by freeze-stops on stage and by a vivid show of hands, outstretched and configured almost as area codes for ethnic identification.

"The Witch" tells about Mirele, a pathetic young girl whose evil stepmother (played by Anna Bess Lank, who is earthy and nagging in both this and another role in the play) plots her riddance with the help of Bobbe Yachne, the witch, represented by Priscilla Quinby as oily, devious and evil. Mirele, whose fragile charm is portrayed by Emily Loesser, is sold to a gypsy (Avery Saltzman) with the voice of Marlon Brando in "The Godfather," and carried off for resale in Constantinople, which leads to a funny cooch dance interlude.

The hero of the piece, Hotzmach, is a shlimazl, that is, a bad-luck, down-at-heels fellow who is played primarily, and comically, by Daniel Neiden; there are two other Hotzmachs just to emphasize that the world is filled with Hotzmach types.

The scenes include homes, a witches' cauldron reminiscent of "Macbeth," the Turkish bazaar, a marketplace and an inn, all cleverly created by Ray Recht. The songs are a motley collection of ballads, folk songs and rather mannered selections reminiscent of art songs.

"The Witch" is a happy, good-humored and nicely paced presentation, and it is more appealing, perhaps, esthetically than viscerally. It is a treat for the eyes, particularly eyes attuned to graceful movement, and ears tuned to refined voices. While it does not attain the personal warmth that was the hallmark of old Yiddish stage folksiness, "The Witch" is a most agreeable and novel theater experience.

1989 N 16, C30:4

The Common Need Onstage and Off

GYPSY, book by Arthur Laurents; music by Jule Styne; lyrics by Stephen Sondheim; original production directed and choreographed by Jerome Robbins; directed by Mr. Laurents; scenery design, Kenneth Foy; costume design, Theoni V. Aldredge; lighting design, Natasha Katz; musical director, Eric Stern; orchestrations, Sid Ramin and Robert Ginzler; dance music arrangements, John Kander; production stage manager, Craig Jacobs; Mr. Robbins's choreography reproduced by Bonnie Walker. Presented by Barry and Fran Weissler, Kathy Levin and Barry Brown. At the St. James Theater, 246 West 44th Street.

Uncle Jocko and Kringelein	Tony Hoty
George and Mr. Goldstone	John Remme
Baby Louise	Kristen Mahon
Baby June	Christen Tassin
Rose	Tyne Daly
Pop and Cigar	Ronn Carroll
Weber and Phil	Mace Barrett
Herbie	Jonathan Hadary
Louise	Crista Moore
June	Tracy Venner
Tulsa	Robert Lambert
Miss Cratchitt and Tessie Tura	
	Barbara Erwin
Agnes	Lori Ann Mahl
Mazeppa	Jana Robbins
Electra	Anna McNeely

WITH: Jim Bracchitta, Demetri Callas, Bobby John Carter, Danny Cistone, Barbara Folts, Teri Furr, Paul Geraci, Jeana Haege, Ned Hannah, Nancy Melius, Jason Minor, Bruce Moore, Michele Pigliavento, Ginger Prince, Robin Robinson, Alec Timerman and Craig Waletzko.

By FRANK RICH

If someone asked me to name the best Broadway musical, I'd gladly equivocate on any side of a debate embracing "Guys and Dolls," "My Fair Lady," "Carousel," "Porgy and Bess" and — well, you know the rest. But I've always had only one choice in the category of favorite musical. It is "Gypsy," and as I sat at its scorching new revival starring Tyne Daly, once again swept up in its goosebump-raising torrents of laughter and tears, I realized why, if anything, this 30-year-old show actually keeps improving with age.

"Gypsy" may be the only great Broadway musical that follows its audience through life's rough familial passages. A wrenching fable about a tyrannical stage mother and the daughters she both champions and cripples — yet also a showcase for

Robert C. Ragsdale
Jonathan Hadary, left, as Herbie, Tyne Daly as Rose and Crista Moore as Louise in "Gypsy" at the St. James Theater.

one classic Jule Styne-Stephen Sondheim song and rousing Jerome Robbins vaudeville routine after another — "Gypsy" is nothing if not Broadway's own brassy, unlikely answer to "King Lear." It speaks to you one way when you are a child, then chases after you to say something else when you've grown up.

•

Like "Lear," it cannot be done without a powerhouse performance in its marathon parental role. Ms. Daly, a television actress who might seem inappropriate to the task, follows Angela Lansbury in proving that not even Ethel Merman can own a character forever. Ms. Daly is not Merman, and she is not Ms. Lansbury. Her vocal expressiveness and attack have their limits (most noticeably in "Mr. Goldstone"), and warmth is pointedly not her forte. But this fiercely committed actress tears into — at times claws into — Mama Rose, that "pioneer woman without a frontier," with a vengeance that exposes the darkness at the heart of "Gypsy" as it hasn't been since Merman.

"Why did I do it? What did it get me?" Ms. Daly shouts as she accelerates into her final number, an aria of nervous breakdown titled "Rose's Turn." Rose is standing on an empty stage, at last deserted by everyone: June, the prized daughter she tried and failed to make into a star; Louise, the unfavored daughter who became Gypsy Rose Lee, queen of burlesque, in spite of years of maternal neglect; Herbie, the gentle agent who wanted only to become Rose's fourth husband.

•

Why did Rose pursue her dream? Why did she push everyone so hard that she drove them all away? Ms. Daly doesn't soften the news that Rose did it for herself. "Just wanted to be noticed," she says a little later. And as Ms. Daly stands there, crying her lungs out, demanding that a phantom audience give her a turn of her own in the spotlight — "Everything's coming up roses this time for *me!*" — one is confronted by a plea for recognition and love so raw and naked that Rose becomes a child again herself, begging as Louise and June once had for "Momma."

Ms. Daly's impressive turn reflects a staging that, as directed by Arthur Laurents, the author of the musical's book, is intent on exposing the primal family drama that always resides just beneath the bygone vaudeville veneer. Not that Mr. Laurents stints on that colorful surface. With the assistance of Bonnie Walker, who reproduced Mr. Robbins's choreography, and the designers Kenneth Foy (scenery) and Theoni V. Aldredge (costumes), he turns the apt St. James Theater into a credible stop on the battered two-a-day road that reaches its dead end in burlesque during the era of talkies and the Depression. From the first rendition of "Let Me Entertain You," led by Christen Tassin's truly hilarious young Baby June, to that recurrent number's last reprise, in which Crista Moore, as the adult Louise, strips her way to the top at Minsky's, Mr. Laurents is in complete command of his show's running parodistic commentary on a vanished pop-culture past.

The thrills really begin with the overture, which, as orchestrated by Sid Ramin and Robert Ginzler, is an invitation to show-biz exhilaration second to none and is played accordingly by Eric Stern's roaring pit band. Mr. Laurents and the three actresses he cast as burned-out strippers (Barbara Erwin, Jana Robbins, Anna McNeely) also pull off the tougher job of making "You Gotta Have a Gimmick" funny and fresh all over again, despite its months of repetition in the neighboring "Jerome Robbins's Broadway." But even in the glitzier numbers, Mr. Laurents burrows into the emotional undertow beneath the turn. When the delightful Robert Lambert — as a hayseed chorus boy with cocky dreams of glory — shows Louise his fantasy dance-team act, "All I Need Is the Girl," it is heartbreaking to watch the forlorn Ms. Moore act out her own doomed romantic fantasy in the shadows of an alleyway stage door.

•

In the meatiest dramatic numbers, Mr. Laurents pays Mr. Styne and Mr. Sondheim the compliment of reminding an audience that songs long assimilated into Broadway lore have a depth of character extending far beyond their unforgettable melodies and effortless verbal wit. "If Momma Was Married" — a comic lament for the grown-up Louise and June (Tracy Venner) — is not only two children's wish for a father but also a pathetic revelation of the sole common bond the very different siblings have enjoyed in their fractured, isolated childhoods. More harrowing still is "Everything's Coming Up Roses," the Act I railroad-platform finale in which Rose finally must switch her allegiance from the vanished June to the ugly-duckling Louise. As Ms. Daly approaches the lyric "We can do it/ Momma is gonna see to it," she hugs the cowering daughter only to toss her instantly and violently aside.

Mr. Styne and Mr. Sondheim are both giants on their own, but in this onetime collaboration they brought out something in each other's talent that cannot quite be found in their extraordinary separate careers. If there's no song as angry as "Some People" in the rest of the Styne canon, neither is there one quite as fragile and vulnerable as "Little Lamb" in the rest of Mr. Sondheim's.

Mr. Laurents's book carries its own weight. In this production, one of the most moving moments occurs when Jonathan Hadary, giving the most

abundantly shaded performance of his career as the warm but weak Herbie, finally summons up the guts to walk out on Rose. When Mr. Hadary leaves Ms. Daly behind in a shabby burlesque dressing room, he does so with the weariness of Willy Loman but with the serenity of a man who has finally found himself after a lifetime of searching.

•

Though much about this staging will be familiar to those who saw the 1974 Lansbury revival, also directed by Mr. Laurents, there is no question that the new Rose radically alters the tone of the result. In a way, it works for "Gypsy" that Ms. Daly is not a glamorous, sexy or sympathetic star — that she could not care less if anyone likes her or not. Rose is a monster, after all, and Ms. Daly is true to the fundamental statement of the piece, which is not a pleasant one.

It's the title character, not Rose, that "Gypsy" asks the audience to root for, and the lovely Ms. Moore, who steadily blossoms from a forgotten child to a self-possessed star, makes it easy to do so. By keeping both mother and daughter in tight and unsentimental focus, the entire production reveals why a musical that might seem so parochially about the small world of show business makes its red-hot connection with the real world beyond. There's never any doubt that the much-married Rose and her lonely, bruised children are driven to perform before an audience, to be gypsies, because that's their only hope of being noticed — of getting the love and acceptance they have been denied in life.

And might not the audience have its own deep needs in that respect? If "Gypsy" is the musical most beloved by theater fanatics, that may be because it forces those on both sides of the footlights to remember exactly why they turned to the theater as a home away from home.

1989 N 17, C5:1

Fighting Men

A WHISTLE IN THE DARK, by Tom Murphy; directed by Charlotte Moore; set design, David Raphel; sound and lighting design, Richard Clausen; costume design, Natalie Walker; production stage manager, Kathe Mull; executive producer, John A. McQuiggan, New Roads Productions. The Irish Repertory Theater, Ciaran O'Reilly, producing director; Ms. Moore, artistic director, presented by The Irish Repertory Theater Company and One World Arts Foundation, in association with South Street Theater Company. At 424 West 42d Street.

Iggy Carney	Chris A. Kelly
Harry Carney	Ciaran O'Reilly
Hugo Carney	Ron Bottitta
Betty	Jean Parker
Mush O'Reilly	Denis O'Neill
Michael Carney	Maurice Sheehan
Dada	W. B. Brydon
Des Carney	Patrick Fitzgerald

By MEL GUSSOW

The furies are unleashed in "A Whistle in the Dark." Tom Murphy's drama, which is being revived at the South Street Theater, centers on the Carneys of County Mayo, a brawling, brutish pack of street fighters who have been brought up to respect their father and their family honor. The fact that both father and family honor are severely tarnished does not lessen the conviction or the ferocity of the characters.

The Carney brothers, who have emigrated from Ireland to Coventry,

England, are the kinds of men who can have a most serious discussion about the comparative advantages of using bottles or fists in combat. As they war with their hated rivals, the Mulryans, and with one another, they seethe with anger at the defeats of their lives.

Last summer, the Abbey Theater in Dublin presented its production of the play as a highlight of the London International Festival of Theater, and the occasion was an exact meeting of play, performance and direction (by Garry Hynes). The Irish Repertory Theater revival is slighter in scale and emotional power. It touches the pulse — but not the heartbeat — of this compelling play.

Though one receives enough emanations of the abusive family to make this production a rewarding theatrical experience, individual characters do not fully resonate, beginning with the most manipulative brother, Harry, a pimp and self-described "thick lad," who in fact has the deepest sense of family loyalty.

In the role, Ciaran O'Reilly communicates Harry's swaggering conceit but misses the menace. In contrast, Sean McGinley, who played Harry for the Abbey Theater, sent shudders through the audience with his threatening presence. Harry is not a man to be encountered in a crowded pub or dark alley. At the same time, his speech about the childhood humiliation he suffered at the hands of a schoolteacher becomes an eloquent cry from an otherwise inarticulate man. Covertly, Harry is the play's pivotal character, the one most harmed by the self-imposed Carney reputation.

In Charlotte Moore's production for the Irish Repertory Theater, the father becomes the dominant figure, principally because of W. B. Brydon's performance. He is colorful, dapper and thoroughly deceitful, both a preener and a pretender, with the actor missing only the hints of a tragic dimension to the character. In common with his sons, the father is entrapped by the role he has chosen to play in life.

Maurice Sheehan is close to the mark in his performance as Michael, the oldest brother and the faded hope of the family. Michael has become mired in his own bitterness. Outwardly he is the articulate voice of reason and conscience. Actually he is a younger version of his cowardly father.

It is the supporting players who have the most notable success, namely Jean Parker as Michael's wife and Patrick Fitzgerald as the youngest brother, the most recent to arrive in England. Ms. Parker has a natural resilience as this English victim of the Carney chaos. To her in-laws, she will always be "the stranger," and wherever she turns in her home, there is a brother underfoot, drinking, smashing a glass or shouting abuse. Mr. Fitzgerald has the requisite blend of innocence and bluffness.

Under Ms. Moore's direction, the actors are convincingly Irish and endemic to their working-class environment. But a larger stage and a more detailed production would help to give a richer feeling of the family explosiveness, the Carney ability to occupy a room as if it were newly claimed enemy territory.

"A Whistle in the Dark" remains one of the most unrelenting of family dramas. Written in the early 1960's, it was the first full-length play by this important dramatist to be produced. Mr. Murphy has continued to be prolific over the years, but his work is seldom performed in New York. With its revival, the Irish Repertory Theater helps to correct that oversight. The play is a worthy example of the company's announced intention to establish an American home for classical and contemporary Irish theater.

1989 N 17, C26:5

Definition of Dilemma

THIN AIR, written and directed by Glyn Vincent; lighting designer, Jan Bael; lighting technician and operator, Joe Murphy; scenic designer, Caroline Gerry; stage manager, Judy Sostek. Presented by Theater for the New City, 155 First Avenue, at 10th Street.

Chantale	Rebecca Chace
Phil	Steven Cook
Greg	Rob Donaldson
Rose	Cecil Mackinnon
Billy	Alan Wynroth

By WILBORN HAMPTON

Rose doesn't pick her men very well. In fact, Rose is probably lucky to be alive, given the two psychopaths she is involved with in Glyn Vincent's "Thin Air," a jumble of a play being presented at the Theater for the New City.

At the beginning of the play, Rose is seeing Greg, a beer-drinking layabout whose idea of a fun Thanksgiving is to shoot road signs with a rifle from a speeding car. He is so serious about building a relationship with Rose that he even gets a job at the Pancake House. But Greg is also pathologically jealous. When Rose returns from the library, for example, he angrily demands to know, "What book did you read?" Needless to say, Greg doesn't take kindly to Rose's budding friendship with Billy.

Billy is your basic pot-smoking, whisky-guzzling, born-again-Christian biker. Billy also is a manipulator, and recognizes a soft touch when he sees one. He soon has Rose singing "Take My Hand, Precious Lord" and sponsoring him in Alcoholics Anonymous, although he doesn't want to stop drinking just yet.

Of course, Rose herself is not exactly a model of stability. Eight years after being jilted and left teaching in a small college town in Missouri, Rose is still trying to gain tenure and has drunk herself into an alcoholic clinic. After leaving the rehab, she begins to read biographies of Karl Malden and seeks salvation for a while with a teen-age lesbian until Greg comes along. But it is only after she undertakes to nurse Billy back to health from a motorcycle accident that her life really becomes unmanageable.

•

Mr. Vincent, who also directed, has piled so many plot contrivances on top of one another that the whole foundation of his play collapses into an implausible muddle before the end of the first act. The main characters are a snarl of contradictions whose selfish, volatile emotions fluctuate so wildly that a manic-depressive would seem a Stoic by comparision.

Mr. Vincent is not without talent as a writer, and a couple of scenes in the second act between Rose and Chantale, her teen-age friend, are genuinely engaging. But by that time one is so inured to the disagreeable nature of Greg and Billy that Rose's woes, many of which she has brought on herself, leave one indifferent.

With the exception of Rebecca Chace, who gives a credible and commendable performance as Chantale, and Cecil Mackinnon, who has her moments as Rose, the acting is somewhat stiff and labored. Caroline Gerry's set looks comfortable and lived in, although I doubt that any of the characters in Mr. Vincent's play could keep an apartment so neat.

1989 N 19, 75:5

STAGE VIEW/Walter Kerr

Of Passion, Politics and Other People's Money

TO MY WAY OF THINKING, which I do not propose as the only way, virtually everything else that's new in town is a relief from "Orpheus Descending."

Consider A. R. Gurney's "Love Letters," a piece of modest proportions which is nonetheless quietly, wittily, irresistibly moving. Its proportions, as you have surely heard by this time, are modest in that the play is permitted only two actors, and these two actors do not spend their time racing about the stage floor making passionate noises but simply sit at a table facing the audience while they read the letters they've exchanged since childhood.

She has, since childhood, nursed a nonconformist streak; when he ventures to send her a Valentine she writes to say that yes, she will be his Valentine provided there's no kissing involved. He is as conventional a lad as his pragmatic, eye-on-the-main-chance father can make him, though he does not allow his sense of propriety to keep him from somehow slipping into the girls' dressing room at the beach.

The letters grow up along with the youngsters, as the girl's divorced mother remarries ("Help! Let me out of here!") and she is packed off to a psychiatrist ("We talk about sex all the time but I think it's worth it"). Along the way, though, she begins to wonder if all their letter writing hasn't "messed us up," functioning as a not very good substitute for some shared life; she wants to see him. He is by no means averse to a passionate interlude, but will defend letter writing to the last; it is only when he writes that he feels he is "giving a piece of myself" to the other. What we are looking at in "Love Letters" is a pair of lovers who are never quite open to each other, never quite can be. With the actors so often facing front, you see, there is more than space between them; there is an ache.

The acting teams at the Edison, by the way, come and go as they did last season Off Broadway, coupling up for a week apiece. I saw Colleen Dewhurst, she of the splendid arrogance, and the forever excellent Josef Sommer in the play.

■

Larry Gelbart's "Mastergate" would seem to be at the furthest possible remove from the firmly compressed, strictly verbal round robin of "Love Letters." Both stage and auditorium are abuzz with the hypertense comings and goings of TV cameramen, committee members, lawyers and witnesses as proceedings get underway in Washington for an investigation into everything that's gone wrong with our Government. As the program note states, "The action is relentless, with no intermission."

Nonetheless. A most able director named Michael Engler is perfectly able to shut all of this off in a finger snap, producing a sharp silence riddled with fading echoes until a stentorian voice pierces the void with a promise that the hearings are going to be fair and square, with no predispositions, no persecutions. "We are not looking for hides to skin nor goats to scape," is what the man says.

The audience is caught off guard. It has laughed, but it wasn't ready for that particular laugh. That laugh doesn't really say anything about Irangate, or contras, or numbered bank accounts, does it? But it *was* funny, wasn't it? Though it's early on to be asking such a question, what exactly is this satirical comedy throwing darts at?

Well, of course it's about politics in some sense: politics we've been through, politics long since satirized by every stand-up and sit-down-a-minute comedian in the funny business. When a witness is asked a question that causes him to wince and clench his teeth before he squeeks out, "I believe that's one of the things I don't know any-

Gerry Goodstein

John Tillinger, center, directs Josef Sommer and Colleen Dewhurst in "Love Letters" by A. R. Gurney at the Edison—never open to each other

Martha Swope

Larry von Bargen as Maj. Manly Battle and Ann McDonough as Mrs. Battle in "Mastergate" by Larry Gelbart at the Criterion—a head full of shrapnel

more," we have no trouble summoning up perfectly real names, names whose bearers have suffered severely from just this planned

On Broadway and Off, tales of lovers, Washington follies, a takeover scheme and a woman unawakened.

aphasia. There's a laugh in that line, too — a bit grimmer, perhaps — but the joke is unmistakably a political joke. Real politics.

As we bubble along into the heart of the evening, however, we begin to notice that we seem more and more to be using politics as background, as milieu, not as target. Mr. Gelbart isn't arguing Irangate or any Gate of his choice all over again; he's taken all that for granted. What he's really after is the damage, possibly irreparable, that all Gates have done to language — to words, syntax, *meaning*.

"Anything that follows will come after," we hear a senator say, and suddenly, unmistakably, we have wandered into Alice in Wonderland, where words do indeed mean what their speakers mean them to say. I love that line. It is so stately, so firmly in control of itself, so treacherously confident. So deliciously, utterly empty.

■

In Switzerland an arms merchant resides in one of "a consecutive series of unnumbered houses." There is reference to a Committee on Hindsight and Déjà Vu, leaving a nice poetic aftertaste on the tongue. As a Secretary of State takes the witness stand, he cautions his interrogators, "I'm sorry, the truth'll have to wait'll after I finish testifying." A Major Manly Battle assures *his* interrogators that he has seen action and has "a head full of shrapnel to prove it." When a man on life supports must be interviewed in a hospital, his responses will necessarily be delayed; short bursts of Muzak are heard during the gaps. "A former podiatrist and his band of foot soldiers" are ready for any eventuality; an actor who strangely resembles Vice President Bush remembers them "leading the attack on Pearl Harbor." "You seem like a nice young man, Mr. Lamb," purrs the chairman to a witness; the witness takes a moment to reflect, then soberly replies, "Yes, sir, I do." Possibly the most honest statement of the evening, and the most ambiguous.

"Mastergate" isn't a play; it is an extended burlesque sketch of a kind that may not have been heard in these parts since the close of Weber and Fields's Music Hall. Neither is it soliciting any votes. Well, not too earnestly. It is about a terrible loss of meaning through the manipulation of syntax and the defiant abuse of words.

A tragedy, if you will. And very, very funny.

■

Jerry Sterner's "Other People's Money," running along for some time now at Off Broadway's Minetta Lane and a good bet to stay a lot longer, is the trimmest, tightest, most suavely self-confident piece of playwriting I've tried to keep up with since everybody stopped devising sleek melodramas.

It *is* a play about money, and most recent plays about money have insisted on placing us on the floor of the market at the peak of trading, where we've had to listen to a full company of actors screaming their greedy hearts out. This one mostly takes place after hours, during the late-afternoon hush, in the offices of an old-fashioned wire-and-cable outfit that steadily loses money but is much beloved by the Old Boy who owns it. The Old Boy makes up its losses out of the profits from his other ventures.

An edgy employee, stirring his cup of coffee as he paces, glances through a dirty window to see a stretch limo pull up outside. Up the stairs and into the obviously valuable property hikes

Peter Cunningham

Kevin Conway and Mercedes Ruehl in "Other People's Money"– a genteel but ruthless threat.

actor Kevin Conway, bearded, obviously proud of his red tie and breast-pocket handerkerchief, seeming to limp a bit but blazing with a thoroughly up-to-date energy. The Old Boy is summoned. Our Mr. Conway informs him that he owns 11 percent of his stock and is on the verge of acquiring enough more to complete a takeover. I shall let you find out for yourself how this genteel, but ruthless, threat works out. I'm not going to tell you *everything.*

This, though. A woman employee who is also the Old Boy's mistress has a daughter who is a lawyer. Per-

'Other People's Money' is about lust, with money as the sex object. In a wholesome way, of course.

haps she can help.

The daughter is brought into the tug of war, she is unmistakably a dish in every respect, and she loves the manipulation of it all as much as Mr. Conway loves the money of it all. In not too long a time it begins to look as though Mr. Conway *could* lose. In which case why is he is dancing that gnomelike little dance just now? So gleefully?

"Other People's Money" turns out to be a play about money, all right, but not a play about greed. It's more nearly a play about lust. Money as a sex object. In a wholesome sort of way, of course. And heading for an interesting switch, you may be sure. Very neat stuff. Uplifting.

■

It seems to me that there are two root things wrong with the Peter Hall

mounting of Tennessee Williams's "Orpheus Descending" and that they are precisely the things that must not go wrong if we are to have a chance of grasping, and taking pleasure in, the play.

The first is a matter of detecting Williams's personal voice at a stage when it was little more than a whisper. "Orpheus" is a reworking of Williams's very first produced play, "Battle of Angels," and the full music of the playwright's imagery — the music that would come from Alma Winemiller and Amanda Wingfield and Blanche DuBois — is simply not there. We are more likely to be hearing guitar-playing Val Xavier's blubbery "Nobody gets to know nobody" instead.

Yet it's *got* to be there, somewhere, in promising fragments. And we are obligated, if the experience is to mean anything at all, to clear away all unnecessary noise, gabble, intrusions from the soundtrack. The Playbill for the Neil Simon Theater quotes Williams: "Poetry doesn't have to be words, you see. In the theater it can be situations, it can be silences." And a director must give us a certain poetry of silence — breathing space, *hearing* space — to catch an oddly characteristic word, a new sound that is a Tennessee Williams sound, when it comes.

But that is most difficult at the Neil Simon these nights, for those pauses that bespeak attentiveness are the very last things you'll find tolerated. The play *is* a noise.

Into a dry-goods store burst five women, not all at once but all direct from the same henhouse, screeching at one another on high, identical pitches as they vie for prominence in a spotlight. They haven't come to this dry-goods store to buy anything; they've come to do exposition, and they do it for 20 minutes, blathering away about the fortunes and misfortunes of a family we haven't met yet and in whom we cannot take the slightest interest. I would make an exception here for Tammy Grimes,

who truly begins to seem a Williams woman as she lets some fluttering hesitation into her insistence that as a good churchgoer and amateur painter, she must have a vision, she *must* have a vision.

■

But director Hall is looking for slam-bang emphases, not protestations of delicacy, and the minute a space opens up it is promptly filled with clatter. The menacing sound of yapping dogs on the street outside (echoes of the Orpheus legend). A giant roll of thunder; can lightning be far behind? Ominous orchestral music. Angel voices in the wings, I swear it. Add to the pandemonium the nuisance of Vanessa Redgrave's bewildering Italian accent. And the hencoup crowd is with us again to give the play a formal touch, though five shrill biddies do not a Greek chorus make.

The other absolute need is to snare the audience into believing in the passion that is developing between Val Xavier and Miss Redgrave, the emotionally deprived wife of the store's owner. Xavier's mission in life, if he has one beyond his guitar-playing along the road, is to save her from the terrible aridity of her loveless state. Say Xavier aloud and you have Savior.

But the play wants to deal with their great coming together mythologically, through symbols. He is akin to dream birds who lack feet and cannot land. They are forever free. Won't she come? He lends her his guitar; next thing you know she's getting out her father's old mandolin, drawn to a new melody. But these things — puns, riddles, dreams — don't do the trick. There's no flesh and blood, let alone desire, in them. As Miss Redgrave toys with the mandolin, we merely feel that we're well on our way toward a string quartet.

Williams *did* overload the play with symbols in the first place: a black "conjur man" appears in rags to offer an incantatory blessing; a neighboring girl whose sexual freedoms have ended in "lewd vagrancy" eats up stage time without being useful to the narrative; the strobe lights arrive.

Most of all, star Vanessa Redgrave looks like a star, all right — an efficient, crisply businesslike star — but not like an unawakened woman. Or at least not like a woman likely to be awakened by this particular visitor: she'd gobble him up in two bites. He has no style of playing that is comparable to hers; they're not a merging twosome. The casting could be better and so, I'm sorry to say, could Miss Redgrave. She is curiously bustling and preoccupied in the part; her swift movements seem mapped. And why is it that I have only a memory of the back of her shoulders, body turned upstage in all crucial moments? That can't be entirely so; yet there is something she does that evades the eye, that keeps her a little bit ahead of herself.

In any case, deep passion doesn't take hold. It doesn't even stir. And that leaves "Orpheus Descending" at the starting gate again, more unfulfilled than its heroine. □

1989 N 19, II:5:1

Correction

A picture caption on page 5 of the Arts and Leisure section today, with the Stage View column, misidentifies the actor who portrays Maj. Manly Battle in "Mastergate." He is Daniel von Bargen.

1989 N 19, 3:1

A Painted Bird

THE SONG OF SHIM CHUNG, conceived and directed by Du-Yee Chang; written by Terrence Cranendonk, in collaboration with Mr. Chang; music composed and played by Mr. Chang; costume designer, James Livingston;

set, mask and puppet designer, Atsushi Moriyasu; lighting designer, Victor En Yu Tan;

stage manager, Sue Jane Stoker. Presented by the Pan Asian Repertory Theater, Tisa Chang, artistic-producing director. At 423 West 46th Street.

Shim Chung	June Angela
Young Man	William Lucas
Blind Shim's Wife	Mary Lee
Blind Shim	Norris M. Shimabuku
Village Bum	Ernest Abuba
The Bird	Donald Li
Mama Setong	Mia Katigbak
Villager; Fisherman	Steve Park
Villagers	
Shigeko, Christen Villamor, Tsuyu Shimizu	

By MEL GUSSOW

As a music-theater adaptation of a traditional Korean folk tale, "The Song of Shim Chung" is a change of pace for the Pan Asian Repertory Theater, allowing the company's proficient actors to experiment in an area distant from contemporary naturalism. The brief play, which opens the Pan Asian season at Playhouse 46 at St. Clement's, is earnest but unimaginative in both conception and execution.

The responsibility is shared by Du-Yee Chang and Terrence Cranendonk. Mr. Chang conceived and directed the work, collaborated with Mr. Cranendonk on the partly colloquialized adaptation and also plays background music of his own composition on percussion and flute.

The story is about a naïve young woman who is exiled from heaven because she has unknowingly fallen in love with a god. Under the name Shim Chung, she becomes the dutiful daughter of a blind man and his wife, and later goes through other transformations, including a return to her earthly life after her presumed death.

Neither the stolid direction nor Atsushi Moriyasu's scenic design (a perfunctory use of puppets and masks) enhance the work, as was the case with Mr. Moriyasu's designs for previous Pan Asian interpretations of Shakespeare ("Shogun Macbeth" and "A Midsummer Night's Dream").

A modicum of interest is offered by Donald Li as a birdman wandering symbolically through the landscape, holding a painted bird at the end of a long stick. Mr. Li, best known as Sam Shikaze, private eye, in Pan Asian's "Yellow Fever" and its sequel, reveals an Ariel-like lightness of movement. The title role is played by June Angela with an appropriate angelic sweetness.

1989 N 19, 76:4

Possible Valedictory Of Regal Irascibility

THE CIRCLE, by W. Somerset Maugham; directed by Brian Murray; scenery design by Desmond Heeley; costume design by Jane Greenwood; lighting design, John Michael Deegan; production stage manager, Mitchell Erickson; general manager, Ralph Roseman.

Presented by Elliot Martin, the Shubert Organization and the Suntory International Corporation. At the Ambassador Theater, 215 West 49th Street.

Arnold Champion-Cheney, M.P.
.... Robin Chadwick
Mrs. Shenstone .... Patricia Conolly
Footman .... Robertson Dean
Elizabeth .... Roma Downey
Edward Luton .... Harley Venton
Clive Champion-Cheney ...... Stewart Granger
Butler .... Louis Turenne
Lady Catherine Champion-Cheney
.... Glynis Johns
Lord Porteous .... Rex Harrison

By FRANK RICH

When Rex Harrison makes his long-awaited star entrance, the evening's last, in the Broadway revival of "The Circle," one can't help wonder: What does he need to do this for?

With more than a half-century of memorable roles behind him, Mr. Harrison hardly must prove himself as an actor anymore. Nor, at age 81, is he likely to show the audience anything new. But here he is on stage at the Ambassador Theater, regal in an Edwardian cream linen suit, playing his part in a 1921 W. Somerset Maugham comedy that seems much older than he is. And Mr. Harrison chooses to undertake this exertion eight times a week.

It doesn't take forever to figure out why. Mr. Harrison, looking fitter than he did last time out on Broadway four years ago, clearly still delights in performing. "The Circle," which he has hinted in interviews will be his valedictory, lets him strut as much as flesh and bones will permit. As Lord Porteous, a once-promising Member of Parliament whose career ended in romantic scandal and exile 30 years ago, Mr. Harrison gets to grind his "damn new teeth," bray insults at his intellectual inferiors and in general carry on as irascibly as ever. Peering across the sitting room at his pompous host's prized, newly bought antique chair, Mr. Harrison raises spectacles to his eyes and immediately declares, "It's a fake!" One hears the same gleeful contempt with which Henry Higgins once dismissed the Hungarian phonetician who crossed Eliza Doolittle at the Embassy Ball.

Yes, Mr. Harrison carries on. So do the somewhat spryer co-stars who have joined him for this occasion, Glynis Johns and Stewart Granger. As for "The Circle," it is merely a convenience that allows a devoted audience to enjoy three troupers enjoying themselves doing what each does best. The result is a theatrical experience of a very specific type, to be sure, but an entirely valid one. Just be certain you understand what you're getting into.

From Desmond Heeley's country-home set, whose sea-green walls almost seem to have acquired a patina of algae with age, to Brian Murray's staging, which mainly consists of draping the actors around the furniture, "The Circle" is a throwback to a distant era in West End boulevard theater. The production almost makes the last Harrison vehicle — Frederick Lonsdale's "Aren't We All?" (1923), seen in 1985 — look avant-garde. It's the kind of relic best encountered on a chilly, rainy, late autumn afternoon; Maugham's writing all but demands the counterpoint of matinee patrons removing their galoshes and adjusting their holiday shopping bags.

The dramaturgical geometry of "The Circle" actually involves two love triangles. Lord Porteous has traveled from Italy to England with Lady Kitty Champion-Cheney (Miss Johns), the married woman for whom he so famously sacrificed his career. As the couple have their reunion with Lady Kitty's son in Dorset, they not only must confront the husband they long ago cuckolded (Mr. Granger), but they also happen upon a new scandal in the brewing. Kitty's pompous son (Robin Chadwick), himself now a rising M.P., may soon lose his wife (Roma Downey) to a sweet-talking tennis-playing house guest from the Malay States (Harley Venton).

Will family history repeat itself and come full circle? I'll hold my peace. The answer would be more interesting, in any case, if the author had something enduring to say about marriage, infidelity and love, or if he expressed his perishable views more wittily. Its occasional laughs and solid construction notwithstanding, "The Circle" isn't about to slow the decline in Maugham's literary reputation since his death in 1965, and it hardly leaves one eager to exhume the 20-odd other plays ("The Constant Wife" most famous among them) that he wrote before abandoning the theater in the 1930's. The flat boilerplate dialogue — "Do you know that I'm awfully in love with you?" or

"You can't serve God and mammon!" — helps one appreciate how excited English audiences must have been when Noël Coward refitted similar sitting rooms with "Hay Fever" and "The Vortex" only a few seasons later.

The most tiresome burdens of "The Circle" fall on the younger characters, here played by decent actors who have been encouraged to accentuate the antiquity of the piece by striking anachronistic, at times campy stock-company attitudes. Their elders play for keeps. Miss Johns, the one member of the company called upon to convey emotion, is a poignant figure: a once-vibrant woman who has been transformed into a silly painted chatterbox by a frivolous life. When she and Mr. Harrison bicker about the disappointments that eventually turned their passionate illicit liaison into a sour parody of marriage, one feels her bitterness even as one exults in the verbal chamber music created by two of the most distinctive speaking voices in the English theater. A later scene, in which Miss Johns confesses to her daughter-in-law that her "smiling eyes" hide an "aching heart," mists over in affecting tears.

Mr. Granger's job is to be a charming consort, and he executes it most handsomely. He also gets to deliver the script's most boisterously received line: "I suppose it's hard for the young to realize that you can be old without being a fool." Actually, it's not so hard as he might think, at least for those who have watched the trio of sly old foxes at play in "The Circle."

1989 N 21, C19:1

Golden Sidewalks

THE LAND OF DREAMS, by Nahum Stutchkoff; adaptation by Miriam Kressyn; translated by Simcha Kruger; directed by Bryna Wortman; music by Raphael Crystal, lyrics by Ms. Kressyn; set design by Brian P. Kelly; costume design by Mimi Maxman; lighting design by Jason Sturm; stage manager, Judith Scher. Presented by the Folksbiene Playhouse, Ben Schechter, managing director; Morris Adler, chairman. At 123 East 55th Street.

Reb Aaren Ziskind .... David Rogow
Helen Ziskind .... Rachel Black
Baile Ziskind .... Zypora Spaisman
Sam Goldwasser .... Yosi Sokolsky
Sidney Ziskind .... Mark Ethan Toporek
Mrs. Katzenelenbogen .... Molly Stark
Cantor Shepsl Katz .... I. W. Firestone
Hymie Ziskind .... Norman Golden
Milton Ziskind .... Richard Carlow
Natalie Katzenelenbogen ...... Shira Flam
Cookie .... Lee Ann Levinson

By RICHARD F. SHEPARD

There was a special texture to life among working-class Jews in New York during the despairing days of the Great Depression, and there is a taste of it in "The Land of Dreams," Nahum Stutchkoff's play now being staged by the Yiddish-speaking Folksbiene Playhouse.

Mr. Stutchkoff in those years was a fixture on radio station WEVD (the station that spoke your language, particularly if it was Yiddish), and he apparently had a keen insight into the things that bothered his public. This play, presented during the 30's under the title "Around the Family Table," starred, among others, Celia Adler. It was not one of the great plays of the Yiddish stage, and yet its affectionate

adaptation by Miriam Kressyn makes it a particularly evocative selection by the Folksbiene, one that recalls a time in history and a period of popular theater that honestly made no pretensions to high art.

After all, audiences knew the Ziskind family from Brooklyn as soon as they all met over the footlights. Hymie, the paterfamilias, has his own garage and is making money, but he's a mule when it comes to deciding things. And he has decided that his son Milton, a doctor who can't find patients, will marry only for money — a big dowry, that is. He insists that his son Sidney, who loves being an auto mechanic, will become a judge, no matter what it costs. And his beautiful daughter, Helen, will marry a lawyer although she's smitten by a fellow who is not only a grease monkey but also a greenhorn.

•

Doesn't sound like too much, this story of strong-minded papa (played with striking credibility by Norman Golden) who, Old World style, insists on calling the shots for his new-world children, But it touches a chord, thanks to an enthusiastic production and a sensitive cast inspired by the direction of Bryna Wortman . The Yiddish and broken English of the dialogue, which runs from the emotive to broad comedy, is studded with references to egg creams, the Bronx, landsman societies and two-cents-plains.

The cast mixes comfortably familiar Folksbiene faces with others that are no less welcome newcomers to this specialized theater. Zypora Spaisman, who plays the mother, is mistress of the glumly comic look and acerbic tongue, assets that don't hide the soft heart underneath and the deep understanding of the world as it is, not as it should be.

And then there is grandpa, 90 years old, who has been made by David Rogow into a quaintly and antiquely wise and funny figure who compares the workings of the clocks he mends to the workings of human life. I. W. Firestone, as an organization-minded cantor, makes one laugh as he applies psychology to get the remorseful father of the house to do what he has sworn never to do.

•

There are good voices sounding off here, among them Rachel Black, who attractively personifies the daughter of the family, and Molly Stark, whose singing in the part of the declassed Russian-Jewish aristocrat brings in a sense of opera.

The music by Raphael Crystal, with lyrics by Ms. Kressyn, is as eclectic as one can get, representing all likely themes of the time, including waltz, cantorial, tango and Yiddish folk tune, and it lends a catchy cachet to the proceedings. Brian P. Kelly's thoughtful set design heightens the sense of the times, with the apartment houses of New York and hints of contemporary street life hovering in the background and on the sidelines.

"The Land of Dreams" finds the Folksbiene in its own dreamy retrospective mode, and its recollections are given to us with charm, humor and no second-generation self-consciousness. It's a fitting gift for the company's own 75th-anniversary year, and evidence that there is a long way to go before this venerable troupe's final candle will be blown out.

1989 N 22, C10:1

Rex Harrison, Glynis Johns and Stewart Granger in a scene from "The Circle."

'We Just Want To Break Its Spirit'

THREE POETS, written and directed by Romulus Linney; set and costume design, Anne C. Patterson; lighting design, David Finley; production stage manager, Ellen Melaver. Presented by the Theater for the New City, George Bartenieff, executive director; Crystal Field, executive artistic director. At 155 First Avenue, at 10th Street.

KOMACHI

Komachi	Adrienne Thompson
Komachi's Voice	Kathleen Chalfant
Shosho	Scott Sowers

HROSVITHA

Gerberga	Ms. Chalfant
Brother William	John MacKay
Hrosvitha	Mary Foskett
Mary	Ms. Thompson
Abraham	Mr. Sowers

AKHMATOVA

Pecdov	Mr. MacKay
Marya	Ms. Thompson
Rudinsky	Mr. Sowers
Klarina	Ms. Foskett
Anna Akhmatova	Ms. Chalfant

By MEL GUSSOW

In "Three Poets," Romulus Linney contemplates three women separated by a millennium and by widely disparate cultures. The characters are united by their individualism and artistry — and by the fact that men were their harshest critics.

The plays at Theater for the New City are small in scale but they ripple with poetic intensity. In each, Mr. Linney adopts the manner of the period in which the poet was writing, and then creates a biographical story illuminating the life and work. He does not press the parallels; they become self-evident. In a time of repression, each artist survived as a secret genius.

The subjects of 'Three Poets' span a millennium.

The first is a Noh-style play about Komachi, a ninth-century Japanese poet, whose art is the essence of graceful understatement. A prince comes to her for advice about his own rhapsodic verse. At the same time, he pursues his romantic inclinations. Rebuffing both the poetry and the passion, she sets herself up as the prince's critic. But the tables are eventually turned, and the play ends with an image of brutal symbolism. In this dramatization, Komachi is masked and her words are spoken by Kathleen Chalfant.

•

After Komachi, Mr. Linney turns to Hrosvitha, the 10th-century nun who was Europe's first female playwright. On request, she describes her play, "Abraham," to a visiting priest in the hope that it can be performed in the Gandersheim convent — and he surprises her and the Mother Superior with his specific objections. Later, in Mr. Linney's imaginative conjecture, the nun revises the play so that the saintly title character plays a manipulative role in the downfall of his virginal niece. It is suggested that Hrosvitha was forced by circumstances to conceal her natural skepticism.

The third and most substantial of the three plays moves to the Soviet Union in the 1950's for a story about

Jonathan Slaff

Kathleen Chalfant as Akhmatova in "Three Poets."

Anna Akhmatova and her confrontation with a censorious minister of culture. In a preliminary series of encounters between the official and others in the poet's life, one can sense the extent of the repressiveness during Stalinist times. In the case of Akhmatova, she waited endlessly for news about her imprisoned son. The agonizing emptiness of that experience inspired her "Requiem." As we are told, as an act of protectiveness, she divided the poem into parcels of words, which were given to friends to memorize.

The official tells the poet, "We don't want to change a word you've written, we just want to break its spirit," a sentiment that echoes through the centuries, back to the time of Komachi and Hrosvitha. All three — and other sisters in art — have been pioneers, suffering at the hands of men for the fact of their gender.

•

In his prolific career, Mr. Linney has specialized in two varieties of plays — interpretations based on history ("The Sorrows of Frederick") and stories about Appalachia ("Tennessee") often involving strong women. "Three Poets" artfully combines both of these dramatic interests. In this trio of cameos, he manages to ennoble his characters without sanctifying them.

Acting as his own director, the playwright has given each play an unadorned production. A few stones denote a path across the water, a rug becomes a room — and the acting reflects the modesty of the staging. There is responsive work by, among others, Mary Foskett as Hrosvitha, John MacKay as the Soviet official and, especially, Ms. Chalfant as Akhmatova, who in her isolation, demonstrates the political power of forbidden words.

1989 N 23, C20:1

Valuing the Libido Despite AIDS

ADAM AND THE EXPERTS, by Victor Bumbalo; directed by Nicholas Deutsch; scenic design, Campbell Baird; costume design, Paul Tazewell; lighting design, Paul Palazzo; music composed by Chris DeBlasio; sound design, Timothy Pritchard; production stage manager, James Latus. Presented by the Three Dollar Bill Theater. At the Apple Corps Theater, 336 West 20th Street.

Adam	John Finch
Sarah	Althea Lewis
Jim	John-Michael Lander
Eddie	Benjamin Evett
Melissa, Mama Mata and Mom	Susan Kaslow
Man	Joseph DiRocco
William, Baba Mata, Dr. Alp, Priest, Ralph and Dad	John Seidman

By STEPHEN HOLDEN

Victor Bumbalo's "Adam and the Experts" may be the most important play to deal with the AIDS crisis in gay society since William Hoffman's "As Is" and Larry Kramer's "Normal Heart" sounded their anguished alarms four and a half years ago.

Since those two dramas were first produced Off Broadway, thousands have died and thousands more who have gotten AIDS fight to survive. Mr. Bumbalo's play expresses a mood of exhaustion, fatalism and embattled determination that, as the decimation continues, has become an overshadowing fact of homosexual life.

It has at least become possible, Mr. Bumbalo's play suggests, to find some bitter humor amid the tragedy. "Adam and the Experts," the first production of the Three Dollar Bill Theater, a new professional Off Broadway gay and lesbian theater company at the Apple Corps Theater, is quite funny in a dry, satiric way. Most of its humor is situational, deployed by the playwright to reveal the pathetic, ludicrous defenses that people adopt to shield themselves from terrifying realities.

•

Within the gay milieu of "Adam and the Experts," actual sex has been all but banished — it is just a nagging memory personified by a recurrent figure, a nameless, leering barechested young man (Joseph DiRocco) who follows the title character around with taunts and propositions. The play begins as Adam (John Finch), a waiter in a SoHo restaurant, learns that his closest friend, Eddie (Benjamin Evett), has AIDS. Adam's immediate response is a desperate, single-minded pursuit of every conceivable avenue of medical and spiritual help. His scramble leads him to drag an unwilling Eddie to a swami swindler and a medical quack whose miracle cure involves injections of ozone.

In "Adam and the Experts," almost everyone, including parents, doctors and a trained counselor from Gay Men's Health Crisis, proves weak, frightened and foolish. The most stinging caricature is of an alcoholic, closeted gay priest who declares he hates God and makes a pass at Adam. The playwright takes special pains to ridicule denial. A main point of the play is that Adam's frantic, obsessive concern for Eddie is itself a hysterical form of denial because it keeps him from confronting his own deepest fears and desires.

•

"Adam and the Experts," though heartfelt, has major structural weaknesses. The play feels like two mismatched one-act stagings, the first comic, the second somber. The deathbed drama of the second act has lessons about remembering the dead and valuing the libido even in the face of AIDS, but the tone of much of the dialogue is poundingly didactic. The director, Nicholas Deutsch, has found a graceful tempo for the first act's social satire, but as the comedy evaporates, the direction becomes tentative. The change of mood affects the performances, especially that of Mr. Finch, who is comfortable projecting a poker-faced comic irony in the early scenes but has difficulty letting go emotionally later in the play.

Bert Andrews

John Finch

As Eddie, Mr. Evett gives the evening's deepest, most consistent performance, one that follows a steady arc from denial to rage to a harrowing acceptance. All the "experts" are played by the same actor, John Seidman, who invents a different, amusingly disagreeable personality for each. Though Mr. DiRocco possesses the right physique and pout to play Adam's lurking libido, his monotonous, bumbling line readings undermine key dramatic moments.

Campbell Baird's handsome scenic design — a spare, robin's-egg blue setting of ruined pillars — gives the action an evocative frame, frayed like the nerves of the characters but as bright as their determination to defy death.

1989 N 23, C20:5

Live and Yearn

THE THREE SISTERS, by Anton Chekhov; translated by Earle Edgerton; directed by Allan Carlsen; set design, Robert Joel Schwartz; lighting, Douglas O'Flaherty; costumes, Barbara A. Bell. Presented by the Pearl Theater Company. At 125 West 22d Street.

Andrei Prozorov	Michael John McGuinness
Natalya	Robin Leslie Brown
Olga	Donnah Welby
Masha	Joanne Camp
Irina	Laura Rathgeb
Kulygin	James Nugent
Vershinin	Stuart Lerch
Tuzenbach	Kurt Ziskie
Solyony	Kevin Hogan
Chebutykin	Frank Geraci

WITH: Sylvia Davis, James Gene Di Lazzaro 2d, Paul Lima and Joseph Warren

By WILBORN HAMPTON

From the very first rehearsals of its initial production at the Moscow Art Theater, Chekhov's "Three Sisters" has been an enigma to directors and actors alike. The play itself is, in Chekhov's own words, "dreary, long and awkward" with "four heroines and a spirit more gloomy than gloom itself." Most of the action seems to take place offstage, and the characters appear to do little but philosophize over the future, longing to be somewhere else while waiting for the samovar to arrive.

Yet "Three Sisters," which is being presented at the Pearl Theater Company, is one of the saddest and most haunting dramas written in this century or any other. Many events do, indeed, happen offstage: a wedding, a fire, a duel, to name only a few. But like so much in life, the real drama of Chekhov lies between the lines, in the common, everyday occurrences of human existence, and the major action is in the internal conflicts within the characters.

•

Modern directors and actors have no less trouble finding a way to portray these inner conflicts than Stanislavsky and the company at the Moscow Art Theater did, and it was from

Martha Swope Associates/Carol Rosegg

Joanne Camp

directing Chekhov that Stanislavsky developed his revolutionary style of acting. In fact, the Russian director cautioned against trying to "act" Chekhov's plays. Rather, he said, an actor must "become part of his plays, live them, have one's being in them."

The Pearl production only partly achieves such an involvement. The three Prosorov sisters are, to varying degrees, successful in realizing the frustrated yearning for life that is the heart of Chekhov's play. Joanne Camp's Masha is a portrait of boredom. When Ms. Camp takes a lover, she does so with little more thought than she might whistle, as a diversion against the unbearable dullness of her life. Donnah Welby's Olga is a study of regret, a portrayal of the spinster schoolteacher who is incapable of stopping the dissolution of their lives, either because she is too tired or has a headache. And Robin Leslie Brown is convincing as Natasha, the bourgeois sister-in-law who usurps the sisters' position and slowly drives them out of their house room by room.

In other roles, there are mixed results. Frank Geraci is good as Chebutykin, the old Nihilist doctor who is content with his vodka and newspaper, and Joseph Warren provides a credible Ferapont. Michael John McGuinness as Andrei, the brother who gambles away the Prozorovs' future, and Laura Rathgeb as Irina, the youngest sister, who extols the joys of work until she gets a job, have their moments, but they are better in some scenes than in others.

What is missing in the Pearl production is the sense of loss which permeates Chekhov's play and which every character in it encounters. Thus, the Pearl's Kulygin becomes a simple cuckold rather than the pitiable, loveless schoolteacher he is, and Solyoni appears as nothing more than a dandy with no hint of the deadly menace that lurks beneath his jesting. Allan Carlsen, the Pearl director, appears to have tried to sidestep this problem by speeding up the pace. Stanislavsky tried the same thing in rehearsals before "Three Sisters" opened in Moscow, but found the quickened tempo destroyed the mood of the play. Several scenes in the Pearl production suffer the same fate.

There is, for example, no feeling for the love of talk that is an essential part of Chekhov's characters and, society. This is especially noticeable in Vershinin and the Baron, both of whom fairly race through their speeches, as though they were talking sports or indulging in idle social chatter instead of discussing the future of the race. The result is a lack of conviction in what they are saying and, the joys of Chekhov's philosophical arguments are lost. Without taking the time to give them the full human dimension, the characters become hollow.

1989 N 23, C20:5

Bitter Fruit

STAND-UP TRAGEDY, by Bill Cain; directed by Ron Link; set design, Yael Pardess; costume design, Carol Brolaski; lighting design, Robert W. Rosentel; dance numbers choreographed by Shabba-Doo; original music, Shabba-Doo and Yutaka Fresh J; sound design, David Budries; dramaturg, Greg Leaming; production stage manager, Ruth E. Sternberg. Produced in association with the Mark Taper Forum. Presented by Hartford Stage, Mark Lamos, artistic director; David Hawkanson, managing director. At Hartford.

Father Ed	Richard Poe
Mitchell James	John C. Cooke
Burke Kendall	Dan Gerrity
Tom Griffin	Jack Coleman
Lee Cortez	Marcus Chong
Marco Ruiz	Anthony Barrile
Henry Rodriguez	Ray Oriel
Carlos	Sixto Ramos
Freddy	Edwin Lugo
Luis	Shabba-Doo

By MEL GUSSOW

Special to The New York Times

HARTFORD, Nov. 21 — Faced with the everyday frustrations of urban education, the playwright Bill Cain responds with "Stand-Up Tragedy," as in the apt title of his corrosive new play. First produced at the Mark Taper Forum in Los Angeles, it is now running in revised form at Hartford Stage. It is an angry work, filled with bitterness about the impossibility of amelioration.

Though the terrain is familiar, Mr. Cain and his director, Ron Link, have taken a novel, highly stylized approach. The play becomes the dramatic equivalent of the jagged, jarring rhythms and the nervous energy of break dancing and rapping, which form a joint background motif. Both the play and the production are resolutely confrontational.

To a certain extent, Mr. Link has staged the play as if it were a classroom variation on a prison melodrama, though of course there are no bars to prevent escape. The performance begins on such a high pitch that it may make theatergoers uncomfortable, which probably is one of the playwright's intentions. A former teacher in a Manhattan elementary school (and, before that, artistic director of the Boston Shakespeare Company), Mr. Cain clearly wants to shake up the system of education and also to aerate what is generally accepted as socially responsive theater. In his outspoken play, he holds everyone up for criticism.

The scene is a rundown Roman Catholic school on the Lower East Side. Through broken windows, we can see a graffiti fresco, a haunting design by Yael Pardess, in which Christ on the cross hovers over urban imagery. Inside the school, the man in charge is the Rev. Ed Larkin, who is like the captain of a ship in polar seas. The point is to stay on a prescribed course, avoid icebergs and keep from capsizing.

In common with everyone else in the play, the priest marks himself as a failure. As he realizes, his obeisance to rules (of religion and of his school) contradicts his natural compassion. Education becomes a waiting game, testing the teachers as well as the students. How long can each side be contained before breaking out?

In a series of clangorous, often comic episodes — some of them like stand-up monologues — we feel the pressures that have reduced the classroom to a battleground. Students are abusive, teachers are dismissive and tests are pointless, except to

prove that there always is a bottom 10 percent. But hope is autumnal, like basketball. The play is all problems and no solutions, one of many ways in which it is in contrast to uplifting films like "Stand and Deliver." The playwright's attitude is more one of fall down and fail, but keep fighting.

A new teacher (Jack Coleman) is a doer rather than a do-gooder, and wise enough to know he is surrounded by obstacles. One veteran of the classroom is far more cynical — his definition of teaching is "casting fake pearls before real swine." Mr. Cain's play is filled with such scathing observations, as many from the students as from the faculty.

There is at least one student with promise, a young Hispanic (Marcus Chong) who lives half of his life in a world of fantasy. As a self-taught artist, he has created and illustrated the adventures of Saga, starring himself in the title role. His comic-strip art is

his means of survival. Saga and other myths, including the Homeric, become the subtext of the play.

The young man is besieged on all sides, especially by the tragedy of his home life, and in a dextrous performance, Mr. Chong plays all the members of his family, switching quickly from one to the other. In such a fashion, the play repeatedly breaks with reality while never losing its credibility.

"Stand-Up Tragedy" is tellingly executed by an energetic and vociferous cast, with especially admirable work by Mr. Chong, Mr. Coleman, Richard Poe as the priest and Ray Oriel as an obstreperous student. The result is a kaleidoscopic portrait of education in extremis, written with an immediacy that makes it seem as if it were faxed from the frontlines.

1989 N 24, C3:4

Small-Scale Circus

BRIGHTNESS, created by Ping Chong, in collaboration with Matthew Yokobosky; set and costumes; Howard Thies, lights; Brian Hallas, sound. Text by Louise Smith after Petronius, Hippocrates and Josephine Baker. Production coordinator, Meryl Vladimer; managing director, Bruce Allardice; assistant director, Virlana Tkacz. Presented by La Mama E.T.C and Ping Chong and Company. At the Annex Theater, 74A East Fourth Street.

WITH: Karen Booth, John Fleming, Dan Froot, Larry Malvern and Louise Smith.

By MEL GUSSOW

For Ping Chong, "Brightness" is an experiment in light and sound, a surrealistic canvas of nonserial images. This new work (at La Mama Annex) is a small play of sensory but not intellectual stimulation. As such, it should be considered a sidelight to Mr. Chong's venturesome career as an author and director of conceptual theater.

This is a fragmented collage, in contrast to earlier performance

pieces like "Kind Ness" and last season's "Skin — a State of Being," both of which operated on wide-ranging metaphorical wavelengths. In the case of "Kind Ness," the title was an intentional pun, referring both to congeniality and divergent species. "Brightness" is what it appears to be, a play of light, using people as sculptural surfaces and focusing on the varieties of illumination in our lives.

The show is structured as a small-scale circus, with Louise Smith, dressed in a white gown and a wizard's hat, acting as ringmistress and offering pointed comments about pre-Christian and post-modern performance art. In this instance, Mr. Chong is less interested in wordplay than in his visual and aural tapestry. Behind Ms. Smith is not a center ring but a square of light, which shifts, changes shape and on occasion blinds us with its intensity.

In a scene aptly entitled "The Glare," three actors are struck still by a white-hot glow, as if stunned by a nuclear explosion. Later, in a lighter

Martha Swope Associates/Carol Rosegg

Ping Chong and Louise Smith in "Brightness."

mood, the so-called Bauhaus twins perform what is described as a folk dance of the 1940's while stars playfully twinkle on the dance floor. In the most balletic sequence, actors interact with a large pendulum that periodically descends like a deus ex machina on a fanciful Miró moonscape.

Mr. Chong's collaborators include not only his acting company but also his designers, Matthew Yokobosky (for the sets and costumes) and Howard Thies, who has the ability to choreograph with light. Brian Hallas's sound design draws freely from various musical sources, including a reinterpretation of a Josephine Baker number by Ms. Smith. Her presence as a kind of clown angel binds the tableaux together. During several attenuated scenes, when the play achieves a state of stasis, one looks forward to her return to the stage. It is a case of the introducer being more evocative than individual acts she is introducing.

1989 N 26, 71:1

Norwegian Threads And Latin American

KATE'S DIARY, by Kathleen Tolan; directed by David Greenspan; set, William Kennon; costumes, Elsa Ward; lighting, David Bergstein. Presented by Joseph Papp. At the Public Theater/Shiva, 425 Lafayette Street.

Kate ....Lizbeth Mackay
Tim and Frank ....Michael Bryan French
Ellen, Angie and Trish ....Laura Hughes
Father Hernandez and Walter
                                           John Griesemer
Pablo .... Rafael Baez

By MEL GUSSOW

In "Kate's Diary" by Kathleen Tolan, characters comment on the deficiencies of a play in progress, indicating that it is melodramatic or self-indulgent or that it causes "the audience's presumed discomfort." The comments are intended to be disarming, but one ends with the belief that the playwright has been astute in her self-criticism.

There are appealing moments in "Kate's Diary," as there were in Ms. Tolan's earlier play, "A Weekend Near Madison." She has a facility for odd eccentricities of dialogue — and Lizbeth MacKay's unself-conscious performance in the title role keeps the work from seeming unduly pretentious. But "Kate's Diary," which opened last night in an austere production at the Public Theater, is less a play than a brief interior monologue on that most unpromising dramatic subject, the interrupted creative process. It is what Ms. Tolan has written in lieu of a play — her stops and starts, her fidgets and footnotes and, far too literally, her diary jottings.

•

Apparently suffering from writer's block after the failure of her first play, the title character is trying to concoct a political thriller. As it unfolds in that dramatic no man's land described as "Kate's bedroom and Kate's imagination," this play within a play is a tale of Central American intrigue involving espionage and border patrols. When a writer friend is called upon for his comments, he accurately pinpoints the weaknesses of the play, but Kate carries on regardless, occasionally interspersing the fiction with selected scenes from her domestic life, in which she does almost all of the talking.

As an alternative to writing an original play, Kate has been commissioned to adapt "A Doll's House." She has decided to trim what she regards as the fat and is setting the adaptation in Greenwich, Conn. Her friend is justifiably horrified at the transplantation and suggests that she create her own Nora instead of tampering with Ibsen's. There is in fact a nubbin of Nora in Kate — a woman dominated by an inexpressive mate.

With work, Kate-as-Nora might have dramatic possibilities, and there is also a hint of an idea in that political story, especially when it moves away from melodrama and a refugee steps forward to tell us about his anguish as an exile from his revolution-

Martha Swope
Lizbeth   MacKay.

torn nation. Both strands remain undeveloped as Ms. Tolan crosscuts from one to the other. After barely 60 minutes, she ends her play precipitately, leaving the audience to wonder if the work has arrived at a conclusion.

•

A certain measure of theatricality is instilled through the performances, especially that of Ms. MacKay, the original Lenny in Beth Henley's "Crimes of the Heart." Sitting on her bed as her characters act out her stories, she remains wide-eyed and attentive. As an observer, she is never shaken even as, inches away, a man smothers a woman with a pillow. The actress takes advantage of the few moments of humor, as in her recitation of the large and small talk that is so integral to her social world.

Under David Greenspan's calm, reasonable direction, the other actors — Michael Bryan French, Laura Hughes, John Griesemer and Rafael Baez — express restraint while populating Kate's psyche with real and imaginary figures.

At one point, the protagonist explains her authorial drive by saying, "I have to write something." One hopes that next time the playwright will write about something more than the marginalia of "Kate's Diary."

1989 N 29, C17:1

Over the Rainbow And Out

BLACK MARKET, by Joe Sutton; directed by Scott Rubsam; set, Jerry Goehring; lighting, Bill Simmons; production stage manager, Tony Luna. Presented by the Primary Stages Company, Casey Childs, artistic director. At 354 West 45th Street.

JoAnn .... Elaine Rinehart
Hatch .... Bruce McCarty
Rosie .... Charlotte Colavin
Bijan .... Christopher McCann

By STEPHEN HOLDEN

In the interminable first act of Joe Sutton's new drama, "Black Market," JoAnn (Elaine Rinehart) and

Hatch (Bruce McCarty), an absurdly naïve young married couple who have recently moved to Manhattan, sit around their tenement and dream of being rich and famous.

JoAnn imagines that through reading tabloid stories about Ann-Margret's early years she can glean the secrets of stardom. Hatch believes that if he can only connect with the right people he will be handed the keys to wealth. As the couple spend their days selling umbrellas and circus toys on a Times Square street corner, Hatch remains certain that it is only a matter of time before they are spotted by well-connected people who will invite them into the big time.

Soon enough JoAnn and Hatch are befriended by Rosie (Charlotte Colavin) and Bijan (Christopher McCann), a scheming prostitute and her Iranian boyfriend, who is a smuggler. Promising the young couple $10,000, they entice them into what seems at first to be a smuggling operation but turns out to be something far more sinister.

•

Although David Mamet might have made a fiendish satiric game from such a premise, Mr. Sutton's play is doggedly earnest in tone. All four characters speak in long, stilted monologues that show no feel for the rhythms of everyday speech. Thoughts that should be expressed only once are numbingly reiterated, and the tedious, repetitive blather fills up space without revealing character.

Though the Primary Stages Company production, directed by Scott Rubsam, has been cast with reputable actors, there's little that Miss Rinehart and Mr. McCarty can do for characters that are written as longwinded ciphers. In the more colorful roles of Rosie and Bijan, Miss Colavin and Mr. McCann make the most of what little they're given and succeed at least in communicating a predatory seediness.

1989 N 29, C17:1

Kentucky Fauna And Family

FEAST HERE TONIGHT, text by Ken Jenkins; songs by Daniel Jenkins; directed by Gloria Muzio; set by William Barclay; costumes by Jess Goldstein; lighting by Phil Monat; musical supervision by Jeff Waxman; production stage manager, Jana Llynn. Presented by the Vineyard Theater, Doug Aibel, artistic director-theater; Barbaa Zinn Krieger, executive director; Jon Nakagawa, managing director. At 108 East 15th Street.

Jesse .... Daniel Jenkins
Sissy .... Susan Glaze
Tolbert .... Patrick Tovatt
Louise ....Cass Morgan
The Band
  Kenny Kosek, Don Brooks, Tom Hanway and Larry Cohen

By MEL GUSSOW

"Feast Here Tonight" is a Kentucky blend of bluegrass music and tales about stranded turtles, lazy dogs, pumpkin pies and angels that speak to mules. The atmosphere is congenial, almost everyone plays a fiddle or a guitar and the sentiment is as thick as the elderberry jam that figures so prominently in the text.

Perhaps if the show were shorter or if it were performed casually in a real kitchen or backyard — rather than simulated ones — its friendliness would override the conceptual limitations. But, as staged by Gloria Muzio

at the Vineyard Theater, it seems somehow displaced.

Although the idea was to be a kind of farm-and-garden "Pump Boys and Dinettes" or "Oil City Symphony," the musical lacks the self-mocking humor and unifying motifs of those other shows. In substitution it offers a collection of songs — singable but with too little variation — interspersed with observations about Kentucky fauna and family, like the one about old Uncle Eli, who found an albino raccoon and gave it to his favorite niece.

The creators of the show are the talented father-and-son team Ken and Daniel Jenkins. Ken Jenkins, an actor-playwright who does not appear on stage, wrote the spoken words. His son, Daniel (Huck Finn in Broadway's "Big River"), wrote the music and lyrics and is one of the busier members of the cast. Cass Morgan, who was an original Dinette, has the most melodic voice in the company.

In an awkward attempt to provide a narrative framework, Daniel Jenkins (playing a character identified as Jesse) invites his friends over to his house after the death of his grandparents. This leads, at least in the first act, to too much coziness as the actors sip coffee and leaf through old photographs to stir their memories. The musicians are also present at the gathering, and they interplay with the actors. This is not as spontaneous as it may sound.

Amid all the various animal and biblical stories there are two one-act monodramas by Ken Jenkins, first presented at the Actors Theater of Louisville. One, "Rupert's Birthday," was memorably performed by Susan Kingsley. At the Vineyard, Ms. Morgan plays the role with suitable affection and reminds us of Mr. Jenkins's felicity for writing shaggy tales (not as evident as it should be in the rest of the show).

Rupert's birthday is the one holiday Ms. Morgan celebrates. The others, she says, are all public works holidays. She has chosen to commemorate the turning point in her life, the day she turned 13 and the day a calf named Rupert was born. In a brief span of time, Mr. Jenkins movingly pictures the rite of passage of a young woman experiencing a life and death cycle. The monologue illustrates what is ostensibly the show's principal theme, the suggestion that man is sometimes called upon to provide assistance to nature.

Sifted through the second act is another Ken Jenkins monologue, "Cemetery Man," delivered by Patrick Tovatt. Though its impact is diluted among the songs, this remains a dryly amusing yarn about a gravedigger fighting progress and dreaming of the good old burial days. Except for these two sketches, "Feast Here Tonight" is fragmentary — songs and homespun impressions in search of a musical.

1989 N 30, C16:3

Babylon in Form And in Spirit

HYDE IN HOLLYWOOD, by Peter Parnell; directed by Gerald Gutierrez; set by Douglas Stein; costumes by Ann Hould-Ward; lighting by Frances Aronson; sound by Scott Lehrer; projection by Wendall K. Harrrington; fight sequence supervised by David Leong; production stage manager, Peter B. Mumford; production manager, Carl Mulert; incidental music by Robert Waldman. Presented by Playwrights Horizons and American Playhouse Theater Productions. At the American Place Theater, 111 West 46th Street.

Julian Hyde .... Robert Joy
Hollywood Confidential .... Keith Szarabajka
Charles Hock .... Stephen Pearlman
Jake Singer .... Peter Frechette
David Hogarth .... Robert Curtis-Brown
Betty Armstrong .... Fran Brill
Lida Todd and Susan .... Julie Boyd
WITH: Derek D. Smith, Kurt Deutsch, Matthew Locricchio, Herbert Rubens, Theresa McElwee, Kenneth L. Marks, Richard Topol, Thomas Eldon, Thia Gartner, Ed Mahler and Rob Richards

By FRANK RICH

Halfway through Peter Parnell's new play, "Hyde in Hollywood," a malevolent 1930's gossip columnist named Harry Babylon tells the audience his nightmare. Harry has dreamed of a phantasmagoric movie premiere at which the stars he helped make famous are all scrambled: Gary Cooper sounds like Marlene Dietrich, Adolphe Menjou is made up like Rita Hayworth, and Deanna Durbin sings "My Bill" to Helen Morgan, who is dressed like Hattie MacDaniel in "Gone With the Wind." Soon the stars turn on Harry and devour him, until finally he finds that his tongue has landed in Bette Davis's purse and that he is "nowhere . . . nothing . . . not anything."

But the nightmare isn't over. Harry, one discovers, really is nothing — he's a movie character played by a legendary actor and director named Julian Hyde (Robert Joy). When a voice shouts "Cut!" he disappears as abruptly as the Toons in the opening scene of "Who Framed Roger Rabbit?"

And only then does the real nightmare begin. In "Hyde in Hollywood," a Playwrights Horizons production staged at the American Place Theater, Mr. Parnell argues that the dreams perpetrated by the dream factory during the movies' golden age were as monstrous as Harry's nightmares but far more lasting and lethal.

Though his play is bounded by glittering Brown Derby dinners and Grauman's Chinese premieres of "The Wizard of Oz" and "The Women," Mr. Parnell quickly rips through the M-G-M tinsel to dramatize the private cowardice of movie

makers all too willing to knuckle under to the reactionary politics of a Louella Parsons or the severe prejudices of scandal-hungry ticket buyers. He wonders if Hollywood's more frivolous screen fantasies might not have reflected that moral abdication and helped foster the atmosphere that encouraged Nazis of all kinds to march in the real world, whether just outside or well beyond the studio gates. "A nation lives by its symbols," says the playwright. Implicit in "Hyde in Hollywood" is the belief that a braver 30's Hollywood might have helped produce a more courageous nation than the one that was tardy in mobilizing against Hitler in one generation and against Joseph McCarthy in the next.

In ambition but not, unfortunately, in follow-through, "Hyde in Hollywood" is of a fascinating piece with Mr. Parnell's previous revisionist look at American cultural iconography, "Romance Language." In that 1984 play, authors and characters of 19th-century literature, from Huck Finn to Emily Dickinson, journeyed to a frontier in which homosexuals, among other minorities, suffered as surely as the Indians.

The West has hardly changed in the Hollywood of "Hyde," where the tyranny of all-American conformity, whether in definitions of patriotism or masculinity or race, is symbolized by Andy Hardy instead of General Custer. Hyde, a homosexual, must hide in a marriage to retain his fans' favor. His screenwriter, Jake Singer (Peter Frechette), is a Communist who also lives in constant fear of informers. Both Hyde and Singer suffer the additional stigma of being unembarrassed Jews in a studio system run by frightened, assimilation-minded Jewish moguls, typified by the L. B. Mayer-like Charles Hock (Stephen Pearlman), who are "American" at any price.

"Hyde in Hollywood" tells what happens when Hyde and Singer, spurred by the mysterious murder of Hyde's film-star wife (Julie Boyd), decide to fight the system. They do so by making "Harry Babylon: His Rise and Fall," a movie that resembles "Citizen Kane" as much as Hyde and Singer at times recall Orson Welles and Herman J. Mankiewicz. And as Welles had to battle Hearst to get

"Kane" to the public, so Hyde must battle Harry Babylon's real-life prototype, a gossip columnist known as Hollywood Confidential and played with nasty wit by Keith Szarabajka. With the insinuating radio voice of

Can the dream world of movies nudge the real world morally?

Father Coughlin and Fascist politics to match, Hollywood Confidential is a crusader for Family, God and Country and the sworn enemy of anti-Americans and "the so-called third sex."

●

As "Romance Language" could not have existed before the literary critic Leslie Fiedler found new romance in the bond between Huck and Jim, so does "Hyde in Hollywood" share its thematic and actual landscape with familiar works of fiction (Nathanael West's "Day of the Locust"), nonfiction (Neal Gabler's "Empire of Their Own") and gossip (Kenneth Anger's "Hollywood Babylon"). Yet Mr. Parnell goes his own inventive way. Not unlike Martin Sherman's "Bent," "Hyde in Hollywood" is a sophisticated attempt to raise the persecution of gay men from the footnotes of mainstream history.

Mr. Parnell also experiments in form. Hyde's film and life eventually merge into a single drama as feverish and open-ended as Harry's nightmare. As the doppelgängers Harry Babylon and Hollywood Confidential inexorably become one, so does Hyde's Jekyll-and-Hyde existence as a closeted homosexual give way to a single, brave identity.

How one wishes the playwright's impressive blueprint were matched by ingenious execution. The movie-within-the-play is half-heartedly sketched, and, like the evening's murder mystery, ends with a thud, not a Rosebud. The characters, too, often seem to have been abandoned on the cutting room floor — especially the dissolute screenwriter, who cannot be rescued from knee-jerk archetype even by the gifted Mr. Frechette.

●

If anything the letdown is compounded by the skill of Gerald Gutierrez's sleek film noir-style production, which, as elegantly acted and designed, promises a finished work. Though one might well quarrel with the casting of Mr. Joy — whose forceful acting cannot disguise his lack of a movie-star presence — "Hyde in Hollywood" generally marches ahead with the conviction of a play that believes, as Hyde hopes, that outspoken art "can really change things."

That confidence is not misplaced, just shortchanged. There have been few new plays this year with as much to say as "Hyde in Hollywood" or with potentially as intriguing a way to say it. Mr. Parnell owes it to himself and his subject to keep working until his dreams are as powerful as those he wants to demolish. Hollywood can never be underestimated, after all. In "The Day of the Locust" — published in the same apocalyptic year, 1939, in which most of "Hyde" is set — West could not rid Babylon of its demons by imagining any nightmare less than that of burning the entire place down.

1989 N 30, C19:3

Large Questions In Whodunit Form

ARTIST DESCENDING A STAIRCASE, by Tom Stoppard; directed by Tim Luscombe; scenery by Tony Straiges; costumes by Joseph G. Aulisi; lighting by Tharon Musser; music and sound effects by Kevin Malpass; production manager, Peter Lawrence; general manager, Leonard Soloway. Presented by the Staircase Company, Emanuel Azenberg, Roger Berlind, Dick Button, Dennis Grimaldi, Robert Whitehead, Roger Stevens and Kathy Levin. At the Helen Hayes Theater, 240 West 44th Street.

Beauchamp .... Harold Gould
Martello .... Paxton Whitehead
Donner .... John McMartin
Sophie .... Stephanie Roth
Young Beauchamp .... Michael Cumpsty
Young Martello .... Jim Fyfe
Young Donner .... Michael Winther

By FRANK RICH

You know you're at a Tom Stoppard play when even the title lends itself to at least three different meanings.

In "Artist Descending a Staircase," a 1972 radio play enjoying a full-dress staging at the Helen Hayes Theater, the title refers, first, to the evening's initial (but unseen) event: an elderly artist named Donner (John McMartin) has fallen down the staircase of his attic studio to his death — possibly after being pushed by one of his closest friends and colleagues of 60 years, Martello (Paxton Whitehead) or Beauchamp (Harold Gould).

As befits a work whose three artists have pursued Dadaist careers since the century's teens, its title is also an allusion to Marcel Duchamp's 1912 painting "Nude Descending a Staircase." Mr. Stoppard's third staircase is to be found in a Playbill step chart that illustrates the story's flashback-flashforward time scheme. The play's first six scenes descend in intervals of hours and finally years from 1972 to 1914; the remaining five scenes take one back up the chronological staircase to 1972. To complete the symmetry, Mr. Stoppard's dramaturgical technique in turn mirrors the advancing, repeated image of Duchamp's Cubist-Futurist nude: the audience sees his characters in a progression of quick sketches that freeze then in isolated moments of time.

●

I don't have to tell you that Mr. Stoppard is clever. In this 85-minute work, that cleverness is not harnessed to a major play but to an often stimulating, sporadically funny and, at one uncharacteristic juncture, genuinely moving investigation of the nature of perception, memory and art. For those who admire the author's "Jumpers" and "Travesties," this piece will offer special illumination. Written between the two, "Artist Descending" echoes "Jumpers" in its use of a whodunit to frame metaphysical questions and it anticipates "Travesties" in its preoccupation with that historic moment when Tristan Tzara, James Joyce and Duchamp (to take Mr. Stoppard's archetypal examples) helped reinvent art to suit a civilization in which rationality and its esthetic corollary, classicism, were being shattered by the Great War.

The evening's whodunit is: Who pushed Donner? The answer, which will not be revealed here, is inextricably bound to Mr. Stoppard's larger inquiry into how people, and artists in particular, see the world (or fail to see it). As it happens, Donner's last moments of life — ambiguous frag-

Gerry Goodstein

Keith Szarabajka, left, and Robert Joy in Peter Parnell's "Hyde in Hollywood."

ments of sounds and words — have been captured by the tape recorder that Beauchamp uses to make the "tonal art" that is his John Cage-like oeuvre. But the meaning of these aural clues, which are replayed and re-examined nearly as assiduously as the tape in Francis Coppola's film "The Conversation," depends on the ear and the character of the listener.

As "Artist Descending" travels back in time — a feat requiring a second, younger set of actors to play the three artists — another, visual mystery of a half-century earlier overlaps Donner's fatal fall. In 1919, at the trio's breakthrough exhibition, "Frontiers in Art," a young woman named Sophie (Stephanie Roth) had fallen in love with one of the men at first sight. But which one? Sophie never had a second sight, because she soon went blind. Though she subsequently has a liaison with Beauchamp, the artist she thinks matches the face she adored, it is possible that Sophie was mistaken, and tragically mistaken at that. The evidence she used to identify Beauchamp was his proximity to an abstract composition that might easily have been confused with another artist's canvas at the same show.

By ingeniously linking his plot questions to his larger themes, Mr. Stoppard turns the play's running debate about art into something more compelling than academic chitchat. He raises the heat another notch by refusing to stack his character's arguments.

Certainly Mr. Stoppard sounds as conservative as Tom Wolfe (in "The Painted Word") when Donner, who has reverted to traditionalism in his dotage, dismisses the avant-garde as "that child's garden of easy victories" or when modern art is fatuously defended as opportunistic narcissism liberated from history, standards and accountability. In the pivotal 1914 sequence, Mr. Stoppard further mocks

---

An inquiry into how people and artists see or do not see the world.

---

the three young artists for spouting frivolous artistic manifestoes while ignoring the bombs detonating around them during a hike through the French countryside.

Yet the playwright gives equal credence to the view that only "nonsense art" that ambushes the mind was possible after the cataclysmic absurdities of a surreal war. What's more, "Artist Descending a Staircase" itself, with its multiple points of view and denial of any naturalistic fix on people and events, adheres to modernist principles as keenly as any painting in the Braque-Picasso show now at the Museum of Modern Art. Even so, Mr. Stoppard keeps one guessing — and thinking — about where he stands by providing a steady stream of rude jokes at the expense of 20th-century artists and critics alike.

The precision of his wit is not consistently equaled by Tim Luscombe's staging, which greets the audience shakily with a phony-looking atelier

(designed by Tony Straiges) and a trio of similarly bogus elderly artists. If only Rex Harrison and Stewart

Sheldon Secunda

Michael Cumpsty in Tom Stoppard's play "Artist Descending a Staircase."

Granger were not otherwise engaged! Mr. Gould, Mr. McMartin and Mr. Whitehead — good actors all — don't remotely pass for octogenerians. Only Mr. Whitehead is credibly British, and Mr. McMartin, who carries the play's largest histrionic burden, is as sloppy with his emotions as he is with his accent. It's a relief when the youthful stand-ins arrive. Michael Cumpsty, Jim Fyfe and, especially, Michael Winther are excellent as the budding geniuses, even if their resemblance to their older selves is confusingly nonexistent.

The heart of the production is Ms. Roth, whose romantic heroine here is as touching as her spinster in the Peter Brook "Cherry Orchard." Women in Stoppard plays have rarely, if ever, been this full-blooded. A scene in which Sophie serves the artists tea — a challenge for her, a lark for them — is imbued with the radiance of spiritual fortitude and devoid of self-pity. Her subsequent fall into loneliness and despair is Expressionism made flesh.

Perhaps Sophie is not the kind of beauty that the arrogant Beauchamp might demand from a model, but Ms. Roth's brilliant acting and Mr. Stoppard's writing make her beautiful in the manner of decidedly pre-Duchamp art. By understanding and embodying love — which she identifies as that "secret in the deep center of my life" — blind Sophie becomes the only person in "Artist Descending a Staircase" who can truly see.

1989 D 1, C3:1

STAGE VIEW/Benedict Nightingale

A Beached Whale And Buttonholes

LONDON

REMEMBER ALBERT FINNEY AS the swaggering lout in the movie "Saturday Night and Sunday Morning"? Recall Peter O'Toole's all-electric "Lawrence of Arabia"? They're well into middle age now, those brash boys who came in the 50's and 60's to beef up British acting in both cinema and live theater, and the passing years have left neither of them untouched. Time has transformed Peter O'Toole into a gangling cadaver, all elbows and cheekbones and floppy silver hair, and done the opposite to Albert Finney, a pretty fleshly, aldermanic figure these days. Yet you still feel something more than nostalgia when the two men respectively rattle and lumber onto the nearby stages they are occupying here this fall. That charisma, that command of the orchestra pit, remains unblighted.

Mark you, one sometimes wonders if the actors have chosen their plays altogether wisely. Both Keith Waterhouse's "Jeffrey Bernard Is Unwell" at the Apollo, in which Mr. O'Toole plays a boozy journalist, and Ronald Harwood's "Another Time" at Wyndham's, with Mr. Finney as a troubled

---

On stage as sot and troubled maestro, respectively, Peter O'Toole and Albert Finney stir up more than nostalgia.

South African pianist, have been enthusiastically embraced by the British critics. Both plays have reportedly attracted the attention of American producers, too. But both need to be thoroughly serviced, perhaps even briefly recalled to the creative factory, if they're to run successfully in New York.

Jeffrey Bernard exists. Indeed, you're quite likely to find him propping up the bar at the Apollo Theater itself. You can certainly read his mischievously anecdotal "low-life" column every week in The Spectator — or, rather, every week he's clearheaded enough to pen it. "Jeffrey Bernard Is Unwell" is actually the genteel euphemism the editor has sometimes had to insert in his magazine's nether regions after one of those weeks in which the low-life correspondent has researched his subject too conscientiously. We're talking here of a man who once published an "author's query" about his projected autobiography in another paper's literary pages: If anyone had any information about what he was doing between 1960 and 1974, would they kindly send it to him?

That autobiography, ghostwritten by Keith Waterhouse, might be the present show at the Apollo. It begins with Mr. O'Toole's Bernard crawling blearily from beneath a table at his favorite Soho pub, only to find the place locked for the night, and it ends with the landlord arriving with the keys to release him. In between, the writer stumbles zigzag through the junkyard of his life, remembering women and drunks and drones and jockeys and one gambler so dedicated that, when the weather got too cold for the horses and greyhounds, he organized indoor races between cats handicapped with weights from the kitchen scales. Doctors, nurses and a succession of wives fail abjectly to reform him. He can't visit a dead girlfriend in a cemetery without provoking a half-heard warning from beneath the tombstone: "Stop staring at that woman in the next grave."

There are quick-change performers, four in all, to embody assorted wives, eccentrics, sinners and straightmen; but essentially this is a monologue for Mr. O'Toole, and one that even he can't prevent seeming a bit long and samey. That big, bony moose face, with its hooded eyes, balances precariously atop an incongruously raffish pink shirt and white jacket. Out of its mouth comes an unexpectedly prim drawl, rising to an aghast whinny as it reminisces about, say, the friend who was officially reported to have choked on his own vomit: "Disgusting phrase! Did you ever hear of anyone who choked on someone else's vomit?" But two and a quarter hours spent being humorously buttonholed by a garrulous gentleman breakfasting on endless glasses of vodka is a bit hard on the mind, not to mention the buttonholes.

What's needed is more variety, maybe more vulnerability. True, there are occasional moments — mourning the death of traditional Soho, or contemplating the pointlessness of that third-rate steeplechase, life — when the eyes ice over, the shoulders sag, and we get a hint of the pain behind the pose. At such times the impression Mr. O'Toole gives is of a character created by P. G. Wodehouse in collaboration with Samuel Beckett, a patrician scarecrow staring at the bottom of some cosmic liquor bottle. But how did the charac-

ter get to feel that way, and when, and why? And isn't there more to say about what Bernard would, one must admit, find pretentious to describe as his existential angst? The entertainment at the Apollo has few if any answers to such questions.

■

In the second and more important half of "Another Time," Albert Finney plays one Leonard Lands: an internationally known pianist, resident in London, and currently plucking up the courage to tell his powerful mother he won't be giving any return concert in his (and her) native South Africa. But it's in the first half, which occurs in Cape Town 35 years earlier,

that Mr. Finney proves more arresting. There, he plays Leonard's father, who suffers from an undiagnosed brain tumor and is thought by his wife, himself and everyone else to be weak, soft and lazy. One wouldn't have expected loss of energy and self-respect to come easily to Mr. Finney, a robust, go-getting actor; but he's found a beached whale somewhere inside himself and brought it twitching to the surface. There aren't many more touching sights in the London theater than this big, tearful mammal, with his florid face and slicked-down hair, awkwardly gabbling at Christien Anholt's young Len, whom he adores and cannot afford to help study abroad.

But Finney the successful yet painfully isolated maestro is a considerably less plausible creation. It isn't just that his hands, build and body language suggest a wizard of the shot put, not the keyboard. And it isn't just that his acting sometimes seems artificial. Since Leonard's own hostile son is on hand to accuse him of emotional hollowness, the slightly stagey swagger may be partly deliberate.

Perhaps the problem is Ronald Harwood's script. Leonard is a skimpy, bland presence in the first half, so it's doubly hard to believe what the second half asks, that the pain of enduring his parents' rancorous marriage has wounded his psyche yet given him his creative juice. Indeed, it's hard to reconcile the boy and the man, or even see the connections between them. Mr. Finney is playing someone with a great void in his personal history, and has yet to fill it.

At all events, the climactic moment in which the desolate pianist covers

his eyes and silently weeps seems empty and even embarrassing: which is a pity, since there's a lot

Peter O'Toole as patrician scarecrow with cosmic liquor bottle.

about the surrounding work to enjoy. As his play "The Dresser" showed, Mr. Harwood is a sensitive, observant writer with a nice sense of humor as well as an intelligent conscience. It happens that he himself was raised in South Africa, and lives in London, and so is well placed to understand the particular pressures facing the exiled Leonard. But the politics that really interest him are more timeless and placeless, those of relationships and the family. And that gives us quite a supporting cast: Janet Suzman's flinty mother, Sara Kestelman as Leonard's culture-vulture aunt, David de Keyser as his amiably dotty uncle -- a trio that causes ripples both emotional and comic wherever it bangs down, Cape Town or London.

It's fun, it's memorable, this chattering crew; but maybe it's too memorable, too much fun, and absorbs too much of everyone's attention, Mr. Harwood's and our own. What's wanted is a deepening of the main character — wanted, and needed, if "Another Time" is to journey beyond London.   □

1989 D 3, II:5:1

Peter O'Toole, left, in "Jeffrey Bernard Is Unwell" by Keith Waterhouse and Albert Finney in "Another Time" by Ronald Harwood—Have these two actors chosen their plays wisely?

Alastair Muir

2 Ways to Deal With the Devil

OH, HELL, two plays directed by Gregory Mosher. Set by John Lee Beatty; costumes by Jane Greenwood; lighting by Kevin Rigdon; sound by Bill Dreisbach; illusionist consultant, George Schindler; general manager, Steven C. Callahan; production manager, Jeff Hamlin. Presented by Lincoln Center Theater, Mr. Mosher, director; Bernard Gersten, executive producer. At the Mitzi E. Newhouse Theater, 150 West 65th Street.

THE DEVIL AND BILLY MARKHAM, by Shel Silverstein.
WITH: Dennis Locorriere.

BOBBY GOULD IN HELL, by David Mamet.
Bobby Gould .... Treat Williams
Interrogator's Assistant .... Steven Goldstein
The Interrogator .... W. H. Macy
Glenna .... Felicity Huffman

By FRANK RICH

Women are a recent addition to the plays of David Mamet, and they really muck up the works. It's not that Mr. Mamet's writing suffers when women are on stage. In his new 45-minute comedy "Bobby Gould in Hell" — the second half of "Oh, Hell," the double bill Mr. Mamet shares with Shel Silverstein at the Mitzi E. Newhouse Theater — the playwright is as funny and pungent as ever. He even gets laughs out of a "Two Jews go into a bar" joke that never reaches its punch line. But women drive the men in Mr. Mamet's plays crazy, even if one of the men happens to be, well, the devil incarnate.

Brigitte Lacombe

W. H. Macy, left, and Treat Williams in "Bobby Gould in Hell".

The title character of "Bobby Gould in Hell" is the Hollywood mogul of "Speed-the-Plow" (in which he was initially played by Joe Mantegna). In that play, Gould made the terrible mistake of letting a sexy woman bamboozle him, at least for 24 hours, into betraying his best male friend, the producer Charlie Fox. The new play finds Gould (now played by Treat Williams) at his day of reckoning. The setting, designed by John Lee Beatty, is hell as Sam Goldwyn might hope it to be: a men's club with tasteful antiques, leather-bound books and "Exorcist" special effects discreetly hidden behind closed mahogany doors. There Bobby must confront the Interrogator (W. H. Macy), a devil who sounds like David Letterman and looks like a walking advertisement for the entire L. L. Bean catalogue of fishing gear.

•

The Interrogator would rather, in truth, be fishing than working. Gould, who describes himself as "a straight B-minus sort of man," insists on pleading his case. Soon the two men's argumentative exchange is abruptly interrupted by Glenna (Felicity Huffman), a medical assistant who arrives in the underworld still clutching TV Guide and a television remote control. Glenna was not well treated by the randy Gould in life. She immediately takes to badgering both him and the Interrogator about the way men "internalize neurotic needs."

"Have you ever thought about counseling?," she asks the devil. It takes only a few minutes of psychobabble-flecked hectoring for Glenna to bring the previously antagonistic Gould and Interrogator together in a male bond as tight as the one shared by Gould and Fox in "Speed-the-Plow." Ms. Huffman, who also played the female spoiler in that play after Madonna left, is most amusing here as she stubbornly and humorlessly stands her ground. When Mr. Williams responds with the exasperated cry, "There was no pleasing her!" he seems to express a masculine bafflement as timeless as the Old Testament imperatives underlying the play's tongue-in-cheek view of heaven and hell.

While the cliché in Mamet criticism is to label him a misogynist, that's not quite the case. For him, women are more the Other than the Enemy, as he makes clear in "Women," an essay whose thinking overlaps

"Bobby Gould in Hell" and which can be found in the writer's new prose collection, "Some Freaks." (Review, page C18.) In "Bobby Gould," Mr. Mamet also extends some of what one might call his theological thinking from "Speed-the-Plow." He has his own idea about how to exorcise what used to be called Jewish guilt — man's intrinsic feeling that he is bad before mothers, wives and God — and it is funnier than any possible ending

Hell hath that fury too, and it drives the boss nuts.

to hoary old stories of "two Jews in a bar."

Despite the fact that "Bobby Gould in Hell" follows so many other Mamet plays (and his latest screenplay, the coming "We're No Angels") in placing two con men at center stage, the director, Gregory Mosher, makes it look as fresh as it sounds. Mr. Williams has been well drilled in the clipped Mamet timing of which Mr. Macy has long been a master, and there is another impeccable performance from Steven Goldstein as an obsequious, bespectacled assistant devil who looks like a Dickensian clerk until that moment when his boss's departure allows him to have a smoke.

•

Shel Silverstein, whose extended monologue, "The Devil and Billy Markham," opens "Oh, Hell," is also a Mamet colleague — whether in one-act bills at the Ensemble Studio Theater, in contributing to the pages of Playboy magazine or in collaborating on the screenplay for "Things Change." Mr. Silverstein, who may be best known for his songs and children's books, can also be an antic playwright. He once reduced "Hamlet" to a country-western ballad (in "The Crate"), and he has also reimagined "Faust" in the terms of contemporary television game shows ("The Lady or the Tiger"). But "The Devil and Billy Markham," however redolent of its author's idiosyncratic voice, quickly proves to be the hell an audience must slog through to get to "Bobby Gould."

The play, performed by the rock singer Dennis Locorriere, is occasion-

ally sung but mostly talked blues (in verse) that recounts the attempts of a Nashville singer to beat the devil in craps, pool and love. There are some inside jokes about the recording industry, many harmless effusions of scatology and, near the end, a playful description of a devil's wedding party at which Catherine the Great is "making a date with the horse of Paul Revere." Just about any five minutes of "The Devil and Billy Markham" would convey enough of its flavor. It goes on for nearly an hour.

Under Mr. Mosher's direction, Mr. Locorriere gives an ingratiating performance, and he works hard enough to break out in a hellish sweat. The audience's sweat is prompted by anxiety. Watching "The Devil and Billy Markham" is like being trapped at a bar with an amiable drunk who simply refuses to let go of your arm or his convoluted, often-told tale. You know the spiel won't end until one of you falls off his stool.

1989 D 4, C15:1

2 Beatles, 1 Stone And No George

UP AGAINST IT, music and lyrics by Todd Rundgren; based on a screenplay by Joe Orton; adapted for the stage by Tom Ross; directed by Kenneth Elliott; choreography by Jennifer Muller; set design, B. T. Whitehill; costume design, John Glaser; lighting design, Vivien Leone; sound design, John Kilgore; orchestrations, Doug Katsaros; vocal arrangements, Mr. Rundgren; musical director, Tom Fay; associate producer, Jason Steven Cohen. Presented by Joseph Papp. At the Public Theater/LuEsther Hall, 425 Lafayette Street.

Father Brodie and The Old Man Stephen Temperley
Miss Drumgoole .... Alison Fraser
Ian McTurk .... Philip Casnoff
The Mayor .... Joel McKinnon Miller
Christopher Low .... Roger Bart
Connie Boon .... Toni DiBuono
Rowena .... Mari Nelson
Bernard Coates .... Tom Aulino
The Man in the Hole and Lilly Corbett
.... Judith Cohen
Georgina .... Marnie Carmichael
Jack Ramsay .... Dan Tubb
Guard .... Scott Carollo
Ensemble
Brian Arsenault, Scott Carollo, Mindy Cooper, Dorothy R. Earle, Julia C. Hughes, Gary Mendelson and Jim Newman

By MEL GUSSOW

In "Up Against It," his unproduced screenplay for the Beatles, Joe Orton tried to combine the irreverent spirit of "A Hard Day's Night" and "Help!" with his own far more mordant sensibility. Since the playwright's death, the screenplay has remained a tantalizing footnote to Orton's career. Although the film script is not in the same class as his plays, the published version exists for reading and imagining, raising the question of what the movie would have been like.

A partial, unrewarding answer is given by the production that opened last night at the Public Theater, a musical stage adaptation by Tom Ross and Todd Rundgren. Perhaps Richard Lester or members of the Monty Python troupe could have realized the script (with revisions), but not the current collaborators and their director, Kenneth Elliott. Together they have obliterated whatever charm existed in the screenplay. The musical itself is emblematic of one of the evening's several unnecessarily repeated songs, "When Worlds Collide." On stage, everything col-

lides — book, score, direction, performances, even the push-me, pull-you plasterboard scenery.

Because "Up Against It" was conceived as a movie musical, there would seem to be a rationale for enlisting someone like Mr. Rundgren, a popular rock composer. Unfortunate-

A tantalizing footnote to Joe Orton's career.

ly, when it came time to create a theatrical score, Mr. Rundgren composed an inferior pastiche of everyone from Brecht and Weill to Gilbert and Sullivan and proves totally unable to transform Orton's wit into lyrics.

One of the most grating songs is the title number, which has the additional misfortune of being sung by the actor with the most unmusical voice, Dan Tubb, in the role that would have been reserved for John Lennon. There is, in fact, only one good song, "Parallel Lines," which, in reprise, is given a plaintive urgency by Philip Casnoff (as Ian McTurk, the Paul McCartney role). In style, "Parallel Lines" seems out of context with the rest of the show.

Following the screenplay, the story chronicles the misadventures of three prodigal friends (Orton had eliminated the George Harrison role after the Beatles turned down the script) who are victimized in a flagrant battle between the sexes. They become involved in a plot to assassinate the first female Prime Minister of Britain. Wherever McTurk turns, on land or at sea, he encounters the entire cast.

The book is spotted with rude Orton remarks about Church, State and sex. In response to a statement that a priest has been wrestling with his conscience all afternoon, McTurk asks, "Who won?" Such moments are far outweighed by the alterations in the script and by the interruption of Mr. Rundgren's score. The show, which is set in the 1960's, also reaches far afield for anachronistic jokes. (In her acceptance speech, the Prime Minister gushes, "You like me, you really like me.")

•

Mistakes are exacerbated in Mr. Elliott's comic strip-style production. Best known for his direction of plays by Charles Busch, he approaches Orton in a similar vein, turning absurdist farce into camp caricature and overplaying the war of genders to the point of misogyny.

One of the pivotal decisions was whether to attempt to imitate the Beatles. The show's response is self-contradictory. The three characters speak in insecure Liverpool accents. Two have Beatle hairdos and mannerisms, while the third, Mr. Casnoff, acts less like a Beatle than like a Rolling Stone. Roger Bart, in the guise of Ringo Starr, is the closest to having a Beatle-mien, but, in common with his colleagues, he is undercut by the circumstances.

The only character to emerge relatively unscathed is Miss Drumgoole, the parlormaid who adores McTurk but whose love remains unrequited until the finale. Alison Fraser plays Miss Drumgoole with a kind of impassioned innocence that is one of the evening's few assets, although in the second act she suffers the indignity of a coarse Spanish number that calls for her to sing to a Yorick-like skull.

Mr. Casnoff carries the primary burden of the score, including the clichéd "If I Have to Be Alone," in which he sounds as if he were still trapped in the musical "Chess." Other actors are even less fortunate, including Toni DiBuono as a strident Chief of Police and Mari Nelson as a bimbo.

After John Tillinger's recent authentic revivals of Orton's three full-length comedies, the author seemed to have achieved his proper recognition and respect as a Wilde for our age. The musical at the Public reminds one that Orton is still up against it, even though in this case the opposition is not from philistines but from misguided admirers.

1989 D 5, C17:3

So Happy In the 1970's

BABA GOYA, by Steve Tesich; directed by Harris Yulin; set, Tom Kamm; lighting, Mal Sturchio; costumes, Candice Donnelly; sound, Gary and Timmy Harris; production stage manager, Camille Calman; stage manager, Edward Phillips. Presented by Second Stage Theater, Robyn Goodman and Carole Rothman, artistic directors. At 2162 Broadway, at 76th Street.

Goya	Estelle Parsons
Mario	Jack Wallace
Old Man	David Clarke
Bruno	Patrick Breen
Sylvia	Martha Gehman
Adolf	Ron Faber
Criminal	Thom Sesma
Client	Irving Metzman

By LAURIE WINER

Baba Goya, the title character and earth mother in the 1973 play by Steve Tesich now being revived at the Second Stage Theater, starts the morning with an Italian love song and a cup of strong Turkish coffee. As long as her household is full of warm bodies, Goya is undaunted by all of the messy problems they can pose.

Her fourth husband, Mario, says he's dying, but he has helpfully taken out a newspaper ad for his replacement. Meanwhile, Goya's daughter, Sylvia, has come home, fleeing a husband who impregnated her only to test the legality of an abortion law. Bruno, Goya's adopted son, is a policeman so overwhelmed with pity for criminals that he forgets to take his socks off in the shower. An old man Goya has recruited as an honorary grandfather is getting really crotchety. If this sounds like "You Can't Take It With You" for the 1970's, hold on.

Other colorful characters flit in and out of Goya's shabby but comfortable Queens home, designed by Tom Kamm with a keen eye for detail, from the worn fabric on the sofa arms to the faint grease stains on the Coldspot refrigerator and the stack of National Geographics under the end table. There's also an unthreatening Japanese criminal whom Bruno has brought home and has chained to the radiator.

Two suitors drop by in response to Mario's ad. Goya rejects one, a stiff German named Adolf who has applied before. But the next applicant is a sad sack with good qualifications: he has no relatives or friends. Goya herself is an orphan, so he's invited to stay.

Goya is all accepting of these characters, who are little more than walking eccentricities. But she does draw the line somewhere. She sympathetically pats Sylvia's head when the girl confesses to having been a shoplifter and an actress in pornographic movies. But when her daughter admits that she voted for Nixon to get back at her husband, Goya pushes her off a chair.

Baba Goya welcomes (almost) everyone.

First produced at the American Place Theater, "Baba Goya" is a period piece now. It evokes a nostalgia for the 1970's as a time when social problems didn't seem so overwhelming, when Americans were more generous about sharing the wealth.

•

In films like "Breaking Away" and "Four Friends," Mr. Tesich, a Yugoslav immigrant, used more realistic characters to embody America's constant striving toward social equality. In his play "The Speed of Darkness," which had its premiere this year at the Goodman Theater in Chicago, Mr. Tesich focused on a loving family whose happiness is seriously threatened by the residue of guilt and rage from the Vietnam War. "Baba Goya" seems like the work of another writer entirely, one who is trying out a lightly absurdist tone that sabotages his sentimental message. The play suffers from an overload of whimsicality.

Under Harris Yulin's direction, the actors turn in some good comic thumbnail sketches. As Goya, Estelle Parsons is a disheveled Mother Courage with a healthy yen for her beefy Mario, played with wide-eyed wonder by Jack Wallace. Thom Sesma's deadpan running commentary as the criminal is refreshing, a harbinger of the more straightforward Tesich characters to come. Ron Faber, as Adolf, delivers a portrait of a punctilious German who manages not to be a cliché.

As the members of her household leave the nest, Goya gets ready for another trip to the orphanage the way other people go down to the dog pound. Mr. Tesich has always liked a happy ending, but this one comes much too easily.

1989 D 6, C21:1

No Exit

BRIAR PATCH, by Deborah Pryor; directed by Lisa Peterson; set, David Birn; costumes, Michael Krass; lighting, Greg MacPherson; original music and sound, Michael Keck; fight choreographer, Ron Piretti; production stage manager, Diane Ward; production supervisor, Kevin Causey; produced by Kate Baggott. Presented by the Ensemble Studio Theater, Curt Dempster, artistic director; Peter Shavitz, managing director. At 549 West 52d Street.

Inez	Elizabeth Berridge
Edgar	Victor Slezak
Flowers	Paul McCrane
Butcher Lee	Connie Ray
Druden	William Ragsdale
Avon	Nancy Franklin

By MEL GUSSOW

The battered bride at the center of Deborah Pryor's "Briar Patch"

stands in the Virginia moonlight and dreams about floating away into outer space. Confined in the tangled brambles of Ms. Pryor's dreary play (opening the season at the Ensemble Studio Theater), theatergoers may feel similarly in need of liberation. There is no exit from this "Briar Patch."

In common with the author's earlier play, "The Love Talker," this is a gnarled, Southern Gothic view of life in ambush. The wife (played by Elizabeth Berridge) is afflicted with a brutalizing husband (Victor Slezak), who regards her as his punching bag. It is unclear why such an outspoken young woman would continue to suffer such daily abuse — or why the theaters (the Arena Stage in Washington as well as the Ensemble Studio) that have presented the play thought it was of dramatic interest.

As a backyard study of dirt-poor people, "Briar Patch" is a late entry in an overworked genre, one that is as old as "God's Little Acre." Only a playwright like Sam Shepard can find new life — and art — in such material. Others, Ms. Pryor included, become mired in tawdry detail. In this case, the wife is chained like a wild dog, punched in the eye (she wears a patch for much of the play) and is frightened out of her dim wits.

As part of his dereliction, the husband allows his creepy friend (Paul McCrane) open access to his home. If anything, the friend is even more disturbed than the husband. They take turns tormenting the wife. She begins to question her domestic incarceration only after she meets a rich young man who rashly, and unbelievably, promises to rescue her.

After an overlong first act, the play finally moves to the crux of the narrative, the fact that the wife has a penchant for exchanging one prison for another, as she is held in thrall by a succession of men. Using an awkwardly platformed set, the director, Lisa Peterson, has difficulty in defining the various indoor and outdoor playing areas and in instilling tension in the predictable play.

The minimal interest in "Briar Patch" derives from Ms. Berridge's performance. Looking about 14, she is completely credible as this baby doll of a wife. One's only reservation about the performance is that it is reminiscent of others delivered by the actress, who has specialized in playing oppressed waifs (as in "Coyote Ugly" and "Crackwalker").

Mr. Slezak and Mr. McCrane are appropriately menacing in their one-dimensional roles, but William Ragsdale is inept as the wife's wealthy suitor. A single spark of common-sense is represented by a fortune-teller named Butcher Lee. The names of the characters are examples of the author's self-conscious attempts at irony. Mr. McCrane's dirt-encrusted villain is named Flowers and a tough-talking policewoman is called Avon. As for the husband and wife, their surname is Macbeth. For the audience as well as the actors, the play boils over with toil and trouble.

1989 D 6, C21:1

The Wicked And the Bad

DR. JEKYLL AND MR. HYDE, by Georg Osterman; directed by Kate Stafford; scenery by Mark Beard; costumes by Susan Young; lighting by Richard Currie; music and sound by James S. Badrak, Alan Gregorie and Jan

Bell; production stage manager, James Eckerle. Presented by the Ridiculous Theatrical Company, at the Charles Ludlam Theater, 1 Sheridan Square.

Minerva	Terence Mintern
Mary Jekyll	Eureka
Henry Jekyll	Everett Quinton
Bernice Braintwain	Mary Neufeld
Lily Gay	Georg Osterman
Aculine	Minnette Coleman

By LAURIE WINER

There's a psychotic killer loose in Coxsackie, N.Y., the setting for the Ridiculous Theatrical Company's new production of "Dr. Jekyll and Mr. Hyde." The killer, a formerly mild-mannered librarian, has dismembered 16½ bodies. Dr. Henry Jekyll of the Coxsackie Medical Institute believes this is no ordinary criminal. No, he declares, this librarian is suffering from quantum synaptic dualism, a theory that Dr. Jekyll's colleague Dr. Braintwain derides as balderdash. But Dr. Jekyll is determined to prove the disease's existence — even if he has to drink a potion that turns him into sleazy little Eddie Hyde, the wickedest man in Coxsackie and a really bad stand-up comic to boot.

In Georg Osterman's slap-happy and very liberal adaptation of Robert Louis Stevenson's short novel, exposition is never subtly interwoven into the text. Dr. Jekyll's faithful maid, Minerva, who looks remarkably like a tall man in a black dress with a little white apron, is plumping the pillows on the doctor's armchair. "Why, I've never met a man as mild and even-tempered as Dr. Jekyll," she says with a sigh to no one in particular.

After that, you can count down the seconds until Everett Quinton, as an anxious, nearly bald Jekyll, makes

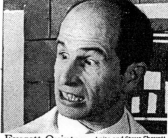

Everett Quinton   Anita and Steve Shevett

his hilarious transformation into the foul Hyde lurking within. In a mad rush to discover the potion, he scrawls formulas on a blackboard in his basement laboratory and simulates elaborate bubbling noises as he pours the contents of a test tube into his coffee cup. After a sip and a pause ("Not bad"), he crosses to the bookcase, where he poses like a crucified martyr and is spun rapidly upside down and in a circle about 50 times. Not even dizzy, he steps down, now sporting a black fright wig, and scurries back to his test tubes. "Hide all evidence, hide all evidence, hide ... I christen you Hyde!" he shouts, clapping himself on the head with a chalk-encrusted eraser.

The next scene finds Hyde at a bohemian hangout called the Fruit Bowl. When the brassy Lily Gay, deliciously played by Mr. Osterman in a beehive hairdo and becoming false eyelashes, takes the microphone to sing "You've Changed," Hyde pelts her with grapes. Soon he'll make Lily his love slave and pour roaches on her and generally torment her. "I've had warts that went away quicker!" poor Lily complains.

"Dr. Jekyll and Mr. Hyde" is full of the gloriously goofy performances and raunchy sight gags cherished by Charles Ludlam, the playwright and

The set as metaphor: Nothing is real if it can be painted on.

rounder of the Ridiculous Company, who died in 1987. Mr. Osterman's writing is not nearly so densely packed with jokes and far-flung cultural allusions as Ludlam's. But if "Dr. Jekyll and Mr. Hyde" does not deliver the frenzied orgy of comedy that Ludlam seemed to achieve so effortlessly, Mr. Osterman creates a madness of his own by interweaving Stevenson's rich Victorian prose with jokes so stupid that a 9-year-old might reject them.

Mr. Quinton, the company's artistic director, plays both the high verbal and low physical comedy with absolute conviction. He wrings his hands, coaxing melodrama from his most florid lines, some of them lifted right from Stevenson. "There's something strange in my sensations," he confides to the audience in one of his bouts of overheated philosophizing. "Something indescribably new, and from its very novelty, incredibly sweet," he says, snapping each hard consonant against his tongue with relish.

•

Under Kate Stafford's direction, both the actors and the designers bring unabashed amateurism to liberating heights. Everyone is good, particularly Mary Neufeld as the suspicious Dr. Braintwain and Terence Mintern in his dual role as the housemaid, Minerva, and a Jehovah's Witness who meets an unfortunate end at the hands of Mr. Hyde. The actress Eureka, so funny earlier this season as the leering alcoholic proprietor of Mr. Ludlam's "Big Hotel," is wasted in the scant role of Mary, Dr. Jekyll's dilettante wife.

Mark Beard's extravagantly phony sets, in which props are never present if they can be painted on, are amusing, and Richard Currie adds some witty lighting touches.

In the end, a lot of the people that Mr. Hyde murders come back to life. But who cares if the moral thread of Stevenson's tale is lost when we get to see Dr. Jekyll nervously hopping around, afraid of the obscenities that Hyde would like to hurl at everyone in sight? When you're in the presence of Mr. Quinton, you've got to root for the re-emergence of that evil Hyde for the pure pleasure of it.

1989 D 8, C3:2

Exorcising In Groups

THE 10th MAN, by Paddy Chayefsky; directed by Ulu Grosbard; set by Santo Loquasto; costume by Jane Greenwood; lighting by Dennis Parichy; sound by Daniel Schreier; poster art by James McMullan; general manager, Steven C. Callahan; production manager, Jeff Hamlin. Presented by Lincoln Center Theater, Gregory Mosher, director; Bernard Gersten, executive producer. At the Vivian Beaumont Theater, Lincoln Center, 150 West 65th Street.

Hirschman-Cabalist	Joseph Wiseman
Schlissel	Bob Dishy
Zitorsky	Jack Weston
Sexton	Sidney Armus
Alper	Ron Rifkin
Foreman	Alan Manson
Evelyn Foreman	Phoebe Cates
Arthur Brooks	Peter Friedman
Harris	Carl Don
Elder Kessler	David Berman
Younger Kessler	Kenny Morris
Rabbi	Michael Mantell
Policeman	Dan Daily

By FRANK RICH

"The 10th Man," Paddy Chayefsky's drama about the dwindling congregation of an Orthodox synagogue on Long Island, is ideal seasonal fare for those who like their holiday plays to go on as long as Hanukkah.

A hit in Tyrone Guthrie's staging at the snug Booth Theater on Broadway in 1959, "The 10th Man" looks forlorn as it strains to fill the vast Vivian Beaumont. Why did Lincoln Center Theater choose so obviously dated a work for exhumation? Perhaps it's because of the modest success achieved by the nostalgic revival of Hy Kraft's equally sentimental but much funnier and far less pretentious "Cafe Crown" (of 1942) at the New York Shakespeare Festival last season.

What's next? Maybe it's time to disinter the Broadway vehicles Leonard Spigelgass wrote for Gertrude Berg 30 years ago, "A Majority of One" and "Dear Me, the Sky Is Falling," so Charles Busch can perform them in repertory.

Like "Cafe Crown," "The 10th Man" is served up with a sizable cast including Bob Dishy and with a realistic set by Santo Loquasto. But this is "Cafe Crown" on a fast. Mr. Dishy, a memorable Second Avenue waiter in the Kraft comedy, can do only so much with the heavier stereotype of a crabby socialist-atheist; Mr. Loquasto's design for a shabby Mineola storefront temple, all too authentically brackish in color, becomes as oppressive as a "Fidelio" dungeon when bloated to Beaumont dimensions.

Even such welcome old-school shtick artists as Jack Weston, Sidney Armus, Ron Rifkin, Alan Manson and Carl Don often fade into the hulking woodwork. The meager wisecracks distributed among them — mainly about burial plots and daughters-in-law — run out well before the end of the first of three acts.

The main business of "The 10th Man" is to reassure the audience of the power of faith — a task Chayefsky undertook with the same sunny alacrity of "The Sound of Music," which opened on Broadway the week after his play (and which, unlike his, at least took pains to acknowledge the shadow of the Holocaust). The evening's catalyst for spiritual renewal is Evelyn (Phoebe Cates), the 18-year-old granddaughter of one of the synagogue's elders.

Evelyn has been diagnosed as a schizophrenic with violent tendencies but just may be possessed by a demon — a dybbuk. In her fits, she has delusions that she is, variously, the whore of Kiev and Susan Hayward. Before modern psychiatry attempts its miracles, the men of the congregation want to give an old-fashioned exorcism a try.

•

For there to be a religious ceremony, however, the straitened synagogue must round up a minyan — or, to use this production's curiously Anglicized diction, a quorum of 10 men. The 10th man is almost literally

blown through the door in the form of Arthur Brooks (Peter Friedman), an ill-shaven young lawyer reeling from

Brigitte Lacombe
Phoebe Cates in "The 10th Man."

a divorce, disenchantment with Communism and an excess of both alcohol and headshrinking. Arthur believes that "life is utterly meaningless." Along with the congregation's new go-getting young Rabbi (Michael Mantell), he is the playwright's symbolic caricature of the ostensibly materialistic, Freud-obsessed, overassimilated American Jews who were fleeing orthodoxy for suburban country clubs, psychoanalysis and color television when "The 10th Man" was written.

You can be sure that Chayefsky, representing the interests of theater-party audiences of his time, will teach a lesson or two to the skeptical Arthur and all those other Reform Jews who "sit around like Episcopalians, listening to organ music." But first he contrives a romantic subplot that reduces both young characters to cooing boulevard-comedy juveniles right out of the Kaufman and Hart plays that the temple's new rabbi hopes to produce for fund-raising purposes.

•

In its eagerness to pander, "The 10th Man" seems as cynical now as the television programming that Chayefsky would later attack in his screenplay for "Network." Everyone on stage is lovable, and the trick ending is so contrived and sentimental that even the cast seems to disbelieve it. The dramaturgy is often as crude as the message. Characters recite their autobiographies at the drop of a prayer shawl. The phone-call traffic is heavy. There is no end to the spelling out of themes ("Here you have the decline of Orthodox Judaism graphically before your eyes") and footnoting of background information (the unenlightened of 1959 are reassured that mental institutions offer "the benefit of trained psychiatric personnel").

Ulu Grosbard, the director, drains any spontaneity from the Old World alter-kakers' kibitzing by insisting on pauses after laugh lines (whether the laughs materialize or not) and by managing to make the most casual

bits of stage business look overrehearsed and fake. The performances are so-so. Though her convulsions are no match for Linda Blair's, Ms. Cates does a fair vocal impersonation of Marlene Dietrich in her whore of Kiev mode; she is made to look preposterous when asked to shift abruptly from madwoman to chirpy ingénue. As her Jewish prince, the exemplary Mr. Friedman, late of "The Heidi Chronicles," works up a frenzy of unmoving passion.

Among the other distinguished but wasted actors in the company is Joseph Wiseman as a long-bearded sonorous-voiced mystic who presides over an exorcism that only dietary laws forbid one from labeling pure ham.

1989 D 11, C13:1

Body Language

PROGRESS, by Doug Lucie; directed by Geoffrey Sherman; set design by Paul Wonsek; light design by Phil Monat; costume design by Pamela Scofield; production stage manager, Melissa L. Burdick. Presented by Hudson Guild Theater, Geoffrey Sherman, producing artistic director; Steven Ramay, associate director. At 441 West 26th Street.

Ronee	Diana Van Fossen
Will	Ivar Brogger
Mark	John Curless
Ange	Anne Bobby
Lenny	Joe Mantello
Bruce	Nelson Avidon
Oliver	Edmund Lewis
Martin	Ray Virta

By LAURIE WINER

In "Progress," the British playwright Doug Lucie argues that peaceful co-existence between the sexes is impossible because almost all men are pigs. But the play, which opened yesterday at the Hudson Guild Theater, takes a sardonic view of its characters' basest motives. Until the final harrowing moments, you don't realize just how depressing a message it contains.

On the surface, Will, a television researcher, has evolved his 1960's activism into a 1980's caring kind of life style. He's supportive when his wife, Ronee, invites Ange, a battered blue-collar wife, to stay in their comfortable North London home. And Will is devoted to his men's consciousness-raising group, which he leads with the goal of "understanding our own maleness" and of "changing attitudes by being open and not resorting to hierarchical structures."

To that end, Will has his group peruse pornographic magazines so they can argue their positions "from experience." But the group members, Oliver, Martin and Bruce, are only nominally interested in the magazines that Will brings home. They're really interested in one another . For Will, the magazines become superfluous when he's confronted with a titillating, real-life pornographic image — the bloodied Ange, whose husband, Lenny, has just raped her.

As long as Will can hide his true nature behind the politically correct language of the day, it's easy for him to feel morally superior to men like Lenny and to Mark, a tabloid journalist and boarder in the house who's a walking compendium of misogynist and antigay jokes. Mr. Lucie takes a wicked pleasure in revealing that Will is in fact a brother under the skin to Mark and Lenny.

Will begins to stalk Ange when Ronee is at work. Unschooled in the ways of middle-class men, Ange

163

recognizes only that Will seems to be nice. She's flattered by his attention, and she rushes to serve him his tea and clean the kitchen. He seduces her over a game of strip backgammon, in which he warns that he'll give her ''a thrashing.'' He does, too, in his way.

In ''Progress,'' men's sexual desires always overcome their best intentions. When romantic entanglements become messy between Oliver, Bruce and Martin, they turn on one another. Will shamelessly uses Ange, and then asks her to seduce Ronee for his further pleasure. Suddenly the words ''understanding our own maleness'' take on new meaning.

The director, Geoffrey Sherman, never asks us to feel sorry for the play's female characters, and that strategy works. He keeps the play taut by focusing on Will's losing struggle to cloak his true nature, and he gets comedy out of the character's hypocrisy.

The cast is excellent. The standouts include John Curless as a joyfully scurrilous Mark, and Anne Bobby, who gives Ange a street-tough edge to cover her little-girl vulnerability. As Bruce, the group member whose stammer keeps him from dissembling as easily as the others, Nelson Avidon uses a forlorn expression that pays off nicely when we discover that he can be as cruel as any of his mates.

The set designer, Paul Wonsek, has created a fashionable and homey town house, with attention to the accouterments of civilized life — plenty of books, elegant molding, pretty striped wallpaper. It's a perfect theater for Will to play out the role of model citizen, comfortable but not ostentatious.

As Will, Ivar Brogger self-destructs in tiny steps, and he makes the progression from confident charm to debauchery smooth and riveting. When, in the last scene, his wife confronts him with undeniable evidence of his moral corrosion, he gets a kick out of finally saying what he really feels. ''Contempt and lust,'' he declares with satisfaction, ''those are my two strongest feelings.''

In the evening's last image, Will takes a sobering, long look at himself in the mirror. His face has the naked intensity of a man fascinated by the horror of the unadorned ego. In a play filled with the chatter of articulate people, the silence of that moment stands out. ''Progress'' details, finally, how little language counts after our actions have said it all.

1989 D 11, C15:1

This Is No Town For the Celestial

CITY OF ANGELS, book by Larry Gelbart; music by Cy Coleman; lyrics by David Zippel; musical numbers staged by Walter Painter; directed by Michael Blakemore; scenery, Robin Wagner; costumes, Florence Klotz; lighting, Paul Gallo; sound, Peter Fitzgerald and Bernard Fox; orchestrations, Billy Byers; vocal arrangements, Mr. Coleman and Yarol Gershovsky; musical direction, Gordon Lowry Harrell; fight staging, B. H. Barry; hair styles, Steve Atha; production stage manager, Steve Zweigbaum; general manager, Ralph Roseman. Presented by Nick Vanoff, Roger Berlind, Jujamcyn Theaters, Suntory International Corporation and the Shubert Organization. At the Virginia Theater, 245 West 52d Street.

Stone .... James Naughton
Alaura Kingsley and Carla Haywood
                                              Dee Hoty
Gabby and Bobbi .... Kay McClelland
Stine .... Gregg Edelman
Buddy Fidler and Irwin S. Irving
                                     Rene Auberjonois
Oolie and Donna .... Randy Graff
WITH: James Cahill, Carolee Carmello, Peter Davis, Shawn Elliott, Tom Galantich, Eleanor Glockner, James Hindman, Gary Kahn, Amy Jane London, Alvin Lum, Jacquey Maltby, Jackie Presti, Keith Perry, Herschel Sparber, Evan Thompson, Doug Tompos, Scott Waara, Raymond Xifo and Rachel York.

By FRANK RICH

There's nothing novel about show-stopping songs and performances in Broadway musicals, but how long has it been since a musical was brought to a halt by riotous jokes? If you ask me, one would have to travel back to the 1960's — to ''Bye Bye Birdie,'' ''A Funny Thing Happened on the Way to the Forum,'' ''How to Succeed in Business Without Really Trying'' and ''Little Me'' — to find a musical as flat-out funny as ''City of Angels,'' the new show about old Hollywood that arrived last night at the Virginia Theater.

This is an evening in which even a throwaway wisecrack spreads laughter like wildfire through the house, until finally the roars from the balcony merge with those from the orchestra and the pandemonium takes on a life of its own. Only the fear of missing the next gag quiets the audience down. To make matters sweeter, the jokes sometimes subside just long enough to permit a show-stopping song or performance or two to make their own ruckus at center stage.

•

Since the musical's principal creators are the writer Larry Gelbart and the composer Cy Coleman — pros who worked separately on ''Forum'' and ''Little Me'' early in their careers — the exhilarating result cannot really be called a surprise. Yet Mr. Gelbart and Mr. Coleman, invigorated with the try-anything brio of first-time collaborators half their age, bring the audience one unexpected twist after another. Only the territory of ''City of Angels'' is familiar: the late 1940's Hollywood romanticized in hard-boiled detective fiction and ruled by tyrannical studio moguls who seemed to give nearly every movie a title like ''Three Guys Named Joe.''

To take comic possession of the entire sprawling cultural landscape — to mock not just the period's movies but also the men behind the movies — Mr. Gelbart stages a two-pronged satirical attack. His hero, Stine (Gregg Edelman), is a novelist trying against considerable odds to turn his own book, ''City of Angels,'' into a screenplay that will not be an embarrassing sellout. But as Mr. Gelbart tracks Stine's travails in the film industry — where the ''envy is so thick you can cut it with a knife lodged in every other back'' — he also presents the hard-knock adventures of Stone, the Philip Marlowe-Sam Spade-like private eye of Stine's screenplay in progress and, in James Naughton's wonderfully wry performance, a comic shamus who is the stuff that dreams are made of.

•

There is no end to the cleverness with which the creators of ''City of Angels'' carry out their stunt of double vision, starting with a twin cast list (a Hollywood Cast and a Movie Cast) in the Playbill. Robin Wagner's extraordinarily imaginative set design — maybe the most eloquent argument yet against coloring old movies — uses the lush black-and-white of a pristine Warner Brothers print for the Stone sequences and candied Technicolor for Stine's off-camera adventures. Because the Stine and Stone narratives have their ironic parallels — fiction's thugs and temptresses often resemble Hollywood's movers and shakers — the ''City of Angels'' actors frequently play dual roles, shifting continually between color and black-and-white settings and characters. In one spectacular turn that rocks the second act, the winning Randy Graff, as a loyal secretary to both Stone and Stine, leaps across the color barrier to belt out her blues as the other woman in two male lives.

Such tricks are brilliantly abetted not just by Mr. Wagner and his fellow designers Florence Klotz and Paul Gallo but also by the director Michael Blakemore, who juggles the farcical collisions between reality and soundstage as deftly as he did the on- and offstage shenanigans of ''Noises Off.'' With occasional injections of stock period film, ''City of Angels'' recreates the swirling flashbacks, portentous tracking shots and swift dissolves of movies like ''The Maltese Falcon'' and ''The Big Sleep'' even as it wallows in the kitschy glamour of nouveau-riche Bel Air mansions where the conversation is ''never at a loss for numbers.''

Mr. Gelbart's jokes come in their own variety of colors. As in his screenplay for ''Movie Movie,'' he is a master at parodying vintage film genres — in this case finding remarkably fresh ways to skewer the sardonic voice-over narration, tough-guy talk and heavy-breathing imagery ('' It's as though I was hit by a wrecking ball wearing a pinky ring'') of the Chandler-Hammett film noir. But the funniest lines in ''City of Angels'' may well be those that assault the movie business — as personified by Buddy Fidler (Rene Auberjonois), an egomaniacal producer and director at Master Pictures, the same fictional studio that Mr. Gelbart accused of money-laundering in his Iran-contra satire, ''Mastergate.''

There are no angels in this show's Hollywood. Next to Fidler's self-serving Goldwynisms — ''You can tell a writer every time: words, words, words!'' he complains — the mixed metaphors of Stone's narration and the obfuscating double talk of the ''Mastergate'' politicians almost make sense. In Mr. Auberjonois's gleefully smarmy performance, Fidler congratulates himself on his philanthropic largess while destroying Stine's script in the interests of commerce or blacklist-era political cowardice. As he revises, the rewrites are carried out in the black-and-white flesh on stage, complete with mimed rewinding of the footage bound for the cutting-room floor. ''You're Nothing Without Me'' goes the title of the high-flying duet for Stine and Stone, but, in Mr. Gelbart's jaundiced view, the writer and his fictional alter ego are both nothing next to the greedy bully with casting approval, screenplay-credit envy and final cut.

•

As the jokes leaven the book's rage until the bitter final number, so does Mr. Coleman's score — a delirious celebration of jazz and pop styles sumptuously orchestrated by Billy Byers and blared out by a swinging pit band led by Gordon Lowry Har-

Martha Swope

Rachel York and James Naughton in ''City of Angels.''

rell. Mr. Coleman uses a scat-singing vocal quartet reminiscent of the Modernaires as a roving chorus; he freely mixes be-bop with wild Count Basie blasts, sentimental radio crooning (well done by Scott Waara) and smoky soundtrack music reminiscent of David Raskin's score for "Laura." The effect is like listening to "Your Hit Parade" of 1946, except that the composer's own Broadway personality remakes the past in his own effervescent, melodic style.

Though the young and talented lyricist David Zippel keeps up with Mr. Coleman's often intricate music, he only occasionally catches up with Mr. Gelbart's endlessly witty wordplay. His biggest success is Ms. Graff's song "You Can Always Count on Me," which recalls the sophisticated sass of the female solos Mr. Coleman once wrote with the lyricists Carolyn Leigh and Dorothy Fields. By contrast, Mr. Zippel's double-entendre duet for Stone and his femme-fatale client (Dee Hoty) is collegiate, and Mr. Auberjonois's big Act I solo isn't as biting about Hollywood as the dialogue surrounding it.

•

For all that's right about "City of Angels," one must also question the casting of Mr. Edelman, a powerful singer whose affable boyishness seems inappropriate and anachronistic for a hard-edged 40's novelist like Stine. It's hard to believe he could have created a character as worldly as Mr. Naughton's Stone, a Bogart incarnation that, for once, is not an impersonation. The show could also use much more dancing, a less arbitrarily plotted and more musical second act and a livelier heroine than the lost love (for Stone) and temporarily lost wife (for Stine) decently played by Kay McClelland.

In the large supporting cast, special attention must be paid — and will be, since she first appears wearing only a sheet — to Rachel York, who sings a torrid seduction number ("Lost and Found") in Act I before serving as a self-promoting starlet in Act II. As Stone says in somber voice-over when describing another Hollywood siren, "Only the floor kept her legs from going on forever." With lines like that, I, for one, would have been happy if "City of Angels" had gone on just as long.

1989 D 12, C19:4

Unbalancing Acts

LAVA, written, directed and designed by Richard Foreman; lighting design, Heather Carson; assistant director, David Herskovits. A co-production of Ontological-Hysteric Theater and the Wooster Group. At 33 Wooster Street.

WITH: Neil Bradley, Matthew Courtney, Peter Davis, Kyle deCamp, Hiedi Tradewell and Richard Foreman.

By MEL GUSSOW

In a program note to "Lava," Richard Foreman suggests that his new play "may at first seem even a bit more perplexing than the 'unbalancing acts' that are performed" in his other works. Theatergoers are forewarned and forearmed. For 20 years, this author and director has been offering ideographic emanations of his inner life. In a sense, he posts road maps without destinations. As with "Lava," the journey is intriguing, although the extent of the interest depends on one's willingness to indulge the playwright's fancifulness.

The plays are mysteries, and some are so elusive as to defeat even the most diligent of private investigators. All a theatergoer can hope to do is to collect clues and leap to conclusions, especially difficult in the case of "Lava."

For this co-production of Mr. Foreman's Ontological-Hysteric Theater and the Wooster Group, the Performing Garage has been turned into a Foreman equivalent of a Joseph Cornell box. Strange objects (and bizarre-looking characters) are firmly fixed in place, but the connection among them is in the eye of the beholder.

•

Before "Lava" begins, there is ample time to contemplate the setting (designed by Mr. Foreman), crisscrossed with his customary string and so crammed with gewgaws as to look like a black magical museum installation. This could be a classroom except that the stage is strewn with feathers. Somewhere, something is molting. Could it be the playwright's imagination?

First clue: Things come in threes. There are three blackboards on which are transcribed versions of the author's sepulchral taped narration. There are three actors, all outfited with hunchbacks, a trio of mad doctors who introduce three categories of thought. Category 1 is reality (regained with our equilibrium when we leave the theater). Category 2 is "random nonsense" (well represented on stage). Category 3 calls for an act of faith as the author attempts to disorient the audience.

With humility, Mr. Foreman admits his inability to communicate, discrediting himself for offering a "mental massage." When the language becomes too self-indulgent, there is a cry for "verbal police," an army of censors who remain unseen.

What one misses in the show is not so much clarity (obfuscation comes with the territory) as humor, which is usually endemic to the author's work — in his recent "Film Is Evil, Radio Is Good" and "Symphony of Rats," as well in his early picaresque tales about his favorite heroine, Rhoda. "Lava" is marked by its sobriety, even as the three actors don long black beards and look like Tatar cousins of the Flying Karamazov Brothers.

One of the play's lingering mysteries is the title, which may, of course, be a volcanic reference or perhaps a nostalgic salute to that soap that was popularized years ago with a commercial that spelled out the product's name with a drum-beating intensity. If one intruded an apostrophe into the title, making it "l'Ava," that might explain all those feathers on stage.

Even as his work becomes more internalized, Mr. Foreman has not lost his ability to awaken an audience's curiosity and to entreat strangers — and admirers — to join him in his own enigmatic quest for self-definition.

1989 D 13, C24:3

When He Was Good . . .

TRU, written and directed by Jay Presson Allen; from the words and works of Truman Capote; set design by David Mitchell; lighting design by Ken Billington and Jason Kantrowitz; costume design by Sarah Edwards; makeup by Kevin Haney; production stage manager, Ruth Kreshka. Presented by Lewis Allen and David Brown, with the Suntory International Corporation and the Shubert Organization, in association with Landmark Entertainment Group. At the Booth Theater, 222 West 45th Street.

WITH: Robert Morse

By FRANK RICH

When the curtain rises on the bloated, jowly bubble of flesh that is the title character of "Tru," Jay Presson Allen's monodrama about Truman Capote, a sentimental theatergoer is not so much startled by the resurrection of Capote, who died in 1984, as shocked by the obliteration of Robert Morse, last seen on Broadway in the mid-1970's. Buried somewhere in that skin-colored tub of Jell-O — the work of makeup man Kevin Haney, whose credits include the movies "Altered States" and "Wolfen" — is the sprite whose grin of impetuous youth charmed a nation in "How to Succeed in Business Without Really Trying" a good quarter-century ago.

Somewhere, but where? As the present Mr. Morse warms to his task at the Booth, dangling his wrists and slurring his words while puttering about the designer David Mitchell's handsome replica of Capote's final home at the United Nations Plaza, it's hard to find the performer one remembers. With his mad shopping-bag woman's cackle and darting lounge lizard's tongue, Mr. Morse so eerily simulates the public Capote of the pa-

Robert Morse struts, putters and slurs, all alone with the telephone.

thetic waning years that he could be a Capote robot, an Audio Animatronic figure in a macabre theme park, Xenonland perhaps, envisioned by Andy Warhol.

As Tru rambles on, however, the actor inside the flab does eventually emerge, and engagingly so. Mr. Morse can still look at an audience as if it were a mirror reflecting his own smiling face back at him. The mischievous twinkle in his eyes is as bright as ever; the rasp in his throat still makes him sound not just like Capote but also like the director Harold Prince (whom he once spoofed in the musical "Say, Darling"). And when, late in Act II, Tru takes to tapping and strutting to a Louis Armstrong recording of "The Sunny Side of the Street," Mr. Morse kicks a loose-limbed leg as high and friskily as he did when joining Bob Fosse's hoedown for the "Brotherhood of Man" finale in "How to Succeed."

•

By then one is glad to have met up with this actor again, is impressed by his command of his technique and his audience, and is moved by the courage that has allowed him to return to a Broadway stage in so unlikely a vehicle. But even then, his two-hour solo flight of celebrity impersonation makes for a very weird night out.

A reunion with Capote — or at least Mrs. Allen's representation of him — may not be everyone's idea of theater. Intentionally or not, "Tru" is a creep show: a hybrid of necrophilia and tame fan-magazine journalism that doesn't so much rekindle fascination with a troubled writer as rea-

waken the willies prompted by those disoriented talk-show appearances (remember "The Stanley Siegel Show"?) that were the desperate final act of his career.

Mrs. Allen sets her discursive monologue in the nights before Christmas 1975, when Tru is reeling from the social ostracism that followed Esquire magazine's publication of "La Côte Basque, 1965," the gossipy excerpt from his never-to-be-finished roman à clef, "Answered Prayers." Tru can no longer get his dearest friends, Babe (Paley) and Slim (Keith), on his heavily trafficked two-line speakerphone and instead must tag along with Ava Gardner to Quo Vadis. His last lover is nowhere in sight. Pills, vodka, cocaine and chocolate truffles all tempt him to oblivion.

Martha Swope
Robert Morse stars in "Tru" at the Booth Theater.

There is, heaven knows, a prospective drama here. Why did the author of such precocious fiction as "Other Voices, Other Rooms" and such adventurous new journalism as "In Cold Blood" betray his muse for the silly full-time job of being famous? Why did he turn on the super rich after two decades as their lap dog? Why did "Answered Prayers" mortally offend the Women's Wear Daily crowd? Speculative answers exist — most prominently in Gerald Clarke's biography "Capote" — but Mrs. Allen rarely explores them.

Tru's defense of "Answered Prayers" — spunky credos about the outlaw role of the writer — is too retroactive and pat to explain his literary death wish. His asides about mortality and suicide are not compelling enough to explain away his self-destruction. Even factual information essential to understanding Capote's current plight is missing, including any description of the actual contents of "Answered Prayers."

•

While Tru announces that everyone loves stories that tell "something horrendous about someone impeccable," Mrs. Allen never does dish much dirt. Perhaps she, unlike Capote, is afraid to offend the living. Nothing truly bitchy is said about the many famous names titilatingly dropped in "Tru"; some major Capote antagonists (most conspicuously Gore Vidal) are not mentioned at all.

Nor does the audience get the measure of the man Capote used to be. It's typical of "Tru" that it offers references to his Christmas shopping at Tiffany's but no recollections about "Breakfast at Tiffany's." A few childhood memories are recounted — complete with a hokey echo-chamber voice from the past — and, for schematic contrast with his grim 1975 holiday season, Capote's memoir "A Christmas Memory" is recited in excerpt. Yet Mrs. Allen's script is unable to evoke the ghost of the driving, eccentric writer who was still flourishing as late as when Mr. Morse was in "How to Succeed."

•

In place of a life portrait with depth, "Tru" settles for its wind-up Mme. Tussaud's caricature of the wrecked 1975 model Capote. This Tru is sporadically funny — if one shares Mrs. Allen's taste for the campiest of anecdotes and one-liners — and rarely boring. But since the soul of the younger Capote doesn't shine through as Mr. Morse's youthful spirit does, the potentially touching drama of decay is lost. The complex, possibly tragic figure of a wasted artist is replaced by a maudlin, some might say antediluvian, stereotype of "Boys in the Band" vintage: the alcoholic moneyed homosexual who, having lost his youth and beauty, is left all alone with his telephone and record collection in his penthouse on Christmas Eve.

A few manufactured tears notwithstanding, the evening's histrionic level is so uniform that any half-hour of "Tru" will probably be enough for most onlookers. True Tru fanatics, of course, will devour it all. Everyone will agree that the star's energy never flags. While Mr. Morse may not succeed in drawing the audience to Truman Capote, he does leave one eager to see a born-again actor inhabit other voices, other rooms.

1989 D 15, C3:1

Rising to the Occasion

THE CRUCIBLE, by Arthur Miller; directed by Arvin Brown; set design by Michael H. Yeargan; costume design by David Murin; lighting design by Ronald Wallace; production stage manager, Pamela Edington. Presented by the Long Wharf Theater, Mr. Brown, artistic director; M. Edgar Rosenblum, executive director. At New Haven.

Betty Parris	Magen Tracy
The Rev. Samuel Parris	Rex Robbins
Tituba	Novella Nelson
Abigail Williams	Ann Dowd
Susanna Wallcott	April Beth Armstrong
Mrs. Ann Putnam	Sarah Peterson
Thomas Putnam	George Guidall
Mercy Lewis	Molly Price
Mary Warren	Pippa Pearthree
John Proctor	Frank Converse
Rebecca Nurse	Joyce Ebert
Giles Corey	Clement Fowler
The Rev. John Hale	Jack Gilpin
Elizabeth Proctor	Maryann Plunkett
Francis Nurse	John Leighton
Ezekiel Cheever	Richard Spore
John Willard	Allen McCullough
Judge Hathorne	John Braden
Deputy Governor Danforth	Charles Cioffi
Sarah Good	Virginia Downing
Hopkins	David Scott Meikle

By MEL GUSSOW
Special to The New York Times

NEW HAVEN, Dec. 13 — "The Crucible" is Arthur Miller's most produced play, for reasons that are chillingly apparent in Arvin Brown's revival at the Long Wharf Theater. The play combines a clear dramatic line with a pronounced moral fervor

that has not lessened in the 36 years since it was first presented.

Written during a time of public hysteria, "The Crucible" used the story of the Salem witch trials as a screen through which the author could speak about what he saw as an eternal illness of mankind, that traitorous instinct that causes people to embrace tyranny and to turn against their neighbors to protect themselves.

In the play, this disease assumes epidemic proportions and results in a perversion of religion as well as of justice. It is Mr. Miller's response that there will always be room for the righteous, people who can bravely transcend their times and, if necessary, lose their lives in pursuit of a higher purpose. In characteristic Miller fashion, he also affirms the residual power of the law as something that will outlive immediate injustices of the judicial system.

Despite the evil that is "loose in Salem," the issues are not black and white, but representative of fallible and suddenly courageous people who rise to heroism. The latter is the case with Giles Corey, the litigious farmer. Facing a slow, agonizing death as rocks are heaped on his chest, he cries, "More weight."

•

At the center of the drama are the Proctors, the upright husband, who desperately tries to keep his world from toppling, and his good wife, a woman who cannot lie (except for the sake of her husband). Frank Converse and Maryann Plunkett are splendid in these roles and in conveying a relationship that allows for severely limited feelings to be transmitted from one to the other.

Mr. Converse's steely concern for his wife and for the principles he honors is exactly partnered with Ms. Plunkett's radiant sense of integrity. In this production, even more than in other versions of the play, Elizabeth Proctor becomes the strong moral center.

T. Charles Erickson

Maryann Plunkett and Frank Converse in "The Crucible."

Allied against the couple are diverse figures of churchly hypocrisy and legalistic pretension, men who far exceed their small authority in order to protect the sanctity of their private domains. Despite the 17th-century dress and the formality of the language, these characters evoke contemporary parallels. It is not a far remove from the covetous Reverend Parris to today's self-aggrandizing television evangelists.

In 'Crucible,' the perversion of religion and justice.

The catalyst of the drama is Abigail Williams, the adolescent whose jealousy sets the delusions in motion. The role is sometimes played in the manner of a willful child. In Ann Dowd's commanding portrayal, the girl has an artful directness. This is a harsher characterization than one customarily sees in the role — and it lifts the battle to a higher dramatic pitch. Ms. Dowd's performance is in contrast to the vibrancy of her character in the Russian play "The Paper Gramophone" last season at Hartford Stage.

•

The work offers theatergoers cold comfort. While following the ineluctable arc of "The Crucible," one looks for a character to try to alter the course of events. The author gives us only the well-intentioned Reverend Hale (Jack Gilpin). Opening his eyes to the reign of terror, he can respond only by asking others to compromise their conscience in quest of survival. Mr. Miller's allegiance — and ours — is not with Hale but with Elizabeth Proctor, whose dutifulness to her God

and to herself keeps her firmly on a course of rectitude.

Not all of the actors in the large cast have the assurance of the principals. Several falter along the way, but there are persuasive performances in supporting roles by, among others, Pippa Pearthree and Clement Fowler. In Mr. Brown's production, there is a firm resolution and understanding, offering further certification of the value of a play that opened the Long Wharf Theater 25 years ago. The atmosphere and Michael H. Yeargan's wood-hewn setting are stark, shadowy and monochromatic, as fits the bleakness of the period. The argument is as timeless as it is disquieting.

1989 D 16, 15:1

The Real World?

LIFE IS A DREAM, by Calderón de la Barca; English version by Roy Campbell; music by Joseph Blunt; directed by Eve Adamson; set designed by Sara Waterbury; costumes designed by Jonathan Bixby; lighting designed by Ms. Adamson. Presented by the Jean Cocteau Repertory, 330 Bowery, at Second Street.

Basilio	Harris Berlinsky
Segismundo	Craig Smith
Astolfo	Robert Ierardi
Estrella	Elise Stone
Clotaldo	James Sterling
Rosaura	Angela Vitale
Clarin	Joseph Menino

Ensemble

Carol Dearman, Grant Neale, Christophr Oden and Lyn Wright.

By WILBORN HAMPTON

The early 17th century was a time of great soul-searching in Europe. Aftershocks from the Reformation and Counter-Reformation still shuddered through cathedrals and palaces, calling into question political alliances, religious convictions and personal beliefs. This introspection inspired a library of dramatic literature that is all too infrequently performed.

In Spain, the two dominant playwrights of that Golden Age were Lope de Vega and Calderón de la Barca. The Cocteau Repertory Theater is now providing a rare opportunity to hear the poetic drama of Calderón with an absorbing production of his masterpiece, "Life Is a Dream."

Calderón, perhaps not wishing to risk the wrath of the Hapsburgs, set his play in an unspecified medieval time when Moscow was a grand duchy on the periphery of Poland's empire, and not the other way around. The main metaphysical argument it addresses is that of free will versus predestination, and the ability of man to overcome his base natural instincts by virtue of reason.

•

But the real strength of "Life Is a Dream" is the dramatic vehicle Calderón employs to move the debate along. The play is wonderfully poetic, especially in Roy Campbell's accomplished translation. Calderón makes lyrical use of simile and metaphor, turning often to nature for his imagery in passages redolent of late Shakespeare.

The story turns on Segismundo, a Polish prince who was born under ominous signs that included his mother's death. His father, King Basilio (Harris Berlinsky), alarmed that he may have sired a monster, orders Segismundo locked in a tower that becomes "both crib and sepulcher" to the prince. "To prevent another being a tyrant," Basilio explains, "I am one myself." Segismundo is raised in seclusion by Clotaldo (James Sterling), the King's regent, who teaches the Prince something of the world and its inhabitants. Now that the King is old, he plans to test Segismundo by bringing him out into society to see if he is fit to abide among humans, perhaps even to rule Poland. To add intrigue, there are other claimants to the throne — Astolfo (Robert Ierardi) and Estrella (Elise Stone), nephew and niece to the King — and a wronged lover arrives in disguise to seek revenge on Astolfo. For comic relief, there is Clarin (Joseph Menino), the self-described "biggest jackanapes who ever lived."

•

In preparation for his introduction to the world, and to assuage his disappointment if he must return to the tower, Segismundo is told that all he experiences may only be a dream. But then perhaps all who live may be dreaming. "Each man dreams what he is until he is awakened by death," Segismundo observes later. "In the end, it is time that will settle all accounts." Segismundo knows some customs of human behavior. "I spoke courteously so thereby I could get my way," he recounts. Other lessons, such as that "even in dreams, nothing is lost by kindness," are harder learned. But surveying the pleasures he finds in the outside world, there is little in the end that surprises him — "nothing I could not have foreseen" he says, "except woman."

Eve Adamson's solid direction has wisely concentrated on the drama itself, keeping the action taut, moving the story along apace and leaving the

Jonathan Slaff

Craig Smith

metaphysics to take care of itself. There is not a weak part in Ms. Adamson's cast. Craig Smith is excellent as Segismundo, holding his innate rage at being robbed of his life by his father on such a tight rein that one waits from moment to moment for it to burst loose. Angela Vitale gives a fine performance as Rosaura, the betrayed lover who captures Segismundo's eye and heart, and James Sterling's Clotaldo also stands out.

1989 D 16, 17:1

Tug of Two Worlds

AWAY ALONE, by Janet Noble; directed by Terence Lamude; music by Larry Kirwan, performed by Black 47; set by David Raphel; lighting by Harry Feiner; assistant lighting by Jon Terry; sound by Tom Gould; costumes by C. Jane Epperson. Presented by Irish Arts Center, Jim Sheridan, artistic director; Nye Heron, executive director. At 553 West 51st Street.

Liam .... Michael Healy
Mario .... Paul Pillitteri
Owen .... Anto Nolan
Paddy .... Barry O'Rourke
Desmond .... Don Creedon
Mary .... Cora Murray
Breda .... Bronagh Murphy
A Girl .... Joelle Martel

By STEPHEN HOLDEN

Almost all the characters in Janet Noble's likable comedy-drama "Away Alone" are illegal Irish immigrants in their 20's who have settled in an area of the Bronx that has been nicknamed the Irish mile.

Employed as waiters, nannies, gardeners and construction workers, in jobs that are usually paid off the books, they nurture essentially the same dreams of affluence as any comparable group of Americans seeking their fortunes in the big city. The most painful difference, of course, is that their status is illegal, and even the most everyday activities have an air of furtiveness.

Miss Noble's play, at the Irish Arts Center, tells the story of Liam (Michael Healy), a typical young Irish immigrant whom word of mouth has steered to a Bronx bar where he can make the connections to find a job and an apartment. Within hours, he is offered a job in construction and a share in a Bainbridge Avenue apartment building that has become a dormitory of sorts for Irish aliens.

•

Most of the scenes in Miss Noble's play are set in the shabby but homey apartment that Liam shares with three other illegal Irish aliens: Owen (Anto Nolan), Paddy (Barry O'Rourke) and Desmond (Don Creedon). Along with Mary (Cora Murray) and Breda (Bronagh Murphy), two young women who are living across the hall in a similar communal setup, the characters make up a finely observed cross section of young Irish immigrants of very diverse personalities and goals who of necessity become an extended family.

Owen has come to America to earn enough money to return to Ireland to start a business. Paddy, who works as an assistant gardener on the Westchester County estate of a wealthy Irish-American family, becomes engaged to the daughter of his employers. Desmond, a misfit, channels his frustration into political consciousness-raising. Liam, quite innocently, keeps bringing home stolen merchandise he has purchased at rock-bottom prices.

The two women are almost opposites in temperament. Mary, in search of personal autonomy and independence, has vowed never to return to Ireland, where she has found it impossible to do anything without the whole town's knowing. Breda, a prudish husband-hunting hysteric with a will of iron, sets her sights on Liam.

•

The play, which spans more than six months, succeeds on many levels. The dialogue, ensemble acting and skillful direction by Terence Lamude create a palpable sense of this small, tightly knit community living under pressure and changing over time. Miss Noble's vision of the plight of her characters is gently comic but hard-headed in its assessment of how tough it is to survive New York in an illegal immigrant's circumstances, even given the advantages of a network of friends and supporters.

One feels the tug between the Old World, with its shabby familiarity and traditions, and the New, with its scary freedom and promise of material well-being. If, by the end of the play, the characters have not revealed their inner souls, they at least have assumed the familiarity of next-door neighbors.

"Away Alone" is well acted, with three outstanding performances. Mr.

Nolan, in the role of Owen, the cook of the house and its unofficial manager, projects the deepest sense of all the tensions underlying the camaraderie. As Mary, a woman trying to balance two very different concepts of womanhood, Miss Murray conveys exactly the right mixture of defiance and sweetness. The play's funniest and most biting portrayal is Miss Murphy's Breda, a young woman whose severe sense of propriety is matched by a haughty self-importance.

1989 D 16, 18:4

STAGE VIEW/Walter Kerr

Two New Musicals Bring Visions of Past and Future

THINK WE CAN TELL OURSELVES that it's going to be all right now.

We did need two things rather desperately in this curious crapshoot we call the American theater. We very much needed an old musical that would remind us of how good we'd been. And we needed a new musical that would function as a promise, saying that we'd be good again. A new start-up — a musical not yet entirely triumphant, perhaps, but one that looked confident and accomplished.

Both have now checked in at their respective stage doors and we can sense the beginning of an end to our long fevered fretting.

"Gypsy" is of course the just plain wonderful powerhouse written in 1959 for Ethel Merman, revived in 1974 for Angela Lansbury, and now taking orders from the earthy presence of the often manic, occasionally thoughtful, forever undefeated Tyne Daly.

"Gypsy" is a fooler. Every time you go to see it you feel that it's got to have lost something since the last time. But it hasn't. So far, it never has. It simply adds its new star to its original weight and height, and lets the composite woman fly. With both fists.

Indeed the only thing at the St. James with anywhere near the ferocity that Miss Daly lavishes on the role of Gypsy Rose Lee's mother is the overture composer Jule Styne has handed musical director Eric Stern. To put the matter mildly, the early bars of this admirable explosion of sound simply blast the audience awake, heavy dinner or no heavy dinner. You can see people sitting up straighter in their seats and blinking themselves to attention all over the house.

It's at this point, pretty early in the overture, that the production declares itself, describing the kind of show it's going to be and hinting at the secret of its continuing, if not actually growing, power. While conductor Stern lashes his men on, strings singing and clarinets tootling, a stealthy light begins to suffuse the visible stage, and we realize that — courtesy of a scrim — we are looking through gauze at a painted brick wall, dim, dusty, soft. So soft that we may have to squint at first to make out the legend on the glass transom, the legend that must of course be read backwards and that says "ROOD EGATS." For the benefit of those who are in a hurry this morning, the lettering, when read forward, says "STAGE DOOR."

But why so dark, why so dusty? What ghosts walk here? Does that musty brown door admit the talented and the untalented, the loving and the greedy only to devour them, whatever they are?

Miss Daly is a stage mother. She will make a star of her younger daughter and, failing that, of her elder. But all the while she wishes to be that star herself, and there's never any mistaking the sudden, feral flare in her eyes as a spotlight inadvertently picks her out, giving her a reasonable excuse to place herself at the end of a high-kicking chorus line, glowing like crazy.

And there is, to tell the truth, a sometime glory about this woman's insane ambition, as there is an equal glory in the drumrolls, the clashing cymbals, the sweet and the stirring sounds that rise from the pit. If this first visual image at the St. James is a shade somber, it is somber because Mama Rose is a monster. But the music Jule Styne has set against it is lively, exciting, martial, happy. It is all of these things, and more, because, monster though Mama Rose be, Mama Rose must be liked, must be understood. And so composer Styne has put these two boldly contrasted elements back to back, or face to face if you like, in the opening surge of the show. He wants us to grasp the two moods simultaneously; after all, they co-exist in Rose.

The arrivals of 'Gypsy' and 'Grand Hotel' are reminders that the future can be as bright as the past.

They also co-exist in Stephen Sondheim's perfectly matched lyrics, in the libretto that Arthur Laurents has fashioned from daughter Gypsy Rose Lee's memoirs, in the fine emotional contrasts of Mr. Laurents's staging, in the blithe choreography originally devised by Jerome Robbins and now restaged by Bonnie Walker.

Structurally, then, this musical is something of a marvel, a fusion of opposites that will haunt us — and Rose, and all her clan — the whole night long. An instance or two:

We can feel the ground shift beneath our feet as we move away from the explosive idiocy of Rose's aging kiddies doing their vaudeville act to a few moments of level-headedness brought on by Jonathan Hadary, a jovial traveling salesman who would like to marry Rose. Rose is not entirely averse; you feel there is something between them.

The feeling is acknowledged, gently nursed, by the simplest, most conversational of Styne-Sondheim tunes, ending:

Small world, isn't it?
Funny, isn't it?
Small, and funny, and fine.

Again, the contradictory insistence that good news is bad news, and probably vice versa, stirs when the troupe's noisy exhilaration over being booked on the Orpheum Circuit is directly cut across — from full lighting to lonely pale moon — by the elder daughter stroking her pet lamb and making a midnight birthday wish. She wishes she knew how old she was. Mother Rose, a principled woman, does not reveal the true ages of her charges, to her charges.

The doubleness is everywhere. Even the show's most striking, best remembered, songs are all intimately bound to the tough narrative thread — "Some People," "Everything's Coming Up Roses," of course "Rose's Turn" — and the wonder of the show's great strength is that there was ever room left over for comedy.

Yet almost everything in it is funny, from Rose's "Children! Go play in the alley!" to the strategically placed triple strip, "You Gotta Have a Gimmick," spotted close to 11 o'clock so that Rose can work the miracle of topping it.

Miss Daly does top it, riding the wind. She is funniest perhaps, when she is being most honest: stealing a glance at that beautiful big white spotlight that makes such a brilliant outline on the backdrop; or borrowing so much and so matter-of-factly that she is accused of stealing someone's ulcers. The actress further pays us all the compliment of building her flaws — most of them well-intentioned — gradually and plausibly instead of shooting the works at first meeting.

She's a lusty, intelligent, hard-driving performer, and she can probably play "Gypsy" for as long as she likes. I hope she will be wise enough to keep Mr. Hadary with her down the course. Apart from a grin that blazes like a windshield reflecting the sun, and it makes him likable before he's got a word out, he's able to infuse a musical comedy role with an uncommon reality. Top drawer.

But of course it's Miss Daly's evening. As it was Miss Merman's, as it was Miss Lansbury's. I came away — again — in some awe of the skill of the builders of "Gypsy," the creative personnel. And I remain staggered by the monumental powers of Miss Daly, who may be ready for Rushmore.

The world may be small, as the song says, but the lady's not. She is big, and funny, and fine.

I find that going back to "Grand Hotel" again, in whatever new shape it may be taking, is a little like reliving my life, or a substantial and reasonably agreeable portion of it. I first saw the piece in play form, adapted from a Vicki Baum novel, when it stopped off in Chicago after a smash Broadway run in 1929-30. Eugenie Leontovich played the fading ballerina and Henry Hull played the Baron who loved her, hotel thief though he might be. I went to see the show

Robert C. Ragsdale ("Gypsy")/Martha Swope ("Grand Hotel")

Jonathan Hadary and Tyne Daly in "Gypsy," at left, and David Carroll and Michael Jeter at the bar in Tommy Tune's "Grand Hotel"—an old musical to remind us of how good we'd been and a new one to promise we'd be good again

because all my friends told me that a spindly little fellow with a high-pitched tremolo and a shock wave of fizzy hair was stealing the show as the dying — Kringelein. The actor's name was Sam Jaffe and my friends were absolutely right. Larceny is what he was up to.

I was around, of course, for the film version of 1932, and managed to catch

Tommy Tune seizes upon the permissiveness of musicals and takes it about as far as it can go.

it at various odd times thereafter in revival houses, just to recheck my opinion of the performances. I seem to stick with my first estimates: that Garbo was surprisingly poor, that Joan Crawford was surprisingly good, and that John Barrymore had done one simple, wonderful thing. He had looked straight into the eyes of his brother Lionel, who probably knew more about him than anyone else living, and said, with utter candor and not a trace of self-pity, "I have no friends." Lionel, not at all incidentally, was playing Kringelein, and Lionel, not at all unexpectedly, stole the film.

And now, at the Martin Beck, we have come to a fully musicalized version of the old warhorse and I found myself watching, with some hope and more doubt, a crumpled little fellow lurch his way into the splendidly filigreed architecture of Berlin's Grand Hotel (1928). He was shivering in an overcoat that had grown far too big for him, popping his head in and out of its massive collar like a turtle checking the road. Aha! Kringelein again, for sure — that pitifully earnest bookkeeper with just enough money tucked away to live the high life until his illness claims him, eager to make friends with anyone who's willing. And I suddenly wondered if Kringelein could possibly steal this one. A play, yes, he could purloin a play. A movie, of course. An opera, probably. But a Broadway musical? I looked up the name of the actor who'd been assigned this impossible chore. Michael Jeter. And I felt for him.

But feeling sorry for either the actors or the characters in the play was a little foolish. Take "Grand Hotel" seriously and you're obliged to feel sorry for absolutely everybody. There's the aging ballerina who is losing her audience. A romantically inclined Baron who keeps himself afloat by stealing jewelry. A business executive losing an important merger and lying about it. A temporary typist forced into driving hard bargains for her after-hours favors. And some 27 helping hands, spinning their ways through the free-standing revolving doors, to keep the merry-go-round going. Except, of course, that it's not merry; a persistent autumnal feeling pervades the dialogue passages.

How does director-choreographer Tommy Tune cope with the rather formidable problem of making a musical of all this?

Preposterously and splendidly. What Mr. Tune does, in effect, is equip every last one of his footloose people with batteries and keep upping the switch that says Go. He refuses to echo, or to join, the dominant mood of the dialogue scenes. Instead, he's gathered the two-steps and the Charlestons (1928, remember), the waltzes and — finally and firmly — the tango and driven them all hard and jazzily against the grain. If this material wants to mope over its sorrows, it's not going to do it on Tune's time. He simply draws on his own supply of audacity and grins as the whole world Goes.

Realistically speaking, there is no way that the role of Kringelein, say, could be a dancing role. Two steps and the man would be dead on the ballroom floor. That's the sense of it. But since when do musical comedies go by the sense of things? Mr. Tune would rather have them go by the sweep of it all, and the soaring.

And so our bookkeeper wanders among the bustling bellhops beneath the triple chandeliers that rise and fall, greeting the girls on the switchboard and dodging the glistening gilt-edged chairs that scoot by, staring at wraparound furs so voluminous they seem to strut by themselves. Naturally, he runs across the typist, who happens to be mellow at the moment because she's had a pleasant date with the Baron. She is mellow enough, in fact, to escort Kringelein onto the dance floor, flustered but happy to have found a friend. Kringelein begins slowly, but that's just because he's never learned the steps and has to keep peering at the floor trying to make out his partner's beat and their tricky behavior. He fumbles, he stumbles, he picks up speed. He laughs at himself and hopes no one else will. He picks up more speed. He learns to glide in a gleeful pattern involving four other couples. He is quite happy, and his collar begins to come loose, or perhaps it is his spirit. You can see him promising himself never to be bashful again. You can also hear him singing "Who Couldn't Dance With You?"

◼

But that's only one of his flings, now that he's got the hang of it. Some six or seven scenes later — lots of other things are going on, of course — you come upon him maddened by the glory of the fox trot and already into the back-kicks and cross-knees of a Charleston. On he plunges, while out of absolutely nowhere a bar — a plain, ordinary bar that might be construed as a barre — rides down from the heavens for him to get a grip on so that his legs can behave ever more eccentrically. And they do, indeed they do. When he has finally outpaced everyone in sight he thinks it would be nice if they all had a drink together.

It seems to me that Mr. Tune has seized upon an aspect of musicals — their *permissiveness* — and taken it just about as far as it can go. And he does it wherever he looks, whatever he sees. He wants the orchestra high overhead, ruling the roost and mak-

Martha Swope

Yvonne Marceau and Pierre Dulaine in "Grand Hotel"— a tango in dazzling shafts of red light

ing a festive flutter of light and shadow the evening long. The furnishings of the Grand Lobby are almost never not in motion; they dance, too. When there is no concluding scene for the Baron and the ballerina, Mr. Tune creates one: Two dancers become unlucky lovers tangoing in dazzling shafts of red light (everything that comes from Jules Fisher's lightboard is stunning).

When it is time for the Baron, David Carroll, to climb the face of the hotel to reach a room he wishes to rob, Mr. Tune isolates him in space, a silhouette dangling high over the city; bold visual effects are everywhere. And when the same Mr. Carroll, whose talents are formidable, declares the intensity of his love by releasing then sustaining a long silvered top note, people in high-rises across the Hudson must hear it. Mr. Carroll's is a considerable talent.

You must be patient about a few things. The opening exposition is overlong and overbusy, with an out-of-place echo of Brecht thrown in to no purpose. And we must all face the fact that the show's dialogue scenes are on the threadbare side now: some were clichés to begin with. But the Robert Wright-George Forrest-Maury Yeston score is pleasantly laced with effective pastiches, and — I wasn't going to mention it — that bookkeeper, Kringelein, is patting his pocket. He's just put the show there.□

1989 D 17, II:7:1

Bitterness And Bananas

KRAPP'S LAST TAPE, by Samuel Beckett; directed by Alan Mokler; costumes designed by Gabriel Berry; environment designed by Kyle Chepulis; site coordinator, Dan Weir; produced by Anne Hamburger. Presented by En Garde Arts and The Talking Band. At 1 Main Street, Brooklyn.

WITH: Paul Zimet

By MEL GUSSOW

In its journey across New York in search of site-specific locations, the nomadic En Garde Arts troupe sets new challenges for theatergoers. In the case of "Krapp's Last Tape," the first question is how to find the temporary theater. The address is 1 Main Street, Brooklyn, a byway by the waterfront in the shadow of the Manhattan Bridge. Inside an unused space in an office building, one can find a table set for "Krapp's Last Tape."

The setting is different, but it is not contrary to Samuel Beckett's specifications. This large dirt-floor, crate-strewn environment could be an approximation of Krapp's solitary den, the repository for the character's journal on tape.

●

Paul Zimet's Krapp remains relatively spry. He does not wheeze as he speaks or shuffle as he walks offstage to pop a cork and sing a tune. As intended, he looks seedy and he is emotionally spent, as haggard as a homeless person who has wandered in from the street.

Seated at his table, Mr. Zimet is surrounded by a towering stack of tapes — the remains of his failed life. Now, on his 69th birthday, he plays back a tape of himself at 39. The elderly Krapp scoffs at his pitiful, middle-aged resolutions and, looking further back, he mocks his aspirations as a "young whelp." Played by Mr. Zimet, Krapp wears his bitterness like a hair shirt, unchangeable no matter what the weather.

Momentarily he finds diversion in eating bananas and in repeating the word spool, which he rolls on his tongue until it sounds like a variation of the word fool. Listening to his younger voice, he responds with derisive laughter and wonders how he could have been so hopeful and so introspective.

●

As directed by Alan Mokler, in this co-production with Mr. Zimet's Talking Band company, the actor is a

Paul Zimet in "Krapp's Last Tape."

Tom Brazil

more sardonic — and a more clown-ish — Krapp than one often sees, but he does not avert a tragic dimension. Mr. Zimet's long, stubbled face and sorrowful voice reflect the despair that is so basic to the character.

His Krapp is defined by his impa-tience. When he hears himself de-scribe a vision of eternal bleakness after "a year of profound gloom and indigence," he has a look of total dis-dain. He cuts off the recollection in

midsentence and speeds the tape for-ward, skipping to a memory of a ro-mantic interlude in a rowboat, the only memory he can bear.

Finally he begins to record his last tape and finds it an impossible task. Returning again to that reverie at sea, he replays it, and in Mr. Zimet's rheumy eyes one can read a distant dream of lost love and a continuing present of vast loneliness.

1989 D 17, 94:5

Living in Glass Booths

SUNSHINE, by William Mastrosimone; di-rected by Marshall W. Mason; sets by David Potts; costumes by Susan Lyall; lights by Dennis Parichy; sound by Stewart Werner and Chuck London; original music by Peter Kater; production stage manager, Fred Rein-glas. Presented by Circle Repertory Compa-ny, Tanya Berezin, artistic director; Connie L. Alexis, managing director. At 99 Seventh Avenue South, at Fourth Street.

Sunshine ....Jennifer Jason Leigh
Robby ....Jordan Mott
Nelson ....John Dossett
Jerry ....Bruno Alberti

By LAURIE WINER

She may not be Gypsy Rose Lee or Blaze Starr, but Sunshine takes pride in her work. From inside her glass

booth in a New Jersey porno house, she says whatever is necessary, via a telephone linkup, to make her cus-tomers feel close to her. "I know how to love you and how to take care of you," she tells a transfixed college student while opening and closing her flimsy robe. Young and attractive be-neath her smeared makeup and tousled hair, Sunshine puts something a little personal in every peep show, to encourage repeat business. "I'm dyin' for love," she whispers with Marilyn Monroe-ish ardor, and you know that she means it.

In "Sunshine," his new play at the Circle Repertory, William Mastrosi-mone soon takes his heroine out of her depressing cage and drops her, improbably, into the home of Nelson,

Madame X
Jordan Mott and Jennifer Jason Leigh are in "Sunshine," a comic drama by William Mastrosimone and directed by Marshall W. Mason about the relationship between a porno star and a young man.

Paula Court

a paramedic who lives, metaphori-cally speaking, in a glass booth of his own.

Nelson seems tersely matter-of-fact and utterly reliable, but in his studio apartment (designed by David Potts), there are the telltale signs of a man in emotional limbo: sheets hang from the windows, and a pile of laun-dry sits on the floor. He sleeps on the sofa. His furniture is unadorned and generic; it is the apartment of a man who does not want to commit himself. Nelson is burned out from his daily contact with the dying. He is recover-ing from the breakup of his marriage. He has had little luck in dating, and he is now considering, in halfhearted fashion, an attempt to woo back his wife.

That is, he is until Sunshine knocks on his window in the middle of a rainy night, begging to be let in. She has jumped from a moving car to escape her husband, who was threatening to kill them both in a high-speed auto crash. The play never tells just why her husband is threatening this. What really interests Mr. Mastrosimone, and what he has previously explored in plays like "The Woolgatherer," "Extremities" and "Shivaree," is the chemical reaction of two strangers shut up in a room together, and how what passes between them will change them forever.

Nelson lets Sunshine in only with the greatest reluctance; at first she is just another victim to him, desperate for care. But she infiltrates his affec-tions with a surprisingly shrewd analysis of his problems. He is touched and aroused by her, but their modes of intimacy clash. When he makes his move, she shrivels away from him, afraid physical contact will degrade their bond. Later, when she turns on her porno house spiel in a show of toughness and indifference,

he is disgusted. But rest assured, Nel-son and Sunshine will spend a long confessional night together that will allow them to demolish the glass booths that confine them.

•

As Sunshine, Jennifer Jason Leigh gives a gutsy performance. If her character is desperate to be loved, Ms. Leigh is not; she makes Sun-shine's neediness annoying. The play fails her, though, in the scenes where a softer quality is needed. Here Mr. Mastrosimone provides warmed-over character quirks that are never as touching or as funny as they are meant to be. For instance, Sunshine keeps a lobster as a pet. She de-scribes how, at home, she puts her face to the glass of its little tank and watches it reach out its claw to her. That is the kind of detail that screams "symbol" and little else to an audi-ence trying to get a fix on a character.

As Nelson, John Dossett has a tense reserve that contrasts nicely with Ms. Leigh's high-pitched edge. The direc-tor Marshall W. Mason brings them together in a smoothly paced dance of attraction and suspicion.

Dennis Parichy cleverly under-scores Sunshine's devotion to crusta-ceans by lighting her, during one mo-ment in her horrid booth, with a splash of pink. She looks like an exotic fish in the aquarium. The costume de-signer, Susan Lyall, gives her the uni-form of a prostitute striving to better herself — there's the ratty fur coat and the sad little red bag, a Chanel knock-off, that speaks of her taste for finer things.

Sunshine is, in the end, a lot like the play that contains her — intermit-tently touching and grating, true and phony.

1989 D 18, C10:4

Three Views of Racism

MY CHILDREN! MY AFRICA!, written and di-rected by Athold Fugard; set and costume de-sign, Susan Hilferty; lighting design, Dennis Parichy; sound design, Mark Bennett; as-sociate director, Ms. Hilferty; production stage manager, Mary Michele Miner; pro-duction manager, George Xenos. Presented by New York Theater Workshop. At the Perry Street Theater, 31 Perry Street.

Mr. M ....John Kani
Isabel Dyson ....Lisa Fugard
Thami Mbikwana ....Courtney B. Vance

By FRANK RICH

In August Wilson's "Fences," Courtney B. Vance had a job to trau-matize any young actor. In the role of a rebellious teen-age son, he had to

Courtney B. Vance, left, and John Kani in a scene from "My Children! My Africa!"

Gerry Goodstein

170

challenge James Earl Jones for supremacy in a household and, by implication, on the stage. Mr. Vance, though not long out of the Yale School of Drama, wasn't fazed. Armed with a baseball bat and a raging desire for justice, he faced down the majestic Mr. Jones in a volatile confrontation of such balanced power that it became the detonation point of one of the decade's most explosive plays.

Mr. Vance has a similar role, albeit in a less exciting context, in "My Children! My Africa!," the new Athol Fugard play produced by the New York Theater Workshop at the Perry Street Theater. This time the actor is cast as Thami Mbikwana, the prized pupil and surrogate son of Mr. M, an aging teacher in a black high school in South Africa, 1984. Because Mr. M is played by John Kani — the memorable co-star, with Winston Ntshona, of "Sizwe Banzi Is Dead" and "The Island" on Broadway in 1975 — he is another father figure of daunting presence. And Mr. Vance is again the rebel, challenging an older generation's cautious approach to change.

For Thami, the moment of revolt comes at the end of Act I, when he delivers a free-associative monologue that is both an autobiography and a polemical call to arms. With inflamed eyes and a voice that roams up and down the scale from a child's soft singsong to a revolutionary's incantatory shout, Mr. Vance charts the rise of his own African consciousness and that of his people, as shaped by modern cataclysms at Sharpeville and Soweto and by a far deeper sense of a continent's history. "The time for whispering is past," says Thami as he raises his voice and fist against apartheid. While the theater is small, Mr. Vance's performance is so impassioned, and still so full of poetic nuance, that one could imagine his Thami commanding the same rapt response from an international stage.

•

It says much about "My Children! My Africa!" that this monologue, by far the play's most ambitious piece of writing, would have nearly the same impact if placed anywhere else in the script or, indeed, if extricated from the text entirely and performed on its own. "My Children! My Africa!" is full of monologues — not a bad thing in itself, but in this case almost palpably an attempt to impose direction and drive on a piece that seems under-written when its characters must actually meet in scenes.

The third of the characters — acted by Lisa Fugard, the author's daughter — is Isabel Dyson, a student from a white prep school who joins Thami and Mr. M in a rare educational venture: the fielding of an integrated team for an extracurricular national literary quiz. But all three players are soon overrun by events as the racial violence and school boycotts of 1984 force South Africans to decide which side they are on. The paternalistic Mr. M, "an old-fashioned traditionalist," holds out for the potency of words and reason in achieving freedom. Thami, unable to keep waiting patiently for long-denied rights, advocates stronger forms of protest and belittles his devoted mentor as what Americans would call an Uncle Tom. Isabel, a well-meaning paragon of white-liberal guilt, is caught in the crossfire and doesn't know "what to think or feel anymore."

"My Children! My Africa!" opens with its actors yelling in debate. For too long thereafter, the inevitable final blowouts are forestalled while the characters inflexibly rephrase their positions, never learning much from one another, barely fluctuating as people. Sometimes they hardly seem to be imagined as people, because Mr. Fugard denies this three-

A father is the symbol of South Africa's reluctance to change its ways.

some the intimate perspective he afforded the trios of " 'Master Harold' ... and the Boys," "A Lesson from Aloes" and "The Road to Mecca." In "My Children! My Africa!," the characters' ideological positions are too often the sum of their psyches.

•

This is particularly disappointing in the cases of Thami and Isabel, teen-agers from antithetical backgrounds whose potentially fascinating and complex relationship, however hostile or harmonious, is stillborn. Given that they are sharing intense afternoons, might there not be some reposeful moments when they put aside politics or literature to share thoughts about some everyday teen-age passion, whether it be pop music or movies or sex? It's almost as if Mr. Fugard were a chaperone afraid to leave the two kids alone in a room, for fear that they might get out of his tight control.

For audiences at Johannesburg's Market Theater, where "My Children! My Africa!" had its premiere in June, the play's disputes about anti-apartheid tactics, and its Act II condemnations of informers, no doubt offered a compensating of-the-moment urgency difficult to replicate here. American audiences may be struck by how much more theatrically Spike Lee engaged some identical issues in the New York context of "Do the Right Thing." The unexceptional quality of Mr. Fugard's political debates — and the hedging of their resolution — might not stand out so much if the writing were graced by the author's usual metaphorical music. But except in Mr. Vance's and Mr. Kani's juiciest speeches about their respective visions of Africa, the pedagogical writing can leave the audience feeling that it, too, is in school.

As directed by the playwright, the stagy production is of a piece with the script. Mr. Kani's mellifluous, self-beatifying teacher and Miss Fugard's strident preppie don't have the depth of related characters in "Master Harold," but it's impossible for an outsider to divide responsibility between the performers and the author. That Mr. Vance is an exceptional talent, and that he is ideally mated with a dramatist of Mr. Fugard's passions, is beyond question. It's to be hoped that their collaboration, like that of Mr. Fugard and Mr. Kani, is built for the long run of history rather than for the passing drama of one particular play.

1989 D 19, C19:3

Deliberate Absurdity

THE BALD SOPRANO and THE CHAIRS, by Eugène Ionesco; translated by Donald Watson; directed by Andrei Belgrader; set design by Anita Stewart; costume design by Candice Donnelly; lighting design by Stephen Strawbridge; sound design by Maribeth Back. Presented by American Repertory Theater, Cambridge, Mass.

WITH: Roberts Blossom, Lynn Chausow, Thomas Derrah, Jeremy Geidt, Rodney Scott Hudson, Tresa Hughes and Deborah Lewin.

TWELFTH NIGHT, by William Shakespeare; directed by Andrei Serban; music by Mel Marvin; set design by Derek McLane; costume design by Catherine Zuber; lighting design by Howell Binkley; sound design by Maribeth Back; fight choreography by William Finlay; assistant to Mr. Serban, Paul Walker.

WITH: Lynn Chausow, Christopher Colt, Kevin Costin, Thomas Derrah, Jeremy Geidt, Rodney Scott Hudson, Cherry Jones, James Lally, Diane Lane, Deborah Lewin, Dan Nutu, Kario Salem, Ross Salinger, Steven Skybell and Robert Stanton.

By MEL GUSSOW

Special to The New York Times

CAMBRIDGE, Mass., Dec. 17 — The influence of transplanted Rumanian artists is being celebrated at the American Repertory Theater, with a pairing of productions — Andrei Belgrader's double-header of Ionesco one-acts and Andrei Serban's radicalization of "Twelfth Night." The two directors have repeatedly enriched the stage with their approaches to classics, although this time with Mr. Serban the result is less edifying than intended. On the other hand, Mr. Belgrader's versions of "The Bald Soprano" and "The Chairs" are invigorating revisits to two seminal works of absurdism.

When it comes to Mr. Belgrader's collaboration with Ionesco, also a Rumanian but a longtime resident of France, there is no barrier of language or of time. The plays seem as vital today as when they were written in the early 1950's. Except for a few minor divergencies, the director (who staged "Rameau's Nephew" last year at the Classic Stage Company in Manhattan) is faithful to his source, in contrast to Mr. Serban, who uses Shakespeare as a stepping stone for footloose perambulation.

"The Bald Soprano" remains an intuitive burst of comic energy, and the fact that other playwrights have elaborated on Ionesco's findings does not detract from the play's originality. Written as a self-parody, or, as the author described it, a "comedy of comedy," this is a vaudeville play about the ineffectuality of language. Words become a barrier to communication as Ionesco's petty bourgeois couple, Mr. and Mrs. Smith, exchange clichés as if they are homeopathic remedies, and then find themselves at cross purposes with their unwelcome dinner guests.

•

In this cuckooland, the clock strikes 17; all male and female members of the same unseen, friendly family are named Bobby Watson; a man and a woman gradually come to the conclusion that their coincident activities prove they must be husband and wife. With careful assurance, Mr. Belgrader bolsters the matter-of-fact realism of the dialogue even as the situation of the two couples seems more and more surrealistic. If accelerated into farce, the comedy might fizzle. Played straight, it echoes with hearty laughter. Lynn Chausow and Thomas Derrah offer model portraits of English middle-class respectability, and Jeremy Geidt and Tresa Hughes, as their guests, are expert at making the implausible seem expected.

"The Chairs" is a more overtly serious play, but it is no less comic, as a nonagenarian couple prepare their island home for an event that never takes place, a speech by a visiting orator. The subject of the play is nothingness, the emptiness of speechifying and, for Ionesco, of life itself. Extending their hospitality to dozens of imaginary guests — chairs are aligned as if in a theater — the husband and wife chat with them in the most personalized and, ultimately, most poignant manner.

•

Though decades short of a convincing 90, Tresa Hughes and Roberts Blossom maintain the requisite balance between rationality and lunacy.

Richard Feldman

Roberts Blossom and Tresa Hughes in "The Chairs."

Ms. Hughes, darting off and on stage to bring on the chairs, lends the work a certain sweet persistence. In this one-act play, Mr. Belgrader allows himself small liberties, sending in a stately emperor's throne and interweaving familiar songs with the old dramatic tune refrained on stage. Taken together, the plays remind us of Ionesco's ineffable humor and his rationality in treating matters of domestic derangement.

In his program notes, Robert Brustein, the theater's artistic director, writes a capsule review of both the Ionesco and Shakespeare plays, declaring that through Mr. Serban's prism one can see "a darker and more dangerous" "Twelfth Night." The prism is more like a cloudy crystal ball; the result is a longer (three and one half hours) and more idiosyncratic version than usual — and the danger is one of self-defeat. The director has, in fact, turned a Shakespearean comedy into a problem play.

Illyria in this instance is more than illusory. Orsino at court looks as if he has wandered into a Grecian mausoleum. He is discovered reclining on top of a stone tablet, resembling — in dark glasses — a brooding Billy Joel. Later he plays an electric guitar. Though the notion of pushing Orsino beyond boredom has possibilities, his speech is overly measured by pauses, and he is not alone as a slow speaker. For the first half-hour, the production crawls, speeding up as the plot winds into action.

•

The clownish subplot is made forcibly anachronistic. A very randy Sir Toby (Mr. Geidt) watches cartoons on television. Sir Andrew (Robert Stanton) does a modified version of Michael Jackson's moonwalk. Sebastian meets Antonio in what appears to be a gay sailors' bar. In the corner sits an actor dressed like Shakespeare, drinking beer from the bottle and transcribing the overheard dialogue with a quill pen. Actually that is a funny sight gag.

Although one stops looking for consistency, it is impossible to ignore the contradictions, the motley line readings, and the Grand Guignol cruelty faced by Malvolio. Humor is sacrificed along with clarity, but incidental moments are intriguing and there are striking scenic effects (by Derek McClane) including a rolling sea that looks like an endless buzz saw. The production is lightened by several vivid performances — by Cherry Jones as Viola and Diane Lane (who made her stage debut years ago in Mr. Serban's "Fragments of a Trilogy") as Olivia; Mr. Derrah as Feste and Ms. Chausow as the maid Maria. Ms. Chausow previously played the role for the Acting Company. In Shakespeare as well as Ionesco, she combines the deadpan with the delirious.

Mr. Serban's errors are of choice, not of happenstance. If anything, he is a director with too many ideas. He is, as always, unpredictable. It was not too long ago that he staged a delightful, straightforward "As You Like It" at La Mama Annex in Manhattan. This time it scarcely helps that he waggishly reverses the label of the play, entitling it "What You Will, or Twelfth Night." One is forced to the conclusion that the production is not what Will would have willed.

1989 D 20, C20:3

The New York Times/Fred R. Conrad

Geraldine James and Dustin Hoffman in Peter Hall's production of "The Merchant of Venice."

Cautious Shylock, Vivid Portia

THE MERCHANT OF VENICE, by William Shakespeare; directed by Peter Hall; designed by Chris Dyer; lighting by Mark Henderson and Neil Peter Jampolis; costumes supervised by Barbara Forbes; associate director, Giles Block; production stage manager, Thomas A. Kelly; music by Robert Lockhart; sound design by Paul Arditti; executive producer, Thelma Holt. Duncan C. Weldon and Jerome Minskoff, in association with Punch Productions, present the Peter Hall Company. At the 46th Street Theater, 226 West 46th Street.

Antonio	Leigh Lawson
Bassanio	Nathaniel Parker
Lorenzo	Richard Garnett
Gratiano	Michael Siberry
Salerio	Donald Burton
Solanio	Gordon Gould
Leonardo	Ben Browder
Shylock	Dustin Hoffman
Jessica	Francesca Buller
Tubal	Leon Lissek
Lancelot Gobbo	Peter-Hugo Daly
Old Gobbo	Leo Leyden
Portia	Geraldine James
Nerissa	Julia Swift
Balthasar	Neal Ben-Ari
Stefano	John Wojda
Prince of Morocco	Herb Downer
Prince Aragon	Michael Carter
Duke of Venice	Basil Henson

By FRANK RICH

Contrary to Broadway gospel, Dustin Hoffman does not have star billing in the new "Merchant of Venice" at the 46th Street Theater. That honor is reserved instead for the Peter Hall Company — or, to put a finer point on it, for Peter Hall. Once you've seen the production, in many ways an unexpected one, you'll understand that Mr. Hall isn't being pretentious and that Mr. Hoffman hasn't suddenly been struck by false modesty. This really is the director's "Merchant" — at times Shakespeare's, too — and Mr. Hoffman plays a supporting role.

It's the modern practice that Shylock dominate any version of "Merchant," whatever the interpretation, despite the fact that he appears in only 5 of 20 scenes. Mr. Hoffman's Shylock — meticulous, restlessly intelligent, emotionally and physically lightweight — does not. His performance is a character actor's polished gem rather than a tragedian's stab at the jugular; it is reminiscent of his fine work in "Death of a Salesman," in which the outsize Willy Loman forged by Lee J. Cobb was whittled down to the humble proportions of a schlemiel. Whether Shakespeare's moneylender can weather the reduction of scale as well as Arthur Miller's salesman did is another question.

•

Wearing a beard, a ponytail, a long gaberdine, a yarmulke, and sometimes a hat emblazoned with a yellow star, Mr. Hoffman presents a proud but long-suffering Jew who has almost become inured to the commonplace bigotry of the Christians around him. When the Venetians spit in his face, as they literally and frequently do in Mr. Hall's staging, Mr. Hoffman thinly masks his rage with a fixed, stoic grin. Shylock knows his gentile antagonists are bullies, but like the brilliant student trying to protect himself in a classroom of hoodlums, he makes deals to survive and doesn't advertise his intelligence. Only when driven to revenge does he fully reveal the sharp wit and sharper knife with which he intends to extract his pound of flesh.

Although Mr. Hoffman has not lost the strange accent (a Bronxish rasp) that, like Vanessa Redgrave's in "Orpheus Descending," is apparently de rigueur for stars in a Hall production, his performance is less tentative than it was early in his London run last summer. Mr. Hoffman is always working, always thinking, always interesting to observe.

Leave it to this actor to make neurotic hay of Shylock's clipped repetitions — the punctuating use of the word "well" through his early lines and the incantatory rhetorical obsession with the size and span of his loan to Antonio (3,000 ducats, three months). Mr. Hoffman's loving but suffocating farewell to Jessica, the daughter who will soon desert him, has the paternal possessiveness of a melancholy Tevye, and his rendition of the "Hath not a Jew eyes?" soliloquy is dignified and searching, more Talmud than Old Testament.

•

But one wants more, and the role's deep notes of blind, distorting rage and vengeance are never sounded. Like it or not, Shylock in the end be-

Dustin Hoffman runs counter to the modern practice.

comes a man driven to collect a debt in blood — whether because he is an anti-Semitic caricature or because, as Mr. Hall properly chooses to stress, his revenge has been provoked by the vicious anti-Semites of Venice. Yet Mr. Hoffman does not rise to the occasion. In his one cheap touch, the actor nudges the audience to milk a laugh in the trial scene — with a Henny Youngman shrug on "These be the Christian husbands!" — and kills any chance that his Shylock will tap into the dark passions of one of the most dramatic scenes in the canon. Even without the lapse into stand-up shtick, Mr. Hoffman looks unprepared to take the dangerous leap of risking an audience's revulsion or condemnation.

The avoidance of risk is uncharacteristic of this imaginative actor; it's the rare Hoffman performance that fails to arouse violent debates pro and con, but this may be one of them. The same may be true of Mr. Hall's impeccable staging, which seems to have been conceived with his star's limited characterization in mind. What does a Shakespearean director do with a cautious Shylock? If he's smart, and few are as smart as Mr. Hall, he stages "Merchant" as the comedy it was once meant to be.

•

Or so Mr. Hall does up to a tasteful point — to go all the way, to mock

Shylock along the lines of Malvolio in "Twelfth Night," would be to give license to the textual anti-Semitism that he and Mr. Hoffman must and do avoid. What the director has done instead is devote full attention to the other elements of Shakespearean comedy in the play. With luminous casting and design (by Chris Dyer), the director gives the sky-crowned Belmont scenes more weight than those in mercantile, copper-hued Venice. The real star of the evening becomes Geraldine James's Portia — the only character to figure prominently in both realms — and her pursuit of pastoral romance is presented as vividly as her prosecution of the urban trial scene.

Miss James is well up to Mr. Hall's demands. Her Portia, who combines the tart intelligence of a Beatrice with the golden glow of a fairy-tale princess, is a delight who drives the production. Mr. Hall has cast her co-conspirators in love vibrantly, too — including Nathaniel Parker's unusually effervescent Bassanio, Richard Garnett's Lorenzo and Francesca Buller's Jessica. Michael Siberry, who previously visited New York as the hero in the Royal Shakespeare Company's return engagement of "Nicholas Nickleby," is an exceptional Gratiano — both a merry jester and a lout. With these actors and others — most notably Leigh Lawson's excellent Antonio, who does not minimize the merchant's grave crush on Bassanio — Mr. Hall can stress the musical poetry of the various lovers' Act V reconciliations, so often trimmed in other productions.

Not all the comic aspects of "Merchant" reward Mr. Hall's tender care. Despite a game cockney turn by Peter-Hugo Daly, Lancelot Gobbo is a lesser buffoon, and the cruelty he inflicts on his pathetic father is not redeemed by dressing Old Gobbo (Leo Leyden) in the dark spectacles and moth-eaten coat of a Beckett clown. The pageantry that Mr. Hall has poured upon the casket scenes — those interludes in which Portia's suitors must play the Shakespearean equivalent of "Let's Make a Deal" — does not add to their thematic importance or humor, let alone accelerate them.

This "Merchant" is also likely to prove a big target for American theater people who routinely deplore British Shakespearean acting and staging. Though the production has gained some American actors since its London inception, its classical look and blander, if well-spoken, secondary performances are ripe for Anglophobic attack. But to criticize Mr. Hall's production as an exercise in fuddy-duddy Shakespeare is beside the point. The results may look conservative, but in this century it is almost a novel idea — even if born of necessity — to restore romance and comedy to "The Merchant of Venice." Which isn't to say that Mr. Hall's novel idea is necessarily the whole idea. His solid, highly watchable production, like Mr. Hoffman's performance, leaves one thinking about this endlessly debated play without for a second being challenged or moved by it.

1989 D 20, C15:1

... and Success in Art

THE ART OF SUCCESS, by Nick Dear; directed by Adrian Noble; scenery and costumes by Ultz; lighting by Beverly Emmons; original music and sound by John Gromada; production stage manager, Ed Fitzgerald. Presented by Manhattan Theater Club, Lynne Meadow, artistic director; Barry Grove, managing director. At City Center, Stage 1, 131 West 55th Street.

Jane Hogarth	Mary-Louise Parker
William Hogarth	Tim Curry
Harry Fielding	Nicholas Woodeson
Frank	Patrick Tull
Oliver	Don R. McManus
Mrs. Needham	Patricia Kilgarriff
Louisa	Suzanne Bertish
Sarah Sprackling	Jayne Atkinson
Robert Walpole	Daniel Benzali
Queen Caroline	Jodie Lynne McClintock

By FRANK RICH

"The Art of Success," the play by Nick Dear at the Manhattan Theater Club, had its premiere at the Royal Shakespeare Company in England in 1986, but an American theatergoer might well assume it had been written in New York this fall. In our year of Mapplethorpe and Serrano, here is a scabrous comedy about the creation, purpose, promotion, merchandising, censorship and government patronage of art — all set forth in a theatrical palette that encompasses rough sex, scatological language, ribald political satire, urine and excrement. The production is, of course, made possible in part by funds from the National Endowment for the Arts.

It's a highly imaginative work, even if by no means a fully achieved one. Rewriting cultural history as Peter Shaffer did in "Amadeus" — but showing even less regard for historical fact — Mr. Dear sets his play on a single night in the 1730's when the artist William Hogarth (Tim Curry) variously paints the portrait of a condemned murderer (Jayne Atkinson), cheats on his wife (Mary-Louise Parker) with a prostitute (Suzanne Bertish), runs around in drag, and attempts to analyze his castration nightmares. During this rake's progress, 10 years of English history are telescoped into the action, including the rise of the politician Robert Walpole (Daniel Benzali) and the advent of laws that permitted the copyrighting of artists' images and the censorship of the English stage.

•

True to his convictions, Mr. Dear honors no truth except his own as a dramatist. The language in "The Art of Success" is contemporary, the footwear is sometimes sneakers and the music is electronic. Hogarth and the play's other famous artist, the writer Henry Fielding (Nicolas Woodeson), are exploited for dialectical purposes. To Mr. Dear, Hogarth is not so much a sharp social commentator as an entrepreneur eager to merchandise his engraved images to a lucrative mass market. He flatters his patrons (his wife is the daughter of one) and is willing to pull his satirical punches with Walpole in exchange for the financial benefits of copyright; lest anyone fail to confuse him with Andy Warhol, Hogarth even dreams of making pornographic Polaroid portraits. By contrast, the uncompromising Fielding believes art should be dangerous, provocative, abusive to the audience. When his plays are silenced, he turns to novels to further the shock of the new.

Gerry Goodstein

Tim Curry and Suzanne Bertish in a scene from "The Art of Success."

I won't be the one to bore you with learned disquisitions on how Mr. Dear has distorted Hogarth's life and sullied his reputation. A more serious problem with his play is its repetitiveness and its British schoolboy sense of humor. The digressions about feminism, marriage and sex, though inoffensive, are neither as witty nor as novel as Mr. Dear seems to think they are; the farcical horseplay that should stitch a sprawling evening together is not so much ingenious as ad hoc.

For balance, there are some highly pointed scenes, the most impressive of which involve Hogarth's confrontations with the condemned murderer, here given the name Sarah Sprackling. (Hogarth actually painted a murderer named Sarah Malcolm.) Sprackling believes that the artist not only misrepresents her in his portrait

A night in the life of the portraitist of the low.

but that he also has no right to appropriate and sell her image. "How can he put the whole of me in a few dollops of paint?" she asks. That and the woman's other questions reverberate through other arts and centuries right up to the New Journalism of crime first championed by Truman Capote in "In Cold Blood."

Mr. Dear touches upon many other issues of art and capital as well: the rise of the art market (Walpole doubles his money on a Titian), an artist's use of publicity, the question of whether art is "property or communication," something "to be owned or to be understood." To raise these matters is not necessarily to explore or dramatize them, however, and

"The Art of Success" often seems like the raw sketch for a work along the lines of Tom Wolfe's "Bonfire of the Vanities" rather than its realization.

Adrian Noble, a gifted Royal Shakespeare director too little known on these shores, makes a virtue of the play's frequently phantasmagoric unruliness. The Manhattan Theater Club's proscenium house has been converted into an arena ringed by flickering candles and Hogarth images and carpeted with straw and less appetizing detritus of the stables. In Ultz's striking design, the stage is itself a flat, white canvas — a suspended, paper-covered platform, actually — on which Hogarthian caricatures carry on in a disruptive, boisterous manner befitting the players in a Fielding novel. If anything, the production is so clever and smart that the play visibly strains to deliver on its promises.

The very good Anglo-American cast also includes Don R. McManus as an indolent fop, Patricia Kilgarriff as a madam who ends up in the stocks and Jodie Lynne McClintock as a lewdly fantasized Queen Caroline. Mr. Curry is outstanding: an actor of intense, vulgar comic energy who also happens to convey fierce intelligence. His Hogarth, like his Mozart in the Broadway "Amadeus," is never quite as loathsome as his worst enemies imply. He's both an artist and a sleaze, but most definitely, most winningly in that order.

1989 D 21, C11:1

A Crime of Science

MISS EVERS'S BOYS, by David Feldshuh; directed by Irene Lewis; set, Douglas Stein; costumes, Catherine Zuber; lighting, Pat Collins; sound, Janet Kalas; choreographer, Dianne McIntyre; music director, Dwight Andrews; dramaturg, Rick Davis. Presented by Center Stage, 700 North Calvert Street, Baltimore.

Caleb Humphries	Delroy Lindo
Hodman Bryan	Damien Leake
Willie Johnson	K. Todd Freeman
Ben Washington	Allie Woods Jr.
Dr. John Douglass	Ethan Phillips
Dr. Eugene Brodus	David Downing
Eunice Evers	Seret Scott

By LAURIE WINER

Special to The New York Times

BALTIMORE, Dec. 17 — When The Associated Press broke the news, it seemed almost incomprehensible. In order to chart the degenerative progress of venereal disease in the human body, the United States Public Health Service withheld treatment from hundreds of poor, black men in rural Alabama. The study lasted from 1932 until it was exposed in 1972. How could something so reminiscent of Nazi medical practices have happened in America?

David Feldshuh, a playwright and physician, tackles that question in his intelligent if schematic new play at Center Stage here. The play, "Miss Evers's Boys," offers a fictional account of the 40 years of experiments, which was entitled "The Tuskegee Study of Untreated Syphilis in the Negro Male."

•

Through the arguments of two Government doctors, Dr. Feldshuh follows the tortuous, bureaucratic justifications that enabled the study to take on a life of its own, continuing even after penicillin became widely available as an effective treatment of the disease. A white doctor (Ethan Phillips), hoping to make "a unique contribution to medical knowledge," is determined to see the study through to the end point, that is, until the autopsies of the subjects. A black doctor (David Downing) has a different goal; he wants to prove a kind of racial equality by demonstrating that the disease is equally devastating to both blacks and whites.

While it's fascinating to follow their increasingly self-deluding logic, the doctors remain only mouthpieces for medical thinking that views humans as subjects rather than patients. In these days of AIDS, it's valuable to illuminate that thinking, particularly as it's applied to people whose lives, in an unspoken but implicit social contract, are deemed dispensable.

But, more dramatically, "Miss Evers's Boys" also chronicles the human cost of that thinking through the characters of four tenant farmers who are subjects in the study and a black nurse caught between her compassion for her patients and her professional vow to aid the physicians in their work.

"I loved those men," says the guilt-racked nurse, Eunice Evers (Seret Scott), as she testifies in 1972 to a Senate committee that is called to investigate the study. "Those men were susceptible to kindness." Dr. Feldshuh intersperses her testimony with scenes from the four decades she spent with the men, who stayed with the study because Miss Evers asked them to.

As embodied by Miss Scott, it's easy to see why the men trust Miss Evers. When she first arrives, in 1932, at the schoolhouse where they are waiting nervously to have their blood tested, she's a slender crusader, a healing angel, aglow with pride at being a nurse. She is convinced that the Public Health Service has sent her to alleviate suffering. Her eyes shining, she promises the men free examinations and a hot lunch.

Dr. Feldshuh has simplified matters by making each of the men good hearted and kind, but the director, Irene Lewis, compensates by extracting vibrant performances from the patients, the only characters unburdened by weighty arguments and guilt. The two most skeptical of getting something free from the Government are the better-educated men: Willie (K. Todd Freeman) and Caleb (Delroy Lindo, who played Herald Loomis in "Joe Turner's Come and Gone" on Broadway). The other patients, Hodman (Damien Leake) and Ben (Allie Woods Jr.) are the most susceptible to the appearance of kindness.

•

But each of these men comes to embrace Nurse Evers as a mother figure and mascot for their Dixieland dance band. She happily enters their lives, driving them to a dance contest they've been rehearsing for and tenderly administering the mercury rubs that were, in 1932, the treatment for the disease.

But later that year, the money for treatment runs out. The doctors inform Nurse Evers that it's better to continue to study the effects of the disease in the men rather than abandon them completely. She is forced to pretend that she's still treating her patients, and she's even asked to sing to calm them during a painful spinal-tap procedure.

As the men's health declines over the years, Nurse Evers's faith in herself erodes also. She begs the doctors to administer penicillin in 1946, but they tell her it's too late. If the men receive the drug at this late stage, they say, their hearts may explode. This she accepts with a dull resignation. "It had become familiar," she says. And so the study goes on.

•

Douglas Stein's gray set, a large country schoolhouse of washed-out wooden planks, underscores the play's bleak message, and so does Pat Collins's stark lighting, which keeps much of the stage in darkness as the disease closes in on the patients.

When the play ends, in 1972, Willie and Caleb are the only two patients still alive to confront Nurse Evers and the doctors, who continue to recite their motivations by rote. "I loved you men," offers the nurse, pathetically. "I got you free medical care."

In the play's dreamlike coda, the four men return to dance with beauty and grace in white tails and top hats. In that moment, "Miss Evers's Boys" attains an eloquence that Dr. Feldshuh has wisely not forced in a final speech. Here the real playwright emerges: what more could words say in the face of that ghostly image of what might have been?

1989 D 21, C16:3

Dashing Memories

PARTING GESTURES, by Rafael Lima; directed by John Ferraro; set, Loren Sherman; lighting, Jackie Manassee; costumes, Jennifer Von Mayrhauser; production manager, Darren Lee Cole. Presented by Intar Hispanic American Arts Center, Max Ferra, founder and artistic director; Jim DiPaola, managing director. At 420 West 42d Street.

Marc	John Leguizamo
Carmen	Ilka Tanya Payan

By STEPHEN HOLDEN

Rafael Lima's one-act drama "Parting Gestures" goes over some very well-worn dramatic territory with mixed success: a death in a family inspires the airing of dirty emotional laundry and leads to a painful catharsis.

In Mr. Lima's variation, Marc (John Leguizamo), the 29-year-old son of a deceased pilot, visits his ailing mother Carmen (Ilka Tanya Payan) in her Miami bungalow. As they reminisce, their happier memories of Marc's dashing daredevil father turn into recriminations. Eventually the son's long-suppressed memories of being brutalized by the man he would rather remember as an idol resurface.

The best thing about Mr. Lima's drama is the specific memories that the two characters share of the glamorous bully who left both mother and son emotionally scarred. One of the most vivid is Carmen's recollection of the time she and her husband got drunk, donned football helmets and lashed themselves to palm trees in the back yard during the full force of a hurricane. Such deeds were typical of a man who was nicknamed Cowboy by his ground crew and who, while courting Carmen, once landed a helicopter in her yard and swept her up into the sky.

Like so many other plays of this type, "Parting Gestures," at Intar Hispanic American Arts Center, begins on a buoyant note and slowly changes in mood as its darker revelations are at first hinted at and then very carefully rationed out. To the playwright's credit, the characters' reminiscences and current peccadillos all have the feel of truth. And most of the dialogue has an easy flow. Yet the doling out of family secrets in such measured, time-released doses makes for dramatic rhythms that feel overly schematized so that play offers no moments of real surprise.

Although Miss Payan seems far too young and vital for the role of the long-suffering mother, Mr. Leguizamo gives a touchingly spontaneous performance as the wounded, repressed son whose legacy of brutality is an intermittent speech impediment.

1989 D 22, C5:4

'Arf!' Said the Box

KINGFISH, by Marlane Meyer; directed by David Schweizer; sets by Rosario Provenza; costumes by Susan Nininger; lighting by Robert Wierzel; music composed by Steven Moshier; projections by Perry Hoberman; associate producer, Jason Steven Cohen. Presented by Joseph Papp. At the Public Theater/Martinson Hall, 425 Lafayette Street.

Wylie	Buck Henry
Hal	Barry Sherman
Finney	Kevin O'Rourke
Wanda	Jacque Lynn Colton
Edward and Mack	Tony Abatemarco
Kingfish	Arthur Hanket

By MEL GUSSOW

The title character in Marlane Meyer's "Kingfish" is a Doberman pinscher portrayed by a black box with a green grin and a rope tail. The dog's bark is supplied by an actor sitting at a microphone. In this play, Ms. Meyer, a playwright with a previously demonstrated talent for gritty realism, has taken a sidestep into self-conscious absurdism.

The play, which opened last night at the Public Theater, is less about the dog than it is about the dog's master, a middle-aged homosexual (played by Buck Henry). He seems to have entered an early dotage. When his Hasselblad is stolen from his car by a hitchhiker, he immediately decides to adopt the thief (Barry Sherman) and make him his heir. Presumably, in his legacy the young man will inherit both the Hasselblad and Kingfish. Only the former is redeemable.

It would be tempting to suggest that, like the title character, the play is all bark and no bite, except that at one point Kingfish does bite back, proving that a black box is not man's best friend — and a dog-as-black-box may be a playwright's worst enemy.

The single mystery is whether the characters know that Kingfish is a box. Apparently they do but continue

Seret Scott, from right, Delroy Lindo, Damien Leake, K. Todd Freeman and Allie Woods Jr. in "Miss Evers's Boys," at Center Stage.

to pretend otherwise. As the author informs the audience, in triplicate, this is "another world, an artificial environment, like a terrarium." Later, Mr. Henry announces that in this environment he is "the king of the fish," which further confuses the species.

•

The brief play has been lengthened through the simple process of having the stage directions read aloud. David Schweizer, the director, himself sits on a lofty perch above the stage, next to Arthur Hanket in the barking role. The director introduces each of the scenes and describes the characters in action. More often than not, the actors totally disregard the stage directions, an attempt at a humorous motif that in practice is unconscionably arch.

In his narration, Mr. Schweizer assumes the tone of an announcer on a radio soap opera, which may be the model for the play, as it wanders through the dreary domestic life of Mr. Henry's character and his bizarre friends, who include a possible C.I.A. agent and a plump, easily seducible nurse (Jacque Lynn Colton). Mr. Sherman willfully intrudes himself into all of their lives.

Mr. Henry, who originated his role when the play was first presented at the Los Angeles Theater Center, takes a dry approach, and Mr. Sherman has the necessary sleaziness for the narcissistic thief. The performance with the most definition is given by Mr. Hanket. He never misses an arf and seems to take genuine pleasure in his nonspeaking lines. Several seasons ago, he played an abominable snowman, among myriad other roles, in Eric Overmyer's "On the Verge"; he is in danger of being typecast as fauna.

"Kingfish" is underproduced, with a single armchair and wall projections as scenery in front of a silhouette of what appears to be the Los Angeles skyline. In her dialogue, Ms. Meyer captures the deadbeat speech of her bored characters, as she did with far greater intensity in her earlier play, "Etta Jenks," presented in New York last year. In "Etta Jenks," the author created a compelling portrait of male oppressiveness. That play was like a Martin Scorsese film on stage. In contrast, "Kingfish" is a black box.

1989 D 22, C5:1

At a time when the world was rushing forward, the New York theater didn't harness itself to history as Mr. Havel did. Only Larry Gelbart, whose "Mastergate" savaged the Iran-contra scandal and its Washington investigators, seemed to be pursuing current events. Let the Berlin Wall crumble or the Mapplethorpe controversy rage; the topics that exercised the New York theater community were the usual matters of parochial self-absorption (Tony Awards and ticket prices and the impact of critics), not the reordering of the world and the potential role of theater art in that new order.

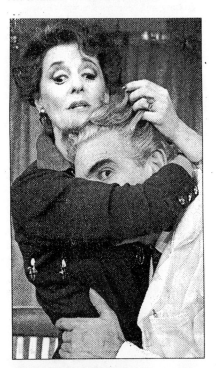

Gerry Goodstein ("Butler," "Aristocrats")

Manhattan Theater Club's outstanding entries included "What the Butler Saw," top, with Carole Shelley and Charles Keating, and "Aristocrats," with Margaret Colin and Niall Buggy

STAGE VIEW/Frank Rich

Personal Voices Made Plays Worth Watching

THERE CAN HARDLY BE ANY doubt that the playwright who mattered most in 1989 was Vaclav Havel. In a year when the world was changing as fast as, if not faster than, at any other time in this century, Mr. Havel was one of the people who changed it — first as a dissident dramatist and now as a political leader shaping the future of Czechoslovakia. But such is the perennial chaos of the New York theater — sometimes a creative chaos, sometimes not — that even Mr. Havel wasn't spared its typically rude shocks in 1989. In April, his play "Temptation" received its American premiere in a wildly distorted production that came and went in a quickly forgotten instant Off Broadway even as its author passed in and out of jail in Prague.

Though the year was noticeably short of major new plays — perhaps reflecting the fact that August Wilson, David Mamet, Richard Greenberg, David Henry Hwang and Michael Weller, among others, had been heard from in 1988 — it was by no means an arid spell for theatergoers. But the fate that befell Mr. Havel's play was typical of a year in which the theater too often reduced the important to the trivial. One thinks back on dazzling names linked to classic titles — Mikhail Baryshnikov in "Metamorphosis," Michelle Pfeiffer in "Twelfth Night," Sting in "Threepenny Opera" — and is hard-pressed to remember a single lively thing about the productions beyond their marquees.

Broadway seemed almost obsessively intent on retreating into the past. Take away Mr. Gelbart's two important contributions — the second being "City of Angels," his collaboration with Cy Coleman and the funniest American musical in years — and the best productions around Times Square in 1989 were often the best of the late 1950's: Peter Hall's crusading revival of Tennessee Williams's "Orpheus Descending" (1957) with Vanessa Redgrave, an electrifying revival of the Arthur Laurents-Jule Styne-Stephen Sondheim "Gypsy" (1959) with Tyne Daly, and "Jerome Robbins's Broadway," a bittersweet anthology of Robbins choreography dominated by a lengthy excerpt from "West Side Story" (1957).

When one turns to the new American plays of 1989, the list may be slender but the two most popular works do, in their very different ways, help define American theater right now for much of the audience: "The Heidi Chronicles" by Wendy Wasserstein and "Other People's Money" by Jerry Sterner. I cannot provide an objective appraisal of "Heidi" because the author is an old friend; I am not among the fanatical fans of "Other

Playwrights, directors and actors managed to enliven productions even when the craft was sloppy or lacking.

People's Money," though I did enjoy parts of it. But, whatever one's opinion of these plays, they do epitomize enduring, opposing strains in American playwriting. It may be in part the peaceful, prosperous coexistence of these disparate hit dramas in 1989 — neither of them carried by stars — that accounts for the happy rise in theatrical production that is creating so much excited anticipation as the year comes to its end.

In the era of television, "Other People's Money" demonstrates that a mass audience will still desert its VCR's for a well-acted, well-made play of the old school, even if only to see an upscale television movie performed live. "Other People's Money" is like television because the personality of the author is almost invisible — subjugated, in this case, to the mechanics of a soundly constructed melodrama that pits two opposing forces in a do-or-die battle for the prize (other people's money) that is central to the ethos of the late 1980's.

If Mr. Sterner had the inclination to dig beneath the surface of his business-takeover story, "Other People's Money" might have made more of its one potentially fascinating human relationship (between the male corporate raider and the female Wall Street attorney) and it might not have so crudely pitted Jewish stereotypes against WASP ones in its financial battle royal. But to appreciate Mr. Sterner's accomplishment — and it *is* an accomplishment — one need only contrast "Other People's Money," an Off Broadway transfer of a play from a resident company (the Hartford Stage), to "A Few Good Men," a similar play produced by the Broadway establishment. Though just as jokey in dialogue, omniscient in tone and stereotypical in characterization as Mr. Sterner's work, "A Few Good Men" is much longer, the price paid for its less efficient con-

struction, and far less in touch with its audience's interests; it's a court-martial drama that assumes a 1989 audience is still gungholier-than-thou (as Larry Gelbart would say) about the cold war.

The kind of playwriting found in "The Heidi Chronicles" is the antithesis of "Other People's Money." To be sure, Wendy Wasserstein deals with an of-the-minute issue: the post-1960's women's movement, its triumphs and its discontents. But her play is a highly idiosyncratic statement in which the mechanics that concern Jerry Sterner (a well-oiled plot, teeth-baring confrontations) are given scant attention and the heroine's thoughts and feelings, sometimes severed from any narrative events whatsoever, come first, even in the bald form of soliloquies. The lawyer in "Other People's Money" could well be a character in "The Heidi Chronicles," but if she were, Ms. Wasserstein would probably tell the audience more about her interior life and leave her legal maneuvers sketchily in the wings. By contrast, if Mr. Sterner had written "Heidi," I suspect we'd see much more of the heroine's tenure battles in academe and not hear any of her most private judgments about the other women in the locker room at her gym.

■

Because I believe that an honest, personal voice is what can make a writer worth listening to — and because I also believe that the craft of playwriting, while an important vehicle for conveying that voice, is a skill, however difficult, that can be acquired — the plays of 1989 that stay with me are those in which the voice is strong even when the craft is too frequently sloppy or lacking. Though these plays sometimes don't "work" — in the sense that "Other People's Mon-

Martha Swope ("Mastergate" and "Angels")

Larry Gelbart savaged the Iran-contra scandal and its investigators in "Mastergate," top, with Daniel von Bargen, and spoofed Hollywood in "City of Angels," with James Naughton, right, and Shawn Elliott

ey" can be said to "work" — they have emotional or intellectual staying power. As usual, such plays have often been developed by institutional theaters Off Broadway (or beyond, as in the case of "Mastergate," a Cambridge import). Outside the commercial theater, a writer's passion still often comes ahead of a producer's hunch as to what the market is most likely to bear.

At the ever more impressive Manhattan Theater Club, where the eclectic spectrum of authors ranged from Richard Wesley ("The Talented Tenth") to Nick Dear ("The Art of Success") this year, audiences were treated to such outstanding works as "Aristocrats," in which the Irish playwright Brian Friel poeticized the brutality of family life; "What the Butler Saw," the 1967 farce that turned out to be the English writer Joe Orton's final and perhaps most uncompromising assault on pieties of church, state and sexual convention; and the still-running "Lisbon Traviata," Terrence McNally's attempt (successful only in Act I, to my mind) to merge the theatrics of grand opera with the gay life of contemporary New York. None of these plays could be mistaken for the work of any other writer. All were directed, whether by Robin Lefèvre (the Friel) or John Tillinger (the Orton and the McNally), with unfailing sensitivity to the authors' intentions and acted accordingly. The lead performers in each production — Niall Buggy (the lost middle-aged son of "Aristocrats"), Joseph Maher (the lunatic asylum's "immediate superior in madness" in "Butler"), Nathan Lane (the prima Callas addict of "Traviata") — can hold their own with any in New York this year.

Other, far more abundantly flawed plays of 1989 whose voices linger include two Circle Repertory Company productions: Paul Zindel's "Amulets Against the Dragon Forces" and Cindy Lou Johnson's "Brilliant Traces," both of which traveled through blind alleys on their way to wrenching showdowns between parents and children, real or surrogate. Like "The Heidi Chronicles," Albert Innaurato's "Gus and Al," Peter Parnell's "Hyde in Hollywood" and Philip Kan Gotanda's "Yankee Dawg You Die" all attest to Playwrights Horizons' affinity for original writers, though the unfinished quality of "Hyde" and "Yankee Dawg" calls into question this company's dramaturgical prowess at seeing scripts through to the Act II curtain.

Everett Quinton's "Tale of Two Cities" and Charles Busch's "Lady in Question" demonstrated that one senior Off Broadway company, the Ridiculous, and one young one, Theater in Limbo, are beginning new chapters in their distinctive histories. While Lincoln Center Theater's first Vivian Beaumont production since "Anything Goes" was another retreat to the 1950's (a gratuitous revival of

The strongest confluence of dramatic voices was in 'Orpheus Descending.'

Paddy Chayefsky's 1959 "Tenth Man"), the company also provided 45

minutes of pungent David Mamet, "Bobby Gould in Hell," in the second half of the Mitzi Newhouse Theater double bill "Oh, Hell."

If directors can be said to be authors — and they can be at least co-authors, sometimes — James Lapine brought some needed magic to the New York Shakespeare Festival's Marathon with a revelatory "Winter's Tale" of a Jungian piece with his contributions (as director and writer) to "Sunday in the Park With George," "Into the Woods" and

"Seven Dreams." At the York Theater Company and later at Circle in the Square, Susan H. Schulman took Stephen Sondheim's familiar "Sweeney Todd" and made it harrowing anew by emphasizing the psychotic horrors, rather than the proletarian anger, shared by the murderous couple played so powerfully by Bob Gunton and Beth Fowler. In "Grand Hotel," the imaginative director Tommy Tune, in collaboration with the designers Tony Walton, Santo Loquasto and Jules Fisher, erected a shimmering Weimar Berlin that is mesmerizing to watch as long as one can disregard the tedious people who have booked rooms.

Actors, too, speak in their own strong voices, particularly when they have sharper personalities than their material. Pauline Collins ("Shirley Valentine"), Bill Irwin ("Largely New York") and the regal triumvirate of Rex Harrison, Glynis Johns and Stewart Granger ("The Circle") were all captivating even when the lines (or, in Mr. Irwin's case, the mime) seemed of less than the first freshness.

But perhaps the strongest confluence of theatrical voices erupting in a highly personal way was "Orpheus Descending," in which the playwright, director and star all spoke up loudly: Williams in the shaky, poetic, frequently confused voice of a great American writer just beginning to skid into the doomed second act of his career; Mr. Hall with a florid Expressionism determined to match the playwright's every wild change of pitch, into Hades, if necessary; and Miss Redgrave with an openhearted directness that challenged audiences to respond to intense, even overbearing, fluctuations of love and hate, often without warning or explanation.

Miss Redgrave's acting, technically inexact (yes, her Sicilian-Southern Lady Torrance sounded like Melina Mercouri) and histrionically dangerous, is out of sync with the digital age of the 1980's, when perfect accents are too often confused with good acting and eruptions of passion are as far from cool as the disorder of a chaotic, half-mad Williams play. It was no surprise that "Orpheus Descending" was the most hotly debated production of 1989. One imagines — and hopes — that there will be much more disruptive theater to argue about now that the 1990's, riding in on winds of previously unimaginable change, are at long last here. ☐

1989 D 24, II:3:1

Robert C. Ragsdale ("Gypsy"); Martha Swope ("Robbins," "Todd")

Broadway seemed intent on retreating into the past, with revivals that included an electrifying "Gypsy," left, with Jonathan Hadary and Tyne Daly, the bittersweet choreographic anthology "Jerome Robbins's Broadway," top, and a harrowing "Sweeney Todd," with Bob Gunton and Beth Fowler

STAGE VIEW/Mel Gussow

Civilization and Savagery Collide in Metaphor

"JUAN DARIEN," THE PUPPET MUsical by Julie Taymor and Elliot Goldenthal, is an eloquent expression of the power of theatrical transformation, which in this case approaches transmutation. As the audience watches, objects and images shift and assume radically different, often metaphorical form. A jaguar cub is reborn as a boy (named Juan Darién), and, suffering at the hands of his fellow man, he is driven back to his beastly origins. In this "carnival Mass," civilization and savagery repeatedly collide. The show is the stage equivalent of the magic realism of novelists like Gabriel García Márquez and Isabel Allende. As in their fiction, the apparently mundane suddenly turns into the miraculous.

For Ms. Taymor, "Juan Darién" is an adventurous leap from such past ventures as her two versions of Thomas Mann's "Transposed Heads" and the various shows she has designed for other directors. She has grown from being an imaginative scenic designer and puppeteer into a conceptual director with a fabulist's view of the mythic possibilities of theater.

The scenery in "Juan Darién" is in constant flux. A church collapses and then evolves into a jungle, which envelops the stage with dense foliage and slithering reptilian forms. The jungle is replaced by a hill town of stuccoed cottages, with a narrow road winding to the top, along which appears a funeral cortege. Foliation occurs on cue and, in a flare of color, the sky is filled with fluttering butterflies. In performance, the show is like an animated film live on stage.

First presented by the Music-Theater Group for a brief engagement early in 1988, "Juan Darién" returns for a six-week run beginning Tuesday at St. Clement's Church.

Making the mundane seem miraculous, the puppet musical 'Juan Darién' reveals the mythic possibilities of theater.

While I have not, of course, seen the present production, the show's representatives indicate that no changes have been made. The revival should approximate the 1988 version.

The musical, which has no spoken words, exists in scenario form, filled with demanding stage directions like "The vulture flies through the space to the sound of loud drums." Characters are played alternately by puppets and actors in masks. Juan Darién himself has five different guises — as rod, hand and Bunraku puppets, as a doll and as a real boy (played by Lawrence A. Neals Jr.).

■

Drawing from diverse sources, Ms. Taymor, designer and director as well as co-author, uses puppets of limitless variety, some minuscule, others as towering as telephone poles. A spindly, parsnip-nosed schoolteacher, whose hairdo is an open book with flapping pages, stares haughtily at his students through five pairs of spectacles — itself a satirical statement about academic shortsightedness. A skeletal symbol of Death does a nervous danse macabre, and, in a flamboyant carnival scene, a tiger tamer leads a Picasso-like parade of saltimbanques, acrobats and aerialists.

In contrast to other examples of performance art that are marked by their coolness and by their emphasis on the visual to the subordination of everything else, "Juan Darién" communicates on an emotional as well as a physical level. It transfixes us with its stage pictures and with its mystical tale of innocence defeated by blind bigotry. The world simply cannot contain a creature as pure as Juan Darién.

In this dramatization of a story by the Uruguayan writer Horacio Quiroga, Juan's ordeal becomes a passion play, a feeling that is enhanced by Mr. Goldenthal's score, which combines liturgical music with pulsating folkloric songs (the lyrics are in Latin and Spanish). The instrumentation is as diverse as the puppetry, using flutes, whistles, gongs, keyboard and the didgeridu from Australia, and the scenic design is influenced by Latin American muralists like Orozco and Rivera.

Ms. Taymor is at the crest of a wave of performance puppeteers who have elevated the craft far beyond children's theater, using it as a bridge between scenery and actors. There is intuitive crossbreeding among these various puppetmasters, who generally act as their own designers.

The tradition in the United States can be traced back to Peter Schumann's Bread and Puppet Theater, whose soulful political pageantry has been a moral presence on our theatrical landscape for many years. Similarly, Ms. Taymor creates pietà-like figures. In contrast to Bread and Puppet's street shows, Theodora Skipitares writes chamber puppet musicals that offer challenging lessons from history, with special emphasis on exploration and scientific discovery (her most recent piece, "Empires and Appetites," was a chronicle of food and famine through the ages).

In "Blue Night," Janie Geiser, an Atlanta-based puppeteer, constructed a walk-through diorama of a walled city. Through lighted windows, one could see scenes of puppet domesticity and intimacy, just as one can on that path to the top of the hill in "Juan Darién." For his one-man shows, Bruce D. Schwartz wears a puppet stage around his body as if it were an overcoat. In effect, he becomes his own stage. In related fashion in "Juan Darién," a walking puppet stage is an ambulatory schoolhouse that swings around and reveals the classroom inside, with puppet children hard at play, Punch and Judy style.

Led by Ms. Taymor, "Juan Darién" is a feat of engineering and synchronization. Primary contributors include G. W. Mercer, who collaborated with her on the sets and costumes, and the team of actors who sing, dance and manipulate puppets.

■

During the show's absence from New York, Ms. Taymor was represented at the New York Public Library branch at Lincoln Center with an exhibition of her theatrical designs (puppets, masks, scenery and sketches). Illustrations of shows that she designed for other directors like Andrei Serban (Carlo Gozzi's "King Stag"), shared space with work for which she bore a greater artistic responsibility. Surrounded by totemic figures emerging from Ms. Taymor's imagination, one could feel the vibrations of "Juan Darién." It was like entering a silent magical forest. Music, drama, actors and living sculptural design are reunited at St. Clement's — with exhilarating results.□

1989 D 24, II:3:1

Carol Rosegg (Toledo); Kenneth Van Sickle (Taymor)

The character Toledo, left, from "Juan Darién," by Julie Taymor, above, and Elliot Goldenthal

Manipulations

THE PUPPETMASTER OF LODZ, by Gilles Ségal; translation by Sara O'Conner; directed by John Driver; set by James Wolk; lighting by Susan A. White; costumes by Victoria Lee; sound by J. Wise; production stage manager, Jon Roger Clark. Presented by American Jewish Theater, Stanley Brechner, artistic director; Lonny Price, associate artistic director. At 307 West 26th Street.

The Concierge	Ann Hillary
Finkelbaum	Sam Tsoutsouvas
Popov	Jay Rubenstein
Spencer	Leo Rovain
Schwartzkopf	Ron Hunter

By MEL GUSSOW

A puppeteer, a survivor of the Holocaust, is living in Germany in 1950 — and is convinced that World War II is still being fought. He believes that if he steps out of his apartment, he will be arrested and returned to the concentration camp from which he escaped. In the privacy of that room, the apparently insane puppeteer acts out plays about his incarceration while his landlady helplessly tries to awaken him to reality.

"The Puppetmaster of Lodz" by Gilles Ségal (at the American Jewish Theater) begins with this interesting premise, but for most of the play, the author indulges in delaying mechanisms. The landlady brings in an assortment of visitors (the same man in various disguises) to the puppeteer's door to convince him that it is safe to come out. At the same time, the protagonist (Sam Tsoutsouvas) has endless, dramatically unrewarding dialogues with his puppets, especially with one representing his wife.

As the play proceeds, one can feel a cloak of inertia descending on the Susan Bloch Theater, unbroken by the landlady's attempt at amelioration. It is only toward the end of the relatively brief work that Mr. Ségal begins to deal more directly with questions about guilt and moral responsibility.

•

A possibility is raised that the puppeteer may himself be in disguise, that he could be an escaped concentration-camp guard, posing as a prisoner to avoid prosecution. The mystery remains, as theatergoers are left to decide if he is suffering from delusions or is acting out of pragmatic self-interest. With such issues under consideration, the play is momentarily thought provoking — until it takes a final turn toward heavy-handed symbolism.

Despite affecting moments — a result of Mr. Tsoutsouvas's subtle performance — the play is more of a contrivance than a well-motivated experience. Watching it, one thinks of a number of other more revealing works (in films as well as on stage) in this area, including Claude Grumberg's "Atelier," a play in which Mr. Ségal appeared as an actor in the original production.

•

Within the limits of the play (using Sara O'Connor's translation), John Driver has staged a reasonably effective production, except for one disconcerting detail. Characters pretend, mime-style, that they are ascending a long flight of stairs to reach the puppeteer's quarters; each boringly treads the same unseen steps. Ron Hunter and Ann Hillary are adept in supporting roles, and Mr. Tsoutsouvas artfully walks a tight-

rope between madness and rationality, while manipulating his puppets with the hand of a master.

1989 D 27, C15:1

An Abundance For the Depression

ROMANCE IN HARD TIMES, written and composed by William Finn; directed by David Warren; choreography by Marcia Milgrom Dodge; scenery by James Youmans; costumes by David C. Woolard; lighting by Peter Kaczorowski; orchestration by Bruce Coughlin; sound by John Kilgore. Presented by Joseph Papp. At Public/Newman, 425 Lafayette Street.

Hennie	Lillias White
Harvey	Lawrence Clayton
Boris	Cleavant Derricks
Zoe	Alix Korey
Polly	J. P. Dougherty
Older Sister	Amanda Naughton
Younger Sister	Stacey Lynn Brass
Gus	Michael Mandell
Eleanor Roosevelt	Peggy Hewett
The Kid	Victor Trent Cook

WITH: Rufus Bonds Jr., Melodee Savage John Sloman and James Stovall.

By FRANK RICH

The real history of the American musical theater in the 1980's began in 1981 with William Finn's "March of the Falsettos," an exuberant show about the love between husbands and wives, parents and children, men and men, and everyone and psychiatrists. Though the story might now have to be revised to accommodate the virus that would later rewrite the lives of its characters, the score and lyrics of "Falsettos" remain as invigorating as ever. Certainly no musical since has offered an opening number to match Mr. Finn's at once merry and neurotic fugue of familial kvetching, "Four Jews in a Room."

It would be nice, not to mention symmetrical, to report that Mr. Finn's new musical at the Public Theater, "Romance in Hard Times," closes the 1980's as brilliantly as "Falsettos" began it. But this show, while giving scattered evidence of its author's special gifts, is a disappointment — not so much a happy farewell to the decade as another symptomatic example of the period's excess in the musical theater and beyond.

•

"Falsettos," which was presented on the small upstairs stage at Playwrights Horizons, was simplicity itself: five actors, a few chairs and a strong point of view that made every moment in a 70-minute show count. "Romance in Hard Times," though unfolding in a Hell's Kitchen soup kitchen during the Depression, reflects the bloated prosperity of 1980's New York. Wildly overproduced on a two-story setting of nearly "Grand Hotel" scale, "Romance" is twice as long as "Falsettos," contains many more performers than it can gainfully employ and is unable to muster a single coherent character, theme or plot development. Given that Mr. Finn has spent much of the decade working on this project in workshops at both Playwrights Horizons and the Public — and given that the evening's stars are two enormous talents, Lillias White and Cleavant Derricks — the waste on view in "Romance in Hard Times" is far more depressing than anything the musical has to say about its nominal subject.

Then again, this show's perspective on the 1930's, to the extent it has any, is almost cheery. After one has taken in the oppressive set (a W.P.A. mural suitable for a post office, in James Youmans's design) and an energetic opening homage to unemployment and bread lines, Mr. Finn seems to forget about hard times. As characters sing repeatedly about good times coming and happy endings in sight, the Walker Evans landscape of

Martha Swope

Cleavant Derricks

"Brother, Can You Spare a Dime?" gives way to a "Happy Days Are Here Again" Depression. By the time a lovably cartoonish Eleanor Roosevelt (Peggy Hewett) has been tossed into the narrative soup, "Romance" has entirely abandoned the hard-edged period tone of, say, Marc Blitzstein's "Cradle Will Rock" for the nostalgia of latter-day Depression musicals like "Flora, the Red Menace" and "Annie."

•

The story that Mr. Finn has set against this background is absurd, if not exactly absurdist. In Act I, Hennie (Ms. White), the doyenne of the soup kitchen, is frustrated by her husband, Harvey (Lawrence Clayton), who refuses to talk until justice comes to the world. In Act II, Harvey's verbiage strike is succeeded by Hennie's maternity strike: She refuses to give birth to her baby until things change for the better. The "romance" of "Romance in Hard Times" is provided by Mr. Derricks, as a ne'er-do-well who spends both acts trying to win Hennie's love and, for cloudy metaphorical reasons, trying to master the saxophone. Meanwhile, Hennie's soup kitchen becomes a soup manufacturer of such uplifting capitalistic prowess that Mr. Finn ends up endorsing the self-help economic credo of Ronald Reagan over that of the New Deal.

Was that his intention? It's hard to know, for very little in "Romance in Hard Times" adds up. For all its powerful black performers, the show has embarrassingly little to say about the particular experience of black people during the Depression. (Its one pungent comment on the subject comes in the form of a running gag about an unemployed actor, amusingly done by Michael Mandell.) With its surreal comic invocations of Supreme Court justices, a pair of handcuffed sisters, Babe Ruth and the First Lady, "Romance in Hard Times" might also have been meant as a sentimental Capra fantasy, a "Pocketful of Miracles." But the tedious, resolutely unerotic love triangle drowns out the fabulist whimsy, especially since Ms. White and Mr. Derricks express their emotions in anachronistic arias reminiscent of their mock-Motown turns in "Dreamgirls."

As always, these two performers sing beautifully — and so does a newcomer named Victor Trent Cook in a cryptic symbolic role known as the

Kid — but this time their big numbers, a lovely initial duet excepted, induce numbness. Too many of the songs are at the same ear-splitting pitch and are vapid in content: Ms. White pulls out the grief-stricken blues stops so frequently, and often with so little motivation, that the pileup of emotional peaks turns her into the gospel singer who cried wolf. It's typical of the evening's wasteful confusions that the musical's most biting song, an autobiographical soliloquy titled "All Fall Down," is not even given to the leads but to a campy second banana (Alix Korey) who shrieks the lyrics into oblivion and otherwise seems, like too many other characters, to have been written out of the show.

•

If "All Fall Down" is a song boasting the specific confessional detail of Mr. Finn at his best, too many songs strain after grandeur with musical and lyrical platitudes. The supple voices of Mr. Derricks and Ms. White often wander up and down the octave as arbitrarily as the underemployed performers, under the direction of David Warren, wander up and down the two levels of the set. It is incredibly frustrating for an audience to watch a musical that keeps advancing — loudly, insistently, with fists pounding the air — without ever arriving anywhere. But the years spent on "Romance in Hard Times" must have been a far more frustrating experience for Mr. Finn, who was wrongly encouraged to march in place during a decade in which he first led the charge.

1989 D 29, C3:1

House Guests

THE FOUNDATION, by Antonio Buero-Vallejo; translated by Marion Peter Holt; directed by James Houghton; set design by E. David Cosier Jr.; lighting design by Amarntha Motte; costume design by Teresa Snider-Stein; sound coordinator, Michael Dalby; stage manager, Carl Skutsch. Presented by Theater for the New City, Crystal Field, executive artistic director; George Bartenieff, executive director. At 155 First Avenue, at 10th Street.

Thomas	Thomas Nahrwold
The Man	Mark Schaller
Berta	Joyce O'Connor
Tulio	John Woodson
Max	Peter G. Morse
Asel	Sean O'Sullivan
Linus	Scott Sowers
The Superintendent	Jeff Sugerman
Aide	Bill Quinlan
Aide	Andrew Fetherolf

By STEPHEN HOLDEN

In the opening scene of Antonio Buero-Vallejo's play "The Foundation," Thomas (Thomas Nahrwold), an aspiring young novelist, paces before the picture window in the lounge of what appears to be a luxurious Alpine spa and exults in the ecstatic music of Rossini wafting through the room he occupies with five other men.

It is Thomas's fantasy that they are all guests of a cultural foundation where their every whim will be gratified. He remains obstinately oblivious to the setting's discordant features. One of the conferees is ill and bedridden on a cot in the corner. The other four seem strangely depressed and taciturn. All of them, including Thomas, wear badges that identify them by number rather than name. When one of the men complains about the stench from a backed-up toilet, Thomas says the management has assured him it will be fixed momentarily. When a meal is served, it is a single minuscule portion of steak with mushroom sauce.

•

As the drama, which is receiving a low-key, Spartan production at Theater for the New City, unfolds, the amenities are gradually withdrawn. The supply of beer, wine and cigarettes runs out, and the telephone disappears. Finally the picture-postcard view of misty mountaintops vanishes, replaced by window bars. When the hotel attendants return they have become prison guards. The man who seemed under the weather has been dead for six days. Instead of distin-

Jonathan Slaff

Thomas Nahrwold in "The Foundation," at Theater for the New City.

guished intellectuals, Thomas learns that his companions are ordinary citizens with everyday jobs who were arrested, as he was, for political dissent. They also tell Thomas that he informed on them while under torture. They have been waiting for days for him to regain his senses.

In Thomas's awakening, the eminent Spanish playwright, who was jailed for five years at the end of the Spanish Civil War, has created a powerful, resounding metaphor for the shaking off of political slumber. But he carries the fable farther and to richer depths, suggesting that imprisonment is a basic condition of life it-

self, and in a final paradoxical stroke, embraces to a degree the sort of fantasy that the play had seemed to deplore.

As the prisoners are taken from their cell for interrogation and possible execution, only one slim possibility for survival is held out — the digging of a tunnel from a different, much less well-appointed cell in the basement of the prison. Each prisoner's actions will depend on his readiness to cling to a faint hope that may be as illusory as Thomas's delusion of the foundation. Without such a hope, there is no future at all. Political and social improvement, the playwright implies, may depend on dreams as unreal as Thomas's possibly schizophrenic delusion.

If "The Foundation" is a drama teeming with ideas, its production, directed by James Houghton, is not especially gripping. The director has wisely avoided treating the fable as a prison melodrama, yet the tone of the production is so distanced that the characters of Thomas and his fellow prisoners never come into very precise focus. While Mr. Nahrworld and John Woodson, Peter G. Morse, Sean O'Sullivan and Scott Sowers succeed in suggesting their characters' personalities, the performances lack an emotional cohesion that would give the production a dramatic core of suspense and apprehension.

1989 D 29, C6:6

Middle-Aged Men And Convent Girls

THE SCHOOL FOR WIVES, by Molière; translated by Earle Edgerton; directed by Joel Bernstein; set by Robert Joel Schwartz; lighting by Douglas O'Flaherty; costumes by Barbara A. Bell. Presented by Pearl Theater Company, Shepard Sobel, artistic director; Mary L. Hurd, general manager. At 125 West 22d Street.

Chrysalde	Stuart Lerch
Arnolphe	James Nugent
Alain	Richard Hart
Georgette	Joanne Camp
Agnès	Robin Leslie Brown
Horace	Kevin Hogan
The Notary, Oronte	Miller Lide

By WILBORN HAMPTON

The word "chauvinist" dates only to the Napoleonic era, but the literary prototype, at least for the male porcine variety, certainly goes back to Molière and his hapless, manipulat-

ing would-be husband Arnolphe in "The School for Wives."

The play, which is being given a passably pleasant revival by the Pearl Theater Company, was Molière's first real comedy of character, discoursing on the role of women and humorously mocking the conceit of middle-aged men who seek the love of younger women. Perhaps not all that coincidentally, Molière wrote it the same year he married, at the age of 40, Armande Béjart, a woman half his age and the youngest sister of his former mistress.

•

At the outset, Arnolphe announces to his friend Chrysalde that he intends to marry his ward, Agnès, a young woman he fell in love with when she was 4 years old and whom he has since had raised in a convent. Arnolphe reasons that if his bride-to-be has been totally unschooled in the ways of the world, she will not know enough to be unfaithful to him. Even now, Arnolphe confides, Agnès is under lock and key at his house, and his servants have orders not to let her see or be seen by any young man.

Chrysalde remarks that Arnolphe basically wants a ninny for a wife. "You would marry her only because she's stupid?" Chrysalde says. "She might betray you and not even know what she's doing." At some point, Chrysalde observes, Arnolphe will have to let Agnès out of the house, and how are you going to keep them in the convent after they've seen Paree?

It is, of course, too late anyway. Agnès has already seen Horace, the handsome young son of Arnolphe's old friend Oronte. And Horace has seen Agnès. And love will overcome all. But not without a struggle. "If that fair-haired boy has her heart," Arnolphe vows, "I'll make sure that's all he has." No one ridicules our human frailties quite so farcically as Molière. "If not to be a cuckold is your only aim," Chrysalde advises Arnolphe, "I suggest you never take a wife."

The Pearl production, which was directed by Joel Bernstein, captures the wit of Molière's text, as rendered by Earle Edgerton's workable if prosaic translation, but is missing that spark of passion necessary to transform the play from the whimsical to the truly hilarious.

James Nugent's Arnolphe, for example, is humorous enough on a cerebral level but lacks any visceral spontaneity. When Arnolphe warns Agnès

Martha Swope Associates/Carol Rosegg

James Nugent of the Pearl Theater Company in Molière's "School for Wives."

that "the vats of hell await a bad wife," Mr. Nugent does so as a man who probably does not really believe in hell himself. And when he states that "a wife is like a bowl of soup," not to be enjoyed by one's neighbors, it is with the fastidiousness of a man who has probably never in his life dribbled a drop of soup down his chin.

Two fine performances are given by Kevin Hogan as the lovesick Horace and Stuart Lerch as the sagacious Chrysalde. Miller Lide also shows flare for classical farce in dual turns as a notary and as Oronde. Robin Leslie Brown's Agnès tries to be demure, but she is a bit too worldly-wise to be the shy country girl who thinks children are begotten through the ear. Joanne Camp and Richart Hart, as Arnolphe's servants, work hard at grabbing a few laughs by running into each other. But they mostly just resemble a couple of people trying to grab a few laughs by running into each other.

Barbara A. Bell's costumes, all satins and feathers and ribbons and bows, would have been the envy of Louis XIV's court.

1989 D 30, 17:1

The New York Times
Theater Reviews
1990

1990

Eating Their Way To Unhappiness

CARBONDALE DREAMS: BETH and BRADLEY, two one-act plays by Steven Sater; directed by Byam Stevens; sets by Jeff Freund; lighting by Stan Pressner; costumes by Rosi Zingales; music by Patricia Lee Stotter; stage managed by Jennifer Gilbert. Presented by Lion King Productions, at the Judith Anderson Theater, 422 West 42d Street.

WITH: Jeff Bender, Deanna DuClos, Anita Keal, James Lish, James Maxson, Navida Stein, Cheryl Thornton and Robert Trumbull.

By RICHARD F. SHEPARD

It is not so much a matter of taste as a taste of matter that creates problems for the chubby housewife whose name gives the title to "Beth," one of the three plays in Steven Sater's "Carbondale Dreams" package of one-acters at the Judith Anderson Theater. The plays, presented two at a time, explore the tensions between family togetherness and individual yearnings.

Beth (Navida Stein) is Jewish, although that has no more relevance, perhaps, than a healthy appetite accompanied by a guilty conscience. She lives in a suburban Illinois town, Carbondale, and even as the curtain rises, the audience sees her compulsively devouring the last contents of a package of Oreos and stealthily stashing the empty box in the bottom of the garbage pail. Her husband (Bob Ari), no sylph himself, rationalizes his own nutritional excesses with a cockamamie theory that one can gain only so much weight in one day; at the same time, he takes sadistic pleasure in discovering and advertising his wife's secret gluttony. Her mother (Anita Keal) is dominating in the most nauseatingly melodramatic way. Beth is obedient, but she is not a happy woman as daughter, wife or mother.

When Beth's brother David (James Lish) arrives for a visit from New York, where he writes poetry, it soon becomes evident that he has left this gourmandizing family in every way: he is pencil thin and into macrobiotics and other health-oriented habits.

●

"Beth" is a study in deterioration and entrapment that makes a strong statement despite its overtones of situation comedy. At the final moment, when a desperate and dispirited Beth has thrown dinner at everyone in the room and, hysterically, is walking out on the family, her husband asks, "Honey, can you stop off at Wolf's and get some ribs?" It is a withering conclusion to a scene that is, at the same time, tragic and comic.

This is a strong cast, with each actor reflecting a clearly etched personality. Byam Stevens has directed the play almost as though it were a choral work, with family scenes played in antiphonal discord — an effective stratagem that calls for mutual awareness of eight characters on stage at once. The well-chosen ensemble also includes Jeff Bender, Cheryl Thornton, Richard Thomsen and Deanna DuClos.

"Beth" is just about the right length for what it has to say, and it is an attractive enough theater piece.

Tensions between togetherness and individual yearnings.

"Bradley" (it and "Arnold" alternate in repertory with "Beth") is a slice of life, and that is a problem. It goes nowhere, although its cast of three — Mr. Bender, Mr. Lish and Ms. Thornton — gives it an illusion of motion. Bradley (Mr. Bender) is a musician by choice, a merchant in the family business by what he deems necessity. He and his wife (Ms. Thornton) have a child, obligations and a drug habit. When brother David (Mr. Lish) comes home and tries vainly to give Bradley the master key to freedom from family servitude — just leave all this, he says — his advice, predictably, is rejected.

Mr. Sater has a keen ear for language and the rare sensitivity of a Paddy Chayefsky to the inflections and stream of consciousness that issue from the mouths of ordinary people. To judge from "Beth" and "Bradley," "Carbondale Dreams" (there are to be five plays in all, with the last two soon to be in production), the voice we are hearing is one that found itself in New York after speaking to itself for formative years in middle America.

1990 Ja 5, C3:1

No Way Out

DE DONDE?, by Mary Gallagher; directed by Sam Blackwell; set by Jay Depenbrock; costumes, by Laura Crow; lighting, by Kirk Bookman; stage manager, Bruce E. Coyle.

Co-produced by Clark, Schaefer, Hackett & Company. Presented by the Cincinnati Playhouse in the Park, Worth Gardner, artistic director; Kathleen Norris, managing director. At Cincinnati.

With: Marie Barrientos, Bill Cwikowski, Betty Miller, Ted Minos, Steve Monés, René Moreno, Enrique Muñoz, John Ortiz, Robert Reilly, Socorro Santiago, Phil Soltanof, Katie C. Sparer and Marta Vidal.

By MEL GUSSOW

●

Special to The New York Times

CINCINNATI, Jan. 5 — Illegal immigration from Mexico to Texas has traditionally been a search for economic opportunity — migrants looking for farm work — but increasingly it has become a case of political necessity, as people run for their lives from repressive Central American regimes. This is the basic premise of Mary Gallagher's compelling new play, "Dé Dónde?," which opened Thursday night at the Cincinnati Playhouse in the Park, as part of the company's 30th anniversary season.

Though the play is drawn from documented sources, gathered during the playwright's research in the Rio Grande Valley in Texas, it has been transformed into visceral theater. While addressing issues, "De Dónde?" does not succumb to polemical techniques and keeps its focus on the humanity and the individuality of its characters. Because of the subject and the economy of execution — 13 actors double in more than 40 roles — the play should have a special appeal to other institutional theaters equally interested in provoking audiences into political awareness.

Crossing the border, the characters in the play are met by a divided reception. There are those who regard the refugees as aliens to be prosecuted, while others consider their escape heroic. Those with the best of motives sometimes blunder, and United States citizens of Hispanic origin can be overcome by snobbery toward the more recent arrivals. Recent world events give Ms. Gallagher's work an additional immediacy. At least indirectly, the play is concerned with United States policy in Central America. In assessing the immigration situation, the author traces the problems to the legal inequities of the naturalization system and its administrators.

The approach is exploratory rather than hortatory — the opposite, in other words, of a Costa-Gavras film. Ms. Gallagher does not lose sight of the abuses of liberty, some of them absurd. One of her strongest suits as a playwright is her sense of irony, which asserts itself even in tense situations.

A young woman (Socorro Santiago) who has fled her country after a threat of rape and acts of violence against her family, is denied asylum. But when a lawyer is told that the woman's brother was tortured to death, he says, unblinkingly, "Him we could get asylum for." "De Dónde?" is filled with such "Catch-22" quandaries, leaving immigrants, many of them unable to speak English, confused about which option to take. Often the easiest course is to return to one's home country, even though retribution awaits.

●

The title of the play is crucial — "De Dónde?," or, freely translated, "Where do you come from?" The unasked question is "A dónde?," or, "Where do you go?" The response would be, "Anywhere but home."

Repeatedly the refugees try to explain to officials the pressing reasons for their flight, and they are met with indifference.

Those who want to provide assistance are trapped by a legalistic bureaucracy. A concerned paralegal (Bill Cwikowski) with a high sense of purpose must accede to the pragmatic wishes of the lawyers who employ him. An elderly nun must weigh questions of conscience against the possibility of reprisals against her sanctuary. As they realize, the most that can be hoped for is not a change of policy but "buying people time."

Under the direction of Sam Blackwell, the actors double on all sides of the battle lines. Scenes are counterpointed and overlap. In the background there are several songs by Rubén Blades (more would give the play added flavor). Demarcations are drawn less by the sparse scenery than by the lighting, as the play moves swiftly from border patrol to internment camp. One could envision a more detailed production, but Mr. Blackwell's staging has an efficiency that does not intrude on the cinematic crosscuts.

Martha Swope Associates/Blanche Mackey

Navida Stein and Jeff Bender in "Beth," part of "Carbondale Dreams."

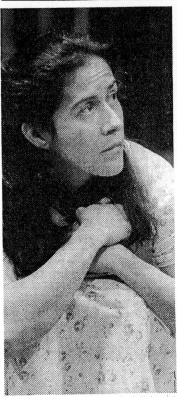

Sandy Underwood

Socorro Santiago in "De Dónde?"

Most of the actors in the largely Hispanic cast skillfully delineate their various characters, including Marie Barrientos, Enrique Muñoz and Betty Miller. Mr. Cwikowski and Ms. Santiago, the only actors who do not double, are particularly moving as the paralegal and the refugee he protects.

Ms. Santiago is so frightened that she remains silent in the face of interrogation, and in so doing unwittingly furnishes herself with a legal defense. If authorities do not know where detainees come from, they may not be able to initiate deportation proceedings. Ms. Santiago's eventual recounting of her ordeal in Central America pierces the play with a cry of helplessness.

Necessarily certain relationships are simplified, as in a romance between a border guard and a young Hispanic woman — and a vaudeville interlude in a holding station does not achieve the desired black comic effect. But Ms. Gallagher's accomplishment is considerable. "De Dónde?" is an outspoken act of social consciousness in a career that, up to now, has been profitably concerned with matters of marriage, home and family (most recently Off Broadway with "How to Say Goodbye").

•

In her work, the playwright has expressed a fierce loyalty to moral principles, even as people are carried away to excessive behavior, as in her satire, "Dog Eat Dog," in which suburbanites combat the recession by becoming supermarket thieves.

"De Dónde?" is a most effective kind of political theater. It encourages the audience to use deductive reasoning to arrive at an inescapable conclusion: in the present handling of illegal immigration to the United States, injustice is being served.

1990 Ja 8, C13:1

Love, Hymns And Rock-and-Roll

JUNON AND AVOS: THE HOPE, book and lyrics by Andrei Voznesensky; music by Aleksei Ribnikov; directed by Mark Zakharov; choreographed by Vladimir Vasilyev; scenery by Oleg Sheintsiss; costumes by Valentina Komolova; sound by Abe Jacob; technical supervisor, Steve Cochrane; narrator, Philip Casnoff; American producer, Lucy Jarvis. Presented by Pierre Cardin. At City Center, 131 West 55th Street.

Count Nikolai Rezanov Nikolai Karachentsev
Conchita .... Yelena Shanina
Burning heretic, Fernando López and the Theatrical narrator .... Aleksandr Abdulov
WITH: Irina Alfiorova, Lyudmila Artemieva, Vladimir Belousov, Boris Chunayev, Tatyana Derbeneva, Villor Kuznetsov, Vladimir Kuznetsov, Yuri Naumkin, Rady Ovchinnikov, Lyudmila Porgina, Tatyana Rudina, Aleksandr Sado, Vladimir Shiryayev, Gennadi Trofimov, Aleksandra Zakharova and Yuri Zelenin.

By STEPHEN HOLDEN

The most exciting moment in "Junon and Avos: The Hope," the Soviet rock musical at City Center, comes late in the first act when the 19th-century Russian explorer Count Rezanov, joined by sailors from the Russian Imperial Navy, sets sail for America.

From the rear of the stage, tiers of bare-chested sailors surge forward in formation doing a mechanical gymnastic dance that carries them down a raked set of illuminated Plexiglas cubes. As the ship's riggings descend around them, they belt out a lusty anthem that blends the international-style art rock of bands like Pink Floyd and Queen with the modality of Russian Orthodox hymns.

In its exuberance and angular kineticism, the scene, splendidly choreographed by Vladimir Vasilyev, suggests a Soviet Socialist answer to a Bob Fosse musical. For a moment, the show's hands-across-the ocean message of international cooperation and brotherhood stirringly comes to life.

"Junon and Avos," the first Soviet rock musical to be produced in America, alas, contains far too few such invigorating moments. In fact, the show, which has been booked for a limited engagement at City Center through Feb. 4, is actually less of a rock musical than an elaborately staged pop pageant.

Intended as a parable for our times, "Junon and Avos" tells the story of the young Count Rezanov (Nikolai Karachentsev), who dreams of opening trade relations between Russia and America and who obtains permission in 1806 from the Czar to sail two ships, the Junon and the Avos, to the Spanish colony of California. Once in San Francisco, he falls in love with the Governor's 16-year-old daughter, Conchita (Yelena Shanina), who helps him sell his Russian goods to a local monastery.

But to marry Conchita, whom he wins after fighting a duel, Count Rezanov must return to Russia to obtain permission from the Russian Orthodox church. While at sea, he falls fatally ill. The faithful Conchita only learns of his death 36 years later, and then becomes a nun.

As staged by Mark Zakharov, the story is told in a sequence of formal tableaux connected by narration. The drama's allegorical implications are underscored by rigidly stylized performances that allow little emotional spontaneity. The climactic love scene between Count Rezanov and Conchita is staged as a series of strained melo-

dramatic clinches. Far too much of the leading performers' time is spent standing center stage and singing while facing the audience.

In the role of Rezanov, the barrel-chested Mr. Karachentsev offers an appropriate sense of heroic command and a wonderfully expressive bass-baritone that revels in the guttural cadences and dynamism of the Russian language as sung. Miss Shanina's portrayal of Conchita, however, seems almost painfully self-conscious. Her singing is pallid, and at moments she appears to be at loose ends.

Aleksei Ribnikov's robust score has big, broad melodies that suggest a more folkish Andrew Lloyd Webber and a bit of Neil Diamond, expansively arranged for keyboard-based rock instruments. The arrangements favor exotic harpsichord-like textures and slogging martial drums. If the score is typical of Soviet rock, it is a genre that has not yet absorbed the more limber African-American influences.

Although "Junon and Avos" is performed in Russian, an English-speaking narrator (Philip Casnoff) delivers brief synopses of events before they happen. The theater program comes with English translations of the major songs. The lyrics were written by Andrei Voznesensky, who adapted the libretto from his poem "What Will Be Will Be." The translation of idiomatic Russian verse into English often bleaches the language of its flavor. That may partly explain why so many of the lyrics seem at once heavy-handed, naïve and sentimental.

The show's final song, "Alleluia," in which the entire cast joins arms and sways, invokes Soviet-American rapprochement as a passionate reunion between two lovers who have waited for each other "for 150 lonely years." "People of the 20th century/Soon your century will be at an end," they sing in Russian. "Will not someone ever find the answer/To why people do not live in peace?"

As good-hearted as "Junon and Avos" may be, the militancy, the oratorical stiffness and the lack of warmth with which it hammers out its message give the show the feel of a humanistic tract instead of an offering of friendship. If this is the contemporary Soviet answer to "Hair," it is woefully lacking in humor or playfulness.

1990 Ja 8, C16:3

The Troubles Of Doubles

20 FINGERS, 20 TOES, book by Michael Dansicker and Bob Nigro; music and lyrics by Mr. Dansicker; directed by Mr. Nigro; setting by Edward T. Gianfrancesco; lighting by Craig Evans; costumes by Gregg Barnes; sound by Aural Fixation; choreography by Ken Prescott; musical direction by Dick Gallagher; production stage manager, K. R. Williams. Presented by WPA Theater, Kyle Renick, artistic director; Donna Lieberman, managing director. At 519 West 23d Street.

Quick Change Artist .... Jonathan Courie
Hanna and Daisy Hilton .... Ann Brown
Helen and Violet Hilton .... Maura Hanlon
Auntie Verna Hilton .... Roxie Lucas
Myer Myers .... Paul Kandel
Bert the Baffling .... Ken Prymus
Musicians
 Dick Gallagher, pianist; Kevin Hayes, bassist; Bobby Kent, drummer.

By MEL GUSSOW

The search for bizarre material for musicals hits barrel bottom with "20

Fingers, 20 Toes," a musical about Siamese twins, in this case the Hilton sisters, who starred in Tod Browning's film "Freaks." Because the show is at the WPA, the company that first presented "Little Shop of Horrors," one begins with expectations of a musical noir. Instead, "20 Fingers, 20 Toes" is merely monstrous, and coming so soon after "Buzzsaw Berkeley," the abominable chain-saw musical, it should make the WPA jettison its so-called Silly Series.

Michael Dansicker (as composer and lyricist) and Bob Nigro (as co-author and director) have taken a dubious idea and managed to plunge into every pitfall, starting with bad taste. The real subject of this backstage musical comedy is child abuse. The music has a sameness and the lyrics are single-edged in their doubleness.

The twins (Ann Brown and Maura Hanlon), joined at the lower back, are brought up by their aunt, who is given a garish performance by Roxie Lucas. Since she left "Forbidden Broadway," where she was noted for her imitation of Mary Martin, Ms. Lucas has turned herself into a caricature. Her Auntie Verna snivels and snarls so much that one wishes a tornado would sweep the wicked witch away on a broomstick.

•

Faced with such a horror for a substitute parent, the girls blithely sing, "We Don't Have a Mother." What they also don't have is a show. Instead they face a series of collusions, as Auntie Verna teams up with an agent (Paul Kandel) of boundless greed and smarminess. Together they force their charges to do four vaudeville shows a day and lock them up at night, offering scant remuneration while they reap huge profits.

The Hiltons sing about "Bluebirds," when they are not singing about fingers, toes and feet. The lyrics are so filled with digital references that one begins to think Mr. Dansicker and Mr. Nigro may be covert chiropodists.

If the sisters do not cooperate, vows Verna, they will be shipped off to Johns Hopkins in Baltimore, where they will be surgically separated, and one will die. This threat momentarily awakens the pair to their plight, but it does not stop them from repeating songs, especially the one about the bluebirds of sappiness.

Finally, in the second act, they find a friend, a hermaphrodite, Bert, who appreciably raises the show's already high camp quotient. Bert urges them to make a break for Hollywood, which they do on a train named Bluebird. Guess which song is reprised.

In dialogue dipped in double-entendre, there is only one line that almost draws a smile: "When it comes to dancing, you girls got four left feet." Siamese twins are not easily choreographable. In response, they sing at the top of their voices. Considering their sibling proximity, Ms. Brown and Ms. Hanlon carry off their roles with a certain aplomb. The show's primary credit should go to the costume designer, Gregg Barnes, who has stitched together a wardrobe of diverse wideness. In other respects, "20 Fingers, 20 Toes" is all thumbs.

1990 Ja 10, C17:1

The Last Word

TERMINAL HIP, written and directed by Mac Wellman. Sets and lights designed by Kyle Chepulis; costumes by Barbara Pohlman; dramaturg, Melissa Cooper; music by Michael Roth. Presented by Performance Space 122, 150 First Avenue, at Ninth Street.

WITH: Stephen Mellor

By MEL GUSSOW

"Terminal Hip," Mac Wellman's "Spiritual History of America Through the Medium of Bad Language," is a post-Joycean Jabberwocky. Expect no exegesis. Just sit back and enjoy the torrent of language, as Mr. Wellman zigzags through time, space and participle.

This riff (at Performance Space 122) is a crazy quilt of slang and circumlocutions, double negatives and oxymorons gathered under a baldachin, or ornamental canopy, of the mind. Listening to it, one repeatedly reaches for a mixed metaphor as steering wheel. "Terminal Hip" is a word processor gone awry, garbling "grammatical shibboleth" on a scrambled screen.

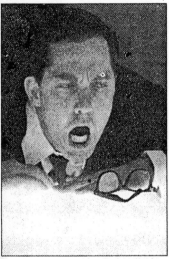

Dona Ann McAdams
Stephen Mellor in "Terminal Hip."

Occasionally, the playwright strikes a note of clarity, trashing beachfront condos, assailing United States foreign policy in Central America (Presidents who "jubilate with successive Somozas") and parsing the component parts of the panda. For fun, there is a replay of Abbott and Costello's "who's on first" routine. If all this sounds illogical, that's for a reason. Think too hard about meaning, or listen for "chtonic murmurs," or primitive sounds, and one might be overcome by vertigo.

Amazingly, the actor Stephen Mellor tones and tames the monologue so that it seems to have an organic flow. Mr. Wellman and Mr. Mellor, who have often worked together, are quite a team, especially as evidenced in this play and in last summer's "Bad Penny." "Bad Penny" made a certain sense, as Mr. Mellor's character summed up a mad tourist's underview of New York. In contrast, "Terminal Hip" whirligigs its way without a thought about destination while taking theatergoers for a wild word-busting ride.

With all its convolutions and neologisms, the text must be impossible to memorize, but then who, except for Mr. Wellman, could tell if Mr. Mellor

missed a word — or made up a word? The dream-of-consciousness principle is the thing, and the actor gives

'Terminal Hip' is a crazy quilt of slang and convolutions.

"Terminal Hip" a kick of kinetic energy. He seems to know what he is saying even when the audience is left musing in the dark. His acting provides punctuation, as when he exclaims, "Why Russia? Why Brooklyn? Why lard?" and punches his fist into the air.

•

Mr. Mellor's expressions are those of a political candidate who believes everything he is told to say. Expostulating and extrapolating, he is sometimes like a hipster version of Prof. Irwin Corey, delivering a doubletalk lecture as the world's greatest authority.

If the play is "a maniacal hubbub," it is a literate, amusing hubbub. It may be true, as the author says, that "any airhead can play an air guitar," but only Mr. Wellman could have written this play and only Mr. Mellor could have imbued it with such histrionic variety.

1990 Ja 12, C3:1

The Promised Land

THE RETURN, by Frederic Glover; directed by Michael Bloom; set design, Scott Bradley; costume design, Edi Giguère; lighting design, Donald Holder; sound design, Gary and Timmy Harris; production stage manager, D. C. Rosenberg. Presented by Jewish Repertory Theater, Ran Avni, artistic director; Edward M. Cohen, associate director. At 344 East 14th Street.

Dr. Chaim Weizmann	Dominic Chianese
Benjamin Weizmann	Bruce Nozick
David Ben-Gurion	Joseph Ragno
Paula Ben-Gurion	Annie Korzen
Vera Weizman	Jennifer Sternberg
Lord Halifax; Capt. Orde Wingate; Lord Lloyd	Graeme Malcolm
Michael Weizmann	Jon Krupp

By RICHARD F. SHEPARD

A note in the program for "The Return," Frederic Glover's play at the Jewish Repertory Theater about conflict between two leading Zionists, alerts the audience to something that is often left unsaid in television docudrama.

The note says: " 'The Return' is dramatic fiction and makes no claim on complete historical accuracy." This is commendable, particularly in a play that deals with a subject about which there is absolutely nothing that is noncontroversial. It is also a statement that gives a writer considerable latitude, perhaps too much, in treating a topic, as fans of King Richard III have complained ever since Shakespeare's docudrama dealt with his reign.

The real hero of "The Return" is Chaim Weizmann, the brilliant chemist who was a key figure in getting the British to endorse the Zionist ideal of a state for the Jews and who then kept struggling with them to implement their promises. In Mr. Glover's play, David Ben-Gurion comes close to being, if not an outright villain, then as unpleasant a fellow as could be found in politics of any kind.

"The Return" is set in the early 1940's. Weizmann, portrayed with dignity, compassion and urbanity by Dominic Chianese, is trying to persuade the British to relent on their plan to restrict Jewish immigration to Palestine, as well as on other backtracking on their announced intentions. Ben-Gurion, played with dramatic intensity by Joseph Ragno, is seen as a scrappy, fiery, impossible leader given to ultimatums, threats and terrorism.

The two men are a study in contrast. Weizmann is tall and dresses as a dignified Englishman should. Ben-Gurion, short and scruffy, dresses sloppily, bolts his meals and hollers a lot. "Dr. Weizmann is a rich chemist, I'm a poor Socialist," he tells his wife, Paula (Annie Korzen), a wise and gabby American woman who puts up with his shenanigans — political and extramarital — with a sort of bitter understanding.

Actually, Ben-Gurion was more complex than "The Return" might indicate. He, no less than Weizmann, believed at first in the possibility of co-existence with Arab neighbors. He was a man who developed depth of character with age, but the play presents him at an early stage of what was to be a long career. Unfortunately, he comes across as a semicomic spouter, in contrast to the sober, insightful Weizmann.

•

The two men were enemies, probably because of differences in personality as well as in politics. Yet both were dreamers and both were pragmatists, a combination inspired by the dreadful European catastrophe they lived through. Weizmann's way was negotiation and persuasion in the old, disappearing European Zionist style; Ben-Gurion was impressed by the more fiery, direct-action tactics of the younger, vigorous American Zionist movement.

Mr. Glover has seized this hot potato of personal relationships and Zionist politics and has cooled it off by depicting the two leading characters in the context of their personal lives. "The Return" is told in a series of short scenes linked by the narration of Weizmann's son, Benjamin (Bruce Nozick), who tells how, as a young man, he hated his father for what he perceived as lack of personal feeling and dedication, instead, to a cause. In the play's momentarily touching conclusion, Weizmann, outmaneuvered by Ben-Gurion, losing his eyesight and rejected by his son, but not by his loving, almost-too-understanding wife (Jennifer Sternberg), emerges as a towering figure of probity and honor who became Israel's first President. (Ben-Gurion was his powerful premier.)

The problem with "The Return" is that it rarely grips the heart. The urgency of the Jewish situation that preoccupies the protagonists make the crises of their personal lives seem almost trivial. The drama, directed by Byam Stevens, comes across as a series of related vignettes without amassing a unified dramatic thrust that develops insight rather than description.

But "The Return" has an interesting and worthy theme. Hopefully some way will be found to give it the human scale that could make it intriguing theater. Meanwhile, it serves to tell of a fascinating episode in history that was to influence the world.

1990 Ja 12, C3:3

One Ring, But Many Acts

MOSCOW CIRCUS, presented by Soyuzgostsirk and Steven E. Leber. Georgi Andrushchenko, General Director; Vyacheslav Sirotkin, chief external relations department; Vsevolod M. Kotik, assistant general director; Yuri Nikulin, special consultant. At Radio City Music Hall, 50th Street and Avenue of the Americas.

WITH: Serebryakov and Popov, Doveyko, The Gugkayevs, Sarvat Begbudi, Raisa and Grant Ibragimov, Aleksandr Frish, the Agayev Family, Olga Denisova, Kherts, Shchmarlovsky, The Gibadullin Jugglers, Tamerlan Nugzarov and Albert Makhtsiyer.

By RICHARD F. SHEPARD

Almost reflecting the way things are going back home, the Moscow Circus moved into Radio City Music Hall on Thursday in a dazzle of spin, whirl and precarious stability.

The company of 120, more than halfway through a North American tour that will have them cavorting about the vast Music Hall through Feb. 4, lacks very little that a circus fancier might admire. There are high-wire acts, tiger acts, clowns, jugglers and horseback riders, all operating at hazardous, breakneck speeds. If anything, the circus functions more brilliantly in its parts than it does as a whole.

It is a one-ring affair, an arrangement that has drawn praise from those who are insufficiently swivelnecked to savor everything in the mind-boggling American three-ring model. But at orchestra-seat level, the one-ring motif does not rivet the eye and what is an arena show elsewhere becomes a stage spectacle of not inconsiderable Music Hall dimensions.

But whatever else it is, the Moscow Circus is circus on a grand scale, and it has made good use of the Music Hall's vast spaces, with the result that the good acts come off magnificently while others lose luster, probably because of the unusual setting. The higher the act, the more strikingly it comes across. The ground-level numbers that benefit from the usual theater-in-the-round circus format, like wild-animal and race-around acts, do not appear to best advantage.

There are any number of venturesome performers who prove that one turns a tough kopek in the circus life. The most vivid practitioners soar in toward the end of the show. The Kherts aerialists are a devil-may-care gang of 10 winched to the top of the Music Hall stage, avoiding the tedious walk-up that such troupes usually start out with. High up, they are bunched in a bewildering cluster

On a one-ring stage, what may be the fastest hands in the East, etc.

of bodies that, like artichoke leaves, peel off from the core and fly to distant hands on other lofty perches.

It is a thrilling, graceful act, one that induces worry in those not reared in a fatalistic tradition. Any sense that the Music Hall is limited as a vertical arena flies right off the trapeze with them. And at the end, after most of the fliers have bounced off the safety net below, the most intrepid of all is tossed for what must be almost half a city block from one side of the stage to the other.

•

Back at ground level, the audience is virtually hypnotized by the Gibadullins, four men and a woman, who make dishes fly in a way that not even the fastest fast-food establishment could approximate. The quintet of jugglers may be the fastest hands in the East, wasting no time in achieving high gear. As peroration, four performers toss the fifth a total of 16 plates, at bullet-speed. The catcher, after several tries and an occasional miss, ends up with the entire batch in his arms.

Sarvat Begbudi has come to New York from Tashkent, where he knew horses before he experienced anything on wheels. He stands on his splendid steed and even as it is loping around the ring juggles hoops and glasses, filled with liquid, that are on a tray perched on a long thin rod that he balances on his head. Finally, he dashes off, trailing a magically produced, enormous, combination U.S.-U.S.S.R. flag.

As reckless as all this seems, it is almost placid compared with Tamerlan Nugzarov and his eight riders, who use their galloping horses as playpens; the one place they never seem to be is in the saddle. At one point, the rider actually keelhauls himself, going overboard on one side of the running horse, hanging on beneath it and then emerging on the other side.

The animal acts, the cute bears and the fierce tigers, are certainly in the tradition of animal comedy and menace, but they do not come off as strikingly in the Music Hall as they might in an arena where the audience surrounds them.

•

The Agayev family of eight work their high wire with extraordinary aplomb. They dance on it, do multiple backward and forward flips and even show that this is a job a savvy guy could do blindfolded. The Gugkayevs play breathtaking seesaw in the air, balancing each other on a fulcrum that seems quite unreliable.

In between the acts, the ringmasters, Aleksandr Frish, speaking in Russian, and Albert Makhtsiyer, who speaks in English, are a charming pair, but would be even more so in an intimate ambience, like the one projected by the Big Apple Circus.

On balance, which is what circus is often all about, the Moscow Circus is a good time, even under a peculiarly New York-type big top. There is movement and color and agility and enough sense of anxiety over the fate of the daredevils to make up for any sense of crisis you may be missing in relations between our two countries.

1990 Ja 13, 13:4

'We' as an Object

JONQUIL, by Charles Fuller; directed by Douglas Turner Ward; set, Charles McClennahan; costumes, Judy Dearing; lighting, Sylvester A. Weaver Jr.; production stage manager, Ed DeShae; company manager, Lauren P. Yates. Presented by the Negro Ensemble Company, Mr. Ward, artistic director/president; Susan Watson Turner, general manager. At Theater Four, 424 West 55th Street.

Jonquil	Cynthia Bond
Klux No. 2 and Isaiah	O. L. Duke
Klux No. 3 and Daniel	Samuel L. Jackson
Sally	Iris Little
Calvin	Charles Weldon
Cable	Tracy Griswold
Judge Bridges	William Mooney
Hannah	Rebecca Nelson
Aunt Bessie	Peggy Alston
Silas	Graham Brown
George Turner	Ed Wheeler
Bobby Williams	William Jay
Woman and Hallie Bridges	Amanda Jobe
Colson	Curt Williams
Black Farmers	
Kenshaka Ali, Tiffany McClinn and Leonard Thomas	

By MEL GUSSOW

With harshness as well as equanimity, Charles Fuller's "Jonquil" reveals the obstacles to full emancipation in the South immediately after the Civil War. Through a voting rights episode in a small South Carolina community, the author views the Reconstruction period as one of the uglier chapters in the nation's history. "Jonquil," the third play in Mr. Fuller's projected five-play series about black Americans in the second half of the 19th century, opened Saturday at the Negro Ensemble Company.

In common with "Sally" and "Prince," the two plays that preceded it, "Jonquil" is not yet a finished work. A tentativeness in some of the characterizations and in Douglas Turner Ward's production lessens Mr. Fuller's argument. But for the first time in this ambitious cycle, the author tellingly dramatizes a complex situation and has a narrative strong enough to carry the play to a tragic conclusion.

Though "Jonquil" makes passing reference to the earlier plays, especially in regard to the absent character of Prince Logan, a charismatic black soldier in the Union Army, the play stands on its own as a portrait of a section of the South totally unable to face its defeat and to discontinue a dehumanizing way of life. The theatergoer need not have seen the first plays in order to follow this one.

At the center is the character named Calvin (Charles Weldon), who is embarking on what he envisions as a political career. Calvin is willfully trying to transform himself into a leader of men. His primary asset appears to be the absence of any others challenging him for that position. In the course of the play, he grows as a candidate for state office, and he also sees the error of his pragmatic ways. Cowardly when his wife, Sally, is attacked by members of the Ku Klux Klan, he is gradually swept into taking a stand.

His allies include a loose assembly of rebels and passivists, from Graham Brown as a man who believes

that only by arming themselves can blacks begin to achieve their rights, to Samuel L. Jackson, who has his mind entirely on the concept of owning property. As in the earlier plays, the author sees economics as a root concern, with blacks demanding equal pay as they did when they served in the army. In the case of "Jonquil," they also claim the right to vote, and that claim sends them into violent collision with whites.

•

Mr. Fuller's white characters include a judge (William Mooney) whose paternalism barely conceals his racism and an apparently well-meaning carpetbagger (Tracy Griswold) with his own ambiguous attitude toward questions of brotherhood. Although some of the minor characters, black and white, become simplistic, these two and others have shadings that make their reactions unpredictable.

The symbolic center is intended to be the title character. Jonquil (Cynthia Bond) is one aspect of the play that needs strengthening. She is blind, but she hears with a mystical intensity. It is she, for example, who can testify with the most certainty about the identity of the hooded assailants who humiliated her friend Sally. Jonquil remains in the background. Whenever she is given prominence, she becomes the embodiment of Mr. Fuller's premise, which is that progress can only come through unity.

•

The comprehensive title of this cycle is "We," a word that the illiterate Jonquil uses in the objective case, as in "Folks are always forgetting what they do to we." Led by Jonquil as concerned conscience, the "we" will presumably consolidate their protest in the next play in the series.

Even as "Jonquil" is the sturdiest of the plays to date, the production is schematic. Charles McClennahan's unfurnished setting is only a step from a workshop. Several of the actors, including Mr. Weldon, still seem to be adjusting themselves to the demands of the play. Iris Little (as Sally), Mr. Mooney, Mr. Brown and, particularly, Ms. Bond are more insightful about delineating characters.

Because of its intelligent perspective on American history, "Jonquil" reminds one of Mr. Fuller's early play "The Brownsville Raid." It is a sign that, as it proceeds, "We" is advancing.

1990 Ja 15, C14:3

Cynthia Bond, left, Samuel L. Jackson and Iris Little in Charles Fuller's "Jonquil."

Intriguing Character, Though Dead

TRAVELER IN THE DARK, by Marsha Norman; directed by D. Lynn Meyer; sets, Joe Tilford; costumes, Becky Senske; lighting, Mary Jo Dondlinger; production stage manager, Victor Lukas; technical director, Norman Frith. Presented by the York Theater Company, Janet Hayes Walker, producing director; Molly Pickering Grose, managing director. At the Church of the Heavenly Rest, 2 East 90th Street.

Sam	Dennis Parlato
Glory	Lynn Ritchie
Stephen	Jeffrey Landman
Everett	Jim Oyster

By MEL GUSSOW

Marsha Norman's "Traveler in the Dark" aims to be a play about a crisis of faith but becomes an unresponsive argument between a skeptic and a believer. The work is didactic when it needs to be humanizing, single-edged when it should be at its most penetrating. First presented in 1984 at the American Repertory Theater in Cambridge, Mass., "Traveler in the Dark" is having its New York premiere at the York Theater Company. It is interesting only as an attempt on Ms. Norman's part to confront metaphysical concerns, but it adds nothing to one's appreciation of her work.

At the root of the difficulty is her choice of protagonist, a surgeon who believes in the power of the mind — his mind. The author has said that the play was motivated by her desire to write about a "sympathetic smart person." Despite that goal, the doctor (played by Dennis Parlato) is self-

Sandy Underwood

Dennis Parlato in Marsha Norman's "Traveler in the Dark."

righteous to the point of smugness, both in his personal relationships and in his attitude toward the medical profession.

Blindly neglectful of his family, he does his greatest harm in his dismissal of the fears of his young son. While stripping him of all illusions, he offers nothing in return except ice-cold intellectualism. He is also given to making metaphorical pronouncements. ("Life is summer camp, and death is lights out.")

The doctor's supposed crisis of faith comes after his childhood friend Mavis dies on his operating table. His supposed genius was not enough to save her, but his questioning goes no further than fragmentary musing about his own possible fallibility.

Though unseen, Mavis is the most intriguing character in the play, as revealed in memories of her youth and her loyalty to the doctor and his family. The characters on stage are unrewarding company, with the possible exception of the doctor's father (Jim Oyster), who is a preacher. One wonders why anyone puts up with the doctor's solipsism; he offers no relief of charm. Early in the play he tells his wife that he is leaving her. That decision is unpersuasively motivated, as is the artificially ameliorative conclusion.

The goal was a 'sympathetic smart person.'

Under the surface, personal issues of parental neglect (including that of the preacher toward his son) remain insufficiently explored, as Ms. Norman superimposes a narrative on a debate and then belabors the symbolism. The title itself derives from an unfamiliar second verse of "Twinkle Twinkle Little Star."

Although the acting is adequate, D. Lynn Meyers's production is marked by a kind of fretfulness, perhaps in an attempt to add detail to the characters. Each actor is busily engaged in activities. Mr. Parlato never stops fussing in the family garden, the play's single setting (an authentic-looking design by Joe Tilford). He unearths small stone figures and brushes away leaves, diverting attention from the dialogue.

The playwright is much more effective — and moving — when drama takes precedence over deliberation, as in "Getting Out" and her Pulitzer Prize-winning " 'Night, Mother."

1990 Ja 16, C13:1

Revenge And Other Lusts

OTHELLO, by William Shakespeare; directed by William Gaskill; music composed by Jeff Langley; set and costumes, Annie Smart; lighting, Frances Aronson; fight direction, David S. Leong; voice and text consultant, Robert N. Williams; associate director, Patrick Kelly; production stage manager, Steven H. Wildern. Presented by Theater for a New Audience, Jeffrey Horowitz, artistic/producing director. At 136 East 13th Street.

Roderigo .... Dan Cordle
Iago .... Brian Reddy
Brabantio .... Max Jacobs
Othello .... Michael Rogers
Cassio .... Craig Wroe
Duke's Officer and First Gentleman •
         Jonathan Nichols
Duke of Venice and Gratiano
        Robert Zukerman
First Senator .... Jonathan Nichols
Second Senator and Montano ... Roger Bechtel
Sailor, Second Gentleman and Lodovico
          P. J. Brown
Desdemona .... Olivia Birkelund
Emilia .... Becky London
Bianca .... Jessica Hecht

By WILBORN HAMPTON

It is something of a mystery why so many directors, often intelligent and talented ones, feel the need to find some gimmick to make the plays of William Shakespeare palatable to the doltish groundlings who make up a modern theater audience.

Happily, William Gaskill is not of like mind. Mr. Gaskill, a veteran director long associated with both the Royal Court Theater in London and the National Theater of Britain, knows the power of raw drama and passion and has mounted a straightforward and commendable production of "Othello" for the Theater for a New Audience at the CSC Theater.

Mr. Gaskill brings the lights up on a bare stage, focusing attention immediately on the characters and the Machiavellian plot as it hatches in Iago's mind. Through the course of the play, only minimal furnishings are brought onstage as they are required — a table or two, two or three chairs, some tankards, a quill and inkstand, a couple of maps of Cyprus and, of course, a bed for the final scene. Mr. Gaskill is a director who moves actors and furniture only to serve the play.

•

"Othello" has proved to be one of Shakespeare's most successful plays, for both audiences and actors. If modern audiences have trouble personally identifying with, say, a mad Scottish thane's guilt over regicide, jealousy is more easily recognizable. It is not an emotion that died with the Elizabethans. For actors, the play offers a wide range of choices for characterization, and the only real mistake for

Gerry Goodstein

Michael Rogers in the title role of the Theater for a New Audience production of "Othello."

an actor (or director) is to be tentative in making them.

Much has been written, for example, about the motives for Iago's perfidy. Samuel Taylor Coleridge wrote of Iago's "motiveless malignity"; William Hazlitt stated that he was driven by a lust for power; G. B. Harrison asserted that Iago acts out of simple revenge at being passed over for promotion by Othello. In the New Audience production, Brian Reddy does not hesitate to portray an Iago as consumed by jealousy as he teaches Othello to be. It is a valid choice, supported by the text in two speeches (one of which Mr. Reddy turns into the most passionate in the production), and supported in this staging by Mr. Gaskill's having Cassio kiss Iago's wife, Emelia, full on the mouth when they arrive in Cyprus.

Mr. Reddy's generally fine performance further illuminates a side of the character that is usually overlooked: Iago as comic relief. In the opening scenes, as Iago begins his manipulation with Roderigo and his duplicity with Othello, there is genuine humor to be mined. The danger, and one from which Mr. Reddy does not always escape, is to avoid turning Iago into a caricature of a Dickensian villain once the bloodletting begins.

•

Michael Rogers's Othello is a quiet study of a soldier clearly more given to speaking with a sword on the battlefield than with flowery phrases in Venetian courts or bedchambers. Mr. Rogers's Moor is a man of action, not of raging. He is loath to believe Iago's insinuations, but once convinced, he becomes a broken man whose first thoughts are of death to those who have betrayed him. Olivia Birkelund presents a strong-willed Desdemona, every inch the daughter of a Venetian nobleman and a young woman clearly used to having her way. This is convincing as she explains her love for Othello and in the scenes in which she pleads for Cassio, but it is less so when she is the naïve innocent who, though facing her death, cannot bring herself to speak the word "whore."

Mr. Gaskill has assembled an able cast that gives a mostly credible reading throughout. Dan Cordle's foppish Roderigo is especially good, and Craig Wroe makes a dashing Cassio. Robert Zukerman and Roger Bechtel also stand out in dual roles. David S. Leong's fights are thoroughly believable — sudden, fierce and quickly over.

Mr. Gaskill creates a great sense of urgency in the pacing of the first half. The intensity flags a bit at moments in the second half, but all in all, this is a faithful and vital "Othello" that is a credit to its author.

1990 Ja 17, C18:4

Wages of Dictatorship

MACBETH, by William Shakespeare; directed by Richard Jordan; set by John Conklin; costumes, Jeanne Button; lighting, Brian Gale; music composed by Daniel Schreier; fight director, Peter Nels; associate producer, Jason Steven Cohen. Presented by Joseph Papp. At the Public/Anspacher Theater, 425 Lafayette Street.

Witch No. 1 .... Mary Louise Wilson
Witch No. 2 .... Jeanne Sakata
Witch No. 3 .... Katherine Hiler
Malcolm .... Thomas Gibson
Duncan and Doctor .... Mark Hammer
Captain and Macduff
      William Converse-Roberts
Ross .... Daniel von Bargen
Macbeth .... Raul Julia
Banquo .... Larry Bryggman
Lady Macbeth .... Melinda Mullins
Porter .... Harry S. Murphy
Lady Macduff .... Harriet Harris
With: Scott Allegrucci, Daniel Berkey, Jesse Bernstein, Reg E. Cathey, Joseph Costa, Peter Jay Fernandez, Rob LaBelle, Christopher McHale, Gabriel Olds, Rene Rivera, Stephen Rowe, Laura Sametz and Matt Bradford Sullivan.

By FRANK RICH

That indelible image of Nicolae Ceausescu's lifeless body lying on the ground could be the final scene in a modern-dress staging of "Macbeth." The earlier images of Ceausescu and his partner in dictatorship, his wife, Elena, staring down a military tribunal could also be taken from Shakespeare's tragedy, as could the entire Rumanian nightmare of a married couple's lust for autocratic power at any brutal price. When Lady Macbeth tells her husband how she would even have "dashed the brains out" of "the babe that milks me" to get what she wants, does not one recall the eyes of that dead baby staring out of the photograph of the massacre at Timisoara?

Nice as it might be were "Macbeth" to go out of fashion, it never does. The Ceausescus may come and go like the Peróns and the Marcoses and so many before them, but there are always successors waiting in the wings. Shakespeare wrote so that audiences might recognize and maybe understand the pathology of evil. What more valuable play could the New York Shakespeare Festival have chosen to greet the 1990's?

•

But if "Macbeth" is sadly and eternally pertinent, it would be hard to imagine a more irrelevant production of it than the one at the Public Theater. Set by the director, Richard Jordan, in a conventionally gray feudal universe and recited with an almost complete absence of passion by a promising cast led by Raul Julia, this "Macbeth" never fires up the play's characters, themes or even its horror-tale atmosphere. While the text trades in supernatural images of warped nature, of scorpion-infested brains and screeching owls and carnivorous wild horses, the evening is so bloodless that theatergoers would get more of the authentic flavor of "Macbeth" by hiking uptown to "Sweeney Todd." A few fog and lightning effects do not constitute hurlyburly.

Mr. Jordan, a good actor, has never directed a Shakespeare play before, and the inexperience shows. He takes the safest route — a by-the-book staging that deals with the logistical management of each scene without ever addressing the larger question of how those scenes come together to present a dramatic portrait of power lust, political terror and madness. The only positive result of Mr. Jordan's workmanlike approach is a lucidity of vocal delivery. One can hear every line, clearly, in this "Macbeth," even if the meaning of the poetry remains unexplored.

•

Though the audience is perched right on top of the action in the intimate, three-quarter arena space, the characters are as remote as any seen from the balcony of a huge Broadway house. Mr. Julia's performance exemplifies the failings of the whole. In fine, resonant voice and full beard, the actor delivers nearly every speech in the same rational tone (sometimes accompanied by the professorial wagging of a finger), whether he is anticipating the murder of Duncan or contemplating his bloody hands following the deed or, much later, acknowledging the death of his wife (who, in one of Mr. Jordan's few flourishes, commits harakiri on stage). When Mr. Julia does raise his voice above its usual declamatory volume, it is usually in blind rage. The "horrible imaginings" prompted by his ambition, the harrowing nights of sleeplessness induced by his crimes, the grief and mental disintegration and abject fear of his final defeats are paid lip service without ever erupting from within.

Among the supporting cast are such excellent players as Larry Bryggman (Banquo), William Converse-Roberts (Macduff), Thomas

Martha Swope Associates/Carol Rosegg

Raul Julia and Melinda Mullins in a scene from the New York Shakespeare Festival's production of "Macbeth."

Gibson (Malcolm) and Daniel von Bargen (Ross). While they are all well-spoken, their characterizations are so vague that probably no one would notice if they gave the identical performances in one another's roles. Harriet Harris injects some tremulous warmth into the self-contained, one-scene part of Lady Macduff, but Melinda Mullins's Lady Macbeth is a conspicuous disaster. When she tries to spur on Mr. Julia's ambition in the early scenes, it is with the peevish inflections and fist-waving tantrums of a spoiled schoolgirl; her subsequent, mechanical sleepwalking scene may be the first to cure an audience's insomnia. Even Mr. Jordan's interpolation of a modest sexual encounter for the Macbeths does not persuade one that this husband and wife are more than passing acquaintants, let alone intimate partners in psychosis and butchery.

•

The production's other odd lapses include a visually obstructed death scene for Mr. Julia, incidental music that turns wistful and lighting that brightens at the play's darkest moments, the periodic brandishment of what looks like a Navajo blanket and a trio of weird sisters who prepare their cauldron stew as if they were hell's answers to Julia Child in a cooking demonstration. (The distinctive comic actress Mary Louise Wilson is a game but wasted lead witch.) Mr. Jordan's most unfortunate yet revealing attempt at a bold stroke is the ending, in which Malcolm and his soldiers celebrate Macbeth's demise with the rah-rah good cheer of a Super Bowl victory demonstration. It's a Pollyanna-ish finale — as if the Scots had instantly forgotten all the suffering inflicted on their nation by the Macbeths. Surely •the wishful point of retelling "Macbeth" — and revisiting the timeless, tragic history it evokes — is that one should never forget.

1990 Ja 17, C13:4

Off to See the Wizard

THE ILLUSION, by Tony Kushner, freely adapted from Pierre Corneille's "Illusion Comique." Director, Mark Lamos; sets, John Conklin; costumes, Martin Pakledinaz; lighting, Pat Collins; sound, ign, Mark Bennett; fight director, Charles Conwell; dramaturg, Greg Leaming; production stage manager, Barbara Reo. Presented by Hartford Stage, Mark Lamos, artistic director; David Hawkanson, managing director. At Hartford.

Pridamant of Avignon	Marco St. John
The Amanuensis	Jarlath Conroy
Alcandre	Frederick Neumann
Calisto, Clindor and Theogenes	J. Grant Albrecht
Melibea, Isabelle and Hippolyta	Ashley Gardner
Elicia, Lyse and Clarina	Bellina Logan
Pleribo, Ad. and the Prince	Andrew Colteaux
Matamore	Philip Goodwin
Musician	Robert Edward Smith

By MEL GUSSOW

Special to The New York Times

HARTFORD, Jan. 16 — Pierre Corneille, France's first great tragic playwright, called "L'Illusion Comique" a strange and capricious "monster" of a play. Coming from the man who is best known as the author of the heroic "Le Cid," it is certainly an oddity — a fanciful comedy on the subject of love, paternity and the art of theater itself.

As elegantly directed by Mark Lamos at Hartford Stage, "The Illusion" (as the play is titled in Tony Kushner's free adaptation) becomes a chimerical vision complete with hidden crannies and mysteries. Though it is presented in its period (the early 17th century, in France), it resonates with modernism, both in style and in commentary. Behind the poetic language and ornate costumes, "The Illusion" is a forerunner of plays by Luigi Pirandello and other masters of theatrical charades.

In it, a father regrets banishing his son and journeys to a magician to find out what befell the youth after he left home. On cue, the magician, Alcandre, conjures scenes from the son's life, which the father greets with increasing amazement.

•

In a play within the play, the son appears as a lovestruck swain, in and out of jeopardy (and in and out of jail). The play is concerned with the illusions of love, repeatedly putting the father — and the audience — on guard to distinguish the real from the feigned. Scenes are stage-managed by Alcandre, a man of wizardly and decidedly unpredictable ways.

One of the father's perplexities is that in the play within the play, the son and other characters keep changing their names and, at times, alter their relationships. Eventually, Alcandre clears up the confusion by revealing that the son is an actor. The scenes from life are scenes from theater, though apparently related to real events and sentiments.

The play operates both as a picaresque romance and as a comedy of love, or, to use Corneille's word, as a caprice. One's enjoyment derives from the father's attitude, the son's adventures and the interference of the diverse characters, especially the son's employer, Matamore, and his love's jealous maid.

Identified by the adapter as a lunatic, Matamore has designs on the

woman the young man adores. When defeated in this pursuit, he reverts to cowardice, barricading himself in an attic until he thinks it is safe to emerge. Others do not behave so self-protectively. The scenes are filled with sword fights as well as incidents of witty verbal abuse, as the son marches merrily through all difficulties with a confidence bordering on arrogance. As he insists, "Obstacles are only obstacles until they are overcome."

In collaboration with the scenic designer, John Conklin, Mr. Lamos has given the play a doubly ingenious production. The magician's cavern is a landscape to delight the eye, decked with sweeping transparent curtains, tilted mirrors, pillars and flying objects from a surrealistic dream. Merlinlike, the magician (Frederick Neumann) animates his lair and his mute manservant, who in moments of stress finds his tongue.

As the father, Marco St. John is alternately astounded and bemused, but he remains a magisterial figure defined by his curiosity. On occasion, he tries to enter the play within the play and has to be restrained by the

T. Charles Erickson

Ashley Gardner in a scene from "The Illusion."

magician. J. Grant Albrecht and Ashley Gardner are suitably impetuous as the romantic partners.

•

All the actors convey the suaveness of language, but two of them are especially diverting: Philip Goodwin as the enlightened lunatic and Bellina Logan as the maidservant. As a trickster, she could give that wizard a run for his magic. Ms. Logan is as guileful and as amusing as any maid in similar circumstances in plays by Shakespeare or Molière.

In his adaptation, Mr. Kushner has excised several characters while retaining the essence of the text. One of his alterations is worthy of special notice. The play no longer concludes with a Corneille salute to the glamour and the value of theater. In this more cynical and realistic version, the father is guarded in his attitude toward his son's choice of acting as a career. In the 17th century, even more than today, theater could provide only an illusion of security.

1990 Ja 18, C21:1

House of Habits

CASA, conceived, directed and performed by Denise Stoklos; assistant director, light designer and operator, Isla Jay; lights realized by Jan Bell; visual consultant, Fabio Namatame; music by Monteverdi, Glasunov and Beethoven; sound design by Miss Stoklos; sound operator, Rachel Whitehead. Presented by La Mama, at the Annex Theater, 74A East Fourth Street.

WITH: Joan Evans, Eli Daruj, Jonathan Slaff, Antonio Herculano, Leticia Monte, Hyunyup Lee, Thais Stoklos Kignel and Piata Stoklos Kignel.

By STEPHEN HOLDEN

Although "Casa," Denise Stoklos's new performance piece at La Mama, bills itself as a comedy, it could just as accurately be called a mystery. In her one-hour play, this Brazilian director, performer and writer, who calls her physically sparse, mimelike style of drama essential theater, heads a cast of eight actors, including her two children, who act out rituals of daily life in surrealistic sequence. "Casa" appears to tell a story about a specific woman, her family, friends and thoughts. But if many details are shown, the actual course of events remains ambiguous.

In Miss Stoklos's witty, postfeminist vision of urban middle-class existence, life is an unending series of mechanical exercises from which escape comes only in solitary reflection, in brief moments shared between parents and children, and in erotic dreams. Miss Stoklos, a vivid stage presence with her spiky white-blond hair, plays a character who has tangled, Chaplinesque relationships with inanimate objects, from keys to handbags to clocks to refrigerators. Her carefully exaggerated pantomimes of daily activities find gentle comedy in commonplace body language.

In the most memorable moment of the piece, Miss Stoklos and an accordion engage in a kind of wrestling match on a couch, as the character figures out first how to wear the instrument and then how to play it. The image of Miss Stoklos struggling with the accordion and then becoming enraptured as she masters its functions becomes a striking metaphor for erotic self-discovery.

The play's other sexual metaphors are glib by comparison. A recurrent character, who appears both as a servant and as a hovering spiritual presence, is an actor in a Japanese woman's kimono who appears to represent a state of androgyny forbidden by the rigid social milieu of the play. In one scene, two women folding a piece of linen begin to fight over it. When two men appear and join the fray, the women take sides against the men in a frantic tug-of-war that becomes a battle of the sexes.

The play's other images of individuals struggling to conform in a regimented society also tend to be hackneyed. The drab gray costumes worn by the adult actors recycle a symbol of conformism that is as old and stale as "The Man in the Gray Flannel Suit." A scene in which the actors, gathered around a table, explode in waves of laughter that subside into edgy paranoia and then become more hysterical, has the feel of a forced acting exercise.

Near the end of the play, the lights dim and a large screen at the rear of the stage is illuminated with a slide of Saturn. As Miss Stoklos and her two children gaze at the image, the sounds of a violin concerto waft

Isla Jay

Denise Stoklos in "Casa."

through the theater. An enigmatic performance piece fades out on a mood of mysticism.

1990 Ja 18, C24:4

Cutting Capers for a 50th Anniversary

By JENNIFER DUNNING

The Ice Capades 50th-Anniversary show, which opened on Friday night for a two-week run at Madison Square Garden, gets off to a surprisingly listless start. But just as one begins to despair of seeing the good, old-fashioned cornball ice dancing on which the show has built its reputation, along comes a second act that lives up to all the hype.

The indisputable star is Richard Dwyer, who at the age of 54 has been skating professionally for 40 years. In a show laced with promotional material, Mr. Dwyer, also known as "Mr. Debonair," is the best advertisement of all — for ice skating. Lean and young-looking, he moves with an easy elegance and ingratiating spirit that puts him into a class by himself as he

sweeps round and round the rink. And in the "cover girl" number, he has an impudently daring duet with Vicki Heasley that is a highlight of the show.

Miss Heasley, a gold medalist in the 1984 United States National and 1988 World Professional Championships, is no slouch herself, skating in a quick-pivoting style that has been compared to that of Sonja Henie. Catarina Lindgren, a Swedish National Skating Champion for four consecutive years, mixes flutters and high, slow kicks distinctively, standing out for her silky solo in the "cover girl" number. And Tom Dickson swings, dips and glides with memorable grace through "All I Need Is a Girl."

Bobby Beauchamp, a gold medalist in the United States Eastern Regional

Championships in the early 1980's, has a sleek and sinuous style of his own. And Jeannine Hoyt and Joe Kalber sail so lyrically through tricky lifts and catches in an adagio number in the "Inside the Golden Ball" routine that it all looks almost too easy. The genuinely funny, slapstick "Hobo Hilarity" routine of Dave 'n' Joey, otherwise known as Dave Pedley and Joey Percelly, was a bright spot in the first act. The show's attractive soloists in the ice dances were Jim Williams, Kacey Yoresen, Steven Rice, Kevin Peeks, Karyl Kawaichi and Shannon Sowers.

•

There is a trapeze and a wild-animal act that suggest that the Ice Capades have run out of ideas for routines, though the Fabulous Fercos' illusionist act, complete with a lion, a tiger and a leopard, is magical enter-

'Mr. Debonair,' animals, and even Barbie and Ken are in the show.

tainment. And the clips of 50 years' worth of shows have a charm that is frequently missing from this anniversary edition. The finale is truly grand, however, with ice dancers soaring high over the rink, their white dresses glowing in black light, and a rinkful of waltzing skaters dwarfed by a huge golden cake that shoots off fireworks at the end.

The children cheered for a clip of Fred Flintstone and most of the way through a Nintendo routine. There was also a plug for Barbie, portrayed by the long-limbed Miss Sowers with a suitably vacuous air. Bring on the Teen-Age Mutant Ninja Turtles.

Choreographed by Sarah Kawahara and directed by Willy Bietak and Tom Scallen, with lighting by Marcia Madeira and costumes by Jef Billings, the Ice Capades show moves to the Meadowlands Arena Jan. 30, where it plays to Feb. 4, and then to the Nassau Coliseum in Uniondale, L.I., from Feb. 6 to 11.

1990 Ja 21, 49:1

Skewed and Skewered

FORBIDDEN BROADWAY 1990, concept, parody lyrics and direction by Gerard Alessandrini; costumes, Erika Dyson; wigs, Teresa Vuoso and Bobby Pearce; production consultants, Pete Blue and Phillip George; production stage manager, Jerry James; associate producer, Chip Quigley. Presented by Jonathan Scharer. At Theater East, 211 East 60th Street.

WITH: Suzanne Blakeslee, Philip Fortenberry, Jeff Lyons, Marilyn Pasekoff and Bob Rogerson.

By MEL GUSSOW

During a dim theatrical season, an actor in "Forbidden Broadway" announced a parody of the current hit shows — followed by a prolonged silence. There is no such dearth of targets in "Forbidden Broadway 1990." With gleeful malice, Gerard Alessandrini, as author and director, mocks Dustin Hoffman, "City of Angels" and that new Tommy Tune musical, "Grim Hotel" and throws comic brickbats at Broadway Brits. The

new version of this four-person musical revue opened last night at Theater East.

Whenever in doubt, there is always Stephen Sondheim, who has consistently inspired Mr. Alessandrini into hilarious assaults. This season, the audience is invited to "attend the tale of 'Teeny Todd,' " in its environmental miniaturization at Circle in the Square on Broadway.

In perfect imitation of the composer, Mr. Alessandrini tells us that the "cast is small and the stage is odd." This button-hole-size musical is so small that the actors keep bumping into one another while the demon barber savagely wields a Bic throwaway razor. There is one topper after another until the cast finally presents the absolutely teeniest "Todd" of all.

•

Equally amusing is the sendup of Jerome Robbins, in which Jeff Lyons (in a bald wig and false beard) bounds on stage to salute himself ("Jerome, Jerome, I'm a hell of a guy") and then cavorts in numbers from his old shows, whipping his dancers into line while saying, "And then I wrote." He corrects himself: "And then I directed."

These two spoofs are 100 proof. In other sketches, there is occasionally more bark than bite, but the satiric quotient remains high. The few reprises from past seasons are evergreen. Most of the material is new and in the case of a dire weather report on "Annie 2," which closed in Washington, it is up to the second.

Contradicting George S. Kaufman's dictum about satire closing on Saturday nights, "Forbidden Broadway" has been running for nine years, through the not so simple maneuver of refreshing itself at the expense of others. For example, there is the rock star of "Der Dreimillionengroschen Opera," whom a mock Lotte Lenya refers to as "Shtink." The hit tune in this Broadway Brecht-Weill is the apt "Song of a Premature Closing."

•

Mr. Alessandrini is at his most fiendish when he checks into "Grim Hotel," where "People come, people go, people move chairs." In this sketch Mr. Lyons plays five roles, including a silverware-jangling scullery worker, Kringelein the bookkeeper, who will soon die of "terminal symbolism" and a jaunty Joel Grey who wanders in from "Cabaret" because "this looked like a quasi-Nazi musical."

The droll Mr. Lyons, the best mimic in a talented cast, also does a withering imitation of Mandy Patinkin, soaring solo in and out of falsetto; a reprise of the sexually confused "M. Butterfly," and Mr. Hoffman. The clever notion, which needs further development, is to mix up Shylock with the actor's movie characters, to Simon and Garfunkel's "Hello, Shakespeare, my old friend."

The other performers, all of them good singers, are Bob Rogerson, who is an appropriately inexpressive Jean Valjean in that frothy French musical comedy,"More Miserable" (in this one, the actors move more stiffly as they are figures in a mechanical clock); Marilyn Pasekoff who is a daffy Glynis Johns sharing a memory loss with Mr. Rogerson's Rex Harrison (in "The Circle"), and Suzanne Blakeslee, who moves from a peppy Judy Garland clunking a trolley in "Meet Me in St. Louis" to a dour Vanessa Redgrave in "Vanessa Descending."

The New York Times/G. Paul Burnett

Shannon Sowers performing Friday night in the Ice Capades at Madison Square Garden.

Carol Rosegg

Jeff Lyons, left, Bob Rogerson, Marilyn Pasekoff and Suzanne Blakeslee, right, in a scene from "Forbidden Broadway 1990."

who draws a smile is the one who posted a sign reading "Cure Guaranteed," and found himself besieged by prospective clients. Before the plot has begun to circulate, the physicians have talked the play to a standstill.

•

The dilemma itself is intriguing though contrived, and deals with a moral, medical question. Ridgeon can add one more patient to a small group he is treating for tuberculosis. There are two candidates, a kindly fellow doctor and Louis Dubedat, a total scoundrel who happens to be a great artist. To save one is to condemn the other. The audience is asked to accept on faith the genius of both Ridgeon and Dubedat.

Gradually, this leads to the play's argument, pitting art against humanity and forcing Ridgeon into the godlike position of weighing the relative importance of individual lives. Around him are characters less bound by ethical strictures, as Shaw punctures various hypocrisies.

The play becomes the author's dilemma as well as that of the central doctor. Clearly, Shaw was more interested in criticizing medical humbug than artistic license. His statements in the latter area barely elaborate on his proclamation in the preface to the play that any artist "may be as selfish as he likes without reproach from the public if only his art is superb."

A limited number of remarks about money and art (as well as doctors) retain their flavor, but they demand a sharper, more Shavian delivery than they receive at the Roundabout. The heavy scenic design is an additional burden. The performances by Charles Keating and Jerome Kilty instill the production with needed moments of buoyancy.

Mr. Keating keeps Ridgeon pleasantly cool even as he confesses to his colleagues that he has fallen in love with the artist's widow-to-be. In the

his death scene, a moment that Shaw believed should be transcendant.

It was the author's assessment that Dubedat's death justified his life, that it gives his wife inspiration with which to carry on his untarnished memory. Such a view is undercut in this production. Very early in the play theatergoers may find themselves rooting for Dubedat's demise — dangerous in a debate that should remain double-edged until the conclusion.

1990 Ja 26, C3:1

The Hes Are Shes And the Shes Hes

LEAR, adaptation and direction, Lee Breuer; score, Pauline Oliveros; lighting, Arden Fingerhut with Lenore Doxsee; costumes, Ghretta Hynd; sound, L. B. Dallas and Eric Liljestrand; fight staging, B. H. Barry; dramatury, Alisa Solomon; stage manager, Elizabeth Valsing; managing director, Anthony Vasconcellos; company manager, Joel Bassin; production manager, Monica Bowin. Presented by Mabou Mines. At the Triplex Performing Arts Center, 199 Chambers Street.

Lear	Ruth Maleczech
The Fool	Greg Mehrten
Gloucester	Isabell Monk
Wilda	Kimberly Scott
Kent	Lola Pashalinski
Elva	Ellen McElduff
Edna	Karen Evans-Kandel
Goneril	Bill Raymond
Regan	Ron Vawter
Albany	Black-Eyed Susan
Cornwall	Honora Fergusson
Cordelion	Lute Ramblin'
France	Clove Galilee
Burgundy	Maya O'Reilly
Henchwomen to Cornwall	Joanna Adler and Allison Dubin
Body Guards to Elva	Frier McCollister and Pedro Rosado

By FRANK RICH

To that perennial list of suspects thought by some to be the true authors of Shakespeare's plays — the Earl of Oxford, Christopher Marlowe, Francis Bacon — one is now tempted to add John Waters, the Baltimore film maker best known for "Hairspray," the classic retro movie about early 1960's rock-and-roll and racial conflict. Or so one might think after taking in the Mabou Mines production of "Lear" at the Triplex Theater.

That raucous Waters sensibility — at once high-minded and low-camp — permeates this adaptation of "King Lear," in which the director, Lee Breuer, reverses the sexes of the characters and moves the setting to backwater Georgia in the late 1950's. Lear (Ruth Maleczech) could be a Tennessee Williams Big Mama. Her evil sons Goneril and Regan are bourbon-swilling good ol' boys who have their way with the bastard Elva (née Edmund), a hot number in tight leather jeans, in the back seat of a convertible. The fool, a transvestite wearing a tatty fur coat and wielding a dildo instead of a coxcomb, is divine, if not exactly Divine. The music of Hank Williams and Elvis competes with the chattering of crickets for dominance of the fetid night air.

This is, at first, a fascinating stunt. In the early scenes, Mr. Breuer reveals a mischievous wit and cooks up a florid Southern Gothic atmosphere redolent of "The Little Foxes," itself a thematic (and sex-reversed) variant on "King Lear." It's fun to watch Lear's disinherited youngest child (now known as Cordelion and portrayed as an unintelligible teen-age rock drummer) be rejected by a spoiled belle in a prom dress (in lieu of the Duke of Burgundy). When Ms.

One of the revue's misfires is with Ms. Redgrave. With a world of accents and acting styles on the firing line, Mr. Alessandrini aims at the actress's politics. Similarly he miscues with his takeoff on Tyne Daly's "Gypsy." Once past the clarion "If Mama Was Merman," he has little to add except for some uneasy jokes at the expense of "Cagney and Lacey." Clearly the revival of "Gypsy" will run long enough for the parodist to

sharpen his saber. These are brief lulls in a mirthful entertainment.

While looking forward to new material, courtesy of Andrew Lloyd Webber, "Forbidden Broadway" is offering its annual retort on the state of theater. The prognosis is laughter, as Mr. Alessandrini and his colleagues deliver their diabolical brand of drama criticism.

1990 Ja 24, C15:1

Whom Would You Save?

THE DOCTOR'S DILEMMA, by George Bernard Shaw; directed by Larry Carpenter; set design by Campbell Baird; costume design by John Falabella; lighting design by Jason Kantrowitz; sound design by Philip Campanella; production stage manager, Kathy J. Faul. Presented by Roundabout Theater Company, Gene Feist, artistic director; Todd Haimes, producing director. At 100 East 17th Street.

Redpenny and Mr. Danby	Adam Redfield
Emmy	Avril Gentles
Sir Colenso Ridgeon	Charles Keating
Leo Schutzmacher	Victor Raider-Wexler
Sir Patrick Cullen	George Hall
Cutler Walpole	Ian Stuart
Sir Ralph Bloomfield Bonington	Jerome Kilty
Dr. Blenkinsop	Gregg Almquist
Jennifer Dubedat	Anne Newhall
Louis Dubedat	Graham Winton
Minnie Tinwell	Cate McNider
The Newspaper Man	Adam LeFevre

By MEL GUSSOW

Although Shaw called "The Doctor's Dilemma" a tragedy, it is of course intended as a comedy, a fact that is not amply in evidence in Larry Carpenter's cumbersome revival of the play at the Roundabout Theater Company.

The fault is shared by Shaw. Despite a contemporary audience's natural predilection to savor criticism of self-important doctors, Shaw's barbs in this 1906 play have been blunted by age — in contrast to his observations about capitalism in "Major Barbara" and politics in "Heartbreak House."

As a quintet of doctors gathers to congratulate Sir Colenso Ridgeon on his knighthood, each defends his own personal quack cure. The only doctor

Stimulating the phagocytes while merrily burbling.

spirit of the author, he speaks about his overwhelming passion in repressed emotional terms. As in last season's revival of "What the Butler Saw," Mr. Keating projects an air of matter-of-fact reality, which works almost as well with Shaw as it did with Joe Orton.

Mr. Kilty finds humor in the self-satisfied Dr. Bonington, whose cure-all, actually a kill-all, is to "stimulate the phagocytes." Mr. Kilty merrily burbles with exclamations that sound like Shaw's wishful self-criticism ("Glorious night! Exquisite scenery!") and falls asleep in one of his more recondite digressions. He reaches a crescendo when he begins to cross-quote Shakespeare, leaping from "tomorrow and tomorrow and tomorrow" to "out, out brief candle."

Although Shaw and Mr. Kilty have fun with Bonington, the other doctors verge on caricature, especially the surgeon who attributes all illness to a poisoning of the bloodstream.

Dubedat, the catalyst for the doctorly disdain, is, in Graham Winton's portrayal, not only a rogue, he is unappealing and lacking in the required cleverness. It is inexplicable that his wife or anyone else could be enthralled by him. The actor is particularly unhelpful as he sinks into

Maleczech bounces back and forth between the low-rent homes of Regan and Goneril, she is a forlorn figure trailed by a battered suitcase and a retinue of dogs, not knights. In Mr. Breuer's eerie first-act conclusion — a sequence reminiscent of Mabou Mines' 1981 deconstruction of film noir, "Wrong Guys" — Lear and her companions flee by car into a crackling Southern thunderstorm defined by a swirl of black umbrellas and by the nocturnal highway iconography of burning headlights and feverish windshield wipers.

•

But to what end? As "Lear" soon trails off into tedium and very sophomoric jokes (a "Singin' in the Rain" routine for the Fool, a pitch 'n' putt range for Gloucester's blind leap), one realizes that Mr. Breuer, whose grandiloquent past works include "The Gospel at Colonus" and "The Warrior Ant," really hasn't thought through this project, his long-anticipated 20th-anniversary effort for the avant-garde company he co-founded.

If the director's good intention is to make the audience see "King Lear" freshly by radically altering its socioeconomic context in a Brechtian fashion, he has failed because Shakespeare's text still overpowers the new setting. If anything, Mr. Breuer's "Lear" seems politically naïve next to "Hairspray" or "The Little Foxes": his rural late 50's Georgia, however cleverly evoked through production design, is incongruously desegregated — a peculiar revisionist view of the Jim Crow South, whatever the esthetic justification. The cosmetic script alterations only nominally reflect the revised casting and setting, and they do so at the price of such vandalized verse as "His voice was ever soft, gentle and low/an excellent thing in a young man." As the English playwright Edward Bond showed in his gutsy post-Marx "Lear" of the 1970's, an icon like "King Lear" may have to be dismantled entirely to make cogent new ideological points.

Mr. Breuer's "Lear" is as long-winded as it is cloudy. At three and a half hours, the production is pretentious in its slavish fidelity to the bulk, if not the meaning, of Shakespeare's text. Though the script changes are not large enough to remake the play's substance, they are just confusing enough to render the story incoherent to any theatergoer new to "King Lear" (which has not received a major New York revival in years). Perhaps the decent rationale for the nearly full text is to give the women in the company a genuine shot at great Shakespearean roles otherwise denied them. Yet a radically rethought script would have better served that mission as well, since the mere reversal of sexual pronouns only superficially reverses the sexual identities of Shakespeare's characters. Even if one does buy Mr. Breuer's simplistic transpositions, the slipshod quality of much of the acting, all of it harshly amplified through distracting facial microphones, undermines those cast members who do go about their challenging assignments seriously.

•

The best performances are in the subplot: Isabell Monk is a dignified and passionate Gloucester, while Ellen McElduff and Karen Evans-Kandel are impressive on their own terms as Elva/Edmund and Edna/Edgar. In lesser roles, Bill Raymond (Goneril), Ron Vawter (Regan) and

The New York Times/Keith Meyers

Isabell Monk, from left, Ruth Maleczech and Karen Evans-Kandel in the Mabou Mines production of "Lear" at the Triplex Theater.

Kimberly Scott (Wilda/Oswald) get away with mild jokeyness. But Lola Pashalinski's Kent and Black-Eyed Susan's Albany jolt the audience out of "Lear" and into the actresses' signature comic turns with directors like Richard Foreman and Charles Ludlam. Mr. Breuer permits such shtick at his own peril, for who wouldn't rather watch Ms. Susan and Everett Quinton in an hour-long Ridiculous Theatrical Company travesty of "Lear" instead of the bloated epic at hand?

Ms. Maleczech, meanwhile, fails to capitalize on her extraordinary opportunity. Hers is a sincere performance of narrow, throaty range. She rails against the elements by letting down her silver hair rather than baring her soul; she relies on a straitjacket and hammy gestures to convey Lear's madness. If Ms. Maleczech demonstrates that the mountainous title role of "King Lear" belongs to both sexes, she does so only by proving that it humbles an ill-equipped actress as ruthlessly as it has blighted the crowning acting ambitions of so many men.

1990 Ja 26, C3:1

STAGE VIEW

For Troubled Tryouts, Few Happy Endings

By FRANK RICH

WASHINGTON

THERE WAS A STANDING OVATION when "Annie 2: Miss Hannigan's Revenge" closed at the Kennedy Center Opera House on Saturday night, Jan. 20. While standing ovations are now more the rule than the exception in American theaters — where audiences often want to salute their own good taste as much as the performers on stage — why "Annie 2"? With a $7 million budget, this was the most costly Broadway production ever to close during its out-of-town tryout and cancel its New York opening. Was the final Washington audience thumbing its nose at Variety and other savage critics of "Annie 2" and proclaiming that the show somehow, somewhere, someday (if not tomorrow) must go on?

Perhaps, and perhaps it is such audiences that have led the musical's management to announce that a revised version of "Annie 2" will be tried out next summer at the Goodspeed Opera House, the Connecticut birthplace of the first "Annie," and brought into New York. Should that plan succeed, it will be an extraordinary turnaround, for plays that fold in their pre-Broadway tryouts almost never come to Broadway, no matter how good (or bad) they might be. Even before "Annie 2" closed in Washington, its troubles were fodder for "Forbidden Broadway," its poster was a candidate for the wall of flops at Joe Allen's theater-district bistro. The initial out-of-town failure of a highly promoted Broadway-bound production leaves a stigma that tends to discourage investors and ticket buyers from a return engagement.

There are odd exceptions. The most distinguished is "A Moon for the Misbegotten," the Eugene O'Neill drama that closed in St. Louis in 1947. It finally arrived on Broadway 10 years later — too late for the author, who died in 1953, to see it — and

failed again. (The 1973 Broadway revival made the play's reputation.) A more typical case is one of the most extravagant musicals to collapse in Washington before "Annie 2," David Merrick's 1967 "Mata Hari." It did turn up in New York the following season — but Off Broadway, not on, and with a new title to replace the tainted original one. As "Ballad for a Firing Squad," it met the executioner after a week at the Theater de Lys.

As it happens, the lyricist of "Mata Hari," Martin Charnin, is also the lyricist and director of "Annie 2." But chaos out of town is the universal dues of being in the Broadway musical theater profession. Larry Gelbart, now known as the author of "City of Angels," but also the battle-scarred author of "The Conquering Hero," another musical with a troubled Washington tryout, famously joked: "If Hitler's alive, I hope he's out of town with a musical." And the nightmare does recur. The star of "Annie 2," Dorothy Loudon, was also the star of the last big musical I watched on the closing night of its pre-Broadway tryout: Alan Jay Lerner's "Lolita, My Love." After folding prematurely in Philadelphia in 1971 and retreating to rehearsal halls in New York, this show made an assault on Boston, which turned out to be its final resting place a few performances later.

To understand the toll of such theatrical misadventures, consider how much frantic revision attended "Annie 2" during its month in Washington. Comparing the closing-night show to the opening-night synopsis of scenes in the program, one finds vanished settings ("The Women's House of Detention, Greenwich Village"), characters (Felix Frankfurter) and songs. Those that didn't jump ship often jumped acts. The many new scenes and numbers were unheralded, but a mimeographed flier in the program did announce the arrival of six orphans and explained that "at this performance, the role of Maurice, which has been renamed Charlie Spinoli, will be played by Scott Robertson." No doubt there are at least three conflicting backstage stories to explain Maurice's rechristening as Charlie alone.

■

Is there any point to the hectic changes? In all likelihood the "Annie 2" I saw was superior to the one that opened in Washington, and, most certainly, it was briefer. Yet its story still hinges on unpleasant developments described in the opening night reviews, including the kidnapping and gagging of a child. Contrary to Broadway myth, huge Broadway musicals cannot be entirely remade in a few weeks during their tryouts — whether the previews are given out of town or in New York. The process is simply too cumbersome. There is not enough time or money to rewrite, rerehearse, re-orchestrate and re-design a complex production that must play eight full-dress performances a week. Tinkering and cutting are possible, not a complete overhaul.

Legend has it that many of the great musicals were written during late-night brainstorming sessions following disastrous openings in New Haven or Boston or Washington. The legend often overstates history. The

Rodgers and Hammerstein hits may have been overlong at their earliest performances ("The King and I") or incomplete or misunderstood ("Oklahoma!"), but at the very least there was a vocal minority that predicted the positive New York reception yet to come. While it's true that "My Fair Lady," "Hello, Dolly!" and "Fiddler on the Roof" — to take three of Broadway's longest-running musicals — added or cut major numbers out of town, all three shows were recognized as hits before those revisions were made.

■

As a young theatergoer in Washington, I witnessed the insertion of "Before the Parade Passes By" into "Dolly" and "Anatevka" into "Fiddler" late in their tryouts — happy additions they were, too — but I did so from standing room, so popular were the shows before the improvements. By contrast, Irving Berlin's final musical of the same period, "Mr. President," was a failure from opening night in Washington and remained one, despite sweeping revisions. Though "A Funny Thing Happened on the Way to the Forum" was damningly reviewed in Washington around that same time, it was nearly as hilarious as the version that triumphed in New York. What made the difference on Broadway was not massive rewriting but the last-minute addition of a mood-setting opening song ("Comedy Tonight") and, perhaps, the greater sophistication of New York audiences and critics than their

Washington counterparts three decades ago.

The "Annie 2" I saw was, as one of its producers told The New York Times when announcing its closing, "not ready yet." It would be silly to review a show that has already been reviewed to death and that is, in any case, unfinished: Anyone could see that the "Annie 2" of closing night

Contrary to myth, huge Broadway musicals cannot be remade in a few weeks on the road.

was an amalgam of two different, perhaps antithetical, musicals — the discarded "Annie 2" that opened in Washington and the embryonic new "Annie 2" promised for Goodspeed. The production ran efficiently despite such inevitable glitches as a conspicuous stagehand or the appearance of all-number phone exchanges on storefront signs ostensibly posted in the New York of 1934.

■

Given that "Everybody in show business listens to anybody" — as Arthur Laurents puts it in "Gypsy" — I

solicited opinions of "Annie 2" from two members of its crucial young audience at the final matinee. The reviews were mixed. "It's just not believable" was the verdict of a nearly 10-year-old boy, who said that the authors would "have to cross out a lot of pages" in further revisions. "The theater is nice, though," he added, referring to the Opera House, which will not be able to travel with subsequent productions of "Annie 2." Another boy of half that age was held rapt and pronounced succinctly at the final curtain: "It's good." The older audience of that night clearly appreciated the spunk of a pilloried show that carried on, at least one more time. The capacity crowd may also have been grateful to see a musical that could never match the gloom of the previous poorly reviewed musical of the Washington tryout season, "Threepenny Opera."

The weekend papers carried advertisements for the next musical that will open in Washington: an Arena Stage production of "Merrily We Roll Along," a revamped revival of the Stephen Sondheim show that underwent its own notoriously chaotic preview period on Broadway in 1982, then closed two weeks after its opening. "Merrily" has been in revision ever since in the country's nonprofit theaters — taking whatever time it takes, rather than obeying the inhuman timetable of Broadway tryouts, as it fights its way back to artistic vindication and, just possibly, to New York.

1990 Ja 28, II:1:3

From Adolescent To Earth Spirit

O PIONEERS!, adapted by Darrah Cloud, from the novel by Willa Cather; music by Kim D. Sherman; directed by Kevin Kuhlke; music director, Brian Russell; scenery by John Wulp; costumes, Ann Roth; lighting, Brian Nason; dialect coach, Nadia Vanesse; sound, Ed McDermid; production stage manager, Diane DiVita; assistant stage manager, C. Renee Alexander; assistant music director, Catherine Stornetta. Presented by the Huntington Theater Company, Peter Altman, producing director; Michael Maso, managing director. At Boston.

Alexandra Bergson	Mary McDonnell
Carl Linstrum	Randle Mell
Emil Bergson	Neil Maffin
Marie Tovesky	Jennifer Rohn
Ivar	John Carpenter
Frank	Thomas Schall
Annie Lee	Kate Phelan
Young Emil	Peter Sokol-Hessner

With: Kate Coffman, Christopher Coucill, Taina Elg, Tad Ingram, Douglas Krizner, Kevin McDermott, Joel Mitchell, Scott Rabinowitz, Brooke Richie, Timothy Sawyer, Eda Seasongood, Maggie Simpson, Jessica Walling

By MEL GUSSOW

Special to The New York Times

BOSTON — For Willa Cather, "O Pioneers!" was the novel in which she spoke for the first time in her own voice, free of influence and literary tradition. In it, she said, she had hit "the home pasture," and the book was to set her off on her creative journey. Written in 1913, "O Pioneers!" remains one of the enduring works of American literature. With its tale of one woman's indomitability, it would seem to be a most natural choice for dramatization, except for the very

important fact that the strength of the book is not in the dialogue but in the poetic depth of the author's narrative and her evocation of characters rooted in environment.

In the adaptation at the Huntington Theater Company, Darrah Cloud has made an ambitious attempt to encompass the entire novel. Her version (to be taped for "American Playhouse" on the Public Broadcasting Service) is faithful in literal detail. She includes all the principal characters and events as well as many of the most memorable of the author's lines. ("There are only two or three human stories, and they go on repeating themselves as fiercely as if they had never happened before.") Ms. Cloud also confronts the book's major themes, starting with the significance of the land in the lives of the homesteaders.

●

In this case, fidelity is not enough. As a playwright, Ms. Cloud has been unable to find a substantial dramatic equivalent for Miss Cather's prose. The result is a series of highlights from the book — "O Pioneers!" in outline. Those unfamiliar with Miss Cather's work will receive only a schematic impression of the vastness of the novel. Using John Wulp's austere set design, the director Kevin Kuhlke has not ameliorated the episodic nature of the adaptation, which covers 17 years in the life of the Bergson family.

Ms. Cloud's previous plays ("The House Across the Street," "The Stick Wife") offer proof of her own theatrical imagination. She could have gone further in asserting her authorial presence, as she might have were this a film rather than a play. She does this in two respects, but with apparent hesitation. In several scenes she uses the character of a quirky hired hand as a commentator, and she approaches a few moments silently with choreographic intent, most effectively in the death of the book's two lovers.

The adaptation is less rewarding in its use of music. Kim D. Sherman's mild background score makes one more aware of the misleading similarities between this show and a musical like "Oklahoma!" The two share a frontier landscape, but the Cather novel is an unrelenting view of survival on a bleak prairie, far closer to the film "The Emigrants," in which stoicism becomes self-denial.

●

The soul of "O Pioneers!" is the heroic character of Alexandra Bergson. As a teen-ager in a barren stretch of Nebraska, she is forced to take charge of her family after the death of her father. She becomes a humane symbol of Miss Cather's conviction that "the history of every country begins in the heart of a man or a woman." At the same time, her youngest brother, Emil, represents the possibilities of the immigrant experience.

The wisest decision in Mr. Kuhlke's production was to cast Mary McDonnell as Alexandra. The role brings out the steeliest and the most sensitive side of this actress and, reflecting her character, she herself becomes the bulwark of the production. In a subtly shaded characterization, she delineates the progression of Alexandra from a willful adolescent to a kind of earth spirit, someone whom Miss Cather identified with the land itself. It is a performance deserving of a more generous adaptation.

Martha Swope

Andrea McArdle, Dick Ensslen and Sandy in "Annie," which opened on Broadway in 1977—It was born at the Goodspeed Opera House, where "Annie 2" is to be tried out next summer.

Richard Feldman

Randle Mell, left, Peter Sokol-Hessner and Mary McDonnell in a scene from the adaptation of Willa Cather's "O Pioneers!"

Randle Mell, playing opposite Ms. McDonnell as her lifelong friend, Carl Linstrum, projects the decency of his searching character. It is a supporting role that echoes throughout the story, expressing the world beyond this small Nebraska town. Neil Maffin and John Carpenter are helpful as Emil and the hired hand (who walks with bare feet even in the coldest weather).

The rest of the large cast is problematic, beginning with Jennifer Rohn, who misinterprets her character's vivacity for artificiality and seems far too contemporary: Thomas Schall, who is unable to don

his character's comprehensive mantle of anger, and Kate Phelan, who turns Alexandra's sister-in-law into a caricature.

Sharper acting would certainly be beneficial, but it would not overcome the limitations of the adaptation or of Mr. Kuhlke's direction. Except for Ms. McDonnell's fine performance, "O Pioneers!" has taken only a tentative step into the theater. What is missing, in Miss Cather's words, is that "acceleration of life" that is so difficult to capture in words — or on stage.

1990 Ja 28, 49:1

Oh! *That* War!

THE STRIKE, by Rod Serling; directed by Thomas Bird; set design, George A. Allison; costume design, Jim Buff; lighting design, Terry Wuthrich; sound design, Scott Sanders; production stage manager, Jerry Bihm. Presented by Vietnam Veterans Ensemble Company, Mr. Bird, artistic director. At the South Street Theater, 424 West 42d Street.

WITH: David Adamson, Anthony Chisholm, Ralph DeMatthews, Russ Ericson, Stephen Lee, Michael Manetta, Brian Markinson, Sean Michael Rice, Ray Robertson, Tucker Smallwood, Matt Tomasino and Jim Tracy.

By WILBORN HAMPTON

In one of the early episodes of the television series M*A*S*H, Col. Henry Blake, the Army surgeon played by McLean Stevenson, bitterly observes that there are two rules of war. The first is that people die. The second is that there is nothing that doctors, chaplains or field officers can do about Rule No. 1. Rod Serling's teleplay "The Strike," which is being given its first stage production by the Vietnam Veterans Ensemble Theater Company at the South Street Theater, examines the agony of conscience of one Army major who must make a battlefield decision that could end in

the death of a score of men he himself has sent out on a reconnaissance patrol.

"The Strike," which was originally presented as a "Studio One" television production in 1954, represents something of a departure for the worthy Vietnam Veterans company. First, it is a play about the Korean War, a conflict that has almost been forgotten in the decades of our national turmoil over Vietnam. Furthermore, it focuses on the soul-searching of an officer, Major Gaylord, as he wrestles with a life-and-death decision. In all the plays, novels or movies about Vietnam there has been little outpouring of sympathy for anyone in uniform above the rank of corporal.

Rod Serling's 'Strike' evokes images of the Korean conflict.

Thomas Bird, the founder of the Vietnam Veterans company and the director of this production, opens the short, stark evening with a brisk staged reading of passages from "The Korean War: An Oral History — Pusan to Chosin" by Donald Knox. It is an imaginative and effective device that provides a quick survey course on the Korean War and cleverly sets the scene for Serling's play.

A group of American G.I.'s recount in rapid, staccato bursts of speech the events of the last six months of 1950 as personal reminiscences — being shipped from the fleshpots of occupied Japan to wartime Korea, the retreat to Pusan, the landing at Inchon, the early successes against the North Koreans, only to be met at the Yalu River by the Chinese Army poised for an invasion of its own. There are references to Gen. Douglas MacArthur's promises that American soldiers would be home by Thanksgiving (a pledge quickly revised to being home for Christmas), and to Bob Hope performing for the troops in Pyongyang.

This gripping tale ends abruptly in a barrage of incoming artillery fire that, once the smoke clears, turns into a snowbound command post for a decimated American battalion. The Americans are in a "fluid situation," which, as Major Gaylord explains, "is what you call it when you're losing and don't want to admit it."

●

Despite some familiar dramatic military terrain — a lost patrol, broken communications, wounded needing evacuation — "The Strike" is a well-crafted play that creates a taut dramatic situation with an economy of action, principally through characterization. That the tension in Serling's play is only partly realized in the Vietnam Veterans production is due mostly to a rather tentative, low-key performance by Tucker Smallwood in the pivotal role of Major Gaylord that only occasionally penetrates much below the surface. "I wish someone with a star on his shoulder would tell me what's right and wrong," the Major says, but there is little sense that the decision presents much of an agonizing quandary. Mr. Smallwood is better in passages recalling his own days before command. The actor delivers a moving account of being ordered to shoot a soldier who refused to give a password only to learn the soldier sacrificed himself for his platoon.

Anthony Chisholm is especially good as Chaplain Walker, whose job of listening to battlefield confessions is like "eavesdropping on death." Ray Robertson is credible as Captain Chick. Matt Tomasino as Lieutenant Peters and Jim Tracy as Captain Franks generate a sense of urgency about the lost patrol that occasionally flags elsewhere onstage. And Brian Markinson delivers a small gem of a performance as Richard Golden, a wounded soldier who can only say his name, address and hometown over and over and over as a plea for help.

George A. Allison's set is simple yet evocative, complete with a 48-star flag, an old hand generator and field phone, some empty ammo crates — all World War II surplus, which is what the G.I.'s in Korea had to fight with.

1990 Ja 29, C18:5

Changing Faces

MOVING TARGETS, by Joe Pintauro; directed by André Ernotte; sets by William Barclay; costumes by Juliet Polcsa; lighting by Phil Monat; sound by Bruce Ellman; associate set designer, Caty Maxey; production stage manager, Edward Phillips. Presented by the Vineyard Theater, Doug Aibel, artistic director; Barbara Zinn Krieger, executive director; Jon Nakagawa, managing director. At 309 East 26th Street.

WITH: Reed Birney, Ned Eisenberg, Ron Faber, Anita Gillette and Mary Mara.

By MEL GUSSOW

Just deserts are on the menu at Joe Pintauro's "Moving Targets." In this amiable anthology of nine brief sketches (at the Vineyard Theater), fathers and sons, friends and lovers come to terms with strained relationships — and couples try to remember what drew them together in the first place.

In his new work, Mr. Pintauro, the author of "Beside Herself" (presented this season at the Circle Repertory Company), faces emotional emergencies with a calmness that is not to be mistaken for dispassion. There is aggravation — sub rosa and sometimes on the surface. A few of the sketches dip into surrealism. The playwright, who is also a novelist and a poet, is most secure and humorous when he holds to the absurdism in everyday life.

Although the plays are slight, and several have contrived endings, dramatic limitations are cosmetized in André Ernotte's free-flowing production, in which five engaging actors quick-change relationships.

Food figures prominently. Confrontation comes in restaurants and kitchens where taste is often at issue, and there are also questions of romantic inclination. Mr. Pintauro pinpoints conflicts in an argument over an old family recipe for a pudding that remains endlessly fresh and at a dinner in which a waiter is the only one solicitous of a woman's bruised feelings.

●

In an amusing tableside dialogue, which, in performance, rises above its familiar framework, Anita Gillette and Mary Mara play actress friends meeting after a separation of several years. Ms. Gillette, as the more tal-

Martha Swope Associates/Carol Rosegg

Mary Mara in "Moving Targets."

ented, is still struggling, while Ms. Mara, who is younger, has soared to celebrity because of an undeserved Oscar. Envy is the shared emotion, though each is reluctant to reveal it.

Ms. Mara, a bright newcomer, has an insouciant vignette as a prostitute who reveals her vulnerability at the same time she denies it. Fathers, not all of them paternally inclined, are played by Ron Faber. In one of the more tender sequences, a recent widower (Reed Birney) forces his garrulous father (Mr. Faber) to relate to his own despondency. In Mr. Pintauro's view, basic insecurities transcend generational and class differences.

•

Ned Eisenberg handles the more offbeat characters, including one who is a smalltime hustler, a match in earthiness with Ms. Mara's prostitute. In the climactic scene, he is a suicidal hairdresser visited by an angel with a musical comedy lineage (Ms. Gillette singing "Tico Tico" and reminding the audience of her own musical comedy talent). Though the episode fluctuates, as in all of "Moving Targets" the actors perform their roles with piquancy.

1990 Ja 30, C14:5

The Soul's Seasons

THE WINTER'S TALE, by William Shakespeare; directed by Frank Galati; set design by John Conklin; costumes by Virgil Johnson; lighting by Jennifer Tipton; sound by Rob Milburn; choreography by Peter Amster; original music composed by Mr. Milburn, Willy Schwarz and Miriam Sturm; dramaturg, Tom Creamer; production stage manager, Lois Griffing; stage manager, Jill Larmett. The Goodman Theater of the Art Institute of Chicago presents a Chicago Theater Group Inc. production; Robert Falls, artistic director; Roche Schulfer, producing director. At Chicago.

Leontes	John Hutton
Hermione	Martha Lavey
Mamillius	Anthony Bravo
Perdita	Sally Murphy
Paulina	Linda Emond
Emilia	Maureen Gallagher
Nurse to Mamillius	Lisa Tejero
Jailer	Maurice Chasse
Officer of the Court	Edward Wilkerson
A Mariner	Ned Mochel
Time	Steve Pickering
Polixenes	David Darlow
Florizel	Bruce Norris
Archidamus	William J. Norris
Autolycus	Skipp Sudduth
Old Shepherd	Tom Aulino
Clown	Ray Chapman
Mopsa	Rebecca MacLean
Dorcas	Treva Tegtmeier

With: Gerry Becker, Keith Byron-Kirk, Patrick Clear, Christa (Cricket) Leigh, Steve Pickering, Terence Plunkett and Ned Schmidtke

By FRANK RICH

Special to The New York Times

CHICAGO, Jan. 28 — A director who chooses "The Winter's Tale," one of the most illogical plays in the canon, as his first Shakespearean assignment has to be a lunatic or a visionary or perhaps a little of both.

On the evidence, Frank Galati, who has staged this romance at the Goodman Theater, does not appear to be crazy. His "Winter's Tale" moves with serene assurance, freely embracing all the quicksilver moods and inexplicable events of the play — from its bleak winter of obsessional jealousy and tragic death to its festive spring of reconciliation and resurrection; from its rampaging bear to its magical unveiling of a living statue. Nothing seems to intimidate this director, whose Steppenwolf

Theater Company adaptation of "The Grapes of Wrath," a hallucinatory treatment of a novel associated with Dust Bowl realism, will introduce his considerable talents to Broadway audiences in March.

•

Far more experienced Shakespearean directors do not possess Mr. Galati's ability to luxuriate in the diversity of late Shakespeare instead of attempting to tame it. The first sound the audience hears in his production is the wind-up mechanism of a cymbal-clashing toy bear belonging to the child prince Mamillius. "Dreams are toys," the nobleman Antigonus says later, shortly before a far larger bear pursues and devours him on the mythical Bohemian coast. Mr. Galati, not the first director to quote Jung in a "Winter's Tale" program, plays with dreams as if they were toys. In keeping with Shakespeare's denouement of rebirth, the evening ends with a joyous mass redemption, a sort of come-as-you-were reunion, to which the entire cast of characters, the bear and his victim included, is welcome.

Like the fantastical text, Mr. Galati's show takes place in all time and no time. John Conklin's lovely classical set, with its sand-colored pillars and deep rear anteroom, seems to echo the august interior of the Art Institute behind the theater. As the play progresses, Mr. Galati and his imaginative design team, which also includes Virgil Johnson (costumes) and Jennifer Tipton (lighting), deck the halls with cultural detritus as far-ranging as that of any contemporary museum. When Leontes (John Hutton), the King of Sicilia, sinks into rage imagining the infidelity of his wife, Hermione (Martha Lavey), he does so at a white-tie court performance of Verdi's "Otello." A television set makes a brief appearance later, and so do 19th-century Romanticism, the spooky 20th-century Surrealism of Magritte, flashes of ageless Japanese stagecraft, swirls of Armani fashion and, in the pastoral sequences, an all-American hoedown. Each turn is bathed by Ms. Tipton in a fairy-tale glow that seamlessly shifts

as the action does from a silvery midwinter dusk to a creamy snowstorm to a verdant harvest dawn.

•

With its post-modern mix of visual and theatrical styles, Mr. Galati's "Winter's Tale" is not so reminiscent of James Lapine's finely spun "Win-

---

Quicksilver moods and inexplicable events abound.

---

ter's Tale" for the Public Theater in New York last year as it is of two controversial recent Shakespeare productions, JoAnne Akalaitis's opaque "Cymbeline," also produced at the Public last season, and Andrei Serban's striking "Twelfth Night" for the American Repertory Theater in Cambridge, Mass., this winter. Mr. Galati, like Mr. Serban, shows that an eclectic approach to Shakespeare isn't a license to practice chaotic self-indulgence but is an opportunity to spin one's own coherent, if irrational, dream logic. Mr. Galati goes both Mr. Serban and Ms. Akalaitis one better by holding his entire cast to a consistent, serious standard of acting even as he takes all kinds of idiosyncratic chances with his staging.

The performances in the Goodman "Winter's Tale" are never less than acceptable. The least interesting of the leading players, Mr. Hutton's Leontes, is sonorous and impassioned even when monotonous. The comic leads — Skipp Sudduth (Autolycus), Tom Aulino (Old Shepherd), Ray Chapman (Clown) — are always ingratiating, even if they are not funny enough (few are) to sustain the very long Bohemia sequences that Mr. Galati has recast in cracker-barrel humor redolent of Mark Twain. (Autolycus is a twangy-voiced guitar-picking riverboat con man in a soiled suit.) Among the superior characterizations are those of Linda Emond and Ned Schmidtke, whose good-hearted Paulina and noble Camillo for once

Steve Leonard

Martha Lavey and Anthony Bravo in Frank Galati's production of "The Winter's Tale," at the Goodman Theater in Chicago.

seem made for each other rather than hastily mated in the final scene. As the more inevitable young lovers, Florizel and Perdita, Bruce Norris and Sally Murphy are tender, picture-book royalty.

•

If there is one performance that dominates the production, it is Ms. Lavey's tremendously affecting Hermione — despite the fact that the queen is absent for much of the play. To testify in the trial scene, she rises from her prison through a trapdoor in a gray smock and bare feet, then argues against her husband's false accusations. As she does so, Ms. Lavey stands completely still, her arms dangling at her side, her raven hair streaming down her back, her eyes glassy with grief but never pleading. She offers the simple dignity of a true martyr, not the melodramatic piety of the self-martyred.

When Hermione reappears much later as a statue — here as a regal figure in a seated, pensive pose — one holds one's breath waiting for. Leontes to discover that the wife he unjustly drove to her ruin 16 years earlier is, by some miracle of forgiveness, still alive. Once the moment at last arrives, the entire audience shares the shiver of rebirth, unmistakably Shakespeare's, that Mr. Galati has found in his own way and in his own winter in "The Winter's Tale."

1990 Ja 31, C15:1

Humor Worn Like a Feathery Boa

RE:JOYCE!, adapted from the works of Joyce Grenfell; by James Roose-Evans and Maureen Lipman; music by Richard Addinsell; directed by Alan Strachan; set by John Lee Beatty; costumes by Ben Frow; lighting by Judy Rasmuson; production stage manager, Anne Keefe. Presented by the Long Wharf Theater, Arvin Brown, artistic director; M. Edgar Rosenblum, executive director. At New Haven.

Joyce Grenfell	Maureen Lipman
Her Accompanist	Denis King

By MEL GUSSOW

Special to The New York Times

NEW HAVEN, Jan. 31 — The spirit of Joyce Grenfell — that of the amateur, the gym teacher, who suddenly finds herself in professional theatrical company — is evoked with congeniality in Maureen Lipman's "Re:Joyce!," now in its United States premiere engagement at the Long Wharf Theater.

What makes the show more than a concert or a cabaret act is Miss Grenfell's life, which is recalled with anecdotes and observations woven through excerpts from the actress's performances. "Re:Joyce!," adapted by Ms. Lipman and James Roose-Evans, evolves into a stage biography, depicting the highlights of an accidental career and illustrating the reasons for Miss Grenfell's notable success.

She was less an actress than a diseuse, an entertainer who performed songs and other special material of her own creation. In her lifetime, largely through her one-woman shows and at least partly because of her efforts entertaining troops during World War II, she became a loved and admired English theatrical figure.

Although "Re:Joyce!" evidently delighted a nostalgic English audience during its recent West End run, it demands a certain degree of familiarity or, at least, acclimatization with the subject. The show is cozy rather than sharply satiric.

Miss Grenfell was not a caricaturist, though one might have received that impression from her film appearances, and she did not pretend to have the sophistication of a Noël Coward, who is represented by one song in the current show. In Ms. Lipman's deft impersonation, she quietly

T.Charles Erickson

Maureen Lipman

enacts stories about seemingly insignificant moments in ordinary lives — those of club ladies, schoolteachers, spinsters and, on occasion, countesses.

There is a kindliness in her satire — if the two words are not incompatible. Malice was not her mantle. She wore her humor gracefully, like a feathery boa, poking fun at quirks and mannerisms while never forgetting her sense of self-ridicule. Among her assets were the aptness of her observations and her gift for mimicry, including the distortions of regional speech.

Though Ms. Lipman appears to be shorter than her gangly role model and has less angular features, she recaptures the essential characteristics of Miss Grenfell in performance. At one point, very much a picture of this unlikely star, she sails across the stage singing "Stately as a Galleon."

The show reprises many of the original monologues — in fact, too many. "Re:Joyce!" needs cutting, especially in the overlong introductory first act. Ms. Lipman sings a selection of Richard Addinsell songs (with lyrics by Miss Grenfell) in a soft, melodic manner. Piano accompaniment and occasional repartee are supplied by Denis King, himself an affable presence, and John Lee Beatty has given the show a plush setting.

Miss Grenfell was an incarnation of a Joyce Grenfell character, a living-room entertainer who made her stage debut without prior experience and became an immediate success. It was her parody lecture, "How to Make a Boutonniere out of Empty Beech Nut Husk Clusters" that led to her first appearance in a "Little Revue" in London. Fifty years later, the stories, including the one about the boutonniere, retain their wryness and their eccentricity.

The play, unobtrusively directed by Alan Strachan, is itself an act of admiration. As Ms. Lipman says in her self-introduction, "I'm not Joyce Grenfell, but that doesn't stop me from wanting to be." Talking to herself, singing with her accompanist

and refraining from overstatement, the actress returns Miss Grenfell to theatrical life.

1990 F 2, C3:1

Music and Memories

CARREÑO, created by Pamela Ross and Gene Frankel; directed by Mr. Frankel; production stage manager, Donald Christy; set design, George A. Allison; light design, Rita Ann Kogler; sound design, David Gervai; costumes, Lois Bewley; production assistant, David Flanigan. Presented by 88 Carrat Productions, in association with the Venezuelan American Association of the United States and the Gene Frankel Theater. At the Intar Theater, 420 West 42d Street.

WITH: Miss Ross

By STEPHEN HOLDEN

"Carreño," Pamela Ross's tribute to the legendary turn-of-the-century pianist Teresa Carreño, is a typical one-person biographical play except for one crucial element. Besides being an actress, Miss Ross is herself a well-regarded concert pianist. Impersonating the Venezuelan-born virtuoso, who was nicknamed the Empress of the Keyboard, she devotes half the evening to playing romantic war horses by Chopin, Grieg, Liszt, Schumann and others on a grand piano placed center stage at the Intar Theater.

Between selections and parts of selections, Miss Ross swivels in her seat to present a sketchy chronological biography in monologues and anecdotes. The story she tells, though in no way revelatory about art, musical history or the role of women in 19th-century musical society, is nevertheless quite engaging.

She was only 9 years old when political unrest drove her family to the United States in 1862, and she quickly made her debut with the Boston Philharmonic Society. When she was 10, she performed in the White House for President Lincoln. Traveling abroad, she met Rossini and Liszt.

•

The personal life recounted is as tempestuous as the Romantic music that formed a major part of Carreño's repertory. During a career that encompassed more than 5,000 concert

A stage biography of stormy Terresa Carreño, played by Pamela Ross.

performances, she still found the time to marry four men and have seven children, two of whom died in infancy.

But the theme of the narration is a sad one. For all of her worldly achievements, Carreño cannot get over the fact that her first child, a daughter who was given up for adoption without her consent while she was on tour, will not acknowledge her.

•

The show, which Miss Ross created with the director Gene Frankel, is more satisfying musically than dramatically. Miss Ross's performances of several Chopin pieces have a

florid grandiosity and cutting percussive ring that seem to reflect her view of Carreño as a bold, sometimes recklessly impulsive virtuoso.

The stitching together of music and dialogue, unfortunately, is far from seamless. The creators have also bitten off more than they can chew in mounting a show that wants to be a concert, a biography and a personal drama all at once. What suffers most is the personal drama of Carreño's search for her daughter and its bitter aftermath, which has the feel of perfunctory soap opera awkwardly larded into the story.

While Miss Ross is a much better pianist than she is an actress, she at least succeeds in conveying some of the fire of a woman who was obviously a trailblazer — and from this account, quite a fearless one — in a profession overwhelmingly dominated by men. Miss Ross's acting is low-key and earnest, allowing only flashes of defiance and fierce pride. The story she tells, however, suggests a woman whose personality was larger and bolder, an artist as expansive and self-dramatizing as the music Miss Ross plays with such a ferocious vivacity.

1990 F 3, 15:4

Down With Pretensions

MANHATTAN PUNCH LINE'S SIXTH ANNUAL FESTIVAL OF ONE-ACT COMEDIES, EVENING A. Set design by David K. Gallo; lighting design by Danianne Mizzy; costume design by Sharon Lynch; sound design by John Bowen. Presented by the Manhattan Punch Line Theater, Steve Kaplan, artistic director. At the Judith Anderson Theater, 422 West 42d Street.
PHILIP GLASS BUYS A LOAF OF BREAD, by David Ives; directed by Jason McConnell Buzas.
PORTFOLIO, by Tom Donaghy; directed by Chris Ashley.
THE SHOW MUST GO ON, by Laurence Klavan; directed by Stephen Hollis.
HOW ARE THINGS IN COSTA DEL FUEGO?, by Rick Louis; directed by Mr. Kaplan; music by Chris Hajian; choreography by William Fleet Lively.
WITH: Michael Aschner, Deryl Caitlyn, Bill Cohen, Kitty Crooks, Randy Danson, Daniel Hagen, Rhonda Hayter, Ryan Hilliard, David Konig, Liz Larsen, Dea Lawrence, Donald Lowe, Theresa McElwee, Robert Montano, Paul O'Brien, Gus Rogerson, Caryn Rosenthal, Nicholas Sadler, Howard Samuelson, Kathrin King Segal, Christopher Wells and Gary Yudman.

By MEL GUSSOW

A bakery is alive and atonal in David Ives's "Philip Glass Buys a Loaf of Bread" as two women, Philip Glass and a baker rap their way through a devastating send-up of this idiosyncratic composer. The play is the first of four in the Manhattan Punch Line's sixth annual festival of one-act comedies.

In imitation of Mr. Glass's lyrics, the linguistic patter is as intricate as it is meaningless. Monosyllables ("you I need," "loaf of bread") become the equivalent of solfege symbols while deadpan actors spoof the self-importance of post-modernist performance art.

Just when the quartet seems on the verge of running repetition into the ground (that in itself is intended as a parody), the actors dance. The tilted, robotic choreography merrily needles Lucinda Childs as well as Mr. Glass's author-director alter ego, Robert Wilson.

There is affection beneath the malice (and the mock-Wilsonian title), as well as an understanding of the art that is being lampooned. A familiarity with Wilson-Glass Einsteinian operas will double a theatergoer's enjoyment, but such is the precision of the sketch that even without prior knowledge, one will laugh along with the spoken music.

choreography of Jason McConnell Buzas, the cast — Randy Danson, Liz Larsen, Ryan Hilliard and Chris Welles in the title role — turns "Philip Glass Buys a Loaf of Bread" into a vintage skit worthy of a "Forbidden Off Broadway."

The other plays in the Evening A of the Punch Line festival are also amusing, but Mr. Ives's curtain-raiser is in a comedy class by itself.

Tom Donaghy's "Portfolio" twits the pretension of fashion models and fashion photographers, as Theresa McElwee strikes awkward glamour poses amid a flock of unseen — and not entirely trained — pigeons. The bird-tender is neatly played by Gary Yudman, but it is the fetching Ms. McElwee, sporting a mini-skirt and a mittel-Streep accent, who steals the scene.

In "The Show Must Go On," Laurence Klavan, a Punch Line regular whose principal territory is sitcom suburbia, takes a devious look at

Martha Swope Associates/William Gibson

Scene from Rick Louis's one-act comedy "How Are Things in Costa del Fuego?" From the left, Howard Samuelson, Caryn Rosenthal, Robert Montano, Dea Lawrence and Paul O'Brien.

everyman's family. The premise is that actors audition for roles in life, and often find themselves out of work. At the dining table, acting "on book," are the Binders, who can only follow prescribed clichés and are unable to improvise dialogue. This is a clever notion that falters in the writing, but Stephen Hollis's staging and the acting have a cartoon sprightliness.

•

Ms. McElwee returns in Rick Louis's "How Are Things in Costa del Fuego?," a frantic travesty of banana dictatorships. Switching to a Roseanne Roseannadanna accent, she plays a rifle-toting radical waitress.

In his first professional production, the author drifts into collegiate humor, but the director, Steve Kaplan, helps him to bridge the lapses. There are funny caricatures by Ms. McElwee; Robert Montano as an honest lawyer (a contradiction, we are told); Paul O'Brien as a callow journalist who files reports about "the war, the poverty and the best places to eat"; and Daryl Caitlin as Major Domo, a smug guardian of civil authority who insists that his hostages do the bunny hop.

Mr. Louis, who is 25 years old, is someone to watch. With "Philip Glass Buys a Loaf of Bread" coming after "Sure Thing" and other plays, Mr. Ives has already certified himself as a witty writer of comedy.

1990 F 4, 60:1

Corrections

Because of a mechanical error, a theater review on Sunday about the Manhattan Punch Line's sixth annual festival of one-act comedies appeared with an incomplete paragraph. It should have read: "Under the clockwork direction and choreography of Jason McConnell Buzas, the cast — Randy Danson, Liz Larsen, Ryan Hilliard and Chris Welles in the title role — turns 'Philip Glass Buys a Loaf of Bread' into a vintage skit worthy of a 'Forbidden Off Broadway.'"

The review also misidentified the actress who plays a radical waitress in "How Are Things in Costa del Fuego?," another play on the program. She is Caryn Rosenthal.

1990 F 10, A3:1

Speaking Her Mind

Martha Swope

Elizabeth Van Dyke

ZORA NEALE HURSTON, by Laurence Holder; directed by Wynn Handman; scenery by Terry Chandler; lighting by Shirley Prendergast; production stage manager, Lloyd Davis Jr.; general manager, Stephen Lisner. Presented by the American Place Theater, Mr. Handman, director. At 111 West 46th Street.

Zora Neale Hurston .... Elizabeth Van Dyke
Herbert Sheen, Langston Hughes, Alain
Locke and Richard Wright .... Tim Johnson

By MEL GUSSOW

Zora Neale Hurston was, in Alice Walker's words, "a genius of the South," a country woman who reinvented herself as a novelist and folklorist and became a leader of the Harlem Renaissance in the 1920's and 1930's. She is certainly a sizable enough figure to command a stage or a movie screen, but as a subject of theatrical biography, she remains elusive.

The latest attempt to dramatize her life, Laurence Holder's "Zora Neale Hurston," which opened yesterday at the American Place Theater, offers a thin storybook portrait. Mr. Holder strikes the high points but not the depths of a fascinating story of success followed by failure and periods of posthumous fame. As written by Mr. Holder, "Zora Neal Hurston" has an excess of pronouncements and a minimum of analysis.

Hurston, who had run away from home at 14, eventually went from Howard University to Barnard College, where she was the only black student. Helped by rich white patrons, she moved onward to a highly individualistic and influential career as the author of, among other books, the novel "Their Eyes Are Watching God." Always speaking her mind, she seemed to court controversy.

Acting more as annotator than as dramatist, Mr. Holder is so busy placing Hurston in company with her peers that he loses sight of the uniqueness of the character. Something similar occurred several seasons ago in Aishah Rahman's musical "The Tale of Madame Zora." Another version of her life, "Zora Is My Name," starring Ruby Dee, will be televised on "American Playhouse" next week.

Mr. Holder's play begins in 1949 with a forlorn Hurston (Elizabeth Van Dyke) in a bus station before she leaves New York for an impoverished life in her native Florida. As the scene flashes back to a headier time, Ms. Van Dyke sheds years along with her drab coat. At several points, she and Tim Johnson (who plays various men in her life) swing into a dance. Shirley Prendergast's lighting and Mr. Johnson's flute playing add atmosphere to Wynn Handman's spare production.

Ms. Van Dyke invests Hurston with a theatricality that enlivens the 90-minute show but also tends to overwhelm the artist's emotional difficulties. For most of its duration — until the downbeat ending — the play seems overly exclamatory,

Here is the youthful Hurston breezing into New York to accept a literary award for a short story. Meeting Langston Hughes (Mr. Johnson) for the first time, she marches him into the ceremony and begins telling him the names of all the famous people in the room, not only Eugene O'Neill and Ethel Waters, but also Carl Van Vechten, Alfred Knopf and others. One can only wonder how she could identify them all so early in her career, unless they were wearing name-tags.

•

Repeatedly the playwright offers names and signposts in lieu of character-revealing detail. Richard Wright briefly appears to denounce Hurston's fiction (an artistic conflict that could bear further dramatic scrutiny) and there are several bland

scenes with her first husband. Hughes is the only man to have anything approaching a sustained role.

Mr. Johnson paints a genteel portrait of the poet, but too often he and Ms. Van Dyke find themselves bickering over their collaboration on the play "Mule Bone" (scheduled to have its first production this year under the auspices of the Lincoln Center Theater Company). When the two writers decide to collaborate, Hughes immediately exclaims, "And we could call it 'Mule! Bone!'" as if he has been struck by double bolts of inspiration. In one especially awkward moment, to dramatize the research involved in an anthropological survey, Ms. Van Dyke steps out of the framework of the performance and interacts with a member of the audience.

The drama stirs during those few interludes when Ms. Van Dyke tells a Hurston folk story. These tales are filled with down-home wisdom about the world and the relationship between men and women. In such glimpses, one has a picture of Hurston's creativity, submerged in the rest of Mr. Holder's play.

1990 F 5, C14:1

He's a Fine Fellow, What There Is of Him

IMAGINING BRAD, by Peter Hedges; directed by Joe Mantello; sets by Loy Arcenas; costumes by Laura Cunningham; lights by Dennis Parichy; sound by Stewart Werner and Chuck London; production stage manager, Denise Yaney. Presented by Circle Repertory Company, Tanya Berezin, artistic director; Connie L. Alexis, managing director. At the Players Theater, 115 Macdougal Street.

Dana Sue Kaye .... Sharon Ernster
Brad's Wife .... Erin Cressida Wilson
Valerie (prologue) .... Melissa Joan Hart

By FRANK RICH

A coupla white chicks, or maybe they're steel magnolias, sit around talkin' in Peter Hedges's "Imagining Brad," a new play presented by the Circle Repertory Company at the Players Theater. The setting is Nashville, and the women's subject is men. Dana Sue Kaye (Sharon Ernster), a bottle blonde with a 90-proof accent, brags about her happy marriage to her high-school sweetie Alex, a devoted breadwinner and "the best looking man in Tennessee." Valerie (Erin Cressida Wilson), a soft-spoken newlywed transplanted from Philadelphia, raves about her own husband, the wealthy, if bedridden, Brad. Though Brad has his drawbacks — he is armless, legless and legally blind, for starters — he has been unfailingly supportive of Valerie's fledgling country-western singing career.

After a brief, introductory flashback, "Imagining Brad" is a string of conversations in which the ingenuous Valerie gradually convinces the complacent Dana Sue that the inert Brad, rather than Alex, is the better mate — "the ultimate man," as she puts it. Brad's supremacy, one hastens to add, is a victory by default, for Alex is eventually unmasked as a wife abuser who enjoys watching women have sex with dogs. In a land of brutal men, the tongue-in-cheek playwright is saying, even a blind "bag of flesh" like Brad is king. A dreamboat he's not, but at least he's incapable of marital violence, if only on technical grounds.

Mr. Hedges's absurdist premise, an amusing one for a sketch, cannot sustain this 65-minute play by itself. What is needed, and not provided, are other surrealistic jokes or narrative twists that might keep the characters, comedy and ideology hopping on the way to the preordained conclusion. Mr. Hedges's grotesque infirmities aside, Mr. Hedges's gags are mild: "Stand By Your Man" is the evening's final, leadenly ironic musi-

Gerry Goodstein

Melissa Joan Hart in Peter Hedges's "Imagining Brad."

cal punch line. In place of outlandish comic invention, the author kills time with the delaying tactics of far more realistic playwrights, withholding the true nature of Alex's character and the complete lowdown on Brad's afflictions until well after most of the audience will have guessed both.

Perhaps it's only coincidence that "Imagining Brad" is the second play of the Circle Rep season (after "Beside Herself") in which a male playwright nobly defends womanhood in the abstract without bothering to examine (and in Mr. Hedges's case even bring on stage) the men held culpable for the heroines' misfortunes. This post-Phil Donahue school

---

Think of the perfect man. Brad, right? It's *Alex?* Think some more.

of playwriting, in which the writer presents himself as an enlightened guy without risking self-examination or any other discernible personal cost, is as sentimental as the macho tradition it replaces. And perhaps its view of women isn't all that different at heart. Mr. Hedges's treatment of Dana Sue — she's a loud, dimwitted vulgarian falling out of a low-cut red dress — is nearly as patronizing as her despised husband's.

•

The production, directed by Joe Mantello and dreamily designed by Loy Arcenas (sets) and Dennis Parichy (lighting), is sufficiently accomplished that one is made all the more aware of the paucity of the dramatic occasion prompting it. Ms. Ernster doesn't find too many surprises in Dana Sue — that's not her fault — but Ms. Wilson's appealing Valerie, calm and beatific nearly to the point of catatonia, could be a double for any of the demure oddballs played by Julie Hagerty. As the 12-year-old Valerie of the prologue — a victim of paternal sexual violence on the very day of her first menstrual period, schematically enough — Melissa Joan Hart delivers a precocious comic monologue with the· worldly show-biz verve of a stand-up comedian more than twice her age. If she's not careful, someone may write her an "Annie 3."

1990 F 7, C15:2

Revenge Fantasy

MEDEA, by Euripides, based on a translation by E. P. Coleridge; directed by Shepard Sobel; stage manager, William Ellis. Presented by the Pearl Theater Company. At 125 West 22d Street.

Nurse of Medea .... Sylvia Davis
Tutor of Medea's Children, Creon, Aegeus and
Messenger .... Frank Geraci
Medea .... Joanne Camp
Choragos .... Erin Martin
Chorus of Corinthian Women
            Lisa Goodman and Laura Rathgeb
Jason .... Michael John McGuinness
The sons of Jason and Medea
            Laura Rathgeb and Lisa Goodman

By STEPHEN HOLDEN

Among the classic Greek tragedies, Euripides' "Medea" probably strikes the brightest sparks in contemporary imaginations. Its story of a woman who lashes back at the man who betrayed her after she had saved his life and engineered his ascent to power is one of the most potent revenge fantasies of all time. And in today's fractious marital climate of child custody battles and warring sexual ideologies, it touches several nerves at once.

Because "Medea" is a drama of pure passion, even the most superficially conceived production ought at least to churn up a froth of soap opera histrionics. But the Pearl Theater Company's "Medea" is so cold, inept and mechanical that the only feelings it awakens are twinges of dismay and embarrassment. The staging of modest but professional productions of theater classics is supposed to be the forte of the Chelsea-based repertory company. Yet its "Medea" has the feel and look of an unfinished amateur production.

As directed by Shepard Sobel, the actors are at such loose ends that they perform mostly without facial expression and often with hands tentatively outstretched as though groping for the very meaning of the words. The line readings of dialogue, based on E. P. Coleridge's translation, rarely break away from the singsong iambic meter of the verse. The stage entrances are so poorly prepared that when a character appears, the actor playing him often has the slightly dazed look of someone who has unexpectedly found himself shoved out from the wings.

The saddest thing about the production is that it involves reputable actors like Joanne Camp, who has distinguished herself in "The Heidi Chronicles" and "Coastal Disturbances." Speaking her lines in a clenched, icy monotone that pre-

cludes any glimpses of fury or sorrow, she doesn't suggest a figure of Greek tragedy so much as a neurotic, emotionally repressed housewife having a prolonged snit.

Ms. Camp's performance is at least consistent with the rest of the ensemble who, even when raising their voices, seem as stiff and impassive as talking statues.

1990 F 8, C15:3

Hare Raising

THE FABULOUS LA FONTAINE, conception, book and lyrics by Owen S. Rackleff; music adapted from "The Carnival of the Animals," by Camille Saint-Saëns; musical arrangements and stage direction by Dennis Deal; production stage manager, John R. Stattel; stage manager, Paul J. Smith; set design, Kaem Coughlin; lighting design, David Finley; costume design, Traci Di Gesu. Presented by CHS Productions and Omar Productions, in association with Riverwest Theater, 155 Bank Street.

WITH: Michael Babin, Maurice Edwards, Thomas Hetmanek, Earl Aaron Levine, Carolyn Marlow, Evan Matthews, Patti Perkins, Michael Shelle and Colby Thomas.

STEPHEN HOLDEN

Few theatrical sights are more forlorn than the bargain-basement staging of a musical costume drama that was obviously conceived for a multi-million-dollar production. The spectacle becomes even sadder when one realizes that all the glitz in the world would still fail to breathe dramatic life into the project. Such a show is "The Fabulous La Fontaine," Owen S. Rackleff's celebration, at the Riverwest Theater, of the life and times of the 17th-century French fabulist Jean de La Fontaine.

Using melodies adapted from Saint-Saëns's "Carnival of the Animals," it interweaves sketches of the writer with clunking musical set pieces depicting his animal fables, while also telling the story of his ban-

Martha Swope Associates/Carol Rosegg

Animal Attraction
Maurice Edwards and Colby Thomas are in Owen S. Rackleff's "Fabulous La Fontaine," with music adapted by Dennis Deal from Saint-Saëns's "Carnival of the Animals."

---

ishment from Versailles after one of his satires pricks the vanity of Louis XIV. This is a show whose major love duet reiterates in all seriousness the entreaty "Please help me, I'm a Pisces."

If the notion of grafting lyrical adaptations of La Fontaine's sly fables onto Saint-Saëns's tunes is theoretically promising, in practice it turns out to be unworkable. The composer's ditties simply can't support the weight of verse that when set to music becomes laboriously singsong and hard to follow. And when performed this poorly by actors who can't keep time with offstage musical accompaniments so gaseous they sound as if they've been pumped through radiator pipes, it becomes insufferable.

1990 F 8, C15:3

Is That All There Is?

SEX, DRUGS, ROCK & ROLL, written and performed by Eric Bogosian; directed by Jo Bonney; set design by John Arnone; lighting by Jan Kroeze; sound by Jan Nebozenko; production stage manager, Pat Sosnow, produced in association with Ethel Bayer and William Suter. Presented by Frederick Zollo and Robert Cole, in association with 126 Second Avenue Corporation and Sine/D'Addario Ltd. At the Orpheum Theater, 126 Second Avenue, at Eighth Street.

By FRANK RICH

It's not news that Eric Bogosian is a great talent, a chameleon actor and penetrating social observer whose one-man shows have staked out their own mean streets in the crowded 1980's theatrical territory inhabited by Lily Tomlin, Spalding Gray, Whoopi Goldberg and so many others, from stand-up comedians to sit-down performance artists. Nor will it be news that "Sex, Drugs, Rock & Roll," Mr. Bogosian's new show at the Orpheum, follows the format of such preceding recitals as "Fun House" and "Drinking in America." Once again the actor appears in black jeans, sneakers and white shirt to take the audience on a nonstop 90-minute tour through the mental states of men who live in these United States.

But there is news at "Sex, Drugs, Rock & Roll," and it is this: with this brilliant show, his funniest and scariest yet, Mr. Bogosian has crossed the line that separates an exciting artist from a culture hero. What Lenny Bruce was to the 1950's, Bob Dylan to the 1960's, Woody Allen to the 1970's — that's what Eric Bogosian is to this frightening moment of drift in our history. With the possible exception of Spike Lee, I know of no one else like him in pop culture right now. He knows which way the wind is blowing, and in "Sex, Drugs, Rock & Roll," those icy currents smack you right in the face.

The show opens just as the day does for so many in the audience. A gimpy, insistent subway panhandler "just released from Rikers Island" announces to the captive straphangers: "This is the situation — I need your money." What follows is a riotous amalgam of the familiar spiels, and Mr. Bogosian, his large green eyes glazed, leaves little doubt that the reformed junkie pleading for spare change is still on drugs. But should the beggar's needs be dismissed because he's lying? Not necessarily. As the man drones on, attempting to flatter his potential benefactors by recycling the jargon he's picked up in a lifetime of contact with the city's social and penal bureaucracies, Mr. Bogosian subtly but even more corrosively indicts the system that greases the skids and blights hope for those

who need help. "Underneath it all," says the subway beggar, "we're exactly the same."

●

Mr. Bogosian's next character — a fatuous, aging English rock star plugging his wares on a talk show — would seem to belie that statement. The musician is an anti-drug crusader who has joined forces with such other public moralists as Dan and Marilyn Quayle. ("She's hot — she's very hot!," the rocker assures his skeptical young fans about the Second Lady). But as he takes deep drags on his cigarette and glamorizes his own drug past in every show-biz reminiscence, it's clear that the rock star is as much a con artist as the subway hustler; only the size of the stakes has changed.

By the time he gets around to pitching his favorite cause, the Amazonian Indians — a charity that seems to be inspired more by the rock star's egomania and unacknowledged racism than by the needs of the third

---

In 'Sex, Drugs, Rock & Roll,' characters enjoy or suffer from the title ingredients.

---

world poor — Mr. Bogosian has come full circle. With only two characters, he has mapped out the entire international cycle of drug dependency, official hypocrisy and economic exploitation that leaves the homeless locked in subterranean hell and the coked-up rich in Hollywood heaven, with everyone else, especially the young, battling the fallout in between.

In the roughly one dozen bits that follow, Mr. Bogosian fills in more and more of the bleak Western landscape of 1990. A raving, phlegm-spewing old man delivers an obsessive but persuasive exegesis of the industrial age's death cycle, the pollution patterns that turn cities into "human septic tanks" and oceans into "giant vats of oil and garbage and dead animals." Yet the monologue is not an environmentalist's boilerplate but rather a baroque fantasy, part Twain and part Ben Jonson, in which the narrative sweep takes in everyone from urinating outdoorsmen to well-heeled passengers vomiting caviar and pâté on an ocean cruise.

Just as far-reaching is the chilling soliloquy that concludes the evening. An unreconstructed 1960's dropout sits cross-legged at stage edge to make the case that the United States is already an "occupied country" run by computers, whether fax machines or supermarket checkout stations, that plot against people all night by jabbering to one another in indecipherable languages. With the aid of television's power to deliver subliminal messages, the machines may already be in charge. How else, the man reasonably asks, can one explain the proliferation of microwave ovens — a superfluous, television-hawked appliance whose only logical use may be to fry the nation's households en masse when the computers stage their coup?

●

This is paranoia, of course, but like the paranoia in a Hitchcock movie, it's a little too close for comfort. And by inhabiting his characters instead of condescending to them, Mr. Bogosian doesn't allow anyone a safe distance from his less philosophical men, like the Mametesque entrepreneur who uses each of four phone lines (and an intercom) to betray a different business associate or loved one, or the self-made exponent of "the good life" showing off his new Olympic-size swimming pool with a pride inextricably bound to a fear of death, or the violent criminal who admiringly likens George Bush to Batman.

Mr. Bogosian's unflaggingly intense impersonations, directed by Jo Bonney on a simple but evocative set designed by John Arnone, are flawless; he doesn't need costume or makeup changes to give each character a distinct face, voice and posture. And as always, Mr. Bogosian is a hilarious wit: there is one line after another, not too many repeatable here, that you will quote to friends. He is also a born storyteller with perfect pitch for the voices of various ethnic, racial and economic backgrounds. A monologue in which an Italian-American hoodlum describes "the best night I ever had in my life" — a pornographic tale of urban mayhem in which he and his drugged pals lay waste to a McDonald's as well as to themselves — is too riveting to dismiss as revolting.

Yet Mr. Bogosian isn't a documentarian, an X-rated Studs Terkel running a tape recorder. And he isn't a public scold of either the left or right, setting political agendas. His sketches don't end with neat moral codas but trail off, like distant radio stations vanishing into the night on a dark highway. The highly original writing in "Sex, Drugs, Rock & Roll" is realer than journalism — and more frightening — and its depth helps boost Mr. Bogosian to a new plateau.

•

This show is much more of a piece than "Talk Radio," his one attempt to

The New York Times/Michelle Agins

Eric Bogosian in rehearsal for "Sex, Drugs, Rock & Roll," at the Orpheum Theater.

collaborate with other actors in a more conventional play. Though the characters don't share scenes, they do share a coherently depicted (if incoherent) civilization (if that's the word for it) where homelessness, guilt and an addictive desire to feel "wonderful" (a state attained with drugs, power, money or sex) are

ubiquitous. The characters we don't see — the abused secretary, the obsequious talk-show host, the tense subway passengers — are often as vivid as the men who do parade across the stage.

The canvas is far broader than the title and quirky cast of characters suggest. Leaving the show, one is struck not so much by the uncanny resemblance between the real-life beggars outside the theater and the fictional ones of Mr. Bogosian's impersonations as by the way "Sex, Drugs, Rock & Roll" as a whole forces the audience to examine its own roles in the larger drama that, however unwillingly, it shares daily with the dispossessed.

The last of Mr. Bogosian's characters argues that the homeless are threatening not just because they evoke suffering and guilt but also because they represent revolt and freedom. They are the people who have been "thrown out of their cages," he says, because they refused to do "what they're supposed to do." At this remarkable historical moment, people all over the world are being thrown out of their cages, and among American writers for the theater, Mr. Bogosian is the first to see his own society as part of the big picture. Using every powerful means available to a theater artist, he shakes the cages of a complacent country engulfed by homelessness to ask just exactly who, if anyone, is at home.

1990 F 9, C3:1

_____

Fertilization and Fights

MANHATTAN PUNCH LINE'S SIXTH ANNUAL FESTIVAL OF ONE-ACT COMEDIES, EVENING B. Set design by David K. Gallo; lighting design by Danianne Mizzy; costume design by Julie Doyle; sound design by John Bowen. Presented by Manhattan Punch Line Theater, Steve Kaplan, artistic director. At the Judith Anderson Theater, 422 West 42d Street.

THE FERTILIZATION OPERA, music and lyrics by Peter Tolan; directed by Jason McConnell Buzas; musical direction and arrangements by Albert Ahronheim; choreographic contributions by the Company.

GRUNIONS, by Barbara Lindsay; directed by Kay Matschulat.

BRUNCH AT TRUDY AND PAUL'S, by Michael Aschner; directed by Louis Scheeder.

FELLOW TRAVELERS, by Jeffrey Hatcher; directed by Jonathon Mintz.

THE ARTISTIC DIRECTION, by Roger Hedden; directed by Greg Johnson.
WITH: Peter Basch, Michael Kelly Boone, Robert Burke, Warren Burton, Mark Chmiel, Charles E. Gerber, Robin Groves, Daniel Hagen, Arthur Hanket, Patricia Hodges, Cheryl Hulteen, Chris A. Kelly, Ken Martin, Janine Leigh Robbins, Anita Rogerson, Linda Wallem and Christopher Wells.

_____

By MEL GUSSOW

A quick, sharp musical curtain-raiser by Peter Tolan begins the second evening in the Manhattan Punch Line festival of one-act comedies. The sketches that follow illustrate the problems and pitfalls of the short-play form.

In "The Fertilization Opera," Mr. Tolan treats human fertilization as a subject for a Gilbert and Sullivan operetta. Three tall, goofy actors sing and dance "Three Little Sperm Are We," then, like sailors in "H.M.S. Pinafore," scan the horizon for a suitable mate. Linda Wallem appears, looking like Bo Peep but playing a character much closer to Humpty Dumpty.

Martha Swope Associates/Carol Rosegg

A scene from "The Fertilization Opera." Clockwise from left: Michael Kelly Boone, Christopher Wells, Mark Chmiel and Linda Wallem.

Because of the cleverness of the author's musical mimicry, this indelicate notion narrowly averts the isle of whimsy. The cameo show is buoyed by the exuberant performances and by Jason McConnell Buzas's swift direction.

•

"The Fertilization Opera" puts one in the mood for more Tolan musical spoofs, as concocted by him and Ms. Wallem in their Off Broadway revue "Laughing Matters." Instead, the evening meanders with four less amusing one-act sketches, which prove that a single character or incident does not necessarily justify a comic situation.

In Barbara Lindsay's "Grunions," a young married couple argue on a beach — an actors' improvisation that goes absolutely nowhere. In Michael Aschner's "Brunch at Trudy and Paul's," a scatterbrained woman, newly deserted by her lover, is forced to entertain her best friends. Listening to the trite dialogue, one understands the reasons for the lover's departure.

For "Fellow Travelers," Jeffrey Hatcher visits a writers' conference in East Berlin, where three Western delegates of different cultural persuasions are trying to agree on a petition asking for the release of Soviet dissidents. The conversation idles with name-dropping until the Soviet representative arrives.

As engagingly played by Daniel Hagen, he is an Americanized extrovert. First, he presents his gifts: pieces of the Berlin wall, bought, naturally, in New York City. He speaks impeccable English except on television, where he affects a thick accent to be a more creditable spokesman. Playfully, the Russian provokes dissension about the disparate delegates, smiling as each reveals his irreconcilable sense of rivalry. Unfortunately, there is not enough of a play to sustain the central character.

•

Something similar could be said about "The Artistic Direction" by Roger Hedden, in which a self-satirizing Off Broadway director takes pride in the fact that in his theater "failure is our lifeblood." Actually he is less interested in art than in womanizing and in selling the cable-television rights to his plays. The character is deftly observed (and

played with a casual flair by Warren Burton), but the narrative that surrounds him is a hindrance.

In a scene that could be described as a playwright's aberration, a drama critic joins the director backstage after a play, has several whiskies and then tells him he is going to "kill" him in print. Mr. Hedden might have gained more comic mileage if he had confronted the director with a wounded playwright.

Evening B alternates with the far funnier Evening A, the two running in repertory until March 4.

1990 F 11, 70:1

_____

Lost in the Woods

A FOREST IN ARDEN, adapted from Shakespeare's "As You Like It" by Christopher Grabowski; directed by Mr. Grabowski; set, Tom Kamm; costumes, Claudia Brown; lighting, Pat Dignan; composer/sound, Scott Killian; production stage manager, Liz Small; production manager, George Xenos. A New York Theater Workshop production at the Perry Street Theater, 31 Perry Street.

The Fool/Oliver	Fanni Green
Orlando	Michael James-Reed
Celia/Aliena	Susan Knight
Rosalind/Ganymede	Michael Liani

_____

By MEL GUSSOW

In this open season on Shakespeare, theatergoers have already encountered a female "King Lear" with a transvestite Fool and a Lady Macbeth committing hara-kiri onstage. It therefore comes as no surprise to see "As You Like It" staged in a wrestling ring, with a bell signaling the beginning and ending of scenes. But the first of many questions that arise is why Orlando is the only one in the ring, wrestling himself to the ground instead of vanquishing Charles the wrestler.

It is possible that Christopher Grabowski, as adapter and director, is trying to make a statement about Orlando's inner demons. More likely Charles simply did not fit into the reduced complement of characters enlisted for this stripped-down production. There are only four actors in the cast of "A Forest in Arden," as Mr. Grabowski titles his work, presumably to differentiate it from the original. Produced by the New York Theater Workshop, the adaptation is at the Perry Street Theater.

For this motley version, Mr. Grabowski has cut the play, re-arranged scenes and eliminated characters while borrowing words from other Shakespearean plays. Most damaging of all, he has interchanged dialogue as if it did not matter which person spoke which lines.

Melancholy clouds the theater as we try to forge a path through Mr. Grabowski's thicket. An actor (Michael Liani) puts on a skirt and plays Rosalind, a most unappealing impersonation that is further complicated by the fact that the actor must pretend to be a woman pretending to be a man. At least Lee Breuer's gender-switching "Lear" has a certain consistency, as did the National Theater's all-male "As You Like It" a number of years ago. In contrast, the current variation is simply aberrant.

●

One may find within the production comments on the varieties and vicissitudes of love, but for "As You Like It," look elsewhere. Submerged along with the poetry and the individuality of the characters is the essential conflict between civilization and the pastoral life.

The four young actors are eager but as yet unready for Shakespeare, with the possible exception of Susan Knight, as Celia et al., who, with textual additions, seems to have the largest role in the play. Michael James Reed doubles as Orlando and a shepherd, marking the change in character by putting on a cowboy suit as if he were a country-western singer. Fanni Green, who plays both Oliver and Touchstone — itself a tricky business — suddenly has to deliver the Seven Ages of Man. Wherefore art thou, Jaques? One assumes he is lost in Arden, along with the play.

1990 F 11, 69:1

Shades of Meaning

ARIANO, by Richard V. Irizarry; directed by Vicente Castro; set design, James Sandefur; costume designer, Toni-Leslie James; lighting designer, Spencer S. Brown; sound designer, Gary and Timmy Harris; producer, Miriam Colon Valle. Presented by the Puerto Rican Traveling Theater, Ms. Colon, artistic director. At 304 West 47th Street.

Ariano	Machisté
Dona Aïda	Graciela Lecube
Soldier	Angel Salazar
Dolores	Denia Brache
Serafin	Jimmy Borbon
Clara	Eileen Galindo
Crystal	Candace Brecker

By RICHARD F. SHEPARD

The Puerto Rican on the American mainland. Who is he? What does he want to be? Identity crisis, the perennial puzzlement of the newcomer in the city, is the issue poignantly and melodramatically at hand in Richard V. Irizarry's "Ariano," now playing at the estimable Puerto Rican Traveling Theater.

The question is more complicated for Puerto Ricans than merely one of "us and them": the rainbow pigmentation of the islanders raises nasty problems of racism in a North American society that tends to see things in unblurred black and white. Ariano, the upwardly mobile hero of the play, who is moving out of the numbers game into a respectable business, is "white," insistently so. His attractive wife is darker and their son is olive-hued.

Peter Krupenye

Candace Brecker and Machisté in a scene from "Ariano."

Ariano instills in his family the idea that they are different from other Puerto Ricans, that they are white, even though the little boy, as the first Puerto Rican in his school, has been getting a hard time from the other children. Ariano wants a "white" child so badly that he has impregnated a trampy blond, blue-eyed woman and is paying her to bear him a child who will have a magazine-cover Anglo-Saxon beauty.

●

There are crises. When the little boy, Serafín, nicely played with wide-eyed, enthusiastic innocence by Jimmy Borbon, draws a picture in dark hues of his family, Ariano flies into a rage and beats the confused child. "Bright colors," he hollers. "No more brown and black. That's the color of dirt. Nobody likes nighttime. Black scares people."

Mr. Irizarry, a New York Puerto Rican who has taught high school here, has a firm understanding of the characters he has created. They are real and their problems are real. His writing is uneven, now giving the audience pleasure with dialogue that is funny and to the point, usually when the comment is at its most acerbic, and then launching into overdrawn expressions of principle. Even in the more inert passages the cast, under the direction of Vicente Castro, portrays a group of believable human beings.

Machisté plays the title role in the English version of the drama (Wednesdays, Thursdays and Fridays) and José Rey has the part in the Spanish staging (Saturdays and Sundays.) Machisté gives us a moody, violent hero, a man who has achieved material success, who believes himself to be doing the right thing and who is more passionate than thoughtful; he is a man who, for lack of esteem for himself and his people, is destroying what he loves most.

●

Denia Brache as the wife projects an optimism and a thorough confidence in being what she is: a woman who is secure in her love and proud of her heritage. Eileen Galindo brings a requisite tartness to the role of a friend, a woman who has broken with the macho culture she was raised in and who has become something of a cynic. Graciela Lecube is outstanding as Dona Aïda, the old friend of Ariano who is an aging neighborhood gossip, spreading bad news in a silkily insidious style, larding her comments with folksy humor.

Candace Brecker portrays Crystal, the blond mother-to-be, in an entirely persuasive manner. Angel Salazar in the part of a numbers runner, bounces on his heels with a swagger in his new garb, which, he confides with pride, a girl said makes him look Italian.

"Ariano" is stronger thematically than it is theatrically. The tidal sweeps from shoes-off down-home comedy to supercharged melodrama are very much in the tradition of folk theater, which is not something always grasped by outsiders. The audience of whites, blacks, Spanish-speakers and English-speakers at a performance of the English version responded enthusiastically to the lines. The play's the thing, to be sure, but audiences are pretty estimable, too.

1990 F 11, 69:2

All the King's Horses

GOOSE! BEYOND THE NURSERY, book by Scott Evans and Austin Tichenor; lyrics by Mr. Evans; music by Mark Frawley; musical director, Joe Baker; choreography and direction by Peter Gennaro; sets, Allen Moyer; costumes, Gregg Barnes; lighting, Mary Louise Geiger; musical supervisor, Michael Rafter; production manager, Randy Lee Hartwig; production stage manager, Ira Mont. Presented by Musical Theater Works, Anthony J. Stimac, artistic director. At St. Peter's Church, 54th Street and Lexington Avenue.

Mary	Jan Neuberger
Simon	Jeff Blumenkrantz
Peter	David Schechter
Jill	Jennifer Leigh Warren
Jack	Mark Lotito
Joan	Adinah Alexander

By STEPHEN HOLDEN

In the opening scene of the new musical revue "Goose! Beyond the Nursery," three men and three women laden with baggage pack themselves into a railroad car, where they snap at each other and complain about their lives.

As their collective peevishness rises to a crescendo, they suddenly break into a frantic chorus of "Three Blind Mice." The ditty becomes a key that unlocks their childhood memories, and they begin spontaneously identifying with characters out of Mother Goose. The men strip down to children's pajamas and sing a song called "Rub-a-Dub" in which "the butcher, the baker and the candlestick maker" become a jazz vocal trio who proclaim themselves "the coolest cats who ever sang in harmony." That claim is painfully unfounded, however, since the trio members, Jeff Blumenkrantz, David Schechter and Mark Lotito, can hardly carry a tune individually let alone make a competent vocal ensemble.

●

"Rub-a-Dub" is the first of more than a dozen songs in the show, presented by Musical Theater Works at St. Peter's Church, in which the rhymes of Mother Goose are turned into show tunes sung by adults playing children singing about adult experience in children's singsong diction. If that sounds confusing, much of what happens on the stage is virtually incomprehensible.

"Goose!" bills itself as a show that brings the nursery rhymes of youth into the 90's. But neither member of the lyrics-and-book-writing team, Scott Evans and Austin Tichenor, seems to know what to do with this odd concept, and the music by Mark Frawley is a workmanlike but shallow pastiche of styles ranging from street-corner doo-wop to Motown to light pop-jazz.

●

Not only have the show's creators overestimated the audience's familiarity with the source material, but they have also overestimated that material's allegorical resonance. No defined characters emerge, and the relationship between childhood and grown-up experience remains unexplored.

In the show's most elaborate number, "Humpty!," which is billed as "a pop opera," a policeman, a psychiatrist and a priest are among the characters who respond to the existential crisis of an offstage Humpty Dumpty, who has threatened to jump off his ledge. The tedious set piece is notable only for its stringing together of witless puns, like the suicidal egg man's address: the corner of Florentine and Benedict.

Under the direction of Peter Gennaro, the cast, dressed in an array of novelty costumes, mugs frantically, behaving as though "Goose!" were a children's theater piece. It wasn't intended to be, and children should find it even more mystifying than adults.

1990 F 11, 69:2

There'll Always Be An Anglophile

SOME AMERICANS ABROAD, by Richard Nelson; directed by Roger Michell; sets and costumes by Alexandra Byrne; lighting by Rick Fisher; original music by Jeremy Sams; poster arts by Edward Sorel; general manager, Steven C. Callahan; production manager, Jeff Hamlin. Presented by Lincoln Center Theater, Gregory Mosher, director; Bernard Gersten, executive producer, by arrangement with the Royal Shakespeare Theater, Stratford-on-Avon, England. At 150 West 65th Street.

Joe Taylor	Colin Stinton
Philip Brown	John Bedford Lloyd
Henry McNeil	Bob Balaban
Betty McNeil	Kate Burton
Frankie Lewis	Frances Conroy
Katie Taylor	Cara Buono
Harriet Baldwin	Jane Hoffman
Orson Baldwin	Henderson Forsythe
Joanne Smith	Ann Talman
An American	John Rothman
Donna Silliman	Elisabeth Shue

By MEL GUSSOW

American literary travelers to Europe in the 19th century often believed that the two cultures were irreconcilable, a response that was typified by Mark Twain, who in "The Innocents Abroad" was rude in the presence of Old World treasures. In Richard Nelson's comedy "Some Americans Abroad," the characters take a more Jamesian approach. The play, which had its United States premiere last night at the Mitzi E. Newhouse Theater, satirizes the American love affair with all things English.

A primary subject of the assault is academia, with Mr. Nelson focusing on a group of American professors of English literature on their annual whirlwind theatrical tour of England. With an attitude related to that of the English novelist David Lodge, the American playwright delivers scathing commentary on the absence of academic morality, cap-and-gown careerism and the need to control traffic on the university "tenure track."

When the play was first presented last summer at the Royal Shakespeare Company — in a splendid all-English production directed by Roger Michell — it seemed to have found its ideal setting and audience, as Americans abroad laughed at their counterparts on stage. The effect was almost like that of an audience of business executives basking in the criticism of themselves in "Other People's Money."

Appreciation of "Some Americans Abroad" can only be enhanced by a familiarity with the cultural landmarks under scrutiny: the National Theater, Stratford-on-Avon and Jamesian Sussex, chosen for retirement by an American academic couple in

Busily dividing their time between eating and admiring.

preference to Dickensian London or Hawthornian Liverpool. As the intrepid travelers divide their time between eating and seeing plays — often in the same place — Mr. Nelson offers food for thought as well as thought for food and theater.

While enjoying the play in London, one questioned how well it would travel. In the show's importation to

the United States, the oddest of sea changes has taken place. Mr. Michell has been brought over by the Lincoln Center Theater Company to restage the play with American actors. Though the text and the crisp stage design are the same, the original London production was far more incisive.

One would not be rash enough to suggest that the English actors were more adept at playing Americans, though, in fact, their accents were faultless. The truth is the English actors were more adept at playing American academics (essential to the play), and, role for role, they were more skillful at conveying both the sardonic comedy and the serious undertones. For this discrepancy, Mr. Michell must share responsibility with his American company.

•

At the center of the play is Joe Taylor, the new head of the English department and the leader of the tour, as cowardly a man of middle management as one is likely to find in any line of business. He will stand up for nothing, least of all his friends, and he turns every dinner conversation into a one-man platform for borrowed ideas and empty ethics.

The character must have, as he did in London, an ingenuous charm, or one may not believe in his authority. At Lincoln Center Colin Stinton plays the role straight down the middle, capturing Taylor's bluff self-confidence but averting subtleties on the periphery.

Even more problematic is the performance of Bob Balaban as a teacher who is being relieved of his position and will do anything to delay the guillotine. Mr. Balaban is appropriately wimpish, but he misses the character's desperation and the pathos of his predicament. Though he is slighted by his colleagues, he is the only one who loves teaching and seems to care about scholarship. The others are so busy publishing their opinions they scarcely have time to read. In this production the wimp's wife, his only loyal defender, is submerged in the crowd.

•

The other performances range from the reasonably accurate (John Bedford Lloyd as the womanizer of the group and the catalyst for the plot) to the unconvincing. In a number of instances the timing is imprecise. Either a pause is too long or a line is thrown away, muffling some of the author's sharpest observations as well as several amusing monologues. The exception is Henderson Forsythe, who is right on the mark as the old retired department head, an incorrigible misanthrope and probable fascist, who is as candid as he is malicious. Exacting in a cameo role is John Rothman as an overly friendly American visitor to Stratford.

In spite of one's disappointment in the New York production, there is still amusement here, as Mr. Nelson exhibits a lighter and more literate touch than evidenced in his earlier plays. He mocks everything from pence-pinching check splitters to compulsive theatergoers who insist on jamming two three-and-one-half-hour Shakespeares into one day (that comment was one of many reasons the play had such a relevance for London audiences).

Even Big Ben wins a laugh, clanging loudly and incessantly as the characters stand in the rain on Westminster Bridge and try to follow up a tribute to Wordsworth with a chorus of "God Save the Queen." When they are finally able to sing, it is with a certain sheepishness, as if someone

might overhear their accents and think they were American tourists rather than scholars on a cultural pilgrimage.

1990 F 12, C17:1

The Dinner Ghosts Who Stay to Bicker

COME AS YOU ARE, written and directed by N. Richard Nash; scenic design by James Morgan; lighting design by Kenneth Posner; costume design by Steven Perry; incidental music by Steven Aprahamian; production stage manager, Alan Fox. Presented by Roger Bowen. At Actors' Playhouse, 100 Seventh Avenue, between Christopher and Grove Streets.

Becky McAlister	Susan Pellegrino
John McAlister	Mark Hofmaier
Cora Briggs	Jane Welch
Lowell Briggs	Donald Symington

By MEL GUSSOW

N. Richard Nash's "Come as You Are" is a potluck dramatic stew centering on a cookbook author with an anorexic past. This might be called a case of overcompensation — or artistic bulimia — although, as one later learns, the cook does not eat her own food.

The play, which opened last night at the Actors' Playhouse, begins with the cook (Susan Pellegrino) alone in her neat country kitchen chopping vegetables for gazpacho, which she does with the wrist action of a gourmet chef. When her husband (Mark Hofmaier) arrives with additional ingredients, the drama starts a downward slide.

In this play, Mr. Nash, the author of "The Rainmaker," certainly has a food fetish. Even when the characters are dining, the conversation continues on the subject of food. In fact, if the word gazpacho were excised from the text, it might save the actors about five minutes, during which time they could check their answering services for more rewarding offers.

The playwright, who is also the director, has a fondness for dropping herbs and spices — saffron, tarragon, sage, but not parsley and thyme — and for having his characters remember such savory morsels as live grasshoppers. For all of the epicurean talk, the cook has written only one book. Suddenly she has another idea — the "Sloppy Sandwich Cookbook," but gets no further than the first few pages.

•

Sharing the menu with all the food references is a sloppy sandwich of a plot about guilt, retribution and two ghosts who come to dinner. The ghosts are the cook's parents, and for specters they are excessively verbal and have insatiable appetites. Together they consume a full share of that gazpacho. After dessert, the mother delivers a rhapsodic review of the meal, announcing that "it delighted the palate." People do not talk like that, but what can one expect from hungry ghosts?

The play is flapdoodle (which one dictionary defines as food for fools) and deals unproductively with relentless intrafamilial bickering. It is the playwright's self-conscious notion that the wife is making up her parents' dialogue; in other words, the play is in her head.

The father's lines are a particular embarrassment — spoken by Donald Symington with an aplomb undeserved by the material. The other ac-

tors simply sink into a morass of self-parody. For theatergoers, "Come as You Are" offers the leanest of dramatic cuisine. Watching it, one wants to send out for another play.

1990 F 15, C26:3

Shadings

WHITE CHOCOLATE FOR MY FATHER, written and directed by Laurie Carlos; lighting, Roma Flowers; set installation, Kevin Hamilton; composer, Don Meissner; costume designer, Sharon Norman; choreography, Jawole Willa Jo Zollar; stage manager, Keith Jones; Presented by BACA Downtown, 111 Willoughby Street, Brooklyn.

Mickey	Avis Brown
Lore	Laurie Carlos
Mama	April Greene
Tony	Dor Green
Emilyn	Evangeline John
Tiny	Susan McKeever
Red Light	Don Meissner
Deola/White Light	Edwina Lee Tyler

By STEPHEN HOLDEN

The eight performers who portray several generations of black women in Laurie Carlos's new theater piece, "White Chocolate for My Father" at BACA Downtown, move about a stage that is bare except for two symbolic structures. One is the sculptural representation of a waterfall, the other a flight of stairs leading nowhere.

During Ms. Carlos's evocative but difficult-to-follow one-hour theatrical collage with music, the voices of a matriarchal lineage mingle and converge in the mind of Lore (Ms. Carlos), a 10-year-old girl growing up in New York City in 1959. Echoes of the soul music of the era mingle with the voices of family members past and present to reflect the adolescent girl's search for identity and roots. Among the women who tell stories are Lore's sisters, Tony (Dor Green) and Tiny (Susan McKeever), her mother, Mickey (Avis Brown), her grandmother Mama (April Greene), and her great-great-grandmother Emilyn (Evangeline John).

•

In its blending of history, poetry, mysticism and and personal testimony into a piece that skips freely around in time, "White Chocolate" has something in common with Ntozake Shange's "For Colored Girls Who Have Considered Suicide/When the Rainbow Is Enuf," in which Ms. Carlos created the role of Lady in Blue. Ms. Carlos's work, however, is lower-keyed and more impressionistic than Ms. Shange's, and not as deeply grounded in language.

The ancestral voices that haunt Lore stretch back to Africa, and their fragmentary testimony balances images of brutality and agonizing struggle with those of endurance and continuity. Some of the sharper images are of the dogs that chewed off the lips of Lore's great-grandmother when she was still in Africa. The recurrent image of "a nose that is too big, too wide, too flat," is one of the play's several references to anxieties among blacks about color and physiognomy. Then there are Mama's stark remembrances of slavery days picking cotton and being paid $1 for 100 pounds and of her being stopped by a white man and beaten when trying to leave Memphis.

Juxtaposed with the ancestral history is the story of a recent incident in an Italian airport when Tony and Tiny were journeying to Zaire. In a financial misunderstanding caused by a language barrier, they are excused for being "Americans who don't speak Italian." As relatively lighthearted as the story is, it further illustrates how one's racial and national identity can change from situation to situation and how confusing and contradictory that can be.

The question that "White Chocolate" circles endlessly is how to piece all these fragments of history, legend and culture into a cohesive identity and where to take it from there.

1990 F 15, C22:3

The Autocrat Of the Classroom

MISS MARGARIDA'S WAY, written and directed by Roberto Athayde; costumes by Santo Loquasto; lighting by Jason Sturm; stage manager, Lisa Ledwich. Presented by Bernard and Toby Nussbaum. At the Helen Hayes Theater, 240 West 44th Street.
Miss Margarida .... Estelle Parsons
One of Her Students .... Koji Okamura
The Rest of Her Students .... The Audience

By MEL GUSSOW

In the 12 years since Miss Margarida held her first class in New York City, demanding blind obedience to her tyrannical rule, dictators have fallen and a dissident playwright has become president of his country. After cataclysmic historical events, seeing Estelle Parsons in "Miss Margarida's Way" in 1990 is like encountering an obstreperous figure from the past, a black sheep returning for a family gathering. As the actress plays the character — should she now be called Ms. Margarida? — it is the comic element of the performance that is principally asserted. The revival of the Roberto Athayde play opened last night at the Helen Hayes Theater.

"Miss Margarida's Way," banned in its first production in Brazil, is, of course, intended as a hortatory political statement, but the polemics and the metaphorical insights are one-dimensional — in contrast to Peter Handke's "Offending the Audience," among other plays.

Addressing the audience as unruly eighth-grade students, Miss Margarida asks if there is a Jesus Christ or a Messiah in the house. Then, clearing that hurdle, she assails religion, education and democracy while assuming the position of omnipotent autocrat. Her remarks draw laughter from a receptive audience, perhaps conditioned to comedy of insult through recent exposure to Eddie Murphy, Roseanne Barr and others. But after about 10 minutes, "Miss Margarida's Way" becomes repetitive. It is heading nowhere, and, like real students, theatergoers may begin to look forward to the bell signaling the end of the class.

What keeps one attentive is Ms. Parsons's performance, which has become even sharper in the intervening years. She is so much in command of her material that the personality of Mr. Athayde, who is the director as well as the author, seems to disappear. Ms. Parsons's Miss Margarida is mean and baleful, but with the spirit of a clown. It is almost as if Hitler had transmogrified into "The Great Dictator" as the actress mocks herself and the character in performance. In fact, whenever she diverges from the text and improvises her dialogue, she is funnier.

There is one actor (Koji Okamura) in the audience, but the other "roles"

are played by the theatergoers themselves. This means that the performance varies from night to night. People talk back, demanding a lecture on

The New York Times/Jim Wilson

Estelle Parsons

sex education instead of one on geography, asserting their own will against that of the teacher. During intermission, they scrawl graffiti on the blackboards.

Ms. Parsons is expert at handling interlopers. She is as quick on the comeback as if she herself had been practicing crowd control during late nights at comedy clubs — or early mornings at New York City schools. But even as she merges with her character, she maintains her actor's perspective.

She does not ignore the fact that this is a theater rather than a classroom. At a preview performance, when the teacher demanded to know what happened to her missing chalk, one woman answered that it had been hidden in the front row of the theater. Ms. Parsons said, "Twelve years ago, nobody would have told me."

That response could mean that people are more apt to tell tales on their neighbors. More likely it demonstrates that audiences have become especially open to environmental, participatory events. After attending "Tony 'n' Tina's Wedding" and trailing "Tamara" and friends through Gabriele D'Annunzio's villa, they may wish to step by Miss Margarida's classroom to be badgered and to return the ridicule. It is entirely possible that theatergoers today are more attuned to Miss Margarida's ways — and means.

1990 F 16, C3:1

Unions

SPECIAL INTERESTS, by Joe Sutton; directed by Mark Lutwak; sets and costumes, Anne C. Patterson; lighting, Spencer Mosse; photographic consultant, Tom Chargin; music, The "Happy" New Yorkers; production and stage manager, Nina Heller; assistant stage manager, Haley Alpiar; general manager, Denise Laffer. Presented by the Working Theater, Bill Mitchelson, artistic director. At the Henry Street Settlement, 466 Grand Street.

Vin .... William Wise
Edna .... Judith Granite
Deb .... Lynn Anderson
Wes .... James DuMont
Fallaci .... Robert Arcaro
Dot .... Lorey Hayes
Yates .... Jude Ciccolella
Nuckles .... Fracaswell Hyman

By RICHARD F. SHEPARD

It's been more than 50 years since plays dedicated to the glory of the labor movement flourished. Those

were strident times that inspired strident playwriting, like Clifford Odets's "Waiting for Lefty," the 1935 drama that became the symbol of the genre.

"Special Interests," Joe Sutton's play now being staged by the Working Theater at the Louis Abrons Art Center of the Henry Street Settlement, is a labor play far removed from its forebears, a play in which the villains and heroes that were so clearly identifiable in the conflict dramas of yesteryear turn out to be decidedly less easy to categorize.

"Special Interests" is about a bus strike called by a local that receives little support from its international. It is a very human play in which the characters are symbols of their situation at the same time they come across as real people. It reflects the influence of the television sitcom, which often mixes affecting situations into its comedy.

Mr. Sutton tells his story through many short scenes. For a long while, the audience may wonder how all of these vignettes are going to come together, but in a way they finally do. What centrality there is revolves about the family of Vin, a veteran bus driver who is enthusiastic about the strike, a good man of strong beliefs and work ethic, if a bit gullible. Living with him and his wife are their daughter and her husband, Wes, and their infant baby. Wes has all but given up looking for work, and he and Vin are in constant conflict, which is sharpened when the young fellow takes a job as a bus driver to replace the strikers, a move intended as much to humiliate his father-in-law as to make money. The denouement is not exactly satisfying but the path to it is lined with eye-catching billboards.

If anything, the play reflects the situation of people caught up in big systems that roll over the individual, but it is by no means a gloomy tale of oppression.

Don't probe too deeply. Mr. Sutton is interested in individuals, and although they are written as types, they emerge with their own personalities. The lines are brisk but there are too many moments that seem taken from old-time broadcast drama where one is told to tune in tomorrow, except that here the periods of suspense and breather come in rapid-fire short order that does not give the audience time to collect its emotions.

•

Under Mark Lutwak's direction, the action mostly spins along at a good clip. It is a well-cast production. Judith Granite, as the bus driver's wife, is notable. She is sharp-tongued and direct, with the manner and appearance of Rhea Perlman playing Carla, the barmaid in "Cheers." William Wise, as the bus driver, gives an excellent portrayal of a working stiff battered by challenges to his belief.

James DuMont makes the son-in-law a callous, malicious man with a hooray-for-me code of ethics. Lynn Anderson gives a sensitive performance as his young and unhappy wife. Robert Arcaro creates a local president who is passionately involved with his union and with his assistant, a self-concerned young woman played by Lorey Hayes. Jude Ciccolella is funny as the board chairman, who is elliptical, monosyllabic and orthodox in all opinions, a man who constantly confounds the labor negotiator he has hired (a role played with appropriate exasperation by Fracaswell Hyman).

"Special Interests" presents sympathetic views of people caught up in

situations that bring out the best and worst in them. It is a traditional play, well told, an observer of how we behave rather than a proponent of how things should be,

1990 F 18, 70:1

Porn Palace With A Heart of Gold

CROWBAR, by Mac Wellman; directed by Richard Caliban; music by David Van Tieghem; slide presentation by James Sanders; sets by Kyle Chepulis; costumes by Claudia Brown; lighting by Brian Aldous; sound by Eric Liljestrand. Presented by En Garde Arts, Anne Hamburger, producer. At the Victory Theater, 209 West 42d Street.

Ghost of David Belasco .... Yusef Bulos
Mr. Rioso .... Reg E. Cathey
First Woman .... Elzbieta Czyzewska
Second Woman .... Nora Dunfee
Second Girl .... Mollie O'Mara
First Girl .... Cordelia Richards
Ghost of Oscar Hammerstein ... Glen Santiago
First Man .... Omar Shapli
Ghost of William Gorman ... Mr. Van Tieghem

By MEL GUSSOW

"Crowbar," the newest site-specific project of Anne Hamburger's En Garde Arts company, is an act of reclamation and renewal. On Sunday, the Mac Wellman play reopened the Victory Theater on West 42d Street as a home for legitimate theater — unfortunately only through March 11.

Built by Oscar Hammerstein in 1899, the theater was originally a grand Broadway palace, a home for stars as well theatrical spectacles. In recent years, it has become a porno movie house. "Crowbar" is part ghost play, part sound-and-light show such as one might see at a chateau in France, echoing with memories of the Victory's illustrious past.

The audience sits on and near the stage while the play takes place throughout the theater — itself a

'Crowbar' evokes ghosts out of the Victory's past.

novel event. The exit signs themselves look like a hundred points of light. As we watch, aisles, balconies and boxes come alive with actors playing out Mr. Wellman's thesis that "all theaters are haunted."

A spotlight strikes the building's dome, with sculptured cherubs that could have flown over from a Boucher painting. Then, with a thud, a sandbag falls to the stage, and Mr. Wellman sails into his archival recreation. "Crowbar" supposedly takes place during the intermission of the play that opened the theater, James A. Hearn's bucolic "Sag Harbor." The narrative revolves circuitously around a father's search for his missing daughter and various factual deaths of the period, including that of a workman who died in an onstage accident.

The tales are wrapped in the author's elliptical, rhapsodic language, aerated by quirky humor. An actress playing a patient theatergoer awaits the end of this "longest intermission" in order to go backstage and ask for an autograph from Lionel Barrymore, "a fine young actor."

For a 90-minute play, there are perhaps too many tangents, with the playwright reaching out to be inclusive of time, place and metaphor ("America is an empty theater"). The show is most intriguing when it holds to the building itself and to the story of Hammerstein and David Belasco, who operated it in the first decade of this century. From accompanying slide projections, arranged by James Sanders, one receives a photographic representation of what the theater was like in its heyday, when it housed everything from Houdini to "Abie's Irish Rose."

At the same time, the play reveals information about the secret apartment that Belasco kept for his mistress above the dome; the roof garden with a Dutch village and a working mill, and the artificial lake beneath the stage. Even when the narrative becomes convoluted, our senses are stimulated by the environmental aspects of the evening, a

Tom Brazil

Omar Shapli

credit both to Mr. Wellman and to the director, Richard Caliban.

In the spirit of En Garde Arts, the two are restlessly inventive in using the vast space, even the great height over the heads of theatergoers on stage. As an actress speaks her lines, three specters parrot her words on three levels of the theater — in the orchestra and the two balconies — and at other moments 20 specters snake through the house. Suddenly, a character appears in a box, followed by a laugh reverberating from the last row of the second balcony. Seated on stage, the audience sees the theater and the theatrical event from the viewpoint of the actor, except, in this case, the theater becomes the protagonist of the play.

Throughout the show is filtered a musical score, written by David Van Tieghem and played by him on various timpanic instruments. The score eerily conveys an air of mystery and Kyle Chepulis's sets and properties and Brian Aldous's lighting effects are additional atmospheric assets.

Bearded and in period costume, Omar Shapli exudes turn-of-the-century theatricality in the leading role of the father of the lost daughter. Reg E. Cathey, Yusef Bulos and Elzbieta Czyzewska evoke the feeling of characters recently released from a state of suspended animation.

Interest is so stimulated in the lost architectural splendor that a second-act tour of the Victory would have seemed most appropriate — from the sky-high dome to the depths of the artificial lake, which, if it still exists, might be a byway for a phantom of 42d Street. Such musings are immediately forgotten when theatergoers exit back into the tawdry street, but for the duration of "Crowbar," our imaginations are heightened along with those of Mr. Wellman and his collaborators.

1990 F 20, C18:1

Fighting Oppression With Art and Sex

WHEN SHE DANCED, by Martin Sherman; directed by Tim Luscombe; set design by Steven Rubin; costumes by Jess Goldstein; lighting by Nancy Schertler; original music and sound design by John Gromada; choreography by Peter Anastos; production stage manager, Roy Harris; production manager, Carl Mulert. Presented by Playwrights Horizons, Andre Bishop, artistic director; Paul S. Daniels, executive director. At 416 West 42d Street.

Isadora	Elizabeth Ashley
Sergei	Jonathan Walker
Jeanne	Jacqueline Bertrand
Mary	Macia Lewis
Miss Belzer	Marcia Jean Kurtz
Alexandros	Robert Sean Leonard
Luciano	Robert Dorfman
Christine	Clea Montville

By FRANK RICH

Isadora Duncan won't dance — don't ask her — in "When She Danced," Martin Sherman's play at Playwrights Horizons. The year is 1923, the place is Paris and the lady is, as she puts it, "extremely kaput." Isadora sees herself as old (45, actually) and fat. Her money and perhaps her inspiration have fled. Her sojourn to Russia has marked her as "a Bolshevik whore" back home in America. Her husband, the poet Sergei Yesenin, is a violent, depressive alcoholic nearly two decades her junior. In four years, Isadora will be dead.

Even so, the fascinating play Mr. Sherman has written is not the gloomy one the dancer's final biographical chapters would suggest. "When She Danced" is a comic portrait of a bohemian salon in both joy and extremis, as the calling of high art meets the low farce of insistent creditors, ludicrous lovers and unexpected guests. Mr. Sherman means to celebrate Isadora as a liberating spirit, an exemplar of creative chaos, rather than as a parochial patron saint of modern dance.

"Anyone can dance — all they have to know is how to listen," says Isadora, here embodied by the formidable Elizabeth Ashley. When Mr. Sherman's heroine rehearses for a recital in "When She Danced," she doesn't move her feet but merely sits meditatively and soaks up a Chopin étude. Later, when a young disciple (Clea Montville) in a tunic drops by to dance a Duncan-inspired solo — a hilarious, parodistic routine choreographed by Peter Anastos — a horrified Isadora quickly gives the girl the hook. She means her legacy to be the license of artistic freedom, not the shackles of specific steps.

As Mr. Sherman makes clear, no one remembers too well exactly what Isadora did on stage anyway. The play's eyewitness accounts are vague. "All she was doing on stage was walking," says one devoted fan, who remembers her own, highly personal psychological associations with a Duncan performance instead of the performance itself. "When I saw Isadora dance for the first time, I saw myself for the first time," says another acolyte. For Duncan's followers, and the playwright is certainly among them, art is a religion whose primary mission is to illuminate the beholder's soul.

In the searing finale of Mr. Sherman's "Bent," two gay prisoners at Dachau triumphed fleetingly over their captors by achieving a mental sexual union. It's a long way from a concentration camp to Duncan's salon of exiles, yet these plays, a decade apart in time, are thematic cousins. To Mr. Sherman, art and sex are passions that speak louder than

Martha Swope

Elizabeth Ashley as Isadora Duncan in "When She Danced."

words and do battle against oppression. It's the principal joke of "When She Danced" that almost no one on stage shares a language with anyone else, Isadora and her Russian husband included. But the man and wife of "When She Danced," as well as the polyglot hangers-on surrounding them, are nonetheless bound together by Isadora's transcendent artistry or sexuality or both. So incandescent is the Duncan spirit that it will later allow her legend to outlast both her husband's published poetry and her own ephemeral choreographic works.

●

Though Mr. Sherman tells a story involving Isadora's money-raising schemes, his play is as freewheeling as its subject. The farcical payoff is an ill-fated lobster-and-champagne dinner party in which Isadora plays host to a nutty assemblage that, along with the usual Americans and Russians, includes an Italian civil servant (Robert Dorfman) and an ingenuous young Greek piano prodigy (Robert Sean Leonard) who is as boastful of what he refers to as his pederasty as he is of his pianism. As written by Mr. Sherman, the scene is an imaginative amalgam of Marx Brothers and Chekhov — a circus of food fights, unrequited lust and ineffectual attempted suicide.

On stage, however, the party is not nearly so rollicking as it should be. Though the English director, Tim Luscombe, has given "When She Danced" a handsome, atmospheric production — Nancy Schertler's lighting alone can evoke the 20's Paris of expatriate artists — his handling of actors is as erratic as it was in the recent "Artist Descending a Staircase." Jonathan Walker's Sergei is convincing as a Russian rake, but his histrionics are too leaden to elevate the poet's self-destructive narcissism and cruelty into Gogolian comedy. Not much funnier are Mr. Dorfman's Italian schlemiel, Jacqueline Bertrand's pouty French maid and Marcia Lewis's American busybody, none of whom transcend type in either writing or performance.

Ms. Ashley is another story. She is right by age and looks for the blowsy Isadora of 1923 and, as always, is a smoldering sexual presence, fun to

watch. But her gesticular repertory of deep sighs, flaring eyebrows and bared teeth is so overworked that she seems to be chain-smoking invisible cigarettes. The tough-as-nails Ashley bravura also seems inappropriate to the somewhat vulnerable heroine of "When She Danced." The Act I finale, in which Isadora collapses to the floor in mournful memory of her drowned children, is a conspicuous emotional thud.

Far more moving are Marcia Jean Kurtz, as a mousey Russian interpreter living vicariously in Isadora's reflected glory, and Mr. Leonard as the Greek musician who longs in vain to see Isadora perform so that he, too, might know "great passion" and "great love." In the play's waning moments, Mr. Leonard recalls asking his mother on her death bed to describe what she saw when Isadora danced. The mother's answer is another failure of words — "I cannot explain" — but so exquisite is Mr. Leonard's smile as he repeats her answer that the very inexplicability of Isadora's art becomes, as "When She Danced" intends, a stirring emblem of its mysterious power to endure.

1990 F 20, C15:1

Nostalgic Figure Eights

WALT DISNEY'S MAGIC KINGDOM ON ICE, produced by Kenneth Feld; theatrical director and writer, Jerry Bilik; skating director and choreographer, Bob Paul; character coordinator, Larry Billman; musical directors, Mr. Bilik and Alan Oldfield; scenic designer, Reid Carlson; costume designer, José Lengson; assistant choreographer, Jill Shipstad Thomas. At Radio City Music Hall, 1260 Avenue of the Americas, at 50th Street.

WITH: J. Scott Driscoll, Shannon Sowers, Grant Noroyan, Toyka Raol, Eric Kerr and the Jackpots.

By RICHARD F. SHEPARD

"Pinocchio," a tale that has mesmerized children both as a story written in 1881 by Carlo Collodi and a feature-length animated film by Walt Disney in 1940, is now live on ice at Radio City Music Hall. It is a good skate in every sense of the word and, particularly if one is entertaining smaller fry, will be worth a visit during its stay, which ends on Sunday.

The spectacle, "Walt Disney's Magic Kingdom on Ice," employs the tale as a framework for nimble and graceful skating. It is a user-friendly show, one that uncomplicatedly sets about entertaining. Ice shows may be spectacular and breathtaking but they are not usually heartwarming; this one does capture some of the spirit of the yarn about the old carver of marionettes and the wooden figure he makes and turns into a real live boy.

This show, celebrating the 50th anniversary of the movie, quite naturally follows the form of the film, but very much on its own imaginative terms. There is Pinocchio, skated winningly by Grant Noroyan, in his peasant vest and feathered hat. Mr. Noroyan neatly mimics the movements of what might very well be an awkward boy and fits this graceful ineptitude closely to the taped sound, which includes music and voice.

There is the introduction, which has a dazzling dance on ice by Kristiina Wegelius, who greets "tourist" characters from the Disney stable, among them Mickey and Minnie Mouse, Donald Duck, Pluto and Goofy, who don't have too much to do with the story itself. One sees Jiminy Cricket, the conscience of Pinocchio; Stromboli, the terrible carnival owner, and Honest John and Gideon, two unabashed villains who lure our hero from the straight and narrow. There can be nothing but joy that the Jackpots, a comedy trio, are given sufficient leeway to strut their stuff, a combination of pratfalls and risky midair leaps, an act that somehow fits into the fabric of the show. And the same goes for Eric Kerr and Toyka Raol and their romantic ice-dancing to the tune of "Arabesque."

There is much familiar music, but "Pinocchio" fans will, of course, resonate most with the likes of "When You Wish Upon a Star" and "Give a Little Whistle."

All of this is lovely, but the real attraction is the overall staging, which is attractive and sometimes overwhelming. The scenes are big, as one expects in Radio City Music Hall, and they are mostly tasteful. Backdrops of an Italian village and of a glittering Coney Island entertainment park catch the eye, but nothing catches it as much as the underwater scenes; they are fantastic, with lights creating watery depths and skaters brilliantly costumed as tropical fish and sea horses, which give reality to the illusion of swimming.

To judge from the enthusiastic screaming of the very young in the audience, "Pinocchio" may still have another hundred years ahead of it.

1990 F 20, C18:4

Desert Song

NEW ANATOMIES, by Timberlake Wertenbaker; dramaturg, Victoria Abrash; lighting, David Bergstein; sets and costumes, Connie Singer; original music, Michele Navazio; production stage manager, Tamara Holt. Presented by Home for Contemporary Theater and Art, in collaboration with the Compass Theater Company. At 44 Walker Street.

Isabelle Eberhardt .... Colette Kilroy
Severine; Antoine; Bou Saadi .... Alison Stair Neet
Verda Miles; Anna; Si Lachmi; Yasmina; Captain Soubiel .... Kate Fuglei
Natalie; Eugenie; Murderer; Judge .... Ching Valdes or Aran
Jenny; Saleh; Lydia; Colonel Lyautey .... Regina Taylor

By MEL GUSSOW

Isabelle Eberhardt drowned in the desert, the victim of a freak flood. This was a bizarre end to a brief, fascinating life. She was a European who transformed herself into an Arab; in the guise of a man, she traveled through the Sahara and lived with with the natives under her adopted name, Si Mahmoud. Dabbling in mysticism, she became an "oblivion seeker," as in the title of one of her short stories.

In the play "New Anatomies," Timberlake Wertenbaker takes a bold though erratic look at this turn-of-the-century adventurer. It is the character more than the play (at the Home for Contemporary Theater and Art) that holds one's interest, in contrast to related works by Caryl Churchill. Ms. Wertenbaker is also the author of "Our Country's Good," the winner of the 1988 Olivier Award as best play in London's West End.

Creating a collage portrait of an obsessive personality, Ms. Wertenbaker draws on her own imaginings as well as on Eberhardt's statements ("I wanted to possess this country and this country has possessed me," she said about North Africa). As exemplified by the play's title, the author emphasizes the gender-switching aspects of the story, viewing Eberhardt as a woman out of her time who believed she could find fulfillment by adopting the clothes and character of a man.

Under the direction of Melia Bensussen, five actresses play a legion of roles, male and female (only Colette Kilroy is limited to one role, that of Eberhardt herself). In performance as well as text, the play is concerned with questions of sexual identity, studying a pre-feminist time with foreknowledge of a changed landscape.

In one satiric episode, the crux of Ms. Wertenbaker's concept, all five actresses appear in a cabaret bar. As one of them observes, four of the women are dressed as men, each with a different motive: one for professional reasons (she is a singer), others for reasons of sexual orientation or willfulness.

"New Anatomies" begins near the end of Eberhardt's life with the character overcome by alcohol and other excesses. The writing veers into overstatement (and an anachronistic tone). In this and other scenes, the play portrays the character as a vulgar eccentric rather than as an original spirit, like Beryl Markham or T. E. Lawrence.

There are revealing flashbacks as hysteria is replaced by reflection and as the playwright studies the biographical roots of the character's disaffection. In quick strokes, we see her ineffectual mother and the strain provided by her siblings, a domineering sister and a brother with whom she had a close, possibly incestuous, relationship.

Shifting back and forth in time and from Europe to North Africa, the play alternates between openness and an authorial detachment. Similarly, the performances waver, with the most agile contributions coming from Alison Stair Neet (as Eberhardt's brother and a journalist) and Regina Taylor (as the brother's bourgeoise wife and a general who protects Eberhardt). Ms. Kilroy is effective in the scenes in Eberhardt's earlier life, but not in the character's decline. Connie Singer's design (sets and costumes) takes a symbolic approach to the desert, using dropcloths to simulate sand. The actresses prove to be adept at their ritualistic handling of Arabian costumes.

Immediately after Eberhardt's death (in 1904 at the age of 27), her reputation was subjected to distortion, but was reaffirmed through the efforts of literary rediscoverers like Paul Bowles. One's curiosity continues to be provoked about a woman who embraced a life as an outcast, taking the most extreme measures in order to assert her demonic sense of self.

1990 F 22, C19:1

Anecdotage

DYLAN THOMAS: RETURN JOURNEY, based on the works of Dylan Thomas; directed by Anthony Hopkins. Presented by Arthur Cantor and Bonnie Nelson Schwartz. At the Hudson Guild, 441 West 26th Street.

WITH: Bob Kingdom

By MEL GUSSOW

On stage in his one-man show, "Dylan Thomas: Return Journey," Bob Kingdom has the look of his subject — short, portly, with a curled lower lip and the general appearance of a fallen cherub. As he begins his performance at the Hudson Guild Theater, the actor also reveals a measure of the disarming Thomas manner. He makes fun of himself while never forgetting that he is, first of all, an artist in love with words.

Mr. Kingdom, who is Welsh, is clear-spoken, but, as the audience soon realizes, he lacks that resonant voice that made Dylan Thomas such a wonderful reader of his own work. It is an attribute that any actor needs in performing Thomas, especially when reciting his poetry.

This is, as Mr. Kingdom explains, a Thomas deep in his "anecdotage." The attempt is not a dramatic biography but a simulation of the poet in performance during his famous tours of the United States in the early 1950's. Those were the tours that confirmed his celebrity and certified his dissolution, as lionization proved to be a crucial step in his self-victimization.

Included in the evening are Thomas's best-known poems, plus a few others not quite so familiar. A full share of the show is devoted to the poetry, and, as it turns out, that is the least persuasive part of the evening.

As Mr. Kingdom delivers the verse, one thinks of other actors who have specialized in reading or acting Thomas. Richard Burton, Alec Guinness and Emlyn Williams all brought more poetry to their performances. Anthony Hopkins directed this one-man show, and one is forced to the conclusion that it might have have been more rewarding if it were the director rather than Mr. Kingdom on stage.

Mr. Kingdom is, however, effective with the informal Thomas, chatting with deliberate casualness while commenting on his career. Even as he mocks European authors on the American lecture circuit, he accepts lecturing as one of his own methods of employment, performing on and off the podium and serving up "bottomless glasses of instant Dylan" for an insatiable audience.

In passing, he makes fun of the BBC, "professional Irishmen," T. S. Eliot and, perhaps most of all, "fat poets with slim volumes" — surrounded, one might add, by attractive, admiring young women on college campuses. It is clear from the selections — from stories and letters as well as poetry — that Thomas not only had a gift for rhapsodic imagery but was an artful craftsman and stylist as well.

The most touching moment in the show is the reading of "Return Journey" itself, describing his homecoming to Swansea. Walking the streets, he stops a series of citizens, asking them if they remember Thomas. None of them recognize him, but each recalls all the badness of his boyhood and never once credits him for his imagination. Finally he meets a man who echoes all the previous disparagement we have heard and then, responding to a question, declares that the exile is "dead, dead, dead." Mr. Kingdom's wince is palpable.

Death was, of course, a hovering presence in Thomas's art, a fatalism allied with the poet's pantheistic attitude toward life. Mr. Kingdom ends his performance on that double-edged note, with "Do Not Go Gentle Into That Good Night" and "Fern Hill."

The actor is not, as one would have hoped, Dylan Thomas restored to life. The portrait is one of sincere homage and moderate verisimilitude.

1990 F 23, C15:1

Freedom Doled Out Like Gruel

SQUARE ONE, by Steve Tesich; directed by Jerry Zaks; set, Tony Walton; lighting, Paul Gallo; costumes, Ann Roth; sound, Aural Fixation; hair, Antonio Soddu; musical director, Norman Weiss; production stage manager, Leslie Loeb; stage manager, Scott Rodabaugh. Presented by Second Stage, Robyn Goodman and Carole Rothman, artistic directors, in association with the A.T.&T. New Plays for the 90's Project. At 2162 Broadway, at 76th Street.

Dianne .... Dianne Wiest
Adam .... Richard Thomas

By FRANK RICH

Steve Tesich doesn't care who knows it: he favors humanity over oppression, individuality over conformity, life over death. These positions are set forth with clocklike regularity in "Square One," a futuristic fable that has attracted such gifted theater people as the actors Richard Thomas and Dianne Wiest, the director Jerry Zaks and the designer Tony Walton to the Second Stage.

A two-character piece staged in a mostly empty space, "Square One" is "Brave New World" reduced to dimensions that would allow it to be performed by any and all casts of "Love Letters." Mr. Thomas is Adam, a "state artist third class" and apparatchik in an unnamed bureaucratic society where he is a regular vocalist on television's wildly popular "Patriotic Variety Hour." Ms. Wiest is Dianne, a daffy free-thinker whom he woos and weds. It is not a happy union. Adam subscribes unblinkingly to a system that confines the elderly to internment centers, refuses to concede a difference between right and wrong, and doles out freedom like meager gruel. Dianne refuses to ignore the unacknowledged suffering around her and decides to take a courageous stand of "noncompliance" against the state that produces it.

Which side are you on?

•

There is much time to wrestle with one's conscience as "Square One" waltzes through its secondhand absurdist jokes. The author of colloquial American comedies like "Division Street" and the film "Breaking Away," Mr. Tesich does not seem comfortable with spaced-out dating scenes and an Albee marriage (complete with symbolic children). His funniest material, all in the second act and usually given to Ms. Wiest as digressionary stand-up shtick, could just as easily have appeared in other Tesich plays as in "Square One": a riff about melodramatic movie music, an updated parable about Jesus Christ's return to earth, a parody of the clichés in political punditry.

The one challenging idea within the knee-jerk portentousness of "Square One" — the notion that artists can be a society's fascists and ordinary civilians its dissidents — is not seriously explored. Clearly Mr. Tesich wants to make a point, and by no means a frivolous one, about the deadening, opportunistic mass culture that exists in the West, where art is more likely to "intimidate life" than imitate it. At a time when totalitarian governments are falling elsewhere, Mr. Tesich perhaps wants self-satisfied Americans to see that television and its many tentacles can strangle freedom, morality and feeling surreptitiously as the heavy-handed state of "Square One" does by force. But by setting this provocative issue within the confines of an arch, vague nowhere land, Mr. Tesich diffuses its urgency, never threatening to hit his audience where it actually lives.

If anything, "Square One" lets the audience off the hook entirely by allowing it always to feel superior to Adam, an intellectual thug and narcissist whose idea of helping the disadvantaged is to sing them a Pollyannaish ditty. Smug laughter was also a byproduct of another recent (and much better) Tesich play, "The Speed of Darkness," seen at the Goodman Theater in Chicago last year. In that sometimes searing reckoning with the Vietnam War, the author frequently presented an all-American family as subhuman, again allowing one to leave the theater blaming other people for national woes whose eradication may require self-examination, not finger-pointing.

Mr. Zaks, as always, directs with animation, and "Square One" keeps spinning about visually while standing in place in other respects. The most dramatic moment is achieved by the lighting designer Paul Gallo as he delicately wraps Mr. Thomas in incriminating, forlorn shadows at that instant when Adam refuses to reach out to the needy, grief-stricken Dianne. This silent, fleeting tableau depicting Adam's pitiful terror of intimacy is also the apex of Mr. Thomas's performance. There is not much this fine actor can do with a chirpy automaton who is as smarmy as a game-show host and is the butt of every joke. For his travails, Mr. Thomas does get to sing two Irving Berlin songs, "Always" and, for ironic purposes, "This Is a Great Country," a patriotic anthem from "Mr. President" that has rarely been disinterred in 30 years.

Susan Cook
Dianne Wiest in "Square One," at Second Stage Theater.

Since Ms. Wiest's character shares her first name, I guess she can't be blamed for playing herself — or at least the public persona created in Woody Allen movies. "Square One" begins with her twittering and squinting to music; later she gets to demonstrate anguish, anger and the comic diction that can produce laughs simply by adding pejorative inflection to a word like genre. But why should Ms. Wiest be milking her mannerisms and packaging emotions as if they were audition routines, untethered to a character? She is much too talented an actress and at far too high a point in her career to go back to square one.

1990 F 23, C3:1

A Boatload Of Gags and Puns

ROUGH CROSSING, by Tom Stoppard, freely adapted from a play by Ferenc Molnar, with music by André Previn. Directed by Steve Stettler; music director, Michael John La Chiusa; production dramaturge, Ulla Backlund; set by James D. Sandefur; lighting by Pat Dignan; costumes by Toni-Leslie James; sound by Tom Gould; production stage manager, Jana Lynn. Presented by the New Theater of Brooklyn, Deborah J. Pope and Mr. Stettler, artistic directors. At 465 Dean Street, Prospect Heights section, Brooklyn.

Dvornichek	David Manis
Turai	Lowry Miller
Adam	Simon Brooking
Gal	Robert Blumenfeld
Natasha	Patricia Norcia
Ivor	Graeme Malcolm

By MEL GUSSOW

When Tom Stoppard's "Rough Crossing" was first presented in London in 1984, it had the shelf life of banana cream pie. Reviews were discouraging and the play, a free-handed adaptation of Ferenc Molnar's comedy "The Play's the Thing," was withdrawn from the National Theater repertory.

With an enterprise suitable to its small storefront space, the New Theater of Brooklyn has dusted off the adaptation and, using Mr. Stoppard's scaled-down, chorus-less touring version, has given the show the theatrical equivalent of the Heimlich maneuver.

While the play may lack Molnar's suaveness (in the P. G. Wodehouse adaptation), it benefits from Mr. Stoppard's breeziness and limber linguistics. Perhaps on the National's large Lyttelton stage, expectations were simply too high. At the tiny New Theater, "Rough Crossing" proves to be a thoroughly amiable trifle. To borrow a line from Mr. Stoppard's protagonist, a playwright, it is written "sine qua nonchalance."

In the original Molnar, the play took place in a castle. Mr. Stoppard has freed the landlocked characters and put them aboard a ship sailing between Southampton and New York. The plot device remains the same. The playwright (Lowry Miller) and his colleagues overhear their leading lady and her co-star in a romantic dalliance. To protect a distraught composer who is in love with the actress, the playwright pretends that the overheard dialogue is a rehearsal of a scene for his new musical comedy. The rest is frivolity involving mistaken identities, running gags and enough puns and plays on words to fill a steamer trunk.

Actually, there are two playwrights, longtime collaborators. The one, Turai (Mr. Miller), is urbane, while the other (Robert Blumenfeld) is a seaborne sybarite. When the ship appears to be in danger of sinking, he rushes to the lifeboats and, to his astonishment, finds that "women and children don't give an inch." In his adaptation, Mr. Stoppard is aiming more for mock-Coward than for pseudo-Wodehouse.

The play within "The Play's the Thing" is now a musical, an impossibly labyrinthine escapade about two cruise ships, one with a boatload of vacationing debutantes (and a jewel thief), the other with a full cargo of French tarts. Naturally the ships are crisscrossed, with everything leading to a madcap, farcical conclusion.

James D. Sandefur's small, stylish set may remind theatergoers of the ship designed for the revival of "Anything Goes" at Lincoln Center. In contrast to that luxurious ocean liner, this one is like a trim tugboat with an

Jessica Katz
David Manis in Tom Stoppard's "Rough Crossing," at the New Theater of Brooklyn.

Art Deco touch. On what must be a minimal budget, the director, Steve Stettler, gives the audience its money's worth.

•

The actors are as nimble as necessary, especially David Manis as the ship's steward, Dvornichek. The steward is Mr. Stoppard's variation on the Molnar-Wodehouse nosy footman. As played by Mr. Manis, Dvornichek is an ingratiating blend of naval naïveté and show business knowhow. Totally at sea at sea, he can't tell stern from starboard, but he turns out to be a sure-fingered plot doctor who can rescue a sinking musical. He also plays the piano, sings and does a quick tap dance (the incidental music is by André Previn, with lyrics by Mr. Stoppard).

This is not to suggest that the result is vintage Stoppard — like "The Real Thing" or "Undiscovered Country," the author's adaptation of Arthur Schnitzler — but with its capable captain and crew, "Rough Crossing" has a relatively smooth sailing.

1990 F 23, C3:4

STAGE VIEW/Ethan Mordden

'Grand Hotel' Through a Kaleidoscope

FIRST THERE WAS VICKI BAUM'S best-selling novel of 1929, then her play, then M-G-M's version, the original all-star Hollywood movie — Garbo, the Barrymore boys, Joan Crawford, Wallace Beery and Lewis Stone. Now, some 60 years after it all began, comes "Grand Hotel" the musical. Of course: the dashing staircase rippling with prestigious entrances! the billowing drapes! the revolving stage to sweep us from suite to suite! Here the joyless ballerina, there the handsome baron! Now the sexy secretary, then the crooked businessman! Look, behind that pillar — it's the dying bookkeeper who wants to "see life"! And there's the grand ballroom, ironically swirling with dancers drunk on the frivolous rapture of the waltz!

This was exactly the show that Tommy Tune knew he *didn't* want to create, when the project was offered to him. "I had five stories

In 'Grand Hotel,' Tommy Tune uses cinematic montage effects to create new visuals out of old.

to tell," he explains. "There was no time for the old layered style. Besides, it's been done already, done beautifully. And haven't today's audiences been spoiled by the television zapper — that constantly shifting image?"

■

It may be that "Grand Hotel" comes with its constantly shifting images all built in. Mr. Tune is fond of a passage in Vicki Baum's autobiography in which she calls her novel and play "probably the first of [their] kind to be written in a sort of moving-picture technique — kaleidoscopic effects, brief, ever-changing scenes, flashes, staccato dialogue." M-G-M's movie, she thought, was "a star-studded wedding cake.'' It's not the *place* she was attracted to, but the life she saw in it — "Menschen im Hotel," she called it: People in a Hotel.

Nevertheless, the "Grand Hotel" musical, in Luther Davis's script and Robert Wright and George Forrest's score (first produced in 1958 in California), honored traditional storytelling techniques — Scene 1, now Scene 2, then Scene 3; songs at regular intervals; and the finale putting forth Grand Hotel's grand lobby for the first time as the public, its breath taken, breaks into Theater Party Ovation With Extreme Prejudice. It was another wedding cake.

That's not *people in a hotel*, thought Mr. Tune. Where's the coming and going? Where's the center of the show, the point of interlock for the five separate stories, the place where ballroom, lobby, suites, orchestra and money and love and death circle around one another? He saw the entire piece flowing as a film flows, dancing through the hotel without having to go anywhere or change scene. "Writing a musical." Mr. Tune says, "is rewriting." So he and his staff and the authors set to work, "to find the form, the essence of the material"; to take the piece from linear narration back to Vicki Baum's kaleidoscope of coming and going, of people in a hotel.

His rewriting is highly collaborative. "The best idea wins," he says. "Nobody owns any one job — we *all* own the show." So the musical supervisor Wally Harper could devise the introductory rhythmic figures that impel the dance numbers. So the designer Tony Walton could provide a platoon of mobile chairs that

function not only architecturally but dramatically, now giving the players room to travel, now hemming them in; the show's big number, "We'll Take a Glass Together," must be the first mass Charleston in history to be performed on a dance floor small enough to suit one or two Dolly Sisters, not Mr. Tune's tensely pulsing ensemble. So Mr. Tune and company jigsawed five numbers and all the exposition dialogue into a preliminary collage of people coming, going — the hotel opened up for us like a dollhouse. So, too, Peter Stone and Maury Yeston could be called in to contribute to, respectively, the book and score during the September Boston tryout when the rewriting moved too slowly. Nobody owns any one job.

Meanwhile, Mr. Tune was compressing, scissoring, dissecting. Music began to course through the show as through a hotel lobby of the 1920's. At the same time, the musical's traditional second and third choruses, its reprises — the familiarizing that makes a score accessible — were pared away. Mr. Tune is his own zapper: the big Charleston peaks so quickly it's almost a sneak preview of itself. A relay race of scenes had been refereed into an intricate tennis of doubles, triples and even a quintet that makes an operatic scene out of dialogue. Five principals are lined up before us in the hotel's phone booths, spilling their secrets as a waltz wheezes faintly in the background. Characters speak over one another, and we hear singing as well, or let's call it a musi-

cal buzzing. It's "Rigoletto" with words.

We overhear; we see through walls. In Boston, Mr. Tune staged a scene (straight out of the novel) in which the Baron irritates his low-life Chauffeur by dressing in front of him, from the nude up. This was too voyeuristic — and it took too long for Baron David Carroll to get into the underpinnings, outerlockings and accessories of a Weimar-era playboy.

But Mr. Tune boldly contrasts sexuality at its most exalted and most brutal in a dazzling visual that gives us four different scenes simultaneously. While the ballerina and Baron forge an ecstatic union in her

Martha Swope

Cast members on the set, from left, Rex D. Hays, John Wylie, Michael Jeter, Jane Krakowski, Charles Mandracchia, Liliane Montevecchi, Karen Akers, Timothy Jerome, David Carroll and Kathi Moss—"Grand Hotel" is so pictorially musical that production becomes inseparable from composition; Mr. Tune has reshuffled the elements of the old-style musical into state of the art.

bedroom, overhead, her companion catalogues her mistress's emotional needs. At stage right, in the hotel conference room, the businessman launches a seduction-rape of the secretary. At stage left, in the lobby, the ogreish hotel manager makes sexual overtures to an intimidated bellboy. At once, Mr. Tune gives us love in pure and corrupt forms, crucial aspects of the "life" we "see" in "Grand Hotel."

∎

Mr. Tune's one-size-fits-all visual can show us anything — the exhausted desperation of the kitchen help, the bullying of petty functionaries, even the morphine addiction of the narrator figure, a doctor who was horribly scarred in World War I and who — in the novel — had treated the wounded Baron, underlining Baum's and Mr. Tune's feeling that fabulous characters have collided to teach us what the world is like. "As It Should Be," the Baron's soaring theme song, directly clashes with the kitchen help's "Some Have, Some Have Not": la dolce vita versus The Grind. This is Mr. Tune's ballroom — the shabbiest angle on the most glamorous clime.

Buffs of the M-G-M version may want to imagine what headline performers might have filled out an all-star musical — Natalia Makarova as the ballerina, Sting as the Baron, Madonna as the secretary, Joel Grey as the bookkeeper, perhaps Michael Douglas as the businessman. Isn't "Grand Hotel" after all a necessarily all-star project because of the brilliant variety of its characters? But this prompts the unanswerable question: Who is the star, the principals' principal?

Mr. Tune was careful to let no single character arrest our attention, holding the show to one act on the ground that whichever of the five intertwined stories brought down the first-act curtain would be taken as the central story. Yet Vicki Baum saw the Baron as something like the big wheel, especially in the novel. A "dilettante amongst rogues," corrupt but irresolutely so, the Baron symbolizes beauty wrecked by war — and he is the sole principal to interact with all the other principals. Mr. Tune's cinematic montage emphasizes this, making the Baron a healing figure, Apollonian, an alchemist, strolling through the action to rejuvenate the weary ballerina, hearten the secretary, initiate the bookkeeper into the high life. People come, people go, but the Baron is permanent, less the hotel's guest than the genius of the place.

∎

Most of the audience probably navigate along with the bookkeeper, "the one," Mr. Tune notes, "whom we pull for. He shows his colors immediately — 'I'm dying and I want to live.'" He's the most sympathetic character, lonely, naïve and clumsy, looking for a little elegance in his last hours on earth — life as it should be. When, after making a killing in the stock market (at the Baron's direction), he throws off his dreary overcoat to reveal a superb tuxedo and step into Mr. Tune's high-concept Charleston, the audience immediately identifies with him. For a moment or so, the

show belongs to the bookkeeper Michael Jeter — especially when he suddenly cannot find his wallet, the embodiment of everything that he owns, the money that gives life. He is hysterical until the Baron returns it to him with a laugh. But the bookkeeper knows the Baron had stolen it — the Baron who had redeemed him, from a dead soul into a bon vivant. The bookkeeper has indeed seen life — not "As It Should Be," but as it is. Everyone is a fake, and all of that elegant coming and going is simply a struggle for money.

A dark show. But Mr. Tune lights it with his peculiar razzmatazz, "something of the old stuff, the show biz that I love" — as in the majestically scaled opening sequence, when the bitter Doctor inveighs against life's

---

'We need new shows,' says Tommy Tune. Without them, how can there be revivals years from now.

---

appalling vanities while the cast parades in splendor through the revolving door into the lobby. It's the vaudevillian's strut and the ironist's satire merged in a flash. "Old plus old equals new," Mr. Tune observes. But "Grand Hotel" is old material presented in an entirely new form. Historians dote on the "musical scene," 8 or 10 minutes of theater made of underscored dialogue, snatches of melody, and outright song — "Show Boat"'s "Make-Believe," "Carousel"'s "If I Loved You," or "West Side Story"'s "Tonight." "Grand Hotel" is like one great musical scene — but so pictorially musical that production becomes inseparable from composition. Mr. Tune has reshuffled the elements of the old-style musical into state-of-the-art.

∎

He had to: "We need new shows," he says. "We have to keep pushing forward, or there won't even be revivals years from now. There won't be anything."

Not everyone is comfortable in "Grand Hotel" and Mr. Tune wonders if the show's mixed reviews after the November opening have fined him for his ambitions. "If you shoot for a 10 and make an 8," he says, "they put you down. But if you aim for a 5 and hit a 5, they love you." "Grand Hotel" may be too fleet and tight for its own good; there is so much to take in that it spins past one even as it dazzles. Perhaps it is a two-visit musical, like "Cabaret," "Pacific Overtures," or "Dreamgirls" — shows which, because of compositional sophistication or textured staging, must be absorbed to be appreciated. That's art as it should be. ⊡

1990 F 25, II:5:1

Can a Dictator Tell Us Something About Ourselves?

BACK IN 1977, WHEN MISS MARgarida, the redoubtable schoolteacher, first strode onto a New York stage, it did not take the audience long to figure out that they were in the hands of a rather unusual tyrant.

Two minutes into "Miss Margarida's Way," the play by the Brazilian writer Roberto Athayde, the protagonist was already getting down to business: abusing the children in her eighth-grade class — that is, the spectators — idiots, she sneered, who had paid to enter and now could not leave. Claiming, as all despots do, to be acting for the good

---

Despite democracy's recent inroads, a Brazilian allegory speaks to all tyrants, great and small.

---

of her defenseless charges, Miss Margarida let it be known that she would tolerate no disobedience, not a breath of independent thought.

The self-control she was preaching to her "children," however, clearly did not apply to her own words or body: two hours of sadistic, hysterical rantings followed, punctuated by profanity, threats of violence and, above all, outbursts of suppressed sexuality. Her lessons were fixated on domination and death: biology ("all of you are going to die"), mathematics ("to divide means that each one of you wants to get more than the others"), history ("everyone wants to be Miss Margarida"), composition (the assignment is "a creative paper describing your own funeral").

As elsewhere around the world, the New York audience embraced the play: besides giving affluent theatergoers a chance to safely experience what it means to live under the frenzied eye and mouth of a schizophrenic autocrat, "Miss Margarida's Way" was darkly, forebodingly hilarious. One month after it opened at the Public Theater, with Estelle Parsons in the title role, it moved to Broadway for a longer run.

Thirteen years later, when Big Sister — played by the same acclaimed actress — stomped back into town for a revival, scheduled to be performed at the Helen Hayes Theater at least through today, she faced a dramatically changed world.

∎

In 1977 — a particularly dismal year — the spectators could identify Miss Margarida with a vast variety of favorite dictatorships, starting with Mr. Athayde's Brazil, or the sad neighboring countries of Argentina, Uruguay, Bolivia, Paraguay or my own Chile. Other United States client dictators abounded: Somoza, the Shah, Duvalier, Marcos and omnipresent generals in Guatemala and South Korea. In the rival camp, one could cast an eye on a genocidal Pol Pot or the beloved leader Kim Il-Sung, or, in Eastern Europe, the gray Brezhnev lookalikes, patriarchal Miss Margaridas, imposing their bureaucratic socialism.

Most of these authoritarian figures have now happily departed from our midst. The most recent and extraordinary changes have, most certainly, been in the Soviet bloc — indeed, Elena Ceausescu's last words at her trial could almost have been lifted verbatim from one of Miss Margarida's monomaniacal monologues. But no less drastic improvements, even if hardly noticed by the media, have been transpiring in Brazil and Chile where the first free presidential elections in many years were held last December.

The question, of course, given these auspicious global developments toward democracy, is whether the play has not aged irrevocably or, as most of the New York critics seem to feel, is politically irrelevant. Can Miss Margarida's ravings continue to inspire and, yes, "instruct" us?

An easy, preliminary answer is that there are plenty of power-starved oppressors still around — in China, in Haiti, in South Africa, in Albania, just to touch on four parts of the world. And those who have been ousted can't wait to get back into the limelight, determining the limits of possible reform by their mere presence; just look at the Philippines or, again, Chile, where the murderous General Pinochet, having lost two successive elections, still intends to remain as Army Commander in Chief in a watchdog capacity for the next eight years. So the play could well symbolize the all too numerous candidates ready to reincarnate Miss Margarida's ghost if offered the slightest provocation. And there is bound to be disorder in the coming years if people in such lands seriously believe that their destiny is now really in their own hands.

This first answer, though true, only validates the theatrical experience "Miss Margarida" provides insofar as it may or may not illuminate dictatorships that are comfortably far away. But it ignores what is most important about the play: that it is a subtle allegorical inquiry into the deepest everyday roots of contemporary domination everywhere, what makes people seek power over others, why those others accept and obey.

■

The metaphorical strength of "Miss Margarida's Way" is paradoxically due to the savage military government that ruled Brazil in 1971, the year the play was written. Barely 21 years old at the time, Roberto Athayde was forced to confront a dilemma that so many other playwrights have faced when they try to write under a dictatorship: how to reach the audience with a political message and not be swallowed up by the very violence they are denouncing. On the one hand are the official demands and pressures for silence, complicity,

frivolous entertainment; on the other, the hunger of local audiences to find onstage a hint of the freedom to think and feel that is absent and forbidden in their lives.

Torn between the fear of being repressed and the fear of being irrelevant, many playwrights — such as Mr. Athayde's compatriot, Augusto Boal — go into exile. Those who stay can choose between scribbling hidden ferocious words which can be produced, if at all, abroad (the case for the last 20 years of the Czechoslovak

An inquiry into what makes people seek power over others and why those others accept and obey.

Vaclav Havel — that is, before he became the president of his country), or they can adopt Roberto Athayde's solution: investigate life under the ubiquitous boot using the wondrous weapon of allegory, roguishly alluding and eluding, hoping the play is indirect enough to keep the secret police away and transparent enough so the public will recognize the connections.

Roberto Athayde was wrong about the police but right about the public. When his play was finally produced in Rio de Janeiro, in early September 1973, the audience quickly — and nervously — understood that the dictatorship itself was on trial. Unfortunately, so did the dictatorship. A few

days after the play opened in a bravura performance by Brazil's most famous actress, Marilia Pera (United States audiences may remember her in "Pixote," the Hector Babenco film), the authorities in Brasilia, acting on complaints from the wives of several generals, banned it. A public scandal ensued and a week later Miss Margarida was back on the boards (and at the blackboard) — though many of the obscenities had been excised along with an unmistakable reference by the crazed schoolteacher to the fact that the students she had sent to the Principal's office "never came back" — in other words, were tortured and executed.

■

Not only did Mr. Athayde manage to finally circumvent the censors, but the very censorship that forced him to hide immediate references and invent a surreal, wild representation of mad power was precisely what afforded the work its universal thrust and allowed it to outlive the dictatorial circumstances that had given it birth. Audiences all over the world saw and may continue to see in Miss Margarida an echo of a darkness that lurks inside their own lives and their own societies, no matter how apparently democratic.

The classroom where Miss Margarida, oozing good intentions, cajoles, threatens, browbeats, belittles, seduces, is meant to multiply an infinite phalanx of replicant Margaridas, tiny dictators in whom crouch and grow tomorrow's petty smiling ravens of power. Miss Margarida's school is not a peculiarly Brazilian institution but one of many contemporary channels for churning out child and country abusers, robotic accomplices of villainy, the conformists who are the backbone of all anti-democratic movements, scared of being different, scared of bucking the system, scared of their values being called into question by people of other races, other sexual preferences, other political options, other social classes.

■

Mr. Athayde knows, as do I and so many other writers who have endured the corrosive everyday invasion of a dictatorship, that imperial longings require obedient people to carry out whims and atrocities — and that the terror of our century would not have been possible if children had not been formed — as adults continue to be formed everywhere — by a grinding, almost invisible, chorus of coercion that disguises itself as self-righteous virtue.

And yet, the play does not show the power of dictatorship to be total. It foretells the demise and vulnerability of tyrants, large and small, their incapacity to stamp out every external and internal flicker of rebellion. In a way, Roberto Athayde does to Miss Margarida what she most fears — and secretly seems to desire: he leaves her exposed in all her nakedness to the audience. As she covers her victims with abuse, she simultaneously and inadvertently strips herself for them. To repress others she has had to repress herself — and what shines through her insensate ramblings is an overwhelming need of company and sex and tenderness,

The New York Times/Jim Wilson

Estelle Parsons as the dictatorial teacher in the revival of "Miss Margarida's Way"—coercion disguised as virtue

the realization that she has lost the magical possibility of using language as a way of freeing people instead of controlling them.

We find ourselves, amazingly, beginning to feel sorry for her. And yet, a word of warning. Before pitying the miserable life she has made for herself, grieving for someone who can only see her own solitary image reflected back in the mirror of other faces, I would suggest that we first make sure we are well rid of the monstrous Miss Margarida. And rid of the Principal, of course. □

1990 F 25, II:5:1

Angel-Hair Pastiche

A SPINNING TALE, book and lyrics, C. E. Kemeny and A. Kemeny; directed by Jack Ross and C. E. Kemeny; music and orchestrations, C. E. Kemeny; choreography, Sally O'Shea; set design, Mariner James Pezza; lighting design, Kevin Connaughton; costumes, Sandora Associates. Presented by Mr. Pezza. At Playhouse 91, 316 East 91st Street.

Melinda	Karen Bianchini
The Elf	Marianne Monroe
Sidney	George Lombardo
King Maximillian	Robert Puleo
Queen Regina	Sherrylee Dickinson
Prince Rupert	Eric Ellisen
Page; Musette	Ruth Lauricella
Ralph	David L. Jackins
Henry	Sean Lawless
Yvette	Sally O'Shea

By STEPHEN HOLDEN

"A Spinning Tale," a new musical at Playhouse 91, announces itself in its press release as "targeted for an adult audience but guaranteed to entertain children." In reality it is targeted for a children's audience and not guaranteed to entertain adults.

As children's entertainment goes, at least, the show, based loosely on the fairy tale "Rumpelstiltskin," is slightly better than average. And in the age of the junk bond and the corporate raider, its cartoonish depiction of greed and deal making in the realm of children's fantasy has an obvious pertinence.

•

Set in the enchanted land of Bim, "A Spinning Tale" tells the story of Sidney (George Lombardo), a mendacious miller who lies his way into a job working for King Maximillian (Robert Puleo), an eccentric, partially deaf monarch, and his avaricious wife, Regina. When the miller casually boasts that his daughter Melinda (Karen Bianchini) can spin straw into gold, she is imprisoned and ordered to come up with the goods immediately.

Through the magical intervention of a chirpy elf (Marianne Monroe), she comes through, and is bethrothed to the royal couple's son, Prince Rupert (Eric Ellisen). But when Melinda is ordered to produce a second shipment, the sprite, whom Miss Monroe plays as a squeaky replica of Sandy Duncan's Peter Pan, makes Melinda promise to hand over her first-born child.

•

The show, which was created by C. E. Kemeny and A. Kemeny, is mugged in a broad children's style by an uneven cast that performs with gusto. The most consistent stage caricature belongs to Mr. Puleo as the perpetually twitching, henpecked king.

The songs in "A Spinning Tale," as in so many for children, seem unnecessarily larded into the story and tend to slow it down. And the music, arranged for three instruments including a cheesy-sounding synthesizer, is strictly formula fare ranging in style from light pop-rock to diluted Gilbert and Sullivan.

1990 F 25, 57:1

Dribbling and Bashing

BOVVER BOYS, by Willy Holtzman; directed by John Pynchon Holms; set design, Philipp Jung; lighting design, Mary Louise Geiger; costume designer, Ellen McCartney; sound design, Tom Gould; stage combat, Jake Turner; associate producer, Herbert H. O'Dell; general manager, Gordon Farrell. Presented by Primary Stages Company, Casey Childs, artistic director; Janet Reed, associate artistic director. At the 45th Street Theater, 354 West 45th Street.

Allie	Jack Gwaltney
Jack	John Plumpis
Gene	Robert Kerbeck
Joyce	Leigh Dillon
John	Keith Langsdale
Ennis	Holt McCallany
Chick	Michael Lewis
Christine	Calista Flockhart

By D. J. R. BRUCKNER

People up front at the 45th Street Theater during performances of Willy Holtzman's "Bovver Boys" must wonder when they will get a soccer ball or a foot in their faces as five of the eight characters kick and butt a ball around a raked stage that ends almost in the laps of front-row patrons. But their anxiety might be a blessing in this case.

"Bovver" is a Cockney word for a rumble, and Mr. Holtzman's theme is that any attempt to improve the lives of people can be dangerous to them in a society where mayhem is the shared culture.

The play is set in 1970, when an American conscientious objector to the Vietnam War turns up as a social worker at a community center in the Scottish city of Dundee. Mr. Holtzman has explored the ways of what used to be called the underclass in several plays, and this setup is a natural.

The teen-age skinheads who hang around the community center have no understanding of or sympathy with pacifism, even if its devotee is a Quaker, and this American Quaker's efforts to improve the morals of these youths is often dangerously wrongheaded. Two older workers at the center utter dire warnings about the consequences, but he persists and in the end an innocent victim suffers as a result of his efforts.

•

But none of the conflicts in the play, not even the beating and rape of a 15-year-old girl, become really dramatic. Characters kick the soccer ball around, dribble a basketball, knock one another down, dance, roll on the floor. But the play is all talk, a kind of back-alley Socratic discussion. And while the seven actors playing Scots manage to hold their accents without a slip, it would take more than a Scots burr and a bit of local dialect to make these limp words fly.

The actors work hard to bring the characters to life, especially Calista Flockhart as the girlfriend of one of the boys, Jack Gwaltney as the leader of a gang, Holt McCallany as his rival, and Robert Kerbeck as the American. And John Pynchon Holms, always an energetic director, keeps everything bouncing. The ballgames and fights serve his purposes; unfortunately, he also sends the characters in and out through the aisle, occasionally speaking behind the backs of half the audience.

Mr. Holtzman has staged works in progress before. In this case one suspects that if he went back to work, dropped all the clichés and tired jokes (including one about a biting dog lifted from a Peter Sellers Pink Panther movie) and let his characters begin to act out their frustrations, suspicions and passions, the ideas he is toying with here might take dramatic form.

After all, his key characters are young gangsters who fear nothing but their own tender feelings; a girl who, subjected to appalling violence, is tougher than any of them, and a stranger who professes he is a Quaker but admits that the war he fled frightened him into dodging the draft. The possibilities are so tantalizing that one leaves "Bovver Boys" really annoyed. That feeling could be a kind of tribute to the playwright.

1990 F 25, 57:3

The Enhancements Of Reduction

Martha Swope Associates/William Gibson

Mike Burstyn

THE ROTHSCHILDS, based on Frederic Morton's biography; music by Jerry Bock; lyrics by Sheldon Harnick; book by Sherman Yellen; directed by Lonny Price; music director, Grant Sturiale; choreographer, Michael Arnold; set designer, E. David Cosier Jr.; costumes, Gail Brassard; lighting, Betsy Adams; assistant musical director, Connie Meng; production stage manager, Rachel S. Levine; assistant director, Daisy Prince; associate artistic director, Mr. Price. Presented by the American Jewish Theater, Stanley Brechner, artistic director. At the Susan Bloch Theater, 307 West 26th Street.

WITH: Mike Burstyn, Leslie Ellis, Sue Anne Gershenson, David Cantor, Evan Ferrante, Joel Malina, Nick Corley, Allen Fitzpatrick, Judith Thiergaard, Bob Cuccioli, Ted Forlow, Ray Wills, Hal Goldberg, Etan and Josh Ofrane and Adam Paul Plotch.

By STEPHEN HOLDEN

There may be no surer test of the sturdiness of a vintage Broadway musical than to be subjected to the kind of spare revival that the American Jewish Theater has given to the 1970 Jerry Bock-Sheldon Harnick show, "The Rothschilds."

Directed by Lonny Price at the tiny, modestly appointed Susan Bloch Theater, the production places the actors practically on top of the audience. Performed with no sets to speak of and with a single piano providing the musical accompaniment, the story of the international banking clan that rose from Frankfurt's ghetto to become a powerful force in European politics emerges toughened and sharpened in tone.

Because it was so overshadowed by "Fiddler on the Roof," "The Rothschilds," which was Bock and Harnick's seventh and last collaboration, has been generally regarded as a tamer sequel to the phenomenally successful show of 1964. If the score of "The Rothschilds" is not so memorable as that of "Fiddler," the effervescent 19th-century folk lilt of its music and Mr. Harnick's acute, colloquial lyrics still give the story a strong narrative push, and Sherman Yellen's libretto is a model of concision and clarity.

On Broadway, where it ran for 505 performances, "The Rothschilds" was a colorful historical pageant that told an uplifting true story of Jewish

Oppression and self-assertion in 'The Rothschilds.'

emancipation. Seen in intimate close-up with the glitz pared away, the pageantry is subsumed into the show's exploration of family psychology, ethnic self-assertion and the politics of oppression. Though "The Rothschilds" still has its homey, sentimental side, its most powerful moments are its confrontations between the irresistible force of the Rothschilds' will to succeed and the disdainful, self-regarding European aristocrats for whom the oppressed Jews are convenient scapegoats.

The fuse lighting the production is the riveting performance of Mike Burstyn as Mayer Rothschild, the enterprising family patriarch who builds a rare-coin collection into a financial empire. Assuming a role originally played by Hal Linden, Mr. Burstyn creates a huge, vibrant portrait of a relentlessly determined salesman, deal maker and empire builder who seems at moments almost consumed by his own unquenchable self-confidence.

Mr. Burstyn's performance doesn't soften the character's demonic edge. Conducting business, he flashes obsequious crocodile smiles, and you can almost feel the gears whir behind his glinting eyes as he calculates his odds. The show's most dramatic scenes are Mayer's do-or-die battles of will with Prince William of Hesse at the beginning of the show and with Austria's Prince Metternich near the end.

Allen Fitzpatrick, who plays both characters, makes a formidable adversary to Mr. Burstyn's Mayer. Responding with no acts to wheedling in an icy drill-instructor's bark, he exudes an arrogance so implacable that Mayer seems warm and vulnerable by comparison. Among the generally strong supporting performances is Bob Cuccioli as Nathan Rothschild. In the role of a son who becomes the family's English emissary during the Napoleonic wars, Mr. Cuccioli really does seem like a chip off the old block — vengeful, avid and righteous all at once.

•

The revival is in some ways comparable to the York Theater's triumphant production last year of "Sweeney Todd," that production proved that a show with strong dramatic content could not only survive, but also be enhanced when presented as an intimate chamber work with good actors.

Though "The Rothschilds" lacks the tragic dimensions of "Sweeney Todd," it is a solid piece of work. Mr. Price, who made his acting debut 17 years ago as one of the sons in a national touring production of the musical, obviously knows the show inside and out and has a deep affection for its characters, warts and all. In putting the audience face to face with the Rothschilds in their living room and presenting them as something like a Jewish European version of the Kennedys, he has revived the show with an exhilarating dash.

1990 F 26, C16:1

Soldiers Who Never Die

A MAN'S A MAN, by Bertolt Brecht; English version by Eric Bentley; music composed by Arnold Black; directed by Robert Hupp; set by George Xenos; lighting by Craig Smith; costumes by Jonathan Bixby; musical direction by Ellen Mandel; choreography by Nicole Fosse. Presented by the Jean Cocteau Repertory, Mr. Hupp, artistic director; David Fishelson, managing director. At 330 Bowery, at Second Street.

Galy Gay	Joseph Menino
Mrs. Gay	Angela Vitale
Uriah Shelley	Christopher Oden
Jesse Mahoney	Carol Dearman
Polly Baker	Robert Ierardi
Jeraiah Jip	James Sterling
Charles Fairchild	Craig Smith
Mr. Wang	Harris Berlinsky
His Sexton	Grant Neale
Widow Leocadia Begbick	Elise Stone
Jobia	Lyn Wright
Jenny	Ellen Mandel

By WILBORN HAMPTON

Galy Gay is an Irish-born waterfront porter in Kilkoa, India, who goes out one day to buy a fish for his dinner and ends up commanding a machine-gun unit in the Imperial Army on the Tibetan front.

Galy's metamorphosis provides the fodder for Bertolt Brecht's cannonades against the militaristic dehumanization of the individual in "A Man's a Man," which is being given an enthusiastic revival by the Jean Cocteau Repertory.

The story, such as it is, involves the recruitment, or shanghaiing, of Galy by three soldiers for their own devious and complicated purposes. But then, plot was never one of Brecht's overriding concerns. "A Man's a Man," as the original "Mann Ist Mann" is entitled in Eric Bentley's accessible translation, marks the beginning of Brecht's expressionist work, and it discourses on the dual nature in each of us and whether anyone can ever know who he really is, "whether he will look into the casket and recognize himself." It is early Brecht, written just before "The Threepenny Opera," as the playwright was developing his concept of epic theater.

For Brecht, the total theatrical effect on an audience was more important than any personal identification its members might find. He sought to challenge an audience, but not to involve them directly in the play. Brecht himself drew up a chart to explain the difference between the more familiar "dramatic" theater, as exemplified by Stanislavsky, and his own epic theater. The dramatic theater, Brecht wrote, "involves the spectator in an action and ... allows him feelings," whereas the epic theater "makes the spectator an observer but ... demands decisions." In order to achieve this "distancing," as he called it, of the audience, Brecht used such devices as songs that comment on the play and placards that describe scenes or the context of the action.

In the Cocteau staging, the director, Robert Hupp, cleverly uses a large television screen above the stage on which tapes of the actors delivering asides to the audience are shown and announcements of scene changes are flashed. In an opening sequence, for example, Harris Berlinsky appears as a recruiting officer delivering a spiel inviting the audience to enlist in the lobby after the play and promising them that as soldiers they'll never die. "The others will die," he says, "but you won't."

The Cocteau production also has some delightful songs composed by Arnold Black and set, very loosely, to Kipling's "Barrack Room Ballads." Ellen Mandel, playing synthesizer and drums, keeps the audience's feet tapping as the cast sings such ditties as "Oh, it's Bill, Bill, Bill/And it's kill, kill, kill," or the bouncy title song ("It's all right, Dan/For a man's a man"), when Brecht's dialectics tend to veer toward tedium.

There are some insightful observations in this Brechtian fable, but it rambles a bit aimlessly in spots and is mostly of interest as a forerunner, albeit an engaging one, of Brecht's later masterpieces. Mr. Hupp's cast brings a lot of energy onstage, and if the idiosyncratic humor of the play is not always fully captured, it is as much the fault of the elephantine vehicle as of those who ride it.

Joseph Menino catches the spirit of Galy Gay, a simple man who cannot say no and who mostly "just wants his name kept out of it." By the end, Galy is "a man who has forgotten who he is," and Mr. Menino's transformation is gradual, seamless and credible. Craig Smith is viciously comic as Sgt. Charles (Bloody Five) Fairchild, a man torn between his urges to kill and to copulate, especially in the monsoon season. Elise Stone gives a solid performance as Widow Begbick, the knowing and strong canteen owner who is a prototype of later Brechtian heroines like Mother Courage and the Good Woman of Szechuan. And Lyn Wright, who always brightens a stage, is pert and sassy as her daughter Jobia.

1990 F 26, C15:4

Will Money Talk?

Bert Andrews

Adam Wade

BURNER'S FROLIC, by Charles Fuller; directed by Douglas Turner Ward; sound, Eric King; costumes, Judy Dearing; lighting, Sylvester A. Weaver Jr.; production stage manager, Ed DeShae; production supervisor, Lisa L. Watson; company manager, Lauren P. Yates. Presented by the Negro Ensemble Company, Mr. Ward, artistic director and president; Susan Watson Turner, general manager. At Theater Four, 424 West 55th Street.

Burner	Adam Wade
Albert Tunes	Ed Wheeler
Ralph Buford	Charles Weldon
Rev. Quash	Graham Brown
Tiche	Sandra Nutt
Miss Charlotte	Cynthia Bond
Mabel Buford	Iris Little
Wade Harris	O. L. Duke
Jim Paine	Samuel L. Jackson
Kimble	William Mooney
Aunt Becky	Peggy Alston
Reed	Wayne Elbert
Vaughn	William Jay
Tommy	Leonard Thomas
Jasper	Mitchell Marchand
Curtis	Gregory Glenn

By MEL GUSSOW

With "Burner's Frolic," the fourth in Charles Fuller's continuing cycle of plays about black Americans in the second half of the 19th century, one has a clearer picture of the playwright's ambitious intention. Through a series of episodes, seemingly tangential in the sweep of American history, the playwright is scrutinizing the economic entrapment of people forced to weigh their pragmatic needs against their desire for complete emancipation and integration. From all four plays, it is also evident that neither Mr. Fuller nor his director, Douglas Turner Ward, has given them the necessary time and care to allow them to speak to their greatest advantage.

In the case of "Burner's Frolic," which opened yesterday at the Negro Ensemble Company, it is 10 years after the Civil War and black citizens in a small Virginia community have risen professionally. Former slaves are now barbers, undertakers and contractors, but they are still severely restricted in their social as well as their business opportunities.

> Emancipation wasn't the same thing as freedom.

•

Each is offered $100 if he will vote for a white man — the owner of a bar — who is running for local office. Led by Burner (Adam Wade), a black businessman and himself a candidate for the same office, a few of the men believe that "a vote is worth more than money." After presenting that argument, the playwright marks time. In common with the three plays that preceded it (in a little more than one year's time), "Burner's Frolic" is schematic. It is less a fully realized play than an intriguing idea awaiting elaboration. Though there are some overlapping characters, each work stands on its own outside of the cycle.

The earlier efforts were as episodic as movie scenarios. "Burner's Frolic" at least has a focus, a single sustained incident, in this case, a backyard party or "frolic" given by the title character in order to win the political support of his friends. During the party, there are flashbacks as well as an ominous nearby gathering of white outsiders waiting to intrude on the festivities.

In the flashbacks, we see the white candidate (William Mooney) campaigning for votes. He tries to convince blacks that he is their only hope for economic betterment, an extremely dubious notion that he encourages through his offer of money. What should emerge from these scenes is a sense of the disparity of the characters and their motivations — the kind of feeling that Mr. Fuller evoked in the interrogation scenes in his "Soldier's Play." Instead one is left with the conclusion that the characters are indistinct and in one instance self-contradictory.

Too much of the play's relatively brief duration is allotted to petty family squabbles involving Burner and his wife. The various female characters remain largely passive personalities, surprising considering the fact that in "Jonquil," the Fuller play that preceded this one, the women were awakened to the necessity of concerted action.

Perhaps the most potentially interesting character is a black soldier (O. L. Duke) who fought in the Union Army and was honored for bravery. Though shellshocked, he has moments of lucidity. Still wearing his uniform, he is a lingering symbol of the war's devastation and the futility of peacetime promises. One regrets that as a character, he is relegated to the sidelines.

Despite Mr. Wade's stalwart performance, Burner himself remains a pallid figure, in contrast, for example, to Prince Logan, the Union soldier who is the protagonist of the first two plays in the cycle and who remains through the other plays an almost reverential, although unseen presence.

In his production, Mr. Ward has been unable to instill tension into the play (even with that offstage threat of violence from opposing whites), but there is a certain smoothness in the transitions from present to past. Given the limitations of the text, performances are effective, with the most forceful contributions from Mr. Wade, Mr. Duke, Iris Little and Sandra Nutt as Burner's wife, who enlivens the frolic with her singing.

Mr. Fuller's cycle (grouped under the title "We") still holds the audience's attention, but none of the plays, with the possible exception of "Jonquil," have had the requisite dramatic intensity. At the same time, the cycle has not evinced a cumulative power that illuminates the playwright's very serious concern with the effects of history on individuals eager to seize control of their own destiny.

1990 F 26, C14:1

A Scoundrel You Hate to Love

MERRILY WE ROLL ALONG, music and lyrics by Stephen Sondheim; book by George Furth; from the play by George S. Kaufman and Moss Hart; directed by Douglas C. Wager; choreography by Marcia Milgrom Dodge; musical direction by Jeffrey Saver; orchestrations by Jonathan Tunick; settings by Douglas Stein; costumes by Ann Hould-Ward; lighting by Allen Lee Hughes; projections by Wendall K. Harrington; dramaturge, Laurence Maslon; sound by Susan R. White; technical director, David M. Glenn; stage manager, Martha Knight. Presented by Arena Stage, Zelda Fichandler, producing director; Mr. Wager, associate producing director; Guy Bergquist, associate producer. In Washington.

Franklin Shepard	Victor Garber
Charley Kringas	David Garrison
Mary Flynn	Becky Ann Baker
Gussie Carnegie	Mary Gordon Murray
Beth Spencer	Marin Mazzie
Joe Josephson	Richard Bauer
Meg	Deanna Wells
Scotty and Maître d'	Tom Hewitt
Terry	Ruth Williamson
Tyler	Erick Devine
Jerome	Rufus Bonds Jr.
K. T. Lewis	Melodee Savage
Dory	Dorothy Yanes
Ruben and Photographer	Thom Sesma
Bunker, TV reporter and Mr. Spencer	John Deyle
TV reporter, Mrs. Spencer and First Auditioner	Ruth Williamson
Frank Jr.	George Alexander
Little Frank	Leo Charles

By FRANK RICH

Special to The New York Times

WASHINGTON, Feb. 25 — At the end of "Merrily We Roll Along," three young people of 1957, all with dreams of theatrical or literary glory, stand on a roof in New York City to spot Sputnik, a repository of their high hopes, as it streaks across a starry sky. Nine years after its failure on Broadway, "Merrily" continues to follow its own alluring, elusive trajectory through the musical theater.

In various revised versions, this Stephen Sondheim-George Furth adaptation of the 1934 play by George S. Kaufman and Moss Hart has been sighted at small companies from Los Angeles to London in recent seasons. Each production raises the hopes of partisans that a resurrected "Merrily" will soon redeem their faith in the show by splashing down triumphantly in New York.

Arena Stage's rendition of the musical at its proscenium house, the Kreeger Theater, is the closest the reworked "Merrily" has gotten to Broadway — geographically, at least. One hopes the authors will not let up now. As it stands in Washington, the much improved "Merrily" still falls short of its exceptional score, whose haunting melodies and dramatic ingenuity were preserved by RCA in a posthumous Broadway-cast recording that has spread the musical's potential to a large audience that never saw the 1981 debacle. While part of the disappointment of the Arena "Merrily" can be attributed to Douglas C. Wager's prosaic production, that is not the whole problem. There's still some work for Mr. Sondheim and Mr. Furth to do.

•

Many of the major flaws of the 1981 "Merrily," starting with its notorious gymnasium setting, have long since been jettisoned or rectified in intervening versions produced in La Jolla, Calif., and in Seattle. It is no longer difficult to follow the show's inverted time scheme, which follows three old friends in reverse chronology, from the pinnacle of jaded show-biz success in 1980 back through their climb to fame and disillusionment during the two decades before. The original production's confusing framing device, a high-school graduation, has been dropped (though a new and counterproductive prologue has been added). Most important, the characters in "Merrily" are now played by adults who appear to get younger as the evening progresses. In 1981, Harold Prince cast too many teen-agers who looked silly impersonating worldly grown-ups.

In Washington, the most crucial role, that of the composer Franklin Shepard, has been given to Victor Garber. It's not an enviable assignment. Franklin has always been the most problematic figure in "Merrily"; he is one of the most unsympathetic leading men in a musical since "Pal Joey." A successful Hollywood film producer when introduced in Act I, he is in every way portrayed as a scoundrel. The audience rapidly learns that Franklin abandoned his musical talent to make schlock movies, that he betrayed two wives, that his closest friend and his son no longer speak to him. Mr. Furth and Mr. Sondheim then ask the audience to spend the next two hours caring about how and why this privileged, callous sellout went wrong.

Mr. Garber is a terrific choice for Franklin, not only because he is a first-rate comic actor who can sing but also because he is so appealing: he always projects intelligence and honesty. If anyone could keep an audience intrigued by Franklin, however expedient his choices in love and art, it is this performer. Mr. Garber's inability to do so in Act I of the Arena's "Merrily" should be a clear indication to the musical's creators that something is still amiss in their conception of the role.

The trouble with Franklin, Mr. Garber's performance makes clear, is not that he is a heel but that he is a passive, clichéd heel until "Merrily" is an hour old. People keep saying terrible things about him at Hollywood parties, and Mr. Garber, lacking a big scene or song of his own for too long, is left to stand around looking battered and forlorn. He doesn't have anything to act. Instead of the drama of character, Mr. Furth provides the noise of melodramatic events: hyperbolic fisticuffs, not intimate moments of anguish or passion, punctuate both of the long Hollywood scenes that establish Franklin.

Nor does Mr. Sondheim come to those scenes' rescue. Act I's early ensemble number, "That Frank," like the 1981 song it replaces ("Rich and Happy"), has Hollywood cynics describe Franklin's spiritual collapse without often letting the man speak for himself. Since the protagonist doesn't fully reveal his own feelings (or even his voice) at the start, it's impossible for the audience to be engaged by his predicament. While it would be disingenuous to soften Franklin's emptiness, is there any reason why he must be so remote?

Joan Marcus
Victor Garber in the Arena Stage's production of "Merrily We Roll Along."

Once "Merrily" has rolled back into Franklin's more animated past, the score and much of the book catch up with its ambitions. But Mr. Wager's production often lags behind. The emotional apex of Act I, "Franklin Shepard Inc.," in which Franklin's collaborator and best friend, the playwright Charley Kringas, tells him off on a television talk show, is muted by David Garrison's low-key, naturalistic delivery of the song's hysterical emotions. Becky Ann Baker's promising performance as Mary Flynn, the platonic (and underwritten) woman in both men's lives, isn't as touching as it should be in lonely laments like "Old Friends/Like It Was" and the reprise of "Not a Day Goes By."

For all its typical Sondheim patina of regret, however, "Merrily We Roll Along" is not Chekhov. While Mr. Wager's production has bright sets (by Douglas Stein) and a Michael Bennett touch or two (choral phalanxes from "Company," a bridge from "Dreamgirls"), it sags under the burdens of a muffled band and ponderous pacing. Act II opens with a new Sondheim gag — the song "Good Thing Going" is expanded into a mock Broadway turn of 1964, a double parody of "Hello, Dolly!" and "Funny Girl" — yet Mr. Wager and his choreographer, Marcia Milgrom Dodge, ask only that its able singer, Mary Gordon Murray, plod through it upstage.

"It's our time, coming through" Franklin and Charley sing later, as they stand on the New York rooftop of 1957, their futures still spread out before them as infinitely as the night sky above. The time is surely coming for "Merrily," too, but, like the ambitious composer and playwright onstage, Mr. Sondheim and Mr. Furth should not be in too much of a hurry while deciding what that future will be.

1990 F 27, C13:1

With Music, President Harding

CAPITOL CAKEWALK, music by Terry Waldo; lyrics by Lou Carter; book by Elmer Kline with Perry Arthur Kroeger; directed by Tom O'Horgan; set design, Mr. Kroeger; costumes, Kathryn Wagner; lighting, Howard Thies; production stage manager, Michael Schaefer; production stage manager, Christophe Pierre; choreography by Wesley Fata. Presented by AMAS Musical Theater, Rosetta LeNoire, founder and artistic director; Jeffrey Solis, managing director. At the Dimson Theater, 108 East 15th Street.

WITH: Adrian Bailey, Minnette Coleman, Philip Gilmore, Sharon Hope, Kimberly Jones, Jack Landron, Miron Lockett, Yoko Matsumura, Aaron Mendelson, Leonard Parker, Jeffery Smith, Marc D. Summers, Jack Waddell and Tena Wilson.

By STEPHEN HOLDEN

It is 1924, and the Harlem Renaissance Theater Company is deep into the final rehearsals of a ragtime musical about the life and times of President Warren G. Harding.

Based on the memories of Alma, a White House maid during the Harding Administration, the show portrays the 29th President as a credulous pawn of his Ohio political cronies and a man who lives by the axiom that what you don't know won't hurt you.

His longtime affair with Nan Britton, whom he meets and makes a pass at while she is still a minor, is presented as a continuing bedroom farce. Rumors of Harding's being of mixed blood are offered as fact, since Alma claims to be directly related to the President through their black great-grandmother.

It is the ingenious conceit of "Capitol Cakewalk," which the AMAS Musical Theater is presenting in this rag-time musical biography a show within a play that has a parallel plot. During breaks in the rehearsal, Big Jim Moses (Adrian Bailey), the theater owner who also portrays Harding, is hoodwinked into secretly selling out his company to bootleggers who want to turn the theater into a speakeasy.

"Capitol Cakewalk," which has a book by Elmer Kline and Perry Arthur Kroeger, lyrics by Lou Carter and music by Terry Waldo, is one of the season's more ambitiously conceived shows and one that along with its clever plot intricacies hints at all kinds of contemporary overtones.

In Mr. Bailey's portrayal, President Harding is an amiable mannequin who fails to grasp the implications of his refusal to mind a store run by his greedy friends. And his motto of a return to normalcy is like the misty-eyed American nostalgia that President Ronald Reagan continually invoked during his eight years in office. If the implications of the black theater company of 1924 claiming the conservative President Harding as one of its own resound with interesting paradoxes, they remain unexplored.

"Capitol Cakewalk," which is energetically directed by Tom O'Horgan, is a stronger show in theory than when seen on the stage. In trying to cover 25 years of Harding's life, it gets bogged down in historical detail. The play that frames the musical is little more than a shell. And the transitions between the two are abrupt and a bit confusing.

Mr. O'Horgan has tried to animate a relatively straightforward musical biography with a vaudevillian zaniness that gives the show a high-spirited zing without pushing things too far toward minstrel-show caricature. Wesley Fata's choreography efficiently arranges the ensemble into chorus lines and production numbers in which the cast plays peekaboo from the corners from Mr. Kroeger's whimsically cartoonish sets. And Mr. Waldo's period tunes maintain a consistent level of craft.

The performances, by a cast that is predominantly black, are robust, both vocally and dramatically. Mr. Bailey imbues his dual roles, especially that of Harding, with a serpentine tongue-in-cheek suavity. Tena Wilson's Nan is an amusingly sassy brat. And Jack Waddell, as Harry Daugherty, Harding's corrupt Attorney General, has a splendidly distinctive bass-baritone voice.

Despite its considerable strengths, "Capitol Cakewalk" is finally not very compelling. The concept of a show with a play, though clever in itself, fails to mesh the parallel stories in a way so that they illuminate each other or make a strong social statement. Far too gentle to work as satire, the show keeps its tongue so firmly in its cheek that one never really knows where its heart lies.

1990 Mr 2, C31:1

An Overture To Chekhov

UNCLE VANYA, by Anton Chekhov; translated by Michael Frayn; conceived and directed by R. Jeffrey Cohen; set by Alexis Siroc; lighting by Michael Gutkin; costumes by Karen Perry; original music by Kevin Scott; technical director, John Harmon and Henry Freeman; stage manager, Katie Davis. Presented by the RAPP Arts Center, Mr. Cohen and Alexis S. Cohen, artistic directors. At 220 East Fourth Street.

By WILBORN HAMPTON

A pervasive pastime for leading playwrights on both sides of the Atlantic these days seems to be rendering new translations of the works of Anton Chekhov. David Mamet and Lanford Wilson have both written American renditions of individual plays and in England, Michael Frayn is translating the entire Chekhov canon.

Mr. Frayn's version of "Uncle Vanya," which enjoyed a fine production in London under Michael Blakemore's direction, with Michael Gambon and Jonathan Pryce as Vanya and Astrov, has been used as the text for a staging by the RAPP Theater Company.

A disquieting credit listing in the RAPP program calls "Uncle Vanya" a "work in progress" and states that the production was "conceived" and directed by R. Jeffrey Cohen. Just what this portends is soon clear. Before a line is spoken in the RAPP production, even before Nanny offers Astrov a cup of tea, a woman in an evening gown walks onstage and lipsyncs a few bars of Mozart's "Exsultate, Jubilate." Why? Your guess is as good as mine.

At the time of its premiere at the Moscow Art Theater, "Uncle Vanya" had indeed been what would today be called a work in progress. Chekhov rewrote the play several times over a period of nearly 10 years, transforming it from an early action-filled melodrama called "The Wood Demon" into the moody, poignant masterpiece that is "Uncle Vanya." But "progress" on this particular work pretty well stopped with its publication in 1897.

Unfortunately, there is little poignancy onstage at the RAPP Theater, and the predominant mood is one of burlesque. A program note further expands on the RAPP director's concept of the play. "Why is Vanya given the title honors of this play?" Mr. Cohen asks, and goes on to suggest that the character is "the family jokester ... gregarious, loud, sometimes obnoxious."

With this view in mind, the RAPP cast takes on Chekhov as though it were a soap opera. Or perhaps the actors have mistaken his admirable translation of "Uncle Vanya" for one of Mr. Frayn's farces. There is a great deal of exaggerated mugging, lustful lurching, bumbling drunkenness and animated gesticulating. When actors continually flail their arms about as if they were "it" in a game of blind man's buff, it is usually a sure sign they are groping for any identity they can find for their characters.

John Bakos has one touching moment as Vanya — in the sad monologue in which he admits his disillusionment with the professor. In that speech, Mr. Bakos catches a hint of the quiet despair in the role, but for the rest of it, he plays Vanya pretty much as the coarse, boorish buffoon that Mr. Cohen describes in his notes. Charls Hall's Astrov is something of a pouting dilettante who doesn't seem to know the difference between a conifer and a birch. As for the mood of this Russian country life, there is a samovar in the first scene, but no one seems to know how it works.

1990 Mr 3, 12:5

Many Shoes to Fill For a Simple Soldier

Martha Holmes

Jenny Robertson and Dennis Parlato in "Violent Peace."

VIOLENT PEACE, by Lavonne Mueller; directed by Bryna Wortman; set design by James Noone; lighting by Victor En Yu Tan; costumes by Mimi Maxmen; sound by Bruce Ellman; production stage manager, Linda Carol Young. Presented by the Women's Project and Productions, Julia Miles, artistic director. At the Apple Corps Theater, 336 West 20th Street.

Kim Denton	Jenny Robertson
Mark Feeny	Dennis Parlato

By MEL GUSSOW

In her plays, "Warriors From a Long Childhood" and "Five in the Killing Zone," Lavonne Mueller wrote with effortless authenticity about men in battle. In "Violent Peace," the third play in her war trilogy, she writes about a man and a woman locked in a lifelong relationship that is part love, part siege. Both characters — a general's daughter and her father's adjutant — are permanently wedded to the military. They are a family within a family.

Ms. Mueller writes with authority about the strictures and rituals and the emotional dress code of Army life. Her two characters are keenly observed and the dialogue has a visceral quality that overcomes occasional moments of artificiality. At the same time, the play, a production of the Women's Project (at the Apple Corps Theater), has unresolved dramatic problems, beginning with a central premise that is unusual to the point of being bizarre.

With the early death of her mother, the general's daughter, Kim, has been placed in the care of the adjutant (Dennis Parlato). Though totally unprepared for the role, the soldier has nurtured the girl (Jenny Robertson) from infancy to adulthood. He has been her mother and father as well as her protector.

•

In the absence of the girl's autocratic four-star father, who has been away fighting wars, Kim has become completely dependent on the young officer, an attachment that eventually leads to a romance. For both characters, the affair is a kind of incest. As we meet the two of them, after a period of separation and on the day of the general's funeral, Kim is forcing the officer to spend a long night with her in order to come to terms with their past.

Having established the conflict, the playwright unwisely intersperses the narrative with brief flashbacks as far back as when Kim was 3 years old. Accompanied by a shift in lighting, the actors play their characters at an earlier age. Although Ms. Robertson does well enough mimicking a child, the interludes are awkward, especially one that takes place in a war zone during an outbreak of violence. The scenes should have been unnecessary. Information offered in them could have come in the body of the play itself, and, in fact, some of it does.

Through the eyes of the characters in the present, we feel both the "violent peace" between them and their shared fidelity to the military. The officer worships the general despite the fact that he has treated him as a servant, and Kim is infatuated with the military milieu. As she recalls, when she was a child she put her father's brass on her snowsuit and pretended to be a general.

As a high-ranking Army brat, she has also been quick to take advantage of the perks of her father's office, beginning with the officer assigned to her. Despite what we learn about the officer's small-town background and his own insecurity over not being a West Point graduate, it stretches credibility to accept that he would have acceded to all the demands of the general and his daughter. Furthermore, the asides about warfare in Central America seem diversionary.

Except for those flashbacks, Ms. Mueller has instilled her play with tension, and it is additionally strengthened by the performances under the direction of Bryna Wortman With his crisp Class A uniform and manners, Mr. Parlato is the essential good soldier, even to doing a quick set of pushups. He also conveys the concerned side of his character, managing to be maternal without becoming unmanly.

Ms. Robertson, who made an impression as a sexy baseball fan in "Bull Durham," has an appealing combination of gaucherie and sophistication. It is as if the character were a child who had learned to play the role of an adult. Alternately cajoling and taunting the officer, she gives a performance that, along with that of her co-star, goes a long way toward anchoring a play with a questionable foundation.

1990 Mr 3, 12:3

Generation Gap

DIVIDENDS, by Gary Richards; directed by Tony Giordano; set design, Ray Recht; costume design, Barbara Bush; lighting design, Jeremy Kumin; incidental music, Elliot Finkel; sound design, Gary and Timmy Harris; production stage manager, D. C. Rosenberg; paintings by Robert Kalaidjian. Presented by Jewish Repertory Theater, Ran Avni, artistic director; Edward M. Cohen, associate director. At 344 East 14th Street.

Neal	James Rutigliano
Bessie	Reizl Bozyk
Bernie	Fyvush Finkel

By RICHARD F. SHEPARD

Bernie, the grandpa, is slowly dying but will survive the play. Bessie, the grandma, is quickly cooking and fussing and will survive grandpa. Neal, the grandson, a modern young man, and you know what *that* adds up to, has decided to immerse himself in the life of his grandparents and even to get grandpa the bar mitzvah ceremony he missed out on when he turned 13.

These are the elements of "Dividends," a new comedy awash in sentimentality that is now at the Jewish Repertory. Gary Richards has written the sort of play one wishes he had only worked on more. Why did grandpa freeze at his tryout with the Dodgers, a moment that shattered his dream and launched him into a career in dry cleaning? Why does Neal, the grandson, say he has trouble establishing a relationship with the old man, who in very short order seems less formidably standoffish than when he first appears? Why do none of the characters refer in any substantial way to the missing generation, the parents of the boy?

T.L. Boston

James Rutigliano, left, and Fyvush Finkel in "Dividends."

For all this, the schmaltz of "Dividends" achieves high-cholesterol level. The author gives us bright lines, funny lines, and he has a sense of human relationships; one may squirm only at such mawkish peaks as the final speech — which grandpa makes at his bar mitzvah — laden with philosophies better said more tightly. But how could anything be bad that puts on stage Reizl Bozyk, the warm and humorous veteran of Yiddish stage who movie audiences will remember from "Crossing Delancy." She putters around the stage avoiding bathos and lightening the evening with her sympathetic stream of chatter spiced with Yiddish. With a simper and a smile, Miss Bozyk does what pages of script cannot.

Fyvush Finkel (the dying grandpa), who played the waiter in the recent revival of "Cafe Crown," puts some of Mr. Richards's lines to best use, in the way of a cranky Lower East Sider. Why wasn't he bar mitzvahed at 13?: "We were too busy being poor." It takes a lifetime of living and performing to get full measure from a line like that, and Mr. Finkel has the proper credentials for the job.

•

Miss Bozyk and Mr. Finkel make an attractive couple, and in several flashback scenes they even make you believe they are coy teen-agers.

Their grandson is played by James Rutigliano. He has no easy job playing an earnest youth, an artist without confidence, a young man who seems to go out only with non-Jewish girls, but he has an engaging personality that quite nicely sees him through as narrator and as a principal performer.

As a play, "Dividends" does not make a big sound, but there is no denying that it touches a chord.

1990 Mr 4, 51:1

Light Blotted Out

WOYZECK, by Georg Büchner; translated by Henry J. Schmidt; directed by Richard Foreman; set design by Mr. Foreman; costume design, Lindsay Davis; lighting design, Heather Carson; dramaturg, Greg Leaming; production stage manager, Ruth E. Sternberg; associate set designer, Nancy Winters; assistant stage manager, Barbara Reo. Presented by Hartford Stage, Mark Lamos, artistic director; David Hawkanson, managing director. In Hartford.

Woyzeck	David Patrick Kelly
Doctor	Michael J. Hume
Andres	Miguel Perez
Marie	Gordana Rashovich
Margret	Tracey Ellis
Karl the Idiot	Brian Delate
Drum Major	William Verderber
Sergeant	Peter Drew Marshall
Carnival Announcer	Daniel Ahearn
Captain	Kenneth Gray
Apprentice	Steven Stahl
Pawnbroker	Edward Seamon
Woyzeck's Son	Hayden Reed Sakow
Children	Hannah Bent and Debbie Jarett

By MEL GUSSOW

Special to The New York Times

HARTFORD, March 1 — Though "Woyzeck" was written in the 1830's, it is a seminal play of the 20th century, the first to articulate the alienation of modern man driven to madness by forces far beyond his control. In a sequence of cumulative scenes, Büchner's play — based on a true story — follows the downward path of a barber who murders his mistress and suffers tragic consequences.

T. Charles Erickson

Michael J. Hume, right, examining David Patrick Kelly in "Woyzeck."

After Büchner came Kafka, Brecht, Camus and Beckett. In fragments, "Woyzeck" survived the playwright's death (at the age of 23) and has become a text to tantalize the imagination — a challenge to which Richard Foreman has responded. In his production at Hartford Stage, Mr. Foreman has unlocked a masterwork through the seemingly simple process of allowing the play to speak for itself. Running barely more than one hour, this is a stark embodiment of the original Büchner.

While staging plays of his own authorship, Mr. Foreman embellishes the text with directorial detail, with ear-piercing buzzers and hot lights. With "Woyzeck," in direct contrast, he has been scrupulous about stressing the play, not the direction or the design (both of which are in fact to his credit). He has stripped the stage of all possible excess, and he has intruded no diversionary notes. Craning one's neck, a theatergoer can see, high overhead, Mr. Foreman's signature — string as long as a trapeze — but the director does not call it into action, and the audience is transfixed by what occurs onstage.

•

The setting is bleak and powerfully evocative, as barren as the exterior of a concentration camp (though without barbed wire). Around the stage runs a wooden track, and in the center is a raised floor padded like a cell. Entering the theater, one hears a throbbing heartbeat of a sound collage.

This could be Woyzeck's pulse as he is held in thrall by events around him, by what the doctor in the play diagnoses as an aberratio mentalis partialis, obsession with a general rational condition. Despite appearances, what happens is irrational. Beyond the fact of Woyzeck's momentary jealousy, there is no moral or even psychological explanation for

his killing of his common-law wife, Marie, but in the context of Büchner's play it is unavoidable. As the author said in a letter to his parents, unconsciously revealing the theme of a play yet to be written, "It lies in no one's power not to become an idiot or a criminal ... because the circumstances lie outside ourselves."

There is something childlike about David Patrick Kelly's Woyzeck, as he converses with his friend Andres, as he moves through his daily drudgeries and as he tries to verbalize his inward feelings of imminent dread. At a distance, watching Marie's seductive behavior with the drum major (in this production, the drum major strides like a majestic lion), he is silent to the point of seeming abstracted. But everything that happens has a direct effect on him. As Woyzeck says, "Everyone is an abyss," and then, proving his point, he plunges on his vertiginous journey.

Again and again, one feels the character's foreboding as in the following exchange with Marie: "We have to go." "Where to?" "How do I know?" Like characters out of Beckett, the two are trapped in a continuum. They have no control of their future or even of their velocity. The carnival scene, barely indicated in the text, is like a brief flash of disequilibrium from the film "The Cabinet of Dr. Caligari."

•

The murder is as vicious as anything in "Macbeth" but the murderer is also his own victim. Having been carried away by his aberrant act, he falls into a daze. He is remorseless but confused, covering the body with a cloth and pretending the death did not take place. Instantly, Woyzeck reminds one of contemporary killers who keep murder within the family. Then, looking down at Marie, Woyzeck asks, "Why is that red thread around your neck?" — a thread that has of course stained his own hands. The play (in Henry J. Schmidt's

translation) resonates with such imagery, up to the moon, which is described as being so red that it is like "a bloody blade."

•

Instead of trying to visualize these images, Mr. Foreman counterpoints the words with the blacks and grays on stage, a landscape of the seemingly mundane and definitively impoverished. Woyzeck is as hapless a creature as one could imagine. Marie and their son are the only brightness in his dreary life, which makes the homicide even more horrendous.

Mr. Kelly's performance as the lonely Woyzeck is the linchpin of the production, with trenchant support from Gordana Rashovich (as Marie who, like Woyzeck, lacks will but not desire), Michael J. Hume (as the self-parodying doctor), William Verderber and Miguel Perez, among others. All of the actors are unified under Mr. Foreman's direction, as the play rushes pell-mell to its foregone, no less chilling conclusion.

1990 Mr 6, C17:1

Reality and Illusion

ACID PARADISE, conceived and directed by Angel Gil Orrios; dramaturgy, Arcadio Ruiz-Castellano and Mr. Gil; sound and lighting, Angel Rivera; graphic design, Deca Graphics. Presented by Instituto Arte Teatral Internacional Inc. At Cuando House, 9 Second Avenue, at First Street.

Jose	Sam Valle
Pedro	Alfredo Ynneco
Leonora	Linda Samantha Fantasia
Cristina	Virginia Cortez
Michele	Soledad Lopez
Hector	Arcadio Ruiz-Castellano
Maria	Eileen Vega
Priest	Sergio Carvajal
Dr. Gomez and Pepe el Cojo	Blas A. Lopez
Domingo	Miguel Brignoni

By JENNIFER DUNNING

"Acid Paradise" tells a familiar story of a likable young man gone wrong in the world of drugs. But the story is given the vivid and committed treatment of good street theater in a production presented by the Instituto Arte Teatral Internacional on Sunday afternoon at the atmospheric little theater of Cuando House, where it will be performed again today and tomorrow at 8 in English and on Saturday at 8 and Sunday at 4 in Spanish.

Conceived and directed by Angel Gil Orrios, "Acid Paradise" is based on improvisations done by cast members in a theater workshop last year. Its cast includes drug addicts and professionally trained actors. And it has the rough and simple ring of truth.

The production makes imaginative use of a few props, among them white netting that figures in the play's powerful sudden ending. Moved by the actors during blackouts between scenes, the props suggest a disco, the interior of a flashy car, two run-down apartments, a church, a drug clinic, a meeting hall and the street where Pedro dies alone of an overdose.

•

The play's anti-drug message is delivered unsentimentally in broad but effective strokes. A natty young drug dealer named Jose, played by Sam Valle, encounters Pedro, a friend, and talks him into selling drugs. Soon Pedro is taking drugs as well, to the consternation of his family and his pretty girlfriend, played by Eileen Vega, who doubles as a clinic nurse. But they cannot save him.

There are standout performances by the incandescent Alfredo Ynneco as Pedro, Virginia Cortez as Pedro's worried but amusingly canny mother, and Blas A. Lopez, a former social worker, as a reformed addict and a clinic doctor with a yen for fast-food chicken and rice. Arcadio Ruiz-Castellano is poignant as a handsome former addict with AIDS.

The fine cast was completed by Linda Samantha Fantasia as Jose's plump, gravely stoic surrogate mother, Sergio Carvajal as a concerned young priest, Miguel Brignoni as a gentle former addict and Soledad Lopez as a gum-chomping dealer. The company also includes Jose Manuel Cotto and Larry Ramos, who perform in the English version, and Mr. Gil, Sasha Jimenez and Santi Suaviro. Angel Rivera designed the lighting.

•

"Acid Paradise" moves to Casa de España (308 East 39th Street) for performances on March 16 at 8 in English and on March 18 at 6 in Spanish.

1990 Mr 8, C24:1

Unlikely Journey

BY AND FOR HAVEL, directed by Vasek Simek; sets by Ed Morrill; costumes by Iris Bazan; lighting and sound by Marc D. Malamud. Presented by Eric Krebs, in association with Raft Theater. At the John Houseman Theater, 450 West 42d Street.

AUDIENCE, by Vaclav Havel.
Brew Master .... Kevin O'Connor
Vanek .... Lou Brockway

CATASTROPHE (FOR VACLAV HAVEL), by Samuel Beckett.
Protagonist .... Lou Brockway
Assistant Director .... Evelyn Tuths
Director .... Kevin O'Connor

By MEL GUSSOW

The two short plays presented under the title "By and for Havel" depict Vaclav Havel in two dehumanizing guises. The first play, "Audience," written by the Czechoslovak playwright and drawn from his life, is an ironic comedy about a dissident writer forced to work as a laborer. The second, "Catastrophe," dedicated to Mr. Havel by Samuel Beckett, is a highly symbolic homage to the author's martyrdom.

Individually, these plays — both seen in New York in 1983 in different productions — are striking works of political theater. They would seem to be the most natural complements to each other, and so they might be in a production other than the one staged by Vasek Simek at the John Houseman Studio Theater. The production performs a double disservice to its authors.

In both halves of the evening, Mr. Simek manages to avert the starkness and the specificity of a playwright's vision. "Audience," which Mr. Simek and his actors previously presented in Prague, becomes a broad — almost a burlesque — comedy, missing the sardonic overtones. "Catastrophe" is mortally wounded by directorial miscalculations and by a stroke of miscasting in the central, silent role.

"Audience" is one of a cycle of plays by Mr. Havel about his alter ego, a writer named Vanek who has been robbed of his freedom, but does not lose his sense of equilibrium. Vanek is a realist as well as a humanist. He sees everything in perspective, as if somewhere in his imagination he knows that all deprivation will eventually pass.

In the play, Vanek is lifting beer barrels in a brewery until the brew master offers him an easier office job if he will perform the simple service of spying on himself. The paradoxical proposal is stupefying, or, one might say, Havelian.

Kevin O'Connor conveys the brew master's bluff, bogus conviviality as he plies his visitor with beer and drinks himself into a stupor, but Lou Brockway's Vanek is a study in blandness. As a result, there is scant sense of the cat-and-mouse game. In Mr. Simek's staging, the play is vulgarized into an extended sketch about a boorish brew master and a reluctant menial.

There is far more in this play than the director allows the audience to experience, beginning with Vanek's suppressed outrage. He is not sullenly discontent, as is the case with Mr. Brockway. What is lost is the character's emotionally charged sense of self-containment. There is nothing that can be done to him that will rob him of his inner dignity.

For his production, Mr. Simek uses an uncredited translation, without the clever wordplay of Vera Blackwell's version used in the original New York production. "Audience" also gains by being performed in tandem with the other Vanek plays, as the audience sees a progression of people reacting to the character's incipient martyrdom.

Martyrdom moves to center stage in "Catastrophe." As Alan Schneider demonstrated in his original New York production, the play is a haunting evocation of the blind power of totalitarianism and of the ennoblement of the individual spirit. Mr. Simek's production is shallow in comparison.

In the play, a character identified as the Director, helped by his Assistant, is preparing to put a martyr on public display as a sacrificial image in the cause of an oppressive state. The Protagonist is unveiled on stage, but in this inhospitable studio theater there is little attempt to approximate a proscenium. That fact alone unmoors the play in an open, brightly lighted space.

Most damaging, the staging misses the fearfulness and the black humor of the play. The Director should be a supreme bureaucrat. His every word should ring with officiousness, with that icy sense that he will allow for no deviation from his prepared ritual. Mr. O'Connor conveys the demanding but not the menacing side of the character.

Despite severe disappointment with this production, one leaves the theater contemplating Mr. Havel. It is astonishing that in less than a year he has gone from confinement, as harrowingly pictured in "Audience" and "Catastrophe," to the Presidency of his nation.

1990 Mr 9, C3:5

Rage, Envy And Seduction

GOING TO NEW ENGLAND, by Ana Maria Simo; directed by Maria Irene Fornes; stage manager, Abigail Koreto; set and costumes, Ms. Fornes; lighting, Stephen Quandt; production manager, Peter J. Davis; general manager, Michael Palma. Presented by Intar Hispanic American Arts Center, Max Ferra, artisitic director; Eva Brune, acting executive director. At 508 West 53d Street.

Tati .... Elizabeth Clemens
Delia .... Divina Cook
Willy .... Rene Rivera
Manolito .... Martin Treat

By STEPHEN HOLDEN

Erotic passion run amok is one of the hardest things to portray on the stage without its seeming either tinnily melodramatic or unintentionally funny. If the Intar Stage 2's production of Ana Maria Simo's heavy-breathing drama, "Going to New England," has moments that seem both shrill and silly, her play still deserves credit for trying to go below the surface of soap opera histrionics to get at the primal emotions that erupt when sexual feelings go out of control.

The story, told in blackout scenes, follows the clandestine but all-too-apparent affair that Delia (Divina Cook), a 40-ish Hispanic housewife, conducts with Willy (Rene Rivera), a 28-year-old laborer and colleague of her husband, Manolito (Martin Treat). Enraged over the deception but also enflamed and envious, Delia's teen-age daughter, Tati (Elizabeth Clemens), seduces the reluctant Willy and becomes pregnant by him. Manolito alternates between complaining of imaginary persecutions and issuing accusations and murderous threats. In the play's most disturbing scene he rails wildly to Tati about hogs who eat their own excrement and untwists a coat hanger, pleading with her to let him demonstrate how she can abort herself.

•

If the production, directed by Maria Irene Fornes, had performances that followed the playwright into the story's seething heart, it might work on the stage as a searing vignette of desire under the elms (or in this case, palm trees) and its tragic outcome. But the performances don't mesh.

Mr. Treat's betrayed husband is a bug-eyed madman who delivers all his lines through clenched teeth while casting crazed-ax-murderer glances. As Delia, Ms. Cook seems more maternal than smoldering. And Mr. Rivera's Willy doesn't exude hot-bloodedness so much as hang-dog victimization.

But even though the production does not sufficiently clarify the individual relationships, it succeeds as a study in physical and emotional claustrophobia. The situation is portrayed as a closed system in which the traditions of Latin American machismo, the family structure and Roman Catholic values reinforce erotic taboos, which, when broken, require unavoidable and violent responses from those who are betrayed.

•

The dim, drab little rooms through which the characters move have the feel of tropical prison cells in which no fresh air ever blows and in which it is almost impossible to enjoy any real privacy. Staring out of his window, Willy coos wistfully at the pigeons who are not trapped by the grim, humorless web of passion in which he finds himself snared.

The tone of the whole production implies that the individuals are not to blame. Given the misery of their existence, a little illicit passion is the only relief they can expect. Even if it kills them, it's better than nothing.

1990 Mr 9, C18:1

An Inner Voice That Speaks Aloud

TINY DIMES, written and directed by Peter Mattei; lighting, Brian Aldous; costumes, Mary Myers; assistant director, Allison McElwain. Presented by Cucaracha Theater, Richard Caliban, artistic director; Janet Paparazzo, producing director. At 429 Greenwich Street.

Neil .... Joey L. Golden
Jane .... Lauren Hamilton
David .... Hugh Palmer
Sara .... Elizabeth Thompson
Richard .... Damian Young
Voice .... Brennan Murphy

By MEL GUSSOW

Challenge, response and then another challenge — Peter Mattei's "Tiny Dimes" is a boardroom-style battle for supremacy, conducted by two married couples and an executive who may or may not all be involved in the same business, what is referred to as "the firm."

Despite all the smart chatter about various transactions being "a virtual certainty" and "a done deal," nothing is readily apparent in this inchoate play at the Cucaracha Theater, least of all what the author is trying to say — in a very elliptical manner and at far too great a length.

With an unsettled mixture of menace and casualness, the two couples sit at a conference table and try to stare — and to talk — one another down. They compare demographics, argue and insinuate, throw things on the floor and push each other around in their chairs.

•

Adding to their own as well as the audience's confusion, they occasionally address one another by the wrong names. The most distinct characters are Jane (Lauren Hamilton), who is exceedingly nervous and has an inner voice that speaks aloud, and David (Hugh Palmer). Prowling the huge warehouse space that is the stage of this experimental downtown

An executive pontificates while pacing.

theater company, Mr. Palmer acts every inch the arrogant executive.

He is both conscience and guide, repeatedly pontificating with information "picked up at the colloquium," while striding to his own tune. His incessant perambulation becomes a counterpoint to the dialogue and seems to be the most dramatic part of the evening. The actors are affable, with the exception of Mr. Palmer, who is, as intended, threatening.

The play has sporadically amusing moments of absurdism, as when one woman says she has forgotten the word for window. Then she remembers it: window. Other times, "Tiny Dimes," written and directed by Mr. Mattei, is static as well as uncommunicative.

1990 Mr 9, C18:1

Stopping Crime (Except for Murder)

CAHOOTS, by Rick Johnston; directed by David Taylor; set by Scott Bradley; lighting by Malcolm Sturchio; costumes by Susan Young; stage manager, Jessica Murrow;

sound design by J. Bloomrosen. Presented by G. G. Productions, the Lerner Rechnitz Group and S. D. K. Productions. At the South Street Theater, 424 West 42d Street.

Jan .... Kathryn Meisle
Lois .... Katherine Leask
Al .... Malachy Cleary
Ken .... James DeMarse
Grant .... John Hickey

By WILBORN HAMPTON

Jan and Ken are a typical New York couple living in a typical East Side apartment with a typical view from the terrace of some steel girders on a construction site. "You've been Trumped," Jan's friend Lois observes later. There are also the typical five locks on the front door.

At the outset of "Cahoots," Rick Johnston's slight but diverting comedy with murder at the South Street Theater, a not-so-typical burglar is breaking into the apartment though the sliding terrace door with a Bloomingdale's charge card. The burglar is no sooner inside, however, than Jan (Kathryn Meisle) and Lois (Katherine Leask) return home to

Gerry Goodstein
James DeMarse and Kathryn Meisle playing a New York couple in a scene from "Cahoots," a comedy by Rick Johnston at the South Street Theater.

prepare dinner for their husbands before the four of them go to a Crime Stoppers block-association meeting.

As it soon turns out, the burglar is none other than Al (Malachy Cleary), Lois's husband, and his unorthodox arrival was meant only as a demonstration of the unexpected dangers of living in a city where crime is rampant. That Al, who also has a newly bought gun in the pocket of his raincoat, may be one of those dangers is not given serious consideration. Al has a lot of other things in the pockets of his dirty, tattered coat (dress defensively, he urges), but it would be giving away too much to list them.

•

By the time Ken (James DeMarse) arrives home, it is established that while Jan and Lois are best friends from way back, Ken and Al share a mutual detestation society. Suffice it to say that when the four sit down to dinner, only three will survive the meal.

Mr. Johnston has worked hard at providing witty, urbane banter for his four main characters that is as contemporary as today's headlines. Jan, for example, is an actress who has just come from an audition for a commercial for a new chain of McDonald's in Czechoslovakia. And Lois, a mass-market book editor, is working on a project to translate Judith Krantz into Polish.

The playwright has also tossed in a bit of New York place name-dropping, like a reference to a restaurant with a "Cross Bronx Expressway décor" and Al's Crime Stopper lecture, "How to Stay Alive on the A

Train." While some of this chatter is mildly amusing, it mostly sounds forced and serves little to further either characterization or plot.

Mr. Johnston is better at plot. The zeal with which he piles on the requisite number of twists also requires acceptance of some fairly implausible coincidences, starting with how Al got out on the terrace in the first place. These little surprises continue right up to the end, though after a certain amount of traffic on the terrace they become somewhat predictable.

But if, as one character observes, "life is not a detective novel," then neither is a comic murder play real life. And if one can accept the behavior of Mr. Johnston's characters in

the first act, the second act provides a payoff. The scene in which the three survivors, now forced into cahoots with one another, greet a security guard (John Hickey) from the building across the street is quite funny.

David Taylor has directed a fine cast in which there is not a weak part. All five actors provide an example of expertly timed ensemble playing and seem to have a lot of fun doing it. Mr. Taylor keeps the action and the bons mots moving at a lively pace that flags only briefly in one or two spots. Scott Bradley's smart, user-friendly set could be a model apartment for a new East Side high-rise.

1990 Mr 10, 16:4

Ah, Those Americans Abroad, So Crassly Pursuing Culture

By FRANK RICH

"I think this is the Pizza Hut where he wrote 'Troilus and Cressida,'" said my theater-fanatic friend during a pre-matinee stroll in Stratford-on-Avon, England, a few summers ago. We had already passed the McDonald's where, we imagined, Shakespeare had written "Twelfth Night." (Or was it "As You Like It" at Burger King?) As we later wolfed down curry just in time to make the curtain at the Royal Shakespeare Company's evening performance of "The Merchant of Venice," we concluded that we had finally found a Stratford restaurant the Bard might have missed. Neither of us could recall a single mention of mango chutney in the banquet scene of "Macbeth."

Such fond memories of being a culturally high-minded American abroad are inevitably revived by "Some Americans Abroad," Richard Nelson's very funny comedy at the Mitzi E. Newhouse Theater about Yankee tourists on an obsessive-compulsive playgoing tour of England. One of Mr. Nelson's scenes, in fact, is set in the Stratford Pizza Hut. By then, his characters are overdosing on the classics — "I think two Shakespeares in one day is asking for trouble," says an exasperated faculty wife, Kate Burton — and they can no longer recall the names of the plays they have seen ("Les Miz" always excepted).

It's Mr. Nelson's despairing point that these tourists, college professors and students on a tight budget, don't

remember the content of the plays either. They are culture vultures who devour everything and digest nothing. The somewhat overheated plot of "Some Americans Abroad" pushes the characters into ethical and sexual conflicts that classic theater, or perhaps even "Les Liaisons Dangereuses" or the latest faculty common-room comedy by Simon Gray, might help illuminate. But to these consumers of literature, plays are valuable only as trophies for one-upmanship at sherry-sipping department socials or as springboards for publishable theses that grease the tenure track. The sole character in "Some Americans Abroad" with a clear conscience and an ability to act decisively in the arena of life — a rebellious student, incandescently played by Elisabeth Shue — is the one who goes AWOL during the plays to romp with a new boyfriend.

Taken to its depressing extreme, Mr. Nelson's play is a sequel to "The Innocents Abroad," Mark Twain's caustic view of pretentious Americans abroad in the last century: both works indict the well-educated American middle class for its supine and superficial relationship to Old World culture in general. Mr. Nelson's characters are particularly marked by a late-20th-century affliction, the "Masterpiece Theater" syndrome: they find it easier to worship all things British than to investigate the intellectual life of their own immediate surroundings.

Not once in "Some Americans Abroad" does any character refer to a play seen back home or to any American writer (except, of course, the expatriate Henry James, an honorary Briton). One feels that these theaterlovers would only go to theater in New York to see a visiting English troupe, just as they favor any book that has been published in

It's an odd thing about theaters. They're all full of ghosts.

paperback by Penguin and purchased on Charing Cross Road. When the time comes for the Anglophilic academics of "Some Americans Abroad" to return to the United States, they gather together on the Westminster Bridge to sing "God Save the Queen."

Home-Grown History

But the British theater doesn't have a monopoly on history. The American theater has a past, too. Even if Mr. Nelson's characters knew that past existed, however, they would probably turn up their noses at it. It's a relatively short past, and, prior to World War I and Eugene O'Neill, a not infrequently trashy one. Pre-modern American theater history usually has more to do with show people (impresarios, actors, actor-managers) than with great native dramatists and enduring plays. Since showmen were more inclined to erect palaces to celebrate their own egos than to build a permanent dramatic literature for the general good, the legacy of American theatrical pioneers can be ephemeral. The productions and performances languish in specialized

Brigette Lacombe
In a scene from "Some Americans Abroad," from left, are Kate Burton, Bob Balaban, Colin Stinton and Frances Conroy.

history books; the theaters have often vanished. American theatergoers don't have a quaint historical theater shrine like Stratford to visit. They have what remains of Times Square.

That being so, why not make the most of it? A new and eccentric theatrical event on the gaudiest and bawdiest block of West 42d Street, the En Garde Arts production of Mac Wellman's play "Crowbar," attempts to do exactly that. It offers an intimate guided tour of a bona fide corner of the American theatrical past. Without waiting for the cloudy Times Square redevelopment scheme to fall into place, En Garde, an itinerant company specializing in site-specific performances, has gone ahead and liberated the oldest surviving theater on the street: the Victory, which was built in 1900 by Oscar Hammerstein as the Theater Republic and was soon leased to David Belasco, who lent the theater his own name for seven years until he built another theater, the beautiful Belasco that now sits mostly dark on West 44th Street.

The Swan or the Globe the Victory is not. Christened with its current name in a quixotic burst of patriotism during World War II, the house has been a home to pornographic movies in recent years. The auditorium has been cleaned up, not renovated, for the limited engagement of "Crowbar." There are holes in the partitions in the men's room. The audience sits on the stage, shrouded by the musty wing and fly space. Though plaster cherubs still ring the domed ceiling, they seem to float in a miasma of mold-colored decay. As imaginatively directed by Richard Caliban, the cast seems to float, too, performing Mr. Wellman's play throughout the house, from the dim second balcony with its red exit signs to the faded boxes to the creepy no man's land beneath the stage's trap doors.

The idea of "Crowbar" is exciting. The play's action unfolds during the intermission of the theater's first attraction, James A. Hearn's "Sag Harbor," which a well-heeled matron in its audience describes as being about the "humble lives" of "simple fisher folk." Mr. Wellman's characters are ghosts — those of the playhouse and those of ordinary New Yorkers whose obituaries were culled from the same September 1900 newspapers that reported on the opening of "Sag Harbor." It's too bad that the execution of this promising premise is often self-indulgent. While Mr. Wellman quotes Djuna Barnes and spins some pretty metaphors — the red-walled theater is like "the inside of a human heart, only bigger and not as empty" — his writing is too solipsistic to allow most of his characters to break loose from his voice and speak in their own.

Yet the theater itself is such a mesmerizing presence that it literally upstages "Crowbar." The evening opens with a slide show, set to spine-tingling music by David Van Tieghem, of photographs of the Victory in its salad days, when its accouterments included a Paradise Roof Garden with a miniature farm village of livestock, cottages, a barn, a pond and watermills. The photographic images bleed into all that follows, allowing the audience's imagination to run riot through the theater's past even as the characters are straitjacketed by tedious verbal arias in an arch contemporary mode. Patience is rewarded at play's end, when Belasco's ghost (Yusef Bulos) delivers a manifesto in favor of "good entertainment" and "good art" that reconnects "Crowbar" with the theater history that shares its stage.

"All theaters are haunted," goes a recurring line in the script. One wishes Mr. Wellman's play made more extravagant use of the many ghosts who haunt the Victory. Belasco's mistress, the actress Mrs. Leslie Carter, once occupied the impresario's studio apartment high above the stage. Blanche Bates performed at the Victory in Belasco's "Girl of the Golden West" — soon to inspire Puccini — and not long after that Mary Pickford and Cecil B. DeMille teamed up on "The Warrens of Virginia" before going Hollywood.

Later still, "Abie's Irish Rose," Broadway's most unexpectedly popular tearjerker, stayed five years at the theater, and, in the 1930's, Minsky's one and only burlesque arrived, trailed by frequent police raids. So haunted is this house that it seems instantly suitable, without the addition of scenery, for a staging of Jack Finney's time-travel novel of Old New York, "Time and Again," or for the Stephen Sondheim-James Goldman musical of a half-demolished, ghost-swept Ziegfeld palace, "Follies."

Spirits at the Kerr

A few blocks up from the Victory, on the marginally more demure 48th Street, stands another old theater that has been reclaimed: the Ritz, built in 1921, lost to radio and television from 1943 to 1970, and restored over the past year by Jujamcyn, the theater owners who will present August Wilson's new play, "The Piano Lesson," there next month. Last week the theater was officially opened with its new name, the Walter Kerr, before an audience that was dazzled by the renovation. Though the Kerr had the same architect, Herbert J. Krapp, as most other handsome Broadway theaters of its period, few, if any, of the others have been restored with such scrupulous fidelity to the original decorative details, from carpet-pattern to pressed-copper marquee.

When the time came for Walter Kerr to take the stage to speak on his namesake theater's opening night, he first paused to luxuriate in the full vista of the glowing house, with its grandiose murals and gold-leaf trim. Then he spoke in a low, awestruck voice that reflected the audience's wonder at finding itself in a time machine: "Welcome to 1921," he said. In the hushed few seconds that followed, you could feel the theater people in the crowd communing with the ghosts who walk the Kerr's boards: Alfred Lunt and Lynn Fontanne, Ina Claire, Katherine Cornell, Leslie Howard, Bette Davis.

Let Americans abroad worship the Elizabethans of Stratford and London. Americans at home can rendezvous with their own exotic theatrical past at the Victory and the Kerr. Either way, pilgrims can grab a bite at ye olde Pizza Hut.

1990 Mr 14, C13:4

Maternal Relations

A MOM'S LIFE, by Kathryn Grody; directed by Timothy Near; scenery by James Youmans; costumes by Holland Vose; lighting by Phil Monat; associate producer, Jason Steven Cohen. Presented by Joseph Papp. At the Susan Stein Shiva Theater of the Public Theater, 425 Lafayette Street.

WITH: Kathryn Grody

By STEPHEN HOLDEN

"How do I teach kids with everything a sense of longing? How do I teach them about kids who long for everything?" asks Kathryn Grody midway in her autobiographical one-woman play, "A Mom's Life." That is one of the more philosophical questions that punctuate a breathless 90-minute monologue evoking, in occasionally smothering detail, the joyous but harrying experience of bringing up two young boys on Manhattan's Upper West Side.

The raising of children, as most parents find out, entails becoming a child again oneself. And in "A Mom's Life," Ms. Grody acts the role not only of mother but of both sons, Isaac and Gideon, who ply her with demands, compete for her attention and wear her down to a loving frazzle.

•

One of the strengths of her performance is the way in which she shows how the lines between parent and child inevitably dissolve in the course of a typical day. In the show's headiest moment, she proudly demonstrates her recipe for bubbles — one-third cup glycerine, three cups water and one cup Joy — then dances about the stage at the Public Theater gleefully wafting soap bubbles through the air. Her performance is winning for its complete absence of narcissism. The actress seems completely comfortable as a homey and disheveled workaday housewife.

In its construction, the intermissionless play, directed by Timothy Near, is as messy as Ms. Grody's antic bubblefest. Consisting of two parts that seem squished together, it begins with the actress's droll reflections on the physical tolls of becoming a mother for the first time: lack of sleep, and bodily changes that make her feel like "those great white whales at Coney Island." Then it lurches forward to the arrival of her second son and follows the mother and two children through an exhausting 12-hour day.

Where another writer might try to organize a monologue about parenting into thematic blocks, Ms. Grody plunges us pell-mell into the minute-by-minute details of bringing up children, from getting them dressed in the morning, to going for an excursion in the park, to reading bedtime stories. Her deeper thoughts are offered as casual asides. The world she inhabits is one in which finding a last-minute sitter becomes a major task and substituting peanut butter for tuna fish in a lunchtime sandwich a matter of emotional urgency.

•

Of all the anxieties that Ms. Grody describes, the most insistent are her worries over safety. Everything from the wildness of the city (the family's apartment building is situated on a major crack corner) to the specter of food additives and pesticides assumes a sharper life-or-death immediacy when the future of one's children is at stake. And without becoming histrionic, she re-enacts the heart-stopping moment when a child impulsively dashes into the street.

The most pensive moments come near the end of the play, when Ms. Grody considers the primal emotions that bind parents and children through the generations. Her own parents died when she was 24, she says. And she still can't quite believe that her children will never meet their grandparents. "I can't bear the possibility that my sons will miss anyone the way I miss my mother and father," she confides.

For all its moments of anxiety, exasperation and sadness, "A Mom's Life" leaves no doubts about the rewards of motherhood. Thoroughly engaging but in no way revelatory, it is a virtual paean to the domestic life.

1990 Mr 15, C22:3

When the Princess Turns Into a Frog

PRELUDE TO A KISS, by Craig Lucas; directed by Norman René; sets by Loy Arcenas; costumes by Walker Hicklin; lighting by Debra J. Kletter; sound by Scott Lehrer; hair and wigs design by Bobby H. Grayson; production stage manager, M. A. Howard. Presented by Circle Repertory, Tanya Berezin, artistic director; Connie L. Alexis, managing director. At Circle Repertory, 99 Seventh Avenue South, at West Fourth Street.

Peter	Alec Baldwin
Rita	Mary-Louise Parker
Taylor	John Dossett
Tom and Jamaican Waiter	L. Peter Callender
Mrs. Boyle	Debra Monk
Dr. Boyle	Larry Bryggman
Minister	Craig Bockhorn
Aunt Dorothy and Leah	Joyce Reehling
Uncle Fred	Michael Warren Powell
Old Man	Barnard Hughes
Party Guests, Barflies, Wedding Guests and Vacationers	Kimberly Dudwitt and Pete Tyler

By FRANK RICH

Peter, the ingenuous hero played by Alec Baldwin in "Prelude to a Kiss," loves the sign at the roller coaster: "Ride at Your Own Risk." It promises a journey into "the wild blue" in which anything can happen. The same sign could be posted at "Prelude to a Kiss," for Craig Lucas, the author of "Reckless" and "Blue Window," has again written a play that propels the audience through hairpin emotional turns, some soaring heavenward and others plummeting toward earth, until one is deposited at the final curtain in a winded and teary yet exhilarating state of disorientation.

I loved this play and the dreamy, perfectly cast Circle Repertory Company production, directed by Norman René, that is inseparable from it. But as the man says, ride at your own risk. "Prelude to a Kiss" takes a most familiar genre, romantic comedy, in directions that are idiosyncratic and challenging. The play's title comes from the Duke Ellington song sung by Ella Fitzgerald that perfumes the evening, and Mr. Lucas follows its prescription that "just a simple melody with nothing fancy, nothing much" can blossom into "a symphony, a Schubert tune with a Gershwin touch." The playwright also takes a cue from his characters' favorite book, "The White Hotel," because "Prelude to a Kiss," though only a prelude compared with D. M. Thomas's novel, is also a psychoanalytic fairy tale that rises from a maze of transference into a cathartic conflict between sex and death.

A brutal universe where everyone is inevitably abandoned.

•

Mr. Lucas is not pretentious, and his play is as airily composed and, at first, as funny as the old-time Holly-

Bob Marshak

Mary-Louise Parker and Alec Baldwin in "Prelude to a Kiss."

wood confections it sometimes paraphrases. Peter, a microfiche specialist at a scientific publishing concern, and Rita (Mary-Louise Parker), a bartender aspiring to be a graphic designer, meet at a Manhattan party, fall under the spell of love and are married at the bride's family home in Englewood Cliffs, N.J. It is a fine romance, with lots of storybook kisses — most of them executed by Mr. Baldwin and Ms. Parker, an enchanting young stage couple made for each other as well as for audiences.

The romance consummated, the trouble begins. During a honeymoon in Jamaica, Peter finds himself increasingly at odds with the wonderful woman he thought he had married. Once he returns to New York, he is convinced that Rita isn't Rita at all. Through a magical plot device that could happen only in a movie — and frequently does — Rita's soul seems to have migrated to another body. The body is that of an old, bespectacled, pot-bellied man, played by Barnard Hughes, who is dying of lung cancer.

"I'm not equipped for this!" Peter cries. While he had sworn to Rita that he would love her even more in old age, when her teeth had yellowed and her breasts had sagged, he had not expected to be put to so blunt a test so soon. Can he love a woman who now looks like an old, decrepit man? What makes "Prelude to a Kiss" a powerful, genuine fairy tale rather than merely a farcical exploitation of the form's narrative devices is that Mr. Lucas insists on playing out Peter's outrageous predicament for keeps. The scenes in which the souls of Peter and Rita merge despite the impediment of Mr. Hughes's undesirable body are as tender and moving as those in which Mr. Baldwin and Ms. Parker strike erotic sparks.

•

It is not difficult to figure out the genesis of "Prelude to a Kiss." Mr. Lucas is also the author of "Longtime

Companion," a much more conventionally written feature film about AIDS that is to open in May, and this play can be taken as an indirect treatment of the same subject. The epidemic is to Mr. Lucas what Babi Yar was to D. M. Thomas, and Peter's fidelity to his true love's soul, even as that soul is trapped in a dying male body, is a transparent metaphor. Yet Mr. Lucas never betrays his play's fantastical tone or sense of humor; its setting is a unspecifically "precarious" New York, and AIDS is never mentioned. The result is a work whose anguish excludes no one. The questions that Mr. Lucas addresses are timeless ones about the powers of compassion and empathy in a brutal universe where everyone is inevitably abandoned by parents, children and lovers and where the only reward for that suffering is to disappear to "no one knows where."

The script's lyrical alchemy of bright comedy and deep feeling is matched by the staging of Mr. René, whose nearly decadelong collaboration with Mr. Lucas and a poetically minded design team has grown into one of the true joys of the American theater. All the performances are excellent, including those of Larry Bryggman and Debra Monk as slightly off-center suburban in-laws and Joyce Reehling as a sad-eyed middle-aged daughter who helps shift the entire play's emotional key in her own confrontation with mortality. Mr. Hughes, repressing a bit of his customary Irish twinkle, turns a role that is not that large into an indelible specter of love lost and found.

For Mr. Baldwin, Peter is a complete, and completely successful, switch on the scurvy contemporary men he has played so amusingly on stage ("Loot," "Serious Money") and screen ("Married to the Mob," "Working Girl"). It is no easy achievement, I'm sure, for an actor with such slick good looks to convey generosity of spirit rather than nar-

cissism. Mr. Baldwin, whose character also serves as the evening's witty narrator, does so with natural ease, never resorting to charming tricks of the leading man's trade. Ms. Parker, recently seen as Jane Hogarth in "The Art of Success," is going places as surely as her co-star is. An uninhibited (but not undisciplined) comic actress whose pouty mouth and big eyes break into unexpectedly radiant smiles, she transcends her own attractive looks to imbue Rita with a soul for which a man might well sacrifice everything.

•

Such is Mr. Lucas's gift that he makes life's sacrifices seem its affirmation, not its burden, even as he by no means underestimates the courage required to make the leap. The leap is not merely figurative. Like "Blue Window" and "Reckless," "Prelude to a Kiss" is dominated by the image of a window. Mr. Lucas often demands that his characters jump through it, leaving home for the unknown of a starry night and the arduous prospect of selfless love, just as he demands that audiences take the leap out of a literal reality and into the imaginative realm of an adult fable.

The amazing part is that if you can go the esthetic distance with this playwright, you may find yourself inspired to take the other, more intimate, much more dangerous leap, too. Though "Prelude to a Kiss" is never more than a heartbeat away from the fearful nightmare of death that inspired it, the experience of seeing it is anything but defeating. Mr. Lucas opens the window on love — true love, not fairy-tale love — so wide that, even in this cynical time, it seems a redemptive act of faith to take a free fall into the wild blue.

1990 Mr 15, C15:1

A Carnival of Music, Acrobatics and Sambas in the Aisles

By JENNIFER DUNNING

It is carnival time at the Marquis Theater, where Franco Fontana's "Oba Oba '90" has settled in through April 22. As colorfully irrepressible as it was when it played in New York in 1988, the revue offers more than two hours of lavish production numbers, spectacular acrobatics and lilting music that take the audience on a somewhat haphazard promotional tour of Brazil.

The dancers are as good looking as ever. The musicians star in a few numbers, often played on exotic native instruments whose warmth and intimacy make them highlights of the show. There are still some tasteless moments, and the miking is nearly unbearable at first. But in what other

show on Broadway does the audience get a chance to samba up and down the aisle with ingratiating young performers, balloons cascading down on them as they dance?

The first act moves from the cheery "Liberation From Slavery" to a giddy tribute to Carmen Miranda, the "Brazilian Bombshell," with stops along the way for an obligatory bow to the lambada and an irresistibly melodic musical homage to the bossanova and Brazilian music of the 1970's.

African gods and goddesses come to life and dance in the glittering, smokey "Macumba," which opens the second act. There is a showstopping number devoted to the capoeira, a wildly acrobatic dance that evolved from slaves' hand and foot fighting. Young men and boys skid on their

Chris Fessler

Members of "Oba Oba '90," a dance and music spectacular,

heads, spin on their elbows, twist into impossible shapes while balancing on one hand and fly through the air like unguided missiles.

The homemade look of the capoeira and of musical numbers like "Rhythm Beaters" is one of the pleasures of "Oba Oba '90." There is not nearly enough time spent with Toco Preto, the wry-faced artist of the caaquinho or small guitar; Maranhão, a tiny, serene singer and triangle player, and Curimã, a laughing drummer. Renny Flores, a charming singer, brought a special touch of class to the show, whose cast of 55 was led by Jaime Santos, Paulo Ramos and the full-voiced Sonia Santos.

The only sour note in "Oba Oba '90" is its heavy-handed attempt to turn up the heat on an already sexy, sultry show with numbers like "Show of Samba Dancers" and a breast-jiggling solo in toe shoes whose naïveté makes it look straight out of a Miss America talent competition. And the sight of the tousled, long-legged Oba Oba Girls struggling to be first, it seemed, to tug up, down or off their costumes was surprisingly unamusing.

But "Oba Oba '90" is otherwise great fun. Wilson Mauro was responsible for the musical direction, Roberto Abrahão for the choreography and Giancarlo Campora for the lighting.

1990 Mr 16, C6:3

Everything That Spins Must Diverge

EVERYTHING THAT RISES MUST CONVERGE, written, directed and designed by John Jesurun. Lighting by Jeffrey Nash; technicians and camera operators, Catherine Gore and Barret Schumacher; production manager and camera operator, Dayton Taylor; technical coordinator and camera operator, David Tumblety. Presented by the Kitchen, 512 West 19th Street.

WITH: Oscar de la Fe Colon, Joe Murphy, Susanne Strenger, Larry Tighe, Michael Tighe, Sanghi Wagner, Phyllis Young, Jane Smith and Jonathan Del Arco.

By MEL GUSSOW

On one level, John Jesurun's "Everything That Rises Must Converge" is an incoherent play on the subject of language. That fact alone says something about the difficulty of communication, which is at the root of Mr. Jesurun's new work, a deeply layered multi-media theater piece that will leave audiences alternately fascinated and exhausted. Fascination wins by a millimeter, because of the playwright's originality and his command of theatrical and electronic techniques.

For the purposes of his play (at the Kitchen, before beginning an international tour), theatergoers are seated on bleachers facing a white wall and a bank of five television monitors. As the show starts, actors on stage address one another as well as other other actors who appear on the screens above their heads.

In characteristic Jesurun fashion, words tumble fast and without apparent logic. With his plays, one often has the feeling of being thrown headlong into a labyrinth from which there is no exit — and no exegesis. The author uses the word "slashback," a neologism denoting the razor-sharp quickness of the images, as the play moves backward, forward and sideways.

Theatergoers naturally will try to find their equilibrium, or, at least, to locate a story. Mr. Jesurun is not interested. Instead of narrative, he offers a kinetic array of kaleidoscopic pictures and journal jottings, principally concerned with people who may be in the "control room of a capital city."

The characters are interpreters translating information from one language to another, information that deals with, among other things, espionage, execution by poisoned glove and a fire that reduces a disco to ashes. Many of these are visions of violence, although they are communicated in a highly civil manner.

•

The actors, some of them familiar from past plays written and directed by Mr. Jesurun, are experts at the author's parrotlike style of performance. Most notable are Larry Tighe, Phyllis Young (who also sings) and Oscar de la Fe Colon. Mr. de la Fe Colon figures prominently in a plot thread concerning the explorer Cabeza de Vaca and the King of Spain. Much of his dialogue is in Spanish (other lines are in German). To an English-speaking audience, even the English may need explanation.

None of this is made easy for the audience, whose best approach is to hold on tight as Mr. Jesurun's roller-coaster swerves to what seems to be no conclusion. This is a more demanding ride than previous Jesurun works like "Deep Sleep" and "Black Maria," other plays in his movies-television-theater cycle that took greater advantage of the author's playful sense of humor.

What holds the audience's attention is the ingenious style of presentation. While we are still trying to correlate the barrage of words and of live and video figures, some of whom appear to be talking to themselves, the rear wall suddenly swings to a perpendicular, revealing an entirely different audience sitting on bleachers on the opposite side of the stage. In a mirror reversal, they have been watching our actors on monitors and our monitor-actors on stage.

•

Later, the wall turns to a diagonal, and oscillates like the blades of a propeller, bisecting our vision and leading to increasing disorientation. In a final coup de théâtre, the wall-as-propeller rotates on fast forward, circulating the play, aerating the theater with a cool breeze and threatening to levitate the actors. Simultaneously the video images are speeded up until voice and picture spin out of control, as in a massive computer glitch.

While putting audiences through a stress test, the play demonstrates that with this theater artist everything that rises converges on the cutting edge of experimentation.

1990 Mr 16, C6:3

Humane Society

HEART OF A DOG, by Deloss Brown, from the novella by Mikhail Bulgakov; directed by Robert Lanchester; scenery, Tom Kamm; costumes, Jane Eliot; lighting, Mary Louise Geiger; sound, Daniel Schreier; production stage manager, Debora Kingston. Presented by CSC Repertory, Carey Perloff, artistic director; Dara Hershman, acting managing director. At 136 East 13th Street.

Pooch/Poochkov	Jace Alexander
Shvonder	Josh Pais
Svetlana	Leslie Geraci
Natasha Petrova	Gwynne Rivers
Professor Preobrazhensky	Bill Raymond
Josef	William Newman
Zina	Anna Levine Thomson
Bormenthal	Anthony Fusco
Colonel Lobchenkov	William Newman
Sonia	Mary Beth Kilkelly

By MEL GUSSOW

Mikhail Bulgakov's novel "Heart of a Dog" is a malicious political parable on what the author envisioned as the inevitable corruption of a socialist state. Written in 1925 (and unpublished in the Soviet Union until 1987), the book follows the rise and fall of a mongrel scientifically transformed into a man but unable to avoid the curse of atavism. Behavior that is acceptable, even ingratiating, in a canine is indecent in a human.

In Deloss Brown's freehanded adaptation, which opened last night at the CSC Repertory, the story is broader and more farcical than the original, but remains faithful to the heart of "Heart of a Dog." As amusingly incarnated by Jace Alexander, a dog-man named Poochkov brings his gross appetites intact into the supposedly civilized world he momentarily inhabits. The actor and the character have bite as well as bark. Because of his determinedly antisocial actions, he clearly deserves his fate, a return trip to the origin of his species.

There are some losses in the novel's metamorphosis to the stage. Though Mr. Brown uses the dog as narrator, as Bulgakov did, he shortchanges the sour sweetness of the animal's wanderings on the streets of Moscow, where he fearfully tries to avert life's kicks. Too suddenly, the title character is a guest in the home of a professor, and an unwitting victim of his surgical experimentation. As played with increasing exasperation by Bill Raymond, the professor is more a nutty doctor than the gentlemanly though Frankensteinian genius of Bulgakov's imagination.

Mr. Brown and his director, Robert Lanchester, move Bulgakov close to French farce — reminding one that one of the Russian author's best-known plays is "Molière in Spite of Himself." In this variation on "Heart of a Dog," the professor's assistant becomes a comely French-style maid (fetchingly played by Anna Levine under her new name, Anna Levine Thomson) who has designs on the professor's lecherous medical colleague (Anthony Fusco).

Although Mr. Lanchester's direction and some of the performances are not marked by their subtlety, the production retains the work's sense of mockery. Tom Kamm's tilted scenic design adds a note of absurdism to the fable. The performance focuses, as it should, on the title character, a role that Mr. Alexander portrays with aplomb.

After his initial mangy appearance, he exchanges his dog suit for the hirsute, looking unkempt and unshaven. He is especially funny in his moments of dogged ingratitude. The canine equivalent of "The Man Who Came to Dinner," he quickly overstays his welcome in the professor's house. At first he slurps from a glass, but soon adapts himself to drinking vodka straight from the bottle. Frequently, he rests his leg on the furniture, assuming a pose that is half-dog, half-Harpo. A self-proclaimed theoretician, he is dogmatic in his didacticism.

Paula Court

Jace Alexander and Anna Levine Thomson in "Heart of a Dog," at CSC Repertory.

The rise and fall of a mongrel that science has made a man, sort of.

Anything he does not like he labels as counter-revolutionary, including the theater (he prefers the circus).

At the mention of the word cat, he loses what remains of his wits. When the professor pleads for humanity toward cats, Poochkov can only respond: "Cats aren't people. Cats are ... pigs." It takes one to know one. Naturally he will find useful employment as the Director of the Purge Section, eliminating stray felines from the city.

Though there are unnecessary Leninist jokes, the adaptation takes advantage of Bulgakov's more general socialist satire, as in the officious tenants' committee, which crams nine people into one apartment, insisting on everyone's equal right to be uncomfortable. In Bulgakov's counter-revolutionary indictment, proletarianism lies down with fleas and literally goes to the dogs.

1990 Mr 16, C3:1

Riding With Punches

I THINK IT'S GONNA WORK OUT FINE, by Ed Bullins; directed by Brian Freeman; original light design by Stephanie Johnson; design realization by Howard Thies; music composed and arranged by Idris Ackamoor, Rhodessa Jones, Peter Fuji and Rock of Edges; costumes by Rene Walker and Pat Stewart; choreography by Roger Dillahunty; original set design by Kemit Amenophis. Presented by La Mama E.T.C. at the Club, 74A East Fourth Street.

By STEPHEN HOLDEN

Midway in "I Think It's Gonna Work Out Fine," a music-theater fable loosely based on the story of Ike and Tina Turner, Rita Golden, the sexy lead singer of the traveling rock-and-roll show Prince Golden and His

Royal Revue, is punched in the face by her husband because she has hidden his gun. Rita, who is portrayed by Rhodessa Jones with a raw, feisty bitterness, turns to the audience and says with a sneer, "Yeah, he hit me! Is that what you all here were waiting for?"

One of several stinging Brechtian asides in the musical, which has the final performance of its current run at 10 o'clock this evening at the Club at La Mama, the remark is a pungent reminder that the story of the Turners (here re-named the Goldens, with many of the biographical details changed) is more than titillating tabloid fare. It is an archetypal American story of social mobility, race and black-on-black violence. Without ranting and railing, the show attributes the brutal, self-destructive ways of Prince Golden, portrayed by Idris Ackamoor as a quintessential hot-tempered street hustler, to simmering resentments of racism.

"I Think It's Gonna Work Out Fine" has an unusually clear-eyed, unsentimental book by the playwright Ed Bullins. The music, by Mr. Ackamoor, Ms. Jones, Peter Fuji and the West Coast group Rock of Edges, skillfully parodies 60's Southern soul music. The show avoids rock-and-roll nostalgia to present the Goldens as a talented but embattled couple fleeing poverty via the only avenue open to them.

When the Prince meets Rita in East St. Louis, she is a gushing farm girl who eagerly abandons her Bible-thumping sharecropper background for the bright lights of show business and under his tutelage quickly becomes the star of his revue. Unable to transcend his resentful hustler's view of the world, the Prince takes out his anger in drugs, promiscuity and wife-beating, while her star ascends. Eventually she leaves him. In their final scene together, they meet near where they first crossed paths, and she coldly pays him off with a check.

The two-person show is crude in many ways. Except for Mr. Ackamoor's saxophone solos, most of the instrumental music is pre-recorded, and Ms. Jones doesn't begin to match Ms. Turner in vocal power or glamor. Yet their depiction of the Goldens' courtship, marital clashes, and the grind of show business has a gritty ring of truth. And Mr. Bullins's caustic streetwise dialogue crackles with an angry, critical edge.

Explaining the roots of Southern soul, the Prince scoffs, "That's where the music came from — we were either down on our knees or we was bendin' our backs," while pantomiming praying and picking cotton.

"I could write a book about the juke joints of America," Rita says with a sigh. "For I have seen the chitlin circuit, and we're not talking Howard Johnson's."

It is the Prince who delivers the show's final bitter epitaph after his wife has been swept up in the big-time white-dominated rock-and-roll world that he was never able to crash himself partly because of his own fears of being exploited. "Rhythm and blues wasn't taken away from us," he announces with defensive sarcasm. "We gave it away."

1990 Mr 17, 18:6

Hers, Hers and Theirs

SPARE PARTS, by Elizabeth Page; directed by Susan Einhorn; scenic designer, Ursula Belden; costumes, Elsa Ward; lighting, Norman Coates; sound, One Dream; production stage manager, Crystal Huntington. Presented by Pamela Kantor, in association with Douglas L. Feldman and Paul A. Kaplan. At Circle in the Square Downtown, 159 Bleecker Street.

Henry	Stephen Hamilton
Lois	Robin Groves
Jax	Donna Haley
Selma	Margo Skinner
Perry	Reed Birney

By STEPHEN HOLDEN

Lois and Jax, the embattled protagonists of Elizabeth Page's comedy "Spare Parts," are a lesbian couple who decide, without really thinking ahead, to have a child. As the play opens, Lois is making love with Henry, a young man she has picked up in a bar and gone home with for the sole purpose of insemination. Neither she nor Jax has bargained for the possibility that the man chosen to be the father will turn out to be a soft-hearted romantic who remains smitten with his date and who, upon discovering she is pregnant with his child, insists on taking on the responsibilities of an expectant father.

"Spare Parts," at Circle in the Square, is a problem play treated as an extended situation comedy. Five characters are programmed to go through a series of changes that make specific points about sexual roles, societal attitudes and tolerance of unconventional family units. The brusque, emotionally possessive Jax, who instigated the plan, has not entertained the possibility that once the insemination was accomplished, she would be furiously jealous of the father. Things go awry when Henry tracks down his dream date and worms his way into the household, making Jax feel so threatened that she walks out.

•

Meanwhile, Lois (Robin Groves) proves to be a helpless wilting violet of vacillating loyalties, prone to anxiety attacks. The only person she trusts completely is her friend Perry (Reed Birney), a pathologically shy homosexual teacher who was once burned in love and is still running away from intimacy. Rounding out the ensemble is Selma (Margo Skinner), the couple's man-hungry next-door neighbor and landlady, who serves as a mouthpiece for the unconscious prejudices of supposedly sophisticated "straight" society. Once Henry has elbowed Jax out of the house, Selma takes his side, even though it is perfectly apparent that Lois and Jax are meant for each other.

As directed by Susan Einhorn, the play, which takes place in Hartford and New Haven, has the pacing of a very leisurely episode of a Norman Lear sitcom, drawn out to more than two hours. The main problem is that the dialogue is only intermittently funny, and when it is not witty "Spare Parts" turns into a soap opera in which the characters nag and snap at one another in a way that undermines one's sympathy for them.

•

Although it is especially hard to warm up to the impulsive, ferocious Jax, a woman who is described as having a fondness for "riding motorcyles with women named Sid," Donna Haley's uncompromisingly ferocious portrayal makes Jax the play's most fully realized character. The haziest creation is Perry, whom even an actor of Mr. Birney's subtlety cannot transform from a shadowy enigma.

While Stephen Hamilton gives the role of Henry an appropriately proprietary air, the character as written is not entirely credible. The way he tracks Lois down and barges into her ménage makes sense only in terms of the most artificial conventions of situation comedy.

Besides Ms. Haley's Jax, the strongest performance is Ms. Skinner's tart-tongued Selma, who condescendingly sets her sights on Henry at a very convenient moment in the plot. A snob, Selma is the kind of person who brings her own perfectly ripened Brie and crackers to a group picnic where everybody else munches on fried chicken and potato salad.

1990 Mr 18, 59:2

What's in a Name?

THE IMPORTANCE OF BEING EARNEST, by Oscar Wilde; directed by Anthony Cornish; set design, Robert Joel Schwartz; lighting design, Stephen Petrilli; costume design, Barbara A. Bell; technical director, Richard A. Kendrick; stage manager, Jennifer E. Boggs. Presented by the Pearl Theater Company, at 125 West 22d Street.

Algernon Moncrieff	Michael John McGuinness
Hon. Gwendolen Fairfax	Donnah Welby
John Worthing	Stuart Lerch
Cecily Cardew	Laura Rathgeb
Lane/Merriman	K. Bruce Harpster
Lady Bracknell	Margaret Hilton
Miss Prism	Joanne Camp
Mr. Chasuble	Frank Geraci

By WILBORN HAMPTON

Oscar Wilde, having been importuned to cut an entire act from "The Importance of Being Earnest," attended one of the final rehearsals before its premiere and remarked: "It is a very good play. I wrote one very like it myself."

Wilde's comment might well apply to the latest in a seeming epidemic of productions this season of what its author called a "trivial play for serious people." The Pearl Theater Company's current staging is an entertaining one, even if it does give more importance to the play's humorous triviality than to the earnestness of its social satire.

Under the direction of Anthony Cornish, the emphasis here is on the romantic coupling of the four principals rather than any deeper examination of the moral hypocrisies of the upper classes. Happily, these four main roles in the Pearl production are ably filled. And if, in the final analysis, the men prove no match for the women, that is only as it should be.

•

Donnah Welby's Gwendolen, all breathy and headstrong, delivers the most fully developed performance. When Miss Welby quietly states "I am never wrong," it is with such confidence that few men, and certainly not Jack Worthing, would dare doubt it, let alone try to convince her otherwise. Here is a wide-eyed and winsome Gwendolyn who knows her own mind and, further, knows she will always get her way.

Michael John McGuinness's Algernon is a first-rate Bumburyist (Wilde's invention for never having to do anything unpleasant) with more than a bit of the profligate in him. Mr. McGuinness presents a man who devoutly adheres to the precept that his "duty as a gentleman has never interfered in my pleasure." And if he has learned that "truth is rarely pure and simple," he has further decided that truth may thus be vastly overrated.

As the objects of these two cousins' affections, Stuart Lerch and Laura Rathgeb provide good foils. Miss Rathgeb's Cecily is no less determined than Miss Welby's Gwendolen and their garden scene over tea seethes with well-bred fury. Mr. Lerch's Jack catches the high moral tone one expects from an English gentleman who would never stoop to

Martha Swope Associates/Carol Rosegg

Donnah Welby in "The Importance of Being Earnest."

read the inscription in another gentleman's cigarette case. K. Bruce Harpster contributes a nice turn in both servant roles, and Margaret Hilton is a credible Lady Bracknell although she occasionally more resembles a stern nanny than a Mayfair matron.

Robert Joel Schwartz's city flat and country garden sets are charming, and Barbara A. Bell's costumes fit the fashion of the times.

1990 Mr 18, 59:1

A la Carte

FEAST OF FOOLS, written and performed by Geoff Hoyle; directorial consultant, Anthony Taccone; scenic designer, Scott Weldin; lighting designer, Neil Peter Jampolis; sound designer, Michael Holten; "Folk Fool" choreographic consultant, Kimi Okada; "Folk Fool" score, Keith Terry; production adviser, Randall Kline. Presented by Raymond L. Gaspard, Charles H. Duggan and Drew Dennett, by arrangement with Mr. Kline. At the Westside Arts Theater, Upstairs, 407 West 43d Street.

By MEL GUSSOW

For the finale of his one-man clown show, "Feast of Fools," Geoff Hoyle does something incomparable with his three legs. All three are trousered and shod and they peep out from under a long greatcoat. Mr. Hoyle walks on stage at the Westside Arts Theater as if it were the most natural thing in the world to be a triped. Then he begins to dance with himself, swirling and dipping, two feet in the air, one on the ground and vice versa, until he becomes an Astaire-and-a-half soaring in ballroom abandon.

If all the comic bits — or lazzi — were as funny and as absurd as this one, the show would be a feast of foolery. A clown, according to Mr. Hoyle, can luxuriate in his own vulgarity, as in an extended interlude about Italian and French jesters. In such sketches,

Allen Nomura

Geoff Hoyle as Mr. Sniff in "Feast of Fools," his one-man clown show.

Mr. Hoyle, an often frazzled Englishman who is a graduate of the Pickle Family Circus in San Francisco, is on the verge of being instructive. One might suggest that he should abbreviate the history and cut to the spontaneous comedy.

As a solo performer, he does not have the easy ingenuousness of such fellow New Vaudevillians as Bill Irwin, Avner Eisenberg and Bob Berky. His work can appear to be effortful and there are questions of taste (bodily functions, such as might appeal to a 5-year-old, figure prominently in his act). In this and other senses, he is a throwback to the classic European clowns whose commedia dell'arte he likes to imitate.

Especially in the second act "Feast of Fools" confirms Mr. Hoyle's own lunatic disposition and his rubber-faced talent for mime and mimicry. He is most amusing when he is at his simplest, not when he is deftly quick-changing behind a screen from an ancient Pantalone to a youthful Arlecchino, but when he is making faces to himself. The latter is the case in one beguiling dialogue in mime in which Mr. Hoyle plays the foil with a replica of himself as puppet-head on a stick. Though the puppet's individual features never move, the puppet's head responds with quizzical expressiveness. The audience receives a very vivid impression of two separate characters or of a single sundered personality.

Similarly, there is Mr. Sniff, his signature character, a scamp who is led by his balloon nose. Smelling his way across the stage, he wiggles his nose so demonstratively that his nose seems to talk. Soon Mr. Sniff finds himself trapped in a hostile environment.

Scenery collapses and the center stage will not hold. He picks up a section of the splintered floor and hands it to a patron in the front row — then mischievously accuses the theatergoer of demolishing the theater. The scene culminates in breakaway de-

lirium. From here, it is one hilarious leap to Mr. Hoyle's final feat of comic legerdemain.

1990 Mr 18, 59:1

Prescriptions Of an Earlier Era

BAD HABITS, by Terrence McNally; directed by Paul Benedict; sets by John Lee Beatty, costumes by Jane Greenwood; lighting by Peter Kaczorowski; sound by John Gromada; production stage manager, Tom Aberger. Presented by the Manhattan Theater Club, Lynne Meadow, artistic director; Barry Grove, managing director. At City Center Stage I, 131 West 55th Street.

DUNELAWN
OttoRalph Marrero
Jason Pepper, M.D. .... Nathan Lane
Dolly Scupp .... Faith Prince
April Pitt .... Kate Nelligan
Roy Pitt .... Robert Clohessy
Hiram Spane .... David Cromwell
Francis Tear .... Bill Buell
Harry Scupp .... Michael Mantell
RAVENSWOOD
Ruth Benson, R.N. .... Ms. Nelligan
Becky Hedges, R.N. .... Ms. Prince
Bruno .... Mr. Clohessy
Mr. Ponce .... Mr. Buell
Dr. Toynbee .... Mr. Cromwell
Mr. Blum .... Mr. Mantell
Mr. Yamadoro .... Mr. Marrero
Hugh Gumbs .... Mr. Lane

By FRANK RICH

Bad habits aren't what they used to be, and neither is "Bad Habits," the twin bill of one-act plays by Terrence McNally that has been given a catch-as-catch-can revival by the Manhattan Theater Club. In the distant year of 1974, when "Bad Habits" made its hilarious New York debut, the characters' vices of chain smoking, high-cholesterol gluttony, martini guzzling and sexual adventurism were regarded more as amusingly naughty acts of rebellion, however self-destructive, than as one-way tickets to

the grave. Today about the only bad habit harmless enough to elicit universal laughter — and be assured Mr. McNally does not neglect it — is the spirited picking of one's nose.

The plays are set in the lavish rest homes of Dunelawn (Act I) and Ravenswood (Act II) where, respectively, warring couples and eccentric individuals seek balms for their ills. While the text's cultural references have been updated to embrace Oprah and Madonna, "Bad Habits" still offers prescriptions closer to Ken Kesey's or R. D. Laing's than to C. Everett Koop's. Mr. McNally implies that his cuckoo inmates would be best off shunning conventional cures and revolting against the status quo, whether by indulging their looniest excesses to the fullest or by taking over the asylum. To do otherwise is to surrender one's humanity to a state of lobotomized conformity, as administered by a fascist nurse brandishing a syringe.

However titillating this point of view was in 1974, it has long since lost its power to startle. Without either an ingenious farcical structure or a smashing production to fill the vacuum, the show has little of the zing audiences rediscovered in the equivalent Joe Orton comedy, the 1967 "What the Butler Saw," revived by the Manhattan Theater Club last season. What survives in "Bad Habits" is not so much a focused evening of theater as a pair of overextended burlesque sketches that live or die from joke to joke.

Mr. McNally is incapable of being completely unfunny, and, in his better moments, he imagines a Dr. Feelgood whose unctuously whispered words of wisdom are babytalk and a skirt-chasing gardener whose libidinal urges are written all over his anatomy, not to mention his face. An egomaniacally competitive show-business couple, an actor and actress known more for the roles they lost than those they actually played, are quintessentially narcissistic McNally buffoons: they battle over possession of a sun-reflector with the same zeal ordinary mortals might bring to a debate over the meaning of life.

The more "Bad Habits" is removed from a show-biz frame of reference and the accompanying insult humor, however, the more Mr. McNally's writing strains. While one crack about seminars on sexual dysfunctions or tobacco "fertilized with hen feces" or a couple known as the Pitts is amusing, two constitutes a bad

habit. And though only the humorless would be offended by a portrait of two prissy, aging male companions locked in an eternal snit-fit, the bitchiness of Mr. McNally's pair is too tame to spice up the cliché.

Perhaps more inspired clowning would help, but the acting does not remotely match that of the two other McNally revivals that preceded this one to the same stage, "It's Only a Play" and "The Lisbon Traviata." Though the director is Paul Benedict, who appeared in the 1974 "Bad Habits" and who sensitively staged the same author's "Frankie and Johnny in the Clair de Lune," he gives this script what can only be called the "Rumors" treatment. As in that Neil Simon production, the cast runs around hyperventilating in bright lighting. The apparent hope is that the frantic simulation of cartoonishness will impress at least some onlookers as the real thing.

•

Such is the generalized hysteria that even the three stellar cast members — Nathan Lane, Kate Nelligan and Faith Prince — struggle uncustomarily. Mr. Lane, occupying an electric wheelchair as a mad doctor in Act I and tumbling out of one as a mad patient in Act II, is easily the funniest performer, though he at times recycles and overdoes his frenzies from "The Lisbon Traviata." (Mr. McNally's comic targets for Mr. Lane in the two plays, like divas and Stephen Sondheim musicals, overlap as well.) Ms. Nelligan is game but seems lost when adopting a Damon Runyon accent as the tacky actress of Act I and is ill at ease as the repressed nurse of Act II. The squeaky-voiced Ms. Prince, though in principle well cast as two unraveling matrons memorably played by Doris Roberts in 1974, is more dizzying than dizzy.

The other performances are at best adequate, and conspicuously less than that in the cases of Robert Clohessy, as the preening actor married to Ms. Nelligan, and Michael Mantell, as a transvestite who worships the hem of Nina Foch. In John Lee Beatty's smart design, the funny farms they and their fellow patients occupy are as witty as the illustrations in children's picture books. "Bad Habits," by contrast, too often succumbs to the merely juvenile.

1990 Mr 21, C13:1

Gerry Goodstein

Nathan Lane and Kate Nelligan in a scene from "Bad Habits."

Parables and Miracles

ST. MARK'S GOSPEL, Alec McCowen performing the Gospel According to St. Mark. Lighting by Lloyd Sobel. Presented by Arthur Cantor. At the Lamb's Theater, 130 West 44th Street.

By MEL GUSSOW

Alec McCowen's "St. Mark's Gospel" is a performance as revelation. Without theatrics, he tells the story of Christ as recounted by Mark. Though Mr. McCowen has given this solo performance innumerable times in the last two decades, his actor's art has kept his delivery extraordinarily fresh. The story is told every time as if for the first time.

His role is primarily that of reporter, filled with awe at the marvelous events and eager to transmit the Gospel·to his listeners. This is not a Bible lesson or a sermon, but a one-man play, in which the actor becomes a conduit of genius. As Shakespeare was to John Gielgud (in his "Ages of Man" recital), St. Mark is to Mr. McCowen.

For his return appearance in the show in New York (a limited run that began last night at the Lamb's Theater), Mr. McCowen has grown a beard and now wears a comfortable sweater rather than a jacket. He looks older and seems more informal, but the performance has not in any sense mellowed through familiarity. If anything, he exudes an even greater empathy with his subject.

●

In his book, "Double Bill," in which he describes his generative process as an actor, Mr. McCowen says about Mark's version of the Gospel, "The events of a great tragic play lead us inexorably to the final catastrophe." Mark is a natural dramatist, but it is the actor's interpretation that brings the book to life on stage. He becomes Mark's creative collaborator, playing all the characters and, through his acting, giving the Gospel atmospheric background as well as dramatic shape.

Alec McCowen in "St. Mark's Gospel" at the Lamb's Theater.

The tragedy is heightened as Mr. McCowen leads us gradually through Christ's days on earth. In his portrait, Jesus is a man before he is seen as a divinity, a man who can rise in anger and even personal irritation, as in his wrathful reaction to the fig tree that refuses to bear fruit.

The actor finds surprising humor within the narrative, partly through his mimicry of characters, but also through his presentation of parables and miracles. Miracles abound as winds are stilled, a blind man regains his sight, and a handful of loaves and fishes feeds a legion.

●

More than anything, it is the wonderment of the experience that is evoked. If at any moment the actor succumbed to histrionics, it would defeat his purpose. The excitement comes, as it must, from the words and the story, and when the most quoted lines are heard in context, they gain resonance.

The performance is self-directed. Mr. McCowen introduces the reading with a few humorous reflections on his long identification with his role, remarking that a theatergoer once asked him where she could find a script. His response: "In almost any hotel room." Then he places a copy of "St. Mark's Gospel" on the table on stage — "just in case." There is, of course, no need to consult it. The performance begins as a feat of memory and becomes an eloquent meeting of actor and text.

1990 Mr 22, C21:1

Fighting the Lies

CAT ON A HOT TIN ROOF, by Tennessee Williams; directed by Howard Davies; scenery, William Dudley; costumes, Patricia Zipprodt; lighting, Mark Henderson; sound, T. Richard Fitzgerald; hair design, Robert DiNiro; music composed by Ilona Sekacz; technical supervisor, Arthur Siccardi; associate lighting designer, Beverly Emmons; production manager, Patrick Horrigan. Presented by Barry and Fran Weissler. At the Eugene O'Neill Theater, 230 West 49th Street.

Maggie	Kathleen Turner
Brick	Daniel Hugh Kelly
Mae	Debra Jo Rupp
Big Mama	Polly Holliday
Sookey	Edwina Lewis
Dixie	Amy Gross
Big Daddy	Charles Durning
Gooper	Kevin O'Rourke
Rev. Tooker	Nesbitt Blaisdell
Dr. Baugh	Jerome Dempseyy
Trixie	Erin Torpey
Polly	Suzy Bouffard
Buster	Seth Jerome Walker
Sonny	Billy L. Sullivan
Brightie	Ron Brice
Lacey	Marcial Howard

By FRANK RICH

It takes nothing away from Kathleen Turner's radiant Maggie in "Cat on a Hot Tin Roof" to say that Broadway's gripping new production of Tennessee Williams's 1955 play will be most remembered for Charles Durning's Big Daddy. The actor's portrayal of a 65-year-old Mississippi plantation owner in festering extremis is an indelible hybrid of red-neck cutup and aristocratic tragedian, of grasping capitalist and loving patriarch. While "Cat" is not the American "King Lear" its author hoped, this character in this performance is a cracker-barrel Lear and Falstaff in one.

Just try to get the image of Mr. Durning — a dying volcano in final, sputtering eruption under a Delta moon — out of your mind. I can't. "Cat" is a curiously constructed work in which the central but sullen character of Brick, the all-American jock turned booze hound, clings to the action's periphery while Act I belongs to his wife, Maggie, Act II to his Big Daddy and the anti-climactic Act III (of which the author left several variants) to no one. Such is Mr. Durning's force in the second act at the O'Neill that he obliterates all that comes after, despite the emergence of Polly Holliday's poignant Big Mama in the final stretch.

●

Mr. Durning's Act II tour de force begins with low comedy: the portly, silver-haired actor, dressed in a sagging white suit and wielding a vaudeville comedian's stogie, angrily dismisses his despised, nattering wife and his bratty grandchildren, those cap-gun-toting "no-neck monsters" who would attempt to lure him into a saccharine birthday party. From that hilarious display of W. C. Fields dyspepsia, it is quite a leap to the act's conclusion. By then, Mr. Durning is white with fear, clutching the back of a chair for support, for he has just learned what the audience has long known: Big Daddy is being eaten away by cancer that "has gone past the knife."

In between comes a father-son confrontation that is not only the crux of Mr. Durning's performance but also the troubling heart of a play that is essential, if not first-rank, Williams. Big Daddy loves Brick (Daniel Hugh Kelly) and would like to favor him when dividing his estate of $10 million and "28,000 acres of the richest land this side of the valley Nile." But there are mysteries to be solved before the writing of the will. Why are Brick and Maggie childless? Why is Brick, once a football hero and later a television sports announcer, now, at 27, intent on throwing away his life as if it were "something disgusting you picked up on the street"? How did Brick break his ankle in the wee hours of the night before?

Mr. Durning will have his answers, even if he has to knock Brick off his crutch to get them. But his Big Daddy, while tough as a billy goat, is not a cartoon tyrant. He wants to talk to his son,.not to badger him. He offers Brick understanding and tolerance in exchange for the truth, even if

---

Big Daddy hasn't much time and he wants straight answers. Now.

---

that truth might be Brick's closeted homosexual passion for his best friend and football buddy, Skipper, now dead of drink. All Big Daddy wants is freedom from the lies and hypocrisy of life that have so long disgusted him. Yet Brick, while sharing that disgust, won't surrender his illusions without a fight.

"Mendacity is the system we live in," the son announces. "Liquor is one way out and death's the other." When the truth finally does emerge — and for both men it is more devastating than any sexual revelation — liquor and death do remain the only exits. Life without the crutch of pipe dreams or anesthesia is too much to take. As the lights dim on Act II, Mr. Kelly is isolated in a stupor and Mr. Durning, his jaw distorted by revulsion and rage, is howling like Lear on the heath. Advancing relentlessly into the bowels of his mansion, the old man bellows an epic incantation of "Lying! Dying! Liars!" into the tall shadows of the Southern Gothic night.

The New York Times/Fred R. Conrad

Kathleen Turner and Charles Durning in Broadway's new production of "Cat on a Hot Tin Roof."

Along with the high drama and fine acting — Mr. Kelly's pickled Adonis included — what makes the scene so moving is Williams's raw sensitivity to what he called (in his next play, 'Orpheus Descending'') man's eternal sentence to solitary confinement. In "Cat," Maggie probably does love Brick, Big Mama probably does love Big Daddy, and Brick loves Skipper and Big Daddy as surely as they have loved him. Yet the lies separating those who would love are not easily vanquished. In this web of familial, fraternal and marital relationships, Williams finds only psychic ruin, as terminal as Big Daddy's cancer and as inexorable as the greed that is devouring the romantic Old South.

In his revival, Howard Davies, the English director last represented in New York by "Les Liaisons Dangereuses," keeps his eye on that bigger picture: Williams's compassion for all his trapped characters and his desire to make his play "not the solution of one man's psychological problem" but a "snare for the truth of human experience." With the exception of Mae (Debra Jo Rupp), Brick's conniving sister-in-law, everyone on stage is human. The playwright doesn't blame people for what existence does to them. He has empathy for the defeated and admiration for those like Maggie who continue the fight for life and cling to the hot tin roof "even after the dream of life is all over."

From her salt-cured accent to her unabashed (and entirely warranted) delight in her own body heat, Miss Turner is an accomplished Maggie, mesmerizing to watch, comfortable on stage and robustly good-humored. Merely to see this actress put on her nylons, a ritual of exquisitely prolonged complexity, is a textbook lesson in what makes a star. Miss Turner is so good as far as she goes that one wishes she'd expose her emotions a shade more — without compromising her admirable avoidance of a campy star turn. Her Maggie is almost too stubbornly a survivor of marital wars; she lacks the vulnerability of a woman "eaten up with longing" for the man who shuns her bed.

Though somewhat more can be made of Brick — and was by Ian Charleson, in Mr. Davies's previous staging of "Cat" in London — Mr. Kelly captures the detachment of defeat, and later the rage, of a man who buried hope in his best friend's grave. When Brick is finally provoked to stand up for the "one great good true thing" in his life, the actor gives an impassioned hint of the noble figure who inspired worship from all who knew him. But it's a major flaw of "Cat" that this character is underwritten. Williams defines the physique of his golden boy — and Mr. Kelly fleshes that out, too — but leaves the soul opaque.

•

Since Brick doesn't pull his weight in any of the playwright's third acts for "Cat," it hardly matters which one is used. Mr. Davies reverts to the unsentimental original draft, which never made it to the stage in Elia Kazan's initial Broadway production. Miss Holliday's Big Mama, an unstrung Amanda Wingfield brought to her own grief by others' mendacity, is a rending figure within the thunderstorm of the denouement. Along with the supporting cast, the designers' vision of a decaying South — from the fading veranda to the intrusion of the latest American innoculation against intimacy, a 1950's console television — thickens the rancid mood of a household where, in Big Mama's words, "such a black thing has come ... without invitation."

But even in Act III, even offstage, Mr. Durning continues to dominate, and, in a way, he gets the big scene with the star that the script denies him. As Maggie tenaciously clings to her tin roof, Big Daddy can be heard from somewhere deep within, his terrifying screams of pain rattling that roof, threatening even at death's doorstep to blow the lid off life's cruel, incarcerating house of lies.

1990 Mr 22, C17:1

The Soul Of a People

THE GRAPES OF WRATH, based on the novel by John Steinbeck; adapted and directed by Frank Galati; scenery and lighting by Kevin Rigdon; costumes by Erin Quigley; sound design by Rob Milburn; original music composed and directed by Michael Smith; production stage manager, Malcolm Ewen. The Steppenwolf Theater Company Production presented by the Shubert Organization, Steppenwolf Theater Company, the Suntory International Corporation and Jujamcyn Theaters. At the Cort Theater, 138 West 48th Street.

Jim Casy .... Terry Kinney
Tom Joad .... Gary Sinise
Ma .... Lois Smith
WITH: Calvin Lennon Armitage, Jeremiah Birkett, Robert Breuler, P. J. Brown, Cheryl Lynn Bruce, Keith Byron-Kirk, Ron Crawford, Nathan Davis, Mark Deakins, Kathryn Erbe, Francis Guinan, Michael Hartman, Terrance MacNamara, Lex Monson, Sally Murphy, James Noah, Lucina Paquet, Jeff Perry, Steve Ramsey, Rondi Reed, Theodore Schulz, William Schwarz, Nicola Sheara, Eric Simonson, L. J. Slavin, Michael Smith, Rick Snyder, Miriam Sturm, Skipp Sudduth, Zoë Taleporos, Jim True and Jessica Wilder.

By FRANK RICH

IT'S not just because audiences must step around homeless people to get to the theater that the time is right for the Steppenwolf Theater Company's majestic adaptation of "The Grapes of Wrath."

When John Steinbeck wrote his novel about dispossessed Okies heading west in search of the promised land of California, he was also writing about a nation in search of itself. After a decade of dog-eat-dog boom and another of Depression, Steinbeck wondered what credo the survivors could still believe in. Fifty years later — after another 1920's-style orgy of greed and with many bills yet to be paid — Americans are once more uncertain in their faith. While an all-night party celebrating democracy is being uncorked around the world, the vast inequities of our own democracy leave some Americans wondering whether they deserve to be invited.

The production at the Cort, an epic achievement for the director, Frank Galati, and the Chicago theater ensemble at his disposal, makes Steinbeck live for a new generation not by updating his book but by digging into its timeless heart. On the surface, "The Grapes of Wrath" is one of the worst great novels ever written. The characters are perishable W.P.A.-mural archetypes incapable of introspection, the dialogue is at times cloyingly folksy and the drama is scant. In any ordinary sense, there's no "play" here (and without Henry Fonda's presence, a sweetened screenplay and Gregg Toland's spectacular on-site cinematography, there would-

The New York Times/Michelle V. Agins
Lois Smith and Gary Sinise in "The Grapes of Wrath," at the Cort Theater.

n't have been a movie, either). But Steinbeck wasn't trying to be Dickens or Hugo or Dreiser. Without embracing either a jingoist's flag or a Marxist's ideology, he was simply trying to unearth and replenish the soul holding a country together. That's the simple, important drama that Steppenwolf, with incredibly sophisticated theatrical technique, brings to the stage.

To be sure, Mr. Galati, as adapter, takes the audience through the narrative of the Joad family's travails by Hudson Super Six truck — a winding trail on Route 66 blighted by abject poverty, deaths, desertions, labor violence, natural disasters. But the evening's dialogue scenes are few and brief, the lines are reduced to a laconic minimum and the many people are defined by their faces and tones of voice rather than by psychological revelations.

Hoping for a generosity of spirit in a brutal land.

What one finds in place of conventional dramatic elements — and in place of the documentary photography possible only on film — is pure theater as executed by a company and director that could not be more temperamentally suited to their task. As Steppenwolf demonstrated in "True West," "Orphans" and "Balm in Gilead" — all titles that could serve for "The Grapes of Wrath" — it is an ensemble that believes in what Steinbeck does: the power of brawny, visceral art, the importance of community, the existence of an indigenous American spirit that resides in inarticulate ordinary people, the spiritual resonance of American music and the heroism of the righteous outlaw. As played by Gary Sinise and Terry Kinney, Tom Joad and the lapsed preacher, Jim Casy — the Steinbeck characters who leave civi-

lization to battle against injustice — are the forefathers of the rock-and-roll rebels in Steppenwolf productions by Sam Shepard and Lanford Wilson just as they are heirs to Huck and Jim. They get their hands dirty in the fight for right.

•

The audience meets Tom and Casy in the parched dust bowl, where they are introduced by the evening's first haunting mating of sight and sound: a fiddler in a lonely spotlight runs a bow across a handsaw, filling the antique Broadway house with the thin, plaintive wail of the barren plains. When the lights come up, the audience finds a set — a deep, barnlike shell of weathered wood, brilliantly designed and lighted by Kevin Rigdon — that will contain the entire event. Aside from the occasional descending wall or sign, the only major piece of scenery is the Joads' mobile truck, piled high with kitchen utensils, bundles of clothes and plucky humanity.

What follows is a stream of tableaux whose mythic power lies in their distillation to vibrant essentials. One's worst fear about a "Grapes of Wrath" adaptation — that it will be a patchwork quilt of sugar-coated Americana — is never realized. Mr. Galati, a director of exquisite taste, strips away sentimentality and cheap optimism. If he has an esthetic model, it is Peter Brook, not "The Waltons." His "Grapes" looks a lot like the Brook "Carmen," for its atmosphere is created with the basic elements of earth, water, fire and air. Even so, Mr. Galati and Mr. Rigdon do not regard homespun simplicity as a license for improvisatory amateurism. Elegance may seem an odd word to apply to "The Grapes of Wrath," but it fits this one. While a stage production cannot compete with the photography of Walker Evans or Pare Lorentz, it can emulate the rigorous, more abstract painterly imagery of Edward Hopper or Thomas Hart Benton or Georgia O'Keeffe.

•

Mr. Galati conveys the loneliness of the open road with headlights burning into an inky night, or with the rotating of the truck under a starry sky to reveal each isolated conversation of its inhabitants. Campfires frequently dot the stage — the ravaged face of Mr. Kinney's itinerant preacher is made to be illuminated by lantern glow — and a sharp duel of flashlights dramatizes the violence of strikebreaking thugs. Equally astringent and evocative is Michael Smith's score, which echoes Woody Guthrie and heartland musical forms and is played by a migrant band on such instruments as harmonica, jew's-harp and banjo. Sometimes salted with descriptive lyrics from Steinbeck, the music becomes the thread that loosely binds a scattered society.

Though trimmed since its premiere in Chicago in 1988, Act I of "The Grapes of Wrath" still requires perseverance. Mr. Galati, like Steinbeck, demands that the audience sink into a jerky, episodic journey rather than be propelled by the momentum of character or story. Act II pays off with the flood sequence — spectacularly realized here with a curtain of rain pouring down on men shoveling for their lives — and in remarkably fresh realizations of some of the novel's most familiar scenes. When Ma Joad — in the transcendent form of the flinty, silver-haired Lois Smith — delivers her paean to the people's ability to "go on," it isn't the inspirational epilogue that won Jane Darwell an Oscar but a no-nonsense, conversational reiteration of unshakable pragmatism. When Mr. Sinise leaves his already disintegrated family to join a radical underground, his "I'll be all around in the dark" soliloquy is not Fonda's Lincolnesque address but a plain-spoken statement of bedrock conviction.

•

Like the superb Miss Smith, Mr. Sinise and Mr. Kinney, the other good actors in this large cast never raise their voices. Such performers as Jeff Perry (Noah Joad) and Robert Breuler (Pa Joad) slip seamlessly

The heirs to Huck and Jim and the forefathers of the rebels of rock.

into folkloric roles that are permanent fixtures in our landscape. They become what Steinbeck believed his people to be — part of a communal soul that will save America from cruelty and selfishness when other gods, secular and religious, have failed.

•

Can they make us believe, too? The evening concludes with the coda the movie omitted, in which the Joad daughter, Rose of Sharon (Sally Murphy), her husband gone and her baby just born dead, offers to breast feed a starving black man (Lex Monson) in a deserted barn. As acted and staged, in a near-hush and visually adrift on the full, lonely expanse of the wooden stage, the tableau is religious theater in the simplest sense. There is no pious sermon — just a humble, selfless act of charity crystallized into a biblical image, executed by living-and-breathing actors, streaked with nocturnal shadows and scented by the gentle weeping of a fiddle string.

Some of the audience seemed to be weeping, too, and not out of sadness, I think. The Steppenwolf "Grapes of Wrath" is true to Steinbeck because it leaves one feeling that the generosity of spirit that he saw in a brutal country is not so much lost as waiting once more to be found.

1990 Mr 23, C1:4

A Man And a Whale

Martha Swope

Jake Ehrenreich

JONAH, adapted, composed and directed by Elizabeth Swados; choreography and musical staging by Bill Castellino; based on the novel "Jonah and the Whale" by Robert Nathan; sets by Michael E. Downs; costumes by Judy Dearing; lighting by Beverly Emmons; whale design by Tobi Kahn; musical director, Michael S. Sottile; associate producer, Jason Steven Cohen. Presented by Joseph Papp. At Martinson Hall of the Public Theater, 425 Lafayette Street.

Jonah .... Jake Ehrenreich
The Jonettes and all other roles and Phyllis Jonette .... Cathy Porter
Marguarita Jonette .... Ann Marie Milazzo
Musicians Paul O'Keefe and Michael S. Sottile

By STEPHEN HOLDEN

For more than two decades, an obligatory set piece in most arena-size rock concerts has been the drum solo. In a typical display of percussive pyrotechnics, the drummer, given 5 to 10 minutes to strut his stuff, attempts to pack as much aggressive grandiosity as he can muster into a thunderous blitz that usually has less to do with music than with simply showing off.

In Elizabeth Swados's new musical, "Jonah," that rock-concert ritual becomes a witty metaphor for the biblical character's ambition, pride and impatience. Whenever Jonah, God's would-be superstar prophet, feels the urge to express himself, he goes to one of several drum kits positioned around the stage of Martinson Hall at the Public Theater and bangs away.

Since Jake Ehrenreich, the actor and singer who portrays Jonah, is a decent rock drummer, the solos are concise and blend smoothly into a score that is one of Ms. Swados's characteristic pastiches of rock styles. Jonah's bushy post-hippie look and demeanor also conform to an image of some 1970's rock musicians as trendy guru-mongers and narcissistic ersatz prophets.

•

Adapted by Ms. Swados from Robert Nathan's novel "Jonah and the Whale," this version of the Jonah story could even be read as a lightly mocking parable of the shallow quick-fix mentality of so many contemporary religious movements.

"Jonah" is the fifth in the series of biblical cantatas Ms. Swados has composed and directed, beginning with "The Haggadah" and continuing with "Esther," "Jersualem" and "Song of Songs." It is also one of the most successful. The show tells Jonah's story entirely in song using a musical vocabulary that shifts easily from 1950's-style rock-and-roll to reggae to rap. Like many of her other scores, the music for "Jonah" is radically stripped down and streamlined into a conversational pop recitative that is deliberately childlike in its simplicity and directness.

In her more somber scores, this style can become monotonous. But in "Jonah," whose score is upbeat and breezy with sparkling electric keyboard and percussion arrangements, it is consistently engaging. One of its strengths is its relaxed narrative flow. "Jonah" tells its story very swiftly — in just an hour — and almost every word can be followed without straining one's ears.

•

Jonah is joined by the Jonettes (Cathy Porter and Ann Marie Milazzo) who amusingly parody the stage movements of rock backup singers. Together they sing the story, which shifts from the third to the first person when Jonah has his little tantrums, punctuated by drum solos.

Though he is not as good a singer as he is a drummer, Mr. Ehrenreich's light folk-pop delivery is more than serviceable. This version of the story is also embellished with whimsical details that are not in the Bible, among them a reluctant whale who is afraid of swallowing Jonah for fear of choking to death.

"Jonah" ends with one of the strongest pieces of music of Ms. Swados's career in her adaptation of I Corinthians 13. This famous passage of the New Testament becomes the soaring folk-rock chorale "I may be able to speak the language of kings and even of angels, but if I have not love I have nothing." The anthem exhilaratingly distills the injunction to compassion that is story's ever-pertinent moral.

1990 Mr 23, C5:1

From Indulgence To Despair

BAAL, by Bertolt Brecht; directed by Robert Woodruff; translation by Peter Tegel; set designed by Douglas Stein; lighting by Rob Murphy; sound by Stephen Santomenna; costumes by Susan Hilferty; original music by Douglas Wieselman. Presented by the Trinity Repertory Company, Anne Bogart, artistic director; Timothy Langan, managing director. At 201 Washington Street, Providence, R.I.

Baal .... Mario Arrambide
Mech .... William Damkoehler
Emilie .... Cynthia Strickland
Pschierer .... Ed Hall
Johannes .... Robert Castro
Dr. Piller, Pianist and Gougou .... Brian McEleney
Young Man and Savettka .... Brian Jucha
Ekart .... Rafael Baez
Johanna .... Josie Chavez
Sophie .... Anne Scurria
Tramp .... Timothy Crowe
Mjurk .... Allen Oliver
WITH: Tony Curotto, Cecilia Engelhardt, Paula McGonagle, Sean Moynihan, Walter Niejadlik and Lisa Welti

By MEL GUSSOW
Special to The New York Times

PROVIDENCE, R.I. March 22 — In Bertolt Brecht's first play, "Baal," written when he was 20 years old, the protagonist is a poet who leads a life of "sensational immorality." The play was indirectly prophetic of what might have become of Brecht himself if he had not continued on his course toward art, philosophy and self-realization. Baal, in contrast, is a portrait of self-indulgence in the extreme, and he ends as a figure of despair.

Though the episodic play is unwieldy and without the powerful political spine of Brecht's later work, it is a compelling piece of theater, filled with vitality and with the insatiable longings of youth. The excesses of the play are inextricable from the assets.

At the Trinity Repertory Company, in a production that opened Wednesday night, Robert Woodruff takes a modernist view of this 1918 play — an interpretation the work can sustain. In this version, Baal is resonant of everyone from Rimbaud to today's hard rockers. He is a man who burns himself out before he has taken the time to be creative.

Mr. Woodruff's production, which sprawls over a three-sided stage that seems as large as a basketball court, has its own directorial excesses, especially in terms of design and disco-style interludes. It lasts more than three hours and could be cut. But by its nature, the play allows for the application of a director's imagination, and Mr. Woodruff responds.

•

Along with Richard Foreman's version of "Woyzeck," presented this season at Hartford Stage, this is a production that extends the boundaries of theater. It is the kind of experimental work more often attempted by regional companies than by New York producers.

For bringing Mr. Woodruff's "Baal" to Providence, Anne Bogart, artistic director of Trinity Repertory, must share credit — as should Mario Arrambide, the actor who plays the title role. Because of the explicit language (in Peter Tegel's translation from the German) and Baal's role as voluptuary, the production may offend some theatergoers, a fact that is intrinsic to the work.

Treating everyone with equal disdain, hypocritical publishers as well as women helplessly in love with him, Baal lies in his lair waiting for victims eager to be degraded. In Mr. Arrambide's portrait — sensual, hedonistic and no longer youthfully trim — Baal looks like a satyr drawn by Picasso. The actor even has a narcissistic smile, indicating that in his eyes he is a benefactor rather than a seducer. There is no doubt that women swim freely into his net. "Don't think the worst of me," says one. "Why not?" he responds with demonic callousness. "You're a woman. Like any other."

•

Though Baal is to be neither admired nor pitied, he is compulsively interesting as a self-betrayer. As we watch, we wonder how far he will go — and then he goes further, adding homicide to his list of sins. At the same time, Brecht never lets the audience forget that Baal is a poet, as demonstrated in flights of rhapsodic verse. Baal refuses to waste his poetry on paper.

Mr. Arrambide incarnates his character without obscuring his roguish charm, as when two not-so-innocent adolescent sisters visit him in his apartment and are interrupted by the entrance of Baal's landlady. The audience shares Baal's laughter at the sudden end of this momentary bedroom farce.

While keeping one foot in the German setting of the original play, Mr. Woodruff creates a more generic environment, which at times has a Hispanic element, as exemplified by the sounds of salsa in Douglas Wieselman's score. Baal performs as a rock singer rather than as a balladeer (as in Brecht), but the purpose is the same — to push his performance so far as to outrage the audience. Baal is meant to be outrageous — and he is. There is no defense of his actions. But the play moves the audience to a disturbing awareness of the emptiness of a life of self-gratification.

•

Mr. Arrambide is the vortex of the production, and there are supportive contributions from members of the large cast, including Cynthia Strickland, Josie Chavez and Anne Scurria as his victims, and from William Damkoehler and Ed Hall.

Brecht wrote the play before the rise of Hitler (whom he later mocked in "Arturo Ui"). Although it would be rash to say that Baal is Hitlerian, his story does demonstrate the horrendous result of unbounded egotism.

Years later the author commented that Baal was in battle against an exploitative world, that he was "antisocial, but in an antisocial society." That position was a case of political hindsight on Brecht's part, but it has application in our time as well as that of the author. One of the points of Mr. Woodruff's visceral production is that there are Baals among us.

1990 Mr 24, 17:1

Peter Cunningham

Kenneth Welsh and Kathy Bates in "Frankie and Johnny."

STAGE VIEW/Mel Gussow

Love and Happiness, Together at Last

IN THE 1930'S AND 40'S, FRED and Ginger and all those other starry-eyed cloudland couples met to the music — sometimes real, sometimes metaphorical — of romantic love. Now there are Peter and Rita, the hero and heroine of "Prelude to a Kiss," Craig Lucas's charming new play at the Circle Repertory Company. As played by Alec Baldwin and Mary-Louise Parker, the two are throwbacks to a more congenial era for romance, in life as well as in art. Recorded musical interludes of the title song and other ballads additionally evoke a nostalgic past. Despite obstacles on their path to marital bliss — arising from Mr. Lucas's use of an intricate plot device — love triumphs, just as it did in Hollywood.

Watching the couple in a most persuasive ritual of courtship, one tries to recall the last time there was such a mutually smitten pair on stage, at least in such serious circumstances. This is not a sitcom but a comedy with sobering undertones.

Most of America's finest playwrights have held romance at a distance. When they deal with it thematically, it can be tormented (a legion headed by Tennessee Williams), incestuous (Sam Shepard) or masochistic (David Rabe). The closest David Mamet has come may be "A Life in the Theater," an affair between an actor and his art.

Other writers are more concerned with generational and family matters. When Beth Henley and Marsha Norman regard the home, they see domestic violence, and Christopher Durang (in "The Marriage of Bette and Boo") sees a history of post-wedding crises. As typified by Wendy Wasserstein's "Heidi Chronicles," love remains elusive, as if waiting for lightning to strike.

This is not to suggest that any of these writers is incapable of writing a love story but, up to now, they have apparently been uninterested — as have their English peers. When Harold Pinter, Simon Gray and David Hare deal with love, they write about betrayal. Alan Ayckbourn frequently writes about a garden-variety infidelity. With Tom Stoppard, in a rare excursion on this terrain earlier this season ("Artist Descending a Staircase"), love leads headlong to suicide.

To find a love story in the American theater, especially that almost extinct sub species, the New York love story, one has to look back to Neil Simon's "Barefoot in the Park." The fact that Mr. Simon's lovers would walk barefoot in the park or could find a low-rent, top-floor studio apartment in Greenwich Village says something about the passage of

Except for Craig Lucas's charming new play, love stories that dare to be positive have been a rarity on stage.

time. In his more recent work, by looking back on the past, the playwright has offered signs of romantic longing if not fulfillment.

Except for "Prelude to a Kiss," American plays this season have been, as usual, barren of romance. Audiences have been asked to share the comic misery of the futuristic couple in Steve Tesich's "Square One"; the discordance in Terrence McNally's "Lisbon Traviata," and the almost lifelong separation of the star-crossed couple in A. R. Gurney's "Love Letters." There is not even a hint of a liaison between the principal male and female characters in "A Few Good Men" by Aaron Sorkin.

Romance is of course a more natural concern of musical theater, as it certainly was in the heyday of Rodgers and Hammerstein and Lerner and Loewe. But in the world of Stephen Sondheim, more often love is an interrupted malady and with Andrew Lloyd Webber love wears a mask to disguise disfigurement (in his new musical, "Aspects of Love," opening in New York next month, there is an attempt to deal more directly with the subject). Both "City of Angels" and "Grand Hotel," musicals that look backward, express a romantic inclination but it is a minor matter next to the more important issues of Hollywood noir and Tommy Tune's dancing hostelry.

Actually there is a connection between "Phantom of the Opera" and "Prelude to a Kiss," and that is in the evocation of the theme of Beauty and the Beast. "Prelude to a Kiss" offers a clever reversal: the prince (or, in this case, the princess) turns into a frog on the wedding day. Mr. Baldwin and Ms. Parker meet at a party and connect on all possible levels. They have amazingly identical taste in food and drink — as if they have memorized each other's computer profile — and they speak the same comic language, a coincidence that Mr. Baldwin underscores with amusing asides to the audience. In a final wish-fulfillment, Rita's father and mother (played with drollness by Larry Bryggman and Debra Monk) turn out to be paragons of parental indulgence. Theatergoers hold their breath while watching the young couple caught up in a dance of love.

The first-act euphoria ends with a most eventful kiss that shifts the play into fantasy and puts the pair to an ultimate test. The husband's love is forced to transcend the fact that his wife has mysteriously switched souls with an elderly man (Barnard Hughes) near the end of his life. In the second act there is a sequence that stretches credibility — even on the author's fanciful terms.

When Mr. Hughes's spirit inhabits Ms. Parker's body he behaves not as an old man rejuvenated into a second life but as an eccentric young woman who simply contradicts all of Ms. Parker's previously established characteristics (as in the purchase of an expensive bracelet). In contrast, the reverse — Ms. Parker inhabiting Mr. Hughes's body — is artfully in character. Such is the strength of the bond Mr. Lucas has created between the lovers that many theatergoers are willing to suspend disbelief and go along with the playwright on his imaginative leap. Much of the willingness is attributable to the endearing performances of Mr. Baldwin and Ms. Parker.

In the American theater over the last dozen years, I can think of only two other such rewarding plays in which dramatists un-self-consciously wrote love stories and dared to close with a happy ending: Lanford Wilson's "Talley's Folly," by the author's intention, "a no-holds-barred romantic story," and Mr. McNally's "Frankie and Johnny in the Clair de Lune." In both instances, apparent opposites are drawn together in a kind of enchantment.

■

With "Talley's Folly," our empathy for Sally Talley and Matt Friedman was deepened by our knowledge that the two were to have a long happy life together (as recounted in the previously produced "Fifth of July"). There is no such assurance with Frankie and Johnny or Peter and Rita, though, having survived the trauma of soul displacement, the latter couple are certainly candidates for that final Fred and Ginger dance of felicity.

■

Other playwrights may prefer to leave the subject of romance to lyricists and those lighter in heart. They may question the narrative validity, wondering if it can sustain a dramatic evening. Two people fall in love — and then a writer searches for a second act. "Talley's Folly" avoided that dilemma by limiting itself to one act. "Prelude to a Kiss" solves it by

whisking the lovers into a fantasy world where souls can be switched like television channels. Rita refers to the old codger who steals her soul as her fairy godfather; actually he is closer to the wicked warlock of the West, at least until he realizes the iniquity caused by his interference in young love.

One of the curiosities of "Prelude to a Kiss" is its provenance. It comes from a playwright who, up to now, has specialized in quirky stories about people unable to connect, as defined by the Sondheim song, "It Wasn't Meant to Happen," in "Marry Me a Little," the collage of the composer's music conceived by Mr. Lucas and his director Norman René. In Mr. Lucas's last play, "Reckless," a wife abandons her home on Christmas Eve in order to avoid being killed by an assassin hired by her husband. Nothing in the playwright's previous work has prepared us for the sheer congeniality of his new play, where love is meant to happen — and does.

Romantic couples on stage are candidates for that final Fred and Ginger dance of felicity.

In films, as on stage, romance seems to be unfashionable. Among those films nominated for an Academy Award this year, only "Driving Miss Daisy" has even a semblance of a love story. One other recent film, "The Fabulous Baker Boys," is singularly unabashed in its regard for

the salutary power of love. As Michelle Pfeiffer and Jeff Bridges regard each other in a rhapsodic gaze — to a background of sultry blues — we are reminded again of Hollywood in the time of the great romantic teams: Tracy and Hepburn, Bogart and Bacall (or Bergman), Gable and Lombard.

They were of course indicative of their period, whether that period was pre-war (escapism) or postwar (optimism). The proliferation was a response to the audience's desire to find a natural romantic order outside of themselves and to live out a dream on a large screen.

"Prelude to a Kiss" may be a harbinger, the first post-yuppie fairy tale in which a young man and woman, terrifically attracted to each other, discover an idyll with a properly pragmatic resolution. The play could be a prelude to a more widespread rediscovery of romance as a subject for dramatization. □

1990 Mr 25, II:5:1

Nature's Indifference

LOST IN A FLURRY OF CHERRIES, original writer, Ango Sakaguchi; script writer and director, Tsunetoshi Hirowatari; set designer, Shigeo Okajima; music, Shinichiro Ikebe; choreography, Takashi Nishida; lighting, Sadahiko Tachiki; costumes, Michiko Kitamura; sound effects, Isao Tamura; Tokyo Engeki Ensemble presented by La Mama E.T.C., with the Agency for Cultural Affairs of Japan (Bunkacho). At 74A East Fourth Street.

WITH: Kisetsu Mano, Mitsuyoshi Yanagawa, Yoko Fujikawa, Setsuko Shimojo, Midori Kinoshita, Yoko Hashimoto, Shizuku Iwao, Makiko Muro, Yoshie Maruoka, Junko Miura, Yoko Kagami and Yoko Nemoto.

By STEPHEN HOLDEN

"Lost in a Flurry of Cherries," the Japanese experimental drama that ends its residence at La Mama E.T.C. today, is only about 70 minutes long. But by its end, the cold, mysterious play with spectacular stage effects leaves one feeling wind-blown and a little breathless from its energy.

Presented by the Tokyo Engeki Ensemble, the drama, directed by Tsunetoshi Hirowatari, a well-known avant-garde director and Brechtian theoretician, is a primal pas de deux based on a 1947 play by Ango Sakaguchi. The play was itself an adaptation of a medieval Japanese fable set in a mythical forest of cherry trees.

As the play opens, the two main characters, a bandit (Mitsuyoshi Yanagawa), and the aristocratic woman he has won (Kisetsu Mano) literally burst through a folding gold-leaf screen at the rear of the stage and tumble over each other in a ferocious life-and-death struggle. Through the hole they have torn, a wind-machine fans dry-ice smoke and billowing swirls of paper cherry blossoms that are released in varying amounts from the ceiling almost continuously throughout the performance.

Performed in Japanese (an English translation is provided in the program), the play presents an image of love as a savage power struggle in which erotic and murderous impulses are inseparable. In the story, the man abducts the woman from her town to the cherry grove where he lives. Once

they arrive, she orders him to kill six of his seven mistresses and keep the seventh as a slave.

All the luxury in the world cannot appease her desire for power, and when they move from the grove back to the town, she demands more severed heads. Eventually she changes into a demon who tries to devour her lover's soul until he strangles her. Later he has a final vision of her inside the demon's body, but as he reaches to touch her, she disappears into the earth, leaving only the echo of her voice through an endless blizzard of cherry blossoms.

●

The enigmatic story is open to any number of interpretations, but on the most obvious level it is a meditation on beauty and cruelty and the indifference of nature dramatized as a quasi-erotic fable. The performances have a ritualistic physical intensity that suggests a fusion of martial arts and Japanese dance traditions. Miss Mano, as the woman whose mane of purple hair clashes with her layers of finery, projects a fierce demonic edge, especially in those moments when she is lifted by wires over the man's head.

Shigeo Okajima's spare, strikingly evocative settings use wind machines and several bushels of paper cherry blossoms to create a whooshing storm of flowers that gathers, ebbs and eventually returns with a renewed fury to leave the stage smothered in a thick pink carpet of petals. Shinichiro Ikebe's background music suggests a modernized, partly electronic pastiche of Stravinsky's "Firebird" and Ravel's "Daphnis et Chloé."

1990 Mr 25, 62:1

Breathing Blue Air

THE NATURE OF THINGS, written and performed by David Cale; a collaboration with Roy Nathanson, Marc Ribot and E. J. Rodriguez; directed by Bill Barnes; lighting, Anne Militello; sound, Richard Kirschner; production stage manager, Elise-Ann Konstantin; production manager, George Xenos. Presented by New York Theater Workshop, James C. Nicola, artistic director; Nancy Kassak Diekmann, managing director. At the Perry Street Theater, 31 Perry Street, west of Seventh Avenue.

By MEL GUSSOW

"I'm a wild animal; no one can tame me," says David Cale, expressing his outsider's vision of the world. There is something undomesticated, almost anti-theatrical about this performance artist. Those unfamiliar with his work might wonder if he had just wandered on stage from the audience, Because the sky is blue, he asks if he is breathing blue air — and he contemplates what birds are thinking about as they fly, leaving the suggestion that thinking might be antithetical to flying. In such a fashion, he tries to project himself into other spheres of existence.

No matter how absurd life can be, he accepts it as a natural order. It is "The Nature of Things," as in the title of his new one-man show (with musical accompaniment) at the Perry Street Theater. He matter-of-factly recounts his dreams, and they become tangible. For the audience it is difficult to separate fact from fancy, which may be Mr. Cale's intention. Though scripted, his musings seem intuitive, even patchwork, as he wanders between wryness and whimsy.

In the first half of his show, he holds a notebook in his hand, and, somewhat in the manner of Spalding Gray, he quotes from his own writings. He offers scenes and snapshots, some as brief as haiku, others longer comic reflections from his boyhood in England. To be excused from compulsory swimming at school, he forged a doctor's note saying that he would "dissolve in water," a phrase that exemplifies Mr. Cale's eccentric humor.

A thin, soft-spoken Englishman, he tells us that his grandmother thought he resembled Prince Charles and that others have confused him with the rock guitarist Mark Knopfler. The comparisons are intriguing but unlikely, as is the case with other references in his rambling monologue. As he searches for quiddities in everyday life, he often finds himself in "dire straits," to borrow the name of Mr. Knopfler's group.

In the middle of "The Nature of Things," he delivers his words to a background of a three-piece jazz combo led by Roy Nathanson (who plays two saxophones at the same time). In common with the tales in Mr. Cale's previous show, "Smooch Music," these fanciful stories are wrapped around music. Some have, in his words, "the ring of truth"; others the ring of self-created myth.

Mr. Cale has expanded his repertory from his earlier monologues like "The Redthroats," and he has polished his performance techniques, changing his voice more skillfully as he moves between characters. Although Spalding Gray and Eric Bogosian surpass him in their contrasting fields, he does combine aspects of both in the process of communicating his own wistful, sometimes cryptic and always affable personality. As a monologuist, he is still defining what it is he does. For Mr. Cale, that continuing search may itself be the nature of things.

1990 Mr 25, 63:1

Rented Land of No Hope

AND THE SOUL SHALL DANCE, by Wakako Yamauchi; directed by Kati Kuroda; lighting design, Tina Charney; costume design, Toni-Leslie James; set design, Robert Klingelhoefer; stage manager, David H. Bosboom. Presented by the Pan Asian Repertory Theater, Tisa Chang, artistic/producing director. At 336 West 20th Street.

Hana Murata	Carol A. Honda
Murata	Ron Nakahara
Masako	Roxanne Chang
Oka	Norris M. Shimabuku
Emiko Oka	Dawn A. Saito
Kiyoko	Yuko Komiyama

By STEPHEN HOLDEN

"And the Soul Shall Dance," Wakako Yamauchi's Depression-era drama, remembers the time when California law forbade Japanese immigrants to own their own land. Farmers who had come to the United States in search of a better life were obliged to sign two-year leases on property they cultivated. Many families found themselves moving from farm to farm eking out a subsistence living. Their treatment as second-class citizens was profoundly demoralizing; added to the language and cultural barriers they faced, it made social and economic assimilation extremely difficult.

Ms. Yamauchi's play had its premiere in Los Angeles in 1977 and was brought to New York two years later by the Pan Asian Repertory Theater,

which is reviving it at the Apple Corps Theater. Her drama is an acutely observant study of how these social pressures affect two neighboring farm families in California. Murata (Ron Nakahara), his wife, Hana (Carol A. Honda), and their 11-year-old daughter, Masako (Roxanne Chang), are the hardier of the two families. Hana, who holds the family together, is a fussing, clucking matriarch with impeccable manners and a stern sense of discipline, who has deferred her own aspirations so her daughter can assimilate and have a better life.

•

Their neighbors are not so resilient. Oka (Norris M. Shimabuku) and his wife, Emiko (Dawn A. Saito), coexist in a state of undeclared war. After the death of Oka's first wife before she could join him in America, her family married him by proxy to her rebellious younger sister, whom they sent abroad against her will.

As portrayed by Ms. Saito, Emiko suggests a Japanese-American answer to one of Tennessee Williams's haunted wraiths. The only things sustaining her are her memories of Japan and her determination to return. A secretive, mercurial woman perpetually drunk on sake, she tiptoes unsteadily about the stage in a trancelike state of suppressed rage and dreamy longing for the past. The marriage explodes when Kiyoko, Oka's 15-year-old daughter by his first marriage, comes to live with them. The tiny nest egg that Emiko fantasized would subsidize her own departure goes to pay for the girl's

Martha Swope Associates/Carol Rosegg

Dawn A. Saito in a scene from "And the Soul Shall Dance."

movie magazines and permanent waves.

•

Although the drama offers sketchy information on the social and legal status of its characters, it is predominantly a psychological study of people struggling to adapt to the stringent traditions and laws of two worlds simultaneously: one they have left and one in which they are trying to forge a new identity. In the playwright's even-handed vision, Oka and Emiko are the largely helpless victims of the squeeze between the two. And the most compelling scenes are those in which the couple's bottled-up feelings explode in violence, followed by excruciating guilt and masochism.

Under Kati Kuroda's direction, the actors give psychologically detailed performances. Ms. Honda and Ms. Saito are especially impressive in their representation of opposed philosophies, one brutally practical, the other crazily romantic. Even the complicated relationship between the two second-generation Japanese-American daughters is carefully elaborated.

The production's main flaw is a lack of momentum, especially in the second act — which peters out in a final scene that seems at once abrupt and tentative. One senses that the production's admirable attempt to be accurate in many small ways inadvertently subverted its overall dramatic sweep.

1990 Mr 25, 63:2

Dreams and Nightmares

EL ETERNO FEMENINO, by Rosario Castellanos; directed by Beatriz Cordoba; assistant director, Aitzpea Goenaga; mime, Michael Trautman; hair stylist, Ana Rojas; production assistants, Rigoberto Obando and Manuel Herrera; production design, Robert Weber Federico. Presented by Repertorio Español, Gilberto Zaldívar, producer; René Buch, artistic director. At the Gramercy Arts Theater, 138 East 27th Street.

WITH: Maria José Alvarez, Birgit Bofarull, Ofelia González, Katerina Lladó, Feiga Martinez, Ana Margarita Martínez-Casado, Carlos Osorio, Virginia Rambal, Diego Taborda, Tatiana Vecinos and David Zúñiga.

By D. J. R. BRUCKNER

Rosario Castellanos took the title of her play "El Eterno Femenino" from Goethe, but nothing else. "The eternal feminine leads us on," the German poet says at the end of "Faust." To the Mexican novelist and poet, this famous tag line was obviously something of a joke, perhaps a bitter one, and her dark comedy supplies a feminist corrective to women's history. But her vision of women's fate might make some feminists uncomfortable.

"El Eterno Femenino" has seldom been produced, even in Mexico. The manuscript dates from 1973, the year before Castellanos died. (She stepped out of a bathtub in Tel Aviv, where she was the Mexican Ambassador to Israel, touched a lamp switch and was electrocuted.) Since it was never staged in her lifetime and thus subjected to revision, it should be considered unfinished.

•

Nonetheless, it has great energy and humor — qualities exploited vigorously in the new production of the work by Repertorio Español under the direction of Beatriz Cordoba. Castellanos herself said it would be a good idea to pay more attention to situation and the rhythm of the plot than to individual characters, and Ms. Cordoba has taken the advice to heart. There may be no other sane approach for a play with 30, 31 or 32 roles (depending on how the director interprets several of them) taken here by 11 actors. (Castellanos defined the cast as "whoever appears.") Six of them play the heroine, Lupita, at 12 different stages of life,

At first glance the story is hardly promising. Lupita, preparing for her wedding, goes to a beauty parlor where a wily salesman has persuaded the owner to try out a dream device attached to the hair dryer. The dream it produces for Lupita is a nightmare of a woman's life in a macho world, from honeymoon to fragile old age.

In the second act she tries on a series of wigs that inspire daydreams of alternative versions of her life. Among other things, she is a ridiculous mistress, a hilariously inept reporter and a triumphant prostitute, and she ends up as Eve in Paradise where the playwright stands the biblical story of the first humans on its head. The Paradise scene best displays the quick turns of Castellanos's caustic wit and her scorn not only for machismo but also for compliant women, even for hesitant feminists.

Ms. Cordoba treats the story as just as unimportant as Castellanos thought it was, and she plays the farcical situations for all they are worth, sometimes more. She is a very successful extortionist of (occasionally nervous) laughter. The script is full of references to Mexican myths about women, history and especially to themes (and sometimes lines) of the great 17th-century Mexican poet Sor Juana, a nun who was nothing if not a precursor of modern feminism. For people who can catch these echos, they are there, but Ms. Cordoba wisely does not emphasize them for her North American audience.

•

In one respect her energy is annoying. In any production the play would not run more than two hours, but this director has shortened it considerably — not so much by cutting as by having the actors rap out lines so fast that some of them must be unintelligible even to people with a perfect ear for Spanish.

As usual, the members of this lively company perform with superb discipline and a kind of courtesy that sets them apart; their rule seems to be that the only mortal sin in theater is upstaging someone. It is a pleasure to watch them zip in and out of different characters in "El Eterno Femenino," and it is a mark of their achievement that the many different Lupitas add up to a single personality. It is beyond anyone to turn this work into a well-made play, but at least they make it all stick together.

1990 Mr 25, 63:1

Passion and Sterility

LETTICE AND LOVAGE, by Peter Shaffer; directed by Michael Blakemore; designed by Alan Tagg; Miss Smith's costumes by Anthony Powell; costumes designed by Frank Krenz; lighting designed by Ken Billington. Presented by the Shubert Organization, Robert Fox Ltd. and Roger Berlind. At the Ethel Barrymore Theater, 243 West 47th Street.

Lettice Douffet	Maggie Smith
Surly Man	Dane Knell
Lotte Schoen	Margaret Tyzack
Miss Framer	Bette Henritze
Mr. Bardolph	Paxton Whitehead
Visitors to Fustian House	

Herb Foster, Prudence Wright Holmes, Patricia Kilgarriff, Barbara Lester, Sybil Lines, Laurine Towler, Tyrone Wilson and Ronald Yamamoto.

By FRANK RICH

There is only one Maggie Smith, but audiences get at least three of her in "Lettice and Lovage," the Peter Shaffer comedy that has brought this spellbinding actress back to Broadway after an indecently long absence and that has the shrewd sense to keep her glued to center stage.

As Lettice Douffet, the most eccentric tour guide ever to lead bored American and Japanese visitors through one of England's dullest stately homes, Miss Smith is, for much of Act I, the dazzling revue

Zoe Dominic

Maggie Smith as Lettice Douffet in "Lettice and Lovage," a comedy by Peter Shaffer.

comedienne she once was, dashing up and down a dark Tudor staircase while dispensing historical arcana and restroom directions with equally mad aplomb. Well, Miss Smith is not running, actually — she just seems to be. Her long arms are in windmill motion, as if she were directing traffic at a rush-hour intersection. Her voice, the only good argument yet advanced for the existence of sinus passages, tucks an extra syllable or two into words already as chewy as "escutcheon." Her moon-shaped eyes, framed by cascading red curls, are as mischievous and wide and darting as those of Lettice's beloved pet cat.

The other Maggie Smiths on view at the Barrymore are no less extravagant, no less endearing. Eventually asked to share the stage, or at least cohabit it, with another actress, the estimable Margaret Tyzack, the star becomes the stylized classicist who can italicize a line as prosaic as "Have you no marmalade?" until it sounds like a freshly minted epigram by Coward or Wilde. Later still, Miss Smith is permitted a moment as a tragedian: she stands in the shadows of Lettice's basement flat — a lonely woman for an instant deserted by her usual ebullience — and reveals her age and isolation through a veil of very small tears.

But that is about the only instance when Miss Smith comes to parade rest in "Lettice and Lovage"; at times this inexhaustible entertainer even switches outrageous costumes in mid-scene. The exertion is needed. Mr. Shaffer's play, his first out-and-out comedy since "Black Comedy" in 1964, is a slight if harmless confection that at first matches Miss Smith's bracing energy but by Act III must be bolstered by it. The jig would be up far earlier in the evening if anyone were so stupid as to ask the star to sit still.

"Lettice and Lovage" is essentially a high camp, female version of the archetypal Shaffer play, most recently exemplified by "Equus" and "Amadeus," in which two men, one representing creativity and ecstatic passion and the other mediocrity and sterility, battle for dominance. In this case, the free spirit is Lettice, a lover of history and theater and a sworn enemy of all in life that is "mere." Lettice, who is inevitably referred to

as incorrigible, loses her tour-guide job because she embellishes the official history of Fustian House in Wiltshire with outlandish Elizabethan fantasies (which are repeated in four riotous variations in Mr. Shaffer's bravura opening scene). The stick-in-the-mud who sacks her, played by Miss Tyzack, is Lotte Schoen, a gray personnel bureaucrat who worships fact as much as Lettice reveres romantic fancy.

What makes this variation on the Shaffer formula less compelling than its predecessors is not so much its comic tone — there are, rest assured, no horses blinded here — as its lackadaisical dramatic structure and its shallow characterizations. The conflict between Lettice and Lotte is resolved fairly early, for it only takes a little lovage, an herb Lettice uses to brew an Elizabethan cordial, to turn them into bosom buddies.

Once these apparently asexual spinsters warm to each other, the author elects to arrest their development. Lotte is stripped of her wig but not down to her soul, thereby robbing Miss Tyzack's flawless performance of the opportunity for a touching metamorphosis. Lettice's relationship to her former adversary remains jokey rather than intimate. The jokes, though written by Mr. Shaffer with a sure sense of the virtuoso instruments at his disposal, deliver more nostalgic tickles than

Female echoes of 'Equus' and 'Amadeus.'

laughter. They're largely impersonal gibes at the dehumanizing modern London the women discover they both deplore: a city full of automated teller machines and the sterile office towers that so nettle the Prince of Wales.

For all of his detestation of automation, Mr. Shaffer is not above using an intercom to keep his play going when all else fails. And too often he provides only a mere pastiche of civilized wit — the kind that impresses American Anglophiles on trust-house tours — by packing in references to

Latin etymologies and the Shakespearean antics of Lettice's actress-mother or by having his characters deliver crowd-pleasing endorsements of yesteryear's values. The zingers promised by the actresses' sharp diction only occasionally materialize, and they're closer in tone to "Auntie Mame" than "The Madwoman of Chaillot." In place of Mame's motto of "Live! Live! Live!" is Lettice's of "Enlarge! Enliven! Enlighten!" and, like Patrick Dennis's heroine, Mr. Shaffer's is dismissed from temporary employment at a department store and must win over a mousy secretary (Bette Henritze) and a stuffy lawyer (Paxton Whitehead) with her bohemian ways.

The staging, by Michael Blakemore, is as airtight as one expects from the director of "City of Angels" and "Noises Off." Or so it is until Act III, which, though given a new and pandering final curtain since the London premiere, still becomes mired in a complex narrative of preposterous offstage events that turn out not to matter anyway. While Alan Tagg's scenic design and Ken Billington's lighting practice an excess of dowdy realism in depicting the gloom of Lettice's Earl's Court flat, Miss Smith's personality so saturates everything around her that, like the character she plays, she instantly floods a world of gray with color. This is idiosyncratic theater acting of a high and endangered order, not to be confused with the actress's tightly minimalistic film work. If "Lettice and Lovage" is but a modest excuse for it, what theaterlover needs any excuse whatsoever to have a rare reunion with Maggie Smith?

1990 Mr 26, C11:1

The Cows Jumped Over the Boom

MAKING MOVIES, by Aaron Sorkin; directed by Don Scardino; sets by David Potts; costumes by Laura Crow; lighting by Dennis Parichy; general management, New Roads Productions; company manager, Laura Heller; consultant to the producer, George Darveris; production stage manager, Fred Reinglas; sound by Aural Fixation; associate producers, Graconn Ltd. and David H. Peipers. Presented by John A. McQuiggan, in association with Lucille Lortel, Promenade Partners Inc. and Pace Theatrical Group Inc. At the Promenade Theater, Broadway and 76th Street.

Jeff	David Marshall Grant
Robert	Michael Countryman
Craig	Kurt Deutsch
Reuben	Christopher Murney
Marty	Sharon Schlarth

By MEL GUSSOW

A first-time film director is making a movie about disgruntled marines on the island of Guam. Naturally he is shooting it on location — on a farm outside Schenectady. Wildly over budget, he hopes to recoup his fortunes with a dramatic final scene, but, as the cameras roll, three cows amble into the picture, adding a jarringly bucolic note to the battlefield.

The reactions — exasperation from the director, desperation from the unseen actors who begin to do "bits of business with the cows" — provide the centerpiece of the second act of Aaron Sorkin's "Making Movies." This new comedy opened last night at the Promenade Theater, revealing a lightly satiric side to the playwright

responsible for the courtroom theatrics of "A Few Good Men" on Broadway.

In this half of "Making Movies," Mr. Sorkin makes a number of pointed remarks about movie careerism and ineptitude, but he precedes it with an attenuated and labored first act about the preproduction problems of the film. "Making Movies" begins by marking time.

Coming after David Mamet's "Speed-the-Plow," Jonathan Reynolds's "Geniuses" and other spoofs, the opening scene is stock footage. This is a case of cinematic déjà vu as the playwright grinds slowly through the prescribed celluloid stops. The dialogue is mock-Mamet, right down to the fact that the director is frequently addressed by his name, Bob or Bobby (as in "Speed-the-Plow").

The director (Michael Countryman) and the screenwriter (David Marshall Grant) are on a sound stage in Queens. Though they are best friends, they are at odds about their movie, trying to plot the illogic of the epic while accommodating the interference of a rising young producer (Sharon Schlarth). The few smiles are provided by two minor characters, a cynical production manager (Christopher Murney) who has seen everything and an ingenuous production assistant (Kurt Deutsch) who knows nothing.

In contrast, the second act is diverting, as it was in 1988 when it was an independent short play titled "Hidden in This Picture," the curtain-raiser on a triple bill of one-acts. The first time around, the sketch starred Nathan Lane as the director and the playwright himself as the screenwriter. Slightly enlarged, the scene still concludes with the frantic film makers grasping for dramatic justification for the screenstruck bovines.

As directed by Don Scardino, Mr. Countryman and Mr. Grant are amusing contrasts in the second half of "Making Movies." Sitting on a hilltop like Cecil B. DeMille on a countdown of "The Ten Commandments," Mr. Countryman exudes auteur authority, so much so that he can casually delegate responsibility to that eager production assistant, or P.A.).

Floating from film to film, the P.A. has never progressed beyond the role of apprentice bagel-fetcher — until now. That gleam in his ambitious eye indicates he will soon be the one to call "Lights, camera, action!" on his own shoot. His imminent ascension in a cutthroat business that deserves him could have been a promising subject for a prophetic postlude to "Making Movies."

Instead, for his expanded version of his one-act play, Mr. Sorkin chose to write that unnecessary prelude. If this were the old studio system, a Hollywood tycoon would have chomped on his cigar and insisted that the movie cut to the chase — and speed the cows.

1990 Mr 28, C17:1

All in the Family

MAMA, I WANT TO SING, PART II book and lyrics by Vy Higginsen and Ken Wydro; original music by Wesley Naylor; directed by Mr. Wydro. Set design, Charles McClennahan; choreographer, Cisco Drayton; lighting design, Marshall Williams; production stage manager, Mark Wagenhurst; assistant stage manager/technical director, Kevin P. Lewis. Presented by Reach Entertainment and Sports, in association with Ms. Higginsen and Mr. Wydro. At the Heckscher Theater, 1230 Fifth Avenue, at 104th Street.

228

Doris Winter ....D'Atra Hicks
The Rev. Julian Simmons .... Norwood
Mama Winter .... Doris Troy
Sister Carrie ....Kathleen Murphy-Palmer
Minister of Music .... Charles Stewart
Little Doris .... Knoelle Higginsen-Wydro
Narrator/Disk Jockey .... Vy Higginsen
WITH: The New York Reach Ensemble

By STEPHEN HOLDEN

"The Story Continues," proclaims the subtitle of "Mama, I Want to Sing, Part II," the sequel to the long-running musical.

Part II, which has just opened at the Heckscher Theater, where the original is still playing on Saturdays at 5 P.M. after seven years, carries forward the biography of the same main character, Doris Winter, a church-trained singer from Harlem who becomes an international pop star. Like Part I, the sequel is crude by Broadway standards but often deeply stirring in its musical depiction of an archetypal American success story.

The "Mama, I Want to Sing" phenomenon is a family affair. The plots for both shows are loosely based on the life of Doris Troy, a singer who, after writing and recording the 1963 hit "Just One Look," spent several years in Britain before returning to her New York roots. Ms. Troy appears in both shows as her mother, Mama Winter, a role she plays with a good-humored, salt-of-the-earth solidity. Ms. Troy's sister, Vy Higginsen, is the narrator for both productions. She is also the co-producer of the show, and the co-author — with her husband Ken Wydro, the show's director — of the book and lyrics.

The format of Part II is identical to that of Part I. Doris's story unfolds as a musical radio serial whose chapters are prefaced with flowery introductions by Ms. Higginsen, a disk jockey for a radio station very much like New York's black-oriented WBLS. A radio program, a gospel service, a theatrical pageant and a soap opera rolled into one, with a little vaudeville thrown in, the show focuses on pivotal scenes from Doris's life, dramatized in song with minimal dialogue.

The score, most of which was composed by the show's conductor, Wesley Naylor, with interpolations of several familiar gospel songs, is sung with an extraordinary exuberance by the cast and the New York Reach Ensemble, an excellent 16-member choir. Again and again, the performances infuse the sketchy, elementary scenario with gusty human passion.

In the original show, Doris, a preacher's daughter who has grown up in the church, survives her beloved father's death and becomes a secular pop star despite her own insecurities and the misgivings of her family and others. Part II covers the subsequent eight and a half years, during which she is married to Julian Simmons, the handsome young preacher who is carrying on her father's ministry, and with whom she has a baby daughter, Little Doris.

The sequel's romance lends the sequel a warmth and sexiness that the original show lacked. In D'Atra Hicks and Norwood, who play Doris and Julian, the director has a team whose vocal and romantic chemistry sizzles. Ms. Hicks, whose good looks, reserve and artful style of pop-gospel declamation recall Whitney Houston, is completely convincing as Doris. Norwood is vocally reminiscent of James Ingram and exudes a brash, crowd-pleasing charm.

The show's dramatic centerpiece, "To Love Is to Serve," is a fiery duet in which the young minister hurls demands at his wife, only to have her reply with even more ferocity that her career is just as valuable as his. As their voices lock in anguished combat, the show reaches an emotional temperature that one rarely finds on the musical stage.

Mr. Naylor's music for the sequel is more sophisticated than that written for the original, which was the work of several composers. The score's three love duets, "Something Pretty," "Long Distance Love" and especially "We Belong Together," wed romantic pop-soul conventions and dramatic narrative to create a heated musical excitement.

•

The show has many weaknesses. It is shameless in the way it pulls heartstrings. The dialogue and line readings sometimes go completely flat. And the flashing of dimly lighted slides to illustrate scenes at the rear of a crude set that is part disk-jockey booth, part choir loft is so ineffective that one quickly stops noticing.

But in an odd way, the show's weaknesses seem inseparable from its strengths. An essentially homemade production, put together by an extended family on a shoestring budget, it has an intimacy that one can't imagine finding in a more conventionally professional production.

The fact that black gospel choirs have served as the music schools and testing grounds for many of today's most successful pop-soul singers is by now so well known that it is practically a cliché. But as both parts of "Mama" remind us, behind the cliché lies a vital social reality. Notwithstanding the incursions of rap, the African-American gospel tradition remains one of American culture's most productive artistic seedbeds.

To attend either production of "Mama" with a typical audience made up largely of church groups, some of which have traveled hundreds of miles by chartered bus to be there, is to be indelibly reminded of the enduring power of that tradition.

1990 Mr 28, C13:1

Martha Swope Associates/Carol Rosegg

D'Atra Hicks, second from left, as Doris Winter in a scene from "Mama, I Want to Sing, Part II," at the Heckscher Theater.

Guilt by Hysteria

THE CRUCIBLE, by Arthur Miller; directed by Gerald Freedman; set design by Christopher H. Barreca; costume design by Jeanne Button; lighting design by Mary Jo Dondlinger; sound design by Philip Campanella; production stage manager, Kathy J. Faul. Presented by the Roundabout Theater, Gene Feist, artistic director; Todd Haimes, producing director. At 100 East 17th Street.

Elizabeth Proctor ....Harriet Harris
John Proctor ....Randle Mell
Abigail Williams .... Justine Bateman
Rev. John Hale .... William Leach
Mary Warren .... Vicki Lewis
Giles Corey .... Maury Cooper
Rebecca Nurse .... Ruth Nelson
Reverend Parris .... Noble Shropshire
Betty Parris .... Julia Gibson
Tituba .... Hazel J. Medina
Susanna Walcott .... Maria Deasy
Mrs. Ann Putnam .... Kathleen Chalfant
Thomas Putnam .... Joseph Costa
Mercy Lewis .... Valorie Hubbard
Francis Nurse ....George Hall
Ezekiel Cheever .... Frank Muller
Marshal Herrick .... Scott Cohen
Judge Hathorne .... Robert Donley
Deputy Governor Danforth .... Neil Vipond
Sarah Good .... Deedy Lederer
Hopkins ....Joe Ambrose

By MEL GUSSOW

"The Crucible" is not only Arthur Miller's most-produced play; it has also become his most continually relevant work of political theater. By focusing on the Salem witch hunts of the 17th century, the playwright placed the outrage of McCarthyism in historical perspective and created a drama that has remained meaningful to succeeding generations. Gerald Freedman's articulate revival at the Roundabout Theater Company is as resolute as the play itself.

Although this is the first New York production since the Lincoln Center version 18 years ago, "The Crucible" is performed with frequency at America's regional theaters (and throughout the world). There were two recent major productions in the Northeast, four years ago at the Trinity Repertory Company in Providence, R.I., and earlier this season at the Long Wharf Theater in New Haven.

In the hands of different directors and actors, and with slight alteration in emphasis, each of the three revivals illustrates the consequential themes of the play: the epidemic of evil, the perversion of religion and civil order and the way that decency can outlive even the most disquieting events. For the playwright, justice and jurisprudence will always triumph over the immediate inequities of the legal system.

Martha Swope

Justine Bateman in "The Crucible," at the Roundabout Theater.

The law in various guises permeates Mr. Miller's work. Plays from "All My Sons" through "After the Fall" and his recent one-acts operate in a courtroom of ideas. In this sense, Salem, at the time of the witch hunt, becomes the crucible for tyranny, as the innocent are considered guilty even in the light of evidence to the contrary. "Black mischief" and fear are loose, and neighbor deserts neighbor. For the time of the play, all reason has absented itself. To be "somewhat mentioned" in a preliminary hearing is tantamount to being condemned to death.

The firm moral center of this insane universe is Elizabeth Proctor, a woman unable to tell a lie, except to try to save her husband's life. Depending on the performance, Elizabeth can seem sanctimonious, a good wife preoccupied with self-denial. In her restrained but moving performance, Harriet Harris avoids that danger, giving Elizabeth a firm individual identity before she has to face their joint crisis.

With equal perspicacity, Randle Mell studiously avoids making Proctor seem heroic or even stoic, at least until his final act of conscience. He is willful and temperamental, a more emotionally highstrung Proctor than is customary. Demanding that Mary Warren, Abigail's acolyte, testify in defense of his wife, he grabs the girl by the throat and lifts her off her feet, holding her aloft as if she were a rag doll. In this and other moments, Mr. Mell becomes a man enraged. The performances by him and Ms. Harris certify the strength of the couple's bond. For Mr. Mell's Proctor, the liaison with Abigail has been an aberration, a misstep but not something to shake his enduring attachment to his wife.

Abigail is character assassin as catalyst. From her first entrance, Justine Bateman — making her New York stage debut — projects the character's nervous intensity, a near demonism that derives from her rebuffed sensuality. A self-dramatizer, she drops her abrasiveness in a quiet plea for Proctor's love. When he rejects her for the last time, she moves unswervingly on her course of vengeance.

Using Christopher H. Barreca's spare, woodhewn set, Mr. Freedman's production is unadorned. Performed within a proscenium, the play loses a sense of a surrounding environment (which it had in the Long Wharf and Providence open-stage versions). No longer do we feel the swirl of predators around their prey. But the production compensates by focusing the audience's attention on the three principal characters and the central dramatic conflict.

The primary change that occurs in the course of the play is in the character of the Reverend Hale, who gradually awakens to the inhumanity around him. Then, to his surprise, he realizes he is contradicting his principles by asking the pure in heart to perjure themselves in order to survive. As Hale, William Leach moves forcefully from good intentions to acts of rebellion. There is watchful support from, among others, Vicki Lewis (as Mary Warren), Maury Cooper and Ruth Nelson.

In Mr. Miller's apt words, the play deals with "one of the strangest and most awful chapters in human history." Though the basic events are true, one always greets them with incredulity. Even today, with formerly repressive nations promoting individual liberty, the scourge that the playwright first identified in the 1950's remains a lingering global presence. In revival, "The Crucible" leaves disturbing reverberations.

1990 Mr 30, C3:1

Meanwhile, Back At Olympus . . .

THE GOLDEN APPLE, composed by Jerome Moross; written by John Latouche; directed by Charles Kondek; choreography and musical staging, David Holdgrive; musical director, Lawrence W. Hill; scenic design, James Morgan; costumes, Maryanne Powell-Parker; lighting, Mary Jo Dondlinger; production stage manager, Bob Foreman; technical director, James E. Fuller Jr. Presented by the York Theater Company, Janet Hayes Walker, producing director; Molly Pickering Grose, managing director. At the Church of the Heavenly Rest, 2 East 90th Street.

Helen	Ann Brown
Lovely Mars/Siren	Mimi Wyche
Mrs. Juniper/Calypso	Mary Stout
Miss Minerva Oliver/The Scientist	
	Cynthia Sophiea
Mother Hare	Muriel Costa-Greenspon
Penelope/Circe	Sylvia Rhyne
Meneleus/Scylla	Gordon Stanley
Ajax	Tim Warmen
Nestor	Alan Souza
Diomede	Glen Pannell
Achilles	John Kozeluh
Petroclus	Bryan Batt
Doc MacCahan	Tim Salce
Ulysses	Robert R. McCormick
Paris	Kelly Patterson
Hector/Charybdis	Kip Niven
The Figurehead	Mary Phillips

Townswomen
Mary Lee Marson, Mary Phillips and Gina Todd

Townsmen
Jim Athens, Mitchel Kantor and Brent Winborn

By STEPHEN HOLDEN

Few vintage musicals have a greater cult reputation than John Latouche and Jerome Moross's cracker-barrel satire of Greek mythology, "The Golden Apple." The 1954 show, which the York Theater Company is reviving for the second time in 12 years, transplants Homer's "Iliad" and "Odyssey" from ancient Greece to the rural village of Angel's Roost, Wash., at the turn of the century.

In the Latouche-Moross deconstruction of Homer, Helen is the village floozy whom Paris, a traveling salesman from the nearby town of Rhododendron, abducts in his balloon. Ulysses, the most pious among a troop of soldiers who have just returned home from the Spanish-American War, decides it is their duty to find Helen and bring her back. Homer's Olympian deities are gossipy biddies from the village who while away their time consulting fortunetellers and entering baking contests.

"The Golden Apple" has a dazzling first act, but its story doesn't quite add up once the momentum of the plot accelerates to the breaking point

Martha Swope Associates/Carol Rosegg
Robert R. McCormick

in Act II. But despite a hurried conclusion, it is still one of the more delightful musical comedies of the era, and its cynically irreverent attitudes toward literature, history, patriotism, and show business have a decidedly contemporary ring. The score — a jaunty pastiche of country tunes, music-hall turns, rustic folk dances and marches all filtered through sensibilities attuned to Gilbert and Sullivan — also remains remarkably fresh.

Because "The Golden Apple" is a continuous sequence of fast-paced production numbers with almost no spoken dialogue, it is difficult to perform. And its conceit of turning Homer into a tongue-in-cheek parody of "Li'l Abner" is so broad that any production must be staged with a very firm control of the tone lest everything deteriorate into campy farce.

Although the York Theater production, directed by Charles Kondek, has many rough edges and the acting runs a bit too much toward caricature, the whimsical edge of the performances is reasonably consistent.

Ann Brown's Helen is an amusingly goofy airhead, though her version of "Lazy Afternoon," the show's most famous song, is not as seductive as it should be. Robert R. McCormick's Ulysses is a quintessential square, and Sylvia Rhyne, who has the cast's prettiest voice, makes an ingenuous Penelope. The strongest acting performance belongs to Kip Niven as Hector, Rhododendron's suave vaudevillian mayor.

The production's most uneven element is the musical direction. An overly percussive ensemble, conducted by Lawrence W. Hill, takes the score at tempos so swift that the singers have trouble keeping pace. While this streamlined approach gives the show a continual boost of energy, it also flattens out the music so that the score's generic parodies lose much of their flavor. The singers are so busy trying catch up with the band that the vocal performances lack personality.

The physical production is witty and inviting. James Morgan's cartoonish cut-out sets make Angel's Roost a bucolic storybook paradise and Rhododendron a fleshpot of ominously inky shadows.

1990 Mr 30, C3:5

The Old Razzmatazz With New Ingredients

RINGLING BROTHERS AND BARNUM & BAILEY CIRCUS, produced by Kenneth Feld; stager, Larry Billman; costume designer, Arthur Boccia; production designer, Keith Anderson; associate producer, Tim Holst; choreographer, Roy Luthringer; music director, Bill Pruyn. At Madison Square, 34th Street and Seventh Avenue.

WITH: Flavio Togni and the Togni family, Lee Stevens, Luis Palacio, Marcia Louise, Carmen Hall, Johnny Peers, the Quiros Troupe, Marquerite, Michelle and Andrea Ayala, the Winns Highwire Motorcycle, the Pellegrini Brothers, the Wee Gets, Jim Ragona, Los Gauchos Latinos, the Flying Morales, the Flying Guttys, Skymasters, the Savio Brothers, the Morales Teeterboard Troupe, the Rotman Teeterboard Troupe and the Helikons.

By RICHARD F. SHEPARD

The weather may not be giving much sign of the season, but New Yorkers who need reassurance that spring is really here will find it at Madison Square Garden, where the circus has moved in for its spring sojourn.

To call the Ringling Brothers and Barnum & Bailey Circus "the" circus

is not to take anything away from other circuses, like the Big Apple, which is a circus for all New York seasons. It is an acknowledgment that the big, venerable visitor at the Garden remains, in its 120th incarnation, an attention-scattering three-ring entertainment whose traditions of hoopla, spangles and ear-shivering decibels are intact.

So, what is new? Well, there is much that has not been seen here before, but the reassuring news is that the additions do not inflict any radical innovation. This is a circus for circus lovers, not for those in search of theater or musical comedy or large-scale night-clubbery. Its pace seems faster than in past years; the ringmaster's whistle has barely blown before the next act comes on. The lighting is more dramatic and brighter than a perennial visitor recalls, but after the sawdust has been swept away, it is still a bracing, refreshing, old-line circus, minus maybe the clowns pouring out of the little car and the people getting shot out of a cannon at the finale.

•

The main new ingredient is an entire circus ingested from Verona, Italy. Ringling has swallowed the Togni family's three-ring Circo Americano, and its family circle includes an ark-sized contingent of fauna, all different breeds but all betraying a common heritage in ham.

The elephants, horses, hyenas, tigers, lions and leopards are put through their paces by Flavio Togni, an engaging 29-year-old who works with a firm but good-humored manner distinguished by a boyish smile and a wink at the audience. Mr. Togni imparts the sense that he and his quadrupeds are all sharing fun at the

Ringling adds a troupe from Italy, with a rhino motivated by food.

circus. His is a performance no less disciplined but not as overawing as those given by Gunther Gebel-Williams, the retiring Ringling star, who often dramatized more the risk of encounters in the cage, making one worry that the issue was in doubt; the Togni touch is a tad more relaxed, although the audience is always aware that there are tons of rippling feline flesh responding to one thin man.

The Togni family performing with the Ringling Brothers and Barnum & Bailey Circus.

The Togni family has a flair for unusual combinations. Four horses and four elephants go through an unlikely dance routine, with the horses stepping delicately and gracefully between the heavy-footed pachyderms. One would be hard-shelled indeed not to warm to the white rhinoceros who runs around the ring with the impassivity of a bureaucrat filling out his time. The rhino doesn't even care that a black panther leaps on and off his back as long as Flavio Togni keeps slipping him nourishment. At the end, the only way to get the rhino offstage is to drag a pot of food in front of him until he trots out the door (it took a few tries to coax him through the exit).

•

The Tognis are by no means the whole circus. There are thrilling acts high above the tanbark. The Quiros are a Spanish quartet that prances about on a high wire; they do hair-raising things, particularly an adventurous routine that calls for one Quiro to sit on a chair balanced on a pole being carried across space between two bicycles. The Skymasters are three fearless high-wire performers whose vaulting ambition has them swaying on many thin and elastic poles 70 feet above the arena. They seem to work best upside down and one was relieved after they had swapped roosting places and slid, rashly, it would seem, to earth.

The production numbers are gaudy and loud, as they should be. The introduction is a colorful concept built around magic, with the ringmaster atop a huge upturned hat. Another spectacle, taking off on "A Chorus Line," fields a line of female dancers against a line of men who are on stilts; it may not reflect the introspective mood of the Broadway show, but it certainly is circus. The clown routines are funny, but the clowns themselves are not the pervasive between-the-act fillers they once were: the price of pace, perhaps, in a fast-moving age.

Your tastes, however, may run more toward the baboons, the tumblers, the women who have found a shtick in hanging by their hair, the trapeze artists, the sound, which comfortingly retains the brassy distortion peculiar to this art form. This circus mixes everything except metaphors, which keeps one from saying that it is a high flyer with its feet firmly on the ground.

1990 Mr 31, 13:1

For Love or Money

I AM A WINNER, by Fred Valle; directed by Melia Bensussen; set designer, Carl Baldasso; lighting designer, Bill Simmons; costume designer, Mary Marsicano; sound designer, Hector Melia; production stage manager, Roger Franklin; producer, Miriam Colon Valle. Presented by the Puerto Rican Traveling Theater, with major support from the Adolph Coors Company. At 304 West 47th Street.

Arturo .... José Rey
Carmela .... Marta Vidal
Héctor .... Jorge Luis Abreu
Tony .... Jack Landron
Cop No. 1 .... Joseph Jamrog
Cop No. 2 .... James Hunt

By D. J. R. BRUCKNER

This appears to be the silly season for the Puerto Rican Traveling Theater, which has put at the top of its 1990 roster Fred Valle's new play, "I Am a

Winner." In performance this farce gives the impression of an improvisation by actors who occasionally forget to stay in character as they develop the wholly unbelievable story. But there has to be a script: on one evening recently an actor was visibly embarrassed when he missed a line and the entire audience could hear a prompter calling it out.

The title tells the story. Arturo, a butcher grown tired of his job, wins $15 million playing Lotto. He becomes a little giddy when he realizes he has the winning ticket, but his termagant of a wife, Carmela, who has grown tired of him, really comes apart at the seams.

•

She and her lover, Tony, scheme to get the money by driving Arturo crazy, but soon they are the ones climbing the walls. Tony, disguised first as a plumber and then as a gay-rights advocate, tries to steal the winning ticket from Arturo. Failing at that, he turns up armed with everything from guns to plastique, but two preposterously incompetent policemen prevent any mayhem except their own.

Melia Bensussen, the director, keeps this mess moving, but not fast enough to make one forget the scores of times every line and every pratfall have been seen in other shows. Mr. Valle, who is new to playwriting, seems to forget that this kind of broad farce has been done by everybody everywhere; it is a tough game in which only practiced masters can come up with new strategies.

•

This production has its moments, largely because of the energetic cast. Many of the best moments are delivered by Jack Landron as Tony the homebreaker in his various guises and voices. His accent can zip from Central European to British to Jamaican without pausing for breath. Marta Vidal as Carmela makes a wonderful shrew who is utterly defeated in the end by the madman she is married to and the one she is having an affair with. And James Hunt and Joseph Jamrog as the policemen are very funny despite the awful lines they have and the slapstick routine the director has handed them; they look respectively like Benny Hill in youth and middle age.

The play, which runs through April 22, is performed in English Wednesdays through Fridays and in Spanish on Saturdays and Sundays.

1990 Ap 1, 52:3

Odd Jobs

NEDDY, by Jeffrey Hatcher; directed by Amy Saltz; sets and costumes by G. W. Mercier; lighting by Frances Aronson; sound by Rob Gorton; production stage manager, Richard Hester; assistant to the producer, Sandra C. Mintz; general manager, Stephen Lisner. Presented by Wynn Handman. At the American Place Theater, 111 West 46th Street.

Elizabeth .... Kristine Nielsen
Fayle .... Colette Kilroy
Raymond .... Kevin Chamberlin
Allan .... John Michael Higgins
David .... Don R. McManus
Ned .... Michael Heintzman

By WILBORN HAMPTON

"Neddy," a rather silly play by Jeffrey Hatcher that opened last night at the American Place Theater, has all the ingredients of a rejected pilot for a television sitcom except for the one thing it badly needs: a laugh track.

There is a banal plot that involves a cast of six stereotypes who speak in a string of vacuous one-liners, none of which bear even a passing resemblance to wit. Neddy (Michael Heintzman), a teacher at a prep school, has just been abandoned by his wife (quite understandably, one might add), and he is not only distraught, but penniless as well. His faculty colleagues decide to undertake his rehabilitation as a sort of sociological project by employing him as a handyman for some odd jobs that crop up around the home and school, and then overpaying him for his services. Ned soon graduates from being a helpless wimp to being an obnoxious young enterpriser of the sort one usually wants to sue.

Eschewing traditional comedic concepts like a whimsical story line or idiosyncratic character development, the playwright mostly relies on one-liners for laughs. Unfortunately, Mr. Hatcher never settles for one gag when six come to mind. Asked by a friend, for example, what his departed wife took, Ned replies: "She took all the furniture ..." (pause). "She took all the light bulbs " (pause). "She took both cars (pause). "She even drained the swimming pool ..." (pause). Some passages remind one of an extended Johnny Carson monologue, although no one in the audience keeps asking, "What else did she take, Neddy?"

The only character one would not immediately avoid if met by chance is David, a cynical chemistry teacher who refuses to give Ned a nickel and who is adroitly played by Don R. McManus. David also has one of the evening's few good lines. Told by a colleague that he should be nice to Ned because the hapless man needs friends, David replies drily, "Robespierre had friends, too."

Amy Saltz's direction is more suited to a soundstage than a theater. For the most part, the actors move to their marks, stand in place, deliver their routines and then exit. The cast makes a game effort. As one character says in quite another context, "I am better than this." One feels that is probably true for all the actors onstage.

1990 Ap 2, C15:1

The Heart Of a Tragedy

KING LEAR, by William Shakespeare; directed by Robert Sturua; translated into Georgian by C. Tcharkviani, Mr. Sturua and L. Popkhadze; first assistant director, Revaz Tchkhaidze; second assistant director, Lily Burbutashvili; designer, Mirian Mshvelidze; composer, Ghia Kancheli; choreography by Georgi Aleksidze; artistic director of the Rustaveli Theater Company, Mr. Sturua. The Rustaveli Theater Company, USSR, presented by the Brooklyn Academy of Music, Harvey Lichtenstein, president and executive producer. At the Majestic Theater, 651 Fulton Street, Brooklyn.

King Lear .... Ramaz Tchkhikvadze
Goneril .... Tatuli Dolidze
Regan .... Daredjan Kharshiladze

Cordelia .... Marina Kakhiani
Gloucester .... Avtandil Makharadze
Edmund .... Ghia Dznelade

Edgar .... Tengiz Ghiorgadze
Albany .... Djemal Ghaghanidze
Cornwall .... Ivan Ghoghitidze
Kent .... Mourman Djinoria

Fool .... Zhanri Lolashvili
Duke of Burgundy .... Guram Sagharadze
King of France .... Soso Laghidze

Oswald .... David Papuashvili
Doctor .... Revaz Tchkhaidze

By MEL GUSSOW

Robert Sturua's extraordinary production of "King Lear" is so unyielding in its intensity that one can see why the Rustaveli Theater Company from Soviet Georgia might regard Shakespeare as its national playwright. This distinguished company began an all too brief one-week engagement on Monday at the Brooklyn Academy of Music's Majestic Theater.

In Mr. Sturua's version, the play begins with everyone waiting for Lear. The court assembles in what appears to be the remains of a once-elegant theater. Standing at attention, the characters become impatient at the interminable delay. The Duke of Albany faints. Finally Lear shuffles onstage, carrying a bird cage and totally oblivious to his court.

Like a dictator in his dotage, Lear publicly indulges his fancies, alternately favoring and badgering his daughter Cordelia. Finally, as he divides his kingdom, he becomes diabolical. He seems to act foolishly, but he is no fool, as the actor Ramaz Tchkhikvadze unveils an unpredictable and penetrating portrait of a king who will never really abdicate.

•

Though the language is Georgian, the actors are in modernized dress and the ending of the play has been altered, this is an essential "Lear." It is not an idiosyncratic interpretation like Lee Breuer's recent gender-switching version (situated in the American state of Georgia), but a splendidly acted production that reaches to the heart of the tragedy of self-deception and of suffering leading to self-knowledge.

Even while conveying the bleakness of "King Lear" (and any comparisons to the Soviet Union under Stalin are there for the audience to make), the actors unearth comedy. At moments, Mr. Tchkhikvadze is disarmingly funny, like the cartoon Little King or a despotic Hollywood tycoon who can and will humiliate anyone he pleases. Anger suddenly replacing affection, he strikes Cordelia as if she were an unruly pet, then he embraces her — and she reciprocates. Within his family, he remains an often inclement force of nature, and Goneril and Regan endure his shenanigans, at least until they assume control.

Once the daughters are in power, they mimic the old man and return his unkindness in full, driving him from court. In Mr. Sturua's interpretation, Goneril and Regan are not wicked witches. They are glamorous creatures, a match in beauty with the fair Cordelia. In their elegant plumage, they stand out against the monochromatic background of Mirian Mshvelidze's scenic design.

•

Without using elaborate devices, the director and designer are imaginative in their production detail and their imagery, creating storms without thundersheets, using lighting to impale characters and taking advantage of the theater-within-a-theater framework. In the starkness of the approach, the production is comparable to that of Peter Brook's "Lear."

In the role of Gloucester, the actor Avtandil Makharadze, portly and bushy-bearded, looks fleetingly like the late Zero Mostel, and in his confusion over which of his two sons to favor one can see a semblance of that American actor at work. He finds comedy within paternal perplexity while not ignoring the man's blind de-

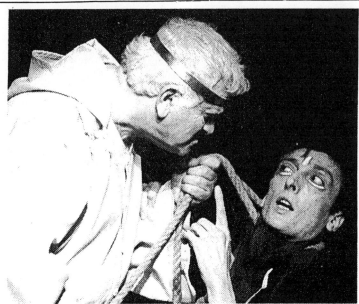

Martha Swope

Ramaz Tchkhikvadze, left, in the title role, and Mourman Djinoria in a scene from Robert Sturua's production of "King Lear."

spair. Naturally Gloucester makes the wrong choice, listening to the crafty Edmund (a jaunty figure in formal attire) rather than Edgar, who seems like a modern version of the young Prince Hal.

Eventually the Gloucester subplot is subordinated as Mr. Sturua focuses on the king and his retinue-in-exile: Edgar transformed into Poor Tom; the worthy Kent (as stalwart as in other productions) and Zhanri Lolashvili's Fool. With great tufts of hair covering each ear, Mr. Lolashvili looks like a clown in alarm. He is more active than pensive (as is the production itself), and not one who easily suffers Lear's abuses.

•

In this three-hour production there are a few questionable directorial choices, beginning with the background music, which sometimes seems like a 1950's movie soundtrack. The translation over headphones becomes more of an encumbrance than an aid. A voice selectively summarizes events and occasionally speaks a soliloquy, in the latter instance re-

minding us of the language we are missing.

For those who do not understand Georgian, this is, of course, a "King Lear" without Shakespeare's words. But as with Ingmar Bergman's "Hamlet" and Akira Kurosawa's film adaptations of Shakespeare, Mr. Sturua's "King Lear" transcends language barriers.

Mr. Bergman ended his "Hamlet" with Fortinbras's storm troopers taking over Elsinore. Mr. Sturua ends his "Lear" with Lear dragging out a dead Cordelia and sitting in the middle of a field of carnage. After his mournful howl, he remains the only man alive, forced to face his own self-victimization and the destruction of his kingdom. With a shudder, the setting — the theater as scenery — begins to fall apart. As expressed by Mr. Sturua, the conclusion of "King Lear" is a fearful vision of the apocalypse.

1990 Ap 4, C17:1

Plays Are Written By Wrights: Festival Returns to Basics

By MEL GUSSOW

Special to The New York Times

LOUISVILLE, Ky., April 1 — After two years of offering encouragement to the latent theatrical inclinations of celebrity authors, the Actors Theater of Louisville has returned this season to first principles. For the 14th annual Humana Festival of New Plays, this regional theater presented a marathon weekend of seven plays by playwrights — some new, some experienced, though not with work of equal quality.

Just as 1979 was the year that Jon Jory's theater discovered Beth Hen-

ley and "Crimes of the Heart," 1990 may be known as the year that Louisville presented the premiere of Romulus Linney's "2," a gripping new drama about Herman Göring and the Nuremberg trials. Mr. Linney was the only male playwright in a festival otherwise devoted to plays by women.

Louisville also saw the welcome return of Jane Martin, the pseudonymous author of "Talking With." Her new play, "Vital Signs," is a vivid collage of 34 glimpses of women at crucial points of their lives. In addition, there were three diverse plays, each of which had its admirers and detrac-

tors among those attending the festival.

Only two of the plays, Elizabeth Egloff's "Swan" and Ellen McLaughlin's "Infinity's House" did not earn their time on stage. Each was the kind of effortful exercise that had theatergoers longing to be elsewhere — perhaps weighing the merits of plays that had merits to be weighed.

At each festival, visiting critics, directors, producers and others less actively involved in theater search for themes and motifs. Frequent travelers here remember the year in which, in play after play, there were baying dogs or the years when country families gathered around dining tables to solve domestic dilemmas and environmental crises.

This year a sign was often posted outside the company's two theaters announcing that the play to be seen inside had incidents of nudity and strong language or that a gun would be fired during the performance. In addition to Göring, there were stage representations of such real people as Henri Matisse and J. Robert Oppenheimer and his colleagues at Alamogordo. Conscience and courage in the face of evil — and the denial of evil — figured prominently. Simultaneously there was a surfeit of symbolism about black holes, time warps and the origin of various species like swans.

•

In Mr. Linney's "2," all emblematic emanations and relevance to more recent political events are left to the audience's imagination. The play is a powerful, personal study of the man who was No. "2" in the Nazi hierarchy. Some may suggest that dramatizing such a figure on stage — except in a savage satire — automatically humanizes him as a character and thereby insufficiently recognizes his inhumanity.

Evidently aware of this possibility, Mr. Linney has been scrupulous about assessing the enormity of Nazi crimes and Göring's complicity in them. To the end, Göring remains arrogant, invidious, vainglorious in his posthumous devotion to Hitler (who deserted him) and aloof from the horrors of the Holocaust.

Seven new works in a marathon Louisville event.

At the same time, through the artistic virtuosity of Mr. Linney and of William Duff-Griffin, the actor incarnating Göring, the audience receives a complex portrait of this contradictory figure — a lover (and plunderer) of great art; a patriot who deceived his nation; a lover of life with a death wish. In creating his drama, Mr. Linney unites his longtime interest in history with his deep concern about questions of morality.

In what certainly is a career high for Mr. Duff-Griffin, his Göring is a man who could charm his executioner. He knows he will be sentenced to death, but he craves his moment in the spotlight and his position (albeit momentary) as No. 1. Mr. Linney has written a full-bodied demonic character and, under the guidance of the director, Thomas Allan Bullard, Mr. Duff-Griffin captures myriad dimensions.

When film of concentration camps is shown in court, Göring is untouched. It was not his concern; as a war hero, he was fighting a war. His

Richard Trigg

William Duff-Griffin in the Actors Theater of Louisville production of Romulus Linney's "2."

German counsel, his ardent defender in court, is himself overcome at the sight of the barbarism. He prods his client. Was he not moved seeing those films? Göring can only answer with a shrug. Were he to demonstrate even a hint of remorse, it would destroy the credibility of the character and of the play.

Nevertheless, the work has its pitfalls. There is a question as to how theatergoers will receive it, whether they will be lulled by Göring's charm (if so, they are not watching). The dialogue could be combed for the few questionable moments (for example, in Göring's exchanges with the two American soldiers guarding him) and the title may seem obscure. But there is every likelihood that the play will finally bring Mr. Linney the major success he so clearly deserves.

The festival's other significant contribution is in giving a stage to Jane Martin, who follows her memorable "Talking With" with "Vital Signs," a series of quick-flowing vignettes about trusting women — flying free, without safety nets — and others trapped in predicaments beyond their control.

The collage, under the direction of Mr. Jory, takes its cue from the opening confession of a character who

A standout is Romulus Linney's '2,' about Göring.

realizes she is better at beginnings but always finds herself inextricably in the middle. Shortly we hear from her sister in spirit who, in reference to romantic relationships, concludes that everyone has 30 hours of conversation and after that it is "all reruns."

A number of the sketches do not draw the desired response (sometimes because of the performance) and others diverge from the central premise. But there is ample indication of the continuing vitality and originality of the author's voice. This is exemplified by a monologue from a black woman (Myra Taylor) who spends her lifetime serving hors d'oeuvres to white people, whom she refers to, generically, as Tiffany and William. She remains blithely philosophical, even though her employers never recognize her away from her serving tray.

Joan Ackermann-Blount's "Zara Spook and Other Lures" fills the familiar Actors Theater category of good ol' boy, or, in this case, good ol' girl comedy. The subject is an all-female fishing contest. Though this was the festival's evident crowd-pleaser, it is less a play than a sitcom pilot on stage. Despite its silliness, "Zara Spook" has colorful characters, including an outrageously jealous husband who is flattered to be considered sensitive.

With "The Pink Studio," Jane Anderson attempts to bring Matisse's art to life. This is a series of imagined scenes that led to the creation of specific paintings. With some works that have a natural narrative element (like "Interior at Nice") the author's suppositions are evocative, but Matisse's frequent still lifes leave too much to the playwright's imagination, which sometimes wanders into the world of domestic comedy.

The play does have pleasurable moments, many of them provided by Paul Owens's Impressionistic scenic design and Peter Michael Goetz's performance as Matisse. The actor captures the artist's single-minded devotion to his art as well as his earnest modesty as a "wild beast."

In contrast to other novelists previously commissioned by Mr. Jory, Joyce Carol Oates has written plays before and has a professed interest in theater. She was represented by a pair of one-acts, allied under the title, "In Darkest America" and dealing with people who become pariahs in their communities.

"Tone Clusters," inspired by the Robert Golub murder case on Long Island, in effect puts an accused killer's parents on trial. As they repeatedly deny their son's guilt, the play leaves the audience little room for empathy. The opposite is true in "The Eclipse," which dramatizes a daughter's devotion to an aging and increasingly deranged mother. "The Eclipse" was enhanced by the performances of Madeleine Sherwood and Beth Dixon. Both plays offer a clear indication that Ms. Oates, if she were not so busy writing fiction, could find a second artistic home in theater.

●

Ms. McLoughlin's "Infinity House" is oppressively amorphous. If anything, it raises too many ideas, as the playwright crosscuts from atomic bomb testing to pioneers traversing America to the railroads to a sermonizing American Indian. It was all too much for the author or her actors (who included herself) to handle.

In contrast, in terms of ideas, Ms. Egloff's "Swan" is minimalist. In this inchoate fantasy, a swan is transmogrified into a naked man. Later he is transfigured along with the play's heroine (if you lie down with a swan, you wake up with wings). Among the many unfathomable questions raised is why the play's third character, a milkman, carries a pistol. Presumably, it is to ward off other feathered creatures or neighborhood doughnut thieves.

While theatergoers freely expressed their interest in — or their discontent with — other plays, it was Mr. Linney's "2" that was the most stimulating aspect of the festival.

1990 Ap 5, C15:1

Ups and Downs And Downs and Downs

Martha Swope Associates/Carol Rosegg

Ellen Greene

STARTING MONDAY, by Anne Commire; directed by Zina Jasper; setting by Edward T. Gianfrancesco; lighting by Craig Evans; costumes by Mimi Maxmen; sound by Aural Fixation; production stage manager, Jana Llynn. Presented by WPA Theater, Kyle Renick, artistic director; Donna Lieberman, managing director. At 519 West 23d Street.

Lynne	Pamela Wiggins
Man, First German, Doctor, Dr. Benberg, Houston Cop and Technican	David Manis
Ellis	Ellen Greene
Jim, Second German, Patient in Wheelchair, Farmer and Male Nurse	Ilo Orleans
Helen	Patricia O'Connell
Nurse Eaton	Paddy Croft
Patient, Farmer's Wife and Blood Nurse	Susan Brenner
Trish	Pamela Tucker-White

By STEPHEN HOLDEN

The grinding, day-to-day realities of terminal illness have rarely been dramatized on the stage with the exhaustive precision that Anne Commire's drama "Starting Monday" brings to a subject that is almost unavoidably depressing.

The play, at the WPA Theater, follows the friendship of Lynne (Pamela Wiggins) and Ellis (Ellen Greene), two young career women who strike up a relationship that undergoes the severest of tests when Ellis is told she has terminal cancer. Unlike the Bette Midler movie "Beaches," which sweetened a similar story with a gauzy, tearjerking sentimentality, "Starting Monday" removes most of the sugar coating to concentrate on the physical and psychic experience of fighting illness and coming to terms with death. The play forcefully shows how a terminal illness can be almost as devastating to a devoted caretaker as to the stricken person.

When Lynne and Ellis first meet on a cruise ship, they forge a bond based on shared neuroses revolving around diets, self-improvement and men. Eventually Ellis, the more fearless of the two, moves to Los Angeles to be a television director. She receives her first ominous diagnosis while Lynne is paying a visit. Because of Ellis's natural combativeness and her willingness to undergo extensive chemotherapy, a prognosis of three months to live stretches to a year and a half, during which time Lynne and Ellis's mother, Helen, join forces to care for her.

The play's strongest element is its sense of documentary fidelity. Cancer is notoriously unpredictable, and the drama captures the terrible uncertainties and roller-coaster ups and downs of fighting the disease. One of most disturbing aspects of the drama is its relentless dwelling on medical detail. In the most hair-raising scene, Lynne, who has vowed to stick with her friend to the end, undertakes for the first time a weekly ritual of infusing medication through a catheter attached to Ellis's chest. She is so nervous that she fumbles the procedure

and Ellis so frightened that the two begin screaming at each other hysterically.

●

In the course of the two-and-a-half-hour play, Ms. Wiggins and Ms. Greene must run a grueling emotional gamut. And under Zina Jasper's direction, both demonstrate an impressive stamina and a chemistry that is often compelling. Ms. Greene's tough-minded portrayal of Ellis carries the character through an emotional and physical spectrum without a false step. Scenes that might have been milked for pathos or an endearing kookiness are played to the truth of a character who, though not unlikable, is impulsive, feisty and insecure. Ms. Wiggins smoothly carries off the subtler but no less difficult task of stepping in and out of the drama to narrate the story. Among the generally strong supporting performances, Patricia O'Connell as Ellis's sweet, flighty mother, and Paddy Croft as a nurse who lives intransigently by the rules, are notable.

The documentary quality of the play is also the source of many of its flaws. A scene of interminable delays in a hospital waiting room seems intended to put the audience through the ordeal but is so protracted it is more likely to drive them out of the theater. Compared to the depiction of Ellis's cancer, the quality and texture of the friendship between the two women remains elusive. An awkward montage of memories, during which the two actresses run back and forth on the stage fails to evoke the cementing of their affection during a vacation at the New Jersey shore. And in the play's lighter moments, banter that is meant to be smartly amusing has little fizz.

In Edward T. Gianfrancesco's spare, effective stage design, the main prop is a single bed surrounded by an arrangement of screens. As the play begins, the bed is an invitingly quilted apartment nest. By the end, it has been exchanged for a hospital bed in which the incontinent, disease-ravaged Ellis can barely sit up. Instead of protecting her, the screens seem to close in and cut her off from the world.

1990 Ap 5, C18:1

Awaiting the Bang With a Whimper

PARADISE FOR THE WORRIED, conceived by Kinematic, Tamar Kotoske, Maria Lakis, Mary Richter with Holly Anderson; directed by Diane Wondisford; music adapted by Jill Jaffe, from a score by Stanley Silverman; text and lyrics by Ms. Anderson; choreography by Kinematic and Eric Barsness; created in collaboration with Mr. Barsness,

Laura Innes and Campbell Scott; music director, Ms. Jaffe; dance director, Pam Critelli; set designed by Victoria Petrovich; costumes designed by Donna Zakowska; lighting designed by Debra Dumas; production manager, Steven Ehrenberg; production stage manager, Barbara Ann O'Leary. Presented by Music-Theater Group, Lynn Austin, producing director; Ms. Wondisford, managing director, in association with Charles Hollerith Jr. At St. Clement's Church, 423 West 46th Street.

Dr. Fellowes	Campbell Scott
Hugo Fellowes	Eric Barsness
Daisy	Laura Innes
Phoebe	Mary Richter
Opal	Maria Lakis
Delphine	Tamar Kotoske
Violin, Viola	Jill Jaffe
Piano	Ted Sperling
Bandoneon	Alfredo Pedernera

By FRANK RICH

According to "Paradise for the Worried," a new dance theater piece presented by Music-Theater Group at St. Clement's, the Upper West Side was in a state of cosmic unrest when Halley's comet streaked through the cosmos on May 10, 1910. Rumors spread that the comet could alter the magnetic field and electrocute bystanders. A doctor hypothesized that the comet's gas could "trigger a vast array of neurological disorders." Hotels and bars served a drink called the Comet Cocktail.

In other words, the Upper West Side was in a frenzy the likes of which would not be seen again until the smoked fish counter opened at Zabar's. And for the creators of "Paradise for the Worried" — the dance trio known as Kinematic and the writer Holly Anderson — this transforming historical moment is a cue for larger meditations. Their piece is in the spirit of Martha Clarke's "Vienna: Lusthaus," a previous Music-Theater Group production, for it mixes words, movement, music and images in the attempt to create an abstract theatrical vision about sex and death in a civilization hurtling into the apocalyptic modern age.

●

Though "Paradise for the Worried" proves too intellectually lightweight and esthetically lazy to make good on its high-minded aims, its un-

Beatriz Schiller

Campbell Scott and Laura Innes in "Paradise for the Worried."

derlying idea is promising. Its Upper West Side indeed belongs to roughly the same centrifugal universe as Martha Clarke's Vienna or E. L. Doctorow's "Ragtime." Political cataclysms, world war included, were soon to splinter the established order. The relationship between men and women was in post-Victorian tumult as sexuality in all its expressions leaped out of the closet. What's more, Halley's comet is a spectacular metaphor for these irrational upheavals — as poetic, erotic and dramatic an image as theater artists might wish.

The show, unlike the comet, never lifts off. Ms. Anderson's text is but a trivial mock-Jungian case study, larded with didactic jokes about sexism, in which a repressed, rigid doctor (Campbell Scott) treats a disturbed patient (Laura Innes) only to discover that he is the one in need of psychic awakening. The patient is named Daisy, but unlike the Henry James and F. Scott Fitzgerald heroines of the same name and overlapping periods, she is less an incandescent exemplar of individualistic American womanhood than a pedantic hallucinator, a clinical archetype. That's too bad, because Ms. Innes, the only person on stage who is equally capable of acting, singing and dancing, has a talent and a glow that the production might have exploited to moving effect.

Even if the text of "Paradise for the Worried" was as substantive as it is pretentious, the evening would still fail to cast a spell. Under the direction, or, more accurately, the routine stage management, of Diane Wondisford, the music, dancing and text of the work do not so much cohere into an imaginative union as constantly interrupt one another in a battle for turf.

•

In the roles of Daisy's eccentric sisters, the able but mostly mute dancers of Kinematic (Tamar Kotoske, Maria Lakis and Mary Richter) trot out at intervals, like a vaudeville specialty act, either to illustrate their characters' emotional states with mime or to dance thematically pertinent tangos and Vernon and Irene Castle flavored ballroom routines. Stanley Silverman's lovely score, which makes its own period references to Scott Joplin, Erik Satie and Victor Herbert, is usually used only as atmospheric aural wallpaper; the composer never gets the chance, as Kurt Weill did in his equivalent Freudian case-study musical of the 1940's ("Lady in the Dark"), to seize the theatrical limelight with his own dreams. A tepid final comet effect notwithstanding, the handsome production design, with its heavy curtains, large observatory window and phallic telescopes, never builds on its initial promise of disorienting perspectives and mysterious culs-de-sac.

Running only 50 minutes, "Paradise for the Worried" is hardly a terrible imposition on its audience, but surely a Comet Cocktail would offer more kick.

1990 Ap 6, C3:1

Cragginess

Martha Swope
Len Cariou

MOUNTAIN, by Douglas Scott; directed by John Henry Davis; sets by Philipp Jung; costumes, David C. Woolard; lighting, Dennis Parichy; score and sound design, John Gromada; production stage manager, James Fitzsimmons; associate producer, Susan Urban Horsey; general management, Darwall von Mayrhauser. Presented by K & D Productions, Margery Klain and Robert G. Donnalley Jr., in association with Lucille Lortel. At the Lucille Lortel Theater, 121 Christopher Street.

William O. Douglas ....Len Cariou
WITH: John C. Vennema and Heather Summerhayes

By MEL GUSSOW

William O. Douglas spent his life on the edge, as an outspoken maverick on the Supreme Court (more than one-third of his 1,306 judicial decisions were dissents) and as a mountaineer and adventurer. From childhood through old age he courted danger, and during his 36½ years as an associate justice, he was often embroiled in controversy. He would seem to be a most likely candidate for dramatization.

Despite the enormous dose of information and quotations provided in Douglas Scott's "Mountain," and the valiant performance by Len Cariou, the subject eludes the playwright. As a biographical drama, "Mountain," which opened last night at the Lucille Lortel Theater, is stubbornly untheatrical. A mountain of fascinating material has yielded a weightless play.

The playwright could have focused on Douglas's court decisions or determined a turning point in his public or private life. Instead, he stands on the horizon and uses the widest possible lens, detailing everything from Douglas's striving childhood through his years teaching law and onward through his judicial exploits, world travels and environmental pursuits.

•

In the play there are hints of the dramatic possibilities, but the structure is self-defeating. The story moves backward in time from 1980 to 1898, skipping decades along the way. The first act concludes with a vow from Mr. Cariou of "I can do anything," which sounds like a cue without a song to follow.

Then the second act plows forward, filling in the missing years and thoroughly befogging chronology. Oddly, in this attempt at total inclusivity, some areas are slighted. From the play, one would never know that John F. Kennedy or Lyndon B. Johnson served as President. Rather than becoming impressionistic, this unnatural order undercuts any sense of momentum.

The play is most interesting when Douglas, as memoirist, tells a favorite anecdote, as in a reminiscence of his journey by freight train from Yakima, Wash., to New York in order to begin his studies at Columbia Law School. The play is least successful in court, where we receive only a scant sense of the passion and the intellectual rigor behind so many judicial conflicts.

•

In an attempt to enliven the drama, the playwright and the director, John Henry Davis, frequently pretend that Douglas is out-of-doors, where he mimes climbing mountains and, at one point, is toppled by an avalanche, moments that would be more effectively described rather than simulated.

Mr. Cariou throws himself headlong into his performance, trying to depict Douglas as the sizable figure that he was. With his craggy features and robust build, the actor resembles the Justice. But with too little help from the playwright, he is forced to breathe theatrical life into a character who does not fully exist on stage.

Background is provided by John C. Vennema and Heather Summerhayes, who portray other characters as sounding boards. Mr. Vennema stands in for everyone from Douglas's son to Presidents Roosevelt and Truman, and finds humor in his occa-

sional turns as Richard M. Nixon. Ms. Summerhayes plays Douglas's mother and wives, which only adds to the audience's confusion.

Belatedly, there is a brief and unconvincing attempt at psychological analysis with the suggestion that a boyhood trauma involving the entrapment of a prostitute led to a prolonged sense of guilt. "Mountain" may have a minimal value as introductory reference, but for the dramatic story of this life of thought and action, one should look to other sources: to books and to the public record.

1990 Ap 6, C29:1

The Road To the Guillotine

A TALE OF TWO CITIES, by Charles Dickens; adapted and directed by Nagle Jackson, after the original staging by Sabin Epstein; sets, Ralph Funicello; costumes, Robert Fletcher; lighting, Jane Reisman; composer, Bruce Odland. Presented by the McCarter Theater, Mr. Jackson, artistic director; John Herochik, managing director. At Princeton, N.J.

Charles Darnay ....Mark Capri
Sydney Carton ....Eric Conger
Jerry Cruncher ....James Coyle
Marquis d'Evremonde ....Edmund C. Davys
Dr. Manette ....Jay Doyle
Jarvis Lorry ....George Ede
Seamstress ....Katherine Heasley
Lucie Manette ....Melissa Hill
Miss Pross ....Kimberly King
Defarge ....Richard Leighton
Gabelle ....Randy Lilly
La Vengeance ....Mary Martello
Madame Defarge ....Jill Tanner
Barsad ....Randolph Walker
WITH: Reathel Bean, John A. Bukovec, Meghan Roberts Cibulskis, Charles Dumas, Elsbeth House Escher, Susan S. Garrett, Rufus C. Gibson, Laurie Huntsman, Cassie Jones, Zoran Kovcic, Frank Lowe, Mark David Murphy, Scott Allen New, F. Robert Stives, Gretchen Liddell Sword and Robin Tate

By WILBORN HAMPTON

PRINCETON, N.J., March 30 — In what is perhaps the most familiar opening paragraph in all English literature, Charles Dickens observed that the best and worst of times just preceding the French Revolution "was so far like the present period that some of the noisiest authorities insisted on its being received, for good or for evil, in the superlative degree of comparison only." Indeed, one of the main reasons epic literature holds its perennial appeal, whether in print or on stage, is the parallels a modern reader can trace to his own time.

Dickens's "Tale of Two Cities," which is being given a worthy new stage production at the McCarter Theater, speaks still to those who struggle against tyranny, whether from exile or underground, and cautions against the bloody abyss to which vengeance may lead. When Madame Defarge asserts, "Nothing we do is done in vain, even if we do not live to see the triumph," one can easily recall the martyrs of the last 30 years in Hungary, Czechoslovakia and Poland, or among the students in Tienanmen Square last summer in China.

Yet tales of melodramatic heroism and morality inevitably provide large targets for criticism. Although Dickens's views of the French Revolution, for example, are authentic as far as they go, they are greatly simplified. And while Nagle Jackson's adaptation of "A Tale of Two Cities" is faithful to the spirit of Dickens's book, it further distills the author's great narrative to the scale of a love story set against a historical background.

The novel is episodic in nature, individual threads knitted together into a complex fabric of intertwined family histories. In his stage adaptation, Mr. Jackson telescopes these episodes into a series of scenes spliced together with asides to the audience to fill in background and move the story along. The result is a mostly fast-moving and action-packed three hours of stagecraft that chronicles the sweep of events but only occasionally captures the human drama of its characters.

There are moments when Mr. Jackson's adaptation goes beyond a simple condensation of the novel to create a confrontation or image that speaks more directly to a theater audience. When the Marquis d'Evremonde is challenged over a dinner table by his nephew, Charles Darnay, that the people of the village are hungry, the Marquis replies: "Yes, but they were never meant to eat partridge. That was never God's plan." The scene conveys the unfeeling arrogance of the nobility more dramatically than a stage carriage clumsily bumping into a child. A vignette in which three little girls laughingly sing a nursery rhyme ditty in praise of "Madame la Guillotine" is a more chilling than any prosaic denunciation of the Reign of Terror. And the touching final scene between Sydney Carton and the Seamstress who shares the tumbril ride to their execution is played against the offstage sound of a heavy blade tearing through the air, followed by a deadly thud. It is further to Mr. Jackson's credit that he has found flashes of humor in a novel not known for its comic relief.

•

As director, Mr. Jackson takes occasional inspiration from other sources. His staging of the storming of the Bastille, for example, bears a striking resemblance to the Act I finale of "Les Misèrables." The McCarter production, a joint venture with the American Conservatory Theater in San Francisco, uses the fine sets Ralph Funicello designed for its premiere there last November.

Most of the dozen or so principals in the cast give credible readings, although a few offer little more than surface characterizations. George Ede is a major asset with a thoughtful and reasoned performance as Jarvis Lorry. Eric Conger is especially good as Sydney Carton, the "man of no convictions" whose sacrifice is the final redemption of Dickens's tale. Edmund C. Davys is thoroughly malicious as the Marquis d'Evremonde. Katherine Heasley makes the most of her cameo as the Seamstress, and Randolph Walker presents a detestably wheedling Barsad.

1990 Ap 7, 16:4

Lusts and Yearnings

ASPECTS OF LOVE, music by Andrew Lloyd Webber; lyrics by Don Black and Charles Hart; based on the novel by David Garnett; book adaptation by Mr. Lloyd Webber; directed by Trevor Nunn; choreography by Gillian Lynne; production design by Maria Bjornson; lighting by Andrew Bridge; sound by Martin Levan; production musical director, Paul Bogaev; orchestrations by David Cullen and Mr. Lloyd Webber. Presented by the Really Useful Theater Company Inc. At the Broadhurst Theater, 235 West 44th Street.

Rose Vibert	Ann Crumb
Alex Dillingham	Michael Ball
George Dillingham	Kevin Colson
Giulietta Trapani	Kathleen Rowe McAllen
Marcel Richard	Walter Charles
Jenny Dillingham, age 12	Deanna Du Clos
Jenny Dillingham, age 14	Danielle Du Clos
Elizabeth	Suzanne Briar
Hugo LeMuenier	Don Goodspeed

WITH: Jane Todd Baird, Philip Clayton, John Dewar, Kurt Johns, Eric Johnson, Marcus Lovett, Gregory Mitchell, Elinore O'Connell, Lisa Vroman and Wysandria Woolsey.

By FRANK RICH

Andrew Lloyd Webber, the composer who is second to none when writing musicals about cats, roller-skating trains and falling chandeliers, has made an earnest but bizarre career decision in "Aspects of Love," his new show at the Broadhurst. He has written a musical about people.

Whether "Aspects of Love" is a musical *for* people is another matter. Mr. Lloyd Webber continues to compose in the official style that has made him an international favorite, sacrificing any personality of his own to the merchandisable common denominator of easy-listening pop music. Though "Aspects of Love" purports to deal with romance in many naughty guises — from rampant promiscuity to cradle-snatching, lesbianism and incest — it generates about as much heated passion as a visit to the bank. Even when women strip to lacy undergarments, the lingerie doesn't suggest the erotic fantasies of Frederick's of Hollywood so much as the no-nonsense austerity of Margaret Thatcher's Britain.

The inspiration for the production's dour game of musical beds is a 1955 novella by David Garnett, a secondary Bloomsbury figure and the son of the great Russian translator Constance Garnett. The tone of the adaptation is more Barbara Cartland than Virginia Woolf. For two acts sprawling over 17 bewildering years, the audience tries to track a young Englishman named Alex (Michael Ball) and his much older Uncle George (Kevin Colson) as they bounce between a French actress (Ann Crumb) and an Italian sculptor (Kathleen Rowe McAllen). The women, named Rose and Giulietta, have a quickie affair of their own along the way, to the extent that anything in "Aspects of Love" can be described as quick.

To find out why everyone is forever taking tumbles in the hay — literally so in a laughable hayloft scene — one must turn to the philosophical lyrics, which were written by the previous Lloyd Webber collaborators Don Black ("Song & Dance") and Charles Hart ("The Phantom of the Opera") and seem to have been translated, though not by Constance Garnett, from the original Hallmark. "Love changes everything, hands and faces, earth and sky," sings Alex. "Life goes on, love goes free," adds Uncle George a little later. "There is more to love than simply making love,"

Ann Crumb and Michael Ball in Andrew Lloyd Webber's "Aspects of Love," a new musical at the Broadhurst Theater.

concludes Giuletta. But perhaps Alex is most to the evening's point when he sings at the outset that love can make "a night seem like a lifetime."

•

Every sentiment in "Aspects of Love," as well as an ever-changing à la carte menu of food and aperitifs, is sung. And sung again and again. Mr. Lloyd Webber, as is his wont, rotates a few tunes throughout his show, some of them catchy and many of them left stranded in musical foreplay. But this time the composer's usual Puccini-isms have been supplanted by a naked Sondheim envy. The first song for the two young lovers, "Seeing Is Believing," echoes "Tonight" in "West Side Story," and a later duet for dueling male rivals recalls "A Little Night Music" (as does much of "Aspects of Love," its staging included). One also encounters the ghosts of Lerner and Loewe's "Gigi" in Uncle George, who is the avuncular, Champagne-sipping Maurice Chevalier boulevardier reincarnated as a truly dirty old man. When men thank heaven for little girls in "Aspects of Love," chances are the girls will turn out to be jail bait.

•

What neither Mr. Lloyd Webber nor his collaborators can provide is a semblance of the humanity that is also, to some, an aspect of love. The misogyny in this show is more transparent than in other Lloyd Webber musicals where the general rule is to present principal female characters as either prostitutes ("Evita," "Cats," "Starlight Express") or sainted virgins ("Jesus Christ Superstar," "The Phantom of the Opera"). Both heroines of "Aspects of Love" frequently behave like bitches and whores, to use the epithets of the male characters. Their men, meanwhile, are overgrown English schoolboys who have no idea that women can be anything other than girls they pick up at Harry's Bar or the nearest stage door.

The sexless casting of the principal roles by the director, Trevor Nunn, only adds to the musical's icy emotional infantilism. From her very first line — a line from "The Master Builder," no less — Ms. Crumb's Rose is a tough cookie, unconvincing as a tempestuous star known for her performances of the classics or as a femme fatale who, in her words, "could have a thousand lovers." With her piercing singing voice and loud, fake laughter, this actress could shatter glass more easily than hearts.

Like Ms. Crumb, Ms. McAllen is an American performer who originated her role last year in the West End. She, too, is a brassy belter who makes no attempt to convey her character's European background and artistic temperament and who is further handicapped by unflattering costumes (by Maria Bjornson) that, in Giulietta's case, announce her Lesbian Tendencies with every pantsuit. While Mr. Colson's silver-maned Uncle George is an amiably drawn cliché — the cultured, moneyed old roué with a "lust for living" — Mr. Ball's Alex cuts a preposterous figure as a libertine. A beefy juvenile who would fit right in with the Trapp Family Singers, Mr. Ball bares his chest for no worthwhile esthetic or prurient reason, but not to the point of dismantling the chest mike from which emanates his entire personality.

With the exception of Andrew Bridge's lighting of mountain vistas, almost nothing in Mr. Nunn's production is appropriate to a work that aspires to romantic Continental finesse. Miss Bjornson, an inspired scenic artist for dark material like "Phantom," fails to lighten up. Her oppressive floor-to-ceiling design of concrete-colored brick and cobblestones suggests two more somber Nunn productions, "Chess" and "Les Misérables," on an enforced holiday in Ceausescu-era Romania. Even at its most bucolic, Uncle George's villa in the Pyrenées looks less like a pleasure dome than a forlorn provincial inn the season after being stripped of its Michelin Guide stars.

As much as its subject invites the spectacle of men and women dancing, "Aspects of Love" offers little,

Combinations, permutations, variations and lusts.

preferring instead to pay a gratuitous, static visit to a shooting gallery at a fairground. Gillian Lynne's scant choreography makes a superfluous circus number seem as grim as a subsequent "Zorba"-like funeral rite. The only steady semblance of movement in the staging is provided by a treadmill that sends people and furniture trundling across the stage with lugubrious monotony. While "Aspects of Love," with its references to Huxley and Turgenev, may be the most high-minded of Lloyd Webber musicals, isn't it also the one in most desperate need of roller skates?

1990 Ap 9, C11:1

Turned Tables

THE BALCONY, by Jean Genet; translated by Bernard Frechtman; directed by Geoffrey Sherman; set and light design by Paul Wonsek; sound by Richard Rose; production stage manager, Gary M. Zabinski. Presented by Raymond J. Greenwald. At the Hudson Guild Theater, 441 West 26th Street.

The Bishop	Charles E. Gerber
Arthur, Photographer, Revolutionary and Slave	Matt Penn
The Penitent, Chantal and Photographer	Valarie Pettiford
The Horse, Revolutionary and Photographer	Mimi Quillin
The General	John Henry Redwood
The Chief of Police	Will Rhys
Mme. Irma	Angela Sargeant
The Beggar and Roger	David Schechter
Carmen	Freda Foh Shen
The Judge	Albert Sinkys
The Thief, Revolutionary and Photographer	Lynne Faljian Taylor
The Envoy	Sharon Washington

By MEL GUSSOW

More than three decades after it was written, "The Balcony" no longer seems so outrageous. In the interval, too much has happened in the world and in art. But Jean Genet's play retains its diabolical originality, and if properly presented on stage, it should still have the power to disturb and even disorient an audience.

"The Balcony" demands a production as audacious as the author's concept and actors who are equipped to handle the earthy, liturgical flights of dialogue and the physical demands of the characters. This was certainly the case in the first New York production directed by Jose Quintero. Unfortunately, Geoffrey Sherman's anniversary production at the Hudson Guild Theater is reductive in every sense. Scene by scene, it diminishes the play, until one wonders why the company chose to stage it in the first place.

In Genet's House of Illusions, clients act out their most bizarre sexual and religious fantasies while, outside, revolutionaries are overthrowing the government. Eventually, the illusionists, led by Mme. Irma as the substitute queen, will be conscripted to play their roles in what masquerades as real life.

"The Balcony" becomes a political fantasy within a fantasy, in which all values are overturned. In their new guises the role players realize that they belong to their fantasies, and not vice versa. They need them as life support. The world, in Genet's distorting mirror, is itself a giant bordello.

The world, in Genet's mirror, is a giant bordello.

Genet insisted that the brothel on stage not be of "petty dimensions," envisioning something on the order of a cathedral and certainly not the chamber version at the Hudson Guild. But the problem is not simply that of a small stage. Neither in the direction nor in the performances does the revival have the required expansiveness or imagination.

This begins with the fact that, in disregard of the author's directive, the actors do not wear cothurni (high platform shoes used in classic tragedy) and heavily padded garments so as to raise little men above mundane reality. Without the necessary costumes and flamboyance, the outlandish roles are cut down to life size. The actors could just as easily be playing in one of the Hudson Guild's more typical naturalistic works than in this larger-than-life ritual.

Angela Sargeant's Mme. Irma is trim and self-disciplined. She might be the manager of a modeling agency, but she is not the grand theatrical impresario of Genet's imagining, a woman formidable enough to take over a kingdom. The actors playing the bishop (actually a gasman), the judge and the general seem as ordinary as the original professions of the characters, though when they indulge their fantasies they are supposed to be transformed into leaders.

•

Mr. Sherman has restored a scene, cut from earlier productions, which clarifies the role of the rebels and their symbolic leader, a kind of St. Joan of the revolution. Doubling in roles, the actors are equally insecure on both sides of the political fence.

For an instant, when Mimi Quillin prances around the stage and pretends to be the general's horse, there is a hint of the desired sensuality, otherwise in very short supply. But the actress does not begin to equal one's memory of Salome Jens, who so strikingly filled the role in the original New York production. Although several of the actors, including Freda

Foh Shen as Mme. Irma's assistant and Will Rhys as a surly police chief, have clues to their characters, they are submerged in a production deficient in decadence and black humor.

It is certainly possible to move too far in the opposite direction, for the acting to become overly stylized. This is what happened several seasons ago in London at the Royal Shakespeare Company, in an elaborate revival that stifled the play in artifice. Mr. Sherman's approach is even less defensible. A prosaic "Balcony" is no "Balcony" at all.

1990 Ap 9, C14:6

Views of the City

LIFETIMES, by Gus Edwards; directed by Douglas Turner Ward; sound and composer, Richard V. Turner; costumes, Judy Dearing; lighting, Sandra Ross; production stage manager, Ed DeShae; sets, Lisa L. Watson; company manager, J. Heather Wiley. Presented by the Negro Ensemble Company, Mr. Ward, artistic director and president; Susan Watson Turner, general manager. At Theater Four, 424 West 55th Street.

WITH: Peggy Alston, Cynthia Bond, Charles Brown, Graham Brown, O. L. Duke, Iris Little, Sandra Nutt, Leonard Thomas, Adam Wade, Douglas Turner Ward and Charles Weldon.

By MEL GUSSOW

Street people, some distraught, others with dreams intact, populate Gus Edwards's "Lifetimes," a gentle anthology of monologues about life today in Harlem. The view is personal rather than political. The wistfulness of Mr. Edwards's play (presented by the Negro Ensemble Company at Theater Four) is represented by a married woman named Mavis who returns to Harlem to look for the sanctuary of a distantly remembered beauty salon and stays to drift into a love affair that becomes increasingly less casual.

As played by Peggy Alston, Mavis knits the vignettes together with her five brief appearances, which are the equivalent of a single short play. Even with Mavis as motif, the monologues remain fleeting glimpses rather than confessions from the heart.

The comparative mildness of "Lifetimes" is partly a result of the audience's exposure to other related stage anthologies and to a film like Spike Lee's "Do the Right Thing," which more vividly conveys the grittiness as well as the unconscious poetry of city streets.

In contrast, Mr. Edwards's 19 monologues often seem familiar (an honest whore, a gardener who has staked out a patch of the city for beautification) or strained (Charles

Brown as a man who worries that he may be a latent homosexual). The show is further shadowed by Mr. Edwards's own plays ("The Offering" and "Old Phantoms," among others), which are more revealing about relationships.

Bert Andrews
Peggy Alston in "Lifetimes," a play about life today in Harlem.

"Lifetimes" does offer acting opportunity to the talented actors on the Negro Ensemble's roster, and individually there are evocative moments, as when Leonard Thomas steps forward as the ultimate collector of returnable empties. He is saving them and imagining a time when he will have accumulated one million cans. Eyes gleaming, he wonders how much that will bring at a nickel apiece, at which point, of course, his burden will be unbearable.

Iris Little, irate over the easy acceptance of black heroes, is quite clear about her own idol, whom she honors with her refrain, "Marvin Gaye Died for Your Sins." O. L. Duke has an amusing sales pitch as a subway panhandler who has contracted a "rare kind of pneumonia that usually only attacks parakeets."

With the help of musical bridges, Douglas Turner Ward has staged the work neatly. Mr. Ward also appears as a homeless relic of Harlem's heyday, which he remembers with nostalgia. He has stayed on to bear witness and to remind newcomers of the music, both real and figurative. It is his prediction that there will be a new ice age that will freeze mankind into immobility — the saddest note in an occasionally poignant collage.

1990 Ap 9, C12:4

Valhallzapoppin

DER RING GOTT FARBLONJET, by Charles Ludlam; directed by Everett Quinton; scenery by Mark Beard; costumes by Susan Young; lighting by Richard Currie; props by Daphne Groos and Sophie Maletsky; hair by Joe Anthony; production stage manager, Ron Murphy; music and sound by Mark Bennett. Presented by the Ridiculous Theatrical Company. At the Charles Ludlam Theater, 1 Sheridan Square.

Twoton	Adam MacAdam
Eartha	H. M. Koutoukas
Siegmund/Siegfried	Jim Lamb
Brunnhilda/Fasdolt	Sophie Maletsky
Ninny/Rossweisse	Stephen Pell
Loge/Grimgerda	Bryan Webster
Hunding/Gutruna	Mary Neufeld
Fricka/Gunther	Eureka
Alverruck and Valtruata	Everett Quinton
Froh/Gerhilda	Ivory
Flosshilde/Ortlinda/Norn	Robert Lanier
Dunderhead/Hagen/Siegruna	Gary Mink
Freia/Sieglinda	Therese McIntyre
Welgunde/Schwertleita	Bobby Reed
Fafner/Helmvige/Norn/Bear	Jean-Claude Vasseux
Woglinde/Forest Bird	Christine Weiss

By MEL GUSSOW

As an irrepressible recycler of other people's art, Charles Ludlam rewrote "The Ring of the Nibelung" to suit the Ridiculous Theatrical Company's purpose. Everett Quinton's revival of "Der Ring Gott Farblonjet," a tragedy turned into a comedy, is the funniest "Ring" cycle one is likely to see. The show, which opened last night at the Charles Ludlam Theater, is a tribute to Ludlam's parodistic virtuosity and to the interpretive alchemy of Mr. Quinton, his successor as artistic director of the Ridiculous company.

A low comic approach to high art that somehow manages to remain true to its source — or at least to the storyline — this is a travesty that even Wagnerians might appreciate. On the simplest level, it could act as a plot-summarizing prelude to the real "Ring," currently in repertory at the Metropolitan Opera House. With four plays abbreviated to two hours and 45 minutes, the Ridiculous "Ring" moves swiftly.

Diving from Valhallan peaks to Nihilumthen depths, "Der Ring" does not miss a Teutonic beat, while adding a few Yiddishisms, as in the title. It is filled with Siegfriedian sangfroid, along with a raving raven, giants that look like a pair of Elephant Men and a dastardly dragon that deserves its deserts. Intricate wordplay and intentional mispronunciations share center stage with gender-bending vaudeville art.

•

The original production in 1977 was ambitious but unwieldy. Mr. Quinton, as director, has tightened the text and given the show a greater cohesiveness while not losing one whit of the outlandish humor. If anything, the revival is more sharply cast and acted.

House of Illusion

Jean Genet's "Balcony," a mocking commentary on the illusion of power, opens tonight in a 30th-year American anniversary production at the Hudson Guild Theater. Directed by Geoffrey Sherman, the cast includes, from left, Valarie Pettiford, Albert Sinkys and Charles E. Gerber.

Gerry Goodstein

Avoiding camp excess, the actors are clear-spoken physical comedians.

Adam MacAdam repeats his original role as Twoton, the one-eyed "Gott" who cherishes his own divinity, and H. M. Koutoukas, himself a pioneer Off Off Broadway playwright, rises from a netherworld as Eartha, the Earth Mother. Both actors hold their own with newer comers to the Ridiculous style.

Jim Lamb doubles heroically as father and son, shifting from a Lancelot-ish Siegmund in love with his twin sister (and the twain meet) to an Arnold Schwarzenegger-like Siegfried, complete with overdeveloped pectorals and accent. He makes his entrance munching a carrot and proclaiming, "Ich bin ein vegetarian," and then gives a properly beefy performance. Sophie Maletsky's Brunnhilda combines beauty with bravura, adding a disarming innocence to her role as warrior queen. There are also daffy characterizations by Stephen Pell, Bryan Webster, Mary Neufeld and Eureka. among others.

It is Mr. Quinton as actor as well as director who anchors the operatic antics. In his principal guise as the toadish Alverruck (read Alberich), he is hilarious, a sniveling Nihilumpen who extols his own villainy. Stealing the Rheingold and overseeing the forging of the title ring, he vows, "Nobody loves me, so I might as well rule the world." The actor also doubles as a Valkyrie, one of a ho-yo-to-ho-ing

Anita and Steve Shevett
Everett Quinton in "Der Ring Gott Farblonjet."

chorus of swinging bikers — "Ring" cyclists of a third kind, who embark on the craziest ride of all.

•

In the background is a pastiche score by Mark Bennett, which confuses "Das Rheingold" with the music for a sudsy beer commercial. A primary contributor is the set designer, Mark Beard, who within a limited budget indulges his scenic imagination and creates a leafy, "Into the Woods" environment in miniature. There is no stinting on the scene

changes — from mountaintop to cave, from rippling Rhein (here come three maidens swimming against the tide) to ring of fire. The climax, narrative and scenic, is a Gibichungen earth quiver. Puppets, masks and costumes (by Susan Young) add their own mischievous note.

The third act, which is devoted to "Siegfried," lapses too long into fractured German, and a few jokes misfire, but these are small deterrents in an evening of unalloyed lunacy. Since Ludlam's death, the Ridiculous company has been searching for identity. The new "Ring" is, one might say, quintessentially Quintonian.

1990 Ap 13, C3:1

Love Quadrangle

FANNY, by S. N. Behrman and Joshua Logan, based on the trilogy of Marcel Pagnol; music and lyrics by Harold Rome; directed by Robert Johanson; scenic design, Michael Anania; costumes, Gregg Barnes; lighting, Mark Stanley; sound, David R. Paterson; hair, Paul Germano; assistant to the director, Larry Grey; production stage manager, Peggy Imbrie; musical director, Jim Coleman; choreographer, Sharon Halley. Presented by the Paper Mill Playhouse, Angelo Del Rossi, executive producer; Mr. Johanson, artistic director. At Millburn, N.J.

Cesar	José Ferrer
Panisse	George S. Irving
Fanny	Teri Bibb
Marius	John Leone
Honorine	Karen Shallo
Cesario	Jonathan Gold
M. Brun	Mitchell Greenberg
The Admiral	Paul Kandel
Escartifique	K. C. Wilson

By STEPHEN HOLDEN

"Fanny," Harold Rome's musical adaptation of Marcel Pagnol's dramatic trilogy, "Marius," "Fanny," and "Cesar," is a quintessential 1950's musical of the more solemnly romantic sort.

Set in the old port of Marseilles, it tells a sentimental story of star-crossed young lovers, Marius and Fanny, their illegitimate child, and the crusty old men who guard their secret and remain their benefactors during the years Marius is off at sea. The show's pace is leisurely, its plot thick, its moral climate of delayed erotic gratification and self-sacrifice very much of its time.

When the show opened on Broadway in 1954, the roles of Panisse, the rich, elderly sailmaker who marries Fanny to give her unborn child a father after Marius has left, and his best friend, Cesar, who is also Marius's father, were portrayed by Walter Slezak and Ezio Pinza. In the Paper Mill Playhouse's revival of the show, they are played with charm and gusto by two distinguished theater veterans, George S. Irving and José Ferrer.

•

With its large cast, exotic French setting and semi-operatic score, "Fanny" is a show that requires a fair amount of grandeur. The Paper Mill Playhouse revival, directed by Robert Johanson, is unstintingly luxurious. Elaborate sets designed by Michael Anania evoke the architecture and narrow streets and courtyards of the French port city. The interior settings also offer a richly atmospheric sense of life in different strata of French society.

In the second-act birthday party scene, a colorful circus of jugglers, tumblers and clowns surges onto the stage, and acrobats descend from the stage into the aisles to twirl on ropes

unfurled above the heads of the audience. In its pomp and pageantry, the show's physical production is of old-time Broadway quality.

The visual opulence is matched in scale by the expansive, open-hearted performance of Mr. Irving as Panisse, the wealthy sailmaker who so yearns for a son that he is happy to bring up the boy, Cesario, so long as no one finds out the truth of his paternity. The portly actor gives a full and moving portrait of a man whose misplaced vanity doesn't preclude an enormous generosity of spirit. And the show's dramatic high point is his enthusiastic and touching rendition of "Panisse and Son," in which he celebrates the realization of his dream of having a male heir. •

The show requires a fair amount of grandeur.

Mr. Ferrer's portrayal of Cesar, though likable, doesn't quite capture the bonhomie of a character whose signature song, "Welcome Home," extols the comforting familiarity of household furniture. And his small, craggy bass-baritone is not on a level with the rest of the voices in the cast.

Mr. Rome's sweepingly romantic score for the show includes four big ballads — "Fanny," "I Have to Tell You," "Restless Heart" and "Welcome Home" — that nearly match in eloquence Rodgers and Hammerstein songs from the same era. Although John Leone and Teri Bibb, the attractive young singers portraying Marius and Fanny, sing the love songs competently, their performances lack the extra fillip of ardor that might have heated up the love story to a sizzle.

Ultimately, however, the flaws of this revival are minor. Under Mr. Johanson's sure-handed direction, the production maintains an energetic flow that is enlivened by a strong ensemble, choral singing and smooth choreography by Sharon Halley. One senses the tug of the sea and the slow passing of time in a city that is deeply set in its ways.

1990 Ap 13, C3:5

A Rabbit And More, Much More

EASTER EXTRAVAGANZA, production conceived and created by Patricia M. Morinelli and William Michael Maher; directed and choreographed by Scott Salmon; sets and costumes designed by Erté; lighting by Ken Billington and Jason Kantrowitz; costume designers, Eduardo Sicangco and Jose Lengson; orchestrators, Michael Gibson, Dick Lieb, Glenn Osser and Jim Tyler; musical director and vocal arranger, Don Pippin; dance-music arrangers, Gordon Lowry Harrell, Mark Hummel, Marvin Laird and Ethyl Will; special musical material by Larry Grossman; special material by Hal Hackady; production stage manager, Howard Kolins; vocal solo recording for "Glory of Easter" by Marilyn Horne. Presented by the Radio City Music Hall Productions, Ms. Morinelli, executive producer; David J. Nash, executive producer for Radio City; Mr. Maher, associate producer for Radio City. At 50th Street and Avenue of the Americas.

WITH: The Rockettes and Wayne Cilento.

By RICHARD F. SHEPARD

The Easter show has returned to Radio City Music Hall, after an 11-

year absence, with all the splendor inherent in both holiday and locale. The brisk and awesome 90-minute "Easter Extravaganza" accords the holiness of the occasion cathedral-like attention at the outset but then goes its own jolly way, celebrating the holiday in particularly New York terms.

To be performed through April 23, the show is presented with such ebullient, overstated animation that only a thoroughly jaded visitor would be inclined to shrug it off as just another one of those music hall spectacles. It is that, of course, but that is what makes one marvel at the ingenuity and stagecraft on display: winter changes into spring, the fable of the hare and tortoise is retold with a surprising twist, and the music hall itself is reproduced on stage, in curvy dimensions that a John Marin might applaud.

First things first. Radio City purists will welcome the return of "The Glory of Easter," the reverent tribute developed by Leon Leonidoff, the first Radio City producer. It was a hardy perennial here from 1933 until 1979, a good run in show-business terms. For this production number, a cathedral is created on the giant music hall stage, with three towering stained glass windows, a stately altar, sprays of lilies and troops of solemn participants in the guise of monks, altar boys, maids and priests.

Then it's on with the revels. Here are scenes of 1890's New York, films recalling old Broadway with horse-cars, bicycles built for two and the outside of St. Patrick's Cathedral on a bygone Easter morn.

The Rockettes, bless them, get a full day's work in this show, appearing in a half-dozen refreshing numbers and garnering cheers with every precise, programmed high kick. Then there are the two scenes and costumes designed by Erté, the venerable artist and designer, whose Art Deco arches in one set and varicolored giant Rorschach blots in another suit Radio City's own lines so splendidly. One of the sprightliest moments arrives with entrance of the odd cartoonlike quintet of instruments called the Musikins, who in jazz song, debate the merits of one instrument over the other.

The continuity, whatever there is to it, is supplied by a character known as the Rabbit, played by Wayne Cilento, who scampers about, sings and is as personable as one might expect in such surroundings. The music hall is more impressive to the eye than to the ear, but the score of the Easter show is liltingly eclectic, ranging from churchlike to barbershop quartet to Gershwin and Irving Berlin, with his indispensable Easter bonnet.

This Easter show, so likable, almost despite its grandeur, makes one wish that the music hall could find a way to celebrate every holiday. What could it not do with Chinese New Year?

1990 Ap 13, C28:4

The Vanishing Point In Perspective

CITIES OUT OF PRINT, by Susan Mosakowski; directed by Ms. Mosakowski; set by Tom Dale Keever; lighting by Pat Dignan; sound by Joe Gallant. Presented by the Creation Production Company at the Westbeth Theater Center, 151 Bank Street.

He	Matthew Maguire
She	Susan Mosakowski

Matthew Maguire and Susan Mosakowski in "Cities Out of Print."

By STEPHEN HOLDEN

One of the many musical fragments that run through Susan Mosakowski's two-character performance
collage, "Cities Out of Print," is Hank
Williams's honky-tonk death wish,
"I'll Never Get Out of This World
Alive." More than any other piece of
music or dialogue in a play that recycles popular myths of violent self-destruction, the song distills the ghoulish glamour of a narcissistic infatuation with death in a speeding car.

In the lively and amusing one-hour
play, which runs through April 22 at
the Westbeth Theater Center, Ms.
Mosakowski and Matthew Maguire
portray a couple so entranced by legendary figures who have died in car
crashes — James Dean, Grace Kelly,
Albert Camus, Jackson Pollock and
many others — that they work themselves into an ecstatic, suicidal frenzy
of fantasized identification.

At its best, the piece recalls "The
Beard," Michael McClure's 1960's
play, which imagines a mythical encounter between Jean Harlow and
Billy the Kid. Instead of inventing one
pop myth, "Cities Out of Print" recycles dozens of familiar ones from life
and from art, swirling them together
into a collage of voices and dialogue
that makes them seem interchangeable and cheap.

The re-enactment of a scene from
the David Lynch movie "Blue Velvet" segues abruptly into a soap-
opera tableau in which Jackson Pollock and an unidentified woman talk
passionately about living on "the
edge." As the actors keep exhanging
characters, accents and wigs, their
dialogues seem phony and hyped up
and the characters foolishly self-
deluded. As such stories have prolif-
erated and been recycled in the age of
the video and audio cassette, the play
strongly suggests, they have lost
their resonance. Both performers obviously relish acting out these games
of charade and dress up. Ms. Mosakowski is especially stinging in her
moments as a mean, goading gun
moll.

Tom Dale Keever's striking set design poses the action between two
visual elements. One is the skeleton of
the death car the couple dreams of
driving into oblivion. The other is a
large painting of an empty highway
that vanishes into the distance. At the
end of the play, the actors fill in that
emptiness, fixing themselves to the
canvas like hungry flies as Hank Williams's fatalistic hymn to extinction
keens in the background.

1990 Ap 14, 16:4

Deathbed Scene

GOGOL, by Roderick O'Reilly; directed by
Stuart Laurence; production stage manager;
Elaine R. O'Donnell; sets and masks, Steve
Carter; lighting, Brian Aldous; costumes,
Elizabeth Huffman; graphic design, Ian Pig-
gott. Presented by the Beacon Project Inc. At
Regenesis Theater, St. Mark's Church-in-the-
Bowery, 131 East 10th Street, at Second Ave-
nue.
WITH: Robert Aberdeen, Ken Bolden, Mi-
chael Fife, Elizabeth Huffman, Nancy Lear-
month, Anthony John Lizzul, Marc F. Nohé,
Larry Reinhardt-Meyer, Robert L. Rowe,
Geraldine Singer and T. Ryder Smith.

By WILBORN HAMPTON

The stage has never been the most
comfortable vehicle for biography,
and the lives of writers, even great
and eccentric ones like Nikolai Gogol,
usually provide fairly flimsy material around which to build a drama.

"Gogol," a jumble of a play by Roderick O'Reilly that is being presented
by the Beacon Project, is no exception. Certainly Gogol was an odd and
troubled man. Vladimir Nabokov
called him "the strangest prose-poet
Russia ever produced." But bizarre
behavior alone cannot support three
hours of traffic on any stage, especially the crazy quilt Mr. O'Reilly has
stitched together from Gogol's writings, letters (mostly to his mother
asking for money) and a lot of hear-
say, the veracity of which is dubious
at best.

The play opens with Gogol on his
deathbed, attended by a physician,
who prescribes leeches and hot baths

with simultaneous cold showers, and
a mad monk of a priest, who counsels
him to renounce everything in his life.
The action then goes back to Gogol's
arrival in St. Petersburg at the age of
19 and proceeds chronologically,
through 23 scenes, none notable for
their brevity, ending up once again at
the author's deathbed, where he finally succumbs after burning the sequel to "Dead Souls" to expiate his
sins.

Mr. O'Reilly seems to have tried to
cram everything he has ever read by
or about Gogol into his play rather
than select representative moments
to dramatize. As a result, the play is
full of awkward transitions that leave
the action darting incomprehensibly
back and forth between Gogol's work
— particularly "The Nose," "The
Overcoat" and "The Government Inspector" — and his life. When Pushkin dies, for example, Mr. O'Reilly
transports Gogol, who was in Rome
at the time, to the poet's side. As
Gogol cradles Pushkin's head in his
lap and reads him the first chapter of
"Dead Souls," Pushkin looks up and
mutters, "One duel too many, eh,
Nikolai?"

Mr. O'Reilly further appears to
take at face value Gogol's later attempts to explain the symbolism that
critics and the reading public had
originally failed to see in both "The
Government Inspector" and "Dead
Souls." But, as Nabokov noted, Gogol
had a penchant for conveniently in-
terpreting his works long after he had
written them, and if Mr. O'Reilly's
version is to be believed, one is faced
with the incredible prospect that one
of history's literary geniuses was little more than a religious fanatic who
totally misunderstood his own life's
work.

The Beacon cast only occasionally
rises above the paucity of the material. Anthony John Lizzul, wearing a
fake ski-nose that would be more appropriate for a Bob Hope impersonation, plays Gogol with such a zealous
intensity one would never suspect
him of ever having a sense of humor.
Robert L. Rowe is the best of the ensemble, all of whom double or triple
in various roles. Marc F. Nohé and
Nancy Learmonth also have credible
moments. The play moves very
slowly in places, and Stuart Laurence's direction does little to help
one through the dull stretches. Elizabeth Huffman's costumes are stunning.

1990 Ap 14, 17:1

At Journey's End

DAY TRIPS, by Jo Carson; directed by Michael Engler; set design, Loy Arcenas; costume design, Catherine Zuber; lighting design, Pat Collins; sound design, David
Budries; dramaturge, Greg Leaming; production stage manager, Barbara Reo; assistant stage manager, Ruth E. Sternberg. Presented by Hartford Stage, Mark Lamos, artistic director; David Hawkanson, managing director. At Hartford.
Pat .... Susan Pellegrino
Storyteller .... Suzanna Hay
Ree and Irene .... Isa Thomas
Rose .... Helen Stenborg

By MEL GUSSOW

Special to The New York Times

HARTFORD, April 12 — Jo Carson's "Day Trips" is personal rather
than issue oriented, but it raises troubling questions about family responsibility and about the prolongation of
life by artificial means. Ms. Carson, a

Texan storyteller and author, approaches her sensitive subject without sentimentality or its opposite,
cynicism.

The play, which is having its East
Coast premiere at the Hartford
Stage, is evidently heartfelt, but it
does have certain limitations. Small
in scale if not in resonance, "Day
Trips" is a mosaic of failing memory
rather than a full-fledged dramatization. It lacks the poetic intensity of a
play like Arthur Kopit's "Wings," and
it has an indefinite destination. After
the last word, the audience waits for a
conclusion or a coda, which, it is suggested, can only come in life.

By not reaching for a statement,
"Day Trips" distinguishes itself from
case history or docudrama. The play
should speak to many families, in
particular to people who are forced to
assume parental control of their
aging parents when serious infirmity
strikes and death seems to be a
hovering but distant presence.

Detailing a woman's concern for
her mother who has Alzheimer's disease and for her grandmother who
suffers from her own delusions, the
play moves from present to past,
from reality to recurrent dreams. In
performance, a potentially fragmented play achieves fluidity.

Michael Engler, the director, and
four talented actresses help to clarify
the sometimes confusing time span.
The scenery by Loy Arcenas removes
the play from rigid domestic confines, creating an impressionistic indoor-outdoor setting in which a bedroom door leads directly to a pastoral
landscape.

The granddaughter is portrayed by
two actresses, Susan Pellegrino as
the character in the play, Suzanna
Hay as storyteller. In Ms. Carson's
hands this method is made to seem
organic, as two voices for a single
character alternate in acting out a
tale of prolonged devotion.

The mother (Isa Thomas) shows
all signs of advancing Alzheimer's.
Her memory is devastated and her
reactions range from the most withdrawn to sudden, willful outbursts of
anger. To add to the granddaughter's
predicament, the grandmother
(Helen Stenborg) combines stubbornness with a selective forgetfulness.

She insists on living alone, barricading herself behind a wall of suspicion (with three locks on every door)
while making excessive demands on
her relatives. Her granddaughter is
forced to become, in the author's
words, a double "care keeper." Shut-
tling (on day trips) from one matriarch to the other, Ms. Pellegrino
scarcely has time to assert her own
identity. Neither older woman is remotely helpful. While they are severely lacking in compassion, the
granddaughter is unable to be less
than dutiful.

If anything, the grandmother, who
still has areas of lucidity, is more of a
hindrance than her more disabled
daughter. In the play's most moving
performance Ms. Stenborg enhances
her character by finding a humor beneath the feistiness, as in her grudg-
ing acceptance of a favorite cake. "I
guess we have to eat some of it," she
says tersely while conveying that the
cake is one of the rare delights of her
declining years.

In one of the play's amusing though
anxious interludes, Ms. Pellegrino
chauffeurs Ms. Stenborg from drugstore to drugstore, searching for the
pharmacist who last filled her prescription. Though the younger woman
is increasingly frustrated by the ex-

Susan Pellegrino in "Day Trips."

perience, she realizes that the repetition of remembered ways is what keeps her grandmother sane.

The need to maintain the status quo, which is, of course, an impossible status to bear, reaches a crisis when the grandmother is hospitalized and the doctors refuse to consider her as a terminal patient. The old woman wants to die; they insist on preserving her life. Agonizingly, the granddaughter wonders, "Can death be a gift?"

One mark of the play's acuity is that such a question seems selfless. It is not the granddaughter who wants to free herself from a burden, but a parent who, in Samuel Beckett's phrase, simply wants to embrace "the close of a long day."

1990 Ap 16, C15:1

Riffs From the Past

THE PIANO LESSON, by August Wilson; directed by Lloyd Richards; scene design by E. David Cosier Jr.; lighting by Christopher Akerlind; costumes by Constanza Romero; musical director/composer, Dwight D. Andrews; sound, G. Thomas Clark; production stage manager, Karen L. Carpenter; general manager, Laurel Ann Wilson; associate producer, Stephen J. Albert. Presented by Mr. Richards, Yale Repertory Theater, Center Theater Group/Ahmanson Theater, Gordon Davidson and the Jujamcyn Theaters with Benjamin Mordecai, executive producer, in association with Eugene O'Neill Theater Center, Huntington Theater Company, Goodman Theater and Old Globe Theater. Presented in New York in association with the Manhattan Theater Club. At the Walter Kerr Theater, 215 West 48th Street.

Doaker	Carl Gordon
Boy Willie	Charles S. Dutton
Lymon	Rocky Carroll
Berniece	S. Epatha Merkerson
Maretha	Apryl R. Foster
Avery	Tommy Hollis
Wining Boy	Lou Myers
Grace	Lisa Gay Hamilton

By FRANK RICH

The piano is the first thing the audience hears in "The Piano Lesson," the new August Wilson play at the Walter Kerr Theater. Three hours later, it seems as if the music, by turns bubbling and thunderous, has never stopped.

Though Mr. Wilson won a Pulitzer Prize last week for this work, no one need worry that he is marching to an establishment beat. "The Piano Lesson" is joyously an African-American play: it has its own spacious poetry, its own sharp angle on a nation's history, its own metaphorical idea of drama and its own palpable ghosts that roar right through the upstairs window of the household where the action unfolds. Like other Wilson plays, "The Piano Lesson" seems to sing even when it is talking. But it isn't all of America that is singing. The central fact of black American life — the long shadow of slavery — transposes the voices of Mr. Wilson's characters, and of the indelible actors who inhabit them, to a key that rattles history and shakes the audience on both sides of the racial divide.

Set in the Pittsburgh of 1936, just midway in time between "Joe Turner's Come and Gone" and "Fences," Mr. Wilson's new play echoes his others by reaching back toward Africa and looking ahead to modern urban America even as it remains focused on the intimate domestic canvas of a precise bygone year. Though "The Piano Lesson" is about a fight over the meaning of a long span of history, its concerns are dramatized within a simple battle between a sister and a brother over the possession of a musical instrument. The keeper of the piano, a family heirloom, is a young widow named Berniece (S. Epatha Merkerson), who lets it languish unused in the parlor of the house she shares with her uncle and daughter. Her brother, Boy Willie (Charles S. Dutton), barges in unannounced from Mississippi, intending to sell the antique to buy a farm on the land his family worked as slaves and sharecroppers.

One need only look at the majestic upright piano itself to feel its power as a symbolic repository of a people's soul. Sculptured into its rich wood are totemic human figures whose knife-drawn features suggest both the pride of African culture and the grotesque scars of slavery. As it happens, both the pride and scars run deep in the genealogy of the siblings at center stage. Their great-grandfather, who carved the images, lost his wife and young son when they were traded away for the piano. Years later, Berniece and Boy Willie's father was killed after he took the heirloom from a new generation of white owners.

In "The Piano Lesson," the disposition of the piano becomes synonymous with the use to which the characters put their ancestral legacy. For Berniece, the instrument must remain a somber shrine to a tragic past. For Boy Willie, the piano is a stake to the freedom his father wanted him to have. To Mr. Wilson, both characters are right — and wrong. Just as Berniece is too enslaved by history to get on with her life, so Boy Willie is too cavalier about his family's heritage to realize that money alone cannot buy him independence and equality in a white man's world. Like all Wilson protagonists, both the brother and sister must take a journey, at times a supernatural one, to the past if they are to seize the future. They cannot be reconciled with each other until they have had a reconciliation with the identity that is etched in their family tree, as in the piano, with blood.

Mr. Dutton and Ms. Merkerson prove to be extraordinary adversaries through every twist of their no-holds-barred dispute. They command equal respect and affection through antithetical acting styles. As he first revealed as Levee, the discordant trumpet player in Mr. Wilson's "Ma Rainey's Black Bottom," the burly, broadly smiling Mr. Dutton is a force of nature on stage: a human cyclone who, as Berniece says, sows noise, confusion and trouble wherever he goes. Here is that rare actor who can announce that he's on fire and make an audience believe he might actually burn down the theater. Yet the impressive Ms. Merkerson remains quiet and dignified holding her ground against him — at least up to a point. In the evening's most devastating scene, she slugs her brother in impotent fury, as if her small fists and incantatory wails might somehow halt the revenge-fueled cycle of violence that killed her father and her husband and their fathers before them.

Although the second act contains its dead ends, repetitions and excessive authorial announcements — an O'Neill-like excess in most of this writer's plays — Mr. Wilson prevents the central conflict in "The Piano Lesson" from becoming too nakedly didactic by enclosing it within an extended household of memorable characters. The ebb and flow of diurnal

Whatever happens to the instrument, the music is not up for sale.

activity in Berniece's home thickens the main theme while offering a naturalistic picture of a transitional black America in an era when movies, skyscrapers and airplanes were fresh wonders of the world. A Wilson play feels truly lived in — so much so in Lloyd Richards's supple production that activities like the cooking of eggs, the washing of dishes, and the comings and goings from an audibly flushed toilet never seem like stage events, but become subliminal beats in the rhythm of a self-contained universe.

Still, the play's real music is in the language, all of which is gloriously served by the ensemble company that Mr. Richards has assembled and

S. Epatha Merkerson and Charles S. Dutton in a scene from August Wilson's "Piano Lesson."

honed during the more than two years that "The Piano Lesson" has traveled to New York by way of the country's resident theaters. Carl Gordon, as an uncle who has spent 27 years working for the railroad, and Lou Myers, as another uncle who has hit his own long road as a traveling musician, trade tall and small tales of hard-won practical philosophy, political wisdom, women and whisky — some of them boisterously funny, others unexpectedly touching. At other moments, their colloquial verbal cadences trail off seamlessly into riffs of actual song, whether piano blues or roof-raising vocal harmonies, that express their autobiographies of pride, defiance and suffering as eloquently as their words.

A younger generation of dispossessed black men with a different set of experiences and aspirations is just as vividly represented by Tommy Hollis, as a Bible-toting elevator man with dreams of leading his own Christian flock, and Rocky Carroll, as a wide-eyed rural drifter dazzled by his first exposure to the big city. A scene in which Mr. Carroll briefly courts Ms. Merkerson by presenting her with a dollar bottle of "French perfume" is, in writing, staging and performance, a masterly romantic duet of crossed signals and unacknowledged longings that seems to float up from a distant, innocent time like a hallucination.

•

While there are no white characters in "The Piano Lesson," the presence of white America is felt throughout — and not just by dint of past history. Boy Willie repeatedly and pointedly announces that he will sell the piano to a white man who he's heard is roaming through black neighborhoods "looking to buy musical instruments." Whatever happens to the piano, however, the playwright makes it clear that the music in "The Piano Lesson" is not up for sale. That haunting music belongs to the people who have lived it, and it has once' again found miraculous voice in a play that August Wilson has given to the American stage.

1990 Ap 17, C13:4

An Unjust Peace At Any Price

THE PEACE OF BREST-LITOVSK, by Mikhail Shatrov; directed by Robert Sturua; designed by Georgi Meskhishvili; lighting designer, Vladimir Amelin; sound designer, Yevgeny Ivanov; music by Guia Kancheli; costumes, Marina Chernyakhovskaya and Emilia Mikhailovskaya. Performed by the Vakhtangov Theater of Moscow, Mikhail Ulyanov, artistic director; Aleksandr Karsov, administrative director. Presented in the Civic Theater in the Civic Center for the Performing Arts, in association with the Court Theater. At 20 North Wacker Drive, Chicago.

Orator .... Maksim Sukhanov
Sidorenko .... Sergei Makovetsky
Widow .... Natalya Moleva

Lenin .... Mr. Ulyanov
Dzerzhinski .... Yevgeny Shersnyov
Bukharin .... Aleksandr Filipenko
Stalin .... Vladimir Koval

Sverdlov .... Vladimir Ivanov
Lomov .... Aleksandr Pavlov
Inessa Armand .... Yelena Ivochkina
Krupskaya .... Alla Parfanyak

Trotsky .... Vasily Lanovoy
"Former People"
 Aleksandr Galevy and Lidiya Konstantinova

By MEL GUSSOW

Special to The New York Times

CHICAGO, April 17 — With an impartiality that has been rare in contemporary Soviet theater, "The Peace of Brest-Litovsk" personalizes history and illuminates a turning point in its nation's past: the 1918 treaty that fixed its signers (post-Czarist Russia and imperialist Germany) on a course that was to have disastrous repercussions.

Mikhail Shatrov's play opened last night at the Civic Theater, beginning its only scheduled engagement in the United States. The highly charged production is presented by the Vakhtangov Theater of Moscow and directed by Robert Sturua, who recently staged the Georgian "King Lear" at the Brooklyn Academy of Music.

"The Peace of Brest-Litovsk" is concerned with men influencing and inflaming other men. It is a play of debate as well as of ideas, raising provocative questions about war and peace and, in particular, about wars undertaken in the name of restoring peace. The drama begins in 1917, after the Czar has been overthrown. At the beginning of the Bolshevik Revolution, Lenin and his colleagues faced the crucial question of whether to continue the war with Germany or negotiate their own peaceful settlement, without regard for their Western allies.

•

At the center of the conflict is Lenin, who, as dramatized, is not the saint of Soviet mythology but a pragmatic politician. He is held back by doubts and fired by his passionate belief in the need to preserve lives and the spirit of the Bolshevik Revolution even at the price of signing a humiliating treaty with Germany. As a result of the treaty, Russia gave up Polish, Baltic and other territory, encouraging German dominance in Europe. With the general armistice of 1918, Germany was forced to renounce the treaty, but it has gone down in history as a most unjust peace.

The historian John W. Wheeler-Bennett, writing about that treaty in his book "The Forgotten Peace," said that it had all the elements of great drama — "tragedy and betrayal, irony and fleeting sardonic wit,' and the inevitable Nemesis of knaves."

All it lacked, he said, was the "element of virtue." Mr. Shatrov's play captures these diverse dimensions.

Though it was written in 1967, the work was not performed in the Soviet Union until two decades later. The reasons are readily apparent. Just as Lenin is a flawed though heroic figure, his principal antagonists, Trotsky and Bukharin, are not the traitors of Soviet tradition but complex characters with their own defensible points of view. Like Lenin, both of these zealots undergo crises of conscience and of dialectics, while waiting in the wings is the figure of Stalin.

The author does not pretend to depict the German position — only Russians are seen on stage — but the play gives weighty issues a theatrical vitality. This is clearly a result of the collaborative efforts of the director and his fine cast, which is headed by Mikhail Ulyanov in the role of Lenin. Mr. Ulyanov (coincidentally, Lenin's real name) is also the artistic director of the Vakhtangov, a 69-year-old Moscow theater. Through artful interweaving of music and cabaret theater techniques and using a striking design by Georgi Meskhishvili, Mr. Sturua creates a portrait of a rising revolutionary government at war with itself.

The characters are in a setting of classical ruin, an imaginary theater. Except for Stalin, there is no attempt at physical impersonation, and even in Stalin's case this is not a waxwork imitation. Mr. Ulyanov's Lenin looks more like Spencer Tracy than Lenin, and he approaches the role naturalistically, without histrionics. This is clearly a plain man who has risen to fill his role in history.

•

In Mr. Ulyanov's authoritative characterization, one can sense the seductiveness of Lenin's oratory (spoken in Russian, and simultaneously translated into English through headphones). For all his steeliness, he remains a politician who is prepared to demean himself to win an argument, at one point dropping to his knees to implore Trotsky's allegiance.

Vasily Lanovoy's Trotsky is, in contrast, a hardline idealist who resolutely reaffirms his impossible compromise: no war but no peace treaty either, a solution that would invite a German invasion of his country. Between the two is Bukharin, who, in Aleksandr Filipenko's portrayal, is as impetuous as he is intractable. He wants war with Germany rather than a separatist peace. It was Trotsky's abstention at a crucial point that led directly to Lenin's victory.

•

A general audience unfamiliar with the intricacies of the treaty may miss some of the subtleties (including Germany's offstage involvement), but the individual Soviet positions are never in doubt. The English translation is a definite asset in following the labyrinthine proceedings. Buoyed with energy and emotion, the actors add an immediacy to what in other authorial hands could have been a textbook treatise. Despite the period trappings, we become witnesses at Brest-Litovsk.

The play carries its audience to a tantalizing conclusion. Two symbolic figures, remnants of the Czarist regime, dance on stage and tip their hats in mockery. A spotlight hits Stalin — up to then a sideline character — and he smiles confidently. That final image is like a flash forward in history, indicating that in a battle for political and ideological supremacy, the worthiest of intentions can lead to the most dire results.

1990 Ap 18, C11:1

Mikhail Ulyanov as Lenin in "The Peace of Brest-Litovsk."

Writers' Blocks

RELATED RETREATS, written and directed by Eduardo Machado; set, Donald Eastman; lights, Stephen Quandt; costumes, E.G. Widulski; stage manager, Thomas George Thomas; assistant directors, Lawrence R. Harris and Beth Nathanson. Presented by Theater for the New City, George Bartenieff, executive director; Crystal Field, executive artistic director. At 155 First Avenue, at 10th Street.

Lis .... Lisa Gluckin
Frank .... Roger Durling
Diane .... Ching Valdes-Aran
Nina .... Kimberly Anne Ryan
Karl .... Jeffery Logan
Tom .... John Finch
Helper .... Ana K. Lon,

By WILBORN HAMPTON

One shudders at the thought that the future of American letters might in any way be influenced by the band of would-be poets that gathers at the writers' workshop that is the setting for "Related Retreats," a new play by Eduardo Machado at the Theater for the New City.

Mr. Machado's play might well be subtitled "Sex, Drugs and Serious Poetry," since all the characters use their ostensible literary pursuits as an excuse to indulge their baser appetites. As the play opens, Frank (Roger Durling) has just arrived at an unnamed writers' conference somewhere near a desert in California. For the first few minutes, everyone walks around reciting his or her poems to anyone who will listen. That the poetry itself is mostly a bad imitation of 1950's coffeehouse verse does not diminish Frank's elation at simply breathing the same air as these literary lions.

The artistic ideals of the commune become clear once the writers start to evaluate one another's work ("It's a good poem except for the part about me," one woman tells another), and the communal ideals of the artists become even more apparent when one impatient couple begin to toss off their clothes with abandon. Frank is ecstatic. "This is life!" he says, watching the couple cavort on the sand. "This is art!"

Sex, in fact, appears to be the main preoccupation of the three men and three women at Mr. Machado's retreat, and the gender of partners is of small concern. Their priorities are summed up by Tom, a famous bisexual who is also a poet, when he meets Frank: "You're young! You're beautiful! Do you write?"

•

The opening scenes are amusing as an affectionate satire of the creative process. As the writers begin their morning exercise — sitting in a circle, recalling their last thought before falling sleep the previous night (if they can remember the previous night), then writing it down — they resemble bratty children fighting in a sandbox. While Frank scribbles furi-

Life and art, sex and egocentric obsessions at a writers' retreat.

ously, as though poetry were some sort of speed-writing contest, a piqued Tom complains, "Frank's pen is making too much noise," and he stalks off.

But all too soon "Related Retreats" begins to take itself seriously and becomes snarled in a tiresome tale of egocentric obsessions. The action degenerates into a lot of shouting, kicking chairs and throwing tantrums, and everyone smokes, snorts or shoots an inordinate amount of drugs. It is all probably meant to be terribly meaningful and shocking, but by the time one character emerges from a three-year writer's block ("Get my pen and paper! I'm going to Write!"), only to attempt suicide when her muse does not return quickly enough, no one really cares.

Mr. Machado, who also directed, has assembled a cast that works hard at making his characters credible. But the exaggerated emotions of the play produce their own histrionics in some roles. John Finch is very funny in the role of Tom. Kimberly Anne Ryan and Lisa Gluckin offer consistently believable performances.

1990 Ap 18, C12:5

Stories Onstage

SPUNK, three tales by Zora Neale Hurston; adapted and directed by George C. Wolfe; choreography by Hope Clarke; music by Chic Street Man; sets by Loy Arcenas; costumes by Toni-Leslie James; lighting by Don Holder; mask and puppet design by Barbara Pollitt; associate producer, Jason Steven Cohen. Presented by Joseph Papp, in association with Crossroads Theater Company, Rick Khan, producer and executive director. At the Public Theater/Martinson Hall, 425 Lafayette Street.

With: Chic Street Man, Ann Duquesnay, K. Todd Freeman, Kevin Jackson, Reggie Montgomery and Danitra Vance.

By FRANK RICH

When writers with clashing personalities share the same stage, the result can often be a tug of war. But in "Spunk," the exuberant show at the Public Theater celebrating the fiction of Zora Neale Hurston, George C. Wolfe, the author of "The Colored

Martha Swope

Danitra Vance and Kevin Jackson in George C. Wolfe's "Spunk."

Museum," submerges his own irreverent sensibility to serve, and serve ingeniously, the spirit of a far different literary voice. When one recalls how much satirical devastation Mr. Wolfe inflicted on Lorraine Hansberry and Ntozake Shange in "The Colored Museum," his selfless devotion to Hurston is all the more impressive.

Mr. Wolfe is not, of course, the first in the theater or anywhere else to pick up the banner for Hurston, the Florida-born novelist, folklorist and anthropologist who was a legendary figure in the Harlem Renaissance, a national literary star and a thorny political ideologue before fading into obscurity and poverty before her death in 1960. In recent years there has been a steady procession of books, essays, plays and television programs about her life and art. Most of Hurston's major works are now back in print and the unproduced play she wrote with Langston Hughes during the Depression, "Mule Bone," is scheduled for production at Lincoln Center in August.

"Spunk," in which three short stories have been adapted for the stage

and folded into a bluesy musical framework, reveals how time has finally caught up with Hurston's view of the Afro-American experience. Once attacked by Richard Wright, among other social realists, as having perpetuated minstrel stereotypes,

The luxuriant spoken language of a multi-layered culture.

she is now seen clearly as an astute observer of a hyphenated black culture merging the African and the American. A connoisseur and zealous reporter of indigenous speech, Hurston lovingly preserved the extravagant black English of the urban and rural America of her time. Yet the people doing the talking were dignified, fully realized characters — in no way minstrels — and the stories containing their verbal improvisations were often narrated in formal, omnis-

cient prose that could swing seamlessly from the caustic to the tragic.

Serving as both writer and director, Mr. Wolfe makes sure that every precious, spiky Hurston word counts. With a company of six performers, two of them singers, he is not only faithful to the dialogue in the stories (and even, at one point, to a comic authorial footnote redefining the word "pimp"), but he also retains the narration, assigning it at will to those members of the free-floating ensemble serving as a chorus or to the characters themselves in mid-scene. The technique rarely seems stagy, because the entire evening, enhanced by the choreography of Hope Clarke and the Noh-like masks and puppets of Barbara Pollitt, has a folklorish gait. The style could anachronistically be likened to magic realism, but whatever one calls it, Mr. Wolfe has created a stage atmosphere in which the rules of conventional realism are suspended in favor of fabulist invention.

•

If there's a subject uniting the stories in "Spunk," it is that of men and women. And the point of view is ideologically balanced. The first tale, "Sweat," is about a physically and spiritually exhausted washerwoman abused and betrayed by her husband; the third, "The Gilded Six-Bits," is about an adoring husband betrayed by his wife. In between the two marital fables comes a small comic masterpiece, "Story in Harlem Slang," in which two sharp male idlers, seeking "wealth and splendor in Harlem without working," try to hustle a meal from a domestic enjoying a payday afternoon off. Along the way to meeting their comeuppance, the men treat the audience to a jamboree of 1940's uptown slang that is perfectly echoed by their burlesque zoot suits and the struts with which they percolate down Lenox Avenue.

The production's elegant stylization extends to the sets, costumes and lighting — handsomely designed by Loy Arcenas, Toni-Leslie James and Don Holder — and to the persistent guitar accompaniment provided by Chic Street Man, who also composed the music for the full-bodied blues interludes gutsily sung by Ann Duquesnay. The cast functions as such a closely knit ensemble that it's almost unjust to single out Danitra Vance's exceptional range in playing a trio of women who are in turn worn to the bone, full of sass and aglow with innocence. (Ms. Vance can sing, too, and does a hilarious impersonation of a "pretty white woman" squealing.) Reggie Montgomery, as an assortment of con artists, and K. Todd Freeman, in broader bits, also make lively contributions. Kevin Jackson, the ingenuous, lovesick husband of "The Gilded Six-Bits," is a young actor of unusual charm and talent.

While the theatrical trimmings that Mr. Wolfe's production pours on Hurston's prose can sometimes be too thick — it takes a while to untangle the narrative thread in "Sweat," for instance — the show seems false to its source only in its repetition of an over-explanatory theme song that champions the characters' grit in corny terms seemingly intended to spoon-feed the stories to white audiences. The show's title is also questionable, for while Hurston did write a story called "Spunk," it isn't dramatized here and its title is hardly the theme of this anthology's unsentimental vignettes, one of which ends with a grisly death.

The fallible people of "Spunk" in fact have no more or less spunk than anyone else, which is one reason why they seem so real and engaging. The true spunk in "Spunk" belongs to Mr. Wolfe, who has gallantly met Zora Neale Hurston in the theater on her own uncompromising terms and, better still, has found the imaginative means to make good on his half of so challenging a collaboration.

1990 Ap 19, C17:4

STAGE VIEW/Walter Kerr

About a Poinsettia And a Woman With Five Hands

Zoe Dominic

Maggie Smith in "Lettice and Lovage"—devilishly accomplished

YES, BUT WHAT IS "LETTICE and Lovage" all about?

It's surely not about Maggie Smith *qua* Maggie Smith, even though the actress — here on a rare respite from London — calls splendiferous attention to herself from time to time in the importation at the Barrymore.

For instance, she makes gestures that require five hands, and she succeeds in displaying all of them simultaneously. I counted. She is further able to deal with a telephone receiver and accompanying coiled wire (left hand) that may or may not become entangled with a rather large, limp cat (right hand and most of right arm). And she is entirely prepared to dress suitably for any and all occasions, in large part due to the fact that her mother, as she tells us, had been an actress and Maggie (here called Lettice) had been her costumer, dresser and inheritor of hand-me-downs.

Thus when she arrives at the headquarters of her employer knowing she is about to be sacked, she is arrayed — quite massively — in a penitential black gown decorated with enough faded lace to suggest a whole winter's supply of hoarfrost. Trailing five or six satiny but essentially downcast bustles, she rather resembles the Armada, after the battle.

She is a quick-change artist, though, and the accouterments of mourning are not with us for long. Leaping from the chair she's sat in, she whips away the dull robes of gloom and lets us see the flame within: head to toe, she is a blazing, silken, fiery red taper of a woman, and the woman's name is Martyr-

You might want to know how a show is going, and a prop's odd service may be able to tell you.

dom. Miss Smith glories in the distinction, and in the knowledge that she's building to a damn good first-act curtain.

Later on, Miss Smith will offer us further transformations, some of which may appeal to us even more. I especially liked her illustration of how her mother had shifted from the role of Richard III into the role of Falstaff simply by making a slight adjustment to the hump. Of course, Miss Smith's mother played all her Shakespeare in French.

But Miss Smith, Miss Smith, Miss Smith! Are we to hear of nothing but the actress, who is wonderful? Nothing of Peter Shaffer's play? Are we even to find his play, under the onrush of captivating tricks?

The play is about the death of color in the British Isles, and in the British eye. Somewhere along the way — the precise "where" will be specified before the evening's done — all of the glory of architecture and dress, of language and heraldry, vanished in England and was never heard of more. The march to a threadbare plainness, to faceless windows and undecorated archways, to muted greetings and monochromatic feasts, had begun. Surely you've had one of those British boiled dinners composed of halibut, cauliflower and potatoes, white on white on white? The march continues today. Or so sayeth "Lettice and Lovage." (Lovage is an herb from which a powerfully giddy 16th-century "quaff" can be brewed. A relic of the richness that's been lost.) Now, the play's points of structure, including most of the bizarre activities of Miss Smith, actually depend on and illustrate playwright Shaffer's plaintiff faces. We first meet Miss Smith on the job, shepherding tourists through an ancient British landmark and wildly elaborating on the historical events that took place there. Or didn't.

Miss Smith, that is to say, is giving them a bit of "color" to brighten them up. She is caught improving on history by overseer Margaret Tyzack — making many and subtle variations on a basic monotone bark — and summoned to the offices of the Preservation House for dismissal.

■

Dismissal it is, except that several months later Miss Tyzack, a most admirable actress, comes ringing at Miss Smith's basement flat with certain amends to make. Miss Tyzack has written Miss Smith a wary letter of recommendation, suggesting that she do guide-work on boat rides, where she will somehow come to less harm. Miss Smith instantly drops to one knee, hand on sword-hilt and ready for knighthood. "Oh, you are good", she exclaims, binding all of the phrase's various meanings into a single soft bundle; amusing *and* affecting.

The two women begin trading life histories. It develops that Miss Tyzack, whom the modern world has made into a dull gray creature with dull gray cheeks and a dull gray jaw, had a father who much lamented the bombing and the dull gray rebuilding of Dresden after the war. He felt that Britain's plight was not a lone plight. The whole world's "communal eye had been put out." And was never going to be recovered.

Miss Tyzack realizes that she is one end product of the loss. Miss Smith, having allowed herself to be carried beyond "the gray of prose and Puritanism," is an active throwback, a wayward spot of color. Improv is her game.

Interesting as it is, there is something about "Lettice and Lovage" that isn't quite in register. The two tones don't precisely fit, don't complement each other, scene to scene. The first act, for instance, contains four variants on a single romantic story that Miss Smith invents for the sightseers staring at a great staircase in the Fustian House [sic] of Wiltshire. But the variants don't vary enough for us to justify the time and space spent on them. And subsequently the "color" theme and the comedy playing around it tend to take turns instead of linking arms and advancing upon us in force.

Incontestably, Miss Smith is devilishly accomplished, whether she is playing with beards, wigs, daggers, little black gloves that turn her hands into fluttering birds, or any other available prop. And whether you go to "Lettice and Lovage" for this incidental fun or for a report on all that Oliver Cromwell has done to us, you'll surely go. You'll go because you'll want to talk about it.

■

I mentioned props a moment ago and that brought back into my head the odd and unusual service a prop may perform. You might want to know how a show is going and a prop may be able to tell you.

Consider, if you will, the case o Robert Morse's one-man evocation o the sassy but sorely troubled las days of Truman Capote. "Tru," at the Booth, is an astonishingly perceptive piece, stunningly played by a performer who has hitherto confined himself to dispensing sunny smiles — stretched ear to ear — along with large gobs of innocence. Here, as Capote, he is backed into the corner o: his New York apartment — sheer glass when it isn't sheer books — and made to confront the fact that he has written a novel filled with thinly disguised or undisguised real people Mr. Capote has tattled on the rich and glamorous folk who have lionized him, and the scandal is about to cost him every last friend he has in the world. We count the losses with him, aware that we seem to be dropping all of the names at once.

In the acting text that Jay Presson Allen has arranged from the "words and works" of Capote, there isn't a lot of hope left in that week before Christmas, 1975, but there's still an

Though the time of the play at the Booth is late, very late, there is still impertinence to be displayed, outrageousness to be savored, humor to be shared. The only thing I miss — and it's inevitable here — is the quiet precise use of his creative intelligence. When he was alone with it, fine things could happen. And in company he could be great fun. That is why he had so many friends to be offended.

About that prop. In "Tru," as the tics threaten to take over and regret rises to the boil, Mr. Morse — see, I almost said Mr. Capote — obviously wants some sort of release that is more flamboyant than wit. Whereupon he snatches up a framed portrait of himself as a younger man and savagely puts his fist through it.

There were gasps from the audience on the night I saw the play, and one of them might well have been mine. Of *course* we knew that the painting was a prop, impersonal and valueless. Given a split second to think, we mightn't have been caught off guard like that. But it is good that we were caught off guard. For what the gasp says, beyond question, is that we'd been believing in what went before.

The prop makes an excellent barometer.

Mr. Morse, palm open and pressed against his midriff as though he were a matador checking his bright red sash, is a fine illusionist. He is just as salty as he used to be while singing preposterous love songs to himself in mirrors ("How to Succeed in Business Without Really Trying," as if you needed to be told). Later, dazedly trimming a Christmas tree in "Tru," he is a troubling figure indeed. He is even touching, I think, when he kicks a poinsettia.

■

Nobody kicks a poinsettia in "Forbidden Broadway 1990," off and running in its eighth edition, but everything else gets it right in the shins.

Start with the disaffected waiters who hustle food and drinks in the

homey East 60th Street basement. Before the onstage performers have so much as opened their crinkly silver revue-curtain to begin mocking this year's old hits like "Gypsy" and new hits like "City of Angels," the hired hands are angry because they haven't been hired as actors, just as table hoppers. What are actors, after all? Actors are people they're just as good as. Except that someone among them happens to know the director's brother-in-law. "Who Do You Know?" rings the plaintive pre-show query.

Show proper begins with that familiar voice on the amplifier: "Both the taking of photographs and the use of recording devices are strictly fine with us."

After which the song from "Meet Me in St. Louis" that has to do with trolley cars gets the revised tunes under way ("Clang! Clang! Clang! went the music!"), and shrill little Baby June from "Gypsy" doesn't ask permission to entertain us. Instead she asks:

*Let me
Break your eardrums.*

With the first blast, mine were gone.

I *could* hear, however, a Walt Whitmanesque question throbbing to a choral beat:

*Do you hear the people sing?
Singing the hit songs from "Les Miz"?*

And I felt that the impersonation of Lotte Lenya was so casually true that I really didn't want people laughing at it. I found myself put off by one thing and one thing only: the business of tagging Vanessa as Vanessa Red-Redgrave. But the show as a whole is unmannerly in the best sense of the word: It's fine, mean-spirited fun. The energy is terrific.

The number I admired most was one in which the alter egos of Rex Harrison and Glynis Johns, melodiously wafting us all the way back to "Gigi" and reaching forward to their current Broadway stand in "The Circle," are to be heard in the happy congratulation of "Ah, Yes, I Remember It Well." Thus:

*It warms my heart
To know that you
Remember your part
And mine, too . . .*

All of this is performed, you understand, with a sound professionalism and much malice. I wonder if it ever occurs to you — for all I know, it occurs to you all the time — that a newspaper reviewer who dared venture into this irreverent territory with just a *pinch* of that malice would likely be dismembered on the spot. There's a double standard here. Why is that?

I guess the difference is that reviewers just aren't funny. ▯

1990 Ap 22, II:5:1

'Forbidden Broadway 1990' and its cast are unmannerly in the best sense of the word.

fee go up?" And he is still very high on St. Teresa of Avila, whose observation that more tears were shed over answered than unanswered prayers had given him the title for his unloved book. "St. Teresa was one sharp little cookie-cutter," he giggles.

irrepressible fondness for phrasemaking. Surveying such Christmas gifts as litter the floor, he murmurs: "I'm giving Tiffany's and getting poinsettias." With sudden urgency, he faces to the phone and briskly calls his agent to ask "when Norman Mailer stabbed his wife, how much did his

Carol Rosegg/Martha Swope Associates

Bob Rogerson spoofs Rex Harrison and "The Circle."

Not Following Orders

THE PRINCE OF HOMBURG, by Heinrich von Kleist; English version by Douglas Langworthy; directed by David Herskovits; set designed by Tom Dale Keever; lighting designed by Trui Malten; costumes designed by Gregory Gale; production stage manager, Laura Himmelein; sound consultant, Thomas Cabaniss; technical director, Lenny Bart. Presented by the Jean Cocteau Repertory, Robert Hupp, director; David Fishelson, managing director. At 330 Bowery, at Second Avenue.

Friedrich Wilhelm .... Joseph Menino
The Electress .... Carol Dearman
Princess Natalia of Oranien ...... Angela Vitale
Lady Bork .... Elise Stone
Prince Friedrich Arthur of Homburg
.... James Sterling
Field Marshal Dörfling .... Craig Smith
Colonel Kottwitz .... Harris Berlinsky
Count Hohenzollern .... Christopher Oden
Count Truchss .... Grant Neale
Captain Golz .... Robert Ierardi
Stranz .... Lyn Wright

By WILBORN HAMPTON

Heinrich von Kleist, a Prussian officer who traded his sword for a pen and became a major light of German Romanticism, could never resolve his ambivalent feelings toward the Prussian fatherland. When he resigned his commission, he wrote a friend that while in uniform he was "always in doubt whether to act as an officer or a human being."

In his final play, "The Prince of Homburg," which is being given a solid and straightforward revival by the Jean Cocteau Repertory company, Kleist dramatized his own conflicting emotions in the dilemma of an officer who must choose honor and death or shame and life, at least as those qualities were defined by the Prussian military code.

If the decision does not seem a particularly difficult one for a predominantly anti-fascist audience, it was nonetheless a burning moral issue of Kleist's day. At the time the play was written, Prussia was under the domination of Napoleon, and any play questioning the justness of Prussian militarism and the willingness of its officers to lay down their lives gladly for the fatherland could be seen as not only in bad taste but also as a document bordering on treason. The play was not performed during the lifetime of Kleist, who committed suicide shortly after its completion in 1811, and it has often been regarded as either an apologia for extreme nationalism or a celebration of heroic independence, depending on one's point of view.

•

The Prince first appears on the eve of the battle of Fehrbellin in 1675, sleepwalking in the Elector of Brandenburg's garden and weaving himself a laurel wreath. The memory of a beautiful maiden whom he met in his sleepwalking haunts the Prince the following morning and makes him inattentive as the Field Marshal goes over the orders of battle.

On the battlefield the Prince, not remembering the battle plan, precipitously leads the calvary charge. Although the battle is won, the Prince is arrested and sentenced to death for disobeying orders. At first he is willing to do anything to save his skin. But when the Elector decides to let the Prince determine his own fate, the Prince has a Teutonic change of heart and insists that the sentence be carried out.

As a philosophical study, "The Prince of Homburg" is almost irrelevent for an audience that has heard about too many horrors at the hands of soldiers who zealously "follow or-

ders." As dramatic poetry, however, especially in the hero's ruminations on life and death, Kleist's play is still masterly, and Douglas Langworthy's translation plays smoothly and adapts well to modern idiom, yet is faithful to the spirit of German Romanticism.

•

The Cocteau company gives a polished reading down to the last soldier and servant. James Sterling is a self-assured Prince with the casual, ramrod military bearing of a man who has probably never even considered the possibility of failure. Joseph Menino, whose engaging performances at the Cocteau this season have ranged from Lady Bracknell in "The Importance of Being Earnest" to Galy Gay in Brecht's "A Man's a Man," is a benevolent but firmly autocratic Elector. Christopher Oden is a sly Count Hohenzollern and Angela Vitale a demure Princess Natalia.

Jonathan Slaff

Angela Vitale and James Sterling in "The Prince of Homburg."

Craig Smith gets more humor than anyone could expect from a Prussian Field Marshal. David Herskovits's direction keeps the action moving at a steady march and Gregory Gale's costumes are so splendid they could have come from a military museum.

1990 Ap 22, 62:1

Audience as Aliens

BEYOND BELIEF, written and directed and music arranged by Fiona Laird; costumes by Julie Speechley; lighting by Cliff Vic and Ms. Laird. The London Small Theater Company presented by Manhattan Punch Line Theater, Steve Kaplan, artistic director. At the Judith Anderson Theater, 422 West 42d Street.

THE CLOUDS, by Aristophanes; adaptation, direction, music and arrangements by Ms.

Laird; produced by Peter Meineck; original lighting design (London), Jacqui Leigh; tour lighting design, Mr. Meineck; costumes by Ms. Speechley.

WITH: Antony James, Fiona Laird, Adrian Schiller, Nicholas Smith, Rachel Spriggs, Jonathan Williams.

By WILBORN HAMPTON

The world holds few surprises more disconcerting than those faced by Dr. Jeremy Peregrine Calthorpe (Jerry Perry to his disrespectful friends), a philosopher, and Jake, an apprentice stand-up comic, who find themselves suddenly transported to an alien dimension in "Beyond Belief," a delightfully zany fantasy.

This 70-minute time warp, a sort of Douglas Adams galactic hitchhiking tour to some cabaret at the end of the universe, is the hilarious concoction of Fiona Laird and the London Small Theater Company, which has brought the show from London's fringe and is presenting it at the Judith Anderson theater on a bill with the Aristophanes comedy "The Clouds." It argues strongly that "what was only hypothetical this morning could become a reality at any moment."

The time is "the Chinese year of the anchovy" and the setting is the terrain of the title, somewhere just beyond belief. The philosopher, deliciously played by Antony James, and the trainee comedian (Nick Smith) are enjoying a healthy difference of opinion when they notice they are somewhere else and being watched by aliens. Peering into the darkness

of the house, Dr. Calthorpe deduces: "It's a theater audience. See, everyone of them is bored." They then proceed to the only reasonable course open to them — they act out a scene from "The Tempest."

Quite soon they come across two women — Belinda and Louise — playing tennis, one of whom mistakes the philosopher for Malvolio (segue into "Twelfth Night"), the women are "major fictional characters" who have been written out of an astonishing number of novels, movies and plays. "I've been cut from 573 plays," Belinda (Rachel Spriggs) boasts. The women are soon joined by David (Jonathan Williams), an extra, who has little to say, of course.

•

The women's conversation consists of dialogue from plays, and the two wayfarers must keep on their literary toes as they move from Shakespeare to T. S. Eliot's "Cocktail Party." They get lost at one point when they mistake a mention of a handbag and rush headlong into Wilde's "Importance of Being Earnest" instead of Joe Orton's "What the Butler Saw," which was the correct cue. And Belinda raises a bit of a fuss by absolutely refusing to follow the men "into a smutty Steven Berkoff play."

Ms. Laird wrote and directed this very clever and imaginative show, which is interspersed with songs from the 1930's like a Dennis Potter teleplay. The company, all quite good singers, perform a cappella and sound like a cross between the King's

Martha Swope Associates/Carol Rosegg

Fiona Laird and Antony James in "Beyond Belief."

College chorus and the New Christy Minstrels.

The entire ensemble is a study in beautifully timed deadpan delivery. Mr. James is a howl and Ms. Spriggs is a pert and sassy character who would be an asset to any novel or play. Ms. Laird, Mr. Williams and Mr. Smith all add to the fun.

The curtain-raiser for "Beyond Belief" is another of the talented Ms. Laird's adaptations, this one of Aristophanes' sendup of Socratic philosophy. Ms. Laird has wisely done little updating of the text but has employed Julie Speechley's outrageous costumes — the women in flower-pot hats or curlers and rubber gloves, and Socrates in a glitter-covered Elton John hat with purple sun glasses and elevator shoes — to help coax the laughter. The result is more of a college lampoon than a satire, but it sets the mood for what follows.

1990 Ap 22, 63:4

Clapping to the Beat Of the Lord

TRULY BLESSED: A MUSICAL CELEBRATION OF MAHALIA JACKSON, conceived and written by Queen Esther Marrow; original music and lyrics by Ms. Marrow; directed by Robert Kalfin; additional music and lyrics by Reginald Royal; choreography by Larry Vickers; musical supervision and orchestrations by Joseph Joubert; scenery and lighting, Fred Kolo; costumes, Andrew B. Marlay; sound, Peter Fitzgerald; executive producers, Philip Rose and Howard Hurst; technical supervisor, Jeremiah J. Harris Associates; general manager, Charlotte Wilcox; production supervisor, Mortimer Halpern; production stage manager, Kenneth Hanson. Presented by Howard Hurst, Philip Rose, Sophie Hurst, in association with Frankie Hewitt. At the Longacre Theater, 220 West 48th Street.

WITH: Queen Esther Marrow, Carl Hall, Lynette G. DuPré, Doug Eskew and Gwen Stewart.

By STEPHEN HOLDEN

In the liveliest scene of the new gospel musical "Truly Blessed: A Musical Celebration of Mahalia Jackson," Queen Esther Marrow, who portrays the legendary gospel singer, endures interrogation by a team of musicologists at a New England symposium.

When one of them poses a fussy question about her vocal technique, she complains good-naturedly, "Help me, Lord, I'm beginning to feel like a Mississippi catfish on a plate with Maine lobster." After another scholar wonders what might be the relationship between jazz and gospel, she chastises him: "Baby, darlin', don't you know the Devil stole the beat from the Lord?" The scene ends as the singer instructs the rhythmically inept academics on how to clap their hands on the offbeat of a gospel song until they finally catch a spirit that brings them to their feet.

This salty, down-home sense of humor is the most distinguishing characteristic of the show, which opened yesterday at the Longacre Theater. "Truly Blessed" was written by Ms. Marrow and has the tone, structure and look of an enlarged cabaret act. An earthy pop-gospel contralto whose voice has marked similarities to that of the legend she is remembering, Ms. Marrow does not command anything like the stupendous power and fervency that Jackson wielded. But if her voice is less than roof-raising, Ms. Marrow still projects a towering dignity and strength and musical intelligence.

"Truly Blessed," which is four-fifths music and one-fifth connective dialogue, includes two dozen gospel songs, some of them written by Ms. Marrow and Reginald Royal, and the rest consisting of gospel hymns associated with Jackson, like her million-selling record, "Move On Up a Little Higher." The music is stuffed casually into the framework of a sketchy chronology of the singer's life, which began in New Orleans in 1911 and ended in Chicago in 1972. As a girl in New Orleans, Jackson listened to the records of Ma Rainey and Bessie Smith, who were her major influences. But as much as she was impressed by these early blues singers, she was not drawn to sing the blues herself. As Ms. Marrow's version of the singer puts it, "When you're through with the blues, honey, you've got nothing left to rest on."

After moving to Chicago as a teenager with dreams of becoming a nurse, Jackson eventually found her calling as a church singer, and as her reputation spread, she began touring the United States. The show's other amusing scene portrays Jackson and her fellow musicians in a car driving through the segregated South singing hymns while searching ever more desperately for a rest stop.

As biography, the show glosses over the singer's formative years and her personal life to concentrate on her roles as a public figure and stalwart keeper of the faith. Explicit references to racial politics and civil rights rarely crop up. After receiving a call from Mayor Richard J. Daley of Chicago asking for her support, she announces, "Here's my chance to

Martha Swope

Queen Esther Marrow in the title role of "Truly Blessed: A Musical Celebration of Mahalia Jackson."

have him in my hip pocket." Recalling the 1963 March on Washington, at which she performed, she declares that to be "a true follower of the Lord" a philosophy of nonviolence is essential.

The show's handling of Jackson's musical career and development is as generalized as its treatment of her life. Beyond citing the singer's blues influences, it gives no sense of the evolution of gospel music or of Jackson's role in that evolution. Ms. Marrow is accompanied on the stage by a four-member instrumental ensemble and four strong gospel singers — Carl Hall, Lynette G. DuPré, Doug Eskew and Gwen Stewart — who double as actors in the vignettes between musical numbers. Their voices make a

bracing contrast to Ms. Marrow's rich contralto. Mr. Hall goes into wild, almost comical falsetto flights, while Ms. DuPré and Ms. Stewart exude the sort of pungent sass associated with singers like Nell Carter.

●

Although the musicians' exuberant, storefront style of gospel is true to the era in which Jackson's voice was in its full glory, significant details are overlooked. Mildred Falls, the great gospel pianist who provided invaluable musical support for Jackson, is not even mentioned. Nor is there any mention of the implications of the singer's signing with Columbia Records in 1954. The commercially shrewd decision earned her a large white audience but also required that she adulterate the power of her records with choirs and strings.

By presenting Jackson as a myth — someone more angelic than human — the character remains firmly affixed on a sanctified pedestal, notwithstanding the show's flashes of humor. In the final scenes, Jackson seems to merge mystically with the gospel songs she sings and to become an icon of goodness and religious faith.

On a trip to the Holy Land, where she bathes ecstatically in the waters of the River Jordan, she finds her unshakable faith is stronger than ever. "People go around saying that God is dead; well, He's not dead," she declares. "He brought me from the swamps of Mississippi to the streets of Paris. Who wouldn't believe in a God like that?"

1990 Ap 23, C13:1

Opposite Versions Of Inversions

THE RUFFIAN ON THE STAIR, by Joe Orton; directed by John Tillinger; set design by James Noone; costumes by Jess Goldstein; lighting by Craig Miller; production stage manager, Ruth M. Feldman. Presented by Long Wharf Theater, Arvin Brown, artistic director; M. Edgar Rosenblum, executive director. At New Haven.

Mike	Nicholas Woodeson
Joyce	Joanne Camp
Wilson	Tate Donovan

THE LOVER, by Harold Pinter.

Richard/Max	Nicholas Woodeson
Sarah	Joanne Camp
John	Tate Donovan

By MEL GUSSOW

Special to The New York Times

NEW HAVEN, April 20 — Though both Joe Orton and Harold Pinter are

playwrights with original, distinct voices, they have similarities as well as disparities. Arriving first, Mr. Pinter became something of a model to Mr. Orton. Just as Pinter plays have a metaphorical weasel lurking under the cocktail table, Mr. Orton's plays are inhabited by carpenter ants insidiously attacking the roofbeams and floorboards. For both playwrights, nothing is as it seems to be as they investigate dualities in everyday life.

The director John Tillinger has had the ingenious idea of pairing two early one-acts by the writers, "The Ruffian on the Stair" by Mr. Orton and "The Lover" by Mr. Pinter. This double bill fills Long Wharf Theater's Stage II with sinister comedy and also offers an arena for versatility to the production's leading actors, Nicholas Woodeson and Joanne Camp.

"The Ruffian" was Mr. Orton's first play (in 1963), broadcast on British radio and subsequently adapted to the stage. Clearly it was influenced by Mr. Pinter, even to Mr. Orton's imitating some of the lines in "The Birthday Party" in the first version of the play. Menace stalks interior rooms as well as the unseen stairwell as a working-class couple's apparent tranquillity barely conceals a predilection for casual mayhem.

A young man of ambiguous sexuality (Tate Donovan) — a forerunner of the author's Mr. Sloane — insinuates himself into the placid household and moves from victimizer to victim. The man of the house (Mr. Woodeson) is a truck driver of vengeful instinct, and his common-law wife (Ms. Camp) has submerged her own shady past in her housewifely present.

On the surface, the two are the most guileless of company as the woman invites the intruder in for a cup of tea. Humor arises from the fact that the characters affect the airs of their so-called betters. The play becomes a reverse comedy of manners.

With an insouciance that was to grow to maturity in his full-length plays, Orton keeps everything matter-of-fact and tongue-in-cheek. As the author wrote about "The Ruffian," "Everything the characters say is true" — no matter how bizarre it may seem. Mr. Tillinger has closely followed the playwright's prescription, right through the doubly murderous conclusion.

In "The Lover," originally written for television, a couple from the professional class belie their social status. As a dapper businessman goes to work, he asks his wife if her lover is

T. Charles Erickson

Nicholas Woodeson and Joanne Camp in a scene from "The Lover."

expected that day, posing the question as calmly as if he were asking her what they were having for dinner. Later, when the lover arrives, he turns out to be the husband, who is supposedly having a tryst with his favorite prostitute.

Conducting this duplicitous charade, the husband and wife awaken each other's libido. Underlying the comedy is a feeling of displacement and sadness, in contrast to "The Ruffian," which manages, despite the malevolence, to seem oddly cheerful. "The Lover" is the more seriously inclined play, but each makes acidulous points at the expense of domestic discord.

Between the plays, the actors are transformed. Mr. Woodeson is amiable as the plebeian truck driver (in the Orton) and suave as the executive (in the Pinter). These are only two sides to this diversely talented actor, who several seasons ago was a Na-

poleonic "King John" at Stratford-on-Avon and was most recently seen in New York as Henry Fielding in "The Art of Success."

In "The Ruffian," Ms. Camp remains convivial as the dowdy housewife (she stops short of being slatternly), padded out to fill the physical dimensions of the role. Then she persuasively becomes the seductress in "The Lover," crossing and uncrossing her legs with a confident sensuality. As demanded, Mr. Donovan is both affable and suspicious as the unfortunate ruffian.

Through a series of productions, Mr. Tillinger has become America's foremost directorial interpreter of Orton. With this double bill, he makes a nimble transition to Mr. Pinter, a playwright with whom he seems to feel an equal compatability — and a taste for conspiratorial humor.

1990 Ap 25, C13:1

muttering a nonstop monologue about the cost of things. His revenge against a $2 hot dog is to pile it high with condiments.

•

The brilliance of these skits begins with the concepts themselves, which find primal states of mind in the mundane activities of life. The precision of Mr. Caesar's body language, especially his intricate and exquisite facial expressions, turns these mental states into comic poetry.

Handily assisting the couple is Mr. Delano, who not only plays the sort of supporting roles Carl Reiner used to play, but who bears a striking physical resemblance to him as well.

1990 Ap 27, C10:4

Fake-Looking Wigs, Facsimile Thriller

ACCOMPLICE, by Rupert Holmes; directed by Art Wolff; scenery by David Jenkins; costumes by Alvin Colt; lighting by Martin Aronstein; special effects by Gregory Meeh; incidental music by Mr. Holmes; music performed by Deborah Grunfeld; sound design by Peter J. Fitzgerald. Presented by Alexander H. Cohen and Hildy Parks, Max Cooper and Normand Kurtz. At the Richard Rodgers Theater, 226 West 46th Street.

WITH: Jason Alexander, Pamela Brüll, Michael McKean and Natalia Nogulich.

By FRANK RICH

In Rupert Holmes's last Broadway whodunit, "The Mystery of Edwin Drood," the audience was invited to vote on the murderer at the end of the second act. In "Accomplice," Mr. Holmes's new whodunit at the Richard Rodgers Theater, the audience should be allowed to vote on the beginning, middle and end of the second act. The winner, in a landslide, would surely be None of the Above.

"Accomplice" is one of those plays — like "Sleuth," "Deathtrap" and "Moose Murders," to name beloved past examples — at which the patrons must be sworn to secrecy lest the author's surprises be ruined for future customers. Those secrets are safe with me because I found "Accomplice" incomprehensible after intermission, even though much of Act II is given over to extended roundtable discussions among the characters as to what has happened or might happen or won't happen or can't happen. These verbose yet unilluminating explanations extend right through the curtain call, which itself is somewhat gabbier than any denouement in Agatha Christie. Theater historians should note that the curtain call of "Accomplice" is additionally distinguished by the appearance of the playwright, who is given his very own bow and takes it with due modesty.

•

What the sepulchral Mr. Holmes, clad in a business suit, is doing on stage is one of those secrets indeed best left undivulged. Suffice it to say that the man is apparently prepared to travel the country with his play for eternity, as his script makes mandatory, should "Accomplice" find favor on the dinner-theater circuit. Some of the evening's other secrets are so poorly kept by the loose-lipped management that one doesn't even have to see the play to guess them: the Playbill gives no character names for its four cast members and includes more biographies for understudies than there ostensibly are roles.

It is also giving away nothing to say that the biggest shocks in "Accomplice" include some special effects unlikely to startle any theatergoer

---

A playwright takes an odd gamble with the danger of success.

---

who has been within 50 yards of a Fourth of July sparkler. Further fireworks of a fashion are provided by a demographically balanced pair of homosexual kisses (one each for male and female couples) that may be becoming de rigueur on Broadway in the season of "Aspects of Love."

•

The kissers, none of them in top form under the overemphatic direction of Art Wolff, include two accomplished clowns, Jason Alexander, late of "Jerome Robbins's Broadway," and Michael McKean, most fondly remembered from "This Is Spinal Tap," and their routine foils, Natalia Nogulich and Pamela Brüll. In Act I, the company dons fake-looking wigs and even faker accents to enact a reasonable though witless facsimile of the sort of West End thriller in which gin-sipping, cigarette-smoking Mayfair twits loll about an isolated weekend cottage (satirically designed by

Martha Swope

Jason Alexander in "Accomplice," at the Richard Rodgers Theater.

David Jenkins) and plot the murder of their own spouses or someone else's. The brittle repartee includes lines like "Medwick may give me insomnia, but I'm not going to lose any sleep over it" and, somewhat funnier in this context, "You should go to the theater more often — there's life in it yet." In Act II, the wisecracks are largely about Broadway show business, with the inevitable butts being Los Angeles actors, backstage unions and Mandy Patinkin.

It's in Act II as well that Ms. Brüll finds herself at the center of a dispute

---

Skits of Sid Caesar and Imogene Coca

By STEPHEN HOLDEN

In "At the Movies," the classic comic skit that is the centerpiece of Sid Caesar and Imogene Coca's reunion show at Michael's Pub (211 East 55th Street) for an open-ended run, Mr. Caesar, without saying a word, turns himself into the movie patron of one's nightmares. Toting a box of popcorn, he makes a conspicuous arrival in the darkened theater, stepping on people's feet to reach his seat. Once he has planted himself, he leans over his row and officiously bids everyone who might impede his sight-lines to slump down so he can have an unobstructed view.

Soon enough, fate delivers his comeuppance in the form of Miss Coca, who plunks herself down in the next seat and begins doing deep breathing and stretching exercises. Before Mr. Caesar can gather his wits to protest, her jealous boyfriend (Lee Delano) storms onto the scene and mistakenly assumes that Mr. Caesar is her date.

By the end of the skit, the quarrelsome lovers have patched it up and departed, and Mr. Caesar has been left thoroughly mauled, his shirt in tatters. One of the many pleasures of "At the Movies" is the thoroughness of its delivery of what might be called an obnoxious nuisance's karmic desserts.

•

At a time when topical stand-up humor is a glut on the entertainment market, Mr. Caesar and Miss Coca offer a reassuring reminder that there is still such a thing as classic comedy. While they are no spring chickens (he is 67 years old, and she is an effervescent 81), one happy discovery of seeing the show is that their brand of comedy is immune to age and time.

Although most of their skits use words, the essence of the humor still lies in a virtuosic command of body language. It is essentially the slapstick physical vocabulary of Hollywood's silent clowns, refined for television.

At the press opening of their show, "Together Again," on Tuesday night, one was also struck by the way the comic chemistry between the two performers is based on stylistic contrast. Miss Coca, with her goofy ear-to-ear grin, buggy eyes and diminutive stature is an eternal innocent beside Mr. Caesar's knowing and beleaguered everyman. And when Miss Coca speaks, her clear, musical

Jack Mitchell

Sid Caesar, who is performing with Imogene Coca, at Michael's Pub.

voice, so evocative of laughter just below the surface, complements her air of purity.

Mr. Caesar, with his heavy-lidded eyes and clown smile touched with just the tiniest hint of sourness, has grown more expressive with the years, especially in his solo turns. In "Man Getting Up in the Morning," he impersonates a shaving man who becomes obsessed to the point of self-destruction with making his sideburns even. In "Mumbler," he is an eccentric ne'er-do-well who wanders around contemporary New York City

as to whether she will bare her breasts on stage. This pressing issue is tabled rather than resolved, but not before it has engendered more tedious debate than a resolution about fishing rights before the United Nations Security Council. For her part, Ms. Nogulich is required to writhe on the floor with Mr. McKean in an exceptionally noisy carnal romp. It's enough to make one long for those predictable old whodunits in which the butlers always did it but at least had the common courtesy to do it quickly with their clothes and mouths both firmly zippered shut.

1990 Ap 27, C5:1

Family Matters

SUGAR HILL, based on an original story by Roberto Fernández; book by Louis St. Louis and Mr. Fernández; music by Mr. St. Louis; lyrics by Mr. Fernández, Mr. St. Louis and Tony Walsh; staging by Carmen de Lavallade; set by James Noone; costumes by Carrie Robbins; lighting by Ken Smith; musical director, Pookie Johnson; production stage manager, Michael Schmalz; production manager, Randy Lee Hartwig. Presented by Musical Theater Works, Anthony J. Stimac, artistic director. At St. Peter's Church, Lexington Avenue at 54th Street.

Beatrice DuBois	Ethel Beatty Barnes
Cassandra DuBois	Cheryl Freeman
Baby Bea	Tatyana Ali
Nettie DuBois	Jeree Palmer Wade
Jaxon DuBois and Boo Brown	Edwin Battle
Cookie Allen	Carol Jean Lewis
Malcolm McDaniels	James Stovall
Blanca Stromburg-Carlson	Marcella Lowery
Eddie Van der Vere	Tony Hoylen

By STEPHEN HOLDEN

It is not every day that one runs across a show as ambitiously conceived as "Sugar Hill," a new musical drama presented by Musical Theater Works at the Theater at St. Peter's Church. Set in the late 1920's to 1970 in the upscale Sugar Hill section of Harlem, the show is a teary-eyed dynastic saga that focuses on the strife between three generations of talented, self-motivating women.

Like "Dreamgirls," to which it bears more than a passing similarity, "Sugar Hill" contemplates black history through the rose-colored lens of show business as it follows the conflicting destinies of headstrong divas. While the story jumps forward in time from 1927 to 1935 to 1954 to 1970, the score reflects a similar historical sweep with songs that change in style from breezy jazz-age swing to belting contemporary pop-soul.

The biggest structural difference between "Sugar Hill" and its successful forerunner is the newer show's sprawling book written by Robert Fernández (who conceived the story) with the composer Louis St. Louis. With Robert Walsh, they also wrote the lyrics. Their pulpy soap opera dialogue augments the old-fashioned tone of a story that looks back to glossy movie tear-jerkers like "Imitation of Life."

•

The essence of the story is how maternal neglect begets maternal neglect. After the sudden onstage death of her entertainer husband, Nettie DuBois (Jeree Palmer Wade), a career-obsessed nightclub star of the Harlem renaissance, leaves the raising of her daughter, Beatrice (Ethel Beatty Barnes), to family friends. The girl's unofficial mentor is an actor and black nationalist sympathizer (James Stovall), who instills Beatrice with a political militancy her mother lacks.

Beatrice eventually becomes a successful lawyer. She also has a daugh-

ter, Cassandra (Cheryl Freeman), whom she rears single-handedly but neglects for her career. When Cassandra decides to go into show business, Beatrice is aghast but Nettie, who lives with them, is supportive. The conflict is expressed in Beatrice's scalding dismissal of Cassandra's aspirations, "Smiling and shuffling is not my idea of a career."

The strongest element of the show, which should still be considered a work in progress, is its handling of the family psychology. The mother-daughter confrontations crackle with a tension that finally explodes in "Where Were You?", the show's most dramatic number.

•

The production by Musical Theater Works, an organization created to develop new shows, is essentially a workshop version. The rudimentary musical accompaniment reveals only the bare bones of songs, which in their present shape demonstrate more passion than polish. Most of the transitions between the songs and the dialogue are still very rough. And Hattie Winston, the singer and actress who is making her directorial debut with "Sugar Hill," doesn't always know how to move the performers smoothly around the stage.

Among the three leading roles, by far the richest is Beatrice, the politically militant lawyer who unconsciously re-enacts with her own daughter the rejection she experienced as a child. Especially in the later scenes, Ms. Barnes, the strongest of the cast's performers, exudes an imposing mixture of bitterness and stubborn strength. Among the several would-be show stoppers, her career woman's lament, "Another Sunday Morning Without Love," which suggests a slightly modernized echo of "Stormy Weather," is the most melodically developed.

The obstacles facing "Sugar Hill" are enormous, for this is the kind of show that could be realized only in a $6 million Broadway production. But the idea is sound, the framework fairly steady. Even in its present half-finished condition, it generates sparks.

1990 Ap 28, 12:6

Parallel Obsessions

RODENTS AND RADIOS, written and directed by Richard Caliban; music composed and performed by John Hoge; lighting by Brian Aldous; costumes by Mary Myers. Presented by the Cucaracha Theater, Mr. Caliban, artistic director; Janet Paparazzo, producing director. At 429 Greenwich Street.

Smith	Damian Young
Mrs. Judd	Sharon Brady
Klari Bogdan	Mollie O'Mara
Beem	Glen M. Santiago
Rand	Lauren Hamilton
Woodard	Mark Dillahunt
Claude	Vivian Lanko
Singers/Voices	
	Christine Deily and Joey L. Golden

By MEL GUSSOW

The characters in Richard Caliban's "Rodents and Radios" are desperately seeking self-realization but settle for a kind of futile escape. At the center of this kaleidoscopic collage are two compulsive young women. One is an athlete who has defected from Romania — a Nadia Comenici of the tennis courts. The other has abandoned a marriage in California for a free-form existence living on the land in the most remote corners of the world. Although the two never meet, their parallel obsessions illuminate each other and also shed a de-

gree of light on the other characters who share the stage in Mr. Caliban's trenchant new play at the Cucaracha Theater.

The tennis pro, Klari Bogdan (Mollie O'Mara), undergoes a punishing regimen in pursuit of her sport, but she is unable to transform herself into a champion. Facing a mental as well as a physical block, she can only work her way to the quarterfinals in the United States Open. As Klari acts out her baseline despair, the tennis racket becomes an extension of her body, a weapon slashing at unseen opponents. At the root of her fear is a recurrent nightmare, in which her identity is erased.

Alternating with this story of statelessness is the journey of a woman named Rand (Lauren Hamilton) who travels from one "apex of spirituality" to another — from a mountaintop in Tibet to a beach in Bali to the headwaters of the Amazon. At each stop, she records her thoughts on tapes that she intends to send home to her husband. Her reports are filled with day-to-day deprivations, all of which seem to give her gratification. Half missionary, half masochist, she has a zeal about living on the edge.

Repeatedly, she vows to sever all of her connections to society, but she is so blissful about her travels — and so oblivious of her desolation — that she cannot bear to stop recording her impressions. Each message, in effect, becomes her last tape, and then she has second thoughts.

While Klari becomes more and more intense, Rand seems to grow increasingly peaceful until it seems as if she might float away on a sea of nirvana. Klari is poignant in her persistence. Rand, who is no less serious, is unconsciously amusing until she casually reveals that she has abandoned two children as well as her husband, a fact that gives her musings a sobering reality.

As portrayed by Ms. O'Mara and Ms. Hamilton, the two women are so vivid that they almost demand to be in a play by themselves. Mr. Caliban, who is the evening's director as well as playwright, has chosen to surround them with contrasting characters.

These people range from a weirdly eccentric tennis fan (Glen M. Santia-

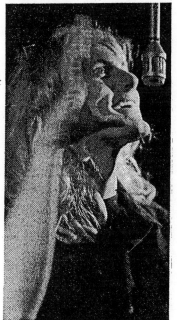

Damian Young in Richard Caliban's "Rodents and Radios."

go), who breaks all rules of court decorum, to a radio talk show host (Damian Young) who is as intemperate as Eric Bogosian's Barry Champlain as he attacks "the root rot of civilization." In varying degrees, each is evocative. The principle disappointment in "Rodents and Radios" deals with the rodents of the title. The other tales may seem irrational, but this is the only one that strains credibility.

With the help of a background score (written and played by John Hoge) and a committed cast, Mr. Caliban has staged his play with fluidity. Characters take turns in the spotlight. Even when their lives intersect, they never directly address one another. This adds to the feeling of compartmentalization, as monologues become confessional — talking postcards as revealing as the tapes of the runaway wife.

1990 Ap 28, 15:1

Strangers in Suburbia

TALES OF THE FORMICANS, by Constance Congdon; directed Gordon Edelstein; set design by James Youmans; lighting by Anne Militello; costumes by Daniele Hollywood; sound by John Gromada; composer, Melissa Shiflett; production stage manager, Susie Cordon. Presented by the Women's Project and Productions, Julia Miles, artistic director. At the Apple Corps Theater, 336 West 20th Street.

Jerry	Michael Countryman
Cathy	Lizbeth Mackay
Jim	Edward Seamon
Eric	Noel Derecki
Evelyn	Rosemary Prinz

By MEL GUSSOW

The aliens in Constance Congdon's "Tales of the Lost Formicans" are as friendly as E. T., but they see no necessity of phoning home or of returning to their extraterrestrial roots. These are resident aliens living somewhere in Colorado, and offering closed-circuit commentary on the plight of suburbia. The equivalent of anthropologists suddenly confronted with a Stone Age tribe, the aliens are thoroughly discombobulated by life on Earth in the 1980's.

It is simple for these newcomers to our strange land to label a four-legged object "a situpon," like Mark Twain's Adam and Eve naming things in the Garden of Eden. But they are easily misled when it comes to such complexities as automobiles ("wheeled sarcophagi used to carry spirits to the next world"), psychiatry or sex. The principal difficulty is in decoding the "loosely structured" unit called a family, which is at the center of Ms. Congdon's intriguing but unfocused play (at the Apple Corps Theater).

Behind the alienization of America — with the playwright's odd and fitfully amusing observations — there is a play about contemporary family problems. A young mother (Lizbeth Mackay) is concerned about her rebellious teen-age son, her husband who has run off with a woman half his age, and her father (Edward Seamon) who is dying.

Ms. Congdon underplays the domestic banalities, but she is so occupied with her satiric subtext about visitors from outer space that she distances the audience from her characters. One knows little more about the heroine after her travail than on first meeting her, and with the exception of her father, her family is unrewarding company.

Lizbeth Mackay and Edward Seamon in a scene from Constan Congdon's "Tales of the Lost Formicans."

Gerry Goods!

There are moments that confirm the play's prospects, especially as the father wanders in and out of his memory. He goes to a restaurant and sees himself and his wife at a younger age. With affecting nostalgia, he remembers his days as a carpenter, constructing houses that were made to last.

The play's other interesting character is a neurotic, suicidal neighbor (Michael Countryman). Roaming on the fringes of the play, this eccentric expounds on assassination theories and his conviction that man did not really land on the moon (the event was staged in a studio). A nurse, he is unable to relate to anyone except those under his medical care and the heroine for whom he has formed a loving but unreciprocated attachment. The aliens regard him as a typical human being (their mistake). If he is any example of life on Earth, it is not surprising that the visitors are disoriented.

Theatergoers may share some of that feeling of unsettlement. Actors double as earthlings and aliens. In the latter role, they put on sunglasses. Occasionally, they also have antennae sprouting from their heads. Wigwagging their confusion, the aliens seem to have arrived from the planet Whimsy. The lead alien offers commentary while standing at a microphone as if introducing a television game show.

The play has gained in intimacy and in clarity since it was first performed a year ago in Kentucky at the Actors Theater of Louisville. Perhaps some of that derives simply from seeing it again, but there are alterations in production values.

On a large stage in Louisville, "Lost Formicans" aspired to epic pretensions. In a trim vest-pocket production, directed by Gordon Edelstein for the Women's Project, the work has an ingenuous appeal. With agility, Ms. Mackay and Mr. Seamon repeat their roles as daughter and father, Mr. Seamon conveying his character's absent-minded wistfulness.

Mr. Countryman is touching as the neighbor who seems even more displaced than the aliens. Though the play remains diffuse, Ms. Congdon takes the audience close to a sedentary community overcome by self-obsolescence and a shopping-mall mentality.

1990 Ap 29, 60:1

Spirit and Serpent

THE BODY BUILDER'S BOOK OF LOVE, by Fernando Arrabal; translated by Lorenzo Mans; directed by Tom O'Horgan; sets, Christina Weppner; lighting, Debra Dumas; costumes, Deborah Shaw; music by Mr. O'Horgan; sound, Bernard Fox and Gene Perla; special effects, Steve Dunnington; production manager, Peter J. Davis; general manager, Michael Palma; stage manager, Robert V. Thurber. Presented at the Intar Hispanic American Arts Center, Max Ferra, founder and artistic director; Eva Brune, acting executive director. At 420 West 42d Street.

Tao	Mark Dold
Job	Saul Philip Stein

By STEPHEN HOLDEN

When Job, a champion weight lifter who is one of two characters in Fernando Arrabal's allegorical comedy "The Body Builder's Book of Love," hoists a barbell to his chest, he prefers not to concentrate on the mechanics of his sport. A mystical ascetic who has committed his spirit to an unseen woman named Phylis, he imagines shucking off his physical being and melting into the universe, guided by her into a celestial sphere beyond pain and desire.

Job, who is portrayed by Saul Philip Stein with a fierce sincerity, recalls Sylvester Stallone in his saintly masochistic mode but run amok in self-flagellating pseudo-heroics. His nemesis appears in the form of a serpentine, androgynous young masseur named Tao (Mark Dold), who at first claims to be a eunuch and later announces that he is Phylis's employee and love-slave. During the breaks in a championship match in which Job has three chances

to break his own world's record, the athlete and his assistant engage in a demented tango of temptation, resistance and cruelty.

While Job blathers on about Phylis, the young man teases and torments the would-be saint with lies and vicious physical challenges. Adding to the tension is the news, broadcast on three video monitors, that the person who recently murdered other weight-lifting champions by hurling scissors into their chests is on the premises and may strike again.

There is nothing subtle about "The Body Builder's Book of Love," which has been given a spicy, idiomatic translation from the French by Lorenzo Mans and which has been energetically staged at the Intar Theater by Tom O'Horgan, who also composed its incidental music. Long before the 1-hour-10-minute play has run its course, its intentions are clear and its outcome apparent.

The comedy, by the prolific multilingual Spanish-Moroccan playwright, who has lived in France since 1955, is also very European in its themes and in its rigid symbolic structure. Taking an age-old motif — the struggle between the spirit and the flesh — the playwright has given it an ironic contemporary twist by reversing the conventional roles and making the beefcake represent the spirit. Naming him Job, after the long-suffering Old Testament figure, and his muse Phylis (after philos, the Greek word for loving), adds another dash of comic-symbolic resonance.

•

Under Mr. O'Horgan's direction, Job's and Tao's struggle unfolds with a knockabout physicality that stops just short of slapstick. When Tao slips Job an aphrodisiac, the pair almost do somersaults as the weight lifter temporarily metamorphoses into a roaring beast. In the play's cruellest charade, Tao pretends to have been shackled and persuades the credulous athlete to break the chains with his teeth, then jeers at the bloody-mouthed strong man as he writhes in agony. Mr. Dold doesn't shy away from portraying Tao as a thoroughly repellent viper.

With all its religious symbolism and mythical associations, "The Body Builder's Book of Love" finally doesn't leave much room for thought. It is an entertaining stunt executed with a rough-and-tumble sense of fun.

1990 Ap 29, 60:1

Send In the Clowns

A CHANGE IN THE HEIR, by George H. Gorham and Dan Sticco; directed and choreographed by David H. Bell; scenery by Michael Anania; costumes by David Murin; lighting by Jeff Davis; orchestrations by Robby Merkin; musical direction and dance arrangements by Rob Bowman. Presented by Stewart F. Lane. At the Edison Theater, 240 West 47th Street.

Aunt Julia	Brooks Almy
Giles	Brian Sutherland
Edwin	J. K. Simmons
Nicholas	David Gunderman
Countess	Connie Day
Lady Enid	Mary Stout
Prince Conrad	Judy Blazer
Princess Agnes	Jeffrey Herbst
Martha	Jan Neuberger
Lady Elizabeth	Jennifer Smith

By STEPHEN HOLDEN

"Do you read Middle Goth?" one minor character asks of another in

the new musical farce "A Change in the Heir."

"I should, but I had mono that semester," comes the reply.

"I had her too," snaps the inquirer.

Such jokes, at once wan and tasteless, exemplify the sad level of wit in the musical fairy tale that limped into the Edison Theater last night, after having been developed at the New Tuners Theater in Chicago, where it was first presented two years ago.

With lyrics by George H. Gorham, music by Dan Sticco and a book by both, "A Change in the Heir" looks and sounds like a campy, nickel-and-dime burlesque of the Stephen Sondheim-James Lapine show "Into the Woods." Whole swatches of its score imitate Mr. Sondheim's musical style with a fidelity that borders on appropriation. The melody of "By Myself," a song in Act II, repeats almost note for note one of the themes in the title song of "Merrily We Roll Along."

Set in a low-rent district of fairyland where the royal garb resembles patterned bed sheets, "A Change in the Heir" tells the story of how two competing branches of the same family, each hoping to inherit the crown, bring a son and a daughter up as the opposite sex. Don't ask why. The conditions by which one or the other might become the monarch are as confusing as they are arbitrary.

The show's one genuine laugh comes early in Act I when Prince Conrad (Judy Blazer) and Princess Agnes (Jeffrey Herbst), the two young rivals, appear at the castle of the kingdom's despotic regent, Aunt Julia (Brooks Almy). Making her entrance, Princess Agnes is quite a sight as she towers incongruously over the rest of the cast. "I'm just not the kind of girl boys chase after," she reflects stoically while twiddling with an itchy chest hair. Agnes, however, soon discovers her true sex after being shown a book of pornographic pictures. Inevitably, the lanky princess and the diminutive prince strike up a romance.

In the show's second act the plot, involving a stolen diary, a forged birth certificate and a bogus marriage contract, becomes so convoluted that it's impossible to figure out what's going on. In the director David H. Bell's slapdash musical staging, the actors tear about the stage in a pointless frenzy of hysterical acrobatics. When they slow down long enough to talk, the tone of their dialogue seldom sinks below a shout.

•

Among the performers one feels the sorriest for is Miss Almy, who, in the role of the wicked Aunt Julia, is required to grimace and spit fire like a stereotypical camp gorgon. As the royal heirs, Miss Blazer and Mr. Herbst are hopelessly bland, both in and out of drag. It is left to Mr. Herbst to deliver the show's clunkiest line. Fed up with all shenanigans, he huffs, "No more princess nice guy!"

"A Change in the Heir" is the kind of show that, were it cut by half and staged in a cabaret, might provide an hour's trashy diversion. Heaven knows what it's doing on Broadway.

1990 Ap 30, C13:1

Prelude to a Kiss

By Craig Lucas; directed by Norman René; sets by Loy Arcenas; costumes by Walker Hicklin; lighting by Debra J. Kletter; sound by Scott Lehrer; hair and wig design by Bobby H. Grayson; production stage manager, James Harker; associate producer, Lawrence J. Wilker. The Circle Repertory Company production presented by Christopher Gould, Suzanne Golden and Dodger Productions. At the Helen Hayes Theater, 240 West 44th Street.

Peter .... Timothy Hutton
Rita ....Mary-Louise Parker
Taylor .... John Dossett
Tom and Jamaican Waiter L. Peter Callender
Mrs. Boyle .... Debra Monk
Dr. Boyle .... Larry Bryggman
Minister ....Craig Bockhorn
Aunt Dorothy and Leah ....Joyce Reehling
Uncle Fred ....Michael Warren Powell
Old Man .... Barnard Hughes
Party Guests, Barflies, Wedding Guests and Vacationers
    Craig Bockhorn, Brian Cousins, Kimberly Dudwitt and Michael Warren Powell.

By FRANK RICH

"The world's a really terrible place — it's too precarious," says Rita, the young heroine of "Prelude to a Kiss," the Craig Lucas play newly arrived on Broadway. Rita (Mary-Louise Parker), a bartender aspiring to be a graphics designer, lives in a modern city whose ills are all too depressingly recognizable. Crack dealers approach first graders, unspeakable diseases consume the bodies of the young and old, and there is never any escape from "the constant fear of being blown up." As Rita warns Peter (Timothy Hutton), the young man with whom she has found love at first sight, the world is so rotten she couldn't even think of bringing children into it.

Yet two hours of stage time later, Rita has reversed her perspective entirely, and not because the world has changed. In this wonderful play, a comic and affecting fairy tale for and about adults, Mr. Lucas acknowledges much that is defeating about civilization as we now know it, then heroically insists on finding a reason to go on living anyway.

Mr. Lucas's reason — that "the miracle of another human being" is

True love in a fairy tale for and about adults.

"never to be squandered" — may sound sentimental, but as dramatized it is not. There's nothing treacly about "Prelude to a Kiss," a play that acknowledges even those modern terrors it leaves unmentioned, like AIDS, by forcing its young lovers to test their bond against the threat of imminent physical decay and death. "My love is a prelude that never dies," sings Ella Fitzgerald in the Duke Ellington song whose nocturnal blues haunts the evening. What this play celebrates, and it's as rare as the moonlight in Ellington's music, is the redemptive power of unselfish love that never dies, of true love that survives transient flesh.

As in any classic fairy tale, Rita and Peter must overcome such terrifying obstacles to seal their union and live happily ever after that their hard-won hope and elation at the final curtain is contagious. It's hard to recall a recent play so suffused with sorrow that sends one home so high; the heady feeling of disorientation that lingers at the denouement, a heightened sensitivity to love and death alike, recalls not only the Grimms but also D. M. Thomas's psychoanalytic fable about the Holocaust, "The White Hotel," that is pointedly Rita and Peter's shared reading.

•

Given Mr. Lucas's transporting dramaturgy, "Prelude to a Kiss" retains much of its spell despite a bumpy transfer from Off Broadway's Circle Repertory Company to its new home at the Helen Hayes. The production's major casting change, the substitution of Mr. Hutton for the Hollywood-contract-bound Alec Baldwin, is far from ideal. While the other acting is, if anything, better than ever, the gifted director, Norman René, has also been sloppy in adjusting his fluid staging from an intimate, open space to a larger proscenium house. Loy Arcenas's abstract setting, its fixed blue window at center stage excepted, now looks as heavy as Stonehenge, and Mr. René sometimes sets the focal point of the action too remotely within its excessive shadows.

To what extent first-time visitors will be bothered by these shortcomings, I couldn't say. Mr. Hutton is an intelligent, sensitive actor and there's nothing wildly off-key about his portrayal. But he's not, as the dazzling Mr. Baldwin was, a prince. What's missing in his performance is the spellbound romantic generosity of a selfless man who sacrifices everything to his lover when she turns, metaphorically at least, into a frog. Like such past Lucas works as "Blue

Window" and "Reckless," this one demands that its lost, orphaned protagonist take a head-over-heels psychic leap into "the wild blue" on his spiritual journey to rebirth. The self-conscious, reserved Mr. Hutton never does plunge into that courageous emotional free fall.

•

The other stars do everything conceivable to mask this void. The change in partners has in no way dulled the airiness of Ms. Parker's lovely Rita, whose big eyes, floating hands and broad, giggly grin imbue her every line and silence with the aura of erotic expectation, likened by Peter to an "extra push of color." As the aged, dying widower who, through the play's pivotal fairy-tale kiss, becomes the unlikely repository of Rita's soul, Barnard Hughes gives "Prelude" its most twinkling comedy and its most touching specter of mortality. His glassy-eyed Irish mournfulness adds a Beckettian lilt to a soliloquy in which he describes life as a long series of abandonments by loved ones that leads only to one's own final mysterious disappearance to "nobody knows where."

Under Mr. René's sensitive hand, the supporting performances also remain sharp: Larry Bryggman and Debra Monk as Rita's slightly off-center suburban parents, Joyce Reehling as a middle-aged daughter in her own rending confrontation with familial grief and John Dossett as Peter's smart-aleck best friend. Reflecting his longtime collaboration with Mr. Lucas, Mr. René orchestrates the entire ensemble to serve the delicate chemistry of a play exquisitely poised between reality and fantasy, anguish and romance.

•

Nothing in "Prelude to a Kiss" is as simple as the director and author make it look. While Act I recounts the courtship, marriage and Caribbean honeymoon of Peter and Rita in the hip terms of contemporary, Manhattan-dry romantic comedy, the laughs never deflate the passion of lovers who are not joking when they exchange sentiments like "I would really, really like to see you with all your clothes off and stuff like that." Meanwhile, the baroque storyteller's diction of Peter's narration — "That night everything was miraculously restored," goes one typical line — helps prepare the audience for its own leap into fantastical plot twists that are no less enchanting for taking place in such prosaic settings as Englewood Cliffs, N.J., and are no less moving for involving such surreal events as a chaste heterosexual love affair between two men.

By the time the laughter subsides, at least temporarily, in Act II, "Prelude to a Kiss" has deftly locked its audience with its characters into what Peter describes as "one of those dreams in which you keep telling yourself 'Hang on!' " because you know that sooner or later you will have to wake up. And so you do. But Mr. Lucas's revivifying dream of love, as beautiful as it is miraculous in these precarious nights, hangs on.

1990 My 2, C15:1

Jack Manning/The New York Times
Mary-Louise Parker and Timothy Hutton in "Prelude to a Kiss."

Some Americans Abroad

By Richard Nelson; directed by Roger Michell; sets and costumes by Alexandra Byrne; lighting by Rick Fisher; original music by Jeremy Sams; production manager, Jeff Hamlin. Presented by Lincoln Center Theater, Gregory Mosher, director; Bernard Gersten, executive producer. At the Vivian Beaumont Theater, Lincoln Center, 65th Street and Broadway.

Joe Taylor ....Colin Stinton
Philip Brown .... John Bedford Lloyd
Henry McNeil ....Nathan Lane
Betty McNeil .... Kate Burton
Frankie Lewis .... Frances Conroy
Katie Taylor .... Cara Buono
Harriet Baldwin ....Jane Hoffman
Orson Baldwin ....Henderson Forsythe
Joanne Smith .... Ann Talman
An American .... John Rothman
Donna Silliman .... Elisabeth Shue
Musicians: Singer, Michelle Johnson; musical director and pianist, Joshua Rosenblum; bassist, Michael Goetz.

By MEL GUSSOW

Richard Nelson's "Some Americans Abroad," which reopened last night on the main stage in the Vivian Beaumont Theater, remains a felicitous comedy about the American penchant for all things English. Mr. Nelson is scathing in his satire, mocking arrogant intellectuals as well as pence-pinching tourists (same people).

As the characters follow the well-traveled cultural route from landmark to landmark, they compulsively consume a high-calorie diet of plays (two long Shakespeares in one day is a gourmandizing experience). Shakespeare, Shaw and Henry James provide a literate subtext of art and morality, repeatedly contradicted in the daily duplicities of the people on stage. Just as academics laugh at their self-portraits in David Lodge's comic novels, they, among others, will be amused by the wit and mordancy of Mr. Nelson's observations.

When the play had its New York premiere in February at the Mitzi E. Newhouse Theater, the production was less incisive than the English one previously staged by Roger Michell at the Royal Shakespeare Company. Now, through a combination of propitious circumstances, the American version is, as it should be, the equal of the London original.

•

The first difference is the welcome entrance into the cast of Nathan Lane. This prodigiously talented character actor now plays Henry McNeil, the hapless professor of English who is about to be rejected by his colleagues and cut loose from the tenure track.

Members of the English department in a New England college are in London on one of those generic winter-session courses in cultural uplift — in other words, a good excuse for a free European trip. Henry and his wife (Kate Burton) have paid their own way, tagging along in the futile hope of winning respect and continued employment. Despite his almost embarrassing humility, Henry is the only one in this group of careerists who really has a commitment to teaching.

Mr. Lane, whose face is one wide worry line, captures his character's need and desperate urgency. For him, everything is at stake, not simply his job but his credibility and, one might say, his soul. He will do anything to survive in academia — short of perjuring himself.

When the department head pompously recites Wordsworth's "Composed Upon Westminster Bridge" while standing on Waterloo Bridge, Henry helplessly corrects him: "Wrong bridge." One can almost feel Mr. Lane biting his tongue as he speaks the truth, a word that is not often in evidence in the whirlwind tour of "Some Americans Abroad." Ms. Burton is his loyal defender; to-

Lincoln Center Theater

Kate Burton and Nathan Lane in "Some Americans Abroad."

ge:her, the actor and actress communicate a loving concern for each other, while those around them are engaged in diverse forms of cheating.

•

Aided by the presence of Mr. Lane and nimbly guided by Mr. Michell, the other actors in this ensemble piece have sharpened their performances and the relationships between the characters. This is especially true in the case of Colin Stinton and John Bedford Lloyd as the department head and his worldly associate, whose womanizing leads to the play's second narrative strand.

Mr. Stinton's character is a cowardly man of middle management — pragmatic rather than principled, ready to offer small bribes (like expenses for dinner) but not real rewards or understanding. Though best friends, he and Mr. Lloyd are antagonists on almost every issue, beginning with questions of politics and theater.

For the production, the newly refurbished Beaumont Theater has been made to resemble the smaller Newhouse and approximates its intimacy. The play and Alexandra Byrne's mobile set adapt easily to the larger stage.

Although the characters are defined by their Anglophilia, in their hearts and manners they are very American. Despite their jeremiads against the vulgarisms of their countrymen — cornered by one such tourist in Stratford-on-Avon, Mr. Stinton pretends to be a naturalized Brit — they are unable to conceal their nationality. There is a wistful insecurity as the academics gather in the rain to sing "God Save the Queen." They sing softly, fearfully worried they might be overheard and identified as some Americans abroad.

1990 My 3, C17:1

Rain. Some Fish. No Elephants.

Directed by Mark Lutwak; written by Y York; set by Russell Parkman; lighting by Howard Werner; costumes by Marianne Powell-Parker; sound by Tom Gould; production stage manager, Lisa Ledwich. Presented by the New Theater of Brooklyn, Deborah J. Pope and Steve Stettler, artistic directors. At 465 Dean Street, in the Prospect Heights section of Brooklyn.

Esther	Angela Pietropinto
Emily	Alice Haining
June	Julia Glander
Gene	Tim Halligan
Julia	Arabella Field
Blackie	Leon Addison Brown

By MEL GUSSOW

In Y York's futuristic comedy, "Rain. Some Fish. No Elephants.," genetic engineering has produced a submissive nation of clones and drones. Everything is gene coded so that all individuality can be obliterated, except for one stubbornly old-fashioned family trying to thaw the perpetual nuclear winter. That winter is actually an endless floodlike rainy season.

The play (at the New Theater of Brooklyn) begins as a kind of science-fiction variation on "You Can't Take It With You," with a wildly eccentric family resolutely staying out of the mainstream. In this case, the father is a crank who has quit his scientific post in a dehumanizing laboratory to go fishing. He neglects his suicidal wife and their two very odd daughters.

In the first act, the playwright spends too much time cataloging the language and the crotchets of behavior brought about by this repressive society. Some comments are amusing, some are merely quirky, and there is an excessively long birthday party involving cardboard cutouts of those title elephants.

Gradually, Ms. York forsakes the whimsy and concentrates on her story. By the second act, she has created a thought-provoking comic parable about mankind's indomitability. As much as anything, the play is concerned with the survival of history itself, a point that the playwright makes by not taking herself too seriously, even as she offers astute observations about environmental, racial and family matters. Using a stark white setting, the director, Mark Lutwak, has given the work a suitably functional production.

The play takes place far in the future in that area of the United States once known as Chesapeake Bay. One receives the impression that here and elsewhere everyone lives identical lives — sans education, entertainment or endearments. Instead of parents, children have male and female elders. This is a world, one might say, populated by a myriad of mutants, a Zeitgeist of zygotes.

The catalyst for renewal is a black man, cloned to be a member of a faceless servant class. Removed from his diet of "stoppers," pills that deny incentive, he becomes a rebel. As conceived by Ms. York and as played by Leon Addison Brown, he is an engaging figure, awakening to his personality as well as to his racial identity.

As with the other, white members of his adoptive family, he is encouraged to choose an individual name. The father searches his selective memory and suggests that in honor of dimly remembered black leaders of long ago, his name should begin with the letter M. Forgetting Martin, Malcolm and Marcus, the father hits upon Morris, and soon the new Morris is marshaling the family and perhaps the nation to overthrow tyranny.

At the same time, the two daughters are realizing their own potential, the younger (Alice Haining) with a cheerful sweetness in the face of adversity, the elder (Julia Glander), her father's successor in the laboratory, with her desire to put science back in the service of humanity. Eventually even the moonstruck mother (Angela Pietropinto) becomes appealing. One of her first acts of dithering rebellion is to abandon housecleaning as a pointless preoccupation.

It is only the father (Tim Halligan) who remains something of an annoyance, slogging around the house in his rain slicker, cleaning fish and singing unmelodically at the top of his voice. If the playwright could find a way to make him less of a misanthrope, the play would be better outfitted for its role as a fanciful domestic comedy for an apocalyptical age.

1990 My 3, C20:5

Ice Cream With Hot Fudge

Two one-act plays by Caryl Churchill; directed by Les Waters; sets and costumes by Annie Smart; lighting by Stephen Strawbridge; fight staged by B. H. Barry; associate producer, Jason Steven Cohen. Presented by Joseph Papp. At the Public/Newman Theater, 425 Lafayette Street.

WITH: Margaret Whitton, John Pankow, Jane Kaczmarek, James Rebhorn, Julianne Moore and Robert Knepper.

By FRANK RICH

Attending a Caryl Churchill play is asking to get one's face slapped, repeatedly, frequently and with vicious force. "Ice Cream With Hot Fudge," as the English writer calls her new pair of one-act comedies at the Public Theater, is short in length but bottomless in its cynicism about citizens of the Thatcher-Reagan 1980's on both sides of the Atlantic. Ms. Churchill doesn't like Americans very much. She may like the English less. "Ice Cream With Hot Fudge" is a livid, hasty piece of work.

Even at its most intellectually vapid, the evening is usually charged with the black humor and esthetic adventurousness one expects from the author of "Cloud 9," "Top Girls," "Fen" and "Serious Money." In past plays, Ms. Churchill has scrambled chronology, allowed overlapping dialogue to erupt into cacophony and asked actors to ricochet between sexes and roles. Some of these techniques resurface here, but so does a new, Mametesque (or Pinteresque) spareness. "Ice Cream," the bill's hourlong main event, and "Hot

Clods, punks, a bad England and a worse America.

Fudge," its 20-odd-minute curtain raiser, hurtle forward in mysterious, strobe-bright, snapshot-quick vignettes of acidic verbal wit and oblique events. The larger dramatic twists -- three grisly deaths in one play alone — are often confined to the shadows offstage.

•

"Ice Cream" at least begins on familiar ground, as another ugly-Americans-abroad play. Lance (James Rebhorn) and Vera (Jane Kaczmarek) are a chatty, Anglophilic middle-aged suburban couple slobbering over castles and pubs while searching for familial roots in the British countryside. They find those roots in Lance's two English third cousins, but the relatives, Phil (Robert Knepper) and his sister, Jaq (Julianne Moore), are themselves rootless. They're alienated, amoral punks living at the dank fringes of the Thatcher economic miracle.

"I completely loathe the United States of America," says the thuggish Phil, who nonetheless wouldn't mind having his way with his American cousin's preppy wife. He darkly adds that Americans, having exported so much cultural and imperialistic "filth" to the rest of the world, should be prepared to have some of it "thrown back." As if to prove the point, he and Jaq lead the square Lance and Vera into a real-life, Ramboesque crime that gives the first half of "Ice Cream" the narrative shape of Alfred Hitchcock's "Man Who Knew Too Much."

In the play's later scenes, the action switches to the United States, with Phil and Jaq becoming the tourists. En route to Yosemite and perhaps Disneyland, they discover a country no less "violent and stupid" than their own England. But the American horrors Ms. Churchill subjects the visitors to — lecherous men, dreary surburbanites, doomsday-fixated evangelicals, all firmly caricatured by John Pankow and Margaret Whitton — seem to have been culled from old Dennis Hopper road movies and television reruns. Ms. Churchill's writing flattens out, a sure sign that her observations are secondhand, and her visions of a poisoned Middle America seem embarrassingly dated and quaint when stacked up against "Twin Peaks."

•

Until it melts, "Ice Cream" is very funny, especially once the previously chipper Mr. Rebhorn and Ms. Kaczmarek sink into panic after unearthing the grotesque England beneath the picturesque tourist vistas. Even in the dud stateside episodes, Ms. Churchill does effectively limn one

The New York Shakespeare Festival

James Rebhorn, left, Julianne Moore and Jane Kaczmarek in Caryl Churchill's "Ice Cream," at the Public Theater.

American trait — the compulsion to confess, whether to shrinks or office-mates — and, as ever, she finds sick laughter in her menacing young British drifters, chillingly embodied by the cruel-eyed Mr. Knepper and the affectless Ms. Moore.

While the title of "Ice Cream" refers to its characters' cultural and linguistic differences, that of "Hot Fudge" is more elusive. Suffice it to say that the characters in this brief, explosive work are on the gravy train. In three dense, fast-talking scenes, set in a pub, wine bar and private club on the same night, Ms. Churchill captures present-day hustlers of several classes and nationalities. The rackets may involve old-fashioned theft, sophisticated credit-card fraud, real-estate speculation or faddish tennis instruction, but to this playwright, they are all part of the same bankrupt new Anglo-American empire of multi-national corporations, "random walks," currency shifts, ecological vandalism and disingenuous corporate public relations.

As is explained in one hilarious speech, even the once-romantic calling of travel agents can now be rationalized in cold market terms because everyone in the world is either "a potential customer" or, as part of a tourist spot's ambiance, "a potential commodity." While Ms. Churchill's rage at greed is familiar from "Serious Money," her stock-exchange comedy, "Hot Fudge" resembles "Top Girls" when it suddenly shifts its setting from the economic arena to the private world where its money grubbers actually live. The play's fourth scene, set in a living room, exposes the sad people shouldering the pyramid schemes of compulsive mercenary success. As harrowingly acted by Ms. Moore and Mr. Pankow, each in a different state of psychological unravelment, this denouement is a nauseating glimpse into a most contemporary void.

•

The director, Les Waters, gives both plays a production as jolting as the writing. Annie Smart's distorted sets, as lighted by Stephen Strawbridge, have the imposing colors and stark, unsettling angularity of Alex

Katz paintings. The six fine actors make fierce impressions in a total of 23 scurvy roles. One doesn't have to swallow all of Ms. Churchill's at times knee-jerk didacticism to find "Ice Cream With Hot Fudge" rich in bracing theatrical bile.

1990 My 4, C5:1

New York 1937

By José Yglesias; directed by Charles Maryan; scenic design, Atkin Pace; costumes. Lana Fritz; lighting, Brian Nason; sound. Gary and Timmy Harris; stage manager, Nina Heller. Presented by the Jewish Repertory Theater, Ran Avni, artistic director; Edward M. Cohen, associate director. At 304 East 14th Street

Sophia	Antonia Rey
Abelardo	Joseph Palmas
Emma	Teresa Parente
Clara	Abigael Sanders
Miguel	Al Rodrigo
Julian	Tim Perez
Mr. Schlein	Michael Egan
Elsie	Ann Dowd
Uncle Raul	Gerald Orange
Mr. Levin	Royce Rich

By RICHARD F. SHEPARD

The name of the play, "New York 1937," sets the scene for José Yglesias's recollective piece being staged at the Jewish Repertory Theater.

The place is Washington Heights at a time when German Jewish refugees were finding their way to that uptown Manhattan neighborhood. At the same time, Hispanic people from Tampa, Fla., where the cigar business had gone bad, had also settled in the Heights, as the family of Mr. Yglesias had. "New York 1937" is about the meeting of the two cultures in one apartment house and an exploration of what they learned about each other.

Their story is one not of confrontation but of similar problems, mostly rooted in financial stress and generation gaps. Along the way, this autobiographical comedy — Mr. Yglesias's first staged work — recalls the hallmarks of the late 1930's. Among them are the "Orphan Annie" radio show, the songs of the supporters of the

Spanish Loyalists, the Christian Front rallies in New York City, the constant quest of tenants for rent concessions, the cafeterias, and the elaborate courtesies of the older new-comers from Florida and Germany.

As a light memoir, "New York 1937" works less easily on stage than, one suspects, it might as a series of prose vignettes that could describe the characters and their ways of thinking. In the play, directed by Charles Maryan, there is too great a rush of action, too little time for the audience to absorb what is happening, what it means. The cast of 10 runs in and out of the living room, the scene of the action, with a speedy artifice reminiscent of an ancient bedroom farce.

•

It is a show not only about the 1930's, but also, in a way, a play of the 1930's. There is a cheery optimism about it that frequently penetrated the cloudy Depression era. William Saroyan had it; even Clifford Odets, and certainly Moss Hart and George S. Kaufman in "You Can't Take It With You." Mr. Yglesias, as playwright, has created characters who are likable and, even when most disaffected by life, upbeat. But they lack depth.

The one who rings truest and is most memorable is Sophia, the Spanish-accented matriarch of the family, portrayed warmly and affectionately by Antonia Rey, who makes her the soul of authenticity. Joseph Palmas is buoyant as the young man proud of his job as counterman in Hector's, the Times Square cafeteria. The elderly German refugee, portrayed by Michael Egan, is too much of a saintly, unsophisticated cardboard type, and his daughter, played by Ann Dowd, could be any young British radical rather than one from a family that has just fled Nazism.

In presenting the apposition of two kinds of refugees, Mr. Yglesias tries to tell all, and consequently tells too little about any one of his characters. In bringing out the simple goodness of people, he has written too many people into the play, and simplicity achieves complexity. Yet the author does have something to say and expresses his thoughts with flashes of charm. It is an attractive idea for a play, this journey to 53 years ago, but Mr. Yglesias, an accomplished writer, might run his comedy through the machine once again and let his characters grow in life as they do in memory.

1990 My 6, 75:4

Once on This Island

Book and lyrics by Lynn Ahrens; music by Stephen Flaherty, based on the novel "My Love, My Love," by Rosa Guy; directed and choreographed by Graciela Daniele; set by Loy Arcenas; costumes by Judy Dearing; lighting by Allen Lee Hughes; sound by Scott Lehrer; orchestrations by Michael Starobin; musical director, Steve Marzullo; production stage manager, Leslie Loeb; music theater program director, Ira Weitzman; production manager, Carl Mulert. Presented by Playwrights Horizons, Andre Bishop, artistic director; Paul S. Daniels, executive director, in association with A.T.&T.: Onstage. At 416 West 42d Street.

Daniel	Jerry Dixon
Erzulie	Andrea Frierson
Mama Euralie	Sheila Gibbs
Ti Moune	La Chanzé
Asaka	Kecia Lewis-Evans
Little Ti Moune	Afi McClendon
Armand	Gerry McIntyre
Agwe	Milton Craig Nealy
Andrea	Nikki Rene
Papa Ge	Eric Riley
Tonton Julian	Ellis E. Williams

By FRANK RICH

In "Once on This Island," the stage has found its own sugar-and-cartoon-free answer to "The Little Mermaid." A 90-minute Caribbean fairy tale told in rousing song and dance, this show is a joyous marriage of the slick and the folkloric, of the hard-nosed sophistication of Broadway musical theater and the indigenous culture of a tropical isle. No doubt the evening will nettle purists who insist that all American musicals be urbane or that all foreign entertainments exhibited in New York be homegrown. Most everyone else is likely to emerge from Playwrights Horizons ready to dance down 42d Street.

The parallel between "The Little Mermaid" and "Once on This Island" is not invoked flippantly. As the songs for the Disney film were provided by Alan Menken and Howard Ashman, who wrote the tongue-in-cheek Off Broadway musical "Little Shop of Horrors," so the authors of this musical are Lynn Ahrens (book and lyrics) and Stephen Flaherty (music), a similarly smart Off Broadway team who made a promising debut with a comic musical, the unsuccessful "Lucky Stiff," at Playwrights Horizons a year ago. What's more, "Once on This Island," which has been adapted from a novel by the Trinidad-born novelist Rosa Guy, owes its own debt to Hans Christian Andersen. Set in the French Antilles, Ms. Guy's deeply felt tale of the romance between a black peasant girl, Ti Moune (La Chanze) and a worldly mulatto aristocrat, Daniel Beauxhomme (Jerry Dixon), is a revisionist "Little Mermaid" in which class and racial differences, rather than the sea, pull the star-crossed lovers asunder.

•

The musical's director and choreographer is Graciela Daniele, who opened this theater season with the short-lived "Dangerous Games" on Broadway and now ends it, show-biz-fairy-tale fashion, with the most effervescent achievement of her career. "Once on This Island" is wall-to-wall dancing, movement and mime. From the mood-setting first number, titled "We Dance" and reminiscent in spirit of Bob Fosse's "Magic to Do" in "Pippin," the audience is drawn into the evening's once-upon-a-time storytelling style and fantastical atmosphere. Yet to come are high-stepping, swivel-hipped calypso routines, ecstatic ritual dances to demanding gods, a rollicking Caribbean counterpart to "Follow the Yellow Brick Road," and even a delicate European waltz in the elegant hotel that serves as Daniel's princely palace.

In a show in which everything is of a piece, the staging is inseparable from the work of three superlative designers: Loy Arcenas (sets), Judy Dearing (costumes) and Allen Lee Hughes (lighting). What the Disney Studios can do with animation or Julie Taymor does with puppets in "Juan Darién," these artists achieve with flesh-and-blood actors. When Daniel races his sports car around the island, Mr. Dixon serves as both vehicle and driver, running about the stage in a white linen suit and sneakers, twin flashlights illuminating his winding road. Rainstorms arrive as a parade of dancers crowned by magical umbrellas dripping silver. Jungle wildlife materializes through costumes, masks and headdresses of hallucinatory design.

Mr. Arcenas, whose flair for fantasy has also been seen this season in

Playwrights Horizons

La Chanze, foreground, performing in "Once on This Island" at Playwrights Horizons on West 42d Street.

"Spunk" and "Prelude to a Kiss," encloses "Once on This Island" within a floor-to-ceiling mural emblazoned with faux-primitive flora and fauna, a tropical setting imagined in the Tahitian idiom of Gauguin, with the palette expanded to the cobalt blues and iridescent fuchsias of Matisse and Bonnard. When a large, lacy white patchwork quilt descends to become a lovers' bed, or when Mr. Hughes dims the sky to twinkling starlight or orange sunsets, "Once on This Island" almost makes one feel its orchid-scented breezes.

That Mr. Arcenas would present the tropics as Post-Impressionists might have imagined them is in keeping with the songs of Mr. Flaherty

An exuberant fantasy brings the Caribbean to 42d Street.

and Ms. Ahrens. Though they have borrowed freely from the musical culture of their setting, the composer and lyricist do not pretend to authenticity, choosing instead to filter the story's environment through their own sensibility. Mr. Flaherty's lush, melodic music goes native in the way Richard Rodgers went "Oriental" when writing "Bali Ha'i" and "The March of the Siamese Children." The score is arranged with an apt transcultural lilt, for flute and bongo drum alike, by Michael Starobin, the orchestrator known for his associations with Stephen Sondheim, Charles Strouse and William Finn.

•

In her lyrics and very spare dialogue, Ms. Ahrens doesn't make the

mistake of writing cutesy mock-dialect, and, except in one rueful song ("Some Girls") about the hero's choosing of a bride, she forsakes the sharp wit apparent in "Lucky Stiff." Her words are simple, direct and poignant. Papa Ge, the Demon of Death played with sinuous Sportin' Life bravura by Eric Riley, declares himself "the secret of life nobody wants to learn . . . the car racing toward distant shores." When Ti Moune leaves home to pursue her love, her heartbroken parents (Sheila Gibbs and Ellis E. Williams) sing a tender yet guilt-inducing farewell: "What you are, we made you/What we gave, you took."

Before the show ends, nearly each performer in the lithe, full-voiced ensemble of 11 breaks out of the chorus to shine. The most golden throats and ethereal presences belong to La Chanze and Nikki Rene as the two very different women with claims to Daniel's love. Kecia Lewis-Evans brings down the house as the gospel-belting earth mother who helps ease Ti Moune into the woods and out again on the path to the fulfillment of her romantic dreams.

•

That path, of course, does not always run smooth. "Once on This Island" has the integrity of genuine fairy tales, in that it doesn't lead to a saccharine ending but to a catharsis, a transcendent acceptance of the dust-to-dust continuity of life and death. "Why We Tell the Story" is the concluding song for the evening's storytellers, and one of those reasons is that "our lives become the stories that we weave." As the story and its tellers at last come full circle in "Once on This Island," the audience feels the otherworldly thrill of discovering the fabric of its own lives in an enchanted tapestry from a distant shore.

1990 My 7, C11:1

Ground People

Directed by Walter Dallas; written by Leslie Lee; sets by Charles McClennahan; costumes by Beth A. Ribblett; lighting by Shirley Prendergast; sound by David Lawson; movement consultant, Bernard J. Marsh; musical arrangements by Robert LaPierre; "Louisiana Mama" by Tajj As-Swaudi; music coordinator, Don Meissner; production stage manager, Lloyd Davis Jr.; general manager, Stephen Lisner. Presented by American Place Theater, Wynn Handman, director. At 111 West 46th Street.

Berlinda .... Bahni Turpin
Singin' Willie Ford .... Ron Richardson
Holly Day .... Denise Burse-Mickelbury
Reggie .... Raymond Anthony Thomas

Viola .... Frances Foster
Bertha .... Erma Campbell
Johnny Hopper .... Kim Sullivan
Musicians Tajj As-Swaudi and Arthur Harper

By MEL GUSSOW

The impoverished lives of black Southern sharecroppers in the 1920's were periodically brightened by visits from black minstrel troupes. It is Leslie Lee's idea, in his play "Ground People," that the nomadic entertainers shared misfortunes similar to those of their rural kinsmen. The farmers and the minstrels were being drawn away from their roots to the opportunities of the industrial North, where they would face inevitable disillusionments.

Mr. Lee's play, which opened last night at the American Place Theater, raises challenging questions about migration, racism and, as exemplified by the title, the importance of the land itself. But the play's validity is clouded by diversionary narrative strands and by a lack of character definition.

In effect, two parallel plays share the stage: one about a dirt-poor farm family, the other about a quartet of entertainers whose cheerful demeanor in their performances is repeatedly contradicted by their offstage arguments. The strength of "Ground People" is in the minstrel half of the evening, vividly personified by the Rabbit Foot Minstrels (the play's original title was "The Rabbit Foot").

The leader of the troupe (Ron Richardson, who was Jim in the musical "Big River") is iron-handed in his domination of his less rigid colleagues. They at least take a semblance of pleasure in their work. But hard times are endemic. Mr. Richardson is fearful of losing his occupation — and there is the competition provided by Ma Rainey and other successful performers who freely journey back and forth from South to North.

•

Mr. Lee captures the ebullience and the musicality of his minstrels, but he is less successful in depicting individuals. The most fully realized character is a lusty blues singer played by

Martha Holmes

Ron Richardson and Erma Campbell in a scene from "Ground People."

Erma Campbell, who is drowning her unhappiness in the jars of moonshine passed hand to hand. The other minstrels and their motivations are more diffuse. One minute, Mr. Richardson is trying to fire an asthmatic younger singer (Denise Burse-Mickelbury); the next minute he is furious at the thought that she and her lover (Kim Sullivan) are leaving the company.

This story alternates with the tale of a World War I veteran (Raymond Anthony Thomas) who returns to an imprisoning life as a Mississippi sharecropper. An incipient labor organizer, he has to face the oppressive rule of his unseen landlord as well as his wife's jealousy. Too easily the veteran and his wife (Bahni Turpin) fall into domestic banalities, relieved by the husband's matriarchal grandmother (Frances Foster), who is intractable about staying in the South. Just sitting in her kitchen, lining the thin soles of her shoes with paper while telling tales of her midwifery, Ms. Foster is a moving presence, as she has been in many other plays, including Mr. Lee's "First Breeze of Summer."

Under the direction of Walter Dallas, the actors add to the work's at-

mospheric authenticity. Charles McClennahan's tree-lined set — giving a tinge of a Chekhovian landscape to the Mississippi Delta — is an evocative environment. Traditional blues, melodically sung by the minstrels troupe and played by Tajj As-Swaudi and Arthur Harper, provide a lively bridge between the two sections of the play.

Since his early, personal dramas, Mr. Lee has frequently investigated the African-American past, with an intelligent eye for pivotal moments in history that have had long-ranging effects. In the case of "Ground People," his authority as a researcher tends to submerge his skills as a playwright.

It is only at the end of "Ground People" that the two halves of the play interact, in a touching encounter that makes it evident how valuable the minstrel shows were to those who were land trapped. It offered them illusions as well as entertainment. The scene makes one wonder why the playwright waited so long before bringing his two stories together.

1990 My 7, C13:1

Sliding, Gliding and Acting Oh So Glamorous

By JACK ANDERSON

All the skating was virtuosic in "Brian Boitano and Katarina Witt Skating," the ice revue directed and choreographed by Sandra Bezic that was presented on Saturday night at Madison Square Garden.

Its stars were the American-born Mr. Boitano, a gold-medal winner at the 1988 Olympic Games, and Miss Witt, an East German who won gold medals at the 1984 and 1988 Olympics. Both were elegant artists whose movements were clear and uncluttered. Mr. Boitano glided smoothly. Miss Witt was glamorous and aloof.

She was also witty enough to make understated jokes with her almost unrelieved remoteness in her solo "Mr. Monotony." She and Mr. Boitano skated together in the grand manner. Even when they wore casual attire in a duet called "Isolation Hotel," they still seemed suave.

Although they looked slightly demure in a choreographically passionate love duet to music from Bizet's "Carmen," the same thing can be

Brian Boitano and Katarina Witt, elegant and aloof.

said about many dancers who have appeared in the various balletic adaptations of that opera. At all times, Miss Witt and Mr. Boitano were in full control, moving with glorious ease.

•

The revue featured an international cast skating to popular, rock and classical music. Yelena Valova and

Oleg Vasilyev, from the Soviet Union, made a duet to Puccini seem to consist of a single, unbroken phrase. Aleksandr Fadeyev, another Soviet artist, was a nimble performer; if he were a ballet dancer, he would surely specialize in jester roles. Yvonne Gómez of Spain turned deftly in a solo to music from the ballet "Don Quixote."

Several American skaters made good impressions. In a solo to music by Saint-Saëns, Caryn Kadavy displayed the way that skating, unlike ballet, is able to combine balances on one leg with sweeps across the floor. Rosalyn Sumners appeared to be propelled by desire in a solo appropriately called "The Power of Love." A duet for Judy Blumberg and Michael Seibert was filled with variations on gliding movements.

Gliding is something skaters can do very well, backward as well as forward. Skaters can also lift their partners while in motion and cover great distances rapidly. Indeed, such difficult movements can be made to look so easy that long sequences of skating may sometimes lack variety.

Therefore, it was especially interesting to see skaters in this revue who had distinctive, and often attractively eccentric, ways of moving. Vladimir Kotin of the Soviet Union, virtually threw himself about the rink.

Gary Beacom of Canada was an outstanding performer who proved capable of investing his actions with a remarkable range of movement qualities. He could be smooth. But his smoothness was impressive because he could also be blunt or rough, and he could look floppy one moment and taut the next.

Paul Martini and Barbara Underhill, also from Canada, were absolutely terrific in a sultry duet. Mr. Martini wore jeans, and both were informal. But he soon literally swept

her off her feet, and she swooned in spectacular backbends.

The revue's performers were never less than proficient. But they were shown at their best when the choreography held surprises. What a pity that although souvenir books with pictures of the skaters were sold, there was no program listing the casts and titles of the show's numbers.

1990 My 8, C17:1

Hamlet

By William Shakespeare; directed by Kevin Kline; scenic design by Robin Wagner; costumes, Martin Pakledinaz; lighting, Jules Fisher; music composed by Bob James; fights staged by B. H. Barry; associate producer, Jason Steven Cohen. Presented by Joseph Papp. At the Public/Anspacher Theater, 425 Lafayette Street.

Bernardo and Player (Lucianus)	Rene Rivera
Francisco, Player (Prologue) and Clown	
	MacIntyre Dixon
Horatio	Peter Francis James
Marcellus and Sailor	Bill Camp
Claudius	Brian Murray
Voltemand and Messenger	Miguel Perez
Laertes	Michael Cumpsty
Hamlet	Kevin Kline
Gertrude	Dana Ivey
Ophelia	Diane Venora
Polonius	Josef Sommer
Ghost and Priest	Robert Murch
Osric	Leo Burmester
Rosencrantz	Philip Goodwin
Guidenstern	Reg. E. Cathey
Player King	Clement Fowler
Player Queen	Susan Gabriel
Fortinbras	Don Reilly
Norwegian Captain	Larry Green
Messenger	Erik Knutsen
Guards, Players, Ladies-in-Waiting, Attendants and Lords	

Claire Beckman, Bill Camp, Susan Gabriel, Larry Green, Curt Hostetter, Erik Knutsen and Rene Rivera

By FRANK RICH

When Kevin Kline is at center stage in a Shakespeare production, New York audiences can for once relax, secure in the knowledge that they will be seeing a classical actor of exceptional gifts and the highest integrity. Mr. Kline does not cruise through the classics to pump up his vanity and earn public-relations brownie points. Is there another star in this country — one whose services are in high demand in New York and Hollywood — who would undertake "Hamlet" twice in four years, as he has now done at the Public Theater?

Given what Mr. Kline stands for — and that he is a natural choice to play a young, witty, intellectually highstrung tragic hero — it is all the more puzzling that his current Hamlet, like the production he has himself directed to surround it, lacks the spark that might make it deeply moving. Mr. Kline's performance has everything else: intelligence, sardonic humor, verbal and physical virility. A born creature of the stage, he is, as Shakespeare would have it, in action like an angel, especially when black costumes set off the pale skin and Byronic features that make him a storybook prince. But if Mr. Kline has something pressing to say about this character, some heartfelt reason to inhabit the role of a hero driven to rendezvous with death, it is not articulated. The man behind Hamlet's various poses remains the wrong kind of mystery throughout, a remote blank rather than a compelling enigma.

•

As one expects, Mr. Kline is at his best when he can be comically, savagely ironic, from his first mocking swipe at Brian Murray's Claudius

("A little more than kin and less than kind!") through the withering tongue lashings in which he likens Polonius (Josef Sommer) to a fishmonger and consigns Ophelia (Diane Venora) to a nunnery. The interlude with the players is an uncommon delight: Mr. Kline is all over the place, leaping up and down from the makeshift stage and waving his arms to direct "The Murder of Gonzago" as if he were making a tongue-in-cheek commentary on his own audacity in directing "Hamlet."

But there comes a point when the hero's antic nature, whether it takes the form of hostile wit or feigned madness, gives way to darker humors. For all his role playing, Hamlet is still sinking into the vertigo of grief and rage and is driven to contemplate murder and suicide. Yet Mr. Kline does not build upon his sweet early sorrow. He strides on to deliver "To be or not to be" as if it were an isolated aria, and most of the evening's soliloquies, though rich in vocal music, sound more or less alike. When Mr. Kline takes a thrilling backward fall after confronting his father's ghost, or clutches his head on "O that this too too solid flesh would melt," or shuts his eyes on "to die, to sleep," the gestures seem like externally affixed illustrations instead of symptoms of profound internal unrest. More than even this role requires, Mr. Kline almost always stands outside himself, appraising his feelings instead of living them.

•

Might a demanding director with a critical eye have pushed the actor further, forcing him to find an interpretation of the part, whatever it might be? Perhaps. The truth is that Mr. Kline's 1990 Hamlet is not that much different from his 1986 one, which was directed unassertively by Liviu Ciulei. This time the star is surrounded by far superior actors — Mr. Kline, like Kenneth Branagh, is a star who likes to share the spotlight with talented peers — but most of the supporting performances prove at least as light as his own in interpretation and psychological weight.

Ms. Venora, who made a brave effort at playing Hamlet on the same stage in 1982, is compulsively watchable as always, but the notes she sounds early are so tremulous that the pitch inevitably has become strained and mannered by Ophelia's mad scene. Mr. Sommer, potentially a brilliant Polonius, does not move beyond the part's avuncular fatuousness; he never seems either a father or a veteran court politician. Mr. Murray, a good choice for Claudius, has his chilling moments, but the Machiavellian power lust and sexual hunger behind his crime are pale. Dana Ivey's stiff Gertrude, her occasional Oedipal embraces with Mr. Kline nothwithstanding, hardly seems related to Hamlet or Claudius; this excellent but brittle character actress is more of an incipient Lady Macbeth. Peter Francis James is an exemplary, tender Horatio, and in less crucial roles, Michael Cumpsty (Laertes), Philip Goodwin (Rosencrantz) and Reg E. Cathey (Guildenstern) are first rate.

Mr. Kline's staging is remarkably consistent with the acting in that it is neutral to a fault. The corruption and decay of the state that parallels the collapse of Hamlet's psyche is no more dramatized in this "Hamlet" than is the disintegration of the play's two familial constellations. Denmark is not rotting so much as suffering from a spell of overcast weather. The action unfolds on a blank space, ably

The New York Shakespeare Festival

Diane Venora and Kevin Kline in "Hamlet."

designed by Robin Wagner (scenery) and Jules Fisher (lighting), that is backed by an ominous North European sky and, for an arras, a towering red-velvet curtain. Even the supernatural nightmarishness of the ghost scenes is pointedly muted.

Blander still are Martin Pakledinaz's modern-dress costumes, which, in keeping with the rest, have no urgent point to make. (Mr. Murray's militaristic tunics, which make him look like a junior skipper on "The Love Boat," are unfortunate exceptions.) While the absence of furniture requires that the actors frequently fall to their knees at dramatic flashpoints, Mr. Kline's staging is impressively well managed for a first-time director and towers over that found in

most of the tragedies seen so far in the Shakespeare Marathon, this season's "Macbeth" included.

Yet a polished, plausibly cast and well-spoken "Hamlet" — one happily free of the catastrophes New York audiences have come to fear at Shakespeare productions — is an empty victory without the excitement that comes from watching a great actor open himself up by wrestling with the soul of a great role. Is it possible that Mr. Kline is that rare star who might need to express more of his ego, even at the risk of looking reckless or foolish, so that he can dig deeper? A rational, poised, controlled Hamlet, no matter how skillfully set forth, is a contradiction in terms.

1990 My 9, C15:4

Dragons and Other Intruders of the Mind

By JACK ANDERSON

If only all of "Dragon's Nest" had been like its best bits and pieces. There were real touches of imagination in the multi-media work that Lee Nagrin presented last Thursday night at La Mama. But between the bits and pieces came long dull stretches.

Ms. Nagrin combined text and movement with scenic effects designed by James Meares. People rode in on the back of a dragon. Other performers flew through the air like Peter Pan. The stage for the last of the work's three acts became a shadowy forest.

Cast as a man obsessed with religion, David Brooks was both amusing

and touching in a series of monologues during which he spoke of life in a mental hospital and of the way the devil had drugged his bananas. In an effective monologue of her own, Ms. Nagrin portrayed a woman patiently trying to speak to her infirm mother on the telephone. As she spoke, she heard prowlers trying to break into her house and her conversation was interrupted when a mysterious toy animal — a combination of rabbit and dinosaur — suddenly flew into the room. That strange beast and the suspicious intruders became symbols of Ms. Nagrin's own mental insecurity.

But most of the work, which lasted nearly three hours, was neither theatrically vivid nor dramatically coherent. The absence of a simple narrative was surely intentional. "Dragon's Nest" was a mosaic of incidents concerning an older woman (Ms. Nagrin) looking back upon her life. Her past unfolded at a glacial pace. Most of the people she encountered were nowhere near as interesting as Mr. Brooks. And her emotional responses to events were usually cryptic. "Dragon's Nest" was a big, imposing production. Unlike most dragons, however, it lacked fire.

1990 My 10, C14:4

The Waves

New York Theather Workshop

Catherine Cox

A musical adaptation of the novel "The Waves" by Virginia Woolf; text adapted by David Bucknam and Lisa Peterson; directed by Ms. Peterson; choreography by Marcia Milgrom Dodge; music and additional lyrics by Mr. Bucknam; musical direction and orchestrations by Helen Gregory; set design, Randy Benjamin; costumes, Michael Krass; lighting, Brian MacDevitt; sound, Bruce Kraemer; text and dialect coach, Robert Neff Williams; stage manager, Liz Small; production manager, George Xenos. New York Theater Workshop, James C. Nicola, artistic director; Nancy Kassak Diekmann, managing director, present the New Directors Series at the Perry Street Theater, 31 Perry Street.

Rhoda	Catherine Cox
Jinny	Diana Fratantoni
Neville	Aloysius Gigi
Louis	John Jellison
Susan	Sarah Rice
Bernard	John Sloman

By MEL GUSSOW

Virginia Woolf wrote the last pages of "The Waves" with "such intensity and intoxication" as to remind her of the times she was overcome by madness. With its torrential language and metaphorical interludes, the novel completely reflects the author's obsessive self-concern. Chronicling the interlocked relationships of six friends in Edwardian England, it is, to borrow the words of one of the characters, "a mysterious illumination" of life unto death.

Until the musical adaptation by David Bucknam and Lisa Peterson (presented by the New York Theater Workshop at the Perry Street Theater), it was difficult to imagine that

anyone could transport this dense novel to the stage with any reasonable degree of fidelity.

In their version, clarification has necessarily led to a certain simplification, particularly in the second act. At the conclusion, the musical unwisely steps back from the abyss of the novelist's despairing vision. But the book, score and lyrics are suffused with a Woolfian intensity and intoxication. Mr. Bucknam (as co-author and composer) and Ms. Peterson (as co-author and director) have distilled the rarefied flavor of the novel, evoked its principal motifs and themes and made the work come alive on stage.

Coincidentally, in a season when Andrew Lloyd Webber has taken a minor Bloomsbury novel, "Aspects of Love," and found no viable theatrical equivalent, Mr. Bucknam and Ms. Peterson have taken one of the great pinnacles of Bloomsbury literature and gone a long distance in reinventing it as musical theater.

•

In direct reaction to Galsworthy and other traditional novelists, Woolf viewed life as a "semi-transparent envelope" through which one receives impressions rather than details of external reality. The adapters approximate the author's stream of consciousness with a collage technique. As overlapping monologues become dialogues, as speech evolves into song, the effect is like that of soul addressing soul. In common with the novel, the musical exists on its own plane of reality. These are six disparate characters in search of oneness.

At the center of "The Waves" is Bernard, an unquenchable storyteller who is flattered to be regarded as a Byronic youth. As an adult, he disappoints himself. None of the characters is remotely content, not even Louis, who achieves notable success in business, or Susan, who embraces a provincial life as wife and mother. All six are haunted by the image of the unseen Perciva!, the golden youth brought to an untimely death in India (the character was based on the author's brother). From estheticism to romantic longing to middle-age regret, the characters share a heightened sense of self-awareness, a fact that makes their singing — and Mr. Bucknam's score — achieve a naturalness.

•

There is a whiff of Sondheim in the structure of the show as well as in the music, but it is combined with an amplitude of the composer's own voice, drawing upon Virginia Woolf as his inspiration. She is, after the fact, his active musical collaborator, with her prose gracefully adapting itself to lyrics. As a heady chamber musical, the show reminds one somewhat of "Goblin Market," with the difference that the novel "The Waves" is far more resonant.

Monologues flow into music, some of it with a lightness (Louis's amusing ode to his daily business duties), others with a passionate introspection (Rhoda's ballad exploring her wish to be the mistress of her own figurative fleet). Occasionally there is a misstep, as in Susan's lullaby to motherhood, a song that belongs in a different show.

In the writing and in the performance (by Catherine Cox), the Rhoda on stage seems even more the author's surrogate as she wrestles with her emotional crises, including a predilection toward suicide. Watching "The Waves," it is impossible to ignore the fact that the novelist herself chose death by drowning.

Each characterization is distinct, with especially strong work (singing as well as acting) by Sarah Rice as Susan, John Jellison as Louis. and John Sloman as Bernard. Led by Ms. Peterson, the actors artfully discover a path through the effulgent prose. But Randy Benjamin's scenic design presents them with unneeded difficulties, layering the small stage into seven levels. Footing is made more precarious by the fact that the floor is covered with a groundcloth, on which are placed tilted chairs. This obstacle course of an environment is somewhat offset by a painterly backcloth of cloudlike waves (or wavelike clouds).

While the adaptation delineates the elation of youth, it is less secure in dealing with the disillusionment of adulthood. The conclusion of the book s Bernard's extended analysis of the six lives. Instead of leaving the reflections in the hands of Bernard, the show sifts his lines among the various characters.

In the novel, Bernard says that to deal with pain, there should be not words but "cries, cracks, fissures," all of which are subordinated at the end of the musical. Having demonstrated earlier that they are unafraid of Virginia Woolf, the adapters should take one further step and offer a final indication of their dramatic fearlessness.

1990 My 10, C16:4

Zoya's Apartment

By Mikhail Bulgakov; translation by Nicholas Saunders and Frank Dwyer; directed by Boris A. Morozov; scenery by James Morgan, based on original designs by Josef Sumbatsivily; lighting by Mary Jo Dondlinger; costumes by Cynthia Doty, based on original designs by Tatyana Gleboya; music by Gregory Gobernik; stage movement by Mina Yakim; hair design by Linda Rice. Presented by Circle in the Square Theater, Theodore Mann, artistic director; Paul Libin, producing director. At 50th Street, west of Broadway.

Zoya Denisovna Peltz	Linda Thorson
Manyushka	Chandra Lee
Anisim Zotikovich Alliuya	Ray DeMattis
Pavel Fyodorovich Abolyaninov	Robert LuPone
Gandzalin	Akira Takayama
Cherubim	Ernest Abuba
Aleksandr Tarasovich Ametistov	Bronson Pinchot
Alla Vadimovna	Lauri Landry
Boris Semyonovich Goose	Robert Stattel

With: Robertson Carricart, Holley Chant, Kevin Crawford, Fiona Davis, Colleen Gallagher, Dana Mills, Joe Palmieri, Talia Paul, Careayre Rambeau, Florence Rowe and David Silber.

By FRANK RICH

It may well be possible for a Soviet director, even one who doesn't speak English, to parachute into the United States and successfully re-create a celebrated Moscow production with American actors unschooled in Russian theatrical styles. But the more likely result of such a hands-across-the-water cultural experiment is typified by Boris A. Morozov's production of Mikhail Bulgakov's "Zoya's Apartment" at the Circle in the Square. Mr. Morozov is resident director of the Maly Theater in Moscow. His New York cast is headed by such actors as Bronson Pinchot, of television's "Perfect Strangers," and Robert LuPone, of "A Chorus Line." In "Zoya's Apartment," East and West do not so much meet as smash their heads against a wall as formidable as Berlin's once was.

This is a well-meaning botch, redeemed only by Linda Thorson, the

Circle in the Square Theater

Russians Are Coming

Bronson Pinchot performs in "Zoya's Apartment," a comedy by Mikhail Bulgakov about outwitting a corrupt Soviet bureaucracy in the 1920's, directed by Boris Morozov.

sole keeper of Bulgakov's flame in a large cast, and by the fascination of the play itself. That fascination will be lost, however, on those who do not arrive at the theater with some knowledge of Soviet politics and drama in the 1920's and of the literary style of Bulgakov, who is best known for his satirical novels "The Master and Margarita" and "Heart of a Dog." When a production is this impotent at revealing the heart of a text, a theatergoer must amuse himself by imagining the director's good intentions rather than by taking seriously the misfires actually occurring on stage.

•

"Zoya's Apartment" was first presented at the Vakhtangov Theater in Moscow in 1926, which was neither the best of times nor the worst in the still-embryonic history of the Soviet Union. The post-Revolution euphoria had dimmed. The Stalinist lid had not quite been nailed shut. The banning of Bulgakov's writing was still three years away. Much as seems to be the case in the Soviet Union now, the mid-1920's was a period of true flux, of mixed emotions, conflicted loyalties, wild uncertainties. That unsettling amalgam of euphoria and fear is bottled in the dark comedy of "Zoya's Apartment."

Set in a clandestine bordello populated by all manner of displaced and newfangled Russian types, from a ruined czarist aristocrat to meddling party bureaucrats, the play is equally sarcastic about the corruption of the old and new regimes and is more than a little worried about the future. The Muscovites of "Zoya's Apartment" dream of emigrating to Paris almost as much as Chekhov's provincials of a quarter-century earlier fantasized about getting to Moscow. And no one more than Ms. Thorson's Zoya. She will stop at nothing, from bribery to flesh-peddling, to escape a society she begins to suspect is a trap.

•

Ms. Thorson brings unexpected depths to this woman, who is at once a brassy comic madam (her brothel is disguised as a dressmaking shop) and a courageous survivor. One believes she has the entrepreneurial flair to recruit "models" and customers as well as the cunning to outsmart the officials who would shut her down. But as the walls close in during the waning scenes, Zoya becomes a braver heroine. Long after her hus-

band, a former count played by Mr. LuPone, retreats into depression and drug addiction, she retains a hunger for life. When Ms. Thorson bids a final, tear-tinged farewell to her smashed apartment, she could be departing Chekhov's cherry orchard, so much does her mixture of regret and triumph suggest the passing of an epoch.

By contrast, Mr. LuPone labors to simulate an Old World nobility, sometimes by walking so rigidly he could have a yardstick for a spine. He fills in the count's melancholy with a repertory of mournful expressions and his snobbishness with sneering intonations. It is, at least, a game effort, and it comes closest to credibility when Mr. LuPone sits at a red piano to sing a sad Russian song. As the bordello's manager, a confidence man who will exploit the Reds and the Whites alike for opportunism's sake, Mr. Pinchot substitutes a monotonous, energetic raising of his voice and arms for comic invention. This talented actor has been and could be much funnier with helpful direction.

•

Aside from Ernest Abuba, who professionally delivers a demeaning Chinese caricature belonging to the play's time, the rest of the acting is dreadful. Mr. Morozov is hardly the first Russian director to fail to mesh with American actors; Yuri Lyubimov's "Crime and Punishment" at Arena Stage in Washington a few years ago was similarly unrealized by most of its cast. Perhaps an American director would have the same problem directing Russian actors to perform David Mamet in Russian in Moscow, unless the rehearsal time was of Moscow Art Theater proportions.

In "Zoya's Apartment," even Mr. Morozov's stagecraft is lost in translation. Those familiar with Soviet theatrical idioms will know what the director is getting at with his stylized use of music and his deployment of ominous extras behind a scrim, but anyone else is likely to be baffled by these flourishes, given their clumsy execution here. As for Bulgakov's wit, about the only humor to survive in this staging are the lowest of bosom and rump gags. It is not praise to say that this is a "Zoya's Apartment" Stalin might have been more inclined to chuckle at than to ban.

1990 My 11, C3:1

Talking Things Over With Chekhov

By John Ford Noonan; directed by Marjorie Mahle; set by Ron Kron; lighting by Tracy Dedrickson; costumes by Gene Lauze; production stage manager, Joe McGuire; associate producers, M. D. Minichiello and Albert Repicci. Presented by Bill Repicci. At the Actors' Playhouse, 100 Seventh Avenue South, near Sheridan Square.

Jeremy M.	John Ford Noonan
Marlene D.	Diane Salinger

By MEL GUSSOW

Ten years ago, John Ford Noonan wrote "A Coupla White Chicks Sitting Around Talking." In his new show, he is once again up to his conversational tricks. This time he is also onstage. In the two-character comedy "Talking Things Over With Chekhov," he plays a playwright drawn to his own dimensions — always amiable and seemingly undisturbed by questions of theatrical form.

Mr. Noonan (as a character named Jeremy Melvin, to move the play one small step from reality) announces that he has come home to find Dr. Chekhov sitting in a rocking chair. Over a glass of kvass, Chekhov chats Chekhovianly — or so we hear. As a character, he remains offstage. The other person in the play (at the Actors' Playhouse) is the playwright's former lady friend (Diane Salinger), a once-promising actress who has retired from the theater.

The playwright and the actress meet again while jogging in Central Park. (Ron Kron's set looks like a New Yorker magazine-cover panorama.) Mr. Noonan reveals that he is no longer a creature of bad habits — one cause of the couple's breakup — and that he has written his first play. The subject of the play is his relationship with Ms. Salinger, and the actress is tempted to return to the stage to portray herself, a role she feels is well within her range. A similar thing could be said about Mr. Noonan. As directed by Marjorie Mahle, both are convincing playing approximations of themselves.

Though this may sound Pirandellian, Mr. Noonan's approach is much more mundane. The apparent purpose is to offer the author a platform for jokes and comments about playwrights, actors, drama critics and anything else that happens to wander into his mind. Except for the fact that

M. D. Minichiello

John Ford Noonan and Diane Salinger in the two-character comedy "Talking Things Over With Chekhov."

the audience knows that Mr. Noonan is himself a playwright, there is scant attempt to shadow truth with illusion. In the Noonan tradition, a couple white people sit around talking.

The play is slight and ephemeral. The conversation repeatedly threatens to float away into the Central Park air. "Talking Things Over With Chekhov" is no match for "The Zoo Story," "Duck Variations" or the other plays that might be taking place on nearby park benches.

In six short vignettes, the two characters are seen over several months, changing clothes to suit each encounter — from jogging suits to formal attire for the opening night of the play within the play. By the end of the show, the bohemian playwright looks like a Broadway bon vivant. Mr. Noonan cuts quite a natty figure as he reads aloud with increasing agitation his mixed review in The New York Times. Ms. Salinger is, as called for by her role, enticing, one of several reasons it is difficult for the playwright to keep his mind on his rewrites.

•

One keeps hoping that Chekhov will make an unannounced appearance. The conversation between the characters on stage is far less interesting than the secondhand stories about the uninvited guest still lurking in the playwright's home. Mr. Noonan reports that Chekhov quotes Gorky and Tolstoy (who, as is well known, told him that he was even a worse playwright than Shakespeare).

Occasionally the Russian offers his American counterpart tips on playwriting. "Writing plays is like baking a cake," he says. "Every step you skip shows up in the end." In his play, Mr. Noonan disregards that recipe. The ingredients are here for an offbeat comedy, but the cake crumbles.

1990 My 13, 44:1

Made in Heaven

By Edward Belling; directed by Stanley Brechner; set designer, James Wolk; costumes, Victoria Lee; lighting, Susan A. White; production stage manager, Benjamin Gutkin; sound, John Wise; associate artistic director, Lonny Price. Presented by the American Jewish Theater, Mr. Brechner, artistic director. At the Susan Bloch Theater, 307 West 27th Street.

Rose Rothenberg .... Grace Roberts
Jack Rothenberg .... Herbert Rubens
Milton Gross .... Jack Aaron
Bunny Gross .... Anita Keal
Richard Rothenberg .... Bruce Nozick
Ellen Rothenberg .... Alexandra Gersten
Harvey Horowitz .... Stuart Zagnit

By STEPHEN HOLDEN

When Rose and Jack Rothenberg first meet Milton and Bunny Gross on a mountaintop in Israel, the vacationing couples quickly discover that they have more in common than just being from New York City. Their children — 27-year-old Richard Rothenberg and 26-year-old Ellen Gross — are unmarried lawyers who live a block apart on the Upper East Side of Manhattan. Once snapshots have been passed around and résumés exchanged, all agree that the two were meant for each other.

The next thing we know, four years have passed, and Richard and Ellen are dividing their possessions in preparation for a divorce. The only apparent problem with their marriage has been career pressures.

Over Richard's objections, Ellen, "the only woman from Forest Hills who doesn't own a fur coat," plans to leave New York to work in Washington as an environmental lawyer.

•

Out of the blue, the four parents appear and barge into Richard and Ellen's apartment with a warning: they intend to lay siege to the place and to refuse all food until Richard and Ellen agree to cancel their divorce. One of their weapons is a list of the phone numbers of television stations. If Richard and Ellen resist, they threaten to turn their hunger strike into an embarrassing media circus.

The premise behind Edward Belling's comedy, "Made in Heaven," which the American Jewish Theater is presenting at the tiny Susan Bloch Theater, is so ingenious that it could have laid the groundwork for a savage cartoon of contemporary New York Jewish life. Instead, the playwright has concocted a mild little comedy that has its charms but that is as predictable as an episode of a situation comedy.

The heart of "Made in Heaven" is an ethical dialogue between generations. The parents, whose side the playwright takes in every argument, believe that marriage and children come first, and they urge Richard and Ellen to "divorce their careers," if necessary, to save the marriage.

In the play's most comically anguished moment, Rose, brandishing a bagel knife, pleads with Ellen and Richard to kill her with it. The moment echoes the opening scene, when the touring couples contemplate events at Masada in the first century that drove Jews to kill themselves and their families rather than become slaves.

"Made in Heaven" is smoothly performed. Grace Roberts and Herbert Rubens, who play Rose and Jack Rothenberg, and Jack Aaron and Anita Keal, who portray the Grosses, imbue their likable stereotypical characters with an appealingly crusty warmth while avoiding glib caricature.

•

Richard and Ellen are also well played by Bruce Nozick and Alexandra Gersten, but as written by the playwright, the characters are selfish, career-obsessed yuppies whose arguments for divorce (even including saving the whales) ring hollow. It's hard to feel much sympathy for their assertion that their jobs are more crucial to their self-esteem than their marriage. And they become the paper tigers in a debate that, had the play taken a more contemplative direction, might have addressed deeper questions about assimilation and the perpetuation of Jewish cultural values and traditions.

Instead the play concentrates on comic trivialities. The playwright's dialogue and Stanley Brechner's deft direction maintain an appropriately snappy tone, but the jokes are too few and too tepid to draw more than occasional laughs.

1990 My 13, 45:1

The Tower of Evil

By Alexandre Dumas père; translated by Michael Feingold; directed by Carey Perloff; scenic design, Donald Eastman; costume design, Gabriel Berry; lighting, Frances Aronson; composer, Elizabeth Swados; production stage manager, Richard Jakiel. Presented by CSC Repertory, Ms. Perloff, artistic director; Dara Hershman, acting managing director. At 136 East 13th Street.

Margaret of Burgundy .... Kathleen Widdoes
Captain Buridan .... Patrick O'Connell
Richard/De Pierrefonds .... Thomas Delling
Simon/Sir Raoul .... Michael Reilly
Gaultier Dolnay .... Bradley Whitford
John/Halberdier .... Ethan Mintz
Gypsy .... Katharine Cohen
Orsini .... Olek Krupa
Philippe Dolnay .... David Bishins
Landry/Sir Guilbert de Marigny
                                                Armand Schultz
A Veiled Woman .... Ellie Hannibal
Charlotte .... Mary Beth Kilkelly
Savoisy/King Louis X .... Frank Raiter
Courtiers . Ellie Hannibal and Gwynne Rivers

By MEL GUSSOW

Though Alexandre Dumas père is best known for his romantic novels "The Three Musketeers" and "The Count of Monte Cristo," he also left a legacy of plays, including "La Tour de Nesle," a bloodthirsty historical melodrama written in 1832. Despite that play's continuing popularity in France, it turns out to be creaky and contrived, not the well-oiled mechanism one would have expected. The fact is attributable to the play itself (entitled "The Tower of Evil" in Michael Feingold's new translation) and also to Carey Perloff's production at the CSC Repertory.

This revenger's tale has the goriness of Grand Guignol as it follows the murderous path of Margaret of Burgundy — the ruler of France whenever her husband, Louis X, is out of town. Margaret and her two sisters take nightly lovers, and then order the men slain and their bodies thrown into the Seine. Justice of a kind triumphs after a plot-heavy narrative involving patricide, incest and a flashback about abandoned twin boys with the sign of a cross on their left arms. Some of this is unintentionally humorous.

•

The dialogue, in Mr. Feingold's version, has its ornate flourishes, as in Margaret's vow, "I would risk the curse of God for you, just as I have risked the contumely of man." Contumely finally forces her into self-defeating measures, but not until she has seriously depleted the population of handsome young soldiers.

Despite the vengeful events, the play does not have the demonic drive found in the best of Jacobean melodrama. As the plot writhes, there are gaps in motivation and glaring coincidences. It would take a Shakespeare to give "The Tower of Evil" coherence, and a far more authentic production than this one to make it entertaining.

What the play demands is a company of swashbuckling actors who can change in an instant from passive observers to slashing cavaliers. What the CSC offers is an ill-suited assort-

---

CSC Reper

Who's Next?

Kathleen Widdoes stars in "The Tower of Evil," a mystery by Alexander Dumas about the Queen of France and a Paris menaced by a serial killer, directed by Carey Perloff

ment of actors who are unable to persuade the audience they are driven to excessive emotions — to say nothing about their lack of bearing in period costumes and their discomfort with the dialogue. Admiring one's fingernails, as one courtier does incessantly, is no substitute for panache.

•

Only two in the cast come close to being exempt from that charge. Fortunately they are playing the leading roles: Kathleen Widdoes as the lustful Margaret and Patrick O'Connell as the officer who becomes her nemesis. Ms. Widdoes exudes authority as she rises in anger to shout "Fiend!" at her foe, and Mr. O'Connell has a semblance of the necessary cunning. But neither is exactly fiendish, as required by their roles.

Other actors, beginning with Bradley Whitford as the captain of the guard, seem peckish rather than strong-willed. Physically the production has an insufficient sense of foreboding, even though Donald Eastman's dungeon-like set is darkly lit. Passion and style are absent from the boiling pot.

1990 My 13, 45:1

The Cemetery Club

By Ivan Menchell; directed by Pamela Berlin; scenery by John Lee Beatty; costumes by Lindsay W. Davis; lighting by Natasha Katz; sound design by Scott T. Anderson; music by Robert Dennis. Presented by Howard Hurst, Philip Rose, David Brown and Sophie Hurst. At the Brooks Atkinson Theater, 256 West 47th Street.

Ida ....Elizabeth Franz
Lucille ....Eileen Heckart
Doris ....Doris Belack
Sam .... Lee Wallace
Mildred ....Judith Granite

By FRANK RICH

If you believe that one good reason for going to the theater is to escape television sitcoms, you may not be tickled to end up at "The Cemetery Club," the new attraction at the Brooks Atkinson. From its peppy canned theme music to its final-scene sermonizing, this comedy about three Jewish widows in Forest Hills, Queens, is "Golden Girls" at four times the length but with at most one-fourth the star wattage. Moving at the leisurely pace of a contentious canasta hand, "The Cemetery Club" could be one of the best arguments yet advanced for cremation.

The author, Ivan Menchell, follows the time-honored rules of his chosen genre: he gives his middle-class senior citizens as many toilet, sexual and anatomical one-liners as he can. Lucille (Eileen Heckart), the randiest of the ladies, sets the evening's tone with her early declaration that "You don't buy a mink because you need it; you buy *support hose* because you need it." Doris (Doris Belack), the pill of the group, issues loud periodic bulletins like "I'm going to the bathroom!" and "Oy, am I going to have gas!" The good-hearted Ida (Elizabeth Franz), suffering from a hangover, opens one scene by rushing offstage to vomit.

•

To stitch these merry episodes together, Mr. Menchell has concocted a story in which the women's so-called cemetery club, a chatty monthly reunion at their beloved husbands' graves, is disrupted by the intrusion of Sam (Lee Wallace), a widower with an eye for Ida. A few misunderstandings, jealous spats, drunken confessions and yahrzeit candles later, order is restored. By then, Ida has delivered the inevitable bit of sentimental boilerplate, "For the first time since Murray died, I felt alive!" and everyone has gotten to dance the cha-cha and eat a little chopped liver.

What's objectionable, as opposed to

Lisa Berg for The New York Times

Eileen Heckart in a scene from "The Cemetery Club."

merely tedious, about Mr. Menchell's writing is the sanctimony in which it cloaks its vulgarity. Not unlike Robert Harling's "Steel Magnolias" — with which it shares its director, Pamela Berlin — "The Cemetery Club" purports to be championing its women's independence even as it alternately patronizes and humiliates them. The play's climax involves the removal of a wig (a stunt also used in the much higher camp of "Lettice and Lovage") and a drink-tossing cat fight. When Mr. Menchell, again echoing "Steel Magnolias," tries to retrieve his seriousness of purpose in Act II by sending a fresh corpse to the grave, the tear-jerking announcement of this untimely passing rings so false that it draws nearly as many titters as the wisecracks about unveilings, perpetual gravesite care and going into remission.

The staging is sluggish, with Ms. Belack's yenta, Ms. Franz's sugary born-again coquette and Mr. Wal-

lace's blandly affable suitor doing nothing to erase one's fond memories of such archetypes as Molly Picon, Gertrude Berg and Sam Levene. The sterling Ms. Heckart has been given especially unflattering (and, for some reason, Day-Glo-hued) costumes by the designer Lindsay W. Davis and must at one point wear a blond wig and florid makeup befitting a Carol Channing impersonator. But such handicaps, let alone the stalled zingers in the script, cannot derail this comedienne's withering sarcasm and impeccable timing. She also is free to smoke in every scene — Ms. Heckart's gravelly voice is no put-on — and at one point she gets to stub out a butt on a tomb.

Such other laughs as there are come from the truly hideous scenery provided by the gifted John Lee Beatty, who seems to be having a giggle at the production's expense. Not only has he given Ida a vast living room of surpassingly realistic drabness, from the ersatz Chagall lithographs on the wall to a towering breakfront crammed with china, but he has also provided a cemetery whose backdrop pictures the cheerless ruins of the Flushing World's Fair as seen through a smoggy haze. During the set changes, the tombstones make such a commotion marching on and off stage that not even the audience is permitted to rest in peace.

1990 My 16, C14:4

Marathon 1990
Festival of New One-Act Plays, Series A

Match Point by Frank D. Gilroy; directed by Billy Hopkins.

Two War Scenes: Cross Patch and Goldberg Street by David Mamet; directed by W. H. Macy.

The Second Coming by Bill Bozzone; directed by Donato J. D'Albis.

Captive by Paul Weitz; directed by Susann Brinkley.
Set design, Paul Wonsek; lighting, Greg MacPherson; sound, Aural Fixation; costumes, David E. Sawaryn; production supervisor, Kent Hoffman; production stage manager, Michael B. Paul. Presented by the Ensemble Studio Theater, Curt Dempster, artistic director; Peter Shavitz, managing director; Kate Baggott, producer, Eric Berkal, associate producer. At 549 West 52d Street.

WITH: Daniel Benzali, Kayla Black, Jude Ciccolella, Christine Farrell, Paul Geier, Greg Germann, Zach Grenier, Andrew Lauer, Anna Levine Thomson, Leslie Lyles, W. H. Macy, Holt McCallany, Mark Metcalf, Kellie Overbey, Martin Shakar, Victor Slezak, Robin Spielberg and Mark Tymchyshyn.

By MEL GUSSOW

The five plays in Marathon 1990, the 13th annual one-act festival at the Ensemble Studio Theater, deal varyingly with retribution and revenge. This concern is amusingly exemplified by comedies from Bill Bozzone and Frank D. Gilroy. Both are skilled practitioners of the short play form. They know that a one-act should never overstay the audience's interest.

Mr. Bozzone is represented by "The Second Coming," a 30-minute sketch about divine improvidence in Perth Amboy, N.J. In this spoof of suburban and spiritual values, a young widow prays to her living-room statue of the Sacred Heart for a suitable young man to rescue her daughter from her punkish inclinations.

Enter Victor Slezak as a born-again divinity — as dashing and convivial a prom date as either mother or daugh-

ter could wish for. He can even dance the lambada better than any of the girl's schoolmates. The playwright has a corsage of surprises on the way to his last indelicate laugh. Under the direction of Donato J. D'Albis, the actors are wryly in caricature, especially Mr. Slezak, and Christine Farrell and Kellie Overbey as the widely disparate mother and daughter.

•

Mr. Gilroy's "Match Point" is as brief as a blackout, a cautionary curtain-raiser about one woman's act of vengeance against her philandering husband. This Machiavellian tale is played out at a resort under the desert sun. On the surface, everything seems so mannerly, but the wife (Leslie Lyles) has a killer instinct.

Billy Hopkins's staging does not overlook a comic beat as Ms. Lyles plots her artful path to equal marital justice. She and Anna Levine Thomson are drollness personified as wives of opposite look and demeanor, with Ms. Lyles's worldly sense of reserve matched against the blithe ingenuousness of Ms. Thomas. W. H. Macy is properly nonplussed as the husband caught in the wife's web.

Paul Weitz's "Captive" is a cat-and-captive game, a variation on "The Collector," vivified through the performances of Kayla Black and Mark Tymchyshyn as temptress and victim. An office mate brought home for what promises to be an evening of romance, he soon finds himself tied up and tied down by Ms. Black and her swaggering co-conspirator. The striking Ms. Black has a kind of sensual self-awareness of her effect on men. Mr. Tymchyshyn maintains his wide-eyed wariness even as he is humiliated.

In contrast to "The Second Coming" and "Match Point," Mr. Weitz's play meanders past several alternative exits before arriving at its inconclusive destination. Using Paul Wonsek's appropriate set design and aided by her actors, Susann Brinkley offers the play a well-modulated production.

In his introduction to a collection of his short plays, David Mamet says the works were written as "emotional meal tickets" that allow him to get through a day without working on a major project "and still think of myself as a writer." This is an apt description of the impetus for short plays. They should be unpretentious and self-sustaining, which is true of the plays in the opening Ensemble Studio evening, with the exception of one of Mr. Mamet's two contributions. Both are linked under the title

"Two War Scenes"and are directed by Mr. Macy.

"Cross Patch" is an enigmatic report on a convention of hard-line conservatives in which lectures are given by an Oliver North-style adventurer and by a man who recalls the Chicago Black Sox scandal in 1919. The relationship between the speeches is hazy, but there is a passing reference to Gen. George S. Patton that echoes in the play's companion piece, "Goldberg Street."

In this father-and-daughter dialogue, a Jewish veteran of World War II recalls a demeaning incident from his military past. In the daughter's concern for her parent (Martin Shakar), the vignette has some of the tenderness of Mr. Mamet's "Dark Pony," in which a parent and child draw close to each other in a bond of memory.

As intended, Evening A in Marathon 1990 offers a diverse taster's menu of short plays by a spectrum of known and lesser-known dramatists. It is the first of a series of three evenings, which will also feature work by, among others, Shel Silverstein, Romulus Linney and Joyce Carol Oates.

1990 My 16, C14:4

Smoke on The Mountain

Directed and conceived by Alan Bailey; written by Connie Ray; scenic design, Peter Harrison; costume design, Pamela Scofield; lighting, Don Ehman; production stage manager, Tom Clewell; musical directors, John Foley and Mike Craver; production manager, Clark Cameron; musical arrangments, Mr. Craver and Mark Hardwick; general manager, Nancy Nagel Gibbs. Presented by the Lamb's Theater Company, Carolyn Rossi Copeland, producing director. At 130 West 44th Street.

Burl Sanders	Reathel Bean
Mervin Oglethorpe	Kevin Chamberlin
Vera Sanders	Linda Kerns
Stanley	Dan Manning
Dennis Sanders	Robert Olsen
Denise Sanders	Jane Potter
June Sanders	Connie Ray

By STEPHEN HOLDEN

It is a June night in 1938 at the Mount Pleasant Baptist Church in the North Carolina backwoods. Presiding over what is announced as the church's first ever Saturday night sing, its portly pastor, Mervin Oglethorpe, reminds the congregation that "God scratches where the world itches."

Ensemble Studio Theater

Kellie Overbey and Andrew Lauer in a scene from "The Second Coming," one of the five plays in Series A of Marathon 1990.

Moments later, the evening's special guests, the Sanders Family Singers, straggle in, a little out of breath because their bus has turned over in a ditch next to the local pickle factory. No sooner have they settled themselves than they launch into William S. Pitts's 1865 chestnut "The Little Brown Church (in the Vale)," accompanying themselves on guitar, banjo, fiddle and other traditional folk instruments.

The song is among the two dozen numbers, many of them vintage pop hymns, that the Sanders family performs in the folk-musical comedy "Smoke on the Mountain," at the Lamb's Theater. The show, conceived and directed by Alan Bailey and written by Connie Ray, is a charming and funny celebration of Americana and white rural church music that also pokes gentle fun at the pious provincialism of an all-but-vanished world.

With its mixture of softened cracker-barrel humor, Christian sweetness and light, and its attitude of gentle amusement at the squareness of it all, "Smoke on the Mountain" creates the same mood, at once sentimental and whimsical, that folk musicals like "Pump Boys and Dinettes" and "Oil City Symphony" have brought to the Off Broadway stage. The resemblance is more than passing, since John Foley, Mike Craver and Mark Hardwick, the evening's musical directors and arrangers, were also associated with the two earlier shows.

"Smoke on the Mountain," which was originally produced at the McCarter Theater in Princeton, N.J., two years ago, also resembles its predecessors in that it is less concerned with sociological accuracy than with evoking a friendly communal spirit. Although the musical is ostensibly set in Depression-era North Carolina, the world it imagines is really a nostalgic never-never land, where the harder physical realities of life remain at a comfortable remove.

The music isn't strictly true to the period. Some songs, like Cindy Walker's "Christian Cowboy" and J. Preston Martinez's "I'll Never Die (I'll Just Change My Address)," are from the 1950's and 60's, and others, including Mr. Bailey's title song and Mr. Craver and Mr. Hardwick's "I'll Walk Every Step of the Way," are contemporary. What they share, however, are uplifting country-folk melodies and words that transform the images from everyday rural life into pungent, often witty spiritual metaphors.

•

The musical performances have a hearty hand-clapping energy, but lack the keening fervency that the best concerts of old-time music can convey. The most authentic-sounding voices belong to Reathel Bean, who plays Burl Sanders, the taciturn paterfamilias, and Dan Manning, who portrays his black-sheep brother, Stanley. Both voices suggest lighter echoes of Johnny Cash's sepulchral drone.

The other four family members include the mother, Vera (Linda Kerns); the eldest daughter, June (Ms. Ray), who doesn't sing but who plays percussion and vigorously signs for the deaf, and the teen-age twins, Dennis and Denise (Robert Olsen and Jane Potter). During the evening, little dramas erupt as each member of the Sanders family takes a solo turn and tells a story.

To her parents' dismay, Denise confesses that she recently took a bus to Charlotte, where David O. Selznick was auditioning would-be Scarlett O'Haras for the movie "Gone With the Wind." When a June bug lands in Mother Vera's lemonade, it inspires a short amusing sermon about how without Jesus we are all June bugs "hitting the screen doors of life and drowning in the refreshments."

•

The show's darkest note is sounded by Mr. Manning as the brother who has just finished serving a sentence of 18 months' hard labor and who guiltily admits, "I know what beer smells like, and I like it." Mr. Bailey has directed the ensemble so that the actors all impart a consistent but subtle edge of caricature to their roles while avoiding any suggestions of hillbilly cartoonishness.

Like "Pump Boys and Dinettes" and "Oil City Symphony," the world of "Smoke on the Mountain" is a sunny place in which a cutegreeting card nostalgia overlaps with a deeper strain of longing for qualities in the American character that can seem very distant in today's embattled urban climate. It's refreshing to rediscover those qualities in Mount Pleasant's mythical little brown church.

1990 My 17, C20:3

Each Day Dies With Sleep

By José Rivera; directed by Roberta Levitow; sets by Tom Kamm; costumes by Tina Cantú Navarro; lighting by Robert Wierzel; New York sound design by Janet Kalas; scenic projection design by Charles Rose; production stage manager, Fred Reinglas. Presented by Circle Repertory Company, Tanya Berezin, artistic director; Connie L. Alexis, managing director, in association with Berkeley Repertory and A.T.&T.: Onstage. At 99 Seventh Avenue South, at Fourth Street.

Johnny .... Randy Vásquez
Nelly .... Erica Gimpel
Augie .... Alex Colón

By FRANK RICH

There probably are not that many playwrights who have both written television shows for Norman Lear and participated in a screenwriting workshop with Gabriel García Márquez, but such is the résumé of José Rivera, whose new play, "Each Day Dies With Sleep," is now at the Circle Repertory Company. The influence of both mentors is apparent in this work, in which glib ethnic comedy battles to a standoff with the metaphorical paraphernalia of magic realism. "Each Day Dies With Sleep" is the kind of evening in which the set is decorated with images from René Magritte while the characters make wisecracks about Sean Penn.

Though it is possible to merge two such divergent sensibilities — one thinks of Jim Jarmusch's film "Mystery Train" and David Henry Hwang's play "F.O.B.," to pick random examples — Mr. Rivera's play comes off merely as weightless and pretentious. At its heart is the not terribly compelling tale of the middle child among 21 Hispanic siblings, Nelly (Erica Gimpel), who escapes the brutal machismo of her impoverished father, Angie (Alex Colón), only to end up in a Hollywood Hills marriage with the equally narcissistic Johnny (Randy Vásquez), a womanizing car mechanic who aspires to the heights of male modeldom.

Such slender dramatic goods do not gain in fascination by being swamped with a cataclysmic hurricane and fire, hifalutinsyntax ("His hands have memories of usefulness and hard work"), ritualistic duels with machetes and guns, jokes about ninja rapists, and surreal hallucinations of carnivorous animals, a severed female hand and a mysteriously expanding ancestral home. Each of the characters' countless days does not so much die with sleep as collapse under its own esthetic dead weight.

For anyone who has been waiting for Mr. Rivera to build on the promise he first revealed in the adventurous, fiercely felt "House of Ramon Iglesia" (at Ensemble Studio Theater, 1983), "Each Day Dies With Sleep" must be considered a serious disappointment. Roberta Levitow's production, tricked up with three-dimensional slide projections and enough sound effects for a "Lethal Weapon" sequel, only accentuates the gulf separating the writing's precious style from its preciously tiny content.

Nor is that content above reproach. Why does a play championing a victimized woman present its heroine's mother as a gross, cackling, sluttish offstage clown? If this running gag is intended to illustrate another poisonous male fantasy, Mr. Rivera is more successful at exploiting the fantasy than at condemning it.

Under Ms. Levitow's direction, the acting only adds to the panic of being trapped in a theater for two acts with three empty characters. Mr. Colón's gruff, one-note ranter of a father is the outstanding irritant. Ms. Gimpel and Mr. Vásquez, though both, as beautiful as the script announces, are a pair of soap-opera juveniles, even when she must grovel theatrically on the floor in accordance with her lowly status as her family's "pinhead" or when he must incantatorily repeat lines like "I play guitar like the wind." It typifies the play's aura of fakery that when Mr. Vásquez actually must play a guitar on stage, he doesn't play like the wind but mimes, all too breezily, to a recording.

1990 My 17, C20:3

Further Mo'

Written and directed by Vernel Bagneris; choreographed by Pepsi Bethel; set design, Charles McClennahan; costumes, Joann Clevenger; lighting, John McKernon; sound, Peter Fitzgerald; musical director, Orange Kellin; musical arrangements, Lars Edegran and Mr. Kellin; vocal arrangements, Topsy Chapman and Mr. Edegran; general management, Frank Scardino Associates; production stage manager, K. R. Williams. Presented by Norzar Productions and Michael Frazier. At the Village Gate, downstairs, Bleecker and Thompson Streets.

Theater Owner .... James (Red) Wilcher
Thelma .... Topsy Chapman
Papa Du .... Vernel Bagneris
Ma Reed .... Frozine Thomas
Big Bertha .... Sandra Reaves-Phillips

By STEPHEN HOLDEN

"Further Mo,'" Vernel Bagneris's rollicking sequel to his successful 1979 blues and jazz revue, "One Mo' Time," returns to the original show's seedy stomping grounds, the Lyric Theater of New Orleans, to catch up with its four vaudevillian troupers. It is a year later (1927), and bawdy blues songs are still the specialty of the house.

Like its forerunner, the sequel offers lusty performances of vintage blues, jazz and popular tunes arranged in a modified Dixieland style for a small jazz ensemble. While the program's high points are its hilariously salacious numbers like "One-Hour Mama" and "Positively No (Construction Gang)," its two dozen songs offer a fairly wide cross section of styles from torch ("My Man") to jazz ("Alabamy Bound").

Two cast members of "One Mo' Time" — Mr. Bagneris and Topsy Chapman — again portray their characters (Papa Du and Thelma) from the original show. The sequel opened last night, downstairs at the Village Gate, where the original show had also opened. As the loose-limbed vaudeville singer and dancer who juggles relationships with two women, Mr. Bagneris has only a passable singing voice, but he dances superbly and projects a cool devil-may-care charisma. Using a minimum of

The Lamb's Theater Company
Dan Manning, foreground, Linda Kerns and Reathel Bean in the folk-musical comedy "Smoke on the Mountain."

fancy footwork, he slinks around the stage with a grace so airy in its confidence that at moments he almost seems to be floating.

●

Ms. Chapman is a versatile pop-blues stylist whose singing suggests a bluesier Nancy Wilson. Frozine Thomas, who plays Ma Reed, the least flamboyant of the four, has a smooth gutbucket blues delivery that contrasts with the more raucous style of the show's most vivid character, Big Bertha.

The role of the huffy blues diva, which was originally played by Sylvia (Kuumba) Williams, has been taken over in the sequel by Sandra Reaves-Phillips, who with her earthy roar seems ideally cast. In "Further Mo,'" the character, who has just returned from a European tour, flounces about the stage fantasizing about imminent stardom in the movies.

In "One Mo' Time," Mr. Bagneris, who conceived, wrote and directed both shows, took a standard nostalgia-revue format and gave it a mild political twist by following its four black vaudevillians backstage. Without seriously dampening the high spirits, he was able to suggest how even in a town as relaxed as New Orleans in the 1920's, blacks were exploited and restricted. And this double vision of euphoric hijinks on the stage and the exploitation and bickering behind the scenes gave the music a historical dimension.

The sequel also insinuates racial politics into the raunchy fun. Early in the evening the Lyric's white owner, played by James (Red) Wilcher, confides to Papa Du that after that evening's performance, the theater, which has not been profitable, will be burned to the ground for the insurance money. The performers will be out of work, and the closest city with a comparable vaudeville house is Mobile, Ala. Though warned in advance of the fire so they can remove their costumes and other belongings, the performers are afraid to leave the theater loaded with baggage lest they be arrested for theft.

●

Because "Further Mo'" crams its story into the nooks and crannies between numbers, its little backstage dramas remain undeveloped, and much remains unclear. In the most enigmatic scene, the theater owner disguises himself in drag to go on an unexplained mission in behalf of his soon-to-be-unemployed troupe.

Although the drama fizzles, the music sails. The singers' voices are well matched, and the five-member New Orleans Blue Serenaders play with verve and fluency. Pepsi Bethel's undemanding choreography gives the show an easygoing lilt without taxing the performers. For those who insist on high-style virtuosity, the show to see for this sort of thing is "Black and Blue" on Broadway. "Further Mo,'" though not as ambitious as its uptown cousin, still offers plenty of hot music, steamy atmosphere and lowdown fun.

1990 My 18, C3:5

The Miser

By Molière; directed by Mark Lamos; translated and adapted by Constance Congdon; set design by John Arnone; costumes by Martin Pakledinaz; lighting by Pat Collins; sound by David Budries; dramaturg and assistant director, Greg Leaming; production stage manager, Ruth E. Sternberg; assistant stage manager, Denise Winter. Presented by Hartford Stage, Mr. Lamos, artistic director; David Hawkanson, managing director. At Hartford, Conn.

Valere	Stephen Caffrey
Elise	Betsy Aidem
Cleante	Tom Wood
Harpagon	Gerry Bamman
La Flèche	Marcus Giamatti
Master Simon and Anselme	Ted van Griethuysen
Frosine	Pamela Payton-Wright
Master Jacques	Jeffery V. Thompson
Brindavoine and Policeman	Kevin Cristaldi
Mariane	Gabriella Diaz-Farrar
Claudine	Donna Mehle

By MEL GUSSOW

Special to The New York Times

HARTFORD, May 16 — For Harpagon, the title character in "The Miser," greed is not only good but it is also essential for his well-being. In Mark Lamos's production of the play at Hartford Stage, Gerry Bamman makes it self-evident that the miser is as obsessive as he is egomaniacal, and, in so doing, the actor carries comedy to diabolical lengths.

The character is far more devoted to his money than he is to his son and daughter, and when his strongbox is stolen, he is crushed beyond relief. At the climax of the play, he is told he can have his fortune back if he will let his son marry the woman he loves, the same woman the aged father had selected for himself.

Confronted with this choice — his money or a wife — Mr. Bamman takes a long Jack Benny-like pause, thinking it over and inducing hearty laughter from the audience before he decides where his interest lies. As the actor knows, Harpagon must end as he begins, as the meanest of skinflints, without any redeeming virtue.

Two seasons ago at Hartford Stage, Mr. Bamman played the complacent master of "The School for Wives." With his role in "The Miser," he reaffirms his comic franchise as a leading interpreter of Molière's self-important, self-deluding protagonists.

The production is fueled by the actor's antic spirit. He has a silent clown's gift for physical comedy as well as a drollness in handling his character's acerbic insults. Even when he is offstage, one can sense his proximity, as if he might leap through a curtain to uncover a devious counterplot.

When he is onstage, he is delightful, asserting his will (and his zeal for his weal). He is especially funny when he falls for the false flattery of Frosine. This wily matchmaker (Pamela Payton-Wright) easily convinces him that it would be impossible for a young woman to prefer a young man when Harpagon himself is available. "You are in your salad days," she tells him. The woebegone Mr. Bamman looks more like a bowl of wilted lettuce.

●

Fawning will get Frosine everywhere when faced with an old fool like Harpagon. He will accept any compliment, now matter how irrational, if it certifies his own lofty opinion of himself. Ms. Payton-Wright is amusing, although her performance is perilously close to a Ruth Gordon imitation.

The miser's worthiest antagonist proves to be his son. At Hartford Stage, that role receives the evening's second most entertaining performance. The lanky Tom Wood, towering over his father (he has to stoop to be badgered), is as impetuous a swain as ever disobeyed the wishes of a parent.

Gabriella Diaz-Farrar is pert as the son's intended, a woman so vulnerable that she faints when she sees the old man to whom she is temporarily affianced. Marcus Giamatti and Ted van Griethuysen are adroit in other roles. Oddly, Mr. Giamatti, as a scheming servant, is the only one in the company who speaks with a French accent.

●

Mr. Lamos's production has its eccentric touches, in an unnecessary attempt to give a contemporary patina to a classic farce. At moments, "The

Hartford Stage

Gerry Bamman

Miser" threatens to emulate the free-wheeling tactics of the Italianate Molière, "Scapino." While Constance Congdon's adaptation wanders into the land of anachronism, it refrains from being heavy-handed.

Lightness and spontaneity are the mode as the actors sweep to the upbeat conclusion. Long-lost children are reunited with their parents, couples are bound together in bliss, and Harpagon once again embraces his true love, his strongbox. Mr. Bamman beams, his exasperation finally replaced by ecstasy: a perfect match of man and money.

1990 My 18, C4:3

F.O.B.

Written and directed by David Henry Hwang; set, Alex Polner; lighting, Victor En Yu Tan; costumes, Eiko Yamaguchi; choreographer, Jamie H. J. Guan; composer and musician, Lucia Hwong; sound design, Robert Barnes; arranger and musician, Yukio Tsuji; stage manager, Sue Jane Stoker. Presented by Pan Asian Repertory Theater, Tisa Chang, artistic and producing director. At Playhouse 46, 423 West 46th Street.

Dale	Stan Egi
Grace	Ann M. Tsuj
Steve	Dennis Dur

By MEL GUSSOW

At the end of the first act of David Henry Hwang's "F.O.B.," there is a mirthful eating scene that summarizes the conflict between an American-born young man of Chinese descent and a newly landed immigrant, fresh off the boat (F.O.B.) from China. The newcomer, played by Dennis Dun, pours a jar of fiery hot sauce over his dinner and eats it as if it were the most savory of delights. The American (Stan Egi) feels forced to compete, but his tastebuds have become accustomed to the blandness of fast food and he is soon gasping for breath. He continues the competition while the F.O.B. smiles — dare one say it? — inscrutably.

Mr. Hwang's play, first produced in New York in 1980, has been revived by the Pan Asian Repertory Theater at Playhouse 46, in a production directed by the author. While the play is not as poetic as his subsequent

---

Comedy and metaphor about assimiliation in an alien environment.

"Dance and the Railroad," it offers a clear indication of Mr. Hwang's nascent talent and his social concern. In contrast to some of his subsequent work, it is free of pretension, even as it enters the world of myth.

●

"F.O.B." begins as a comedy about the possibilities and perils of assimilation, but it aspires to a deeper metaphorical level. The F.O.B. regards himself as an incarnation of Gwan Gung, a legendary Chinese warrior. In response to his acting-out of a Gwan Gung story, his American friend (Ann M. Tsuji) assumes the air of a warrior queen.

Mixing ritual and music, the play enlarges the portrait of a people trying to determine its place in an alien environment. Each of the three characters has a disparate response. Mr. Egi, already racing on the fast track to economic success, has become overly Americanized. He is determined to remove himself from the "yellow ghosts" of his past. Ms. Tsuji seeks to combine ancient and modern traditions while going to college and working in her father's restaurant. Mr. Dun, as the mysterious F.O.B., is clownishly deceptive, pretending to be the rawest of greenhorns while actually being a man of intellectual mettle.

●

While one misses the balletic grace of John Lone, who played the title role in the original New York production, the author has given his play a stylish, highly professional production. Mr. Egi, as a man climbing up from the upper middle class, is an amusing picture of sleek American consumerism. His opposite, Mr. Dun — familiar to television audiences for his role on "Midnight Caller" — slips neatly out of his assumed naïveté with his mission as cool master of martial arts.

In the pivotal role, Ms. Tsuji is charming. She is a born peacemaker trying to referee the conflict (over ethnicity as well as hot sauce) without discouraging the attention she receives from both young men. In common with Mr. Dun, she is agile in her stage movements, as choreographed by Jamie H. J. Guan. Alex Polner's scenic design for the back room of a family restaurant adds a necessary note of reality, but it is almost too detailed for a small stage. On opening

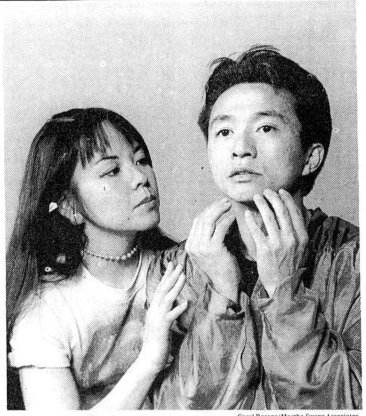

Carol Rosegg/Martha Swope Associates

Ann M. Tsuji and Dennis Dun in "F.O.B.," at Playhouse 46.

night, the preponderance of properties turned the setting into an obstacle course for the actors.

•

Mr. Hwang, who also wrote "M. Butterfly," has said that one of his inspirations for "F.O.B." was Maxine Hong Kingston's book "The Woman Warrior." Ms. Kingston returned the compliment in her foreword to a collection of Mr. Hwang's plays, expressing her wonder that through his work "our private Chinese lives and secret language can be communally understood."

In "F.O.B.," the playwright entreats theatergoers to leave all preconceptions behind and to open their minds to the warring subdivisions in what would appear to be a homogeneous community. The fact of these differences within the Asian-American culture is itself a moving commentary, especially during a time of increased tension between races.

1990 My 20, 60:1

The B. Beaver Animation

Written and directed by Lee Breuer; original design, Tina Girouard; set adapted by Marcia Altieri; costumes adapted by Gabriel Berry; lighting design, David Tecson; music, Jimmy Harry and Steve Peaboy; production manager, Monica Bowin; stage manager, Jack Doulin; company manager, Frier McCollister; managing director, Anthony Vasconcellos. The Mabou Mines production presented by Joseph Papp. At the Public/Shiva Theater, 425 Lafayette Street.

B. Beaver .... Frederick Neumann
Chorus
         Honora Fergusson, Clove Galilee, Ruth Maleczech, Greg Mehrten, David Neumann and Terry O'Reilly
Musicians
         Steve Peabody and Frier McCollister

By MEL GUSSOW

After Lee Breuer's imposing "Warrior Ant" and his version of "King Lear," with the men as women and the women as men, it is refreshing to return to Breuer past, to the modesty and the crazy-quilt humor of "The B. Beaver Animation." Originally produced in 1974, this work is having a brief revival at the Public Theater as part of the Mabou Mines' 20th-anniversary season.

"B. Beaver" and its companion pieces, "The Red Horse Animation" and "The Shaggy Dog Animation," are small, abstruse comedies about anthropomorphized animals faced with people-size problems. As written and directed by Mr. Breuer, the plays are like animated cartoons onstage, while keeping a foot (or a flipper) in experimental theater.

There are several disparate approaches to "B. Beaver." One can regard the protagonist's Beckett-like stream of consciousness as a sea of words and images that wash over an audience. Impressions are snared on the wing. On the other hand, exegesis is possible, if not certifiable fact. There is a freewheeling quality to the narrative that makes it open to diverse interpretations.

The title character, played as in earlier productions by Frederick Neumann, is a portly beaver trying to protect his family from destruction by snowstorm and icebergs. Raging at the elements, he is a practitioner of the lost art of damnation (one of the multitudinous puns that populate the play). He is a survivor beaver as well as an expert sailor and mathematician, able to traverse any hypotenuse. As his home — a clever set designed by Tina Girouard — collapses, he looks for a new equilibrium. That set is like a self-destroying sculpture, reconstructed for every performance.

On a metaphorical level, the beaver without a dam could be regarded as the equivalent of the writer without an idea, or as a clear case of beaver's block. "B. Beaver" could even have autobiographical implications. This analysis may be excessive and certainly it is inessential for enjoyment of the show.

In performance, as directed by Mr. Breuer, "B. Beaver" has a vaudeville spontaneity. Mr. Neumann (who is dressed like a man, not a beaver) conducts a chorus of garishly costumed castaways, presumably his family, including Ruth Maleczech and Greg Mehrten, the King and her Fool in Mr. Breuer's recent "King Lear." They

Mabou Mines

Frederick Neumann in Lee Breuer's "B. Beaver Animation."

all capsize along with B. Beaver, as the stage appears to become a ship sinking far from port. A thunder sheet, used like a bed sheet, offers some small protection against the elements.

At one point, Ms. Maleczech plays a most unmusical musical saw. In the background is a two-piece combo, whose sound is a tin-pan cross between Kabuki and Ernie Kovacs's Nairobi Trio. As much as anything, there is a Kovacs-like nuttiness in the air as the members of the Mabou Mines cut up, cool down and have a hectic, inventive hour.

1990 My 24, C19:1

The Cherry Orchard

By Anton Chekhov; a newly revised version in English by Jean-Claude Van Itallie; directed by Luke Yankee; scenic design, James Morgan; costumes, Kerri Lea Robbins; lighting, A. C. Hickox; original music by Dennis Holly; choreography by Hal Simons; technical director, James E. Fuller Jr.; production stage manager, Kim Vernace. Presented by the York Theater Company, Janet Hayes Walker, producing director; Molly Pickering Grose, managing director. At the Church of the Heavenly Rest, 2 East 90th Street.

Lopakhin .... Paul Hecht
Dunyasha .... Corliss Preston
Yepikhodov ....Michael Nostrand
Anya ....Cynthia Nixon
Ranevskaya ... .Penny Fuller
Varya .... Louise Roberts
Gayev .... David Canary
Charlotta Ivanovna ....Merle Louise
Simenov-Pischik ....Victor Raider-Wexler
Yasha .... Paul Schoeffler
Firs ....Phillip Pruneau
Trofimov .... Tim Loughrin
A Vagrant ....Scott Barton
Station Master ....Robert Warren

By STEPHEN HOLDEN

Anton Chekhov's dramas are easier to ruin in performance than those of most other major playwrights because so much depends upon finding and sustaining a delicate balance between pathos and humor. "The Cherry Orchard," the last of his comedies, is especially challenging because its effete, self-deluded characters are so easily turned into cartoons. Unless their angst is given a social and historical dimension, the play doesn't convey much resonance.

In the York Theater Company's new production, directed by Luke Yankee, the comedy is played so broadly that the tone of the performances often verges on raucous sit-com. From the very opening scene in which the down-at-the-heels aristocrat Mme. Ranevskaya and her party return from Paris to her Russian country estate, the conversation has a hyped-up, almost farcical ring.

Lacking a unifying vision of "The Cherry Orchard," Mr. Yankee has elicited performances that seem unsynchronized and in which frantic physicality and self-conscious grimacing substitute for a deeper revelation of character. The most glaring of many bad performances is David Canary as Ranevskaya's sentimental and ineffectual brother, Gayev.

Paul Hecht's mumbling portrayal of Lopakhin is so self-effacing that the role of the ferocious entrepreneur who buys out the aristocrats almost disappears from the drama. Penny Fuller's one-dimensional Ranevskaya is a vain, dithering fool whose dreaminess seems more eccentric than poetic. When called upon to simulate tears, her emoting is transparently false. But then this is a production in which all the characters' outbursts seem dry-eyed, both literally and in their lack of conviction.

1990 My 24, C19:3

Forever Plaid

Written, directed and staged by Stuart Ross; musical continuity, arrangements and musical direction, James Raitt; scenery, Neil Peter Jampolis; lighting, Jane Reisman; costumes, Debra Stein; assistant director, Larry Raben. Presented by Gene Wolsk, in association with Steven Suskin. At Steve McGraw's, 158 West 72d Street.

WITH: Stan Chandler, David Engel, Jason Graae and Guy Stroman.

By STEPHEN HOLDEN

When the Plaids, a mythical 1950's male quartet from eastern Pennsylvania, perform a piece of vintage kitsch like "Three Coins in the Fountain," they don't merely sing it in smooth four-part harmonies that echo the Four Aces; they physically illustrate the lyrics with a painstaking literalness. A line like "See the ripples,how they shine" is accompanied by hilariously synchronized arm wrigglings meant to simulate little wavelets.

This is just the sort of thing that squeaky-clean harmony groups of the 1950's like the Four Lads, the Crew Cuts, the Four Aces and the Ames Brothers actually used to do in their performances. But the Plaids exaggerate it just enough to make it all seem as playfully surreal as their own fateful biography.

That biography begins in the opening moments of their show, "Forever Plaid," at Steve McGraw's, when the quartet, carrying candles and looking lost and frightened, stumbles into the club, literally from out of the past. It seems that a time warp and a hole in the ozone layer have combined to catapult them 26 years into the future from the moment on Feb. 9, 1964, when they died in a collision with a bus full of parochial-school girls on their way to see the Beatles on "The Ed Sullivan Show."

"Forever Plaid," which was written directed and choreographed by Stuart Ross, has had previous lives, in regional theater and as a cabaret revue, but this is the first time it has been an Off Broadway show. Expanded and rewritten from its cabaret version, which opened last year at the same club, it is a thoroughly amusing, lightheaded spoof of the more insipid side of 50's pop culture.

Over the course of the evening, the group, which sports matching plaid cummerbunds and bow ties, fantasizes the musical career it might have enjoyed had it not been cut short. Among many funny bits, the group offers its version of the Beatles' "She Loves You" (in which "yeah, yeah, yeah" becomes "yes siree, Bob") and tell the story of "the golden cardigan," the sweater that Perry Como left behind after he was stranded in their hometown. The cardigan has become an icon to which the Plaids croon letter-perfect renditions of the Como hits "Papa Loves Mambo" and "Catch a Falling Star."

Donning sombreros and playing bongos and maracas, the Plaids also "go calypso," leading the audience through a sing-along of "Matilida, Matilda," under Christmas-tree lighting augmented with bunches of illuminated bananas. The show reaches a pinnacle of goofiness with the group's three-minute capsule version of "The Ed Sullivan Show." In that time, the Plaids become jugglers, fire-eaters, folk dancers, plate-

spinners and Judy Garland, all while "Lady of Spain" is played on an accordion.

Underneath its mockery of 50's squareness, "Forever Plaid" oozes nostalgia for the decade of the button-down mind and affection for its ultra-sanitized pop. Stan Chandler, David Engle, Jason Graae and Guy Stroman, the singers who portray the Plaids, have refined a harmonic blend that is as tonally precise and dynamically controlled as that of any of their 50's antecedents.

While James Raitt's arrangements do not exactly duplicate those of the original hit records, they offer a skillful pastiche of a style that the Plaids explain they developed at the Osterizer School of Harmonic Theory. It was there that they learned the four basic modes of vocal harmony: blend, puree, mix and chop. This sweet, funny little revue shows them to be more than adept at all four functions.

1990 My 25, C3:1

What a Man Weighs

By Sherry Kramer; directed by Carole Rothman; set design by Andrew Jackness; lighting by Dennis Parichy; costumes by Susan Hilferty; sound by Gary and Timmy Harris; hair by Antonio Soddu; production stage manager, Pamela Edington; stage manager, Lori Lundquist. Presented by Second Stage Theater, Robyn Goodman and Ms. Rothman, artistic directors. At 2162 Broadway, at 76th Street.

Joan	Christine Estabrook
Ruth	Harriet Harris
The Debbie	Katherine Hiler
Haseltine	Richard Cox

By MEL GUSSOW

The characters in Sherry Kramer's "What a Man Weighs" are employees in a book conservation laboratory devoted to insuring the continuing life of words in print. The playwright provides the audience with intriguing details of this profession, raising questions that apply to art as well as literature. She describes, for example, how the pursuit of perfect restoration can lead to forgery. But books and the conservation of books are not the principal subjects of her play at Second Stage.

Unfortunately, Ms. Kramer is far more interested in the ardor of a

young woman (Christine Estabrook) for a compulsive womanizer (Richard Cox), the head of the university laboratory in which she works. The author makes some pithy observations ("The first thing a woman says after an accident is, 'Where's my purse?' "). But often, flippancy substitutes for wit. There is also a serious question about the heroine's undervaluing of herself. It is impossible to understand what she sees in the book restorer, who is untrustworthy in love (and possibly in his occupation). In the relationship between Ms. Estabrook and Mr. Cox, "What a Man Weighs" is perilously close to television comedy.

There are indications that Ms. Kramer intended to integrate the bookbinding background and the romantic foreground beyond the fact that the characters work in the same lab. She may have wanted to make a statement about the permanence of literature, in contrast to the impermanence of relationships. But metaphorical matters are subordinated to the brittle surface where almost every statement is a retort.

In one sequence, Mr. Cox re-enacts a typical seduction, explaining to Ms. Estabrook the step-by-step intricacies of each of his romantic maneuvers. The object of his siege is a nubile student, the kind of woman he generically characterizes as "a Debbie." Ms. Estabrook is fascinated by his conquest, but as a sophisticated woman, she is at least one step ahead of him — as is the audience. She has his number but refuses to assert herself, preferring to be demeaned into Debbie-hood. It is astonishing to think that women today

Second Stage

Heavy Duty "What a Man Weighs," Sherry Kramer's ruminations on sexual politics in the 90's and its effect on three university workers.

could fall for Mr. Cox's obvious line. All supposed Debbies might rise in protest.

Working within an awkward set by Andrew Jackness (the laboratory turns into Ms. Estabrook's apartment), Carole Rothman has drawn deft performances from her cast, especially in the case of Ms. Estabrook. Her deadpan delivery enhances her character, the only fully developed one in the play. Mr. Cox is

suitably pompous as the smug conservator, Harriet Harris adds flavor to her underwritten role as Ms. Estabrook's lab-mate and Katherine Hiler is amusing as various Debbies who move with rapidity through the revolving door of Mr. Cox's romantic life.

In a final twist, Ms. Kramer asks the audience to believe that the cad really has a heart. That scene is not convincing, and it is a sign of a wider dramatic problem in a play in which the author expresses mixed emotions about her allegiance to her heroine.

1990 My 25, C3:2

Happy End

Gerry Goodstein

Molly Hickok and Steve Cross of the Irondale Ensemble Project performing in "Happy End" at the House of Candles Theater.

Lyrics by Bertolt Brecht; music by Kurt Weill; original German play by Dorothy Lane; translated and adapted by Michael Feingold; directed by James Niesen. A collaboration of the Irondale Ensemble Project. At the House of Candles Theater, 99 Stanton Street, one block below Houston Street.

WITH: Mr. Niesen, Josh Broder, Annie-B Parson, Paul Lazar, Steve Osgood, Steve Cross, Montana Lattin, Terry Greiss, Hilarie Blumenthal, Ken Rothchild, Barbara Mackenzie-Wood, Jody Reiss, Nicole Potter, Gerry Goodstein, Molly Hickok, Elena Pelliciaro, Michael Cain and Ann Delaney. Associates: Carrie Owerko, Janet O'Hair and Umit Celebi.

By STEPHEN HOLDEN

The House of Candles Theater, the ramshackle storefront site on the Lower East Side of Manhattan where the Irondale Ensemble Project is performing the 1929 Brecht-Weill show, "Happy End," is an appropriately atmospheric space in which to stage the team's followup to "Three Penny Opera."

"Happy End," whose setting alternates between Bill's Beer Hall, a gangster's hangout in old Chicago, and a nearby Salvation Army mission, is a knockabout street musical that revels in seediness. And as staged by the Irondale Ensemble Project, a seven-year-old experimental company of youthful actors and technicians, it erupts with the freewheeling energy of a rough-and-tumble vaudeville show. The audience, seated at the rear of the theater on elevated platforms under which members of the orchestra are tucked, looks down on the action that the director James Niesen has staged as a sort of Keystone Cops comedy with singing and dancing.

Unlike many other Irondale productions, "Happy End" is not wildly iconoclastic. One recent Irondale show, "Peter Panic," fused "Peter Pan" with the story of the late Abbie Hoffman's life as a fugitive. Another, "Outside the Law," blended Shakespeare's "As You Like It" with the

Gene Wolsk

From left, David Engle, Guy Stroman, Stan Chandler and Jason Graae in "Forever Plaid," at Steve McGraw's.

legend of the 1930's outlaw Pretty Boy Floyd. This show attempts no such juxtapositions. It is a straightforward, fast-paced production that uses the original orchestrations for keyboard, percussion, banjo and brass that are the only arrangements officially sanctioned by the Kurt Weill Foundation. And they are very well played by the seven musicians from the Walter Thompson Orchestra.

•

"Happy End," whose story has strong resemblances to "Guys and Dolls," is a spirited fable of crime and redemption that becomes so relentlessly upbeat that its high spirits become facetiously ironic. While the show lacks the dramatic richness of "Three Penny Opera," its score includes several classic Brecht-Weill numbers, including "The Bilbao Song," "The Sailor's Tango" and "Surabaya Johnny." And in the musical numbers, especially the stirringly sung choral ensemble pieces, the production surges with adrenaline.

The rest of the time the Irondale troupe plays "Happy End" as a lighthearted old-time movie spoof. In several sequences, including a bank robbery, the actors adopt the jerky, accelerated body language of silent movies.

The lead performances har'; back to vintage movie archetypes. Montana Lattin as the Fly, the homicidal gang leader, slinks about the stage like a classic silent screen vamp, fingering a blood-red cigarette holder. Paul Lazar, who portrays the unsavory gangster known as the Governor, imbues his character with a Peter Lorre-like creepiness.

Steve Cross, who plays the show's strapping antihero, Bill Cracker, and Molly Hickok, as Lillian Holiday, the woman who would redeem him, also suggest wholesome all-American Hollywood types from the 30's. Their strong singing voices match their images in a production whose effervescence almost makes up for its many unpolished edges.

1990 My 26, 11:1

Spanish Eyes

By Eduardo Iván López; translated by Graciela Lecube; directed by Roger Franklin; sets, Robert Klingelhoefer; lighting, Bill Simmons; costumes, Mary Marsicano; sound designer, Héctor Milia; producer, Miriam Colón Valle. Presented by the Puerto Rican Traveling Theater, with major support from the Adolph Coors Company. At 304 West 47th Street.

Esteban Salazar	Eddie Andino
Young Esteban	Jimmy Borbón
Abuelo	Edouard de Soto
Myra	Alexandra Reichler
Francisco/Foreman/Priest/Mr. Sleazak/ Doctor/André Ramírez	Christofer de Oni

By D. J. R. BRUCKNER

After seeing Eduardo Iván López's "Spanish Eyes" at the Puerto Rican Traveling Theater, an audience could conclude that love and loyalty, if they are virtues at all, are very dangerous ones. The play has some laughs and a few poignant moments, but it is emotionally exhausting and more than a little bewildering.

It is the story of an orphaned Puerto Rican boy who is rescued from indifferent, even hostile, relatives by his eccentric abuelo (grandfather), who brings him to New York City in the belief that he will have a

better life on the mainland than he would at home.

•

And he probably has. Once he grows up and learns that success in America is a bit of a con game, this grandson marries a beautiful woman,

A grandfather refuses to assimilate, and ruins a marriage.

sets himself up in the construction business, and quickly moves up and out into the suburbs. But the grandfather, who remains stubbornly isolated from the language and culture of his new country, moves along with the young couple and virtually destroys their marriage.

Mr. López peppers his play with funny stories told by the old man about his family in Puerto Rico, comic scenes of frustrated passion between the young man and his wife, and a couple of hilarious confrontations between this odd family and unsuspecting outsiders. And he writes moving lines in which the young man expresses his gratitude and devotion to his grandfather, and his frustration with the material comfort and spiritual emptiness of modern life.

•

But after a while these things seem mere distractions in what is essentially a painful story. The bond between the old man and his grandson may be noble to them, but the young man's wife becomes its victim — and at the end the audience is left feeling that she is an unpitied one.

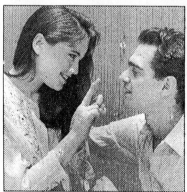

The Puerto Rican Traveling Theater
Tough Town Alexandra Reichler and Eddie Andino star in "Spanish Eyes," a drama by Eduardo Iván López about love and assimilation in New York City.

It would be impossible to impose dramatic unity on this piece, but the director, Roger Franklin, and the cast do what they can. In a brief appearance as the grandson in childhood, Jimmy Borbón is a very confident boy indeed: he does not simply occupy the stage; he owns it. Alexandra Reichler as the young wife, Myra, exposes her character's pain effectively, but the few chances she is given at humorous exchanges suggest that her real talent lies in comedy. Eddie Andino as Esteban, her husband, has to play two roles: straight man in comic encounters with both Myra and the grandfather,

and suffering man as he confronts the failure of his marriage and his dreams. He never fuses the two into one character, but maybe no one could.

Edouard de Soto, a character actor for stage, film and television for many years, makes the grandfather an engaging old mischief-maker who seems utterly unaware of the havoc he creates. And Christofer de Oni, who has a keen eye for absurdity, is greatly amusing in several roles, especially as a beer-drinking blue-collar suburbanite and as a fussy and very nervous Cuban barber.

1990 My 27, 56:3

Is He Still Dead?

Directed by Charles Nelson Reilly; written by Donald Freed; set design, Marjorie Bradley Kellogg; costume design, Noel Taylor; lighting, Marc B. Weiss; music, David Fox; sound, Brent Evans; production stage manager, Anne Keefe. Presented by Long Wharf Theater, Arvin Brown, artistic director; M. Edgar Rosenblum, executive director. At the Long Wharf Theater, New Haven.

Nora Joyce	Julie Harris
James Joyce	Ronny Graham

By MEL GUSSOW

Special to The New York Times

NEW HAVEN, May 18 — Nora Barnacle Joyce, the wife of James Joyce, has gradually grown in critical esteem. In Brenda Maddox's authoritative 1988 biography, "Nora," she is depicted as a person of considerable distinction and importance in her husband's life and art. Not only was she the inspiration for Molly Bloom; her voice, as the voice of Irish women, resonates throughout Joyce's work.

Donald Freed's new play about Nora and James Joyce, "Is He Still Dead?" (at the Long Wharf Theater), is misguided in all respects, impeding one's understanding of the couple. This is in contrast to Mr. Freed's "Secret Honor," a one-man play about Richard M. Nixon. Perhaps the playwright is simply on firmer ground dealing with political figures rather than literary ones. In any case, he has nothing of interest to say about either Joyce.

This is in spite of the fact that Julie Harris and Ronny Graham, as directed by Charles Nelson Reilly, offer reasonable facsimiles of the couple. Ms. Harris has a proven talent for incarnating historical characters (Emily Dickinson and Charlotte Brontë). Mr. Graham, the evening's single surprise, bears a fleeting resemblance to Joyce, and in common with his co-star has a certain Irish authenticity. But the actors' readiness is all there is. They would have been better advised to do a reading from Joyce's novels or letters.

•

For the purposes of this two-character play, Mr. Freed focuses on the couple in late 1940. They are living in a hotel near Vichy, France, while waiting for their visas so they can leave for safety in Switzerland. This was a particularly crucial period in their lives. Their schizophrenic daughter was confined in a sanitarium. They had abandoned many of their possessions in Paris. "Finnegans Wake," which was to be Joyce's last novel, had been published the previous year and he had not begun another project. As it turned out, Joyce had barely a month to live. He was to die in Zurich after an operation for his ulcers.

Instead of treating these and other events insightfully or creating a kaleidoscopic portrait flashing back to earlier days, Mr. Freed has written an attenuated short play about people marking time. Dialogue is sparse, and pauses are prolonged. The two sing Irish songs and talk interminably about food. The second act begins at a crawl, with Mr. Graham padding around the room and shouting at airplanes flying overhead.

The dialogue is an unsettling amalgam of Mr. Freed and borrowed Joyce (Nora as well as James), with lines taken out of context, including Nora's remark that "This place is not fit to wash a rat in." Jarringly, Joyce paraphrases the famous comment referring to his first sexual encounter with Nora in Dublin, "And you'd make a man of me."

•

The least is yet to come, and that is with the uses Mr. Freed makes of Samuel Beckett, a friend of the couple and one of their visitors in Vichy. Under the misapprehension that the

Stephen Castagneto for The New York Times
Ronny Graham and Julie Harris at a rehearsal of Donald Freed's "Is He Still Dead?" at the Long Wharf Theater in New Haven.

Joyces were models for Beckett's Gogo and Didi, he suddenly has them indulging in an insult contest (as in "Waiting for Godot"), culminating with Nora's epithet, "Pornographer!", and Joyce's countercharge, "Critic!" Perhaps Mr. Freed wants the audience to believe that Beckett is hiding in the closet taking notes and cribbing dialogue for his own play in progress.

The title of Mr. Freed's play, "Is He Still Dead?," is the punch line of a joke, which becomes an endless running gag. After watching this woeful attempt at biographical drama, one may well ask the title question in reference to James Joyce. The answer is yes, but his bones are rattling.

1990 My 27, 58:1

A Chorus Line Plus,
in the Leningrad Tradition

By ANNA KISSELGOFF

The music-hall tradition has died out in this country, supplanted by television specials. But with the best dog act in decades, creative aerialists and acrobat-contortionists, a brilliant Michael Jackson impersonator-cum-juggler and its one-sketch comedians, the Leningrad State Music Hall declares that there is still room for a be-plumed chorus line and the old variety show.

The Soviet production, which made its United States debut on Saturday night for a run through Sunday at the City Center (131 West 55th Street), is a family show. The performers, it is true, are uneven, and the ragged glitz in the production values bespeaks a provincialism that goes with the music-hall territory of today. For another example, see the Folies-Bergère in Paris.

Leningrad's long-legged beauties bare less flesh than those in the City of Light, but they constantly change into scanty costumes with veils and folk motifs that transform them into everything from peacocks to hussars. Their choreographer is Igor Belsky, who was the artistic director of the Kirov Ballet from 1973 to 1977, and he is at his best in a revue-style gypsy number.

A precision line with Rockette-style discipline may not fit preconceptions about Soviet entertainment in the past. Yet this program itself testifies to how much has changed: one vocalist sings in Yiddish, and many of the dancers, as well as a lead singer, openly wear crosses on gold chains around their necks.

Founded in 1967 by its director, Ilya Rakhlin, the Leningrad State Music Hall is as good as its specific programs. The best numbers in this one cut across language barriers.

In "Butterfly and Flower," Tatyana Korolyova and Albert Rogatsky are the invisible manipulators of a Day-Glo butterfly and flower. Their little drama in the "black theater" style of Czechoslovakia is technically perfect, with a moral of mutual help; when the wind-blown flower is reduced to a petal, the butterfly flies in the pollen for a botanic rebirth.

A spectacular number comes from Galina Mikhalevich and Dmitri Kostylyov in "Oriental Legend." He is a strongman, carrying a round sack above his head; she, a fabulous contortionist, is a serpent in a green leotard. George Balanchine, who worked in Leningrad variety shows before 1925, would recognize the creature who holds her own ankles and forms a coil around her partner. (Balanchine

put her in his "Prodigal Son.") The sack, the audience finally realizes, contained the doubled-up form of the "snake."

No illusions are left. This current state of mind in the Soviet Union is metaphorically embodied in the program. The comedy team of Yevgeny Shpitko and Yevgenya Vlasova offers the image of the illusionist exposed when the woman reveals how a magician's trick is no trick at all.

Along these lines, Shamkhal Abakarov's tightrope act is all act. And Igor Zheltkov, a small, wiry man with amazing coordination, never hides his quick-change artistry. As he doffs different disguises on stage, his hat tricks and accelerated ball-juggling make way for witty impersonations. His twitching and moonwalking Michael Jackson captures the essence of kinetic nuance.

There are two breathtaking acts in which secrets are not revealed. Olga and Irina Lobanov are fine aerialists caught with heart-stopping suddenness by Anatoly Yarosh. Natalya Peretyatko and Aleksandr Kozlovsky are superbly creative acrobats; repeatedly they mold themselves into an assemblage of overlapping forms or a Rodinesque embrace.

What is there to say about Mikhail Gubanov, unicyclist and dog trainer, except that his long-haired, tail-wagging partner is adorable as it tries to share an umbrella and then brings along a friend with a parasol of its own?

Among the singers, Anatoly Tukish has an annoying manner, both hoarse and breathy, but Galina Kuznetsova, singing in Ukrainian, Yiddish and Russian, has a refined folk style that many will find familiar.

1990 My 28, 11:1

German Requiem

Directed by Judith Malina; written by Eric Bentley; music by Patrick Grant; set by Ilion Troya; lighting by Joseph Errante; costumes by Bénédicte Leclerc; assistant director, Rob Press; stage manager, Andrea Malloy; combat choreography, Erica Bilder, technical director, Henry Freeman; executive producer, Hanon Reznikov. Presented by the Living Theater, 272 East Third Street.

Count Rupert .... Tom Walker
Eunice .... Amber
Otto .... Gary Brackett
Johann .... Philip Brehse
Aldo and Fintenring .... Alan Arenius
Santing .... Henry Freeman
Klaus .... Thomas Hinckley
Count Sylvius .... Bob Paton
Count Sylvester .... Robert Projansky
Gertrude .... Laura Kolb
Agnes .... Pat Russel

By WILBORN HAMPTON

Familial quarrels, especially those incited by greed, sometimes degenerate into bloodletting, and in "German Requiem," Eric Bentley's new play at the Living Theater, they may even portend the end of the world.

Inspired by Heinrich von Kleist's first known work, "Die Familie Schroffenstein," Mr. Bentley's play is actually more parable than drama, a sort of medieval fairy tale, complete with a moral at the end, intended as a sort of modern-day ethical and political lesson.

At the outset, the Rosset branch of the Schroffenstein family is burying Count Rupert's youngest son, a boy they have cause to believe was killed by agents of the Varvand branch of the family, arch rivals who live on the other side of a mountain. At the root of this suspicion is an ancient legacy stipulating that if one branch of the family dies out, the surviving branch gets it all — both castles and the mountain in between.

Count Rupert of Rosset forces his eldest son, Otto, to swear revenge on the Varvands by killing Agnes, the beautiful young daughter of Count Sylvester. An heir for an heir. But Otto, of course, duly falls in love with Agnes. Each side has its own contingent of vassals and there is an out-of-town cousin who may or may not be double-crossing the Rossets and Varvands. Allegiances among the Schroffensteins are ambiguous at best. It all gets rather complicated.

There is an awful lot of simple misunderstanding to fuel this family feud. Protestations of love are mistaken for attempted rape, and a suicide threat is misconstrued as attempted murder. As with so many plays condemning violence, there is no shortage of butchery and mayhem — a beheading, a stoning and several sword fights. Yet there are no real surprises, and the play has the sound of a somewhat simplistic sermon delivered mostly for the benefit of the converted.

"German Requiem" does not have here the benefit of a polished production. The acting is rarely up to classroom level, and any humor in Mr. Bentley's text is lost in the melodramatic performances. In Living Theater tradition, the action moves in and around the audience, resulting in some of its members ducking stones and dodging swords during a couple of murders. Judith Malina directed.

1990 My 28, 14:5

Elbers Johan for The New York Times

Dancers from the Leningrad State Music Hall at City Center, where they are performing through Sunday.

The Merry Wives of Windsor

By William Shakespeare; directed by Michael Kahn; set, Derek McLane; costumes, Catherine Zuber; lighting, John McLain; composer, Steven Rydberg; stage manager, James Latus; production manager, John W. Kingsbury. Presented by the Shakespeare Theater at the Folger, Mr. Kahn, artistic director; Mary Ann de Barbieri, managing director, in association with the University of South Carolina. At Washington.

Justice Shallow	Emery Battis
Abraham Slender	Matt Bradford Sullivan
Sir Hugh Evans	John Thomas Waite
Master Page	Francis Kane
Sir John Falstaff	Pat Carroll
Anne Page	Tonia Rowe
Mistress Page	Franchelle Stewart Dorn
Mistress Ford	Caitlin O'Connell
Host of the Garter Inn	Richard Dix
Mistress Quickly	Marilyn Sokol
Doctor Caius	Floyd King
Fenton	Michael MacCauley
Master Ford	Edward Gero

With: Hunter Boyle, Mark Douglas, Conrad Feininger, C. W. Hardy, Carter Jahncke, Drew Kahl, Jason Kravits, Lisa Ann Miller, Areesah Mobley, Edward Morgan, Natalie Simone, Margo West, Baakari Askia Wilder, Cornell Womack and Robert Zalkind

By FRANK RICH

Special to The New York Times

WASHINGTON, May 28 — Not even the metamorphosis of Robert Morse into Truman Capote can match that of the comic actress Pat Carroll into Sir John Falstaff for "The Merry Wives of Windsor." When Ms. Carroll makes her first entrance, a nervous silence falls over the audience at the Shakespeare Theater at the Folger here, as hundreds of eyes search for some trace of the woman they've seen in a thousand television reruns. What they find instead is a Falstaff who could have stepped out of a formal painted portrait: a balding, aged knight with scattered tufts of silver hair and whiskers, an enormous belly, pink cheeks and squinting, froggy eyes that peer out through boozy mists. The sight is so eerie you grab onto your seat.

Then comes the walk. The first business Ms. Carroll must carry out in Michael Kahn's staging of Shakespeare's comedy is the simple descent of a staircase. As the actress negotiates her bulk down the steps, waddling and gasping all the way, one realizes that it is Shakespeare's character, not a camp parody, that is being served. Here is a weary, cynical clown, out of resources and near death, a shadow in every way but girth of the witty royal sidekick of "Henry IV," Parts I and II. Legend has it that Shakespeare brought Falstaff back in "Merry Wives" at Queen Elizabeth's request. Whatever the truth, the obligatory Falstaff of this play is a pathetic buffoon, the butt of its most extravagant jokes. And that's the person, "a man of continual dissolution and thaw," that Ms. Carroll creates as she wheezes down those stairs: a hot-air balloon waiting to be burst, a pickled Humpty Dumpty riding for a fall.

The fall will come — the Falstaff of "Merry Wives" has "a kind of alacrity in sinking," whether into a laundry basket or the Thames — and Ms. Carroll will handle that, too, with the comic aplomb she has honed through a long career. Her performance is a triumph from start to finish, and, I think, a particularly brave and moving one, with implications that go beyond this one production. Ms. Carroll and Mr. Kahn help revivify the argument that the right actresses can perform some of the great classic roles

traditionally denied to women and make them their own. It's not a new argument, to be sure; female Hamlets stretch back into history. But what separates Ms. Carroll's Falstaff from some other similar casting experiments of late is that her performance exists to investigate a character rather than merely as ideological window dressing for a gimmicky production.

As it happens, Mr. Kahn's production, though not gimmicky, leaves much to be desired itself. Ms. Carroll aside, his "Merry Wives" simply isn't as funny as it has to be. Unlike "Twelfth Night," which Mr. Kahn staged so buoyantly with Kelly McGillis to open the Folger season, this Shakespeare text is not bolstered by feeling, ideas and poetry. Everything rides on a series of farcical pranks in which Falstaff and some lesser fools are humiliated as they attempt to seduce either the merry wives Page and Ford or the Page daughter, Anne. In the funniest "Merry Wives" I've seen, directed by Bill Alexander for the Royal Shakespeare Company in 1986, the setting was advanced to prosperous 1950's suburbia, and no wonder: the pratfalls of this play are a perfect stylistic fit with the "Carry On" movies and "I Love Lucy."

Mr. Kahn knows this. Though he keeps the setting firmly Elizabethan, his staging is as knockabout, and as mindful of the bourgeois complacency of the Windsor community, as was Mr. Alexander's. It's the execution, not the interpretation, that fails: Mr. Kahn's Windsor isn't populated by natural clowns but by straining actors simulating clowning with stock vocal and facial exaggerations, augmented by jokey props (a skeleton, a breakaway hat). The more energetic performers, led by Marilyn Sokol (Mistress Quickly), Edward Gero (Master Ford) and Floyd King (Doctor Caius), generally offer three broad gestures when a single sharp one would do, while the others, with the exceptions of Franchelle Stewart Dorn (Mistress Page) and Emery Battis (Justice Shallow), are too bland to register at all.

Perhaps the director put most of his energy into his collaboration with

The Shakespeare Theater

Pat Carroll as Falstaff in "The Merry Wives of Windsor."

his star, and, for once, that may be achievement enough. Falstaff is played so convincingly as a man (yet without any phony lowering of the actress's voice) that he still seems masculine when the plot requires him to adopt the drag outfit of a witch. Ms. Carroll's unambiguous manliness is appropriate, because "Merry Wives," in contrast to "Twelfth Night" or "As You Like It," does not take sexual identity as a subject. Falstaff's designs on the Mistresses Page and Ford have mainly to do with money, not flesh.

●

But Ms. Carroll invests her performance with an extra dimension anyway. The success of her male camouflage makes the decrepit knight's isolation from the conventional folk of Windsor seem doubly pronounced. When this Falstaff receives his final comeuppance, in the Act V forest masquerade that requires him to don a deer's head and be "made an ass," the ridicule he suffers carries an unusually cruel aftertaste.

As befits a comedy, of course, the knight is soon forgiven for his misdeeds and is invited to join the townfolk to "laugh this sport o'er by a country fire." But not before Ms. Carroll, still cowering in antlers, has stood alone and abandoned at the forest's shadowy edge, her eyes revealing just how lonely and humiliating it has been for her particular Falstaff to be dismissed as a freak. And not before the audience has seen a fearless comic actress hit a tragic note that promises to extend her Shakespearean range even further than this remarkable embodiment of the opposite sex.

1990 My 30, C13:1

A Quiet End

By Robin Swados; directed by Tony Giordano; scenery by Philipp Jung; costumes by David Murin; lighting by Dennis Parichy; sound by Tony Meola; production stage manager, Alan Fox; general manager, Joseph Piazza; original music composed and performed by Mr. Swados. Presented by Theater Off Park, Albert Harris, artistic director. At 224 Waverly Place, one block west of Seventh Avenue.

Max	Lonny Price
Tony	Philip Coccioletti
Billy	Jordan Mott
Doctor	Paul Milikin
Jason	Rob Gomes

By STEPHEN HOLDEN

"A Quiet End," Robin Swados's drama of three gay men suffering through the final stages of AIDS, is suffused with an anguished tenderness toward its characters. Unlike other recent plays dealing with the impact of AIDS on homosexual life in New York, it eschews the history and politics of the epidemic to explore at some depth the inner lives of desperately ill men from varying backgrounds. Impending death forces men — two are Catholic and one is Jewish — to confront their fears and to grapple with the meaning of existence.

Max (Lonny Price), Tony (Philip Coccioletti) and Billy (Jordan Mott)

Martha Swope/Theater Off Park

Lonny Price

share an apartment on Manhattan's Upper West Side as part of a hospice program that provides shelter and psychological counseling for the terminally ill. Max, the most vivid and complicated of the three, is a hyperkinetic bundle of neuroses with low self-esteem and a very short fuse. Tony is a failed actor and sexual athlete obsessed with the idea of himself as a sexual murderer. Billy, an innocent who only recently arrived in Manhattan from the heartland, longs to go home to his religious family but fears their rejection.

●

For a play that deals with life and death, "A Quiet End," directed by Tony Giordano at the Theater Off Park, is surprisingly low-key. Most of the characters' revelations occur in interior monologues in which the stage suddenly goes dark and each man remembers an interview with the program's psychiatrist (Paul Milikin), a character who is heard but not seen.

The only real fighter among the three is Max, who combats his terror with an unending stream of sarcasm and hysterical sniping. In Mr. Price's virtuosic portrayal, the character seems to survive through sheer force of will and a mental energy that carries him forward a mile a minute, even in his physically weakened state. And by infusing the character's shtick with a sharp, self-knowing humor, he makes him sympathetic. The main action of the play occurs when his sometime lover, Jason (Bob Gomes), arrives unexpectedly at the apartment, and Max realizes that if he acts out his self-loathing instincts one more time, he will lose his last chance at a kind of salvation.

●

Although the production has its touching moments, its power is severely diminished by directorial timidity. All three major characters are in the terminal stages of illness, yet their extreme physical condition is acknowledged only by token signs of distress. And the production's inability to deliver even a semblance of medical versimilitude renders absurd the notion that the three men share an apartment because they can no longer cope by themselves. The worst symptoms exhibited suggest that one of the three has a mild case of bronchitis and the other two the sniffles. The second act includes a preposterously perfunctory death scene that comes almost out of the blue and is over in five minutes.

It's a shame that a drama that ought to grab one by the throat has been staged as mild-mannered, almost soothing AIDS soap opera.

1990 My 31, C16:6

Kiss of the Spider Woman

Book by Terrence McNally; music by John Kander; lyrics by Fred Ebb; directed by Harold Prince; choreography by Susan Stroman; based on the novel by Manuel Puig; scenic design, Thomas Lynch; costumes, Florence Klotz; lighting, Peter A. Kaczorowski; sound, Alan Stieb; hair and makeup, Robert DiNiro; musical director and conductor, Donald Chan; orchestrations, Michael Gibson; dance arangements, David Krane; production stage manager, Beverley Randolph; assistant to Mr. Prince, Ruth Mitchell; musical coordinator, John Monaco. Presented by New Musicals, in association with the Performing Arts Center of the State Univesity College at Purchase, N.Y.

Valentin	Kevin Gray
Warden	Harry Goz
Molina	John Rubinstein
Aurora	Lauren Mitchell
Señora Molina	Barbara Andres
Armando	Donn Simione

With: Jonathan Brody, Bill Christopher-Myers, Karen Giombetti, Ruth Gottschall, Harry Goz, Philip Hernandez, Dorie Herndon, David Koch, Rick Manning, Carl Maultsby, Lauren Mufson, Casey Nicholaw, Aurelio Padron, Forest Dino Ray, Lorraine Serabian, John Norman Thomas, Wendy Waring, Matt Zarley and Greg Zerkle.

By FRANK RICH

Special to The New York Times

PURCHASE, N.Y., May 29 — Almost 25 years ago, the director Harold Prince pushed Broadway a significant step forward with "Cabaret," a show that folded Brechtian storytelling, abstract theatrical metaphors and the history of Nazism into the sophisticated glitter of a mainstream Broadway musical. In "Kiss of the Spider Woman," his first musical since "Phantom of the Opera," Mr. Prince reunites with John Kander and Fred Ebb, the composer and lyricist of "Cabaret," with far more radical ideas in mind.

"Spider Woman," an adaptation of the 1978 Manuel Puig novel that also inspired the 1985 film with William Hurt and Raul Julia, is the first large-scale American musical told from an unapologetic and unsentimental gay point of view. In Terrence McNally's script, the entire narrative is seen through the eyes of Molina (John Rubinstein), a homosexual window dresser incarcerated in a Latin American prison, while the perspective of his cellmate, a political prisoner named Valentin (Kevin Gray), is reduced to the barest essentials. "Spider Woman" isn't shy about taking chances. It depicts torture with the grueling ferocity missing from

Mr. Prince's "Evita," has a morphine-fueled dream sequence of dancing hypodermic needles and simulates an involuntary act of defecation. The evening culminates with the image of its title, a blood-spattering kiss of death.

The show is the first offering of New Musicals, a production company that has announced a season of four new American musicals at the State University College here. New Musicals informed the press that its attractions are works in progress and asked that drama critics not review them. "Spider Woman," however, is presented to the audience as a full-dress commercial production rather than a workshop.

If anything, the tragedy of "Spider Woman" is that New Musicals, which describes itself as a "new Broadway" in its promotional literature, has not allowed the work to develop slowly in a laboratory staging, as nonprofit, Off Broadway companies have helped develop adventurous musicals like "A Chorus Line" or "Sunday in the Park With George." Instead, "Spider Woman" arrives already burdened with the full, and in this case crushing, weight of Broadway extravagance. It is as overproduced as other seriously intentioned Prince musicals of the past decade like "Grind" and "A Doll's Life." But unlike those failures, "Spider Woman" has the kernel of an exciting idea, and it also has, in Mr. Kander and Mr. Ebb, superb, if often underrated, songwriters who are clearly hungering to rise to a challenge.

The show's potential virtues are being held hostage by a staging so overgrown that major esthetic reconsiderations, as opposed to cosmetic nips and tucks, are already foreclosed in this production. Though the musical's story is fundamentally an intimate one about two people — men of opposite sensibilities who teach each other about self-respect and self-sacrifice while in captivity — it is often difficult to find Molina and Valentin within the bloated trappings. As in its other incarnations, this "Spider Woman" intersperses its grim prison scenes with Molina's campy recounting of an old, fondly embroidered Hollywood movie that is his imaginary escape from present despair. But in this case, the fantasy film — here fittingly changed to an old movie musical — overwhelms the reality so completely that the compelling story of Molina and Valentin seems a mild, often incoherent intrusion.

•

Part of the problem may be endemic to Prince musicals that follow the "Cabaret" format of alternating realistic scenes with show-biz production numbers that comment thematically upon them. As recent revivals of "Cabaret" and "Follies" have demonstrated, those musicals' ironic cabaret and vaudeville turns hold up far better than the realistic scenes they are meant to annotate, and "Spider Woman" shares that shortcoming. Yet the new show has a graver defect: the lengthy movie-musical sequences of Molina's fantasies have only a nominal and repetitive relationship to his jail-cell reality. In contrast with the Joel Grey numbers in "Cabaret," the glitzy routines of "Spider Woman" detract from, rather than enhance, the work's dramatization of fascist repression.

Though Mr. Kander and Mr. Ebb have written some typically amusing parodies for their movie musical,

Martha Swope/"Kiss of the Spider Woman"

John Rubinstein, left, and Kevin Gray in "Kiss of the Spider Woman," at the Performing Arts Center in Purchase, N.Y.

even their better numbers are defeated by the routine choreography of Susan Stroman and by the performance of Lauren Mitchell as the star of Molina's celluloid visions. What is needed in this role is not, perhaps, a mysterious reincarnation of Rita Hayworth (which is what Sonia Braga brought to the film version) but a dazzling musical-comedy presence of the Chita Rivera sort who has always ignited the flashiest Kander-Ebb songs. Ms. Mitchell has neither the personality nor the vocal authority for the task.

The casting of Molina and Valentin is even more damaging. The window dresser now sounds remarkably like the opera fanatic played by Nathan Lane in Mr. McNally's "Lisbon Traviata," and Mr. Rubinstein, not a natural comedian, pushes himself so hard that he crosses the line into retrograde gay caricature. Worse, his singing range is now so narrow that he cannot be given the big emotional arias that his character must have, and that Mr. Kander and Mr. Ebb are prepared to write, as they demonstrate in a haunting early quartet. Without those songs, Molina becomes an outsider in his own story. While Mr. Gray's Valentin has a stronger voice, his character remains, in writing and performance, too vague to fill the vacuum, a poster-flat radical who looks like Che in "Evita" and sings an anthem, "The Day After That," as generic as "One Day More" in "Les Misérables."

By evening's end, when Molina and Valentin are supposed to be achieving a redemptive symbiosis, the male stars hardly seem to have met each other. Instead of concentrating on the performances crucial to this psycho-drama, Mr. Prince seems fixated on the big production numbers and scenic effects, as if he felt obligated to warp his show to placate Broadway audiences' presumed insistence on spectacle even when he is ostensibly working away from the commercial dictates of Broadway. And the spectacle falls short. The jailhouse choruses, though as grimly conceived as "Fidelio," still have an antiseptic musical-comedy sheen. Thomas Lynch's scenic design, an inversion of the Hollywood-versus-reality color scheme of Robin Wagner's sets for "City of Angels," is more busy than ingenious.

It's all frustrating because somewhere in "Kiss of the Spider Woman" is the compelling story its creators

want to tell, which is nothing less than an investigation of what it means to be a man, in the highest moral sense, whatever one's sexual orientation. That story begins with two men in a tiny room, and if the creators of "Kiss of the Spider Woman" are to retrieve the intimate heart of their show, they may have to rescue it from the voluminous web in which it has so wastefully become ensnared.

1990 Je 1, C3:1

Marathon 1990: Festival of New One-Act Plays, Series B

Hamlet, by Shel Silverstein; directed by Curt Dempster.

The Eclipse, by Joyce Carol Oates; directed by Mr. Dempster.

Eulogy for Mister Hamm, by Michael John LaChiusa, directed by Kirsten Sanderson; musical direction by David Loud.

The Stalwarts by Oyamo; directed by Jack Gelber. Set design, Mark Fitzgibbons; light design, Greg MacPherson; sound design, Aural Fixation; costume design, Lauren Press; production supervisor, Kent Hoffman; production stage manager, Sarah Pickett; unit set design, Linda Balmuth Giering. Presented by the Ensemble Studio Theater, Mr. Dempster, artistic director, Peter Shavitz, managing director. Kate Baggott, producer, Eric Berkal, associate producer. At 549 West 52d Street.

WITH: Pepe Douglas, Dean Irby, Vicki Lewis, Karen Looze, Heather Lupton, William Parry, Alice Playten, Madeleine Sherwood, Pamala Tyson and Melvin Van Peebles.

By MEL GUSSOW

In Shel Silverstein's hipster "Hamlet," Melvin Van Peebles rises from a front stoop and tells a loopy tale of royal Danish duplicity, replete with contemporary flourishes. Both the writer and the actor are in fine comic fettle, an antic disposition shared by Curt Dempster as director. Mr. Silverstein's Shakespearean rewrite is the curtain raiser of Evening B in the Ensemble Studio Theater's continuing "Marathon 1990" of one-act plays.

Somewhat in the manner of Mr. Silverstein's "Devil and Billy Markham," presented this season at Lincoln Center, this is a monologue in verse. It is a kind of street rap that imitates the rhythms of Robert Service and Clement Moore.

In the author's plot-twisting compression, the Ghost has a tattoo that says Gertrude Forever, Yorick's skull makes an appearance before Polonius is planted behind the arras, and Ophelia is much more of a designing woman. But the high points are in place as is a healthy share of contumely.

The most mirthful digression is Hamlet's instruction to the recalcitrant Players. The Player King has paid his dues (to Actors' Equity and otherwise). He is aghast at the suggestion that he re-enact a murder to an audience including the murderer, but accepts the assignment after the director meets all of his demands (billing above the title and seats for all his friends to the performances of the play within the play).

•

When moodiness strikes, Mr. Van Peebles (who plays all the roles) delivers a curve ball of a soliloquy, finding rhyme even if there is no reason and adding modern meaning to Hamlet's Oedipal complexity. Mr. Silverstein's version of "Hamlet" gets the Ensemble Studio evening off to a rousing start, matched by Michael John LaChiusa's "Eulogy for Mister Hamm," a delirious little chamber musical.

Mr. LaChiusa's show moves recitative to new depths of mundaneness, chronicling a moment in the lives of three single people waiting in line to use a bathroom in a New York tenement. Led by William Parry's quarrelsome bachelor, they sing self-mockingly about daily drudgeries and about the inept superintendent of their building (the Hamm of the title). Musical inventiveness and even a cloud-clearing coda come from such seemingly unpromising material.

Under Kirsten Sanderson's direction, Mr. Parry, Alice Playten and Karen Looze form a melodic trio. With this one act, the third part of a musical trilogy, Mr. LaChiusa erases one's memory of his score for "Buzzsaw Berkeley."

"The Eclipse," by Joyce Carol Oates, is a wounding series of vignettes about a woman's devotion to her aging, delusional mother. This devotion severely damages the daughter's assertion of self. Outside her home she is depicted as a feminist role model, but when she is with her mother she faces increasing helplessness and desperation.

The Ensemble Studio production sacrifices some intensity that the play had in its premiere in March at the Actors Theater of Louisville in Kentucky, but Madeleine Sherwood repeats her moving portrayal of the willful mother forcing herself more deeply into a dream world.

In "The Stalwarts," Oyamo slashes stereotypes of the black urban professional variety, as represented by a prosperous married couple trapped on a fast treadmill. This cartoon is too long and wordy, but it is filled with humorous touches in the dialogue, in the performances by Pamala Tyson and Dean Irby and in Mark Fitzgibbons's Pop Art set design. "The Stalwarts," directed by Jack Gelber, is an amusing bookend to an evening that begins with a streetwise "Hamlet."

1990 Je 1, C8:5

Hannah . . . 1939

Music, lyrics and book by Bob Merrill; directed by Douglas Aibel; choreography by Tina Paul; set design by G. W. Mercier; costumes by James Scott; lighting by Phil Monat; orchestrations by Bob Goldstone; production stage manager, Ira Mont; sound by Bruce Ellman. Presented by the Vineyard Theater, Mr. Aibel, artistic director, theater; Barbara Zinn Krieger, executive director; Jon Nakagawa, managing director. At 108 East 15th Street.

Hannah Schuler	Julie Wilson
Lieut. Kurt Wald	Tony Carlin
Commandant Baumann	Richard Thomsen
Janos	Yusef Bulos
Luba	Patti Perkins
Toby	Lori Wilner
Mina	Deirdre Lovejoy
Vera	Leah Hocking
Reuben	Allan Heinberg
Paulina	Mary Setrakian
Jules	Mark Ankeny
Esther	Neva Small
Leah	Nicolette Salas
Young Hannah	Kathleen Mahoney-Bennett
Gerte Baumann	Leigh Beery
German Soldiers	Paul Klementowicz and Kirk Lombard

By MEL GUSSOW

"Hannah ... 1939," the new Bob Merrill musical at the Vineyard Theater, takes place in Prague on the eve of World War II, but there is so much affability afoot that this could almost be the Budapest of "She Loves Me." In tone, the show should have been closer to "Cabaret." Though "Hannah" has its assets, beginning with Julie Wilson in the title role as a Jewish dress designer of international reputation, it is a soft-edged

---

Complex feelings of love for the oppressor delay a realization.

---

musical on a momentous subject.

A new manager, Kurt Wald, has been installed in Hannah Schuler's dress factory, and she has to put up with his unknowing but insistent ways. Gradually, with her encouragement, he loses his irascibility. But Kurt happens to be a German officer, and Hannah and her employees (all of them Jewish) are effectively his captives, sewing German uniforms instead of fancy dresses.

For too long, Hannah accommodates herself to the new regime, reprising a song about her fondness for Germans and pretending that Kurt could have been her son if her son had lived beyond infancy. An unconvincing equation is also made between the soldier and a sculptor Hannah loved in her youth (the actor Tony Carlin plays both roles).

•

All this romanticization fogs the main issues — the imminence of the Holocaust, Hannah's formidability and her growing sense of self-knowledge. For dramatic and musical purposes, Hannah's eventual heroic stand comes too late — and too suddenly — after she has easily succumbed to the favors of a rich German patron.

Despite that fact, the show holds the audience's interest, largely because of Miss Wilson, who makes Hannah a stylish embodiment of a fading European sensibility. With a Chanel-like self-assurance, she is sharp-tongued and aware of her talents as a negotiator. Miss Wilson captures seemingly contradictory

Carol Rosegg/Martha Swope Associates/"Hannah...1939"
Julie Wilson as Hannah Schuler in "Hannah . . . 1939."

aspects of this charismatic personality. Dressed in black, she exudes her own quiet elegance.

She acts and sings with authority, especially "Who is Hannah?," a self-questioning analysis that arrives at the end of the show. But some songs are unsupportive of the show's material (Mr. Merrill wrote the book as well as the music and lyrics). Several pretty tunes would seem more at home in such other Merrill shows as "Take Me Along" and "Carnival" than in this presumably harsher environment.

Occasionally the score veers toward Kurt Weill but quickly retreats to a more homogenized sound. The music is, however, several steps ahead of the lyrics, which can descend to banalities. In the second act, the composer begins to move forward, with the help of the director, Douglas Aibel, and the choreographer, Tina Paul, in a misty dance in which the factory workers evoke memories of a life left behind.

•

Though the setting is intended to be hermetic, there is little sense of a political context — a radio broadcast about the fall of Poland, occasional references to restricted zones of travel. The villainy of the Nazis remains on the outskirts. When realities are confronted, the result is unbelievably mild, as represented by the German commandant, whom his wife (Leigh Beery) refers to, in one of the show's more unfortunate though accurate lyrics, as "mush."

Ms. Beery, Neva Small, Yusef Bulos and others play peripheral roles to those of Miss Wilson and Mr. Carlin. Mr. Carlin is suitably rigid as the soldier, although, as with other characters on stage, there is no attempt to assume an accent. In awkward flashbacks, Kathleen Mahoney-Bennett plays Hannah as a young woman.

Mr. Aibel has given the show an elaborate production, one that could fill a Broadway stage — with a cast of 17, a seven-piece orchestra and, through the windows of G. W. Mercier's evocative set, an aura of Prague itself. But these are trappings in a musical that is not amply reflective of a life-threatening dramatic situation.

1990 Je 2, 16:3

The Grand Guignol

EXPERIMENT AT THE ASYLUM, by Annie G. and Mitch Hogue, directed by Richard Galgano.

THE TREATMENT OF DR. LOVE, by William Squier, directed by Linda Feinberg and Martin Fluger.

ORGY IN THE AIR-TRAFFIC CONTROL TOWER, by Sean Bruke and Steve Nelson, directed by Michael Hillyer.

Sets by Vicki R. Davis, light by Ken Davis, costume consultant, Mary Myers, original music by Robert Montgomery. Presented by Aboutface and Mr. Burke. At Playhouse 91, 316 East 91st Street.

WITH: Robert Alexander, Dina Corsetti, Gary Evans, Leslie R. Hollander, Kelleigh McKenzie, Ellen McQueeney, Gina Menza, Chuck Pooler, J. J. Reap, J. Kelly Salvadore, Nomi Tichman and David D. Yezzi.

By STEPHEN HOLDEN

"Orgy in the Air-Traffic Control Tower," the meatiest of the three one-act plays presented at Playhouse 91 under the title "The Grand Guignol," tells a nasty Christmas Eve horror story.

It is 1981 at La Guardia Airport after an air-traffic controllers' strike, and three controllers are having a holiday party while on duty in their observatory. Joined by two tough floozies, they stoke themselves with booze and cocaine and goad one another into wild, rolling-around-the-floor sex. By the time a potential disaster looms, they are too far gone to avert it. Amid the catastrophe, one of the three goes murderously berserk.

In the moments when this holiday nightmare, concocted by the mem-

Aboutface Theater Company

Gary Evans and Kelleigh McKenzie in part of "The Grand Guignol."

bers of the young, experimental theater company Aboutface, succeeds, it presents one of the meaner visions of contemporary American life to be seen on a New York stage this year. The dialogue, by Sean Burke and Steve Nelson, shows a sharp ear for hostile, bullying banter among people for whom instant gratification is related to cruelty. The play also insinuates a political subtext dealing with labor, boredom and violence in the land of opportunity. And the performances of Gary Evans and Kelleigh McKenzie, as the sort of yahoos one might find chortling at the sexual jokes at an Andrew Dice Clay show, have a realistic chill.

Unfortunately, the play and its two companions are all tied to a pretentious concept that the company fails to bring off. The evening's three one-acts are intended to be modern American representations of Grand Guignol, the kind of short horror play crammed with gore and titillation that flourished in France in the 1890's and in England a bit later. In the curtain raiser, William Squier's "Treatment of Dr. Love," a demented gynecologist who as the guest on a television talk show is confronted by a patient he once mutilated. Annie G. and Mitch Hogue's "Experiment at the Asylum" is a grisly story of rape, abortion and insanity.

The satire in the first play is so exaggerated that it has no edge. And the comic tone of the second is oddly goofy in "The Bride of Frankenstein" mode. In all three plays, the gore is also treated far too perfunctorily, with the several stabbings transparently fake and undramatic. Ultimately, the evening can't begin to match in shock value and in bloody realism the modern horror movie, which is the true contemporary descendant of the Grand Guignol sensibility.

1990 Je 2, 18:1

The Chocolate Soldier

Based on the play "Arms and the Man," by George Bernard Shaw; music by Oscar Straus; original book and lyrics by Stanislaus Stange; directed by Larry Carpenter; musi-

cal adaptation and musical direction by Albin Konopka; new lyrics by Ted Drachman; new book by Mr. Carpenter; choreography by Daniel Pelzig; scenery by James Leonard Joy; costumes by John Falabella; lighting by Craig Miller; production manager, William Chance; stage manager, Michael Brunner; assistant musical director, Steven Silverstein; associate artistic director, Dan Siretta; associate producer, Sue Frost; orchestrations by Larry Moore; produced by Michael P. Price. Presented by the Goodspeed Opera House, East Haddam, Conn.

Raina	Victoria Clark
Catherine	Susan Cella
Masha	Joanna Glushak
Louka	Anna Bess Lank
Bluntschli	Paul Ukena Jr.
Captain Massakroff	Richard Malone
Stephen	Robert Torres
Petkoff	Kurt Knudson
Sergius	Max Robinson

With: Jonathan Cerullo, Kelly Corken, Richard Costa, Pamela Dayton, Peter Flynn, Deborah Geneviere, J. Kathleen Lamb, Rose McGuire, Glenn Sneed, Robert Torres, Stephen Lloyd Webber and Leigh-Anne Wencker

By STEPHEN HOLDEN

Special to The New York Times

EAST HADDAM, Conn., May 27 — "My Hero," by far the most famous song from Oscar Straus and Stanislaus Stange's 1909 operetta "The Chocolate Soldier," is one of the most wildly romantic ballads to have survived as a standard from the early part of the century. In a paroxysm of dreamy fantasy, the narrator of this overheated waltz actually proclaims, "Thou art divine," to the image of a lover who is not present. Rarely in pop have romantic and religious fervor been more thoroughly blended.

•

In the Goodspeed Opera House's revival of the show, which was very loosely adapted from George Bernard Shaw's play "Arms and the Man," the song is revealed as the caricature it was intended to be. Sung by the leading ingénue of the piece, a Bulgarian aristocrat named Raina (Victoria Clark), to a portrait of her soldier-fiancé, Sergius (Max Robinson), it is part of the show's very gentle spoof of the worship of the military.

Miss Clark, who balances the show's romantic and comic sides

more comfortably than the rest of the cast, is the best singer and actor in a production that leans a bit too heavily toward farce. Her sweet lyric soprano is matched by a simpering, twinkly demeanor that can shift from sweet to silly with just the small adjustment of a smile. Though the rest of the cast tries harder than Miss Clark to be funny, their performances by comparison seem a little forced.

Although "The Chocolate Soldier" is a quintessential operetta of its period, its muted Shavian satire of military pomp has prompted a production in which comedy counts for more than musical refinement. For this production, the show has a new book, by Larry Carpenter, and new lyrics, by Ted Drachman, that give the story of late-19th-century Bulgaria a more contemporary comic flavor. Mr. Carpenter, who also directed, has staged the show as knockabout musical comedy with a lot of mugging. That tone is augmented by James Leonard Joy's cartoonish storybook sets and by Daniel Pelzig's choreography, which broadly spoofs Eastern European folk dances and military drills.

•

The approach, though entertaining, seems a little coarse and at odds with the delicacy of the music, with which not enough care has been taken. A listener frequently senses the singers struggling to keep time with the brisk tempos of the orchestra. And with the exception of Miss Clark, their vocal performances are less than outstanding.

Paul Ukena Jr., who portrays Bluntschli, the admittedly frightened and nonheroic soldier-hero who wins Raina's heart, is the performer who seems most out of tune with the show. With his goofy Joe E. Brown smile

Diane Sobolewski/The Goodspeed Opera House

Victoria Clark in a revival of the 1909 operetta "The Chocolate Soldier" at the Goodspeed Opera House.

and a singing voice that is too plain for the operetta, he does not make a very credible romantic lead. Mr. Ukena is the latest in a long string of Goodspeed leading men who don't quite match their leading ladies in finesse.

1990 Je 3, 62:2

Comedy and Satire Open Experimental Festival

By ALLAN KOZINN

A dark comedy by Tom Judson and a timely, defiant satire by Kevin Malony opened the seventh annual Tweed (Theater Works: Emerging Experimental Directions) New Works Festival on Thursday evening. The works made up the first of five programs in the festival, which runs through Sunday at the Ohio Theater, 66 Wooster Street.

Mr. Judson's work, "The Blue Piano," begins as a parody of a 1930's film musical, with characters that burst into song at the slightest provo-

---

'Pornsongspiel' is part of a larger work still unseen.

---

cation. The piece is set on the patio of the Hotel Caesar Augustus, on Capri, where one Dimitri Dimitrovich (Mr. Judson), a concert pianist, is recuperating after collapsing during a tour.

With him are Isabella (Liz Prince), a waitress who humors him and fetches cocktails, and Bruno (Billy Swindler), an accordionist. The piece

cruises along breezily until Dimitri goes for a swim and Isabella tells his real story. He is indeed a concert pianist, but a washed-up one who has had a nervous breakdown.

A second twist occurs later: Intent on returning to the concert stage, Dimitri is strapped to his lounge chair by Bruno, and Isabella returns as a nurse, with a syringe instead of a cocktail. The dual perspective Mr. Judson has constructed works nicely, with Dimitri's outbursts making sense enough in his illusory world, but taking on different meanings in the light of clinical reality.

The songs are an eclectic lot. "Aimless," sung by Mr. Judson, is a comic blues tune in the manner of Loudon Wainwright 3d. Isabella's aria, "The Saga of Dimitri Dimitrovich," is a mock melodrama not unlike the Kinks' "Alcohol." There are brushes with bossa nova and other styles, which Mr. Judson delivers with flair, to Mr. Swindler's stylish accompaniment.

Mr. Malony's "Pornsongspiel" is part of a larger work, "The History of Pornography," which is to have its premiere next February. A multimedia effort, with video sequences, projections and song and dance numbers, the work peeks at the parallel extremes of sexual overdrive and repression, presenting both in streams of catch phrases and exaggerated character types.

Both sides are portrayed as emotionally dysfunctional, and the likelihood that censorship advocates would miss that point amid the welter of nude images and recitations of unprintable terms seemed one of the show's leitmotifs.

How these fragments are related to the complete work remains to be seen, but they suggest a show inspired equally by "Mahagonny" and "Hair" — more daring and current, but less polished, than either. The half-dozen songs composed by Carol Lipnik and choreographed by John O'Malley range from nightclub parodies to 1950's doo-wop, and have some clever touches. Stephen Pell as a lowlife crooner and Jerry Kernion as a porn-shop owner were distinguished among the fine ensemble cast.

1990 Je 4, C22:1

The Cry of the Body

Written, directed and performed by Benito Gutmacher. Presented by La Mama E.T.C, 74A East Fourth Street.

By STEPHEN HOLDEN

The most indelible image in Benito Gutmacher's "Cry of the Body," a solo performance piece inspired by the writings of Antonin Artaud, is its opening sequence called "The Plague." Entering from the back of the audience at La Mama, the emaciated mime and acrobat from Argentina appears in a gas mask and staggers down the center aisle, wheezing desperately for air while stopping now and then to bang one hand violently on the floor.

The portrayal of the human being as a gasping fish out of water is the scariest of the 10 explorations of

---

The man and the beast, 2 halves of the self, meet in absurdist combat.

---

primal feeling that Mr. Gutmacher enacts in a show that he has performed across Latin America and Europe. When at the end of "The Plague," he removes his mask, the face one encounters has blazing fanatic eyes and a parched, thin little mouth. For the rest of the evening, he toys with the audience, posing riddles in several languages, and acting out eccentric, difficult-to-perform physical feats.

•

Mr. Gutmacher's characteristic theatrical games portray bestial instinct and civilized training going eye to eye. And if civilized training wins out, it is only by a hair. In "No Violence," the performer announces "No violence" and then counters, "But why not violence?" before lunging down the center aisle with a sword. Quivering with homicidal fury, he lays its tip on the shoulder of a spectator and barely restrains himself from committing murder. The piece is so carefully choreographed, however, that it is not particularly threatening.

A virtuoso of movement, Mr. Gutmacher, in "People," compresses many of the rituals of daily life into an accelerated montage of grimaces and twitches. "Mommy Why?" parodies birth, as the performer claws and kicks his way out of an orange sack at the center of the stage, to emerge quivering and squalling in a Donald Duck voice.

•

Unlike so many other clowns and mimes, whose distillation of primal feelings uses humor to create a warm sense of the human community, Mr. Gutmacher is an absurdist with streak of sadism. "What is the point?" he asks repeatedly in "The Point Is," then bounces like a human pogo stick between two platforms on which he does a pointless acrobatic turns while screaming his head off. Answering his own question, he shouts "to be" repeatedly and devours imaginary food with the voracity of a wild animal, then caps the display with some noisy belches.

"The Cry of the Body," reduces human existence to appetite and purposeless activity.

1990 Je 5, C15:1

A Perfect Diamond

By Don Rifkin; directed by Philip D. Giberson; scenic design, Robert Klingelhoefer; lighting, William J. Plachy; costumes, Jo-Dee Mercurio; sound, Neal Arluck; production stage manager, Michael Perreca. Presented by Apple Corps Theater, 336 West 20th Street.

Buck Beauregard	Dennis Sook
Gentleman Jim Wilson	Daryl Edwards
Legs Lannigan	Michael Cullen
Mark Haftel	Milton Elliott
Tess Gallagher	Iona Morris
The Kid	Earl Whitted
Buster Ziltz	Paul O'Brien
Dollar Bill Brunowski	Josh Mostel

By WILBORN HAMPTON

The season is not going well for the Nationals, the home team in "A Perfect Diamond," Don Rifkin's mild baseball comedy at the Apple Corps Theater. They've just dropped a 13-3 squeaker to the Cubs in which the Nats pitching staff gave up 15 hits and the defense committed 7 errors. But if the team's manager, Legs Lannigan, thinks he's got troubles on the diamond, it's nothing compared to what's waiting for him in the clubhouse.

Legs, who before becoming a manager built a lifetime .295 batting average by beating out infield hits, must make room on the roster for his ace starter who is coming off the disabled list. The club's general manager, Dollar Bill Brunowski, thinks he can trade Buster Ziltz, an aging slugger who is now hitting .204 and just stranded seven men on base, to the Yankees. But Legs doesn't want to trade Ziltz, a popular player with the fans who owns a chain of restaurants in town. "Why do you want to keep Ziltz?" Dollar Bill asks Legs. "He can't run; he can't hit, and he can't throw." "He's got intangibles," Legs snaps back.

•

But even Legs doesn't know Buster's biggest intangible: the affection in which the veteran is held by the Kid, a young center fielder who is already so close to superstardom that he barely has time to play ball between his television appearances and attending to his 900-number call-in business. The Kid, in fact, is so upset at the news Buster may be traded that he comes out of the locker, con-

fesses his love for the veteran and threatens to kill himself if Legs sends Ziltz to the Yankees.

Complicating all this are two sports writers — one male (Milton Elliott) and one female (Iona Morris) — a pitching coach (Daryl Edwards) who keeps nipping into the clubhouse between innings for a shot of Jack Daniels, and a tobacco-chewing coach (Dennis Sook) who wants a Nintendo game for the club's computer.

Yet for all the promise of its lineup, "A Perfect Diamond" has as much trouble scoring as the slumping Nationals. Mr. Rifkin has loaded the bases with some humorous characters, but it's not until the second act that he manages to get some laughs across the plate. Too much of the dialogue in the first act is peppered with baseball jargon and stats and is given to dated jokes about female reporters in the locker room and nostalgic talk about baseball "not being the game it used to be."

•

There are some funny moments in the second act when Legs tries to adjust to the Kid's bisexuality and Dollar Bill Brunowski starts making plans to hold a shotgun media wed-

Martha Holmes/"A Perfect Diamond"

Josh Mostel and Michael Cullen in "A Perfect Diamond."

ding for the Kid with the altar at home plate and an umpire performing the ceremony.

But even if one overlooks such improbables as the Nationals' coaching staff and veteran spending their entire careers with one team, or a female reporter having a romance going with both the club's manager and star player at the same time, or a newspaper with a 6 P.M. deadline for its sports section, "A Perfect Diamond" often has little more punch than a broken bat.

Philip D. Giberson, the director, has put together an able cast that brings a lot of energy and enthusiasm to the play. Josh Mostel is deliciously crass and sarcastic as Dollar Bill and Michael Cullen strikes a credible note of exasperation as the beleaguered Legs. Earl Whitted as the Kid has the strut and attitude of a .400 hitter and Paul O'Brien offers a fine turn as the slumping Ziltz. Robert Klingelhoefer's set is major league.

1990 Je 6, C18:1

Prin

By Andrew Davies; directed by John Tillinger; sets by John Lee Beatty; costumes by Jane Greenwood; lighting by Richard Nelson; sound by Bruce Ellman; production stage manager, Travis DeCastro. Presented by Manhattan Theater Club, Lynne Meadow, artistic director; Barry Grove, managing director. At City Center Stage I, 131 West 55th Street.

Prin	Eileen Atkins
Dibs	Amy Wright
Boyle	John Curless
Walker	John Christopher Jones
Kite	Remak Ramsay
Melanie	Wendy Makkena

By FRANK RICH

Since there is no new Simon Gray play in sight at the moment, the Manhattan Theater Club has imported a reasonable facsimile of one, "Prin," by another British writer, Andrew Davies. Like Mr. Gray's "Butley," "Prin" recounts a disastrous day in the midlife crisis of an arrogant, self-destructive academic. Its cast includes American specialists in the Gray canon, Remak Ramsay ("Quartermaine's Terms") and John Christopher Jones ("Otherwise Engaged"). John Tillinger's genteel production, from the wood paneling and Gothic spires of John Lee Beatty's set to the incidental touches of Benjamin Britten choral music, will leave Anglophiles longing to be in England now that New York's summer humidity is here.

"Prin" is second rate but at times entertainingly so. Though the dramaturgy is predictable and the intellectual content is limited to the dropping of modestly trendy literary names like Terry Eagleton and Alison Lurie, Mr. Davies has written a few crackling scenes and sprinkled the others with the slick, practiced wit of "Masterpiece Theater." (The playwright was, fittingly, the adaptor of R. F. Delderfield's "To Serve Them All My Days" for the television series.) The most formulaic patches, some of them classroom lectures and faculty meetings, are usually enlivened by the excellent cast. The company is led by a rare and welcome visitor, Eileen Atkins, who recalls her peers over at "Lettice and Lovage" with her fierce concentration and her absolute instinct for knowing exactly when to raise an eyebrow or descend an octave for maximum comic effect.

•

It's hardly her fault that her character, the teachers' college principal of the play's title, is a pill. Like the schoolteacher heroine played by Glenda Jackson in "Rose," the previous Davies play seen in New York, Prin is arch and ice cold. Even Miss Atkins cannot always succeed in riveting the audience's attention to the predicaments of a starchy tyrant who treats everyone with withering contempt: her faculty, her students and most particularly her vice principal and lover, Dibs, played by Amy Wright.

Prin champions "the pursuit of excellence," and, in the Jean Brodie manner, exhorts her charges to "be extraordinary," but such attributes are overshadowed by her ability to zero in sadistically on any human frailty she encounters. Once the audience has watched Prin treat her "little Dibs" as an indentured servant or seen her repeatedly mock a science teacher named Boyle (John Curless) by addressing him as Bile, it is hard to get caught up in her defense of "civilized values" and in her rightminded attacks on Thatcher-era "asset stripping" of educational institutions.

Given Prin's behavior, it's no wonder that her claims on both her authoritarian power and her lover are in jeopardy. Mr. Davies tips off these pending upheavals in the opening scenes, then practices a variety of delaying tactics before handing Prin her inevitable comeuppance. The most invigorating digressions involve Mr. Jones, who gives an exceptionally vivid account of a sad-sack English teacher caught in a hapless affair with a student. All too keenly aware that his life is a squalid botch beyond his limited means of understanding, Mr. Jones breaks into increasingly

Gerry Goodstein/"Prin"

Eileen Atkins, top, and Amy Wright in "Prin."

hysterical, red-cheeked laughter as his woes pile up. Wendy Makkena, as his equally pathetic yet likable paramour, and Mr. Ramsay, as the faculty bureaucrat who happens to be the student's scandalized father, are so tantalizingly quirky as well that one wonders why Mr. Davies won't break out of Prin's rigid procession of office consultations to give them a scene of their own.

•

As the principal's acolyte, Ms. Wright has more to do and makes the most of it. Dibs is a part eerily similar to the one that introduced Miss Atkins to Broadway audiences in Frank Marcus's "Killing of Sister George" in the 1960's — a girl-woman ready to revolt against her older female keeper. An uncertain accent notwithstanding, Ms. Wright's puckish eyes and retreating chin convey Dibs's growing independence with birdlike tentativeness and self-deprecating good humor. Her revolt against her mentor finally emerges not as a trivial gesture of romantic pique but as a courageous act of self-realization.

Until Dibs's revolt comes, Miss Atkins has very few opportunities to break through Prin's hard exterior. In one of them, she berates Anthony Blunt and other "silly old queens" of her leftist Oxbridge circles of the 1930's for betraying England to the Soviet Union while "it was us who stayed, us dykes," who did the hard, unglamorous work of trying to remake society from within. But this potentially fascinating line of inquiry, like others in "Prin," is quickly dropped for the next sarcastic bon mot. Only at the play's coda, as Prin stands alone surveying the wreckage of her well-intentioned life, can Miss

Atkins raise the curtain entirely on her character's conflicted soul. The actress ends the evening with a chilling, virtuoso soliloquy delivered in a hush at stage edge — a revelation of high internal drama with which a deeper play might have chosen to begin.

1990 Je 7, C18:5

Sisters

By Marsha A. Jackson; based on a short story by Barbara Neely; directed by Thomas W. Jones 2d; original set and lighting design, John Harris; costume design by Debi Frye Barber; sound design by Craig Cousins; stage manager, Kimberly Harding; production manager, Ms. Barber; assistant stage manager, Vantony Jenkins; technical assistants, Lou Bailey and Tony Loadholt. Presented by the Joyce Theater Foundation Inc., in association with Jomandi Productions. At 175 Eighth Avenue, at 19th Street.

Olivia .... Marsha A. Jackson
Cassie .... Andrea Frye

By MEL GUSSOW

In Marsha A. Jackson's "Sisters," two disparate women are snowbound on New Year's Eve on the 20th floor of an office building in downtown Atlanta. For dimly stated reasons, they decide not to challenge the elements. Instead, they try to stretch the audience's credulity. Repeatedly, the question arises why the two women do not leave the building. The tie that binds them there is Ms. Jackson's contrived play.

The broad two-character comedy arrived at the Joyce Theater Tuesday night after an engagement at the Jomandi Theater of Atlanta and a tour of 20 other cities.

Remaining in that office, the women behave according to dramatic formula. Olivia (played by the author) is a high-rising, uptight advertising executive who is jumping off the fast track — before she is pushed. Cassie (Andrea Frye), undereducated and openhearted, is a cleaning woman.

In her pursuit of worldly success, the loveless Olivia has jettisoned her personal life. In saintly contrast, Cassie is dedicated to taking care of her son and her wise old grandmother while neglecting her own chances for self-improvement.

•

The play follows a predictable path from divisiveness (snobbishness on Olivia's part) to sisterly feelings of mutual support. The playwright stops short of having the two women switch jobs, though that might not have been a bad idea. From the advertising campaigns Olivia offers as samples of her ability, she may not have deserved that promotion she sought. Cassie, in contrast, is at least high in common sense.

Cassie provides the play with its single glimmer of interest, She has some pungent lines — along with others that are heavyhanded. We are supposed to laugh at her lack of polish. Fortunately, Ms. Frye is an appealing performer and she plays her role tongue in cheek. Olivia is a walking résumé, offering her credentials along with the names of authors whose books she has supposedly read. Having given herself the least amusing lines, Ms. Jackson, as an actress, underlines Olivia's disagreeableness with a stridency.

•

"Sisters" moves sideways, shifts into reverse, repeats itself, then rumbles to its foregone conclusion. As director, Thomas W. Jones 2d is unable

to instill momentum or to convince us of the reality of the situation. At one point, he sends the two women walking over and around the cluttered set in an awkward attempt to simulate their descent to the lobby of the office

Worldly and unworldly, snowbound in an office building.

building — and their unwarranted return up the long staircase.

Hidden in the picture is a brief comedy sketch or a pilot for a sitcom. "Sisters" would, in fact, be more at home on television than in a theater, but there is a serious question what the show would do for a second episode.

1990 Je 7, C19:3

Elliot Loves

By Jules Feiffer; directed by Mike Nichols; set design by Tony Walton; costumes by Ann Roth; lighting by Paul Gallo; sound by Tom Sorce; production supervisor, Peter Lawrence; associate producers, Susan MacNair. Presented by Roger Berlind. At the Promenade Theater, 2162 Broadway, at 76th Street.

Elliot .... Anthony Heald
Joanna .... Christine Baranski
Vera .... Latanya Richardson
Phil .... David Pierce
Larry .... Oliver Platt
Bobby .... Bruce A. Young

By FRANK RICH

Though Jules Feiffer is always thought of first as an iconoclastic political cartoonist, it is his words for film and theater that really get people hopping mad. It's still possible to find fans of Feiffer cartoons arguing about whether "Carnal Knowledge," his 1971 movie about eternally adolescent American men, was mysogynist, or whether "Grown Ups," his 1981 play about an imploding Jewish American family, was an act of Jewish anti-Semitism. The anger is hardly likely to subside with "Elliot Loves," the bleak and unsatisfying comedy that Mr. Feiffer and his "Carnal Knowledge" collaborator, the director Mike Nichols, have brought to the Promenade Theater.

Only at the outset does the play offer fairly uncomplicated laughter: Elliot (Anthony Heald), a divorced pollster in Chicago, delivers a classic Feiffer soliloquy, a sequence of cartoon panels really, in which he declares his devotion to Joanna (Christine Baranski), a twice-divorced real-estate broker, while simultaneously revealing all his fear and loathing of women, sex and love. Two hours later, Elliot and Joanna are shrieking at each other on the phone with vitriol worthy of "The Dance of Death": He now describes an evening with her as "one of the classic bad times of the century" while she says that their argument leaves her feeling "as if I'd been mugged." In between, Joanna and the audience journey to a Near North Side apartment to meet Elliot's three best friends, variously damaged, crude and violent men who regard women as objects of pornographic fantasies at best and of homicidal daydreams at worst.

These are not nice people, nor are they meant to be, and because the men outnumber and outtalk the women, "Elliot Loves" may strike some as an implicit endorsement of its male characters' grotesquely piggish views. Speaking as a fervent admirer of both "Carnal Knowledge" and "Grown Ups," I would argue that Mr. Feiffer is ecumenical in his misanthropy, and that the disappointment of "Elliot Loves" has less to do with partisanship in sexual politics than with the hollowness of all the people in the play, regardless of their sex. On this occasion, Mr. Feiffer asks theatergoers to spend an evening with empty characters without offering the payoff of insight. His script often seems like a catchall into which he has deposited a pile of unsorted dirty psychic laundry, and by the end it is the depressed but still unenlightened audience that is left holding the bag.

What is missing from the writing — and from Mr. Nichols's muddled production — are the specificity and empathy of Mr. Feiffer at his best. It is clear from Tony Walton's handsome penthouse setting, which looks well beyond the economic means of its occupants, and even from the opening monologue that essential, potentially telling character details are being fudged. Though Mr. Heald's age is around 40, Elliot identifies himself early on as a member of the generation initiated into the battle of the sexes by James Thurber. In truth, a man of his years would more likely have learned about sexual warfare from "Carnal Knowledge" than from Thurber, and when we meet Elliot's friends, also 40-ish, they also sound like men who entered manhood in the 1950's, not the 1960's.

Why are the male characters presented as at least a decade younger than they are written? A forced, slightly snide digression about "Glengarry Glen Ross" leaves one wondering if Mr. Feiffer and Mr. Nichols mistakenly and resentfully feel that their closed-off men have to be contemporaneous with David Mamet's to be marketable. It is similarly jarring that Mr. Feiffer differentiates Elliot's cronies mainly by a pollster's demographics, as if they were descendants of the cartoon poker players in "The Odd Couple": the nerdy accountant (David Pierce), the beefy entrepreneur (Oliver Platt) and the overassimilated black (Bruce A. Young).

A deeper failing in Elliot's case is Mr. Feiffer's inability to locate the origins of this protagonist's vicious behavior, not just to Joanna but to an alcoholic among his pals. Elliot is a generic collection of traits (he's a worrywart) and attitudes rather than someone with a clear and convincing past and present. The tightly wound Mr. Heald, one of our best comic actors, tries here, as he did in "The Lisbon Traviata," to fill in an ill-defined role's dark gaps by exaggerating neuroses into psychoses. Even in his initial stand-up routine, he has the distorted features of an incipient serial killer.

•

Ms. Baranski's Joanna is also confused. When she first appears in Act I, Mr. Nichols brings her on as an Elaine May comic type, with busy shtik involving chain-smoking and hair spray and ditsy line readings of the sort the gifted Ms. Baranski can and does do to perfection. But in Act II, Joanna becomes first, a cool verbal seductress out of Pinter's "Homecoming" and second, a no-holds-barred fighter out of "Who's Afraid of

Martha Swope/"Elliot Loves"
Anthony Heald in "Elliot Loves," at the Promenade Theater.

Virginia Woolf?" Neither the acting nor the lines, a last-minute mea culpa included, fill in the transitions needed to transform a clownish saleswoman with two (offstage) children into a desperately lonely, world-class emasculator. The sympathy and emotional weight given to the wife in "Grown Ups" and the pinup played by Ann-Margret in "Carnal Knowledge" are sorely missed.

While the play's one major farcical plot development, involving a call-girl service, also lacks follow-through, there are some extremely witty passages lightening the heavy weather of "Elliot Loves" throughout. Yet the funniest riffs and jokes, whether about Richard Nixon, Frank Sinatra or the ethnicity of alcoholics, seem arbitrarily draped onto the main action and, revealingly, often belong to the fine supporting players, not the principals.

•

Mr. Feiffer does have some funny, biting and highly quotable things to say about the evening's real subject, too — about the cruelties men and women perpetrate in the name of marriage, about the terrors of intimacy, about a culture that turns to Oprah and Phil for answers that must be found within. But much as Elliot has a nasty, belittling habit of identifying Joanna's jokes instead of laughing at them, the author is better at identifying his characters' ailments than investigating them. Though there is genuine anguish underlying this play, it is paraded about the stage rather than harnessed to a provocative end. The anguish the audience finally shares at "Elliot Loves" is not Elliot's purported pain of self-examination but Joanna's numbing sensation of having been mugged.

1990 Je 8, C3:1

Circus Oz

From Australia. Artistic director, Tim Coldwell; administrator, Susan Provan; production manager, Georgine Sparks; stage manager, Steven Richardson; sound, Bill Vickers; lighting, Carmel Duffy. Presented by City Center Theater, 131 West 55th Street.

WITH: Mr. Coldwell, Scott Grayland, Stephen Burton, Anni Davey, Natalie Dyball, Tanya Cavanagh, Julie McInnes, Matthew Hughes, Melissa Reeves, Lisa Small, Elaine Stevens and Tom Lycos.

By MEL GUSSOW

At Circus Oz, almost everyone, no matter how daring, intends to be funny: jumpers, gymnasts and aerialists who crowd a trapeze so that they become as close-quartered as straphangers on a subway car during rush hour. In this Australian circus, clowns can fly.

The signature act of the zany troupe calls for three performers to be transformed into human flies. With the help of hidden magnets, they hang by their feet and walk upside down on the ceiling (at City Center Theater, where the company began a three week engagement on Wednesday). Not satisfied with this odd accomplishment, the three hangers reveal individual topsy-turvy talents. One plays the flute, another the drums and the third, Natalie Dyball, puts out the garbage — all at a death-defying height above the stage.

Like a team of Pythons, the company goes about the business of obstreperous tomfoolery, mocking themselves as well as circus arts. The show never moves far from new (or old) vaudeville. Occasionally a stunt misfires, so the unabashed performers do it again — and keep trying until they get it right. Though some of the conversational byplay is overly whimsical, in terms of physical comedy the show retains its informality. In so doing, it should appeal to children as well as adults.

The key is in the company's versatility. There are specialists, but everyone can do at least a little bit of everything else. Acrobats scramble up a tall pole as speedily as if they are stealing second base — and then, with barely a pause, they return to the stage and stand on each other's shoulders. Matthew Hughes, one of the

Johan Elbers
Scott Grayland, of the Circus Oz, performing the 'cloud swing' at City Center Theater.

aerial catchers, doubles as an expert on the trampoline, a jumping jester who always ends in an upright position.

•

Beyond the feats there are interludes of sketch comedy, as in a musical number in which a cellist finds herself accompanied by her chair (an upholstered chair concealing a rival cellist with long arms and a way with a bow). There is an irresistible urge toward doing things together — lawn bowling on the hardwood stage, forming human pyramids (four teetering tiers) and holding a group conference while simultaneously riding a single bicycle. The performers reach their height with hoops, diving and twisting their bodies through these circles until they choreograph themselves into a hoop de théâtre.

While the clowns are cavorting on and off the stage, a rock-inclined combo provides a rhythmic background and Tim Coldwell, the ringmaster and artistic director, intrudes, deadpan, in various routines. At one point, he plays a musical solo on an instrument called the thong-a-phone. Most notable in the cast are the pixielike Ms. Dyball (playing a Girl Guide), Mr. Hughes and Anni Davey, a fire eater who finds comedy by being inflammatory. There are no animals and little of a circus's traditional paraphrenalia.

This is Circus Oz's first visit to the United States in six years, during which time the company has polished most of the rough edges and has clarified its purpose. With this merry band of theatrical pranksters, laughter is the first priority.

1990 Je 8, C7:1

Chelsea Walls

Directed by Ed Sherin; written by Nicole Burdette; produced by Merrill Holtzman; set design, George Xenos; lighting design, Stephen Quandt; sound design, David Ferdinand; costume design, Rosalyn Evans; prop design, Michele Mayas. Presented by Naked Angels. At the Space, 114 West 17th Street.

WITH: Jon Robin Baitz, Patrick Breen, Kevin Corrigan, William Duff-Griffin, Paul Eckstein, Richard Edson, Margaret Eginton, Aaron Forste, Gina Gershon, Brett Goldstein, Christina Haag, Julianne Hoffenberg, Merrill Holtzman, Tim Guinee, Catherine Lloyd, Marisa Tomei, Gary McCleary, Trina McGee, Lisa Beth Miller, Geoffrey Nauffts, Pippin Parker, Timothy Britten Parker, Richard Joseph Paul, Barry Sherman, Billy Strong, Melinda Wade, Jack Wallace, Gareth Williams and Jeff Williams.

By MEL GUSSOW

People come and people go, but most of all, people stay. This is the Chelsea Hotel, the legendary West Side home of writers and artists, a building fallen from its former glory and surviving in memories conjured up by newer, younger residents and by the few who have been left in place. The play, Nicole Burdette's "Chelsea Walls," at the Naked Angels theater, is filled with energy and theatrical imagination.

In literary quality, Ms. Burdette's writing is not to be confused with that in Lanford Wilson's related, environmental plays, "The Hot l Baltimore" and "Balm in Gilead." But her quick-moving collage of vignettes has its own evocative power and Ed Sherin, leading a company of 29 actors, has given the sprawling work cohesiveness and room to breathe.

"What peace and lament these rooms knew," says one character, quoting Edgar Lee Masters, one of the many famous Chelsea Hotel ten-

ants. As the audience realizes, both those elements exist in abundance in the play.

•

A writer (Patrick Breen) bashes out a novel, talking to himself as he types on an old-fashioned typewriter. For inspiration, he plays a recording of "Rhapsody in Blue" at full volume. Next door, a dancer (the lovely Margaret Eginton) dances, attuning Gershwin to her own ethereal balletic spirit. Suddenly, the novelist stops writing and cuts off the music, and Ms. Eginton is so surprised she nearly loses her balance. Later, the two meet, and she tells him of the mystique of "dancing to someone else's music." But they remain isolated individuals united only by their place of residence.

Other stories overlap and a few intersect, but most remain compartmentalized. A courtly trainer (William Duff-Griffin) instructs a boxer, an actor practices soliloquies, a wandering lover returns home. Two newcomers arrive from Minneapolis, one a guitarist (Gary McCleary) with aspirations of becoming a new Bob Dylan. A prostitute, a blind gambler and outcasts of various kinds pay their calls while two policemen discover the suicide of a composer. Two young women think they see an electrical fire burning in the wall; it turns out to be a piece of sparkling tinsel left from Christmas. Small moments become meaningful, and no scene lasts too long.

Among the prominent characters is a flashy stand-up comedian (Timothy Britten Parker), who works in a nearby club. In a clever twist, his chorus of red-hot dancing girls pays homage to the pride of the old Chelsea — Thomas Wolfe, Brendan Behan, Dylan Thomas and Masters. The comic turns out to be the night clerk at the hotel.

Everyone does what has to be done to pay the bills, and there is even a young artist who gives the hotel manager paintings in lieu of rent. In such a fashion, an aura of the past overlooks the present. Despite the seediness (vividly conveyed in George Xenos's elaborate, open-walled set), one receives an impression of what the hotel was in its heyday and how New York itself was once an open academy for artists. In this sense, "Chelsea Walls" is related to Mac Wellman's "Crowbar," which performed a similar service for derelict theaters on West 42d Street this year.

Ms. Burdette's play has its sentimental side. A sweet couple settles down to a game of Scrabble. An editor (the playwright Jon Robin Baitz) is overly solicitous of the self-destructive novelist. Even these glimpses have their point. There is nostalgia as well as hope in the air. But dreams become delusions and ghosts threaten to become corporeal.

•

In England, a play like "Chelsea Walls" might be staged as a promenade walk-through event (as was the case with Jim Cartwright's "Road"). Mr. Sherin keeps theatergoers seated, although they are dispersed in various areas throughout the large theater. The action unfolds around them, as rooms double and triple for occupants. One refrigerator at center stage serves all, and myriad musical sounds eventually emanate from the novelist's stereo.

Under Mr. Sherin's confident direction, and with the actors inhabiting the environment, the play achieves an organic flow. Those Chelsea walls are resonant with life.

1990 Je 9, 12:5

Philadelphia, Here I Come!

By Brian Friel; directed by Paul Weidner; set design, David Raphel; sound and lighting, Richard Clausen; costumes, Natalie Walker; production stage manager, Chris A. Kelly. Presented by the Irish Repertory Theater and One World Arts Foundation Inc., in association with the South Street Theater. Producing director, Ciaran O'Reilly; artistic director, Charlotte Moore. At South Street Theater, 424 West 42d Street.

Madge	Pauline Flanagan
Gareth O'Donnell (Public)	Patrick Fitzgerald
Gareth O'Donnell (Private)	Ciaran O'Reilly
S. B. O'Donnell	W. B. Brydon
Kate Doogan	Madeleine Potter
Senator Doogan	Chris Carrick
Master Boyle	Frank McCourt
Lizzy Sweeney	Paddy Croft
Con Sweeney	Bernard Frawley
Ben Burton	John William Short
Ned	Colin Lane
Tom	Brian F. O'Byrne
Joe	Denis O'Neil
Canon Mick O'Byrne	Dermot McNamara

By WILBORN HAMPTON

It has been 25 years since "Philadelphia, Here I Come!" established Brian Friel as a vibrant new voice in the English-speaking theater, and it is New York's loss that his work is so infrequently staged here. Perhaps that is changing. Last season the Manhattan Theater Club mounted a splendid production of Mr. Friel's "Aristocrats," and now the Irish Repertory Theater is staging a poignant revival of "Philadelphia, Here I Come!" at the South Street Theater.

If "Aristocrats" was evocative of Chekhov's "Cherry Orchard," then "Philadelphia" recalls Tennessee Williams's "Glass Menagerie" inasmuch as both are memory plays and each tells the story of a young man who finds he must flee to escape the narrow confines of his home, where comfortable predictability and little mendacities make life bearable for those who stay. In Mr. Friel's play, Gareth O'Donnell spends his last night in Ballybeg, Ireland, trying to settle some emotional accounts.

•

Gar's routine is unchanged by the fact that the morrow will take him away forever. Gar, played with disarming boyish sensitivity, cowlick and all, by Patrick Fitzgerald, takes refuge from his bleak world in fantasy. With his Walter Mitty imagination, Gar flies jetliners across the Atlantic, scores game-winning goals in international soccer matches and conducts an orchestra in Mendelssohn's Violin Concerto while simultaneously playing solo. Shadowing Gar at all times is his alter ego, the Private Gar, played with guileless charm and humor by Ciaran O'Reilly, who provides a running commentary on Gar's life and who offers frequent advice that the Public Gar only rarely follows.

The usual nightly parade of visitors call at the O'Donnell house. There is the local schoolmaster (Frank McCourt), on his way to the pub, who asks to "borrow" 10 shillings from a Gar he will never see again. There are Gar's mates, who were never friends and who in truth never even spoke to the long list of girls they boast they've had. There is the Canon (Dermot McNamara), who always "waits till the Rosary is over and the kettle is on" before stopping for his nightly cup of tea and game of checkers. And there is Kate (Madeleine Potter), the colleen Gar planned to marry and have 14 children with but for whose hand he was afraid to ask. And in the background is always

Irish Repertory Theater

Phillie Bound

Deirdre Moore and Patrick Fitzgerald star in the Irish Repertory Theater's production of "Philadelphia, Here I Come!," a comedy by Brian Friel about an Irishman on the eve of his departure to the New World.

Madge (Pauline Flanagan), the aging O'Donnell housekeeper, who *can never be the mother Gar never had*.

•

But what Gar most wants he knows he will never find in Ballybeg. He wants a father who will say something, anything other than "Another day over. I guess we can't complain" when he comes home to tea every evening. He wants to know about his mother, a "young, gay girl from behind the mountains who sometimes cried herself to sleep" and who died three days after he was born. He wants his father to ask him to stay. And once he knows that will not happen, he at least wants him to remember taking his son out in a blue boat when Gar was a child, putting his coat around him and singing to him. But there is nothing but silence, and as Private Gar tells Public Gar, "It's the silence that's the enemy." There is no rancor here. Gar's farewell will be a wave to a face behind a lace-curtained window, not the slamming of a door.

Gar has no illusions about what awaits him. He is going to a blathering aunt whose fondness for gin has rendered her incapable of seeing a sentence through to its end and who wants Gar to come live with her and her long-suffering husband only to fill the childless void in their lives. When Gar accepts it is not for the promise of a television in his room or a job at a hotel, but because it is his last chance for some semblance of familial love. And Gar knows the price he will have to pay. As a tired Madge shuffles off to bed, he tries to photograph the image in his mind so he can recall it later. "Watch every move," the Private Gar tells Public Gar. "Keep the camera whirring."

•

Paul Weidner's direction is studiously low key, and his able cast does not have a weak link in it. Mr. Fitzgerald and Mr. O'Reilly work together with a facility that is hard to achieve on stage. Although Mr. Fitzgerald never directly acknowledges Mr. O'Reilly's presence, the latter is such a part of Gar's character that the two actors seem inseparable even when they're at opposite sides of the stage. W. B. Brydon is absorbing as Gar's father, a stolid man for whom heaven will be a cup of tea and a checkerboard. Paddy Croft gives a fine reading of the loquacious Aunt

Lizzy, and Colin Lane provides a strong turn as Ned, the bully ringleader of Gar's circle of mates.

1990 Je 13, C15:1

Price of Fame

By Charles Grodin; directed by Gloria Muzio; set by David Jenkins; costumes by Jess Goldstein; lighting by Tharon Musser; sound by Philip Campanella; production stage manager, Kathy J. Faul. Presented by Roundabout Theater, Todd Haimes, producing director; Gene Feist, founding director. At 100 East 17th Street.

Roger	Charles Grodin
Pete	W. J. Paterson
Matt	Jace Alexander
Mario	Joseph R. Sicari
Karen	Lizbeth Mackay
Evelyn	Jeannie Berlin
Cappy	Michael Ingram
Bob	Sam Groom

By FRANK RICH

Charles Grodin is one of those actors whom audiences are always glad to see — whether he is appearing as the wry star of an independent-minded film comedy ("Real Life") or the saving grace of a Hollywood turkey ("Ishtar") or an island of civility on a late-night television talk show. Even so, some theatergoers may find their affectionate regard for Mr. Grodin put to a more strenuous test than usual by "Price of Fame," the flimsy new play at the Roundabout for which the actor serves as both leading man and playwright.

This is an it's-lonely-at-the-top comedy as only someone at or near the top could write it. Its hero is Roger, a movie star played by Mr. Grodin, who spends two successive mornings whining in his dressing room, a commodious trailer on a Hollywood back lot, while waiting for his latest picture to overcome mechanical delays and commence shooting. Roger is in both professional and personal funks. His last film has just opened to soft grosses; his pending one is an undignified sci-fi potboiler; his lover is about to give him the shove, and his son, a gofer on the set, is so alienated that even the fruits of nepotism have lost all meaning.

For reasons that are not immediately clear, Roger confides his woes to a stranger, Karen (Lizbeth Mack-

ay), an interviewer from Vanity Fair who has transparently come to do a hatchet job but soon cannot bury the hatchet quickly enough. It is one of the odder aspects of "Price of Fame" that Karen is presented as an exemplar of sleazy journalism in Act I, then is magically redeemed by means of a ludicrous plot coincidence into a blameless, indeed selfless, romantic heroine in Act II. The play accordingly breaks into conflicting halves, with the first act's somber yet frivolous debate about press ethics giving way incongruously to a hide-and-seek sex farce after intermission. It is as if a scenario by Janet Malcolm, that tireless crusader against journalistic transgressions, were abruptly revised by Bernard Slade, the author of Mr. Grodin's last Broadway vehicle, "Same Time, Next Year."

•

What is missing from both acts is any serious introspection by Roger, his son or Karen on their way to a jerry-built sentimental resolution of their various crises. The script instead digresses into Hollywood anecdotes and wisecracks that, however knowing and sporadically funny, cannot inject drama into a play in which the exposition is often recited into a handy cellular phone or tape recorder and the character development is mandated by authorial whim.

As directed by Gloria Muzio on David Jenkins's perhaps overzealous rendering of a mobile home, the cast seems to chew over the more sober dialogue as if it were handed down from Mount Sinai, as befits a play in which the author is in constant attendance. Though Mr. Grodin is his typically charming self when delivering jokes, one wishes he had an objective collaborator at hand to slap him out of his glassy-eyed, tight-jawed spells of self-martyrdom.

In addition to the hard-working Ms. Mackay, the supporting cast includes Jace Alexander as the blank, long-suffering son, Joseph R. Sicari and Michael Ingram as exceptionally irritating back-lot sycophants and a good-natured Jeannie Berlin as the co-star of Roger's stalled movie. Fans of "The Heartbreak Kid" will recall that Ms. Berlin was also Mr. Grodin's hilarious co-star in that film, which was directed by her mother, Elaine May. On this occasion, Ms.

Jim Wilson/The New York Times

Lizbeth Mackay and Charles Grodin in "Price of Fame."

Berlin is in view only long enough to reveal how distractingly she has come to resemble her mother, a price of fame potentially more fascinating than any other in "Price of Fame."

1990 Je 14, C17:1

Marathon 1990, Festival of New One-Act Plays, Series C

Mere Mortals by David Ives; directed by Jason Mc-Connell Buzas.

Death and the Maiden by Susan Kim; directed by Lisa Peterson.

Tonight We Love by Romulus Linney; directed by John Stix.

Stay Away a Little Closer by John Ford Noonan; directed by Bill Roudebush.
Sets, Linda Giering Balmuth; lighting, Greg MacPherson; costumes, Leslie McGovern; sound, Aural Fixation; production supervisor, Kent Hoffman; production stage manager, Diane Ward. Presented by the Ensemble Studio Theater; Curt Dempster, artistic director; Peter Shavitz, managing director; Kate Baggott, producer; Eric Berkal, associate producer. At 549 West 52d Street.

WITH: Janet Busser, Hope Cameron, Chris Ellis, Frank Girardeau, Zach Grenier, Stephen Hamilton, Baxter Harris, Sakina Jaffrey, Anthony LaPaglia, Anne O'Sullivan, Emmett O'Sullivan-Moore, Jesse Sage Noonan, Robert Pastorelli, Robert Sedgwick, Brian Smiar, Phyllis Somerville and Adrienne Thompson.

By STEPHEN HOLDEN

Club Nirvana, the South American singles' resort that is the setting of Susan Kim's provocative one-act play "Death and the Maiden," could be a nightmare version of Club Med. The place is surrounded by barbed wire, and a popular recreational sport is a game called "combat," in which the battle of the sexes is waged with camouflage and toy rifles.

In "Death and the Maiden," the most engrossing of the four short plays in Series C of the Ensemble Studio Theater's one-act marathon, Club Nirvana is also a metaphor for the world as seen through the eyes of its morbid protagonist, Margery (Anne O'Sullivan). While everyone else is obsessed with finding attractive sexual partners, she dreams only of self-annihilation. The first question she asks upon meeting a man is what his favorite mode of suicide would be. She is more than happy to offer a voluptuously detailed dramatization of her own imaginary drowning in a nearby cove.

As the play slowly swings from satiric comedy toward a darker surrealism, Margery attempts to fend off the attentions of two men. One is Doyle (Robert Sedgwick), an empty-headed body builder who eventually settles for her slatternly roommate, Michelle (Sakina Joffrey). The other is a heavy-lidded seducer, Laurence (Zach Grenier), who speaks with a thick Latin American accent but claims to be from Englewood Cliffs, N.J.

As the gunfire from the evening's war games becomes more insistent and a distant explosion rocks the hotel, Margery and Laurence's dialogue turns into a life-and-death battle of wills. Confidently directed by Lisa Peterson, "Death and the Maiden" is a stylish if vague little allegory whose political and social reverberations are emphasized just enough to deepen the mood without being pushed into pretentiousness.

Magic, both sinister and benign, also touches the lives of the four char-

acters in John Ford Noonan's "Stay Away a Little Closer," the longest and most ambitious play in the series. Set in a remote Vermont cabin in the middle of a blizzard, the drama is a contemporary ghost story in which a young married couple on the verge of going stir-crazy are visited by the cabin's former owner and his psychically gifted 12-year-old daughter.

•

The visitors, though very down-to-earth, also exude the radiant good will of angels who have been sent to save the soul of the young husband, Manny (Frank Girardeau), a drunkard consumed by paranoid fantasies that his wife, Wilma (Janet Busser), is unfaithful. While Mr. Noonan's characters make a lively quartet (in one scene the two men do competing Elvis imitations), the playwright doesn't seem to know quite what to do with them beyond using them to build an intriguing psychological puzzle that doesn't carry much weight. Among the four performances, by far the most authoritative is Mr. Girardeau's grim, clenched portrayal of a man possessed by demons.

Some of the same surreal devices enliven David Ives's comedy, "Mere Mortals," which is set on a girder on the 50th floor of an unfinished skyscraper. During a lunch break, three construction workers (superbly acted by Robert Pastorelli, Brian Smiar and Anthony LaPaglia) swap outlandish stories of their exotic "real" identities. The one with the most detailed fantasy is convinced that he is the kidnapped baby of Charles and Anne Morrow Lindbergh.

•

Romulus Linney's "Tonight We Love," the most conventional play in the series, is an entertaining comedy that might easily be adapted into an episode of the television series "Mama's Family." Set in a Tennessee nursing home, the play is an unabashed polemic for the humane treatment of the elderly that pits lovable heroes against hissable villains. On the side of the angels are a young nurse and the two aged sweethearts who wish to marry and leave the nursing home. Their antagonists are the would-be bride's greedy children, a brother and sister whom Mr. Linney paints as savage caricatures of curdled Southern gentility. The old folks are played with a quivering poignancy by Emmett O'Sullivan-Moore and Hope Cameron. Phyllis Barbow and Baxter Harris bite into their thoroughly nasty roles with an almost gleeful zest.

If none of the four plays in Series C are close to masterpieces, all four are thoroughly entertaining. Even for Ensemble Studio Theater's usually impressive annual marathon, that is a high batting average.

1990 Je 14, C20:3

Six Degrees of Separation

By John Guare; directed by Jerry Zaks; sets, Tony Walton; costumes, William Ivey Long; lighting, Paul Gallo; sound, Aural Fixation; production manager, Jeff Hamlin. Presented by Lincoln Center Theater, Gregory Mosher, director; Bernard Gersten, executive producer. At the Mitzi E. Newhouse Theater, Lincoln Center.

Ouisa	Stockard Channing
Flan	John Cunningham
Geoffrey	Sam Stoneburner
Paul	James McDaniel
Hustler	David Eigenberg
Kitty	Kelly Bishop
Larkin	Peter Maloney
Detective	Brian Evers
Tess	Robin Morse
Woody	Gus Rogerson
Ben	Anthony Rapp
Dr. Fine	Stephen Pearlman
Doug	Evan Handler
Policeman/Doorman	Philip LeStrange
Trent	John Cameron Mitchell
Rick	Paul McCrane
Elizabeth	Mari Nelson

By FRANK RICH

Ouisa Kittredge, the Upper East Side hostess at the center of John Guare's "Six Degrees of Separation," delights in the fact that it only takes a chain of six people to connect anyone on the planet with anyone else. But what about those who are eternally separated from others because they cannot find the right six people? Chances are that they, like Ouisa, live in chaotic contemporary New York, which is the setting for this extraordinary high comedy in which broken connections, mistaken identities and tragic social, familial and cultural schisms take the stage to create a hilarious and finally searing panorama of urban America in precisely our time.

For those who have been waiting for a masterwork from the writer who bracketed the 1970's with the play "House of Blue Leaves" and the film "Atlantic City," this is it. For those who have been waiting for the American theater to produce a play that

captures New York as Tom Wolfe did in "Bonfire of the Vanities," this is also it. And, with all due respect to Mr. Wolfe, "Six Degrees of Separation" expands on that novel's canvas and updates it. Mr. Guare gives as much voice to his black and female characters as to his upper-crust white men, and he transports the audience beyond the dailiness of journalistic storytelling to the magical reaches of the imagination.

Though the play grew out of a 1983 newspaper account of a confidence scheme, it is as at home with the esthetics of Wassily Kandinsky as it is with the realities of Rikers Island. The full sweep of the writing — 90 nonstop minutes of cyclonic action, ranging from knockabout farce to hallucinatory dreams — is matched by Jerry Zaks's ceaselessly inventive production at Lincoln Center's Mitzi E. Newhouse Theater. A brilliant ensemble of 17 actors led by Stockard Channing, John Cunningham and James McDaniel is equally adept at fielding riotous gags about Andrew Lloyd Webber musicals and the shattering aftermath of a suicide leap. As elegantly choreographed by Mr. Zaks, the action extends into the auditorium and rises through a mysterious two-level Tony Walton set that is a fittingly abstract variation on the designer's "Grand Hotel."

The news story that sparked "Six Degrees of Separation" told of a young black man who talked his way into wealthy white Upper East Side households by purporting to be both Sidney Poitier's son and the Ivy League college friend of his unwitting hosts' children. In Mr. Guare's variation, the young man (Mr. McDaniel), who calls himself Paul Poitier, lands in the Fifth Avenue apartment of Ouisa (Ms. Channing) and her husband, Flan (Mr. Cunningham), a high-rolling art dealer. Paul is a charming, articulate dissembler on all subjects who has the Kittredges in thrall. He is also a petty thief who invites a male hustler into the guest room he occupies while waiting for his "father" to take up residence at the Sherry-Netherland Hotel.

Much as this situation, a rude twist on "Guess Who's Coming to Dinner," lends itself to the satirical mayhem Mr. Wolfe inflicted on white liberals in "Radical Chic," Mr. Guare has not written a satire about race relations. Paul, the black man whose real identity the Kittredges never learn, becomes the fuse that ignites a larger investigation of the many degrees of separation that prevent all the people in the play from knowing one another and from knowing themselves.

It is not only blacks and whites who are estranged in Mr. Guare's New York. As the action accelerates and the cast of characters expands, the audience discovers that the Kittredges and their privileged friends don't know their alienated children, that heterosexuals don't know homosexuals, that husbands don't know their wives, that art dealers don't know the art they trade for millions. The only thing that everyone in this play's Manhattan has in common is the same American malady that afflicted the working-class Queens inhabitants of "House of Blue Leaves" — a desire to bask in the glow of the rich and famous. Here that hunger takes the delirious form of a maniacal desire to appear as extras in Sidney Poitier's purported film version of "Cats," a prospect Paul dangles in front of his prey.

•

Yet these people hunger for more as well, for a human connection and

perhaps a spiritual one. It is Paul, of all people, who points the way, by his words and his deeds. In a virtuoso monologue about "Catcher in the Rye," he decries a world in which assassins like Mark David Chapman and John W. Hinckley Jr. can take Holden Caulfield as a role model — a world in which imagination has ceased to be a means of self-examination and has become instead "something outside ourselves," whether a handy excuse for murderous behavior or a merchandisable commodity like van Gogh's "Irises" or an escapist fashion promoted by "The Warhol Diaries." Intentionally or not, Paul helps bring Ouisa into a reunion with her imagination, with her authentic self. His trail of fraud, which ultimately brushes against death, jolts his hostess out of her own fraudulent life among what Holden Caulfield calls phonies so that she might at last break through the ontological paralysis separating her from what really matters.

•

Among the many remarkable aspects of Mr. Guare's writing is the seamlessness of his imagery, characters and themes, as if this play had just erupted from his own imagination in one perfect piece. "There are two sides to every story," says a comic character, a duped New York Hospital obstetrician (Stephen Pearlman), and every aspect of "Six Degrees of Separation," its own story included, literally or figuratively shares this duality, from Paul's identity to a Kandinsky painting that

twirls above the Kittredge living room to the meaning of a phrase like "striking coal miners." The double vision gives the play an airy, Cubist dramatic structure even as it reflects the class divisions of its setting and the Jungian splits of its characters' souls.

Mr. Guare is just as much in control of the brush strokes that shift his play's disparate moods: In minutes, he can take the audience from a college student who is a screamingly funny personification of upper-middle-class New York Jewish rage (Evan Handler) to a would-be actor from Utah (Paul McCrane) of the same generation and opposite temperament. Though Mr. Guare quotes. Donald Barthelme's observation that "collage is the art form of the 20th

century," his play does not feel like a collage. As conversant with Cézanne and the Sistine Chapel as it is with Sotheby's and "Starlight Express," this work aspires to the classical esthetics and commensurate unity of spirit that are missing in the pasted-together, fragmented 20th-century lives it illuminates.

That spirit shines through. Great as the intellectual pleasures of the evening may be, it is Mr. Guare's compassion that allows his play to make the human connections that elude his characters. The people who walk in and out of the picture frames of Mr. Walton's set are not satirical cartoons but ambiguous, full-blooded creations. There's a Gatsby-like poignance to the studied glossy-magazine aspirations of Mr. McDaniel's

Paul, a Willy Loman-ish sadness to the soiled idealism of Mr. Cunningham's art dealer. As the one character who may finally see the big picture and begin to understand the art of living, the wonderful Ms. Channing steadily gains gravity as she journeys flawlessly from the daffy comedy of a fatuous dinner party to the harrowing internal drama of her own rebirth.

•

"It was an experience," she says with wonder of her contact with the impostor she never really knew. For the author and his heroine, the challenge is to hold on to true experience in a world in which most human encounters are bogus and nearly all are instantly converted into the disposable anecdotes, the floating collage scraps that are the glib currency of urban intercourse. In "Six Degrees of Separation," one of those passing anecdotes has been ripped from the daily paper and elevated into a transcendent theatrical experience that is itself a lasting vision of the humane new world of which Mr. Guare and his New Yorkers so hungrily dream.

1990 Je 15, C1:2

Stockard Channing, left, James McDaniel, center, and John Cunningham in "Six Degrees of Separation" at the Mitzi E. Newhouse Theater.

Brigitte Lacombe/"Six Degrees of Separation'

Ghosts

Univ. at Stony Brook

Conor Mullen, left and Doreen Hepburn in "Ghosts," at Staller Center for the Arts.

A new version of Ibsen's classic by Thomas Kilroy; directed by Michael Scott; set and cotumes, Geraldine O'Malley; lighting, Leslie Scott; production manager, Trevor Dawson. The Abbey Theater, presented by the Staller Center for the Arts. At the State University at Stony Brook, L.I.

Jacko English .... Kevin Flood
Regina English .... Noelle Brown
Father Manning .... David Kelly
Mrs. Helen Aylward .... Doreen Hepburn
Oliver Aylward .... Conor Mullen

By STEPHEN HOLDEN

STONY BROOK, L.I., June 12 — In updating Henrik Ibsen's "Ghosts," what could be flashier than to change the disease that represents an upper-class family's tragic curse from syphilis to AIDS?

That is exactly what the Abbey Theater of Ireland has done in its adaptation of Ibsen's gloomy drama. The play, whose five-night run at the Staller Center here concludes tomorrow evening, is the first of six events to be presented in the next month as the center's International Theater Festival. But if the production represents an honorable attempt to inject some contemporary resonance into a classic, its efforts to be both of the moment and respectful toward the original's tone and symbolic structure never harmonize.

•

In adapting "Ghosts," the playwright Thomas Kilroy has moved the play's setting from late 19th-century

Norway to contemporary Ireland and renamed the characters. Helene and Osvald Alving, the original play's mother and son, are now Helen and Oliver Aylward. Its venal, duplicitous cleric, Pastor Manders, is called Father Manning. The original play's orphanage is changed to a home for unwed mothers.

By making AIDS instead of syphilis the disease that is the play's metaphor for the family's tragic inheritance, Mr. Kilroy has tampered with the drama's central concept: that the sins of the fathers are literally passed on to their sons. In Ibsen, Osvald acquired his venereal disease as a little boy by smoking his father's pipe. In Mr. Kilroy's adaptation, the son returns from a trip to Europe and informs his mother that he is HIV positive. Although he defends homosexuality as a way of life, his sexual orientation is never made clear. In the new version, the father's vices are also painted more vividly. Helen describes her dead husband as a brutal sadist who "tried every variation of human sexuality." Father Manning has been made an emblem of conservative repression who pontificates about "the fight against modern secular humanism" and warns against "elements of the media hellbent on destroying the faith."

The trouble with Mr. Kilroy's adaptation is that these modern touches have been slapped onto the play like buzzwords. They may elicit little jolts of recognition, but they are still only superficial references in an adaptation that maintains a ponderous late-19th--century tone. That ponderousness is exacerbated by dialogue and performances that emphasize Ibsen's oratorical tendencies at the expense of genuine passion.

•

As directed by Michael Scott, the five actors deliver labored, stentorian performances that keep all the emotions frozen and at a distance. Doreen Hepburn plays Helen as a regal grande dame whose agonized confessions of concealed family secrets are delivered with an affected huffiness. As Oliver, Conor Mullen conveys only a fraction of his character's desperation and rebellious spirit. Although David Kelly's scheming priest exudes a dry, cadaverous creepiness, the actor conveys few signs of the character's deeper moral squalor.

The woodenness of the performances is underscored by static staging that often places the actors yards apart even in the heat of an argument. Far too many speeches are directed straight at the audience. Even with its contemporary touches, this production of "Ghosts" has the airless atmosphere of a 19th-century melodrama played without conviction.

1990 Je 15, C13:1

THEATER VIEW/Mel Gussow

Other Ways at the Shakespeare Festival

WITH THE RECENT NAMing of JoAnne Akalaitis as artistic associate, and the possibility that she will succeed Joseph Papp as artistic director, the New York Shakespeare Festival has taken a bold step into the future. For years, Ms. Akalaitis, a founding member of the Mabou Mines experimental theater company, has been one of the most innovative — and one of the most controversial — figures in the American theater. Nothing she does is safe and in no sense is she a director in the mainstream.

She has a full share of detractors and partisans. Her production of Samuel Beckett's "Endgame" at the American Repertory Theater in Cambridge, Mass., in 1984, which relocated the play in an abandoned subway station, provoked a protest from the author's spokesmen and, at a remove, from Beckett himself, accusing her of tampering with the text. Last season she had her first, bruising, encounter with Shakespeare, directing "Cymbeline" as her contribution to Joseph Papp's cycle of Shakespeare's complete works.

It seemed evident from her production that she had scant regard for the text, treating it — uncharacteristically — as an opportunity for directorial self-indulgence, which extended from miscasting to a misreading of the play, transposed to a world that was a cross between the Celtic and the Victorian. In answer to those who might wrongly regard "Cymbeline" as minor Shakespeare, there were Mark Lamos's version at Hartford Stage and Peter Hall's more recent produc-

tion at London's National Theater, both of which realized the imaginative potential within the play.

But just as directors can place their signature on theater companies, companies can al-

> **JoAnne Akalaitis, the Public's new artistic associate, has a reputation for a kind of feisty individualism.**

ter directors by offering them a wider platform and artistic independence. In any case, it is unlikely that Ms. Akalaitis would turn the Shakespeare Festival into a large-scale equivalent of Mabou Mines. Mabou Mines is sui generis. It thrives from the fact that it has no single artistic head, that it is an ensemble of directors, writers, actors and artists working together in democratic fashion.

One would hope that any Shakespeare Festival, under Mr. Papp or Ms. Akalaitis, will always find room for such troupes as Mabou Mines. But the company's mission is both broader and deeper in purpose — to produce new plays, with the emphasis on what is socially conscious, and to do Shakespeare and other classics. Ms. Akalaitis is not the first director to achieve administrative prominence at the Shakespeare Festival. Gerald Freedman and Wilford Leach were both principal directors, but not with the autonomy that Mr. Papp has promised his new associate.

In her new role at the Shakespeare Festival Ms. Akalaitis will direct plays and will also be instrumental in selecting plays for others to direct. This suggests that she will have to open herself to a world of dramatic literature — to Chekhov, Ibsen and others as well as to today's playwrights. In her favor is her lack of rigidity in matters of art. As she

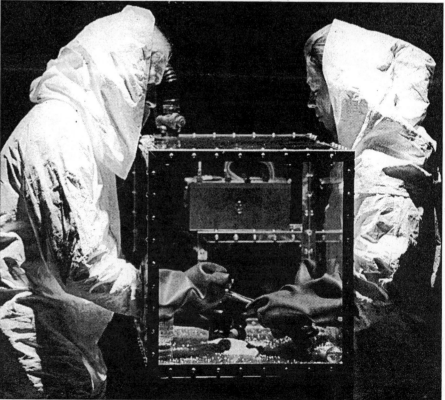

Carol Rosegg-Martha Swope Associates/"Dead End Kids"

George Bartenieff and Ruth Maleczech in the Mabou Mines production of "Dead End Kids," created by JoAnne Akalaitis

said several years ago, she has neither "a master career or esthetic agenda" in mind.

In her two decades with Mabou Mines and, more recently, as a freelance director (and occasional playwright) at the Public Theater and in regional theaters, Ms. Akalaitis has achieved a reputation for a kind of feisty individualism, as expressed through her plays and not through public utterances. In contrast to producers she has worked for, she has wisely refrained from a public battle of words and has instead confined herself to creating art (a healthy sign, given her emergence as a company leader). The range of her art is wide though often rarefied. It is also — and this is where she has been subject to criticism — freely interpretive.

When she took Samuel Beckett's brief radio play "Cascando" and turned it into a stage play, finding visual correlatives for what was entirely an auditory experience, there was general appreciation of her efforts, but when she had the temerity to attempt "Endgame," there were outcries. Overlooked was the fact that, except for the altered setting, Ms. Akalaitis's production was true to the words as well as the essential spirit of the play. Similarly, she has been faithful — though interpretive — to the work of Franz Xaver Kroetz, most notably with "Through the Leaves" (which she did at the Public in 1984 and which is scheduled to be revived there in the fall) and "Request Concert," that haunting, wordless document of a woman's suicide. Admittedly, Kroetz's plays are like scenarios, allowing and even encouraging directorial collaboration.

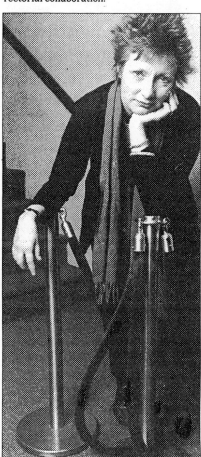

Robin Holland

JoAnne Akalaitis—In her favor is a lack of rigidity in matters of art.

In her own work as a playwright, she has been equally imaginative while remaining responsive to her source, especially so in the case of "Dressed Like an Egg." This dramatic collage drawn from the life and work of Colette, remains a paradigm of literary adaptation. Presented in 1977 at the Public Theater, "Dressed Like an Egg" was neither a biographical drama nor a compilation of Colette stories, but an impressionistic canvas of visual and verbal imagery inspired by Colette. That same year, Ms. Akalaitis casually filled in "a dream test" in a newspaper and was categorized as "a transformative dreamer," a description that she took quite seriously.

This is in fact a most appropriate label for her role as theater artist, as she combines art objects and moves them from one medium to another, as she transforms dreams into stage reality. The title "Dressed Like an Egg" came from an actual Akalaitis dream, in which she saw a beautiful dress with a pattern of eggs on it, and decided the image was very romantic and feminine — like Colette. In "Southern Exposure," she fantasized about Antarctic exploration, and in "Dead End Kids" she looked to the past and found the future. "Dead End Kids," which is a documentary vaudeville show about atomic experimentation and radiation, is an example of the avant-garde using its resources for political purposes.

She has had her share of failures, on the smallest of scale with "Red and Blue" some seasons ago at the Public Theater, a void for voices (no actors, no action, no point), not of her authorship, and on a grand scale with "Cymbeline."

Ms. Akalaitis has staged major productions of more modern classics, including her well-reviewed versions of Büchner's "Leonce and Lena" and Genet's "Screens," both at the Guthrie Theater in Minneapolis. With the exception of "Cymbeline," her New York productions have been chamber-size works. If Shakespeare were beyond her grasp, she would certainly be an anomaly as a key force at the New York Shakespeare Festival. One would hope that "Cymbeline" was a learning experience and that next time she would be more judicious in honoring the intention of the author. Having laid the necessary groundwork, she could then — in Akalaitis fashion — approach a play as a transformative dream. □

1990 Je 17, II:5:1

Florida Girls

Written and performed by Nancy Hasty; directed by Robert Stewart; set and production management, E. F. Morrill; sound, J. Bloomrosen; stage manager, Lloyd Davis Jr. Presented by Eric Krebs. At the Arielle Theater, 432 West 42d Street.

By STEPHEN HOLDEN

In "Florida Girls," Nancy Hasty's autobiographical memory play set in Crestview, Fla., in 1965, Ms. Hasty, a big-boned, deep-voiced actress, portrays all eight members of the Van Helms family, a blue-collar clan that includes five sisters and their loony, Bible-toting grandmother.

The play, which is divided into 10 short scenes, is really an evening-length dramatic monologue similar in style to one of Eric Bogosian's solo sketches. But instead of purveying searing sociological insights, it basks in a mood of barbed, comic nostalgia.

Ms. Hasty is neither a brilliant vocal mimic like Mr. Bogosian nor an instinctive comic actress like Lily Tomlin, who is able to distill eccentric personalities through refined caricature. More of a storyteller than an actress, she is at least able to distinguish characters from one another by altering the tone of her voice. But in the 90-minute show, at the Theater Arielle, she never completely transforms herself into someone else.

The strongest element of "Florida Girls" is Ms. Hasty's writing. Her detailed descriptions of a small-town world where everybody is in everyone else's hair make the boredom and claustrophobia of belonging to a large family and living in a small town almost palpable. In the most vivid scenes, two of the younger Van Helms daughters are dropped off by their parents for the weekend at the home of their fundamentalist Christian grandmother, who assigns them absurd tasks like scrubbing used hairpins. The old woman also takes them to church, where they are treated to a fire-and-brimstone sermon denouncing the local beauty contest in which the two oldest Van Helms girls are both contestants.

Another sharply drawn scene introduces Bobbi, a family friend and a former beauty contestant who is regarded as a local celebrity because she once worked as a model in Atlanta. Bobbi demonstrates how to "rotate" when walking by imagining a

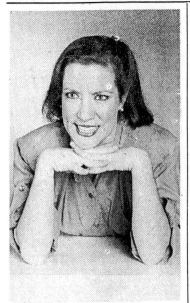

Carol Rosegg/Martha Swope Associates/"Florida Girls"

Nancy Hasty in her autobiographical play, "Florida Girls."

penny clenched between the buttocks. She also demonstrates how to leave a room without showing her back and offers useful tips on pageant attire, the most important being that "the hem of the gown should kiss the shoe." The action of the play builds to the beauty contest, at which one of competing sisters recites an awkward biblically inspired answer to the question "When does a person become an adult?" and the other warbles an off-pitch rendition of "I Enjoy Being a Girl."

If Ms. Hasty's play shows a comic affection for the world it describes, its portrait of Crestview suggests a place so provincial and narrowminded that it would drive anyone with ambition and imagination to flee at the earliest opportunity. The level of culture is evoked by a parade of insipid 50's hit records by Doris Day, Perry Como and others that punctuate the scenes. One leaves "Florida Girls" reminded that family ties not only bind but often constrict.

1990 Je 21, C20:1

Maids of Honor

Blanche Mackey/Martha Swope Associates

Elizabeth McGovern

By Joan Casademont; directed by Max Mayer; set by Edward T. Gianfrancesco; lighting by Craig Evans; costumes by Mimi Maxmen; sound by Aural Fixation; production stage manager, Denise Laffer. Presented by WPA Theater, Kyle Renick, artistic director; Donna Lieberman, managing director. At 519 West 23d Street.

Isabelle Bowlin	Elizabeth McGovern
Annie Bowlin	Kyra Sedgwick
Monica Bowlin	Laila Robins
Pat Weinhardt	Kristine Nielsen
Harry Hobson	John Michael Higgins
Joel Silverman	Jake Weber
Roger Dowling	Joe Urla

By WILBORN HAMPTON

It is one of the myths of matrimony that both bride and groom suffer last-minute misgivings the night before the wedding. But rarely does an epidemic of panic infect an entire family as in Joan Casademont's "Maids of Honor," a new play at the WPA Theater that is, to be quite honest, a bit of a mess.

At the center of what becomes a great deal of sound and fury is Monica Bowlin (Laila Robins), a vain television talk-show host who is about to marry a millionaire stockbroker named Chuck. Monica, who boasts of being "a bitch" and has been through seven therapists, has ordered 2,058 orchids and an enormous tent for the ceremony, and her main worry seems to be getting her makeup right for the outdoor lighting that the television crew has set up. Lest anyone think Monica is totally self-centered, however, she confesses that she wants to have children. She just wants *her* babies to be born with trust funds.

But Monica's kid sister, Isabelle (Elizabeth McGovern), has some bad news. Izzy, as she is known, is a news assistant for a big-city newspaper, and she has been helping an investigative reporter nail down a story naming Chuck as an insider trader. The reporter (Jake Weber) even shows up at the Bowlin house in Marblehead, Mass., to offer Monica proof that her intended mate is soon to be

Three sisters, two ex-beaus and one bridegroom headed for jail.

an inmate. The icing on this multi-layered wedding cake is the arrival of Roger (Joe Urla), an ex-boyfriend of Monica's who has driven up to return a diary that Monica left when she moved out on him, and to rake over some old coals to see if there are any sparks left between them. For a subplot, the caterer for the weddding, Harry Hobson (John Michael Higgins), is an old flame of Annie (Kyra Sedgwick), the middle Bowlin sister, and he tries to woo her back.

•

Some gaps in Ms. Casademont's tale strain credulity from the start. But even if one overlooks the author's scant understanding of journalism and accepts the device of having a crucial plot twist come from a lost diary that conveniently falls into the wrong hands, there are other problems. Not least among them is that very little of what is said or happens in "Maids of Honor" is even mildly amusing. The dialogue is littered with lines like "Life is full of compromises." And the play seems to support the absurd romantic notion that a man and a woman who argue and shout at one another must be truly in love.

There is a subtext to "Maids of Honor" that surfaces briefly in a couple of scenes, and one wishes Ms. Casademont had explored it more deeply. The three sisters are the daughters of an alcoholic father and an abused mother, both now dead. When the sisters examine the sense of guilt they were made to feel for their father's alcoholism and their inherent

sense of being unlovable, the characters come alive and the play begins to take on some meaning. But this flash of real drama is quickly abandoned to the futile pursuit of laughter.

One has a feeling through most of "Maids of Honor" that Ms. Casademont was writing with a television camera in mind rather than a proscenium stage. She seems to adopt the premise that it is the situation that makes the comedy, rather than the people involved in it, and the little plot surprises that she plants throughout the play spring up at regular intervals as though timed for commercial breaks. What emerges is a quite predictable story and characters who for the most part are shallow individuals with little to say of genuine wit or insight.

The performances vary widely. Ms. McGovern is a natural actor and always a joy to watch. Her Izzy testifies to Ms. McGovern's ability to breathe some life into the weakest of roles. As Harry the caterer, Mr. Higgins presents a sympathetic guy who is just trying to get his girl back. Izzy and Harry, in fact, are about the only people in this wedding party one would want to go have a beer with. Ms. Robins tries hard between tantrums to find something likable in Monica, but her character may after all be more temperamentally suited to Roger, who in Mr. Urla's hands is potentially violent if not actually homicidal. Max Mayer has directed as though zaniness is somehow synonymous with frenzy. The result is closer to shrill.

1990 Je 22, C3:3

Love Life

Music by Kurt Weill; book and lyrics by Alan Jay Lerner; directed by Barry Harman; choreographed by Christopher Chadman; music director, Robert Kapilow; additional book materials by Thomas Babe; orchestrations and arrangements by Mr. Weill; set design, Loren Sherman; lighting, Beverly Emmons; costumes, Randy Barcelo; sound, Alan Stieb; production stage manager, Renee Lutz. Presented by A.T.&T.: Onstage and American Music Theater Festival, Marjorie Samoff, producing director; Eric Salzman, artistic director. At the Walnut Street Theater, Philadelphia.

Swank	Neal Ben-Ari
Samuel Cooper	Richard Muenz
Susan Cooper	Debbie Shapiro

WITH: Dennis Callahan, David Enriquez, Tony Field, Nicole Fosse, Don Hoshko, Kathryn Kendall, Betsy Ann Leadbetter, Don Mayo, Michael McCoy, Maureen McNamara, Mike Paternostro, Jamie Dale Sheppard, Steven Sophia, Lynn Sterling, Christopher Vettel and Valerie Wright.

By STEPHEN HOLDEN

Special to The New York Times

PHILADELPHIA, June 16 — "Love Life," a 1948 Kurt Weill-Alan Jay Lerner musical that is being given its first major revival by the American Music Theater Festival in Philadelphia, is a fascinating, odd duck of a show.

Created nearly 20 years before the term "concept musical" was invented to describe thematic shows like "Company" and "Follies," "Love Life" was far ahead of its time both in form and subject matter. Subtitled "A Vaudeville," it counterpoints the story of an all-American couple's unraveling marriage with comic production numbers, introduced by a clown-nosed master of ceremonies named Swank, that comment ironically on the story.

The troubled union of Samuel and Susan Cooper, moreover, isn't just

any marriage, but rather an alliance loaded with historical weight. The story begins in 1792 in the small Connecticut town of Mayville, where the young couple has just set up house. It ends more than 150 years later in contemporary Manhattan where they are on the verge of a divorce. In between, a chronological sequence of historical tableaux carries them and their two children to the factories of Bridgeport in the 1890's and the decks of the Queen Elizabeth in 1929.

Samuel Cooper's metamorphosis from honest carpenter to wheeler-dealer businessman becomes the show's central metaphor for the crumbling of the American dream, in which historical events that include the Industrial Revolution, the women's rights movement and the rise of radio and television conspire to alienate this prototypical American couple from each other.

In the American Music Theater Production that runs through Sunday at the Walnut Street Theater here, "Love Life" emerges as an absorbing but flawed work whose ambitions far exceed its accomplishments. Its biggest weakness is the strained symbolism by which the Coopers' marriage is contorted into a metaphor for America's failing spiritual health. Ultimately the two ideas just don't mesh. And in a final sequence, a minstrel show in which the Coopers are tempted by Swank to console themselves with dangerous illusions (fortunetelling, cynicism, and faith in "Mr. Right"), the show runs out of wind.

Still, "Love Life" has many strengths, not the least of which is the Weill-Lerner score. In Weill's seventh Broadway show after emigrating from Germany to the United States, the composer's tunes demonstrate a sure mastery of American vernacular styles tinged with a residual European formality. The two loftiest songs are the glowing ballad "Here I'll Stay" and Samuel's final bitter soliloquy, "This Is the Life." Among the vaudevillian numbers, "Women's Club Blues," a 20's-style bump-and-grind in which Lerner's cheeky lyric compares a woman's right to work with sexual liberation, is the wittiest.

As the Coopers, Richard Muenz, who possesses a baritone of striking richness and warmth, and Debbie Shapiro, who can sound disconcertingly like Eydie Gormé, give strong, full-bodied vocal performances. Barry Harman, who directed, has taken a cautious approach to a show that might well have benefited from a more surreal one. Although the vaudevillian ringmaster, Swank (Neal Ben-Ari), who sets the tone for the evening, has plenty of demonic potential, the character's dark side is masked under a kindly bonhomie.

Christopher Chadman's skillful choreography in the production numbers is similarly cautious in its avoidance of overtly satirical and expressionistic touches. There is a cheery martial energy in his deployment of the ensemble in strutting and kicking formations that make efficient use of the set's several staircases.

"Love Life" may be a flawed work, but it is never dull. And in the festival's workmanlike production, one can sense the feverish heat of its creators' imaginations as they broke musical-theater ground that wouldn't be built upon until "Cabaret" 18 years later. If Weill and Lerner couldn't figure out how to bring their experiment to a satisfying conclusion, "Love Life" remains a show of unusual conceptual audacity and flair.

1990 Je 22, C15:1

Swim Visit

By Wesley Moore; directed by William Partlan; set, Robert Klingelhoefer; lighting, Tina Charney; costumes, Amanda J. Klein; sound, Gayle Jeffery; fight choreography, Jake Turner; associate producer, Herbert H. O'-Dell; general manager, Gordon Farrell. Presented by Primary Stages Company Inc., Casey Childs, artistic director; Janet Reed, associate artistic director. At 354 West 45th Street.

Izz ....Caroline Lagerfelt
Beth ....Alice Haining
Ted ....Pirie MacDonald
Clay ....Mark Metcalf

By WILBORN HAMPTON

Perhaps there's a play to be written about four people sitting around a backyard swimming pool in the Midwest on a sunny Sunday in May discussing the vagaries of the fiberglass business between dips, but Wesley Moore's "Swim Visit," the current production at Primary Stages, is not it.

At the outset, Izz (Caroline Lagerfelt) and her friend Beth (Alice Haining) are relaxing on chaise longues, soaking up the first rays of summer, while Ted (Pirie MacDonald), Izz's husband, sits nearby reading a magazine and waiting for Clay (Mark Metcalf) to arrive. Clay is the quality control manager at Ted's fiberglass plant, and he has come to tell his boss that their fiberglass trays aren't selling as well as they used to and that the company will soon go bankrupt unless they retool and come up with a better line of trays. For reasons never exactly made clear, Ted adamantly opposes this plan.

That's about it for the drama, a duel fought with hedge clippers and a beach towel notwithstanding. There is a lot of dialogue about whether there is enough chlorine in the water and whether to put on more suntan lotion. In fact, Mr. Moore's characters offer one another suntan oil the way Noël Coward's characters offer one another cigarettes or highballs. While this may achieve a certain verisimilitude of poolside conversation, it is not the stuff of memorable drama. Or comedy either, for that matter.

•

In fact, "Swim Visit" is not so much a play as a quartet of character sketches, and rather flimsy ones at that, occupying the same stage. Izz is full of sarcasm, a woman whose normal speaking tone can most flatteringly be described as snide. In Ms. Lagerfelt's hands, she can turn a question like, "What are you reading, Ted?" into a sneering accusation. But the reasons for Izz's nasty sarcasm toward everyone else remain a mystery. Beth, on the other hand, is introduced as a rather demure, withdrawn and even shy young widow. About two minutes after meeting Clay, however, Beth confides to this stranger how her mean alcoholic husband died in a car crash on the first day of his sobriety. She no sooner finishes this personal confession than she invites Clay to take off his shirt, and he barely gets it unbuttoned before she asks him to rub suntan oil on her back ("You have such strong hands"), and then, not one to waste time, to hold her ("You have strong arms"). Ted is a bore whose thoughts seem to be elsewhere through most of the two acts. And strong-handed and strong-armed Clay appears to be totally perplexed as to why he is there.

The cast of four works hard at trying to generate some tension onstage, but the only real question by the end is what are four talented actors, especially Ms. Lagerfelt and Mr. Metcalf, doing here in the first place. William Partlan directed.

1990 Je 23, 12:4

What's Wrong With This Picture?

By Donald Margulies; directed by Larry Arrick; sets, Ray Recht; costumes, Jeffrey Ullman; lights, Brian Nason; stage manager, Nina Heller. Presented by Jewish Repertory Theater, Ran Avni, artistic director; Edward M. Cohen, associate director. At 344 East 14th Street.

Artie ....Stephen Mailer
Mort ....Michael Lombard
Bella ....Dolores Sutton
Sid ....Salem Ludwig
Ceil ....Barbara Spiegel
Shirley ....Lauren Klein

By RICHARD F. SHEPARD

There is something about the phrase "coping with loss" that conjures a television melodrama in which people bravely learn to deal with a future that's minus someone near and dear. "What's Wrong With This Picture?," a new comedy by Donald Margulies at the Jewish Repertory Theater, takes off on this theme, but instead of evoking tears it goes for the laughs, and certainly gets them.

Shirley, the wife and mother of this Brooklyn household, has died, and the family is just winding up the weeklong Jewish mourning period. She choked on a piece of pork at a Chinese restaurant, and Mort, her adoring husband, reproaches himself for letting her talk him out of taking her to the deli. He hollers at Artie, the son who shouted "liar" at the rabbi during the excessive eulogy, to find the laundry ticket for his shirts. "I have no wife, I have no shirts," he observes, no less pathetic for grieving in material rather than spiritual terms.

He tells Artie he would like a simple funeral for himself, and Artie says,"I'll leave you on the F train."

Grandma Bella sighs and says of Shirley, "Maybe if she cooked a little more, she'd be alive today."

Absent-minded Grandpa Sid tells Artie that his own mother died when he was 57 and that he couldn't stop himself from crying like a baby. Artie is still strong, he says: "Better it should happen while you're young."

The relatives exit, leaving father and son alone, and they still can't get over the loss. Mort won't give away Shirley's dresses and won't leave the house, and makes Artie wear his mother's flashy red gown. There doesn't seem much else to all this

> ## 'Maybe if she cooked a little more, she'd be alive today.'

until, toward the end of Act I, Shirley walks in the door, disheveled and tired but ready to clean the house. How did she get here from there, Mort asks. "The B.Q.E.?"

Shirley is cheerful but she feels cold. Somebody asks her, "You're a ghost, right?" Shirley barely pauses before saying, with steeply soaring inflection, "So?"

The second act moves at somewhat slower pace, getting a little deeper into the business of living with fantasy and hope rather than reality, but each time things seem on the verge of going over the brink into schmaltz, Mr. Margulies pulls it back with deft dialogue and wit. His is the perfect ear for New York speech, an ideal understanding that gets inside the calloused exterior of people who are not given to exploring themselves. Under Larry Arrick's deft direction, there are no lulls, no awkward waits for moralizing.

Although this is a new comedy, it was performed as a workshop production at the Manhattan Theater Club in 1985.

The play is felicitously cast: one might meet all the players outside the mourning room at a local funeral home. Michael Lombard is splendid as the bereaved husband who, mercurial and rough-cut, cannot accept Shirley's death. Stephen Mailer, as Artie, is a persuasive young man who can't stand much of the family even though he is obviously greatly attached to them.

Dolores Sutton, as Bella, is the personification of a shrewd, if vapid, woman who rambles on with almost peasant imperturbility and is unwittingly hilarious. Salem Ludwig makes of the doddering grandfather not only a funny character but one

with surprising depths of feeling as well — not an easy trick. Then there is Shirley, the ghost, played with rosy practicality and infinite optimism by Lauren Klein. Filling out ths family circle is Barbara Spiegel as Ceil, an aunt who is hurrying to leave the mourning session for a date and another chance at meeting the perfect fellow.

"What's Wrong With This Picture?" is a very pleasant interlude of theater, and if it's not Ibsen or O'Neill or Pinter, it tackles troubles from another angle and uses just the right words to tell about it.

1990 Je 23, 14:1

Falsettoland

Conceived by William Finn and James Lapine; music and lyrics by Mr. Finn; directed by Mr. Lapine; set design by Douglas Stein; costume design by Franne Lee; lighting design by Nancy Schertler; sound design by Scott Lehrer; musical theater program director, Ira Weitzman; production stage manager, Kate Riddle; musical direction and arrangements by Michael Starobin. Presented by Playwrights Horizons, Andre Bishop, artistic director; Paul S. Daniels, executive director. At 416 West 42d Street.

Mendel ....Chip Zien
Marvin ....Michael Rupert
Jason ....Danny Gerard
Whizzer ....Stephen Bogardus
Trina ....Faith Prince
Dr. Charlotte ....Heather MacRae
Cordelia ....Janet Metz

By FRANK RICH

Nearly 10 years after its debut, the electric opening number of William Finn's breakthrough musical, "March of the Falsettos," remains emblazoned in memory: A handful of leapfrogging young performers, backed by a jazzy band, charged forward on a red stage at Playwrights Horizons to sing merrily about the neurotic plight of "Four Jews in a Room Bitching."

What followed was just as unorthodox. "March of the Falsettos" told of Marvin (Michael Rupert), who left his wife and son for a man named Whizzer (Stephen Bogardus) only to lose Whizzer and to watch his psychiatrist, Mendel (Chip Zien), move in on his abandoned family. Mr. Finn and his collaborator, the director James Lapine, told this story in 70 minutes of songs that were far more melodious and touching than titles like "My Father's a Homo" and "Marvin at the Psychiatrist (a Three-Part Mini-Opera)" might immediately suggest.

•

You can't go home again, of course, yet right at the beginning of "Falsettoland," Mr. Finn's bracing new installment of the Marvin trilogy that began in 1978 with "In Trousers," that surge of excitement is uncannily re-created. And on the surface, little has changed. "Falsettoland" is set in 1981-82, right after its predecessor. The theater is again Playwrights Horizons, the director is again Mr. Lapine, the running time is again 70 minutes, the stage remains red, the three terrific lead actors are back in place (looking no worse for wear) and, best of all, the music and lyrics still ignite. As a mobile red door twirls about — another emblem of "Falsettos" — the company exuberantly welcomes us to Falsettoland, a figurative precinct whose landmarks include homosexuals, women with children, "a teeny tiny band" and "one bar mitzvah" — for Marvin's

Carol Rosegg/Martha Swope Associates/"What's Wrong With This Picture?"
Michael Lombard and Lauren Klein in a scene from "What's Wrong With This Picture?" at the Jewish Repertory Theater.

son, Jason (Danny Gerard) — "that is scrupulously planned."

But just as it would be tedious for "Falsettoland" to keep mimicking "March of the Falsettos," so it soon proves impossible. An intervening decade cannot be stuffed into a closet. While Mr. Finn is blissfully back in full voice after several projects of esthetic drift, that voice has inevitably been tempered by time; some of his ethnic humor seems a bit strained even as his sentiments about romance in hard times are more deeply felt. Mr. Lapine, perhaps reflecting his post-"Falsettos" Broadway success with Stephen Sondheim ("Sunday in the Park With George," "Into the Woods"), seems to be directing with more dazzling assurance than ever, creating a kaleidoscopic world of comedy and heartbreak with only seven performers, that red door and, as before, a few rolling chairs.

The biggest changes, however, are those that befall Marvin and Whizzer. "Falsettoland" is only a few numbers old when the happy reconciliation of these two lovers is clouded by the hospital observations of their friend Dr. Charlotte (Heather MacRae), an internist who lives nearby with her lover, a kosher caterer (Janet Metz). "Something very bad is happening . . . spreading round" sings Ms. MacRae's doctor in a voice of unsettling, ethereal sweetness: "Bachelors arrive sick and frightened/They leave, weeks later, unenlightened."

•

What is happening is so bad "that words have lost their meaning," she adds. In 1981, the word to describe what is "spreading round" had, in fact, yet to spread. But Mr. Finn finds his own words. Without losing the sense of humor that made "March of the Falsettos" levitate, he has written an achingly articulate musical that copes with AIDS much as its characters do — with denial, rage, empathy and even some small hope that what Marvin's son, Jason, calls a "miracle of Judaism" will come to the rescue. Never maudlin, clinical or didactic — but always, in some hard-won way or another, high-spirited — "Falsetto-

land" is a musical of jubilance and courage, not defeat. It must have taken exceptional fortitude to write, and it is by turns entertaining and devastating to witness.

"This story needs an ending," sings the chipper company in the opening number. There are hilarious passages on the way to an ending none could have foretold. Jason's extended family, who can turn even a catering debate into a conga line, visits a Little League game and sings of "watching Jewish boys who cannot play baseball play baseball." Jason and Mendel perform a high-stepping vaudeville number titled "Everybody Hates His Parents" in which Mr. Zien's delightfully circumspect psychiatrist reassures his stepson that "you grow up, you get old, you hate less." Even after the curtain dominating Douglas Stein's sleek set has become a hospital curtain, "Falsettoland" does not surrender its right to a joke. The evening builds to a bar mitzvah in the Philip Roth mode, though in Jason's case the ceremony also proves to be the stirring spiritual initiation into manhood that satirical bar mitzvahs seldom are.

Mr. Finn's more sober songs reflect a cultural sea change from "Falsettos," in which "pretty boys" were instructed to "check for acne" and the death of passion was the only one its young lovers feared. There are several full-throated ballads here, led by "Unlikely Lovers," a soaring quartet of devotion in which the musical's paired homosexual couples vow to "be scared together." In "You Gotta Die Sometime," Mr. Bogardus caps an altogether superlative performance with the ferocious, unsentimental blues of a man in his prime facing mortality. When the moment comes for Marvin to give in to "tears and schmaltz" — and to take the audience with him — Mr. Rupert does so with his characteristic, eternally boyish tenderness in "What Would I Do?," a song that both mourns and resurrects the adored lover for whom he left his wife and child.

The soul-searching interludes for the heterosexual characters in "Falsettoland" sometimes seem forced

by comparison, especially the schematic anthem, heartily delivered by Faith Prince, in which Marvin's former wife rises too easily to saintliness. Nor is the relationship between Marvin and his son so intimately dramatized here as it was in "Falsettos." This time, Mr. Finn seems to broaden his characters a bit to keep them on their best behavior — as if AIDS really did bring out the nobility in everyone — and the consequences spill into his score, which, for all the shimmer of Michael Starobin's arrangements, could at times use more variety and vinegar.

Such flaws do not seriously diminish the overall achievement, which culminates in a chilling finale that inverts the charged opening number so completely that everything from the performers' emotional and physical gravity to the set's red door to the meaning of playful lyrics ("we're a teeny tiny band") is transformed by the disease that has in the interim transformed a society. "This is where we take a stand," sings Mr. Zien as he welcomes the audience to a new Falsettoland where lovers no longer just come and go but "live and die fortissimo." That stand is a defiant one for music, love, laughter and miracles, Jewish or otherwise, in a world where something very bad has been happening for so very long.

1990 Je 29, C3:1

Jekyll and Hyde

Book and lyrics by David Crane and Marta Kauffman; music by Michael Skloff; directed by Jay Harnick; choreographed by Helen Butleroff; musical arrangements by Steve Orich; sets by Vaughn Patterson; costumes by Anne-Marie Wright; musical direction by Wayne Abravanel; production stage manager, Ronald A. Koenig; lighting by Mathew J. Williams; sound consultants, Gary and Timmy Harris. Presented by Theaterworks USA, Mr. Harnick, artistic director; Charles Hull, managing director. At the Promenade Theater, Broadway and 76th Street.

Henry	Christopher Scott
Stuart	Eric Ruffin
Marissa/Mother	Amanda Green
Chelsea	Emily Bear
Vernicker/Father	Fredrick Einhorn

By STEPHEN HOLDEN

"Jekyll and Hyde," which opens Theaterworks/USA's second four-week season of free Off-Broadway summer theater for young people, is a musical that wants to entertain while putting over a serious message about the perils of substance abuse. Until it ends with an abrupt, heavy-handed clunk, the hourlong show at the Promenade Theater succeeds ad-

mirably in maintaining the precarious balance between being fun and conveying its warning against the pitfalls of quick chemical fixes.

Loosely adapted from Robert Louis Stevenson's classic tale, the musical, which has a book and lyrics by David Crane and Marta Kauffman and music by Michael Skloff, tells the story of Henry Meckler, a shy, insecure high school student and amateur chemist who concocts what initially seems to be a magic potion. With one tiny swig, the nerdy Henry is able to turn himself into his fearless, swaggering alter-ego, Eddie.

Heroic and charming at first, Eddie substitutes for Henry in his high school classes. He makes a fool of the school bully who used to extort Henry's lunch money, and wins the heart of Chelsea (Emily Bear), the girl of Henry's dreams. But as Henry continues to take the potion, Eddie changes from cocky to reckless and threatening. He proposes a weekend outing involving car theft and breaking-and-entering, breaks the confidence of Henry's best friend by revealing a family secret, and sabotages a critical interview for a scholarship. Henry's parents become alarmed when they receive word from the high school that their son has been absent for days.

"Jekyll and Hyde" demonstrates an unusually high degree of workmanship for a show aimed at children (in this case between 10 and 17 years). The book deftly negotiates the tricky transposition of the story from late-19th-century London to a high school in contemporary Cleveland. From the opening number, in which Henry longingly envisions the liberation of "a very different me," Mr. Skloff's pop-rock music echoes Andrew Lloyd Webber, scaled-down and Americanized for the occasion.

Jay Harnick has directed the cast of five, some of whom play multiple roles in a breezy, informal style. Christopher Scott, who plays Henry/Eddie, has the challenging task of changing personalities, sometimes in mid-scene. In a performance that includes a lot of humor below the surface, he makes the prissy-nerdy Henry and his frantically hyped-up alter-ego seem like two sides of the same coin. Mr. Scott's only weakness is a wavering, whiny singing voice.

Because the show ends suddenly with the acknowledgement of Henry's problem but with no solutions in sight, the story seems frustratingly half-finished. The audience is left cut off, waiting for a second act that never arrives.

1990 Jl 1, 48:1

Gerry Goodstein/Playwrights Horizons/Falsettoland

Stephen Bogardus, left, and Michael Rupert in William Finn and James Lapine's "Falsettoland," at Playwrights Horizons.

STAGE VIEW/FRANK RICH

A Guidebook to the Soul Of a City in Confusion

TOWARD THE END OF JOHN GUARE'S NEW play, "Six Degrees of Separation," a young man named Rick takes center stage to describe the horrors that have befallen him in New York City. Rick, played by Paul McCrane, is a struggling actor who had hit town from Utah with visions of stardom. But now his eyes fight back tears, his mouth weakens with revulsion. Seduced and then discarded by a flashy confidence man who did him out of his money and sexual innocence at the Rainbow Room, Rick finds himself without means, without prospects, without self-respect and possibly without the devoted girl-friend he shunted aside for a reckless one-night stand.

"I came here to have experience," says Mr. McCrane, a shattered figure peering at the audience from beneath a lonely spotlight. "I didn't come here to be *this*."

Rick is only one dupe — the saddest — on a stage full of dupes in Mr. Guare's remarkable play, which was loosely inspired by the actual, 1983 confidence schemes of a young black man who fleeced New Yorkers by passing himself off as Sidney Poitier's son. In Mr. Guare's version, "Paul Poitier" (James McDaniel) also talks his way into the lives of a New York Hospital obstetrician (Stephen Pearlman) whose parents were Holocaust victims, a visiting South

John Guare's 'Six Degrees of Separation' moves beyond headlines to take the psychic pulse of a population.

African magnate (Sam Stoneburner), a warring married couple (Peter Maloney and Kelly Bishop) and, most promi-nently, Flan Kittredge (John Cunningham), a WASP-y, high-rolling private art dealer, and his devoted, terribly social wife, Ouisa (Stockard Channing). These are the smart, sophisticated, tough New Yorkers who populate the pages of the city's newspapers and glossy magazines — the folk one might meet in William Hamilton cartoons, Louis Auchincloss stories or Stephen Sondheim musicals. Yet they, like the hick actor, open their homes to a stranger with a gift for Ivy League gab and an infinite supply of clever lies.

Why is everyone so easily fooled? The answer to that question gives "Six Degrees of Separation" its searing substance, which, combined with its hugely entertaining surface, makes this play not only the long-awaited fulfillment of a playwriting career that promised so much with the 1971 "House of Blue Leaves," but also the outstanding American play in an outstanding sea-son for American plays. Mr. Guare has given the theater a work that runs only 90 minutes but that should linger, on stage and in its audience's consciousness, for years to come.

I haven't stopped thinking about 'Six Degrees' in the week since I first saw it at the Mitzi E. Newhouse

Sara Krulwich/The New York Times

nes McDaniel—playing an impostor ose true identity is never revealed

Theater at Lincoln Center, and a sec-ond viewing has only heightened my admiration for Mr. Guare's writing, Jerry Zaks's direction and the acting of a large cast. In this production, ev-ery collaborator helps create an ex-quisite balance between high comedy and rending pathos, all the better to give airy life to a densely packed text whose tone can flip instantly from the madcap humor of "Hellzapoppin' " to the astringent domestic warfare of "Who's Afraid of Virginia Woolf?" to the hallucinatory lyricism of past Guare works like "Landscape of the Body," "Bosoms and Neglect" and the film "Atlantic City."

■

Better still, this range is fitted to a canvas worthy of such sweep — New York. As "The House of Blue Leaves" apotheosized Vietnam-era Queens at the time the Pope visited Yankee Sta-dium, so "Six Degrees of Separation" captures the divided Manhattan of the year in which Nelson Mandela made the same pilgrimage. Using his impostor as a catalyst, Mr. Guare has created a Baedeker to the soul of a chaotic city and its people, a play as central to the deflated and confused post-crash New York of 1990 as Tom Wolfe's "Bonfire of the Vanities" was to the immediately preceding go-go years of junk-bond boom. But "Six Degrees," in contrast to the Wolfe novel, owes nothing to journalism — it rises above daily headlines, includ-ing the newspaper stories that in-spired it, to take the population's psy-chic pulse. The play has an insinuat-ing subconscious afterlife that can make you, like its characters, bolt up-right at 3 in the morning.

More interested in meaning than in facts, Mr. Guare never does reveal the true identity of "Paul Poitier." But Paul's identity doesn't matter

any more than that of Rosebud in "Citizen Kane," or that of James Gatz, the "penniless young man with-out a past," who reinvents himself as Jay Gatsby to crash society in Scott Fitzgerald's novel. Like the unknow-able Kane and Gatsby, Paul is a suc-cessful con man precisely because he parrots and mirrors the America he cons. In Paul's case, that America is a fractionalized metropolis teeming with debt, show-biz fantasies of fame and fortune, passionless couplings and love-starved families of habit and convenience.

What makes Paul's scams moving as well as farcical, and Mr. Guare's play compassionate rather than mean, is that the victims, financially overprivileged but emotionally un-dernourished, yearn for what is miss-ing in their lives. The well-heeled Flan and Ouisa Kittredge are not the cartoonish white liberal satirical foils of, say, Mr. Wolfe's "Radical Chic." No less than the actor Rick, Ouisa hungers for "experience" — some sort of genuine human connection in a city crowded with people trying on new identities as easily as actors take on roles. Even the more opaque Flan still hasn't quite forgotten the beauty of the art he exchanges for cash. "Six Degrees" is most of all the story of how the Kittredges' devastation by a fraud forces them at last to begin sorting out what is authentic from what is fraudulent in themselves and in their world.

The Kittredges' story becomes a city's story because of Mr. Guare's ability to merge theme, character, language and plot into a large and seamless theatrical fabric. It is no small achievement to pack 17 vividly drawn people and a breathless plot embracing knockabout mistaken-identity farce and tragic death into 90 minutes of stage time. Mr. Guare goes well beyond that impressive feat

by deftly extending the interior dra-ma of the Kittredges prismatically through layer after layer of his play until finally the plight of his charac-ters seems to be imprinted on every line and action in the entire work.

■

As both Paul and his prey are schizophrenically divided against themselves, presenting false faces to the world while burying their true identities and feelings, so everything in "Six Degrees" is two-faced, dou-ble-sided. The metaphor extends

In John Guare's new play, no one knows anybody, and an impostor takes charge.

from a two-sided Kandinsky painting that twirls in the half-light above the Kittredge living room to a mother and daughter's conflicting readings of the phrase "cruelty-free cosmet-ics" to an angry father's protestation that "There are two sides to every story'" after being dismissed as "a cretin" by his collegiate son.

In the urbanscape beyond the char-acters, Mr. Guare finds a bifurcated New York in which not only are whites ignorant of blacks, but hetero-sexuals don't know homosexuals, the rich don't know the poor, husbands don't know their wives, and parents don't know their alienated offspring. If no one in New York knows anybody else, it is no wonder that an impostor can take charge, especially one who purports to be the son of a movie star and a college classmate of his vic-tims' absent children.

Sara Krulwich/The New York Times

Stockard Channing—In the new play at Lincoln Center, her character seeks authenticity in a world of fraud.

Swoosie Kurtz in the 1986 revival of "The House of Blue Leaves."
In Mr. Guare's new play, "Six Degrees," the promise is fulfilled.

Brigitte Lacombe/Lincoln Center

John Guare—unpolemic passion

The city's schisms reflect a cultural schizophrenia as well. As Paul explains in a soliloquy inspired by "The Catcher in the Rye," we live in a time when imagination has become "something outside ourselves" — not an integral part of our identities, a tool for the essential act of self-examination, but an anesthetizing escape from the inner life we should be embracing and exploring. So topsy-turvy is our definition of culture, in Paul's view, that J. D. Salinger's "touching, beautiful, sensitive story" has been turned into "a manifesto of hate" by assassins like Mark David Chapman and John Hinckley who use Holden Caulfield's social estrangement as an excuse to commit murder. The death of introspection has similarly allowed such antihuman fads as "Star Wars," "The Andy Warhol Diaries" and "Cats" — the butt of Mr. Guare's most scalding running gag — to pass for works of imagination while a Cézanne canvas is merely a "piece of meat" that passes briefly and uncontemplated through Sotheby's on its way to new owners in Tokyo.

But Mr. Guare is not offering the audience anything as pat as a neoconservative, Allan Bloom-style diatribe about the decline of cultural standards. He doesn't really have anything against pop culture: his play's form, after all, owes as much to the campy Sidney Poitier film "Guess Who's Coming to Dinner?" which it devilishly subverts, as it does to Cézanne's use of structure and color. What is really at stake in "Six Degrees" is humanity itself, which must regain the harmonious composition and spiritual self-awareness that inspired high culture in the first place.

For all the modern jump-cuts and absurdist devices of his play, Mr. Guare holds out for the classical unities in both life and art. When his characters discuss Salinger, Chekhov and Beckett and their "great modern theme" of "emotional and intellectual paralysis," it is not because Mr. Guare wants to endorse the theme. Nor is the playwright championing the disjunctive 20th-century art of collage when he sets it in rhetorical opposition to Ouisa's memories of visiting the Sistine Chapel. Like the reawakened Ouisa, who finds in Paul a sense of family her own children

never gave her, Mr. Guare hungers for the city's disjointed collage of pasted-together, fragmented lives to be exchanged for a family — a community of lives that touch one another and, figuratively at least, touch the hand of God.

■

How does one achieve that family? "In a world of destruction one must hold fast to whatever fragments of love are left," wrote Dawn Powell (1897-1965) in "The Locusts Have No King" (1948), her postwar Manhattan comic novel that was reissued (by Yarrow Press) with an introductory essay by Mr. Guare last fall. The playwright quotes Powell's line approvingly in his essay, and it could be a prescription for the characters of "Six Degrees," which he was writing at roughly the same time. Mr. Guare wants people to rebel against modern paralysis, to move on as the tramps of "Waiting for Godot" cannot at their final curtain. He wants people to reunite with their souls. He wants people to stop reducing experience to newspaper and cocktail-party anecdotes as impersonally entertaining as "Cats." If Ouisa Kittredge is to move on at play's end — if she is to walk through "new doors opening up into other worlds" — she must plug into what she calls the "six degrees of separation," the hypothetical trail of six people, authentic people, who can connect anyone on the planet with anyone else. But to plug in, she must find "the right six people" — people who know who they are, not frauds.

Mr. Guare isn't sentimental or polemical about the importance of making that human connection. He is impassioned. "Six Degrees" never seems like an illustrated theory and always feels like a fully inhabited play, in which whites, blacks, Jews, WASP's, men, women, young, old, the wealthy and the homeless are all given their voice. Some of the characters are filled in by simply a few well-chosen brush strokes, just as the city is evoked by verbal snapshots of the Strand Book Store and the old Madison Square Garden and "traffic on the F.D.R." rather than by realistic scenery. (The designer Tony Walton provides two levels of haunted doorways bordered by gilt picture frames.) Mr.

Zaks's actors do the rest, with Ms. Channing's Ouisa setting the tone in a performance that can bring a laughing audience to a tear-stained hush as smoothly as if she were turning down the volume of a radio.

"I didn't come here to be this," says Rick, the young man who car to New York from Utah in search experience and roles in plays onl o find himself hating the role he is laying in real life. What finally allows "Six Degrees of Separation" to become a touching, beautiful, sensitive work is that Mr. Guare doesn't waste time assigning the predictable political blame for all the separations that turn a city's people into what Holden Caulfield called phonies. Instead the playwright points the way — by the lustrous examples of Ouisa's redemptive spiritual journey to authenticity and his own elevated act of art — to a transcendent alternative to the inhuman urban collage. This play invades an audience's soul by forcing it to confront the same urgent question asked of its New Yorkers: If we didn't come here to be this, then who do we intend to be? ☐

1990 Jl 1, II:1:1

A Silent Thunder

Austin Turett/Apple Corps Theater/A Silent Thunder

Suzen Murakoshi, left, and Nestor Carbonell

Written by Eduardo Ivan Lopez; directed by John Cappelletti; scenic design by Randy Benjamin; lighting design by William J. Plachy; costume design by MaryAnn D. Smith; sound design by Neal Arluck; production stage manager, Ken Simmons. Presented by the Apple Corps Theater, John Raymond and Michael Tolan, artistic directors; Neal Arluck, managing director. At 336 West 20th Street.

Joe Santana .... Nestor Carbonell
Kimiyo .... Suzen Murakoshi

By WILBORN HAMPTON

At the outset of "A Silent Thunder," Eduardo Ivan Lopez's sentimental romance at the Apple Corps Theater, Kimiyo, an Okinawan teen-ager working in her uncle's tailor shop, takes a man's suit off the rack and dances around the room softly singing Simon and Garfunkel's "Condor Pasa." She is interrupted in this reverie by the arrival of Cpl. Joe Santana, U.S.M.C., who has come to collect his suit — as it happens, the very suit Kimiyo is waltzing with. Kimiyo's fantasy suddenly expands its horizons.

From this plausible version of meeting cute in Okinawa, circa 1966, when the island was still under United States military control, Mr. Lopez moves to a rather implausible scenario for seducing cute. The seduction, of course, being Kimiyo's of Corporal Santana. How Kimiyo goes from being scandalized by the corporal's invitation to a teahouse to spending the night in his hotel room occupies the entire first act of "A Silent Thunder," and is not without a certain charm and humor even if somewhat overwritten. Instead of pursuing what might have been a light romantic encounter, Mr. Lopez wants to make something more serious.

●

Through the requisite exchange of biographies, here over tea and sake, the playwright tries to turn a seemingly average American marine and Okinawan teen-ager into innocent victims of their respective class, racial and sexual struggles. Kimiyo's father has begun negotiations for her marriage to a man she has never seen, and she wants to leave home and run away to Japan to make a new life for herself. Corporal Santana is an orphan who could not assimilate into his unknown father's Puerto Rican background and whose search for an identity led him to the Marine Corps, the only family he has ever known.

Two obvious questions that arise from this somewhat trite situation are never really explored — whether Corporal Santana is anything more to Kimiyo than a possible ticket to Tokyo and whether the marine has any inkling that he is being manipulated and outflanked by an Okinawan schoolgirl. By the second act, Mr. Lopez has led his characters into the uncharted mine field of true love and it is in this foray into darker territory that "A Silent Thunder" is really ambushed.

The corporal awakes from a nightmare induced by a thunderstorm and, after lengthy encouragement from Kimiyo (nothing happens in the play without a lot of discussion first), relates a harrowing war story that not only strains credulity but is also supposed to explain why the marine believes he is unworthy of love, marriage or family — things that we are asked to believe Kimiyo is prepared to offer and the shellshocked marine is yearning to accept.

There is no real conflict on which to build let alone sustain any of this as drama. To fill in time onstage there are several travelogue scenes, presumably meant to illustrate the cultural gap between a half-Puerto Rican orphan and an Okinawan schoolgirl, but which end up becoming repetitious. There is, for example, a foot washing, two massages — one complete with Kimiyo walking on the corporal's back — and a few discourses on tea ceremony etiquette.

The whole tale is wrapped up in a saccharine ending worthy of a Danielle Steel novel.

•

It is mostly through the polish of the performances by both actors in this two-hander that the play achieves the credibility it has. Suzen Murakoshi as Kimiyo is a study of knowing naïveté while Nestor Carbonell's Joe Santana is a portrait of naïve worldliness. Ms. Murakoshi's Kimiyo, one moment blushing and shy and the next wide-eyed and disarming, is especially a delight. Her modesty is made more becoming by her boldness. When Ms. Murakoshi demurely undresses for bed behind the protection of her kimono, and *then* puts on her lipstick before climbing between the sheets, it seems almost chaste. Mr. Carbonell tries hard to bring some tension to the stage in the second act, but it is forced.

John Cappelletti's direction is for the most part relaxed and fluid. There are occasional stretches of dead time onstage, when one actor is left alone with nothing to do or say, for far too long. Randy Benjamin's set is authentic right down to its tatamis.

1990 Jl 6, C11:1

Father Was a Peculiar Man

By Reza Abdoh and Mira-Lani Oglesby; directed by Mr. Abdoh; music by Eric Liljestrand; sets by Kyle Chepulis; costumes by Claudia Brown; lighting by Brian Aldous; choreography by Maggie Rush and Ken Roht; production manager, David Waggett; stage manager, Dan Weir. Presented by En Garde Arts, Anne Hamburger, producer. Performed indoors and outdoors, Ninth Avenue and Little West 12th Street.

WITH: A cast of 60.

By STEPHEN HOLDEN

Near the beginning of "Father Was a Peculiar Man," an exhilarating evening of environmental street theater presented by En Garde Arts, an actor from the company of more than 60 performers approaches the audience and excitedly offers his theory of the significance of Madonna. By suggesting that sex is possible in the age of AIDS, he says, she is "trying to become a Christ — she will link us together."

The speech is only a tiny satiric element of the sprawling theatrical pageant, staged in the meat-packing district of Manhattan, in the vicinity of Little West 12th Street and Ninth Avenue. Yet it touches on the themes of spirituality, corruption and redemption, which the two-and-a-half-hour, intermissionless play explores with a profusion of epic images drawn both from literature and popular culture.

Although Madonna never appears, Jesus does, as do the Kennedys, Marilyn Monroe and Dostoyevsky's Karamazov family, along with a colorful gallery of allegorical eccentrics. The play, which is the New York debut of the Iranian-born director Reza Abdoh and his longtime collaborator, the playwright Mira-Lani Oglesby, is every bit as enjoyable, though not as high styled, as "Tamara," the long-running environmental play at the Park Avenue Armory. What they have created, under auspices of the producer Anne Hamburger's En Garde Arts, is an exuberant, often savagely satirical theatrical work

Tom Brazil

Meg Kruzewska in a scene from "Father Was a Peculiar Man."

that uses the characters and plot of "The Brothers Karamazov" to evoke the decline of the American family, in both the specific and broadest meanings of the word "family."

•

"Father Was a Peculiar Man" keeps the audience moving from site to site around four square blocks. Leading the way and setting the brisk pace is the wonderful Walter Thompson Marching Band, an ensemble that plays everything from improvisatory free jazz to New Orleans-style Mardi Gras music. There are always several things going at once in the show, which combines the participatory swirl of "Tamara" and "Tony 'n' Tina's Wedding" with the oversized funny-grotesque street theater imagery of the Bread and Puppet Theater.

The one character who unites pop icons and literary characters alike is Fyodor Pavlovich Karamazov, the brutal paterfamilias from the Dostoyevsky novel. Outfitted in a top hat, cutaway and riding boots, and played with snarling glee by Tom Fitzpatrick, he also bears a close physical resemblance to the mythical image of Uncle Sam.

One of the goals of En Garde Arts's site-specific journeys through New York neighborhoods is to use the local architecture as a theatrical set while at the same time evoking the history of the neighborhood. The half-deserted cobblestone streets of the meat-packing district enhance the play's 19th-century aspect. And the neighborhood's history as both a meat-packing area and a former cen-

ter for after-hours sex clubs merge in spectacular tableaux of gluttony and lust.

•

In one of the most striking of the evening's eight sections, the audience is led through the fetid streets to a gigantic banquet table that occupies nearly half a block on West 12th Street and over which is suspended a huge meat cleaver. During the rowdy banquet scene in which a dozen things happen simultaneously, Pavlovich sodomizes one of his sons and has a fistfight with another in what is announced as "the fight of the century." Miss Arizona, a beauty queen, strolls down the center of the table, lecturing on toxic waste and joking bitterly about having earned the title of Miss Congeniality because she shared her drugs. On the fringes, characters chase one another with chainsaws.

The play's most intense moments occur during its only indoor section, near the end of the evening. The audience is led into an empty warehouse that has been transformed into a prisonlike gallery of surrealistic tableaux in which the major characters do everything from singing Christmas carols to engaging in torture. This powerful vision of heaven and hell concludes with a funeral procession in which the entire company troops up the street singing "Dream a Little Dream of Me," one of several pop tunes that punctuate the often violent action with a note of ironic cheer.

•

Theatergoers in search of finely polished drama should be warned about the crudeness of the produc-

tion. In scenes where the characters speak through microphones, it is sometimes hard to discern the dialogue or even to tell who is speaking. And there are moments when the simultaneous jamming together of so many images and ideas seems more confusing than stimulating.

What is finally so winning about the show, which plays through July 21, is its sheer vitality. The performances are as large and passionate as the audacity of the conception. And the surrealistic costumes and design make the audience participants in a literary and historical carnival out of "Alice in Wonderland." Surprisingly light-hearted despite its darker elements, it is great fun.

1990 Jl 11, C13:1

The Taming of the Shrew

By Shakespeare; directed by A. J. Antoon; scenery by John Lee Beatty; costumes by Lindsay W. Davis; lighting by Peter Kaczorowski; music by Claude White; fights staged by B. H. Barry; associate producer, Jason Steven Cohen. Presented by Joseph Papp. At the Delacorte Theater, Central Park West, enter at 81st Street.

Lucentio	Graham Winton
Tranio	Robert Joy
Baptista Minola	George Guidall
Katherina	Tracey Ullman
Bianca	Helen Hunt
Gremio	Mark Hammer
Hortensio	Tom Mardirosian
Biondello	Peter Appel
Petruchio	Morgan Freeman
Grumio	Jose Perez
Bartender	Royal E. Miller
Curtis	Michael Gaston
Nathaniel	Joe Zaloom
Joe Bob	Wade Williams
Walter	Timothy Perez
Sugarsop	Timothy D. Stickney
Beau	Peter Ryan
A Traveling Actor	William Duff-Griffin
Tailor	Norris M. Shimabuku
Vincentio	Thomas Barbour
Widow	Leah Maddrie

By FRANK RICH

If Cole Porter and company could transplant "The Taming of the Shrew" to sedate, late 1940's Baltimore, why can't the New York Shakespeare Festival let Kate and Petruchio have their standoff in the wild, late 19th-century West? A. J. Antoon's rambunctious production of Shakespeare's comedy, at the Delacorte Theater in Central Park, turns out to be its own best argument. With Morgan Freeman and Tracey Ullman, a theoretically unlikely yet entirely winning couple, at center stage, the entertainment is consistently more engaging than it may sound on paper. Were Mr. Antoon's "Shrew" a musical, it would be too broad to be "Kiss Me Kate" perhaps, but it could happily pass for "Annie Get Your Gun."

As he proved in the 1970's with his radiant Teddy Roosevelt-era "Much Ado About Nothing" in Central Park, and more recently with his Bahia "Midsummer Night's Dream," the inaugural show of Joseph Papp's Shakespeare Marathon, Mr. Antoon does not settle for merely dreaming up new settings for Shakespeare's comedies; he carries out his schemes to the finest details. Even before an actor appears in "Shrew," the audience takes in John Lee Beatty's high-spirited Main Street set, a Hollywood-backlot facade decorated with a mock-Remington mural of stampeding horses, and watches some tumbleweeds dance about to a musi-

Martha Swope/New York Shakespeare Festival/The Taming of the Shrew

Tracey Ullman and Morgan Freeman in "The Taming of the Shrew," at the Delacorte Theater in Central Park.

cal score (by Claude White) reeking of manifest destiny in the "Bonanza" key.

•

For all the chaps, buckskins and spurs of Lindsay W. Davis's costumes and cumulus clouds of Peter Kaczorowski's lighting scheme, Mr. Antoon's staging soon proves more than a matter of fine decorative touches. While the director has rewritten and cut some of Shakespeare's text (most disappointingly the "Arabian Nights"-inspired prologue), he has also inventively coupled its action to his own merry purposes. When Kate plays a prank on her better behaved and more marriageable younger sister, Bianca (Helen Hunt), in this

Kate claws, spits and shrieks. And Petruchio is going to try *kindness*.

"Shrew," she uses the poor girl as the centerpiece of a balloon-popping marksmanship exhibition. Bianca's rival suitors draw guns at the saloon, and, to be sure in a work that invites slapstick, at least one Paduan gets a good dunking at the town water trough. In one lovely, wintry nocturnal scene, Petruchio's servant, Grumio (Jose Perez), recounts his master's and mistress's misadventures while his audience of cowpokes thaws out by a warm stove.

Mr. Antoon's inspiration seems to be the airiest of Hollywood westerns. His "Shrew" never quite becomes a

parody like, say, "Cat Ballou" or "Blazing Saddles," but it does evoke the bucolic interludes of John Ford movies, which themselves had a bawdy Elizabethan sense of rustic comedy. For the "Shrew" subplot, in which Bianca's many suitors, led by Lucentio (Graham Winton), all but trip over one another in a maze of disguised identities, Mr. Antoon has recruited comic actors who recall such grizzled, idiosyncratic Ford stock players as Strother Martin, Andy Devine and Woody Strode. Tom Mardirosian's deadpan Hortensio (who doubles as the town sheriff) and Robert Joy's cigar-chomping Tranio stand out among the younger generation of Paduan clowns, though even they are upstaged by a delightful pair of older pros: Mark Hammer as the creaky, unreconstructed · skirt-chaser Gremio, and William Duff-Griffin as a tipsy, itinerant ham actor made up to resemble W. C. Fields at his most pink-cheeked and Dickensian.

•

Given the large number of slammable doors in Mr. Beatty's set, there are times when Mr. Antoon might have gone further with his farcical choreography. Some of the staging is static and some of the ludicrous vocal twangs wear out their welcome. But every time the whole stunt seems about to pall, Mr. Freeman and Ms. Ullman ride to the rescue, tongues and pistols ablazing. They not only fit in handily with the western scheme but they also help Mr. Antoon finesse the problematic sexual politics of a play that humorless contemporary audiences might regard as an endorsement of male supremacy and female submissiveness.

Mr. Freeman does everything brilliantly, whether he is falling on the

floor in knockabout comic emulation of one of Ms. Ullman's temper tantrums or standing quietly in a soft spotlight to savor a reflective passage of verse or modeling an outlandish wedding costume that makes him look like a hybrid of Davy Crockett, Pancho Villa and Sitting Bull. He is one of those rare actors whose easeful command of his art seems to inspire a higher level of performance from everyone around him. His highest achievement here, though, is to rescue Petruchio from piggishness without any sacrifice of masculine strength or wit. His proud, intelligent shrew-tamer is genial and firm, not vindictive and cruel, even when roping in his bonny Kate with a lasso or, in one hilarious bit of business, good-naturedly countering her well-aimed volley of spit. One always believes that this Petruchio is out to "kill a wife with kindness" and "curb her mad and headstrong humor" rather than to brutalize and subjugate her.

While Ms. Ullman's Kate could use a few more notes, especially in the ill-tempered brawls preceding her wedding, her fierce presence and sardonic comic attack usually rivet the attention. Once Kate's transformation from swaggering malcontent to affectionate spouse does occur, the actress rises to the occasion. Her climactic speech championing wifely duties is delivered with just the right twinkle of irony and is capped by an ingeniously managed physical gag that allows Kate to have her man and her feminist independence, too.

The real point of the production, however, is stated earlier by Petruchio, who notes that "where two raging fires meet together, they do consume the thing that feeds their fury." By the time Ms. Ullman ends up in Mr. Freeman's arms — in a romantic embrace both passionate and erotic — Mr. Antoon's "Shrew" hardly seems a war between the sexes, a shootout between heroes and villains. Kate and Petruchio are instead laughing together as equals, a true couple at last, excited to consummate their marriage ("Come, Kate, we'll to bed," says the text) and euphoric to share private jokes at an intimate remove from the rest of the world. If this "Taming of the Shrew" imparts the same lift as old-fashioned westerns, that's because Mr. Freeman and Ms. Ullman leave the audience with the unambiguous feeling that the good guys, man and woman alike, have won.

1990 Jl 13, C3:1

___

Hanging the President

By Michele Celeste; directed by Julian Webber; set design, Stephan Olson; costume design, Patricia Sarnataro; lighting designer, Donald Holder; sound design, Eric Liljestrand; stage manager, Barbara Lynn Rice; stage combat, Jim Manley; production manager, David Waggett; dialect consultant, Nora Dunfee. Presented by SoHo Repertory Theater, Marlene Swartz and Mr. Webber, artistic directors. At the Alma Shapiro Theater, 605 West 115th Street.

Chief Warder .... Dan Moran
Nak van der Merwe .... Peter Drew Marshall
Stoffel Le Grange .... Peter Crombie
Zwanini ....◆............ Themba Ntinga

By STEPHEN HOLDEN

It would be hard to imagine a more detestable pair of louts than Stoffel Le Grange and Nak van der Merwe, the Afrikaner protagonists of Michele Celeste's grim political allegory "Hanging the President."

Cellmates who share a filthy, airless hole on death row in the central prison of Pretoria, South Africa, the pair are awaiting execution for murder. While they wait, each hoping for a last-minute reprieve from the President, P. W. Botha, they torment each other and are, in turn, tormented by a guard who administers beatings and who chortlingly regales them with the grisly details of previous hangings.

The 90-minute, intermissionless play, which the SoHo Repertory Theater is presenting in its American première engagement at the Alma Shapiro Theater, caused a stir when it was performed last summer at the Edinburgh Festival. One of the more brutal plays to be seen in New York lately, it has lots of foul language and graphic sadism.

Although "Hanging the President" begins naturalistically, it quickly turns into a forced allegory about the evils of apartheid in which the prison pecking order symbolizes the South African power structure under Mr. Botha. Stoffel, who is revealed as the prison's strongman by dint of his sheer brute force, periodically dons the red cover of a candy box, which he treats as a kind of crown while impersonating the former South African President.

As king of the prison, Stoffel has also turned Nak into his abused prison "wife." One of the nastier ways in which he likes to humiliate his cellmate is by vociferously making love to a snapshot of Nak's wife. And in a metaphorical plot twist borrowed from Jean Genet, Stoffel is also desired as a lover by the very same guard who beats him.

The symbolism becomes even more explicit late in the play when a third prisoner, Zwanini, a black South African freedom fighter and hero, is thrown into the cell. The two white cellmates are outraged at having to share their space with a black man. While Stoffel beats up Zwanini, Nak tries to coax him into revealing negotiable political secrets. Zwanini, an all-too-obvious Christ symbol, endures his humiliations silently.

As much as one might admire the playwright's moral zeal, his use of sexual metaphors to dramatize the degradation of apartheid seems increasingly exploitative as the play unfolds. He has taken the metaphor of fiendish perversion that has been long used as a convenient shortcut for evoking the moral squalor of Nazism and applied it in a shallow, sensationalistic manner to South African politics.

"Hanging the President," though well acted, is not ideally cast. Peter Crombie, who plays Stoffel with a fine cackling defiance, lacks the physical stature of a prison bully. Peter Drew Marshall and Dan Moran, who portray Nak and the guard, also give intense, charged performances. But under Julian Webber's uneven direction, the performances only skim the play's surface.

The director has supervised the words far more confidently than he has the action. The play's many savage punches are weak and poorly choreographed and its sexual shenanigans are staged with a queasy timidity. As a result, a drama jam-packed with violence is completely lacking in visceral clout.

1990 Jl 13, C17:1

Romeo and Juliet

By Shakespeare; directed by Bill Homewood; producer, Barry Nettleton; designer, Andrea Carr; lighting, Jeremy Newman-Roberts; production manager, John Merrylees. Presented by Hull Truck Productions, John Godber, artistic director; Mr. Nettleton, administrator. At the Staller Center for the Arts, State University at Stony Brook, L.I.

Peter	David Barber
Nurse	Claire Benedict
Prince Escalus	Neil Boorman
Mercutio	Paul Brennen
Tybalt	Guy Burgess
Lady Capulet	Shirley Anne Field
Old Montague	Kenneth Gardnier
Romeo	Roland Gift
Paris's Page	Beverley Jordan
Friar Lawrence	Colin Kaye
Juliet	Daphne Nayar
Abram	Robert Warren Payne
Benvolio/Paris	Miles Richardson
Lord Capulet	Madhav Sharma

By STEPHEN HOLDEN
Special to The New York Times

STONY BROOK, L.I., July 10 — Lured by the pop-star glamour of Roland Gift, an unusually youthful theater audience swarmed through the Staller Center for the Arts at the State University here this evening for the first of five performances of Shakespeare's "Romeo and Juliet."

The 29-year-old lead singer of the English pop group Fine Young Cannibals is no stranger to acting, having played a leading role in the 1987 English film "Sammy and Rosie Get Laid." Even though he may be a trifle too old for Romeo, Mr. Gift has always exuded a smoldering, sulky contrariness that would make him an intriguing choice for the part. And in the wildly uneven nontraditional production of the play at Stony Brook by the Hull Truck Theater Company of England — the fourth of five events in the 1990 International Theater Festival — Mr. Gift's Romeo is the evening's strongest asset. Rather than striving for heroism, his Romeo swings from arrogant brattiness to petulant whining, with his most appealing quality being the consistency of his ardor.

With brattiness, whining and always ardor.

With casting that covers a broad ethnic spectrum, the Hull Truck troupe's modern-dress version of the play has a lot of the look but only a little of the feel of a Stephen Frears movie like "Sammy and Rosie," which depicts London as a seething multinational city. The production, directed by Bill Homewood, is iconoclastic from its very opening scenes, in which the actors seated around the edge of the stage hum during the prologue and throw out slangy interjections. For the rest of the evening, the cast members slip in and out from the wings to sit on folding chairs on either side of the stage, waiting for their cues. In the drama's tenser moments they stamp together on the floor in an ominous marching rhythm.

The best thing about the direction is the loose, breezy athleticism of the first half of the evening. The camaraderie of Romeo, Benvolio (Miles Richardson) and Mercutio (Paul Brennen) is played as loose, easygoing farce. In Mr. Richardson's hands, Benvolio is a buffoonishly impulsive kid who goes overboard on every-

thing. Mr. Brennen's Mercutio is comparably comedic, a know-it-all who, even while dying, tries to put a flippant, wise-guy face on the situation. Guy Burgess's Tybalt is contrastingly grim, an implacable, infuriated avenger.

●

The flashiest performance is Claire Benedict's Nurse. Miss Benedict is much younger than most actresses cast as a character who is often interpreted as a prurient old busybody. The actress, who speaks with a pronounced West Indian accent and does a lot of eyeball-rolling, plays her as a hot-blooded, squealing flirt. A major weakness of the production is Daphne Nayar's Juliet. The actress, who totes around a teddy bear, has the fresh pubescent looks for the role, but her outbursts seem more infantile than erotically heated.

The sparse production unfolds on a stage painted with geometrical patterns and strewn with large, movable blocks. Overlooking the action are two glowing moons, one red, the other white. The visual starkness extends to costumes that dress the Montagues in black and the Capulets in white. Mr. Gift wears a black hooded sweatshirt and sneakers.

If the production has a number of clever notions, it doesn't build a consistent social, psychological or political vision of the play. And as it goes along, its energy steadily diminishes. Even the boldest departures from Shakespeare lack a sense of purpose. Instead, they have the weight of clever improvisations complementing a star turn.

1990 Jl 14, 10:1

Jersey City

Directed by Risa Bramon; written by Wendy Hammond; set design, James Youmans; lighting design, Anne Militello; costume design, Sharon Sprague; sound design, Bruce Ellman; hair design, Antonio Soddu; fight coordinator, Robert Goodwin; production stage manager, Liz Small; stage manager, Elise-Ann Konstantin. Presented by Second Stage Theater, Robyn Goodman and Carole Rothman, artistic directors. At 2162 Broadway, at 76th Street.

Magaly	Alison Bartlett
David	Eddie Castrodad
Pa	Jude Ciccolella
Esther	Adina Porter

By WILBORN HAMPTON

As the audience meets Magaly and Pa in "Jersey City," Wendy Hammond's jarring new play at the Second Stage Theater, they are finishing their evening meal with a game of baseball trivia. Magaly, still tomboy enough at age 15 to prefer a catcher's mitt to a new dress for a present, knows what year Willie Mays and Mickey Mantle broke in as rookies, then stumps her dad with a question about what outfielder is named after a fruit (until she starts chanting "Dar-ryl" to give him a clue). They seem quite happy, father and daughter sharing a love of our national pastime. Moments later, Magaly's dad knocks her around the kitchen and rapes her.

Of all the crimes that can be committed in the family not one is more unspeakable, both in the sense that it is at once the most heinous and the most hidden, than incest. It is one of the oldest sins and, if statistics are accurate, far more common than one might suppose. Neither Ms. Hammond nor her fine director, Risa Bramon, flinch from bringing the

brutality of the act full force to the stage. But the tragedy of incest is not confined to the violence of the act itself. It is in the damage that remains with the victim long after the abuse has ceased, the psychological and the physical handicaps that may scar her for life. In seeking to dramatize these residual injuries, Ms. Hammond only partly succeeds.

●

Immediately after violating his daughter, Magaly's father tearfully begs her forgiveness. Once Magaly grants her father absolution, he goes into the living room and turns on the ball game. It is clearly a scene they have played out for years. On this night, however, Magaly has found the courage to leave home.

Magaly (Alison Bartlett) has heard someone at her school describe Jersey City as a beautiful town, full of parks and grass, a place, as she puts it, "where I can feel clean." Staying one step ahead of her father, Magaly ends up in the restroom of a strip joint in Jersey City. There she makes friends with a dancer named Esther (Adina Porter) and a young Salvadoran named David (Eddie Castrodad), who fled his war-torn homeland after his brother was killed and who reluctantly takes Magaly in. Magaly's father (Jude Ciccolella) manages to follow her to David's apartment, but then in one of the more inexplicable of several contrivances in Ms. Hammond's story, he abruptly leaves.

Once Magaly crosses the Hudson, until a final harrowing confrontation with her father, the structure of "Jersey City" becomes more of a docudrama than a play, a sort of case study of one victim of incest. It is soon apparent that Magaly expects all men to behave like her father. In her first argument with David, she slaps him, then shouts tauntingly, "If you were a man you'd hit me back!" It is when she learns that the years of incest have left her with tendencies toward masochism that Magala fears she has lost forever the ability for happy sexual relations.

Ms. Hammond is a writer capable of both raw power and quiet tenderness, and some of the scenes between Magala and David are touchingly drawn. But there are stretches of "Jersey City" that sound like the writer has been trying to force a dramatic conflict to fill out a play.

Magaly and David, for example, have a propensity to argue at great length over anything, including whether to turn out the lights, or even to remain under the same roof. (Magaly: "You want me to leave." David: "I don't want you to leave." Repeat four times). While this may have the ring of truth for normal teen-age conversation, it quickly dilutes whatever intensity has been built onstage and risks losing the attention of any audience, however compelling the subject matter.

Ms. Bartlett and Mr. Castrodad head the good cast. Their strong and sensitive peformances go a long way toward covering up some of the play's weaknesses. Ms. Bartlett's splendid Magaly is an unsentimental study of the wordly innocence and indomitable spirit of a teen-ager at bay. And Mr. Castrodad draws a complex portrait of a boy being rushed into adulthood. They work very well together. Robert Goodwin, the play's fight coordinator, directed the violence with teeth-clenching realism but without resorting to sensationalism.

1990 Jl 15, 40:3

Ann Magnuson, a Cast All by Herself

By STEPHEN HOLDEN

At a time when New York City edges steadily toward chaos, it's no coincidence that Thornton Wilder's "Our Town" should exert a special fascination on local theater artists. Wilder's evocation of New England small-town life at the turn of the century serves as a central text for "Route 1 and 9," the Wooster Group's theatrical collage about the decline of the New York. A full-scale revival of "Our Town" was subsequently mounted by the Lincoln Center Theater. And now the performance artist Ann Magnuson's one-woman show "You Could Be Home Now," which opened Lincoln Center's Serious Fun festival, uses the same play as a crucial point of departure.

●

In the opening scenes of the delightful but messy 90-minute show that Ms. Magnuson performed at Alice Tully Hall on Friday and Saturday, she offers her own comic variations on two of the play's principal characters, the Stage Manager and Emily Gibbs. In Ms. Magnuson's comic gallery of ultra-modern urban types, the Stage Manager has become a lumberjack-capped lesbian named Babe Wrangler whose Broadway duties include being on call to repair the Joad family truck in "The Grapes of Wrath." Her updated Emily is a television-addicted teen-ager who leans over the top of a stepladder and excitedly tells her diary about the "very trippy MTV-style" television movie of the week she has just watched in which a dog "gets squished" by a truck. "I guess 'Twin Peaks' has revolutionized TV," she sighs admiringly.

When 'Our Town' becomes her town, some decidedly odd things happen.

An endearing theatrical chameleon who has as many characters at her fingertips as Lily Tomlin does, Ms. Magnuson portrays at least a dozen other personalities in a satiric show in which she also dances and sings (from operetta style to folk), hilariously lip-syncs, and scatters up-to-the-minute cultural references ranging from the Utne Reader and Romeo Gigh to Pat Carroll's Falstaff. Ms. Magnuson is not afraid to depart from her script to offer ad-libs inspired by the tabloid headlines of the day. In the middle of Friday's show, she pointed at a spectator in the front row and exclaimed: "It's Dart Man! Who put up your bail?"

The slickest in Ms. Magnuson's parade of dreamers and eccentrics is a smooth-talking real estate agent who proudly describes her work as "the buying selling of the American dream" while peddling suburban properties named Brittany Woods and Camelot. The saleswoman is one of the more well-heeled in a cast of characters, several of whom have no fixed abode. Ms. Magnuson mischievously implies, however, that even those who have a place to live have no real sense of security or rootedness. For in the television junk culture that she dissects with deadpan satiric contempt, nothing much is really worth owning, nor can anything be expected to last.

Toward the end of the show, the merriment takes on a plaintive undercurrent. Dropping her masks, Ms. Magnuson picks up a guitar and plays "Hello Death, Goodbye Avenue A," an extended one-chord song that suggests one of Bob Dylan's surrealist epics deflated of self-importance and reduced to buzzword symbolism. "Joseph Campbell gave me hope/And now I have been saved," goes one ironic fragment. The song, which ridicules President Bush's "lizard lips" and expresses outrage at Senator Jesse Helms, goes on to describe a bad drug experience in Joshua Tree National Park spent watching "Berlin Alexanderplatz" on PBS and to reflect on how easy it would be to believe in a Jesus who looks like Willem Dafoe.

The embattled Lower East Side — where Ms. Magnuson first made her name — and the plagues of homelessness and of AIDS are evoked in words

Marilynn K. Yee/The New York Times
Ann Magnuson

that inject the show with strong notes of sadness and anger. Even if you could be home now, Ms. Magnuson suggests, that home, whether it be New York City, Grover's Corners, N.H., or some anonymous suburban Camelot, is not at all what it used to be.

1990 Jl 17, C16:1

Ed Linderman's Broadway Jukebox

Production conceived and supervised by Ed Linderman; directed and choreographed by Bill Guske; scenic design by James Morgan; costume design by Barbara Forbes; lighting design by Stuart Duke; sound design and production management, E. F. Morrill; production stage manager, Michael J. Chudinski. Presented by Eric Krebs, in association with Joanne Macan and Carol Wernli. At the John Houseman Theater, 450 West 42d Street.

WITH: Robert Michael Baker, Susan Flynn, Beth Leavel, Gerry McIntyre, Amelia Prentice and Sal Vivano.
Musicians: Mr. Linderman and Ken Lundie.

By STEPHEN HOLDEN

"Ed Linderman's Broadway Jukebox" has a nifty concept. On entering the John Houseman Theater, patrons

are handed a list of 85 songs chosen mostly from unsuccessful shows of the last three decades and given slips of paper on which to vote for the ones they would like to hear.

Over the course of the evening, Mr. Linderman, who created the show and serves as its master of ceremonies, musical director and first pianist, leads a cast of 8 through a 30-song program that interweaves the audience's choices with preselected numbers. The show, in which no performance theoretically will be the same as any other, strives to create the atmosphere of a cheery but sophisticated living-room musicale.

The roster of tunes, performed by six singers and two keyboard players, is shrewdly chosen. Although the selections date from as far back as the mid-1940's and from as recently as the late 1980's (numbers from "Chess" and "Carrie"), the bulk of the material has been taken from unsuccessful shows from the 1960's and 70's, with John Kander and Fred Ebb the songwriters most heavily represented. The roster pointedly avoids popular standards from flop shows to concentrate on worthy material that is for the most part obscure.

One comic high point at the performance I attended on Tuesday evening was Alan Menken's hilarious "Pink Fish," from "Big Apple Country," a 1976 cabaret revue. The song describes an aspiring actor's arrival in New York City and his appalled discovery of a local tribal food that at first seems untouchable but that he gradually comes to terms with. The dish, which he describes as pink fish on a big stale doughnut, turns out to be lox and bagels.

Richard Rodgers's and Stephen Sondheim's "What Do We Do? We Fly!" from "Do I Hear a Waltz?" offers some of Mr. Sondheim's most scintillating light verses about the woes of air travel. Another high point is Stan Daniels's bawdy "Butler's Song," from "So Long, 174th Street," a 1976 flop show based on Joseph Stein's play "Enter Laughing." In the song, the haughty servant of a 1930's Hollywood bigwig attempts to find a place for Greta Garbo in his employer's star-studded schedule of sexual appointments.

If "Broadway Jukebox" is a wonderful idea, Mr. Linderman and the show's director and choreographer Bill Guske haven't developed it much beyond a piano-bar level of sophistication. Robert Michael Baker, Susan Flynn, Beth Leavel, Gerry McIntyre, Amelia Prentice and Sal Viviano, the show's singers, all possess good voices. None, however, are outstanding.

The singers, who smile tightly throughout the show, are barely introduced, and Mr. Guske's uninspired 60's revue-style choreography only increases the tension of an evening that is intended to be relaxing. Instead of dishing out interesting lore about the histories of the songs and their shows, Mr. Linderman wastes precious time reading dedications from audience members. He is also a merely functional theater pianist, and the arrangements for two pianos (spiced with synthesizer) are perfunctory run-throughs that don't permit the singers' much dramatic elaboration.

If the best comic numbers in "Broadway Jukebox" can withstand such treatment, the ballads and love songs tend to fall flat. These deficiencies shrivel an evening of potential show stoppers into a agreeable little revue devoid of revelations.

1990 Jl 20, C3:1

Finley Mocks Her Critics In Her Art

By STEPHEN HOLDEN

Early in her powerful one-woman show, "We Keep Our Victims Ready," Karen Finley mocks conservative critics who have denounced her work as obscene by offering her own satirical portrait of an American cultural landscape stripped bare by arts censorship.

In "It Was Only Art," a savagely funny polemic that is the evening's prologue, she imagines a country whose museums have been emptied because their contents were considered offensive: Jasper Johns's paintings desecrated the flag, van Gogh encouraged psychedelia, Mary Cassatt painted nude children, and even Edward Hopper suffered from "repressed lust." Extrapolating from there, Ms. Finley goes on to describe a culture in which even hot dogs have been outlawed for being "too phallic" and where the only actor allowed on television is Charlton Heston.

The cultural landscape denuded by censorship.

Like everything else Ms. Finley performed on Sunday evening at Alice Tully Hall, where she gave the first of her two shows in the Serious Fun series (the second is tomorrow), "It Was Only Art" drew gusts of applause and laughter from the sold-out house. Some people were no doubt attracted by Ms. Finley's notoriety. She was recently one of four performance artists denied grants by the National Endowment for the Arts, and a nationally syndicated column by Rowland Evans and Robert Novak ridiculed "Victims," which has toured the country, as the performance of "a nude, chocolate-smeared woman." Sunday's performance found the hall packed with supporters who gave her a sustained ovation at the end of the evening.

Although "We Keep Our Victims Ready" uses both partial nudity and incendiary, often profane language, they underscore a disquieting, nightmarish view of a society controlled by white heterosexual men wreaking violence and oppression on women, racial minorities and homosexuals. Her raw vocabulary is disturbing precisely because it reminds us that even today a sexual double standard applies to profanity.

Typically, Ms. Finley adopts the voice of a socially victimized woman unleashing her pent-up fury in a ritualized poetic diatribe. Her poems interweave horrifying descriptions of mental and physical degradation, including rape, with searing broadsides that indict the sexism of a patriarchal society and its attitudes toward abortion, child care and other issues. Ms. Finley traces much of the trouble to a deeply instilled loathing of the body and to primal fears of blood and excrement.

The impact of Ms. Finley's writing is extraordinarily magnified by her shamanistic style of performance, in which she becomes a lightning rod for the spirits of women who seem almost to speak through her. Delivered in a style that combines the ritualized tone of evangelical preaching with a raving hysteria that deliberately and uncomfortably flirts with madness, she works on a raw emotional plane that even in these sophisticated times touches nerves and piques subconscious anxieties. In their most feverish moments, her monologues suggest the exhortations of a faith healer. But instead of the physical, her territory is the psyche and its poisons.

"We Keep Our Victims Ready" has three sections performed without intermission. During the show's 90 minutes, the performer moves from a public space into an increasingly private and personal realm. It is during the second act, on a kitchen set, that Ms. Finley strips to her panties and smears chocolate over her body from the neck down. Not a comic or sexual

Dona Ann McAdams
Karen Finley

gesture, this ritual signifies the mortification of the body by a psychically battered character whose self-image is so damaged that she thinks of herself as nothing more than excrement.

The centerpiece of the third act, which takes place beside an empty bed, is Ms. Finley's rapt recitation of "The Black Sheep," an anguished ode to a recently deceased AIDS patient who becomes a symbolic figure for all those alienated from their families. Gentler in tone than the two earlier acts, "Black Sheep" is a griefstricken meditation on death, absence and memory. Its final verses hold out hope for a mystical reunion of family members and ultimately of the larger human family. Ms. Finley calls this state of feeling, which forms the emotional and moral core of her art, "unconditional love."

1990 Jl 24, C13:1

Pal Joey

Book by John O'Hara; music by Richard Rodgers; lyrics by Lorenz Hart; directed and choreographed by Dan Siretta; scenery, Kenneth Foy; costumes, Jose Lengson; lighting, Kirk Bookman; production manager, William Chance; stage manager, Michael Brunner; assistant choreographer, Ken Leigh Rogers; assistant musical director, Steven Silverstein; associate artistic director, Mr. Siretta; associate producer, Sue Frost; musical direction by Tim Stella; dance music and vocal arrangements by Tom Fay; additional orchestrations by Mr. Stella and Mr. Fay; produced for the Goodspeed Opera House by Michael P. Price. Presented by the Goodspeed Opera House, East Haddam, Conn.

Joey Evans	Peter Reardon
Mike Spears	Kurt Knudson
Vera Simpson	Florence Lacey
Linda English	Anne Allgood
Ludlow Lowell	Jerry Grayson
Melba	Valerie Dowd
Gladys	Kari Nicolaisen

WITH: David Arthur, Quin Baird, Keith Robert Bennett; Maria Calabrese, Kelly Crafton, Jan Downs, Jack Eldon, Tim Foster, Michael Hayward-Jones, Pam Klinger, Tom Kosis, Elizabeth Palmer, Jane Sonderman and Susan Trainor.

By FRANK RICH

Special to The New York Times

EAST HADDAM, Conn., July 21 — When the musical "Pal Joey" opened in 1940, Brooks Atkinson ended his review in The New York Times with a rhetorical question that remains one of the most quoted lines in the annals of Broadway theater criticism: "Can you draw sweet water from a foul well?"

Atkinson admired the professionalism of the Richard Rodgers-Lorenz Hart score, George Abbott staging and Robert Alton choreography, but he couldn't stomach the sleazy title character taken from John O'Hara's epistolary novel, a second-rate Chicago nightclub emcee who provides sexual companionship to a wealthy matron in exchange for monetary favors. "If it is possible to make an entertaining musical comedy out of an odious story," Atkinson wrote in the lead of his respectful, equivocal notice, "'Pal Joey' is it."

With a cast led by Gene Kelly and Vivienne Segal, "Pal Joey" did well enough in 1940, but not until its 1952 Broadway revival, pairing Harold Lang with Miss Segal, did it become a smash hit, recognized as a classic by the public and a circumspect Atkinson alike. What happened in the intervening 12 years? Perhaps postwar America had finally caught up with O'Hara's gin-soaked cynicism. Perhaps Rodgers, in his subsequent collaborations with Oscar Hammerstein 2d, had succeeded in educating Broadway audiences about the possibilities of musicals that were not unalloyed fluff. When "Pal Joey" had its debut in 1940, "Oklahoma!" was still three years in the offing. When the revival opened at the Broadhurst in 1952, its 44th Street block housed a pair of long-running Rodgers and Hammerstein attractions, "South Pacific" (at the Majestic) and "The King and I" (at the St. James), with morally blemished characters of their own.

Even so, the durability of "Pal Joey" remains ambiguous at its 50th anniversary, as the wildly variable new production at the Goodspeed Opera House here attests. Since the early 1960's, when Bob Fosse starred in a pair of revivals at City Center, successful major productions of this musical have been hard to come by. A 1976 Circle in the Square attempt, in which Edward Villella vacated the lead role during previews, was a fiasco. An updated version of the show titled "Pal Joey '78," featuring Lena Horne, languished on the road. A 1988 production at the Goodman Theater in Chicago, starring Kevin Anderson, did not have an extended life. Though no one any longer disputes a musical's right to tell the odious tale of a gigolo, is it possible that a work once ahead of its time is now in need of a revamp?

The Goodspeed production, ragged as it is, conscientiously attempts to address this issue. The director, Dan Siretta, has given the staging the harsh Brechtian look of Harold Prince's "Cabaret" and Fosse's "Chicago," with an onstage band, which allows the nightclub turns at Chez Joey to blend more naturally into the plot scenes. There has been some gingerly tinkering with the book. One production number has been cut ("The Flower Garden of My Heart") and another has been repositioned ("Do It the Hard Way"). The final duet for Joey's women, "Take Him," has been replaced by another Rodgers and Hart song, the lovely but less dramatically appropriate "He Was Too Good to Me" and a modest song cut from the original "Pal Joey" during its Philadelphia tryout, "I'm Talking to My Pal," has been exhumed.

Clearly some revisions are in order: O'Hara's book does move in fits and starts, reflecting the pre-"Oklahoma!" division of script and songs in Broadway musicals, and Act II bogs down in some half-comic underworld shenanigans as tiresome as those prompting "Slaughter on 10th Avenue" in a preceding breakthrough Rodgers and Hart musical, "On Your Toes."

But Mr. Siretta's alterations, however promising in principle, are compromised by sloppy execution. Kenneth Foy's set is grotesque beyond the call of duty — it looks like the skeletal, fire-charred remains of a stock "Cabaret" — and Jose Lengson's cheap, unflattering costumes mock all the women in the company, from the brassy strippers in the chorus to the vocally adept but erotically undercharged heroines, Florence Lacey (as Joey's sponsor, Vera) and Anne Allgood (as Linda, the all-good also-ran for his affections). Mr. Siretta's obsessive, generic tap-dance routines, more appropriate to sunny "42d Street" than to the lurid smoke-filled precincts of "Pal Joey," further compromise any attempt to sustain an acrid atmosphere.

Still, the director has done one important thing well: he has coaxed a terrific Joey from a gifted young performer named Peter Reardon. Mr. Reardon's unexpectedly moving portrayal, along with the evening's undying progression of great songs ("You Mustn't Kick It Around," "I Could Write a Book," "Bewitched, Bothered and Bewildered," "Zip" and "Den of Iniquity," for starters), leave one feeling far from hopeless about the prospects of "Pal Joey" with the right staging and a rethought, possibly streamlined libretto. The core of a powerful, adult musical is always in view, even when swamped by this revival's wrong notes.

Though Mr. Reardon is a singer, not the dancer of "Pal Joey" tradition — a trait he shares with Frank Sinatra's bowdlerized screen Joey — it is his acting that is most telling. As he swaggers about in the role's trademark trench coat and raffishly tilted hat, he cuts the cocky figure of a crude yet charming heel whose lying and narcissism never become oily and hateful to an audience and whose sexual magnetism to women is as irresistible as advertised.

There's an aura of danger to this Joey, and some pathos, too. When he tries to seduce a woman with "I Could Write a Book," the genuine romantic longing in the melody and the con man's flattery in the lyric are each kept in sharp focus. Mr. Reardon captures the complexity of the character O'Hara created, and he il-

luminates the sophistication with which Rodgers and Hart fleshed out that character in a score that is far more than a hit parade. For all the failings of the Goodspeed production, there's never any doubt that "Pal Joey" draws sweet water from a foul well. The esthetic question to be answered now is: How can you make it flow?

1990 Jl 24, C13:3

English Theater Quick on Political Trigger

By MEL GUSSOW

Special to The New York Times

LONDON — In the 1970's, during the heyday of the Joint Stock Company and other politically inclined theatrical organizations, English playwrights like Caryl Churchill, David Hare and Howard Brenton often reacted immediately to public issues. Faced with urgent political questions, the writers reached for their quill cudgels.

Except for the agitprop days of the Living Newspaper in the 1930's, playwrights in the United States have traditionally left such quick commentary in the hands of stand-up comics and monologuists. Although in the 1980's this kind of political theater was on the wane in London — possibly because theaters were worried about losing financial support — this summer in London there has been a reawakening of interest in what could be called Theater of the Moment.

As in previous years, the playwrights are led by Miss Churchill, whose new play, "Mad Forest," is an insightful investigation of the revolution in Romania last December that

toppled the regime of Nicolae Ceausescu and led to the execution of the Communist dictator and his wife. Simultaneously, the Royal Court Theater sponsored a six-week season of 15 issue-oriented dialogues, under the title "May Days."

Max Stafford-Clark, the company's artistic director, has explained the impetus for the dialogues: "The swift course of events in Eastern Europe at the end of 1989 and the end of a decade of Thatcherism here in Britain prompted a wish for a kind of 'Royal Court Instant Response Unit,' able to give a theatrical platform to the immediate debate of political issues."

The immediacy of the playwrights' response does not necessarily insure wide public attention. The Churchill play is performed on a small stage in the Embassy Theater in North London by students at the Central School of Speech and Drama — a long way from the customary venues of the author of such trans-Atlantic successes as "Cloud Nine," "Top Girls" and "Fen." The show is scheduled to conclude its run this weekend. The May Days series, which ended this month, played to embarrassingly small audiences, a fact that was variously attributed to a dearth of publicity, mixed notices and public apathy.

Nevertheless, the plays — in particular, "Mad Forest" and Doug Lucie's Royal Court one-act, "Doing the Business" — are provocative in the extreme.

Miss Churchill's play, commissioned by the Central School, is an incendiary piece of theater, which moves beyond reportage into a kind of historical analysis. As a play, it still has rough edges. Some scenes are either underdeveloped or overextended. But it has a visceral sense of events happening as the audience watches and a feeling of first-hand truthfulness.

Together with her director, Mark Wing-Davey, Ms. Churchill visited Bucharest in March, amassing information and images. Two months later, the playwright had finished

Nigel Norman/Mad Forest

The cast of "Mad Forest," Caryl Churchill's new play about the Romanian revolution last December.

writing the play and it was in production, without the delays found in the commercial and even the institutional theater.

Sitting on hard concrete blocks, theatergoers are uncomfortable witnesses to the Romanian revolution, as it detonates and then is eventually surrounded by questions. In the first act there are glimpses of the repressiveness of the Ceausescu regime and the economic and political deprivations suffered by Romanian citizens. The view is through the eyes of two families, one working class, one representing the intelligentsia — about to be united through marriage.

The second act offers a collage of snapshot reactions to the revolution. As in a mystery play, people with limited knowledge try to piece together what actually happened. In the third and most amorphous act, the playwright describes the seismic tremors

Playwrights hold forth on Eastern European and domestic issues.

that continue after the initial revolution. Especially in this final section, there are indications of Miss Churchill's more imaginative side, as she creates a sardonic encounter between a dapper Transylvanian vampire and a fleabitten dog, a stand-in for the bedeviled common man. Wisely, the playwright has refrained from sealing her play with a conclusion. Like the revolution itself, the play remains in progress.

The confused nature of the uprising, as Miss Churchill sees it, is reflected in the title. "Mad Forest" refers to the name of a forest outside Bucharest, considered to be "impenetrable for the foreigner who did not know the paths." In other words, Miss Churchill believes one would have to be Romanian to understand the intricacies of the events of the last year, and even then the view might be obstructed. Guided by the playwright, we begin to understand the political and moral complexity. In one of many bitterly comic interludes, the play's Ceausescu explains why he is mightier than God. God created the sun, the moon, the stars and mankind "out of chaos"; Ceausescu boasts, "I created the chaos."

The student actors are a closely allied ensemble, offering indications of their nascent theatrical talent. Similarly, there is a feeling of potential in the play — incomplete but far more evocative than the author's last effort ("Ice Cream," produced last season at the Public Theater in New York). With work, "Mad Forest" could become the Eastern European political equivalent of Miss Churchill's "Fen," a play that far transcended its journalistic origins.

Coincidentally, at Miss Churchill's customary habitat, the Royal Court, there was the rotating repertory of one-act political dialogues, commissioned from a wide diversity of people, some of them playwrights, some of them public figures not previously involved in writing for the theater. The nonprofessional roster included one of Prime Minister Margaret Thatcher's advisers, a member of the Labor Party's shadow government, the Bishop of Durham and even a theater critic. Free to choose subjects, they focused on a diversity of contemporary issues.

The plays on one bill were "The Wall-Dog," by Manfred Karge, a polemical conversation about German reunification; "How Now Green Cow," a very funny assault on environmentalism by Julie Burchill, a newspaper columnist and pop novelist, and Mr. Lucie's "Doing the Business," a comedy about the dangers inherent in private financing of the arts.

In the caustic Burchill comedy, a trendy woman (deftly played by Lesley Manville) committed to the self-indulgences of city life assails a liberal friend, who has retreated to the country and adopted a save-the-rain-forest missionary zeal. The author's anti-Green spokeswoman says, "Nature is the biggest serial killer the world has ever seen." Theater of the Moment can, of course, derive from conservative as well as liberal hands.

The most incisive of the dialogues was "Doing the Business." Mr. Lucie, the author of "Progress" and "Fashion," is no latecomer in responding to public issues. But "Doing the Business" sets something of a record for a play hot off the presses. It was performed just as both England and the United States faced crises in financing of the arts. The crises outlasted the run of the play.

Those who are opposed to government support indicate that organizations and individual artists would be able to substitute private sponsorship for public support and this presumably would free them from restraints of censorship. With malevolent wit, Mr. Lucie concludes that the opposite is true. If anything, private financing, he says, will lead to more interference and a greater loss of artistic freedom.

The instruments for the author's debate are two former university classmates, a forward-looking theater director (Nick Dunning) and a fund raiser (Nicholas Woodeson) who brokers partnerships between art and business, something long in evidence in both countries. Mr. Woodeson, genial even as he is insidious, plays a diabolical dissembler who believes in "creative funding" — code words for censorship and sponsor control. In particular, the broker objects to two plays on the director's schedule, one by an Irishman (therefore, Mr. Woodeson concludes, he only writes "Irish plays"), the other by a lesbian and dealing with child abuse. In the current English climate, the lesbian is more acceptable than the Irishman.

In order to guarantee jobs for members of his company, the director trims and rationalizes while trying to maintain his artistic conscience. Eager to please his own constituency, Mr. Woodeson dilutes the other's intentions through a series of guileful maneuvers, suggesting that he cast a famous "alternative comedian" in a leading role in a play to boost ticket sales. Art is sacrificed in the name of "doing business" and "compromise is the language of progress." The sensibility is not too far removed from the crass commercialism of the movie executives in David Mamet's "Speed-the-Plow."

Mr. Lucie's short sharp satire has a particular resonance during a time when the National Endowment for the Arts is being subjected to heavy criticism. In this excoriating example of Theater of the Moment, audiences could be watching what may happen in the American arts if grants by the endowment are further restricted. •

1990 Jl 25, C11:3

The Men's Room

Presented by Lincoln Center for the Performing Arts. At Alice Tully Hall.

WIPE THE DIRT OFF YOUR LIPS AND STROKE THE MYSTERY created and performed by Christian Swenson.

A SHORT HISTORY OF ROMANCE created by Tom Cayler, Kay Cummings and Clarice Marshall; performed by Tom Cayler and Clarice Marshall; lighting by Dan Kotlowitz; costumes by Martin Pakledinaz

HARRY SHEARER songs and vocals by Mr. Shearer; Greg Cohen, musical director.

By MEL GUSSOW

Harry Shearer's transition from comedy writer and stand-up comic to performance artist seems trapped in a holding pattern. As the closing act in "The Men's Room," a three-part show on Saturday in the Lincoln Center Serious Fun festival, Mr. Shearer sought satiric mileage at the expense of public figures — with wavering results.

His jokes about Nicholas Ridley, the British Trade Secretary who resigned this month after making anti-German remarks, were woefully imprecise. Something similar was true when Mr. Shearer dealt with German reunification. On the other hand, as a collector of television outtakes, he can be on target. But there is something wrong when the most amusing moments in a live show are those on a television screen.

In one clip, President Ronald Reagan was seen practicing a coin toss for the Super Bowl (toss, toss, until he got it right), and in another there was a glimpse of the usually unflappable Peter Jennings in a moment of television self-consciousness. With tongue-in-cheek commentary, Mr. Shearer also took the audience inside the mind of Dan Rather, worrying less about his on-scene reporting than about the look of the collar on his field jacket.

In person, talking and singing to the tune of a backup combo, Mr. Shearer has neither the force of mimicry nor his own distinctive personality in performance. At Lincoln Center his routine was additionally marred by a flawed audio system. Nothing in his act was as clever as "This Is Spinal Tap," which Mr. Shearer co-wrote and appeared in, That satiric film about a rock-and-roll band would still seem to be the high point of his comic career so far, a fact that was reaffirmed with his encore rendition of a Spinal Tap song, "Big Bottom."

"The Men's Room," presented at Alice Tully Hall, began with "Wipe the Dirt Off Your Lips and Stroke the Mystery," a brief exercise in animalistic movements and sounds by Christian Swenson. Imitating apes and birds in flight, Mr. Swenson demonstrated that he has a limber body and a limited theatrical vocabulary.

The most evocative of the three performers was Tom Cayler, who is an actor as well as performance artist. "A Short History of Romance," created by Mr. Cayler, Kay Cummings and Clarice Marshall, was both wry and whimsical as it paralleled modern romance with the tragedy of Tristan and Isolde.

The words were less important than the physical comedy, as Mr. Cayler and Ms. Marshall pratfalled through a pas de deux. Every time Ms. Marshall leaped into the actor's arms, he toppled to the floor, a running gag with countless variations. In the background were popular lyrics like "Who stole my heart away?" providing a gently ironic background to Mr. Cayler's love-struck shenanigans on stage.

1990 Jl 26, C13:3

The English Only Restaurant

By Silvio Martinez Palau; directed by Susana Tubert; music and lyrics by Sergio Garcia-Marruz and Saul Spangenberg; music directors, Mr. Garcia-Marruz and Mr. Spangenberg; set and costumes, Michael Sharp; lighting, Rachel Budin; choreography, Ron Brown; production stage manager, Roger Franklin; producer, Miriam Colon Valle. Presented by the Puerto Rican Traveling Theater, 304 West 47th Street.

Mr. Martinezz	Alberto Guzman
Henry	Al D. Rodriguez
Jorg	Miguel Sierra
John Table	Jose Rey
Eugenica Heads and Reporter	Emma Mio
Sam Peters	Hal Blankenship
Mrs. Peters	Sheila Kay
Henryque Curly	Adriano Gonzalez
William F. Fartley	David J. Seatter
Johnny Garcia	Miguel Sierra
Patricia Rodriguez	Jeanette Toro
Language Policemen	Jose Rey and Adriano Gonzalez

By D. J. R. BRUCKNER

By the time "The English Only Restaurant" ends, you wonder what language, if any, you have been hearing during its 90 minutes. It hardly matters; the meaning is beyond mere words. This wild musical farce by Silvio Martinez Palau, with music and lyrics by Sergio Garcia-Marruz and Saul Spangenberg, mauls the English and Spanish languages and lampoons the pretensions of upwardly mobile Latinos, the snobberies of English-speaking Americans, critics, the police, reporters, high fashion, trendy restaurants and many other absurdities that happened to catch the attention of the playwright and lyricists.

The farce is being presented by the Puerto Rican Traveling Theater at its home at 304 West 47th Street through this week and then, throughout August, in parks and other settings in the five boroughs and in Newark and Jersey City.

The perpetrators of the mayhem that passes for action in this play gather sometime in the future at a Queens restaurant just after the Spanish language has been outlawed and a language police force has been established. Obviously, much of the humor involves the effort of the Latino proprietor and his Spanish-speaking customers to adopt English-sounding names and speak an artifical English they associate with high society. They are joined by several English-speaking customers who maul their own language and make alphabet soup of Latin American dishes on the menu.

Some fun is also made of what many New Yorkers take to be ordinary English, especially by Jose Rey as a policeman describing a crime scene to a television reporter and Miguel Sierra as a neighborhood punk who totes a pistol designed by Calvin Klein and speaks a hilarious version of New Yorkese.

This is old stuff, but Mr. Martinez Palau has given much of it new twists. And Susana Tubert, the director, keeps it all moving so fast that it seems surprisingly fresh.

Anything is fair game. The Latin beat comes in for some wonderfully malicious mimicking in song and dance, especially in the involuntary jerks and lunges of a waiter who breaks into snappy body rhythm from dead repose. The funniest dancing is by Adriano Gonzalez. He is very tall, thin and rangy and, as a character who realizes he can pass directly into the upper reaches of society because he has blue eyes, he breaks into a number that can only be called Tommy Tune out of control.

On the whole the music is serviceable. While only half the songs move the action along, the others don't interfere with it. And a couple of tunes are memorable: "Brown-Eyed Blues" and "So Ama Speaking Español, So What?"

In the end it is the good humor of everyone involved that makes the farce work. The playwright and lyricists step on hundreds of toes but break none, and the members of the cast have so much fun with one another that the cheer spreads to the audience, as does some of the boisterousness and the beat.

There is one moment toward the end when Mr. Martinez Palau seems to have thought he ought to have a plot, and things turn very briefly serious. That is a small and forgivable intrusion of common sense into what is otherwise a short evening of good nonsense.

1990 Jl 27, C4:5

Das Vedanya Mama

Written and directed by Ethyl Eichelberger; lighting design by David Ferri; stage management by Pedro Posado and Mike Taylor; costumes by Mr. Fashion. Presented by Performance Space 122, 150 First Avenue, at Ninth Street.

WITH: Ethyl Eichelberger, Gerard Little, Miss Joan Marie Moossy, Helen Shumaker and Black-Eyed Susan.

By MEL GUSSOW

When Ethyl Eichelberger is at his sharpest, his theatrical spoofs are sendups without being put-downs. This was the case with his one-man version of "King Lear" and his feminization of "Hamlet" (starring Black-Eyed Susan). With his new show, "Das Vedanya Mama" (at Performance Space 122), the result is less delirious than fragmented. As author, director and star, he has not clearly designated his target before making his assault.

Ostensibly the subject is Chekhov, and the cast of characters promises more amusement than is delivered. Mr. Eichelberger is the eldest sister, Olga, and Black-Eyed Susan plays "the three sisters," which, with the exclusion of Olga, become Masha, Irina and Maude.

As the show's chief adornment, Black-Eyed Susan wears two extra heads on her shoulders (puppets that resemble the face in Edvard Munch's "Scream"). She plays all three siblings at once, altering her voice for each while always keeping Masha in the moody middle. One of the other sisters has a lisp, causing her to say, "How I long to return to the patht." Watching the actress, it is impossible not to remember her own patht as Hamlette and as countless besieged heroines in plays by Charles Ludlam. In "Das Vedanya Mama" she is often left to her own comic devices.

Into the Eichelberger blender go "The Three Sisters," "The Seagull," "The Cherry Orchard" and the Bolshoi ballet, as well as random borrowings from Shakespeare and a soupçon of Greek tragedy. One excuse for these perambulations is that Olga is not a small-town schoolteacher as in Chekhov, but a grande dame of an actress from Minsk.

The story centers on the return home of Olga's prodigal son, Vaslav. Gerard Little, who plays that role, draws a single laugh with his opening line, "When is dinner?" and then marks time until he sings an Eichelberger song toward the end of the evening. The other characters add clutter — Miss Joan Marie Moossy's

suicidal Nina, who has a dead gull attached to her train; Helen Shumaker as "Fierz, the butler," who appears at one point in a tutu (certainly a first for Chekhov).

At various moments, Mr. Eichelberger seems to become restless in Russia, but his digressions can be droll. He offers commentary on everything from the National Endowment for the Arts to his own performance in the ill-fated Broadway revival of "The Threepenny Opera." Finally, he throws up his hands in mock anger and banters with his leading lady about her failure to use Method acting in her performance. As director, he says he wants her to be more like Marlon Brando. Black-Eyed Susan's justified response: "You've never seen Marlon Brando play Masha in 'The Three Sisters.'" Explaining her approach, she says she is "playing on intuition."

The show itself needs less intuition and more ingenuity (and Performance Space 122 desperately needs air-conditioning). But for diehard Eichelberger admirers, there is always the sight of him rising on point and in posture and losing his wig because of his too florid gestures. Olga dies before the play has concluded, a fact that does not stop the irrepressible Mr. Eichelberger from offering one final, prone accordion solo.

1990 Jl 28, 12:5

Dueling Lears and a Fascist Richard III

By FRANK RICH

Special to The New York Times

LONDON, Aug. 7 — No one here would be so vulgar as to acknowledge anything so crude as a theatrical rivalry, but any visiting theatergoer can see that this is the summer of dueling King Lears on the English stage. The country's two pre-eminent repertory companies, the Royal National Theater in London and the Royal Shakespeare Company in Stratford-on-Avon, have each just opened major productions of Shakespeare's most epic tragedy. Both stagings feature star actors, and both are the work of ascending-star directors in their 30's: Deborah Warner directs Brian Cox at the National, while Nicholas Hytner directs John Wood at the Royal Shakespeare. As if this were not enough "King Lear" to fill the dog days of August, Kenneth Branagh will soon bring his touring Renaissance Theater Company edition of the play, in which he plays Edgar to Richard Briers's King, to the West End.

The two competing Lears at hand expose an English classical theater seeking to redefine itself in the era after the one dominated by the directors Peter Hall and Trevor Nunn. Miss Warner, who is passionately committed to the minimalism of Peter Brook, and Mr. Hytner, a highly regarded opera director who staged the hit musical "Miss Saigon," have very different sensibilities, yet their productions have some revealing traits in common. Both directors use full four-hour versions of the text, both set the play in an abstract modern limbo rather than any particular period, both practice some gingerly nontraditional casting, and both have

failed to elicit solid performances in such crucial roles as the Fool, Edmund, Goneril and Regan. By accentuating the tormented father-daughter relationships and the humbling infirmities of age — each Lear is as quickly given a wheelchair as a throne — the directors emphasize the decline of a domineering patriarch over the fall of a powerful king.

New York audiences who recall Mr. Cox from his appearances in "Rat in the Skull" and the Glenda Jackson "Strange Interlude" may be startled to encounter the actor in his current form, with a stooped, thickened torso and a feral mane of silver hair to go with his bushy beard. As

---

An amplitude of Shakespeare, from spartan to operatic to creepy.

---

befits his role, he looks far older than his age (44), but the power of his body and voice remain formidable. His is a battering ram of a Lear whose wild eyes peer out searchingly from beneath a heavy brow. In the storm scene, he twirls and cracks a whip, as if somehow his brute force might tame the elements that besiege him. There is some vaudeville clowning in the characterization — Mr. Cox first wheels across the stage wearing a bright paper party hat — and, fleetingly, some pathos. The actor's Scottish bark dwindles into the plaintive lilt of second childhood by the time his elder daughters' cruelty prompts him to ask, "Is there any cause in nature that makes these hard hearts?" In madness, he becomes but a bag of mud-splattered flesh and bones, deposited in a wheelbarrow.

The spartan production surrounding Mr. Cox inevitably arouses memories of the landmark Brook "King Lear" of 1962, in which Paul Scofield's King was set down in the empty Beckettian landscape of "Endgame." Miss Warner uses only a few tarpaulins for scenery in a design redolent of L. L. Bean. The storm is simulated by flashlights and a pair of visible percussionists, one of whom lends Lear a cymbal for an umbrella. The burlesque relationship between the king and his fool echoes Beckett's Hamm and Clov.

What's missing, unfortunately, is the depth of acting needed to draw us to the people adrift in an indifferent absurdist universe of cruelty and nothingness. Mr. Cox's performance, while more affecting than such dry English Lears of the 1980's as Michael Gambon's and Anthony Hopkins's, is not yet up to his highest standard, and some of his fellow players are dreadful. It's hard to imagine how Miss Warner, a champion of intimate ensemble acting, could tolerate, among others, a Gloucester who never loses his cool elocutionary diction even when losing his eyes.

Though Mr. Hytner has better luck with his supporting cast, to the extent that his Gloucester (Norman Rodway) and Edgar (Linus Roache) almost run away with the show, his "King Lear" mainly leaves one with greater appreciation for Miss Warner's, flaws and all. Despite David Fielding's Magritte-like scenic design, which encloses the storm scene within a big fun-house box spinning out of control against a kaleidoscopic sky, the production feels mannered and busily old-fashioned. The tall, vig-

orous Mr. Wood — who looks as much like Don Quixote as Mr. Cox does like Sancho Panza — reveals little of the fiery intellectual quirkiness that has so distinguished his acting in Tom Stoppard plays. His Lear, a doting father who declines into red-faced tantrums, is most of all a spectacular vocal display. The oral fireworks reach their culmination near the end, when Mr. Wood's cries of "Howl!" boom through the large Stratford auditorium even before his final entry from the wings and are then followed by grief-stricken odes to Cordelia just as impressively pitched at the opposite, pianissimo end of his range.

Such displays of technique are entertaining, especially to a visitor from New York, where the only home-grown "Lear" in years has been the heavily amplified Southern-Gothic cartoon version staged by the Mabou Mines last season. But Mr. Hytner and Miss Warner, as well as their stars, too often seem to be climbing this Shakespearean mountain mainly because it is there, rather than because they have anything compelling to say about the play. The eight, largely cerebral hours spent with their Lears yield more insights into English theatrical careers than into Shakespeare's canvas of a universe in decay.

The difference between a Shakespearean production that is committed to ideas about the world as opposed to ideas simply about the theater is brought into dramatic relief by the companion piece presented in alternating repertory with Miss Warner's "King Lear" on the National's Lyttelton stage, Richard Eyre's "Richard III" with Ian McKellen. Mr. Eyre, who succeeded Peter Hall as the National's artistic director in 1988, is roughly midway between Mr. Hall and Miss Warner in age and esthetics. Using the same company as the "Lear" — in which Mr. McKellen serves unpersuasively as Kent — Mr. Eyre gets far more exciting results even as he works from a far less profound text.

Certainly there's nothing startling about the basic notion of his "Richard III," which transplants the despot's tale to the fascist realms of the 1930's. Yet Mr. McKellen's dictator is not a distanced Hitler or Mussolini: he's unambiguously an Englishman. Regal in posture rather than humpbacked, with a paralyzed left arm whose deformity is matched by the unnaturally white left temple of his hair, this patrician, cigarette-smoking blackshirt vaguely recalls the Duke of Windsor. And not for nothing is the British fascist Oswald Mosley quoted along with Stalin and Göring in the program. With the aid of the designer Bob Crowley, who tops his Albert Speer-minded vistas with rows of inquisition lamps, Mr. Eyre ushers the audience into a creepy official England all too ready to collaborate with a strongman.

The atmosphere, thick with behind-closed-doors intrigue along corrupt corridors of power, recalls both Alfred Hitchcock movies and Graham Greene novels from the eve of World War II. The elegant, chalky-voiced Mr. McKellen, whose other dark recent Shakespearean roles have included Coriolanus and Iago, is chilling in a manner not quite like any Richard I've seen. Kinkily obsessed with horses long before he would exchange his kingdom for one, his Richard conveys evil with a bloodless equine hauteur, an intellectual aggressiveness that runs roughshod over the foolish and the weak. He easily outargues and outmaneuvers

Photographs by Alastair Muir

LEFT Brian Cox as King Lear
ABOVE John Wood as King Lear
BELOW Ian McKellen as Richard III

everyone in his court, revealing the satanic madness beneath the facade only at the first-half climax, when his spine and sickly grin twist for an instant into the distorted figure of a grotesque George Grosz caricature marshaling a neo-Nazi salute.

•

What makes Mr. Eyre's direction of "Richard III" so impressive are his striking stage pictures, in which brutal executions sometimes share the stage with shadowy background tableaux of ineffectual Westminster political conferences, and his supple orchestration of the supporting company, which is led by Mr. Cox's Buckingham. Actors who fare poorly in "King Lear" — Peter Jeffrey, Clare Higgins, David Bradley — are so good here that one imagines their performances for Miss Warner will improve with further playing time. What makes this "Richard III" alarming are the plausibility and urgency with which it charts totalitarianism's easy, inky spread through a genteel world close to home. While Mr. Eyre's staging is scarcely Brechtian, his fiercely cautionary tone is of a piece with "The Resistible Rise of Arturo Ui."

In the months ahead, the National's Shakespeare double bill will be touring in Europe and Asia, with stops contemplated for cities like Prague and Bucharest, where Richards have only recently been toppled. As a piece of stagecraft, Miss Warner's stripped-to-basics "King Lear" is likely to strike audiences abroad as the more esthetically advanced of the two productions, but it is Mr. Eyre's "Richard III" that has the terrifying march of history on its side.

1990 Ag 8, C11:3

Death Takes a Holiday

By Alberto Casella; rewritten for the American stage by Walter Ferris; directed by Peter Hunt; settings, Hugh Landwehr; costumes, David Murin; lighting, Arden Fingerhut; original music, Arthur B. Rubinstein; sound, Darron West; special makeup, Joe Rossi; dialect and voice coach, Elizabeth Carlin. The Williamstown Theater Festival presented by the Williamstown Theater Foundation. At Williamstown, Mass.

Cora	Jenny Greenberg
Fedele	Robert Brolli
Duke Lambert	George Morfogen
Alda	Maria Tucci
Duchess Stephanie	Giulia Pagano
Princess of San Luca	Blythe Danner
Baron Cesarea	John Franklyn-Robbins
Rhoda Fenton	Christina Rouner
Eric Fenton	Patrick Boll
Corrado	James Phoenix
Grazia	Calista Flockhart
Prince Sirki	Christopher Reeve
Major Whitred	Robert Hogan

By MEL GUSSOW

Special to The New York Times

WILLIAMSTOWN, Mass., Aug. 10 — As the title character in "Death Takes a Holiday," Christopher Reeve has another role commensurate with his larger-than-life presence. Replacing his bright Superman cape with a cloak of spectral darkness, he is a not-so-Grim Reaper. More than anything, it is the actor's drollness that helps invigorate this creaky vehicle, revived at the Williamstown Theater Festival.

Walter Ferris's adaptation of the Alberto Casella original was a Broadway success in 1929 and was the subject of a 1934 film starring Fredric March. Peter Hunt has chosen to exhume it as part of his first season as head of the Williamstown company.

Mr. Reeve, Maria Tucci, Blythe Danner and their colleagues are clearly more than the play deserves. Together, led by Mr. Hunt, they turn "Death Takes a Holiday" into a diverting summer's entertainment, though even they cannot disguise the work's contrivances. In a curious fashion, the play does have a certain modishness as a period piece foreshadowing all those ghostly romantic comedies currently filling movie screens.

From his entrance in a death's head mask, Mr. Reeve is an ominous figure. A phantom without an opera, he sends a shudder through the theater and the Villa Happiness, the mansion in which he has decided to spend a three-day holiday. This is his first jaunt away from his deadly office.

It is Death's notion that to improve his on-the-job performance he must experience life. Most of all he must experience love, a definite conflict of interest considering the demands of

his profession. As the uninvited guest at a weekend soirée, he privately reveals his identity to the host (George Morfogen). He decides to stand in for Prince Sirki, apparently the last man to die before Death has declared a hiatus.

As substitute Prince, Mr. Reeve sheds his macabre mien for the actor's own visage. He becomes the soul of conviviality and the subject of all female attention. A newcomer to life, he is not without his ingenuousness. After all, he tells the other guests, "I am not of your world." They surmise that he is of Siberia. Actually Transylvania would be closer to the mark. With his Dracula-like accent and commanding manner, Mr. Reeve could next move on to vampires.

•

In "Death Takes a Holiday," he repeatedly has to sidestep the play's pretension. Philosophical interludes

Richard Feldman

Christopher Reeve in "Death Takes a Holiday"

about the loneliness of power make the title character sound like the beleaguered C.E.O. of a multi-national company. To his credit, Mr. Reeve can be as foreboding as Ingmar Bergman's cosmic chess player and also as antic as the character in Woody Allen's short play "Death Knocks." With deadly timing, he announces his world weariness, "I have not slept," pause, "for ages."

In his production, Mr. Hunt emphasizes realism and avoids melodramatic excesses. The tone is set with Hugh Landwehr's clever design. A black curtain rises to reveal a dark old house in which are gathered the host and his friends, all of whom have amazingly averted disasters, mostly of a vehicular variety. Later we learn that a man has leaped from the Eiffel Tower and walked away alive.

•

Concealing his dread with a patina of company manners, Mr. Morfogen plays the role of host as if he were the captain of a capsizing ship. In the only role with a dash of cynicism, John Franklin-Robbins strikes a Shavian posture (without the Shavian lines to support him). The other actors are left to their own inventions, which on one level means dressing well in David Murin's elegant costumes.

Ms. Danner is so glamorous as the mother of the ingénue (Calista Flockhart) that one wonders why Mr. Reeve does not make a play for her. Ms. Tucci shares an intense romantic scene with Mr. Reeve in which they transfix each other. The nubile Ms. Flockhart is so smitten with the tall, handsome stranger that she is willing to forgo all other considerations. Her character gives new meaning to the idea of being in love with death.

Mr. Hunt's first season has skipped eclectically from "Harvey" to "Marat/Sade" and will end with "A Moon for the Misbegotten." These plays have nothing in common except that they draw from the festival's extended roster of accomplished actors, amply in evidence in "Death Takes a Holiday."

1990 Ag 13, C11:1

Sin Testigos

By Sofiya Prokofyeva. Translated by Nina Miller; directed by Inda Ledesma; set design by Tito Egurza; costumes by Jorge Ferreri; lighting by Tito Egurza and Inda Ledesma. Associate producer, Jason Steven Cohen. Festival Latino in New York, Oscar Ciccone and Cecilia Vega, directors, presented by Joseph Papp. At the Public/Newman Hall, 425 Lafayette Street, at Astor Place.

Woman	Susu Pecoraro
Man	Miguel Angel Sola

By STEPHEN HOLDEN

Near the start of the Soviet writer Sofiya Prokofyeva's two-character drama "Sin Testigos" ("Without Witnesses") the wife in a marriage that came apart nine years earlier declares in a soliloquy that the submergence of her personality in her husband's became a kind of death. Now she feels nothing. The husband, for his part, complains bitterly about his wife's being a noble victim. "Nobody marries a victim," he sneers.

Over the course of the one-act, one-hour-and-15-minute play, which has performances through Friday at the Public Theater as part of the Festival Latino, the man and woman who have been separated for nine years circle each other warily while peeling away family secrets. The play, adapted and directed by the Argentine writer Inda Ledesma, suggests a muted chamber version of Ingmar Bergman's epic cinematic portrait of domestic upheaval, "Scenes From a Marriage." Simultaneous translation from the Spanish is available on Thursday and Friday evenings.

•

Unlike so many other dramas that explore similar territory "Sin Testigos" does so with a minimum of explosive passion. As the couple sort out their lives, we learn that they have a 14-year-old son who lives with the mother. The boy, whom the neglectful father refers to as an imbecile, drinks and likes heavy metal rock and boxing. The deeper secrets shared by the couple are all embarrassing to the husband. He established his scientific career through deceit and treachery involving an anonymous letter. His new domestic arrangements are a disaster. The son is really the offspring of one of his flings.

Miguel Rajmil/New York Shakespeare Festival

Miguel Angel Sola and Susu Pecoraro in "Sin Testigos."

He is in fact so accustomed to deceit that when the wife tells him she plans to marry one of his colleagues, he suspects her of lying to ensnare him. What little suspense the drama engenders lies in the cat-and-mouse games he plays to try to call her bluff. The play is staged as a kind of miniature domestic symphony in which the conversation and the interior monologues mingle with sounds of the telephone, elevator, appliances and fragments of an uncredited musical sound track.

Susu Pecoraro and Miguel Angel Sola give beautifully detailed, understated performances as the embattled couple. Miss Pecoraro brings a sanctimonious hush to the role of the unsmiling wife, who is largely unaware of her moral advantage and of the way it oppresses her husband. In the more dramatically varied role of the husband, Mr. Sola is convincing, although he fails to convey the depths of self-loathing and disappointment that are suggested by the character's most revealing confessions.

If "Sin Testigos" is a far from transcendent evocation of ties that bind, it rings true. But in its modest way, it succeeds as an almost clinical study of the way two people's knowledge of each other can create an inescapable bond that, however poisoned, still must be counted as a kind of love.

1990 Ag 14, C16:1

The Old Maid/Daisy Miller

Dennis Krausnick's stage adaptations of "The Old Maid," by Edith Wharton, directed by Gary Mitchell, and "Daisy Miller," by Henry James, directed by Dennis Krausnick; costumes by Kate Morrison; technical director, Stephen D. Ball; production stage manager, K. Dale White. Presented by Shakespeare & Company, Tina Packer, artistic director; Mr. Krausnick, managing director. At the Mount Theater, Lenox, Mass.

THE OLD MAID
Dr. Lanskell	Mr. Krausnick
Delia	Andrea Haring
Charlotte	Corinna May
Jim Ralston	James Goodwin Rice
Joe Ralston	Walton Wilson
Tina	Ruth Callahan

DAISY MILLER
Frederick Winterbourn
Christopher von Baeyer

Randolph Miller	Luke Breslin
Daisy Miller	Gillian Hemstead
Mrs. Costello	Heather Peterson
Mrs. Miller	Karen Beaumont
Eugenio	Dan Mufson
Mrs. Walker	Adrienne Robbins
Giovanelli	Brad Kimmelman

By MEL GUSSOW

Special to The New York Times

LENOX, Mass., Aug. 11 — Visitors to the Mount, Edith Wharton's former country house, can receive emanations not only of the resident author but also of her close friend, Henry James. Together they walked the paths and terraces of this beautiful estate. It was in 1910, several years after first seeing the Mount, when James wrote that the two novelists "would be more and more never apart."

This summer at the Mount, the Shakespeare & Company theatrical troupe has evoked that celebrated literary relationship with adaptations of works by both writers — Wharton's "Old Maid" and James's "Daisy Miller," one of Mrs. Wharton's favorite stories. The two plays are staged on a terrace and in an adjoining room in the restored Wharton home. They can be seen, with an interval, on the same day.

It is a most interesting dramatic juxtaposition. "The Old Maid" is resonant with the morality of old New York in the mid-19th century, with the characters bound by the Puritanical predilections of their time. The title character rejects marriage and allows her illegitimate daughter to be brought up by her married cousin. Humanity suffers in the name of outward respectability.

With a greater spontaneity, "Daisy Miller" chronicles the life of travelers in the latter half of the same century, following a family of wealthy Americans on a grand tour in which their incipient vulgarity comes into conflict with Old World traditions.

As he has in the past with Wharton stories, Dennis Krausnick has adapted the two with a certain efficacy, linking dialogue from a book with the not overly intrusive voice of a narrator. The approach falls somewhere between full dramatization and storytelling. It is a hospitable way to encounter these tales in a theatrical environment.

There is, however, a definite difference between the two as works of theater. The Wharton is shadowed both by the book and by the Bette Davis movie in which Miss Davis incarnated the self-sacrificing "old maid" and Miriam Hopkins played her cousin.

This might not matter as much if the performances were polished, but Gary Mitchell, as director, has allowed his cast to stray into paths of histrionic excess. This is true not only of Corinna May in the title role, but also of Mr. Krausnick himself as the family doctor, who heavily italicizes his narration. One has to look behind the performance to ascertain the poignant story. Coming to Lenox after seeing Blythe Danner and Maria Tucci in small roles in "Death Takes a Holiday" at the Williamstown Theater Festival, one can fantasize what these fine actresses would bring to a production of "The Old Maid."

Though "Daisy Miller" also suffers from amateurish acting in several roles and Mr. Krausnick, as adapter and director, has made a few unwarranted additions to the text, the story makes a smoother transition to the stage. This is with the help of Christopher von Baeyer, who plays the role of Frederick Winterbourn, the young expatriate American who is so taken with the ebullient Daisy Miller. Though Gillian Hemstead does not have the striking appearance of Cybill Shepherd, her cinematic prede-

Richard Feldman/Shakespeare & Company/Daisy Miller

Gillian Hemstead and Christopher von Baeyer in Shakespeare & Company's adaptation of Henry James's "Daisy Miller."

cessor as Daisy, she captures the character's flirtatious behavior as well as her inescapable penchant for injuring her own reputation.

•

Both plays fit neatly on the improvised stage at the Mount, where they benefit from their architectural surroundings. Again, it is "Daisy Miller" that has the easier adaptability. The terrace becomes the hotel in Vevey, Switzerland, where Winterbourn first encounters Daisy and invites her to explore the castle at Chillon.

In the second act, the scene shifts indoors to a simulation of Daisy's life in Rome. There, she is caught up in a social whirl that shocks more prudent observers, except for Winterbourn, who continues to be charmed by her freshness. The Mount's "Daisy Miller" conveys the Jamesian mood as the tragic story leads to Winterbourn's youthful conclusion that he has already lived "too long in foreign parts."

1990 Ag 16, C14:4

Quiet on the Set

By Terrell Anthony; directed by A. C. Weary; scenic designer, Rick Dennis; lighting, Nancy Collings; costumes, Colleen McFarlane. The Westbeth Theater Center Production presented by Coup de Grace Productions, in association with 126 Second Avenue Corporation. At the Orpheum Theater, 126 Second Avenue, at St. Marks Place.

Judith Petri/Barbara Stewart.... Kate Collins
Taylor Lydell/John Whittington
.... Robert Newman
Tamra Lydell/Bridget Stewart...Beth Ehlers
Bruce Mitchell/Bart Whittington
.... Trent Bushey
Director/Characters............ .... Matt Servitto

By WILBORN HAMPTON

Early in the second act of "Quiet on the Set," Terrell Anthony's frothy parody of daytime television at the Orpheum Theater, two actresses are discussing that age-old conundrum, "Do the soaps imitate life, or does life imitate the soaps?" The answer, they decide, is that "both imitate commercials." Whatever your personal belief, if you ever watched a soap opera, you'll very likely enjoy "Quiet on the Set."

The set of the title is Sound Stage 3 of "Sunset," a top-rated daytime television drama, and the action takes place during a long evening shoot. The plot revolves around four principal actors on the series whose off-camera lives are only slightly less complicated and intertwined than those of the characters they play on the home screen.

This soap-within-a-soap can become rather muddled. There are two newcomers to the "Sunset" cast: Tamra, who is returning after a two-year absence to play Bridget, and Taylor, a serious film actor who is creating a character named John. Tamra and Taylor are brother and sister in real life. Then there is Judith, a hard-bitten veteran soap star who plays Barbara. Off the set, Judith is the embittered ex-girlfriend of Taylor. Finally, there is Bruce, who plays a character named Bart and whose main concern, apart from remembering his lines, is how his hair looks. In the "Sunset" plot, Bridget and Barbara are sisters, while John and Bart are brothers, although Bridget (who has had an illegitimate child by Bart but is in love with John) doesn't know that yet. All these characters have

last names, but it's confusing enough as it is.

•

It's not essential, or even desirable, to remember any of this. As one character observes about the soaps, "people can tune in once a week and not miss a thing, or even once a month and not get confused." In "Quiet on the Set," like the soap operas it affectionately parodies, very little of consequence actually happens.

In fact, it is at this level that the play falters slightly. Mr. Anthony seems to have aimed at farce, and if he falls a bit short of that mark it is mainly because the off-camera plot fails to provide the comic intricacies or satirical characterizations (such as in Larry Gelbart and Murray Schisgal's screenplay for "Tootsie" or Michael Frayn's stage play "Noises Off") that genuine farce requires. In "Quiet on the Set" the laughs come mostly from the scenes being taped for "Sunset."

•

To his credit, Mr. Anthony takes the time to construct an elaborate situation in the first act that pays some funny dividends in the second act, and a first-rate cast of soap-opera regulars from ABC's "All My Children" and CBS's "Guiding Light" makes the most of them. Under A. C. Weary's crisp direction, the actors resist any temptation to caricature themselves, taking their directorial cue from the soap actor's credo: "Open your mouth. Say your line. Get off the set."

Trent Bushey is hilarious as the vain, slow-witted Bruce/Bart, especially in one scene in which he jots his lines on his hands, only to become hopelessly lost when his palms start to sweat under the studio lights. Mr. Bushey gives one of those deadpan performances in which, by the end, he can get a laugh simply by walking onstage. Kate Collins is amusingly vicious as the chain-smoking, hard-boiled Judith/Barbara. Robert Newman as Taylor/John captures the manic intensity of a serious actor who takes relaxation exercises on the set and shouts for more time to study his character even as the director is counting down the start of a scene. Beth Ehlers is engaging as Tamra/Bridget, and Matt Servitto provides some humorous turns (and one or two exaggerated ones) as a hairdresser, makeup man, deli delivery boy, wardrobe mistress, electrician and director.

Even if you don't watch daytime television, "Quiet on the Set" can provide an evening of fun, although at the end you may ask yourself this slightly edited version of another age-old question about soaps: "Who writes this stuff, anyway?"

1990 Ag 16, C17:1

The Tragedy of King Richard III

By William Shakespeare; directed by Robin Phillips; scenery and costumes by Elis Y. Lam; lighting by Louise Guinand; music by Louis Applebaum; fights staged by Martino N. Pistone; associate producer, Jason Steven Cohen. Presented by Joseph Papp. At the Delacorte Theater, Central Park (entrance at West 81st Street).

Richard, Duke of Gloucester
.... Denzel Washington
George, Duke of Clarence........Joseph Ziegler
William, Lord Hastings.......... JeffreyNordling
Lady Anne..........................Sharon Washington

Queen Elizabeth	Nancy Palk
Lord Rivers	Philip Moon
Marquess of Dorset	David Aaron Baker
Duke of Buckingham	Daniel Davis
Earl of Derby	Ben Hammer
Queen Margaret	Mary Alice
Sir William Catesby	Jake Weber
First Murderer	Wade Williams
Second Murderer	Tim Nelson
King Edward IV	Sam Tsoutsouvas
Sir Richard Ratcliffe	Jonathan Fried
Duchess of York	Virginia Downing
Edward Plantagenet	Reese Madigan
Margaret Plantagenet	Jenny Nichols
Prince Edward	Seth Gilliam
Lord Mayor of London	Peter McRobbie
Earl of Richmond	Armand Schultz

By MEL GUSSOW

THE tragedy of "Richard III" is in the title character's perverted brilliance. In a world of dissemblers, he appears to be the only one with a comprehension of the abuses of politics, as he manipulates his way to the crown and, inevitably, falls to his doom. Any actor attempting this awesome role must be able to convey Richard's demonic sense of purpose and self-worth.

Denzel Washington, an actor of range and intensity, is expert at projecting a feeling of controlled rage, as demonstrated in his Academy Award-winning performance in the film "Glory." Such an attitude, if used, would suit him particularly well in undertaking the role of Richard, a man who can barely contain his hostility. Surprisingly, Mr. Washington's performance in the version that opened last night at the Delacorte Theater in Central Park, is muted. That constraint is reflected in other aspects of Robin Phillips's disappointing production for the New York Shakespeare Festival.

Beginning with the actor's physical approach to the role, the characterization is less than a concept. Led by the director, Mr. Washington plays Richard almost at a crouch, contorting his body and concealing his face. This means that he is forced to play scenes while peering over his left shoulder. The choices an actor makes in articulating Richard's deformity should help to liberate his performance. Here the choices restrict the performance, cramping Mr. Washington's movements and also his voice, a voice that seems well able to encompass Shakespearean verse.

Martha Swope/Richard III
Denzel Washington in the title role of Shakespeare's "Richard III."

"Richard III" is of course open to diverse interpretation, while always retaining the character's villainous core. Laurence Olivier might have seemed to monopolize the franchise, until Antony Sher astonished audiences in England in 1984 with his daring performance for the Royal Shakespeare Company. Mr. Sher's Richard walked with crutches, which became both a symbol and an extension of his twisted body. The actor was the bottled spider of Shakespeare's imagination. Currently at London's National Theater, there is Ian McKellen's provocative intellectualization of the character as a steely, fascistic fanatic. Both of these actors and others (including Americans like George C. Scott and Kevin Kline) have discovered self-definition within the role.

Mr. Washington's characterization remains undefined, a fact that is evident from his entrance. In trying to add a freshness to his first soliloquy, he arbitrarily breaks the lines into staccato rhythms. Soon, as he courts Lady Anne (a graceful portrayal by Sharon Washington), he misses Richard's zest for his own performance. Richard should silently revel in his ability to woo, win and discard such a lovely foe. In Mr. Washington's case, even the misogyny seems superimposed.

When Buckingham stage-manages Richard's call to power, the actor in Richard should emerge as he gauges the audience response before laying claim to a grand public appearance. Richard's presence should cause those around him to quaver with trepidation. This is not the case in Mr. Phillips's production. Mr. Washington is persuasive in certain confrontations, as in his scenes with Queen Margaret, who is given a passionate performance by Mary Alice. But the actor frequently misses the feral and emotional assertiveness so essential to his role.

Mr. Phillips must bear at least equal responsibility. In contrast to so many other directors who have participated in Joseph Papp's Shakespeare cycle, he is a director of proven Shakespearean mettle, as demonstrated during his years as head of the Stratford Festival in Canada.

To his credit, he presents the play in period, taking advantage of an impressive castle-like design by Elis Y. Lam. Using a slightly abridged text, the production proceeds with a certain dispatch. There is strength in the physical surroundings and in Mr. Phillips's deployment of the large company of actors in and out of bat-

Mary Alice fiercely evokes the enraged Queen Margaret.

tle. The fights are sharply staged by Martino N. Pistone. Characters have been cast without regard to color, a principle that is smoothly accomplished. But there is no sense of the production having a through-line or specific conceptual purpose.

One might not be as conscious of the vagueness were the acting all on Miss Alice's plane. She offers a fierce evocation of the enraged queen, savagely assailing her nemesis. When Richard kisses her (an interpolation in this version), she looks startled — as if she had just tasted poison. In Miss Alice's performance, this is a queen to command a kingdom. Daniel Davis also consistently elevates his scenes as a crafty Buckingham, who outwits himself rather than his liege. In small roles, there are admirable contributions from Sam Tsoutsouvas and Seth Gilliam.

Counterbalancing these performances are ineffectual ones from, among others, Virgina Downing, Joseph Ziegler, David Aaron Baker and Armand Schultz. The conspirators

against Richard and those who are his allies tend to blur into faceless antagonists.

At the problematic center is Mr. Washington. While it is ambitious of him to attempt a major Shakespearean role at this high point of his career, he has not yet gathered his character's furies into a cohesive dramatic assault. "Richard III" remains for the actor to conquer.

Performances of "Richard III" will continue through Sept. 2.

1990 Ag 17, C1:1

El Huésped

By Pedro Juan Soto; directed by Beatriz Córdoba. Presented by Repertorio Español, Gilberto Zaldívar, producer; René Buch, artistic director. At the Gramercy Arts, 138 East 27th Street.

Padre.. Ricardo Barber
Victoria.................................... Birgit Bofarull
Doña Antonia .... Virginia Rambal
Irma... Adriana Sananes
Hombre.................................... René Sánchez
Lucía..Tatiana Vecino

Los Jíbaros Progresistas

Based on a tale by Ramón Méndez Quiñones; music by Manuel González; musical direction by Pablo Zinger; directed by René Buch; production design by Robert Weber Federico; assistants to the director, María José Alvarez and Kristine Horner; technical director, Rigoberto Obando; production assistant, Manuel Herrera.

Antón ....Francisco Chahin-Casanova
Chepa.. Brenda Feliciano
Cleto.. George Maldonado
Juaniya .... Nell Snaidas

By D. J. R. BRUCKNER

Repertorio Español has constructed an improbable double bill at the Gramercy Arts Theater: a play about a family tragedy among Puerto Ricans in New York City today and a musical about rural Puerto Rico 130 years ago. The fit is, at best, imperfect, but the musical has great charm and one leaves the pair, somewhat miraculously, with little emotional confusion.

Calling the second piece a musical is inadequate. "Los Jíbaros Progresistas," by the Puerto Rican composer Manuel González, with a libretto drawn from a play by Ramón Méndez Quiñones, is really a little comic opera. A literal translation of the title is

A dreaming, aging parent of today and rural life 130 years ago.

misleading. "Jíbaros" is distinctly a Puerto Rican word referring to country people; depending on the tone of voice it can range from demeaning to downright rude. And "progresso" in Spanish is as ambiguous as "progress" is in English. Mr. González has no malice; the title really suggests something like "savoir-faire in the sticks."

The story is timeless and universal. Cleto, a jíbaro with a roguish sense of humor, wants to take Chepa, his wife, and Juaniya, their daughter, to a fiesta in the town of Ponce that is advertised on a handbill he has picked up.

Juaniya flies into bel canto ecstasies, and Chepa hardens into stony resistance as she ponders what moral dangers there are in a city of teeming hundreds, or more.

•

Her suspicions double when her husband proposes that a neighbor, Antón, who is in love with Juaniya, go along. Romance is perilous enough; in an air of urban laxity it may explode. So the game becomes seduction of the mother; she has to be won over to the cause of civilization, and the fiesta in Ponce, by slippery and funny arguments from the others about the wonders of progress.

Mr. González's music deliberately calls to mind familiar 18th-century- and 19th-century comic opera scores. It is rendered energetically by Pablo Zinger at the piano and sung — every line but one — by a quartet of actors who rejoice in the absurd. The grandeur of the score and a clever baroque proscenium frame for the stage by Robert Weber Federico make a fine ironic joke of this tale of climbing molehills and other heights. And René Buch's direction keeps it as light as a feather.

Nell Snaidas and Brenda Feliciano sound perfectly like daughter and mother: the one with a light soprano that can languish, cajole, laugh and pout, and the other with a big operatic voice that makes the Repertorio's small auditorium ring and can drop from the clouds into the basement at a beat.

•

George Maldonado as the father makes up with shrewd acting what he lacks in vocal power; he knows how to give every syllable, smile and step a special meaning. There are times when Francisco Chahin-Casanova's tenor can pin your ears back, and

while his Antón is a confused and somewhat self-important young man, the singer's outbursts occasionally introduce a hilarity that is not in the libretto.

It might have been nice to be able to buy a libretto, incidentally. Even people who understand Spanish perfectly can miss some words in these songs. They shouldn't be missed; the songs were good enough to send at least a few people out singing snatches of them.

In stark contrast, the opener, "El Huésped" (the Guest) by Pedro Juan Soto, is an unsettling 40-minute play about three women gathered in the New York apartment of one of them to discuss ways of getting their old

Francisco Chahin-Casanova in "Los Jíbaros Progresistas."

Photographs by Gerry Goodstein/Repertorio Español

Ricardo Barber and Virginia Rambal in a scene from "El Huésped."

and sick father off their hands and into the care of two unmarried relatives.

While they talk, the father, apparently sleeping in the next room, is alert, but to other voices: he hears the daughters in their youth persuading him to take them from Puerto Rico to New York after their mother dies. Fatefully, he also hears his wife asking him to go away with her, with the help of a bottle of sleeping pills.

It is a mark of the achievement of Beatriz Córdoba, the director, and the seasoned members of this cast that "El Huésped" is not unbearably painful. It is played almost like a dream, an enchantment. Indeed, the scenes in which the dead wife reaches out with compassion to the old man are enchanting.

•

But there is real bitterness here. For the daughters who give such pain to the old man are themselves driven by pain and disappointment. The last memorable words are spoken by their dead mother, who tells her husband he should die, to make them "realize their mistake." "In this way you can save them," she tells him. What kind of salvation we are left to imagine, with no help from the playwright.

Maybe the reason these two plays make an almost tolerable pair is simple: after such bleakness, a sunny island backwater where the rustics have great hopes, however deluded they are, is heaven.

1990 Ag 18, 15:1

El Palomar ("The Pigeon House")

By Carlos Catania; translated by Melia Bensussen; directed by Alfredo Catania; assistant producer, Rodolfo Araya; set design by Pilar Quirós; costume design by Mercedes González; lighting design, Jody Steiger; set construction by Federico Solís. Associate producer, Jason Steven Cohen. Teatro Encuentro de Costa Rica. Festival Latino in New York, Oscar Ciccone and Cecilia Vega, directors, presented by Joseph Papp. At the Public Theater/LuEsther Hall, 425 Lafayette Street.

Hermógena Vilesia	Eugenia Chavarri
Arístides	Carlos Ovares
El General	Rubén David Pagura
Silvina Hernández	Grettel Cedeno
Lucrecia Iturraspe Finch	Jacqueline Stellar
Nerasio Prisco	Juan Carlos Calderón
Gaspar Zabaleta	Rodolfo Araya
Atenor Pistacho	Luis Fernando Gómez

By RICHARD F. SHEPARD

It's not always easy for an outsider to grasp that he is being presented with a metaphor, but that is not a prime consideration in the case of "El Palomar" ("The Pigeon House"), a play being offered by Teatro Encuentro de Costa Rica at the Public Theater as part of the Festival Latino in New York. The new Costa Rican troupe is giving New York a refreshing lesson in stagecraft where language works in tandem with mood and motion.

The metaphor in this drama by Carlos Catania, an Argentine playwright, whose brother, Alfredo Catania, is the director, would seem to be about strong government and the people who go along with it. It is set in a boarding house whose owner, played by Eugenia Chavarri, is a dominating yet apparently benevolent overseer of her guests, a mixed, even eccentric lot representing various classes and temperaments.

The landlady controls rents and demands obedience, which is enforced by her armed son (Carlos Ovares). She is also rather gracious when need be, solicitous and generous with her meals. There is also the ghost of an old general (Rubén David Pagura), seen by nobody else but the audience, who was killed on a battlefield where this house now stands; he would represent the old military elite that perhaps founded the country or at least fought to establsh it.

A new tenant arrives, a professor of literature (Luis Fernando Gómez), and he is curious about a tenant whose room he is taking; a man who organized the tenants to protest and then died under questionable circumstances. There is a heightening of tensions and then a strange ending in which the landlady and her son apparently die at the hands of the rebellious boarders, but is she really dead?

•

What will attract the outsider is the style of presentation. Miss Chavarri projects such a strong personality that her very changes from sweet and sociable to sharp and severe transcend language. Grettel Cedeno, as a pretty young ballerina used and abused by men, is not a central figure in the script, but she becomes one under Mr. Catania's direction.

He employs lots of music and dance, and Miss Cedeno does the tango and Andean mountain dance and ballet movement with a sinuous and sexy virtuosity, maintaining at the same time the stance of a young woman who is right-minded and intent on career.

Juan Carlos Calderón, as a South American Indian and former circus entertainer, plays pipes, bangs drums and projects a hearty if fatalistic acceptance of his life. Mr. Gomez creates the intrusive newcomer as a man who is not a hero but refuses to let go of anything that might smack of a wrongdoing.

"El Palomar" is a one-act play that promotes change, but in so doing it illustrates the unvarying principle of

Miguel Rajmil/Festival Latino

Eugenia Chavarri and Rodolfo Araya in "El Palomar."

showmanship that in terms of theater, the medium may very well outshine the message.

1990 Ag 19, 53:1

The Man Who Fell in Love With His Wife

By Ted Whitehead; directed by Will Lieberson and Kevin Conway; lighting and sound designer, Graeme F. McDonnell; set designer, Jeff Read Freund; costume designer, V. Jane Suttell; stage manager, David O'Connell; production associate, Joyce Korbin Bell. Presented by Mr. Lieberson, producing artistic director. At Theater 808, Lexington Avenue at 62d Street.

Tom Fearon	Kevin Conway
Mary Fearon	Mila Burnette
Susy Fearon	Julia Gibson
Julia	Holly Barron

By WILBORN HAMPTON

During the blackouts between scenes in Ted Whitehead's play "The Man Who Fell in Love With His Wife," excerpts of golden oldies ranging from Nat (King) Cole to the Beatles to David Bowie are played over the Quaigh Theater's sound system. This hit parade from the past is the best part of an otherwise tedious tale of a Liverpool docker's midlife crisis, which he is handling rather badly.

Tom Fearon (Kevin Conway) met and married Mary (Mila Burnette) when both were in their teens. Emotionally, Tom hasn't grown a day since. Although they have a daughter, Susy (Julia Gibson), who is now at college and about to move out of the house, and Tom has become a supervisor on the docks, mentally he's still stuck somewhere in late adolescence. He's the one who constantly plays all those old favorites we hear during scene breaks, and he seems to have derived his concept of love entirely from the lyrics of 1960's rock songs.

Tom has some other quirks. His idea of romance, for example, is to take Polaroid snapshots of his wife in

lace underwear, and to insist on making love on the living room couch when Mary would prefer the bedroom. Tom's conversation tends to ruminations about their courtship 20 years ago and he becomes piqued when Mary wants to talk about such mundane contemporary matters as their daughter's leaving home.

Mary can be something of a pill herself. When Tom suggests on the spur of the moment that they take a holiday in Marrakesh, Mary admits she would rather stay home and run the vacuum cleaner.

•

When Mary takes a civil service job, Tom's peculiarities take a turn for the worse. He becomes obsessed with the idea that his wife is having an affair with her boss. On one occasion he bursts into the boss's office and warns him to stay away from her; on another he confronts the hapless man in a pub with a similar threat. Unfortunately for the play, which badly needs some livening up, both those scenes take place offstage.

It is of little surprise to anyone except Tom that Mary soon chucks him out. Tom immediately adopts the role of betrayed martyr, complaining frequently and at length to anyone who will listen — his daughter, his wife's best friend, Julia (Holly Barron), the audience — that he is a man whose only fault is that "he fell in love with his wife." The problem is that he has apparently confused pathological jealousy with love.

Mr. Conway, who shares directing credits with Will Lieberson, raises his voice in a couple of scenes in a vain attempt to stir up some audience interest in what amounts to a humdrum play about humdrum people.

1990 Ag 19, 55:1

Voces de Acero (Voices of Steel)

Collective creation by Pregones Theater Group; directed by Alvan Colon Lespier; music, Pregones Theater Group; lighting, Mr. Lespier; set design, Jorge Merced and Mr. Lespier; costumes, Rosalba Rolon and Fanny Hutter. Festival Latino in New York, Oscar Ciccone and Cecilia Vega, directors. Presented by Joseph Papp. At the Public/Susan Stein Shiva Theater, 425 Lafayette Street.

Wilma	Sandra Berrios
Samuel	Jose Joaquin Garcia
Angel	Jorge B. Merced
Evangelina	Judith Rivera
Marta	Rosalba Rolon

By D. J. R. BRUCKNER

The sensuous music and movement in "Voces de Acero" (Voices of Steel) by the Pregones Theater, presented as part of the Festival Latino at the Public Theater, might make some viewers think the experience of prison is not all bad.

Indeed, who is to say that that is not the message of this entrancing but puzzling performance by the innovative New York Puerto Rican ensemble? The program declares: "'Voices of Steel' is a collective creation that offers a different view on imprisonment in the United States. Pregones has created the characters from research and testimony gathered from current and past Puerto Rican political prisoners."

The last two words give one the group's point of view. But in a time when, at least in a large city, it is difficult to avoid meeting at least one or two people with personal tales of jail to tell, the audience may not be able to distinguish what is different about these "political" prisoners and those locked up for reasons that are not political, whatever they may be.

•

Actually, none of that need matter. What is most striking about the Pregones performance is the movement and the music. There are some words, in English and Spanish, but those that can be understood hardly add up to a message. Basically, "Voices of Steel" is an improvised ballet, perhaps the most effective kind of theater in an age when speech is no longer the most commonly shared language.

The company assumes that no translation is needed, and for the most part it is not. But in a few places it might have helped, especially in a kind of catalogue song ridiculing all the wonders to be seen and pleasures to be felt by the immigrant who makes it to the promised land of America.

Otherwise, the few words there are — about terrorism, seditious conspiracy and the like — get in the way. The intricate, stylized movements of the five actors in the piece convey elegantly the physical and mental torment of being totally deprived of freedom. The famous old poem notwithstanding, iron bars *do* a prison make, and one comes away from "Voices of Steel" wondering whether there might not be some other way for humanity to express its disapproval of unlicensed conduct. Whatever the intentions of the company, the piece speaks to the human condition, not merely a political situation. And that is what makes it worthwhile.

•

Except for a few moments of explosive percussion, it also provides an hour of haunting and intriguing music, performed by Cristina Hernandez, Ricardo Pons and Cesar Rodriguez, on what sometimes sound like hundreds of instruments. It is tempting at times just to close the eyes and listen to it as a concert. Of course, doing that might frustrate the intentions of the Pregones company, for the music is on the whole uplifting, upbeat, a sound that gives your toes a life of their own, a very free life.

1990 Ag 20, C14:1

Light Up the Sky

Written by Moss Hart; directed by Larry Carpenter; set design, Andrew Jackness; costume design, Martin Pakledinaz; lighting, Dennis Parichy; sound, Philip Campanella; production stage manager, Roy W. Backes. Presented by the Roundabout Theater Company, Todd Haimes, producing director; Gene Feist, founding director. At the Roundabout Theater, 100 East 17th Street.

Miss Lowell ..... Elaine Bromka
Carleton Fitzgerald ..... Charles Keating
Frances Black ..... Betsy Joslyn
Owen Turner ..... Humbert Allen Astredo
Stella Livingston ..... Peggy Cass
Peter Sloan ..... John Bolger
Sidney Black ..... Bruce Weitz
Sven ..... Paul Nielsen
Irene Livingston ..... Linda Carlson
Tyler Rayburn ..... John C. Vennema
Max, a Shriner ..... Max Robinson
Shriners ..... Peter Robinson, Paul Nielsen
William H. Gallegher ..... Bill McCutcheon
A Plainclothes Cop ..... Peter Robinson

By MEL GUSSOW

Moss Hart's love affair with the theater, so movingly chronicled in his memoir, "Act One," did not blind him to the inequities of his profession. In the theater, a private or collaborative act of creativity is subjected to the capriciousness of actors, producers, audiences and, of course, critics.

All accusatory feelings are accounted for in Hart's "Light Up the Sky," revived at the Roundabout Theater Company more than 40 years after its Broadway premiere. This is a backstage comedy in which everything is intended to undercut the poor, pitiable playwright. He puts his heart into his play, only to have it eviscerated by his colleagues on opening night in Boston. But being a satirist, Hart knew he had to spoof to conquer. Even the playwright is a figure of fun; his integrity is matched by his naïveté.

As a play, "Light Up the Sky" does not have the sustained vitality of Hart's earlier collaborations with George S. Kaufman. Their "Once in a Lifetime" did to Hollywood what the later solo play aspires to do to Broadway. "Light Up the Sky" does have some amusing lines, and it survives as an insider's comic valentine to a kind of theater that disappeared decades ago. Today, the play within the play, an elaborate allegory that includes Mount Rushmore in its stage design, would never get as far as Boston. If it did, it is unlikely that critics, even the most provincial, would be so ecstatic about such hot air.

•

Any revival of "Light Up the Sky" has to disguise this and other departures from reality, including the sentimentality into which the play eventually slides, as all hands roll up sleeves to repair the unrepairable for Broadway. Unfortunately, when it counts most, Larry Carpenter's Roundabout production trips. There is a broadness afoot that diminishes the play's wryness.

Linda Carlson, as the temperamental actress at the center of the evening (a role reportedly based on Gertrude Lawrence), takes a heavy-handed approach. All that is missing is a laugh track or a pie in the eye, as she turns the character into a caricature.

To a somewhat lesser degree, Betsy Joslyn overplays the Billie Dawn dumbness of the producer's wife, until intelligence dawns (and the actress improves). John Bolger is one dimensional as the first-time playwright and Charles Keating, who is stylish in the plays of Joe Orton, is too mannered in his role as a narcissistic director. Mr. Keating does draw a laugh, however, when, delivering an insult about audiences of the period, he directly faces theatergoers at the Roundabout.

As the producer, Bruce Weitz steps into shoes originally worn on Broadway by Sam Levene, and fills the role handsomely. With his dapper manner, he adds a necessary note of calmness to the farcical activity that is characteristic of the production. Bill McCutcheon also inserts a note of low-pressure lunacy with his late arrival in a cameo role as a visiting Shriner who desperately wants to get into the theater.

•

As the star's cranky mother, the role with the most acerbic dialogue, Peggy Cass effectively uses her patented deadpan delivery. With her raspy voice, she describes how she sneaked into the theater against the director's orders to watch a run-through of the play. She posed as a cleaning lady, and, with mop and pail, lingered in the balcony. Her advice is, "See this show on an empty stomach." Miss Cass's account is topped by her astonished reaction as Mr. Keating tells his very disparate version of the same event.

Hart tried to have it both ways, to make fun of the playwright and the play within the play — and then, in the third act, to show up the cynics for their small-mindedness. By the end of the play we are not sure to whom the playwright owes his allegiance. Although the conclusion is less convincing than the beginning, there is enough humor here to make the comedy a staple on the summer stock stage — in or out of Manhattan. But Mr. Carpenter's production is only intermittently able to lighten up "Light Up the Sky."

1990 Ag 22, C10:5

O Doente Imaginario
(The Imaginary Invalid)

By Molière; translated by Marcia Abujamra; directed by Caça Rosset; translation and adaptation into Portuguese by Mr. Rosset; set and costumes, José De Anchieta; choreography, Lala Deheinzelin; musical director, Hector Gonzalez; lighting, Abel Kopanski. Associate producer, Jason Steven Cohen. Teatro Do Ornitorrinco. Festival Latino in New York, Oscar Ciccone and Cecilia Vega, directors, presented by Joseph Papp. At the Public Theater/Newman Hall, 425 Lafayette Street.

WITH: Andre Caldas, José Rubens Chachá, Paulo Contier, Edson Cordeiro, Loren Dae, Ary Franca, Tereza Freire, Marina Mesquita, Monica Monteiro, Marshall Netherland, Caça Rosset, Christiane Tricerri, Guto Vasconcelos and Maria Alice Vergueiro.

By STEPHEN HOLDEN

Deep into end of "O Doente Imaginario" ("The Imaginary Invalid"), the Teatro do Ornitorrinco's rollicking, irreverent version of the classic 17th-century farce, Molière's archetypal hypochondriac, Argan, has a dream about dying.

Onto the stage of the New York Shakespeare Festival's Newman Theater parade members of the Brazilian company dressed as skeletons with faces that glow green in ultraviolet light. From ropes strung to the rafters, more skeletons appear, acrobatically hanging by their heels and leering like happy zombies. One of the most spectacular scenes in the iconoclastic production by the experimental theater company from São Paulo, the dream sequence is true to the spirit of Molière, if not to the letter. For it suggests that not even nightmares will be allowed to dampen the ebullience of an evening that treats the farce as a Brazilian carnival circus.

The production, which continues through Sunday at the Public Theater's Festival Latino, is a madcap extravaganza that conveys the atmosphere of a sumptuous carnival revue even though it was obviously put together with modest resources. The closest American equivalent of the Brazilian company's approach to a classic is Robert Woodruff's vaudevillian version of Shakespeare's "Comedy of Errors" for the Lincoln Center Theater, which featured the Flying Karamazov Brothers.

•

For the two-hour production, which has no intermission, Molière's dialogue, translated into Portuguese by Marcia Abujamra, has been drastically cut, although the story of a hypochondriac who is tricked out of his obsession with doctors by his resourceful maid has been kept intact. That already funny story is regularly and amusingly interrupted by bawdy rough-and-tumble production numbers and circus stunts that are executed with exhilarating comic enthusiasm.

In the production, directed by Caça Rosset, who also plays Argan, Molière's characters are cartoonish hybrids of 17th-century aristocrats and circus clowns. All but 2 of the 14 actors play multiple roles, many of which are athletic, ranging from Egyptian dancers to apothecaries cavorting on stilts.

The notion of treating "The Imaginary Invalid" as a musical circus is not so far-fetched, for the play is one of two Molière farces that were con-

Ary Brandi/New York Shakespeare Festival

Caça Rosset playing the role of Argan in "O Doente Imaginario," at the Festival Latino.

ceived as "comedy ballets." The production uses the score composed for the play by Marc-Antoine Charpentier but augments it with zany interpolations of Duke Ellington's "Caravan" and Albert W. Ketelbey's "In a Persian Market," and even a fragment of "I Left My Heart in San Francisco," among other additions.

The show's antic mood extends to the lead performances by Mr. Rosset; Maria Alice Vergueiro as his servant, Toinette; Christiane Tricerri, who plays his wife, Berlinne; and especially Ary Franca as Tomas Diaforius, who may be the most ignorant and reckless physician in the history of drama. In Mr. Franca's portrayal, a primal instinct for mischief-making glints from eyes that at the same time express an impenetrable stupidity. Along with a dangerously fixed smile, the character wears a hideous brown hat that spirals to a point several feet over his head. Lurching idiotically around the stage, he is an irresistibly hilarious figure of comic menace.

1990 Ag 23, C20:1

Mondo Mambo

Conceived and directed by Adal Alberto Maldonado; written by Pedro Pietri; music arranged and composed by Tito Puente; choreogrpahy by Eddie Torres; set design by Marsha Ginsberg; lighting design by Peggy Eisenhauer; costumes supervised by Mr. Maldonado; costumes for the dancers designed by Mr. Torres and Maria Torres; hairstyles for Divino la Bangó by Riah; assistant director, Juan Fischer; mambo videos from the archives of Henry Medina. Associate producer, Jason Steven Cohen. Festival Latino in New York, Oscar Ciccone and Cecilia Vega, directors, presented by Joseph Papp. At the Public/Anspacher Theater, 425 Lafayette Street.

Divino la Bongó ..... Edwin de Asis
Tito Puente ..... Tito Puente

By STEPHEN HOLDEN

In a poem by Pedro Pietri that runs like a hallucinatory thread through the first half of the revue "Mondo Mambo," the Puerto Rican-born writer compiles a series of surreal images to evoke the transcendental mysteries of mambo music. The train of associations, recited by Edwin de Asis, begins with images of an "absent-minded alarm clock," rain that falls upward and "colors that no one can name." As the narration continues, the imagery turns religious. The mambo beat is praised as a "pure and supernatural rhythm that can keep you alive."

Mr. Pietri's poem, which forms the spine of "Mondo Mambo," the singing and dancing revue that plays through Sunday at the New York Shakespeare Festival's Anspacher Theater, is ambitious in an overheated, post-Beat sort of way. Unfortunately, it has to compete with the music it is praising. And the poetic hyperbole is simply no match for the power of the music itself, which as played by Tito Puente and his orchestra is really beyond words.

For "Mondo Mambo," which was conceived and directed by Adal Alberto Maldonado, the domed three-story Anspacher has been partly converted into a Latin American dance palace called the Mango Mambo, complete with a bandstand, cardboard palm trees and dance floor with cabaret seating. The Mango Mambo is supposed to be a fictional echo of the Palladium, a popular 1950's dance club at Broadway and 52d Street in Manhattan. And Mr. de Asis, who exudes a jivey, slippery charm, plays a mythical master of revels known as Divino la Bongó.

In the first half of the show, the narration and musical numbers accompany the Eddie Torres Dancers, a superb three-couple ensemble whose graceful glides and twirls convey a contagious physical exhilaration. Over the course of the evening, Mr. Puente and his band perform nine numbers, including famous songs like "Babarabatiri" and "Ove Como Va." The Anspacher Theater, with its roomy acoustics, proves an ideal setting for hearing the band's precisely punctuated Afro-Cuban swing, which is as classic a style of big band music as Count Basie's. At Thursday's opening night performance, Joseph Papp presented Mr. Puente with a proclamation from Gov. Mario M. Cuomo naming him "King of Mambo Day, Aug. 23, 1990."

For all its musical vigor, "Mondo Mambo" doesn't amount to much as a revue. It has no story, developed theme or characters except for the enigmatic Divino who simply disappears shortly after the intermission. That's when the show stops being a revue. The audience is invited to leave its seats and go down to the tiny stage for half an hour of dancing to Mr. Puente's music.

1990 Ag 25, 16:5

It's Still My Turn

By Terry Sweeney; directed by Bill Lovejoy; accompanist, Mark Hampton; lighting, Tracy Dedrickson. Presented by Bill Repicci and M. D. Minichiello, in association with the Performing Arts Preservation Association. At Actors' Playhouse, 100 Seventh Avenue South, at Bleecker Street.

Nancy Reagan........................Terry Sweeney

By STEPHEN HOLDEN

Nancy Reagan may be out of the public eye, but one person who hasn't forgotten her is Terry Sweeney.

The comic, whose amusing caricatures of the former First Lady on "Saturday Night Live" provided some of the show's brighter spots during its mid-1980's slump, recently published "It's Still My Turn," a slim volume of satirical "Nancy Reaganesque poetry." And in his one-person show, also called "It's Still My Turn," at the Actor's Playhouse, the comedian and actor intersperses readings from the collection with amusingly catty anecdotes.

Mr. Sweeney's stage caricature is considerably more biting than his television impression, although it essentially works off the same farcical notion of Mrs. Reagan as an unflappably demure monster. Early in the show, the character polls the audience to see how many have read her autobiography. When few hands show, she haughtily announces that she is going to have Senator Jesse Helms introduce legislation that would make "It's My Turn" mandatory reading for everyone over the age of 12. She also announces her new Revlon perfume, named Nancy, and its slogan: "Finally a fragrance that says I'm better than you!"

Among the longer anecdotes, the funniest describes a tryst with Mikhail S. Gorbachev during a state visit to the Soviet Union. "He looked at me like a starving peasant looks at a cold bowl of borscht," she exults before going on to take credit for bringing about the dissolution of the Communist system. While Mr. Gorbachev was sleeping, she explains, she whispered the words "multi-party system" over and over, and the next morning he woke up with the idea fixed in his head.

•

The character reserves special scorn for her White House successor, Barbara Bush, whose autobigraphy she dismisses as "the most powerful tranquilizer you can get without a prescription."

Terry Sweeney in his one-man show at the Actors' Playhouse.

If Mr. Sweeney, even wearing a red imitation-Adolfo suit, doesn't look much like Mrs. Reagan, he offers a creditable spoof of her physical man-

nerisms, from her eye-popping stare to her tight, arms-to-the-body way of slinking around. Since humor this mean can pall quickly, he keeps his performance short; the show lasts barely an hour.

Near the end, the character bursts into song with a musical setting of Mr. Sweeney's poem "If I Ruled the World," which sums up the comedian's unsparingly nasty Mrs. Reagan as a would-be empress: "If I ruled the world/Ronald Reagan would be President for life/Only one person could take his place: his wife!"

1990 Ag 26, 67:5

Indecent Materials

Two one-act plays, "Indecent Materials" and "Report From the Holocaust," adapted by Edward Hunt and Jeff Storer from text by Jesse Helms and from Larry Kramer's book "Reports From the Holocaust: The Making of an AIDS Activist." Directed by Mr. Storer; choreography by Barbara Dickinson; photographic design by Alan Dehmer; stage manager, Andrea Ball; associate producer, Jason Steven Cohen. Presented by Joseph Papp. At the Public/Shiva Theater, 425 Lafayette Street, at Astor Place.

WITH: Patricia Esperon, David Ring and Rebecca Hutchins.

By MEL GUSSOW

The borderline between politics and political theater is crossed with polemical results in "Indecent Materials," two one-act plays that opened last night at the Public Theater. The plays, one dealing with AIDS, the other with Senator Jesse Helms's attack on the National Endowment for the Arts, come to New York from the Manbites Dog Theater Company of Durham, N.C. Evidently there is a rumbling of protest in Senator Helms's home territory.

A definite distinction should be drawn between the two plays. The main piece, an adaptation of the title essay in Larry Kramer's collection "Reports From the Holocaust," speaks with anger and urgency about the AIDS epidemic. With equally worthy intentions, the curtain raiser — extracts from Senator Helms's Congressional speeches — vitiates its own purpose.

Mr. Kramer, the author of "The Normal Heart," is a fiercely committed AIDS activist. In his essay (as adapted for the stage by Edward Hunt and Jeff Storer and directed by Mr. Storer), he places his battle in a historical context while stressing the traumatic personal consequences, including the impact of his activism on his family.

•

Though "Report From the Holocaust" is a spoken version of a published text, it achieves a dramatic momentum as the author, with a sense of growing futility, tries to awaken others to his cause. On the personal side we hear two especially moving stories, the first about the funeral of one of Mr. Kramer's friends in which a minister labels the deceased a sinner — to the horror of his mourners — and the other about Mr. Kramer's brief estrangement from his brother. That estrangement ends with a dialogue between the playwright and his sister-in-law as they reach across a restaurant table — and a chasm of difference — to try to arrive at a community of feeling.

In his performance, David Ring makes no attempt to impersonate the author, playing him with a soft South-

ern accent. The "report" might have been more effectively delivered as a speech by the author himself, but there is something to be said for distancing the role from the real-life character. It is as if Mr. Ring were saying that he and others can be "a Larry Kramer."

The evening's other author is less well served. Senator Helms is listed in the program under "Who's Who in the Cast" as a onetime "broadcaster and editorialist from Raleigh" who "was first elected to the United States Senate in 1972." That listing is surely a first in the American theater, although it is doubtful that the Senator is receiving royalties for his dramatic contribution.

As adapters, Mr. Hunt and Mr. Storer have spliced together statements from the Senator in which he assails what he calls "esthetic art" — to distinguish it from the non-esthetic variety — and discovers obscenities wherever he turns. "Bosh and nausea" are favorite terms of opprobrium.

Instead of having Mr. Ring stand in for Senator Helms, the role is played

David Ring in "Indecent Materials," two one-act plays at the Public Theater.

by an actress, Patricia Esperon, who offers a shrill rendering of his lines. Watching this performance is a bit like being in the courtroom when a policeman delivered Lenny Bruce's comic monologue. The words begin to lose all meaning, which may of course be the point.

As symbolic counterpoint, photographs are projected on a screen, Robert Mapplethorpe images alternating with views of war and racism. The point is made with the heaviest of hands. Additionally diminishing the effectiveness, a dancer, Rebecca Hutchins, interrupts the monologue to strike severe choreographic poses, seeming like a gate-crasher who has forced her way into the senatorial chambers. It is an unnecessary intrusion of "esthetic art" into a didactic statement.

Together the two plays run barely one hour. They are followed by a curtain speech from Mr. Ring, in which he tells the audience, calmly but with conviction, that Senator Helms's political career will be terminated in the next election. Mr. Ring is even more persuasive in this "performance" than he is when portraying Mr. Kramer. Perhaps in the future other actors will portray "David Ring" in a re-creation of his hortatory act of theatrical politics.

1990 Ag 28, C14:3

Comedy, Heartbreak And Offbeat Casting On London Stages

By FRANK RICH

Special to The New York Times

LONDON — Two summers ago the Gate Theater, Dublin, jolted New York audiences with the festering, dark-brewed, tragic reality of its "Juno and the Paycock," a brief Broadway tenant courtesy of the New York International Festival of the Arts. Now the Gate is offering Londoners an equivalent thrill with its visiting production of "The Three Sisters": a stunning collaboration between Ireland's acting dynasty — Cyril Cusack and a trio of his daughters — and the English director Adrian Noble, the newly named artistic leader of the Royal Shakespeare Company. This is Chekhov in the true Russian manner — soulful, gloomy, neurotic, inward — as it could be performed only by a cast schooled in the poetic delicacy of the Irish.

Without question the sister act adds a whole field of depth to the play; the communality and prickliness of Chekhov's siblings could not be more transparently served. Even so, it's hard to take one's eyes off the family patriarch whenever he pads into view. Cyril Cusack has achieved an esthetic suppleness reminiscent of the latter-day Ralph Richardson; even his perfunctory cameo appearance at the end of "My Left Foot" has the twinkle of magic. As Chebutykin, the aging and alcoholic doctor who hangs about the Prozorov household, he gives a perfectly calculated minimalist performance that, besides being a thing of beauty in itself, dramatizes the cultural linkage between Chekhov and Ireland's pre-eminent modern playwright, Samuel Beckett.

When Chebutykin inadvertently smashes a clock, Mr. Cusack, adrift in a private haze, could be a Beckett tramp stuck in time and meaninglessness as he argues that he didn't really break the clock but created "just the illusion" of breaking it. In the final scene, which calls upon the doctor to deliver to Irina the tragic news of her fiancé's offstage death, he mutters "Your man's been killed" matter-of-factly from the rear of the bleak outdoor set, the words no louder than the rustle of his omnipresent newspaper or the dead autumn leaves smoldering beside him. Grizzled, soft-featured and slight of stature, Mr. Cusack looks almost like an intricate ink sketch of himself. In wry voice, pixieish gait and choked emotion he is the perfect inhabitant for those peripheries of life where the comedy and heartbreak of Chekhovian theater most often unfold.

•

Sinead Cusack, best remembered by Broadway audiences for her pairing with Derek Jacobi in the itinerant Royal Shakespeare repertory of "Much Ado About Nothing" and "Cyrano de Bergerac," is a wounding Masha, all black cynicism until she gives herself to Colonel Vershinin, whose dogged optimism about posterity is tempered by the ineffable sadness of the here and now in Nicky Henson's haunting portrayal. When the colonel must finally ship out of town, the previously taut Miss Cusack shatters like glass. As she collapses in a heap of grief, Mr. Henson backs offstage with the repetition of a simple word into which he packs all the feeling of the scene and perhaps the play: "late ... late."

The other Misses Cusack — Sorcha (as Olga) and Niamh (as Irina) — are also fine, as is Lesley Manville's icy, understated characterization of their predatory sister-in-law, Natasha, and most of a company in which even the aged servants have unforgettably weathered faces. Mr. Noble, whose skills as a director were seen by Manhattan Theater Club audiences last spring in "The Art of Success," seems to be sensitive to every last Chopin-like modulation of one of the most nuanced texts in theatrical literature, refusing either to rejigger Chekhov in the present-day fashion or to be a slave to Moscow Art Theater naturalism. The evening's tone is conversational throughout — which requires a house as intimate as the Royal Court, where the production plays through September — and yet every aspect of the staging is highly theatrical.

In this, Mr. Noble's key collaborator is the brilliant set designer Bob Crowley, who did "Les Liaisons Dangereuses" on Broadway and who is responsible for the elegant designs of both David Hare's "Racing Demon" and the Ian McKellen "Richard III" in London this season. Here he has designed four classic sets, three of which dramatize the increasing diminishment of the inexorably suffocating Prozorov household from within and the last of which, viewing the house from outside, crunches it to the dimensions of a doll's house. Mr. Crowley and Mr. Noble reach a creative peak perhaps in Act III, in which the offstage fire slowly bleeds into and contaminates the bright colors of Olga and Irina's room, heightening the nightmarishness implicit in the set's jarring forced perspectives. By the scene's end, the dispossessed sisters are visually consumed by their close and cluttered quarters, reduced to dreaming of Moscow from beds cramped behind folding screens, heard but no longer seen by the audience.

Modern classics are in perpetual revival in London: This fall there will be yet another familial "Three Sisters," starring the Redgrave sisters and Vanessa Redgrave's daughter Joely Richardson. Somewhat more popular than Chekhov, however, is Arthur Miller. Despite a seeming glut of revivals in recent years, including the landmark Alan Ayckbourn-directed "View From the Bridge" with Michael Gambon, the Miller appetite remains so large here that the Young Vic has even mounted "The Man Who Had All the Luck," the play whose four-performance run marked the writer's Broadway debut in 1944. (Mr. Miller himself labels the Young Vic production "joyous" in a quote on its posters.)

•

At the National Theater, Howard Davies's acclaimed staging of "The Crucible" has now been joined by the local debut of the 1964 "After the Fall," which has been received only slightly more warmly in London than it traditionally has been in New York. The director is the Australian-born Michael Blakemore, who was responsible for two classic American revivals at the National in the 1970's, "The Front Page" and the Laurence Olivier-Constance Cummings "Long Day's Journey Into Night," and who is currently represented on Broadway by both British and American hits, "Lettice and Lovage" and "City of Angels."

The big news about Mr. Blakemore's "After the Fall" is his casting

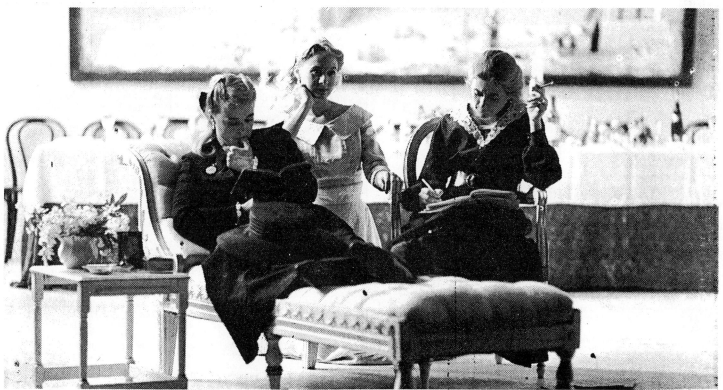

Sinead, Niamh and Sorcha Cusack, real-life sisters, from left, in a scene from the London production of "The Three Sisters."

Josette Simon as Maggie in "After the Fall" in London.

Alastair Muir

of a black actress, Josette Simon, in the role of Maggie, a self-destructive pop singer modeled after Mr. Miller's second wife, Marilyn Monroe. In interviews, Mr. Blakemore has said he hopes the unorthodox casting will help audiences forget about the play's notorious autobiographical connections and start focusing instead on its larger themes, which its author has described as "a world of political and ethical dilemmas," including the Great Depression, McCarthyism and the Holocaust.

Miss Simon's performance is so exciting that, if anything, her intended mission has boomeranged: one is more aware than ever of how hollow the play surrounding her is. When she is offstage, it is hard to take the self-importance and pretentions of the soliloquizing protagonist, Quentin (James Laurenson), a Jewish lawyer who wraps himself in a half-century's worth of guilt only to absolve himself of all blame by the final curtain. As a piece of writing, "After the Fall" seems alive only when it stoops from high-flown philosophizing to tabloid gossip, invoking not just Monroe but also Elia Kazan and Lee Strasberg. The play is at its most humane, as opposed to grandiloquently humanitarian, when Miss Simon has her circumscribed turns, first as the most defenseless (and erotic) of lost women and later as an insecure, battered show-biz monster indulging herself in booze-fueled temper tantrums.

Lithe, sharp-humored and in total command of a formidable vocal and physical range, Miss Simon is the first Maggie I've seen who is totally convincing as a pop superstar; not for a second does she relinquish her grip on the audience at the National's Cottesloe Theater. She is also one of the few members of Mr. Blakemore's cast who seem credibly American. (In fact — and amazingly, given her perfect mid-Atlantic pitch — she is of Caribbean descent and grew up in Leicester, England.) It's too bad "After the Fall" is so self-absorbed that Mr. Miller never honestly bothers to dramatize Maggie's fall or to see life from her point of view, but one imagines that another playwright or screenwriter will soon write a role of Monroe-like or larger dimensions for this extraordinary young actress.

Though Henrik Ibsen is the chief inspiration, and sometimes the author of the ur-text, of Mr. Miller's

plays, the Norwegian dramatist's complexity has been flattened in so many wooden productions that New York audiences tend to consign him to the theatrical dustheap. In this context — and, for that matter, in the context of the humorless moralizing of "After the Fall" — Peter Hall's West End revival of "The Wild Duck" was a revelation. The director's mission was to fulfill Shaw's famous description of watching the play in 1897: "to look in horror and pity at a profound tragedy, shaking with laughter all the time at an irresistible comedy." Mr. Hall got the laughs, horror and pity by seeing the fanatical truth-teller Gregers and the man his revelations destroy, the would-be inventor Hjalmar, in the round. He presented both men as ridiculously self-deluded and egotistically well meaning, as sympathetic victims of their fathers' harsh psychological legacies and callous victimizers of their own prey.

I saw "The Wild Duck" on the last

Chekhov, Ibsen and Arthur Miller are being treated with honor.

night of its three-month run at the Phoenix Theater, when the cast seemed ignited by Ibsen's fire. The two equally matched young leads — David Threlfall (the original Smike of "Nicholas Nickleby," here playing Gregers) and Alex Jennings (Hjalmar) — went after each other with maniacal conviction and were memorably supported by Nichola McAuliffe as Hjalmar's long-suffering wife, Maria Miles as his tragic young daughter and Terence Rigby as the misanthropic neighboring doctor who can diagnose all the symptoms of a fatally flawed human race. Unlike the previous two productions of the Peter Hall Company — the Vanessa Redgrave "Orpheus Descending" and the Dustin Hoffman "Merchant of Venice" — "The Wild Duck" lacks the marquee star required to float nearly any serious play on Broadway. Troubled as the London theater may be

economically right now, the West End can never be completely bankrupt as long as drama as uncompromising as this "Wild Duck" can fly.

1990 Ag 30, C15:1

Strides for Asian Actors

By MEL GUSSOW

The conflict over the casting of Jonathan Pryce as a Eurasian character in the musical "Miss Saigon" has focused rare attention on Asian-American actors and their presence in the theater, in movies and on television.

Listening to the arguments about casting the musical, one might conclude that the actor B. D. Wong and the playwright David Henry Hwang were the only ones of their ethnic background to have made an impact on the public consciousness. Together they shared a success on Broadway with "M. Butterfly," but they represent only one aspect of an expanding artistic movement.

Through the Pan Asian Repertory Theater in New York, the East West Players in Los Angeles, other ethnic troupes and the New York Shakespeare Festival's policy of cross-casting, Asian-American actors have made breakthroughs. They have played major roles Off Broadway, in television series and in feature movies running all the way from "The Karate Kid" to "The Last Emperor." A few, like Pat Morita, have become stars, and Wayne Wang has become an important director. Many Asian-American actors are less widely known than some of their colleagues because of their limited opportunities. But within those limits they have come a long way from Hollywood and Broadway stereotypes.

While black actors were playing servants in 1940's movies, Asians were typecast as dragon ladies, geisha girls, Zero pilots and prison camp commandants. Richard Loo became the quintessential Japanese-American actor in films during World War II, usually playing villains who relished bombing hospitals or orphanages. Principal Asian roles like Charlie Chan were reserved for white actors like Sidney Toler, although the subsidiary part of the detective's wimpish No. 1 son was given to Keye Luke.

On Broadway, for many years it was the practice for white actors to play Asians (as Yul Brynner in "The King and I" and David Wayne in "The Teahouse of the August Moon"), except in rare cases (Miyoshi Umeki and Pat Suzuki in "Flower Drum Song"). As recently as 1970, when the Repertory Theater of Lincoln Center was presenting Bertolt Brecht's "Good Woman of Szechwan," Asians were not cast in the Asian roles. (The title character was portrayed by Colleen Dewhurst.) In 1973, in response to a suit by a group of Asian-American actors, the New York State Human Rights Appeal Board ruled that the casting policy at the Lincoln Center theater was discriminatory.

•

Since then, there have been considerable career advances among

Asian-American performers, although success has not always been commensurate with individual artistry.

John Lone, an actor of balletic grace and riveting stage presence, first came to public prominence in two plays by Mr. Hwang, "F.O.B." and "The Dance and the Railroad." He has gone on to a rewarding movie career, playing the title role in both "Iceman" and "The Last Emperor," the Academy Award-winning Bernardo Bertolucci film.

For 25 years, Sab Shimono has been demonstrating his versatility on Broadway (as the original houseboy in "Mame"), Off Broadway and in films. Last year, in Philip Khan Gotanda's "Yankee Dawg You Die," he played a role that was almost too true to life — as a movie actor forced to play houseboys and evil Japanese officers. Currently he can be seen as the bumbling medical examiner in the film "Presumed Innocent."

Joan Chen, who was also in "The Last Emperor," has become well known through her appearances as the mysterious owner of the lumber mill in "Twin Peaks," and Lauren Tom, who was appearing in Off Broadway plays, is finding a growing celebrity through her roles on television.

During the 1970's, Randall Duk Kim played leading roles Off Broadway and for the New York Shakespeare Festival. His authoritative "Pericles" stands as a high point in that company's Shakespeare in the Park history. Finding his chances limited as a classical actor in New York — true for actors of any ethnic minority — he moved to Spring Green, Wis., where for some years he has been the artistic director and a principal actor at the American Players Theater. New York has missed Mr. Kim, but clearly he found a home in which to nurture his talent.

•

A number of years ago, Alvin Lum had a showstopping song in the New York Shakespeare Festival's musical version of "Two Gentlemen of Verona" and has gone on to a career as a character actor. Jodi Long was a regal Hippolyta and Titania in the Pan Asian Mandarin Chinese production of "A Midsummer Night's Dream." Ernest Abuba, who is also a playwright, was fearsome in the title role of the Pan Asian's "Shogun Macbeth" and demonstrated his musical versatility as the narrator in the York Theater Company's revival of "Pacific Overtures." (His part was played by Mako in the original Broadway production.)

In pursuit of roles, actors have certainly been helped by the proliferation of Asian-American playwrights, dozens of whom have had their works produced by the Pan Asian Rep and other companies, including Mr. Hwang, Mr. Gotanda, R. A. Shiomi, Ping Chong, Momoko Iko, Wakako Yamauchi, Frank Chin and Genny Lim.

Many are second- and third-generation Asian-Americans who look at the United States and their place in its culture from a special vantage. Their heritage is Asian, their sensibility American, and the combination leads to contradictions. For Japanese-American writers, there are frequent attempts to come to terms with the internment of Americans of Japanese descent during World War II — and with its traumatic effects on succeeding generations.

Others have dealt with warring currents within families, assimilation within communities and the trans-

THEATER REVIEWS

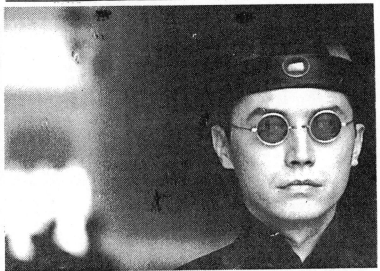

Angelo Novi

John Lone as Emperor Pu Yi in Bernardo Bertolucci's "Last Emperor."

Gerry Goodstein/Playwrights Horizons

Sab Shimono in "Yankee Dawg You Die."

ABC

Joan Chen as Josie Packard in the ABC series "Twin Peaks."

Columbia Pictures

Pat Morita has found stardom in the United States.

plantation of Japanese industry to the United States. Many of these plays, like Mr. Hwang's "Sound and Beauty" and Mr. Chong's performance pieces, have operated on a mythic plane; others are satirical or farcical.

•

Plays are inspired by a search for a national identity, as if to be Asian in America is to be homeless. The proliferation of these plays is not an isolated event. In fiction as well, people with an Asian family background,

like Maxine Hong Kingston and Amy Tan in the United States and Timothy Mo and Kazuo Ishiguro in England, have looked to history (as well as to their own lives) for enlightenment.

The Pan Asian Rep will start its 14th year in October. With characteristic eclecticism, it will begin with two very different plays, Jon Shirota's "Lucky Come Hawaii," a comedy that takes place on the eve of Pearl Harbor, and Elizabeth Wong's "Letters to a Student Revolutionary," dealing with the killing of students in Tiananmen Square.

Every year, actors meet the challenge of Asian-American plays — Donald Li as Sam Shikaze, the dashing private eye in Mr. Shiomi's caper comedy, "Yellow Fever," and Henry Yuk as his amiable sidekick; Ron Nakahara in a variety of character roles, including the White Rabbit in Mr. Chong's "Noiresque: The Fallen Angel," a variation on "Alice in Wonderland"; Raul Aranas, Ching Valdes, Keenan Shimizu and Freda Foh Shen.

In the introduction to "Between Worlds," a recent anthology of Asian-American plays, Misha Berson explains her title by saying that the characters in the plays are "suspended between countries of origin and adopted homelands." Even as the characters are suspended, they are serving as a bridge between cultures.

The diverse ethnicity of Asian-American theater — of the actors and the playwrights — is one of its greatest strengths.

1990 S 3, 11:1

Camille

By Charles Ludlam; directed by Everett Quinton; costumes by Elizabeth Michal Fried; scenery by Mark Beard; lighting by Terry Alan Smith; hair by Joseph Boggess; jewelry by Larry Vrba; sound by Mark Bennett; props coordinators, Daphne Groos and Sophie Maletsky; production stage manager, James Eckerle. Presented by the Ridiculous Theatrical Company, Mr. Quinton, artistic director; Steve Asher, managing director. At the Charles Ludlam Theater, 1 Sheridan Square.

Baron de Varville	H. M. Koutoukas
Nanine	Stephen Pell
Marguerite Gautier	Everett Quinton
Joseph	Kevin Scullin
Nichette Fondue	Carl Clayborn
Olympe de Taverné	Cheryl Reeves
Saint Gaudens	Bobby Reed
Prudence Duvernoy	Eureka
Gaston Roué	Jim Lamb
Armand Duval	Georg Osterman
Duval Sr.	Jean-Claude Vasseux
Molnik	James Eckerle

By STEPHEN HOLDEN

The biggest artistic challenge that the Ridiculous Theatrical Company has had to face since the death of its founding father, Charles Ludlam, may be its revival of "Camille," the playwright, director and actor's drag travesty of Dumas fils's theatrical warhorse.

Probably no role is more closely identified with Ludlam, who died three years ago, than his famous caricature of the tubercular courtesan Marguerite Gautier. Hairy-chested, his head dripping with Garboesque ringlets, his eyes ablaze, he was simultaneously hilarious and heartbreaking and left many in the audience in tears.

If "Camille," which was first seen in 1973, is not the wittiest Ridiculous Theatrical creation ("The Mystery of Irma Vep" and "Bluebeard" are more amusing as literature), it became one of the company's biggest hits, playing more than 500 performances in seven years. After "Camille" opened, it was a full decade before Ludlam played another female character, the Maria Callas-like diva in "Galas," in which he again found a complicated, compelling balance between comedy and pathos.

In the revived "Camille," now at the Charles Ludlam Theater, Everett Quinton, Ludlam's partner and successor, has dared to step into a role that it has been difficult to imagine anybody else carrying off with the same bravura grandeur. That Mr. Quinton, in his own way, creates a memorable Marguerite is good news, not only for the revival, but for the Ridiculous Theatrical Company's future. Though not perfect, the production proves once and for all that Ludlam created a style that was not ultimately dependent on his flamboyant, brilliant presence both on the stage and behind the scenes — a style that, for all its extravagance, seems both enduring and surprisingly malleable.

•

As much as Mr. Quinton has learned from Ludlam, the kind of energy he gives off when performing is quite different. Where Ludlam invented an insouciant camp style of

Anita and Steve Shevett/"Camille"

Everett Quinton in "Camille" at the Charles Ludlam Theater.

physical caricature that crackled with a maniacal spontaneity, Mr. Quinton, using the same vocabulary, imparts an air of considered, classical precision. Mr. Quinton's air of underlying austerity — the sense that his every gesture, right down to the twitch of an eyebrow and the curl of a cherry-red lip, is not wasted — lends a very different tone to this production.

In this revival, the cross-dressing, along with the script's occasional ribaldry and pointed gay references, has the feel of familiar and cherished conventions rather than being the expressions of an antic sexual and theatrical defiance. But what is lost in pure merriment is gained in a sense of the play as a classic comic ritual whose rhythms have been minutely calibrated by a theater artist with a clear and careful mastery of design.

Mr. Quinton, with his distinctively harsh voice and pronounced New York accent, makes a severe Marguerite, one who at moments suggests Leona Helmsley in a tragic mode. If not quite operatic in scale, his performance is consistently commanding. He brings a special poignancy to a ballroom dancing scene in the first act when the ailing Marguerite defies good sense and cavorts about the stage with a mad desperation. Over the following two acts, the performance builds in size to a death scene that echoes with a touching nobility.

•

The surrounding performances run a wide gamut of styles that mesh fairly well, though not all are as finely tuned as they might be. Georg Osterman's Armand Duval is an ingenuous, apple-cheeked schoolboy who stumbles and blushes before the great courtesan. In the role of the Baron de Varville, H. M. Koutoukas resembles an exotic purple-lipped gorgon with red hair that stands straight out from his head in three grotesque clumps. When he kisses Marguerite's arm, he leaves an ominous Draculan imprint.

The actress Eureka, who plays Marguerite's bubbly milliner, Prudence Duvernoy, delivers an especially rich caricature, as does Stephen Pell in his robust portrayal of Marguerite's faithful servant, Nanine. It is Nanine who has the play's last comic words once the histrionics have subsided. On her knees beside her dead mistress, she bids her an almost cheery farewell: "Toodle-oo, Marguerite." There, in a nutshell, is the essence of the Ridiculous Theatrical Company's zany slant on love, death, art and all things serious.

1990 S 7, C3:1

Money Talks

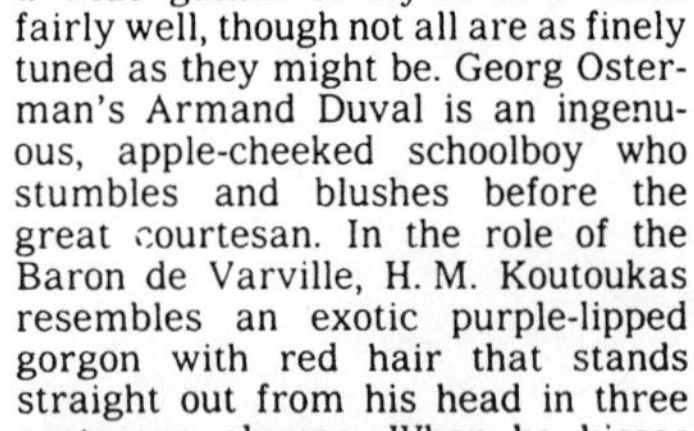

Promenade Theater/"Money Talks"

Helen Gallagher

By Edwin Schloss; directed by David Kaplan; continuity by Cindy Adams; set design by James Noone; costume design by David Woolard; lighting design by Dan Kotlowitz; sound design by Aural Fixation; company manager, Laura Heller; production stage manager, J. P. Elins. Presented by Arthur Cantor. At the Promenade Theater, Broadway and 76th Street.

Phyllis Stein	Dolores Gray
Vivian Newhouse	Helen Hanft
Adrienne	Judith Cohen
Irma Katzenbach	Janet Sarno
Lucille Blumenthal	Lucille Patton
Natalie Kilroy Axelrod	Helen Gallagher
Morty Drexler	Arnie Kolodner
Allan Rothenberg	Ted Neustadt
Claudia Stein	Julie Halston
Carla Axelrod	Jill Wisoff
Cesare Rotini	John Braden

By WILBORN HAMPTON

Some years ago on "Saturday Night Live," a regular skit featured Dan Aykroyd playing a television host whose weekly program "Bad Theater" celebrated some of the worst plays ever written. "Money Talks," a comedy by Edwin Schloss at the Promenade Theater, would have been a prime candidate for Mr. Aykroyd's scrutiny.

As the lights come up on a posh Upper East Side apartment, a voice-over of a radio gossip show being broadcast from atop the Plaza Mitsubishi Hotel tells listeners they are about to be given a tour of the home of the socialite Phyllis Steen. At that point, the character herself enters and corrects the pronunciation. "That's Phyllis *STEIN!*" The play goes downhill from there.

What passes for a plot in this homage to Philistinism revolves around five members of the Wealthy Widows Investment Club, whose only concern, between rubbers of bridge and canasta tournaments, is their stock portfolios. These women go through brokers the way more adventuresome rich widows might go through gigolos. As a subplot, two of the cattiest members of the club try to palm off their daughters on a couple of Wall Street dealers. Widows, wealthy or poor, deserve better than this.

•

The level of humor ranges from the insults these vain women toss at one another to their disparagement of domestics. The director's idea of hilarity seems to be having a stageful of fatuous females, panicked when a burglar alarm trips and the lights go out, waving their arms and shouting "Is everything all right?" In fact, the shrill tone that permeates the whole exercise tempts one to rename the play "Money Shrieks."

Even if one overlooks the dropped lines (after all, who would want to memorize this play) and the exaggerated delivery, most of the performances are an embarrassment, and the best ones are little more than caricature. Dolores Gray's Phyllis Stein is perpetually on the verge of hysteria. Helen Gallagher is almost believable as Natalie, Phyllis's old friend and adversary, and gets a laugh from the old line: "You're looking very well. I almost didn't recognize you." But it's doubtful anyone on or off stage will want this effort on their résumés.

The antics of these vacuous, wealthy widows, their daughters, maids and stockbrokers did elicit some scattered titters at a recent preview and more than half the audience even returned for the second act. One surmises they were friends of the cast, offering support. Or possibly enemies, gloating. "Money Talks," as Mr. Aykroyd might say, gleefully rubbing his hands together and beaming his most winning smile, is "exquisitely bad theater."

1990 S 7, C3:5

Romeo and Juliet

By William Shakespeare; indigenous version adapted, designed and directed by María Alicia Martínez Medrano; translated by Martín Pérez Dzul and Carlos Yocupicio; music by Guillermo Briseno; associate producer, Jason Steven Cohen. Festival Latino directors, Oscar Ciccone and Cecilia Vega. Laboratorio de Teatro Campesino y Indígena, presented by Joseph Papp. Delacorte Theater, Central Park West, enter at 81st Street.

Romeo	Octavio Cervantes
Juliet	Lesvi Vázquez
Montague	Gavino Campos
Capulet	Juan Francisco Tun
Mercutio	Víctor Bacasehua
Paris	Eusebio Peñuelas
Juliet's nurse	Luz Emilia Vázquez

By WILBORN HAMPTON

Shakespeare might not immediately recognize it. But for sheer theatricality, he would probably have enjoyed the "Romeo and Juliet" that Joseph Papp has imported from Mexico for his Festival Latino.

The production, which is being performed free at the Delacorte Theater in Central Park through this weekend, is the creation of María Alicia Martínez Medrano and her Laboratorio de Teatro Campesino y Indígena.

Miss Martínez Medrano has taken Shakespeare's tragedy, borrowed a bit from "West Side Story," inserted some Greek-style choruses and turned it all into a production that is more a pageant than a play, but that offers such a visual spectacle that only those with a serious attention-span deficiency can fail to be fascinated. The basic plot is still Shakespeare's tale of star-crossed lovers, but it has been so elaborately embroidered with dance, mime, movement and music that it takes on the appearance of a sort of Mayan fable rather than an Elizabethan drama.

•

The director has transported the tale of feuding Veronese nobles to 1908 Yucatan and transformed the Capulet and Montague families into Mayan and Mayon clans. Although the program says the play is performed in those American Indian languages, only some of the characters, like old Capulet and the priest, speak in those ancient tongues. Most of the scenes are played in Spanish, and anyone with high-school fluency in the language should be able to understand a good deal of what is said.

But the poetry of Miss Martínez Medrano's "Romeo and Juliet" comes more from the visual imagery she parades nonstop across the stage than from the verbal imagery of the text. Throughout the three hours of the performance there is almost perpetual movement — whether it is a chorus of candle-bearing maidens, a torchlight procession of funeral biers or a Mayan wedding dance. It is all expertly choreographed, giving audience members something to watch even if they don't understand the words.

The dancing is exhilarating. In the great fight scene, which Jerome Robbins turned into a gang rumble in "West Side Story," Miss Martínez Medrano stages a dancing duel between the fractious families. After a brief clash of machetes, the men, in boots with jangling spurs, are joined by women in sandals. Two score men and women on each side face off across the stage, battling one another with ever more elaborate steps, their pounding feet raising billows of dust above the theater and quickening the tempo of the dance to create a tension as taut as any swordfight. Later, in the wedding scene, the company joins in an exotic Mayan dance that slowly becomes more sensual than any norteamericano's dirty dancing.

Miss Martínez Medrano's adaptation consistently emphasizes sensory impressions over words. At the outset, a character dressed as Death, with stone-gray hair, black-rimmed eyes and trailing a 30-foot black train, slowly enters, circles the stage and climbs to the top of a giant tower. At the same time, a dozen or so men and women march from the back of the theater carrying large candles, which they place on the apron of the stage. All this happens before a line is spoken and effectively sets the tone for all that follows. In various scenes, candles and torches are carried on and off while clouds of incense rise into the night sky from small braziers. In other scenes, choruses appear in colorful masks and costumes for both revels and mourning.

A variety of sounds infiltrate each scene — from male dancers with spurs, seashell leggings, gourds, clashing machetes that literally make sparks fly — and Guillermo Briseno has spliced together occasional music that ranges from orchestrations that could go on a movie soundtrack to native drums, flutes and whistles. The whole production is dressed by Miss Martínez Medrano in a wardrobe of simple yet colorful Mayan dresses, bandanas and yards and yards of cloth. Bolts of material are swirled about the stage and unfurled for trains, shrouds, drapes and bunting.

•

Parts of the Mexican company's "Romeo" move slowly, and it would be easy for the impatient to suggest some trims, especially in the second act. Much of the drama is narrated by the choruses, and some of the performances in the straight scenes tend toward the declamatory. None of this, however, is a major detraction from the effect Miss Martínez Medrano is trying to achieve. Lesvi Vásquez is a most winning Juliet. With her waist-length raven hair and disarming smile, Miss Vásquez is a joy to watch, and the way she tilts her head to cast a fond look at Romeo speaks more of Juliet's love than any verse. Her Romeo (and real-life husband), Octavio Cervantes, makes a dashing hero. Víctor Bacasehua's Mercutio and Luz Emilia Vásquez's Nurse also stand out, and their second-act confrontation would be funny in any language.

1990 S 15, 15:1

Skelton's 1-Man Band Of Comical Characters

By LAWRENCE VAN GELDER

A fellow named Lou went into a synagogue one day and asked the Lord to make him a lottery winner.

The next week, having failed to win, he was back — again beseeching the Lord to make him a lottery winner.

The third week, he asked once more.

And finally he heard a voice. "Lou," it said, "Meet me halfway. Buy a ticket."

Lou was onstage at Carnegie Hall on Wednesday night. So were assorted drunks, an American Indian, an old woman, several old men, a salad maker in a Greek restaurant, a little boy, a new father and a rustic named Clem Kadiddlehopper. The occasion, naturally, was a one-man show — starring Red Skelton.

•

In 2 hours 15 minutes, Mr. Skelton, who is 77 years old, kept a near-capacity audience in near-constant laughter with jokes, anecdotes and character sketches on subjects that ranged from New York City and crime to Donald Trump, television evangelists, wives, old age and musings about the afterlife.

"People in hell," Mr. Skelton wondered. "Where do they tell people to go?"

On New York City: "I never saw so much construction in my life. The state bird must be the crane. There's one in every vacant lot."

Lawlessness: "You think New York is bad? You ought to go to Detroit. You can go 10 blocks and never leave the scene of the crime."

Drugs: "How can a kid 10 years old find a dope pusher and the F.B.I. can't?"

Donald Trump and the beautiful view from his penthouse: "On a clear day, he can see the poorhouse."

Television evangelists: "I bought Oral Roberts's Christmas album, but I couldn't play it. The hole healed up."

Wives: "Webster wouldn't have written his dictionary if it wasn't for his wife. She was always saying, 'What's that supposed to mean?'"

Old age: "'For a guy your age,'" Mr. Skelton said his doctor told him, "'you're sound as a dollar.' That scared the devil out of me."

•

If there was a jarring note in the almost ceaseless merriment, it came almost at the end, when Mr. Skelton, turning serious, injected his own political opinion by terming "idiots" the Supreme Court justices who upheld the constitutional right to burn the flag and calling for members of the High Court to be elected rather than appointed. The suggestion was met by cheers and a couple of boos, but it was a moment that clashed with the mood of evening.

Mr. Skelton might have taken his cue from Clem Kadiddlehopper. "I don't pick on politicians," Clem told the audience. "They ain't done nothin'."

Still, "An Evening With Red Skelton," as the show was titled, was great good, clean fun. Mr. Skelton's performance — which was signed for the hearing-impaired — was backed by an orchestra conducted by Frank Leone.

Mr. Skelton began his career in 1923 and has worked in everything from tent shows and circuses to films, radio and television. The combination of talent and experience makes him a formidable comedian. Audiences like the one at Carnegie Hall, which gave him standing ovations at his entrance, during the show and at the finish, surely hope that Mr. Skelton will grow older. But they can scarcely hope that he can grow much better.

1990 S 16, 66:3

STAGE VIEW/David Richards

When Going Too Far Is Not Far Enough

IN THESE DAYS WHEN DEMOLITION is usually a matter of cold-blooded expediency or worse, Charles Ludlam's "Camille" qualifies as an act of loving sabotage.

There's no question that it wants to bring down that old war horse of French romanticism, "La Dame aux Camélias," from which it is freely and raucously adapted. Inflating already dangerously inflated sentiments to the bursting point, exaggerating the sort of noble stances that once made tender sensibilities weep, it could easily pass for a work of bald — and ribald — cynicism.

The notion of the consumptive demimondaine, gallantly renouncing her lover so that he can enjoy a happier, more respectable life in someone else's arms, was eminently mockable in 1973, when "Camille" was first produced with Ludlam himself careering about the stage — heart all a-pitter pat, eyelashes all a-flutter — as the emotion-wracked Marguerite Gautier. Supposedly, we've since weathered the Me Decade and come out more or less safely on the other side, but I can't say self-sacrifice has made a significant comeback. "La Dame aux Camélias" still seems to be asking for it, and in the revival at the Charles Ludlam Theater, "Camille" continues to dish it out.

And yet, funny as I recall "Camille" being the first time around, what elevated it above

the level of an extended put-on, was that by the end you actually believed in this outrageous creature, whose thirst for life was not unlike that of the bum for his jug wine and who was exulting drunkenly, "I'm not suffer-

The revival of Charles Ludlam's 'Camille' is all joke. 'Money Talks' was no joke at all.

ing any more... I am going to live," only seconds before she coughed a final cough and croaked. Believed in her even though the generous décolletage of Camille's gowns exposed a fair expanse of Ludlam's hairy chest. Believed even though Ludlam's size, his voice and his great glowering eyebrows argued that you really shouldn't.

I suspect that's because Ludlam himself believed, however crude or cartoonish matters got on stage. Taste was purposefully being violated, perhaps, but a reckless theatricality — not only unashamed, but eager to speak its name — was also being gleefully pursued. This Marguerite Gautier was part monstre sacrée, part Hollywood goddess and part incorrigible showoff, and Ludlam's delight in taking her to the edge of her tremulous destiny was apparent. But he never pushed her over the brink. The actor in him wanted it both ways. Inviting our laughter with a lurch, a fierce moue, a growled rejoinder, he then proceeded to overturn all rational expectations by provoking a genuine sadness for a wasted woman with too much rouge on her cheeks.

The odd sense of disorientation that resulted is, unfortunately, not imparted by the Ridiculous Theatrical Company's current production. The actors certainly chase after laughs with Punch and Judy vigor. Several of them could even be mistaken for puppets — and none more so than H. M. Koutoukas, who plays the disreputable Baron de Varville. In guise of hair, waves of flame-red surf appear to be breaking over his head. His eyebrows are green and his teeth give every indication of having been polished with an emery board. Mr. Koutoukas doesn't deliver lines, he issues them rather like marching orders.

■

Fetes at Marguerite's are gross-outs, after which her retinue of garish opportunists hoist their hoop skirts and hitch up their trousers and dance the "Beer-Barrel Polka." Pies get flung; champagne gets gargled. The revelry is broad and boisterous. And when true love finally strikes the heroine, it is with the force of acute indigestion and many of the same outward manifestations. The characterizations are unapologetically two-dimensional, in keeping with the cardboard scenery and the cutout cow that is trotted across the stage at one point to establish the properly bucolic mood. Belief is not being courted; it is being intentionally flouted.

The role of Marguerite has been inherited by the Ridiculous Theatrical Company's artistic director, Everett Quinton, who endows her with a feverish giddiness and ripples of petulant laughter that invariably degenerate into foul hacking. The abundant sausage curls that dangle about his long, horsy face suggest so many sprung bedsprings. But quite the most distinctive aspect of Mr. Quinton's performance is a formidable sneer, made even more imposing by thick coats of lipstick, unless it is fire-engine paint.

"Have you no heart?" asks the smitten Armand Duval, to whom Marguerite has been

Anita and Steve Shevett/The Ridiculous Theatrical Company

Everett Quinton, Eureka, and Cheryl Reeves in "Camille"—True love strikes with the force of acute indigestion and many of the same outward manifestations.

showing a distinctly cold shoulder. Appropriating the sassy attitude from Mae West and the clipped tone from Bette Davis, Mr. Quinton retorts crisply, "I'm traveling light." This wilting flower is also one tough cookie and the actor plays the two halves off each other — bounces them off each other, actually — with some entertaining results. But that's as far as it goes, which is not quite far enough.

If the production, which Mr. Quinton also directed, grows wearisome in the long run, it's because the sabotage is straightforward, unrelenting, unambiguous. No sudden, surprising fissures open up in this comic landscape. Buffoonery dogs the heroine to her deathbed and her final dramatic shudder. "Toodle-loo, Marguerite," sobs a girlfriend over the warm corpse. The transparent blitheness of the adieu underscores the evening's comic tactics. No emotion is so holy that it can't be soundly tweaked.

Ludlam, however, could catch you up short with his zigzagging artistry and, every so often, the joke didn't seem like a joke. (Little wonder Marguerite remained one of his most popular creations right up to his death.) Now that Mr. Quinton has slipped into the poor lady's fancy wardrobe, the joke is a joke to the end.

As for "Money Talks," the comedy which gave quickly up the ghost at the Promenade Theater, it was no joke at all, but one of those calamities that leave a flummoxed audience wondering how it could have come about. Was there no one to blow the whistle, run up a red flag, counsel the performers to make tracks for the border? The script was by one Edwin Schloss, whose professional life up to now has had to do, according to the program, with investments "focusing on undervalued securities." The best of his quips — "Nature abhors a vacuum." "So does my cleaning lady." — did not suggest a change of career was advisable.

Making out Mr. Schloss's plot was akin to reading tea leaves, but it seemed to revolve about two feuding Upper East Side widows (Dolores Gray and Helen Gallagher) who were determined to outmaneuver each other

on the stock market and match their daughters up with the same oily investment counselor. Ms. Gray, seemingly outfoxed, declared bankrupty in Act I and then, although she had acquired no new assets in the interim, declared it again in Act II.

A scornful Italian art dealer, called in to liquidate her extensive modern-art collection, proclaimed it worthless, but in one of those stunning reversals that make the theater the wonder it is, wound up asking for her hand. Somehow, this gave way to a last scene, in which Ms. Gray and her wealthy friends, not long back from a funeral and still draped in black, donned festive chapeaux and sang Irving Berlin's "Marrying for Love."

It was the sort of deliriously surrealistic ending that Ludlam might well have concocted for "Camille." But it seems to have been appended to "Money Talks" only because Mr. Schloss didn't have a curtain line handy and things had dragged on quite long enough as it was.

Sabotage never entered into this one. What you had, I fear, was a clear-cut case of self-destruction. ☐

1990 S 16, II:7:1

Gypsy

Book by Arthur Laurents; suggested by the memoirs of Gypsy Rose Lee; music by Jule Styne; lyrics by Stephen Sondheim; directed by Mr. Laurents; original production directed and choreogrpahed by Jerome Robbins; scenery, Keneth Foy; costumes, Theoni V. Aldredge; lighting, Natasha Katz; sound, Peter Fitzgerald. Produced in association with Tokyo Broadcasting System International Inc. and Pace Theatrical Group. Presented by Barry and Fran Weissler, Kathy Levin and Barry Brown. At the St. James Theater, 246 West 44th Street.

Uncle Jocko	Stan Rubin
Baby Louise	Kristen Mahon
Baby June	Christen Tassin
Rose	Linda Lavin
Herbie	Jonathan Hadary
Louise	Crista Moore
June	Tracy Venner
Tulsa	Robert Lambert
Miss Cratchitt and Tessie Tura	
	Barbara Erwin
Mazeppa	Jana Robbins
Electra	Anna McNeely

By FRANK RICH

Tyne Daly, a television cop with scant musical-theater experience, sounded like a terrible idea for the role of Rose in "Gypsy." Linda Lavin, who has succeeded Ms. Daly in the revival of the landmark 1959 musical at the St. James, sounds like a natural. Early in her career, Ms. Lavin belted out sprightly numbers in brash New York musicals — "The Mad Show," the Harold Prince "Superman" — and only a few seasons ago she gave a memorable serious performance as another resolute, Depression-forged mama of starry-eyed children in Neil Simon's "Broadway Bound."

So why is it that Ms. Daly's Rose was a triumph and Ms. Lavin's Rose, which was officially presented to the press over the weekend, proves a washout? As Rose herself says in "Gypsy," "That's show business." If the theater were an exact science, it would be dead. One of the many moving stories told in Arthur Laurents's book for "Gypsy" is that a gawky, no-talent child performer in a bankrupt vaudeville act would grow up against all odds to be Gypsy Rose Lee, Minsky's Queen of Burlesque. Anything can happen on a stage, and that includes Ms. Lavin's odd predicament at the St. James. This actress works hard, with ample resources of concentration and energy, yet she rarely seems a participant in the pulsating production (still in pristine shape, by the way) spinning around her.

•

Ms. Lavin — presumably in league with Mr. Laurents, who serves as director — has a method of sorts for attacking her assignment. The actress comes on talking very fast as she connives to get her daughters out of Seattle and onto the Orpheum circuit. Whenever she hatches a new scheme, she abruptly slows down, her button eyes flickering out of focus, to give the audience an intimate glimpse of her mind's shifting gears. But if such painstaking kitchen-sink realism can pay off in a musical like "Gypsy" — in which the emotions are uncommonly real and primal, to be sure, but the characters are extravagantly theatrical — Ms. Lavin never makes the case. By trying to create a lifelike Rose, she ends up, in the work's epic context, looking smaller than life.

Though part of this stage mother's tragedy is that she could never be a star, and so tries to realize her dreams through her children, the role has nonetheless required star presence since Ethel Merman created it. That aura is entirely missing here. Ms. Lavin's acting is of a piece with her slight, taut physical appearance: thin, tight-jawed, pinched. While Rose is a steamroller — "a pioneer woman without a frontier" — who would knock down anyone to get her way, Ms. Lavin seems more like a scrappy, pugnacious terrier snapping at everyone's heels; she's pushy rather than driven, a nag instead of a power-house. Given her similarly clenched vocalism — a screechy singing voice and a wavering, nasal Brooklyn ac-

Anything can happen on a stage, as 'Gypsy' proves.

cent reprised from the Simon play — Ms. Lavin often leaves the impression that one's Aunt Ceil is performing Rose, or might as well be.

A theatergoer who loves "Gypsy" is let down with Ms. Lavin's first song, that masterly Jule Styne-Stephen Sondheim firecracker "Some People." In this version, Rose's unyielding battle plan for success comes out not as the scorched-earth policy it must be, but merely as perky determination. Under these circumstances, there is little hope for the "King Lear"-like cataclysms that close each act, "Everything's Coming Up Roses" and "Rose's Turn," both of which eventually receive shrill renditions in which Ms. Lavin parrots some of Ms. Daly's gestures but little of the volcanic feeling that accompanied them. Above all else, "Gypsy" is a musical about a parent and her children, and, even as she alternately coddles, terrorizes and reviles her daughters in these two soliloquies, Ms. Lavin never truly seems the mother, however monstrous, of the girls she relentlessly shoves into the spotlight.

•

No wonder one spends much of the evening focused on the periphery of "Gypsy," and with far happier results. Jonathan Hadary, as the weak but gentle agent who might become

Rose's fourth husband, remains a fount of generosity, deferentially giving all he can to Ms. Lavin even as his deeper passion salvages both of their duets ("Small World" and "You'll Never Get Away From Me"). Crista Moore, as Gypsy, and Robert Lambert, as a hoofer she loves unrequitedly, are as touching as ever in "All I Need Is the Girl," a Jerome Robbins stage-door-alley dance that both dramatizes their mutual isolation and deconstructs a Fred Astaire routine in a manner anticipating the choreographer's New York City Ballet gem, "I'm Old-Fashioned." The three fad-ed strippers who instruct Gypsy in their art — Barbara Erwin, Jana Robbins and Anna McNeely — outshine those who performed the same show-stopper, "You Gotta Have a Gimmick," in the now-departed "Jerome Robbins's Broadway."

It says much about "Gypsy" that no matter how many times one sees it, there is always something new to discover and admire in its interwoven saga of a family's dead end and an innocent American era's demise. With the possible exception of "Guys and Dolls," it may be the only vintage Broadway musical that never for a moment seems dated in form or content. The transitions between song and script are seamless; the emotional terrain is always adult. That's why "Gypsy" is indestructible, even when there's a void where its red-hot center should be. First-time visitors seeing this production will still marvel at the classical architecture even as they can only guess at the heartbreaking passions locked away inside.

1990 S 18, C11:1

Through the Leaves

By Franz Xaver Kroetz; translated by Roger Downey; directed by JoAnne Akalaitis; scenery by Douglas Stein; lighting by Frances Aronson; costumes by Teresa Snider-Stein; sound by L. B. Dallas; stage manager, Jack Doulin; production management, Bella Via Productions; technical adviser, Richard Meyer; artistic

director Interart Theater, Margot Lewitin. Interart Theater and Mabou Mines production presented by Joseph Papp. At the Public/Newman Theater, 425 Lafayette Street.

Annette	Ruth Maleczech
Victor	Frederick Neumann

By D. J. R. BRUCKNER

Annette and Victor have returned to Queens and, if anything, they are even more lonely and isolated, and more disturbing, than they were six years ago.

The female butcher and her abusive companion are the whole cast of Franz Xaver Kroetz's play "Through the Leaves," first presented here in 1984 by Mabou Mines at the Interart Theater and now having a revival at the Public Theater through Oct. 14.

All the people involved in the production are the same as in 1984. But the actors have changed enough to make the play more poignant than before. Ruth Maleczech and Frederick Neumann have aged into a more convincing Annette and Victor. Miss Maleczech is less brassy, but tougher. And Mr. Neumann has perfected Victor's crude wrestlings with Annette into movements so precise they have the character of a repulsive ballet.

If only Annette's loneliness would turn to hopelessness, there might be some relief from the intensity of Mr. Kroetz's exploration of isolation. But from the first scene she makes it clear she will do literally anything he wants if only Victor will keep coming around to her shop, and keep touching her. Their copulations make sex dirty beyond the imagination of any hell-fire preacher, but the only real gift he gives her is the contamination of his rudeness. Nonetheless, the insistent voice of her diary, calling out like a disembodied chorus, is a litany of longing so great that anger, shame and disgust have no power against it.

The point the Bavarian playwright seems to want to make in this grim piece is that time has changed the human condition in the 300 years since John Locke specified just how awful it was; thanks to economic, scientific and dietary improvements, life is now solitary, nasty, brutish and long.

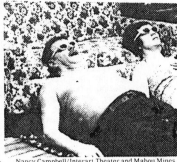

Nancy Campbell/Interart Theater and Mabou Mines

Frederick Neumann and Ruth Maleczech in a revival of Franz Xaver Kroetz's drama, "Through the Leaves."

Mr. Kroetz often writes as though he derives his greatest pleasure from watching actors turn his works into dramas that will grab an audience and not let go, no matter how much viewers might want to flee. Ms. Maleczech and Mr. Neumann realize his purposes perfectly. They excite not disgust or pity, but fear and astonishment — fear that they have mirrored a truth about human isolation that it would be better not to know, and astonishment that such characters can hold one's rapt attention for 75 minutes without engaging one's sympathy.

Why this production transposes to Queens remains as much a mystery as ever. Mr. Kroetz had put them where they belong, in a south German backwater 20 years ago. If anything, they seem more out of place in this production's Queens setting than they did in 1984. Then the concept seemed simply wrongheaded; by now it begins to look ridiculous. It is a tribute to the playwright, and the actors, that "Through the Leaves" survives such mischief.

1990 S 18, C18:1

The 1990 Young Playwrights Festival

Sets by Allen Moyer; costumes by Claudia Stephens; lighting by Pat Dignan; sound by Jane Kalas; production manager, Tom Aberger; production stage manager, James FitzSimmons. Presented by the Foundation of the Dramatists Guild, Nancy Quinn, producing director; Sheri M. Goldhirsch, managing director. At Playwrights Horizons, 416 West 42d Street.

MUTTERSCHAFT, by Gregory Clayman; directed by Michael Mayer.
BELIEVING, by Allison Birch; directed by Clinton Turner Davis; fights by B. H. Barry.
PSYCHONEUROTIC PHANTASIES, by Gilbert David Feke; directed by Gloria Muzio.
HEY LITTLE WALTER, by Carla D. Alleyne; directed by Mark Brokaw.
WITH: Jane Adams, Walter Bobbie, Lisa Carson, Seth Gilliam, Natalia Harris, Zakee Howze, Kevin Jackson, Marjorie Johnson, Mia Korf, Leslie Lyles, Bruce MacVittie, Cynthia Martells, Sasha Mujica, Sean Nelson, Harold Perrineau, Wendell Pierce, Angela Pietropinto, Tonya Pinkins, Kevin Rock, Michael Rogers, Merlin Santana, Christopher Shaw, Victor Slezak, Jill Tasker, Lenny Venito and Chandra Wilson.

By MEL GUSSOW

Of the four writers in the 1990 Young Playwrights Festival, two keep their ambition in check — and tongue in cheek — and demonstrate their promise with comedy. The two others, tackling more overtly dra-

Jack Manning/The New York Times

Linda Lavin, left, and Crista Moore in a scene from the revival of "Gypsy" at the St. James Theater.

matic material, are overcome by their ambition and veer into melodrama. The festival is at Playwrights Horizons under the sponsorship of the Foundation of the Dramatists Guild.

The most engaging of the plays is the satiric curtain raiser, "Mutterschaft," by Gregory Clayman. In this zestful variation on the mother-daughter relationship, it is the mother (Leslie Lyles) who is the mess, the teen-age daughter (Jane Adams) who is both competent and supervisory. She keeps trying to encourage her mother to straighten out her life, and to straighten up her room. Because the mother is played by Ms. Lyles, the character has a blithe spontaneity.

Conflict arises with the entrance of the mother's suitor (Victor Slezak), an empty-headed avant-garde artist who might easily be mistaken for a Nazi. Dressed in black and issuing curt orders, he quickly shifts his attentions from the mother to the daughter. On the sidelines is Harold Perrineau as one of Ms. Adams's schoolmates. The bearer of good sense, he notices that the daughter is getting back at her mother "by turning into her."

The author demonstrates an insightfulness into family attachments and rivalries, though occasionally he settles for an easy joke. Rough edges in the play are polished in the performance by the quartet of actors, nimbly led by Michael Mayer as director.

Gilbert David Feke's "Psychoneurotic Phantasies" is a breezy and at times sophomoric spoof of post-Freudian psychology, in which Freud himself (Walter Bobbie) plays a pivotal role. Two youngsters (Ms. Adams and Christopher Shaw) have wild fantasies, which are acted out by a vociferous team of cartoonlike players.

Freud frequently frolics, psychoanalyzing a patient on the kitchen table, and popping up in the classroom. At one point, he becomes the emcee of a television game show called "Family Freud," which pits the Adlers against the Jungs. As directed by Gloria Muzio, some of this is amusing, in the "Saturday Night Live" mode. But the funniest bit has nothing to do with teen-age sexuality or Freud. The scene takes place at breakfast as Mr. Shaw is bedeviled by a frozen waffle that insists on talking back to him from the toaster.

Each of the over-reaching plays, Allison Birch's "Believing" and Carla D. Alleyne's "Hey Little Walter," has enough plot to be full-length combined with a chaotic sense of theater. The setting for "Believing" is a West Indian community where women are subjugated to male domination and repression. The play plunges from wife abuse to rape to murder.

There are sparks of local flavor, but the play, as conceived, is too much for the playwright to handle, especially in 45 minutes. Clinton Turner Davis, as director, tries to make the melodrama plausible, but it is an uphill climb, as it is for the actors. Chandra Wilson gives a touching performance as a young woman victimized by adults.

With "Hey Little Walter," the family trauma moves to the city for a story of a young man's self-abandonment. Blockaded by poverty, the title character (played by Mr. Perrineau) takes up drug selling as an easy road to remuneration, and he pays a heavy price. Though the subject is worn through familiarity, it always needs restating.

Unfortunately, Ms. Alleyne is unable to sustain our interest even for the play's brief duration. She does have an ear for urban language, just as the actors (as directed by Mark Brokaw) have a feeling for urban characters. In addition to Mr. Perrineau, there is a pungent performance by Natalia Harris as the protagonist's diminutive sister, who seems more knowing than all of her elders.

The four playwrights, who were under 19 when they submitted their works, come from a diversity of geographic and educational backgrounds. It is worth noting that Mr. Clayman studied playwriting at St. Ann's School in Brooklyn, under the tutelage of Nancy Fales Garrett, who has been responsible for many of the winners during the nine years of the Young Playwrights Festival.

1990 S 21, C14:6

My Father, My Son

By Ken Wolf and Henry E. Wolf; directed by Frank Trezza; lighting, Jeff Nash; production stage manager, Paul A. Kochman; set and costumes, Ina Mayhew; music by Rodger Davidson; company manager, Michael Barreiro; choreography by Dan Hogan; sound design, David Lawson. Presented by My Father, My Son Productions. At the South Street Theater, 424 West 42d Street.

Harry Fox...................................Steve Parris
Ted...Ken Wolf

By WILBORN HAMPTON

Filial affection and devotion may be admirable qualities, but they are not in themselves ingredients that make engaging theater.

"My Father, My Son," a play by Ken Wolf and Henry E. Wolf at the South Street Theater, is little more than a homage to the friendship between the father-and-son authors and a eulogy to the memory of the elder Mr. Wolf, who died during the writing of it.

In the play, Ted Fox and his father, Harry, who was divorced from Ted's mother when the boy was 12 years old, decide during one of their regular lunch meetings at an Upper West Side Chinese restaurant to write a play together. They can't agree on a vehicle so they decide to write a play about a father and son writing a play. "Has this ever been done before?" the father asks. "Never," enthuses the son. Someone should have cautioned them that if something has never been done before, there's usually a reason.

•

What follows is a rather repetitious chronicle of the divorced father's relationship with his son. The prologue even has some childhood photographs that are flashed on a screen above the stage while a country-and-western song about "Daddy" plays in the background.

The entire play is like spending an evening being shown the Wolf/Fox family snapshot album while the son provides a commentary on each scene in asides to the audience. Some of these recollections are simply tiresome. The son, for example, has a habit of excusing himself to the men's room and bursting into tears whenever he feels any emotion, a personality trait that is played out about half a dozen times. Other reminiscences are probably too personal to have much meaning to an audience unacquainted with the authors.

But there are more serious problems facing "My Father, My Son" than its inherent sentimentality. The closest thing to a conflict comes when the two men argue over who will pay the check at the Chinese restaurant. The wife and mother is never seen or even heard from and the parents' divorce is never examined. The father and son discuss at some length whether to include the divorce in their play, and the father, after some initial reluctance, finally agrees. But when he starts to talk about it, all he can tell his son is, "It was tough, really tough," and that it was the mother's fault.

There are several morals and parables scattered throughout, and by the end, as the son finishes writing the play after his father's death, the father's religiosity and generosity take on the proportions of a candidate for beatification. It is all very earnest and heartfelt, as are the performances of Steve Parris as the father and Ken Wolf, who plays the son. And dull. Frank Trezza directed.

1990 S 23, 65:3

Lilith

By Allan Havis; directed by Robert Bailey. Presented by Home for Contemporary Theater and Art. At 44 Walker Street.

Adam and Arnold .... Zach Grenier
Lilith and Claire....................... Allison Janney
Voice (Archangel)............................Joel Rooks
Eppy .... Lindsey Margo Smith
Earl...Carl Purcell

By MEL GUSSOW

Before there was Eve there was Lilith. In his new play, "Lilith" (at the Home for Contemporary Theater and Art), Allan Havis has placed Adam's legendary first wife at the center of a parable about marriage. Springing Lilith loose in our age, the play is as devious as it is diabolical.

The first act is in biblical times, the second in present-day New York, but the distinction is not intended to be clear-cut. John Lee Beatty's design for both halves of the play is clinically modern. Adam (Zach Grenier) sits in a room or near the Garden of Eden and is interrogated by an offstage Archangel acting as counsel in divorce proceedings between Adam and Lilith (Allison Janney).

Eve, we are told, is on the drawing board and Lilith is trying to warn Adam against his forthcoming marital entrapment. He is eager to move on to a calmer life than he has had with this she devil. Despite the air of menace, there is lightness afoot. Speaking about the division of property, Adam says, "I want" — pause — "the Garden," as if it were a Jacuzzi or tickets to the Super Bowl. Gradually Mr. Havis weaves an intricate web of lustfulness and deceit, laying the groundwork for the expulsion from Eden.

•

In the second act, eons after the Fall, the story repeats itself in reverse. Adam is a self-involved New York trial lawyer with an Eve-like wife (Lindsey Margo Smith). They have one son and a seemingly durable marriage, and he has no memory of his former relationship. Enter the demon, according to myth, a child-killer as well as eternal temptress.

The scene is Strindbergian, as in "The Stronger." The wife is sitting silently in a cafe when Lilith (now called Claire) intrudes on her privacy and begins to insinuate herself into her marriage. The sardonic language could have been written by a contemporary counterpart of the Swedish playwright.

Lilith casually demands possession of the husband — her ex-husband — for a day. The wife is astonished, then oddly receptive and finally resistant to all of the other woman's maneuvers. Lilith never lets up and the play spirals into stranger and more dangerous territory as amulets are raised against creatures of the night.

•

Under Robert Bailey's adroit direction, the three actors are tightly bound in a balancing act. No histrionics intrude on the cool urbanity of the dialogue. Mr. Grenier's unassuming Adam is less wimpish than a man enthralled. The incredulous look on his face adds amusement to Lilith's machinations. As the modern Eve, Ms. Smith rises to bar the family door

Zach Grenier and Allison Janney in Allan Havis's play "Lilith."

to invaders; the actress wisely keeps her defensiveness matter-of-fact.

In the title role, Ms. Janney is both fiendish and seductive, with a mischievous sense of humor. Even as she threatens retaliation, she maintains her poise (along with her provocative poses). "It's witchcraft," sings Frank Sinatra on a record and, to broaden the musical references, there are also songs from Sinead O'Connor, all of which underscores the character's sorcery.

As in his earlier plays, "Mink Sonata" and "Morocco," Mr. Havis shows a mordant wit, used this time to ask the question, who is Lilith and what is her fatal attraction

1990 S 23, 67:4

STAGE VIEW/Elie Wiesel

The Secret Wealth Of 'The Rothschilds'

FIVE HUNDRED AND FIVE PERformances on Broadway in 1970 and 1971 and a vivid "chamber" revival in 1990: the Rothschilds are lucky. That is undeniable. Anyone will confirm it. Their name lives as a virtual guarantee of good quality. Is that why a considerable public is still interested in them? Is it because now, as always, people revel in success stories or, as some put it, the Frankfurt ghetto of the 19th century prefigures the modern "Dallas"? We must forgive them their misguided humor. Obviously, for the Jewish family we come to know in this very Jewish play, the danger is not corruption of morals and traditions by money, but rather isolation, oppression and death. For them, evil lies not within the family, but outside it. Their story is not of a clan's decline, but of its flowering, in the context of a great adventure in war-torn Europe.

■

Haloed by legend, the name of Rothschild made me daydream, as it did many Jewish children. In my little shtetl, nestled in the Carpathian Mountains, it summoned up distant journeys and prodigious challenges, luxurious chateaux and magnificent banquets, and all that we were deprived of: stability, security, liberty and power. Envied by the high society that accepted them reluctantly, the Rothschilds were our princes and protectors, recalling the glory and pride of ancient days. Innumerable stories about them circulated, and still do, each more picturesque and improbable than the others. On the highest rung of the social ladder, they could seek anything, win anything, permit themselves anything. Aware of their power, they spoke to earthly potentates as equals. A word from them, a gesture, sufficed to free prisoners,

Because vibrant life has been transposed into theater, the musical stirs up forgotten yearnings that include us all.

Carol Rosegg-Martha Swope Associates/"The Rothschilds"

Father & Sons: Mike Burstyn, center, with, left to right, Bob Cuccioli, Joel Malina, David Cantor, Nick Corley and Ray Wills as his sons in "The Rothschilds"—Their story is not of a clan's decline, but of its flowering.

victims unjustly condemned, from their gloomy dungeons. Their fortune? It was said that they owed it to the blessing of a Hasidic rabbi, a miracle worker. Or to the prophet Elijah himself. But I've already said it. The Rothschilds seem to have been born under a lucky star, the best money can buy: our worst enemies could do them no harm.

"Ah, if I were a Rothschild," exclaims Tevye in "Fiddler on the Roof," Tevye whose melodies, if not his philosophical reflections, have swept the world. And not only him. Poor merchants and weary porters, starving students and vagabond beggers, meeting to exchange a word between two errands or two prayers, let themselves go in ardent fantasy: What would they do if they were a Rothschild? One would eat a real meal, another would sleep in a real bed, a third would pass out cakes and candies to every child in the village, if not the world, and maybe to everybody else, too.

How do we explain the singular, privileged place occupied by the Rothschilds in Jewish legend? Other families acquired fortunes and titles. Some were feared, others respected. They can be found in our historic annals, but not in our fables. The play that sets forth the Rothschilds' phenomenal destiny — currently in the American Jewish Theater production at the Circle in the Square Downtown — may reveal a reason buried in our collective unconscious: of all our famous families and dynasties, the Rothschilds remained most closely attached and faithful to their Jewish roots.

■

Their philanthropic endeavors extended to all the European communities. Everywhere hospitals and homes for the elderly bear their name. When financial aid was needed, or political intervention, pious Jews turned first to God, and then to the Rothschilds. The others, the other way around.

How well is this musical, the last collaboration of the Jerry Bock-Sheldon Harnick-"Fiddler on the Roof" team, documented and corroborated by facts? I confess I have no idea. Does it correspond, in all its aspects, to historic reality? The play tells us that the founder, Mayer Rothschild, has five children, all boys: Is that true, or is it to contrast with poor Tevye, who had the same number of children, but all girls? Mayer had daughters, too, but that's another story. The Rothschilds we see are all exemplary Jews: Were they in fact? All wear the yarmulke, even in the presence of somewhat anti-Semitic monarchs and generals: Is that conceivable? Did the aged father really don the tallith (the ritual shawl) to read his will to his sons? And the financial blackmail that the sons dared to practice upon Metternich, to win more freedom for the Jews: Isn't that a bit exaggerated? Mayer was not present at the 1818 victorious powers conference in Aix-la-Chapelle: he had died earlier

The truth is, it doesn't matter. Here art is more powerful — and more important — than life. What does matter is the play, the rest belongs to biographers. Here the imaginary should not yield to the sort of eyewitness account that must serve, in other areas, as the vehicle of memory. This play is only a play. But it is also life transposed into theater, and because it is vibrant life, we respond in kind as it stirs up ancient, forgotten yearnings. Now light and droll, now solemn and overwhelming, it carries us from the ghetto in Frankfurt to the Prince of Hesse's palace, from Hamburg to Paris and London: it is Jewish history on the move. The father, played by Mike Burstyn, drives the play: stubborn, nervous, obsessed, he is, as Stephen Holden said in The

Times, riveting. In fact, all the actors are fervent in their parts. As the audience is in its.

The play includes us all. We care, we are touched by these precocious children matured by the demands of life in exile. We follow them step by step. They sing and dance, never at rest, creating and re-creating plans and projects, daring to challenge a system that rejects them. Mayer's sons are "Rothschilds" very early on, financial wizards. Their residences and clothes will change, but not their essence.

A 19th-century etching depicts William of Hesse-Cassel entrusting his wealth to Mayer Rothschild during the Napoleonic Wars.

How can we explain the continuing success of "The Rothschilds"? This play is not trendy. Beating against the current, it includes no daring scenes, no eroticism, no sexual innuendo, no crude remarks. The characters are not caricatures; they suffer none of the complex neuroses that seem to afflict so many of their counterparts in current novels and plays. No self-hate, no fleeing to "the other side," no desire to assimilate.

The five sons of the first Rothschild, projected onto the international scene, know that they are Jews and want to remain so; not one repudicates his origins. Not one is a renegade. The seductions of the other side have little effect on them. They do not forget that they came from the ghetto. For them, being a Jew is not a "problem," but an awareness, a commitment. At no time do they consider breaking the chain that links them to a past made up of suffering.

A strange play — it would shock a Freud, Oedipus and all the other complexes as much as it would scandalize a Gide, whose cry, "Families, I hate you," became famous — strange because it praises three elements that have had a rather bad press these last few years.

■

First, the family. It remains united, close-knit, sustained by a common purpose. Even when it is scattered geographically, it will not permit itself to be torn apart. The sons quarrel now and then about tactics, but even when they clash it is to protect the family — by which they themselves are protected — not to break it down. That can only astound today's audience, so accustomed to broken families motivated by hatred and rancor, whether in matters of inheritance or psychology. The most moving aspect

of this play comes when we realize that we have been present at a true celebration of the family, any family, irrespective of its ethnic origins.

The second element is money and the characters' attitude toward it. Mayer's sons, following their father's example, want it, and lots of it, and do

This strange play is most moving when it is seen as a celebration of the family, irrespective of ethnic origins.

not hide their desire. They intend to get rich and dare to admit it. But for them money is the means and not an end. A means of proving to the world that Jews are as smart and as vulnerable as other people; and that they know how to deal with humiliation, of which poverty is only one painful aspect.

And finally, the third element: the mother. Her sons show her respect and affection, sometimes going so far as to ask her advice on business matters. What? Portray a Jewish mother and not make fun of her? Love a Jewish mother without being ridiculed?

Apparently you can. That is the secret and the magic of the theater: You can do anything. If you have talent, of course. And luck. A little luck never hurts. If you don't believe me, ask Tevye. He'll tell you; he, who never had any, except of course on stage. ▯

1990 S 23, II:5:1

STAGE VIEW/David Richards

Mama Rose in 'Gypsy' Needs Sharp Thorns

T IS OFTEN ADVANCED AS A RULE of life that if you take care of the little things, the big things will take care of themselves. But that's a rule of the theater, too, isn't it?

Attend to the little moments assiduously enough and before long you'll have a big moment on your hands. Why else, when they enter rehearsals, are actors wont to break down their scenes, dissect their lines and search relentlessly for those elusive "beats" that can suddenly lend life to lifeless words? You don't go for broke the first time out. Get the second-to-second details right, and if they *are* right, they'll add up by themselves. Naturally. Inexorably. And there's your big moment, present and accounted for.

After seeing Linda Lavin in "Gypsy," I'm not so sure.

■

Ms. Lavin, in case you hadn't noticed, is now the featured name on the marquee at the St. James Theater, where she recently took over the role of Mama Rose. Ms. Lavin handles lots of little moments persuasively. The trouble is, they don't seem to be adding up. The performance stays little to the end. The dimensions we keep looking for, yearning for, never materialize.

It isn't just Ethel Merman who's responsible for our expectations, although there's no doubt that her native effrontery and the sheer, blistering power of her voice marked Mama Rose from the start. Still, if we had to wait around for someone of Merman's special gifts before taking "Gypsy" off the shelf, revivals would be few and far between. There are other ways of getting Mama Rose up to size.

Angela Lansbury, for one, brought a ruthless intelligence and a kind of blowzy glamour to the proceedings. Her face, which could have been that of a fallen kewpie doll, projected an astonishing innocence, even as Mama Rose was concocting brazen lies or hatching cockeyed schemes to put her daughters' names in lights. The guilelessness was mesmerizing. You were taken in.

■

I caught Tyne Daly on the road, when the current production was still finding its shape and establishing its rhythms. Her characterization wasn't in place yet, but by the time the production reached New York, the critical consensus held that it was. Ms. Daly's emotions were naked and her nerve endings raw, and the raging desperation helped put a Tony award in her pocket.

The point is that in Mama Rose's case, little won't do, even for starters. Extraordinary measures are called for.

Arthur Laurents's book, of course, charts the destiny of the stripper Gypsy Rose Lee and how she emerged from a lowly backup position in her sister June's vaudeville act to become the country's first lady of tease. But the spotlight never strays far from Mama Rose, the stage mother to end all stage mothers. What Medea is to Greek tragedy and Lady Macbeth is to the Shakespearean canon, Mama Rose is to the Broadway musical: a monster of ambition and vengeance in a cloche hat. She claims she's got her children's welfare at heart — and the cheesy act that is supposed to catapault them to stardom — but she's really servicing her own greedy needs and fooling no one in the process. Only herself.

The character comes on like a steamroller and builds from there. The first song out of her mouth is that defiant declaration of independence, "Some People." By the end of Act I, her dreams have collapsed and she's arguing against all evidence that "Everything's Coming Up Roses." And lying in wait at the evening's end, is the toughest challenge of all — "Rose's Turn," which is the equivalent of having a nervous breakdown on a bare stage. Rose's accumulated frustrations come clattering garishly to the surface and the full depths of her battered soul are there for all to see.

The Jule Styne-Stephen Sondheim score is a classic, full of gutsy melodies and fast lyrics. But we know that already. What you'll discover at the St. James is that the gutsiest numbers are those in which Ms. Lavin does her least convincing work. In fact, you're primarily aware of all the work she's putting into them. Repeatedly, the actress tucks her tongue in the corner of her mouth, screws up her face and shakes out her body like a nervous athlete before the race, as if she could

What Medea is to Greek tragedy, this heroine is to the Broadway musical, but in the role, Linda Lavin comes up short.

thereby will the requisite power into being. But the windup eclipses the delivery, and her stamina tends to give out before the number does.

Martha Swope/"Gypsy"

Jonathan Hadary, Linda Lavin as Mama Rose and Christa Moore in the revival at the St. James Theater

She is visibly more comfortable warbling "Small World," "You'll Never Get Away From Me" and "Together," and not just because Jonathan Hadary or Crista Moore, engaging performers both, happen to be by her side. They're "Gypsy's" smaller numbers. They permit a playful giggle, a peekaboo flirtatiousnes, a wry mockery — all of which Ms. Lavin handles with charm. More important, they can be sidled up to; no frontal attack is called for.

In Neil Simon's 1986 comedy, "Broadway Bound," her last Broadway appearance, Ms. Lavin also portrayed an embittered mother with ambitions for her children and a dream locked away in her past. But the role called for her to digest the anger, sidestep the harsh feelings in her soul and get on with the housework. When her younger son finally coaxed her into recounting that long ago episode from her youth when George Raft asked her to dance at the Primrose Ballroom, the years of drudgery fell away quietly and for a shimmering instant she was a girl again.

■

The story was unbearably poignant and Ms. Lavin relived it beautifully. But, you see, the actress was playing against the grain, letting herself slip into a golden memory despite her better judgment, which said she really should be polishing the dining room table. She had to be prodded to reveal herself, and the reluctance made the eventual revelation more precious.

Mama Rose needs no such encouragement. To the contrary, she's the one doing all the prodding. Neither common manners nor the uncommon love of a decent man hold her back — which may be why Ms. Lavin appears at odds with the role. Letting it all hang out doesn't come naturally to the actress, who operates far more effectively under the cover of restraint. In the great, gaudy world of "Gypsy," however, half steps can seem like no steps at all.

As a result, a strapping production of a strapping musical now finds itself without a spine.

On the other hand, rampaging egos are crawling all over "Forbidden Broadway," Gerard Alessandrini's very funny (and largely futile) crusade to keep show folk humble. Spoofing the town's star players and smash shows (plus a few that aren't so starry) constitutes the prime order of business. The current edition at Theater East certainly

manages to hit "Grand Hotel," for instance, smack in the puss. ("People come. People go. People move chairs," solemnly entones the drugnumbed narrator of what has become "Grim Hotel.") "Love Changes Everything," the proud refrain of Andrew Lloyd Webber's "Aspects of Love," has been transmuted into "I Sleep With Everyone," which not only neatly disposes of the song, but mischievously reduces the show to a game of musical beds.

If, however, you put the impertinent specifics aside, it seems to me that "Forbidden Broadway" really is a show about megalomania. Megalomania and bad wigs. The wigs, maliciously styled by Teresa Vuoso, qualify as a kind of character assassination in themselves, allowing the players to pass for ludicrous versions of Dustin Hoffman, Carol Channing, Rex Harrison, Colleen Dewhurst, Glynis Johns and Karen Akers, among others. Then it's simply a question of releasing the megalomania and letting it rise to stratospheric heights.

Almost any number would serve as an example, but since "Forbidden

But at 'Forbidden Broadway,' the megalomania rises to stratospheric heights.

Broadway" makes a concerted effort to remain timely, consider its take on the "Miss Saigon" flap. Midway through the first act, the lights come up on a Jonathan Pryce stand-in, peering out at the audience from under a coolie hat. His eyes clearly depend on makeup for their almond shape, and old racial clichés would appear to be the inspiration for the subservient clasp of his hands, the quizzical tilt of the head.

■

To the tune of "I'm an Indian Too" (from "Annie Get Your Gun"), the

surrogate Mr. Pryce proceeds to explain that "Just like Ho Chi Minh, Chiang Kai-shek, Mao Zedong, like those Chinamen, I'm an Asian, too." The claim is outrageous, but for the moment it's being made with deference and the semblance of sweet reason. When, though, the actor, pressing his argument, expands the comparisons to include "Connie Chung, B. D Wong, Nancy Kwan in a musical," preposterousness rears its head. Indeed, by the end of the number, sanity has been cast to the winds, and he's no longer content with Asian roles. He's vehemently asserting his right to play characters of any and all persuasion — young, old, male, female, *lesbian*.

And "just when 'Miss Saigon' is done," he vows by way of a parting sally, "I'll star in 'Raisin in the Sun.'"

Whether it's Jerome Robbins, proclaiming (to "New York, New York") "Jerome, Jerome, I'm a helluva guy"; or Mandy Patinkin, exulting in weird gestures and weirder vocal arabesques; Liza Minelli, all but sticking a mike in her throat and screaming down the house; or Kathleen Turner, flipping her hair back, the better to cover her shoulders with kisses — the ferocious drive is hilarious. "Forbidden Broadway" understands something important about these people. If they didn't have show business to keep themselves busy, they'd be invading countries, seizing television stations and toppling governments.

The cast of four is wonderfully nimble, but the nimblest to my mind is Jeff Lyons. If ever someone chooses to revive "Banjo Eyes," he's a shoo-in for the Eddie Cantor role. Since the wait risks being long, you'd do best to catch his furrowed scowls, slow burns and manic leaps in the inspired context of "Forbidden Broadway." □

1990 S 23, II:5:1

Ivanov

By Anton Chekhov; translated by Robert W. Corrigan; adapted and directed by Oleg Yefremov; sets by David Borovsky; costumes by Jess Goldstein; lighting by Geoff Korf; sound by Jamie Anderson; associate director, Victor Steinbach. Presented by Yale Repertory Theater, Lloyd Richards, artistic director; Benjamin Mordecai, managing director. At University Theater, 222 York Street, New Haven, Conn.

Yegorushka	Bernard Jaffe
Pavel Kerylovich Lebedev	Austin Pendleton
Avdotya Nazarovna	Anne Pitoniak
Gavrila	Tom McGowan
First Guest	Liev Schreiber
Second Guest	Malcolm Gets
Third Guest	Tom Whyte
Sasha	Mary Mara
Marfa Yegorovna Babakina	Joyce Van Patten
Zinaida Saveshna	Susan Kellermann
Visitors	Ann Hutchinson, Martha Johnson, Maggie Roberts & Kimberly Squires
Old Women	Ruth Jaffe and Carol Lowrance
Housemaid	Sarah Long
Nikolai Alexeyevich Ivanov	William Hurt
Mihail Mihailovich Borkin	Leo Burmester
Anna Petrovna	Frances Conroy
Matvyey Semyonich Shabyelsky	Lee Richardson
Yevgeny Konstantinovich Lvov	Zeljko Ivanek
Pyotr	Bill Nesta
Dimitri Nekitovich Kosykh	William Mesnik

By FRANK RICH

Special to The New York Times

NEW HAVEN, Sept. 21 — Most American directors would kill to get

the high-powered acting company that the Yale Repertory Theater has handed over to Oleg Yefremov, the artistic director of the Moscow Art Theater, for his first assignment in the United States. The cast for Mr. Yefremov's production of Chekhov's "Ivanov" here includes William Hurt, Frances Conroy, Zeljko Ivanek, Lee Richardson, Austin Pendleton and Anne Pitoniak. A major force in the Soviet theater for more than two decades, Mr. Yefremov is the happy beneficiary of the American hospitality showered on most visitors from the Soviet Union in our age of Gorbachev. It seems almost churlish to point out that this particular cultural exchange is not nearly so salutary for the audience, or, for that matter, for Chekhov.

The trouble with the evening has nothing to do with its intentions, which are the highest, or with the talent of Mr. Yefremov and his actors, which is indisputable. Rather, this "Ivanov" suffers from the mistaken conviction that a brilliant Soviet director can drop into a foreign theater and, in a rehearsal period that would no doubt seem laughably brief by Russian standards, re-create a celebrated Moscow production with actors whose language, careers and theatrical idiom he scantly knows. Even glasnost and the unquenchable American faith in instant results have their limits. Though it speaks well of Mr. Yefremov and his cast that this "Ivanov" is superior to similar recent experiments at other American theaters — Yuri Lyubimov's "Crime and Punishment" at the Arena Stage in Washington, Boris A. Morozov's "Zoya's Apartment" at the Circle in the Square in New York — the results still fail to fulfill the play at hand and the highest standards of either the Soviet or American artists involved.

●

From the evocative production design, the canny textual jugglings and the tragicomic lilt of the staging, one can easily see why Mr. Yefremov's "Ivanov" has captivated audiences in Moscow, where it has been in repertory for more than a decade. David Borovsky's set is a stunning exercise in corroded classicism that in itself conveys the torpid atmosphere of provincial late-19th-century Russia — a grim, rotting country house whose shuttered facade and peeling pillars are overrun by twisted branches and barren vines. Mr. Yefremov further heightens the mood of social petrifaction by opening the play with transposed vignettes of party gossip and by sprinkling its entire expanse with swirling images of eavesdropping and empty, raucous revelry. Nearly every scene is haunted by a ghoulish, vodka-proffering manservant and the Diane Arbusesque specter of two seated, chalkfaced old women staring numbly into space.

Mr. Yefremov's stage pictures can be chilling. When Ivanov, the depressed, self-lacerating intellectual played by Mr. Hurt, has a final confrontation with his dying wife (Ms. Conroy), their faces and a candle are the only flickering dabs of light in a velvety expanse of darkness. Right after that, the director uses that waning candle, eerie apparitions of white floral bouquets and solitary strains of a cello to dramatize wordlessly the play's sweeping transition from the wife's subsequent funeral to Ivanov's incipient taking of a new bride. The violent denouement that follows is nearly as spooky.

But nonverbal theatrics can go only so far in Chekhov. "Ivanov," the writer's first produced full-length play

(1887), is of a piece in content, if not in achievement, with the masterworks that follow it. Highly populated by bored, educated souls in varying degrees anguished by existence, it is full of the articulate chatter, by turns brave and ridiculous and pathetic, of stalled lives. While there are lapses into melodrama and broad characterizations in "Ivanov," Chekhov still comes very close to his goal of dramatizing life as it is. When he fails, it is all the more incumbent on the cast to provide the fine brush strokes essential to his canvas.

•

Quite understandably, Mr. Yefremov has not been able to achieve such intricately detailed performances from his pickup company, or to knit its members into a true ensemble. He has to settle for an approximate Chekhovian mood in a play in which, as he knows better than most, specificity of character is almost all. While most of the actors are well cast — with the glaring exceptions of Joyce Van Patten, as the young widow, Babakina, and Mary Mara as Ivanov's younger paramour, Sasha — the performances are all over the map in achievement and at times even in accent.

In the largest role, Mr. Hurt is the largest disappointment. The solipsistic, guilt-ridden Ivanov should be a natural for this actor, who has a special gift for conveying disillusioned intelligence, wry despair and brooding introspection. His early Circle Repertory Company performances — in Lanford Wilson's "Fifth of July" and as Hamlet — were much in the spirit of Ivanov, a man who dreams of rising above his purposeless life yet lacks the will to do so. But this time it is hard to find authentic passion in Mr. Hurt, the buried self that might grip the audience with Ivanov's strangled and finally suicidal yearnings. Instead the actor offers pretentious, obfuscatory mannerisms (squinting eyes, muttered sentences, tossed hair) that, if little else, will give Mr. Yefremov an illustration of the time-honored American tradition of garbling the legacy of the Moscow Art Theater's patriarch, Stanislavsky.

•

Since it is impossible to get close to Ivanov's suffering, the production spins into centrifugal entropy, rising or falling from scene to scene and rarely engaging the emotions. Along the way, one finds some excellent actors giving one-note performances (Mr. Ivanek as the narrow doctor Lvov, Leo Burmester as the vulgar estate manager Borkin) and others giving wrong-note performances (Ms. Pitoniak's benign local busybody, Susan Kellermann's toothlessly parsimonious bourgeois matron). It is the actors who actually make contact with the play's depths, however, who most tantalize a theatergoer with the prospect of what might have been.

Mr. Pendleton, as the drunken County Council chairman, Lebedev, and Mr. Richardson, as Shabyelsky, the buffoonish count who wants only to "sink into the muck," both capture the weary, humorous sense of futility that marks Chekhov's most acutely self-aware burned-out cases. They earn the evening's warmest laughter and tenderest sympathies. Nearly as affecting is Ms. Conroy, who exploits her flowing red hair and alabaster skin as well as her talent to heighten the loneliness of the consumptive Anna Petrovna. But even these superb actors could use fine-tuning, as well as more support from their fel-

low players. Their plight is indicative of a cross-cultural "Ivanov" that is better savored as a sweet episode in post-glasnost brotherhood than as a serious Soviet-American collaboration in the art of the stage.

1990 S 25, C13:3

The Death of the Last Black Man in the Whole Entire World

Written by Suzan-Lori Parks; directed by Beth A. Schachter; set designer, Sharon Sprague; lighting designer, Brian MacDevitt; costume designer, Toni-Leslie James; production stage manager, Elise-Ann Konstantin. Presented by BACA Downtown, 111 Willoughby Street in downtown Brooklyn.

Black Woman With Fried Drumstick	Pamala Tyson
Black Man With Watermelon	Leon Addison Brown
Lots of Grease and Lots of Pork	Willy Corpus
Yes and Greens Black-Eyed Peas Corn Bread	Fanni Green
Voice on Thuh Tee V	Ann Harada
Before Columbus	James Himelsbach
And Bigger and Bigger and Bigger	Michael Jayce
Prunes and Prisms	Patrice Johnson
Ham	Jasper McGruder
Old Man River Jordan	John Steber
Queen-Then-Pharaoh Hatshepsut	Ching Valdez-Aran

By MEL GUSSOW

In Suzan-Lori Parks's new play, "The Death of the Last Black Man in the Whole Entire World," the author's admonition is self-evident. She warns, "Write that down," before it disappears. Write it down, or we do not exist.

From Ms. Parks's point of view, the acculturation of blacks in the United States can lead to the obliteration of signs and symbols of character. If the last black man should die tomorrow, what would the artifacts of his existence be? Her mission: find the signature behind the stereotype. "The Death of the Last Black Man" (at BACA Downtown) becomes an act of ecology as well as a prophecy of mourning. That death, when it comes, occurs again and again.

Last season at this same Brooklyn theater, Ms. Parks was introduced with "Imperceptible Mutabilities in the Third Kingdom," a quartet of compelling vignettes about the black experience from slavery to modern times. Covering similar territory, her new play lacks the precision of "Mutabilities," but in common with the earlier work it has a rapturous feeling for the flow of ethnicity through language. Ms. Parks transforms patois into poetry.

The playwright's kinship with Adrienne Kennedy and Ntozake Shange is again readily apparent. The three share a dreamlike drift of imagery and a lyrical intensity. In reading Ms. Parks's play, it might seem like automatic writing tumbling in an endless cycle of broken and disconnected words. But as performed by this persuasive company of actors, the writing becomes the spoken equivalent of a musical riff. As intended, the play is a "requiem mass in the jazz esthetic." "The Death of the Last Black Man" is as recondite as it is elliptical.

The open stage is set for symbols (by its designer, Sharon Sprague). In the background are stones from a graveyard, and off to one side is a framework of a country church. The pulpit is a television set on which is perched a watermelon, the primal symbol of the play, and, without em-

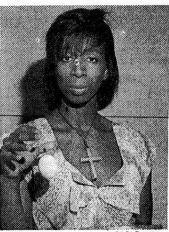

BACA Downtown

Pamala Tyson in "The Death of the Last Black Man in the Whole Entire World."

---

barrassment, a kind of life sign. In one amusing combination of clichés, an actor shines a watermelon as if it were a big shoe.

Sitting on a porch at the center of the stage are two representative figures, identified as a Black Man With Watermelon (Leon Addison Brown) and a Black Woman With Fried Drumstick (Pamala Tyson).

The archetypal black man, who was "born a slave" and "rose to become a spearhead in the civil rights movement," dies a dozen *deaths by falling and hanging. He dies to live again*, while the woman (wife, earth mother) continues to offer him soul food as a kind of wishbone for survival. "Re-member me," urges Ms. Tyson, seeking a verbal reconstruction of her story and of history.

Around them flow characters from fiction and mythology: Bigger Thomas from "Native Son," Ham (as in "Ham Bone, Ham Bone, where you been?") and others back to the time of the Pharaohs. Each becomes a motif, orchestrated into limber linguistic patterns.

With down-home humor, Ms. Parks skirts pretension and pokes fun at stereotypes. Under the choreographic direction of Beth A. Schachter, the actors (most prominently, Ms. Tyson, Mr. Brown and Jasper McGruder as a dancing man) exult in the idiomatic dialogue and instill a sense of order. Freewheeling and earthy, the play confirms Ms. Parks's indigenous theatrical talent.

1990 S 25, C15:1

Whatnot

Conceived and written by Mark Waldrop and Howard Crabtree; direction and musical staging by Mr. Waldrop; music and lyrics by Dick Gallagher; set design, James Noone; special effects and design, Mr. Crabtree; lighting, Kendall Smith; sound, One Dream; musical director, Mr. Gallagher; production stage manager, Ira Mont. Presented by Musical Theater Works, Anthony J. Stimac, artistic director, by arrangement with Michael Unger. At St. Peter's Church, 54th Street and Lexington Avenue.

WITH: Howard Crabtree, John Treacy Egan, Mark Lazore and Jennifer Smith

By WILBORN HAMPTON

"Whatnot" is a mishmash.

Billed as "the new musical vaudeville" and opening the seventh season of the Musical Theater Works at the Theater at St. Peter's Church, "Whatnot" is a collection of musical bric-a-

brac that its creators and their friends might find cute but that may seem more like a hodgepodge of attic junk to an outsider.

Three of the dozen songs in the show are sung by insects — a lightning bug, a moth and a fly — and another is a hymn to the joys of entomology. Only the lightning bug figures in the story.

The showcase chosen by Mark Waldrop and Howard Crabtree, who conceived and wrote it, to display this accumulation of curios is a variety show being produced to raise money to save the local Whatnot Shelf Factory, the economic backbone of Whatnot Springs, from bankruptcy. The authors have also thrown in a bit of science fiction, or perhaps biblical parable (a giant fish swallows a boat with a boy and his grandpa inside), a feud among three eccentric sisters, an invisible family that has formed a dance troupe, a nefarious knickknack manufacturer who tries to sabotage the fund drive, and a romance that detours the plot through Las Vegas, Nev.

•

The aim of all this appears to be a folksy cabaret parody of Smalltown, U.S.A., but there is little of the empathy or affection for its targets that, for example, "Oil City Symphony" so brilliantly achieved a few seasons back. The music, credited to Dick Gallagher, includes some rather silly rhymes set to some very familiar tunes that range from country and western to 1960's rock to Broadway musicals to the Maguire Sisters.

Four game actors play about 14 roles and pour a lot of energy into the show, not the least of which is spent in an awesome number of quick costume changes. Mark Lazore gets the most out of all his roles, whether in drag or pants, and Jennifer Smith is especially good as the fly singing a torch song. John Treacy Egan has one of the more amusing turns delivering radio ads for knickknacks of Michelangelo's "Last Supper" in biodegradable plastic or an endangered species series "made from the skins of the animals they immortalize."

Some of the numbers, which are lavishly costumed by Mr. Crabtree, might be found diverting in the way a college fraternity house skit is, provided one has had a few beers first and is an acquaintance of someone in the cast. But for most of it, "Whatnot" is defined by its title — a nondescript object.

1990 S 25, C16:3

The Video Store Owner's Significant Other

Adapted by the Cornerstone Theater Company, with additional inspiration by Dyann Simile. From "The Shoemaker's Prodigious Wife" by Federico García Lorca, as translated by James Graham-Lujan and Richard L. O'Connell. Directed by Bill Rauch; producer, James Bundy; assistant director, Rachel Wineberg; set and costume designer, Lynn Jeffries; lighting, Mary-Ann Greanier. Presented by Cornerstone Theater Company, at St. Clement's Church, 423 West 46th Street.

WITH: Amy Brenneman, Christopher Moore, Ashby Semple, Peter Howard, Alison Carey and Jeff Branion.

By MEL GUSSOW

The purpose of the Cornerstone Theater Company is to bring classic theater to the people. Like a portable circus, this nomadic troupe moves into a town, casts members of the community in some of the roles and reworks a play to make it more relevant to local concerns. In this manner, the Cornerstone has taken Shakespeare to Port Gibson, Miss., and performed "Pier Gynt" on the Maine coast.

The company has presented its version of "The Shoemaker's Prodigious Wife" (by Federico García Lorca) under a variety of titles in a diversity of locations. Retitled "The Video Store Owner's Significant Other" for its New York engagement, the show is playing through this weekend at St. Clement's Church. In this case, all the actors are members of the company. The play has been drastically altered, and García Lorca has been left somewhere on the road.

The author labeled the work a "violent farce." It is both antic and surrealistic — as if Pirandello had rewritten Ben Jonson in Spanish. In this comedy of imagined infidelity, an aging cobbler becomes outrageously jealous of his faithful teen-age bride.

•

By transplanting the setting from provincial Spain to a shopping mall in an unspecified suburb of middle America and by changing the shoemaker into the owner of a video store, the troupe vitiates García Lorca's sense of small-town character. Other mistakes of interpretation follow, until the company paints itself into a corner. In its touring capacity, Cornerstone may have a beneficial effect on grass-roots theater. But the New York production of "The Video Store Owner's Significant Other" is a lesson in how to denature a classic.

The dialogue is a makeshift collage of contemporary references and wisecracks, with occasional lines of García Lorca, which in this case seem out of context. The single notion behind Bill Rauch's staging is to mix the sexes to demonstrate that any romantic relationship can result in disharmony. This means that the four principal actors (two men and two women) take turns at playing the store owner, his "significant other" and a neighborhood pizza deliverer (or mall boy).

One actor will start a sentence, then duck behind a counter or display case, and another member of the company will pop up, puppet-style, and continue the dialogue. This endless round robin clutters the story and the stage. It is not always clear which character is being personified. If the actors were a quick-changing band of clowns, as found in companies like the San Francisco Mime Troupe, this might result in a certain zaniness. In this instance, there is no arte in the commedia, too little verve in the vaudeville.

•

At the end of the first act, the storekeeper leaves home and after the intermission returns in disguise. In the Cornerstone version, he is inexplicably posing as Santa Claus. To switch roles, the actors have to change wigs, beards and red jackets, which slows down the performance and leads to a surfeit of Santas. In the circumstances, it is difficult to assess the actors' talent, although none seem overly adept at mime and mimicry.

One wishes that the earnest company had followed García Lorca's stage directions as well as his dialogue. Within the play, the author offers the following helpful suggestion to prospective players: "No one should exaggerate Farce always demands naturalism." The advice is over-

looked, along with the author's intention. Perhaps the show was funnier when it was performed in Schurz, Nev., under the title, "The Cowpoke's Persnickety Spouse."

1990 S 26, C9:5

Big, Fat and Ugly With a Mustache

By Christopher Widney; directed by Stone Widney; scenic design, George Allison; lighting, Michael Stiller; costumes, Traci Di Gesu; sound, Scott Widney; production stage manager, Greg P. Weiss; production manager, Kathleen Mary. Presented by the Perry Street Theater Company's Prima Artists, in association with Buzzhead Productions. At 31 Perry Street.

Spike	Alison Martin
David	David Beach
Zeke	Brian Howe
Tyler	Evan O'Meara
Kathleen	Jane Gabbert
Frank Krutchik	Gordon Stanley

By WILBORN HAMPTON

"Big, Fat and Ugly With a Mustache," a new play by Christopher Widney at the Perry Street Theater, has all the right ingredients for a television movie of the week with an option for a series.

A couple of serious, socially revelant issues are given a slick, superficial treatment. The good guys are easily distinguished from the one bad guy. There is some slightly risqué dialogue that is meant to be adult and funny (although a laugh track would come in handy and the banter about genitalia would probably have to be edited out). And everyone can feel that love and justice have once again triumphed in a happily-ever-after ending.

The story concerns a gay couple who want to adopt a baby. Or rather David, the domestic/songwriter half of this pair, wants a baby. Tyler, his fitness buff/schoolteacher partner, is not so sure. In fact, Tyler's not sure about a lot of things, including just how far he wants to come out of the closet or whether he plans to stay with David long enough to change a diaper. For balance, David and Tyler's closest friends are a heterosexual couple, Spike and Zeke, who have just had a baby of their own. Zeke is a lawyer, which is convenient for the plot later on.

•

Although David and Tyler's chances of adopting a healthy white baby are slim to none, Zeke has read a newspaper article about the possibility of adopting "at risk" babies, mostly nonwhite infants whose mothers are addicts or prostitutes or who may have AIDS. When a case worker arrives to interview David and Tyler, she cautions them about the children she has to offer. "We're not talking the pick of the litter here," she says.

Mr. Widney has carefully crafted his play. Each of the seven scenes includes a small confrontation that is wrapped with some light, hopefully humorous patter. Unfortunately, these little dramas are all too predictable and too easily resolved, and the small talk that serves as filler is forced and weak.

•

The major failing of the play, however, is the glibness with which it tries to deal with such heart-rending issues as the plight of homeless babies born either drug-addicted or with AIDS, or questions about the qualifications of homosexual or lesbian couples for adopting children. Any hint of an honest, raw emotion is quickly

smothered with some silly slapstick stab at comedy. As with too much television (and film and drama, for that matter), Mr. Widney seems to write from the point of view that nothing is as bad as it first seems. The baby David and Tyler adopt (the title character, by the way) doesn't have AIDS or a heroin addiction after all — just a heart defect that an operation can cure. "Big, Fat and Ugly" supports the notion that as long as one's heart and sense of humor are in the right place, everything will turn out all right in the end.

Under the direction of Stone Widney, the playwright's father, the performances are for the most part facile as the play. One exception is Brian Howe, who is quite good as Zeke, the lawyer friend.

1990 S 29, 14:6

Lusting After Pipino's Wife

By Sam Henry Kass; directed by Casey Childs; set, Ray Recht; lighting, Deborah Constantine; costumes, Amanda J. Klein; sound, Gayle Jeffery; production stage manager, Tony Luna. Presented by Primary Stages Company Inc., Mr. Childs. artistic director; Janet Reed, associate artistic director. At 354 West 45th Street.

Vinnie	Joseph Siravo
Patsy	Wayne Maugans
Lorraine	Alexandra Gersten
Rita	Debra Riessen

By WILBORN HAMPTON

The Pipino in the title of Sam Henry Kass's "Lusting After Pipino's Wife" at Primary Stages is an immigrant dishwasher who speaks no English and who has made love to his wife every single night of their marriage. Pipino's wife and the mother of his dozen or so children has never known another man and is so accommodating to Pipino's every whim that she doesn't even object to his fooling around with a waitress on the side.

That, at any rate, is the mental picture of Pipino's domestic life based solely on the somewhat warped imagination of Vinnie, the owner of the bar and restaurant where Pipino washes dishes. Neither Pipino nor his wife actually appears in Mr. Kass's caustic comedy, a sort of dispatch from the battle front in the war of the

sexes. But for Vinnie, Pipino's wife represents the ultimate ideal of a woman — subservient, silent, submissive.

Vinnie, who by his own definition is "cut from a different loin of cloth," is the kind of guy who can get into a flaming row with a woman two minutes after he introduces himself and tries to start a conversation with her in a museum. The facility with which such an argument erupts is abetted by the fact that his intended pickup is Lorraine, a feisty paralegal who develops an obsessive fondness for guns and whose idea of a fun weekend is to go squirrel-hunting. Lorraine discourages gentlemen callers by firing a .38-caliber revolver point blank through her front door. In the particular sexual skirmish fought in "Lusting After Pipino's Wife," Vinnie and Lorraine are the opposing generals, and the soldiers in the trenches are Patsy and Rita, their respective best friends.

Patsy, a bartender at Vinnie's who aspires to be a shoe salesman, meets Rita in a grocery store checkout line and recognizes her as the lifeguard who once saved him from drowning. About five minutes later, they are in bed, and before the act is out they are in the county clerk's office happily waiting to be married. Neither, of course, reckoned on the resources of Vinnie and Lorraine.

Mr. Kass spins out his tale in a series of quick scenes that begin plausibly enough and then take almost surreal twists. The dialogue is mostly sharp and witty, nearly Mametesque at times, and the characterizations avoid falling into simple misogynist or militant feminist stereotypes. Opposing philosophies of life and love are at war here. Sex just happens to be the chosen weapon.

•

Vinnie, who describes himself as being "filled with a lack of self-aggrandizement," is by nature dubious of anything that might be construed as happiness (except, of course, Pipino's marriage). When Patsy tells Vinnie he is in love, Vinnie immediately asks, "You running a background check on this girl?" and then advises him: "Give it enough time. Everything passes." When it comes to men and women, Vinnie explains to Patsy, "There are no rules, no logic and no winner." Lorraine is ever more certain that everything in life

William Gibson/Martha Swope Associates/"Lusting After Pipino's Wife"
Wayne Maugans, left, and Joseph Siravo in Henry Kass's "Lusting After Pipino's Wife," presented by the Primary Stages Company.

will end badly, and she does not hesitate to express her anger. "Act as miserable as you really are," she urges Rita. "You'll be a better person for it."

There are weaknesses in the play. By the second act, when Rita and Patsy are fighting in every scene, some of the humor is based on nothing more than the cleverness of insults the combatants hurl. Another scene, involving the reading of a newspaper account of bestiality, is silly and tasteless. But through most of this fast-paced account of one encounter in the battle of sexes, Mr. Kass's observations, although bitterly drawn, are bitingly sharp.

The playwright is fortunate in a first-rate cast. In less able hands, the pungency of the humor could easily deteriorate into shrillness, even crassness, and possibly prompt protests from women's rights groups. Joseph Siravo is hilarious as Vinnie, a pompous and obnoxious would-be lecher who is very difficult not to like. Alexandra Gersten is every bit his match as Lorraine, the gun-toting crusader who has her own ideas about romance. Debra Riessen as Rita and Wayne Maugans as Patsy are believable both as lovers and as lovers quarreling. Casey Childs's fine direction quickly glides over the slow spots.

1990 S 30, 57:4

SUNDAY VIEW/David Richards

Learning to Live When Life Is a Welsher

MIDWAY THROUGH "FALSETtoland," the stirring musical by William Finn at the Lucille Lortel Theater, a beleaguered housewife named Trina sings of the difficulty of "holding to the ground, as the ground keeps shifting."

Truths crumble. Relationships come apart. Rules change. All she's trying to do, she says, is stay sane, keep up her head "as my heart falls out of sight," and convince herself that "everything will be all right." But she's confused and angry, and at the song's end, the best she can muster by way of reassurance is that "everything will be . . ."

While Trina is not the principal character in Mr. Finn's work, the concluding installment of his trilogy about coming out and coming of age, her bewilderment, I think, cuts very close to its core. How do you maintain your balance, when the world is behaving like a Tilt-A-Whirl and each mad spin puts the calm center of things a little farther out of your reach?

Nothing, you'll notice, stays put for long in "Falsettoland" — the props no more than the people. The designer, Douglas Stein, has mounted the various bits and pieces of scenery on wheels, so that if a door is needed, a door can be rolled into place in a flash. An

> ### William Finn's 'Falsettoland' is a strong, clear-eyed work that imparts the overwhelming sense of the fragility of our lives.

armchair traces a few crisp circles on the bright red floor, before skidding off into the wings, while a hospital bed speeds on stage, as if it were a matter of life or death, which, in fact, it is.

Mr. Finn's musical, which first saw light last spring at Playwrights Horizons, moves restlessly through dozens of locales in 70 short minutes and, obviously, someone had to figure out a quick way of getting from here to there. But more than efficiency is at stake.

The "Falsettoland" family: Danny Gerard, right, and, from left, Michael Rupert, Lonny Price, Heather MacRae, Faith Prince, Janet Metz and Stephen Bogardus

Carol Rosegg-Martha Swope Associates/"Falsettoland"

The scenery is really behaving no differently than Mr. Finn's characters — coming together, breaking apart, recombining in new patterns that will hold a brief while before invariably breaking apart again. The story takes place in New York in 1981, just as a mysterious virus is about to make its terrible ravages felt. But you could also say that flux itself is the relentless setting.

Paradoxes abound. "Falsettoland" is one of those strong, clear-eyed works that impart an overwhelming sense of the fragility of our lives. It is concisely told in what approaches dramatic shorthand, yet the stage always seems full to overflowing. It is a hard evening to take, dealing as it does with AIDS and mortality. (In general, audiences prefer death in the picturesque mode of "Les Misérables.") Nonetheless, it is very likely to leave you exhilarated.

For more than a decade now, Mr. Finn has been chronicling the fortunes of his hero, a certain Marvin — young, Jewish and compulsive — and edging him with each successive work in the trilogy a little closer to maturity. The introductory episode, "In Trousers" (1978), depicted him alternately as a kid and a married man, wrestling with his sexual identity. In "March of the Falsettos" (1981), he left his wife, Trina, and son, Jason, for love and games with another man. By the end of those 70 minutes, his life was in a shambles. Whizzer, the lover, had bolted. Jason, worried that maybe his father's homosexuality was catching, was seeing a psychiatrist, who, for his part, was busy scoring points with Trina, soon to be his spouse. Presumably, in the course of the hullabaloo, Marvin was shedding some of his selfishness and learning how to love. I was never particularly convinced, but no matter. The third time's the charm.

Now, Marvin is reaping the rewards and paying the costs of his love, and both prove greater than he could have expected. A more generous work than its predecessors, "Falsettoland" is also more consequential. Marvin himself (Michael Rupert) signals the change in the air early on, when he notes, as much for his own benefit as ours, that "it's about time to grow up, don't you think, and face the music."

Initially, the territory seems familiar enough. Most of the old characters are back, and the two new ones — Dr. Charlotte (Heather MacRae), an internist, and her lover, Cordelia (Janet Metz), a kosher caterer — have no trouble fitting right in. When they gather at the ball park to watch "Jewish boys play baseball who cannot play baseball," Whizzer (Stephen Bogardus) turns up, too, ready to reactivate his affair with Marvin.

A jittery neuroticism and flip humor are very much a part of the scene. Mr. Finn's characters have always been riddled with insecurities and complaining comes easily to them. Indeed, Trina (Faith Prince) still can't bring herself to accept Marvin's ways. Marvin has difficulties tolerating Trina's psychiatrist husband. Jason's impending bar mitzvah offers them all a convenient pretext to keep up the bickering, especially since Jason isn't sure he wants a bar mitzvah. As for Marvin and Whizzer, once again they find their passion fanned by a faintly sadistic rivalry that extends, this time, to the racquetball court.

We're all primed for a repeat performance. Then Dr. Charlotte announces after a day at the hospital that "something bad is happening." "Bachelors arrive sick and frightened," she explains, passingly, in song. "They leave weeks later unenlightened."

Your stomach sinks. Whizzer starts stumbling on the racquetball court and it sinks a little more. We have nine years on Mr. Finn's characters — nine long years of dread and anger that leave little doubt about what is go-

Carol Rosegg-Martha Swope Associates/"Falsettoland"

Stephen Bogardus and Michael Rupert—a faintly sadistic rivalry

ing on. The characters may try to pretend that "there's nothing to fear." We know better, and we're braced for a downhill ride. Miraculously, "Falsettoland" follows another trajectory entirely. By weaving together Whizzer's progressive decline and Jason's on-again, off-again bar mitzvah, Mr. Finn manages to surprise us with the inevitable. The ending is yours to discover. Let me assure you only that it is an exultant affirmation of life, even when life is callously welshing on its promises.

Whether or not "Falsettoland" is rooted in biography, I cannot say. It certainly appears to derive its authenticity from lived, not imagined experience. You get the distinct impression that Mr. Finn, the director and co-author of the book James Lapine and a superlative cast are not merely creating a musical. They are honoring a trust that has called forth the very best in all of them. In the past, something seemed to be holding Mr. Finn's abundant gifts in check. Just when you most wanted his numbers to expand and assert their full lyric potential, they tended to beat a retreat. Here, the music soars, as if it had been liberated from any demands to be clever or arty and were desirous only of rising to a worthy occasion.

■

"What More Can I Say?" which Mr. Rupert voices with hushed reverence to the slumbering body at his side, is a love song of simple, plaintive beauty, while "You Gotta Die Sometime," a protest in pounding waltz time, permits Mr. Bogardus to fight his way through the fury of one who cannot believe his fate to the courage of one who accepts it. But the most exquisite number is "Unlikely Lovers," in which the two men, joined by Ms. MacRae and Ms. Metz, vow to stand together and, since gallow's humor is not beyond them, to "buy the farm arm in arm."

In "March of the Falsettos," a distraught Marvin repeatedly expressed his ragged desire to have a tight-knit family, all the while his wife, son and lover were slipping away from him. In "Falsettoland," he gets his wish. It's not the traditionally cozy unit he once may have pictured, but it's no less a family for that. In times of upheaval, basic definitions change, too.

Family is whoever chooses to be there — proud and unyielding — when the plague strikes. □

1990 S 30, II:5:1

The Caucasian Chalk Circle

By Bertolt Brecht; translated by Ralph Manheim; directed by Tazewell Thompson; music composed by Fabian V. Obispo Jr.; scenic design by Loy Arcenas; costume design by Paul Tazewell; lighting design by Nancy Schertler; musical direction by George Fulginiti-Shakar; vocal consultant, Ralph Zito; dramaturg, Laurence Maslon; sound by Susan R. White; technical director, David M. Glenn; stage manager, Maxine Krasowski Bertone. Presented by Arena Stage in Washington; Zelda Fichandler, producing director; Douglas C. Wager, associate producing director; Guy Bergquist, associate producer.

The Storyteller .... Jane White
Grusha Vachnadze .... Gail Grate
Azdak.. Lewis J. Stadlen
WITH: Teagle F. Bougere, Tony Carlin, Jarlath Conroy, Ralph Cosham, Terrence Currier, Tana Hicken, Michael W. Howell, Jurian Hughes, Thomas Ikeda, Saul Stein, Henry Strozier, Jeffrey V. Thompson and Halo Wines.

By MEL GUSSOW

Special to The New York Times

WASHINGTON, Sept. 27 — In "The Caucasian Chalk Circle," Bertolt Brecht dramatized the purest of heroic acts, as a servant, Grusha, sacrifices her own safety to preserve the life of an abandoned child. The play is one of Brecht's most emotionally engaging works, a description not normally associated with this intellectual playwright. Tazewell Thompson's imaginative production opened the 40th season at the Arena Stage here last night, the final year that the Arena will be headed by its founding director, Zelda Fichandler.

In the debate about property, ownership and the meaning of parenthood, it is the individual who is triumphant, the state that is infinitely fallible. Because this is Brecht, Grusha's journey to a happy ending is seasoned with cynicism. All politicians are venal, revolution is followed by more revolution and the most judicious man in the country is a buffoon. Enter Azdak, zestfully portrayed by Lewis J. Stadlen.

Though Azdak does not appear until the play is more than half-over, he is a full comic creation and immediately assumes control of all the

Lewis J. Stadlen, left, and Richard Charles Lowe

Arena Stage

events of the evening. He is the local drunk who has been conscripted to play the role of judge (and jury). Even as he opens his hands to solicit bribes, he is unswervable in bending the law — and in using low comedy — in pursuit of a higher justice.

Events leading up to his Solomonic decision about Grusha's foundling are a mirthful mockery of courtroom procedure, made doubly amusing by Mr. Stadlen's shenanigans. The actor has not had such apparent fun with a role since he played Pangloss in the musical "Candide." Azdak is an equally wily figure.

The last time that the Arena did "The Caucasian Chalk Circle" (in 1977), Robert Prosky was a Falstaffian Azdak. Physically, Mr. Stadlen is the opposite. He is ferretlike as he eats away at the tenets of the legal system. But he shares with his predecessor an Azdakian impudence. He is fearless, even though the courtroom is shrouded by the hanging bodies of all his less prudent predecessors. Mr. Stadlen is, as Brecht intended, a wise man who consciously plays the fool.

Grusha is gullible but no fool. As touchingly played by Gail Grate, she has a willful determination. Like Little Eva crossing the ice, a character to whom Grusha bears some resemblance, she exudes a single-minded sense of purpose. In her care is a princely infant, deserted by his monstrous mother. Facing impossible obstacles, Grusha flees across what appears to be half of China, never losing her footing or the audience's sympathy.

As the soldier who loves her, Tony Carlin underplays the formality of his character's dialogue so that it seems to derive from reserve rather than from pretension. He and Ms. Grate are an appealing couple, and in common with the other principals they are singers as well as actors.

Using Ralph Manheim's translation and a new score by Fabian V. Obispo Jr., Mr. Thompson stresses the folkloric nature of the piece, a Chinese legend reinterpreted to make a modern political statement. Spread over the Arena's wide stage, the tale unfolds with a storybook simplicity.

For clarity, narration in words and song is supplied by a storyteller. In the role that was to be played by Ethyl Eichelberger, Jane White adds a distinctive silky touch, her voice blending well with her songs. Mr. Obispo's tingling music moves the play one step closer to becoming the Brecht-Weill musical Weill did not write.

On one level, the play is a spectacle and, helped by Loy Arcenas's subtle scenery and Paul Tazewell's cos-

tumes, Mr. Thompson artfully suggests panoply. A narrow bridge across a chasm is represented by a simple shadow and, as instructed by Brecht, the villains are masked.

In a program insert, it is announced that the prologue, in which Brecht framed the play within a play, was cut during rehearsals. The director's original plan was to update the prologue to comment on events in Eastern Europe. Though Brechtians may shudder at the excision, the core of the work remains firmly in place.

In revival, "The Caucasian Chalk Circle" reveals its durability and its air of prophecy. There is something heartening about seeing it when previously suppressed nations are espousing principles of democratic reform. Just as the child belongs to the woman who mothers it, the valley belongs "to those who water it," not to those who claim it as a birthright or as a result of political conquest.

1990 O 1, C14:1

Richard III

By William Shakespeare; directed by Michael Kahn; set, Derek McLane; costumes, Merrily Murray-Walsh; lighting, Howell Binkley; presented by the Shakespeare Theater at the Folger, Mr. Kahn, artistic director; Mary Ann de Barbieri, managing director, in association with the University of South Carolina. At Washington.

King Edward IV................................ Floyd King
George, Duke of Clarence.........Edward Gero
Richard, Duke of Gloucester.......Stacy Keach
Duchess of York .... Rebecca Thompson
Queen Margaret................. Rosemary Murphy
Lady Ann.....................................Lynnda Ferguson
Queen Elizabeth......Franchelle Stewart Dorn
Lord Grey and Sir James Blunt
                              Gregory L. Williams
Lord Hastings.............................K. Lype O'Dell
Duke of Buckingham.... Ted van Griethuysen
Lord Stanley................................. Emery Battis
Sir William Catesby.................Michael Gaston
Sir Richard Ratcliffe.....A. Benard Cummings

By MEL GUSSOW

Special to The New York Times

WASHINGTON, Sept. 27 — Stacy Keach leaps into the role of "Richard III" with diabolical delight and the gleefulness of an actor who knows he has a captive audience. A smile turns into a sneer as he begins his exploration at the Shakespeare Theater at the Folger in Washington.

Mr. Keach's Richard seems to stage manage the action as well as his own performance, and his confidence is such that one fully expects him to give himself a good review. Moving quickly from the winter of his

discontent to his seduction of Lady Anne, he taunts her into submission.

Dressed in black, wearing a single glove in the manner of Michael Jackson, he is more jackal than bottled spider, and he cannot resist that extra wink of self-approval, cueing the audience into every step of his treachery. The flamboyance of his performance is in refreshing contrast to Denzel Washington's recent, undemonstrative "Richard" for the New York Shakespeare Festival.

The Folger "Richard" reminds us that earlier in his career Mr. Keach delivered a probing "Hamlet" and "Peer Gynt" for the New York Shakespeare Festival. His movie and television work has not lessened his stage authority. He has the voice and articulation for classics.

It would, in fact, be easy to overpraise his "Richard." But for all of his playful malice, he is not fearsome. He is almost too entertaining. Nor does he approach the role with a fully sustained concept, as was the case with Antony Sher (for the Royal Shakespeare Company) or Ian McKellen (in his recent fascistic version at London's National Theater). One feels that Mr. Keach can play Richard any which way he chooses, and that this time he has chosen to play it more for the fun of its parts than for the whole.

Those scenes that especially engage his interest, like Richard's dismissal of Buckingham, generate enthusiasm. Others of more courtly complexity are brushed by. To keep the performance brisk, Michael Kahn, as director, has pared the text to under three hours of playing time. Neither Mr. Keach's performance nor the production builds to Richard's tragic declamation on Bosworth Field. A stronger sense of self-discipline and a tighter directorial hand from Mr. Kahn might have led the actor further into the depths of this demonic role.

Still, this is a performance that fills the small Folger stage with theatricality, and it is encouraging that an actor of Mr. Keach's ability would choose to return to his classical roots and work with a regional company. There are, in passing, insightful personalized touches. Mr. Keach wears a metal brace on one leg, but, buoyed by his own successful climb to the throne, he removes it and decides to march upright without encumbrance. But, taking a step, he feels a pain shoot through his body. Within minutes he has unobtrusively replaced his support. This Richard needs his crutch.

When Mr. Keach is offstage, there is a serious sag in the proceedings. He is very nearly the entire show. Unwisely, Mr. Kahn prefaces the play with a scene-setting prologue that succeeds in delaying Richard's entrance. Among the women who are allied against him only Franchelle Stewart Dorn, as Queen Elizabeth, has the steeliness for hand-to-hand combat. Rosemary Murphy and Rebecca Thompson as mad Margaret and Richard's mother are simply shrewish and Lynnda Ferguson is out of her depth as Lady Anne.

The usually reliable Ted van Griethuysen overplays Buckingham's oiliness and others in smaller roles seem uneasy, as if surprised to find themselves on stage in a costume drama. The souffle-like hats many of them wear are a particular distraction. Edward Gero is a resilient Clarence and there is also commendable support from K. Lype O'Dell and Emery Battis (as old Stanley).

Derek McLane's cage-and-crate set design makes the court seem more like a prison, which is appropriate for some of the scenes. After all, Richard has cornered the other characters; he is their keeper. Because of

Joan Marcus/The Shakespeare Theater

Stacy Keach in the title role of "Richard III" at the Shakespeare Theater at the Folger.

their disarray, he can easily assert himself at their expense.

There was no question that Mr. Keach pleased theatergoers with his histrionics at a recent student matinee. If he were a little less pleasing, the performance might be more challenging, to this estimable actor as well as to the audience.

1990 O 2, C12:3

The Iceman Cometh

By Eugene O'Neill; directed by Robert Falls; set by John Conklin; costumes, Merrily Murray-Walsh; lighting, James F. Ingalls; sound, Rob Milburn; dramaturg, Tom Creamer; production stage manager, Lois Griffing; stage manager, Kimberly Osgood. The Goodman Theater of the Art Institute of Chicago presents a Chicago Theater Group, Inc. production, Mr. Falls, artistic director; Roche Schulfer, producing director. At Chicago.

Harry Hope.................................. Jerome Kilty
Ed Mosher .... Bill Visteen
Rocky Pioggi.................................Ron Dean
Chuck Morello.........................Peter Siragusa
Piet Wetjoen...........................Bruce M. Fischer
Cecil Lewis .... Derek Murcott
James Cameron.....................Larry McCauley
Joe Mott................................. Ernest Perry Jr.
Larry Slade .... James Cromwell
Hugo Kalmar .... Dennis Kennedy
Willie Oban ....Denis O'Hare
Don Parritt.................................Jim True
Pearl.......................................Rengin Altay
Margie......................................Hope Davis
Cora ....Kate Buddeke
Theodore Hickman (Hickey)
                              Brian Dennehy
Moran..Dev Kennedy
Lieb.. Tom Webb

By FRANK RICH

Special to The New York Times

CHICAGO, Sept. 29 — Brian Dennehy, most visible these days on film as Harrison Ford's treacherous boss in "Presumed Innocent," is one of those indelible character actors who could very profitably spend the rest of his career in the movies playing crusty Irish pols and cops. But not unlike his most gifted predecessors in the same Hollywood niche, Charles Durning and the late Kenneth McMillan, Mr. Dennehy cannot keep away from the stage. A few seasons back he earned acclaim at the Goodman Theater here for his title performance in Brecht's "Galileo." Later he proved an exceptionally sensitive Lopakhin in the Peter Brook "Cherry Orchard" that visited Brooklyn. Now Mr. Dennehy has returned to the Goodman in a Eugene O'Neill role that is made for him — Hickey, in "The Iceman Cometh" — and his shattering turn leaves one hungry to see his Falstaff, his Macbeth and, when the time is ripe, his Lear and his James Tyrone.

•

Mr. Dennehy is a big bear of a man, but sometimes more of a teddy bear than a grizzly. There's a buried, dainty tenderness in his burly frame as well as a hint of festering violence. As Hickey, a hardware salesman who comes to Harry Hope's end-of-the-line gin mill and flophouse on a deranged evangelical mission, the actor shows off a spectrum of passions that runs from love to hate, from a drummer's forced optimism to a condemned man's sweaty vertigo. His Hickey seems to encapsulate all the salesmen in American theatrical literature, from Meredith Willson's ebullient Harold Hill to Arthur Miller's weary Willy Loman. At the same time, O'Neill's four-and-a-half-hour play, written in 1939 and first presented on Broadway in 1946, bridges the illusion-stripping theatrics of early moderns like Ibsen and Strindberg and the bleak, godless terrain of post-war Beckett dramas that were still to come.

In "The Iceman Cometh," Hickey is the man who, for guilty reasons of his own, elects to show the soused bums of Hope's sad establishment that there is no hope for the long-held pipe dreams that allow them to fantasize about someday redeeming their misbegotten lives. When Mr. Dennehy, in chalk-stripe suit and vest, first enters the dank saloon, he practices a soft sell, working the room with the wide, well-practiced grin and extravagant handclasps of a gregarious party hack. (He's big enough to embrace three giggling prostitutes at once.) Hickey assures his old drinking cronies that his only ambition now is to offer them the peace and salvation that comes from shaking off the haze of booze and the lies of self-delusion to face one's true self in the mirror. But for all his warm effusions, there is, as one skeptical observer puts it, "the touch of death" about this would-be angel of mercy. Mr. Dennehy's curtain line in Act I — "All I want is to see you happy" — is delivered in an exhausted, broken cadence, with a quizzical half-smile that curls into a demonic grin just as the lights go down.

•

The meaning of that grin and the truly Herculean test in this role arrive much later, in the Act IV soliloquy that made a star of Jason Robards in the landmark José Quintero "Iceman Cometh" revival of 1956. Neither fighting the Robards characterization nor imitating it, Mr. Dennehy gives his own riveting account of the marathon speech in which Hickey's sales pitch for personal salvation becomes intertwined with cruel autobiography and, finally, a confession of murder. The actor's mood swings are shocking. As Hickey describes how his wife, Evelyn, loved him, and his self-revulsion at betraying that love with whoring and drinking, Mr. Dennehy's voice becomes plaintive, his expression almost baby-faced; he recalls his marital bond facing forward from a center-stage seat, hat in hand, with a tender intimacy that brings him and the audience near tears. In the circumspect account of Evelyn's murder that follows, he stands and raises his voice just slightly, to acknowledge Hickey's light-headed feelings of relief in the immediate aftermath of the crime.

But dark laughter quickly dissolves into sheer blackness. Mr. Dennehy bellows to the rafters and smashes a chair into the floor when he reaches the moment of truth in which Hickey suddenly refers to the dead Evelyn as a "damned bitch." The full power of the actor's physique and voice, summoned at last after four hours of restraint, reveal a killer — and symbolically re-enact a killing — on the spot where only moments earlier had stood a sympathetic O'Neill braggart with a touch of the poet.

•

By that point the surrounding production, directed by Robert Falls, is ready to meet Mr. Dennehy's Hickey in that O'Neill abyss from which the only deliverance is death. Earlier, especially in the hour or so of ham-fisted exposition that precedes the star's first entrance, this "Iceman Cometh" tries the patience somewhat. The younger derelicts in Hope's living morgue, the father-obsessed Harvard Law alumnus Willie Oban and the informer Don Parritt, are given stock renderings here, as are most of the elder inmates (with Larry McCauley's somnambulent Jimmy Tomorrow being a notable exception). In the final act, however, Mr. Falls and his two best supporting players, Jerome Kilty as the pickled Hope and James Cromwell as the terminally detached and lapsed anarchist Larry Slade, join with the set designer John Conklin and the lighting designer James F. Ingalls to give this staging its own corrosive identity.

The design plays a crucial role, with Mr. Conklin varying the standard set in each act to help push "The Iceman Cometh" out of kitchen-sink realism and into the timeless, trance-like realm it must finally inhabit. The third act, in which the barflies don their Sunday best in a doomed effort to return to the outside world, unfolds in a spooky, tilted barroom whose gates open into a blank Magritte sky. For Act IV, the full depth of the large stage is revealed for the first time, filled with gloomy row upon row of tables. The isolated patrons, no longer able to find the kick in their booze, stare straight ahead like mannequins and, in a surrealistic touch, are stripped of some clothes along with all their illusions.

When Hickey's final departure allows the bar's denizens to emerge from that stupor and retrieve their sustaining pipe dreams once more, they return to demented life by slamming all the tables together and drinking, stomping, singing and dancing their way back to oblivion. The stage picture could be from Daumier, and the din accompanying it builds to such an obscene crescendo that not even the sound and sight of a suicide leap can upstage the ruckus. Mr. Falls can only extinguish the grotesque spectacle with an abrupt blackout that, like Mr. Dennehy's performance, puts the kick into a ferocious American classic that has lost none of its power to send one shaking into the middle of the night.

1990 O 3, C13:4

The Goodman Theater

Brian Dennehy and Kate Buddeke in "The Iceman Cometh" at the Goodman Theater in Chicago.

Carol Lawrence and Larry Kert Together . . . Again!

Direction and staging by Dennis Grimaldi; costumes courtesy of Adolfo and Bob Mackie; arrangements by Brian Lasser; orchestrations by Tom Kochen. Piano, Mark Hummel; bass, Mark Minkler; drums, James Saparito. Presented by the B. E. Rock Corporation at Rainbow and Stars, 30 Rockefeller Plaza.

By MEL GUSSOW

Remember the photograph on the cover of the original cast album of "West Side Story?" With her arms raised, a smiling Carol Lawrence leads an equally happy Larry Kert through the streets of Manhattan. It is a youthful portrait exemplifying one aspect of the musical — an exhilarating merging of drama, music and dance. In their show at Rainbow and Stars, the two actors mime their pose on that photograph with surprising verisimilitude. The audience laughs and then sits back to enjoy this well-deserved reunion of the original Tony and Maria.

It has been 33 years since "West Side Story" opened at the Winter Garden Theater and entered Broadway history, establishing the careers of its creators and beginning the careers of its two stars. After that, Mr. Kert and Ms. Lawrence went their individual ways. Despite offers, they have not appeared together in another musical until now.

•

The show, which runs through Oct. 13, promises nostalgia and delivers it. But there is soon something else in the air, an enthusiasm for a kind of musical theater that unfortunately has gone out of fashion. That enthusiasm is not limited to "West Side Story." The two sing an hour of numbers from a selection of Broadway's popular songwriters, including Rodgers and Hart, Lerner and Loewe and Burton Lane.

Home base is Stephen Sondheim. Mr. Kert gives an impassioned rendition of "Being Alive," which he sang in "Company," and Ms. Lawrence gives a cloak-and-dagger stealth to the composer's "Sooner or Later." With the Kander and Ebb "Broadway My Street," they salute their profession and the indomitability of performers who can play eight shows a week.

The two exchange memories of "West Side" and other stories, of opportunities accepted and roles not taken. All of this is convivial, although Ms. Lawrence has a touch of coyness, especially as she sings "I'm the Greatest Star" from "Funny Girl," which she calls her favorite show other than you know what. There are also a few too many references to the couple's advancing

Jessica Willer
Carol Lawrence and Larry Kert in their show at Rainbow and Stars.

years, as if they are about to move to a home for retired actors. Both performers are in excellent voice and are especially harmonious in a brief trilogy of songs about marriage that ends with Richard Maltby Jr. and David Shire's "Could We Have Loved Like That."

Eventually they respond to audience anticipation and bring back "West Side Story," offering a medley with a twist. They sing the songs they never got to sing, the music they heard while sitting in their dressing rooms. Mr. Kert begins with an antic chorus of "I Feel Pretty," and together they do a rousing version of "America." One almost expects Chita Rivera to dance on stage and assert her proprietary rights and follow up with "Tonight." The notion is a clever one. Perhaps it is time for Julie Andrews to do a show in which she sings "On the Street Where You Live" and "I've Grown Accustomed to Her Face."

As it should be, the high point in the Kert-Lawrence cabaret show is a re-

prise of their signature numbers from "West Side Story." When an audience hears those imperishable Leonard Bernstein-Stephen Sondheim songs, sung by those who first brought them to stage life, three decades become a blink in time.

1990 O 4, C21:1

Stand-Up Tragedy

By Bill Cain; directed by Ron Link; set design by Yael Pardess; costume design by Carol Brolaski; lighting design by Michael Gilliam; sound design by Jon Gottlieb; original music by Craig Sibley; rap choreography by Charles Randolph-Wright. The Center Theater Group/Mark Taper Forum and Hartford Stage Company Production, presented by Charles B. Moss Jr., Brent Peek and Donald Taffner. At the Criterion Center Stage Right, 45th Street and Broadway.

Marco Ruiz	Anthony Barrile
Lee Cortez	Marcus Chong
Father Ed Larkin	Charles Cioffi
Tom Griffin	Jack Coleman
Mitchell James	John C. Cooke
Freddy	Robert Barry Fleming
Burke Kendall	Dan Gerrity
Carlos Cruz	Darrin DeWitt Henson
Henry Rodriguez	Ray Oriel

By FRANK RICH

Act I of "Stand-Up Tragedy," the new play by Bill Cain at the Criterion Center, is labeled "First Semester" in the Playbill. Act II is "Second Semester." Make no mistake about it: The audience is in school, and there's no use praying for early dismissal.

The school in question is a small Roman Catholic institution for Hispanic boys on the present-day Lower East Side. The lesson Mr. Cain wishes to impart is sadly perennial: the impotence of inner-city schools in their front-line battle to rescue young lives from the ravages of poverty, absent and abusive parents and drugs. Who would doubt that the crisis in urban education is the most pressing American tragedy? That makes it all the more painful to report that "Stand-Up Tragedy" — whether viewed as a serious effort to illuminate its issues or merely as pop entertainment with a conscience — is so often a farce.

The author, who himself taught at a school like the one in his play, is

A school portrait, presumably drawn from life.

obviously sincere in his frustration. The story he tells, however familiar from fiction, is presumably drawn from first-hand experience: The only faculty member hip enough to wear Nikes, a Georgetown-educated yuppie named Tom Griffin (Jack Coleman), sets out to salvage an unexpectedly gifted student, Lee Cortez (Marcus Chong), who might otherwise be devoured by his violent family or lost in the housing-project maze or the educational morass. Yet Mr. Cain never takes this premise or its characters any further than the archetypal tableaux that have been served up with far more vigor in works as various as "Blackboard Jungle," "Up the Down Staircase," "To Sir With Love," "Open Admissions" and even "Room 222."

At a time when authors like Diane Ravitch and Samuel G. Freedman, among others, are prominently examining the same classrooms seen in this play, seeking to learn from their small victories and big defeats, Mr. Cain merely restates the obvious, parading the familiar symptoms of a social calamity before the audience without offering any diagnosis or, at the very least, fresh observations. Rather than risk offending anyone by raising any controversial questions about the church's exact educational role in a city riddled by AIDS and racism, he settles instead for the middlebrow theater's sentimental boilerplate of moral concern, as typified by a monologue in which the school's presiding priest (Charles Cioffi) argues his students' need for "a better God." (Not for nothing does this play share an originating theater, the Mark Taper Forum in Los Angeles, with "Children of a Lesser God.") Finally Mr. Cain just throws up his hands in despair, disposing of as many characters as possible in a denouement that, for all its tragic pretensions, proves laughably melodramatic.

Were it not for the stylization of the writing and Ron Link's production, "Stand-Up Tragedy" would merely be another innocuously topical television movie that had somehow strayed onto a Broadway stage. But the gimmickry of the script, which attempts to appropriate the hard-edged styles of both stand-up comedy and rap music, and the noisy busyness of the staging, in which synthetic rap numbers and gruntingly gymnastic choral recitations are punctuated by the incessant banging of lockers and ringing of school bells, do succeed in insinuating "Stand-Up Tragedy" into a theatergoer's mind — if not as an intellectual or emotional stimulant, then as the relentless source of a throbbing headache.

"Stand-Up Tragedy" lowers the volume of its assault only when some of its actors, most notably Mr. Cioffi, wait for laughter at the end of a punch line. Unfortunately, Mr. Cain just isn't a witty enough writer to score with the teachers-lounge wisecracks he uses to avoid an actual dramatization of what happens in his play's school. The gags, like the frequently inaudible and always white-bread rap lyrics, are filler.

•

An even more irritating jokeyness is injected by the arbitrary assignment of multiple roles to the principal actors. Mr. Chong, a promising performer in need of editing and direction, is asked to interrupt and compromise his portrayal of the sensitive Lee by repeatedly impersonating Lee's mother in a manner more appropriate to a "Forbidden Broadway" spoof of Rita Moreno. Mr. Coleman, an ingratiating figure as the earnest teacher, is in turn asked to adopt an embarrassingly ersatz Hispanic accent to impersonate Lee's brother — even as Mr. Chong sometimes plays Lee's brother, too, in tandem. This is theatricality, I guess, but other than providing acting exercises for an enthusiastic young cast, what goal does it serve?

A cynic might assume that the real point of the awkward and confusing piggybacking of roles is to save money on actors, but if so, the economies have not extended to the employment of two black performers who, though costumed as students and always used in the rap routines, remain patronizingly undifferentiated as characters throughout. It's rather bizarre

Jay Thompson/Criterion Center Stage Right
Marcus Chong.

to find a contemporary slice-of-life high school drama emulating a Mickey Rooney-Judy Garland vehicle of yesteryear by padding the class with faceless chorus boys. But once they and other members of the all-male cast gratuitously start stripping to the waist late in Act II, one can at least relax in the happy knowledge that the school in "Stand-Up Tragedy" is finally adjourning for summer camp.

1990 O 5, C3:1

World Without End

Written and performed by Holly Hughes; directed by Kate Stafford; original music by Sharon Jane Smith (with Vincent Girot and B. Bronson); original lighting design by Lori E. Seid. Presented by Performance Space 122, 150 First Avenue, at Ninth Street.

By STEPHEN HOLDEN

Late in her solo performance piece, "World Without End," Holly Hughes reimagines the story of Adam and Eve as a semiautobiographical, hard-boiled B-movie set in the bohemian environs of the Lower East Side. As the primal couple make love, Ms. Hughes wonders aloud to her partner: "Buddy, do you have any idea who I am? I am the premier lesbian performance artist from Michigan."

At once funny and feisty, self-affirming and self-mocking, the scene exemplifies Ms. Hughes's iconoclastic brand of feminist art. In subverting sexual and social stereotypes, she rejects the more solemn, mystical tone of much feminist literature to present a cheerful, rough-and-tumble portrait of unloosed female sexuality. Introducing her version of Adam and Eve, she goes out of her way to address the word "whore" and an anti-lesbian epithet with a double-edged good humor. Somewhat ironically, she suggests that they be seen as positive labels for women who are good at sex.

The Adam and Eve story is only one strand of "World Without End," which plays irregularly through Oct. 28 at P.S. 122 (150 First Avenue, at Ninth Street). A 90-minute monologue whose explicit content caused Ms. Hughes to be denied a grant by the National Endowment for the Arts, the work slaps together surrealistic autobiography, feminist polemics and comic asides in a very helter-skelter manner. Though messy in its construction and too long by at least 20 minutes, the piece crackles with verbal energy and a disarming humor. And Ms. Hughes, demurely clad in a party dress and black pumps, performs it with a mischievous comic glint in her eye.

•

The monologue, directed by Kate Stafford, opens with Ms. Hughes sitting mostly out of sight of the audience behind an armchair under a surrealistic map of the world. Over the course of the evening, she emerges from hiding to talk about growing up in Michigan and about her mother, who died of emphysema. As the tone becomes progressively less formal, Ms. Hughes's attitude toward the audience turns increasingly confrontational, though she is never overtly hostile.

The show's most memorable writing deals with the death of her mother, who becomes a powerful, mystical symbol of female sexual autonomy. The portrait that emerges, told in a mixture of surreal poetry and slangy conversation, is of an eccentric, larger-than-life woman whose half-hidden inner life contrasted sharply with the drab middle-class world of Saginaw that Ms. Hughes describes in cuttingly sarcastic detail.

The evening's most recurrent image is of an apple. At the beginning of the piece, Apple Mountain is mentioned as the name of a Michigan landfill. Later, it becomes Eve's apple of temptation, and by the end it is a symbol of an indomitable erotic spirit that Ms. Hughes has accepted as a proud inheritance.

1990 O 6, 11:3

East Texas

Written by Jan Buttram; directed by Alex Dmitriev; scenic design, James Morgan; costumes, Holly Hynes; lighting, Mary Jo Dondlinger; sound, David Oberon; technical director, Matt Goldin; production stage manager, Mary Ellen Allison. Presented by the York Theater Company, Janet Hayes Walker, producing director; Molly Pickering Grose, managing director. At the Church of the Heavenly Rest, 2 East 90th Street.

Naomi Ludlam .... Venida Evans
Billy Swagger .... Peter Brouwer
Joan Ann Buford Percy .... Susanne Marley
Lucy Buford .... Dorothy Lancaster
Sheriff Sly Rubins .... Page Johnson

By WILBORN HAMPTON

One of the most instructive lectures that a popular English professor at the University of Texas used to give taught that literature knew no geography. "People in Paris, Texas," the lesson went, "experience the same joys and sorrows, cherish the same hopes and confront the same fears as people in Paris, France." Obviously the prof never dreamed of "East Texas," a new play by Jan

Buttram at the York Theater Company that brings a new depth of meaning to banality.

It is hard to imagine that a play in which a paroled convict shoots his stepmother, breaks into a former girlfriend's house, and persuades her to give him money and even run away with him could be so devoid of any hint of drama or humor.

•

Despite all the commotion that takes place in Joan Ann Buford Percy's kitchen one evening and morning somewhere in East Texas, not far, one presumes, from Paris, the characters are simply tiresome. The major event in the entire first act, apart from someone running over a dog in the driveway, is built around an incident in which Joan Ann insulted Sissy Butz at the Baptist Church choir practice. Most of the two scenes is given to debating whether Joan Ann should call Sissy to apologize.

Although Billy Swagger, a local ne'er-do-well on whom Joan Ann had a crush in junior high school, sneaks into the kitchen with a hunting rifle early on, he quickly hides in a pantry and never really emerges until the second act (some man-in-the-closet-with-a-gun gags notwithstanding). The only real question about Billy by the time the intermission finally comes is why he hasn't shot himself after listening to Joan Ann and her mother talk for three-quarters of an hour.

•

The playwright has tried to make the characters interesting by giving them some quirky habits. Joan Ann is partial to milk-and-vodka cocktails, for example, and is sculpturing a papier-mâché bust of her husband, Connally, who has just gone to prison himself for fraud.

The more complicated Ms. Buttram's plot becomes, the more it unravels. Billy, one first gathers, has been paroled from the state prison in Huntsville, while Joan Ann's husband is serving his time on a low-security work farm where he even has a telephone and a cooler in his room. Yet in the second act, much of the plot turns on the fact that Billy had been occupying a cell adjoining that of Joan Ann's husband. By this time, however, such inconsistencies are of little consequence.

Neither Alex Dmitriev's direction nor the cast makes any appreciable contribution to salvaging "East Texas," although Peter Brouwer at least brings some badly needed energy onstage in the second act as Billy. There is also an old piece of valid playwriting advice that anytime you bring a gun onstage, it has to go off sometime. That's the least of Ms. Buttram's problems, but a little gunfire would at least have livened things up a bit.

1990 O 7, 70:4

SUNDAY VIEW/David Richards

Three Faces of Richard III
In a One-Man Display of Evil

I N THE COURSE OF HIS ROLLICKING performance in "Richard III," Stacy Keach comes close to accounting for that character's popularity with a single brazen gesture. For the saturnine creature is decidedly popular right now.

Mr. Keach happens to be performing the title role in Shakespeare's history at the Shakespeare Theater at the Folger in Washington. But this summer, if you'd dropped by the Delacorte Theater in Central Park, you'd have found Denzel Washington, eliciting squeals of excitement from young women in the audience, who were as much drawn to the

---

Three actors – Stacy Keach, Ian McKellen and Denzel Washington – take on Shakespeare's chief villain.

---

handsome actor as they were taken aback by the diabolical actions required of him. (Pretty little pickle, that.)

Meanwhile, across the Atlantic, Ian McKellen is endowing Richard with icy scorn in a stunning production which the National Theater in London has recently taken on a world tour. So far, North America is not on the itinerary, but if you're in Cairo in December . . .

Stacy Keach as Richard

But back to Mr. Keach, who has opted to give us a monstrously misshapen Richard and, in fact, could probably step into the role of Quasimodo without so much as a change of makeup. The character, of course, has never pretended to grace. He's scarcely been on stage a minute — and in Mr. Keach's case, had time to scramble down from a metal catwalk, winking at spectators as he goes — than he has informed us that he is "rudely stamped" and "cheated of feature." Since Nature has so ill-equipped him for fair deeds, his reasoning goes, it is only natural that he should distinguish himself in foul exploits.

Mr. Keach and his equally vigorous director, Michael Kahn, are not content to leave it at that, though. They've expanded the opening monologue to include some of Richard's lines from "Henry VI, Part 3." This allows Mr. Keach to tick off the deformities one by one — the arm "like a wither'd shrub," the "envious mountain on my back," the "legs of an unequal size." As if that were not enough, he is, he further boasts, disproportioned "in *every* part" — the lascivious leer leaving little doubt about just what part he really means.

Then comes that gesture I mentioned. Having proudly exhibited himself as the unappetizing lump that he is, Mr. Keach throws his arms wide — like a vaudevillian who's successfully executed a cheap trick — smiles a broad smile and lets out a triumphant hiss, as if to say "Tah-dah!" Yes, Richard is a tyrant in the making. But he's also an unapologetic showman, raring to make a spectacle of himself. The manic glint in Mr. Keach's eyes and the brief eruption of razzle-dazzle are rife with the promise of bloody entertainments to come. Whatever we may think of the monarch's morals, we are bound to appreciate him for his unabashed theatricality.

Glee infuses every warped and crooked inch of Mr. Keach's performance. Let him successfully woo Lady Anne — over the corpse of her father-in-law, no less — and he explodes in uncontrollable laughter. Amazed that she could find him "a marv'lous proper man," he promptly covers himself with congratulatory kisses. Hatching his lethal plots, he adopts a tone that suggests they are no more than clever pranks, and there's enough leftover boyishness in his face so that he almost gets away with it.

When the young Prince of Wales, his rival for the throne, arrives in London, Richard is there to welcome him with a colorful gift. Up pops a jack-in-the-box to the Prince's manifest disinterest. Even though Richard intends to have the boy murdered, he is genuinely crestfallen that the offering has fallen flat. How can anyone not like a good surprise, he seems to be wondering? (What, after all, are the reversals and betrayals he's been busy fomenting, if not surprises raised to a deadly power?)

Moments later, the Prince and his brother are packed off to the Tower of London, and the gates in Derek McLane's steel and wire set clang shut. Mr. Keach can't contain himself: he waves bye-bye, as he would to toddlers on their way to school, and then permits himself a delicious chortle. If he weren't promoting so much bloodshed, wreaking so much misery, he would make an adorable troll, perched on the right garden wall.

Only in the end does the revelry drain out of him. The laughing mouth drops open dully, the eyes take on a fishlike glaze and you're left with a hollow man, reeling. Mr. Keach, quite splendid at the devious merriment, makes a grand transformation to the numbness of the lurching dead. It's a wild performance, encouraged at every bend, I dare say, by Mr. Kahn, who wields buckets of blood and a severed head with trick-or-treat flair. For some, it may smack too much of Grand Guignol, but there's no contesting that director and actor are keeping the stage of the Folger in a state of zesty turmoil.

Ian McKellen as Richard

Mr. Keach's performance couldn't be further from the austere, patrician approach that Mr. McKellen is taking, yet Mr. McKellen is no less theatrical. The National Theater's production, masterfully conceived by the director Richard Eyre, moves the action forward to modern times and a grim police state, in which standing out is risky business. When he's not deigning to take us into his confidence, Mr. McKellen is doing as much as he can to mel avize the gray, bureaucratic landscape. His gnarled hand is neatly tucked away in a pocket. He would rather no one noticed the limp. And when he slings a greatcoat over his shoulders, the hunch is hardly detectable. As for the odd, cauliflower-shaped growth on his left temple, he disregards it entirely, finding it unworthy of the proud notice that Mr. Keach takes of his imperfections.

Not for Mr. McKellen the peals of crazed delight or the forthright winks of complicity. Where Mr. Keach flashes a mad grin, Mr. McKellen is more likely to let the sides of his mouth curl up ironically. He's a cool intellectual, wrapped in tendrils of blue cigarette smoke. The emphasis is on the inner man who, Mr. McKellen would probably argue, is far more deformed than his outer self. The role is exquisitely spoken, with a clarity that sometimes eludes Mr. Keach. But that only enhances the danger. This Richard relishes words because he knows the damage they can do when they are properly shaded and artfully placed. Mr. McKellen dominates the stage by the sheer force of

> ## If Richard doesn't carry the play, no one else will; you can't count on the plot.

his submerged will. The control is breathtaking.

Denzel Washington As Richard

Mr. Washington, on the other hand, visibly in over his head this summer, didn't make much of a dent in the production that Robin Phillips directed as part of Joseph Papp's continuing Shakespeare marathon. Granted, Mr. Washington's sleek physical presence came in handy for the wooing scene with Lady Anne, whose capitulation to Richard at least gained some credibility on sexual grounds. Stalking the fringes of the action, Mr. Washington projected a certain feral cunning. But he wasn't very effective at the center of things. If Richard is a double-dealer, Mr. Washington was never more than a single-dealer. Still, there were insights to be gleaned. Because the actor failed to fill up the role, you were all the more aware of how big and demanding it is.

If Richard doesn't carry the play, no one else will. You can't count on the plot — a headlong rush to power, really, through the brambles of Lancastrian and Yorkist politics. A vendor, peddling plot summaries for $1 outside the Delacorte, was not merely trying to hype sales when he advised potential customers, "You might just want one before Act II." I have yet to see a production of "Richard III" that didn't leave at least half the audience casting about at intermission for a family tree. No wonder we instinctively turn to the hunchback. He's a rock of infamy in a sea of confusions. No other character begins to impress us as he does. For a play teeming with bodies, we're perilously close to a one-man show.

■

I'm not sure how you go about establishing a semblance of balance. The National Theater gets around the issue somewhat by setting the play in

Joan Marcus/Shakespeare Theater

Theme and variations: Stacy Keach, above, a gleeful tyrant in the making at the Folger in Washington, and Ian McKellen, an icy bureaucrat in a grim police state at the National Theater in London earlier this year—a brutal game of fascination

Alastair Muir/National Theater, London

Martha Swope/"Richard III"

Denzel Washington—projecting a certain feral cunning

a Fascist state in the 1930's. As the designer Bob Crowley sees it, it's a world of endless corridors, vast ceremonial rooms, police stations hung with metal lamps and, way upstage, a door half-cracked to let in a shaft of chilly, white light. In such a society, men *are* insignificant, fodder for a coup or a grilling. The Shakespeare Theater at the Folger has no equivalent conceit in mind and consequently a noticeable gulf separates Mr. Keach from the supporting players. I'm afraid that includes Rosemary Murphy, whose Queen Margaret is flat and lusterless, for all the imprecations she is hurling about. The chief exception is Ted van Griethuysen, who plays Buckingham as a priss secretly in love with Richard (or at least, seriously infatuated by him). The performance benefits from its ambiguous proximity to the villain. But when the character undergoes a change of conscience, he, too, quickly loses his theatrical allure.

■

I know it should operate the other way around. Goodness is supposed to raise a man in our eyes. But in our playhouses, evil generally has a much better time of it. Goodness is what it is — pure, exemplary, open. It has no secret agenda to spring on us. No about-faces. It interests us only when it's under siege, caught in a

compromising position and struggling to stay good.

Evil, for its part, is unpredictable, misleading, seductive. Since role-playing is one of its chief tactics, it takes naturally to the stage. It says yes, when it means no; masks treason with a smirk; and shores up the baldest of lies with the purest of oaths. It is forever luring us down the garden path and, while we're by no means certain a mugging doesn't await us at the end, each time we follow eagerly, our curiosity inflamed.

Tah-dah, indeed.

1990 O 7, II:5:1

Yesterdays

By Reenie Upchurch; directed by Woodie King Jr.; stage manager, Antoinette Tynes. Presented by the National Black Touring Circuit Inc., Mr. King, producer with Art D'Lugoff. At Top of the Gate Cabaret Theater, 160 Bleecker Street.

Billie Holiday .... Reenie Upchurch
Drummer .... Herb Lovelle
Pianist .... Weldon Irvine

By STEPHEN HOLDEN

Among show-business legends who have inspired posthumous stage and film impersonations, Billie Holiday has proved to be one of the most stubbornly inimitable. Perhaps be-

cause her life and her art embodied such extreme contradictions — she was simultaneously regal and coarse, strong and victimized — those who have chosen to portray the singer have usually emphasized only one aspect of a complex personality.

Diana Ross concentrated on Holiday's surface glamour in the film "Lady Sings the Blues." Lonette McKee, in the Off Broadway show "Lady Day at Emerson's Bar and Grill," focused on Holiday's simmering anger. And in "Yesterdays," a new musical revue remembering Lady Day, at the Top of the Village Gate, Reenie Upchurch stresses Holiday's bitter, self-lacerating humor.

"Yesterdays," which was written by Ms. Upchurch and is directed by Woodie King Jr., is set in a New York nightclub in May 1959, two months before the singer's death. Between performances of around a dozen of her best-known numbers, Holiday grows progressively tipsier and more combative as she free-associates autobiographical vignettes and rails at the policemen in the audience who are about to arrest her for drug possession.

The many brutalizing experiences recounted include Holiday's rape at the age of 10, her later enslavement to drugs by a womanizing lover and numerous instances of humiliating racial discrimination. There are also tender moments of remembrance of Bessie Smith, the blues singer who was Holiday's greatest influence, of the tenor saxophonist Lester Young, with whom she felt a mystical kinship, and of her mother.

●

As blood-chilling as some of the vignettes are, the sequencing of the songs and stories is so haphazard that the evening accumulates little dramatic momentum. The attempt to pack an entire biography in between

"Yesterdays"
Reenie Upchurch as Billie Holiday in musical revue "Yesterdays."

numbers seems so awkward and forced that "Yesterdays" often has the feel of two shows, one a jazz concert, the other an evening of storytelling, jammed together.

Dressed in a white gown, with a white gardenia tucked behind one ear, Ms. Upchurch bears some physical resemblance to Holiday. Her act-

ing is very uneven. Although she is able to communicate Holiday's earthy humor, the deeper pathos of Holiday's life is missing.

Vocally, her re-creation of the singer's slippery intonation, guttural accents and stealthy behind-the-beat phrasing is more accurate than that of many Holiday impersonators. Her performances of two Holiday signature ballads — "Don't Explain" and "My Man" — strikingly capture the air of masochistic pride that Holiday brought to songs describing sexual betrayal and physical abuse. In the uptempo numbers, however, her grasp of Holiday's style is tenuous.

1990 O 8, C14:

Endangered Species

Conceived and directed by Martha Clarke created with the Company. Text: "Leaves of Grass" by Walt Whitman, adapted by Robert Coe; sound by Richard Peaslee and Stanley Walden; sets and costumes, Robert Israel; lighting, Paul Gallo; production stage manager, Steven Ehrenberg. Presented by the Brooklyn Academy of Music, Harvey Lichtenstein, president and executive producer, and Music-Theater Group, Lyn Austin, producing director; Diane Wondisford, managing director, in association with Circus Flora, Ivor David Balding, artistic director and producer. At Brooklyn Academy of Music, Majestic Theater, 651 Fulton Street, Brooklyn.

WITH: Michael J. Anderson, Felix Blaska, Alistair Butler, Courtney Earl, Lisa Dalton, David Grausman, Paul Guilfoyle, Valarie Eileen Henry, Judy Kuhn, Peter McRobbie and Frank Raiter.

By FRANK RICH

Flora, a charming half-grown elephant with Dumbo-sized ears, is not the only thing that is elephantine about "Endangered Species," the Martha Clarke theater piece that has opened the Next Wave Festival at the Majestic Theater of the Brooklyn Academy of Music. In this show, a few unobjectionable, ecologically sound old-wave ideas — war is hell, man is cruel, animals are nice — have been inflated past the bursting point by grand scenic effects, a large cast of humans and circus animals, fractionalized quotations from Walt Whitman and, presumably, big bucks. It's almost as if Ms. Clarke, the one-time Pilobolus dancer and the wildly imaginative creator of "The Garden of Earthly Delights" and "Vienna: Lusthaus," has been afflicted by Broadway-itis. "Endangered Species" is Billy Rose's "Jumbo" with pieties instead of peanuts.

●

As in "Miracolo d'Amore" and "The Hunger Artist," the two disappointing Clarke works that preceded it, this production is short on dance and heavy on mimetic interludes of bestiality, sexual and otherwise. The most evocative choreographic movement is provided by the horses, who periodically circle the vast, wood-chip-carpeted stage in a fleet image out of a Seurat circus painting, and by the performers Lisa Dalton and Felix Blaska, who contribute agile acrobatic stunts with or without animal collaborators. The rest of the time, people come and go reciting sound-bite-sized snippets from "Leaves of Grass" that strip down the poetry to simplistic moral-mongering, or sing a capella musical fragments that range from obscure Sondheim to wobbly Pergolesi. Much of the singing is done by the Broadway belter Judy Kuhn, a specialist in playing the walking wounded, who wanders about wearing rags and a hollow-eyed expression that are presumably meant to emblemize the Holocaust.

Even so, history's nightmares have rarely looked so handsome. As designed by Ms. Clarke's brilliant team of Robert Israel (sets and costumes) and Paul Gallo (lighting), "Endangered Species" has a sumptuous, at times candlelit elegance that not even such thunderous recorded sound effects as a Nazi rally and the slaughter of screaming children can blot. The stage is backed by an exquisitely cloudy sky that thickens in direct proportion to the heaviness of the message. A towering pair of white doors stands center stage, a classical visual element that turns surrealistic when the doors blow open to reveal Flora in a fetching if enigmatic pose. It says much about "Endangered Species" that from the show's opening moments to the curtain call, it is the elephant that earns the audience's raptest attention and warmest applause.

The human content, meanwhile, evaporates. In these prettified circumstances, the depictions of a white man beating a black man, or of a man roughing up a woman, look sanitized. "Endangered Species" seems to be purveying its tame images of racial and sexual violence to advertise its own self-importance rather than to add to the audience's knowledge or sense of urgency about these horrors. When, in a quasi-finale, the cast members run into a wall in a repeated, Robert Wilson-like frenzy paralleling the recorded sounds of a massacre — an aural apocalypse that seems to culminate in the dropping of a bomb, no less — one is more inclined to admire the stylized athleticism of the performers than to contemplate Dachau, Gettysburg or Hiroshima. Almost every aspect of the piece is too blandly archetypal to wound, with Ms. Kuhn's wandering victim being matched in leaden sym-

bolism by a curiously speechless black couple dressed like slaves out of "Roots."

Given that "Vienna: Lusthaus," Ms. Clarke's masterwork about the cataclysmic fin-de-siècle crossroads of the 20th century, also dealt with sex, death, oppression and genocide, and with some of the same theatrical techniques, the decline in esthetic achievement is all the more pronounced. How does one account for it? Perhaps the ever-accelerating, fever-dream anxiety of "Vienna" was enhanced by the unifying waltz of dance and movement, by the shrewd, kaleidoscopic collage of old and new texts (by the playwright and historian Charles L. Mee Jr.) and by a fully integrated musical score (by Richard Peaslee, who is given a credit this time only for co-creating "sound").

Though "Endangered Species" runs roughly as long as "Vienna" — about 65 minutes — it seems much longer, largely because it doesn't expand as it goes along but keeps repeating itself with literal-minded statements of the obvious. Complacent pretension has overtaken the earlier work's mysterious spirit of adventure and discovery. In "Vienna," the audience's imagination was given the mental space to find its own connections with Ms. Clarke's abstract Freudian dreams and performers were given room to metamorphose into the snarling beasts of a Darwinian human kingdom. This time the predictable meaning is handed down didactically, if not directly, and the performers, whatever their species, are usually segregated by task.

On its own terms, the spectacle is expertly executed, as befits its long period of gestation and Ms. Clarke's uncompromising precision as a director: But what is visionary theater without an agitated artist's fresh, personal and challenging vision at its heart? In "Endangered Species" the

animal sideshows can be cute and the big top is striking, but for all the transcendental huffing and puffing in the center ring, I could not find anyone there.

1990 O 9, C13:1

Louisville Takes Clowning Seriously

By MEL GUSSOW

Special to The New York Times

LOUISVILLE, Ky., Oct. 7 — The breadth of clowning from 16th-century Italian zanni to 20th-century American zanies like Bill Irwin was explored this weekend with wit and erudition in Commedia dell'Arte and the Comic Spirit at the Actors Theater of Louisville.

In this three-day festival of performances, lecture-demonstrations, panels and exhibitions, it was difficult to distinguish the audience from the participants, as several hundred professionals — clowns, actors and theatrical academics — gathered to expand their knowledge about this long-running phenomenon. This was the latest in the Actors Theater's annual Classics in Context series, in which Louisville cultural institutions join in a citywide celebration of an aspect of the performing arts.

Mr. Irwin was himself in Louisville, with his fellow clown Geoff Hoyle, apparently as representatives of the second half of the festival title, "the comic spirit." While acknowledging a kinship with Commedia dell'Arte, Mr. Irwin said it was "a source of inspiration better left a little distant." But the inspiration is there, as it is with mimes, music-hall performers and silent-film comedians.

The tradition was represented by two European masters, the Italian actor Ferruccio Soleri and the French teacher of mime and masked acting Jacques Lecoq. As performers, both emphasized the demonstrative side of their lectures and their own comedic roots.

In his masked presentation, Mr. Soleri quick-changed from a rich, randy old Pantalone to an obstreperous Arlecchino and then stepped aside to play the pompous Dottore, a man of letters who pontificates — a figure not in attendance at the festival.

Mr. Lecoq, who has run his celebrated Paris school for more than 30 years, explained his theory of theater of gesture with differing walks. With a minimal shift in body language, he seemed to gain or lose height and weight and to change nationality, profession and sex. Then, adding masks to his image-making, he became an emblematic entourage of characters, which he traced from commedia to Molière and on to Laurel and Hardy.

In these and other events, it was clear that Arlecchino (Harlequin) was the servant of many masters, a fact that was immediately apparent from an exhibition at the J. B. Speed Art Museum in which Jacques Callot's 17th-century engravings shared space with a Picasso Harlequin and Meissen figurines. In passing, in his demonstration, Mr. Lecoq made it clear that it was inadvisable for actors to try to imitate the poses in those Callot pictures. Commedia is stylized, but the spontaneity of performance must be preserved.

●

The festival opened with a lively workshop in physical comedy, conducted by Steve Smith from the Clown College of the Ringling Brothers and Barnum & Bailey Circus. While insisting that any cheap gag worth doing is worth doing three times, he demonstrated the demands of physical comedy, especially when

Martha Swope/Brooklyn Academy of Music

A scene from "Endangered Species," the Martha Clarke theater piece that has opened the Next Wave Festival at the Brooklyn Academy of Music.

playing in a large arena where some of the audience may be a quarter of a mile away.

Clowning is not easy, but it should look easy, which certainly is the case with Chaplin and Keaton, whose movies began one morning of the festival with a cascade of laughter. In "A Night at the Show," in an instance of wish-fulfillment for some members of the audience, Chaplin interrupts a dire stage performance, revealing in this and other scenes a violent streak beneath his sentimentality. In "Cameraman," Buster Keaton tries to break into the movies but finds himself stymied by bad luck. On his way to photograph a fire, he jumps aboard a fire engine — and almost smiles at his sudden good fortune — as the vehicle speeds straight back into the firehouse.

•

Uniting past and present was Jon Jory's production of "The Three Cuckolds," an adaptation by various hands, including that of Bill Irwin. This door-slamming farce, unevenly acted but sparked by Peter Zapp as a mischievous Arlecchino, was updated with references to local Louisville politics, a fact that kept the piece in the Commedia spirit of evolution.

In his lecture on the "The Origins of American Slapstick Comedy," Laurence Senelick vividly described the 18th-century roots before he moved on to George L. Fox, the first indigenous American clown, who believed in "slap and counterslap, uncontaminated by plot." Mr. Senelick is himself at least half a performer, even to putting on a red nose to make a comic point. Describing a clown who did a split on stilts, he wondered how he got up, something that continued to puzzle later participants. In response to a question from the audi-

D. Lecoq/Actors Theater of Louisville

Jacques Lecoq performing in a mask at the festival.

ence, he said he did not know who threw the first custard pie in America. He added that "the research was ongoing."

•

The research was never more ongoing or more amusing than in the contribution of Mr. Irwin and Mr. Hoyle, a clown show masquerading as a lecture demonstration. Years

before their individual success, they shared the ring at the Pickle Family Circus in San Francisco. The partnership was in the nature of a reunion, Mr. Irwin's innocence deftly paired with his partner's insouciance. They turned talk into performance, and that performance seemed a culmination of all the clown colloquy that surrounded it.

Putting on his favorite minimalist mask (glasses and a hat), Mr. Irwin tripped, tap danced and pratfalled as he discussed his perpetual search for comic dilemmas. In contrast to Mr. Irwin, Mr. Hoyle said he was obsessed with Commedia dell'Arte masks and went "to the Library of Congress and looked at 17th-century videotapes" on the subject. Then he performed his Pantalone and an Arlecchino so ravenous that he eats an imaginary fly as if it were the tastiest of delicacies.

Together the two reactivated their own classic clown characters, Mr. Irwin's Willie the Clown (gullible but ultimately triumphant) and Mr. Hoyle's meddling Mr. Sniff. With the help of a false-bottom trunk, they provided the audience with a double dose of hilarity.

Between visits to the Speed Museum and the Louisville Ballet, where the Commedia highlight was a performance of George Balanchine's "Sonnambula," with its alternate version of Arlecchino, visitors gathered at the Actors Theater for a vigorous panel discussion extending Commedia into the area of contemporary political theater. Insisting that political satire was unquenchable, Joan Holden, from the San Francisco Mime Troupe, said the reason for continuing to ridicule politicians was that "laughter gives us power over them." Comedy, she said, is "basically insubordinate" — whether it concerns senatorial chambers or an Italian boudoir.

A darker side of comedy was approached by Ronlin Foreman in his "Pigeon Show," which managed to weave "Madama Butterfly," E. E. Cummings and one man's mania into a chaotic collage. The play ended in the dark with the actor-author demol-

ishing his set, the centerpiece of which was a door. When the lights came on, the door was flat on the floor and from under it came an appeal for someone to turn the knob. Someone did and Mr. Foreman exited upward.

The next day the identical gag appeared on screen in Laurel and Hardy's "Busy Bodies." Clearly, Mr. Foreman had borrowed the joke, but then, one wondered, what had been the source of Laurel and Hardy's inspiration. Had they borrowed it from George Fox, who in turn might have been in debt to an English vaudevillian or a French mime?

•

During the weekend, one kept looking for lassi, impromptu comic interludes such as occurred in the real Commedia. Finally one, or an approximation, happened. While Mr. Foreman performed, one member of the audience, a writer for Pravda, repeatedly and vocally expressed his displeasure with the show. As it ended, he said aloud, "Don't encourage him!"

Seated next to the Pravda man was the actor, Max Wright, who could not contain his irritation at the theatergoer's behavior. He said if he did not like the show, he should have exited. As Mr. Wright's voice rose and as he assumed histrionic command of the situation, the other theatergoers stood and watched, as if it might turn into a Punch and Judy show. Mr. Wright concluded by accusing the other man of expressing "contempt prior to investigation." The actor later said he had borrowed the rather formal insult from William James, who thereby earned a position in the history of Commedia dell'Arte.

At the end of the weekend, one of the guests who had also attended last year's salute to the Moscow Art Theater at the Actors Theater, said, "This was more laughs than Gorky." It certainly was, and the Commedia is not finita. As the clowns in context festival demonstrated, the research and the fun are ongoing.

1990 O 9, C14:4

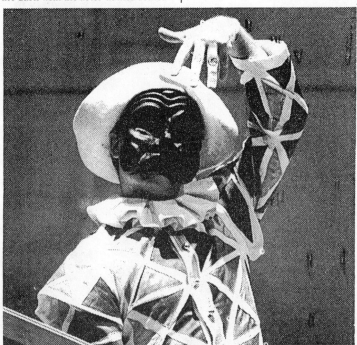

David S. Talbott/Actors Theater of Louisville

Peter Zapp in "The Three Cuckolds" in the Commedia dell'Arte and the Comic Spirit festival at the Actors Theater of Louisville.

About Time

Written by Tom Cole; directed by Tony Giordano; set by Kent Dorsey; lighting, Mr. Dorsey and Neil Peter Jampolis; costume, Christine Dougherty; executive producer, Roger Alan Gindi; sound supervisor, Tom Gould; production stage manager, Christine Michael. Presented by Eric Krebs. At the John Houseman Theater, 450 West 42d Street.

Old Man .... James Whitmore
Old Woman .... Audra Lindley

By MEL GUSSOW

Onstage in "About Time," James Whitmore and Audra Lindley are an endearing couple, as they act their way through and around the slight play that Tom Cole has created for them. Portraying two people generically identified as Old Man and Old Woman, they chat, argue and begin to ameliorate their differences.

Mr. Cole, the author of "Medal of Honor Rag," has written some amusing lines and a few scenes that verge on being touching, but the play itself lacks the variety and depth that would demand that it be a full-length work. For all its performance virtues, "About Time," which opened this week at the John Houseman Theater, is a one-act sketch with a dimension that exceeds its aspiration.

•

Problems begin with the decision to focus on the characters only at mealtime. In four vignettes we see them in the kitchen of their condominium, where there is entirely too much talk about food, about Mr. Whitmore's ravenous appetite and Miss Lindley's inability to eat.

His favorite food is chopped vegetables with sour cream and, for her, the preparation has become increasingly difficult. What once took her a brief time now takes the entire afternoon. The kitchen, a neatly functional set design by Kent Dorsey, is up to date with modern electronic conveniences, but there is no Cuisinart in sight. If used, such a utensil would have sliced 20 minutes of the play's redundant dialogue.

When Old Man and Old Woman are not talking about food, the subject is often sex, and here "About Time" strays into the land of "The Golden Girls." Having considered the geriatric options, Miss Lindley indicates that nymphomania may be her mania of choice. Further attenuating the show, the two play games in which each exhibits an encyclopedic knowledge, with references as ancient as the Romans. A little of this goes a long way if the pursuit is intended to be dramatic rather than trivial.

•

Character development is minimal and scarcely anything is revealed about the couple's life outside the play or beyond the walls of the kitchen. The two have grown children. Mr. Whitmore ran a successful business, but regrets that he did not help the poor. As for Miss Lindley, her dreams remain her secret and there is no serious contemplation of how or why she became so subservient in this long-running marriage.

Still there are interludes in which Mr. Cole raises evocative questions about the triumph of routine over affection, about death and the extension of life by artificial means. But whenever the play shows signs of progressing, it takes a step backward into that ubiquitous bowl of vegetables.

Under the knowing direction of Tony Giordano, the actors are able to disguise some of the work's flaws. Even as he buries his nose in a newspaper and keeps his mind on himself,

Mr. Whitmore remains a foxy pretender, while Miss Lindley seasons her sweetness with a playful humor. Together they have a timing that must derive from acting consanguinity, but the play denies them life support.

"About Time" is scheduled to be joined in repertory by another two-character play, William Gibson's "Handy Dandy."

1990 O 11, C18:6

he Miser

y Molière; directed by Stephen Porter; enic design, James Morgan; costume esign, Gail Brassard; lighting design, Mary Dondlinger; production stage manager, illiam Hare. Presented by Circle in the quare Theater, Theodore Mann, artistic rector; Paul Libin, producing director. At 33 Broadway, at 50th Street.

ame Claude	Jennifer Roblin
alère	Christian Baskous
Elise	Mia Dillon
Cléante	Thomas Gibson
Harpagon	Philip Bosco
La Flèche	Adam Redfield
Maître Simon and Officer's Assistant	Bill Buell
Frosine	Carole Shelley
Maître Jacques	John Christopher Jones
Brindavoine	Willis Sparks
La Merluche	Joseph Jamrog
Marianne	Tracy Sallows
Police Officer	Tom Brennan
Anselme	John MacKay

By FRANK RICH

The spitting up of phlegm may not be everyone's idea of a laugh riot, but it is unmistakably the comic peak in the Circle in the Square's catch-as-catch-can revival of "The Miser."

The eruption comes shortly after Philip Bosco, cast in the title role of Harpagon, has been bamboozled by a double-dealing matchmaker into believing he has won the affections of a young woman who is actually pining for his son. Harpagon, an elderly man with a stoop, a bespectacled squint and a lifeless mop of silver hair, is so eager to believe this genuinely incredible news that he starts to strut about like a rake, all but breaking into a jig in celebration of his newly discovered sexual appeal. But the exertion activates his catarrh, and he is soon reduced to his usual decrepit posture by a coughing fit so loud that not even the accompanying uproar of the audience can drown it out.

What's so funny? Part of the laughter can be attributed to Mr. Bosco's masterly technique: Just when it seems he can put away his extravagantly soiled white handkerchief, another roar rises from deep within his lungs, more explosively gutteral than the one before. Yet Molière

Martha Swope/"The Miser"

Philip Bosco — A Harpagon that is more Shylock than cartoon?

deserves credit, too. The character of Harpagon, as self-deluded as he is avaricious, is all the more ridiculous — and hilarious — for not having the remotest inkling of just how big a fool he is, even when the evidence stares him in the face. The coughing fit, by arriving at precisely that moment when Harpagon's vanity has become most overweening, functions like a banana peel, sending the old skinflint flat just as he presumes to pump himself up.

If there were more such moments in this staging of "The Miser," the occasion would be a happier one. But the production has been guided with uncharacteristic sloppiness by the Molière and Shaw expert (and frequent Bosco collaborator) Stephen Porter. Too often the director and his star seem to forget what they remember in the coughing scene — that Harpagon, the evening's butt, must not be let in on the joke, if the joke is to be funny. Mr. Bosco deflates much of the evening by wailing and sobbing in grave self-pity over Harpagon's travails, as if he were somehow imbued with a tragic awareness more appropriate to Shylock than to a role with roots in commedia dell'arte. (Is the actor's mind already preoccupied by the King Lear he will be playing at the Folger in Washington this season?) While Harpa-

Martha Swope/"Miser"

John Christopher Jones

gon is undeniably pathetic — he would rather sell out both of his children than part with a sou — such pathos as Molière will allow the man can follow only if the comedy comes first. "The Miser" lacks the dark shadows of "Tartuffe" and "The Misanthrope," and this production is far too willing to mortgage the play's comic franchise to plumb for depths that are not there.

"The Miser" is a cartoon, not a slice of naturalistic life, or a psychological character study. The author would rather toss in the farcical old Roman gag about separated twins reunited with the aid of a signet ring than, say, explore Harpagon's feelings about his late wife or the sources of his paranoia. The play's tone is defined by the fact that nearly everyone in it is a liar, scheming in some way or another to pry a lover or a fortune from the geezer's tight grasp. The false flattery, disguised identities and con games that ensue give the dialogue the high gloss of sheer facetiousness and turn disingenuousness into comic art. In one representative exchange, Harpagon and the steward Valère debate the dispensation of a "treasure" at considerable length without realizing that they are speaking at cross-purposes about two entirely different treasures. It is typical of the production that Mr. Bosco and Christian Baskous deliver this volley with the whine of escalating exasperation, not the effervescence of spiraling absurdity.

One cannot really blame the cast for such heaviness of attack, because its good actors seem to have been left to their own devices by Mr. Porter. The director's few attempts at establishing a high-comic sheen — a dumb show to open the evening, an exaggerated war of bows and curtsies between Harpagon and his daughter — are crudely managed, and the acting comes in a myriad of conflicting styles. Mia Dillon, as that sorely tried daughter, and Adam Redfield, as the servant La Flèche, seem to be winging their roles with a generalized jolliness, while Thomas Gibson, with longer blond ringlets than Ms. Dillon, ascends into camp of near-Cyril Ritchard extremis in his broad reading of Harpagon's son, Cléante. Better are Carole Shelley, who brings her crisp professionalism (if an excess of vulgarity) to the matchmaker, Frosine, and, especially, John Christopher Jones, as Maître Jacques, Harpagon's cook and coachman. Mr. Jones is so funny as he mournfully describes his boss's underfed horses

— "they are no more than ghosts or shadows or ideas of horses" — that it seems unsporting to question why he is the only American actor in this French play to affect an English accent.

Such other high points as there are usually emanate from the text's slapdash plot shenanigans or from Mr. Bosco, when he elects to lighten up. His funniest second-half bit is the long, eye-rolling pause he takes when he finally must choose once and for all between love of money and love for a woman. This is a Jack Benny or Phil Silvers moment if ever there was one, and Mr. Bosco squeezes it, as he had his coughing fit, for all the burlesque clownishness it is worth. Surely it would not have violated Harpagon's miserly spirit if this fine comic actor had been unleashed to hunt down some more cheap laughs.

1990 O 12, C1:1

Happy Days

By Samuel Beckett; directed by Carey Perloff; scenic design, Donald Eastman; costume design, Julie Weiss; lighting design, Frances Aronson; production stage manager, Carol Dawes. Presented by CSC Repertory, Ms. Perloff, artistic director; Patricia Taylor, managing director. At 136 East 13th Street.

Winnie	Charlotte Rae
Willie	Bill Moor

By MEL GUSSOW

Despite her cheerful demeanor, Winnie in "Happy Days" (revived at the CSC Repertory Theater) knows the limits and defeats of her life. Her way to endure the day, and the day after that, is "laughing wild amid severest woe." Laughter shares the stage with sorrow.

As Winnie (Charlotte Rae) primps and fusses over herself, it is as if she is sitting at her dressing table. She is, of course, buried up to her waist in a large mound of earth and, by the second act of Samuel Beckett's masterly existential comedy, she is buried up to her neck. In the unwritten third act, she might have become the distant voice of someone symbolically entombed in life.

Peggy Ashcroft has called the role "a summit part," like Hamlet. Any actress attempting it must find her path through a minefield of detailed stage directions and must single-handedly sustain the drama. Although her husband, Willie, appears, he seldom speaks, leaving the stage to his wife and her one-woman show. Necessarily the role lends itself to interpretation, but no performance should neglect the essential adaptability of Winnie. Though her stage movements are rigidly restricted, emotionally she is unbound.

In Carey Perloff's thoughtful production, Miss Rae holds firmly to the author's inclinations — the pauses, stops and starts and poetic lilt of language. With an ebullience that seems to spring from conviction, she goes about her everyday life, undeterred by the fact of her entrapment.

This is a Winnie who is unswerving in her ability to come through wars as well as personal deprivations.

Best known for her comic performances, Miss Rae aims for lightness and achieves it as called for in the first act, which benefits from the actress's expressive face and gestures. She also catches a measure of second act sobriety, when Winnie's soliloquy begins to resemble the delirium of later Beckett works like "Not I."

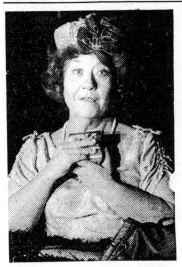

Paula Court/Happy Days

Charlotte Rae in "Happy Days."

For the audience, she becomes a cozy chatterer such as one might encounter in an English pub. She engages us with her refrain, as she tries to recall happy beginnings as well as endings. Other actresses from Ruth White in the original Off Broadway production to Irene Worth have uncovered the gentility beneath the extroverted behavior. That aspect of Winnie eludes Miss Rae, who is most adept at projecting the character's earthy humor.

At the CSC, the audience is seated on three sides of a small stage. Donald Eastman's set places Winnie in the center of a volcanolike hill. The surface looks seared. In the close surroundings, Miss Rae keeps her performance within the framework of intimacy. Bill Moor is apt as Willie, her crusty companion, in top hat and tails looking like a remnant from another, more formal epoch.

•

Miss Perloff previously directed "Happy Days" (with Miss Rae and Mr. Moor) at the Mark Taper Forum in Los Angeles as part of that company's recent retrospective of plays of the 1950's and 1960's. The production arrives here with a sense of surety, except in one respect. In a sudden flash, Winnie's parasol is supposed to be consumed by flames, but when the moment came during a critics' preview, the fire fizzled. Spontaneous combustion resulted in a puff of smoke.

The director and the actress are careful about keeping the dialogue conversational, even when it is alluding to Milton, Dante and Shakespeare. Ever eclectic, Winnie remembers literary references as a kind of artifact of a cultural heritage she does not possess.

Because of Winnie's persistence, some may regard her as an eternal optimist. Her role is more that of perpetual pragmatist. As she passes the minutes with remembered routines and favorite distractions, "Happy Days" becomes a partial reflection of "Waiting for Godot." Neither salvation nor cessation await her; one dawn is like another. Searchingly, Winnie looks for daily mercies as her helpmate for survival.

1990 O 13, 17:1

Misalliance

By George Bernard Shaw; directed by Casey Kizziah; set and lighting by Giles Hogya; costumes by Jonathan Bixby; music by Ellen Mandel; production stage manager, Julie Bleha. Presented by the Jean Cocteau Repertory, 330 Bowery, at Second Avenue.

Johnny Tarleton	Joseph Menino
Bentley Summerhays	David Cheaney
Hypatia Tarleton	Jeanne Demers
Mrs. Tarleton	Angela Vitale
Lord Summerhays	Craig Smith
John Tarleton	Harris Berlinsky
Joey Percival	Mark Waterman
Lina Szczepanowska	Elise Stone
Gunner	Grant Neale

By WILBORN HAMPTON

Politics and business have long been known to make very strange bedfellows, but they are nothing compared with the bizarre alliances formed in the name of love. And no playwright in the past century, or very likely any other, has been so adept at exposing the absurdities of our most cherished romantic notions as George Bernard Shaw. As its first offering of the season, the Jean Cocteau Repertory is staging a diverting if somewhat uneven revival of "Misalliance."

In the course of one pleasant May afternoon at John Tarleton's country house in Surrey, Shaw goes hunting for the hypocrisies that hide out in every corner of society and bags the limit. No one escapes Shaw's withering wit in "Misalliance" — from the aristocracy to shopkeepers, philanthropists to clerks, chivalrous gentlemen, emancipated young women, anarchists and Edwardian yuppies.

As with so much of Shaw, the overall success of "Misalliance" depends on the strength of the entire ensemble. The Cocteau production is spotty. Some performances sparkle. Others are flat. The predictable result is a revival that is delightful in some scenes yet disappointing in others.

•

The best part of the Cocteau staging is happily one of the most essential — Elise Stone's no-nonsense reading of Lina Szczepanowska, the acrobat whose turn it is to risk her life to save the family honor. Lina is the St. Joan of "Misalliance," a thoroughly Shavian heroine who drops out of the sky into John Tarleton's stuffy country house with all the quiet, determined fervor of a religious force, showing the inhabitants one by one the error of their romantic ways.

Ms. Stone, employing a melodious contralto that translates into a convincing Polish accent, conveys the

Jonathan Slaff/"Misalliance"

Elise Stone in "Misalliance."

grave disapproval of all the conventions that keep the others earthbound without becoming superior herself. She is indignant without being haughty when all the men in the house try to make love to her. Ms. Stone presents Shaw's completely liberated woman, refusing to sell herself into marriage anymore than she would sell herself into slavery, and not drawing too fine a line between the two.

Harris Berlinsky's John Tarleton is more problematic. Mr. Berlinsky is a fine actor, and his performance finds a measure of the humor in Tarleton, a shopkeeper who has made a fortune in underwear and now occupies himself giving away public libraries. Tarleton is not a man troubled by doubts. Whether confronted with an airplane falling into his greenhouse or a gunman emerging from his Turkish bath, Tarleton is never at a loss for words or an author to quote and does not hesitate to express whatever opinion pops into his head. Shaw once advised Wilfrid Lawson, who played the role in a London revival: "Tarleton picks up everything like a shot. You should not be able to get in a knife edge between his cue and his answer." Under Casey Kizziah's direction, however, there is little of Tarleton's commanding self-assurance in Mr. Berlinsky's interpretation. And in some scenes he is downright reflective.

•

Other performances are mixed. Craig Smith is splendid as Lord Summerhays, who is spending his declining years proposing marriage to every young woman he meets, and Mark Waterman has some fun with Joey Percival, the young aviator who is much too well brought up to be truthful when a lady's honor is at stake. Grant Neale's Gunner is amusing as a stereotypical frightened gunman, an outraged clerk viewing upper-class mores. But there is little evidence of the angry bastard and anarchist lurking in Mr. Neale's performance. Jeanne Demers portrays Hypatia, Tarleton's upstart daughter, more as a vamp than a liberated young woman who wants "to live life as an active verb."

1990 O 14, 56:4

SUNDAY VIEW/David Richards

Stalking One's Fate With an Alarm Clock

In 'Stand-Up Tragedy,' an inner-city student tries to beat the odds; in 'About Time,' an elderly couple play hide-and-seek with death.

AMONG THE MORE IRRITATING creatures in a world full of them are those theatergoers who tell you, just after the curtain has come down, "You really should have seen the London production." Or, "It was a lot better *before* the producer moved it uptown." Or, "Trust me. With the original lead, it was a different show entirely."

The unmistakable message is that they were in the right place for the right production, whereas you, bumbling into the wrong place, have succeeded only in catching the wrong production. What's more, you're probably still going to that little French bistro that's been passé for months now.

Under the circumstances, I am hesitant to note that Bill Cain's "Stand-Up Tragedy," which opened recently at the Criterion Center, struck me as a worthy endeavor when I saw it in the round last January at the Arena Stage in Washington. But it did. I said so then and I'll say so again, although anyone who beholds the overbearing evidence on the Criterion stage will probably be sorely pressed to believe me.

The chronicle of an academic year in a Roman Catholic high school on New York's Lower East Side, where it is considered a minor achievement if a student even shows up for class, "Stand-Up Tragedy" doesn't pretend for an instant that educational conditions are any less appalling than they are. As one of the faculty members quips, "Somebody has to be the bottom 10 percent on standardized tests. And if our kids don't do it, the people on Staten Island will be very upset." At the Criterion, however, what is meant to be relentlessly hard-hitting is merely relentless, and then it is off-putting.

Mr. Cain recounts a familiar enough saga — that of Tom Griffin (Jack Coleman), an idealistic young teacher fresh on the job and eager to save a soul, whatever the costs. In Lee Cortez (Marcus Chong), he seems to have the perfect candidate —- a talented artist, whose home life is so traumatic he can express himself only in comic book fantasies. Remove him from the abuse of a drunken mother and the violence of a drug-addicted brother, Griffin reasons, and Lee is bound to flower.

It doesn't take a huge imagination to guess what comes to pass. And even if it did, the gruff priest (Charles Cioffi) who runs the school provides an early tip-off when he warns Griffin that there is "an ecology of evil." Once its subtle balance is altered, who knows what destruction will be unleashed? No, you callously play the odds, teach the teachable, and if only one boy gets out of the neighborhood, pedagogy is vindicated for the year. Griffin disobeys orders. But the more he tries to change Lee, the more enmeshed he finds himself in the student's chaotic family life.

"Your family's your fate," explains Lee helplessly, and while I'm not sure that's necessarily how a withdrawn and brutalized Hispanic student would put it, there's the nub of Mr. Cain's play in a phrase.

∎

What makes "Stand-Up Tragedy" unusual is its aggressive, jumpy form, with no more than a sharp school bell to mark the transition from one scene to the next. "The Star-Spangled Banner," as the students sing it on opening day of classes, is reduced to "O say can you see by the dawn's early light and the home of the brave." The ensuing scenes — in and out of the classroom — are similarly condensed. Periodically, the students function as a latter-day Greek chorus, barking out rap lyrics, undertaking some seam-splitting leaps and generally bringing the raw energy of the street to bear on matters.

Every time "Stand-Up Tragedy" starts to follow the more conventional laws of playwriting, Mr. Cain takes a sledgehammer to it. The pieces go flying. The splintered dramaturgy, of course, is meant to mirror the uneasy, jagged lives of the students themselves. (That may be why the play took so well to the round. When it exploded, it exploded outward in all directions.) But just to clinch the notion at the Criterion, Yael Pardess's high school set — rusted lockers serving as columns; panes of dirty glass overhead filtering out anything so salubrious as sunshine — could easily pass for a medium-security prison.

"Stand-Up Tragedy" was originally developed last year at the Mark Taper Forum in Los Angeles, after which the same creative team continued to refine it at the Hartford Stage Company. The Broadway production, I presume, represents a culmination of that process. Arena Stage mounted a separate version on its own with the understanding that it would be for Washington alone. But if you'll allow me to use that production as a yardstick, something clearly went awry on the way to the Criterion.

Under Ron Link's direction, frenzy is the bottom line. It's not just the sound that is painfully overamplified. So are the emotions. Simple exchanges are elevated to confrontations and lines of passing import are delivered as if they were written in capital letters. In brief, a full-fledged assault is under way (guess who the target is), as often happens

Jay Thompson/"Stand-Up Tragedy"

Martha Swope/"About Time"

Marcus Chong, left, and Jack Coleman in "Stand-Up Tragedy"—a year at a Lower East Side school, where just showing up is an achievement; right, Audra Lindley and James Whitmore in "About Time"—nattering on about aches, pains and the end in a gleaming condo kitchen

when the theater decides to grapple with social issues. Not surprisingly, given all the tumble and din, the play's humanity is virtually drummed out of existence.

As the hard-bitten priest who hasn't allowed reality to overwhelm his faith completely, Mr. Cioffi is the most successful in resisting the tidal wave of urgency that engulfs the stage. Mr. Coleman's teacher, however, never seems more than a sanctimonious crusader on sabbatical from the Ivy League, and the qualities that might lend some complexity to the part — a boyish naïveté, a stubborn pride, a willful derring-do perhaps — are noticeably lacking. The play's flashiest assignment goes to Mr. Chong, who not only portrays an introverted youth coming out of his shell, but is also called upon, at the flick of a wrist, to play his spitfire mother and his drug-crazed brother, too. When all three characters fall to arguing, Mr. Chong is a very busy man.

The triple-pronged role is not just a theatrical gimmick on Mr. Cain's part. Lee's family is an ineradicable part of him. Their voices are lodged in his head. Wherever he goes, they go. Mr. Chong, long on intensity and fervor, is nonetheless short on the sort of technique that makes such a challenge appear effortless. What you see is an actor sweating through some quick changes, not a character so possessed he has nowhere to turn.

In retrospect, I now recognize it was not the fierce energy that made "Stand-Up Tragedy" work at Arena Stage, although it may have seemed so at the time. The key was what spelled the explosions — the fleeting expressions of friendship and understanding, the reaching out, the rueful moments of self-reflection. Give "Stand-Up Tragedy" its head and its natural tendency is to race out of control. It demands a restraining hand. After watching the production at the Criterion, I am tempted to conclude that Mr. Link's solution to the problem of a runaway car would be to step on the gas.

'About Time'

By way of contrast, Tom Cole's "About Time," one half of the two-play repertory at the John Houseman Theater (William Gibson's "Handy Dandy," which opens Oct. 22, is the other half), goes nowhere slowly. If, perish the thought, Samuel Beckett had ever tried to write a sitcom about a married couple in their sunset years, he might have produced something akin to this morose drama, in which Old Man (James Whitmore) and Old Woman (Audra Lindley) idle away a day and night in their gleaming condo kitchen. They remember bits of their past, but forget the ravioli in the oven, natter on about their aches and pains, split semantic hairs, quibble, sulk, make up and make love. All the while, however, they're really playing hide-and-seek with death.

He may not be waiting for Godot — a telephone call from one of their children would do — but the silent wall phone nonetheless induces in him that characteristically Beckettian blend of hope and anguish. "Telephone, television — you keep wanting messages from afar," she observes tartly. Her recurring complaint is how long it takes her these days to chop the veggies for lunch. Lunch hour's well over by the time she's through. Her system needs oiling. Slowing down, she is. Or is it slowing *up*?

◼

"What happens to our dentures when we die?" he wonders.

"Life starts with a cry for warm milk in the middle of the night and ends with a cry for warm milk in the middle of the night," she muses.

A power failure is the big event in Act II, and when the lights come back on, blindingly bright, it may occur to you, as it did to me, that the characters have died and gone to heaven. But no. There are more veggies to be chopped. More word games to be played. More angst to be waded through.

In that Ms. Lindley and Mr. Whitmore both appear to have aged rather splendidly, their participation in this lugubrious enterprise seems oddly inappropriate. An enchanting schoolgirl blush is, apparently, hers forever, while a substantial part of him remains a bright-eyed cub scout, eager to embark on a brisk 20-mile hike. "About Time" subjects them to the indignity of old age. What we can't help wanting to know is how they've avoided it. ☐

1990 O 14, II:5:1

Calvin Trillin's Words, No Music

Written and performed by Calvin Trillin; directed by Wynn Handman; stage design by Bill Stabile; lighting by Andrew James Meyer; production stage manager, Lloyd Davis Jr. Presented by American Place Theater, Mr. Handman, director; Stephen Lisner, general manager. At 111 West 46th Street.

By MEL GUSSOW

Calvin Trillin is the Buster Keaton of performance humorists. As droll as he is deadpan, he never once suggests that he thinks he is as funny as we know he is. He lets the audience do the laughing as he ambles onstage at the American Place Theater and begins his mirthful commentary.

In his new show, "Words, No Music," he is both a wordsmith and a word collector, savoring expressions brought home by his daughters, his explorers in the linguistic field. He likes the sound of "SNAG" ("sensitive new-age guy"), the kind of man who takes courses in women's studies and goes on pro-choice marches. One might propose that Mr. Trillin is himself a "SMAG" ("sensitive middle-aged guy"), a man steadfastly in favor of all the right rights.

Equally he is angry about public wrongs, about anything that suppresses individualism or makes life more difficult for people like himself. Because he has given up on learning irregular French verbs, he wants to be identified in his obituary as "monolingual reporter." He is proud of being a reporter, although his wife gives a higher rating to his role as writer. The subjects of his satire range from social injustices to the problem of maintaining an automobile in Manhattan. In his imaginary résumé, he lists the editorship of Beautiful Spot, the Magazine of Parking.

•

When Mr. Trillin is talking, politicians should run for cover (and not for office). In the author's story, President Bush takes President Gorbachev aside and asks, "Where'd ya prep?" If anyone is thinking about a possible White House successor, Mr. Trillin is quick to add that there should be a constitutional amendment making a C average a requirement for the Presidency. At one point, he threatens to sing a chorus of "If you knew what Sununu" but then remembers the vow in his show's title. He promises not to hum and whistle at the same time, his response whenever he is asked, Miss America-style, to "do your talent."

As a famous feinschmecker from Kansas City, he tells about his far-flung culinary adventures, eating bull foot soup and noticing "the unmistakable presence of the foot." Sibling rivalry shares the stage with the tale of how two tuxedos can be amortized to last a lifetime. We learn a few pertinent facts about marriage and family, but he is less interested in autobiography than in attitude, in how he relates to a world that always seems to be moving counterclockwise.

He is trying to save that world the best way he can, which is with humor. Deflating pretension wherever he finds it, he reserves a special niche for all those who assume they represent a higher authority — beginning with editors he has served.

•

The last time he appeared at the American Place Theater, he pretended he was in a classroom and had a map and blackboard to sustain that image. In his new show he has a set (including a door), a director (Wynn Handman) and changes of lighting. These accouterments do not detract from the informality of the entertainment.

"It's new material but the same costume," he says, and by costume he means his blue blazer. (Where'd ya prep?) This is new material only if one is unfamiliar with Mr. Trillin's

David Rothenberg Associates

Calvin Trillin

articles, magazine columns and books. But acting as his own ecologist, he has recycled his words and fine-tuned them into theatrical form. In his hands, words in print become performance. As author and actor, he knows how to punctuate a pause. Even sitting down, Jackie Mason is a stand-up comic. Even standing up, Mr. Trillin is a wry armchair monologuist. His ease and professionalism in facing his public should be an inspiration to writers who hide behind hard covers.

1990 O 15, C15:1

Machinal

By Sophie Treadwell; directed by Michael Greif; sets by David Gallo; costumes by Sharon Lynch; lighting by Kenneth Posner; original music and sound by John Gromada; associate producer, Jason Steven Cohen. Presented by Joseph Papp. At the Public Theater, LuEsther Hall, 425 Lafayette Street.
Announcer, Bellboy, Waiter, Defense Attorney and Jailer. Timothy Britten Parker
Adding Clerk, Prosecuting Attorney and First Barber.....................Ralph Marrero
Filing Clerk, Neighbor, Boy at Speakeasy Table No. 3 and Reporter..........Omar Carter
Stenographer, Neighbor, Nurse, Final Speakeasy Woman and Reporter
.....................Linda Marie Larson
Telephone Girl, Neighbor and Court Stenographer.................Kristine Nielsen
Husband................................John Seitz
Young Woman.......................Jodie Markell
Mother...................... Marge Redmond
Singer and Neighbor..........Darby Rowe
Doctor, Salesman at Speakeasy Table No. 1, Neighbor, Reporter and Second Barber...........................Christopher Fields

Lover..William Fichtner
Man at Speakeasy Table No. 3, Priest and
Neighbor..Rocco Sisto
Woman at Speakeasy Table No. 2, Neighbor
and Matron..Regina Taylor
Man at Speakeasy Table No. 2, Neighbor,
Bailiff, Reporter and Guard Gareth Williams
Judge, Final Speakeasy Man and
Convi t.......................................Michael Mandell

By FRANK RICH

When the American theater dusts off forgotten Broadway plays from the 1920's and 30's, it is usually with the hope of finding a charming period piece, like Paul Osborn's "Morning's at Seven" or Charles MacArthur's "Johnny on a Spot," that might give hardy perennials like "The Front Page" and "You Can't Take It With You" a run for the box-office gold. A young director named Michael Greif, making a sensational debut at the New York Shakespeare Festival, has quite another idea in mind in his resuscitation of "Machinal," a 1928 Broadway success by Sophie Treadwell that has languished in oblivion except for one fleeting Off Broadway revival 30 years ago.

Mr. Greif has no interest in nostalgia. He has taken a tough work about an ordinary woman who is destroyed by a world of men, money and machines — "a tragedy in 10 episodes," in its author's conception — and given it an imaginative, unpatronizing production that would befit a play written only yesterday. The result is a startling collision of past and present. Like an archeological treasure preserved in a subterranean air pocket, "Machinal" (pronounced mock-en-AHL) is both an authentic artifact of a distant civilization and a piece of living art that seems timeless.

The civilization to which the play belongs is that of the late 20's, on the eve of the crash, when the overweening business of America was business. Treadwell (1885-1970) loosely adapted her play from the scandalous Snyder-Gray murder trial, a suburban love-triangle case that led to the first execution of a woman in an electric chair. "Machinal" charts that woman, played by Jodie Markell and known simply as "young woman," as she progresses from anonymous secretary to wife of the boss to young mother, adulterer and, finally, murder defendant. From the first scene, in which office life is presented as a dehumanizing clatter of number-crunching machines and clerks, to

the last, in which the power of industry is harnessed to the task of electrocution, "Machinal" dramatizes urban America as an unrelenting assembly line, carrying the blank but thrashing heroine from one cruel way station to the next as if she were a lost lamb being led to slaughter.

As the critic Brooks Atkinson noted in The New York Times after attending the 1928 opening at the Plymouth Theater, both the style and content of "Machinal" owe something to "The Adding Machine," Elmer Rice's play of 1923, and to Dreiser's "American Tragedy" (1925) as well as to "the whole mad tumble of Expressionist drama." One can also see the influences of Henry Adams (in "The Virgin and the Dynamo"), of early O'Neill, earlier Dreiser (starting with "Sister Carrie") and the Sacco-Vanzetti case. Yet even as Atkinson pointed out the play's "resemblances" to other works, he found it "a triumph of individual distinction, gleaming with intangible beauty." For once, at least, a drama critic was right.

What makes "Machinal" individual and distinct from some similarly themed fiction written by men in the same period is simple enough: Treadwell sees her stifled female protagonist from the inside. More fascinating still, she writes in a deadpan tone that keeps both sentimentality and ideological boilerplate at bay. Her spiky use of language and stylized theatrical technique and her refusal to preach, even when challenging the masculine hierarchies of obstetrics and Christianity, make "Machinal" seem far more contemporary than the social-protest plays that would soon be ushered in by the Depression. Treadwell strips everything bare, from dialogue to characterization to narrative, as she pours out her fable in the streamlined cadences of a modernist hallucination.

When the nameless people talk about business in "Machinal," it is in the repetitive, staccato shorthand of Babbitt-era salesmanship — "he signed on the dotted line" or "I put it over" — that today would be labeled Mamet-ese. The characters preying on the heroine are boiled down to their essential animal drives. The boorish vice president who becomes the young woman's husband (John Seitz) is summed up by his repeated, mercantile ambition to one day buy a Swiss watch in Switzerland; her sour working-class mother (Marge Redmond) is interested only in the hand-

outs her new son-in-law might provide. The murder that drives the plot is presented unmelodramatically offstage, within the blackouts separating the play's "episodes," as simply a naturalistic matter of fact.

Yet there is terror everywhere in this evening. In keeping with Treadwell's original intentions, Mr. Greif folds each scene within the "purgatory of noise" that marks the urban jungle: jackhammers and subway trains and grinding manufacturing machinery. With the collaboration of a gifted new design team — David Gallo (sets), Sharon Lynch (costumes) and Kenneth Posner (lighting) — he places the entire action within a skeletal factory that is constantly and subtly reconfigured to serve such settings as a speakeasy, a furnished room, a resort hotel, a maternity ward and a courtroom. The tall green window shades, the chiaroscuro of stark lamplight and shadows, the spooky silhouettes that rise in the smoky glass panel of an office door all conspire to re-create the lonely, sometimes surreal, often macabre American cityscapes found in the contemporaneous paintings of Sheeler, Shahn and Hopper. The stage pictures are completed by the director's shimmering use of extras to suggest a jazz-age ballroom or the buzzing domestic hive of a tenement apartment house.

Mr. Greif's relentless theatricality, which rightly leads him to eliminate an intermission, carries "Machinal" even when the acting is merely competent or an occasional scene (notably the trial) goes into overdrive. William Fichtner, who plays the heroine's illicit lover (a role originated by the young Clark Gable), does not reveal much personality, for instance, but it hardly matters, given the sweaty darkness, relieved only by a cigarette's solitary glow, with which Mr. Greif evocatively shrouds his mechanical bedroom technique. When the acting is distinguished — as it is in the key roles played by Ms. Markell, Mr. Seitz and Ms. Redmond and in ghoulish cameos contributed by Rocco Sisto — "Machinal" becomes nightmarish. Particularly chilling is the honeymoon night in which the sinister Mr. Seitz, a smiling pig with fat hands and a traveling salesman's crude bonhomie, bounces the flinching Ms. Markell on his knee while trying to coax her to a grotesquely pink bed. His bride ends up shivering and sobbing on the floor, begging in vain for "somebody" to rescue her.

That scene notably excepted, Ms. Markell sometimes could be a shade less tentative in her portrayal of an Everywoman, however ordinary, swept up in forces beyond her control. Even so, her anguished cries for peace and freedom are so affecting that they never fail to overwhelm the churning mechanical sounds of the hellish city engulfing her. What the audience hears, of course, is not just the passion of a young actress, but the piercing voice of a forgotten writer who, in an act of justice unknown to her tragic heroine, has been miraculously reborn.

1990 O 16, C13:1

Martha Swope/"Machinal"
John Seitz and Jodie Markell in Sophie Treadwell's "Machinal."

By MEL GUSSOW

The setting for "Jackie Mason: Brand New" (at the Neil Simon Theater) is an approximation of a television studio. Behind Mr. Mason is a battery of television monitors on which are projected images of politicians, astronauts and — a bulletin from Israel — Charlton Heston parting the Red Sea. The stand-up comedian is now standing in for a television anchor. He is also doing his own commercials, as in his confident aside to the audience, "It's a wonderful thing to see me in person."

Mr. Mason's audience, which is an integral part of his act, returns the compliment. With this comedian, there is no sense of indecisiveness. He is sharp, pungent and self-assured. Yet his humor is not without its moments of subtlety. He does not batter an audience into submission, but informally amuses them with shticks of recognition.

"Brand New" is an exact meeting of performer and material. He is wound up and ready for action, with the same targets but with a different arsenal of jokes. He never moves very far from what he regards as eternal differences betweens Jews and Gentiles, differences that are social, marital and, perhaps above all, culinary.

Jay Thompson
Jackie Mason in his new show.

There is a high caloric content in his comedy. In his view, you eat what you are. This leads him to a withering discussion of health-food stores, whose patrons have sickly looks on their faces from eating too much alfalfa, a word he pronounces with disdain. As a confirmed hot-pastrami fancier, he offers a shrewd comment on changing nutritional patterns: no food is considered good to eat for two weeks in a row.

For him, there is something especially suspect about sushi, the food served by restaurateurs who have no room in their establishments for a kitchen. Chauvinistically, he questions the elevation of everything Japanese while reserving surprisingly virulent remarks for the French. He prefers seltzer to Perrier and, as a tip to bottlers, suggests that sparkling-water sales would soar if the beverage were pronounced seltzier.

The comic style — a spritz followed by a topper — derives from the Catskills via Las Vegas, but in his heart, Mr. Mason has the retaliatory in-

Jackie Mason: Brand New

Executive producer, Jyll Rosenfeld; production design and lighting, Neil Peter Jampolis; sound design, Bruce Cameron. Presented by Old Friends Group. At the Neil Simon Theater, 250 West 52d Street.

stincts of a political commentator. Despite the controversy he aroused during last year's mayoral campaign, he still makes jokes about Mayor David N. Dinkins's wardrobe (photo of the natty Mayor on the television screen). He surmises that if the Brooklyn Korean market had sold jackets instead of vegetables, the Mayor would have immediately broken up the boycott. Not one to play favorites, he also spoofs former Mayor Edward I. Koch and Mr. Mason's own defeated mayoral candidate, Rudolph W. Giuliani ("He's a brilliant crime fighter. He puts people in jail whether they're guilty or not").

In the equivalent of an extended opening monologue on the Johnny Carson show, he needles George Bush, Ronald Reagan and Mayor Marion S.Barry Jr. of Washington who "said he would get drugs off the street and did." The assault is ecumenical, as he imitates a gallery of Israeli leaders as well as William F. Buckley Jr. When he mimics someone he does not ape a voice but rather a manner — and mannerisms — that reveal his own diabolical gift as a caricaturist.

•

This time there is perhaps excessive interaction with the audience, which only reminds one that the show would be equally at home in a nightclub. Those seated in front rows should be prepared to become the object of Mr. Mason's mockery. On the other hand, he seems more concerned than in his previous Broadway show about giving the audience its money's worth. During the intermission, theatergoers can remain in their seats and watch Daffy Duck and Porky Pig cartoons on those monitors. This bizarre touch may be an attempt to broaden his already wide audience.

Despite his apparent parochialism, there is a universality in his comic assault. He cuts everyone down to size, including himself, as in his comment, "At the stage of life when most people are passing away, I became a star." Admirers will laugh and skeptics will smile. Mr. Mason is one of a kind, a stand-up comic who has found a hospitable home on Broadway.

1990 O 18, C21:1

Remembrance

By Graham Reid; directed by Terence Lamude; lighting, John McLain; sound, Tom Gould; set designer, Duke Durfee; props and scenic artist, Pearl Broms; technical director, David Raphel; costume designer, C. Jane Epperson; production stage manager, Kurt Wagemann; produced in association with Stamford Theater Works. Presented by the Irish Arts Center, Jim Sheridan, artistic director; Nye Heron, executive director. At 553 West 51st Street.

Bert Andrews......................... Malachy McCourt
Victor Andrews.................................. John Finn
Theresa Donaghy...................... Aideen O'Kelly
Joan Donaghy....................................... Ann Dowd
Deirdre Donaghy........................ Terry Donnely
Jenny.. Ellen Tobie

By WILBORN HAMPTON

It has been more than 20 years since the arrival of British troops in Northern Ireland to quell rioting in Londonderry and Belfast signaled the beginning of the latest round of what the Irish so quaintly call the Troubles. The legacy of rancor, suspicion and hatred bred in those two decades of strife has now passed to the next generation, poisoning the lives of all it touches. Death still waits in driveways, at street corners or sometimes

even knocks at the front door. Children who have grown to adulthood amid this terror assuage their sense of guilt with anger, and they spite their parents any glimmer of happiness.

"Remembrance," an absorbing, powerful and touching play by Graham Reid that is being presented at the Irish Arts Center, focuses on two Belfast families whose lives become intertwined through the courtship of an elderly widow and widower.

Bert Andrews, a Protestant, and Theresa Donaghy, a Roman Catholic, meet while visiting their respective sons' graves. They become acquainted chatting about the circumstances of those sons' deaths. Bert's boy Sam was gunned down in the driveway of his father's home. Theresa's Peter was killed by a Protestant vigilante. "Did they shoot him?" Bert asks. "Eventually," Theresa replies. In such a place and time, where else should love begin but in a cemetery.

But the differences in their own backgrounds are the least of Bert's and Theresa's problems as their friendship turns to affection during picnics they share in the graveyard. Each has a grown child living at home and knows too well the reception those children would give each other. Victor, Bert's surviving son, is an Ulster policeman who is separated from his wife and lives with the belief that his father wished he had died instead of his brother. Joan, Theresa's younger daughter, is convinced she was responsible for her brother's death and obsessively cleans her mother's kitchen as penance. Her elder sister, Diedre, whose husband, an Irish Republican Army gunman, is in prison at Her Majesty's pleasure, wants a man in her bed and is willing to leave her children and run away to London to get one. Jenny, Victor's estranged wife, cried for the last six months of her marriage and now looks forward to a trip to the supermarket as a highlight of her life.

At first reading, it might seem that Mr. Reid has simply crafted a well-made play that serves as a microcosm for the tragedy of Ulster. But that does not do justice to the strength of this poignant drama. Through the complexity and unflinching honesty of his characters, believably realized by a splendid cast under Terence Lamude's direction, Mr. Reid's 1984 play becomes a gripping account of the brutality of bigotry that knows no geography.

When Joan finally learns her mother might consider marrying a Protestant, she first explodes with anger. "Will it be church or chapel?" she sneers.

"Do you hate them all?" Theresa asks her daughter sadly.

"Yes," Joan replies reflectively. "I suppose I do."

Victor, who is rapidly sinking into self-loathing alcoholism, talks of emigrating to South Africa, where police cruelty is considered a virtue. "In South Africa, they don't care if you're Protestant or Catholic," he explains. "Just whether you're black."

Through all of this, Mr. Reid never takes sides or indulges in politics or moralizing. "Remembrance" is about how people on both sides succeed or fail at their lives in the circumstances given them and find the faith to continue. As Theresa tells her daughter: "Today I believe in me. Mother Ireland will have to take a back seat." Mr. Reid suggests no remedies, offers no solutions to any of this.

In one moving scene, Theresa asks Bert to write her a letter. "I'd love to

receive a love letter," she says. "All the letters of my life are in one shoe box."

Bert nods. "They won't have to sit up at night sorting out what we leave behind," he says. But by the end, a simple exchange of letters can hold out as much hope as a cease-fire.

Through the thoroughly credible performances in this production, one comes to know these characters as one knows neighbors, and with that familiarity one begins to care about them. Mr. Lamude never lets any one actor's individual objectives get in the way of Mr. Reid's story, which he moves smartly along. Malachy McCourt and Aideen O'Kelly capture the quiet desperation with which Bert and Theresa yearn for companionship in their remaining years. John Finn is superb as Victor, the once intelligent young man hiding his fear and longing for love behind a curtain of rage. Ann Dowd is excellent as Joan, the "clever girl with clever talk" who must confront her own suppressed emotions. Terry Donnely's Diedre is full of unquenched desire, and Ellen Tobie's Jenny is a sad portrait of a woman who has simply given up on her love of life.

1990 O 18, C22:5

The Sum of Us

By David Stevens; directed by Kevin Dowling; sets by John Lee Beatty; lighting by Dennis Parichy; costumes by Therese A. Bruck; sound by Darren West; stage manager, Larry Bussard; associate producers, Jay Hass and Donald R. Stoltz. Presented by Dowling Entertainment, Duane Wilder, Gintare Seleika Everett and in association with Chantepleure Inc. At the Cherry Lane Theater, 38 Commerce Street.

Jeff.. Tony Goldwyn
Harry... Richard Venture
Greg.. Neil Maffin
Joyce....................................... Phyllis Somerville

By STEPHEN HOLDEN

In one of the noisier scenes in David Stevens's quiet, affecting drama, "The Sum of Us," Harry Mitchell, a

widower in his late 50's, nags his 24-year-old gay son, Jeff, to be more aggressive about finding a lover. "Don't put off till tomorrow what you should do today!" he harangues. One day, he warns, Jeff could wake up all alone and regret not having taken action.

With their affectionate bickering, Harry and Jeff, who share a small house in an industrial suburb of Melbourne, Australia, suggest a new variation of "The Odd Couple." But the oddest and most refreshing thing about them is their utter normalcy. Harry (Richard Venture), who is heterosexual, dreams of remarrying one day and methodically sets about meeting prospective wives through a dating service. Jeff (Tony Goldwyn), a plumber who plays on the local rugby team, is a shy young man who is still smarting from the recent breakup of a relationship. At the start of the play, he is preparing for a date with Greg (Neil Maffin), a young gardener he has met in a local pub and on whom he has already pinned many hopes and fantasies.

If Harry is wistful about the fact that he will have no grandchildren, he has also gone out of his way to understand his son's world. He has allowed Jeff to take him on a tour of gay bars, in one of which the patrons, assuming Harry to be gay, dubbed him "Harriet." The father's concern for his son's health in the age of AIDS has even prompted him to bring home gay pornography depicting safe sex. The magazines lie casually about the Mitchell living room.

•

A relationship that could easily be the basis of situation comedy full of stock gags and cute double-entendres has been turned by Mr. Stevens, an Australian playwright and director, into a poignant, psychologically rich exploration of family ties and the conflicts between those loyalties and the formation of outside relationships. The story revolves around the problems that ensue with the arrival of potential new mates into Harry and Jeff's closed domestic existence.

When Greg visits, the young gardener, whose own father is so intoler-

Martha Swope Associates

Tony Goldwyn, left, and Richard Venture in "The Sum of Us."

ant of homosexuality that his son must hide it, finds himself smothered by Harry's coziness and matchmaking maneuvers. That scene is echoed later when Harry brings home a prospective wife, Joyce (Phyllis Somerville). The one thing he has neglected to discuss with her is his son's homosexuality. As much as Harry loves and supports Jeff, his omission suggests that he still feels a lingering sense of shame about his son. And his speeches to Joyce in which he explains his feelings about fatherhood are among the drama's most touching moments.

The playwright, whose credits include co-writing the screenplay for the film "Breaker Morant," has scrupulously detailed two of the richer and more complex characters to be found in a contemporary play. At the same time, he has bent over backward to avoid sensationalism and melodrama. If the play has a fault, it is that the mundane exchanges between father and son drag on a bit too long in the first act, so that the cheery atmosphere begins to seem stifling.

•

Both the direction and the acting in the production at the Cherry Lane Theater are exceptional in their understatement and precision. It would have been easy enough to treat the father-son banter and the monologues in which the characters reveal their inner thoughts as shticks. Instead, the director, Kevin Dowling, has found a seamless dramatic rhythm for all of the dialogue. It is a rhythm that finds serious undertones beneath the lightest chatter and a spiritual buoyancy underlying the gloomier reflections.

From the first moment they are onstage together, Mr. Venture and Mr. Goldwyn create a palpable father-son bond that grows steadily more powerful as the play progresses to its surprising, bittersweet finale. Mr. Venture's Harry suggests a more refined Australian answer to Archie Bunker, stripped of his prejudices but still a little rough around the dges.

As Jeff, Mr. Goldwyn, who played Patrick Swayze's duplicitous best friend in the film "Ghost," is equally impressive in a role that calls for him to be at once physically appealing but unsure of himself and somewhat inarticulate. In playing against his own smooth handsomeness, the actor has adopted a hesitant, slightly gawky body language. In their supporting roles, Mr. Maffin and Ms. Somerville are also flawness. The four actors' Australian accents are as consistent as they are finely tuned.

"The Sum of Us" has no epic ambitions. But as such small-scale realistic dramas go, it is an unusually sturdy and well-made play whose humane vision of decent people struggling to find love in a treacherous universe strikes a deep, warmly resonant chord.

1990 O 20, 16:4

Our Country's Good

By Timerlake Wertenbaker; based on the novel "The Playmaker," by Thomas Keneally; directed by Mark Lamos; set design,Christopher Barreca; costumes, Candice Donnelly; lighting, Mimi Sherin; sound, David Budries; dramaturg, Greg Leaming; dialect coach, Elizabeth Smith; production stage manager, Barbara Reo; stage manager, Denise Winter; assistant director, Rob Greenberg. Presented by Hartford Stage, Mr. Lamos, artistic director; David Hawkanson, managing director. At Hartford.

WITH: Amelia Campbell, Helen Carey, Michael Cumpsty, Herb Downer, Tracey Ellis, Adam LeFevre, Richard Poe, Stephen Rowe, J. Smith-Cameron, Sam Tsoutsouvas and Gregory Wallace.

By MEL GUSSOW

HARTFORD, Oct. 16 — Timberlake Wertenbaker's "Our Country's Good" is an enlightening exploration of the inhumanity of the penal system in New South Wales, the British colony that became Australia. Ms. Wertenbaker's drama is now running at Hartford Stage in a perceptive production directed by Mark Lamos.

In this free-handed adaptation of Thomas Keneally's novel "The Playmaker," the author uses inventive stage devices to bring a distant world to life and to view it in historical perspective. By extension, the play is prescient about the founding of Australia itself. First presented in London at the Royal Court Theater, "Our Country's Good" received an Olivier Award as best play of 1988.

Both the novel and the play deal with events in the late 1780's in the ultimate penal colony, a final station for the dregs and outcasts of British society. For the most minor crimes, convicts, some of them adolescents, are made to pay disproportionate consequences. Arriving by prison ship, the convicts continue to be brutalized in their new encampment.

•

Suddenly there is a ray of hope with the announcement by the settlement's Governor that a play will be presented with the convicts as actors. A stage-struck lieutenant in the Royal Marines is named the director, and he chooses George Farquhar's Restoration comedy "The Recruiting Officer" for the simple reason that he has two copies of the play. This much of the story is true — the play turned out

to be the first ever presented in Australia — and many of the characters are based on real people.

From here, the playwright lets her imagination expand. "Our Country's Good" becomes a backstage play with a social conscience, demonstrating the redemptive power of theater and of education. While making political points, Ms. Wertenbaker underlines the humanity of her characters and the grotesque humor that is so endemic to their daily existence.

The thought of being onstage energizes the convicts. As Mr. Keneally wrote in his novel, they sensed "that their best chance out of hunger and lovelessness and a bad name was to capture the first primitive stage of this new earth."

The lieutenant finds himself besieged by competitive candidates, at least one of them insane, and beset by the rigid strictures of the military community. As he tries to put together a production with this motley troupe of misfits, many of them illiterate, art is repeatedly imperiled by life.

•

In Christopher Barreca's haunting scenic design, the roof of the Hartford Stage sprouts a field of nooses waiting to ensnare the convicts, who go about their acting as their sole escape. Eventually they become actors, with temperaments as well as talent, and the lieutenant begins to play the role of actor-manager. At one point, he becomes the audience's guide, admonishing that "people who can't pay attention should not go to the theater."

Several factors elevate the play: the use of "The Recruiting Officer" as reflective subtext confronting convicts with roles seemingly contradictory to those they play in life, and Ms. Wertenbaker's artfulness in moving among the various stages of reality,

for example. In her adaptation, she wisely underplays the native symbolism and focuses on the play within the play. The lieutenant's faith in his actors is confirmed. Acquiring a sense of selfworth, they begin to see a path through the wilderness.

As director, Mr. Lamos meets the challenge with a theatricality matching that of the playwright. Because of the elements of role-playing, this is one play that can support the concept of cross-casting. Ten actors double in roles, playing officers as well as convicts, men and women, blacks and whites.

Only Michael Cumpsty portrays a single character, the stalwart director of "The Recruiting Officer," a man who marches on his own interior journey in the course of the narrative. In particular, one prisoner (Tracey Ellis) makes him realize the iniquities within the penal colony as well as the moralistic limits the officer has imposed on his own life.

At times, Mr. Cumpsty overplays the pietism, but he grows with his character, as does Ms. Ellis. Both are movingly at the center of the drama, and there are also penetrating performances by Sam Tsoutsouvas (as the convict who in real life subsequently founded Australia's first theater), Stephen Rowe, Amelia Campbell, and, especially, Helen Carey as a woman rescued by theater from her own desperation.

It is left to Richard Poe, portraying the potential playwright of the troupe, to articulate the meaning behind the title of the play. In his character's invented prologue to Farquhar, he says the convicts have left England "for our country's good," not as exiles but as patriots. The irony in that declaration resonates throughout Ms. Wertenbaker's compelling drama, even as the new prologue is censored for being too provocative. The play ends, as it should, with the audience eager to see an actual performance of these actor-convicts in "The Recruiting Officer." At the Royal Court, both plays were performed in repertory.

1990 O 21, 59:3

Theme and Variations

By Samuil Alyoshin; English translation by Michael Glenny; directed by Geoffrey Sherman; set and lighting design, Paul Wonsek; costumes, Marianne Powell Parker; sound design, Richard Rose; production stage manager, Randy Lawson. Presented by Chelsea Stage, 441 West 26th Street; Mr. Sherman, artistic director; Dara Hershman, managing director.

Igor Mikhailovich......................Ethan Phillips
Lyubov (Lyuba) Sergeyevna Kathleen McCall
Dmitri Nikolayevich..................:William Wise

By WILBORN HAMPTON

There is a surprise plot twist at the end of the first act of "Theme and Variations," a play by the Soviet writer Samuil Alyoshin at the Chelsea Stage that is built solely around a faintly amusing case of mistaken identity.

This error, which goes uncorrected and undetected through much of the second act because of the lust and self-interest of the misidentified, alters the lives of all three characters in the play. Unfortunately, this unexpected turn of events comes only after a tedious introduction of the other two characters, told mostly in the exchange of a series of rather mundane letters.

T. Charles Erickson

Richard Poe and Tracey Ellis in a scene from "Our Country's Good," at the Hartford Stage in Connecticut.

The story evolves out of a chance meeting between two Muscovite lawyer friends near a statue of Pushkin in Simferopol, the old Crimean city that has built a small cottage industry out of the fact that Russia's great poet once spent three weeks there on his way from St. Petersburg to somewhere else. The two men make the acquaintance of Lyuba (Kathleen McCall), a beautiful young tour guide who gives her entourage a 10-minute break to take photographs of the Pushkin statue. Dmitri (William Wise), the older lawyer, quotes Pushkin with the young woman. Igor (Ethan Phillips), the younger lawyer, tries to impress her in a more traditional way, and fails. He does, however, manage to get her home address.

Back in Moscow, Dmitri writes to the young woman, and the rest of the first act is a recitation of their correspondence. The world of letters may be the grandfather of all literature, but, with a few exceptions, it is not a literary device that transfers successfully to the stage. Mr. Alyoshin uses it in "Theme and Variations" for character exposition. The trouble is that the characters these epistles expose are ordinary people living commonplace lives filled with familiar problems. Lyuba turns out to be a complainer of the "it's always something" school. She's bored; her husband wants her to give dinner parties to help his career; her mother-in-law

Gerry Goodstein/"Theme and Variations"
Ethan Phillips and Kathleen McCall in a scene from "Theme and Variations."

is always criticizing her; she gets so angry that she slams a door.

•

Dmitri is one of those older men who are full of understanding; he is supportive; he has an aphorism for every occasion. "Don't slam doors," he advises Lyuba. "It's not the door's fault."

The deeper problem with the play, however, is that none of this really leads anywhere, even after the inadvertent mistake in identity leads to a second-act spiral of deception, betrayal and accusation. As an illustration of the darker side of human nature and the ironies present in the process of self-discovery, "Theme and Variations" has all the ingredients for a good short story.

Despite energetic and animated performances, especially by Miss McCall and Mr. Phillips, neither the cast nor Geoffrey Sherman's lively direction can overcome the mediocrity and sedentary nature of so much of the material.

1990 O 21, 62:3

Hello, Bob

Written and directed by Robert Patrick. Presented by LaMama E. T. C., at 74A East Fourth Street.

WITH: Carol Nelson, Edmond Ramage, Jeffrey J. Albright and Stephen Engle.

By STEPHEN HOLDEN

One of the sadder scenes in "Hello, Bob," a montage of monologues written and directed by Robert Patrick and set in the late 1970's, features a character named Tennessee who speaks with a courtly Southern accent and bears a striking resemblance to Tennessee Williams. Talking on the telephone to a playwright named Robert, Tennessee complains about the indignity of peddling his memoirs and offers condolences to Robert, whose artistic reputation he has been told was "squelched" by the media.

Tennessee's monologue is not the only moment in the play, at La Mama, in which Mr. Patrick, who never appears, portrays himself as a writer persecuted by enemy forces. In another scene, a fawning journalist apologizes over the phone to the playwright for having been assigned to do a "kill job" on him.

This strain of paranoia, which runs through "Hello, Bob," gives the play a queasy undertone. Among 21 monologues, delivered by four actors, more than half are one-sided conversations with the invisible playwright. The speakers range from a New York cab driver to a theater producer in Iowa to a male prostitute in Wisconsin. Taken together, they represent a very rough cross-section of Americans in the late 1970's.

•

On a more personal level, some of them appear to represent people Mr. Patrick knew around the time his only Broadway play, "Kennedy's Children," was produced and gave him a fleeting moment of fame. The production won Shirley Knight a 1976 Tony Award for best featured actress. And sure enough, another speaker is an actress named Shirley.

The monologues trace the unseen Robert's path from New York to the heartland of America on a lecture tour of high schools and colleges. Here, the playwright discovers to his dismay that what little theater exists is synonymous with "Arsenic and Old Lace" and "Hello, Dolly!" Ultimately, Robert concludes that artistically he is "a token liberal to assuage the guilt of a lot of fascist fools," as one character quotes him as saying.

As in his other plays, Mr. Patrick shows a flair for histrionic dialogue and crude caricature. But with few exceptions, his creations don't have the feel of autonomous individuals but seem instead like authorial mouthpieces and paper tigers equipped with appropriate clothing and regional accents.

Carol Nelson, who plays 11 female characters ranging from a philistine drama teacher in Georgia to a New York City street person, is the most effective of the four performers. The actress, who has appeared in many of Mr. Patrick's plays, bites into these caricatures with a fearless avidity that fits the spirit of his high-pitched, exhibitionistic and often cantankerous writing.

1990 O 21, 62:3

One Good Laugh That Deserves Another

NORMALLY, I DON'T KEEP track of protracted laughs in the theater, but the production of "The Miser" at the Circle in the Square provokes so few that I feel fairly safe in giving you my personal count.

I'm not talking about the sudden attack of the giggles that sometimes overtakes a single spectator, often to the bewilderment of everybody else. Or the sporadic chortling that can break out in one row, while the row behind sits blank-faced. (In the round, you notice these things.) No, I'm talking about the laugh that starts out solidly, then builds on itself a couple of times, extending its dominion in the process, so that when it finally crests, the entire audience is caught up in its embrace.

There is one.

I don't think I'm spoiling it for you by revealing what brings it about. That estimable actor Philip Bosco, who is playing Harpagon, the title character in Molière's indestructible farce, has simply surrendered to a catarrh and embarked on a colossal coughing jag. That's it. Since Molière's script provides far ampler opportunities for revelation and merriment — including one of the most celebrated monologues in 17th-century French theater — an explanation may be in order here.

As a 60-year-old skinflint, Mr. Bosco does not present a pretty picture. Nor is he meant to. The drab olive of his threadbare britches and vest casts an unhealthy pallor over his face (unless it is the other way around). The cost of a wig being to his mind shockingly prohibitive, he prefers to let his hair hang straight down, rather like wet string, while his sharp squint suggests that he is trying to economize on his vision, as well. That doesn't take into account his disposition, which is less attractive.

Having no sense of himself, it has occurred to Harpagon, as it does to so many of Molière's elderly autocrats, that a fresh young wife might be an appropriate companion in his advanced years. To facilitate the alliance, he has engaged a matchmaker (Carole Shelley). But he's beginning to nurture a doubt or two. What if his intended really prefers a handsome swain her own age?

How could she, scoffs Ms. Shelley, eager to collect her fee and therefore quick to dismiss any and all callow swains with an airy wave of the hand. What could youth possibly offer to compare with the magnificence of old age? (Biting off her consonants as if they were celery, while grandly extending her vowels, Ms. Shelley may remind you of Maggie Smith in "Lettice and Lovage." No harm there. They both are engaged in similar endeavors: lending luster to crumbling monuments.)

■

As Ms. Shelley ladles out the flattery, Mr. Bosco's chest swells, his heavy step grows springy and he permits himself a little jig. That's when the cough begins to well up deep inside him. When it breaks, it is thunderous. Here he is, determined to play the peacock and prove himself the match of any randy 20-year-old in wig and ribbons. But he's hacking like a tubercular ward and his arthritic bones are bearing up badly under the onslaught. The tug of war is hilarious.

The rest of Mr. Bosco's performance is nowhere near so entertaining and it's no mystery why: nothing else, not even his devotion to the almighty sou, seizes him with the full-bodied fury of that cough. Money, however, is not just the overriding consideration in Harpagon's life; it is the only consideration.

He's ready to give away his daughter (Mia Dillon) to the first comer who'll take her without a dowry. His son (Thomas Gibson) is reduced to consorting with usurers to keep himself in threads. For want of oats, the horses in his stable are skin and bone. The furniture's falling apart and every creak in the house arouses his fear of robbers. No one is immune from his suspicions.

"Show me your hands," he orders a cowering servant (Adam Redfield), who has no sooner obeyed than Harpagon barks, "Now the others." This is not someone to let logic stand in his way.

You'll find, however, that Mr. Bosco steadfastly refuses to be as single-minded as the character. He wants to plumb the man's mind, investigate the depths of his obsession and shade his mania, even as it's mushrooming out of control. His Harpagon is reflective, calculating, deliberate. There is, in fact, a great deal of Shylock in him. Psychologically, the approach may be defensible. But if Harpagon is allowed to sit back, coolly appraising people and events, you end up depriving the play of the whirlwind at its center. Blind recklessness is what makes him a fool. But just as significantly, it is also what turns his household topsy-turvy. In an effort to accommodate him, all the other characters are forced into unnatural postures and hypocritical stances. Take away the zeal and they're left high and dry.

◼

That's just what's happening at the Circle in the Square, which suffers the added drawback of a generally mediocre supporting cast. Mr. Gibson, looking in his 17th-century finery not unlike a supercilious poodle, is a notable exception. His high-strung performance as the impetuous son strikes me as perfectly pitched. Given the prevailing torpor, most people are apt to conclude he's going over the top. But that's precisely the impact Harpagon should have on his beleaguered entourage.

Martha Swope/"The Miser"

Thomas Gibson and Philip Bosco in "The Miser"—rampant suspicion

Philip Bosco is a reflective skinflint in Molière's 'Miser'; Charlotte Rae an optimist with angst in Beckett's 'Happy Days.'

Mr. Bosco certainly knows how to propel himself expertly — and apoplectically — through the madness of farce, as he demonstrated most recently in "Lend Me a Tenor." So the choice to rein in Harpagon and let him ruminate is clearly a conscious one, abetted by the director Stephen Porter, whose staging is uncharacteristically listless. The unfortunate consequences are never more evident than in that monologue I mentioned.

Learning late in the second act that his precious strongbox has been stolen, Harpagon reels on stage — short of breath, shorter of reason, so beside himself with loss that at one point he actually mistakes his own hand for the thief's. He hectors. He pleads. And when that fails to produce his gold, he announces melodramatically, "I'm dying. I'm dead," sinks to the floor and adds, once he gets there, "I'm buried." Not for long, though. The mere thought of revenge stirs new life into his spent body and he's back on his feet, threatening to hang every member of the audience. If *that* doesn't bring his fortune back, he concludes deliriously, "I'll hang myself."

It's not wholly Mr. Bosco's fault that he never gets up to speed or that his raving pays only minor comic dividends. You can't just jump into Harpagon's monologue at a moment's notice. You need a running start. And a running start is, regrettably, the very thing this inwardly focused production refuses to give him.

'Happy Days'

Unlike Mr. Bosco, Charlotte Rae *is* rising to the occasion, although not right off the bat, not for an act, not until the playwright Samuel Beckett has her, so to speak, by the throat. Ms. Rae is playing Winnie, that inexhaustible font of optimism in "Happy Days" at the CSC Theater and the first act shows her buried up to her waist in a mound of desiccated earth. Not that that's anything to be discouraged about.

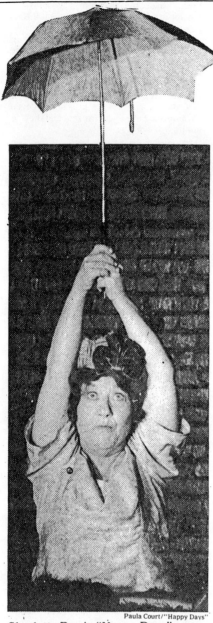

Paula Court/"Happy Days"

*Charlotte Rae in "Happy Days"—
chirps before the oncoming dark*

"Another heavenly day," she gushes. And
so much to be done: teeth to be brushed,
makeup to be applied, pieties to be uttered,

old memories to be savored. Of course, she'll want to sound out Willie (Bill Moor), her decrepit mate who lives in a burrow just out of sight, although she can hear him if he grunts, which he is occasionally wont to do. There's her song to be sung, but not immediately (some things should be saved for later in the blazing day) and, lest she be thought an ingrate, thanks to be given for so many "great mercies."

In Act II, the earth has reclaimed all but her head. And yet Winnie jabbers on, struggling to put a rosy interpretation on her wretchedness. If she can no longer see anyone, perhaps she is still seen. Willie could be looking on. Or God. Or an emmet. (There's a consolation.) She can't budge, but isn't that the faint stirring of a zephyr she feels on her face? (Another consolation.) When Willie, dressed in a tattered tux, crawls out of his hole, to bid her adieu — or maybe just pay tribute to their long-ago courting days — her ecstasy is

complete and the song in her heart bubbles up. It's the waltz from "The Merry Widow," which is ironic enough. But as Ms. Rae delivers it — shrilly, raucously even — it sounds a lot like a dirty barroom ballad.

Panic is in the air and Ms. Rae's tone is richer for that.

We're leagues removed from the transcendent elegance and feathery grace that the great French actress Madeleine Renaud brought to the role. Under the guidance of CSC Rep's artistic director Carey Perloff, Ms. Rae's Winnie is loud and vulgar — an Irish washerwoman who has elbowed her way into the bourgeois

class, but can't always keep her roots from showing. Her generous features, especially the rubbery mouth, are made for mugging, of which there is rather too much in the first act. And her voice sometimes tears into Beckett's lines like a buzz saw.

The conditions of the second act, however, work in Ms. Rae's favor, restraining her broader impulses. Stripped of makeup, her face is sad and vulnerable. Her silly purple hat, once an adornment, has become a humiliation now that it's squashed down low on her head. Fear has crept into the eyes and seemingly drained them of their blueness. The lips are thinner, tighter. If, an act earlier, Ms. Rae was chirping dutiful praises of a world without end, the thought has since occurred to her that an end is nigh, after all. The jubilation has lost its confidence, panic is in the air, and the actress's tone is richer for that.

Inside this garish and overbearing performance, you see, is a moving one. Watching it emerge, as night closes in and the human race closes down, is not the least of the stark fascinations in "Happy Days," but surely one of the more surprising. □

1990 O 21, II:5:1

The Colorado Catechism

By Vincent J. Cardinal; directed by Mark Ramont; sets by James Youmans; costumes by David C. Woolard; lighting by Pat Dignan; sound by Stewart Werner and Chuck London; production stage manager, Denise Yaney; production manager, Jody Boese. Presented by Circle Repertory Company; Tanya Berezin, artistic director; Terrence Dwyer, managing director. At 99 Seventh Avenue South, at West Fourth Street.

Ty .... Kevin James O'Connor
Donna .... Becky Ann Baker

By FRANK RICH

Until Craig Lucas started shaking up the joint with otherworldly comedies like "Reckless" and "Prelude to a Kiss," a season at the Circle Repertory Company was not complete without a play set on a whitewashed, Victorian, all-American porch. The porches were always designed by that master of heartland lyricism John Lee Beatty, and they would usually be the setting for moonlit revelations of family scars and ambisexual love triangles, reliably punctuated by the nattering of crickets. For one playwright — Lanford Wilson, in the Talley trilogy — the Circle Rep porches were a platform for myth, history and passion. You could take the measure of the country in a play like "The Fifth of July." But for lesser writers, the porch was often just a handy place to park adolescent feelings and hope that someone might mistake them for poetic truths.

•

The porch has been dusted off in "The Colorado Catechism," the opening attraction of the Circle Rep's new season, and students of this company's history may be shocked to discover that appearances notwithstanding, the porch's designer is James Youmans, not Mr. Beatty. The evening's jolts end there. The play's author, a much honored 1990 graduate of the Yale School of Drama, Vincent J. Cardinal, clearly has the

makings of a professional dramatist, and "The Colorado Catechism," a two-hander about recovering alcoholics, is hard to fault on such grounds as structure, sincerity, literacy and seriousness of intent. What's missing are depth of emotion and originality of expression, which is why the play, like its high-altitude setting, seems so short of oxygen. Much as one may appreciate the scenery, it's hard to escape the sensation of suffocation.

Written as a memory piece, "The Colorado Catechism" is narrated in the present by Ty (Kevin James O'Connor), a young, self-destructive New York painter of the go-go 1980's who recalls his life-saving rehabilitation three years earlier at a drug-and-alcohol clinic in Cripple Creek. There he found salvation with the help of a fellow patient, Donna (Becky Ann Baker), a wrecked Middle American wife and mother who captured his heart for a time. In his soliloquies to the audience, Ty explains that he wants to enshrine his feelings for Donna by capturing her on canvas "in a single pose." Yet Mr. Cardinal does not really confront his hero's feelings on his way to an upbeat ending that leaves the painter waving a fist in victory while Donna remains as faceless as a waxy apple in a still life.

•

Though "The Colorado Catechism" is pumped up with the clinical terminology of 12-step programs and some cultural name-dropping, its roots can be found in two-character romantic comedies like "Two for the Seesaw" and "Same Time, Next Year." Opposites except for their alcoholism and lapsed Catholicism, Ty and Donna meet cute, exchange histories, have a crisis and reach an understanding. In this case, the crisis concerns the hero's revelation of a past homosexual affair with an art-world mentor named Artie. While Ty calls himself a bisexual, and Donna seems to accept him as such, he seduces her only to pull away. Why? Mr. Cardinal does not say. Thorny issues are swept under the rug so that Ty can send the audience home with the happy news that he somehow learned "for the first time" how to "love a person." Who such a person might be is left so vague that his affections might as well be addressed to "Occupant."

Mr. Cardinal is much more painstaking about marshaling his dramatic effects than penetrating his characters' psyches. Metaphors — portraiture, a house of cards, shooting stars — are carefully set up, then cashed in. For flavoring, there are tortured Tennessee Williamsisms ("I will play my memory like solitaire for two") and a few offhand jokes. The author's inexperience can be found in that bane of two-character plays, the lengthy accounts of offstage figures, an all-male crew that in addition to Artie, most prominently includes the clinic's director, Roger, and Donna's estranged husband, Brad. (Given this play and last season's "Imagining Brad," the Circle Rep might declare at least a temporary moratorium on imagined Brads.) The director, Mark Ramont, leans on his lighting designer, Pat Dignan, to create the illusion of movement while busily yanking the action back and forth between Ty's downtown present and Cripple Creek past.

•

Like the script, the actors are better at attending to surface details than the substance of passion and suffering. The sexual and emotional

328

Gerry Goodstein/Circle Repertory Company

Kevin James O'Connor and Becky Ann Baker in the play "The Colorado Catechism."

charge between them is nil. That said, the bearded, unkempt Mr. O'Connor uses a Nicholson-Malkovich vocal fissure and intense little eyes to create a persuasive portrait of the narcissistic artist as a young Mary Boone discovery. While Ms. Baker's wisecracking, chainsmoking and round-faced Donna at first seems a bit too close to Roseanne Barr for comfort, her comic timing does bring crusty verve to a heroine who, as written, approaches sentimental camp.

By the end, both she and Mr. O'Connor get to bask in a display of colored lights prompted by the sudden, gratuitous arrival of Independence Day. As Circle Rep porch plays go, "The Colorado Catechism" may be no "Fifth of July" but at least no one can accuse it of failing to give the audience the Fourth.

1990 O 22, C13:1

Ninagawa Macbeth

By Shakespeare; translated by Yushi Odashima from the English; directed by Yukio Ninagawa; scenery by Kappa Senoh; lighting by Sumio Yoshii; music arrangement, Masato Kai; sound effects, Akira Honma; choreography, Kinnosuke Hanayagi; fight arranger, Masahiro Kunii; costumes, Jusaburo Tsujimura. Produced by Tadao Nakane for the Point Tokyo Company in association with Noriko Sengoku/Inter-Arts, New York. The Ninagawa Company presented by the Brooklyn Academy of Music, Harvey Lichtenstein, president and executive producer. At the Opera House, 30 Lafayette Avenue, at Ashland Place, Fort Greene section.

Duncan	Mizuho Suzuki
Malcolm	Norihiro Inoue
Donalbain	Eiichi Seike
Macbeth	Masane Tsukayama
Banquo	Kazuhisa Seshimo
Macduff	Haruhiko Joh
Ross	Masafumi Seno
Fleance	Tomoyuki Yamada
Siward/Old Man	Tatsumi Aoyama
Lady Macbeth	Komaki Kurihara
Lady Macduff	Hitomi Kageyama
Three Witches	Tokusaburo Arashi, Goro Daimon and Matanosuke Nakamura

By MEL GUSSOW

The central symbol in the image-laden "Ninagawa Macbeth" is a large cherry tree spreading its blossoms and shimmering in the light. As the play progresses and as Macbeth's plot fails, spring turns autumnal and the petals begin to fall. When Birnam Wood moves, branches of that tree are carried across the stage. As directed in Japanese by Yukio Ninagawa, "Macbeth" becomes a tale of tragic loss and of lamentation.

The classically centered experimental Ninagawa Company opened Saturday in the Next Wave Festival at the Brooklyn Academy of Music with a production that exudes an exotic beauty.

This is not simply a matter of historical relocation, of moving the play from 11th-century Scotland to 16th-century Japan; it is a question of style and sensibility. While adhering to Shakespeare's text (which we hear in English over headsets), the director turns "Macbeth" into a samurai play and in so doing underlines its universality.

Something similar occurred in the director's all-male "Medea," presented several years ago at the Delacorte Theater in Central Park. In this fiery version, Euripides was transformed into a Japanese playwright. In both "Medea" and "Macbeth," the merging of Western literary tradition and Eastern theatrical techniques results in an original work of performance art.

•

Mr. Ninagawa does not offer a radical reinterpretation of Shakespeare, as was the case with Ingmar Bergman's fascistic "Hamlet" and the Georgian tragicomic "King Lear," both staged in previous seasons at the Brooklyn Academy of Music. Instead, Mr. Ninagawa holds firmly to Shakespearean intention while stressing the timelessness of the story.

Macbeth becomes a Japanese warrior who slashes his way to the crown. Before Lady Macbeth has prodded him into assassinating the king, he is already determined on a course to assume power. There is a perverse rationality to their monstrous acts, even as their "unnatural deeds ... breed unnatural troubles."

All this is communicated in highly ritualized acting and in the stage pictures that hauntingly fill Mr. Ninagawa's canvas. Those pictures are often seen through a scrim. The garish weird sisters and the bloody battles, as well as the cherry blossoms, are viewed in a frame, adding an aura of magic.

Two stoop-backed old women act as stagehands and silent chorus, parting a screen to reveal a Buddhist shrine that serves as the principal setting for the stateliness of court. Seamlessly the play alternates between close-ups and wide screen images, giving the work a cinematic texture. In the vastness of its pictorial imagery, the production is closer to Akira Kurosawa's "Ran" that it is to that director's "Throne of Blood" (an earlier Japanese adaptation of "Macbeth"). From the "Ninagawa Macbeth," one receives a feeling of what the world is like beyond the cataclysmic events at the center.

•

Repeatedly theatergoers are tantalized. Seen at a distance through that scrim, two horses momentarily look real, then as the screen opens, it is clear that they are artful mock-ups, men in opulent equine costumes. Kappa Senoh's scenery and Josaburo Tsujimura's costumes are integral to the directorial concept.

The acting adds its own distinction. Masane Tsukayama's Macbeth is a proud young general. When he becomes a killer, he is overcome by stunned disbelief at his own action. With one stroke, he has sundered his world, and the daggers seem glued to his hands. Recovering, he remains a demon in combat. The battle scenes as well as the murders are strikingly staged, benefiting from the actors' command of martial arts. In contrast to her husband, Komaki Kurihara's Lady Macbeth is cool to the point of seeming serene. Between moments of violence, she strokes a violin-like stringed instrument. Even more than Macbeth, she is possessed by a fury.

Jack Manning/The New York Times

Masane Tsukayama, left, in the title role and Kazuhisa Seshimo as Banquo in an interpretation of "Macbeth" performed in Japanese at the Brooklyn Academy of Music.

Both actors rise to their mad scenes, Mr. Tsukayama when he is confronted by Banquo's ghost (Japanese style, the characters sit on the floor rather than at a table for the banquet scene), Miss Kurihara as she sleepwalks through her insanity.

Naturally an English-speaking audience will miss hearing the actors deliver Shakespeare's words, but in his simultaneous translation, Faubion Bowers has the diction of a trained actor. The translation holds to the text, except for an occasional passing reference, as to Macbeth's "battle fan." Only in Japan would such an object be carried into combat.

While there are no significant shifts in scenes, there are atmospheric interpolations. When Malcolm and Macduff meet, the palace is filled with huge sculptural figures looking like icons of warriors past. Macbeth delivers "Tomorrow, and tomorrow" surrounded by a circle of glowing and inextinguishable candles.

At the Brooklyn Academy, we hear Shakespeare and we see "Ninagawa Macbeth," a theatrical experience that is doubly enriching.

1990 O 22, C20:1

Handy Dandy

By William Gibson; directed by Tony Giordano; set and lighting by Neil Peter Jampolis; costume design by Barbara Forbes; sound supervisor, Tom Gould; executive producer, Roger Alan Gindi; production stage manager, Christine Michael. Presented by Eric Krebs. At the John Houseman Theater, 450 West 42d Street.

Molly Egan.................................Audra Lindley
Henry Pulaski.....................James Whitemore

By MEL GUSSOW

As he demonstrated in "Two for the Seesaw," William Gibson has a sure touch with two-character plays, but his new dialogue, "Handy Dandy," is less a genuine two-hander than a case of dramatic underpopulation. When the couple at the center of the piece address unseen characters, one is led to the conclusion that economics rather than artistic necessity determined the size of the cast.

James Whitmore and Audra Lindley are alternating "Handy Dandy" with Tom Cole's "About Time" at the John Houseman Theater. While the fact of two actors doing two plays in repertory is admirable, one must question the validity of each work, except as exercises for acting. Mr. Whitmore and Ms. Lindley are infinitely resourceful, and as a result, "Handy Dandy" holds the audience interest longer than one might expect.

Following the established principle that opposites attract theatrically, Mr. Gibson has positioned a crusty, conservative New England judge against a high-flying liberal nun. Arrested in a protest march against a nuclear missile plant, she insists on acting as her own counsel and refuses to let the judge dismiss her case.

•

The author has contrived a collision of ideas and personalities, with Mr. Whitmore stubbornly holding out for the law even if it leads to injustice. Above all, he wants order in his courtroom, while Ms. Lindley strikes repeated blows for conscience and civil liberties. She is relentless in her desire to awaken the judge from his judicial slumber.

For added drama, we learn that the nun was married three times before she found her calling and that the judge continues, late in life, as a ladies' man. Eventually he softens to the point where he begins to fall in love with the obstreperous sister. All this and the ending itself are as predictable as the fact that no other characters are going to walk on stage.

Because of Mr. Gibson's intelligence and the appeal of the actors, there are moments with warmth and humor. Mr. Whitmore could be a real judge as well as an acting judge. In fact he is so congenial in the role that one keeps wanting to hear another case in his courtroom instead of following this one through several post-judgment permutations. Ms. Lindley gives an equally persuasive portrait of a nun with a sense of morality as well as faith. She is feisty without being overbearing.

In contrast to "About Time," a play about the hermetic world of an elderly married couple, there is at least an effort to depict the background of the characters and life outside the court, a life that is sparingly simulated in Neil Peter Jampolis's setting. Given the limits of the play, Tony Giordano's staging achieves a certain fluidity.

As it stands, "Handy Dandy" could be shortened without dramatic impairment, which could also be said about its companion play. Instead of two self-supporting two-handers, what is offered is a pair of attenuated one-act plays. If each were distilled to half its length, "Handy Dandy" and "About Time" might make a single contrasting evening in the theater.

1990 O 23, C20:1

Gonza the Lancer

By Chikamatsu Monzaemon; translated by Donald Keene; directed by David Greenspan; set design by William Kennon; costume design by Elsa Ward; lighting by David Bergstein; fights staged by B. H. Barry; associate producer, Jason Steven Cohen. Presented by Joseph Papp. At the Public/Susan Stein Shiva Theater, 425 Lafayette Street.

WITH: Ron Bagden, Fanni Green, Koji Okamura, Tim Perez, Keenan Shimizu, Mary Shultz and Ching Valdes/Aran

By MEL GUSSOW

As the author of 130 plays performed by both Kabuki and Bunraku theaters, Chikamatsu Monzaemon was the first Japanese playwright to make heroic figures out of common men. His tales often deal with acts of domestic violence, as is the case with "Gonza the Lancer," which opened Tuesday night in a misguided production at the Public Theater.

Chikamatsu's artistry is inextricable from performance and production techniques, that combination of highly formalized acting, movement and scenic panoply that so distinguishes the work of classic Japanese theater. Specifically, he wrote "Gonza" and other plays for the puppet theater, a choice, it has been said, provoked by his feeling that puppets would be more faithful to his intentions than actors ever could be. One wonders what the playwright (1653-1725) would have thought of David Greenspan's aberrant version.

The director's aim may have been to put Chikamatsu to the test of modernism, to see if this story of ambition, adultery and vengeance would

have a relevance to today's world and today's theater. The result is a deconstruction of the text. Reduced to its basic narrative (in Donald Keene's authoritative translation) and staged in campy contemporary style, "Gonza" moves dangerously close to self-parody. At the same time, it does not take a further comic step and embrace the world of ridiculous theater.

Anyone who has not seen a Chikamatsu play as done in the classic mode of Kabuki or Bunraku may well question the author's creativity. From this production, it would be impossible to comprehend how this epic playwright could be regarded as Shakespeare's equal in Japan.

Gonza is more a villain than a hero, though his final act of self-sacrifice could be seen as heroic. An 18th-century samurai, the "pride of the martial profession," he is a man of high-vaulted ambition. He wants to be a master of the highly prized art of the tea ceremony.

Through his own duplicity, he becomes affianced to two women. Simultaneously, the mother of one of the young women has her own romantic designs on Gonza, and in the play's pivotal moment, the mother and her prospective son-in-law are caught in an act of seeming infidelity. Around these two are various vicious rivals in love and battle, all of them driving the unfortunate couple to their doom.

In Mr. Greenspan's production, 7 actors perform 20 roles, with crosscasting of the most debilitating kind. A tall, gawky actor plays a simpering governess, a short actress with a painted moustache pretends to be an aged grandfather and Keenan Shimizu, who has done notable work with the Pan Asian Repertory Theater, is hamstrung by a gallery of characters, including small children and Gonza's dewy-eyed first love.

Though two narrators introduce the characters and tell the story, theatergoers may find themselves frequently consulting the program to see who is saying what to whom. Except for Ching Valdes/Aran as a narrator and, at odd moments, Koji Okamura and Mary Shultz in the central roles, the performances are self-conscious.

Further divorcing the play from its source, the scenery is sparse and the costumes are a motley collection of T-shirts and trousers that give the play an air of a workshop rather than that of a finished production. Occasionally, Mr. Greenspan tries to adapt a Japanese technique. The puppetry is especially ineffective. The production would certainly have benefited from the collaboration of an imaginative puppeteer or mask maker. The atmospheric barrenness is in stark contrast to the visual splendor of the current "Ninagawa Macbeth" at the Brooklyn Academy of Music.

The evening begins with a prologue, written and performed by Mr. Greenspan. His writing has an elliptical lilt but adds nothing to one's understanding of "Gonza the Lancer." In the past, he has been an evocative director of his own plays, but Chikamatsu proves to be beyond his reach. Mr. Greenspan, one of four directors in residence this season at the Public Theater, has made an unfortunate choice for his debut production.

1990 O 25, C20:5

The Voysey Inheritance

By Harley Granville Barker; directed by Arvin Brown; set design by John Lee Beatty; costume design by David Murin; lighting by Arden Fingerhut; production stage manager, Anne Keefe. Presented by Long Wharf Theater, Arvin Brown, artistic director; M. Edgar Rosenblum, executive director. At New Haven.

Peacey.................................Ralph Williams
Voysey Sr...........................James Noble
Edward Voysey.....................Boyd Gaines
Maj. Booth Voysey................Doug Stender
Evans Colpus.................William Swetland
George Booth......................William Prince
Denis Tregoning..........T. Scott Cunningham
Ethel Voysey.....................Louise Roberts
Alice Maitland....................Caris Corfman
Honor Voysey.....................Jeanne Ruskin
Beatrice Voysey.............Ann McDonough
Phoebe...............................Jody Rowell
Mary..................................Ashley Voos
Mrs. Voysey........................Joyce Ebert
Emily Voysey................Rebecca Nelson
Trenchard Voysey.................Tom Hewitt
Hugh Voysey....................Michel R. Gill

By FRANK RICH

Special to The New York Times

NEW HAVEN, Oct. 23 — Devotees of television's prime-time disasters may well recall "Beacon Hill," the 1975 CBS series that tried to knock off public television's hit English import "Upstairs Downstairs" for fun and profit. Though lavishly produced with the best New York character actors that network capital could buy, "Beacon Hill" died a sorry Nielsen death in 13 weeks. The rigorous class distinctions of the British social order looked silly when superimposed even on the snootiest neighborhood of democratic Boston. As Sally Bedell Smith reports in her new biography of the CBS chairman William S. Paley ("In All His Glory," Simon & Schuster), network surveys revealed that "the American public just didn't believe that one household could have that many servants."

"Beacon Hill," long faded to a dull blur on this television viewer's consciousness, came leaping back to mind during Arvin Brown's staging of "The Voysey Inheritance" at the Long Wharf Theater here. Written at the beginning of this century, the play is the best-known drama by Harley Granville Barker (1877-1946), the dazzling English director, actor and critic who played a crucial role in modernizing Shakespeare production and in shepherding new plays by his friend and mentor George Bernard Shaw to the stage. The only thing remotely American about Barker was his second wife, but this has not stopped Mr. Brown and an adapter, James Luse, from transplanting "The Voysey Inheritance" from England to Boston. The Voyseys, a large Edwardian family, now talk of Adams instead of Cromwell, refer to such American institutions as Nash Motors and Kidder, Peabody and, of course, have been moved from Chislehurst to Chestnut Hill. All things considered, it's a wonder that the play's title wasn't changed to "The Kennedy Loot."

•

If the Englishness of "The Voysey Inheritance" were only a matter of proper names, the switch in setting would be an innocuous gimmick. But Barker's play, whose serious themes of money and conscience are prompted by the revelation of a scandal within the ancestral Voysey law firm, is as indigenously English as "Bleak House." Its Edwardian nuances of class, sex and Fabian economics cannot be Americanized with such simple tools as white-out and a ballpoint pen. And even if they could be, Mr. Brown's production would have wilted anyway, because his approach to the play's substance is consistent with the superficial overhaul of its setting.

The intent seems to be to jolly up "The Voysey Inheritance" into a quaint period piece, a sentimental domestic comedy with darker melodramatic overtones along the lines of "Ah, Wilderness!" Barker's delicate theatricality, which relies more on ideas, moral ambiguities and psychological undercurrents than on plot or surface charms, simply cannot deliver such crowd-pleasing goods, and his play's genuine virtues are bulldozed in the attempt to broaden the text into something it's not. Only John Lee Beatty's set and David Murin's costumes — a "Magnificent Ambersons"-style celebration of dark wood paneling, crimson velvet curtains and aristocratic turn-of-the-century fashions — consistently fulfill the production's aspirations to nostalgic entertainment.

•

In a large company, a few actors try to get at the author's real meaning and would be worth recruiting for a more heartfelt version. The most important by far is Boyd Gaines, who originated the role of the heroine's best male friend in "The Heidi Chronicles" and here plays Edward Voysey, a priggish young man who learns in the first scene that his true family "inheritance" is a dirty secret: for years his father (a miscast James Noble) has been secretly speculating

T. Charles Erickson/"The Voysey Inheritance"

William Prince, left, and Boyd Gaines in "The Voysey Inheritance" in New Haven.

with the trust funds of clients. Mr. Gaines's heavy-browed air of troubled conscience serves him well as he copes with the ramifications of his disillusioning discovery. His final transformation into a mature man — one of heart and soul as well as rigid principles — is also nicely handled. As a broad smile breaks through Edward's perpetual gloom, so Mr. Gaines's stiff posture at last unbends in a flamboyant collapse into the nearest chair.

It is not this actor's fault that he is earlier robbed of the play's comic apex — the scene in which Edward reveals the family scandal to all his relatives right after his father's funeral. By turning a properly bourgeois Edwardian family into Gilded Age vulgarians, most of the cast, led by Joyce Ebert's brassy matriarch, flattens the scene's exquisitely mixed emotions of mourning, materialism and shock into cheap farce. It's as if Debussy — a composer to whom critics have rightly likened Barker — were being blared out by the horn section of the Boston Pops. Only two supporting players share Mr. Gaines's grasp of the text's spirit: Ann McDonough as a sardonic aspiring author and William Prince as a rich old Voysey client whose utter decadence adds shades of gray to Edward's black-and-white moral perspective on his father's crimes.

The few bright spots cannot salvage the evening's lost opportunity to reclaim a neglected writer. Barker's plays, which have received loving revivals in England over the last decade or so, are so little known in the United States that "The Voysey Inheritance" is said to have never been seen on a professional American stage before the Long Wharf production. It still hasn't been.

1990 O 26, C3:1

Polygraph

Written by Marie Brassard and Robert Lepage; directed by Mr. Lepage; music, Pierre Brousseau and Yves Chamberland; set design, Mr. Lepage; props manager, Steve Lucas; translation, Gyllian Raby; lighting design, Eric Fauque and Mr. Lepage; assistant set designer, Jean Hazel; stage manager, Mr. Fauque; slides, Dave Lepage. Music performed live by Mr. Brousseau. Le Théâtre Repère presented by the Brooklyn Academy of Music, Harvey Lichtenstein, president and executive producer. At Lepercq Space, 30 Lafayette Avenue, Brooklyn.

WITH: Pierre Auger, Marc Béland and Marie Brassard.

By STEPHEN HOLDEN

In the opening sequences of "Polygraph," a play that is billed by its creators as a "metaphysical detective story," many striking but seemingly unrelated images are introduced onto the stage. A skeleton lies in front of a low brick wall behind which a criminologist (Pierre Auger) engages in an overlapping conversation with a waiter (Marc Béland). Their monologues merge into a dialogue that compares the flow of blood to the human heart to the traffic routes in and out of East Berlin. Moments later, an actress (Marie Brassard) auditioning for a movie, confesses that her goal is to play the title role in "Hamlet." The waiter reappears in a restaurant frantically clearing tables and sniffing cocaine and later in a bar practicing bondage and flagellation.

Over the next 90 minutes, the criminologist, the actress and the waiter are revealed to be enmeshed in a triangle. The actress has been chosen to play the lead role in a movie depicting the unsolved murder of a woman in Montreal several years earlier. It emerges that the waiter, who lives in an apartment on the other side of a wall from the actress, was originally suspected of the crime. It also emerges that the polygraph test that helped clear him of suspicion was administered by the criminologist, who in an attempt to trick him had lied to him about the results. The criminologist, who learned his techniques of interrogation in East Berlin, becomes romantically involved with the actress, who in turn has an affair with the waiter.

Handsomely staged by the French-Canadian company Le Théâtre Repère at the Brooklyn Academy of Music, "Polygraph" is a fascinating attempt to make a play that has the form and texture of a film. The script, written by Miss Brassard and the experimental director Robert Lepage, divides the drama into 20 short "sequences" in which theatrical equivalents are found for film-making techniques like dissolves, cross-cutting, montage, flashbacks, dream sequences and slow-motion action.

If Mr. Lepage is hardly the first director to attempt a synthesis of the vocabularies of film and theater, his particular blend shows an exceptional visual flair, rhythmic energy and deftness in the manipulation of symbols. As Mr. Lepage demonstrated in his six-hour theater work, "The Dragons' Trilogy," he also has a special talent for finding symbols that at first seem arbitrary but that through intensive reworking assume an epic richness and significance. In "Polygraph," the most prominent symbol is the wall, which is the wall between the two apartments, the Berlin wall, the barriers between men and women, and finally an obstacle to the truth.

The production also skillfully integrates ritualistic athletic movement into the drama. Scenes in which the three actors climb over, slide down and writhe against the wall in various states of terror and erotic engagement have a compelling visceral drive. The three actors — but especially Miss Brassard — move from conventional narrative into expressionistic pantomime and back with a seamless sense of dramatic flow.

It is a measure of the success of "Polygraph" that the work it recalls the most strongly is not a play but Michelangelo Antonioni's mystery film "Blow Up," which was set in swinging London in the late 1960's. If "Polygraph," with its expressionistic use of slide patterns, shadow and computerized music, suggests a futuristic film noir, it brings the same obsessed fascination to a particular crime. As in "Blow Up," the more one learns of what might have taken place, the deeper the mystery becomes.

1990 O 27, 12:5

SUNDAY VIEW/David Richards

There Is Warmth To Be Found In 2 Gentle Fables

'Once on This Island' derives its appeal from passing details; 'The Sum of Us' has an emotional impact that lifts the play beyond particulars.

"**O**NCE ON THIS ISLAND," THE cinnamon-flavored musical at the Booth Theater, is a lovely piece of handiwork, with much to admire. But I suspect your enjoyment will depend largely on your ability to keep its passing details foremost in your mind.

Although it begins with a booming thunderstorm, its overall effect is more that of a tropical breeze that lulls and caresses, but never threatens to blow off your hat. Lynn Ahrens, who wrote the book and lyrics, and Stephen Flaherty, who is responsible for the score, aspire to the familiarity of an oft-told folk tale. That they achieve it may be the evening's chief accomplishment and its principal drawback: there just aren't a whole lot of surprises here.

The setting is a luxuriant island in the French Antilles, where the division between the dark-skinned peasants and the lighter-skinned aristocrats is sharply drawn. "Two

Sara Krulwich/The New York Times

The 11-member cast of "Once on This Island," shown in part above, doesn't move from place to place. It undulates. No hip remains unswiveled for long, no pelvis goes unrotated.

Martha Swope Associates/"The Sum c

Richard Venture, right, and Tony Goldwyn as father and son in "The Sum of Us"— performances that seem to spring directly from life with no interim stop in a rehearsal hall

different worlds never meant to meet," we're informed in the opening number. That pretty much suggests what happens, when the two worlds do come together — in the persons of Ti Moune, a radiant peasant girl, and Daniel, the fine-boned "grand homme" she rescues from a car crash, nurses back to health and then pursues to the other end of the island.

The gods, who preside over her destiny — and a cheerfully meddlesome bunch they are — may pretend to a hands-off policy. Presumably, they're undertaking an experiment to determine which is stronger — love or death. But we're not fooled. The ending is implicit in the beginning. I suppose that's the lure of fables — knowing their contours from the start reassures us. (Why else do children try to stave off the darkness with plaintive requests to hear their favorite bedtime story just once more?)

Still, familiarity doesn't do much for theatrical tensions. And after you've grown accustomed to the rhythms of Mr. Flaherty's score — calypsos mostly, spelled by the occasional waltz — the problem becomes more acute. The 90 minutes of "Once on This Island" can seem very much of a kind, if you don't keep your eyes peeled for the details. They provide the needed seasoning.

The production, which originated last season at Playwrights Horizons, is confined to a box, exquisitely decorated by the set designer Loy Arcenas and glowingly lit by Allen Lee Hughes, but a box nonetheless. Marrying story-theater techniques to the dances of a Caribbean night, the director and choreographer Graciela Daniele transforms the space into a rain-washed forest or a grand ballroom. The 11-member cast doesn't move

from place to place. It undulates. No hip remains unswiveled for long, no pelvis goes unrotated. (Somewhere up there, Bob Fosse must be looking down, beaming.) Merely having the actor Jerry Dixon hold a flashlight in each hand and kick back his legs, as if he were skating on hot ice, is enough to convince us that Daniel is streaking across the stage in his Mercedes.

If he proves to be something of a dolt ("We could *never* marry," he tells Ti Moune, snootily), well, fairy tale princes usually do. It doesn't help his case that Ti Moune is played by La Chanze, an endearing actress who appears to be opening innocent eyes on the world's wonders for the very first time. The gods, however, most caught my fancy, perhaps because what passes for wit and wisdom in this piece falls primarily to them.

As Erzulie, Goddess of Love, Andrea Frierson looks as much like a box of candy as anyone could reasonably expect and, futhermore, delivers a luscious rendition of the show's most insinuating number, "The Human Heart." Kecia Lewis-Evans is the salt of the earth, which is appropriate since she is playing the Mother of the Earth. Even Eric Riley, death's representative, has his charm as he goes about doing the demonic work of Papa Ge — extending fingers long as spiders' legs and flashing a grin that would be the envy of a jack-o'-lantern. Of course, he's defeated in the end, but am I really spilling any beans by telling you that?

Think big and you're likely to be disappointed by "Once on This Island." Think small. You'll stand a better chance of coming away sufficiently beguiled.

'The Sum of Us'

Whenever the drama turns to the father-son relationship, nine times out of ten it's because a playwright wants to record the damages: misunderstandings, misplaced ambitions, rifts that only widen with age and love that never gets spoken or gets spoken too late. The resulting work (O'Neill's "Long Day's Journey Into Night," Miller's "Death of a Salesman," Anderson's "I Never Sang for My Father") is, at least in part, an attempt to exorcise the lingering pain and to forgive, if not to forget. We are so used, in fact, to the head-to-head confrontations that the playwright David Stevens seems to be staking out fresh territory merely by showing us a father and son who care for each other and pull actively for each other's happiness.

At the outset of "The Sum of Us," Mr. Stevens's warm and touching play at the Cherry Lane Theater, the father (Richard Venture) lets us know exactly how he feels. Momentarily putting aside the frozen lasagna he's preparing for their dinner, he assures us his son is "a good lad," "an honest lad with a heart as big as Western Australia." And if the boy appears just a little wound up tonight, that's because he'll be going out later and he's always a bit edgy "if he thinks he's meeting Mr. Right."

There, with no fuss whatsoever, you have the second distinguishing characteristic of Mr. Stevens's play: the son, Jeff (Tony Goldwyn), a 24-year-old plumber in an industrial suburb of Melbourne, is homosexual. When his father first learned the truth, he felt compelled to purchase some porno magazines and visit a few gay bars. "I thought I'd better try to find out what it was about," he explains. "I wanted to know who his friends were. I didn't want him to have to keep them secret from his Dad." But the two have so few secrets now that when Jeff brings home someone to spend the night, he's not sure his father won't march into the bedroom the next morning to ask how the stranger takes his tea for breakfast.

"There's such a thing as being too well adjusted," Jeff admits with a sheepishness that verges on impatience. (Mr. Goldwyn, you'll notice, is very adept at locating the fine line where one emotion abuts another.)

The father is not without regrets, although Mr. Venture doesn't want us to confuse disappointments with judgments. He's sad he won't have grandchildren. And he's pretty sure Jeff will never know the kind of love he enjoyed with his late wife, and "most of all, making him, making a baby, knowing I'd put the seed in there and watching it grow." But that doesn't matter. Jeff is his only son and he wants him to be as happy as possible. If anything angers him, it's that his offspring is so shy and easily hurt he doesn't put enough effort into finding Mr. Right.

No, not your average father-son relationship. Mr. Stevens is certainly laying himself wide open to charges of being sentimental and starry-eyed. Cynics will find "The Sum of Us" the product of wishful thinking — as much a fable in its way as "Once on This Island." It dawdles for stretches and the characters spend far too much time talking to the audience, when you'd rather they talk to one another. But such flaws are redeemed to an extraordinary degree by Mr. Venture and Mr. Goldwyn, who are giving performances that seem to spring directly from life with no interim stop in a rehearsal hall.

Mr. Goldwyn's ability to project bedrock decency is put to devious uses in the current hit film "Ghost," in which he plays Patrick Swayze's Wall Street buddy. Here the decency is allowed to be its own disarming self with no hidden agenda. Mr. Venture, on the other hand, displays the kind of affectionate nature that tends to overstep itself, and then has to pull back and apologize for the mess. The pairing is ideal. Under the direction of Kevin Dowling, the performers are operating in an atmosphere of palpable trust, further authenticating a play which is about acceptance, after all.

The plot, to the extent that there is one, chronicles how father and son set about trying to fill the void in their hearts — the father with a jittery widow he's met through "Desiree's Introduction Agency," the son with a

gardener he's been eyeing at the pub. But the outsiders aren't ready for the openness they find in the snug working-class bungalow. The love between father and son actually gets in the way of their dealings with others. That's the evening's main dramatic irony and it's not a huge one, granted.

■

"The Sum of Us" is really no more than the relationship itself, observed from different angles, commented upon by each of the participants, but essentially unchanging. Whatever the reversals — and Mr. Stevens finally hits the father with a wallop in the last scene — the bond holds fast.

That very constancy, however, lifts the play beyond its particulars and gives it considerable emotional appeal. Mr. Goldwyn and Mr. Venture's generous performances are large enough to speak to any child who failed to measure up to a parent's expectations and every parent who was obliged to change the yardstick. Which includes, I would think, a fair number of us.   □

1990 O 28, II:5:1

Lucky Come Hawaii

Written by Jon Shirota; directed by Ron Nakahara; set design, Robert Klingelhoefer; costume design, Maggie Raywood; sound design, Ty Sanders; lighting design, Victor En Yu Tan; stage manager, Sue Jane Stoker. Presented by Pan Asian Repertory Theater, Tisa Chang, artistic and producing director. At Playhouse 46, 423 West 46th Street.

Ishi	Tom Matsusaka
Tengan	Mel Duane Gionson
Kama Gusuda	Norris M. Shimabuku
Tsuyu	Kati Kuroda
Ikehara-san	Les J. N. Mau
Kimiko	Ann M. Tsuji
Bob Weaver	James Jenner
Kenyei	Stan Egi
Specks	Joe Fiske

By MEL GUSSOW

Jon Shirota's "Lucky Come Hawaii" is a rambunctious, good-natured romp that deals with a most unlikely subject for comedy, the reaction of people to the Japanese attack on Pearl Harbor. The play, which opened the Pan Asian Repertory Theater's 14th season on Saturday at Playhouse 46, somehow manages to avoid bad taste. For one thing, the author studiously keeps the war itself far offstage. The play benefits from both local color and period flavor.

The scene is a bucolic community on the island of Maui, Hawaii, in which, at the outbreak of World War II, a community of transplanted Okinawans tries to come to terms with mixed loyalties. Some characters retain a close allegiance to their ancestral Okinawa, which is under Japanese control, while others are firmly committed to their new American home. This was, of course, long before Hawaii became a state.

●

Over the years, Tisa Chang's Pan Asian theater has introduced plays with a wide ethnic diversity. This is the first whose cultural crosscurrents are Okinawan, Japanese and Hawaiian, and also the first comedy on this particular subject. Mr. Shirota, who is from Maui, finds humor in the differences between these cultures, in regard to marriage, business, politics and patriotism.

The play becomes a Pan-Asian comedy of errors, with many errors deriving from a collision of language barriers. Quite early, it is observed that whenever two Okinawans talk over the telephone, no one can understand them. Even in their home, a husband and wife can seem linguistically incompatible.

When the prosperous pig farmer (Norris M. Shimabuku), who is at the center of the play, socializes with a friendly American sergeant stationed in Maui, each is bound to misunderstand the other, especially as each tries to practice counterintelligence. The playwright is ecumenical in his humor. All partisans are equally ineffectual in their mock war effort.

The play takes place in around the pig farmer's house, neatly designed by Robert Klingelhoefer. Mr. Shimabuku is eager to please everyone, except for his repressed wife whom he treats as his servant, and his pretty Americanized daughter (Ann M. Tsuji). He has arranged a marriage for her with a young self-proclaimed island politician (Stan Egi), a reject from the Japanese Imperial Army with delusions of martial and marital grandeur.

●

On the sidelines, acting as a kind of chorus, are two local layabouts who prefer to drink sake and play cards but find themselves unwitting pawns in Maui's pseudomilitary shenanigans. In these roles, Tom Matsusaka and Mel Duane Gionson maintain a playfully amusing balance between innocence and skepticism. It is innocence that propels them to run from house to house on Dec. 7, 1941, with the breathless news that the Chinese have attacked Pearl Harbor.

●

Later, it is skepticism and common sense that encourage them to mind their own business while others are undertaking private little wars. These two cronies are clownish but neither is a baka (or fool, in Japanese-Okinawan, says the program's glossary). That role is reserved for the daughter's suitor. Playing that nearsighted character, Mr. Egi offers

Carol Rosegg/Martha Swope Associates/"The Sum of Us"

Neil Maffin and Tony Goldwyn in "The Sum of Us"—operating in an atmosphere of trust in a play about acceptance

Carol Rosegg/Martha Swope Associates/"Lucky Come Hawaii"

Norris M. Shimabuku, left, and Stan Egi in "Lucky Come Hawaii."

a self-mocking portrait of a man who is as dimwitted as he is vain.

Though the play is farcical by intention, Ron Nakahara, as director, does not broaden it beyond belief. A few actors try too hard to turn their characters into stereotypes, but most remain only slightly exaggerated for comic effect. "Lucky Come Hawaii" nimbly spoofs its absurdities while moving toward an ameliorative epilogue.

1990 O 29, C16:1

Yiddle With a Fiddle

Carol Rosegg/"Yiddle With a Fiddle"

Emily Loesser

A musical based on the 1936 Yiddish movie by Joseph Green; book and lyrics by Isaiah Sheffer; music by Abraham Ellstein; director, Ran Avni; set design, Jeffrey Schneider; costume design, Karen Hummel; lighting design, Robert Bessoir; sound design, David Smith; production stage manager, D.C. Rosenberg; musical direction and orchestration, Lanny Meyers; choreogrpaher, Helen Butleroff. Presented by Raymond Ariel and Lawrence Toppall. At Town Hall, 123 West 43d Street.

Yiddle .... Emily Loesser
WITH: Robert Michael Baker, Susan Flynn, Mitchell Greenberg, Michael Ingram, Patricia Ben Peterson, Rachel Black, Steven Fickinger, Andrea Green, Danny Rutigliano and Steve Sterner.

By RICHARD F. SHEPARD

Before getting into the sort of profundities that come with the territory of Jewish theater, it must be said that "Yiddle With a Fiddle" is as good a time at the theater as one with an eye and ear for musical comedy might wish. The show at Town Hall simply sparkles with fun and music, and its star, Emily Loesser, presides over it with an all-embracing bright-eyed impishness.

In staging, performance and music, "Yiddle" is very much its own theatrical bauble and only tangentially rubs against the original that inspired it. This "Yiddle" is in English and it is live, very live, on a stage. The original was in Yiddish, a great motion picture made in 1936 in Poland, a musical that starred Molly Picon, she of the flashing ganeyvishe oygn, or fun-loving "thievish eyes."

•

Linking past and present versions are the thread of plot and, most of all, the music of Abraham Ellstein, a New York-born composer (1907-1963) and Juilliard graduate who in a short lifetime became one of the leading creators of scores for theaters on Second Avenue, that street of hits once known as the Yiddish Broadway. What Isaiah Sheffer, who has written the book and lyrics for the new show, has done is to hang 17 Ellstein songs on the story line of a young woman who passes as a boy, Yiddle, to play in an impoverished quartet of wandering musicians.

The movie was an eloquent pastoral (with a Warsaw conclusion) re-

calling life in the shtetl, and it fit into a time and place that is no more ("Yidl Mitn Fidl" has recently been issued as a videotape by Ergo, a Teaneck, N.J., concern). This new version has made "Yiddle" into a Second Avenue musical, a cavalcade of Ellstein melody, but one that finds humor in itself. Under the direction of Ran Avni, the cast, a particularly ingratiating one, romps through Jeffrey Schneider's colorful sets, which in a colorful cartoon-like way give us the essence of a shtetl, a Warsaw street and a rich man's wedding party with all sorts of cardboard contrivances from horse-drawn wagon to truck and limousine getting people on and off stage.

To the tune of a five-piece band, "Yiddle" sings and dances to a bumper crop of Ellstein beats, including tango and doo-wop, recollections of the Andrews Sisters and that special difficult-to-define music that is a recognizable Yiddish area code. Mr. Sheffer's lyrics are in Yiddish-flavored English (the movie's lyrics were written by the Yiddish poet Itzik Manger) and, like the music, they reflect what is more a New York style of entertainment a half-century ago than Jewish life in Poland.

As the girl in boy's clothing, the petite Ms. Loesser has an infectious smile, a talent for good-humored mugging and, in putting over a song or a mood, a charm that is wide enough to warm Broadway down the block. Robert Michael Baker, a romantic lead within the vague parameters of the story, has a mellow, attractive voice and becomes part of a merry twosome when he clowns and clogs with his fellow musician, the very comical Michael Ingram. Patricia Ben Peterson and Susan Flynn are two singers whose voices bolster the production, the first as a serious lover, the second as a comic one. Mitchell Greenberg is the sympathetic father of the young fiddler, and others, like Steve Sterner, do yeoman work as a complete minyan of characters.

"Yiddle With a Fiddle" is a retrospective peek at worlds that have vanished, both in New York and in Poland. If it weren't so much fun, it could make you cry.

1990 O 30, C14:5

Abundance

By Beth Henley; directed by Ron Lagomarsino; sets by Adrianne Lobel; costumes by Robert Wojewodski; lighting by Paulie Jenkins; music by Michael Roth; fight director, J. Allen Suddeth; production stage manager, Ruth Kreshka. Presented by Manhattan Theater Club, Lynne Meadow; artistic director; Barry Grove, managing director. At City Center, Stage I, 131 West 55th Street.

Bess Johnson........................Amanda Plummer
Macon Hill ....Tess Harper
Jack Flan ....Michael Rooker
William Curtis ....Lanny Flaherty
Prof. Elmore Crome................Keith Reddin

By FRANK RICH

In most American frontier sagas, the thrill is to be found in the relentless drive west of the men who are forging a nation. Beth Henley, the author of "Crimes of the Heart" and "The Miss Firecracker Contest," has no such brawny celebrations of Manifest Destiny in mind in "Abundance," her new play at the Manhattan Theater Club.

"Abundance" is a Western epic, all right, complete with mountainous

scenic vistas, two-fisted brawls, lust in the dust, rampaging Indians and a 25-year narrative that finally deposits its characters in a newly tamed America hurtling by train into the 20th century. But Ms. Henley's play begins and ends with paired scenes foreign to her chosen genre — intimate conversations between two women. "Abundance" is a revisionist western that no one will confuse with the classics of John Ford and Howard Hawks.

•

Ms. Henley, who has previously confined her unreconstructed Southern sensibility to the eccentric precincts of small-town Mississippi and environs, is lighting out for new territory this time. And a welcome development that is. It has been a decade since audiences fell in love with this writer's voice, but in such recent disappointments as "The Lucky Spot" and the film "Nobody's Fool," the style that had once seemed as fresh and spiky as Eudora Welty's started to thicken into a syrupy formula. Have Ms. Henley's misadventures in Hollywood, whether with "Nobody's Fool" or the film version of "Crimes of the Heart," reawakened her muse, or is it just coincidence that "Abundance" is a fiercely held parable about the evils that befall women (an author among them) who sell out their identities to men, commerce and celebrity in the golden West? Whatever the explanation, this is its author's most provocative play in years, a departure to be cherished even when it falls short of its highest ambitions.

The two women at center stage, who meet by chance at a lonely depot, are mail-order brides, Bess (Amanda Plummer) and Macon (Tess Harper). Instant best friends and then homesteading neighbors, they quickly prove submissive wives to the unappetizing men fate has dealt them — a brutal tyrant (Michael Rooker) in Bess's case, an awkward widower with a scarred face and eye patch (Lanny Flaherty) in Macon's. Ms. Henley has not forsaken her usual

comic attack, and at first "Abundance" percolates with dark laughter as the women accept the primitive ways of frontier domesticity and of men who treat them like chattels. In an archetypal Henley touch, Mr. Flaherty proudly gives his wife a Christmas card signed not by him but by a favorite cow named Brown Spot; the play's most persistent running gag is a series of disfiguring accidents with thrashing and shearing machines. Even so, the fable's melancholy breaks through the Gothic humor. The abundance Bess and Macon seek so fervently upon arrival in the Wyoming Territory — freedom and love as boundless as the tabula rasa of the Western sky — is betrayed and forgotten as the men around them mine the material abundance of the earth.

•

Given Ms. Henley's ability to spin the tallest of tales, "Abundance" sometimes has the tone of a rambunctious tongue-in-cheek Twain story, with echoes of Thomas Berger's "Little Big Man." The four principal characters are alternately driven apart and reunited by such extravagant events as an Indian kidnapping, a love triangle, the booms and busts of the economy and finally Bess's unexpected collaboration on a bestselling memoir that makes her the sensation of the Lyceum Lecture Circuit and even the subject of a hit play by Dion Boucicault. But if this is Twain, it is late, bitter Twain refracted through a contemporary woman's point of view. The more Macon and Bess are driven to emulate the entrepreneurship of men, whether by building a farm or a literary career, the less human they become, forsaking sexual pleasure, children, love and their own friendship on the way to a chilling denouement that leaves them both literally and figuratively indistinguishable from tent-show freaks. The jokes about mutilated limbs notwithstanding, it is the specter of disfigured dreams and values that haunts the play.

So committed is the author to unearthing the dark underside of Amer-

Gerry Goodstein/Manhattan Theater Club

Tess Harper, left, and Amanda Plummer in "Abundance."

ican mythology, while all the while, remaining true to her own oddball theatrical cadences, that one keeps wishing "Abundance" were more fully realized than it is. Though its ideological reach tries to extend to sexual, economic and racial warfare alike, the play seems small and scattershot, more like a patchwork quilt than a large, ingeniously conceived canvas that is all of a piece. There are too many deadpan vignettes of equal length and dramatic weight, too many repetitions, too many prosaic transitions between time frames, too many endings to each act. The director, Ron Lagomarsino, though exemplary in his handling of his cast, accentuates the evening's episodic rhythm and diminishes its capacity to jolt by piling on naturalistic frills in the form of languorous set changes and incidental music. While Adrianne Lobel's scenery, all two turntables' worth of it, is handsome, "Abundance" seems weighed down by an overabundance of production.

•

Yet even when the play seems to be spinning its wheels along with the turntables, the performers hold the attention, the leading men included. Mr. Rooker's abusive husband, a beery thug who feigns ignorance of his own cruelty, is so revolting that his nastiness becomes outlandishly funny, especially after age and circumstances knock the fight out of him. The more benign Mr. Flaherty not only makes the most of the greatest number of sick glass-eye gags since Joe Orton's "Loot" but also becomes a source of pathos: his ex-

pression seems as dead as his cigarette in a late-evening tableau in which he is finally forced to survey the loveless terrain of his bankrupt life.

It says everything about the superb leading women of "Abundance" that they come across not as simple martyrs or heroines but as free young spirits who are gradually but inexorably corrupted by time and treachery. Ms. Harper, known for her film appearances in "Crimes of the Heart" and "Tender Mercies," turns out to be a first-rate stage actress, evolving from a giddy beauty with literary airs to a broken, syphilitic crone hardened by disappointment and whisky. Ms. Plummer, at her unmannered best, conveys Bess's doltish naïveté with sweet ingenuousness before moving on to such other, more vibrant guises as abused wife, involuntary Indian squaw and hard-nosed, self-merchandising tycoon.

The first sound one hears in "Abundance" is the plaintive lilt of Ms. Plummer's girlish singing voice, and almost everything that follows is emblemized by that voice's steady descent, initially farcical, later harrowing and finally grotesque, through sorrow and derangement into nasty, cold-blooded manliness. Much as one wishes that "Abundance" had the artistic size of its vast frontier landscape, there is no escaping its tight, disturbing close-ups of the women who lost while the West was won.

1990 O 31, C15:3

Oh, Kay!

Music by George Gershwin; lyrics by Ira Gershwin; book by Guy Bolton and P. G. Wodehouse; directed and choreographed by by Dan Siretta; adaptation by James Racheff; concept by Mr. Siretta; scenery by Kenneth Foy; costumes, Theoni V. Aldredge; lighting, by Craig Miller; musical director, vocal and additional dance arrangements by Tom Fay; orchestrations by Arnold Goland; dance arrangements by Donald Johnston; sound by Jan Nebozenko; hair design by Robert DiNiro; assistant choreographer, Ken Leigh Rogers; production stage manager, Harold Goldfaden; executive producer, Natalie Lloyd; associate producer, Leo K. Cohen. Presented by David Merrick. At the Richard Rodgers Theater, 226 West 46th Street.

Bill Lyles	Gregg Burge
Dolly Greene	Kyme
Duke	Stanley Wayne Mathis
Nick and Sam	David Preston Sharp
Joe	Fracaswell Hyman
Waiter and Jake	Frantz Hall
Larry Potter	Kevin Ramsey
Shorty	Helmar Augustus Cooper
B. J.	Keith Robert Bennett
Floyd	Frederick J. Boothe
Zeke	Ken Roberson
Jimmy Winter	Brian Mitchell
Constance DuGrasse	Tamara Tunie Bouquett
Chauffeur	Byron Easley
Kay Jones	Angela Teek
Janson	Mark Kenneth Smaltz
Rev. Alphonse DuGrasse	Alexander Barton

By FRANK RICH

IF there is any serious doubt that David Merrick is one of the greatest showmen in Broadway history, it can be dispelled by the fact that his flops are as fabled as his hits. Nearly as much theatrical lore attends the ill-fated "Mata Hari," "Breakfast at Tiffany's," "Mack and Mabel" and "Subways Are for Sleeping" as it does "Hello, Dolly!," "Gypsy" and "42d Street." Mr. Merrick, like most other high-rolling, larger-than-life impresarios, was rarely one to mess with the in-between, which is why "Oh, Kay!," his new show at the Richard Rodgers Theater and his first since "42d Street" a decade ago, is an anomaly. This loose adaptation of the Gershwins' 1926 musical is a chintzy, innocuous slab of stock that is likely to leave more than a few theatergoers shrugging their shoulders and asking, "Didn't I doze through that a couple of summers ago in a barn?"

Actually, "Oh, Kay!" bills itself as "inspired by" a well-received production mounted at the Goodspeed Opera House in Connecticut last year with a mostly different cast. I didn't see the Goodspeed "Oh, Kay!," but Mr. Merrick has undoubtedly had his way with the project since

then: faint quotations from his happier past achievements filter like ghosts through the evening's haze.

Music by the Gershwins, a Bolton-Wodehouse book and an all-black cast.

Dan Siretta's opening and closing dance routines (and surely the word routine was coined to describe them) are would-be clones of the Gower Champion numbers that bracketed "42d Street," though this time the size of both the chorus and the choreographer's imagination seem about half that of the originals. The Merrick legacy also figures in this production's "concept," credited in the program to Mr. Siretta. Just as the producer brought Pearl Bailey, Cab Calloway and company into the long-running "Hello, Dolly!" a quarter-century ago, so he fields an all-black cast in "Oh, Kay!," first written by Guy Bolton and P. G. Wodehouse for the English star Gertrude Lawrence.

Even in its time, Mr. Merrick's black "Dolly" was attacked in some churlish quarters as a minstrel show, but history should more kindly regard it as an exhilarating example of what current parlance calls non-traditional casting. "Hello, Dolly!" was not rewritten for its black performers, and Ms. Bailey and Mr. Calloway were given the same free rein to play Dolly Gallagher Levi and Horace Vandergelder as Carol Channing and David Burns, among others, had been before them. "Oh, Kay!," by contrast, does seem like a minstrel show. An adapter, James Racheff, has clumsily transported the libretto to an ersatz Jazz Age Harlem, with eye-

Angela Teek and Brian Mitchell — A fine romance?

Jim Estrin for The New York Times

popping gags and stereotypes that are less redolent of the Cotton Club than of "Amos 'n' Andy."

But "Oh, Kay!" is so deficient in more mundane theatrical areas that debating its curious racial politics is a critical luxury. Little in this show makes sense, starting with a vertigo-inducing opening scene in which a cry of "Raid!" sends chorus performers at the Paradise Club running around in circles while various curtains rise and fall to beat the band. Shortly after that, the entire company delivers cases of bootleg booze to a millionaire's town house while performing a song ("When Our Ship Comes Sailing In") that, as staged, might be mistaken for the hurricane sequence in "Porgy and Bess."

When the town house's millionaire (Brian Mitchell) returns home soon after, he almost marries a preacher's daughter only to find himself falling instead for an intruder who must be the real love interest since her name is Kay (Angela Teek). This romantic triangle is then rehashed almost verbatim during the long opening scene of Act II before being abruptly resolved. The end of the plot is not the end of "Oh, Kay!," however, for the show loiters in the Paradise Club for three gratuitous scenes more, among them a three-man comedy act of the sort that didn't so much kill vaudeville as drive it to suicide.

For punctuation along the way, there are hoary jokes masquerading as campy wisecracks ("If brains was a boulevard, you wouldn't even make an alley") and, more occasionally, such lovely Gershwin tunes as "Maybe," "Do, Do, Do" and "Dear Little Girl." Certainly it's not necessary for anyone to sing Gershwin's praises at this late date, but it says much about his music's durability that "Someone to Watch Over Me" still exerts a pull here, despite the fact that the muffled-sounding orchestration (by Arnold Goland) is trashy and the singer (Ms. Teek) is strident of voice and mechanical of gesture.

•

Most of the other songs are excuses for Mr. Siretta's dances, in which noisy tapping, frantic arm waving and constantly accelerating speed exhaust an audience's spirits in the

Jim Estrin for The New York Times

Gregg Burge

name of raising them. This choreographer seems to impose the same style on every show — even one as different from "Oh, Kay!" as "Pal Joey," last summer at Goodspeed — and one can fully expect to find tap dancers having a go at the "Ascot Gavotte" some day when "My Fair Lady" rolls off his assembly line.

As director, Mr. Siretta does not show off his company to good advan-

tage. There is no romantic rapport between the ice-cold Ms. Teek and Mr. Mitchell, the robotic leading man. The rest of the acting is outrageously broad by any measure this side of the circus. Only the dancer Gregg Burge's sharply defined, time-stopping leaps and turns in "You've Got What Gets Me" elevate "Oh, Kay!" to an elegant Broadway standard.

•

That standard was more or less defined by Mr. Merrick for a couple of decades. Who could have imagined then that he would later produce a musical in which most of the first act is imprisoned in a gloomy Victorian parlor (muddily designed by Kenneth Foy) suitable for "Arsenic and Old Lace"? "Oh, Kay!" can be labeled a Merrick enterprise only because of the size of his billing and the ubiquitousness of a shade of red that has been standard issue in all his productions since "Hello, Dolly!"

Romantically or not, I would like to believe that this legendary showman, notoriously the toughest of audiences, is seeing another kind of red as he surveys the pallid entertainment to which he has unaccountably lent his name.

1990 N 2, C1:1

The Big Apple Circus

Conceived and directed by Paul Binder; musical director, Rik Albani; original music by Linda Hudes; clown coordinator, Michael Christensen; scenic design by James Leonard Joy; lighting design by Jan Kroeze; costume design by Donna Zakowska; associate director, Dominique Jando; choreographer, Mónica Levy; performance director, Guillaume Dufresnoy; ring crew chief, Bryan Fox. Presented by the Big Apple Circus. At Damrosch Park, Lincoln Center.

WITH: The Alexis Brothers, Marie Pierre Benac, David Casey, David Dimitri, Annie Dugan, Carlos Guity, John Lepiarz, Barry Lubin, Melinda Merlier, Olivier Merlier, Panteleenko Brothers, Katja Schumann, Taso Stavrakis, the Svensons Jr., Vanessa Thomas and Ben Williams.

By MEL GUSSOW

With its portrait of a ballerina on point on the bare back of a white horse, Georges Seurat's final, unfinished painting, "Le Cirque," stands as an emblem of the celebrated one-ring European circus. And the Big Apple Circus, in its grand new show, "Ballerinas, Horses and Clowns: The Golden Age," pays tribute to Seurat and other period artists who immortalized the circus on canvas.

As the "ballerina on horseback," Susanna Svenson glides around the Big Apple's single ring, arms raised high, as if she is standing on air. Encircling the horse and rider are colorful streamers that turn the ring

into a moving Maypole. The moment is as lovely as it is simple, and it is one of a number of impressionistic interludes in this year's show. The Big Apple is in residence in a heated tent at Lincoln Center through Jan. 6.

In this return to a classic-style circus, Paul Binder, the Big Apple's founder and master of ceremonies, has placed the emphasis on horses rather than on spectacle and daredevilry. Leading six horses, Katja Schumann re-creates a Degas day at the Longchamps racetrack in Paris. Jumping through hoops and over bars, the horses are precise enough in their close-quartered movements to turn on a centime.

•

Then, to lighten the mood, three not so little pigs oink their way into the spotlight. Pigs are inherently funny creatures; imitating horses, they become quintessential clowns. Instead of prancing and assuming positions of equipoise, they wiggle their tails and skid across the ring. Skirting the hoops, they nudge each other to the exit as if they are commuters trying to get off a crowded subway during rush hour.

One of the show's motifs is mimicry. Just as pigs pretend to be horses, elephants ape people. David Dimitri, who performs on a low wire, stands in for a string puppet in a version of "Petrushka," and Susanna and Carlos Svenson, equine equilibrists billed as the Svensons Jr., pose as tourists who accidently find themselves caught up in the circus. Pratfalling on horseback, they suavely simulate ineptitude.

If there is any deficiency in the current show, it is in the clown department. In particular, a raw-egg-tossing act is less funny than messy, spattering circusgoers as well as the ring itself. Children find this amusing, as they do the ubiquitous Grandma (Barry Lubin), a perennial favorite with Big Apple regulars.

•

As in past seasons, the top banana is Anna May, a 47-year-old elephant

who does not show an inch of her middle age. Performing with pachydermic panache, she plays the tambourine and does agile hoof- and handstands. This year she is accompanied by an elephantine newcomer, 6-year-old Baby Ned, already an expert at imitating his elder.

The ballerina on horseback typifies the classic single-ring show.

Ben Williams, Anna May's longtime human partner, is joined by his wife and their two daughters, turning the routine into a captivating two-family act. Mite-size Stormy Williams enters riding Baby Ned, and then is succeeded by her tinier sister Skye. Both little girls are the epitome of graceful concentration. Together the elephants and the Williamses dance to the music of the Rolling Stones' "Start Me Up."

Leading the nonanimal brigade are two teams of European gymnasts. The Alexis Brothers, who are from Portugal, balance on each other's hands and heads. Strongmen siblings, they seem to have the body control of bionic men. The Panteleenko Brothers, who twist and turn on cables, are Soviet acrobats as closely twinned as Castor and Pollux.

A final bow is justifiably reserved for Baby Ned, an elephant with a trunkful of promise — a sign of the Big Apple's constant self-replenishment.

1990 N 3, 13:4

Patricia Lanza/Big Apple Circus

The Alexis Brothers balancing on each other's hands and heads.

Famine Plays

Written and directed by Richard Caliban; music by John Hoge; lighting by Brian Aldous; costumes by Mary Myers; projections by Tony Jacobs; sound by John Huntington; stage manager, J. Tori Evand; assistant director, Daniel Tharau; production manager, Janet Paparazzo. Presented by Under One Roof and Cucaracha. At the Triplex Theater, 199 Chambers Street, between Greenwich and West Streets.

WITH: Steven Bland, Lia Chang, Mark Dillahunt, Corinne Edgerly, Lauren Hamilton, Vivian Lanko, Mollie O'Mara, Brennan Murphy, Hugh Palmer, Glen Santiago, David Simonds and George Tynan.

By MEL GUSSOW

In Richard Caliban's "Famine Plays," the center of the country cannot hold. America's heartland has become a disaster area. Facing unemployment and poverty, people move from street to highway, looking for a resting zone. Some grasp a livelihood in crime. No one has enough to eat, and there is no solace on the horizon. The once-sedentary become eternal nomads, as the Okies did in the 1930's.

As written and directed by Mr. Caliban, "Famine Plays," at the Triplex Theater, is an ambitious attempt at creating a "Grapes of Wrath" for modern, depressed times. The period is undated, but it seems more like the near future than anything futuristic. Each of the images in the collage is evocative, and at the same time each is overextended. The play runs more than two and a half hours, and half the length would have been an improvement.

•

As Mr. Caliban has shown in his previous work, he is a venturesome playwright and director, but "Famine Plays" is marred by self-indulgence. It needs editing, which was not the case last season with his "Rodents and Radios." Dealing with a related theme, the disorientation of young people living on the edge of life, that play had an exactitude that had one looking forward to each of the interlocking episodes.

The similarly structured "Famine Plays" is an earlier work, first presented several years ago at the Cucaracha Theater and brought back for a return engagement in the company's new downtown home. Having seen the later play first, as well as Mr. Caliban's staging of Mac Wellman's "Crowbar," one knows the breadth of his talent, varyingly in evidence in the current production.

On a broad, open stage, slashed by a crossroad of light, the characters tramp their way into oblivion. A young mother leaves her family to look for work, and a street urchin treats her as an adoptive parent. The son of a suicide turns mugger. A married couple pack remnants of a once-stable life; they become the equivalent of a walking tag sale.

In the background as counterpoint are pictures of artworks by everyone from Andrew Wyeth to Edvard Munch, and striding through the play is a choral figure acting as the specter of Norman Rockwell. His presence reminds us that before famine, America's image of itself was a Saturday Evening Post cover of a bountiful Thanksgiving dinner.

•

The narrative is most enveloping when it is least pretentious, especially during moments of eccentric humor. Two dirt-encrusted wanderers become partners in crime. One, apparently an immigrant, carries a cudgel, with which he beats his victims. He also strikes them with a verbal curse of "Walt Whitman! Walt Whitman!" — words that somehow, irrationally, force them into submission.

Wandering through the evening is a buffoon, who comments on the action with pronouncements like "God is an omnipotent waiter." He and others are accompanied by cultural detritus from a former existence; carless travelers remember a verse of "See the U.S.A. in Your Chevrolet."

The show, labeled a "downtown opera," is at least partly a musical, with a score written and played by John Hoge. Moving from neo-liturgical to recitative, the songs help to capture the vagrancy of the open road.

The fact that a number of the actors appeared in contrasting roles in "Rodents and Radios" certifies their range. Lauren Hamilton, poignant as that scruffy urchin, previously played the opposite, a self-styled visionary. Mollie O'Mara, Vivian Lanko, Glen Santiago and Lia Chang also appear, to advantage, and Steven Bland adds an affable touch of tomfoolery. The actors have the makings of an ensemble.

As the characters crisscross the stage, they become routeless. None has a sense of destination, and, in an odd, ironic note, neither does the play. It wanders prodigally on Mr. Caliban's endless road, moves past several possible exits and never quite arrives at a conclusion.

1990 N 3, 14:5

El Abanderado

By Alberto Heiremans; directed by Guillermo Semler; technical director, Rigoberto Obando; production assistant, Manuel Herrera; assistant director, Beatriz Cordoba; percussionist, Virginia Rambal; designer, José Luis Plaza; lighting, Mr. Semler. Presented by Repertorio Español, Gilberto Zaldivar, producer, René Buch, artistic director, Robert Weber Federico, artistic designer. At the Gramercy Arts Theater, 138 East 27th Street.

El Abanderado	Diego Taborda
Tordo	Carlos Osorio
Cornelia	Maria José Alvarez
Riquelme	Birgit Bofarull
Cornelio	José Luis Ferrer

WITH: Ricardo Barber, Irma Bello, Katerina Llado, Alfonso Manosalvas, Ana Margarita Martínez-Casado, José Cheo Oliveras, Carlos Osorio, René Sánchez, Tatiana Vecino and Lilia Veiga.

By D. J. R. BRUCKNER

A bandit with a record of crimes longer than the years of his life is the hero of "El Abanderado" ("The Standard Bearer") by the Chilean playwright Alberto Heiremans. And in the production by the Repertorio Español at the Gramercy Arts Theater, under the direction of Guillermo Semler, he becomes not only a believable hero, but the victim of the society bent on bringing him to justice.

The text of this 30-year-old work, without specifically drawing parallels, invites many comparisons of the life of the captured young criminal with the New Testament account of Jesus. But the political developments in Chile in the last couple of decades have made other connections possible, and Mr. Semler, a Chilean director, has enlarged the play's few allusions to repression.

•

In this tale the man called El Abanderado, the son of a woman who operates a brothel in a typical isolated town in the Central Valley of Chile, flees from home in his youth and becomes a symbol of fear and romance to the surrounding countryside as he is often seen riding in the mountains, his white bandanna flowing in the breeze as a kind of flag or standard.

During a local festival of the cross, he returns one night to his mother's place, where he is captured after one of his associates in crime, Tordo, betrays him. He is carried off by the police and the military, presumably to his death, but not before he gets the comfort of the compassion of one of his young guards and a declaration of love from a young woman who sees in him a spirit of adventure that gives her hope she too might escape her mountain-ringed valley and see the great world beyond.

Mr. Semler, engaged by the Repertorio Español in a continuing three-year program to showcase work by leading Latin American directors, takes an aggressive approach to this material. He leaves the impression he regards the playwright as a colleague, the play as inspiration more than set text, and the characters as symbols.

He eliminates a few minor roles and prunes dialogue, occasionally turning it into dumb show. He ignores the changing scenes of the play and presents all the action on an empty black stage. He moves his gaudily costumed characters like ceremonial dancers who, when they speak, seldom address one another or even face one another.

He limits the music called for in the text to the thumps and rings of one tympanist and gives the play's folk songs a metallic and slightly discordant sound. And he emphasizes change in characters by action rather than words — as when El Abanderado (Diego Taborda), in an extraordinary feat of illusion, seems to be bent, snapped and crushed as his indictment is recited.

Perhaps Mr. Semler's most crucial decision is to make most of the play's policemen and soldiers instruments of oppression. This is especially effective in the case of one minor male character, Riquelme, turned by Mr. Semler into a woman who might have sprung live from a Richard Lindner painting of booted heavy-metal menaces.

Altogether, the effect is pointed, sharp, even overwhelming, and much of the action can be understood even by viewers who know no Spanish. But this is achieved at the cost of most of the gentle humor of the play — in which the members of the constabulary are for the most part ignorant, vain and foolish and El Abanderado is the victim of prejudice, selfishness and blindness and not necessarily of a system of oppression.

As usual, the members of this company respond to the director's challenges with enthusiasm and skill. In addition to Mr. Taborda's, outstanding performances are given by Maria José Alvarez as the young woman who falls in love with El Abanderado, Carlos Osorio as the treacherous Tordo, and José Luis Ferrer as Cornelio, the young cadet who, assigned to stand guard on the manacled bandit, becomes his protector.

1990 N 4, 72:1

Spinoza

By Dimitri Frenkel Frank; translated by Martin Cleaver; directed by Robert Kalfin; sets, Richard Hoover; costumes, Gail Cooper-Hecht; lights, John Gisondi; composer, John Clifton; stage manager, Nina Heller. Presented by Jewish Repertory Theater, Ran Avni, artistic director; Edward M. Cohen, associate director. At 344 East 14th Street.

Spinoza	Diego Matamoros
Rembrandt	W. B. Brydon
Rabbi Saul Levi Morteira	Salem Ludwig
Italian Countess	Pamela Burrell
Hendrickje	Karen McLaughlin
Zacuto	Jeffery Logan
Magistrate	William Duff-Griffin
Polish Girl	Funda Duyal

By STEPHEN HOLDEN

Near the end of Dimitri Frenkel Frank's stimulating dramatic study of the life and times of Benedict Spinoza, the 17th-century Dutch philosopher and his friend Rembrandt van Rijn find themselves down and out in their home city of Amsterdam. Spinoza, the brilliant but rebellious free thinker, has been excommunicated by the local rabbinate for his heretical views. And Rembrandt, a high-living sensualist 27 years Spinoza's senior, is out of fashion as a painter, bankrupt and about to lose his house and possessions.

In a final meeting before Spinoza leaves Amsterdam, the philosopher and the painter have a discussion about values that reveals them to be polar opposites. When Rembrandt informs Spinoza that he is bankrupt, the philosopher, who has no strong ties to the material world, replies flippantly, "Is that all?" Spinoza's philosophy, boiled to down to four words, insists that "It's better to think." To which Rembrandt retorts, "It's better to feel — you're too cold."

•

In the view of the playwright, who died two years ago at the age of 60, both have valid points to make, but Rembrandt may be closer to the truth. The drama, directed by Robert Kalfin at the Jewish Repertory Theater, is a respectful but detached portrait of the philosopher and theologian whose rationalist beliefs were too much even for a city as enlightened as 17th- century Amsterdam. Spinoza came from an affluent Jewish family that had fled the Portuguese Inquisition and settled in Calvinist Holland, which offered both religious freedom and commercial opportunity to Jews. Recognized early as an intellectual Wunderkind, the brilliant young scholar became a freethinker who began questioning the veracity of events in the Bible and spouting his rationalist concept of God with a vehemence that caused him to be deemed a threat to public order.

"Spinoza," which was originally performed in the Netherlands in 1964, is having its first American production. With its carefully structured dia-

Carol Rosegg/Martha Swope Associates/"Spinoza"

W. B. Brydon in "Spinoza."

logues woven into a historical framework that tries to give all points of view a fair hearing, the play is the product of an era when religious and ideological conflicts seemed simpler and less heated than they do today. And in Martin Cleaver's elegant but occasionally stiff translation from the Dutch, the debates have a high-flown aphoristic ring and clarity.

As written by Mr. Frank and portrayed by Diego Matamoros with a

---

Rembrandt and Spinoza debate intellect versus emotion.

---

beady-eyed, darting impatience, the title character is an arrogant brat who is so consumed with his own brilliance that he is unable to comprehend the feelings of others. After a fling with an Italian countess (Pamela Burrell), who has also been Rembrandt's mistress, he unwittingly insults her with his icy analysis of the mechanics of desire.

Mr. Kalfin's production is true to the play in giving all the characters' points of view an equal weight. Mr. Matamoros's spiky performance is well balanced by W. B. Brydon's roaring, robust Rembrandt and by Salem Ludwig's quietly authoritative portrayal of the common-sensical, politically savvy rabbi who is pressured into excommunicating his star pupil.

Working in a small space, the director has done a workmanlike job of organizing a spare, handsome production in which miniature replicas of 17th-century architecture are used as both furniture and background décor on a checkerboard floor. But if the drama presents an absorbing intellectual portrait of a brilliant fanatic, some of its dramatic ingredients fail to jell. Most seriously, Rembrandt's chaotic battles with his wife, Hendrickje, (Karen McLaughlin), erupt without adequate preparation or explanation.

"Spinoza" is too schematic a play of ideas for the passions of its characters to engage the audience very deeply. Yet its view of the interactions of the workaday world and its unruly geniuses is astute and well-balanced enough to make its intellectual crossfire consistently interesting.

1990 N 4, 72:4

SUNDAY VIEW/David Richards

Sunday at the Dacha With Rooster

'Cerceau' bores deeply into one generation's discontents; the Abbey's 'Playboy' is a darlin' Irish photo opportunity.

WASHINGTON

IF YOU WERE OF A MIND TO APPEND a subtitle to Viktor Slavkin's "Cerceau," it seems to me that "A Little Soviet Night Music" wouldn't be too far off the mark.

In this wryly melancholic drama, receiving its English-language premiere here in Arena Stage's Kreeger Theater, a 40-year-old Moscow engineer named Rooster invites a group of his contemporaries to spend a weekend in the country at the dacha he's just inherited from his great-aunt. An aimless bunch, they philosophize and flirt and dance the boogie-woogie barefoot on the grass. They don old clothes from the attic, and when the attic also yields up the implements of cerceau — hoops to be tossed in the air and wooden swords to catch them with — they try their hand at the old French game, too.

But the vital connections they yearn for never get made. While nobody sings "Send In the Clowns," by the end of the weekend, they've all behaved a little foolishly, desper-

ately even, and the smiles of a late summer's eve have begun to harden into grimaces of middle-aged resignation.

■

Written before the Gorbachev-induced thaw, "Cerceau" attracted considerable attention when Moscow's Taganka Theater performed it in Russian as part of the 1987 London International Festival of Theater. If glasnost has robbed the work of its more revelatory aspects, it still bores deep into one generation's discontents. Mr. Slavkin has no large dramatic event to disturb the drift of time, only futile flurries of activity that inevitably recall Chekhov. The play is all texture. Nonetheless, using a translation by Fritz Brun and Laurence Maslon, the Romanian director Liviu Ciulei artfully layers dreams and reality, past and present, indoors and outdoors. The overlapping makes for a tantalizingly dense climate, which Mr. Slavkin's characters will come to find almost as suffocating as the one-room city flats from which they so eagerly want to escape.

Rooster hopes to constitute a community of unattached adults like himself — who will live together and enjoy one another's company — when he issues his invitation to the country. Among the prospective "colonists," as he likes to view them, are: his boss and fellow engineer; a former lover, none the fresher for a decade of wear; a giggly neighbor he refers to as his "trash-chute mate"; a Swedish gadabout he encountered 24 hours earlier on a Moscow street corner; and a lapsed intellectual who's abandoned the pursuit of knowledge for the more lucrative practice of door upholstering. (The padding, apparently, serves the practical purpose of soundproofing overcrowded apartment buildings. But it is also a convenient symbol for a society that forces people to live in close proximity, while failing to unite them in any significant way.)

No sooner have they all settled into the dacha than Koka, an aged gentleman sporting a Rip van Winkle beard, shows up on the doorstep. A remnant of Russia's prerevolutionary past, he was the lover of Rooster's great-aunt and a man of expansive romantic gestures.

Joan Marcus/Arena Stage

A scene from the English-language premiere of Viktor Slavkin's "Cerceau," with, from left, Pamela Nyberg, Richard Bauer and Randy Danson—The Romanian director Liviu Ciulei layers dreams and reality, past and present, indoors and outdoors.

As he stirs the dead embers of his long-ago affair, the others can't help seeing in him the very intensity they lack. "Nowadays, love means living together, not dying together," notes Rooster's ex-flame, her sardonic tone leaving little doubt that the former prospect is hardly worth the effort.

In an attempt to contain them and their mood swings, Mr. Ciulei, who is an architect, too, has designed a lovely white-pine, two-story dacha, although I suspect the image of a maze, or even a funhouse, also lurks somewhere in the back of his head. With its multiple porches and bay windows, pillars and cubbyholes, it is the ideal locale for hide-and-seek. Exploring the premises in the first act, the guests could be cavorting in a thick forest.

In the play's second act — the richest of the three — Mr. Ciulei splits the dacha down the middle, banishes the two halves to the wings and takes us into the garden. Seated at a long dining table, dappled with candlelight, the characters pore over a sheaf of love letters that Koka and Rooster's great-aunt exchanged six decades earlier. Touched by the past, they turn reflective and we hear what they're thinking. Mr. Slavkin, however, puts their thoughts in the form of formal letters — the letters they might have sent to one another had they lived in an earlier age of exalted passions and epistolary elegance.

In turn, each character, unheard by the others, recites the ardent missive in his soul. But there is no breakthrough when Mr. Slavkin brings them all back to reality. Exaltation degenerates into giddiness, and the best anyone can think to do is play cerceau. A diaphanous curtain is drawn across the stage. Behind it, as if in a memory, the wooden hoops arch silently back and forth, from one delighted player to the next. The image is breathtaking. All the sad evanescence and foolish beauty of life itself seem to be momentarily captured in the graceful flight of rings through the darkling sky

■

Mr. Ciulei made his directorial debut at Arena Stage in 1974 with a dazzlingly anarchic production of Georg Buchner's "Leonce and Lena." In recent years, however, his work has become increasingly introspective, Koka's notion that life is a crossword puzzle that takes decades to fill in — and even then the answers may not be right — is obviously one that speaks to him. If he is moved and amused by Mr. Slavkin's characters, it is with the detached emotion that the wise reserve for the young and the reckless

The Arena cast blossoms under his care Charles Geyer endows Rooster with a goofy ineffectualness that extends to his stumbling walk. You get the impression he thinks no one much likes him and he's probably right. As his onetime lover, Randy Danson suggests with the sullen set of her mouth and the weary rasp of her voice that she's done little more with her life than accumulate disappointments.

The fullest performance, however, is given by Richard Bauer, who has long been one of Mr. Ciulei's favorite actors. As Koka, a silly old anachronism in a wrinkled suit and Borsalino hat, Mr. Bauer injects a frittering gallantry into the proceedings. "My life, I missed it," he confesses, with a chortle that could be a sob. Part of him wants to believe that his youthful amours were as intense as Rooster and his friends think. But even as his eyes are twinkling with remembered pleasure, you can see the regret shining through. The performance is filled with such telling double exposures.

Mr. Slavkin's play is not quite so blessed. After the glorious second-act peak, it's mostly downhill. The complaints grow repetitious and, the characters, recognizing that no connections will be forged, give in to testiness. All that's really left to do in the third act is the packing up.

But if the play falters, Mr. Ciulei's vision holds until the end. He's put the dacha back

Roma Downey and Frank McCusker in the Abbey's "Playboy"

together again. The windows have been boarded up and the door padlocked against intruders. As the guests leave, the headlights of their automobile wash the walls with ghostly white light. Then, the deserted building takes its place once again in the blackness — its secrets inviolate, its offer of sanctuary still no more than an unclaimed promise.

I wouldn't swear to it. But in the silence, I might have heard the creak of a floorboard or the stir of the wind.

'The Playboy of The Western World'

"In a good play," the Irish poet and playwright John Millington Synge observed, "every speech should be as fully flavored as a nut or an apple." There's no better illustration of that proposition than his own 1907 masterpiece "The Playboy of the Western World," which the Abbey Theater, in its first American tour in 55 years, is currently taking to selected cities across the country. (If this is Sunday, it must be Scottsdale, Ariz.) Few stage characters speak with such natural pungency as Synge's peasants — and that's before they've had a drink or three. It matters little if you can tell "a streeler" (a vagrant) from "a peeler" (a policeman), or know that "a loy" is a spade, while "a lep" is a leap. Synge's poetry will work its spell on you anyway.

Such, at any rate, is the operating premise of the director Vincent Dowling, and up to a point it is valid. As spoken by the Dublin-based players, all in a state of high brogue, this "Playboy," which I caught at the Kennedy Center, is music to the ears. I'm not sure the other senses are so fully satisfied, however. The Abbey production prolongs a stodgy theatrical tradition that holds the Irish to be a picturesque lot, as darlin' in their anger as in their merriment. This is the travel poster school of thinking: You can't see the garbage cans for the hollyhocks.

■

"Playboy" is a far tougher play than Mr. Dowling and company are letting on. Synge is writing, after all, about a cowardly young man who, in

This 'Playboy' is music to the ears, but the other senses are not so satisfied.

a fit of spite, rises up and hits his father over the head with a shovel, then takes to the roads, boasting of the murder he's committed. The County Mayo villagers, who welcome him into their midst, give themselves over to mindless hero worship, only to turn on him later with the collective hysteria of a lynch mob. After Pegeen Mike, Synge's headstrong heroine, betrays the lad, who is probably the one true love of her life, the stage directions call for her to break out into "wild lamentations."

It would take a far more visceral production than this one to tap the play's latent power and unleash its rollicking humor. While Roma Downey makes a handsome Pegeen Mike, she can hardly be said to possess "the divil's own temper." Frank McCusker, as the unintentional patricide, has the wimpish side of the character down pat, but he never acquires the swaggering statute of the braggart. Meanwhile, most of the supporting players are posturing so quaintly that you half expect a bus load of tourists to stroll onstage and begin taking snapshots.

The lilting accents, entrancing as they are, are deceptive. They're covering up for a multitude of cruelties, large and small. □

1990 N 4, II:5:1

Buddy
The Buddy Holly Story

Written by Alan Janes; directed by Rob Bettinson; designed by Andy Walmsley; costumes by Bill Butler and Carolyn Smith; lighting by Graham McLusky; sound by Rick Price; musical consultant, Bruce Welch; musical director, Paul Jury; executive producer, Brian Sewell; associate producer, Contracts International Ltd. From an original idea by Laurie Mansfield. Presented by Paul Elliott, Ms. Mansfield and Greg Smith (for International Artistes) and David Mirvish. At the Shubert Theater, 225 West 44th Street.

Hipockets Duncan	Fred Sanders
Buddy Holly	Paul Hipp
Joe B. Mauldin	Bobby Prochaska
Jerry Allison	Russ Jolly
Norman Petty and KRWP DJ	Kurt Ziskie
Vi Petty	Jo Lynn Burks
Fourth Cricket	Ken Triwush
Maria Elena	Jill Hennessy

Murray Deutch and Jack Daw. Steve Steiner Big Bopper and Decca Producer David Mucci Ritchie Valens and WWOL DJ Philip Anthony WITH: Sandra Caldwell, Demo Cates, Caren Cole, Alvin Crawford, Melanie Doane, Kevin Fox, Denese Matthews, Paul McQuillan, Tom Nash, Lorraine Scott, Jerome Smith Jr., Liliane Stilwell, Don Stitt and James H. Wiggins Jr.

By FRANK RICH

"Let's rock and roll!" is the inevitable battle cry of the sainted hero of "Buddy: The Buddy Holly Story." And who would go anywhere near the new musical at the Shubert for any reason other than rock-and-roll? The nostalgia-seeking audience at "Buddy" knows what it wants — golden oldies pounded out the way they used to be — and the people who have concocted this entertainment know how to give it to them. In its final 40 minutes or so, "Buddy" unveils a torrential simulation of a hard-driving yet senior-prom-sweet rock concert of the 1950's in which Buddy (Paul Hipp), the Big Bopper (David Mucci), Ritchie Valens (Philip Anthony), a hyperkinetic band and a fervent choir of backup singers turn back the clock by blasting out "Chantilly Lace," "Maybe Baby," "Peggy Sue Got Married," "La Bamba" and more.

For those who remember the 50's — and I do, just — this self-contained concert is bound to touch a nerve. The director, Rob Bettinson, and his designers have gotten the details right, from the typography of the fliers passed out by the ushers to the acres of low-cut satin draped around the bouncing girl singers. While no one will confuse the stand-in rock icons for their prototypes, Mr. Hipp and his colleagues do have a youthful enthusiasm, a raw rock-and-roll talent and an obvious affection for the music that help diminish the ghoulish aura of necrophilia that has given Elvis impersonations a bad name.

●

Not that death escapes the scene: the concert being re-created — a Winter Dance Party at the Surf Ballroom in Clear Lake, Iowa, on Feb. 2, 1959 — is the tragic one of rock-and-roll lore. Hours later, Buddy Holly, 22 years old and only 18 months a rock phenomenon, would be killed along with his companions in a plane crash while trying to fly through a snowstorm to the next stop on their tour. Though "Buddy" eventually fills in the details of that calamity, even then it finds a way to keep its now levitated audience from crashing down at the curtain call. Broadway being Broadway, the music is not allowed to die with the leading man.

It is too bad that the beginning of "Buddy" is not nearly so happy as the ending. To get to the simulated concert, one must slog through two hours of simulated musical comedy much the way contemporary rock audiences must endure interminable warm-up acts before the headliner arrives. Not content to give its customers the 1950's equivalent to "Beatlemania" that they came for, the creators of "Buddy" pad the evening with a superficial, extremely talky biographical drama that makes the puffy 1940's Hollywood biographies of Tin Pan Alley composers look like "Citizen Kane."

The evening's author, Alan Janes, seems to be trying to emulate two other works: Michael Bennett's brilliant, fictionalized musical about the Supremes, "Dreamgirls," and the film "The Buddy Holly Story," which made a deserved star of Gary Busey in 1978. A few of Bennett's theatrical devices are crudely reprised here — notably when Holly is in the Apollo Theater's wings or is heading up the Billboard charts — and the narrative structure is often the same as that of the Busey picture's pedestrian screenplay. But Mr. Janes seems incapable of writing a scene that is dramatic or funny or revealing of character, and he lacks the technical skill to integrate the songs into such scenes as he does write. The result is a series of primitive, predictable vignettes — Buddy revolts against country music, Buddy wears his glasses on stage, Buddy gets married, etc. — in which the actors announce events rather than inhabit them, like the androids in a Disney World pageant.

To keep the audience from mounting an insurrection, the first act and a half of "Buddy" is punctuated by a few songs and a lot of tantalizing song fragments; just before intermission there is a brief preliminary concert occasioned by Holly's famous accidental booking among black acts at the Apollo. But the bad acting and clichéd dialogue — Buddy is forever vowing to play his music "my way" — are wearying and finally laughable. By the time the fateful plane ride is being telegraphed in lines exclaimed by both Valens ("I got to get on that plane tonight!") and the Big Bopper ("Thanks for saving me a seat on that plane!"), "Buddy" has aroused as much nostalgia for Carol Burnett's satirical sketches as it has for vintage rock-and-roll.

●

It seems unconscionable for this show to rave on for nearly three hours without trying to reveal, however speculatively, the soul of the man behind the songs of joyous true love. Mr. Janes is content to portray Holly instead as a perfectly normal American boy who was a "stubborn son of a gun" about his music and, despite his conventional West Texas upbringing, something of a visionary about racial tolerance. Surely there is more than that to the tale of this enduring pop artist. There is also more to the story of how rock-and-roll transformed American culture and society in the 1950's, but such history seems lost on Mr. Janes, an Englishman who first wrote this show for the West End. The new teen-age America that was being parodied on Broadway as long ago as "Bye Bye Birdie," a year after Holly's death, is presented in deadly earnest here, and the Populuxe period billboards of Andy Walmsley's slick set seem infinitely more knowing than the show they decorate.

Aside from Holly's songs, the production's strongest asset is Mr. Hipp, an American performer who originated his role in London. An occasional raspiness notwithstanding, he does everything that is asked, vocal hiccups and yodels included, to capture the vocal manner and shy, gangly persona of the script's Buddy. But there is enough of an edge to his personality, especially as he breaks into the sexual gymnastics of the final concert, to suggest that he, like Gary Busey, could eventually rise to meet a more demanding acting challenge. That'll be the day for Mr. Hipp. In the meantime, "Buddy" is for him and the audience alike as much countdown as blastoff.

1990 N 5, C13:1

The Lady From Havana

By Luis Santeiro; directed by Max Ferra; set and costume design, Campbell Baird; lighting design, Debra Dumas; sound design, Fox/Perla Ltd.; musical arrangements, Fernando Rivas; hair and makeup design, Bobby Miller. Presented by Intar Hispanic American Arts Center, Mr. Ferra, artistic director; Eva Brune, managing director. At 420 West 42d Street.

Marita/Rosa	Olga Merediz
Mama/Gloria	Xonia Benguria
Zoila/Isabel	Alina Troyano

By D. J. R. BRUCKNER

Not exile, poverty, loneliness or age, not even death can defeat the indomitable women of Luis Santeiro's new comedy, "The Lady From Havana," at the Intar Theater.

Mr. Santeiro, who has won many awards for his writing for "Sesame Street" on television, first tried his hand at theater only three years ago, with a faltering comedy about a family finding the image of the Virgin Mary on a tortilla.

He has grown a great deal in a short time. There is not a wasted line

Martha Swope Associates

Paul Hipp in the title role of "Buddy: The Buddy Holly Story."

in "The Lady From Havana," and the author's good humor and warm feelings for his characters suffuses the cast and flows right out into the audience.

Thirty years after the Cuban revolution a woman in her 70's finally escapes and arrives at the Miami home of her daughter, bringing with her a young woman who had been her maid before the old woman turned her into a subverter of good socialist order. It turns out, in a series of hilarious revelations, that this grande dame had become the queen of the black market in Havana. And, to her daughter's growing horror, she quickly learns how to adapt her royally larcenous methods to a capitalist society.

•

Of course, mother and daughter find they have much less in common than they expected and they become formidable foes in family combat despite the former maid's tireless efforts at peacemaking. The playwright keeps all this lighter than air. The anger of the characters is real and so are their verbal blows, but Mr. Santeiro, keeping his eye steadfastly on the absurdity of the human condition, makes it all ridiculous.

Evidently enjoying that kind of challenge, he sets his second act in a funeral home. Ten years have passed. The old woman has died and three friends from Havana days who are also exiles in Miami have come to her wake.

This has to be one of the funniest funerals ever staged. As these women pray, take pokes at one another with mild and delicious malice, and complain about the air-conditioning — "the young ones make it a social occasion and just come and leave; it's the old ones who really love the dead and stay all night who get pneumonia" — their remembrances reveal a story that enfolds the one told in the first act and gives it depth. At the end their recitation of the rosary is overwhelmed by their memories and prayer gives way to a marvelous song they sing, about an old tree remembering a young woman who carved her name on it decades ago.

Max Ferra's direction of this fine comic piece is as taut and delicate as Mr. Santeiro's writing. And Olga Merediz, Xonia Benguria and Alina Troyano, each taking two roles, not only take obvious delight in their characters but set up a certain resonance by occasionally sharing with the audience their amusement in upstaging one another.

Ms. Benguria, who plays the lady from Havana in Act I and a friend who was once a nightclub singer in Act II, has a great gift for comedy. With a glance, a shrug, an arched eyebrow, the movement of a hip, the very slightest misstep, she can extort laughter, and her peeves and resentments are monumentally ridiculous.

1990 N 5, C14:4

Elephant Memories

Conceived and directed by Ping Chong; created in collaboration with the performers and designers. Choreography and text by Mr. Chong, John Fleming, Brian Hallas, Jeannie Hutchins, Larry Malvern, Johanna Melamed, Ric Oquita and Louise Smith. "Afternoon Melodies" composed by Meredith Monk. Presented by La Mama E.T.C. and Ping Chong and Company. At 74A East Fourth Street.

By MEL GUSSOW

As a theatrical explorer, Ping Chong once again ventures into the

Carol Rosegg/Martha Swope Associates/"Elephant Memories"
Louise Smith, left, and Jeannie Hutchins in "Elephant Memories."

future in his enticing, elliptical "Elephant Memories." The time is distant in this new performance piece at La Mama Annex. But it could be closer than one thinks as a race of humans — or are they humanoids? — obeys their daily rules and rituals while receiving Big Brotherly orders from a ubiquitous voiceover.

Though the title of the play duplicates that of Cynthia Moss's fascinating book about her life with elephants in Amboseli National Park in Kenya, there is not an elephant on stage. Nor does the animal appear in the text (prepared by Mr. Chong in collaboration with his company). There is, however, a turtle, or a turtle-like creature, in a photograph that hangs over the cast like an emblem, next to a picture of what appears to be a nuclear plant.

The emphasis in the play is on the elephantine quality of man's memory, lingering through the ages with thoughts of civilizations lost and cultural detritus regained. Or, in the author's words, "Man felt lonesome so he reinvented the past."

•

Mr. Chong is not concerned with repeating brand names and buzzwords, which was also true of his other forward-looking pieces like "A Race" and "The Games" (created with Meredith Monk). Instead his interest is in evoking an aura of what he thinks would remain of our life in an ecologically depleted epoch. It is a time, we are told, of climatic crisis. The sky will be "a beautiful fool's gold today," and if the heat doesn't kill you, the lack of water will.

"Elephant Memories" acknowledges inspiration from sources as diverse as George Orwell ("Animal Farm" as well as "1984"), Fritz Lang ("Metropolis") and the cyberpunk fiction of William Gibson. Mr. Chong's grave new world is more cyber than punk.

Man and his thoughts are controlled by computers. There is no freedom (especially of choice) and people called "no-joys" populate the world. The "long wars" are long over, but peace is no picnic. Every surface has a false facade. Behind the gravity is Mr. Chong's puckish humor and gentleness of spirit. Crossing the fanciful with the cynical, he spoofs our time as well as the indeterminate future while keeping aspects of the play abstruse.

The style is more than half the fun. Mr. Chong draws freely from his background in the graphic and choreographic arts, with an additional musical assist from Meredith Monk. As designed by Mr. Chong and Matthew Yokobosky, the set is striated with string, forming a striking cat's cradle.

The ensemble of actors is dressed in their sci-finery, a space-age version of striped pajamas. With a stiff-legged but graceful walk, they move across the stage, threatening to break into a tap dance, just as the play itself seems on the verge of becoming a musical comedy.

It is easy to lose one's place in the nonlinear narrative as the words cascade through the tightly compressed atmosphere, but the message is unmistakable. "Elephant Memories" is a warning against mankind's drift toward self-denial and self-destruction.

1990 N 6, C15:1

Subfertile

Gerry Goodstein/Playwrights Horizon
Tom Mardirosian

By Tom Mardirosian; directed by John Ferraro; set design by Rick Dennis; costumes, Abigail Murray; lighting, Brian MacDevitt; sound, Frederick Wessler; production stage manager, Karen Armstrong. Presented by Playwright's Horizons, André Bishop, artistic director, Paul S. Daniels, executive director. At 416 West 42d Street.

WITH: Tom Mardirosian, Richard Council, Kitty Crooks, Susan Knight and Frederica Meister.

•

By MEL GUSSOW

Desperation is at the root of Tom Mardirosian's comedy. In "Saved From Obscurity," he chronicled his life as an actor looking for work in the desert of New York theater. In his new play, "Subfertile," he graphically — and amusingly — describes the

anguish of a husband with a low sperm count who will do almost anything in order to improve his chances of fatherhood. The would-be father is named Tom and he is played by the author, facts that move the play (at Playwrights Horizons) two steps closer to autobiography.

If art is imitating life, then Mr. Mardirosian is unabashed and candid in his confessional. That the play is also funny says more about his talent as a writer and actor than it does about the subject matter. One would not have thought so much humor could be derived from so indelicate a theme.

Is there a doctor in the house? Mr. Mardirosian needs help. What he receives in the play is expensive advice and endless pain, with the accent on the latter. The suggestion "this will hurt a little," ricochets through the comedy. Actually, everything hurts a lot, as the hero's body becomes a target zone for testing.

Theatergoers, especially the men in the audience, will wince as they laugh. Mr. Mardirosian certainly evokes empathy for his dilemma. As he undergoes a surfeit of embarrassments in active pursuit of paternity, he remembers with lightning-clear clarity the nights of his youth when he was mortally afraid of "getting girls pregnant."

"Subfertile" is essentially an extended comedy sketch, and the padding shows, as in a fantasy sequence in which the hero imagines he is Mr. Spock, not the baby doctor, on "Star Trek." At another juncture, the play suddenly begins to take itself too seriously as a study of marital discord. For unconvincing reasons, the framework of the story is a visit that Tom makes to the natural history museum on the occasion of his 40th birthday. He converses with a skeleton of a dinosaur that reminds him of his late grandfather.

Beneath this wool-gathering is an acerbic comedy of a special sort. Mr. Mardirosian has a clever way with self-revealing dialogue and a keen eye for apt detail, even when he is digressionary, as in his casual reference to 47th Street Photo as "that place on 45th Street."

This is at least partly a comedy about doctors. Tom sees one doctor after another, including a referral from "my wife's cousin's hairdresser's doorman." Each office visit is more excruciating than the last, and the diagnoses become increasingly dire. If the doctors are not overtly harmful, they are certainly insensitive.

There are, of course, alternative, non-surgical solutions — like adoption and sperm adoption. Or his wife could have an affair with his best friend (who is both fertile and willing). But Tom, devoted to his manhood, will have none of that. He wants to father his own child.

Mr. Mardirosian is about as unprepossessing a heroic figure as one could imagine — balding, standing at a slouch, with a perpetual look of glumness. His appearance enhances a theatergoer's concern. He becomes a kind of everyman, or at least an everyman with a fertility problem. Mr. Mardirosian's deadpan, Bob Newhart-style of delivery is a mirthful asset. As an actor, he is the author's best surrogate.

As directed in a sprightly manner by John Ferraro, the other actors populate the stage (and Tom's nightmares) with comic oddments. Richard Council, Susan Knight and Kitty Crooks play assorted friends, doctors and nurses, all of whom are unconsciously allied in making the hero's life more miserable. Long-suffering is too mild a term to describe Tom's wife (Frederica Meister), married to a man with perpetual testicular anxiety.

To paraphrase the words of Tom's own favorite television show, "Star Trek," in his search for comedy Mr. Mardirosian has decided to boldly go where no playwright has gone before.

1990 N 8, C20:5

The Wash

Gerry Goodstein

Nobu McCarthy, left, and Sab Shimono in "The Wash."

By Philip Kan Gotanda; directed by Sharon Ott; scenery by James Youmans; costumes by Lydia Tanji; lighting by Dan Kotlowitz; original music and sound by Stephen LeGrand; production stage manager, Renée Lutz. Presented by Manhattan Theater Club. At City Center, Stage 2, 131 West 55th Street.

Nobu Matsumoto	Sab Shimono
Masi Matsumoto	Nobu McCarthy
Marsha Matsumoto	Diane Takei
Judy Adams	Jodi Long
Kiyoko Hasegawa	Shizuko Hoshi
Blackie	Marshall Factora
Sadao Nakasato	George Takei
Chiyo Froelich	Carol A. Honda

By MEL GUSSOW

In "The Wash" by Philip Kan Gotanda, a wife abruptly leaves her husband after more than 40 years of marriage, but she continues to do his laundry, visiting him regularly in what is now his seedy bachelor home. She has been totally subservient in marriage and remains dutiful during their separation. The laundry becomes the central symbol of a wife's self-subjugation and the hesitancy with which she assumes a role of independence. For the Matsumotos, the Japanese-American couple at the heart of the play, habit is indeed a great deadener.

The two are trapped not only by that long, lingering marriage but also by the memory of their confinement in an internment camp during World War II. That experience casts a continuing shadow over their lives and over the play itself.

In his attitude toward the characters in "The Wash" (at Manhattan Theater Club's Stage II), Mr. Gotanda is both sensitive and fair-minded. His purpose is not to apportion blame but to lead the audience to an understanding of the wide disparities among these seemingly close-knit people. The result is a play that is small in scale but has a broader relevance for families, especially Asian-Americans.

•

Both the husband and wife undertake new relationships, but their approaches could not be in greater contrast. The wife (Nobu McCarthy) meets a widower who treats her as his equal partner. Overcoming years

of timidity, she renews her hopefulness and her feeling that life can have possibilities. At the same time, her husband (Sab Shimono) becomes involved with the owner of his favorite neighborhood restaurant, a worldly widow who accepts his glumness as a challenge. Increasingly, she finds herself unable to break through the barriers he has erected, some of which trace back to that wartime internment.

Mr. Gotanda artfully shifts between the two couples and their overlapping lives. He also reserves time to paint cameo portraits of minor characters, including the two Matsumoto daughters, who are helpless in their brief attempts to ameliorate their parents lives. Repeatedly the father's stubbornness proves to be greater than his compassion.

There is a quietude and even a fragility about many of the scenes, a fact that makes the few emotional outbursts by the husband carry even more weight, as when he belatedly tries to persuade his wife to return. With the help of Mr. Shimono's resolute performance, the play embraces understatement and avoids sentimentality.

•

As director, Sharon Ott has given the work a fluidity on James Youmans's open set, which serves interchangeably for all locations. Abetted by his director, Mr. Gotanda is gently effective in evoking character through atmosphere, as in the juxtaposition of Mr. Shimono and his rival (George Takei) — the loneliness of the former preparing a perfunctory solitary dinner and the expansiveness of the latter making breakfast for himself and Miss McCarthy. With a smile, Mr. Takei mixes waffles while announcing proudly that everything in the meal is low in cholesterol, "except for the Cool Whip." Then he adds a dash of MSG.

Food becomes an underlying motif in several lives (along with kite-making and fishing). Mr. Shimono freely accepts the hospitality of the restaurant owner (Shizuko Hoshi) while severely limiting his emotional reciprocity. In the background is the cook, whose language is as highly seasoned as his food.

The play arrives in New York relatively late. In the 1980's, it was presented at several California theaters and was filmed for public television (starring some of the members of the present company). As appealingly performed under Ms. Ott's direction, it remains a touching slice of life. It is also a sign of Mr. Gotanda's range as a playwright. His talent encompasses satiric comedies ("Yankee Dawg You Die"), surrealism ("Bullet Headed Birds") and more personalized group portraits like "The Wash."

1990 N 8, C28:4

The Playboy of the Western World

By J. M. Synge; directed by Charlotte Moore; set design, David Raphel; costumes, Natalie Walker; sound and lighting, Richard Clausen; production stage manager, J. Andrew Burgreen; fight director, J. Steven White; original music by Larry Kerwin, performed by Black 47. The Irish Repertory Theater, Ciaran O'Reilly, producing director; Ms. Moore, artistic director, presented by the Irish Repertory Theater Company, South Street Theater Company and One World Arts Foundation. At South Street Theater, 424 West 42d Street.

Christy Mahon	Patrick Fitzgerald
Pegeen Mike	Madeleine Potter
Widow Quin	Caroline Winterson
Shawn Keogh	Ciaran O'Reilly
Old Mahon	Stephen Joyce
Michael James Flaherty	Brendan Burke
Jimmy Farrell	Chris Carrick
Philly Cullen	Brian F. O'Byrne
Susan Brady	Mac Orange
Honor Blake	Miriam Foley
Sara Tansey	Laura Hughes
Town Crier	Adrian O'Byrne

By STEPHEN HOLDEN

Among comic protagonists of 20th-century drama, Christy Mahon, the title character of John Millington's Synge's satirical masterpiece "The Playboy of the Western World," is one of those most open to interpretation. At once loutish and poetic, cowardly and dashing, the young man who seduces the imagination of a poor Irish village with his story of having murdered his father can be played as everything from a dolt to a slippery con man to a flawed romantic hero. It depends on the actor playing him and on how harshly the director wishes to rub the audience's noses in Synge's satiric vision of the brutish life of the Irish peasantry in 1900.

In the Irish Repertory Theater's sturdy production of the play at the South Street Theater, Patrick Fitzgerald plays Christy as a little bit of each. When he first appears, covered from head to toe in mud, there is an opportunistic gleam in his eye. Later, as he embellishes his tale of having murdered his tyrannical father by hitting him over the head with a hoe, he seems more like a fool who is just beginning to wake up to his storytelling powers. Later still, when his flowery cadences win Pegeen's heart, he exudes a princely charisma.

•

If the figure Mr. Fitzgerald cuts on the stage ultimately seems a bit too polished, his performance still synchronizes smoothly with a production that doesn't camouflage the darkness of Synge's humor. After all, one reason Christy's tale of patricide is greeted with such enthusiasm is that the poachers, thieves and drunkards he charms are no more virtuous than he. The Widow Quin (Caroline Win-

Martha Swope Associates/Irish Repertory Theater

Patrick Fitzgerald

terson), the most persistent of the women who swarm around him like flies to a pot of jam, has killed a husband who was once imprisoned for maiming sheep. In the pecking order of brutal acts, justifiable patricide seems positively heroic.

As directed by Charlotte Moore, this production of "Playboy' moves swiftly, propelled by a good-humored knockabout energy. The portrayals of characters who could easily be played as grotesque caricatures maintain a confident middle ground between the sentimental and the savagely satirical. When Christy's father, Old Mahon (Stephen Joyce), stumbles into the village, his head swathed in bloody bandages, his menacing physicality is tempered with a strain of pathos. Ciaran O'Reilly, who plays Pegeen's bumbling fiancé,

Shawn Keogh, also injects a subtle note of yearning into the role of a dullard.

•

With the exception of Madeleine Potter's spirited Pegeen, the production is a little kinder to its male characters than to its women. The village girls who throw themselves at Christy are played as giggling, half-demented harpies by Mac Orange, Miriam Foley and Laura Hughes. Ms. Winterson's Widow Quin is a cold, ruthless schemer whose interest in Christy has less to do with sexual desire than with a competitive drive to beat out the other women and win him.

It is Miss Potter's seething portrayal of Pegeen that brings the rest of the performances into perspective. Her feisty flashing-eyed performance evokes a woman whose toughened surface only partially conceals a bitter idealism that is momentarily sparked to life by Christy's eloquence before it is smashed. The rending cry with which she ends the play is a brilliant flourish of grief-stricken passion.

1990 N 8, C28:1

Six Degrees of Separation

By John Guare; directed by Jerry Zaks; sets, Tony Walton; costumes, William Ivey Long; lighting, Paul Gallo; sound, Aural Fixation; hair, Angela Gari; production manager, Jeff Hamlin. Presented by Lincoln Center Theater, Gregory Mosher, director; Bernard Gersten, executive producer. At the Vivian Beaumont Theater, Lincoln Center, 65th Street and Broadway.

Ouisa	Stockard Channing
Flan	John Cunningham
Geoffrey	Sam Stoneburner
Paul	Courtney B. Vance
Hustler	David Eigenberg
Kitty	Kelly Bishop
Larkin	Peter Maloney
Detective	Brian Evers
Tess	Robin Morse
Woody	Gus Rogerson
Ben	Anthony Rapp
Dr. Fine	Stephen Pearlman
Doug	Evan Handler
Policeman/Eddie	Philip LeStrange
Trent	John Cameron Mitchell
Rick	Robert Duncan McNeil
Elizabeth	Mari Nelson

By FRANK RICH

"How do we *keep* the experience?" asks an anguished Stockard Channing, fighting back anger and tears near the end of "Six Degrees of Separation," the John Guare play that reopened in a new and larger Lincoln Center theater, the Vivian Beaumont, with a new co-star, Courtney B. Vance, last night.

Ms. Channing, in the role of an Upper East Side matron named Ouisa Kittredge, has just had the experience of her life: A young black man, posing as the son of Sidney Poitier, bamboozled his way into her home, family and heart and then, just as abruptly, vanished. Ouisa is not the same person she was before she met the impostor, who called himself Paul and is played by Mr. Vance. The encounter has jolted her out of her insular sophistication, sending her through "new doors opening into other worlds." But now she' fears her cathartic reawakening may be slipping away to become merely another New York dinner-party anecdote "with no teeth and a punch line you'll mouth over and over for years to come." And if Ouisa has learned anything from Paul, it is that she wants to hold onto experience, to connect at last to the people around her, to stop being one of "these human jukeboxes spilling out these anecdotes."

Returning to "Six Degrees" nearly

A new co-star, Courtney Vance, adds a sexual edge.

five months after its premiere, I worried whether it, too, might have been reduced by time to glib anecdotal status. Certainly this play, like any other hot ticket on the New York cultural scene, has been masticated by le tout Manhattan. People dined out on Mr. Guare's smartest lines all summer. The real-life con man whose 1983 scams inspired the play resurfaced in the press, and so did his prominent victims. The work's meaning has been debated by all manner of pundits, its creators have been exhaustively interviewed, its title has passed into the language. To be a full-fledged New York phenomenon, "Six Degrees" lacks only a strong critical backlash, and surely this, too, will come.

But not here. Watching "Six Degrees" again, with full knowledge of where its laughs are and where its bodies (three of them) are buried, I found it as funny and moving and provocative as ever — still a fresh experience, not last season's calcified hit. Part of this is a tribute to the high quality of the production's transfer. The director, Jerry Zaks, and the set designer, Tony Walton — the only team ever to have consistent success in the vast Beaumont — have duplicated their initial staging meticulously, re-creating the same living-room intimacy they achieved downstairs at the tiny Mitzi E. Newhouse Theater and sacrificing nothing, including the use of the auditorium's first row as a bench for the temporary parking of the large supporting cast. Mr. Vance, younger than James McDaniel, his predecessor as Paul, proves a fine addition to the company, revealing a wit and a sexual edge that had not surfaced in his impassioned previous appearances in plays by August Wilson and Athol Fugard.

If Mr. Vance alters the chemistry of "Six Degrees" slightly, it is to accentuate the bond that inexorably develops between Paul and Ouisa — a connection at once emotional, intellectual and erotic linking two such seemingly disparate characters as a poor, gay, young black man of unknown identity and a rich, WASP-y, middle-aged wife with a pedigree. The emphasis helps focus the play, perhaps because above all else, above even its hilarious jokes about money and art and the musicals of Andrew Lloyd Webber, "Six Degrees" is an unlikely, chaste, covert love story in which Paul and Ouisa reach out for each other as surely as do those hands in Ouisa's beloved Sistine Chapel. The real if buried plot of "Six Degrees" deals not with Paul's fraudulent identity but with the authenticity of spirit that allows him and Ouisa to break through those degrees of separation that isolate people in a dehumanizing metropolis overpopulated by all kinds of phonies.

It's possible as well that the raised temperature between Paul and Ouisa has contributed to the evening's other new phenomenon — the growth in

Martha Swope/Lincoln Center Theater

Stockard Channing, left, and Courtney B. Vance in "Six Degrees of Separation" at the Vivian Beaumont Theater.

Stockard Channing's performance. This actress, who was merely brilliant in June, now cuts so close to the bone that she straddles the territory between heart-stopping fragility and comic radiance that theater lovers talk about when they remember Laurette Taylor in "The Glass Menagerie" or Irene Worth's Ranevskaya in "The Cherry Orchard." In fact, I found myself thinking of Ranevskaya's farewell to her ancestral estate when, in the final moments of "Six Degrees," Ms. Channing, alone in a dim spotlight and dissolved in the spiritual memory of a visit to the Sistine Chapel, slowly swivels her head so that her glassy, imploring eyes can take in every corner of the audience. Some actresses, one is often told, have a greatness that demands a large house. Here — in our own time, incredibly enough — is one of them.

•

As Ms. Channing would surely be the first to agree, great acting cannot exist in a vacuum. The rest of the ensemble, led by John Cunningham's miraculously human account of Ouisa's patrician yet hustling art-dealer husband, is as sharp as ever, if not sharper: Sam Stoneburner as a visiting South African magnate, Kelly Bishop and Peter Maloney as a warring married couple, Stephen Pearlman as an obstetrician with a deceptively avuncular bedside manner. While all of these figures could be cartoons, each is rewarded by playwright and actor with compassion and a burst of color.

In the flat-out funny roles of children — riotous cameos that recall Mr. Guare's collaboration on "Taking Off," the Milos Forman film about 1960's runaways — Evan Handler, Robin Morse, Gus Rogerson and John Cameron Mitchell remain some of the most articulately hostile teenagers ever to pass through the East's finer institutions of higher eductation. As their ingenuous opposites — a couple of starry-eyed young innocents who travel to New York from Utah in search of acting careers — Robert Duncan McNeill, another cast

newcomer, and Mari Nelson play crucial, late-evening roles in switching the play's tone from the farcical high pitch of a hip "Guess Who's Coming to Dinner" to that of its final chapters of tragic death and final visions of ecstatic rebirth.

•

The play that nurtures these and the other good actors each night rewards repeat visitors just as plentifully. Running only 90 minutes in one act that Mr. Zaks takes at a breakneck pace, "Six Degrees" is extraordinarily dense with ideas and feelings that can be picked apart and analyzed individually after the fact but that somehow coalesce into an elegant composition on stage.

If there is one image that dominates, it can be found in the play's final words — "It's painted on two sides." The line refers to a Kandinsky canvas that twirls above the action in the Kittredge home, but it emblemizes the two-sided metaphors of a play that pointedly defines schizophrenia as "a horrifying state" where what is inside the psyche "doesn't match up with what's out there." In the fractionalized New York of "Six Degrees," the bust town that followed the boom town of "Bonfire of the Vanities," families, classes, races and sexes are all divided, just as each individual is divorced from the imagination that might yet be his means to introspection and salvation.

As that Kandinsky canvas hangs above "Six Degrees," so does Kandinsky's artistic principle, recited early on, that there can be a "harmony of form" in a painting only if the choice of each object is dictated by "a corresponding vibration in the human soul." Mr. Guare yearns against all odds for the same redemptive harmony from his New Yorkers. The set for his play is a series of doorways — some at ground level leading to the rooms of a Fifth Avenue apartment, others above opening to the characters' dreams, all of them bordered by the gilt frames of art. What prevents this searing comedy from becoming another disposable New York anec-

dote is that, for all the perfection of Mr. Guare's own art within those frames, it is ourselves, imperfect and bloodied and as hungry as Ouisa for that transcendent vibration, whom we meet once we walk through those doors.

1990 N 9, C5:1

Daytrips

By Jo Carson; directed by Billie Allen; scenery by James Noone; lighting, Anne Militello; costumes, Barbara Beccio; sound, Lia Vollack; production stage manager, Robert Daley. Presented by the Women's Project and Productions, Julia Miles, artistic director. At the Judith Anderson Theater, 422 West 42d Street.

Pat...Linda Atkinson
Irene/Ree..................................Barbara Barrie
Pat...Beth Dixon
Rose..Helen Stenborg

Martha Holmes

Helen Stenborg in "Daytrips."

By MEL GUSSOW

Jo Carson's "Daytrips" is a collage of events, memories and fantasies, as a granddaughter moves back and forth between her demanding, often abusive elders. She is the sole attendant for her mother, who is suffering from Alzheimer's disease, and for her grandmother, who is subject to her own delusions as well as to the infirmities of old age.

In effect, parents become completely dependent on their offspring. The granddaughter is put to a severe test. With desperation but with unabated tenderness, she tries to alleviate family pressures. The play, which is having its first New York production under auspices of the Women's Project, is heartfelt in its concern for its characters. It is also revealing about the wounding effects of those who are ill on those who are devoted "care keepers." But Ms. Carson has not enveloped her people in a fully conceived drama.

The playwright is best known as a Texas storyteller and "Daytrips" bears the marks of the oral tradition. Two actresses play the protagonist, one (Beth Dixon) introducing the story and standing in for minor characters, the other (Linda Atkinson) portraying the granddaughter in life.

Even though the play has had prior productions, the narrative still seems to be evolving. This is especially evident in Billie Allen's staging at the Judith Anderson Theater. In a version last season at Hartford Stage, Michael Engler unmoored the play from realism. Using an imaginative indoor-outdoor set by Loy Arcenas, the director enhanced the work by making it more of a dream play. The audience could feel that it was entering the minds and sharing the delusions of the characters.

•

Ms. Allen's version is far more stolid and emotionally unyielding. The device of the storyteller reveals its awkwardness just as the staging emphasizes the work's roots as family case history. In the New York production, the play is fragmentary.

Three of the four actresses appear to be at a remove from their characters, particularly so in the case of Barbara Barrie as the mother, an adult who has regressed into childlike behavior. Her spasms of violence seem less-steadily unnerving than repetitive. Ms. Allen has been unable to capture the underlying strain of melancholy that characterizes the mother-daughter relationships.

What the production does have is Helen Stenborg, repeating her Hartford Stage performance as the grandmother. That performance is distinguished by both its gravity and its humor. As written by Ms. Carson and as personified by Ms. Stenborg, this is a complex portrait of a woman whose mind is outliving her physical capability, in spite of the fact that she confuses names with a merry abandon. Her feisty humor comes out in

her own storytelling (including one amusing tale about a man who lived in a tree) and in her craving for the continuation of routine.

•

In one of the play's most moving sequences, the granddaughter drives her grandmother to the drugstore to fill a prescription. The older woman's favorite pharmacist seems to have disappeared and the trail leads through a maelstrom of shopping malls, with Ms. Stenborg firmly holding out for the familiar as her last ballast. The granddaughter comes to realize that the grandmother's stubbornness is the primary factor in preserving her sanity, even as she tries to will her own death. Ms. Stenborg gives "Daytrips" a resilience and a clarity otherwise lacking in the current production.

1990 N 10, 16:1

SUNDAY VIEW/David Richards

The Gershwins' 'Oh, Kay!' Dances to Harlem

"OH, KAY!" — THE GERSHWIN brothers' 1926 opus, David Merrick's 88th Broadway production and the first big splash of the season — is the one thing an escapist musical can't afford to be: hard-working.

The effort is everywhere — from a tap-dancing ensemble that is pounding the floor like so many human jackhammers, to a leading lady who conducts herself with the lac-

quered grit of a Miss America contestant determined to smile her way to the top. A Gershwin song is second to none, and the "Oh, Kay!" score counts among its treasures "Clap Yo' Hands," "Do, Do, Do" and "Someone to Watch Over Me." But the prevailing view at the Richard Rodgers Theater seems to be that they, too, have to be pushed, as if they belonged to that category of goods (raffle tickets, vacation land, light-up bow ties) that don't naturally sell themselves.

David Merrick's musical works hard; Beth Henley's 'Abundance' tackles the American dream; at 'Buddy,' it's prom night again.

Collectively, the cast must be expending between 10 and 20 million calories per performance, and while it looked none the worse for wear at the curtain call the other night, I was exhausted. A musical with no letup, paradoxically, can be a big letdown. As directed and choreographed by Dan Siretta, this one appears to be coming at you on a conveyor belt, jammed in forward gear and doomed to constant acceleration, so that the performers are all but thrust into the final production number.

Putting together "Show Me the Town" and "Sleepless Nights," Mr. Siretta has fashioned one of those paeans to the loneliness and frenzy of the city, after the deep purple falls. I suspect it is supposed to do for "Oh, Kay!" what the title number did for Mr. Merrick's megahit, "42d Street." (Someone, lurking in the wings, even tells the heroine to "knock

Jim Estrin for The New York Times

Kevin Ramsey, center, in "Oh, Kay!"—The musical appears to be coming at you on a conveyor belt, jammed in forward gear and doomed to constant acceleration.

'em dead,'' as she pulls herself together and prepares to brave center stage.) But Mr. Siretta possesses a second-rate imagination, and the heaviness of his hand, not to mention his feet, is never more apparent.

Vintage musical comedies have enough built-in problems as it is. The songs are usually splendid, but the books are terrible and the jokes worse. Until "Oklahoma!" the form never took itself too seriously — or too coherently — and "Oh, Kay!" certainly wasn't out to alter history. Originally, it involved a rum-running English duke and his sister, Kay (Gertrude Lawrence and, from all accounts, radiant), who stash their illegal hooch in the basement of a palatial Long Island summer cottage. Unexpectedly, the owner, a dashing millionaire, pops up with his new bride. Since Kay is instantly smitten with the young man, getting rid of the booze *and* disposing of the bride loom as the plot's biggest hurdles.

They still do. Mr. Siretta, however, has had an idea. An idea is generally referred to as a concept these days, merits billing in the program (as in "Concept by . . . ") and for all I know increases your share of the royalty pool. What would happen, he has asked himself, if you were to transfer the action to Harlem and make the characters black? Accordingly, in the adaptation by James Racheff, the duke is now Duke, who runs the snazzy Paradise Club with a team of goofy bootleggers in tuxedos. Kay is a songstress at the club. And the sleek millionaire inhabits a Victorian mansion on Striver's Row — far enough removed, symbolically, from Lenox Avenue to keep some of the show's class distinctions intact.

This does not make the book any better, mind you; it merely allows it to be awful in another setting. Whatever new quips Mr. Racheff has concocted for the occasion, they are indistinguishable from those Guy Bolton and P. G. Wodehouse pitched at audiences in 1926. "What's a poltergeist?" "Almost any geist that polters," is a groaner for all seasons.

More to the point, Mr. Siretta has not really followed through on his concept. The production is black only to the extent that it employs a black cast. In no significant way does it reflect a black sensibility or illuminate, however passingly, the black world in which it is presumably taking place. If you were to close your eyes, the notion of color probably wouldn't even occur to you. The production's spiritual ancestor is the all-black version of "Hello, Dolly!" which Mr. Merrick hit upon in the late 1960's to prolong what was already shaping up as a very long run. One team was substituted for another, but the game remained the same. The changes Mr. Siretta has wrought on "Oh, Kay!" strike no deeper.

His choreography seems to owe its existence to a Cuisinart, into which he has fed such popular dances as the Charleston, the black bottom, the cakewalk and the shimmy. What comes out is all flapping legs and jutting elbows. But it never goes any place. Mr. Siretta's notion of building a dance number is simply to have everyone do the same step more intensely, while heating up the lights.

As the comic lovers, asserting that "You've Got What Gets Me," Kyme and Gregg Burge rise above the banality by sheer force of personality. All the while they're making goo-goo eyes at each other, their limbs are flying — now in unison, now at cross purposes, but never without devilish bravado. The duo gives "Oh, Kay!" its best shot at a show-stopper. Mr. Siretta's staging of "Fidgety Feet" is so suggestive of passengers on the deck of a storm-tossed ocean liner, however, that the number might be more aptly titled "Queasy Stomachs."

For the most part, the cast does not bring out the best in the material, any more than the material brings out the best in the cast. As one of the bootleggers, obliged to pass himself off as a butler, Helmar Augustus Cooper has great reserves of joviality and a warm pudding of a face. But he's saddled with the evening's hoariest material and it's his good sportsmanship, more than his comic aplomb, you end up applauding. Brian Mitchell's matinee-idol looks and smooth singing voice serve him well as the millionaire, although they don't exactly make for a characterization. The missing person in this production, however, is Kay herself.

Angela Teek comes to the role straight from 10 consecutive wins as

Gerry Goodstein/Manhattan Theater Club
Amanda Plummer, left, and Tess Harper in "Abundance"—friendship put to the test

best female vocalist on television's "Star Search '90." Surely that prepares you for a great deal in life, if not a Broadway musical. On the legitimate stage, Ms. Teek is stiff and forced, and she displays little comic flair when, caught red-handed in the millionaire's home, she must pretend to be the maid. "Someone to Watch Over Me" also goes to the performer, and while I have no doubt she could deliver a gutsy rendition of the classic (you can hear a soul singer's wail lapping at the ends of her lyrics), that is not the plaintive interpretation Mr. Siretta is after.

As a result, much of Ms. Teek's hard work in "Oh, Kay!" seems to be devoted to holding herself back. The strain shows.

'Abundance'

I won't say that Tess Harper's performance is the major hitch in "Abundance," but it prevented me from getting a clear bead on Beth Henley's new play at the Manhattan Theater Club. Abandoning her usual turf — the small Southern town, where much of the animal population is stuck to the roads and the human population stands as a warning against the perils of inbreeding — Ms. Henley has struck out for the wide-open spaces of the Wyoming Territory, circa 1860. She's charting the see-sawing fortunes of two mail-order brides, who vow at the outset of their adventure to be best friends, but find men and events putting their friendship to the test.

For the first half of the play, outgoing Macon Hill (Ms. Harper) and her glass-eyed husband prosper, while clumsy Bess Johnson (Amanda Plummer) and her brutish mate undergo progressively harder times and are reduced to sifting through a straw-filled mattress for slivers of wheat to eat. ("Early disappointments are embittering my life," notes Bess, and she hasn't even been carried away by Indians, yet.)

The second act turns the tables. Rescued after years in the wilderness, Bess, now tattooed and missing a small patch of her scalp, converts her experiences as the concubine of an Indian chief into a best-selling book and a prosperous career on the

lecture circuit. Meanwhile, drought hits Macon's spread, the bank forecloses, her husband bolts (handing

Martha Swope/"Buddy"
Paul Hipp in the title role of "Buddy"—more rock concert than story

over his glass eye as a parting gesture), and she slowly sinks to the bottom of the social ladder.

Is Ms. Henley commenting ironically on the mythical abundance of the American dream? Spinning a tall tale about the odd things odd people do to get by? Is her concern female bonding, the physical and spiritual disfigurement of women or the loopy ways of destiny, which never closes one trapdoor that it doesn't open another?

Probably all of the above. "Abundance" has epic ambitions, although it lacks the epic thrust that would bind its multiple episodes together.

The focus keeps shifting and more than once you get the nagging sensation that Ms. Henley is being weird just to be weird. But I can't·say that stopped me. Ms. Harper did.

In a play about the dark side of the 19th-century West, she has sunny Southern California written all over her. There's something about her extroverted presence that turns life into a pep rally and reduces grief to a form of foot-stamping petulance. Ms. Plummer, quivering as strangely as ever, and the men in the cast (Michael Rooker, Lanny Flaherty and Keith Reddin) have no trouble fitting into Ms. Henley's vision of America, the macabre. But only a time machine could have transported Ms. Harper there.

'Buddy'

Although "Buddy," the musical at the Shubert Theater, purports to tell "The Buddy Holly Story," there's not a whole lot of story to be told. Good-natured·lad from Lubbock, Tex., just

Is Ms. Henley commenting on female bonding, or the loopy ways of destiny?

out of his teens, sets the rock-and-roll world agog in 1957 with "That'll Be the Day." Career takes off, future looks bright. Then, as any Holly fan knows, it all comes to a cruel end on Feb. 3, 1959, when Holly and his fellow performers, the Big Bopper and Ritchie Valens, go down in a plane crash. Holly was 22.

With no point of view other than that of the acolyte toward his god, the writer Alan Janes puts this brief life into a series of seemingly endless scenes, rife with the clichés of show business. ("I think you'll find I'm different from the others. Buddy Holly does things his way.") Despite all the scenery, five va-va-vooming motorcycles and a cast of characters that numbers more than 75, the musical is just a Buddy Holly concert in disguise, with Paul Hipp doing a remarkably convincing Holly impersonation. If such songs as "Peggy Sue," "Oh Boy," "Raining in My Heart," "Maybe Baby" and "Rave On" are inextricably linked to your past — or constitute a· meaningful part of your present — you know what to do.

The final half hour of "Buddy" gives up any claims at story-telling and re-creates Holly's last engagement, the Winter Dance Party, in the Surf Ballroom at Clear Lake, Iowa. Programs are handed out. There's a drawing for a door .prize. The Big Bopper (David Mucci) and Ritchie Valens (Philip Anthony) contribute their big hits, "Chantilly Lace" and "La Bamba." The refracted light from a mirrored ball blankets the auditorium with a swirl of snowflakes, just like on prom night. Every five minutes or so, someone shouts out, "Are you having a good time?" and if the audience response is not

sufficiently rousing, the question gets asked again.

To my mind, the best of "Buddy" can be found on the original-cast recording. But critical judgments are probably irrelevant. You don't consult the guidebooks before deciding whether or not to visit Graceland, do you? □

1990 N 11, II:5:1

Shadowlands

By William Nicholson; directed by Elijah Moshinsky; designed by Mark Thompson; lighting by John Michael Deegan; general manager, Ralph Roseman; production stage manager, Elliott Woodruff. Presented by Elliot Martin, James M. Nederlander, Brian Eastman, Terry Allen Kramer and Roger L. Stevens. At the Brooks Atkinson Theater, 250 West 47th Street.

C. S. Lewis	Nigel Hawthorne
Christopher Riley	Paul Sparer
The Rev. Harry Harrington	Robin Chadwick
Dr. Oakley	Hugh A. Rose
Alan Gregg	Edmund C. Davys
Maj. W. H. Lewis	Michael Allinson
Douglas	Lance Robinson
Joy Davidman	Jane Alexander
Registrar	Mary Layne

By FRANK RICH

Jack is a crusty, remote middle-aged Oxford don, a devout Anglican who is more comfortable chatting to God than to the opposite sex. Joy is a 40-ish New Yorker, a Jewish convert to Christianity with a big mouth and a failing marriage. Jack and Joy strike up an unlikely epistolary friendship, rendezvous in Oxford and, overcoming all obstacles, fall in love. No sooner do these opposites attract, however, than tragedy, in the form of terminal illness, tears them asunder.

Thus in rough outline goes "Shadowlands," and who could imagine a tidier recipe for a television movie? The audience gets to have an odd-couple comic romance — a sort of May-September, trans-Atlantic "Bridget Loves Bernie" — and a disease of the week, too. "Shadowlands" in fact began its life as a television drama, but because Jack is the nickname for C. S. Lewis (1898-1963), the scholarly proselytizer for Christianity and the author of the evergreen Narnia fantasies for children, and because Joy was Joy Davidman, the American poet he married near the end of both their lives, it was produced by the tony British television,

not the usual Hollywood suspects. Starring Joss Ackland and Claire Bloom, the 52-minute film was broadcast in the United States on public television in 1986.

Now "Shadowlands" is a play of considerably more than twice that length that has arrived on Broadway at the Brooks Atkinson Theater via the West End. The stars are Nigel Hawthorne, a rightly beloved fixture on the British comedy series "Yes Minister," and Jane Alexander, whose spunky Joy may remind many of her appearance as another strong-willed wife in another nonfiction TV romance, "Eleanor and Franklin."

How you will feel about "Shadowlands" depends a great deal on your degree of Anglophilia. The play, by William Nicholson, has little more intellectual or emotional depth than a tear-jerker set in two-car-garage suburbia, but it does boast a certain rarefied British atmosphere. This is the kind of work that is often described as "literate," especially by nonreaders, because its characters frequently mention works of literature. As at "84 Charing Cross Road," its London theatrical prototype, no visitor to "Shadowlands" need worry that anyone on stage will be so boorish as to discuss the actual substance of the books and authors whose names are bandied about.

Even those who find "Masterpiece Theater" as resistible as I do are likely to be charmed by the endearing Englishness of Mr. Hawthorne, who happens to be South African. With a rumpled, well-worn face and ginger-snap voice to match his tweed jacket, Marks & Spencer sweater and corduroy pants, his C. S. Lewis is Mr. Chips, Dr. Doolittle and the shaggy professor once played by Michael Hordern in Tom Stoppard's "Jumpers" all in one.

Never pretending that Jack is anything other than an old softie at heart, Mr. Hawthorne is a joy to watch as "Shadowlands" lumbers toward the inevitable scenes in which Ms. Alexander's Joy penetrates his confirmed bachelorhood. In the play as in life, Jack first marries Joy "technically" — so she can settle in England with her young son after her divorce — and then marries her in earnest, as she lies in a hospital bed, a victim of bone cancer. In between these two benchmarks, Mr. Hawthorne migrates from absent-mindedness to passion. His performance reaches an exquisite peak of comic turmoil when he finds himself torn between the gesture he always uses to put off

Joy's affection — a random, reflexive search of his many pockets for some unspecified object — and his ravenous hunger for a kiss.

•

When suffering overwhelms his spirit, Mr. Hawthorne goes further still, spitting out his grief in pink-faced rage. The actor makes one see how "Shadowlands" might have been as moving as Lewis's own memoir, "A Grief Observed." But Mr. Nicholson and Ms. Alexander undercut the actor by refusing to bring his romantic partner to life. As written, Joy is a generic, wisecracking literary broad, a Dorothy Parker wind-up doll.

While Ms. Alexander's comic timing is expert, notably during a Greek honeymoon that is the play's funniest interlude, she is never given a chance to act the rest of this woman, whose renunciations of Judaism and leftism were central to her character. (Can one imagine an American playwright reducing Joy Davidman's discarded Judaism to a gag, as Mr. Nicholson does?) The heroine's deeper feelings are usually sidestepped entirely, often by having the actress turn away from the audience or dart offstage at emotional climaxes. When Joy succumbs to love, Ms. Alexander lets down her hair, not her guard; her descent toward death is delineated most persuasively by her makeup and declining posture.

Perhaps to compensate for the absence of any real psychological intimacy — the couple's sex life, or lack of same, is never mentioned — "Shadowlands" turns to Lewis's Narnia books for mystical scenic tableaux that, in the most literal-minded fashion, periodically equate Jack's new domestic ecstasy with the world of wonder discovered by children in "The Lion, the Witch and the Wardrobe" and its sequels. In lieu of fleshing out his characters, Mr. Nicholson also piles on touristic local color, padding the evening with repetitive anecdotes about the high-table clubbiness of Jack's masculine academic circle at Oxford. The weak American supporting cast, typified by Paul Sparer's buffoonish caricature of a misogynistic don, compromises what wit these scenes offer and also vitiates the authenticity of Mark Thompson's handsome scenery and the lighting designer John Michael Deegan's wonderfully exact wintry Oxbridge gloom.·

•

Unlike most of his casting, Elijah Moshinsky's staging is graceful, except when he and the designers are playing with the set's front scrim or hammering in the Narnia-inspired metaphor of the title. The director has elicited one excellent supporting performance, too, from Michael Allinson, as Jack's devoted older brother and housemate. But the Lewises' fraternal bond, like the play's other important secondary relationship, between Joy's son and Jack, is so sketchily drawn that it cannot carry the dramatic weight it must in the evening's waning scenes.

•

The same superficiality attends the play's potentially fascinating philosophical conflict: How can Lewis reconcile his belief in a benevolent God's Heaven with the pain and suffering he experiences on earth? Mr. Nicholson raises such questions only to resolve them happily and instantaneously, before anyone might be tempted to turn the channel. In "Shadowlands," even death becomes the stuff of genteel entertainment, no more troubling

Martha Swope

Jane Alexander and Nigel Hawthorne in "Shadowlands."

r surprising than a patch of gray during an otherwise sunny West End afternoon.

1990 N 12, C11:1

The Christmas Spectacular

Directed by Scott Salmon; set design, Charles Lisanby; "Carol of the Bells" and "We Need a Little Christmas" choreography by Scott Salmon and costume designs, Pete Menefee. "Christmas in New York" choreography by Marianne Selbert; additional choreography Violet Holmes and Linda Lemac. Original costume designs, Frank Spencer; additional costume designs, Jose Lengson; lighting design, Ken Billington; music director and conductor, Don Pippin; orchestrations, Michael Gibson, Jim Tyler and Bob Wheeler. Presented by Radio City Music Hall Productions, David J. Nash, executive producer. At 50th Street and the Avenue of the Americas.

By RICHARD F. SHEPARD

If you ever doubted that life in New York was on the fast track consider this: less than a week ago we were in the midst of Election Day and today we are already in full celebration of Christmas. Not all of us, of course, but certainly the people up at the Radio City Music Hall, where the venerable "Christmas Spectacular" has opened, just moments, it feels, after the mercury learned how to spell Jack Frost.

"The Christmas Spectacular," no less venerated than venerable, rarely shows its age because it is spruced up annually. This year it has 3 new acts among the 11 that fill that extraterrestrial floating stage for 90 minutes. They are new, but you might never notice because they fit so seamlessly into the texture of this hardy institutional perennial, which started life in 1933 and took on its present shape in 1979 with revisions in 1985.

What keeps it young, in addition to the trim production itself, is the constant influx of young audiences who may not have seen it before and, for all the technical sophistication of the newer generations, cannot be anything but impressed by the grandeur of mechanical motion seen live on something larger than a television screen.

•

The marvelous tingly elements of the show are the magnificent scene-stealing backdrops, the colorful props and the lavish use of space and lighting, which transport not only the players, including the symphony-sized orchestra, back and forth and up and down, but also, in spirit, the audience. Two of the new acts are musical numbers, one of them with a handsome view of New York as seen from atop a skyscraper, the Chrysler Building twinkling across the way and giant jack-in-the-box figures that rise high above the dancers; the other is a lavish bell-ringer, with all sorts of chimes.

•

Also new is a rewrite of "A Christmas Carol," which in previous editions took up the Ebenezer Scrooge story from the time he decided to become a good fellow. The update takes the Dickens tale from the top, throws in three Christmas spirits, one of them a Christmas tree and the others creatures that float down from on high. It does not add much to what it replaced, but again it doesn't hurt.

The familiar show stoppers are still in evidence, including the Rockettes and their "Parade of the Wooden Soldiers," which, no matter how often you may have seen it, remains a marvel of human, if faceless, precision and is doubtless the surest-fire hit of the program. Everything else is pretty much as it has been, so one can relive one's past, or the show's past, once again at the Music Hall. Don't worry about message. The last act, "The Living Nativity," a truly solemn and awesome spectacle in which the loneliness of a desert is created with a cast of scores, plus camels, sheep, donkeys as only the Music Hall can produce, takes care of the religiosity. For the rest, it has the cheer of a holiday as it is observed in midtown Manhattan.

1990 N 13, C20:1

The March on Russia

By David Storey; directed by Josephine R. Abady; lighting by Marc B. Weiss; costumes by Linda Fisher; sound by Jeffrey Montgomerie; production stage manager, Robert Bennett. Presented by Chelsea Stage, Geoffrey Sherman, artistic director; Dara Hershman, managing director, in association with the Cleveland Play House, Ms. Abady, artistic director; Dean R. Gladden, managing director. At 441 West 26th Street.

Colin	Sean Griffin
Mr. Pasmore	John Carpenter
Mrs. Pasmore	Bethel Leslie
Wendy	Carol Locatell
Eileen	Susan Browning

By MEL GUSSOW

In David Storey's novel "Pasmore," the title character is troubled by a recurrent dream. Running in a race, he finds himself overtaken by everyone, even the "idlers and dullards." Suddenly awakening, he feels an "undiminished sense of terror."

That fear — that life itself has passed one by — shadows Mr. Storey's new play, "The March on Russia," a seemingly becalmed but quietly turbulent drama about Colin Pasmore, a university lecturer and author, and his family. For the Pasmores, fulfillment is no longer even a wishful fantasy. All that the characters can see on the horizon is more of the same, followed by "full stop."

The play was first presented last year at the Royal National Theater in London, in a production reuniting the playwright with his symbiotic director, Lindsay Anderson. In May, Josephine Abady staged it with an American company at the Cleveland Play House, and that production opened this week at Chelsea Stage.

•

Though one would never suggest that the American actors could duplicate the authenticity, especially the Yorkshire accents, of their English predecessors, Ms. Abady's production is exactingly shaded and subtle in its delineation of these regional characters. Led by John Carpenter and Bethel Leslie as the father and mother, the actors capture the underlying humor as well as the sadness. The uncredited scenic design is overly spare, but the production achieves a greater intimacy on the small stage at the Hudson Guild Theater than it did on a vast stage at the National.

Each of the three younger actors, Carol Locatell and Susan Browning as the daughters and Sean Griffin as Colin, is sensitive to the disparities as well as the similarities of these siblings. Together the five actors evoke a moving family portrait.

In more hopeful times, there were happier dreams. The father recalls, with poignancy, his youthful military service invading the Crimea around the time of the Russian Revolution (his march on Russia). It was a moment of adventure, followed immediately by marriage and 45 years of work in a Yorkshire coal mine. The father's life has been more forcefully circumscribed than the lives of his wife and children, but each one has been trapped within a self-limiting world.

Family rivalries become family rituals. Old stories and old sayings are repeated, as in the father's answer to a crossword puzzle clue: "Put-upon man. Seven letters. Husband." Which child was loved most? To the audience, it should be clear that each was equally unloved, despite signs of occasional favoritism, and that the elder Pasmores have moved past their own despair to a kind of barely controlled disharmony.

•

At least for the first act, the story may seem deceptively light as the three adult offspring arrive separately at the parents' retirement cottage to help them celebrate their 60th wedding anniversary. There are no character revelations, as in Mr. Storey's "In Celebration," which deals with a related family situation 20 years earlier. But "The March on Russia" is suffused with sorrow and understanding as the characters find themselves unable to achieve a sense of kinship or of mutual support.

The play becomes elegiac, a longing for lost times that never were, except perhaps for the father's "march on Russia," and even that story seems to be disappearing from his memory. At the end of the play, his wife has to prod him to remember the facts (and perhaps the fiction) of his tale, the thought of which has become as important to her as it is for him.

•

In his plays and novels, Mr. Storey has tellingly explored the nature of families, especially those with working-class backgrounds, in which the offspring are educated and elevated to a higher social and economic level. The generational chasm between a father who has worked with his hands as a collier and a son who works with his mind cannot be bridged. People in Storey plays may embrace, but they are unable to touch one another emotionally. Instead, they either repress their feelings (like the mother) or suffer breakdowns (like Colin).

For Mr. Storey, "The March on Russia" is a return to an earlier mode. After "In Celebration," he moved on to the poetic symbolism of "The Contractor" and "Home," and in more recent years he has concentrated on fiction. Some may regard the new work as overly traditional, but their plays are always viable when they are as deeply felt as this one and when they are written with such lyrical understatement. Though the Pasmores are definably from Yorkshire, they are recognizable wherever sons and daughters are encouraged to excel and then do not realize their own ambitions and the expectations of their parents.

1990 N 14, C24:3

Those Were the Days

Concept and continuity, Zalmen Mlotek and Moishe Rosenfeld; directed and choreographed by Eleanor Reissa; musical director, Mr. Mlotek; lighting, Tom Sturge; costumes, Gail Cooper-Hecht; sound, Jim Badrak and Alan Gregorie. Presented by Moe Septee, in association with Victor H. Potamkin, Mr. Mlotek and Mr. Rosenfeld. At the Edison Theater, 240 West 47th Street.

WITH: Bruce Adler, Mina Bern, Eleanor Reissa, Robert Abelson, Lori Wilner and the Golden Land Klezmer Orchestra.

By RICHARD F. SHEPARD

Like a glass of cold seltzer, "Those Were the Days," the new revue at the Edison Theater, brings sparkle to the eye and a tickle to the throat. It's in Yiddish and English, practically a self-translating effusion of song and dance. Yiddish, a dead language? At the Edison, it bounces like a baby.

There is no plot, no set, maybe a prop or two and an image on the backdrop, and that is all to the good because one is too busy taking in the superb performances of the troupe of five performing to the tune of an orchestra equipped to play anything, from lean to schmaltz. "Survey" is an off-putting word with overtones of seminars and droning, so although "Those Were the Days" covers a lot of musical ground and time in its romp from shtetl to Lower East Side, let's call it a cavalcade. Whatever it is, it is a humdinger of a hum-along.

•

This is third revue of its kind fashioned by Zalmen Mlotek and Moishe Rosenfeld, who, with "The Golden Land" and "On Second Avenue," pioneered a way to stage programs of old Yiddish song in contemporary theatrical modes. This mating of the ages naturally puts one in the mood of a wedding, and it is an especially happy marriage at the Edison.

And why not? There is something old ("Romania, Romania," delivered with stunning dexterity of tongue by Bruce Adler); something, er, nu? ("Litvak/Galitsyaner," the ancient north-south Polish conflict, fought in wounding words by Mr. Adler and Eleanor Reissa); something borrowed ("Figaro's Aria," sung operat-

Martha Swope/"Those Were the Days"

Eleanor Reissa performing in "Those Were the Days."

ically, with neat Yiddish lyrics, by the resonant Robert Abelson); and something blue ("My Yiddishe Mama," hauntingly crooned by Ms. Reissa and still as blue as it was when sung by the red-hot mama, Sophie Tucker).

Ms. Reissa, who is also director and choreographer of the undertaking, keeps the cast in constant motion, from the batting of an eye to an ensemble dance in which the five can conjure up a mass celebration. She and her stage mates are an unusual assortment of young and not so young, of Yiddish-born fluent in English, of those born to English and fluent in Yiddish. Mina Bern, the seasoned veteran of the Yiddish stage, emerges as a superlative comic. She gives a hilarious, if sometimes painfully accurate, monologue of the old mother who proudly tells of her three children, none of whom let her live with their families for more than a few months at a time. Ms. Bern is beguilingly manipulative as she leads the audience in a sing-along, tartly chiding a man up front for just nodding his head and not singing out.

Lori Wilner, a woman for all seasons, manifests uncommon versatility in characters from a shtetl child playing out "Who Will Laugh First?" to a femme fatale giving a sexy rendition of "Shpil Gitar." Mr. Abelson, a real-life cantor with credits from opera and Sammy's Famous Romanian Restaurant on the Lower East Side, is a sonorous musical presence who doubles nicely in comedy. As for Mr. Adler, what is there that this anchor man can't do? He kazotskys, he softshoes, he fandangos, or something in reasonable facsimile. He makes the oldest jokes fresh and funny in his nonstop hoofer break-two-three-four vaudeville routine, "Hootsatsa." He plays the bemused restaurant customer who can't find anything to eat in a Sholom Aleichem skit. Yiddish, English, whatever, he sets a funny pace.

If one good turn deserves another, the many good theater turns of "Those Were the Days" amount to the ultimate good turn, a musical mitzvah.

1990 N 14, C26:1

Monster in a Box

Directed by Renee Shafransky; general manager, Steven C. Callahan; production manager, Jeff Hamlin. Presented by Lincoln Center Theater, Gregory Mosher, director; Bernard Gersten, executive producer. At the Mitzi E. Newhouse Theater, Lincoln Center.

WITH: Spalding Gray

By FRANK RICH

To hear him tell it — and we do, for 90 delicious minutes — Spalding Gray was starting to worry that he might be pandering to the audience with his autobiographical monologues. "Swimming to Cambodia," his soliloquy about his adventures as an actor in the movie "The Killing Fields," was so successful on stage that Jonathan Demme adapted it into a hit film. Mr. Gray's answering machine was soon clogged with show-biz offers, with everyone from the Mark Taper Forum to HBO to Creative Artists Agency ("the Mafia of talent agencies") on the prowl. Maybe it was time to escape. Should he get away from his "self-deprecating, ironic voice" and look for a Jimmy Stewart role "with heart"? Should he stop performing altogether and write a book?

•

"Monster in a Box," Mr. Gray's 13th and latest stage monologue, tells of how he sort of found that role and sort of wrote that book while enduring countless interruptions. The "monster" — one of the few props he requires on the bare stage of the Mitzi E. Newhouse Theater at Lincoln Cen-

Paula Court/Lincoln Center Theater

Spalding Gray in his 13th monologue, "Monster in a Box."

ter — is his manuscript, a novel called "Impossible Vacation" about "a New England puritan" named Brewster North who has trouble enjoying vacations. The "box" is the corrugated cardboard box that contains the monster, which was "due to be published by Knopf two years ago." Mr. Gray explains that he was inspired to write by the example of Thomas Wolfe, and judging from the imposing size of his manuscript, which makes even the Manhattan phone directory look wimpy, one assumes that Knopf will have to unearth Maxwell Perkins to edit it. In the meantime, Mr. Gray performs the airtight "Monster in a Box," which he describes in the program as a piece "about the dizziness that comes from too much possibility" and which he describes from the stage as a "monologue about a man who can't write a book about a man who can't take a vacation."

Whatever happens with Mr. Gray's book, or, for that matter, with his vacations, there can be no doubt that "Monster in a Box" is a triumph for him as both writer and performer. Despite the addition of a director — Renee Shafransky, the companion who frequently turns up in his tales — he still addresses us informally from behind a table, on which sit a spiral notebook, a glass of water and a microphone. As always, his talk is a mixture of personal confession, journalistic observation, sermon and digression. There are stories within stories, anecdotes within anecdotes and jokes within jokes, yet the whole sprawling narrative eventually comes full circle to fall into the same effortless unity that distinguished "Swimming to Cambodia" from its predecessors. "Monster in a Box" is a play, not a comedian's routine or improvisation, though it is a play probably best performed by its author, a silver-haired master of deadpan with a WASP's Rhode Island accent.

•

Not every actor can accomplish what Mr. Gray does here, which is to whip an audience abruptly yet gently

from offhand reflections about his mother's suicide (a perennial Gray subject, at least as far back as "Rumstick Road") to hilarious memories of his life in the theater. Such juxtapositions are central to Mr. Gray's particular humor and vision of the world; only in "Monster in a Box" could one hope to find links between the MacDowell Colony and "Psycho," between "The World of Sholom Aleichem" and flatulence, between Pilot Pens and a Soviet film festival attended by Richard Gere and Daryl Hannah. Little is off-limits. "Monster in a Box" may be the first play to make fun of low-risk heterosexual men whipping themselves into a frenzy of self-indulgent hypochondria about AIDS.

Though a few of Mr. Gray's observations about well-worn subjects (psychoanalysis and sun-dried Hollywood lunch menus) are tired, even they are redeemed by the freshness of their context. In the several years covered by this installment of Mr. Gray's perpetual Bildungsroman, our hero encounters everyone from a Nicaraguan nun to Charles Manson's lawyer to the anonymous Cambodian refugees and elderly shut-ins he tracks down while conducting a search for those citizens of Los Angeles who have yet to write a screenplay. Mr. Gray's most unforgettable character, however, is still himself, though the identity of that self remains open to question.

•

Within the funny autobiographical tales lies a poignant drama, and just the one that Mr. Gray promises at the evening's outset. Here is a man who is trying "to relate" to others in a "nonperformance mode," to discover what is authentic beneath the armor of his role as a theatricalized commodity known as Spalding Gray. The search for the man under the pose leads him not only into therapy and fiction writing but also to accepting the part of the Stage Manager in the recent Broadway revival of Thornton Wilder's "Our Town," directed by Gregory Mosher. After first resisting the offer and suggesting Garrison

Keillor for the assigment, Mr. Gray comes to see the play as his own Tibetan Book of the Dead, as a touchstone for getting back to his own roots as a child of New England and the son of a troubled mother. (Surely Brewster North, the hero of Mr. Gray's suspended novel, is as much an allusion to a Wilder character name as it is to a railroad station.) In "Our Town," Mr. Gray decides, "I could speak from the heart if I could memorize those lines."

He did memorize the lines, and the payoff for his hard work was terrible reviews. In "Monster in a Box," Mr. Gray recounts the experience of his Broadway opening and its aftermath with a Twain-like sense of absurdity that made even the author of one of those unflattering reviews laugh until he cried. To refute his critics, Mr. Gray finally slips back into Wilder again, reciting once more the lines he proudly memorized. And once more he seems too boxed into the role of Spalding Gray, too much of an edgy, contemporary urban ironist, to pass for an inhabitant of Grovers Corners.

So maybe the more homespun Garrison Keillor would have been a better casting choice after all for the Stage Manager for "Our Town." As a stage manager for our town, Mr. Gray is right now without peer.

1990 N 15, C19:1

King Lear

By William Shakespeare; directed Gerald Freedman; scenic design by John Ezell; costume design by Robert Wojewodski; lighting design by Thomas R. Skelton; music composed by John Morris; sound design by Tom Mardikes; fight direction by Robert L. Behrens; production stage manager, Kathy J. Faul; general manager, Ellen Richard. Presented by the Roundabout Theater Company, Todd Haimes, producing director; Gene Feist, founding director. At 100 East 17th Street.

King Lear...................................... Hal Holbrook
WITH: Peter Aylward, Gloria Biegler, Andrew Boyer, Simon Brooking, John Buck Jr., Suzy Hunt, John Hutton, Michael James-Reed, Henry LeBlanc, Richard Long, Christopher McCann, Kevin McCarty, Patrick Mulcahy, Margery Murray, Eric Nolan, Ron Randell, Stephan Roselin, David Ruckman, Andrew M. Segal, Gary Sloan, Darrell Starnik, Eric Vogt, William Wilson and John Woodson.

By MEL GUSSOW

In the title role of "King Lear," Hal Holbrook has a magisterial grace and the agility of a mountain climber, capturing the sudden, mercurial turns in his character. Dividing his kingdom and activating his wrath against Cordelia, he becomes mean-spirited and abusive. At home and in court, he is a monarch who insists on having his own way. His bitter humor, one of the strongest elements in the actor's performance, eventually turns inward into self-mockery as he falls into despair. In the course of the play (at the Roundabout Theater), Mr. Holbrook's characterization grows and deepens.

With the exception of several minor players, Mr. Holbrook is the only asset in Gerald Freedman's production, and the absence of a supporting con-

---

A production in which a lot of labor's lost amid much ado.

---

text is steadily debilitating. Mr. Freedman has directed a number of notable productions of Shakespeare, including both "Love's Labor's Lost" and "Much Ado About Nothing" for the New York Shakespeare Festival's marathon. This is not one of them.

The production of "King Lear," which began last May at the Great Lakes Shakespeare Festival, is marked by its slackness and its artificiality. Despite the fact that the play is performed in its historical period, there is an odd sense of dislocation.

In pursuit of atmosphere, actors go about indeterminate tasks as if they have wandered on stage to participate in a re-creation of daily life in pagan Britain. For no defensible reason, Goneril and Regan plait Cordelia's hair — badly — before she is banished from the kingdom. Everyone is so busy crisscrossing the stage with activity that words are lost in the wind. This is most definitely the case with some major speeches, as when Edgar delivers his final statement on the perdurability of mankind ("Ripeness is all").

As the play opens, soldiers slowly file on stage and form a circle for what could be a Druid ritual. Instead, nothing happens. We wait patiently for Lear to appear, thinking perhaps

---

he will rise, magically, in the center of the ring. After much too long a time, the soldiers walk off stage. Then Mr. Holbrook enters, and immediately invigorates the play. Even as the production abandons him, he is relentless in his intensity.

Ron Randell is a stalwart Gloucester and Gloria Biegler has the freshness for Cordelia, but the other actors never rise above the level of competence, and in pivotal cases fall below. There is a kind of infectious wimpishness afoot, as typified by Michael James-Reed's Edgar, and John Woodson's Kent is bland, two roles that demand a princely bearing and an ability to dissimulate.

John Hutton's Edmund is only a slight improvement, but he is victimized in his relationship with Suzy Hunt's Goneril, who affectionately twists a scarf around his neck as though she wants to choke him. Ms. Hunt and Margery Murray (as Regan) are one-dimensional vixens. Along with other members of the company, they are so occupied with histrionics that they obscure the complexity of their characters.

•

The most dubious performance is given by Christopher McCann as the Fool. Mousy, with a pinched voice, he mangles the comedy and misplaces the tragedy. In this production, Lear's report of the Fool's death comes as a relief rather than as a moment of ineffable sadness.

In collaboration with his scenic, sound and lighting designers, Mr. Freedman is effective in reproducing laser beams of lightning and crashes of thunder, but the battle scenes, conducted with banners feebly waving, have a picture-book childishness. The stage is decorated with ropes hanging from the ceiling, tied together, unbound and thoroughly obtrusive. In a particularly obvious touch, the rear wall of John Ezell's set splits further in twain as the play progresses and as the king sinks into madness. There is never a sense of lives and reigns being at stake. The production is loud sound and imagined fury.

Roger Mastroianni/Roundabout Theater
Hal Holbrook in "King Lear."

This is the fifth "King Lear" I have seen this year, ranging widely from John Wood's wounded patriarch at Stratford-on-Avon to the Soviet Georgian version (at the Brooklyn Academy of Music), which uncovered the black comedy within the tragedy. The Roundabout production is the first to reveal that the play's richness can be finite.

•

Encountering Mr. Randell's Gloucester after his fantasized fall, Mr. Holbrook performs with another actor equal to his role. The two old men are twinned ruined pieces of nature. Garlanded with blossoms, his white hair askew, Mr. Holbrook looks like an aged flower child momentarily restored to life.

This is not in any sense a case of Mark Twain grown old and Shakespearean, but a distinctive individualization of a self-vanquishing king. There is more than a measure of Prospero in his Lear; he is a sorcerer without revels. In extremis, Mr. Holbrook extends his first howl to the breaking point, a cry of urgency in a "King Lear" in which the actor is left to forge his own path through the wilderness.

1990 N 16, C3:1

Catch Me If I Fall

Martha Swope/Promenade Theater
Laura Dean

Book, music and lyrics by Barbara Schottenfeld; directed by Susan Einhorn; additional staging by Stuart Ross; settings and costumes by G. W. Mercier; lighting by Richard Nelson; sound by Gary and Timmy Harris; musical supervision and direction, Joseph Church; orchestrations, Joe Gianono; production stage manager, John C. McNamara; general manager, Paul B. Berkowsky; associate producers, Frederick Schultz and Terry A. Johnston. Presented by the Never or Now Company. At the Promenade Theater, 2162 Broadway, at 76th Street.

Lonny Simon .... James Judy
Brian Simon ....David Burdick
Laurie Simon .... Jeanine Morick
Peter Bennington........................... Sal Viviano
Godiva Harris...........................Ronnie Farer
Domnica Gruia.............................Laura Dean
Andrei Gruia................................A. D. Cover

By MEL GUSSOW

Barbara Schottenfeld's previous musicals, "I Can't Keep Running in Place" and "Sit Down and Eat Before Our Love Gets Cold," were collage-style shows dealing principally with questions of feminism. Her new musical, "Catch Me if I Fall," continues the composer's fondness for conversational titles. But this time she has both a central story line and a male protagonist. Unfortunately, "Catch Me if I Fall" is decidedly lacking in character.

Ostensibly, the musical, at the Promenade Theater, is about a green card marriage of convenience between a 40-year-old divorced New Yorker and a young Romanian woman who wants to remain in the United States. Actually, it offers the slimmest of excuses for Ms. Schottenfeld to write songs about anything that catches her fancy — marriage, divorce, yuppie values and the fall of the Berlin wall. Politics repeatedly and awkwardly intrudes on the romantic interludes.

At the center of the show is James Judy as the indecisive hero, who has given up his ambitions as a sculptor for a career as a corporate headhunter. Though he is hangdog and slightly overweight, he is surrounded by three women clamoring to control his life. They are his rancorous ex-wife, a neurotic veterinarian (devoted to her pet patients) and the Romanian émigré, who is both intelligent and attractive. Which one will Mr. Judy choose? The outcome is incontestable, but it takes 14 songs for the characters to arrive at the pat ending.

•

As the plot gets thicker, the show becomes thinner, rambling to the heroine's predictable television bulletin: "It's on the news. The revolution in Romania is beginning." Ms. Schottenfeld is as casual in her treatment of Nicolae Ceausescu's despotism as she is about immigration problems, the hero's latent artistic impulses and endangered species. Almost everything is reduced to a joke or a subject for sentimentality.

The music has a pseudo-Sondheim sameness and the lyrics are a match in blandness, with one song, "Timing and Lighting," also disregarding rules of grammar ("Timing and lighting is all that it was"), and another, "Isn't It Strange," sounding like a lesser lead in to "Send in the Clowns." The dialogue makes unprofitable use of fractured English, as practiced by educated Romanians. The heroine's uncle, visiting from the old country, suggests that her niece and her maritally convenient husband are "still wedlynews." Ms. Schottenfeld wrote the book, music and lyrics.

Laura Dean (remembered from the musical, "Doonesbury") is engaging as the émigré and gives her character a certain buoyancy. Mr. Judy makes the unprepossessing hero likable. Both have melodic voices. But the direction (by Susan Einhorn, with "additional staging" by Stuart Ross) pushes the show further into caricature. Jeanine Morick and Ronnie Farer overdo the predatory nature of the ex-wife and the veterinarian. Ms. Farer is additionally encumbered with a scene in which she crudely compares the hero's sexuality with that of a Romanian beast of burden. As required by his role as Mr. Judy's craven employer, Sal Viviano is a shallow yuppie, singing his most passionate love song to his beach house.

•

G. W. Mercier has designed a twinkling backdrop of city lights, but in other respects his contributions are not helpful. The stage is cluttered with a revolving kiosk that restricts the mobility of the actors, forcing them to play their scenes in a tightly confined space.

The three women share an amusing number called "Chaperone," and there is one tuneful ballad, "Never or Now," which is supposed to sum up the show's carpe diem philosophy. The two songs are scant compensation for a musical that aims for an up-to-the-minute, sophisticated view of urban life — and misfires.

1990 N 17, 16:5

Father's Inheritance

Adaptation, lyrics and music by Emil Gorovets; based on "The Charlatan," by Jacob Gordin. Directed by Yevgeny Lanskoye; choreographer, Felix Fibich; dancers, Mane Rebelo and Fausto Matias; set design, Brian P. Kelly; costume design, Susan Sigrist; lighting design, Thomas Goldberg and Janet Clancy; musical director, Nikolas Levinowsky; translator, Simcha Kruger; stage manager, Judith Scher; assistant stage manager, Richard Carlow. Presented by the Folksbiene Playhouse, Ben Schechter, managing director; Morris Adler, chairman. At 123 East 55th Street.

Esther-Rokhl	Zypora Spaisman
Benish-Lemakh	Semyon Grinberg
Oliyetchke	Julie Alexander
Mendele	Shira Flam
Shloimke	Emil Gorovets
Misha	Ira Sakolsky
Simon Kozlin	Sandy Levitt
Golde	Irina Fogelson

By RICHARD F. SHEPARD

It speaks Yiddish only, but the Folksbiene Theater is the oldest continuing theatrical company in New York, in any language. The Folksbiene, even when it does comedy, as in its new 75th-anniversary production, a musical called "Father's Inheritance," has always been serious about its undertakings; after all, its first production, in 1915, was a Yiddish version of Ibsen's "Enemy of the People."

Anyone who is devoted to the Yiddish language, who will travel to hear a well-spoken Yiddish word, will, of course, beat a path to the comfortable Folksbiene Playhouse, in the Central Synagogue's modern building on East 55th Street. Those whose Yiddish is faltering may resort to renting the simultaneous translation device, which presents the action in complete, almost scholarly detail, explaining the genesis of terms used, like "pogrom," or references to persons, like Shulamit, the Biblical beauty.

"Father's Inheritance" is a musical comedy adapted by Emil Gorovets, who also wrote the lyrics and music and who stars in it. Mr. Gorovets has taken it from "Shloimke the Charlatan," a play by the Yiddish playwright Jacob Gordin that was first staged in New York in 1896.

•

As for the plot, what is there to say? A poor actor in Odessa, a man of most vices, learns that his father has died, but when he gets back to his hometown, his sister hoodwinks him out of his inheritance. Suddenly it's 20 years later and he has come home again, just in time to prevent his niece's wedding to an American fraud and insure her betrothal to a man who turns out to be the son he never knew.

"Mr. Gorovets is a substantial presence in the lead, although, with a voice that makes a lyric do more than merely speak, he comes across more convincingly as singer than as actor.

But he does project a sort of lugubrious likeability.

The performer who sets the pace is Zypora Spaisman, that wonderful stalwart of the Folksbiene and other Yiddish theaters whose deadpan shoulder-shrugging acidity adds a necessary comic touch to the proceedings. Sandy Levitt also infuses a fortunate spirit of overstated comedy in his burlesque interpretation of the American villain's role. Irina Fogelson, as the maid, Golde, is an upbeat voice in the proceedings both in song and dialogue.

Yevgeny Lanskoye, the director, has done some imaginative staging of a show that might otherwise founder in static talk and heavy artifice. The insertion of a Purim play within the play itself is charming. The dances choreographed by Felix Fibich and performed by Mane Rebelo and Fausto Matias also enhance the play.

If the plot is a frail vehicle, it does carry Mr. Gorovets's lines well enough. Some of them are clever and observant, like the observation that a Jew without money in London is a poor Jew, while a Jew without money in Russia is a "Kasrilivke bourgeois," referring to the fabled town created by Sholom Aleichem; the segment that compares English with Yiddish is also amusing, as when "eye" is equated with "Ay, yi, yi." The music has the traditional Yiddish theater beat, and those with a tendency to keep time with their feet will find it as comfortable as an old shoe.

"Father's Inheritance" is a new musical, but also a veritable revival of shows that no longer exist. Over the years, the Folksbiene has demonstrated an uncommon theatrical versatility and, on its 75th birthday, one can only say, as they do in Yiddish circles, "Bis 120," which translates, very loosely, as "May you live until 120."

1990 N 18, 75:1

The Mud Angel

By Darrah Cloud; directed by Kevin Kuhlke; sets, Clay Snider; lighting, Mary Louise Geiger; costumes, Marina Draghici; fights coached by David S. Leong; sound, Scott Steidl; production stage manager, Kristin Nieuwenhuis; assistant stage manager, Jeffrey Pajer. Presented by Theater for a New Audience, Jeffrey Horowitz, artistic and producing director, in association with Home for Contemporary Theater and Art. At 44 Walker Street.

Jenny	Seane Corn
Shadow	Alyssa Breshnahan
Sonny	Andrew Weems
Burt	David Neipris
Mrs. Malvetz	Sofia Landon

By MEL GUSSOW

Strange things are happening on the Malvetz family farm in Sturgeon Bay, Wis. "The Mud Angel" is a play knee-deep in symbolism and sexuality, as Darrah Cloud studies the interwoven relationships among a mother, her three children and a horse named Shadow. In this bizarre middle-American Gothic tale, the horse has all the best lines.

Shadow is played by an actress, Alyssa Breshnahan. Prancing, whinnying and straining at her halter, Ms. Breshnahan evokes an equine sensibility, just as Salome Jens did many years ago in "The Balcony." The actress's expert anthropomorphism is not enough to overcome the sheer quirkiness and the confusion of Ms. Cloud's play. In several senses, "The Mud Angel" is a nightmare.

While one son (Andrew Weems) manhandles the horse, his younger brother (David Neipris) is crawling around the farm on his stomach, pretending to be a snake. "When you crawl," he says, "you got no shadow." That's lower-case, shadow. The upper-case Shadow is standing up and looking for a hint of human kindness, even if it is only a cube of sugar. Because Ms. Breshnahan is playing an actual horse, for a while one thinks that Mr. Neipris may really be a snake. When he stands up, one knows differently. In the background is the

sister (Seane Corn) who walks by night, immerses herself in the horse's trough and then makes a mud equivalent of snow angels.

•

As written, and as performed at the Home for Contemporary Theater and Art, the play lingers on the edge of lunacy. The mother (Sofia Landon) may be the most unbalanced of all, wandering around the house in a daze and deciding to sell the horse despite the protests of her children.

At first, the characters seem to be talking to themselves, but soon one realizes they are mutually responsive, even to barnyard animals. In Sturgeon Bay, there seems to be nothing unusual about talking to a horse — and having the horse talk back.

There has always been a Surrealistic streak in Ms. Cloud's plays, but perhaps never as overtly as in "The Mud Angel." No sun rises over the Malvetz farm. That family name is clearly intended as a pun, as each character, even the concerned younger brother, acts to damage the horse's well-being. There is a bleakness as the play moves very far away from a children's story into Ms. Cloud's darkening vision.

•

Despite the weirdness of the material, Kevin Kuhlke has managed to give the play a reality on stage, helped by Clay Snider's scenic design, which takes advantage of several truckloads of earth. Each of the actors performs with a seriousness of purpose, even when the demands are onerous — none more than Ms. Breshnahan, who moves her character close to verisimilitude.

"The Mud Angel" does not have the scope of "The Stick Wife," Ms. Cloud's drama about the 1963 church bombing in Birmingham, Ala. Nor is it clear what she is trying to say about the various subjects she raises, including parental negligence, sibling rivalry and animal husbandry. But as a study in primal behavior — and as an exercise in acting — it nuzzles its way into the imagination.

Rebecca Lesher/Martha Swope Associates/Folksbiene Theater

Zypora Spaisman and Emil Gorovets in "Father's Inheritance."

SUNDAY VIEW/David Richards

Why Breaking Up Is Hard to Do

In Britain's 'Shadowlands,' a good cry is not bad form; in 'The Wash,' a Japanese marriage of 42 years falls apart.

HAVE YOU NOTICED THAT THE tear-jerker rarely gets its due? It is considered perfectly acceptable to laugh in the theater, laugh until the buttons pop, laugh until the spectator in front of you can't stand it any longer and has to turn around and stare. There's no shushing reproval in the look. Just shared pleasure, and a touch of amazement, that someone is having so much fun.

It is equally acceptable to be moved at the theater. Moved to the very quick. As long as it doesn't show, no shame there. People are always announcing loudly, "Very moving. Very touching," as they tug on their coats and elbow their way up the aisles. Crying is another matter, however. Somehow it's deemed bad form.

The house lights have only to come up and spectators who were awash in tears minutes earlier are doing all they can to wipe away the traces. Or they're busying themselves in the search for a lost glove or a dropped program. Anything that will allow them to keep their heads down long enough to regain a semblance of composure.

Laughter tends to be a collective response and there's safety — even superiority — in numbers. But crying is a private undertaking and we are reluctant to be caught with our feelings down. It makes for a curious double standard. The more we guffaw at a comedy, the more successful we judge it to be. But let a play leave us weeping and it's immediately suspect. The dramaturgy is said to be manipulative, rigged, sneaky. The greatest offenders are dismissed as tear-jerkers.

But I wonder if that doesn't really mean that they're doing precisely what they're supposed to.

Take "Shadowlands," the British drama by William Nicholson at the Brooks Atkinson Theater, since that is what has prompted my musings this morning. Superlatively acted by Nigel Hawthorne and Jane Alexander, it represents the tear-jerker in full glory, and I say that admiringly. Oh, you can look down your nose at it and accuse it of middlebrow preten-

sions, if you wish. You can fault it for not always sidestepping the clichés of love and regret, for saying nothing that hasn't been said before. But in the end, you'll probably conclude that your reservations count for precious little. Like the play's middle-aged, paunchy and altogether unlikely protagonist — the British author and Christian apologist C. S. Lewis (Mr. Hawthorne) — the only course of action is to give in to the mounting grief so that you can come out the other side.

For most of his life, Jack Lewis, as friends called him, was the quintessential, pipe-smoking Oxford don, as committed to his bachelorhood as he was to the scratchy tweed jacket, which modesty, as much as habit, prevented him from removing in the presence of women. As it was, women generally brought out acute embarrassment in him. He shared his house with his older brother, Warnie, and his social life revolved about a group of like-minded scribes and intellectuals who dubbed themselves the Inklings. Such books as "The Screwtape Letters" and "The Lion, the Witch and the Wardrobe" had won Lewis a fair measure of celebrity when he received his first letter from Joy Davidman (Ms. Alexander), a minor American poet whose marriage was heading for the rocks.

The correspondence flowered, not in the least because of Joy's sparring wit and independent spirit. So when she visited England in 1952, it was appropriate, if decidedly awkward, that she should have tea with her pen pal. That is where Mr. Nicholson's play takes up, although it's no impediment if you don't know C. S. Lewis from Jerry Lewis or are making your first acquaintance with Ms. Davidman. Stripped of its literary adornments, which are hardly forbidding to begin with, "Shadowlands" is a story of love against all odds.

A man, set in his ways and not especially eager to change them, learns that he has a heart. The forthright woman who brings him to that realization is unexpectedly stricken with bone cancer. Their platonic union blossoms into a real marriage. But their time together is short. Then, their time is no more. The man, who once lectured confidently on the purpose of pain ("God's megaphone to rouse a deaf world"), is confronted with the inadequacy of his definitions. In his bewilderment, he is like a child again.

That final transformation is rendered with wrenching simplicity. On her deathbed, Joy has made Lewis promise he will take care of her son. (In reality, she had two children, but the script settles for one.) Although Lewis has barely accustomed himself to the role of lover and husband, he must now assume that of father, too. As the director Elijah Moshinsky has envisioned the ensuing scene, Mr. Hawthorne retreats in a daze to one side of the stage. The twitching features that all evening long have made him look rather like an amiable rabbit are uncharacteristically still. An aimless drift has seized his hands.

Facing him from the other side of the stage, standing as tall as only a youngster can stand when he's trying to act grown-up, is Lance Robinson — the son who dearly wants an explanation for his mother's death, but doesn't want to ask for it. The silence is unbearable. When words are finally spoken, they prove halting and inadequate. Suddenly, the youth rushes forward and buries his face in the stomach of the adult.

Stunned, Mr. Hawthorne throws his hands high in the air. There they stay, limp and useless, as he himself is consumed by great convulsive sobs. Then, almost as if they had a will of their own, the hands come down slowly, search out the child and catch him up in a clumsy embrace. The moment is operatic in its power. Helplessness hasn't just united man and boy, it has erased the distinctions between them. In the presence of death, they can only hold on to each other for dear life.

No one, you see, is backing off from "Shadowlands" or soft-pedaling its call to the emotions. The fullness of the acting exonerates what could be, in lesser performances,

greeting-card sentiments. Lest this make the play sound like one long wallow, I should point out that much of the time it is crisply funny. Wit was a happy exercise for Lewis, when it did not provide him with protective camouflage. And Joy was not one to suffer fools gladly. ("I need a little guidance here," she says to a particularly patronizing professor. "Are you being offensive or merely stupid?") But humor accompanies them only so far, before it, too, must bow before the spreading cancer.

During a final idyll in Greece, Lewis can't help thinking ahead to the inevitable separation. "That pain then is part of this happiness now," Joy says to him, forthright as ever. "That's part of the deal." It is also the deal that the playwright strikes with the audience.

Ms. Alexander has long played heroic women, but the gallantry has rarely seemed as unassuming as it does here. She asks for no pity and offers no apologies (unless it be for some of Joy's early poems about the Spanish Civil War). A lively intelligence makes her attractive, but it's unflinching honesty that makes her affecting. Mr. Hawthorne fidgets and squirms and rocks on ungainly feet, as if someone had spilled itching powder down his back. His discovery of love comes as both a miraculous awakening and a fearful surrender.

But when we last see him — alone on the stage, clinging to the memory of what was and the tiny, tentative hope of what might lie hereafter — it is clear that hurt has made him whole. The old saw has it that if you laugh, the world laughs with you. Cry, and you cry alone. Not so. Cry at "Shadowlands" and you'll find yourself in good company.

'The Wash'

The principal characters in "The Wash" (at the Manhattan Theater Club's Stage II at City Center) are as

Jane Alexander has long played heroic women, but the gallantry has rarely seemed as unassuming as it does here.

hesitant about acknowledging what's happening to them as those in "Shadowlands." But whereas Mr. Nicholson is chronicling a late-in-life coming together, the playwright Philip

Kan Gotanda is dramatizing the breaking apart of a Japanese-American couple after 42 years of marriage. Don't look for confrontations and recriminations, however. There are very few, and then only when every possible face-saving alternative has been tried. What gives this drama its subtle fascination are the lengths to which the characters go to avoid saying what lies heavy on their hearts and to pretend that the gathering unpleasantness doesn't exist.

∎

Masi (Nobu McCarthy) has moved out on the husband who has always blamed her for his own misery and hasn't slept with her in years. A widowed pharmacist is courting her, making her laugh, and she's begun to entertain the unthinkable — the possibility of happiness. Nonetheless, once a week, she drops by her old home in San Jose, Calif., to pick up her husband's dirty laundry and deliver a stack of clean clothes. Out of delicacy and the residual subservience of the traditional Japanese wife, she is loath to meet the issue of divorce head-on.

Nobu (Sab Shimono), the autocratic husband, won't even allow himself to consider it. The good-natured proprietress of the restaurant where he regularly has his meals — the same meal every day, actually — would take up with him in a minute, if he'd show some interest. But he has shut himself up in a self-contained world of intolerance and bitterness that dates from his incarceration in an internment camp during World War II. Asking his wife to come back would merely add to the ignominy he perceives as his lot. Besides, in his recalcitrant mind, she hasn't really left.

∎

Only the characters on the fringe — the couple's children, a sassy hair-

dresser, a slovenly restaurant cook — speak their minds. Nobu and Mas belong to a generation for which any discussion of relationships would be unseemly. Her discretion and his stubborn silence are not made for battling, only uneasy coexistence.

That, you may be thinking, doesn't leave a lot of maneuvering room for drama. In the revelatory performances of Ms. McCarthy and Mr. Shimono, however, the unspoken emotions run deep. What the script doesn't tell you, their magnificent faces do — his as much a defiant rejection of feeling as hers is a transparently lovely reflection of it.

An exquisite actress, Ms. McCarthy flickers and shimmers like sunlight on a pond. Liberation does not come easy to her. She is constantly catching herself mid-emotion, cutting her anger short or nipping joy in the bud, as if she were waiting for permission to experience what she's already visibly experiencing. Indeed, snuggling in bed with the pharmacist, she is so confused by the surge of happiness that she confesses ingenuously, "I think something is wrong with me." Does happiness really go on and on, she wonders. Assured i

What the script of 'The Wash' doesn't tell you, the magnificent faces of the two main actors do.

can, Ms. McCarthy gives out with ripple of laughter — surprised, coquettish, childish all at once. (Th

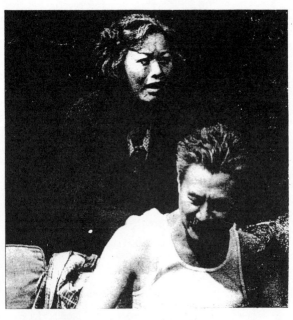

Gerry Goodstein/Manhattan Theater Club

Martha Swope/"Shadowlands"

"Shadowlands," left, with Nigel Hawthorne and Jane Alexander as C. S. Lewis and Joy Davidman, doesn't soft-pedal its call to the emotions; in "The Wash," with Nobu McCarthy and Sab Shimono, unspoken emotions run deep.

scene is the play's most entrancing; not coincidentally, it is also the most protracted.)

Mr. Shimono's brooding performance, on the other hand, suggests the pond's dark waters. He has fierce jowls and his left eyebrow is higher than his right, which only accentuates the suspicion with which he views others. Everything in him is dense, constricted, packed down hard. When the ache in his heart proves too much to bear, the best he can do to communicate the tumult is to lay a shotgun before his wife, point at it and walk away.

Mr. Gotanda began "The Wash" as a play, turned it into a low-budget movie that was widely admired in 1988 and now has turned it back into a play. The movie still shows. The story is told in a succession of vignettes, some containing no more than a few lines of dialogue. On the whole, the climaxes are visual, rather than verbal. (Whenever the director, Sharon Ott, isolates her performers in a spotlight, you get the notion she's doing so to compensate for the close-ups that are no longer possible.) Compared to Mr. Gotanda's slyly subversive 1989 comedy, "Yankee Dawg You Die," "The Wash" is slight and impressionistic, which leaves plenty of blank spaces for Mr. Shimono and Ms. McCarthy to fill in.

Although they succeed eloquently, you still end up with a loose-leaf notebook of scenes about people who will do anything *not* to make a scene. That's not quite a contradiction, but almost. ☐

1990 N 18, II:5:1

Fiddler on the Roof

Book by Joseph Stein; music by Jerry Bock; lyrics by Sheldon Harnick; original production directed and choreographed by Jerome Robbins; choreography reproduced by Sammy Dallas Bayes; direction reproduced by Ruth Mitchell; scenery by Boris Aronson; costumes based on original designs by Patricia Zipprodt; lighting by Ken Billington; sound by Peter J. Fitzgerald; hair design by Robert DiNiro; orchestrations by Don Walker; musical director and vocal arrangements by Milton Greene; music coordinator, John Monaco; technical supervisor, Arthur Siccardi; general managers, Charlotte Wilcox and Connie Weinstein; production stage manager, Martin Gold; associate producer, Alecia Parker; produced in association with C. Itoh & Company/Tokyo Broadcasting System International; A. Deshe (Pashanel). Presented by Barry and Fran Weissler and Pace Theatrical Group. At the Gershwin Theater, 222 West 51st Street.

Tevye	Topol
Golde	Marcia Lewis
Tzeitel	Sharon Lawrence
Hodel	Tia Riebling
Chava	Jennifer Prescott
Motel	Jack Kenny
Perchik	Gary Schwartz
Lazar Wolf	Mark Zeller
Yente	Ruth Jaroslow
Rabbi	Jerry Matz

WITH: Judy Dodd, Jerry Jarrett, David Masters, Mike O'Carroll, David Pevsner, Kathy St. George and Stephen Wright.

By MEL GUSSOW

In the 26 years since it was first produced on Broadway, "Fiddler on the Roof" has become a universally cherished folk musical. With countless versions performed throughout the world, it is part of our musical heritage, just as the Sholom Aleichem stories on which the show is based derive from an earlier European literary heritage. As the revival that opened last night at the Gershwin Theater proves, "Fiddler on the Roof" has not lost an ounce of its charm or its emotional power.

From the Chagall-inspired settings by the late Boris Aronson to Topol's performance as Tevye the dairyman, this is a heartwarming production. It is presented on Broadway by Barry and Fran Weissler, who have produced it with the same care and attention to detail that they demonstrated last season with their revival of "Gypsy."

When Fruma-Sarah, the ghost of the butcher's wife, scurries across the stage in Jerome Robbins's dream ballet, sending a tremor of terror through the superstitious characters, "Fiddler" levitates, like those figures in the scenic backdrops that fill the landscape with the ambiance of Anatevka.

•

As everyone knows, Anatevka is a little town next to nowhere, a bucolic Russian community in which Jewish residents at the turn of the century hold fast to their religion and their traditions, even as their world collapses. The tone of the show is established by Tevye's opening number, "Tradition." Despite its familiarity, that song retains its elemental wisdom, as does the show that revolves around it.

Historically, the primary question facing Tevye is how far he is prepared to go in forsaking — or re-evaluating — the old ways as he tries to preserve his feelings of fatherhood and moral responsibility. As intended, "Fiddler" is not simply the story of a father and his five daughters, but of the end of a way of life and an assumption of the principles of a new freedom.

All this is captured in Jerry Bock's music, Sheldon Harnick's lyrics, Joseph Stein's book and the original stage conception, direction and choreography by Mr. Robbins (reproduced with fidelity in the current production, as staged by Ruth Mitchell, with the choreographic assistance of Sammy Dallas Bayes).

The score liltingly evokes folk and liturgical strains while never losing sight of the show's obligations as a work of popular theater. Both the lyrics and book convey Sholom Aleichem's homespun philosophies. The musical has a seamless fluidity, songs flowing into story into dance. Even the settings seem to dance as Tevye's cottage swirls in time to the music and as, in the song "Sabbath Prayer," the skies are lined with an aurora borealis of families lighting candles.

•

In the apportionment of responsibility, the creative team deserves the highest credit. But one must not overlook another figure of importance,

Robert Ragsdale

Topol as Tevye in the Broadway revival of "Fiddler on the Roof."

Zero Mostel, who first gave the musical Tevye such extraordinary stage life. In the original production (and in the 1976 Broadway revival), Mr. Mostel turned a poor, put-upon country dairyman into a larger-than-life hero with human-size impulses. It was a most difficult, double-edged feat.

Great roles, in the musical theater as well as in drama, exist to be reinterpreted, true of Tevye as it is of Rose in "Gypsy" and Henry Higgins. Topol, who has his own history with the character and toured the United States last year with this production, has grown considerably since he played Tevye in the 1971 film. It is not simply a matter of his age, which is now approximately that of his character, but of his maturing in the role. On the other hand — as Tevye would say — Topol is not hilarious like Mr. Mostel, nor as expressive a musical performer. On the other hand, he never neglects the warmth or the drollness of his character.

Most important, Topol's Tevye is deeply embedded in Anatevka, where he wearily accommodates his bossy wife and their marriageable daughters, all with minds of their own, while on the horizon there is a pogrom that will remove what little stability remains in the shtetl. Topol is playful rather than sentimental, a self-dramatizer, but with an appealing humanity, and a believer who is skeptical enough to hold his own in man-to-God conversations.

The actor also has a natural gift for melody, as he demonstrates in the wishful "If I Were a Rich Man" and in "Sunrise, Sunset," that poignant Bock-Harnick acceptance of the effects of the passage of time. Topol does have a tendency to talk down into his beard, which, with the Gershwin Theater's dubious acoustics, sometimes makes it sound as if he is speaking into a microphone muffled beneath the bristle. In all significant respects, he is an authoritative Tevye, and when he sings "Chavaleh," about a daughter who has challenged tradition, he once agains reveals a tenderness.

Marcia Lewis as his wife, Golde, has a piercing voice that automatically sets her husband's body trembling, and it may have a similar effect on theatergoers. A little toning-down would make her performance more in keeping with those of her colleagues. She does, however, seem like the mother of her daughters, each of whom is winningly personified (Sharon Lawrence, Tia Riebling and Jennifer Prescott as the three oldest).

Ms. Riebling and Gary Schwartz are most engagingly matched as Hodel and the radical teacher Perchik. In addition, there are sympathetic performances by Jack Kenny as Motel the timid tailor, Ruth Jaroslow (who has made a career of playing Yente the matchmaker) and Stephen Wright as the ubiquitous fiddler on and off the roof.

•

"Fiddler" is an enduring work of musical theater, simultaneously a comedy and a drama, retaining its sense of wonder as it spins to its moving conclusion. As Anatevka is abandoned, Aronson's palette of Chagall colors is suddenly replaced by a monochromatic horizon more resonant of Rothko, conveying an aura of the unknown. Topol as Tevye harnesses himself to his milk wagon and becomes a Father Courage leading the remainder of his family to the more promising land of America.

1990 N 19, C13:1

Shogun
The Musical

Based on James Clavell's novel; book and lyrics by John Driver; music by Paul Chihara; directed and choreographed by Michael Smuin; scenery by Loren Sherman; costumes by Patricia Zipprodt; lighting by Natasha Katz; orchestrations by David Cullen; musical director, Edward G.

Robinson; co-choreographer, Kirk Peterson; fight instructor, Masahiro Kunii; production supervision by Jeremiah J. Harris. Presented by Mr. Clavell, Joseph Harris and Haruki Kadokawa. At the Marquis Theater, Broadway and 46th Street.

John Blackthorne	Philip Casnoff
Pieterzoon	Lee Lobenhofer
Father Alvito	John Herrera
Lord Buntaro	Joseph Foronda
Omi	Eric Chan
Gyoko	Freda Foh Shen
Kiku	JoAnn M. Hunter
Lord Toranaga	Francis Ruivivar
Sazuko	Jenny Woo
Osagi and Ishido's General	Jason Ma
Lady Mariko	June Angela
Lord Ishido	Alan Muraoka
Fujiko	Leslie Ishii
Chimmoko	Kiki Moritsugu

By FRANK RICH

Had the actor Philip Casnoff not been beaned by a falling slab of scenery at a press preview last week, "Shogun: The Musical" might have been best remembered as the first Broadway musical extravaganza to beguile an audience with a song about a dildo. But Mr. Casnoff's accident and his speedy recovery upstaged all else in the show — and justly so. Mr. Casnoff is something. "Shogun," with or without sexual toys, is something else.

I was at the fateful preview in which the actor was abruptly knocked flat, bringing screams from the audience and causing the immediate suspension of the show, which delayed its opening until last night. When I returned to the Marquis Theater a few days later to see the complete second act, I was struck not only by Mr. Casnoff's physical resilience but also by a remarkable change in his performance. Before he was injured, Mr. Casnoff, a gifted young New York actor little known outside the profession, was giving a dutiful but hardly stellar performance — well sung, agile, bland — in the role of John Blackthorne, the English sea captain who finds himself marooned in the civil-war-torn Japan of 1598. After his recovery, Mr. Casnoff had the swaggering self-assurance of a star in complete command of a vast production. He was enjoying himself as he had not been before, and, of course, the audience was adoring him in return.

Had the actor's brush with a possibly career-ending injury inspired him to take a gutsier stance on stage? Had all the publicity attending the incident pumped up his ego, forcing him to behave like a big deal rather than like just another unsung New York actor who happened to land a large part in a forgettable show? Whatever the explanation, Mr. Casnoff's accident, painful and terrifying as it must have been, can be seen from the vantage point of its happy ending as the biggest break of his career. And if that's not show biz, what is?

•

As for the rest of "Shogun: The Musical," I suspect it is best appreciated by fans of its James Clavell source, "Shogun: The Novel," or perhaps by viewers of "Shogun: The Mini-Series" or even wearers of "Shogun: The T-shirt." "Shogun" aficionados will presumably experience the stage version as a progression of recognizable tableaux inspired by a sacred text. For those unfamiliar with the Clavell tale, the musical's book, by John Driver, is mostly incomprehensible, and the synopsis in the Playbill is itself in need of synopsis. ("Ishido schemes with the three Catholic Daimyos and passes a resolution demanding that Toranaga re-

Carol Rosegg/Martha Swope Associates/Shogun
Philip Casnoff, left, June Angela and Francis Ruivivar in "Shogun."

main as a 'guest' in Osaka Castle, thus making Toranaga a virtual prisoner," goes one typical passage.) The Playbill is also equipped with a glossary of Japanese expressions, such as "kampai," which means "bottoms up," and "seppuku," which refers to the "ritual suicide" one samurai or shogun or another is threatening to commit in every other scene.

Curiously, the glossary does not list "pillowing," which is the term "Shogun" gives its medieval Japanese characters as a synonym for copulation. It is in Mr. Driver's lyrics for the song "Pillowing" that female characters describe the joys of a portable phallus ("It never tires of women like a lazy, jaded man") with a gleeful prurience that almost makes one nostalgic for the relatively benign sexism of "I Enjoy Being a Girl" in Rodgers and Hammerstein's "Flower Drum Song." Of the 30-odd other musical numbers composed by Paul Chihara for "Shogun," few are memorable except "Karma," this show's inevitable if ludicrous opening number, and a ballad titled "Born to Be Together" that, between its constant repetition and its orchestration by the Andrew Lloyd Webber arranger David Cullen, might as well be piped in from "Aspects of Love" around the corner.

Given its poverty in other departments, "Shogun" is the kind of show at which it is de rigueur to praise the physical production — if only because that's where the big budget was most conspicuously spent. Patricia Zipprodt, a costume designer second to none, has indeed done beautiful work here, turning out enough kimonos and other more extravagant ceremonial robes to make the silkworm an endangered species. Loren Sherman, a witty miniaturist in his scenic assignments Off Broadway, has not made the leap to Broadway overproduction too gracefully. The black-and-gold folding screens used as a front cur-

tain look like the sort of heavy, ersatz chinoiserie that was popular in middle-class American homes in the 1950's, and a big earthquake effect is less redolent of Kabuki or Kurosawa than of "Godzilla." The delicacy of Japanese esthetics is apparent only in a late-evening "Winter Battle" sequence, hauntingly lighted by Natasha Katz, in which warriors on silver horses advance from within a cloud of fog and snow.

By then, "Shogun" is almost three hours old, and it has not exactly flown by under the direction of Michael Smuin. A snazzy choreographer of period American dancing ("Sophisticated Ladies," "Anything Goes"), Mr. Smuin seems to have little luck with actors. June Angela, the leading lady, who pillows with Mr. Casnoff in various Kama Sutra positions near the end of Act I, has a squeaky soprano, a professional smile and scant presence. Francis Ruivivar's jolly, rotund Shogun, John Herrera's shifty-eyed priest and Joseph Foronda's monotoned villain all seem to be refugees from a Gilbert and Sullivan tour of the provinces, and not necessarily the Japanese provinces.

Mr. Smuin's choreography includes a stormy opening shipwreck sequence that, with its spangled, gyrating furies and fabric waves, looks like the Trump casino edition of Jerome Robbins's "Small House of Uncle Thomas" ballet from "The King and I." The post-intermission dance treat is an utterly gratuitous "Festival of the Fireflies" that is best applauded not for its Crazy Horse Saloon onslaught of scantily clad "insects" but for its temporary forestalling of Act II's turgid scenes of exposition. After that, "Shogun" may leave all except its most fiercely committed partisans longing for a pillow of the old-fashioned, G-rated kind.

1990 N 21, C9:1

Carnal Knowledge

By Jules Feiffer; directed by Martin Charnin; scenery by Alan Kimmel; lighting by Ken Billington; sound design by Abe Jacob; production stage manager, Brandon E. Doemling; general management, Marshall B. Purdy; associate producer, Bill Repicci. Presented by Martin R. Kaufman. At the Kaufman Theater, 534 West 42d Street.

Sandy	Jon Cryer
Jonathan	Judd Nelson
Susan	Justine Bateman
Bobbie	Karen Byers
Cindy	Mimi Quillin
Daisy	Laura Rogers
Louise	Arminae Azarian

By MEL GUSSOW

Watching Jules Feiffer's "Carnal Knowledge" in its long delayed New York theatrical premiere at the Kaufman Theater, one reaches the conclusion that with work and revisions this might be the basis for a provocative film. The odd thing is that the film, which preceded the play's production by 19 years, uses a script that is nearly identical to that of the play. The difference is that of direction, performance and perception.

"Carnal Knowledge" was originally written as a play, which Mr. Feiffer then adapted into a screenplay for Mike Nichols as director. Both the play and the film deal with cruel sexual games that masquerade as mating rites. The tone is comic yet unrelentingly harsh.

The film is a small-scale dead-on time capsule of a pre-feminist period when men routinely subjugated women and both sexes were trapped by their desire for carnal knowledge and experience. The author is critical of all his characters. The women contribute to their predicament, and the men become their own impotent victims.

•

As stylishly directed by Mr. Nichols and heightened by Jack Nicholson's performance as the more manipulative of two close male friends, the film has the fascination of a highway collision. Moviegoers become voyeurs to twinned catastrophic cases of self-delusion. Onstage, in an unadorned production directed by Martin Charnin, the play seems spasmodic. In performance, the vignettes in quickly changing settings suffer from the loss of cinematic crosscuts and artful atmospheric selectivity.

The opening is a dormitory dialogue between two preppy Amherst students in the 1940's, with Jon Cryer in the Art Garfunkel role and Judd Nelson in the Nicholson role. Mr. Nelson is the overbearing sexual savant next to Mr. Cryer's innocent. Their initial conversation is fast and funny (in the film, the lines are heard over the titles), amusingly performed by the two actors in a low-key confidential mode.

The effect onstage is like a period version of David Mamet's "Sexual Perversity in Chicago" as a guidebook lesson on how young men try to exploit women. While Mr. Mamet's comedy retains its immediacy, Mr. Feiffer's leaps ahead several decades between the play's two acts. Mr. Cryer has married the woman (Justine Bateman) both men loved, but will soon jettison the marriage along with other aspects of his life.

Mr. Nelson has become even more obsessive and empty minded in his search for bed mates. The play slips into a story that by now seems familiar, not only from the Nichols film but also from other movies that came after it. Actually, the most dated aspect of the play — an Aquarian celebration of open love — was among several scenes wisely deleted from the film.

In the film, Mr. Nicholson was snakelike in his insidiousness, but with a residual sense of helplessness. He was an adult only by age, stalled forever in adolescence. In the play, Mr. Nelson simply seems caddish, and beyond his character's willfulness one wonders why the others tolerate his outrageous behavior.

Mr. Cryer is more persuasive as is Ms. Bateman in the role created in the film by Candice Bergen, but together the two actors are unable to convey the desperation of their movie predecessors. As the woman who becomes Mr. Nelson's sexual slave, Karen Byers does not dislodge one's image of Ann-Margret as a figure of male wish fulfillment.

•

The screen presence of Mr. Nicholson and his co-stars should not be underestimated in terms of its contribution to the film's success. But the disappointment of the play has less to do with the change in actors than with the concept. Opened up on screen, "Carnal Knowledge" gained intensity. Stripped down to dialogue onstage, it becomes schematic and verges on caricature. There is a limit to what the actors or Mr. Charnin can do to give the play its own validity.

After the film was released, Mr. Feiffer said some time would have to pass before the play could be performed, but time and Mr. Feiffer's own career as a playwright (of "Knock Knock" and "Grown Ups") have passed it by. Seen today, the play "Carnal Knowledge" has only marginal interest. The trip to the stage was unnecessary.

1990 N 21, C15:1

Jelly Belly

By Charles Smith; directed by Dennis Zacek; set and lighting, Richard Harmon; costumes, Judy Dearing; sound, Jacqui Casto; production stage manager, Jesse Wooden Jr. Presented by the New Federal Theater, Inc., Woodie King Jr., producer; the Victory Gardens Theater, Mr. Zacek, producer. At the Louis Abrons Art Center of the Henry Street Settlement, 466 Grand Street.

Barbara .... Gina Torres
Mike .... Weyman Thompson
Bruce .... Donald Douglass
Kenny .... Ramon Melindez Moses
Jelly Belly .... Tony Smith

By STEPHEN HOLDEN

Early in Charles Smith's despairing drama "Jelly Belly," the title character, a drug dealer who has returned to his old stomping grounds after serving a six-month prison term for murder, describes his vision of a world in which people are either shepherds, sheep or lamb chops.

•

The portly ex-convict's audience consists of Mike (Weyman Thompson), an old friend who has given up his criminal ways for a low-level job in construction, Mike's young protégé, Kenny (Ramon Melindez Moses), and Bruce (Donald Douglass), a jibbering drug addict who follows Jelly Belly (Tony Smith) around begging for handouts of angel dust. In Jelly Belly's universe, shepherds are people like himself who give orders, and Mike and Kenny are sheep who are foolish enough to take them. "You'd break your backs for people who would rather spit at you than look at you," he sneers and warns that Kenny will wind up a lamb chop, someone

who is devoured by a system he compares to slavery.

"Jelly Belly," which the New Federal Theater is co-producing with a Chicago organization, the Victory Gardens Theater, at the Louis Abrons Art Center, offers an unremittingly bleak portrait of inner-city life and of the enormous pressures on working-class black men to be gangsters. The central conflict is a battle waged between Jelly Belly and Mike for the soul of Kenny. Mike has partly convinced the young man, who also used to deal drugs, that if the two of them are patient and work hard, they will someday own their own construction company.

The evil shepherd, who dispenses beer and free "toots" of angel dust, sets about undermining Kenny's fragile hopes while trying to regain some control over Mike. He reminds Mike that he owes him for all the drugs they did together in the old days and for covering up his involvement in the murder of Jelly Belly's brother-in-law. In appealing to Kenny, Jelly Belly challenges the young man's shaky machismo. Producing a gun, he urges him to "be a man" and slay the local hoodlum who recently robbed him of his drugs.

Although "Jelly Belly" doesn't try to explore the roots of the social horrors it portrays, its unblinking, almost matter-of-fact depiction of a world whose values have turned upside down is credible and at moments, even funny in a ghastly way. In one of its most outrageous yarns, Jelly Belly glamorizes the experience of prison by telling the story of Frosty the Snowman, a rebellious inmate who emerged from 91 days in solitary confinement with a suntan and claiming to have been on vacation in the Bahamas.

The most disturbing thing about the play is the fact that while Jelly Belly is presented as a walking nightmare, his arguments against the straight-and-narrow life have a kernel of truth. The barriers of race and class to Mike's realization of his dream, the play suggests, are nearly insurmountable. And without the love of his fiery wife, Barbara (Gina Torres), the playwright suggests, Mike himself would relapse into criminality.

•

The play, which unfolds on the front porch of Mike's decrepit house, has been directed by Dennis Zacek with a low-keyed efficiency that keeps a very firm lid on the characters' passions. Mr. Zacek is a producer and director at the Victory Gardens Theater, where the play originated. The performances — especially Mr. Smith's alternately roaring and cajoling Jelly Belly — add dimension to characters that in a less confident production might not have transcended the playwright's portrayal of them as social stereotypes.

1990 N 22, C13:3

World of Adventure in a Monologue

By STEPHEN HOLDEN

One of the two strands of the playwright John O'Keefe's vivid, chargingly energetic performance mono-

logue "Vid," at Performance Space 122, is his description of being both the player and the protagonist of his own video game.

A science-fiction adventure whose breakneck action makes even a movie like "Star Wars" seem sluggish by comparison, it is filled with such images as riding on surf that is actually a river of snakes, playing with a "razor Frisbee" and being set upon by flocks of birds that leave the playwright covered with blood that turns into phosphorescent designs.

Interwoven with Mr. O'Keefe's breathlessly paced video adventure are picaresque tales of his life in the mid-1970's in the San Francisco Bay area. After working briefly for the Magic Theater, he recalls, he lived hand to mouth in a van that he kept illegally in a hospital parking area. In the funniest of several amusing stories, he describes a conference in Denver on Buddhism and the theater

---

John O'Keefe's words provide more action than 'Star Wars.'

---

at which Robert Wilson "took an hour to cross a room while a girl counted to 10," the Open Theater performed American Indian chants, and the Buddhist guru who was the guest of honor condescended to everyone.

As the "true" story continues, the narrator takes up with assorted colorful street people and bohemians, including two primal-scream aficionados. For entertainment, he spends hours in his van following the activities of the Oakland police on a short-wave radio. He has nightmares about literally ending up a carnival sideshow attraction. It becomes clear that the "real" experience Mr. O'Keefe recounts is in its way even crazier than his imaginary video game.

"Vid," which has its final three performances tomorrow, Saturday and Sunday at P.S. 122, 150 First Avenue, at Ninth Street, is a riskier but no less gripping piece than "Shimmer," Mr. O'Keefe's monologue about his adolescent escape from an Iowa work farm, which also began at P.S. 122 and was later produced by the Second Stage. As the monologue winds up, the playwright expertly pulls the two strands of his story together so that the two stories become corollaries of each other.

If there are obvious similarities between Mr. O'Keefe and Spalding Gray, who is also drawn to the surreal, their styles of performance are very different. Where Mr. Gray maintains an air of New England gentility much of the time and talks in a dry, ironic tone, Mr. O'Keefe is a wild Irish storyteller who acts out his tales with a feverish though disciplined physical intensity. Both storytellers have the gift of making the audience see the world new.

1990 N 22, C18:4

Spectacle With a Ninja Twist

'Shogun' – even an earthquake can't stop it; Spalding Gray remains the master of digression; 'Fiddler' has hardly changed a bit.

AT THE OUTSET OF "SHOGUN," the sumptuous musical that has been wrested — and I do mean wrested — from James Clavell's sprawling novel about feudal Japan, a crackle of lightning dances across the black lacquered screen that serves as a curtain at the Marquis Theater.

As the wind howls, the screen parts to reveal a galleon in the grip of an angry ocean. The captain is clinging desperately to the wheel, and the ship is pitching violently from side to side, so violently that one crew member after another is hurled off the deck into the foaming waters. Then a fierce swell sends the captain himself flying and the unmanned vessel disappears from sight.

It's an astonishing beginning. From that point on, however, I'd be hard-pressed to tell you what's going on. Illicit love, yes. Intrigue, yes. Coups, battles, betrayals, pursuits, ritual suicides, yes. But how they all link up, what's cause and what's effect and who's who in the exotic scheme of things are matters beyond my understanding.

You can't accuse the playwright and lyricist John Driver of stinting on the action in his dramatization of Mr. Clavell's saga. A little stinting, in fact, would have gone a long way toward solving the evening's problems. So many incidents are clamoring to happen that when one does make it on stage, it is given no time to acquire any dramatic weight before it is elbowed into the wings by the next eager incident, raring to stake its claim. (Acting auditions, from what I'm told, obey a similar dynamic and are similarly frustrating.)

"Shogun" is a Gordian knot of confusions, and you'll just have to accept that if you intend to enjoy what's best about the show: some impressive special effects, an exquisite wardrobe courtesy of Patricia Zipprodt, and one haunting love song, "Born to Be Together," that Andrew Lloyd Webber might have written if Paul Chihara hadn't beaten him to it. There are times when you won't believe your eyes. But there are more times when you won't believe your ears.

■

Of course, we are living in an age that deems any subject fit for musicalization, as long as you can rustle up the financing. I don't know if it was "Cats" that first flung the door wide open in the early 1980's. But once you had a litter of felines singing and dancing in a junk heap — and one of them ascending to heaven on a giant automobile tire — a line had definitely been crossed. In the musicals that followed, trains were engaging in a cross-country race, heroic Frenchmen were mounting the barricades and a masked

phantom was scampering all over the Paris Opera House and under it, as well. The problem of who might logically deliver a song in a musical had been effectively laid to rest. *Anyone* could.

But I suspect it was really a play — the Royal Shakespeare Company's extraordinary 8½-hour production of "Nicholas Nickleby" in 1980 — that gave the green light to the current rash of epic thinking in musicals. After all, Charles Dickens's novel runs more than 800 pages, counts hundreds of characters and wanders over a large patch of Victorian England. Supposedly, this was the province of the movies or the television miniseries, and yet here was the stage, bringing it all vitally and imaginatively alive. Another barrier down.

To look at "Shogun," as it has turned out at the Marquis, is to wonder why anybody thought for an instant that it would make a viable musical. But in light of the past, nothing could be more comprehensible. "Miss Saigon" has crowds thrilling to the doomed romance between an American G.I. and a lovely Vietnamese bar girl, so why shouldn't they respond to the passion between "Shogun's" hero, John Blackthorne, the dashing English sea captain, shipwrecked off the coast of Japan, and Lady Mariko, the lovely Japanese aristocrat who serves as his translator, his guide and — for one delicious night, which we view through a curtain gauzily — his secret consort?

If the nasty Inspector Javert can pursue Jean Valjean through the Paris sewers in "Les Misérables," why can't a band of ninjas chase Blackthorne and Mariko through the labyrinthian corridors of Osaka Castle? "The Phantom of the Opera" may send a crystal chandelier crashing spectacularly t the floor. "Shogun" will go it one better witl a full-fledged earthquake, belching smoke and fire and threatening to swallow up Toranaga, the rotund "overlord of the Central Province," who aspires to the shogunate an is behind the evening's machinations. It

Martha Swope Associates/Carol Rosegg/"Shogun"

John Herrera, at center left, Francis Ruivivar and June Angela in "Shogun"—kindred spirit to the one that found Grauman's Chinese Theater a monument to the East

makes sense, if you're sitting in a board room or a bar or wherever it is that musicals get dreamed up.

■

In practice, however, the confusions of the narrative are compounded by the stylistic mishmash that is Michael Smuin's direction and choreography. Although black-hooded prop men scurry industriously about the stage, as they do in traditional Japanese theater, much of "Shogun" is closer in spirit to the Hollywood that found Grauman's Chinese Theater a fitting monument to the East.

"Tonight we celebrate the festival of the fireflies. Enjoy it," thunders Toranaga to his court in what well may be the baldest lead-in to a production number in recent times. What ensues is pure camp — six ever-so-lithe maidens, diaphanously dressed, cavorting with six bare-chested lads, while the prop men dart among them waving illuminated wands in the night air, thereby simulating all the twinkling magic of the fireflies themselves.

The show's most bewitching image — Toranaga and his men advancing on horseback into a whirling snowstorm — is so utterly convincing it could be coming to you on film. Not a hint of artifice shows, as men and beasts, magnificently girded for battle, push forward through the gray, wintry mists. But the death of Mariko is all artifice — red ribbons exploding up from the stage like a geyser of blood and wrapping themselves around her expiring body. (I seem to recall Peter Brook doing something of the sort in "The Mahabharata.") In the course of what is shaping up as a realistic fight sequence, a warrior is apt to leap acrobatically on the scene, turn a flip in midair, and bound off.

The staging is forever switching back and forth between a literal and a nonliteral rendering of events. And although I didn't mention it earlier, just when the opening illusion of a sinking ship is strongest, a band of water sprites, decked in silver and seaweed, trips on to whip the waves to even greater frenzy.

A towering performance or two might dispel some of the chaos. But as Blackthorne, Philip Casnoff (the victim of falling scenery during the show's previews) is neither strapping nor magnetic enough for the job, although he sings nicely. As Toranaga, a character Mr. Clavell describes as "the almighty puppeteer," Francis Ruivivar is more of a Jolly Green Giant, Eastern variety, and never more so than when he hitches up his skirts and joins Blackthorne in a spirited English hornpipe. (I seem to recall Yul Brynner doing something of the sort in "The King and I.") June Angela's Mariko manages to project grace and dignity with appealing delicacy, until she has to put a knife between her teeth and engage in hand-to-hand combat with villains. Then she looks foolish.

Those supporting players, who do not appear to be on missions of utmost secrecy, give the understandable impression that they are overwhelmed by the whiz of activity. "Karma" frequently crops up as an explanation for the twists and turns of the plot and even merits a song of its own. "Karma does its dance,/ Buddhist game of chance," go the lyrics, if that helps.

It didn't help me.

And I just read Mr. Clavell's book.

'Monster in a Box'

I don't know if Spalding Gray is having a more interesting life than the rest of us, but he certainly is telling it better. "Monster in a Box," his 13th autobiographical monologue, is a thoroughly entertaining account of the

Martha Swope Associates/Carol Rosegg/"Fiddler"

Topol's Tevye—He knows what he's doing every second.

difficulties he has encountered completing a novel that is "due to be published by Knopf ... two years ago."

Five minutes from anyone else on the subject of writer's block would be more than enough. Mr. Gray takes 90 minutes in the Mitzi E. Newhouse Theater at Lincoln Center and leaves you thinking that he has barely scratched the surface. As his prior monologues have amply illustrated, he is a master of digression. Or else it's his life that keeps digressing. At any rate, the shortest distance between two points is definitely not Mr. Gray talking.

After he has explained how he came to undertake his novel, "Impossible Vacations," a first-person narrative about a man who doesn't know how to take vacations, his monologue consists of the endless diversions and distractions that have kept him from the work. Mr. Gray is seated, as usual, at a wooden table, on which can be found a microphone, a glass of water and the nettlesome novel in question in all its 1,600 pages of unedited glory. (Normally, it's stored in a cardboard box, hence the monologue's title.) All evening long, the manuscript functions as a silent reproach to Mr. Gray, who, despite the years he has spent cultivating what he describes as a self-deprecating, ironic New York voice, is still a dyed-in-the-wool Puritan from Rhode Island and therefore highly susceptible to reproach.

In one respect, "Monster in a Box" is a wonderful picaresque tale that takes Mr. Gray and his companion, Renee Shafransky (who has directed the production), to the board rooms of Hollywood, the slums of Nicaragua and a film festival in Moscow, before winding up on the stage of the Lyceum Theater, where the silver-haired actor played the role of the stage manager in "Our Town" to somewhat less than unanimous critical acclaim a few seasons back.

■

If there are oddballs in the vicinity, it's sure he'll meet them — not that that's such a chore in Los Angeles. Still, while there, he's quick to pick up on the trend for "passion fruit mango mousse." Researching a film in Nicaragua, he ends up bunking with a paranoid "pedantics major from Berkeley," who thinks the C.I.A. is speaking through his teeth. When he throws open a discussion of his film, "Swimming to Cambodia," to a group

of Russian film enthusiasts, the first question he is asked is, "Why did Dustin Hoffman make 'Tootsie'?" Mr. Gray's world is perpetually askew.

On the other hand, what gives his monologues their dramatic tension is a battle that rages within himself. Confidential as he gets — and no subject, from his sweaty feet to the fear that he's contracted AIDS, is taboo — he can't entirely shake the heritage of the uptight New Englander, schooled in the virtues of fortitude and reserve. Born guilty, he's been lugging about a hyperactive conscience ever since.

All the while he's relating what's happened to him in the last three years, he's struggling to justify himself to himself. After all, a man can't have the kind of topsy-turvy, Alice-in-Wonderland existence he has without sooner or later posing that most profound of questions. Am I imagining things, or are the words "Why me?" beginning to etch themselves into Mr. Gray's aimiably furrowed brow?

'Fiddler on the Roof'

Here's what you should know about "Fiddler on the Roof," which has pulled into the Gershwin Theater for a limited run, after a lengthy tour of the country. No one is out to trash your memories. Boris Aronson's scenery, Patricia Zipprodt's costumes and Jerome Robbins's direction and choreography have all been faithfully "reproduced," as the program puts it, so that the show looks and behaves much as it did 26 years ago. Tradition is being served, as well it should, when the very theme of the musical is how tradition binds a beleaguered community together.

Here's what else you should know. The whole enterprise seems just a little musty, rather like a historic home that has been preserved exactly as it was during the occupant's lifetime, right down to the teacup he was holding when the croup carried him off. This "Fiddler" is in the hands of curators, not creators, and authenticity is their greatest concern. To that end, Tevye, the indomitable milkman in Anatevka, is played by Chaim Topol, who starred in the original London production, the film version and a 1984 London revival. He's not the boisterous Tevye that Zero Mostel was, and his voice has a strangulated quality that suggests he's swallowed something more tangible than life's indignities.

But he's obviously got the role down pat and knows what he's doing every second he's on stage. Not a laugh eludes him, and when it's time for pathos, pathos is what he delivers. I'm sure I was the only person in the audience to think he was watching one of those incredibly lifelike, talking mannequins Disney makes so well these days. □

1990 N 25, II:5:1

Major Barbara

By George Bernard Shaw; directed by Anthony Cornish; sets, Robert Joel Schwartz; lighting, Stephen Petrilli; costumes, Barbara A. Bell; sound, Arthur C. Mortensen; stage manager, Lynn Bogarde. Presented by the Pearl Theater Company. At 125 West 22d Street

Stephen Undershaft and Snobby Price
.... Stuart Lerch
Lady Britomart Undershaft and Rummy Mitchens.................................. Margaret Hilton
Major Barbara Undershaft
.... Robin Leslie Brown
Sarah Undershaft and Jenny Hill
.... Laura Rathgeb
Adolphus Cusins............................ Tom Bloom
Charles Lomax and Bill Walker Arnie Burton
Morrison, Peter Shirley and Bilton
.... Woody Sempliner
Andrew Undershaft..................... Frank Geraci
Mrs. Baines .... Sylvia Davis

By WILBORN HAMPTON

It is always something of a surprise to rediscover how timely Shaw's early plays remain. And few are more germane to the social problems of the 1990's than "Major Barbara," Shaw's witty and wise discourse on politics, arms, greed, poverty and other crimes that is being given a mostly worthwhile revival at the Pearl Theater Company.

There are two essential ingredients to a successful staging of "Major Barbara": strong performances in the two central roles of Barbara, the Belgravia-bred missionary who tries to bring salvation to the poor through an East End soup kitchen, and Andrew Undershaft, her father, whose only religion is "money and gunpowder" and whose cannon foundry's motto is "Unashamed."

The Pearl production has at least one of those requirements in a solid reading of the title character by Robin Leslie Brown. The character of Major Barbara Undershaft is a forerunner of Shaw's St. Joan, and Ms. Brown captures all the fiery zeal of an evangelist, especially in the third act when Barbara visits her father's cannon factory and undergoes her own conversion. If Ms. Brown seems a bit tentative earlier among her flock at the Salvation Army shelter, it is only in anticipation of the fervor with which she accepts her true vocation.

•

It is here that Ms. Brown manages to deliver what is the real point of Shaw's sermon in "Major Barbara." The play is not, as it is often presented, a simple homily on what Shaw saw as the crime of poverty, but rather a lesson on who is in actual need of salvation in a materialistic and industrial society. After watching her father buy off the Salvation Army, Barbara becomes a proselyte to the view that it is the wealthy and the middle classes who must be saved from their own greed and complacency. After Ms. Brown's conversion one can only pity the Undershaft Cannon Foundry workers.

Unfortunately, Frank Geraci's Andrew Undershaft is more problematic. To make the conflict of this play any kind of contest, Andrew Undershaft should be every bit as charming and winning in his devotion to money and gunpowder as Barbara is in helping the poor and homeless with a Bible and treacle soup. It is not that he is against mercy and compassion

The Pearl Theater Company
Robin Leslie Brown in a revival of Shaw's "Major Barbara."

Who is that nice chap offering a better life on a law-away plan?

for the less fortunate, it's just that he sees them only as luxuries that a nation with lots of money and gunpowder can afford. If he knows he can buy the Salvation Army, he also knows he cannot buy his daughter with anything so trifling as money. Nor will he bully or frighten her. Mr. Geraci's Undershaft is a suavely sinister arms merchant, more in the school of Dr. No, or even Dr. Strangelove, oily and evil behind a tight-lipped smile and given to flashes of anger. As Shaw would be the first to point out, if the Devil comes among us, it will not be as a menacing Mephistopheles but as a polite, friendly chap promising a better life on a lay-away plan.

•

There are also a couple of fine performances from Tom Bloom as Barbara's long-suffering fiancé, Adolphus Cusins, the Greek scholar who finds he can believe in all religions and whom Undershaft must also convert, and from Arnie Burton, who doubles excellently as both the dandy Charles Lomax and the threatening Salvation Army intruder Bill Walker. Woody Sempliner is also good as Peter Shirley, another denizen of the shelter, and Margaret Hilton delivers a credible Lady Britomart, the imperious matriarch of the Undershaft household who could be twin sister to Lady Bracknell in Wilde's "Importance of Being Earnest."

The Pearl production, which was directed by Anthony Cornish, starts out slowly, and there are some awkward bumps and silences in the opening act (not the best way to get an

audience into a Shavian drawing room). But once the play hits stride in the second act, "Major Barbara" is still as entertaining a religious, economic, political or sociological debate as one is likely to hear.

1990 N 28, C17:1

The Fever

A one-man show with Wallace Shawn. Presented by Joseph Papp. At the Public/Shiva Theater, 425 Lafayette Street.

By FRANK RICH

"This is a piece I've been doing mostly in people's apartments since January," says the actor and playwright Wallace Shawn by way of introducing "The Fever," the one-hour-45-minute monologue he is now reciting at the Public Theater. But which people, which apartments and, for that matter, which January?

•

Perhaps out of fear that an aspiring Tom Wolfe, reporter's pad in hand, might record one of these private performances for public sport, Mr. Shawn isn't saying. And no wonder. "The Fever" is nothing if not a musty radical-chic stunt destined to be parodied: a brave, sincere and almost entirely humorless assault on the privileged class by one of its card-carrying members. In an orgy of self-flagellation that even Woody Allen might find a bit rich, Mr. Shawn naively tells the audience of his guilt about enjoying ice cream and good hotel rooms while peasants make do with beans; he didactically deplores the injustice of a capitalist economy that rewards an actor more extravagantly than a chambermaid or a beggar. All of which leaves one wondering: Were there any beggars and chambermaids in the apartments where Mr. Shawn honed "The Fever" — aside from those serving drinks and emptying ashtrays — or did he merely preach to other devotees of Häagen-Dazs?

•

Don't get me wrong: I admire Mr. Shawn's idiosyncratic comic gifts as both a writer and performer. "Aunt Dan and Lemon," a play so scabrous it managed to offend the ideologically antithetical drama critics of The New Republic and The New Criterion alike, was one of the most daring political comedies produced by the American theater in the 1980's, a work in which a civilized, well-educated heroine "defended" Hitler so that Mr. Shawn might argue how fascism could happen here and now. But while "The Fever" aspires to be similarly outrageous — it unfashionably defends Marxism during Communism's lowest ebb — it has less in common with the mordantly funny "Aunt Dan and Lemon" than with the obvious, if intensely argued, essay about morality that Mr. Shawn appended to that play's published text. "The Fever" arrives at unassailable conclusions — "There's no piece of paper that justifies what the beggar has and what I have" — by a circuitous route that passes through dense thickets of syllogism unrelieved by vivid characters, dramatic anecdotes, arresting language or even wisecracks.

•

Mr. Shawn delivers his earnest, scripted speech while remaining seated in a plain chair on an empty stage. In keeping with the new proletarian austerity he espouses, there

are no Playbills, no stagehands, no lighting cues, no curtain call, no intermission, only drab colors in his wardrobe and a low ticket price ($10).

Martha Swope/"Fever"
Wallace Shawn in "Fever."

Next to "The Fever," Spalding Gray's "Monster in a Box" and Eric Bogosian's "Sex, Drugs, Rock & Roll" look like Ziegfeld extravaganzas. Presumably these spartan conditions will prevail when "The Fever" moves on from the Public to other scheduled engagements at the Royal Court Theater in London and at the Second Stage, La Mama and Lincoln Center Theater in New York. Yet the studied informality does not re-create the casual experience of sitting in someone's living room. Mr. Shawn, his voice at an unvaried high pitch and his face sweating under the bright overhead lights, looks uncomfortable, like a Feiffer cartoon figure squirming before an inquisitor.

That's partly the point. The title of "The Fever" refers to the condition in which Mr. Shawn finds himself at the beginning of his talk. He has awakened "shaking and shivering" in "a strange hotel room in a poor country where my language isn't spoken." In between fever dreams and bouts of vomiting, he alternately offers selective accounts of his life to date, describes incidents of torture in "revolutionary" nations and, at his most amusing, provides Marxist critiques of "The Cherry Orchard," pornographic magazines and "commodity fetishism." Along the way he marshals arguments both for and against leaving his own comfortable, selfish world "to fight on the other side" of the class struggle. With an honesty that is more admirable than intellectually compelling, he is still sitting on the fence, and in his chair, at evening's end.

•

What makes "The Fever" lulling rather than a challenging or inspiring act of social protest is not so much its unexceptional ideological content as its flat, unspecific mode of expression. Though an occasional phrase pricks the ear — an upper-middle-class childhood is emblemized by "orange juice on a table in a glass pitcher" — too much of the writing painstakingly attempts to imitate the archetypal diction of Kafka, as if any unnamed trial could pass for "The Trial" or any heavily symbolic waterbug might turn out to be Gregor Samsa. Just as the audience never learns the identity of those "people's apartments" where "The Fever" was first performed, so the specifics of the speaker's family, career and friends — and those of the unnamed poor countries he visits — remain vague and generic. For a piece that presents itself as a self-critical, autobiographical confession, the monologue seems resolutely unrevealing and risk free. It's socialist art of the official, instructional kind.

Perhaps, like Eric Bogosian or, say, the well-heeled, conscience-ridden movie director in Preston Sturges's "Sullivan's Travels," Mr. Shawn would retrieve his fanatical comic voice by gaining a more intimate knowledge of the downtrodden he wishes to apotheosize but fails to bring to life on stage. "The Fever" is a strangely insular event, charged with intelligence and a desire to do good, yet rendered nearly inert by its author's solipsism. For a play that condemns decadence, it is itself a luxurious exercise in escapism: whether the arena is the theater or an apartment, Mr. Shawn's replay of old battles is a safe refuge from a real world poised at the brink of war.

1990 N 29, C17:1

Lake No Bottom

By Michael Weller; directed by Carole Rothman; sets, Adrianne Lobel; lighting, Kevin Rigdon; costumes, Jess Goldstein; sound, Mark Bennett; hair design, Antonio Soddu; production stage manager, Pamela Edington; stage manager, Elise-Ann Konstantin. Presented by Second Stage Theater, Robyn Goodman and Ms. Rothman, artistic directors. At 2162 Broadway, at 76th Street.

Petra.............................Marsha Mason
Will.................................Robert Knepper
Rubin...............................Daniel Davis

By FRANK RICH

I didn't realize I had been missing Marsha Mason until I saw her — radiant, good-humored, emotionally and sexually voluptuous — in Michael Weller's "Lake No Bottom," the new play at the Second Stage. The actress one fondly remembers from the films "Cinderella Liberty" and "The Goodbye Girl," a two-fisted comedienne with a desperately vulnerable undertow, has returned to the stage with her gifts intact and matured. It seems a waste that Ms. Mason reaches Mr. Weller one play too late. The racy, hard-nosed, flamboyantly neurotic mother played so brilliantly by Kate Nelligan in the author's "Spoils of War" would be a great role for this star as well.

"Lake No Bottom" is not nearly so rewarding, for the actress or for the audience, and it is not particularly representative of Mr. Weller, whose other works include the plays "Moonchildren" and "Loose Ends" and the screenplays for the Milos Forman films "Hair" and "Ragtime." "Lake No Bottom" is a stab at a pastoral play, set on a vaguely Walden-ish lake front at no tightly defined time,

Susan Cook/Second Stage Theater

Marsha Mason and Robert Knepper in Michael Weller's "Lake No Bottom," at the Second Stage Theater.

by a writer whose best works have always played out before vividly drawn and profoundly understood sociopolitical backdrops. ("Context is everything," goes one of Mr. Weller's lines here, but on this occasion he ignores his own advice.) The new effort is also a get-the-critics play, and this genre, too, proves not to be this writer's forte. A dramatist of unusual compassion who can empathize with both camps in a broken marriage and even with both sides of the Vietnam-era generation gap, Mr. Weller is utterly unpersuasive in affecting the bitchy tone he does in "Lake No Bottom."

•

He also seems to have temporarily lost his senses of humor and dramatic proportion. The program's advisory that "a gun will be fired during the performance" is no put-on: the play ultimately devolves into a duel between Rubin (Daniel Davis), a lofty literary critic who has retired to the woods to write his magnum opus, and his overnight house guest, Will (Robert Knepper), a former student who has hit the jackpot with his fourth novel, a Jay McInerney excursion into chic Manhattan. Are Rubin and Will, who had always been mutual admirers, doing battle now because Will has made it as an artist and Rubin is jealous? Or is the real problem that Will has fooled around with Rubin's wife, Petra, a onetime film actress played by Ms. Mason? Mr. Weller entertains both possibilities at random intervals without investing much energy in either, and he also leaves open the additional option that the critic is simply a murderous psychopath.

Both men are so empty, and so incapable of loving Petra or anyone, that it is hard to choose sides in any case. Sounding like a hammy road-company stand-in for Frank Langella, Mr. Davis does nothing to soften Mr. Weller's stereotyped portrait of the critic as bitter, preening windbag; the actor's mellifluous cadences, casual rustic fashions and wavy silver hair remain immaculately in place even when he is fighting to

the death. The young novelist — seemingly too young to have published four books, as embodied by the otherwise credible Mr. Knepper — proves to be a narcissistic denizen of Elaine's who is frequently caught in lies. Ms. Mason notwithstanding, even Petra sometimes loses her appeal as she alternately encourages both men with apparently arbitrary abandon.

•

In Carole Rothman's production, the characters' mixed motives and ambiguous loyalties, whether romantic or esthetic, never crystallize into coherence. Both the play's narrative and its style seem unfocused and fragmented. Act I, peppered heavily with double-entendres and the word "darling," could pass for an arch pastiche of an adulterous Pinter love triangle; the melodramatic violence of Act II, cleverly choreographed with the aid of Adrianne Lobel's imaginative sets, Kevin Rigdon's lighting and Mark Bennett's sound, could be an outtake from "Deathtrap." On the way to a fudged denouement, one also encounters a single funny joke (Rubin threatens to relegate Will's books to the syllabic purgatory of "suggested additional reading") and more than a few water images. (Didn't Mr. Weller get them out of his system in "Fishing"?)

There is also one moving passage, in which a sobbing Ms. Mason, torn between memories of an abortion and hunger for a new life, grabs greedily at Mr. Knepper as if happiness were something that could be seized from another's arms and thin, moonlit air. "Lake No Bottom," sad to say, never returns to the bottomless feelings plumbed in this scene, but one remains haunted by the image of the exposed and defenseless Ms. Mason, ready and eager to follow a playwright who will take her into the deep.

1990 N 30, C3:1

The Lunatic, the Lover and the Poet

Created by Brian Bedford; lighting design, Jack Jacobs; production stage manager, Murray Gitlin. Presented by the York Theater Company, Janet Hayes Walker, producing director; Molly Pickering Grose, managing director. At the Paul Mazur Theater, 555 East 90th Street.

WITH: Brian Bedford

By MEL GUSSOW

Brian Bedford's one-man show, "The Lunatic, the Lover and the Poet," is both an actor's celebration of Shakespeare and an act of Shakespearean scholarship. This enlightening anthology (presented by the York Theater Company at the Mazur Theater) chronicles Shakespeare's life through his words.

Exploring what few facts are known about the playwright, Mr. Bedford links art with emotion, tracing Shakespeare's romantic inclinations and familial concerns and his obsessions, emphasizing, above all, his commitment to the art of theater. This is in contrast to Ian McKellen's one-man show, which analyzed the nature of Shakespearean verse.

Mr. Bedford's approach is impressionistic rather than documentary. This is decidedly an actor's view, and, as such, it is free from pedantry. As was also true of Mr. McKellen's anthology, Mr. Bedford's show evidently derives from a deep familiarity with the work itself.

•

With the actor as our guide, we visit Kenilworth Castle in the company of John Shakespeare and his young son on the occasion of a visit from the Queen. The pageants that were presented for her benefit may have been William Shakespeare's first theatrical experiences, and Mr. Bedford amusingly demonstrates how they were parodied in the tragical mirth of "A Midsummer Night's Dream." As expected, the coda to the anthology is Prospero's farewell in "The Tempest," equated with Shakespeare's own retirement from the Globe Theater.

Following a chronological route, Mr. Bedford parallels the sonnets and the plays and plumbs texts for revelations and for opportunities for commentary, as in his playful suggestion that Shakespeare made "a fleeting personal appearance" as William, the rustic youth in "As You Like It." He makes the persuasive argument that Hamlet's advice to the Players is actually Shakespeare rehearsing his own company of actors.

•

Though most of the selections have a direct bearing on the central thesis (the balcony scene in "Romeo and Juliet" as an emblem of Shakespeare's youthful ardor), several seem at a distance. Mr. Bedford, who devised and directed the production, is not about to exclude a favorite soliloquy even if it does not fit strictly within the premise. This leaves time enough for "To be or not to be" and "Tomorrow, and tomorrow," in each case delivered with the actor's articulate inflections. On at least one occasion, he courts hubris: his distillation of "King Lear," in which he rashly leaps across several scenes to follow "Kill, kill, kill" with a cry of "Howl, howl, howl."

Although it employs no scenery and only minimal changes in lighting, the show achieves a theatricality, principally because of Mr. Bedford's zest for his subject and his versatility as a classical actor. This allows him to move from Romeo to the Old Shepherd in "The Winter's Tale," and to play both the low comedy of Bottom and the wit of Berowne in "Love's Labor's Lost."

•

It is no surprise that the choicest moments come in roles with which he is closely identified: "Richard II," whom he portrays with a lyrical self-awareness, and Malvolio (in "Twelfth Night"), who is hilarious in his lack of self-knowledge. For his one-man show, he extracts the essence of his Malvolio, seen in its entirety at the Stratford Festival in Canada, reproducing the scene in which the lovestruck steward is encouraged to make a cross-gartered fool of himself.

Mr. Bedford has performed Molière with great success in New York, but until now local audiences have been deprived of his performances in Shakespeare. "The Lunatic, the Lover and the Poet" is partial compensation for that oversight, presenting this fine actor in tragical, comical and historical guises.

1990 D 1, 16:5

The Infernal Machine

By Jean Cocteau; translated by Albert Bermel; directed by Robert Hupp; set design by Robert Joel Schwartz; costume design by Gregory Gale; lighting by Craig Smith; music by Ellen Mandel. Presented by the Jean Cocteau Repertory, Mr. Hupp, artistic director; David Fishelson, managing director. At 330 Bowery.

Oedipus......................................Mark Waterman
Jocasta.................................Elise Stone
Tiresias....................................Harris Berlinsky
The Sphinx................................Pascale Roger
Anubis..................... Keith Hamilton Cobb
WITH: David Cheaney, Jeanne Demers, Jenny Matthews, Joseph Menino, Abby Mentzer, Grant Neale, Craig Smith, Angela Vitale and Christopher Zaborowski.

By STEPHEN HOLDEN

In "The Infernal Machine," Jean Cocteau's 1934 adaptation of the story of Oedipus, the playwright and director lifted characters familiar from Greek tragedy off their pedestals and wittily humanized them while remaining true to Sophocles' plot.

Oedipus, instead of a tragic hero, is a cocky, virginal youth whose arrogance is matched by his colossal naïveté. In one of the play's key scenes he meets the deadly Sphinx, a bored young girl who becomes so infatuated with him that she slips him the answer to the riddle that will enable him to escape death and ascend the Theban throne. Without a word of thanks, he dashes off to claim his destiny, leaving her fuming. Later, in telling Jocasta of this fateful encounter, he embellishes the story to make himself look more heroic.

The relationship of Oedipus and Jocasta is treated as an extended Freudian joke. A vain, insecure woman obsessed with age, Jocasta has an eye for handsome young men, while Oedipus is drawn to older women who will cradle him like a child. On their wedding night, the newlyweds are constantly nodding off in the middle of conversation, as though they had to return to a Freudian dream to get their bearings. In its first act, the play also pointedly alludes to "Hamlet" in a scene in which two soldiers on the ramparts of Thebes encounter the ghost of King Laius.

•

If today Cocteau's arch modernism seems more playful than audacious,

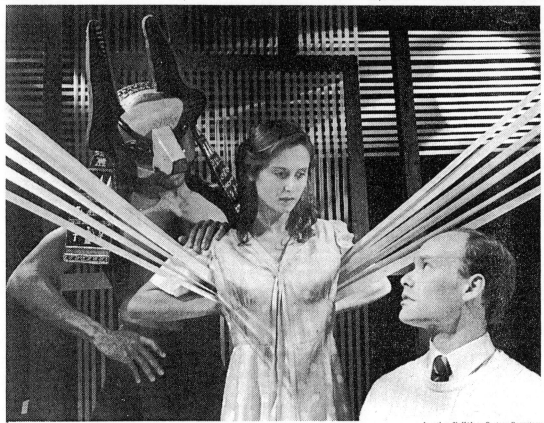

Jonathan Slaff/Jean Cocteau Repertory

Pascale Roger with Mark Waterman, right, and Keith Hamilton Cobb in Jean Cocteau's "Infernal Machine."

"The Infernal Machine" still conveys a good deal of energy and wit. And in its workmanlike revival by Jean Cocteau Repertory, the director Robert Hupp sustains a delicate balance be-

The Greek tragedy's main characters are part of a Freudian joke.

tween tragedy and farce. Without doing away with the tragic dimensions of the story, the production finds a lot of mordant humor in the story of mortals who are self-deluded enough to think they have outwitted fate and found lasting happiness.

The acting is consistent, though by no means brilliant. Mark Waterman may be too old for the role of a conquering 19-year-old prince, but his portrayal of Oedipus as a silly, hot-headed teen-ager who roughs up Tiresias (Harris Berlinsky) and displays the ego of a star athlete has an almost goofy energy. Elise Stone's Jocasta is equally self-centered. A honey-voiced diva, the character is as oblivious as Oedipus to all the ominous portents as she goes on fussing about her appearance. Pascale Roger's Sphinx has the look and air of a Victorian milkmaid whose spirit is going sour.

Robert Joel Schwartz's economical set and Gregory Gale's costumes evoke a zany neo-classicism that suits the mood of the play, which is, after all, still a tragedy, despite its comic frills.

1990 D 2, 83:1

Mambo Mouth
A Savage Comedy

Written and performed by John Leguizamo; directed by Peter Askin; lighting, Graeme F. McDonnell; production manager, Andrew Meyer; production stage manager, Joseph A. Onorato. Presented by the American Place Theater, Wynn Handman, director; Stephen Lisner, general manager. At 111 West 46th Street.

By STEPHEN HOLDEN

"You, too, can be a crossover success," announces the conservatively dressed Japanese lecturer in "Crossover Seminar," the final monologue of John Leguizamo's brutally funny one-man show, "Mambo Mouth." Crossing over, he explains, is "the art of passing for something you are not" to climb the corporate ladder. From a "loud, obnoxious Latino, holding my crotch for self-assurance," he says proudly, he has transformed himself into an affluent "Japanese warrior who listens to Lite FM." He proceeds to show before-and-after photos of other formerly flamboyant Latinos who have taken his course and emerged looking like drab corporate cogs.

The studious Asian lecturer is one of seven characters created by Mr. Leguizamo, a 26-year-old writer and actor of Colombian and Puerto Rican descent. Appropriately subtitled "A Savage Comedy," the 90-minute show at the American Place Theater finds Mr. Leguizamo portraying a spectrum of Latino men, most of whom are pathetic losers, trapped by poverty and driven by an obsessive machismo.

Mr. Leguizamo's hard-edged caricatures are offered without sentimental or intellectual cushioning. With the exception of the crossover lecturer, they reinforce negative stereotypes of Latino men as shallow, strutting roosters for whom every woman is a "mommy."

The American Place Theater

John Leguizamo in a scene from "Mambo Mouth."

A typical character is Agamemnon, the unctuous, self-aggrandizing host of a phone-in show on cable television, who advertises his availability as a lover to the women in the audience by boasting, "I'm not omnipresent; I'm only omnipotent." Agamemnon's teen-age counterpart is Loco Louie, a sex-crazed 14-year-old who meticulously re-enacts for his younger brother the loss of his virginity with an obese prostitute at Nilda's Bodega and Bordello.

Other characters include an illegal alien being transported across the Mexican border, a young drug dealer being arrested for the first time, a homeless drug addict, and a transvestite prostitute who describes taking revenge on a faithless Prince Charming by wielding an iron and some Krazy Glue.

"Mambo Mouth," directed by Peter Askin, recalls the earlier work of

Eric Bogosian, before he had refined his writing and performing into a kind of verbal martial art. Mr. Leguizamo is a promising writer with an ear sharply attuned to several vernaculars. What he hasn't learned yet is how to structure and edit his monologues so that each word has its own precisely calculated weight.

As a performer, however, Mr. Leguizamo is a master of body language and vocal inflection. His metamorphoses from adolescent boy to angry drag queen to make-believe Japanese businessman are eerily convincing. And, like Eddie Murphy at his best, he communicates with the audience a shared sense of reveling in his sheer, overflowing talent.

1990 D 2, 83:1

SUNDAY VIEW/David Richards

Laughing – Hard – Through the Pain

'Marvin's Room' treats mounting horrors with tenderness; 'Carnal Knowledge' is a true period piece.

HARTFORD

LOGICALLY SPEAKING, "MARVIN'S Room," the new play by Scott McPherson, shouldn't work. It is a black comedy with a big heart, and had I not seen it at the Hartford Stage Company in a wonderful production, all sharp and tender, I would have thought that was a contradiction in terms.

In what is only his second, full-length effort, the 31-year-old Ohio-born playwright is writing about a middle-aged spinster, who has devoted her life to taking care of her bedridden father and her dotty aunt, only to learn that she herself has leukemia. You can imagine how such a work could be compassionate, the way a TV drama is compassion-

ate, when it depicts the fight against a terminal disease or a horrible handicap for inspirational purposes. Or else it could be sardonically funny, the way the late Joe Orton's plays were funny, when they set about exploiting the indignities and miseries of the flesh for farcical ends.

But how could it be both? You can't have "The Miracle Worker" if you're going to make cracks about walking into the walls. And if Mr. Sloane is an altruist, there's no "Entertaining Mr. Sloane."

Black humor, after all, operates only when the object of its ridicule is at a certain remove. The closer you get, the more you feel the pain, and there go your laughs. On the other hand, compassion depends on the ability to put yourself in another's skin and that is about as close as close can get. Mr. McPherson's play should be coming apart at the seams from all the shifting back and forth. Instead, "Marvin's Room" advances un-

T. Charles Erickson/Hartford Stage Company

Laura Esterman, left, and Janet Zarish in "Marvin's Room," by Scott McPherson—Just holding on is a triumph of sorts.

Martha Swope/"Carnal Knowledge"

Judd Nelson and Justine Bateman in Jules Feiffer's "Carnal Knowledge"—The sexual games have become all too familiar.

erringly on its multiple fronts as Bessie (Laura Esterman), the evening's uncomplaining heroine, goes about her decidedly grim, decidedly comical, decidedly touching chores as the family nurse and general caretaker. We never get to see Bessie's father, Marvin, who lies inside his room — a glass-block cube, center stage, that could pass for a Con Edison substation. But we hear enough about him.

For the last 20 years, Bessie explains stalwartly, he's been dying "real slow so I don't miss anything." While he's lost the use of most of his vital organs, he retains a full head of hair and a zest for sucking on Yahtzee dice. Usually, he's "white as a bedsheet, unless he's choking," Bessie continues, before looking on the bright side and adding, "then he gets a little color."

As for Ruth, Bessie's flibbertigibbet aunt, she has three collapsed vertebrae in her back, which caused her enormous suffering until medical technicians outfitted her brain with tiny electrodes. Now she twists a dial in the box at her waist and the pain stops immediately, but the garage door flies open.

Exhausted from keeping everyone's spirits up, Bessie repairs to an absent-minded doctor who can't tie a tourniquet without someone else to put a finger on the knot and would probably be right at home in a Marx Brothers movie. Once he's drawn enough blood to appease a medium-sized vampire, he confirms her worst suspicions: she has leukemia, and a bone-marrow transplant from a close relative offers the only chance for survival.

Sobering as that news is, it gets worse. Bessie is estranged from the most likely matchup, her sister, Lee, an aspiring cosmetician with two obstreperous sons and enough problems of her own as it is. Ever since the elder son, Hank, burned down the family home — and a few adjacent dwellings — he's been on lithium in what Lee refers to pointedly as either "the nut house" or "the loony bin," but not "the mental institution," because she wants "to show we have a sense of humor about it."

Still, a crisis is a crisis and family is family, crazy or not. Mr. McPherson brings all his characters together at Bessie's place on the Gulf coast of Florida, where they try to sort out their prospects for the future, mend injured feelings and keep Marvin content, if only by bouncing the light from his bed lamp onto the walls with a compact mirror.

∎

I won't tell you how their saga comes out, but you'd be wrong to get your hopes up. "Marvin's Room," which originated last season at the Goodman Studio Theater in Chicago, is about living with minimal expectations and discovering that under such circumstances a little love can go a long way. However, you'd also be wrong to conclude, as you've no doubt already been sorely tempted, that "Marvin's Room" is a downer.

Just why this should be is best indicated by Mr. McPherson himself in a program note about his grandmother, the first "dying" person he ever knew. As he was growing up in Columbus, he recounts, she was wasting away from cancer "in the upstairs bedroom where the only TV in the house stood at the foot of her bed. If you wanted to watch Ed Sullivan, and I did, you also had to watch grandmother, commercials and morphine injections coming at regular intervals. It was a situation that, to a child, seemed neither odd nor morbid."

That matter-of-factness in the face of mortality runs throughout "Marvin's Room." "Can I go watch grandpa breathe?" asks Lee's younger son, as offhandedly as if he were asking to go outside and play. Aunt Ruth figures God has reasons for everything,

and if her body has begun to resemble a question mark, it could be because He wants to teach her "how to dress without standing up." (Until more satisfactory answers are forthcoming, she'll watch the soaps on television.) No one, you see, treats the mounting horrors in "Marvin's Room" as particularly unusual. They're accepted as part of the crazy-quilt fabric of life and that acceptance is strangely comforting.

There is certainly nothing heroic about Ms. Esterman, who looks like the stick-figure that children produce when they set about drawing their mothers. Yet, by refusing to be daunted by the magnitude of her tasks — she treats them rather as if they were items on a grocery list (detergent, potatoes, *injections*) — she suggests enormous reserves of courage. Sometimes panic flickers across her wide, luminous eyes, but mostly her eyes are wide with love for her odd brood.

Even Bessie's most humiliating moment is free of self-pity, as Ms. Esterman plays it. The character has taken to wearing an unflattering red wig to hide the ravages of chemotherapy. As a gesture of reconciliation, Lee (Janet Zarish, and she's perfect in her prickliness) offers to restyle it. Not wanting to reject the overture, but embarrassed to reveal the humiliating spareness of her own hair, Bessie hesitates, before her feelings for

the other person win out, as they usually do. Slowly, she tugs off the wig and, with a helplessness that desperately wants to convert itself to trust, hands it over to her sister. Ms. Esterman's exquisite performance — strappingly frail and cheerfully downcast — is no less a marriage of apparent contradictions than the play itself.

But then, the director, David Petrarca, has maintained a delicate balance all down the line — making sure that Mark Rosenthal's explosive anger as Hank doesn't overwhelm the confused decency underneath; or that Tim Monsion's buffoonish antics, as the inept Dr. Wally, don't defuse the gravity of his diagnosis. Like Mr. McPherson, Mr. Petrarca appears instinctively attuned to an absurd world that allows, for example, a happy-go-lucky carnival worker to go under for the third time because to bystanders on the shore "laughing and choking looked the same on Clarence." The director also knows just how much sentiment it takes to keep the black humor from degenerating into cruelty.

By the end, fate hasn't changed its harsh tune, but the characters are holding on, which is a triumph of sorts. Bessie is comforting her father, as she does every night. We see the reflections from the compact dancing over the glass-brick walls and hear the warm gurgle of laughter from within. And suddenly we're confronted with the loveliest contradiction of all: the surrealistic bunker that is Marvin's room actually houses something very close to joy.

'Carnal Knowledge'

Jules Feiffer's "Carnal Knowledge" was one of the more memorable, if unsavory films of 1971. With minor adjustments to the screenplay and the restoration of a few passages excised the first time around for their frankness, it makes for a perfectly forgettable stage play in 1990. The automatic response is to blame the young performers (Judd Nelson, Jon

Cryer, Justine Bateman) whom the director, Martin Charnin, has assembled Off Broadway at the Kaufman Theater. More experienced in the ways of television than in those of the legitimate stage, they can't begin to counter the impressions that Jack Nicholson, Art Garfunkel and Candice Bergen made in the film.

But I suspect the battle was lost from the start. "Carnal Knowledge"

David Petrarca, the director of 'Marvin's Room,' appears attuned to an absurd world.

may survive as a marker of where we once stood in the sexual revolution. But its banality as drama is increasingly apparent. It's become all too familiar — these sexual games played by men who grow older, but never grow up; and by women whose consciousness has yet to be raised and who therefore go along with the charade. As a bimbo who wants a marriage ring more than anything — and will grovel for it if she has to — Ann-Margret was hailed for a bruising movie performance that turned her image as a sex kitten inside out. Today, the character just seems dumb and indolent, an all too compliant victim.

On the tiny stage of the Kaufman, the scenery has been reduced to a few cubes and pillows and most of the props are mimed. The concrete details that would help pin down matters to a specific period and place are in woefully short supply. Furthermore, Mr. Charnin thinks nothing of keeping his performers on the premises, curled up in a ball or slumped over a book, while they're waiting for their next scene to begin. As a result, the production ends up looking curiously abstract.

If this stripped-down approach is meant to emphasize the timelessness of "Carnal Knowledge," it is a severe miscalculation. The time is very much mid-1940's to mid-1960's — an era that began coy and ended up permissive. Why ever would you choose limbo for the setting, unless it was to save a few bucks?   —□

1990 D 2, II:5:1

The Caucasian Chalk Circle

By Bertolt Brecht; adapted by Thulani Davis; from the translation by William R. Spiegelberger; directed by George C. Wolfe; choreography by Hope Clarke; music and vocal arrangements by Kweyao Agyapon; additional vocal arrangements by Carol Maillard; sets by Loy Arenas; costumes by Toni-Leslie James; lighting by Don Holder; mask and puppet design by Barbara Pollitt and Stephen Kaplin; associate producer, Jason Steven Cohen. Presented by Joseph Papp. At the Public/Martinson Hall, 425 Lafayette Street.

Storyteller, Woman Cook, Mon Oncle and House Servant ....Novella Nelson
Casbeque, Corporal, Laurent, the Landlord and the Odd Couple............L. Peter Callender
Mme. Le Gouverneur, Peasant Woman and Anique ....Sharon Washington
Simon Chachava, Landlord, Shadow Puppeteer, the Fugitive and the Lame Man......................................Kevin Jackson
Grusha Vasne ....Charlayne Woodard
Azdak................................ Reggie Montgomery
WITH: Fanni Green, Cynthia Martells, Patrick P. Mathieu, Luis A. Ramos, M. W. Reid and Raymond Anthony Thomas

By FRANK RICH

A friend who had never shown any interest in the plays of Bertolt Brecht announced that he was rushing to catch "Mother Courage" in London over the summer. Why? "It may be my last chance," he said. "Now that the Berlin wall has come down, I don't think people will bother to do them anymore."

Martha Swope/New York Shakespeare Festival
Charlayne Woodard as Grusha in "The Caucasian Chalk Circle."

He was half joking, of course, but who can doubt that the democratization of Eastern Europe and the end of the cold war have rattled the theatrical as well as the geopolitical order? Some of Brecht's plays, no less than Franz Xaver Kroetz's or Vaclav Havel's, are going to hit audiences differently in a world where Marx has been relegated to the back burner. More than ever, Brecht the poet, showman and theatrical innovator may upstage Brecht the political activist.

Whether by serendipity or shrewd design, that is most certainly the case in the highly imaginative, if at times sluggishly executed, adaptation of "The Caucasian Chalk Circle" that the director George C. Wolfe and the writer Thulani Davis have brought to the Public Theater. There is nothing Caucasian about this "Chalk Circle." Brecht's Caucasus setting has been switched to the oppressed, black, civil-war-torn Haiti of Papa Doc Duvalier and his heirs, and the original text's prologue, which sets up the entire evening as a Marxist parable about ownership, has been discarded. Written in the mid-1940's while Brecht was living in exile in Santa Monica, Calif., "The Caucasian Chalk Circle" has, one might cheekily say, been brought back to the beach by Mr. Wolfe and Ms. Davis.

•

They and their designers — the same inventive team that worked on "Spunk," Mr. Wolfe's dazzling adaptation of stories by Zora Neale Hurston — have done an irreproachable job of serving Brechtian theatricality within the context of their chosen setting. Ms. Davis's script, based on a translation from the German by William R. Spiegelberger, effortlessly remakes the play's language in the flavorful cross-cultural tongue of a Caribbean peasantry with a French colonial legacy. The story, in which a maid named Grusha (Charlayne Woodard) rescues and then spirits away the abandoned child of a deposed ruler, remains as universal as the biblical and Chinese legends that Brecht drew upon in the first place. Here as always, the tale reaches its

'The Caucasian Chalk Circle' in the Haiti of Duvalier and his heirs.

culmination in a farcical post-post-revolutionary courtroom, where Grusha must prove that she, not the child's biological parent, is the mother who truly merits custody.

It's with the stylized devices of epic theater in the evening's fabulist first half, however, that Mr. Wolfe can really run riot. The folkloric masks and puppets, designed by Barbara Pollitt and Stephen Kaplin, are spectacular, allowing even the Governor's Mercedes limousine (the hood ornament included) and the Black Shirts' motorcycles to materialize through jazzy mime and mixed-media collage. In one choice touch of magic realism, a sinuously entwined couple holding leaves stands in for a tree; a delicate shadow play projected onto a translucent quilt conveys the melodrama of Grusha's Eliza-like flight across a rickety bridge. Toni-Leslie James's costumes, especially the campy ones for the gilded, Marcos-style royal household, often contribute their own biting social commentary, reaching a witty peak with a pair of pseudobohemian, quasi-cubist court architects.

The set designer is Loy Arenas, who happens to be represented by another fairy-tale Caribbean island, right now, in the musical "Once on This Island." It says much about Mr. Arenas's artistry that he doesn't repeat himself at all here, for his "Chalk Circle" setting, a dusty village square crowned with a log canopy, is no less atmospheric than the last one, but far darker and earthier, a more credible environment for a society eternally shadowed by terror.

Even so, this production could use some of the musical-theater zip of Graciela Daniele's "Island" staging. Kweyao Agyapon's percussion-driven score, however authentic, is wearyingly austere, and it squanders the powerhouse singing voices of Ms. Woodard and Novella Nelson, the play's commanding storyteller (or, in this version, griot). While Hope Clarke's choreography is pleasing as far as it goes — especially in an early, twirling lovers' duet — the dancing is also kept on a tight leash until someone yells "Let's dance!" just before the curtain call.

•

If stronger song and dance might have diminished the repetitiveness in this three-hour show, so, in the second half, might have a knockout star performance in the role of Azdak, the buffoonish yet judicious judge who is at once a Brecht stand-in and a comic type alternately reminiscent of Falstaff and Groucho Marx. (Though Brecht specifically wrote this play in "revulsion against the commercialized dramaturgy of Broadway," he was hardly antipathetic to Chaplin and vaudeville.) The energetic Azdak here, Reggie Montgomery, becomes increasingly frenetic as his routine progresses, pounding in the character's message but rarely getting his laughs. This accomplished actor is just not the sort of natural clown

required for Azdak — one who can bring down the house with a simple smirk or a delicious pratfall in his judicial robes.

The rest of the acting by a hardworking cast of 12 is lovely, with Kevin Jackson proving a sweet suitor for Grusha and Sharon Washington, in a typical multiple assignment, having antic fun with female characters of various classes and dispositions. Ms. Woodard, a performer better known for her singing than her acting, proves a lustrous heroine, a tenacious yet hearty mother courage with a stage personality expansive enough to embrace Brecht's old world and this show's brave new third world, too.

1990 D 3, C13:3

Nightingale

By Elizabeth Diggs; directed by John Rubinstein; scenic design by William Barclay; lighting design, Phil Monat; costume design by James Scott; original music by Robert Waldman; sound design, Bruce Ellman; production stage manager, Kate Broderick; musical staging by Jane Lanier. Presented by Vineyard Theater, Douglas Aibel, artistic director-theater; Barbara Zinn Krieger, executive director; Jon Nakagawa, managing director. At 108 East 15th Street.

William Edward Nightingale and Dr. Hall .... James A. Stephens
Florence Nightingale..............Kathryn Pogson
Parthenope Nightingale........Pippa Pearthree
Fanny Nighingale.....................Sloane Shelton
Sidney Herbert ....John Curless

WITH: Robertson Carricart, Jane Lanier, Edmund Lewis, Elizabeth Logun, Jodie Lynne McClintock, Emily Arnold McCully, Patrick O'Connell, Greg Porretta and Diana Van Fossen.

By MEL GUSSOW

For Lytton Strachey, Florence Nightingale was a "woman of action" rather than the "saintly, self-sacrificing" Lady With a Lamp out of a Victorian dream. The truth is her life was closer to a nightmare. Possessed by demons, she threw herself into battle against disease, male priggishness and her own despair about ever being able to accomplish her goals.

It is this very human — and very heroic — Florence Nightingale who is the subject of Elizabeth Diggs's bold new play, "Nightingale." By defeating the storybook image, Ms. Diggs sheds a clear intense light on a true pioneer for women's rights and medical reform.

Ms. Diggs's play opened Sunday nightat the Vineyard Theater, after a previous engagement under the title "St. Florence" at the Capital Repertory Theater in Albany. Though some of the supporting players lack the necessary resolution for their roles, John Rubinstein's production is an improvement over the earlier version.

The production is especially fortunate in its casting of the title role with Kathryn Pogson. Ms. Pogson, who was the exceedingly impressionable Lemon in Wallace Shawn's "Aunt Dan and Lemon," reveals a steeliness and a firm sense of purpose as Florence Nightingale. In her striking performance, she merges aspects of Lewis Carroll's Alice and Bernard Shaw's St. Joan.

•

Her passion to be a nurse (a profession previously dominated by prostitutes) leads her into a black, comic wonderland, where practically everyone seems anxious to undermine her. In common with St. Joan, she is drawn to a divine calling and exudes

Kathryn Pogson, right, in the title role of "Nightingale" with, from left, Elizabeth Logun, Jane Lanier and Jodie Lynne McClintock.

a blind faith in her ability to transcend what others would call realities. In the case of Ms. Pogson, all this is combined with a nervous intensity. While family and friends toss quoits and exchange platitudes in a symbolic parody of courtly manners, she looks as if she is about to explode.

She is oppressed by a restrictive society, which treats women as chattel and soldiers as sacrifices. Some may look at this play and wonder if things really have changed very much. Look again. Victorian times were desperate, and it is only through dedicated people like Nightingale that changes occurred.

Her charge is first of all against the pigeonholing of "young ladies in mindless pursuits." They are meant to marry, have children and lead ornamental lives — and she will have none of it. In this regard her father is for a time her encourager (at least he allows her to learn Latin and Greek) and her mother remains her foe.

•

The most complex familial relationship is with her older sister, who is bitterly envious of Florence's strength of will at the same time she is fearful of her penchant for breaking rules. In the play's second resonant performance, Pippa Pearthree makes it evident that the sister has been as victimized by her sibling as she is by herself and her time.

Ms. Pogson moves from fretful child to uncompromising adult. The young woman who blithely declares, "I'm going to marry myself" carries out that solipsistic role as she matures. While avoiding marriage, she never for an instant fits the spinsterish stereotype. This Florence is a woman of great conviction and energy. It is her immoderation that leads to her triumph as a nurse during the Crimean War. Told that "war and medicine are jealously guarded male preserves," she breaks through locked doors. Singlehandedly she raises hygiene as a flag in battle, and reduces the hospital death rate from 76 percent to 2 percent.

Along the way she finds a faithful foot soldier in a high position, Sidney Herbert, who, as Secretary of War,

becomes the political pragmatist the idealistic Florence needs to further her cause. In one of the play's most moving scenes, she pushes her mentor beyond his own endurance. Unfortunately, Sidney Herbert is given a tentative rendition by John Curless, one of several actors in the company who are not equal to the demands of their roles. One exception is Edmund Lewis as a wounded soldier. Despite revisions, the play is still less trenchant about the male characters than it is about Florence herself.

In its style and spirit, "Nightingale" is not unrelated to "The Elephant Man," dealing as it does with the inhumanity of English traditions. As the play shifts between reality and dream, William Barclay's set design breaks free from the strictures of naturalism, flowing from Victorian parlor to battlefield hospital. During her time at the front, Florence communicates with Sidney Herbert by letters, which are artfully dramatized as dialogue. Scenes are defined without the help of projections or other visuals.

By disavowing sentimentality, the playwright makes her story even more inspirational. The focus remains riveted on the figure of Florence Nightingale, a visionary given life-size dimension in Ms. Diggs's play and Ms. Pogson's performance.

1990 D 4, C16:3

Sincerity Forever

By Mac Wellman; directed by Jim Simpson; costume design by Claudia Brown; set and lighting design by Kyle Chepulis; music by David Van Tieghem; production stage manager, Dan M. Weir. Presented by BACA Downtown, Charlene Victor, executive director; Chuck Reichenthal, program director. At 111 Willoughby Street, Brooklyn. (718) 596-2222.

Judy	Amy Brenneman
Molly	Leslie Nipkow
Tom	Zach Grenier
Hank	Patrick Kerr
George	Dan Moran
Lloyd	David Van Tieghem
Melvin	Frank Deal
Furball #1	Stephen Mellor
Furball #2	Jan Leslie Harding
Jesus H. Christ	Kenya Scott

By MEL GUSSOW

In "Sincerity Forever," Mac Wellman's savage comedy about everyday lunacies in America, two adolescent girls in a dirt-poor Southern town calmly accept the order of the universe. God must have a plan, says one, or why else would He keep both of them "ignorant forever in absolute sincerity."

Like everyone else in Hillsbottom, the two are wearing Ku Klux Klan costumes. They are blissful in their brainlessness, confessing they cannot tell good art from bad art and do not know why junk bonds are junky: The conversation dwells on important matters like boyfriends rather than on child abuse or the plutonium-poisoned water that is killing their community.

Mr. Wellman's view of contemporary society is dire but not doleful. In his headlong search for social and political commentary, he never neglects his comical instincts, starting with the fact that the play is dedicated to Jesse Helms. Though not mentioned in the text, Senator Helms is as omnipresent as air; the characters exist in an age of "infinite regress."

Sincerity is the key to that infinitude. The message is that one can do anything and say anything as long as it is said with conviction. This goes equally for questions of racism, religion and art, and, of course, confuses sincerity with truth.

•

While pursuing polemics, the author retains his role as a theatrical conjurer. "Sincerity Forever" (at BACA Downtown) is very much a heightened act of the imagination, the success of which is shared by Mr. Wellman's director, Jim Simpson, and by their droll, cone-headed cast.

The framework of the play is fantasy. A "mystic furball" has infected Hillsbottom. What, you may ask, are furballs? They are foul-mouthed aliens that look like partly plucked chickens. The two who have landed (or have emerged from Hell) are played in full comic plumage by Stephen Mellor and Jan Leslie Harding.

The grand furball design is to glitch Hillsbottom. Those two teen-agers (Amy Brenneman and Leslie Nipkow) are succeeded on stage by two crude dudes, and as the furball effect occurs, their dialogues are cross-pollinated. Deviously, Mr. Wellman churns the words into a Babel, so that the teen-age girls talk like beer-bellied rednecks, and vice versa.

"Sincerity Forever" does not follow a straight narrative path, but is brambled with digressions and allusions to Wotan and other figures from legend and mythology. A theatergoer may be mystified, especially by the sudden appearance of a character identified as Jesus H. Christ (who is black and female), carrying a staff and a lead-heavy suitcase that may contain the secrets of the universe. Behind the seeming blasphemy is a deeper sense of morality and a knowledge that a Messiah would be greeted with cynicism by these natives.

What connects the scenes is the evocative power of Mr. Wellman as word-spinner. As in his other plays ("Bad Penny," "Terminal Hip"), he writes a kind of rapturous rap — street language mixed with metaphorical flights of fancy.

Over the evening hangs an atmospheric dread. As David Van Tieghem's score curls around the dialogue, one realizes that those furballs could be fugitives from a David Lynch dream. But "Sincerity Forever" is very much its own thing, just as it is

becoming increasingly clear that, as a playwright, Mr. Wellman is sui generis.

In all respects, he is abetted by his company, beginning with Mr. Simpson, who keeps everything both eerie and matter of fact, a combination that enhances the menace — in the performance and in Kyle Chepulis's setting. The lighting is dim; the acting is bright. No one dashes for laughs. Instead, all the actors play with sincerity, absolutely necessary under the mysterious circumstances. Ms. Brenneman and Ms. Nipkow are twinned in their charm, blending innocence with insouciance, Zach Grenier is properly bullheaded as a redneck and, as the furballs, Mr. Mellor and Ms. Harding are a delirious double act.

•

Because of the play's graphic language and its approach to piety, some theatergoers may find "Sincerity

Amy Brenneman wearing a Ku Klux Klan hood in "Sincerity Forever" at BACA Downtown.

Forever" offensive, a fact that should please the playwright. Mr. Wellman does not play anything safe as he does his danse macabre far out on the cutting edge.

Mr. Wellman, who received a grant from the National Endowment for the Arts in 1990, had initially acknowledged the endowment along with other foundations as providers of support in the creation of his new play, but he removed the credit at the request of endowment officials. For the record, "Sincerity Forever" is the Wellman play that "was not made possible by the generous assistance of the N.E.A."

1990 D 8, 17:3

Generations of the Dead in the Abyss of Coney Island Madness

By Michael Henry Brown; directed by L. Kenneth Richardson; set design by Donald Eastman; costume design by Judy Dearing; lighting design by Anne Militello; sound design by Rob Gorton; fight director, David Leong; production stage manager, Ruth M. Feldman. Presented by the Long Wharf Theater, Arvin Brown, artistic director; M. Edgar Rosenblum, executive director. At 222 Sargent Drive, New Haven.

Reed	Isaiah Washington
Lena	Kimi 'Sung
Lenore	Lorey Hayes

Job	William Jay Marshall
Cody Cooper	Jeff Caldwell Williams
The Butterman	Jerome Preston Bates
Marlene Cooper	Petie Trigg Seale

By MEL GUSSOW

Special to The New York Times

NEW HAVEN, Dec. 4 — In contrast to Lawrence Ferlinghetti's poem "A Coney Island of the Mind," the world in Michael Henry Brown's play "Generations of the Dead in the Abyss of Coney Island Madness" is tangible, depicting a threatening portrait of urban insanity. A drug lord is king, corruption is endemic and parents instill offspring with perverse values. In Mr. Brown's Coney Island, everything is for sale.

As a work of theater, "Generations of the Dead" goes wildly awry. It is like a rollercoaster out of control, flying off its track in the middle of the ride. Melodrama collides with metaphor and the play's crackup is total. At the end of the evening, audiences at Stage II of the Long Wharf Theater may wonder why they have stayed so long on this journey while the playwright, in a series of events, undermines his characters and finally transforms the play into an unbelievable bloodbath.

Until that happens, Mr. Brown reveals a talent for conjuring characters and considerable insight into what has become a recurrent contemporary nightmare, verified every day in the news, of race turning against race and parents and children finding themselves in a family war zone. With bitter humor, Mr. Brown pictures various levels of black life, moving from the streets into the projects and to suburbia, where financial success can be wrongly regarded as a certification of social acceptance.

At the center of the play is a welfare mother (Lorey Hayes) who, though only 34, has already survived a lifetime of degradation in order to free her teen-age daughter (Kimi 'Sung) from making the same mistakes she did. But her idea of freedom is the opposite of uplifting. She encourages her daughter to entrap a cleancut young man from Long Island into marriage, so that the two women can share his inheritance.

Around them swirl a swaggering drug dealer and Ms. 'Sung's drugged-out twin brother. Each of these people and others are revealed with the pungency and the poetry of the vernacular. The characters are played with a visceral self-awareness, especially so in the case of Ms. Hayes. The performances by Ms. 'Sung and Isaiah Washington as the twins and L. Kenneth Richardson (who is also the director) as the drug dealer are permeated with authenticity, as each tries to perpetuate a self-designated image.

In Ms. Hayes's portrayal, her character is both irascible and ravenous, a grotesque apparition of motherhood and mother love. She will do anything to get her way, and there are no limits to her rudeness. Even as she goes through her monstrous acts, she is amusing and seductive — a gargoyle counterbalanced with common sense. Each of the characters, including the daughter's suitor and his snobbish mother, is defeated by a twisted purpose. In the author's equation, drug pushers are entrepreneurs and businessmen are con men, and it is a simple step from one to the other.

With "Generations of the Dead," two plays inhabit the stage simultaneously. One half is naturalistic, with a firm grip on credibility even as the behavior becomes increasingly bizarre. The other half is overwrought and heavily symbolic, and that is the play that unfortunately takes precedence. Clues to the work's eventual self-abandonment are planted early,

T. Charles Erickson/Long Wharf Theater

Kimi 'Sung in a scene from "Generations of the Dead in the Abyss of Coney Island Madness."

as Mr. Brown strives for a mythic level that is not within his grasp.

As director, Mr. Richardson is effective at handling his actors and maintaining a balance between playful humor and menace. He might also have acted as a stabilizing editorial influence on the play itself, guarding against the author's penchant for leaping into pretentious language and for activating violence. As Mr. Brown manipulates his characters, they lose their distinctiveness and are converted into clichés.

1990 D 9, 82:3

Love and Anger

By George F. Walker; directed by James C. Nicola and Christopher Grabowski; set design by James Schuette; costume design by Gabriel Berry; lighting design by Christopher Akerlind; music and sound design by Adam Guettel and Mark Bennett; fight director, David Leong; production stage manager, Liz Small. Presented by New York Theater Workshop, James C. Nicola, artistic director; Nancy Kassak Diekmann, managing director; Stephen Graham, executive director. At 31 Perry Street, West of Seventh Avenue.

Peter (Petie) Maxwell	Saul Rubinek
Gail Jones	Tonia Rowe
Eleanor Downey	Kristine Nielsen
John (Babe) Conner	Arthur Hanket
Sean Harris	Steve Ryan
Sarah Downey	Deirdre O'Connell

By MEL GUSSOW

Alan Dershowitz has said that while there is equal justice for the very rich (who can pay for it) and for the very poor (who, with luck, may receive it free), it does not exist for the broad middle class of America. The lawyer who is the protagonist of George F. Walker's black comedy "Love and Anger," apparently subscribes to that thesis — and has decided to do something about it. After suffering a stroke, he feels reborn as a renegade in the legal profession. Any deceitful means will justify his supposedly altruistic ends.

The view is unrelentingly cynical. For the play (a New York Theater Workshop production at the Perry Street Theater), it is also self-defeating. As the lawyer (Saul Rubinek) sinks deeper into misanthropy and into sermonizing, he becomes increasingly tiresome.

Mr. Walker, a prolific Canadian playwright, specializes in comedies about criminals and detectives, written, as in this case, in superheated, exclamatory style. As co-directors, James C. Nicola and Christopher Grabowski emphasize the cartoon nature of the work, leaving little breathing space between the verbal punch-ups, the moments of simulated violence and the offstage cacophony of urban sounds.

The lawyer's hectoring is partly relieved by the characters in his orbit — in particular, by two women who form an alliance to fight corruption in his name. Tonia Rowe is Mr. Rubinek's client — seemingly his sole client — who is trying to get her wrongfully convicted husband out of prison. Deirdre O'Connell is a former mental patient and a close friend. Despite (or because of) her dementia, Ms. O'Con-

Gerry Goodstein/New York Theater Workshop

Deirdre O'Connell in "Love and Anger," about a renegade lawyer.

nell makes more sense and wins more laughs than anyone else in the play.

While Mr. Rubinek is offstage concocting evidence in order to reverse the husband's conviction, the women find themselves cornered in the law office by two seemingly civilized figures of villainy. Led by Ms. O'Connell, assuming powers of attorney, they badger the invaders into retreat.

The tactics are intellectual (Ms. O'Connell pretends to be fully briefed on legal matters) and, finally, physical. Under the guidance of David Leong as fight director, the dynamic team demolishes its opponents as well as aspects of James Schuette's seedy set, a garage not fully converted into an office.

Ms. O'Connell is appealing in her dottiness. Like a sprite from another planet, she has the quirkiest of habits. Eating pizza for what may be the first time, she is disturbed by the clutter of ingredients on the topping. Her solution is to wash the pizza. This is of course about as hopeless a task as that search for equal justice. One of Ms. O'Connell's other wryly misguided notions is that she is a black person, a feeling she expresses with such conviction as to put the other characters in a quandary. Together Ms.

O'Connell and Ms. Rowe energize the play and define the legal argument.

Eventually, Mr. Rubinek returns and continues his machinations. On the side of his desk is a sticker reading, "High on Stress," which, as much as anything, sums up "Love and Anger." It is a highly stressful comedy that, like its hero, hyperventilates and ultimately succumbs to an anxiety attack.

1990 D 9, 82:3

The Gifts of the Magi

Book and lyrics by Mark St. Germain; music and lyrics by Randy Courts; directed by Carolyn Rossi Copeland; costumes, Hope Hanafin; lighting, Heather Carson; orchestrations, Douglas Besterman; musical director, Steven M. Alper; production stage manager, Robin Anne Joseph. Presented by Lamb's Theater, Carolyn Rossi Copeland, producing director; Clark Cameron, production manager. At 130 West 44th Street.

Willy	Richard Blake
City Her	Sarah Knapp
City Him	Gordon Stanley
Jim Dillingham	Paul Jackel
Della Dillingham	Lyn Vaux
Soapy Smith	Ron Lee Savin

By RICHARD F. SHEPARD

For the goggle-eyed, New York institutions seem best known for their large scale: a Metropolitan Museum of Art, a Lincoln Center, a rush hour and a Christmas spectacular at Radio City Music Hall. But for most New Yorkers, Christmas is a family-sized festivity rather than a Cecil B. DeMille production, and that is where one of the city's more modest traditions, the annual staging of "The Gifts of the Magi," comes into play.

This modest musical is making its seventh annual appearance at the Lamb's Theater on West 44th Street, and seven years, which has been long enough to establish something as an institution. The word "modest" is appropriate; it is not a great musical. The — book and lyrics by Mark St. Germain and the music and some lyrics by Randy Courts are pleasant enough, but nothing that will have you whistling as you leave the third-floor theater; at times, the volume produced by the two-member band blotted out the lyrics of the songs, which are not quite patter songs but lean in that direction.

The performance on the whole is not riveting, but there is something beguiling and attractive in the very good cheer and humor with which the whole affair comes across. Perhaps it is the theme, which has been taken from two New York Christmas stories by O. Henry and made into a confederated musical unity. Maybe it is the attractive personalities of the six players who radiate a warmth even when the parts do not fan it. Whatever it is, the one-act, 90-minute production, under the direction of Carolyn Rossi Copeland, works.

Richard Blake, a teen-ager who gets top billing, plays a Manhattan newsboy at the turn of the century. In that role, he serves, appealingly, as narrator, changing the scenes with a snap of his fingers and singing the songs. Paul Jackel and Lyn Vaux are the impoverished young couple who sell their best-loved assets to buy each other a Christmas gift. Sarah Knapp and Gordon Stanley are particularly gifted and funny in roles that require quick-change bits as restaurateurs, police, secretary, butcher, landlord and entire street crowd. And Ron Lee Savin is entertaining as the bum — that's a term that has disappeared from the lexicon in recent decades — who is determined to find a warm berth in jail for the winter.

In the evening, you can also buy a meal at the Lamb's before the show, a repast served beside a "roaring fire." For those who enjoy theater best on a full stomach, "The Gifts of the Magi" can make an evening that will generate a contented purr, if not the roar of a theatrical experience.

1990 D 9, 82:3

Telltale Hearts

By Joe Barnes; directed by Dean Irby; set by Charles McClennahan; costumes by Terry Leong; lighting by Ron Burns; sound by Joel Foster; production stage manager, Kathleen Mahoney. Presented by Frederick Douglass Creative Arts Center, Fred Hudson, president and artistic director. At 45th Street Theater, 354 West 45th Street.

Janet..Iona Morris
Michael..Tony Evans
James..Count Stovall
Charlene..Petronia Paley
Lola..Elain Graham
Marie...Kim Sykes
Kevin...Jack Landron
Bob..Fred Anderson

By STEPHEN HOLDEN

Joe Barnes's "Telltale Hearts" is one of the more ambitious plays in recent years to explore the mating rituals of young, single urban professionals in New York City. The two-and-a-half-hour comedy, which ends its run today at the Frederick Douglass Arts Center, follows six months in the emotional lives of four men and four women, all of them black and in their late 20's and 30's, who pair off and develop sexual partnerships. Eventually they must face the question of where they want their new relationships to go.

With an elaborate structure that crosscuts among the four couples and eventually brings them together in the same singles bar, "Telltale Hearts" has the form of an extended television play. Not the least of its accomplishments is its creation of eight characters who are simultaneously credible and engaging. Sev-

eral, like the gawky, gangling Bobby (Fred Anderson), who sneaks off from his girlfriend for weekly sessions with a therapist, and Lola (Elain Graham), a sassy Southerner with a rich fantasy life, are craftily conceived as comic caricatures.

The main drama revolves around the relationships that two brothers, James (Count Stovall) and the younger, Michael (Tony Evans), develop with Charlene (Petronia Paley) and Janet (Iona Morris), both strong, autonomous women who have everything except the perfect mates to which they they feel entitled. Bitter, cynical and wary of commitment, James has a history of leaving women at the first sign of pressure to commit. By contrast, the idealistic, slightly prudish Michael entertains the sort of old-fashioned romantic notions of courtship and happily-ever-after that the female characters daydream about.

Two parts situation comedy to one part soap opera, "Telltale Hearts" almost completely skirts any larger social issues to concentrate on its characters' psychological vicissitudes. The milieu it depicts, with its shortage of eligible men and its emphasis on material success and personal fulfillment, is almost identical in its values to its white middle-class equivalent. And the play doesn't question those values.

●

Overly studious in its effort to give equal time to everybody, "Telltale Hearts" is at least a half-hour too long. While its director, Dean Irby, has given the dialogue a tone that is appropriately hard edged and chatty, the pace of the production is sluggish, with the transitions between scenes often labored.

"Telltale Hearts," however, is consistently well acted, with the outstanding performances belonging to Mr. Stovall and Ms. Paley. Portraying complicated, strong-willed lovers in an intense power struggle that occasionally explodes with pent-up fireworks, they evoke the growing pains of an adult relationship that, despite its tensions, is finally too valuable to be abandoned.

1990 D 9, 82:6

SUNDAY VIEW/David Richards

Brecht Dons a Mad Party Hat

EVERYBODY'S WORKING OVERtime at the Public Theater to make Bertolt Brecht's "Caucasian Chalk Circle" vibrant and eye-catching. Everyone, that is, except Brecht himself.

The director, George C. Wolfe, has relocated the action from Soviet Georgia to a Caribbean island very much like Papa Doc's Haiti and treated the play as if it were a phantasmagorical bal masqué. Loy Arcenas, who seems to be the set designer of choice these days when it comes to the tropics, has taken the idyllic kingdom he created for "Once on This Island" and subjected it to the ravages of revolution and poverty, although it's no less picturesque for that. Toni-Leslie

James's costumes, raffish and wittily ostentatious, are the stuff of a dozen Mardi Gras floats.

And if people and puppets are often interchangeable in this epic saga of greed and motherhood, it's in no small measure due to Barbara Pollitt and Stephen Kaplin. They're responsible for the half-masks that turn the actors' faces into bold, porcine caricatures, just as they are for the various dolls and mannequins that come miraculously alive sometimes with no more than a wistful tilt of the head. Even Brecht's script has been given a good going-over by the playwright Thulani Davis, who has altered the vocabulary to fit the new latitude, added a lovely lilt and strewn mon dieu's, merci's and n'est-ce pas's all over the premises.

Then, there's Brecht, suffering the mad party hat that has been plopped on his head, perhaps, but otherwise being his same old pedagogical self. I know that's heresy. "The Caucasian Chalk Circle" is supposed to be one of his most playful works. If he is determined to discuss the nature of property and the obligations of ownership, he is also acknowledging in his fashion that entertainment can be a viable teacher's aid.

Presumably, the first half, which recounts the travails of Grusha (Charlayne Woodard), the plucky serving girl who takes an abandoned baby under her motherly wing, unfolds with the charm of a storybook fable. And the second half, which focuses on Azdak (Reggie Montgomery), the drunken chicken thief who becomes a high court judge in spite of himself, is claimed to abound in broad buffoonery. (The two parts, of course, come together

'The Caucasian Chalk Circle' heats up in the hands of George C. Wolfe and Thulani Davis; 'Lake No Bottom' pits writer against critic.

when Azdak is called upon to determine who gets the child — the aristocrat who birthed it or the peasant who reared it.) The charm has always eluded me, however, and the buffoonery, I dare say, is buffoonery as only an intellectual could conceive it.

Exercising boundless imagination, however, Mr. Wolfe and his company have raised the play's temperature about 50 degrees and actually got its pulse pounding in places. The act of resuscitation is never finished — a minute's inattention and you lose the patient — but Mr. Wolfe is vigilant. Nothing — neither people nor places — is allowed to stand for long before undergoing a metamorphosis. Using sheets on a wash line and a swatch of blue fabric off the back of the play's narrator, for example, he easily establishes the remote river valley in which Grusha is hiding out. But no sooner has the illusion taken, than he whips away the sheets to reveal, as if in a nightmare, the Black Shirts who are in furious pursuit of her and her high-born foundling.

There is also another explanation for the liveliness of the staging, and it has to do with Mr. Wolfe's predilection for constantly altering the scale of things. When you take into account her gold platform heels and her conical Far Side coiffure, Madame Le Gouverneur (Sharon Washington) checks in at over 6 feet, while her arms have been accordingly elongated, the better, I would imagine, to grasp the world's goodies. At that, she's dwarfed by Le Gouverneur, a scarecrow in full military regalia held high by one of the actors. The baby she so absent-mindedly leaves behind in the confusion of revolution, however, is a puppet, puny and helpless.

Fleeing into the mountains with the child, Grusha comes to the edge of a deep chasm and, although warned that the rope bridge ahead is frayed and ready to snap, decides courageously to push on. That much is life-size. But the crossing is depicted by shadow puppets, whose frail and stumbling forms are projected onto an upright quilt, and they could be miles away. Sometimes, it's simply Don Holder's lighting that skews the perspective, making villains loom large and humble folk look small. Other times, this being a land of voodoo and vengeance, the bodies are dangling from the end of a noose, which, needless to say, gives a man height.

When you further consider that a cast of only 12 is portraying more than 40 characters, that the masks are going on and coming off, and that the actor on all fours, snarling and baring fangs in one scene, is back on two feet not much later as a hired hand, then you may have a notion of the swirl that Mr. Wolfe has orchestrated.

And still, I hate to say it, some of Brecht's ponderousness pokes through, particularly when the play shifts to Azdak and his cockamamie conduct of justice. I wouldn't blame Mr. Montgomery, who is forever rocking on his haunches and giggling into his hand and generally giving out every indication that he is as good-natured as a clam. But Brecht's way with broad comedy is so close to bullying that it's never very funny. Earlier this fall, in the production of "Chalk Circle" that opened Arena Stage's 40th season in Washington, Lewis J. Stadlen tried another tack by making Azdak into a reeling ironist and succeeded only in conveying the impression that he was playing the role entirely out of one side of his mouth. I conclude it takes a very special clown to triumph over the part.

Ms. Woodard, bright-eyed and generous-hearted, has a far better time of it as Grusha and she matures convincingly from a coquettish girl to a fiercely protective mother. Ms. Washington's spidery Madame Le Gouverneur, and L. Peter Callender's Casbeque, a thug drawn from the ranks of the Tonton Macoute, make for grand heavies. Novella Nelson presides over the production as the narrator, and her graceful dignity defuses a lot of the schoolmarmish aspects of a character who is there, after all, to tell us to note that and now hear this and don't forget what it adds up to, either.

But that's Brecht for you. Not one to neglect a moral. The astute Mr. Wolfe is far more willing to let goblins be goblins.

'Lake No Bottom'

There's no love lost, I'm here to tell you, between the artist and the critic. But never before have I seen the contentious relationship depicted as a duel. Oh, I don't mean a

Martha Swope/New York Shakespeare Festival

In the cast of "The Caucasian Chalk Circle" are, from left, Patrick P. Mathieu, M. W. Reid, L. Peter Callender, Cynthia Martells and Luis A. Ramos—People and puppets are often interchangeable in this epic saga of greed and motherhood.

duel of words. Insults fly back and forth all the time in this business. I mean a real duel with real pistols, armed and at the ready, and a critic and a writer circling each other warily in the woods and just waiting for the chance to get off an unobstructed shot.

This, however, is the climax of "Lake No Bottom," Michael Weller's new drama at the Second Stage, which, I am hesitant to note under the circumstances, strikes me as petulant and overheated. But what the deuce. There is no way a critic isn't going to get into hot water with this one.

Quite understandably, Mr. Weller's allegiances lie with Will (Robert Knepper), a long-struggling writer who's finally produced a blockbuster novel to the disdain (and, quite possibly, the envy) of Rubin, the critic who championed him early on. Public clamor has pushed the book into its eighth printing and isn't that what counts in the end? Mr. Weller's case for the critic is not so strong, although, arch and superior as he is, Rubin (Daniel Davis) appears once to have functioned as a voice of conscience, holding Will to his best qualities.

Still, a critic and an artist hashing over their differences is the stuff of panel discussions, not plays. To complicate matters, Mr. Weller introduces Petra (Marsha Mason), a seductive ex-actress, into the equation. Rubin's wife, she was also Will's mistress for a while and seems prepared to reactivate the affair at a moment's notice. When Will is invited to spend the day at Rubin's isolated country estate — and the day extends to a night — professional animosities are quickly compounded by sexual betrayals. And before long, out come the pistols.

■

"Armed to the teeth under heavy camouflage. I'm reminded of Elaine's," quips Rubin before lurching into the woods, where the rivals

Before long, out come the pistols in 'Lake No Bottom.'

exchange as many insults as they do shots. "What you are, Rubin, is weather," bellows Will. "Sunshine one day, drizzle the next. Something to put up with until we can duck indoors and make new work." For his part, Rubin retaliates by predicting that future generations will find Will's name listed under "suggested additional reading."

It's all very, well, Slavic. — this muddle of jealousy, despondency and recrimination, played out by Lake No Bottom, the unfathomable depths of which are equated with Petra's enigmatic soul. In fact, Mr. Weller's dialogue is stilted enough to bring to mind those painstakingly academic translations of Chekhov that strain so hard for significance they mangle the poetry. This is not what one expects from the playwright who in "Moonchildren" (1971) and "Loose Ends" (1979) showed that he knows exactly how his generation speaks.

Under Carole Rothman's direction, the performers have adopted a slightly heightened tone that lends a vague sense of import to lines conspicuously lacking in urgency. For all their efforts, though, I never once believed that these characters had lives of their own. Mr. Weller is simply using them to get something off his chest. The drama is perilously close to bellyaching.

Effectively as Ms. Rothman has staged the duel, with multiple sets of curtains continuously opening and closing to suggest the endless forest, it, too, is rigged symbolically to make a point. Will's gun, you see, is loaded with blanks, which cause a loud noise but injure no one. The critic gets the ammunition and draws the blood.

So I should probably resist the unworthy urge to describe "Lake No Bottom" as "Chatty Chatty Bang Bang." □

1990 D 9, II:5:1

I Stand Before You Naked

By Joyce Carol Oates; directed by Wynn Handman; stage design by Bill Stabile; lighting design by Andrew James Meyer; costume consultant, Sally J. Lesser; production stage manager, Lloyd Davis Jr. Presented by American Place Theater, Wynn Handman, director; Stephen Lisner, general manager. At 111 West 46th Street.

Little Blood Button................Bronwen Booth
Wife of.....................Marguerite Kuhn
The Boy ....Penny Templeton
Wealthy Lady...............Nancy Barrett
The Orange.................Bronwen Booth
Good Morning, Good Afternoon
                              Marguerite Kuhn
Darling, I'm Telling You (Angel Eyes)
                              Annie McGreevey
Nuclear Holocaust............Nancy Barrett
Slow Motion.............Penny Templeton
Pregnant.....................Elizabeth Alley

By MEL GUSSOW

In an afterword to "The Assignation," a 1988 collection of short prose pieces, Joyce Carol Oates refers to the numerous vignettes as "miniatures" and "radical distillations of story." The origin of each, she said, lay in "desire inchoate, uncertain, unnameable." Ms. Oates's newest work for the stage, "I Stand Before You Naked," which opened last night at the American Place Theater, is an attempted dramatization of some of those miniatures and of others that derive from related sources.

In typical Oates fashion, the characters are women with desire; they are betrayed, sometimes by themselves. But what is effective in prose is not necessarily theatrical. In performance, the pieces seem flat and unfulfilled, as if each is preparing for a flight that never occurs. The stories lack the imagistic intensity necessary to bring them to theatrical life. The anthology falls short not only of Ms. Oates's longer fiction but also of her original plays, like the two recent one-acts paired under the title "In Darkest America."

"I Stand Before You Naked" consists of 10 monologues, delivered by women in moments of confessional reflection, in Ms. Oates's words, "waiting to be loved." The subjects include infidelity, bulimia and homicide and have an undercurrent of sensuality and religious fanaticism. In one case a woman has a conversation with her unborn child (whose voice is provided by an adult actor) — territory that has been pre-empted by the movie "Look Who's Talking."

Despite the title of the anthology, none of the pieces have a deep sense of emotional unveiling, the feeling that these are stories that are told from the heart. The model in the genre is Jane Martin's "Talking With," a distinctive montage in which a diversity of women reveal the obsessions that rule their dreams and their lives.

Ms. Oates's work would be marginally more effective if the production and performance had merit. But the actresses assembled under Wynn Handman's utilitarian direction (on the American Place's sub-basement studio stage) are for the most part unskilled in the soliloquy form. There is an amateurishness in the acting that makes the scenes seem as if they are, at best, hopeful audition pieces. In particular one story from "The Assignation," about a substitute school teacher's fleeting (and failed) sexual encounter with one of her teen-

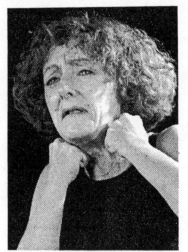

Martha Holmes/"I Stand Before You Naked"

Annie McGreevey in one of Joyce Carol Oates's 'miniatures.'

age students, reads better than it stages.

Only one actress, Annie McGreevey, is able to communicate an empathy with her character. In "Darling, I'm Telling You," the earliest written and the most sustained of the vignettes, she plays a murdered go-go dancer, speaking after her death and moving the audience back into the loose ends of her life. The actress does this with a naïveté that counterpoints the morbidity of the material.

In the prolific line of Ms. Oates's valuable contribution to literature and her continuing potential as a playwright, "I Stand Before You Naked" is peripheral.

1990 D 10, C14:1

The Big Funk

Written and directed by John Patrick Shanley; set by Nancy Winters; costume, Lindsay W. Davis; lighting, Arden Fingerhut; sound, John Gromada; associate producer, Jason Steven Cohen. Presented by Joseph Papp. At the Public/Anspacher Theater, 425 Lafayette Street.

Jill......................Jeanne Tripplehorn
Fifi..........................Jayne Haynes
Omar........................Graham Beckel
Austin.........................Jake Weber
Gregory......................Skipp Sudduth

By FRANK RICH

Whatever the ultimate fate of "The Big Funk," John Patrick Shanley's new play at the Public, you can be sure that people are going to be talking about the incidents that end its first act, henceforth to be known, I suspect, as "the Vaseline scene" and "the bath scene."

Shall we start with the Vaseline? Jill (Jeanne Tripplehorn), an attractive young woman dressed in red vinyl, is having a drink with Gregory (Skipp Sudduth), a seemingly nondescript young businessman with a British accent. After sadistically flirting with Jill by preying on every pathological childhood wound he can uncover in a first encounter, Gregory suddenly removes a "family-sized jar of Vaseline petroleum jelly" from a brown paper bag and sets it on the table. "I think you want to get a little shining," he says. Then Gregory rolls up a sleeve, and, sticking his hand all the way to the bottom of the jar, removes great globs of Vaseline that he methodically smears over the passive Jill's face and hair.

So, naturally, it's only a matter of time before Jill must take a bath.

•

The bath is given to her by another suitor of sorts, a young actor named Austin (Jake Weber), who fills a marble tub with water and bubbles as an Olympian orchestral arrangement of "Born Free" floods the scene. Jill hardly knows Austin, but he reassures her of his propriety by remaining dressed in a suit and tie

Being clean. Getting greasy. Being clean. Getting greasy.

while attending to her. He gives her a shampoo to the beat of "The Girl From Ipanema." He provides yellow plastic ducks and a white terry-cloth robe. "This is so much better than fighting with people," says Austin. "This is like another world," says Jill. And so she is liberated from grease until the Act II dinner-party scene in which she smears her face with olive oil.

But that's another story, and I must try not to be as digressional as Mr. Shanley, a writer with a gift for blarney who will try anything and sometimes gets away with it. With or without Vaseline, "The Big Funk" is very much of a piece with both the well-known screenplays ("Moonstruck," "Joe vs. the Volcano") and less familiar stage works of its author's career. The archetypal Shanley hero, as represented by Austin here and by characters acted by John Turturro in the plays "Danny and the

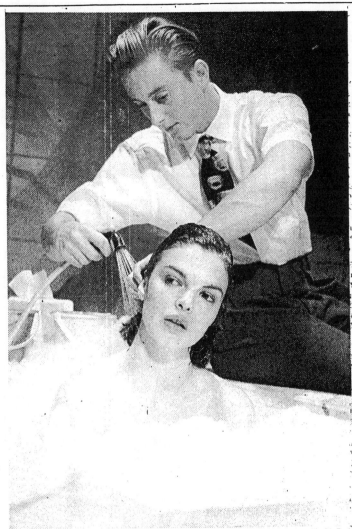

Martha Swope/"The Big Funk"

Jeanne Tripplehorn being bathed by Jake Weber in "The Big Funk."

Deep Blue Sea" and "Italian-American Reconciliation," is the one-handed pizza baker played by Nicolas Cage in "Moonstruck": a young man who has been maimed by the past and must realize an obsessive romantic fantasy to be made whole again. The archetypal Shanley heroine — whether played by the very appealing Ms. Tripplehorn or by Cher — must get past her own damaging childhood so she can grab that big-hearted guy. "Grease is not love," Austin instructs Jill late in "The Big Funk," as he helps her overcome a neurosis that traces back to her father's peculiar use of butter. The play's governing metaphor is that of a cleansing storm that will wash away the self-defeating funk of the entire world.

"The Big Funk" is a very uneven evening, alternately grabbing the attention and relinquishing it. But its faults do not reflect so much on the author's talent, which is real, as on his control of that talent, which can be lax. If Jill's misadventures with grease are the play's most memorable incidents, that is because they are also the most dramatic: with his heroine, Mr. Shanley works out his theme in visceral, not to mention viscous, action and images, and imaginative ones at that. The rest of the time he settles too easily for having his other characters, a one-time knife-thrower named Omar (Graham Beckel) and his pregnant wife, Fifi (Jayne Haynes), deliver his messages directly in cute, at times well-written but finally static soliloquies

that work overtime to be ingratiating. Listening to these overripe arias is often like being licked at length by a big, sloppy, watery-eyed pooch.

Here, as always, Mr. Shanley's philosophical ruminations do not benefit by being presented in unadulterated form. This playwright is in awe of love and the miracle of childbirth. He believes that "human beings are the absolute home of the unexpected." He believes, with Freud, that one must unearth the roots of one's destructive patterns to outgrow them. He believes, with Jung (who is quoted in the Playbill), that existence boasts "meaningfulness" as well as meaninglessness. The big funk engulfing society will go away if only all its alienated citizens might join Jill in that purifying bath, choosing love and life over defeatist neuroses and death.

●

So breathlessly and egomaniacally are these sentimental bromides declaimed in Mr. Shanley's work that one fears he thinks he coined them. Now that he serves as his own director, both in the theater and in film, there may be no one around to tell him the rude truth. Yet even as his sermons narrow into greeting-card messages, Mr. Shanley's ideas about the theater are expanding. "The Big Funk" takes all sorts of chances in technique, drawing on classical theater for its set, costumes and use of choral address while simultaneously mining absurdism for its bizarre, funny plot twists and Pirandellian shufflings of on- and off-stage realities.

As energetically acted by its entire company, "The Big Funk" is a play that can usually keep an audience intrigued even as it numbs the intelligence. The split between banal content and arresting style is typified by the uplifting coda in which Mr. Weber wanders on stage to deliver a reassuring pep talk about the delicacy of life, the precious "phenomenon of being a man" and the possibilities of hope. Though the words are no more inspiring than the lyrics of "Born Free," this epilogue is strikingly theatrical nonetheless, and pure Shanley in both its inventiveness and narcissism: The actor delivers his ode to personal salvation standing completely nude, now and again gazing in a mirror to contemplate his own private parts.

1990 D 11, C15:4

Two Gentlemen of Verona

Irene Haupt/The Acting Company

Jeffrey Guyton, left, and Rainn Wilson

By Shakespeare; directed by Charles Newell; sets, Derek McLane; costumes, Catherine Zuber; lighting, Marcus Dilliard; music, Kim D. Sherman; movement, Jim Calder; assistant director, John Rando; production stage manager, George Darveris; stage manager, Chet Leaming; company manager, Patricia Frey. Presented by the Acting Company, Margot Harley and John Houseman, co-founders. At the Borough of Manhattan Community College, 199 Chambers Street.

Valentine	Laurence Drozd
Proteus	William D. Michie
Speed	Rainn Wilson
Duke of Milan	John Michalski
Silvia	Stephanie Erb
Julia	Diana LaMar
Lucetta	Trish Jenkins
Thurio	Andrew Prosky
Crab	Maggie

WITH: Dan Berkey, Ethan T. Bowen, Matthew Edwards, David Eichman, Ben Eric, Mark Stewart Guin, Jeffrey Guyton, Mark Kincaid and Kathleen Mary Mulligan.

By MEL GUSSOW

The Acting Company has turned "Two Gentlemen of Verona" into an evening of comic horseplay — and the double meaning in that last word is intentional. Under the direction of Charles Newell, the production (at the Triplex Theater) is a far-West, free-range version of Shakespeare with cowboy references that roam from the Lone Ranger to "Blazing Saddles."

Not satisfied with the possibilities of a sagebrush setting, Mr. Newell has also made the comedy into a clown show. There are more red noses and floppy shoes than one would find at the circus. As a third layer of reference, there is a brief homage to the 1960's, with one of the play's two heroines, Julia, wearing a spire-high beehive hairdo. This means that when Julia poses as a

man in order to spy on her prodigal lover, she pops a ten-gallon hat atop the beehive, and later removes it in order to reveal her femininity — the show's funniest, double-barreled sight gag.

More than most other Shakespearean comedies, "Two Gentlemen" is an open-ended farce that lends itself to improvisation, as demonstrated a number of years ago in the delightful New York Shakespeare Festival musical version. The Acting Company is less disciplined in its approach. Win a laugh, and Mr. Newell's cast repeats the joke and then, vaudeville style, tries for a triple.

●

At times, the show seems top-heavy with low comedy, and certainly there is a surfeit of clowns on stage. But the zestfulness of the company never slackens. There is an imagination afoot, or, rather, a-horse. The actors are having fun with Shakespeare and the audience eases into the merriment.

One of the production's cleverest notions is to make the Two Gentlemen, Valentine and Proteus, white-hat-black-hat cowboys, respectively. Laurence Drozd's Valentine walks and talks with a swagger and William D. Michie's Proteus is unabashed about his deceitful shenanigans. Both actors are deft parodists who are also at home with Shakespeare's words.

The romantic rivalry between these two best friends is clear-cut and leads theatergoers to cheer Valentine and hiss Proteus, a fact that is in keeping with the participatory style of performance. Stephanie Erb's Silvia is a glamorous golden girl of the West and Diana LaMar is her opposite, a gamin-like Julia. They all act like castaways from a Hollywood western. When we first hear the strains of Shakespeare's "Who Is Silvia?," it sounds more like a wind named Maria. As composer, Kim D. Sherman has strewn cowboy tunes from Verona to Milan.

The Duke of Milan is played by John Michalski with the shiftiness of a movieland villain, and his choice of a suitable suitor for his daughter, Silvia, is the goofiest of bumblers (Andrew Prosky). There are a few inexplicable oddities, like giving Julia's maid (the amusing Trish Jenkins) one permanently raised eyebrow. But just when one wishes the company would cut down on the tomfoolery, along come four outlaws, a zany quartet of madcaps with fractured accents that turn the frontier into a mirthful melting pot.

Derek McLane's desert landscape makes colorful use of cacti, and Catherine Zuber has designed an odd bin of crazy-quilt costumes. One additional credit is worth noting. Maggie, the dog that plays Crab, is a canny Shakespeare canine. Maggie's companions on stage studied acting at a diversity of academic institutions including the Tisch School of the Arts at New York University, Southern Methodist University and Juilliard, the last the springboard for the traveling troupe. Together, the actors are a fresh, young Acting Company. Unfortunately, they are only visiting New York this week, performing "Romeo and Juliet" today and tomorrow, and "Two Gentlemen" on Saturday, before returning to the road.

1990 D 13, C16:5

Search and Destroy

By Howard Korder; directed by David Chambers; sets by Christopher Barreca; costumes by Dunya Ramicova; lighting by Chris Parry; sound by David Budries; production photography by Joel Greenberg. Presented by Yale Repertory Theater, Lloyd Richards, artistic director; Benjamin Mordecai, managing director. At New Haven.

Martin Mirkheim....................................Joe Urla
Accountant and Dr. Waxling...Jarion Monroe
Lauren......................................Claudia Feldstein
Robert and Ron....................Anthony Forkush
Jackie, Terry and Voice of Radio
Announcer.......................................Amy Povich
Kim..Keith Szarabajka
Marie...Welker White
Roger...Jeffrey Wright

By FRANK RICH

Special to The New York Times

NEW HAVEN, Dec. 11 — Martin Mirkheim — whose name is surely not meant to be confused with Michael Milken's — is an ambitious young man with no principles, no skills, no roots and a due bill from the State of Florida for $91,756, exclusive of penalties and interest, in back taxes. In "Search and Destroy," Howard Korder's new play at the Yale Repertory Theater, Martin (Joe Urla) does what any self-respecting man would do in such a predicament. He flees the law, his estranged wife, his Boca Raton condo and eventually even his name to journey across the country in search of a career in the movie business.

Martin is an American everyman with a dream, some might say, but that's not quite the way that Mr. Korder sees it. The hint of violence in the title of this pitch-black comedy is no joke. As Martin travels through the landscape in search of self-fulfillment, fast cash and show-biz glory, "Search and Destroy" unfurls a progressively more violent panorama of American life in which drugs, sadism, white-collar theft and murder finally converge in an almost pornographic shootout in a polluted swamp in industrial New Jersey. Only then is Martin at last ready to produce his first movie: a brain-spilling, guts-ripping exploitation quickie titled "Dead World."

"Search and Destroy" is a very adventurous play by a very talented young dramatist whose past works include "Boys' Life" (seen at Lincoln Center Theater last year) and "Lip Service" (seen on public television). Writing in a pungent staccato that recalls both his sometime associate, David Mamet, and hard-boiled novelists like Jim Thompson and James M. Cain, Mr. Korder tries this time to create an Expressionist hallucination about social corruption. Sometimes, especially in Act II, he pulls it off, achieving echoes of such highly stylized cinematic prototypes as Orson Welles's "Touch of Evil" and Roman Polanski's "Chinatown." The evening as a whole is not a success, however, in part because of the knee-jerk thinking and writing in the script's weaker episodes and in part because of the mostly inadequate acting in David Chambers's production.

The play's more inventive conceits leave one excited about its prospects for further development. (Yale is the second stop on the resident-theater circuit for "Search and Destroy," which had its premiere last winter at South Coast Repertory in Costa Mesa, Calif.) Certainly the character of Martin is a new breed of American monster for the 1990's, however little of Mr. Korder's conception is realized in Mr. Urla's frantic, inexact lead

performance. Martin is not so much greedy for money or power as eager to be "strong" for the sake of sheer strength, like a mindless predator near the bottom of the Darwinian hierarchy. He does not have bad values; he has no values.

"I believe in myself," he says constantly, repeating the credo of an evangelical self-realization crackpot named Dr. Waxling (Jarion Monroe), whom he worships in league with an insomniac populace of late-night cable-television viewers. But who is that self he believes in? Martin is empty, a blank. Though aspiring to be a leader, he could just as easily become a faceless follower of any other strongman who comes along, whether a manipulative cult figure like Dr. Waxling or a fascist Presidential candidate for 1992.

What makes Mr. Korder's vision scarier still is his ability to portray his protagonist's emptiness as symptomatic of a larger, national condition. While the plot of "Search and Destroy" sends Martin to as many destinations as Cary Grant visits in "North by Northwest," each locale is as faceless as he is. "It's an easy country to disappear in," Martin observes, for it is a country that has bulldozed its past and, with that, its moral legacy. As the cynical Dr. Waxling says, the only remaining American heritage is a theme park populated by Elvis impersonators and "200 personnel managers looking for a salad bar."

"Everyone here is from everywhere," explains a resident of Dallas after Martin wonders why no one he meets there has a Texas accent. This bleak homogenization is superbly visualized in Christopher Barreca's sleek set design, Chris Parry's light-

Gerry Goodstein/Yale Repertory Theater
Joe Urla in "Search and Destroy,"

ing and Joel Greenberg's slide projections: the hard angles, fluorescent glow and glossy surfaces of the country's new generation of post-modern, freeway-straddling office buildings and motels are ubiquitous, whether or not a scene is set in an "Omni atrium hotel" or a Rodeway Inn.

The hard edges of "Search and Destroy" soften considerably when Mr. Korder makes conventional connections between political and business chicanery, or when he mimics the Mamet tic of repeating a line of dialogue two or three times in succession, adding scatological punctuation with each repetition. But one wonders if even the weaker vignettes might not shine with more distinctive acting. Though Mr. Chambers's staging is fluent, most of his large supporting cast blurs Mr. Korder's acidly etched

caricatures as much as Mr. Urla does.

There are two exceptions. Welker White, the young actress who plays the dim-witted drug courier in the Martin Scorsese film "Goodfellas," contributes an eerie cameo as a blank-voiced receptionist with a gruesome screenplay under her arm. In the much larger role of an elegantly dressed "freelance consultant" who becomes Martin's entrepreneurial Svengali, Keith Szarabajka uses his cool good looks, dead eyes, an omnipresent curl of cigarette smoke and a deep, old-time-radio voice to create a soulless mystery man. His character has no discernible home, sexuality or precise job description; yet he seems to control all of Martin's actions from the shadowy periphery of every scene.

"It's a dead little planet we are standing on," Mr. Szarabajka concludes with sinister finality as he stands in the burning nocturnal haze of a refinery field, surveying his own criminality in a country where "polite young white men in well-cut suits" can sometimes get away with murder. When he is speaking, at least, "Search and Destroy" is not just a diatribe against that dead world, but a chilling horror tale about the living dead who plunder its grave.

1990 D 14, C3:1

Peter Pan

A musical production of the play by Sir James M. Barrie; lyrics by Carolyn Leigh; music by Moose Charlap; additional lyrics by Betty Comden and Adolph Green; additional music by Jule Styne; original production conceived, directed and choreographed by Jerome Robbins; directed by Fran Soeder; musical supervision and direction by Kevin Farrell; choreographed by Marilyn Magness; costumes by Mariann Verheyen; lighting by Natasha Katz; sound by Peter J. Fitzgerald; Neverland scenery by James Leonard Joy; flying mechanics by Flying by Foy; wigs by Rick Geyer; additional arrangements by M. Michael Fauss and Mr. Farrell; production stage manager, John M. Galo. James M. Nederlander and Arthur Rubin present the Thomas P. McCoy and Keith Stava production, in association with P. P. Investments Inc. and Jon B. Platt. At the Lunt-Fontanne Theater, 205 West 46th Street.

Wendy Darling ....Cindy Robinson
John Darling ....Britt West
Michael Darling ....Chad Hutchison
Mrs. Darling..........................Lauren Thompson
Mr. Darling................................Stephen Hanan
Peter Pan....................................Cathy Rigby
Mr. Smee...Don Potter
Tiger Lily...Holly Irwin

By MEL GUSSOW

"Peter Pan" is the musical that never grew up. It is locked in a time warp in which children can dream about breaking loose from their families and searching for lofty adventure, and adults can feel nostalgic about their lost dreams of childhood. When Peter Pan persuades Wendy and her brothers to fly with him to the world of the Lost Boys — in a Jerome Robbins aerial ballet — children in the audience may feel a similar surge to the open windows of experience.

For many, the musical will continue to serve as an initial exposure to the theater. This is in spite of the work's defects, which include an opening half-hour of exposition that may lull children (and adults) into thinking about other matters; a depiction of an insufferably patriarchal society, and a stage load of stereotypes and sentimentalities.

"Peter Pan," which began a limited engagement last night at the Lunt-Fontanne Theater in a produc-

tion starring Cathy Rigby in the title role, is not a musical classic. But as a theatrical fairy tale it seems to be perdurable, and there is enough entertainment value to make it an appropriate holiday diversion, at least for the very youngest members of the audience.

•

What it needs to fly is a magical central performance, such as it received from Mary Martin (in the original Broadway version and on television) and from Sandy Duncan in the Broadway revival in 1979. In both cases, the show was elevated by the

Carol Rosegg/Martha Swope Associates/"Peter Pan"
Cathy Rigby stars in the title role of "Peter Pan" at the Lunt-Fontanne Theater.

force of a star's personality, which did not soften the character's edges but made him seem like the kind of natural scamp one would follow straight on till morning.

Ms. Rigby, a world-class gymnast turned actress, has stage presence and a pleasant singing voice and, as one might expect, her physical capability in flight exceeds that of her predecessors. Maneuvered on wires by Flying by Foy, those masters of aerial theatrical engineering, she soars high above the stage, back and forth, in dizzying patterns that would dismay actresses without her gymnastic training.

On the ground, she is a resolute down-to-earth Peter, and it is a long delay between flights. She does not inspire wonder, and although that may sound like an elusive attribute, it is essential in projecting a Peter Pan in all his fantastical dimensions. When Ms. Rigby sings "I've Got to Crow," one vividly remembers Mary Martin's joyful cry (at this point, Ms. Rigby's voice sounds dubbed or, at least, overamplified). When she asks the children in the audience to applaud and re-energize Tinker Bell's fading wattage, the charge seems more that of a team captain than charismatic conjurer.

Still, the children at the preview matinee on Wednesday applauded, and Tinker was rescued once more. As an act of faith, the belief in fairies apparently extends to anyone playing the title role.

Even in its earliest incarnation, the show was an unsettled combination of ingredients, an uncredited adaptation of James M. Barrie's original play and songs (and additional songs) by a

This time around, Cathy Rigby's the one with the urge to crow.

quintet of composers and lyricists. The seams in the score show, just as they do in the book. It is a long step down from lilting songs like "Neverland" (by Betty Comden, Adolph Green and Jule Styne) and "I'm Flying" (by Carolyn Leigh and Moose Charlap) to "Ugg-a-Wugg." This is a show in which one looks forward to every reprise. One might say that the musical seems best when excerpted.

Stephen Hanan offers a broad, lip-smacking impersonation of Captain Hook, the hammiest of Hooks, which is not necessarily unsuitable. He is far less comfortable in the role of Mr. Darling, who in his hands seems too much a villain of the nursery. Tear off his paternal disguise and there would be Captain Hook. Lauren Thompson and Cindy Robinson are on a more even keel as Mrs. Darling and Wendy. Neither overplays the confectionary content of their roles. Children should also be amused by fluffy Nana, the dog as nanny, and the ticking crocodile.

The scenery (uncredited except for James Leonard Joy's cluttered Neverland) is serviceable. Fran Soeder's production is a reconstitution rather than any attempt at re-invention. This version is for traveling, which the show has been doing around the United States for the last year.

Were Mr. Robbins to have selected a second dance from the musical to include in his recent choreographic collage, "Jerome Robbins's Broadway," he would have found it exceedingly difficult. The flying ballet is a clear first choice. The other dance numbers seem to consist mostly of pirates and Indians jumping around in clusters. The portrait of Indians, which includes a simulated scalping, is one that should not endear itself to admirers of Kevin Costner's "Dances With Wolves."

Actually, it is another current movie that comes to mind while watching "Peter Pan," and that is "Home Alone," in which Macaulay Culkin fulfills his fantasies without benefit of a Peter Pan. His attitude is not so distant from that of the Lost Boys, who have fallen from their prams and have then discovered a life unencumbered by parental guidance. It is that feeling of childlike independence and disrespect that gives "Peter Pan" — the original story and play as well as the musical — its resilience.

1990 D 14, C3:4

SUNDAY VIEW/David Richards

Disenchanted, Yes, But Trying to Laugh

In John Patrick Shanley's 'Big Funk,' soap is the solution; in George F. Walker's 'Love and Anger,' the goal is getting even.

WHATEVER ELSE IT'S REmembered for — and that will probably not be a great deal — "The Big Funk" by John Patrick Shanley may nonetheless take credit for momentarily elevating the bubble bath to a position of prominence in the theater.

The cinema has always appreciated the peekaboo possibilities of suds, of course, and television soap commercials are forever showing us how mountains of foam make for a happy all-American family. But the last time I saw someone luxuriating in a tub on stage was a revival of "The Women" by Clare Booth Luce. The woman in question was a catty husband-stealer, and her willingness to loll about all day in hot water was equated with her brazen lack of morals.

Mr. Shanley has far sweeter purposes in mind, when the curtains at the Public The-

ater's Anspacher Theater part to reveal a pink and rose marble tub and in it, a very recalcitrant young woman named Jill (Jeanne Tripplehorn) whose experiences with the opposite sex have tended up to this point to be highly degrading. Only a few scenes earlier, in fact, we are privy to a characteristically disastrous date — this one with a British lout, who plops a family-size jar of Vaseline on the cafe table and then says in a tone Rasputin would have applauded, "I think you want to get a little shiny. I think you want to get a little greasy."

■

Thereupon, while she sits passively and he hums "It's a Long Way to Tipperary," he proceeds to smear her face and hair with petroleum jelly. She is eventually saved from this humiliation by Austin (Jake Weber) — an unemployed actor, the self-proclaimed hero of the play and, it would appear, Mr. Shanley's mouthpiece, although I should point out that all the characters spend a large part of their time sharing their musings on life and death with the audience. Viewing himself as something of a constructive person, Austin convinces Jill to come home with him and let him clean her up. Which is more or less how she winds up in that tub — her teeth on edge and her body steeled against who knows what perversity to come.

But no. Austin is just what he says he is — a man who's only trying to tidy up a small corner of a messy universe every day — and he's put on a blue suit to show his honorable intentions. "This is so much better than fighting with people in the street," he reassures Jill, as he squeezes a wet sponge over her head and lathers up her hair. "The Girl From Ipanema" is playing on the tape deck, his touch is gentle and after a while even she has begun to wiggle her toes with enjoyment. Once she's whistle-clean, Austin helps her out of the tub, dusts her down with a circus-sized powder puff, then, surveying his work, proclaims proudly, "Good as new."

■

As Mr. Shanley himself has staged the scene and Mr. Weber and the beauteous Ms. Tripplehorn play it, it's oddly beguiling — a little bit of Eden reclaimed from what the playwright clearly sees as a neurotic, self-destructive world, suffering from near terminal paralysis.

Were it not for a persistent optimism-in-spite-of-it-all (Mr. Shanley is, we shouldn't forget, the author of the buoyant screenplay for "Moonstruck"), "The Big Funk" could easily be mistaken for any number of anxious plays that came to be known collectively as the theater of the absurd a few decades ago. In them, language was turned inside out and shown to be useless. Human behavior was deemed unfathomable — which reduced people to the status of puppets or automatons. Society was degenerating into chaos, God was apparently dead, and the big void, if not the big funk, was lapping up against life's very edges.

Mr. Shanley would seem to have no argument with that. He has even adapted many of the standard practices of the absurdists, discarding traditional narrative for a topsy-turvy structure that is held together as much by free association as anything else. Among his unconventional characters are Omar, "a family man," who for a living throws knives at a one-inch black dot from 35 paces; and Fifi, Omar's wife, who announces abruptly that she is pregnant with twins which she'll be birthing tomorrow. When Omar admits, "I'm trying to like break into a new way of speaking that'll rip the television set outta my head," we may presume that he's also expressing Mr. Shanley's ambitions as well.

Well, television "The Big Funk" isn't. But it isn't particularly captivating theater, either. Mr. Shanley's sense of the ridiculous and his social conscience make for a very uneasy blend. Off-the-wall reflections exist side by side with grand pronouncements on everything from fate ("a miracle that gives you a job") to happiness ("a side issue . . . it comes to you while you do other things . . . like grace"). The two don't complement each other so much as they tug the play in opposite directions.

The dinner party that constitutes most of Act II comes close to pure surrealism. Omar's wearing Viking horns. Fifi, the dutiful hostess, is armed with a four-foot pepper grinder. Jill is facing enough salad to feed an army of rabbits. The conversation is decidedly screwy. Before the coffee has been served, Austin excuses himself, disappears off stage and then reappears soon after, naked as a jaybird. We've all had dreams like that, although, unlike Austin, we don't necessarily cap them off by delivering a long, socially relevant speech.

Austin wants us to know, however, that we're tense and sweating and living our lives as if death were imminent, when we're the very ones, not destiny, who are responsible for this big thundercloud, this big funk, overhead. And just as we've created it with our anxieties, we can dispel it, if we "relax" and "be casual." I'm not sure the speech amounts to much more than Roosevelt's "The only thing we have to fear is fear itself," retooled for the dazed 1990's. But Mr. Weber delivers the message genuinely under difficult working conditions.

Mixed signals are coming at us all evening long, however. Strangely as it sometimes behaves, "The Big Funk" is never giddy enough to defy gravity. Insightful as it wants to be, it is loath to admit to preaching, when that's precisely what it's doing. The most charming interlude is a wash. So, I'm afraid, is the rest of the play.

'Love and Anger'

In "Filthy Rich," his zesty 1979 tribute to all the grade-B detective flicks you ever saw, the Canadian playwright George F. Walker drafted a hard-boiled, ex-investigative reporter to fight the forces of corruption in The Big City. At best, the battle ended in a stalemate. Now in his comedy "Love and Anger," which is being given its American premiere by the New York Theater Workshop at the Perry Street Theater, he has put a lawyer on the job. But you can't call it a draw this time.

Either the privileged classes are becoming more entrenched or Mr. Walker's crusaders are becoming more inept. Actually, I suspect it's a matter of both. Mr. Walker is no less disenchanted with the times than Mr. Shanley is, although he relies on a more straightforward dramaturgy to depict chicanery in places high and low. His heavy is the ruthless publisher of The World Today, a big-circulation rag, who doesn't like anyone defacing his vending machines, let alone his reputation. Opposing him on wobbly pins is Peter (Petie) Maxwell, a high-octane corporate lawyer until a stroke reordered his priorities and brought him around to the side of the downtrodden.

Petie has no more principles than before, mind you. He's just decided to apply the lack of them to the goal of undermining "the entire institutional bias of our culture." Proclaiming himself a citizen of a new era, he explains with a feistiness that threatens his already shaky equilibrium, "I call this the age of getting even."

■

As played by Saul Rubinek, a schmoo-shaped dynamo when he isn't momentarily having one of his dizzy spells, Petie could be the fifth Marx Brother — Pinko. He's got a pit bull's tenacity, an anarchist's madness and a tent preacher's indignation, and he's quite funny — careering about the hole in the wall he calls an office or charging up the steps and out the door in pursuit of the evidence that will bring the publisher to his knees. (When it is pointed out that his pitiful evidence boils down to a few flagrantly doctored photos, Petie doesn't blink. "They can be improved," he snaps.)

Even funnier is Sarah (Deirdre O'Connell), a schizophrenic who has just been released from a mental institution and turns up in Petie's office, where she has little trouble fitting right in. Sarah believes deeply in the conspiracy of "beefy white guys" who surround small towns with their tractor-trailer trucks before taking them over. She tends to confuse males in evening dress with vampires and is not comfortable in the presence of pizza. Despite a tumble of red hair and a complexion that would be the envy of any Irish milkmaid, Sarah also thinks she is black.

Martha Swope/New York Shakespeare Festival

Surrealism on the menu in "The Big Funk": from left, Graham Beckel, Jayne Haynes, Jake Weber and Jeanne Tripplehorn—a persistent optimism-in-spite-of-it-all

Gerry Goodstein/New York Theater Workshop

From left, Tonia Rowe, Saul Rubinek and Steve Ryan in "Love and Anger"—chicanery in places high and low

This makes her a natural ally, if an altogether unpredictable one, in Petie's assault on the citadels of power.

There is a lot of the young Sandy Dennis in Ms. O'Connell, who can inject a sudden gurgle of laughter into a lamentation or bring the tone of sweetest reason to bear on the most outlandish observation. The performance zigzags all over the lot, but hewing to some wild, emotional logic of her own, the actress never leaves you behind. In the play's best scene, she and the newspaper publisher (Arthur Hanket, adroitly walking the fine line separating sleek from oily) come to a meeting of the minds, although it's clear to us, if not immediately to him, that her mind has the general consistency of fruitcake.

Sanity is not quite so colorfully depicted by Mr. Walker. Still, you're

In 'Love and Anger,' the rich and mighty are only temporarily at bay.

not apt to overlook Steve Ryan, as an aspiring politican, well bred and better connected, who promises, "If I am elected, I'll keep a ... what's that

thing? ... Open mind!" Or Kristine Nielsen, who was so vivid presiding over the switchboard in "Machinal" earlier this season and is here having an understandably rougher time, maintaining order as Petie's Gal Friday. Or Tonia Rowe, who gets the whole play rolling when she enlists Petie to help spring her innocent husband from jail. ("Innocent?," he snorts. "More and more I hear that word less and less.")

Mr. Walker's characters are far and away what is most vigorous about "Love and Anger." In Act I they sound one another out, draw up sides and face off in a stupendous cat and dog fight that threatens to demolish Petie's office and put them in traction for the next six months. From then on, though, a lot of steam goes out of the tale and the directors James C. Nicola and Christopher Grabowski don't seem to be able to do much about it.

Act II is given over to a mock trial of the newspaper baron and a second fight that can't hold a baseball bat to the first. By this time, Petie is growing short of breath and his eyes are glassing over. His tirades have turned to whimpers. All he and his unlikely cohorts have done is hold the rich and mighty temporarily at bay.

"This has got to be a place for winners," barks the publisher, with the authority of the victorious.

"We've got to keep up the momentum. Let the slower people pick up the jet stream. That's our only choice. We've got to get richer. The only alternative is to get poorer."

Sound familiar? Consider "Love and Anger" a fitting addendum to the Reagan years. And know that the first half, at least, is nutty, knockabout fun. □

1990 D 16, II:5:1

The American Plan

By Richard Greenberg; directed by Evan Yionoulis; sets by James Youmans; costumes by Jess Goldstein; lighting by Donald Holder; sound and original music, Thomas Cabaniss; production stage manager, Richard Hester. Presented by Manhattan Theater Club, Lynne Meadow, artistic director; Barry Grove, managing director. At City Center, 131 West 55th Street.

Lili Adler	Wendy Makkena
Nick Lockridge	D. W. Moffett
Eva Adler	Joan Copeland
Olivia Shaw	Yvette Hawkins
Gil Harbison	Jonathan Walker

By FRANK RICH

The time is 1960, the place the Catskills, and Nick Lockridge of all people finds himself summering in a Jewish hotel where the food is dished out round the clock according to the American plan. Nick (D. W. Moffett), a handsome young Time magazine writer whose square jaw and Darien manners match his F. Scott Fitzgeraldesque name, has never seen such an excessive regimen of meals and snacks. "What Americans live like this?" he asks in affable disbelief.

But in "The American Plan," Richard Greenberg's first play since "Eastern Standard," the American plan isn't just a matter of enforced menus for resort vacationers. The American plan is instead symptomatic of a larger fate that finally engulfs each of Mr. Greenberg's five very different characters, the golden Nick not excluded. Set for most of its length during the last summer of the Eisenhower years, this sorrowful comedy tells of people who are in one way or another at odds with the ethnic, intellectual or sexual codes by which Americans of their time are required to live. When the play ends a decade later — in an epilogue set in a Central Park West parlor pointedly overlooking a Vietnam-era demonstration — the conformist American plan may be under attack, but not soon enough to rescue Mr. Greenberg's characters from the tragedy of assimilation.

I have some serious reservations about "The American Plan" — about both the play itself and Evan Yionoulis's staging of it at the Manhattan Theater Club — but none of them prevented me from being devastated by Mr. Greenberg's denouement or from being awestruck once again by his precocious talent. (He is still in his early 30's.) As this playwright has demonstrated since his earliest works at the Ensemble Studio Theater, "The Bloodletters" and "Life Under Water" (later seen on public television), he remains a tender, ecumenical champion of individualists who are crushed by society, whether they be Jews or lonely post-adolescents or homosexuals or artists or even outwardly self-assured WASP's like Nick. Yet Mr. Greenberg would rather exercise his highly articulate wit and boundless empathy than moralize, which is one reason why "East-

ern Standard," a screwball comedy in which not unsympathetic yuppies foolishly adopted a bag lady, went right over the heads of its more pompous critics.

"The American Plan" is more melancholy in tone. And given its author's concern for fragile souls who are destroyed by the world's mendacity, it is not surprising that its basic premise owes something to "The Glass Menagerie": Nick is a gentleman caller who crosses a Catskill lake to rescue Lili (Wendy Makkena), the lonely, oppressed daughter of the widowed Eva Adler (Joan Copeland), a wealthy refugee from Hitler's Germany. After that, most resemblances to Tennessee Williams end. Mr. Greenberg's voice — he describes Time magazine as "the weekly cultural epiphany" and a domineering Jewish mother as a "late Ibsenesque figure with mah-jongg tiles" — is purely his own. This play, though, is kept so firmly in period that it at times seems a literary cousin of such roughly contemporaneous phenomena as Herman Wouk's "Marjorie Morningstar" and J. D. Salinger's stories of the Glass family.

If Lili is a Laura Wingfield, she is a decidedly Jewish one, a Sarah Lawrence dropout who is too smart for her own good and so sensitive she seems to court psychological collapse whenever exposed to any environment more volatile than "rooms heavy with damask and Sabbath light." Nick, her putative savior, is no ordinary Joe but "a prince," an aspiring architect who would "like to build a whole city" once he has left behind his transient post-collegiate career in Luce journalism. While Lili feels that "everything I've ever done was something that happened to me," the buoyant Nick looks as if "nothing ever happened" to him. "I cause happiness — that's what I do," he says.

The problem for these soon rhapsodic young lovers — and to some extent the problem of the play — is Eva, who is not merely a suffocating mother but a liar and manipulator who will stop at nothing to keep Lili from leaving home for Nick. Eva's nasty intrigues add a lot of flabby narrative repetitiveness to "The American Plan," too much of it laborious subterfuge to camouflage another buried plot that won't be revealed here. Nor do Mr. Greenberg or Ms. Copeland bring enough balance to the mother, once her initially amusing Eastern European worldliness gives way to pure destructiveness. Though the playwright provides an intellectual rationale for Eva's behavior, she remains that rare Greenberg character whom the audience does not see compassionately, from the inside.

Even so, Eva's defeatist view of life, a legacy of her narrow escape on the last boat out of Germany, is provocative. "The world has a wish of its own for you, and it's never good," she says definitively. Eva sees figurative Nazis everywhere in her adopted country and blames gentile businessmen for the destruction of her husband, an inventor. Under her philosophy, even the perennial Catskills game of Simon Says can be interpreted as a sublimated replay of Jewish annihilation.

The sadness of "The American Plan" is not only that Eva holds her daughter a hostage to the neurotic patterns of her grim history lesson, but that her fatalistic view of an intolerant and unyielding world is also borne out by the lives of Ameri-

Gerry Goodstein/Manhattan Theater Club

Wendy Makkena as Lili Adler and D. W. Moffett as Nick Lockridge in a scene from "The American Plan."

cans as disparate as Nick and the Adler household's loyal but sphinx-like black maid, played with buried bitterness by Yvette Hawkins. "Happiness exists, but it's for other people" — Eva's credo — becomes a universal one for Mr. Greenberg's characters by the play's 1970 coda. Only the demonstrators in Central Park offer any small hope for a new order of justice for those who do not fit in with those "other people," the American majority.

The urgency of what "The American Plan" has to say is not always conveyed by Ms. Yionoulis's direction. The lethargic pacing and nostalgic tone of Act I — reinforced by James Youmans's realistic woodsy setting and the dithering woodwinds of Thomas Cabaniss's incidental music — are too ironic by half. An audience should not have to wait until well after intermission for a play to stop being coy about its intentions. Ms. Yionoulis can be congratulated, however, on her guidance of the acting partnership of Ms. Makkena and Mr. Moffett, who make an enchanting pair of unlikely lovers in Act I before lighting out for other territory in Act II.

Lili and Nick show off Mr. Greenberg's range — in depicting women and men, Jews and WASP's — and the playwright, in turn, gives two young actors a chance to show off theirs. Lili, the victimized overgrown girl to whom things always happened, finally must make a choice in "The American Plan," and once she does, Ms. Makkena metamorphoses harrowingly from a difficult, teary child into a resigned adulthood choked by pearls. For his part, Nick, the privileged boy to whom nothing ever happened, is visited by life at last, and he, too, enters a defeated adulthood, which Mr. Moffett conveys by seeming just a shade too small for his broad smile and Brooks Brothers suit.

"It's such a relief to find your place in life, don't you think?" he says to Ms. Makkena as they reach the resolution of their story. But there is no relief for the audience, only a kind of horror at seeing exactly what that place is. The all-American portrait, suitable for framing, in which Mr. Greenberg leaves his characters trapped at the end of "The American Plan" looks too inhuman to be mistaken for anything other than a deadly lie.

1990 D 17, C11:1

The Voice of the Prairie

By John Olive; directed by John Daines; scene design by Randall Etheredge; lighting, Philip Monat; costumes, Kathryn Wagner; sound, Richard Rose; sound consultant, Stuart Bernstein; production stage manager, Randy Lawson. Presented by Chelsea Stage, Geoffrey Sherman, artistic director; Dara Hershman, managing director. At 441 West 26th Street.

Actor 1 .... Kevin Geer
Actor 2 .... Jack Cirillo
Actor 3 .... Wendy Barrie-Wilson

By MEL GUSSOW

"The Voice of the Prairie" (at Chelsea Stage) is both an affectionate hymn to the early days of radio and a requiem for a country's loss of innocence. The time of John Olive's play is the 1920's before there were networks and federal regulating agencies. Barnstorming broadcasters were like traveling pilots or baseball players. They crisscrossed the United States, beaming blues, banjo music, hog prices and shaggy stories to people previously isolated from home entertainment.

As a Nebraskan farmer named Davey Quinn spins tales on the radio about his Huck Finn boyhood, he be-

comes an overnight celebrity, just as other performers would subsequently become stars in the movies. At the same time, the play takes a Twain-like look at America's changing landscape, in which rural communities are about to be irrevocably linked to the cities.

The unlicensed broadcaster who discovers Davey and dubs him "the voice of the prairie" often says that radio, or "the magic of ether," is the wave of the future, but even he has no idea of its limitless potential. Significantly, the turning point in Davey's life — and one of the most dramatic moments in the play — comes with a call from General Sarnoff inviting him to New York. The move east represents the end of one era and the beginning of that wave of the future.

The play was commissioned by Artreach as a touring show in the Middle West, with three actors taking on numerous roles. In a more fully staged, six-actor version, the work was presented in 1987 at the Hartford Stage. Instead of repeating, or equalling, Norman René's impeccably cast Hartford production, the Chelsea Stage has returned the play to its schematic roots.

John Daines's production uses three actors, and two of them, Kevin Geer and Jack Cirillo, are overworked in personifying diverse characters. Mr. Cirillo takes a broad approach to the itinerant broadcaster (and mixes other identities while changing costumes and accents). In the earlier production, David Schramm gave a memorable performance as this ambitious harbinger of the radio revolution.

To enjoy "The Voice of the Prairie," one has to overlook the limits of the current staging (and the play's slow beginning) and concentrate on the author's words and the evocative emanations of radio-on-the-run, as represented by the character of Da-

vey Quinn. Davey, played country-boy-style by Mr. Geer, first nurtures his imagination just before the turn of the century. As a youth, he lives off the land with his grandfather — the world's worst con man — and, later, with a runaway blind girl named Frankie (a feisty performance by Wendy Barrie-Wilson).

Many years afterward, these three become the inspiration for Davey's radio reminiscences, which are rich with local color and aphoristic observations. For the new listening audience, the stories become a storyteller's serial as, day by day, those at home follow the escapades of their favorite renegades.

●

These stories and the world of amateur broadcasting are brought to life by Mr. Olive, who writes in a foot-loose, lyrical manner that reflects the material. In its openness, "The Voice of the Prairie" is a step beyond the author's previous works ("Clara's Play," "Standing on My Knees").

The period of "The Voice of the Prairie" is decades before that of Woody Allen's "Radio Days," but the play shares with that film a sense of optimism at the birth of a new medium. Watching these pioneers of communication, the audience has the hindsight of the television and computer age.

The hero's grandfather always told him, "Never turn down an unexpected invitation to travel." Even in this flawed production, "The Voice of the Prairie" offers that kind of invitation, entreating theatergoers to join Davey on an elegiac journey back in time.

1990 D 18, C18:5

Love Diatribe

By Harry Kondoleon; directed by Jorge Cacheiro; sets by G. W Mercier; costumes by Walker Hicklin; lighting by Dennis Parichy; sound by Scott Lehrer; production stage manager, Fred Reinglas; production manager, Jody Boese. Presented by Circle Repertory Company, Tanya Berezin, artistic director; Terrence Dwyer, managing director. At 99 Seventh Avenue South, at West Fourth Street.

Frieda .... Martha Gehman
Orin .... Barry Sherman
Sandy .... Amy Aquino
Mrs. Anderson .... Jane Cronin
Dennis .... Edward Seamon
Mike .... Michael Rispoli
Gerry .... Lynn Cohen

By FRANK RICH

The title of Harry Kondoleon's new comedy at the Circle Repertory Company is "Love Diatribe," but one need only glance at the grotesque family-room setting, a Naugahyde-upholstered shrine to suburban tchotchkes, and the grotesque family inhabiting it to know that more conventional diatribes, the angry kind, are what will make this evening tick.

No matter how much its author tries to embrace love and other noble sentiments, "Love Diatribe" is always at its best when it is a get-the-parents play in the vengeful modern American tradition that runs from Edward Albee to Christopher Durang. This is a work, after all, in which the "emotionally stingy" Dad (Edward Seamon) is rarely seen without the inflatable toilet cushion he uses when tending to his hemorrhoids, and in which Mom, a nurse (Lynn Cohen), snaps at her daughter that "women who died at the hospital do more with their hair than you do." Mr. Kondoleon's attempts to transcend such rancor by folding the play within a fairy-tale format, a "Sleeping Beauty" happy ending included, are less convincing. Compassion toward one's parents is not, alas, something that can be suddenly cooked up for the final curtain, even if one subscribes, as Mr. Kondoleon's characters occasionally do, to the therapeutic shortcuts that constitute our supposed new age.

•

Like their parents, the adult children in this play are also at their most entertaining when they are at their nastiest. Orin (Barry Sherman), a befuddled, 30-ish librarian, and Sandy (Amy Aquino), aptly described by her father as "a sarcastic malcontent," have returned to their childhood home, at least temporarily, after losing their respective mates to suicide and divorce. But home remains, as Orin puts it, "an unalterably mad world where all communication is for nothing." He still cannot forgive his parents for the way they treated Tippy, the family dog, during the pet's declining years. His sister, meanwhile, never misses a chance to make humiliating sport of her father's tendency to hog the bathroom. When Mr. Kondoleon gets a familial fugue of diatribes going — all ably handled by a cast adept at farcical apoplexy — "Love Diatribe" actually wages some fresh battles in the oldest war known to the human race.

The evening's unlikely agent of peace and reconciliation is a mysterious intruder into the household, an exchange student named Frieda (Martha Gehman) who may or may not be the German of high-school age she claims to be. She brings with her both a magic potion and a sermon. "Love is the great power of the world," Frieda instructs anyone who will listen. "One well-placed kiss can cause a turnaround just when you thought there was no God." Though Mr. Kondoleon has employed fairies before in his work, this one sounds not unlike a refugee from Craig Lucas's "Prelude to a Kiss," which occupied the same stage earlier this year. Frieda's feats of magic even seem to be introduced by the same tingling chimes that punctuated Mr. Lucas's fantasy.

"Love Diatribe" further recalls "Prelude to a Kiss" by being a pointed response to the age of AIDS (as was Mr. Kondoleon's fascinating previous play, "Zero Positive"). The death of a meanly treated neighbor-

hood AIDS victim haunts the family in "Love Diatribe"; Frieda's potion is presented as an antidote to disease and bigotry alike. "If you don't love someone sufficiently, you end up killing them," goes one of Mr. Kondoleon's homilies, to which is later added the corollary, "When you are nice to people, they do not die." While the playwright is hardly asking the audience to take such sentiments literally, he is trying to posit a more humane world in which trust and kindness must begin at home.

Sincere as the message undoubtedly is, Mr. Kondoleon has not succeeded in making it compelling on stage. A major stumbling block is the conception of Frieda, both as written and performed: Starting with an introductory soliloquy that is bizarrely similar to the one that recently opened John Patrick Shanley's "Big Funk," Ms. Gehman has been encouraged to play the do-gooder as a camp comedienne rather than as a genuine spirit an audience might have faith in. However many laughs may result from this strategy — and not that many do, in fact — the jokiness sends mixed signals that prove fatal to the

The message: Trust and kindness must begin at home.

play's serious intentions. When the time comes for Frieda to reawaken hardened hearts, her feel-good spiel isn't remotely touching; it seems instead like a snide put-on or, worse, a cloying attempt to pander.

That Mr. Kondoleon's aims were loftier can be seen in the character of the next-door neighbor, the mother of the AIDS victim, affectingly acted by Jane Cronin. In a play full of images of food and nutrition, Ms. Cronin is constantly whipping up meals for others, practicing the selfless, redemptive love that Mr. Kondoleon preaches, but with a spirit that is truly healing, not facetious or syrupy. If she, rather than Frieda, were the center-stage patron saint of "Love Diatribe," the playwright's benevolent passions might have come through as forcefully as his vindictive wit.

Jorge Cacheiro, the director, and his cast do serve Mr. Kondoleon's comic schemes well. Mr. Cacheiro is also in tune with his author's brand of extravagant theatricality, typified here by his use of Frieda as a Greek chorus, by his insistence on a plush front curtain (a rarity at the Circle Rep) and by the constant rounds of food and drink. At 90 minutes without an intermission, "Love Diatribe" is itself best devoured as a seasonal trifle, one more spiked than sweet.

1990 D 19, C15:1

Township Fever

Book, music and lyrics by Mbongeni Ngema; conceived, choreographed and directed by Mr. Ngema; set and costumes by Sarah Roberts; lighting by Mannie Manim; sound by Rick Rowe; original sound (South Africa) by Mark Malherbe; musical arrangements and orchestrations by Mr. Ngema; horn arrangements by Brian Thusi and Eric Norgate; additional choreography by Clara Reyes. The Committed Artists, Voza Rivers, executive director, Duma Ndlovu, trustee; production presented by Lincoln Center Theater, Gregory Mosher, director; Bernard Gersten, executive producer, in association with Brooklyn Academy of Music, Harvey Lichtenstein, executive producer. At the Majestic Theater, 651 Fulton Street, Brooklyn.

Jazz Mngadi	Brian Mazibuko
Tonko Mnisi	Sindiswa Dlathu
Mr. Sibisi	Bhoyi Ngema
Bra Cobra	Bheki Mqadi
Hostel workers	Faca Khulu, Mabonga Khumalo and Sbusiso Ngema
Philadelphia	John Lata
Priest	David Manqele
Mrs. Mngadi	Mamthandi Zulu
American Molefe	Themba Mbonani
Manyewu Mnisi	Dieketseng Mnisi
Dzehwe	Mike Motsogi
Fireman	Sduduzo Mthethwa
Master of Ceremony	Sphamandla Ngcamu
Kiriman	Siphiwe Nkosi
News Presenter/Pregnant Woman	Clara Reyes
Policeman	Mabonga Khumalo

By MEL GUSSOW

The continuing battle against apartheid in South Africa is the urgent subject of the theater of Mbongeni Ngema. In "Sarafina!" he dramatized the student participation in the Soweto rebellion of 1976 and in his new musical, "Township Fever," he broadens his canvas to study the 1987 transport workers' strike, which pitted black laborers against their white employers — and also brother against brother.

The primary instrument for the indictment is mbaqanga, that surging hybrid of rock, jazz and tribal music that reverberates across the large stage at the Majestic Theater in Brooklyn just as it did several seasons ago in "Sarafina!" The score of "Township Fever," more than two dozen songs, all of them written or adapted by Mr. Ngema, has both vitality and musicality. The songs are a call to arms and to conscience, celebrating the bravery of heroes like Oliver Tambo and Nelson Mandela at the same time that they mourn the tragedies that befall South Africans in their journey toward freedom.

In this Lincoln Center production (in collaboration with the Brooklyn Academy of Music) the score is sung by a melodic, township-size cast (often performing as massed chorale) and it is played with a driving syncopation by a large, on-stage band. Musicians, singers and score exude authenticity.

•

Unfortunately, this represents only half the show. More an insecure platform for Mr. Ngema's didacticism than a play with a life of its own, "Township Fever" is agit-propped with polemical sloganeering.

Certainly Mr. Ngema deserves full credit for ambition and moral purpose. He has taken a recent, still pressing case and has tried to present it with immediacy. The story concerns a railway workers' strike in a country in which such strikes are illegal. Enraged by the dismissal of one of their co-workers, employees of the South African Transport Services walked out. While attempting to break up the strike, officials killed three workers. Rebellion flared, reaching its culmination when the

Ruphin Coudyzer/"Township Fever"
Brian Mazibuko in a scene from "Township Fever."

strikers executed a group of scabs who had assumed their positions.

The show's approach owes a debt to Brecht (as well as to Clifford Odets), even down to the message, "South Africa belongs to all the people in it," which sounds like a variation on the message in "The Caucasian Chalk Circle" — that the valley belongs to the people who water it. Dramatically the book of "Township Fever" is undeveloped. We learn far more about the intricacies of the strike from the detailed program notes than from anything seen on stage.

Mr. Ngema's previous work had a certain simplicity, but at least in the

Gerry Goodstein/Circle Repertory Company
Edward Seamon, left, Barry Sherman and Lynn Cohen in Harry Kondoleon's "Love Diatribe."

case of "Sarafina!," conviction was elevated to a kind of eloquence, as the youngsters in the cast made theatergoers feel they were witnessing a re-enactment of a real-life passion. This is not the case with the new show.

Despite the 21-month workshop process, the musical has rough textual edges. Mr. Ngema wrote the book, music and lyrics, conceived, choreographed and directed the production and also assumed responsibility for the musical arrangements and the orchestrations. In Mr. Ngema's case this would seem to be too much for one man to handle. The staging carries informality to the point of chaos, and the choreography simply adds another hectic element. On the other hand, the set by Sarah Roberts, a simulation of a tin-roofed shantytown, is one of the evening's assets.

"Township Fever" begins in a Johannesburg prison where workers are awaiting punishment for the killing of the scabs, a punishment that still has not come (four are still on death row). The play then flashes back to the beginnings of the labor protest and the election of a chairman to lead the fight.

That chairman (Bhoyi Ngema) is a most reluctant choice. For too much of the play, he appears to be in a state of catatonia, and it is not clear if that stolidity should be attributed to the character or to the actor. In direct contrast, there is the chairman's hyperkinetic partisan (Bheki Mqadi) who boisterously inhabits the stage for the entire musical, intruding in songs and distracting the audience's attention, especially during the more touching moments. One keeps wishing that the director would guide Mr. Mqadi offstage where he could sit quietly while the others performed.

Watching the scenes in prison (and subsequent ones in a workers' hostel), one remembers related and far more compelling sequences in "The Island" by Athol Fugard and also in Mr. Ngema's own "Asinamali!" In addition, the action is awkwardly interrupted by a simulated CBS correspondent offering instant updates on the progress of the strike.

The drama somewhat improves in those scenes involving the families of the strikers, as in the wedding of two of the village's young people, played by Brian Mazibuko and Sindiswa Dlathu. Mr. Mazibuko portrays the show's protagonist, a hopeful musician, who is carried along on the wave of the strike until he discovers his own fierce commitment to justice. He and Ms. Dlathu are an appealing couple, and, as they become devastated by events beyond their control, they earn the audience's empathy.

In a characteristic juxtaposition, the slaying of strikers is followed by a sorrowful song of bereavement, a call to ancestors to "wake up and help us win the war," as beautifully sung by two women in the chorus, Nomasonto Khumalo and Khululiwe Sithole. If all aspects of "Township Fever" had the impassioned intensity of this number and its performance, the musical would have come closer to realizing its worthy intentions.

1990 D 20, C11:1

Valued Friends

By Stephen Jeffreys; directed by Robin Lefèvre; set and costumes by Sue Plummer; lighting by Marc B. Weiss; production stage manager, Tammy Taylor. Presented by Long Wharf Theater, Arvin Brown, artistic director; M. Edgar Rosenblum, executive director. At New Haven.

Sherry	Jill Tasker
Howard	Bill Camp
Paul	John Benjamin Hickey
Marion	Liann Pattison
Scott	Mark Vietor
Stewart	Ian Trigger

By MEL GUSSOW

Special to The New York Times

NEW HAVEN, Dec. 13 — In Stephen Jeffreys's "Valued Friends," four young working-class Londoners renting an unfashionable basement flat suddenly find themselves surrounded by gentrification. By holding fast to their tenancy, they become increasingly wealthy, at least on paper. The play (at the Long Wharf Theater) opens up into a study of the effect of real estate on individuals, of property values on friendship. At the root is a question of colonization: people living together in pursuit of a common goal but divided by self-interest.

The play, which was first presented at the Hampstead Theater in London, is trenchant in its exploration of the group living arrangements, especially in matters of economics. Mr. Jeffreys is somewhat less revealing about the original connection of the characters. One has to accept on faith that these disparate people are such close friends (two are on-again, off-again lovers).

Individually the characters are scrutinized with empathy and humor. There is something to be said about each point of view, from the most altruistic to the most egocentric. The latter position is represented by a pert, would-be alternative comedian (Jill Tasker), always in need of cash and lightheaded in all matters of responsibility.

When the first offer for a buy out comes from the landlord, Ms. Tasker is quick to suggest that the quartet take the money. Her flat-mates want to proceed cautiously, knowing that a collaborative hesitation would provoke a higher offer. Finally when three of them agree to buy the flat at an insider's price, they buy Ms. Tasker's share and she flies around the world, a spree that is bound to leave her penniless and in need of lodging.

In various ways the others are each self-sustaining: Liann Pattison as an executive on the rise, Bill Camp as a scholar and John Benjamin Hickey as the play's principal character, a rock critic who gradually finds himself caught up in his new role as homesteader.

Forsaking his work as well as his romance with Ms. Pattison, Mr. Hickey immerses himself in renovation. It becomes his compulsive preoccupation, as he undertakes painting, carpentry and plumbing, and finds that he enjoys it. When Ms. Pattison decides the new kitchen should be built by an outside professional, Mr. Hickey is crestfallen. Such is the credibility of the play and the performances that one feels the weight of his disappointment.

It might be said that the play is of specialized interest. A similar charge might have been raised against Michael Frayn's "Benefactors" or Margaret Drabble's novel "The Ice Age," both related in their concern with urban redevelopment. On the other hand, it should appeal to all those who are either tenants or landlords; in other words, almost everyone trying to live in a city.

Important issues are at stake, such as survival in a sinkable economy and how to get the most for one's money. There is an amusing second-

T. Charles Erickson/"Valued Friends"
Bill Camp in "Valued Friends."

act cameo performed by Ian Trigger as a disk jockey turned construction worker, who pitches in to help Mr. Hickey. Together they do the backbreaking manual labor as well as the architectural planning, because it is Mr. Trigger's conclusion that "the whole building trade is an enormous rip-off."

Although there is not an excess of plot, there is conflict as the tenants ally themselves against Mark Vietor as the increasingly frustrated landlord and as each tries to maximize the return on his investment. The play is more than just a group case history. It becomes a highly informative slice of contemporary life and an object lesson for prospective householders.

"Valued Friends" is firmly situated in London but achieves a more widespread relevance. One could find similar stories in New York. To make its point, the play has to have a localized foundation. Robin Lefèvre, who directed the London production of the play, leads an expert American cast (Mr. Trigger is one English exception) into Anglicized waters. Accents, attitudes and characteriztions are exacting.

The authenticity extends to the scenic design. Sue Plummer, the play's original designer, turns the Long Wharf stage into a run-down Victorian flat. Between scenes, the apartment is converted into a stylish lair, a before-and-after transformation that could earn a spread in House and Garden. In fact, the final setting looks as cool and contained as Ms. Pattison's character is supposed to be, as she waits alone to entertain her guests. Enter Ms. Tasker with an aerosol can of reverse intention. With it, she gives the place a natural cooking smell — to restore life into an environment that is now as antiseptic as it is fashionable.

1990 D 20, C20:4

Romeo and Juliet

By William Shakespeare; directed by Charles Keating; set designed by David P. Gordon; lighting designed by Sam Scripps; costumes designed by Martha Hally; music by James Keating; fight choreography by J. Allen Suddeth; assistant director, Sean Keating; production stage manager, Paul A. Kochman. Presented by Riverside Shakespeare Company, Timothy W. Oman, artistic director. At Playhouse 91, 316 East 91st Street.

WITH: Wendy Allegaert, Brian Byrnes, Michael Connor, Margot Dionne, Debra England, Beth Fowler, Jeremy Johnson, Lynellen Kagen, Youssif Kamal, Cuivan Kelly, Tom Kelly, Herb Klinger, John Leighton, Robert Sean Leonard, Joanne Lessner, Brian Mulligan, Andrew Palmer, Gary Piquer, John Plumpis, Gerit Quealy, Will Rhys, James Ryan, Stephen Schnetzer, Ian Stuart and Andy Taylor.

By STEPHEN HOLDEN

The greatest strength of the Riverside Shakespeare Company's new production of "Romeo and Juliet" at Playhouse 91 is its clarity. Even in the most stellar productions of Shakespeare, the Elizabethan locutions tend to impede perfect comprehension. But in this new "Romeo and Juliet," directed by Charles Keating (a former actor with the Royal Shakespeare Company), the line readings have a conversational ease and a sure sense of direction that are matched by precise delineations of the characters and their relationships.

The director's vision of the play revolves around the very believable concept of Romeo as a supersensitive adolescent who has just discovered the opposite sex and is in love with the idea of love as much as he is with Juliet herself. As portrayed by Robert Sean Leonard, who was so memorable in the role of an oppressed, suicidal adolescent in the film "Dead Poets Society," Romeo becomes a gangling, starry-eyed youth given to self-dramatizing fits in which he sometimes seems about to choke on his own words. Mr. Leonard's decidedly nonheroic Romeo is also a shameless crybaby. In his scene with Friar Laurence following his banishment, he comes completely unstrung, breaking down in hysterical sobs.

The neurasthenic intensity of Mr. Leonard's portrayal is supported by the production's depiction of his parents as ineffectual, sensitive introverts. Debra England's Lady Montague, in particular, is a quivering ethereal presence. The Capulets, by contrast, are pushy social climbers whose daughter appears to be a fairly robust adolescent motivated as much by rebellion as by passion. Margot Dionne's Lady Capulet is a haughty grande dame, while Jeremy Johnson depicts her husband as a coarse, grasping materialist.

•

Where Mr. Leonard's Romeo goes on crying jags, Gerit Quealy's Juliet merely pouts when things don't go her way. Her balcony scene with Romeo, instead of focusing on the young lovers' ardor, is played as a sweet romantic comedy. Miss Quealy does not embody her role as comfortably as Mr. Leonard does his. She sometimes gives the uneasy appearance of a mature woman aping a young girl's mannerisms. Ultimately, the two performances don't completely harmonize, and the relationship seems less like a mutually all-consuming passion than the dramatic springboard for a very social comedy.

Conceptually, the production's most unusual touch is its suggestion that Mercutio is secretly in love with Romeo. And Stephen Schnetzer, an actor who resembles the young Robert Taylor, imbues the character with an air of suave, sensual knowingness. Among the generally strong supporting performances, Beth Fowler's Nurse is especially fine. Her Nurse is a shallow prurient busybody who for all her dithering, has no deep attachment to the young woman she serves.

The Riverside Company's spare production sets most of the action around an iron gate at the center of the stage. It also effectively uses the theater aisles for several dramatic entrances. As is often the case with productions of "Romeo and Juliet," the first half the play is richer and more imaginatively developed than the second half, in which the lovers'

deaths and the resolution of their families' feud are treated in a rushed, almost perfunctory manner. Yet all things considered, this "Romeo and Juliet" is to be recommended. Without pushing too hard for relevance, the fresh, smart production maintains a bracingly contemporary point of view.

1990 D 21, C20:6

SUNDAY VIEW/David Richards

This Time, A Different Cry In South Africa

'Sarafina!'s' author draws on a violent strike for 'Township Fever'; 'Peter Pan' soars in; and Daugherty and Field sing for their supper.

I KNOW ABOUT LIGHTNING. BUT there's no law that says jubilation can't strike twice in the theater. Conditions have to be favorable, but favorable conditions aren't entirely a matter of chance. They can be created, controlled, manipulated. So why, I am wondering, isn't "Township Fever," the new musical by Mbongeni Ngema at the Brooklyn Academy of Music's Majestic Theater, as exhilarating as "Sarafina!," the hugely successful freedom ride that Mr. Ngema took us on three years ago.

Once again, Mr. Ngema is exploring the fabric of South Africa's racially torn society. His starting point this time is the 1987 strike against the Government-owned South African Transport Services (SATS) — a protest that was triggered when a black employee was summarily dismissed for a minor accounting offense. Very quickly thousands of railway and bus workers swelled the ranks and their confrontations with the police were brutal and bloody before the authorities bowed to their demands. Not content merely to flail injustice, Mr. Ngema once again wants to plant the seeds of hope and reconciliation in the smoldering wreckage.

Like "Sarafina!," "Township Fever" unfolds to the assertive rhythms of mbaqanga, the indigenous music of South Africa that

Martha Swope Assoc.-Carol Rosegg/"Peter Pan"

Cathy Rigby as that boy from Neverland—nothing to apologize for

Ruphin Coudyzer/Lincoln Center Theater

Cast members in Mbongeni Ngema's "Township Fever" in Brooklyn—The fervor is always disciplined, the plea is never permitted to degenerate into a harangue.

blends tribal chants with American gospel, jazz and more than a touch of brass to come up with its proud sound. The on-stage band is seated among the corrugated metal dwellings of a shantytown, wrapped in the lazy smoke of a dozen outdoor cooking fires. If anything, the set and costume designer, Sarah Roberts, has coaxed even more beauty out of the impoverished landscape of "Township Fever" than she did from the bleak schoolyard that was "Sarafina!'s" stomping ground.

■

The first act culminates with the marriage of Jazz (Brian Mazibuko), a striking worker and aspiring musician, and his village sweetheart (Cindy Dlathu). A full moon shines down on the wedding guests, vibrantly garbed in native dress. Everywhere, bright oranges are vying with golden yellows, especially when the performers take lighted candles in hand and begin crisscrossing the stage in various geometric patterns, like a slow-motion marching band at halftime. Then, one by one, the guests go their separate ways, the newlyweds disappear into their makeshift home and only the moonlight is left behind. The interlude is as magical as anything Mr. Ngema has put on the stage.

Drafting his performers directly from South Africa's townships and villages, he trains them long and rigorously. Here, as before, the effort shows. The singing is heart-rendingly beautiful (what Joshua did with a trumpet blast, I suspect this cast could do with a single, sonorous "Amen"). The dancing approaches a joyful frenzy with none of frenzy's disorderliness. And if the acting lacks professional sheen, it is nonetheless almost painstakingly sincere. Many of the speeches in "Township Fever" are delivered directly to the audience, and there is such earnestness in the performers' desire to communicate the pain in their land that you are willing to overlook what amounts to outright sermonizing.

"Township Fever," after all, belongs to the realm of street theater, even if you don't feel, as you did watching the home-grown variety in the 1960's, that things could get out of hand and turn messy. The fervor is always disciplined, the plea is never permitted to degenerate into a harangue. An inherent good humor, in fact, tends to prevail far longer than the grim circumstances would dictate.

On the whole, "Township Fever" really isn't behaving any differently than "Sarafina!" did. So where is the exultation "Sarafina!" tossed up in the face of oppression? Shouldn't we be just as elated this time by the clarion call for liberty at the show's end?

■

We're not, and the reason, I suspect, is that Mr. Ngema leaves us grappling with some slippery moral issues. "Sarafina!," you may remember, pitted the students of Morris Issacson High School in Soweto against the Government. As we came to know them, the schoolchildren were disarming, hardly the incipient radicals the secret police claimed. So when army troops burst into the classroom, machine guns blazing, we seemed to be witnessing a massacre of innocents. There was nothing equivocal about the situation.

Mr. Ngema has considerably enlarged his canvas in "Township Fever," but in doing so, a certain ambiguity has crept into the picture. As the protest against SATS heated up, the Government intervened with predictable force. But in this instance, the strikers' retaliation extended to their own — five replacement workers, who, it was felt, seriously jeopardized union solidarity. By way of example, four were killed on April 28, 1987. The fifth escaped and turned informant. "Town-

ship Fever" begins in prison, where the men convicted in the case are awaiting execution. Then flashing back, it tells their interlocking stories, as "Sarafina!" did, in rudimentary scenes and explanatory monologues.

In the course of researching events surrounding the killings, Mr. Ngema has said he came to realize that "I, or indeed any one of us, who was caught up in that situation, might well have participated in the deed." But he never proves that on stage. Basically, the strikers are presented as a rowdy, good-tempered lot. The pot-bellied driver they elect as their leader (Bhoyi Ngema) is as leery of power as he is sickened by the devastation it unleashes. It is society itself that is being held accountable. "Politicians are corrupt. Nobody seems to care," sings the cast in what is, ironically, one of the show's catchier numbers. The "system," you see, is forcing decent, common folk to act against their better natures.

■

While no one would deny the horrors of apartheid, that kind of blanket indictment goes only so far as sociology and not much farther as drama. To my mind, Jazz draws the more honest, if disquieting conclusion. On trial as an accomplice to murder, he is allowed a few words in his defense. Bewildered, he shrugs an aimless shrug and says, "What I remember is that I was angry. I was confused, but I don't know why. Magistrate, I don't know that world. All I know is G seventh, B flat or C major."

Mr. Mazibuko is an appealing performer and his helplessness in the cold judicial spotlight is troubling. What it implies is a dark, unfathomable pool at the heart of human behavior, which the rhetoric of politics and protest cannot begin to plumb. Had he chosen to expand upon that idea, Mr. Ngema would have come up with a different musical entirely. And, probably a better one. Still, the notion is out of the bag, and the only way "Township Fever" can end with a display of exuberant tribal dancing is to forget it was ever mentioned in the first place.

The characters in "Sarafina!" had the untarnished idealism of youth on their side. When, in a prophetic finale, they imagined the release of Nelson Mandela from prison, the show's clumsy mechanics no longer mattered. What emerged was pure celebration. "Township Fever" also implores Mr. Mandela to "show us the way to freedom," but the words, boldly sung out, register more like a cry in the night. Despite Mr. Ngema's best efforts to keep spirits up, a black and white universe has acquired sobering shades of gray.

'Peter Pan'

As you might well expect, the former gymnast Cathy Rigby flies with considerably more daring than any of her celebrated predecessors in the musical version of "Peter Pan." But she has nothing to apologize for when her feet are on the ground. She sings with assurance, moves rambunctiously, walks on her hands and generally makes a perfectly convincing scamp. (Perky as Mary Martin was in the role, did we ever really think she was a boy? I mean, really?)

■

In what is being billed as the 35th-anniversary production of the musical, "Peter Pan" has taken time out from a national tour to play a limited engagement at the Lunt-Fontanne Theater. Unlike "Fiddler on the Roof," which came in from the road half-embalmed, the production has a

lot of gusto. The director, Fran Soeder, has no qualms about tinkering with tradition and he's set about reducing the show's cuteness quotient by 50 percent, which still leaves more than enough to go around.

The scenery for Neverland is almost lurid. The pirate crew can't seem to make up its mind whether it's appearing in "The Three Musketeers" or "The Pirates of Penzance," and consequently carries on with either drunken panache or snooty punctiliousness — both equally amusing states. Stephen Hanan's Captain Hook clearly spent his apprenticeship in a third-rate Shakespearean company, perfecting the sneers and flourishes of villainy. (You're never quite sure he isn't going to throw himself up against the proscenium arch and mangle a famous soliloquy.) The approach is a welcome change from the effete interpretation established by Cyril Ritchard, who, even when he was brandishing a sword, seemed to be taking after Peter with a teacup.

I was also content to see Tinkerbell restored to her state as a flickering ball of light. The last time around (the 1979 revival with Sandy Duncan), the poor thing was portrayed by a green laser beam that, frankly, looked as if it could have burned a hole in the sets.

'Daugherty & Field Off Broadway'

Daugherty and Field (that's the boyish-faced singer Bill Daugherty and his wry pianist and partner in song, Robin Field) admit to being anachronisms. Their act is made up of vintage show tunes and easygoing bickering, and you can see how they would have been right at home on "The Colgate Comedy Hour" or in one of Leonard Sillman's New Faces revues.

But an old-fashioned musical comedy revue hasn't been sighted on Broadway in years, while the chances of two guys in tuxedos going on television and singing the entire score of "South Pacific" (albeit in abbreviated form) were greatly reduced the day "You Asked for It" went off the air. No matter. Mr. Daugherty and Mr. Field have done what has to be done: They've set themselves up in the Double Image Theater in lower Manhattan for the holidays, which are bound to be cheerier because of that.

■

Accuracy bids me note that Mr. Field favors the show tunes. Mr. Daugherty says he wants to be a big-band singer when he grows up. So in their opening medley, while Mr. Field is delivering such numbers as "Lost in the Stars," "Over the Rainbow" and "Tea for Two," Mr. Daugherty is swinging and swaying through the likes of "Stars Fell on Alabama," "Skylark" and "The White Cliffs of Dover." Some Swiss clocks don't mesh this well.

Whether they're re-creating the glory days of radio, paying homage to the great vaudeville teams of the past (Abbott and Costello, Mr. Gallagher and Mr. Sheen, Jim and Tammy Faye Bakker) or examining the imprint of classical composers on popular music, the interaction between the two performers is never less than nimble. Mr. Field is older and wiser, and tends to have to explain things to Mr. Daugherty, who is younger and daffier and given to impertinence. But that's all part of the give and take.

Good company, the pair would seem to be headed places. Savoring the prospect, Mr. Field asks his partner, "Where do all the stars go when they've made it really big?" Mr. Daugherty has no trouble fielding that one. "The Betty Ford Clinic," he answers, confidently. □

1990 D 23, II:5:1

The Sea Gull
The Hamptons: 1990

Directed and adapted from Chekhov. by R. Jeffrey Cohen; set design by Alexis Siroc; lighting design by Jim Kellough; costume design by Karen Perry; music composed by Kevin Scott; technical director, Mr. Kellough; stage manager, Rebecca Nestle. Presented by the RAPP Arts Center, Mr. Cohen and Alexis S. Cohen, artistic directors. At 220 East Fourth Street.

Masha Shamrayev	Karen Millard
Simon Medvedenko	Sheridan Crist
Paulina Shamrayev	Lucille Rivin
Dr. Eugene Dorn	John Bakos
Constantine Treplev	D. B. Sweeney
Peter Sorin	Howard Wesson
Nina Zarechny	Laura Linney
Irina Arkadina	Carol Lynley
Ilya Shamrayev	Michael Twaine
Boris Trigorin	George McGrath

By STEPHEN HOLDEN

The characters in "The Sea Gull: The Hamptons: 1990," R. Jeffrey Cohen's contemporary adaptation of Chekhov's classic drama at the RAPP Arts Center, are an immediately recognizable bunch of modern-day malcontents.

Irina Arkadina (Carol Lynley) has starred in several television miniseries, appeared on "Murder, She Wrote" and near the end of the play crows about her recent triumph playing Desirée Armfeldt in a Los Angeles production of "A Little Night Music." Constantine (D. B. Sweeney), her self-hating son, is an aspiring East Village performance artist whose play within the play in the first act is a didactic broadside about ecology that involves a toilet and some pornographic photos.

Nina (Laura Linney), whose role in that performance consists mostly of letting forth bloodcurdling screams, is the daughter of working-class eastern Long Island natives. Upon striking out on an unpromising acting career, her first steady job is touring the Carolinas in a nonunion road company of "Pippin." Trigorin (George McGrath), her seducer, is a literary smoothie who realizes to his chagrin that he is not as good a writer as Norman Mailer.

The biggest surprise about Mr. Cohen's updating of "The Sea Gull" from 19th-century Russia to present-day America is that what might sound in theory like a gimmicky "Forbidden Broadway"-style parody of Chekhov actually has substance. Despite the contemporary references and slangy up-to-the-minute dialogue, Mr. Cohen's adaptation sticks fairly close to Chekhov in its interpretation of the characters and keeps their key monologues more or less intact. If the Americans aren't as poetic sounding as their Russian forerunners, as a group they evoke the same peevish sense of social anomie.

●

The production, on a cramped stage where the principal piece of scenery is an impressionistic canvas of a seascape, is spare and rhythmically very jumpy but teeming with energy. Mr. Cohen, who is the director as well as the adapter, rushes his characters on and off and often with no preparation, sometimes trapping individuals in the spotlight to create soliloquies where they don't exist in the text. Live solo cello music adds an extra, unnecessary, layer of Chekhovian mood.

Although the acting is uneven, much of it has a ferocious vitality. The production's one disastrous mistake is the casting of Miss Lynley as Irina. The actress is incapable of projecting either the grandiosity or the mercurial charm of a vain, aging actress. Physically ungainly and vocally unrefined, Miss Lynley simply shouts her lines. Her Irina is a flailing, self-obsessed, no-talent slob.

Some of the other performances, however, contain brilliant moments. Karen Millard's sullen, kohl-eyed Masha brings a recognizably punkish demeanor to the character. Instead of taking snuff, she sniffs cocaine and swigs Jack Daniel's out of the bottle for breakfast. Yet her continual teetering between hostility and despair contains genuine pathos.

Mr. Sweeney's even more volatile Treplev is an overgrown baby who is totally at the mercy of his own emotions and given to uncontrollable tantrums. In his fight with his mother, a scene played with strong incestuous overtones, he momentarily regresses

into infantile blubbering. During his final scene with Nina, he becomes so abject that he literally kisses the ground she walks on. If his tumultuous performance goes off in too many directions, it is still bold and exciting to watch.

Best of all is Miss Linney's Nina. From a naïve, idealistic artist's groupie with a streak of crazy determination, her Nina emerges as a woman who is a lot stronger and more complicated than the terminally wounded bird-woman that is the character's traditional interpretation. Though deeply embittered at the end of the play, she is also fortified by a hard-won self-knowledge. Miss Linney projects the character's ambiguities with stinging force and clarity. She is clearly a talent of enormous potential.

1990 D 24, 21:1

The Fine Art of Finesse

By Pierre de Marivaux; translated by Alex Szogyi; directed by Richard Morse; set design, Robert Joel Schwartz; lighting, Richard A. Kendrick; costumes, Barbara A. Bell; sound, John Wise; production stage manager, Ernest L. Williams. Presented by Pearl Theater Company, Kenneth J. Rotman, president; Shepard Sobel, artistic director. At 125 West 22d Street, Manhattan.

The Countess	Robin Leslie Brown
Frontin	Hank Wagner
The Marquise	Donnah Welby
The Chevalier	Matthew Loney
Dorante	Ahvi Spindell
Blaise	Frank Geraci
Harlequin	Stuart Lerch
Lisette	Laura Rathgeb
Lackey/Notary	Christopher Cook

By MEL GUSSOW

Though his works have long been in the repertory of the Comédie Française, Pierre de Marivaux wrote principally for the Comédie-Italienne. One can detect in plays like "The Fine Art of Finesse" ("L'Heureux Stratagème") an elegant Italian hand. In the playwright's time, the 18th century, his bantering manner was labeled marivaudage, a word that was at first used derisively but then became a mark of approbation.

In Alex Szogyi's felicitous translation, the play (at the Pearl Theater Company) is frothy and filled with commedia dell'arte touches, as servants fool their masters and lovers collide simply for the sport of romance. Proclaiming that "jealousy is praise," the play's heroine, the Countess, goes out of her way to make each of her two lovers as jealous of the other as possible, and the men respond by flaunting their own dalliances, real and pretended.

●

The Pearl Theater is to be complimented for doing Marivaux (along

with other classic writers), and the scenery and costumes, by Robert Joel Schwartz and Barbara A. Bell, respectively, are congenial to the cozy surroundings. But Richard Morse's production is middling. The marivaudage is intermittent, barely conveying the gamelike aspect of the comedy, one of the hallmarks of Marivaux, whose other plays also have self-defining titles like "The Game of Love and Chance" and "The False Confession." Only at odd moments do Mr. Morse's actors tantalize the audience with the intricacies of the playwright's highly stylized humor.

Fortunately, the evening's most diverting performance comes from Robin Leslie Brown as the fickle Countess. Saucily moving between her admirers, she admits to a certain coquettishness while resisting the label of coquette. Nothing can raise her ire more than knowledge that either suitor is unfaithful to her. Each character, male and female, wants exclusivity in matters of infidelity.

●

The actors playing the suitors are no match for the leading lady. Ahvi Spindell is supercilious as the more easily enraged of the two men, and Matthew Loney, though he wins a few smiles, is hampered by the choice of a thickly lisping foppish accent and by an eagerness to overplay double-entendres. In one case, the joke is re-

Carol Rosegg/Martha Swope Associates/Pearl

Robin Leslie Brown in "The Fine Art of Finesse."

peated three times, each less funny than the last.

Minor comic relief is provided by Hank Wagner as a servant with clownish resources and the instincts of a mime. He and Ms. Brown bring a piquancy to the performance, which in other respects is not notable for its finesse.

1990 D 28, C5:1

Reality Intruded In a Paradoxical Year

By FRANK RICH

IF YOU BELIEVE EVERYTHING HAPpens for a reason, then why was the star of the year's second-most boring Broadway musical, "Shogun," knocked cold by a piece of falling scenery during a press preview? Why was New York's angriest theatrical controversy of the year about a performance — by Jonathan Pryce, in "Miss Saigon" — that has only been seen in London and even there by few, if any, of those leading the debate about it? Why in an exceptional year for new American plays — "Six Degrees of Separation," "The Piano Lesson," "Prelude to a Kiss" — did December find three prime Shubert playhouses on West 45th Street (the Plymouth, the Royale, the Golden) sitting dark, with no bookings in sight for the New Year?

Don't look here for simple answers to any of these questions. (The answer to an easier question — Which Broadway musical was more boring than "Shogun"? — can be more quickly provided: "Aspects of Love.") This has been a more paradoxical year than usual in the eternally irrational world of the theater. The high quality of new productions has been undermined by the low number of new productions, particularly on Broadway, where the output has slowed to a trickle. The American musical, having revived in 1989 with "City of Angels" and "Grand Hotel," dropped dead once again on Broadway in 1990, only to have a small renaissance at one theater company Off Broadway, Playwrights Horizons (which originated "Falsettoland" and "Once on This Island" and is now previewing the new Stephen Sondheim-John Weidman "Assassins"). The gala relighting of two antique Broadway houses — the Walter Kerr (with "The Piano Lesson") and, briefly, the Victory (with "Crowbar") — has been overshadowed by the perpetual darkness of so many of their neighbors in the half-redeveloped, half-abandoned, increasingly surreal theater district.

More pressing still, this was a year in which some of the real-life dramas preoccupying the audience attending the theater — racial conflict and recession, for starters — permeated not only the year's outstanding plays but also racked the theater community, dividing it and depleting it. And sometimes the New York theater's own backstage story

Martha Swope/"Once on This Island"

"Once on This Island," the happiest fairy tale of the year, announces the arrival of the young songwriting team of Stephen Flaherty and Lynn Ahrens—Broadway babies.

was as compelling as anything happening on stage.

Take, as one representative example, "The Grapes of Wrath," Frank Galati's epic adaptation of John Steinbeck's Depression novel, as performed by the Steppenwolf Theater Company of Chicago. Watching this work, one could not ignore the parallels between the homeless Okies of the 1930's and the homeless New Yorkers of 1990, some of whom were begging for change outside the theater at intermission. But "The Grapes of Wrath" itself soon became a sad casualty of hard times, despite winning the Tony Award for best play, traditionally a sure box-office boon to any production in any year. The audience for the show, though by no means meager, was simply not big enough to support its populous payroll, and within weeks of its Tony victory, "The Grapes of Wrath" closed.

Bob Marshak/Circle Repertory Company

"Prelude to a Kiss," with Barnard Hughes and Mary-Louise Parker—bottomless love as a defense

Gerry Goodstein/"The Piano Lesson"

"The Piano Lesson," with Charles Dutton starring in August Wilson's Pulitzer Prize winner—a successful run

DECEMBER 30, 1990

Thus did a play about a distant depression become in death a symbolic victim of a new economic tailspin, adding its own large company at least temporarily to the ranks of the unemployed and leaving another darkened midtown marquee to serve as a makeshift shelter for New York's destitute. Where did art end and real life begin?

But as the country reeled from its various crises, Americans seemed to want to believe in any world other than this one.

The "Miss Saigon" dispute was also part of a sociopolitical drama far weightier and broader than any single play. Ostensibly the battle was about Jonathan Pryce's right, as a white British actor, to repeat his London performance as a Eurasian pimp in the Broadway production of a West End hit. In reality Mr. Pryce wasn't the issue at all but a symbol, merely the wrong man in the wrong place at the wrong time, rather like Sherman McCoy in Tom Wolfe's "Bonfire of the Vanities." Mr. Pryce's case proved to be a catalyst for the release of racial tensions that had been building up for some time and were bound to explode sooner or later in the theater industry, with or without "Miss Saigon."

As is now history, Actors' Equity shot itself in the foot by attempting to bar Mr. Pryce: The union both unjustly slurred a colleague's performance, inaccurately branding it a "minstrel" routine, and unwisely set itself up as a censor, restricting the creative freedom of theater artists who want to cast whoever they think will best serve their show. (The Equity position was a particularly embarrassing one in a year when the theatrical

profession was fighting government censorship of the arts.) But while Equity's quixotic stand on Mr. Pryce was eventually reversed, the wounds opened up by the episode are not going to heal so easily. Though "Miss Saigon" was an absurdly ill-chosen battleground for a debate about racial equality in the theater — the show is likely to employ more minority performers for more months than any Broadway production in decades — the debate continues to be a real and challenging one, as yet attracting more demagoguery than solutions.

No Solomon, this observer included, has emerged with a plan about how to resolve the legitimate complaints of minority actors, especially Asians, who feel they have not had a fair shake in pursuing their art on the professional stage. There are more questions than answers. What does one say about a musical like "Oh, Kay!," which gives employment to dozens of black performers but often treats them in a patronizing fashion? What is one to make of the white theater establishment, which often supports nontraditional, or colorblind, casting with its big mouths but not with its bigger productions?

In a letter to the editor published in The New York Times during the Pryce controversy, and typical of the discourse the affair engendered, a half-dozen prominent white

Martha Swope/New York Shakespeare Festival
"Machinal," a sensational revival at the Public Theater, with Jodie Markell and Rocco Sisto

Paula Court/Lincoln Center Theater
"Monster in a Box," a cool star turn courtesy of Spalding Gray—sheer escapism

Peter Cunningham/"The Grapes of Wrath"
"The Grapes of Wrath," with the Steppenwolf Theater Company, became a victim of hard times itself when it closed within weeks of winning a Tony.

381

actors and playwrights argued that affirmative action is the best route for improving a New York casting system in which "actors of color are silently and automatically excluded from consideration for the majority of offered roles simply because they would be 'inappropriate.'" The three playwrights who signed this letter — Craig Lucas, Terrence McNally and Larry Kramer — are all the authors of recent hits ("Prelude to a Kiss," "Frankie and Johnny in the Clair de Lune," "The Normal Heart") in which the lead roles, all of them repeatedly re-cast during the plays' lengthy New York runs, have been exclusively played by white actors.

Talk is cheap, and, heaven knows, there has been plenty of it. One of the few leaders in the theater who tends to back up his pronouncements with deeds, Joseph Papp, helped improve the climate by taking actual affirmative action, both by continuing his career-long practice of nontraditional casting (Morgan Freeman in the summer's "Taming of the Shrew") and by installing George C. Wolfe, the young black author (of "The Colored Museum") and director, as an artistic leader of the New York Shakespeare Festival. (This year Mr. Papp also practiced his convictions on another front by refusing much needed National Endowment funds rather than submit to strictures on their use.) The results of Mr. Wolfe's tenure at the Public so far have included "Spunk," a selflessly imaginative theatrical homage to the fiction of Zora Neale Hurston, and "The Caucasian Chalk Circle," an adaptation of Brecht's epic in which the writer Thulani Davis reset the story in Duvalier's Haiti.

Whatever the individual achievements of the Wolfe productions, they are even more notable for their lavishly executed and uncompromising African-American esthetics, realized by an informal, floating company of young actors and adventurous designers. When one considers the successful Broadway run of "The Piano Lesson," August Wilson's latest, Depression-era installment in his cycle of plays about black America in this century, it is clear that this year, at least, black theater art had far more than a token representation in the major venues of New York theater. But color-blind casting — whether of blacks, Asians, Hispanics or any other minority — is another cause entirely, and one that is likely to continue to erupt not just in the theater but in television and film as well.

■

As the real-life dramas of racial division and economic hardship pressed on the theater in 1990, so again did the tragedy of AIDS. Both in "Falsettoland," the musical by William Finn and James Lapine, and in Mr. Lucas's "Prelude to a Kiss," writers unearthed beauty and heroism in a story of hideous suffering.

"Falsettoland," whose principal lovers were bracingly played by Stephen Bogardus and Michael Rupert, is the more explicit of the two shows, charting the path of the disease in New York in the early 80's, when, as one lyric goes, "something very bad" was happening but the something still lacked a name and identity. By contrast, "Prelude to a Kiss," which initially featured Alec Baldwin and Mary-Louise Parker as its spellbinding couple, never mentions AIDS but is just as moving in its depiction of bottomless love as the only defense in a "precarious" world where the young join the old in being tested by death. Usually I am tempted to run the other way from plays that try to be uplifting about terminal illness — see "Shadowlands" for a treacly case in point — but "Falsettoland" and "Prelude" do leave one feeling, as Mr. Lucas puts it, that "the miracle of another human being" is "never to be squandered."

I would be harder pressed to argue that the two best of the most overtly polemical productions of the season left one with such a full heart. Eric Bogosian's "Sex, Drugs, Rock & Roll," a brilliant solo performance touring nearly every urban battlefront in contemporary America, and the director Michael Greif's sensational Public Theater revival of Sophie Treadwell's forgotten "Machinal," a 1928 "tragedy in 10 episodes" in which a mercantile New York grinds up its proletarian heroine, leave one high about the power of theater rather than sanguine about humanity. For sheer escapism, a 1990 theatergoer would be better off watching Maggie Smith's outrageous star turn of the old school in Peter Shaffer's well-mannered "Lettice and Lovage," or Spalding Gray's cool star turn of

the narcissistic new school in his autobiographical comic monologue "Monster in a Box." The happiest fairy tale of the year is "Once on This Island," a show that announces the arrival of the young songwriting team Stephen Flaherty and Lynn Ahrens.

In a class by itself in 1990 is "Si Degrees of Separation," the Joh Guare play that is an alternately h larious and moving attempt to uncov er what feelings, ideas and peopl might still be authentic in a cit where the con artist is king. In only 9 minutes, Mr. Guare surveys a Nev

"Aspects of Love," the London import by Andrew Lloyd Webber, featuring Ann Crumb and Michael Ball, won the most-boring-musical competition.

"Shogun," with Francis Ruivivar, placed second to "Aspects."

"*Six Degrees of Separation,*" *with Stockard Channing, in a triumphant performance, and Courtney B. Vance*

Martha Swope/Lincoln Center Theater

Michelle Agins/The New York Times

"*Sex, Drugs, Rock & Roll,*" *a brilliant solo turn by Eric Bogosian that covers nearly every urban battlefront*

Gerry Goodstein/Playwrights Horizons

"*Falsettoland,*" *with Danny Gerard, charted the tragedy of AIDS in the early 80's through beauty and heroism.*

York landscape that stretches from the Upper East Side to Rikers Island and that encompasses everything from racism, recession and homelessness to the spiritual qualities of art and love to the cultural significance of Sidney Poitier, Wassily Kan-

No Solomon has emerged with a plan about how to resolve the legitimate complaints of minority actors.

dinsky, J. D. Salinger and "Cats." As directed by Jerry Zaks, "Six Degrees" is also a dizzying feat of stagecraft blessed with its own triumphant star performance, by Stockard Channing. In a year that has seen classical theater descend to a still lower estate in New York — Kevin Kline's intelligent, almost passionless "Hamlet" was by default the best of a lot that included the Mabou Mines's crossgender "Lear" and a disappointing Philip Bosco "Miser" — Mr. Guare and Mr. Zaks have given the theater what looks like a new classic.

■

About the only up-to-the-minute phenomenon missing from "Six Degrees of Separation" is the supernatural. As the country reels from its various crises, not the least of which is the threat of war, Americans seem to want to believe in any world other than this one. Not for nothing was "Ghost" the most popular movie in the country this year. Is it coincidence that ghosts, poltergeists and miracles figure in so many plays this season, often to facilitate happy endings, whether in "Prelude to a Kiss," "The Piano Lesson," "Crowbar" or "Once on This Island"?

If things do happen for a reason, and if one wants to be superstitious — and I'm half-kidding, but only half — maybe a message was being sent when the screen fell and beaned Philip Casnoff during that fateful preview of "Shogun." The effect of the inci-

dent on the audience in the Marquis Theater that November night, much of it theater people, was shocking. "Shogun" itself had been numbing most everyone from its opening number, "Karma," but Mr. Casnoff's accident roused the crowd to the loudest screams I've heard in a theater in memory, followed by an equally stunned silence. It was as if an alarm of some sort had sounded.

A karma alarm, perhaps? Mr. Casnoff got a happy ending, recovering from his injury within days. But the prognosis for the theater, like that for the world the stage inevitably reflects, is less clear. The deep divisions and economic darkness spreading throughout the New York theater were hardly abating as 1990 reached its final curtain. If the bizarre calamity at "Shogun" somehow seemed the perfect denouement for this whole disquieting theatrical year, so one cannot rule out the possibility that more than scenery might come crashing down in the months to come.   □

1990 D 30, II:5:1

383

Theater Awards
and Prizes
1989-1990

Included in this section are Times
articles covering the following awards
and prizes.

Pulitzer Prizes
for original American plays

New York Drama Critics Circle Awards

Antoinette Perry (Tony) Awards

Obie (Off-Broadway) Awards

Drama Desk Awards

1989

PULITZER PRIZE

The Pulitzer Prize Winners: Excellence in Journalism, Letters and the Arts

By MICHAEL T. KAUFMAN

Echoes of the dramatic turbulence of the 1960's dominated the 73d annual Pulitzer Prize awards as Neil Sheehan's book about the Vietnam War and Taylor Branch's study of the civil-rights struggle gained honors, along with "The Heidi Chronicles," Wendy Wasserstein's play about a child of the 60's alienated from the consciousness of the 80's.

Drama

Wendy Wasserstein
"The Heidi Chronicles"

With her most recent play, Wendy Wasserstein, continued her exploration of women. But this time she delved deeper, examining one woman and her relationships over a quarter-century as a way to discuss the women's movement in the 1960's and 70's and the desires and disappointments it spawned. Ms. Wasserstein was born in New York City and graduated from Mount Holyoke and the Yale School of Drama. She has previously received a 1983 Guggenheim Fellowship. Her plays include "Any Woman Can't," "Montpelier Pazazz," "Tender Offer," "Uncommon Women and Others" and "Isn't It Romantic."

1989 Mr 31, B4:3

NEW YORK DRAMA CRITICS CIRCLE AWARDS

'Heidi Chronicles' Wins Critics Circle Prize

By MEL GUSSOW

"The Heidi Chronicles" by Wendy Wasserstein was named the best new play of the 1988-1989 season by the New York Drama Critics Circle at a meeting held yesterday at the Algonquin Hotel. The critics also named Brian Friel's "Aristocrats" as the best new foreign play and voted a special citation to Bill Irwin for his show "Largely New York."

By a 15-1 vote, it was decided not to give an award for best new musical.

The winners will be honored on Monday, when a check for $1,000, given annually by the producer Lucille Lortel, will be presented to Ms. Wasserstein. The playwright has won a number of awards for "The Heidi Chronicles," including the Pulitzer Prize for Drama, the Susan Smith Blackburn Prize and the Hull-Warriner Award given by the Dramatists Guild. Her play, originally presented at Playwrights Horizon, is now at the Plymouth Theater.

"The Heidi Chronicles" won on the first ballot, with 10 votes from the 18 voting members. Two votes each went to Richard Greenberg's "Eastern Standard," Jon Robin Baitz's "Film Society" and Jerry Sterner's "Other People's Money," with single votes for Michael Weller's "Spoils of War" and Joshua Sobol's "Ghetto."

"Aristocrats," presented by the Manhattan Theater Club at Theater Four, won on a weighted second ballot, with the runners-up headed by Willy Russell's "Shirley Valentine," Barry McGovern's "I'll Go On" and "Ghetto." There were also votes for David Williamson's "Emerald City," David Mercer's "No Limits to Love," Tadeusz Kantor's "I Shall Never Return" and Ray Cooney's "Run for Your Wife."

"Largely New York," which Mr. Irwin wrote, directed and co-choreographed (with Kimi Okada) and in which he stars, is at the St. James Theater.

These are the voting members:

Clive Barnes, The New York Post.
John Beaufort, The Christian Science Monitor.
Michael Feingold, The Village Voice.
Julius Novick, The Village Voice.
William A. Henry 3d, Time.
Richard Hummler, Variety.
Howard Kissel, The Daily News.
Douglas Watt, The Daily News.
Don Nelsen, The Daily News.
Michael Kuchwara, The Associated Press.
Jacques le Sourd, Gannett Newspapers.
Edith Oliver, The New Yorker.
Mimi Kramer, The New Yorker.
William Raidy, Newhouse.
John Simon, New York.
Edwin Wilson, The Wall Street Journal.
Sylviane Gold, The Wall Street Journal.
Linda Winer, Newsday.

1989 My 16, C22:1

TONY AWARDS

'Heidi' and 'Jerome Robbins's Broadway' Win the Top Tonys

By MERVYN ROTHSTEIN

"Jerome Robbins's Broadway" won the Tony Award for best musical last night and Wendy Wasserstein's "Heidi Chronicles" was named best play.

The Robbins show, a compilation of numbers from 20 years of Mr. Robbins's Broadway musicals, won the most Tonys, six, including ones for Jason Alexander as best actor and Mr. Robbins himself as best director of a musical.

"Black and Blue," a jazz, blues and tap-dancing revue, won three. "Heidi," the Pulitzer Prize-winning serio-comic saga of 25 years in the

Philip Bosco and Pauline Collins are named the best actor and actress.

life of a modern woman, won two, as did "Lend Me a Tenor," Ken Ludwig's farce about an opera singer in 1930's Cleveland.

The 43d annual awards were presented at the Lunt-Fontanne Theater, with Angela Lansbury, a four-time Tony winner, as the host for the third year in a row. They were broadcast live on CBS.

Philip Bosco was named best actor in a play for his role as an opera impresario in "Lend Me a Tenor." The best actress prize went to Pauline Collins for her performance as "Shirley Valentine" in Willy Russell's one-woman play about an unhappy Liverpool housewife who leaves home for a Greek isle.

Best Actor in Musical

Mr. Alexander of "Jerome Robbins's Broadway" won as best actor in a musical for his tour de force performance in multiple roles, including those of Pseudolus from "A Funny Thing Happened on the Way to the Forum" and Tevye from "Fiddler on the Roof."

Best actress in a musical was Ruth Brown, for her torchy and comic jazz and blues numbers in "Black and Blue." In accepting the prize, Ms. Brown glanced over to the steps she had just walked up and said, "It's taken me 42 years to climb those eight steps." Among the other nominees were her co-star, Linda Hopkins and Charlotte d'Amboise of the Robbins show.

There were few surprises at the tightly orchestrated black-tie event. The show opened with Ms. Lansbury singing "Everything's Coming Up Roses," which was perhaps a classic case of hyperbole considering the quality of much of the season. Back in 1960, "Gypsy," the origin of "Roses," didn't even win the Tony, losing out to two other musicals that tied for the prize, "Fiorello!" and "The Sound of Music."

Later in the evening, there was a medley of showstoppers — Betty Buckley singing "Memories" from "Cats," Larry Kert doing "Being Alive" from "Company" and Ms. Lansbury performing "Send in the Clowns" from "A Little Night Music." They also brought back remembrance of better things past.

The often difficult task of fitting the 19 regular awards and the one special prize into the roughly two-hour television time slot was made easier this year because two categories were eliminated, cutting the 19 to 17. Because of the paucity of good musicals during the Broadway season, there were no nominations for best book or best original score of a musical.

Also, there were only three nominees for best musical instead of the usual four. Since excerpts are shown from each nominee, the producers were left with a little extra air time.

Presenters and others who appeared included John Lithgow, B. D. Wong, Nell Carter, Leslie Uggams, Barry Bostwick, Swoosie Kurtz, Steve Martin, Zoe Caldwell, Colleen Dewhurst, Gwen Verdon, Tommy Tune, August Wilson, James Earl Jones, Jerry Herman and Carol Channing.

The New York Times/Sara Krulwich

Jerome Robbins with his Tony Award and members of the cast of "Jerome Robbins's Broadway."

The prize for best direction of a play went to Jerry Zaks for "Lend Me a Tenor." In winning the musical direction award, Mr. Robbins said with a smile that as the director, he would have to thank his choreographer. Mr. Robbins, who of course was also the choreographer, last won the direction award 24 years ago, in 1965, for "Fiddler on the Roof."

'Our Town' Wins Award

The Robbins show was not eligible for the choreography award or for the scenic and costume design prizes because those elements were considered reproductions of previous work. The choreography prize was won by Cholly Atkins, Henry LeTang, Frankie Manning and Fayard Nicholas of "Black and Blue," with Mr. Robbins presenting the Tony.

Lincoln Center Theater's production of Thornton Wilder's "Our Town" won the award for best revival.

The featured acting awards for plays went to Boyd Gaines of "The Heidi Chronicles" and Christine Baranski of Neil Simon's "Rumors."

"Yesterday I bet my producer, Manny Azenberg, a million dollars that I would lose tonight," Ms. Baranski said. "Perhaps I can borrow the money from Neil Simon."

Mr. Gaines thanked Victor Garber — himself a nominee for best actor in a play, for "Lend Me a Tenor" — "for not taking the part."

The Robbins show took both featured acting awards for musicals, with the prizes going to the singer Debbie Shapiro and the dancer Scott Wise.

Claudio Segovia and Héctor Orezzoli of "Black and Blue" won the costume award.

The Tony for best scenic design went to Santo Loquasto, for creating a 1940's New York cafeteria that was next door to a Yiddish theater, in a revival of "Cafe Crown."

Bill Irwin's "Largely New York" was nominated for five Tonys, and Mr. Irwin himself for four — best play, acting, direction and choreography (with Kimi Okada) — but both he and the play won none. On the musical side, "Starmites" came up empty despite six nominations.

The Hartford Stage Company was given a special Tony for best regional theater. The Tony Awards were presented by the American Theater Wing and the League of American Theaters and Producers.

The Winners Of the Awards

BEST PLAY: "The Heidi Chronicles"

BEST MUSICAL: "Jerome Robbins's Broadway"

BEST REVIVAL: "Our Town"

LEADING ACTOR IN A PLAY: Philip Bosco ("Lend Me a Tenor")

LEADING ACTRESS IN A PLAY: Pauline Collins ("Shirley Valentine")

LEADING ACTOR IN A MUSICAL: Jason Alexander ("Jerome Robbins's Broadway")

LEADING ACTRESS IN A MUSICAL: Ruth Brown ("Black and Blue")

FEATURED ACTOR IN A PLAY: Boyd Gaines ("The Heidi Chronicles")

FEATURED ACTRESS IN A PLAY: Christine Baranski ("Rumors")

FEATURED ACTOR IN A MUSICAL: Scott Wise ("Jerome Robbins's Broadway")

FEATURED ACTRESS IN A MUSICAL: Debbie Shapiro ("Jerome Robbins's Broadway")

DIRECTION OF A PLAY: Jerry Zaks ("Lend Me a Tenor")

DIRECTION OF A MUSICAL: Jerome Robbins ("Jerome Robbins's Broadway")

BEST SCENIC DESIGN: Santo Loquasto ("Cafe Crown")

BEST COSTUME DESIGN: Claudio Segovia and Héctor Orezzoli ("Black and Blue")

BEST LIGHTING DESIGN: Jennifer Tipton ("Jerome Robbins's Broadway")

BEST CHOREOGRAPHY: Cholly Atkins, Henry LeTang, Frankie Manning and Fayard Nicholas ("Black and Blue")

1989 Je 5, C13:1

1990

PULITZER PRIZE

'Piano Lesson' Wins Drama Pulitzer

By ROBERT D. McFADDEN

"The Piano Lesson," August Wilson's Broadway-bound play about the black experience in America as seen through a prism of conflict between a brother and sister over their family's slavery-era heirloom piano, won the 1990 Pulitzer Prize for drama yesterday.

The play, which has toured the nation to large audiences and vibrant reviews and was a Pulitzer finalist last year, began previews this week and opens at the Walter Kerr Theater Monday night. It was Mr. Wilson's second Pulitzer. In 1987, he won the prize for "Fences," another in his series of dramas on black American life in the 20th Century.

1990 Ap 13, A16:1

Drama
August Wilson
"The Piano Lesson"

Mr. Wilson's award for "The Piano Lesson" is his second Pulitzer Prize for drama; he won his first in 1987 for "Fences." "It adds fuel to the fire," Mr. Wilson said yesterday. "It makes me want to do more work." Until less than a decade ago, he was a little-known poet; then the manuscript of a play he had written was discovered by the director Lloyd Richards at the Eugene O'Neill Theater Center in Connecticut. That play was "Ma Rainey's Black Bottom," which opened on Broadway in the 1984-85 season and won much critical praise. "Ma Rainey" was followed on Broadway by "Fences" — which won the Tony Award for best play as well as the Pulitzer — and "Joe Turner's Come and Gone." They and "The Piano Lesson" — the story of a dispute between a brother and sister over a piano that has involved their family since the days of slavery — are part of a series of plays that Mr. Wilson is writing, one for each decade, on the life of black Americans in the 20th century. The newest, "Two Trains Running," is now at the Yale Repertory Theater. Mr. Wilson, who will be 45 years old on April 27, lives in St. Paul, Minn.

1990 Ap 13, A17:4

DRAMA DESK AWARDS

"Jerome Robbins's Broadway" was selected by the Drama Desk yesterday as the outstanding musical of the 1988-89 theater season. Wendy Wasserstein's "Heidi Chronicles" was named best new play and "Our Town" best revival. The Drama Desk, formed in 1949, is an association of New York City critics, editors and reporters.

Ken Ludwig's "Lend Me a Tenor" won the most awards — four — including those for Philip Bosco as best actor in a play, Tovah Feldshuh for featured actress, Jerry Zaks for direction and William Ivey Long for costume design.

"Jerome Robbins's Broadway" won three awards, including ones to Jason Alexander for best actor in a musical and Jennifer Tipton for lighting design. Ms. Tipton's award also included her work on "Long Day's Journey Into Night" and "Waiting for Godot."

Pauline Collins was named best actress in a play for "Shirley Valentine." Best featured actor was Peter Frechette in "Eastern Standard."

Toni DiBuono of "Forbidden Broadway" was chosen as best actress in a musical. There were no awards for featured actors in a musical, direction of a musical and music, book, lyrics, choreography and orchestration.

The set-design prize went to Santo Loquasto for his work on "Cafe Crown" and "Italian American Reconciliation." Bill Irwin's "Largely New York" was given an award for "unique theatrical experience," and special awards went to the Manhattan Theater Club, Bernard Gersten and Gregory Mosher of Lincoln Center Theater, Jerome Robbins, Paul Gemignani and John McGlinn.

1989 My 23, C14:5

NEW YORK DRAMA CRITICS CIRCLE AWARDS

Critics Honor 'Piano Lesson'

"The Piano Lesson," by August Wilson, was selected as best new play of the 1989-90 season by the New York Drama Critics Circle. "City of Angels" was named best new musical. The critics also voted an award to Peter Nichols for "Privates on Parade" as best new foreign play. The Circle's annual award meeting was held yesterday at the Algonquin Hotel.

The winners are to be honored next Monday evening at the Algonquin, with Mr. Wilson receiving a check for $1,000, given annually by Lucille Lortel.

This is the fourth Critics Circle award to Mr. Wilson, who won for all his previous Broadway plays, "Ma Rainey's Black Bottom," "Fences" and "Joe Turner's Come and Gone." This ties the record for plays, set by Tennessee Williams. Stephen Sondheim won six for musicals.

"The Piano Lesson," which deals with the family legacy of a finely carved piano, is at the Walter Kerr Theater, in a production directed by Lloyd Richards. The play was first presented at the Yale Repertory Theater and, earlier this year, won the Pulitzer Prize for drama.

"City of Angels," a musical satire of Hollywood and private-eye movies, was written by Larry Gelbart, Cy Coleman and David Zippel. It is playing at the Virginia Theater. "Privates on Parade," a 1977 play by Mr. Nichols, received its New York premiere last August at the Roundabout Theater Company.

1990 My 15, C20:4

TONY AWARDS

The Winners of the 1990 Tonys

The Tony Awards were presented by the American Theater Wing on Sunday night at the Lunt-Fontanne Theater, with Kathleen Turner as host. These were the categories and the awards:

BEST PLAY: "The Grapes of Wrath"

BEST MUSICAL: "City of Angels"

BEST REVIVAL: "Gypsy"

LEADING ACTOR IN A PLAY: Robert Morse, "Tru"

LEADING ACTRESS IN A PLAY: Maggie Smith, "Lettice and Lovage"

LEADING ACTOR IN A MUSICAL: James Naughton, "City of Angels"

LEADING ACTRESS IN A MUSICAL: Tyne Daly, "Gypsy"

FEATURED ACTOR IN A PLAY: Charles Durning, "Cat on a Hot Tin Roof"

FEATURED ACTRESS IN A PLAY: Margaret Tyzack, "Lettice and Lovage"

FEATURED ACTOR IN A MUSICAL: Michael Jeter, "Grand Hotel"

FEATURED ACTRESS IN A MUSICAL: Randy Graff, "City of Angels"

DIRECTION OF A PLAY: Frank Galati, "The Grapes of Wrath"

DIRECTION OF A MUSICAL: Tommy Tune, "Grand Hotel"

BEST BOOK OF A MUSICAL: Larry Gelbart, "City of Angels"

BEST ORIGINAL MUSICAL SCORE: Cy Coleman and David Zippel, "City of Angels"

BEST SCENIC DESIGN: Robin Wagner, "City of Angels"

BEST COSTUME DESIGN: Santo Loquasto, "Grand Hotel"

BEST LIGHTING DESIGN: Jules Fisher, "Grand Hotel"

CHOREOGRAPHY: Tommy Tune, "Grand Hotel"

1990 Je 5, C15:1

Index

This index covers all the reviews included in this volume. It is divided into three sections: Titles, Personal Names, and Corporate Names.

Citations in this index are by year, month, day, section of newspaper (if applicable), page, and column; for example, 1989 Ja 11,II:12:1. Since the reviews appear in chronological order, the date is the key locator. The citations also serve to locate the reviews in bound volumes and microfilm editions of The Times.

In the citations, months are abbreviated as follows:

Ja - January	F - February	Mr - March
Ap - April	My - May	Je - June
Jl - July	Ag - August	S - September
O - October	N - November	D - December

TITLE INDEX

All plays reviewed are listed alphabetically. Articles that begin titles are inverted. Titles that begin with a number are alphabetized as though the number was spelled out. Whenever possible, foreign plays are entered under both the English and foreign-language titles. Plays reviewed more than once and plays with identical titles are given multiple listings.

PERSONAL NAMES INDEX

All persons included in the credits are listed alphabetically, last name first. Their function in the play is listed in parentheses: Playwright, Director, Producer, Choreographer, Composer, Lyricist, Scenic Designer, Lighting Director, Costume Designer, Original Author, Translator. Other functions (such as Sound Designer, Stage Manager, etc.) are listed as Miscellaneous. Where no such qualifier appears, the person was a performer (actor, actress, singer, dancer, musician). A person with multiple functions will have multiple entries.

Names beginning with Mc are alphabetized as if spelled Mac.

Names beginning with St. are alphabetized as if spelled Saint.

Entries under each name are by title of play, in chronological order.

CORPORATE NAME INDEX

All corporate bodies and performance groups mentioned in reviews as involved in the production of the play or in some other function connected with it are listed here alphabetically. Names that begin with a personal name are inverted (e.g., Kennedy, John F., Center for the Performing Arts). The function of the organization is given in parentheses as either Prod. (for Producer) or Misc. (for Miscellaneous). A company that has more than one function is listed twice.

Entries under each name are by title of play, in chronological order.

Q

R

S

T

10th Man, The 1989,D 24,II:3:1
Terminal Hip 1990,Ja 12,C3:1
Theme and Variations 1990,O 21,62:3
Thin Air 1989,N 19,75:5
Thirteenth Chair, The 1989,Ap 16,61:1
Those Were the Days 1990,N 14,C26:1
Three Cuckolds, The 1990,O 9,C14:4
Three Poets (Komachi; Hrosvitha; Akhmatova) 1989,N 23,C20:1
Three Sisters 1989,Ja 24,C16:4
Three Sisters, The 1989,Je 12,C13:1
Three Sisters, The 1989,Jl 23,II:5:5
Three Sisters, The 1989,N 23,C20:5
Three Sisters, The 1990,Ag 30,C15:1
Threepenny Opera 1989,N 6,C13:4
Thrill a Moment, A 1989,My 4,C23:1
Through the Leaves 1990,S 18,C18:1
Tiny Dimes 1990,Mr 9,C18:1
Titus Andronicus 1989,Je 12,C13:1
Titus Andronicus 1989,Ag 21,C13:1
Together Again 1990,Ap 27,C10:4
Tomfoolery 1989,Ja 14,10:4
Tone Clusters (In Darkest America) 1990,Ap 5,C15:1
Tonight We Love (Marathon 1990: Festival of New One-Act Plays, Series C) 1990,Je 14,C20:3
Tour de Nesle, La (Tower of Evil, The) 1990,My 13,45:1
Tower of Evil, The (Tour de Nesle, La) 1990,My 13,45:1
Township Fever 1990,D 20,C11:1
Township Fever 1990,D 23,II:5:1
Traveler in the Dark 1990,Ja 16,C13:1
Travesties 1989,N 3,C29:1
Treatment of Dr. Love, The (Grand Guignol, The) 1990,Je 2,18:1
Triplets in Uniform 1989,F 12,70:4
Tru 1989,D 15,C3:1
Tru 1990,Ap 22,II:5:1
Truly Blessed: A Musical Celebration of Mahalia Jackson 1990,Ap 23,C13:1
Twelfth Night 1989,Jl 10,C13:1
Twelfth Night 1989,O 4,C17:1
Twelfth Night 1989,D 20,C20:3
20 Fingers, 20 Toes 1990,Ja 10,C17:1
Twice Shy (Young Playwrights Festival) 1989,S 22,C5:4
2 1990,Ap 5,C15:1
Two Gentlemen of Verona 1990,D 13,C16:5
Two War Scenes: Cross Patch and Goldberg Street (Marathon 1990: Festival of New One-Act Plays, Series A) 1990,My 16,C14:4

U

Ubu 1989,Je 26,C14:1
Ulysses in Nighttown 1989,Ja 15,44:1
Uncle Vanya 1990,Mr 3,12:5
Unguided Missile, The 1989,F 13,C16:3
Up Against It 1989,D 5,C17:3
Up 'n' Under 1989,Je 13,C17:1

V

Valued Friends 1990,D 20,C20:4
Vid 1990,N 22,C18:4
Video Store Owner's Significant Other, The 1990,S 26,C9:5
Violent Peace 1990,Mr 3,12:3
Visit, The 1989,F 5,56:5
Vital Signs 1990,Ap 5,C15:1
Voces de Acero (Voices of Steel) 1990,Ag 20,C14:1
Voice of the Prairie, The 1990,D 18,C18:5
Voices of Steel (Voces de Acero) 1990,Ag 20,C14:1
Vortex, The 1989,Je 27,C15:4
Voysey Inheritance, The 1990,O 26,C3:1

W

Walkers 1989,Ap 16,60:1
Wall-Dog, The 1990,Jl 25,C11:3
Walt Disney's Magic Kingdom on Ice 1990,F 20,C18:4
Ward No. Six 1989,Jl 29,16:1
Wash, The 1990,N 8,C28:4
Wash, The 1990,N 18,II:5:1
Water Music (Marathon '89, Series C) 1989,Je 29,C14:5
Waves, The 1990,My 10,C16:4
We Keep Our Victims Ready 1990,Jl 24,C13:1
Welcome to the Club 1989,Ap 14,C3:1
What a Man Weighs 1990,My 25,C3:2
What the Butler Saw 1989,Mr 9,C21:1
What the Butler Saw 1989,Mr 29,C17:1
What the Butler Saw 1989,D 24,II:3:1
Whatnot 1990,S 25,C16:3
What's Wrong with This Picture? 1990,Je 23,14:1
When She Danced 1990,F 20,C15:1
When We Are Married 1989,Ja 28,14:3
Whistle in the Dark, A 1989,Ag 28,C13:4
Whistle in the Dark, A 1989,N 17,C26:5
White Boned Demon 1989,Mr 5,68:1
White Chocolate for My Father 1990,F 15,C22:3
Widow's Blind Date, The 1989,N 8,C23:1
Wild Duck, The 1990,Ag 30,C15:1
Wink-Dah (Marathon '89, Series A) 1989,My 30,C19:1
Winter's Tale, The 1989,Mr 22,C19:4
Winter's Tale, The 1989,D 24,II:3:1
Winter's Tale, The 1990,Ja 31,C15:1
Wipe the Dirt Off Your Lips and Stroke the Mystery (Men's Room, The) 1990,Jl 26,C13:3
Witch, The 1989,N 16,C30:4
Without Apologies 1989,F 19,74:4
Wizard of Oz, The 1989,Mr 24,C3:1
Woman Floating Out a Window (Marathon '89, Series B) 1989,Je 15,C14:5
Wonderful Party! (Manhattan Punch Line's Fifth Annual Festival of One-Act Comedies, Series A) 1989,Ja 26,C16:1
Wonderful Town 1989,O 8,64:1
Words, No Music 1990,O 15,C15:1
Working One-Acts '89 (Closer, The; Floor Above the Roof; Freeze Tag; Sand Mountain Matchmaking) 1989,Je 25,45:4
World Without End 1990,O 6,11:3
Woyzeck 1990,Mr 6,C17:1

Y

Yankee Dawg You Die 1989,My 15,C13:4
Yankee Dawg You Die 1989,D 24,II:3:1
Year of the Baby, The 1989,Ag 17,C14:6
Yesterdays 1990,O 8,C14:3
Yiddle with a Fiddle 1990,O 30,C14:5
Yoshitsune and the Thousand Cherry Trees (Yoshitsune Senbonzakura) 1989,S 8,C3:4
Yoshitsune Senbonzakura (Yoshitsune and the Thousand Cherry Trees) 1989,S 8,C3:4
You Could Be Home Now 1990,Jl 17,C16:1
Young Playwrights Festival (Twice Shy; Peter Breaks Through; Painted Rain; Finnegan's Funeral Parlor and Ice Cream Shoppe) 1989,S 22,C5:4
Young Playwrights Festival 1990 (Mutterschaft; Believing; Psychoneurotic Phantasies; Hey Little Walter) 1990,S 21,C14:6
Young Rube 1989,Ap 21,C3:4
Your Handsome Captain 1989,N 12,71:6

Z

Zara Spook and Other Lures 1990,Ap 5,C15:1
Zora Neale Hurston 1990,F 5,C14:1
Zoya's Apartment 1990,My 11,C3:1

A

Aarif, N. Richard
Titus Andronicus 1989,Ag 21,C13:1
Aaron, Caroline
Self-Torture and Strenuous Exercise (Marathon '89, Series A) 1989,My 30,C19:1
Aaron, Jack
Made in Heaven 1990,My 13,45:1
Abady, Josephine R. (Director)
Born Yesterday 1989,Ja 30,C11:1
Better Days (New Music) 1989,N 4,16:3
March on Russia, The 1990,N 14,C24:3
Abady, Josephine R. (Miscellaneous)
New Music 1989,N 4,16:3
March on Russia, The 1990,N 14,C24:3
Abajian, Chris (Composer)
White Boned Demon 1989,Mr 5,68:1
Abakarov, Shamkhal
Leningrad State Music Hall 1990,My 28,11:1
Abatemarco, Tony
Kingfish 1989,D 22,C5:1
Abbott, George (Director)
Frankie 1989,O 10,C18:3
Abbott, George (Playwright)
Frankie 1989,O 10,C18:3
Abdoh, Reza (Director)
Father Was a Peculiar Man 1990,Jl 11,C13:1
Abdoh, Reza (Playwright)
Father Was a Peculiar Man 1990,Jl 11,C13:1
Abdulov, Aleksandr
Junon and Avos: The Hope 1990,Ja 8,C16:3
Abel, Ron (Miscellaneous)
Blame It on the Movies 1989,My 18,C22:3
Abel, Ron (Musical Director)
Blame It on the Movies 1989,My 18,C22:3
Abelson, Robert
Those Were the Days 1990,N 14,C26:1
Aberdeen, Robert
Gogol 1990,Ap 14,17:1
Aberger, Tom (Miscellaneous)
Aristocrats 1989,Ap 26,C15:1
All God's Dangers 1989,O 23,C15:3
Bad Habits 1990,Mr 21,C13:1
Young Playwrights Festival 1990 1990,S 21,C14:6
Abrahao, Roberto (Choreographer)
Oba Oba '90 1990,Mr 16,C6:3
Abrams, Helene
God's Policemen 1989,O 22,64:4
Abramson, Barbara (Scenic Designer)
White Boned Demon 1989,Mr 5,68:1
Abrash, Victoria (Miscellaneous)
New Anatomies 1990,F 22,C19:1
Abravanel, Wayne (Musical Director)
Jekyll and Hyde 1990,Jl 1,48:1
Abreu, Jorge Luis
I Am a Winner 1990,Ap 1,52:3
Abuba, Ernest
Song of Shim Chung, The 1989,N 19,76:4
Zoya's Apartment 1990,My 11,C3:1
Abuba, Ernest (Director)
Play Ball 1989,F 12,68:4
Abujamra, Marcia (Translator)
Doente Imaginario, O (Imaginary Invalid, The) 1990,Ag 23,C20:1
Ackamoor, Idris
I Think It's Gonna Work Out Fine 1990,Mr 17,18:6
Ackamoor, Idris (Composer)
I Think It's Gonna Work Out Fine 1990,Mr 17,18:6
Ackerman, Robert Allan (Director)
Madhouse in Goa, A 1989,Je 27,C15:4
Ackermann-Blount, Joan (Playwright)
Zara Spook and Other Lures 1990,Ap 5,C15:1
Acosta, Elizabeth
Adios, Tropicana 1989,Ag 10,C16:5
Adam, Ben (Miscellaneous)
Ambassador, The 1989,O 22,63:1
Adams, Betsy (Lighting Director)
Education of H*Y*M*A*N K*A*P*L*A*N, The 1989,Ap 6,C22:4
Rothschilds, The 1990,F 26,C16:1
Adams, Cindy (Miscellaneous)
Money Talks 1990,S 7,C3:5
Adams, David (Miscellaneous)
Skin—A State of Being 1989,Ja 12,C15:1

Adams, David (Scenic Designer)
Dionysus Filius Dei 1989,Mr 5,69:1
Adams, Dianne (Miscellaneous)
Starmites 1989,Ap 28,C3:1
Adams, Jane
Young Playwrights Festival 1990 1990,S 21,C14:6
Adams, Kent
Red Sheets (Manhattan Class Company, One-Act Play Festival, Series A) 1989,Mr 11,16:1
Adams, Mary Kay
In Her Own Words (A Portrait of Jane) 1989,Ag 17,C18:3
Adamson, David
Ambassador, The 1989,O 22,63:1
Strike, The 1990,Ja 29,C18:5
Adamson, Eve (Director)
Three Sisters 1989,Ja 24,C16:4
Life Is a Dream 1989,D 16,17:1
Adamson, Eve (Lighting Director)
Life Is a Dream 1989,D 16,17:1
Addinsell, Richard (Composer)
Re:Joyce! 1990,F 2,C3:1
Adkins, David
New Music 1989,N 4,16:3
Adler, Bruce
Bone-the-Fish 1989,Ap 5,C19:4
Those Were the Days 1990,N 14,C26:1
Adler, Joanna
Lear 1990,Ja 26,C3:1
Adler, Morris (Miscellaneous)
Land of Dreams, The 1989,N 22,C10:1
Father's Inheritance 1990,N 18,75:1
Adolfo (Costume Designer)
Carol Lawrence and Larry Kert Together . . . Again! 1990,O 4,C21:1
Adolphe, Bruce (Composer)
Love's Labor's Lost 1989,My 26,C4:5
Adshead, Patricia (Costume Designer)
Phantom Lady, The 1989,Ap 16,60:1
Aedo, Cesar
Grandma Goes West 1989,N 3,C4:1
Affoumado, Ralph (Composer)
Ad Hock 1989,Ja 20,C11:1
Agyapon, Kweyao (Composer)
Caucasian Chalk Circle, The 1990,D 3,C13:3
Ahearn, Daniel
Hollywood Scheherazade 1989,O 1,60:5
Woyzeck 1990,Mr 6,C17:1
Ahrens, Lynn (Lyricist)
Once on This Island 1990,My 7,C11:1
Once on This Island 1990,O 28,II:5:1
Ahrens, Lynn (Playwright)
Once on This Island 1990,My 7,C11:1
Once on This Island 1990,O 28,II:5:1
Ahronheim, Albert (Miscellaneous)
Fertilization Opera, The (Manhattan Punch Line's Sixth Annual Festival of One-Act Comedies, Evening B) 1990,F 11,70:1
Ahronheim, Albert (Musical Director)
Fertilization Opera, The (Manhattan Punch Line's Sixth Annual Festival of One-Act Comedies, Evening B) 1990,F 11,70:1
Aibel, Douglas (Director)
Hannah . . . 1939 1990,Je 2,16:3
Aibel, Douglas (Miscellaneous)
Feast Here Tonight 1989,N 30,C16:3
Moving Targets 1990,Ja 30,C14:5
Hannah . . . 1939 1990,Je 2,16:3
Nightingale 1990,D 4,C16:3
Aidem, Betsy
Night Hank Williams Died, The 1989,Ja 25,C16:4
Miser, The 1990,My 18,C4:3
Aitken, Maria
Vortex, The 1989,Je 27,C15:4
Akalaitis, JoAnne (Director)
Cymbeline 1989,Je 1,C15:1
Through the Leaves 1990,S 18,C18:1
Akerlind, Christopher (Lighting Director)
Piano Lesson, The 1990,Ap 17,C13:4
Love and Anger 1990,D 9,82:3
Akers, Karen
Grand Hotel 1989,N 13,C13:3
Grand Hotel 1990,F 25,II:5:1
Alasa, Michael
Peggy and Jackson 1989,Ag 10,C16:5
Alasa, Michael (Director)
Peggy and Jackson 1989,Ag 10,C16:5
Alasa, Michael (Playwright)
Peggy and Jackson 1989,Ag 10,C16:5

Albani, Rik (Musical Director)
Grandma Goes West 1989,N 3,C4:1
Big Apple Circus, The 1990,N 3,13:4
Albert, Stephen J. (Producer)
Piano Lesson, The 1990,Ap 17,C13:4
Alberti, Bruno
Sunshine 1989,D 18,C10:4
Albrecht, J. Grant
Illusion, The 1990,Ja 18,C21:1
Albright, Jeffrey J.
Hello, Bob 1990,O 21,62:3
Alchourron, Rodolfo
Dangerous Games 1989,O 20,C3:3
Alchourron, Rodolfo (Miscellaneous)
Dangerous Games 1989,O 20,C3:3
Aldous, Brian (Lighting Director)
Indiana Dog 1989,S 26,C17:1
Hyde Park 1989,N 12,73:1
Crowbar 1990,F 20,C18:1
Tiny Dimes 1990,Mr 9,C18:1
Gogol 1990,Ap 14,17:1
Rodents and Radios 1990,Ap 28,15:1
Father Was a Peculiar Man 1990,Jl 11,C13:1
Famine Plays 1990,N 3,14:5
Aldous, Brian (Miscellaneous)
Night Breath 1989,Ap 9,57:2
Aldredge, Theoni V. (Costume Designer)
Gypsy 1989,N 17,C5:1
Gypsy 1990,S 18,C11:1
Oh, Kay! 1990,N 2,C1:1
Aldrich, Janet
Starmites 1989,Ap 28,C3:1
Alejandro, Jorge
No + (No More) 1989,Ag 12,14:4
Aleksidze, Georgi (Choreographer)
King Lear 1990,Ap 4,C17:1
Alessandrini, Gerard (Director)
Forbidden Broadway 1989,Ap 16,II:7:1
Gigi 1989,My 28,57:1
Forbidden Broadway 1990 1990,Ja 24,C15:1
Forbidden Broadway 1990,S 23,II:5:1
Alessandrini, Gerard (Lyricist)
Forbidden Broadway 1989,Ap 16,II:7:1
Forbidden Broadway 1990 1990,Ja 24,C15:1
Forbidden Broadway 1990,S 23,II:5:1
Alessandrini, Gerard (Miscellaneous)
Forbidden Broadway 1990 1990,Ja 24,C15:1
Alexander, Adinah
Young Rube 1989,Ap 21,C3:4
Madame Sherry 1989,Jl 30,57:1
Goose! Beyond the Nursery 1990,F 11,69:2
Alexander, Bill (Director)
Cymbeline 1989,Ag 6,II:5:1
Alexander, C. Renee (Miscellaneous)
O Pioneers! 1990,Ja 28,49:1
Alexander, Erika
Forbidden City, The 1989,Ap 7,C3:1
Alexander, George
Merrily We Roll Along 1990,F 27,C13:1
Alexander, Jace
Good Coach, The 1989,Je 13,C18:5
Heart of a Dog 1990,Mr 16,C3:1
Price of Fame 1990,Je 14,C17:1
Alexander, Jane
Approaching Zanzibar 1989,My 5,C3:1
Shadowlands 1990,N 12,C11:1
Shadowlands 1990,N 18,II:5:1
Alexander, Jason
Jerome Robbins's Broadway 1989,F 27,C13:1
Accomplice 1990,Ap 27,C5:1
Alexander, Julie
Father's Inheritance 1990,N 18,75:1
Alexander, Randolph (Scenic Designer)
Tomfoolery 1989,Ja 14,10:4
Alexander, Randy (Miscellaneous)
Three Sisters 1989,Ja 24,C16:4
Alexander, Robert
Grand Guignol, The 1990,Je 2,18:1
Alexander, Terry
Some Sweet Day 1989,Mr 27,C13:1
Alexis, Connie L. (Miscellaneous)
Brilliant Traces 1989,F 6,C11:1
Dalton's Back 1989,F 10,C3:1
Amulets Against the Dragon Forces 1989,Ap 6,C17:4
Florida Crackers 1989,Je 2,C3:1
Beside Herself 1989,O 18,C15:1
Sunshine 1989,D 18,C10:4
Imagining Brad 1990,F 7,C15:2
Prelude to a Kiss 1990,Mr 15,C15:1

Arcade, Penny
Quiet Evening with Sid and Nancy, A (At the Chelsea) 1989,Ja 20,C3:1
Arcade, Penny (Playwright)
Quiet Evening with Sid and Nancy, A (At the Chelsea) 1989,Ja 20,C3:1
Arcaro, Robert
Sand Mountain Matchmaking (Working One-Acts '89) 1989,Je 25,45:4
Special Interests 1990,F 18,70:1
Arcenas, Loy (Scenic Designer)
For Dear Life 1989,Ja 11,C17:1
Heiress, The 1989,Je 16,C3:1
Glass Menagerie, The 1989,O 16,C19:1
Mountain Language 1989,N 9,C21:3
Birthday Party, The 1989,N 9,C21:3
Imagining Brad 1990,F 7,C15:2
Prelude to a Kiss 1990,Mr 15,C15:1
Day Trips 1990,Ap 16,C15:1
Spunk 1990,Ap 19,C17:4
Prelude to a Kiss 1990,My 2,C15:1
Once on This Island 1990,My 7,C11:1
Caucasian Chalk Circle, The 1990,O 1,C14:1
Once on This Island 1990,O 28,II:5:1
Caucasian Chalk Circle, The 1990,D 3,C13:3
Caucasian Chalk Circle, The 1990,D 9,II:5:1
Ard, Ken
Dangerous Games 1989,O 20,C3:3
Ardila, Jorge (Scenic Designer)
Paso o Parabola del Camino, El (Parable of the Path, The) 1989,Ag 20,62:1
Arditti, Paul (Miscellaneous)
Orpheus Descending 1989,S 25,C15:4
Merchant of Venice, The 1989,D 20,C15:1
Arenberg, Lee
Carnage, A Comedy 1989,S 18,C14:1
Arenius, Alan
I & I 1989,S 24,72:3
German Requiem 1990,My 28,14:5
Ari, Bob
Cardondale Dreams 1990,Ja 5,C3:1
Aridjis, Homero (Original Author)
Suenos 1989,F 23,C13:3
Ariel, Raymond (Producer)
Yiddle with a Fiddle 1990,O 30,C14:5
Aristophanes (Playwright)
Clouds, The 1990,Ap 22,63:4
Ariza, Patricia
Paso o Parabola del Camino, El (Parable of the Path, The) 1989,Ag 20,62:1
Arlen, Harold (Composer)
Wizard of Oz, The 1989,Mr 24,C3:1
Arlt, Lewis
Orpheus Descending 1989,S 25,C15:4
Arluck, Neal (Miscellaneous)
Perfect Diamond, A 1990,Je 6,C18:1
Silent Thunder, A 1990,Jl 6,C11:1
Armitage, Calvin Lennon
Member of the Wedding, The 1989,Ap 1,16:3
Grapes of Wrath, The 1990,Mr 23,C1:4
Armstrong, April Beth
Crucible, The 1989,D 16,15:1
Armstrong, Karen (Miscellaneous)
Subfertile 1990,N 8,C20:5
Armstrong, Richard (Director)
Malady of Death, The 1989,Ja 28,13:1
Armus, Sidney
10th Man, The 1989,D 11,C13:1
Arnold, Jennifer (Costume Designer)
Lady in Question, The 1989,Jl 26,C17:1
Arnold, Michael (Choreographer)
Rothschilds, The 1990,F 26,C16:1
Arnone, John (Scenic Designer)
Winter's Tale, The 1989,Mr 22,C19:4
Sex, Drugs, Rock & Roll 1990,F 9,C3:1
Miser, The 1990,My 18,C4:3
Aronson, Boris (Scenic Designer)
Jerome Robbins's Broadway 1989,F 27,C13:1
Fiddler on the Roof 1990,N 19,C13:1
Fiddler on the Roof 1990,N 25,II:5:1
Aronson, Frances (Lighting Director)
Kathy and Mo Show, The: Parallel Lives 1989,F 1,C21:1
Niedecker 1989,Mr 19,61:1
Don Juan of Seville (Burlador de Sevilla y Convidado de Piedra, El) 1989,Ap 7,C3:5
Brimstone and Treacle 1989,Ap 18,C15:3
Blessing, The 1989,My 22,C12:1
Hyde in Hollywood 1989,N 30,C19:3

Othello 1990,Ja 17,C18:4
Neddy 1990,Ap 2,C15:1
Tower of Evil, The (Tour de Nesle, La) 1990,My 13,45:1
Through the Leaves 1990,S 18,C18:1
Happy Days 1990,O 13,17:1
Aronson, Henry (Miscellaneous)
Starmites 1989,Ap 28,C3:1
Aronson, Henry (Musical Director)
Starmites 1989,Ap 28,C3:1
Aronstein, Martin (Lighting Director)
Accomplice 1990,Ap 27,C5:1
Arrabal, Fernando (Playwright)
Body Builder's Book of Love, The 1990,Ap 29,60:1
Arrabal, Miguel
Dangerous Games 1989,O 20,C3:3
Arrambide, Mario
Measure for Measure 1989,Mr 10,C3:1
Baal 1990,Mr 24,17:1
Arrick, Larry (Director)
What's Wrong with This Picture? 1990,Je 23,14:1
Arrucci, John
Suenos 1989,F 23,C13:3
Arsenault, Brian
Up Against It 1989,D 5,C17:3
Artemieva, Lyudmila
Junon and Avos: The Hope 1990,Ja 8,C16:3
Arthur, David
Pal Joey 1990,Jl 24,C13:3
Ascher, Tamas (Director)
Three Sisters, The 1989,Jl 23,II:5:5
Aschner, Michael
Manhattan Punch Line's Sixth Annual Festival of One-Act Comedies, Evening A 1990,F 4,60:1
Aschner, Michael (Playwright)
Brunch at Trudy and Paul's (Manhattan Punch Line's Sixth Annual Festival of One-Act Comedies, Evening B) 1990,F 11,70:1
Ash, Jeffrey (Producer)
Other People's Money 1989,F 17,C3:4
Ashe, Jennifer
Hollywood Scheherazade 1989,O 1,60:5
Asher, Jane
Henceforward 1989,Ja 15,II:1:4
Asher, Steve (Miscellaneous)
Camille 1990,S 7,C3:1
Ashkenasi, Danny (Miscellaneous)
Witch, The 1989,N 16,C30:4
Ashley, Christopher (Director)
Night Hank Williams Died, The 1989,Ja 25,C16:4
Buzzsaw Berkeley 1989,Ag 21,C14:3
Portfolio (Manhattan Punch Line's Sixth Annual Festival of One-Act Comedies, Evening A) 1990,F 4,60:1
Ashley, Christopher (Miscellaneous)
Buzzsaw Berkeley 1989,Ag 21,C14:3
Ashley, Elizabeth
When She Danced 1990,F 20,C15:1
Askin, Peter (Director)
Beauty Marks 1989,O 29,63:5
Mambo Mouth: A Savage Comedy 1990,D 2,83:1
Asner, Edward
Born Yesterday 1989,Ja 30,C11:1
Born Yesterday 1989,F 19,II:5:1
Assaf, Michele (Choreographer)
Starmites 1989,Ap 28,C3:1
As-Swaudi, Tajj
Ground People 1990,My 7,C13:1
As-Swaudi, Tajj (Composer)
Ground People 1990,My 7,C13:1
Astrachan, Joshua (Miscellaneous)
Sleeping Dogs 1989,Mr 23,C17:1
Apocalyptic Butterflies 1989,Je 17,12:3
Astredo, Humbert Allen
Light Up the Sky 1990,Ag 22,C10:5
Atha, Steve (Miscellaneous)
City of Angels 1989,D 12,C19:4
Athayde, Roberto (Director)
Miss Margarida's Way 1990,F 16,C3:1
Athayde, Roberto (Playwright)
Miss Margarida's Way 1990,F 16,C3:1
Miss Margarida's Way 1990,F 25,II:5:1
Athens, Jim
Golden Apple, The 1990,Mr 30,C3:5
Atkins, Cholly (Choreographer)
Black and Blue 1989,Ja 27,C3:1
Atkins, Eileen
Prin 1990,Je 7,C18:5
Atkinson, Jayne
Heiress, The 1989,Je 16,C3:1

Art of Success, The 1989,D 21,C11:1
Atkinson, Linda
Daytrips 1990,N 10,16:1
Atwood, Kathryn
Indiana Dog 1989,S 26,C17:1
Auberjonois, Rene
Metamorphosis 1989,Mr 7,C15:1
City of Angels 1989,D 12,C19:4
Auder, Alexandra
Little House on the Prairie (At the Chelsea) 1989,Ja 20,C3:1
Auger, Pierre
Polygraph 1990,O 27,12:5
Augustus, Nicholas
Gigi 1989,My 28,57:1
Aulino, Tom
Ubu 1989,Je 26,C14:1
Up Against It 1989,D 5,C17:3
Winter's Tale, The 1990,Ja 31,C15:1
Aulisi, Joseph G. (Costume Designer)
Jerome Robbins's Broadway 1989,F 27,C13:1
Run for Your Wife! 1989,Mr 8,C17:1
Artist Descending a Staircase 1989,D 1,C3:1
Aulisi, Joseph G. (Miscellaneous)
Jerome Robbins's Broadway 1989,F 27,C13:1
Austin, Lyn (Miscellaneous)
Ladies 1989,Ap 7,C3:1
Paradise for the Worried 1990,Ap 6,C3:1
Endangered Species 1990,O 9,C13:1
Avan (Miscellaneous)
Over Forty 1989,My 16,C17:1
Boochie 1989,Jl 30,57:2
Every Goodbye Ain't Gone 1989,Jl 30,57:2
Avidon, Nelson
Progress 1989,D 11,C15:1
Avni, Ran (Director)
Yiddle with a Fiddle 1990,O 30,C14:5
Avni, Ran (Miscellaneous)
Bitter Friends 1989,F 14,C16:3
Sunshine Boys, The 1989,My 14,49:1
Double Blessing 1989,Jl 2,38:1
Witch, The 1989,N 16,C30:4
Return, The 1990,Ja 12,C3:3
Dividends 1990,Mr 4,51:1
New York 1937 1990,My 6,75:4
What's Wrong with This Picture? 1990,Je 23,14:1
Spinoza 1990,N 4,72:4
Ayala, Andrea
Ringling Brothers and Barnum & Bailey Circus 1990,Mr 31,13:1
Ayala, Marquerite
Ringling Brothers and Barnum & Bailey Circus 1990,Mr 31,13:1
Ayala, Michelle
Ringling Brothers and Barnum & Bailey Circus 1990,Mr 31,13:1
Ayala, Nohora
Paso o Parabola del Camino, El (Parable of the Path, The) 1989,Ag 20,62:1
Ayckbourn, Alan (Director)
Henceforward 1989,Ja 15,II:1:4
Revengers' Comedies, The 1989,Je 22,C17:1
Ayckbourn, Alan (Miscellaneous)
Revengers' Comedies, The 1989,Je 22,C17:1
Ayckbourn, Alan (Playwright)
Henceforward 1989,Ja 15,II:1:4
Revengers' Comedies, The 1989,Je 22,C17:1
Aylward, Peter
King Lear 1990,N 16,C3:1
Ayres, Mary-Helen (Translator)
Paper Gramophone, The 1989,Mr 4,11:4
Azar, Rick (Producer)
All God's Dangers 1989,O 23,C15:3
Azarian, Arminae
Carnal Knowledge 1990,N 21,C15:1
Azenberg, Emanuel (Producer)
Jerome Robbins's Broadway 1989,F 27,C13:1
Artist Descending a Staircase 1989,D 1,C3:1

B

Babe, Thomas (Director)
Sleeping Dogs 1989,Mr 23,C17:1
Peter Breaks Through (Young Playwrights Festival) 1989,S 22,C5:4
Finnegan's Funeral Parlor and Ice Cream Shoppe (Young Playwrights Festival) 1989,S 22,C5:4

Casa 1990,Ja 18,C24:4
Bell, Jan (Scenic Designer)
Tale of Two Cities, A 1989,Ja 18,C15:4
Bell, Jennifer
Step into My World 1989,F 19,76:4
Bell, Joyce Korbin (Miscellaneous)
Man Who Fell in Love with His Wife, The 1990,Ag 19,55:1
Bell, Neal (Playwright)
Sleeping Dogs 1989,Mr 23,C17:1
Open Boat, The (Marathon '89, Series B) 1989,Je 15,C14:5
Bell, Ralph
Henry Lumper 1989,F 5,53:1
Bella, Robert
Measure for Measure 1989,Mr 10,C3:1
Bella-Joa, Ricardo
Sueno de una Noche de Verano (Midsummer Night's Dream, A) 1989,Ag 16,C16:1
Bellamy, Amanda
Midsummer Night's Dream, A 1989,Ag 6,II:5:1
Bellamy, Ned
Carnage, A Comedy 1989,S 18,C14:1
Bellamy, Terry E.
Walkers 1989,Ap 16,60:1
Belling, Edward (Playwright)
Made in Heaven 1990,My 13,45:1
Bello, Irma
Abanderado, El (Standard Bearer, The) 1990,N 4,72:1
Bello, Miriam
Sueno de una Noche de Verano (Midsummer Night's Dream, A) 1989,Ag 16,C16:1
Bello-Joa, Jorge
Sueno de una Noche de Verano (Midsummer Night's Dream, A) 1989,Ag 16,C16:1
Belousov, Vladimir
Junon and Avos: The Hope 1990,Ja 8,C16:3
Belsky, Igor (Choreographer)
Leningrad State Music Hall 1990,My 28,11:1
Benac, Marie Pierre
Big Apple Circus, The 1990,N 3,13:4
Ben-Ari, Neal
Education of H*Y*M*A*N K*A*P*L*A*N, The 1989,Ap 6,C22:4
Merchant of Venice, The 1989,D 20,C15:1
Love Life 1990,Je 22,C15:1
Bender, Jeff
Cardondale Dreams 1990,Ja 5,C3:1
Benedict, Claire
Romeo and Juliet 1990,Jl 14,10:1
Benedict, Elizabeth
Uncle Vanya 1990,Mr 3,12:5
Benedict, Paul (Director)
Kathy and Mo Show, The: Parallel Lives 1989,F 1,C21:1
Prelude and Liebestod (Manhattan Class One-Acts, Series B) 1989,Mr 19,61:4
Anthony Rose 1989,O 30,C16:3
Bad Habits 1990,Mr 21,C13:1
Benet, Stephen Vincent (Playwright)
John Brown's Body 1989,Je 27,C14:5
Ben Gal, Nir (Miscellaneous)
Ghetto 1989,My 1,C11:1
Benguria, Xonia
Lady from Havana, The 1990,N 5,C14:4
Benham, Dorothy
Jerome Robbins's Broadway 1989,F 27,C13:1
Benjamin, Randy (Scenic Designer)
Immigrant, The: A Hamilton County Album 1989,F 8,C19:1
Education of H*Y*M*A*N K*A*P*L*A*N, The 1989,Ap 6,C22:4
Waves, The 1990,My 10,C16:4
Silent Thunder, A 1990,Jl 6,C11:1
Benjamin, Shawn
Red Sneaks, The 1989,Je 29,C13:1
Bennett, Alan
Single Spies 1989,Ja 15,II:1:4
Single Spies 1989,Ag 20,II:5:1
Bennett, Alan (Director)
Single Spies 1989,Ag 20,II:5:1
Bennett, Alan (Playwright)
Single Spies 1989,Ja 15,II:1:4
Single Spies 1989,Ag 20,II:5:1
Bennett, Beate Hein (Translator)
I & I 1989,S 24,72:3
Bennett, Keith Robert
Oh, Kay! 1989,N 1,C22:3

Pal Joey 1990,Jl 24,C13:3
Oh, Kay! 1990,N 2,C1:1
Bennett, Lynette
Gigi 1989,My 28,57:1
Bennett, Mark (Composer)
Ring Gott Farblonjet, Der 1990,Ap 13,C3:1
Love and Anger 1990,D 9,82:3
Bennett, Mark (Miscellaneous)
Nest, The 1989,Mr 2,C26:1
Working One-Acts '89 1989,Je 25,45:4
My Children! My Africa! 1989,D 19,C19:3
Illusion, The 1990,Ja 18,C21:1
Ring Gott Farblonjet, Der 1990,Ap 13,C3:1
Camille 1990,S 7,C3:1
Lake No Bottom 1990,N 30,C3:1
Bennett, Robert (Miscellaneous)
Meet Me in St. Louis 1989,N 3,C3:1
March on Russia, The 1990,N 14,C24:3
Bennion, Alan
Macbeth 1989,Mr 21,C19:1
Apart from George 1989,Mr 21,C19:1
Benson, Jodi
Welcome to the Club 1989,Ap 14,C3:1
Benson, Raymond (Composer)
Hyde Park 1989,N 12,73:1
Benson, Sally (Original Author)
Meet Me in St. Louis 1989,N 3,C3:1
Benstein, Susan
Slay It with Music 1989,O 24,C20:6
Bensussen, Melia (Director)
How It Hangs (Equal 'Wrights) 1989,My 18,C20:3
New Anatomies 1990,F 22,C19:1
I Am a Winner 1990,Ap 1,52:3
Bensussen, Melia (Translator)
Sueno de una Noche de Verano (Midsummer Night's Dream, A) 1989,Ag 16,C16:1
Palomar, El (Pigeon House, The) 1990,Ag 19,53:1
Bent, Hannah
Woyzeck 1990,Mr 6,C17:1
Bentley, Eric (Playwright)
German Requiem 1990,My 28,14:5
Bentley, Eric (Translator)
Man's a Man, A 1990,F 26,C15:4
Benzali, Daniel
Art of Success, The 1989,D 21,C11:1
Marathon 1990: Festival of New One-Act Plays, Series A 1990,My 16,C14:4
Berenger, Tom
National Anthems 1989,Ja 1,II:5:1
Berezin, Tanya (Miscellaneous)
Brilliant Traces 1989,F 6,C11:1
Dalton's Back 1989,F 10,C3:1
Amulets Against the Dragon Forces 1989,Ap 6,C17:4
Florida Crackers 1989,Je 2,C3:1
Beside Herself 1989,O 18,C15:1
Sunshine 1989,D 18,C10:4
Imagining Brad 1990,F 7,C15:2
Prelude to a Kiss 1990,Mr 15,C15:1
Each Day Dies with Sleep 1990,My 17,C20:3
Colorado Catechism, The 1990,O 22,C13:1
Love Diatribe 1990,D 19,C15:1
Berg, Tracey
Midsummer Nights 1989,S 24,71:3
Bergquist, Guy (Miscellaneous)
Glass Menagerie, The 1989,O 16,C19:1
Merrily We Roll Along 1990,F 23,C13:1
Caucasian Chalk Circle, The 1990,O 1,C14:1
Bergstein, David (Lighting Director)
II Samuel 11, Etc. 1989,O 7,13:1
Kate's Diary 1989,N 29,C17:1
New Anatomies 1990,F 22,C19:1
Gonza the Lancer 1990,O 25,C20:5
Berkal, Eric (Miscellaneous)
Manhattan Class Company, One-Act Play Festival, Series A 1989,Mr 11,16:1
Manhattan Class One-Acts, Series B 1989,Mr 19,61:4
Marathon 1990: Festival of New One-Act Plays, Series A 1990,My 16,C14:4
Marathon 1990: Festival of New One-Act Plays, Series B 1990,Je 1,C8:5
Marathon 1990: Festival of New One-Act Plays, Series C 1990,Je 14,C20:3
Berkey, Daniel
Twelfth Night 1989,Jl 10,C13:1
Titus Andronicus 1989,Ag 21,C13:1
Macbeth 1990,Ja 17,C13:4
Two Gentlemen of Verona 1990,D 13,C16:5
Berkoff, Steven (Director)
Metamorphosis 1989,Mr 7,C15:1

Berkoff, Steven (Playwright)
Metamorphosis 1989,Mr 7,C15:1
Berkowsky, Paul B. (Miscellaneous)
Catch Me If I Fall 1990,N 17,16:5
Berlin, Irving (Miscellaneous)
Jerome Robbins's Broadway 1989,F 27,C13:1
Berlin, Jeannie
Price of Fame 1990,Je 14,C17:1
Berlin, Pamela (Director)
Early One Evening at the Rainbow Bar and Grille 1989,Ap 14,C34:5
Cemetery Club, The 1990,My 16,C14:4
Berlind, Roger (Producer)
Jerome Robbins's Broadway 1989,F 27,C13:1
Blame It on the Movies 1989,My 18,C22:3
Artist Descending a Staircase 1989,D 1,C3:1
City of Angels 1989,D 12,C19:4
Lettice and Lovage 1990,Mr 26,C11:1
Elliot Loves 1990,Je 8,C3:1
Berlinsky, Harris
Three Sisters 1989,Ja 24,C16:4
Good 1989,F 25,18:4
Importance of Being Earnest, The 1989,O 5,C19:1
Travesties 1989,N 3,C29:1
Life Is a Dream 1989,D 16,17:1
Man's a Man, A 1990,F 26,C15:4
Prince of Homburg, The 1990,Ap 22,62:1
Misalliance 1990,O 14,56:4
Infernal Machine, The 1990,D 2,83:1
Berman, Brook
Summerfolk 1989,O 14,15:4
Berman, David
10th Man, The 1989,D 11,C13:1
Berman, Donald
Phantom Lady, The 1989,Ap 16,60:1
Self-Torture and Strenuous Exercise (Marathon '89, Series A) 1989,My 30,C19:1
Berman, Heather
Madame Sherry 1989,Jl 30,57:1
Berman, Irene B. (Translator)
Peer Gynt 1989,My 28,14:5
Berman, Norman L. (Composer)
Amulets Against the Dragon Forces 1989,Ap 6,C17:4
Bermejo, Luz
Suenos 1989,F 23,C13:3
Bermel, Albert (Translator)
Infernal Machine, The 1990,D 2,83:1
Bermingham, Gigi
Twelfth Night 1989,Jl 10,C13:1
Bern, Mina
Those Were the Days 1990,N 14,C26:1
Bernstein, Douglas
Showing Off 1989,My 28,57:1
Bernstein, Douglas (Playwright)
Showing Off 1989,My 28,57:1
Bernstein, Jesse
Winter's Tale, The 1989,Mr 22,C19:4
Macbeth 1990,Ja 17,C13:4
Bernstein, Joel
Born Yesterday 1989,Ja 30,C11:1
Bernstein, Joel (Director)
School for Wives, The 1989,D 30,17:1
Bernstein, Leonard (Composer)
On the Town 1989,My 12,C3:4
Wonderful Town 1989,O 8,64:1
Bernstein, Leonard (Miscellaneous)
Jerome Robbins's Broadway 1989,F 27,C13:1
Bernstein, Stuart (Miscellaneous)
Voice of the Prairie, The 1990,D 18,C18:5
Berridge, Elizabeth
Briar Patch 1989,D 6,C21:1
Berrios, Sandra
Voces de Acero (Voices of Steel) 1990,Ag 20,C14:1
Berry, Gabriel (Costume Designer)
Betty Bends the Blues 1989,Ja 28,13:1
Don Juan of Seville (Burlador de Sevilla y Convidado de Piedra, El) 1989,Ap 7,C3:5
New Cities 1989,My 7,74:3
Investigation of the Murder in El Salvador, The 1989,My 23,C14:4
Abel and Bela 1989,O 1,61:1
Architruc 1989,O 1,61:1
Mountain Language 1989,N 9,C21:3
Birthday Party, The 1989,N 9,C21:3
Krapp's Last Tape 1989,D 17,94:5
Tower of Evil, The (Tour de Nesle, La) 1990,My 13,45:1
Love and Anger 1990,D 9,82:3
Berry, Gabriel (Miscellaneous)
B. Beaver Animation, The 1990,My 24,C19:1

German Requiem 1990,My 28,14:5
Bradbury, Stephen
Few Good Men, A 1989,N 16,C23:4
Braden, John
Home Games 1989,O 2,C16:3
Crucible, The 1989,D 16,15:1
Money Talks 1990,S 7,C3:5
Bradford, Don
Tomfoolery 1989,Ja 14,10:4
Bradford, Mark (Playwright)
Anulah, Let Them Eat Cake 1989,S 17,79:4
Bradley, Carol
Henry Lumper 1989,F 5,53:1
Bradley, David
Silent Woman or Epicoene, The 1989,Ag 6,II:5:1
Dr. Faustus 1989,Ag 6,II:5:1
King Lear 1990,Ag 8,C11:3
Richard III 1990,Ag 8,C11:3
Bradley, Maureen
Indiana Dog 1989,S 26,C17:1
Bradley, Neil
Lava 1989,D 13,C24:3
Bradley, Scott (Miscellaneous)
At the Chelsea 1989,Ja 20,C3:1
Bradley, Scott (Scenic Designer)
Prisoner of Second Avenue, The 1989,N 5,96:1
Return, The 1990,Ja 12,C3:3
Cahoots 1990,Mr 10,16:4
Brady, Atticus
Our Town 1989,Mr 28,C15:1
Brady, Patrick Scott
Closer Than Ever 1989,N 7,C19:1
Brady, Patrick Scott (Musical Director)
Closer Than Ever 1989,N 7,C19:1
Brady, Sharon
Rodents and Radios 1990,Ap 28,15:1
Bramon, Risa (Director)
Jersey City 1990,Jl 15,40:3
Brand, Oscar (Composer)
Education of H*Y*M*A*N K*A*P*L*A*N, The
1989,Ap 6,C22:4
Brand, Oscar (Lyricist)
Education of H*Y*M*A*N K*A*P*L*A*N, The
1989,Ap 6,C22:4
Brandenberg, Jon E.
Largely New York 1989,My 2,C15:1
Brandt, Ariane
Rose Tattoo, The 1989,Jl 28,C3:4
Branion, Jeff
Video Store Owner's Significant Other, The 1990,S
26,C9:5
Branton, Michael
Rose Tattoo, The 1989,Jl 28,C3:4
Brass, Stacey Lynn
Romance in Hard Times 1989,D 29,C3:1
Brassard, Gail (Costume Designer)
Rothschilds, The 1990,F 26,C16:1
Miser, The 1990,O 12,C1:1
Brassard, Marie
Polygraph 1990,O 27,12:5
Brassard, Marie (Playwright)
Polygraph 1990,O 27,12:5
Braugher, Andre
Twelfth Night 1989,Jl 10,C13:1
Brauner, Leon I. (Costume Designer)
S. J. Perelman in Person 1989,My 18,C22:4
Bravo, Anthony
Winter's Tale, The 1990,Ja 31,C15:1
Braxton, Brenda
Midsummer Nights 1989,S 24,71:3
Bray, Barbara (Translator)
Architruc 1989,O 1,61:1
Brechner, Stanley (Director)
Made in Heaven 1990,My 13,45:1
Brechner, Stanley (Miscellaneous)
Immigrant, The: A Hamilton County Album 1989,F
8,C19:1
Education of H*Y*M*A*N K*A*P*L*A*N, The
1989,Ap 6,C22:4
Call Me Ethel! 1989,Je 10,14:3
Prisoner of Second Avenue, The 1989,N 5,96:1
Puppetmaster of Lodz, The 1989,D 27,C15:1
Rothschilds, The 1990,F 26,C16:1
Made in Heaven 1990,My 13,45:1
Brecht, Bertolt (Lyricist)
Threepenny Opera 1989,N 6,C13:4
Happy End 1990,My 26,11:1
Brecht, Bertolt (Playwright)
Threepenny Opera 1989,N 6,C13:4
Man's a Man, A 1990,F 26,C15:4

Baal 1990,Mr 24,17:1
Caucasian Chalk Circle, The 1990,O 1,C14:1
Caucasian Chalk Circle, The 1990,D 3,C13:3
Caucasian Chalk Circle, The 1990,D 9,II:5:1
Brecker, Candace
Ariano 1990,F 11,69:2
Breen, Patrick
Baba Goya 1989,D 6,C21:1
Chelsea Walls 1990,Je 9,12:5
Brehm, Heide
People Who Could Fly, The 1989,Ag 3,C20:3
Brehse, Philip
I & I 1989,S 24,72:3
German Requiem 1990,My 28,14:5
Brennan, Stephen Vincent
Ulysses in Nighttown 1989,Ja 15,44:1
Brennan, Tom
Miser, The 1990,O 12,C1:1
Brenneman, Amy
Video Store Owner's Significant Other, The 1990,S
26,C9:5
Sincerity Forever 1990,D 8,17:3
Brennen, Paul
Romeo and Juliet 1990,Jl 14,10:1
Brenner, Janet (Producer)
Closer Than Ever 1989,N 7,C19:1
Brenner, Susan
Starting Monday 1990,Ap 5,C18:1
Breshnahan, Alyssa
Mud Angel, The 1990,N 18,75:1
Breslin, Luke
Daisy Miller 1990,Ag 16,C14:4
Breuer, Lee (Director)
Lear 1990,Ja 26,C3:1
B. Beaver Animation, The 1990,My 24,C19:1
Breuer, Lee (Playwright)
Lear 1990,Ja 26,C3:1
B. Beaver Animation, The 1990,My 24,C19:1
Breuler, Robert
Grapes of Wrath, The 1990,Mr 23,C1:4
Breyer, Christopher (Miscellaneous)
Blessing, The 1989,My 22,C12:1
Briar, Suzanne
Aspects of Love 1990,Ap 9,C11:1
Brice, Ron
Cat on a Hot Tin Roof 1990,Mr 22,C17:1
Brickhill, Joan (Choreographer)
Meet Me in St. Louis 1989,N 3,C3:1
Bridge, Andrew (Lighting Director)
Aspects of Love 1990,Ap 9,C11:1
Brielle, Jonathan (Composer)
Florida Crackers 1989,Je 2,C3:1
Beside Herself 1989,O 18,C15:1
Briggs, Bunny
Black and Blue 1989,Ja 27,C3:1
Briggs, David
Sleeping Dogs 1989,Mr 23,C17:1
Brignoni, Miguel
Acid Paradise 1990,Mr 8,C24:1
Brill, Fran
Hyde in Hollywood 1989,N 30,C19:3
Brinkley, Susann (Director)
Captive (Marathon 1990: Festival of New One-Act
Plays, Series A) 1990,My 16,C14:4
Brinkmann, Katrin
Sunspot 1989,Mr 18,14:4
Briseno, Guillermo (Composer)
Romeo and Juliet 1990,S 15,15:1
Brites, Zunilda (Miscellaneous)
Nelson 2 Rodrigues 1989,O 15,65:1
Brito, Adrian
Dangerous Games 1989,O 20,C3:3
Broadbent, Jim
Flea in Her Ear, A 1989,Ag 20,II:5:1
Broadhurst, Jeffrey Lee
Jerome Robbins's Broadway 1989,F 27,C13:1
Broadhurst, Kent
Early One Evening at the Rainbow Bar and Grille
1989,Ap 14,C34:5
Brockway, Adrienne (Scenic Designer)
Before Dawn 1989,Ag 31,C20:5
Brockway, Lou
Audience (By and for Havel) 1990,Mr 9,C3:5
Catastrophe (By and for Havel) 1990,Mr 9,C3:5
Broder, J. Scott (Miscellaneous)
Sid Caesar & Company: Does Anybody Know What
I'm Talking About? 1989,N 2,C19:3
Broder, Josh
Happy End 1990,My 26,11:1

Broderick, Kate (Miscellaneous)
Nightingale 1990,D 4,C16:3
Brody, Jonathan
Kiss of the Spider Woman 1990,Je 1,C3:1
Brogger, Ivar
Up 'n' Under 1989,Je 13,C17:1
Progress 1989,D 11,C15:1
Brohn, William D. (Miscellaneous)
Jerome Robbins's Broadway 1989,F 27,C13:1
Brokaw, Mark
Twice Shy (Young Playwrights Festival) 1989,S
22,C5:4
Brokaw, Mark (Director)
Heaven on Earth 1989,N 12,71:5
Hey Little Walter 1990,S 21,C14:6
Brolaski, Carol (Costume Designer)
Stand-Up Tragedy 1989,N 24,C3:4
Stand-Up Tragedy 1990,O 5,C3:1
Brolli, Robert
Death Takes a Holiday 1990,Ag 13,C11:1
Bromelmeier, Martha (Costume Designer)
Brimstone and Treacle 1989,Ap 18,C15:3
Bromka, Elaine
Light Up the Sky 1990,Ag 22,C10:5
Broms, Pearl (Scenic Designer)
Remembrance 1990,O 18,C22:5
Bronson, B. (Composer)
World Without End 1990,O 6,11:3
Brooking, Simon
Manhattan Class One-Acts, Series B 1989,Mr
19,61:4
Rough Crossing 1990,F 23,C3:4
King Lear 1990,N 16,C3:1
Brooks, David
Dragon's Nest 1990,My 10,C14:4
Brooks, Don
Feast Here Tonight 1989,N 30,C16:3
Brooks, Donald L. (Director)
Best Friends 1989,Ag 13,57:6
Brooks, Eric
Wonderful Town 1989,O 8,64:1
Brooks, Hewitt
Thirteenth Chair, The 1989,Ap 16,61:1
Brooks, Jeff
Lend Me a Tenor 1989,Mr 3,C3:1
Lend Me a Tenor 1989,Mr 29,C17:1
Brousseau, James (Miscellaneous)
Meet Me in St. Louis 1989,N 3,C3:1
Brousseau, Pierre
Polygraph 1990,O 27,12:5
Brousseau, Pierre (Composer)
Polygraph 1990,O 27,12:5
Brouwer, Peter
East Texas 1990,O 7,70:4
Browder, Ben
Merchant of Venice, The 1989,D 20,C15:1
Brown, A. Whitney
A. Whitney Brown's Big Picture (in Words) 1989,Mr
31,C36:1
Brown, A. Whitney (Playwright)
A. Whitney Brown's Big Picture (in Words) 1989,Mr
31,C36:1
Brown, Amelda
Macbeth 1989,Mr 21,C19:1
Apart from George 1989,Mr 21,C19:1
Brown, Ann
20 Fingers, 20 Toes 1990,Ja 10,C17:1
Golden Apple, The 1990,Mr 30,C3:5
Brown, Arvin (Director)
Crucible, The 1989,D 16,15:1
Voysey Inheritance, The 1990,O 26,C3:1
Brown, Arvin (Miscellaneous)
When We Are Married 1989,Ja 28,14:3
Some Sweet Day 1989,Mr 27,C13:1
Heiress, The 1989,Je 16,C3:1
Flea in Her Ear, A 1989,O 13,C15:1
Dance Lesson, A 1989,N 11,16:5
Crucible, The 1989,D 16,15:1
Re:Joyce! 1990,F 2,C3:1
Ruffian on the Stair, The 1990,Ap 25,C13:1
Lover, The 1990,Ap 25,C13:1
Is He Still Dead? 1990,My 27,58:1
Voysey Inheritance, The 1990,O 26,C3:1
Generations of the Dead in the Abyss of Coney
Island Madness 1990,D 9,82:3
Valued Friends 1990,D 20,C20:4
Brown, Avis
White Chocolate for My Father 1990,F 15,C22:3
Brown, Barry (Producer)
Gypsy 1989,N 17,C5:1

Ground People 1990,My 7,C13:1
Burstyn, Ellen
  Shirley Valentine 1989,Ag 10,C13:1
Burstyn, Mike
  Prisoner of Second Avenue, The 1989,N 5,96:1
  Rothschilds, The 1990,F 26,C16:1
  Rothschilds, The 1990,S 23,II:5:1
Burt, John (Producer)
  Starmites 1989,Ap 28,C3:1
Burton, Arnie
  Major Barbara 1990,N 28,C17:1
Burton, Donald
  Privates on Parade 1989,Ag 23,C13:3
  Merchant of Venice, The 1989,D 20,C15:1
Burton, Kate
  Measure for Measure 1989,Mr 10,C3:1
  Some Americans Abroad 1990,F 12,C17:1
  Some Americans Abroad 1990,Mr 14,C13:4
  Some Americans Abroad 1990,My 3,C17:1
Burton, Miriam
  Sunshine Boys, The 1989,My 14,49:1
Burton, Stephen
  Circus Oz 1990,Je 8,C7:1
Burton, Warren
  Manhattan Punch Line's Sixth Annual Festival of
    One-Act Comedies, Evening B 1990,F 11,70:1
Buscemi, Steve
  Sunspot 1989,Mr 18,14:4
Busch, Charles
  Lady in Question, The 1989,Jl 26,C17:1
Busch, Charles (Playwright)
  Lady in Question, The 1989,Jl 26,C17:1
  Lady in Question, The 1989,D 24,II:3:1
Bush, Barbara (Costume Designer)
  Dividends 1990,Mr 4,51:1
Bushey, Trent
  Quiet on the Set 1990,Ag 16,C17:1
Bushler, David (Composer)
  Abel and Bela 1989,O 1,61:1
  Architruc 1989,O 1,61:1
Bussard, Larry (Miscellaneous)
  Sum of Us, The 1990,O 20,16:4
Busser, Janet
  Marathon 1990: Festival of New One-Act Plays,
    Series C 1990,Je 14,C20:3
Butler, Alistair
  Endangered Species 1990,O 9,C13:1
Butler, Bill (Costume Designer)
  Buddy: The Buddy Holly Story 1990,N 5,C13:1
Butler, Bruce
  Play to Win 1989,Jl 21,C3:2
Butler, Dan
  Early One Evening at the Rainbow Bar and Grille
    1989,Ap 14,C34:5
  Lisbon Traviata, The 1989,Je 7,C21:1
  Lisbon Traviata, The 1989,N 1,C22:3
Butler, Paul
  Few Good Men, A 1989,N 16,C23:4
Butleroff, Helen (Choreographer)
  Jekyll and Hyde 1990,Jl 1,48:1
  Yiddle with a Fiddle 1990,O 30,C14:5
Butterfield, Richard
  Saint Joan 1989,Ag 19,14:1
Button, Dick (Producer)
  Artist Descending a Staircase 1989,D 1,C3:1
Button, Jeanne (Costume Designer)
  In a Pig's Valise 1989,F 15,C15:1
  Showing Off 1989,My 28,57:1
  Twelfth Night 1989,Jl 10,C13:1
  Macbeth 1990,Ja 17,C13:4
  Crucible, The 1990,Mr 30,C3:1
Buttram, Jan (Playwright)
  East Texas 1990,O 7,70:4
Buzas, Jason McConnell (Director)
  Pillow Talk (Manhattan Punch Line's Festival of
    One-Act Comedies, Series B) 1989,F 11,12:3
  Ancient History 1989,My 18,C29:3
  Philip Glass Buys a Loaf of Bread (Manhattan Punch
    Line's Sixth Annual Festival of One-Act
    Comedies, Evening A) 1990,F 4,60:1
  Fertilization Opera, The (Manhattan Punch Line's
    Sixth Annual Festival of One-Act Comedies,
    Evening B) 1990,F 11,70:1
  Mere Mortals (Marathon 1990: Festival of New One-
    Act Plays, Series C) 1990,Je 14,C20:3
Byers, Billy (Miscellaneous)
  City of Angels 1989,D 12,C19:4
Byers, Karen
  Carnal Knowledge 1990,N 21,C15:1

Byrne, Alexandra (Costume Designer)
  Some Americans Abroad 1990,F 12,C17:1
  Some Americans Abroad 1990,My 3,C17:1
Byrne, Alexandra (Scenic Designer)
  Some Americans Abroad 1990,F 12,C17:1
  Some Americans Abroad 1990,My 3,C17:1
Byrnes, Brian
  Romeo and Juliet 1990,D 21,C20:6
Byron, John
  Gigi 1989,My 28,57:1
Byron-Kirk, Keith
  Winter's Tale, The 1990,Ja 31,C15:1
  Grapes of Wrath, The 1990,Mr 23,C1:4

C

Caballero, Christophe
  Jerome Robbins's Broadway 1989,F 27,C13:1
Cabaniss, Thomas (Composer)
  American Plan, The 1990,D 17,C11:1
Cabaniss, Thomas (Miscellaneous)
  Prince of Homburg, The 1990,Ap 22,62:1
Cacheiro, Jorge (Director)
  Love Diatribe 1990,D 19,C15:1
Cade, Mark Daniel
  Funny Thing Happened on the Way to the Forum, A
    1989,Ag 6,49:3
  Saint Joan 1989,Ag 19,14:1
Caesar, Sid
  Sid Caesar & Company: Does Anybody Know What
    I'm Talking About? 1989,N 2,C19:3
  Together Again 1990,Ap 27,C10:4
Caffey, Marion J.
  Oh, Kay! 1989,N 1,C22:3
Caffrey, Stephen
  Miser, The 1990,My 18,C4:3
Cahill, James
  Twelfth Night 1989,Jl 10,C13:1
  Lady in Question, The 1989,Jl 26,C17:1
  City of Angels 1989,D 12,C19:4
Cahn, Sammy (Miscellaneous)
  Jerome Robbins's Broadway 1989,F 27,C13:1
Cain, Bill (Playwright)
  Stand-Up Tragedy 1989,N 24,C3:4
  Stand-Up Tragedy 1990,O 5,C3:1
  Stand-Up Tragedy 1990,O 14,II:5:1
Cain, Michael
  Happy End 1990,My 26,11:1
Cain, William
  Forbidden City, The 1989,Ap 7,C3:1
  Mastergate 1989,O 13,C3:1
Caird, John (Director)
  Midsummer Night's Dream, A 1989,Ag 6,II:5:1
Caitlyn, Deryl
  Measure for Measure 1989,Mr 10,C3:1
  Titus Andronicus 1989,Ag 21,C13:1
  Manhattan Punch Line's Sixth Annual Festival of
    One-Act Comedies, Evening A 1990,F 4,60:1
Calabrese, Maria
  Pal Joey 1990,Jl 24,C13:3
Calamates, Andy (Miscellaneous)
  Passion of Narcisse Mondoux, The 1989,Je 18,50:1
Caldas, Andre
  Doente Imaginario, O (Imaginary Invalid, The)
    1990,Ag 23,C20:1
Calder, Jim (Miscellaneous)
  Two Gentlemen of Verona 1990,D 13,C16:5
Calderon, Juan Carlos
  Palomar, El (Pigeon House, The) 1990,Ag 19,53:1
Calderon de la Barca, Pedro (Playwright)
  Phantom Lady, The 1989,Ap 16,60:1
  Life Is a Dream 1989,D 16,17:1
Calderone, Michael
  People Who Could Fly, The 1989,Ag 3,C20:3
Caldwell, George (Musical Director)
  Step into My World 1989,F 19,76:4
Caldwell, Sandra
  Buddy: The Buddy Holly Story 1990,N 5,C13:1
Cale, Bennett
  Starmites 1989,Ap 28,C3:1
Cale, David
  Nature of Things, The 1990,Mr 25,63:1
Cale, David (Playwright)
  Nature of Things, The 1990,Mr 25,63:1
Caliban, Richard (Director)
  Crowbar 1990,F 20,C18:1

Crowbar 1990,Mr 14,C13:4
Rodents and Radios 1990,Ap 28,15:1
Famine Plays 1990,N 3,14:5
Caliban, Richard (Miscellaneous)
  Indiana Dog 1989,S 26,C17:1
  Tiny Dimes 1990,Mr 9,C18:1
  Rodents and Radios 1990,Ap 28,15:1
Caliban, Richard (Playwright)
  Rodents and Radios 1990,Ap 28,15:1
  Famine Plays 1990,N 3,14:5
Callahan, Dennis
  Love Life 1990,Je 22,C15:1
Callahan, Ruth
  Old Maid, The 1990,Ag 16,C14:4
Callahan, Steven C. (Miscellaneous)
  Measure for Measure 1989,Mr 10,C3:1
  Our Town 1989,Mr 28,C15:1
  Oh, Hell 1989,D 4,C15:1
  10th Man, The 1989,D 11,C13:1
  Some Americans Abroad 1990,F 12,C17:1
  Monster in a Box 1990,N 15,C19:1
Callan, Jeff
  Murder in the Cathedral 1989,S 9,13:1
Callas, Demetri
  Gypsy 1989,N 17,C5:1
Callas, Ellen (Scenic Designer)
  Seeing Double 1989,N 16,C28:4
Callen, Chris
  Prince of Central Park 1989,N 10,C3:1
Callender, L. Peter
  Twelfth Night 1989,Jl 10,C13:1
  Prelude to a Kiss 1990,Mr 15,C15:1
  Prelude to a Kiss 1990,My 2,C15:1
  Caucasian Chalk Circle, The 1990,D 3,C13:3
  Caucasian Chalk Circle, The 1990,D 9,II:5:1
Callow, Simon
  Single Spies 1989,Ja 15,II:1:4
Callow, Simon (Director)
  Shirley Valentine 1989,F 17,C3:1
  Shirley Valentine 1989,Ag 10,C13:1
  Single Spies 1989,Ag 20,II:5:1
Callow, Simon (Translator)
  Jacques and His Master 1989,N 16,C28:5
Calman, Camille (Miscellaneous)
  Baba Goya 1989,D 6,C21:1
Camera, John
  Lark, The 1989,My 29,20:5
Cameron, Bruce (Miscellaneous)
  Sid Caesar & Company: Does Anybody Know What
    I'm Talking About? 1989,N 2,C19:3
  Jackie Mason: Brand New 1990,O 18,C21:1
Cameron, Clark (Miscellaneous)
  Smoke on the Mountain 1990,My 17,C20:3
  Gifts of the Magi, The 1990,D 9,82:3
Cameron, Hope
  Marathon 1990: Festival of New One-Act Plays,
    Series C 1990,Je 14,C20:3
Camp, Bill
  Twelfth Night 1989,Jl 10,C13:1
  Titus Andronicus 1989,Ag 21,C13:1
  Hamlet 1990,My 9,C15:4
  Valued Friends 1990,D 20,C20:4
Camp, Joanne
  Hedda Gabler 1989,Ja 25,C18:5
  Midsummer Night's Dream, A 1989,O 15,67:1
  Three Sisters, The 1989,N 23,C20:5
  School for Wives, The 1989,D 30,17:1
  Medea 1990,F 8,C15:3
  Importance of Being Earnest, The 1990,Mr 18,59:1
  Ruffian on the Stair, The 1990,Ap 25,C13:1
  Lover, The 1990,Ap 25,C13:1
Campanella, Philip (Miscellaneous)
  Enrico IV 1989,Ja 19,C22:3
  Member of the Wedding, The 1989,Ap 1,16:3
  Arms and the Man 1989,Je 5,C12:4
  Doctor's Dilemma, The 1990,Ja 26,C3:1
  Crucible, The 1990,Mr 30,C3:1
  Price of Fame 1990,Je 14,C17:1
  Light Up the Sky 1990,Ag 22,C10:5
Campanella, Philip (Musical Director)
  Privates on Parade 1989,Ag 23,C13:3
Campbell, Amelia
  Member of the Wedding, The 1989,Ap 1,16:3
  Our Country's Good 1990,O 21,59:3
Campbell, Bill (Costume Designer)
  Wizard of Oz, The 1989,Mr 24,C3:1
Campbell, Christine
  Wonderful Town 1989,O 8,64:1
Campbell, Erma
  Ground People 1990,My 7,C13:1

D

Egi, Stan
Yankee Dawg You Die 1989,My 15,C13:4
F.O.B. 1990,My 20,60:1
Lucky Come Hawaii 1990,O 29,C16:1
Eginton, Margaret
Largely New York 1989,My 2,C15:1
Largely New York 1989,My 14,II:5:1
Chelsea Walls 1990,Je 9,12:5
Eginton, Margaret (Choreographer)
Largely New York 1989,My 2,C15:1
Egloff, Elizabeth (Playwright)
Swan 1990,Ap 5,C15:1
Egurza, Tito (Lighting Director)
Sin Testigos 1990,Ag 14,C16:1
Egurza, Tito (Scenic Designer)
Sin Testigos 1990,Ag 14,C16:1
Ehlers, Beth
Quiet on the Set 1990,Ag 16,C17:1
Ehlers, Heather
Born Yesterday 1989,Ja 30,C11:1
Ehlers, Stephen (Scenic Designer)
Wizard of Oz, The 1989,Mr 24,C3:1
Ehman, Don (Lighting Director)
Smoke on the Mountain 1990,My 17,C20:3
Ehn, Erik (Playwright)
Red Sheets (Manhattan Class Company, One-Act
Play Festival, Series A) 1989,Mr 11,16:1
Ehrenberg, Steven (Miscellaneous)
Ladies 1989,Ap 7,C3:1
Prince of Central Park 1989,N 10,C3:1
Paradise for the Worried 1990,Ap 6,C3:1
Endangered Species 1990,O 9,C13:1
Ehrenreich, Jake
Jonah 1990,Mr 23,C5:1
Eichelberger, Ethyl
Measure for Measure 1989,Mr 10,C3:1
Herd of Buffalo 1989,Jl 6,C18:4
Buzzsaw Berkeley 1989,Ag 21,C14:3
Threepenny Opera 1989,N 6,C13:4
Das Vedanya Mama 1990,Jl 28,12:5
Eichelberger, Ethyl (Director)
Herd of Buffalo 1989,Jl 6,C18:4
Das Vedanya Mama 1990,Jl 28,12:5
Eichelberger, Ethyl (Playwright)
Herd of Buffalo 1989,Jl 6,C18:4
Das Vedanya Mama 1990,Jl 28,12:5
Eichman, David
Two Gentlemen of Verona 1990,D 13,C16:5
Eigenberg, David
Young Playwrights Festival 1989,S 22,C5:4
Six Degrees of Separation 1990,Je 15,C1:2
Six Degrees of Separation 1990,N 9,C5:1
Eigenberg, Julie Anne
Ghetto 1989,My 1,C11:1
Einhorn, Fred
Sunshine Boys, The 1989,My 14,49:1
Jekyll and Hyde 1990,Jl 1,48:1
Einhorn, Susan (Director)
Spare Parts 1990,Mr 18,59:2
Catch Me If I Fall 1990,N 17,16:5
Eisenberg, Avner
Ghetto 1989,My 1,C11:1
Eisenberg, Ned
Moving Targets 1990,Ja 30,C14:5
Eisenhauer, Peggy (Lighting Director)
In a Pig's Valise 1989,F 15,C15:1
Dangerous Games 1989,O 20,C3:3
Mondo Mambo 1990,Ag 25,16:5
Elbert, Wayne
Burner's Frolic 1990,F 26,C14:1
Elder, Eldon (Scenic Designer)
Hizzoner! 1989,F 24,C3:1
Eldon, Jack
Pal Joey 1990,Jl 24,C13:3
Eldon, Thomas
Hyde in Hollywood 1989,N 30,C19:3
Elethea, Abba
Mythos Oedipus 1989,Mr 5,69:1
Dionysus Filius Dei 1989,Mr 5,69:1
Elg, Taina
O Pioneers! 1990,Ja 28,49:1
El-Hajjar, Nabil
Story of Kufur Shamma, The 1989,Jl 28,C17:1
Elins, J. P. (Miscellaneous)
Money Talks 1990,S 7,C3:5
Elio, Donna Marie
Jerome Robbins's Broadway 1989,F 27,C13:1
Eliot, Drew
Visit, The 1989,F 5,56:5

Eliot, Jane (Costume Designer)
Heart of a Dog 1990,Mr 16,C3:1
Eliot, T. S. (Playwright)
Murder in the Cathedral 1989,S 9,13:1
Elledge, David
Grand Hotel 1989,N 13,C13:3
Elliott, Kenneth
Lady in Question, The 1989,Jl 26,C17:1
Elliott, Kenneth (Director)
Lady in Question, The 1989,Jl 26,C17:1
Up Against It 1989,D 5,C17:3
Elliott, Kenneth (Producer)
Lady in Question, The 1989,Jl 26,C17:1
Elliott, Milton
Perfect Diamond, A 1990,Je 6,C18:1
Elliott, Paul (Producer)
Run for Your Wife! 1989,Mr 8,C17:1
Buddy: The Buddy Holly Story 1990,N 5,C13:1
Elliott, R. Bruce
Leave It to Jane 1989,Mr 23,C17:1
Hamlet 1989,Je 2,C3:5
Elliott, Shawn
City of Angels 1989,D 12,C19:4
Ellis, Chris
Marathon 1990: Festival of New One-Act Plays,
Series C 1990,Je 14,C20:3
Ellis, Leslie
Rothschilds, The 1990,F 26,C16:1
Ellis, Richard (Scenic Designer)
Fifth of July 1989,F 16,C34:3
Cradle Song 1989,Mr 19,61:1
Ellis, Tracey
Woyzeck 1990,Mr 6,C17:1
Our Country's Good 1990,O 21,59:3
Ellis, William (Miscellaneous)
Medea 1990,F 8,C15:3
Ellisen, Eric
Spinning Tale, A 1990,F 25,57:1
Ellison, Julian (Miscellaneous)
Macbeth 1989,Mr 21,C19:1
Apart from George 1989,Mr 21,C19:1
Ellison, Nancy (Producer)
Threepenny Opera 1989,N 6,C13:4
Ellman, Bruce (Miscellaneous)
Magic Act, The 1989,Mr 16,C21:1
Niedecker 1989,Mr 19,61:1
Beauty Marks 1989,O 29,63:5
Moving Targets 1990,Ja 30,C14:5
Violent Peace 1990,Mr 3,12:3
Hannah . . . 1939 1990,Je 2,16:3
Prin 1990,Je 7,C18:5
Jersey City 1990,Jl 15,40:3
Nightingale 1990,D 4,C16:3
Ellstein, Abraham (Composer)
Yiddle with a Fiddle 1990,O 30,C14:5
Elm, Louise
God's Policemen 1989,O 22,64:4
Emery, Lisa
Dalton's Back 1989,F 10,C3:1
Emmet, Robert
Hamlet 1989,Je 2,C3:5
Emmons, Beverly (Lighting Director)
Winter's Tale, The 1989,Mr 22,C19:4
Mountain Language 1989,N 9,C21:3
Birthday Party, The 1989,N 9,C21:3
Art of Success, The 1989,D 21,C11:1
Jonah 1990,Mr 23,C5:1
Love Life 1990,Je 22,C15:1
Emmons, Beverly (Miscellaneous)
Cat on a Hot Tin Roof 1990,Mr 22,C17:1
Emond, Linda
Winter's Tale, The 1990,Ja 31,C15:1
Emonts, Ann (Costume Designer)
Beside Herself 1989,O 18,C15:1
Engel, David
Forever Plaid 1990,My 25,C3:1
Engelhardt, Cecilia
Baal 1990,Mr 24,17:1
England, Debra
Romeo and Juliet 1990,D 21,C20:6
Engle, Stephen
Hello, Bob 1990,O 21,62:3
Engler, Michael (Director)
Mastergate 1989,F 14,C17:1
Mastergate 1989,O 13,C3:1
Mastergate 1989,N 19,II:5:1
Day Trips 1990,Ap 16,C15:1
English, Ellia
Frankie 1989,O 10,C18:3

Eno, Terry
Prince of Central Park 1989,N 10,C3:1
Enriquez, David
Love Life 1990,Je 22,C15:1
Ensler, Eve (Playwright)
Ladies 1989,Ap 7,C3:1
En Yu Tan, Victor (Lighting Director)
Play Ball 1989,F 12,68:4
Song of Shim Chung, The 1989,N 19,76:4
Violent Peace 1990,Mr 3,12:3
F.O.B. 1990,My 20,60:1
Lucky Come Hawaii 1990,O 29,C16:1
Epperson, C. Jane (Costume Designer)
Sunday Promenade, The 1989,Mr 12,68:1
Jacques and His Master 1989,N 16,C28:5
Away Alone 1989,D 16,18:4
Remembrance 1990,O 18,C22:5
Epps, Christian (Lighting Director)
Over Forty 1989,My 16,C17:1
Boochie 1989,Jl 30,57:2
Every Goodbye Ain't Gone 1989,Jl 30,57:2
Epps, Sheldon (Miscellaneous)
Oh, Kay! 1989,N 1,C22:3
Epstein, Alvin
Mastergate 1989,F 14,C17:1
Threepenny Opera 1989,N 6,C13:4
Epstein, Sabin (Miscellaneous)
Tale of Two Cities, A 1990,Ap 7,16:4
Erb, Stephanie
Two Gentlemen of Verona 1990,D 13,C16:5
Erbe, Kathryn
Grapes of Wrath, The 1990,Mr 23,C1:4
Erde, Sara
Don Juan of Seville (Burlador de Sevilla y
Convidado de Piedra, El) 1989,Ap 7,C3:5
Eric, Ben
Two Gentlemen of Verona 1990,D 13,C16:5
Erickson, Michael (Playwright)
Water Music (Marathon '89, Series C) 1989,Je
29,C14:5
Erickson, Mitchell (Miscellaneous)
Circle, The 1989,N 21,C19:1
Ericson, Russ
Strike, The 1990,Ja 29,C18:5
Ermides, Peter
Prizes 1989,My 18,C22:4
Ernotte, Andre (Director)
Moving Targets 1990,Ja 30,C14:5
Ernster, Sharon
Early One Evening at the Rainbow Bar and Grille
1989,Ap 14,C34:5
Ambassador, The 1989,O 22,63:1
Imagining Brad 1990,F 7,C15:2
Errante, Joseph (Lighting Director)
German Requiem 1990,My 28,14:5
Erte (Costume Designer)
Easter Extravaganza 1990,Ap 13,C28:4
Erte (Scenic Designer)
Easter Extravaganza 1990,Ap 13,C28:4
Erwin, Barbara
Gypsy 1989,N 17,C5:1
Gypsy 1990,S 18,C11:1
Esbjornson, David (Director)
August Snow (New Music) 1989,N 4,16:3
Night Dance (New Music) 1989,N 4,16:3
Escher, Elsbeth House
Tale of Two Cities, A 1990,Ap 7,16:4
Eschweiler, Paula
Hamlet 1989,Je 2,C3:5
Eshelman, Drew
Funny Thing Happened on the Way to the Forum, A
1989,Ag 6,49:3
Eskew, Doug
Truly Blessed: A Musical Celebration of Mahalia
Jackson 1990,Ap 23,C13:1
Eskra, Donna
Member of the Wedding, The 1989,Ap 1,16:3
Esperon, Patricia
Indecent Materials 1990,Ag 28,C14:3
Esposito, Mark
Jerome Robbins's Broadway 1989,F 27,C13:1
Esposito, Vickie (Costume Designer)
People Who Could Fly, The 1989,Ag 3,C20:3
Anthony Rose 1989,O 30,C16:3
Essmann, Jeffrey
Triplets in Uniform 1989,F 12,70:4
Essmann, Jeffrey (Playwright)
Triplets in Uniform 1989,F 12,70:4
Estabrook, Christine
For Dear Life 1989,Ja 11,C17:1

F

Graae, Jason
Forever Plaid 1990,My 25,C3:1
Grabber, Ariel
Starmites 1989,Ap 28,C3:1
Grabowski, Christopher (Director)
Forest in Arden, A 1990,F 11,69:1
Love and Anger 1990,D 9,82:3
Love and Anger 1990,D 16,II:5:1
Grabowski, Christopher (Playwright)
Forest in Arden, A 1990,F 11,69:1
Grace, Brian (Miscellaneous)
Night Breath 1989,Ap 9,57:2
Graff, Randy
City of Angels 1989,D 12,C19:4
Graham, Bruce (Playwright)
Early One Evening at the Rainbow Bar and Grille
1989,Ap 14,C34:5
Graham, Elain
Talented Tenth, The 1989,N 10,C3:1
Telltale Hearts 1990,D 9,82:6
Graham, Rachael
Meet Me in St. Louis 1989,N 3,C3:1
Graham, Ronny
Is He Still Dead? 1990,My 27,58:1
Graham, Stephen (Miscellaneous)
Love and Anger 1990,D 9,82:3
Graham-Lujan, James (Translator)
Video Store Owner's Significant Other, The 1990,S
26,C9:5
Gralek, Jerzy
Hamlet 1989,Jl 11,C13:1
Granaroli, Ty
Genesis: Music and Miracles from the Medieval
Mystery Plays 1989,Ja 18,C20:5
Granger, Stewart
Circle, The 1989,N 21,C19:1
Granite, Judith
Special Interests 1990,F 18,70:1
Cemetery Club, The 1990,My 16,C14:4
Grant, David Marshall
Making Movies 1990,Mr 28,C17:1
Grant, Micki (Composer)
Step into My World 1989,F 19,76:4
Grant, Micki (Lyricist)
Step into My World 1989,F 19,76:4
Grant, Patrick (Composer)
German Requiem 1990,My 28,14:5
Grant, Richard
Playboy of the West Indies, The 1989,My 21,II:5:1
Grant, William H., 3d (Lighting Director)
Thrill a Moment, A 1989,My 4,C23:1
God's Trombones 1989,O 11,C17:1
Granville, Bernard
Gigi 1989,My 28,57:1
Grate, Gail
Caucasian Chalk Circle, The 1990,O 1,C14:1
Grausman, David
Endangered Species 1990,O 9,C13:1
Graves, Rupert
Madhouse in Goa, A 1989,Je 27,C15:4
Graves, Shannon (Miscellaneous)
Phantasie 1989,Ja 4,C15:5
Gray, Allan
Three Sisters, The 1989,Je 12,C13:1
Gray, David Barry
Young Playwrights Festival 1989,S 22,C5:4
Gray, Dean (Miscellaneous)
Open Boat, The (Marathon '89, Series B) 1989,Je
15,C14:5
Jacques and His Master 1989,N 16,C28:5
Gray, Dolores
Money Talks 1990,S 7,C3:5
Money Talks 1990,S 16,II:7:1
Gray, Kenneth
Woyzeck 1990,Mr 6,C17:1
Gray, Kevin
Kiss of the Spider Woman 1990,Je 1,C3:1
Gray, Paula (Miscellaneous)
In a Pig's Valise 1989,F 15,C15:1
Gray, Sam
Bitter Friends 1989,F 14,C16:3
Woman Floating Out a Window (Marathon '89,
Series B) 1989,Je 15,C14:5
Gray, Spalding
Monster in a Box 1990,N 15,C19:1
Monster in a Box 1990,N 25,II:5:1
Monster in a Box 1990,D 30,II:5:1
Gray, Spalding (Playwright)
Monster in a Box 1990,N 15,C19:1
Monster in a Box 1990,N 25,II:5:1

Monster in a Box 1990,D 30,II:5:1
Grayland, Scott
Circus Oz 1990,Je 8,C7:1
Grayman, Dwayne
Thrill a Moment, A 1989,My 4,C23:1
Grayson, Bobby H. (Miscellaneous)
Beside Herself 1989,O 18,C15:1
Prelude to a Kiss 1990,Mr 15,C15:1
Prelude to a Kiss 1990,My 2,C15:1
Grayson, Jerry
Pal Joey 1990,Jl 24,C13:3
Greanier, Mary-Ann (Lighting Director)
Video Store Owner's Significant Other, The 1990,S
26,C9:5
Green, Adolph (Lyricist)
On the Town 1989,My 12,C3:4
Wonderful Town 1989,O 8,64:1
Peter Pan 1990,D 14,C3:4
Green, Adolph (Miscellaneous)
Jerome Robbins's Broadway 1989,F 27,C13:1
Green, Amanda
Jekyll and Hyde 1990,Jl 1,48:1
Green, Andrea
Yiddle with a Fiddle 1990,O 30,C14:5
Green, Brian Lane
Starmites 1989,Ap 28,C3:1
Green, Dor
White Chocolate for My Father 1990,F 15,C22:3
Green, Fanni
Playboy of the West Indies, The 1989,My 11,C17:1
Playboy of the West Indies, The 1989,My 21,II:5:1
Forest in Arden, A 1990,F 11,69:1
Death of the Last Black Man in the Whole Entire
World, The 1990,S 25,C15:1
Gonza the Lancer 1990,O 25,C20:5
Caucasian Chalk Circle, The 1990,D 3,C13:3
Green, Gretchen (Miscellaneous)
Mythos Oedipus 1989,Mr 5,69:1
Green, Joseph (Original Author)
Yiddle with a Fiddle 1990,O 30,C14:5
Green, Larry
Love's Labor's Lost 1989,My 26,C4:5
Hamlet 1990,My 9,C15:4
Greenberg, Helen
Double Blessing 1989,Jl 2,38:1
Greenberg, Jenny
Death Takes a Holiday 1990,Ag 13,C11:1
Greenberg, Joel (Miscellaneous)
Search and Destroy 1990,D 14,C3:1
Greenberg, Mitchell
Threepenny Opera 1989,N 6,C13:4
Fanny 1990,Ap 13,C3:5
Yiddle with a Fiddle 1990,O 30,C14:5
Greenberg, Richard (Playwright)
Eastern Standard 1989,Ja 1,II:5:1
American Plan, The 1990,D 17,C11:1
Greenberg, Rob (Miscellaneous)
Our Country's Good 1990,O 21,59:3
Greenberg, Rob (Scenic Designer)
Cobb 1989,Mr 31,C3:3
Greenblatt, Kenneth D. (Producer)
Grand Hotel 1989,N 13,C13:3
Greene, April
White Chocolate for My Father 1990,F 15,C22:3
Greene, Arthur M. (Musical Director)
Frankie 1989,O 10,C18:3
Greene, Ellen
Starting Monday 1990,Ap 5,C18:1
Greene, Lyn
Freeze Tag (Working One-Acts '89) 1989,Je 25,45:4
Prisoner of Second Avenue, The 1989,N 5,96:1
Greene, Milton (Musical Director)
Fiddler on the Roof 1990,N 19,C13:1
Greenhill, Susan
Pathological Venus (Marathon '89, Series B) 1989,Je
15,C14:5
Greenleaf, John
Love's Labor's Lost 1989,My 26,C4:5
Greenspan, David (Director)
II Samuel 11, Etc. 1989,O 7,13:1
Kate's Diary 1989,N 29,C17:1
Gonza the Lancer 1990,O 25,C20:5
Greenspan, David (Playwright)
II Samuel 11, Etc. 1989,O 7,13:1
Greenwald, Raymond J. (Producer)
Welcome to the Club 1989,Ap 14,C3:1
Balcony, The 1990,Ap 9,C14:6
Greenwood, Jane (Costume Designer)
What the Butler Saw 1989,Mr 9,C21:1

Our Town 1989,Mr 28,C15:1
Aristocrats 1989,Ap 26,C15:1
Lisbon Traviata, The 1989,Je 7,C21:1
Flea in Her Ear, A 1989,O 13,C15:1
Secret Rapture, The 1989,O 27,C3:1
Lisbon Traviata, The 1989,N 1,C22:3
Circle, The 1989,N 21,C19:1
Oh, Hell 1989,D 4,C15:1
10th Man, The 1989,D 11,C13:1
Bad Habits 1990,Mr 21,C13:1
Prin 1990,Je 7,C18:5
Gregg, Clark
Few Good Men, A 1989,N 16,C23:4
Gregg, Jacqueline
People Who Could Fly, The 1989,Ag 3,C20:3
Gregg, Stephen (Playwright)
Sex Lives of Superheroes (Manhattan Punch Line's
Fifth Annual Festival of One-Act Comedies,
Series A) 1989,Ja 26,C16:1
Gregio, Mario (Miscellaneous)
Nelson 2 Rodrigues 1989,O 15,65:1
Gregorie, Alan (Composer)
Dr. Jekyll and Mr. Hyde 1989,D 8,C3:2
Gregorie, Alan (Miscellaneous)
Big Hotel 1989,S 29,C3:1
Those Were the Days 1990,N 14,C26:1
Gregory, Helen (Musical Director)
Waves, The 1990,My 10,C16:4
Gregory, Michael Scott
Jerome Robbins's Broadway 1989,F 27,C13:1
Gregus, Lubitza
Sid Caesar & Company: Does Anybody Know What
I'm Talking About? 1989,N 2,C19:3
Greif, Michael (Director)
Lost Colony, The (Manhattan Class Company, One-
Act Play Festival, Series A) 1989,Mr 11,16:1
Machinal 1990,O 16,C13:1
Machinal 1990,D 30,II:5:1
Greig, Grace
Wizard of Oz, The 1989,Mr 24,C3:1
Greiss, Terry
Happy End 1990,My 26,11:1
Grenfell, Joyce (Lyricist)
Re:Joyce! 1990,F 2,C3:1
Grenfell, Joyce (Original Author)
Re:Joyce! 1990,F 2,C3:1
Grenier, Zach
Water Music (Marathon '89, Series C) 1989,Je
29,C14:5
Mastergate 1989,O 13,C3:1
Marathon 1990: Festival of New One-Act Plays,
Series A 1990,My 16,C14:4
Marathon 1990: Festival of New One-Act Plays,
Series C 1990,Je 14,C20:3
Lilith 1990,S 23,67:4
Sincerity Forever 1990,D 8,17:3
Grey, Larry (Miscellaneous)
Fanny 1990,Ap 13,C3:5
Griesemer, John
Our Town 1989,Mr 28,C15:1
Kate's Diary 1989,N 29,C17:1
Griffin, Sean
March on Russia, The 1990,N 14,C24:3
Griffing, Lois (Miscellaneous)
Speed of Darkness, The 1989,My 9,C15:1
Winter's Tale, The 1990,Ja 31,C15:1
Iceman Cometh, The 1990,O 3,C13:4
Griggs, Robert (Miscellaneous)
Prizes 1989,My 18,C22:4
Grigorescu, Simone
Ice Capades 1989,Ja 21,17:4
Grilikhes, Michel M. (Director)
Wizard of Oz, The 1989,Mr 24,C3:1
Grilikhes, Michel M. (Playwright)
Wizard of Oz, The 1989,Mr 24,C3:1
Grilikhes, Michel M. (Producer)
Wizard of Oz, The 1989,Mr 24,C3:1
Grimaldi, Dennis (Director)
Carol Lawrence and Larry Kert Together . . . Again!
1990,O 4,C21:1
Grimaldi, Dennis (Producer)
Other People's Money 1989,F 17,C3:4
Artist Descending a Staircase 1989,D 1,C3:1
Grimes, Tammy
Orpheus Descending 1989,S 25,C15:4
Orpheus Descending 1989,N 19,II:5:1
Grimm, Timothy
Mill Fire 1989,O 19,C22:3
Grinberg, Semyon
Father's Inheritance 1990,N 18,75:1

H

Easter Extravaganza 1990,Ap 13,C28:4
Harrell, Gordon Lowry (Musical Director)
City of Angels 1989,D 12,C19:4
Harrington, Nancy (Miscellaneous)
Largely New York 1989,My 2,C15:1
Mill Fire 1989,O 19,C22:3
Harrington, Wendall K. (Miscellaneous)
Hyde in Hollywood 1989,N 30,C19:3
Merrily We Roll Along 1990,F 27,C13:1
Harris, Albert (Miscellaneous)
Quiet End, A 1990,My 31,C16:6
Harris, Baxter
Marathon 1990: Festival of New One-Act Plays,
Series C 1990,Je 14,C20:3
Harris, Bill (Playwright)
Every Goodbye Ain't Gone 1989,Jl 30,57:2
Harris, Christopher (Playwright)
Pixie Led, The 1989,Jl 21,C3:5
Harris, Estelle
Prisoner of Second Avenue, The 1989,N 5,96:1
Harris, Gary (Miscellaneous)
Bitter Friends 1989,F 14,C16:3
In a Pig's Valise 1989,F 15,C15:1
Quintuplets 1989,Ap 2,51:1
Approaching Zanzibar 1989,My 5,C3:1
Conversation Among the Ruins 1989,Je 4,64:6
Lisbon Traviata, The 1989,Je 7,C21:1
Play to Win 1989,Jl 21,C3:2
Chinese Charade (Chino de la Charada, El) 1989,Ag
13,57:3
Lisbon Traviata, The 1989,N 1,C22:3
Baba Goya 1989,D 6,C21:1
Return, The 1990,Ja 12,C3:3
Ariano 1990,F 11,69:2
Dividends 1990,Mr 4,51:1
New York 1937 1990,My 6,75:4
What a Man Weighs 1990,My 25,C3:2
Jekyll and Hyde 1990,Jl 1,48:1
Catch Me If I Fall 1990,N 17,16:5
Harris, Harriet
Flea in Her Ear, A 1989,O 13,C15:1
Macbeth 1990,Ja 17,C13:4
Crucible, The 1990,Mr 30,C3:1
What a Man Weighs 1990,My 25,C3:2
Harris, Jeremiah J. (Miscellaneous)
Shogun: The Musical 1990,N 21,C9:1
Harris, Jessica (Translator)
Your Handsome Captain 1989,N 12,71:6
Harris, John (Lighting Director)
Sisters 1990,Je 7,C19:3
Harris, John (Scenic Designer)
Sisters 1990,Je 7,C19:3
Harris, Joseph (Producer)
Shogun: The Musical 1990,N 21,C9:1
Harris, Julie
Is He Still Dead? 1990,My 27,58:1
Harris, Lawrence R. (Miscellaneous)
Related Retreats 1990,Ap 18,C12:5
Harris, Natalia
Young Playwrights Festival 1990 1990,S 21,C14:6
Harris, Niki (Choreographer)
Leave It to Jane 1989,Mr 23,C17:1
Harris, Niki (Director)
Leave It to Jane 1989,Mr 23,C17:1
Harris, Ratzo B.
Suenos 1989,F 23,C13:3
Harris, Rosalind
Double Blessing 1989,Jl 2,38:1
Harris, Roy (Miscellaneous)
When She Danced 1990,F 20,C15:1
Harris, Timmy (Miscellaneous)
Bitter Friends 1989,F 14,C16:3
In a Pig's Valise 1989,F 15,C15:1
Quintuplets 1989,Ap 2,51:1
Approaching Zanzibar 1989,My 5,C3:1
Conversation Among the Ruins 1989,Je 4,64:6
Lisbon Traviata, The 1989,Je 7,C21:1
Play to Win 1989,Jl 21,C3:2
Lisbon Traviata, The 1989,N 1,C22:3
Baba Goya 1989,D 6,C21:1
Return, The 1990,Ja 12,C3:3
Ariano 1990,F 11,69:2
Dividends 1990,Mr 4,51:1
New York 1937 1990,My 6,75:4
What a Man Weighs 1990,My 25,C3:2
Jekyll and Hyde 1990,Jl 1,48:1
Catch Me If I Fall 1990,N 17,16:5
Harris, Viola
Bitter Friends 1989,F 14,C16:3

Harrison, Gregory (Producer)
Blame It on the Movies 1989,My 18,C22:3
Harrison, Llewellyn (Scenic Designer)
God's Trombones 1989,O 11,C17:1
Harrison, Peter (Scenic Designer)
Smoke on the Mountain 1990,My 17,C20:3
Harrison, Rex
Circle, The 1989,N 21,C19:1
Harrison, Tony (Translator)
Misanthrope, The 1989,Ag 20,II:5:1
Harry, James (Composer)
White Boned Demon 1989,Mr 5,68:1
B. Beaver Animation, The 1990,My 24,C19:1
Hart, Caitlin
Sunday Promenade, The 1989,Mr 12,68:1
Hart, Charles (Lyricist)
Aspects of Love 1989,Je 27,C15:4
Aspects of Love 1990,Ap 9,C11:1
Hart, Charles (Playwright)
Aspects of Love 1989,Je 27,C15:4
Hart, Cynthia (Miscellaneous)
Anthony Rose 1989,O 30,C16:3
Hart, Dan
Seeing Double 1989,N 16,C28:4
Hart, Dan (Composer)
Seeing Double 1989,N 16,C28:4
Hart, Dan (Musical Director)
Seeing Double 1989,N 16,C28:4
Hart, Ed
Tempest, The 1989,N 15,C18:3
Hart, Joe (Director)
People Who Could Fly, The 1989,Ag 3,C20:3
Hart, Joe (Miscellaneous)
People Who Could Fly, The 1989,Ag 3,C20:3
Hart, Linda
Sid Caesar & Company: Does Anybody Know What
I'm Talking About? 1989,N 2,C19:3
Hart, Lorenz (Lyricist)
Pal Joey 1990,Jl 24,C13:3
Hart, Melissa Joan
Beside Herself 1989,O 18,C15:1
Imagining Brad 1990,F 7,C15:2
Hart, Moss (Original Author)
Merrily We Roll Along 1990,F 27,C13:1
Hart, Moss (Playwright)
Man Who Came to Dinner, The 1989,Ag 1,C13:3
Light Up the Sky 1990,Ag 22,C10:5
Hart, Richard
Midsummer Night's Dream, A 1989,O 15,67:1
School for Wives, The 1989,D 30,17:1
Hartenstein, Frank (Miscellaneous)
Sid Caesar & Company: Does Anybody Know What
I'm Talking About? 1989,N 2,C19:3
Hartley, Jan (Miscellaneous)
Skin—A State of Being 1989,Ja 12,C15:1
House of Horror, The 1989,O 19,C26:1
Hartley, Susan
Leave It to Jane 1989,Mr 23,C17:1
Hartman, Michael
Grapes of Wrath, The 1990,Mr 23,C1:4
Hartwig, Randy Lee (Miscellaneous)
Goose! Beyond the Nursery 1990,F 11,69:2
Sugar Hill 1990,Ap 28,12:6
Harvey, Don
Titus Andronicus 1989,Ag 21,C13:1
Harwood, Ronald (Playwright)
Another Time 1989,D 3,II:5:1
Hashimoto, Kazuakira (Composer)
Takarazuka 1989,O 27,C21:1
Hashimoto, Kazuakira (Miscellaneous)
Takarazuka 1989,O 27,C21:1
Hashimoto, Yoko
Lost in a Flurry of Cherries 1990,Mr 25,62:1
Hass, Jay (Producer)
Sum of Us, The 1990,O 20,16:4
Hastings, John (Lighting Director)
Manhattan Class Company, One-Act Play Festival,
Series A 1989,Mr 11,16:1
Manhattan Class One-Acts, Series B 1989,Mr
19,61:4
New Music 1989,N 4,16:3
Hasty, Nancy
Florida Girls 1990,Je 21,C20:1
Hasty, Nancy (Playwright)
Florida Girls 1990,Je 21,C20:1
Hatcher, Jeffrey (Playwright)
Fellow Travelers (Manhattan Punch Line's Sixth
Annual Festival of One-Act Comedies, Evening
B) 1990,F 11,70:1

Neddy 1990,Ap 2,C15:1
Hauser, Frank (Director)
Arms and the Man 1989,Je 5,C12:4
Havel, Vaclav (Playwright)
Temptation 1989,Ap 10,C13:1
Audience (By and for Havel) 1990,Mr 9,C3:5
Havis, Allan (Playwright)
Lilith 1990,S 23,67:4
Hawkanson, David (Miscellaneous)
Paper Gramophone, The 1989,Mr 4,11:4
Importance of Being Earnest, The 1989,O 11,C15:1
Stand-Up Tragedy 1989,N 24,C3:4
Illusion, The 1990,Ja 18,C21:1
Woyzeck 1990,Mr 6,C17:1
Day Trips 1990,Ap 16,C15:1
Miser, The 1990,My 18,C4:3
Our Country's Good 1990,O 21,59:3
Hawkins, Yvette
Some Sweet Day 1989,Mr 27,C13:1
American Plan, The 1990,D 17,C11:1
Hawthorne, Nigel
Shadowlands 1990,N 12,C11:1
Shadowlands 1990,N 18,II:5:1
Hay, Rosemary (Director)
Brimstone and Treacle 1989,Ap 18,C15:3
Hay, Suzanna
Day Trips 1990,Ap 16,C15:1
Hayama, Kiyomi (Choreographer)
Takarazuka 1989,O 27,C21:1
Hayes, Kevin
20 Fingers, 20 Toes 1990,Ja 10,C17:1
Hayes, Lorey
Special Interests 1990,F 18,70:1
Generations of the Dead in the Abyss of Coney
Island Madness 1990,D 9,82:3
Haynes, Jayne
Big Funk, The 1990,D 11,C15:4
Big Funk, The 1990,D 16,II:5:1
Haynes, Robin
Max and Maxie 1989,Ja 18,C14:6
Hays, Rex D.
Grand Hotel 1989,N 13,C13:3
Grand Hotel 1990,F 25,II:5:1
Hayter, Rhonda
Manhattan Punch Line's Sixth Annual Festival of
One-Act Comedies, Evening A 1990,F 4,60:1
Hayward-Jones, Michael
Pal Joey 1990,Jl 24,C13:3
Hazel, Jean (Miscellaneous)
Polygraph 1990,O 27,12:5
Heacock, Richard (Composer)
Apart from George 1989,Mr 21,C19:1
Head, Terry
Ice Capades 1989,Ja 21,17:4
Heald, Anthony
Lisbon Traviata, The 1989,Je 7,C21:1
Lisbon Traviata, The 1989,N 1,C22:3
Elliot Loves 1990,Je 8,C3:1
Healy, Katherine
Skating for Life—A Celebration of Champions
1989,N 8,C25:1
Healy, Michael
Away Alone 1989,D 16,18:4
Heard, Denise
Oh, Kay! 1989,N 1,C22:3
Heard, Lynise
Oh, Kay! 1989,N 1,C22:3
Hearn, George
When We Are Married 1989,Ja 28,14:3
Ghetto 1989,My 1,C11:1
Meet Me in St. Louis 1989,N 3,C3:1
Heasley, Katherine
Tale of Two Cities, A 1990,Ap 7,16:4
Heasley, Vicki
Ice Capades 1990,Ja 21,49:1
Hebron, Paul
Born Yesterday 1989,Ja 30,C11:1
Hecht, Jessica
Othello 1990,Ja 17,C18:4
Hecht, Lawrence
Saint Joan 1989,Ag 19,14:1
Hecht, Paul
Enrico IV 1989,Ja 19,C22:3
Cherry Orchard, The 1990,My 24,C19:3
Heckart, Eileen
Eleemosynary 1989,My 10,C15:3
Cemetery Club, The 1990,My 16,C14:4
Hedden, Roger (Playwright)
Artistic Direction, The (Manhattan Punch Line's

Buddy: The Buddy Holly Story 1990,N 11,II:5:1

irowatari, Tsunetoshi (Director)
Lost in a Flurry of Cherries 1990,Mr 25,62:1

irowatari, Tsunetoshi (Playwright)
Lost in a Flurry of Cherries 1990,Mr 25,62:1

irsch, Andy
Speed of Darkness, The 1989,My 9,C15:1

irschfeld, Abe (Producer)
Prince of Central Park 1989,N 10,C3:1

irschfeld, Susan (Costume Designer)
Starmites 1989,Ap 28,C3:1

irsh, Jody (Playwright)
Seeing Double 1989,N 16,C28:4

oberman, Perry (Miscellaneous)
Kingfish 1989,D 22,C5:1

obson, Anne Marie (Miscellaneous)
Ambassador, The 1989,O 22,63:1

obson, Jade (Costume Designer)
Laughing Matters 1989,My 21,68:1

ocking, Leah
Hannah . . . 1939 1990,Je 2,16:3

odge, Mike
Some Sweet Day 1989,Mr 27,C13:1

odges, Patricia
Manhattan Punch Line's Sixth Annual Festival of One-Act Comedies, Evening B 1990,F 11,70:1

odgins, Marilyn
Prince of Central Park 1989,N 10,C3:1

offenberg, Julianne
Chelsea Walls 1990,Je 9,12:5

offman, Avi
Songs of Paradise 1989,Ja 24,C16:3

offman, Avi (Director)
Songs of Paradise 1989,Ja 24,C16:3

offman, Dustin
Merchant of Venice, The 1989,Je 21,C15:3
Merchant of Venice, The 1989,D 20,C15:1

offman, Jane
Some Americans Abroad 1990,F 12,C17:1
Some Americans Abroad 1990,My 3,C17:1

offman, K. Robert (Lighting Director)
Heart Outright, The 1989,My 21,68:2

offman, Kent (Miscellaneous)
Marathon 1990: Festival of New One-Act Plays, Series A 1990,My 16,C14:4
Marathon 1990: Festival of New One-Act Plays, Series B 1990,Je 1,C8:5
Marathon 1990: Festival of New One-Act Plays, Series C 1990,Je 14,C20:3

offman, Miriam (Playwright)
Songs of Paradise 1989,Ja 24,C16:3

ofmaier, Mark
Come As You Are 1990,F 15,C26:3

ofvendahl, Steve
Mastergate 1989,O 13,C3:1

ogan, Dan (Choreographer)
My Father, My Son 1990,S 23,65:3

ogan, Kevin
Three Sisters, The 1989,N 23,C20:5
School for Wives, The 1989,D 30,17:1

ogan, Robert
Few Good Men, A 1989,N 16,C23:4
Death Takes a Holiday 1990,Ag 13,C11:1

ogan, Tessie
Babel on Babylon (Plays in the Park) 1989,Je 20,C15:4

ioge, John
Rodents and Radios 1990,Ap 28,15:1

ioge, John (Composer)
Rodents and Radios 1990,Ap 28,15:1
Famine Plays 1990,N 3,14:5

iogue, Annie G. (Playwright)
Experiment at the Asylum (Grand Guignol, The) 1990,Je 2,18:1

iogue, Mitch (Playwright)
Experiment at the Asylum (Grand Guignol, The) 1990,Je 2,18:1

iogya, Giles (Lighting Director)
Importance of Being Earnest, The 1989,O 5,C19:1
Travesties 1989,N 3,C29:1
Misalliance 1990,O 14,56:4

iogya, Giles (Scenic Designer)
Importance of Being Earnest, The 1989,O 5,C19:1
Travesties 1989,N 3,C29:1
Misalliance 1990,O 14,56:4

Hoisington, Eric A.
Jerome Robbins's Broadway 1989,F 27,C13:1

Holbrook, Hal
King Lear 1990,N 16,C3:1

Holbrook, Ruby
Amulets Against the Dragon Forces 1989,Ap 6,C17:4

Holden, Arthur (Playwright)
Seeing Double 1989,N 16,C28:4

Holden, Joan (Playwright)
Seeing Double 1989,N 16,C28:4

Holder, Donald (Lighting Director)
Cezanne Syndrome, The 1989,F 3,C3:5
Phantom Lady, The 1989,Ap 16,60:1
Return, The 1990,Ja 12,C3:3
Spunk 1990,Ap 19,C17:4
Hanging the President 1990,Jl 13,C17:1
Caucasian Chalk Circle, The 1990,D 3,C13:3
Caucasian Chalk Circle, The 1990,D 9,II:5:1
American Plan, The 1990,D 17,C11:1

Holder, Laurence (Playwright)
Zora Neale Hurston 1990,F 5,C14:1

Holdgrive, David (Choreographer)
Golden Apple, The 1990,Mr 30,C3:5

Holgate, Ron
Lend Me a Tenor 1989,Mr 3,C3:1
Lend Me a Tenor 1989,Mr 29,C17:1

Holger (Lighting Director)
Unguided Missile, The 1989,F 13,C16:3

Holger (Scenic Designer)
Unguided Missile, The 1989,F 13,C16:3

Hollander, Leslie R.
Grand Guignol, The 1990,Je 2,18:1

Hollerith, Charles, Jr. (Miscellaneous)
Paradise for the Worried 1990,Ap 6,C3:1

Holliday, Polly
Cat on a Hot Tin Roof 1990,Mr 22,C17:1

Hollis, Stephen (Director)
Show Must Go On, The (Manhattan Punch Line's Sixth Annual Festival of One-Act Comedies, Evening A) 1990,F 4,60:1

Hollis, Tommy
Solid Gold Cadillac, The 1989,S 21,C28:1
Piano Lesson, The 1990,Ap 17,C13:4

Holly, Buddy (Composer)
Buddy: The Buddy Holly Story 1990,N 5,C13:1

Holly, Buddy (Lyricist)
Buddy: The Buddy Holly Story 1990,N 5,C13:1

Holly, Dennis (Composer)
Cherry Orchard, The 1990,My 24,C19:3

Hollywood, Daniele (Costume Designer)
Tales of the Lost Formicans 1990,Ap 29,60:1

Holman, Robert (Playwright)
Across Oka 1989,Ag 28,C13:4

Holman, Stephen
Breakfast with the Moors Murderers 1989,F 2,C18:4

Holmes, Ed
Seeing Double 1989,N 16,C28:4

Holmes, Prudence Wright
Lettice and Lovage 1990,Mr 26,C11:1

Holmes, Rupert (Composer)
Accomplice 1990,Ap 27,C5:1

Holmes, Rupert (Playwright)
Accomplice 1990,Ap 27,C5:1

Holmes, Violet (Choreographer)
Christmas Spectacular, The 1989,N 13,C20:5
Christmas Spectacular, The 1990,N 13,C20:1

Holms, John Pynchon (Director)
Floor Above the Roof (Working One-Acts '89) 1989,Je 25,45:4
Bovver Boys 1990,F 25,57:3

Holpit, Penny (Scenic Designer)
Showing Off 1989,My 28,57:1

Holst, Tim (Producer)
Ringling Brothers and Barnum & Bailey Circus 1990,Mr 31,13:1

Holt, Marion Peter (Translator)
Foundation, The 1989,D 29,C6:6

Holt, Shannon
Carnage, A Comedy 1989,S 18,C14:1

Holt, Tamara (Miscellaneous)
Year of the Baby, The 1989,Ag 17,C14:6
Indiana Dog 1989,S 26,C17:1
New Anatomies 1990,F 22,C19:1

Holt, Thelma (Producer)
Merchant of Venice, The 1989,D 20,C15:1

Holten, Michael (Miscellaneous)
Feast of Fools 1990,Mr 18,59:1

Holtzman, Merrill
Mastergate 1989,O 13,C3:1
Chelsea Walls 1990,Je 9,12:5

Holtzman, Merrill (Miscellaneous)
Chelsea Walls 1990,Je 9,12:5

Holtzman, Willy (Playwright)
Closer, The (Working One-Acts '89) 1989,Je 25,45:4

Bovver Boys 1990,F 25,57:3

Homewood, Bill (Director)
Romeo and Juliet 1990,Jl 14,10:1

Honda, Carol A.
And the Soul Shall Dance 1990,Mr 25,63:2
Wash, The 1990,N 8,C28:4

Honegger, Gitta (Director)
Solid Gold Cadillac, The 1989,S 21,C28:1

Honey, Susan
Member of the Wedding, The 1989,Ap 1,16:3

Honig, Edwin (Translator)
Phantom Lady, The 1989,Ap 16,60:1

Honma, Akira (Miscellaneous)
Ninagawa Macbeth 1990,O 22,C20:1

Hoodwin, Rebecca
Fifth of July 1989,F 16,C34:3

Hook, Cora
Empires and Appetites 1989,My 25,C18:4

Hooker, Brian (Translator)
Cyrano de Bergerac 1989,Jl 7,C19:1

Hooks, Lumengo Joy
Spirit Time 1989,Jl 14,C18:1

Hooks, Lumengo Joy (Playwright)
Spirit Time 1989,Jl 14,C18:1

Hooks, Stephen
Spirit Time 1989,Jl 14,C18:1

Hooks, Stephen (Composer)
Spirit Time 1989,Jl 14,C18:1

Hoon, Barbara
Jerome Robbins's Broadway 1989,F 27,C13:1

Hoover, Paul
Prizes 1989,My 18,C22:4

Hoover, Richard (Scenic Designer)
Spinoza 1990,N 4,72:4

Hooyman, Babs
Thirteenth Chair, The 1989,Ap 16,61:1

Hope, Sharon
Capitol Cakewalk 1990,Mr 2,C31:1

Hopkins, Anthony (Director)
Dylan Thomas: Return Journey 1990,F 23,C15:1

Hopkins, Billy (Director)
Match Point (Marathon 1990: Festival of New One-Act Plays, Series A) 1990,My 16,C14:4

Hopkins, David
Ghetto 1989,My 1,C11:1

Hopkins, Linda
Black and Blue 1989,Ja 27,C3:1

Horen, Bob
Thirteenth Chair, The 1989,Ap 16,61:1

Hori, Teruaki (Producer)
Karakuri Ningyo: Ancient Festival Puppets 1989,S 15,C28:4

Horne, J. R.
Night Hank Williams Died, The 1989,Ja 25,C16:4

Horne, Marilyn
Easter Extravaganza 1990,Ap 13,C28:4

Horner, Kristine (Miscellaneous)
Jibaros Progresistas, Los 1990,Ag 18,15:1

Horovitz, Israel (Director)
Widow's Blind Date, The 1989,N 8,C23:1

Horovitz, Israel (Playwright)
Henry Lumper 1989,F 5,53:1
Widow's Blind Date, The 1989,N 8,C23:1

Horowitz, Jeffrey (Miscellaneous)
Red Sneaks, The 1989,Je 29,C13:1
Othello 1990,Ja 17,C18:4
Mud Angel, The 1990,N 18,75:1

Horrigan, Patrick (Miscellaneous)
Metamorphosis 1989,Mr 7,C15:1
Cat on a Hot Tin Roof 1990,Mr 22,C17:1

Horsey, Susan Urban (Producer)
Mountain 1990,Ap 6,C29:1

Horsman, Kim
Henry V 1989,Je 12,C13:1

Horton, John
Love's Labor's Lost 1989,F 23,C15:1

Horton, Louisa
Blessing, The 1989,My 22,C12:1

Horvath, Jan
Threepenny Opera 1989,N 6,C13:4

Horvitz, Wayne (Composer)
Mountain Language 1989,N 9,C21:3

Hoschna, Karl (Composer)
Madame Sherry 1989,Jl 30,57:1

Hoshi, Shizuko
Wash, The 1990,N 8,C28:4

Hoshko, John
Love Life 1990,Je 22,C15:1

Hostetter, Curt
Hamlet 1990,My 9,C15:4

James, Harold Dean
Mastergate 1989,O 13,C3:1
James, Henry (Original Author)
Heiress, The 1989,Je 16,C3:1
Daisy Miller 1990,Ag 16,C14:4
James, Jerry (Miscellaneous)
Forbidden Broadway 1990 1990,Ja 24,C15:1
James, Peter Francis
Enrico IV 1989,Ja 19,C22:3
Cymbeline 1989,Je 1,C15:1
Hamlet 1990,My 9,C15:4
James, Toni-Leslie (Costume Designer)
Play Ball 1989,F 12,68:4
Suenos 1989,F 23,C13:3
Ariano 1990,F 11,69:2
Rough Crossing 1990,F 23,C3:4
And the Soul Shall Dance 1990,Mr 25,63:2
Spunk 1990,Ap 19,C17:4
Death of the Last Black Man in the Whole Entire
World, The 1990,S 25,C15:1
Caucasian Chalk Circle, The 1990,D 3,C13:3
Caucasian Chalk Circle, The 1990,D 9,II:5:1
James-Reed, Michael
Forest in Arden, A 1990,F 11,69:1
King Lear 1990,N 16,C3:1
Jamison, David
Ice Capades 1989,Ja 21,17:4
Jampolis, Neil Peter (Lighting Director)
Black and Blue 1989,Ja 27,C3:1
Orpheus Descending 1989,S 25,C15:4
Sid Caesar & Company: Does Anybody Know What
I'm Talking About? 1989,N 2,C19:3
Merchant of Venice, The 1989,D 20,C15:1
Feast of Fools 1990,Mr 18,59:1
About Time 1990,O 11,C18:6
Jackie Mason: Brand New 1990,O 18,C21:1
Handy Dandy 1990,O 23,C20:1
Jampolis, Neil Peter (Scenic Designer)
Sid Caesar & Company: Does Anybody Know What
I'm Talking About? 1989,N 2,C19:3
Forever Plaid 1990,My 25,C3:1
Jackie Mason: Brand New 1990,O 18,C21:1
Handy Dandy 1990,O 23,C20:1
Jamrog, Joseph
Henry Lumper 1989,F 5,53:1
I Am a Winner 1990,Ap 1,52:3
Miser, The 1990,O 12,C1:1
Janasz, Charles
Gus and Al 1989,F 28,C17:1
Jando, Dominique (Miscellaneous)
Grandma Goes West 1989,N 3,C4:1
Big Apple Circus, The 1990,N 3,13:4
Jandova, Elena
I & I 1989,S 24,72:3
Janes, Alan (Playwright)
Buddy: The Buddy Holly Story 1990,N 5,C13:1
Buddy: The Buddy Holly Story 1990,N 11,II:5:1
Jani, Robert F. (Miscellaneous)
Christmas Spectacular, The 1989,N 13,C20:5
Janney, Allison
Ladies 1989,Ap 7,C3:1
Lilith 1990,S 23,67:4
Jaramillo, Florencio
No + (No More) 1989,Ag 12,14:4
Jared, Robert (Lighting Director)
Gus and Al 1989,F 28,C17:1
Jarett, Debbie
Woyzeck 1990,Mr 6,C17:1
Jarkowsky, Andrew
Hamlet 1989,Je 2,C3:5
Jaroslow, Ruth
Fiddler on the Roof 1990,N 19,C13:1
Jarred, Joseph (Miscellaneous)
Legends in Concert 1989,My 14,49:3
Jarrett, Jerry
Fiddler on the Roof 1990,N 19,C13:1
Jarry, Alfred (Playwright)
Ubu 1989,Je 26,C14:1
Jarvis, Lucy (Producer)
Junon and Avos: The Hope 1990,Ja 8,C16:3
Jason, Mitchell
Grand Hotel 1989,N 13,C13:3
Jasper, Zina (Director)
Starting Monday 1990,Ap 5,C18:1
Jay, Brian
Meet Me in St. Louis 1989,N 3,C3:1
Jay, Isla (Lighting Director)
Casa 1990,Ja 18,C24:4
Jay, Isla (Miscellaneous)
Casa 1990,Ja 18,C24:4

Jay, William
Jonquil 1990,Ja 15,C14:3
Burner's Frolic 1990,F 26,C14:1
Jayce, Michael
Don Juan of Seville (Burlador de Sevilla y
Convidada de Piedra, El) 1989,Ap 7,C3:5
Death of the Last Black Man in the Whole Entire
World, The 1990,S 25,C15:1
Jbara, Gregory
Born Yesterday 1989,Ja 30,C11:1
Privates on Parade 1989,Ag 23,C13:3
Jeffery, Gayle (Miscellaneous)
Marathon '89, Series A 1989,My 30,C19:1
Marathon '89, Series B 1989,Je 15,C14:5
Marathon '89, Series C 1989,Je 29,C14:5
Swim Visit 1990,Je 23,12:4
Lusting After Pipino's Wife 1990,S 30,57:4
Jeffrey, Peter
King Lear 1990,Ag 8,C11:3
Richard III 1990,Ag 8,C11:3
Jeffreys, Stephen (Playwright)
Valued Friends 1990,D 20,C20:4
Jeffries, Kevin
Fifth of July 1989,F 16,C34:3
Jeffries, Lynn (Costume Designer)
Video Store Owner's Significant Other, The 1990,S
26,C9:5
Jeffries, Lynn (Scenic Designer)
Video Store Owner's Significant Other, The 1990,S
26,C9:5
Jellison, John
Waves, The 1990,My 10,C16:4
Jenkins, Daniel
Feast Here Tonight 1989,N 30,C16:3
Jenkins, Daniel (Composer)
Feast Here Tonight 1989,N 30,C16:3
Jenkins, Daniel (Lyricist)
Feast Here Tonight 1989,N 30,C16:3
Jenkins, David (Scenic Designer)
Kathy and Mo Show, The: Parallel Lives 1989,F
1,C21:1
Other People's Money 1989,F 17,C3:4
Welcome to the Club 1989,Ap 14,C3:1
Accomplice 1990,Ap 27,C5:1
Price of Fame 1990,Je 14,C17:1
Jenkins, Ken (Playwright)
Feast Here Tonight 1989,N 30,C16:3
Jenkins, Lillian
I & I 1989,S 24,72:3
Jenkins, Paulie (Lighting Director)
Abundance 1990,O 31,C15:3
Jenkins, Trish
Two Gentlemen of Verona 1990,D 13,C16:5
Jenkins, Vantony (Miscellaneous)
Sisters 1990,Je 7,C19:3
Jenner, James
Play Ball 1989,F 12,68:4
Lucky Come Hawaii 1990,O 29,C16:1
Jennings, Alex
Wild Duck, The 1990,Ag 30,C15:1
Jennings, Ken
Grand Hotel 1989,N 13,C13:3
Jensen, Brian
Florida Crackers 1989,Je 2,C3:1
Jepson, J. J.
Grand Hotel 1989,N 13,C13:3
Jerome, Timothy
Grand Hotel 1989,N 13,C13:3
Grand Hotel 1990,F 25,II:5:1
Jerry, Philip
Dangerous Games 1989,O 20,C3:3
Jesurun, John (Director)
Sunspot 1989,Mr 18,14:4
Everything That Rises Must Converge 1990,Mr
16,C6:3
Jesurun, John (Playwright)
Sunspot 1989,Mr 18,14:4
Everything That Rises Must Converge 1990,Mr
16,C6:3
Jesurun, John (Scenic Designer)
Sunspot 1989,Mr 18,14:4
Everything That Rises Must Converge 1990,Mr
16,C6:3
Jeter, Michael
Grand Hotel 1989,N 13,C13:3
Grand Hotel 1989,D 17,II:7:1
Grand Hotel 1990,F 25,II:5:1
Jiler, John
Sunday Promenade, The 1989,Mr 12,68:1

Jimenez, Jose (Lighting Director)
Coronel No Tiene Quien le Escriba, El (No One
Writes to the Colonel) 1989,Ag 3,C17:1
Jirousek, Julie
Gigi 1989,My 28,57:1
Jo, Haruhiko
Tempest, The 1989,Ja 1,II:5:1
Jo, Haruhiko (Miscellaneous)
Tempest, The 1989,Ja 1,II:5:1
Jobe, Amanda
Jonquil 1990,Ja 15,C14:3
Joh, Haruhiko
Ninagawa Macbeth 1990,O 22,C20:1
Johanson, Robert (Director)
Fanny 1990,Ap 13,C3:5
Johanson, Robert (Miscellaneous)
Fanny 1990,Ap 13,C3:5
John, Evangeline
White Chocolate for My Father 1990,F 15,C22:3
John, Joseph (Miscellaneous)
House of Horror, The 1989,O 19,C26:1
John, Joseph (Scenic Designer)
House of Horror, The 1989,O 19,C26:1
Johns, Glynis
Circle, The 1989,N 21,C19:1
Johns, Kurt
Aspects of Love 1990,Ap 9,C11:5
Johnson, Alan (Musical Director)
Cymbeline 1989,Je 1,C15:1
Johnson, Ann (Miscellaneous)
Moon over Miami 1989,F 24,C3:1
Johnson, Arch
Other People's Money 1989,F 17,C3:4
Johnson, Bertina
Winter's Tale, The 1989,Mr 22,C19:4
Johnson, Cindy Lou (Playwright)
Brilliant Traces 1989,F 6,C11:1
Brilliant Traces 1989,D 24,II:3:1
Johnson, Cullen
Henry Lumper 1989,F 5,53:1
Johnson, Daniel Timothy
Cyrano de Bergerac 1989,Jl 7,C19:1
Johnson, Eric
Aspects of Love 1990,Ap 9,C11:1
Johnson, Ethan (Miscellaneous)
Carnage, A Comedy 1989,S 18,C14:1
Johnson, Geordie
Titus Andronicus 1989,Je 12,C13:1
Comedy of Errors, The 1989,Je 12,C13:1
Johnson, Greg (Director)
Artistic Direction, The (Manhattan Punch Line's
Sixth Annual Festival of One-Act Comedies,
Evening B) 1990,F 11,70:1
Johnson, Grey Cattell (Director)
Henry Lumper 1989,F 5,53:1
Johnson, James Weldon (Original Author)
God's Trombones 1989,O 11,C17:1
Johnson, Jeremy
Romeo and Juliet 1990,D 21,C20:6
Johnson, John (Musical Director)
Funny Thing Happened on the Way to the Forum, A
1989,Ag 6,49:3
Johnson, Larry
Oh, Kay! 1989,N 1,C22:3
Johnson, Linda
Wizard of Oz, The 1989,Mr 24,C3:1
Johnson, Marjorie
Young Playwrights Festival 1990 1990,S 21,C14:6
Johnson, Martha
Ivanov 1990,S 25,C13:3
Johnson, Mary Lee (Producer)
Grand Hotel 1989,N 13,C13:3
Johnson, Michelle
Some Americans Abroad 1990,My 3,C17:1
Johnson, Page
East Texas 1990,O 7,70:4
Johnson, Patrice
Death of the Last Black Man in the Whole Entire
World, The 1990,S 25,C15:1
Johnson, Paul (Miscellaneous)
Leave It to Jane 1989,Mr 23,C17:1
Johnson, Paul (Musical Director)
Gigi 1989,My 28,57:1
Johnson, Pookie (Musical Director)
Sugar Hill 1990,Ap 28,12:6
Johnson, Richmond
Hamlet 1989,Je 2,C3:5
Johnson, Stephanie (Lighting Director)
I Think It's Gonna Work Out Fine 1990,Mr 17,18:6

ohnson, Sy (Miscellaneous)
Black and Blue 1989,Ja 27,C3:1
ohnson, Sy (Musical Director)
Black and Blue 1989,Ja 27,C3:1
ohnson, Tim
Zora Neale Hurston 1990,F 5,C14:1
ohnson, Virgil (Costume Designer)
Winter's Tale, The 1990,Ja 31,C15:1
ohnston, Donald (Miscellaneous)
Oh, Kay! 1989,N 1,C22:3
Oh, Kay! 1990,N 2,C1:1
ohnston, John Dennis
Blood Issue 1989,Ap 5,C19:4
ohnston, Rick (Playwright)
Cahoots 1990,Mr 10,16:4
ohnston, Ron
Born Yesterday 1989,Ja 30,C11:1
ohnston, Terry A. (Producer)
Catch Me If I Fall 1990,N 17,16:5
olly, Russ
Buddy: The Buddy Holly Story 1990,N 5,C13:1
ones, B. J.
Mill Fire 1989,O 19,C22:3
ones, Bronwen (Miscellaneous)
Peggy and Jackson 1989,Ag 10,C16:5
Adios, Tropicana 1989,Ag 10,C16:5
ones, Cassie
Tale of Two Cities, A 1990,Ap 7,16:4
ones, Cherry
Mastergate 1989,F 14,C17:1
Twelfth Night 1989,D 20,C20:3
ones, Clayton Barclay
Approaching Zanzibar 1989,My 5,C3:1
ones, Dexter
Prizes 1989,My 18,C22:4
Oh, Kay! 1989,N 1,C22:3
ones, Herman LeVern (Miscellaneous)
Macbeth 1989,Mr 21,C19:1
Apart from George 1989,Mr 21,C19:1
ones, Jeffrey M.
Bad Penny (Plays in the Park) 1989,Je 20,C15:4
ones, John Christopher
Aristocrats 1989,Ap 26,C15:1
Prin 1990,Je 7,C18:5
Miser, The 1990,O 12,C1:1
ones, Keith (Miscellaneous)
White Chocolate for My Father 1990,F 15,C22:3
ones, Kimberly
Capitol Cakewalk 1990,Mr 2,C31:1
ones, Mark (Miscellaneous)
Ladies 1989,Ap 7,C3:1
ones, Meachie (Director)
Spirit Time 1989,Jl 14,C18:1
ones, Rhodessa
I Think It's Gonna Work Out Fine 1990,Mr 17,18:6
ones, Rhodessa (Composer)
I Think It's Gonna Work Out Fine 1990,Mr 17,18:6
ones, Richard (Director)
Flea in Her Ear, A 1989,Ag 20,II:5:1
ones, Simon
Privates on Parade 1989,Ag 23,C13:3
ones, Thomas W., 2d (Director)
Sisters 1990,Je 7,C19:3
ones, Walker
Moon over Miami 1989,F 24,C3:1
Wonderful Town 1989,O 8,64:1
onson, Ben (Playwright)
Silent Woman or Epicoene, The 1989,Ag 6,II:5:1
ordan, Beverley
Romeo and Juliet 1990,Jl 14,10:1
ordan, Richard (Director)
Macbeth 1990,Ja 17,C13:4
ory, Jon (Director)
Blood Issue 1989,Ap 5,C19:4
Seagull, The 1989,O 19,C19:3
Vital Signs 1990,Ap 5,C15:1
Three Cuckolds, The 1990,O 9,C14:4
Jory, Jon (Miscellaneous)
Stained Glass 1989,Ap 5,C19:4
Bone-the-Fish 1989,Ap 5,C19:4
Blood Issue 1989,Ap 5,C19:4
Autumn Elegy 1989,Ap 5,C19:4
Tales of the Lost Formicans 1989,Ap 5,C19:4
Seagull, The 1989,O 19,C19:3
Children of the Sun 1989,O 19,C19:3
2 1990,Ap 5,C15:1
Vital Signs 1990,Ap 5,C15:1
Zara Spook and Other Lures 1990,Ap 5,C15:1
Pink Studio, The 1990,Ap 5,C15:1

In Darkest America 1990,Ap 5,C15:1
Infinity House 1990,Ap 5,C15:1
Swan 1990,Ap 5,C15:1
Joseph, Robin Anne (Miscellaneous)
Gifts of the Magi, The 1990,D 9,82:3
Joslyn, Betsy
Light Up the Sky 1990,Ag 22,C10:5
Joubert, Joseph (Miscellaneous)
Truly Blessed: A Musical Celebration of Mahalia
Jackson 1990,Ap 23,C13:1
Jovovich, Scott
Jerome Robbins's Broadway 1989,F 27,C13:1
Joy, James Leonard (Scenic Designer)
Grandma Goes West 1989,N 3,C4:1
Chocolate Soldier, The 1990,Je 3,62:2
Big Apple Circus, The 1990,N 3,13:4
Peter Pan 1990,D 14,C3:4
Joy, Robert
Hyde in Hollywood 1989,N 30,C19:3
Taming of the Shrew, The 1990,Jl 13,C3:1
Joyce, Heidi
Leave It to Jane 1989,Mr 23,C17:1
Joyce, James (Original Author)
Ulysses in Nighttown 1989,Ja 15,44:1
Joyce, Stephen
Playboy of the Western World, The 1990,N 8,C28:1
Joyner, Kimble
Young Playwrights Festival 1989,S 22,C5:4
Jozefowicz, Januez (Choreographer)
Dybbuk, The 1989,Jl 11,C13:1
Juana Ines de la Cruz (Original Author)
Suenos 1989,F 23,C13:3
Jucha, Brian
Baal 1990,Mr 24,17:1
Judd, Jacqueline (Producer)
Reno: In Rage and Rehab 1989,Mr 16,C20:4
Judson, Tom
Blue Piano, The 1990,Je 4,C22:1
Judson, Tom (Playwright)
Blue Piano, The 1990,Je 4,C22:1
Judy, James
Catch Me If I Fall 1990,N 17,16:5
Julia, Raul
Macbeth 1990,Ja 17,C13:4
Jung, Philipp (Scenic Designer)
Mastergate 1989,F 14,C17:1
Ancient History 1989,My 18,C29:3
Lisbon Traviata, The 1989,Je 7,C21:1
Mastergate 1989,O 13,C3:1
Lisbon Traviata, The 1989,N 1,C22:3
Closer Than Ever 1989,N 7,C19:1
Bovver Boys 1990,F 25,57:3
Mountain 1990,Ap 6,C29:1
Quiet End, A 1990,My 31,C16:6
Jurasz, Marta
Dybbuk, The 1989,Jl 11,C13:1
Jury, Paul (Musical Director)
Buddy: The Buddy Holly Story 1990,N 5,C13:1

K

Kaczmarek, Jane
Ice Cream with Hot Fudge 1990,My 4,C5:1
Kaczorowski, Peter (Lighting Director)
Forbidden City, The 1989,Ap 7,C3:1
Importance of Being Earnest, The 1989,O 11,C15:1
Romance in Hard Times 1989,D 29,C3:1
Bad Habits 1990,Mr 21,C13:1
Kiss of the Spider Woman 1990,Je 1,C3:1
Taming of the Shrew, The 1990,Jl 13,C3:1
Kadavy, Caryn
Skating for Life—A Celebration of Champions
1989,N 8,C25:1
Brian Boitano and Katarina Witt Skating 1990,My
8,C17:1
Kadokawa, Haruki (Producer)
Threepenny Opera 1989,N 6,C13:4
Shogun: The Musical 1990,N 21,C9:1
Kadri, Ron (Scenic Designer)
People Who Could Fly, The 1989,Ag 3,C20:3
Kafka, Franz (Original Author)
Metamorphosis 1989,Mr 7,C15:1
Kagami, Yoko
Lost in a Flurry of Cherries 1990,Mr 25,62:1
Kagan, Diane
Enrico IV 1989,Ja 19,C22:3

Kagan, Lois
I & I 1989,S 24,72:3
Kagen, Lynellen
Romeo and Juliet 1990,D 21,C20:6
Kageyama, Hitomi
Ninagawa Macbeth 1990,O 22,C20:1
Kahl, Drew
Merry Wives of Windsor, The 1990,My 30,C13:1
Kahn, Gary
City of Angels 1989,D 12,C19:4
Kahn, Madeline
Born Yesterday 1989,Ja 30,C11:1
Born Yesterday 1989,F 19,II:5:1
Kahn, Michael (Director)
As You Like It 1989,My 13,10:5
Twelfth Night 1989,O 4,C17:1
Merry Wives of Windsor, The 1990,My 30,C13:1
Richard III 1990,O 2,C12:3
Richard III 1990,O 7,II:5:1
Kahn, Michael (Miscellaneous)
Twelfth Night 1989,O 4,C17:1
Merry Wives of Windsor, The 1990,My 30,C13:1
Richard III 1990,O 2,C12:3
Kahn, Tobi (Miscellaneous)
Jonah 1990,Mr 23,C5:1
Kai, Masato (Miscellaneous)
Ninagawa Macbeth 1990,O 22,C20:1
Kaikkonen, Gus (Miscellaneous)
Cyrano de Bergerac 1989,Jl 7,C19:1
Kakhiani, Marina
King Lear 1990,Ap 4,C17:1
Kalaidjian, Robert (Miscellaneous)
Dividends 1990,Mr 4,51:1
Kalas, Janet (Miscellaneous)
Young Playwrights Festival 1989,S 22,C5:4
Miss Evers's Boys 1989,D 21,C16:3
Each Day Dies with Sleep 1990,My 17,C20:3
Young Playwrights Festival 1990 1990,S 21,C14:6
Kalber, Joe
Ice Capades 1990,Ja 21,49:1
Kalcheim, Lee (Director)
Friends 1989,Je 11,67:1
Kalcheim, Lee (Playwright)
Friends 1989,Je 11,67:1
Kalfin, Robert (Director)
Truly Blessed: A Musical Celebration of Mahalia
Jackson 1990,Ap 23,C13:1
Spinoza 1990,N 4,72:4
Kalfin, Robert Mark (Miscellaneous)
In a Pig's Valise 1989,F 15,C15:1
Dangerous Games 1989,O 20,C3:3
Kalita, Marek
Dybbuk, The 1989,Jl 11,C13:1
Hamlet 1989,Jl 11,C13:1
Kalt, Melissa
Murder in the Cathedral 1989,S 9,13:1
Kamal, Youssif
Romeo and Juliet 1990,D 21,C20:6
Kamlot, Robert (Miscellaneous)
Lend Me a Tenor 1989,Mr 3,C3:1
Kamm, Tom (Scenic Designer)
Investigation of the Murder in El Salvador, The
1989,My 23,C14:4
Baba Goya 1989,D 6,C21:1
Forest in Arden, A 1990,F 11,69:1
Heart of a Dog 1990,Mr 16,C3:1
Each Day Dies with Sleep 1990,My 17,C20:3
Kanai, Shunichiro (Scenic Designer)
Yoshitsune Senbonzakura (Yoshitsune and the
Thousand Cherry Trees) 1989,S 8,C3:4
Kurozuka (Black Mound, The) 1989,S 8,C3:4
Kancheli, Ghia (Composer)
King Lear 1990,Ap 4,C17:1
Peace of Brest-Litovsk, The 1990,Ap 18,C11:1
Kandel, Paul
20 Fingers, 20 Toes 1990,Ja 10,C17:1
Fanny 1990,Ap 13,C3:5
Kander, John (Composer)
Kiss of the Spider Woman 1990,Je 1,C3:1
Kander, John (Miscellaneous)
Gypsy 1989,N 17,C5:1
Kane, Bradley
Titus Andronicus 1989,Ag 21,C13:1
Kane, Donna
Meet Me in St. Louis 1989,N 3,C3:1
Kane, Francis
Merry Wives of Windsor, The 1990,My 30,C13:1
Kane, Mary
Good Coach, The 1989,Je 13,C18:5

And the Soul Shall Dance 1990,Mr 25,63:2
Spanish Eyes 1990,My 27,56:3
Perfect Diamond, A 1990,Je 6,C18:1
Swim Visit 1990,Je 23,12:4
Lucky Come Hawaii 1990,O 29,C16:1
Klinger, Herb
Romeo and Juliet 1990,D 21,C20:6
Klinger, Pam
Pal Joey 1990,Jl 24,C13:3
Klingler, Rebecca
Seeing Double 1989,N 16,C28:4
Klion, Jenny
Grandma Goes West 1989,N 3,C4:1
Klotz, Florence (Costume Designer)
City of Angels 1989,D 12,C19:4
Kiss of the Spider Woman 1990,Je 1,C3:1
Knapp, Sarah
Gifts of the Magi, The 1990,D 9,82:3
Knell, Dane
Lettice and Lovage 1990,Mr 26,C11:1
Knepper, Robert
Ice Cream with Hot Fudge 1990,My 4,C5:1
Lake No Bottom 1990,N 30,C3:1
Lake No Bottom 1990,D 9,II:5:1
Knight, Jonathan (Miscellaneous)
Suenos 1989,F 23,C13:3
Knight, Martha (Miscellaneous)
Merrily We Roll Along 1990,F 27,C13:1
Knight, Michael E.
Home Games 1989,O 2,C16:3
Knight, Susan
Apocalyptic Butterflies 1989,Je 17,12:3
Titus Andronicus 1989,Ag 21,C13:1
New Music 1989,N 4,16:3
Forest in Arden, A 1990,F 11,69:1
Subfertile 1990,N 8,C20:5
Knight, Wayne
Mastergate 1989,O 13,C3:1
Knudson, Kurt
Without Apologies 1989,F 19,74:4
Chocolate Soldier, The 1990,Je 3,62:2
Pal Joey 1990,Jl 24,C13:3
Knutsen, Erik
Tempest, The 1989,N 15,C18:3
Hamlet 1990,My 9,C15:4
Kobart, Ruth
Funny Thing Happened on the Way to the Forum, A
  1989,Ag 6,49:3
Kobayashi, Kohei (Producer)
Takarazuka 1989,O 27,C21:1
Koch, David
Kiss of the Spider Woman 1990,Je 1,C3:1
Kochen, Tom (Miscellaneous)
Carol Lawrence and Larry Kert Together . . . Again!
  1990,O 4,C21:1
Kochman, Paul A. (Miscellaneous)
My Father, My Son 1990,S 23,65:3
Romeo and Juliet 1990,D 21,C20:6
Kociolek, Ted (Musical Director)
Madame Sherry 1989,Jl 30,57:1
Kodama, Ai
Takarazuka 1989,O 27,C21:1
Koenig, Ronald A. (Miscellaneous)
Jekyll and Hyde 1990,Jl 1,48:1
Koeppe, Sarah Cornelia
Apart from George 1989,Mr 21,C19:1
Koeppe, Sarah Cornelia (Miscellaneous)
Macbeth 1989,Mr 21,C19:1
Kogler, Rita Ann (Lighting Director)
Carreno 1990,F 3,15:4
Koherr, Bob
Triplets in Uniform 1989,F 12,70:4
Kohl, Daniel
Indiana Dog 1989,S 26,C17:1
Kolasinska, Ewa
Dybbuk, The 1989,Jl 11,C13:1
Kolb, Laura
I & I 1989,S 24,72:3
German Requiem 1990,My 28,14:5
Kolins, Howard (Miscellaneous)
Easter Extravaganza 1990,Ap 13,C28:4
Kolo, Fred (Director)
Unguided Missile, The 1989,F 13,C16:3
Kolo, Fred (Lighting Director)
Truly Blessed: A Musical Celebration of Mahalia
  Jackson 1990,Ap 23,C13:1
Kolo, Fred (Scenic Designer)
Truly Blessed: A Musical Celebration of Mahalia
  Jackson 1990,Ap 23,C13:1

Kolodner, Arnie
Lady in Question, The 1989,Jl 26,C17:1
Money Talks 1990,S 7,C3:5
Koloskov, N. (Miscellaneous)
My Big Land 1989,Ag 17,C15:1
Komiyama, Yuko
And the Soul Shall Dance 1990,Mr 25,63:2
Komolova, Valentina (Costume Designer)
Junon and Avos: The Hope 1990,Ja 8,C16:3
Kondek, Charles (Director)
Golden Apple, The 1990,Mr 30,C3:5
Kondoleon, Harry (Playwright)
Self-Torture and Strenuous Exercise (Marathon '89,
  Series A) 1989,My 30,C19:1
Love Diatribe 1990,D 19,C15:1
Konieczny, Zygmunt (Composer)
Dybbuk, The 1989,Jl 11,C13:1
Konig, David
Manhattan Punch Line's Sixth Annual Festival of
  One-Act Comedies, Evening A 1990,F 4,60:1
Konopka, Albin (Musical Director)
Chocolate Soldier, The 1990,Je 3,62:2
Konstantin, Elise-Ann (Miscellaneous)
At the Chelsea 1989,Ja 20,C3:1
Nature of Things, The 1990,Mr 25,63:1
Jersey City 1990,Jl 15,40:3
Death of the Last Black Man in the Whole Entire
  World, The 1990,S 25,C15:1
Lake No Bottom 1990,N 30,C3:1
Konstantinova, Lidiya
Peace of Brest-Litovsk, The 1990,Ap 18,C11:1
Kopache, Thomas
Big Frogs (Marathon '89, Series C) 1989,Je 29,C14:5
Orpheus Descending 1989,S 25,C15:4
Kopanski, Abel (Lighting Director)
Doente Imaginario, O (Imaginary Invalid, The)
  1990,Ag 23,C20:1
Kopit, Arthur (Playwright)
Bone-the-Fish 1989,Ap 5,C19:4
Korbich, Eddie
Sweeney Todd: The Demon Barber of Fleet Street
  1989,Ap 8,11:5
Sweeney Todd 1989,S 15,C3:1
Korder, Howard (Playwright)
Wonderful Party! (Manhattan Punch Line's Fifth
  Annual Festival of One-Act Comedies, Series A)
  1989,Ja 26,C16:1
Search and Destroy 1990,D 14,C3:1
Koreto, Abigail (Miscellaneous)
Going to New England 1990,Mr 9,C18:1
Korey, Alix
Romance in Hard Times 1989,D 29,C3:1
Korf, Geoff (Lighting Director)
Ivanov 1990,S 25,C13:3
Korf, Mia
Young Playwrights Festival 1990 1990,S 21,C14:6
Kornfeld, Eric
Midsummer Nights 1989,S 24,71:3
Korolyova, Tatyana
Leningrad State Music Hall 1990,My 28,11:1
Korp, Pamela (Costume Designer)
Year of the Baby, The 1989,Ag 17,C14:6
Korzen, Annie
Return, The 1990,Ja 12,C3:3
Kosek, Kenny
Feast Here Tonight 1989,N 30,C16:3
Kosis, Tom
Pal Joey 1990,Jl 24,C13:3
Kostylyov, Dmitri
Leningrad State Music Hall 1990,My 28,11:1
Kotik, Vsevolod M. (Miscellaneous)
Moscow Circus 1990,Ja 13,13:4
Kotin, Vladimir
Brian Boitano and Katarina Witt Skating 1990,My
  8,C17:1
Kotlowitz, Dan (Lighting Director)
Yankee Dawg You Die 1989,My 15,C13:4
Slay It with Music 1989,O 24,C20:6
Short History of Romance, A (Men's Room, The)
  1990,Jl 26,C13:3
Money Talks 1990,S 7,C3:5
Wash, The 1990,N 8,C28:4
Kotoske, Tamar
Paradise for the Worried 1990,Ap 6,C3:1
Kotoske, Tamar (Miscellaneous)
Paradise for the Worried 1990,Ap 6,C3:1
Kourilsky, Francoise (Director)
Alive by Night 1989,My 18,C22:3
Your Handsome Captain 1989,N 12,71:6

Kourilsky, Francoise (Miscellaneous)
Alive by Night 1989,My 18,C22:3
Koutoukas, H. M.
Big Hotel 1989,S 29,C3:1
Ring Gott Farblonjet, Der 1990,Ap 13,C3:1
Camille 1990,S 7,C3:1
Camille 1990,S 16,II:7:1
Koval, Vladimir
Peace of Brest-Litovsk, The 1990,Ap 18,C11:1
Kovcic, Zoran
Tale of Two Cities, A 1990,Ap 7,16:4
Kowal, James
Dangerous Games 1989,O 20,C3:3
Kowal, James (Musical Director)
Dangerous Games 1989,O 20,C3:3
Kozak, Irina (Miscellaneous)
Cinzano 1989,Je 29,C15:1
Kozak, Roman (Director)
Cinzano 1989,Je 29,C15:1
Kozeluh, John
Golden Apple, The 1990,Mr 30,C3:5
Kozlov, Igor
My Big Land 1989,Ag 17,C15:1
Kozlovsky, Aleksandr
Leningrad State Music Hall 1990,My 28,11:1
Kraemer, Bruce (Miscellaneous)
Waves, The 1990,My 10,C16:4
Krag, James
Mill Fire 1989,O 19,C22:3
Krakowski, Jane
Grand Hotel 1989,N 13,C13:3
Grand Hotel 1990,F 25,II:5:1
Kramer, Larry (Original Author)
Report from the Holocaust (Indecent Materials)
  1990,Ag 28,C14:3
Kramer, Rob
Dance Lesson, A 1989,N 11,16:5
Kramer, Sherry (Playwright)
What a Man Weighs 1990,My 25,C3:2
Kramer, Terry Allen (Producer)
Shadowlands 1990,N 12,C11:1
Krane, David (Miscellaneous)
Kiss of the Spider Woman 1990,Je 1,C3:1
Krane, David (Musical Director)
Sweeney Todd: The Demon Barber of Fleet Street
  1989,Ap 8,11:5
Sweeney Todd 1989,S 15,C3:1
Krascella, Jed
Visit, The 1989,F 5,56:5
Krasker, Tommy (Miscellaneous)
Madame Sherry 1989,Jl 30,57:1
Krasnansky, Jennifer
People Who Could Fly, The 1989,Ag 3,C20:3
Krass, Ellen M. (Producer)
Kathy and Mo Show, The: Parallel Lives 1989,F
  1,C21:1
Reno: In Rage and Rehab 1989,Mr 16,C20:4
Krass, Michael (Costume Designer)
Briar Patch 1989,D 6,C21:1
Waves, The 1990,My 10,C16:4
Kraszelnicki, Pawel
Dybbuk, The 1989,Jl 11,C13:1
Krausnick, Dennis
Old Maid, The 1990,Ag 16,C14:4
Krausnick, Dennis (Director)
Daisy Miller 1990,Ag 16,C14:4
Krausnick, Dennis (Miscellaneous)
Old Maid, The 1990,Ag 16,C14:4
Daisy Miller 1990,Ag 16,C14:4
Krausnick, Dennis (Playwright)
Old Maid, The 1990,Ag 16,C14:4
Daisy Miller 1990,Ag 16,C14:4
Krauss, Marvin A. (Producer)
Grand Hotel 1989,N 13,C13:3
Kravets, Laura (Miscellaneous)
Manhattan Class Company, One-Act Play Festival,
  Series A 1989,Mr 11,16:1
Manhattan Class One-Acts, Series B 1989,Mr
  19,61:4
Kravits, Jason
Merry Wives of Windsor, The 1990,My 30,C13:1
Krebs, Eric (Producer)
Ad Hock 1989,Ja 20,C11:1
People Who Could Fly, The 1989,Ag 3,C20:3
By and for Havel 1990,Mr 9,C3:5
Florida Girls 1990,Je 21,C20:1
Ed Linderman's Broadway Jukebox 1990,Jl 20,C3:1
About Time 1990,O 11,C18:6
Handy Dandy 1990,O 23,C20:1

reindel, Mitch
  Metamorphosis 1989,Mr 7,C15:1
remer, Daniel
  Funny Thing Happened on the Way to the Forum, A
    1989,Ag 6,49:3
  Saint Joan 1989,Ag 19,14:1
renz, Frank (Costume Designer)
  Lettice and Lovage 1990,Mr 26,C11:1
reshka, Ruth (Miscellaneous)
  Eleemosynary 1989,My 10,C15:3
  Tru 1989,D 15,C3:1
  Abundance 1990,O 31,C15:3
ressyn, Miriam (Lyricist)
  Land of Dreams, The 1989,N 22,C10:1
ressyn, Miriam (Miscellaneous)
  Land of Dreams, The 1989,N 22,C10:1
rich, Gretchen
  Three Sisters 1989,Ja 24,C16:4
  Good 1989,F 25,18:4
richevsky, Aleksandr (Miscellaneous)
  Cinzano 1989,Je 29,C15:1
rieger, Barbara Zinn (Miscellaneous)
  Feast Here Tonight 1989,N 30,C16:3
  Moving Targets 1990,Ja 30,C14:5
  Hannah . . . 1939 1990,Je 2,16:3
  Nightingale 1990,D 4,C16:3
ristic, Angie
  God's Policemen 1989,O 22,64:4
rizner, Douglas
  Love's Labor's Lost 1989,My 26,C4:5
  O Pioneers! 1990,Ja 28,49:1
roeger, Perry Arthur (Playwright)
  Capitol Cakewalk 1990,Mr 2,C31:1
roeger, Perry Arthur (Scenic Designer)
  Capitol Cakewalk 1990,Mr 2,C31:1
roetz, Franz Xaver (Playwright)
  Nest, The 1989,Mr 2,C26:1
  Through the Leaves 1990,S 18,C18:1
roeze, Jan (Lighting Director)
  Genesis: Music and Miracles from the Medieval
    Mystery Plays 1989,Ja 18,C20:5
  Grandma Goes West 1989,N 3,C4:1
  Sex, Drugs, Rock & Roll 1990,F 9,C3:1
  Big Apple Circus, The 1990,N 3,13:4
ron, Ron (Scenic Designer)
  Talking Things Over with Chekhov 1990,My 13,44:1
ruger, Simcha (Translator)
  Land of Dreams, The 1989,N 22,C10:1
  Father's Inheritance 1990,N 18,75:1
rupa, Olek
  Ubu 1989,Je 26,C14:1
  Tower of Evil, The (Tour de Nesle, La) 1990,My
    13,45:1
rupp, Jon
  Return, The 1990,Ja 12,C3:3
ruschke, Gerhard
  Shenandoah 1989,Ag 9,C13:1
ruszelnicki, Pawel
  Hamlet 1989,Jl 11,C13:1
ruzewska, Meg
  Father Was a Peculiar Man 1990,Jl 11,C13:1
rynkin, Gennady
  Ward No. Six 1989,Jl 29,16:1
ubala, Michael
  Jerome Robbins's Broadway 1989,F 27,C13:1
ucera, Vaclav (Lighting Director)
  White Boned Demon 1989,Mr 5,68:1
uhlke, Kevin (Director)
  O Pioneers! 1990,Ja 28,49:1
  Mud Angel, The 1990,N 18,75:1
uhn, Judy
  Endangered Species 1990,O 9,C13:1
uhn, Kevin (Composer)
  Midsummer Nights 1989,S 24,71:3
uhn, Marguerite
  I Stand Before You Naked 1990,D 10,C14:1
ulerman, Ruth
  Quintessential Image, The 1989,Ag 17,C18:3
  In Her Own Words (A Portrait of Jane) 1989,Ag
    17,C18:3
umin, Jeremy (Lighting Director)
  Dividends 1990,Mr 4,51:1
undera, Milan (Playwright)
  Jacques and His Master 1989,N 16,C28:5
unii, Masahiro (Miscellaneous)
  Ninagawa Macbeth 1990,O 22,C20:1
  Shogun: The Musical 1990,N 21,C9:1
urdyumova, N. (Lighting Director)
  My Big Land 1989,Ag 17,C15:1

Kurihara, Komaki
  Ninagawa Macbeth 1990,O 22,C20:1
Kuroda, Kati
  Noiresque: The Fallen Angel 1989,My 5,C3:4
  Lucky Come Hawaii 1990,O 29,C16:1
Kuroda, Kati (Director)
  And the Soul Shall Dance 1990,Mr 25,63:2
Kurshal, Raymond
  Winter's Tale, The 1989,Mr 22,C19:4
Kurth, Juliette
  Love's Labor's Lost 1989,F 23,C15:1
Kurtz, Marcia Jean
  Loman Family Picnic, The 1989,Je 22,C24:1
  When She Danced 1990,F 20,C15:1
Kurtz, Normand (Producer)
  Accomplice 1990,Ap 27,C5:1
Kuschner, Jason (Miscellaneous)
  Jacques and His Master 1989,N 16,C28:5
Kuser, Hulya
  Mythos Oedipus 1989,Mr 5,69:1
  Dionysus Filius Dei 1989,Mr 5,69:1
Kushner, Tony (Playwright)
  Illusion, The 1990,Ja 18,C21:1
Kutsevalov, S. (Scenic Designer)
  My Big Land 1989,Ag 17,C15:1
Kux, Bill
  Minny and the James Boys (Plays in the Park)
    1989,Je 20,C15:4
Kuznechenko, Roman
  My Big Land 1989,Ag 17,C15:1
Kuznetsov, Villor
  Junon and Avos: The Hope 1990,Ja 8,C16:3
Kuznetsov, Vladimir
  Junon and Avos: The Hope 1990,Ja 8,C16:3
Kuznetsova, Galina
  Leningrad State Music Hall 1990,My 28,11:1
Kyle, Barry (Director)
  Dr. Faustus 1989,Ag 6,II:5:1
Kyme
  Black and Blue 1989,Ja 27,C3:1
  Oh, Kay! 1990,N 2,C1:1
  Oh, Kay! 1990,N 11,II:5:1

L

LaBelle, Rob
  Macbeth 1990,Ja 17,C13:4
LaBourdette, Katie
  Legends in Concert 1989,My 14,49:3
Labow, Hilary
  Run for Your Wife! 1989,Mr 8,C17:1
Lacey, Florence
  Pal Joey 1990,Jl 24,C13:3
Lach, Mary Ann (Costume Designer)
  Step into My World 1989,F 19,76:4
La Chanze
  Once on This Island 1990,My 7,C11:1
  Once on This Island 1990,O 28,II:5:1
LaChiusa, Michael John
  Triplets in Uniform 1989,F 12,70:4
LaChiusa, Michael John (Composer)
  Triplets in Uniform 1989,F 12,70:4
  Buzzsaw Berkeley 1989,Ag 21,C14:3
LaChiusa, Michael John (Lyricist)
  Buzzsaw Berkeley 1989,Ag 21,C14:3
LaChiusa, Michael John (Musical Director)
  Rough Crossing 1990,F 23,C3:4
LaChiusa, Michael John (Playwright)
  Eulogy for Mister Hamm 1990,Je 1,C8:5
Lackey, Skip
  Young Rube 1989,Ap 21,C3:4
Lacy, Tom
  Architruc 1989,O 1,61:1
Laffer, Denise (Miscellaneous)
  Sunday Promenade, The 1989,Mr 12,68:1
  Equal 'Wrights 1989,My 18,C20:3
  Friends 1989,Je 11,67:1
  Special Interests 1990,F 18,70:1
  Maids of Honor 1990,Je 22,C3:3
La Fosse, Robert
  Jerome Robbins's Broadway 1989,F 27,C13:1
La Fosse, Robert (Choreographer)
  Positive Me 1989,N 16,C28:5
Lagerfelt, Caroline
  Lend Me a Tenor 1989,Mr 3,C3:1
  Swim Visit 1990,Je 23,12:4

Laghidze, Soso
  King Lear 1990,Ap 4,C17:1
Lagomarsino, Ron (Director)
  Abundance 1990,O 31,C15:3
Lagond, Charlie
  In a Pig's Valise 1989,F 15,C15:1
LaGuerre, Irma-Estel
  Suenos 1989,F 23,C13:3
Lahti, Christine
  Heidi Chronicles, The 1989,O 9,C13:1
Laird, Fiona
  Beyond Belief 1990,Ap 22,63:4
  Clouds, The 1990,Ap 22,63:4
Laird, Fiona (Composer)
  Clouds, The 1990,Ap 22,63:4
Laird, Fiona (Director)
  Beyond Belief 1990,Ap 22,63:4
  Clouds, The 1990,Ap 22,63:4
Laird, Fiona (Lighting Director)
  Beyond Belief 1990,Ap 22,63:4
Laird, Fiona (Miscellaneous)
  Beyond Belief 1990,Ap 22,63:4
  Clouds, The 1990,Ap 22,63:4
Laird, Fiona (Playwright)
  Beyond Belief 1990,Ap 22,63:4
Laird, Marvin (Miscellaneous)
  Easter Extravaganza 1990,Ap 13,C28:4
Lakis, Maria
  Paradise for the Worried 1990,Ap 6,C3:1
Lakis, Maria (Miscellaneous)
  Paradise for the Worried 1990,Ap 6,C3:1
Lally, James
  Solid Gold Cadillac, The 1989,S 21,C28:1
  Twelfth Night 1989,D 20,C20:3
Lam, Elis Y. (Costume Designer)
  Richard III 1990,Ag 17,C1:1
Lam, Elis Y. (Scenic Designer)
  Richard III 1990,Ag 17,C1:1
LaMar, Diana
  Two Gentlemen of Verona 1990,D 13,C16:5
Lamb, J. Kathleen
  Chocolate Soldier, The 1990,Je 3,62:2
Lamb, Jim
  Big Hotel 1989,S 29,C3:1
  Ring Gott Farblonjet, Der 1990,Ap 13,C3:1
  Camille 1990,S 7,C3:1
Lamb, Larry
  Madhouse in Goa, A 1989,Je 27,C15:4
Lamb, Mary Ann
  Jerome Robbins's Broadway 1989,F 27,C13:1
Lambermont, Jeannette (Director)
  Titus Andronicus 1989,Je 12,C13:1
Lambert, Juliet
  Meet Me in St. Louis 1989,N 3,C3:1
Lambert, Robert
  Gypsy 1989,N 17,C5:1
  Gypsy 1990,S 18,C11:1
Lambie, Joseph
  For Dear Life 1989,Ja 11,C17:1
Lamos, Mark
  Importance of Being Earnest, The 1989,O 11,C15:1
Lamos, Mark (Director)
  Measure for Measure 1989,Mr 10,C3:1
  Peer Gynt 1989,Ap 11,C17:1
  Importance of Being Earnest, The 1989,O 11,C15:1
  Illusion, The 1990,Ja 18,C21:1
  Miser, The 1990,My 18,C4:3
  Our Country's Good 1990,O 21,59:3
Lamos, Mark (Miscellaneous)
  Paper Gramophone, The 1989,Mr 4,11:4
  Importance of Being Earnest, The 1989,O 11,C15:1
  Stand-Up Tragedy 1989,N 24,C3:4
  Illusion, The 1990,Ja 18,C21:1
  Woyzeck 1990,Mr 6,C17:1
  Day Trips 1990,Ap 16,C15:1
  Miser, The 1990,My 18,C4:3
  Our Country's Good 1990,O 21,59:3
Lamude, Terence (Director)
  Away Alone 1989,D 16,18:4
  Remembrance 1990,O 18,C22:5
Lan, David (Translator)
  Ghetto 1989,My 1,C11:1
Lancaster, Dorothy
  East Texas 1990,O 7,70:4
Lanchester, Robert (Director)
  Heart of a Dog 1990,Mr 16,C3:1
Lander, John-Michael
  Adam and the Experts 1989,N 23,C20:5
Landesman, Heidi (Scenic Designer)
  Approaching Zanzibar 1989,My 5,C3:1

Landman, Jeffrey
Traveler in the Dark 1990,Ja 16,C13:1
Landon, Sofia
Mud Angel, The 1990,N 18,75:1
Landrieu, Nelson
Happy Birthday, Mama 1989,F 9,C22:3
Landron, Jack
Chinese Charade (Chino de la Charada, El) 1989,Ag 13,57:3
Capitol Cakewalk 1990,Mr 2,C31:1
I Am a Winner 1990,Ap 1,52:3
Telltale Hearts 1990,D 9,82:6
Landry, Lauri
Zoya's Apartment 1990,My 11,C3:1
Landwehr, Hugh (Scenic Designer)
When We Are Married 1989,Ja 28,14:3
Rose Tattoo, The 1989,Jl 28,C3:4
Dance Lesson, A 1989,N 11,16:5
Death Takes a Holiday 1990,Ag 13,C11:1
Lane, Allen Walker
Prizes 1989,My 18,C22:4
Lane, Colin
Philadelphia, Here I Come! 1990,Je 13,C15:1
Lane, Diane
Twelfth Night 1989,D 20,C20:3
Lane, Dorothy (Playwright)
Happy End 1990,My 26,11:1
Lane, Eddie
Before Dawn 1989,Ag 31,C20:5
Lane, Nathan
In a Pig's Valise 1989,F 15,C15:1
Lisbon Traviata, The 1989,Je 7,C21:1
Lisbon Traviata, The 1989,N 1,C22:3
Lisbon Traviata, The 1989,D 24,II:3:1
Bad Habits 1990,Mr 21,C13:1
Some Americans Abroad 1990,My 3,C17:1
Lane, Sara Beth
Oh, Kay! 1989,N 1,C22:3
Lane, Stewart F. (Producer)
Change in the Heir, A 1990,Ap 30,C13:1
Lane, William (Costume Designer)
Summerfolk 1989,O 14,15:4
Lang, Stephen
Speed of Darkness, The 1989,My 9,C15:1
Few Good Men, A 1989,N 16,C23:4
Lang, William H. (Miscellaneous)
At the Chelsea 1989,Ja 20,C3:1
Nest, The 1989,Mr 2,C26:1
Investigation of the Murder in El Salvador, The 1989,My 23,C14:4
Plays in the Park 1989,Je 20,C15:4
Love Letters 1989,Ag 25,C3:1
Langan, Timothy (Miscellaneous)
Summerfolk 1989,O 14,15:4
Baal 1990,Mr 24,17:1
Langan, William
Titus Andronicus 1989,Ag 21,C13:1
Solid Gold Cadillac, The 1989,S 21,C28:1
Lange, Anne
Heidi Chronicles, The 1989,O 9,C13:1
Lange, Doug (Miscellaneous)
Hizzoner! 1989,F 24,C3:1
Langella, Frank
Tempest, The 1989,N 15,C18:3
Langley, Jeff (Composer)
Othello 1990,Ja 17,C18:4
Langsdale, Keith
Bovver Boys 1990,F 25,57:3
Langworthy, Douglas (Translator)
Prince of Homburg, The 1990,Ap 22,62:1
Lanier, Jane
Jerome Robbins's Broadway 1989,F 27,C13:1
Nightingale 1990,D 4,C16:3
Lanier, Jane (Miscellaneous)
Nightingale 1990,D 4,C16:3
Lanier, Robert
Ring Gott Farblonjet, Der 1990,Ap 13,C3:1
Lank, Anna Bess
Witch, The 1989,N 16,C30:4
Chocolate Soldier, The 1990,Je 3,62:2
Lanko, Vivian
Indiana Dog 1989,S 26,C17:1
Rodents and Radios 1990,Ap 28,15:1
Famine Plays 1990,N 3,14:5
Lanovoy, Vasily
Peace of Brest-Litovsk, The 1990,Ap 18,C11:1
Lansbury, David
Young Playwrights Festival 1989,S 22,C5:4
Lansbury, Edgar (Director)
Without Apologies 1989,F 19,74:4

Lansing, Robert
John Brown's Body 1989,Je 27,C14:5
Lanskoye, Yevgeny (Director)
Father's Inheritance 1990,N 18,75:1
Lanteri, Joe (Choreographer)
Buzzsaw Berkeley 1989,Ag 21,C14:3
Lanzener, Sonja
Hamlet 1989,Je 2,C3:5
New Music 1989,N 4,16:3
LaPaglia, Anthony
Marathon 1990: Festival of New One-Act Plays, Series C 1990,Je 14,C20:3
Lapchinski, Larissa
Three Sisters, The 1989,Je 12,C13:1
Lapham, Kenneth J. (Lighting Director)
Tomfoolery 1989,Ja 14,10:4
LaPierre, Robert (Miscellaneous)
Ground People 1990,My 7,C13:1
Lapine, James (Director)
Winter's Tale, The 1989,Mr 22,C19:4
Winter's Tale, The 1989,D 24,II:3:1
Falsettoland 1990,Je 29,C3:1
Falsettoland 1990,S 30,II:5:1
Falsettoland 1990,D 30,II:5:1
Lapine, James (Playwright)
Falsettoland 1990,Je 29,C3:1
Falsettoland 1990,S 30,II:5:1
Falsettoland 1990,D 30,II:5:1
Larmett, Jill (Miscellaneous)
Speed of Darkness, The 1989,My 9,C15:1
Winter's Tale, The 1990,Ja 31,C15:1
LaRon, Ken
Glass Menagerie, The 1989,O 16,C19:1
Larsen, Liz
Starmites 1989,Ap 28,C3:1
Manhattan Punch Line's Sixth Annual Festival of One-Act Comedies, Evening A 1990,F 4,60:1
Larsen, Robert R. (Producer)
Welcome to the Club 1989,Ap 14,C3:1
Larson, Jayne Amelia
Ulysses in Nighttown 1989,Ja 15,44:1
Larson, Jens
Pickle Family Circus, The 1989,Jl 24,C12:3
Larson, Linda Marie
Bikini Snow (Manhattan Class Company, One-Act Play Festival, Series A) 1989,Mr 11,16:1
Machinal 1990,O 16,C13:1
Lasker-Schuler, Else (Playwright)
I & I 1989,S 24,72:3
Lassek, Ewa
Hamlet 1989,Jl 11,C13:1
Lasser, Brian (Miscellaneous)
Carol Lawrence and Larry Kert Together . . . Again! 1990,O 4,C21:1
Laszczyk, Grazyna
Dybbuk, The 1989,Jl 11,C13:1
Lata, John
Township Fever 1990,D 20,C11:1
Latham, Bradley
Christmas Spectacular, The 1989,N 13,C20:5
Latham, Stacy
Christmas Spectacular, The 1989,N 13,C20:5
Latouche, John (Lyricist)
Golden Apple, The 1990,Mr 30,C3:5
Latouche, John (Playwright)
Golden Apple, The 1990,Mr 30,C3:5
Latta, Richard (Lighting Director)
Young Rube 1989,Ap 21,C3:4
Lattin, Montana
Happy End 1990,My 26,11:1
Latus, James (Miscellaneous)
Adam and the Experts 1989,N 23,C20:5
Merry Wives of Windsor, The 1990,My 30,C13:1
Lauer, Andrew
Marathon 1990: Festival of New One-Act Plays, Series A 1990,My 16,C14:4
Laurel, Peggy (Miscellaneous)
Big Frogs (Marathon '89, Series C) 1989,Je 29,C14:5
Laurence, Stuart
Hyde Park 1989,N 12,73:1
Laurence, Stuart (Director)
Gogol 1989,Ap 14,17:1
Laurenson, Diana
Dangerous Games 1989,O 20,C3:3
Laurenson, James
After the Fall 1990,Ag 30,C15:1
Laurents, Arthur (Director)
Gypsy 1989,N 17,C5:1
Gypsy 1989,D 17,II:7:1

Gypsy 1990,S 18,C11:1
Laurents, Arthur (Miscellaneous)
Jerome Robbins's Broadway 1989,F 27,C13:1
Laurents, Arthur (Playwright)
Gypsy 1989,N 17,C5:1
Gypsy 1989,D 17,II:7:1
Gypsy 1990,S 18,C11:1
Gypsy 1990,S 23,II:5:1
Lauria, Dan (Producer)
Bronx Tale, A 1989,O 22,63:5
Lauricella, Ruth
Spinning Tale, A 1990,F 25,57:1
Lauze, Gene (Costume Designer)
Talking Things Over with Chekhov 1990,My 13,44:1
Laverdiere, Renee
Madame Sherry 1989,Jl 30,57:1
Lavey, Martha
Mill Fire 1989,O 19,C22:3
Winter's Tale, The 1990,Ja 31,C15:1
Lavezzo, Giulietta
Witch, The 1989,N 16,C30:4
Lavin, Linda
Gypsy 1990,S 18,C11:1
Gypsy 1990,S 23,II:5:1
Law, Mary Kate
Starmites 1989,Ap 28,C3:1
Lawless, Rick
Magic Act, The 1989,Mr 16,C21:1
Lawless, Sean
Spinning Tale, A 1990,F 25,57:1
Lawless, Sue (Director)
Ad Hock 1989,Ja 20,C11:1
Lawless, Wendy
Cymbeline 1989,Je 1,C15:1
Lawrence, Burke
Shenandoah 1989,Ag 9,C13:1
Lawrence, Carol
Carol Lawrence and Larry Kert Together . . . Again! 1990,O 4,C21:1
Lawrence, Dea
Manhattan Punch Line's Sixth Annual Festival of One-Act Comedies, Evening A 1990,F 4,60:1
Lawrence, Elizabeth
Beauty Marks 1989,O 29,63:5
Lawrence, Peter (Miscellaneous)
Artist Descending a Staircase 1989,D 1,C3:1
Elliot Loves 1990,Je 8,C3:1
Lawrence, Sharon
Fiddler on the Roof 1990,N 19,C13:1
Laws, Holly (Miscellaneous)
Empires and Appetites 1989,My 25,C18:4
Lawson, David (Miscellaneous)
Visit, The 1989,F 5,56:5
Ground People 1990,My 7,C13:1
My Father, My Son 1990,S 23,65:3
Lawson, Leigh
Merchant of Venice, The 1989,D 20,C15:1
Lawson, Randy (Miscellaneous)
Theme and Variations 1990,O 21,62:3
Voice of the Prairie, The 1990,D 18,C18:5
Lawson, Richard
Talented Tenth, The 1989,N 10,C3:1
Lawyer, Russell
Lark, The 1989,My 29,20:5
Lay, Richard (Playwright)
God's Policemen 1989,O 22,64:4
Layne, Mary
Importance of Being Earnest, The 1989,O 11,C15:1
Shadowlands 1990,N 12,C11:1
Lazar, Paul
Happy End 1990,My 26,11:1
Lazarus, Frank
Brimstone and Treacle 1989,Ap 18,C15:3
Lazarus, Paul (Director)
Sex Lives of Superheroes (Manhattan Punch Line's Fifth Annual Festival of One-Act Comedies, Series A) 1989,Ja 26,C16:1
Lazore, Mark
Whatnot 1990,S 25,C16:3
Leach, Nancy
Wonderful Town 1989,O 8,64:1
Leach, William
Crucible, The 1990,Mr 30,C3:1
Leadbetter, Betsy Ann
Love Life 1990,Je 22,C15:1
Leake, Damien
Some Sweet Day 1989,Mr 27,C13:1
Miss Evers's Boys 1989,D 21,C16:3
Leaming, Chet (Miscellaneous)
Two Gentlemen of Verona 1990,D 13,C16:5

Your Handsome Captain 1989,N 12,71:6
Rothschilds, The 1990,F 26,C16:1
Levinowsky, Nikolas (Musical Director)
Father's Inheritance 1990,N 18,75:1
Levinson, Lee Ann
Land of Dreams, The 1989,N 22,C10:1
Levitin, Nicholas
Manhattan Punch Line's Festival of One-Act
Comedies, Series B 1989,F 11,12:3
Levitow, Roberta (Director)
Each Day Dies with Sleep 1990,My 17,C20:3
Levitt, Sandy
Father's Inheritance 1990,N 18,75:1
Levy, Franklin R. (Miscellaneous)
Blame It on the Movies 1989,My 18,C22:3
Levy, Franklin R. (Producer)
Blame It on the Movies 1989,My 18,C22:3
Levy, Monica (Choreographer)
Grandma Goes West 1989,N 3,C4:1
Big Apple Circus, The 1990,N 3,13:4
Levy, Ted
Black and Blue 1989,Ja 27,C3:1
Lew, Karen
Funny Thing Happened on the Way to the Forum, A
1989,Ag 6,49:3
Lewin, Deborah
Bald Soprano, The, and The Chairs 1989,D 20,C20:3
Twelfth Night 1989,D 20,C20:3
Lewis, Althea
Adam and the Experts 1989,N 23,C20:5
Lewis, Bobo
Heaven on Earth 1989,N 12,71:5
Lewis, Carol Jean
Sugar Hill 1990,Ap 28,12:6
Lewis, Edmund
Without Apologies 1989,F 19,74:4
Up 'n' Under 1989,Je 13,C17:1
Flea in Her Ear, A 1989,O 13,C15:1
Progress 1989,D 11,C15:1
Nightingale 1990,D 4,C16:3
Lewis, Edwina
Cat on a Hot Tin Roof 1990,Mr 22,C17:1
Lewis, Irene (Director)
Rose Tattoo, The 1989,Jl 28,C3:4
Miss Evers's Boys 1989,D 21,C16:3
Lewis, Jayne
Kiss Me Kate 1989,Je 12,C13:1
Lewis, Jim (Playwright)
Dangerous Games 1989,O 20,C3:3
Lewis, Kevin P. (Miscellaneous)
Mama, I Want to Sing, Part II 1990,Mr 28,C13:1
Lewis, Marcia
Orpheus Descending 1989,S 25,C15:4
When She Danced 1990,F 20,C15:1
Fiddler on the Roof 1990,N 19,C13:1
Lewis, Matthew
Apocalyptic Butterflies 1989,Je 17,12:3
Lewis, Michael
Bovver Boys 1990,F 25,57:3
Lewis, Vicki
Buzzsaw Berkeley 1989,Ag 21,C14:3
Crucible, The 1990,Mr 30,C3:1
Marathon 1990: Festival of New One-Act Plays,
Series B 1990,Je 1,C8:5
Lewis-Evans, Kecia
Once on This Island 1990,My 7,C11:1
Once on This Island 1990,O 28,II:5:1
Lewitin, Margot (Miscellaneous)
Brimstone and Treacle 1989,Ap 18,C15:3
Through the Leaves 1990,S 18,C18:1
Leyden, Leo
Merchant of Venice, The 1989,D 20,C15:1
Leys, Bryan D. (Lyricist)
Midsummer Nights 1989,S 24,71:3
Leys, Bryan D. (Playwright)
Midsummer Nights 1989,S 24,71:3
Li, Donald
Song of Shim Chung, The 1989,N 19,76:4
Liani, Michael
Forest in Arden, A 1990,F 11,69:1
Libbon, Robert (Miscellaneous)
Grandma Goes West 1989,N 3,C4:1
Libertini, Richard
Love's Labor's Lost 1989,F 23,C15:1
Libin, Andrea Clark
Ghetto 1989,My 1,C11:1
Libin, Paul (Miscellaneous)
Ghetto 1989,My 1,C11:1
Sweeney Todd 1989,S 15,C3:1

Zoya's Apartment 1990,My 11,C3:1
Miser, The 1990,O 12,C1:1
Lichte, Richard (Director)
Wink-Dah (Marathon '89, Series A) 1989,My
30,C19:1
Lichtefeld, Michael (Choreographer)
Sweeney Todd: The Demon Barber of Fleet Street
1989,Ap 8,11:5
Sweeney Todd 1989,S 15,C3:1
Lichtenstein, Harvey (Miscellaneous)
Stuff as Dreams Are Made On 1989,N 2,C22:4
King Lear 1990,Ap 4,C17:1
Endangered Species 1990,O 9,C13:1
Ninagawa Macbeth 1990,O 22,C20:1
Polygraph 1990,O 27,12:5
Township Fever 1990,D 20,C11:1
Lide, Miller
School for Wives, The 1989,D 30,17:1
Lieb, Dick (Miscellaneous)
Easter Extravaganza 1990,Ap 13,C28:4
Lieberman, Donna (Miscellaneous)
Night Hank Williams Died, The 1989,Ja 25,C16:4
Early One Evening at the Rainbow Bar and Grille
1989,Ap 14,C34:5
Buzzsaw Berkeley 1989,Ag 21,C14:3
Heaven on Earth 1989,N 12,71:5
20 Fingers, 20 Toes 1990,Ja 10,C17:1
Starting Monday 1990,Ap 5,C18:1
Maids of Honor 1990,Je 22,C3:3
Lieberson, Will (Director)
Before Dawn 1989,Ag 31,C20:5
Man Who Fell in Love with His Wife, The 1990,Ag
19,55:1
Lieberson, Will (Miscellaneous)
Before Dawn 1989,Ag 31,C20:5
Man Who Fell in Love with His Wife, The 1990,Ag
19,55:1
Life, Regge (Miscellaneous)
Play to Win 1989,Jl 21,C3:2
Liljestrand, Eric
Investigation of the Murder in El Salvador, The
1989,My 23,C14:4
Liljestrand, Eric (Composer)
Father Was a Peculiar Man 1990,Jl 11,C13:1
Liljestrand, Eric (Miscellaneous)
Investigation of the Murder in El Salvador, The
1989,My 23,C14:4
Lear 1990,Ja 26,C3:1
Crowbar 1990,F 20,C18:1
Hanging the President 1990,Jl 13,C17:1
Lilly, Randy
Tale of Two Cities, A 1990,Ap 7,16:4
Lilly, T. Scott
Alive by Night 1989,My 18,C22:3
Lima, Paul
Three Sisters, The 1989,N 23,C20:5
Lima, Rafael (Playwright)
Parting Gestures 1989,D 22,C5:4
Lindblad, Alan (Choreographer)
White Boned Demon 1989,Mr 5,68:1
Linderman, Ed
Ed Linderman's Broadway Jukebox 1990,Jl 20,C3:1
Linderman, Ed (Miscellaneous)
Ed Linderman's Broadway Jukebox 1990,Jl 20,C3:1
Lindgren, Catarina
Ice Capades 1990,Ja 21,49:1
Lindley, Audra
About Time 1990,O 11,C18:6
About Time 1990,O 14,II:5:1
Handy Dandy 1990,O 23,C20:1
Lindo, Delroy
Cobb 1989,Mr 31,C3:3
Miss Evers's Boys 1989,D 21,C16:3
Lindsay, Barbara (Playwright)
Grunions (Manhattan Punch Line's Sixth Annual
Festival of One-Act Comedies, Evening B) 1990,F
11,70:1
Lines, Sybil
Lettice and Lovage 1990,Mr 26,C11:1
Link, Ron (Director)
Stand-Up Tragedy 1989,N 24,C3:4
Stand-Up Tragedy 1990,O 5,C3:1
Stand-Up Tragedy 1990,O 14,II:5:1
Linney, Laura
Sea Gull, The: The Hamptons: 1990 1990,D 24,21:1
Linney, Romulus (Director)
Sand Mountain Matchmaking (Working One-Acts
'89) 1989,Je 25,45:4
Three Poets 1989,N 23,C20:1

Linney, Romulus (Playwright)
Sand Mountain Matchmaking (Working One-Acts
'89) 1989,Je 25,45:4
Three Poets 1989,N 23,C20:1
2 1990,Ap 5,C15:1
Tonight We Love (Marathon 1990: Festival of New
One-Act Plays, Series C) 1990,Je 14,C20:3
Linzalone, Anthony
Arrivederci Papa 1989,Je 22,C15:3
Lion, Margo (Producer)
Threepenny Opera 1989,N 6,C13:4
Lipman, Maureen
Re:Joyce! 1990,F 2,C3:1
Lipman, Maureen (Playwright)
Re:Joyce! 1990,F 2,C3:1
Lipnik, Carol (Composer)
Pornsongspiel 1990,Je 4,C22:1
Lipp, Larry (Producer)
Aunts, The 1989,O 8,64:1
Lippencott, Catherine
Peggy and Jackson 1989,Ag 10,C16:5
Lisanby, Charles (Scenic Designer)
Christmas Spectacular, The 1989,N 13,C20:5
Christmas Spectacular, The 1990,N 13,C20:1
Lish, Becca
Summerfolk 1989,O 14,15:4
Lish, James
Cardondale Dreams 1990,Ja 5,C3:1
Lisner, Stephen (Miscellaneous)
Zora Neale Hurston 1990,F 5,C14:1
Neddy 1990,Ap 2,C15:1
Ground People 1990,My 7,C13:1
Words, No Music 1990,O 15,C15:1
Mambo Mouth: A Savage Comedy 1990,D 2,83:1
I Stand Before You Naked 1990,D 10,C14:1
Liss, Richard
Shenandoah 1989,Ag 9,C13:1
Lissek, Leon
Merchant of Venice, The 1989,D 20,C15:1
Litkei, Ervin (Producer)
Aunts, The 1989,O 8,64:1
Little, Cleavon
All God's Dangers 1989,O 23,C15:3
Little, Gerard
Herd of Buffalo 1989,Jl 6,C18:4
Das Vedanya Mama 1990,Jl 28,12:5
Little, Gerard (Costume Designer)
Herd of Buffalo 1989,Jl 6,C18:4
Das Vedanya Mama 1990,Jl 28,12:5
Little, Iris
Jonquil 1990,Ja 15,C14:3
Burner's Frolic 1990,F 26,C14:1
Lifetimes 1990,Ap 9,C12:4
Lively, William Fleet (Choreographer)
How Are Things in Costa del Fuego? (Manhattan
Punch Line's Sixth Annual Festival of One-Act
Comedies, Evening A) 1990,F 4,60:1
Livingston, James (Costume Designer)
Song of Shim Chung, The 1989,N 19,76:4
Lizardo, Maribel
Suenos 1989,F 23,C13:3
Lizzul, Anthony John
Hyde Park 1989,N 12,73:1
Gogol 1990,Ap 14,17:1
Llado, Katerina
Nelson 2 Rodrigues 1989,O 15,65:1
Eterno Femenino, El 1990,Mr 25,63:1
Abanderado, El (Standard Bearer, The) 1990,N
4,72:1
Llompart, Jose M. (Miscellaneous)
Gran Circo E.U. Craniano, El (Great U.S. Kranial
Circus, The) 1989,Ag 4,C15:1
Llompart, Jose M. (Scenic Designer)
Gran Circo E.U. Craniano, El (Great U.S. Kranial
Circus, The) 1989,Ag 4,C15:1
Lloyd, Catherine
Chelsea Walls 1990,Je 9,12:5
Lloyd, Natalie (Producer)
Oh, Kay! 1990,N 2,C1:1
Lloyd, Robert Langdon
Don Juan of Seville (Burlador de Sevilla y
Convidado de Piedra, El) 1989,Ap 7,C3:5
Lloyd Webber, Andrew (Composer)
Aspects of Love 1989,Je 27,C15:4
Aspects of Love 1990,Ap 9,C11:1
Lloyd Webber, Andrew (Miscellaneous)
Aspects of Love 1990,Ap 9,C11:1
Lloyd Webber, Andrew (Playwright)
Aspects of Love 1990,Ap 9,C11:1

Lund, Kenny
Red Sneaks, The 1989,Je 29,C13:1
Lundell, Kurt (Scenic Designer)
Shenandoah 1989,Ag 9,C13:1
Lundle, Ken
Ed Linderman's Broadway Jukebox 1990,Jl 20,C3:1
Lundquist, Lori (Miscellaneous)
What a Man Weighs 1990,My 25,C3:2
Lundy, Nicholas (Scenic Designer)
Gigi 1989,My 28,57:1
LuPone, Robert
Zoya's Apartment 1990,My 11,C3:1
LuPone, Robert (Miscellaneous)
Manhattan Class Company, One-Act Play Festival,
Series A 1989,Mr 11,16:1
Manhattan Class One-Acts, Series B 1989,Mr
19,61:4
Lupton, Heather
Marathon 1990: Festival of New One-Act Plays,
Series B 1990,Je 1,C8:5
Lurenz, Betty (Costume Designer)
Legends in Concert 1989,My 14,49:3
Luscombe, Tim (Director)
Artist Descending a Staircase 1989,D 1,C3:1
When She Danced 1990,F 20,C15:1
Luse, James (Miscellaneous)
Voysey Inheritance, The 1990,O 26,C3:1
Luthringer, Roy (Choreographer)
Ringling Brothers and Barnum & Bailey Circus
1990,Mr 31,13:1
Lutwak, Mark (Director)
Special Interests 1990,F 18,70:1
Rain. Some Fish. No Elephants. 1990,My 3,C20:5
Lutz, Renee (Miscellaneous)
Loman Family Picnic, The 1989,Je 22,C24:1
Man Who Shot Lincoln, The 1989,S 24,72:6
Love Life 1990,Je 22,C15:1
Wash, The 1990,N 8,C28:4
Lyall, Susan (Costume Designer)
Dalton's Back 1989,F 10,C3:1
Sunshine 1989,D 18,C10:4
Lycos, Tom
Circus Oz 1990,Je 8,C7:1
Lyles, Leslie
Sleeping Dogs 1989,Mr 23,C17:1
Marathon 1990: Festival of New One-Act Plays,
Series A 1990,My 16,C14:4
Young Playwrights Festival 1990 1990,S 21,C14:6
Lyman, Andrea
Gigi 1989,My 28,57:1
Lynch, Michael
Jerome Robbins's Broadway 1989,F 27,C13:1
Lynch, Sharon (Costume Designer)
Manhattan Punch Line's Sixth Annual Festival of
One-Act Comedies, Evening A 1990,F 4,60:1
Machinal 1990,O 16,C13:1
Lynch, Thomas (Scenic Designer)
Speed of Darkness, The 1989,My 9,C15:1
Kiss of the Spider Woman 1990,Je 1,C3:1
Lynley, Carol
Sea Gull, The: The Hamptons: 1990 1990,D 24,21:1
Lynn, Jana (Miscellaneous)
Rough Crossing 1990,F 23,C3:4
Lynn, Jess (Miscellaneous)
Sleeping Dogs 1989,Mr 23,C17:1
Gigi 1989,My 28,57:1
Lynne, Gillian (Choreographer)
Aspects of Love 1989,Je 27,C15:4
Aspects of Love 1990,Ap 9,C11:1
Lyons, Jeff
Forbidden Broadway 1990 1990,Ja 24,C15:1
Forbidden Broadway 1990,S 23,II:5:1

M

Ma, Jason
Prince of Central Park 1989,N 10,C3:1
Shogun: The Musical 1990,N 21,C9:1
Mabon, Paul
Mill Fire 1989,O 19,C22:3
MacAaron, Francesca
Adios, Tropicana 1989,Ag 10,C16:5
MacAdam, Adam
Ring Gott Farblonjet, Der 1990,Ap 13,C3:1
McAllen, Kathleen Rowe
Aspects of Love 1990,Ap 9,C11:1

Macan, Joanne (Producer)
Ed Linderman's Broadway Jukebox 1990,Jl 20,C3:1
McArt, Jan (Producer)
Prince of Central Park 1989,N 10,C3:1
McAuliffe, Nichola
Wild Duck, The 1990,Ag 30,C15:1
McBride, Tom
Hollywood Scheherazade 1989,O 1,60:5
McCabe, Richard
Silent Woman or Epicoene, The 1989,Ag 6,II:5:1
Dr. Faustus 1989,Ag 6,II:5:1
Midsummer Night's Dream, A 1989,Ag 6,II:5:1
McCafferty, Nell (Original Author)
Now and at the Hour of Our Death 1989,Je 1,C18:4
McCall, Kathleen
Theme and Variations 1990,O 21,62:3
McCall, Robert
Skating for Life—A Celebration of Champions
1989,N 8,C25:1
McCallany, Holt
Bovver Boys 1990,F 25,57:3
Marathon 1990: Festival of New One-Act Plays,
Series A 1990,My 16,C14:4
McCann, Christopher
Black Market 1989,N 29,C17:1
King Lear 1990,N 16,C3:1
McCann, Elizabeth Ireland (Producer)
Orpheus Descending 1989,S 25,C15:4
McCarthy, Nobu
Wash, The 1990,N 8,C28:4
Wash, The 1990,N 18,II:5:1
McCarthy, Theresa
Love's Labor's Lost 1989,My 26,C4:5
Summerfolk 1989,O 14,15:4
McCartney, Ellen (Costume Designer)
Heaven on Earth 1989,N 12,71:5
Bovver Boys 1990,F 25,57:3
McCarty, Bruce
Black Market 1989,N 29,C17:1
McCarty, Conan
Man Who Shot Lincoln, The 1989,S 24,72:6
McCarty, Kevin
King Lear 1990,N 16,C3:1
McCarty, Michael
Sweeney Todd 1989,S 15,C3:1
McCauley, James
Titus Andronicus 1989,Ag 21,C13:1
McCauley, Larry
Iceman Cometh, The 1990,O 3,C13:4
MacCauley, Michael
Love's Labor's Lost 1989,My 26,C4:5
Merry Wives of Windsor, The 1990,My 30,C13:1
McCleary, Gary
Chelsea Walls 1990,Je 9,12:5
McClellan, Maggie
Cyrano de Bergerac 1989,Jl 7,C19:1
McClelland, Kay
City of Angels 1989,D 12,C19:4
McClendon, Afi
Once on This Island 1990,My 7,C11:1
McClennahan, Charles (Scenic Designer)
Talented Tenth, The 1989,N 10,C3:1
Jonquil 1990,Ja 15,C14:3
Mama, I Want to Sing, Part II 1990,Mr 28,C13:1
Ground People 1990,My 7,C13:1
Further Mo' 1990,My 18,C3:5
Telltale Hearts 1990,D 9,82:6
McClinn, Tiffany
Jonquil 1990,Ja 15,C14:3
McClintock, Jodie Lynne
Art of Success, The 1989,D 21,C11:1
Nightingale 1990,D 4,C16:3
McClinton, Marion Isaac (Director)
Walkers 1989,Ap 16,60:1
McClinton, Marion Isaac (Playwright)
Walkers 1989,Ap 16,60:1
McClure, Spike
Love's Labor's Lost 1989,F 23,C15:1
Ghetto 1989,My 1,C11:1
McCollister, Frier
Lear 1990,Ja 26,C3:1
B. Beaver Animation, The 1990,My 24,C19:1
McCollister, Frier (Miscellaneous)
B. Beaver Animation, The 1990,My 24,C19:1
McComb, Bill (Miscellaneous)
Aunts, The 1989,O 8,64:1
McConeghey, David B.
Indiana Dog 1989,S 26,C17:1
McCormick, Michael
In a Pig's Valise 1989,F 15,C15:1

McCormick, Robert R.
Madame Sherry 1989,Jl 30,57:1
Golden Apple, The 1990,Mr 30,C3:5
McCourt, Frank
Philadelphia, Here I Come! 1990,Je 13,C15:1
McCourt, Malachy
Remembrance 1990,O 18,C22:5
McCowen, Alec
St. Mark's Gospel 1990,Mr 22,C21:1
McCoy, Kerry (Musical Director)
Legends in Concert 1989,My 14,49:3
McCoy, Michael
Love Life 1990,Je 22,C15:1
McCoy, Thomas P. (Producer)
Peter Pan 1990,D 14,C3:4
McCrane, Paul
Briar Patch 1989,D 6,C21:1
Six Degrees of Separation 1990,Je 15,C1:2
Six Degrees of Separation 1990,Jl 1,II:1:1
McCray, Jennifer (Miscellaneous)
Love's Labor's Lost 1989,My 26,C4:5
McCullers, Carson (Playwright)
Member of the Wedding, The 1989,Ap 1,16:3
McCullough, Allen
Crucible, The 1989,D 16,15:1
McCullum, Kim
Heart Outright, The 1989,My 21,68:2
McCully, Emily Arnold
Nightingale 1990,D 4,C16:3
McCusker, Frank
Playboy of the Western World, The 1990,N 4,II:5:1
McCutcheon, Bill
Light Up the Sky 1990,Ag 22,C10:5
McDade, Innes-Fergus
Sunday Promenade, The 1989,Mr 12,68:1
McDaniel, James
Six Degrees of Separation 1990,Je 15,C1:2
Six Degrees of Separation 1990,Jl 1,II:1:1
McDermid, Ed (Miscellaneous)
O Pioneers! 1990,Ja 28,49:1
MacDermot, Galt (Composer)
Moon over Miami 1989,F 24,C3:1
McDermott, Kevin
O Pioneers! 1990,Ja 28,49:1
McDermott, Phelim
Flea in Her Ear, A 1989,Ag 20,II:5:1
McDermott, Tom
Investigation of the Murder in El Salvador, The
1989,My 23,C14:4
Mastergate 1989,O 13,C3:1
MacDevitt, Brian (Lighting Director)
A. Whitney Brown's Big Picture (in Words) 1989,Mr
31,C36:1
Equal 'Wrights 1989,My 18,C20:3
Lark, The 1989,My 29,20:5
Wonderful Town 1989,O 8,64:1
Waves, The 1990,My 10,C16:4
Death of the Last Black Man in the Whole Entire
World, The 1990,S 25,C15:1
Subfertile 1990,N 8,C20:5
McDonald, Antony (Scenic Designer)
Hamlet 1989,Ag 6,II:5:1
McDonald, Beth
Ancient History 1989,My 18,C29:3
Macdonald, James G.
Water Music (Marathon '89, Series C) 1989,Je
29,C14:5
MacDonald, Jason
Tempest, The 1989,N 15,C18:3
McDonald, Marilyn
Uncle Vanya 1990,Mr 3,12:5
MacDonald, Pirie
Swim Visit 1990,Je 23,12:4
McDonald, Tanny
Temptation 1990,Ap 10,C13:1
Titus Andronicus 1989,Ag 21,C13:1
McDonnell, Graeme F. (Lighting Director)
Man Who Fell in Love with His Wife, The 1990,Ag
19,55:1
Mambo Mouth: A Savage Comedy 1990,D 2,83:1
McDonnell, Graeme F. (Miscellaneous)
Man Who Fell in Love with His Wife, The 1990,Ag
19,55:1
McDonnell, James
Young Playwrights Festival 1989,S 22,C5:4
McDonnell, Mary
National Anthems 1989,Ja 1,II:5:1
O Pioneers! 1990,Ja 28,49:1
McDonough, Ann
Mastergate 1989,O 13,C3:1

Martin, Michael X.
Funny Thing Happened on the Way to the Forum, A 1989,Ag 6,49:3
Martinez, Barbara
Suenos 1989,F 23,C13:3
Martinez, Feiga
Eterno Femenino, El 1990,Mr 25,63:1
Martinez, Francisco
Paso o Parabola del Camino, El (Parable of the Path, The) 1989,Ag 20,62:1
Martinez, Miguel Angel
Sueno de una Noche de Verano (Midsummer Night's Dream, A) 1989,Ag 16,C16:1
Martinez-Casado, Ana Margarita
Eterno Femenino, El 1990,Mr 25,63:1
Abanderado, El (Standard Bearer, The) 1990,N 4,72:1
Martinez Medrano, Maria Alicia (Director)
Romeo and Juliet 1990,S 15,15:1
Martinez Medrano, Maria Alicia (Miscellaneous)
Romeo and Juliet 1990,S 15,15:1
Martinez Medrano, Maria Alicia (Scenic Designer)
Romeo and Juliet 1990,S 15,15:1
Martinez Palau, Silvio (Playwright)
English Only Restaurant, The 1990,Jl 27,C4:5
Martini, Paul
Skating for Life—A Celebration of Champions 1989,N 8,C25:1
Brian Boitano and Katarina Witt Skating 1990,My 8,C17:1
Martins, Rita (Miscellaneous)
Nelson 2 Rodrigues 1989,O 15,65:1
Maruoka, Yoshie
Lost in a Flurry of Cherries 1990,Mr 25,62:1
Marvin, Mel (Composer)
Measure for Measure 1989,Mr 10,C3:1
Twelfth Night 1989,D 20,C20:3
Maryan, Charles (Director)
Aunts, The 1989,O 8,64:1
New York 1937 1990,My 6,75:4
Marzullo, Steve (Musical Director)
Once on This Island 1990,My 7,C11:1
Mashkov, Vladimir
My Big Land 1989,Ag 17,C15:1
Maslon, Laurence (Miscellaneous)
Merrily We Roll Along 1990,F 27,C13:1
Caucasian Chalk Circle, The 1990,O 1,C14:1
Maslon, Laurence (Translator)
Cerceau 1990,N 4,II:5:1
Maso, Michael (Miscellaneous)
O Pioneers! 1990,Ja 28,49:1
Mason, Jackie
Jackie Mason: Brand New 1990,O 18,C21:1
Mason, Jackie (Playwright)
Jackie Mason: Brand New 1990,O 18,C21:1
Mason, Marsha
Lake No Bottom 1990,N 30,C3:1
Lake No Bottom 1990,D 9,II:5:1
Mason, Marshall W. (Director)
Sunshine 1989,D 18,C10:4
Masson, Linda J. K. (Director)
Hamlet 1989,Je 2,C3:5
Masters, David
Fiddler on the Roof 1990,N 19,C13:1
Masters, Patricia
Tomfoolery 1989,Ja 14,10:4
Mastrantonio, Mary Elizabeth
Twelfth Night 1989,Jl 10,C13:1
Mastrosimone, William (Playwright)
Sunshine 1989,D 18,C10:4
Matamoros, Diego
Spinoza 1990,N 4,72:4
Mathieu, Kent (Scenic Designer)
Seeing Double 1989,N 16,C28:4
Mathieu, Patrick P.
Caucasian Chalk Circle, The 1990,D 3,C13:3
Caucasian Chalk Circle, The 1990,D 9,II:5:1
Mathis, Stanley Wayne
Oh, Kay! 1989,N 1,C22:3
Oh, Kay! 1990,N 2,C1:1
Matias, Fausto
Father's Inheritance 1990,N 18,75:1
Matlack, Deborah (Lighting Director)
Before Dawn 1989,Ag 31,C20:5
Matschulat, Kay (Director)
Grunions (Manhattan Punch Line's Sixth Annual Festival of One-Act Comedies, Evening B) 1990,F 11,70:1
Matsudaira, Toshiko
Kiyotsune: The Death of a Warrior 1989,My 19,C3:4

Matsumoto, Yuri
Takarazuka 1989,O 27,C21:1
Matsumura, Yoko
Capitol Cakewalk 1990,Mr 2,C31:1
Matsusaka, Tom
Privates on Parade 1989,Ag 23,C13:3
Lucky Come Hawaii 1990,O 29,C16:1
Mattei, Peter (Director)
Tiny Dimes 1990,Mr 9,C18:1
Mattei, Peter (Playwright)
Tiny Dimes 1990,Mr 9,C18:1
Matthews, Denese
Buddy: The Buddy Holly Story 1990,N 5,C13:1
Matthews, Edward R. F. (Lighting Director)
Ulysses in Nighttown 1989,Ja 15,44:1
Matthews, Evan
Step into My World 1989,F 19,76:4
Fabulous La Fontaine, The 1990,F 8,C15:3
Matthews, Jenny
Infernal Machine, The 1990,D 2,83:1
Matthiessen, Joan
Hedda Gabler 1989,Ja 25,C18:5
Matura, Mustapha (Playwright)
Playboy of the West Indies, The 1989,My 11,C17:1
Playboy of the West Indies, The 1989,My 21,II:5:1
Matz, Jerry
Ghetto 1989,My 1,C11:1
Fiddler on the Roof 1990,N 19,C13:1
Matz, Peter (Miscellaneous)
Grand Hotel 1989,N 13,C13:3
Mau, Les J. N.
Lucky Come Hawaii 1990,O 29,C16:1
Maugans, Wayne
Lusting After Pipino's Wife 1990,S 30,57:4
Maugham, W. Somerset (Playwright)
Circle, The 1989,N 21,C19:1
Maultsby, Carl
Kiss of the Spider Woman 1990,Je 1,C3:1
Mauro, Wilson (Musical Director)
Oba Oba '90 1990,Mr 16,C6:3
Maxey, Caty (Miscellaneous)
Moving Targets 1990,Ja 30,C14:5
Maxmen, Mimi (Costume Designer)
Early One Evening at the Rainbow Bar and Grille 1989,Ap 14,C34:5
Land of Dreams, The 1989,N 22,C10:1
Violent Peace 1990,Mr 3,12:3
Starting Monday 1990,Ap 5,C18:1
Maids of Honor 1990,Je 22,C3:3
Maxson, James
Cyrano de Bergerac 1989,Jl 7,C19:1
Cardondale Dreams 1990,Ja 5,C3:1
Maxwell, Roberta
Our Town 1989,Mr 28,C15:1
May, Corinna
Old Maid, The 1990,Ag 16,C14:4
Mayans, Nancy A.
Jacques and His Master 1989,N 16,C28:5
Mayas, Michele (Miscellaneous)
Chelsea Walls 1990,Je 9,12:5
Mayer, Max (Director)
Self-Torture and Strenuous Exercise (Marathon '89, Series A) 1989,My 30,C19:1
Maids of Honor 1990,Je 22,C3:3
Mayer, Michael (Director)
Mutterschaft (Young Playwrights Festival 1990) 1990,S 21,C14:6
Mayes, Sally
Welcome to the Club 1989,Ap 14,C3:1
Closer Than Ever 1989,N 7,C19:1
Mayhew, Ina (Costume Designer)
My Father, My Son 1990,S 23,65:3
Mayhew, Ina (Scenic Designer)
My Father, My Son 1990,S 23,65:3
Mayo, Don
Measure for Measure 1989,Mr 10,C3:1
Love Life 1990,Je 22,C15:1
Mazer, Elizabeth
Dangerous Games 1989,O 20,C3:3
Mazibuko, Brian
Township Fever 1990,D 20,C11:1
Township Fever 1990,D 23,II:5:1
Mazzie, Marin
Merrily We Roll Along 1990,F 27,C13:1
Mbonani, Themba
Township Fever 1990,D 20,C11:1
Mbonika, Oisaa (Miscellaneous)
Empires and Appetites 1989,My 25,C18:4
Mead, David M. (Miscellaneous)
Marathon '89, Series B 1989,Je 15,C14:5

Marathon '89, Series C 1989,Je 29,C14:5
Mead, Winter
Don Juan of Seville (Burlador de Sevilla y Convidado de Piedra, El) 1989,Ap 7,C3:5
Meadow, Lynne (Director)
Eleemosynary 1989,My 10,C15:3
Meadow, Lynne (Miscellaneous)
What the Butler Saw 1989,Mr 9,C21:1
Aristocrats 1989,Ap 26,C15:1
Eleemosynary 1989,My 10,C15:3
Lisbon Traviata, The 1989,Je 7,C21:1
Loman Family Picnic, The 1989,Je 22,C24:1
Lisbon Traviata, The 1989,N 1,C22:3
Art of Success, The 1989,D 21,C11:1
Bad Habits 1990,Mr 21,C13:1
Prin 1990,Je 7,C18:5
Abundance 1990,O 31,C15:3
American Plan, The 1990,D 17,C11:1
Meares, James (Scenic Designer)
Dragon's Nest 1990,My 10,C14:4
Medina, David
Twelfth Night 1989,O 4,C17:1
Medina, Hazel J.
Crucible, The 1990,Mr 30,C3:1
Medina, Henry (Miscellaneous)
Mondo Mambo 1990,Ag 25,16:5
Medina, Roberto
Quintuplets 1989,Ap 2,51:1
Medoff, Mark (Playwright)
Heart Outright, The 1989,My 21,68:2
Mee, Charles L., Jr. (Playwright)
Investigation of the Murder in El Salvador, The 1989,My 23,C14:4
Meeh, Gregory (Miscellaneous)
Accomplice 1990,Ap 27,C5:1
Mehle, Donna
Miser, The 1990,My 18,C4:3
Mehrbach, Glenn (Composer)
Bronx Tale, A 1989,O 22,63:5
Mehrten, Greg
Investigation of the Murder in El Salvador, The 1989,My 23,C14:4
Lear 1990,Ja 26,C3:1
B. Beaver Animation, The 1990,My 24,C19:1
Meikle, David Scott
Flea in Her Ear, A 1989,O 13,C15:1
Crucible, The 1989,D 16,15:1
Meineck, Peter (Lighting Director)
Clouds, The 1990,Ap 22,63:4
Meineck, Peter (Producer)
Clouds, The 1990,Ap 22,63:4
Meisle, Kathryn
Cahoots 1990,Mr 10,16:4
Meissner, Don
White Chocolate for My Father 1990,F 15,C22:3
Meissner, Don (Composer)
White Chocolate for My Father 1990,F 15,C22:3
Meissner, Don (Miscellaneous)
Ground People 1990,My 7,C13:1
Meister, Frederica
Magic Act, The 1989,Mr 16,C21:1
Subfertile 1990,N 8,C20:5
Mejia, Angel
Sueno de una Noche de Verano (Midsummer Night's Dream, A) 1989,Ag 16,C16:1
Melamed, Johanna
Elephant Memories 1990,N 6,C15:1
Melamed, Johanna (Choreographer)
Elephant Memories 1990,N 6,C15:1
Melamed, Johanna (Playwright)
Elephant Memories 1990,N 6,C15:1
Melaver, Ellen (Miscellaneous)
Sand Mountain Matchmaking (Working One-Acts '89) 1989,Je 25,45:4
Three Poets 1989,N 23,C20:1
Melia, Hector (Miscellaneous)
Leave It to Jane 1989,Mr 23,C17:1
I Am a Winner 1990,Ap 1,52:3
Melia, Joe
Some Americans Abroad 1989,Ag 1,C13:3
Melian, Antonio
Nelson 2 Rodrigues 1989,O 15,65:1
Melici, Sarah
Temptation 1989,Ap 10,C13:1
Melius, Nancy
Gypsy 1989,N 17,C5:1
Mell, Randle
O Pioneers! 1990,Ja 28,49:1
Crucible, The 1990,Mr 30,C3:1

Miller, Monique (Miscellaneous)
Ulysses in Nighttown 1989,Ja 15,44:1
Miller, Nina (Translator)
Coronel No Tiene Quien le Escriba, El (No One
Writes to the Colonel) 1989,Ag 3,C17:1
Paso o Parabola del Camino, El (Parable of the Path,
The) 1989,Ag 20,62:1
Sin Testigos 1990,Ag 14,C16:1
Miller, Royal E.
Taming of the Shrew, The 1990,Jl 13,C3:1
Miller, Susan (Playwright)
For Dear Life 1989,Ja 11,C17:1
Millrose, Peter (Composer)
Positive Me 1989,N 16,C28:5
Millrose, Peter (Miscellaneous)
Positive Me 1989,N 16,C28:5
Mills, Dana
Zoya's Apartment 1990,My 11,C3:1
Mills, Robert P. (Composer)
Estate, The 1989,F 18,18:1
Minami, Roger (Choreographer)
Takarazuka 1989,O 27,C21:1
Mineo, John
Dangerous Games 1989,O 20,C3:3
Miner, Kohl
Wink-Dah (Marathon '89, Series A) 1989,My
30,C19:1
Miner, Mary Michele (Miscellaneous)
My Children! My Africa! 1989,D 19,C19:3
Minichiello, M. D. (Miscellaneous)
Talking Things Over with Chekhov 1990,My 13,44:1
Minichiello, M. D. (Producer)
It's Still My Turn 1990,Ag 26,67:5
Mink, Gary
Big Hotel 1989,S 29,C3:1
Ring Gott Farblonjet, Der 1990,Ap 13,C3:1
Minkler, Mark
Carol Lawrence and Larry Kert Together . . . Again!
1990,O 4,C21:1
Minor, Jason
Gypsy 1989,N 17,C5:1
Minor, John Hugh (Miscellaneous)
Madame Sherry 1989,Jl 30,57:1
Oh, Kay! 1989,N 1,C22:3
Minos, Ted
De Donde? 1990,Ja 8,C13:1
Minskoff, Jerome (Miscellaneous)
Orpheus Descending 1989,S 25,C15:4
Minskoff, Jerome (Producer)
Merchant of Venice, The 1989,D 20,C15:1
Minskoff, Lee (Director)
Prizes 1989,My 18,C22:4
Minsky, Greta (Miscellaneous)
Night Hank Williams Died, The 1989,Ja 25,C16:4
Buzzsaw Berkeley 1989,Ag 21,C14:3
Mintern, Terence
Big Hotel 1989,S 29,C3:1
Dr. Jekyll and Mr. Hyde 1989,D 8,C3:2
Minton, Nina
Hyde Park 1989,N 12,73:1
Mintz, Ethan
Tower of Evil, The (Tour de Nesle, La) 1990,My
13,45:1
Mintz, Jonathon (Director)
Fellow Travelers (Manhattan Punch Line's Sixth
Annual Festival of One-Act Comedies, Evening
B) 1990,F 11,70:1
Mintz, Sandra C. (Miscellaneous)
Without Apologies 1989,F 19,74:4
Neddy 1990,Ap 2,C15:1
Mio, Emma
English Only Restaurant, The 1990,Jl 27,C4:5
Mironchik, James (Musical Director)
Songs of Paradise 1989,Ja 24,C16:3
Mironov, Yevgeny
My Big Land 1989,Ag 17,C15:1
Mirvish, David (Producer)
Buddy: The Buddy Holly Story 1990,N 5,C13:1
Mr. Fashion (Costume Designer)
Das Vedanya Mama 1990,Jl 28,12:5
Mitchell, Aleta
Approaching Zanzibar 1989,My 5,C3:1
Mitchell, Brian
Oh, Kay! 1990,N 2,C1:1
Oh, Kay! 1990,N 11,II:5:1
Mitchell, David (Miscellaneous)
Young Rube 1989,Ap 21,C3:4
Mitchell, David (Scenic Designer)
Tru 1989,D 15,C3:1

Mitchell, Deborah
Black and Blue 1989,Ja 27,C3:1
Mitchell, Gary (Director)
Old Maid, The 1990,Ag 16,C14:4
Mitchell, Gregory
Dangerous Games 1989,O 20,C3:3
Aspects of Love 1990,Ap 9,C11:1
Mitchell, Jerry (Miscellaneous)
Jerome Robbins's Broadway 1989,F 27,C13:1
Mitchell, Joel
O Pioneers! 1990,Ja 28,49:1
Mitchell, John Cameron
Six Degrees of Separation 1990,Je 15,C1:2
Six Degrees of Separation 1990,N 9,C5:1
Mitchell, Lauren
Kiss of the Spider Woman 1990,Je 1,C3:1
Mitchell, Ruth (Miscellaneous)
Kiss of the Spider Woman 1990,Je 1,C3:1
Fiddler on the Roof 1990,N 19,C13:1
Mitchelson, Bill (Miscellaneous)
Working One-Acts '89 1989,Je 25,45:4
Special Interests 1990,F 18,70:1
Mitterhoff, Barry
Ghetto 1989,My 1,C11:1
Mitzman, Marcia
Welcome to the Club 1989,Ap 14,C3:1
Miura, Junko
Lost in a Flurry of Cherries 1990,Mr 25,62:1
Mixon, Christopher
Cyrano de Bergerac 1989,Jl 7,C19:1
Miyake, Kiki (Producer)
Threepenny Opera 1989,N 6,C13:4
Mizzy, Danianne (Lighting Director)
Manhattan Punch Line's Fifth Annual Festival of
One-Act Comedies, Series A 1989,Ja 26,C16:1
Manhattan Punch Line's Festival of One-Act
Comedies, Series B 1989,F 11,12:3
Manhattan Punch Line's Sixth Annual Festival of
One-Act Comedies, Evening A 1990,F 4,60:1
Manhattan Punch Line's Sixth Annual Festival of
One-Act Comedies, Evening B 1990,F 11,70:1
Mlotek, Zalmen (Miscellaneous)
Those Were the Days 1990,N 14,C26:1
Mlotek, Zalmen (Musical Director)
Those Were the Days 1990,N 14,C26:1
Mlotek, Zalmen (Producer)
Those Were the Days 1990,N 14,C26:1
Mnisi, Dieketseng
Township Fever 1990,D 20,C11:1
Mobley, Areesah
Merry Wives of Windsor, The 1990,My 30,C13:1
Mochel, Ned
Winter's Tale, The 1990,Ja 31,C15:1
Moffat, Donald
Titus Andronicus 1989,Ag 21,C13:1
Moffett, D. W.
American Plan, The 1990,D 17,C11:1
Mohn, Leslie (Director)
White Boned Demon 1989,Mr 5,68:1
Mohn, Leslie (Playwright)
White Boned Demon 1989,Mr 5,68:1
Moinot, Michel
Grand Hotel 1989,N 13,C13:3
Mokler, Alan (Director)
Krapp's Last Tape 1989,D 17,94:5
Moleva, Natalya
Peace of Brest-Litovsk, The 1990,Ap 18,C11:1
Moliere (Playwright)
Misanthrope, The 1989,Ag 20,II:5:1
School for Wives, The 1989,D 30,17:1
Miser, The 1990,My 18,C4:3
Doente Imaginario, O (Imaginary Invalid, The)
1990,Ag 23,C20:1
Miser, The 1990,O 12,C1:1
Miser, The 1990,O 21,II:5:1
Molina, Arnold
Few Good Men, A 1989,N 16,C23:4
Mollenhauer, Heidi
Prizes 1989,My 18,C22:4
Molnar, Ferenc (Original Author)
Rough Crossing 1990,F 23,C3:4
Molnar, Robert
Ulysses in Nighttown 1989,Ja 15,44:1
Monaco, John (Miscellaneous)
Dangerous Games 1989,O 20,C3:3
Kiss of the Spider Woman 1990,Je 1,C3:1
Fiddler on the Roof 1990,N 19,C13:1
Monaco, Marylin
Gigi 1989,My 28,57:1

Monat, Phil (Lighting Director)
Phantasie 1989,Ja 4,C15:5
Feast Here Tonight 1989,N 30,C16:3
Progress 1989,D 11,C15:1
Moving Targets 1990,Ja 30,C14:5
Mom's Life, A 1990,Mr 15,C22:3
Hannah . . . 1939 1990,Je 2,16:3
Nightingale 1990,D 4,C16:3
Voice of the Prairie, The 1990,D 18,C18:5
Moncure, Lisa
Carnage, A Comedy 1989,S 18,C14:1
Monczka, Jan
Dybbuk, The 1989,Jl 11,C13:1
Hamlet 1989,Jl 11,C13:1
Mones, Steve
De Donde? 1990,Ja 8,C13:1
Monette, Richard (Director)
Comedy of Errors, The 1989,Je 12,C13:1
Monge, Julio
Jerome Robbins's Broadway 1989,F 27,C13:1
Monk, Debra
Young Playwrights Festival 1989,S 22,C5:4
Prelude to a Kiss 1990,Mr 15,C15:1
Prelude to a Kiss 1990,Mr 25,II:5:1
Prelude to a Kiss 1990,My 2,C15:1
Monk, Isabell
Ladies 1989,Ap 7,C3:1
Lear 1990,Ja 26,C3:1
Monk, Meredith (Composer)
Elephant Memories 1990,N 6,C15:1
Monroe, Jarion
Search and Destroy 1990,D 14,C3:1
Monroe, Marianne
Spinning Tale, A 1990,F 25,57:1
Monsion, Tim
Marvin's Room 1990,D 2,II:5:1
Monsod, Trinket
Empires and Appetites 1989,My 25,C18:4
Monson, Lex
God's Trombones 1989,O 11,C17:1
Grapes of Wrath, The 1990,Mr 23,C1:4
Mont, Ira (Miscellaneous)
Marathon '89, Series B 1989,Je 15,C14:5
Midsummer Nights 1989,S 24,71:3
Goose! Beyond the Nursery 1990,F 11,69:2
Hannah . . . 1939 1990,Je 2,16:3
Whatnot 1990,S 25,C16:3
Montagna, Juan Carlos
No + (No More) 1989,Ag 12,14:4
Montano, Robert
Manhattan Punch Line's Sixth Annual Festival of
One-Act Comedies, Evening A 1990,F 4,60:1
Monte, Leticia
Casa 1990,Ja 18,C24:4
Monteiro, Monica
Doente Imaginario, O (Imaginary Invalid, The)
1990,Ag 23,C20:1
Montevecchi, Liliane
Grand Hotel 1989,N 13,C13:3
Grand Hotel 1990,F 25,II:5:1
Monteverdi, Claudio (Composer)
Casa 1990,Ja 18,C24:4
Montgomerie, Jeffrey (Miscellaneous)
New Music 1989,N 4,16:3
March on Russia, The 1990,N 14,C24:3
Montgomery, Reggie
Measure for Measure 1989,Mr 10,C3:1
Spunk 1990,Ap 19,C17:4
Caucasian Chalk Circle, The 1990,D 3,C13:3
Caucasian Chalk Circle, The 1990,D 9,II:5:1
Montgomery, Robert (Composer)
Grand Guignol, The 1990,Je 2,18:1
Montgomery, Robert (Lyricist)
Genesis: Music and Miracles from the Medieval
Mystery Plays 1989,Ja 18,C20:5
Montgomery, Robert (Playwright)
Genesis: Music and Miracles from the Medieval
Mystery Plays 1989,Ja 18,C20:5
Monthertrand, Carine
Cyrano de Bergerac 1989,Jl 7,C19:1
Montilla, Micky
Sueno de una Noche de Verano (Midsummer Night's
Dream, A) 1989,Ag 16,C16:1
Montville, Clea
When She Danced 1990,F 20,C15:1
Monzione, David
Madame Sherry 1989,Jl 30,57:1
Moon, Marjorie (Miscellaneous)
Boochie 1989,Jl 30,57:2

N

Nason, Brian (Lighting Director)
  Metamorphosis 1989,Mr 7,C15:1
  Threepenny Opera 1989,N 6,C13:4
  O Pioneers! 1990,Ja 28,49:1
  New York 1937 1990,My 6,75:4
  What's Wrong with This Picture? 1990,Je 23,14:1
Nassau, Paul (Composer)
  Education of H*Y*M*A*N K*A*P*L*A*N, The
    1989,Ap 6,C22:4
Nassau, Paul (Lyricist)
  Education of H*Y*M*A*N K*A*P*L*A*N, The
    1989,Ap 6,C22:4
Nassivera, John (Miscellaneous)
  Without Apologies 1989,F 19,74:4
Nastasi, Frank
  Enrico IV 1989,Ja 19,C22:3
Nasution, Arswendi
  Anulah, Let Them Eat Cake 1989,S 17,79:4
Nathan, Robert (Original Author)
  Jonah 1990,Mr 23,C5:1
Nathanson, Beth (Miscellaneous)
  Related Retreats 1990,Ap 18,C12:5
Nathanson, Roy
  Nature of Things, The 1990,Mr 25,63:1
Nations, Denise (Miscellaneous)
  Crossin' the Line 1989,My 14,48:1
Nauffts, Geoffrey
  Few Good Men, A 1989,N 16,C23:4
  Chelsea Walls 1990,Je 9,12:5
Naughton, Amanda
  Romance in Hard Times 1989,D 29,C3:1
Naughton, James
  Rose Tattoo, The 1989,Jl 28,C3:4
  City of Angels 1989,D 12,C19:4
Naumkin, Yuri
  Junon and Avos: The Hope 1990,Ja 8,C16:3
Navarro, Tina Cantu (Costume Designer)
  Each Day Dies with Sleep 1990,My 17,C20:3
Navazio, Michele (Composer)
  Anulah, Let Them Eat Cake 1989,S 17,79:4
  New Anatomies 1990,F 22,C19:1
Nayar, Daphne
  Romeo and Juliet 1990,Jl 14,10:1
Naylor, Marcus
  Every Goodbye Ain't Gone 1989,Jl 30,57:2
Naylor, Wesley (Composer)
  Mama, I Want to Sing, Part II 1990,Mr 28,C13:1
Nazzal, Nidal (Playwright)
  Seeing Double 1989,N 16,C28:4
Ndlovu, Duma (Miscellaneous)
  Township Fever 1990,D 20,C11:1
Neal, John (Miscellaneous)
  Wizard of Oz, The 1989,Mr 24,C3:1
Neale, Grant
  Life Is a Dream 1989,D 16,17:1
  Man's a Man, A 1990,F 26,C15:4
  Prince of Homburg, The 1990,Ap 22,62:1
  Misalliance 1990,O 14,56:4
  Infernal Machine, The 1990,D 2,83:1
Nealy, Milton Craig
  Once on This Island 1990,My 7,C11:1
Near, Timothy (Director)
  Mom's Life, A 1990,Mr 15,C22:3
Nebgen, Stephen (Miscellaneous)
  Crossin' the Line 1989,My 14,48:1
Nebozenko, Jan (Miscellaneous)
  Sex, Drugs, Rock & Roll 1990,F 9,C3:1
  Oh, Kay! 1990,N 2,C1:1
Nederlander, James M. (Producer)
  Orpheus Descending 1989,S 25,C15:4
  Dangerous Games 1989,O 20,C3:3
  Threepenny Opera 1989,N 6,C13:4
  Shadowlands 1990,N 12,C11:1
  Peter Pan 1990,D 14,C3:4
Needle, William
  Henry V 1989,Je 12,C13:1
Neely, Barbara (Original Author)
  Sisters 1990,Je 7,C19:3
Neenan, Maria
  Jerome Robbins's Broadway 1989,F 27,C13:1
Neet, Alison Stair
  Love's Labor's Lost 1989,My 26,C4:5
  New Anatomies 1990,F 22,C19:1
Neff, Debra (Playwright)
  Twice Shy (Young Playwrights Festival) 1989,S
    22,C5:4
Neiden, Daniel
  Witch, The 1989,N 16,C30:4

Neipris, David
  Mud Angel, The 1990,N 18,75:1
Neipris, Janet (Playwright)
  Agreement, The (Equal 'Wrights) 1989,My 18,C20:3
Nelligan, Kate
  Bad Habits 1990,Mr 21,C13:1
Nels, Peter (Miscellaneous)
  Macbeth 1990,Ja 17,C13:4
Nelson, Bill
  Bitter Friends 1989,F 14,C16:3
Nelson, Carol
  Hello, Bob 1990,O 21,62:3
Nelson, Judd
  Carnal Knowledge 1990,N 21,C15:1
  Carnal Knowledge 1990,D 2,II:5:1
Nelson, Mari
  Twelfth Night 1989,Jl 10,C13:1
  Up Against It 1989,D 5,C17:3
  Six Degrees of Separation 1990,Je 15,C1:2
  Six Degrees of Separation 1990,N 9,C5:1
Nelson, Mark
  Few Good Men, A 1989,N 16,C23:4
Nelson, Novella
  Ladies 1989,Ap 7,C3:1
  Crucible, The 1989,D 16,15:1
  Caucasian Chalk Circle, The 1990,D 3,C13:3
  Caucasian Chalk Circle, The 1990,D 9,II:5:1
Nelson, Rebecca
  Jonquil 1990,Ja 15,C14:3
  Voysey Inheritance, The 1990,O 26,C3:1
Nelson, Richard (Lighting Director)
  Twelfth Night 1989,Jl 10,C13:1
  Secret Rapture, The 1989,O 27,C3:1
  Prin 1990,Je 7,C18:5
  Catch Me If I Fall 1990,N 17,16:5
Nelson, Richard (Playwright)
  Some Americans Abroad 1989,Ag 1,C13:3
  Some Americans Abroad 1990,F 12,C17:1
  Some Americans Abroad 1990,Mr 14,C13:4
  Some Americans Abroad 1990,My 3,C17:1
Nelson, Ruth
  Crucible, The 1990,Mr 30,C3:1
Nelson, Sean
  Young Playwrights Festival 1990 1990,S 21,C14:6
Nelson, Steve (Playwright)
  Orgy in the Air-Traffic Control Tower (Grand
    Guignol, The) 1990,Je 2,18:1
Nelson, Tim
  Richard III 1990,Ag 17,C1:1
Nemeth, Sally (Playwright)
  Mill Fire 1989,O 19,C22:3
Nemoto, Yoko
  Lost in a Flurry of Cherries 1990,Mr 25,62:1
Nesbit, Pat
  Agreement, The (Equal 'Wrights) 1989,My 18,C20:3
Nesta, Bill
  Ivanov 1990,S 25,C13:3
Nestle, Rebecca (Miscellaneous)
  Sea Gull, The: The Hamptons: 1990 1990,D 24,21:1
Netherland, Marshall
  Doente Imaginario, O (Imaginary Invalid, The)
    1990,Ag 23,C20:1
Nettleton, Barry (Miscellaneous)
  Romeo and Juliet 1990,Jl 14,10:1
Nettleton, Barry (Producer)
  Romeo and Juliet 1990,Jl 14,10:1
Neuberger, Jan
  Goose! Beyond the Nursery 1990,F 11,69:2
  Change in the Heir, A 1990,Ap 30,C13:1
Neufeld, Mary
  Dr. Jekyll and Mr. Hyde 1989,D 8,C3:2
  Ring Gott Farblonjet, Der 1990,Ap 13,C3:1
Neumann, David
  Cymbeline 1989,Je 1,C15:1
  B. Beaver Animation, The 1990,My 24,C19:1
Neumann, Frederick
  Niedecker 1989,Mr 19,61:1
  Cymbeline 1989,Je 1,C15:1
  Illusion, The 1990,Ja 18,C21:1
  B. Beaver Animation, The 1990,My 24,C19:1
  Through the Leaves 1990,S 18,C18:1
Neustadt, Ted
  Money Talks 1990,S 7,C3:5
Neville, David (Lighting Director)
  Max and Maxie 1989,Ja 18,C14:6
Neville, John (Director)
  Three Sisters, The 1989,Je 12,C13:1
Neville, John (Miscellaneous)
  Henry V 1989,Je 12,C13:1

Kiss Me Kate 1989,Je 12,C13:1
  Three Sisters, The 1989,Je 12,C13:1
  Titus Andronicus 1989,Je 12,C13:1
  Comedy of Errors, The 1989,Je 12,C13:1
Nevins, Kristine
  Midsummer Nights 1989,S 24,71:3
New, Scott Allen
  Tale of Two Cities, A 1990,Ap 7,16:4
Newcomb, Don (Costume Designer)
  Buzzsaw Berkeley 1989,Ag 21,C14:3
Newell, Charles (Director)
  Two Gentlemen of Verona 1990,D 13,C16:5
Newhall, Anne
  Doctor's Dilemma, The 1990,Ja 26,C3:1
Newkirk, Eunice
  Over Forty 1989,My 16,C17:1
Newman, Jim
  Up Against It 1989,D 5,C17:3
Newman, Robert
  Quiet on the Set 1990,Ag 16,C17:1
Newman, William
  Heart of a Dog 1990,Mr 16,C3:1
Newman-Roberts, Jeremy (Lighting Director)
  Romeo and Juliet 1990,Jl 14,10:1
Newton, John
  Max and Maxie 1989,Ja 18,C14:6
Ngcamu, Sphamandla
  Township Fever 1990,D 20,C11:1
Ngema, Bhoyi
  Township Fever 1990,D 20,C11:1
  Township Fever 1990,D 23,II:5:1
Ngema, Mbongeni (Composer)
  Township Fever 1990,D 20,C11:1
  Township Fever 1990,D 23,II:5:1
Ngema, Mbongeni (Choreographer)
  Township Fever 1990,D 20,C11:1
Ngema, Mbongeni (Director)
  Township Fever 1990,D 20,C11:1
  Township Fever 1990,D 23,II:5:1
Ngema, Mbongeni (Lyricist)
  Township Fever 1990,D 20,C11:1
  Township Fever 1990,D 23,II:5:1
Ngema, Mbongeni (Miscellaneous)
  Township Fever 1990,D 20,C11:1
Ngema, Mbongeni (Playwright)
  Township Fever 1990,D 20,C11:1
Ngema, Sbusiso
  Township Fever 1990,D 20,C11:1
Nicholas, Fayard (Choreographer)
  Black and Blue 1989,Ja 27,C3:1
Nicholas, Lisa
  Hamlet 1989,Je 2,C3:5
Nicholaw, Casey
  Kiss of the Spider Woman 1990,Je 1,C3:1
Nichols, Jenny
  Richard III 1990,Ag 17,C1:1
Nichols, Jonathan
  Measure for Measure 1989,Mr 10,C3:1
  Othello 1990,Ja 17,C18:4
Nichols, Mike (Director)
  Elliot Loves 1990,Je 8,C3:1
Nichols, Peter (Lyricist)
  Privates on Parade 1989,Ag 23,C13:3
Nichols, Peter (Playwright)
  Privates on Parade 1989,Ag 23,C13:3
Nichols, Tom
  Lark, The 1989,My 29,20:5
Nicholson, Danny
  Ice Capades 1989,Ja 21,17:4
Nicholson, William (Playwright)
  Shadowlands 1990,N 12,C11:1
  Shadowlands 1990,N 18,II:5:1
Nickalaus
  Indiana Dog 1989,S 26,C17:1
Nicola, James C. (Director)
  Love and Anger 1990,D 9,82:3
  Love and Anger 1990,D 16,II:5:1
Nicola, James C. (Miscellaneous)
  Nature of Things, The 1990,Mr 25,63:1
  Waves, The 1990,My 10,C16:4
  Love and Anger 1990,D 9,82:3
Nicolaisen, Kari
  Prizes 1989,My 18,C22:4
  Pal Joey 1990,Jl 24,C13:3
Niejadlik, Walter
  Baal 1990,Mr 24,17:1
Nielsen, Kristine
  Ubu 1989,Je 26,C14:1
  Flea in Her Ear, A 1989,O 13,C15:1

451

Neddy 1990,Ap 2,C15:1
Maids of Honor 1990,Je 22,C3:3
Machinal 1990,O 16,C13:1
Love and Anger 1990,D 9,82:3
Love and Anger 1990,D 16,II:5:1
Nielsen, Paul
Light Up the Sky 1990,Ag 22,C10:5
Niesen, James
Happy End 1990,My 26,11:1
Niesen, James (Director)
Happy End 1990,My 26,11:1
Nieuwenhuis, Kristin (Miscellaneous)
Mud Angel, The 1990,N 18,75:1
Nigro, Bob (Director)
20 Fingers, 20 Toes 1990,Ja 10,C17:1
Nigro, Bob (Playwright)
20 Fingers, 20 Toes 1990,Ja 10,C17:1
Nikulin, Yuri (Miscellaneous)
Moscow Circus 1990,Ja 13,13:4
Ninagawa, Yukio (Director)
Tempest, The 1989,Ja 1,II:5:1
Ninagawa Macbeth 1990,O 22,C20:1
Nininger, Susan (Costume Designer)
Kingfish 1989,D 22,C5:1
Nipkow, Leslie
Investigation of the Murder in El Salvador, The
1989,My 23,C14:4
Sincerity Forever 1990,D 8,17:3
Nishida, Takashi (Choreographer)
Lost in a Flurry of Cherries 1990,Mr 25,62:1
Nishizaki, Mayumi (Choreographer)
Takarazuka 1989,O 27,C21:1
Nissenson, Gloria (Lyricist)
Frankie 1989,O 10,C18:3
Prince of Central Park 1989,N 10,C3:1
Niven, Kip
Golden Apple, The 1990,Mr 30,C3:5
Nixon, Cynthia
Cherry Orchard, The 1990,My 24,C19:3
Nixon, Ken (Director)
Play to Win 1989,Jl 21,C3:2
Nkosi, Siphiwe
Township Fever 1990,D 20,C11:1
Noah, James
Grapes of Wrath, The 1990,Mr 23,C1:4
Noble, Adrian (Director)
Art of Success, The 1989,D 21,C11:1
Three Sisters, The 1990,Ag 30,C15:1
Noble, James
Voysey Inheritance, The 1990,O 26,C3:1
Noble, Janet (Playwright)
Away Alone 1989,D 16,18:4
Noda, Ryo
Kiyotsune: The Death of a Warrior 1989,My 19,C3:4
Noda, Ryo (Composer)
Kiyotsune: The Death of a Warrior 1989,My 19,C3:4
Noda, Ryo (Director)
Kiyotsune: The Death of a Warrior 1989,My 19,C3:4
Nogulich, Natalia
Accomplice 1990,Ap 27,C5:1
Nohe, Marc F.
Hyde Park 1989,N 12,73:1
Gogol 1990,Ap 14,17:1
Nolan, Anto
Away Alone 1989,D 16,18:4
Nolan, Eric
King Lear 1990,N 16,C3:1
Noling, David (Lighting Director)
No Limits to Love 1989,My 4,C21:1
Noonan, Jesse Sage
Marathon 1990: Festival of New One-Act Plays,
Series C 1990,Je 14,C20:3
Noonan, John Ford
Talking Things Over with Chekhov 1990,My 13,44:1
Noonan, John Ford (Playwright)
Talking Things Over with Chekhov 1990,My 13,44:1
Stay Away a Little Closer (Marathon 1990: Festival
of New One-Act Plays, Series C) 1990,Je
14,C20:3
Noone, James (Scenic Designer)
Niedecker 1989,Mr 19,61:1
Midsummer Nights 1989,S 24,71:3
Bronx Tale, A 1989,O 22,63:5
Violent Peace 1990,Mr 3,12:3
Ruffian on the Stair, The 1990,Ap 25,C13:1
Lover, The 1990,Ap 25,C13:1
Sugar Hill 1990,Ap 28,12:6
Money Talks 1990,S 7,C3:5
Whatnot 1990,S 25,C16:3
Daytrips 1990,N 10,16:1

Norcia, Patricia
Rough Crossing 1990,F 23,C3:4
Nordling, Jeffrey
Don Juan of Seville (Burlador de Sevilla y
Convidado de Piedra, El) 1989,Ap 7,C3:5
Cymbeline 1989,Je 1,C15:1
Richard III 1990,Ag 17,C1:1
Norgate, Eric (Miscellaneous)
Township Fever 1990,D 20,C11:1
Norman, Marsha (Playwright)
Traveler in the Dark 1990,Ja 16,C13:1
Norman, Sharon (Costume Designer)
White Chocolate for My Father 1990,F 15,C22:3
Noroyan, Grant
Walt Disney's Magic Kingdom on Ice 1990,F
20,C18:4
Norris, Bruce
What the Butler Saw 1989,Mr 9,C21:1
Winter's Tale, The 1990,Ja 31,C15:1
Norris, Kathleen (Miscellaneous)
De Donde? 1990,Ja 8,C13:1
Norris, William J.
Winter's Tale, The 1990,Ja 31,C15:1
Norwood
Mama, I Want to Sing, Part II 1990,Mr 28,C13:1
Noseworthy, Jack
Jerome Robbins's Broadway 1989,F 27,C13:1
Nostrand, Michael
Cherry Orchard, The 1990,My 24,C19:3
Noth, Christopher
Arms and the Man 1989,Je 5,C12:4
Novack, Kathleen (Miscellaneous)
Don Juan of Seville (Burlador de Sevilla y
Convidado de Piedra, El) 1989,Ap 7,C3:5
Nozick, Bruce
Return, The 1990,Ja 12,C3:3
Made in Heaven 1990,My 13,45:1
Nri, Cyril
Macbeth 1989,Mr 21,C19:1
Ntinga, Themba
Hanging the President 1990,Jl 13,C17:1
Nugent, James
Hedda Gabler 1989,Ja 25,C18:5
Midsummer Night's Dream, A 1989,O 15,67:1
Three Sisters, The 1989,N 23,C20:5
School for Wives, The 1989,D 30,17:1
Nugzarov, Tamerlan
Moscow Circus 1990,Ja 13,13:4
Null, Panchali
Manhattan Class One-Acts, Series B 1989,Mr
19,61:4
Nunes, Jose (Costume Designer)
Nelson 2 Rodrigues 1989,O 15,65:1
Nunez, Luis Alberto
Nelson 2 Rodrigues 1989,O 15,65:1
Nunn, Trevor (Director)
Aspects of Love 1989,Je 27,C15:4
Othello 1989,S 24,II:5:1
Aspects of Love 1990,Ap 9,C11:1
Nussbaum, Bernard (Producer)
Miss Margarida's Way 1990,F 16,C3:1
Nussbaum, Toby (Producer)
Miss Margarida's Way 1990,F 16,C3:1
Nutt, Sandra
Burner's Frolic 1990,F 26,C14:1
Lifetimes 1990,Ap 9,C12:4
Nutu, Dan
Twelfth Night 1989,D 20,C20:3
Nyberg, Pamela
Cerceau 1990,N 4,II:5:1
Nye, Carrie
Without Apologies 1989,F 19,74:4
Nye, Hope
Don Juan of Seville (Burlador de Sevilla y
Convidado de Piedra, El) 1989,Ap 7,C3:5

O

Oates, Joyce Carol (Playwright)
In Darkest America 1990,Ap 5,C15:1
Eclipse, The (Marathon 1990: Festival of New One-
Act Plays, Series B) 1990,Je 1,C8:5
I Stand Before You Naked 1990,D 10,C14:1
Obando, Rigoberto (Miscellaneous)
Eterno Femenino, El 1990,Mr 25,63:1
Jibaros Progresistas, Los 1990,Ag 18,15:1

Abanderado, El (Standard Bearer, The) 1990,N
4,72:1
Oberon, David (Miscellaneous)
East Texas 1990,O 7,70:4
Obispo, Fabian V., Jr. (Composer)
Caucasian Chalk Circle, The 1990,O 1,C14:1
O'Brien, Liam
Saint Joan 1989,Ag 19,14:1
O'Brien, Paul
Henry Lumper 1989,F 5,53:1
Sand Mountain Matchmaking (Working One-Acts
'89) 1989,Je 25,45:4
Widow's Blind Date, The 1989,N 8,C23:1
Manhattan Punch Line's Sixth Annual Festival of
One-Act Comedies, Evening A 1990,F 4,60:1
Perfect Diamond, A 1990,Je 6,C18:1
O'Brien, Quentin
Dance Lesson, A 1989,N 11,16:5
O'Byrne, Adrian
Playboy of the Western World, The 1990,N 8,C28:1
O'Byrne, Brian F.
Philadelphia, Here I Come! 1990,Je 13,C15:1
Playboy of the Western World, The 1990,N 8,C28:1
O'Carroll, Mike
Young Rube 1989,Ap 21,C3:4
Fiddler on the Roof 1990,N 19,C13:1
Ochlan, P. J.
Love's Labor's Lost 1989,F 23,C15:1
Ochoa, Steve
Jerome Robbins's Broadway 1989,F 27,C13:1
O'Connell, Caitlin
Merry Wives of Windsor, The 1990,My 30,C13:1
O'Connell, David (Miscellaneous)
Man Who Fell in Love with His Wife, The 1990,Ag
19,55:1
O'Connell, Deirdre
Love and Anger 1990,D 9,82:3
Love and Anger 1990,D 16,II:5:1
O'Connell, Elinore
Aspects of Love 1990,Ap 9,C11:1
O'Connell, Patricia
Starting Monday 1990,Ap 5,C18:1
O'Connell, Patrick
Tower of Evil, The (Tour de Nesle, La) 1990,My
13,45:1
Nightingale 1990,D 4,C16:3
O'Connell, Richard L. (Translator)
Video Store Owner's Significant Other, The 1990,S
26,C9:5
O'Conner, Sara (Translator)
Puppetmaster of Lodz, The 1989,D 27,C15:1
O'Connor, Joyce
Foundation, The 1989,D 29,C6:6
O'Connor, Kevin
Heart Outright, The 1989,My 21,68:2
Audience (By and for Havel) 1990,Mr 9,C3:5
Catastrophe (By and for Havel) 1990,Mr 9,C3:5
O'Connor, Kevin James
Colorado Catechism, The 1990,O 22,C13:1
Odashima, Yushi (Translator)
Ninagawa Macbeth 1990,O 22,C20:1
O'Dell, Herbert H. (Miscellaneous)
Ancient History 1989,My 18,C29:3
Bovver Boys 1990,F 25,57:3
O'Dell, Herbert H. (Producer)
Swim Visit 1990,Je 23,12:4
O'Dell, Herbert H. (Scenic Designer)
Hollywood Scheherazade 1989,O 1,60:5
O'Dell, K. Lype
Richard III 1990,O 2,C12:3
Oden, Christopher
Three Sisters 1989,Ja 24,C16:4
Good 1989,F 25,18:4
Importance of Being Earnest, The 1989,O 5,C19:1
Travesties 1989,N 3,C29:1
Life Is a Dream 1989,D 16,17:1
Man's a Man, A 1990,F 26,C15:4
Prince of Homburg, The 1990,Ap 22,62:1
Odland, Bruce (Composer)
Tale of Two Cities, A 1990,Ap 7,16:4
Odo, Maureen Fleming
Mythos Oedipus 1989,Mr 5,69:1
Dionysus Filius Dei 1989,Mr 5,69:1
Odo, Maureen Fleming (Choreographer)
Mythos Oedipus 1989,Mr 5,69:1
O'Donnell, Elaine (Miscellaneous)
Henry Lumper 1989,F 5,53:1
Night Breath 1989,Ap 9,57:2
Hyde Park 1989,N 12,73:1

Death of the Last Black Man in the Whole Entire
  World, The 1990,S 25,C15:1
Parlato, Dennis
  Lark, The 1989,My 29,20:5
  Traveler in the Dark 1990,Ja 16,C13:1
  Violent Peace 1990,Mr 3,12:3
Parnell, Peter (Playwright)
  Hyde in Hollywood 1989,N 30,C19:3
  Hyde in Hollywood 1989,D 24,II:3:1
Parris, Steve
  My Father, My Son 1990,S 23,65:3
Parry, Chris (Lighting Director)
  Search and Destroy 1990,D 14,C3:1
Parry, William
  Cymbeline 1989,Je 1,C15:1
  Marathon 1990: Festival of New One-Act Plays,
    Series B 1990,Je 1,C8:5
Parson, Annie-B
  Happy End 1990,My 26,11:1
Parsons, Estelle
  Unguided Missile, The 1989,F 13,C16:3
  Baba Goya 1989,D 6,C21:1
  Miss Margarida's Way 1990,F 16,C3:1
  Miss Margarida's Way 1990,F 25,II:5:1
Partlan, William (Director)
  All God's Dangers 1989,O 23,C15:3
  Swim Visit 1990,Je 23,12:4
Pasekoff, Marilyn
  Forbidden Broadway 1990 1990,Ja 24,C15:1
Pashalinski, Lola
  Lear 1990,Ja 26,C3:1
Paslawsky, Gregor
  Phantom Lady, The 1989,Ap 16,60:1
Passeltiner, Bernie
  Sunshine Boys, The 1989,My 14,49:1
Pastorelli, Robert
  Marathon 1990: Festival of New One-Act Plays,
    Series C 1990,Je 14,C20:3
Paternostro, Mike
  Love Life 1990,Je 22,C15:1
Paterson, David R. (Miscellaneous)
  Fanny 1990,Ap 13,C3:5
Paterson, W. J.
  Price of Fame 1990,Je 14,C17:1
Paterson, William
  Saint Joan 1989,Ag 19,14:1
Patinkin, Laura
  Education of H*Y*M*A*N K*A*P*L*A*N, The
    1989,Ap 6,C22:4
Patinkin, Mandy
  Winter's Tale, The 1989,Mr 22,C19:4
Paton, Bob
  German Requiem 1990,My 28,14:5
Patrick, Robert (Director)
  Hello, Bob 1990,O 21,62:3
Patrick, Robert (Playwright)
  Hello, Bob 1990,O 21,62:3
Patterson, Anne C. (Costume Designer)
  Working One-Acts '89 1989,Je 25,45:4
  Three Poets 1989,N 23,C20:1
  Special Interests 1990,F 18,70:1
Patterson, Anne C. (Scenic Designer)
  Working One-Acts '89 1989,Je 25,45:4
  Three Poets 1989,N 23,C20:1
  Special Interests 1990,F 18,70:1
Patterson, Jay
  Early One Evening at the Rainbow Bar and Grille
    1989,Ap 14,C34:5
  Tempest, The 1989,N 15,C18:3
Patterson, Julie
  Ice Capades 1989,Ja 21,17:4
Patterson, Kelly
  Jerome Robbins's Broadway 1989,F 27,C13:1
  Golden Apple, The 1990,Mr 30,C3:5
Patterson, Vaughn (Scenic Designer)
  Jekyll and Hyde 1990,Jl 1,48:1
Patti, John
  Gigi 1989,My 28,57:1
Pattison, Liann
  Valued Friends 1990,D 20,C20:4
Patton, Lucille
  Money Talks 1990,S 7,C3:5
Patton, Theresa
  Suenos 1989,F 23,C13:3
Paul, Bob (Choreographer)
  Walt Disney's Magic Kingdom on Ice 1990,F
    20,C18:4
Paul, Michael B. (Miscellaneous)
  Marathon 1990: Festival of New One-Act Plays,
    Series A 1990,My 16,C14:4

Paul, Richard Joseph
  Chelsea Walls 1990,Je 9,12:5
Paul, Stephanie
  Summerfolk 1989,O 14,15:4
Paul, Steve (Miscellaneous)
  White Boned Demon 1989,Mr 5,68:1
Paul, Talia
  Crossin' the Line 1989,My 14,48:1
  Zoya's Apartment 1990,My 11,C3:1
Paul, Tina
  Genesis: Music and Miracles from the Medieval
    Mystery Plays 1989,Ja 18,C20:5
  Dangerous Games 1989,O 20,C3:3
Paul, Tina (Choreographer)
  Love's Labor's Lost 1989,F 23,C15:1
  Dangerous Games 1989,O 20,C3:3
  Hannah . . . 1939 1990,Je 2,16:3
Pavlov, Aleksandr
  Peace of Brest-Litovsk, The 1990,Ap 18,C11:1
Payan, Ilka Tanya
  Parting Gestures 1989,D 22,C5:4
Payne, Erica
  Suenos 1989,F 23,C13:3
Payne, Robert Warren
  Romeo and Juliet 1990,Jl 14,10:1
Payton-Wright, Pamela
  Miser, The 1990,My 18,C4:3
Peabody, Steve
  B. Beaver Animation, The 1990,My 24,C19:1
Peabody, Steve (Composer)
  White Boned Demon 1989,Mr 5,68:1
  B. Beaver Animation, The 1990,My 24,C19:1
Peachena, Lady
  Over Forty 1989,My 16,C17:1
Peacock, Lucy
  Three Sisters, The 1989,Je 12,C13:1
Pearce, Bobby (Miscellaneous)
  Forbidden Broadway 1990 1990,Ja 24,C15:1
Pearlman, Stephen
  Hyde in Hollywood 1989,N 30,C19:3
  Six Degrees of Separation 1990,Je 15,C1:2
  Six Degrees of Separation 1990,Jl 1,II:1:1
  Six Degrees of Separation 1990,N 9,C5:1
Pearson, Sybille (Playwright)
  Phantasie 1989,Ja 4,C15:5
Pearthree, Pippa
  Crucible, The 1989,D 16,15:1
  Nightingale 1990,D 4,C16:3
Peaslee, Richard (Miscellaneous)
  Endangered Species 1990,O 9,C13:1
Pechenkina, E. (Costume Designer)
  My Big Land 1989,Ag 17,C15:1
Peck, Bob
  In Lambeth 1989,Ag 28,C13:4
Peck, Jonathan Earl
  Glass Menagerie, The 1989,O 16,C19:1
Pecktal, Lynn (Miscellaneous)
  Without Apologies 1989,F 19,74:4
Pecoraro, Susu
  Sin Testigos 1990,Ag 14,C16:1
Pedernera, Alfredo
  Paradise for the Worried 1990,Ap 6,C3:1
Pederson, Rose (Costume Designer)
  Largely New York 1989,My 2,C15:1
Pedley, Dave
  Ice Capades 1990,Ja 21,49:1
Peek, Brent (Producer)
  Stand-Up Tragedy 1990,O 5,C3:1
Peek, Jenny (Miscellaneous)
  Triplets in Uniform 1989,F 12,70:4
Peeks, Kevin
  Ice Capades 1990,Ja 21,49:1
Peers, Johnny
  Ringling Brothers and Barnum & Bailey Circus
    1990,Mr 31,13:1
Peet, Paris
  As You Like It 1989,My 13,10:5
Pehlivanian, Raffi (Playwright)
  Prizes 1989,My 18,C22:4
Peil, Mary Beth
  Cymbeline 1989,Je 1,C15:1
Peipers, David H. (Producer)
  Making Movies 1990,Mr 28,C17:1
Peldon, Courtney
  Henry Lumper 1989,F 5,53:1
  Meet Me in St. Louis 1989,N 3,C3:1
Pelikan, Lisa
  Immigrant, The: A Hamilton County Album 1989,F
    8,C19:1

Pell, Amy (Miscellaneous)
  Run for Your Wife! 1989,Mr 8,C17:1
Pell, Stephen
  Big Hotel 1989,S 29,C3:1
  Ring Gott Farblonjet, Der 1990,Ap 13,C3:1
  Pornsongspiel 1990,Je 4,C22:1
  Camille 1990,S 7,C3:1
Pellegrino, Susan
  Cyrano de Bergerac 1989,Jl 7,C19:1
  Come As You Are 1990,F 15,C26:3
  Day Trips 1990,Ap 16,C15:1
  Agreement, The (Equal 'Wrights) 1989,My 18,C20:3
Pelletier, Carol Ann (Costume Designer)
  Alive by Night 1989,My 18,C22:3
  Your Handsome Captain 1989,N 12,71:6
Pellicciaro, Elena
  Happy End 1990,My 26,11:1
Pelzig, Daniel (Choreographer)
  Privates on Parade 1989,Ag 23,C13:3
  Chocolate Soldier, The 1990,Je 3,62:2
Pena, Manuel
  No + (No More) 1989,Ag 12,14:4
Pendleton, Austin
  Hughie (Serious Company—An Evening of One-Act
    Plays) 1989,Ap 19,C19:1
  Hamlet 1989,Je 2,C3:5
  Ivanov 1990,S 25,C13:3
Pendleton, Austin (Miscellaneous)
  John Brown's Body 1989,Je 27,C14:5
  Rose Tattoo, The 1989,Jl 28,C3:4
Pendleton, Wyman
  Peer Gynt 1989,Ap 11,C17:1
Pene du Bois, Raoul (Costume Designer)
  Jerome Robbins's Broadway 1989,F 27,C13:1
Penn, Matt
  Balcony, The 1990,Ap 9,C14:6
Penn, Matthew (Director)
  Big Frogs (Marathon '89, Series C) 1989,Je 29,C14:5
Pennington, Mark (Choreographer)
  Adios, Tropicana 1989,Ag 10,C16:5
Pennington, Mark (Composer)
  Adios, Tropicana 1989,Ag 10,C16:5
Pennington, Mark (Director)
  Adios, Tropicana 1989,Ag 10,C16:5
Penuela, Fernando
  Paso o Parabola del Camino, El (Parable of the Path,
    The) 1989,Ag 20,62:1
Penuelas, Eusebio
  Romeo and Juliet 1990,S 15,15:1
Percelly, Joey
  Ice Capades 1990,Ja 21,49:1
Pereira, Gustavo
  Suenos 1989,F 23,C13:3
Pereiras, Manuel (Playwright)
  Chinese Charade (Chino de la Charada, El) 1989,Ag
    13,57:3
Perelman, S. J. (Original Author)
  S. J. Perelman in Person 1989,My 18,C22:4
Peretyatko, Natalya
  Leningrad State Music Hall 1990,My 28,11:1
Perez, Jose
  Taming of the Shrew, The 1990,Jl 13,C3:1
Perez, Josie
  Gran Circo E.U. Craniano, El (Great U.S. Kranial
    Circus, The) 1989,Ag 4,C15:1
Perez, Lazaro
  Enrico IV 1989,Ja 19,C22:3
Perez, Luis
  Jerome Robbins's Broadway 1989,F 27,C13:1
  Dangerous Games 1989,O 20,C3:3
Perez, Luis (Miscellaneous)
  Dangerous Games 1989,O 20,C3:3
Perez, Michael
  Don Juan of Seville (Burlador de Sevilla y
    Convidado de Piedra, El) 1989,Ap 7,C3:5
Perez, Miguel
  Mountain Language 1989,N 9,C21:3
  Woyzeck 1990,Mr 6,C17:1
  Hamlet 1990,My 9,C15:4
Perez, Tim
  New York 1937 1990,My 6,75:4
  Taming of the Shrew, The 1990,Jl 13,C3:1
  Gonza the Lancer 1990,O 25,C20:5
Perez Dzul, Martin (Translator)
  Romeo and Juliet 1990,S 15,15:1
Perillo, Robert (Director)
  Importance of Being Earnest, The 1989,O 5,C19:1
Perkins, Kathy (Lighting Director)
  Spirit Time 1989,Jl 14,C18:1

Perkins, Patti
Fabulous La Fontaine, The 1990,F 8,C15:3
Hannah . . . 1939 1990,Je 2,16:3
Perkins, Phineas (Miscellaneous)
Apocalyptic Butterflies 1989,Je 17,12:3
Perkis, Phil (Miscellaneous)
Imperceptible Mutabilities in the Third Kingdom 1989,S 20,C24:4
Perl, Joshua
Titus Andronicus 1989,Ag 21,C13:1
Perla, Gene (Miscellaneous)
Body Builder's Book of Love, The 1990,Ap 29,60:1
Perlman, Bonnie
Prince of Central Park 1989,N 10,C3:1
Perloff, Carey (Director)
Don Juan of Seville (Burlador de Sevilla y Convidado de Piedra, El) 1989,Ap 7,C3:5
Mountain Language 1989,N 9,C21:3
Birthday Party, The 1989,N 9,C21:3
Tower of Evil, The (Tour de Nesle, La) 1990,My 13,45:1
Happy Days 1990,O 13,17:1
Happy Days 1990,O 21,II:5:1
Perloff, Carey (Miscellaneous)
Don Juan of Seville (Burlador de Sevilla y Convidado de Piedra, El) 1989,Ap 7,C3:5
Heart of a Dog 1990,Mr 16,C3:1
Tower of Evil, The (Tour de Nesle, La) 1990,My 13,45:1
Happy Days 1990,O 13,17:1
Happy Days 1990,O 21,II:5:1
Perman, Dennis (Lyricist)
Witch, The 1989,N 16,C30:4
Perreca, Michael (Miscellaneous)
Perfect Diamond, A 1990,Je 6,C18:1
Perretta, Laura
Love's Labor's Lost 1989,My 26,C4:5
Perrineau, Harold
Midsummer Nights 1989,S 24,71:3
Young Playwrights Festival 1990 1990,S 21,C14:6
Perry, Alvin B. (Costume Designer)
Talented Tenth, The 1989,N 10,C3:1
Perry, Ernest, Jr.
Iceman Cometh, The 1990,O 3,C13:4
Perry, Jeff
Grapes of Wrath, The 1990,Mr 23,C1:4
Perry, Karen (Costume Designer)
Uncle Vanya 1990,Mr 3,12:5
Sea Gull, The: The Hamptons: 1990 1990,D 24,21:1
Perry, Keith
City of Angels 1989,D 12,C19:4
Perry, Lynnette
Grand Hotel 1989,N 13,C13:3
Perry, Steven (Costume Designer)
Come As You Are 1990,F 15,C26:3
Perry, Steven (Scenic Designer)
Songs of Paradise 1989,Ja 24,C16:3
Perryman, Dwayne B., 3d (Miscellaneous)
Spirit Time 1989,Jl 14,C18:1
God's Trombones 1989,O 11,C17:1
Peszek, Jan
Dybbuk, The 1989,Jl 11,C13:1
Hamlet 1989,Jl 11,C13:1
Peter, Sinai (Playwright)
Seeing Double 1989,N 16,C28:4
Peters, Charlie (Playwright)
Hollywood Scheherazade 1989,O 1,60:5
Peters, Donna Marie
Estate, The 1989,F 18,18:1
Peters, Wes (Scenic Designer)
S. J. Perelman in Person 1989,My 18,C22:4
Peterson, Heather
Daisy Miller 1990,Ag 16,C14:4
Peterson, Kirk (Choreographer)
Shogun: The Musical 1990,N 21,C9:1
Peterson, Lisa (Director)
Essence of Margrovia, The (Marathon '89, Series A) 1989,My 30,C19:1
Briar Patch 1989,D 6,C21:1
Waves, The 1990,My 10,C16:4
Death and the Maiden (Marathon 1990: Festival of New One-Act Plays, Series C) 1990,Je 14,C20:3
Peterson, Lisa (Playwright)
Waves, The 1990,My 10,C16:4
Peterson, Michael
Summerfolk 1989,O 14,15:4
Peterson, Pam (Miscellaneous)
Imperceptible Mutabilities in the Third Kingdom 1989,S 20,C24:4

Peterson, Patricia Ben
Yiddle with a Fiddle 1990,O 30,C14:5
Peterson, Sarah
Crucible, The 1989,D 16,15:1
Petherbridge, Edward
Misanthrope, The 1989,Ag 20,II:5:1
Petit, Christopher
People Who Could Fly, The 1989,Ag 3,C20:3
Petrarca, David
Marvin's Room 1990,D 2,II:5:1
Petrarca, David (Director)
Mill Fire 1989,O 19,C22:3
Petratos, Eleni (Translator)
Dionysus Filius Dei 1989,Mr 5,69:1
Petrilli, Stephen (Lighting Director)
Hedda Gabler 1989,Ja 25,C18:5
Importance of Being Earnest, The 1990,Mr 18,59:1
Major Barbara 1990,N 28,C17:1
Petrilli, Stephen (Miscellaneous)
Hedda Gabler 1989,Ja 25,C18:5
Petrovich, Victoria (Scenic Designer)
Ladies 1989,Ap 7,C3:1
Summerfolk 1989,O 14,15:4
Paradise for the Worried 1990,Ap 6,C3:1
Petrushevskaya, Lyudmila (Playwright)
Cinzano 1989,Je 29,C15:1
Cinzano 1989,O 19,C19:3
Pettiford, Valarie
Balcony, The 1990,Ap 9,C14:6
Pevsner, David
Fiddler on the Roof 1990,N 19,C13:1
Pezza, Mariner James (Producer)
Spinning Tale, A 1990,F 25,57:1
Pezza, Mariner James (Scenic Designer)
Spinning Tale, A 1990,F 25,57:1
Pfeiffer, Michelle
Twelfth Night 1989,Jl 10,C13:1
Phelan, Kate
O Pioneers! 1990,Ja 28,49:1
Philippi, Michael S. (Lighting Director)
Speed of Darkness, The 1989,My 9,C15:1
Phillips, Andy (Lighting Director)
Threepenny Opera 1989,N 6,C13:4
Phillips, Brad (Miscellaneous)
Sunspot 1989,Mr 18,14:4
Phillips, David
Mythos Oedipus 1989,Mr 5,69:1
Dionysus Filius Dei 1989,Mr 5,69:1
Indiana Dog 1989,S 26,C17:1
Phillips, Edward (Miscellaneous)
Minny and the James Boys (Plays in the Park) 1989,Je 20,C15:4
Baba Goya 1989,D 6,C21:1
Moving Targets 1990,Ja 30,C14:5
Phillips, Ethan
Miss Evers's Boys 1989,D 21,C16:3
Theme and Variations 1990,O 21,62:3
Phillips, Lloyd (Producer)
Threepenny Opera 1989,N 6,C13:4
Phillips, Mary
Sweeney Todd: The Demon Barber of Fleet Street 1989,Ap 8,11:5
Sweeney Todd 1989,S 15,C3:1
Golden Apple, The 1990,Mr 30,C3:5
Phillips, Mary Bracken
Cradle Song 1989,Mr 19,61:1
Phillips, Mary Bracken (Lyricist)
Cradle Song 1989,Mr 19,61:1
Phillips, Mary Bracken (Playwright)
Cradle Song 1989,Mr 19,61:1
Phillips, Robin (Director)
Richard III 1990,Ag 17,C1:1
Richard III 1990,O 7,II:5:1
Phillips, Tommy
Arrivederci Papa 1989,Je 22,C15:3
Philpot, Mark
As You Like It 1989,My 13,10:5
Twelfth Night 1989,O 4,C17:1
Phoenix, James
Death Takes a Holiday 1990,Ag 13,C11:1
Piazza, Joseph (Miscellaneous)
Quiet End, A 1990,My 31,C16:6
Piazzolla, Astor (Composer)
Dangerous Games 1989,O 20,C3:3
Picciotto, Henri (Playwright)
Seeing Double 1989,N 16,C28:4
Pickering, Steve
Titus Andronicus 1989,Ag 21,C13:1
Winter's Tale, The 1990,Ja 31,C15:1

Pickett, Sarah (Miscellaneous)
Marathon 1990: Festival of New One-Act Plays, Series B 1990,Je 1,C8:5
Pielmeier, John
Seagull, The 1989,O 19,C19:3
Pierce, David
Heidi Chronicles, The 1989,O 9,C13:1
Elliot Loves 1990,Je 8,C3:1
Pierce, Wendell
Cymbeline 1989,Je 1,C15:1
Young Playwrights Festival 1990 1990,S 21,C14:6
Pierre, Christophe (Miscellaneous)
Step into My World 1989,F 19,76:4
Prizes 1989,My 18,C22:4
Capitol Cakewalk 1990,Mr 2,C31:1
Pietri, Pedro (Playwright)
Mondo Mambo 1990,Ag 25,16:5
Pietropinto, Angela
Rain. Some Fish. No Elephants. 1990,My 3,C20:5
Young Playwrights Festival 1990 1990,S 21,C14:6
Piggott, Ian (Miscellaneous)
Gogol 1990,Ap 14,17:1
Pigliavento, Michele
Gypsy 1989,N 17,C5:1
Pilbrow, Fred (Scenic Designer)
Macbeth 1989,Mr 21,C19:1
Apart from George 1989,Mr 21,C19:1
Pillitteri, Paul
Away Alone 1989,D 16,18:4
Pinchot, Bronson
Zoya's Apartment 1990,My 11,C3:1
Pineda, Pedro
Coronel No Tiene Quien le Escriba, El (No One Writes to the Colonel) 1989,Ag 3,C17:1
Pinget, Robert (Playwright)
Abel and Bela 1989,O 1,61:1
Architruc 1989,O 1,61:1
Pinhasik, Howard
Frankie 1989,O 10,C18:3
Pinkins, Tonya
Young Playwrights Festival 1990 1990,S 21,C14:6
Pinkney, Mikell (Director)
Over Forty 1989,My 16,C17:1
Boochie 1989,Jl 30,57:2
Every Goodbye Ain't Gone 1989,Jl 30,57:2
Pintauro, Joe (Playwright)
Beside Herself 1989,O 18,C15:1
Moving Targets 1990,Ja 30,C14:5
Pinter, Harold (Playwright)
Mountain Language 1989,Ja 15,II:1:4
Mountain Language 1989,N 9,C21:3
Birthday Party, The 1989,N 9,C21:3
Lover, The 1990,Ap 25,C13:1
Pinto, Chickie (Costume Designer)
Arrivederci Papa 1989,Je 22,C15:3
Pinto, Dan
Bitter Friends 1989,F 14,C16:3
Piontek, Michael
Florida Crackers 1989,Je 2,C3:1
Threepenny Opera 1989,N 6,C13:4
Pippin, Don (Miscellaneous)
Easter Extravaganza 1990,Ap 13,C28:4
Pippin, Don (Musical Director)
Easter Extravaganza 1990,Ap 13,C28:4
Christmas Spectacular, The 1990,N 13,C20:1
Piquer, Gary
Romeo and Juliet 1990,D 21,C20:6
Pirandello, Luigi (Playwright)
Enrico IV 1989,Ja 19,C22:3
Six Characters in Search of an Author 1989,Jl 24,C13:1
Piretti, Ron (Miscellaneous)
Briar Patch 1989,D 6,C21:1
Piro, Sal (Director)
Arrivederci Papa 1989,Je 22,C15:3
Piro, Sal (Playwright)
Arrivederci Papa 1989,Je 22,C15:3
Pisoni, Larry (Miscellaneous)
Pickle Family Circus, The 1989,Jl 24,C12:3
Pisoni, Lorenzo John
Pickle Family Circus, The 1989,Jl 24,C12:3
Pistone, Martino N. (Miscellaneous)
Richard III 1990,Ag 17,C1:1
Pitoniak, Anne
Blood Issue 1989,Ap 5,C19:4
Rose Tattoo, The 1989,Jl 28,C3:4
Solid Gold Cadillac, The 1989,S 21,C28:1
Ivanov 1990,S 25,C13:3
Pittman, Richard (Miscellaneous)
Suenos 1989,F 23,C13:3

Maids of Honor 1990,Je 22,C3:3
Robinson, Bernita (Miscellaneous)
Wonderful Town 1989,O 8,64:1
Robinson, Cindy
Peter Pan 1990,D 14,C3:4
Robinson, Dean
Carnage, A Comedy 1989,S 18,C14:1
Robinson, Edward G. (Musical Director)
Shogun: The Musical 1990,N 21,C9:1
Robinson, Hal
Grand Hotel 1989,N 13,C13:3
Robinson, Lance
Shadowlands 1990,N 12,C11:1
Shadowlands 1990,N 18,II:5:1
Robinson, Lewis
Red Sneaks, The 1989,Je 29,C13:1
Robinson, Mary B. (Director)
Painted Rain (Young Playwrights Festival) 1989,S
22,C5:4
Robinson, Max
Chocolate Soldier, The 1990,Je 3,62:2
Light Up the Sky 1990,Ag 22,C10:5
Robinson, Meghan
Lady in Question, The 1989,Jl 26,C17:1
Robinson, Peter
Light Up the Sky 1990,Ag 22,C10:5
Robinson, Robin
Gypsy 1989,N 17,C5:1
Roblin, Jennifer
Miser, The 1990,O 12,C1:1
Rocamora, Carol (Miscellaneous)
Anthony Rose 1989,O 30,C16:3
Rock, Kevin
Young Playwrights Festival 1990 1990,S 21,C14:6
Rodabaugh, Scott (Miscellaneous)
Square One 1990,F 23,C3:1
Rodgers, Richard (Composer)
Pal Joey 1990,Jl 24,C13:3
Rodgers, Richard (Miscellaneous)
Jerome Robbins's Broadway 1989,F 27,C13:1
Rodrigo, Al
New York 1937 1990,My 6,75:4
Rodrigues, Nelson (Playwright)
Nelson 2 Rodrigues 1989,O 15,65:1
Rodriguez, Al
Don Juan of Seville (Burlador de Sevilla y
Convidado de Piedra, El) 1989,Ap 7,C3:5
English Only Restaurant, The 1990,Jl 27,C4:5
Rodriguez, Alvaro
Paso o Parabola del Camino, El (Parable of the Path,
The) 1989,Ag 20,62:1
Rodriguez, Cesar
Voces de Acero (Voices of Steel) 1990,Ag 20,C14:1
Rodriguez, E. J.
Nature of Things, The 1990,Mr 25,63:1
Rodriguez, Fabian
Coronel No Tiene Quien le Escriba, El (No One
Writes to the Colonel) 1989,Ag 3,C17:1
Rodriguez, Ignacio
Paso o Parabola del Camino, El (Parable of the Path,
The) 1989,Ag 20,62:1
Rodriguez, Ignacio (Composer)
Paso o Parabola del Camino, El (Parable of the Path,
The) 1989,Ag 20,62:1
Rodriguez, Steven
Heaven on Earth 1989,N 12,71:5
Rodway, Norman
King Lear 1990,Ag 8,C11:3
Rogatsky, Albert
Leningrad State Music Hall 1990,My 28,11:1
Roger, Pascale
Infernal Machine, The 1990,D 2,83:1
Rogers, Cynthia
Mythos Oedipus 1989,Mr 5,69:1
Dionysus Filius Dei 1989,Mr 5,69:1
Rogers, Gil
Frankie 1989,O 10,C18:3
Rogers, Ken Leigh
Oh, Kay! 1989,N 1,C22:3
Rogers, Ken Leigh (Miscellaneous)
Pal Joey 1990,Jl 24,C13:3
Oh, Kay! 1990,N 2,C1:1
Rogers, Laura
Carnal Knowledge 1990,N 21,C15:1
Rogers, Michael
Playboy of the West Indies, The 1989,My 11,C17:1
Othello 1990,Ja 17,C18:4
Young Playwrights Festival 1990 1990,S 21,C14:6

Rogers, Poli (Choreographer)
Chinese Charade (Chino de la Charada, El) 1989,Ag
13,57:3
Rogerson, Anita
Manhattan Punch Line's Sixth Annual Festival of
One-Act Comedies, Evening B 1990,F 11,70:1
Rogerson, Bob
Forbidden Broadway 1990 1990,Ja 24,C15:1
Forbidden Broadway 1990 1990,Ap 22,II:5:1
Rogerson, Gus
Manhattan Punch Line's Sixth Annual Festival of
One-Act Comedies, Evening A 1990,F 4,60:1
Six Degrees of Separation 1990,Je 15,C1:2
Six Degrees of Separation 1990,N 9,C5:1
Rogow, David
Land of Dreams, The 1989,N 22,C10:1
Rohn, Jennifer
O Pioneers! 1990,Ja 28,49:1
Roht, Ken (Choreographer)
Father Was a Peculiar Man 1990,Jl 11,C13:1
Roi, Tony
Legends in Concert 1989,My 14,49:3
Rojas, Ana (Miscellaneous)
Eterno Femenino, El 1990,Mr 25,63:1
Rojas, Rosalinda
Pickle Family Circus, The 1989,Jl 24,C12:3
Rojo, Jerry (Scenic Designer)
Temptation 1989,Ap 10,C13:1
Rolfe, Mickey (Miscellaneous)
Unguided Missile, The 1989,F 13,C16:3
Blessing, The 1989,My 22,C12:1
Rolle, Esther
Member of the Wedding, The 1989,Ap 1,16:3
Rolon, Rosalba
Voces de Acero (Voices of Steel) 1990,Ag 20,C14:1
Rolon, Rosalba (Costume Designer)
Voces de Acero (Voices of Steel) 1990,Ag 20,C14:1
Roman, Elsa
Gran Circo E.U. Craniano, El (Great U.S. Kranial
Circus, The) 1989,Ag 4,C15:1
Rome, Harold (Composer)
Fanny 1990,Ap 13,C3:5
Rome, Harold (Lyricist)
Fanny 1990,Ap 13,C3:5
Romero, Constanza (Costume Designer)
Piano Lesson, The 1990,Ap 17,C13:4
Romero, Constanza (Scenic Designer)
Indiana Dog 1989,S 26,C17:1
Ronan, Brian (Miscellaneous)
Aunts, The 1989,O 8,64:1
Rooker, Michael
Abundance 1990,O 31,C15:3
Abundance 1990,N 11,II:5:1
Rooks, Joel
Lilith 1990,S 23,67:4
Rooney, Deborah (Costume Designer)
Ambassador, The 1989,O 22,63:1
Roos, Casper
Shenandoah 1989,Ag 9,C13:1
Frankie 1989,O 10,C18:3
Roose-Evans, James (Playwright)
Re:Joyce! 1990,F 2,C03:1
Root, Melina (Costume Designer)
Apocalyptic Butterflies 1989,Je 17,12:3
Rosado, Pedro
Lear 1990,Ja 26,C3:1
Rosado, Pedro (Lighting Director)
Herd of Buffalo 1989,Jl 6,C18:4
Rosaire, David
Grandma Goes West 1989,N 3,C4:1
Rosario, Carmen
Happy Birthday, Mama 1989,F 9,C22:3
Rosati, Christina (Miscellaneous)
Equal 'Wrights 1989,My 18,C20:3
Rose, Charles (Miscellaneous)
Each Day Dies with Sleep 1990,My 17,C20:3
Rose, David
Thirteenth Chair, The 1989,Ap 16,61:1
Rose, Hugh A.
Shadowlands 1990,N 12,C11:1
Rose, Ian
Cyrano de Bergerac 1989,Jl 7,C19:1
Rose, Ian (Miscellaneous)
Cyrano de Bergerac 1989,Jl 7,C19:1
Rose, Jeff
Sunday Promenade, The 1989,Mr 12,68:1
Rose, Philip (Director)
Shenandoah 1989,Ag 9,C13:1

Rose, Philip (Playwright)
Shenandoah 1989,Ag 9,C13:1
Rose, Philip (Producer)
Truly Blessed: A Musical Celebration of Mahalia
Jackson 1990,Ap 23,C13:1
Cemetery Club, The 1990,My 16,C14:4
Rose, Richard (Miscellaneous)
Balcony, The 1990,Ap 9,C14:6
Theme and Variations 1990,O 21,62:3
Voice of the Prairie, The 1990,D 18,C18:5
Roselin, Stephan
King Lear 1990,N 16,C3:1
Roseman, Ralph (Miscellaneous)
Hizzoner! 1989,F 24,C3:1
Metamorphosis 1989,Mr 7,C15:1
Circle, The 1989,N 21,C19:1
City of Angels 1989,D 12,C19:4
Shadowlands 1990,N 12,C11:1
Rosen, Louis (Composer)
Titus Andronicus 1989,Ag 21,C13:1
Rosenbaum, David
Ghetto 1989,My 1,C11:1
Rosenberg, D. C. (Miscellaneous)
Bitter Friends 1989,F 14,C16:3
Quintuplets 1989,Ap 2,51:1
Double Blessing 1989,Jl 2,38:1
Return, The 1990,Ja 12,C3:3
Dividends 1990,Mr 4,51:1
Yiddle with a Fiddle 1990,O 30,C14:5
Rosenblum, Joshua
Some Americans Abroad 1990,My 3,C17:1
Rosenblum, Joshua (Musical Director)
Some Americans Abroad 1990,My 3,C17:1
Rosenblum, M. Edgar (Miscellaneous)
When We Are Married 1990,Ja 28,14:3
Some Sweet Day 1989,Mr 27,C13:1
Heiress, The 1989,Je 16,C3:1
Flea in Her Ear, A 1989,O 13,C15:1
Dance Lesson, A 1989,N 11,16:5
Crucible, The 1989,D 16,15:1
Re:Joyce! 1990,F 2,C3:1
Ruffian on the Stair, The 1990,Ap 25,C13:1
Lover, The 1990,Ap 25,C13:1
Is He Still Dead? 1990,My 27,58:1
Voysey Inheritance, The 1990,O 26,C3:1
Generations of the Dead in the Abyss of Coney
Island Madness 1990,D 9,82:3
Valued Friends 1990,D 20,C20:4
Rosenfeld, Jyll (Producer)
Jackie Mason: Brand New 1990,O 18,C21:1
Rosenfeld, Moishe (Miscellaneous)
Those Were the Days 1990,N 14,C26:1
Rosenfeld, Moishe (Producer)
Those Were the Days 1990,N 14,C26:1
Rosengarten, Theodore (Original Author)
All God's Dangers 1989,O 23,C15:3
Rosengarten, Theodore (Playwright)
All God's Dangers 1989,O 23,C15:3
Rosenstock, Milton (Miscellaneous)
Meet Me in St. Louis 1989,N 3,C3:1
Rosentel, Robert W. (Lighting Director)
Stand-Up Tragedy 1989,N 24,C3:4
Rosenthal, Caryn
Manhattan Punch Line's Sixth Annual Festival of
One-Act Comedies, Evening A 1990,F 4,60:1
Rosenthal, Lisa (Miscellaneous)
Murder in the Cathedral 1989,S 9,13:1
Rosenthal, Mark
Marvin's Room 1990,D 2,II:5:1
Roshchkovan, Lyudmila (Miscellaneous)
Cinzano 1989,Je 29,C15:1
Ross, Bertram (Choreographer)
Aunts, The 1989,O 8,64:1
Ross, Blair
Wonderful Town 1989,O 8,64:1
Ross, Jack (Director)
Spinning Tale, A 1990,F 25,57:1
Ross, Jamie
Approaching Zanzibar 1989,My 5,C3:1
Ross, Lola
I & I 1989,S 24,72:3
Ross, Pamela
Carreno 1990,F 3,15:4
Ross, Pamela (Playwright)
Carreno 1990,F 3,15:4
Ross, Sandra (Lighting Director)
Lifetimes 1990,Ap 9,C12:4
Ross, Stephen (Lighting Director)
Shenandoah 1989,Ag 9,C13:1

S

Sabin, David
Twelfth Night 1989,O 4,C17:1
Sablow, Jane (Scenic Designer)
Prizes 1989,My 18,C22:4
Saddler, Donald (Choreographer)
Kiss Me Kate 1989,Je 12,C13:1
Saddler, Donald (Director)
Kiss Me Kate 1989,Je 12,C13:1
Frankie 1989,O 10,C18:3
Sadler, Nicholas
Manhattan Punch Line's Sixth Annual Festival of
One-Act Comedies, Evening A 1990,F 4,60:1
Sado, Aleksandr
Junon and Avos: The Hope 1990,Ja 8,C16:3
Sadusk, Maureen
Madame Sherry 1989,Jl 30,57:1
Saex, Robin (Director)
Requiem for a Heavyweight (Manhattan Punch
Line's Festival of One-Act Comedies, Series B)
1989,F 11,12:3
Marathons (Equal 'Wrights) 1989,My 18,C20:3
Saez, Isabel
Suenos 1989,F 23,C13:3
Sagharadze, Guram
King Lear 1990,Ap 4,C17:1
Saint, David (Director)
Midsummer Nights 1989,S 24,71:3
Saint Clair, Michael
I & I 1989,S 24,72:3
St. George, Kathy
Fiddler on the Roof 1990,N 19,C13:1
St. Germain, Mark (Lyricist)
Gifts of the Magi, The 1990,D 9,82:3
St. Germain, Mark (Playwright)
Gifts of the Magi, The 1990,D 9,82:3
St. John, Gregory
Murder in the Cathedral 1989,S 9,13:1
St. John, Marco
Illusion, The 1990,Ja 18,C21:1
St. Louis, Louis (Composer)
Sugar Hill 1990,Ap 28,12:6
St. Louis, Louis (Lyricist)
Sugar Hill 1990,Ap 28,12:6
St. Louis, Louis (Playwright)
Sugar Hill 1990,Ap 28,12:6
Saint-Saens, Camille (Composer)
Fabulous La Fontaine, The 1990,F 8,C15:3
Saire, Rebecca
Hamlet 1989,Ag 6,II:5:1
Saito, Dawn A.
And the Soul Shall Dance 1990,Mr 25,63:2
Saka, Haruhiko (Miscellaneous)
Takarazuka 1989,O 27,C21:1
Sakaguchi, Ango (Original Author)
Lost in a Flurry of Cherries 1990,Mr 25,62:1
Sakata, Jeanne
Macbeth 1990,Ja 17,C13:4
Sakolsky, Ira
Father's Inheritance 1990,N 18,75:1
Sakow, Hayden Reed
Woyzeck 1990,Mr 6,C17:1
Saks, Gene (Director)
Rumors 1989,Mr 29,C17:1
Man Who Came to Dinner, The 1989,Ag 1,C13:3
Salas, Nicolette
Hannah . . . 1939 1990,Je 2,16:3
Salata, Gregory
Jacques and His Master 1989,N 16,C28:5
Salazar, Angel
Ariano 1990,F 11,69:2
Salce, Tim
Golden Apple, The 1990,Mr 30,C3:5
Salem, Francois Abu (Director)
Story of Kufur Shamma, The 1989,Jl 28,C17:1
Salem, Francois Abu (Miscellaneous)
Story of Kufur Shamma, The 1989,Jl 28,C17:1
Salem, Francois Abu (Playwright)
Story of Kufur Shamma, The 1989,Jl 28,C17:1
Salem, Kario
Twelfth Night 1989,D 20,C20:3
Salerno, Mary Jo
Unguided Missile, The 1989,F 13,C16:3
Salinger, Diane
Phantasie 1989,Ja 4,C15:5

Stronger, The (Serious Company—An Evening of
One-Act Plays) 1989,Ap 19,C19:1
Talking Things Over with Chekhov 1990,My 13,44:1
Salinger, Ross
Twelfth Night 1989,D 20,C20:3
Sallows, Tracy
Miser, The 1990,O 12,C1:1
Salmon, Scott (Choreographer)
Easter Extravaganza 1990,Ap 13,C28:4
Christmas Spectacular, The 1990,N 13,C20:1
Salmon, Scott (Director)
Easter Extravaganza 1990,Ap 13,C28:4
Christmas Spectacular, The 1990,N 13,C20:1
Saltz, Amy (Director)
Neddy 1990,Ap 2,C15:1
Saltzman, Avery
Witch, The 1989,N 16,C30:4
Salvadore, J. Kelly
Grand Guignol, The 1990,Je 2,18:1
Salzberg, Marc (Miscellaneous)
Mastergate 1989,O 13,C3:1
Salzman, Eric (Miscellaneous)
Love Life 1990,Je 22,C15:1
Sametz, Laura
Macbeth 1990,Ja 17,C13:4
Samoff, Marjorie (Miscellaneous)
Love Life 1990,Je 22,C15:1
Sams, Jeremy (Composer)
Some Americans Abroad 1990,F 12,C17:1
Some Americans Abroad 1990,My 3,C17:1
Sams, Jeremy (Lyricist)
Ghetto 1989,My 1,C11:1
Samuelsohn, Howard
Midsummer Nights 1989,S 24,71:3
Samuelson, Howard
Manhattan Punch Line's Sixth Annual Festival of
One-Act Comedies, Evening A 1990,F 4,60:1
Sananes, Adriana
Nonna, La 1989,S 1,C12:1
Huesped, El 1990,Ag 18,15:1
Sanchez, George Emilio (Lyricist)
Suenos 1989,F 23,C13:3
Sanchez, Luis Rafael (Playwright)
Quintuplets 1989,Ap 2,51:1
Sanchez, Rene
Nonna, La 1989,S 1,C12:1
Nelson 2 Rodrigues 1989,O 15,65:1
Huesped, El 1990,Ag 18,15:1
Abanderado, El (Standard Bearer, The) 1990,N
4,72:1
Sandefur, James (Scenic Designer)
Ariano 1990,F 11,69:2
Rough Crossing 1990,F 23,C3:4
Sanders, Abigael
New York 1937 1990,My 6,75:4
Sanders, Fred
Buddy: The Buddy Holly Story 1990,N 5,C13:1
Sanders, Fred (Director)
Seven Menus (Manhattan Punch Line's Fifth Annual
Festival of One-Act Comedies, Series A) 1989,Ja
26,C16:1
Sanders, James (Miscellaneous)
Crowbar 1990,F 20,C18:1
Sanders, Jay O.
Heaven on Earth 1989,N 12,71:5
Sanders, Scott (Miscellaneous)
Manhattan Punch Line's Fifth Annual Festival of
One-Act Comedies, Series A 1989,Ja 26,C16:1
Manhattan Punch Line's Festival of One-Act
Comedies, Series B 1989,F 11,12:3
Equal 'Wrights 1989,My 18,C20:3
Strike, The 1990,Ja 29,C18:5
Sanders, Ty (Miscellaneous)
Lucky Come Hawaii 1990,O 29,C16:1
Sanderson, Austin (Costume Designer)
Hyde Park 1989,N 12,73:1
Sanderson, Kirsten (Director)
Eulogy for Mister Hamm 1990,Je 1,C8:5
Sandifur, Virginia
Slay It with Music 1989,O 24,C20:6
Sandt, Severn (Producer)
Starmites 1989,Ap 28,C3:1
Santana, Merlin
Young Playwrights Festival 1990 1990,S 21,C14:6
Santana, Norman
Coronel No Tiene Quien le Escriba, El (No One
Writes to the Colonel) 1989,Ag 3,C17:1
Santaniello, Eric (Miscellaneous)
Tempest, The 1989,N 15,C18:3

Santareni, Gene
Hamlet 1989,Je 2,C3:5
Santeiro, Luis (Playwright)
Lady from Havana, The 1990,N 5,C14:4
Santiago, Glen
Indiana Dog 1989,S 26,C17:1
Crowbar 1990,F 20,C18:1
Rodents and Radios 1990,Ap 28,15:1
Famine Plays 1990,N 3,14:5
Santiago, Renoly
Suenos 1989,F 23,C13:3
Santiago, Socorro
Anthony Rose 1989,O 30,C16:3
De Donde? 1990,Ja 8,C13:1
Santini, Bruno (Scenic Designer)
Shirley Valentine 1989,F 17,C3:1
Shirley Valentine 1989,Ag 10,C13:1
Santomenna, Stephen (Miscellaneous)
Summerfolk 1989,O 14,15:4
Baal 1990,Mr 24,17:1
Santore, Regina B. (Miscellaneous)
Buzzsaw Berkeley 1989,Ag 21,C14:3
Santoriello, Alex
Threepenny Opera 1989,N 6,C13:4
Santos, Jaime
Oba Oba '90 1990,Mr 16,C6:3
Santos, Sonia
Oba Oba '90 1990,Mr 16,C6:3
Saparito, James
Carol Lawrence and Larry Kert Together . . . Again!
1990,O 4,C21:1
Sappington, Margo (Choreographer)
Prizes 1989,My 18,C22:4
Sargeant, Angela
Balcony, The 1990,Ap 9,C14:6
Sargeant, Greg
Estate, The 1989,F 18,18:1
Sarnataro, Patricia (Costume Designer)
Hanging the President 1990,Jl 13,C17:1
Sarno, Janet
Money Talks 1990,S 7,C3:5
Sata, Warren
Seeing Double 1989,N 16,C28:4
Sater, Steven (Playwright)
Cardondale Dreams 1990,Ja 5,C3:1
Saunders, Donald
Shenandoah 1989,Ag 9,C13:1
Saunders, Nicholas
Visit, The 1989,F 5,56:5
Saunders, Nicholas (Translator)
Zoya's Apartment 1990,My 11,C3:1
Savage, Keith
Young Rube 1989,Ap 21,C3:4
Savage, Keith (Miscellaneous)
Madame Sherry 1989,Jl 30,57:1
Oh, Kay! 1989,N 1,C22:3
Savage, Melodee
Romance in Hard Times 1989,D 29,C3:1
Merrily We Roll Along 1990,F 27,C13:1
Saver, Jeffrey (Musical Director)
Merrily We Roll Along 1990,F 27,C13:1
Savin, Ron Lee
Gifts of the Magi, The 1990,D 9,82:3
Sawaryn, David E. (Costume Designer)
Magic Act, The 1989,F 16,C21:1
Marathon '89, Series C 1989,Je 29,C14:5
Marathon 1990: Festival of New One-Act Plays,
Series A 1990,My 16,C14:4
Sawyer, David (Composer)
Mythos Oedipus 1989,Mr 5,69:1
Sawyer, Ken
Love's Labor's Lost 1989,My 26,C4:5
Sawyer, Mark
Showing Off 1989,My 28,57:1
Sawyer, Timothy
O Pioneers! 1990,Ja 28,49:1
Saxon, Don (Producer)
Legends in Concert 1989,My 14,49:3
Scales, Prunella
Single Spies 1989,Ja 15,II:1:4
Single Spies 1989,Ag 20,II:5:1
Scallen, Tom (Director)
Ice Capades 1989,Ja 21,17:4
Ice Capades 1990,Ja 21,49:1
Scallen, Tom (Producer)
Ice Capades 1989,Ja 21,17:4
Scanlan, John
Pathological Venus (Marathon '89, Series B) 1989,Je
15,C14:5

T

U

V

W

Wilson, William
King Lear 1990,N 16,C3:1
Wiltse, David (Playwright)
Dance Lesson, A 1989,N 11,16:5
Winborn, Brent
Golden Apple, The 1990,Mr 30,C3:5
Wincott, Michael
Secret Rapture, The 1989,O 27,C3:1
Wineberg, Rachel (Miscellaneous)
Video Store Owner's Significant Other, The 1990,S 26,C9:5
Wines, Halo
Caucasian Chalk Circle, The 1990,O 1,C14:1
Wing-Davey, Mark (Director)
Mad Forest 1990,Jl 25,C11:3
Wingfield, Betsy J. (Miscellaneous)
Ulysses in Nighttown 1989,Ja 15,44:1
Winkler, Henry
Solid Gold Cadillac, The 1989,S 21,C28:1
Winn, David (Producer)
Pixie Led, The 1989,Jl 21,C3:5
Winn, Krystyna (Producer)
Pixie Led, The 1989,Jl 21,C3:5
Winn, Marie (Translator)
Temptation 1989,Ap 10,C13:1
Winslow, Michele
Ulysses in Nighttown 1989,Ja 15,44:1
Winston, Hattie (Director)
Sugar Hill 1990,Ap 28,12:6
Winter, Denise (Miscellaneous)
Miser, The 1990,My 18,C4:3
Our Country's Good 1990,O 21,59:3
Winters, Nancy (Miscellaneous)
Woyzeck 1990,Mr 6,C17:1
Winters, Nancy (Scenic Designer)
Big Funk, The 1990,D 11,C15:4
Winterson, Caroline
Playboy of the Western World, The 1990,N 8,C28:1
Wintersteller, Lynne
Closer Than Ever 1989,N 7,C19:1
Winther, Michael
Artist Descending a Staircase 1989,D 1,C3:1
Winton, Graham
Winter's Tale, The 1989,Mr 22,C19:4
Twelfth Night 1989,Jl 10,C13:1
Doctor's Dilemma, The 1990,Ja 26,C3:1
Taming of the Shrew, The 1990,Jl 13,C3:1
Wirthner, Naomi
Cymbeline 1989,Ag 6,II:5:1
Wise, John (Miscellaneous)
Immigrant, The: A Hamilton County Album 1989,F 8,C19:1
Prisoner of Second Avenue, The 1989,N 5,96:1
Puppetmaster of Lodz, The 1989,D 27,C15:1
Made in Heaven 1990,My 13,45:1
Fine Art of Finesse, The (Heureux Stratageme, L') 1990,D 28,C5:1
Wise, Scott
Jerome Robbins's Broadway 1989,F 27,C13:1
Wise, William
Early One Evening at the Rainbow Bar and Grille 1989,Ap 14,C34:5
Special Interests 1990,F 18,70:1
Theme and Variations 1990,O 21,62:3
Wiseman, Joseph
10th Man, The 1989,D 11,C13:1
Wisniski, Ron
Frankie 1989,O 10,C18:3
Wisoff, Jill
Money Talks 1990,S 7,C3:5
Wisti, Toni
Largely New York 1989,My 2,C15:1
Witt, Howard
When We Are Married 1989,Ja 28,14:3
Witt, Katarina
Brian Boitano and Katarina Witt Skating 1990,My 8,C17:1
Wittenbauer, John
Tempest, The 1989,N 15,C18:3
Wittmer, Mary Lou
Positive Me 1989,N 16,C28:5
Witto, Marcelo
No + (No More) 1989,Ag 12,14:4
Wodehouse, P. G. (Playwright)
Leave It to Jane 1989,Mr 23,C17:1
Oh, Kay! 1989,N 1,C22:3
Oh, Kay! 1990,N 2,C1:1
Oh, Kay! 1990,N 11,II:5:1
Wojda, John
Merchant of Venice, The 1989,D 20,C15:1

Wojewodski, Robert (Costume Designer)
Abundance 1990,O 31,C15:3
King Lear 1990,N 16,C3:1
Wolf, Henry E. (Playwright)
My Father, My Son 1990,S 23,65:3
Wolf, Ken
My Father, My Son 1990,S 23,65:3
Wolf, Ken (Playwright)
My Father, My Son 1990,S 23,65:3
Wolfe, George C. (Director)
Spunk 1990,Ap 19,C17:4
Caucasian Chalk Circle, The 1990,D 3,C13:3
Caucasian Chalk Circle, The 1990,D 9,II:5:1
Wolfe, George C. (Playwright)
Spunk 1990,Ap 19,C17:4
Wolff, Art (Director)
Accomplice 1990,Ap 27,C5:1
Wolk, James (Scenic Designer)
Manhattan Punch Line's Fifth Annual Festival of One-Act Comedies, Series A 1989,Ja 26,C16:1
Manhattan Punch Line's Festival of One-Act Comedies, Series B 1989,F 11,12:3
Equal 'Wrights 1989,My 18,C20:3
Slay It with Music 1989,O 24,C20:6
Anthony Rose 1989,O 30,C16:3
Puppetmaster of Lodz, The 1989,D 27,C15:1
Made in Heaven 1990,My 13,45:1
Wolos-Fonteno, David
Floor Above the Roof (Working One-Acts '89) 1989,Je 25,45:4
Wolpe, David (Playwright)
Unguided Missile, The 1989,F 13,C16:3
Wolsk, Gene (Producer)
Mastergate 1989,O 13,C3:1
Forever Plaid 1990,My 25,C3:1
Womack, Cornell
Merry Wives of Windsor, The 1990,My 30,C13:1
Wondisford, Diane (Director)
Paradise for the Worried 1990,Ap 6,C3:1
Wondisford, Diane (Miscellaneous)
Ladies 1989,Ap 7,C3:1
Paradise for the Worried 1990,Ap 6,C3:1
Endangered Species 1990,O 9,C13:1
Wong, B. D.
Tempest, The 1989,N 15,C18:3
Wonsek, Paul (Lighting Director)
Without Apologies 1989,F 19,74:4
Walkers 1989,Ap 16,60:1
Up 'n' Under 1989,Je 13,C17:1
Balcony, The 1990,Ap 9,C14:6
Theme and Variations 1990,O 21,62:3
Wonsek, Paul (Scenic Designer)
Walkers 1989,Ap 16,60:1
Up 'n' Under 1989,Je 13,C17:1
Home Games 1989,O 2,C16:3
Progress 1989,D 11,C15:1
Balcony, The 1990,Ap 9,C14:6
Marathon 1990: Festival of New One-Act Plays, Series A 1990,My 16,C14:4
Theme and Variations 1990,O 21,62:3
Woo, Jenny
Shogun: The Musical 1990,N 21,C9:1
Wood, John
Tempest, The 1989,Ja 1,II:5:1
Tempest, The 1989,Je 21,C15:3
Man Who Came to Dinner, The 1989,Ag 1,C13:3
King Lear 1990,Ag 8,C11:3
Wood, John (Director)
Henry V 1989,Je 12,C13:1
Wood, Tom
Miser, The 1990,My 18,C4:3
Woodall, Sandra (Costume Designer)
Saint Joan 1989,Ag 19,14:1
Woodard, Alfre
Winter's Tale, The 1989,Mr 22,C19:4
Woodard, Charlayne
Twelfth Night 1989,Jl 10,C13:1
Caucasian Chalk Circle, The 1990,D 3,C13:3
Caucasian Chalk Circle, The 1990,D 9,II:5:1
Wooden, Jesse, Jr. (Miscellaneous)
Jelly Belly 1990,N 22,C13:3
Woodeson, Nicholas
Art of Success, The 1989,D 21,C11:1
Ruffian on the Stair, The 1990,Ap 25,C13:1
Lover, The 1990,Ap 25,C13:1
Doing the Business 1990,Jl 25,C11:3
Woodruff, Elliott (Miscellaneous)
Shadowlands 1990,N 12,C11:1

Woodruff, Robert (Director)
Baal 1990,Mr 24,17:1
Woods, Allie, Jr.
Forbidden City, The 1989,Ap 7,C3:1
Miss Evers's Boys 1989,D 21,C16:3
Woods, Eileen
Gigi 1989,My 28,57:1
Woodson, John
Foundation, The 1989,D 29,C6:6
King Lear 1990,N 16,C3:1
Woodsono, Deborah
Step into My World 1989,F 19,76:4
Woolard, David C. (Costume Designer)
Gus and Al 1989,F 28,C17:1
Few Good Men, A 1989,N 16,C23:4
Romance in Hard Times 1989,D 29,C3:1
Mountain 1990,Ap 6,C29:1
Money Talks 1990,S 7,C3:5
Colorado Catechism, The 1990,O 22,C13:1
Woolf, Virginia (Original Author)
Waves, The 1990,My 10,C16:4
Woolsey, Wysandria
Aspects of Love 1990,Ap 9,C11:1
Worby, Joshua
Enrico IV 1989,Ja 19,C22:3
Workman, Jason
Meet Me in St. Louis 1989,N 3,C3:1
Worley, Jo Anne
Prince of Central Park 1989,N 10,C3:1
Worrall, Tom (Musical Director)
Wizard of Oz, The 1989,Mr 24,C3:1
Wortman, Bryna (Director)
Land of Dreams, The 1989,N 22,C10:1
Violent Peace 1990,Mr 3,12:3
Wray, Peter
Incommunicado 1989,Mr 3,C3:1
Wright, Amy
Prin 1990,Je 7,C18:5
Wright, Anne-Marie (Costume Designer)
Jekyll and Hyde 1990,Jl 1,48:1
Wright, Barbara (Translator)
Abel and Bela 1989,O 1,61:1
Wright, Doug (Miscellaneous)
Ubu 1989,Je 26,C14:1
Buzzsaw Berkeley 1989,Ag 21,C14:3
Wright, Doug (Playwright)
Buzzsaw Berkeley 1989,Ag 21,C14:3
Wright, Elaine
Jerome Robbins's Broadway 1989,F 27,C13:1
Wright, Jeffrey
Playboy of the West Indies, The 1989,My 11,C17:1
Search and Destroy 1990,D 14,C3:1
Wright, Lyn
Importance of Being Earnest, The 1989,O 5,C19:1
Travesties 1989,N 3,C29:1
Life Is a Dream 1989,D 16,17:1
Man's a Man, A 1990,F 26,C15:4
Prince of Homburg, The 1990,Ap 22,62:1
Wright, Nicholas (Playwright)
Mrs. Klein 1989,Ja 15,II:1:4
Wright, Robert (Composer)
Grand Hotel 1989,N 13,C13:3
Grand Hotel 1989,D 17,II:7:1
Grand Hotel 1990,F 25,II:5:1
Wright, Robert (Lyricist)
Grand Hotel 1989,N 13,C13:3
Grand Hotel 1989,D 17,II:7:1
Grand Hotel 1990,F 25,II:5:1
Wright, Samuel E.
Welcome to the Club 1989,Ap 14,C3:1
Wright, Stephen
Fiddler on the Roof 1990,N 19,C13:1
Wright, Tim
I & I 1989,S 24,72:3
Wright, Valerie
On the Town 1989,My 12,C3:4
Love Life 1990,Je 22,C15:1
Wroe, Craig
Tempest, The 1989,N 15,C18:3
Othello 1990,Ja 17,C18:4
Wulp, John (Scenic Designer)
Without Apologies 1989,F 19,74:4
O Pioneers! 1990,Ja 28,49:1
Wuthrich, Terry (Lighting Director)
Ambassador, The 1989,O 22,63:1
Strike, The 1990,Ja 29,C18:5
Wyche, Mimi
Golden Apple, The 1990,Mr 30,C3:5

Wydro, Ken (Director)
Mama, I Want to Sing, Part II 1990,Mr 28,C13:1
Wydro, Ken (Lyricist)
Mama, I Want to Sing, Part II 1990,Mr 28,C13:1
Wydro, Ken (Playwright)
Mama, I Want to Sing, Part II 1990,Mr 28,C13:1
Wydro, Ken (Producer)
Mama, I Want to Sing, Part II 1990,Mr 28,C13:1
Wyeth, Zoya (Miscellaneous)
Starmites 1989,Ap 28,C3:1
Wylie, John
Born Yesterday 1989,Ja 30,C11:1
Pixie Led, The 1989,Jl 21,C3:5
Grand Hotel 1989,N 13,C13:3
Grand Hotel 1990,F 25,II:5:1
Wyn Davies, Geraint
Henry V 1989,Je 12,C13:1
Wynkoop, Christopher
Aunts, The 1989,O 8,64:1
Wynne, Daniel, Jr. (Miscellaneous)
Spirit Time 1989,Jl 14,C18:1
Wynroth, Alan
Thin Air 1989,N 19,75:5

X

Xenos, George (Miscellaneous)
My Children! My Africa! 1989,D 19,C19:3
Forest in Arden, A 1990,F 11,69:1
Nature of Things, The 1990,Mr 25,63:1
Waves, The 1990,My 10,C16:4
Xenos, George (Scenic Designer)
Man's a Man, A 1990,F 26,C15:4
Chelsea Walls 1990,Je 9,12:5
Xifo, Raymond
City of Angels 1989,D 12,C19:4

Y

Yakim, Mina (Miscellaneous)
Zoya's Apartment 1990,My 11,C3:1
Yamada, Taku (Choreographer)
Takarazuka 1989,O 27,C21:1
Yamada, Tomoyuki
Ninagawa Macbeth 1990,O 22,C20:1
Yamaguchi, Eiko (Costume Designer)
Mythos Oedipus 1989,Mr 5,69:1
F.O.B. 1990,My 20,60:1
Yamamoto, Ronald
Lettice and Lovage 1990,Mr 26,C11:1
Yamauchi, Wakako (Playwright)
And the Soul Shall Dance 1990,Mr 25,63:2
Yanagawa, Mitsuyoshi
Lost in a Flurry of Cherries 1990,Mr 25,62:1
Yancey, Kim
Don Juan of Seville (Burlador de Sevilla y
Convidado de Piedra, El) 1989,Ap 7,C3:5
Yancey, Terence
Suenos 1989,F 23,C13:3
Yanes, Dorothy
Merrily We Roll Along 1990,F 27,C13:1
Yaney, Denise (Miscellaneous)
Dalton's Back 1989,F 10,C3:1
Beside Herself 1989,O 18,C15:1
Imagining Brad 1990,F 7,C15:2
Colorado Catechism, The 1990,O 22,C13:1
Yankee, Luke (Director)
Cherry Orchard, The 1990,My 24,C19:3
Yankovsky, Filip
My Big Land 1989,Ag 17,C15:1
Yarosh, Anatoly
Leningrad State Music Hall 1990,My 28,11:1
Yates, Lauren P. (Miscellaneous)
Jonquil 1990,Ja 15,C14:3
Burner's Frolic 1990,F 26,C14:1
Yazbeck, David (Composer)
Wonderful Party! (Manhattan Punch Line's Fifth
Annual Festival of One-Act Comedies, Series A)
1989,Ja 26,C16:1
Yeager, Barbara
Jerome Robbins's Broadway 1989,F 27,C13:1

Yeargan, Michael (Costume Designer)
Paper Gramophone, The 1989,Mr 4,11:4
Yeargan, Michael (Scenic Designer)
Nothing Sacred 1989,Ja 13,C5:1
Paper Gramophone, The 1989,Mr 4,11:4
Some Sweet Day 1989,Mr 27,C13:1
Playboy of the West Indies, The 1989,My 11,C17:1
Importance of Being Earnest, The 1989,O 11,C15:1
Crucible, The 1989,D 16,15:1
Yearsley, Alice
Jerome Robbins's Broadway 1989,F 27,C13:1
Prince of Central Park 1989,N 10,C3:1
Yee, Kelvin Han
Saint Joan 1989,Ag 19,14:1
Yefremov, Oleg (Director)
Ivanov 1990,S 25,C13:3
Yefremov, Oleg (Miscellaneous)
Ivanov 1990,S 25,C13:3
Yekimov, Yuri
My Big Land 1989,Ag 17,C15:1
Yellen, Sherman (Playwright)
Rothschilds, The 1990,F 26,C16:1
Yellow Robe, William, Jr. (Playwright)
Wink-Dah (Marathon '89, Series A) 1989,My
30,C19:1
Yelshevskaya, Liya
My Big Land 1989,Ag 17,C15:1
Yenque, Teresa
Conversation Among the Ruins 1989,Je 4,64:6
Yeremin, Yuri (Director)
Paper Gramophone, The 1989,Mr 4,11:4
Ward No. Six 1989,Jl 29,16:1
Yeremin, Yuri (Miscellaneous)
Ward No. Six 1989,Jl 29,16:1
Yeremin, Yuri (Playwright)
Paper Gramophone, The 1989,Mr 4,11:4
Yermakov, Aleksandr
Ward No. Six 1989,Jl 29,16:1
Yeston, Maury (Composer)
Grand Hotel 1989,N 13,C13:3
Grand Hotel 1989,D 17,II:7:1
Grand Hotel 1990,F 25,II:5:1
Yeston, Maury (Lyricist)
Grand Hotel 1989,N 13,C13:3
Grand Hotel 1989,D 17,II:7:1
Grand Hotel 1990,F 25,II:5:1
Yezzi, David D.
Grand Guignol, The 1990,Je 2,18:1
Yglesias, Jose (Playwright)
New York 1937 1990,My 6,75:4
Yionoulis, Evan (Director)
American Plan, The 1990,D 17,C11:1
Ynneco, Alfredo
Acid Paradise 1990,Mr 8,C24:1
Yocupicio, Carlos (Translator)
Romeo and Juliet 1990,S 15,15:1
Yokobosky, Matthew (Costume Designer)
Skin—A State of Being 1989,Ja 12,C15:1
Noiresque: The Fallen Angel 1989,My 5,C3:4
Brightness 1989,N 26,71:1
Yokobosky, Matthew (Scenic Designer)
Brightness 1989,N 26,71:1
Elephant Memories 1990,N 6,C15:1
Yonekawa, Toshiko (Composer)
Takarazuka 1989,O 27,C21:1
Yoresen, Kacey
Ice Capades 1990,Ja 21,49:1
York, Rachel
City of Angels 1989,D 12,C19:4
York, Y (Playwright)
Rain. Some Fish. No Elephants. 1990,My 3,C20:5
Yoshii, Sumio (Lighting Director)
Ninagawa Macbeth 1990,O 22,C20:1
Yoshizaki, Kenji (Composer)
Takarazuka 1989,O 27,C21:1
Youmans, James (Scenic Designer)
Triplets in Uniform 1989,F 12,70:4
Gus and Al 1989,F 28,C17:1
Romance in Hard Times 1989,D 29,C3:1
Mom's Life, A 1990,Mr 15,C22:3
Tales of the Lost Formicans 1990,Ap 29,60:1
Jersey City 1990,Jl 15,40:3
Colorado Catechism, The 1990,O 22,C13:1
Wash, The 1990,N 8,C28:4
American Plan, The 1990,D 17,C11:1
Youmans, William
When We Are Married 1989,Ja 28,14:3
Young, Bruce A.
Elliot Loves 1990,Je 8,C3:1

Young, Damian
Tiny Dimes 1990,Mr 9,C18:1
Indiana Dog 1989,S 26,C17:1
Rodents and Radios 1990,Ap 28,15:1
Young, Linda Carol (Miscellaneous)
Niedecker 1989,Mr 19,61:1
Violent Peace 1990,Mr 3,12:3
Young, Phyllis
Everything That Rises Must Converge 1990,Mr
16,C6:3
Young, Susan (Costume Designer)
Tale of Two Cities, A 1989,Ja 18,C15:4
Big Hotel 1989,S 29,C3:1
Dr. Jekyll and Mr. Hyde 1989,D 8,C3:2
Cahoots 1990,Mr 10,16:4
Ring Gott Farblonjet, Der 1990,Ap 13,C3:1
Young, Victor A.
Kiss Me Kate 1989,Je 12,C13:1
Youngman, Christina
Largely New York 1989,My 2,C15:1
Yudman, Gary
Manhattan Punch Line's Sixth Annual Festival of
One-Act Comedies, Evening A 1990,F 4,60:1
Yuhasz, Steve (Miscellaneous)
Legends in Concert 1989,My 14,49:3
Yulin, Harris
Approaching Zanzibar 1989,My 5,C3:1
Yulin, Harris (Director)
Baba Goya 1989,D 6,C21:1
Yurman, Lawrence
Moon over Miami 1989,F 24,C3:1
Yurman, Lawrence (Miscellaneous)
Moon over Miami 1989,F 24,C3:1
Yurman, Lawrence (Musical Director)
Moon over Miami 1989,F 24,C3:1
Yutaka Fresh J (Composer)
Stand-Up Tragedy 1989,N 24,C3:4

Z

Zabinski, Gary M. (Miscellaneous)
Up 'n' Under 1989,Je 13,C17:1
Balcony, The 1990,Ap 9,C14:6
Zaborowski, Chriztopher
Infernal Machine, The 1990,D 2,83:1
Zacek, Dennis (Director)
Jelly Belly 1990,N 22,C13:3
Zacek, Dennis (Miscellaneous)
Jelly Belly 1990,N 22,C13:3
Zachwatowicz, Krystyna (Costume Designer)
Dybbuk, The 1989,Jl 11,C13:1
Zachwatowicz, Krystyna (Miscellaneous)
Hamlet 1989,Jl 11,C13:1
Zagnit, Stuart
Made in Heaven 1990,My 13,45:1
Zahler, Adam (Director)
News from St. Petersburg (Manhattan Punch Line's
Festival of One-Act Comedies, Series B) 1989,F
11,12:3
Zaionz, Craig R. (Miscellaneous)
Walkers 1989,Ap 16,60:1
Up 'n' Under 1989,Je 13,C17:1
Zakharov, Mark (Director)
Junon and Avos: The Hope 1990,Ja 8,C16:3
Zakharova, Aleksandra
Junon and Avos: The Hope 1990,Ja 8,C16:3
Zakowska, Donna (Costume Designer)
Ladies 1989,Ap 7,C3:1
Grandma Goes West 1989,N 3,C4:1
Paradise for the Worried 1990,Ap 6,C3:1
Big Apple Circus, The 1990,N 3,13:4
Zaks, Jerry (Director)
Lend Me a Tenor 1989,Mr 3,C3:1
Lend Me a Tenor 1989,Mr 29,C17:1
Square One 1990,F 23,C3:1
Six Degrees of Separation 1990,Je 15,C1:2
Six Degrees of Separation 1990,Jl 1,II:1:1
Six Degrees of Separation 1990,N 9,C5:1
Six Degrees of Separation 1990,D 30,II:5:1
Zaldivar, Gilberto (Miscellaneous)
Nonna, La 1989,S 1,C12:1
Nelson 2 Rodrigues 1989,O 15,65:1
Eterno Femenino, El 1990,Mr 25,63:1
Huesped, El 1990,Ag 18,15:1
Jibaros Progresistas, Los 1990,Ag 18,15:1

Each Day Dies with Sleep 1990,My 17,C20:3
Colorado Catechism, The 1990,O 22,C13:1
Love Diatribe 1990,D 19,C15:1
Circus Flora (Prod.)
Endangered Species 1990,O 9,C13:1
City Center Theater (Prod.)
Circus Oz 1990,Je 8,C7:1
Civic Center for the Performing Arts (Prod.)
Peace of Brest-Litovsk, The 1990,Ap 18,C11:1
Claridge Productions (Prod.)
Man Who Shot Lincoln, The 1989,S 24,72:6
Clark, Schaefer, Hackett & Company (Prod.)
De Donde? 1990,Ja 8,C13:1
Cleveland Play House (Prod.)
Born Yesterday 1989,Ja 30,C11:1
New Music 1989,N 4,16:3
March on Russia, The 1990,N 14,C24:3
Clurman, Harold, Theater (Prod.)
Ulysses in Nighttown 1989,Ja 15,44:1
Cocteau, Jean, Repertory (Prod.)
Three Sisters 1989,Ja 24,C16:4
Good 1989,F 25,18:4
Importance of Being Earnest, The 1989,O 5,C19:1
Travesties 1989,N 3,C29:1
Life Is a Dream 1989,D 16,17:1
Man's a Man, A 1990,F 26,C15:4
Prince of Homburg, The 1990,Ap 22,62:1
Misalliance 1990,O 14,56:4
Infernal Machine, The 1990,D 2,83:1
Cole Theatrical Enterprises (Prod.)
Pixie Led, The 1989,Jl 21,C3:5
Columbia Artists Management (Prod.)
Born Yesterday 1989,Ja 30,C11:1
Comco Productions Inc. (Prod.)
S. J. Perelman in Person 1989,My 18,C22:4
Committed Artists, The (Misc.)
Township Fever 1990,D 20,C11:1
Community Association for the Preservation of Festival Floats in Inuyama (Misc.)
Karakuri Ningyo: Ancient Festival Puppets 1989,S 15,C28:4
Community Association for the Preservation of Festival Floats in Kamezaki (Ishibashigumi) (Misc.)
Karakuri Ningyo: Ancient Festival Puppets 1989,S 15,C28:4
Community Association for the Preservation of Festival Floats in Kamezaki (Nishigumi) (Misc.)
Karakuri Ningyo: Ancient Festival Puppets 1989,S 15,C28:4
Compass Theater Company (Prod.)
New Anatomies 1990,F 22,C19:1
Concept Fabrication (Misc.)
Seeing Double 1989,N 16,C28:4
Contracts International Ltd. (Prod.)
Buddy: The Buddy Holly Story 1990,N 5,C13:1
Coors, Adolph, Company (Misc.)
I Am a Winner 1990,Ap 1,52:3
Spanish Eyes 1990,My 27,56:3
Cornerstone Theater Company (Misc.)
Video Store Owner's Significant Other, The 1990,S 26,C9:5
Cornerstone Theater Company (Prod.)
Video Store Owner's Significant Other, The 1990,S 26,C9:5
Coup de Grace Productions (Prod.)
Quiet on the Set 1990,Ag 16,C17:1
Court Theater (Prod.)
Peace of Brest-Litovsk, The 1990,Ap 18,C11:1
Creation Production Company (Prod.)
Cities Out of Print 1990,Ap 14,16:4
Crossroads Theater Company (Prod.)
Spunk 1990,Ap 19,C17:4
CSC Repertory (Prod.)
Don Juan of Seville (Burlador de Sevilla y Convidado de Piedra, El) 1989,Ap 7,C3:5
Birthday Party, The 1989,N 9,C21:3
Mountain Language 1989,N 9,C21:3
Heart of a Dog 1990,Mr 16,C3:1
Tower of Evil, The (Tour de Nesle, La) 1990,My 13,45:1
Happy Days 1990,O 13,17:1
Happy Days 1990,O 21,II:5:1
Cucaracha Theater (Prod.)
Indiana Dog 1989,S 26,C17:1
Tiny Dimes 1990,Mr 9,C18:1
Rodents and Radios 1990,Ap 28,15:1
Famine Plays 1990,N 3,14:5

D

Dance Theater Workshop's Suitcase Fund (Prod.)
Story of Kufur Shamma, The 1989,Jl 28,C17:1
Deca Graphics (Misc.)
Acid Paradise 1990,Mr 8,C24:1
Design Associates (Miscellaneous)
Peggy and Jackson 1989,Ag 10,C16:5
Design Industries Foundation for AIDS (Misc.)
Skating for Life—A Celebration of Champions 1989,N 8,C25:1
Disney, Walt, Studios (Prod.)
Largely New York 1989,My 2,C15:1
Dodger Productions (Prod.)
Prelude to a Kiss 1990,My 2,C15:1
Douglass, Frederick, Creative Arts Center (Prod.)
Telltale Hearts 1990,D 9,82:6
Dowling Entertainment (Prod.)
Sum of Us, The 1990,O 20,16:4
Duo Theater (Misc.)
Adios, Tropicana 1989,Ag 10,C16:5
Peggy and Jackson 1989,Ag 10,C16:5

E

Edinburgh Festival (Misc.)
Tempest, The 1989,Ja 1,II:5:1
88 Carrat Productions (Prod.)
Carreno 1990,F 3,15:4
El-Hakawati Theater Company (Misc.)
Story of Kufur Shamma, The 1989,Jl 28,C17:1
En Garde Arts (Prod.)
At the Chelsea 1989,Ja 20,C3:1
Plays in the Park 1989,Je 20,C15:4
Krapp's Last Tape 1989,D 17,94:5
Crowbar 1990,F 20,C18:1
Crowbar 1990,Mr 14,C13:4
Father Was a Peculiar Man 1990,Jl 11,C13:1
Ennosuke's Kabuki (Misc.)
Kurozuka (Black Mound, The) 1989,S 8,C3:4
Yoshitsune Senbonzakura (Yoshitsune and the Thousand Cherry Trees) 1989,S 8,C3:4
Ensemble Studio Theater (Prod.)
Magic Act, The 1989,Mr 16,C21:1
Marathon '89, Series A 1989,My 30,C19:1
Marathon '89, Series B 1989,Je 15,C14:5
Marathon '89, Series C 1989,Je 29,C14:5
Briar Patch 1989,D 6,C21:1
Marathon 1990: Festival of New One-Act Plays, Series A 1990,My 16,C14:4
Marathon 1990: Festival of New One-Act Plays, Series B 1990,Je 1,C8:5
Marathon 1990: Festival of New One-Act Plays, Series C 1990,Je 14,C20:3
EPI Products (Prod.)
Meet Me in St. Louis 1989,N 3,C3:1
Equity Library Theater (Prod.)
Tomfoolery 1989,Ja 14,10:4
Fifth of July 1989,F 16,C34:3
Leave It to Jane 1989,Mr 23,C17:1
Thirteenth Chair, The 1989,Ap 16,61:1
Gigi 1989,My 28,57:1
Wonderful Town 1989,O 8,64:1

F

Fabulous Fercos (Misc.)
Ice Capades 1990,Ja 21,49:1
Festival Floats in Arimatsu (Misc.)
Karakuri Ningyo: Ancient Festival Puppets 1989,S 15,C28:4
Festival Latino in New York (Misc.)
Coronel No Tiene Quien le Escriba, El (No One Writes to the Colonel) 1989,Ag 3,C17:1
Gran Circo E.U. Craniano, El (Great U.S. Kranial Circus, The) 1989,Ag 4,C15:1
Adios, Tropicana 1989,Ag 10,C16:5
Peggy and Jackson 1989,Ag 10,C16:5
No + (No More) 1989,Ag 12,14:4

Sueno de una Noche de Verano (Midsummer Night's Dream, A) 1989,Ag 16,C16:1
Paso o Parabola del Camino, El (Parable of the Path, The) 1989,Ag 20,62:1
Sin Testigos 1990,Ag 14,C16:1
Palomar, El (Pigeon House, The) 1990,Ag 19,53:1
Voces de Acero (Voices of Steel) 1990,Ag 20,C14:1
Doente Imaginario, O (Imaginary Invalid, The) 1990,Ag 23,C20:1
Mondo Mambo 1990,Ag 25,16:5
Romeo and Juliet 1990,S 15,15:1
Flying Alejandros (Misc.)
Ringling Brothers and Barnum & Bailey Circus 1989,Mr 25,13:1
Flying by Foy (Misc.)
Peter Pan 1990,D 14,C3:4
Flying Guttys (Misc.)
Ringling Brothers and Barnum & Bailey Circus 1990,Mr 31,13:1
Flying Lunas (Misc.)
Ringling Brothers and Barnum & Bailey Circus 1989,Mr 25,13:1
Flying Morales (Misc.)
Ringling Brothers and Barnum & Bailey Circus 1990,Mr 31,13:1
Folksbiene Playhouse (Prod.)
Land of Dreams, The 1989,N 22,C10:1
Father's Inheritance 1990,N 18,75:1
Foundation of the Dramatists Guild (Prod.)
Young Playwrights Festival 1989,S 22,C5:4
Young Playwrights Festival 1990 1990,S 21,C14:6
14th Street Stage Lighting (Misc.)
I & I 1989,S 24,72:3
Fox, Robert, Ltd. (Prod.)
Lettice and Lovage 1990,Mr 26,C11:1
Fox/Perla Ltd. (Misc.)
Lady from Havana, The 1990,N 5,C14:4
Frankel, Gene, Theater (Prod.)
Carreno 1990,F 3,15:4
Franklin Furnace (Prod.)
Breakfast with the Moors Murderers 1989,F 2,C18:4
Fraternity Society for the Preservation of Temmansha Shrine (Prod.)
Karakuri Ningyo: Ancient Festival Puppets 1989,S 15,C28:4

G

G. G. Productions (Prod.)
Cahoots 1990,Mr 10,16:4
Gate Theater, Dublin (Misc.)
Three Sisters, The 1990,Ag 30,C15:1
Gauchos Latinos, Los (Misc.)
Ringling Brothers and Barnum & Bailey Circus 1990,Mr 31,13:1
Gibadullin Jugglers (Misc.)
Moscow Circus 1990,Ja 13,13:4
Glines (Prod.)
In Her Own Words (A Portrait of Jane) 1989,Ag 17,C18:3
Quintessential Image, The 1989,Ag 17,C18:3
Gloucester Stage Company (Prod.)
Henry Lumper 1989,F 5,53:1
Golden Land Klezmer Orchestra (Misc.)
Those Were the Days 1990,N 14,C26:1
Goodman Theater, The (Prod.)
Speed of Darkness, The 1989,My 9,C15:1
Winter's Tale, The 1990,Ja 31,C15:1
Piano Lesson, The 1990,Ap 17,C13:4
Iceman Cometh, The 1990,O 3,C13:4
Goodspeed Opera House (Prod.)
Madame Sherry 1989,Jl 30,57:1
Oh, Kay! 1989,N 1,C22:3
Chocolate Soldier, The 1990,Je 3,62:2
Pal Joey 1990,Jl 24,C13:3
Gorky, M., Moscow Art Theater (Misc.)
My Big Land 1989,Ag 17,C15:1
Graconn Ltd. (Prod.)
Making Movies 1990,Mr 28,C17:1
Great Jones Repertory Company (Misc.)
Dionysus Filius Dei 1989,Mr 5,69:1
Mythos Oedipus 1989,Mr 5,69:1
Gugkayevs (Misc.)
Moscow Circus 1990,Ja 13,13:4

H

Hall, Peter, Company (Misc.)
Orpheus Descending 1989,S 25,C15:4
Merchant of Venice, The 1989,D 20,C15:1
Hall, Peter, Company (Prod.)
Orpheus Descending 1989,Ja 15,II:1:4
Wild Duck, The 1990,Ag 30,C15:1
"Happy" New Yorkers, The (Misc.)
Special Interests 1990,F 18,70:1
Harris, Jeremiah J., Associates (Misc.)
Truly Blessed: A Musical Celebration of Mahalia
Jackson 1990,Ap 23,C13:1
Hartford Stage (Misc.)
Other People's Money 1989,F 17,C3:4
Stand-Up Tragedy 1990,O 5,C3:1
Hartford Stage (Prod.)
Nothing Sacred 1989,Ja 13,C5:1
Paper Gramophone, The 1989,Mr 4,11:4
Peer Gynt 1989,Ap 11,C17:1
Importance of Being Earnest, The 1989,O 11,C15:1
Stand-Up Tragedy 1989,N 24,C3:4
Illusion, The 1990,Ja 18,C21:1
Woyzeck 1990,Mr 6,C17:1
Day Trips 1990,Ap 16,C15:1
Miser, The 1990,My 18,C4:3
Our Country's Good 1990,O 21,59:3
Marvin's Room 1990,D 2,II:5:1
Helikons (Misc.)
Ringling Brothers and Barnum & Bailey Circus
1990,Mr 31,13:1
Holiday, Billie, Theater (Prod.)
Boochie 1989,Jl 30,57:2
Every Goodbye Ain't Gone 1989,Jl 30,57:2
Home Box Office (Prod.)
Kathy and Mo Show, The: Parallel Lives 1989,F
1,C21:1
Reno: In Rage and Rehab 1989,Mr 16,C20:4
Home for Contemporary Theater and Art (Prod.)
Year of the Baby, The 1989,Ag 17,C14:6
II Samuel 11, Etc. 1989,O 7,13:1
New Anatomies 1990,F 22,C19:1
Lilith 1990,S 23,67:4
Mud Angel, The 1990,N 18,75:1
Hudson Guild Theater (Prod.)
Without Apologies 1989,F 19,74:4
Walkers 1989,Ap 16,60:1
Up 'n' Under 1989,Je 13,C17:1
Home Games 1989,O 2,C16:3
Progress 1989,D 11,C15:1
Hull Truck Productions (Prod.)
Romeo and Juliet 1990,Jl 14,10:1
Humana Festival of New American Plays (Misc.)
Autumn Elegy 1989,Ap 5,C19:4
Blood Issue 1989,Ap 5,C19:4
Bone-the-Fish 1989,Ap 5,C19:4
Stained Glass 1989,Ap 5,C19:4
Tales of the Lost Formicans 1989,Ap 5,C19:4
2 1990,Ap 5,C15:1
In Darkest America 1990,Ap 5,C15:1
Infinity House 1990,Ap 5,C15:1
Pink Studio, The 1990,Ap 5,C15:1
Swan 1990,Ap 5,C15:1
Vital Signs 1990,Ap 5,C15:1
Zara Spook and Other Lures 1990,Ap 5,C15:1
Huntington Theater Company (Prod.)
O Pioneers! 1990,Ja 28,49:1
Piano Lesson, The 1990,Ap 17,C13:4

I

Instituto Arte Teatral Internacional Inc. (Prod.)
Acid Paradise 1990,Mr 8,C24:1
Intar Hispanic American Arts Center (Prod.)
Suenos 1989,F 23,C13:3
Don Juan of Seville (Burlador de Sevilla y
Convidado de Piedra, El) 1989,Ap 7,C3:5
Parting Gestures 1989,D 22,C5:4
Going to New England 1990,Mr 9,C18:1
Body Builder's Book of Love, The 1990,Ap 29,60:1
Lady from Havana, The 1990,N 5,C14:4
Interart Theater (Misc.)
Through the Leaves 1990,S 18,C18:1

Interart Theater (Prod.)
Brimstone and Treacle 1989,Ap 18,C15:3
International Artistes (Prod.)
Buddy: The Buddy Holly Story 1990,N 5,C13:1
**International Performing Arts Consultants Inc.
(Prod.)**
Story of Kufur Shamma, The 1989,Jl 28,C17:1
Irish Arts Center (Prod.)
Now and at the Hour of Our Death 1989,Je 1,C18:4
Away Alone 1989,D 16,18:4
Remembrance 1990,O 18,C22:5
Irish Repertory Theater (Prod.)
Whistle in the Dark, A 1989,N 17,C26:5
Philadelphia, Here I Come! 1990,Je 13,C15:1
Playboy of the Western World, The 1990,N 8,C28:1
Irondale Ensemble Project (Prod.)
Happy End 1990,My 26,11:1
Itoh, C., & Company (Prod.)
Fiddler on the Roof 1990,N 19,C13:1

J

Jackpots (Misc.)
Walt Disney's Magic Kingdom on Ice 1990,F
20,C18:4
Jackson Family Quartet (Misc.)
God's Trombones 1989,O 11,C17:1
Jewish Repertory Theater (Prod.)
Bitter Friends 1989,F 14,C16:3
Sunshine Boys, The 1989,My 14,49:1
Double Blessing 1989,Jl 2,38:1
Witch, The 1989,N 16,C30:4
Return, The 1990,Ja 12,C3:3
Dividends 1990,Mr 4,51:1
New York 1937 1990,My 6,75:4
What's Wrong with This Picture? 1990,Je 23,14:1
Spinoza 1990,N 4,72:4
Jomandi Productions (Prod.)
Sisters 1990,Je 7,C19:3
Joseph, Stephen, Theater in the Round (Prod.)
Revengers' Comedies, The 1989,Je 22,C17:1
Joyce Theater Foundation Inc. (Prod.)
Sisters 1990,Je 7,C19:3
Jujamcyn Theaters (Prod.)
Grand Hotel 1989,N 13,C13:3
City of Angels 1989,D 12,C19:4
Grapes of Wrath, The 1990,Mr 23,C1:4
Piano Lesson, The 1990,Ap 17,C13:4

K

K & D Productions (Prod.)
Mountain 1990,Ap 6,C29:1
Katona Jozsef Theater (Prod.)
Three Sisters, The 1989,Jl 23,II:5:5
**Kennedy, John F., Center for the Performing Arts
(Prod.)**
Largely New York 1989,My 2,C15:1
Kherts (Misc.)
Moscow Circus 1990,Ja 13,13:4
Kinematic (Misc.)
Paradise for the Worried 1990,Ap 6,C3:1
Kitchen, The (Prod.)
Sunspot 1989,Mr 18,14:4
Everything That Rises Must Converge 1990,Mr
16,C6:3

L

La MaMa E.T.C. (Prod.)
Skin—A State of Being 1989,Ja 12,C15:1
Triplets in Uniform 1989,F 12,70:4
Dionysus Filius Dei 1989,Mr 5,69:1
Mythos Oedipus 1989,Mr 5,69:1
New Cities 1989,My 7,74:3
Positive Me 1989,N 16,C28:5
Brightness 1989,N 26,71:1
Casa 1990,Ja 18,C24:4
I Think It's Gonna Work Out Fine 1990,Mr 17,18:6

Lost in a Flurry of Cherries 1990,Mr 25,62:1
Dragon's Nest 1990,My 10,C14:4
Cry of the Body, The 1990,Je 5,C15:1
Hello, Bob 1990,O 21,62:3
Elephant Memories 1990,N 6,C15:1
La MaMa Set Construction Group (Misc.)
Skin—A State of Being 1989,Ja 12,C15:1
Laboratorio de Teatro Campesino y Indigena (Misc.)
Romeo and Juliet 1990,S 15,15:1
Lamb's Theater Company (Prod.)
Crossin' the Line 1989,My 14,48:1
Smoke on the Mountain 1990,My 17,C20:3
Gifts of the Magi, The 1990,D 9,82:3
Landmark Entertainment Group (Prod.)
Tru 1989,D 15,C3:1
Lawlor/Shovestull (Misc.)
Immigrant, The: A Hamilton County Album 1989,F
8,C19:1
Lerner Rechnitz Group (Prod.)
Cahoots 1990,Mr 10,16:4
Lincoln Center for the Performing Arts (Prod.)
You Could Be Home Now 1990,Jl 17,C16:1
We Keep Our Victims Ready 1990,Jl 24,C13:1
Men's Room, The 1990,Jl 26,C13:3
Lincoln Center Theater (Prod.)
Measure for Measure 1989,Mr 10,C3:1
Our Town 1989,Mr 28,C15:1
Ubu 1989,Je 26,C14:1
Oh, Hell 1989,D 4,C15:1
10th Man, The 1989,D 11,C13:1
10th Man, The 1989,D 24,II:3:1
Bobby Gould in Hell 1989,D 24,II:3:1
Some Americans Abroad 1990,F 12,C17:1
Some Americans Abroad 1990,My 3,C17:1
Six Degrees of Separation 1990,Je 15,C1:2
Six Degrees of Separation 1990,Jl 1,II:1:1
Six Degrees of Separation 1990,N 9,C5:1
Monster in a Box 1990,N 15,C19:1
Township Fever 1990,D 20,C11:1
Lion King Productions (Prod.)
Cardondale Dreams 1990,Ja 5,C3:1
Little Prince Productions Ltd. (Prod.)
Born Yesterday 1989,Ja 30,C11:1
Living Theater (Prod.)
I & I 1989,S 24,72:3
German Requiem 1990,My 28,14:5
London, Chuck, Media (Misc.)
Amulets Against the Dragon Forces 1989,Ap 6,C17:4
London International Festival of Theater (Prod.)
Three Sisters, The 1989,Jl 23,II:5:5
Whistle in the Dark, A 1989,Ag 28,C13:4
London Small Theater Company (Misc.)
Beyond Belief 1990,Ap 22,63:4
Clouds, The 1990,Ap 22,63:4
Long Wharf Theater (Prod.)
National Anthems 1989,Ja 1,II:5:1
When We Are Married 1989,Ja 28,14:3
Some Sweet Day 1989,Mr 27,C13:1
Heiress, The 1989,Je 16,C3:1
Flea in Her Ear, A 1989,O 13,C15:1
Dance Lesson, A 1989,N 11,16:5
Crucible, The 1989,D 16,15:1
Re:Joyce! 1990,F 2,C3:1
Lover, The 1990,Ap 25,C13:1
Ruffian on the Stair, The 1990,Ap 25,C13:1
Is He Still Dead? 1990,My 27,58:1
Voysey Inheritance, The 1990,O 26,C3:1
Generations of the Dead in the Abyss of Coney
Island Madness 1990,D 9,82:3
Valued Friends 1990,D 20,C20:4
Loyal-Suarez Troupe (Misc.)
Grandma Goes West 1989,N 3,C4:1

M

M. M. G. Arena Productions (Prod.)
Wizard of Oz, The 1989,Mr 24,C3:1
Mabou Mines (Misc.)
Through the Leaves 1990,S 18,C18:1
Mabou Mines (Prod.)
Suenos 1989,F 23,C13:3
Lear 1990,Ja 26,C3:1
B. Beaver Animation, The 1990,My 24,C19:1
McCarter Theater (Prod.)
Tale of Two Cities, A 1990,Ap 7,16:4

Manbites Dog Theater Company (Misc.)
Indecent Materials 1990,Ag 28,C14:3
Manhattan Class Company (Prod.)
Manhattan Class Company, One-Act Play Festival,
Series A 1989,Mr 11,16:1
Manhattan Class One-Acts, Series B 1989,Mr
19,61:4
Manhattan Punch Line (Prod.)
Manhattan Punch Line's Fifth Annual Festival of
One-Act Comedies, Series A 1989,Ja 26,C16:1
Manhattan Punch Line's Festival of One-Act
Comedies, Series B 1989,F 11,12:3
Equal 'Wrights 1989,My 18,C20:3
Friends 1989,Je 11,67:1
Manhattan Punch Line's Sixth Annual Festival of
One-Act Comedies, Evening A 1990,F 4,60:1
Manhattan Punch Line's Sixth Annual Festival of
One-Act Comedies, Evening B 1990,F 11,70:1
Beyond Belief 1990,Ap 22,63:4
Clouds, The 1990,Ap 22,63:4
Manhattan Theater Club (Prod.)
What the Butler Saw 1989,Mr 9,C21:1
What the Butler Saw 1989,Mr 29,C17:1
Aristocrats 1989,Ap 26,C15:1
Eleemosynary 1989,My 10,C15:3
Aristocrats 1989,My 21,II:5:1
Lisbon Traviata, The 1989,Je 7,C21:1
Loman Family Picnic, The 1989,Je 22,C24:1
Lisbon Traviata, The 1989,N 1,C22:3
Talented Tenth, The 1989,N 10,C3:1
Art of Success, The 1989,D 21,C11:1
Aristocrats 1989,D 24,II:3:1
Lisbon Traviata, The 1989,D 24,II:3:1
What the Butler Saw 1989,D 24,II:3:1
Bad Habits 1990,Mr 21,C13:1
Piano Lesson, The 1990,Ap 17,C13:4
Prin 1990,Je 7,C18:5
Abundance 1990,O 31,C15:3
Wash, The 1990,N 8,C28:4
Abundance 1990,N 11,II:5:1
Wash, The 1990,N 18,II:5:1
American Plan, The 1990,D 17,C11:1
Martel Media Enterprises (Prod.)
Kathy and Mo Show, The: Parallel Lives 1989,F
1,C21:1
Media Innovations (Misc.)
Legends in Concert 1989,My 14,49:3
Mitsubishi (Misc.)
Takarazuka 1989,O 27,C21:1
Morales Teeterboard Troupe (Misc.)
Ringling Brothers and Barnum & Bailey Circus
1990,Mr 31,13:1
Music-Theater Group (Prod.)
Ladies 1989,Ap 7,C3:1
Juan Darien 1989,D 24,II:3:1
Paradise for the Worried 1990,Ap 6,C3:1
Endangered Species 1990,O 9,C13:1
Musical Theater Works (Prod.)
Cradle Song 1989,Mr 19,61:1
Young Rube 1989,Ap 21,C3:4
Midsummer Nights 1989,S 24,71:3
Goose! Beyond the Nursery 1990,F 11,69:2
Sugar Hill 1990,Ap 28,12:6
Whatnot 1990,S 25,C16:3
My Father, My Son Productions (Prod.)
My Father, My Son 1990,S 23,65:3

N

Naked Angels (Prod.)
Chelsea Walls 1990,Je 9,12:5
National Black Touring Circuit, Inc. (Prod.)
Spirit Time 1989,Jl 14,C18:1
Yesterdays 1990,O 8,C14:3
Negro Ensemble Company (Prod.)
Jonquil 1990,Ja 15,C14:3
Burner's Frolic 1990,F 26,C14:1
Lifetimes 1990,Ap 9,C12:4
**Nemirovich-Danchenko, Vladimir I., Studio-School
(Misc.)**
My Big Land 1989,Ag 17,C15:1
Never or Now Company (Prod.)
Catch Me If I Fall 1990,N 17,16:5
New Arts Theater (Prod.)
Sleeping Dogs 1989,Mr 23,C17:1

Apocalyptic Butterflies 1989,Je 17,12:3
New Directors Series (Misc.)
Waves, The 1990,My 10,C16:4
New Federal Theater (Prod.)
Thrill a Moment, A 1989,My 4,C23:1
Goree 1989,S 24,72:3
God's Trombones 1989,O 11,C17:1
Jelly Belly 1990,N 22,C13:3
New Musicals (Prod.)
Kiss of the Spider Woman 1990,Je 1,C3:1
New Roads Productions (Misc.)
Making Movies 1990,Mr 28,C17:1
New Theater of Brooklyn, The (Prod.)
Sunday Promenade, The 1989,Mr 12,68:1
No Limits to Love 1989,My 4,C21:1
Jacques and His Master 1989,N 16,C28:5
Rough Crossing 1990,F 23,C3:4
Rain. Some Fish. No Elephants. 1990,My 3,C20:5
New Wave of Quebec Festival (Misc.)
Cezanne Syndrome, The 1989,F 3,C3:5
New York Reach Ensemble, The (Misc.)
Mama, I Want to Sing, Part II 1990,Mr 28,C13:1
New York Shakespeare Festival (Prod.)
For Dear Life 1989,Ja 11,C17:1
Genesis: Music and Miracles from the Medieval
Mystery Plays 1989,Ja 18,C20:5
Love's Labor's Lost 1989,F 23,C15:1
Winter's Tale, The 1989,Mr 22,C19:4
Forbidden City, The 1989,Ap 7,C3:1
Temptation 1989,Ap 10,C13:1
Twelfth Night 1989,Jl 10,C13:1
Coronel No Tiene Quien le Escriba, El (No One
Writes to the Colonel) 1989,Ag 3,C17:1
Gran Circo E.U. Craniano, El (Great U.S. Kranial
Circus, The) 1989,Ag 4,C15:1
Adios, Tropicana 1989,Ag 10,C16:5
Peggy and Jackson 1989,Ag 10,C16:5
No + (No More) 1989,Ag 12,14:4
Sueno de una Noche de Verano (Midsummer Night's
Dream, A) 1989,Ag 16,C16:1
My Big Land 1989,Ag 17,C15:1
Paso o Parabola del Camino, El (Parable of the Path,
The) 1989,Ag 20,62:1
Titus Andronicus 1989,Ag 21,C13:1
Carnage, A Comedy 1989,S 18,C14:1
Kate's Diary 1989,N 29,C17:1
Up Against It 1989,D 5,C17:3
Kingfish 1989,D 22,C5:1
Winter's Tale, The 1989,D 24,II:3:1
Romance in Hard Times 1989,D 29,C3:1
Macbeth 1990,Ja 17,C13:4
Mom's Life, A 1990,Mr 15,C22:3
Jonah 1990,Mr 23,C5:1
Spunk 1990,Ap 19,C17:4
Ice Cream with Hot Fudge 1990,My 4,C5:1
Hamlet 1990,My 9,C15:4
B. Beaver Animation, The 1990,My 24,C19:1
Taming of the Shrew, The 1990,Jl 13,C3:1
Sin Testigos 1990,Ag 14,C16:1
Richard III 1990,Ag 17,C1:1
Palomar, El (Pigeon House, The) 1990,Ag 19,53:1
Voces de Acero (Voices of Steel) 1990,Ag 20,C14:1
Doente Imaginario, O (Imaginary Invalid, The)
1990,Ag 23,C20:1
Mondo Mambo 1990,Ag 25,16:5
Indecent Materials 1990,Ag 28,C14:3
Romeo and Juliet 1990,S 15,15:1
Through the Leaves 1990,S 18,C18:1
Machinal 1990,O 16,C13:1
Gonza the Lancer 1990,O 25,C20:5
Fever, The 1990,N 29,C17:1
Caucasian Chalk Circle, The 1990,D 3,C13:3
Big Funk, The 1990,D 11,C15:4
New York Theater Workshop (Prod.)
Nest, The 1989,Mr 2,C26:1
Investigation of the Murder in El Salvador, The
1989,My 23,C14:4
My Children! My Africa! 1989,D 19,C19:3
Forest in Arden, A 1990,F 11,69:1
Nature of Things, The 1990,Mr 25,63:1
Waves, The 1990,My 10,C16:4
Love and Anger 1990,D 9,82:3
Love and Anger 1990,D 16,II:5:1
New Yorkers, The (Misc.)
Christmas Spectacular, The 1989,N 13,C20:5
Next Wave Festival (Misc.)
Empty Places 1989,O 6,C3:1
Stuff as Dreams Are Made On 1989,N 2,C22:4
Endangered Species 1990,O 9,C13:1

Ninagawa Macbeth 1990,O 22,C20:1
Ninagawa Company (Misc.)
Ninagawa Macbeth 1990,O 22,C20:1
Ninagawa Company (Prod.)
Tempest, The 1989,Ja 1,II:5:1
Noriko Sengoku/Interarts, New York (Prod.)
Ninagawa Macbeth 1990,O 22,C20:1
Norstar Bank International Theater Festival (Misc.)
Cinzano 1989,Je 29,C15:1
Pickle Family Circus, The 1989,Jl 24,C12:3
Norzar Productions (Prod.)
Further Mo' 1990,My 18,C3:5

O

Old Friends Group (Prod.)
Jackie Mason: Brand New 1990,O 18,C21:1
Old Globe Theater (Prod.)
Piano Lesson, The 1990,Ap 17,C13:4
Old Vic (Prod.)
Tempest, The 1989,Ja 1,II:5:1
Flea in Her Ear, A 1989,Ag 20,II:5:1
Omar Productions (Prod.)
Fabulous La Fontaine, The 1990,F 8,C15:3
One Dream (Misc.)
Spare Parts 1990,Mr 18,59:2
Whatnot 1990,S 25,C16:3
126 Second Avenue Corporation (Prod.)
Sex, Drugs, Rock & Roll 1990,F 9,C3:1
Quiet on the Set 1990,Ag 16,C17:1
One World Arts Foundation (Prod.)
Whistle in the Dark, A 1989,N 17,C26:5
Philadelphia, Here I Come! 1990,Je 13,C15:1
Playboy of the Western World, The 1990,N 8,C28:1
O'Neill, Eugene, Theater Center (Prod.)
Piano Lesson, The 1990,Ap 17,C13:4
Ontological-Hysteric Theater (Prod.)
Lava 1989,D 13,C24:3

P

P. P. Investments Inc. (Prod.)
Peter Pan 1990,D 14,C3:4
Pace Theatrical Group (Prod.)
Jerome Robbins's Broadway 1989,F 27,C13:1
Making Movies 1990,Mr 28,C17:1
Gypsy 1990,S 18,C11:1
Fiddler on the Roof 1990,N 19,C13:1
Pan Asian Repertory Theater (Prod.)
Play Ball 1989,F 12,68:4
Noiresque: The Fallen Angel 1989,My 5,C3:4
Song of Shim Chung, The 1989,N 19,76:4
And the Soul Shall Dance 1990,Mr 25,63:2
F.O.B. 1990,My 20,60:1
Lucky Come Hawaii 1990,O 29,C16:1
Panteleenko Brothers (Misc.)
Big Apple Circus, The 1990,N 3,13:4
Paper Mill Playhouse (Prod.)
Fanny 1990,Ap 13,C3:5
Papp, Joseph, Yiddish Theater (Prod.)
Songs of Paradise 1989,Ja 24,C16:3
Paramount Pictures (Prod.)
Shirley Valentine 1989,Ag 10,C13:1
Grand Hotel 1989,N 13,C13:3
Pearl Theater Company (Prod.)
Hedda Gabler 1989,Ja 25,C18:5
Midsummer Night's Dream, A 1989,O 15,67:1
Three Sisters, The 1989,N 23,C20:5
School for Wives, The 1989,D 30,17:1
Medea 1990,F 8,C15:3
Importance of Being Earnest, The 1990,Mr 18,59:1
Major Barbara 1990,N 28,C17:1
Fine Art of Finesse, The (Heureux Stratageme, L')
1990,D 28,C5:1
Pellegrini Brothers (Misc.)
Ringling Brothers and Barnum & Bailey Circus
1990,Mr 31,13:1
Pepsico Summerfare (Prod.)
Dybbuk, The 1989,Jl 11,C13:1
Hamlet 1989,Jl 11,C13:1
Six Characters in Search of an Author 1989,Jl
24,C13:1

Ward No. Six 1989,Jl 29,16:1
Performance Space 122 (Prod.)
  Shimmer 1989,Ja 16,C15:1
  Herd of Buffalo 1989,Jl 6,C18:4
  Terminal Hip 1990,Ja 12,C3:1
  Das Vedanya Mama 1990,Jl 28,12:5
  World Without End 1990,O 6,11:3
  Vid 1990,N 22,C18:4
Performing Arts Center of the State Univ. College at Purchase (Misc.)
  Kiss of the Spider Woman 1990,Je 1,C3:1
Performing Arts Preservation Association (Prod.)
  It's Still My Turn 1990,Ag 26,67:5
Perry Street Theater Company's Prima Artists (Prod.)
  Big, Fat and Ugly with a Mustache 1990,S 29,14:6
Philadelphia Festival Theater for New Plays (Prod.)
  Anthony Rose 1989,O 30,C16:3
Pickle Family Circus, The (Misc.)
  Pickle Family Circus, The 1989,Jl 24,C12:3
Play Troupe of Port Washington (Misc.)
  Murder in the Cathedral 1989,S 9,13:1
Playwrights Horizons (Prod.)
  Heidi Chronicles, The 1989,Ja 1,II:5:1
  Gus and Al 1989,F 28,C17:1
  Yankee Dawg You Die 1989,My 15,C13:4
  Hyde in Hollywood 1989,N 30,C19:3
  Gus and Al 1989,D 24,II:3:1
  Heidi Chronicles, The 1989,D 24,II:3:1
  Hyde in Hollywood 1989,D 24,II:3:1
  Yankee Dawg You Die 1989,D 24,II:3:1
  When She Danced 1990,F 20,C15:1
  Once on This Island 1990,My 7,C11:1
  Falsettoland 1990,Je 29,C3:1
  Falsettoland 1990,S 30,II:5:1
  Once on This Island 1990,O 28,II:5:1
  Subfertile 1990,N 8,C20:5
Point Tokyo Company (Prod.)
  Ninagawa Macbeth 1990,O 22,C20:1
Pregones Theater Group (Misc.)
  Voces de Acero (Voices of Steel) 1990,Ag 20,C14:1
Primary Stages Company (Prod.)
  Ancient History 1989,My 18,C29:3
  Hollywood Scheherazade 1989,O 1,60:5
  Black Market 1989,N 29,C17:1
  Bovver Boys 1990,F 25,57:3
  Swim Visit 1990,Je 23,12:4
  Lusting After Pipino's Wife 1990,S 30,57:4
Producciones Cisne (Misc.)
  Gran Circo E.U. Craniano, El (Great U.S. Kranial Circus, The) 1989,Ag 4,C15:1
Promenade Partners Inc. (Prod.)
  Making Movies 1990,Mr 28,C17:1
Puerto Rican Traveling Theater (Prod.)
  Happy Birthday, Mama 1989,F 9,C22:3
  Quintuplets 1989,Ap 2,51:1
  Conversation Among the Ruins 1989,Je 4,64:6
  Chinese Charade (Chino de la Charada, El) 1989,Ag 13,57:3
  Ariano 1990,F 11,69:2
  I Am a Winner 1990,Ap 1,52:3
  Spanish Eyes 1990,My 27,56:3
  English Only Restaurant, The 1990,Jl 27,C4:5
Punch Productions (Prod.)
  Merchant of Venice, The 1989,D 20,C15:1
Pushkin Theater of Moscow (Misc.)
  Ward No. Six 1989,Jl 29,16:1

Q

Quaigh Theater (Prod.)
  Before Dawn 1989,Ag 31,C20:5
  Man Who Fell in Love with His Wife, The 1990,Ag 19,55:1
Quiros Troupe (Misc.)
  Ringling Brothers and Barnum & Bailey Circus 1990,Mr 31,13:1

R

Radio City Music Hall Productions (Prod.)
  Takarazuka 1989,O 27,C21:1
  Christmas Spectacular, The 1989,N 13,C20:5
  Easter Extravaganza 1990,Ap 13,C28:4
  Christmas Spectacular, The 1990,N 13,C20:1
Raft Theater (Prod.)
  By and for Havel 1990,Mr 9,C3:5
Rajatabla (Misc.)
  Coronel No Tiene Quien le Escriba, El (No One Writes to the Colonel) 1989,Ag 3,C17:1
RAPP Arts Center (Prod.)
  Uncle Vanya 1990,Mr 3,12:5
  Sea Gull, The: The Hamptons: 1990 1990,D 24,21:1
Reach Entertainment and Sports (Prod.)
  Mama, I Want to Sing, Part II 1990,Mr 28,C13:1
Really Useful Theater Company (Prod.)
  Shirley Valentine 1989,F 17,C3:1
  Lend Me a Tenor 1989,Mr 3,C3:1
  Aspects of Love 1990,Ap 9,C11:1
  Shirley Valentine 1989,Ag 10,C13:1
Red Eye Collaboration (Misc.)
  White Boned Demon 1989,Mr 5,68:1
Repertorio Espanol (Prod.)
  Nonna, La 1989,S 1,C12:1
  Nelson 2 Rodrigues 1989,O 15,65:1
  Eterno Femenino, El 1990,Mr 25,63:1
  Huesped, El 1990,Ag 18,15:1
  Jibaros Progresistas, Los 1990,Ag 18,15:1
  Abanderado, El (Standard Bearer, The) 1990,N 4,72:1
Ridiculous Theatrical Company (Prod.)
  Tale of Two Cities, A 1989,Ja 18,C15:4
  Big Hotel 1989,S 29,C3:1
  Dr. Jekyll and Mr. Hyde 1989,D 8,C3:2
  Tale of Two Cities, A 1989,D 24,II:3:1
  Ring Gott Farblonjet, Der 1990,Ap 13,C3:1
  Camille 1990,S 7,C3:1
  Camille 1990,S 16,II:7:1
Rios Brothers (Misc.)
  Grandma Goes West 1989,N 3,C4:1
Riverside Shakespeare Company (Prod.)
  Hamlet 1989,Je 2,C3:5
  Cyrano de Bergerac 1989,Jl 7,C19:1
  Romeo and Juliet 1990,D 21,C20:6
Riverwest Theater (Prod.)
  Fabulous La Fontaine, The 1990,F 8,C15:3
Rock of Edges (Misc.)
  I Think It's Gonna Work Out Fine 1990,Mr 17,18:6
Rockettes, The (Misc.)
  Christmas Spectacular, The 1989,N 13,C20:5
  Easter Extravaganza 1990,Ap 13,C28:4
  Christmas Spectacular, The 1990,N 13,C20:1
Rotman Teeterboard Troupe (Misc.)
  Ringling Brothers and Barnum & Bailey Circus 1990,Mr 31,13:1
Roundabout Theater Company (Prod.)
  Enrico IV 1989,Ja 19,C22:3
  Member of the Wedding, The 1989,Ap 1,16:3
  Arms and the Man 1989,Je 5,C12:4
  Privates on Parade 1989,Ag 23,C13:3
  Tempest, The 1989,N 15,C18:3
  Doctor's Dilemma, The 1990,Ja 26,C3:1
  Crucible, The 1990,Mr 30,C3:1
  Price of Fame 1990,Je 14,C17:1
  Light Up the Sky 1990,Ag 22,C10:5
  King Lear 1990,N 16,C3:1
Royal Canadian Aerial Ski Squadron (Misc.)
  Ringling Brothers and Barnum & Bailey Circus 1989,Mr 25,13:1
Royal Court Theater (Prod.)
  Doing the Business 1990,Jl 25,C11:3
  How Now Green Cow 1990,Jl 25,C11:3
  Wall-Dog, The 1990,Jl 25,C11:3
Royal National Theater (Misc.)
  Apart from George 1989,Mr 21,C19:1
  Macbeth 1989,Mr 21,C19:1
Royal National Theater (Prod.)
  Tempest, The 1989,Ja 1,II:5:1
  Mountain Language 1989,Ja 15,II:1:4
  Mrs. Klein 1989,Ja 15,II:1:4
  Single Spies 1989,Ja 15,II:1:4
  Secret Rapture, The 1989,Ja 15,II:1:4
  Hamlet 1989,Je 21,C15:3

Hamlet 1989,Ag 20,II:5:1
Hedda Gabler 1989,Ag 20,II:5:1
Misanthrope, The 1989,Ag 20,II:5:1
King Lear 1990,Ag 8,C11:3
Richard III 1990,Ag 8,C11:3
After the Fall 1990,Ag 30,C15:1
Richard III 1990,O 7,II:5:1
Royal Shakespeare Company (Misc.)
  Some Americans Abroad 1990,F 12,C17:1
Royal Shakespeare Company (Prod.)
  Tempest, The 1989,Ja 1,II:5:1
  King John 1989,Je 21,C15:3
  Tempest, The 1989,Je 21,C15:3
  Man Who Came to Dinner, The 1989,Ag 1,C13:3
  Some Americans Abroad 1989,Ag 1,C13:3
  Cymbeline 1989,Ag 6,II:5:1
  Dr. Faustus 1989,Ag 6,II:5:1
  Hamlet 1989,Ag 6,II:5:1
  Midsummer Night's Dream, A 1989,Ag 6,II:5:1
  Romeo and Juliet 1989,Ag 6,II:5:1
  Silent Woman or Epicoene, The 1989,Ag 6,II:5:1
  Across Oka 1989,Ag 28,C13:4
  Othello 1989,S 24,II:5:1
  King Lear 1990,Ag 8,C11:3
Royston Company (Prod.)
  Murder in the Cathedral 1989,S 9,13:1
Rustaveli Theater Company, USSR (Misc.)
  King Lear 1990,Ap 4,C17:1

S

Sage Theater Company (Prod.)
  God's Policemen 1989,O 22,64:4
San Francisco Mime Troupe (Prod.)
  Seeing Double 1989,N 16,C28:4
Sandora Associates (Misc.)
  Spinning Tale, A 1990,F 25,57:1
Savio Brothers (Misc.)
  Ringling Brothers and Barnum & Bailey Circus 1990,Mr 31,13:1
Scardino, Frank, Associates (Misc.)
  Further Mo' 1990,My 18,C3:5
S.D.K. Productions (Prod.)
  Cahoots 1990,Mr 10,16:4
Second Stage Theater (Prod.)
  In a Pig's Valise 1989,F 15,C15:1
  Approaching Zanzibar 1989,My 5,C3:1
  Baba Goya 1989,D 6,C21:1
  Square One 1990,F 23,C3:1
  What a Man Weighs 1990,My 25,C3:2
  Jersey City 1990,Jl 15,40:3
  Lake No Bottom 1990,N 30,C3:1
  Lake No Bottom 1990,D 9,II:5:1
Serious Fun! (Misc.)
  You Could Be Home Now 1990,Jl 17,C16:1
  We Keep Our Victims Ready 1990,Jl 24,C13:1
  Men's Room, The 1990,Jl 26,C13:3
Shakespeare & Company (Prod.)
  Daisy Miller 1990,Ag 16,C14:4
  Old Maid, The 1990,Ag 16,C14:4
Shakespeare Theater at the Folger (Prod.)
  As You Like It 1989,My 13,10:5
  Twelfth Night 1989,O 4,C17:1
  Merry Wives of Windsor, The 1990,My 30,C13:1
  Richard III 1990,O 2,C12:3
  Richard III 1990,O 7,II:5:1
Shoestring Players, The (Misc.)
  People Who Could Fly, The 1989,Ag 3,C20:3
Shubert Organization (Prod.)
  Jerome Robbins's Broadway 1989,F 27,C13:1
  Secret Rapture, The 1989,O 27,C3:1
  Few Good Men, A 1989,N 16,C23:4
  Circle, The 1989,N 21,C19:1
  City of Angels 1989,D 12,C19:4
  Tru 1990,D 15,C3:1
  Grapes of Wrath, The 1990,Mr 23,C1:4
  Lettice and Lovage 1990,Mr 26,C11:1
Sine/D'Addario Ltd. (Prod.)
  Sex, Drugs, Rock & Roll 1990,F 9,C3:1
Skymasters (Misc.)
  Ringling Brothers and Barnum & Bailey Circus 1990,Mr 31,13:1
Skysaver Productions (Prod.)
  Empires and Appetites 1989,My 25,C18:4
Soho Rep (Prod.)
  Cezanne Syndrome, The 1989,F 3,C3:5

Phantom Lady, The 1989,Ap 16,60:1
Hanging the President 1990,Jl 13,C17:1
Source Foundation (Prod.)
Serious Company—An Evening of One-Act Plays 1989,Ap 19,C19:1
South Street Theater (Prod.)
People Who Could Fly, The 1989,Ag 3,C20:3
Whistle in the Dark, A 1989,N 17,C26:5
Philadelphia, Here I Come! 1990,Je 13,C15:1
Playboy of the Western World, The 1990,N 8,C28:1
Soyuzgostsirk (Prod.)
Moscow Circus 1990,Ja 13,13:4
Spoleto Festival U.S.A. (Misc.)
Eleemosynary 1989,My 10,C15:3
Staircase Company (Prod.)
Artist Descending a Staircase 1989,D 1,C3:1
Staller Center for the Arts (Prod.)
Cinzano 1989,Je 29,C15:1
Pickle Family Circus, The 1989,Jl 24,C12:3
Ghosts 1990,Je 15,C13:1
Stamford Theater Works (Prod.)
Remembrance 1990,O 18,C22:5
Stary Theater of Cracow (Misc.)
Dybbuk, The 1989,Jl 11,C13:1
Hamlet 1989,Jl 11,C13:1
Steppenwolf Theater Company (Misc.)
Grapes of Wrath, The 1990,Mr 23,C1:4
Grapes of Wrath, The 1990,D 30,II:5:1
Steppenwolf Theater Company (Prod.)
Grapes of Wrath, The 1990,Mr 23,C1:4
Strada Entertainment Trust (Prod.)
Run for Your Wife! 1989,Mr 8,C17:1
Stratford Festival of Canada (Prod.)
Comedy of Errors, The 1989,Je 12,C13:1
Henry V 1989,Je 12,C13:1
Kiss Me Kate 1989,Je 12,C13:1
Three Sisters, The 1989,Je 12,C13:1
Titus Andronicus 1989,Je 12,C13:1
Straus, Robert V., Productions Inc. (Misc.)
Heart Outright, The 1989,My 21,68:2
Laughing Matters 1989,My 21,68:1
Suntory International Corporation (Prod.)
Jerome Robbins's Broadway 1989,F 27,C13:1
Few Good Men, A 1989,N 16,C23:4
Circle, The 1989,N 21,C19:1
City of Angels 1989,D 12,C19:4
Tru 1989,D 15,C3:1
Grapes of Wrath, The 1990,Mr 23,C1:4
Svensons, Jr. (Misc.)
Big Apple Circus, The 1990,N 3,13:4

T

Takarazuka Revue Company (Misc.)
Takarazuka 1989,O 27,C21:1
Talking Band (Misc.)
Betty Bends the Blues 1989,Ja 28,13:1
Malady of Death, The 1989,Ja 28,13:1
New Cities 1989,My 7,74:3
Talking Band (Prod.)
Krapp's Last Tape 1989,D 17,94:5
Taller de Investigacion Teatral (Misc.)
No + (No More) 1989,Ag 12,14:4
Teatro do Ornitorrinco (Misc.)
Doente Imaginario, O (Imaginary Invalid, The) 1990,Ag 23,C20:1
Teatro Encuentro de Costa Rica (Misc.)
Palomar, El (Pigeon House, The) 1990,Ag 19,53:1
Theater Chelovek, U.S.S.R. (Misc.)
Cinzano 1989,Je 29,C15:1
Theater for a New Audience (Prod.)
Red Sneaks, The 1989,Je 29,C13:1
Othello 1990,Ja 17,C18:4
Mud Angel, The 1990,N 18,75:1
Theater for the New City (Prod.)
Betty Bends the Blues 1989,Ja 28,13:1
Malady of Death, The 1989,Ja 28,13:1
White Boned Demon 1989,Mr 5,68:1
Heart Outright, The 1989,My 21,68:2
Empires and Appetites 1989,My 25,C18:4
Anulah, Let Them Eat Cake 1989,S 17,79:4
Thin Air 1989,N 19,75:5
Three Poets 1989,N 23,C20:1
Foundation, The 1989,D 29,C6:6
Related Retreats 1990,Ap 18,C12:5

Theater in Limbo (Prod.)
Lady in Question, The 1989,D 24,II:3:1
Theater of Comedy, The (Misc.)
Run for Your Wife! 1989,Mr 8,C17:1
Theater of Fine Arts of the Dominican Republic (Misc.)
Sueno de una Noche de Verano (Midsummer Night's Dream, A) 1989,Ag 16,C16:1
Theater Off Park (Prod.)
Quiet End, A 1990,My 31,C16:6
Theaterworks/USA (Prod.)
Play to Win 1989,Jl 21,C3:2
Jekyll and Hyde 1990,Jl 1,48:1
Theatre Repere, Le (Misc.)
Polygraph 1990,O 27,12:5
Thompson, Walter, Marching Band (Misc.)
Father Was a Peculiar Man 1990,Jl 11,C13:1
Thompson, Walter, Orchestra (Misc.)
Happy End 1990,My 26,11:1
Three Dollar Bill Theater (Prod.)
Adam and the Experts 1989,N 23,C20:5
TNT. See New Theater of Brooklyn, The
Togni Family (Misc.)
Ringling Brothers and Barnum & Bailey Circus 1990,Mr 31,13:1
Tokyo Broadcasting System International (Prod.)
Gypsy 1990,S 18,C11:1
Fiddler on the Roof 1990,N 19,C13:1
Tokyo Engeki Ensemble (Misc.)
Lost in a Flurry of Cherries 1990,Mr 25,62:1
Torres, Eddie, Dancers (Misc.)
Mondo Mambo 1990,Ag 25,16:5
Torture Chorus (Misc.)
Breakfast with the Moors Murderers 1989,F 2,C18:4
T.O.T.A.L. (Prod.)
Best Friends 1989,Ag 13,57:6
Trinity Repertory Company (Prod.)
Summerfolk 1989,O 14,15:4
Baal 1990,Mr 24,17:1
Trouble and Strife Theater Company (Prod.)
Now and at the Hour of Our Death 1989,Je 1,C18:4
Tweed (Theater Works: Emerging Experimental Directions) New Works Festival (Misc.)
Blue Piano, The 1990,Je 4,C22:1
Pornsongspiel 1990,Je 4,C22:1

U

Ubu Repertory Theater Inc. (Prod.)
Alive by Night 1989,My 18,C22:3
Abel and Bela 1989,O 1,61:1
Architruc 1989,O 1,61:1
Your Handsome Captain 1989,N 12,71:6
Under One Roof (Prod.)
Famine Plays 1990,N 3,14:5
Unicorn Entertainment (Prod.)
Hizzoner! 1989,F 24,C3:1
Union 212 (Prod.)
Pixie Led, The 1989,Jl 21,C3:5
University of South Carolina (Misc.)
Merry Wives of Windsor, The 1990,My 30,C13:1
Richard III 1990,O 2,C12:3

V

Vakhtangov Theater of Moscow (Misc.)
Peace of Brest-Litovsk, The 1990,Ap 18,C11:1
Venezuelan American Association of the United States (Prod.)
Carreno 1990,F 3,15:4
Victory Gardens Theater (Prod.)
Jelly Belly 1990,N 22,C13:3
Video Studios (Misc.)
Largely New York 1989,My 2,C15:1
Vietnam Veterans Ensemble Theater Company (Prod.)
Ambassador, The 1989,O 22,63:1
Strike, The 1990,Ja 29,C18:5
Vineyard Theater (Prod.)
Phantasie 1989,Ja 4,C15:5
House of Horror, The 1989,O 19,C26:1
Feast Here Tonight 1989,N 30,C16:3

Moving Targets 1990,Ja 30,C14:5
Hannah . . . 1939 1990,Je 2,16:3
Nightingale 1990,D 4,C16:3

W

Warner/Chappel Music (Prod.)
Hizzoner! 1989,F 24,C3:1
Warp and Woof Theater Company (Misc.)
People Who Could Fly, The 1989,Ag 3,C20:3
Wee Gets (Misc.)
Ringling Brothers and Barnum & Bailey Circus 1990,Mr 31,13:1
Westbeth Theater Center (Misc.)
Quiet on the Set 1990,Ag 16,C17:1
Williamstown Theater Festival (Misc.)
Death Takes a Holiday 1990,Ag 13,C11:1
Williamstown Theater Foundation (Misc.)
John Brown's Body 1989,Je 27,C14:5
Rose Tattoo, The 1989,Jl 28,C3:4
Death Takes a Holiday 1990,Ag 13,C11:1
Wilma Theater (Prod.)
Incommunicado 1989,Mr 3,C3:1
Winns Highwire Motorcycle (Misc.)
Ringling Brothers and Barnum & Bailey Circus 1990,Mr 31,13:1
Women's Project and Productions (Prod.)
Niedecker 1989,Mr 19,61:1
Ladies 1989,Ap 7,C3:1
Mill Fire 1989,O 19,C22:3
Violent Peace 1990,Mr 3,12:3
Tales of the Lost Formicans 1990,Ap 29,60:1
Daytrips 1990,N 10,16:1
Wooster Group (Prod.)
Lava 1989,D 13,C24:3
Working Theater (Prod.)
Henry Lumper 1989,F 5,53:1
Working One-Acts '89 1989,Je 25,45:4
Special Interests 1990,F 18,70:1
WPA Theater (Prod.)
Night Hank Williams Died, The 1989,Ja 25,C16:4
Early One Evening at the Rainbow Bar and Grille 1989,Ap 14,C34:5
Good Coach, The 1989,Je 13,C18:5
Buzzsaw Berkeley 1989,Ag 21,C14:3
Heaven on Earth 1989,N 12,71:5
20 Fingers, 20 Toes 1990,Ja 10,C17:1
Starting Monday 1990,Ap 5,C18:1
Maids of Honor 1990,Je 22,C3:3

Y

Y in Terms of X (Prod.)
Imperceptible Mutabilities in the Third Kingdom 1989,S 20,C24:4
Yale Repertory Theater (Prod.)
Moon over Miami 1989,F 24,C3:1
Cobb 1989,Mr 31,C3:3
Playboy of the West Indies, The 1989,My 11,C17:1
Playboy of the West Indies, The 1989,My 21,II:5:1
Solid Gold Cadillac, The 1989,S 21,C28:1
Piano Lesson, The 1990,Ap 17,C13:4
Ivanov 1990,S 25,C13:3
Search and Destroy 1990,D 14,C3:1
YIVO Institute for Jewish Research (Misc.)
Songs of Paradise 1989,Ja 24,C16:3
York Theater Company (Prod.)
Max and Maxie 1989,Ja 18,C14:6
Sweeney Todd: The Demon Barber of Fleet Street 1989,Ap 8,11:5
Sweeney Todd 1989,Ap 19,C15:1
Lark, The 1989,My 29,20:5
Frankie 1989,O 10,C18:3
Sweeney Todd 1989,D 24,II:3:1
Traveler in the Dark 1990,Ja 16,C13:1
Golden Apple, The 1990,Mr 30,C3:5
Cherry Orchard, The 1990,My 24,C19:3
East Texas 1990,O 7,70:4
Lunatic, the Lover and the Poet, The 1990,D 1,16:5

Z

Zebra Promotions (Prod.)
  Apart from George 1989,Mr 21,C19:1
  Macbeth 1989,Mr 21,C19:1